IEEE Technology Update Series

Neural Networks Theory, Technology, and Applications

IEEE Technology Update Series

Neural Networks Theory, Technology, and Applications

Patrick K. Simpson
EDITOR

IEEE Technical Activities Board

A Selected Reprint Volume under the sponsorship of the Products Council of the IEEE Technical Activities Board

The Institute of Electrical and Electronics Engineers, Inc.
New York City, New York

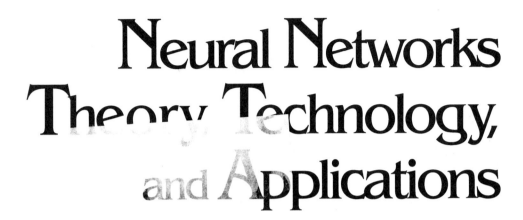

Library of Congress Cataloging-in-Publication Data

Neural networks theory, technology, and applications / Patrick K. Simpson, editor.
p. cm.— (IEEE technology update series)
"IEEE Technical Activities Board."
"A selected reprint volume . . . ."
Includes indexes.
ISBN 0-7803-2564-8 (alk. paper)
1. Neural networks (Computer science) I. Simpson, Patrick K.
II. Institute of Electrical and Electronics Engineers. Technical Activities Board. III. Series.
QA76.87.N488 1996
006.3—dc2 95-11170
CIP

FOREWORD

Technology advances and applications in a wide variety of both consumer and industrial products has led to rapid growth in the field of neural networks. Neural networks applications can be found in many, if not most, of the fields of electrotechnology. In 1995, fifteen IEEE Societies have shown interest in the field through their participation in the IEEE Neural Networks Council.

For these reasons, neural networks was selected as the topic of this edition of the IEEE Technology Update Series. This Series was developed by the IEEE Technical Activities Board (TAB) and the TAB Book Broker Committee to furnish readers with up-to-date information in specific fields of interest. "Neural Networks Theory, Technology, and Applications" contains material from IEEE conferences and journals, and is of value to electrotechnology professional around the world. A second volume will be published later this year.

I would like to thank Patrick K. Simpson for his skilled efforts as Editor-in-Chief of "Neural Networks Theory, Technology, and Applications." Mr. Simpson served as Chair of the IEEE Neural Networks Council in 1994. His paper, "Foundations of Neural Networks" serves as a tutorial to this volume.

For their guidance and work with the Technology Update Series, I would like to recognize the support of Dr. Bruce Eisenstein, IEEE Vice President —Technical Activities, and Dr. Jan Brown, Chair of the TAB Book Broker Committee.

Finally, I acknowledge the Technical Activities Department staff who gathered the materials for this volume. Thanks to Tania Skrinnikov, Harry Strickholm, Jayne F. Cerone, Lois J. Pannella, Eileen M. Reid, Patricia Thompson and Mark A. Vasquez-Jorge for their editorial input. I would also like to thank Ann Burgmeyer of the IEEE Publishing Department.

Robert T. Wangemann
Staff Director - IEEE Technical Activities

CONTENTS

EDITOR'S INTRODUCTION

In 1987, the IEEE sponsored the First International Conference on Neural Networks (ICNN 87) in San Diego CA. Over 1200 scientists and engineers attended that historic meeting, which included several tutorials, standing room only plenary sessions, and the presentation of over 400 papers. This meeting served as a catalyst for the community. Several government and industry funded efforts emerged as a result of this meeting. In addition, the field began to take shape. Leaders emerged, technical challenges were identified, and literally hundreds of applications were proposed or already being developed.

Since 1987, the IEEE has remained very active in neural networks. There has been at least one ICNN (or IJCNN) each year since. In addition, well over half of the IEEE sponsored meetings held each year includes at least one paper concerned with some aspect of neural networks. Special issues or special sections on neural networks have appeared in sixteen of the 92 archival IEEE publications ranging from Communications to Oceanic Engineering. In 1988, the IEEE formed a Technical Committee that served as the focal group for IEEE neural networks activities. This committee grew and in 1990 became the IEEE Neural Networks Council (NNC). In 1994, the NNC directly involved 15 of the 35 IEEE Societies. The NNC publishes two Transactions (*Transactions on Neural Networks and Transactions on Fuzzy Systems*), has sponsored over a half-dozen books and video tutorials, and honors the best in the field with awards, promotes local activities through regional interest groups and distinguished lecturers, and supports Fellow activities.

A close examination of the neural networks field reveals continued growth. In his September 1993 editorial,[1] Prof. Robert J. Marks II chronicled the growth of neural networks in two areas: archival papers and patents. Using the INSPEC database of archival papers, Marks reported the number of papers published in 1990, 1991, and 1992 was 2720, 4336, and 5574, respectively. Almost half of these INSPEC entries were associated with IEEE activities. In a similar fashion, using the CASSIS database of U.S. Patents, Marks reported 36, 66, and 119 neural network related patents were issued in 1990, 1991, and 1992, respectively.

Clearly, the field of neural networks is expansive and diverse. Each year it becomes more difficult to follow all the advances being made. In recognition of this problem, this book's objective is to provide the practicing engineer with a snapshot of the latest theory, technology, applications, and implementations of neural networks. To achieve this goal, the IEEE Technical Activities Board has collected all of the papers dealing with any aspect of neural networks from any IEEE sponsored or co-sponsored meeting during 1993. Over 1200 papers were published in these IEEE conference records in 1993. This collection included at least one paper in 87 of 137 IEEE sponsored or co-sponsored meetings during the year. Due to the sheer diversity of this field, and the quality of papers presented, it was not possible to reduce 1200 papers to a single volume. As such, a second volume was needed. Two volumes was enough, but just barely.

The paper selection process was done in three steps. First, each of the 1200 papers was reviewed for accuracy, clarity, and completeness. Also, duplicate papers (nearly identical papers presented at two or more different meetings) were eliminated. This process reduced the original 1200 papers to 803 papers. The second pass through the papers was used to create index terms and organize the papers into categories. The results of this second pass included two theory categories, seven technology categories, three implementation categories, and seven application categories. The third and final pass was used to reduce the collection of papers to those found in these first two "Neural Networks Technology and Applications" volumes. The final selection of

---

1 Marks, R. (1994). Intelligence: Computational vs. Artificial, *IEEE Trans. on Neural Networks,* Vol. 4, No. 5, pp. 737-739.

papers emphasized diversity and new results. This volume covers theory, technology, and implementations, and includes 139 conference papers. A second volume is dedicated to applications and includes approximately the same number of papers.

THE STATE OF NEURAL NETWORKS

I have had the privilege of being involved with neural networks since 1986. Over these past nine years, I have witnessed several changes in the field. I have watched the funding for neural network technology dramatically grow. I have seen changes and trends in the technical emphasis of the field. And, I still see many challenges that remain ahead. The following three sections provide my perspectives in each of these areas.

A. Funding

There has been a significant investment in neural network technology since 1987. *Electronic Engineering Times* (March 29, 1993) reported the U.S. Department of Defense has spent $71 M developing neural network technology. Of this $71 M, the Advanced Research Projects Agency has spent $35 M. *Federal Computer Week* (February 15, 1993) reported this number could double by 1996. Neural network programs also exist within the National Science Foundation (basic research), Department of Energy (adaptive control), Department of Transportation (Intelligent Vehicle Highway System), Department of Commerce (process control), Department of Health and Human Services (diagnostic technologies), Federal Bureau of Identification (fingerprint recognition), Internal Revenue System (character recognition), Postal Service (handwriting recognition), and the Environmental Protection Agency (environment monitoring). Neural network programs have also emerged within other countries. The European Community funded a large effort under ESPRIT entitled Pygmalion. In addition, the Japanese have been aggressively funding several efforts in speech processing, control, and character recognition, and Australia has also been very active.

Private industry has also embraced the application of neural networks. When looking at industry's involvement, I am reminded of a comment made by Prof. Robert Hecht-Nielsen during one of his neural network short courses I attended in 1987. When asked to prognosticate and describe where the biggest applications of neural networks would be, Hecht-Nielsen offered a list he felt had good potential, but concluded his answer by stating that the applications with the greatest pay-off may not even be envisioned yet. Hecht-Nielsen proved to be prophetic. Two areas where neural networks are enjoying success are financial forecasting and process control. To my knowledge, neither of these applications were highly touted in 1987, yet both receive strong industrial support today.

B. Trends

There have been many changes over the past eight years. The following list represents some of the trends that I have observed during this period of time. Introductions to the chapters will expand on these items where appropriate.

- **Associative Memory Obsolescence.** Associative memory research has lost its momentum. Although there are still some researchers attempting to shine a spotlight into corners of a well-lit room, this area of research has never met the potential originally projected. Cellular neural networks represent one possible exception to this observation.

- **Optical Implementation Decline**. Optical and Electro-Optical implementations of neural networks have almost disappeared. Only one paper of the 1200 dealt with this area. Through the late 1980s, this was considered to be the implementation of choice. It was felt that light intensity could encode connection weights and dense packaging could be achieved because light nondestructively interferes with itself. Some of this attention deficit can be attributed to the reduction in associative memory interest.

- **MLP Proliferation.** Multi-Layer Perceptrons (MLPs) trained using the backpropagation algorithm encompasses almost half of the 1200 papers reviewed. Many scientists and engineers first exposed to the field are not aware there are other neural network paradigms beyond MLPs trained with backpropagation.

Unfortunately, those that have followed such a path and have met limited success might have discarded this approach and retained a poor perspective of neural networks on a whole.

- **Analytical Rigor.** The analytical rigor has steadily improved each year. In particular, this volume will examine sensitivity, fault tolerance, generalization, and approximation in detail.

- **Analog Versus Digital.** The link between digital signal processing (DSP) and neural networks seems to be growing stronger. In particular, DSP chips are used for neural network applications in increasing numbers, resulting in a reduced need for special purpose neural network chips. Neural network integrated circuits have been emphasizing analog operations and the digital operations are being performed by DSP chips.

- **Software Simulations.** There are several excellent neural network simulation packages that are available in the public domain. As a result, companies that provide neural network software are emphasizing full solutions more than a software package.

- **Synergistic Hybrids.** The synergism between neural networks and other technologies is on the rise. Three notable areas include expert systems, fuzzy sets, and evolutionary computation. Expert systems and neural networks are combined to allow *a priori* knowledge to be efficiently and effectively combined with information that is attained through adaptation. Fuzzy sets and neural networks are now regularly combined for pattern recognition and control tasks, and evolutionary computation is often used for network design and training.

C. Challenges

Although the field of neural networks has matured, there are still many challenges that remain. The following list represents some of the most pressing problem areas.

- **Biological Ignorance**. Most of the scientists and engineers in the field of neural networks are biologically ignorant. There is a great body of knowledge in neuroscience that is available that has not been tapped by this community. With a few notable exceptions (such as Terrance Sejnowski, Stephen Grossberg, and Carver Mead), the gap between what is biologically relevant and what is being simulated has not been closed. To achieve truly intelligent machines, there must be more collaboration between engineering and neuroscience.

- **Rapid Learning.** Although there have been notable improvements, neural networks still are not learning fast enough to be of practical use in a great many applications, including adaptive control and communications. The neural networks community is still waiting for an algorithm that trains a three-layer nonlinear neural network as fast as a two-layer linear network.

- **Explanation Facility**. The explanation facilities that are available to neural networks are still primitive. Currently, fuzzy neural networks are closest to achieving this goal.[2] The papers found in Chapter 1: Design give an indication of the progress being made in this area. Until this problem is solved, neural networks will continue to be perceived as an impenetrable black box that provides no hint of how it makes decisions. For many applications, especially in diagnostics, this proves to be a significant barrier.

---

2 Bezdek, J. & Pal, S. Eds., (1992). Fuzzy Models for Pattern Recognition, IEEE Press, Piscataway, NJ.

- **Construction Theorem**. There are several existence theorems that prove some neural networks can approximate a broad class of functions to any desired degree of accuracy.[3] Examples of this work are found in this volume. Knowing that a neural network can approximate a function is an important step, but now a prescription on how to build a network to achieve the mapping is needed. These construction theorems are the next big hurdle for neural networks.

- **Incremental Learning**. With only a few exceptions, if you have new data that you would like to train an existing neural network with, you must add the new data to the old data and completely retrain. This is clearly not how humans learn. New information is added incrementally to the old information immediately. In many neural network applications, incremental learning is an important property. As examples, often an engineer will want to add a new class to an existing neural network classifier, or additional data in a time-series modeling problem will become available and she will want to improve the model with the new data. With the exception of Reduced Coulomb Energy (RCE) networks,[4] Probablistic Neural Networks (PNN),[5] Fuzzy Min-Max (FMM) Neural Networks,[6] and Adaptive Resonance Theory (ART) networks,[7] this property is not widely available. In particular, the most popular neural networks today, the Multi-Layer Perceptron (MLP),[8] the Radial Basis Function (RBF) network,[9] and the Learning Vector Quantization (LVQ) network,[10] are not incremental learning networks.

- **Sparse Data Generalization**. One area of neural network analysis that has made significant progress over the past few years has been the study of generalization.[11] Using the theory of Probably Almost Correct (PAC) learning,[12] bounds on the number of training patterns needed for sufficient generalization have been

---

3 Poggio, T. & Girosi, F. (1990). Networks for approximation and learning, Proceedings of the IEEE, Vol. 78, No. 9., pp. 1481-1497.

4 Reilly, D., Cooper, L., & Elbaum, C. (1982). A neural model for category learning, Biological Cybernetics, Vol. 45, pp. 35-41.

5 Specht, D. (1990). Probablistic neural networks, Neural Networks, Vol. 3, No. 5, pp. 109-118.

6 Simpson, P. (1992). Fuzzy Min-max neural networks - Part 1: Classification, Vol. 3, No. 5, pp. 776-786; Simpson, P. (1993). Fuzzy Min-max neural networks - Part 2: Clustering, Vol. 1, No. 1, pp. 32-45.

7 Carpenter, G. (1989) Neural network models for pattern recogntion and associative memory, Neural Networks, Vol. 2, No. 4, pp. 243-258.

8 Haykin, S. (1994). Neural Networks: A Comprehensive Foundation, IEEE Press, Piscataway, NJ.

9 Leonard, J., Kramer, M. & Unger L. (1992). Using radial basis functions to approximate a function and its error bounds, IEEE Trans. on Neural Networks, Vol. 3, No. 4, pp. 624-626.

10 Kohonen, T. (1990). Self-Organization and Associate Memory, Springer-Verlag, Berlin.

11 Hush, D. & Horne, B. (1993). Progress in supervised neural networks, IEEE Signal Processing Magazine, Vol. 10, No. 1, pp. 8-39

12 Vapnik, V. & Chervonenkis, A. (1971). On uniform convergence of relative frequencies of events to

derived. That is the good news. The bad news is that the number of training patterns needed relative to the number of free parameters (neural network weights) grows large very quickly. A new challenge now emerges. Although there are some neural network applications that are abundant with data, there are large number that are not. Training techniques for existing (or new) neural networks need to be devised that will allow good generalization from sparse data sets.

- **Recurrent Network Analysis**. Recurrent neural networks present a whole new class of problems. The foremost problem is learning while remaining stable. When is it best to learn in a recurrent neural network? Once the network has stabilized? While it is stabilizing? What if it is not stable? In addition, learning in recurrent neural networks is slower, sometimes much slower, than learning in purely feedforward systems. How can the learning speed be improved? A special issue of the *IEEE Transactions on Neural Networks*[13] recently addressed many of these issues. Some of the papers found in this volume begin to work on this problem, but a good solution still remains to be found.

---

their probabilities, Theory of Probability and its Applications, Vol. 16, No. 2, pp. 264-280; Baum, E. & Haussler, D. (1989). What size net gives valid generalization?, Neural Computation, Vol. 1, pp. 151-160.

13 Giles, C., Kuhn, G. & Williams, R. (1994). Guest Editorial: special Issue on Dynamic Recurrent Neural Networks, IEEE Trans. on Neural Networks, Vol. 5, No. 2, pp. 153-156.

ORGANIZATION

This volume is organized into three parts: Theory, Technology, and Implementations. Each of the three parts has individual chapters. Preceding Part 1 is a tutorial paper entitled "Foundations of Neural Networks" that provides an overview of neural networks. A description of each part and the corresponding chapters is as follows:

- **Part 1: Theory**. There are two aspects of theory examined in this volume: Design and Analysis. Design (Chapter 1) specifically addresses modifications of existing neural networks or new neural network paradigms. Topics covered in this chapter include time-delay neural networks, hierarchical neural networks, Multi-Layer Perceptrons (MLPs), Radial Basis Function (RBF) networks, Wavelet networks, cascade correlation (CC) neural networks, Reduced Coulomb Energy (RCE) neural networks, Self-Organizing Feature Maps (SOFMs), fuzzy neural networks, evolutionary computation, biological neural networks, and new neural network paradigms. Analysis (Chapter 2) addresses issues in learning, recall dynamics, fault tolerance, function approximation, classification, and biological analogy.

- **Part 2: Technology**. Technology, as defined within this volume of papers, is the development of a set of capabilities that are not specific to an application but are targeting a broad application area. As an example, there are many neural networks that are proposed as nonlinear extensions of linear filtering techniques in signal processing. In this sense, the technology area is signal processing. There are seven technology topic areas (in alphabetical order): Control (Chapter 3), Data Fusion (Chapter 4), Forecasting (Chapter 5), Image Processing & Vision (Chapter 6), Optimization (Chapter 7), Signal Processing (Chapter 8), and Virtual Reality (Chapter 9).

- **Part 3: Implementations.** There are three categories of neural network implementations defined in this volume. Array Processor Implementations (Chapter 10) describes the use of special purpose hardware, multi-purpose hardware, and digital signal processing hardware for neural network applications. Integrated Circuit Implementations (Chapter 11) focuses on neural network implementations on a single device. Software Simulations (Chapter 12) reviews some of the software packages that are currently available for simulating a large number of neural network paradigms on conventional computers.

IEEE Technology Update Series

Neural Networks Theory, Technology, and Applications

Foundations of Neural Networks

PATRICK K. SIMPSON

GENERAL DYNAMICS ELECTRONICS DIVISION, SAN DIEGO, CA 92138

1. Introduction

Building intelligent systems that can model human behavior has captured the attention of the world for years. So, it is not surprising that a technology such as neural networks has generated great interest. This paper will provide an evolutionary introduction to neural networks by beginning with the key elements and terminology of neural networks, and developing the topologies, learning laws, and recall dynamics from this infrastructure. The perspective taken in this paper is largely that of an engineer, emphasizing the application potential of neural networks and drawing comparisons with other techniques that have similar motivations. As such, mathematics will be relied upon in many of the discussions to make points as precise as possible.

The paper begins with a review of what neural networks are and why they are so appealing. A typical neural network is immediately introduced to illustrate several of the key features. With this network as a reference, the evolutionary introduction to neural networks is then pursued. The fundamental elements of a neural network, such as input and output patterns, processing element, connections, and threshold operations, are described, followed by descriptions of neural network topologies, learning algorithms, and recall dynamics. A taxonomy of neural networks is presented that uses two of the key characteristics of learning and recall. Finally, a comparison of neural networks and similar nonneural information processing methods is presented.

2. What are neural networks, and what are they good for?

Neural networks are information processing systems. In general, neural networks can be thought of as "black box" devices that accept inputs and produce outputs. Some of the operations that neural networks perform include

- Classification—an input pattern is passed to the network, and the network produces a representative class as output.
- Pattern matching—an input pattern is passed to the network, and the network produces the corresponding output pattern.
- Pattern completion—an incomplete pattern is passed to the network, and the network produces an output pattern that has the missing portions of the input pattern filled in.
- Noise removal—a noise-corrupted input pattern is presented to the network, and the network removes some (or all) of the noise and produces a cleaner version of the input pattern as output.
- Optimization—an input pattern representing the initial values for a specific optimization problem is presented to the network, and the network produces a set of variables that represents a solution to the problem.
- Control—an input pattern represents the current state of a controller and the desired response for the controller, and the output is the proper command sequence that will create the desired response.

Neural networks consist of processing elements and weighted connections. Figure 1 illustrates a typical neural network. Each layer in a neural network consists of a collection of processing elements (PEs). Each PE in a neural network collects the values from all of its input connections, performs a predefined mathematical operation (typically a dot product followed by a PE function), and produces a single output value. The neural network in Fig. 1 has three layers: F_X, which consists of the PEs $\{x_1, x_2, x_3\}$; F_Y, which consists of the PEs $\{y_1, y_2\}$; and F_Z, which consists of the PEs $\{z_1, z_2, z_3\}$ (from bottom to top, respectively). The PEs are connected with weighted connections. In Fig. 1 there is a weighted connection from every F_X PE to every F_Y PE, and there is a weighted connection from every F_Y PE to every F_Z PE. Each weighted connection (often synonymously referred to as either a connection or a weight) acts as both a label and a value. As an example, in Fig. 1 the connection from the F_X PE x_1 to the F_Y PE y_2 is the connection weight w_{12} (the connection from x_1 to y_2). The connection weights store the information. The value of the connection weights is often determined by a neural network learning procedure (although sometimes they are predefined and hardwired into the network). It is through the adjustment of the connection weights that the neural network is able to learn. By performing the update operations for each of the PEs, the neural network is able to recall information.

There are several important features illustrated by the neural network shown in Fig. 1 that apply to all neural networks:

- Each PE acts independently of all others—each PE's output relies only on its constantly available inputs from the abutting connections.
- Each PE relies only on local information—the informa-

The author is now with ORINCON Corporation, 9363 Towne Centre Drive, San Diego, CA 92128.

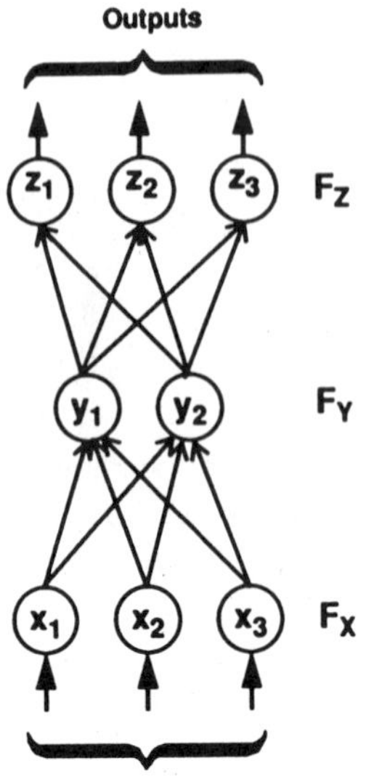

Fig. 1.

tion that is provided by the adjoining connections is all a PE needs to process; it does not need to know the state of any of the other PEs where it does not have an explicit connection.

- The large number of connections provides a large amount of redundancy and facilitates a distributed representation.

The first two features allow neural networks to operate efficiently in parallel. The last feature provides neural networks with inherent fault-tolerance and generalization qualities that are very difficult to obtain from typical computing systems. In addition to these features, through proper arrangement of the neural networks, introduction of a nonlinearity in the processing elements (i.e., adding a nonlinear PE function), and use of the appropriate learning rules, neural networks are able to learn arbitrary nonlinear mappings. This is a powerful attribute.

There are three primary situations where neural networks are advantageous:

1. Situations where only a few decisions are required from a massive amount of data (e.g., speech and image processing)
2. Situations where nonlinear mappings must be automatically acquired (e.g., loan evaluations and robotic control)
3. Situations where a near-optimal solution to a combinatorial optimization problem is required very quickly (e.g., airline scheduling and telecommunication message routing)

The foundations of neural networks consist of an understanding of the nomenclature and a firm comprehension of the rudimentary mathematical concepts used to describe and analyze neural network processing. In a broad sense, neural networks consist of three principle elements:

1. *Topology*—how a neural network is organized into layers and how those layers are connected.
2. *Learning*—how information is stored in the network.
3. *Recall*—how the stored information is retrieved from the network.

Each of these elements will be described in detail after discussing connections, processing elements, and PE functions.

3. Dissecting Neural Networks

Each neural network has at least two physical components: connections and processing elements. The combination of these two components creates a neural network. A convenient analogy is the directed graph, where the edges are analogous to the connections and the nodes are analogous to the processing elements. In addition to connections and processing elements, threshold functions and input/output patterns are also basic elements in the design, implementation, and use of neural networks. After a description of the terminology used to describe neural networks, each of these elements will be examined in turn.

3.1. Terminology

Neural network terminology remains varied, with a standard yet to be adopted (although there is an effort to create one (cf. Eberhart, 1990)). For clarity in further discussions, the terminology used within this paper will be described where appropriate. To illustrate some of the terminology introduced here, please refer to Fig. 2.

Input and output vectors (patterns) will be denoted by subscripted capital letters from the beginning of the alphabet. The input patterns will be denoted

$$A_k = (a_{k1}, a_{k2}, \cdots, a_{kn}); \qquad k = 1, 2, \cdots, m$$

and the output patterns

$$B_k = (b_{k1}, b_{k2}, \cdots, b_{kp}); \qquad k = 1, 2, \cdots, m.$$

The processing elements in a layer will be denoted by the same subscript variable. The collection of PEs in a layer form a vector, and these vectors will be denoted by capital letters from the end of the alphabet. In most cases, three layers of PEs will suffice. The input layer of PEs is denoted

$$F_X = (x_1, x_2, \cdots, x_n)$$

where each x_i receives input from the corresponding input pattern component a_{ki}. The next layer of PEs will be the F_Y PEs, then the F_Z PEs (if either layer is necessary). The dimensionality of these layers depends on its use. For the network in Fig. 2, for example, the second layer of the network is the output layer, so the number of F_Y PEs must match the dimensionality of output patterns. In this instance,

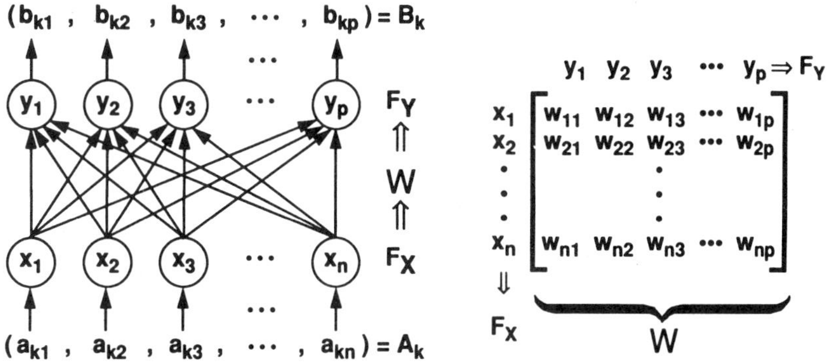

Fig. 2.

the output layer is denoted

$$F_Y = (y_1, y_2, \cdots, y_p)$$

where each y_j is correlated with the jth element of B_k.

Connection weights are stored in weight matrices. Weight matrices will be denoted by capital letters toward the middle of the alphabet, such as U, V, and W. For the example in Fig. 2, this two-layer neural network requires one weight matrix to fully connect the layer of n F_X PEs to the layer of p F_Y PEs. The matrix in Fig. 2 describes the full set of connection weights between F_X and F_Y, where the weight w_{ij} is the connection weight from the ith F_X PE, x_i, to the jth F_Y PE, y_j.

3.2. *Input and Output Patterns*

Neural networks cannot operate unless they have data. Some neural networks require only single patterns, and others require pattern pairs. Note that the dimensionality of the input pattern is not necessarily the same as the output pattern. When a network only works with single patterns, it is an autoassociative network. When a network works with pattern pairs, it is heteroassociative.

One of the key issues when applying neural networks is determining what the patterns should represent. For example, in speech recognition there are several different types of features that can be employed, including linear predictive coding coefficients, Fourier spectra, histograms of threshold crossings, cross-correlation values, and many others. The proper selection and representation of these features can greatly affect the performance of the network.

In some instances the representation of the features as a pattern vector is constrained by the type of processing the neural network can perform. Some networks can only process binary data, such as the Hopfield network (Hopfield, 1982; Amari, 1972), binary adaptive resonance theory (Carpenter and Grossberg, 1987a), and the brain-state-in-a-box (Anderson et al., 1977). Others can process real-valued data such as backpropagation (Werbos, 1974; Parker, 1982; Rumelhart, Hinton, and Williams, 1986), and learning vector quantization (Kohonen, 1984). Creating the best possible set of features and properly representing those features is the first step toward success in any neural network application (Anderson, 1990).

3.3. *Connections*

A neural network is equivalent to a directed graph (digraph). A digraph has edges (connections) between nodes (PEs) that allow information to flow in only one direction (the direction denoted by the arrow). Information flows through the digraph along the edges and is collected at the nodes. Within the digraph representation, connections serve a single purpose: they determine the direction of information flow. As an example, in Fig. 2 the information flows from the F_X layer through the connections W to the F_Y layer. Neural networks extend the digraph representation to include a weight with each edge (connection) that modulates the amount of output signal passed from one node (PE) down the connection to the adjacent node. For simplicity, the dual role of connections will be employed. A connection both defines the information flow through the network and modulates the amount of information passing between to PEs.

The connection weights are adjusted during a learning process that captures information. Connection weights that are positive-valued are *excitatory* connections. Those with negative values are *inhibitory* connections. A connection weight that has a zero value is the same as not having a connection present. By allowing only a subset of all the possible connections to have nonzero values, sparse connectivity between PEs can be simulated.

It is often desirable for a PE to have an internal bias value (threshold value). Part (a) of Fig. 3 shows the PE y_j with three connections from F_X $\{w_1, w_2, w_3\}$ and a bias value Θ_j. It is convenient to consider this bias value as an extra connection w_0 emanating from the F_X PE x_0, with the added constraint that x_0 is always equal to 1, as shown in part (b). This mathematically equivalent representation simplifies many discussions. Throughout the paper this method of representing the bias (threshold) values will be intrinsically employed.

3.4. *Processing Elements*

The PE is the portion of the neural network where all the computing is performed. Figure 3 illustrates the most com-

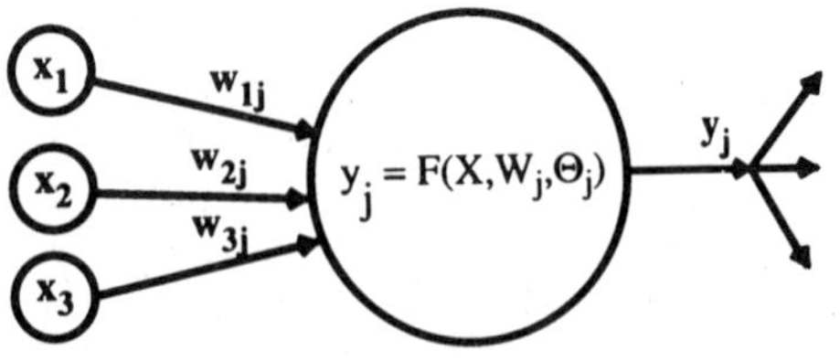

(a)

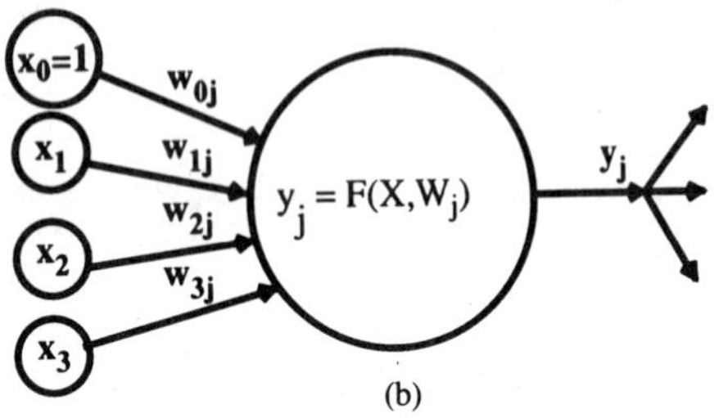

(b)

Fig. 3.

mon type of PE. A PE can have one input connection, as is the case when the PE is an input-layer PE and it receives only one value from the corresponding component of the input pattern, or it can have several weighted connections, as is the case of the F_Y PEs shown in Fig. 2, where there is a connection from every F_X PE to each F_Y PE. Each PE collects the information that has been sent down its abutting connections and produces a single output value. There are two important qualities that a PE must possess:

1. PEs require only local information. All the information necessary for a PE to produce an output value is present at the inputs and resides within the PE. No other information about other values in the network is required.
2. PEs produce only one output value. This single output value is propagated down the connections from the emitting PE to other receiving PEs, or it will serve as an output from the network.

These two qualities allow neural networks to operate in parallel. As was done with the connections, the value of the PE and its label are referred to synonymously. For example, the jth F_Y PE in Fig. 2 is y_j, and the value of that PE is also y_j.

There are several mechanisms for computing the output of a processing element. The output value of the PE shown in Fig. 3(b), y_j, is a function of the outputs of the preceding layer, $F_X = X = (x_1, x_2, \cdots, x_n)$ and the weights from F_X to y_j, $W_j = (w_{1j}, w_{2j}, \cdots, w_{nj})$. Mathematically, the output of this PE is a function of its inputs and its weights,

$$y_j = F(X, W_j). \tag{1}$$

Three examples of update functions follow.

3.4.1. Linear Combination. The most common computation performed by a PE is a linear combination (dot product) of the input values X with the abutting connection weights W_j, possibly followed by a nonlinear operation (cf. Simpson, 1990a; Hecht-Nielsen, 1990; Maren, Harston, and Pap, 1990). For the PE in Fig. 3(b), the output y_j is computed from the equation

$$y_j = f\left(\sum_{i=0}^{n} x_i w_{ij}\right) = f(X \cdot W_j) \tag{2}$$

where $W_j = (w_{1j}, w_{2j}, \cdots, w_{nj})$ and f is one of the nonlinear PE functions described in Section 3.4. The dot product update has a very appealing quality that is intrinsic to its computation. Using the relationship $A_k \cdot W_j = \cos(A_k, W_j)/\|A_k\|\,\|W_j\|$, one sees that the larger the dot product (assuming fixed length A_k and W_j), the more similar are the two vectors. Hence, the dot product can be viewed as a similarity measure.

3.4.2. Mean-Variance Connections. In some instances a PE will have two connections interconnecting PEs instead of just one, as shown in Fig. 4. One use of these dual connections is to allow one set of the abutting connections to represent the mean of a class and the other, the variance of the class (Lee and Kil, 1989; Robinson, Niranjan, and Fallside, 1988). In this case, the output value of the PE depends on the inputs and both sets of connections; that is, $y_j = F(X, V_j, W_j)$, where the mean connections are represented by $W_j = (w_{1j}, w_{2j}, \cdots, w_{nj})$ and the variance connections $V_j = (v_{1j}, v_{2j}, \cdots, v_{nj})$ for the PE y_j. With this scheme, the output of y_j is calculating the difference between the input X and the mean W_j, divided by the variance V_j, squaring the resulting quantity, and passing this value through a Gaussian nonlinear PE function to produce the final output value as follows:

$$y_j = g\left(\sum_{i=1}^{n}\left(\frac{w_{ij} - x_i}{v_{ij}}\right)^2\right) \tag{3}$$

where the Gaussian nonlinear PE function is

$$g(x) = \exp\left(\frac{-x^2}{2}\right) \tag{4}$$

Note that it is possible to remove one of the two connections in a mean-variance network, if the variance is known and

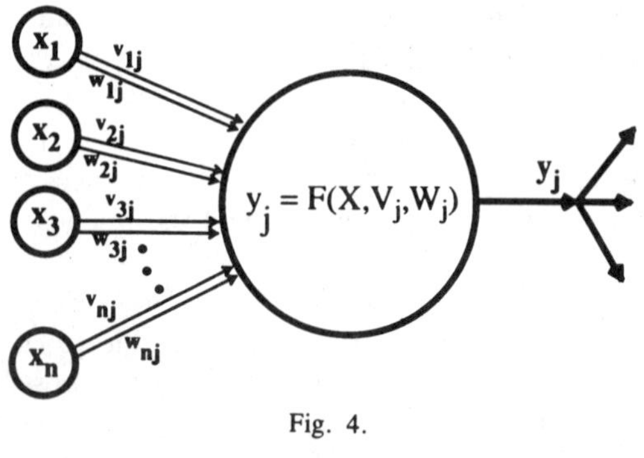

Fig. 4.

stationary, by dividing by the variance prior to neural network processing. Section 3.5.5 describes the Gaussian nonlinear PE function in greater detail.

3.4.3. Min–Max Connections. Another less common use of dual connections is to assign one of the abutting vectors, say V_j, to become the minimum bound for the class and the other vector, W_j, to become the maximum bound for the same class. Measuring the amount of the input pattern that falls within the bounds produces a min–max activation value (Simpson, 1991a). Figure 5 illustrates this notion by a graph representation for the min and the max points. The ordinate of the graph represents the value of each element of the min and max vectors, and the abscissa of the graph represents the dimensionality of the classification space. The input pattern X is compared with the bounds of the class. The amount of disagreement between the class bounds, V_j and W_j, and X is shown in the shaded regions. The measure of these shaded regions produces an activation value y_j.

Referring once again to Fig. 5, note that the max bound W_j is the maximum point allowed in class j and the min bound V_j is the minimum point allowed in class j. Measuring the degree to which X does not fall between V_j and W_j is done by measuring the relative amount of X that falls outside class j. One measure that was proposed (Simpson, 1990c) used Kosko's (1990a) fuzzy subsethood measures, which resulted in the equation

$$y_j = (1 - \text{supersethood}(X, W_j))(1 - \text{subsethood}(X, V_j)) \tag{5}$$

When $y_j = 1$, X lies completely within the min–max bounds. When $y_j = 0$, X falls completely outside of the min–max bounds. When $0 < y_j < 1$, the value describes the degree to which X is contained by the min–max bounds. Although this is only one of many possible equations (cf. (59) and (60)), it does illustrate the use of min–max connections.

3.5. PE Functions

PE functions, also referred to as activation functions or squashing functions, map a PE's (possibly) infinite domain to a prespecified range. Although the number of PE functions possible is infinite, five are regularly employed by the majority of neural networks:

1. Linear PE function
2. Step PE function
3. Ramp PE function
4. Sigmoid PE function
5. Gaussian PE function

With the exception of the linear PE function, all of these functions introduce a nonlinearity in the network dynamics by bounding the output values within a fixed range. Each PE function is briefly described and shown in parts (a)–(e) of Fig. 6.

3.5.1. Linear PE Function. The linear PE function (see Fig. 6(a)) produces a linearly modulated output from the input x as described by the equation

$$f(x) = \alpha x \tag{6}$$

where x ranges over the real numbers and α is a positive scalar. If $\alpha = 1$, it is equivalent to removing the PE function completely.

3.5.2 Step PE Function. The step PE function (see Fig. 6(b)) produces only two values, β and δ. If the input to the PE function x equals or exceeds a predefined value θ, then the step PE function produces the value β; otherwise it produces the value $-\delta$, where β and δ are positive scalars. Mathematically this function is described as

$$f(x) = \begin{cases} \beta & \text{if } x \geq \theta \\ -\delta & \text{if } x < \theta \end{cases} \tag{7}$$

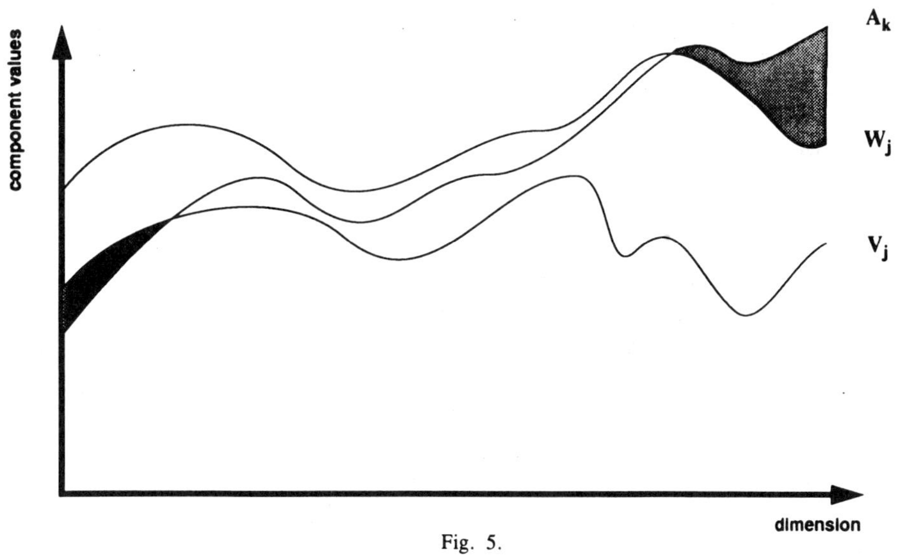

Fig. 5.

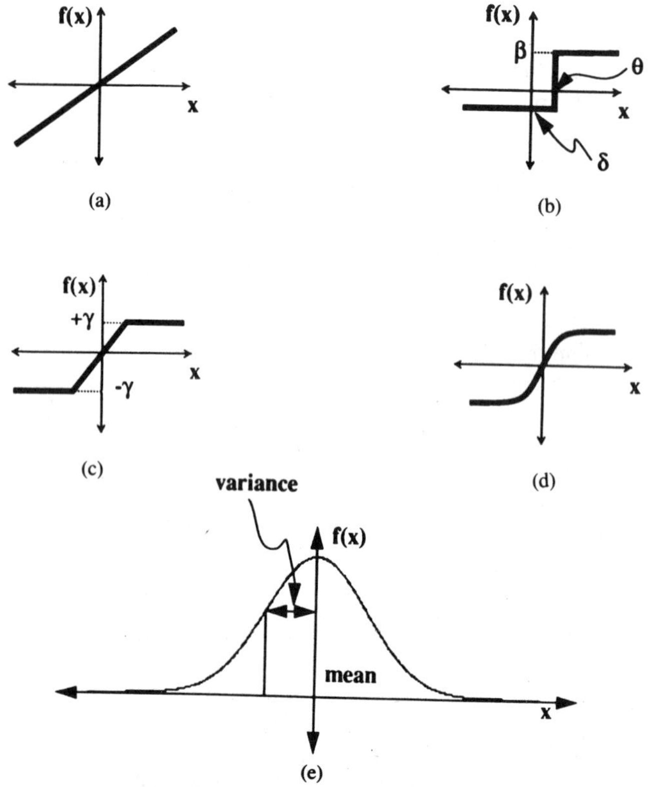

Fig. 6.

Typically, the step PE function produces a binary value in response to the sign of the input, emitting +1 if x is positive and 0 if it is not. For the assignments $\beta = 1$, $\delta = 0$, and $\theta = 0$, the step PE function becomes the binary step function

$$f(x) = \begin{cases} 1 & \text{if } x \geq 0 \\ 0 & \text{otherwise} \end{cases} \tag{8}$$

which is common to neural networks such as the Hopfield neural network (Amari, 1972; Hopfield, 1982) and the bidirectional associative memory (Kosko, 1988). One small variation of (8) is the bipolar PE function

$$f(x) = \begin{cases} 1 & \text{if } x \geq 0 \\ -1 & \text{otherwise} \end{cases} \tag{9}$$

which replaces the 0 output value with a -1. In punish–reward systems such as the associative reward–penalty (Barto, 1985), the negative value is used to ensure changes, whereas a 0 will not.

3.5.3. Ramp PE Function. The ramp PE function (see Fig. 6(c)) is a combination of the linear and step PE functions. The ramp PE function places upper and lower bounds on the values that the PE function produces and allows a linear response between the bounds. These saturation points are symmetric around the origin and are discontinuous at the points of saturation. The ramp PE function is defined as

$$f(x) = \begin{cases} \gamma & \text{if } x \geq \gamma \\ x & \text{if } |x| < \gamma \\ -\gamma & \text{if } x \leq -\gamma \end{cases} \tag{10}$$

where γ is the saturation value for the function, and the points $x = \gamma$ and $x = -\gamma$ are where the discontinuities in f exist.

3.5.4. Sigmoid PE Function. The sigmoid PE function (see Fig. 6(d)) is a continuous version of the ramp PE function. The sigmoid (S-shaped) function is a bounded, monotonic, nondecreasing function that provides a graded, nonlinear response within a prespecified range.

The most common sigmoid function is the logistic function

$$f(x) = \frac{1}{1 + e^{-\alpha x}} \tag{11}$$

where $\alpha > 0$ (usually $\alpha = 1$), which provides an output value from 0 to 1. This function is familiar in statistics (as the Gaussian distribution function), chemistry (describing catalytic reactions), and sociology (describing human population growth). Note that a relationship between (11) and (8) exists. When $\alpha = \infty$ in (11), the slope of the sigmoid function between 0 and 1 becomes infinitely steep and, in effect, becomes the step function described by (8).

Two alternatives to the logistic sigmoid function are the hyperbolic tangent

$$f(x) = \tanh(x) \tag{12}$$

which ranges from -1 to 1, and the augmented ratio of squares

$$f(x) = \begin{cases} \dfrac{x^2}{1 + x^2} & \text{if } x > 0 \\ 0 & \text{otherwise} \end{cases} \tag{13}$$

which ranges from 0 to 1.

3.5.5. Gaussian PE Function. The Gaussian PE function (see Fig. 6(e)) is a radial function (symmetric about the origin) that requires a variance value $v > 0$ to shape the Gaussian function. In some networks the Gaussian function is used in conjunction with a dual set of connections as described by (3), and in other instances (Specht, 1990) the variance is predefined. In the latter instance, the PE function is

$$f(x) = \exp(-x^2/v) \tag{14}$$

where x is the mean and v is the predefined variance.

4. Neural Network Topologies

The building blocks for neural networks are in place. Neural network topologies now evolve from the patterns, PEs, connections, and PE functions that have been described. Neural networks consist of layer(s) of PEs interconnected by weighted connections. The arrangement of the PEs, connections, and patterns into a neural network is referred to as a topology. After introducing some terminology, we describe six common neural network topologies.

4.1. Terminology

4.1.1. Layers. Neural networks are organized into layers of PEs. Within a layer, PEs are similar in two respects: 1) The connections that feed the layer of PEs are from the same source: for example, the PEs in the F_X layer in Fig. 2 all receive their inputs from the input pattern and the PEs in the layer F_Y all receive their inputs from the F_X PEs. 2) The PEs in each layer utilize the same type of update dynamics; for example, all the PEs will use the same type of connections and the same type of PE function.

4.1.2. Intralayer versus Interlayer Connections. There are two types of connections that a neural network employs: intralayer connections and interlayer connections. Intralayer connections (*intra* is Latin for "within") are connections between PEs in the same layer. Interlayer connections (*inter* is Latin for "among") are connections between PEs in different layers. It is possible to have neural networks that consist of one, or both, types of connections.

4.1.3 Feedforward versus Feedback Networks. When a neural network has connections that feed information in only one direction (e.g., input to output) without any feedback pathways in the network, it is a feedforward neural network. If the network has any feedback paths, where feedback is defined as any path through the network that would allow the same PE to be visited twice, then it is a feedback network.

4.2. Instars, Outstars, and the ADALINE

The two simplest neural networks are the instar and the outstar (Grossberg, 1982). The instar (see Fig. 7(a)) is the minimal pattern-encoding network. A simple example of an encoding procedure for the instar would take the pattern $A_k = (a_{k1}, a_{k2}, \cdots, a_{kn})$, normalize it, and use the values as the weights $W_j = (w_{1j}, w_{2j}, \cdots, w_{nj})$, as shown by the equation

$$v_{ij} = \frac{a_{ki}}{\sum_{i=1}^{n} a_{ki}} \tag{15}$$

for all $i = 1, 2, \cdots, n$.

The dual of the instar is the outstar (see Fig. 7(b)). The outstar is the minimal pattern recall neural network. An output pattern is generated from the outstar by using the equation

$$z_i = y_j w_{ji} \tag{16}$$

for all $i = 1, 2, \cdots, p$, where the weights are determined from (15) or one of the learning algorithms described in Section 5.

The ADALINE (ADAptive LInear NEuron, Widrow and Hoff, 1960) has the same topology as the instar (See Fig. 7(a)), but the weights V_j are adjusted by using the least-mean-square (LMS) algorithm (see Section 5.7.1). In the framework of adaptive signal processing, a similar topology with the same functionality is referred to as a finite impulse response (FIR) filter (Widrow and Stearns, 1985). Applications of the FIR filter to noise cancellation, echo cancellation, adaptive antennas, and control are numerous (Widrow and Winter, 1988).

4.3. Single-Layer Networks: Autoassociation, Optimization, and Contrast Enhancement

Beyond the instar/outstar neural networks, the minimal neural networks are the single-layer intraconnected neural networks. Figure 8 shows the topology of a one-layer neural network that consists of n F_X PEs. The connections are from each F_X PE to every other F_X PE, yielding a connection matrix with n^2 entries. The single-layer neural network accepts an n-dimensional input pattern in one of three ways:

1. PE initialization only—the input pattern is used to initialize the F_X PEs, and the input pattern does not influence the processing thereafter.
2. PE initialization and constant bias—the input pattern is used to initialize the F_X PEs, and the input remains as a constant valued-input bias throughout processing.
3. Constant bias only—the PEs are initialized to all zeroes, and the input pattern acts as a constant valued bias throughout processing.

One-layer neural networks are used to perform four types of pattern processing: pattern completion, noise removal, optimization, and contrast enhancement. The first two opera-

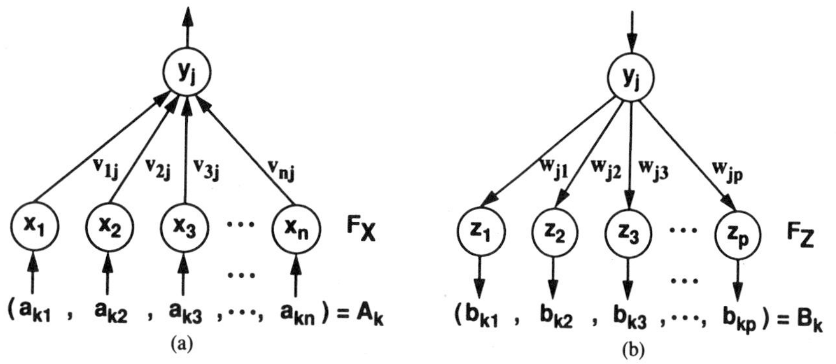

Fig. 7.

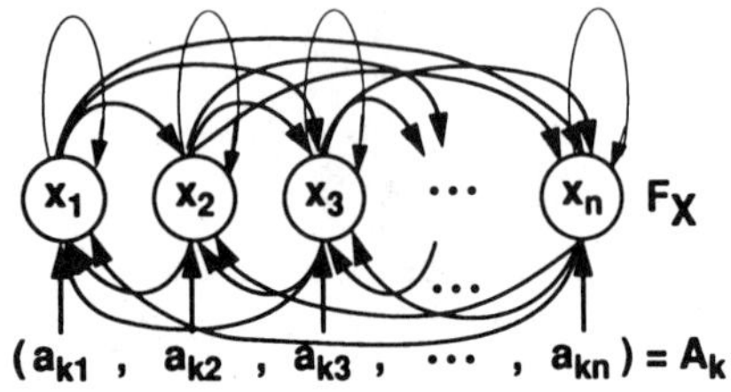

Fig. 8.

tions are performed by autoassociatively encoding patterns and (typically) using the input pattern for PE initialization only. The optimization networks are dynamical systems that stabilize to a state that represents a solution to an optimization problem and (typically) utilizes the inputs for both PE initialization and as constant biases. Contrast enhancement networks use the input patterns for PE initialization only and can operate in such a way that eventually only one PE remains active. Each of these one-layer neural networks is described in greater detail in the following paragraphs.

4.3.1. Pattern Completion. Pattern complction in a single-layer neural network is performed by presenting a partial pattern initially, and relying upon the neural network to complete the remaining portions. For example, assume a single-layer neural network has stored images of human faces. If half of a face is presented to the neural network as the initial state of the network, the neural network would complete the missing half of the face and output a complete face.

4.3.2. Noise Removal. Noise cancellation is similar to pattern completion in that a complete, noise-free response is desired from a pattern corrupted by noise. Fundamentally there is no difference between noise removal and pattern completion. The difference tends to be entirely operational. For the previous image-storage example, if a blurry or splotchy image is presented to the neural network, the output would be a crisp, clear image. Single-layer neural networks designed for pattern completion and noise cancellation include the discrete Hopfield network (Hopfield, 1982), the brain-state-in-a-box (Anderson et al., 1977), and the optimal linear associative memory (Kohonen, 1984).

4.3.3. Neural Optimization. One of the most prevalent uses of neural networks is neural optimization (Hopfield and Tank, 1985; Tank and Hopfield, 1986). Optimization is a technique for solving a problem by casting it into a mathematical equation that, when either maximized or minimized, solves the problem. Typical examples of problems approached by an optimization technique include scheduling, routing, and resource allocation. The neural optimization approach casts the optimization problem into the form of an energy function that describes the dynamics of a neural system. If the neural network dynamics are such that the network will always seek a stable state when the energy function is at a minimum, then the network will automatically find a solution. The inputs to the neural network are the initial state of the neural networks, and the final PE values represent the parameters of a solution.

4.3.4. Contrast Enhancement. Contrast enhancement in single-layer neural networks is achieved using on-center/off-surround connection values. The on-center connections are positive self-connections (i.e., $w_{ii} = \alpha (\alpha > 0)$ for all $i = 1, 2, \cdots, n$) that allow a pattern's activation value to grow by feeding back upon themselves. The off-surround connections are negative neighbor connections (i.e., $w_{ij} = -\beta$ $(\beta > 0)$ for all i not equal to j) that compete with the on-center connections. The competition between the positive on-center and the negative off-surround activation values are referred to as competitive dynamics. Contrast-enhancement neural networks take one of two forms: locally connected and globally connected. If the connections between the F_X PEs are only connected to a few of the neighboring PEs (see Fig. 9(a)), the result is a local competition that can result in several large activation values. If the off-surround connections are fully interconnected across the F_X layer (see Fig. 9(b)), the competition will yield a single winner.

4.4. *Two-Layer Networks: Heteroassociation and Classification*

Two-layer neural networks consist of a layer of n F_X PEs fully interconnected to a layer of p F_Y PEs, as shown in Fig. 10. The connections from the F_X to F_Y PEs form the $n \times p$ weight matrix W, where the entry w_{ij} represents the weight for the connection from the ith F_X PE, x_i, to the jth F_Y PE, y_j. There are three common types of two-layer neural networks: feedforward pattern matchers, feedback pattern matchers, and feedforward pattern classifiers.

4.4.1. Feedforward Pattern Matching. A two-layer feedforward pattern-matching neural network maps the input patterns A_k to the corresponding output patterns B_k, $k = 1, 2, \cdots, m$. The network in Fig. 10(a) illustrates the topology of this feedforward network. The two-layer feedforward neural network accepts the input pattern A_k and produces an output pattern $Y = (y_1, y_2, \cdots, y_p)$, which is the network's best estimate of the proper output, given A_k as the input. An optimal mapping between the inputs and the outputs is one that produces the correct response B_k when A_k is presented to the network, $k = 1, 2, \cdots, m$.

Most two-layer networks are concerned with finding the optimal linear mapping between the pattern pairs (A_k, B_k) (cf. Widrow and Winter, 1988; Kohonen, 1984), but there are other two-layer feedforward networks that also work with nonlinear mappings by extending the input patterns to include multiplicative combinations of the original inputs (Pao, 1989; Maren, Harsten, and Pap, 1990).

4.4.2. Feedback Pattern Matching. A two-layer feedback pattern-matching neural network, shown in Fig. 10(b), accepts inputs from either layer of the network, either the F_X or F_Y layer, and produces the output for the other layer (Kosko, 1988; Simpson, 1990a and b).

4.4.3. Feedforward Pattern Classification. A two-layer pattern classification neural network, shown in Fig. 10(c), maps an input pattern A_k to one of p classes. Representing

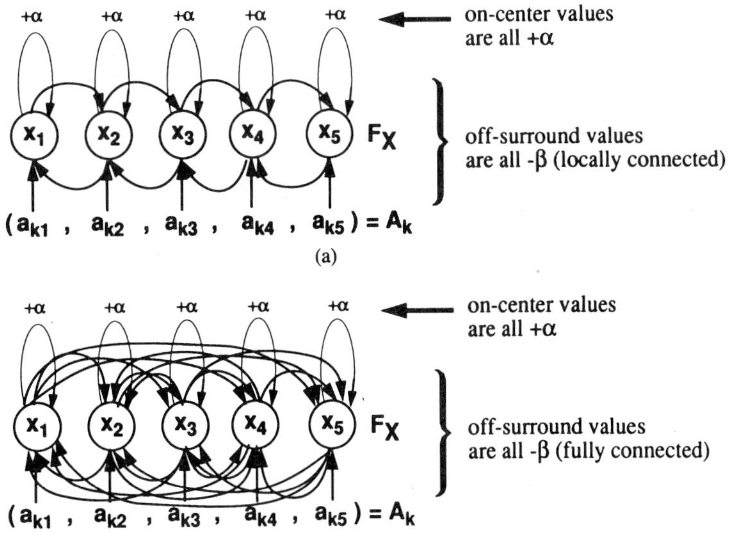

Fig. 9.

each class as a separate F_Y PE reduces the pattern classification task to selecting the F_Y PE that best responds to the input pattern. Most two-layer pattern classification systems utilize the competitive dynamics of global on-center/off-surround connections to perform the classification.

4.5. Multilayer Networks: Heteroassociation and Function Approximation

A multilayer neural network has more than two layers, possibly many more. A general description of a multilayer neural network is shown in Fig. 11, where there is an input layer of PEs, F_X, L hidden layers of F_Y PEs (Y_1, $Y_2, \cdots, Y_L$), and a final output layer, F_Z. The F_Y layers are called hidden layers because there are no direct connections between the input/output patterns to these PEs, rather they are always accessed through another set of PEs such as the input and output PEs. Although Fig. 11 shows connections only from one layer to the next, it is possible to have connections that skip over layers, that connect the input PEs to the output PEs, or that connect PEs together within the same layer. The added benefit of these PEs is not fully understood, but many applications are employing these types of topologies.

Multilayer neural networks are used for pattern classification, pattern matching, and function approximation. By adding a continuously differentiable PE function, such as a Gaussian or sigmoid function, it is possible for the network to learn practically any nonlinear mapping to any desired degree of accuracy (White, 1989).

The mechanism that allows such complex mappings to be acquired is not fully understood for each type of multilayer neural network, but in general the network partitions the input space into regions, and a mapping from the partitioned regions to the next space is performed by the next set of connections to the next layer of PEs, eventually producing an output response. This capability allows some very complex decision regions to be performed for classification and pattern-matching problems, as well as applications that require function approximation.

Several issues must be addressed when working with multilayer neural networks. How many layers are enough for a given problem? How many PEs are needed in each hidden layer? How much data is needed to produce a sufficient

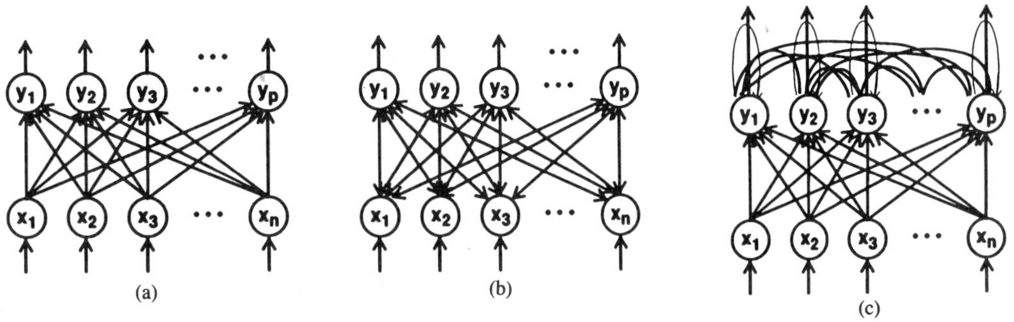

Fig. 10.

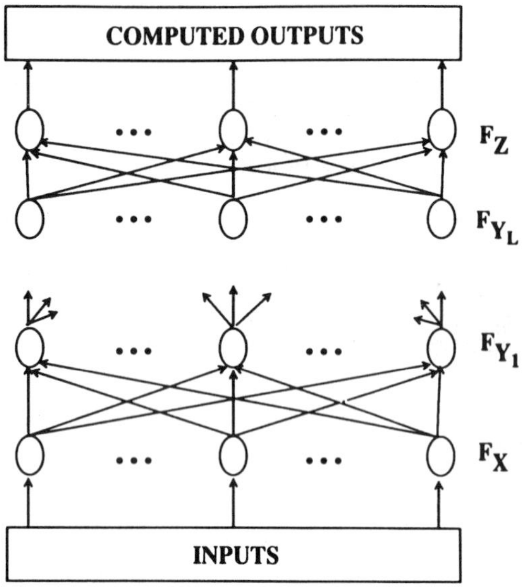

Fig. 11.

mapping from the input layer to the output layer? Some of these issues have been dealt with successfully. As an example, several researchers have proven that three layers are sufficient to perform any nonlinear mapping (with the exception of a few remote pathological cases) to any desired degree of accuracy with only one layer of hidden PEs (see White, 1989, for a review of this work). Although this is a very important result, it still does not indicate the proper number of hidden-layer PEs, or if the same solution can be obtained with more layers but fewer hidden PEs and connections overall.

There are several ways that multilayer neural networks can have their connection weights adjusted to learn mappings. The most popular technique is the backpropagation algorithm (Werbos, 1974; Parker, 1982; Rumelhart, Hinton, and Williams, 1986) and its many variants (see Simpson, 1990a for a list). Other multilayer networks include the neocognitron (Fukushima, 1988), the probabilistic neural network (Specht, 1990), the Boltzmann machine (Ackley, Hinton, and Sejnowski, 1985), and the Cauchy machine (Szu, 1986).

4.6. Randomly Connected Networks

Randomly connected neural networks are networks that have connection weights that are randomly assigned within a specific range. Some randomly connected networks have binary-valued connections. Realizing that a connection weight equal to zero is equivalent to no connection being present, binary-valued random connections create sparsely connected networks. Randomly connected networks are used in three ways:

1. Initial weights—The initial connection values for the network prior to training are preset to random values within a predefined range. This technique is used extensively in error-correction learning systems (see Sections 5.5–5.6).
2. Pattern preprocessing—A set of fixed random binary-valued connections are placed between the first two layers of a multilayer neural network as a pattern preprocessor. Such random connections can be used to increase the dimensionality of the space that is being used for mappings in an effort to improve the pattern-mapping capability. This approach was pioneered with the early Perceptron (Rosenblatt, 1962) and has been used recently in the sparse distributed memory (Kanerva, 1988).
3. Intelligence from randomness—Early studies in neural networks exerted a great deal of effort analyzing randomly connected binary-valued systems. The model of the brain as a randomly connected network of neurons prompted this research. These fixed-weight, nonadaptive systems have been studied extensively by Amari (1971) and Rozonoer (1969).

5. Neural Network Learning

Arguably the most appealing quality of neural networks is their ability to learn. Learning, in this context, is defined as a change in connection weight values that results in the capture of information that can later be recalled. Several procedures are available for changing the values of connection weights. After an introduction to some terminology, eight learning methods will be described. For continuity of discussion, the learning algorithms will be described in pointwise notation (as opposed to vector notation). In addition, the learning algorithms will be described with discrete-time equations (as opposed to continuous-time). Discrete-time equations are more accessible to digital computer simulations.

5.1. Terminology

5.1.1. Supervised versus Unsupervised Learning. All learning methods can be classified into two categories: supervised learning and unsupervised learning. Supervised learning is a process that incorporates an external teacher and/or global information. The supervised learning algorithms discussed in the following sections include error correction learning, reinforcement learning, stochastic learning, and hardwired systems. Examples of supervised learning include deciding when to turn off the learning, deciding how long and how often to present each association for training, and supplying performance (error) information. Supervised learning is further classified into two subcategories: structural learning and temporal learning. Structural learning is concerned with finding the best possible input/output relationship for each individual pattern pair. Examples of structural learning include pattern matching and pattern classification. The majority of the learning algorithms discussed on the following pages focus on structural learning. Temporal learning is concerned with capturing a sequence of patterns necessary to achieve some final outcome. In temporal learning, the current response of the network is dependent on previous inputs and responses. In structural learning, there is no such dependence. Examples of temporal learning include prediction and control. The reinforcement learning algorithm to be discussed is an example of a temporal learning procedure.

Unsupervised learning, also referred to as self-organization, is a process that incorporates no external teacher and relies upon only local information during the entire learning process. Unsupervised learning organizes presented data and discovers its emergent collective properties. Examples of unsupervised learning in the following sections include Hebbian learning, principal component learning, differential Hebbian learning, min–max learning, and competitive learning.

5.1.2. Off-line versus On-line Learning. Most learning techniques utilize off-line learning. When the entire pattern set is used to condition the connections prior to the use of the network, it is called off-line learning. For example, the backpropagation training algorithm (see Section 5.7.2) is used to adjust connections in multilayer neural network, but it requires thousands of cycles through all the pattern pairs until the desired performance of the network has been achieved. Once the network is performing adequately, the weights are frozen and the resulting network is used in recall mode thereafter. Off-line learning systems have the intrinsic requirement that all the patterns have to be resident for training. Such a requirement does not make it possible to have new patterns automatically incorporated into the network as they occur; rather these new patterns must be added to the entire set of patterns and a retraining of the neural network must be done.

Not all neural networks perform off-line learning. Some networks can add new information "on the fly" nondestructively. If a new pattern needs to be incorporated into the network's connections, it can be done immediately without any loss of prior stored information. The advantage of off-line learning networks is they usually provide superior solutions to difficult problems such as nonlinear classification, but on-line learning allows the neural network to learn in situ. A challenge in the future of neural-network computing is the development of learning techniques that provide high-performance on-line learning without extreme costs.

5.2. Hebbian Correlations

The simplest form of adjusting connection-weight values in a neural network is based upon the correlation of PE activation values. The motivation for correlation-based adjustments has been attributed to Donald O. Hebb (1949), who hypothesized that the change in a synapses' efficacy (its ability to fire or, as we are simulating it in our neural networks, the connection weight) is prompted by a neuron's ability to produce an output signal. If a neuron A was active and A's activity caused a connected neuron B to fire, then the efficacy of the synaptic connection between A and B should be increased.

5.2.1. Unbounded PE Values and Weights. This form of learning, now commonly referred to as Hebbian learning, has been mathematically characterized as the correlation weight adjustment

$$w_{ij}^{\text{new}} = w_{ij}^{\text{old}} + a_{ki} b_{kj} \tag{17}$$

where $i = 1, 2, \cdots, n$, $j = 1, 2, \cdots, p$; x_i is the value of the ith PE in the F_X layer of a two-layer network; y_j is the value of the jth F_Y PE; and the connection weight between the two PEs is w_{ij}. In general, the values of the PEs can range over the real numbers, and the weights are unbounded. When the PE values and connection values are unbounded, these two-layer neural networks are amenable to linear systems theory. Neural networks like the linear associative memory (Anderson, 1970; Kohonen, 1972) employ this type of learning and analyze the capabilities of these networks with linear systems theory as a guide. The number of patterns that a network trained using (17) with unbounded weights and connections can produce is limited to the dimensionality of the input patterns (cf. Simpson, 1990a).

5.2.2. Bounded PE Values and Unbounded Weights. Recently, implementations that restrict the values of the PEs and/or the weights of (17) have been employed. These networks (called Hopfield networks because John Hopfield had excited people about their potential (Hopfield, 1982)), restrict the PE values to either binary $\{0, 1\}$ or bipolar $\{-1, +1\}$ values. Equation (17) is used for these types of correlations.

These discrete-valued networks typically involve some form of feedback recall, resulting in the need to show that every input will produce a stable response (output). Limiting the PE values during processing introduces nonlinearities in the system, eliminating some of the linear systems theory analyses that had previously been performed. Adding feedback into the recall process forms a discrete-valued, nonlinear, dynamical system. The single-layer versions of this learning rule are described as Hopfield nets (Hopfield, 1982), and two-layer versions as the bidirectional associative memory (Kosko, 1988). Some of the earlier analysis of these networks was performed by Amari (1972, 1977), who used the theory of statistical neurodynamics to show these networks were stable. Later, Hopfield (1982) found an alternative method to prove stability. Also, the number of patterns that neural networks of this form can store is limited (McEleice et al., 1987).

5.2.3. Bounded PE Values and Weights. Sometimes both the PE values and the weights are bounded. There are two forms of such systems. The first form is simply a running average of the amount of correlation between two PEs. The equation

$$w_{ij}^{\text{new}} = \frac{1}{k}\left(a_{ki} b_{kj} + (k-1) w_{ij}^{\text{old}}\right) \tag{18}$$

describes the average correlation during the presentation of the kth pattern pair (A_k, B_k), where $A_k = (a_{k1}, a_{k2}, \cdots, a_{kn})$; $B_k = (b_{k1}, b_{k2}, \cdots, b_{kp})$; and k is the current pattern number, $k = 1, 2, \cdots, m$. The same information that was stored using (17) is stored using (18), the connection weights being simply bounded to the unit interval in the latter case.

The other example of the correlation neural network learning equation with bounded PE values and bounded weights is the sparse encoding equation, defined

$$w_{ij}^{new} = \begin{cases} 1 & \text{if } a_{ki}b_{kj} = 1 \\ 1 & \text{if } w_{ij}^{old} = 1 \\ 0 & \text{otherwise} \end{cases} \quad (19)$$

This equation assigns a binary value to a connection if the PEs on each end of the connection have both had the value of 1 over the course of learning. The learning equation is equivalent to performing the logic operation

$$w_{ij}^{new} = (a_{ki} \cap b_{kj}) \cup w_{ij}^{old} \quad (20)$$

where $\cap$ and $\cup$ are the intersection and union operations, respectively.

Neural networks that have utilized this form of learning include the Learnmatrix (Steinbuch and Piske, 1963) and the Willshaw associative memory (Willshaw, 1980). This learning equation had a great deal of potential. Through the encoding of information in a binary vector (say, for example, only 32 components out of 1 million were set to 1, the others being set to 0), it is possible to store a tremendous amount of information in the network. The problem lies in creating the code necessary to perform such dense storage (cf. Hecht-Nielsen, 1990).

5.3. Principal Component Learning

Some neural networks have learning algorithms designed to produce, as a set of weights, the principal components of the input data patterns. The principal components of a set of data are found by first forming the covariance (or correlation) matrix of a set of patterns and then finding the minimal set of orthogonal vectors that span the space of the covariance matrix. Once the basis set has been found, it is possible to reconstruct any vector in the space with a linear combination of the basis vectors. The value of each scalar in the linear combination represents the "importance" of that basis vector (Lawley and Maxwell, 1963). It is possible to think of the basis vectors as feature vectors, and the combination of these feature vectors is used to construct patterns. Hence, the purpose of a principal component network is to decompose an input pattern into values that represent the relative importance of the features underlying the patterns.

The first work with principal component learning was done by Oja (1982), who reasoned that Hebbian learning with a feedback term that automatically constrained the weights would extract the principal components from the input data. The equation Oja uses is

$$w_{ij}^{new} = w_{ij}^{old} + b_{kj}(\alpha a_{ki} - \beta b_{kj} w_{ij}^{old}) \quad (21)$$

where a_{ki} is the ith component of the kth input pattern A_k, $i = 1, 2, \cdots, n$; b_{kj} is the jth component of the kth output pattern B_k, $j = 1, 2, \cdots, p$; $k = 1, 2, \cdots, m$; and α and β are nonzero constants.

A variant of the work by Oja has been developed by Sanger (1989) and is described by the equation

$$w_{ij}^{new} = w_{ij}^{old} + \gamma_k \left(a_{ki}b_{kj} - b_{kj} \sum_{h=1}^{i} y_h w_{jh} \right) \quad (22)$$

where the variables are similar to those of (21) with the exception of the nonzero, time-decreasing learning parameter γ_k. Equations (21) and (22) are very similar; the key difference is that (22) includes more information in the feedback term and uses a decaying learning rate. There have been many analyses and applications of principal component networks. For a review of this work, see Oja (1989). It should be noted that both Oja's and Sanger's principal component networks only extract the first "one" principal component, and they are limited to networks with linear PEs.

5.4. Differential Hebbian Learning

Hebbian learning has been extended to capture the temporal changes that occur in pattern sequences. This learning law, called differential Hebbian learning, has been independently derived by Klopf (1986) in the discrete-time form, and by Kosko (1986b) in the continuous-time form. The general form, some variants, and some similar learning laws are outlined in the following sections. Several other combinations have been explored beyond those presented here. A more thorough examination of these Hebbian learning rules and others can be found in Barto (1984) and Tesauro (1986).

5.4.1. Basic Differential Hebbian Learning. Differential Hebbian learning correlates the changes in PE activation values with the equation

$$w_{ij}(t+1) = w_{ij}(t) + \Delta x_i(t) + \Delta y_j(t-1) \quad (23)$$

where $\Delta x_i(t) = x_i(t) - x_i(t-1)$ is the amount of change in the ith F_X PE at time t, and $\Delta y_j(t-1) = y_j(t-1) - y_j(t-2)$ is the amount of change in the jth F_Y PE at time $t-1$.

5.4.2. Drive-Reinforcement Learning. Klopf (1986) uses the more general case of (23) that captures changes in F_X PEs over the last k time steps and modulates each change by the corresponding weight value for the connection in a two-layer neural network. Klopf's equation is

$$w_{ij}(t+1) = w_{ij}(t) + \Delta y_j \sum_{h=1}^{k} \cdot \alpha(t-h) \, | w_{ij}(t-h) | \, \Delta x_i(t-h) \quad (24)$$

where $\alpha(t-h)$ is a decreasing function of time that regulates the amount of change, and $w_{ij}(t)$ is the connection value from the x_i to y_j at time t. Klopf refers to the presynaptic changes $\Delta x_i(t-h)$, $h = 1, 2, \cdots, k$, as drives and to the postsynaptic change $\Delta y_j(t)$ as the reinforcement; hence the name drive-reinforcement learning.

5.4.3. Covariance Correlation. Sejnowski (1977) has proposed the covariance correlation of PE activation values in a two-layer neural network using the equation

$$w_{ij}^{\text{new}} = w_{ij}^{\text{old}} + \mu[(a_{ki} - \bar{x}_i)(b_{kj} - \bar{y}_j)] \qquad (25)$$

where the bracketed terms represent the covariance, the difference between the expected (average) value of the PE activation values (x_i and y_j) and the input and output pattern values (a_{ki} and b_{kj}), respectively. The parameter $0 < \mu < 1$ is the learning rate. The overbar on the PE values represents the average value of the PE.

Sutton and Barto (1981) have proposed a similar type of covariance learning rule, suggesting the correlation of the expected value of x_i with the variance of y_j as expressed by the equation

$$w_{ij}^{\text{new}} = w_{ij}^{\text{old}} + \mu\bar{x}_i(b_{kj} - \bar{y}_j) \qquad (26)$$

5.5 Competitive Learning

Competitive learning, introduced by Grossberg (1970) and Malsburg (1973) and extensively studied by Amari and Takeuchi (1978), Amari (1983), and Grossberg (1982), is a method of automatically creating classes for a set of input patterns. Competitive learning is a two-step procedure that couples the recall process with the learning process in a two-layer neural network (see Fig. 12). In Fig. 12 each F_x PE represents a component of the input pattern, and each F_Y PE represents a class (see also Section 4.3.4).

Step 1: Determine winning F_Y PE. An input pattern A_k is passed through the connections from the input layer F_X to the output layer F_Y in a feedforward fashion by using the dot-product update equation

$$y_j = \sum_{i=1}^{n} x_i w_{ij} \qquad (27)$$

where x_i is the ith PE in the input layer F_X, $i = 1, 2, \cdots, n$, y_j is the jth PE in the output layer F_Y, $j = 1, 2, \cdots, p$, and w_{ij} is the value of the connection weight between x_i and y_j. Each set of connections that abut an F_B PE, say y_j, is a reference vector $W_j = (w_{1j}, w_{2j}, \cdots, w_{nj})$ representing the class j. The reference vector W_j closest to the input A_k should provide the highest activation value. If the input patterns A_k, $k = 1, 2, \cdots, m$, and the reference vectors W_j, $j = 1, 2, \cdots, p$, are normalized to Euclidean unit length, then the following relationship holds:

$$0 \leq \left(y_j = A_k \cdot W_j = \sum_{i=1}^{n} a_{ki} w_{ij} \right) \leq 1 \qquad (28)$$

where the more similar A_k is to W_j the closer the dot product is to unity (see Section 3.4.1). The dot-product values y_j are used as the initial values for winner-take-all competitive interactions (see Section 4.3.4). The result of these interactions is identical to searching the F_Y PEs and finding the PE with the largest dot-product value. Using the equation

$$y_j = \begin{cases} 1 & \text{if } y_j > y_k \text{ for all } j \neq k \\ 0 & \text{otherwise} \end{cases} \qquad (29)$$

it is possible to find the F_y PE with the highest dot-product value, called the winning PE. The reference vector associated with the winning PE is the winning reference vector.

Step 2: Adjust winning F_Y PE's connection values. In competitive learning with winner-take-all dynamics like those previously described, there is only one set of connection weights adjusted—the connection weights of the winning reference vector. The equation that automatically adjusts the winning reference vector and no others is

$$w_{ij}^{\text{new}} = w_{ij}^{\text{old}} + \alpha(t) y_j (a_{ki} - w_{ij}) \qquad (30)$$

where $\alpha(t)$ is a nonzero, decreasing function of time. The result of this operation is the motion of the reference vector toward the input vector. Over several presentations of the data vectors (on the order of $O(n^3)$ (Hertz, 1990)), the reference vectors will become the centroids of data clusters (Kohonen, 1986).

There have been several variations of this algorithm (cf. Simpson, 1990a), but one of the most important is the conscience mechanism (DeSieno, 1988). By adding a conscience to each F_Y PE , an F_Y PE is only allowed to become a winner if it has won equiprobably. The equiprobable winning constraint improves both the quality of solution and the learning time. Neural networks that employ competitive learning include self-organizing feature maps (Kohonen, 1984), adaptive resonance theory I (Carpenter and Grossberg, 1987a), and adaptive resonance theory II (Carpenter and Grossberg, 1987b).

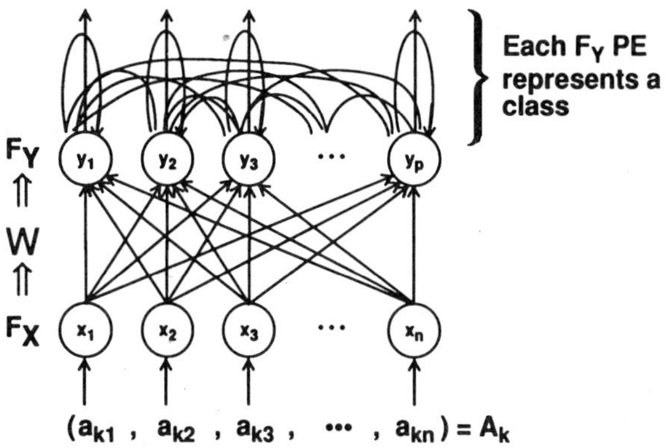

Fig. 12.

5.6. Min-Max Learning

Min-max classifier systems utilize a pair of vectors for each class (see Section 3.4.3). The class j is represented by the PE y_j and is defined by the abutting vectors V_j (the min vector) and W_j (the max vector). Learning in a min-max neural system is done with the equation

$$v_{ij}^{\text{new}} = \min\left(a_{ki}, v_{ij}^{\text{old}}\right) \tag{31}$$

for the min vector and

$$w_{ij}^{\text{new}} = \max\left(a_{ki}, w_{ij}^{\text{old}}\right) \tag{32}$$

for the max vector. The min and max points are treated as bounds for a given membership/transfer function, providing a mechanism to easily adjust and analyze classes being formed in a neural network (Simpson, 1991a and 1992).

5.7. *Error Correction Learning*

Error correction learning adjusts the connection weights between PEs in proportion to the difference between the desired and computed values of each output layer PE. Two-layer error correction learning is able to capture linear mappings between input and output patterns. Multilayer error correction learning is able to capture nonlinear mappings between the inputs and outputs. In the following two sections, each of these learning techniques will be described.

5.7.1. Two-Layer Error Correction Learning. Consider the two-layer network in Fig. 13. Assume that the weights W are initialized to small random values (see Section 4.6). The input pattern A_k is passed through the connection weights W to produce a set of F_Y PE values $Y = (y_1, y_2, \cdots, y_p)$. The difference between the computed output values Y and the desired output pattern values B_k is the error. The error for each F_Y PE is computed from the equation

$$\delta_j = b_{kj} - y_j \tag{33}$$

The error is used to adjust the connection weights by using the equation

$$w_{ij}^{\text{new}} = w_{ij}^{\text{old}} + \alpha \delta_j a_{ki} \tag{34}$$

where the positive-valued constant α is the learning rate.

The foundations for the learning rule described by (33) and (34) are solid. By realizing that the best solution can be attained when all the errors for a given pattern across all the output PEs, y_j, is minimized, we can construct the following

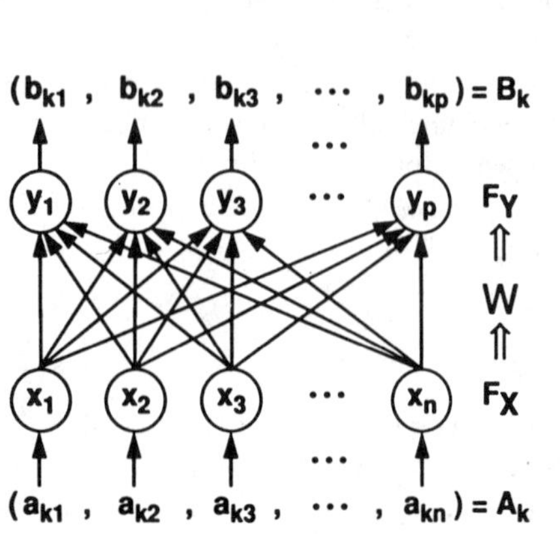

Fig. 13.

cost function:

$$E = \frac{1}{2} \sum_{j=1}^{p} \left(b_{kj} - y_j\right)^2 \tag{35}$$

When E is zero, the mapping from input to output is perfect for the given pattern. By moving in the opposite direction of the gradient of the cost function with respect to the weights, we can achieve the optimal solution (assuming each movement along the gradient α is sufficiently small). Restated mathematically, the two-layer error correction learning algorithm is computed as follows:

$$\begin{aligned} \frac{\partial E}{\partial w_{ij}} &= \frac{\partial}{\partial w_{ij}} \left[\frac{1}{2} \sum_{j=1}^{p} \left(b_{kj} - \sum_{i=1}^{n} a_{ki} w_{ij} \right)^2 \right] \\ &= \left(b_{kj} - \sum_{i=1}^{n} a_{ki} w_{ij} \right) a_{ki} \\ &= \left(b_{kj} - y_j \right) a_{ki} \end{aligned} \tag{36}$$

Although the cost function is only with respect to a single pattern, it has been shown (Widrow and Hoff, 1960) that the motion in the opposite direction of the gradient for each pattern, when taken in aggregate, acts as a noisy gradient motion that still achieves the proper end result.

The Perceptron (Rosenblatt, 1962) and the ADALINE (Widrow and Hoff, 1960), two of the most prominent early neural networks, employed error correction learning. In addition, the brain-state-in-a-box (Anderson et al., 1977) uses the two-layer error correction procedure previously described for one-layer autoassociative encoding.

5.7.2. Multilayer Error Correction Learning. A problem that once plagued error correction learning was its inability to extend learning beyond a two-layer network. With only a two-layer learning rule, only linear mappings could be acquired. There had been several attempts to extend the two-layer error correction learning algorithm to multiple layers, but the same problem kept arising: How much error is each hidden-layer PE responsible for in the output-layer PE error? Using the three-layer neural network in Fig. 14 to explain, the problem of multilayer learning (in this case three-layer learning) was to calculate the amount of error that each hidden-layer PE, y_j, should be credited with for an output-layer PE's error.

This problem, called the credit assignment problem (Barto, 1984; Minsky, 1961), was solved through the realization that a continuously differentiable PE function for the hidden-layer PEs would allow the chain rule of partial differentiation to be used to calculate weight changes for any weight in the network. For the three-layer network in Fig. 14, the output error across all the F_Z PEs is found by using the cost function

$$E = \frac{1}{2} \sum_{j=1}^{q} \left(b_{kj} - z_j\right)^2 \tag{37}$$

The output of an F_Z PE, z_j, is computed by using the

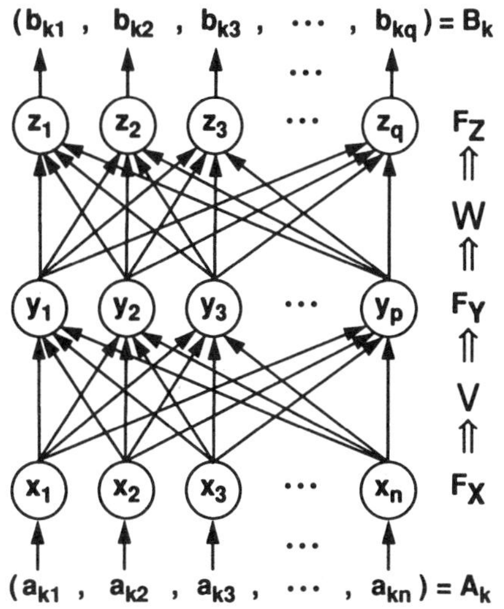

Fig. 14.

equation

$$z_j = \sum_{i=1}^{p} y_i w_{ij} \tag{38}$$

and each F_Y (hidden-layer) PE, y_i, is computed by using the equation

$$y_i = f\left(\sum_{h=1}^{n} a_{kh} v_{hi}\right) = f(r_i); \qquad r_i = \sum_{h=1}^{n} a_{kh} v_{hi} \tag{39}$$

The hidden-layer PE function is

$$f(\gamma) = \frac{1}{1 + e^{-\gamma}} \tag{40}$$

Using the same principle as described in the previous section, we perform the weight adjustments by moving along the cost function in the opposite direction of the gradient to a minimum (where the minimum is considered to be the input/output mapping producing the smallest amount of total error). The connection weights between the F_Y and F_Z PEs are adjusted by using the same form of the equation derived earlier for two-layer error correction learning, thereby yielding

$$\begin{aligned}\frac{\partial E}{\partial w_{ij}} &= \frac{\partial}{\partial w_{ij}}\left[\frac{1}{2}\sum_{j=1}^{q}(b_{kj} - z_j)^2\right] \\ &= (b_{kj} - z_j) y_i \\ &= \delta_j y_i \end{aligned} \tag{41}$$

where the positive, constant-valued learning rate α has been added to adjust the amount of change made with each move down the gradient (see (43)).

Next, the adjustments to the connection weights between the F_X and F_Y PEs are found by using the chain rule of partial differentiation:

$$\begin{aligned}\frac{\partial E}{\partial v_{hi}} &= \frac{\partial E}{\partial y_i}\frac{\partial y_i}{\partial r_i}\frac{\partial r_i}{\partial x_h}\frac{\partial x_h}{\partial v_{hi}} \\ &= \sum_{l=1}^{p}(b_{kl} - y_l) y_l w_{hl} f'(r_i) a_{kh}\end{aligned} \tag{42}$$

where β is a positive, constant-valued learning rate (see (44)). The multilayer version of this algorithm is commonly referred to as the backpropagation of errors learning rule, or simply backpropagation. Utilizing the chain rule, we can calculate weight changes for an arbitrary number of layers. The number of iterations that must be performed for each pattern in the data set is large, making this off-line learning algorithm very slow to train. From (41) and (42), the weight adjustment equations become

$$w_{ij}^{\text{new}} = w_{ij}^{\text{old}} - \alpha\frac{\partial E}{\partial w_{ij}} \tag{43}$$

and

$$v_{hi}^{\text{new}} = v_{hi}^{\text{old}} - \beta\frac{\partial E}{\partial v_{hi}} \tag{44}$$

where α and β are positive-valued constants that regulate the amount of adjustments made with each gradient move.

Extending the backpropagation to utilize mean-variance connections (see Section 3.4.2) between the F_X and F_Y PEs is straightforward (Robinson, Niranjan, and Fallside, 1988). Figure 15 shows the topology of a three-layer mean-variance version of the multilayer error correction learning algorithm. The hidden layer F_Y PE values are computed with the equation

$$y_l = g(r_i); \qquad r_i = \sum_{h=1}^{n}\left(\frac{u_{hi} - a_{kh}}{v_{hi}}\right)^2 \tag{45}$$

where u_{hi} represents the mean connection strength between the hth F_X and ith F_Y PEs, v_{hi} is the variance connection strength between the hth F_X and ith F_Y PEs, and the PE function is the Gaussian function

$$g(x) = e^{-x/2} \tag{46}$$

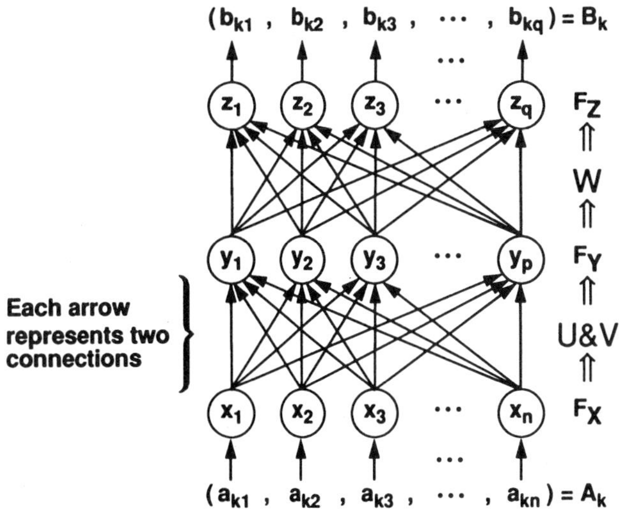

Fig. 15.

The output PE, F_Z, values are then formed from the linear combination of the hidden-layer Gaussians by using the equation

$$z_j = \sum_{i=1}^{p} y_i w_{ij} \tag{47}$$

where w_{ij} is the connection strength between the ith F_Y and jth F_Z PEs. Computing the gradients for each set of weights yields the following set of equations:

$$\frac{\partial E}{\partial u_{hi}} = \frac{\partial E}{\partial z_j}\frac{\partial z_j}{\partial y_i}\frac{\partial y_i}{\partial r_i}\frac{\partial r_i}{\partial u_{hi}} = \sum_{j=1}^{q} (b_{kj} - z_j) w_{ij} g'(r_i) \left(\frac{u_{hi} - a_{ki}}{v_{hi}^2} \right) \tag{48}$$

$$\frac{\partial E}{\partial v_{hi}} = \frac{\partial E}{\partial z_j}\frac{\partial z_j}{\partial y_i}\frac{\partial y_i}{\partial r_i}\frac{\partial r_i}{\partial v_{hi}} = \sum_{j=1}^{q} (b_{kj} - z_j) w_{ij} g'(r_i) \left(\frac{u_{hi} - a_{ki}}{v_{hi}^3} \right) \tag{49}$$

$$\frac{\partial E}{\partial w_{ij}} = (b_{kj} - z_j) y_i \tag{50}$$

From these equations, the update equations are found to be

$$u_{hi}^{\text{new}} = u_{hi}^{\text{old}} - \alpha \frac{\partial E}{\partial u_{hi}} \tag{51}$$

$$v_{hi}^{\text{new}} = v_{hi}^{\text{old}} - \beta \frac{\partial E}{\partial v_{hi}} \tag{52}$$

$$w_{ij}^{\text{new}} = w_{ij}^{\text{old}} - \gamma \frac{\partial E}{\partial w_{ij}} \tag{53}$$

where α, β, and γ are nonzero constants.

The backpropagation algorithm was introduced by Werbos (1974) and rediscovered independently by Parker (1982) and Rumelhart, Hinton, and Williams (1986). The algorithm presented here has been brief. There are several variations on the algorithm (cf. Simpson, 1990a), including alternative multilayer topologies, methods of improving the learning time, methods for optimizing the number of hidden layers and the number of hidden-layer PEs in each hidden layer, and many more. Although many issues remain unresolved with the backpropagation of errors learning procedure, such as proper number of training parameters, existence of local minima during training, extremely long training time, and optimal number and configuration of hidden-layer PEs, the ability of this learning method to automatically capture nonlinear mappings remains a significant strength.

5.8. Reinforcement Learning

The initial idea for reinforcement learning was introduced by Widrow, Gupta, and Maitra (1973) and has been championed by Williams (1986). Reinforcement learning is similar to error correction learning in that weights are reinforced for properly performed actions and punished for poorly performed actions. The difference between these two supervised learning techniques is that error correction learning utilizes more specific error information by collecting error values from each output-layer PE, while reinforcement learning uses nonspecific error information to determine the performance of the network. Whereas error correction learning has a whole vector of values that it uses for error correction, only one value is used to describe the output layer's performance during reinforcement learning. This form of learning is ideal in situations where specific error information is not available, but overall performance information is, such as prediction and control.

A two-layer neural network such as that in Fig. 16 serves as a good framework for the reinforcement learning algorithm (although multilayer networks can also use reinforcement learning). The general reinforcement learning equation is

$$w_{ij}^{\text{new}} = w_{ij}^{\text{old}} + \alpha(r - \theta_j) e_{ij} \tag{54}$$

where r is the scalar success/failure value provided by the environment, θ_j is the reinforcement PE value for the jth F_Y PE, e_{ij} is the canonical eligibility of the weight from the ith F_X PE to the jth F_Y PE, and $0 < \alpha < 1$ is a constant-valued learning rate. In error correction learning, gradient descent is performed in error space. Reinforcement learning performs gradient descent in probability space. The canonical eligibility of w_{ij} is dependent on a previously selected probability distribution that is used to determine if the computed output value equals the desired output value, and is defined as

$$e_{ij} = \frac{\partial}{\partial w_{ij}} \ln g_i \tag{55}$$

where g_i is the probability of the desired output equaling the computed output, defined as

$$g_i = \Pr(y_j = b_{kj} \mid W_j, A_k) \tag{56}$$

which is read as the probability that y_j equals b_{kj} given the input A_k and the corresponding weight vector W_j.

Neural networks that employ reinforcement learning include the adaptive heuristic critic (Barto, Sutton, and Anderson, 1983) and the associative reward–penalty neural network (Barto, 1985).

5.9. Stochastic Learning

Stochastic learning uses random processes, probability, and an energy relationship to adjust connection weights in a multilayered neural network. For the three-layer neural network in Fig. 14, the stochastic learning procedure is described as follows:

1. Randomly change the output value of a hidden-layer PE (the hidden-layer PEs utilize a binary step PE function).

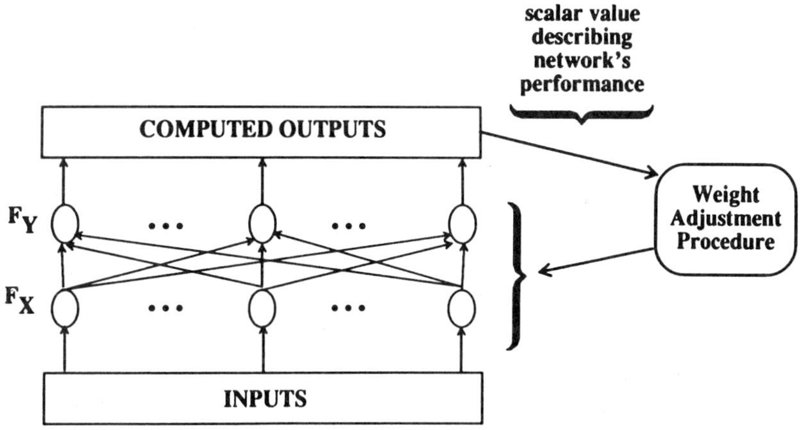

Fig. 16.

2. Evaluate the change by using the resulting difference in the neural network's energy as a guide. If the energy after the change is lower, keep the change. If the change in energy is not lower after the random change, accept the change according to a prechosen probability distribution.
3. After several random changes, the network will eventually become "stable." Collect the values of the hidden-layer PEs and the output-layer PEs.
4. Repeat steps 1–3 for each pattern pair in the data set; then use the collected values to statistically adjust the weights.
5. Repeat steps 1–4 until the network performance is adequate.

The probabilistic acceptance of higher energy states, despite a temporary increase in energy, allows the neural network to escape local energy minima in favor of a deeper energy minimum. This learning process, founded in simulated annealing (Kirkpatrick, Gelatt, and Vecchi, 1983), is governed by a "temperature" parameter that slowly decreases the number of probabilistically accepted higher energy states.

The Boltzmann machine (Ackley, Hinton, and Sejnowski, 1985) was the first neural network to employ stochastic learning. Szu (1986) has refined the procedure by employing the Cauchy distribution function in place of the Gaussian distribution function, thus resulting in a network that converges to a solution much quicker.

5.10. Hardwired Systems

Some neural networks have their connection weights predetermined for a specific problem. These weights are "hardwired" in that they do not change once they have been determined. The most popular hardwired systems are the neural optimization networks (Hopfield and Tank, 1985). Neural optimization works by designing a cost function that, when minimized, solves an unconstrained optimization problem. By translating the energy function into a set of weights and bias values, the neural network becomes a parallel optimizer. Given the initial values of the problem, the network will run to a stable solution. This technique has been applied to a wide range of problems (cf. Simpson, 1990a), including scheduling, routing, and resource optimization (see Section 4.3.3).

Two other types of hardwired networks include the avalanche matched filter (Grossberg, 1969; Hecht-Nielsen, 1990) and the probabilistic neural network (Specht, 1990). These networks are considered hardwired systems because the data patterns are normalized to unit length and used as connection weights. Despite the lack of an adaptive learning procedure, each of these neural networks is very powerful in its own right.

5.11. Summary of Learning Procedures

Several attributes of each of the neural network learning algorithms have been described. Table 1 describes six key attributes of the learning procedures discussed:

1. *Training time*—How long does it take the learning technique to adequately capture information (quick, slow, very slow, or extremely slow)?
2. *On-line / off-line*—Is the learning technique an on-line or an off-line learning algorithm?
3. *Supervised / unsupervised*—Is the learning technique a supervised or unsupervised learning procedure?
4. *Linear / nonlinear*—Is the learning technique capable of capturing nonlinear mappings?
5. *Structural / temporal*—Does the learning algorithm capture structural information, temporal information, or both?
6. *Storage capacity*—Is the information storage capacity good relative to the number of connections in the network?

The information provided in Table 1 is meant as a guide and is not intended to be a precise description of the qualities of each neural network. For a more detailed description of each neural network learning algorithm, please refer to Simpson,

TABLE 1

Learning Algorithm	Training Time	On-Line/ Off-Line	Supervised/ Unsupervised	Linear/ Nonlinear	Structural/ Temporal	Storage Capacity
Hebbian learning	Fast	On-line	Unsupervised	Linear	Structural	Poor
Principal component learning	Slow	Off-line	Unsupervised	Linear	Structural	Good
Differential Hebbian learning	Fast	On-line	Unsupervised	Linear	Temporal	Undetermined
Competitive learning	Slow	On-line	Unsupervised	Linear	Structural	Good
Min–max learning	Fast	On-line	Unsupervised	Nonlinear	Structural	Good
Two-layer error correction learning	Slow	Off-line	Supervised	Linear	Both	Good
Multilayer error correction learning	Very slow	Off-line	Supervised	Nonlinear	Both	Very good
Reinforcement learning	Extremely slow	Off-line	Supervised	Nonlinear	Both	Good
Stochastic learning	Extremely slow	Off-line	Supervised	Nonlinear	Structural	Good
Hardwired systems	Fast	Off-line	Supervised	Nonlinear	Structural	Good

(1990a), Hecht-Nielsen (1990), or Maren, Harsten, and Pap (1990).

6. Neural Network Recall

The previous section emphasized the storage of information through a wide range of learning procedures. In this section, the emphasis is on retrieving information already stored in the network. Some of the recall equations have been introduced as a part of the learning process. Others will be introduced here for the first time. The recall techniques described here fall into two broad categories: feedforward recall and feedback recall.

6.1. Feedforward Recall

Feedforward recall is performed in networks that do not have feedback connections. The most common feedforward recall technique is the linear combiner (see Section 3.4.1) followed by a PE function.

$$y_j = f\left(\sum_{i=1}^{n} x_i w_{ij}\right) \tag{57}$$

where the PE function f is one of those described in Section 3.5.

For a feedforward network using dual connections (see Section 3.4.2) where one set of connection weights W represents the mean and the other set of connection weights V represents the variance, the recall equation is

$$y_j = g\left(\sum_{i=1}^{n}\left(\frac{w_{ij} - x_i}{v_{ij}}\right)^2\right) \tag{58}$$

where g is the Gaussian PE function (see Section 3.5.5).

For a feedforward network using dual connections where one set of connection weights V represents the min vector and the other set of connection weights W represents the max vector (see Section 3.4.3), and the system is confined to the unit hypercube, there are two possible recall equations: the first is the "product of complements" based equation (Simpson, 1991b)

$$y_j = \left[1 - \frac{1}{n}\sum_{i=1}^{n} \max(0, \min(1, \gamma(v_{ji} - x_i)))\right] \times \left[1 - \frac{1}{n}\sum_{i=1}^{n} \max(0, \min(1, \gamma(x_i - w_{ji})))\right] \tag{59}$$

and the other is the productless relative (Simpson, 1992)

$$y_j = \frac{1}{2n}\sum_{i=1}^{n} [\max(0, 1 - \max(0, \gamma \min(1, x_i - w_{ji}))) + \max(0, 1 - \max(0, \gamma \min(1, v_{ji} - x_i)))] \tag{60}$$

where x_i is the input layer F_X PE value, γ is a value regulating the sensitivity of the membership functions, and y_j is the output value of the jth F_Y PE. Referring to Fig. 5, (59) measures the degree to which the input pattern A_k falls between the min and max vectors of class j, where a value of 1 means that A_k falls completely between V_j and W_j, and the closer y_j is to 0 the greater the disparity between A_k and the class j, with a value of 0 meaning that A_k is completely outside of the class. Note that there are many other possible functions that can be used here. Also note that the relationship between neural networks and fuzzy sets is realized when each PE is seen as a separate fuzzy set (Simpson, 1992).

6.2. Feedback Recall

Those networks that have feedback connections employ a feedback recall equation of the form

$$x_j(t+1) = (1-\alpha)x_j(t) + \beta\sum_{i=1}^{n} f(x_i(t))w_{ij} + a_{ki} \tag{61}$$

where $x_j(t+1)$ is the value of the jth element in a single-layer neural network at time $t+1$, f is a monotonic nondecreasing function (e.g., sigmoid function), α is a positive constant that regulates the amount of decay a PE value has during a unit interval of time, β is a positive constant that regulates the amount of feedback the other PEs provide the jth PE, and a_{ki} is the constant-valued input from the ith component of the kth input pattern.

One issue that arises in feedback recall systems is stability. Stability is achieved when a network's PEs cease to change in value after they have been given an initial set of inputs, A_k, and have processed for a while. If the network did not stabilize, it would not be of much use. Ideally, the initial inputs to the feedback neural network would represent the input pattern, and the stable state that the network reached would represent the nearest-neighbor output of the system.

An important theorem was presented by Cohen and Grossberg (1983), which proved that, for a wide class of neural networks under a set of minimal constraints, the network would become stable in a finite period of time for any initial conditions. This theorem dealt with systems that had fixed weights. In an extension to the Cohen-Grossberg theorem, Kosko (1990b) showed that a neural network could learn and recall at the same time and yet remain stable.

6.3. *Interpolation versus Nearest-Neighbor Responses*

In addition to recall operations being either feedforward or feedback, there is another important attribute associated with recall, namely output response. There are two types of neural network output response: nearest-neighbor and interpolative. Figure 17 illustrates the difference. Assume that the three face/disposition pairs in Fig. 17(a) have been stored in a neural network. If an input that is a combination of two of the faces is presented to the network, there are two ways that a neural network might respond. If the output is a combination of the two correct outputs associated with the given inputs, then the network has performed an interpolation (see Fig. 17(b)). On the contrary, the network might determine which of the stored faces is most closely associated with the input and respond with the associated output for that face (see Fig. 17(c)). The feedforward pattern-matching neural networks are typically interpolative response networks (e.g., backpropagation and linear associative memory). The feedforward pattern classification networks (e.g., learning vector quantization) and the feedback pattern-matching networks (e.g., Hopfield network and bidirectional associative memory) are typically nearest-neighbor response networks.

7. Neural Network Taxonomy

Several different topologies, learning algorithms, and recall equations have been described. Attempts at organizing the various configurations quickly become unwieldy unless some simple, yet accurate, taxonomy can be applied. The two most prevalent aspects of neural networks, learning supervision and information flow, seem ideally suited to address this need. Table 2 utilizes these criteria to organize the neural networks.

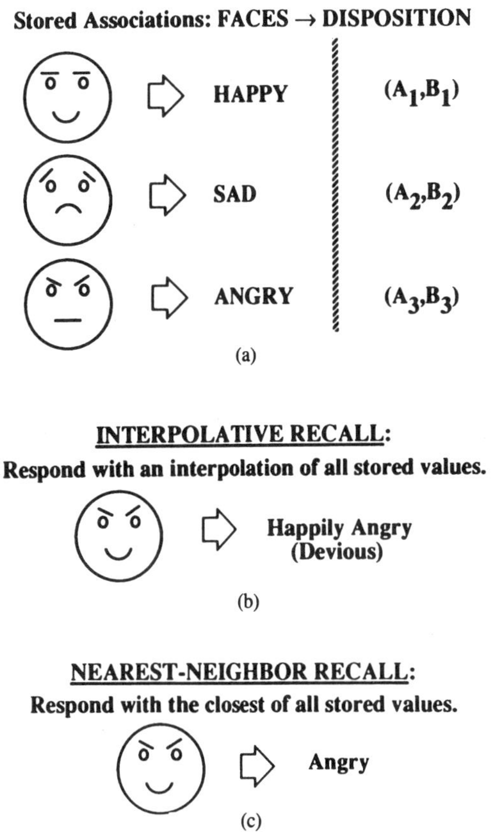

Fig. 17.

8. Comparing Neural Networks and Other Information Processing Methods

Several information processing techniques have capabilities similar to the neural network learning algorithms described. Despite the possibility of equally comparable solutions to a given problem, several additional aspects of a neural network solution are appealing, including fault-tolerance through the large number of connections, parallel implementations that allow fast processing, and on-line adaptation that allows the networks to constantly change according to the needs of the environment. The following sections briefly describe some of the alternative methods that are used for pattern recognition, clustering, control, and statistical analysis.

8.1. *Stochastic Approximation*

The method of stochastic approximation was first introduced by Robbins and Monro (1951) as a method for finding a mapping between inputs and outputs when the inputs and outputs are extremely noisy (i.e., the inputs and outputs are stochastic variables). The stochastic approximation technique has been shown to be identical to the two-layer error correction algorithm presented in Section 5.7.1 (Kohonen, 1984) and the three-layer error correction algorithm presented in Section 5.7.2 (White, 1989).

TABLE 2

Learning	RECALL INFORMATION FLOW: Feedback	Feedforward
Unsupervised	Hopfield networks (Amari, 1972; Hopfield, 1982) ART1 & ART2 (Carpenter and Grossberg, 1987a, b) Bidirectional associative memory (Kosko, 1988; Simpson, 1990b) Principal component networks (Oja, 1982; Sanger, 1989)	Linear associative memory (Anderson, 1970; Kohonen, 1972) Associative reward-penalty (Barto, 1985) Adaptive heuristic critic (Barto, Sutton, and Anderson, 1983) Drive-reinforcement learning (Klopf, 1986) Learning vector quantization (Kohonen, 1984) Fuzzy min-max classifier (Simpson 1991a) Learnmatrix (Steinbuch and Piske, 1963; Willshaw, 1980)
Supervised	Brain-state-in-a-box (Anderson et al., 1977) Neural optimization (Hopfield and Tank, 1985)	Boltzmann machine (Ackley, Hinton, and Sejnowski, 1985) Neocognitron (Fukushima, 1988) Avalanche matched filter (Grossberg, 1969; Hecht-Nielsen, 1990) Sparse distributed memory (Kanerva, 1988) Gaussian potential function network (Lee and Kil, 1989) Backpropagation (Werbos, 1974; Parker, 1982, Rumelhart et al., 1986) Perceptron (Rosenblatt, 1962) Probabilistic neural network (Specht, 1990) Cauchy machine (Szu, 1986) ADALINE (Widrow and Hoff, 1960)

8.2. Kalman Filters

A Kalman filter is a technique for estimating, or predicting, the next state of a system based upon a moving average of measurements driven by additive white noise. The Kalman filter requires a model of the relationship between the inputs and the outputs to provide feedback that allows the system to continuously perform its estimation. Kalman filters are primarily used for control systems. Singhal and Wu (1989) have developed a method of using a Kalman filter to train the weights of a multilayer neural network. In some recent work, Ruck et al. (1990) have shown that the backpropagation algorithm is a special case of the extended Kalman filter algorithm, and have provided several comparative examples of the two training algorithms on a variety of data sets.

8.3. Linear and Nonlinear Regression

Linear regression is a technique for fitting a line to a set of data points such that the total distance between the line and the data points is minimized. This technique, used widely in statistics (Spiegel, 1975), is similar to the two-layer error correction learning algorithm described in Section 5.7.1.

Nonlinear regression is a technique for fitting curves (nonlinear surfaces) to data points. White (1990) points out that the PE function used in many error correction learning algorithms is a family of curves, and the adjustment of the weights that minimizes the overall mean-squared error is equivalent to curve fitting. In this sense, the backpropagation algorithm described in Section 5.7.2 is an example of an automatic nonlinear regression technique.

8.4. Correlation

Correlation is a method of comparing two patterns. One pattern is the template and the other is the input. The correlation between the two patterns is the dot product. Correlation is used extensively in pattern recognition (Young and Fu, 1986) and signal processing (Elliot, 1987). In pattern recognition the templates and inputs are normalized, allowing the dot-product operation to provide similarities based upon the angles between vectors. In signal processing the correlation procedure is often used for comparing templates with a time series to determine when a specific sequence occurs (this technique is commonly referred to as cross-correlation or matched filters). The Hebbian learning techniques described in Section 5.2 are correlation routines that store correlations in a matrix and compare the stored correlations with the input pattern by using inner products.

8.5. Bayes Classification

The purpose of pattern classification is to determine to which class a given pattern belongs. If the class boundaries are not clearly separated and tend to overlap, the classification system must find the boundary between the classes that minimizes the average misclassification (error). The smallest possible error is referred to as the Bayes error, and a classifier that provides the Bayes error is called a Bayes classifier (Fukunuga, 1986). Two methods are often used for designing Bayes classifiers: the Parzen approach and k-nearest neighbors. The Parzen approach utilizes a uniform kernel (typically the Gaussian function) to approximate the probability density function of the data. A neural network implementation of this approach (see Section 4.5) is the probabilistic neural network (Specht, 1990). The k-nearest-neighbors approach uses k vectors to approximate the underlying distribution of the data. The learning vector quantization network (Kohonen, 1984) is similar to the k-nearest-neighbors approach (see Section 5.5).

8.6. *Vector Quantization*

The purpose of vector quantization is to produce a code from an n-dimensional input pattern. The code is passed across a channel and then used to reconstruct the original input with minimal distortion. There have been several techniques proposed to perform vector quantization (Gray, 1984), with one of the most successful being the LBG algorithm (Linde, Buzo, and Gray, 1980). The learning vector quantization (see Section 5.5) is a method of developing a set of reference vectors from a data set and is very similar to the LBG algorithm. A comparison of these two techniques can be found in Ahalt et al. (1990).

8.7. *Radial Basis Functions*

A radial basis function is a function that is symmetric about a given mean (e.g., a Gaussian function). In pattern classification, a radial basis function is used in conjunction with a set of n-dimensional reference vectors, where each reference vector has a radial basis function that constrains its response. An input pattern is processed through the basis functions to produce an output response. The mean-variance connection topologies that employ the backpropagation algorithm (Lee and Kil, 1989; Robinson, Niranjan, and Fallside, 1988) as described in Section 5.7.2 are methods of automatically producing the proper sets of basis functions (by adjustment of the variances) and their placement (by adjustment of their means).

8.8. *Machine Learning*

Neural networks are not the only method of learning that has been proposed for machines (although they are the most biologically related). Numerous machine learning procedures have been proposed during the past 30 years. Carbonell (1990) classifies machine learning into four major paradigms (p. 2):

> [I]nductive learning (e.g., acquiring concepts from sets of positive and negative examples), analytic learning (e.g., explanation-based learning and certain forms of analogical and case-based learning methods), genetic algorithms (e.g., classifier systems), and connectionist learning methods (e.g., nonrecurrent "backprop" hidden layer neural networks).

It is possible that some of the near-term applications might find it useful to combine two or more of these machine learning techniques into a coherent solution. It has only been recently that this type of approach has even been considered.

References

Ackley, D., G. Hinton, and T. Sejnowski (1985), "A learning algorithm for Boltzmann machines," *Cognitive Sci.*, vol. 9, pp. 147-169.

Ahalt, S., A. Krishnamurthy, P. Chen, and D. Melton (1990), "Competitive learning algorithms for vector quantization," *Neural Networks*, vol. 3, pp. 277-290.

Amari, S. (1971), "Characteristics of randomly connected threshold-element networks and network systems," *Proc. IEEE*, vol. 59, pp. 35-47, Jan.

Amari, S. (1972), "Learning patterns and pattern sequences by self-organizing nets of threshold elements," *IEEE Trans. Computer*, vol. C-21, pp. 1197-1206, Nov.

Amari, S. (1977), "Neural theory of association and concept formation," *Biol. Cybernet.*, vol. 26, pp. 175-185.

Amari, S. (1983), "Field theory of self-organizing neural nets," *IEEE Trans. Systems, Man, Cybernet.*, vol. SMC-13, pp. 741-748, Sept./Oct.

Amari, S. and M. Takeuchi (1978), "Mathematical theory on formation of category detecting nerve cells," *Biol. Cybernet.*, vol. 29, pp. 127-136.

Anderson, J. (1970), "Two models for memory organization using interactive traces," *Math. Biosci.*, vol. 8, pp. 137-160.

Anderson, J. (1990), "Knowledge representation in neural networks," *AI Expert*, Fall.

Anderson, J., J. Silverstein, S. Ritz, and R. Jones (1977), "Distinctive features, categorical perception, and probability learning: Some applications of a neural model," *Pysch. Rev.*, vol. 84, pp. 413-451.

Barto, A. (1984), "Simulation experiments with goal-seeking adaptive elements," Air Force Wright Aeronautical Laboratory, Technical Report AFWAL-TR-84-1022.

Barto, A. (1985), "Learning by statistical cooperation of self-interested neuron-like computing units," *Human Neurobiol.*, vol. 4, pp. 229-256.

Barto, A., R. Sutton, and C. Anderson (1983), "Neuron-like adaptive elements that can solve difficult learning control problems," *IEEE Trans. Systems, Man, Cybernet.*, vol. SMC-13, pp. 834-846, Sept./Oct.

Carbonell, J. (1990), "Introduction: Paradigms for machine learning," in *Machine Learning: Paradigms and Methods*, J. Carbonell, Ed., Cambridge, MA: MIT/Elsevier, pp. 1-10.

Carpenter, G. and S. Grossberg (1987a), "A massively parallel architecture for a self-organizing neural pattern recognition machine," *Computer Vision, Graphics, and Image Understanding*, vol. 37, pp. 54-115.

Carpenter, G. and S. Grossberg (1987b), "ART2: Self-organization of stable category recognition codes for analog input patterns," *Appl. Optics*, vol. 26, pp. 4919-4930.

Cohen, M. and S. Grossberg (1983), "Absolute stability of global pattern formation and parallel storage by competitive neural networks," *IEEE Trans. Systems, Man, Cybernet.*, vol. SMC-13, p. 815-825, Sept./Oct.

DeSieno, D. (1988), "Adding a conscience to competitibe learning," in *Proc. 1988 Int. Conf. Neural Networks*, vol. I, pp. 117-124.

Eberhart, R. (1990), "Standardization of neural network terminology," *IEEE Trans. Neural Networks*, vol. 1, pp. 244-245, June.

Elliot, D., Ed. (1987), *Handbook of Digital Signal Processing: Engineering Applications*, San Diego, CA: Academic Press.

Fukunuga, K. (1986), "Statistical pattern classification," in *Handbook of Pattern Recognition and Image Proc.*, T. Young and K. Fu, Eds., San Diego, CA: Academic Press, pp. 3-32.

Fukushima, K. (1988), "Neocognitron: A hierarchical neural network capable of visual pattern recognition," *Neural Networks*, vol. 1, pp. 119-130.

Gray, R. (1984), "Vector quantization," *IEEE ASSP Mag.*, vol. 1, no. 2, pp. 4-29, Apr.

Grossberg, S. (1969), "On the serial learning of lists," *Math. Biosci.*, vol. 4, pp. 201-253.

Grossberg, S. (1970), "Neural pattern discrimination," *J. Theoret. Biol.*, vol. 27, pp. 291-337.

Grossberg, S. (1982), *Studies of Mind and Brain*, Boston: Reidel.

Hebb, D. (1949), *Organization of Behavior*, New York: Wiley.

Hecht-Nielsen, R. (1990), *Neurocomputing*, Reading, MA: Addison-Wesley.

Hertz, J. et al. (1990), *Introduction to the Theory of Neural Computation*, Reading, MA: Addison-Wesley.

Hopfield, J. (1982), "Neural networks and physical systems with emergent collective computational abilities," *Proc. Nat. Acad. Sci. U.S.A.*, vol. 79, pp. 2554–2558.

Hopfield, J. and D. Tank (1985), "'Neural' computation of decisions in optimization problems," *Biol. Cybernet.*, vol. 52, pp. 141–152.

Kanerva, P. (1988), *Sparse Distributed Memory*, Cambridge, MA: MIT Press.

Kirkpatrick, S., C. Gelatt, and M. Vecchi (1983), "Optimization by simulated annealing," *Science*, vol. 220, pp. 671–680.

Klopf, A. (1986), "Drive-reinforcement model of a single neuron function: An alternative to the Hebbian neuron model," in *AIP Conf. Proc. 151: Neural Networks for Computing*, J. Denker, Ed., New York: American Institute of Physics, pp. 265–270.

Kohonen, T. (1972), "Correlation matrix memories," *IEEE Trans. Computer*, vol. C-21, pp. 353–359, Apr.

Kohonen, T. (1984), *Self-organization and Associative Memory*, Berlin: Springer-Verlag.

Kohonen, T. (1986), "Learning vector quantization for pattern recognition," Helsinki University of Technology, Technical Report No. TKK-F-A601.

Kosko, B., (1986a), "Fuzzy entropy and conditioning," *Information Sci.*, vol. 40, pp. 165–174.

Kosko, B. (1986b), "Differential Hebbian learning," in *AIP Conf. Proc. 151: Neural Networks for Computing*, J. Denker, Ed., New York: American Institute of Physics, pp. 277–282.

Kosko, B. (1988), "Bidirectional associative memories," *IEEE Trans. Systems, Man, Cybernet.*, vol. SMC-18, pp. 42–60, Jan./Feb.

Kosko, B. (1990a), "Fuzziness vs. probability," *Int. J. General Systems*, vol. 17, pp. 211–240.

Kosko, B. (1990b), "Unsupervised learning in noise," *IEEE Trans. Neural Networks*, vol. 1, pp. 44–57, Mar.

Lawley, D. and A. Maxwell (1963), *Factor Analysis as a Statistical Method*, London: Butterworths.

Lee, S. and R. Kil (1989), "Bidirectional continuous associator based on Gaussian potential function network," in *Proc. IEEE/INNS Int. Joint Conf. Neural Networks*, vol. I, pp. 45–54.

Linde, Y., A. Buzo, and R. M. Gray (1980), "An algorithm for vector quantizer design," *IEEE Trans. Communications*, vol. 28, no. 1, pp. 84–95.

Malsburg, C. v. d. (1973), "Self-organization of orientation sensitive cells in the striate cortex," *Kybernetik*, vol. 14, pp. 85–100.

Maren, A., C. Harston, and R. Pap (1990), *Handbook of Neural Computing Applications*, San Diego, CA: Academic Press.

McEliece, R., E. Posner, E. Rodemich, and S. Venkatesh (1987), "The capacity of the Hopfield associative memory," *IEEE Trans. Information Theory*, vol. IT-33, pp. 461–482, July.

Minsky, M. (1961), "Steps toward AI," *Proc. of the IRE*, vol. 49, pp. 5–30.

Oja, E. (1982), "A simplified neuron model as a principal component analyzer," *J. Math. Biol.*, vol. 15, pp. 267–273.

Oja, E. (1989), "Neural networks, principle components, and subspaces," *Int. J. Neural Networks*, vol. 1, pp. 61–68.

Pao, Y. (1989), *Adaptive Pattern Recognition and Neural Networks*, Reading, MA: Addison-Wesley.

Parker, D. (1982), "Learning logic," Stanford University, Dept. of Electrical Engineering, Invention Report 581-64, Oct.

Robbins, H. and S. Monro (1951), "A stochastic approximation method," *Ann. Math. Statist.*, vol. 22, pp. 400–407.

Robinson, A., M. Niranjan, and F. Fallside (1988), "Generalizing the nodes of the error propagation network," Cambridge University Engineering Department, Technical Report CUED/F-INENG/TR.25.

Rosenblatt, F. (1962), *Principles of Neurodynamics*, Washington, DC: Spartan Books.

Rozonoer, L. (1969), "Random logic networks I, II, III," in *Automatic Remote Control,* vols. 5–7, pp. 137–147, 99–109, and 129–136.

Ruck, D., S. Rogers, M. Kabrisky, P. Maybeck, and M. Oxley (1990), "Comparative analysis of backpropagation and the extended Kalman filter for training multilayer perceptrons," *IEEE Trans. Pattern Anal. Machine Intelligence*, in review.

Rumelhart, D., G. Hinton, and R. Williams (1986), "Learning representations by backpropagating errors," *Nature*, vol. 323, pp. 533–536.

Sanger, T. (1989), "Optimal unsupervised learning in a single-layer linear feedforward neural network," *Neural Networks*, vol. 2, pp. 459–473.

Sejnowski, T. (1977), "Storing covariance with nonlinearly interacting neurons," *J. Math. Biol.*, vol. 4, pp. 303–321.

Simpson, P. (1990a), *Artificial Neural Systems: Foundations, Paradigms, Applications and Implementations*, Elmsford, NY: Pergamon Press.

Simpson, P. (1990b), "Higher-ordered and intraconnected bidirectional associative memories," *IEEE Trans. Systems, Man, Cybernet.*, vol. 20, pp. 637–653, May/June.

Simpson, P. (1990c), "Fuzzy adaptive resonance theory," presented at Southern Illinois Neuroengineering Workshop, Sept., and published as General Dynamics Technical Report GDE-ISG-PKS-010, Apr. (revised Nov. 1990).

Simpson, P. (1991a), "Fuzzy min–max classification with neural networks," *Heuristics*, vol. 4, no. 7, pp. 1–9.

Simpson, P. (1991b), "Fuzzy min-max neural networks," in *Proc. 1991 Int. Joint Conf. Neural Networks* (Singapore), pp. 1658–1669.

Simpson, P. (1992), "Fuzzy min-max neural networks: I. Classification," *IEEE Trans. Neural Networks*, in press.

Singhal, S. and L. Wu (1989), "Training multi-layer perceptrons with the extended Kalman algorithm," in *Advances in Neural Information Processing Systems 1*, D. Touretzky, Ed., San Mateo, CA: Kaufmann, pp. 133–140.

Specht, D. (1990), "Probabilistic neural networks," *Neural Networks*, vol. 3, pp. 109–118.

Spiegel, M. (1975), *Schaum's Outline of Theory and Problems of Probability and Statistics*, New York: McGraw-Hill.

Steinbuch, K. and U. Piske (1963), "Learning matrices and their applications," *IEEE Trans. Electronic Computers*, vol. EC-12, pp. 846–862, Dec.

Sutton, R. and A. Barto (1981), "Toward a modern theory of adaptive networks: Expectation and prediction," *Psych. Rev.*, vol. 88, pp. 135–171.

Szu, H. (1986), "Fast simulated annealing," in *AIP Conf. Proc. 151: Neural Networks for Computing*, J. Denker, Ed., New York: American Institute of Physics, pp. 420–425.

Tank, D. and J. Hopfield (1986), "Simple 'neural' optimization networks: A/D convertor, signal decision circuit, and a linear programming circuit," *IEEE Trans. Circuits Systems*, vol. CAS-33, pp. 533–541, May.

Tesauro, G. (1986), "Simple neural models of classical conditioning," *Biol. Cybernet.*, vol. 55, pp. 187–200.

Werbos, P. (1974), "Beyond regression," Ph.D. dissertation, Harvard University, Cambridge, MA.

White, H. (1989), "Learning in neural networks: A statistical perspective," *Neural Computation*, vol. 1, pp. 425–464.

White, H. (1990), "Neural network learning and statistics," *AI Expert*, Fall.

Widrow, B. and M. Hoff (1960), "Adaptive switching circuits," in *1960 WESCON Convention Record: Part IV*, pp. 96–104.

Widrow, B., N. K. Gupta, and S. Maitra (1973), "Punish/reward: Learning with a critic in adaptive threshold systems," *IEEE Trans. Syst., Man, Cybernetics*, vol. SMC-3, no. 5, pp. 455–465.

Widrow, B. and S. Stearns (1985), *Adaptive Signal Processing*, Englewood Cliffs, NJ: Prentice-Hall.

Widrow, B. and R. Winter (1988), "Neural nets for adaptive filtering and adaptive pattern recognition," *IEEE Computer Mag.*, pp. 25–39, Mar.

Williams, R. (1986), "Reinforced learning in connection to networks: A mathematical analysis," University of California, Institute for Cognitive Science, Technical Report No. 8605.

Willshaw, D. (1980), "Holography, associative memory, and inductive generalization," in *Parallel Models of Associative Memory*, J. Anderson and G. Hinton, Eds., Hillsdale, NJ: Lawrence Erlbaum, pp. 103–122.

Young, T. and K. Fu, Eds. (1986), *Handbook of Pattern Recognition and Image Processing*, San Diego, CA: Academic Press.

Part I: Theory

Theory is the fundamental building block for all engineering applications. Ideas spawn theories; theories are then realized as applications. In Part 1 of this edited volume, two aspects of theory are addressed. Chapter 1 focuses on design. Many of these designs are extensions of existing neural networks, but some represent new designs that could provide significant performance improvement over previous techniques. Chapter 2 emphasizes theoretical analysis. This chapter includes papers that try to answer the hard questions in neural networks, such as: How long will it take to train? How well will the net generalize to the data? And, how sensitive is the net to perturbations?

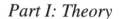

Chapter 1: Design

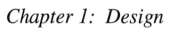

CHAPTER 1

Design

The design of neural networks is a topic of great interest to all engineers. Developing more capable neural networks has become increasingly difficult and the progress seems to slow each year. As such, most of the thirty-three papers included in this chapter represent enhancements or modifications to previously existing neural networks. Two areas that have gained more attention recently include hierarchical neural networks and wavelet networks. This chapter is organized into twelve areas. The first eleven areas focus on recent design innovations of specific types of neural networks. The papers included in each area are described below.

1. Time-Delay Neural Networks (TDNNs). TDNNs were introduced several years ago by Waibel and his colleagues for speech processing applications. Unlike most neural networks that have one or two connections from one processing element to the next, TDNNs encode the temporal structure of a problem with several connections between processing elements. Since their introduction, these neural networks have been used for many other signal processing applications. In **Paper 1.1**, a technique entitled Optimal Brain Damage (OBD) is applied to a TDNN. OBD is a pruning technique that attempts to improve generalization by reducing the number of connections.

2. Hierarchical Neural Networks. Hierarchical processing in neural networks has been in existence for a long time. Fukushima's Neocognitron had several hierarchical levels of processing within a single character recognition neural network. Recently, the concept of hierarchical neural networks has been extended to included hierarchies of neural network modules. **Paper 1.2** describes a recurrent hierarchical neural network that generates waltzes. **Paper 1.3** looks at hierarchies of oscillatory neural networks used to learn trajectories.

3. Multi-Layer Perceptrons (MLPs). There have been thousands of papers written on every variation of the MLP that can be imagined. In this chapter, two design papers have been included that present relatively new ideas within this vast sea of paper. **Paper 1.4** compares two methods of training MLPs with hard limiting neurons. Comparisons with sigmoid neurons are made for convergence speed, training efficiency, architecture size, and generalization. **Paper 1.5** describes a technique for optimizing neural network size using a pruning technique similar to OBD. Analysis of the weights following pruning illustrates the effectiveness of this design technique.

4. Radial Basis Functions (RBFs). RBF neural networks have grown in popularity over the past few years. These networks are faster and easier (i.e., fewer parameters to adjust) to train than a MLP, they offer more insight into the mapping that is produced, and they offer the same function approximation capability. Three design papers look at different aspects of this paradigm. **Paper 1.6** designs RBFs that perform classification with missing and uncertain data. **Paper 1.7** describes an incremental learning RBF that replaces the traditional Gaussian basis functions with a response function. The performance of this RBF configuration is compared with a MLP on a 4-class 2-dimensional classification problem. **Paper 1.8** extends RBFs to a wider range of functions that can be approximated. The basis functions used in this paper include splines and regularization.

5. Wavelet Networks. One of the recent innovations in neural networks is the use of wavelets as basis functions in multilayer function approximation networks. **Paper 1.9** describes a hierarchical wavelet neural network for modeling time series data. **Paper 1.10** examines function approximation using Chui-Wang wavelets.

6. Cascade Correlation Networks (CCN). CCNs are an example of an incremental learning neural network that has shown great promise for many function approximation applications. **Paper 1.11** enhances recurrent neural networks by adding a CCN to improve the prediction performance of a highly nonlinear time-series. **Paper 1.12** extends the current CCN architecture to allow it to learn a wide range of regular grammars using a collection of smaller architectures.

7. Reduced Coulomb Energy (RCE) Networks. The RCE network is a classification network that uses hyperspherical nodes and is capable of incremental learning. Two recent extensions of RCE provide this network with greater capabilities. **Paper 1.13** introduces a technique for learning production rules from a RCE hyperspherical node network and demonstrates the technique for diagnosing diabetes. **Paper 1.14** describes an extension of RCE that replaces hyperspherical nodes with fuzzy sets to produce a fuzzy RCE network.

8. Self-Organizing Feature Maps (SOFMs). The SOFM is arguably the second most popular neural network for applications (behind MLPs). One of the strengths of this neural network is its ability to create 2-dimensional maps from n-dimensional data (actually p-dimensional maps, where p is commonly 2). **Paper 1.15** describes a technique called grid growing that incrementally adds nodes to a 2-dimensional self-organizing feature map that reflects the underlying distribution of a high dimension space. This is an important concept as it extends SOFMs into an incremental learning network. It has been argued by many researches that the SOFM is closely linked to actual biological processes. **Paper 1.16** provides new insights into this discussion by examining these biological connections relative to the SOFM's ability to learn with low accuracy data.

9. Fuzzy Neural Networks. In addition to the aforementioned wavelet networks, fuzzy neural networks have recently emerged as a promising new neural network technique, especially for the development of neural networks with an explanation facility. This chapter includes six papers that describes the recent work in this expanding branch of neural networks. **Paper 1.17** describes a translation from a fuzzy rule base to a neural network. Once the rule base is translated, rule refinement is achieved through a stochastic learning technique. The use of this technique is demonstrated for a mobile robot navigation problem. **Paper 1.18** outlines a supervised learning technique that enhances the Fuzzy ART neural network. The utility of this approach is analyzed on a classification problem and its performance is compared with the MLP. **Paper 1.19** describes an extension of fuzzy min-max neural networks to function approximation. **Paper 1.20** proposes a fuzzy neural network that uses fuzzy numbers for connection values and demonstrates its ability to perform function approximation. **Paper 1.21** shows how expert system operations such as inference, inquiry, and explanation can be implemented in a fuzzy neural network. **Paper 1.22** outlines a fuzzy error backpropagation algorithm used to construct a fuzzy neural network for control applications.

10. Evolutionary Computation. Evolutionary computation is an umbrella term that describes survival-of-the-fittest techniques of computation. The three primary evolutionary computation techniques include evolutionary programming, genetic algorithms, and evolutionary strategies. Although the roots of evolutionary computation reach back more than two decades, the branches have only recently begun to sprout. One area where evolutionary computation is having an impact is in the construction and training of neural networks. Two examples of this work are included in this chapter. **Paper 1.23** demonstrates the use of evolutionary programming to build an MLP capable of playing tic-tac-toe. **Paper 1.24** shows how genetic algorithms can be used to create sparse-connected neural networks with the same function approximation capability as their densely connected counterparts.

11. Biological Neural Networks. There are several neural networks that emphasize strong biological connections. Four examples of this work are included in this chapter. **Paper 1.25** describes tensor network theory, a technique introduce many years ago that models cerebellum operations. In **Paper 1.26,** a biologically inspired spatiotemporal neural network is described for saccade generation within a vision system. **Paper 1.27** examines a biologically inspired oscillatory neural network that implements rhythm for locomotion. **Paper 1.28** introduces the notion of a self-architecture neural network based on the growth of neurons on oxide strips.

12. Other Neural Networks. There are five other papers in this chapter that did not fit neatly within any of the previous categories, but are clearly of value. **Paper 1.29** compares the concepts of self-generation and self-organization. **Paper 1.30** describes a multilayer associative memory. **Paper 1.31** proposes a neural-logic belief network that represents knowledge in a framework that allows commonsense reasoning. **Paper 1.32** extends the dyna framework of neural networks toward a more efficiently learning technique. **Paper 1.33** outlines a homotopy approach to determining the weights of a neural network.

On Design and Evaluation of Tapped-Delay Neural Network Architectures

Claus Svarer, Lars Kai Hansen, and Jan Larsen
CONNECT, Electronics Institute, B349
Technical University of Denmark,
DK-2800 Lyngby, Denmark
emails: claus, lars, jan@eiffel.ei.dth.dk

Abstract— **We address pruning and evaluation of Tapped-Delay Neural Networks for the sunspot benchmark series. It is shown that the generalization ability of the networks can be improved by pruning using the Optimal Brain Damage method of Le Cun, Denker and Solla. A stop criterion for the pruning algorithm is formulated using a modified version of Akaike's Final Prediction Error estimate. With the proposed stop criterion the pruning scheme is shown to produce succesful architectures with a high yield.**

I. Introduction

Needless to say, processing of time series is an important application area for neural networks, and the quest for application-specific architectures penetrates current network research. While the ultimate tool may be fully recurrent architectures, many problems arise during adaptation of these. Even worse, the generalization properties of recurrent networks are not well understood, hence, model optimization is difficult. However, the conventional Tapped-Delay Neural Net (TDNN) [11] may be analysed using statistical methods and the results of such analysis can be applied for model optimization. Here we demonstrate the power of this strategy within time series prediction. We aim at designing compact TDNN's using the so-called *Optimal Brain Damage* (OBD) method of Le Cun *et al.* [5]. The benefits from compact architectures are three-fold: They generalize better, they carry less computational burden, and they are faster to adapt if the environment changes. Further we show that the generalization ability of the network may be estimated, without extensive cross-validation, using a modification of Akaike's *Final Prediction Error* (FPE) estimate [1].

II. Time Series Prediction

The possibility of predicting the future fascinates. The techniques invoked through history cover oracles, crystal balls, feed forward neural networks and many more. While we can rule out long time predictions for chaotic systems; short time predictions may still be viable. Recent work by Priestly [9], and Weigend *et al.* [11] have established the *sunspot series* as a benchmark for time series prediction algorithms. The series is a scaled record of the yearly average sunspot activity for the period 1700-1979. The sunspot series is believed to be generated by a noisy, chaotic, dynamical system. The spectrum is dominated by a frequency corresponding to a 12 year period. Weigend *et al.* applied a weight decay scheme to design feed-forward networks that generalize better than conventional algorithms from the training set to an independent test set. In this work the OBD *pruning* method is shown to produce very compact networks for this problem, having only around 15 free parameters. The networks that we obtain use around one third of the parameters of the network published by Weigend *et al.* while having comparable performance.

We start the pruning procedure from the same initial network configuration as in [11]. The network is a *tapped delay line* architecture with 12 input units, 8 hidden sigmoid units and a single linear output unit, see Fig. 1. The initial network is fully connected between layers and implements a non-linear mapping from lag space $\mathbf{z}(k) = [x(k-1), ..., x(k-L)]$, $L = 12$, to the real axis:

$$\widehat{x}(k) = F_{\mathbf{u}}(\mathbf{z}(k)) \qquad \widehat{x} \in \mathcal{R}, \tag{1}$$

where $\mathbf{u}=(w, W)$ is the N-dimensional weight vector and $\widehat{x}(k)$ is the prediction of $x(k)$.

The non-linear mapping can be written as:

$$F_{\mathbf{u}}(\mathbf{z}(k)) = \sum_{j=1}^{n_H} W_j \tanh\left(\sum_{i=1}^{L} w_{ij} x(k-i) + w_{i0}\right) + W_0, \tag{2}$$

where n_H is the number of hidden units. W_j are the hidden-to-output weights while w_{ij} connect the input and hidden units.

0-7803-0999-5/93/$03.00 ©1993 IEEE

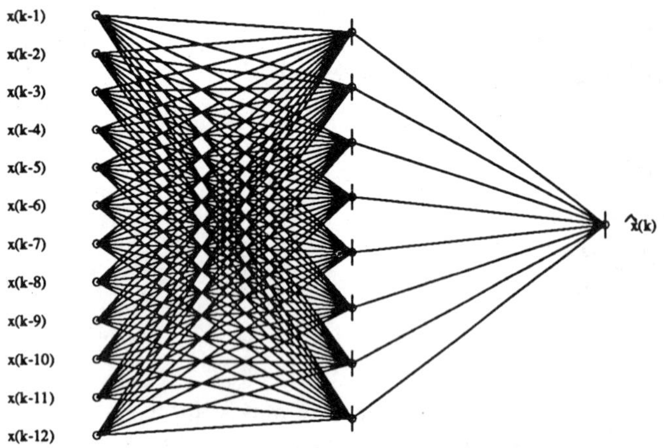

Fig. 1 Fully connected network used as a starting point for the pruning procedure. A vertical bar through a unit indicates an active threshold.

III. Training

The objective of the training procedure is single-step prediction. Hence, the network weights, **u**, are trained to recognize the short time structure of the chaotic time series. We use the sum of squared errors to measure the prediction ability of the current network:

$$E_{train} = \frac{1}{p} \sum_{k=1}^{p} \left[x(k) - F_{\mathbf{u}}(\mathbf{z}(k))\right]^2 , \qquad (3)$$

where p is the number of training examples.

A state of the art simulator has been developed based on *batch mode*, second order local optimization. The second order scheme is implemented as a direct matrix-inversion identification of the hidden-to-output weights [2], while a pseudo Gauss-Newton method is used for identification of input-to-hidden weights, see e.g. [3].

To ensure numerical stability and for assisting the pruning procedure we augment the cost-function with a weight decay term. The cost-function can then be written as:

$$E = E_{train} + \frac{\alpha_w}{p} \sum_{ij}^{N_w} w_{ij}^2 + \frac{\alpha_W}{p} \sum_{j}^{N_W} W_j^2, \qquad (4)$$

where N_w, N_W are the numbers of weights and thresholds in hidden and output units, respectively.

The second order pseudo Gauss-Newton method used for identification of input-to-hidden weights can be written as:

$$\Delta w_{ij} = -\eta \left(\frac{\partial E_{train}}{\partial w_{ij}} + \frac{2\alpha_w}{p} w_{ij} \right) \Big/ \left(\frac{\partial^2 E_{train}}{\partial w_{ij}^2} + \frac{2\alpha_w}{p} \right) \qquad (5)$$

where the parameter η is used to secure that all the weight updates lead to a decrease in the cost-function. η is initialized to 1 before each step, and iteratively dimished by powers of two, until the step leads to a decrease in the cost-function. As in [5] we approximate the second derivative by the positive semi-definite expression:

$$\frac{\partial^2 E_{train}}{\partial w_{ij}^2} \approx \frac{2}{p} \sum_{k=1}^{p} \left(\frac{\partial F_{\mathbf{u}}(\mathbf{z}(k))}{\partial w_{ij}} \right)^2 . \qquad (6)$$

IV. Pruning by Optimal Brain Damage

The OBD scheme proposed by Le Cun *et al.* [5] was succesfully applied to reduce large networks for recognition of handwritten digits [6]. The basic idea is to estimate the effect on the *training error* when deleting weights. The estimate is formulated in terms of weight saliencies s_l:

$$\delta E_{train} = \sum_{l \in D} s_l \equiv \sum_{l \in D} \left(\frac{2\alpha}{p} + \frac{1}{2} \frac{\partial^2 E_{train}}{\partial u_l^2} \right) u_l^2, \qquad (7)$$

where u_l is a component of **u**. The saliency definition used here takes into account that the weight decay terms force the weights to depart from the minimum of the training set error. The sum runs over the set of deleted weights D.

The following assumptions enter the derivation of OBD:

- The terms of third and higher orders in the deleted weights can be neglected.
- The off-diagonal terms in the Hessian, $\frac{\partial^2 E_{train}}{\partial u_l \partial u_{l'}}$, can be neglected.

Computationally the second order (diagonal) terms are reused from the training scheme (5), in particular we refrain from working on the full Hessian, which would scale poorly for large networks.

The recipe allows for *ranking* the weights according to saliency. The question of how many weights it may be possible to delete was not answered in [5]. To evaluate a network, hence, formulate a pruning *stop criterion*, we note that there are three objectives of pruning:

- Improve the generalization performance by limiting the network resources.
- Reduce the computational burden of prediction.
- Allow for fast on-line adaptation.

In this presentation we emphasize the first of these objectives. However, since the generalization error by definition, involves test on an independent data set, we cannot directly use the error on the training set, as estimated by OBD, to formulate a stop criterion. We may indeed accept an increased error on the training set if better generalization is obtained. Also, among networks with the same estimated test error we still prefer the minimal, because it has a lower computational burden, and typically needs less training examples for retraining if the environment changes. The latter is very important for on-line adaptation. If data are abundant we can formulate a stop criterion based on a validation set (an independent subset of the training set). This approach was criticized by Weigend *et al.*: The training data set is scarce for the sunspot series – and indeed for many other applications. We support their conclusion by the observation that even for the (90%)/(10%) splitting of the training set (in training and validation sets, respectively), as used by [11], the estimated validation error is an extremely noisy quantity.

In the usual case of limited data sets we follow the standard approach within *system identification* [7] and estimate the generalization error of the pruned networks using statistical arguments. In particular, we apply Akaike's FPE estimate [1, 7] of the test error in terms of the training error. In its standard form it reads:

$$\widehat{E}_{test} = \frac{p+N}{p-N} E_{train}, \qquad (8)$$

where p is the number of training samples, and N is the number of parameters in the model. The left hand side of (8) is the average generalization error, averaged over all possible training sets of size p. The estimate is based on linearization of the networks as regards the fluctuations in the weights resulting from different training sets. The relation express the fact that the training error is a biased estimate of the noise level because each parameter during training has "absorbed" some of the noise in the training samples.

Since we have regularized the training procedure by weight-decay terms α_w, α_W, hence, suppressed the ability of the (otherwise) ill-determined parameters to model noise, we need to modify the classical FPE estimate by replacing the total number of parameters with the *effective* number of parameters see e.g. [4, 8]:

$$\widehat{E}_{test} = \frac{p+N_{eff}}{p-N_{eff}} E_{train}, \qquad (9)$$

$$N_{eff} = \sum_{ij}^{N_w} \left(\frac{\lambda_{ij}}{\lambda_{ij} + 2\alpha_w/p} \right)^2 + \sum_{j}^{N_W} \left(\frac{\Lambda_j}{\Lambda_j + 2\alpha_W/p} \right)^2 . \qquad (10)$$

Where the λ's are the second derivatives already computed in (7), $\lambda_{ij} \equiv \partial^2 E_{train}/\partial w_{ij}^2$, $\Lambda_j \equiv \partial^2 E_{train}/\partial W_j^2$.

In brief, the following assumptions enter the derivation of (8-10):

- Independence of input and error on output.
- Sufficient capacity, i.e., the network must be able to implement the rule.
- Many examples pr. weight: $N/p \to 0$.
- The off-diagonal elements of the second derivative matrix can be neglected.

With the above tool we can obtain a generalization error estimate for each pruned network. By selecting the network with the lowest estimated generalization error we have developed the stop criterion sought.

V. Experiments

Following Weigend *et al.* [11], the sunspot data are partioned into a training set (1700-1920) and a test set (1921-1979), and further we compute the test error for two separate sets, namely the periods 1921-1955 and 1956-1979. The sunspot series is rather non-stationary and the latter period is atypical for the series as a whole. The normalized errors on the training set and on the two test sets are calculated as:

$$E_{set} = \frac{1}{\sigma_{total}^2 \cdot p_{set}} \sum_{k=1}^{p_{set}} \left[x(k) - F_{\mathbf{u}}(\mathbf{z}(k)) \right]^2 , \qquad (11)$$

where p_{set} is the number of examples in the data set in question. The squared errors of each data set are normalized as in [11] by the variance of the total data set σ_{total}^2.

An ensemble of 11 networks were trained and pruned. The weight decay parameters were set as: $\alpha_w = 0.02$ and $\alpha_W = 0.01$.

Fig. 2 shows the normalized training error and the two test set errors during training of the fully connected network. Note that the training set error decreases monotonously, while the error on the test sets start out decreasing, but after some training increase again. This is a generic *over-training scenario* in which the network overfits the training set.

In order to prevent the network from overfitting we limit its resources by pruning. We use OBD, rank the remaining weights according to saliency, and delete a number of these determined by $|D| = \lceil 0.02 \cdot N_{remaining} \rceil$, in a simple iterative procedure. The evolution of training and test errors during pruning are recorded for a specific network in Fig. 3. Further this figure shows the estimated test error as given by (9). The FPE estimate of the test error lies

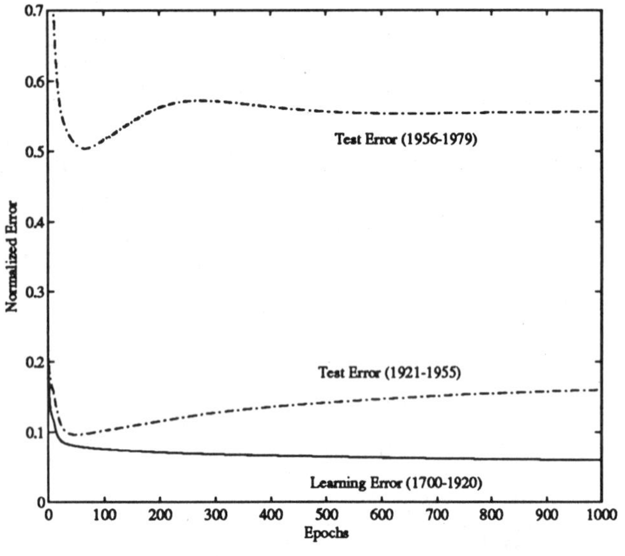

Fig. 2 Training and test error when training the fully connected network. An 'Epoch' is a full sweep through the training set.

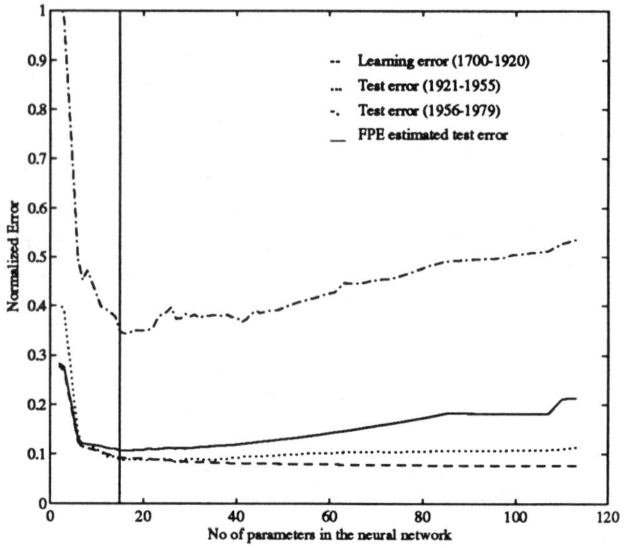

Fig. 3 The evolution of training and test errors during pruning. The FPE estimate of the test error is based on equation (9). The vertical line indicates the network for which the *estimated* test error is minimal.

between the two test sets. Most importantly, the estimate reproduce the common trend of the test sets, sharing a generalization error minimum just below 20 parameters, indicating that the statistical approach is viable. In the particular run, the stop criterion selects a network having 12 weights and 3 thresholds as indicated by the vertical line in Fig. 3.

Among the eleven networks pruned, the procedure selected 9 nets with a number of parameters in the range $12-16$, and two nets with more than 25 parameters. The 9 small architectures were considered succesfully pruned, and used as an ensemble for computing significance levels for the procedure. In order to fine tune the nine small networks, they were retrained without weight decay, resulting in the normalized errors on the three data sets: 0.090 ± 0.001 (1700-1920), 0.082 ± 0.007 (1921-55), and 0.35 ± 0.05 (1956-79). Four nets had 15 parameters, another four nets had 16 parameters, while one net had 12 parameters. The latter appears to be overpruned and carried higher errors than the rest. In Table I we compare our findings with other reported results for the sunspot series.

We illustrate the properties of one of the compact networks (presented in Fig. 4 and in Table II), in two ways: First we show, in Fig. 5, the retraining history of this network after pruning. As expected we see no overtraining. Both the training error and the two test errors are monotonously decreasing.

It is interesting to note that the network does not use

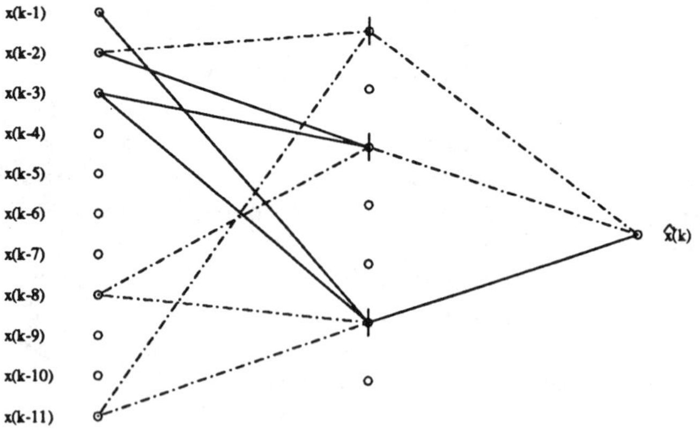

Fig. 4 Pruned network with 12 weights and 3 thresholds. Note that the network only uses a subset of the Tapped-Delay line. Dash-dotted lines indicate negative weights, and solid lines positive weights. The network parameters are given in Table II.

the full set of inputs. We interpret this to be a result of the finite training set. Within the noise level of the sunspot time series it is harmful to use more than a carefully selected subset of the available lag space. Among the succesfully pruned networks there is some consensus regarding which inputs to use. They all use the two most recent inputs, and one or more inputs among the "oldest" part of lag space.

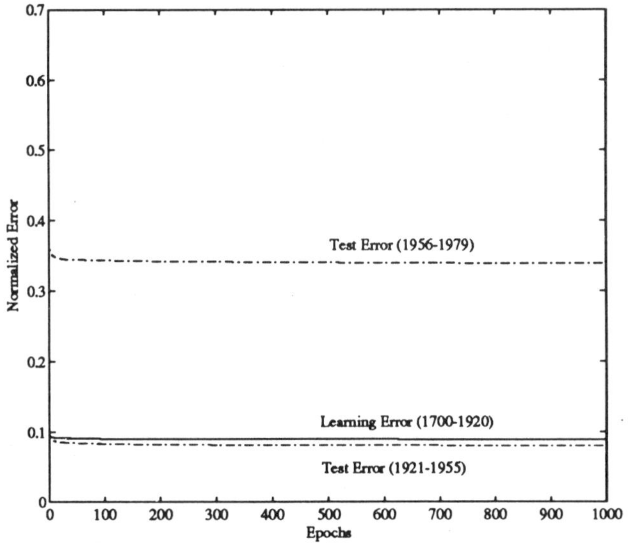

Fig. 5 Training and test error when re-training the pruned network without weight decay.

Secondly, in Fig. 6, the predicted sunspot activity using the pruned and fine tuned network is shown. We note that the variance of the sunspot activity is increased significantly in the period after about 1960.

In Fig. 7 we show the effective number of parameters as computed from (10). Judged from this figure the weight decays are important in the initial pruning phase where they limit the number of parameters to about 85. With higher weight decays we were unable to train the networks to error levels like those reported. On the other hand, with smaller weight decays the second order optimization scheme is plagued by numerical problems also leading to higher errors and a lower yield of useful architectures.

VI. Conclusion

We have discussed pruning and evaluation of Tapped-Delay Neural Networks. We have shown that the generalization ability on the sunspot data can be improved by pruning using the Optimal Brain Damage method. In particular, we have identified a set of compact networks with three hidden units employing around 15 weights and thresholds. These networks generalize well compared to

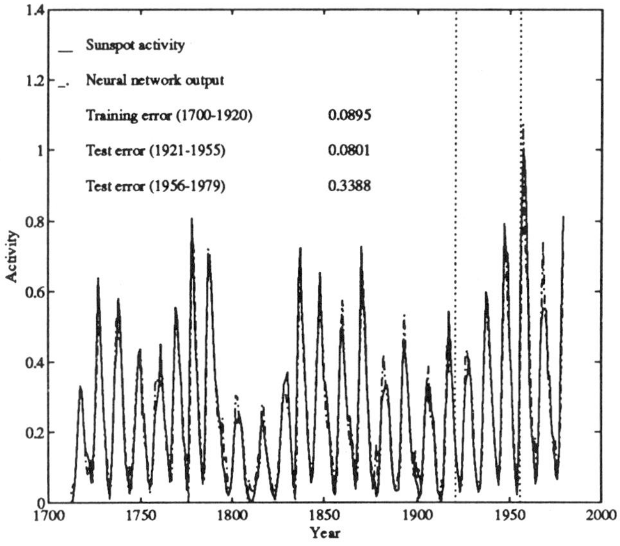

Fig. 6 Predicted sunspot activity using the pruned feed-forward network shown in Fig. 4.

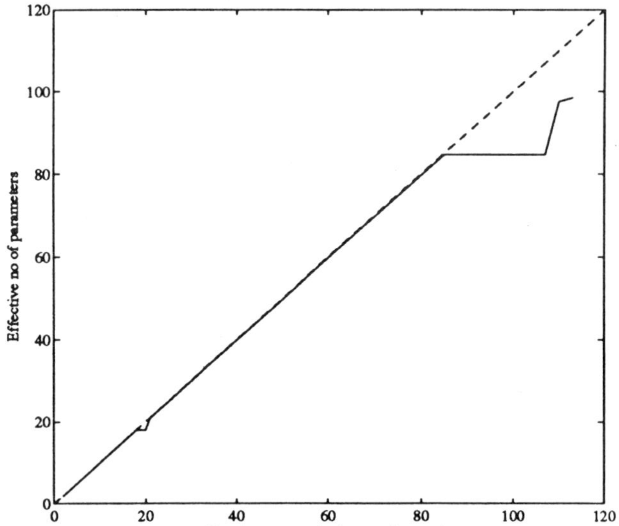

Fig. 7 The effective number of parameters in the neural network during the pruning session.

TABLE I
NORMALIZED ERROR

Model	Train (1700-1920)	Test (1921-55)	Test (1956-79)	Number of parameters
Tong and Lim [10]	0.097	0.097	0.28	16
Weigend *et al.* [11]	0.082	0.086	0.35	43
Linear model[1]	0.132	0.130	0.37	13
Fully connected network[2]	0.078 ± 0.002	0.104 ± 0.005	0.46 ± 0.07	113
Pruned network[3]	0.090 ± 0.001	0.082 ± 0.007	0.35 ± 0.05	$12 - 16$

1) Linear model is a single linear unit. 2) The initial pre-pruned networks, trained with the same weight decay terms as used during pruning. 3) Pruned networks retrained without weight decay. The mean and standard deviation are based on the networks selected for retraining (90 % of the initial set of networks).

TABLE II
PRUNED NETWORK WEIGHTS

Input	Hidden unit 1	Hidden unit 3	Hidden unit 6
Lag 1	0	0	1.399
Lag 2	-0.562	0.944	0
Lag 3	0	1.035	1.068
Lag 8	0	-0.435	-0.408
Lag 11	-0.279	0	-0.259
Threshold	0.192	0.236	0.411

Hidden	Output unit
Unit 1	-1.1544
Unit 3	-1.5537
Unit 6	1.5636
Threshold	0

previous studies. Further we have shown that the network performance may be evaluated using statistical methods and that the trend (in error versus number of parameters) of the estimate is in good agreement with those of the test sets. We have shown how the estimated generalization error may be used for selection of the optimal network architecture during a pruning session. The yield of the procedure was 90%: Out of eleven networks the procedure found nine useful architectures.

For the sunspot series we note that non-stationarity is a problem insofar that the normalized test error for the period 1956-1979 is four times higher than the test error on the more representative test set comprising the period 1921-1955. This means, that it is important to corroborate our results on other problems and time series, such work is in progress.

Acknowledgments

This research is supported by the Danish Natural Science and Technical Research Councils through the Computational Neural Network Center (CONNECT).

References

[1] H. Akaike: "Fitting Autoregressive Models for Prediction". *Ann. Inst. Stat. Mat.* , vol. 21, 243-247, (1969).

[2] S.A. Barton: "A Matrix Method for Optimization a Neural Network". *Neural Computation*, vol. 3, 450-459 (1990).

[3] J. Hertz, A. Krogh and R.G. Palmer: *Introduction to the Theory of Neural Computation*, Addison Wesley, New York (1991).

[4] J. Larsen: *Design of Neural Network Filters*. Ph. D. Thesis, Electronics Institute, Technical University of Denmark. In preparation, (1993).

[5] Y. Le Cun, J.S. Denker, and S.A. Solla: "Optimal Brain Damage". In *Advances in Neural Information Processing Systems 2*, 598-605, Morgan Kaufman. (1990).

[6] Y. Le Cun, B. Boser, J.S. Denker, D. Henderson, R.E. Howard, W. Hubbard, and L.D. Jakel: "Handwritten Digit Recognition with a Back-Propagation Network", In *Advances in Neural Information Processing Systems 2*, 396-404. Morgan Kaufman. (1990)

[7] L. Ljung: *System Identification: Theory for the user*, Prentice-Hall, Information and System Sciences series (1987).

[8] J.E. Moody: "Note on Generalization, Regularization and Architecture Selection in Nonlinear Systems". In *Neural Networks For Signal Processing*; Proceedings of the 1991 IEEE-SP Workshop, (Eds. S.Y. Kung, B.H. Juang, and C. Kamm), IEEE Service Center, 1-10, (1991).

[9] M.B. Priestly: *Non-linear and Non-stationary Times Series Analysis*, Academic Press (1988).

[10] H. Tong and K. S. Lim: "Threshold autoregression, limit cycles and cyclical data". *Journ. Roy. Stat. Soc. B*, vol. 42, 245 (1980).

[11] A.S. Weigend, B.A. Huberman, and D.E. Rumelhart: "Prediction the future: A Connectionist Approach", *Int. J. of Neural Systems*, vol. 3, 193-209 (1990).

HIERARCHICAL RECURRENT NETWORKS FOR LEARNING MUSICAL STRUCTURE

D. J. Burr
Bellcore, Morristown, NJ 07962
djb@bellcore.com

Y. Miyata
Chukyo University, Toyota, 470-03 Japan
miyata@sccs.chukyo-u.ac.jp

Abstract. Interest in automatic music composition by computer dates back to the 1950's when Markov chains were used to generate melodies. Recently layered neural networks employing feedback links have been proposed for certain sequential pattern tasks. A hierarchical version of this type of network has been studied by one of the authors. We investigate the use of such a hierarchical neural network for modeling coarse and fine temporal structure in music. We trained this network on two classical waltzes and then used it to generate novel waltzes. The generated waltzes contained both novel phrases and phrases from the original scores. More importantly, they exhibited an overall structure which has been difficult to learn using conventional methods. We argue that it is the synaptic *links* of artificial neural networks which allow them to learn the relationship between coarse and fine temporal structure.

1. INTRODUCTION

The possibility of automatically composing music with computers has intrigued researchers from the very earliest days of computing. Since music students often learn composition by *example*, early approaches were based on analysis of patterns in existing music. Markov chains appeared suitable for generating melodic sequences, but the sequences lacked long-range or global structure typical of Western music.

We are proposing a neural network model which has several features naturally suited to learning music. One feature, similar to Markov chain models, is the ability to predict a future event based on a past history of events. The second feature is a variable resolution capability which models temporal events at both coarse and fine levels of detail. Fine details consist of individual note events. Coarse details consist of note patterns which reappear through the melody as melodic *units* or phrases. These units, which are different for each melody, are learned

0-7803-0928-6/93$03.00

by the network during training. The structural relationships between units are also learned. After assimilating the unit patterns of a few different melodies, the network can reshape and combine them in novel ways to produce different melodies.

2. CONVENTIONAL MODELS

Chance has played an important role in the design of composing automatons. This dates as far back as 1024 AD, when Guido D'Arezzo devised a correspondence table for generating pitches from vowels in arbitrary text (Loy [7]). It is said that Mozart also applied rules of chance to compose his *Musikalische Wurfelspiel* or Musical Dice Game (Potter [14]). Pinkerton [13] described a clever ring structure for generating nursery tunes in which note decisions were made by tossing a coin. Recently Langston [6] composed tunes by concatenating stored *riffs*. The choice of which riff to select at any time was determined by pitch continuity considerations. This is similar in concept to Mozart's system, which was organized by strict compositional rules.

Hiller and Isaacson [2] are credited as the first to use a computer to automatically compose music. They applied a Markov chain technique which chose a new note based on the context from the N previous notes. The main objection to Markov chain music is that it has a tendency to *wander*. Brooks et. al. [1] studied window length effects and showed that for long windows (up to 8 notes) the Markov chain regenerated complete phrases from the training music. For an alternative model see Kohonen [5], who applied dynamically expanding context to learn deterministic patterns in music.

A later attempt to generate music from examples was based on interpolating between melodies. Mathews and Rosler [8] encoded note values and durations of two melodies and then computed a running interpolation between them. This generated a melody which started with the first melody and ended with the second.

3. NEURAL MODELS

Neural networks have recently received attention as tools for statistical sequence analysis. In particular, recurrent neural networks have been proposed as natural models for sequence learning. In the simplest sense a (linear) neuron with a single recurrent connection can be viewed as a variable duration memory. Jordan [4] describes such a model based on self-recurrent connections. Such networks are dynamical by their nature and are attractive for modeling sequential problems such as motor dynamics and speech. Todd [16] showed that this kind of network could learn musical scales. Mozer and Soukup [12] applied a similar style of recurrent network to learn Bach melodies. They used a psychological representation for pitch based on a circle of fifths. A recent variation of a recurrent network uses multiple levels of feedback to model coarse and fine details of sequence planning [9,10,11].

4. TODD'S NETWORK

Our work was strongly influenced by Todd's [16] recurrent network. He showed that a neural network could be used to predict the next note in a melody from previous notes. This can be viewed as a neural implementation of a kind of Markov chain. In Todd's model (shown in Figure 1) a decaying memory of the melody up to the current note is implemented with self-recurrent connections. Connection weights are fixed to produce a short term memory of recent notes. Feedback connections from the output to the input merely transfer the predicted note code to the input. Recurrent connections are discrete instead of continuous and switch on at every beat. After training, the hidden units learn to predict the next note from the context of previous notes.

5. SELF SIMILARITY OF MUSIC

Western music is highly structured. Similar tonal and rhythmic patterns reoccur at regular time intervals. Time intervals are generally related by simple power-of-two ratios. This hierarchy of temporal structure, though important for the perception of coherence, has not been successfully incorporated into automatic music learning systems. Similarities can occur within the same time scale or across different time scales (Hofstadter [3]).

Since self similarity is an important feature of Western music, a music composing system should be able to learn this. Fortunately, because self similarities occur as simple binary ratios, time scales can be arranged accordingly. This order is common for units larger than a musical measure (a measure is the interval between two vertical bars). However, within a measure, time scales can be non-binary ratios of three (waltzes) or six (certain marches in 6/8 time).

Markov models have not succeeded in modeling both the coarse and fine temporal structure of music, though they have been around for many years. Perhaps the missing link is in fact the *synaptic* link which allows artificial neural networks to learn a *symbolic* code in a layer of hidden units. A different symbolic code is generally learned for each of the melodic phrases or *units* in the melody. It is for this reason we have chosen to investigate the neural network paradigm.

6. A HIERARCHICAL RECURRENT NETWORK FOR MUSIC

We propose to apply a hierarchical recurrent network to the problem of learning music self similarity. A hierarchical recurrent network consists of a collection of *subnetworks* each of which operates on a different time scale. For example, if the smallest time unit is a quarter note (1 beat), then the lowest subnet cycles every *beat*, and the next higher (measure) subnet cycles every *three* beats. The next higher (phrase) subnet cycles every 12 beats, and the highest subnet, every 24 beats. Our example shows only the two lowest subnets, though larger hierarchies could be used.

To generate a melody, an input vector, called a plan, is presented to the highest level subnetwork (largest time scale). This subnetwork generates a sequence of vectors representing small segments of the melody. These vectors are then given as plans to the subnetwork one level below. They are converted to smaller segments by successively lower level subnetworks until the outputs representing individual notes are generated at the lowest level.

This network overcomes the difficulty of generating a long complex sequence by a single sequential network, because each subnetwork needs to generate a sequence of only a few output vectors. More importantly, such a network may be well suited to capture structural regularity at different time scales: By training such a network on example scores of a particular style we may capture the local and global regularities present in the style. After the network has been trained on a set of melodies, we let the network generate novel melodies by giving it new plan vectors. The new plan vectors can be randomly chosen, or can be mixtures of plan vectors associated with the original melodies. If enough example scores have been provided, then we expect the network to generate new scores which reflect the structural properties of the original scores.

7. A TWO-LEVEL HIERARCHICAL NETWORK

Figure 2 shows the structure of a two-level hierarchical recurrent network. A note is represented as a 1-of-N code as shown. The subnetwork on the left predicts a note from the recent history of notes in a decaying memory. This is essentially Todd's network. The right subnetwork encodes patterns at a coarser time interval into a symbol sequence representing similarities at the measure level. The time interval of the left subnetwork is a quarter note, and the time interval of the right subnetwork is three quarter notes (waltz tempo). That is, feedback connections are turned on every note in the left subnetwork and every three notes in the right. Nodes with self-recurrent connections are linear units. All other nodes are nonlinear units with sigmoid activation.

Our hierarchical recurrent network can be viewed as two Markov chains operating at different time scales. They are linked in a natural way using weighted synaptic links. The right subnet is performing the same function as the left subnet, but predictions are done at the 3-note time scale. In the right subnet the hidden units are labeled *measure hidden units*. The measure hidden units learn to encode their outputs (i.e. *note* hidden units) at the slower 3-note time scale.

8. ENCODING MELODIES

The plan units at the far right produce a unique input code for each melody being trained. Two input plan units can encode four different melodies. In synthesis mode, plan units are activated with arbitrary real numbers to generate novel combinations of the trained melodies.

Melodies to be used for training are selected to have the same metric pattern (e.g. waltzes) and length (e.g. 32 measures). All melodies are initially transposed to the key of C. In our experiment we limited the melodies to a two octave range above middle C. A separate neuron exists for each note of this 24 note range. The neuron corresponding to a note is turned on and all others are turned off. This is inherently a parallel encoding scheme, allowing chords to be naturally encoded by turning on the multiple neurons representing the chord notes.

Time is represented by itself, with basic unit selected beforehand as the smallest interval needed for the melodies. In our example we chose the quarter note as the basic time interval. Todd used an additional input unit to signal note begin and end, so that consecutive notes of the same pitch could be re-keyed. We omitted that feature for simplicity in our present study – consecutive notes of the same pitch are tied. A nice feature for chords would be the ability to hold some notes of a chord while re-keying others. Therefore, Todd's note-begin concept might be incorporated, but it may need to be extended.

9. FEEDBACK AND SHORT TERM MEMORY

Feedback connections include two types of weights: those from output neurons to input neurons in each hierarchical subnetwork, and recurrent connections from input units to themselves. Weights of the first type are fixed to the value 1 since their purpose is only to transfer the output to the input for next-note prediction. Self-recurrent weights, in contrast to Todd's model, are trainable using a simulator developed by the second author. However, for expediency, they may be fixed a-priori to constant values (typically 0.5) to provide fixed short term memories. Variable weights are more powerful as they allow for variable duration memories.

10. MELODY LEARNING AND GENERATION

The network is trained using backward error propagation [15]. To expedite training the true note rather than the feedback note may be used as input to the network after each cycle. This was the choice in our examples. Training is completed after the error is sufficiently small.

After training, new melodies can be generated by first choosing some arbitrary plan input vector. Since these may be real numbers, they represent a particular *mixture* of the plan vectors used in training. The network is initialized by setting all units to zero. A note is decoded by choosing the output neuron which is most strongly activated. If the activation of the strongest neuron is not sufficiently high, then that beat is interpreted as a rest.

This is a purely deterministic scheme, however, stochastic variability can be introduced if needed by selecting the output note in a different way. The output activations can be interpreted as likelihoods that the corresponding note is generated. The actual note can be selected by a Monte Carlo scheme which picks the note randomly according to the distribution indicated by the activations. For example, if the note F has an activation three times that of C, F would be chosen three times more frequently than C on an average basis. In this scheme all notes could have some likelihood of being selected. The Monte Carlo scheme is normally used in Markov chain implementations.

11. EXPERIMENT

The network in Figure 2 was trained on two classical waltzes using plan vectors {1,0} and {0,1}. Figure 3 shows an example of a melody generated by the network using a plan vector {0.7,0.3}. The first melody was emphasized in this plan by giving it higher weight. Figure 4 shows another example of a melody generated with a different plan vector {0.5,0.5}. This plan vector was chosen to provide an equal balance between the two trained melodies.

Sections marked with solid bars indicate phrases identical in *both* note and rhythmic patterns. In addition, they were *newly created* phrases not seen in the training melodies. Sections marked with shaded bars in Figure 3 indicate newly created phrases in which *only* the rhythmic pattern repeats. A slight variation at the end of a phrase (second shaded bar) is normal and occurs in human compositions.

Alternatively, the plan vector may be allowed to vary with time, producing melodies which contain dynamic variation of the mix. However, in order to encourage self similar pattern generation, the plan vector should be kept constant within phrases, and switch only between a preset inventory of plan vectors at phrase boundaries.

12. LEARNING GLOBAL PATTERNS

One can speculate on how the hierarchical network learns global structure. One theory is that during the measure interval, evidence is accumulated linking the notes to a *symbolic* code generated in the *measure* subnet. That is, all the notes in the measure contribute to the learning of the weights in the measure subnet, since it is fixed (no recurrent feedback) during the entire measure. Recurrent connections are then switched on for the next measure. During the measure interval the hidden unit encodings of the notes are correlated with the encoding of the measure. This ultimately results in a symbolic code in which similar note patterns in different measures are encoded as chord sequences (or AABA patterns). The histogram *signature* of the number of notes versus pitch is what discriminates melodic phrases.

One can also speculate on how melodies are actually created. One view is that different melodies are created by *interpolations* of those melodies that have been encoded during training. It is also an important point to ask whether the generated melodies are musically useful in that they satisfy many of the normal constraints of harmony and global structure that are characteristic of the training melodies. These questions can only be answered with a more thorough training of such networks with many more melodies. However, the simple experiment does suggest that characteristic local and global patterns of music appear to be preserved.

13. FUTURE

An important extension is in the direction of adding more hierarchical subnets (four- and eight-measure phrases). We are interested in how many melodies our network must to learn so its compositions would not have easily distinguishable segments from the original melodies. Unfortunately, this is a characteristic shared also by high order Markov chains (Brooks et al [1]). Perhaps one could constrain the self-recurrent weights so they would not grow too large and thus prevent long memories. Low order Markov chains do not have this problem.

To ensure correct timing information, we have used for training data direct translations of scores entered by hand. However, larger data bases may be needed to allow the network to capture regularities in a particular *style* of music. Later we envision using live input via a MIDI keyboard in order to gather large amounts of data and to learn dynamic patterns such as key velocity.

14. CONCLUSIONS

We have trained a hierarchical recurrent network on two classical waltzes and we have demonstrated the network's ability to generate novel waltzes. Waltzes generated by the network consisted of phrases from the training melodies as well as novel phrases. This experiment is encouraging as it demonstrates that a hierarchical recurrent network can organize melodic patterns in a structured manner useful for melody generation. This has been difficult in conventional approaches due to lack of a flexible way to link Markov chains operating at different time scales. Linking is accomplished in a straightforward manner by using trainable synapses of artificial neural networks. The experiment represents a start toward understanding the relationships between melody and structure in automatic music composition.

REFERENCES

[1] F. P. Brooks, Jr., A. L. Hopkins, Jr., P. G. Neumann, and W. V. Wright, "An Experiment in Musical Composition," IRE Trans. Elec. Comp., EC-6, 1957.

[2] L. A. Hiller, Jr. and L. M. Isaacson, Experimental Music, McGraw-Hill, New York, 1959.

[3] D. R. Hofstadter, Godel, Escher, Bach: An Eternal Golden Braid, Vintage Books, Random House, New York, 1989.

[4] M. I. Jordan, Serial Order: "A Parallel Distributed Processing Approach," in Advances in Connectionist Theory: Speech, J. Elman and D. Rumelhart, eds., Erlbaum, 1989.

[5] T. Kohonen, "A Self-Learning Musical Grammar, or Associative Memory of the Second Kind," Proc. Intl. Joint Conf. Neural Networks, 1-5, 1989.

[6] P. Langston, "Eedie and Eddie on the Wire -- an Experiment in Music Generation," Proc. USENIX Conference, 1986.

[7] G. Loy, "Composing with Computers -- A Survey of Some Compositional Formalisms and Music Programming Languages," in Current Directions in Computer Music Research, M. Mathews and J. Pierce, eds., MIT Press, 1989.

[8] M. V. Mathews and L. Rosler, "Graphical Language for the Scores of Computer Generated Sounds," Perspectives of New Music, 6(2), 1968.

[9] Y. Miyata, "Organization of Action Sequences in Motor Learning: a Connectionist Approach," Proc. Ninth Ann. Conf. Cognitive Science Soc., 1987.

[10] Y. Miyata, "The Learning and Planning of Actions," PhD thesis, Psychology Department, University of California, San Diego, 1988.

[11] Y. Miyata, "A PDP Model of Sequence Learning that Exhibits the Power Law," Proc. Eleventh Ann. Conf. Cognitive Science Soc., 1989.

[12] M. Mozer and T. Soukup, "Connectionist Music Composition Based on Melodic and Stylistic Constraints," in Advances in Neural Information Processing Systems 3, D. Touretzsky, ed., Morgan Kaufmann, 1991.

[13] R. C. Pinkerton, "Information Theory and Melody," Scientific American, February, 1956.

[14] G. M. Potter, "The Role of Chance in Contemporary Music," Ph. D. Dissertation, Indiana University, 1971.

[15] D. E. Rumelhart, G. E. Hinton, and R. Williams, "Learning Internal Representation by Error Propagation," Nature, 1986.

[16] P. Todd, "A Sequential Network Design for Musical Applications," Proc. Connectionist Models Summer School, Carnegie Mellon, 1988.

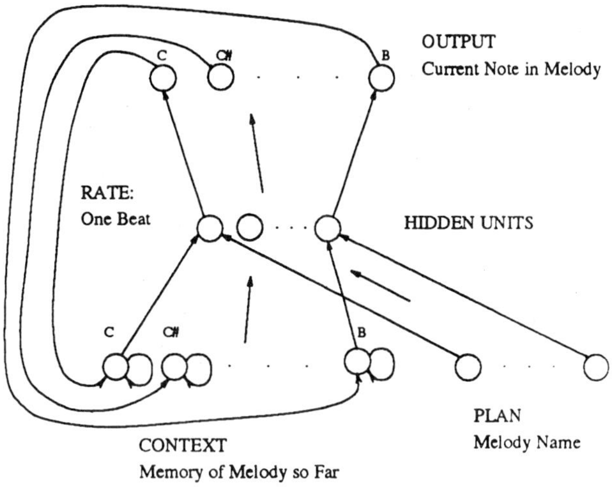

Figure 1. Todd's recurrent network architecture.

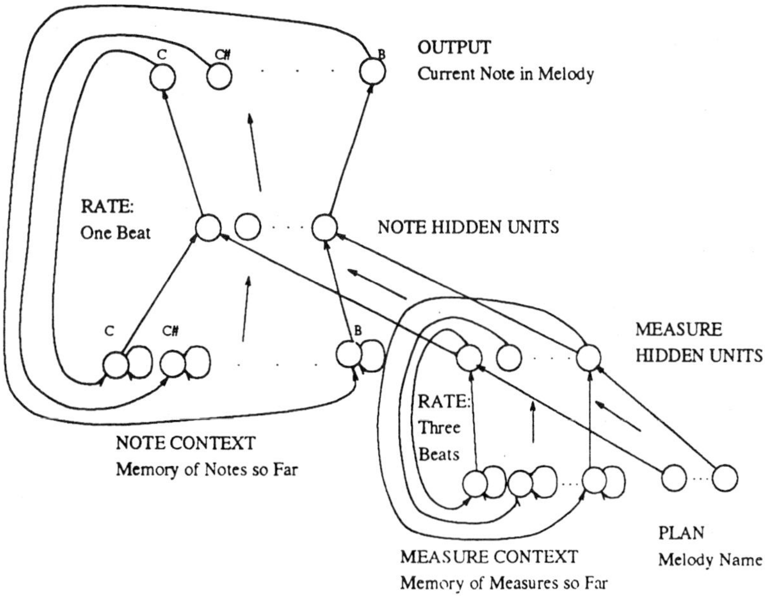

Figure 2. Hierarchical recurrent net with two temporal levels.

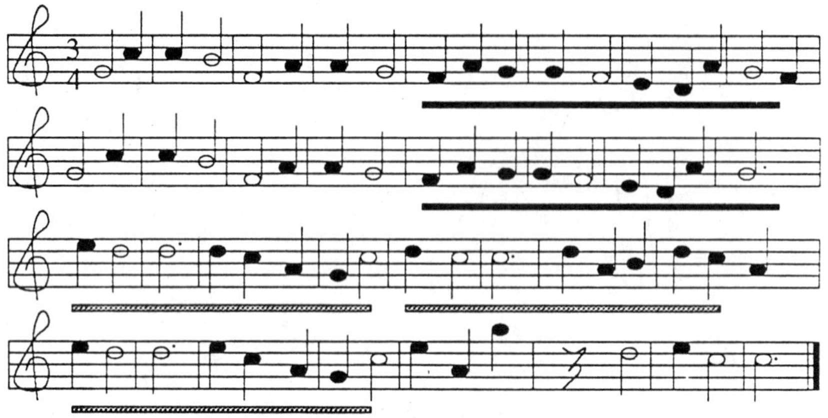

Figure 3. Example melody generated by Figure 2 network using plan {0.7,0.3}.

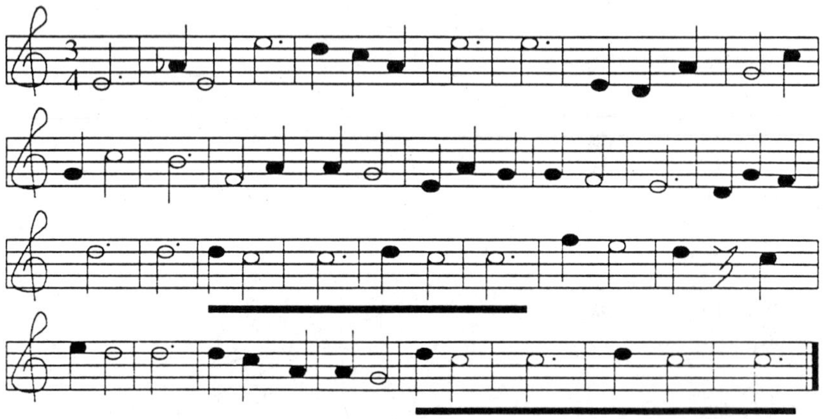

Figure 4. Example melody generated by Figure 2 network using plan {0.5,0.5}.

Learning Trajectories with a Hierarchy of Oscillatory Modules

Pierre Baldi* and Nikzad Benny Toomarian
Jet Propulsion Laboratory
California Institute of Technology
Pasadena, CA 91109

***Abstract*—To this date, the most successful approaches to learning has been the back-propagation method. Although very powerful on relatively simple problems, theoretical analysis and simulations show that this approach breaks down as soon as sufficiently complex problems are considered. To overcome this fundamental limitation, we suggest a hierarchical and modular approach, directly inspired from biological networks, whereby a certain degree of structure is introduced in the learning system. This approach is applied to a simple example of trajectory learning of a semi-figure eight. The ideas involved, however, extend immediately to more general computational problems.**

I. Introduction

Learning is a fundamental ability of biological systems. Understanding its principles is also key to the design of intelligent circuits, computers and machines of various kinds. To this date, the most successful approach to learning, from an engineering standpoint, has been the back-propagation approach [12] or gradient descent approach. In this framework, in the course of learning from examples, the parameters of a learning system, such as a neural network, are adjusted incrementally so as to optimize, by gradient descent, a suitable function measuring the performance of the system at any given time. Although very powerful on relatively simple problems, theoretical analysis and simulations, (see [4-5]), show that this approach breaks down as soon as sufficiently complex problems are considered. Gradient descent learning applied to an amorphous learning system is bound to fail. To overcome this fundamental limitation, we have suggested a hierarchical and modular approach, directly inspired from biological networks, whereby a certain degree of structure is introduced in the learning system. The basic organization of the system consists of a hierarchy of modules. The lowest levels of the hierarchy serve as primitives or basic building blocks for the successive levels. A very concrete example is described next for the basic problem of trajectory learning in neural networks (see also [9] and [13]). The ideas involved, however, extend immediately to more general computational problems.

*and Division of Biology, California Institute of Technology

0-7803-0999-5/93/$03.00 ©1993 IEEE

II. Trajectory Learning

Consider the problem of synthesizing a neural network capable of producing a certain given non-trivial trajectory. To fix the ideas, we can imagine that the model neurons in the network satisfy the usual additive model equations (see, for instance, [1] and [6])

$$\frac{du_i}{dt} = -\frac{u_i}{\tau_i} + \sum_j w_{ij} f(u_j) + I_i \tag{1}$$

The learning task is to find the right parameter values, for instance for the synaptic weights w_{ij}, the charging time constants τ_i and the amplifiers gains, so that the output units of the network follow a certain prescribed trajectory $u^*(t)$ over a given time interval $[t_0, t_1]$. For instance, a typical benchmark trajectory in the literature is a circle or a figure eight. Networks such as (1) have been successfully trained, although through lengthy computer runs, on figure eights using a form of gradient descent learning for recurrent networks [10-11,14]. Consider now the problem of learning a more complicated trajectory, such as a double figure eight (i.e. a set of four loops joined at one point). Although the task appears only slightly more complicated, simulations show that a fully interconnected set of units will not be able to learn this task by indiscriminate gradient descent learning on all the parameters. Thus a different approach is needed.

III. Modular Hierarchical Approach

Biology seems to have overcome the obstacles inherent to gradient descent learning through evolution. Learning in biological organisms is never started from a tabula rasa. Rather, a high degree of structure is already present in the neural circuitry of newly born organisms. This structure is genetically encoded and the result of evolutionary tinkering over time scales several times larger than those of continental drift. Little is known of the interaction between the prewired structure and the actual learning. One reasonable hypothesis is that complex tasks are broken up into simpler modules and that learning, perhaps in different forms, can operate both within and across modules. The modules in turn can be organized in a hierarchical way, all the way up to the level of nuclei or brain areas. The difficult problem then becomes how to find a suitable module decomposition and whether there are any principles for doing so (in particular, the solutions found by biology are probably not unique). One trick used by evolution seems to have been the duplication, by error, of a module together with the subsequent evolution of one of the copies into a new module somehow complementary of the first one. But this is far from yielding any useful principle and may, at best, be used in genetic type of algorithms, where evolutionary tinkering is mimicked in the computer. Whether in our search of solutions to complex problems we can avoid or significantly accelerate a long evolutionary process for each problem remains to be seen.

We have taken inspiration from these ideas, to tackle the problem of creating specific complex trajectories in a neural network. Although it is difficult at this stage to keep a close analogy with biology, it may be useful to think of the problem of central pattern generation or motor control in natural organisms. In order to construct a neural network capable of producing a double figure eight, we are going to introduce a certain degree of organization in the system prior to any learning. The basic organization of the system consists of a hierarchy of modules. Related but different ideas on hierarchical and modular decomposition, applied to a different class of problem, can be found in [7-8]. In this particular example, each module can be viewed essentially as an oscillator. The modules, in turn, are organized in a hierarchical way. For the time being, all the modules within one level of the hierarchy control the output of the modules located in the previous layer.

At the bottom of the hierarchy, in the first level, one finds a family of simple and possibly independent modules, each one corresponding to a circuit with a small number of units capable of producing some elementary trajectory, such as a sinusoidal oscillation. In the case of the additive model, these could be simple oscillator rings with two or three neurons, an odd number of inhibitory connections and sufficiently high gains [2-3]. Thus, in our example, the first level of the hierarchy could contain four oscillator rings, one for each loop of the target trajectory. The parameters in each one of these four modules can be adjusted, by gradient descent or random descent or some

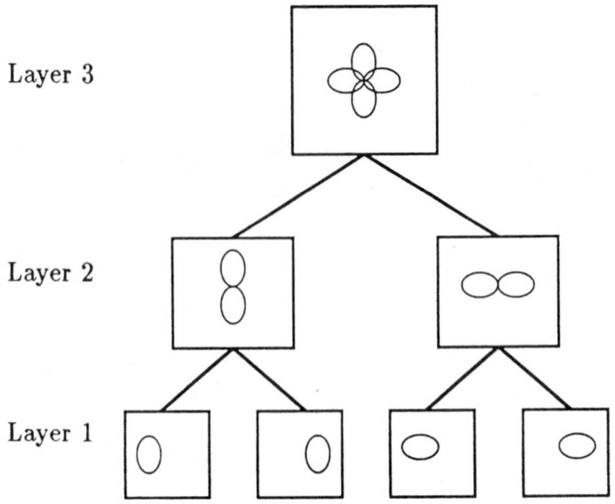

Figure 1: Symbolic representation of a modular and hierarchical network for double figure eight.

other optimization procedure, in order to match each one of the loops in the target trajectory.

The second level of the pyramid should contain two control modules. Each one of these modules controls a distinct pair of oscillator networks from the first level, so that each control network in the second level ends up producing a simple figure eight (see fig .1). Again, the control networks in level two can be oscillator rings and their parameters can be adjusted. In particular, after the learning process is completed, they should be operating in their high-gain regimes and have a period equal to the sum of the periods of the circuits each one controls.

Finally, the third layer, consist of another oscillatory and adjustable module which controls the two modules in the second level so as to produce a double figure eight. The third layer module must also end up operating in its high-gain regime with a period equal to four times the period of the oscillators in the first layer. In general, the final output trajectory is also a limit cycle because it is obtained by superimposition of limit cycles in the various modules. If the various oscillators relax to their limit cycles independently of one another, it is essential to provide for adjustable delays between the various modules in order to get the proper harmony among the various phases. In this way, a sparse network with 20 units or so can be constructed which can successfully execute a double figure eight. The importance of the effects of delays and adjustable delays in these architectures and their ubiquitous presence in natural neural systems has also lead us to conduct an analytical study of the effect of delays on neural dynamics (especially oscillatory properties) and learning

[3]. The main result there is that delays tend to increase the period of oscillations and broaden the spectrum of possible frequencies in a quantifiable way. A recurrent back-propagation learning algorithm can be derived for adjustable delays.

There are actually different possible neural network realizations depending on how the action of the control modules is implemented. For instance, if the control units are gating the connections between corresponding layers, this amounts to using higher order units in the network. The number of layers in the network then becomes a function of the order of the units one is willing to use. Alternatively, one could assume the existence of a fast weight dynamics on certain connections governed by a corresponding set of differential equations.

In the terminology used in [7-8], the four oscillators in the first level can be regarded as four experts, each one of them being knowledgeable about one of the four loops of the double figure eight. In their framework, the two output units of the network would be linear combinations of the corresponding outputs of the experts. The weights of the linear combinations, would come from the outputs of a gating network which has access to some input, for instance a representation of periodic time. The weights form a Gibbs distribution. These authors propose a back-propagation scheme to train the entire architecture simultaneously in a supervised way. Successful training should lead both to proper experts and proper Gibbs distribution which select only one of the experts at a time, in the right order. It remains to be seen if their algorithm can be used dynamically.

It is clear that this approach which combines a modular hierarchical architecture together with some simple form of learning can be extended to general trajectories. At the very least, one could always use Fourier analysis[1] to decompose a target trajectory into a superimposition of sinusoidal oscillations of different frequencies and use, in the first level of the hierarchy, a corresponding large bank of oscillators networks (although this decomposition may not be the most economical). One could also use damped oscillators to perform some sort of wavelet decomposition. Although we believe that oscillators with limit cycles present several attractive properties (stability, short transients, biological relevance...), one can conceivably use completely different circuits as building blocks in each module. Another observation is that the problem of synthesizing a network capable of certain given trajectories is more general than what would seem at first sight. In fact, any computation can be viewed as some sort of trajectory in the state space of a computing device, whether digital or analog.

The modular hierarchical approach leads to architectures which are more structured than fully interconnected networks, with a general feedforward flow of information and sparse recurrent connections to achieve dynamical effects. The sparsity of units and connections are attractive features for hardware design; and so is also the modular organization and the fact that learning is much more circumscribed than in fully interconnected systems. In these architectures, some form of learning remains essential, for instance to fine tune each one of the modules. This, in itself, is a much easier task than the one a fully interconnected and random network would have been faced with. It can be solved by gradient or random descent or other methods. Yet, fundamental open problems remain in the overall organization of learning across modules and in the origin of the decomposition. In particular, can the modular architecture be the outcome of a simple internal organizational process rather than an external imposition and how should learning be coordinated in time and across modules (other than the obvious: modules in the first level learn first, modules in the second level second,...)? How successful is a global gradient descent strategy applied across modules? How can the same modular architecture be used for different trajectories, with short switching times between trajectories and proper phases along each trajectory?

IV. Example of Numerical Simulations

The learning paradigm, presented in the preceding section, can be applied to the problem of learning a figure eight trajectory. Results referring to this problem can be found in the literature [10,14]. We assumed that the desired trajectory of a semi-figure eight is composed of two circles and given by:

$$D_1 = C_1\ [x_{10} + cos(t)]\ +\ (1 - C_1)[y_{10} - cos(t)] \quad (2a)$$

$$D_2 = C_1\ [x_{20} + sin(t)]\ +\ (1 - C_1)[y_{20} + sin(t)] \quad (2b)$$

in which C_1 is a square wave with a period of 4π, given by the following equation;

$$C_1 = sign[sin(t/2)] \quad (3)$$

and $x_{10}, x_{20}, y_{10}, y_{20}$ are the coordinates of the center of the left and right circles respectively. Plotting D_1 vs. D_2 will produce the desired semi-figure eight, as shown in fig. 2.

The basic module of the hierarchical approach for this trajectory is a simple oscillatory ring network with four

[1] Actually, in classical Fourier analysis, functions are expressed as superposition of sinusoidal oscillations with evenly spaced frequencies over the entire real line. This decomposition is not very "neural" and should be replaced by one where the frequencies of the oscillations are concentrated in a relatively narrow band, but can take arbitrary values within this band.

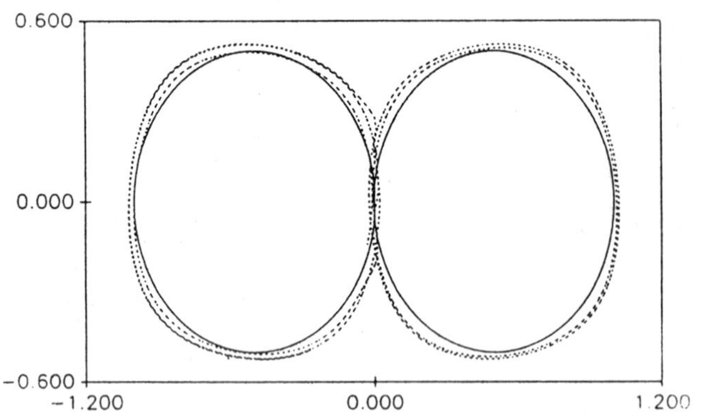

Figure 2: Desired semi-figure eight (solid line) and the one produced by the network (dashed line).

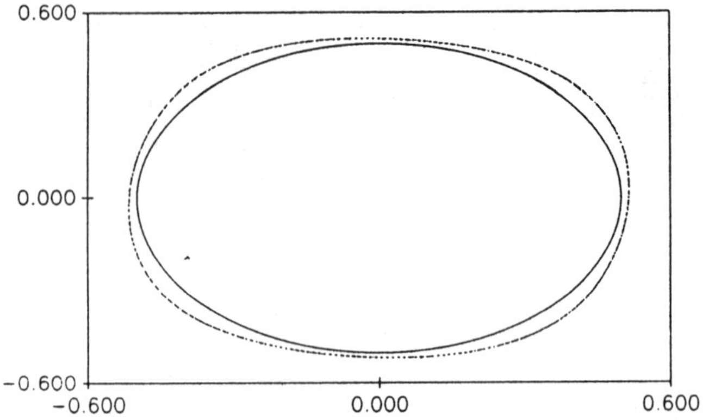

Figure 3: Desired circle (solid line) and the one produced by the basic module in the first layer (dashed line).

neurons. The activation dynamics of each unit in the module is given by:

$$\frac{du_i}{dt} = -\frac{u_i}{\tau_i} + w_{i-1}V_{i-1} \quad i = 1, \cdots, 4 \tag{4}$$

where $V_0 = V_4$ and V_i is the output of neuron i given by;

$$V_i = tanh(\gamma_i \ u_i) \tag{5}$$

An odd number of inhibitory connections is required for stable oscillations [2]. At this stage for simplicity, we assume that $w_i = w$ for $i = 1,3,4$, $w_2 = -w$ and $\tau_i = \tau, \gamma_i = \gamma$ for $i = 1, \cdots, 4$. The module is trained to produce a circle through a sinusoidal waive with period of 2π. Following the analysis in [2], the initial value of the network parameters, i.e., w, τ and γ are set to one at the beginning of the learning procedure. To update the network parameters, a gradient descent algorithm based upon the forward propagation of the error is used [15]. After the training, the network parameters converge to the following values, $w = 1.025, \tau = 0.972$ and $\gamma = 1.526$. With these values, after a brief transition period, the module converges to a limit cycle where each unit has a quasi-sinusoidal activation. The phase shift between two consecutive neurons is about $\pi/4$. Therefore, plotting the activity of neuron 1 and 3 in the module against each other will produce a circle which is close to the desire one as illustrated in Fig. 3.

At the second level of the hierarchy is the control module. This module is also chosen to be a simple oscillatory ring network with four neurons. This network is operating in the high gain regime and its period is twice that of the basic modules, i.e., 4π. The network parameters at the beginning of the learning are set to $w = 0.9, \gamma = 10$, and $\tau = 2.58$.

The overall network has two output at any time, Z_1 and Z_2. Their value is given by:

$$Z_1 = 0.5\{[1+VC(1)]\cdot[x_{10}+VN1(1)]+[1-VC(1)]\cdot[y_{10}+VN1(3)]\} \tag{6a}$$

$$Z_2 = 0.5\{[1+VC(1)]\cdot[x_{20}+VN2(1)]+[1-VC(1)]\cdot[y_{20}+VN2(3)]\} \tag{6b}$$

in which $VN1(i)$ and $VN2(i)$ are the output of ith neuron in the first and second modules in the first level of the hierarchy, respectively, where $VC(1)$ is the output of the first neuron in the control module. Figure 4 shows the semi-figure eight obtained be plotting Z_1 vs. Z_2.

The convergence time of different modules to their limit cycle may vary. Therefore, it is essential to have a synchronization mechanism that aliens the activity of different units at various modules and levels. One such mechanism that has been adapted in this example is based upon time delays. The value of these delays is adjusted by using gradient descent approach such that the network outputs are in harmony with the desired output.

V. Conclusions

In conclusion, a new hierarchical approach for supervised neural learning of time dependent trajectories is presented. The modular hierarchical methodology leads to architectures which are more structured than fully interconnected networks, with a general feedforward flow of information and sparse recurrent connections to achieve dynamical effects. The sparsity of the connections as well as the modular organization makes the hardware implementation of the methodology very easy and attractive.

ACKNOWLEDGMENTS

This research was carried out at the Center for Space Microelectronics Technology, Jet Propulsion Laboratory, California Institute of Technology under contract with the National Aeronautics and Space Administration. Support for the work came from agencies of the U.S. Department of Defense, including Air-Force Office of Scientific Research and Army's APO techbase program.

REFERENCES

[1] S. Amari, "Characteristics of random nets of analog neuron-like elements," *IEEE Transactions on Systems, Man and Cybernetics*, Vol. **SMC-2**, 5, 643-657, 1972.

[2] A. Atiya and P. Baldi, "Oscillations and synchronization in neural networks: an exploration of the labeling hypothesis," *International Journal of Neural Systems*, Vol. **1**, 2, 103-124, 1989.

[3] P. Baldi and A. Atiya, "How delays affect neural dynamics and learning," *IEEE Trans. On Neural Networks*, in Press, 1993. unpublished.

[4] P. Baldi, " Learning in dynamical systems: gradient descent, random descent and modular approach," JPL Technical Report, California Institute of Technology, 1992.

[5] S. Geman, E. Bienenstock and R. Doursat, "Neural networks and the bias/variance dilemma," *Neural Computation*, Vol. **4**, 1-58, 1992.

[6] J. J. Hopfield, "Neurons with graded response have collective computational properties like those of two-state neurons," *PNAS USA*, Vol. **81**, 3088-3092, 1984.

[7] R. A. Jacobs, M. I. Jordan, S. J. Nowlan and G. E. Hinton, "Adaptive mixture of local experts," *Neural Computation*, Vol. bf 3, 79-87, 1991.

[8] M. I. Jordan and R. A. Jacobs, "Hierarchies of adaptive experts," *Neural Information Processing Systems*, Vol. bf 4, J. Moody, S.Hanson and R. Lippmann Eds., Morgan Kaufmann, 1992.

[9] D. Kleinfeld, "Sequential state generation by model neural networks." *PNAS*, Vol. **83**, 9469-9473, 1986.

[10] B. Pearlmutter, "Learning state space trajectories in recurrent neural networks," *Neural Computation*, Vol. **1**, 2, 263-269, 1989.

[11] F. J. Pineda, "Generalization of back-propagation to recurrent neural networks," *Physical Review Letters*, Vol. **59**, 19, 2229-2232, 1987.

[12] D. E. Rumelhart, G. E. Hinton and R. J. Williams, "Learning internal representations by error propagation," *Parallel Distributed Processing*, Rumelhart, D. E. and McClelland, J. L. eds. MIT Press, 1986.

[13] H. Sompolinsky and I. Kanter, "Temporal association in asymmetric neural networks," *Physical Review Letters*, Vol. **57**, 22, 2861-2864, 1986.

[14] N. B. Toomarian and J. Barhen, "Learning a trajectory using adjoint functions and teacher forcing," *Neural Networks*, Vol. **5**, 3, 473-484, 1992.

[15] R. J. Williams and D. Zipser, " A learning algorithm for continually running fully recurrent neural networks," *Neural Computation*, Vol. bf 1, 2, 270-280, 1989.

Comparisons of Four Learning Algorithms for Training the Multilayer Feedforward Neural Networks With Hard-limiting Neurons

Xiangui Yu[1], Nan K. Loh[2], G. A. Jullien[1], W. C. Miller[1]

1. Dept. of Electrical Engineering, University of Windsor
Windsor, Ontario N9B 3P4
Tel: (519)253-4232, Ext:3393 Fax: (519)973-7062
e-mail: xianguy@engn.uwindsor.ca

2. Center for Robotics and Advanced Automation
Dodge Hall of Engineering
Oakland University
Rochester, Michigan 48309-4401, U. S. A.

Abstract

In this paper, two kinds of learning algorithms that have been developed for training the multilayer feedforward neural networks with hard-limiting neurons are reviewed. For the modified backpropagation algorithms, their numerical performances of convergence speed, training efficiency are compared; For the architecture generating methods, the architecture sizes of the neural network generated are compared and their generalization ability were discussed. For any given application problem, some criteria for selecting the suitable training algorithm are also discussed.

1. Introduction

Hard-limiting neurons were always used in the artificial neural networks as early as this area was emerged several decades ago [1]. For one layer perceptron, the perceptron learning algorithm is very efficient to classify the linear separable training sets. For linear non-separable training set, the one layer perceptron cannot classify the input-output pattern pairs correctly. Thus, the multilayer feedforward neural networks were proposed to cope this difficulty [2]. If hard-limiting neurons are used in the multilayer perceptrons, the input-output relationship is a non-continuous, non-linear function, no efficient learning algorithm was developed for training the multilayer feedforward neural networks with hard-limiting neurons. Although the famous backpropagation algorithm is very efficient for training the multilayer feedforward neural networks with analog sigmoidal neurons, because of the non-continuity and absence of derivatives of the hard-limiting activation functions, training this kind of neural network with hard-limiting neurons by means of the standard backpropagation algorithm was thought almost impossible [3]. In recent years, several methods were developed for training the multilayer feedforward neural networks with binary or bipolar neurons. All of them could be classified into two categories: the modified backpropagation algorithms and the architecture generating algorithms. In 1990, D.J. Toms proposed a modified backpropagation algorithm which used hybrid neurons in all the hidden layers. The activation function of the hybrid neurons is defined as the linear combination of the continuous sigmoidal one and the binary hard-limiting one [4]. The transformation from analog sigmoidal-like neuron into discrete hard-limiting one is controlled by a coefficient λ, which is 1 at initial training process to 0 after some training steps. The authors of this paper improved Toms' algorithm by updating the coefficient λ with the sum-squared-error [5]; In addition, another form of modified backpropagation algorithm was developed which used the transforming neurons in all the hidden layer. The transforming neuron activation function is defined as the analog sigmoidal one with an adaptive steepness factor. By adjusting this steepness factor in the learning process adaptively, a multilayer feedforward neural network can be trained with the resultant architecture is only composed of hard-limiting neurons.

Although the backpropagation-based algorithms are very efficient in training multilayer feedforward neural networks, there are some problems they could not solve efficiently. For a given pattern recognition problem, we only know the number of the input nodes and the number of output neurons, there is no prior knowledge about the architecture of the neural network. Although it is shown [6] that a three layer perceptron with sigmoid-type nonlinearity at cells can approximate any arbitrary nonlinear function and generate any complex design region needed for classification and recognition tasks, but we don't know how many hidden layers, and how many neurons in each hidden layer should be used for a given problem.

The network architecture is a very important consideration for the optimal trainability and generalization ability. In recent years, a few researchers proposed some learning algorithms which can generate the neural network architecture dynamically in the learning process. In 1989, Mezard *et al* [8] proposed a tiling algorithm, which adds hidden layers, and hidden neurons in each layer, at will until convergence, and the system error is guaranteed to zero after the neural network was fully trained. In 1990, M. Frean proposed an upstart algorithm [9], which build hidden layers from the input outward until convergence, new units are interpolated between the input layer and the output neuron. The role of these units is to correct mistakes made by the output unit [9]. In 1991, R. Zollner *et al* proposed a fast iterative algorithm [10] for construction and training of a neural network with only one hidden layer, since one hidden layer is enough to classify any training patterns. Their algorithm construct and train the system from bottom to top of the network other than feedforward [10].

This paper studies the above two kinds of algorithms--the modified backpropagation algorithms and the architecture generating algorithms. For the modified BP algorithms, we compared their convergence speed, studied the effects of the transforming coefficients on its trainability; For the architecture generating methods, the size of the architecture of the neural networks generated were compared and their generalization ability were discussed. For any given application problem, some criteria for selecting the suitable training algorithm are also reviewed.

The paper is organized as follows: In the following Section 2, the modified backpropagation algorithms are reviewed and their numerical performance are compared; In

CCECE/CCGEI '93

0-7803-1443-3/93 $3.00

the Section 3, three architecture generating methods were reviewed; and some comments on their implementation are presented; In the Section 4, the numerical simulations are presented to show their advantages and disadvantages respectively; In the final Section 5, conclusions are given and future research directions are recommended.

2. The Modified Backpropagation Algorithms

The two modified backpropagation algorithms are similar to the standard backpropagation algorithm, just the hidden neuron activation functions and their derivatives are changed. Consider a L-layer fully connected feedforward neural network. Suppose that the network has N_0 input notes, N_l neurons in the lth layer, where $l=1, 2, \cdots, L$. Furthermore, suppose that the pth input pattern in the training set is:

$$x_p = (x_{1p}\ x_{2p}\ \cdots\ x_{N_0 p})^T \tag{1}$$

The pth output pattern in the training set is:

$$y_p^{[L]} = (y_{1p}^{[L]}\ y_{2p}^{[L]}\ \cdots\ y_{N_L p}^{[L]})^T \tag{2}$$

Corresponding to the pth input pattern, the output vector of the lth hidden layer is:

$$y_p^{[l]} = (y_{1p}^{[l]}\ y_{2p}^{[l]}\ \cdots\ y_{N_l p}^{[l]})^T \tag{3}$$

then the relationship between the output of all neurons in the lth layer and the jth neuron in the $(l+1)$th layer is:

$$y_{jp}^{[l+1]} = f(\sum_{i=1}^{N_l} w_{ij}^{[l+1]} y_{ip}^{[l]} + \vartheta_j^{[l+1]}) \tag{4}$$

where, $\vartheta_j^{[l+1]}$ is the threshold of jth neuron in the $(l+1)$th layer; $w_{ij}^{[l+1]}$ is the connection strength (weight) from the ith neuron in the lth layer to the jth neuron in the $(l+1)$th layer; $i=1, 2, \cdots, N_l$, $j=1, 2, \cdots, N_{l+1}$, $l=0, 1, 2, \cdots, L-1$. when $l=0$, $y_{ip}^{[0]} = x_{ip}$, $i=1, 2, \cdots, N_0$. $f(\ )$ is the neuron activation function, it is nondecreasing and differentiable.

The standard backpropagation algorithm can be found in [5],[11].

In 1990, D.J. Toms proposed a modified backpropagation algorithm which used hybrid neurons in the hidden layers. The activation function of the hybrid neuron is defined as:

$$f(x) = \lambda \cdot s(x) + (1-\lambda)\cdot h(x) \tag{5}$$

where $s(x)$ is the sigmoidal function which is defined as:

$$s(x) = \frac{1}{1+e^{-x}} \tag{6}$$

and $h(x)$ is the hard-limiting function which is defined as:

$$h(x) = \begin{cases} 1 & x \ge 0 \\ 0 & x < 0 \end{cases} \tag{7}$$

and $0 \le \lambda \le 1$. Obviously, when $\lambda = 1$, the hybrid neuron is purely analog sigmoidal one; When $\lambda = 0$, the hybrid neuron becomes purely discrete hard-limiting one. For intermediate value of $0 < \lambda < 1$, the neuron is a hybrid one, with a hidden unit activation function that is differentiable everywhere except at $\lambda = 0$:

$$f'(x) = \lambda s(x)(1-s(x)) \qquad \lambda \ne 0 \tag{8}$$

The Toms' algorithm is just substituting (5), (8) with the corresponding parts in the standard backpropagation algorithm. It is initialized with $\lambda=1$, in the training process, λ is gradually reduced to zero in a few steps. Thus the trained multilayer feedforward neural network is composed of hard-limiting neurons.

Although this simple modification can train the binary neural networks, it often stuck in the local minima. In addition, since λ is linearly decreased to zero, the learning speed is also affected by the updating way of this coefficient. If we update this coefficient according to the following way:

$$\lambda(n) = e^{-1/SSE} \tag{9}$$

where SSE is the Sum-Squared-Error. Then in the initial training process, since sum-square-error is very great, $\lambda(n)$ is nearly 1; with the training proceeds, $\lambda(n)$ will decreased to 0 with the convergence of the sum-square-error. This updating could guarantee the final error is absolutely zero.

The second modification is using the following sigmoidal neuron activation function with a adaptive steepness factor α in the hidden layers:

$$f(x) = \frac{1}{1+e^{-\alpha x}} \tag{10}$$

Its derivative is:

$$f'(x) = \alpha \cdot f(x)(1-f(x)) \tag{11}$$

The coefficient α is related to the steepness of the sigmoidal function. Obviously, with the increase of α, the sigmoidal function defined by (10) will approach to hard-limiting one. In the initial steps, α is selected as a small positive value, with the training proceeds, it will increase gradually. The best way is to update the α with the decrease of the sum-square-error . When the SSE is great, α is selected as a small value, when SSE is small, α is updated to a great value, and the hidden neurons are transformed into hard-limiting ones. Thus the updating of α can choose the following form:

$$\alpha(n) = 0.5 \cdot e^{1/SSE} \tag{12}$$

Thus the second modified backpropagation algorithm is just substitute (10), (11) with the corresponding parts in the standard backpropagation algorithm.

The comparisons of their numerical properties were discussed in [5] in detail.

3. Architecture Generating Algorithms

There are several algorithms which could generate the architecture of the neural network in the training process. In which most of them are suitable for only one neuron in the output layer. In the following we listed three of them:

3.1: The Improved Tiling Algorithm

The tiling algorithm was first proposed in 1989. The architecture generated by the original tiling algorithm is every big. The authors of this paper improved the tiling algorithm by assigning the target output value of the added neurons with a new method [7]. It is summarized as follows:

1. START with a one-layer perceptron with N_0 input nodes, N_t output neurons;
2. Train this neural net using pocket algorithm [14],[15] until it converges;
3. Classify the input-output pattern pairs into some groups according to the kinds of actual output pattern:

take those input-output pattern pairs with same actual output pattern into same group. In each group, count up the number of kinds of target output patterns, let M is the maximum value of these numbers;

4. A: If $M=1$, check each group if the actual output pattern equal to the corresponding target output pattern;

   a: If yes, go to 6;

   b: If not, let P_h is the number of kinds of the actual output patterns, form the P_h different actual-target output pattern pairs, go to 5;

   B: If $M>1$, add $N=\log_2 M$ ancillary neurons, carefully define the target output values of these added neurons in order to sure in each group, those input patterns corresponding to different target outputs must have different output values for the added neurons. Let $N_t=N_t+N$, go to 2);
5. Generate a one-layer perceptron with N_h input nodes, N_t output neurons, it has P_h input-output pattern pairs to be trained, go to 2);
6. The previously trained neural net is the network what we want, print out the weights and threshold values in each layer;
7. STOP

3.2: The Upstart Algorithm

The upstart algorithm interpolate the new units between the input layer and the output layer instead of building layers from the input outward. It can be described as follows [9]:

1 START with a one-layer perceptron with N_0 input nodes, one output neuron;

2 Train this neural net using pocket algorithm until it converges; Let T_1 is the total number of patterns with recall output is 1 but the target output is 0; T_2 is the total number of patterns with recall output is 0 but the target output is 1;

3 If $T_1 \neq 0$, add one neuron X connected to the input nodes, define the target output of X is:

$$t_X = \begin{cases} 1 & t_Z = 0 \ \ and \ \ o_Z = 1 \\ 0 & otherwise \end{cases}$$

If $T_2 \neq 0$, add one neuron Y connected to the input nodes, define the target output of Y is:

$$t_Y = \begin{cases} 1 & t_Z = 1 \ \ and \ \ o_Z = 0 \\ 0 & otherwise \end{cases}$$

4 Connect the outputs of X and Y to the original output neuron Z, train X, Y, Z again. This time Z should be fully trained. For X and Y, doing the same process as Z, until every neuron are fully trained.

3.3: The Fast Generating Algorithm

The main idea of the fast generating algorithm is to collect the set of patterns with the target output 1 into several subsets, every subset will be treated as a simple perceptron architecture. Let p^+ patterns with a desired output of +1 and p^- patterns with a desired output of 0. we try to divide the p^+ patterns into some subsets, for every subset, there exist a hypercone which contains and only contains some patterns in this subset. Define the desired output for the corresponding intermediate unit in the following way: only patterns inside the hypercones should be 1 and all the other patterns outside the hypercone, including those of the other subsets, which should have finally output 1, should have output 0 at the intermediate unit considered. Then the output simply achieves an OR Boolean function on the results of the intermediate units: if for a given input at least one hidden neurons with output 1, then the target output is also 1, On the other hand, if every hidden neuron with output 0, then the target output is also 0.

Construction of those subsets can employs the modified Hebbian method to decompose the p^+ patterns iteratively. Other methods are also feasible. This paper only used the modified Hebbian method in the numerical simulations.

4. Numerical Simulations

We have tested the above four algorithms with a lot of problems. The comparison criteria are: the number of neurons added in the intermediate layers, the generalizations ability of the generated neural networks..

4.1: The comparison of the synthesized architecture

Take the random Boolean function as an example to compare the ability of the above 4 architecture generating methods. The binary classification of a random Boolean function is obtained by assigning each of the 2^{N_0} input patterns with target 0 or 1 with equal probability. It is a difficult problem due to the absence of correlation and structure in the input for the network to exploit. The number of neurons generated by the above 4 methods for different N_0 are summarized in Figure 1.

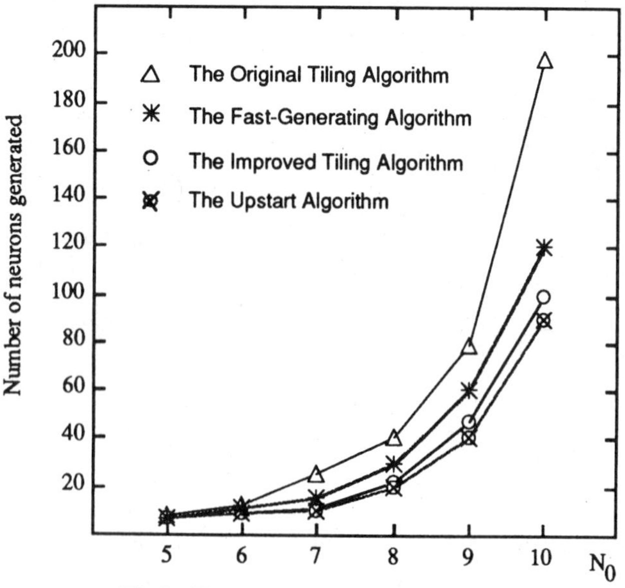

Fig.2: The comparisons of 4 methods

From Fig.1, we know that for a given application problem, the upstart algorithm generally obtains a small number of neurons, the original tiling algorithm gets more neurons. But in fact, the upstart algorithm generally produces more layers than other methods, and the fast generating algorithm only produces one hidden layer.

4.2: The comparison of the generalization ability

Once a network has been built, it performs the correct mapping for all the patterns in the training set. How does it perform on new patterns not presented in the training set is the neural network generalization problem. Here we also take an example to show the generalization ability of the above 4 algorithms. One of the difficult problem for neural network is the parity problem, in which for N_0 Boolean units the output should be 1 if the number of input units in the "on" states are even, 0 if the number of input units in the "off" states are odd. For this problem, there is a solution consisting of a single hidden layer of N_0 hidden neurons that would solve the problem exactly. Using the above 4 methods, it is very difficult to get the theoretical solutions for $N_0 \geq 10$. Take $N_0 = 12$ as a special case, the number of complete input patterns is $2^{15} = 4096$. Randomly selecting some number of patterns, using the 4 methods to construct the neural network, then take the whole pattern set as testing patterns. Figure 2 shows the percentage of correct generalization as the size of the training set is increased.

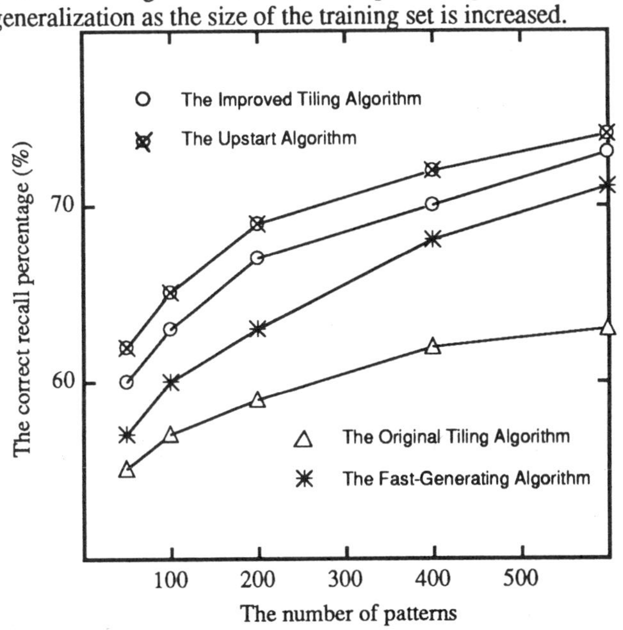

Fig.4: The generalization ability comparison

It can be concluded that for a given problem, with the increase of the size of the neural network, the generalization ability will decrease. It is same as the theoretical results.

5. Conclusions

In this paper, two kinds of learning algorithms that have been developed for training the multilayer feedforward neural networks with hard-limiting neurons are reviewed. For the modified backpropagation algorithms, their numerical properties is similar to the standard BP algorithm. Some methods can be used to improve its numerical performance. Using some newly developed methods to generate the minimum neural network architecture using the modified BP algorithms is also possible. For the architecture generating methods, is there any possibility to combine them together is also an interesting topic. In addition, how to generate a neural network with multi-output neurons and how to minimize the number of hidden neurons and the number of connections (weights) for a given application problem is also very challenging.

References

[1] B. Widrow and M.A. Lehr, "30 years of adaptive neural networks: Perceptron, Madaline, and Backpropagation," *Proc. of the IEEE,* Vol.78, No.9, pp.1415-1442, September 1990

[2] M. Minsky, and S. Papert. *Perceptron: An introduction to Computational geometry,* M.I.T. Press, 1969.

[3] D. Rumelhart, D. Hinton, and G. Williams, "Learning internal representations by error propagation." In D. Rumelhart and F. McCelland, eds., *Parallel Distributed Processing,* Vol.1, Cambridge, MA, MIT Press, 1969

[4] D. J. Toms, "Training binary node feedforward neural networks by back propagation of errors," *IEE Electronics Letters,* Vol.26, No.21, pp.1745-1746, 1990

[5] Xiangui Yu, Nan K. Loh, G.A. Jullien and W. C. Miller, "Modified backpropagation algorithms for training the multilayer feedforward neural networks with hard-limiting neurons," *1993 Canadian Conference on Electrical and Computer Engineering,* Vancouver, Sept. 14-17, 1993.

[6] R. P. Lippmann, "An Introduction to Computing with Neural Nets", *IEEE ASSP Magazine,* April 1987, pp. 4-22.

[7] Xiangui Yu, Nan K. Loh and W. C. Miller, "A new algorithm for training the multilayer feedforward neural networks," *1993 International Symposium on circuits and systems,* Chicago, May 4-6, 1993.

[8] M. Mezard, and J. P. Nadal, "Learning in feedforward layered networks: the tiling algorithm," Journal of Physics A: Mathematical and General, Vol.22, pp.2191-2203, 1989

[9] M. Frean, "The upstart algorithm: a method for constructing and training feedforward neural networks," *Neural Computation,* Vol.2, pp198-209, 1990

[10] R. Zollner, H.J. Schmitz, F. Wunsch and U. Krey, "Fast generating algorithm for a general three-layer perceptron," *Neural Networks,* Vol.5, pp.771-777, 1992

[11] J.M. Zurada, *Introduction to artificial neural systems,* West Publishing Company, 1992

[12] S. I. Gallant, "Perceptron-based learning algorithms," *IEEE Trans. on Neural Networks,* Vol.1, No.2, pp.179-191, 1990

[13] M. Frean, "A 'thermal' perceptron learning rule," *Neural Computation,* Vol.4, pp.946-957, 1992

[14] M. Biehl, and M. Opper, "Tiling like Learning in the parity machine," *Physical Review A,* Vol.44, No.10, pp.6888-6894, 1991

Optimal Brain Surgeon and General Network Pruning

Babak Hassibi*
Ricoh California Research Center and
Department of Electrical Engineering
Stanford University
Stanford, CA 94305

David G. Stork
Ricoh California Research Center
2882 Sand Hill Road Suite 115
Menlo Park, CA 94025-7022
stork@crc.ricoh.com

Gregory J. Wolff
Ricoh California Research Center
2882 Sand Hill Road Suite 115
Menlo Park, CA 94025-7022
wolff@crc.ricoh.com

***Abstract*— We investigate the use of information from all second order derivatives of the error function to perform network pruning (i.e., removing unimportant weights from a trained network) in order to improve generalization, simplify networks, reduce hardware or storage requirements, increase the speed of further training, and in some cases enable rule extraction. Our method, Optimal Brain Surgeon (OBS), is significantly better than magnitude-based methods and Optimal Brain Damage, which often remove the wrong weights. OBS permits pruning of more weights than other methods (for the same error on the training set), and thus yields better generalization on test data. Crucial to OBS is a recursion relation for calculating the inverse Hessian matrix $\mathbf{H}^{-1}$ from training data and structural information of the net. OBS permits a 76%, a 62%, and a 90% reduction in weights over backpropagation with weight decay on three benchmark MONK's problems. Of OBS, Optimal Brain Damage, and a magnitude-based method, only OBS deletes the correct weights from a trained XOR network in every case. Finally, whereas Sejnowski and Rosenberg used 18,000 weights in their NETtalk network, we used OBS to prune a network to just 1,560 weights, yielding better generalization.**

I. Introduction

A central problem in machine learning and pattern recognition is to minimize the system complexity (description length, VC-dimension, etc.) consistent with the training data. In neural networks this regularization problem is often cast as minimizing the number of connection weights. Without such weight elimination overfitting problems and thus poor generalization will result. Conversely, if there are too few weights, the network might not be able to learn the training data.

If we begin with a trained network having too many weights, the questions then become: Which weights should be eliminated? How should the remaining weights be adjusted for best performance? How can such network pruning be done in a computationally efficient way?

One possible magnitude based method [3] eliminates weights that have the smallest magnitude. This simple, plausible idea unfortunately often leads to the elimination of the wrong weights – small weights can be necessary for low error. Optimal Brain Damage [6] uses the criterion of minimal increase in training error for weight elimination. For computational simplicity, OBD assumes that the Hessian matrix is diagonal; in fact, however, Hessians for every problem we have considered are strongly non-diagonal, and this leads OBD to eliminate the wrong weights. The method described here – Optimal Brain Surgeon (OBS) – accepts the criterion used by Le Cun et al., but makes no restrictive assumptions about the form of the network's Hessian. OBS thereby eliminates the correct weights. Moreover, unlike other methods, OBS does not demand (typically slow) retraining after the pruning of a weight.

II. Optimal Brain Surgeon

In deriving our method we begin, as do Le Cun, Denker and Solla [6], by considering a network trained to a local minimum in error. The functional Taylor series of the error with respect to weights (or parameters, see below) is:

$$\delta E = \left(\frac{\partial E}{\partial \mathbf{w}}\right)^T \cdot \delta \mathbf{w} + \frac{1}{2}\delta \mathbf{w}^T \cdot \mathbf{H} \cdot \delta \mathbf{w} + O(\| \delta \mathbf{w} \|^3) \quad (1)$$

*Supported in part by grants AFOSR 91-0060 and DAAL03-91-C-0010 to T. Kailath, who in turn provided constant encouragement. Deep thanks go to Jerome Friedman (Stanford) for pointers to relevant statistics literature.

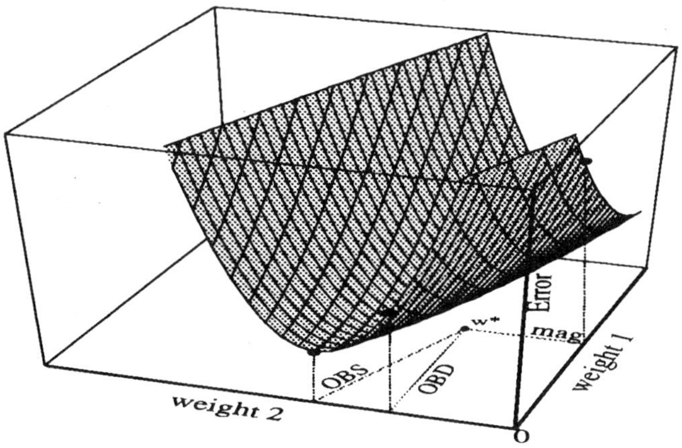

Figure 1: Error as a function of two weights in a network. The (local) minimum occurs at weight w*, found by gradient descent or other learning method. In this illustration, a magnitude based pruning technique (mag) then removes the smallest weight, weight 2; Optimal Brain Damage (OBD) before retraining removes weight 1. In contrast, our Optimal Brain Surgeon method (OBS) not only removes weight 1, but also automatically adjusts the value of weight 2 to minimize the error, without retraining. The error surface here is general in that it has different curvature (second derivatives) along different directions, a minimum at a non-special weight value, and a non-diagonal Hessian (i.e., principal axes are not parallel to the weight axes). We have found (to our surprise) that every problem we have investigated has strongly non-diagonal Hessians - thereby explaining the improvement of our method over that of Le Cun et al.

where $\mathbf{H} \equiv \partial^2 E/\partial \mathbf{w}^2$ is the Hessian matrix (containing all second order derivatives) and the superscript T denotes vector transpose. For a network trained to a local minimum in error, the first (linear) term vanishes; we also ignore the third and all higher order terms. Our goal is then to set one of the weights to zero (which we call w_q) to minimize the increase in error given by Eq. 1. Eliminating w_q is expressed as $\delta w_q + w_q = 0$ or more generally:

$$\mathbf{e}_q^T \cdot \delta\mathbf{w} + w_q = 0 \tag{2}$$

where $\mathbf{e}_q$ is the unit vector in weight space corresponding to (scalar) weight w_q. Our goal is then to solve:

$$\min_q \{ \min_{\delta\mathbf{w}} (\frac{1}{2} \delta\mathbf{w}^T \cdot \mathbf{H} \cdot \delta\mathbf{w}) \mid \mathbf{e}_q^T \cdot \delta\mathbf{w} + w_q = 0 \} \tag{3}$$

To solve Eq. 3 we form a Lagrangian from Eqs. 1 and 2:

$$L = \frac{1}{2} \delta\mathbf{w}^T \cdot \mathbf{H} \cdot \delta\mathbf{w} + \lambda(\mathbf{e}_q^T \cdot \delta\mathbf{w} + w_q) \tag{4}$$

where λ is a Lagrange undetermined multiplier. We take functional derivatives, employ the constraints of Eq. 2, and use matrix inversion to find that the optimal weight change and resulting change in error are:

$$\delta\mathbf{w} = -\frac{w_q}{[\mathbf{H}^{-1}]_{qq}} \mathbf{H}^{-1} \cdot \mathbf{e}_q \tag{5}$$

$$L_q = \frac{1}{2} \frac{w_q^2}{[\mathbf{H}^{-1}]_{qq}} \tag{6}$$

Note that neither $\mathbf{H}$ nor $\mathbf{H}^{-1}$ need be diagonal (as is assumed by Le Cun et al.); moreover, our method recalculates the magnitude of all the weights in the network, by Eq. 5. We call L_q the "saliency" of weight q – the increase in error that results when the weight is eliminated – a definition more general than Le Cun et al.'s, and which includes theirs in the special case of diagonal $\mathbf{H}$. Thus we have the algorithm of Table 1.

Table 1: *Optimal Brain Surgeon procedure*

1. Train a "reasonably large" network to minimum error.
2. Compute $\mathbf{H}^{-1}$.
3. Find the q that gives the smallest saliency $L_q = w_q^2/(2[\mathbf{H}^{-1}]qq)$. If this candidate error increase is much smaller than E, then the qth weight should be deleted, and we proceed to step 4; otherwise go to step 5. (Other stopping criteria can be used too.)
4. Use the q from step 3 to update *all* weights (Eq. 5). Go to step 2.
5. No more weights can be deleted without large increase in E. (At this point it may be desirable to retrain the network.)

Figure 1 illustrates the basic idea. The relative magnitudes of the error after pruning (before retraining, if any) depend upon the particular problem, but to second order obey: E(mag) $\geq$ E(OBD) $\geq$ E(OBS), which is the key to the superiority of OBS. In this example OBS and OBD lead to the elimination of the same weight (weight 1). In many cases, however, OBS will eliminate *different* weights than those eliminated by OBD (cf. Sect. VI). We call our method Optimal Brain Surgeon because in addition to deleting weights, it calculates and changes the strengths of other weights without the need for gradient descent or other incremental retraining.

III. Computing the inverse Hessian

The difficulty appears to be step 2 in the OBS procedure, since inverting a matrix of thousands or millions of terms seems computationally intractable. In what follows we shall give a general derivation of the inverse Hessian for a fully trained neural network. It makes no difference whether it was trained by backpropagation, competitive learning, the Boltzmann algorithm, or any other method, so long as derivatives can be taken (see below). We shall show that the Hessian can be reduced to the sample covariance matrix associated with certain gradient vectors. Furthermore, the gradient vectors necessary for OBS are normally available at small computational cost; the covariance form of the Hessian yields a recursive formula for computing the inverse.

Consider a general non-linear neural network that maps an input vector, in, of dimension n_i into an output vector, o, of dimension n_o, according to the following:

$$\mathbf{o} = \mathbf{F}(\mathbf{w}, \mathbf{in}) \qquad (7)$$

where $\mathbf{w}$ is an n-dimensional vector representing the neural network's weights or other parameters. We shall refer to $\mathbf{w}$ as a weight vector below for simplicity and definiteness, but it must be stressed that $\mathbf{w}$ could represent any continuous parameters, such as those describing neural transfer function, weight sharing, and so on. The mean square error on the training set is defined as:

$$E = \frac{1}{2P}\sum_{k=1}^{P}(\mathbf{t}^{[k]} - \mathbf{o}^{[k]})^T(\mathbf{t}^{[k]} - \mathbf{o}^{[k]}) \qquad (8)$$

where P is the number of training patterns, and $\mathbf{t}^{[k]}$ and $\mathbf{o}^{[k]}$ are the desired response and network response for the kth training pattern. The first derivative with respect to $\mathbf{w}$ is:

$$\frac{\partial E}{\partial \mathbf{w}} = -\frac{1}{P}\sum_{k=1}^{P}\frac{\partial \mathbf{F}(\mathbf{w}, \mathbf{in}^{[k]})}{\partial \mathbf{w}}(\mathbf{t}^{[k]} - \mathbf{o}^{[k]}) \qquad (9)$$

and the second derivative or Hessian is:

$$\mathbf{H} \equiv \frac{1}{P}\sum_{k=1}^{P}\left[\frac{\partial \mathbf{F}(\mathbf{w}, \mathbf{in}^{[k]})}{\partial \mathbf{w}} \cdot \frac{\partial \mathbf{F}(\mathbf{w}, \mathbf{in}^{[k]})^T}{\partial \mathbf{w}} - \frac{\partial^2 \mathbf{F}(\mathbf{w}, \mathbf{in}^{[k]})}{\partial \mathbf{w}^2} \cdot (\mathbf{t}^{[k]} - \mathbf{o}^{[k]})\right] \qquad (10)$$

Next we consider a network fully trained to a local minimum in error at $\mathbf{w}^*$. Under this condition the network response $\mathbf{o}^{[k]}$ will be close to the desired response $\mathbf{t}^{[k]}$, and hence we neglect the term involving $(\mathbf{t}^{[k]} - \mathbf{o}^{[k]})$. Even late in pruning, when this error is not small for a single pattern, this approximation can be justified (see next Section). This simplification yields:

$$\mathbf{H} = \frac{1}{P}\sum_{k=1}^{P}\frac{\partial \mathbf{F}(\mathbf{w}, \mathbf{in}^{[k]})}{\partial \mathbf{w}} \cdot \frac{\partial \mathbf{F}(\mathbf{w}, \mathbf{in}^{[k]})^T}{\partial \mathbf{w}} \qquad (11)$$

If our network has just a single output, we may define the n-dimensional data vector$\mathbf{X}^{[k]}$ of derivatives as:

$$\mathbf{X}^{[k]} \equiv \frac{\partial \mathbf{F}(\mathbf{w}, \mathbf{in}^{[k]})}{\partial \mathbf{w}} \qquad (12)$$

Thus Eq. 11 can be written as:

$$\mathbf{H} = \frac{1}{P}\sum_{k=1}^{P}\mathbf{X}^{[k]} \cdot \mathbf{X}^{[k]T} \qquad (13)$$

If instead our network has *multiple* output units, then $\mathbf{X}$ will be an n x n_o matrix of the form:

$$\mathbf{X}^{[k]} \equiv \frac{\partial \mathbf{F}(\mathbf{w}, \mathbf{in}^{[k]})}{\partial \mathbf{w}} = \frac{\partial \mathbf{F}_1(\mathbf{w}, \mathbf{in}^{[k]})}{\partial \mathbf{w}}, \ldots, \frac{\partial \mathbf{F}_{n_o}(\mathbf{w}, \mathbf{in}^{[k]})}{\partial \mathbf{w}} = (\mathbf{X}_1^{[k]}, \cdots, \mathbf{X}_{n_o}^{[k]}) \qquad (14)$$

where $\mathbf{F}_i$ is the ith component of $\mathbf{F}$. Hence in this multiple output unit case Eq. 11 generalizes to:

$$\mathbf{H} = \frac{1}{P}\sum_{k=1}^{P}\sum_{l=1}^{n_o}\mathbf{X}_l^{[k]} \cdot \mathbf{X}_l^{[k]T} \qquad (15)$$

Equations 13 and 15 show that $\mathbf{H}$ is the sample covariance matrix associated with the gradient variable $\mathbf{X}$. Equation 13 also shows that for the single output case we can calculate the full Hessian by sequentially adding in successive "component" Hessians as:

$$\mathbf{H}_{m+1} = \mathbf{H}_m + \frac{1}{P}\mathbf{X}^{[m+1]} \cdot \mathbf{X}^{[m+1]T} \qquad (16)$$

with $\mathbf{H}_0 = \alpha \mathbf{I}$ and $\mathbf{H}_P = \mathbf{H}$.

But Optimal Brain Surgeon requires the *inverse* of $\mathbf{H}$ (Eq. 5). This inverse can be calculated using a standard matrix inversion formula [4]:

$$(\mathbf{A} + \mathbf{B} \cdot \mathbf{C} \cdot \mathbf{D})^{-1} = \mathbf{A}^{-1} - \mathbf{A}^{-1} \cdot \mathbf{B} \cdot (\mathbf{C}^{-1} + \mathbf{D} \cdot \mathbf{A}^{-1} \cdot \mathbf{B})^{-1} \cdot \mathbf{D} \cdot \mathbf{A}^{-1} \qquad (17)$$

applied to each term in the analogous sequence in Eq. 17:

$$\mathbf{H}_{m+1}^{-1} = \mathbf{H}_m^{-1} - \frac{\mathbf{H}_m^{-1} \cdot \mathbf{X}^{[m+1]} \cdot \mathbf{X}^{[m+1]T} \cdot \mathbf{H}_m^{-1}}{P + \mathbf{X}^{[m+1]T} \cdot \mathbf{H}_m^{-1} \cdot \mathbf{X}^{[m+1]}} \qquad (18)$$

with $\mathbf{H}_0^{-1} = \alpha^{-1}\mathbf{I}$ and $\mathbf{H}_P^{-1} = \mathbf{H}^{-1}$ and α $(10^{-8} \leq \alpha \leq 10^{-4})$ a small constant needed to make $\mathbf{H}_0^{-1}$ meaningful, and to which our method is not especially sensitive [2]. Actually, Eq. 18 leads to the calculation of the inverse of $(\mathbf{H} + \alpha\mathbf{I})$, and this corresponds to the introduction of a penalty term $\alpha||\delta\mathbf{w}||^2$ in Eq. 4. This effective weight decay has the benefit of penalizing large candidate jumps in weight space, and thus helping to insure that the neglecting of higher order terms in Eq. 1 is valid.

Equation 18 permits the calculation of $\mathbf{H}^{-1}$ using a *single* sequential pass through the training data $1 \leq m \leq P$. It is also straightforward to generalize Eq. 19 to multiple outputs: in this case Eq. 16 is generalized to have recursions on both the indices m and l giving:

$$\mathbf{H}_{m\,l+1} = \mathbf{H}_{m\,l} + \frac{1}{P}\mathbf{X}_{l+1}^{[m]} \cdot \mathbf{X}_{l+1}^{[m]T}$$

$$\mathbf{H}_{m+1\,l} = \mathbf{H}_{m\,n_o} + \frac{1}{P}\mathbf{X}_{l}^{[m+1]} \cdot \mathbf{X}_{l}^{[m+1]T} \qquad (19)$$

To sequentially calculate $\mathbf{H}^{-1}$ for the multiple output case, we use Eq. 17 , as before.

IV. THE $(\mathbf{t} - \mathbf{o}) \to 0$ APPROXIMATION

The approximation used for Eq. 11 can be justified on computational and functional grounds, even late in pruning when the training error is not negligible. From the computational view, we note first that normally H is degenerate – especially before significant pruning has been done – and its inverse not well defined. The approximation guarantees that there are no singularities in the calculation of $\mathbf{H}^{-1}$. It also keeps the computational complexity of calculating $\mathbf{H}^{-1}$ the same as that for calculating H, $O(Pn^2)$. In Statistics the approximation is the basis of Fisher's method of scoring and its goal is to replace the true Hessian with its expected value and hence guarantee that H is positive definite (thereby avoiding stability problems that can plague Gauss-Newton methods) [9].

Equally important are the functional justifications of the approximation. Consider a high capacity network trained to small training error. We can consider the network structure as involving both signal and noise. As we prune, we hope to eliminate those weights that lead to "overfitting," i.e., learning the noise. If our pruning method did *not* employ the $(\mathbf{t} - \mathbf{o}) \to 0$ approximation, every pruning step (Eqs. 9 and 5) would inject the noise back into the system, by penalizing for noise terms. A different way to think of the approximation is the following. After some pruning by OBS we have reached a new weight vector that is a local minimum of the error (cf. Fig. 1). Even if this error is not negligible, we want to stay as close to that value of the error as we can. Thus we imagine a new, effective teaching signal $\mathbf{t}^*$, that would keep the network near this new error minimum. It is then $(\mathbf{t}^* - \mathbf{o})$ that we in effect set to zero when using Eq. 11 instead of Eq. 10.

V. OBS AND BACKPROPAGATION

Using the standard terminology from backpropagation [8] and the single output network of Fig. 2, it is straightforward to show from Eq. 12 that the derivative vectors are:

$$\mathbf{X}^{[k]} = \begin{pmatrix} \mathbf{X}_v^{[k]} \\ \mathbf{X}_u^{[k]} \end{pmatrix} \qquad (20)$$

where

$$[\mathbf{X}_v^{[k]}]^T = \left(f'(net^{[k]})o_{j=1}^{[k]}, \cdots, f'(net^{[k]})o_{n_j}^{[k]}\right) \qquad (21)$$

refers to derivatives with respect to hidden-to-output weights v_j and

$$\begin{aligned}[\mathbf{X}_u^{[k]}]^T = \ & (f'(net^{[k]})f'(net_1^{[k]})v_1^{[k]}o_{i=1}^{[k]}, \cdots, \qquad (22)\\ & f'(net^{[k]})f'(net_1^{[k]})v_1^{[k]}o_{n_i}^{[k]}, \cdots,\\ & f'(net^{[k]})f'(net_{n_j}^{[k]})v_{n_j}^{[k]}o_1^{[k]}, \cdots,\\ & f'(net^{[k]})f'(net_{n_j}^{[k]})v_{n_j}^{[k]}o_{n_i}^{[k]})\end{aligned}$$

refers to derivatives with respect to input-to-hidden weights u_{ji}, and where lexicographical ordering has been used. The neuron nonlinearity is $f(\cdot)$.

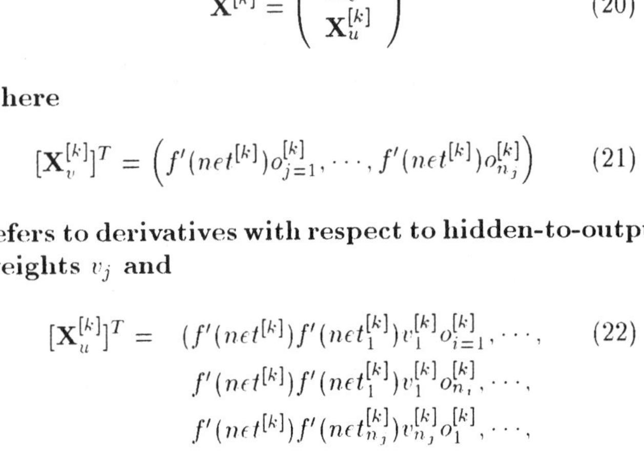

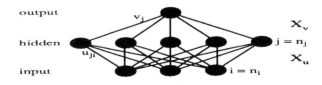

Figure 2: Backpropagation net with n_i inputs and n_j hidden units. The input-to-hidden weights are u_{ji} and hidden-to-output weights v_j. The derivative ("data") vectors are $\mathbf{X}_v$ and $\mathbf{X}_u$ (Eqs. 20 and 21).

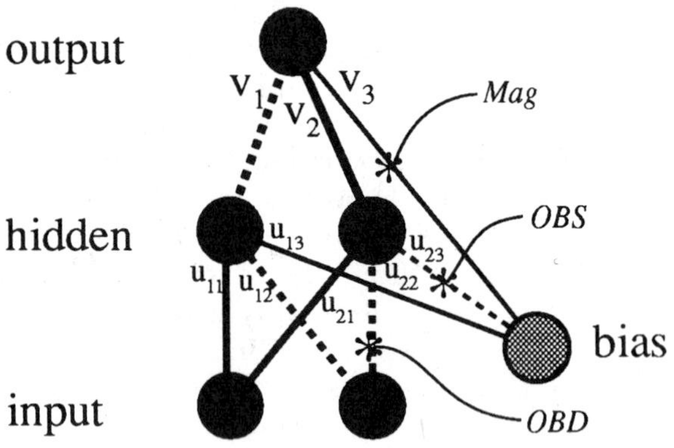

Figure 3: A nine weight XOR network trained to a local minimum. The thickness of the lines indicates the weight magnitudes, and inhibitory weights are shown dashed. Subsequent pruning using a magnitude based method (Mag) would delete weight v_3; using Optimal Brain Damage (OBD) would delete u_{22}. Even with retraining, the network pruned by those methods cannot learn the XOR problem. In contrast, Optimal Brain Surgeon (OBS) deletes u_{23} and furthermore changed all other weights (cf. Eq. 5) to achieve zero error on the problem.

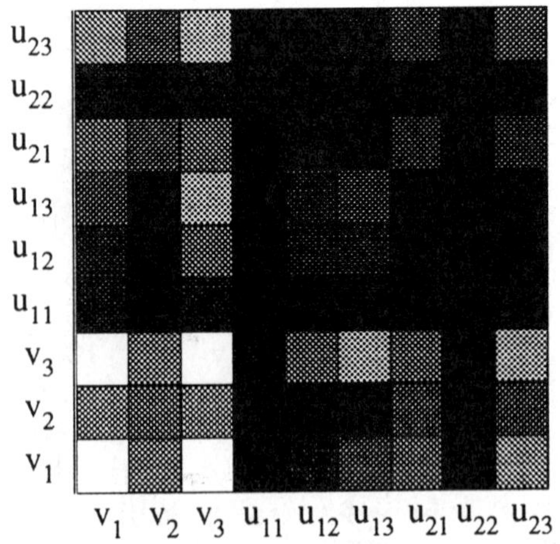

Figure 4: The Hessian of the trained but unpruned XOR network, calculated by means of Eq. 13. White represents large magnitudes and black small magnitudes. The rows and columns are labeled by the weights shown in Fig. 3. As is to be expected, the hidden-to-output weights have significant Hessian components. Note especially that the Hessian, while symmetric, is far from being diagonal. The Hessians for all problems we have investigated, including the MONK's problems, are far from being diagonal.

VI. Simulation results

We have found that OBS performs better than OBD and magnitude-based method on illustrative problems. We applied all three methods to the 2-2-1 network trained on the XOR problem. The network was first trained to a local minimum, which had zero error, and then each methods was used to prune a single weight. Depending on the actual minimum found in the initial training, the three methods sometimes chose identical weights to prune, but oftentimes chose different weights. A typical run is shown in Fig. 3, where each of the methods has selected a different weight to be deleted. In this particular case, both OBD and the Magnitude based methods have made a fatal mistake: they have deleted a crucial weight, such that *no amount* of retraining can reduce the error back to 0. OBS on the other hand, never deletes such a crucial weight. In fact, in every case we observed, applying OBS to delete a weight and alter the remaining weights (Eq. 5) resulted in a networked that maintained perfect performance on the XOR problem. So, even in cases where the other pruning methods delete an incorrect weight (i.e. the resulting net can *never* relearn the problem), OBS provides a network which maintains perfect performance *without any retraining* by gradient descent.

Figure 4 shows the Hessian of the trained but unpruned XOR network of Fig. 3. It is clear that the off-diagonal terms do contribute significantly to the error of the network. This has been true of every problem we have looked at.

Figure 5 shows two-dimensional "slices" of the nine-dimensional error surface in the neighborhood of a local minimum at w* for the XOR network. The cuts compare the weight elimination the Magnitude method (left) and OBD (right) with the elimination and weight adjustment given by OBS. After pruning by OBS all network weights are updated by Eq. 5 and the system is at zero error (not shown).

It is especially noteworthy that for this error minimum w*, the resulting networks after pruning by OBD or by the Magnitude method cannot achieve zero error, even after retraining. In short, magnitude methods and Optimal Brain Damage delete the wrong weights, and their mistake cannot be overcome by further network training. Only Optimal Brain Surgeon deletes the correct weight.

We also applied OBS to larger problems, three MONK's problems, and compared our results to those of Thrun et al. [11], whose backpropagation network outperformed all other approaches (network and rule-based) on these benchmark problems in an extensive machine learning competi-

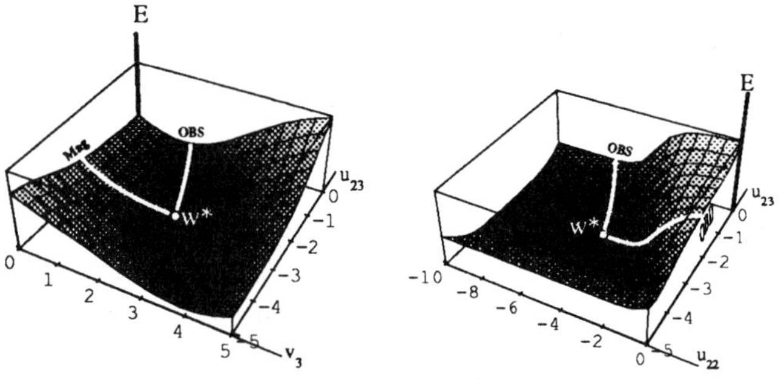

Figure 5: (Left) the XOR error surface as a function of weights v_3 and u_{23} (cf. Fig. 4). A magnitude based pruning method would delete weight v_3 whereas OBS deletes u_{23}. (Right) The XOR error surface as a function of weights u_{22} and u_{23}. Optimal Brain Damage would delete u_{22} whereas OBS deletes u_{23}. For this minimum, only deleting u_{23} will allow the pruned network to solve the XOR problem.

tion. The Hessians for all three MONKs problems are far from diagonal.

Table 2 shows that for the same performance, OBS (without retraining) required only 24%, 38% and 10% of the weights of the backpropagation network, which was already regularized with weight decay (Fig. 6). The error increase L (Eq. 5) accompanying pruning by OBS negligibly affected accuracy.

		Accuracy		
		training	testing	# weights
MONK1	**BPWD**	100	100	58
	OBS	100	100	14
MONK2	**BPWD**	100	100	39
	OBS	100	100	15
MONK3	**BPWD**	93.4	97.2	39
	OBS	93.4	97.2	4

Table 2: The accuracy and number of weights determined by backpropagation with weight decay (BPWD) found by Thrun et al., and by OBS on three MONK's problems.

The dramatic reduction in weights achieved by OBS yields a network that is simple enough that the logical rules that generated the data can be recovered from the pruned network, for instance by the methods of Towell and Shavlik [12]. Hence OBS may help to address a criticism often levied at neural networks: the fact that they may be unintelligible.

We applied OBS to a three-layer NETtalk network. While Sejnowski and Rosenberg [10] used

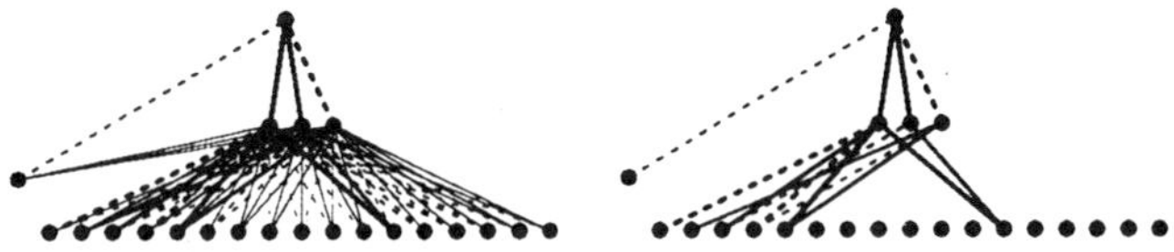

Figure 6: Optimal networks found by Thrun using backpropagation with weight decay (Left) and by OBS (Right) on MONK 1, which is based on logical rules. Solid (dashed) lines denote excitatory (inhibitory) connections; bias units are at left.

18,000 weights, we began with just 5,546 weights, which after backpropagation training had a sum-squared test error of 5,259. After pruning this net with OBS to 2,438 weights, and then retraining and pruning again, we achieved a net with only 1,560 weights and test error of only 4,701 – a significant improvement over the original, more complex network. Thus OBS can be applied to real-world pattern recognition problems such as speech recognition and optical character recognition, which typically have several thousand parameters.

VII. Analysis and conclusions

Why is Optimal Brain Surgeon so successful at reducing excess degrees of freedom? Conversely, given this new standard in weight elimination, we can ask: Why are the simplest magnitude based methods so poor? Consider again Fig. 1. Starting from the local minimum at w*, a magnitude based method deletes the wrong weight, weight 2, and through retraining, weight 1 will *increase*. The final "solution" is weight 1 → large, weight 2 = 0. This is precisely the *opposite* of the solution found by OBS: weight 1 = 0, weight 2 → large. Although the actual difference in error shown in Fig. 1 may be small, in large networks differences from many incorrect weight elimination decisions can add up to a significant increase in error. But most importantly, it is simply wishful thinking to believe that after the elimination of many incorrect weights by magnitude methods the net can "sort it all out" through further training and reach a global optimum, especially if the network has already been pruned significantly (cf. XOR discussion, above).

We have also seen how the approximation employed by Optimal Brain Damage – that the diagonals of the Hessian are dominant – does not hold for the problems we have investigated. There are

typically many off-diagonal terms that are comparable or larger than their diagonal counterparts. This explains why OBD often deletes the wrong weight, while OBS deletes the correct one.

We note too that our method is quite general, and subsumes previous methods for weight elimination. In our terminology, magnitude based methods assume isotropic Hessian ($H \propto I$); OBD assumes diagonal H; FARM [5] assumes linear $f(net)$ and only updates the hidden-to-output weights. We have shown that none of those assumptions are valid nor sufficient for optimal weight elimination.

We should also point out that our method is even more general than presented here [2]. For instance, rather than pruning a weight (parameter) by setting it to zero, one can instead reduce a degree of freedom by projecting onto an *arbitrary plane*, e.g., $w_q = C$ a constant, though such networks typically have a large description length [7]. The pruning constraint $w_q = 0$ discussed throughout this paper makes retraining (if desired) particularly simple. Several weights can be deleted simultaneously; bias weights can be exempt from pruning, and so forth. A slight generalization of OBS employs cross-entropy or the Kullback-Leibler error measure, leading to Fisher Information matrix rather than the Hessian [2]. We note too that OBS does not by itself give a criterion for when to stop pruning, and thus OBS can be utilized with a wide variety of such criteria. Moreover, gradual methods such as weight decay during learning can be used in conjunction with OBS.[1]

REFERENCES

[1] Hassibi, B. and Stork, D. G. (1992). Second order derivatives for network pruning: Optimal Brain Surgeon, in Proceedings of the Neural Information Processing Systems-5, S. J. Hansen, J. D. Cowan, and C. L. Giles (eds.), Morgan-Kaufmann.

[2] Hassibi, B. Stork, D. G. and Wolff, G. (1993b). Optimal Brain Surgeon, Information Theory and network capacity control (in preparation)

[3] Hertz, J., Krogh, A. and Palmer, R. G. (1991). Introduction to the Theory of Neural Computation Addison-Wesley.

[4] Kailath, T. (1980). Linear Systems Prentice-Hall.

[1] This is a revised and expanded version of Hassibi and Stork [1].

[5] Kung, S. Y. and Hu, Y. H. (1991). A Frobenius approximation reduction method (FARM) for determining the optimal number of hidden units, Proceedings of the IJCNN-91 Seattle, Washington, vol. II 163-172.

[6] Le Cun, Y., Denker, J. S. and Solla, S. A. (1990). Optimal Brain Damage, in Proceedings of the Neural Information Processing Systems-2, D. S. Touretzky (ed.) 598-605, Morgan-Kaufmann.

[7] Rissanen, J. (1978). Modeling by shortest data description, Automatica 14, 465-471.

[8] Rumelhart, D. E., Hinton, G. E., and Williams, R. J. (1986). Learning internal representations by error propagation, Chapter 8 (318-362) in Parallel Distributed Processing I D. E. Rumelhart and J. L. McClelland (eds.) MIT Press.

[9] Seber, G. A. F. and Wild, C. J. (1989). Nonlinear Regression 35-36 Wiley.

[10] Sejnowski, T. J., and Rosenberg, C. R. (1987). Parallel networks that learn to pronounce English text, Complex Systems 1, 145-168.

[11] Thrun, S. B. and 23 co-authors (1991). The MONK's Problems - A performance comparison of different learning algorithms, CMU-CS-91-197 Carnegie-Mellon U. Department of Computer Science Tech Report.

[12] Towell, G. and Shavlik, J. W. (1992). Interpretation of artificial neural networks: Mapping knowledge-based neural networks into rules, in Proceedings of the Neural Information Processing Systems-4, J. E. Moody, D. S. Touretzky and R. P. Lippmann (eds.) 977-984, Morgan-Kaufmann.

Classification with Missing and Uncertain Inputs

Subutai Ahmad
Siemens Research, ZFE ST SN61,
Otto-Hahn Ring 6, 8000 Munich 83, Germany.
ahmad@icsi.berkeley.edu

Volker Tresp
Siemens Research, ZFE ST SN41,
Otto-Hahn Ring 6, 8000 Munich 83, Germany.
tresp@inf21.zfe.siemens.de

Abstract--In many classification tasks the ability to deal with missing or uncertain inputs is crucial. In this paper we discuss some Bayesian techniques for extracting class probabilities given only partial or noisy inputs. The optimal solution involves integrating over the missing dimensions weighted by the local probability densities. We then show how to obtain closed-form approximations to the Bayesian solution using gaussian basis function networks. Simulation results on the complex task of 3D hand gesture recognition validate the theory. Using the Bayesian technique significant information can be extracted even in the presence of a large amount of noise. The results also show that a classifier that works well with perfect inputs is not necessarily very good at dealing with missing or noisy inputs.

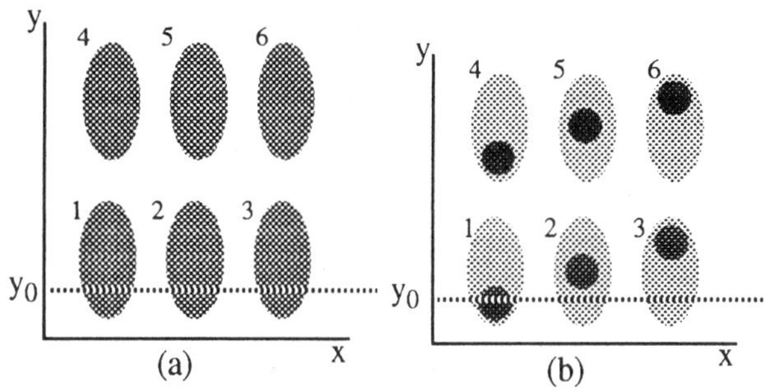

Fig. 1. The images show two possible situations for a 6-class classification problem. (Dark shading denotes high-probability regions.) If the value of feature x is unknown, the correct solution depends both on the classification boundaries along the missing dimension and on the distribution of exemplars.

I. Introduction

The ability of classifiers to deal with missing inputs or features is vital in many real-world situations. To date this issue has not been dealt with in neural networks in a systematic way. Instead the usual practice is to substitute a single value for the missing feature (e.g. *0*, the mean value of the feature, or a pre-computed value) and use the network's output on that feature vector. With noisy values the usual practice is to just use the measured noisy features directly. The point of this paper is to show that this approach is not optimal. By applying standard statistical techniques to neural networks, we can in fact do much better.

A simple example serves to illustrate why one needs to be careful in dealing with this problem. Consider the situation depicted in Fig. 1(a). It shows a *2-d* feature space with *6* possible classes. Assume a network has already been trained to correctly classify these regions. During classification of a novel exemplar, only feature *y* has been measured, as y_0; the value of feature *x* is unknown. For each class C_i, we would like to compute $p(C_i=1|y=y_0)$. One possibility would be to simply substitute zero (or perhaps the mean value of x) in place of the missing value. This would result in the classifier assigning a probability near 1 to class 1 (or 2 if the mean is used). Since nothing is known about x, the classifier should assign classes 1-3 a uniform probability *1/3* and classes 4-6 a probability of 0. Note that substituting any *single* value will always produce the wrong result. For example, if the mean value of x is substituted, the classifier would assign a probability near 1 for class 2. To obtain the correct posterior, it is necessary to integrate the network output over all values of x. But there is one other fact to consider: the probable values of x may be highly constrained by the known feature y. With a distribution as in Fig. 1(b) the classifier should assign class 1 the highest probability. Thus it is necessary to *integrate over the values of x along the line* $y=y_0$ *weighted by the joint distribution p(x,y).* When features are uncertain (i.e. $y=y_0$ and $x=x_0$ + *noise*) the solution is similar except that the integration should also be weighted according to the noise model.

Correct solutions incorporating the above intuitions would be important. In real-world applications features often highly constrain each other so classifiers must be able to deal with unusual distributions. We will consider one such example in our simulations in Section IV.

II. Missing and Uncertain Inputs

We first show how the intituitive arguments for missing inputs can be formalized using Bayes rule. Let $\vec{x}$ represent a complete feature vector. We assume the classifier outputs reasonable estimates of $p(C_i|\vec{x})$. In a given instance, $\vec{x}$ can be split up into $\vec{x}_c$, the vector of known (certain) features, and $\vec{x}_u$, the unknown features. When features are missing the task is to estimate $p(C_i|\vec{x}_c)$. Computing marginal probabilities:

$$p(C_i|\vec{x}_c) = \frac{\int p(C_i, \vec{x}_c, \vec{x}_u)\, d\vec{x}_u}{p(\vec{x}_c)}$$

$$= \frac{\int p(C_i|\vec{x}_c, \vec{x}_u)\, p(\vec{x}_c, \vec{x}_u)\, d\vec{x}_u}{p(\vec{x}_c)} \quad (1)$$

Note that $p(C_i|\vec{x}_c, \vec{x}_u)$ is approximated by the network output and that in order to use (1) effectively we need estimates of the joint probabilities of the inputs.

A. Uncertain Inputs

In many situations feature values are noisy. The standard approach has been to simply use the noisy value, but as with the missing inputs case, using any single value is suboptimal. In particular, if some information about the noise is available, it is possible to obtain a better estimate. The missing feature scenario can be extended to deal with noisy inputs. (Missing features are simply noisy features in the limiting case of complete noise.) Let $\vec{x}_c$ be the vector of features measured with complete certainty, $\vec{x}_u$ the vector of measured, uncertain features, and $\vec{x}_{tu}$ the true values of the features in $\vec{x}_u$. $p(\vec{x}_u|\vec{x}_{tu})$ denotes our knowledge of the noise (i.e. the probability of measuring the (uncertain) value $\vec{x}_u$ given that the true value is $\vec{x}_{tu}$). We assume that this is independent of $\vec{x}_c$ and C_i, i.e. that $P(\vec{x}_u|\vec{x}_{tu}, \vec{x}_c, C_i) = P(\vec{x}_u|\vec{x}_{tu})$. (Of course the value of $\vec{x}_{tu}$ is dependent on $\vec{x}_c$ and C_i.)

We want to compute $p(C_i|\vec{x}_c, \vec{x}_u)$. This can be expressed as:

$$p(C_i|\vec{x}_c, \vec{x}_u) = \frac{\int p(\vec{x}_c, \vec{x}_u, \vec{x}_{tu}|C_i)\, p(C_i)\, d\vec{x}_{tu}}{p(\vec{x}_c, \vec{x}_u)}$$

$$= \frac{\int p(\vec{x}_c, \vec{x}_u, \vec{x}_{tu}, C_i)\, d\vec{x}_{tu}}{p(\vec{x}_c, \vec{x}_u)} \quad (2)$$

According to our assumption:

$$p(\vec{x}_c, \vec{x}_u, \vec{x}_{tu}, C_i) = p(\vec{x}_u|\vec{x}_c, \vec{x}_{tu}, C_i)\, p(\vec{x}_c, \vec{x}_{tu}, C_i)$$

$$= p(\vec{x}_u|\vec{x}_{tu})\, p(C_i|\vec{x}_c, \vec{x}_{tu})\, p(\vec{x}_c, \vec{x}_{tu})$$

and:

$$p(\vec{x}_c, \vec{x}_u) = \int p(\vec{x}_u|\vec{x}_c, \vec{x}_{tu})\, p(\vec{x}_c, \vec{x}_{tu})\, d\vec{x}_{tu}$$

$$= \int p(\vec{x}_u|\vec{x}_{tu})\, p(\vec{x}_c, \vec{x}_{tu})\, d\vec{x}_{tu}$$

Substituting back into (2) we get:

$$p(C_i|\vec{x}_c, \vec{x}_u) = \frac{\int p(C_i|\vec{x}_c, \vec{x}_{tu})\, p(\vec{x}_c, \vec{x}_{tu})\, p(\vec{x}_u|\vec{x}_{tu})\, d\vec{x}_{tu}}{\int p(\vec{x}_c, \vec{x}_{tu})\, p(\vec{x}_u|\vec{x}_{tu})\, d\vec{x}_{tu}} \quad (3)$$

As before, $p(C_i|\vec{x}_c, \vec{x}_{tu})$ is given by the classifier. (3) is almost the same as (1) except that the integral now has to be weighted by the noise model. As with the missing feature case using any single value (such as the measured values) is suboptimal. Note that in the case of complete uncertainty about the features (i.e. the noise is uniform), the equations reduce to the missing feature case.

III. Two Common Classifiers

The above discussion shows how to optimally deal with missing and uncertain inputs in a statistical sense. We now show how these equations can be approximated using two common neural network classifiers.

A. Gaussian Basis Function Networks

Let us consider networks with Gaussian basis functions (GBF nets) with diagonal covariance matrices [4]. Such networks have proven to be useful in a number of real-world applications [7]. Each hidden unit is characterized by a mean vector $\vec{\mu}_j$ and by $\vec{\sigma}_j$, a vector representing the diagonal of the covariance matrix. The network output is:

$$y_i(\vec{x}) = \frac{\sum_j w_{ij} b_j(\vec{x})}{\sum_j b_j(\vec{x})} \quad (4)$$

with $b_j(\vec{x}) = \pi_j n(\vec{x}; \vec{\mu}_j, \vec{\sigma}_j^2)$

$$= \frac{\pi_j}{(2\pi)^{\frac{d}{2}} \prod_k^d \sigma_{kj}} exp\left[-\sum_i \frac{(x_i - \mu_{ji})^2}{2\sigma_{ji}^2}\right]$$

w_{ji} is the weight from the j'th basis unit to the i'th output unit, π_j is the probability of choosing unit j, and d is the dimensionality of $\vec{x}$. Under certain training regimes such as Gaussian mixture modeling, EM or "soft clustering" [1-2, 4] or an approximation as in [3] the hidden units adapt to represent local probability densities. For our purposes, a major advantage of this architecture is that the densities required in (3) are directly approximated. In particular $y_i(\vec{x}) \approx p(C_i|\vec{x})$ and $p(\vec{x}) \approx \sum_j b_j(\vec{x})$. In this section we show how this can be exploited to obtain closed form solutions to (1) and (3). Substituting into (3):

$$p(C_i|\vec{x}_c, \vec{x}_u) =$$

$$\frac{\int y_i(\vec{x}_c, \vec{x}_{tu}) \left(\sum_j b_j(\vec{x}_c, \vec{x}_{tu})\right) p(\vec{x}_u | \vec{x}_{tu})\, d\vec{x}_{tu}}{\int \left(\sum_j b_j(\vec{x}_c, \vec{x}_{tu})\right) p(\vec{x}_u | \vec{x}_{tu})\, d\vec{x}_{tu}}$$

$$= \frac{\int \left(\sum_j w_{ij} b_j(\vec{x}_c, \vec{x}_{tu})\right) p(\vec{x}_u | \vec{x}_{tu})\, d\vec{x}_{tu}}{\int \left(\sum_j b_j(\vec{x}_c, \vec{x}_{tu})\right) p(\vec{x}_u | \vec{x}_{tu})\, d\vec{x}_{tu}} \quad (5)$$

As noted before, (1) is simply (3) with $p(\vec{x}_u | \vec{x}_{tu})$ uniform. The indefinite integral along each dimension of a multivariate normal density is one so (5) can now be computed directly. So for the case of missing features we get:

$$p(C_i | \vec{x}_c) \approx \frac{\sum_j w_{ji} b_j(\vec{x}_c)}{\sum_j b_j(\vec{x}_c)} \quad (6)$$

(Here $b_j(\vec{x}_c)$ denotes the same function as in (4) except that it is only evaluated over $\vec{x}_c$.) Equation (6) is appealing since it gives us a closed form solution. Intuitively the solution is nothing more than projecting the Gaussians onto the dimensions which are available and evaluating the resulting network.

B. GBF Networks with Uncertain Features

With noisy features the situation is a little more complicated and the solution depends on the form of the noise. If the noise is known to be uniform in some region $[\vec{a}, \vec{b}]$ then (5) becomes:

$$P(C_i | \vec{x}_c, \vec{x}_u) = \frac{\int_{\vec{a}}^{\vec{b}} \left(\sum_j w_{ij} b_j(\vec{x}_c, \vec{x}_{tu})\right) d\vec{x}_{tu}}{\int_{\vec{a}}^{\vec{b}} \left(\sum_j b_j(\vec{x}_c, \vec{x}_{tu})\right) d\vec{x}_{tu}}$$

$$= \frac{\sum_j w_{ij} b_j(\vec{x}_c) \int_{\vec{a}}^{\vec{b}} b_j(\vec{x}_{tu})\, d\vec{x}_{tu}}{\sum_j b_j(\vec{x}_c) \int_{\vec{a}}^{\vec{b}} b_j(\vec{x}_{tu})\, d\vec{x}_{tu}} \quad (7)$$

$$\int_{\vec{a}}^{\vec{b}} b_j(\vec{x}_{tu})\, d\vec{x}_{tu} = \prod_{i \in U} \int_{a_i}^{b_i} n(x_i; \mu_{ij}, \sigma_{ij}^2)\, dx_i$$

$$= \prod_{i \in U} [N(b_i; \mu_{ij}, \sigma_{ij}^2) - N(a_i; \mu_{ij}, \sigma_{ij}^2)] \quad (8)$$

Here $\vec{\mu}_{ij}$ and $\vec{\sigma}_{ij}^2$ select the i'th component of the j'th mean and variance vectors. U ranges over the noisy feature indices. Good closed form approximations to the normal distribution function $N(x; \mu, \sigma^2)$ are available [5].

In the case of Gaussian noise we can also write down a closed form solution. In this case we have to integrate a product of two Gaussians. If the variance of the noise is σ_u^2 we end up with:

$$p(C_i | \vec{x}_c, \vec{x}_u) = \frac{\sum_j w_{ij} b'_j(\vec{x}_c, \vec{x}_u)}{\sum_j b'_j(\vec{x}_c, \vec{x}_u)}$$

where $b'_j(\vec{x}_c, \vec{x}_u) = n(\vec{x}_u; \vec{\mu}_{ju}, \vec{\sigma}_u^2 + \vec{\sigma}_{ju}^2)\, b_j(\vec{x}_c)$

C. Backpropagation Networks

As the number of samples tends to infinity, the outputs of a network trained with back-propagation using the LMS error function converges to the optimal Bayes *a posteriori* estimates of the class memberhips [6]. Let $B_i(\vec{x})$ be the output of the i'th output unit when presented with input $\vec{x}$. Then, assuming the network has been trained on a large enough training set, $B_i(\vec{x}) \approx p(C_i | \vec{x})$. Unfortunately, unlike basis function networks, access to the input distribution is not available with backpropagation. However (3) can still be exploited to provide some information. If we assume that the input distribution is uniform, the right hand side of (3) can be simplfied to:

$$p(C_i | \vec{x}_c) \approx \frac{\int p(C_i | \vec{x}_c, \vec{x}_{tu})\, p(\vec{x}_u | \vec{x}_{tu})\, d\vec{x}_{tu}}{\int p(\vec{x}_u | \vec{x}_{tu})\, d\vec{x}_{tu}} \quad (9)$$

If the noise is uniform in an interval $[\vec{a}, \vec{b}]$, then this reduces to (ignoring normalizing constants):

$$p(C_i | \vec{x}_c) \approx \int_a^b p(C_i | \vec{x}_c, \vec{x}_{tu})\, d\vec{x}_{tu} \quad (10)$$

This equation is appealing since only an estimate of $p(C_i | \vec{x})$ is required. (The intergral may be approximated using standard Monte Carlo techniques [5].) Strictly these are only valid in restricted situations but even a degraded estimate using (9) or (10) should be better than random guessing. With missing features the integral in (10) should be computed over the entire range of each missing features.

IV. An Example Task: 3D Hand Gesture Recognition

A simple realistic example serves to illustrate the utility of the above techniques. We consider the task of recognizing a set of hand gestures from single 2D images independent of 3D orientation (Fig. 2). As input, each classifier is given the 2D polar coordinates of the five fingertip positions relative to the 2D center of mass of the hand (so the input space is 10-dimensional). Each classifier is trained on a training set of 4368 examples (624 poses for each gesture) and tested on a similar independent test set.

The task forms a good benchmark for testing performance with missing and uncertain inputs. The classification task itself is non-trivial. The classifier must learn to deal with hands (which are complex non-rigid objects) and with perspective transformation. In fact it is impossible to obtain a perfect score since in certain poses some of the gestures are indistinguishable (e.g. when the hand is pointing directly at the screen). Moreover, the task is characteristic of real vision problems. The position of each finger is highly (but not completely) constrained by the others resulting in a very non-uniform input distribution. Finally it is often easy to see what the classifier should output if features are uncertain. For example suppose the real gesture is "five" but for some reason the features from the thumb are not reliably computed. In this case the gestures "four" and "five" should both get a positive probability whereas the rest should get zero. (No other class in the training set contains a gesture with the other four fingers extended.) In many such cases only a single class should get the highest score, e.g. if the features for the little finger are uncertain the correct class is still "five".

The theory predicts that classifiers with knowledge about the probability distribution would perform best with missing or uncertain features. To test this we tried out three different classifiers on this task: standard sigmoidal networks trained with backpropagation (BP), and two types of gaussian networks as described in (4). In the first (Gauss-RBF), the gaussians were radial and the centers were determined using k-means clustering as in [3]. σ^2 was set to twice the average distance of each point to its nearest gaussian (all gaussians had the same width). After clustering, π_j was set to:

$$\pi_j = \sum_k \left[\frac{n(\vec{x}_k; \vec{\mu}_j; \vec{\sigma}_j^2)}{\sum_i n(\vec{x}_k; \vec{\mu}_i; \vec{\sigma}_i^2)} \right]$$

The output weights were then determined using LMS gradient descent. In the second (Gauss-G), each gaussian had a unique diagonal covariance matrix. The centers and variances were determined using gradient descent on all the parameters [7]. With this type of training, even though gaussian hidden units are used, there is no guarantee that the distribution information will be preserved. Both BP and Gauss-G were very good at learning the task. The best BP network (60 hidden units) managed to score 95.3% and 93.3% on the training and test sets, respectively. Gauss-G with 28 hidden units scored 94% and 92%. Gauss-RBF scored 97.7% and 91.4% but required 2000 units to achieve it. (Larger numbers of hidden units led to overtraining.)

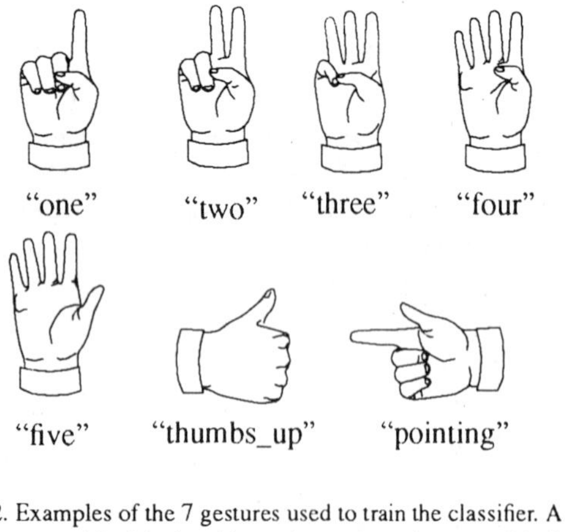

Fig. 2. Examples of the 7 gestures used to train the classifier. A 3D computer model of the hand is used to generate images of the hand in various poses. For each training example, we choose a 3D orientation, compute the 3D positions of the fingertips and project them onto 2D. For this task we assume that the correspondence between image and model features are known, and that during training all feature values are always available.

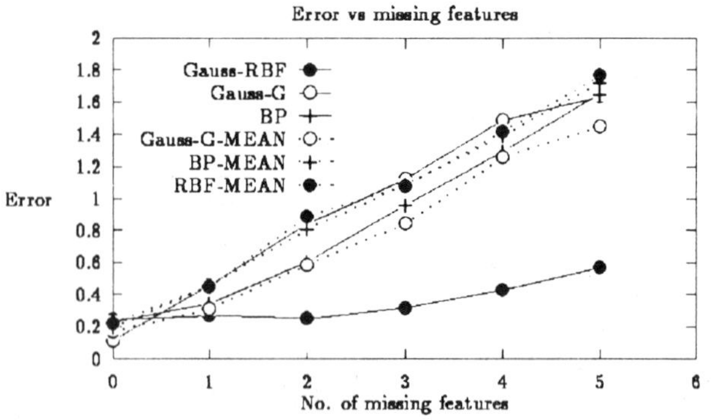

Fig. 3. The error of various classifiers when dealing with missing features. Each data point denotes an average over 1000 random samples from an independent test set. For each sample, random features were considered missing. The graph plots the average number of classes that were ranked above the correct class.

A. Performance with Missing Inputs

We tested the performance of each network in the presence of missing features. For backpropagation we used a numerical approximation to (10). For both gaussian basis function networks we used (6). To test the networks we randomly picked samples from the test set and deleted random features. We calculated an error score as the average number of classes that were ranked above the correct class. Fig. 4 displays the results. For comparison we also tested each classifier by substituting the mean value of each missing feature and using the normal update equation.

It is clear from the figure that the performance of Gauss-RBF was consistently better than the others. BP and Gauss-G performed relatively poorly. This agrees well with the theory which predicts good performance when the input distribution is taken into account. Perhaps most astonishing (and encouraging) is the result that even with 50% of the features missing, Gauss-RBF chooses the correct class about half the time. Further inspection shows that, in fact, Gauss-RBF ranks the correct class among the top two scores almost 90% of the time. This clearly shows that if the distribution is taken into account, and the missing features are integrated out, then a significant amount of information can be extracted.

B. Performance with Noisy Inputs

We also tested the performance of each network in the presence of noisy features. We randomly picked samples from the test set and added uniform noise to random features. The noise interval was calculated as $[x_i - 2\sigma_i, x_i + 2\sigma_i]$ where x_i is the feature value and σ_i is the standard deviation of that feature over the training set. (For all features, $2\sigma_i$ corresponded to about 1/3 of the entire range of feature values so the noise interval was quite large.) The error measure was the same as the missing feature case. For BP we used to (10) evaluated over the noise interval. For both gaussian basis function networks we used (8) evaluated over the noise interval. Fig. 4 displays the results. For comparison we also tested each classifier by substituting the noisy value of each noisy feature and using the normal update equation.

As with missing features, the performance of Gauss-RBF was much better than the others with a large number of noisy features. BP and Gauss-G both performed poorly when the number of noisy features was large. The error y substituting the measured noisy value was consistently the worst indicating that, in the presence of some noise, the integration step might be crucial. As would be expected, overall performance was better than with missing features (note the change in scale from Fig. 4). Again, the performance of Gauss-RBF under a large amount of noise is quite encouraging.

V. Discussion

In our opinion the performance of Gauss-RBF clearly shows the advantages of estimating the input distribution and computing the integrals. The results are not due to the use of gaussian hidden units over sigmoidal units since both BP and Gauss-G performed poorly. However on complete input vectors Gauss-RBF was not the best. To get the best of both worlds, one could possible use an alternate "hybrid" technique: e.g. numerically integrate (9) and use Gauss-RBF to estimate the probabilities combined with either BP or Gauss-G for classification.

One way to improve the performance of BP and Gauss-

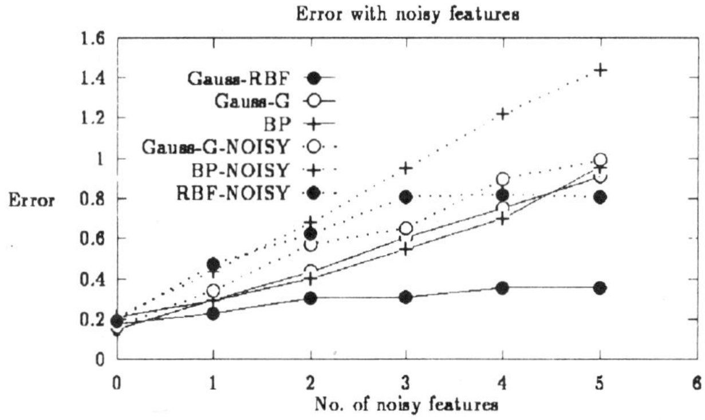

Fig. 4. The error of various classifiers when dealing with noisy features. Each data point denotes an average over 1000 random samples from an independent test set. For each sample, random features were considered missing. The graph plots the average number of classes that were ranked above the correct class.

G might be to use a training set that contained missing features. Given the unusual distributions that can arise in real-world applications, in order to guarantee accuracy such a training set should include every possible combination of missing features. In addition, for each such combination, enough patterns must be included to accurately estimate the posterior density. In general this type of training is impractical since the number of combinations is exponential in the number of features. Note that if input distribution is available (as in Gauss-RBF), then such a training scenario is unnecessary.

There are a number of tradeoffs which must be considered in deciding which classifier to use. Although Gauss-RBF performed well in this task, these types of networks encounter problems if the input dimensionality is high. Even with 10 inputs the network required a large number of hidden units for good performance. (Although this would decrease if a diagonal covariance matrix was used, it is unclear whether the total number of parameters would decrease.) Due to this problem, in higher dimensions BP or Gauss-G might be the tool of choice despite the lack of distribution information.

Note that we have assumed in the discussion that enough training data is available to estimate the required densities. In some applications this can be a problem as little training data is available. In such cases some sort of prior information needs to be incorporated. We have not addressed this issue here but see [8] for one approach to this problem.

Acknowledgment

We thank D. Goryn, C. Maggioni, S. Omohundro, A. Stolcke, and R. Schuster for helpful discussions, and also B. Wirtz for providing the computer hand model. V.T. is supported in part by a grant from the Bundesministerium für Forschung und Technologie.

REFERENCES

[1] A.P. Dempster, N.M. Laird, and D.B. Rubin. Maximum-likelihood from incomplete data via the EM algorithm. *J. Royal Statistical Soc. Ser. B*, **39**:1-38, 1977.

[2] R. O. Duda and P. E. Hart. *Pattern Classification and Scene Analysis*. New York: John Wiley & Sons., 1973.

[3] J. Moody and C. Darken. Learning with localized receptive fields. In: D. Touretzky, G. Hinton, T. Sejnowski, (eds.), *Proceedings of the 1988 Connectionist Models Summer School*, San Mateo, CA: Morgan Kaufmann, 1988.

[4] S. Nowlan. Maximum Likelihood Competitive Learning. In: *Advances in Neural Information Processing Systems 4*, pages 574-582, 1990.

[5] W.H. Press, B.P. Flannery, S.A. Teukolsky, and W.T. Vetterling. *Numerical Recipes: The Art of Scientific Computing*, Cambridge, UK: Cambridge University Press, 1986.

[6] M. D. Richard and R.P. Lippmann. Neural Network Classifiers Estimate Bayesian *a posteriori* Probabilities, *Neural Computation*, **3**:461-483, 1991.

[7] M. Röscheisen, R. Hofman, and V. Tresp. Neural Control for Rolling Mills: Incorporating Domain Theories to Overcome Data Deficiency. In: *Advances in Neural Information Processing Systems 4*, pages 659-666, 1992.

[8] V. Tresp, J. Hollatz, and S. Ahmad. Network Structuring and Training Using Rule-based Knowledge. In: S. J. Hanson, J.D. Cowan, and C. L. Giles (eds.), *Advances in Neural Information Processing Systems 5*. San Mateo, CA: Morgan Kaufmann, 1993.

Proceedings of the 1993 IEEE/RSJ International Conference on Intelligent Robots and Systems Yokohama, Japan July 26-30, 1993

Recognition System by Neural Network for Additional Learning

Shigetoshi SHIOTANI, Toshio FUKUDA and Takanori SHIBATA

Dept. of Mechano-Informatics and Systems, Nagoya University

Furo-cho 1, Chikusa-ku, Nagoya 464-01, Japan

Abstract

This paper proposes a new neural network (NN) model for the pattern recognition, which can learn new patterns additionally without losing memorized patterns in the past. This NN model is called Neural network based on distance between patterns (NDP). The NDP uses the radial basis function (RBF) as the response function in place of the sigmoid function. The response function is a smooth function similar to the Gaussian base function and the probability dencity function. The response function learns patterns faster than multi-layered perceptron (MLP) as well as other RBF-NNs. The most salient architecture of the NDP is to self-organize the networks by adding nodes in the output layer one by one. That is, the NDP has the structure with variable nodes different from the conventional NNs. Besides, the NDP varies the curve of the response function by tuning the center and the width of the response function, and separates the input space into regions for each category appropriately.

1.Introduction

Recently automatic systems are needed to decrease works of human in many fields. The automatic systems requires many kinds of sensory information to recognize the fields of the works. The sensory informations are vision, voice and so on. This paper deals with pattern recognition to obtain the visual information. The pattern recognition for vision is performed as follows. At first, image processing measures characteristics of objects in images through a CCD camera. The characteristics are often area, length and so on. Then artificial neural networks [1-11] or data bases classify objects based on the characteristics.

The artificial neural network deals with much numerical information in parallel using parallel distributed processing [2]. The artificial neural network processes much information more quickly than data bases. For classification, the artificial neural network learns training patterns which consist of input patterns and output patterns using back propagation algorithm. The trained artificial neural network can classify input patterns which are not used in the learning to some degree. This ability is referred to as generalization. As artificial neural networks for pattern recognition, multi layered perceptron (MLP), radial basis function neural network (RBF-NN) and ART model have been reported. However, the MLP [2] and the RBF-NN [3-7] need much computing cost in additional learning. The **additional learning** is to memorize new patterns or categories additionally. The MLP and the RBF-NN must learn both a pattern and training patterns which they learned before in order to memorize a pattern which they could not classify. Thus, the MLP and RBF-NN are ineffective due to learning many patterns in additional learning.

The ART model [8,9] learns patterns using back propagation algorithm and Reilly's algorithm [11]. Thus, the ART model can perform additional learning more efficiently than the MLP and RBF-NNs. That is, the ART model can perform additional learning by learning new patterns or categories. However, the ART model cannot distinguish patterns with same input vectors due to response function using cosine function between patterns.

This paper introduces a neural network which has a new structure for the additional learning [12]. This neural network is referred to as ***Neural network based on distance between patterns*** (***NDP***). The NDP is a RBF-NN which learns patterns using Reilly's algorithm and back propagation algorithm. The NDP has two layers and uses radial basis functions. The NDP learns patterns one by one by addition of new nodes or variation of weights between nodes using back propagation algorithm. The NDP can add new regions and vary regions in input space without breaking other regions a lot. Thus, the NDP performs additional learning more efficiently than the MLP and other RBF-NNs. Moreover, the NDP classifies patterns with same input vectors due to using radial basis function. Thus, the NDP is superior to the ART model with respect to classification ability. Experiments are performed to show the efficiency of the NDP. In the experiment, the NDP is compared with the MLP with respect to additional learning abilities for condition of plant cells.

The paper is organized as follows. Section 2 shows the architecture of the NDP. Section 3 describes the additional learning scheme. Section 4 shows experiments in additional learning. Section 5 describes the conclusion.

2. Architecture of the Neural Network Based on Distance between Patterns

After structures and separation methods of the input space for some typical neural networks are described, those of the NDP are shown.

0-7803-0823-9/93/$3.00 (C) 1993 IEEE

2.1 Conventional Neural Networks

The MLP updates weights of all linear connections in the network entirely by back propagation algorithm to decrease the whole error for patterns:

$$E=\sum_{p=1}^{P}\sum_{i=1}^{I}\frac{1}{2}(T_{pi}-O_{pi})^2 \qquad (1)$$

where Tpi, Opi, P and I indicate the teaching signals, outputs of nodes in output layer, the number of training patterns and the number of inputs respectively. The structure and the separation of the input space in the MLP are shown in fig.1. The MLP has yielded success to the category classification, while the MLP needs many learning times and cannot describe its inner processing clearly. Moreover, the MLP is ineffective in additional learning.

The RBF-NN has two layers shown in fig.2. The regions formed by the RBF arc very visible. The learning styles of the RBF-NN are the local tuning and the entire tuning of connection weights in the network. The locally-tuned algorithm can learn training patterns faster than the MLP. The RBF has a single maximum at the center and drops off rapidly to zero at large radii. Overall the RBF is expressed by the following equations:

$$R_j(\vec{X})=\alpha_j|\vec{X}-\vec{W_j}|/\sigma$$
$$X=(X1,...,XI),\ Wj=(Wj1,...,WjI) \qquad (2)$$

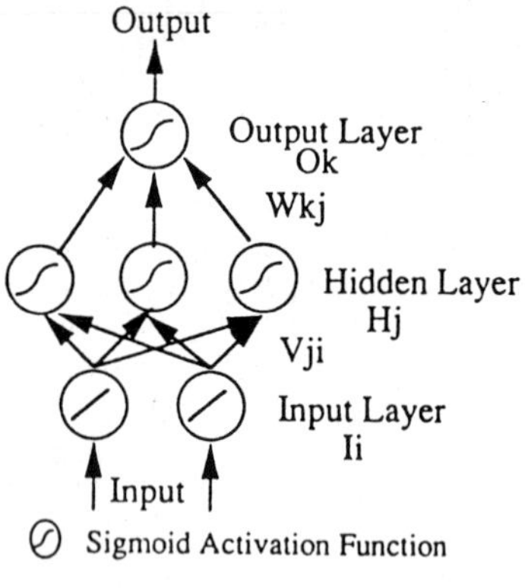

Fig.1 (A) Structure of Multi-Layered Perceptron

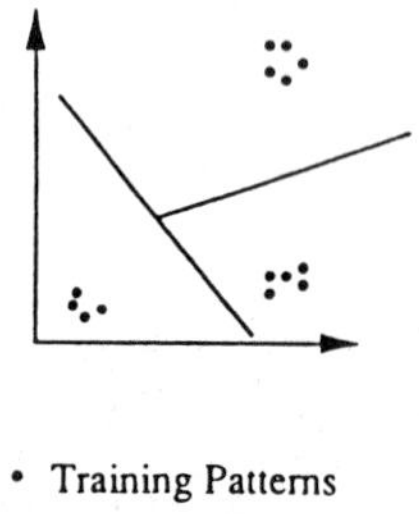

Fig. 1(B) Region Formed by Multi-Layered Perceptron

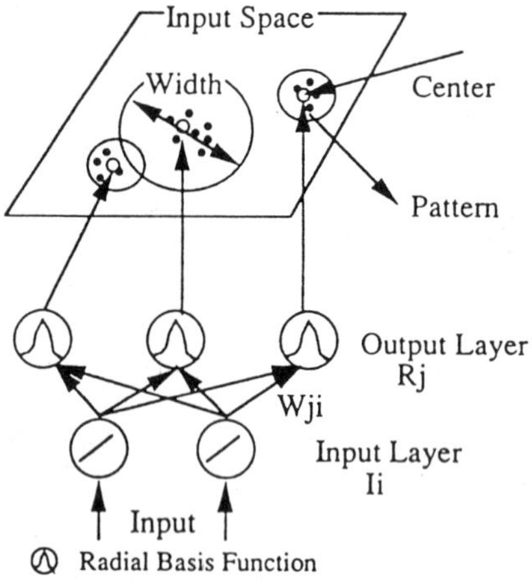

Fig. 2(A) Structure of Radial Basis Function Neural Network (RBF-NN)

Here, Rj is the RBF of j-th node, X is a real-valued input vector in the input space, Wj and αj are the center vector and the amplitude of the RBF. The width of the RBF varies by σ. The probability density function (PDF) and the Gaussian function are proposed as similar response functions to the RBF. As the RBF-NN for the category classification, we survey Probabilistic Neural Networks (PNN) [3]. The PNN has both linear connections as the Perceptron and nonlinear connections, learns faster than the MLP. However, the PNN is ineffective in the separation ability as compared with the NDP because of the learning algorithm without varying the center and width (called smoothing parameter in his paper) of the response function (called PDF).

The adaptive resonance theory (ART) model [8,9] has two layers (which are F1 and F2 Layer in fig.4) is similar to Reilly's model except 2/3 matching rule. The response function is expressed by the following equations:

$$Y_j=\frac{(\vec{X},\vec{Z_j})}{|\vec{X}|\,|\vec{Z_j}|}=\cos\theta_j$$
$$X=(X1,...,XI),\ Zj=(Zj1,...,ZjI) \qquad (3)$$

Here X, Zj and Yj indicate input vector, the weight vector of connection between F1 and F2, and output value respectively. The ART model divides the input space into many regions as shown in fig.3 by the angle between the input vector X and the weight vector Zj. The ART model varies only Zj associated with a node with maximum output value in the F2 layer locally by the following equation:

$$\vec{Z_j}(t+1)=\beta\vec{X_i}+(1-\beta)\vec{Z_j}(t) \quad (|\beta|<1) \qquad (4)$$

The ART model can learn training patterns fast than the Perceptron because of the locally-tuned learning.

However, the ART model cannot distinguish patterns with same input vectors and is inferior to the MLP and RBF-NN in separation ability.

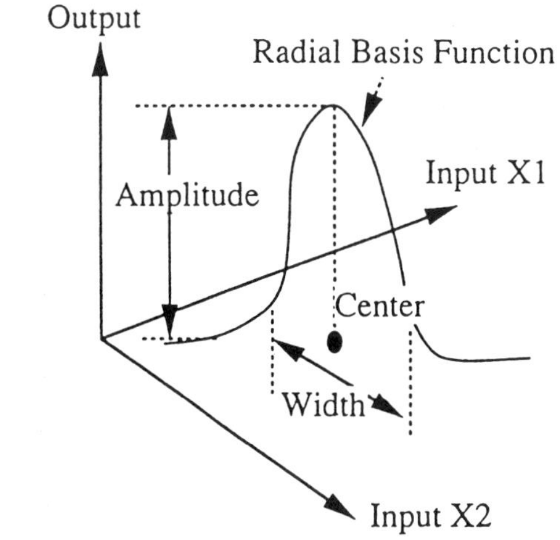

Fig. 2(B) Curve of Radial Basis Function

2.2 Neural Network Based on Distance between Patterns (NDP)

The NDP is two-layered hierarchical network as shown in fig.4. The NDP trains categories of patterns one by one by the supervised learning. The inputs of the NDP are parameters expressed characteristics of the patterns. The output of the NDP is a category of inputted pattern. The NDP has RBF expressed by the following equation:

$$O_j = \frac{1}{1+\alpha_j\sqrt{(I_i - W_{ji})^2}} \qquad (5)$$

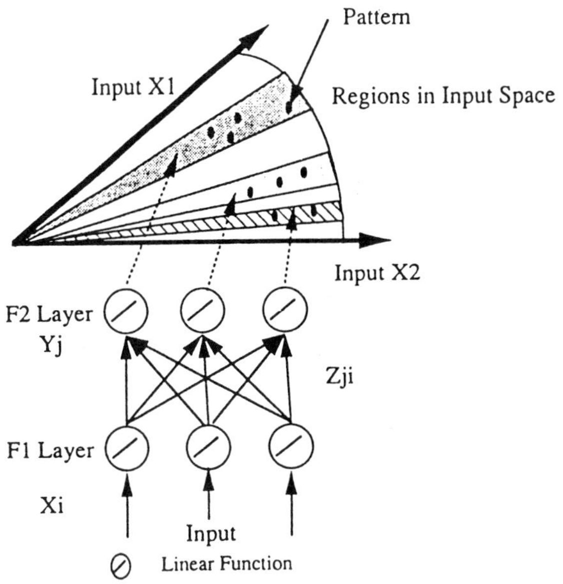

Fig. 3 Adaptive Resonance Theory (ART) Model

where αj, Ii, Wji and Oj imply the parameter relative to the width of the response function, inputs, connection weights indicating the center of the response function and outputs. Each output node memorizes a category of patterns. The learning process of the NDP is described as follows. The NDP learns a category of a pattern one by one by supervised learning. If a pattern is inputted

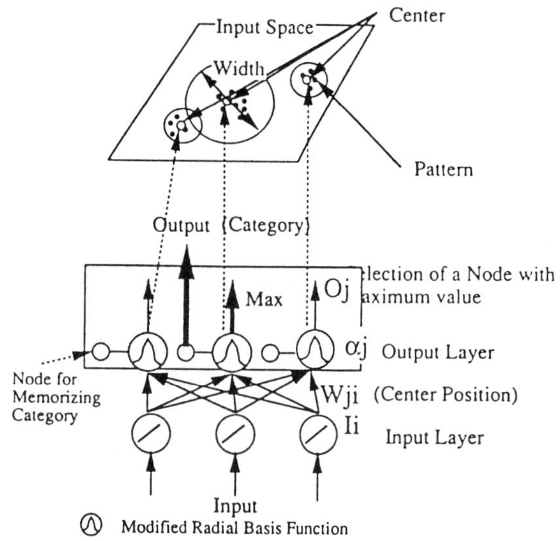

Fig. 4 Neural Network Based on Distance between Patterns (NDP)

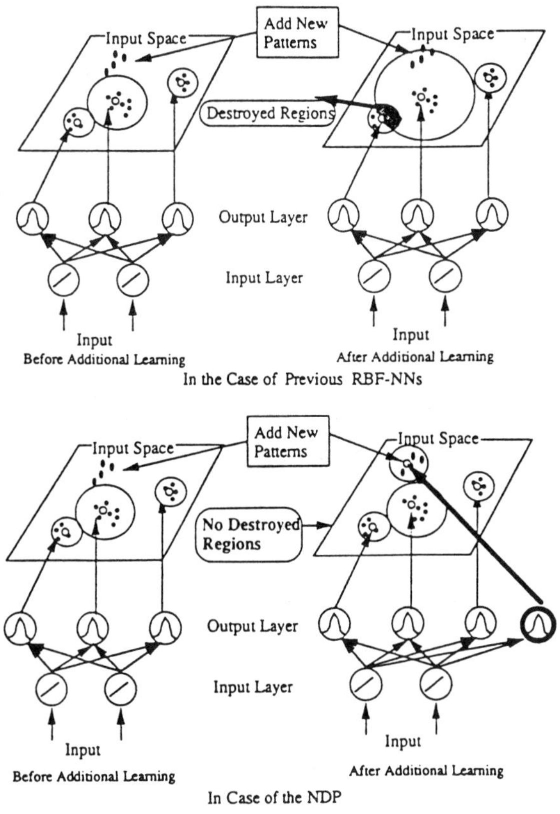

Fig. 5 Variation of Regions in Input Space by Additional Learning

into the NDP, the NDP selects a output node with the maximum value and recognizes the pattern as a category of the selected node. If the NDP can not recognize the pattern correctly, the NDP learns only the pattern by additional learning algorithm in section 3. The NDP performs additional learning more effectively than conventional RBF-NNs with respect to computing cost. The NDP performs additional learning by varying curve and position of response functions or adding a new node in the output layer. Figure 5 indicates effect that the NDP adds a new node in the output layer. The conventional RBF-NNs break the regions more largely than the NDP in additional learning.

3. Additional Learning Scheme

This section describes an additional learning scheme for the NDP. The NDP learns teaching patterns to classify patterns. The NDP is inputted patterns one by one. Then the NDP learns in the case that the NDP fails to classify the patterns. The NDP learns patterns additionally by varying curve and position of response functions or adding a new node. The NDP memorizes categories of patterns by nodes in the output layer. At first, the NDP learns training patterns with one node in the output layer and self-organizes networks by the following cases:

case 1:

If the maximum output value Ot in output nodes is less than threshold θ, the NDP adds a new node in the output layer. The new node memorizes a category of inputted pattern and is connected to all input nodes. The connection weights of the new node are determined by the following equations:

$$W_{ji}=I_i \quad (6)$$

$$\alpha_j=\alpha I \quad (7)$$

where aI is a initial value with respect to αj.

Case 2:

If the largest output value Ot in output nodes is more than the threshold θ, the NDP updates curves and positions of response function in output nodes. The learning is continued until the node selected in following case (a) outputs the maximum value in all output nodes. The NDP perform learnings in both case (a) and case (b).

case (a): The NDP selects a node with the maximum output value in nodes which memorizes a category of an inputted pattern. Then the NDP varies the response function of the selected node by following equations (8)-(10). Where, Tj in equation (8) is 1.

case (b): The NDP selects nodes with output value more than that of the node selected in case (a). The NDP varies response functions of their nodes by following equations (8)-(10). Where, Tj in equation (8) is 0.

$$E_j=(T_j - O_j)^2 \quad (8)$$

$$\alpha_j(t+1)=\alpha_j(t) - A\frac{\partial E_j}{\partial \alpha_j} \quad (9)$$

$$W_{ji}(t+1)=W_{ji}(t) - B\frac{\partial E_j}{\partial W_{ji}} \quad (10)$$

where,

Ej:	Error,
A and B:	learning rate,
t :	learning time,
Tj:	1 (in the case of (a))
	0 (in the case of (b)).

In the learning of case 1, the NDP avoid destroying regions shown fig. 5 by adding a new region. In the learning of case 2, the NDP selects regions to tune in the input space, then learns inputted patterns by tuning selected regions locally without destroying other regions. Thus, the NDP performs additional learning efficiently without losing past memory by learning only inputted patterns.

4. Experiments of Additional Learning

In order to show the effectiveness of the NDP, two kinds of pattern recognition are performed.

4.1 Classification of patterns in two dimensional space

The NDP and the MLP learned 16 patterns shown in fig. 6. After the NDP and the MLP learned three categories 1, 2 and 3, they did only category 4 incrementally. Each category has four patterns. Therefore, two neural networks trained 16 patterns.

The MLP has three layers. Input layer has 2 nodes and output layer has 4 nodes. We varied the number of the nodes in the MLP 's hidden layer in the range from 2 to 10. We selected the number of nodes in hidden layer with the best accuracy on the classification. The nodes in output layer memorize a category respectively. The teaching data for the MLP were described in 0 or 1. For example, the teaching data of the category 1 are "1, 0, 0, 0". The inputted pattern is recognized as the category which the node with the maximum output value memorizes.

The NDP has 2 nodes in input layer and a node in the output layer at first. The number of nodes in the output layer varies by learning patterns. In the initial learning conditions of the NDP, $\alpha = 2.5$, $A = 0.01$, $B = 0.01$, and $\theta = 0.6$.

According to the result shown in table 1, the NDP memorized all patterns, while the MLP forgot 12 patterns of categories 1,2 and 3 except four patterns of category 4. Figure 7 and 8 show the variation of the regions in the input space with respect to the NDP and the MLP respectively. Before additional learning, the NDP divided the input space into three regions for the category 1,2 and 3. After additional learning, the NDP added a new region for the category 4 without varying regions a lot. The MLP forgot three categories because the MLP broke

3 regions for the categories 1, 2 and 3 in the additional learning. The result of this simulation indicate that the NDP is superior to the MLP with respect to additional learning ability.

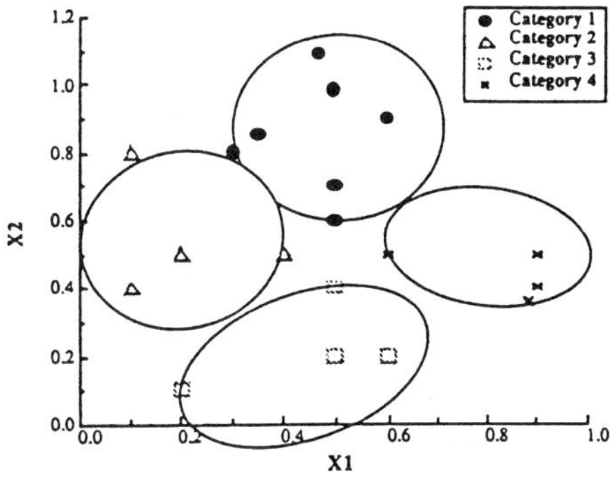

Fig. 6 Space Including Four Categories

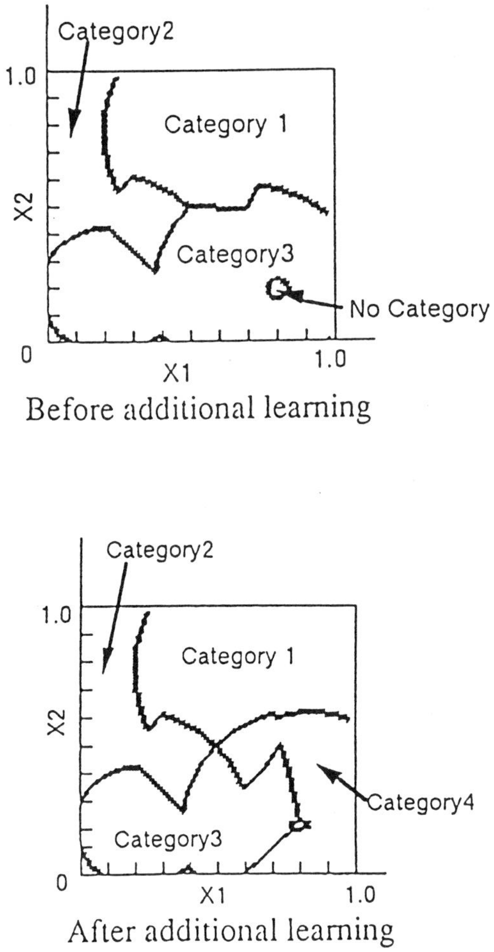

Fig. 7 Variation of Regions in the Input Space by the NDP

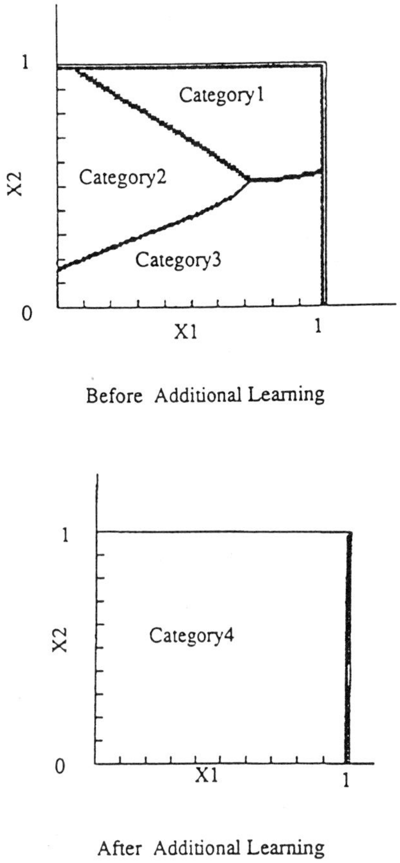

Fig. 8 Variation of the Regions in the Input Space by the MLP

Table 1 Result of the Category Classification Fig. 6

(Recognized Number / Total Number)

Neuron Model	Number of recognized patterns	Number of used neurons in each layer		
		Input layer	Hidden layer	Output layer
MLP	4 / 16	2	3	4
NDP	16 / 16	2		8

4.2 Image Recognition

Besides the NDP performed the additional learning of cell recognition shown in fig.9. The NDP and the MLP classify the cells into three types which are the protoplast regenerating cells and colonies shown in fig.10 [13]. Image processing describes the shape and colors of the cells by 22 parameters numerically. These parameters are area, ratio of width to length, length of the contour and so on.

Those values of the parameters are normalized in the range from 0 to 1 and inputted into the NDP and the MLP.

The NDP was compared with the MLP in the generalization ability for the cell recognition. After the NDP and the MLP trained 41 cells, those neural networks recognized untraining 66 cells. As a result shown in table 2, the MLP could not recognize 7 cells, while the NDP could not do 3 cells. As for the generalization of the neural network on this cell recognition, the NDP was superior to the MLP.

Then the NDP was compared with the MLP in additional learning ability. After those two neural networks learned only 23 patterns of the protoplasts, they did only 57 patterns of the regenerating cells. Moreover, they trained only 27 patterns of the colonies. Therefore they learned 107 patterns. According to a result shown in table 2, the NDP memorized 105 patterns (98 percents), while the MLP did 69 patterns (64 percents). The NDP was superior to the MLP with respect to the additional learning ability. Table 3 indicates the experimental results of the category classification with respect to the number of the nodes in the MLP's hidden layer.

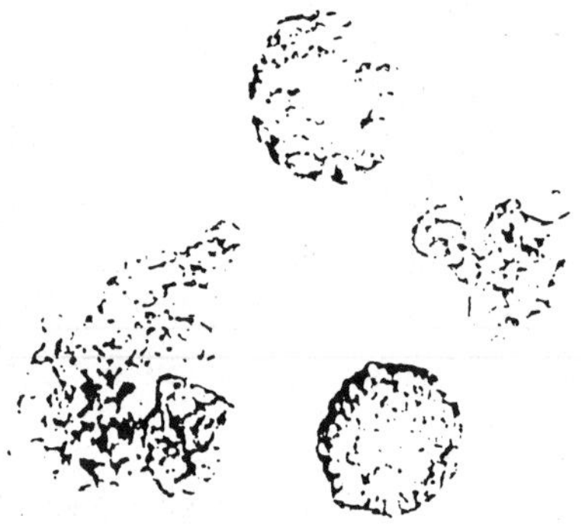

Fig. 9 Image of the Plant Cell in the Culture Solution

Protoplast Regenerating Cell Colony

Fig. 10 Growing Process of the Plant Cell

5. Conclusions

This paper introduces a new radial basis function neural network (RBF-NN) for additional learning, i.e., Neural network based on distance between patterns (NDP). The NDP learns patterns faster than the MLP as well as other RBF-NNs due to the locally-tuned learning. The NDP had superior generalization ability to the MLP on the cell recognition. The most noticeable architecture of the NDP is a structure with variable nodes and distinct from conventional RBF-NNs. The NDP adds new regions in the input space without breaking other regions almost. Thus, the NDP performs additional learning. It is shown by the results on the experiments of the cell recognition that the NDP has both the generalization ability and the additional learning ability. Because the NDP varies the curve of the response function by tuning the center and the width of the response function, the NDP overcomes the problem of the initial parameters to some degree. Our next try is to construct the NDP for the saccadic movement.

Table 2 Experimental Results on the Plant Cell Recognition

(Recognized Number / Total Number)

Outline of Experiments on Plant Cell Recognition	Recognition Accuracy	
	MLP	NDP
Recognition accuracy of untraining patterns (66 patterns) by NNs which learned training patterns (41 patterns)	59 / 66	63 / 66
Recognition Accuracy on the additional learning in which NNs which learn three categories one by one	69 /107	105/107

Table 3 Experimental Results of the MLP with respect to Number of Nodes in Hidden Layer

[Recognized Number (Total Number)]

Outline of Experiments on Plant Cell Recognition	Recognition Accuracy								
	Number of Nodes in Hidden Layer of the MLP								
	2	3	4	5	6	7	8	9	10
Recognition accuracy of untraining patterns (66 patterns) by MLP which learned training patterns (41 patterns)	61 (66)	61 (66)	61 (66)	61 (66)	61 (66)	61 (66)	61 (66)	61 (66)	61 (66)
Recognition accuracy on the additional learning in which MLP which learns three categories one by one	18 (107)	18 (107)	23 (107)	69 (107)	44 (107)	68 (107)	69 (107)	37 (107)	68 (107)

References

[1] Rosenblat F., "Principles of neurodynamics, Spartan, 1961

[2] Rumelhart D.E., Himton, G.E. and Williams R.J., "A learning Internal Representation by Error

Propagation", Rumelhart D.E. and McCllelland J.L. eds, Parallel Distributed Processing, MIT Press, Cambridge, Mass, 1986
[3] Donald F. Specht, "Probabilistic Neural Networks", Neural Networks, vol.3, pp.109-118, 1990
[4] Moody J. and Darken C.J., "Fast learning in networks of locally-tuned processing units", Neural Computation, 1, pp.281-294, 1989
[5] Poggio T. and Girosi F., "Regularization algorithm for learning that are equivalent to multilayer networks", Science, 247, pp.978-982, 1990
[6] Hartmann E.J., Keler J.D. and Kowalski J.M., "Layered neural networks with Gaussian hidden units as universal approximations", Neural Computation, 2, pp.210-215, 1990
[7] Bishop C.M., "Improving the generalization properties of radial basis function neural networks", Neural Computation, 3, pp.579-588, 1991
[8] Carpenter G.A., Grossberg S and Rosen D.B., "ART2-A: An adaptive resonance algorithm for rapid category learning and recognition", Neural Networks, 4, pp.493-504, 1991
[9] Carpenter G.A., Grossberg S. and Reynold J.H., "ARTMAP: Supervised real-time learning and classification of nonstationary data by a self-organizing neural network, "Neural Networks", 4, pp.565-588, 1991
[10] Fukushima K., "Neocognitron: A self-organizing neural network model for a mechanism of pattern recognition unaffected by shift in position, Biol. Cybern. 36, pp.193-202, 1980
[11] Reilly D. L., Cooper L.N. and Elbaum C., "A neural model category learning", Biol. Cybern. vol.45, pp. 35- 41
[12] Fukuda T., Shiotani S. and Arai F, "A new neuron model for additional learning", IJCNN Baltimore 1992 June, vol. 1, pp. 938-943
[13] Bruce Alberts, Dennis Bray and so on, "Molecular biology of the cell", Garland Publishing Inc. New York & London, pp.1142-1143, 1983

FROM REGULARIZATION TO RADIAL, TENSOR AND ADDITIVE SPLINES

Tomaso Poggio, Federico Girosi and Michael Jones
Artificial Intelligence Laboratory
Massachusetts Institute of Technology
Cambridge, MA 02139 USA

We had previously shown that regularization principles lead to approximation schemes which are equivalent to networks with one layer of hidden units, called *Regularization Networks*. We summarize here some recent results (Girosi, Jones and Poggio, 1993) that show that regularization networks encompass a much broader range of approximation schemes, including many of the popular general additive models and some of the neural networks. In particular, additive splines as well as some tensor product splines can be obtained from appropriate classes of smoothness functionals. Furthermore the same extension that extends Radial Basis Functions to Hyper Basis Functions leads from additive models to ridge approximation models, containing as special cases Breiman's hinge functions and some forms of Projection Pursuit Regression. We propose to use the term *Generalized Regularization Networks* for this broad class of approximation schemes that follow from an extension of regularization.

INTRODUCTION

In recent papers we and others have argued that the task of learning from examples can be considered in many cases to be equivalent to multivariate function approximation, that is to the problem of approximating a smooth function from sparse data – the examples. The interpretation of an approximation scheme in terms of networks – and viceversa – has also been extensively discussed (Barron and Barron, 1988; Poggio and Girosi, 1989, 1990; Broomhead and Lowe, 1988).

In a series of papers we have explored a specific - albeit quite general – approach to the problem of function approximation. The approach is based on the recognition that the ill-posed problem of function approximation from sparse

[1]This paper has also been submitted to the International Joint Conference on Neural Networks to be held in Nagoya, Japan, October 1993.

0-7803-0928-6/93$03.00 © 1993 IEEE

data must be constrained by assuming an appropriate prior on the class of approximating functions. Regularization techniques typically impoose smoothness constraints on the approximating set of functions.

In Poggio and Girosi (1989) we showed that regularization principles lead to approximation schemes which are equivalent to networks with one "hidden" layer, that we call *Regularization Networks* (RN). In particular, we described how a certain class of radial stabilizers – and the associated priors in the equivalent Bayes formulation – lead to a subclass of regularization networks, the already known Radial Basis Functions (Powell, 1987; Micchelli, 1986) that we have extended to Hyper Basis Functions. In this paper we show that an extension of Regularization Networks, that we propose to call *Generalized Regularization Networks* (GRN), encompasses an even broader range of approximation schemes, including tensor product splines and many of the general additive models and some of the neural networks..

REGULARIZATION NETWORKS

Suppose that the set $g = \{(\mathbf{x}_i, y_i) \in R^d \times R\}_{i=1}^N$ of data has been obtained by random sampling a function f, belonging to some space of functions X defined on R^d, in presence of noise, and suppose to be interested in recovering the function f, or an estimate of it, from the set of data g. This problem is clearly ill-posed, since it has an infinite number of solutions.

Regularization solves the problem by choosing the function that minimizes the following functional:

$$H[f] = \sum_{i=1}^{N} (f(\mathbf{x}_i) - y_i)^2 + \lambda\phi[f] \ . \qquad (1)$$

where λ is a positive number that is usually called *regularization parameter*. The first term is enforcing closeness to the data, and the second smoothness, while the regularization parameter controls the trade off between these two terms.

Here we consider smoothness functionals of the form:

$$\phi[f] = \int_{R^d} ds \, \frac{|\tilde{f}(\mathbf{s})|^2}{\tilde{G}(\mathbf{s})} \qquad (2)$$

where $\tilde{}$ indicates the Fourier transform, $\tilde{G}$ is some positive function that falls off to zero as $||\mathbf{s}|| \rightarrow \infty$ (so that $\frac{1}{\tilde{G}}$ is an high-pass filter) and for which the class of functions such that this expression is well defined is not empty. Under some mild conditions the function that minimizes the functional (1) has the form:

$$f(\mathbf{x}) = \sum_{i=1}^{N} c_i G(\mathbf{x} - \mathbf{x}_i) + \sum_{\alpha=1}^{k} d_\alpha \psi_\alpha(\mathbf{x}) \qquad (3)$$

where $\{\psi_\alpha\}_{\alpha=1}^k$ is a basis in the k dimensional null space $\mathcal{N}$ and the coefficients d_α and c_i satisfy the following linear system:

$$(G + \lambda I)\mathbf{c} + \Psi^T \mathbf{d} = \mathbf{y}$$

$$\Psi \mathbf{c} = 0$$

where I is the identity matrix, and we have defined

$$(\mathbf{y})_i = y_i \ , \quad (\mathbf{c})_i = c_i \ , \quad (\mathbf{d})_i = d_i \ ,$$

$$(G)_{ij} = G(\mathbf{x}_i - \mathbf{x}_j) \ , \quad (\Psi)_{\alpha i} = \psi_\alpha(\mathbf{x}_i)$$

The approximation scheme of (3) has a simple interpretation in terms of a network with one layer of hidden units, which we we call *Regularization Network* (RN).

In the past we have mainly considered radial stabilizers originating Radial Basis Functions approximation techniques. We show now that there exist two other broad classes of stabilizers. Each of them corrsponds to different a priori assumptions on the smoothness of the function that has to be approximated.

Most of the commonly used stabilizers have radial simmetry, that is satisfy the following equation:

$$\phi[f(\mathbf{x})] = \phi[f(R\mathbf{x})]$$

An alternative to choosing a radial function $\tilde{G}$ in the stabilizer is a *tensor product* type of basis function, that is a function of the form

$$\tilde{G}(\mathbf{s}) = \Pi_{j=1}^d \tilde{g}(s_j) \tag{4}$$

where s_j is the j-th coordinate of the vector $\mathbf{s}$, and $\tilde{g}$ is an appropriate one dimensional function. Stabilizers with $\tilde{G}(\mathbf{s})$ as in (4) have the form

$$\phi[f] = \int_{R^d} ds \frac{|\tilde{f}(\mathbf{s})|^2}{\Pi_{j=1}^d \tilde{g}(s_j)}$$

which leads to a *tensor product* basis function

$$G(\mathbf{x}) = \Pi_{j=1}^d g(x_j)$$

where x_j is the j-th coordinate of the vector $\mathbf{x}$ and $g(x)$ is the Fourier transform of $\tilde{g}(s)$.

Additive approximations on the other hand have the form

$$f(\mathbf{x}) = \sum_{\mu=1}^d f_\mu(x^\mu) \tag{5}$$

where x^μ is the μ-th component of the input vector $\mathbf{x}$ and the f_μ are one-dimensional functions that will be defined as the *additive components* of f (from now on greek indices will be used in association to components of the input vectors). The simplest way to obtain such an approximation scheme from regularization is to choose a stabilizer that corresponds to an additive basis function:

$$G(\mathbf{x}) = \sum_{\mu=1}^{n} \theta_\mu g(x^\mu) \tag{6}$$

where θ_μ are certain fixed parameters. Such a choice, in fact, leads to an approximation scheme of the form (5) in which the additive components f_μ have the form:

$$f_\mu(x) = \theta_\mu \sum_{i=1}^{N} c_i G(x^\mu - x_i^\mu) \tag{7}$$

We would like to write stabilizers corresponding to the basis fuction (6), where $\tilde{G}(\mathbf{s})$ is the Fourier Transform of $G(v\mathbf{x})$. It is possible to do so considering the limit (in two dimensions) for the variance going to zero of the stabilizer:

$$\phi[f] = \int_{R^d} ds \; \epsilon \frac{|\tilde{f}(\mathbf{s})|^2}{\theta_x \tilde{g}(s_x) e^{-(\frac{s_y}{\epsilon})^2} + \theta_y \tilde{g}(s_y) e^{-(\frac{s_x}{\epsilon})^2}} \tag{8}$$

This corresponds to a basis function of the form:

$$G(x, y) = \theta_x g(x) e^{-\epsilon^2 y^2} + \theta_y g(y) e^{-\epsilon^2 x^2} \; . \tag{9}$$

In the limit of ϵ going to zero the basis function (9) approaches a basis function that is the sum of one dimensional basis functions.

GENERALIZED REGULARIZATION NETWORKS

A fundamental problem in almost all practical applications in learning and pattern recognition is the choice of the the relevant variables. It may happen that some of the variables are more relevant than others, or some variables are just totally irrelevant, or that the relevant variables are linear combinations of the original ones. It can therefore be useful to work not with the original set of variables $\mathbf{x}$, but with an arbitrary linear transformation of them, $\mathbf{W}\mathbf{x}$, where $\mathbf{W}$ is a possibily rectangular matrix. In the framework of regularization theory, this can be taken in account making the assumption that the approximating function f has the form $f(\mathbf{x}) = F(W\mathbf{x})$ for some smooth function F. The smoothness assumption is now made directly on F, through a smoothness functional $\phi[F]$. The regularization functional is now expressed in terms of F as

$$H[F] = \sum_{i=1}^{N} (y_i - F(\mathbf{z}_i))^2 + \lambda\phi[F]$$

where $\mathbf{z}_i = \mathbf{W}\mathbf{x}_i$. The function that minimizes this functional is of the form:

$$F(\mathbf{z}) = \sum_{i=1}^{N} c_i G(\mathbf{z} - \mathbf{z}_i) \ .$$

(plus eventually a polynomial in $\mathbf{z}$). Therefore the solution for f is:

$$f(\mathbf{x}) = F(\mathbf{W}\mathbf{x}) = \sum_{i=1}^{N} c_i G(\mathbf{W}\mathbf{x} - \mathbf{W}\mathbf{x}_i) \tag{10}$$

Usually the matrix $\mathbf{W}$ is unknown, and it has to be estimated from the examples. Estimating both the coefficients c_i and the matrix $\mathbf{W}$ by least squares is probably not a good idea, since we would end up trying to estimate a number of parameters that is larger than the number of data points (though one may use regularized least squares). Therefore we proposed to replace the approximation scheme of eq. (10) with a similar one, in which he basic shape of the approximation scheme is retained, but the number of basis functions is decreased. The resulting approximating function that we call *Generalized Regularization Network* (GRN) is:

$$f(\mathbf{x}) = \sum_{\alpha=1}^{n} c_\alpha G(\mathbf{W}\mathbf{x} - \mathbf{W}\mathbf{t}_\alpha) \ . \tag{11}$$

where $n < N$ and the *centers* $\mathbf{t}_\alpha$ are chosen according to some heuristic, or are considered as free parameters. The coefficients c_α and the elements of the matrix $\mathbf{W}$ are estimated accordingly to a least squares criterion. The elements of the matrix $\mathbf{W}$ could also be estimated through crossvalidation, which may be a formally more appropriate technique.

In the case in which the basis function is radial, the approximation scheme of eq. (11) becomes:

$$f(\mathbf{x}) = \sum_{\alpha=1}^{n} c_\alpha G(\|\mathbf{x} - \mathbf{t}_\alpha\|_{\mathbf{W}}) \tag{12}$$

where we have defined the weighted norm:

$$\|\mathbf{x}\|_{\mathbf{W}} \equiv \mathbf{x} \cdot \mathbf{W}^T\mathbf{W}\mathbf{x} \ . \tag{13}$$

In the case in which the bais function is "additive" we introduce a linear transformation of the inputs $\mathbf{x} \rightarrow \mathbf{W}\mathbf{x}$, where $\mathbf{W}$ is a $d' \times d$ matrix. Calling $\mathbf{w}_\mu$ the μ-th column of W, Girosi, Jones and Poggio (1993) show how to derive an approximation scheme of the form

$$f(\mathbf{x}) = \sum_{\alpha=1}^{n} \sum_{\mu=1}^{d'} c_\alpha^\mu G(\mathbf{w}_\mu \cdot \mathbf{x} - t_\alpha^\mu) \ . \tag{14}$$

which is similar to the Projection Pursuit Regression technique: in both schemes the unknown function is approximated by a linear superposition of one dimensional variables, that are projections of the original variables on certain vectors that have to been estimated.

In summary, a large number of approximation techniques can be written as multilayer networks with one hidden layer. In past papers we showed how to derive a large subset of such approximation schemes from regularization principles of the form used to deal with the ill-posed problem of function approximation. In particular, RBF, HBF and many forms of multidimensional splines can be justified in terms of regularization. We had not used regularization to yield approximation schemes of the additive type, such as additive splines, ridge approximation of the PPR type and hinges. In Girosi, Jones and Poggio (1993) we have succeeded in showing that appropriate stabilizers can be defined to justify such additive schemes. Our Generalized Regularization Networks include, depending on the stabilizer (that is on the associated prior), HBF networks, ridge approximation and tensor products splines. Figure (1) shows a diagram of the relationships. Notice that HBF networks and ridge regression networks are directly related in the special case of normalized inputs (Maruyama, Girosi and Poggio, 1992).

We feel that there is now a theoretical framework that justifies a large spectrum of approximation schemes in terms of different smoothness constraints imposed within the same regularization functional to solve the ill-posed problem of function approximation from sparse data. The claim is thus that all the different networks and corresponding approximation schemes can be justified in terms of the variational principle

$$H[f] = \sum_{i=1}^{N} (f(\mathbf{x}_i) - y_i)^2 + \lambda\phi[f] \ . \tag{15}$$

They differ because of different choices of legal stabilizers ϕ, which correspond to different assumptions of smoothness. In this context, we believe that the Bayesian interpretation is one of the main advantages of regularization: it makes clear that different network architectures correspond to different prior assumptions of smoothness of the functions to be approximated. To our knowledge this is also the first attempt to provide a Bayesian interpretation of techniques such as PPR.

The common framework we have derived suggests that differences between the various network architectures are relatively minor, corresponding to different smoothness assumptions. One would expect that each architecture will work best for the class of function defined by the associated prior (that is stabilizer) an expectation which is consistent with numerical results.

References

[1] A. R. Barron and Barron R. L. Statistical learning networks: a unifying view. In *Symposium on the Interface: Statistics and Computing Science*, Reston, Virginia, April 1988.

[2] D.S. Broomhead and D. Lowe. Multivariable functional interpolation and adaptive networks. *Complex Systems*, 2:321–355, 1988.

[3] C. A. Micchelli. Interpolation of scattered data: distance matrices and conditionally positive definite functions. *Constr. Approx.*, 2:11–22, 1986.

[4] T. Poggio and F. Girosi. A theory of networks for approximation and learning. A.I. Memo No. 1140, Artificial Intelligence Laboratory, Massachusetts Institute of Technology, 1989.

[5] T. Poggio and F. Girosi. Networks for approximation and learning. *Proceedings of the IEEE*, 78(9), September 1990.

[6] T. Poggio and F. Girosi. Regularization algorithms for learning that are equivalent to multilayer networks. *Science*, 247:978–982, 1990.

[7] M. J. D. Powell. Radial basis functions for multivariable interpolation: a review. In J. C. Mason and M. G. Cox, editors, *Algorithms for Approximation*. Clarendon Press, Oxford, 1987.

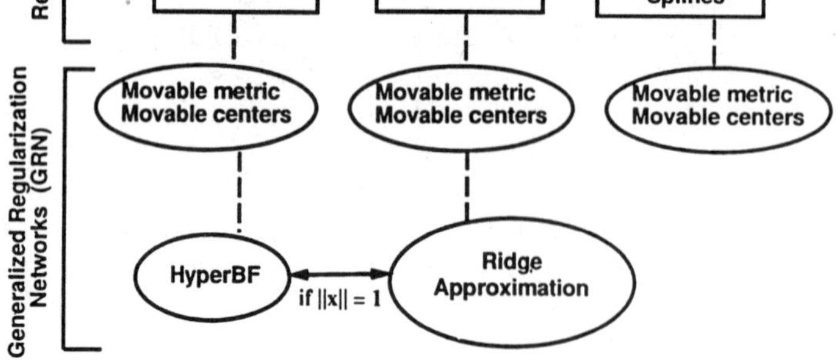

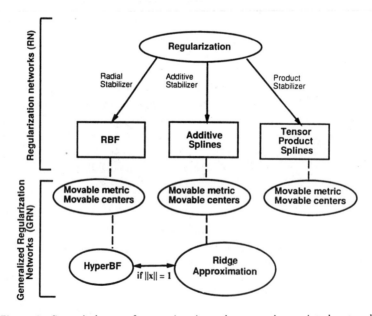

Figure 1: Several classes of approximation schemes and associated network architectures can be derived from regularization with the appropriate choice of smoothness priors and corresponding stabilizers and Greens functions

Hierarchical Wavelet Neural Networks

Sathyanarayan S. Rao and Ravikanth S. Pappu
Department of Electrical and Computer Engineering
Villanova University, Villanova, PA 19085.
phone: (215) 645-4971; fax: (215) 645-4436
email: pappu@vu-vlsi.vill.edu

Abstract: Neural Networks are capable of learning highly complex, nonlinear input-output mappings. This characteristic of neural networks enables them to be used in nonlinear system modelling and prediction applications. The wavelet decomposition, on the other hand. provides a method of examining a signal at multiple scales. In this paper, we draw upon the recently established connection between these two fields. A method is outlined which exploits the localized, hierarchical nature of wavelets in the learning of time series. This is achieved by having a dynamic network - one in which nodes are added to the network so as to progressively reduce the modelling error. This cascade correlation approach overcomes some of the disadvantages of a static network architecture. The learning algorithm is outlined and its performance is demonstrated using simulations.

INTRODUCTION

Time series prediction has important applications in many fields. The majority of commonly occurring time series are nonlinear in nature and hence can be approximated by neural networks. Since [1], neural networks have been increasingly employed for such tasks. Multilayer Perceptrons trained using backpropogation and Radial Basis Function Networks have been used successfully to predict nonlinear and chaotic data [2], [3].

Wavelet techniques have generated tremendous interest among the signal processing community in recent years. Wavelet decomposition involves representing arbitrary functions in terms of simpler basis functions at different scales and positions. In other words, the wavelet decomposition represents the signal as the sum of contributions of components at different scales. By its very definition, the wavelet decomposition is hierarchical in nature. For more details on wavelet theory and applications, the reader is referred to any of the number of books and articles which have appeared in the literature ([4-7]).

Wavelet neural networks represent a fruitful synthesis of ideas from neural networks and wavelet analysis. Recently the utility of wavelets in nonlinear system modelling and approximation was demonstrated in [8], [9], and [10]. In [10] the authors show that any arbitrary time series may be approximated by using wavelets as activation functions in a typical 1+1/2 layer network. Our work draws upon ideas from [10] to provide an alternate method of using wavelets as activation functions. The algorithm presented in this paper is inspired by the hierarchical nature of the wavelet decomposition and cascade-correlation learning [13]. Hidden units are progressively added to the existing network to model the residual error from the previous approximation. This method overcomes the problem of selecting the number of hidden units in advance and also allows explicit control over the global approximation error.

This paper is organized as follows. The next section provides a brief introduction to wavelet networks. Then the proposed scheme is outlined and we illustrates how it overcomes some of the disadvantages of a static wavelet network. Details of the simulations are presented here. The last section summarizes the key results of this paper.

LEARNING IN WAVELET NETWORKS

In this section of the paper, we provide a concise description of the structure and learning ability of the wavelet network. The material in this section is, for the most part, is along the lines of [10].

Structure

Cybenko [11] proved the following result. If $\sigma(\ )$ is a continuous, discriminatory function, then finite sums of the form

$$f(x) = \sum_{i=1}^{N} w_i \sigma(a_i^T x + b_i) \tag{1}$$

are dense in the space of continuous functions defined on $[0,1]^n$ - where $w_i, b_i \in R$ and $a_i \in R^n$. This implies that any continuous function $f(\ )$ may be approximated by a weighted sum of $\sigma(\ )$ functions. The parameters w_i, b_i, and a_i may be determined by some optimization technique, such as backpropagation.

There is an analogous result in wavelet theory that enables arbitrary functions to be written as weighted sums of dilated and translated wavelets. This states that the sum

$$f(\boldsymbol{x}) = \sum_{i=1}^{N} w_i det(D_i^{1/2}) \psi(D_i \boldsymbol{x} - t_i) \tag{2}$$

is dense in $L^2(R^n)$. Here the t_i's are translation vectors and the $D_i = diag(d_i)$, where d_i's are the dilation vectors. $\psi(\ )$ is the basic wavelet whose translates and dilates form the basis for the space $L^2(R^n)$. Equation (2) immediately suggests the network structure shown in Fig.(1).
The primary advantages which wavelets have to offer over other activation

functions are:

- They guarantee the universal approximation property, i.e., (2).
- Initial values for the learning algorithm may be obtained from the continuous or discrete wavelet transform coefficients and thus enable faster convergence.
- If orthogonal wavelets are used, then adding or removing nodes from the network does not affect those weights which have already been trained. This is true since components at different scales lie in orthogonal subspaces.

These features lead to fast, localized, and hierarchical learning - in the spirit of [12].

Learning Algorithm

Learning in the network of Fig.(1) is accomplished by the stochastic gradient algorithm. We present the flow chart in Fig.(2) for a 1-D function (3), with the understanding that this procedure may be easily extended to higher dimensions. In 1-D, (2) reduces to

$$f(x) = \sum_{i=1}^{N} w_i \psi\left(\frac{x - t_i}{s_i}\right) + \bar{f} \tag{3}$$

where $\bar{f}$ is the estimated mean of $f(x)$ from the available samples and s_i is the scale parameter. The algorithm proceeds as shown in Fig.(2).

Let Θ be the vector containing all the parameters to be evaluated i.e., $[w_i, t_i, s_i, \bar{f}]$, $N_\Theta(x_k)$ be the output of the network for input x_k, and $J(\Theta, x_k, y_k)$ be the objective function to be minimized. This is defined as follows.

$$J(\Theta, x_k, y_k) = \frac{1}{2}[N_\Theta(x_k) - y_k]^2 \tag{4}$$

The gradient of $J(\Theta, x_k, y_k)$ with respect to the various parameters are computed and Θ is changed in the opposite direction of the gradient of the objective function. Further details of the training algorithm may be found in [10].

Observations

The above method prescribes an algorithm which uses wavelets as activation functions in a neural network. Admittedly, the selection of the number of hidden units (N) poses a problem. It is difficult to select a value of N directly from the data that will guarantee good approximation performance. Several statistical criteria such as the Akaike Criterion or the Minimum Description Length Principle have been suggested to determine the value of N. This problem may be rectified by approaching the problem from a cascade-correlation point of view. This is a powerful method which provides explicit control over the error and also exploits the hierarchical character of the wavelet decomposition. This is the inspiration for the modified scheme proposed below.

PROPOSED SCHEME

As an alternative to the fixed network structure above, a dynamic network structure based on cascade correlation is proposed in this section. The principles of cascade correlation learning architecture are simple. It is a supervised learning architecture that builds a near-minimal multilayer network topology during the course of training. The key word here is "build". Initially the network contains only inputs, output units and the connections between them. The single layer of connections is trained repeatedly till there is no change in the error. The network's performance is evaluated at this stage. If the error is small enough, then we stop. Otherwise a new hidden unit is added in an attempt to reduce the error further.

Cascade correlation eliminates the need for the user to guess the size of the network and its topology in advance. A reasonably small network is built automatically. The learning is also faster than backpropagation for several reasons. First only a single layer of weights is being trained at any given time. There is no need to propagate any errors backwards as in backprop. Another reason is that this is a 'greedy" algorithm. Each node "grabs" as much of the residual error as it can. Thus, each node has a well defined role to play in the scheme of things. This is the motivation for adopting a variant of this method for the wavelet neural network.

In our method, the network begins learning by having a single "wavelon" - a combination of a translation, dilation, and wavelet lying along the same path from input to output. This wavelon is trained according to the algorithm in Fig.(2) till the error does not decrease any further. Then a new node is added and trained to model the residual error from the previous approximation. This process is repeated till the modelling error performance is satisfactory. Intuitively, it is clear that this hierarchical method of learning a time series is very well matched to the use of wavelets as activation functions. The hierarchical nature of the wavelet decomposition enables each wavelon to optimally complete its assigned task - i.e., to model the residual error from the previous approximation - before a new wavelon is added.

Simulation Results

In this section, we present two examples of wavelets based hierarchical learning. In the first example, a sinusoid is approximated by translations and dilations of a basic wavelet defined by

$$\psi(x) = -xe^{-\frac{1}{2}x^2} \tag{5}$$

Graph 1 is the approximation at the largest scale and graphs 2 through 5 are the added details. The approximation at different scales is clearly observed by examining the y-axis of each plot. Graph 6 shows the sum of all the components at different scales along with the desired output. In this example the learning rate γ was 1. The final network had 5 wavelons and the sum of squared error (SSE) was 0.1026. Each wavelon was trained for 10 epochs of the training data. Comparable performance was achieved using a static network only after the network was trained for about 10^4 epochs.

The second example involves prediction of the logistic map. This is a quadratic map defined by the equation

$$x(t+1) = \alpha x(t)(1-x(t)) \qquad (6)$$

This system is known to be chaotic for values of $\alpha > 3$. We use $\alpha = 4$ for which the system is guaranteed to be chaotic. The initial condition $x(0) = 0.1$. The inputs were $x(t)$ and the desired outputs were $x(t+1)$. The nonlinear map is shown in graph 7 along with the training data pairs. Daubechies' wavelets of order 2 were used as activation functions. Graphs 8 through 10 show the approximation of the training data at various scales and graph 11 shows the predicted time series. It is clear from the graphs that large structures in the input data are approximated by wavelets at large scales and detail is added at lower scales. The table below provides figures for the approximation and the prediction SSE at various levels.

	L=9 (ψ_9)	L=8 (ψ_8)	L=7 (ψ_7)	L=6 (ψ_6)	L=5 (ψ_5)
Approximation Error	0.3699	0.1766	0.1123	0.0942	0.0940
Prediction Error	0.3971	0.2409	0.1543	0.1694	0.1688

Table 1: APPROXIMATION AND PREDICTION SSE FOR THE LOGISTIC MAP

DISCUSSIONS AND SUMMARY

In summary, we have shown that a time series may be approximated by using a dynamic wavelet neural network. This method of learning a time series offers the advantage of having control over the error and eliminates the need to select the number of hidden units before the training phase begins. Simulation results have shown that the proposed algorithm is indeed well matched to the hierarchical character of wavelets. There are two issues which merit further investigation. First, it is likely that a more efficient algorithm will have a scale dependent learning rate - with large scales having a large rate and small scales having a smaller rate. In other words, the approximation of large structures is done quickly and the detail is added at a rate proportional to the scale of approximation. Another issue is the choice of the wavelet family. There are several families of wavelets available and one has to choose one of them. It appears that continuous, orthogonal wavelets offer the most advantages. Desirable properties of wavelets for prediction applications have to be established and various families have to be compared. These ideas are deferred to future work.

REFERENCES

[1] Alan Lapedes and Robert Farber, "Non Linear Signal Processing Using Neural Networks: Prediction and System Modelling", Los Alamos National Laboratory Report LA-UR-87-2662, 1987.

[2] M. Casdagli, "Nonlinear Prediction of Chaotic Time Series", Physica D, vol. 35, pp. 335-356, 1989.

[3] M. Niranjan et. al., "A Nonlinear Model for Time Series Prediction and Signal Interpolation", Proceedings of ICASSP 1991, pp. 1713-1716.

[4] S. G. Mallat, "A Theory for Multiresolution Decomposition: The Wavelet Representation", IEEE Transactions on Pattern Analysis and Machine Intelligence, vol. 2, pp. 674-693, July 1989.

[5] I. Daubechies, "Orthonormal Bases of Compactly Supported Wavelets", Communications on Pure and Applied Math., vol. 41, pp. 909-996, 1988.

[6] J. M. Combes et. al., editors, Wavelets: Time-Frequency Methods in Phase Space, Springer-Verlag, 1989.

[7] C. K. Chui, editor, Wavelets: A Tutorial in Theory and Applications, Academic Press, 1992.

[8] B. Bakshi et. al, "Wave-Net: A Multiresolution, Hierarchical Neural Network with Localized Learning", American Institute of Chemical Engineers Journal, July 1992.

[9] S. S. Rao et. al, 'Nonlinear Time Series Prediction Using Wavelet Networks', Proceeding of the World Congress on Neural Networks, 1993 (to appear).

[10] Q. Zhang et. al, "Wavelet Networks", IEEE Transactions on Neural Networks, vol. 3, pp. 889-898, November 1992.

[11] G. Cybenko, "Approximation by Superposition of a Sigmoidal Function", Mathematics of Control, Signals and Systems, vol. 2, pp. 303-314, 1989.

[12] J. Moody, "Fast Learning in Multiresolution Hierarchies", Research Report, Yale University, YALEU/DCS/RR-681, 1989.

[13] S. Fahlman et. al, "The Cascade-Correlation Learning Architecture", Technical Report CMU-CS-90-100, School of Computer Science, Carnegie Mellon University, August 1992.

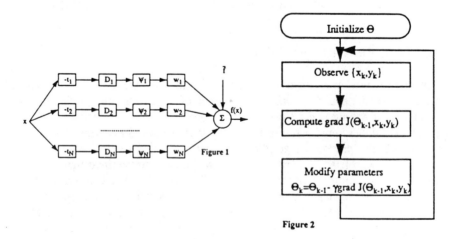

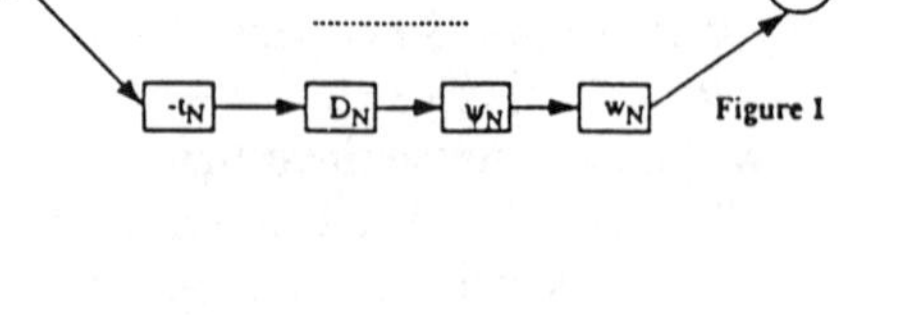

Figure 1

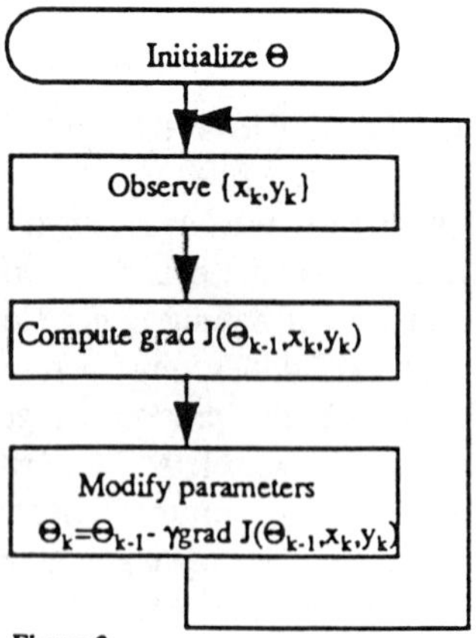

Figure 2

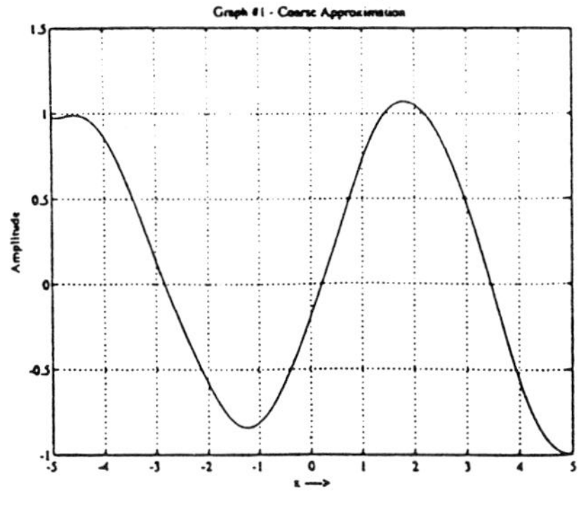
Graph #1 - Coarse Approximation
Amplitude
x --->

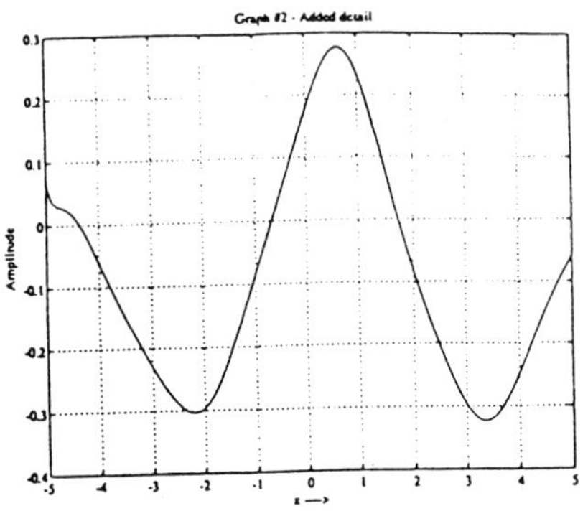
Graph #2 - Added detail
Amplitude
x --->

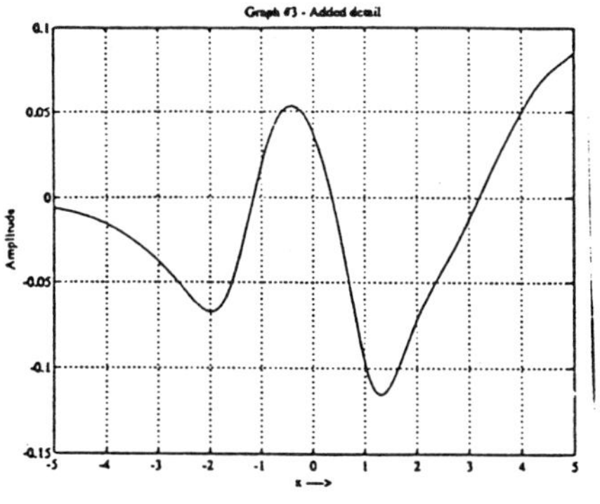
Graph #3 - Added detail
Amplitude
x --->

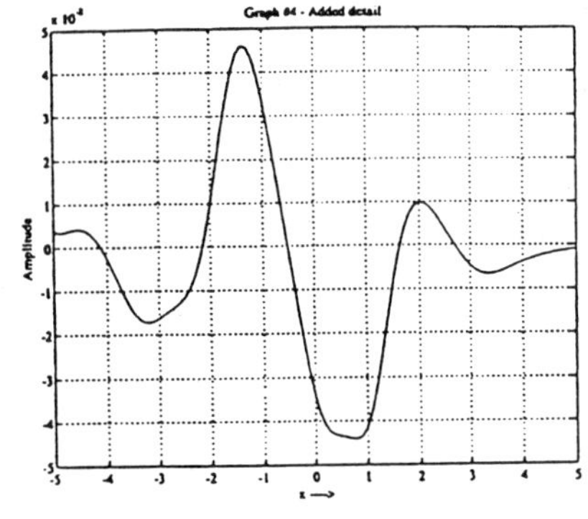
Graph #4 - Added detail
Amplitude
x --->

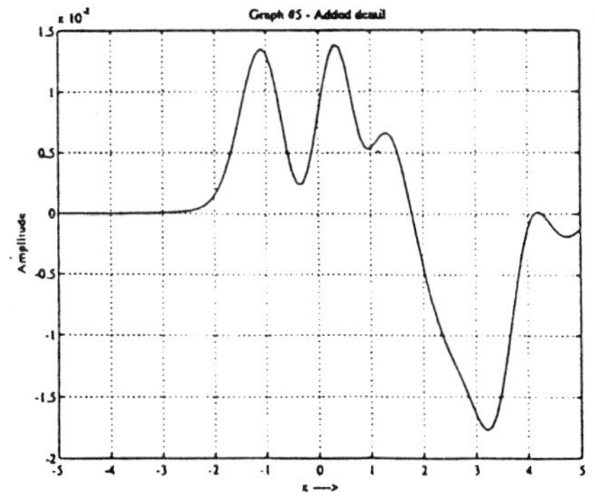
Graph #5 - Added detail
Amplitude
x --->

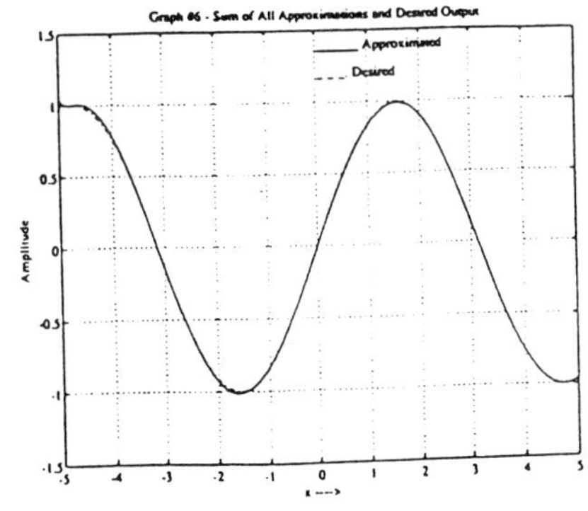
Graph #6 - Sum of All Approximations and Desired Output
Approximated
Desired
Amplitude
x --->

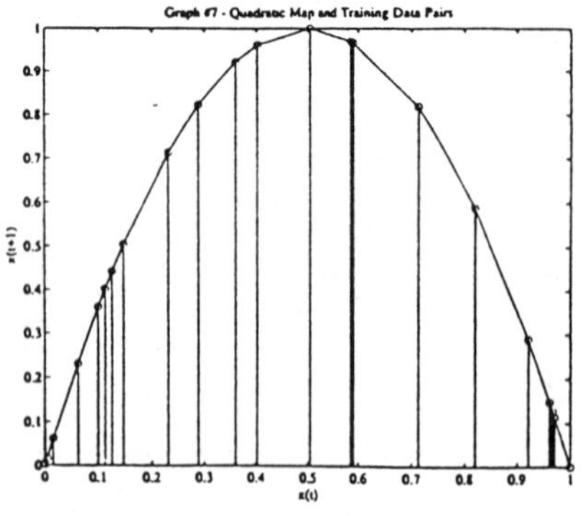

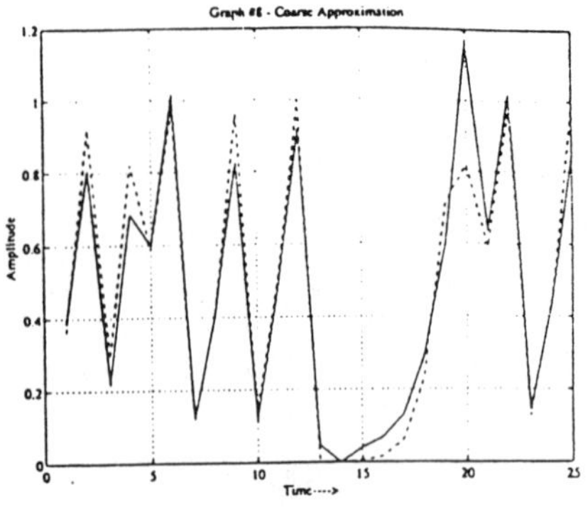

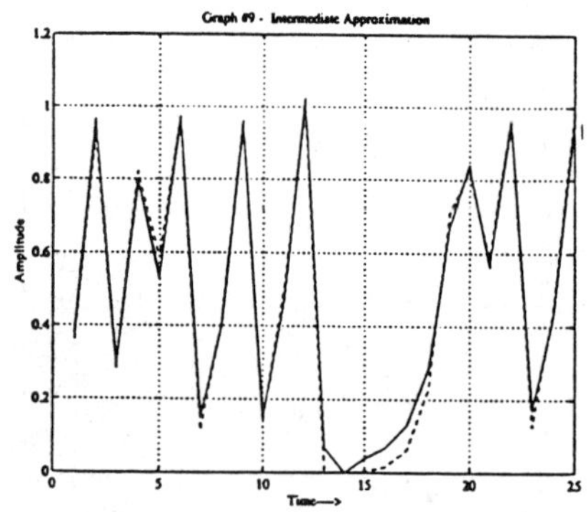

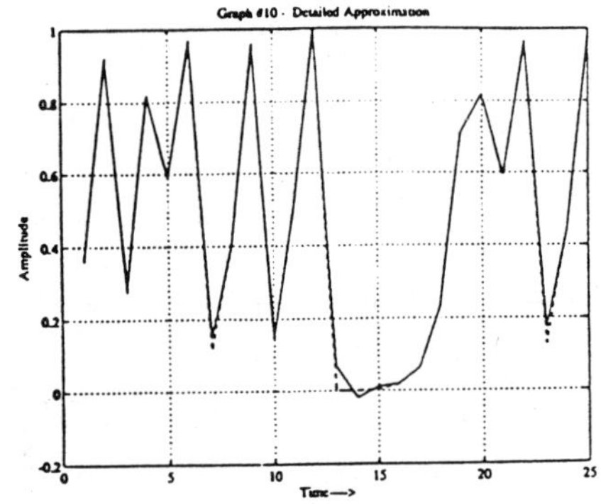

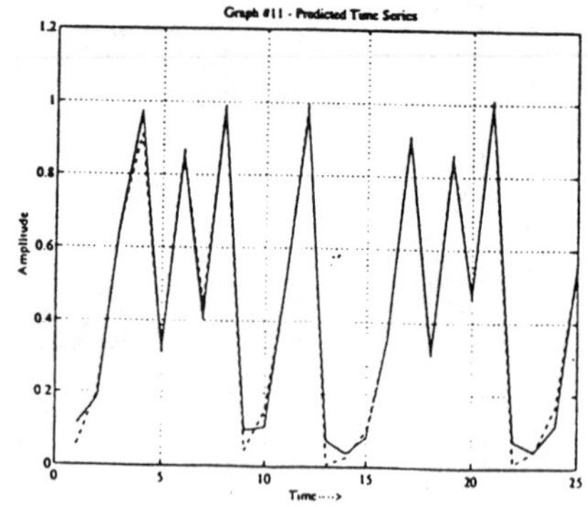

Approximation and prediction of the logistic map.
Dashed lines represent true values.

NEURAL NETWORKS FOR LOCALIZED APPROXIMATION OF REAL FUNCTIONS

H. N. Mhaskar
Department of Mathematics, California State University,
Los Angeles, CA 90032, U.S.A.
email: hmhaska@atss.calstatela.edu

Abstract. We discuss the problem of constructing universal networks capable of approximating all functions having bounded derivatives. We demonstrate that using standard ideas from the theory of spline approximation, it is possible to construct such networks to provide localized approximation. The networks can be used to implement multivariate analogues of the Chui-Wang wavelets and also for simultaneous approximation of a function and its derivative. The number of neurons required to yield the desired approximation at any point does not depend upon the degree of accuracy desired.

INTRODUCTION

In recent years, many authors [1, 3, 4, 7, 9, 11, 12, 15, 18, 19] have studied the question of approximating a given real function of several real variables on compact subsets of a Euclidean space. Poggio and Girosi [16] have pointed out that the training of a feedforward network can be thought of as approximating a real function given its values, which serve as the training examples. Hornik, Stinchcombe, White [11] and Cybenko [7] have proved that a network with one hidden layer and a sigmoidal activation function can always approximate a given continuous function on any compact subset to any degree of accuracy. Mhaskar and Micchelli [15] have shown that practically any non-polynomial activation function has this property.

In the same paper, they have given specific algorithms to achieve this approximation and estimated the rate of approximation in terms of the smoothness of the function being approximated and the number of neurons (principal elements) in the network. The present author [13]

0-7803-0928-6/93$03.00 © 1993 IEEE

has also given specific algorithms using networks with more than one layer to achieve an asymptotically optimal order of approximation. In the case when the function to be approximated is analytic, it is shown in [13] that a network with n neurons arranged in $\mathcal{O}(\log n)$ layers can be constructed to give a near geometric rate of approximation; this rate being substantially independent of the dimension of the input space.

It is well known that any algorithm that aims to approximate an r-times continuously differentiable function on $Q := [0,1]^s$ with n parameters depending continuously on the function cannot, in general, give a degree of approximation better than $\mathcal{O}(n^{-r/s})$ (cf. [8]). This rate was obtained in [13] with a network with multiple hidden layers. It is readily seen that as the dimension s of the input space increases, the size of the network which seeks to approximate a function to even a modest degree of accuracy will have to be outrageously large.

In this paper, we suggest an alternative approach for approximating functions with networks of modest sizes. The idea is to construct a network to provide local approximation to the function. Thus, instead of trying to construct a network that will approximate the function on the entire cube Q, we construct a network with a fixed size that will approximate the function 'pointwise'. More precisely, given a function f and a point $\mathbf{x} \in Q$, the network will utilize only a few examples in the vicinity of $\mathbf{x}$ to train itself to approximate $f(\mathbf{x})$. In a recent paper [2], Bottou and Vapnik have described the advantages of a local network trained with examples close to the point $\mathbf{x}$, but their perspective is entirely different as the following discussion will demonstrate.

CONSTRUCTION OF NETWORKS

The construction of our networks is based on the notion of spline functions. Let $m \geq 1$ be an integer. A univariate (cardinal) spline function of order m is an $m-2$ times continuously differentiable function whose restriction to any interval of the form $[i, i+1]$ is an algebraic polynomial of degree at most $m-1$. (A spline function of order 1 is merely a piecewise constant.) While an algebraic polynomial cannot be zero on an interval without being identically zero everywhere, a spline function can easily be constructed so as to be zero outside a compact interval. The (univariate, cardinal) B-spline of order m is defined by the formula

$$N_m(x) := \frac{1}{(m-1)!}\sum_{j=0}^{m}(-1)^j\binom{m}{j}(x-j)_+^{m-1}, \qquad x \in \mathbf{R}, \tag{1}$$

where the truncated power function x_+^{m-1} is defined by

$$x_+^{m-1} := \begin{cases} x^{m-1}, & \text{if } x \geq 0, \\ 0, & \text{if } x < 0. \end{cases} \tag{2}$$

The B-splines have many interesting properties (cf. [17]). In particular, $N_m(x) = 0$ if $x \notin [0, m]$. Therefore, at any point $x \in \mathbf{R}$, at most m B-splines are nonzero. Several efficient algorithms exist for the evaluation of B-splines as well as their derivatives.

The easiest way to extend the notion of spline functions to the multivariate setting is to use tensor product splines. For each integer $m \geq 1$ and $\mathbf{x} = (x_1, \cdots, x_s) \in \mathbf{R}^s$, the tensor product B-spline of order m is defined by the formula

$$N_m^s(\mathbf{x}) := \prod_{j=1}^{s} N_m(x_j). \tag{3}$$

A tensor product spline of order m is simply defined as a linear combination of the tensor product B-splines of order m. Naturally, in any such expression, at most m^s terms are nonzero at any given point $\mathbf{x} \in \mathbf{R}^s$.

The idea behind our construction of the networks is to use an activation function σ which satisfies the following conditions. (Here, $k \geq 2$ is a fixed integer and $M \geq 1$ is a real constant.)

$$\lim_{x \to \infty} \frac{\sigma(x)}{x^k} = 1, \qquad \lim_{x \to -\infty} \frac{\sigma(x)}{x^k} = 0, \tag{4}$$

$$|\sigma(x)| \leq M(1 + |x|)^k, \qquad x \in \mathbf{R}. \tag{5}$$

Using this activation function, it can be shown (cf. [5], [13]) that a tensor product B-spline of any order m can be approximated arbitrarily closely using a network with a size depending only on m, k and the dimension s of the input space, but independent of the degree of approximation desired. Standard results in spline approximation theory can then be used to construct the networks.

We illustrate with a simple example where $\sigma(x) := x_+^3$ and $s = 2$. The univariate B-spline N_4 can be implemented by the formula

$$N_4(x) = \frac{1}{6}\{\sigma(x) - 4\sigma(x-1) + 6\sigma(x-2) - 4\sigma(x-3) + \sigma(x-4)\}. \tag{6}$$

We may also write $x^3 = \sigma(x) + \sigma(-x)$. The function $N_4^2(\mathbf{x})$ of two variables $\mathbf{x} = (x_1, x_2)$ can be implemented by the formula

$$\begin{aligned} N_4^2(\mathbf{x}) = \frac{1}{4}\{&(N_4(x_1) + 1 + N_4(x_2))^3 + (N_4(x_1) - 1 - N_4(x_2))^3 \\ &- (N_4(x_1) + 1 - N_4(x_2))^3 - (N_4(x_1) - 1 + N_4(x_2))^3\}. \end{aligned} \tag{7}$$

The implementation (7) requires 48 neurons. For a univariate function f, and integers ν, n we define

$$\lambda_\nu(f) := \frac{28}{3} f(\frac{\nu - 3}{n}) - \frac{109}{6} f(\frac{\nu - 2}{n}) + \frac{40}{3} f(\frac{\nu - 1}{n}) - \frac{7}{2} f(\frac{\nu}{n}). \tag{8}$$

For a function f of two variables, and a multi-integer $\mathbf{k} = (k_1, k_2)$, we define $\lambda_{\mathbf{k}}(f)$ as the value obtained by applying first λ_{k_2} to f in its second variable and then applying λ_{k_1} to the resulting function of x_1 (cf. [13]). It can be shown that the spline function defined by

$$S_n(f, \mathbf{x}) := \sum_{\mathbf{k} \in \mathbf{Z}^2} \lambda_{\mathbf{k}}(f) N_4^2(n\mathbf{x} - \mathbf{k}) \tag{9}$$

provides an optimal approximation order of $\mathcal{O}(n^{-4})$ for all functions having continuous fourth order partial derivatives on $[0,1]^2$. It is important to note that at any point $\mathbf{x} \in \mathbf{R}^2$, only 16 terms in the formula (9) are nonzero. Therefore, the network can be implemented by 768 neurons at any point $\mathbf{x}$, independent of the accuracy desired. The accuracy is controlled by the parameter n. The number of neurons can be reduced by allowing the calculations to proceed serially rather than in parallel and saving all the intermediate results. The same network can be used to calculate the approximate derivatives of the function as discussed in [14].

We note that the univariate Chui-Wang wavelets [6] are defined in terms of the B-splines. Their multivariate analogues are easy to obtain using tensor products. The above idea can then be used to implement these wavelets using neural networks. This is done in detail in [5].

In the case when the functions cannot be sampled at equidistant points, one may still use the cardinal B-splines, but instead of using the functionals as indicated, use other quasi-interpolants [17]. This changes the order of approximation somewhat; but unless the sample points are too close together, does not affect the performance in the asymptotic sense. In addition, one may ignore the samples which are not close to the point where the approximation is desired.

FEATURES OF THE NETWORKS

Interesting features of our network are the following.

1. The network is trained non-iteratively, without back- propogation and, in fact, without considering the error surface at all. The training time and the number of examples needed to train the network at any point is constant independent of the degree of accuracy desired. However, the degree of accuracy will depend upon how close the examples are to the point in question.
2. The network is universal, i.e., the architecture of the network is the same regardless of the function being approximated; only the weights at the outermost layers need to be changed if the function is changed. In the simulation, this amounts to changing a parameter in the program.

3. The network can be easily modified to calculate the derivatives of the function at the point in question. Moreover, the rate of approximation of the function value as well as the derivatives can be estimated in advance.
4. Several networks can be combined easily to yield global approximation if desired. Of course, the number of networks necessary to yield a given degree of approximation will then suffer the 'curse of dimensionality'.

RESULTS OF A NEGATIVE NATURE

An essential feature of our networks is that they have necessarily at least two hidden layers. In [15], Mhaskar and Micchelli have constructed a network with one hidden layer that gives the approximation order $\mathcal{O}(n^{-r/(2s+1)})$ for functions having r continuous derivatives on Q. Their research in progress shows that a network with a single hidden layer having a sufficiently smooth activation function can give a near optimal order of approximation, but this approximation is not local. Our joint work with Chui and Li suggests that a network with one hidden layer and a sigmoidal activation function cannot provide a localized approximation (cf. [5]). With a Heavyside activation function, the minimal number of neurons required to provide localized approximation to all functions with a bounded gradient within an accuracy of $\mathcal{O}(1/n)$ seems to be n^{2s}.

CONCLUSIONS

We have constructed neural networks with multiple hidden layers that provide an asymptotically optimal order of approximation for functions which are known to have a certain number of bounded derivatives. The networks can be trained non-iteratively using only a fixed number of neurons, independent of the accuracy desired, and provide localized approximation at any point. The networks can be effectively used to implement the multivariate analogues of the Chui-Wang wavelets as well as to obtain a simultaneous approximation of a function and its derivatives. Some negative results in this direction are also discussed.

ACKNOWLEDGEMENTS

I wish to thank Professor Dr. F. Girosi for his very helpful comments on an initial draft of this paper. The work was supported in part by AFOSR grant 2-26 113.

REFERENCES

[1] A. R. Barron, "Universal approximation bounds for superposition of a sigmoidal function", preprint, November, 1990.

[2] L. Bottou and V. Vapnik, "Local learning algorithms", Neural Computation, **4** (1992), 888-900.

[3] C. K. Chui and X. Li, "Approximation by ridge functions and neural networks with one hidden layer", Texas A & M University CAT Report # 222, 1990.

[4] C. K. Chui and X. Li, "Realization of neural networks with one hidden layer", Texas A & M University CAT Report # 244, March, 1991.

[5] C. K. Chui, X. Li and H. N. Mhaskar, "Neural networks for localized approximation", Preprint, 1993.

[6] C. K. Chui and J. Z. Wang, "On compactly supported spline wavelets and a duality principle", CAT Report 213, May, 1990.

[7] G. Cybenko, "Approximation by superposition of sigmoidal functions", Mathematics of Control, Signals and Systems, **2**, # 4 (1989), 303-314.

[8] R. DeVore, R. Howard and C. A. Micchelli, "Optimal nonlinear approximation", Manuscripta Mathematica, **63** (1989), 469-478.

[9] K. I. Funahashi, "On the approximate realization of continuous mappings by neural networks", Neural Networks, **2** (1989), 183-192.

[10] R. Hecht-Nielsen, Neurocomputing, Addison Wesley, New York, 1989.

[11] K. Hornik, M. Stinchcombe, and H. White, H., "Multilayer feedforward networks are universal approximators", Neural Networks, **2** (1989), 359-366.

[12] B. Irie, and S. Miyake, "Capabilities of three layored perceptrons", IEEE International Conference on Neural Networks, **1** (1988), 641-648.

[13] H. N. Mhaskar, "Approximation properties of a multilayered feedforward artificial neural network", To appear in Advances in Computational Mathematics.

[14] H. N. Mhaskar, "Noniterative training algorithms for mapping networks", Manuscript, 1993.

[15] H. N. Mhaskar and C. A. Micchelli, "Approximation by superposition of a sigmoidal and radial basis functions", Advances in Applied Mathematics, **13** (1992), 350-373.

[16] T. Poggio and F. Girosi, "Regularization algorithms for learning that are equivalent to multilayer networks", Science, **247** (1990), 978-982.

[17] L. L. Schumaker, Spline functions : Basic Theory, John Wiley and Sons, New York, 1981.

[18] M. Stinchcombe and H. White, "Universal approximation using feedforward network with non–sigmoid hidden layer activation functions", in Proceedings of the International Joint Conference on Neural Networks, (1989), 613-618, San Diego, SOS printing.
[19] M. Stinchcombe and H. White, "Approximating and learning unknown mappings using multilayer feedforward networks with bounded weights", IEEE International Conference on Neural Networks, **3** (1990), III-7-III-16.

A HYBRID TECHNIQUE TO ENHANCE THE PERFORMANCE OF RECURRENT NEURAL NETWORKS FOR TIME SERIES PREDICTION

Sathyanarayan S. Rao and Viswanath Ramamurti
Department of Electrical and Computer Engineering
Villanova University, Villanova, PA 19085
Ph: (215)- 645-4971 Fax: (215)-645-4436
email: {rao / viswa}@vu-vlsi.vill.edu

Abstract-The recurrent neural network trained by the real time recurrent learning (RTRL) algorithm is one of the more popular networks used for time series prediction.When there is a strong non-linear relationship connecting the adjacent samples of the time series the network is trying to predict, the prediction performance of the network deteriorates. In this paper we propose a scheme to overcome this drawback. This scheme incorporates cascade-correlation into the recurrent network learning after the network has been trained using RTRL.This scheme does not suffer from the defects of one other scheme which was proposed to counter the above drawback. In addition, we have incorporated Fahlman's quickprop algorithm into the RTRL learning to make the network converge faster. Simulation results with the above enhancements are presented at the end of the paper. The improvement in the prediction performance is found to be considerable.

I. INTRODUCTION

Most of the commonly encountered time series are non-linear in nature, i.e, the systems that create these time series are non-linear. Neural networks have proved to be capable of producing highly non linear mappings. Since Lapedes and Farber's technical report [1], neural networks are increasingly being employed for non-linear system modelling and prediction. Multilayer perceptrons trained using the backpropagation algorithm and radial basis functions trained using least squares fitting have been used successfully to predict chaotic and real time series data [2],[3],[6]. But the serious drawback with such feedforward networks is that they lack the ability to retain information about the infinite past. Hence several past samples have to be provided at the input in order to predict one or more steps into the future. This, in a way, requires the knowledge of the model order of the time series data, which in general is difficult to estimate. On the other hand, the recurrent network, based on the real time recurrent learning algorithm of Williams and Zipser [8] possesses the capability of retaining information about the infinite past. Hence it is ideally suited for the prediction problem. The information about the past is stored in the network due to the recurrent connections. Hence, it is sufficient to provide to the trained network just one sample at the input and predict the next sample at the output. Several researchers have confirmed the superiority of recurrent neural networks over the feedforward networks, for the non-linear time series prediction problem [4],[5],[7]. In [11], we have compared the performance of the recurrent network with classical techniques such as state dependent Kalman filters and Volterra filters. This comparison showed us that the recurrent network performed as good or sometimes better than the classical methods. In addition, recurrent networks are simpler to use when compared to the model dependent classical methods.

In this paper we propose certain enhancements to go with the recurrent network for the prediction problem. The paper is organized as follows. Section II explains how the original quickprop algorithm[14] has been extended to the recurrent network learning algorithm. Convergence speed comparison in learning to predict a benchmark non-linear time series, the sunspot series, is also given in this section. Section III discusses a major drawback of the recurrent network in the prediction context and the defects of one other scheme which was proposed to counter the drawback. Section IV describes the new scheme being proposed. Simulation results with the new scheme are presented in section V and the conclusions are captured in section VI.

II. NEED FOR ACCELERATED LEARNING

The real time recurrent learning algorithm is based on the gradient descent method and proceeds in a manner similar to the backpropagation algorithm. Hence it suffers from the same major drawback that is present in the backpropagation algorithm - the slow learning. This slowness is largely due to the lack of knowledge of the right step size to be taken to reach the global minima. For certain prediction problems, we need the learning time to be very short and therefore cannot afford to take infinitesimal steps. But if the step size is chosen to be large, there is fear of the network diverging. For a good step size to be chosen, knowledge of the curvature at the vicinity of weight space is needed.

Fahlman's quickprop algorithm is one of the more well

0-7803-0999-5/93/$03.00

known algorithms to take care of the step size problem. Quickprop's weight update procedure depends on two approximations: first, that small changes in one weight have relatively little effect on the error gradient observed at other weights; second, that the error function with respect to each weight is locally quadratic. For each weight, a copy of the previous value of slope $\delta J/\delta w(t-1)$ and the present value $\delta J/\delta w(t)$ is stored. The change in the weight in the last update cycle, $\Delta w(t-1)$ is also retained. The two slopes and the step between them are used to jump to the minimum value of a parabola.

$$\Delta w(t) = \frac{\frac{\partial J}{\partial w(t)}}{\frac{\partial J}{\partial w(t-1)} - \frac{\partial J}{\partial w(t)}} \Delta w(t-1)$$

Due to the above mentioned approximations, the new point is usually not the minimum and the procedure is continued iteratively. Certain complications as in [12] are added to the simplified algorithm presented here to make it work in practice.

Figure 1 shows the comparison between the learning speeds of the recurrent network and the quickprop incorporated recurrent network. The graphs indicate the number of epochs taken to learn single step prediction for the sunspot series. Sunspot series is a popular non-linear time series and is a series of values denoting the number of sunspots every year from 1700 to 1979. The first 100 samples of the series were considered for training. For both the training rules, the weight update was performed once every epoch. Figure 1. shows dotted learning curve corresponding to the original algorithm with the largest (best) learning rate such that the mean squared error does not diverge. It is seen from the graph that quickprop learning is more than a magnitude faster than the regular RTRL learning. One more desirable feature in incorporating the quickprop algorithm is that it avoids getting stuck at a local minima. In all the runs that were performed, it converged reliably to a good answer - same was not the case with the original algorithm. However, it should be mentioned that the quickprop weight update rule does not perform well if the weights are updated after the presentation of every pattern.Yet, even the comparison of 'pattern learning' with the original algorithm and 'epoch learning' with quickprop algorithm has revealed that the latter is considerably faster.

III. Drawback Of The Recurrent Network In The Prediction Context

In the recurrent network based on the RTRL algorithm, any node produces an output only one time instant after the input is presented to that node. In the prediction problem, the input is one of the samples from the time series and the output is the predicted value of the next sample.The output node is any one of the recurrent nodes. Hence in a time series, if $x(n)$ is the input and $x^p(n+1)$ is the predicted output, the influence of $x(n)$ on $x^p(n+1)$ is only due to the direct connection between the input node and the output node, due to the unit time delay through a node assumption. Therefore $x^p(n+1)$ will be only a simple non-linear function of $x(n)$ and a complex non-linear function of $x(n-1)$, $x(n-2)$, ... etc. Furthermore, if we expect to capture the entire dynamic range of the time series, the output unit will have to be linear. In this case, $x^p(n+1)$ will be just a constant times $x(n)$ plus a non-linear function of the samples prior to $x(n)$. Therefore if the adjacent samples of the time series have a highly non-linear relationship, the best prediction performance cannot be expected from the recurrent network.

In [12] it was suggested that a feedforward network be trained in parallel with the recurrent network to overcome this adjoining samples non-linearity problem. The idea was to have the input nodes (including the bias) and the output node common to both the recurrent network and the feedforward network. The feedforward network was trained using the backpropagation algorithm. The target value for the feedforward network was assumed to be the true target minus the output produced by the recurrent network and the target value for the recurrent network was assumed to be the true target minus the output produced by the feedforward network.

The above scheme works well when a sample in a time-series depends very strongly on the previous sample like for example the samples in the logistic map time series. But this scheme fails to perform even as well as the original recurrent network when the dependence between adjacent samples is not so strong like for example the samples from the Mackey-Glass time series or the Canadian-Lynx series. The reason for this failure is that the targets for the recurrent network as well as the feedforward network do not represent the true targets. Consider the extreme case when $x(n+1)$ is not dependent upon $x(n)$ and dependent only upon $x(n-1)$ and its past values. This then will mean that, there is no need for a parallel network and the target for the recurrent network while being trained should be equal to the true target. But the target that is assumed by the recurrent network is the true target minus the output of the parallel network. Similarly the target for the feedforward network is also not the one which will make its weights go to zero. Hence the presence of the feedforward network actually hinders the learning of the recurrent network. So we are in need of an approach which will not affect the learning of the recurrent network. There is also an additional drawback with the above scheme; if the current sample being fed to the network is associated in the form of a product with its past samples, the parallel network can not model this non-linearity.

IV. Proposed Technique

In the scheme that is considered here, we first train the network with the RTRL algorithm and make it learn the prediction task as well as possible. For training, a portion of the time series is considered. The present sample is fed as the input and the network is trained to predict the next sample. This is continued till the segment of the time series considered for training is exhausted. This operation is construed as one epoch. Weight updates are made after each epoch and the procedure is continued iteratively. The training is performed by 'teacher-forcing', i.e., the output from the output node is replaced by the value that was desired at the output when it is fed back to the network at the next time instant. The reason for employing 'teacher-forcing' will be explained shortly. Once the network has learned the prediction task as well as it can, the training is stopped. We then adopt a procedure based on the cascade-correlation algorithm[15]. The weights of the network which has been trained so far are frozen and the network is run one more epoch to collect the residual error at the output node for each input. An additional node is then created which has as its inputs, connections from the inputs and all the recurrent units of the recurrent network [figure 2.]. The output of this new unit is not yet connected to the recurrent network. With the weights of the recurrent network frozen, we run a number of epochs over the training segment adjusting the new unit's input weights after each epoch. The goal of the adjustment is to maximize the magnitude of the correlation between v, the new unit's output and the output error E observed at the output unit of the recurrent network.

Let us define

$$S = \left| \sum_p (v_p - \bar{v}) (E_p - \bar{E}) \right|$$

where p is the training sample and the bars over v and E represent the average values of v_p and E_p respectively, averaged over all samples in an epoch.

The partial derivative of S with respect to each of the new unit's incoming weights, w_i is given by,

$$\frac{\partial S}{\partial w_i} = \sigma \sum_p (E_p - \bar{E}) f'_p I_{i,p}$$

where σ is the sign of the correlation between the new unit's output and the output unit of the recurrent network, f'_p is the derivative for sample p of the new unit's activation function with respect to the sum of its inputs and $I_{i,p}$ is the input, the new unit receives from unit i for pattern p.

By computing the partial derivative for each incoming connection, a gradient ascent is performed to maximize S. Quickprop algorithm is once again employed for this purpose. The 'teacher-forced' value of the output node of the recurrent network is fed to the new unit while training.

After having trained the new unit as well as possible, its input weights are frozen and the unit is connected to the output node of the recurrent network. Now the entire set of weights that have been obtained so far except those which come inwards to the output unit, are frozen. The weights which are connected to the output unit are then trained to reduce the prediction error. Training in this manner does not affect what the recurrent network had originally learned. This is because only the weights coming inwards to the output unit are altered. This affects the value produced by the output unit to hopefully produce a better prediction. When the output value is fed back to the network, it is replaced by the teacher forced version which does not change with training and hence the dynamics the original network had learned, are still preserved. Also we now have a non-linear contribution from the input sample via the new node. If there is a feeling that the prediction error can still be reduced, another new node is created with inputs from all the other existing nodes and the routine that was described above is once again followed. Nodes are added one after another till the prediction error reduces no further.

V. Simulation Results

We have considered two time series data to test our proposed scheme here. One is the Sunspot series and the other is a series based on the exponential autoregressive (AR) model given in [10].

$$x(n) = \sum_{i=1}^{N} \left(\Gamma_i + \lambda_i e^{-(\gamma x(n-1)^2)}\right) x(n-i) + e(n)$$

The parameters for the exponential AR time series are given by

N=5; $\Gamma 1 = 0.4$; $\lambda 1 = 0.8$ $\gamma = 0.4$; $\Gamma 2 = -0.3$; $\lambda 2 = -0.7$; $\Gamma 3 = 0$; $\lambda 3 = 0.1$; $\Gamma 4 = 0.0$; $\lambda 4 = 0.2$; $\Gamma 5 = 0.0$; $\lambda 5 = -0.3$.

The Sunspot series has been chosen here as it is a classical example of a non-linear time series. It has also been analyzed extensively in [10]. The exponential AR time series has been chosen because it contains an explicit relationship between adjacent samples.

The Sunspot series is 280 points long. It was scaled down by a factor of 100 to reduce its dynamic range. The first 100 samples were taken for training and the remaining 180 samples were used for testing. For the exponential AR series, 1500 points were generated based on the model. The first 400 of them were used for training and the remaining were used for testing. The number of inputs to the network was two including the bias and the number of recurrent units in the network was ten. All the recurrent units except the output unit had sigmoidal transfer functions. The output unit had a linear transfer function. Training was performed as was detailed before. The mean squared error was taken as the index of prediction performance.

Figure 3. shows a segment of test data and the corresponding predictions for the Sunspot series and the exponential AR series. In the graphs for the exponential AR series, actual time series implies the original time series minus the innovations residual since that is the best any predictor can predict. Figures 3a. and 3c. indicate MSEs with just the recurrent network. Figure 3b. indicates the MSE for the Sunspot series with one new node based on the proposed scheme. The Sunspot series has been tested with different neural network as well as conventional predictors in connection with [11] and [12]. This value of MSE = 0.0269 is the best we have obtained among all these predictors (MSE values for the other predictors have been tabulated in [13]). Further addition of nodes did not help in improving the prediction performance.

Figures 3d. and 3e. show the prediction performance with one and two extra nodes respectively for the exponential AR series. We see that we achieve a considerable reduction in the MSE from the one obtained using the original recurrent network. This drastic enhancement in performance is due to the elimination of the drawbacks mentioned in section III.

VI. Conclusions

In this paper, we have proposed certain enhancements to the basic method of using a recurrent network for non-linear time series prediction. We have first of all incorporated the quickprop type of learning into the RTRL algorithm and found the network to converge considerably faster. We then make use of the principle of cascade correlation to eliminate a major shortcoming of the recurrent network in the prediction context. This scheme also eliminates the shortcomings of one other scheme which was proposed to counter the original drawback[12]. Simulations performed have shown to validate our claims.

References

1. Alan Lapedes & Robert Farber, "Non linear signal processing using neural networks: prediction & system modeling", *Los Alamos National Laboratory Report*, LA-UR-87-2662.
2. M. Casdagli, "Nonlinear prediction of chaotic time series", *Physica D*, Vol.35, pp.335-356, 1989.
3. M. Niranjan & K. Kadirkamanathan, "A nonlinear model for time series prediction & signal interpolation, *Proceedings of ICASSP '91*, pp.1713-1716.
4. J. Connor & L. Atlas, "Recurrent neural networks and time series prediction", *Proceedings of IJCNN '91*, pp.301-306.
5. R. Hecht-Nielsen, "Application of feedforward and recurrent neural networks to chemical plant predictive modeling", *Proceedings of IJCNN '91*, pp.373-378.
6. Xiangdong He and Alan Lapedes, "Nonlinear modeling and prediction by successive approximation using radial basis functions", *Los Alamos National Laboratory Report*, LA-UR-91-1375.
7. David R. Seidl & Robert D. Lorenz, "A structure by which a recurrent neural network can approximate a nonlinear dynamic systems", *Proceedings of IJCNN '91*, Vol.II, pp.709-714.
8. R. J. Williams & David Zipser, "A learning algorithm for continually running fully recurrent neural networks", *Neural Computation*, Vol.1, MIT Press, 1989.
9. S. Chen, et. al, "Non-linear system identification using neural networks", *Int. J. of Control*, vol.51,No.6, 1990
10. M. B. Priestley, "*Non-linear and nonstationary time series analysis*", Academic Press, Chapter 4 & 5, 1988
11. S. S. Rao, S. Sethuraman & V. Ramamurti, 'A recurrent neural network for nonlinear time series prediction - A comparative study', *Proceedings of the IEEE NNSP workshop*, Copenhagen, Denmark, 1992.
12. S. S. Rao & S. Sethuraman, 'A modified recurrent learning algorithm for nonlinear time series prediction', *Proceedings of Artificial Neural Networks in Engineering (ANNIE) '92*.
13. S. Sethuraman, "*Application of neural networks to signal detection and non linear time series prediction*", Master's thesis report, Villanova University, December 1992
14. S. E. Fahlman, 'An empirical study of learning speed in back-propagation networks', *Technical Report CMU-CS-88-162*, Carnegie Mellon University, School of Computer Science, Pittsburgh, PA, Sept. 1988.
15. S. E. Fahlman and C. Lebiere. 'The cascade-correlation learning architecture', *Technical Report CMU-CS-90-100*, Carnegie Mellon University, School of Computer Science, Pittsburgh, PA, August 1991.

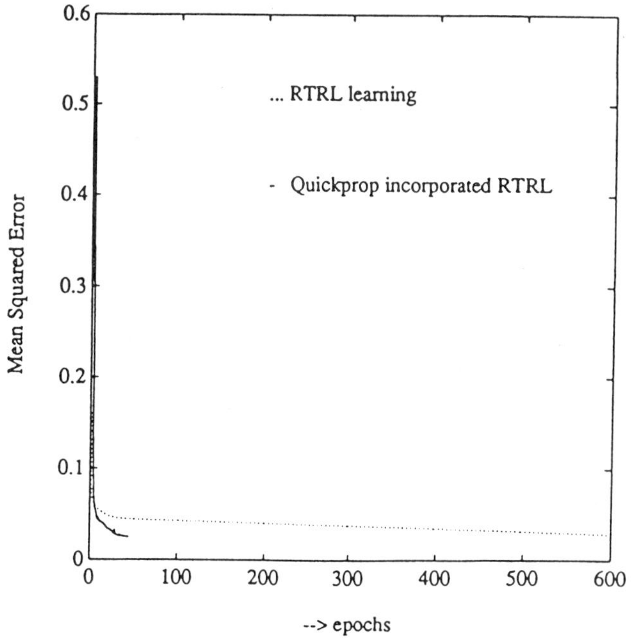

Figure 1. Learning curves for the sunspot series prediction problem.

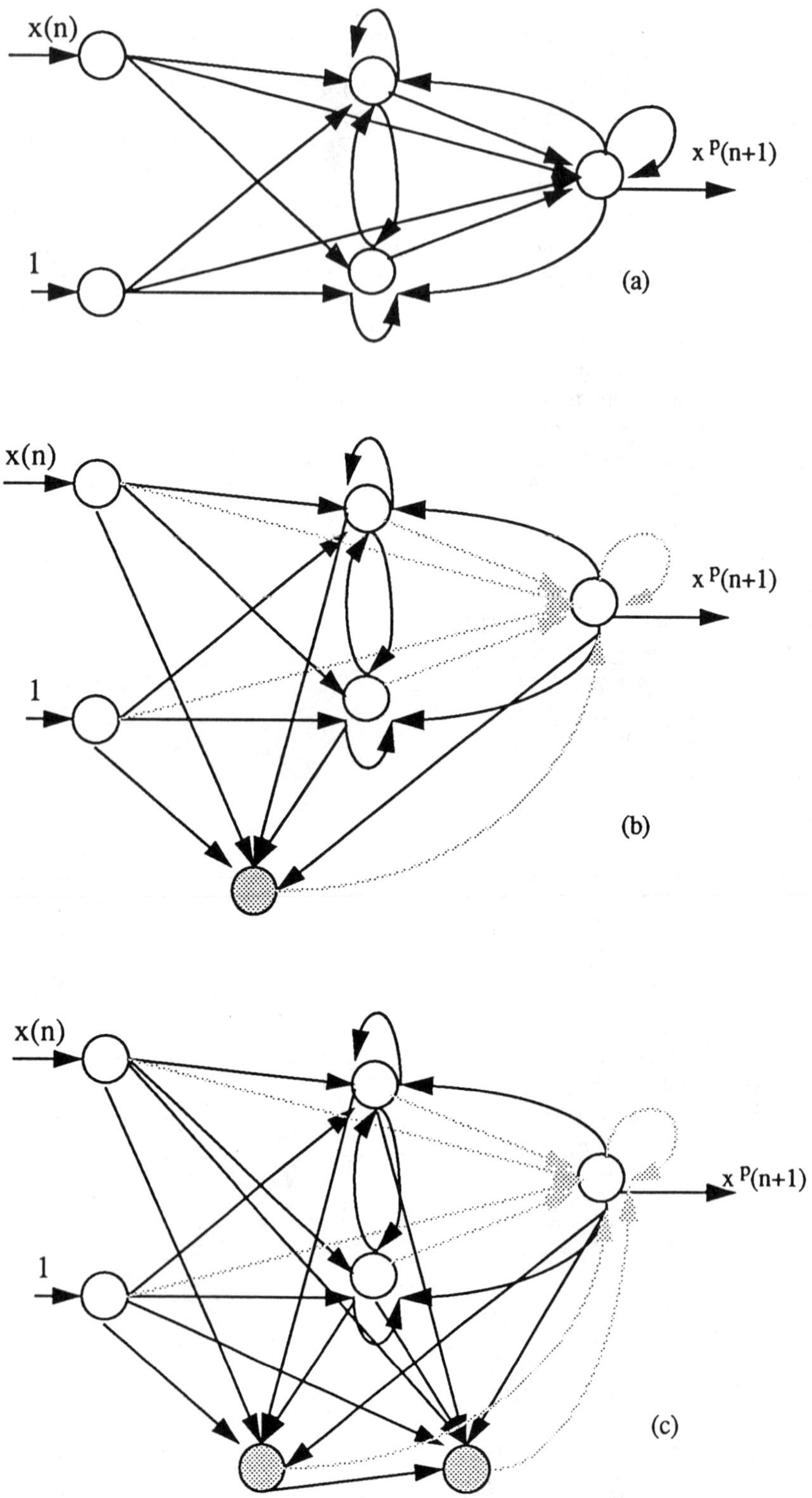

Figure 2. The proposed scheme for the prediction problem (assuming three recurrent nodes), (a) after the recurrent network training (b),(c) after the addition of one and two new units respectively. The solid connections are frozen. The dotted connections are trained repeatedly.

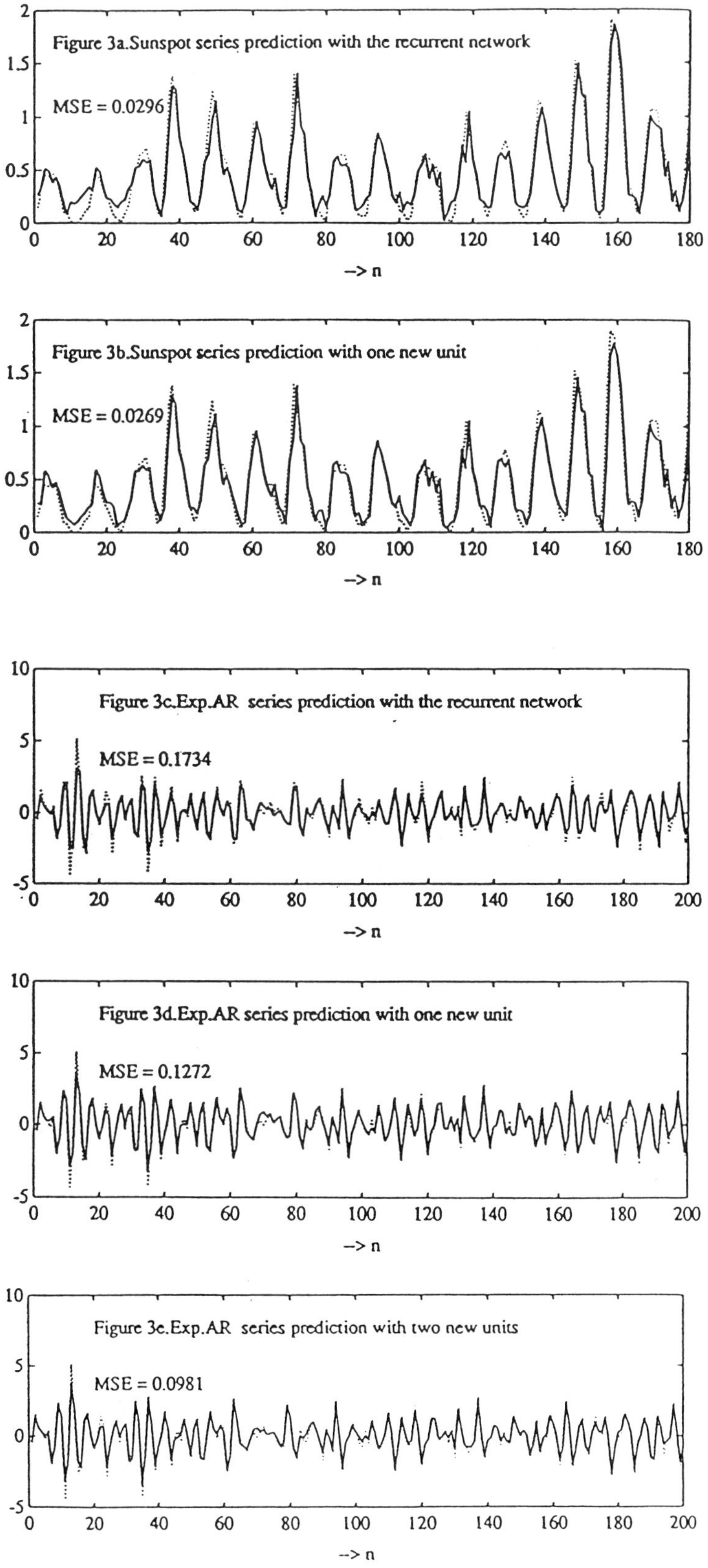

Figure 3. Prediction curves for the Sunspot series and the Exponential AR time series. The dotted curve corresponds to the actual time series and the solid curve corresponds to the single step predicted time series.

Constructive Learning of Recurrent Neural Networks

D. Chen[a], C.L. Giles[a,b], G.Z. Sun[a], H.H. Chen[a], Y.C. Lee[a], M.W. Goudreau[b,c]

[a]Institute for Advanced Computer Studies
University of Maryland
College Park, MD 20742

[b]NEC Research Institute
4 Independence Way
Princeton, NJ 08540

[c]Department of Electrical Engineering
Princeton University
Princeton, NJ 08544

***Abstract*— Recurrent neural networks are a natural model for learning and predicting temporal signals. In addition, simple recurrent networks have been shown to be both theoretically and experimentally capable of learning finite state automata [Cleeremans 89, Giles 92a, Minsky 67, Pollack 91, Siegelmann 92]. However, it is difficult to determine what is the minimal neural network structure for a particular automaton. Using a large recurrent network, which would be versatile in theory, in practice proves to be very difficult to train. Constructive or destructive recurrent methods might offer a solution to this problem. We prove that one current method, Recurrent Cascade Correlation, has fundamental limitations in representation and thus in its learning capabilities. We give a preliminary approach on how to get around these limitations by devising a "simple" constructive training method that adds neurons during training while still preserving the powerful fully recurrent structure. Through simulations we show that such a method can learn many types of regular grammars that the Recurrent Cascade Correlation method is unable to learn.**

I. Introduction

Recurrent Neural Networks have been studied extensively, because of their ability to store and process temporal information and sequential signals; for a summary of these issues see [Hertz 91, Narendra 90]. For example recent studies have shown that various order recurrent networks are able to infer small regular grammars from grammatical examples [Cleeremans 89, Giles 92a, Watrous 92].

For the purpose of good generalization, Occam's Razor would likely conclude that a small a network as possible would give the best generalization; this is also in keeping with the results of systems theory [Ljung 87]. [Alon 91] has given an upper limit on the size of a first order network needed to represent a regular grammar or a state automaton. However, in practice, we often do not have enough information about the nature of the target sequence in order to decide the network size before training. In addition for a particular problem, a much smaller network than that given by the theoretical upper bound solution usually exists.

One way to solve this problem is to train different size networks and find the smallest one that learns the training sequences. In practice this can be very time consuming since each different network is trained independently and there are too many different network architectures to choose from.

Another problem associated with recurrent networks is that the training scales badly with both network and problem size. The convergence can be very slow and training errors are not always guaranteed to reduce to previously defined tolerances. By using constructive training methods, one can hope that the neural network could possibly build itself little by little, and speed up the whole training process. In this paper, we show that an existing constructive method, Recurrent Cascade Correlation, has fundamental limitations. We propose an alternative method which eliminates these limitations and give some encouraging preliminary training results.

II. Simple Driven Recurrent Network

For our purposes a simple driven recurrent neural network consists of three parts (figure 3). We term the recurrent network "driven" to denote that it responds

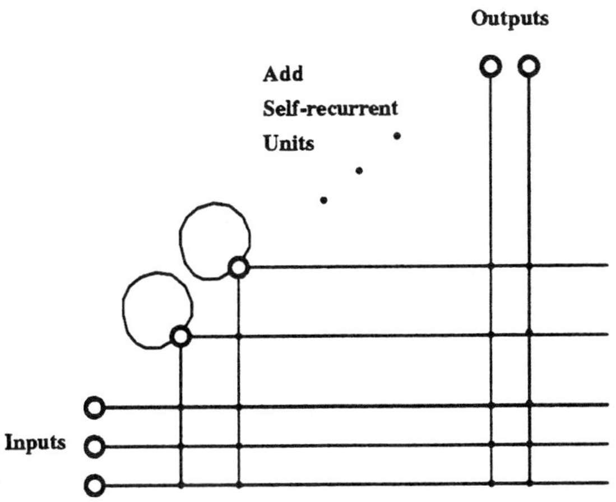

Figure 1: Recurrent Cascade-Correlation Network. The hidden neurons are self-recurrent, and only connect to previously existing neurons.

temporally to inputs. The hidden recurrent layer is activated by both the input neurons and the recurrent layer itself. The output neurons are in general activated by the input and recurrent neurons or, in a special case, by only the recurrent neurons.

Connections between layers can be first, second, or even higher orders: see [Giles 92a, Pollack 91, Sun 90, Watrous 92] for more discussion. In general, the updating rule can be written as,

$$\mathbf{S}^{t+1} = \mathcal{F}(\mathbf{W}, \mathbf{S}^t, \mathbf{I}^t)$$
$$\mathbf{O}^{t+1} = \mathcal{G}(\mathbf{U}, \mathbf{S}^t, \mathbf{I}^t).$$

where $\mathbf{I}^t, \mathbf{S}^t, \mathbf{O}^t$ are the values of input, recurrent and output neurons at time step t and $\mathbf{W}, \mathbf{U}$ are the respective connection weights. The typical learning rule uses gradient decent [Williams 89] to adjust the weights $\mathbf{W}, \mathbf{U}$ so as to minimize the error function:

$$E = \sum_t (\mathbf{T}^t - \mathbf{O}^t)^2.$$

III. "Simple" Constructive Learning

In general a constructive method dynamically changes the network structure during the training - [Gallant 86], [Hanson 90] and for a summary of other methods [Hertz 91]. In addition to the normal updating rule and learning rule of the neural network, a constructive training scheme also requires:

1. a criterion for when the changing takes place,
2. how to connect the newly created neurons to the existing system,
3. how to assign initial values to the newly added connections.

(For simplicity we ignore methods which are both constructive and destructive.) To speed up the training, we hypothesize that in addition to these criteria we must also satisfy the principle that the network preserves previously acquired knowledge *while* the network is changing. Previous work where a priori knowledge such as rules are encoded directly into recurrent networks have shown this to be the case [Frasconi 91, Giles 92b]. Various constructive learning schemes have been proposed for feed-forward networks [Ash 89, Fahlman 90, Gallant 86]. These methods find a minimal structure for the problem and reduce the computational complexity. However, to our knowledge little work besides [Fahlman 91] has focused on recurrent networks.

A. Limitations of the Recurrent Cascade-Correlation Architecture

[Fahlman 91] proposed a constructive training method — a Recurrent Cascade-Correlation (RCC) network (Figure 1). Regardless of the training procedure, this network can be topologically viewed as in Figure 2. It differs from a fully connected recurrent network in the sense that the recurrent connection of the old neurons to the newly added neurons are restricted - *i.e.* nonexistent. Even though this self recurrent restriction simplifies the training (each neuron can be trained sequentially), it *significantly* restricts the representational power of the network. We will show that this type of structure with a *sigmoid updating function* is **not** capable of representing all finite state automata.

To understand the limitations of RCC, we first examine the hard-limit threshold case, where each neuron is only allowed to take on binary values, *e.g.* $\{0, 1\}$ or $\{-1, 1\}$. Suppose we have a constant input sequence, say all 1's. The activation function of the first neuron S_1 then simplifies to

$$S_1^{t+1} = \Theta(W_{11} * S_1^t + \theta_1),$$

where Θ is the threshold function and the constant input term I is implicit. It is easy to verify that under such an update function, S_1 will either remain constant or oscillate at each time step between the two values $0, 1$ or $-1, 1$, since S_1 only depends only on its value at the previous time step. We define this oscillation at each time step as an oscillation of period 2. Oscillations that occur at two or more time steps have a period greater than 2, and a constant value is a period 1 oscillation. An example of all such sequences of period 2 or less is: $\{0000000\cdots, 1111111\cdots, 0101010\cdots\}$.

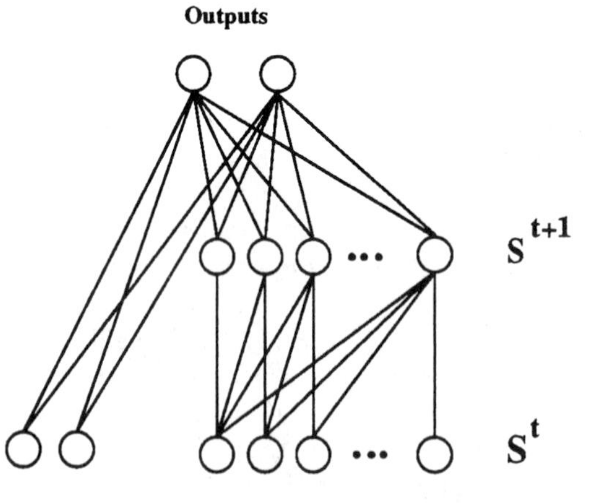

Figure 2: Re-drawing of RCC in figure 1.
The input and output neurons are connected to all hidden recurrent neurons. The hidden neurons are not fully connected to each other.

The activation function for the nth RCC neuron S_n can be written as

$$S_n^{t+1} = \Theta(W_{n1} * S_1^{t+1} + W_{n2} * S_2^{t+1} + \cdots + W_{nn} * S_n^t + \theta_n).$$

Or,

$$S_n^{t+1} = \Theta(\Lambda + W_{nn} * S_n^t), \qquad (1)$$

where

$$\Lambda = W_{n1} * S_1^{t+1} + W_{n2} * S_2^{t+1} + \cdots + W_{n(n-1)} * S_{n-1}^{t+1} + \theta_n.$$

We prove this by induction. Assume $S_1, \cdots, S_{n-1}$ at each time step all oscillate with period 2 or remain constant. As Λ is a linear function of $S_1, \cdots, S_{n-1}$, it will at most oscillate at period 2. If Λ remains constant all the time, then S_n will be a constant or oscillate at period 2, the same as for S_1. If Λ oscillates at period 2, then by examining all 14 possible mappings of equation 1 (see Appendix), we find that S_n can only oscillate at period 2 or remains constant all the time. This proves that the binary RCC structure is not be able to represent or to simulate all possible finite state machines, *e.g.* a machine consists of part that has period greater that 2 under a same input. It can also be shown that for an analog RCC network with a constant input signal, the activities of the recurrent neurons will asymptotically become either constant or oscillate at period 2. [There results hold for both first and second order recurrent neural networks. See [Pao 89] for a discussion of order and [Lee 86] for order in recurrent networks.]

It is arguable that the analog RCC network can have more complex dynamics during the transient period. However, a typical finite state automaton can accept infinitely long strings. Thus, the RCC type of network structure (with sigmoid thresholds) will fail at some point (beyond the transient period) after a periodic input sequence is presented. For example, numerical simulations have shown the RCC network is unable to learn the simple double parity grammar. The number of added neurons grow as a function of the longest string length of the training examples!

It should be noted that the sigmoid type updating function is *essential* to the above proof. If the activity function is Gaussian or another non-monotonic shape, or if the activity function is of high order in terms of the hidden neurons, i.e. based on terms such as $S_i * S_j$; much more complicated behavior can occur and the above conclusions may not hold.

B. Simple Expanding Recurrent Neural Network

In order to get around the interconnect restriction imposed by RCC, we propose a very simple scheme to dynamically construct a recurrent network. In this method, the network is the same as the simple driven recurrent structure discussed in Section II. In this method the number of neurons in the recurrent layer is allowed to expand whenever needed. The only criterion for expansion is that the network spend some time learning. As the network is always fully-connected, it does not have the restriction of RCC. Theoretically it has been shown that a fully connected recurrent network is capable of representing any finite state automaton [Minsky 67].

The importance of using a priori knowledge in neural network learning has been described by many, see for example [Towell 90, Giles 92b, Frasconi 91]. We further assume that it is important to effectively maintain some of the networks knowledge acquired during training. To do this we require the network to be expanded smoothly, *i.e.* the newly added weights should remain zero or very small random numbers. Thus, the new network behaves very similar to the old one immediately after the expansion.

First, we present a simple example of the above method. For our example we train a recurrent neural network to be a deterministic finite state automaton. For training we use a second-order fully-recurrent neural network that uses full gradient, real-time recurrent learning [Williams 89]. For detail description see [Giles 92a]. We examine if the network can take advantage of its previous knowledge. We first train the network to learn a 10-state randomly generated deterministic finite state automaton (DFA) (figure 4) as in [Giles 92c]. We use the incremental training method, where the network reads through

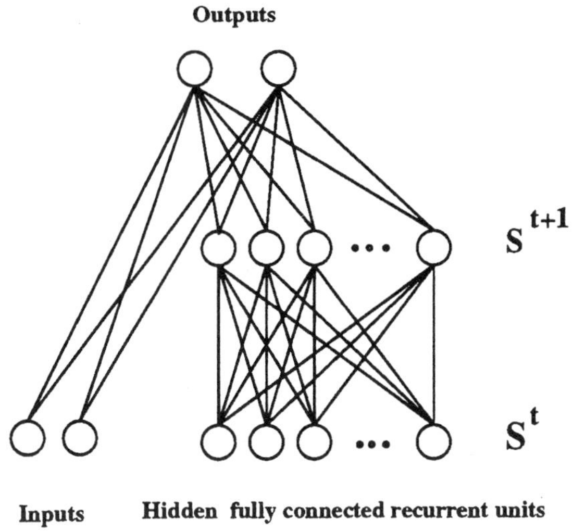

Figure 3: Fully recurrent neural network.
The input and output neurons are connected to all hidden recurrent neurons.

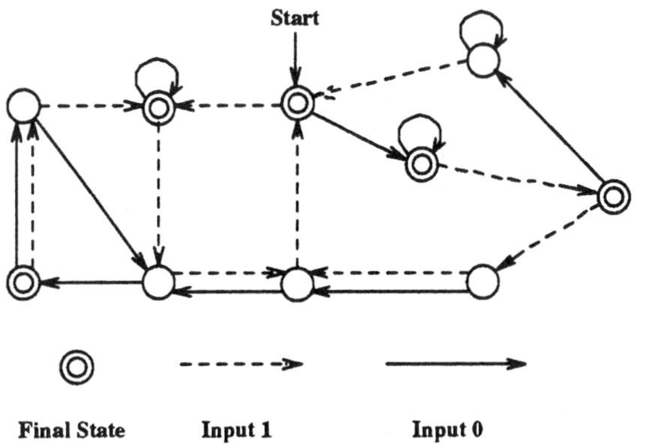

Figure 4: A 10-state finite state automaton, which is randomly generated.

the ordered training samples until the accumulated error exceeds the preset value or all training samples are classified correctly. When training with a fixed size 8 neuron fully-recurrent network, the network converged in 72 epoches after using 10000 positive and negative training examples. However, if we train a similar network with only 7 recurrent neurons for 150 epoches first and then expand the network to 8 recurrent neurons, the network takes only 32 more epoches to converge. Here an epoch is defined as a training cycle in which the network starts again at the beginning of the training samples after finding 5 errors. This indicates that the network does take advantage of previous knowledge and converges faster than a network with no a priori knowledge and random initial weights.

Choosing the criterion for when the network expands is very important. A simple method is to determine if the training error reaches the local minimum. More complex methods based on entropy measure, network capacity, or neuron activity distribution would be more feasible.

In other preliminary experiments, we add one more neuron to the recurrent layer after every 50 epoches, until the network learns all the training samples. This is a very simple constructive criterion; a more sophisticated constructive criterion might generate a smaller network. In training very small grammars (those of [Tomita 82]), we found that the constructive method converges very fast when the network size grows up to the minimal size required. However the convergence speed was not significantly less than that obtained by training the corresponding fixed size networks. This is understandable since for a very simple problem, the fixed size network can learn the training samples very quickly assuming a large enough network is provided. However, by avoiding training all different size networks, the constructive method does appear to save time in finding the smallest size network for each of these grammars.

IV. Conclusions

We presented some preliminary results on a "simple" constructive learning method for recurrent neural networks. This method relies on using some of the knowledge of a partially trained neural network, and more importantly, expands the network in a fully recurrent manner. The constructive learning method permits the network to build itself up from scratch. This type of training method is necessary when only very limited information about the problem to be solved is available. The recurrent cascade-correlation network is certainly a step in the right direction, but it is incapable of representing and thus learning many finite state automata. The simple constructive method proposed avoids the limitations of Recurrent Cascade-Correlation (RCC) networks. We illustrate this method by learning some small grammars of Tomita and a randomly generated 10-state grammar. The reason this simple constructive method outperforms RCC easily explained - the full recurrence of the growing network is preserved. Admittedly, the experiments described are preliminary. Further experiments might show inherent limitations in such a "simple" method, such as uncontrolled neuron growth. Other questions are what are good criteria for expansion? What amount of "captured" knowledge is necessary for effective learning? However, the lesson of maintaining the full recurrence in the "added" neurons seems an important one, especially if the full representational power of the recurrent network is needed.

APPENDIX BINARY RECURRENT CASCADE CORRELATION NETWORK

Without loss of generality, assume the binary neuron is either 0 or 1. Recall equation 1,

$$S_n^{t+1} = \Theta(\Lambda + W_{nn} * S_n^t).$$

If Λ oscillates with period 2, *i.e.*

$$\Lambda = \begin{cases} \lambda_1 & \text{if } t = \text{odd} \\ \lambda_2 & \text{if } t = \text{even} \end{cases}$$

we can list all possible outcomes of the above equation.

Λ	S^t	S^{t+1}	possible sequences
λ_1	0	0	
λ_1	1	0	*00000000···*
λ_2	0	0	
λ_2	1	0	*10000000···*

Λ	S^t	S^{t+1}	possible sequences
λ_1	0	1	
λ_1	1	0	*01010101···*
λ_2	0	0	
λ_2	1	0	*10010101···*

Λ	S^t	S^{t+1}	possible sequences
λ_1	0	0	
λ_1	1	1	*00000000···*
λ_2	0	0	
λ_2	1	0	*11000000···*

Λ	S^t	S^{t+1}	possible sequences
λ_1	0	1	
λ_1	1	1	*01010101···*
λ_2	0	0	
λ_2	1	0	*11010101···*

Λ	S^t	S^{t+1}	possible sequences
λ_1	0	0	
λ_1	1	0	*00101010···*
λ_2	0	1	
λ_2	1	0	*10101010···*

Λ	S^t	S^{t+1}	possible sequences
λ_1	0	1	
λ_1	1	0	*01010101···*
λ_2	0	1	
λ_2	1	0	*10101010···*

Λ	S^t	S^{t+1}	possible sequences
λ_1	0	1	
λ_1	1	1	*01010101···*
λ_2	0	1	
λ_2	1	0	*10101010···*

Λ	S^t	S^{t+1}	possible sequences
λ_1	0	0	
λ_1	1	0	*00000000···*
λ_2	0	0	
λ_2	1	1	*10000000···*

Λ	S^t	S^{t+1}	possible sequences
λ_1	0	0	
λ_1	1	1	*00000000···*
λ_2	0	0	
λ_2	1	1	*11111111···*

Λ	S^t	S^{t+1}	possible sequences
λ_1	0	1	
λ_1	1	1	*01111111···*
λ_2	0	0	
λ_2	1	1	*11111111···*

Λ	S^t	S^{t+1}	possible sequences
λ_1	0	0	
λ_1	1	0	*00101010···*
λ_2	0	1	
λ_2	1	1	*10101010···*

Λ	S^t	S^{t+1}	possible sequences
λ_1	0	1	
λ_1	1	0	*01101010···*
λ_2	0	1	
λ_2	1	1	*10101010···*

Λ	S^t	S^{t+1}	possible sequences
λ_1	0	0	
λ_1	1	1	*00111111···*
λ_2	0	1	
λ_2	1	1	*11111111···*

Λ	S^t	S^{t+1}	possible sequences
λ_1	0	1	
λ_1	1	1	*11111111···*
λ_2	0	1	
λ_2	1	1	*11111111···*

Two combinations of S^{t+1}

Λ	S^t	S^{t+1}
λ_1	0	0
λ_1	1	1
λ_2	0	1
λ_2	1	0

Λ	S^t	S^{t+1}
λ_1	0	1
λ_1	1	0
λ_2	0	0
λ_2	1	1

are not listed above. This is because the linear threshold function cannot solve the XOR problem. It is easy to see that the sequence of S will either be a constant or oscillate at period 2.

REFERENCES

[Alon 91] N. Alon, A.K. Dewdney, T.J. Ott, Efficient simulation of finite automata by neural nets, *J. A.C.M.* 38, p. 495 (1991).

[Ash 89] T. Ash, Dynamic Node Creation in Backpropagation Networks, it Connection Science, vol 1, No. 4, p. 365 (1989).

[Cleeremans 89] A. Cleeremans, D. Servan-Schreiber, J. McClelland, Finite State Automata and Simple Recurrent Recurrent Networks, *Neural Computation*, 1(3), p. 372 (1989).

[Fahlman 90] S.E. Fahlman, C. Lebiere, The Cascade-Correlation Learning Architecture, *Advances in Neural Information Systems 2*, D.S. Touretzky (ed), Morgan Kaufmann, San Mateo, Ca, (1990).

[Fahlman 91] S.E. Fahlman, The Recurrent Cascade-Correlation Architecture, in *Advances in Neural Information Processing Systems 3*, R.P. Lippmann, J.E. Moody, D.S. Touretzky (eds), Morgan Kaufmann, San Mateo, Ca., p.190 (1991).

[Frasconi 91] P. Frasconi, M. Gori, M. Maggini, G. Soda, An Unified Approach for Integrating Explicit Knowledge and Learning by Example in Recurrent Networks, *Proceedings of the International Joint Conference on Neural Networks* IJCNN-91-SEATTLE, Vol. I, p. 811, (1991).

[Gallant 86] S.I. Gallant, Three Constructive Algorithms for Network Learning, in *Proceedings, 8th Annual Conference of the Cognitive Science Society*, p. 652 (1986)

[Giles 92a] C.L. Giles, C.B. Miller, D. Chen, H.H. Chen, G.Z. Sun, Y.C. Lee, Learning and Extracting Finite State Automata with Second-Order Recurrent Neural Networks, *Neural Computation*, 4(3), p. 393 (1992).

[Giles 92b] C.L. Giles, C.W. Omlin, Inserting Rules into Recurrent Neural Networks *Neural Networks for Signal Processing II, Proceedings of the 1992 IEEE-SP Workshop*, S.Y. Kung, F. Fallside, J. Aa Sorenson C.A. Kamm (eds), IEEE92TH0430-9, p.13 (1992).

[Giles 92c] C.L. Giles, C.B. Miller, D. Chen, G.Z. Sun, H.H. Chen, Y.C. Lee, Extracting and Learning an Unknown Grammar with Recurrent Neural Networks, *Advances in Neural Information Processing Systems 4*, J.E. Moody, S.J. Hanson and R.P. Lippmann (eds), Morgan Kaufmann, San Mateo, Ca., (1992).

[Hanson 90] S.J. Hanson, Meiosis Networks, in *Advances in Neural Information Processing Systems 2*, D. Touretzky (ed), Morgan Kaufmann, San Mateo, Ca., p.533 (1990)

[Hertz 91] J. Hertz, A. Krogh, R.G. Palmer, *Introduction to the Theory of Neural Computation*, Addison-Wesley, Redwood City, CA., p. 163 (1991).

[Lee 86] Y.C. Lee, G. Doolen, H.H. Chen, G.Z. Sun, T. Maxwell, H.Y. Lee, C.L. Giles, Machine Learning Using a Higher Order Correlational Network, *Physica D*, Vol.22-D, No.1-3, p. 276 (1986).

[Ljung 87] L. Ljung, *System Identification - Theory for the User*, Prentice-Hall, Englewood Cliffs, N.J. (1987).

[Minsky 67] M.L. Minsky, *Computation: Finite and Infinite Machines*, Ch 3.5, Prentice-Hall, Englewood Cliffs, N.J. (1967).

[Narendra 90] K.S. Narendra, K. Parthasarathy, Identification and Control of Dynamical Systems Using Neural Networks, *IEEE Trans. on Neural Networks*, Vol. 1, No. 1, page 4 (1990).

[Pao 89] Y-H. Pao, *Adaptive Pattern Recognition and Neural Networks*, Addison-Wesley Publishing Co., Inc., Reading, MA (1989).

[Pollack 91] J.B. Pollack, The Induction of Dynamical Recognizers, *Machine Learning*, vol 7, p. 227 (1991).

[Siegelmann 92] H.T. Siegelmann, E.D. Sontag, On the computational power of neural nets, in *Proc. Fifth ACM Workshop on Computational Learning Theory*, Pittsburgh PA, ACM Press, p. 440 (1992).

[Sun 90] G.Z. Sun, H.H. Chen, C.L. Giles, Y.C. Lee, D. Chen, Connectionist Pushdown Automata that Learn Context-Free Grammars, *Proceedings of the International Joint Conference on Neural Networks*, IJCNN-90-WASH-DC, Lawrence Erlbaum, Hillsdale, N.J., Vol I, p. 577 (1990).

[Tomita 82] M. Tomita, Dynamic Construction of Finite-state Automata from Examples Using Hill-climbing, *Proceedings of the Fourth Annual Cognitive Science Conference* p. 105 (1982).

[Towell 90] G.G. Towell, J.W. Shavlik, M.O. Noordewier, Refinement of Approximately Correct Domain Theories by Knowledge-Based Neural Networks, *Proceedings of the Eighth National Conference on Artificial Intelligence*, Boston, MA, p. 861, (1990).

[Watrous 92] R.L. Watrous, G.M. Kuhn, Induction of Finite-State Languages Using Second-Order Recurrent Networks, *Neural Computation* 4(3), p.406 (1992).

[Williams 89] R.J. Williams, D. Zipser, A Learning Algorithm for Continually Running Fully Recurrent Neural Networks, *Neural Computation*, Vol.1, No.2, p.270, (1989).

A Neural Network Based Approach to Knowledge Acquisition and Expert Systems[1]

Nicholas DeClaris and Mu-Chun Su
School of Medicine and College of Engineering
University of Maryland in Baltimore and College Park
U.S.A

Abstract **Often a major difficulty in the design of expert systems is the process of acquiring the requisite knowledge in the form of production rules. This paper presents a novel class of neural networks which are trained in such a way that they provide an appealing solution to the problem of knowledge acquisition. The value of the network parameters, after sufficient training, are then utilized to generate production rules on the basis of preselected meaningful coordinates. Futhere, the paper provides a mathematical framework for achieving reasonable generalization properties via an appropriate training algorithm (supervised decision-directed learning) with a structure that provides acceptable knowledge representations of the data. The concepts and methods presented in the paper are illustrated through one practical example from medical diagnosis.**

I. INTRODUCTION

Neural networks are attracting a lot of interest in the scientific community because of their dynamical nature: robustness, capability of generalization and fault tolerance. Neural networks have already proven useful in low level information processing (*e.g.* signal analysis). An area where neural networks find exciting applications is in medicine in cases where statistical methods can not be used such as when incomplete, or insufficient amount of data. In medical diagnose, clinicians make a series of inferences about the nature of the physiological abnormality derived from existing observations (*e.g.* historical data, physical findings, and routine laboratory tests). There are diagnostic processes which are guided by precompiled production rules. In such cases the use of rule-based expert systems is helpful.

Rule-based expert systems are rather practical development in the artificial intelligence (AI) field. They are based on the premise that expert knowledge can be encapsulated in a set of **IF...THEN...** statements. Traditionally, the design of rule-based expert systems involves a process of interaction between a domain expert and a knowledge engineer who formalizes the expert's knowledge as inference rules and encodes it in a computer. However, there are several difficulties in obtaining an adequate set of rules from human experts. Experts may not know, or may be unable to articulate, what knowledge they actually use in solving their problems. Often, the development of an expert system is time-consuming. Thus, the process of building an expert system requires much effort. Another important problems is that it is difficult to determine whether the knowledge base is correct, consistent and/or incomplete. One way to alleviate these problems is to use machine learning to automate the process of knowledge acquisition [1].

An appealing aspect of neural networks is that they can inductively acquire concepts from examples. A set of labeled examples is provided to the neural networks for training. After the process of training, the network can classify inexperienced patterns. Training procedure is accomplished by appropriately modifying its adjustable weights so that the training data is more correctly classified. Neural networks have shown promise in classification and diagnostic tasks. Nevertheless, there are still some obstacles lying in the combination of neural networks and expert systems: 1) lengthy training time; 2) no systematic way to set up a good network topology; and 3) difficulty in interpreting trained networks [2]. The difficulty in interpreting, in physiological meaningful ways, trained networks is one of the greatest problem of neural networks. A neural network can not justify its response on the bases of explicit rules or logical reasoning process. This feature is particularly important in medicine where medical experts require detailed justification for any diagnosis, whether it issues from nature or artificial intelligence.

There have been several attempts to overcome these problems. One approach is to interpret or extract rules from a trained backpropagation networks [3]. Other researchers focused on refining coarse knowledgebase by adjusting weights of neural networks [4], [5]. Sestito and Dillon [6] and Goodman, Higgins and Miller [7] considered problems of extracting rules that relate to a set of binary (or discrete) feature variables. However, there are rules which can not be extracted by such algorithms. In this paper, an architecture and algorithm of neural networks is discussed that insures the extraction of all applicable rules. Our approach is based on a new concept of utilizing "intermediate rules", by which the final decision rules are represented. Specifically, intermediate rules are represented in the form of a hyperspherical type description. A final decision rule is represented as a disjunction of intermediate rules. The training algorithm results in

Manuscript received July 8, 1993. This footnote is not numbered.

1 Supported in part under NIH Grant # 510 RR06460-01, Nicholas DeClaris, Principle Investigator

a two-layer hyperspherical composite neural network shown in Fig. 1. Each intermediate rule corresponds to a distinct node. An important feature is that the final neural network is required to learn correctly all training data.

II. REPRESENTATIONS AND PROPERTIES

Knowledge representation in expert systems must be as clear to human users as possible. The knowledge of a trained backpropagation network lies in its inter-node weights [8], in this respect, it differs from the high level representation obtained through traditional knowledge acquisition methods.

The construction of a rule-based expert system involves the process of acquiring the production rules. The production rules are often represented as "IF *condition* THEN *act*". Backpropagation networks do not always arrive to this type of representation. A suitable class are hyperspherical composite networks because production rules can be easily extracted from them. The symbolic representation of a hyperspherical neural node is shown in Fig. 2 and it is described by the following equations,

$$net(X) = d^2 - \sum_{i=1}^{n} (x_i - c_i)^2 \tag{1}$$

and

$$Out(X) = f(net(X)) \tag{2}$$

where

$$f(x) = \begin{cases} 1 & if\ x \geq 0 \\ 0 & if\ x < 0 \end{cases}, \tag{3}$$

c_i, and $d \in \mathbf{R}$ are adjustable weights, $\mathbf{R}$ is the set of real number, n is the dimensionality of input variables, $x_i \in \mathbf{R}$, X is an n-component column vector of x_i and $Out(X) : R^n \rightarrow \{0, 1\}$ is an output function of a hyperspherical neural node.

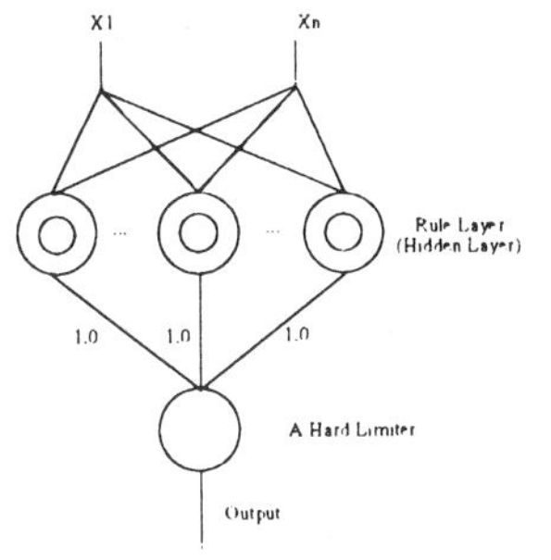

Fig. 1 A two-layer hyperspherical composite neural network

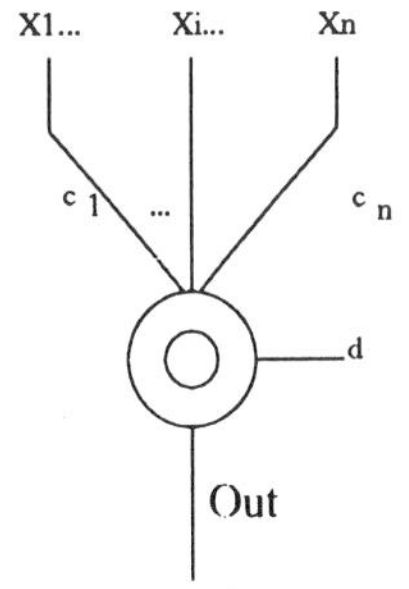

Fig. 2 A hyperspherical neural node

According to (1) & (2), we know the network outputs one only under the following condition:

$$\sum_{i=1}^{n} (x_i - c_i)^2 \leq d^2. \tag{4}$$

Then the classification knowledge can be described in the form of a production rule. The *if-then* rule corresponds to the following statement

$$IF \left(\sum_{i=1}^{n} (x_i - c_i)^2 \leq d^2 \right) \quad THEN\ Out = 1. \tag{5}$$

The domain defined by (5) is an n-dimensional hypersphere. DeClaris and Su have done considerable works with this class of quadratic junction neural-type networks [9]. The decision region formed by a neural node with quadratic junctions is in general a hyperellipsoid whose axes may be oblique with respect to the axes of the input space in n-dimensional space. Use of a nondiagonal covariance matrix allows each general hyperellipsoid to tilt in the direction of the maximum data spread. However, the inclusion of correlation coefficients for each general hyperellipsoid increases the numbers of parameters. The class of neural nodes studied in this paper uses constrained quadratic junctions—a trade-off between the flexibility of hyperellipsoids and the number of parameters.

Owing to characteristics of data, such as *dispersion characteristic*, it may be not adequate to use a simple classification rule represented as a hypersphere to solve all pattern recognition problems. Dispersion characteristic of data leads to an existence of many distinct clusters in input space. A reasonable idea of clustering data would be in the form of a hyperspherical or hyperellipsoidal "cluster" of patterns. In this way a complex concept is represented as *intermediate concepts* explicitely extracted by the set of hyperspheres. In the two-layer neural network configuration as shown in Fig. 1, input variables are assigned input nodes, intermediate concepts are assigned hidden nodes (rule nodes), and the induced concept (final classification decision rule) is assigned an output node. Each hidden node is connected, with weight value

1.0, to the output node. The output node is just a hard limiter. The network outputs one whenever there exists one hidden node whose output is one. Fig. 3 illustrates decision regions formed by hyperspherical composite neural networks. Therefore, if there are k hidden nodes, a decision rule can be represented as

$$
\begin{aligned}
&IF\left(\sum_{i=1}^{n}(x_i - c_{1i})^2 \le d_1^2\right)\\
&THEN\ output = 1,\\
&\dots\\
&ELSE\ IF\left(\sum_{i=1}^{n}(x_i - c_{ki})^2 \le d_k^2\right)\\
&THEN\ output = 1.
\end{aligned}
\tag{6}
$$

III. TRAINING ALGORITHM FOR HYPERSPHERICAL COMPOSITE NEURAL NETWORKS

Fig. 4 shows the algorithm called supervised decision-directed learning algorithm for training hyperspherical composite neural networks. Here, we apply the idea of inductive machine learning into the training procedure of the class of hyperspherical composite neural networks. In setting up the network topology, this algorithm generates a two-layer feed-forward network in a sequential manner by adding hidden nodes as need. After the training procedure, all training patterns are correctly recognized. At the same time the decision rule can be easily extracted. The algorithm is based on a concept of division of the domain of inputs into appropriate subsets.

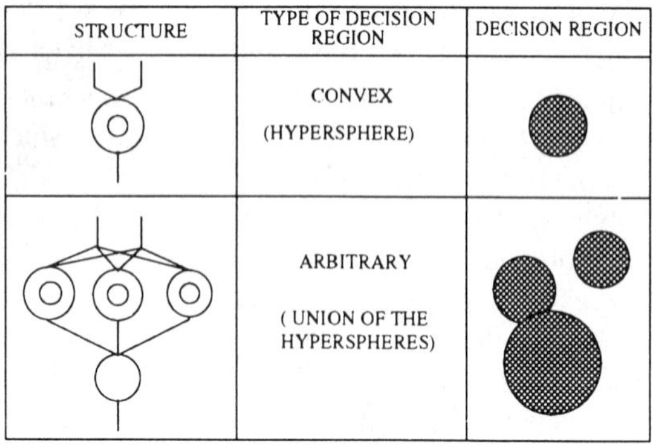

STRUCTURE
TYPE OF DECISION REGION
DECISION REGION
CONVEX
(HYPERSPHERE)
ARBITRARY
(UNION OF THE HYPERSPHERES)

Fig. 3 Decision regions formed by hyperspherical composite neural networks

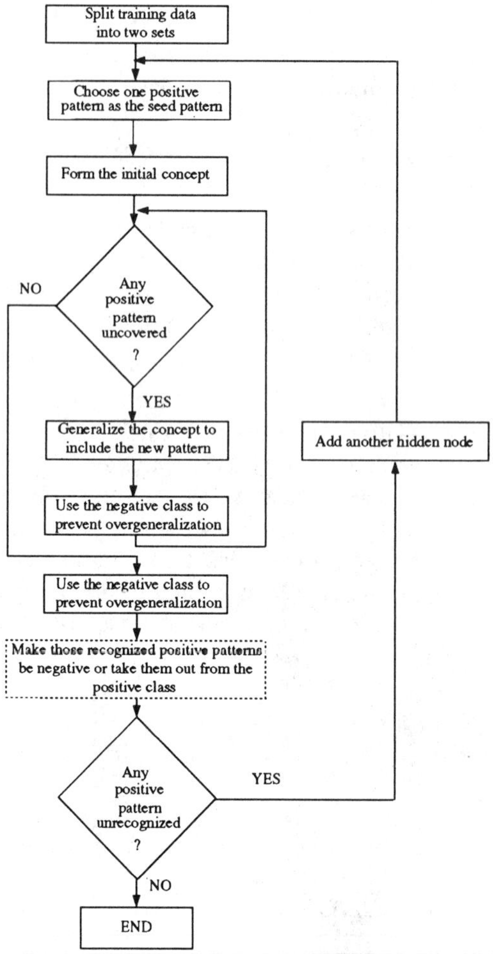

Fig. 4 Flowchart of the training algorithm for hyperspherical composite neural networks

Often inputs (features) are measured on different units. For instances, in medical diagnostic process, data are derived from nature existing observations such as historical data, physical findings, and routine laboratory tests. Therefore, patterns need to be normalized so that no single input overwhelms data merely because of scale. The method of normalization used in this paper is that data have been normalized to zero mean and unit variance in each direction. Thus, a hypersphere in normalized input space is indeed a hyperellipsoid in original input space as shown followed

$$
\begin{aligned}
&\sum_{i=1}^{n}(x_i' - c_i')^2 \le d^2 \quad x_i' = \frac{x_i - m_i}{\sigma_i}\\
&\Leftrightarrow \sum_{i=1}^{n}\frac{(x_i - c_i)^2}{\sigma_i^2} \le d^2 \quad c_i = m_i + \sigma_i c_i'
\end{aligned}
\tag{7}
$$

where m_i and σ_i are mean value and squared variance of x_i, and x_i' is the normalized input.

In this training algorithm, we want to find a set of hyperspheres which cover all patterns belonging to the same categories. To begin with, training patterns are divided into two sets: 1) a *positive class* from which we want to extract (induce) the **concept** and 2) a *negative class* which provides counterexamples with respect to the concept. Then a *seed* pattern X' is used as the basis of an initial concept (the seed pattern is any one chosen from the positive class). Then weights are initialized in the following manner:

$$\begin{cases} c'_i(0) = x'_i & 1 \leq i \leq n \\ d(0) = \delta & \delta \; is \; a \; small \; positive \; number. \end{cases} \tag{8}$$

Next we use all counterexamples to prevent overgeneralization (the induced concept should not be so general as to include any of counterexamples) formed by the initialization of weights. The following step is to fetch the next positive pattern and to generalize the initial concept to include the new positive pattern. This process involves growing the original hypersphere to make it larger to include the new positive pattern. The size and position of the present hypersphere is adapted from a better knowledge of the local distribution of positive patterns falling inside the present hypersphere. The way of computing a new center and radius is shown as follows:

$$c'_i(t+1) = \left(\sqrt{\sum_{i=1}^{n} (x'_i - c'_i(t))^2} + d(t)\right) \cdot \frac{(c'_i(t) - x'_i)}{2\sqrt{\sum_{i=1}^{n} (x'_i - c'_i(t))^2}} + x'_i \quad 1 \leq i \leq n. \tag{9}$$

and

$$d(t+1) = \frac{\left(\sqrt{\sum_{i=1}^{n} (x'_i - c'_i)^2} + d(t)\right)}{2} + \epsilon \tag{10}$$

where ϵ, a small positive number, is the control parameter which decides the degree of generalization contributed by a positive pattern. After the process of generalization, again we use counterexamples to validate the size of the expanded hypersphere. Here let us assume X' is the nearest counterexample to the center of the original hypersphere (*i.e.* at time t). Then

$$c'_i(t+2) = \left(\sqrt{\sum_{i=1}^{n} (x'_i - c'_i(t))^2} + d(t)\right) \cdot \frac{(c'_i(t) - x'_i)}{2\sqrt{\sum_{i=1}^{n} (x'_i - c'_i(t))^2}} + x'_i \quad 1 \leq i \leq n. \tag{11}$$

and

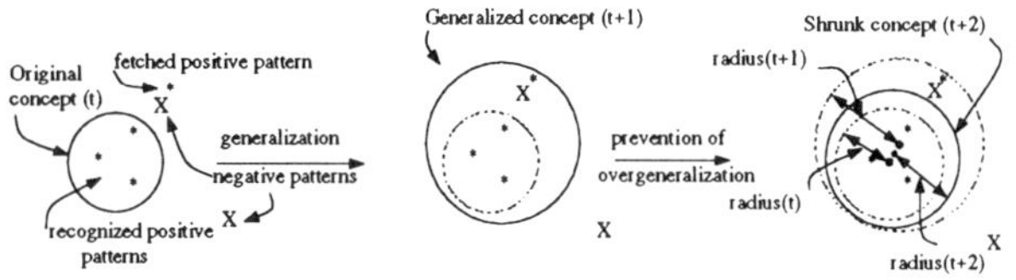

Fig. 5 Process of learning in hyperspherical composite neural networks

$$d(t+2) = \frac{\left(\sqrt{\sum_{i=1}^{n} (x'_i - c'_i(t))^2} + d(t)\right)}{2} - \epsilon \tag{12}$$

Fig. 5 illustrates this process of learning. This process is repeated for all the remaining positive patterns.

Here, we want to point out that during the process of preventing overgeneralization, a most important consideration is that whenever we shrink the expanded hypersphere (at time t+1) in order to exclude counterexamples, the shrunk hypersphere should include the original hypersphere (at time t). This criteria can guarantee that at least one positive pattern (*e.g.* seed pattern) is correctly recognized after the training procedure. In other words, it prevents the new learning from washing away the memories of prior learning. Thus if there exists any unrecognized positive pattern, another hidden node is self-generated and the process of learning is repeated again and again until all positive patterns are recognized correctly. In the worst case, the number of the hidden nodes is equal to the number of positive patterns, however, if the data clusters well, the number of hidden nodes will be as small as possible.

A multi-output system can always be separated into a group of single-output systems. Therefore, we may break down a large training task into pieces of small tasks. Finally, each hidden node is associated with a value, V, representing the total number of positive examples explained (covered) by the respective intermediate concept. The V-value may be interpreted as a measure of its representativeness of the intermediate concept as a concept description.

The RCE networks also adopt the representation of hyperspheres [10]. During its training procedure, each new pattern that is not correctly recognized results in the creation of a new hypersphere whose center is defined by the new pattern. Misclassifications reduce the size of the created hyperspheres, but they are not moved, nor deleted. Thus the number of hyperspheres created by the RCE networks does not reflect the number of underlying clusters of data. Nevertheless, in our training algorithm, we do attempt to minimize the number of hyperspheres in normalized input space. On the other hand, a popular choice for choosing radial basis units for the radial basis function (RBF) networks is the K-means algorithm [11], [12]. It require the number of units be predetermined, nevertheless, this predetermined number may not the right number of clusters. Our algorithm provides another choice for training RBF networks.

IV. Example: A Medical Diagnosis Expert Network

Diabetes mellitus is one of the major non-communicable chronic diseases and as such it constitutes a major medical challenge. Diabetes is a syndrome involving both metabolic and vascular abnormalities. It results in a range of complications which affect circulatory systems, eyes, and nerves. There are two primary categories of diabetes mellitus: type I—insulin dependent diabetes mellitus (IDDM); and type II—non-insulin dependent diabetes mellitus (NIDDM) [13]. The pathogenesis of IDDM is well understood, but, little progress has been made in discovering the mechanisms which trigger NIDDM. In hopes of discovering a method of early detection of future NIDDM onset, and ultimately, a means to delay or avert the onset of this catastrophic metabolic disorder, Hansen and Bodkin [14] are studying its pathogenesis in Rhesus monkeys. Currently, nine *phases* of progression have been identified in the development of the type II diabetes mellitus. These phases are identified by fluctuations in various measurements taken on the monkeys. Unfortunately, these relationships are rather complex and difficult to be described by human experts. Lin [15] used a multilayer backpropagation network to classify the data in order to decide on which phase the monkey is. The result was satisfactory. However, the classification knowledge can not be articulated as comprehensible diagnosis rules so its use is rather limited. We shall use hyperspherical composite neural networks to elicit the knowledge required to identify the phases on the basis of physiological variable.

In collaboration with Hamsen we used data from 42 monkeys which had been followed through the course of various phases of diabetes mellitus. The set of physiological variables used for phase identification is as follows:

1. age (C_{ge})—monkey's age (years),
2. wgt (C_{gt})—monkey's weight (kg),
3. fpg (C_{pg})—fasting plasma glucose (mg/dl),
4. fpi (C_{pi})—fasting plasma insulin (μU/ml),
5. gpr (C_{pr})—glucose disappearance rate.

The above five measurements, age, wgt, fpg, fpi, and gdr, were used as physiological coordinates in our expert system. 479 observations were used in our training algorithm. All of the data entries contain five parameters and the corresponding diabetes phase classification identified by experts. Because there are low numbers of data points per phases, it was decided to partition the complete data set in a 90%/10% ratio for training and testing, respectively. This partitioning was felt to be good compromise between having training patterns to fully described the decision regions during training and having enough patterns in the testing set to yield meaningful generalization tests.

Phases	Train	Test	# of rules	Compression Rate
1	100%	91.7%	7	9 : 479
2	100%	90.0%	38	38 : 479
3	100%	88.1%	21	21 : 479
4	100%	94.9%	17	17 : 479
5	100%	84.7%	17	17 : 479
6	100%	91.7%	11	11 : 479
7	100%	83.1%	17	17 : 479
8	100%	94.9%	11	11 : 479
9	100%	96.7%	11	11 : 479
average	100%	90.6%	16.7	1 : 28.5

Table 1 Performance of the hyperspherical composite neural networks as diagnosis expert systems for diabetes mellitus: 479 is the total number of observations and total set (100%) = training set (90%) + testing set (10%)

Generalization performance is evaluated by presenting testing patterns to the trained networks, and comparing the networks classification with the desired classification. Table 1 depicts the successful generalization performance of the hyperspherical composite neural networks as a diabetes mellitus diagnosis expert system. The average successful performance shown in the last row of Table1 is around 90% which is very encouraging. The number of extracted intermediate diagnosis rules for each phase is not as small as we expected, however, the average compression rate (defined as the number of extracted intermediate rules divided by the total data) shown in the last column of Table1 is acceptable. The large number of hidden nodes is due to the following two reasons: 1) The diabetes mellitus data do not cluster in the form of hyperspherical subspaces. and 2)During training procedure, each hypersphere, at its initial creation, migrates in the input space and generally tends toward the most near mode of the data distribution. As hyperspheres move toward modes, and latter positive patterns create hyperspheres at position from which older hyperspheres have migrated, there will always be hyperspheres which cover few positive patterns [16].

The training procedure was implemented as a C program and run on a SUN-IPX. It took less than 20 minutes for all phases to converge. This is significantly faster than running C programs based on the backpropagation approach, which took several hours to converge. However the important advantage of the hyperspherical composite neural networks is the fact that the classification knowledge can be represented

Phase	age	wgt	fpg	fpi	gpr	d
1	6.4	7.7	63.8	45.2	3.8	0.7
2	7.6	9.6	67.9	31.8	2.7	0.4
3	6.9	9.3	67.3	23.7	6.0	0.3
4	9.2	10.7	63.7	60.0	5.0	0.2
5	10.7	9.5	65.3	23.0	3.3	0.2
6	8.1	10.4	70.1	67.7	4.5	0.1
7	8.9	11.4	69.2	51.5	3.7	0.1
deviation	5.7	4.8	62.9	105.3	1.3	—

Table 2 The seven extracted intermediate rules for phase 1

as production rules in the following form:

$$IF\ (\left(\frac{C_{ge} - age}{5.7}\right)^2 + \left(\frac{C_{gt} - wgt}{4.8}\right)^2 + \left(\frac{C_{pg} - fpg}{62.9}\right)^2 + \left(\frac{C_{pi} - fpi}{105.3}\right)^2 + \left(\frac{C_{pr} - gpr}{1.3}\right)^2 \leq d^2)$$
$$THEN\ \ the\ monkey\ is\ on\ phase\ 1$$
$$\ldots$$
$$ELSE\ IF\ (\ldots)$$
$$THEN\ the\ monkey\ is\ on\ \ldots \qquad (13)$$

where d is the radius of the hypersphere and each denominator represents the deviation of each variable, respectively. Table 2 depivts all seven extracted intermediate rules for phase 1.

V. DISCUSSIONS AND CONCLUSIONS

In this paper, we provide a new approach that brings together two distinct methodologies: rule-based expert systems and neural networks. The most important characteristic of this approach is that classification knowledge embedded in numerical weights of networks is extracted and represented as sets of production rules for human users or automated by algorithmic digital computers. It promised to be of high promise in medical diagnosis requiring pathophysiological explanations.

REFERENCES

[1] R. S. Michalski and R. L. Chilausky, Learning by being told and learning from examples: an experimental comparison. International Journal of Policy Analysis and Information Systems, vol. 4, no. 2, pp. 125–160, 1980.

[2] J. W. Shavlik and G. G. Towell, An approach to combining explanation-based and neural learning algorithm. In N. G. Bourbakis, Ed. Applications of Learning & Planning Methods, pp. 71–98, 1991.

[3] L. M. Fu, "Rule learning by searching on adapted nets," AAAI'91, pp. 590–595, 1991.

[4] G. G. Towell and J. W. Shavlik, "Using symbolic learning to improve knowledge-based neural networks," AAAI'9, pp. 177–182, 1992.

[5] R. C. Lacher, S. I. Hruska, and D. C. Kumcicky, "Back-propagation learning in expert networks," IEEE Trans. on Neural Networks, vol. 13, pp. 62–72, 1992.

[6] S. Sestito and T. Dillon, "Machine learning using single-layered and multi-layered neural networks," IEEE 2nd Int. Conf. on Tools for Art. Intell., pp. 269–275, 1990.

[7] R. M. Goodman, C. M. Higgins, and J. W. Miller, "Rule-based neural networks for classification and probability estimation," Neural Computation, vol. 4, pp. 781–804, 1992.

[8] D. Rumelhart, J. McClelland, and PDP Research Group, Explanation in the Microstructure of Cognition, in Parallel Distributed Processing, MIT Press, 1986.

[9] N. DeClaris and M.-C. Su, A novel class of neural networks with quadratic junctions, in IEEE Int. Conf. on Systems, Man, and Cybernectics, pp. 1557–1562, 1991 (Received the 1992 Franklin V. Taylor Award).

[10] D. L. Reilly, L. N. Cooper, and C. Elbaum, "A neural network for category learning," Biol. Cybern. vol. 45, pp. 35–41, 1982.

[11] J. Moody and C. J. Darken, "Fast learning in networks of locally-tuned processing units," Neural Computation, vol. 1, pp. 281–293, 1989.

[12] R. O. Duda and P. H. Hart, *Pattern Recognition and Scene Analysis. Wiley. New York, NY, 1973.*

[13] M. B. Davidson, Diabetes Mellitus Diagnosis and Treatment. New York, Wiley & Sons, 1986.

[14] B. C. Hansen and N. L. Bodkin, "Heterogeneity of insulin responses: phases leading to Type 2 (non-insulin-dependent) diabetes mellitus in the rhesus monkey," Diabetologia, vol. 29, pp. 713–719, 1986.

[15] S. C. Lin, "Implementation of a novel neural network design for a demanding medical problem," Master's thesis, Univ. of Maryland, College Park, 1991.

[16] G. Sebestyen and J. Edie, "An algorithm for non-parametric pattern recognition," IEEE Trans. on Electronic Computers, vol. 15, pp. 908–915, Dec. 1966.

Fuzzy RCE Neural Network

Sing-Ming Roan, Cheng-Chin Chiang and Hsin-Chia Fu
Department of Computer Science and Information Engineering
National Chiao-Tung University
Hsinchu, Taiwan 300, R.O.C.
E-mail: hcfu@hsinchu.csie.nctu.edu.tw

***Abstract*— This paper proposes a supervised fuzzy neural network called *Fuzzy Restricted Columb Energy* (Fuzzy RCE) network for classification problems. In Fuzzy RCE, each hidden neuron is a fuzzy prototype which can be used to represent one or many training patterns. At the learning stage, the fuzzy membership functions of prototype neurons can be automatically adjusted according to the training data. The simulation results on the handwritten alphanumeric characters show that the proposed model learns very fast and has good recognition performance.**

1 Introduction

In these years, neural networks have been more and more attractive for various application domains. In general, a neural network involves only simple arithmetic operations with a simple control structure. They usually can be either implemented on standard sequential machines, or can be easily parallelized on connection machine. Besides, the self-adjusting property of neural networks also makes neural networks more suitable for modeling of unknown systems. Therefore, neural networks have good potential to become feasible tools for information processing.

Simutaneously, the study on fuzzy set theory also gets much attention from researchers [1, 3]. Particularly, the theories of fuzzy sets have a strong impact on techniques of pattern recognition [4]. In comparison with the conventional crisp sets, the concepts of fuzzy sets provides more robust representations to model real-world objects. Therefore, this paper is to integrate the techniques of neural networks with the concepts of fuzzy pattern recognition such that we can develop a more feasible system for classification problems.

Following this introduction is a brief descriptions on the concepts of fuzzy recognition. In Section 3, a neural network called *Fuzzy Restricted Columb Energy* (Fuzzy RCE) network, which combines the fuzzy

0-7803-0614-7/93$03.00 ©1993IEEE

recognition concepts with the RCE neural network model [2], together with its learning procedure and retrieving procedure are proposed. In Section 4, experimental results of the application on handwritten alphanumberic character recognition are presented. The final section provides some concluding remarks on this research.

2 Concepts of Fuzzy Recognition

Using the formal definition of fuzzy sets presented by Klir [3], let U denote a universal set. Then, the membership function μ_A of a fuzzy set A is usually defined as

$$\mu_A : U \rightarrow [0,1], \qquad (1)$$

where $[0,1]$ denotes the interval of real numbers from 0 to 1. In fuzzy pattern recognition, an input is composed of one or many features. The space of each feature is assumed to be an universal set U. Within each feature, many fuzzy sets may be defined. For example, each tree has the height feature. The space of a tree's height may be any value in the interval (10cm,1000cm). Thus, the universal set U is the interval (10cm,1000cm). For this feature, we can define four fuzzy sets such as "very high", "high", "short", and "very short". For each fuzzy set, we need to define its membership function over U. Thus, given a height, we can compute its corresponding degrees of membership for these four fuzzy sets.

The process of pattern classification is to assign an input to a category. Let $\mathbf{f} = [f_1, f_2, \ldots, f_n]$ be an input vector, where f_i's are its features. In general, a category of objects may contains several representative prototypes. For example, the category of coconut trees generally contains a prototype with properties "*very high*", "*with large fruits*", etc. On the other hand, the category of orange trees may contain a prototype with properties "*short*", "*with small fruits*", etc. For the above two example prototypes, the words 'very', 'large', 'short' have introduce the fuzzy concepts into its features. Thus, we can use fuzzy sets to represent the prototypes of a categories of objects. Now, consider a prototype P_i of a category C. Assume that P_i has fuzzy properties in each feature. Let A_i's $(1 \leq i \leq n)$ denotes the fuzzy sets which represents the fuzzy properties. Thus, we need n membership functions, which is denoted as μ_{A_i}, for P_i. When an input vector $\mathbf{f}$ is given, all these n membership functions are evaluated according to f_i's. Then, we can define a "goodness of fit" (say $\mathcal{G}_i(\mathbf{f})$) for P_i with respect to $\mathbf{f}$ as

$$\mathcal{G}_i(\mathbf{f}) \quad = \quad \sum_{j=1}^{n} \mu_{A_j}(f_j). \qquad (2)$$

With the goodness of fit defined on each prototype of each category, we can assign an input vector $\mathbf{f}$ to category C, if there exist a prototype P_k of category C such that $\mathcal{G}_k(\mathbf{f}) = \max_i\{\mathcal{G}_)(\mathbf{f})\}$. Of course, we can also reject $\mathbf{y}$ if the maximum goodness of fit does not exceed a prespecified threshold.

The process of fuzzy pattern recognition stated above needs an important step to define the membership functions for each fuzzy properties of prototypes in each category.

Since it may be impossible to known what fuzzy properties a prototype should have, we cannot directly define the membership functions by observing the feature vector of training patterns. Thus, the self-adjusting capability of neural network can be utilized to handle this problem. Through the learning process of neural networks, the prototypes together with their membership functions can be generated automatically for all categories. In the next section, a fuzzy neural network together with its learning and retrieving procedure is proposed.

3 Fuzzy RCE Neural Network

RCE [2] network is one of the neural network models which had been used as a pattern classifier for forming nonlinear boundaries of pattern classes. Using the concepts of RCE, each hidden neuron can be used to represent a prototype. The network architecture of the model is shown in Fig. 1. In this network, there are three layers, input layer (I), prototype layer (P) and output layer (O). The neurons of input layer present the feature vector of input pattern. Each neuron in output layer represents one category. As stated earlier, each prototype neuron must define its fuzzy sets together with their corresponding membership functions for fuzzy properties. In our model, all membership functions are triangular functions which are of the form shown in Fig. 2. Each triangular membership function has two parameters a and b which are used to determines the center and the width of this function, respectively.

The triangular membership function can be formally defined as:

$$\mu(x) = \begin{cases} \frac{1}{b}(-|x-a|+b), \\ \text{if } (a-b) < x < (a+b) \\ 0, \qquad \text{otherwise.} \end{cases} \tag{3}$$

Given that the dimension of input feature vectors is n, then n fuzzy membership functions $(\mu_{i,j}(x_j))$ should be defined within each prototype. In other words, we need parameters $\{a_{i,j}|1 \leq j \leq n\}$ and $\{b_{i,j}|1 \leq j \leq n\}$ for those membership functions in each hidden neuron i. However, to simplify the network model, we use only one common b_i, instead of $\{b_{i,j}|1 \leq ji \leq n\}$, in each neuron. Thsu, the internal structure of each prototype neuron is shown as Fig. 3.

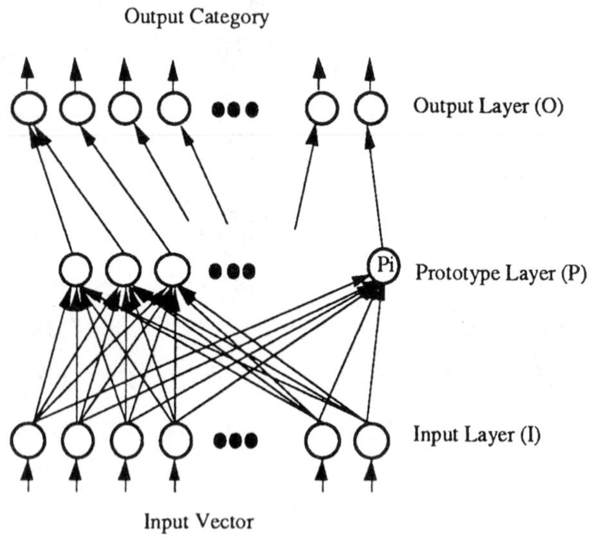

Figure 1: Fuzzy RCE net topology.

A. *Fuzzy RCE Learning*

Fuzzy RCE net is a supersived learning neural model. Each pattern presented to the net-

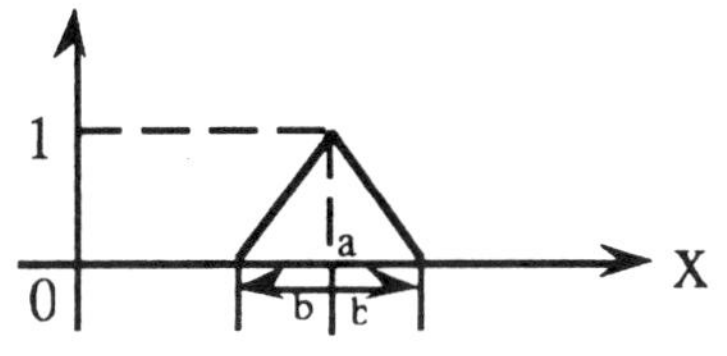

Figure 2: A fuzzy set with triangular membership function.

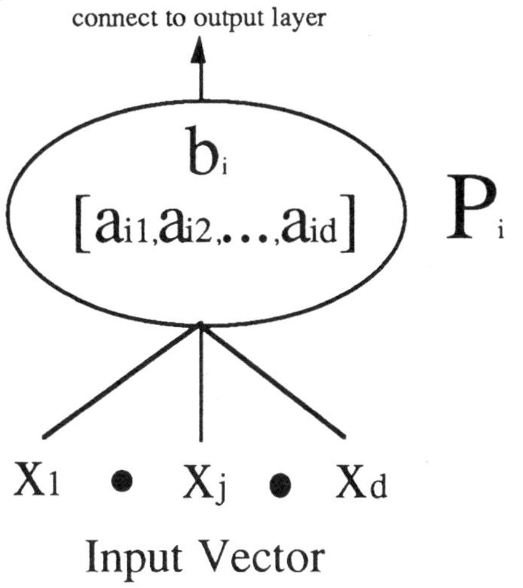

Figure 3: The structure of one prototype neuron in Fuzzy RCE.

work must contain the input feature vector as well as its associated class output. Given a training input vector $\mathbf{f} = [x_1, x_2, \ldots, x_n]$ belonging to the Kth class, the learning procedure of fuzzy RCE network is described as follows:

1. calculate the output of all prototype neurons by

$$OUT_{P_i} = \Phi(\frac{1}{n}\sum_{j=1}^{n} \mu_{i,j}(x_j)), \qquad (4)$$

where

$$\mu_{i,j}(x_j) = \begin{cases} \frac{1}{b_i}(-|x_j - a_{i,j}| + b_i), \\ if(a_{i,j} - b_i) < x_j < (a_{i,j} + b_i) \\ 0, otherwise \end{cases}$$

$$\Phi(x) = \begin{cases} 0, & \text{if } x \leq TH \\ x, & \text{if } x > TH \end{cases} \qquad (5)$$

The "TH" is a prespecified threshold. If $OUT_{P_i} > 0$, then we say that prototype P_i is "fired".

2. Modify the parameters of prototype neurons according to the following steps.

   (a) *New Classification*
   If none of the prototype neurons in the Kth category is fired, then a new prototype P_j which connects to the Kth output neuron is created in prototype layer. The parameters of fuzzy set in prototype

P_j are set as follows:

$$\begin{bmatrix} a_{j,1} \\ a_{j,2} \\ \vdots \\ a_{j,n} \end{bmatrix} = \begin{bmatrix} x_1 \\ x_2 \\ \vdots \\ x_n \end{bmatrix} \quad (6)$$

$$b_j = b_0 \quad (7)$$

The b_0 is a prespecified initial value for all membership functions.

(b) *Confusion*

If any prototype P_i which does not connect to the Kth output neuron is fired, then the parameter b_i is reduced to b_i' such that the prototype P_i cannot be fired. The value of b_i' can be derived by solving the equation $OUT_{P_i} = TH$. Thus

$$b_i' = \frac{\sum_{j=1}^{n} f(x_j)}{(n-k) - n * TH} \quad (8)$$

where

$$f(x_j) = \begin{cases} |x_j - a_{i,j}|, \\ \text{if } (a_{i,j} - b_i) < x_j < (a_{i,j} + b_i) \\ 0, \text{otherwise} \end{cases}$$

k is the number of $f(x_j)$'s such that $f(x_j) \neq 0$, $j = 1, 2, \ldots, n$.

These two rules for prototype acquisition and modification will guarantee the network to learn the geography of the pattern categories.

B. *Fuzzy RCE Retrieving*

The network retrieving procedure for an input feature vector **f** is described as follows:

1. Calculate the output of all prototype neurons in prototype layer according to Eq.(4).
2. Find the prototype neuron with the maximum output value. If this found prototype neuron connects to the Kth output neuron, then assigned **f** to the Kth category. If no prototype neuron is fired, then **f** is rejected.

4 Experimental Fuzzy RCE Recognizer and Testing Results

To applied the Fuzzy RCE network to a practical application, an experimental recognizer is built on a PC-386 AT based on the Fuzzy RCE network. This recognizer is used to recognize the handwritten alphanumberic characters. The characters input to this recognizer is through a digitizer. All sampled characters are transformed to their bit array representations. After normalizing the input bit array, the features are extracted from this bit array. The main features utilized for each character are the strokes in eight orientations. The technique for stroke extraction is based on the pixel density in each orientation [5] instead of based on tracing each stroke in the bit array. This approach reduces much computation complexity in feature extraction.

In order to demonstrate the performance of this recognizer, we present the testing results in the following. The experimental is to recognize on-line handwritten alphanumeric characters. We prepared 8 data sets each of which contains $36 \times 5(=180)$ characters as the database. In this experiment, we try to train the recognizer with different sizes of training sets and evaluate the recognition performance on the remained untrained training set. Table 1 shows the testing results. In Table 1, the training set s1-i denotes a training set which containing i training data sets chosen from the eight training data sets. The second row of this table shows the number of prototypes generated after the training. The third row is the number of iterations used for the training. The fourth row shows the rejection rates. The fifth and sixth rows denote the recognition rate with rejection rate and without rejection rate, respectively.

Table 1: The testing results of the Fuzzy RCE recognizer.

	s1	s1-2	s1-3	s1-4	s1-5	s1-6
Prototype	116	179	216	259	317	364
Iteration	5	5	5	5	6	5
Reject	10.16	6.67	5.84	5.56	3.43	2.23
Correct_1	92.54	94.03	94.37	95.64	96.55	98.16
Correct_2	83.18	87.83	88.89	90.35	93.24	95.97

5 Conclusions

A new neural network model, called fuzzy RCE is presented. The advantages of fuzzy RCE include

1. The training time of fuzzy RCE is very short and limited.
2. The membership degree measures has good tolerance for input pattern variety.
3. The calculation of outputs for prototype neurons involves no exponential operations, thus the compuation complexity is reduced.
4. The parameters of network have their physical meaning and can be easily interpreted.

References

[1] L. Zadeh, "Fuzzy sets," Information and control, Vol.8, pp.338-353, 1965.

[2] D.L. Reilly, L.N. Cooper, C. Elbaum, "A Neural Model for Category Learning," Biological Cybernetics v.45,pp. 35-41,1982.

[3] G.J. Klir, T.A. Folger, "Fuzzy sets, Uncertainty, and Information," Prentice-Hall International,Inc. 1988.

[4] W. Pedrycz, "Fuzzy sets in pattern recognition: Methodology and Methods," Pattern Recog. Vol.23,pp.121-146, 1990.

[5] S.M. Roan, "The study of neural network for on-line handwritten alphanumeric character recognition," Master Thesis, NCTU Taiwan ROC, 1992.

Incremental Grid Growing: Encoding High-Dimensional Structure into a Two-Dimensional Feature Map

Justine Blackmore and Risto Miikkulainen
Department of Computer Sciences
The University of Texas at Austin, Austin, TX 78712-1188
justine,risto@cs.utexas.edu

***Abstract*— Knowledge of clusters and their relations is important in understanding high-dimensional input data with unknown distribution. Ordinary feature maps with fully connected, fixed grid topology cannot properly reflect the structure of clusters in the input space—there are no cluster boundaries on the map. Incremental feature map algorithms, where nodes and connections are added to or deleted from the map according to the input distribution, can overcome this problem. However, so far such algorithms have been limited to maps that can be drawn in 2-D only in the case of 2-dimensional input space. In the approach proposed in this paper, nodes are added incrementally to a regular, 2-dimensional grid, which is drawable at all times, irrespective of the dimensionality of the input space. The process results in a map that explicitly represents the cluster structure of the high-dimensional input.**

I. Introduction

The self-organizing feature map's [6, 7] primary use as a computational tool is in forming a mapping from a high-dimensional input space to two dimensions. How useful the map is for a given task depends on how accurately it represents the input space. In general, the input space may be arbitrarily nonconvex and discontinuous, and may contain high-dimensional clusters. A good representation of the space should somehow capture such topological properties. However, accurately representing high-dimensional structure on a continuous, fully connected $n \times m$ grid is problematic. Discontinuities in the input space may appear bridged in the map. The map may have connections that span the disjoint clusters, or it may have nodes situated within the discontinuity where the input probability is 0 (Fig. 1). In other words, the final feature map sometimes misrepresents the topology of the input data.

Real world data sets often contain distinct but non-obvious subsets of data. Determining the set of classifications that optimally describes such subgroupings is a primary goal of many standard clustering methods. Because gaps become bridged, the standard self-organizing algorithm does not naturally delineate the boundaries of such groupings. A feature map application that depends on an accurate representation of neighborhood boundaries would thus need to perform further analysis to determine if discontinuities have been inaccurately spanned in the map.

This paper describes an incremental grid-growing algorithm for incorporating such information directly into the structure of the map. During organization, non-convexities, discontinuities and clusters in the data set become explicitly represented in the 2-dimensional structure of the map. Thus the algorithm can yield an accurate, low-dimensional description of the structure in high-dimensional input.

II. An incremental approach

In order to develop an accurate representation of the topology, the self-organizing algorithm must either recognize and correct misrepresentations that develop in the map, or else prevent such incorrect topology from being encoded in the first place. Completely preventing the development of inaccurate structure is impossible without a priori knowledge of the input space. On the other hand, fully organizing a map and then modifying it so that unwanted structures are removed may require much extra computational effort. In general, an algorithm must be equipped with some effective heuristics to accomplish both ends: to guide the development of structure actually present in the data set, and to detect and correct any "false" topology in the map as early as possible during organization.

These considerations suggest an incremental approach to building and organizing the map. Such an approach would initially organize a small number of nodes in the structure, then use a heuristic to find and remove any potentially inaccurate nodes or connections. Another heuris-

Fig. 1: **Representing nonconvex input distributions with ordinary feature maps.** The input space consists of 2-dimensional vectors uniformly distributed in the shaded region. The black dots indicate locations of the feature map weight vectors after the map has been organized. Weight vectors of neighboring nodes in the map are connected with lines. Note that nodes are allocated to areas where there is no input. Similarly, connections sometimes span these areas, suggesting that the connected nodes represent neighboring vectors in the input space although in reality they belong to different clusters.

tic could be used to add nodes to the structure. The new structure would be re-organized, and the process continued. At every epoch, the algorithm would guide the map toward representing the high-dimensional properties of the data set accurately.

Approaches that employ such heuristics to some extent include [1, 2, 3, 4, 5, 8, 10, 12, 13]. Fritzke's growing cell structure algorithm [1, 2, 3] is particularly interesting because it incorporates methods for both the incremental build-up and the periodic correction of the network structure. The basic layout of the map, however, is not a 2-dimensional grid of nodes, but rather a structure whose connections at all times define a system of triangles (i.e., every node must always be a member of a triangle). During organization, a heuristic measure is used to determine areas of the map that inadequately represent their corresponding areas of the input space, and new nodes are added in these areas. Also, nodes that rarely respond maximally to the input are periodically removed from the map.

The algorithm results in a network structure that represents an arbitrarily connected graph $G = (V, E)$, where V is the set of nodes, and E is the set of connections between them. In the case of 2-dimensional input, it is easy to verify that the network accurately represents the input by plotting the weight vectors in 2-D. When the input is high-dimensional, however, such an arbitrary structure may not have a simple low-dimensional description (that is, it cannot easily be drawn in 2 dimensions). Fritzke [3] presents a drawing method based on a physical force analogy that works reasonably well when the input space is low-dimensional (e.g., 3-D), but is not guaranteed to produce a planar drawing. Also, the arbitrary connectivity makes topological neighborhoods ambiguous beyond directly connected nodes. Any node may be connected to any number of neighbors, so a neighborhood of a given radius in the structure (i.e., the number of connections outward in any direction) has little topological meaning. Thus, extracting the overall topological relationships of the input space from this structure may not be easy. The algorithm does explicitly represent clustering of the input data by removing connections between the clusters in the structure. However, the topology within clusters and across continuous data sets may be difficult to determine.

The incremental grid-growing algorithm described in this paper is also based on the incremental approach, but it avoids the difficulties of an arbitrarily connected graph structure. The map retains a regular 2-dimensional grid at all times. At any point during the organization, the map has a simple 2-dimensional description, and topological relations are easily examined by plotting the nodes and connections of the map in 2-D.

III. The grid-growing algorithm

Initially, the feature map grid consists of four connected nodes with weight vectors chosen at random from the input (Fig. 2a). Each main iteration of the algorithm consists of three steps:

1. Adapting the current grid to the input distribution through the usual feature map self-organizing process.
2. Adding nodes to those areas in the perimeter of the grid that inadequately represent their corresponding input area.
3. Examining the weight vectors of neighboring nodes and determining whether a connection between the nodes should be deleted from the map, or whether a new connection should be added.

The new structure is re-organized, and the process continues until a predetermined maximum number of nodes has been reached.

Each step will now be described in more detail. A boundary node is defined as any node in the grid that has at least one directly neighboring position in the 2-dimensional grid space not yet occupied by a node. Each boundary node of the current structure maintains an error

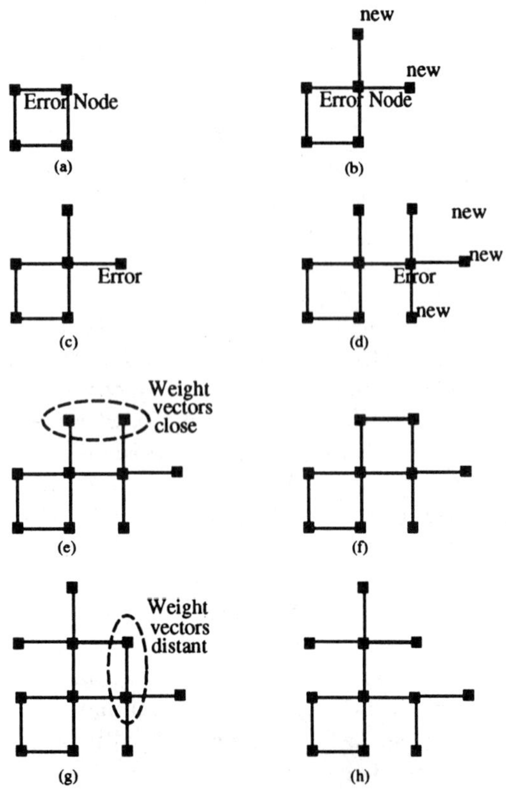

Fig. 2: **Growing the feature map grid.** Figure (a) shows the initial structure after the first organization stage; the boundary node with the highest error value is marked. (b) New nodes are "grown" into any open grid location that is an immediate neighbor of the error node. (c) After organizing the new structure with the standard self-organization process, a new error node is found. (d) Again, new nodes are grown into any open grid location that is an immediate neighbor of the error node. (e) During self-organization of this new structure, the algorithm detects that the circled nodes have developed weight vectors very close in Euclidean distance. (f) These "close" nodes are connected. (g) After further organization, the algorithm discovers connected neighboring nodes whose weight vectors occupy distant areas of the input (i.e., the nodes have a large Euclidean distance). (h) These "distant" nodes are then disconnected in the grid.

value E over its organizational stage. During each iteration within the organizational stage, whenever a boundary node wins an input presentation (i.e., the Euclidean distance between the node's weight vector and the input vector is minimum for the map), the square of the distance between its weight vector and the input is added to the error value:

$$E(t) = E(t-1) + \sum_k (x_k - w_k)^2, \qquad (1)$$

where E is the cumulative error and $\mathbf{w}$ the weight vector of the winning unit, and $\mathbf{x}$ is the input vector.

At the end of each iteration, the boundary node with the greatest cumulative error can be said to represent the area of the input space most inadequately represented in the map. This node "grows" new nodes in all unoccupied grid locations in its immediate neighborhood (Figures 2a-d). New nodes are directly connected to the error node. If any other directly neighboring grid spots are occupied (as in Fig. 2d), the new node's weight vector is initialized to be the average value of all the neighboring weight vectors:

$$w_{NEW,k} = 1/n \sum_{i \in \mathcal{N}} w_{i,k}, \qquad (2)$$

where $w_{NEW,k}$ is the kth component of the new unit's weight vector and $\mathcal{N}$ is the set of the n neighboring nodes of the new unit. Otherwise (as in Fig. 2b), the new node's weight vector is initialized so that the weight vector of the error node is the average of the new node's vector and the vectors of any already existing neighbors of the error node:

$$w_{ERR,k} = 1/(m+1)\left(w_{NEW,k} + \sum_{i \in \mathcal{M}} w_{i,k}\right), \qquad (3)$$

where $w_{ERR,k}$ is the kth component of the error node's weight vector and $\mathcal{M}$ is the set of the m already existing neighbor units of the error node.

Initially, the new nodes are connected to the structure only through the error node. As the structure continues to organize, these new nodes may develop weight vectors that are close to the weight vectors of neighbors to which they have not been connected. If this is the case, it is desirable to add a new connection joining these nodes. An adjustable threshold parameter is used to decide if a new connection should be grown. After each organizational iteration, the Euclidean distance between unconnected neighboring nodes in the map is examined. If the distance is below the "connect" threshold parameter, a connection between the nodes is added to the structure (Figures 2e-f).

Similarly, a "disconnect" threshold parameter is used to determine if there are two nodes in the map that are connected even though they represent points that are distant in the input space. Exceeding such a threshold may indicate that a connection spans a discontinuity in the input, and should be removed from the map (Figures 2g-h).

If the input distribution forms a connected area (as do the four arms of the cross in Fig. 1), in practice it is rarely necessary to delete connections from the grid. But it is possible to have disjoint input clusters in the data set—for example, the four arms might be separated by gaps. In general, Euclidean distances between clusters are greater than the intra-cluster distances. The clusters become separated from each other when the connections that span the inter-cluster gaps are removed by the algorithm. If the disconnect threshold is selected properly, distinct clusters will become separated in the map. The portions of the grid representing the independent clusters will continue to develop according to the topologies of the individual data clusters.

Adding nodes only at the perimeter allows the map to develop an arbitrary topology. Further, adding nodes only to areas that inadequately represent the input encourages the map to develop only those topological structures that are actually present in the data. Disconnecting nodes that span an apparent discontinuity allows clusters to separate and to continue to develop independently. The clusters that automatically develop this way may represent categories or sub-sets within the data set. Capturing such properties of the input space in the 2-dimensional structure of the map can greatly assist the interpretation of the input data.

IV. Examples

The topology of an arbitrary high-dimensional space is difficult to visualize without a dimensionality-reducing tool such as a feature map. On the other hand, the topology of a 2-dimensional data set is trivial to visualize. Thus, for illustrative purposes, an experiment where the incremental grid-growing algorithm developed a feature map of a 2-dimensional input space is presented in Fig. 3. As in Fig. 1, 2-dimensional vectors were chosen with uniform probability from the cross-shaped shaded area. The grid developed four arms connected through an area that represents the central portion of the cross. Each arm is represented by approximately the same number of nodes, and the central region is represented by a proportionately lower number of nodes. The clusters in this input space are joined in the central region; this structure is duly reflected by the continuity of the resulting grid. Note that the grid structure itself, even without any labelling of nodes, follows the overall topology of the input space. The structure of the data set and its overall probability density are encoded in the structure of the map.

Let us now extend this example to higher-dimensional input. Consider the case where each of the arms is a 4-dimensional "box" along one of 4 coordinate axes. Three of these arms are connected to a 4-dimensional area surrounding the origin, while the fourth region is separated from the origin by a gap. That is, the input vectors (x_1, x_2, x_3, x_4) are uniformly distributed within the 4-dimensional area defined by the union of the following 5 areas:

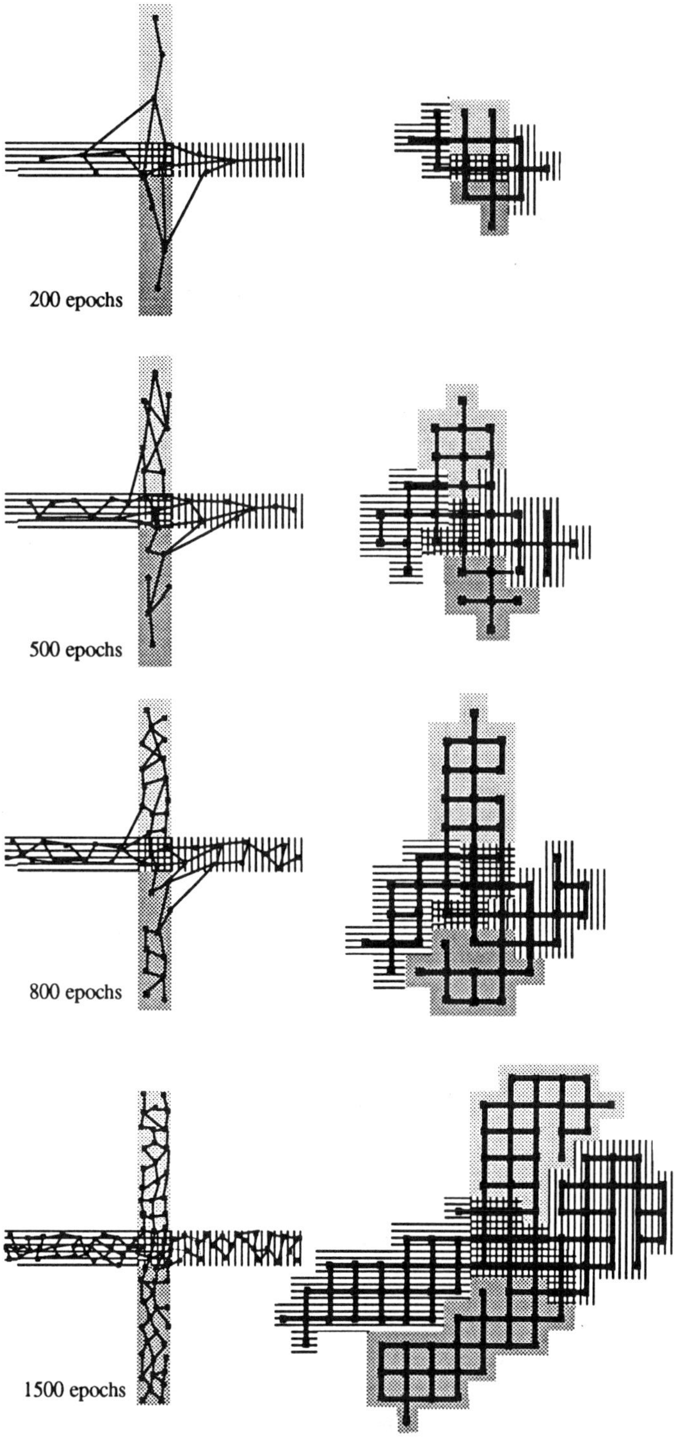

Fig. 3: **Snapshots of the grid evolution for a 2-dimensional cross input.** On the left, the weight vectors are plotted on the 2-d input space. On the right, the corresponding grid structure is shown. Shading of the area around a node indicates the arm of the cross where that node's weight vector is located. The four arms are separated in the grid, with a common center.

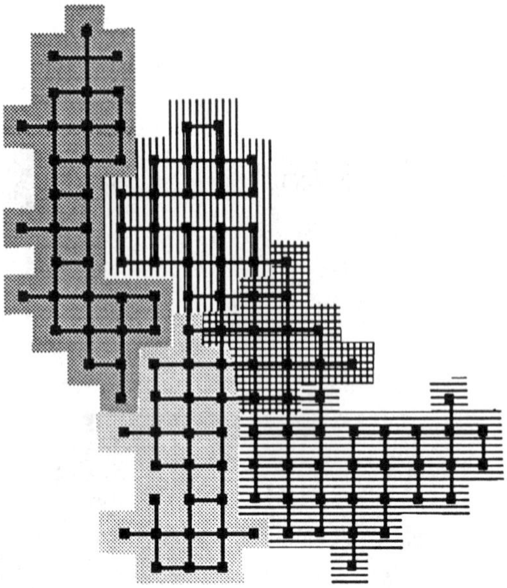

▦	Weights $(w_1, w_2, w_3, w_4) : 0 \leq w_1, w_2, w_3, w_4 < 1$
▤	Weights $(w_1, w_2, w_3, w_4) : 0 \leq w_2, w_3, w_4 < 1; 1 \leq w_1 < 5$
░	Weights $(w_1, w_2, w_3, w_4) : 0 \leq w_1, w_3, w_4 < 1; 1 \leq w_2 < 5$
▥	Weights $(w_1, w_2, w_3, w_4) : 0 \leq w_1, w_2, w_4 < 1; 1 \leq w_3 < 5$
▒	Weights $(w_1, w_2, w_3, w_4) : 0 \leq w_1, w_2, w_3 < 1; 2 \leq w_4 < 6$

Fig. 4: **Final grid structure for 4-dimensional, disjoint input space.** The common center (the first area) and the first three arms are connected, while the fourth arm is fully separated.

$$\text{Area } 1 = \{(x_1, x_2, x_3, x_4) : 0 \leq x_1, x_2, x_3, x_4 < 1\}$$
$$\text{Area } 2 = \{(x_1, x_2, x_3, x_4) : 0 \leq x_2, x_3, x_4 < 1; 1 \leq x_1 < 5\}$$
$$\text{Area } 3 = \{(x_1, x_2, x_3, x_4) : 0 \leq x_1, x_3, x_4 < 1; 1 \leq x_2 < 5\}$$
$$\text{Area } 4 = \{(x_1, x_2, x_3, x_4) : 0 \leq x_1, x_2, x_4 < 1; 1 \leq x_3 < 5\}$$
$$\text{Area } 5 = \{(x_1, x_2, x_3, x_4) : 0 \leq x_1, x_2, x_3 < 1; 2 \leq x_4 < 6\}$$

The final map representing this structure is shown in Fig. 4. As in the 2-dimensional case above, the first three arms are connected through the central region and extend outward. The fourth arm is fully separated from the first three. The relative numbers of nodes throughout the structure reflect the uniform distribution of the input. Again, the overall topology and distribution of the input space is apparent in the simple 2-dimensional structure of the grid.

The final example, the "spanning tree" of [7], demonstrates the algorithm's ability to develop arbitrarily complex topologies for discrete inputs. In this example, the input consists of the 5-dimensional vectors listed in Fig. 5a.

A	B	C	D	E	F	G	H	I	J	K	L	M	N	O	P	Q	R	S	T	U	V	W	X	Y	Z	1	2	3	4	5	6
1	2	3	4	5	3	3	3	3	3	3	3	3	3	3	3	3	3	3	3	3	3	3	3	3	3	3	3	3	3	3	3
0	0	0	0	0	1	2	3	4	5	3	3	3	3	3	3	3	3	3	3	3	3	3	3	3	3	3	3	3	3	3	3
0	0	0	0	0	0	0	0	0	0	1	2	3	4	5	6	7	8	3	3	3	3	6	6	6	6	6	6	6	6	6	6
0	0	0	0	0	0	0	0	0	0	0	0	0	0	0	0	0	0	1	2	3	4	1	2	3	4	2	2	2	2	2	2
0	0	0	0	0	0	0	0	0	0	0	0	0	0	0	0	0	0	0	0	0	0	0	0	0	0	1	2	3	4	5	6

(a)

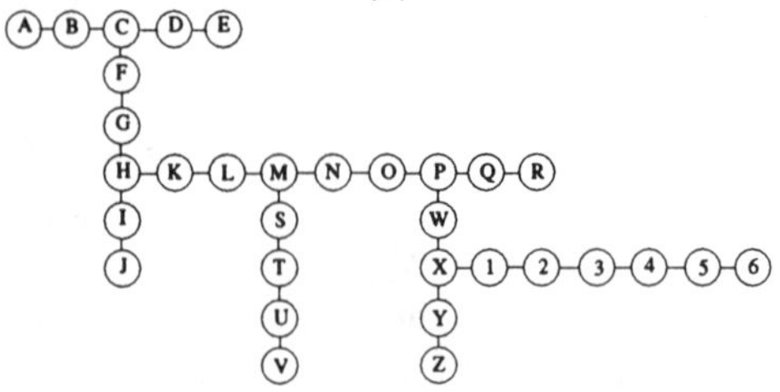

(b)

Fig. 5: **(a) The input set for Kohonen's spanning tree example [7]. (b) The minimal spanning tree of the data.** Although the example may seem artificial, it illustrates the self-organizing feature map's capacity to represent the general topology of difficult-to-describe data sets. The data has no obvious or easily discernible description, but the minimal spanning tree is one relational description that might be derived.

The high-dimensional topology of this data set is difficult to describe, but a minimum spanning tree is one possible structure that could be used to represent it (Fig. 5b). Indeed, if one knows what to look for, it is easy to see that the map developed through the standard self-organizing algorithm displays the spanning tree (Fig. 6a). However, the full connectivity of the map makes it difficult to discern a true tree or graph structure from the map alone.

The incremental grid-growing algorithm applied to the same data set derives a map that makes the arrangement much clearer (Fig. 6b). The arms of the spanning tree are clustered in delineated regions of the map. Also, the relationships between the clusters are narrowly specified by the limited connectivity between them. The structure of the map obviates the need for a priori knowledge of the spanning tree. Interestingly, "conventional" clustering methods (e.g., merge clustering) do not naturally derive such graph-like relationships in this type of data.

V. Conclusion and Future Work

The incremental grid-growing algorithm constructs 2-D drawable feature maps of arbitrary nonconvex and discontinuous high-dimensional input distributions. The algorithm addresses a primary shortcoming of the standard SOFM: deciding where the boundaries of clusters and specific regions are on the map. The overall topology of the input space is encoded in the continuity of the network structure alone, before any node labelling has been done.

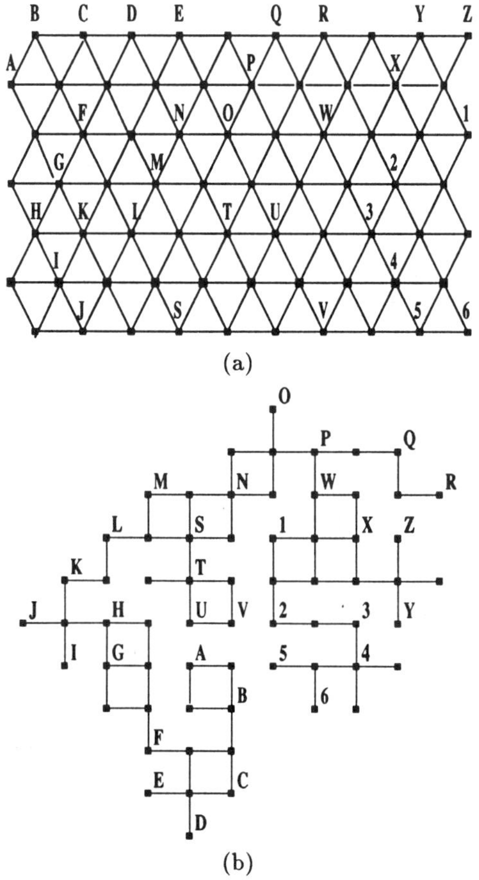

Fig. 6: **Feature map representation for the spanning tree data.** (a) Map derived by the standard self-organizing algorithm [7]. The map is hexagonally connected. The spanning tree structure is clearly present in the map; however, the full connectivity makes it difficult to extract exact neighborhood relations between units. (b) Map derived by the grid growing algorithm. The limited connectivity between clusters in the map closely resembles the structure of the spanning tree.

Because the 2-dimensional clusters that develop can be interpreted as categories, the grid is a useful tool for data classification. Furthermore, it can extract and represent tree- and graph-like structures, which makes it useful in visualizing the relationships in complex high-dimensional data sets.

Our ongoing work on grid growing includes fine-tuning the basic algorithm and applying it to real-world problems. Like any other feature map algorithm, the incremental grid algorithm could be improved by a method for setting the threshold values automatically (removing the need for parameter tuning). It would also be desirable to develop a computational measure that could be used decide when a map has developed a good representation for an arbitrary data set.

In addition, the application of the algorithm to various complex high-dimensional data sets is being investigated. For example, the algorithm should be useful in developing clusters for the representation of semantic features of words (e.g. [9, 11]). Data interpretation and knowledge representation in general is a most promising application of feature map algorithms, and incremental grid growing should prove particularly useful in such tasks.

References

[1] B. Fritzke. "Let it grow—Self-organizing feature maps with problem dependent cell structure." *Proceedings of the International Conference on Artificial Neural Networks* (Espoo, Finland). Amsterdam; New York: North-Holland, 1991, pp. 403–408.

[2] B. Fritzke. "Unsupervised clustering with growing cell structures." *Proceedings of the International Joint Conference on Neural Networks* (Seattle, WA), volume II. Piscataway, NJ: IEEE, 1991, pp. 531–536.

[3] B. Fritzke. *Wachsende Zellstrukturen—ein selbstorganisierendes neuronales Netzwerkmodell.* PhD thesis, Technischen Fakultät, Universität Erlangen-Nürnberg, Erlangen, Germany, 1992.

[4] S. Jokusch. "A neural network which adapts its structure to a given set of patterns." Rolf Eckmiller, Georg Hartmann, and Gert Hauske, Eds., *Parallel Processing in Neural Systems and Computers.* Amsterdam; New York: North-Holland, 1990, pp. 169–172.

[5] J. Kangas, T. Kohonen, and J. Laaksonen. "Variants of self-organizing maps." *IEEE Transactions on Neural Networks*, 1:93–99, 1990.

[6] T. Kohonen. *Self-Organization and Associative Memory*, 3rd ed. Berlin; Heidelberg; New York: Springer, 1989.

[7] T. Kohonen. "The self-organizing map." *Proceedings of the IEEE*, 78:1464–1480, 1990.

[8] T. M. Martinetz and K. J. Schulten. "A 'neural gas' network learns topologies." *Proceedings of the International Conference on Artificial Neural Networks* (Espoo, Finland). Amsterdam; New York: North-Holland, 1991, pp. 397–402.

[9] R. Miikkulainen and M. G. Dyer. "Natural language processing with modular neural networks and distributed lexicon." *Cognitive Science*, 15:343–399, 1991.

[10] H. J. Ritter. "Learning with the self-organizing map." *Proceedings of the International Conference on Artificial Neural Networks* (Espoo, Finland). Amsterdam; New York: North-Holland, 1991, pp. 379–384.

[11] H. J. Ritter and T. Kohonen. "Self-organizing semantic maps." *Biological Cybernetics*, 61:241–254, 1989.

[12] J. S. Rodriques and L. B. Almeida. "Improving the learning speed in topological maps of patterns." *Proceedings of the International Neural Networks Conference* (Paris, France). Dordrecht; Boston: Kluwer, 1990, pp. 813–816.

[13] L. Xu and E. Oja. "Adding top-down expectation into the learning procedure of self-organizing maps." *Proceedings of the International Joint Conference on Neural Networks* (Washington, DC), volume II. Hillsdale, NJ: Erlbaum, 1990, pp. 531–534.

Things You Haven't Heard about the Self-Organizing Map

Teuvo Kohonen
Helsinki University of Technology
Laboratory of Computer and Information Science
Rakentajanaukio 2 C, SF-02150 Espoo, Finland

***Abstract*— This presentation has been inspired by two new findings. First, it quite recently turned out that the Self-Organizing Map (SOM) algorithm can be related to a biological neural network in many essential known details; even a cyclic behavior automatically ensues from a simple nonlinear neural model, whereby these cycles correspond to the steps of the discrete-time SOM algorithm. Second, compared with the other traditional neural-network algorithms, the SOM alone has the advantage of tolerating a very low accuracy in the representation of its signals and synaptic weights; this has been proven by simulations. Such a property ought to be shared by any realistic neural-network model. While the SOM can thus be advanced as a genuine neural-network paradigm, it has also been shown in this presentation how the basic algorithm can be generalized and made more efficient computationally in several ways.**

I. Introduction

The *Self-Organizing Map (SOM)* [1,2] is a neural-network model that usually implements a peculiar nonlinear "projection" from the high-dimensional space of sensory or other input signals onto a two-dimensional array. This mapping often automatically finds and displays characteristic features or other abstractions from the raw data.

There exist many kinds of such maps in the brain. The SOM then has a twofold role in neural-network research: first, it models certain brain structures in idealized form, and second, it can be used for many practical applications to visualize interrelationships in complex data, such as process states.

The SOM belongs to the competitive-learning category of neural-network algorithms. Its cells usually form a two-dimensional array, and in principle at least, they receive the same input information in terms of a spatial activity pattern. Every cell acts as a selective decoder of a different pattern, by comparison of its weight vector with the input vector. Learning of the proper weight vector values is somewhat similar to high-dimensional regression, where a finite number of *reference vectors*, corresponding to the weight vectors, is adaptively placed into the input signal space to approximate to the samples. During adaptation, the corrections made in the reference vectors of neighboring cells in the array are correlated, as if the set of reference vectors formed an elastic net in the signal space. Self-organization means that this net becomes oriented and adaptively assumes a form by which it best describes the input vectors *in an ordered, structured fashion.*

I start this presentation with an overview of the SOM algorithms, pointing out how they look in different metrics.

Since most of the neural-network research is still based on software methods, a new idea to compute the SOM is introduced in this paper. The so-called *Batch Map algorithm* is a parameter-free and very fast version of the SOM. With special unsymmetric weighting of the learning rate at the borders of the map, this algorithm can be made to follow time-variable density functions accurately and very fast; a straightforward application is in telecommunications engineering, in the adaptive detection of discrete signal states.

An attempt to generalize the SOM for arrays of *operators* that may not even be differentiable with respect to any parameters is also made.

This paper was actually inspired by two important new findings. First, although these algorithms are usually advanced only as effective computational methods without reference to biology, it has recently turned out that the "short-cut" SOM algorithms may not be so abstract and nonbiological after all: there seems to exist a rather detailed *physiological interpretation* of the SOM process, which is described by system equations, the solutions of which behave very similarly with those of the "short-cut" SOM. Second, we have recently carried out extensive simulations on high-dimensional speech data, whereby it also turned out that the vector-quantization methods (to which the SOM belongs) tolerate *very coarse numerical*

0-7803-0999-5/93/$03.00

accuracies, three or four bits. This result too favors the SOM as a biological model and might be particularly interesting to researchers aiming at *analog hardware implementation* of artificial neural networks.

II. Many Different Algorithmic Descriptions of the SOM

A. The "Dot-Product Map"

Let us start with an algorithmic model that may have its biological counterpart in the brain as explained in Sec. IV. This algorithm is related to a two-dimensional array of interacting cells as depicted in Fig. 1.

Signal inputs to the cells of the SOM network can be defined in many ways. Consider first that the cells are activated in proportion to the dot product $m_i^T x$, where $x \in \Re^n$ is the input data vector, and $m_i \in \Re^n$ the reference vector of cell i, respectively.

In Sec. IV we shall show how a *Winner-Take-All (WTA) function* can be implemented by a simple distributed network. Its effect is to find the cell c ("winner") for which the activation is highest, i.e.,

$$m_c^T x = \max_i \{m_i^T x\} \ . \tag{1}$$

During learning, the corrections on adjacent cells are made to depend on their *relative distances*, and the degree of interaction is defined by the function $h_{ci}(t)$ below. The idealized updating or "learning" rule relative to (1) is expressed in discrete-time coordinates as

$$m_i(t+1) = \frac{m_i(t) + h_{ci}(t) \cdot x(t)}{\text{Norm of the numerator}} \tag{2}$$

where $h_{ci}(t)$ is the so-called (scalar-valued) *neighborhood function* relating to the "winner" and another arbitrary cell i in the array. This function has high values when $||i - c||$ is small and decreases with increasing distance. It

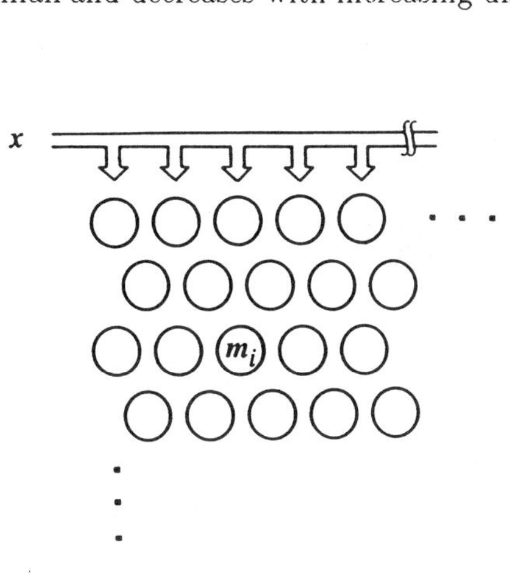

Fig. 1. Layout of a Self-Organizing Map.

has been shown that self-organization is most effective if the average width of $h_{ci}(t)$ decreases during the course of learning.

For a high learning power of this version of the SOM, $h_{ci}(t)$ for $i = c$ ought to assume rather high values during the first steps, say, >> 1. Naturally the process also works for low $h_{ci}(t)$, although slower, whereby we can use the approximate series expansion of (2),

$$m_i(t+1) \approx m_i(t) + h_{ci}(t) \cdot [x(t) - m_i(t) m_i^T(t) x(t)] \ . \tag{3}$$

This law will be found similar to the one discussed in Sec. IV.

B. The "Euclidean-Distance Map"

While above the matching criterion and updating were referred to dot products of high-dimensional vectors, an almost similar self-ordering process is implemented in high-dimensional Cartesian coordinates by the following pair of equations:

$$||x - m_c|| = \min_i \{||x - m_i||\} \ , \tag{4}$$

$$m_i(t+1) = m_i(t) + h_{ci}(t)[x(t) - m_i(t)] \ . \tag{5}$$

In this algorithm we must have $0 < h_{ci}(t) < 1$. The reference vectors $m_i(t)$ are not normalized. This may be the most familiar version of the SOM.

C. The SOM for a General Differentiable Distance Measure

Let now $d(x, m_i)$ be a general distance measure between x and m_i in the signal space. Assume that $d(x, m_i)$ is differentiable with respect to m_i. The "winner" is defined by

$$c = \arg \min_i \{d(x, m_i)\} \tag{6}$$

Let us next introduce a global objective or weighted-error function

$$E = \int \sum_i h_{ci} f(d(x, m_i)) p(x) dx \ , \tag{7}$$

where some function f of the quantization error $d(x, m_i)$ is first weighted by the neighborhood function h_{ci} and then averaged; here $p(x)$ is the probability density function of x. It has to be emphasized that in the following discussion, E need not be a potential function. If we would know an effective method for to minimize E, we could accept the optimal values of the m_i as a solution that would represent a generalized SOM. A severe problem is caused, however, by the subscript c being not constant but variable, $c = c(x; m_1, \ldots, m_k)$, where k is the number of all reference vectors, as discussed in depth in [4]. Therefore the solution method chosen here, the *Robbins-Monro stochastic approximation* [4, 5] only finds approximate optima. The class of these solutions has been studied with mathematical rigor and especially the convergence properties are thoroughly known. In applying this method we first define the *sample function* $E_1(t)$:

$$E_1(t) = \sum_i h_{ci}(t) f(d(x(t), m_i(t))) \ . \tag{8}$$

An approximate solution is then obtained as the last term of a sufficiently long sequence defined by

$$m_i(t+1) = m_i(t) - \lambda(t) \text{grad}_{m_i(t)} E_1(t) \ , \tag{9}$$

where $\lambda(t)$ defines the step size, or learning rate. The learning rate sequence must always fulfil the following conditions:

$$\sum_{t=0}^{\infty} \lambda(t) = \infty \, , \sum_{t=0}^{\infty} \lambda^2(t) < \infty \ . \tag{10}$$

Notice that "optimization" in this method only means "local gradient" steps, not the steepest descent in the E "landscape."

For instance, if $d(x, m_i) = ||x - m_i||$ and $f(d) = d^2$, and we denote $\alpha(t) = 2\lambda(t)$, we obtain the "Euclidean Distance" SOM algorithm written as

$$m_i(t+1) = m_i(t) + \alpha(t) h_{ci}(t)[x(t) - m_i(t)] \ . \tag{11}$$

Naturally, $\alpha(t)$ can be combined with $h_{ci}(t)$.

Although the Robbins-Monro method is only approximate, it anyway facilitates derivation of various practical algorithms with different choices of f and d. For instance, in applications one might often want to experiment with different Minkowski metrics [1]. In particular, for hardware reasons, the Minkowski metric with power 1 (the so-called city-block or Manhattan distance) is sometimes used in learning circuits. Above we would then have $f(d) = d = \sum_j |\xi_j - \mu_{ij}|$, where $x = (\xi_1, \ldots, \xi_n)^{\mathrm{T}}$ and $m_i = (\mu_{i1}, \ldots, \mu_{in})^{\mathrm{T}}$, and the "optimal" (actually, almost optimal) adaptation rule relating to this metric would read

$$\mu_{ij}(t+1) = \mu_{ij}(t) + h_{ci}(t) \cdot \text{sgn}[\xi_j(t) - \mu_{ij}(t)] \ . \tag{12}$$

The learning rate $h_{ci}(t)$ must now be normalized in a different way than in the previous cases, to guarantee a proper convergence.

D. The "Batch Map" Algorithm

The following observation leads to further computational simplification of the "Euclidean Distance" SOM algorithm. In the convergence limit every $m_i = m_i^*$ must satisfy the equilibrium condition

$$\mathrm{E}\{h_{ci}(x - m_i^*)\} = 0 \ , \tag{13}$$

whereby, in the averaging over the x space, the subscript c of the "winner" is a function $c = c(x; m_1^*, \ldots, m_k^*)$. An alternative way of writing (13) is

$$m_i^* = \frac{\int h_{ci} x p(x) dx}{\int h_{ci} p(x) dx} \ , \tag{14}$$

where $p(x)$ is the probability density function of x. It has to be noted that m_i^* has thereby not been solved explicitly; the index c on the right side still depends on x and all the m_i^*. Nonetheless (14) may be regarded as an expression from which the m_i^* can be solved *iteratively*, as shown shortly.

It has further been shown [1, 2] that the following simple definition of h_{ci} is effective enough in practice and saves much computing time: $h_{ci} = 1$ if i belongs to some *topological neighborhood set* N_c of cell c in the cell array, whereas otherwise $h_{ci} = 0$. With this h_{ci} there follows

$$m_i^* = \frac{\int_{V_i} x p(x) dx}{\int_{V_i} p(x) dx} \ , \tag{15}$$

where V_i means the following domain of values of x: Let some cell c be selected by values of x that belong to domain V_c around c, and let N_c be the topological neighborhood set of c (as referred to cell indices). If cell i is a common member of several neighborhood sets N_c, the union of the corresponding V_c is then called V_i. In [1] it was called the "influence region of cell i," i.e., *the set of those values of x that directly, or indirectly through the neighborhood function, select cell i for updating.*

Both (14) and (15) are already in the form in which the so-called *iterative contraction mapping* used in the solving of nonlinear equations is directly applicable. If z is an unknown vector that has to satisfy the equation $f(z) = 0$, then, since it is always possible to write the equation as $z = g(z)$, the successive approximations of the root can be computed as a series $\{z_n\}$ where

$$z_{n+1} = g(z_n) \ . \tag{16}$$

We shall not discuss any convergence problems here. If there would exist any, they can be overcome by the so-called Wegstein modification of (16). The iterative process in which a number of samples of x is first classified into the respective V_i regions, and the updating of the m_i^* is made iteratively as defined by (15) and (16), can be expressed as the following steps. The algorithm dubbed *"Batch Map"* resembles the familiar K-means algorithm [3], where all the training samples are assumed to be available when learning begins. The learning steps are defined as follows:

1. For the initial reference vectors, take, for instance, the first K training samples, where K is the number of reference vectors.
2. For each map unit i, collect a list of copies of all those training samples x, whose nearest reference vector belongs to the topological neighborhood set N_i of unit i.
3. Take for each new reference vector the mean over the respective list.
4. Repeat from 2 a few times.

This algorithm is particularly effective if the initial values of the reference vectors are already roughly ordered, even though they would not yet approximate to the distribution of the samples. It should be noticed that the above algorithm contains no learning-rate parameter; therefore it seems to yield stabler asymptotic values for the m_i than the original SOM. We shall revert to this algorithm in Sec. III.

Definition of the size of the neighborhood set N_i can be similar as in the basic SOM algorithms. "Shrinking" of N_i in this algorithm means that the neighborhood size is decreased while the steps 2 and 3 are repeated . At the last iterations, N_i may contain the element i only, and the last steps of the algorithm are then equivalent with the K-means clustering.

E. The SOM for Operators with Nonobservable Parameters or Nondifferentiable Similarity Measures

The SOM philosophy can actually be much more general than discussed so far. For instance, in a two-dimensional array it is possible to associate with each cell any complex *operator*, like a filter for dynamic signals, whereby the filter parameters may not directly be observable or controllable. Still it would be possible to run an input sequence $\{x(t)\}$ through each filter and compare the integrated responses; the cell with the maximum integral or energy of response can be characterized as the "winner". But how can we make such cells learn, to develop an *ordered* SOM?

The solution to this problem is a kind of "evolution" or "natural choice" that resembles the genetic algorithms. Let us denote the operator associated with cell i in the array by F_i. Denote the input information, eventually a process, by X. The "winner" with respect to X is now denoted by F_c. In the first method we assume that new candidates or versions for the F_i operators called G can be generated easily; for instance, if they belong to some category that is parametrized, by a random choice of the parameters one can easily generate one or several candidates G, although these parameters were not observable later on. During one "learning" step, the same input process X is operated by both the F_i and a number of tentative G, and among these tests one eventually finds the best operator G_c that is better (in terms of some criterion) than F_c. Then F_c is *replaced* by G_c *with a probability* P, where P corresponds to the learning rate $h_{cc}(t)$ in the other SOM models. Moreover, every other F_i (or eventually operators in a bounded neighborhood N_c around cell c) will similarly be replaced by G_c with the probability $h_{ci}(t)$. These replacements shall be statistically independent, i.e., the decisions concerning replacements in the neighboring cells are drawn independently, but with the given probabilities.

It may also be self-evident that the F_i and G must somehow be *normalized*. For instance, one might require that the impulse responses of every F_i and G should have the same integral or energy.

If the operators are so complex that their on-line generation as described above is time-consuming, one may keep up another table, eventually a nonordered linear list that contains precomputed operators denoted by G_j. The G_j list can also be updated with new items intermittently. In order that the "learning" procedure explained below were gradual enough, it is important that the size of the G_j list is all the time much greater than the size of the F_i array, so that the G_j list contains plenty of gradual intermediate cases of the F_i. Now X is operated by every F_i and every G_j, and the best matches in the two tables, according to some criterion, are indexed by c in the F_i array, and by d in the G_j list, respectively. Assume that the G_d functional of X represents a better match than the F_c functional of X. The substitution of F_c and its neighbors by G_d is then made as explained in connection with the first method.

It might turn out that this kind of operator array, without preprocessing, were directly applicable, e.g., to the recognition or analysis of time-domain signals such as continuous speech. Filters sensitive to temporal features might be defined, e.g., as linear or nonlinear recursive expressions of the time-domain samples. The input process X might be taken from a sufficiently long time interval that extends over a few phonemes, to take the temporal context effects into account, too. The next sample X would then be taken from another interval that *overlaps* with the previous one, etc. In this way the different cells of the map become trained, say, to different *sequences* of the speech waveforms, in analogy with the methods reported in [12].

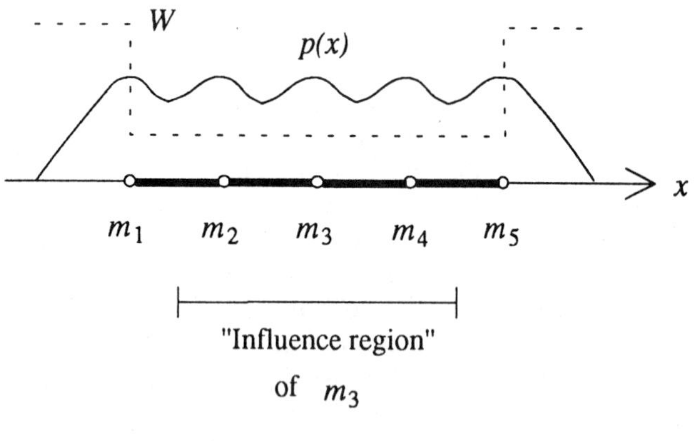

Fig. 2. One-dimensional SOM with five reference "vectors" m_i that approximate to the probability density function $p(x)$, and delineation of the weighting function W.

III. Elimination of Border Effects and Application of the Batch Map to Telecommunications

In the transmission of digitally encoded signals, the discrete signal states are often represented by amplitude modulation. In the QAM (quadrature amplitude modulation) method, the same frequency channel transmits two carrier waves that have a relative phase shift of 90 degrees. If each carrier has k possible discrete amplitude states, the whole channel can transmit one of k^2 digital states at a time. Such discrete signal states form a k by k lattice in a two-dimensional signal space. A SOM array, with k^2 reference vectors, can be made to follow and detect (demodulate) such signal vectors: if the signals are corrupted by noise and time-variable transmission properties of the channel, the SOM follows the corrupted states adaptively, and each of its cells acts as a decoder of the respective signal state. In practice, the SOM must be preceded by an equalizer, which first compensates for the general transfer properties of the channel, whereby the SOM can be used to control the equalizer [6]. In the present context, however, we shall omit the equalizer and concentrate on the problem of adaptive detection.

Consider first a single carrier wave that is amplitude-modulated by one of k discrete states. Consider also a one-dimensional SOM with k reference "vectors" (scalars) $m_i(t) \in \Re$; each of the $m_i(t)$ can be made to follow one particular signal state. One property of the simple SOM, which is harmful in this application, is occurrence of border effects, on account of which the $m_i(t)$ do not accurately approximate to $p(x)$, the density function of input. The compensation method used in [6] was not yet quite effective. Contrary to that, the solution presented in this paper seems to be very close to ideal.

Inspection of Fig. 2 may facilitate understanding of the reason for the border effects. Let every cell of the SOM have two neighbors, except one at the ends. For instance, the "influence region" of cell i ($i > 2$ and $i < k - 1$) (or the range of x values that can affect cell i) is $R_i = [\frac{1}{2}(m_{i-2} + m_{i-1}), \frac{1}{2}(m_{i+1} + m_{i+2})]$. In the asymptotic equilibrium, according to (13), every m_i must coincide with the centroid of $p(x)$ over the respective R_i. The definition of the "influence regions" near the borders of the SOM is different, however, and therefore the m_i do not approximate to $p(x)$ everywhere in the same way.

In computing the centroids, it is now possible to provide the x samples with *conditional weights* W that depend on index i and the relative magnitude of x and m_i. This weighting can be used both in the old stepwise SOM algorithm (with the given definition of the neighborhood set N_c), and with the Batch Map, too. In the former case, the weight should be applied to the learning rate α, not to x. For to guarantee stability, one must then have $\alpha W < 1$, so this trick is not applicable during the first steps when α is still large. In the Batch Map algorithm, however, the x samples are always weighted directly, so no such restriction exists. Henceforth we assume that the Batch Map is used.

The following rules may first sound a bit complicated, but they are simple to program, and in practice they are also very effective and robust in eliminating the border effects to a large extent. Assume that the m_i values are already ordered.

Weighting Rule for the One-Dimensional SOM:

> *In updating, each x sample is provided with weight W. Normally $W = 1$, but $W > 1$ for the border (end) cells in the case that x is bigger than the biggest m_i or smaller than the smallest m_i, AND when the updating of the border cell (but not of its neighbors) is due.*

Consider the special case that $p(x)$ is *uniform* over some connected domain of x and zero outside it. It may then be easy to deduce on the basis of Fig. 2 and the Weighting Rule that if we select for the special weight a value of $W = 9$, all the m_i will become equidistant in the asymptotic equilibrium; then they describe $p(x)$ in an unbiased way. Naturally, for other forms of $p(x)$, we should take other values for W. In those practical cases that occur in signal detection, however, the default value $W = 9$ compensates for the most part of the border effects in general.

It is possible to eliminate the border effects *totally*, if after a couple Batch Map iterations the neighborhood set N_i is replaced by i, i.e., having a couple of simple K-means iterations at the end. It is known that the K-means clustering is unbiased for static data, but it cannot be used to follow stochastically occurring time-variable signal states as such, because it does not "notice" if one signal state does not occur for some time; the algorithm tries to approximate to the rest of the states (cf. Fig. 3). The Batch Map algorithm, on the contrary, is more stable, because when any m_i is updated, the neighboring m_i values are updated, too, which has a regularizing effect on the m_i. The m_i are thus much less sensitive to missing signal states. Combination of a couple weighted Batch Map iterations and a couple K-means iterations is robust and usually leads to a totally unbiased result, as demonstrated in Fig. 3 (b).

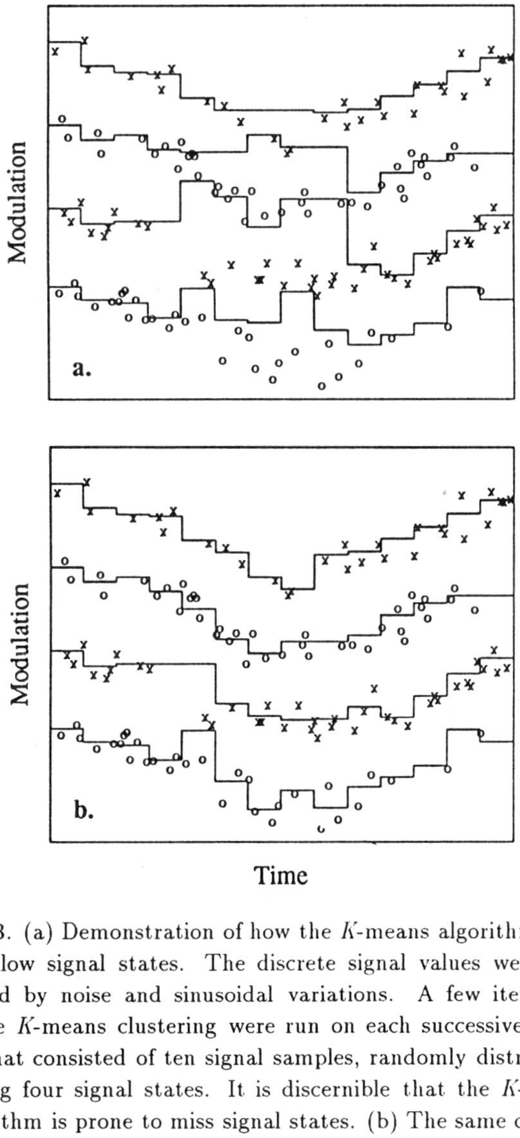

Fig. 3. (a) Demonstration of how the K-means algorithm tries to follow signal states. The discrete signal values were corrupted by noise and sinusoidal variations. A few iterations of the K-means clustering were run on each successive interval that consisted of ten signal samples, randomly distributed among four signal states. It is discernible that the K-means algorithm is prone to miss signal states. (b) The same demonstration for two iterations of the Batch Map followed by two iterations of the K-means algorithm. The number of errors has radically reduced.

In the QAM method with a two-dimensional SOM, the weighting rules are slightly different. While we used, say, the value of $W = 9$ for the end cells in the one-dimensional array, in the updating of the two-dimensional array we must have a different weight W_1 for the corner cells, and another value W_2 for edge cells that are not in the corner. Inside the array, the weight is equal to unity.

Weighting Rules for the Two-Dimensional SOM:

> *The value W_1 is applied if both of the following two conditions are satisfied: A1. The value of x is in one of the four "outer corner sectors," i.e. outside the array and such that the m_i of some corner cell is closest. A2. Updating of this selected m_i (but not of any other of its topological neighbors) is due.*
>
> *The value W_2 is applied if both of the following two conditions are satisfied: B1. The value of x lies outside the m_i array, but the closest m_i does not belong to any corner cell. B2. Updating of the selected edge cell or any of its topological neighbors, which must be one of the edge cells (eventually even a corner cell) is due.*

If $p(x)$ in the two-dimensional signal space were uniform over a square domain and zero outside it, it will be easy to deduce, in analogy with the one-dimensional case, that for equidistant equilibrium distribution of the m_i values we must have $W_1 = 81$, $W_2 = 9$. Again, for other $p(x)$ the compensation is not total with these weights. Then, as earlier, the Batch Map process may be run a couple iterations, followed by a couple K-means iterations. Such a combination of methods is again both robust and unbiased and follows the two-dimensional signal states very effectively.

IV. Physiological Interpretation of the SOM

It is possible to ask just how "neural" the SOM algorithms are. The same question could be posed about the other traditional feedforward and feedback "neural networks", too, the analytical descriptions of which are developed further in the computational than in the biological direction. Therefore it may be of special interest to note that the SOM can be related to a biological neural network in many essential details, as shown below.

A comprehensive discussion of this new physiological SOM model can be found in [7]; let only its main features be reviewed here.

A. The WTA Network

Consider a planar neural network (Fig. 4) where each cell receives input from some external sources, and the cells are

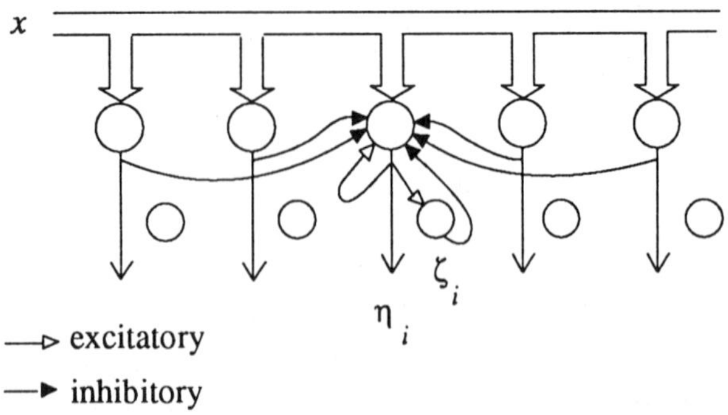

Fig. 4. Simplified model of a distributed neural network (cross section of a two-dimensional array). Each location consists of an excitatory principal input neuron and an inhibitory interneuron that feeds back locally. The lateral corrections between the principal input neurons may or may not be made via interneurons.

further interconnected by abundant lateral feedbacks. In the simplest case the same set of input signals is connected to all cells in this piece of network.

Assume that the output activity η_i (spiking frequency) of the input neuron i in the network is described [7, 8] by

$$d\eta_i/dt = I_i - \gamma(\eta_i) , \tag{17}$$

where I_i is the combined effect of all inputs, i.e. afferent inputs as well as lateral feedbacks, on cell i embedded in the layered network. Let $\gamma(\eta_i)$ describe the net effect of all loss or leakage effects that oppose to I_i. This is an abbreviated way of writing: since $\eta_i \geq 0$, (17) only holds when $\eta_i > 0$, or when $\eta_i = 0$ and $I_i - \gamma(\eta_i) \geq 0$, whereas otherwise $d\eta_i/dt = 0$.

If we write $I_i = I_i^e + I_i^f$, where the superscript e means "external" or afferent input, and f the lateral feedback, respectively, then in the simplest model we have

$$I_i^e = m_i^{\mathrm{T}} x = \sum_j \mu_{ij}\xi_j , \tag{18}$$

$$I_i^f = \sum_k g_{ik}\eta_k . \tag{19}$$

Here $x = (\xi_1, \xi_2, \ldots, \xi_n)^{\mathrm{T}} \in \Re^n$ again means the input data vector, or the vector of signal activities on a set of axons that is assumed to be connected in parallel to all cells of this network, and $m_i = (\mu_{i1}, \mu_{i2}, \ldots, \mu_{in})^{\mathrm{T}} \in \Re^n$ is redefined to be the corresponding vector of synaptic strengths of cell i. The $g_{ik} \in \Re$ describe effective lateral coupling strengths of cells in the planar array. For simplicity, it is assumed that g_{ii} is independent of i, and the g_{ik}, $k \neq i$ are mutually equal.

In the above system of equations, the only and rather general further restrictions shall be $\mu_{ij} > 0$, $\xi_j > 0$ (i.e., the external inputs are mainly excitatory), $g_{ii} > 0$, $g_{ik} < 0$ for $k \neq i$, $|g_{ik}| > |g_{ii}|$, $\gamma > 0$, and $d^2\gamma/d\eta^2 > 0$.

Starting with arbitrary (nonnegative) different m_i and $\eta_i(0) = 0$, the output η_c of that cell for which $m_i^{\mathrm{T}}x$ is maximum ("winner") will converge to an asymptotic high value, whereas the other η_i, $i \neq c$ tend to zero. This convergence property and the uniqueness of the winner can be proved mathematically [7].

As this network must respond to new inputs continually, the output state $\{\eta_i\}$ must be *reset* before application of a new input. In this model resetting is done automatically by providing each cell with an extra local inhibitory integrating feedback loop, eventually through an interneuron with feedback variable ζ_i (Fig. 4) described by the system equation

$$d\zeta_i/dt = b\eta_i - \theta , \tag{20}$$

where b and θ are scalar parameters. Also here we must state that (20) only holds if $\zeta_i > 0$, or if $\zeta_i = 0$ and $b\eta_i - \theta \geq 0$, whereas otherwise $d\zeta_i/dt = 0$. The complete equation corresponding to (17) reads

$$d\eta_i/dt = I_i - a\zeta_i - \gamma(\eta_i) , \tag{21}$$

where a is another scalar parameter.

This WTA circuit operates in *cycles* like a multivibrator, and each cycle can be thought to correspond to one discrete-time phase in (2) or (3). Normally the input is also thought to be changed at each new cycle; however, if the input is steady for a longer time, the next cycle selects the "runner-up", after which the "winner" is selected again, etc.

The cyclic operation of this WTA circuit is illustrated in Fig. 5.

B. Almost-Hebbian Learning

Most neural-network models, in one way or another, make use of the synaptic adaptation law named *Hebb's hypothesis.* If ξ is a presynaptic signal and η the output (spiking) activity of a neuron, the efficacy (strength, weight) of the synapse is thereby assumed to increase in proportion to $\xi\eta$.

At least two severe problems have now to be mentioned. First, since ξ, $\eta \geq 0$, then the efficacy can only grow or stay constant. In order that adaptation be reversible, some extra stabilizing term or terms should be subtracted from $\xi\eta$. Second, one has to take into account that neural cells are usually ramified, and the postsynaptic effect (proportional to η) must be propagated unattenuated even to the most distal branches and synapses.

If it is essential, as it seems, that the plasticity (modifiability) of a synapse is a function of the cell's output, then the quickest and most uniform retrograde messenger for this information would be a chemical agent that is

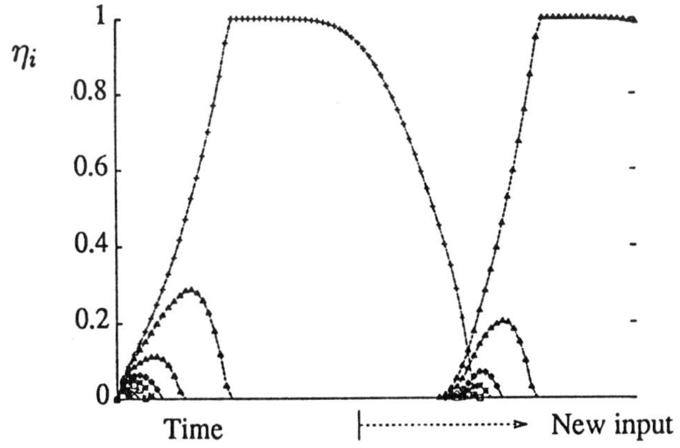

Fig. 5. Demonstration of the WTA function provided with automatic reset. The first inputs were applied at time zero. New inputs were applied as indicated by the dotted arrow. The network consisted of 20 cells, and the inputs $I_i^e = m_i^T x$ were selected as random numbers from the interval (0, 1). The g_{ii} were equal to 0.5 and the $g_{ij}, i \neq j$, were -2.0, respectively. The loss function had the form $\gamma(\eta) = 0.1 \ln \frac{1+\eta}{1-\eta}$; other simpler laws can also be used. The feedback parameters were $a = b = 1, \theta = 0.5$. The network operates as follows: The first "winner" is the cell that receives the largest input; its response will first stabilize to a high value, while the other outputs tend to zero. When the activity of the "winner" is temporarily depressed by the dynamic feedback, the other cells continue competing. The solution was obtained by the classical Runge-Kutta numerical integration method, using a step size of 10^{-5}.

produced in proportion to the postsynaptic activity and spreads back to the synaptic sites extracellularly. As a matter of fact, plenty of experimental evidence for such agents, of which the most primary one is nitric oxide (NO), has accumulated in a couple of recent years (cf., e.g., [9]). Among the numerous chemicals that are present at the cells, there probably also exist other similar factors, which have not yet been detected, however. Such chemicals can spread evenly over the cells' surfaces, even in their most distal branches.

An even more important aspect of the above diffuse chemical interaction is that due to diffusion, the postsynaptic chemical messenger can also affect *nearby* cells, not only the active cell itself. This property is central in the SOM process where the "winner", or the cell with the highest activation, is supposed to control adaptation in its *neighboring cells*, too. Attempts to explain such an interaction through collateral synaptic control have not been particularly successful, and one must also note that the anatomy of the biological neural networks is not isotropic enough for to define a symmetric neighborhood function $h_{ci}(t)$. If, on the other hand, the lateral interaction during learning were implemented by diffuse chemical substances, its geometric form would be rather isotropic, independent of the microanatomy of the network, and thus very beneficial for the SOM process.

We are now ready to set up the adaptation equation corresponding to (2) or (3), which we write:

$$d\mu_{ij}/dt = (\xi_j - \lambda \mu_{ij} \sum_r \mu_{ir} \xi_r) \sum_l h_{il} \eta_l \,, \qquad (22)$$

where λ and h_{il} are system parameters. This equation can be justified in the following way. The rate of change of the synaptic efficacy, $d\mu_{ij}/dt$, is *modulated* by $\sum_l h_{il}\eta_l$, a weighted sum of the activities of the nearby cells, which describes the strength of the diffuse chemical effect of cell l on cell i; h_{il} is a function of the distance of these cells. Synaptic changes shall be proportional to ξ_j like in the Hebb synapses, but their reversibility is guaranteed by the active "forgetting" effect, or disturbance due to the adjacent synapses. Typically, forgetting effects are proportional to the variable itself (here μ_{ij}), and if the disturbance caused by synaptic site r is mediated through the postsynaptic potential, such an effect must further be proportional to $\mu_{ir}\xi_r$. Naturally this effect would be some function of the distance between sites j and r, too, but for simplicity we "compartmentalize" a subset of synapses that are located near each other, and approximately act as one collectively interacting set. If the interaction between synapses is mediated chemically, say, by nitric oxide, the size of such an interacting synaptic subset at the cell is then roughly defined by the diffusion length of this chemical.

If we now think that the factor $\sum_l h_{il}\eta_l$ corresponds to the time-variable neighborhood function $h_{ci}(t)$ in the SOM algorithm, if we realize that only the speed of the ordering process depends on this factor, and if we further assume that the range of index r defines those input signals that are regarded to constitute the input vector x relating to this particular ordering process, then (22), which is expressed in continuous time, and (3), which is a discrete-time approximation, can easily be found equivalent.

The most important message of the above discussion is that it motivates biologically the following "idealized" features of the SOM theory: 1. A natural, robust way for the implementation of the WTA function. 2. A realistic interpretation of the Hebb-like law of synaptic plasticity. 3. Automatic normalization of *subsets* of synaptic vectors. 4. A natural explanation of the lateral interaction (neighborhood function) between neurons in learning.

A more rigorous discussion of the physiological SOM model can be found in [7].

V. Using Low-Accuracy Signals in Vector Quantization

The SOM and the *Learning Vector Quantization (LVQ)* [1, 2] are two "neural network" algorithms that are closely related. Learning in the SOM is unsupervised, while the LVQ is a supervised method. The cells in the SOM interact (during learning) in the lateral direction, while the LVQ cells are updated independently. In principle, both the SOM and the LVQ could be used for pattern recognition (classification); however, if supervised learning is possible, the LVQ is usually two to three times more accurate.

It is a general notion that the traditional neural-network algorithms need a numerical accuracy of three to four decimal digits. It will now be shown that the LVQ and SOM tolerate much worse accuracies.

The experiments reported in this section were actually performed by the LVQ, but similar results may be obtained for the SOM, too. In short, it has been shown that if the dimensionality of the m_i vectors is high (> 100), their component values *during classification* (or determination of the "winner") can be approximated by as few as three or four *bits*, without noticeable reduction in recognition accuracy. Thus, if learning is made off-line, preferably with a higher accuracy, the approximations of the m_i values can be loaded onto very simple hardware devices. The low accuracy demands also make it possible to apply special solutions, such as replacement of arithmetic circuits by precomputed tables or memories, from which the values of the classification functions can be *searched* rapidly.

One of the problems studied in our laboratory over the years has been speech recognition, whereby we have collected a large database of Finnish speech. The speech states are represented every 10 ms by 20 cepstral coefficients [10]. To someone unfamiliar with this task it may not be quite clear how much statistical variance the same phonemes, even for the same speaker, may have. For this reason, increasing accuracy in feature detection, e.g., in cepstral amplitude detection is reasonable only up to a certain limit, whereas increasing the number of different feature variables is much more effective in improving statistical accuracy [11, 12]. For instance, picking the cepstral coefficients from the 220-ms "time window" (Fig. 6) and concatenating them into a 140-dimensional feature vector yields an about 14-fold accuracy in phonemic recognition compared with recognition of single 20-dimensional feature vectors.

It is now demonstrated in the present paper that (i) a very similar recognition accuracy is achievable, although the feature *amplitudes* are *quantized* to a few, say, eight or 16 levels, (ii) with such a quantization, a very high computing power is achievable in decisions, using quite conventional circuit technology but unconventional architectures.

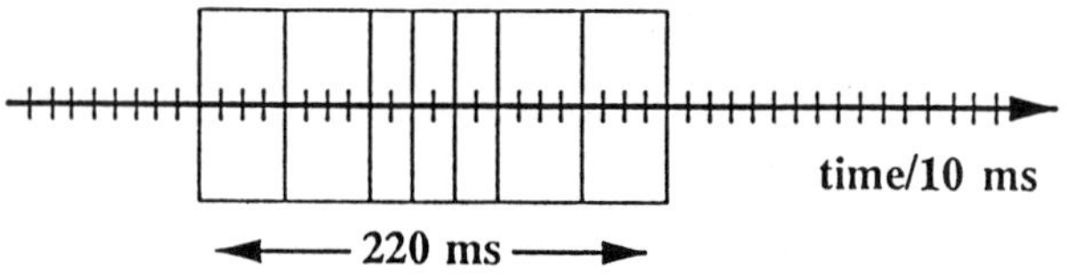

Fig. 6. Time window for phonemes.

First we evaluate how much the phonemic recognition results are reduced if the component values of the feature vectors, and those of the reference vectors are represented in a quantized scale. These figures describe the *average* accuracy taken over all the Finnish phonemes (for a single speaker): even /*k*/, /*p*/, and /*t*/ were recognized individually!

The quantization levels were selected to be equidistant, and the level values were set experimentally to approximate to the dynamic range of the cepstral coefficients. (Determination of optimal quantization levels for each vectorial component separately by the so-called scalar quantization, i.e., minimizing the average expected quantization errors was also tried, but the results were not much different.)

The cases studied were: (i) 20-dimensional input feature vectors formed of the coefficients of single cepstra taken over 10 ms intervals and using 200 reference vectors, (ii) 140-dimensional input feature vectors taken from the "time window" (cf. Fig. 6) and using 2000 reference vectors, respectively.

Table I
Effect of quantization: recognition accuracy, per cent

No. of bits	No. of quantization levels	Dimensionality of input and number of reference vectors: 20 times 200	140 times 2000
1	2	50.1	90.1
2	4	72.1	97.3
3	8	82.6	98.7
4	16	84.9	99.0
	Floating-point computing accuracy	85.9	99.0

The basic and most frequently computed expression in classification, based on vector quantization methods (such as the SOM or the LVQ) is

$$c = \arg\min_i \left\{ \sum_{j=1}^{n} (\xi_j - \mu_{ij})^2 \right\} \quad (23)$$

Here the ξ_j are the components of vector x, and the μ_{ij} the components of vector m_i, respectively. It is to be noted that if the ξ_j and μ_{ij} are quantized, there exists only a finite and generally rather small number of their discrete-value combinations, for which the function $(\xi_j - \mu_{ij})^2$ can be tabulated completely. For instance, with 3-bit accuracy such a table contains 64 rows, and with 4 bits, 256 rows, respectively.

The curled-bracket expression in (23) may be computed by tabular search depicted in Fig. 7, whereas the $\min_i(\cdot)$ operation could best be left to software. The ξ_j and μ_{ij} can be loaded from a bus into the buffers, from which they are read cyclically. The expressions $(\xi_j - \mu_{ij})^2$ may be added in a fast accumulator, from which the result can be copied into the bus. Counting of loop indices, reading the arguments, and performing the table-look-up can be done by an autonomous control circuit of this hardware. If we have k reference vectors with dimensionality n, and T is the length of the clock cycle, then the computing time is roughly $k \cdot n \cdot T$. For instance, for the 140×2000 array and a typical clock frequency $1/T = 66$ MHz, classification time would be 4.2 msec.

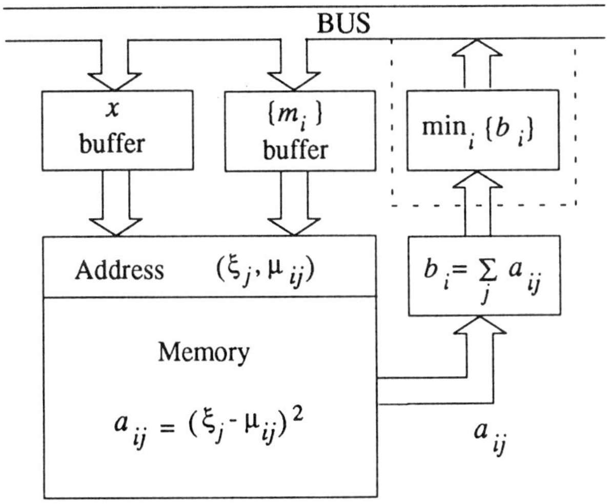

Fig. 7. Block scheme of the pattern-recognition architecture that makes use of tabular search in the evaluation of the classification function.

VI. Available Software

Recently, two software packages, the LVQ_PAK and the SOM_PAK, were released by us. They are available free of charge at the Internet address cochlea.hut.fi (130.233.168.48).

The LVQ_PAK contains near-Bayesian pattern recognition methods, whereas the SOM_PAK can be used, e.g., for the visualization of complex process states.

References

[1] T. Kohonen, *Self-Organization and Associative Memory*, 3rd ed. Heidelberg: Springer, 1989.

[2] T. Kohonen, "The self-organizing map," *Proc. IEEE*, vol. 78, pp. 1464-1480, September 1990.

[3] J. Makhoul, S. Roucos, and H. Gish, "Vector quantization in speech coding," *Proc. IEEE*, vol. 73, pp. 1551-1588, 1985.

[4] T. Kohonen, "Self-organizing maps: optimization approaches," in *Artificial Neural Networks*, T. Kohonen, K. Mäkisara, O. Simula, and J. Kangas, Eds. Amsterdam: Elsevier (North-Holland), 1991, vol. 2, pp. 981-990.

[5] H. Robbins and S. Monro, "A stochastic approximation method," *Ann. Math. Statist.*, vol. 22, pp. 400-407, 1951.

[6] T. Kohonen, K. Raivio, O. Simula, and J. Henriksson, "Start-up behaviour of a neural network assisted decision feedback equalizer in a two-path channel," *Proc. IEEE Int. Conf. on Communications* (Chigago, Ill., USA, 1992) pp. 1523-1527.

[7] T. Kohonen, "Physiological interpretation of the self-organizing map algorithm," *Neural Networks*, in press.

[8] T. Kohonen, "An introduction to neural computing," *Neural Networks*, vol. 1, pp. 3-16, 1988.

[9] M. S. Fazeli, "Synaptic plasticity: on the trail of the retrograde messenger," *Trends in Neuroscience*, vol. 15, pp. 115-117, 1992.

[10] K. Torkkola et al., "Status report of the Finnish phonetic typewriter project," in *Artificial Neural Networks*, T. Kohonen, K. Mäkisara, O. Simula, and J. Kangas, Eds. Amsterdam: Elsevier (North-Holland), 1991, vol. 1, pp. 771-776.

[11] T. Kohonen, "New developments of Learning Vector Quantization and Self-Organizing Map," in *SYNAPSE'92, Symposium on Neural Networks; Alliances and Perspectives in Senri 1992* (Osaka, Japan, 1992).

[12] J. Mäntysalo, K. Torkkola, and T. Kohonen, "LVQ-based speech recognition with high-dimensional context vectors," *Proc. ICSLP, 1992 Int. Conf. on Spoken Language Processing* (Banff, Alberta, Canada, 1992) vol. 1, pp. 539-542.

FUN: Optimization of Fuzzy Rule Based Systems Using Neural Networks

Sandra M. Sulzberger
Institute of Robotics
ETH Zurich
8092 Zurich (Switzerland)
<sandra@ifr.ethz.ch>

Nadine N. Tschichold-Gürman
Institute of Robotics
ETH Zurich
8092 Zurich (Switzerland)
<nadine@ifr.ethz.ch>

Sjur J. Vestli
Institute of Robotics
ETH Zurich
8092 Zurich (Switzerland)
<vestli@ifr.ethz.ch>

Abstract---**This paper describes a method for optimization of fuzzy rule based systems using neural networks. A new neural network model with special neurons has been developed so that the translation of fuzzy rules and membership functions into the network is possible. The performance of this network and hence the quality of the original rule base is then improved by training the network using a combination of neural network learning algorithms. The optimized rules and membership functions can be extracted from the net and used in normal fuzzy inference tools. This net has been tested on the "WallJumperOver"[1] and the problem of local navigation for mobile robots.**

I. Introduction

Many complex processes are difficult to model mathematically because of their nonlinear and time varying behaviors. The local navigation of a mobile robot is one of these processes, where it is difficult to find an accurate model. Different information processing methods like fuzzy logic, neural networks and their combinations are under evaluation at the Institute of Robotics, for application on this and similar problems.

As an example, consider the case of a mobile robot designed to perform a specific indoor task. This places some requirements on the robot motion control: it must be robust (i.e. have extensive error recovery features), adapt to changes in the environment and it cannot rely upon an exact model of the robot or its environment. If there are unmodeled obstacles on the path taken by the robot, it must be able to detect them with its sensors and to avoid them.

Neurocontrollers are robust and adaptive, however the main disadvantage compared to other controllers is that the operation cannot be stated explicitly. On the other hand, in fuzzy logic based systems the operation is given through the rules and the membership functions. Furthermore, fuzzy controllers are also robust, but not adaptive.

For several problems within the field of robotics it is desirable to have all the features described above (robust, adaptive, and possibility of explicitly stating the operation) for the implementation of controllers. FUN (FUzzy Net), a development of the Institute of Robotics, is a step in this direction.

Experience with Fuzzy Logic show that this technique allows a fast development of controllers. However, due to the large number of parameters and little knowledge about their exact influence on the behavior of the controller optimization is difficult.

Research on the possibilities of combining these two techniques has been done for several years in Japan. Fuzzy neurons have been proposed [4] that are able to calculate a conjunction for linguistic variables. There are nets, that are used to calculate the inference [8]. Many neural networks have been tested on the possibility to extract rules from them [6]. There have also been attempts to use neural networks to learn multidimensional membership functions [11]. A method for learning fuzzy rules in a net is described in[5].

The common factor of these methods is that they do not allow a simple bijective mapping from the rulebase into the net. Where a learning method is used, as in [11], there is no possibility to extract the result from the net. There is no solution to the problem, where both rules and membership functions are to be learned simultaneously.

II. Fuzzy Net FUN

A new neural network model has been developed which is very well suited to represent logic expressions. In order to enable an unequivocal translation of fuzzy rules and membership functions into the network, special neurons have been defined, which, through their activation functions, can evaluate logic expressions. Similar neurons have also been proposed in [4], however these are very restricted in their use. The neurons proposed here are for multi purpose use.

A. Architecture of FUN

The network consists of an input, an output and three hidden layers. The neurons of each layer have different activation functions representing the different stages in the calculation of fuzzy inference. The activation functions can be chosen individually for different problems (e.g. AND can be implemented as the MIN-function, the dot product function, or any other function).

The network is initialized with a fuzzy rulebase and the corresponding membership functions. As an example, in Fig. 1. the structure of a net is shown, which represents a rulebase with two variables and one rule.

The input variables are stored in the input neurons. The neurons in the first hidden layer contain the membership functions and thus perform a fuzzification of the input values. In the second hidden layer, the conjunctions (fuzzy-AND) are calculated. In the nodes of the third hidden layer, the

1. The "WallJumperOver" is explained in section (IV.) .

0-7803-0999-5/93/$03.00 ©1993 IEEE

Structure:

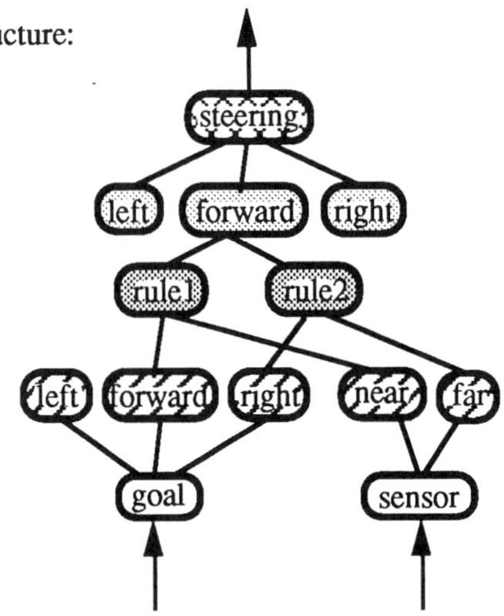

Activation functions per layer:

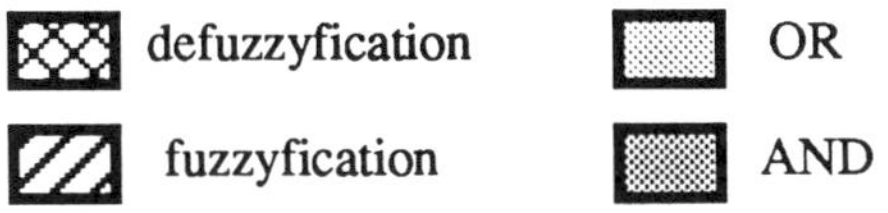

Rule:

IF (goal IS forward AND sensor IS near)
OR (goal IS right AND sensor IS far) THEN
steering := forward
END

Fig. 1. Structure of FUN, and the corresponding rule base.

membership functions of the output variables can be found. Their activation function is a fuzzy-OR. The output neurons contain the output variables and have a defuzzification as activation function. Therefore the propagation of the input values through FUN is equivalent to making fuzzy inference with the given rule base.

III. LEARNING STRATEGIES

The rules and the membership functions are used to construct an initial FUN network. The rulebase can then be optimized by changing the structure of the net or the data in the neurons. To learn the rules, the connections between the rules and the fuzzy values are changed. To learn the membership functions, the data of the nodes in the first and thirs hidden layers are changed. The net can be trained with the standard neural network training strategies such as reinforcement or supervised learning (Fig. 2) as described in [10], [9], [1].

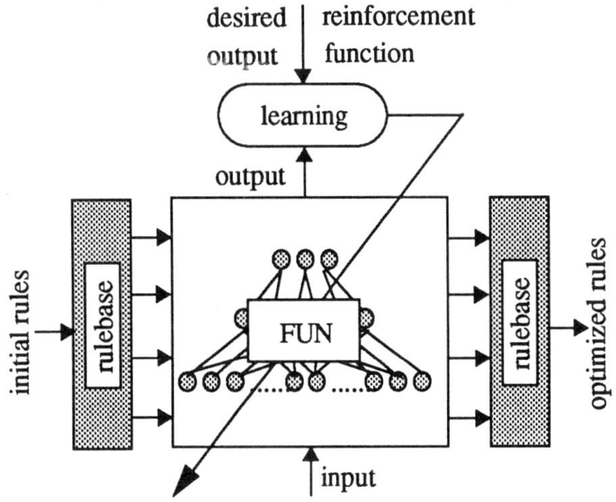

Fig. 2. Learning strategies for FUN

A. Learning of the Rules

The rules are represented in the net through the connections between the layers. The learning of the rules is implemented as a stochastic search in the rulespace: a randomly chosen connection is changed and the new network performance is verified with a cost function. If the performance is worse, the change is undone, otherwise it is kept and some other changes are tested, until the net shows the desired input- output behavior.

In the example below (Fig. 3), a change is made in the connections between the first and the second hidden layers for a modification of the conjunction.

As the learning algorithm should preserve the semantic of the rules, it has to be controlled that no two values of the

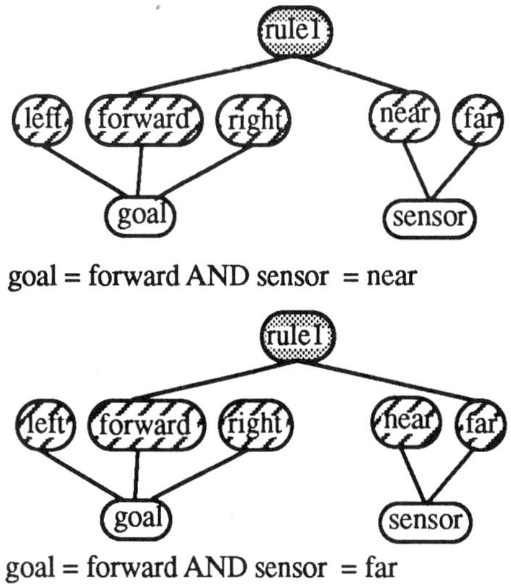

Fig. 3. Connections between the first and second hidden layers before and after a change.

same variable appear in the same rule. This is achieved by swapping connections between the values of the same variable.

B. Learning of the Membership Functions

Manual optimizations of rulebases have shown, that the overlap of the membership functions have a big influence on the performance of the contoller [12]. This means that the position and the width of the membership functions have a big influence on the inference.

In FUN the membership functions are represented by triangles (Fig. 4). These triangles are specified with three membership function descriptors (MFDs); it is presumed, that the membership functions are normalised, i.e. they always have a constant height of 1. Other shapes could also be represented, without major change to the system.

The learning algorithm for the membership function is a combination of gradient descent and a stochastic search. A maximum change in a random direction is initially assigned to all MFDs. In a random fashion one MFD of one linguistic variable is selected, and the network performance is tested with this MFD altered according to the allowable change for this MFD. If the network performs better according to a given cost function, the new value is accepted and the next time another change is tried in the same direction (Fig. 5). If the network gets worse, the change is reversed and the following tests are done in the other direction.

To guarantee convergence, the changes are reduced after each training step and shrink asymptotically towards zero. The learning rate specifies the speed at which this is reduced (Fig. 6).

It might often be desirable that the size of the values should stay within a given range (max, min), and the condition $w_{left} \leq w_{middle} \leq w_{right}$ must hold at all times. In this implementation, only those changes are carried out, which do not violate the restrictions imposed on the MFDs.

Representation as a curve:

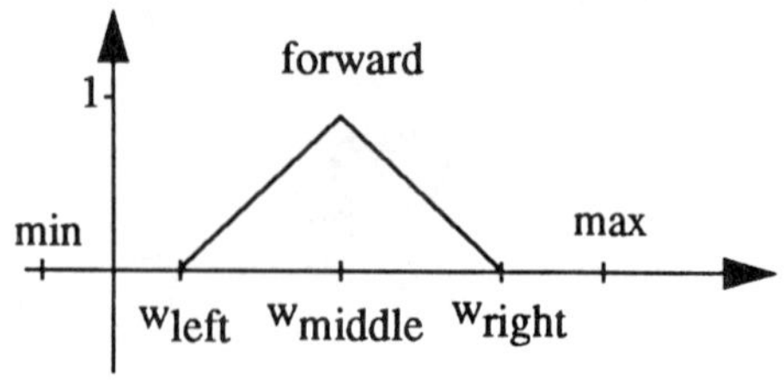

Representation with three MFDs:

VALUE forward =

(wleft , wmiddle, wright)

Fig. 4. Representation of the membership function as a triangle.

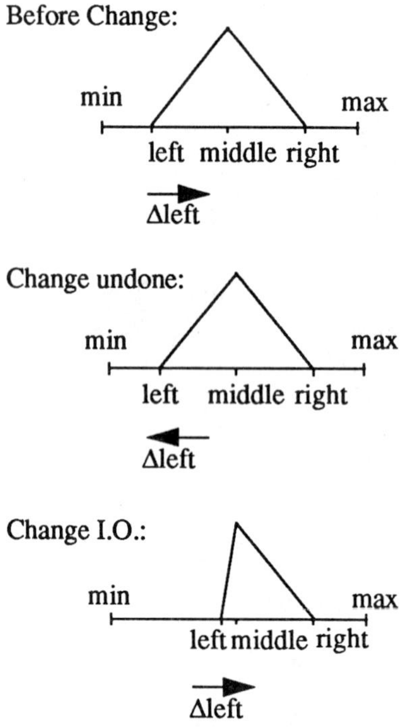

Fig. 5. Optimization of the membership functions by changing position and width of the curve.

With this learning method, an optimal size of a value is also found if it lies very close to a given border.

IV. Examples

The ability of the FUN to optimize a given rulebase with corresponding membership functions is demonstrated at two examples.

A. The WallJumperOver

In this example, a given rulebase is optimized using a supervised learning strategy. The rulebase specifies how to jump over a wall. The height of the wall and the horizontal speed of the jumper are given. The controller should then

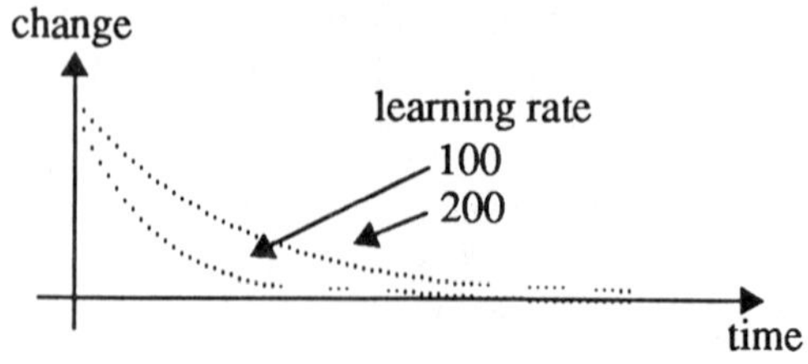

$$change(t) = change(t-1) - \frac{change(t-1)}{learningrate}$$

Fig. 6. Reduction of the change according to the learning rate.

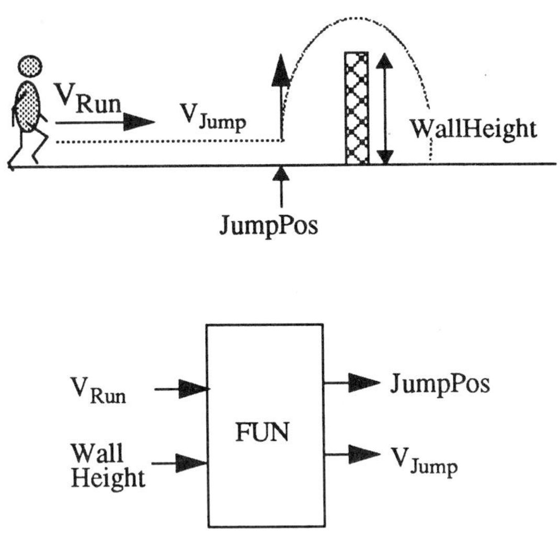

Fig. 7 The WallJumperOver and associated controller.

calculate the vertical speed and jump position at which the WallJumper will safely jump over the wall (Fig. 7).

This example was chosen, since learning examples can be easily created using two simple physical formulas. Still there is no easy or obvious connection between the input- and output values. With this example, the learning ability of the FUN-net was tested.

As learning examples could be generated, a supervised learning was used to optimize this net. The cost function was defined as below:

$$Cost = \sum_{AllExamples} (DesiredOutput - ActualOutput)^2$$

With this example could be shown that FUN is able to optimize a given solution with supervised learning. The net is capable of optimizing the given set of rules and membership functions within a couple of thousand learning cycles (Fig. 8). It generates rules that let the WallJumper jump over the wall in almost all situations.

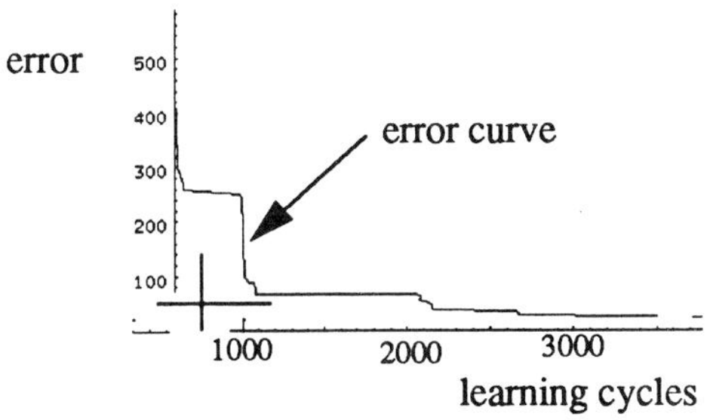

Fig. 8. Error curve for the "WallJumperOver."

B. Local Navigation for Mobile Robot Using FUN

A mobile robot should be able to drive from a start to a goal position and to avoid obstacles, if there are any. The controller for the local navigation has as input the sensor data and the direction, in which the goal lies. As output it should produce a steering angle (Fig. 9).

It is very difficult to create learning examples for the mobile robot navigation problem. Thus the supervised learning strategy used in the previous example is replaced with a reinforcement learning (RL) strategy. For RL a cost function must be defined. The cost function provides us with an evaluation of the path, and hence the rule base. The learning algorithm then attempts to optimize the cost function by adapting the network / rule base. The execution continues until either: the goal is reached, or the robot collides with an obstacle, or a predefined time, T, has elapsed. At the end of the execution the cost function is calculated as given below:

$$Cost = \begin{cases} Constant & \text{if robot drives into wall} \\ |\overrightarrow{Goal} - \overrightarrow{ActualPos}| & \text{otherwise} \end{cases}$$

An untrained net with an a priori defined rule base would typically perform as seen in Fig. 10 a), after optimization the controller performed as in Fig. 10 b). The oscillation in Fig. 10 a) is a result of contradictory rules in the rule base. A more demanding environment and the corresponding performance of the (optimized) controller can be seen in Fig. 11. The path produced by the controller for the environment given in Fig. 11 is clearly not optimal with respect to length. However, since the cost function takes no account of the path length this was expected. In order to optimize the performance of the controller even further than demonstrated in this paper, a different cost function taking more characteristics of the path into account must be devised.

V. Discussion and Future Work

In this paper the possibility of optimizing a fuzzy logic rulebase and membership functions with a new neural network model FUN has been demonstrated. The performance of FUN has been evaluated on two different problems. The learning capability of this network is clearly dependant on the quality of the learning examples (in the case of supervised learning) and the quality of the cost function (in the case of reinforcement learning).

Future work will include: enhancement of the learning algorithms with the option of adding new neurons in the

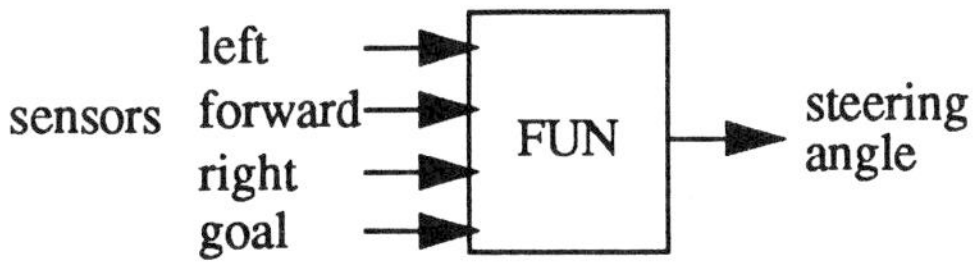

Fig. 9. Input and Output values for the mobile robot.

a)

b)

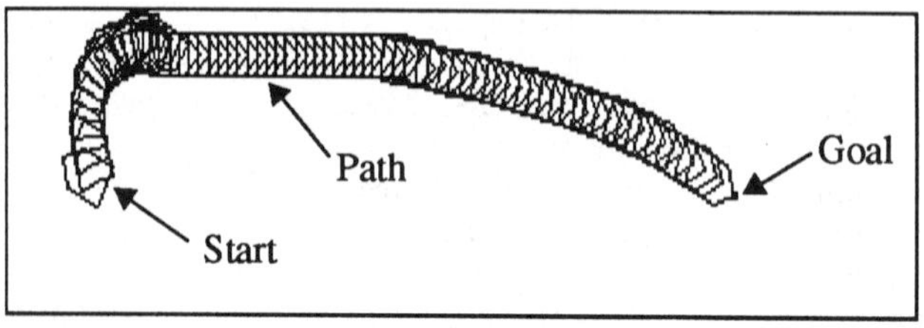

Fig. 10. Path of the mobile robot before (a) and after (b) learning

hidden layers (i.e. adding new rules and new membership functions to the rule base), introduction of weighted connections between the layers which allows differentiating between important and unimportant features, and evaluation of altenrative learning algorithms.

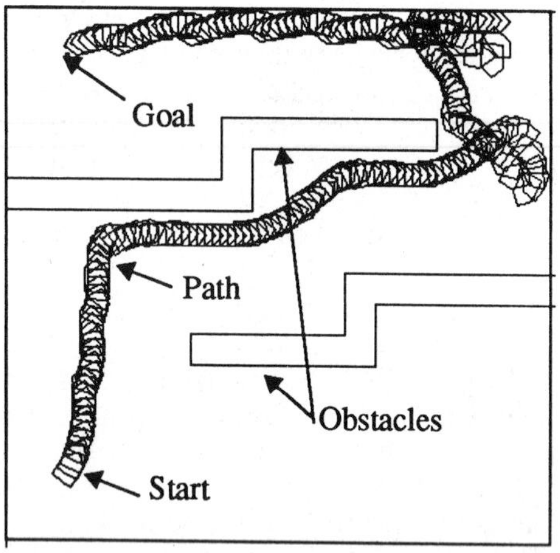

Fig. 11. Path of mobile robot in a complex environment (after optimization).

A method to analyze the consistency and the completeness of the rule base is also under development.

For the mobile robot navigation problem enhanced cost functions will be defined and tested. Further applications within the field of robotics are also under evaluation for possible utilization of FUN.

VI. References

[1] Bernasconi J., "Informationsverarbeitung in Neuronalen Netzwerken" Lecture notes, ETH Zuerich, 1990.

[2] Boviere S., Demaya B., Titli A.,"Fuzzy logic control compared with other automatics control approaches", 30. IEEE-CDC, Brighton, December 11-13, 1991.

[3] Enbutsu I., Baba K., Hara N., "Fuzzy Rule Extraction from a Multilayered Neural Network", International Joint Conference on Neural Networks, Seattle, WA, July 8-12, 1991, pp. II 461 - II 465.

[4] Gupta M.M., Qi, J., "On Fuzzy Neuron Models", International Joint Conference on Neural Networks, Seattle, WA, July 8-12, 1991, pp. II 431 - II 435.

[5] Kosko B., "Neural Networks and Fuzzy Systems", Prentice Hall, 1992.

[6] Lau, C., "Neural Networks", IEEE Press, 1992.

[7] Mamdani, E.H., "Applications of fuzzy algorithms for control of simple dynamic plant", Proceedings of IEE, vol.121(12), pp.1585-1588, 1974.

[8] Patrikar A., Provenc, J., "Neural Network Implementation of Linguistic Controllers", in: Hamza, M.H.(ed.): IASTED Proceedings on Robotics and manufacturing, Acta Press, 1989.

[9] Ritter H., et al.,"Neuronale Netze,Bonn/München" , Addison-Wesley, 1991.

[10] Rumelhart D.E. , Jamse L. McClelland et. al, Parallel Distributed Processing, MIT Press, 1988.

[11] Takagi H., Hayashi I., "NN-Driven Fuzzy Reasoning", International Journal of Approximate Reasoning, Vol 5, No 3, May 1991, pp. 191-212.

[12] Zadeh, L.A., "Fuzzy Sets", Information and Control, vol. 8, pp. 338-353, 1965.

[13] Zadeh, L.A., "Fuzzy algorithm", Inform and Control, vol. 12, pp. 94-102, 1068.

[14] Zimmermann, H.-J.,"Fuzzy Set Theorie- and its Applications", by Kluver in Boston, 1991.

Supervised Fuzzy ART: Training of a Neural Network for Pattern Classification via Combining Supervised and Unsupervised Learning

Hahn-Ming Lee and Chia-Shing Lai
Department of Electronic Engineering
National Taiwan Institute of Technology
Taipei, Taiwan
E-mail: HMLEE@TWNNTIT.BITNET

Abstract— A neural network model that incorporates a supervised mechanism into a fuzzy ART is presented. In any time, the training instances may or may not have desired outputs, that is, this model can handle supervised learning and unsupervised learning simultaneously. The unsupervised component finds the cluster relations of instances, then the supervised component learns the desired associations between clusters and categories. In addition, this model has the ability of incremental learning. It works equally well when instances in a cluster belong to different categories. This situation can not be handled well in unsupervised learning models, since they are unable to distinguish those instances in different categories with only the superficial input information. Moreover, multi-category and nonconvex classifications can also be dealt with.

I. Introduction

Artificial neural network training strategies can be identified as supervised and unsupervised learning [1]. In supervised learning, a target output pattern is associated with each training input pattern. On the other hand, the information to the network during unsupervised learning is just the input pattern. This two learning strategies have their specific environments and applications [2]. In this paper, we try to integrate these two approaches.

A neural network model that incorporates a supervised mechanism into the fuzzy ART [3] is presented here. It utilizes a learning theory called Nested Generalized Exemplar (NGE) theory [4]. The modified fuzzy ART subsystem quantizes the input vectors. A category node in this subsystem represents a cluster of the same category. It has a geometric representation of hyper-rectangle in feature space. Instances in a hyper-rectangle belong to the same category. Instances, belonging to different categories, in a cluster can be distinguished by nested hyper-rectangles [4]. A layer of Grossberg's Outstars [5] are used to learn the desired associations between categories and output patterns. In any time, the training instances may or may not have desired outputs. When the desired output is present, the model learns the desired association. When the desired output is absent, the model makes a prediction and generalization based on its learned associations. It also has the ability of incremental learning. In addition, multi-category and nonconvex classifications can be solved.

Though we derive our net from the fuzzy ART, there are some differences between them. The fuzzy ART is essentially a vector quantizer, forming categories according to the clusters of input vectors. In addition to the vector quantization, the supervised fuzzy ART can take supervised learning of categorical maps between analog vector pairs. In addition, the fuzzy ART stores only the concept (represented by the hyper-rectangle) in each category. In contrast, the supervised fuzzy ART stores both the concept and the prototype in each category. By including the statistic character (prototype) of clusters, the predictions for novel inputs are more reliable. On the other hand, the fuzzy ART recognizes only the regularities in input data. In contrast, the supervised fuzzy ART detects both the regularities and the exceptions. Exceptions are represented by nested hyper-rectangles. Thus, it can relieve the overgeneralization problems of neural net [6].

II. System Architecture

The network architecture is shown in Fig. 1. The two lower layers are essentially fuzzy ART with complement coding [3], but with different bottom-up weights and match control. The input vector is transmitted through the bottom-up connections from $F1$ input field to $F2$ category field. Then, a node in $F2$ is chosen as a candidate category for the input vector according to the choice function. Next, the concept contained in the category is read out and transmitted through the top-down connections from $F2$ to $F1$. If the category is accepted by the match control, the concept will be generalized via including the input vector into the original concept.

A layer of Grossberg's Outstars is superimposed on the

0-7803-0999-5/93/$03.00 ©1993 IEEE

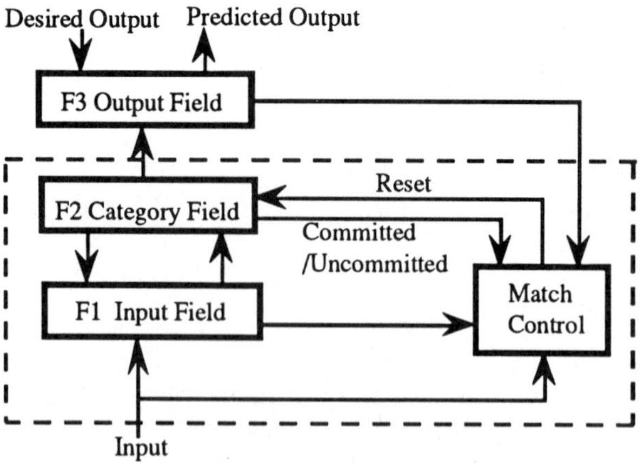

Fig. 1. System architecture of Supervised Fuzzy ART

top of $F2$ layer. During learning, the Outstar connection weights learn the desired output for the category chosen on $F2$. Initially, all categories are said to be uncommitted. After a category is selected and meets the match criteria, it becomes committed. If the chosen category is committed, $F3$ layer will read out the predicted output corresponding to the category. During learning, match signals that reflect the match degree between desired output and predicted one are computed in $F3$. The point is that another category must be chosen for the input if the desired output is different from the predicted one. The match control unit takes care of this. In what follows, we will detail the system architecture.

Input Vector: The input vector can be binary or analog. The components of analog input are in the interval [0,1]. The N-dimensional input vectors are preprocessed by complement coding [3]. The complement of the original input vector $\boldsymbol{I}$ is denoted by $\boldsymbol{I}^c$, where

$$\boldsymbol{I} = (i_1, ..., i_i, ..., i_N),$$
$$\boldsymbol{I}^c = (i_1^c, \cdots, i_i^c, \cdots, i_N^c),$$
$$\text{and } i_i^c = 1 - i_i . \tag{1}$$

Bottom-Up Connection Weights: There are bottom-up connections from those $F1$ nodes corresponding to the original input vector to every $F2$ node. The weight on the connection between the ith $F1$ node and the jth $F2$ node is denoted by b_{ji}. The weight vector $\boldsymbol{b}_j$ represents a prototype vector in the jth category. It supports the similarity measure between categories and the input vector (described in the choice function subsection). Initially, all bottom-up connection weights are set to 1. They are updated during learning (outlined below).

Top-Down Connection Weights: Unlike bottom-up connections, top-down connections connect every $F2$ node to every $F1$ node. The weight on the connection between the jth $F2$ node and the ith $F1$ node in $\boldsymbol{I}$ part is denoted by u_{ji}. Let v_{ji}^c denote the weight on the connection between the jth $F2$ node and the ith $F1$ node in $\boldsymbol{I}^c$ part. Each node j in $F2$ corresponds to a weight vector [3]

$$w_j = (u_j , v_j^c), \text{ where}$$
$$u_j = (u_{j1} , \cdots, u_{ji} , \cdots, u_{jN}),$$
$$v_j^c = (v_{j1}^c , \cdots, v_{ji}^c , \cdots, v_{jN}^c). \tag{2}$$

Each weight vector $\boldsymbol{w}_j$ corresponds to a N-dimensional hyper-rectangle [3]. The vectors $\boldsymbol{u}_j$ and $\boldsymbol{v}_j$ are two vertices of the hyper-rectangle with the minimum and the maximum values in every dimension, respectively. For the specific two-dimensional case, the rectangle associated with a weight vector is shown in Fig. 2. The same hyper-rectangle corresponds to the same cluster in the feature space. Nevertheless, input vectors in one cluster may not be associated with the same output vector. Nested hyper-rectangles are allowed to deal with this situation [4]. The inner hyper-rectangle represents an "exception" to the outer one. Within a hyper-rectangle, another hyper-rectangle is created for the input vectors mapped to different outputs (outlined in the learning subsection). Initially,

$$u_{ji} = v_{ji}^c = 1, \text{ for } 1 \le i \le N,\ 1 \le j \le M. \tag{3}$$

Outstar Connection Weights: For each $F2$ node, there are Grossberg's Outstar connections to $F3$ nodes. The weight vector $\boldsymbol{t}_j$ corresponds to the jth $F2$ node. During learning, the weight vector learns the activation pattern in $F3$ layer. In this way, input vectors in one hyper-rectangle are mapped to the desired output by the Outstar connections. Initially,

$$t_{jk} = 0, \text{ for } 1 \le j \le M,\ 1 \le k \le P. \tag{4}$$

Choice Function: For each input vector $\boldsymbol{I}$, $F2$ node J is chosen for candidate category according to the choice function

$$T_j = \beta * \sqrt{\sum_{i=1}^{N} (dif_{ji})^2} + (1 - \beta) * \sqrt{\sum_{i=1}^{N} (i_i - b_{ji})^2}$$

where

$$dif_{ji} = \begin{cases} i_i - v_{ji} & \text{,when } i_i > v_{ji} \\ u_{ji} - i_i & \text{,when } i_i < u_{ji} \\ 0 & \text{, others} \end{cases} \tag{5}$$

The parameter β is set in [0,1]. In terms of geometric interpretation, the first term of the choice function calculates the Euclidean distance between the input vector $\boldsymbol{I}$ and the hyper-rectangle corresponding to the jth node in $F2$.

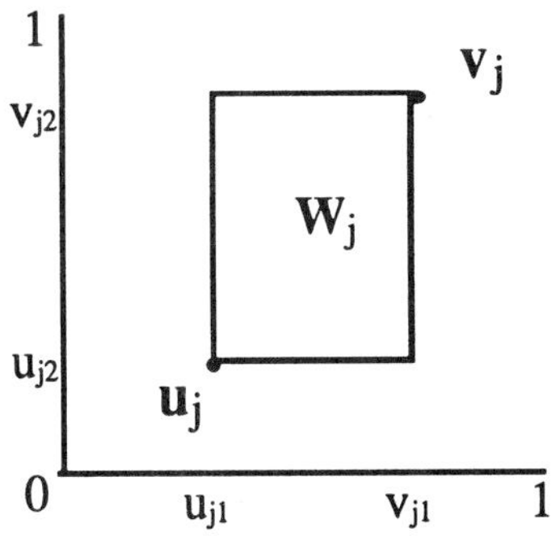

Fig. 2. Rectangle corresponding to a weight vector in two-dimensional feature space

Whenever the input vector $\boldsymbol{I}$ locates in this hyper-rectangle, the distance is zero. In addition, the second term of the choice function calculates the distance between the input vector and the prototype vector $\boldsymbol{b}_j$. Thus, the choice function takes account of the learned concept and the statistic character in the hyper-rectangle. The chosen category is indexed by J, where

$$T_J = \min \{ T_j : j = 1 \dots M \} \tag{6}$$

All uncommitted $F2$ nodes have the maximum value for this choice function. If the input vector $\boldsymbol{I}$ locates in nested hyper-rectangles, the node J corresponding to the innermost hyper-rectangle is selected unless its prototype is farther from $\boldsymbol{I}$. The selected node has activation value of one, and the other nodes are set to be zero.

Matching Criteria: If the chosen node is uncommitted, it is not necessary to check the matching criteria. Since the search for committed node to include input $\boldsymbol{I}$ fails, the first chosen uncommitted node is the right choice beyond question. There are three criteria the candidate category must satisfy. The first is that the chosen category must meet the vigilance criterion [3]; that is,

$$|(I \vee v_J) - (I \wedge u_J)| \leq N * (1 - \rho) \tag{7}$$

where the fuzzy OR operator $\vee$ is defined as

$$(x \vee y)_i \equiv \max (x_i, y_i), \tag{8}$$

the fuzzy AND operator $\wedge$ is defined as

$$(x \wedge y)_i \equiv \min (x_i, y_i), \tag{9}$$

the norm is defined as

$$|x| \equiv \sum_{i=1}^{N} |x_i| \tag{10}$$

and the vigilance parameter $\rho \in [0,1]$.
If the candidate category is accepted, the corresponding hyper-rectangle will be expanded during learning to include the input vector $\boldsymbol{I}$ (described below). The left term in the above vigilance criterion reflects the size of the expanded hyper-rectangle. This criterion guards the size of every hyper-rectangle below some threshold and defines the similarity between the learned concept and the input vector [3]. If the chosen category represents a inner nested hyper-rectangle, the following condition must also be met.

$$|(I \vee v_J) - (I \wedge u_J)| \leq \alpha \, |v_J^{(outer)} - u_J^{(outer)}| \tag{11}$$

,where $v_J^{(outer)}$ and $u_J^{(outer)}$ are vertices of the outer hyper-rectangle.

The constant α (nesting parameter) is suggested to be not greater than 0.25. This condition means that the inner hyper-rectangle can not be expanded to cover too much of the outer one. The reason is given in the learning subsection below.

The second criterion is that the expanded hyper-rectangle can not overlap with other hyper-rectangles; that is, the expanded hyper-rectangle must meet some conditions for all committed node k. The entire algorithm is attached in the appendix for detail. The checking equation shown in [7] is not sufficient. Some nonoverlap situations would be recognized as overlaps. We derive the conditions from the point of mathematics to avoid neglect. This criterion avoids confusion in recognition phase. If this condition fails, the system will search another nearby hyper-rectangle or create a new category (select another uncommitted $F2$ node) if necessary.

The last criterion is that the candidate category must make a correct prediction. The chosen node makes a prediction on $F3$ output pattern through Grossberg's Outstar connections. This prediction must match the desired output of input vector $\boldsymbol{I}$. This criterion is implemented by incorporating a matching mechanism into each $F3$ node. Fig. 3 shows the processing. The output of the equivalence logic is 1 if the predicted output matches the desired output within some small threshold. The threshold equals 0 for binary inputs. This matching criterion is to check

$$\sum_{k=1}^{P} m_k = P \tag{12}$$

It guards that inputs within the same hyper-rectangle are mapped to the same output pattern.

If any of the matching criteria described above is violated, the chosen node is reset and the search process continues. In other words, if all criteria are met or one uncommitted node is selected, the system enters resonance state.

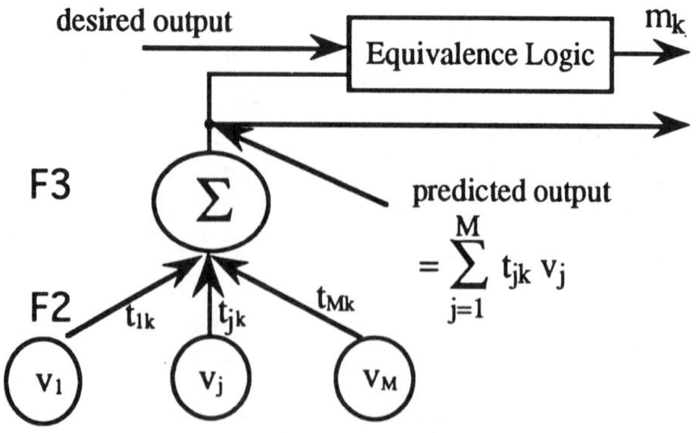

Fig. 3. The processing within each F3 node

Learning: Whenever resonance occurs, learning takes place. There are three kinds of weights to be updated during learning. In the bottom-up connections from $F1$ to $F2$, the weights are updated by the learning rule of the Cluster Euclidean algorithm [8],

$$b_{Ji} = (1 - \lambda)\ b_{Ji} + \lambda\, i_i, \tag{13}$$

where λ is the learning rate.

The weight vector b_j is moved toward the input vector. Eventually, the weight vector will be the prototype vector in the Jth category. It participates in the similarity measure between the input vector and categories. By including the statistic character of clusters, the choice function could compensate for the overgeneralization by the hyper-rectangle.

In the top-down connections from $F2$ to $F1$, the weight vector is updated by the learning rule [3]:

$$u_J^{(new)} = I \wedge u_J\ ,\ v_J^{(new)} = I \vee v_J \tag{14}$$

The hyper-rectangle is expanded by this learning rule to encapsulate the input vector I. The vectors, $v_J^{(new)}$ and $u_J^{(new)}$, are new vertices of the expanded hyper-rectangle. A two-dimensional case is shown in Fig. 4. If the chosen node is uncommitted, the expanded hyper-rectangle is a point in feature space located by I. This is obvious since $I \wedge 1 = I$ and $I \vee 0 = I$.

According to the matching criteria, if the input vector I is mapped to different desired output from that of the hyper-rectangle containing I, a new category is created. Initially, the new category represents an exception point in the original hyper-rectangle. The point will expand to a hyper-rectangle if another such input vector near the point exists. Thus, nested hyper-rectangles are constructed. Fig. 5 shows the two-dimensional case. The depth of nest is unlimited. With nested hyper-rectangles, any noncovex classification can be solved.

In the Outstar connections, the weight vector t_J corresponding to the chosen node J learns the desired output pattern O^*. The learning rule,

$$t_{Jk} = O_k^*\ , \tag{15}$$

effects if the chosen node J is uncommitted. Because all inputs within one category are mapped to the same output pattern, the desired output is learned only when the new category is created. In any time, the training instances may or may not have desired outputs. When the desired output is present, the model learns the desired association (supervised learning). One candidate category is chosen for the input vector. If the output pattern of the chosen category is different from the desired one, the category is reset. Searching process continues until a category with the same output pattern is selected or a new category (uncommitted node) is created. The hyper-rectangle of the selected category may be expanded by the input vector. On the other hand, when the desired output is absent, the model makes a prediction and generalization based on its learned associations (unsupervised learning). If the chosen category is not reset by the matching criteria, the output pattern of the category is read out and the hyper-rectangle may be expanded by the input vector. If a new category is created, the system will request the user to support the desired output for this novel input vector. This new association will be made another training example to train the system. Therefore, this system has the ability of incremental learning.

One problem may occur in the expanded inner hyper-rectangle. As shown in Fig. 6, the inner rectangle will be expanded to cover region A. Some instances, belonging to the category of outer rectangle, in region A may have previously been learned. If one of these instances is present again, the model will predict incorrectly. Therefore, the size of the inner hyper-rectangle is limited by matching criteria

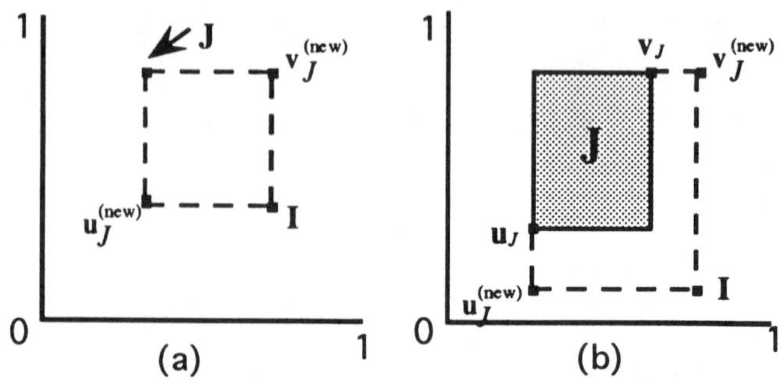

Fig. 4. During learning, the rectangle J expands to the smallest rectangle that includes the input vector I. (a) Rectangle is a point initially. (b) Rectangle represents a category.

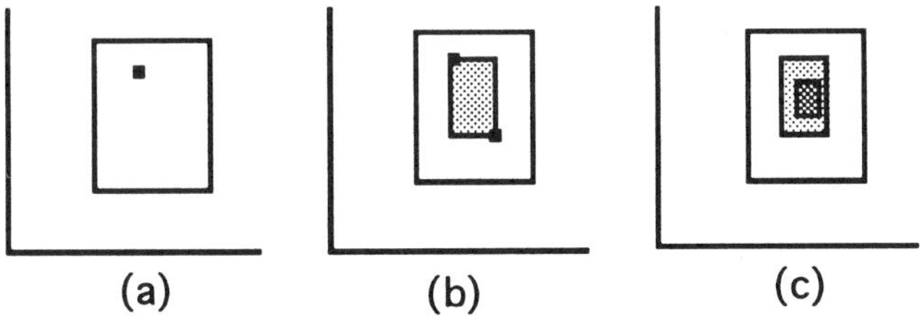

Fig. 5. Nested rectangles (a) One exception occurs within a rectangle. (b) The exception point expands to a rectangle with another exception. (c) In the inner rectangle, some exceptions occur.

to decrease the chance of misclassifications. The second term in the choice function has the same effect. Similar problem also exists in [4] and [7].

III. EXPERIMENTAL RESULTS

The example given here is the IRIS plant classification [4]. This problem is to classify a set of IRIS flowers into three classes: Virginica, Setosa, and Versicolor. The data set consists of 150 instances, 50 for each class. One class is linearly separable from the other two, but the other two are not linearly separable from each other. Therefore, it is suitable for evaluating the performance of the supervised fuzzy ART.

The simulation program was coded in C under the software environment of PDP programs [9]. It was run on the IBM PC and the Sun Workstation. In the following experiments, the net parameters: learning rate, vigilance parameter, and nest parameter, were set to 0.1, 0.2, and 0.25, respectively. The data set is obtained from the UCI Repository of Machine Learning Databases and Domain Theories, maintained by Murphy (e-mail: ml-repository @ics.uci.edu). In order to evaluate the generalization ability, the data set was partitioned into a training set and a test set, 75 instances for each set. The net was trained using the training set for only one epoch and then tested on the test set. The error rate obtained is shown in Table I for two cases -- the training instance is taken from the training set in sequence and at random, respectively. The result for random order case is the average of 30 trials. After one single pass through the training set, a 100% success rate was obtained for the training set and a 94.7% success rate was gotten for the novel test set. From these indications, we have confidence in its ability of generalization.

In addition, we made a few experiments to compare the performance of the supervised fuzzy ART with Backpropagation. Two error rates [10] were measured. The first one is the apparent error rate that is measured by testing the same 150 instances as those of training set. The second one is the leaving-one-out error rate. In this case, the net is trained using 149 instances and then tested on the remaining instance. This process is repeated 150 times, one time for each instance as the testing data. The error rate is the number of errors divided by 150. Table II shows the apparent error rate. The result for random order case is the average of 20 trials. The corresponding error rate of Backpropagation in [11] was attached for comparison. Apparently, supervised fuzzy ART is superior to Backpropagation in this respect. Table III shows the leaving-one-out error rate resulted from the average of 5 complete leaving-one-out trials. In the leaving-one-out trials, an average of 5 errors occurred in Backpropagation and an average of 1.5 errors took place in supervised fuzzy ART. By the comparisons, supervised fuzzy ART took only one epoch to get superior performance than that of Backpropagation trained for 1000 epochs.

Lastly, we made experiments to evaluate the incremental learning ability of supervised fuzzy ART. In these experiments, each of the 150 instances was utilized to train the net one by one. After the incoming instance had been learned, each of the previously learned instances was utilized to test the net. The number of recognized instances at each iteration was shown in Fig. 7. The learning of newcome instance did not corrupt the learned memory. Thus, its ability of incremental learning was demonstrated.

IV. CONCLUSION

The combined learning model presented in this paper is superior to purely supervised or unsupervised models in generalization ability and performance. It can deal with the classification problems, such as the above example, which unsupervised models can not do well. In addition, since it learns the cluster relations between instances, its ability of abstraction and generalization is superior to that of supervised models. According to its operation environment, it can take both supervised learning and unsupervised learning. Since the desired output for each instance may or may not be known during operation, the proposed model is of great flexibility. It also has the ability of incremental learning. In order to correctly classify all the input vectors, additional training passes may be required, depending on the distribution of categories.

Although we are confident that our method can be used for many applications well, there are a number of issues which need to be further investigated. The first one is that the overlap checking of expanding hyper-rectangle is a tedious work when the number of hyper-rectangles increases. Efficient match control methods will be studied. The other one is that the number of hyper-rectangles created depends on the sequence of training data. The optimization of the number of the hyper-rectangles is left a future work. Nowadays we are planning to do the handwritten Chinese character recognition using this model.

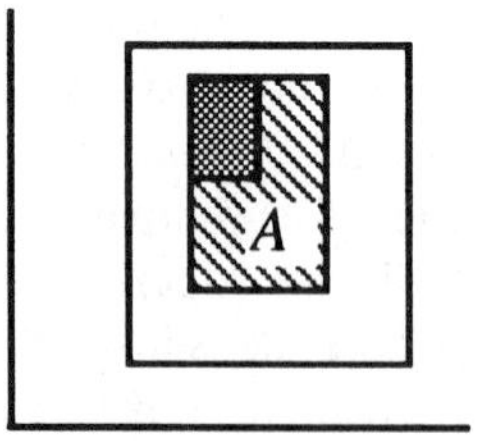

Fig. 6. The problem that may occurs in expanded inner rectangle

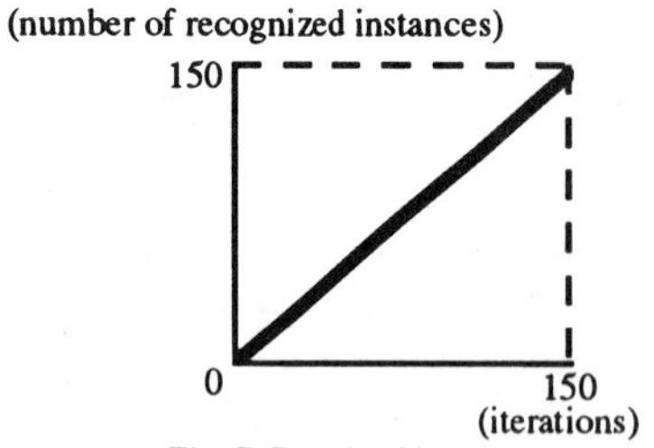

Fig. 7 Result of incremental learning test

REFERENCES

[1] G. E. Hinton, "Connectionist learning procedures," *Artificial Intelligence*, vol. 40, pp. 185-234, 1989.

[2] Richard P. Lippmann, "An introduction to computing with neural nets," *IEEE ASSP MAGAZINE*, vol. 4, pp. 4-22, 1987.

[3] G. A. Carpenter, Stephen Grossberg, and D. B. Rosen, "Fuzzy ART: Fast stable learning and categorization of analog patterns by an adaptive resonance system," *Neural Networks*, vol. 4, pp. 759-771, 1991.

[4] Steven Salzberg, "A nearest hyperrectangle learning method," *Machine Learning*, vol. 6, pp. 251-276, 1991.

[5] Gail A. Carpenter, "Neural network models for pattern recognition and associative memory," *Neural Networks*, vol. 2, pp. 243-257, 1989.

[6] Mohammad Bahrami, "Recognition of rules and exceptions by neural networks," *International Journal of Neural Systems*, vol. 2, pp. 341-344, 1992.

[7] P. K. Simpson, "Fuzzy min-max neural networks," *International Joint Conference on Neural Networks*, Singapore, 1991, pp. 1658-1669.

[8] B. Moore, "ART1 and pattern clustering," *Proceedings of the 1988 Connectionist Models Summer School*, San Mateo, CA, 1989, pp. 174-185.

[9] J. McClelland and D. Rumelhard, *Explorations in Parallel Distributed Processing*, Cambridge: Bradford Books/MIT Press, 1988.

[10]S. M. Weiss and I. Kapouleas, "An empirical comparison of pattern recognition, neural nets, and machine learning classification methods," *Proceeding of Eleventh International Joint Conference on Artificial Intelligence*, Detroit, MI, 1989, pp. 781-787.

TABLE I
GENERALIZATION ABILITY TEST OF SUPERVISED FUZZY ART

order	number of category nodes	misclassifications training set	misclassifications test set	success rate
sequent	4	0	4	94.7%
random	mean = 4.6 max. = 7 min. = 4	mean = 0 max. = 0 min. = 0	mean = 4.0 max. = 5 min. = 3	94.7%

TABLE II
APPARENT ERROR TESTS OF SUPERVISED FUZZY ART AND BACKPROPAGATION

order	number of category nodes	misclassifications	success rate
sequent	9	0	100%
random	mean = 8.7 max. = 10 min. = 8	mean = 0 max. = 0 min. = 0	100%
Backpropagation: 1 trial = 1000 epochs ave. of 5 trials			98.3%

TABLE III
LEAVING-ONE-OUT TESTS OF SUPERVISED FUZZY ART AND BACKPROPAGATION

number of category nodes	misclassifications	success rate
mean =8.09 max. = 12 min. = 6	mean = 1.5 max. = 3 min. = 0	99.0%
Backpropagation: 1 trial = 1000 epochs 1 leaving-one-out trial = 150 trial ave. of 5 leaving-one-out trials		96.7%

APPENDIX

<u>Hyper-rectangle Overlap Checking Algorithm</u>

expanding hyper-rectangle J
other hyper-rectangle k
$v_J^{(new)}$, $u_J^{(new)}$: new vertices of hyper-rectangle J
$\mathbf{v}_k$, $\mathbf{u}_k$: vertices of hyper-rectangle k
a: any vector in hyper-rectangle J

To check if J overlaps with k, there are some conditions to be investigated, as following.

[*Condition1*] $\forall$ i, $u_{ki} \le v_{Ji}^{(new)} \le v_{ki}$
[*Condition2*] $\forall$ i, $u_{ki} \le u_{Ji}^{(new)} \le v_{ki}$

The following two rules can be derived.

[*Rule1*] If condition 1 and condition 2 are satisfied, hyper-rectangle J nests in the hyper-rectangle k.

[*Rule2*] If only one of the above two conditions is satisfied, overlap occurs.

On the other hand,

[*Condition3*] $\exists$ p, $u_{kp} \le v_{Jp}^{(new)} \le v_{kp}$
[*Condition4*] $\exists$ p, $u_{kp} \le u_{Jp}^{(new)} \le v_{kp}$

Because overlap $\Leftrightarrow \forall$ i, $\exists$ a, $u_{ki} \le a_i \le v_{ki}$

nonoverlap $\Leftrightarrow \exists$ i, $\forall$ a, $a_i < u_{ki}$ or $a_i > v_{ki}$

and $\forall$ i, $u_{Ji}^{(new)} \le a_i \le v_{Ji}^{(new)}$

[*Condition5*] $\exists$ q ($q \neq p$), $v_{Jq}^{(new)} < u_{kq}$ or $u_{Jq}^{(new)} > v_{kq}$

therefore we get the rule

[*Rule3*] If either condition 3 or condition 4 is satisfied, nonoverlap if and only if condition 5 is true.

Fuzzy Min-Max Neural Networks for Function Approximation

Patrick K. Simpson
Gary Jahns
ORINCON Corporation
9363 Towne Centre Drive
San Diego, CA 92121

Abstract - The fuzzy min-max function approximation neural network is introduced and results of its performance on a sample problem are presented. The function approximation network is realized by modifying the previously developed fuzzy min-max clustering network to include an ouput layer that sums and thresholds the hidden layer membership functions. Approximation of a test function to a small tolerance and robustness when trained on sparse data is demonstrated.

I. INTRODUCTION

Fuzzy min-max neural networks represent a synergism of fuzzy sets and neural networks in a unified framework. The use of fuzzy sets as classes (Zadeh, 1965) and as clusters (Ruspini, 1969) has been well known for over twenty years. Fuzzy min-max neural networks create fuzzy set classes and clusters in a similar fashion with a membership function based on a hyperbox core. Fuzzy min-max neural network classification (Simpson, 1992a) creates classes from the union of fuzzy sets. Fuzzy min-max neural network clustering (Simpson, 1990a & 1992b) creates clusters from individual fuzzy sets. This paper presents the next evolution of fuzzy min-max neural networks where fuzzy sets are used as the basis set for function approximation. Recently it has been shown that fuzzy sets can be used for universal approximation where fuzzy rules and Gaussian membership functions act as the basis functions (Wang, 1992). This paper will present a fuzzy neural network that is capable of approximating functions by first finding a basis set of fuzzy sets and then finding the linear combination of these clusters that provides the necessary functional mapping. Each fuzzy set in the basis set is treated as an individual cluster that is found using the fuzzy min-max neural network cluster learning. The use of a linear combination of clusters to perform function approximation is not new. Radial basis functions (Poggio & Girosi, 1990) are an important example of this technique.

This paper is organized as follows. In section two is a review of fuzzy sets and the hyperbox membership functions used by fuzzy min-max neural networks. Section three reviews fuzzy min-max neural network clustering. Section four builds on section three by forming linear combinations of fuzzy hyperbox clusters to form function approximation. Examples of the function approximation capabilities and advantages of this approach are also presented. Section five provides a list of the references cited throughout this paper.

II. FUZZY SETS AND FUZZY MIN-MAX CLUSTERS

A. Fuzzy Set Definition

A fuzzy set α is defined as an ordered pair

$$\alpha = \{x, m_\alpha(x)\} \ \forall x \in X \tag{1}$$

where X is the entire space of objects, x is an object from X, and $0 \le m_\alpha(x) \le 1$ is a membership function that describes that degree to which x belongs to the set α.

B. Fuzzy Sets as Clusters

Fuzzy sets bring a new dimension to traditional clustering systems by allowing a pattern to belong to multiple clusters to different degrees. Each fuzzy set is a separate cluster. In the fuzzy min-max clustering neural network, a fuzzy set is defined as a membership function that uses a hyperbox core. If the patterns being clustered have only one dimension, the hyperbox membership function collapses to the common trapezoid membership function.

To make the computations simpler, the pattern space is rescaled to the unit hypercube. As such, hyperboxes lie within the unit hypercube. A hyperbox is completely defined by a min-point and a max-point. The hyperbox membership function for the j'th hyperbox, b_j, is defined as

$$\begin{aligned} b_j &= f(A_h, V_j, W_j) \\ &= \frac{1}{n}\sum_{i=1}^{n}\big[1 - g(v_{ji} - a_{hi}, \gamma) \\ &\qquad - g(a_{hi} - w_{ji}, \gamma)\big] \end{aligned} \tag{2}$$

where g is the common ramp transfer function defined as

$$g(x,\gamma) = \begin{cases} 1 & \text{if} \quad x\gamma > 1 \\ x & \text{if} \quad 0 \le x\gamma \le 1 \\ 0 & \text{if} \quad x < 0 \end{cases} \tag{3}$$

0-7803-0999-5/93/$03.00

and where the remaining parameters are defined as follows:

$A_h \in [0,1]^n$	h'th input pattern $A_h = (a_{h1}, a_{h2}, ..., a_{hn})$,
h	index for the patterns. The number of patterns is not specified here. It is not necessary for the algorithm to have this information because it is an on-line learning clusterer,
n	number of dimensions for the input patterns and the input layer,
p	number of fuzzy set hyperboxes (i.e. number of clusters),
γ	*the slope of the membership function.* A value of $\gamma = 1.0$ will guarantee that the membership function will cover the entire space. Values greater than 1 will sharpen the sides of the trapezoidal membership function,
$V_j \in [0,1]^n$	min vector for the j'th hyperbox fuzzy set, $V_j = (v_{j1}, v_{j2}, ..., v_{jn})$, $j = 1, 2, ..., p$, and
$W_j \in [0,1]^n$	max vector for the j'th hyperbox fuzzy set $W_j = (w_{j1}, w_{j2}, ..., w_{jn})$, $j = 1, 2, ..., p$.

III. FUZZY MIN-MAX NEURAL NETWORK CLUSTERING

The fuzzy min-max neural network clusterer adds new hyperbox fuzzy sets as they are needed. The maximum size of a hyperbox is bound above by the parameter θ. This value represents the upper bound of the average length of the side of a hyperbox. The learning algorithm will only briefly be described here. For details, please refer to Simpson (1992b). Clustering differs from classification in that there are no labels associated with input patterns and the objective is to find the natural structure of the data. In the following sections it will be assumed that we are clustering a set of patterns $A = \{A_1, A_2, ..., A_m\}$.

A. Learning

Fuzzy min-max clustering neural network learning proceeds in three steps: (1) find a hyperbox that will allow expansion (or add a new hyperbox if one can not be found), (2) expand the hyperbox, and (3) eliminate overlap with other hyperboxes. Each of these steps is outlined below.

1. *Expansion Test.* Given the input pattern A_h, find a hyperbox that can be expanded to include this hyperbox. The hyperbox expansion test is defined as

$$\theta \leq \frac{1}{n}\sum_{i=1}^{n} [\max(a_{hi}, w_{ji}) - \min(a_{hi}, v_{ji})] \quad (4)$$

If a hyperbox can not be found that satisfies (4), then a new hyperbox, b_J, is created that has its min and max points defined as follows

$$V_J = (1, 1, ..., 1) \quad (5)$$

$$W_J = (0, 0, ..., 0) \quad (6)$$

which will ensure that the expansion steps taken below will result in the input pattern, A_h, becoming the initial min point and max point (initially all hyperboxes have zero volume).

2. *Expansion.* Assume that the hyperbox that will be expanded to include the input pattern, A_h, is b_j. The expansion of the min point is performed using

$$v_{ji}^{new} = \min(v_{ji}^{old}, a_{hi}) \quad (7)$$

and the expansion of the max point is performed using

$$w_{ji}^{new} = \max(w_{ji}^{old}, a_{hi}) \quad (8)$$

3. *Overlap Test.* The fuzzy min-max clustering neural network does not allow any point to have full membership (a membership value of 1) in more than one hyperbox. To eliminate the overlap between hyperboxes, the expanded hyperbox is compared with each of the existing hyperboxes. If overlap is found, it is eliminated along each dimension. Although the operations that perform the overlap elimination are not difficult to implement, their exposition is beyond the scope of this paper. Please refer to Simpson (1992b) for details of the hyperbox overlap elimination procedure.

B. Neural Network Implementation

The implemention of a fuzzy set hyperbox and its membership function fits very naturally into a neural network framework. As **Figure 1** shows, the input pattern, A_h, is represented as n input nodes, the min and max points, V_j and W_j, are represented as dual connections, and the membership function, $f(A_h, V_j, W_j)$, becomes the j'th cluster's output value, b_j. This network represents a fuzzy set.

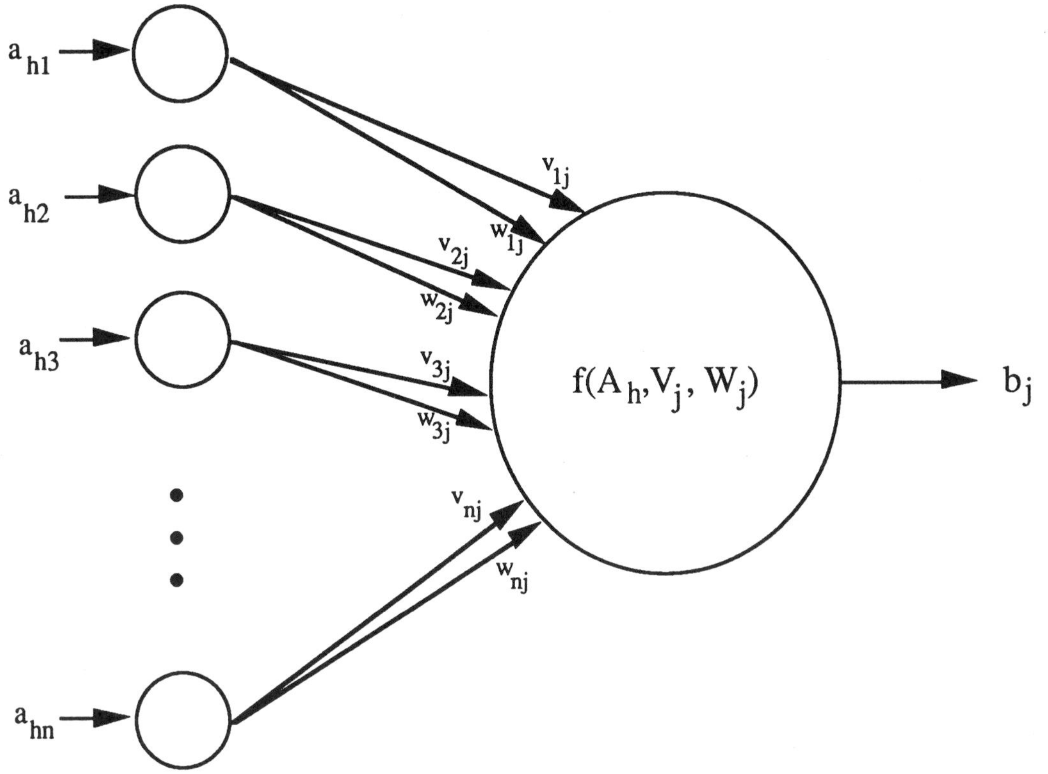

Fig. 1. Neural network implementation of fuzzy set hyperbox cluster.

IV. Fuzzy Min-Max Neural Network Function Approximation

Function approximation is mathematically described as $| F(A_h) - G(A_h) | < \varepsilon \ \forall A_h$ where $F(A_h)$ is the true (and often unknown) function, $G(A_h)$ is the approximation of the true function (computed here by the fuzzy min-max function approximation neural network), and $\varepsilon > 0$. The ability of neural networks to perform function approximation for a broad class of functions is clearly one of their greater strengths. Recently, the use of fuzzy sets to perform function approximation has also been introduced (Wang, 1992). In the following sections, the learning algorithm for the fuzzy min-max function approximation neural network will be described. Throughout this section, it is assumed that the input patterns are $A_h \in [0,1]^n$, the output patterns are $F(A_h) = D_h \in \Re^q$, and the data set is the collection of pattern pairs $D = \{(A_h, D_h): h = 1, 2, ..., m\}$.

A. Fuzzy Clusters as Basis Functions

The radial basis function network has been shown to be very good for function approximation (Poggio & Girosi, 1990). Radial basis functions are typically constructed in three steps: (1) represent the data as a set of clusters, (2) assign a radial basis function to the centroid of each cluster -- typically this will be a gaussian function, and (3) approximate the function from a linear combination of the basis functions. The approach taken here will be similar. Hyperbox fuzzy sets will be formed using the algorithm described in section 3 and linear combinations of these fuzzy sets will be used to approximate a function.

To perform function approximation requires an alteration to the trapezoidal membership function given by (2). The flat region between the min and max of the membership function does not provide a continuous graded response that a triangular membership function would, so the membership function described by (2) is replaced with the membership function

$$b_j = f(A_h, V_j, W_j) = \frac{1}{n}\sum_{i=1}^{n}\left[1 - g(|z_{ji} - a_{hi}|, \gamma)\right] \quad (9)$$

where z_{ji} is defined as

$$z_{ji} = \frac{w_{ji} + v_{ji}}{2} \quad (10)$$

for all hyperboxes $j = 1, 2, ..., p$ and all dimensions $i = 1, 2, ..., n$. The vectors $Z_j = (z_{j1}, z_{j2}, ..., z_{jn})$ represent the mid-points of the hyperboxes that are defined by the min point and the max point. Note that the min and max points are preserved and the mid-point is computed from these values.

B. *Fuzzy Min-Max Function Approximation Neural Network Topology*

The fuzzy min-max function approximation neural network has three layers: (1) the input layer F_A, (2) the fuzzy hyperbox cluster layer F_B, and (3) the output layer F_C. **Figure 2** shows a fuzzy min-max function approximation neural network with four F_A nodes, five F_B nodes (including the bias node), and three F_C nodes. Each of the hidden nodes is a fuzzy hyperbox node like that shown in **Figure 1**. The connections between the F_A and F_B nodes are the min-max dual connections described in the previous section. The connections between the F_B and F_C nodes are real-valued connections $U = u_{jk}, j = 1, 2, ..., p$ and $k = 1, 2, ..., q$, where u_{jk} represents the single connection from b_j to c_k. In addition to the F_B and F_C connections, each F_C node has a bias input, denoted as u_{0k}, which can be treated like an F_B node that is held constant at 1.

C. *Fuzzy Min-Max Function Approximation Learning*

Fuzzy min-max function approximation learning occurs in two steps. First, the input data is clustered into a set of hyperbox fuzzy set clusters using the algorithm described in section III. When the clustering process is completed, the first two layers and their associated connections are held fixed for the second phase of the learning process.

Each F_B node produces an output value, b_j, using (9) defined above. The F_C nodes, c_k, produce output values using the equation

$$c_k = \sum_{j=1}^{p} b_j u_{jk} + u_{0k} \tag{11}$$

for all $k = 1, 2, ..., q$. The F_B to F_C connections are adjusted using the LMS (Least Mean Square) algorithm as follows:

1. A_h is presented to F_A.
2. Each F_B node computes its membership value using (9).
3. The value of the F_B nodes are propagated through the U connections and the computed output values, c_k, are produced using (11).
4. The computed output values are compared with the desired output values. The difference is used to adjust the U connections using the equation

$$u_{jk}^{new} = u_{jk}^{old} + \alpha(d_{hk} - c_k)b_j \tag{12}$$

5. Steps 1-4 are repeated until the sum of the errors has reached the desired level.

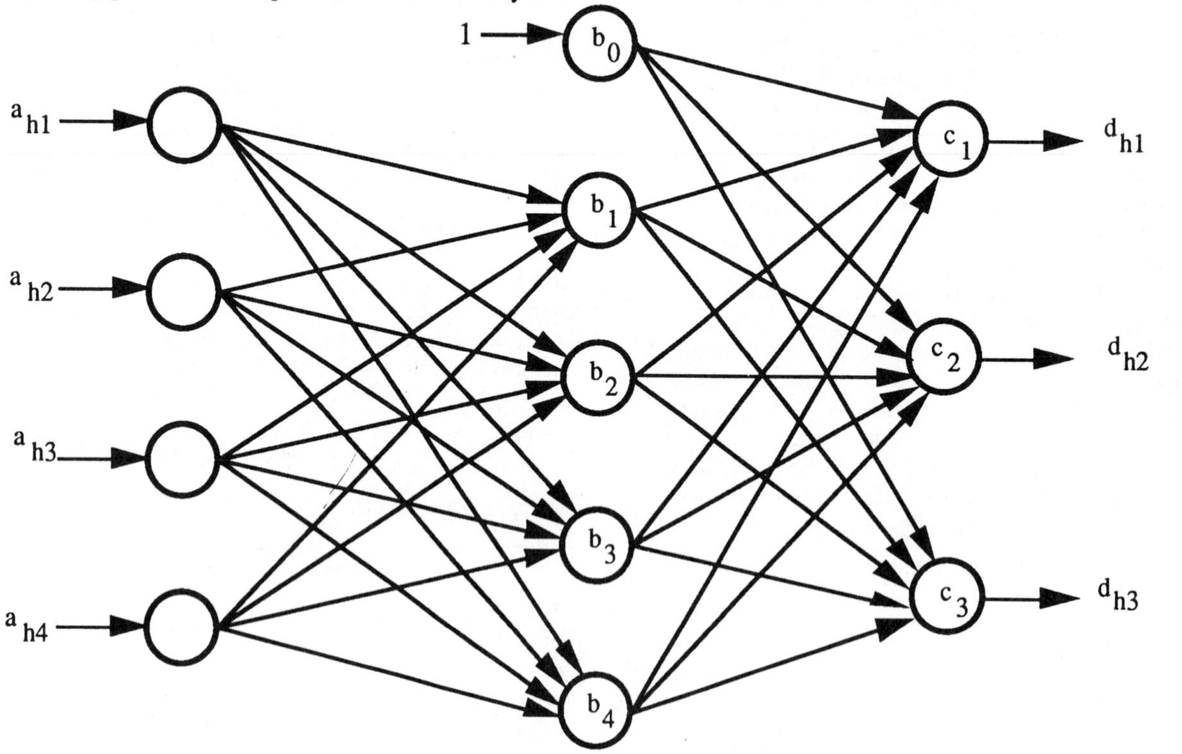

Fig. 2. Topology of the Fuzzy Min-Max Function Approximation Neural Network.

D. Results

For the sake of illustration, a one-dimensional nonlinear function was arbitrarily chosen to demonstrate the function approximation capabilities of the fuzzy min-max neural network. The following sigmoid function was approiximated

$$f(x) = \frac{2x}{1+x^2} \tag{13}$$

A set of 300 exemplars was generated randomly with an equiprobable distribution over the interval [-1,+1], producing an input of x and an output f(x). **Figure 3** shows a scatterplot of the data produced for this function.

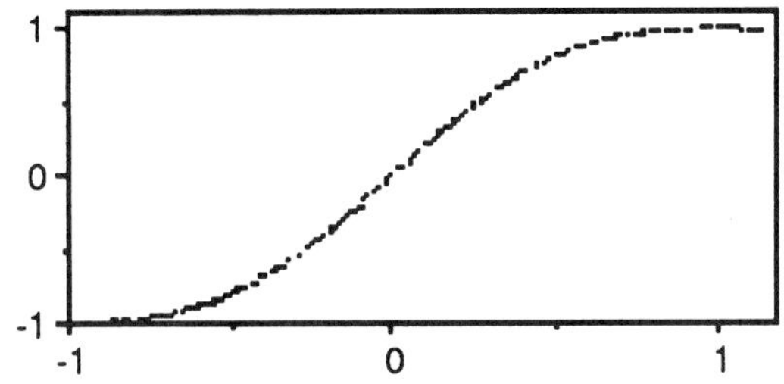

Fig. 3. Scatterplot of the data used for function approximation.

The fuzzy min-max function approximation neural network used to encode this function had one input (x) and one output. The input values where rescaled to the range [0,1], but the outputs remained untouched. Two experiments were conducted. First, using all 300 data points, determine if the fuzzy min-max function approximation neural network can approximate the sigmoid function. Second, reduce the data set to determine how the function approximation capability suffers when sparse data is used

The first experiment clustered the input data into 12 hyperbox fuzzy sets using a hyperbox size of 0.10. The LMS algorithm iterated 10,000 times at a learning rate of 0.10 and was stopped with an average error of 0.00465 and a maximum error of 0.0376 for any given exemplar. A scatterplot of the resulting function is shown in **Figure 4** with the original function lying underneath each scatterplot to illustrate where the function approximation was in error.

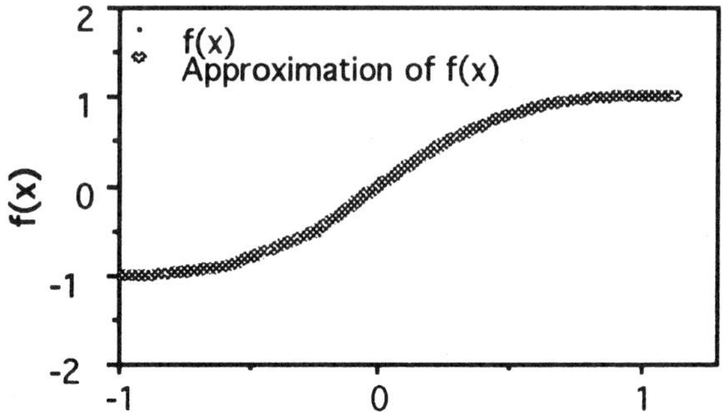

Fig. 4. Scatterplot of the function approximation of the sigmoid using 300 exemplars.

The second experiment tested the function approximation ability of the network with sparse data. If the function approximation is being performed using fuzzy sets as basis functions, the degradation in performance should be gradual. The first part of this experiment reduced the number of exemplars by an order of magnitude, using only 30 for training and all 300 for testing. The 30 exemplars were clustered into 10 hyperbox fuzzy sets using a hyperbox size of 0.10. The LMS algorithm iterated 10,000 times at a learning rate of 0.10 and was stopped with an average error of 0.0030 and a maximum error of 0.0136 for any given exemplar. A scatterplot of the resulting function is shown in **Figure 5** with the original function lying underneath each scatterplot to illustrate where the function approximation was in error. As the scatterplot shows, the function approximation did not suffer at all, and in fact performed better.

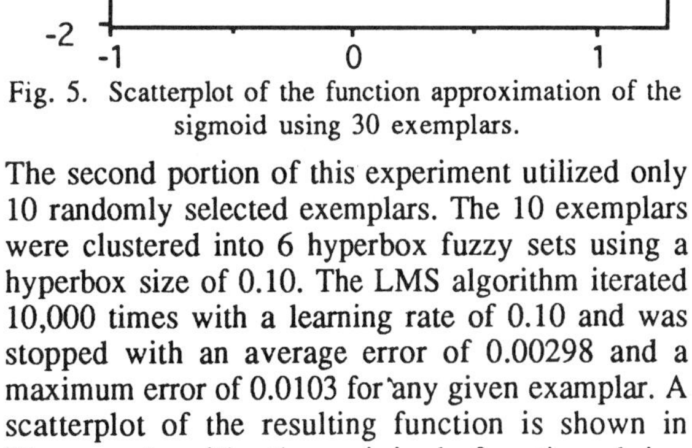

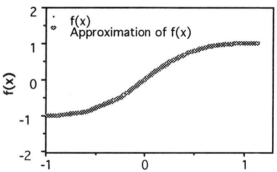

Fig. 5. Scatterplot of the function approximation of the sigmoid using 30 exemplars.

The second portion of this experiment utilized only 10 randomly selected exemplars. The 10 exemplars were clustered into 6 hyperbox fuzzy sets using a hyperbox size of 0.10. The LMS algorithm iterated 10,000 times with a learning rate of 0.10 and was stopped with an average error of 0.00298 and a maximum error of 0.0103 for any given examplar. A scatterplot of the resulting function is shown in **Figure 6** with the original function lying underneath the scatterplot to illustrate where the function approximation was in error. As the scatterplot shows, the function approximation did degrade significantly. What was interesting was how the function approximation degraded. It is visibly noticable that a piecewise linear approximation of the function resulted from the sparse data.

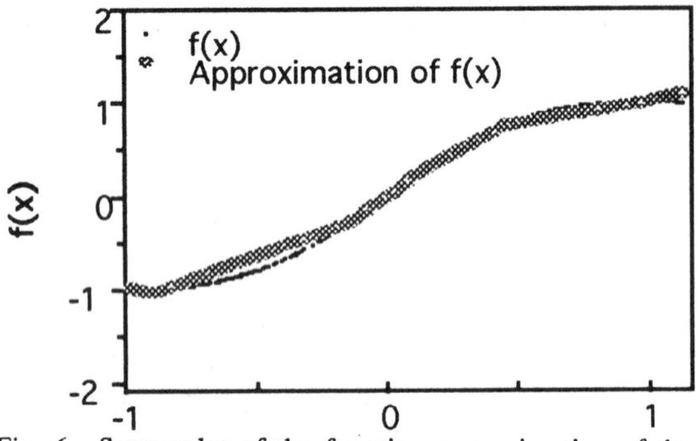

Fig. 6. Scatterplot of the function approximation of the sigmoid using 10 exemplars.

V. Conclusions And Future Work

The fuzzy min-max function approximation neural network has been introduced and an example of its function approximation capability has been briefly examined. The fuzzy min-max function approximation network is similar in many ways to radial basis function networks in that a basis set of functions is first defined and then a linear combination of these functions is then found. In addition to properties listed for the clustering portion of the function approximation process described in section 3.3, the use of the LMS algorithm makes this technique relatively fast to train.

There are several areas where this work will continue. First, a proof that this function approximation approach is valid for a large range of functions will be explored. Second, the application of this function approximation technique to other function approximation problems needs to be explored, including forecasting and control. Finally, a methodology for the extraction of fuzzy rules from a trained fuzzy min-max network will be investigated.

References

Bezdek, J. (1981). *Pattern Recognition with Fuzzy Objective Function Algorithms*, Plenum Press, New York.

Bezdek, J. (1987). Some non-standard clustering algorithms, *NATO ASI Series, vol. G14: Developments in Numerical Ecology*, P; Legendre & L. Legendre, Eds., Springer-Verlag, Berlin.

Ignizio Burke, L. (1991). Clustering characteriaion of adaptive resonance, *Neural Networks*, **4**, pp. 485-492.

Kohonen, T. (1990). *Self-Organization and Associative Memory: Third Edition*, Springer-Verlag, Berlin.

Poggio, T. & Girosi, F. (1990). Networks for approximation and learning, *Proceedings of the IEEE*, **78**, pp. 1481-1497.

Ruspini, E. (1969). A new approach to clustering, *Information and Control*, **15**, pp. 22-32.

Simpson, P. (1990a). Fuzzy adaptive resonance theory, *SIUC Neuroengineering Workshop*, Sept. 6-7, Carbondale, IL. Also, General Dynamics Electronics Division, Technical Report, GDE-ISG-PKS-11.

Simpson, P. (1990b). *Artificial Neural Systems: Foundations, Paradigms, Applications, and Implementations*, Pergamon Press: Elmsford, NY.

Simpson, P. (1991). Fuzzy min-max classification with neural networks, *Heuristics*, **4**, No. 1, pp. pp. 1-9.

Simpson, P. (1992a). Fuzzy min-max neural networks: 1. classification, *IEEE Trans. on Neural Networks*, **3**, PP. 776-786.

Simpson, P. (1992b). Fuzzy min-max neural networks: 2. clustering, *IEEE Trans. on Fuzzy Systems*, in review.

Simpson, P.& Perlow, D (1992c). Feature analysis with the fuzzy min-max clustering neural network, in preparation.

Wang, L & Mendel, J. (1992). Universal approximation with fuzzy sets, *Proceedings of the First IEEE International Conference on Fuzzy Systems*, San Diego, CA, March 8-12.

Zadeh, L. (1965). Fuzzy sets, *Information and Control*, **8**, pp. 338-353.

Fuzzy Neural Networks with Fuzzy Weights and Fuzzy Biases

Hisao Ishibuchi, Hideo Tanaka
Department of Industrial Engineering, University of Osaka Prefecture
Gakuencho 1-1, Sakai, Osaka 593, JAPAN

Hidehiko Okada
Kansai C&C Research Laboratory, NEC Corporation
Shiromi 1-4-24, Chuo-ku, Osaka 540, JAPAN

***Abstract*— In this paper, we propose an architecture of multi-layer feedforward neural networks whose weights and biases are given as fuzzy numbers. The fuzzy neural network with the proposed architecture maps an input vector of real numbers to a fuzzy output. The input-output relation of each unit is defined by the extension principle. We derive a learning algorithm of the fuzzy neural network for real input vectors and fuzzy target outputs. Moreover, the derived learning algorithm is extended to the case of fuzzy input vectors and fuzzy target outputs.**

I. INTRODUCTION

From the viewpoint of the principle of incompatibility[1], which asserts that high precision is incompatible with high complexity in dealing with humanistic systems by computers, several methods have been proposed for deriving inexact models from input-output data. For example, Tanaka et al.[2] proposed the concept of fuzzy regression analysis where the following fuzzy model with fuzzy parameters was employed:

$$Y(\boldsymbol{x}) = A_0 + A_1x_1 + \cdots + A_nx_n, \tag{1}$$

where $\boldsymbol{x} = (x_1, \cdots, x_n)$ is an n-dimensional real input vector and A_i is a fuzzy parameter given as a symmetric fuzzy number. Thus the output $Y(\boldsymbol{x})$ from the fuzzy model (1) is also a symmetric fuzzy number. The fuzzy parameters in (1) can be easily obtained using a linear programming technique. We show an example of fuzzy model with a single input in Fig.1 where fuzzy outputs corresponding to eight input values are depicted.

Several methods for deriving non-linear fuzzy models from input-output data were also proposed. For example, Ishibuchi & Tanaka[3,4] proposed a method for obtaining a non-linear interval model using two standard BP networks[5].

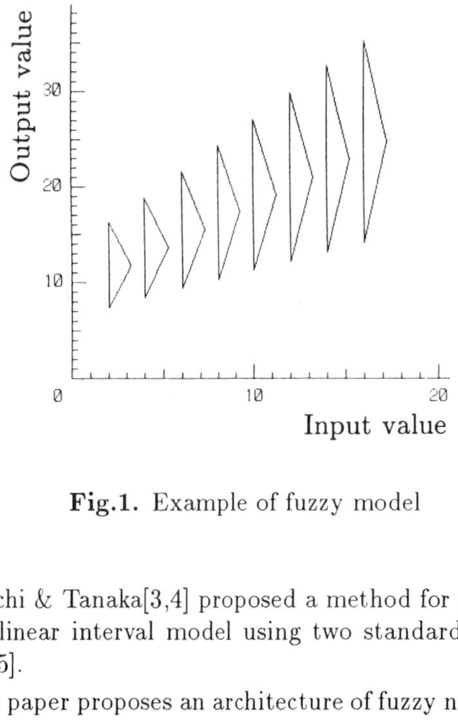

Fig.1. Example of fuzzy model

This paper proposes an architecture of fuzzy neural networks with fuzzy weights and fuzzy biases, and derives its learning algorithm for the modelling of non-linear fuzzy systems which map a real input vector to a fuzzy output. First we define the input-output relation of each unit of the fuzzy neural network by the extension principle[1]. Next we derive a learning algorithm from a cost function defined by the level sets of a fuzzy actual output and a fuzzy target output. Last we show that the derived learning algorithm can be applied to the case of fuzzy input vectors and fuzzy target outputs by slightly modifying it.

Hayashi et al.[6] also proposed a similar architecture of neural networks with fuzzy weights but the learning

0-7803-0999-5/93/$03.00 ©1993 IEEE

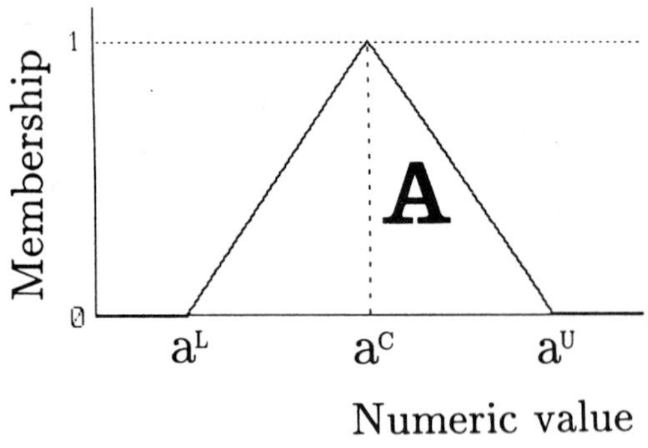

Fig.2. Triangular fuzzy number A

algorithm in [6] was totally different from our approach. In Hayashi et al., the BP algorithm[5] is directly fuzzified based on a fuzzy-valued cost function (i.e., the rule for changing fuzzy weights is also defined by fuzzy numbers), while a learning algorithm is derived from a non-fuzzy cost function in this paper.

II. ARCHITECTURE OF FUZZY NEURAL NETWORKS

A. Fuzzy Weights and Fuzzy Biases

We extend the standard BP networks in Rumelhart et al.[5] to fuzzy neural networks with fuzzy weights and fuzzy biases. We use symmetric triangular fuzzy numbers for fuzzy weights and fuzzy biases.

Let us denote a triangular fuzzy number A as $A = (a^L, a^C, a^U)$ where a^L, a^C and a^U are the lower limit, the center and the upper limit of A (see Fig.2). The membership function of A is defined as

$$\mu_A(x) = \begin{cases} 0, \; for \; x \leq a^L \\ (x - a^L)/(a^C - a^L), \; for \; a^L < x \leq a^C \\ (a^U - x)/(a^U - a^C), \; for \; a^C < x \leq a^U \\ 0, \; for \; a^U < x \end{cases} \tag{2}$$

The membership function of A is 1 at the center a^C and positive in the open interval (a^L, a^U), that is, (a^L, a^U) is the support of the fuzzy number A.

We propose an architecture of fuzzy neural networks that have fuzzy weights and fuzzy biases. The proposed architecture is shown in Fig.3 where the fuzzy weights and the fuzzy biases are as follows (in Fig.3, biases are omitted).

$$W_j = (w_j^L, w_j^C, w_j^U), \quad W_{ji} = (w_{ji}^L, w_{ji}^C, w_{ji}^U), \tag{3}$$

$$\Theta = (\theta^L, \theta^C, \theta^U), \quad \Theta_j = (\theta_j^L, \theta_j^C, \theta_j^U). \tag{4}$$

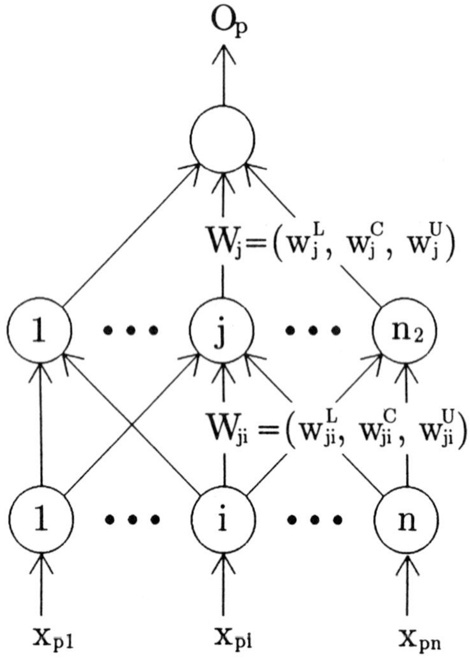

Fig.3. The proposed architecture of neural networks with fuzzy weights and fuzzy biases

Since we use symmetric triangular fuzzy numbers for the fuzzy weights and the fuzzy biases, the following relations hold:

$$w_j^C = (w_j^L + w_j^U)/2, \quad w_{ji}^C = (w_{ji}^L + w_{ji}^U)/2, \tag{5}$$

$$\theta^C = (\theta^L + \theta^U)/2, \quad \theta_j^C = (\theta_j^L + \theta_j^U)/2. \tag{6}$$

The level sets of fuzzy numbers are defined as

$$[A]_h = \{x : \mu_A(x) \geq h\}, \tag{7}$$

where $[A]_h$ is the h-level set of the fuzzy number A. Since the level sets of fuzzy numbers are closed intervals, we denote $[A]_h$ by its lower limit $[A]_h^L$ and its upper limit $[A]_h^U$ as

$$[A]_h = [[A]_h^L, \; [A]_h^U]. \tag{8}$$

Since the fuzzy weights W_j and W_{ji} are symmetric fuzzy numbers, the h-level sets can be calculated as

$$[W_j]_h^L = w_j^L(1 - h/2) + w_j^U h/2, \tag{9}$$

$$[W_j]_h^U = w_j^L h/2 + w_j^U(1 - h/2), \tag{10}$$

$$[W_{ji}]_h^L = w_{ji}^L(1 - h/2) + w_{ji}^U h/2, \tag{11}$$

$$[W_{ji}]_h^U = w_{ji}^L h/2 + w_{ji}^U(1 - h/2). \tag{12}$$

The h-level sets of the biases Θ and Θ_j can be calculated in the same manner.

B. Definition of Input-Output Relation of Each Unit

When an n-dimensional real input vector $\boldsymbol{x}_p = (x_{p1}, x_{p2}, \cdots, x_{pn})$ is presented to the input units of the fuzzy neural network in Fig.3, the input-output relation of each unit can be written as follows.

Input units :

$$o_{pi} = x_{pi},\ i = 1, 2, ..., n. \tag{13}$$

Hidden units :

$$O_{pj} = f(Net_{pj}),\ j = 1, 2, ..., n_2, \tag{14}$$

$$Net_{pj} = \sum_{i=1}^{n} W_{ji} o_{pi} + \Theta_j,\ j = 1, 2, \cdots, n_2. \tag{15}$$

Output unit :

$$O_p = f(Net_p), \tag{16}$$

$$Net_p = \sum_{j=1}^{n_2} W_j O_{pj} + \Theta. \tag{17}$$

This definition is the same as the standard BP network[5] except that the weights W_{ji}, W_j and the biases Θ_j, Θ are fuzzy numbers. In (13)-(17), uppercase letters and lowercase letters denote fuzzy numbers and real numbers, respectively. The activation function in the hidden units and the output unit is the sigmoid function: $f(x) = 1/\{1 + \exp(-x)\}$.

The fuzzy input-output relation in (13)-(17) is defined by the extension principle[1]. For example, the fuzzy input-output relation by the activation function $f(\cdot)$ is defined as follows (see Fig.4).

$$\mu_{f(Net)}(y) = \max_x\{\mu_{Net}(x) : y = f(x)\}, \tag{18}$$

where Net is a fuzzy input and $f(Net)$ is the corresponding fuzzy output.

While the input-output relation of each unit is defined by the extension principle, the calculation of actual fuzzy outputs are performed using interval arithmetic[7] for level sets. For example, the fuzzy output $f(Net)$ in Fig.4 is calculated by interval arithmetic for 50 level sets ($h = 0.02, 0.04, \cdots, 1.00$). This approach was applied to the calculation of fuzzy outputs corresponding to fuzzy input vectors to the standard BP network in Ishibuchi et al.[8-10].

The input-output relation of each unit for the h-level sets can be derived from (13)-(17) as follows.

Input units :

$$o_{pi} = x_{pi},\ i = 1, 2, \cdots, n. \tag{19}$$

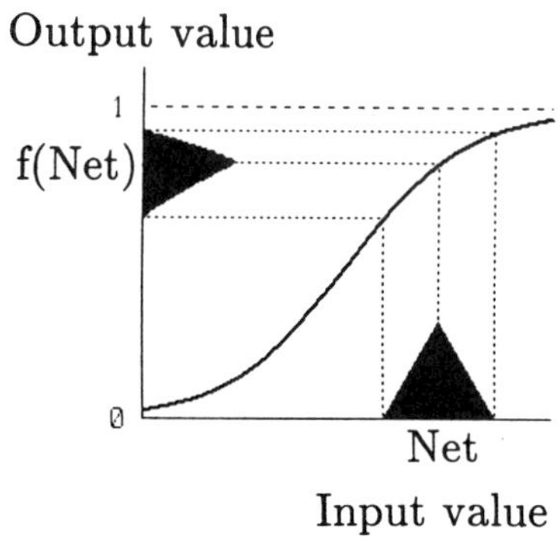

Fig.4. Fuzzy input-output relation

Hidden units :

$$\begin{aligned}[O_{pj}]_h &= [f(Net_{pj})]_h \\ &= f([Net_{pj}]_h),\ j = 1, 2, \cdots, n_2,\end{aligned} \tag{20}$$

$$[Net_{pj}]_h = \sum_{i=1}^{n} [W_{ji}]_h o_{pi} + [\Theta_j]_h,\ j = 1, 2, \cdots, n_2. \tag{21}$$

Output unit :

$$[O_p]_h = [f(Net_p)]_h = f([Net_p]_h), \tag{22}$$

$$[Net_p]_h = \sum_{j=1}^{n_2} [W_j]_h [O_{pj}]_h + [\Theta]_h. \tag{23}$$

These input-output relations for h-level sets are similar to those of the neural network with interval weights and interval biases in Ishibuchi et al.[11].

III. LEARNING ALGORITHM OF FUZZY NEURAL NETWORKS

A. Training Data

Let us assume that m input-output pairs $(\boldsymbol{x}_p, T_p)$, $p = 1, 2, ..., m$, of the real input vector $\boldsymbol{x}_p$ and the corresponding fuzzy target output T_p are given. We also assume that the target output T_p is a triangular fuzzy number:

$$T_p = (t_p^L, t_p^C, t_p^U). \tag{24}$$

It should be noted that the fuzzy target output T_p may be non-symmetric while the fuzzy weights and the fuzzy biases are symmetric triangular fuzzy numbers.

B. Definition of Cost Function

Let us denote the h-level sets of the fuzzy actual output O_p and the corresponding fuzzy target output T_p as

$$[O_p]_h = [[O_p]_h^L, [O_p]_h^U], \quad [T_p]_h = [[T_p]_h^L, [T_p]_h^U], \quad (25)$$

where $[\cdot]_h^L$ and $[\cdot]_h^U$ denote the lower limit and the upper limit of the h-level set. For the h-level sets, we define the following cost function (i.e., error measure) to be minimized in the learning of the proposed fuzzy neural network.

$$e_{ph} = ([T_p]_h^L - [O_p]_h^L)^2/2 + ([T_p]_h^U - [O_p]_h^U)^2/2. \quad (26)$$

This cost function satisfies the relation:

$$e_{ph} = 0 \;\; if \;\; [O_p]_h = [T_p]_h. \quad (27)$$

In the learning for the p-th input-output pair $(\boldsymbol{x}_p, T_p)$, we can use several values of h. Therefore the cost function for $(\boldsymbol{x}_p, T_p)$ is defined as

$$e_p = \sum_h h \cdot e_{ph}, \quad (28)$$

where the cost function e_{ph} for the h-level sets is weighted by the value of h in order to attach the greater importance to the higher level. This cost function satisfies the relation:

$$e_p = 0 \;\; if \;\; O_p = T_p. \quad (29)$$

Moreover, if we use an infinite number of values of h in (28), the cost function defined by (28) satisfies the relation:

$$e_p = 0 \;\; if\ and\ only\ if \;\; O_p = T_p. \quad (30)$$

Therefore the actual fuzzy output O_p approaches the fuzzy target output T_p as the cost function e_p approaches zero. In computer simulations, we use five values of h, i.e., $h = 0.2, 0.4, 0.6, 0.8, 1.0$.

C. Derivation of Learning Algorithm

In the learning of the fuzzy neural network, we adjust the lower limits and the upper limits of the fuzzy weights W_j, W_{ji} and the fuzzy biases Θ, Θ_j. In a similar manner to the BP algorithm[5], the learning rules for the fuzzy weights W_j, W_{ji} can be written as

$$\Delta w_j^L(t+1) = -\eta \cdot h(\partial e_{ph}/\partial w_j^L) + \alpha \Delta w_j^L(t), \quad (31)$$

$$\Delta w_j^U(t+1) = -\eta \cdot h(\partial e_{ph}/\partial w_j^U) + \alpha \Delta w_j^U(t), \quad (32)$$

$$\Delta w_{ji}^L(t+1) = -\eta \cdot h(\partial e_{ph}/\partial w_{ji}^L) + \alpha \Delta w_{ji}^L(t), \quad (33)$$

$$\Delta w_{ji}^U(t+1) = -\eta \cdot h(\partial e_{ph}/\partial w_{ji}^U) + \alpha \Delta w_{ji}^U(t), \quad (34)$$

where η is a learning constant and α is a momentum constant. In computer simulations of this paper, we specify η and α as $\eta = 0.5$ and $\alpha = 0.9$. The derivatives $\partial e_{ph}/\partial w_j^L$, $\partial e_{ph}/\partial w_j^U$, $\partial e_{ph}/\partial w_{ji}^L$ and $\partial e_{ph}/\partial w_{ji}^U$ in (31)-(34) can be derived from the cost function (26) using (9)-(12) and (19)-(23). For example, $\partial e_{ph}/\partial w_j^L$ is derived as follows.

i) If $0 \le [W_j]_h^L \le [W_j]_h^U$ then

$$\begin{aligned}
\frac{\partial e_{ph}}{\partial w_j^L} &= \frac{\partial e_{ph}^L}{\partial w_j^L} + \frac{\partial e_{ph}^U}{\partial w_j^L} \\
&= \frac{\partial}{\partial [O_p]_h^L}\{([T_p]_h^L - [O_p]_h^L)^2/2\} \\
&\quad \cdot \frac{\partial [O_p]_h^L}{\partial [Net_p]_h^L} \frac{\partial [Net_p]_h^L}{\partial [W_j]_h^L} \frac{\partial [W_j]_h^L}{\partial w_j^L} \\
&\quad + \frac{\partial}{\partial [O_p]_h^U}\{([T_p]_h^U - [O_p]_h^U)^2/2\} \\
&\quad \cdot \frac{\partial [O_p]_h^U}{\partial [Net_p]_h^U} \frac{\partial [Net_p]_h^U}{\partial [W_j]_h^U} \frac{\partial [W_j]_h^U}{\partial w_j^L} \\
&= -([T_p]_h^L - [O_p]_h^L)[O_p]_h^L \\
&\quad \cdot (1 - [O_p]_h^L)[O_{pj}]_h^L (1 - h/2) \\
&\quad -([T_p]_h^U - [O_p]_h^U)[O_p]_h^U \\
&\quad \cdot (1 - [O_p]_h^U)[O_{pj}]_h^U h/2 \\
&= -\delta_{ph}^L [O_{pj}]_h^L (1 - h/2) \\
&\quad -\delta_{ph}^U [O_{pj}]_h^U h/2, \qquad (35)
\end{aligned}$$

where

$$\delta_{ph}^L = ([T_p]_h^L - [O_p]_h^L)[O_p]_h^L (1 - [O_p]_h^L), \quad (36)$$

$$\delta_{ph}^U = ([T_p]_h^U - [O_p]_h^U)[O_p]_h^U (1 - [O_p]_h^U). \quad (37)$$

ii) If $[W_j]_h^L \le [W_j]_h^U < 0$ then

$$\partial e_{ph}/\partial w_j^L = -\delta_{ph}^L [O_{pj}]_h^U (1 - h/2) - \delta_{ph}^U [O_{pj}]_h^L h/2. \quad (38)$$

iii) If $[W_j]_h^L < 0 \le [W_j]_h^U$ then

$$\partial e_{ph}/\partial w_j^L = -\delta_{ph}^L [O_{pj}]_h^U (1 - h/2) - \delta_{ph}^U [O_{pj}]_h^U h/2. \quad (39)$$

After the adjustments of the fuzzy weights by (31)-(34), it is undesirable but may happen that the lower limits of the fuzzy weights exceed the upper limits. In order to cope with this undesirable situation, we define new fuzzy weights after the adjustments as

$$w_j^L = \min\{w_j^L(t+1), w_j^U(t+1)\}, \quad (40)$$

$$w_{ji}^L = \min\{w_{ji}^L(t+1), w_{ji}^U(t+1)\}, \quad (41)$$

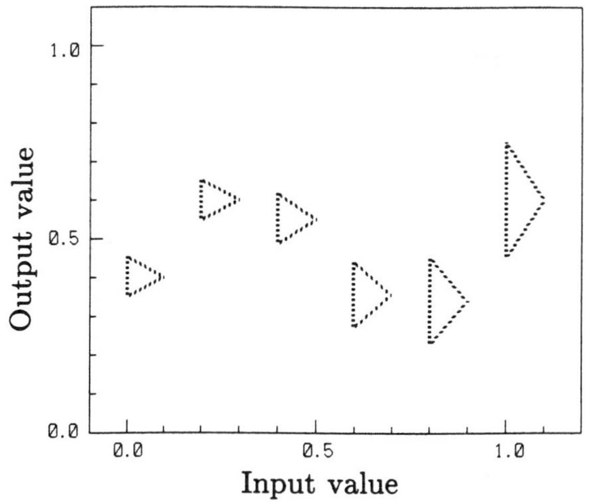

Fig.5. Training data for the learning of the neural network

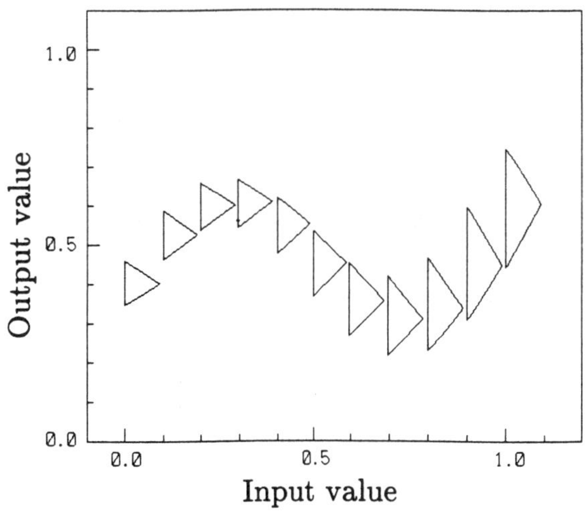

Fig.6. Fuzzy actual outputs from the trained neural network

$$w_j^U = \max\{w_j^L(t+1), w_j^U(t+1)\}, \quad (42)$$

$$w_{ji}^U = \max\{w_{ji}^L(t+1), w_{ji}^U(t+1)\}. \quad (43)$$

The centers w_j^C and w_{ji}^C are determined from w_j^L, w_j^U, w_{ji}^L and w_{ji}^U by (5). The fuzzy biases are changed in the same manner as the fuzzy weights.

D. Numerical Example

We show a simulation result of the learning of the proposed fuzzy neural network. The training data is shown in Fig.5. In Fig.5, fuzzy target outputs corresponding to six input values: $x = 0.0, 0.2, \cdots, 1.0$, are given as triangular fuzzy numbers. Using the proposed learning algorithm, we trained the fuzzy neural network with a single input unit, five hidden units and a single output unit. The learning algorithm was iterated 10,000 times, i.e., 10,000 epochs. The sum of the cost function e_p over the given six training patterns was 0.0082 after 10,000 iterations. In Fig.6, we show the actual fuzzy outputs from the trained neural network corresponding to 11 input values: $x = 0.0, 0.1, ..., 1.0$. From this figure, we can see that good fitting to the six fuzzy target outputs and good interpolation for the five new inputs were accomplished.

IV. EXTENSION TO FUZZY INPUT VECTORS AND FUZZY TARGET OUTPUTS

The proposed approach can be extended to the case of fuzzy input vectors and fuzzy target outputs. Let $(\boldsymbol{X}_p, T_p)$ be the p-th input-output pair where $\boldsymbol{X}_p$ is an n-dimensional fuzzy input vector and T_p is a fuzzy target output. In this case, the input-output relation in (13)-(17) is modified as follows.

Input units :

$$O_{pi} = X_{pi}, \; i = 1, 2, \cdots, n. \quad (44)$$

Hidden units :

$$O_{pj} = f(Net_{pj}), \; j = 1, 2, \cdots, n_2, \quad (45)$$

$$Net_{pj} = \sum_{i=1}^{n} W_{ji} O_{pi} + \Theta_j, \; j = 1, 2, \cdots, n_2. \quad (46)$$

Output unit :

$$O_p = f(Net_p), \quad (47)$$

$$Net_p = \sum_{j=1}^{n_2} W_j O_{pj} + \Theta. \quad (48)$$

The input-output relation of the output unit is the same as the case of a real input vector in Section II.

Using the fuzzy input vector $\boldsymbol{X}_p$ and the fuzzy target output T_p, the fuzzy neural network can be trained by the learning algorithm defined by (31)-(34) and (40)-(43). That is, we can also use the cost function e_{ph} in (26) for this case. The derivatives $\partial e_{ph}/\partial w_j^L$, $\partial e_{ph}/\partial w_j^U$, $\partial e_{ph}/\partial w_{ji}^L$ and $\partial e_{ph}/\partial w_{ji}^U$ can be derived from the cost function e_{ph} in (26) using the input-output relation for h-level sets in a similar manner as the case of the real input vector $\boldsymbol{x}_p$ ($\partial e_{ph}/\partial w_j^L$, $\partial e_{ph}/\partial w_j^U$ are the same and $\partial e_{ph}/\partial w_{ji}^L$, $\partial e_{ph}/\partial w_{ji}^U$ are more complicated.)

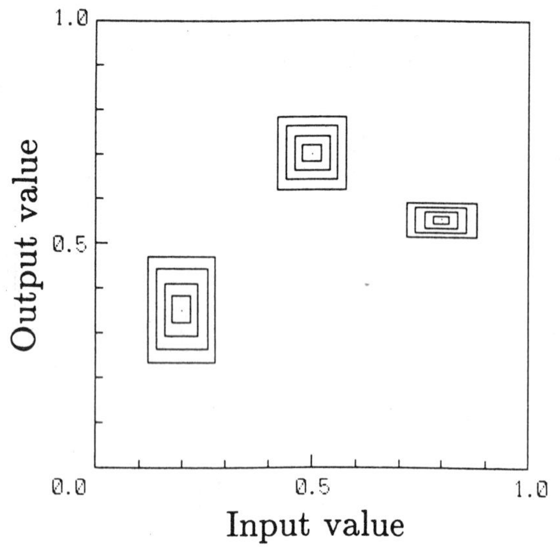

Fig.7. Training data

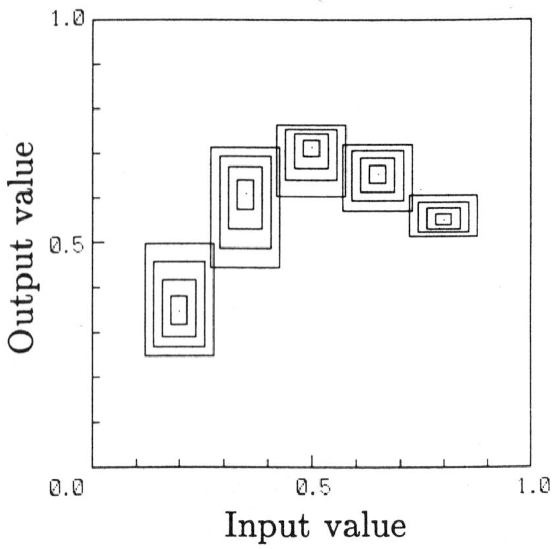

Fig.8. Fuzzy actual outputs

In Fig.7 and Fig.8, we show a simulation result. Fig.7 is the training data and Fig.8 is the fuzzy actual outputs from the trained fuzzy neural network after 10,000 iterations. In these figures, five level sets corresponding to $h = 0.2, 0.4, 0.6, 0.8, 1.0$, are depicted.

V. CONCLUSION

In this paper, we proposed an architecture of fuzzy neural networks with fuzzy weights and fuzzy biases. For the input-output pairs of real input vectors and fuzzy target outputs, a learning algorithm is derived from a cost function defined by the level sets of a fuzzy actual output and the corresponding fuzzy target output. The derived learning algorithm was extended to the case of fuzzy input vectors and fuzzy target outputs.

REFERENCES

[1] L.A.Zadeh, "The concept of a linguistic variable and its application to approximate reasoning - I, II and III," Information Sciences, vol.8, pp.199-249, pp.301-357 and vol.9, pp.43-80, 1975.

[2] H.Tanaka, S.Uejima and K.Asai, "Linear regression analysis with fuzzy model," IEEE Trans. on System, Man and Cybernetics, vol.12, pp.903-907, 1982.

[3] H.Ishibuchi and H.Tanaka, "Regression analysis with interval model by neural networks," Proc. of IJCNN'91 (November 18-21, 1991, Singapore) pp.1594-1599.

[4] H.Ishibuchi and H.Tanaka, "Fuzzy regression analysis using neural networks," Fuzzy Sets and Systems, vol.49, pp.257-265, 1992.

[5] D.E.Rumelhart, J.L.McClelland and the PDP Research Group, Parallel Distributed Processing, vol.1. MIT Press, Cambridge, 1986.

[6] Y.Hayashi, J.J.Buckley and E.Czogala, "Direct fuzzification of neural network and fuzzified delta rule," Proc. of the 2nd International Conference on Fuzzy Logic & Neural Networks (July 17-22, 1992, Iizuka, Japan) pp.73-76.

[7] G.Alefeld and J.Herzberger, Introduction to Interval Computations. Academic Press, New York, 1983.

[8] H.Ishibuchi, R.Fujioka and H.Tanaka, "An architecture of neural networks for input vectors of fuzzy numbers," Proc. of FUZZ-IEEE'92 (March 8-12, 1992, San Diego) pp.1293-1300.

[9] H.Ishibuchi, R.Fujioka and H.Tanaka, "Neural networks that learn from fuzzy if-then rules," IEEE Trans. on Fuzzy Systems, in press, 1993.

[10] H.Ishibuchi, H.Okada and H.Tanaka, "Learning of neural networks from fuzzy inputs and fuzzy targets," Proc. of IJCNN'92 (November 3-6, 1992, Beijing, China) vol.III, pp.507-511 and pp.481.

[11] H.Ishibuchi, H.Okada and H.Tanaka, "A neural network with interval weights and its learning algorithm," Proc. of IJCNN'92 (November 3-6, 1992, Beijing, China) vol.III, pp.447-452.

INFERENCE, INQUIRY AND EXPLANATION IN EXPERT SYSTEMS BY MEANS OF FUZZY NEURAL NETWORKS

Ricardo José Machado
IBM Rio Scientific Center
Av. Presidente Vargas, 824
20071-001 Rio de Janeiro, Brasil

Armando Freitas da Rocha
Instituto de Biologia - UNICAMP
13081 Campinas, Brasil

Abstract — **A new field of research focus on integrating the paradigms of expert systems and neural networks. In this paper we show how basic functions of expert systems, such as inference, inquiry and explanation can be implemented by means of fuzzy neural networks.**

I. INTRODUCTION

Hybrid architectures for intelligent systems is a new field of Artificial Intelligence research concerned with the development of the next generation of intelligent systems. Current research interests in this field focus on integrating the computational paradigms of expert systems and neural networks in a manner that exploits the strengths of both systems expanding the applications to which either system could be applied individually. Such systems are called *Connectionist Expert Systems* (CES) [4,18].

The ability to learn in uncertain or unknown environments is an essential component of any intelligent system and is particularly crucial to its performance. This ability, which is lacking in traditional expert systems, can be achieved by incorporating neural network learning mechanisms into expert systems. These learning techniques enable expert systems to modify and/or enrich their knowledge structures autonomously. As pointed out by Kandel and Langholz [9], intelligent hybrid systems offer the means to overcome some of the major drawbacks of conventional expert systems, such as: 1) their total reliance on consultation with human experts for knowledge acquisition (the knowledge acquisition bottleneck), 2) their inability to synthesize new knowledge, 3) their inability to allow for dynamic environments by modifying knowledge whenever it becomes necessary.

However, in combining such methods we should take care of not violating basic characteristics of expert systems [8], such as:

- the ability of receiving and representing knowledge elicited from human experts,
- the capability of dealing with data absence, and inquiring the user when additional data is necessary,
- the intelligibility of the knowledge base,
- the capability of explaining and justifying solutions or recommendations to convince the user that its reasoning is in fact correct.

Unfortunately this list of requirements imposes severe restrictions on the use of classical artificial neural networks for constructing CESs. Neural networks cannot directly encode structured knowledge. This makes difficult for them to receive knowledge elicited from an expert, and also to justify their conclusions. Neural nets superimpose several input-output samples on a black-box web of synapses. It is quite hard to know what a neural net has learned or forgotten. Many models (e.g., Backpropagation) are unable to perform incremental learning (that is imperative for a neural net being able to receive an initial load of expert knowledge, and to refine it with the experience [17]). It is also difficult (or impossible) for most neural net models to represent and deal with data absence, which is crucial for the inquiry process.

Fuzzy Neural Networks (FNN) appear as a solution able to meet all the above mentioned requirements [5,6,7,10,12,14,20,21]. Such networks, based on the fuzzy logic theory, encode directly structured knowledge, but in a numerical framework. They have been studied recently by many researchers. In this paper we will describe the FNN model introduced by Machado and Rocha for building CES, called *Combinatorial Neural Model* (CNM) [16,17], aimed at solving classification tasks.

As an additional advantage, FNNs provide to CESs powerful uncertainty management procedures for approximate reasoning. The fuzzy logic framework allows CESs to deal systematically with the vagueness, inaccuracy, incompleteness, and inconsistency frequently associated to the human reasoning [10]. This would enable CESs to better emulate human decision-making processes as well as allow for imprecise information and/or uncertain environment.

The purpose of present paper is to introduce some measures of uncertainty to be used by the connectionist inference machine of a classification expert system when performing inference, inquiry and explanation. Here, we

0-7803-0614-7/93$03.00 ©1993IEEE

do not describe the neural network structure in detail, nor the techniques for building/training them, because it was done before in [14,16,17], but we will focus our attention upon the uncertainty processing by the different elements of the network.

To accomplish this task, the paper is divided in the following sections: Fuzzy Neural Networks, which gives a summarized description of the CNM connectionist model, and introduces the uncertainty measures employed in this model; Consultation, which describes the control strategy used during consultation; Inference, which describes how classification is performed by FNNs; Inquiry, where the algorithm for the inquiring process is discussed in detail; Explanation, where the algorithms allowing the system to justify how a conclusion was achieved, or why an evidence was asked are introduced.

II. FUZZY NEURAL NETWORKS

In CESs, the knowledge base is replaced by a fuzzy neural network called the *Connectionist Knowledge Base* (CKB). The concepts of the problem domain are represented by neurons whose activations can be interpreted as their degrees of possibility. The neurons are connected by synapses whose weights represent the degree of adhesion between the corresponding neuron concepts. The resulting network constitutes the CKB [15,18].

The fuzzy neural network associated to a classification task assumes a feedforward topology with three or more layers: the *Input layer* for evidences, *Hidden layers* for intermediate abstractions and the *Output layer* for hypotheses. It uses several types of neurons: *Fuzzy-Number* at the input layer, *Fuzzy-AND* at hidden layers, *Fuzzy-OR* at the output layer.

The Fuzzy-Number cells located at the input layer may receive input data in a symbolic or numeric form. In the second case, such neurons will perform the fuzzification of the input numeric data into possibility degrees, using the membership functions corresponding to their associated concepts [15].

The fuzzy-AND cells of the hidden layers implement a fundamental characteristic in the reasoning of humans: to chunk input evidences into clusters of information for representing regular patterns of the environment. These clusters are intermediate abstractions, used to reduce the computational complexity of performing the classification task.

The fuzzy-OR cells of the output layer compute the degree of possibility of each hypothesis, i.e., the degree of membership of the object under analysis to each class of a classification task. Note that every pathway reaching a fuzzy-OR neuron can be seen as an independent module competing with other modules for establishing the decision of the case.

Each class of the classification task has an independent network called *Hypothesis Network.* For example, Figure 2-I presents one hypothesis network in a FNN. The FNN architecture is strongly inspired in the *knowledge graphs* elicited from experts by the application of the knowledge acquisition technique of Rocha et al. [11,13]. In this technique, experts express their knowledge about each hypothesis of the problem domain by selecting a set of appropriate evidences and building an acyclic weighted AND-OR graph (called *Knowledge Graph*) to describe how these evidences must be combine to support decision making. The similitude between knowledge graphs and fuzzy neural nets allows the direct and easy translation of expert knowledge into the FNNs of the CKB [17,18].

A. Uncertainty Management in FNNs

A FNN is capable of reasoning with three types of uncertainty: Fuzziness, Imprecision and Incompleteness [15]. For coping with these uncertainties, the FNN computes for every neuron (and consequently for every problem domain concept) a *Possibility Value Interval* (PVI), which contains its unknown possibility value. The PVI's lower bound represents the minimal degree of confirmation for the possibility value assignment. The PVI's upper bound represents the degree to which the evidence failed to refute the possibility value assignment. The interval's width represents the amount of ignorance associated with the possibility value assignment. Consummate concepts have PVI of width equal to zero. The absence of information is represented by the PVI [0, 1]. The fuzzy negation of an evidence presenting a PVI: [a, b] is given by the interval [1-b, 1-a]. A similar approach was used in the system PRIMO [1].

The above uncertainty management scheme can be easily implemented in fuzzy neural networks by defining two different activations for neurons: *Current Activation* (CA) representing the PVI's lower bound, and *Potential Activation* (PA) representing the PVI's upper bound, which is the maximum degree of activation a neuron will reach. We define the *Ignorance* (IG) of a neuron: IG = PA - CA. At the input layer, IG expresses the imprecision of input data. Neurons corresponding to unmeasured input concepts present IG equal to 1. At the hidden and output layers, IG expresses the maximum gain that neurons can obtain in their CA's if ignorance is solved at all neurons of the input level.

III. THE CONSULTATION

The consultation process in a CES follows the hypothetico-deductive approach [19] mimicking human information processing characteristics. The consultation is organized in two different phases: the *passive* and the *active phase.* During the passive phase the user enters a set of triggering data into the system, which will be used to trigger hypotheses, forming the *Consultation Focus* (also called *Context* or *Differential*). Hypotheses that present, at the end of the passive phase, CA larger than a pre-defined *Triggering Threshold* are included into the consultation focus.

During the active phase the system tries to prove or refute the hypotheses belonging to the focus by actively inquiring the user. Only hypotheses with possibility degree larger than a predefined *Acceptance Threshold* (T_{acc}) are presented to the user as the problem solution. The focus may be revised periodically to account for new data.

The processes of *Inference, Inquiry*, and *Explanation* are required during the consultation. They are described in the following sections.

A. Inference

The goal of the inference process is to compute the degree of possibility of each hypothesis, and to point those classes having possibilities greater than the Acceptance Threshold as the problem solution. This is done by propagating the available input evidences forward in the network through two information flows. We define the *Current Evidential Flow* (CEF_{ij}) and the *Potential Evidential Flow* (PEF_{ij}) in a synapsis (i,j) as

$$CEF_{ij} = CA_i \cdot w_{ij} \qquad PEF_{ij} = PA_i \cdot w_{ij}$$

where CA_i = current activation of neuron i, PA_i = potential activation of neuron i, w_{ij} = weight of the synapsis (i,j). If the synapsis (i,j) is inhibitory (fuzzy negation) then

$$CEF_{ij} = (1 - PA_i) \cdot w_{ij} \qquad PEF_{ij} = (1 - CA_i) \cdot w_{ij}$$

The inference process performs the forward propagation of the current and potential activations of the neurons of the input layer, according to the fuzzy evidence aggregation rules of the neurons in the network. The Fuzzy-AND and Fuzzy-OR neurons aggregate the incoming evidential flows according to the classical rules (minimum and maximum) of fuzzy logic, shown below:

For Fuzzy-AND neurons:

$$CA_x = \min_{i \in R_x} (CEF_i) \qquad PA_x = \min_{i \in R_x} (PEF_i)$$

For Fuzzy-OR neurons:

$$CA_x = \max_{i \in R_x} (CEF_i) \qquad PA_x = \max_{i \in R_x} (PEF_i)$$

where R_X is the set of neurons that can send directly messages to the neuron X. Other norm and co-norms can be used for implementing Fuzzy-AND and Fuzzy-OR [3].

In FNNs based on CNM, if the PVIs of the input neurons are not divergent intervals across time, then the PVIs of the output neurons also will not be divergent intervals with time (See proof at appendix). Figure 1 shows the evolution of CA and PA of a hypothesis neuron H with time as evidences are measured. At time t, CA represents the support achieved for concept H, MA-PA is the concept refutation (MA being the potential activation at the beginning of the consultation), and PA-CA is the ignorance of H. When the curves of PA and CA meet, it means that there is no more ignorance to be solved in relation to the neuron H.

Only hypotheses exhibiting $CA \geq T_{acc}$ are accepted by the system as the problem solution. Hypotheses having $PA < T_{acc}$ are rejected by the system. Hypotheses showing $CA < T_{acc}$ and $PA \geq T_{acc}$ are considered undecided, requiring additional information for decision making. Figure 2 shows for example the inference calculation in two different networks. (Synaptic weights are denoted at the side of arcs. In both nets the hypotheses remained undecided for T_{acc}).

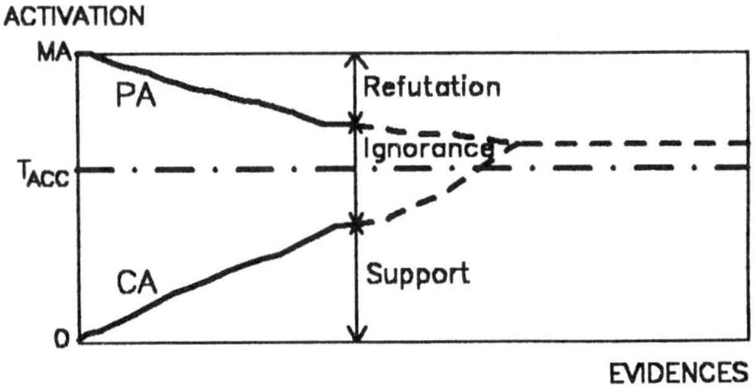

Fig. 1 - Potential and current activations of a hypothesis as a function of the evidences measured during a consultation.

B. Inquiry

The inquiry process has as goal to find the best question to be asked next to the user, among the input nodes having ignorance. If a neuron located at any level presents IG > 0, it implies that there is ignorance at the input layer, that if solved can potentially improve the current activation of this neuron. This makes possible to determine the best question through local decisions, producing a very efficient inquiry algorithm (no backtracking required), which is shown next:

Algorithm INQUIRY

1- Select the hypothesis H of the focus with PA > T_{acc} and the largest IG
2- BACKWARD (QUERY, H)
3- If QUERY is not empty then ask to the user the question QUERY.
4- Stop

Algorithm BACKWARD(QUERY, N)

0- Comment. N: neuron from which we want to determine the best question QUERY: input node selected as the best question
1- Determine R = $\{X \mid (PEF_{XN} - CEF_{XN} > 0)$ and $(PEF_{XN} > CA_N)\}$
2- Select $X \in R$ that presents minimum PA if N is a Fuzzy-AND neuron, or the maximum PA if N is a Fuzzy-OR neuron
3- If X is an input node
   then QUERY ← X
      Stop
   else BACKWARD(QUERY,X)
      Stop

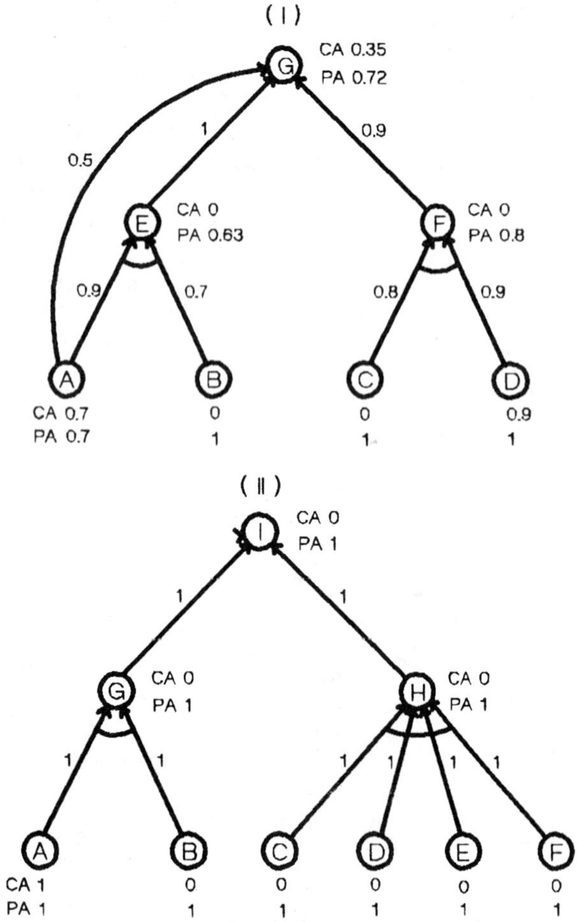

Fig. 2 - Inference process. In the network I the evidences B and C are unknown and the evidence D is imprecise. In the network II only the evidence A is known.

This algorithm can be applied to general networks using Fuzzy-AND and Fuzzy-OR nodes at any layers. The heuristic rules employed in this algorithm provide a powerful pruning mechanism, avoiding to make questions and to perform tests that cannot contribute to solve the problem. Hypotheses of the focus whose PA's become smaller than T_{acc} are not more investigated during a consultation (rejected hypotheses). For instance, in Figure 2-I if the neuron C receives CA = PA = 0.9 then the evidence associated to the neuron B will not be more asked to the user (assuming T_{acc} = .7). The algorithm pursues all hypotheses of the focus, being able to deal with multiple fault problems. Sometimes the algorithm may ask the user to repeat a previous measurement, which was early informed with too much imprecision. If we are interested in stopping the investigation of hypotheses as soon as they are accepted, the step 1 of the algorithm Inquiry should be replaced by:

1- Select the undecided hypothesis of the Focus with the largest IG.

This inquiry algorithm takes into consideration only the informational power of the neurons. This can produce some troubles. For instance, at the node I in the network II of the figure 2, the system does not have any information to select between B or C. However, the choice B is clearly more adequate, because it suffices to make one question to the user to eventually solve the problem. In the network I of the figure 2, if B represents a X-Ray and C a biopsy, the natural choice should be the X-Ray, a procedure of lower cost and risk. However the presented algorithm would choose the biopsy. To avoid this problem, it is fundamental to make the system sensitive to the costs (and or risks) associated to the measurement procedures. With this intent, we will define for every neuron a variable called *Neuron Utility* (NU), that expresses the utility associated to to solving the ignorance associated to the neuron. To be able to make local decisions we need to propagate the utility information of input evidences in the network. This is done defining a third flow in the synapses, called the *Utility Flow* (UF):

$$UF_{ij} = NU_j \cdot s(PA_i - CA_i) = \text{utility flow at synapsis } (i,j)$$

where $s(x) = s(PA_i - CA_i)$ is the unitary step function: $s(x) = 1$ if $x > 0$, $s(x) = 0$ if $x \leq 0$. Each neuron computes its utility aggregating the utility flows received from other neurons. Fuzzy-AND neurons aggregate cost utilities according to

$$NU_j = \sum_{i \in R_{AND}} UF_{ij} \qquad \text{where } R_{AND} = \{ i \mid CEF_{ij} < PA_j \}$$

Fuzzy-OR neurons aggregate cost utilities according to

$$NU_j = \min_{i \in R_{OR}} \{ UF_{ij} \}$$

where $R_{OR} = \{ i \mid (PEF_{ij} > T_{acc}) \text{ and } (PEF_{ij} > CA_j) \text{ and } (PEF_{ij} - CEF_{ij} > 0) \}$

These aggregation functions should be modified if we intend to work with risks rather than costs.

To be able to describe the benefit/cost relation of a pathway, we define the variable *Merit* (M_{ij}) of an arc (i,j)

$$M_{ij} = (PEF_{ij} - CEF_{ij}) / UF_{ij}.$$

This division is defined equal to 0 if the numerator and the denominator become simultaneously equal to 0.

Now a *Utility Conscious Inquiry Algorithm* can be easily obtained by replacing the line 1 of the algorithm INQUIRY by:

1- Select the hypothesis H of the focus with PA > T_{acc} and the largest ratio IG/NU and by replacing the lines 1 and 2 of the algorithm BACKWARD by:

1- Determine R = R_{AND}, or R_{OR} depending on the type of the neuron N.
2- Select X ∈ R that presents the largest merit M_{XN}.

For example, assuming NU=1 for every input neuron in the network II of Figure 2, the algorithm INQUIRY will select the node B to be inquired first.

C. Explanation

We provide explanations for the following two types of user inquiries during a consultation: those that ask HOW a particular conclusion was reached, and those that ask WHY a particular question was formulated [8].

The structure of FNNs is highly modular making easy to justify their conclusions and questions. Each hypothesis network is formed by a set of pathways that compete for sending the largest evidential flow to the hypothesis neuron. Since each neuron in a pathway can be seen as a heuristic fuzzy rule, it is quite simple to provide a trace style explanation of the system response just by showing the structure of the winning pathway as a chain of pseudo-production rules.

A pseudo-production rule is a practical way of describing neurons in the winning pathway. For a hidden neuron it has the following format:

If $Y_1(w_1,t_1)$ Ψ ... Ψ $Y_n(w_n,t_n)$ then N

where

- X = hidden neuron that is being described
- Y_i = code (or name of the associated concept, if available) of the ith neuron of the fan-in of X
- (w_i,t_i) = weight and synaptic type (excitatory or inhibitory) of the synapsis connecting Y_i to X
- Ψ = logical connective associated to neuron X (fuzzy-AND or fuzzy-OR)
- N = Neuron to which X is connected in the pathway under consideration

For an input neuron belonging to a pathway linking it directly to the hypothesis neuron, the pseudo-production rule is expressed as:

If $X(w_X, t_X)$ then H

where (w_X,t_X) = weight and synaptic type of the synapsis from X to N.

An algorithm for HOW-inquiries, based on this approach, is presented next:

Algorithm HOW(H)
0- Comment: Justification of the acceptance of hypothesis H
1- Present CA_H and show that $CA_H \geq T_{acc}$
2- Select the neuron X sending the largest CEF to H
3- If X is an input neuron
then Present its pseudo-production rule and show CA_X
else Trace(X, H)
4- Stop

Algorithm TRACE(X,N)
0- Comment: Display of the synapsis X→N and its antecedents
1- Present the pseudo-production rule describing neuron X
2- Present the CA of neurons belonging to the fan-in R of X
3- For each neuron Y ∈ R do
- If Y does not belong to the input layer
then TRACE(X, N)
Endfor
4- Stop

The algorithm for answering WHY an evidence E is being asked by the system in the context of a hypothesis H is presented next:

Algorithm WHY(E, H)
0- Comment: Justification why E is needed in the context of H
1- Justify why H is being investigated: it belongs to the focus, it was not yet rejected, and it presents the best ratio IG/NC
2- Justify why in this context E was selected to be inquired, showing the sequence of selections of synapses with largest merit, that were made departing from H and going backwards in direction of evidence E.
3- Show the PVI that H will have if we receive a PVI equal to [1, 1] for E.
4- Stop

The algorithm HOW may be invoked by the user at the end of the consultation, whereas the algorithm WHY may be invoked after every question formulated by the system.

IV. CONCLUSION

Expert systems and neural networks represent complementary approaches to knowledge representation: the logical, cognitive, and mechanical nature of expert systems versus the numeric, associative, and self-organizing nature of the neural network. The use of fuzzy neural networks for building connectionist expert systems has several advantages. Besides the capabilities of easy construction of the FNN from expert knowledge, incremental learning, and knowledge base readability, it provides an easy implementation of basic functions of expert systems, such as inference, inquiry, and explanation, as well as the ability to deal with the vague, uncertain and partial data, commonly found in practical applications.

The inference, inquiry, and explanation processes in CESs present low computational cost because they are performed using local decisions on an acyclic network. No backtracking is required. Local decisions in the inquiry process were made possible by propagating simultaneously in the network three different informations: the current evidential flow, the potential evidential flow and the utility flow. The complexities for the above mentioned processes are:
$O(n+s)$ for inference, where n = number of neurons and s = number of synapses;
$O(f.l+h)$ for inquiry, where l = number of layers, f = maximum size of the fan-in of a hidden neuron (usually limited to the number 7 of Miller) and h = number of hypotheses;

$O(l.f+h+n)$ for HOW explanation;
$O(l.f+h)$ for WHY explanation.

In the sense of the Dreyfus' definition [2], we can tell that the system seems to have intuition: "the ability of effortlessly and rapidly to associate with one's present situation an action or decision which experience has shown to be appropriate". The utility conscious inquiry process introduced in this paper allows to lower significantly the consultation cost/risk and can give to the system the common sense property presented by experts when selecting tests to be performed.

The CES scheme described in this paper may be seen as a building block for construction of more complex expert systems, whose cognitive task can be decomposed in different interconnected elementary classification tasks. For instance, in the medical domain the physician usually performs a diagnostic task, before proceeding the treatment prescription and the prognostic tasks. Each of these tasks should be implemented by a different FNN.

The model and the methods described in this paper were implemented successfully in the system NEXTOOL [18], a shell for building classification expert systems able to learn from experience.

REFERENCES

[1] J.K. Aragones, P.J. Bonissone, and J. Stillman, "PRIMO: a tool for reasoning with incomplete and uncertain information," *Proceedings of the Third International Conference IPMU*, Paris, 1990, pp. 325-327.

[2] R. Davis, (1989). "Expert systems: how far they can go?," *AI Magazine*, pp. 65-84, Spring 1989.

[3] D. Dubois, and I.I. Prade, "A class of fuzzy measures based on triangular norms," *Int. J. General Systems*, vol.8, pp. 43-61, 1992.

[4] S.I. Gallant, "Connectionist expert systems," *Communications of the ACM*, vol. 31, pp. 152-169, 1992.

[5] T. Hashiyama, T. Furuhashi, Y. Uchikawa, "An interval fuzzy model using a fuzzy neural network," *International Joint Conference on Neural Networks*, Baltimore, 1992.

[6] Y. Hayashi, "A neural expert system using fuzzy teaching input," *IEEE International Conference on Fuzzy Systems*, San Diego, 1992.

[7] L.S. Hsu, H.H. Teh, P.Z. Wang, and K.F. Loe, "Fuzzy neural-logic system," *International Joint Conference on Neural Networks*, Baltimore, 1992.

[8] P. Jackson, *Introduction to Expert Systems*, Workingham: Addison Wesley, 1990.

[9] A. Kandel, and G. Langholz, *Hybrid Architectures for Intelligent Systems*, Boca Raton, Fl: CRC Press, 1992.

[10] B. Kosko, *Neural Networks and Fuzzy Systems*, Englewood Cliffs, NJ: Prentice Hall Inc., 1992.

[11] B.F. Leão, "Proposed methodology for knowledge acquisition - a study on congenital heart diseases diagnosis," *Methods of Inf. in Medicine*, vol. 29, pp. 30-40, 1990.

[12] C.T. Lin, and C.S.G. Lee, "Real-time supervised structure / parameter learning for fuzzy neural network," *IEEE International Conference on Fuzzy Systems*, San Diego, 1992.

[13] R.J. Machado, A.F. Rocha, and B.F. Leão, "Calculating the mean knowledge representation from multiple experts," in *Multi-person Decision Making Models Using Fuzzy Sets and Possibility Theory*, J. Kacprzyk and M. Fedrizzi, Eds. Dordrecht: Kluwer Academic Publishers, 1990, pp. 113-127.

[14] R.J. Machado, and A.F Rocha, "The combinatorial neural network: a connectionist model for knowledge based systems," in *Uncertainty in Knowledge Bases*, B. Bouchon, L. Zadeh and R. Yager, Eds. Berlin: Springer Verlag, 1991, pp. 578-587.

[15] R.J. Machado, and A.F. Rocha, "A hybrid architecture for fuzzy connectionist expert systems," in *Hybrid Architectures for Intelligent Systems*, A. Kandel, G. Langholz, Eds. Boca Raton, Fl: CRC Press Inc, 1992, pp. 136-152.

[16] R.J. Machado, and A.F. Rocha, "Evolutive fuzzy neural networks," *IEEE International Conference on Fuzzy Systems*, San Diego, 1992.

[17] R.J. Machado, C. Ferlin, A.F. Rocha , and G.J. Erthal, "Incremental learning in fuzzy neural networks," *International Conference on Information Processing and Management of Uncertainty in Knowledge-Based Systems, IPMU*, Palma de Mallorca, 1992.

[18] R.J. Machado, A.F. Rocha, and C. Ferlin, "NEXTOOL - an environment for connectionist expert systems," *Third Annual Symposium of the International Association of Knowledge Engineers*, Washington, 1992.

[19] R.S. Patil, "Artificial intelligence techniques for diagnostic reasoning on medicine," in *Exploring Artificial Intelligence: Surveys Talks from the National Conference on AI*, H.E. Schrobe and AAAI, Eds. San Mateo: Morgan Kauffmann, 1988, pp. 347-379.

[20] S.G. Romaniuk, and L.O. Hall, "Learning fuzzy information in a hybrid connectionist, symbolic model," *IEEE International Conference on Fuzzy Systems*, San Diego, 1992.

[21] F. Yuan, A. Feldkamp, L.I. Davis, and G.V. Puskorios, (1992). "Training a hybrid neural-fuzzy system," *International Joint Conference on Neural Networks*, Baltimore, 1992.

APPENDIX

Theorem 1: The partial derivatives of activations of output neurons with respect to the activations of input neurons in a FNN based on the CNM model are positive or null.

Proof: Let H be an output neuron, and X an input neuron of a FNN with activations p_H and p_X respectively. Let i be anyone of the pathways towards H departing from the neuron X.

$$CEF_i = w_i \cdot \min(w_1 \cdot p_1, \ldots, w_X \cdot p_X, \ldots, w_n \cdot p_n)$$

$$p_H = \max(CEF_1, \ldots CEF_i, \ldots)$$

Let Δp_X be a positive variation on p_X. It will produce

$\Delta CEF_i \geq 0$ and $\Delta p_H \geq 0$

Hence we have the ratio $\Delta p_H / \Delta p_X \geq 0$

For $\Delta p_X \to 0$ the theorem is proved.

Theorem 2: If the PVIs of input neurons of a FNN based on CNM are not divergent across time, then the same will happen with the PVIs of output neurons.

Proof: Let X be an input neuron presenting at time t a PVI $= [p'(t), p''(t)]$, and H be an output neuron presenting at this time PVI $= [\pi'(t), \pi''(t)]$.

At time $t+\Delta t$ we will have $p'(t+\Delta t) \geq p'(t)$ and $p''(t+\Delta t) \leq p''(t)$ (non-divergent PVI),

and by theorem 1:

$\pi'(t+\Delta t) \geq \pi'(t)$ and $\pi''(t+\Delta t) \leq \pi''(t)$

Hence the PVI of H is not divergent.

A Fuzzy Neural Network Learning Fuzzy Control Rules and Membership Functions by Fuzzy Error Backpropagation

Detlef Nauck Rudolf Kruse

Department of Computer Science

Technical University of Braunschweig

W-3300 Braunschweig, Germany

***Abstract*— In this paper we present a new kind of neural network architecture designed for control tasks, which we call fuzzy neural network. The structure of the network can be interpreted in terms of a fuzzy controller. It has a three-layered architecture and uses fuzzy sets as its weights. The fuzzy error backpropagation algorithm, a special learning algorithm inspired by the standard BP-procedure for multilayer neural networks, is able to learn the fuzzy sets. The extended version that is presented here is also able to learn fuzzy-if-then rules by reducing the number of nodes in the hidden layer of the network. The network does not learn from examples, but by evaluating a special fuzzy error measure.**

I. Introduction

Neural Networks and Fuzzy Controllers are both capable of controlling nonlinear dynamical systems. The disadvantage of neural control is that it is not obvious how the network solves the respective control task. It is not possible in general to retrieve any kind of structural knowledge from the network that could be formulated e.g. in some kind of rules, or to use prior knowledge to reduce the learning time. The network has to learn from scratch, and might have to do so again if substantial parameters of the dynamical system change for some reason.

The use of a fuzzy controller on the other hand allows to interpret the control behavior due to the explicit linguistic rules the controller consists of. The design problems of a fuzzy controller are the choice of appropriate fuzzy if-then-rules, and membership functions, and the tuning of both in order to improve the performance of the fuzzy controller. The disadvantage of this method is the lack of suitable learning algorithms retaining the semantics of the controller.

We propose to overcome these disadvantages by using a special feed-forward neural network architecture with fuzzy sets as its weights. The weights are membership functions and represent the linguistic values of the input variables and the output variables, respectively. Due to its structure the network can be interpreted as a fuzzy controller, where the nodes of the hidden layer represent fuzzy if-then-rules. The input layer consists of nodes for the variables describing the state of the dynamical system, and the output layer contains the node(s) representing the control action to drive the system towards a desired state. A learning algorithm utilizing a fuzzy error measure, valuating the output of the fuzzy neural network, is able to learn fuzzy rules by deleting hidden nodes, and to adapt the membership functions. We call this learning procedure fuzzy error backpropagation (FEBP).

We refrained from just inserting neural networks in fuzzy controllers to tune some weights scaling the rules or the fuzzy sets [3], or from using neural networks to identify fuzzy rules to build a fuzzy controller [9]. We use instead a new architecture which we call fuzzy neural network (FNN) that is able to learn both fuzzy if-then-rules and fuzzy sets by changing its structure and its weights. The network converges to a state that can be easily interpreted and has clear semantics. Our model is able to learn, to use prior knowledge, and has no black box behavior. Its structure can be interpreted in terms of membership functions and fuzzy-if-then rules. The learning procedure is an extension to our fuzzy error propagation algorithm for neural fuzzy controllers [6, 7]. A learning procedure that uses examples is considered in [2].

II. The Fuzzy Neural Network

We consider a dynamical system S that can be controlled by one variable C and whose state can be described by n variables $X_1, \dots, X_n$. For each variable we consider measurements in a subinterval $H = [h_1, h_2]$ of the real line. The imprecision is modelled by mappings $\mu : [h_1, h_2] \to [0, 1]$ in the sense of membership functions with the obvious interpretation as representations of linguistic values.

The control action that drives the system S to a desired state is described by the well-known concept of fuzzy if-

0-7803-0999-5/93/$03.00 ©1993 IEEE

then rules [10] where a conjunction of input variables associated with their respective linguistic values determines a linguistic value associated with the output variable. All rules are evaluated in parallel, and their outputs are combined to a fuzzy set which has to be defuzzified to receive the crisp output value.

As the T-norm operator for the conjunction of the input values usually the min-operator is used, and as the S-norm for aggregating the output values of the rules the max-operator is used, as it is done by the well known Zadeh-Mamdani procedure [10, 5].

For the evaluation of fuzzy rules the defuzzification-operation constitutes a problem that cannot be neglected. It is not obvious which crisp value is best suited to characterize the output fuzzy set of the rule system. In most of the fuzzy control environments the center-of-gravity method is used [4]. Using this method, it is difficult to determine the individual part that each rule contributes to the final output value.

To overcome this problem we use Tsukamoto's monotonic membership functions, where the defuzzification is reduced to an application of the inverse function [1]. Such a membership function μ is characterized by two points a, b with $\mu(a) = 0$ and $\mu(b) = 1$, and it is defined as

$$\mu(x) = \begin{cases} \frac{-x+a}{a-b} & \text{if } (x \in [a,b] \wedge a \leq b) \\ & \vee\ (x \in [b,a] \wedge a > b) \\ 0 & \text{otherwise} \end{cases}$$

The crisp value x belonging to the membership value y can be easily calculated by

$$x = \mu^{-1}(y) = -y(a-b) + a$$

with $y \in [0,1]$.

In Fig. 1 a simple fuzzy neural network is shown that incorporates the two fuzzy-if-then rules

R_1: **IF** X_1 is PL **AND** X_2 is PL **THEN** C is PL,
R_2: **IF** X_1 is PL **AND** X_2 is PM **THEN** C is PM,

where PL and PM represent the usual linguistic expressions *positive large* and *positive medium*. The circles represent the nodes, and the squares represent the fuzzy weights.

The network consists of three layers. The first layer, the input layer, contains one node for each input variable. The states of these nodes reflect the crisp values of the variables. The intermediate layer is called the *rule layer*. It contains one node for each fuzzy-if-then rule. The state of each *rule node* represents the membership value obtained by the conjunction of the rule antecedents. The crisp input values are sent over the respective connections to the rule nodes. Each connection has a fuzzy weight attached to it that is combined with the input value. In our case these weights are membership functions μ_{ik_i} representing the linguistic values of the input variables. The combination of the weight μ_{ik_i} and the crisp input value x_i simply results in the membership value $\mu_{ik_i}(x_i)$. If an input variable takes part with the same linguistic value in more than one rule antecedent, it is connected to the respective rule nodes by connections that share a common weight (see Table I and Fig. 1, weight μ_{11}). The sharing of the fuzzy weights is an important aspect of the architecture. We want to interpret the behavior of the network, and so we need identical membership functions for identical linguistic values.

The rule nodes R_j collect all incoming membership values and use a T-norm (e.g. min-operation) to calculate the conjunction of their antecedents. This is done by all rule nodes in parallel, and then they pass their states on to the output layer that contains one or more nodes describing the control action for the next time step. The weights attached to the connections between the intermediate and the output layer are membership functions ν_k representing the linguistic values of the rule consequents. The calculations that are carried out on the connections represent a fuzzy implication (e.g. Mamdani's minimum operation as fuzzy implication) resulting in fuzzy sets $\nu^*_{R_j}$ describing the output of each rule R_j. Nodes representing rules with an identical linguistic output value share a common

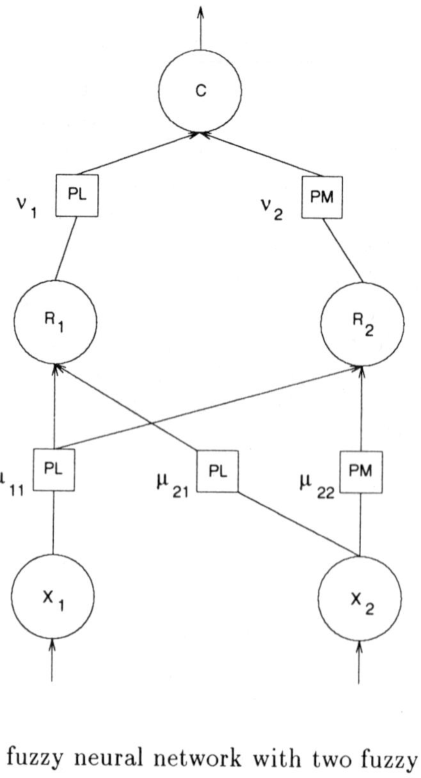

Fig. 1: A fuzzy neural network with two fuzzy rules

TABLE I:
TYPES OF CONNECTIONS IN A FUZZY NEURAL NETWORK

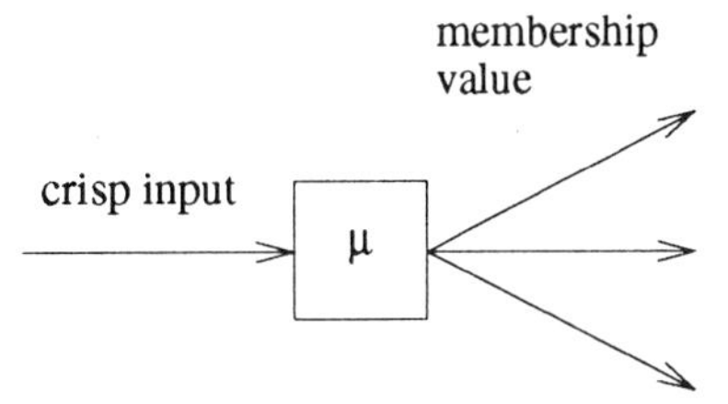	A connection from an input variable to three different rule nodes, which use the same linguistic value of this input variable in their antecedents.
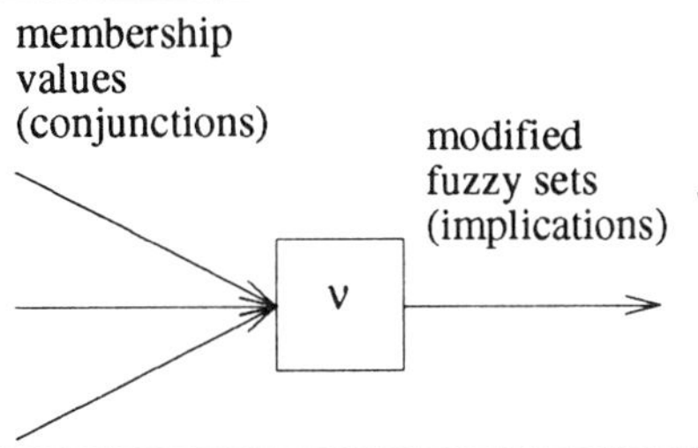	A connection from three rule nodes with the same linguistic value for their consequences to an output node. The output node receives three different signals from this connection.

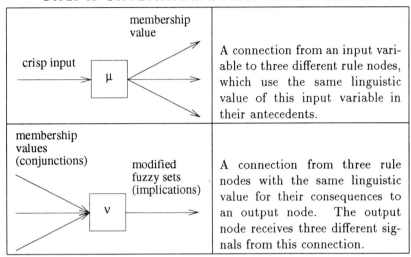

weight on their connection to the respective output node. In this case more than one value travels on the connection to the output node (see Table I).

Each output node collects the incoming fuzzy sets, aggregates them, and determines a crisp output value with the help of an appropriate defuzzification procedure D.

The learning algorithm for the fuzzy neural network needs to know the part each rule contributes to the final output value, and therefore the use of monotonic membership functions in the consequence parts of the fuzzy rules is required. This results in Tsukamoto's method for fuzzy reasoning [4] where the aggregation and the defuzzification are carried out in one step. The crisp output value c (activation of the output node) is calculated by

$$c = \frac{\sum_{j=1}^{m} r_j \nu_{R_j}^{-1}(r_j)}{\sum_{j=1}^{m} r_i},$$

where m is the number of rules, and r_j is the result inferred from rule R_j. This is a simplified reasoning method based on Mamdani's minimum operation rule that is usually used in fuzzy controllers [4].

If the fuzzy rules are known, the learning algorithm has just to tune the membership functions. This situation is described in [6]. In the case that the rules are unknown, the learning algorithm has to be extended, so they can be learned, too.

To build a fuzzy neural network we have to identify the input and output variables. Then for each variable a number of initial non-optimal fuzzy sets have to be chosen describing such linguistic terms as *positive large, negative small,* etc. If we assume that the fuzzy if-then-rules that are necessary to control the dynamical system are not known, we have to create a network, that represents every possible rule that can be created from the number of fuzzy sets attributed to the variables. If we have a MISO (multiple input single output) system with two input variables and five linguistic variables for each variable we have to create a fuzzy neural network with 2 input nodes, 1 output node, and $5^3 = 125$ intermediate rule nodes. An example of our fuzzy neural network where three fuzzy sets are attributed to each variable is depicted in Fig. 2. During the learning procedure the network has to remove those rule nodes that are not needed or that are counterproductive.

III. FUZZY ERROR BACKPROPAGATION AND RULE LEARNING

Our goal is to tune the membership functions of the fuzzy neural network by a learning algorithm. Because it is usually not possible to calculate the optimal control action by other means parallel to the network so we can derive the error directly, we have to obtain a measure that adequately describes the state of the plant under consideration.

The optimal state of the plant can be described by a vector of state variable values. That means, the plant has reached the desired state if all of its state variables have reached their value defined by this vector. But usually we are content with the current state if the variables have roughly taken these values. And so it is natural to define the goodness of the current state by a membership function from which we can derive a fuzzy error that characterizes the performance of the fuzzy neural network.

Consider a system with n state variables $X_1, \ldots, X_n$. We define the fuzzy-goodness G_1 as

$$G_1 = \min\left\{\mu_{X_1}^{optimal}(x_1), \ldots, \mu_{X_n}^{optimal}(x_n)\right\},$$

where the membership functions $\mu_{X_i}^{optimal}$ have to be defined according to the requirements of the plant under consideration.

In addition of a near optimal state we also consider states as good, where the incorrect values of the state variables compensate each other in a way, that the plant is driven towards its optimal state. We define the fuzzy-goodness G_2 as

$$G_2 = \min \{\mu^{compensate_1}(x_1, \ldots, x_n), \ldots, \mu^{compensate_k}(x_1, \ldots, x_n)\}$$

where the membership functions $\mu^{compensate_j}$ again have to be defined according to the requirements of the plant. There may be more than one $\mu^{compensate_j}$ and they may depend on two or more of the state variables.

The overall fuzzy-goodness is defined as

$$G = g(G_1, G_2),$$

where the operation g has to be specified according to the actual application. In some cases a min-operation may be appropriate, and in other cases it may be more adequate to choose just one of the two goodness measures, perhaps depending on the sign of the current values of the state variables, e.g. we may want to use G_1 if all variables are positive or negative and G_2 if they are both positive and negative.

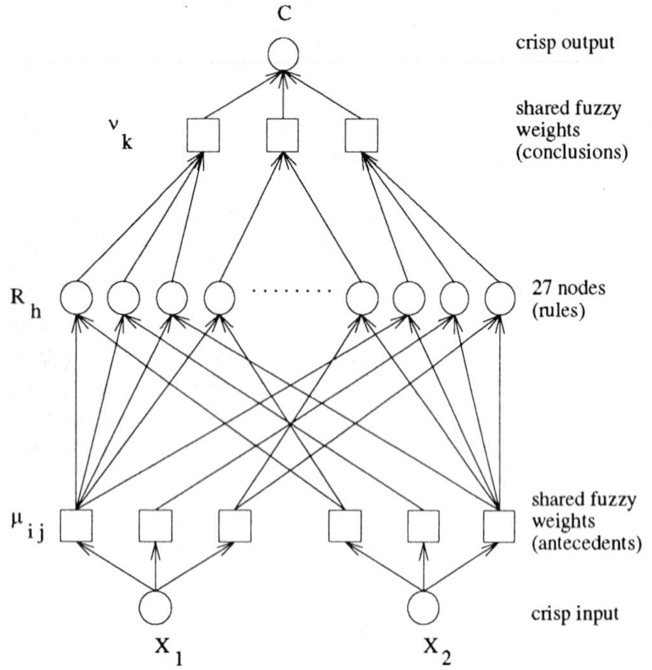

Fig. 2: The initial state of a fuzzy neural network

The fuzzy-error of the fuzzy neural network is defined as

$$E = 1 - G,$$

and it is needed to tune the membership functions.

In addition to this error measure we need an additional measure that helps to determine the rule nodes that have to be deleted from the network. We have to define when we conceive a transition between two states as desirable. By this we can derive a *fuzzy transition error* E_t to punish those rule nodes that contribute to overshooting or those nodes that apply a force that is too small to drive the system to a desired state.

The fuzzy transition error is defined as

$$E_t = 1 - min\{\tau_i(\Delta x_i) | i \in \{1, \ldots, n\}\},$$

where Δx_i is the change in variable X_i, and τ_i is a membership function giving a fuzzy representation of the desired change for the respective variable.

We are now able to define our learning algorithm. For each rule node R_j the value r_j of the conjunction of its antecedent and the value c_{R_j} of its consequence is known. Because we are using monotonic membership functions, c_{R_j} is already crisp. After the control action has been determined in the output node, applied to the plant, and its new state is known, we propagate the fuzzy-error E, the fuzzy transition error E_t and the current values of the state variables back through the network. The output node can determine for each rule node R_j that has contributed to the control output, i.e. $r_j \neq 0$, whether its conclusion would drive the system to a better or to a worse state. For the first case the rule node has to be made more sensitive and has to produce a conclusion that increases the current control action, i.e. makes it more positive or negative respectively. For the second case the opposite action has to be taken.

The learning procedure is divided in three phases:

Phase I: During phase I all rule nodes that have produced a counterproductive result, i.e. a negative value where a positive value is required and vice versa, are deleted instantly. Furthermore each rule node maintains a counter that is decremented each time the rule node does not fire, i.e. $r_j = 0$. In the other case, i.e. $r_j > 0$, the counter is reset to a maximum value.

Phase II: At the beginning of phase II there are no

rule nodes left that have identical antecedents and consequences that produce output values of different directions. To obtain a sound rule base, from each group of rules with identical antecedents only one rule node must remain. During this phase the counters are evaluated and each time a counter reaches 0 the respective rule node is deleted. Furthermore each rule node now maintains an individual error value that accumulates the fuzzy transition error. If the rule produced a counterproductive result, E_t is added unscaled, and if not, E_t is weighted by the normalized difference between the rule output value and the control output value of the whole network. At the end of this phase from each group of rule nodes with identical antecedents, only the node with the least error value remains, all other rule nodes are deleted. This leaves the network with a minimal set of rules needed to control the plant under consideration.

Phase III: During phase III the performance of the fuzzy neural network is enhanced by tuning the membership functions. Consider that we are using Tsukamoto's monotonic membership functions. Each membership function can be characterized by a pair (a,b) such that $\mu(a) = 0$ and $\mu(b) = 1$ hold. A rule is made more sensitive by increasing the difference between these two values in each of its antecedents. That is done by keeping the value of b and changing a. That means the membership functions are keeping their positions determined by their b-values, and changing a such that their ranges determined by $|b-a|$ are made wider. To make a rule less sensitive the ranges have to be made smaller. In addition to the changes in its antecedents, for firing rule the membership function of its conclusion have to be changed. If a rule has produced a good control value, this value is made better by decreasing the difference $|b-a|$, and a bad control value is made less worse by increasing $|b-a|$.

The output node C has to know the direction of the optimal control value c_{opt}. The value itself is unknown, of course, but from the observation of the current state it can be determined if e.g. a positive or a negative force had to be applied, i.e. $\text{sgn}(c_{\text{opt}})$ is known. The output node calculates an individual rule error e_{R_j} for each rule node R_j according to

$$e_{R_j} = \begin{cases} -r_j \cdot E & \text{if } \text{sgn}(c_{R_j}) = \text{sgn}(c_{\text{opt}}), \\ r_j \cdot E & \text{if } \text{sgn}(c_{R_j}) \neq \text{sgn}(c_{\text{opt}}). \end{cases}$$

The changes in the membership functions ν_k of the connections from the intermediate layer to the output layer are determined as follows:

$$a_k^{\text{new}} = \begin{cases} a_k - \sigma \cdot e_{R_j} \cdot |a_k - b_k| & \text{if } (a_k < b_k), \\ a_k + \sigma \cdot e_{R_j} \cdot |a_k - b_k| & \text{otherwise}, \end{cases}$$

where σ is a learning factor and rule node R_j is connected through ν_k to C. If a weight ν_k is shared, it is changed by the output node as often as rule nodes are connected to it through this weight.

The rule errors are now propagated back to the intermediate layer, where the rule nodes change the membership functions of their antecedents:

$$a_{ik_i}^{\text{new}} = \begin{cases} a_{ik_i} + \sigma \cdot e_{R_j} \cdot |a_{ik_i} - b_{ik_i}| & \text{if } (a_{ik_i} < b_{ik_i}), \\ a_{ik_i} - \sigma \cdot e_{R_j} \cdot |a_{ik_i} - b_{ik_i}| & \text{otherwise}, \end{cases}$$

where input node X_i is connected to R_j through $\mu_{ik_i}, k_i \in \{1, \ldots, s_i\}$, s_i is the number of linguistic values of X_i. If a weight μ_{ik_i} is shared, it is changed by as much rule nodes as X_i is connected to through this weight.

At the end of the learning process we can interpret the structure of the network. The remaining rule nodes identify the fuzzy if-then-rules that are necessary to control the dynamical system under consideration. The fuzzy weights represent the membership functions that suitably describe the linguistic values of the input and output variables.

IV. Simulation Results

The fuzzy neural network has been simulated and applied to the control of an inverted pendulum. Although it is too early to present final results of the performance, and more tests have to be run, first experiments gave promising results. For the inverted pendulum a simplified version was used that is described by the differential equation

$$(m + \sin^2\theta)\ddot{\theta} + \frac{1}{2}\dot{\theta}^2 \sin(2\theta) - (m+1)\sin\theta = -F\cos\theta.$$

The movement of the rod is simulated by a Runge-Kutta procedure with a timestepwidth of 0.1.

There are eight linguistic values attributed to each of the three variables. This are the common values PL, PM, PS, PZ, NZ, NS, NM, NL. Because we use monotonic membership functions that are not symmetric, we model the value Zero as Positive Zero and Negative Zero. This leads to an initial state of the network with $8 \cdot 8 \cdot 8 = 512$ possible rules. Several tests have been run under these

TABLE II:

The Rule Base After the Learning Process

	NL	NM	NS	NZ	PZ	PS	PM	PL
NL	NZ	NZ	NZ	NZ				
NM	NZ	NZ	NZ	NZ				
NS	NZ	NZ	NZ	NZ				
NZ	NZ	NM	NM	NS				
PZ					PS	PM	PM	PZ
PS					PM	PZ	PZ	PZ
PM					PZ	PZ	PZ	PZ
PL					PZ	PZ	PZ	PZ

TABLE III:

The Membership Functions Before and After the Learning Process

	angle			*angle velocity*			*force*		
	b	d	d'	b	d	d'	b	d	d'
NL	-45	45	43.9	-4.0	4.0	3.6	-30	30	15.0
NM	-30	30	30.0	-2.5	2.5	2.2	-20	20	14.9
NS	-15	15	14.9	-1.0	1.0	1.0	-10	10	8.0
NZ	0	-45	-14.9	0.0	-4.0	-1.0	0	-30	-8.0
PZ	0	45	14.5	0.0	4.0	0.9	0	30	8.0
PS	15	-15	-14.9	1.0	-1.0	-0.9	10	-10	-8.4
PM	30	-30	-29.9	2.5	-2.5	-2.1	20	-20	-15.0
PL	45	-45	-43.9	4.0	-4.0	-3.6	30	-30	-15.0

conditions. One result is shown in the Tables II and III, where the final fuzzy rule base (remaining hidden nodes) and the initial and final state of the membership functions can be found. In Table III d denotes the difference $b - a$. As we stated above a monotonic membership function is adapted by changing its parameter a to a' during the learning process.

The system was able to balance the pendulum with this configuration. In our experiments the learning process succeeded in about 90% of all cases resulting in different rule bases and fuzzy sets depending on internal parameters describing the error measures.

V. Conclusions

The presented fuzzy neural network is able to learn fuzzy-if-then rules by deleting nodes of its intermediate layer, and it learns membership functions that are used as its weights by fuzzy error backpropagation. The structure of the network can be easily interpreted in terms of a fuzzy controller.

The network has not to learn from scratch as it is presented here, but knowledge in the form of fuzzy if-then rules can be coded into the system. The learning procedure does not change this structural knowledge. It tunes the membership functions in an obvious way, and the semantics of the rules are not blurred by any semantically suspicious factors or weights attached to the rules [6, 7]. If some parameters of the controlled plant change, the fuzzy neural network can be easily changed, e.g. by adding additional rule nodes, and by restarting the the learning process to change the membership functions, if necessary.

Berenji has presented a similar approach [1] combining two neural networks into a system that behaves like a fuzzy controller. A comparison between Berenji's and our approach is presented in [8].

References

[1] Hamid R. Berenji: A reinforcement learning-based architecture for fuzzy logic control. Int. J. Approx. Reas., vol. 6, no. 2, 267-292 (1992)

[2] P. Eklund, F. Klawonn, D. Nauck: Distributing errors in neural fuzzy control. Proc. IIZUKA'92, 1139-1142, (1992)

[3] B. Kosko: Neural Networks and Fuzzy Systems. Prentice–Hall, Englewood Cliffs (1992)

[4] C.C. Lee: Fuzzy logic control systems: Fuzzy logic controller. IEEE Trans. Syst. Man Cybern., vol. 20, no. 2, 404-418 (Part I), 419-435 (Part II), (1990)

[5] E.H. Mamdani: Applications of fuzzy algorithms for a simple dynamic plant. Proc. IEE vol. 121, 1585-1588 (1974)

[6] D. Nauck, R. Kruse: A neural fuzzy controller learning by fuzzy error propagation. Proc. NAFIPS'92, 388-397 (1992)

[7] D. Nauck, R. Kruse: Interpreting the changes in the fuzzy sets of a self-adaptive neural fuzzy controller. Proc. IFIS'92 (1992)

[8] D. Nauck, F. Klawonn, R. Kruse: Combining neural networks and fuzzy controllers. Submitted for publication (1993)

[9] H. Takagi, I. Hayashi: NN–driven fuzzy reasoning. Int. J. Approx. Reas. vol. 5 no. 3, 191-212 (1991)

[10] L.A. Zadeh: Outline of a new approach to the analysis of complex systems and decision processes. IEEE Trans. Syst. Man Cybern., vol. SMC-3, 28–44 (1973)

Using Evolutionary Programming to Create Neural Networks that are Capable of Playing Tic-Tac-Toe

David B. Fogel
ORINCON Corporation
9363 Towne Centre Dr.
San Diego, CA 92121
fogel@sunshine.ucsd.edu

Abstract - All intelligent systems are evolutionary. Simulating evolution provides a method for generating machine intelligence. To date, there have been three main efforts in simulating evolution: genetic algorithms, evolution strategies, and evolutionary programming. The current research focuses on the use of evolutionary programming for adapting the design and weights of a multi-layer feed forward perceptron in the context of machine learning. Specifically, it is desired to evolve the structure and weights of a single-hidden layer perceptron such that it can achieve a high level of play in the game tic-tac-toe without the use of heuristics or credit assignment algorithms. Conclusions from the experiments are offered regarding the relative importance of specific mutation operations, the necessity for credit assignment procedures and the efficiency and effectiveness of evolutionary search.

I. INTRODUCTION

Intelligence is that property which allows a system to adapt its behavior to meet desired goals in a range of environments. There are three naturally-occurring organizational forms of intelligence: phylogenetic (arising within the line of descent), ontogenetic (arising within the individual) and sociogenetic (arising within the group) [1,2]. Phylogenetic learning is the most ancient form of intelligence and gave rise to ontogenetic and sociogenetic forms. All intelligent systems are evolutionary. Each possesses a reservoir of learned behavior and a unit of mutability [2]. It is natural to simulate evolutionary processes in order to create machine intelligence.

The biological foundation for such simulations is the neo-Darwinian paradigm [3,4]. This argument asserts that the history of life can be accounted for by processes acting on and within populations and species. These processes are reproduction, mutation, competition and selection. Reproduction is an obvious property of all extant species. Mutations in any positively entropic system must occur. Competition is a natural consequence of existing populations expanding to fill a finite resource space. Selection is the result of competition for the finite available resources. Under such conditions, evolution becomes an inevitable process.

Mayr [3] succinctly summarizes some of the more important characteristics of the neo-Darwinian paradigm. These include:

1. The individual is the primary target of selection,
2. Genetic variation is largely a chance phenomenon and stochastic processes play a significant role in evolution,
3. Genotypic variation is largely a product of recombination and "only ultimately of mutation,"
4. "Gradual" evolution may incorporate phenotypic discontinuities,
5. Not all phenotypic changes are necessarily the consequences of *ad hoc* natural selection,
6. Evolution means changes in adaptation and diversity and not merely a change in gene frequencies, and
7. Selection is probabilistic, not deterministic.

Simulations of evolution, whether they are implemented as methods of machine learning or simply to solve a specific problem, should rely on these foundations.

II. PREVIOUS EFFORTS IN SIMULATED EVOLUTION

Simulated evolution has a long history. Speculation on the evolutionary nature of intelligence goes back at least to Cannon [5] and Turing [6], with the first simulations being performed by Fraser [7,8], Friedberg [9], Friedberg et al. [10], Bremermann [11], Fogel and colleagues [12,13], Schwefel and colleagues [14,15], and Holland and colleagues [16,17]. More complete descriptions of efforts in the field can be found in [18-21,27]. There are three widely researched paradigms in simulated evolution: genetic algorithms, evolution strategies and evolutionary programming. These approaches can be compared and contrasted.

The genetic algorithm and evolutionary programming have some obvious similarities. Both algorithms operate

0-7803-0999-5/93/$03.00 ©1993 IEEE

on a population of candidate solutions, both algorithms subject these solutions to modifications, and both algorithms employ a selection criterion to determine which solutions to maintain for future generations. As proposed in [17], the genetic algorithm differs from evolutionary programming in the following regards:

1. Genetic algorithms use a coding (e.g., a bit string) of the parameters to be evolved, not the parameters themselves [22],
2. The number of offspring to be created from each parent is exponentially related to the parent's fitness relative to all other members of the current population [17, pp. 87-88], and
3. Parents create offspring through the use of genetic operators such as one-point crossover and inversion [17, pp. 89-120].

In contradistinction, in evolutionary programming [18]:

1. The representation for a problem follows in a top-down fashion from the problem. Rather than try to fit a single coding structure to every problem, each problem is regarded as being unique,
2. The number of offspring per parent is generally unimportant and successful simulations need not create more than a single offspring per parent, and
3. Offspring are created through various mutation operations that follow naturally from the chosen problem representation. No emphasis is put on specific genetic operations such as crossover and inversion. Selection is then made a probabilistic function of fitness.

Many of Holland's [17] original proposals have undergone significant revision since first defined. Much of the current research in genetic algorithms has forgone the use of bit strings (e.g. [23]). Experiments in [24] have indicated the inferiority of the one-point crossover and two-point crossover to uniform crossover, although these conclusions have received criticism in [25]. Other research [26] has indicated a greater role for mutation in evolutionary search than was admitted in [17], and illustrated cases where crossover can be detrimental to search.

The evolution strategies paradigm [14] is very similar to that of evolutionary programming. Both methods operate on a population of solutions, subject those solutions to changes through random mutation and compete existing solutions with respect to an objective function. In real-valued parameter optimization, both methods typically apply Gaussian perturbations to all components [27,28] and extensions to self-adapting variances of these perturbations have been made [27,29]. There is no requirement for specific mutation operations that follow the form of genetic transfer in biota, although Schwefel [27] has experimented with various forms of recombination. Evolutionary programming and evolution strategies both emphasize phenotypic changes [18,30].

III. Method & Materials

The current experiments focus on the use of evolutionary programming. Consider the problem of evolving multi-layered feed forward perceptrons capable of playing tic-tac-toe. The game is well-known but will be described in detail for completeness. There are two players and a three by three grid. Initially, the grid is empty. Each player moves in turn by placing a marker in an open square. By convention, the first player's marker is "X" and the second player's marker is "O." The first player moves first. The object of the game is to place three markers in a row. This results in a win for that player and loss for the opponent. Failing a win, a draw may be earned by preventing the opponent from placing three markers in a row. It can be shown by enumerating the game tree that at least a draw can be forced by the second player.

Attention will be devoted to evolving a strategy for the first player (an equivalent procedure could be used for the second player). A suitable coding structure must be selected. It must receive a board pattern as input and yield a corresponding move as output. The coding structure utilized in these experiments was a multi-layered feedforward perceptron (see Figure 1). Each hidden or output node performs a sum of the weighted input strengths, subtracts off an adaptable bias term and passes the result through a sigmoid filter $1/(1+\exp(-x))$. Only a single hidden layer was incorporated. This architecture was selected because: (1) variations can be shown to be universal function approximators [31], (2) it was believed to be adequate for the task, (3) the response to any stimulus could be evaluated rapidly, and (4) the extension to multiple hidden layers is obvious.

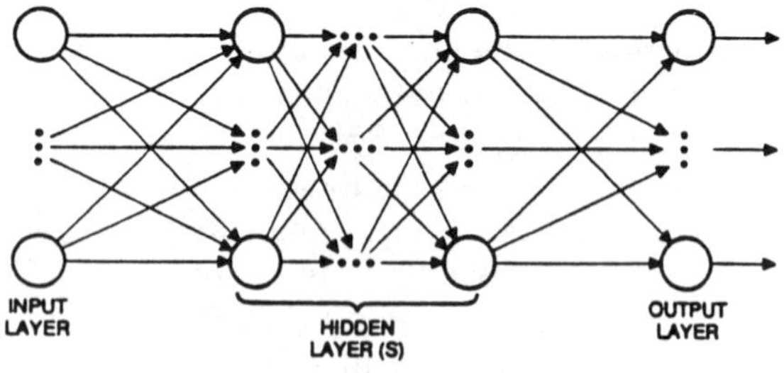

Figure 1. A Multi-Layer Feed Forward Perceptron

There were nine input and output units. Each corresponded to a square in the grid. An "X" was denoted by the value 1.0, an "O" was denoted by the value -1.0, and an open space was denoted by the value 0.0. A move was determined by presenting the current board pattern to the network and examining the relative strengths of the nine output nodes. A marker was placed in the empty square with the maximum output strength. This procedure guaranteed legal moves. The output from nodes associated with squares in which a marker had already been placed was ignored. No selection pressure was applied to drive the output from such nodes to zero.

The initial population consisted of 50 parent networks. The number of nodes in the hidden layer was chosen at random in accordance with a uniform distribution over the integers [1,...,10]. The initial weighted connection strengths and bias terms were randomly distributed according to a uniform distribution ranging over [-0.5,0.5]. A single offspring was copied from each parent and modified by two modes of mutation:

1. All weight and bias terms were perturbed by adding a Gaussian random variable with zero mean and a standard deviation of 0.05, and
2. With a probability of 0.5, the number of nodes in the hidden layer was allowed to vary. If a change was indicated, there was an equal likelihood that a node would be added or deleted, subject to the constraints on the maximum and minimum number of nodes (10 and one, respectively). Nodes to be added were initialized with all weights and the bias term being set equal to 0.0.

A rule-based procedure that played nearly perfect tic-tac-toe was implemented in order to evaluate each contending network. The execution time with this format was linear with the population size and provided the opportunity for multiple trials and statistical results. The evolving networks were allowed to move first in all games. The first move was examined by the rule-base with the eight possible second moves being stored in an array. The rule-base proceeded as follows:

1. From the array of all possible moves, select a move that has not yet been played.
2. For subsequent moves:
   a) with a 10 percent chance, move randomly, else
   b) if a win is available, place a marker in the winning square, else
   c) if a block is available, place a marker in the blocking square, else
   d) if two open squares are in line with an "O", randomly place a marker in either of the two squares, else
   e) randomly move in any open square.
3. Continue with (2) until the game is completed.
4. Continue with (1) until games with all eight possible second moves have been played.

The 10 percent chance for moving randomly was incorporated to maintain a variety of play in an analogous manner to a persistence of excitation condition. This feature and the restriction that the rule-base only looks one move ahead makes the rule-base nearly perfect, but beatable.

Each network was evaluated over four sets of these eight games. The payoff function varied in several sets of experiments. Due to space limitations, only the experiments with the payoff function {+1, -10, 0} will be described here, where the entries are the payoffs for winning, losing and playing to a draw, respectively. Other results are described in [18]. The maximum possible score over any four sets of games was 32. But a perfect score in any generation did not necessarily indicate a perfect algorithm because of the random variation in play generated by step 2a, above. After competition against the rule-base was completed for all networks in the population, a second competition was held in which each network was compared to 10 other randomly chosen networks. If the score of the chosen network was greater than or equal to its competitor, it received a win. Those networks with the greatest number of wins were retained to be parents of the next generation. Twenty trials were conducted. Evolution was halted after 800 generations in each trial.

IV. Experimental Results

The mean learning rate over all 20 trials when using {+1, -10, 0} is indicated in Figure 2. There is an initially rapid increase in performance as strategies that lose are quickly purged from the evolving population. After this first-order condition is satisfied, optimization continues to sort out strategies with the greatest potential for winning rather than drawing. The approximate 95 percent confidence limits around the mean are close to the average performance across all 20 trials. Figure 3 indicates the tree of possible games when competing the best evolved network from the first trial against the rule-based player, omitting random moves from step 2a. The tree is typical of the results across all trials. This selected network possessed 10 hidden nodes. It does not force a win in any branch of the tree when the rule-base makes no errors. But it also never loses.

V. Conclusions

These results and those offered in [18] indicate a capability for general problem solving. No information regarding the object of the game was offered to the evolutionary program. No hints regarding appropriate moves were given, nor were there any attempts to assign values to various board patterns. The final outcome (win, lose, draw) was the only available information regarding the quality of play. Heuristics regarding the environment were limited to:

1. There were nine inputs,
2. There were nine outputs, and
3. Markers may only be placed in empty squares.

Evolutionary programming was able to adjust the architecture and connections of the single hidden layer

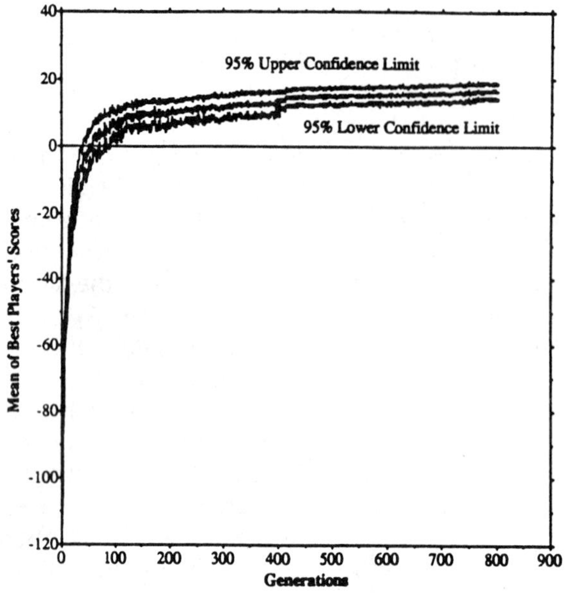

Figure 2. The Mean and Upper/Lower Confidence Limits of the Best Players' Scores Averaged Over All 20 Trials Using the Payoff Function {+1, -10, 0}.

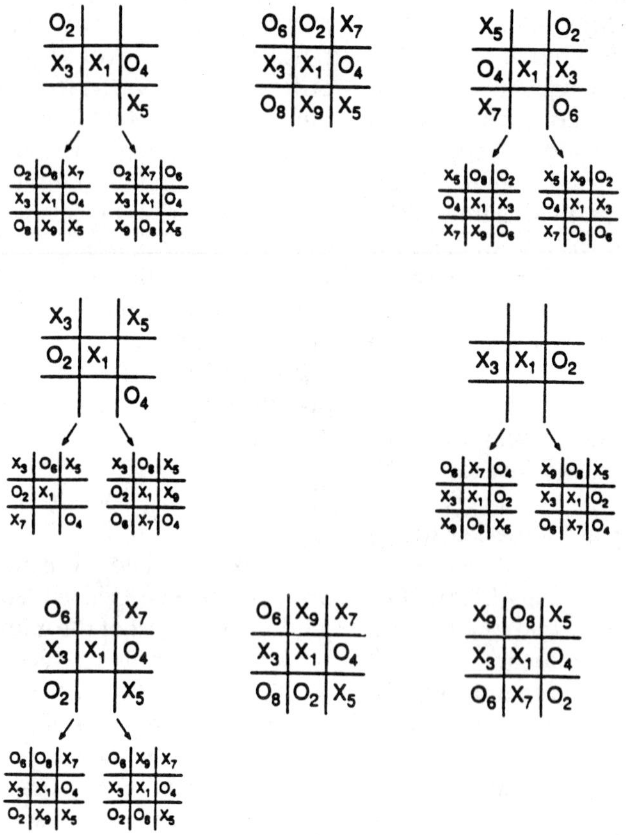

Figure 3. The Tree of All Possible Games When the Best Network from Trial #1 is Played Against the Rule-Based Opponent. The Network Plays as "X", the Rule-Base Plays as "O". The Subscripts Indicate the Order of Play.

perceptrons in order to adapt behavior in light of the given goal. While single hidden layer networks were sufficient for tic-tac-toe, other problems may be more easily addressed by more complex stimulus-response structures. But the evolutionary procedure is robust and no fundamental alteration of the basic algorithm is required to address problems of arbitrary complexity.

The results also illustrate how connectionist and rule-based systems can be supplemented with evolutionary learning. Testing the effectiveness of the evolving networks provided an absolute measure of performance. Evolution may surpass the performance of the available rule-base and then continue to generate even more effective strategies.

If it were desired to create a truly perfect tic-tac-toe algorithm using neural coding structures, a population of evolved first players could be put in competition against a population of evolved second players, with evolutionary programming essentially generating a minimax search over both populations. Alternatively, a single coding structure could be required to act both as first and second player. Or, following [32,33], the coding structure could be an explicit rule base of conditions and actions. Evolutionary programming does not restrict the form of the stimulus-response coding; the researcher is free to select a structure that appears most suitable for the task.

As recently as [34], it was still claimed that mutation does not generally advance a search for optimal solutions and that such searches require carefully structured rules of recombination. These claims are not correct. As indicated in the above experiments, abstractions of specific genetic mechanisms such as crossover, inversion and other recombinatory methods are not required for successful evolution. This follows similar evidence presented in other evolutionary studies ([20,28,35] and others).

In expressing his belief that intelligent, conscious systems could not arise strictly through evolution, Penrose [36] stated, "Any selection process of [the type illustrated by evolution] could act only on the *output* of the algorithms and not directly on the ideas underlying the actions of the algorithms. This is not simply extremely inefficient; I believe that it would be totally unworkable." The evidence reported here indicates that not only is such a method workable, it is also efficient.

ACKNOWLEDGMENTS

The author would like to thank W. Atmar, T. Bäck, L. J. Fogel, B. Scurlock, A.V. Sebald, and P.K. Simpson for their helpful comments and suggestions regarding this research.

REFERENCES

[1 N. Wiener, *Cybernetics*, Part II, MIT Press, Cambridge, MA, 1961.

[2] J.W. Atmar, "Speculation on the Evolution of Intelligence and Its Possible Realization in Machine Form," Doctoral Dissertation, New Mexico State University, 1976.

[3] E. Mayr, *Toward a New Philosophy of Biology: Observations of an Evolutionist*, Belknap Press, Cambridge, MA, 1988.

[4] A. Hoffman, *Arguments on Evolution: A Paleontologist's Perspective*, Oxford Univ. Press, New York, 1989.

[5] W. D. Cannon, *The Wisdom of the Body*, Norton & Co., New York, 1932.

[6] A.M. Turing, "Computing machinery and intelligence," *Mind*, Vol. 59, pp. 433-460, 1950.

[7] A.S. Fraser, "Simulation of genetic systems by automatic digital computers. I. Introduction," *Australian J. of Biol. Sci.*, Vol. 10, pp. 484-491, 1957.

[8] A.S. Fraser, "Simulation of genetic systems by automatic digital computers. II. Effects of linkage on rates of advance under selection," *Australian J. of Biol. Sci.*, Vol. 10, pp. 492-499, 1957.

[9] R.M. Friedberg, "A learning machine: Part I," *IBM J. of Res. & Dev.* Vol. 2, pp. 2-13, 1958.

[10] R.M. Friedberg, B. Dunham, and J. H. North, "A learning machine: Part II," *IBM J. of Res. & Dev.*, Vol. 3, pp. 282-287, 1959.

[11] H.J. Bremermann, "The evolution of intelligence. The nervous systems as a model of its environment," Technical Report No. 1, Contract No. 477(17), Dept. of Mathematics, Univ. of Washington, Seattle, July, 1958.

[12] L.J. Fogel, "Autonomous automata," *Industrial Research*, Vol. 4, pp. 14-19, 1962.

[13] L.J. Fogel, A.J. Owens and M.J. Walsh, *Artificial Intelligence Through Simulated Evolution*, John Wiley & Sons, New York, 1966.

[14] H.-P. Schwefel, "Kybernetische Evolution als Strategie der Experimentellen Forschung in der Strömungstechnik," Diploma Thesis, Tech. Univ. of Berlin, 1965.

[15] I. Rechenberg, *Evolutionsstrategie: Optimierung Technischer Systeme nach Prinzipien der Biologischen Evolution*, Frommann-Holzboog Verlag, Stuttgart, 1973.

[16] J.H. Holland, "Adaptive plans optimal for payoff-only environments," *Proc. of 2nd Hawaii Int. Conf. on System Sciences*, pp. 917-920, 1969.

[17] J.H. Holland, *Adaptation in Natural and Artificial Systems*, Univ. of Michigan Press, Ann Arbor, MI, 1975.

[18] D.B. Fogel, "Evolving Artificial Intelligence," Doctoral Dissertation, Univ. Cal. San Diego, 1992.

[19] D.E. Goldberg, *Genetic Algorithms in Search, Optimization & Machine Learning*, Addison-Wesley, Reading, MA, 1989.

[20] D.B. Fogel and W. Atmar (eds.), *Proc. of the First Annual Conference on Evolutionary Programming*, Evolutionary Programming Society, La Jolla, CA, 1992.

[21] H.-P. Schwefel and R. Männer, *Proc. of the First Conf. on Parallel Problem Solving from Nature*, Springer, Berlin, 1991.

[22] D.E. Goldberg and C.H. Kuo, "Genetic algorithms in pipeline optimization," *J. Comp. Civ. Eng.*, Vol. 1:2, pp. 128-141, 1987.

[23] L. Davis (ed.), *Handbook of Genetic Algorithms*, Van Nostrand Reinhold, New York, 1991.

[24] G. Syswerda, "Uniform crossover in genetic algorithms," *Proc. of the Third Int. Conf. on Genetic Algorithms*, J.D. Schaffer (ed.), George Mason Univ., pp. 2-9, 1991.

[25] R. Das and D. Whitley, "The only challenging problems are deceptive: Global search by solving order-1 hyperplanes," *Proc. of the Fourth Int. Conf. on Gen. Algs.*, R.K. Belew and L.B. Booker (eds.), Morgan Kaufmann, pp. 166-173, 1991.

[26] J.D. Schaffer and L.J. Eshelman, "On crossover as an evolutionarily viable strategy," *Proc. of the Fourth Int. Conf. on Gen. Algs.*, R.K. Belew and L.B. Booker (eds.), Morgan Kaufmann, pp. 61-68, 1991.

[27] H.-P. Schwefel, *Numerical Optimization of Computer Models*, John Wiley, Chichester, 1981.

[28] D.B. Fogel and J.W. Atmar, "Comparing genetic operators with Gaussian mutations in simulated evolutionary processes using linear systems," *Biol. Cyb.*, Vol. 63, pp. 111-114, 1990.

[29] D.B. Fogel, L.J. Fogel, W. Atmar and G.B. Fogel, "Hierarchic methods of evolutionary programming," *Proc. of the First Ann. Conf. on Evol. Prog.*, D.B. Fogel and W. Atmar (eds.), Evolutionary Programming Society, La Jolla, CA, pp. 175-182, 1992.

[30] T. Bäck and F. Hoffmeister, "Extended selection mechanisms in genetic algorithms," *Proc. of the Fourth Intern. Conf. on Gen. Algs.*, R.K. Belew and L.B. Booker (eds.), Morgan Kaufmann, pp. 92-99, 1991.

[31] A.R. Barron, "Statistical properties of artificial neural networks," *Proc. of the 28th Conf. on Decision and Control*, Tampa, FL, pp. 280-285, 1989.

[32] S.H. Rubin, "Case-based learning: A new paradigm for automated knowledge acquisition," *ISA Transactions*, Vol. 31:2, pp. 181-209, 1992.

[33] D.B. Fogel, "An evolutionary approach to representation design," *Proc. of the First Ann. Conf. on Evol. Prog.*, D.B. Fogel and W. Atmar (eds.), Evolutionary Programming Society, La Jolla, CA, pp. 163-168, 1992.

[34] J.H. Holland, "Genetic algorithms," *Scientific American*, July, 1992.

[35] T. Bäck, F. Hoffmeister, and H.-P. Schwefel, "A survey of evolution strategies," *Proc. of the Fourth Intern. Conf. on Gen. Algs.*, R. K. Belew and L. B. Booker (eds.), Morgan Kaufmann, pp. 2-9, 1991.

[36] R. Penrose, *The Emperor's New Mind: Concerning Computers, Minds, and the Laws of Physics*, Penguin Books, New York, 1989.

Applications of GA-Based Optimization of Neural Network Connection Topology

E. Smuda, K. KrishnaKumar

Box 870280, Department of Aerospace Engineering
The University of Alabama, Tuscaloosa, AL 35487

Abstract

This paper employs a genetic algorithm (GA) to explore the connection space of an artificial neural network (ANN) with the objective of finding a sparsely connected network that yields the same accuracy as a fully connected network. Such sparsity is desired as it improves the generalization capabilities of the mapping. The ANN with the GA-chosen set of connections is then trained using a supervised mode of learning known as backpropagation of error. Using this technique, three different applications are analyzed.

1. Introduction

The smallest part of an ANN is it's micro-structure, which consists of a single neuron. A neuron, which can be represented by a transfer function, receives signals that have been weighted by other neurons connected to it. The output of this neuron is then weighted and passed to other neurons. A neural network consists of a collection of interconnected neurons. An advantage to using ANN is that the neural network will adapt to a given set of patterns, thus no situation dependent programming is required. Furthermore, nonlinear systems can be accurately modeled and analyzed. One of the important requirements of ANN is its robustness to a set of patterns not seen during training. In applications related to neuro-control, the robustness of the neuro-model is critical. Here the interest is in obtaining a generalized copy (neuro-model) of the system to be controlled. A robust (i.e., generalized) copy of the model will then provide a robust controller design. In this paper, ANN is combined with an optimization technique known as genetic algorithms (GA) to arrive at an ANN that is more robust than a fully forward-connected ANN [3]. Combinations of GAs with ANN have been examined before [1,2]. GAs have been used previously to optimize ANN weights, as well as both connections and weights. Experiments have also been performed that utilize GA in determining ANN architecture that uses fewer connections yet learns quickly and accurately [2].

This paper first presents the general concepts of neural networks and genetic algorithms. The use of these concepts to find a generalized set of ANN connections is described next. Finally, the resulting technique is applied to two systems which are required to be robust to facilitate a robust controller design.

1.1. The Concepts of Neural Networks

For the generalized ANN used in this research, it is assumed that each neuron can be connected to neurons to the right of it. Such a general, forward-connected network is shown in Figure 1.

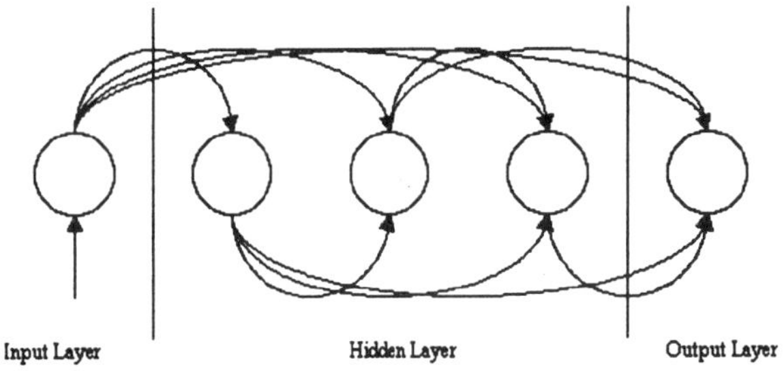

Figure 1. Fully Forward-Connected Network

The net input of the ith neuron is

$$net_i = \sum_{j=1}^{i-1} W_{ij} * X_j, \qquad 1 \le i \le N \qquad (1)$$

where X_j are the inputs and W_{ij}s are the weights. This net input is then turned into an activation value with the use of a transfer function. This transfer function is a key aspect of the ANN, and varies for different neurons in a network. For the network used in this research, a sigmoidal function was chosen for the hidden units, and a linear function was chosen for the input and output units. The sigmoidal transfer function used for the hidden units is

$$f(x) = \frac{1-e^{(-\alpha x)}}{1+e^{(-\alpha x)}} \qquad (2)$$

and the linear function used for the input and output units is $f(x) = x$ (3)

The output for an individual neuron is calculated in a procedure called the forward pass. At the end of the forward pass, a total error is calculated for all the network outputs. This is done by comparing the ANN output (Y) to the desired system output (D). To train the network a supervised mode of learning known as the backpropagation of error is used (see Figure 2). Complete equations for ANN implementation can be found in references [3] and [4].

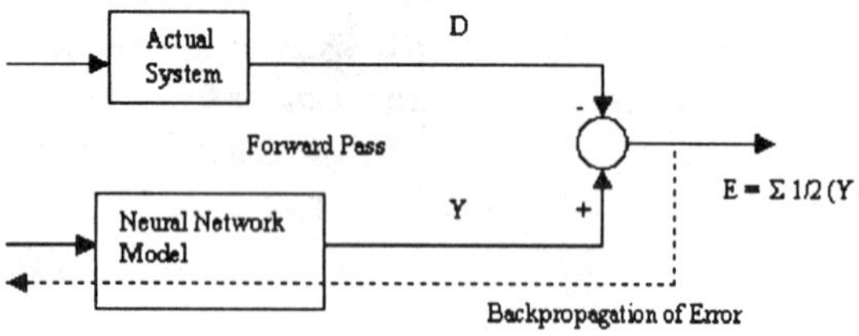

Figure 2. ANN with backpropagation of error

In this method of learning, the partial derivatives of the error with respect to the weights are used to adjust the weights of the network until a minimum error is achieved. In using backpropagation of error, each data point is sampled, an error is calculated, and the weights are adjusted. When all data points have been sampled, one epoch is complete.

1.2. The Concepts of Genetic Algorithms

GAs differ from other optimization techniques in that they work with a coding of the parameter set instead of with the parameters themselves. They search from a population of points rather than from a single point. Also, GAs use objective function information in the search rather than the derivative of the function.

A GA starts by generating a random population of binary strings, where each string is the binary form of a possible solution. The GA undergoes several generations, or iterations, in which three operators, reproduction, crossover, and mutation alter the population in the search for an optimal solution. The first of these operators, reproduction, is a process in which the binary strings are copied from one generation to the next according to their objective function values. Copying strings according to how good a solution they yield, or how fit they are, means that strings that are more fit have a greater probability of contributing to the next generation. This operator is therefore a model of natural selection. The end result of reproduction is that highly fit strings are copied into a mating pool. Once a mating pool has been formed the second GA operator, crossover, proceeds to randomly choose two members from the mating pool. A random location along the string is chosen, and the two strings swap the characters from that location to the end of the string. Through crossover, a new population of strings is formed from the most fit strings of the previous generation. The third operator, mutation, ensures a global search by randomly flipping a bit in a string to it's opposite value. With the use of a random population of strings, and the operators of reproduction, crossover, and mutation, a GA finds an optimal solution by searching for similarities among strings called schema that yield high fitness [5].

2. Exploring the Connection Space of an ANN

The objective of this paper is to use genetic algorithms to explore the connection space of an ANN. The desired final result of this exploration is to find a sparsely connected network that will yield the same accuracy as a fully connected network. This is desirable because the sparsity of the ANN improves the generalization capabilities of the mapping. To achieve the above objective, a generalized neural network structure [3], was configured within a GA code on an IBM RS6000 system. During the first step of this system, the GA would interpret each bit in the binary string as an ANN connection. The total connection pattern is then defined by a binary string. This is illustrated as follows. If a connection between nodes exists, it is represented by a one in the binary string. If that connection does not exist, it is represented by a zero. Figure 3 presents this concept. The solid lines represent connections and the dotted lines represent no connections.

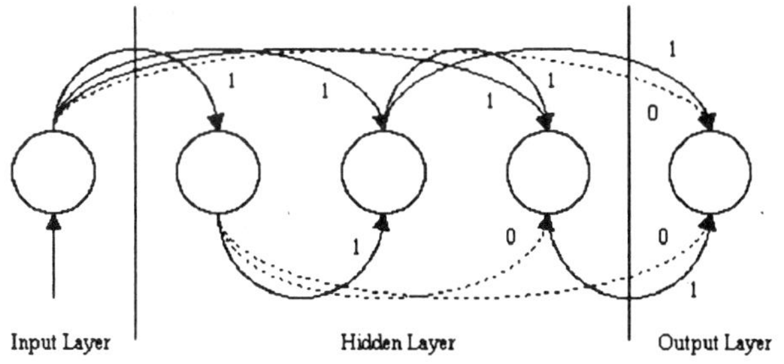

Figure 3.GA representation for the ANN connections

With the connections chosen by the GA, a random number generator was used to input a set of random weights to the ANN in the range $-1<W<1$. A forward pass was then executed for each of the samples associated with that particular application. During the forward pass calculations the total error between the calculated ANN output and the desired output over all samples was calculated. This value was then minimized by the GA, and the set of connections associated with the minimum total output error of the network is the optimal set of connections. With a optimal set of connections known, the network was trained using the backpropagation algorithm, which adjusted the weights to further reduce the total error between the calculated ANN output and the desired output. The final result is a well trained ANN.

A nonlinear test function was used as an initial model for comparison using the above technique. The ANN consisted of five input units, one output unit and twenty hidden units. The test function used was:

$$f(x) = \frac{x_1 x_2 x_3 x_5 (x_3 - 1) + x_4}{1 + x_3^2 + x_2^2} \tag{4}$$

where x_1, x_2, x_3, x_4, and x_5 are the net inputs and f(x) is the desired output. The next step was to use the GA to optimize the connections as already discussed. For the GA optimization a population size of thirty , and a tournament selection size of two was used [5]. Several different experiments were performed to determine which probabilities of crossover and mutation would yield the best result. This was done by running the GA for thirty generations to optimize the connections, then passing these connections to the backpropagation algorithm which adjusted the weights for two hundred epochs. After two hundred epochs, all data points have been sampled two hundred times. The result was that a crossover probability of 0.75 and a mutation probability of 0.01 yielded the best GA solution of minimum total error for the system. These probabilities as well as the population size and tournament selection size were then held constant throughout all experiments. Since it was realized that the GA might find a better set of connections for a given ANN with a better set of weights than a random set, an additional experiment that was performed was one in which the backpropagation algorithm was first run for ten epochs to improve the system weights, then these weights were used by the GA in optimizing the connections. The resulting connections and weights were then passed to the backpropagation algorithm a second time for a larger number of epochs. For the nonlinear test function shown in equation 4, the results are compared with a fully forward connected ANN in Figure 4.

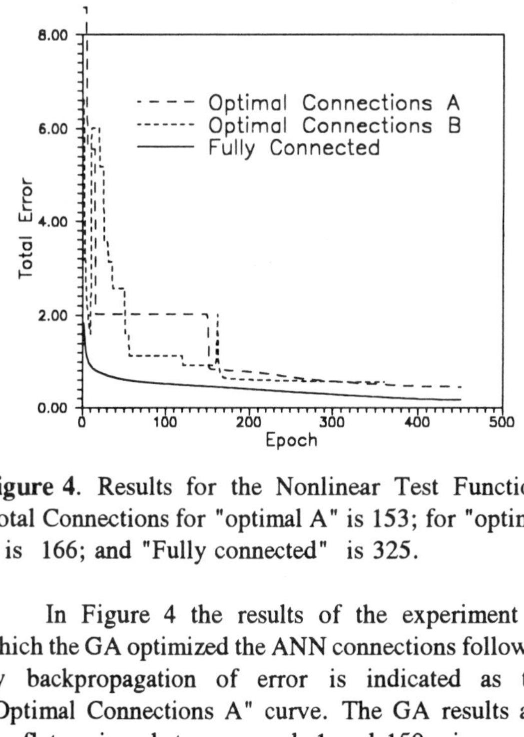

Figure 4. Results for the Nonlinear Test Function. Total Connections for "optimal A" is 153; for "optimal B is 166; and "Fully connected" is 325.

In Figure 4 the results of the experiment in which the GA optimized the ANN connections followed by backpropagation of error is indicated as the "Optimal Connections A" curve. The GA results are the flat regions between epoch 1 and 150, since each generation is equivalent to five epochs and thirty generations were performed. In a similar fashion, the curve labeled "Optimal connections B" represents the experiment in which backpropagation was first performed for ten epochs to obtain a good set of weights. It is recalled that these weights are then used by the GA for connection optimization. As seen from the figure, the number of total ANN connections are greatly reduced from the fully connected network when the GA chooses the connections. It can also be seen from Figure 4 that the case in which learning occurred for a few epochs before GA optimization yielded a set of ANN connections that produced a much lower total error for the system than without this learning. This ultimately resulted in a slightly lower total error after backpropagation.

3. Applications

To continue examining the techniques described above, two additional applications related to robust system modeling were examined. The first of these is modeling an input-output relationship of a large space structural system. A mathematical model of an existing structure, the Advanced Control Evaluation for Systems (ACES) test article located at NASA/Marshall Space Flight Center Large Space Structures Ground Test Facility (LSS GTF), Huntsville, Alabama was used for this purpose.

The ACES structure is characteristic of a long, slender, lightweight, lightly damped, flexible beam and is vertically suspended within the LSS GTF. The test article had once served as a backup Astromast for the Voyager spacecraft. Furthermore, a three meter diameter antenna is affixed to the lower end of the suspended beam to better simulate realistic disturbance scenarios. Actuators and sensors are positioned over the entire length of the ACES test article. Reference 6 presents greater details of this model.

The ACES math model has 11 inputs and 27 outputs. The scope of this study did not involve modeling the entire system, but instead was limited to a single actuator/sensor combination (DET-X and the LMED-1X, respectively, see reference 6). The neural network model for this problem had four input units, one output unit, and ten hidden units. Three of the four input units are time-delayed outputs, which explicitly introduce dynamics into the network. The fourth input represents a single actuator control signal, and the single output represents a sensor signal. An actuator/sensor input-output relationship is, thus, defined by the ANN.

For this system the same experiments were performed as in the case of the nonlinear test function. The results are shown below in Figure 5. It is first noted that the format of this graph is the same as that of Figure 4. As in the case of the nonlinear test function, the experiment in which learning occurred for a few epochs before GA optimization yielded a set of ANN connections with a much lower total error for the system than without this learning. It can also be seen in Figure 5 that for both experiments in which an optimal set of connections was found, the ANN yielded an accuracy that was approximately the same as that of the fully connected network. It is noted that this has been done with a reduction of at least half of the original number of connections.

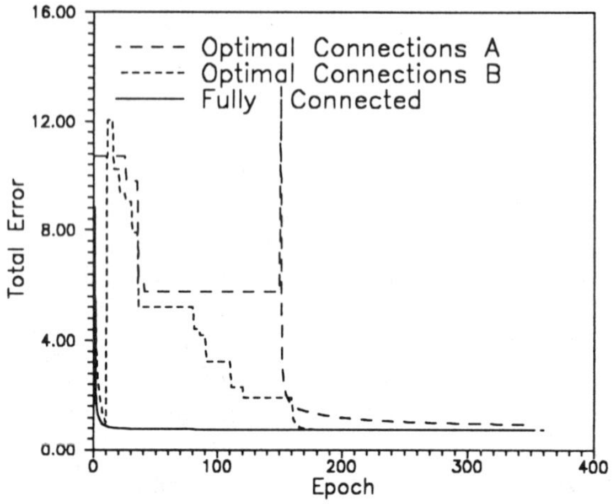

Figure 5 Results for the structural system ACES. Total Connections for "optimal A" is 50; for "optimal B is 38; and "Fully connected" is 105.

Another application that was examined using this technique was modeling of the space station freedom non-linear dynamics [7]. The ANN model of this highly non-linear system had eight inputs: the three angles of rotation, their angular velocities, the pitch control torque input, and a bias. The system had one output, the pitch angle of the spacecraft. Sixteen hidden units were used for a total of twenty five nodes. The results of exploring the connection space are shown in Figure 6.

Here only those epochs after GA optimization are shown so that the end effect can be seen more clearly. It is apparent from this figure that a set of GA-optimized ANN connections does indeed yield the same accuracy as the fully connected network. To compare the error between the desired output (pitch angle of SSF) and the ANN output for the fully and optimally connected cases, Figure 7 is provided.

For the optimally connected network the average error was -0.00144 and the standard deviation was 0.016697. The average error and standard deviation for the fully connected network were -0.00032 and 0.0182667 respectively. From these numbers it is clear that these two networks are of similar accuracy, but the generalization is better (by examining the standard deviation) for the sparsely connected network (less than half of the original number of connections).

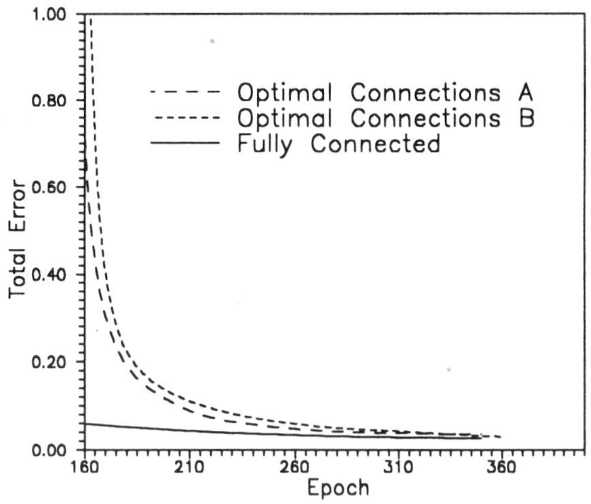

Figure 6. Results for the Space Station Freedom. Total Connections for "optimal A" is 130; for "optimal B is 137; and "Fully connected" is 300.

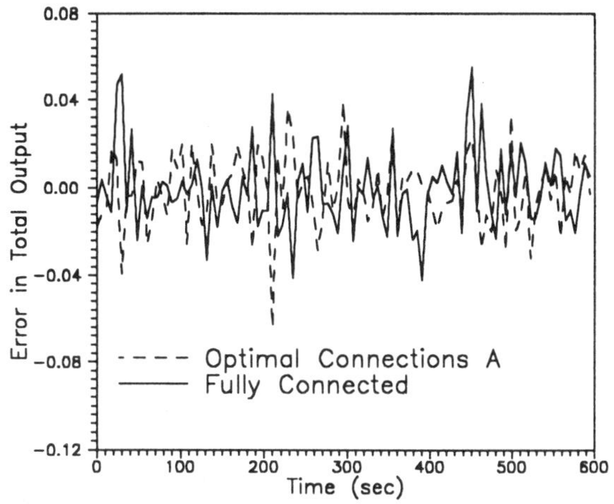

Figure 7. ANN output error comparison for the Space Station Freedom modeling

4. Summary and Discussion

In this paper, a sparsely connected artificial neural network (ANN) that yields similar accuracy to the fully connected net was found using a genetic algorithm (GA) optimization technique. This was accomplished by allowing the GA to find a set of optimal connections associated with the minimum total error between the desired output of the system and the ANN output. The ANN with this set of connections was then trained with a supervised mode of learning known as backpropagation of error. Network sparsity is desired as it improves the generalization capabilities of the mapping.

The solutions of the GA/ANN combination for three applications were then compared with a fully forward-connected network. The results showed that the generalized set of connections yielded approximately the same total error in output as the fully forward-connected networks. In a continuing effort to find a generalized set of connections using a GA, current research is focussed on finding a set of connections that are relatively insensitive to changes in their connection strengths (weights).

ACKNOWLEDGEMENT

This material is based upon work partly supported by the National Science Foundation under Grant No. ECS-9113283.

References

[1] Whitley, D., Starkweather, T., Bogart, C., "Genetic Algorithms and neural networks: optimizing connections and connectivity", Parallel Computing, 1990, Vol.14, p347-361.

[2] Schaffer, J., Whitley, D., Eshelman, L., "Combinations of Genetic Algorithms and Neural Networks: A Survey of the State of the Art", 1992 proceedings of the International Workshop on Combinations of Genetic Algorithms and Neural Networks.

[3] Krishnakumar, K., "Backpropagation Algorithm for a General Neural Network Structure", IEEE Southeastern Conference, 1992.

[4] Freeman, James A., Skapura, David M., Neural Networks: Algorithms, Applications, and Programming Techniques, (Addison-Wesley Publishing Company, Reading, MA, 1991).

[5] Goldberg, David E., Genetic Algorithms in Search, Optimization, and Machine Learning, (Addison-Wesley Publishing Company, Reading, MA, 1989).

[6] KrishnaKumar, K. and Montgomery, L., "Adaptive Neuro-control for Large Flexible Structures, Journal of Smart Materials and Structures, 1993.

[7] KrishnaKumar, K., Bartholomew, S., and Rickard, S., "Adaptive neuro-control for the Space Station Freedom", AIAA 93-0407.

Artificial Cerebellum ACE: Tensor Network Transformer Enabling Virtual Movement in Virtual Environment; Facilitating Teleoperation in Telepresence

Andras J. Pellionisz, David L. Tomko [$] and Charles C. Jorgensen
NASA Ames Research Center *, Information Sciences Division, 269-3
[$] Vestibular Research Facility, 242-3
Moffett Field, CA 94035 USA

Abstract - An electronic implementation of cerebellar neural network theory (an artificial cerebellum) serves to both utilize our neurobiology-based knowledge, as well as test quality and usefulness of theory. A cerebellum implemented as a tensor network transformer and realized by dedicated parallel processors such as Transputers can be used to transform intentional movements specified through a virtual environment, into teleoperative execution signals. The cerebellum thus matches, by a crucial transformation, funtional geometries intrinsic to telepresence and to teleoperation systems.

I. Introduction

A. *Emergence of Cerebellum in Natural Evolution*

Brain theory and its application in neurobotics [14] can undergo an "evolution", similar to how biological sensorimotor neural systems have been perfected in the course of *natural evolution*. At the earliest evolutionary stages, sensorimotor neural networks were only direct connections of receptors to motor executors. About 400 million years ago (at the time of emergence of sharks) a separate co-processor appeared between sensory and motor systems, the cerebellum [9]. According to its name, this "little brain" protrudes as an addition to the "rest of the brain", and performs a transformation that made the sensorimotor system of the shark distinctly better coordinated than that of other aquatic animals. Faster and more precisely coordinated sharks could thus outperform their peers and could "survive as one of the fittest" [12].

It is evident from the "architecture" of biological sensorimotor systems, that a cerebellar "co-processor" adds a transformation to the basic sensorimotor loop [16]. This can be studied by removing the entire organ (cerebellar ablation), which does not disrupt sensorimotor performance but makes performance uncoordinated; *dysmetric* [5].

The question is: What mathematically is nature's invention? The question is important, since the cerebellum, later in evolution, was the "enabling technology" that permitted fish to crawl onto hard terrain and to purposefully operate fins as limbs. It was this same cerebellar coordinator that enabled terrestrial animals become birds (the cerebellum amounting to a full 1/3 of the total mass of the brain). In fact, the cerebellum became a neurocomputer, for coordinated dynamic flight control [23].

While awaiting a "Newtonian revolution in neuroscience" [30], one theory of the cerebellum (for review of others, see [17], [16]) yields a concise mathematical answer to this question. The cerebellum, by incorporating the functional geometry (metric tensor) of the motor system serves as a "secretary" that transforms goals, given in intentional (sensory) terms, into signals specified in executive (motor) terms [21]. This theory was elaborated for about a dozen (mostly gaze-control) neural nets in various species (see review in [24]) and yielded biologically testable predictions that were experimentally confirmed [26], [7]. In this paper, further implications of the theory are outlined, primarily in the domain of implementation and application.

B. *"Evolution" of Human Interactions from "Hands On" Manipulation to Teleoperation in Telepresence*

Human "sensorimotor" performance *employing man-made sensory and motor systems*, can be brought into alignment with natural evolution. "Hands on" manipulation, when the brain's sensors and effectors are directly connected to the operandi requires only the biological "neural network". Humans, however, long ago evolved from "hands on" interaction with the world. Passive sensory representations advanced from cave-paintings to oil-paintings, photographs, motion-pictures and *television)*. "Telepresence" by purely passive means does not permit, however, either "look around" or the possibility of exerting motor action (there is no *teleoperation)*.

Active telepresence evolved only in the last few years, with the development of "virtual environment" techniques (also called "artificial or virtual reality" [11]). Since teleoperation, using a human central nervous system to control man-made motor effectors at remote sites, is useless without a sensory representation to the human operator, teleoperation and telepresence must be matched seemlessly. *However, matching sensory representation by telepresence to motor representation by teleoperation emerges as a theoretical "neural net" problem.*

* This paper gives personal views and does not reflect official positions of NASA. All ideas expressed are within the public domain.

0-7803-0999-5/93/$03.00 ©1993 IEEE

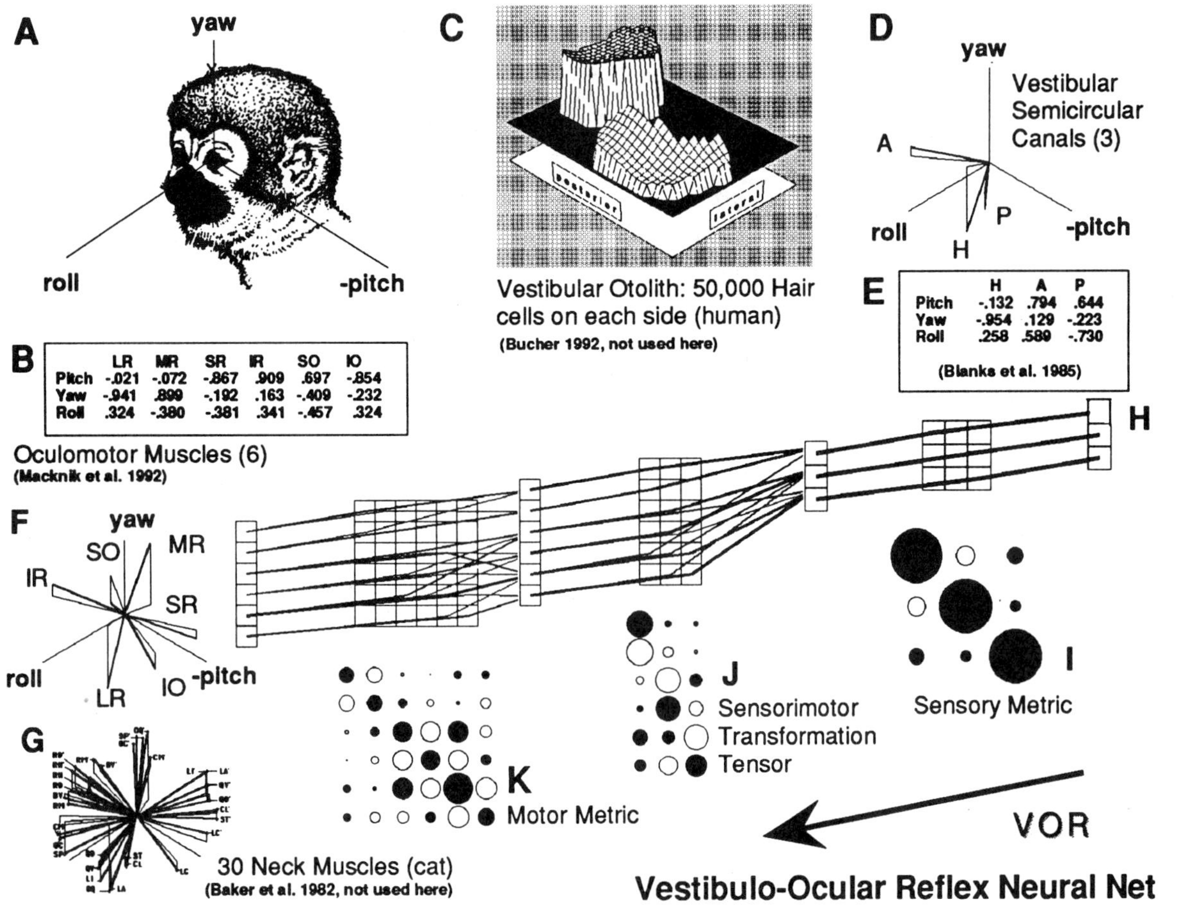

Fig. 1. Neural Network of the Vestibulo-Ocular Reflex of the squirrel monkey. A: Coordinate system in which axes of intrinsic frames are expressed. B: Coordinates intrinsic to eye muscles. C: Curved surfaces of the otolith organs, accomodating 50,000 hair cells. D-E: Vestibular coordinate system of the Anterior, Posterior and Horizontal semicircular canals. F: Oculomotor coordinate axis directions, G: 30 axis neck-motor coordinate system. H:Simplified set of connections from three vestibular canals to six oculomotor muscles. I-J-K Tensor transformation matrices (shown by filled and empty circles representing positive and negative matrix-components)

A practical example of this problem can be observed when a surgeon operates using sensory feedback supplied by television (e.g. micromanipulation in endoscopic surgery). The human nervous system is sandwiched by this between an active sensory representation, involving a moving camera, and operation in atelepresented environment. If telepresence and teleoperation are left uncoordinated, as in general, their conflict calls for, at the least, an arduous learning process (measurable by many months)- and outright impossible for some surgeons.

While "virtual environment" techniques for active sensory representation and "robot control" by remote computers (teleoperation) are advanced fields in the information sciences, their integration poses the task of *matching the geometry of active sensory representation to the geometry of active motor representation.*

II. Linear Vestibulo-Ocular Reflex as a Neural Network Prototype for Matching Sensory and Motor Geometries

The role of the cerebellum in solving, in an adaptive fashion, such problems of a conflict of sensory and motor geometries can be demonstrated by a gaze-stabilization neural network, the so-called (linear) vestibulo-ocular reflex [13, 28]. To stabilize gaze when fixating to a visual target while the head is in motion, the sensory apparatus measures head-movement in the 3 axis coordinate systems of vestibular semicircular canals (as well in the 50,000-axis coordinate system of the otolith organ (see Fig.1). Sensory information, expressed in covariant vector-components [20], then has to be transformed into compensatory motor information, expressed as a contravariant vector in the six-dimensional oculomotor system (as well as in a thirty-dimensional neck-motor coordinate system). It is both physically evident that the sensory coordinate systems are vastly different from that of the motor apparatus, and it has also been elaborated, for a number gaze reflexes of a number of species, that neural networks performing generalized vector (tensor) transformations can resolve the conflict of sensory and motor geometries [15],[19],[4],[24].

Analysis of Neural Geometry

A

by fractal analysis of morphology

B

C

Fractal Template
of Geometry of
Purkinje Cells

by multielectrode electrophysiology

D firing of neurons   time windows

F_1
F_2
F_n

E Covariant Metric Tensor g Compared
to the Correlation-Coefficient r

F
$$r_{ab} = \frac{\sum\limits_{i=1}^{4}(a_i - \overline{a})(b_i - \overline{b})}{\{\sum\limits_{i=1}^{4}(a_i - \overline{a})^2 \cdot \sum\limits_{i=1}^{4}(b_i - \overline{b})^2\}^{1/2}}$$

G
$$g_{ab} = \sum\limits_{n=1}^{2} \frac{\partial x^n}{\partial y^a} \cdot \frac{\partial x^n}{\partial y^b} = \cos(\varphi_{ab})$$

H Metric of the
Curved Manifold
of Neural Firings

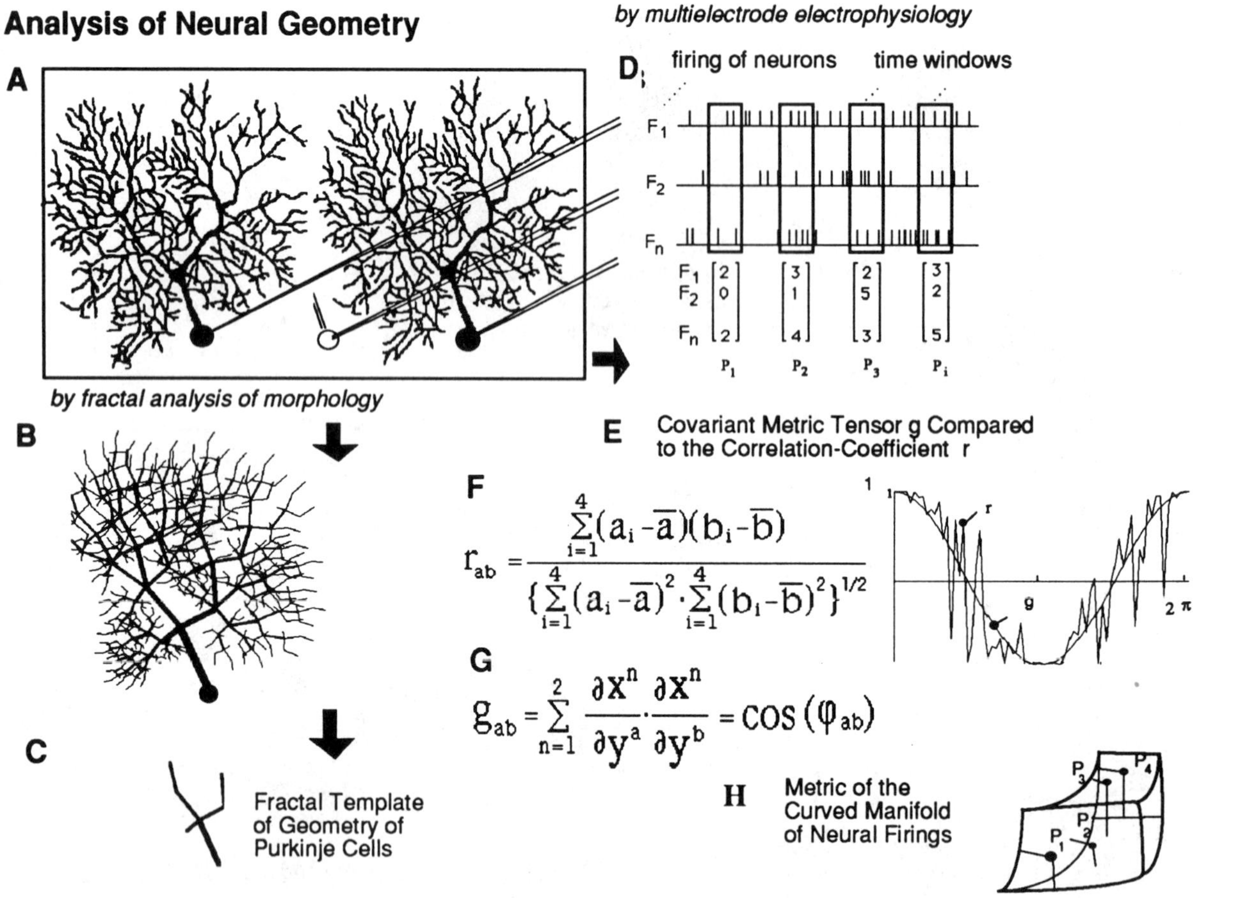

Fig. 2. Non-Euclidean fractal and metrical neural geometries revealed by the cerebellum. Fractal geometry is expressed by the cerebellar Purkinje cells in Guinea-pig (A) and in the computer model (B). Complexity of the dendritic tree is comprised by fractal template shown in (C). Metrical neural geometry of firings of cerebellar Purkinje cells can be revealed by the mathematical technique, cf. [18], of correlation analysis (F) followed by calculation of Moore-Penrose inverse of covariant metric (G)

As shown in Fig. 1. tensorial neural nets transform a) sensory coordinates to motor coordinates (where not only the direction of axes may be different but also the number of dimensions can change, even increase), b) changing from mathematically covariant (sensory intentional) components to mathematically contravariant (motor execution) components. As elaborated earlier, it is the cerebellar neural network that enables adaptablity to such sensorimotor reflexes, in effect by altering the cerebellum as the metric tensor of the motor geometry [21].

III. DISCERNING NON-EUCLIDEAN NEURAL GEOMETRIES FROM THE CEREBELLUM

A geometrical concept of neural network research [20],[6],[2], therefore has at least three major thrusts of direction; (1) discerning the exact nature of neural geometry, (2) implementation of neural geometries by artificial (electronic) means, (3) application of implemented neural geometries, as in the case of the cerebellum, for sensorimotor tasks such as to geometrically match telepresence to teleoperation. Fig.2. outlines the complexity of

the task of discerning neural geometry. First, metrical geometries (such as that of overall sensorimotor operation) can be measured by multielectrode-means (for theoretical foundation see [18], for methods and results see [22],[25]) and Figs. 3-4). It must be emphasized, that neural geometry, even at the coarsest level of granularity, as in overall sensorimotor performance of movement-directions and amplitudes, is non-Euclidean (the functional geometry is curved since its metric is position-dependent). Its experimental measurement calls for the mathematical procedure of correlation-analysis followed by the calculation of Moore-Penrose generalized inverse of covariant metric tensor [18]. Experimentally, this requires multielectrode-techniques [27] as well as a dedicated parallel processor, in effect an electronic neurocomputer facing the biological neurocomputer. (Features of such a transputer-based, Macintosh-IIfx hosted neurocomputer are shown in Fig.3.).

It is also evident that from the same cerebellar structure, at a finer level of granularity, a *fractal neural geometry* can be revealed (Fig. 2B,C). This implies that geometrical primitives of neural networks may well be grossly non-Euclidean fractals, not

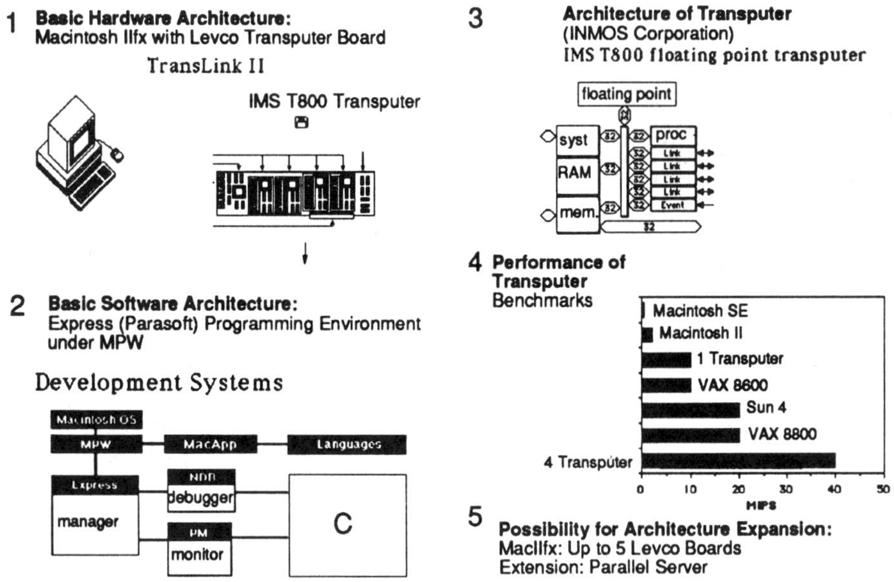

Fig. 3. Ffeatures of the Transputer-architecture of the neurocomputer developed for analysis and implementation of neural geomety [25].

only in a structural sense as shown by dendritic trees of neurons, but also functionally. For instance, contrary to classical experiments [8], the geometrical primitives of biological vision (pattern recognition, especially recognition of textures [10]) are likely to be fractals. This latter geometrical approach already yields dramatic bandwith-reduction techniques for robotic vision and virtual environment-techniques [3], and may well revolutionize experimentation on neurobiological vision.

Fig. 4 presents a display of the Transputer-based neurocomputer, to be used for discerning from the firing-patterns of cerebellar Purkinje neurons the position-dependent metric tensors of the functional geometry of musculo-skeletal system of an eye-head-neck apparatus of the squirrel monkey [25].

IV. Artificial Cerebellum ACE for Aerospace Applications of Adaptive Sensorimotor Control

The cerebellum provides a "secretariat-type" interface between one type of geometry, governing the world of intentions specified by sensory type representation, and another governing the world in which precise execution commands are given in terms of another functional geometry, specified by the constraints of the motor effectors. Thus, implementation of such a generic "interface" between sensory and motor geometries will find its usefulness in a variety of particular cases of adaptive sensorimotor control. Most importantly, it is expected to be crucial to the economic feasibility of the human settlement of space [1], which will require new control technologies in transportation [29] and an improvement in telerobotics techniques so as to permit the cost-effective exploitation of non-terrestrial materials and planetary exploration and monitoring. The Artificial Cerebellum ACE project is a framework within which NASA, together with other agencies such as NSF and NIH-NIMH could effectively target such goals of telepresence and teleoperation.

While presently the Artificial Cerebellum ACE Neural Network is implemented only on the Macintosh IIfx experimental platform (using Transputer parallel processor), the suitability of other dedicated processors, such as the Draper INCA (with JPL neurochip), and INTEL's Ni1000 processor are also explored.

As for general types of application of the Artificial Cerebellum ACE, three major areas appear as the most important (see Fig. 5). In conformance with the original goal for which nature developed biological neurocomputers, flight control emerges as one of the most potent ultimate application. In nature the fast and precise coordination required by forward-swept wings is resolved by an existing neurocomputer that features both an architecture with

Fig. 4. (See following page!) Representative display from the Macintosh IIfx-hosted, Ttransputer-based neurocomputer, developed by AJP and DLT on NASA DDF-T4967, to discern neural geometry from vestibular and cerebellar neurons of the squirrel monkey. Panel A displays the eye-head-neck skeletomuscular system of the squirrel monkey as it tracks a moving target. The neural network scheme shows the vestibular nucleus (B) and the cerebellum (C) from which Purkinje cell activities are recorded (panel D). Bottom panels show the computation of the metric tensors of the geometry of the curved functional space. Panel E shows the coordinate axes of the sensory system and its covariant metric tensor (matrix elements shown by proportional circles). Contravariant sensory metric tensor is shown in F. Axes and covariant motor metric is shown in panel G, contravariant metric as calculated from the axis is shown in H. Panels I and J display the metric tensors calculated from neural firings. Note that tensor I closely corresponds to G, while tensor J is virtually identical with the one in H. Also note, that all of the metric tensors discerned have non-zero off-diagonals!

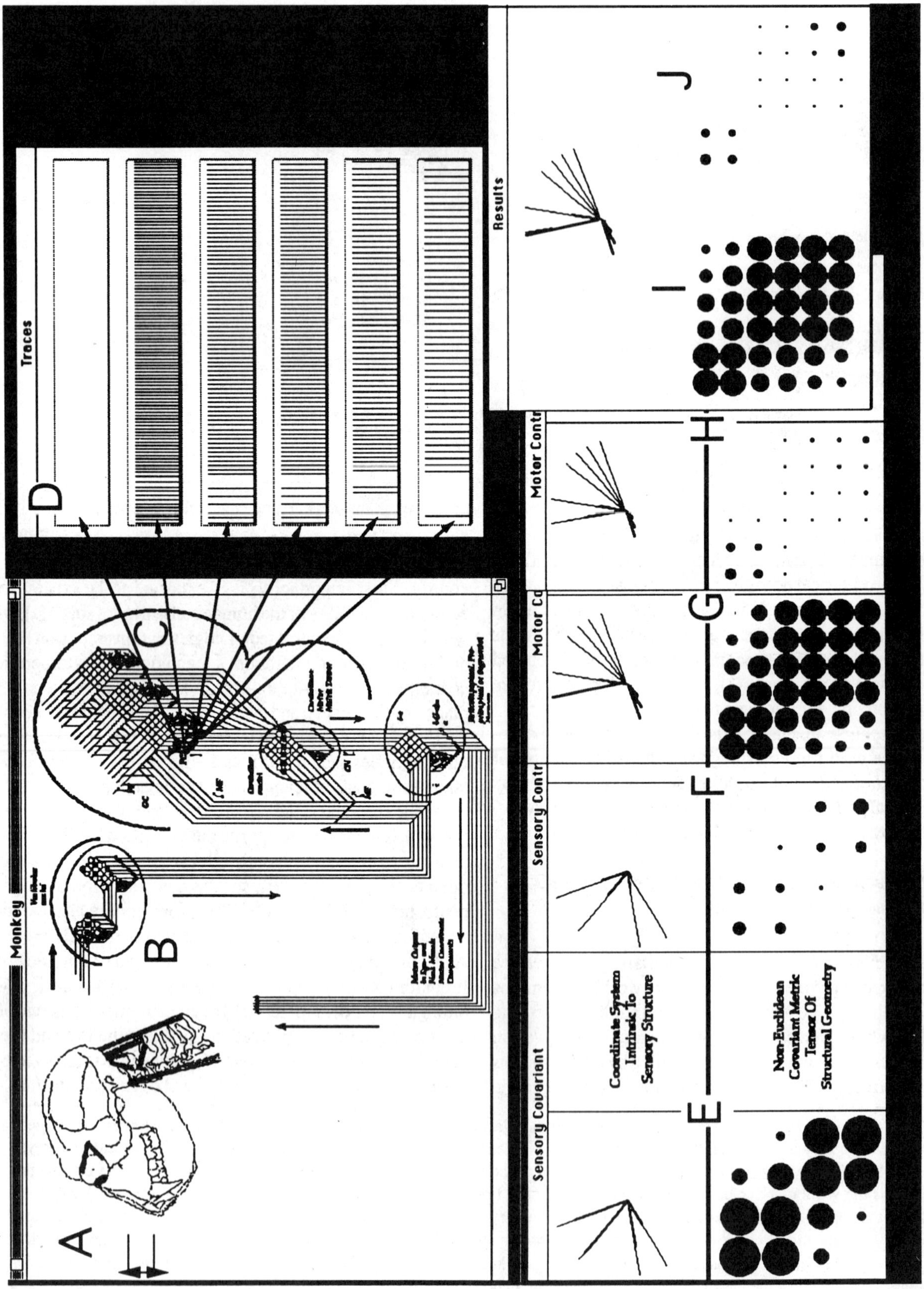

A
B
C
D
E
F
G
H
I
J
Monkey
Traces
Results
Sensory Covariant
Sensory Contr
Motor Co
Motor Contr
Coordinate System Intrinsic To Sensory Structure
Non-Euclidean Covariant Metric Tensor Of Structural Geometry

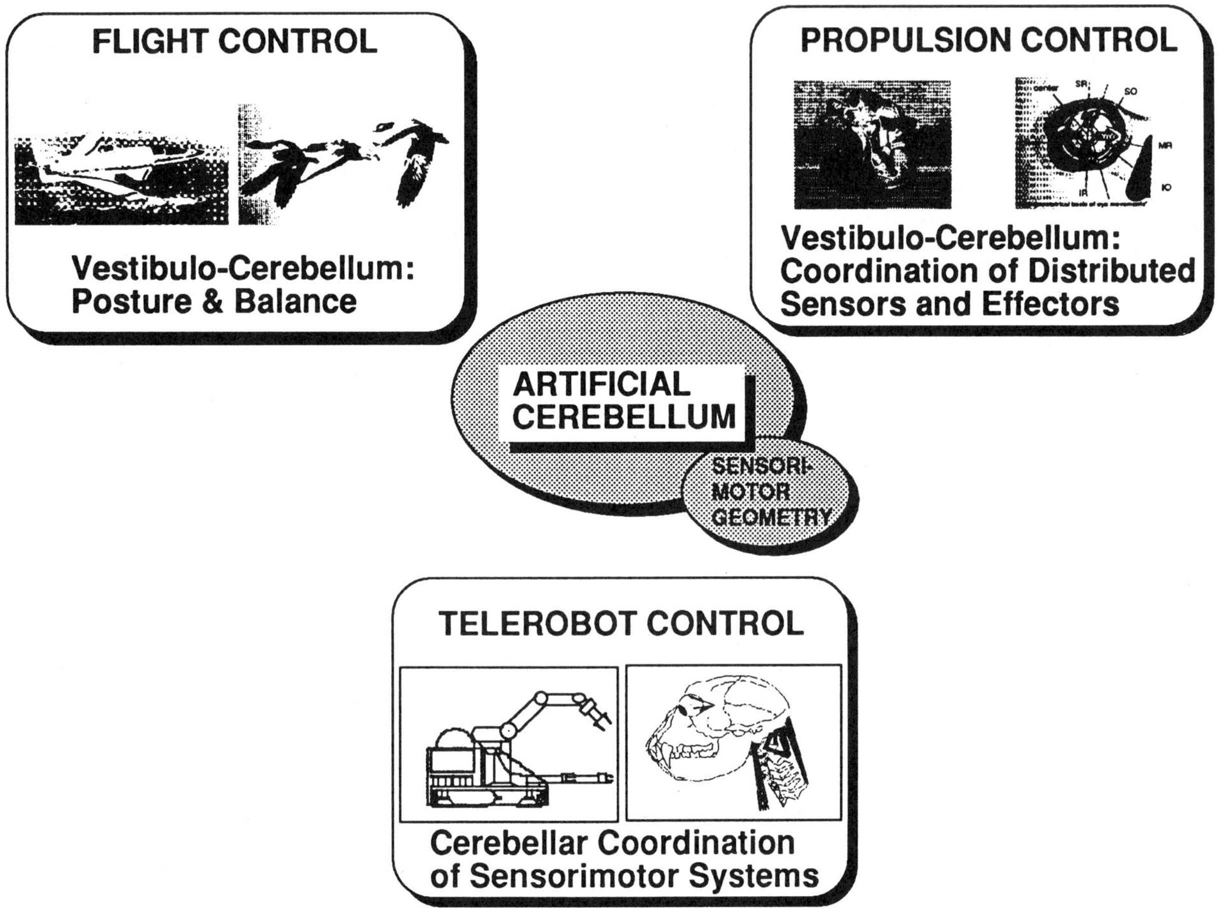

Fig. 5. Three major targeted fields of application of the Artificial Cerebellum (ACE) project for (1) Flight control (coordination and control of forward-swept winged craft), (2) Propulsion control of vectored thrusters, (3) Telerobot control in telepresence. These applications are based on the close parallel of existing neuronal network solutions in biology and technological utility.

built-in error tolerance as well as adaptive, self-organizing "software". While tackling such flight-control tasks with electronic neurocomputers is still its very early planning stages, the ultimate advantages of parallel, error-tolerant architecture destine neurocomputing for such role. Propulsion control of vectored thrusters is another potential application, where close parallel between non-orthogonally arranged and movable effectors (such as eye-muscles) are controlled by a biological neural net, and such natural solutions lend themselves for use in control of similar vectored thrusters.

One of the most obvious parallel between biological and artificial neural net sensorimotor control exists between telerobot control in telepresence and the actual neural control of skeletomuscular apparatus (e.g. that of eye-head-neck system) under visual and vestibular coordination.

Government support (especially by NIH) has long resulted in vast knowledge and has started to yield mathematical understanding of biological neural networks. Likewise, civilian neuroengineering programs (e.g. by NSF) have also been in place for some time to provide the technology needed for implementation of artificial neural nets. Specific application-oriented NASA programs were therefore required that delineate the most promising projects that can integrate the hitherto separate civilian efforts. This was the rationale for aiming at an "Artificial Cerebellum, ACE-Neurocontroller", as a framework of an interdisciplinary and interagency program by NASA-NSF-NIH-NIMH.

Acknowledgment

This research was supported by NASA-DDF-T4967 to AJP and DLT, and NASA-NRC-A8967730 to AJP

References

[1] "Settling Space." *AMERICA'S future in space: a briefing book.* National Space Society. Washington, D.C. 1989.

[2] S. Amari. Dualistic Geometry of the Manifold of Higher-Order Neurons. *Neural Networks.* 4(4): 443-451, 1991.

[3] M. F. Barnsley and A. D. Sloan. A better way to compress images. *Byte.* (Jan.): 215-223, 1988.

[4] W. Daunicht and A. Pellionisz. Spatial arrangement of the vestibular and the oculomotor system in the rat. *Brain Res.* 435: 48-56, 1987.

[5] J. C. Eccles, M. Ito and J. Szentágothai. *"The cerebellum as a neuronal machine."* Springer-Verlag. Berlin, New York, Heidelberg. 1967.

[6] R. Eckmiller. "Concerning the emerging role of geometry in neuroinformatics." *Parallel Processing in Neural Systems and Computers.* Eckmiller, Hartmann and Hauske ed. Elsevier Science Publishers B.V (North Holland). 5-8, Amsterdam. 1990.

[7] C. C. A. M. Gielen and E. J. van Zuylen. Coordination of arm muscles during flexion and supination: Application of the tensor analysis approach. *Neuroscience.* 17: 527-539, 1986.

[8] D. Hubel and T. Wiesel. Receptive fields, binocular interaction and functional architecture in the cat's visual cortex. *J. Physiol.*160: 106-154, 1962.

[9] M. Ito. *"The cerebellum and neural control."* Raven Press. New York. 1984.

[10] B. Julesz. *"Foundations of Cyclopean Perception."* The University of Chicago Press. Chicago. 1971.

[11] M. W. Krueger. *"Artificial Reality II."* Addison-Wesley. Reading, MA. 1991.

[12] R. Llinás, D. E. Hillman and W. Precht. "Functional aspects of cerebellar evolution." *The Cerebellum in Health and Disease.* Green ed. 269-291, St. Louis. 1966.

[13] G. D. Paige and D. L. Tomko. Linear vestbular-ocular reflex of squirrel monkey: I. Basic Characteristics *J. Neurophysiol.* 65(5); 1170-1182. 1991

[14] A. Pellionisz. Brain Theory: Connecting Neurobiology to Robotics. Tensor Analysis: Utilizing Intrinsic Coordinates to Describe, Understand and Engineer Functional Geometries to Intelligent Organisms. *J. Theoret. Neurobiol.* 2: 185-211, 1983.

[15] A. Pellionisz. "Tensorial aspects of the multidimensional approach to the vestibulo-oculomotor reflex and gaze." *Adaptive Mechanisms in Gaze Control.* Berthoz and Melvill-Jones ed. Elsevier. 281-296, Amsterdam. 1985.

[16] A. Pellionisz. Tensorial brain theory in cerebellar modeling. In: *Cerebellar Functions.*, ed. by J. Bloedel et al., Springer Verlag, 201-229, Berlin-Heidelberg-New York 1985.

[17] A. Pellionisz. "David Marr's theory of the cerebellar cortex: A model in brain theory for the "Galilean combination of simplification, unification and mathematization"." *Brain Theory.* G. and Aertsen ed. Springer Verlag. 253-257, Berlin-Heidelberg-New York. 1986.

[18] A. Pellionisz. "Vistas from Tensor Network Theory: A horizon from reductionalist neurophilosophy to the geometry of multi-unit recordings." *Computer Simulation in Brain Science.* Cotterill ed. Cambridge Univ. Press. 44-73, Cambridge. 1988.

[19] A. Pellionisz and W. Graf. Tensor network model of the "three-neuron vestibulo-ocular reflex-arc" in cat. *J. Theoret. Neurobiol.* 5: 127-151, 1987.

[20] A. Pellionisz and R. Llinás. Tensorial approach to the geometry of brain function: Cerebellar coordination via metric tensor. *Neurosci.* 5: 1125-1136, 1980.

[21] A. Pellionisz and R. Llinás. Tensor Network Theory of the metaorganization of functional geometries in the CNS. *Neurosci.* 16: 245-274, 1985.

[22] A. J. Pellionisz and J. R. Bloedel. *Functional Geometry of Purkinje Cell Population Responses as Revealed by Neurocomputer Analysis of Multi-Unit Recordings.* Soc. Neurosci Absts. 21: 920,1991.

[23] A. J. Pellionisz, C. C. Jorgensen and P. J. Werbos. *Cerebellar Neurocontroller Project, for Aerospace Applications, in a Civilian Neurocomputing Initiative in the "Decade of the Brain"*. IJCNN 92. III: 379-384,1992.

[24] A. J. Pellionisz, B. W. Peterson and D. L. Tomko. "Vestibular Head-Eye Coordination: A Geometrical Sensorimotor Neurocomputer Paradigm." *Advanced Neurocomputing.* Eckmiller ed. Elsevier, North-Holland. 126-145, Amsterdam. 1990.

[25] A. J. Pellionisz, D. L. Tomko and J. Bloedel R. "Neural Geometry Revealed by Neurocomputer Analysis of Purkinje Cell Responses". *Computing by Neural Systems.* C.Ploegert, 1-5, Kluever, Boston. 1992.

[26] B. W. Peterson and F. J. R. Richmond. *"Control of head movements."* Oxford University Press. 1988.

[27] H. J. Reitboeck and G. Werner. Multi-electrode recording system for the study of spatio-temporal activity pattern of neurons in the central nervous system. *Experientia.* 19: 339-341, 1983.

[28] D. L. Tomko and G. D. Paige. Linear vestibular-ocular reflex in squirrel monkey: II. Visual-vestibular interactions and kinematic considerations. *J. Neurophysiol.* 65(5) 1183-1196. 1991

[29] P. J. Werbos. Backpropagation and neurocontrol: a review and prospectus. *IJCNN.* : I-209, 1989.

[30] P. J. Werbos and A.J. Pellionisz. Neurocontrol and Neuro-biology: New Developments and Connections. *IJCNN. 92.* III.373-378, 1992

A Spatio-temporal Neural Network Model of Saccade Generation

K. Arai[1], E. L. Keller, and J. A. Edelman
Smith-Kettlewell Eye Research Institute and University of California, Berkeley
2232 Webster Street, San Francisco, CA 94115

Abstract—In this article we present a new spatio-temporal neural network model of the superior colliculus. The model uses lateral excitatory and inhibitory connections to help control both the dynamic and static behavior of saccadic eye movements. In simulations the model succeeds in replicating accurate saccades of a variety of sizes. Simulation results and the model's relation to neurophysiological findings are discussed.

I. Introduction

Saccadic eye movements are among the most rapid yet precise of all movements produced by higher mammals. This type of movement is only fully developed in humans and monkeys, both animals with high-acuity foveal vision. An understanding of the neurological organization that underlies this unique type of behavior has long been a goal of neuroscientists.

Saccades move the line of sight of the eyes to the spatial location of visual targets in the peripheral retinal field. Thus target location in retinal coordinates is the sensory input that determines the goal of the saccadic movement, but because of processing delays in the visual system (on the order of 100 msec or more), this visual feedback cannot be used during the actual saccade to control the accuracy of its trajectory, since the duration of a typical saccade is less than 60 ms. At first, their brevity suggested that saccades were ballistic movements in which the commands necessary to move the line of sight were pre-computed. However, later physiological experiments revealed that saccades were executed by a closed-loop feedback system residing in primate brainstem [1].

Single-unit recordings in alert monkeys have shown that saccades are encoded by neural maps in the deeper layers of the superior colliculus (SC), a laminar structure on the roof of the brainstem. In the deeper layers of the SC, the location of the center of a large population of active cells determines the change in line of sight, or saccadic vector. Within the map the discharge of the particular population of active cells is relatively the same for saccades of different sizes, only the location changes. Thus, a two-degree saccade is coded by the activity of a population of cells located in the rostral SC as shown in Fig. 1 and a 20-degree saccade is coded by the activity of another population of cells in the caudal SC. Furthermore, a visual map in the SC lies in spatial register with this motor map. Indeed, many cells in the deeper layers of the SC fire both in response to a visual stimulus at the appropriate spatial location and immediately before saccades with the corresponding saccadic vector.

Cells in the SC project to other regions in the brainstem with eye movement related properties. Studies in the brainstem reticular formation have revealed a class of neurons that discharge intensely during saccades in a preferred direction with a duration of activity equal to the duration of the saccade. Thus, this interface between the SC and reticular formation converts a signal encoded spatially into one encoded temporally. Neurons in the reticular formation in turn project to motoneurons innervating the eye muscles.

In the past two decades a number of workers have proposed models of this brainstem saccade generator. The main purpose of these models has been to show how a closed-loop system could produce realistic saccades without the use of visual feedback. Robinson proposed that an efference copy of the motor signal used to drive motoneurons served as a feedback signal [2]. He and his colleagues later provided a local feedback model of saccadic control that produced simulated dynamics and accuracies very similar to those found experimentally [3]. This model is a standard engineering idealization composed of interconnected transfer functions and nonlinearites.

Unfortunately, the nature of the input to this brainstem saccade generator, as well as the role the SC plays in providing this input, have not been modelled extensively. The Van Gisbergen - Robinson model assumes as input a

---

[1]supported in part by Mitsubishi Kasei Corporation

0-7803-0999-5/93/$03.00 ©1993 IEEE

single analog signal whose magnitude codes desired saccade size, and does not address how the spatio-temporal transformation takes place. Recently, two models of saccade generation using population coding from a topographically organized neural map of the SC have appeared [4,5]. They produce spatially accurate saccades from a distributed collicular input which is summed in the brainstem reticular formation, but do not address the control of saccadic dynamics or the firing patterns of cells during saccades. Another model using a neural network approach has appeared, but its focus was directed toward short term visual memory and the spatial frame of reference used to compute target position and not the dynamic modelling of collicular cell discharge during saccades [6].

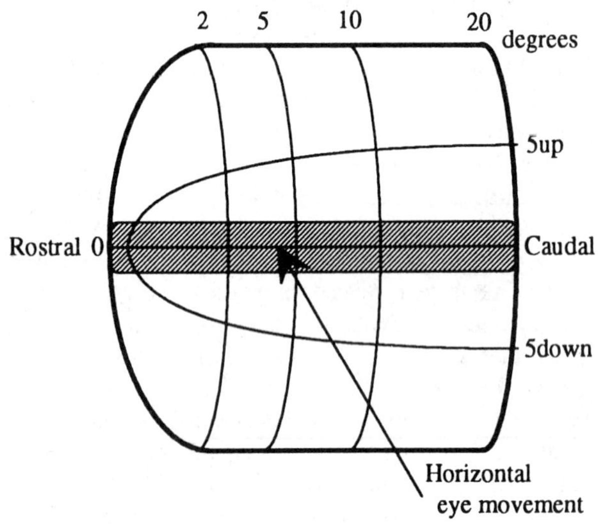

Fig. 1. The spatial map in the superior colliculus. Stippled region shows the area active for horizontal, contralateral saccades modelled in the present paper.

II. Neural Network Model

Neurophysiological experiments have shown that the receptive fields of cells in both the superficial and deeper layers of the SC have suppressive surrounds, suggesting the presence of lateral inhibitory connections between collicular cells [7, 8]. Other studies have shown the presence of excitatory interconnections over shorter intercollicular distances [9]. This pattern of excitatory and inhibitory influences, often called a Mexican hat function, has been shown to produce interesting spatio-temporal dynamic properties in neural network models. Depending on the relative widths of the excitatory and inhibitory regions and on the pattern of the inputs to the network, these properties can include a dramatic lengthening of the network time constant over that associated with single cells as well as a form of modified winner take all behavior [10,11]. Thus these connections may play a role in controlling the dynamics as well as the static behavior of saccadic eye movements.

Here we propose a new spatio-temporal neural network model of the SC using these lateral interconnections. For simplicity we have concentrated on a one-dimensional realization as shown in Fig. 2 that produces realistic horizontal saccade eye movements. The model's two layers represent the superficial and the deeper layers of the SC. In the model's superficial layer, pools of neurons, indicated by V_i, respond to visual stimuli and project to neuron pools in the deeper layer, indicated by M_i, with a delay. Neuron pools in the deeper layer discharge just before the saccade. The output of this layer is in turn sent as a distributed input to a local feedback model of the type previously discussed [3]. Each layer has five neuronal pools that represent a map of saccade sizes 2 to 20 degrees. Thus, the distributed discharge in the deeper layer codes for the particular size of eye movement (spatial coding). The dynamics of each neuronal pool is described by a first-order equation:

$$\tau_v \frac{dx_{vi}}{dt} = -x_{vi} + I_i - h_{vi} \quad (1)$$

$$\tau_m \frac{dx_{mi}}{dt} = -x_{mi} + w_{ii} y_{mi} + \sum_{j \neq i} w_{ij}(\lambda) y_{mj} + y_{vi}(t-d) - h_{mi} \quad (2)$$

$$y_{vi} = f(x_{vi}),\ y_{mi} = f(x_{mi}) \quad (3)$$

where x_{vi} and x_{mi} are state variables describing the membrane properties of the ith neuron pool, τ_v and τ_m are time constants, I_i is visual input from the retina, w_{ii} is the weight of local self-excitation, $w_{ij}(\lambda)$, which is set to have nearby excitation and remote inhibition, is the weighting function of interconnections, y_{vi} and y_{mi} are outputs of the neuron pools, f(x) is a non-linear output function, h_{vi} and h_{mi} are threshold levels, and d is the delay between the two layers.

The crucial feature of this model is that the weight of self-excitation, w_{ii}, is effectively reduced during inter-saccadic intervals of fixation by a shunting global inhibition, P, hypothesized to originate in a higher level of the brain [12]:

$$w_{ii} = \frac{w_0}{P} \qquad (4)$$

where w_0 is a default value of low self-excitation. This inhibition dramatically changes dynamic behavior of the entire layer of neuron pools by reducing the network time constant close to that of the individual pool during the fixation interval. Low level membrane potentials remain, but no neuron pool in the deeper layer can generate a saccadic burst. Once the global inhibition turns off (P=1), the neuron pool receiving the largest visual input will rapidly increase its discharge to a saturation level. Neighboring pools are recruited at low rates because of local excitatory connections. The global inhibition turns on (P>1) again when pause cells, which control saccadic burst cells in the brain stem, resume their discharge after the eye movement is complete.

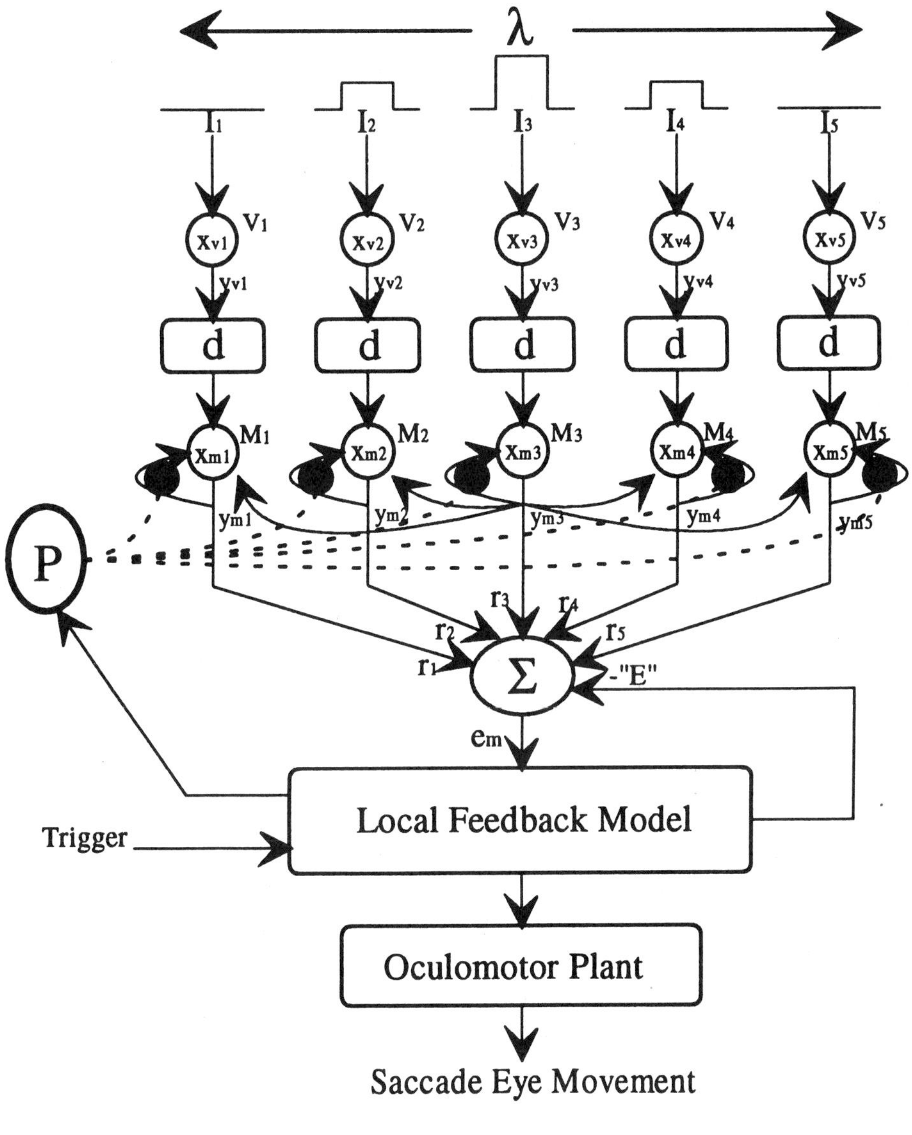

Fig. 2. The saccadic spatio-temporal neural network with lateral interconnections. Upper layered structure represents a spatially coded structure like the SC. Lower structure is the temporally coded saccadic burst generator. The filled circles from P represent global shunting (presynaptic) inhibition of the lateral interconnections.

III. SIMULATION RESULTS

In this section we illustrate that the model described above produces realistic saccades dynamics and SC cellular discharge. The desired eye position, E_d, and the dynamic motor error, e_m, in the local feedback model are calculated by the following equations:

$$E_d=\sum_{i=1}^{5} r_i y_{mi} \quad (5)$$

$$e_m=E_d-''E'' \quad (6)$$

where r_i is the weight of the saccade size and "E" is the efferent copy feedback of the motor signal.

The proper weights, r_i, were adjusted during learning sessions using the gradient-descent method so that the actual final eye positions corresponded to visual inputs of 2, 5, 10, 15, and 20 degrees. The input, I_i, is a square function in time and spreads in space as shown in Fig. 2, which means that neighboring inputs, I_{i-1} and I_{i+1}, also have small values. Fig. 3 and Table I show simulation results and the parameter list used for saccadic eye movements, respectively. The model succeeds in making accurate saccadic eye movements of a variety of sizes.

IV. DISCUSSION

The global shunting inhibition and lateral interconnections used in our model serve to rapidly transform the network between two states. With inhibition present, the network acts as a leaky capacitor, preventing visual-induced activity in the upper layer from causing any location in the deeper layer to burst. When this inhibition is removed activity rapidly increases in one of the deeper layer pools, providing the brainstem saccade generator with the input necessary to create a saccade. This global inhibition may represent activity in the substantia nigra, a part of the basal ganglia known to inhibit the SC during intersaccadic intervals [13]. Removing the inhibition allows the model to create saccades immediately after the arrival of the visual input in the deeper layer, a situation comparable to the extremely short latencies of "express" saccades.

Waitzman and his colleagues have suggested that many motor layer collicular cells carry a signal correlated with dynamic motor error, the instantaneous difference between the desired eye position and the efferent copy of eye position [14]. This hypothesis places the SC within the local feedback loop. In contrast, our model places the SC outside this loop, providing a input to a local feedback loop located in the brainstem saccade generator. Neuron pools in the deeper layers send a desired eye position signal to the feedback loop until the saccade ends. However, in our simulations,

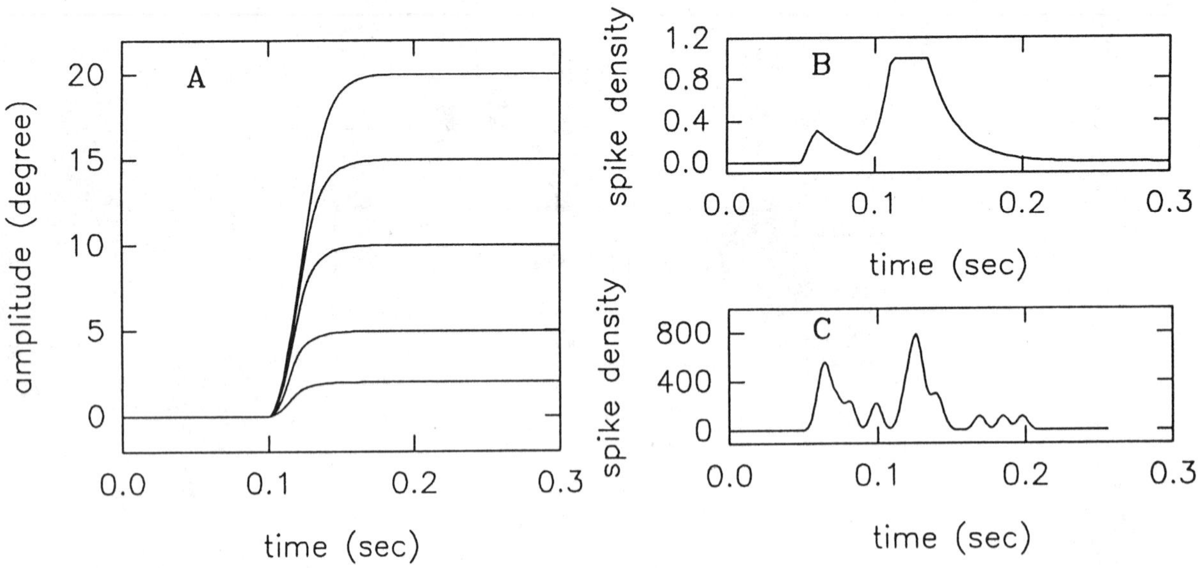

Fig. 3. (A) Simulated results of saccade eye movements (2, 5, 10, 15, and 20 degrees). (B) Simulated discharge of the deeper layer cells active for a 10-deg saccade. (C) Actual discharge of a deeper layer cell during a 10-deg saccade in monkey.

TABLE I

PARAMETER LIST

Time Constant	τ_v=1msec, τ_m=5msec
Weight(lateral interconnection)	w_o=1.5, $w_{ii-1}=w_{ii+1}$=0.5, $w_{ii-2}=w_{ii+2}$=-3.5, others=0, (i=1~5)
Global Inhibition	P=1, (no inhibition), P=2.5, (global inhibition)
Threshold Level	$h_{vi}=h_{mi}$=0, (i=1~5)
Delay	d=40msec
Input	I_1=0.2, I_2=0.06, others=0, (2 deg.), I_2=0.2, $I_1=I_3$=0.06, others=0, (5 deg.) I_3=0.2, $I_2=I_4$=0.06, others=0, (10 deg.), I_4=0.2, $I_3=I_5$=0.06, others=0, (15 deg.) I_5=0.2, I_4=0.06, others=0, (20 deg.)
Output Function	f(x)= x ($0 \le x \le 1.0$), 0 (otherwise)
Weight (saccade size)	r_1=1.42, r_2=3.49, r_3=7.63, r_4=10.5, r_5=18.0

deeper layer activity does start to decline before the end of the saccade. Our future work with the model will explore if the SC needs to be included inside the feedback loop in order to create realistic discharge profiles as motor error declines and the saccade ends.

It has been well documented that accurate saccades can be made to the location of flashed targets even after extensive intervals of time have passed. The present model is able to replicate these results because even the extremely low residual levels of local activity present in the deeper layer (x_{mi}) is able to reexcite the winner-take-all mechanism when the global inhibition is removed. Activity then builds up at the appropriate spatial site in the colliculus to guide the correct saccade. This feature of the model constitutes a type of short-term memory. A similar mechanism was proposed recently by Droulez and Berthoz [6].

REFERENCES

[1] Hepp, K., Henn, V., Vilis, T., and Cohen, B. (1989) Brainstem regions related to saccade generation. In: "The Neurobiology of Saccadic Eye Movements", Wurtz, R. and Goldberg, M., eds., Elsevier, Amsterdam. pp. 105-212.

[2] Robinson, D. A. (1975) Oculomotor control signals. In: "Basic Mechanisms of Ocular Motility and Their Clinical Implications", Lennerstrand, G. and Bach-y-Rita, P., eds., Pergammon Press, Oxford, England. pp. 337-374.

[3] Van Gisbergen, J. A. M., Robinson, D. A., and Gielen, S. (1981) A quantitative analysis of generation of saccadic eye movements by burst neurons. J. Neurophysiol. 45, 417-442.

[4] Lee, C., Rohrer, W. H., and Sparks, D. L. (1988) Population coding of saccadic eye movements by neurons in the superior colliculus. Nature. 332, 357-360.

[5] Van Gisbergen, J. A. M., Van Opstal, A. J., and Tax, A. A. M. (1987) Collicular ensemble coding of saccades based on vector summation. Neuroscience. 21, 541-555.

[6] Droulez, J., and Berthoz, A. (1991) A neural network model of sensoritopic maps with predictive short-term memory properties. Nat.Acad.Sci.,USA. 88, 9653-9657.

[7] Cynader, H., and Berman, N. (1972) Receptive-field organization of monkey superior colliculus. J. Neurophysiol. 35, 187-201.

[8] Goldberg, M. E., and Wurtz, R. H. (1972) Activity of superior colliculus in behaving monkey: I. Visual receptive fields of single neurons. J. Neurophysiol. 35, 542-559.

[9] McIlwain, J. (1982) Lateral spread of neural excitation in intermediate gray layer of cat's superior colliculus. J. Neurophysiol. 47, 167-178.

[10] Cannon, S. C., Robinson, D. A., and Shamma, S. (1983) A proposed neural network for the integration of the oculomotor system. Biol. Cybern. 49, 127-136.

[11] Yuille, A. L., and Grzywacz, N. M. (1989) A winner-take-all mechanism based on presynaptic inhibition feedback. Neural Comp. 1, 334-347.

[12] Torre, V., and Poggio, T. (1978) A synaptic mechanism possibly underlying directional selectivity to motion. Proc. R. Soc.(London). B202, 409-416.

[13] Hikosaka, O., and Wurtz, R. H. (1983) Visual and oculomotor functions of monkey substantia nigra pars reticulata. I. Relation of visual and auditory responses to saccades. J. Neurophysiol. 49, 1230-1253.

[14] Waitzman, D., Ma, T., Optican, L., and Wurtz, R. (1988) Superior colliculus neurons provide the saccadic motor error signal. Exp. Brain Res. 72, 649-652.

Generation of Traveling Wave Mode in A Chained Neural Oscillator Network Model

Hirofumi Nagashino, Koji Kakuyama and Yohsuke Kinouchi

Department of Electrical and Electronic Engineering, Faculty of Engineering,
The University of Tokushima, Tokushima 770 JAPAN

Abstract We analyzed a chained neural oscillator network model for a possible mechanism of generation of biological rhythm such as locomotion and peristaltic movement. Each oscillator unit is inhibited by its nearest neighbors. Numerical analysis emplying Poincaré map and computer simulation of the model have clarified characteristics of oscillation. It has been found out that among multi-stable oscillatory solutions traveling wave mode is generated by the chained networks of ring and linear structures and it can occur not only by setting proper initial conditions but also by transition from other mode with change of a parameter.

1. INTRODUCTION

The central nervous system of vertebrates and invertebrates generates and controls various rhythmic activities such as locomotion and peristaltic movement. It has been found out in a number of species that such behaviors are produced by central pattern generators (CPGs) which are believed to involve collections of oscillators [1,2]. It is considered that CPGs generate fundamental rhythmic patterns without any periodic inputs or feedback from peripheral systems.

The time scale of period of the rhythms is seconds, which is much longer than the firing interval of a single neuron. Most of the models for the mechanism of the rhythm generation incorporate the time scale with intrinsic property of a neuron [3-6]. Nagashino et al. [7,8] proposed a possible alternative mechanism. It produces the long period by the coupling of a number of elements in the model network. The network is composed of neurons that have impulse generation characteristics and inhibit reciprocally nearest neighbors. The mechanism is based on the phase difference of firing between neurons. Under the consifderable fluctuations of biological states, however, it is more appropriate to develop a model that generates such rhythmic activities by collective variables.

We have analyzed a neural network model whose element is a neural oscillator coupled in chained structures. In this paper, we show multi-phase mode and traveling wave mode as multi-stable oscillatory solutions in the present model. The multi-phase mode is the same kind of oscillation as have been reported in some networks of coupled oscillators [9,10]. On the other hand, oscillatory behaviors such as the traveling wave mode have not been reported before. The traveling wave mode gives much longer period of oscillation than that of a single oscillator approximately proportional to the number of oscillators. It occurs in the linear structure as well as in the ring structure. These results are similar to the firing modes in reciprocal inhibition neural networks composed of a number of pulse generating neurons. We show a) the existence regions and b) the transitions of the oscillatory solutions with respect to coupling coefficient of oscillators in the ring networks and c) initial conditions for generation of the traveling wave mode.

2. A CHAINED NEURAL OSCILLATOR NETWORK MODEL

Fig. 1 shows the neural oscillator model that is the unit of a chained neural oscillator network model in the present work. Each oscillator unit is composed of an excitatory and an inhibitory neuron. Each "neuron" is assumed to represent the average behavior of a number of neurons. These two neurons are coupled to each other forming a negative feedback loop. The excitatory neuron has a self-excitatory connection forming a positive feedback loop. Without both of the loops, there is no oscillation. This self-excitatory connection does not mean the recurrent connection of a neuron to itself, which has not been observed in general, but rather simplifies the interconnection of a number of excitatory neurons. Existence of bi-directional connections of excitatory neurons has been reported [11,12]. For suitable ranges of coupling coefficients, the unit generates a rhythmic output without any tonic external input. The oscillators are assumed to be identical.

Fig. 2 shows a chained neural oscillator network model with reciprocal inhibition to nearest neighbors. The excitatory neuron in an oscillator unit receives inhibition from the inhibitory neuron of two adjacent oscillators. The coupling coefficient is denoted by c_o and uniform in the network for simplicity of analysis. Let u_{ek} and u_{ik} denote the membrane potential of the excitatory neuron E_k and the inhibitory neuron I_k respectively in k-th unit. Their dynamics is expressed as

$$\tau_e \dot{u}_{ek} + u_{ek} = c_{ee} z_{ek} - c_{ei} z_{ik} - c_o(z_{ik-1} + z_{ik+1}) \qquad (1a)$$

and

$$\tau_i \dot{u}_{ik} + u_{ik} = c_{ie} z_{ek}\ , \qquad (1b)$$

where k=1, 2, ... , N and z_{rk} (r=e or i) is the output of the neuron expressed as

$$z_{rk} = \frac{2}{\pi} \tan^{-1} u_{rk}\ , \qquad (2)$$

0-7803-0999-5/93/$03.00 ©1993 IEEE

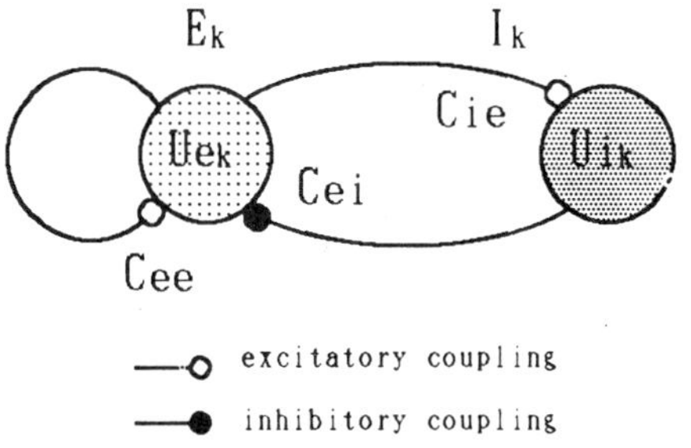

Fig. 1 A neural oscillator model.

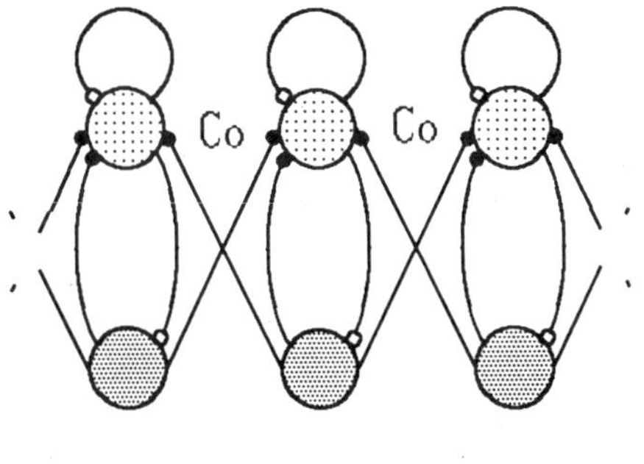

Fig. 2 A chained neural oscillator network model with reciprocal inhibition.

where $|z_{rk}| < 1$. These outputs are assumed to be the average values of the impulse frequencies of the neurons over a certain period of time. They increase monotonically and are saturated at ± 1. For ring structure, when k=1, N takes the place of k-1 and when k=N, 1 replaces k+1. For linear structure, when k=1, z_{k-1}=0 and when k=N, z_{k+1}=0. Symbol $\dot{}$ denotes the derivative with respect to time. The time constants of the membranes of the excitatory and inhibitory neurons are denoted by τ_e and τ_i respectively. In the following for simplicity of analysis, they are assumed to be equal and set to one. The coupling coefficients of the coupling from neuron r' to neuron r within each oscillator are denoted by $c_{rr'}$, where r, r'=e or i.

3. ANALYSIS OF A SINGLE NEURAL OSCILLATOR

In this section, we show the stable solutions of the single neural oscillator with different coupling coefficients by linear approximation analysis. The dynamics of the single oscillator is described as

$$\dot{u}_e + u_e = c_{ee}z_e - c_{ei}z_i \tag{3a}$$

and

$$\dot{u}_i + u_i = c_{ie}z_e\ , \tag{3b}$$

where u_e and u_i are the membrane potential of the excitatory and the inhibitory neuron respectively. The linearized system of (3a) and (3b) at the origin has a single equilibrium, the origin. The analysis of the stability of the equilibrium gives eigenvalues λ as

$$\lambda = \frac{c_{ee}}{\pi} - 1 \pm \frac{1}{\pi}\sqrt{c_{ee}^2 - 4c_{ei}c_{ie}}\ . \tag{4}$$

The equilibrium is stable when

$$c_{ee} < \pi \tag{5a}$$

and

$$c_{ee} < \frac{\pi^2 + 4c_{ei}c_{ie}}{2\pi}\ . \tag{5b}$$

Eigenvalues are real and at least one of them is positive when

$$c_{ee} > \frac{\pi^2 + 4c_{ei}c_{ie}}{2\pi}\ , \tag{6}$$

or

$$c_{ee} > \pi \tag{7a}$$

and

$$c_{ee} > 2\sqrt{c_{ei}c_{ie}}\ . \tag{7b}$$

In this case, (3) has two stable equilibria, one of which is positive, the other negative. Their absolute values are equal. When

$$\pi < c_{ee} < 2\sqrt{c_{ei}c_{ie}}\ , \tag{8}$$

the egenvalues are conjugate comlex numbers and have positive real part and an oscillatory solution exists in (3). Fig. 3 shows these three regions of coupling coefficients c_{ee} and c_{ei} when c_{ie}=1. From (4), angular frequency ω of the oscillation is given as

$$\omega = \frac{1}{\pi}\sqrt{4c_{ei}c_{ie} - c_{ee}^2}\ . \tag{9}$$

In the following, the coupling coefficients inside each oscillator are fixed as c_{ee}=4, c_{ei}=5 and c_{ie}=1, which gives the oscillatory solution. We analyzed the chained network with different values of mutual inhibitory coupling coefficient c_o of the oscillators, which is uniform throughout the network.

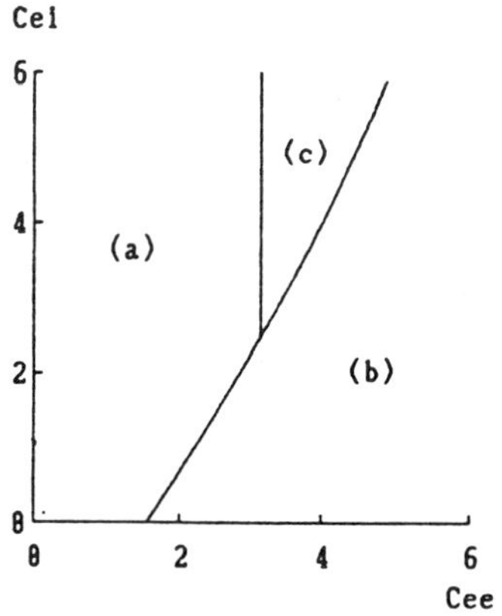

Fig. 3 Relationship between coupling coefficients and the stable solutions of the neural oscillator unit. (a) monostable equilibrium at the origin, (b) bistable equilibria, (c) oscillatory solution.

4. MULTI-PHASE MODE

In the chained neural oscillator network of the ring structure, for relatively weak mutual coupling, there exist rhythmic patterns in which the waveform is nearly sinusoidal (The stronger the mutual coupling is, the greater the distortion of the waveform is.) and the phase difference between adjacent oscillators is uniform. We call this type of oscillatory solutions multi-phase mode. The number of patterns depends on the number of oscillators in the network.

4. 1 Classification of multi-phase mode

The number of solutions of the multi-phase mode is equal to the number of oscillators in the network, as is shown below. The number of phases is confined to the divisors of the number of oscillators. In the individual solution of the multi-phase mode, the adjacent oscillators have the same phase difference. Solutions with different phase differences may exist which have the same number of phases. For example, when the number of oscillators N is 5, there are synchronized mode and 5 phase mode. In the synchronized mode, all the oscillators are synchronized in oscillation and the membrane potentials of excitatory and inhibitory neurons are equal respectively;

$$u_{e1}=u_{e2}=u_{e3}=u_{e4}=u_{e5}$$

and

$$u_{i1}=u_{i2}=u_{i3}=u_{i4}=u_{i5}\,.$$

The synchronized mode exists in networks of any number of oscillators. One example of 5 phase mode is illustrated in

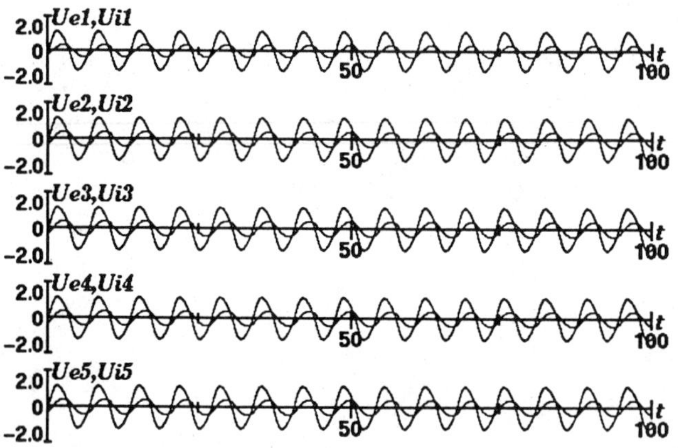

Fig. 4 Multi-phase mode in the ring structure. N=5.

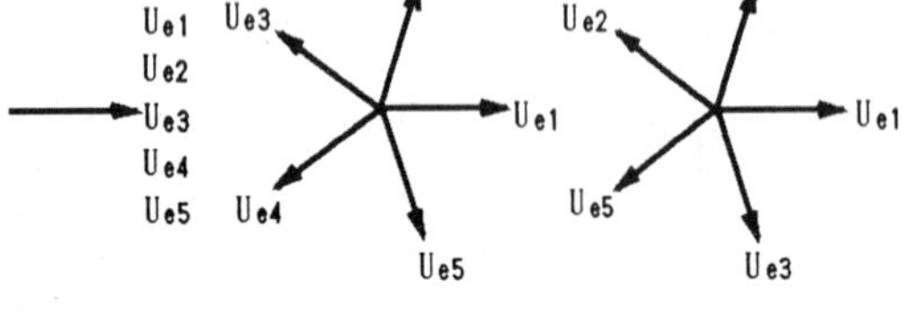

Fig. 5 The phase of each oscillator in the multi-phase mode, N=5. (a) Synchronized mode, (b) 5 phase mode I, (c) 5 phase mode II.

Fig. 4. In this solution, the phase difference between the adjacent oscillators is $-2\pi/5$. There are symmetric pairs of 5 phase mode; in one solution, the phase shift rotates clockwise and in the other counter-clockwise in the ring structure. In one pair, the order of the phase shift is oscillator 1, 2, 3, 4, 5 or oscillator 1, 5, 4, 3, 2. Phase difference is $\pm 2\pi/5$. We call this pair 5 phase mode I. In the other pair, the order of the phase shift is oscillator 1, 3, 5, 2, 4 or oscillator 1, 4, 2, 5, 3. Phase difference is $\pm 4\pi/5$. We call this pair 5 phase mode II. As is shown below, for arbitrary N, the phase difference of the adjacent oscillators are $2j\pi/N$ (j =0 , ±1, ... , $\pm N'$), where

$$N' = \left\{ \begin{array}{l} N/2 \;\; (N: \text{even}) \\ (N-1)/2 \;\; (N: \text{odd}) \end{array} \right\}. \tag{10}$$

4. 2 Analysis of oscillation phase by linear approximation

We analyze the relationship between the angular frequency of the oscillation and the oscillation phase of each oscillator by linear approximation of (2) at the origin. The dynamics of the linearized network model in case N>2 is expressed as

$$\dot{u}_{ek} + u_{ek} = \frac{2}{\pi}c_{ee}u_{ek} - \frac{2}{\pi}c_{ei}u_{ik} - \frac{2}{\pi}c_o(u_{ik-1} + u_{ik+1}) \tag{11a}$$

and

$$\dot{u}_{ik} + u_{ik} = \frac{2}{\pi}c_{ie}u_{ek}\,. \tag{11b}$$

The eigenvalues of (11) are

$$\lambda = \frac{c_{ee}}{\pi} - 1 \pm \frac{1}{\pi}\sqrt{c_{ee}^2 - 4c_{ie}(c_{ei} + 2c_o\cos\frac{2\pi}{N}j)}\;, \tag{12}$$

where j=0, 1, ... , N-1. For N=2, $2c_o$ is replaced by c_o, as is also the case below. Therefore, the condition for oscillation is given as

$$c_{ee} > \pi \tag{13}$$

and

$$c_{ee}^2 - 4c_{ie}(c_{ei} + 2c_o\cos\frac{2\pi}{N}j) < 0\,. \tag{14}$$

The angular frequencies ω are obtained as

$$\omega = \frac{1}{\pi}\sqrt{4c_{ie}(c_{ei} + 2c_o\cos\frac{2\pi}{N}j) - c_{ee}^2}\,. \tag{15}$$

The number of these angular frequencies is $N/2+1$ when N is even and $(N+1)/2$ when N is odd.

We calculate the angular frequencies of oscillation by an alternative method which employs the phase relation of the periodic solution obtained from computer simulation. The waveform is assumed to be sinusoidal. Denote the phases of k-1-th, k-th and k+1-th oscillators by ϕ_{k-1}, ϕ_k and ϕ_{k+1} respectively. The membrane potential u_{ek} of the excitatory neuron in k-th oscillator is expressed as

$$u_{ek} = a\cos(\omega t + \phi_k)\,, \tag{16}$$

where k=1, 2, ..., N. Amplitude a and angular frequency ω are unknown. From (11b), the membrane potential u_{ik} of the inhibitory neuron is expressed as

$$u_{ik} = b\cos(\omega t + \phi_k - \theta)\,, \tag{17}$$

where

$$b = \frac{2ac_{ie}}{\pi\sqrt{1+\omega^2}} \tag{18}$$

and

$$\theta = \tan^{-1}\omega \,. \tag{19}$$

Substituting (16) and (17) into (11a), rearranging it in terms of $\cos\omega t$ and $\sin\omega t$ and setting the coefficients zero, we obtain that the amplitude a is arbitrary and the angular frequency ω is expressed as

$$\omega = \frac{1}{\pi}\sqrt{4c_{ie}(c_{ei} \pm 2c_o \cos\frac{\phi_{k+1} - \phi_{k-1}}{2}) - c_{ee}^2}\,, \tag{20}$$

where

$$(\phi_{k+1}-\phi_{k-1})/2 = \phi_k \text{ or } \phi_k + \pi \tag{21}$$

from computer simulation. By comparing (20) with (15), from the compound signs, positive sign is selected when

$$(\phi_{k+1}-\phi_{k-1})/2 = \phi_k$$

and negative sign is selected when

$$(\phi_{k+1}-\phi_{k-1})/2 = \phi_k + \pi \,.$$

The phase ϕ_k is expressed as

$$\phi_k = \frac{2\pi}{N} j(k-1)\,, \tag{22}$$

where $j = 0, \pm 1, \ldots\ldots, \pm N'$ and N' is expressed in (10). The greater the absolute value of j is, the greater are the phase difference of the adjacent oscillators and the period of oscillation. The relationship between the value of j and $x = \cos 2\pi j/N$ is illustrated in Fig. 6. For example, when N=5, j=0 corresponds to the synchronized mode, $j=\pm 1$ to 5 phase mode I and $j=\pm 2$ to 5 phase mode II. Taking the nonlinearity of (2) into account, whether the angular frequency is larger or smaller than the value obtained from (15) depends on the value of j.

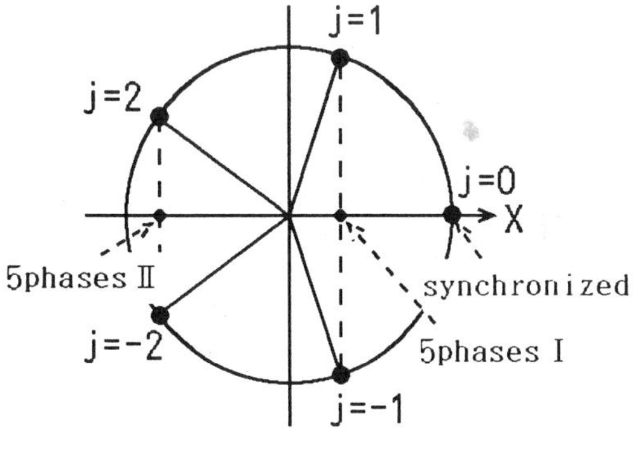

Fig. 6 Multi-phase mode and x, j

5. TRAVELING WAVE MODE

While the multi-phase mode occurs for relatively weak mutual coupling of oscillators in the ring structure, another type of oscillatory behaviors is seen for certain regions of stronger mutual coupling. This kind of oscillatory solutions exists in the linear structure as well as in the ring structure. Since these patterns can be regarded as traveling wave as is shown below, we call this mode traveling wave mode. Traveling wave mode exits in the network in which the number of oscillators is large enough.

The traveling wave mode occurs by the following mechanism. Suppose that infinite number of oscillators are arranged in a chained line with inhibitory coupling as is shown in Fig.7. The coupling coefficient is assumed to be suitable for the generation of the traveling wave mode. For this region of the coupling coefficient, there also exists a stable equilibrium in which membrane potentials are ...... , $+\bar{U}_r$ $-\bar{U}_r$, $+\bar{U}_r$, $-\bar{U}_r$, ... in order, where $\bar{U}_r$ is positive and r=e, or i . Suppose that the initial conditions of the potentials are given as ...... , $+\bar{U}_r$, $-\bar{U}_r$, U_r $+\bar{U}_r$, $-\bar{U}_r$, ... Let k denote the oscillator number whose initial values of potentials are given U_r , that is $u_{ek}(0)$=U_e and $u_{ik}(0)$=U_i [Fig. 7(a)].

Roughly speaking, if U_e is larger than U_i [Fig. 7(b)], positive feedback has more effect than negative feedback on the excitatory neuron, so that u_{ek} , then as a result u_{ik}, goes to a positive value, then u_{ek-1} and u_{ik-1} go to negative values

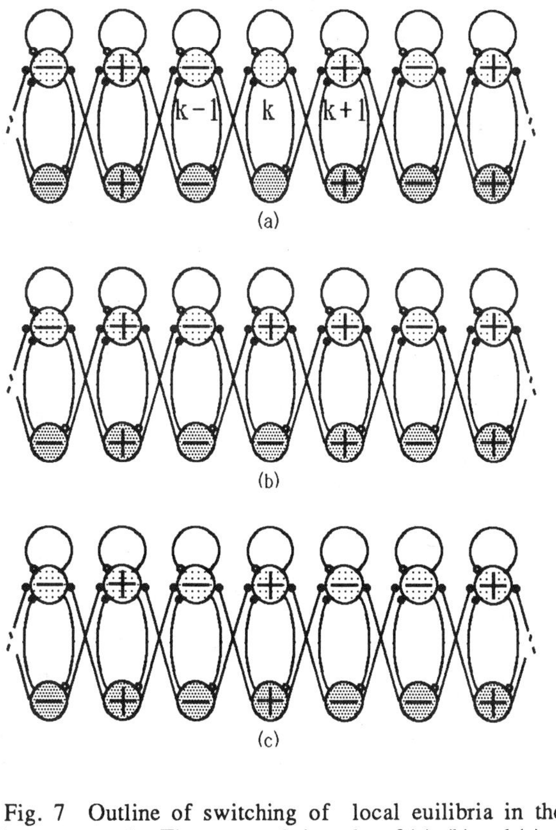

Fig. 7 Outline of switching of local euilibria in the traveling wave mode. Time proceeds in order of (a), (b) and (c).

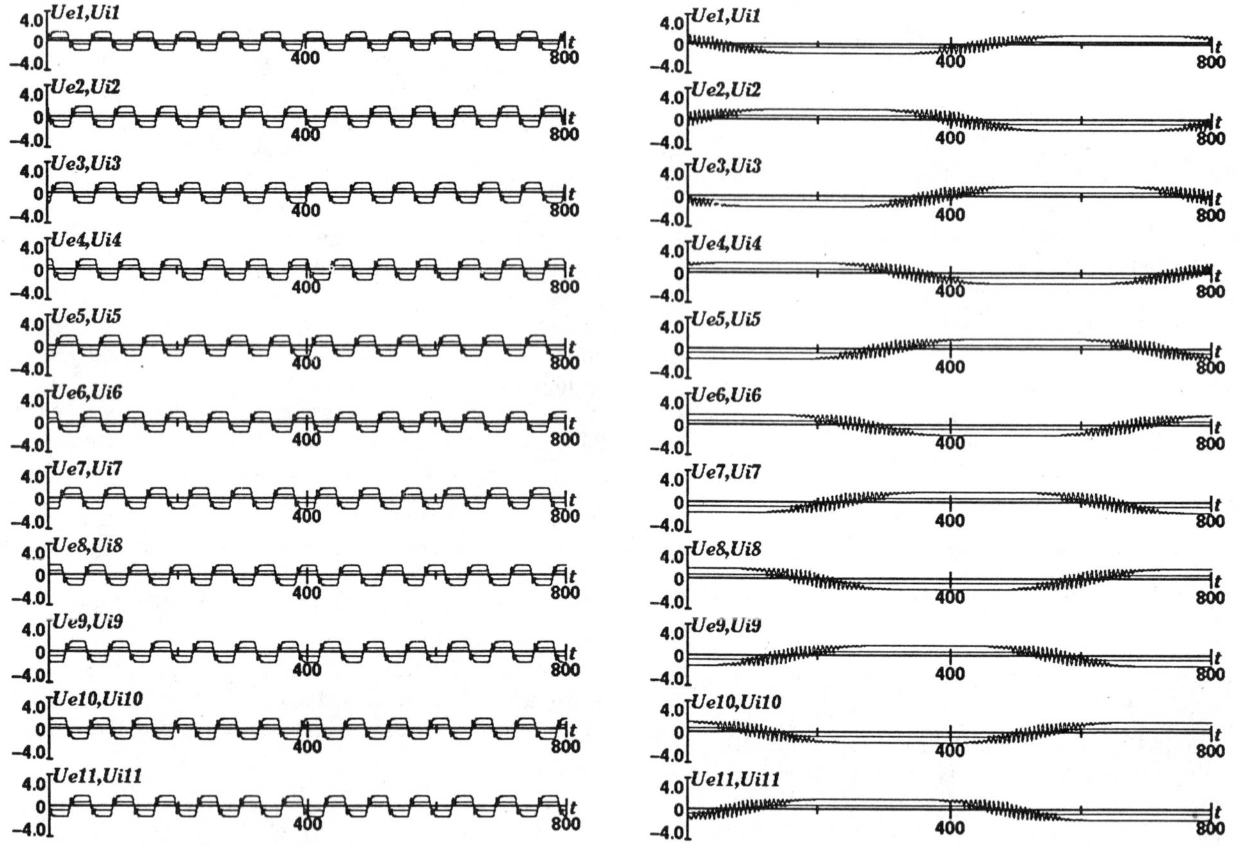

(a) (b)

Fig. 8 Traveling wave mode in the ring structure. N=11. (a) traveling wave mode I, (b) traveling wave mode II.

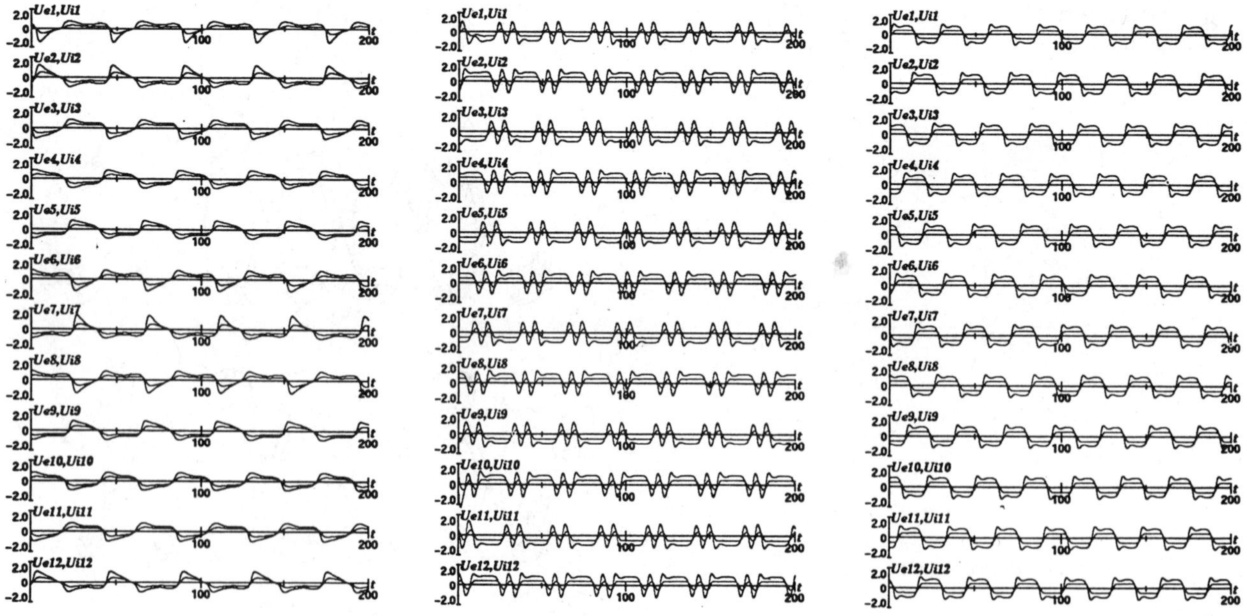

(a) (b) (c)

Fig. 9 Traveling wave mode in the ring structure. N=12. (a) traveling wave mode I-a, (b) traveling wave mode I-b, (c) traveling wave mode I-c.

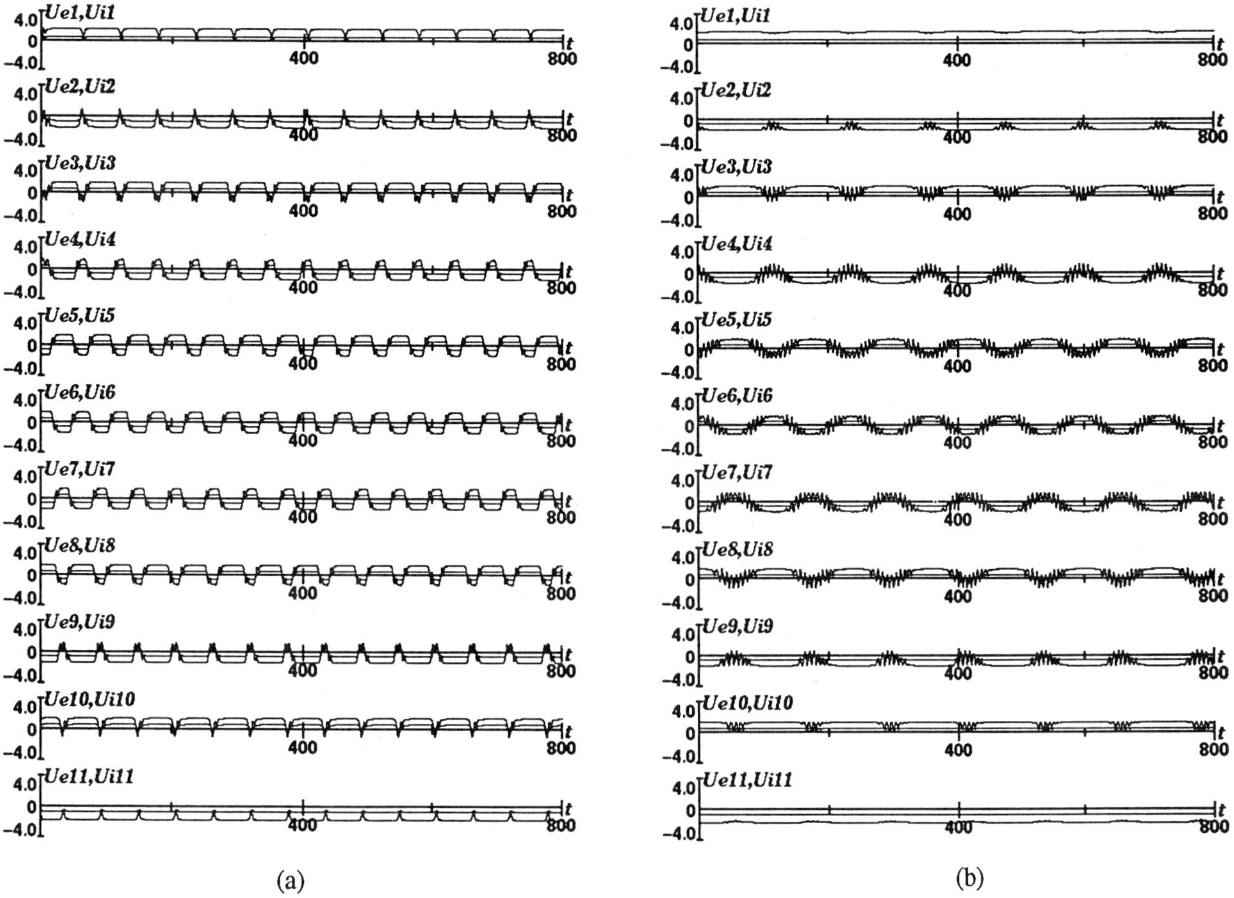

Fig. 10 Traveling wave mode in the linear structure, N=11. (a) traveling wave mode I, (b) traveling wave mode II.

[Fig. 7(c)]. In this way, switching from positive to negative or from negative to positive local equilibrium occurs in succession along the network. If U_e is smaller than U_i, opposite switching occurs; that is u_{ek} , then as a result u_{ik}, goes to a negative value, then u_{ek-1} and u_{ik-1} go to positive values and so on. The period of the traveling wave mode is much longer than that of the oscillation of the oscillator unit. It is approximately proportional to the number of oscillators.

5. 1 Ring structure

For the ring structure composed of odd (even) number of oscillators, the switching described above at odd (even) number of locations gives a periodic solution. The switching rotates through the network. In other words, it is considered that traveling waves are propagated along the oscillators. Fig. 8 shows the examples of the oscillatory solutions of the traveling wave mode in the network containing 11 oscillators. There are two patterns of the traveling mode; one is the pattern in which the switching is completed in a short period [Fig. 8(a)] and the other is the pattern in which the switching occurs with a number of cycles of transient oscillation [Fig. 8(b)]. We call the former one traveling wave mode I and the latter traveling wave mode II. Fig. 9 shows three solutions of traveling wave mode I in the network composed of 12 oscillators.

5. 2 Linear structure

In the linear structure, the waveforms of the potentials of the neurons in the oscillators are not the same since the oscillators at the both ends receive inhibition only from one side, so that the multi-phase mode does not exist. However, you can generate the traveling wave mode in which the switching goes back and forth repeatedly from one end to the other. The traveling wave mode can occur with suitable tonic inputs to the oscillators at the both ends and proper initial conditions to the membrane potentials for the switching. Fig. 10 shows the traveling wave mode I and II in the network of the linear structure. The number of oscillators N is 11 and constant input -1.36 is given to u_{e1} and 1.36 to u_{e11}.

In this way, the traveling wave mode can occur not only in the ring structure but also in the linear structure. It is reasonable to consider that the traveling wave mode is characteristic to the chained structure of oscillators. These results are similar to the firing modes in reciprocal inhibition neural networks composed of a number of neurons [7,8].

6. EXISTENCE REGIONS AND TRANSITIONS OF OSCILLATORY SOLUTIONS

We obtained the existence regions of oscillatory solutions of multi-phase mode, traveling wave mode and other modes in a network of ring structure with respect to the coupling coefficient c_o between adjacent oscillators by numerical analysis employing Poincaré map [13]. First, we obtained a fixed point of each periodic solution by Newton's method. Then, we calculated the characteristic multipliers of the solution with different values of c_o and examined its stability and bifurcation from it. We also obtained the initial conditions for generation of the traveling mode among multi-stable solutions at a certain coupling coefficient. The mode transition with bifurcation was studied by computer simulation.

6. 1 Existence regions

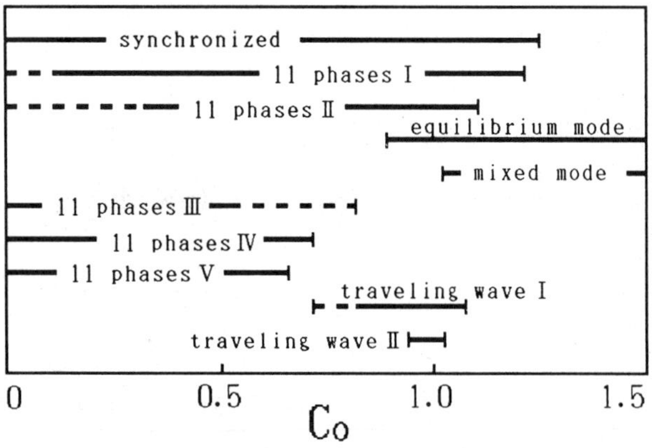

Fig. 11 Existing regions of oscillatory modes in the ring strcture. N=11.

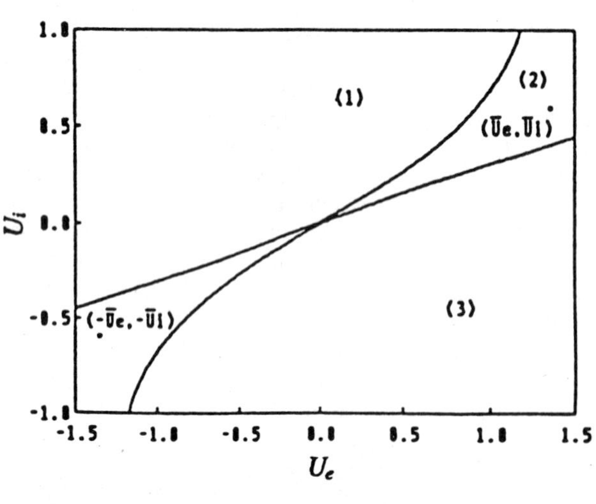

Fig. 12 Initial conditions and generation of traveling wave mode in the ring structure. N=11.

Fig. 11 shows the existence regions of oscillatory modes and equilibrium mode with respect to the coupling coefficient c_o in the ring network composed of 11 oscillators. There are a number of solutions of equilibrium mode with different initial conditions. In a solution of equilibrium mode, the membrane potential of each neurons has a stable equilibrium which differs depending on oscillators. Mixed mode is a kind of oscillatory solutions. The waveforms of the oscillation differ in different oscillators. The number attached to 11 phase mode corresponds to the absolute value of j in (22). The solid lines in the figure denote the regions where the stable periodic solutions exist. The dashed lines denote the existence regions for quasi-periodic solutions that emerge by Hoph bifurcation from the periodic solutions. The region for the traveling wave mode II is included by that for the traveling wave mode I.

6. 2 Initial conditions and generation of oscillatory solutions of traveling wave mode

As shown in Fig. 11, the regions of oscillatory solutions overlap with each other. For an identical value of coupling coefficient c_o, a certain number of periodic solutions exist stably. Which solution comes out depends on the initial conditions of the network. It is extraordinarily troublesome to elucidate completely the relation between the initial conditions and solutions because the dimension of the state space is $2N$ and the relation is very complicated. We are particularly interested in whether the traveling wave mode I and II can occur with easy setting of initial conditions. Therefore, we investigated the generation of the traveling wave mode I and II with limited initial conditions, in which only 2 state variables, the membrane potentials of the neurons in oscillator 1, were varied and the rest of the state variables are set to the local equilibrium in which every other oscillator keeps the same values of membrane potentials, positive for one group and negative for the other.

Fig. 12 shows the result of computer simulation when N=11. The initial values of membrane potentials except those in oscillator 1 are given as

$$u_{r3} = u_{r5} = u_{r7} = u_{r9} = u_{r11} = \bar{U}_r,$$
$$u_{r2} = u_{r4} = u_{r6} = u_{r8} = u_{r10} = -\bar{U}_r \quad (r=e \text{ or } i),$$

where

$$\bar{U}_e = 1.356 \text{ and } \bar{U}_i = 0.5956.$$

Initial values $u_{e1}(0)=U_e$ and $u_{i1}(0)=U_i$ are varied. For the initial conditions in region (1), the traveling wave mode I occurs in which the wave is propagated in order of oscillator 1, 3, 5, ... For region (3), also traveling wave mode I occurs, but the order of wave propagation is opposite, oscillator 1,10,8, ... For region (2), traveling wave mode II occurs. In this way, the traveling wave mode can occur with easy setting of initial conditions among multi-stable solutions.

6. 3 Transitions of oscillatory solutions

It is also our great concern whether the traveling wave mode can occur by transitions from other modes when the coupling coefficient of oscillators are varied beyond the

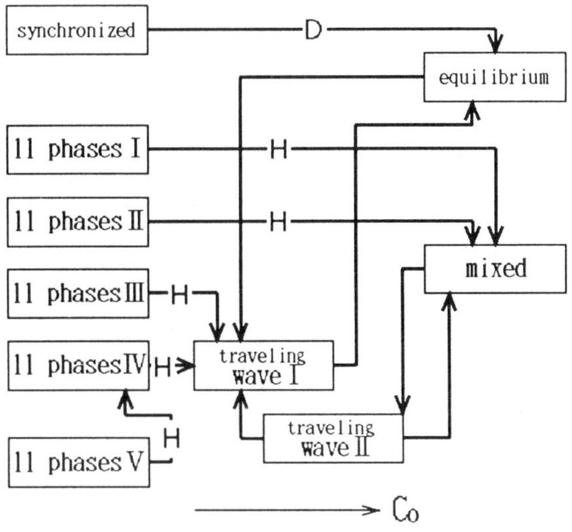

Fig. 13 Mode transitions in the ring structure. N=11.

existing regions of those modes. Fig. 13 shows the mode transition obtained by computer simulation when N=11. Transition with Hoph bifurcation is denoted by simbol H and transition with D-type of branching by symbol D. D-type of branching occurs in degenerated systems. It occurs in the present model because the oscillators are identical and their coupling is uniform. Traveling wave mode I occurs by transition from 11 phases IV when the coupling coefficient c_o increases and from equilibrium mode when c_o decreases. Traveling wave mode II occurs by transition from mixed mode when c_o decreases.

7. Conclusions

In this paper, we proposed a chained neural oscillator network model for a mechanism of rhythm generation in biological neural networks and showed generation of not only well-known multi-phase mode but also traveling wave mode as multi-stable oscillatory solutions by numerical analysis employing Poincare map. The period of the traveling wave mode is much longer than that of the oscillation of the oscillator unit. It is approximately proportional to the number of oscillators. The traveling wave mode is classified in two categories. One of them has a long transient period with a number of cycles of oscillation in switching from one local equilibrium to the other. These results are similar to the firing modes in reciprocal inhibition neural networks composed of a number of neurons. The traveling wave mode might exist in various chained oscillator networks. It has been found out that the traveling wave mode occurs by transitions from other modes. The initial conditions which bring the generation of the traveling wave mode have also been obtained. The traveling wave mode in the ring networks composed of even number of oscillators and in the linear networks is open to future analysis.

In the present work, the mutual coupling of oscillators is confined to be uniform and only for nearest neighbors. The oscillators are identical. The traveling wave mode will occur also in more complicated networks since the solutions have a certain measure of existence regions for the coupling coefficient and the traveling wave mode occurs due to the local coupling properties. More detailed analysis of such cases is necessary in the future.

Acknowledgments

We are grateful to Prof. H. Kawakami and Dr. T. Yoshinaga for their helpful advice.

This work is partly supported by Grant-in-Aid for Science Research of Ministry of Education, Japan, No. 03805028.

References

[1] A. H. Cohen, S. Rossignol and S. Grillner, Eds. *Neural control of rhythmic movements in vertebrates* , John Wiley & Sons, New York, 1988.

[2] J. W. Jacklet, Ed., *Neuronal and cellular oscillators* , Marcel Dekker, New York, 1989.

[3] R. F. Reiss, "A theory and simulation of rhythmic behavior due to reciprocal inhibition in small nerve nets," *Proc. 1962 AFIPS Spring Joint Computer Conference*, pp. 171-193, 1962.

[4] R. Suzuki, I. Katsuno and K. Matano, "Dynamics of 'Neuron Ring', Computer simulation of central nervous system of starfish," *Kybernetik*, vol. 8, pp. 39-45, 1971.

[5] A. I. Selverston, "A consideration of invertebrate central pattern generators as computational data bases," *Neural Networks*, vol. 1, pp. 109-117, 1988.

[6] P. A. Getting, "Reconstruction of small neural networks," in *Methods in Neuronal Modeling*, C. Koch and I. Segev Eds., The MIT Press, Cambridge, 1989, pp. 171-194.

[7] H. Nagashino, H. Tamura and T. Ushita, "Firing modes in reciprocal inhibitory neural networks and their analysis," *Electronics and Communications in Japan*, vol. 61, pp. 27-35, 1978.

[8] H. Nagashino, H. Tamura and T. Ushita, "Existence and control of rhythmic activities in reciprocal inhibition neural networks," *Trans. IECE Japan*, vol. E62, pp. 768-774, 1979.

[9] D. A. Linkens, "Analytical solution of a large number of mutually coupled nearly sinusoidal oscillators," *IEEE Trans. Circuits and Systems,* vol. CAS-21, pp. 294-300, 1974.

[10] T. Endo and S. Mori, "Mode analysis of a ring of a large number of mutually coupled van der Pol oscillators," *IEEE Trans. Circuits and Systems,* vol. CAS-25, pp. 7-18, 1978.

[11] S. M. Ahn,. and W. J. Freeman, "Steady -state and limit cycle activity of mass of mass of neurons forming simple feedback loops (I): Lumped circuit model," *Kybernetik*, Vol. 16, pp. 87-91, 1974.

[12] P. A. Getting, "Emerging principles govering the operation of neural networks", in *Annual Review of Neuroscience*, vol. 12, W. M. Cowan, et al. eds., Annual Reviews Inc., Palo Alto, 1989, pp. 185-204.

[13] H. Kawakami and K. Kobayashi, "A computation of periodic solutions of nonlinear autonomous systems," *Proc. 1979 Int. Sym. Circuits and Systems*, pp. 44-45, 1979.

Self-Architecture
Theory and Experiment of Biological Neural Networks*

Harold Szu, ^Jung Kim, and +Insook Kim,
Naval Surface Warfare Center, Code R44, Silver Spring MD 20903
^Center for Advanced Computer Studies, and +Department. of Biology
Univ. of SW Louisiana, Lafayette, LA 70504

ABSTRACT

Live neuron behavior on an electronic chip was recorded with a time-lapsed video under the microscope. By an image processing technique, we discovered the smallest size of intelligent biological neural networks (BNN). The dissociated chick embryonic brain neurons were experimentally placed on silicon glass plates deposited with metal oxide strips about 10 μm width for possible electronegativity neurite guidance. The neurite growth connecting other neurons was accomplished intentionally through selective paring in time rather than mechanically following the external electronegativity guidance.

We have theoretically mapped to artificial neural networks (ANN) to determine whether the connectivity patterns dictate the information processing efficiency, or vice versa. A dynamic interconnection model is based on the energy landscape $E(v_i, W_{ij})$, which is a function of both the individual neuron output firing rates v_i and the pair synaptic weights W_{ij} of which a linear Hebbian rule becomes a special case, and general convergence theorem is proven. Consequently, a nonlinear backprop-like learning rule associated with slopes of the singlet sigmoidal function and the pair-correlation function is derived.

Keywords: Self-Architecture, Neurite Growth, Morphology, VLSI, Chip
*Supported NSWCDD Independent Research and Board of regents of Louisiana of Grant LEQSF-RD-A-28, and NSF Grant NSF-ADP-04

1. Biological Neural Network (BNN) Formations

The computational properties of BNN can be observed by in vitro systems that consist of the bottom up: electronic chips, the top-down: time-lapsed Video microscopic, and the middle: neurochemical control of synaptic growth (namely phosphoproteins: Synapsin IIb discovered by Han & Greengard in 1991 which promised to unlock the secret of memory). This paper describes how in real time dissociated chick embryonic brain neurons form live BNN on a silica glass plate revealing an intelligent behavior despite the external metal oxide guidance. A minimally intelligent BNN, called Peter-Paul-Mary, has been discovered with time-frozen frame analysis[Szu92].

The paper is organized as follows. A brief review of international research groups is given in Sect.1. Then, a time analysis of live dynamics follows in Sect.2, discussion about mathematical models in Sect.3, and further research perspectives in Sect.4.

Extracellular matrices have been known to guide the growth direction of nerve fibers. Kleinfeld et. al. have reported the hydrophilic guidance of live neural nets on pattern chip substrates [Klei88]. Gross has patterned live neural nets over weeks by trimming the dense interconnections with laser surgery [Gros91]. Kawana et. al.[Kawa90] have successfully applied the electronegativity of the metal (in the metal oxide pattern deposited on a silica glass) to guide live neurons into definite interconnection patterns. Neurons were then placed on substrates which had metal oxide patterns about 10 μm size. Metal oxide patterns were made by standard optical lithography with lift-off.

2. Time Analysis Dynamics

In the video imaging experiment [Szu92], three dissociated chick brain neurons were seeded on metal oxides on silicon glass plate At time t = 0:00, then the neuron connection patterns was video-recorded under the microscope at a fixed delay, say every 10 or 15 min. The play back rate is compressed at 30 video frames per second. Such a time-lapsed video-microscope-chip

0-7803-0999-5/93/$03.00

technique is proved to be powerful to analyze live neuron dynamics.

Step 1) Figure 1.A shows the culturing process at time t = 3:40. One neuron (named Peter denoted as a) of three dissociated neurons has been producing neurite outgrowth towards another neuron (named Paul denoted as b) located about twenty body lengths away below its own metal oxides strip about ten mm width.

Step 2) At time t = 6:49 (Figure 1.B), the neurite of Peter which has been growing along the axial direction of the metal oxides strip, starts crossing the non-metal oxides strip towards Paul's direction, instead of following the guided axial direction of the metal oxides strip.

Step 3) At time t = 8:10 (Figure 1.C), the neurite of Peter has just crossed the non-metal oxides strip.

Step 4) At time t = 8:22 (Figure 1.D), Peter-to-Paul contact has been made.

Step 5) At time t = 9:02 (Figure 1.E), the neurite of Mary has crossed the non-metal oxides strip. Interestingly, the initial neurite of Mary is not following the metal oxides strip.

Step 6) At time t = 9:46 (Figure 1.F), the neurite of Mary has been growing along the axial direction of the metal oxides strip.

Step 7) At time t = 11:38 (Figure 1.G), Paul started to produce its neurite outgrowth towards Mary. It took 3:16 time for Paul to initiate its neurite outgrowth, after the contact from Peter.

Step 8) At time t = 12:57 (Figure 1.H), Paul began the growing of neurites along the existed interconnection pathway built early by Peter-to-Paul and moving quickly toward Mary rather to Peter.

This preference becomes self-evident at later video frames. It is further supported by the detailed time analysis of the neurite outgrowth rate as shown in the sum up [Szu92], where Mary growth time from t = 11:38 to t = 14:03 is reduced about in half compared to that from t = 8:22 to t = 11:38,.

Step 9) At time t = 14:03 (Figure 1.I), the Paul-to-Mary interconnection is intentionally made because Paul has deliberately bypassed Peter and contacted Mary behind him.

Step 10) At time t = 14:42 (Figure 1.J), the neurite growth of Mary is almost stopped in the previous direction, and Mary starts to produce another neurite in the new direction (see the arrow in Figure 1.J).

Step 11) At time t = 22:10, Figure 1.K shows that the new nuerite of Mary grows very slowly while the old neurite of Mary is retracting.

Step 12) At time t = 23:50 (Figure 1.L), Mary is getting separated from Peter, while the old neurite of Mary is more retracted (see the arrow in Figure 1.L).

3. Theory of Self-Architectures

The minimal intelligence is the ability of comparisons and decision making ranging from the small perturbation of Hebbian learning to the drastic change of nonlinear dynamics of interconnections[Szu90]. We begins with the video observation that the smallest sizes of BNN that has exhibited a self-architecture are those associated with three live neurons [Szu92]. A single neuron alone has no choice in the connectivity pattern except to itself. Two neurons have only two choices, connected or not. Among three neurons, they can collectively have any one out of six possible interconnections as demonstrated in the above video frames.

Dynamic Interconnection Convergence Theorem.

From the BNN viewpoint, the probablity of ith neuron neurite outgrowth reaching at jth neuron (from Peter to Paul) defines the axonic pair correlation function T_{ij} which obviously requires a different notation than the dendritic synaptic junction weight W_{ij} before the formation of synapse. Given that distinction, we have generalized the linear Hebbian synaptic learning rule to the nonlinear dynamics learning rule as described below.

Convergence Theorem

Let the network energy $E(v_i,W_{ij})$ be both the output firing rates v_i and the synapatic weights W_{ij}. Then, without Hebbian rule,a local minimum of an N neurons architecture is given at

$$dE(v_i, W_{ij})/dt \le \quad 0, \tag{1}$$

provided the condition that both the singlet sigmoidal function σ_1 and the synapse formation pair correlation function σ_2 are defined to have non-negative logic slopes as follows;

$$v_i = \sigma_1 (u_i) = (1 + \exp(-u_i))^{-1}; \qquad \sigma'_1 = (dv_i/du_i) \approx G(u_i - \theta_i) \ge 0, \tag{2}$$

$$W_{ij} = \sigma_2(T_{ij}) \approx \text{step}(T_{ij} - \theta_{ij})/(1-\theta_{ij}); \sigma'_2 = (dW_{ij}/dT_{ij}) \approx \delta(T_{ij} - \theta_{ij})/(1-\theta_{ij}) \ge 0, \tag{3}$$

Although it is not necessary, but convenient to assume that all N neurons are initially connected together, and u_i is the net input (above the threshold value θ_i) collected initially from all N neuron outputs v_j passing through the synaptic weights W_{ij} which are subsequently pruned.

$$u_i \quad = \quad \Sigma^N{}_{j=1} W_{ij}\, v_j \; - \quad \theta_i, \tag{4}$$

Furthermore, condition (ii) is the local energy descents:

Input firing rate dynamics: $\partial u_i/\partial t \;\approx -\; \partial E/\partial v_i$ (5),

Output Axon dynamics: $\partial T_{ij}/\partial t \approx - \; \partial E/\partial W_{ij}$ (6),

The mathematical proof is based on the universal truth of real positive quadratic expression obtained by chain rule of differentiations and substitution of gradient descents Eqs(5,6) as follows:

$$\begin{aligned} dE(v_i, W_{ij})/dt &= \Sigma^N{}_{i=1} (\partial E/\partial v_i)(\partial v_i/\partial t) \quad + \Sigma^N{}_{i,j=1} (\partial E/\partial W_{ij})(\partial W_{ij}/\partial t) \\ &= \Sigma^N{}_{i=1} (\partial E/\partial v_i)(\partial v_i/\partial u_i)(\partial u_i/\partial t) \quad + \Sigma^N{}_{i,j=1} (\partial E/\partial W_{ij})(\partial W_{ij}/\partial T_{ij})(\partial T_{ij}/\partial t) \\ &\approx - \Sigma^N{}_{i=1}\, \sigma'_1 (\partial E/\partial v_i)^2 \quad - \Sigma^N{}_{i,j=1}\, \sigma'_2 (\partial E/\partial W_{ij})^2 \\ &\le 0 \end{aligned} \tag{7}$$

where the primes denote the nonnegative slopes of singlet and pair correlation functions Eqs(2,3). Thus, by definition of nonnegative logic Eqs(2,3) the energy landscape is always monotonously convergent for every quadratic term independent of the energy slope value and the size N. This independence is important as the network size changes through a dynamic interconnect.

The sigmoidal slope σ'_1 is known to be a radial base function or Gaussian-like window cnetered around θ_i. Since the pair correlation function T_{ij} has been approximately modeled as a "use-or-loss"probability function (properly normalized between 0 and 1). $\sigma_2(T_{ij})$ is a step function above the frequency threshold θ_{ij}.whose value can be statistically estimated about how often an existed pair of connection is ultilized from ith neuron to jth neuron when compared with other pairs. Note that the approximate Kronecker/Dirac delta function $\delta(T_{ij} - \theta_{ij})$ has a normalization constant appears in the denominator $(1-\theta_{ij})$ which could make the second window function σ'_2 a factor 10 bigger than the first Gaussian-like window if θ_{ij} =0.9 for an infrequently used pair of interconnect.

Now, we derive the synaptic weight chnage in a backprop-like algorithm as follows:

$$\begin{aligned} \Delta W_{ij} &= (\partial W_{ij}/\partial t)\Delta t = (\partial W_{ij}/\partial T_{ij})(\partial T_{ij}/\partial t)\Delta t = -(\partial W_{ij}/\partial T_{ij})(\partial E/\partial W_{ij})\Delta t \\ &= -(\partial W_{ij}/\partial T_{ij})(\partial E/\partial v_i)(dv_i/du_i)(\partial u_i/\partial W_{ij})\Delta t\,. \end{aligned} \tag{8}$$

Substituting these results into Eq(8), one finds that the linear Hebbian learning rule

$$\Delta W_{ij} \approx v_i\, v_j$$

is a special case modified by means of both Gaussian and weighted Dirac windows:

$$\Delta W_{ij} = -\ G(u_i)(\partial \mathbf{E}/\partial v_i)v_j\ \delta(T_{ij} - |\theta_{ij}|)/(1-|\theta_{ij}|)\Delta t \qquad (9)$$

Without the synaptic pruning window σ'_2 of Eq(3), the learnig rule Eq(8) is the traditional delta rule,which takes a long computational time to find itself within the Gaussian window of opportunity for a small weight change. Furthermore, the change is rarely large enough to nullify the interconnection weight in order to prune a specific interconnection weight. Thus, one expects that the modified delta formula, that has divided the backprop delta rule by a samll number $(1-|\theta_{ij}|) \leq 1$ and controlled by the second window, becomes efficient. The pair correlation probability function is also self-updated by

$$\Delta T_{ij} = (\partial T_{ij}/\partial t)\ \Delta t \quad = -\ (\partial \mathbf{E}/\partial W_{ij})\Delta t$$

$$= -(\partial \mathbf{E}/\partial v_i)(dv_i/du_i)(\partial u_i/\partial W_{ij})\Delta t = -G(u_i)(\partial \mathbf{E}/\partial v_i)v_j\ \Delta t \qquad (10)$$

In a feedforward layer architecture, if a quadratic cost energy is chosen $\mathbf{E} = (d_i - v_i)^2/2$ is chosen for the supervised training in terms of the actual output v_i departed from the desired output d_i, then

$$(\partial \mathbf{E}/\partial v_i) = (v_i - d_i); \qquad i = 1,2,3,\text{ output layer neurons} \qquad (11)$$

$$(\partial \mathbf{E}/\partial v_i) = -\partial u_i/\partial t; \qquad i = 1,2,3,\text{ all other neurons} \qquad (12)$$

Eq(12) can be further feedbacked via the net input change Δu_i of Eq(4) and synaptic change ΔW_{ij} of Eq(9). Thus, the set of Eqs(8,12) may be useful for the self-organization in an architecture.

4. Conclusions

In this report, the synergism between electronics and neurosciences has been demonstrated. Much more work is needed. One shall investigate functional-specific neurons, such as those associated with hearing, seeing, sensing, moving, controlling, communicating, etc. and to observe the connectivity patterns on chips with real time measurements. As an interesting by-product of the architectural taxonomy study, one can quantitatively measure the single neuron sigmoidal function, that was done early by McCullouch and Pitts almost five decades ago, statistically in parallel via the chip technology. One can also generalize the Hebbian synaptic strength learning rule for new born networks by parallel and direct measurements of singlet and pair correlation function. These functions might reveal the major learning rule through the morphology change theorem, as opposed to the minor learning via linear Hebbian rule upon a fixed architecture.

We believe that the trend of modern neural network study will be centered around the learning with dynamic interconnections, which is capable of self-adapting from one architecture to another to accommodate both the hardware fault tolerance and the necessary software inference.

References

[Gros91] Gross, G.W. & Kowalski, J.M. 1991 Experimental and Theoretical Analysis of Random Nerve Cell Network Dynamics, Neural Networks: Concepts, Applications, and Implementations, Prentice Hall

[Han91] Han, H, Nichols, R.A, Rubin, M.R, Bahler,M, Greengard, P.1991.Induction of formation of presynaptic terminals in neuroblastoma cells by synapsin IIb, Nature 349:697-700.

[Kawa90] Torimitsu, K. and Kawana A. 1990. Selective Growth of Sensory Nerve Fibers on Metal Oxide Pattern in Culture,Devel. Brain. Res. 51:128-131.

[Klei88] Kleinfeld, D., Kahler, K.H., and Hockberger, P.E. 1988. Controlled Outgrowth of Dissociated Neurons on Patterned Substrates, J. Neuros. 8:4098-4120.

[Szu90] Szu, H.H. 1990. Neural Networks Based on Peano Curves and Hairy Neurons, Telematics and Informatics, 7: 403-430, Pergamon Press.

[Szu92] Szu, H.H.,Kim, J., Kim, I. 1992. Live Neural Network Formations on Electronic Chips, IJCNN-92 Beijing; Also appear INNS Appalanchian Conf.Radford VA

[Tana91] Tanaka, E.M. and Kirschner, M. 1991. Microtubule Behavior in the Growth ones of Living Neurons During Axon Elongation, Jour. Cell Biol. 115:345-363.

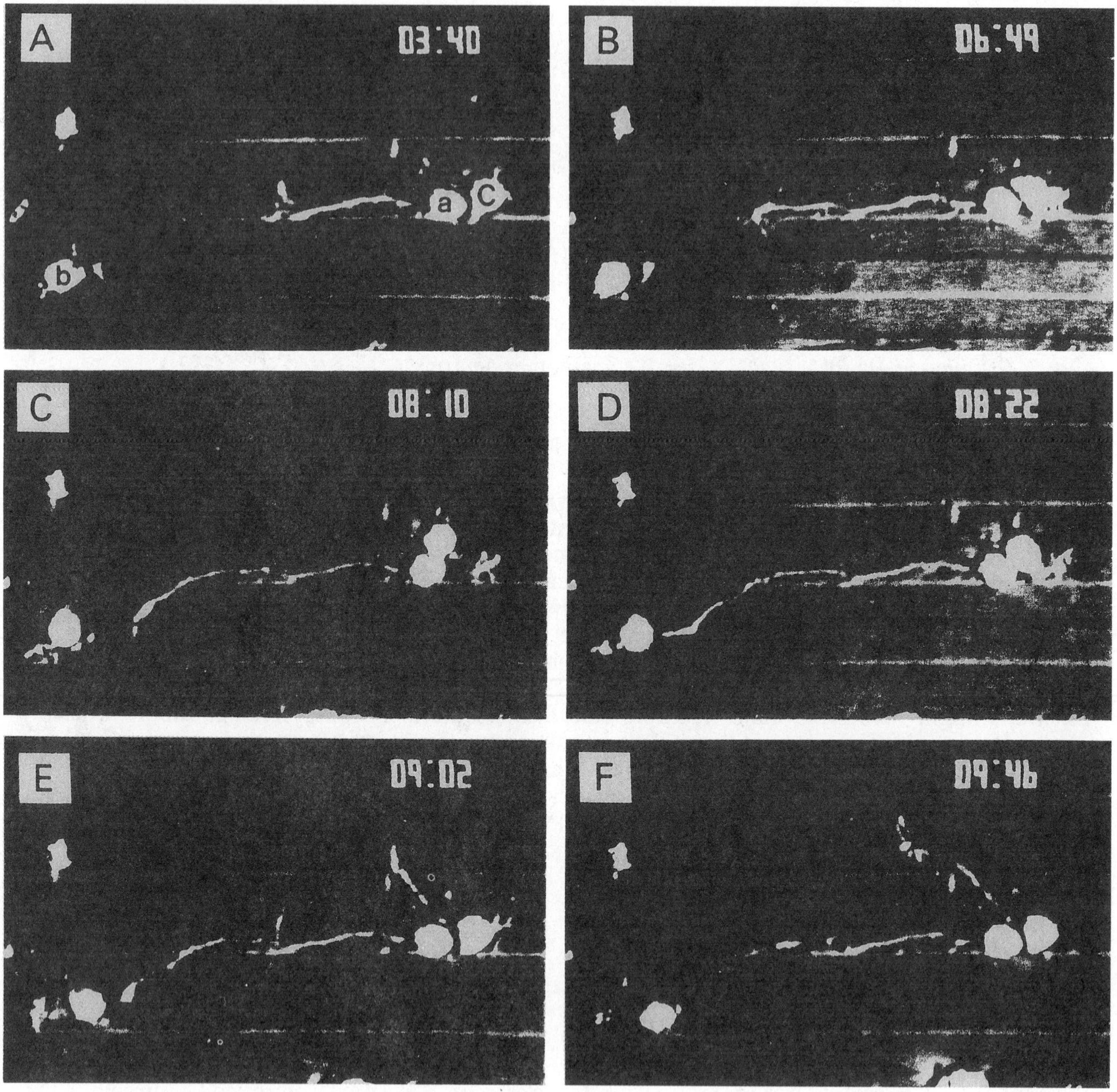

Figure 1. Snapshot pictures taken from a video tape showing the formation of live neural networks from 3 dissociated chick embryonic neurons cultured on a VLSI chip.
(Neuron a is named as Peter; Neuron b is named as Paul; Neuron c is named as Mary.)

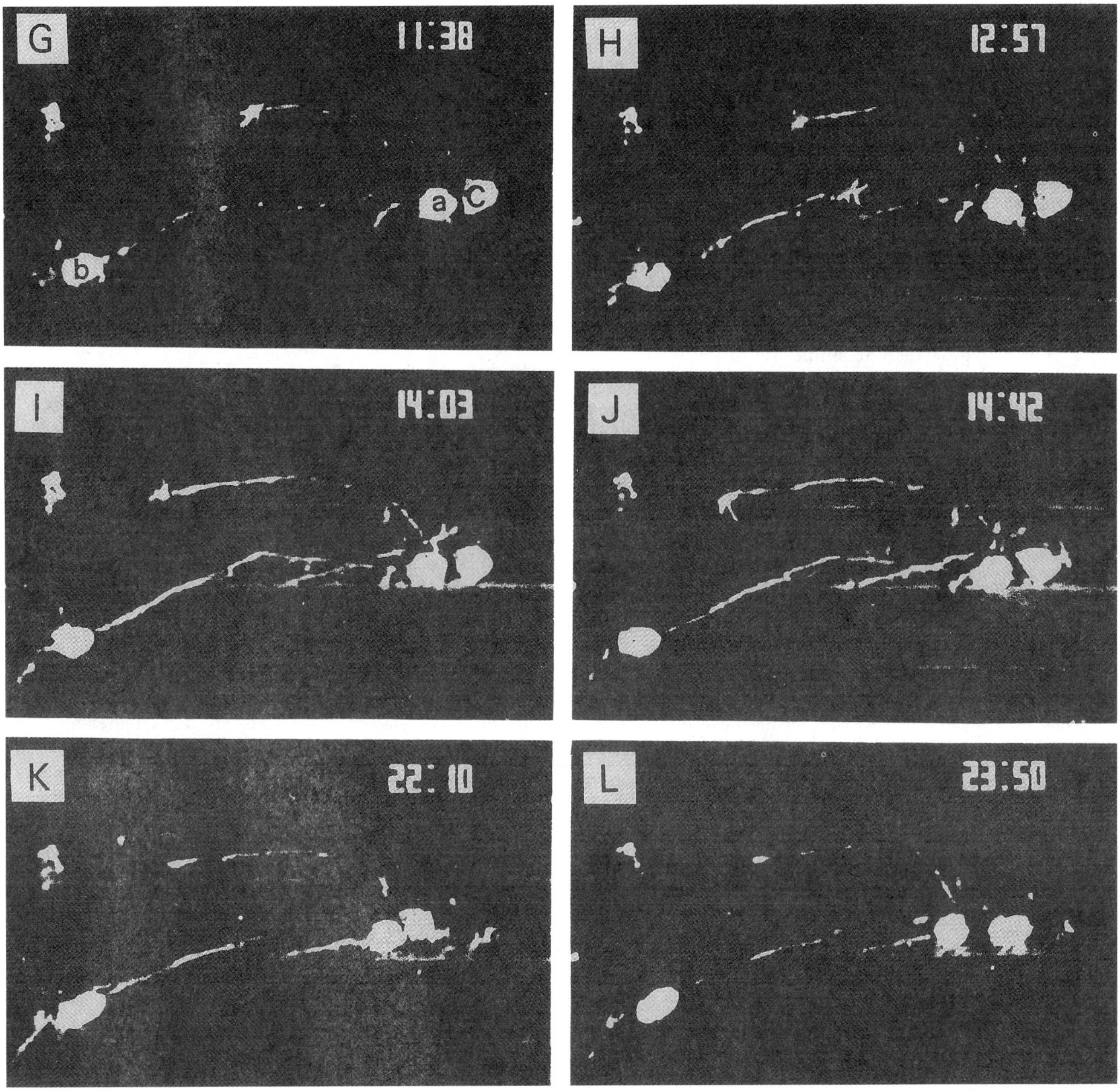

Figure 1.(Continued) Snapshot pictures taken from a video tape showing the formation of live neural networks from 3 dissociated chick embryonic neurons cultured on a VLSI chip. (Neuron a is named as Peter; Neuron b is named as Paul; Neuron c is named as Mary.)

Self-Generating vs. Self-Organizing, What's Different?

W.X. Wen, V. Pang, and A. Jennings
AISS/TSSS, Telecom Research Labs.
Clayton, Victoria 3168, Australia

Abstract

Comparisons between the Self-Generating Neural Network (SGNN) and the Self-Organizing Neural Network (SONN) are performed. Although the SGNN concept was developed from SONN, the results obtained show that it has quite a few significant advantages when compared with SONN. These include simplicity of design methodology, greater speed for both training and testing, higher accuracy of clustering/classification, and better generalization capability. An analysis is also conducted to investigate why SGNN is superior to SONN.

1 Introduction

The SGNN (Self-Generating Neural Network) method proposed in [13, 10] is based on both SONN (Self-Organizing Neural Network) [4] and traditional AI unsupervised learning methods, such as COBWEB and ARACHINE [2, 5]. It has been applied to different applications such as image coding, diagnostic expert systems and document/information retrieval systems [12, 6]. Two SGNN systems have been developed on SUN SPARC stations and IBM-PC/AT with X-window/MS-window 3 interfaces, respectively. Comparisons have been given in [11] to show the advantages of the SGNN method over COBWEB/CLASSWEB/ARACHINE.

The purpose of this paper is to give a comparative analysis between the performances of a type of SGNN, Self-Generating Neural Trees (SGNT), and SONN to show the difference between them and the reasons for this difference. The MONK problems [9] – a de facto standard benchmark set for testing supervised/unsupervised learning methods are used for comparison. The result of the comparison shows that SGNN/SGNT is superior to SONN in aspects such as the simplicity of design, speed of training and testing on conventional computer systems, better clustering/classification results, and better generalization capability.

2 The SGNT Algorithm

Neural networks are usually designed by human experts. It is quite tricky to choose the right structure of the neural network suitable for a particular application at hand. In this section, we briefly discuss the SGNT method proposed in [13] to generate a neural tree [1] automatically from training examples without any other human intervention.

For this kind of network, not only the weights of the network connections but also the structure of the whole network are all learned from the training examples directly. These include:

1. the number of the neurons in the network,
2. the interconnections among the neurons,
3. the weights on the connections.

A neural tree [1] generated in this way is called a Self-Generating Neural Tree (SGNT). The algorithm to generate an SGNT is basically a hierarchical clustering algorithm. Before we describe the SGNT algorithms, some related definitions are given below:

Definition 1: An *instance* e_i is a real vector of attributes: $e_i = < a_{i1}, ..., a_{in} >$.

Definition 2: A *neuron* n_j is a ordered pair $< W_j, C_j >$, where W_j is the real weight vector of the neuron: $W_j = < w_{j1}, ..., w_{jn} >$, and C_j is the child neuron set of n_j.

Definition 3: An *SGNT* is a tree $< \{n_j\}, \{l_k\} >$ of neurons generated automatically from a set of training instances by the algorithm given below, where $\{n_j\}$ is the neuron/node set and $\{l_k\}$ is the link set of the tree. There is a directed link from neuron n_i to n_j, if and only if $n_j \in C_i$.

Definition 4: A neuron n_k in a neuron set $\{n_j\}$ is called a *winner* for an instance e_i if $\forall j, d(n_k, e_i) \leq d(n_j, e_i)$ where $d(n_j, e_i)$ is the distance between neuron n_j and instance e_i.

0-7803-0999-5/93/$03.00 ©1993 IEEE

Any distance measure can be used, but we use a modified Euclidean distance measure:

$$d(n_j, e_i) = \sqrt{\frac{\sum_{k=1}^{n}(a_{jk} - a_{ik})^2}{n}}.$$

The SGNT algorithm is a hierarchical clustering algorithm given in a pseudo-C language as follows:

Algorithm 1 (SGNT Generation/Training):

Input:

1. A set of training instances $E = \{e_i\}$, $i = 1, ..., N$.
2. A threshold $\xi \geq 0$.
3. A distance measure for each attribute/weight in instances/neurons.

Output: An SGNT generated from E.

Method:

```
Method:    copy(root,e0);
    for(i=1,j=1;i<=N;i++) {
        minmumDistance = distance(ex,root);
        winner = oldWinner = root;
        minimumDistance = test(ei,root);
        if(minimumDistance>ξ) {
            if(leaf(winner)) {
                copy(nj,winner);
                connect(nj,winner);
                j++;
            }
            copy(nj,ei);
            connect(nj,winner);
            j++;
        }
        update(winner,ei);
    }
```

where the routines are defined as follows:

1. copy(n,e): create a neuron n and copy the attributes/weights in the instance/neuron e to n.
2. distance(e,n): return the distance between instance e and neuron n.
3. test(e,subRoot): find a winner in the current SGNT/sub-SGNT rooted by subRoot for instance e and return the distance between the winner and e.
4. leaf(n): check a neuron n to see whether it is a leaf neuron in the current SGNT. A neuron in an SGNT is called a leaf neuron if it has no child neuron.
5. connect(n_0, n_1): connect neuron n_0 to n_1 making n_0 as a child neuron of n_1.
6. update(n_i, e_{k+1}): update the weight vector of neuron n_i by the attribute vector of e_{k+1} according to the updating rule (1) below.

$$w_{ij,k+1} = w_{ij,k} + \frac{1}{k+1} \cdot (a_{k+1,j} - w_{ij,k}). \qquad (1)$$

where $w_{ij,k}$ is the j-th weight of n_i after having seen the first k examples covered by n_i.

After an initial network has been built, some optimizations (called horizontal and vertical optimizations) are performed to improve the performance of the network. As the network is trained, the dead branches which stop growing are pruned away to reduce the size of the network. An SGNT branch is called dead if the number of examples covered by its root does not increase during repeated training. Finally, it is possible to simplify an SGNT by a method similar to Quinlan's method of decision tree simplification [7]. For more detailed information about the SGNT algorithm, optimization, pruning, and simplification, see [13].

3 SGNN/SGNT vs. SONN

Although the SGNN/SGNT bears much resemblance to SONN, it has many of its own features. To compare SGNT/SGNN with SONN, we conducted a systematic performance analysis for both methods. The benchmark that we chose was the MONK's problems [9]. The reasons for this choice are

1. MONK's tests have been performed for many (at least 20) well-known supervised/unsupervised learning methods at the 2nd European Summer School on Machine Learning during the summer of 1991. This makes an independent comparison of different methods possible.

2. The training and test data and the test results for other well-known methods are easily accessed.

3. The MONK's problems are not too complicated or time-consuming to test but are reasonably difficult to solve.

The MONK's problems [9] rely on an artificial robot domain, in which robots are described by six different attributes:

x_1:	head_shape	$\in$	round, square, octagon
x_2:	body_shape	$\in$	round, square, octagon;
x_3:	is_smiling	$\in$	yes, no
x_4:	holding	$\in$	sword, balloon, flag;
x_5:	jacket_color	$\in$	red, yellow, green, blue;
x_6	has_tie	$\in$	yes, no.

The learning tasks of the three MONK's problems are binary classification tasks, each of them is given by the following logical description of a class.

- Problem M_1: (head_shape = body_shape) or (jacket_color = red). From 432 possible examples, 124 were randomly selected for the training set. No noise is present.
- Problem M_2: Exactly two of the six attributes have their first value. From 432 examples, 169 were selected randomly. No noise is present.
- Problem M_3: (Jacket_color is green and holding a sword) or (jacket_color is not blue and body_shape is no octagon). From 432 examples, 122 were selected randomly. and among them there were 5% misclassifications, ie. noise in the training set.

The results given in [11] show that SGNN/SGNT outperforms the most popular unsupervised learning methods, such as ECOBWEB and CLASSWEB, and is significantly faster than all those competitors. In this paper, we will use MONK's problems again to compare SGNN/SGNT and SONN. The comparison is conducted in three aspects: simplicity of network design, accuracy of classification/clustering and generalization capability, and the training/testing speed.

3.1 Design Efforts

As implied by the name Self-Generating, the design of an SGNT/SGNN requires much less effort from the designer. For the design of an SONN, such as LVQ [4], to handle a particular application, the designer has to decide

1. how many neurons the network needs,
2. how the neurons are arranged in the networks,
3. what is the neighbourhood size to use and how the neighbourhood should shrink during the training,
4. the usage count arrangement to make better use of the neurons, and
5. the appropriate learning rate for training the network and the strategy to reduce it.

Some of these system parameters affect the performance of the SONN significantly. This means that if they are selected improperly, the final system performance may not be as good as expected. Too many neurons or links will obviously waste the system resources and also cause unnecessary delay because of the exhaustive search strategy of SONN during both training and testing. Once the structure of the network has been determined, it remains fixed. Any change of the application requirement will lead to a complete re-design and re-training of the network. The rest of the decisions that the network designer has to make are very tricky and there is no standard way to choose these parameters convincingly. The usual practice is to perform multiple experiments to choose them empirically. Therefore, this is often a tedious and fruitless design task.

For MONK's problems, we performed experiments with 6×6, 8×8, 12×12, and 14×14 LVQ grids. The 12×12 and 14×14 networks did not give significantly better performance than that of 8×8 network for MONK's problems, but 8×8 network was significantly better than 6×6 network. There was a severe penalty when increasing the network size because training time would become longer due to the number of nodes needed to be searched. In addition, the neighbourhood size for training must be initially large and this will further add to the length of the training schedule. Therefore, we decided to use the 8×8 network for our comparisons with SGNT/SGNN. Because there is no standard way of choosing the diameters of the neighborhoods and their shrinking strategy for LVQ network training, we chose them empirically according to experience accumulated in previous experiments (see Table 1). The learning rates used in the LVQ networks is also given in Table 1. Neuron usage counters were not used because we were not concerned with making the best use of the neurons. We used two metrics, city block and Euclidean distance, for LVQ net training and testing. Our results seem to show that city-block is on average slightly better for the MONK's problems. This might be because an Euclidean metric requires the computation of a square of the sum followed by a square root, whereas a city block requires only the sum of the absolute differences. The networks were trained using 110 epochs in total.

learning rate	neighbourhood diameter	epochs
0.06	4	10
0.06	3	30
0.05	2	20
0.04	1	20
0.025	0	30

Table 1: The training schedule for LVQ nets

In the case of SGNN/SGNT, all that needs to be done is to choose an appropriate parameter ξ and if we are lazy to do so, we can always choose $\xi = 0$. The SGNN/SGNT system will do everything else for the development of the neural network. According to our experiences, the system does this quite well. For the MONK's problems, SGNT generated three networks with 156, 168, and 82 neurons, respectively. These figures are greater than the 64 neurons used by an 8×8 LVQ network, but it should be noted that for MONK's problems there was no significant difference in performance between 8×8 and $14 \times 14 (= 196)$ LVQ networks except that the former was significantly faster to train/test than the latter. The generated SGNT networks had 5 levels and each of them was generated in only 5 epochs.

3.2 The accuracy of classification / clustering

The results of SGNT, SONN, and some other unsupervised methods for the MONK problems are given in Table 2. The results of LVQ nets show the averages of 10 runs with different initial weight sets. The results show that SGNT is better than SONN for the easier tasks such as M_1 and M_3. For the harder task M_2, the performance of SGNT is much better than SONN, as is the average performance of SGNT. This comparison shows that the fixed uniform structure (such as a grid structure) of SONN cannot be a perfect panacea for all applications. For different applications, ideally, different networks structures should be carefully designed. SGNN/SGNT gives a possible alternative to heavily handcrafted network methods, such as Neocognitron[3]. It automatically adjusts the neuron/link density in different parts of the network according to the training sample distribution for a particular application, whereas SONN treats all applications uniformly and consequently, wastes neurons/links in some parts of the network while has too few neurons/links to use in other parts even in a big network.

Learning method tested	Test results		
	M_1	M_2	M_3
SGNT	82.6%	78.2%	84.5%
8 × 8 LVQ (CB)	76.1%	63.0%	81.2%
8 × 8 LVQ (Eu)	72.5%	64.4%	75.7%
CLASSWEB 0.10	71.8%	64.8%	80.8%
CLASSWEB 0.15	65.7%	61.6%	85.4%
CLASSWEB 0.20	63.0%	57.2%	75.2%
ECOBWEB l.p.	71.8%	67.4%	69.1%

Table 2: Accuracy comparisons for unsupervised learning methods

3.3 The training speed

For the MONK's problems, speed comparisons between the SGNT and SONN are given in Table 3. The results show that the SGNT is significantly faster than SONN. The problem here for SONN is that an exhaustive search of the whole network is performed to find a winner no matter how large the network is. Furthermore, as mentioned earlier, there are often redundant neurons in SONN, thus extra delays are added to the search. SGNT/SGNN avoids the pitfalls of SONN by only searching a very small part of the network hierarchically. For SGNT, this becomes a very efficient tree search ($O(\log_b N)$). The SGNN/SGNT algorithm generates neurons/links only when they are really needed and the pruning and simplification of the network further reduce redundancy. Therefore, it is not surprising that SGNN/SGNT should be much faster to train/test than SONN.

Learning method tested	Training time (in sec)		
	M_1	M_2	M_3
SGNT	1.47	2.37	2.69
8 × 8 LVQ (CB)	62.74	85.72	62.04
8 × 8 LVQ (Eu)	86.12	117.01	84.56
CLASSWEB 0.10	1406.47	2013.78	1311.25
CLASSWEB 0.15	867.47	977.04	822.09
CLASSWEB 0.20	499.94	646.06	521.21
COBWEB's	Not available		

Table 3: Speed comparisons for unsupervised learning methods

4 Discussion

"The thought that my mind is really nothing but an empty sieve - often this, too, disconcerts me."

Logan Pearsall Smith,

"All Trivia"

There are a great many neural network researchers concerned with the issue of "scaling up" neural networks to tackle large problems, and more difficult problems than pattern recognition. A task such as target identification in the presence of noise and clutter is fairly well treated by current networks, but a more difficult task such as handwritten text is still fairly difficult. In all practical cases of network application to large problems, a strict network structure is constructed by the network designers. For example the AT&T zip code network has seven layers and a complex hierarchical structure [8]. More well known is the Neocognitron [3]. The success of the neocognitron derives very much from its structure and its careful training regime wherein the feature set is at a progressively higher level of abstraction towards the top of the network.

So it appears that to tackle large problems some structuring of the problem is necessary. The key question then becomes: how do such networks arise in nature? There is no designer present carefully feeding examples to the network in such a way that it has tractable and computationally feasible learning tasks at each layer. To resolve this question we can proceed in two ways: we can look in nature for how the networks develop, or attempt to construct models that emulate the biological capability. Our work on SGNT follows this second path, and the results on standard problems show that it is a powerful mechanism. SONN shows some promise in delivering a network solely on the basis of the sensory data. For example Kohonen's network [4] is quite successful at developing a network for pattern recognition. It gives the appearance of "principle free" learning: that the network structure arises solely on the basis of the training data.

However, Kohonen's network incorporates a neighbourhood measure that is reduced as the training of the network proceeds, which plays a major part in the network structure. Even though this is not a "principle based" method, it is still giving the network designer considerable control over the end result. So we argue that SONN's are developed with influence from the designer in selecting this schedule.

The SGNT approach is quite different: there are guiding principles and constraints that influence the formation of the network structure. These principles are derived from traditional AI concept formation/decision tree methods, so they have apparently little in common with biological mechanisms.

What are the biological equivalents of our pruning rules? Given that artificial neural networks are a greatly abstracted view of neural networks, we cannot say at this stage. But on the surface it does appear reasonable to limit the number of poorly formed hierarchies. Perhaps we can discover biological mechanisms that are similar. Even though speed of training is not of great importance in itself, it does show economy of computation which may imply evolutionary advantage for the corresponding biological network. There is considerable evidence that network development is not from a "blank sheet".

Acknowledgement

Discussions with Huan Liu and Maureen Molloy assisted in the preparation of the discussion. The permission of the Director of Telecom Australia Research Laboratories to publish this paper is acknowledged.

References

[1] L. Fang, A.Jennings, W.Wen, K.Li, and T.Li. Unsupervised learning in a self-organizing tree. In *Proc. IJCNN'91 (International Joint Conf. on Neural Networks)*, Singapore, Nov. 1991.

[2] D. Fisher. Knowledge acquisition via incremental conceptual slustering. *Machine Learning*, 2:139–172, 1987.

[3] K. Fukushima and N. Wake. Handwritten alphanumeric character recognition by the neocognition. *IEEE Trans. on Neural Networks*, 2, No. 3:355–365, 1991.

[4] T. Kohonen. *Self-Organization and Associative Memory*. Springer-Verlag, Berlin, 1984.

[5] K. McKusick and P. Langley. Constrains on tree structure in concept formation. In *Proc. IJCAI'91*, volume 2, pages 810–816, Sydney, Aug. 1991. Morgan Kaufmann.

[6] M. Moloy, W. Wen, V. Ciesielski, and A. Jennings. Neuopsychological diagnosis using a neural netowrk. In *preparation (submitted to Australian Cognitive Conference)*, Sept. 1992.

[7] J. Quinlan. Simplifying decision trees. *Int.J.Man-Machine Studies*, 27:221–234, 1987.

[8] E. Sackinger et al. Application of the ANNA neural network chip to high-speed character recognition. *IEEE Trans. on Neural Networks*, 3, No. 3:498–505, 1992.

[9] S. Thrun et al. The MONK's problems: A performance comparison of different learning algorithms. Tech Report CMU-CS-91-197, Carnegie Mellon University, Dec. 1991.

[10] W. X. Wen, A. Jennings, and H. Liu. Learning a neural tree. In *Proc. IJCNN'92 (International Joint Conf. on Neural Networks), Beijing, China*, Nov. 1992.

[11] W. X. Wen, A. Jennings, and H. Liu. A performance analysis for self-generating neural networks. In *Proc. IJCNN'92 (International Joint Conf. on Neural Networks), Beijing, China*, Nov. 1992.

[12] W. X. Wen, A. Jennings, and H. Liu. Self-generating neural networks and their applications to telecommunications. In *Proc. ICCT'92 (International Conference on Communication Technology)*, Beijing, China, 9 1992.

[13] W. X. Wen, H. Liu, and A. Jennings. Self-generating neural networks. In *Proc. IJCNN'92 (International Joint Conf. on Neural Networks)*, Baltimore, June 1992.

Multi-layer Associative Neural Networks (M.A.N.N.):

Storage Capacity vs. Noise-free Recall

Hoon Kang

Dept. of Control & Instrumentation Eng., Chung-Ang University
221 Huksuk-dong Dongjak-gu, Seoul 156-756, Korea

Abstract

The objective of this paper is to to resolve important issues in artificial neural nets – **exact recall** and **capacity** in multilayer associative memories. These problems have imposed restrictions on coding strategies. We propose the following triple-layered neural network: the first synapse is a one-shot associative memory using the modified Kohonen's adaptive learning algorithm with arbitrary input patterns; the second one is Kosko's bidirectional associative memory consisting of orthogonal input/output basis vectors such as **Walsh series** satisfying the strict continuity condition; and finally, the third one is a simple one-shot associative memory with arbitrary output images. A mathematical framework based on the relationship between energy local minima (capacity of the neural net) and noise-free recall is established. The **robust** capacity conditions of this multi-layer associative memory are derived and it leads to forming the energy local minima at the exact training pairs. The proposed strategy not only maximizes the total number of stored images but also completely relaxes any code-dependent conditions of the learning pairs.

1 Introduction

Kosko's Bidirectional Associative Memory (BAM) [1,2] has been and is being investigated by many researchers. In a BAM, as the required – perhaps arbitrary – number of training pairs increases, success in recalling the training pairs is to be questioned and even unanticipated or complementary patterns begin to appear as shown in Figure 1. Moreover, some of the original patterns might be buried in the slopes of the energy wells and bidirectional stability[1] does not always imply exact recall in noise. The key problem is the unsolved relationship between the capacity of a BAM and the energy local minima for each learning pair. This is a fundamental issue on learning of neural network for error-free recovery as well as an alternate to backpropagation. The idea can be extended to a code-independent strategy to a BAM for perfect recovery of data in noise.

The objective of this paper is

- to relax any conditions or coding problems for exact recall of the stored learning pairs $\{w_k, z_k\}$ from noisy data,
- to solve the capacity problems for noise-free recall, and
- to utilize this paradigm as an alternate to backpropagation.

Two code-dependent strategies has been proposed in Wang et al.[3] where noise-free recall is possible with sufficient conditions enforced on the coding technique of input/output learning pairs. Here, we suggest a Multi-layer Associative Neural Network (MANN) with three layers as shown in Figure 2, so as to eliminate the sufficient conditions and to achieve code-independent associative memories. Thus, we don't have to deal with complex coding problems from the continuity condition of a BAM when we need to add many different learning data that might not follow the continuity condition. In Figure 2, a MANN consists of three processing units:

- 1st Synapse: Optimal Discrete Associative Memory (ODAM)
- 2nd Synapse: Bidirectional Associative Memory (BAM)
- 3rd Synapse: Unidirectional Associative Memory (UAM)

The main idea is to put hard restrictions on predetermined hidden data and thus to relax limitations on code-dependent learning pairs. The learning cycles of a MANN are predetermined by the hidden training data, the Walsh vectors. A MANN has two more one-shot associative memories as interfaces to both ends of a BAM but the capacity of a MANN increases maximally while exact recall is guaranteed through noisy channels. As an example, a MANN is applied to robust recognition of noisy patterns. Each unit will be described in detail in the next section.

2 Main Results – M.A.N.N.

2.1 Learning/Retrieving Mechanisms

In this section, we consider the learning structure of a MANN and show how one of the output learning data $\{z_k\}$ can be recalled from the noisy input data $\{w = w_k + \tilde{w}\}$. First, the first processor plays a role of matching arbitrary input data with orthogonal series of data. These orthogonal data have exactly one half of the number of elements with each other which we may call the ***strict continuity*** condition. In fact, the first correlation matrix, M_1 associates a noisy input image with its closest orthogonal vector in an optimal least squares sense. Therefore, M_1 matrix is an optimal discrete associative memory (ODAM).

The second processor utilizes a bidirectional stability of a BAM. The continuity condition is inevitable for noise-free recall in a BAM so that the learning pairs can preserve the maximum Hamming distance with one another [1]. Without this condition, a cross talk will appear when recalling a trained pair. In this paper, we employ a strong rule (strict continuity) in the second layer. Therefore, we circumvent this burden imposed on the original learning pairs by prescribing the **strict continuity** condition for predetermined hidden Walsh patterns in the second/third neuronal fields as follows:

$$\frac{H(a_i,a_j)}{m} \simeq \frac{H(b_i,b_j)}{p} \simeq \frac{1}{2} \tag{1}$$

where m, p stand for the numbers of elements for input and output fields, respectively; $H(\cdot,\cdot)$ denotes a Hamming distance between two binary vectors; a_i, b_j are the binary vectors of hidden input/output fields, respectively; and furthermore, these hidden data will be orthogonal if we employ Walsh series[4] such that

$$x_i^T x_j = m\delta_{ij}, \qquad y_i^T y_j = p\delta_{ij} \tag{2}$$

where x_i, y_j are the bipolar vectors of hidden input/output data in the second synapse, BAM, and δ_{ij} is the Kronecker-delta function.

Threshold Function for Neurons in MANN: Consider a vector $x = (x[1], \cdots, x[m])^T$ with $x[i]$ representing the i-th bipolar element of x. A binary vector a is described in terms of a bipolar representation x,

$$a = \frac{1}{2}(x + \mathbf{1}) \tag{3}$$

where $\mathbf{1} = (1, \cdots, 1)^T \in \mathcal{N}^m$. We take the following threshold function ϕ for every layer of neurons:

0-7803-0999-5/93/$03.00

$$y = \phi(\xi), \qquad \xi = Mx. \tag{4}$$

The threshold function $\phi(\cdot)$ is defined as follows:

$$y[i] = \phi(\xi[i]) = \begin{cases} +1 & if \ \xi[i] > 0 \\ -1 & if \ \xi[i] \leq 0 \end{cases} \tag{5}$$

Here, the threshold level is chosen so that only positive action potential can excite the nerve cells. Let us consider the learning/recalling mechanism of a MANN in detail.

First Synapse (M_1): The first unit, M_1, utilizes and modifies Kohonen's Optimal Linear Associative Memory (OLAM) [5]. The difference is that the elements of the correlation matrix M_1 are integers for the purpose of implementation and that the synaptic strength of the weights is enhanced. A modified learning algorithm for this optimal discrete associative memory (ODAM) is proposed as follows:

First of all, the neurons of the first and the second fields are

input learning patterns: $w_k \in \{-1,1\}^m$
output Walsh patterns: $x_k \in \mathcal{W}\{-1,1\}^m$

where $\mathcal{W}\{-1,1\}^m$ denotes a set of Walsh series. An m-bit Walsh matrix W_m has $(m-1)$ possible candidate vectors satisfying orthogonality as well as strict continuity.

Learning Algorithm for M_1 ODAM:

1. Initialize:
(i) $M_1(0) = 0$, $P(0) = I$ where $M_1(k) \in \mathcal{N}^{m\times m}$, $P(k) \in \Re^{m\times m}$.
(ii) $N \gg m$, $N \in \mathcal{N}^1$ is a design parameter of the synaptic strength for M_1.
where $\mathcal{N}, \Re$ are sets of integers and real numbers, respectively.

2. Repeat: for $k = 0$ to $n-1$ do
begin

$$\begin{aligned} s_{k+1} &= P(k)w_{k+1} \\ e_{k+1} &= Nx_{k+1} - M_1(k)w_{k+1} \\ d_{k+1} &= 1 + w_{k+1}^T s_{k+1} \\ P(k+1) &= P(k) - \frac{s_{k+1}s_{k+1}^T}{d_{k+1}} \\ M_1(k+1) &= M_1(k) + f_r\left[\frac{e_{k+1}s_{k+1}^T}{d_{k+1}}\right] \end{aligned} \tag{6}$$

end.
where $f_r[\cdot]$ denotes a round-off function; s_k, e_k are real-valued vectors in $\Re^m$; d_k is a real number; and n is the total number of learning pairs.

3. Download $M_1 = M_1(n)$ into the ODAM.

It is remaked that the input training patterns $\{w_k\}$ need not follow the continuity condition nor any other coding strategies. The learning structure of this first layer (ODAM) is shown in Figure 3.

Lemma 2.1 (M_1 ODAM) *Given M_1 ODAM, let the input training patterns $\{w_k : k = 1..n\}$ form a subset of linearly independent basis vectors $(n < m)$ then $\{x_k : k = 1..n\}$ is recalled perfectly from $\{w_k\}$ in a one-shot manner.*

Proof: see Kohonen's OLAM[5].

The possible errors are the round-off errors in $M_1(n)$ due to discretization function $f_r[\cdot]$, however, this would be avoided if the design parameter N for the synaptic strength is chosen to be sufficiently large.

Second Synapse (M_2): M_2 correlation matrix is just a BAM with the following training mechanism which is based on the discrete hetero-associative Hebbian learning:

input Walsh patterns: $x_k \in \mathcal{W}\{-1,1\}^m$
output Walsh patterns: $y_k \in \mathcal{W}\{-1,1\}^p$

Learning Algorithm for M_2 BAM:

1. Initialize: $M_2(0) = 0$, $M_2(k) \in \mathcal{N}^{p\times m}$.

2. Repeat: for $k = 0$ to $n-1$ do

$$M_2(k+1) = M_2(k) + y_{k+1}x_{k+1}^T \tag{7}$$

3. Download $M_2 = M_2(n) = \sum_{k=1}^n y_k x_k^T$ into the BAM.

As the orthogonal pairs $\{x_k, y_k\}$ follow the strict continuity condition, it is true that energy local minima will be formed at the exact location of each pair. The forward path for x_i pattern is described by

$$\begin{aligned} M_2 x_i &= y_i x_i^T x_i + \sum_{i\neq j} y_j \delta_{ij} \\ &= m y_i \xrightarrow{\phi} y_i \end{aligned} \tag{8}$$

However, the size of a Walsh function should be always 2^ℓ with an integer ℓ. Therefore, in a practical sense, we will use the Walsh series-like patterns satisfying either strict continuity or orthogonality.

$$\begin{aligned} M_2 x_i &= y_i x_i^T x_i + \sum_{j\neq i} y_j x_j^T x_i \\ &= m y_i + \sum_{j\neq i} y_j[m - 2H(a_i, a_j)] \xrightarrow{\phi} y_i \end{aligned} \tag{9}$$

where a_i is the binary version of the bipolar vector x_i. The second term of the right side of (9) will vanish if the strict continuity condition holds for the forward direction, i.e., $H(a_i, a_j) = m/2$. Reversely, the backward path for y_i pattern is

$$\begin{aligned} M_2^T y_i &= x_i y_i^T y_i + \sum_{j\neq i} x_j y_j^T y_k \\ &= p x_i + \sum_{j\neq i} x_j[p - 2H(b_i, b_j)] \\ &= p x_i \xrightarrow{\phi} x_i \end{aligned} \tag{10}$$

if $H(b_i, b_j) = p/2$ where b_i is the binary version of the bipolar vector y_i. The noise input image x will match with the corresponding output image y bidirectionally.

An energy Lyapunov function $E(x,y)$ is defined for M_2 BAM as follows [1]:

$$E(x,y) = -b^T M_2 a \tag{11}$$

where a and b are the binary vectors of the bipolar Walsh patterns, x and y, respectively. How the state changes in x_k or y_k would result in the behavior of a BAM? It is shown by Kosko[1] that a BAM is bidirectionally stable and always has local minima at $\{x_f, y_f\}$ which depend on the learning patterns $\{x_k, y_k\}$, in our case, learning pairs of a Walsh subspace. It is shown here that orthogonality and strict continuity of $\{x_k, y_k\}$ guarantee local minima at the exact Walsh pairs $\{x_k, y_k\}$, i.e., noise-free recall.

First of all, we consider the state changes in x_k or y_k. The correlation matrix M_2 of a BAM is

$$M_2 = \sum_{i=1}^n y_i x_i^T = \{m_{jk}\}, \qquad m_{jk} = \sum_{i=1}^n y_i[j]x_i[k] \tag{12}$$

where $x_i = (x_i[1], \cdots, x_i[m])^T$, $y_i = (y_i[1], \cdots, y_i[p])^T$, or we can rewrite

$$M_2 = Y_n X_n^T \tag{13}$$

where $X_n = [x_1 \cdots x_n] \in \mathcal{N}^{m\times n}$ and $Y_n = [y_1 \cdots y_n] \in \mathcal{N}^{p\times n}$. Since x_k is a vector in $\mathcal{W}\{-1,1\}^m$ (the Walsh space),

$$\sum_{j=1}^m x_i[j] = 0 \qquad \forall i \in \{1..n\} \tag{14}$$

and using (3)

$$\begin{aligned} x_i^T a_k &= \sum_{j=1}^{m} x_i[j] a_k[j] = \frac{1}{2} x_i^T (x_k + \mathbf{1}) \\ &= \frac{1}{2} x_i^T x_k + \frac{1}{2} \sum_{j=1}^{m} x_i[j] = \frac{1}{2} x_i^T x_k \end{aligned} \tag{15}$$

and similarly, for y_k, we get

$$y_i^T b_k = \frac{1}{2} y_i^T y_k.$$

In fact, x_k and y_k are subsets of Walsh series, and therefore,

$$x_i^T a_k = \frac{m}{2}\delta_{ik}, \qquad y_i^T b_k = \frac{p}{2}\delta_{ik}. \tag{16}$$

Now, suppose that the k-th state in x_i is changed (bit-reversed) then the energy change due to $x_i[k]$ will be

$$\begin{aligned} \frac{\Delta E}{\Delta a_i[k]} &= -\sum_{j=1}^{p} b_i[j] m_{jk} = -\sum_{j=1}^{p} b_i[j] \sum_{\ell=1}^{n} y_\ell[j] x_\ell[k] \\ &= -\sum_{\ell=1}^{n}\sum_{j=1}^{p} b_i[j] y_\ell[j] x_\ell[k] = -\sum_{\ell=1}^{n} (b_i^T y_\ell) x_\ell[k] \quad (17) \\ &= -\sum_{\ell=1}^{n} \frac{p}{2}\delta_{i\ell} x_\ell[k] = -\frac{p}{2} x_i[k] \end{aligned}$$

It is obvious that $\Delta E = -\frac{p}{2} x_i[k] \Delta a_i[k]$ and we recognize that, if $x_i[k]$ is changed from $(+1)$ to (-1) then $\Delta a_i[k] = -1 < 0$, and if $x_i[k]$ is changed from (-1) to $(+1)$ then $\Delta a_i[k] = 1 > 0$. Thus, the energy changes due to the state changes in x_i will always result in $\Delta E < 0$. The same is true for the state changes in y_i and $\Delta E < 0$ always holds as Kosko[1,2] mentioned. In a MANN, the second synapse M_2 is a special case since the training pairs in a BAM consists of Walsh series. Therefore, a pattern applied to the second unit will be bidirectionally stable and converge to some equilibrium pair in the energy potential terrain where $\Delta E = 0$.

Now, consider the following important lemma for M_2 BAM which is a special case of a BAM:

Lemma 2.2 **(M_2, Capacity Condition for Noise-Free Recall)** *If $\{x_k, y_k\}$ constitutes a Walsh subspace in $\mathcal{W}\{-1,1\}^m$ and $\mathcal{W}\{-1,1\}^p$, respectively, then the following inequality holds for all $\{x_i, y_i\}$ pairs and for some bit-reversal noise vectors $\{\tilde{x}, \tilde{y}\}$ such that*

$$E(x_k, y_k) < E(x_k + \tilde{x}, y_k + \tilde{y}) \tag{18}$$

if the robust capacity condition holds where $x_k + \tilde{x} \neq x_i$ and $y_k + \tilde{y} \neq y_i$ for $i \neq k$. Let the number of bit-reversal be $\ell_{(k,\tilde{a})}$ for $x \cong x_k$, $\ell_{(k,\tilde{b})}$ for $y \cong y_k$, then the robust capacity condition for noise-free recall is stated as follows:

$$n \leq \min\left\{\frac{m}{\ell_{(k,\tilde{a})}}, \frac{p}{\ell_{(k,\tilde{b})}}\right\} \tag{19}$$

where $\ell_{(k,\tilde{a})}, \ell_{(k,\tilde{b})}$ are

$$\ell_{(k,\tilde{a})} = \sum_{i=1}^{m} |\tilde{a}[i]|, \qquad \ell_{(k,\tilde{b})} = \sum_{i=1}^{p} |\tilde{b}[i]|.$$

Proof: see Appendix.

It is noted that the capacity of this special BAM will generally increase by the efficient use of Walsh series because the corresponding corrupted bits change in turn for the other Walsh patterns. Also, the capacity condition is equivalent to the noise-free recall condition.

Third Synapse (M_3): The final matrix is unidirectional with Walsh patterns in the third neuron field. The learning mechanism for M_3 UAM is similar to M_2 BAM except that M_3 UAM is a one-shot associative memory.

input Walsh patterns: $y_k \in \mathcal{W}\{-1,1\}^p$
output learning patterns: $z_k \in \{-1,1\}^p$

Learning Algorithm for M_3 UAM:

1. Initialize: $M_3(0) = 0$, $M_3(k) \in \mathcal{N}^{p\times p}$.
2. Repeat: for $k = 0$ to $n-1$ do

$$M_3(k+1) = M_3(k) + z_{k+1} y_{k+1}^T \tag{20}$$

3. Download $M_3 = M_3(n) = \sum_{k=1}^{n} z_k y_k^T$ into the UAM.

and for a given pattern y_i with strict continuity, $H(b_i, b_j) = p/2$, the association mechanism is

$$\begin{aligned} M_3 y_i &= z_i y_i^T y_i + \sum_{i\neq j} z_j [p - 2H(b_i, b_j)] \\ &= p z_i \xrightarrow{\phi} z_i \end{aligned} \tag{21}$$

Therefore, for each y_i, exact recall is guaranteed.

Remark: Note that neither the continuity condition in [1] nor the sufficient condition proposed in [3] is imposed on the patterns of the original training pairs $\{w_i, z_i\}$ absorbed in a MANN.

This final synapse plays a role of one-shot association from convergent data in the third neuronal field to the resultant output image.

Lemma 2.3 **(M_3 UAM)** *Given M_3 UAM established by n-pairs $\{y_k, z_k\}$, let y_k be applied to M_3 then the output image z is equal to z_k.*

Proof: It is obvious from (21).

Theorem 2.1 **(MANN)** *Let a pattern w be applied to a MANN and let a MANN satisfy the noise-free recall condition in (19). Then, a MANN retrieves (recalls) one among $\{w_k, z_k\}$ pairs, the nearest convergent pair $\{w_k, z_k\}$ even if the initial condition w is corrupted by noise.*

Proof: The proof is straightforward if we use Lemmas 2.1, 2.2, and 2.3. But, when $w \cong w_k$ is subject to noise, the nearest hidden pattern (y, resonance pattern) will be obtained in the second layer from Lemma 2.2 and finally M_3 UAM filters y and extracts the pattern z closest to z_k. The noise-free recall is guaranteed if the robust capacity condition holds for a finite number of training pairs.

2.2 Capacity Conditions vs. Exact Recall

(Worst-case Capacity & Approximate Robust Capacity of MANN)
The capacity of Hopfield nets is rigorously investigated by McEliece et al.[6] where the restriction of training patterns is $n < \frac{m}{2\log_2 m}$ for exactly recoverable patterns. The amount of information for randomly selected patterns is $n < \frac{m^2}{2\log_2 m}$ bits. In the case of the non-homogeneous BAM, Haines et al.[7] demonstrated that a storage capacity is $n < 0.68\frac{m^2}{[(\log_2 m)+4]^2}$ from randomly chosen sparce coded bipolar vectors.

In a MANN, The capacity for noise-free recall in (19) is a rough estimate in the worst case. Let ℓ_1, ℓ_2 be the numbers of bit-reversal errors in the hidden input/output pair, respectively, then we can interpret this worst-case capacity condition

$$n < \min\left\{\frac{m}{\ell_1}, \frac{p}{\ell_2}\right\} \tag{22}$$

as two instances of noise-free recall that is always guaranteed both for small bit-reversal noise and for large number of stored pairs, or vice versa, with sufficient margins. The denominator is the number of bit-reversal occuring at the layers of M_2 BAM. If we define bit-reversal noise probabilities, $pr_1 = \frac{\ell_1}{m}$ and $pr_2 = \frac{\ell_2}{p}$, then the noise-free recall capacity condition (22) is $n < \min\{1/pr_1, 1/pr_2\}$. If the bit-reversal probabilities of input/output channels are less than $\frac{1}{m}$ and $\frac{1}{p}$, the capacity of a MANN is equal to Kosko's original conjecture in [1] such that $n < \min\{m, p\}$. The true estimate of capacity for noise-free recall is

$$n < \min\left\{1 + \frac{\ell_2(m-\ell_1)}{\ell_2'\ell_1'}, 1 + \frac{\ell_1(p-\ell_2)}{\ell_1'\ell_2'}\right\} \quad (23)$$

where ℓ_1', ℓ_2' are defined subsequently. An important point of view in capacity of MANN is that the capacity of a MANN is equal to that of M_2 BAM, and that with Walsh patterns $\{x_k, y_k\}$ it is true that the effect of bit-reversal on the other Walsh patterns is (see Appendix (28))

$$\ell_1' = \Delta_{(i,\tilde{a})} < \ell_1, \qquad \ell_2' = \Delta_{(i,\tilde{b})} < \ell_2 \qquad (for\ i \neq k).$$

Therefore, the robust capacity of a MANN increases in general since we obtain an approximate estimate if, on the average, $\ell_1'\ell_2' = \frac{1}{2}\ell_1\ell_2$ holds then

$$n < \min\left\{\frac{2m}{\ell_1} - 1, \frac{2p}{\ell_2} - 1\right\}. \quad (24)$$

Table 1 shows the worst-case capacity n for error-free recorvery in terms of bit-reversal noise, $\ell_1 = \ell_2$, based on (22). With the approximate robust capacity condition, we can store the training pairs twice as much as those of the worst-case capacity condition with the same bit-reversal probabilities. When we know the signal-to-noise bit-ratios, we can decide the robust capacity for noise-free recall (the maximum number of recoverable learning pairs).

	$m = p = 100$	$m = p = 150$	$m = p = 200$
$\ell_1 = \ell_2 = 5$	20/39	30/59	40/79
$\ell_1 = \ell_2 = 10$	10/19	15/29	20/39
$\ell_1 = \ell_2 = 20$	5/9	7.5/13	10/19

Table 1: Storage Capacity of MANN (Worst-case Capacity/Approximate Robust Capacity)

3 Example of Pattern Recognition

A MANN can be applied to various pattern recognition systems or image classifiers especially when the system suffers from a noise environment. We consider a pattern recognition problem using the Korean and the English characters.

Example: We want to match the international characters, from a Korean character to an English one, on the basis of pronunciation. A digital communication channel is subject to noise with the bit-reversal probabilities of 10 ~ 25%. Fourteen Korean consonants are chosen and their corresponding like-sound English characters are shown together in Figure 4. The number of pattern pixels are selected as $m = 100$ (Korean) and $p = 96$ (English).

From random bit-reversal noise injected into input patterns w_k such as $pr_1 = pr_2 = 0.1 \sim 0.25$, the worst-case capacity for noise-free recall is

$$n = \min\{\frac{1}{pr_1}, \frac{1}{pr_2}\} = 4 \sim 10.$$

However, as mentioned, this estimate is rough and is a lower bound of the noise-free recall capacity. In general, the true capacity of a MANN will be larger as shown in (23). The approximate capacity is found to be $n = 7 \sim 19$ from (24). In this example, fourteen pattern pairs of the Korean and the English characters are stored in a MANN. Figure 5 demonstrates a MANN as a robust pattern recognition system showing recall processes in noise. The sizes of pixels are $m = 100$ for Korean characters and $p = 96$ for English ones, and the design parameter N is chosen to be 10^4. All fourteen characters were recovered exactly if there is no bit-reversal error. The noise-affected characters have their origin in the second synapse because some parasitic energy local minima have been reached by a noise-corrupted internal pattern pair. Figure 6 shows the average success rate of "G" for different numbers of learning pairs ($n = 4, 9, 14$) collected from approximately 300 different uniform noise sets for each bit-reversal noise (%). When ℓ_1 is 7%, the success rates for "G" are 100% for 4 training pairs, 96.3% for 9 pairs, and 84.7% for 14 pairs.

4 Conclusions

In this paper, the robust capacity condition is derived for MANN nets using the Lyapunov energy function. The MANN recalls an exact output learning pattern from any uncertain input patterns via noisy channels and this is a one-way association. Our strategy is better in the performance point of view since the multi-layer concept is more efficient than the magnification of the correlation matrix or the increase in the number of neurons and processing units. Moreover, as we put more learning pairs into a MANN, the old learning pairs would be still recalled perfectly without any intervention of new learning pairs until the capacity limit is reached. Even if the original pattern is disturbed heavily, the nearest output pattern is obtained as a result of optimality and bistability.

Like the BAM structure, we can add two more one-shot associative memories in order to recall a input/output learning pair bidirectionally as shown in Figure 7. This Bidirectional MANN (BMANN) can be represented by the bidirectional data flows. The strongest advantages of a MANN or a BMANN are as follows:

- Learning pairs do not depend on any coding strategies and virtually no restrictions are imposed on the input/output learning patterns.
- The capacity of a MANN or a BMANN is increased maximally as we add more learning pairs indepedently of existing learning pairs in a MANN.

The difference between MLP nets and MANNs is that MANNs use the optimality concept in the weights of the first synapse instead of using the backpropagation concept in MLP nets[8]. A holographic memory[4] has a simpler structure than that of a MANN but it requires additional logic circuits to compute the maximum correlation during recall processes. Examples show very promising applications of a MANN or a BMANN to robust image recognition systems under noise.

Appendix

Proof of Lemma 2.2: The patterns $\{x_k, y_k\}$ satisfy either orthogonality or strict continuity, and therefore,

$$H(a_i, a_j) = \frac{m}{2} \ (i \neq j), \qquad x_i^T x_j = m - 2H(a_i, a_j) = m\delta_{ij} \quad (25)$$

$$H(b_i, b_j) = \frac{p}{2} \ (i \neq j), \qquad y_i^T y_j = p - 2H(b_i, b_j) = p\delta_{ij}. \quad (26)$$

First of all, we will investigate three cases near the energy local minima:

(case i): First, we consider the local minimum of $\{x_k, y_k\}$. The energy function in a bipolar pair $\{x_k, y_k\}$ or in a binary pair $\{a_k, b_k\}$ is represented by

$$E_i(x_k, y_k) = -b_k^T M_2 a_k = -\sum_{i=1}^{n} b_k^T y_i x_i^T a_k.$$

From (16), we know that

$$x_i^T a_k = \frac{1}{2} m\delta_{ik}, \qquad y_i^T b_k = \frac{1}{2} p\delta_{ik}$$

since x_k, y_k are Walsh series. Therefore, we can find the energy local minimum E_i,

$$E_i(x_k, y_k) = -\frac{1}{4}\sum_{i=1}^{n} pm\delta_{ik}^2 = -\frac{1}{4}pm.$$

(case ii): Second, a class of noisy patterns $\{x, y\} = \{x_k + \tilde{x}, y_k\}$ or $\{a, b\} = \{a_k + \tilde{a}, b_k\}$ are considered, and in this case, the energy function is

$$E_{ii}(x_k + \tilde{x}, y_k) = -b_k^T M_2(a_k + \tilde{a}) = -\frac{1}{4}pm - \frac{1}{2}p(x_k^T \tilde{a})$$

since it is found that

$$-b_k^T M_2 \tilde{a} = -\frac{1}{2}\sum_{i=1}^{n}(y_k^T y_i)(x_i^T \tilde{a}) = -\frac{1}{2}\sum_{i=1}^{n} p\delta_{ik}(x_i^T \tilde{a}).$$

Here, let $x[i] = -1$ (noise-affected) then we realize that $x_k[i] = +1$ and $\tilde{x} = -2$ ($a_k[i] = +1$ and $\tilde{a} = -1$), and let $x[i] = +1$ (noise-affected) then $x_k[i] = -1$ and $\tilde{x} = +2$ ($a_k[i] = -1$ and $\tilde{a} = +1$). Therefore, $x_k^T \tilde{a} < 0$ for every bit-reversal process in this case. Let $\Delta_{(k,\tilde{a})} = -x_k^T \tilde{a} > 0$ then the energy function is

$$E_{ii}(x,y) = -\frac{1}{4}pm + \frac{1}{2}p\Delta_{(k,\tilde{a})} > E_i(x_k, y_k).$$

Similarly, in the case of $\{x, y\} = \{x_k, y_k + \tilde{y}\}$ or $\{a, b\} = \{a_k, b_k + \tilde{b}\}$, let $\Delta_{(k,\tilde{b})} = -y_k^T \tilde{b} > 0$ then it is straightforward that

$$E'_{ii}(x,y) = -\frac{1}{4}pm + \frac{1}{2}m\Delta_{(k,\tilde{b})} > E_i(x_k, y_k).$$

(case iii): Finally, let us consider more complex case for another class of noisy pattern $\{x_k + \tilde{x}, y_k + \tilde{y}\}$ or $\{a_k + \tilde{a}, b_k + \tilde{b}\}$. The energy function E_{iii} is

$$E_{iii}(x,y) = -\frac{1}{4}pm + \frac{1}{2}p\Delta_{(k,\tilde{a})} + \frac{1}{2}m\Delta_{(k,\tilde{b})} - \sum_{i=1}^{n}\Delta_{(i,\tilde{b})}\Delta_{(i,\tilde{a})}. \quad (27)$$

It is easy to realize that, with first three terms, the energy function E_{iii} is less than the local minimum E_i, but we cannot anticipate the general behavior of E_{iii} due to the last term,

$$\Delta^* = \sum_{i=1}^{n}\Delta_{(i,\tilde{b})}\Delta_{(i,\tilde{a})}.$$

However, we introduce the capacity condition for noise-free recall and will subsequently prove that

$$E_{iii} > E_i.$$

<u>**Capacity Condition for Noise-Free Recall**</u>: The number of bit-reversal is directly related to the probability of bit-reversal. Let the number of bit-reversal in $x \cong x_k$ and $y \cong y_k$ be $\ell_{(k,\tilde{a})} < m$ and $\ell_{(k,\tilde{b})} < p$, respectively, then it is realized that

$$\Delta_{(k,\tilde{a})} = -x_k^T \tilde{a} = \ell_{(k,\tilde{a})}$$

and for the other patterns x_i $(i \neq k)$,

$$|\Delta_{(i,\tilde{a})}| = |-x_i^T \tilde{a}| < \ell_{(k,\tilde{a})} \qquad (i \neq k) \quad (28)$$

according to the characteristics of Walsh series since we recognize that, on the average, bits of the Walsh patterns alternate element by element and vector by vector. $\Delta_{(i,\tilde{a})}$, $\Delta_{(i,\tilde{b})}$ take the values of

$$-\ell_{(k,\tilde{a})} < \Delta_{(i,\tilde{a})} < \ell_{(k,\tilde{a})}, \qquad -\ell_{(k,\tilde{b})} < \Delta_{(i,\tilde{b})} < \ell_{(k,\tilde{b})}.$$

where $i \neq k$. Therefore,

$$\Delta^* = \ell_{(k,\tilde{a})}\ell_{(k,\tilde{b})} + \sum_{i \neq k}\Delta_{(i,\tilde{b})}\Delta_{(i,\tilde{a})}$$

and Δ^* will take the value of

$$\ell_{(k,\tilde{a})}\ell_{(k,\tilde{b})}[1-(n-1)] < \Delta^* < \ell_{(k,\tilde{a})}\ell_{(k,\tilde{b})}[1+(n-1)].$$

In the worst case, we get

$$\Delta^* = n\ell_{(k,\tilde{b})}\ell_{(k,\tilde{b})}$$

and from (27) the energy function becomes

$$\begin{aligned} E_{iii}(x,y) &= -\frac{1}{4}pm + \frac{1}{2}p\ell_{(k,\tilde{a})} + \frac{1}{2}m\ell_{(k,\tilde{b})} - n\ell_{(k,\tilde{a})}\ell_{(k,\tilde{b})} \\ &= E_i(x_k, y_k) + \frac{1}{2}\ell_{(k,\tilde{a})}\left(p - n\ell_{(k,\tilde{b})}\right) + \frac{1}{2}\ell_{(k,\tilde{b})}\left(m - n\ell_{(k,\tilde{a})}\right). \end{aligned}$$

Therefore, if the following capacity condition holds

$$n < \min\left\{\frac{m}{\ell_{(k,\tilde{a})}}, \frac{p}{\ell_{(k,\tilde{b})}}\right\} \quad (29)$$

then $E_i = E(x_k, y_k)$ is the local minimum for a pair $\{x_k, y_k\}$ and it holds that there exist local minima for all pairs $\{x_k, y_k : k = 1..n\}$,

$$E(x_k, y_k) = E_i < E_{iii} = E(x, y) \qquad x \neq x_i, y \neq y_i \qquad (i \neq k)$$

for sufficiently small number of bit-reversal in $\{x, y\}$. Furthermore, these local minima are distinct with each other.

□

References

[1] B. Kosko, "Adaptive bidirectional associative memories," *Applied Optics*, vol. 26, pp. 4947–4960, Dec 1987.

[2] B. Kosko, "Bidirectional associative memories," *IEEE Trans. Syst. Man Cybern.*, vol. 18, pp. 49–60, Jan/Feb 1988.

[3] Y. F. Wang, J. B. Cruz, and J. H. Mulligan Jr., "Two coding strategies for bidirectional associative memory," *IEEE Trans. Neural Networks*, vol. 1, pp. 81–92, Mar 1990.

[4] Y. H. Pao, *Adaptive Pattern Recognition and Neural Networks.* Massachusetts: Addision-Wesley, 1989.

[5] T. Kohonen, *Self-Organization and Associative Memory.* New York: Springer-Verlag, 1984.

[6] R. J. McEliece, E. C. Posner, E. R. Rodemich, and S. S. Venkatesh, "The capacity of the hopfield associative memory," *IEEE Trans. Inform. Theory*, vol. IT-33, pp. 461–482, July 1987.

[7] K. Haines and R. Hecht-Nielsen, "A bam with increased information storage capacity," in *Proc. IJCNN 88*, pp. 181–190, 1988.

[8] D. E. Rumelhart and J. L. McClelland, *Parallel Distributed Processing.* Massachusetts: MIT Press, 1986.

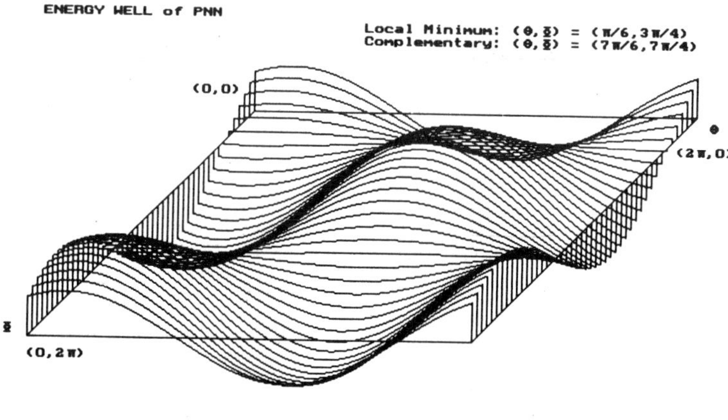

Figure 1: Energy Well of Phase Neural Network with One Learning Pair and One Complimentary Pattern

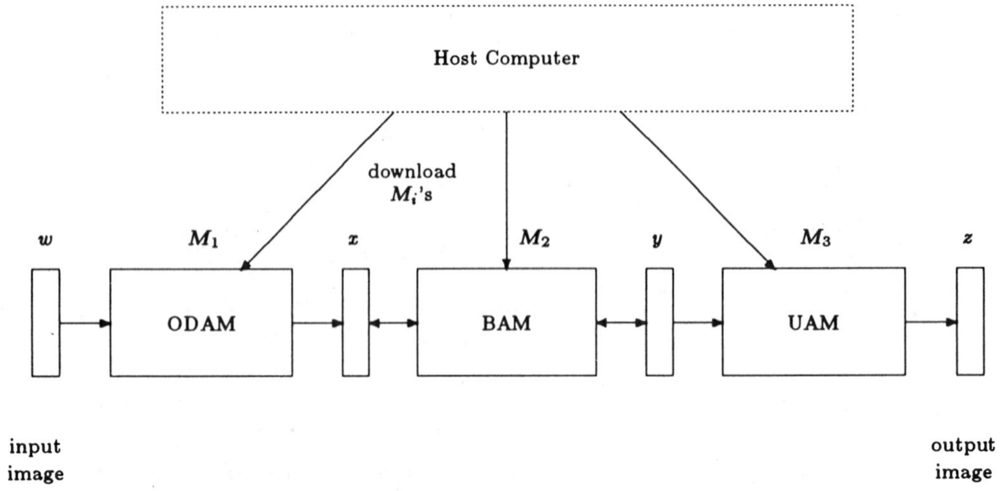

Figure 2: Block Diagram of MANN

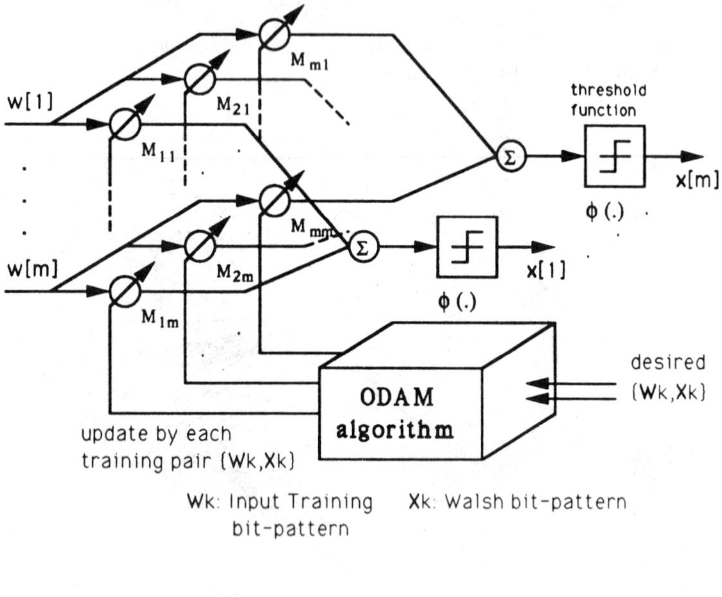

Figure 3: Learning Structure of First Synapse (ODAM)

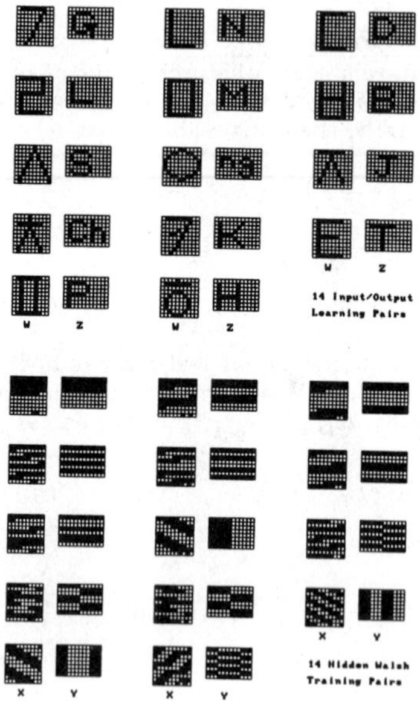

Figure 4: 14 Training Pairs of English and Korean Characters with 14 Hidden Walsh Trainee Pairs

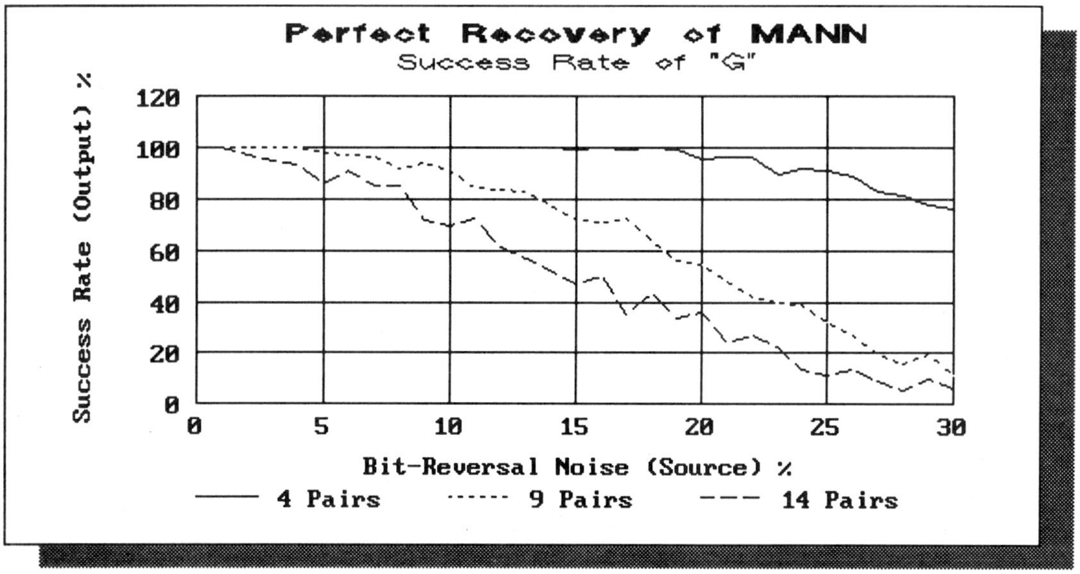

Figure 6: Success Rate (%) of MANN Given Source-side Bit-reversal Noise

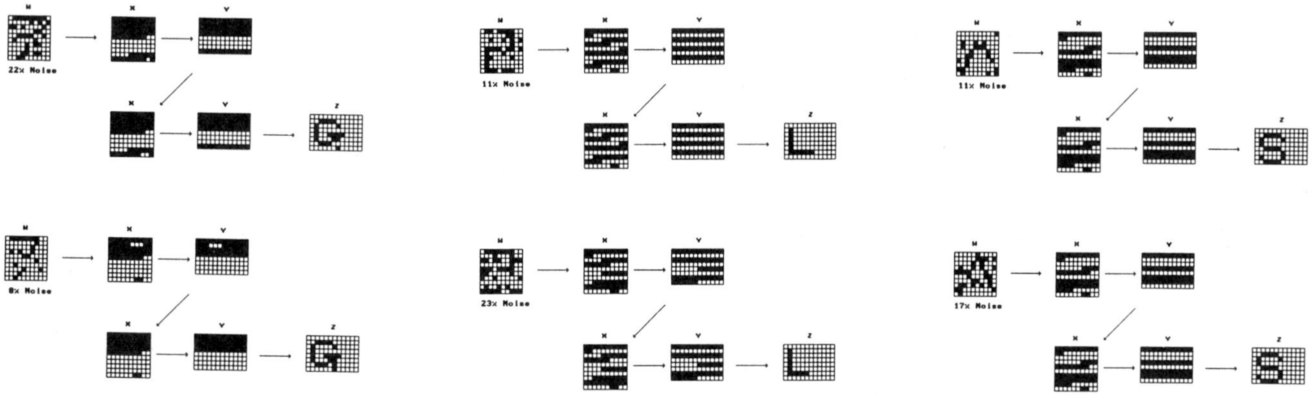

Figure 5: Recall Processes in Noise (with 14 Training Pairs Stored)

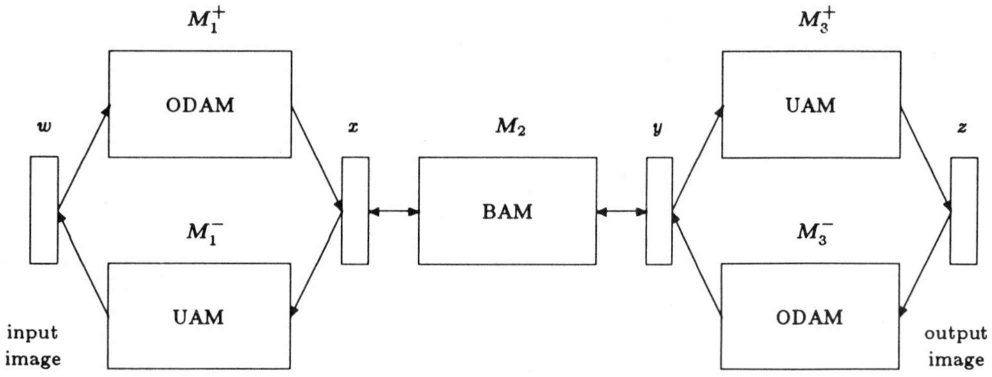

Figure 7: Block Diagram of Bidirectional MANN

Proc. of the 1993 IEEE
Int.'l Conf. on Tools with AI,
Boston, Massachusetts, Nov. 1993

Neural-Logic Belief Networks—a Tool for Knowledge Representation and Reasoning

Boon Toh LOW boontoh@cs.su.oz.au
Knowledge Systems Group, Basser Department of Computer Science
University of Sydney, NSW 2006, Australia

Abstract

This paper sketches a new architecture for representing knowledge and performing commonsense reasoning. It is an acyclical directed graph formalism with a neural network computation model and a Prolog-style unification mechanism called Neural-Logic Belief Network. In this representation, a concept is either believed, its negation is believed, unknown, or in the state of contradiction. Each proposition also has a degree-of-belief value to represent its reliability and/or certainty. Every directed link carries a tuple of real numbers to model a three-valued logic and other relations such as the commonsense IF-THEN rules. Due to the nature of network computation, it has an extreme level of tolerance to contradictory input knowledge.

1 Introduction

With a definite clause selection sequence and performs resolutions over Horn-clauses, Prolog—a logic programming language (e.g. [9], [1]), has been a popular AI knowledge representation and problem solving tool. However, its inheritance from classical logic and adoption of negation handling strategies bring about several limitations. One may question about its insistence on two-valued logical representation where vagueness and uncertainty of knowledge has no part to play, or does its logical consistency too strict for human commonsense reasoning? Neural networks (e.g. [8], [2]), which are recognized as good formalisms in performing pattern matching/classifications, do not posses some of these limitations. But one major criticism is their sub-symbolic nature of knowledge representation which makes commonsense reasoning within the systems extremely difficult, if not impossible.

In this paper, we try to solve these problems by incorporate ideas from both formalisms into the new knowledge representation system. This system is based on an acyclical finite directed network formalism with four belief truth values and it is called *Neural-Logic Belief Network.* On the one hand, it resembles the basic computational structures of a neural net; on the other hand, with a fixed computation model and semantic interpretation for each node and group of links in the networks, symbolic knowledge is represented explicitly and a more general than Prolog-liked programming environment is created.

2 Neural-Logic Belief Networks

A *Neural-Logic Belief Network* [6][1], or *belief network* for short, is a finite acyclical directed graph (nodes and directed links) with a neural network computation model. To represent knowledge with variables, we need a three-level belief network: the lower *propositional net*, the *predicate net* and the upper *variable layer.*

The propositional net represents basic beliefs for commonsense reasoning where predicate layer allows us to lift knowledge from plain propositions up to abstract predicated form where we can reason about knowledge with variables. When some of the variables are instantiated, part of the predicate net (i.e. the grounded nodes) is transformed into propositions and it can be duplicated onto the propositional layer. The variable layer represents binding relations of variables in predicate net. Figure 1 shows a typical three-layer Neural-Logic Belief Network.

In the propositional layer, there are two types of nodes: *input nodes* and *propositional base nodes.* Each node represents a *proposition* and has a *node value* to indicate its current belief state. Input nodes receive input knowledge (propositions) and propagate them via directed input links to the relevant base nodes. As we allow incomplete and inconsistent input knowledge, input nodes can represent different views of the same proposition from different sources. For propositional base nodes, each proposition is uniquely repre-

[1] [6] describes the details of propositional belief networks.

1063-6730/93 $03.00 © 1993 IEEE

sented by one node and the collection of all base nodes (including all higher layer base nodes) represents the belief state, usually denoted as S.

A node value is an ordered pair: (proposition-value, degree-of-belief value). There are three possibilities for the proposition-value (t, f): (1, 0) means that the proposition associated with the node is believed, (0, 1) that the negation of the proposition is believed, and (0, 0) that it is neither believed nor not-believed. The degree-of-belief values (written as deg[(proposition)]) induce a total asymmetric order (TAO) on the strength or certainty of the propositions. For example, we may have a total order for beliefs such as

0 <weakly<normally<strongly<surely<definitely

If we let "0" denotes the weakest value then ((0, 0), 0) is the default node value of beliefs including those currently not represented by the network (i.e. unknown beliefs). In a belief state S, a base node a ((0, 0), 0) means both $a \notin S$ and $\neg a \notin S$. A base node a ((0, 0), deg[a]>0) means that a currently has contradictory beliefs at deg[a], i.e. $a \in S$ and $\neg a \in S$. A base node "a" having a node value of ((1, 0), deg[a]) means that $a \in S$ while a node value of ((0, 1), deg[a]) means $\neg a \in S$.

In the predicate layer, every node is a *predicate base node* (with a default node value of ((0, 0), 0) unless fully instantiated) and they each represents a *predicate* with *n variables* (n-ary predicate where $n \geq 1$). Here, we employ the usual interpretations of predicates and individuals of classical first order logic. Unary predicates are used to represent class membership and other n-ary predicates ($n \geq 2$) are used to express relations among variables. For example, we may have a node to represent the class of dogs denoted as *"(X)_is_a_dog"* where X is a variable which can be instantiated to *a name of an individual* from some input propositions so that this particular individual belongs to the class of *is_a_dog*. There is one unique *prototypical predicate* for each n-ary predicate represented by the predicate layer. All other n-ary predicates with the same predicate name (but with different group of variable-links to other nodes) are assumed to carry the same semantic as their prototypical predicate. These nodes only represent co-existence of different instantiations of their prototypical predicate. Two such nodes for the relation *"(A)_is_the_parent_of_(B)"* have to be created in the commonsense rules *"IF (X)_is_the_parent_of_(Y) and (Y)_is_the_parent_of_(Z) THEN (X)_is_the_grandparent_of_(Z)"*..

For each proposition base node at the propositional layer, if it is an instance of a predicate base node, an

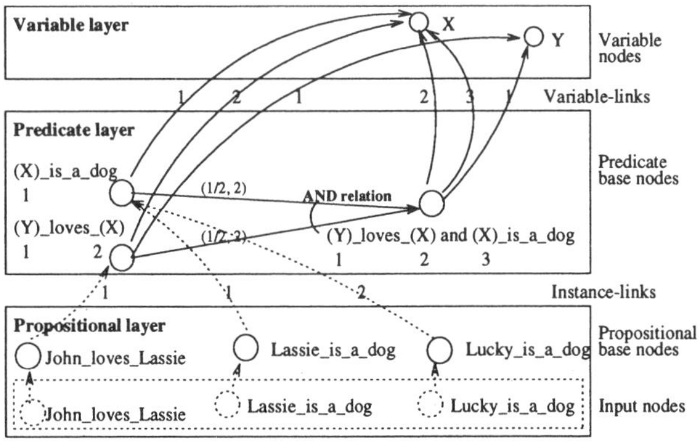

Figure 1: Construction of inter-layer links.

instance-link is linked from the proposition base node to its corresponding prototypical predicate base node. These are inter-layer connections from propositional layer to predicate layer. A prototypical predicate base node may have multiple proposition instances, i.e. propositional base nodes with the same predicate name but different individuals. To differentiate these instances, each instance-links pointing to a prototypical predicate base node is assigned with a different ascending instance number *inst* starting from 1 (one series of numbers per prototypical predicate base node). Figure 1 shows that there are two instances for the prototypical predicate base node *"(X)_is_a_dog"* and one instance for *"(Y)_loves_(X)"*.

The variable layer consists of a finite set of disconnected *variable nodes*. There is no node value attached to them and they contain empty slots which can be filled by instantiated individual names during network computation. Variable-links are used to transmit the correct binding of variables for predicate base nodes during instantiations (from predicate base nodes in predicate layer to variable nodes in variable layer or vice versa). Each variable in a predicate base node is indexed to a natural number p ($p \geq 1$) according to its position appeared in the naming of the predicate. One variable node is created for each variable and and it is linked by a variable-link with the index number p from the predicate base node. For example, a predicate base node *(Y)_loves_(X)* will have the variable Y indexed to 1 and X indexed to 2. From this node a variable-link carrying an index number of 1 is linked to a variable node representing variable Y in the variable layer and another variable-link with an index number of 2 to a variable node representing variable X (see figure 1).[2]

[2]Variables with the same symbol within a belief expression are assumed to represent the same individuals.

3 Instantiation

Instantiation is the process of temporarily assigning individual names to the variable nodes for any instance of computation. Here we adopt the same principle of unification from Prolog (e.g.[9]). Firstly, from the predicate base node considered, an input instance (a proposition in the propositional layer) with an instance number of *inst* is selected and the individual names are mapped to the positions p of the variables in the predicate base node. These names are put into the appropriated variable nodes in the variable layer via the correspondingly indexed variable-links p. When node value computations for other predicate base nodes take place, if they are of the same instance, the individual names carried by variable nodes are mapped down to the predicates accordingly. When computation for a particular instance cease, the variable nodes are made empty (the default state) for further instantiations. In figure 1, if instance 1 of *"(X)_is_a_dog"* is selected, then X in the variable layer will be instantiated to *"Lassie"*. Reasoning of co-existing instances of a predicate at a single instance is also possible under this formalism.

4 Links within each layer

Within the propositional layer, there are three types of links [6]:

- *Combinative-links* are the most basic links in the network to make all kinds of relations among base nodes.
- *Rule-links* are used to connect the premise nodes of the rules to the conclusion nodes.
- *Input-links* are used to propagate input values from input nodes to propositional base nodes.

These directed links serve as signal transmission channels from one node to another within the same layer of belief networks. The strength of information passing through any link is controlled (reduced or amplified) by an ordered pair of link weights (u, v), $u, v \in$ {Real Numbers}. Analogous to the proposition-values of nodes, the first weight u is an excitatory value and the second weight v is an inhibitory value. In the predicate layer, only combinative- and rule- links are used, and there is no inter-node link within the variable layer.

5 Network computation and representing relations

Basically, the computation functions of belief networks are similar to that of a neural-net where at each node, a summation function totals the inputs from incoming combinative-links, i.e. the products of the link-weights and the incoming node's proposition-value. This value then goes through a thresholding function which decides the node value for the node. For input- and rule- links, instead of summing all inputs, each incoming link is considered as alternative input and computed accordingly. A selection function is then used to pick up the strongest input among the computed alternative values. Due to space constraint, please refer to [6] for details.

Predicate base nodes are computed in the same way except for every instance of computation, a particular instance of proposition for the predicate under consideration has to be selected and Prolog-style instantiation matching is carried out across the network. Only successfully instantiated predicate base nodes are assigned with the computed node values.

Neural-Logic Belief Networks are capable of representing many different types of classical logical connectives as well as other relations using directed links [6]. Logical expressions are constructed by combinative-links and they follow Kleene's strong three-valued logic [4]. For example, a two input OR relation $a \vee b$ and a two input AND relation $c \wedge d$ are represented as:

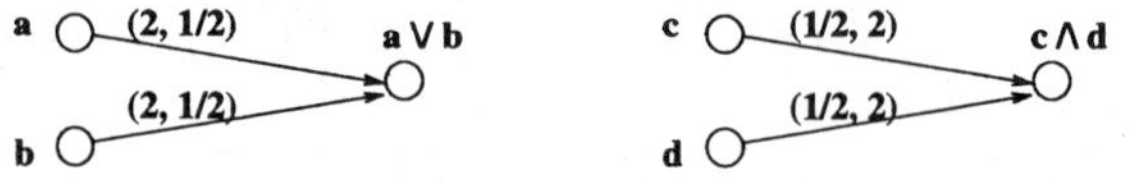

where (2, 1/2) and (1/2, 2) are the corresponding link weights. For an n-input OR, each link weight is $(2, \frac{1}{n})$ and for n-input AND relations, the link weights are $(\frac{1}{n}, 2)$. Details and other logical expressions such as the Material Implication, Negation, IF-AND-ONLY-IF, Exclusive OR, etc., are given in [6].

In addition to classical logical relations, commonsense defeasible rules are represented explicitly by rule-links from the condition base nodes to the conclusion base nodes. The interpretation of a rule e.g. *"IF a THEN b"* is straight forward and it does not acquire the sometimes undesirable property of $\neg b \rightarrow \neg a$ which is automatically associated with a material implication $a \rightarrow b$. Typical link weights carried by a rule-link for an IF-THEN rule is (1, 0). Other combinations such as IF-THEN-Not, IF-Not-THEN, etc., are possible. Direct representation of general relations such as human biases and human subjectivities can also be easily represented [6]. As belief networks accept inconsistent knowledge, *Inconsistency Reasoning* [7] is performed to ensure that all resulting belief states are consistent.

6 Knowledge update and network propagation

There is a set of network update operators for belief networks: *Add, Update, Remove, Forget, Revise* and *Not-to-Conclude.* This set of operators together with the procedures for creating inter-layer links and variable nodes are the means for building a belief network. They are used for incorporating new knowledge into the belief state or expelling existing knowledge that are no longer believed. The belief state after any update operations will remain consistent as consistency reasoning algorithms are part of the update procedures. Detailed characteristics of each of the update operator and a comparison with the AGM Belief Revision operators [3] are given in [5].

In the propositional layer, a belief network could be propagated (using the computation functions) in two modes: Forward Propagation and Backward Chaining. In Forward Propagation mode, node values are propagated from all the input nodes to all the propositional base nodes using the computation functions defined until the whole net settles at a stable state. In Backward Chaining mode we will have a set of propositions of interest and the respective base nodes (base node with the some proposition) are selected. To have the node value of each of these base nodes, network computation is carried out for each incoming node in a backward manner. This backward chaining process terminates when it reaches the input node(s). In the predicate layer, only backward chaining similar to that of Prolog's backward chaining is applicable.

7 Conclusions

Neural-Logic Belief Network is a generalization of logic programming.[3] With the ability to represent four truth values (believe, not believe, unknown and contradiction) and the knowledge certainty value (degree-of-belief value), it provides proper treatment to negations and can be use to represent expert knowledge base with incomplete information, vagueness and/or uncertainties. Relations among knowledge in this formalism such as AND, OR, etc., are considered as competitive and co-operative inputs. The direct representation of non-classical and more complex relations in the links opens up a convenient way for creating expert systems. This system adopts Prolog-style unification but variable bindings from instances to instances can be easily revealed from the variable layer. The set of update operators and consistency reasoning enforce overall consistency of the knowledge base represented although inputs may be contradictory to each other.

We would like to investigate the possibility of introducing temporal reasoning into this belief network formalism. This may open up the scope for Temporal Neural-Logic Belief Network to be used for reasoning about actions and as the platform for more elaborated expert systems such as real-time robotic and process control.

[3] Part of the Neural-Logic Belief Network system has been implemented using Prolog on a unix machine.

Acknowledgement

This research is supported in part by an EMSS grant. I would like to thank members of Knowledge Systems Group, especially Norman Foo, for their invaluable suggestions and criticisms.

References

[1] Ivan Bratko. *Prolog Programming for Artificial Intelligence.* Addison-Wesley, Wokingham, England, 1986.

[2] Joachim Diederich, editor. *Artificial Neural Networks:Concept Learning.* IEEE Computer Society Press, Los Alamitos, California, 1990.

[3] Peter Gardenfors. *Knowledge in Flux.* MIT Press, Cambridge, Massachusetts, 1988.

[4] Stephen Cole Kleene. *Introduction to Metamathematics.* North Holland, Amsterdam, 1964.

[5] Boon Toh Low and Norman Y. Foo. Towards a network for representing beliefs. In *Proceedings of the Second International Computer Science Conference*, pages 85–91, Hong Kong, 1992. IEEE.

[6] Boon Toh Low and Norman Y. Foo. A network formalism for commonsense reasoning. In *Proceedings of the Sixteenth Australian Computer Science Conference*, pages 425–434, Brisbane, 1993.

[7] Boon Toh Low and Norman Y. Foo. Towards human-like consistency reasoning. Submitted to a special issue of "Annals of Mathematics and Artificial Intelligence", 1993.

[8] David E. Rumelhart. *Parallel Distributed Processing: Explorations in the Microstructure of Cognition.* MIT Press, Cambridge, Massachusetts, 1986.

[9] Leon Sterling and Ehud Shapiro. *The Art of Prolog.* The MIT Press, Cambridge, Massachusetts, 1986.

Efficient Learning and Planning Within the Dyna Framework *

Jing Peng and Ronald J. Williams
College of Computer Science
Northeastern University
Boston, MA 02115
jp@corwin.ccs.northeastern.edu
rjw@corwin.ccs.northeastern.edu

Abstract

Sutton's Dyna framework provides a novel and computationally appealing way to create integrated learning, planning, and reacting systems. Examined here is a class of strategies designed to enhance the learning and planning power of Dyna systems by increasing their computational efficiency. The benefit of using these strategies is demonstrated on some simple abstract learning tasks.

1 Introduction

Many problems faced by an autonomous agent in an unknown environment can be cast in the form of *reinforcement learning* tasks. Recent work in this area has led to a clearer understanding of the relationship between algorithms found useful for such tasks and asynchronous approaches to dynamic programming (Bertsekas & Tsitsiklis, 1989), and this understanding has led in turn to both new results relevant to the theory of dynamic programming (Barto, Bradtke, & Singh, 1991; Watkins & Dayan, 1991; Williams & Baird, 1990) and the creation of new reinforcement learning algorithms, such as *Q-learning* (Watkins, 1989) and *Dyna* (Sutton, 1990; 1991). Dyna was proposed as a simple but principled way to achieve more efficient reinforcement learning in autonomous agents, and this paper proposes enhancements designed to improve this learning efficiency still further.

*We wish to thank Rich Sutton for his many valuable suggestions and continuing encouragement. This work was supported by Grant IRI-8921275 from the National Science Foundation.

0-7803-0999-5/93/$03.00 ©1993 IEEE

2 Q-Learning and Dynamic Programming

As Barto, Sutton, and Watkins (1989) have pointed out, an appropriate formal framework for studying reinforcement learning algorithms is the theory of *dynamic programming* (Bertsekas, 1987). as applied to *Markov decision problems.* A Markov decision problem has the following general form. At each discrete time step, the agent observes its current state x, uses this information to select action a, receives an immediate reward r and then observes the resulting next state y, which becomes the current state at the next time step. In general, r and y may be random, but their probability distributions are assumed to depend only on x and a.

At each time step k we would like the learning system to select action $a(k)$ so that the *expected total discounted reward*

$$E\left\{\sum_{j=0}^{\infty} \gamma^j r(k+j)\right\}$$

is maximized, where $r(l)$ represents the reward received at time step l and γ is a fixed discount factor between 0 and 1. A function that assigns to each state an action maximizing the expected total discounted reward is called an *optimal policy.*

Dynamic programming methods for finding such a policy entail first determining the *optimal state-value function* V, which assigns to each state the expected total discounted reward obtained when an optimal policy is followed starting in that state. Following Watkins (1989), we can define a closely related function that assigns to each state-action pair a value measuring the expected total discounted reward obtained when the given action is taken in the given state and the optimal policy is followed thereafter. That is, using the notation given above, with x the current state, a the current action, r the resulting immediate reward, and y the resulting next state,

$$\begin{aligned} Q(x,a) &= E\{r + \gamma V(y) | x, a\} \quad (1) \\ &= R(x,a) + \gamma \sum_y P_{xy}(a) V(y), \end{aligned}$$

where $R(x,a) = E\{r|x,a\}$, $V(x) = \max_a Q(x,a)$, and $P_{xy}(a)$ is the probability of making a state transition from x to y as a result of applying action a. Note that once we have this Q-function it is straightforward to determine the optimal policy. For any state x the optimal action is simply $\arg\max_a Q(x,a)$.

Watkins's *Q-learning* algorithm is based on maintaining an estimate $\hat{Q}$ of the Q-function and updating it so that (1), with estimated values substituted for the unknown actual values, comes to be more nearly satisfied for each state-action pair encountered. More precisely, the algorithm is as follows: At each transition from one time step to the next, the learning system observes the current state x, takes action a, receives immediate reward r, and observes the next state y. Assuming a tabular representation of these estimates, $\hat{Q}(x,a)$ is left unchanged for all state-action pairs not equal to (x,a) and

$$\hat{Q}(x,a) \leftarrow \hat{Q}(x,a) + \alpha \left[r + \gamma \hat{V}(y) - \hat{Q}(x,a) \right], \quad (2)$$

where $\alpha \in (0,1]$ is a learning rate parameter and $\hat{V}(y) = \max_b \hat{Q}(y,b)$. An estimate of the optimal action at any state x is obtained in the obvious way as $\arg\max_a \hat{Q}(x,a)$.

This algorithm is an example of what Sutton (1988) has called a *temporal difference* method because the quantity $r + \gamma\hat{V}(y) - \hat{Q}(x,a)$ can be interpreted as the difference between two successive predictions of an appropriate expected total discounted reward. The general effect of such algorithms is to correct earlier predictions to more closely match later ones.

Throughout this paper we will usually use the term *backup* to refer to a single application of equation (2). Each backup leads to updating of the Q-estimate for a single state-action pair. There are other related reinforcement learning algorithms in which a corresponding set of estimates of state values or state-action values are maintained and updated in a similar fashion, and the term *backup* is frequently applied in these cases as well, but we will the more self-explanatory term *value function estimate update* when referring generically to the corresponding step of any such algorithm.

3 Dyna

A key feature of the Q-learning algorithm is that when combined with sufficient exploration it can be guaranteed to eventually converge to an optimal policy without ever having to learn and use an internal model of the environment (Watkins, 1989; Watkins & Dayan, 1992), From an AI point of view, what is interesting about this is that the eventual behavior of the system is as good as might be obtained if the system had carried out explicit *planning,* which can be thought of as simulation of possible future agent-environment interactions in an internal model to determine long-range consequences.

However, the cost of not using an internal model is that convergence to the optimal policy can be very slow. In a large state space, many backups may be required before the necessary information is propagated to where it is important. To correct this weakness, Sutton (1990; 1991) has introduced the *Dyna* class of reinforcement learning architectures, in which a form of planning is performed in addition to learning. This means that such an architecture includes an internal world model along with mechanisms for learning it. But the novel aspect of this approach is that planning is treated as being virtually identical to reinforcement learning except that while learning updates the appropriate value function estimates according to experience as it actually occurs, planning differs only in that it updates these same value function estimates for simulated transitions chosen from the world model. It is assumed that there is computation time for several such updates during each actual step taken in the world, and the algorithm involves performing some fixed number of total updates during each actual time step. The organization of a Dyna system is shown on the top of Figure 1.

In this paper we focus on a version (called *Dyna-Q* by Sutton) whose underlying reinforcement learning algorithm is Q-learning. By performing several backups at each time step and avoiding the restriction that these backups occur only at current state transitions, such a system can perform much more effectively than simple Q-learning. In Sutton's work the learned world model was simply a suitably indexed record of (state, action, next-state, immediate-reward) 4-tuples actually encountered in the past, and simulated experiences were obtained for planning purposes by selecting uniformly randomly from this record. His simulations demonstrated that such a system improves its performance much faster than a simple Q-learning system.

4 Queue-Dyna

Although Sutton's (1990; 1991) demonstrations of Dyna showed that use of several randomly chosen

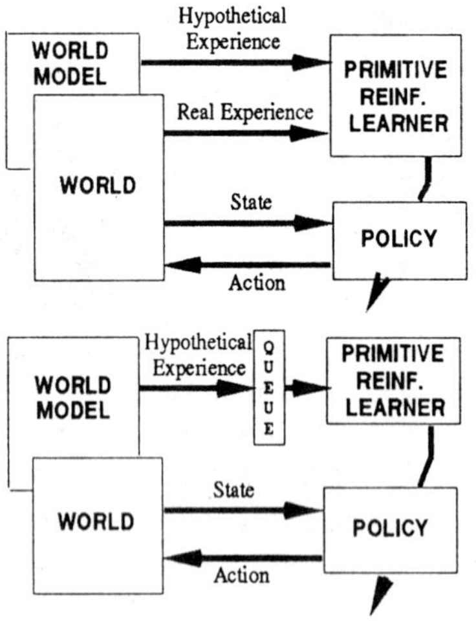

Figure 1: Overview of the Dyna architecture (on the top) and the queue-Dyna architecture (on the bottom). The primitive reinforcement learner represents an algorithm like Q-learning. Not shown is the data path allowing the world model to learn to mimic the world.

past experiences along with the current experience for value function estimate updates outperforms the use of current experience only, it is natural to ask whether a more focused use of simulated experiences could lead to even better performance. This is the motivation for proposing *queue-Dyna*, a version of Dyna in which value function estimate updates are prioritized and only those having the highest priority are performed at each time step. The organization of a queue-Dyna system is shown on the bottom of Figure 1.

Here we examine two specific versions of this strategy employing slightly different criteria for prioritizing the potential updates. One of these applies to both deterministic and stochastic tasks, although the details of the respective algorithms differ somewhat, and the other currently applies only to deterministic tasks.

In all cases, an important aspect of the algorithm is the identification of places where the value function estimates may require updating, as will be more fully explained below. We call these places *update candidates*. In the Q-learning version we use here, these are state-action pairs for which a resulting next state and immediate reward prediction can be made. As in the work of Sutton, we take these to be simply state-action pairs that have been experienced at least once in the world.

4.1 Deterministic Environment

For any state-action pair (x, a) under consideration, define the *prediction difference* to be

$$r + \gamma \hat{V}(y) - \hat{Q}(x, a),$$

where r is the immediate reward and y the next state known from the model to result from state-action pair (x, a). Each update candidate is first checked to see if there is any significant prediction difference (based on comparison with an appropriate threshold). If there is, then its priority is determined and it is placed on the queue for eventual updating. The top several update candidates are then removed from the queue on each time step and the backup

$$\hat{Q}(x, a) \leftarrow r + \gamma \hat{V}(y) \quad (3)$$

actually performed for each. Note that this is the same as equation (2) with $\alpha = 1$.

New update candidates are obtained from two main sources on each time step. For any backup actually performed, if the state-value estimate for the corresponding predecessor changes, then all transitions into that state become update candidates. The current transition is also made an update candidate, and this represents a further subtle difference between this approach and that investigated by Sutton. While one of the several backups performed during a single time step was always reserved for the current state-action pair in his system, in our approach it is given no special priority.

One other interesting source of update candidates that can be used effectively in this approach is externally provided information about changes in the environmental reward or transition structure, as we examine later.

4.1.1 Priority Based on Prediction Difference Magnitude

One straighforward way to assign priority to an update candidate, also recently explored extensively in independent work of Moore and Atkeson (1992), is to simply use the magnitude of the prediction difference. The larger the difference, the higher the priority. In the type of task studied in the experiments reported below, the effect of this strategy is a breadth-first spread of value estimate updates outward from a high-reward goal state following its discovery.

4.1.2 Priority Based on Effect on Start-State Value

Another interesting strategy that is appropriate for problems having a well-defined start state s is to try to estimate what the effect of any update would be on the estimated long-term reward at this start state. Our efforts at developing a general approach for this are preliminary at this point, so we sketch the details here only for one useful subclass of problem where we have identified a sensible algorithm for this: deterministic environments having a single terminal positive reward, with all other rewards being zero. If we also assume that all initial value estimates are overly pessimistic, it then makes sense to use

$$\gamma^{d(x)}[r + \gamma \hat{V}(y)]$$

as the priority for updating $\hat{Q}(x, a)$, where $d(x)$ is an estimate of the minimum number of time steps required to go from s to x. There are various choices for $d(x)$ that one might sensibly use. For example, if the state space is equipped with a metric, one might choose $d(x)$ to be proportional to the metric distance between s and x. An even more interesting choice is to try to maintain an estimate of the length of the shortest path from s to x in a manner that is entirely analogous to the manner in which discounted total rewards are estimated. In particular, we can use another priority queue for the necessary updates and thereby maintain fairly accurate estimates of the actual proximity of states visited to the start state very efficiently.

The overall effect of a priority scheme of this type is that backups are directed in a more focused way. In the type of task studied in the experiments reported below, the effect of this strategy is to perform value estimate updates in the same order as an A^* search would proceed from the high-reward goal state backwards toward the start state, with the d function serving as the heuristic estimate of remaining path length (backward) to the start state.

4.2 Stochastic Environment

Starting from equation (1) we can write

$$\begin{aligned} Q(x,a) &= E\{r + \gamma V(y) | x, a\} \\ &= \sum_y P_{xy}(a) E\{r + \gamma V(y) | x, a, y\} \\ &= \sum_y P_{xy}(a) [E\{r | x, a, y\} + \gamma V(y)] \quad (4) \end{aligned}$$

For an environment which may be stochastic, it then makes sense to form a learned model by storing all past experiences together with appropriate counters and using this to compute estimates $\hat{P}_{xy}(a)$ of the relevant transition probabilities as well as estimates $\hat{R}_y(x, a)$ of $E\{r|x, a, y\}$, the expected immediate rewards conditioned on next state. We can then maintain estimates $\hat{Q}_y(x, a)$ of the bracketed expression on the right-hand side of (4) and update them using

$$\hat{Q}_y(x,a) \leftarrow \hat{R}_y(x,a) + \gamma \hat{V}(y), \quad (5)$$

with Q-value estimates computed using

$$\hat{Q}(x,a) = \sum_y \hat{P}_{xy}(a) \hat{Q}_y(x,a).$$

In this case a natural choice of prediction difference is

$$\hat{P}_{xy}(a) \left[\hat{R}_y(x,a) + \gamma \hat{V}(y) - \hat{Q}_y(x,a) \right],$$

and it is appropriate to count a single application of (5) as one backup.

Just as in the deterministic case, one useful way to assign priority to any update candidate (x, a) is to set it equal to the magnitude of this prediction difference and this is used in one of the experiments described below. However, it is not straightforward to generalize the more focused method described earlier for tasks with a single starting state to stochastic environments, since both the probability of landing at a state and the number of actions taken must be taken into account in general.

5 Experimental Demonstrations

Here we describe the results of several experiments designed to test the performance of the methods proposed. In particular, the following three algorithms were used in these experiments: (1) Dyna with updating along randomly chosen transitions, together with the current transition, as in Sutton's (1990; 1991) work; (2) queue-Dyna with priority determined by prediction difference magnitude; and (3) queue-Dyna with priority determined by estimated value of the start state. For this last algorithm, estimates of minimum distance from the starting state were maintained using an additional queue, as outlined above. In the interest of brevity, henceforth we refer to these algorithms as *random-update Dyna*, *largest-first Dyna*, and *focused Dyna*, respectively.

All tasks studied involved discrete 2-dimensional maze navigation tasks of the kind studied by Sutton (1990; 1991). Some of the mazes used are shown in Figures 2, 4, and 5. Shaded cells in these figures represent barriers, and the agent can occupy any other cell within such a maze and can move about by choosing one of four actions at each discrete time step. Each of these actions has the effect of moving the agent to an adjacent cell in one of the four compass directions, north, east, south, or west, except that any action that would ostensibly move the agent into a barrier cell or outside the maze has the actual effect of keeping the agent at its current location. All tasks studied here have a well-defined start state (marked S in the figures) and a single goal state (indicated by G), with all rewards equal to 0 except upon arrival at the goal state, when a reward of 100 was delivered. After arrival at the goal state the agent is always placed back at the start state.

In every experiment, the agent's efficiency at negotiating the maze from the start state to a goal state at various points in the learning process was measured by interspersing test trials with the normal activities of the agent. Each such test trial consisted of placing the agent at the start state and letting it execute its currently best action for each state visited until a goal state was reached (or until an upper limit on number of moves allowed was reached). At the end of such a test trial the agent resumed its usual activities from the state it had been in before the test trial began. These test trials were performed solely to obtain this data and no learning took place during them. Also, the normal activity of the agent included some random overriding of its current policy in order to foster exploration, and this was shut off during testing.

In all cases each system was allowed 5 updates for every action taken in the world (excluding actions taken during test trials). The discount parameter used throughout was $\gamma = 0.95$, and the queue-Dyna threshold parameter was set to 0.0001. The learning rate parameter for Dyna was set at $\alpha = 0.5$, which was found experimentally to optimize its performance across tasks. All Q-values were initialized to 0 at the start of each experiment.

One set of experiments was performed on a series of related tasks, each using essentially the same deterministic maze environment except for the coarseness of representation of the states and actions. The number of states ranged from 47 for the coarsest partitioning to 6016 for the finest. Two of these state spaces are shown in Figure 2 and another is shown in Figure 5. Results of some of these experiments are displayed in Figure 3. Both forms of queue-Dyna clearly show slower growth with respect to state space size than random-update Dyna. While there appears to be no clear difference between focused Dyna and largest-first Dyna in their ability to discover an optimal path, examination of the actual learning curves suggests that focused Dyna generally gives much more rapid improvement in the early stages of learning. The nature of the exploration strategy used may play a role in the specific results obtained, but this is an issue we have not addressed systematically in this work.

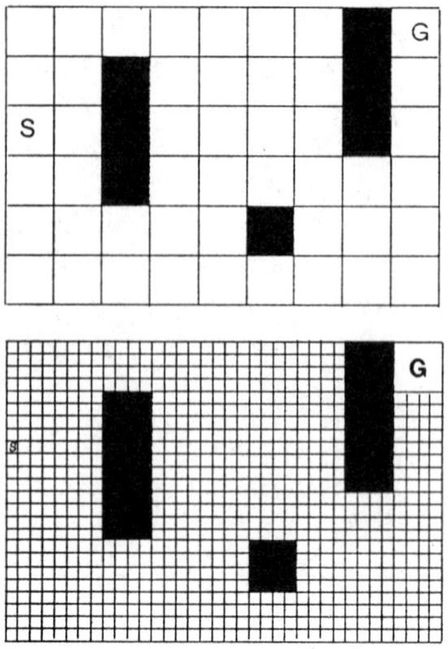

Figure 2: Two maze tasks. The one on the bottom is a more finely quantized version of the one on the top.

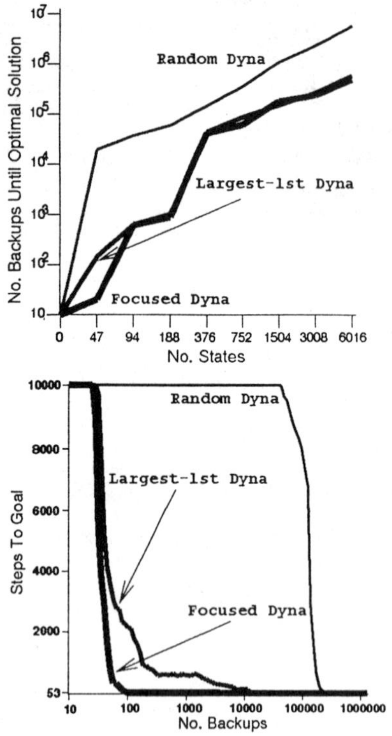

Figure 3: The graph on the top shows the number of backups required until optimal performance was obtained as a function of state space size. These numbers represent averages over 10 runs. On the bottom are learning curves for the 752-state task shown on the right of Figure 2, averaged over 100 runs.

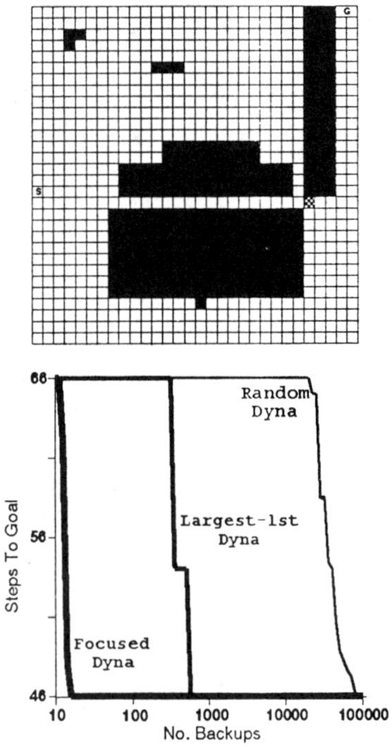

Figure 4: In this experiment, the agent first learned the shortest path to the goal with the cross-hatched block in place. This path, of length 66, goes along the bottom. Then this block was removed, creating a path of length 46, and the agent was "told" about this change in the environmental transition structure. Performance as a function of number of additional backups is shown on the bottom.

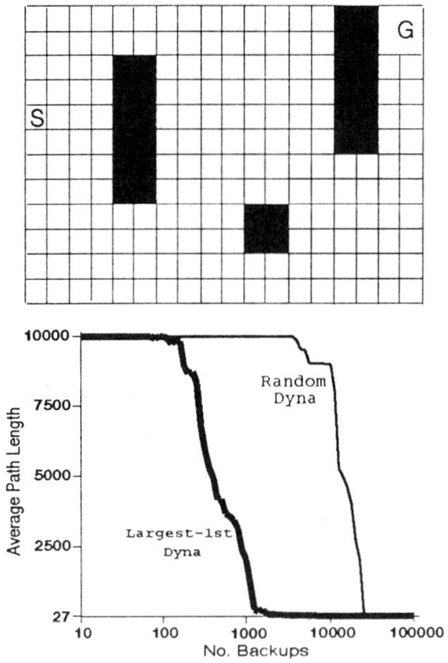

Figure 5: Maze used for the stochastic environment experiments and performance results obtained using the largest-first and random-update Dyna systems. The numbers plotted are averages over 10 runs.

It is also possible in any Dyna system to make use of externally provided information about changes in the environmental reward or transition structure. In one interesting experiment along these lines, we first let an agent learn to find the shortest path to the goal state in the maze shown on the top of Figure 4, with the cross-hatched cell occupied by a barrier. Then we opened up this cell and "told" the agent about it. More precisely, we updated its model to correctly reflect the effects of the 3 actions that could now move the agent into this cell and the 4 actions that could be taken from inside this cell. For queue-Dyna, we also placed these on the priority queue as if these actions had just been taken by the agent itself, and for the version that focuses backups toward the start state, we also placed these on the queue for updating of the minimum distance from the start state. Performance results for the 3 algorithms are shown on the bottom of Figure 4.

We also performed an experiment with a stochastic environment using the maze shown on the top of Figure 5, with the actions having a random effect. In particular, the direction of actual movement matched that of the action selected with a $\frac{2}{3}$ probability but there was a $\frac{1}{3}$ probability that the actual motion would be in one of the two adjacent compass directions instead, with the two "noisy" results being equally likely. For example, if the agent picked the action corresponding to the northward direction, its actual movement would be northward with probability $\frac{2}{3}$, westward with probability $\frac{1}{6}$, and eastward with probability $\frac{1}{6}$ (where these represent "virtual" directions in the sense that they result in no movement at all whenever such movement is illegal). Results of this experiment are shown on the bottom of Figure 5.

6 Issues and Further Directions

There are a number of relevant issues that we have not addressed here. Of substantial importance in realistic environments is the need for generalization in the world model. This presents some interesting challenges for the techniques investigated here, at least in their current form.

An additional aspect considered in some depth by Moore and Atkeson (1992) in their work with this approach is the issue of efficient exploration. While we have highlighted the efficiency of queue-Dyna in terms of number of backups required and have emphasized its relationship to backwards search from the goal, it is worth noting that a somewhat different behavior emerges when the initial value function estimates are overly optimistic when compared with the actual reward structure. With priority based on prediction difference magnitude, more backups are required but exploration occurs automatically as a result of following the current policy. As Moore and Atkeson have emphasized, the efficiency with which queue-Dyna propagates value function updates leads to much more purposeful exploration in such cases, and the agent can thus much more rapidly discover high-reward states.

7 Conclusion

We have proposed prioritizing the backups to be performed in Dyna in order to improve its efficiency and we have demonstrated on simple tasks that use of some specific prioritizing schemes can indeed lead to drastic reductions in computational effort and corresponding dramatic improvements in learning performance. Thus we argue that not only does the Dyna framework represent a useful conceptual basis for integrated learning, planning, and reacting systems, but we are also optimistic that simple improvements like those we have examined here can help give it sufficient power to allow it to serve as the basis for creating reinforcement learning systems that can adapt quickly to more complex and realistic environments.

References

Barto, A. G., Bradtke, S. J., & Singh, S. P. (1991). *Real-time learning and control using asynchronous dynamic programming* (COINS Technical Report 91-57). Department of Computer Science, University of Massachusetts, Amherst, MA.

Barto, A. G., Sutton, R. S., & Watkins, C. J. C. H. (1989). *Learning and sequential decision making* (COINS Technical Report 89-95). Department of Computer and Information Science, University of Massachusetts, Amherst, MA.

Bertsekas, D. P. (1987). *Dynamic Programming: Deterministic and Stochastic Models.* Englewood Cliffs, NJ: Prentice Hall.

Bertsekas, D. P. & Tsitsiklis, J. N. (1989). *Parallel and Distributed Computation: Numerical Methods.* Englewood Cliffs, NJ: Prentice Hall.

Moore, A. W. & Atkeson, C. G., (1992) Memory-based reinforement learning: Converging with less data and less real time, *Proceedings of NIPS*92.*

Sutton, R. S. (1988). Learning to predict by the methods of temporal differences. *Machine Learning, 3*, 9-44.

Sutton, R. S. (1990). Integrated architectures for learning, planning, and reacting based on approximating dynamic programming. *Proceedings of the Seventh International Conference in Machine Learning*, 216-224.

Sutton, R. S. (1991). Planning by incremental dynamic programming. *Proceedings of the 8th International Machine Learning Workshop.*

Sutton, R. S., Barto, A. G., & Williams, R. J. (1992). Reinforcement learning is direct adaptive optimal control. *IEEE Control Systems Magazine, 12*, 19-22.

Watkins, C. J. C. H. (1989). *Learning from delayed rewards.* Ph.D. Dissertation, Cambridge University, Cambridge, England.

Watkins, C. J. C. H. & Dayan, P. (1992). Q-learning. *Machine Learning, 8*, 279-292.

Williams, R. J. & Baird, L. C., III (1990). A mathematical analysis of actor-critic architectures for learning optimal controls through incremental dynamic programming. *Proceedings of the Sixth Yale Workshop on Adaptive and Learning Systems*, August 15-17, New Haven, CT, 96-101.

A Geometric View of Neural Networks Using Homotopy [1]

Frans M. Coetzee Virginia L. Stonick
Electrical and Computer Engineering Department
Carnegie Mellon University
Pittsburgh, PA 15213

Abstract – We formulate a homotopy approach for solving for the weights of a network, and show how this leads simply to a geometric interpretation of the weight optimization problem. The homotopy approach accounts for non-distinct sets of weights and infinite weights. The geometric interpretation further aids in explaining the appearance of local minima in the network, the appearance of infinite weights and the similarities and differences between optimizing the weights in a nonlinear network, and the weights in a linear network.

INTRODUCTION

While neural networks have been very successful in a number of applications, in theory learning by example requires *global optimization* of network parameters[1, 2], and approximating arbitrary input/output mappings requires *infinitely large* networks[3, 4]. Exploiting the potential of realizable neural networks to solve challenging nonlinear signal processing applications requires characterizing the input-output mappings for finite neural networks, and determining methods to compute the globally optimal parameter estimates. To begin accomplishing these objectives, we draw upon the powerful geometric projection operator perspective used in signal processing. For linear systems, the insight resulting from the development of this projector operator/error surface view has resulted in a number of very successful signal processing algorithms, particularly in adaptive filtering, e.g.[5]. In this work, we begin to bridge the gap between neural network theory and practice by using homotopy approaches to explore the geometrical properties of performance surfaces produced by finite neural networks.

Our work differs from previous homotopy approaches[6, 7] in that the homotopy equations are formulated to address the properties of the neural network directly.

[1] This research was funded in part by NSF Grant number MIP-9157221.

0-7803-0928-6/93$03.00

In this previous work, the node nonlinearity was approximated as a polynomial or a rational function, and established polynomial homotopy methods were used to solve for the weights. In this approach the number of solutions depends on how the nonlinearity is defined, equations can correspond to networks with unbounded nonlinearities, and little insight into the mapping performed by the network results. Further, these methods track the distinct roots of polynomials, while our approach allows the tracking of non-distinct sets of weights.

In work published after acceptance of this paper, a homotopy apparently similar to the one that will be presented here was evaluated by Yang et al[8]. However, as will be detailed in this paper, they do not account for the structure of the weight solutions nor do they attempt to characterize the mappings performed by the neural network.

This paper has the following outline: First a brief introduction to homotopy describes the requirements inherent to current homotopy approaches, after which the predictor setup and natural homotopy approach are defined. The results of analysis and implementation of the natural homotopy is then described, and examples illustrating theoretical concepts are presented.

HOMOTOPY METHODS

Homotopy methods find the solutions to a set of equations by mapping the known solutions from a simple initial system to the desired solution of the unsolved system of equations. Given certain restrictions, the procedure corresponds to tracking paths of solutions as the initial system is gradually transformed into the system for which a solution is desired. In general, homotopy methods are advantageous as they are globally convergent and can be constructed to be exhaustive.

Mathematically, the basic homotopy method is described as follows: Given *final* equations $\boldsymbol{f}(\boldsymbol{x}) = \mathbf{o}, \boldsymbol{f} : \boldsymbol{D} \subset \Re^n \rightarrow \Re^n$ to which a solution is desired, an initial system $\boldsymbol{g}(\boldsymbol{x}) = \mathbf{o}, \quad \boldsymbol{g} : \boldsymbol{D} \subset \Re^n \rightarrow \Re^n$ is chosen. A *homotopy* function $\boldsymbol{h} : \boldsymbol{D} \times T \rightarrow \Re^n$ is defined in terms of an embedded parameter $\tau \in T \subset \Re$, such that

$$\boldsymbol{h}(\boldsymbol{x}, \tau) = \begin{cases} \boldsymbol{g}(\boldsymbol{x}) & \text{when } \tau = 0 \\ \boldsymbol{f}(\boldsymbol{x}) & \text{when } \tau = 1 \end{cases} \tag{1}$$

In *natural* homotopy methods, the parameter τ represents some fundamental property of the system. The objective is to solve the final equations by solving $\boldsymbol{h}(\boldsymbol{x}, \tau) = \mathbf{o}$ numerically for $\boldsymbol{x}$ for increasing values of τ, starting at $\tau = 0$

and continuing to $\tau = 1$. The problem reduces to finding the solution to a differential equation, for which efficient numerical techniques exist[9, 10]. This method is successful if solutions for $h(x, \tau)$ exist for all τ and form paths that connect the initial solutions to the final solutions.

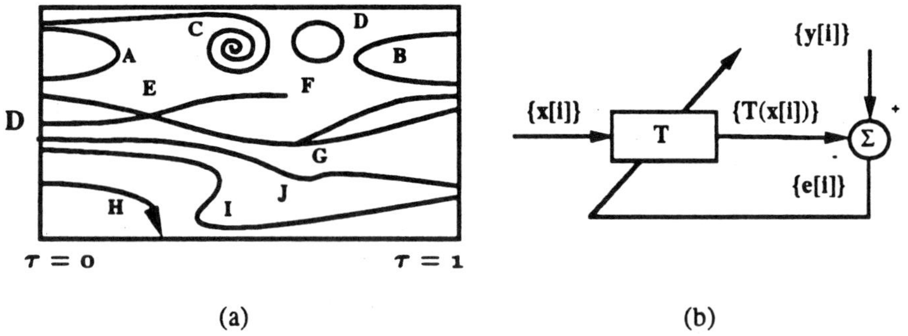

Figure 1: (a) Types of homotopy paths, (b) The general predictor problem

Possible paths are shown in Fig 1(a). Restrictions are imposed to obtain the desired types of paths, those similar in form to (I) and (J). Full rank and continuity conditions on the Jacobian of $\mathbf{h}$ prevent paths of the form (C), (E), (F) and (G)[10]. Paths of the form (D) are usually disregarded because they do not directly affect the results at $\tau = 0$ and $\tau = 1$. Divergence to infinity (H) can be prevented by restricting paths to the interior of D and is usually evaluated on a case by case basis, often by exploiting physical restrictions[11]. If the above restrictions are satisfied and the initial and final systems have the same number of solutions, then each initial solution maps onto a final solution such that the method is exhaustive.

While these methods are intuitively appealing and have significant potential benefit, establishing a homotopy relationship for a specific set of equations that result in well behaved paths is, in general, nontrivial. In particular, for neural networks the weight solutions are not isolated and therefore do not form paths, and infinite weights cannot be avoided. We now proceed to describe how a suitable homotopy can be formulated to overcome these problems.

PROBLEM STATEMENT AND NATURAL HOMOTOPY FORMULATION

The basic signal prediction problem formulation is shown in Fig 1(b). Given input data $\{x[i] \in \Re^n | i = 1, 2, ..L\}$ and desired outputs $\{y[i] \in \Re^m | i = 1, 2, ..L\}$, the objective is to find the optimal network weights $\{w\}$ so that T maps $x[i]$ into $y[i]$ while minimizing the stochastic mean square error

$$\epsilon = E\left\{\frac{1}{2}[y - T(x)]^T[y - T(x)]\right\}. \quad (2)$$

In this work we develop a natural homotopy mapping between linear and nonlinear networks. Through this mapping we gain insight into how the nonlinearities of the network influence the optimal parameter values and the performance of the predictor. This natural homotopy is defined by parametrizing the neural network node nonlinearity in terms of τ such that

$$\sigma(x) \equiv \sigma(x;\tau) = \begin{cases} x & \text{when } \tau = 0 \\ \sigma_f(x) & \text{when } \tau = 1 \end{cases} \quad (3)$$

where σ_f is the node nonlinearity of the final network. Through this approach we are able to establish consistent homotopy relationships between all equations and performance measures pertaining to the linear network and the corresponding equations of the final neural network.

RESULTS AND IMPLEMENTATION FOR A SINGLE PERCEPTRON

Although the natural homotopy formulation described represents a viable approach for finding a set of weights for a multi-layer perceptron, for brevity and clarity only the results for a single layer perceptron are presented below. The most important proofs referred to for this case are contained in the appendix. The extension to multilayer networks will briefly be discussed later in the paper.

For the problem defined by Fig 1(b) and performance measure (2) the input and output data matrices $\mathbf{X} \in \Re^{n \times L}$ and $\mathbf{y} \in \Re^L$, respectively, are defined as

$$X = [\ x[1] \ \ x[2] \ \ \ldots \ \ x[L]\ ] \quad y = [\ y[1] \ \ y[2] \ \ \ldots \ \ y[L]\ ]^T. \quad (4)$$

The output $y'[i]$ for an input $x[i]$ of a single layer perceptron with weight w is described by $y'[i] = \sigma(r[i])$ where the activation $r[i] = w^T x[i]$. The necessary equations for an extremum point of the error criterion are then given by

$$Xq = \mathrm{o} \quad (5)$$

$$\text{where } q = [\ \epsilon[1]\sigma'(r[1]) \ \ \epsilon[2]\sigma'(r[2]) \ \ \ldots \ \ \epsilon[L]\sigma'(r[L])\ ]^T \quad (6)$$

$$\epsilon[i] = y[i] - \sigma(r[i]) \ \ i = 1, 2 \ldots L \quad (7)$$

This implies that $q \in \eta(X) = \text{Im}\left(X^T\right)^{\perp}$ and since $\sigma'(r) > 0 \ \forall\, r \in \Re$

$$\epsilon \;=\; y - \sigma(r) \;=\; \left[\; v_1 \oslash \sigma'(r) \quad v_2 \oslash \sigma'(r) \quad \ldots \quad v_{L-s} \oslash \sigma'(r) \;\right] \eta \qquad (8)$$

where span $\{V\} = \eta(X)$, $\eta \in \Re^{L-s}$ and $\oslash$ denotes the *inverse Schur product* of two matrices, formed by appropriately dividing the matrices element by element. If X is not full rank, there are an infinite number of solutions to the perceptron weights. These solutions define affine subspaces in $\Re^n$, since, as in the linear case, if a weight vector w_0 solves the necessary equations, then $w = w_0 + w'$ where $w' \in \text{Im}(X)^{\perp}$ is also a solution. Homotopy approaches can only track isolated solutions. We are able to track a whole affine subspace by tracking only a particular solution in each plane.

This particular solution in turn is defined by performing a reduced QR decomposition of the rank s input data matrix $X^T = QR$, to obtain the parameters $\beta = Rw \in \Re^s$. These parameters also form an allowable set of *nonlinear* curvilinear coordinates for the nonlinear perceptron mapping. Mathematically, the map $\Sigma : \Re^s \rightarrow \Re^L$ defined by $\Sigma(\beta) = \sigma(Q\beta)$ is a one-to-one immersion of $\text{Im}\left(X^T\right)$ in $\Re^L$ (Theorem 1).

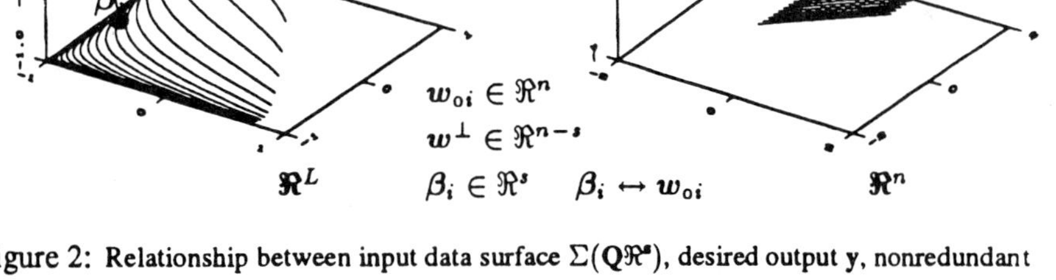

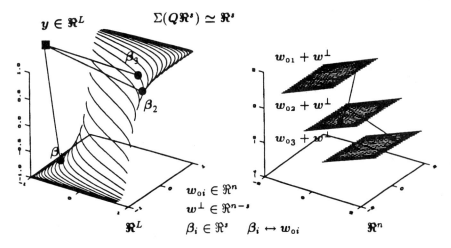

Figure 2: Relationship between input data surface $\Sigma(Q\Re^s)$, desired output y, nonredundant particular solutions β_i, particular neural network weight solutions w_{oi} and general solution $w = w_0 + w^{\perp}$.

This formulation makes it easy to see how the weight solutions are related to the data. Specifically, there exists a solution to the optimization problem if an orthogonal projection of the desired output signal vector $y \in \Re^L$ onto the hypersurface $\Sigma(Q\Re^s)$ defined by the data exists (Theorems 2,3). The point on $\Sigma(Q\Re^s)$ where such an orthogonal projection exists corresponds to an *unique and distinct* solution $\beta \in \Re^s$(Theorem 4). Every solution β in turn is related to a specific *hyperplane* (affine subspace) of weights in $\Re^n$ that solves the necessary equations. The point β on $\Sigma(Q\Re^s)$ with the shortest error vector defines the global minimum of the problem. Fig 2 illustrates the relationships between these quantities for a case where $L = 3$, $s = 2$, and the perceptron has three weights ($n = 3$). Solutions at infinite weights occur when the desired vector $\mathbf{y}$ is far enough from $\Sigma(\mathbf{Q}\Re^s)$ that the closest point on the surface to $\mathbf{y}$ is an edge point when $\tau = 1$. In this case $\Sigma(Q\Re^s)$ is a compact set in $\Re^L$ since the final sigmoidal function results in a bounded output. In our homotopy approach these weights are handled by tracking on *finite coordinates* on the compact surface $\Sigma(\mathbf{Q}\Re^s)$ when divergence is detected.

Example. To illustrate these results, consider the case where $\mathrm{Im}\left(X^T\right) = \mathrm{span}\left\{[1 \;\; \alpha]^T\right\}$. The desired vector is $[-R\sin(\tan^{-1}(\alpha)) \quad R\cos(\tan^{-1}(\alpha))]^T$, where $R = 2$ and $\alpha = 4$. Then $L = 2$ and $s = 1$. The surface $\mathcal{W} = \Sigma\{Q\Re\}$ is parametrized in terms of β by $\left[\, \sigma(\beta) \;\; \sigma(\alpha\beta) \,\right]^T$. The relative locations of the point $\mathbf{y}$ and the surfaces $\mathcal{W}$ corresponding to different values of τ are shown in Fig 3(a), while the error power surfaces ϵ corresponding to different values of τ are shown in Fig 3(b). Fig 4 shows the homotopy paths which are defined by the critical points of the error surface for each $\tau \in [0, 1]$.

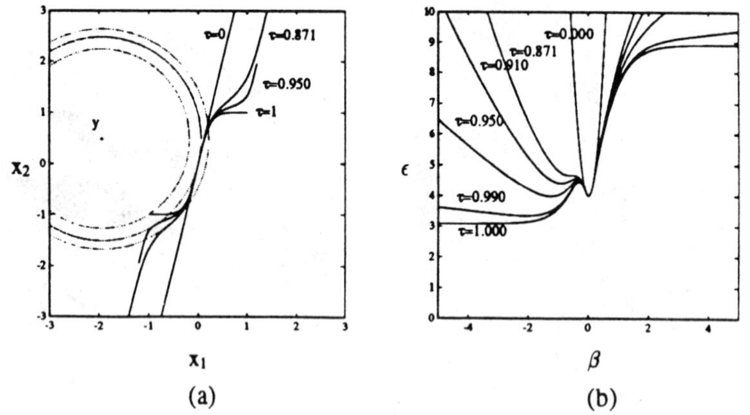

(a) (b)

Figure 3: (a) $\Sigma(Q\Re)$ for different τ, (b) Error vs β for different values of τ

Note from Fig 3(a) that when $\tau = 0$, $\mathcal{W}$ is a straight line and thus there exists a unique orthogonal projection of $\mathbf{y}$ onto this surface. Thus the performance surface shown in Fig 3(b) is quadratic and has a unique minimum at $\beta = 0$. As τ is increased from $\tau = 0$ to $\tau = 0.871$, the performance surface is no longer quadratic, but the global minimum at $\beta = 0$ is still the only critical point (region [1] in Fig 4). At $\tau = 0.871$, an inflection point appears in the performance surface at $\beta = -0.545$, corresponding to critical point (D) where $\mathcal{W}$ has been deformed such that another point of $\mathcal{W}$ is tangent to a circle centered at $\boldsymbol{y}$. As τ is increased, a local minimum appears at specific values of $\beta < -0.54$, and a local maximum appears between the two local minima. For $0.871 < \tau < 0.907$, the second local minimum located at $\beta < -0.54$ has higher error than that of the minimum located at $\beta = 0$. This corresponds to region [2] in Fig 4. When $\tau = 0.907$, the two minima are located at $\beta = 0$ and $\beta = -0.884$, and have equal error (points (B) and (G) in Fig 4). For $\tau > 0.907$, the minimum at $\beta = 0$ is no longer the global minimum; in this case the global minimum is the second minimum (region [3] of Fig 4). When $\tau = 1$, there are three critical points; a local minimum (C), a local maximum at (F) and the global minimum is located at $\beta = -\infty$, indicated by (H).

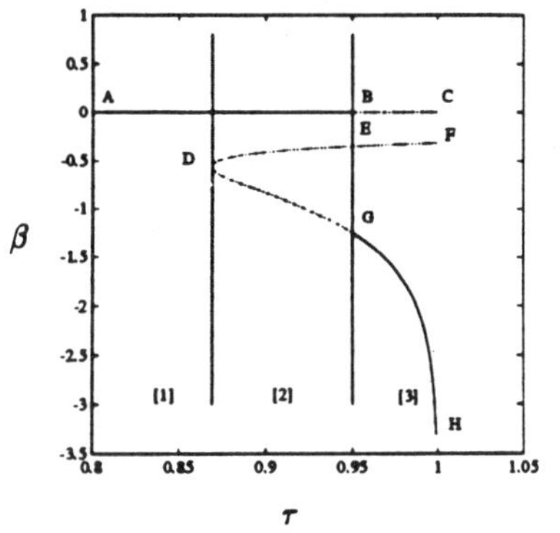

Figure 4: Homotopy paths: Critical points for different values of τ

The results in the previous sections can be extended to perceptron networks with one hidden layer and linear output nodes. In this case the weights in the output layer are found using a suitable pseudoinverse, and the problem of finding the weights in the first layer once again reduces to a projection problem. The surface onto which a desired vector is projected, however, is more complex and involves pseudoinverses of data matrices. In general, allowable curvilinear coordinates can be defined only locally.

DISCUSSION

Based on the above results and demonstrations, a number of observations are made regarding the homotopy solution procedure.

The existence of a path from $\tau = 0$ to $\tau = 1$ has not been proven (for the real-valued weight case), i.e. it has not been shown that the method always leads to a solution. However, based on the physical interpretation of projection, and the fact that the curvilinear data surface coordinates are infinitely differentiable, it seems plausible that such a path always exists. The weight solution that is finally tracked by the homotopy is uniquely specified by the solution to the linear network optimization problem (and therefore the input and output data). There is no element of randomness. The path corresponding to the solution of the linear system ($\tau = 0$), does not necessarily lead to the solution corresponding to the global minimum of the final homotopy equations. Multiple critical points can appear as τ is varied, and a specific homotopy path can correspond to either a global or a local extremum at various values of τ. Infinite weight solutions are fundamental and do not indicate algorithm divergence, as claimed in [8], and can be handled in this formulation by tracking on finite coordinates.

Ensuring that the homotopy method tracks distinct paths is of critical theoretical and numerical importance[5, 9, 10]. This is a fundamental difference between the formulation above and that in [8].

In many cases, the number of projections can be determined based on the geometric properties of the data surface. Then an initial system of equations having the same number of solutions can be formulated, enabling all solutions to be computed. Similarly, differential geometric analysis of the data surface can further provide an understanding of when a nonlinear network will outperform a linear network. By calculating the curvature of the data surface as τ is varied, it can be determined whether the surface will bend towards the desired data point, or away from the surface. Similarly, calculation of the maximum curvature of the data surface can provide bounds on the distance of the desired data point to the data plane that will result in a unique minimum.

CONCLUSION

We have described how a natural homotopy can be defined for perceptron networks. The homotopy tracks an infinite number of weights by transforming coordinates and characterizing all solutions by a finite number of distinct and unique solutions. The formulation provides a natural geometric perspective on the weight optimization problem, providing insight on appearance of and convergence to local extremum points, infinite weights and performance of neural networks.

APPENDIX. SINGLE LAYER HOMOTOPY ANALYSIS

Theorem 1 *The map* $\Sigma : \Re^s \rightarrow \Re^L$ *defined by* $\Sigma(\beta) = \sigma(Q\beta)$ *is a one-to-one immersion of* $\mathrm{Im}\left(X^T\right)$ *in* $\Re^L$.

The Jacobian of the mapping is given by

$$J = \frac{\partial \sigma(Q\beta)}{\partial \beta} = \left[\frac{\partial \sigma(Q\beta)}{\partial \beta_1} \; \frac{\partial \sigma(Q\beta)}{\partial \beta_2} \; \ldots \; \frac{\partial \sigma(Q\beta)}{\partial \beta_s}\right] = \sigma'(r) \circ Q \qquad (9)$$

Here $\circ$ denotes the *Schur product* of two matrices, formed by appropriately multiplying element by element. However, since $\sigma'(x) > 0 \; \forall \; x \in \Re$, the rank of the Jacobian is equal to $\mathrm{rank}(Q) = s$. Therefore the mapping is an immersion. Now suppose there are two points β and β' and $\sigma(Q\beta) = \sigma(Q\beta')$. Considering the vectors component by component, this implies that for $i = 1, 2 \ldots L$,

$$\begin{aligned} \sigma(Q_i'^T\beta) = \sigma(Q_i'^T\beta') \; \Leftrightarrow \; Q_i^T\beta \; = \; \sigma^{-1}(\sigma(Q_i^T\beta')) \; \Leftrightarrow \; Q_i^T\beta \; = \; Q_i^T\beta' \\ \Leftrightarrow \; Q(\beta - \beta') \; = \; 0 \end{aligned} \qquad (10)$$

where Q_i is the ith row of Q. However, the matrix Q has orthonormal columns, and therefore the coordinates of the linear combination of the columns has to be zero. Therefore $\beta = \beta'$ and Σ is one-to-one. ■

Theorem 2 *The orthogonal subspace* $\mathcal{U}$ *to the tangent space spanned by the columns of* J, *is the column space of*

$$U \; = \; \left[\Psi_1 \oslash \sigma'(r) \;\; \Psi_1 \oslash \sigma'(r) \;\; \ldots \;\; \Psi_{L-s} \oslash \sigma'(r)\right] \qquad (11)$$

where the columns of Ψ *span* $\eta(X)$, *and* $\oslash$ *denotes the* inverse Schur product *of two matrices, formed by appropriately dividing element by element.*

Considering the s-dimensional surface in $\Re^L$ generated by $\Sigma(Q\Re^s)$, the tangent hyperplane at each point is spanned by the columns of the Jacobian J, and has dimension s. The orthogonal subspace $\mathcal{U}$ to the tangent is of dimension $L - s$. Consider a matrix $U \in \Re^{L \times (L-s)}$ whose columns form a basis (not necessarily orthogonal) for $\mathcal{U}$. Using the inner product

$$\begin{aligned} U^T J \; = \; 0 \; \Leftrightarrow \; U^T\{\sigma'(r) \circ Q\} \; = \; 0 \; \Leftrightarrow \; \Psi^T Q \; = \; 0 \\ \text{where } \Psi \; = \; \left[\sigma'(r) \circ U_1 \;\; \sigma'(r) \circ U_2 \;\; \ldots \;\; \sigma'(r) \circ U_{L-s}\right] \end{aligned} \qquad (12)$$

Since $\Psi^T Q = 0$ and $\mathrm{rank}(\Psi) = L - s$, it follows that $\mathrm{span}\{\Psi\} = \mathrm{Im}\left(X^T\right)^{\perp} = \eta(X) = \mathrm{span}\{V\}$. Similarly, the orthogonal subspace to the tangent is spanned by the columns of any matrix Ψ whose columns are constructed of linearly independent vectors spanning $\eta(X)$ appropriately divided by the elements of $\sigma'(r)$. ■

Theorem 3 *There exist at least one solution* $[\beta_0^T \;\; \eta_0^T]^T$ *to (8) for all points* $y \in \Re^L$ *that have a* normal *projection onto* $\Sigma(Q\Re^s)$.

The result of Theorem 2 can now be applied to interpret the necessary equation (8). The necessary equation will be satisfied for a desired signal $y \in \Re^L$ if and only if y can be written as the sum of two vectors in $\Re^L$, one vector connecting the origin to a point in the hypersurface $\Sigma(Q\Re^s)$, and the other lying in the normal subspace of dimension $L-s$ at this particular point in the hypersurface. In that case there exists a set of coordinates $\beta \in \Re^s$ from which a hyperplane of possible weights of dimension $n-s$ can be reconstructed in $\Re^n$, and $L-s$ coordinates η describing the vector in $\mathcal{U}$ that ensures that (8) can be satisfied. ■

Theorem 4 *The solutions $[\beta_0^T \;\; \eta_0^T]^T$ to (8) for a given point $y \in \Re^L$ are isolated almost everywhere on $\Sigma(Q\Re^s)$*

We briefly sketch the solution. If the solutions β_i are not isolated for a given value of τ, then in a sufficiently small region, a curve of solutions can be found on the surface $\Sigma(Q\Re^s)$ such that the normal along the curve, in $\Re^L$, passes through y. This implies that the curve on $\Sigma(Q\Re^s)$ is a curve on a hypersphere. However, general sigmoidal functions $\sigma(x)$ cannot generate portions of surfaces $\Sigma(Q\Re^s)$ that are locally described everywhere by hyperspheres. ■

References

[1] D. Haussler, "Generalizing the PAC model for neural net and other applications," Tech. Report UCSC-CRL-89-30, UCSC Computer research laboratory, September 1989.

[2] H. White, "Learning in artificial neural networks: a statistical perspective," Neural Computation, vol. 1, pp. 425–464, 1989.

[3] K.-I. Funahashi, "On the approximate realization of continuous functions by neural networks," Neural Networks, vol. 2(3), pp. 183–92, 1989.

[4] K. Hornik, M. StinchCombe, and H. White, "Multilayer feedforward networks are universal approximators," Neural Networks, vol. 2, pp. 359–366, 1989.

[5] S. Alexander, Adaptive Signal Processing. New York: Springer-Verlag, 1986.

[6] J. Chow, L. Udpa, and S. Udpa, "Homotopy continuation methods for neural networks," in Proc. ISCAS Singapore, IEEE, 1991.

[7] W. D. Miller, "Homotopy analysis of recurrent neural nets," Digital Signal Processing, vol. 2, pp. 33–38, 1992.

[8] L. Yang and W. Yu, "Backpropagation with homotopy," Neural Computation, vol. 5, pp. 363–366, 1993.

[9] L. T. Watson, S. C. Billups, and A. P. Morgan, "HOMPACK: A suite of codes for globally convergent algorithms," Tech. Report GMR-5344, GM Research Institute, 1986.

[10] C. B. Garcia and W. I. Zangwill, Pathways to solutions, fixed points and equilibria. Prentice-Hall, 1981.

[11] L. Trajković, R. C. Melville, and S.-C. Fang, "Passivity and no-gain properties establish global convergence of a homotopy method for DC operating points," in Proc. Int. Symp. Circuits Systems, IEEE, 1990, pp. 914–917.

Chapter 2: Analysis

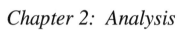

CHAPTER 2

Analysis

In Chapter 1, the emphasis was on the design and development of new neural networks or the extension of existing neural networks. In this chapter, the emphasis is on the analysis of existing neural network paradigms. The papers in this chapter deal with several issues, including:

- **Functional Analysis.** Once the neural network has been trained, properties such as sensitivity, fault tolerance, generalization, and function approximation are examined.

- **Recall Analysis.** In a feedback neural network (or recurrent neural network), aspects of the resulting neural network are examined such as the placement and number of domains of attraction, the stability of recall operations, and the presence of bifurcation.

- **Learning Analysis.** There are several aspects of learning that are of importance, including how rapid learning can occur, the effectiveness of incremental learning, and learning with minimal error information (such as reinforcement learning).

- **Topological Analysis.** Analyzing the resulting neural network topologies provides insight into how the neural network is performing its computational task. Issues such as pruning for improved generalization and rule-extraction for explanation are analyzed to provide insights in this area.

- **Comparative Performance.** A great deal can be learned about a neural network by comparing its performance against other techniques used to solve the same problem. Comparative performance with traditional techniques as well as emerging techniques deepens our understanding of the learning process and provides confidence in the resulting neural network.

The papers in this chapter are organized into eleven areas that deal with various aspects of learning, recall, approximation, and comparative performance. A review of the papers in each area follows.

1. Backpropagation. The backpropagation learning algorithm is the most popular method of adjusting the connections in a MLP. Backpropagation is a gradient descent technique that is slow and it often gets trapped in local minima. This chapter includes four papers that analyze various aspects of this learning procedure. **Paper 2.1** derives an optimum time-varying learning rate adjusting the weights. **Paper 2.2** introduces the notion of terminal attractors to improve the convergence rate of learning. **Paper 2.3** analyzes several variants of the backpropagation algorithm for recurrent neural networks. **Paper 2.4** analyzes overtraining in the presence of noise.

2. Kalman Filters. A relatively recent innovation in the training of MLPs is the use of Kalman filters as a quicker method of determining the weights. This method treats the weights as a state vector that is modified over time. **Paper 2.5** analyzes a decoupled extended Kalman filter used to train recurrent neural networks with an emphasis on the application to control problems (an application that requires quick adaptation).

3. Reinforcement Learning. Reinforcement learning requires only a single scalar performance measure during learning (often good/bad). Similar in many respects to condition-response learning found in behavioral psychology, this method has received a great deal of attention in the cognitive science communities. Over the past few years, the utility of reinforcement learning has become appreciated in the area of control. **Paper 2.6** describes improvements to reinforcement learning algorithms with emphasis on control problems.

4. Radial Basis Function (RBF) Learning. Neural networks formed from a linear combination of radially symmetric basis functions (e.g. splines, Gaussians) have been growing in favor. These neural networks learn faster than MLPs, they provide greater insight into the mapping that is learned, and they (like MLPs) are proven universal approximators. **Paper 2.7** proves the convergence of a modified gradient descent algorithm used to train RBFs. **Paper 2.8** analyzes the conditions under which real-valued functions of several variables can be approximated arbitrarily well by finite linear combinations of elliptical basis functions. **Paper 2.9** shows that a Gaussian basis function network provides the best function approximation capability under certain conditions. **Paper 2.10** describes a fuzzified RBF and compares its performance with a fuzzy rulebase for a blood pressure control problem.

5. Cerebellar Model Articulation Controller (CMAC) Learning. The CMAC neural network combines hashing with linear approximation to provide a fast nonlinear function approximator that has enjoyed great success in many control and pattern recognition applications. **Paper 2.11** uses Fourier analysis to show that CMAC is capable of learning any discrete input-output mapping. Further analysis of CMAC shows that its learning is governed by a single parameter.

6. Unsupervised Learning. Unsupervised learning refers to learning without any performance information. Most unsupervised learning techniques focus on clustering data to form codes that are useful as feature extractors and basis functions. **Paper 2.12** analyzes a biologically motivated method of creating feature maps and shows that this approach develops "Mexican hat" shaped basins of attraction around each reference vector. **Paper 2.13** shows that a single neural network can be trained to produce three distinctly different functions: principle component analysis, orthogonal projection, and novelty filtering.

7. Recall Dynamics. Feedback (recurrent) neural networks require specific analysis of the stability of recall. If learning occurs within a feedback neural network, the analysis process is further complicated. **Paper 2.14** proves that a multilayer recurrent neural network is absolutely stable under certain conditions. **Paper 2.15** analyzes a two-layer feedback network with hysteresis, proving stability and showing that the number of equilibria is governed by only three parameters. **Paper 2.16** shows that a discrete associative memory with a bias vector is globally stable. **Paper 2.17** investigates bifurcation in cellular neural networks; showing that the adjustment of a single parameter can move a stable system into a periodic attractor.

8. Fault Tolerance. One of the most appealing properties of neural networks is the fault tolerance afforded to these computational paradigms through massive interconnectivity. Recently, a great deal of analysis has focused on measuring the amount of fault tolerance exhibited by a given neural network. **Paper 2.18** analyzes a method of training neural networks for greater fault tolerance to weight perturbations. **Paper 2.19** presents a technique for measuring and improving the robustness of neural networks and introduces the concepts of link sensitivity and node sensitivity. **Paper 2.20** characterizes classification performance with missing, unknown, and ambiguous inputs using a two-stage system; the first stage classifies and the second stage characterizes the classification. **Paper 2.21** compares the fault tolerance of the MLP and RBF using a rigorously derived fault tolerance metric.

9. Function Approximation. Several neural networks have been shown to have function approximation capabilities under a wide variety of conditions. The next step to be taken is the development of a construction theorem that defines exactly how a neural network can be built to achieve a known level of performance from a fixed data set. The following papers represent steps in this direction. **Paper 2.22** examines the capability of multilayer perceptrons in approximation functions and their derivatives. **Paper 2.23** places bounds on the valid range of prediction performance of a neural network by examining the invertability of neural network approximations. In **Paper 2.24,** spectral domain techniques are applied to determine the most appropriate basis functions for a given problem.

10. Classification Performance. There are many neural networks that perform classification. The following collection of papers examine neural network classification performance from several different aspects. **Paper**

2.25 compares neural networks and discriminant analysis for classification problems using several different performance metrics. **Paper 2.26** compares the MLP and RBF networks with and without recurrent connections for a speech classification task. **Paper 2.27** compares a PNN and a pruned PNN network on a benchmark classification problem. **Paper 2.28** compares the LVQ with a variant of the LVQ for a set of benchmark classification problems. **Paper 2.29** compares the Volterra connectionist model with the Bayes decision theory for time series classification. **Paper 2.30** shows that differential learning can produce the most efficient classifier for the discrimination of handwritten characters.

11. Biological Analogy. Although the biological ignorance quotient is high for most of the neural network community, there are a few examples of true biological modeling. **Paper 2.31** compares a biological model of ionic permeability of a neuron with a living preparation.

OPTIMUM LEARNING RATE FOR BACKPROPAGATION NEURAL NETWORKS

N.Kandil, K. Khorasani, R.V. Patel, and V. K. Sood
Dept. of Electrical & Computer Engineering
Concordia University, Montreal, Quebec
Canada H3G 1M8

Abstract - Backpropagation (BP) is a systematic method for training multi-layer artificial neural networks (NNs). Although it has dramatically expanded the range of problems to which NNs can be applied, BP networks suffer from slow learning mainly due to a constant, non-optimum learning rate (a fixed step size) η. In this paper, an optimum, time-varying learning rate for multi-layer BP networks is analytically derived. Results show that training time can be reduced significantly while not causing any oscillations during the training process.

INTRODUCTION

Training a NN is adjusting its weights vector (**W**) in the direction of minimizing the error E(**W**) between its outputs and the targets to be learned. During its training, BP uses the Steepest Descent (SD) method in minimizing this error. The SD method is the fundamental first order method which uses the Jacobien gradient vector **g**(**W**) to determine a suitable direction of movement i.e. at the kth iteration

$$\Delta \mathbf{W}_k = -\eta_k (dE/d\mathbf{W}) = -\eta_k g_k(\mathbf{W}) \qquad (1)$$

where η_k is the step size which minimizes the error at the next iteration i.e its value is determined by minimizing $E(\mathbf{W}_k - \eta_k g_k)$ with respect to η_k. This is a single variable optimisation problem. If E(**W**) is a quadratic function, η_k^* can be found analytically, otherwise, a single variable search technique can be used [1]. However, because of the nonlinear activation functions used by NNs, an analytical derivation of η_k^* is very difficult. In addition, single variable search techniques are computationally expensive, especially for large scale problems. Therefore, according to the BP algorithm, η is given a constant positive value, usually between 0 and 1.

The choice of the learning rate is still a non-trivial problem in BP theory. A low value of η results in slow learning while a large value of η corresponds to rapid learning but might also result in oscillations which leads to no learning at all. In addition, if the NN is to be trained on-line, the choice of η becomes more critical. Applications have shown that the stability of the total system depends heavily on the choice of this value [2].

Two types of methods have been proposed to speed up the BP algorithm without leading to oscillations. The first, so called second order methods [3], use second order gradient information to guide in the search for a suitable minimum. However, these methods are computationally expensive, so that in many cases they are not appropriate. The second type are heuristic methods that produce empirically acceptable results. Among these methods, the momentum [4] and step size variation methods [5,6,7] are commonly used.

In [4], it is suggested that a momentum term be included at each iteration to incorporate past weight changes on the current weight change. This effect is determined by a constant, α, which has a value between 0 and 1. Applications have shown that a finite value of α tends to dampen some oscillations but can also serve to slow down the learning process. A large value of momentum causes divergence and (in case of on-line training) total instability [2]. Therefore, the choice of α is a problem in itself.

For step size variations, [5] introduced heuristic arguments such that every weight has its own step size, and is varied under consideration of gradient polarities. However, in the implementation of the above algorithm, the author underestimated the possibility of slow initial convergence due to a small initial step size and of divergence due to the large step size in the learning process.

To avoid these difficulties, [6] introduced a scheme where, at first, the step size is set to its maximum value (which is assumed to be known) and as the error becomes smaller the step size is decreased to its minimum value exponentially. This method gives fast initial convergence and prevents the entire learning process from diverging by limiting the step size within its maximum value. However, using this method there may be a situation where, due to the larger initial step size, the learning process may bounce back and forth between the two opposite hills of a narrow valley of the mean square error surface instead of following its bottom trail. Therefore, a zig-zagging or local trapping problem may occur. To solve this problem, the authors [6] adopted a gradient averaging term in the weight updates instead of the instantaneous gradient itself. This gradient averaging method turned out to be essentially identical to the so called momentum algorithm.

In [7], an adaptive learning rate algorithm is introduced. This procedure increases η, but only to the extent that the network can learn without large error increases. Thus a near optimum learning rate is obtained for the local terrain. When a larger η could result in stable learning, η is increased. Otherwise, it is decreased until stable learning is resumed.

In this paper, an analytical derivation for an optimum step size is obtained by linearizing the NN around $\mathbf{W}_k$ at each iteration k.

OPTIMUM LEARNING RATE FOR BP

The NN used for this derivation (Figure 1) consists of 5 layers: the input layer X, three hidden layers A, B, C, and the output layer Y. The number of neurons in these layers are respectively n_x, n_a, n_b, n_c, and n_y. The inputs, outputs, and the connecting weights of these layers are represented by vectors and matrices which are described and defined in the Appendix. However, the methodology is general and can be applied to NNs consisting of any numbers of hidden layers and neurons.

The derivation (see Appendix) is based on linearizing the NN at each iteration i.e. at every iteration k where

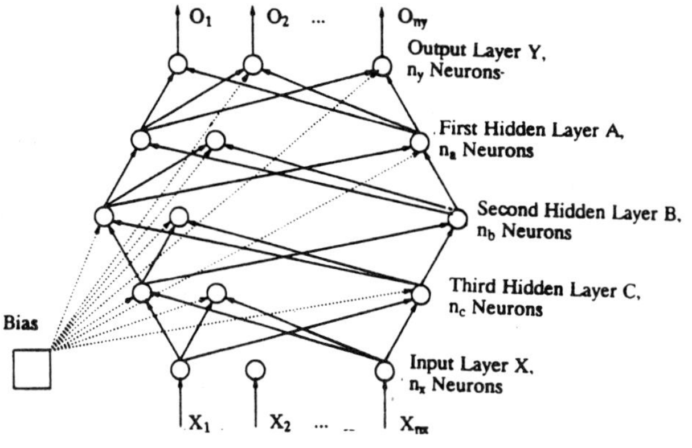

Figure 1 The Neural Network used for this derivation

0-7803-1443-3/93 $3.00 © 1993 IEEE

$O_y = F(Net_y)$ gives $\Delta O_y = F'(Net_y)\,\Delta Net_y$ (2)
$O_a = F(Net_a)$ gives $\Delta O_a = F'(Net_a)\,\Delta Net_a$
$O_b = F(Net_b)$ gives $\Delta O_b = F'(Net_b)\,\Delta Net_b$
$O_c = F(Net_c)$ gives $\Delta O_c = F'(Net_c)\,\Delta Net_c$

and the **Net** vectors are:

$Net_y = W_y^t O_a + B_y$ giving $\Delta Net_y = \Delta W_y^t O_a + W_y^t \Delta O_a + \Delta B_y$
$Net_a = W_a^t O_b + B_a$ giving $\Delta Net_a = \Delta W_a^t O_b + W_a^t \Delta O_b + \Delta B_a$
$Net_b = W_b^t O_c + B_b$ giving $\Delta Net_b = \Delta W_b^t O_c + W_b^t \Delta O_c + \Delta B_b$
$Net_c = W_c^t X + B_c$ giving $\Delta Net_c = \Delta W_c^t X + \Delta B_c$ (3)

From the above equations, it can be shown that

$$\begin{aligned}\Delta O_y = {} & F'(Net_y)\,\Delta W_y^t O_a \\ & + F'(Net_y) W_y^t F'(Net_a) \Delta W_a^t O_b \\ & + F'(Net_y) W_y^t F'(Net_a) W_a^t F'(Net_b) \Delta W_b^t O_c \\ & + F'(Net_y) W_y^t F'(Net_a) W_a^t F'(Net_b) W_b^t F(Net_c) \Delta W_c^t X \\ & + F'(Net_y) W_y^t F'(Net_a) W_a^t F'(Net_b) W_b^t F(Net_c) \Delta B_c \\ & + F'(Net_y) W_y^t F'(Net_a) W_a^t F'(Net_b) \Delta B_b \\ & + F'(Net_y) \Delta W_y^t F'(Net_a) \Delta B_a \\ & + F'(Net_y) \Delta B_y\end{aligned} \quad (4)$$

where ΔW_y, ΔW_a, ΔW_b, ΔW_c, ΔB_y, ΔB_a, ΔB_b, and ΔB_c are the adjustment of the Weights and Biases given, according to BP, by

$$\begin{aligned}\Delta W_y &= \eta\, O_a Dy^t \quad (5)\\ \Delta W_a &= \eta\, O_b [F'(Net_a) W_y Dy]^t \\ \Delta W_b &= \eta\, O_c [F'(Net_b) W_a F'(Net_a) W_y Dy]^t \\ \Delta W_c &= \eta\, X [F'(Net_c) W_b F'(Net_b) W_a F'(Net_a) W_y Dy]^t \\ \Delta B_y &= \eta\, Dy \\ \Delta B_a &= \eta\, F'(Net_a) W_y D_y \\ \Delta B_b &= \eta\, F'(Net_b) W_a F'(Net_a) W_a D_y \\ \Delta B_c &= \eta\, F'(Net_c) W_b F'(Net_b) Wa\, F(Net_a) W_y Dy\end{aligned}$$

Dy is the delta vector given by; $Dy = F'(Net_y)\,e$.

Now, substituting these values into equation (4) gives

$$\begin{aligned}\Delta O_y = {} & \eta\, F'(Net_y)\, [\, I_{ny}^t I_{ny} (O_a^t O_a + 1) \\ & + W_y^t F'(Net_a) F'(Net_a) Wy\, (O_b^t O_b + 1) \\ & + W_y^t F'(Net_a) W_a^t F'(Net_b) F'(Net_b) W_a F'(Net_a) W_y (O_c^t O_c + 1) \\ & + W_y^t F'(Net_a) W_a^t F'(Net_b) W_b^t F'(Net_c) * \\ & F'(Net_c) W_b F'(Net_b) W_a F'(Net_a) W_y (X^t X + 1)]\, Dy\end{aligned} \quad (6)$$

where I_{ny} is an (n_y, n_y) identity matrix. By setting

$$\begin{aligned}R_y &= I_{ny} \quad (7)\\ R_a &= F'(Net_a) W_y \\ R_b &= F'(Net_b) W_a F'(Net_a) W_y \\ R_c &= F'(Net_c) W_b F'(Net_b) W_a F'(Net_a) W_y\end{aligned}$$

and

$$\begin{aligned}H_y &= R_y^t R_y (O_a^t O_a + 1) \quad (8)\\ H_a &= R_a^t R_a (O_b^t O_b + 1) \\ H_b &= R_b^t R_b (O_c^t O_c + 1) \\ H_c &= R_c^t R_c (X^t X + 1) \text{ and} \\ H &= H_y + H_a + H_b + H_c \quad (9)\end{aligned}$$

then eq. (6) may be written as

$$\Delta O_y = \eta\, F'(Net_y)\, H\, Dy \quad (10)$$

Since H_y is positive definite, and H_a, H_b, H_c can only be positive definite or positive semi definite. Therefore **H** is a positive definite matrix. **Dy** was defined by the delta vector as

$$\Delta O_y = \eta\, F'(Net_y)\, H\, F'(Net_y)\, e \quad (11)$$

Using $S = F'(Net_y)\, H\, F'(Net_y)$ (12)

hence $\Delta O_y = \eta\, S\, e$ (13)

The matrix **S** is positive definite since **H** is positive definite, and $F'(Net_y)$ is a diagonal matrix with positive elements. The objective here now is to derive an optimum learning rate (step size, η). That is at iteration k, an optimum value of the step size, η_k^*, which minimizes E_{k+1} is to be obtained. Since the target vector **T** is constant, we have

$$e_{k+1} = e_k - (\Delta O_y)_k$$

giving

$$E_{k+1} = 0.5[\, e_k - (\Delta O_y)_k\,]^t\, [\, e_k - (\Delta O_y)_k\,] \quad (14)$$

Using eq.(13), and the fact that S is symmetric, it can be shown that eq.(14) may be written as

$$E_{k+1} = 0.5\, e\, e_k^t - \eta_k\, e_k^t S_k e_k + 0.5\, \eta^2_k\, e_k^t S_k^2 e_k \quad (15)$$

which gives the error e, at iteration k+1, as a function of the step size, η_k. To determine an optimum value of η_k which minimizes E_{k+1}, we use the first and second order conditions

$$dE_{k+1}/d\eta_k \Big|_{\eta_k = \eta_k^*} = -e_k^t S e_k + \eta_k e_k^t S_k^2 e_k = 0 \quad (16)$$

and

$$d^2E_{k+1}/d\eta_k^2 \Big|_{\eta_k = \eta_k^*} = e_k^t S_k^2 e_k > 0 \quad (17)$$

Since S is positive definite, the second condition is met and the optimum value of the step size is found to be

$$\eta_k^* = e_k^t S_k e_k / e_k^t S_k^2 e_k \quad (18)$$

Discussion : Two things need to be considered:

No.1 - There is some approximation involved in linearizing the outputs of the neurons, at each iteration k, about the point $\mathbf{Net_k}$. For example, eq. (2) is not exact because, according to theTaylor series expansion of the function F(net) about a point net_k,

$$F(net_k + \Delta net_k) = F(net_k) + F'(net_k)\,\Delta net_k + 0.5\, F''(net_k)\, \Delta net_k^2 + (\text{higher order terms}) \quad (19)$$

which gives

$$\Delta F(net_k) = F'(net_k)\,\Delta net_k + 0.5\, F''(net_k)\,\Delta net_k + (\text{higher terms})$$

Our derivation is based on a first order approximation by considering only the first term and dropping the higher order terms. This is acceptable since, for the sigmoid and hyperbolic activation functions (used by NNs), it can be shown that higher order derivatives are smaller than the first order derivative.

No.2 - From the computational point of view, η is a function of **e** and **S**. The latter is a function of **H** which is a function of R_y, R_a, R_b, and R_c. Since these matrices need to be computed anyway to determine the delta vectors for the weights adjustment, the computational overhead appears to be reasonable.

CASES STUDIED

To test the proposed approach and compare it with other methods, two cases were studied:

Case1 : Simple Case, F(x,y) = x y

In this case, a BP NN (having one hidden layer with 5 neurons) is trained to learn the multiplication of two variables i.e. F(x,y) = xy where $0<x<1$ and $0<y<1$. The NN was trained, first, with a constant learning rate (fixed step size). Figures 2. shows the Sum Squared Error (SSE) during the training for two values of η. For $\eta = 0.1$, the learning is very slow and the error is still large even after 5000 iterations. For a larger value of $\eta = 0.9$, the learning is faster but it still takes about 3000 iterations to bring the error down to the accepted minimum value. However, by using an optimum time-varying step size the training was found to be much faster and reduced to an acceptable value within a few hundred epochs.

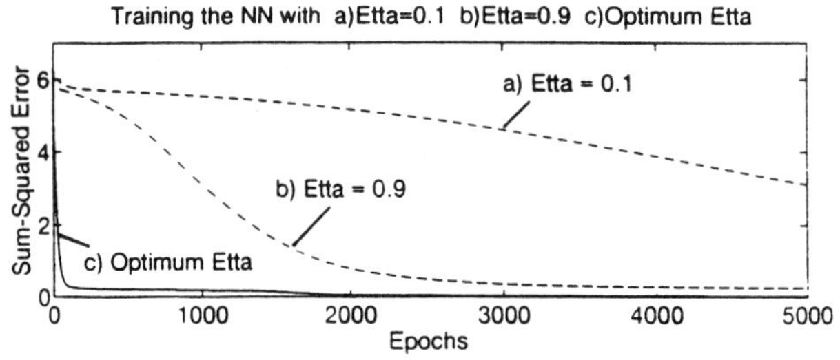

Figure 2 : The error, E, during training of the NN (case 1)

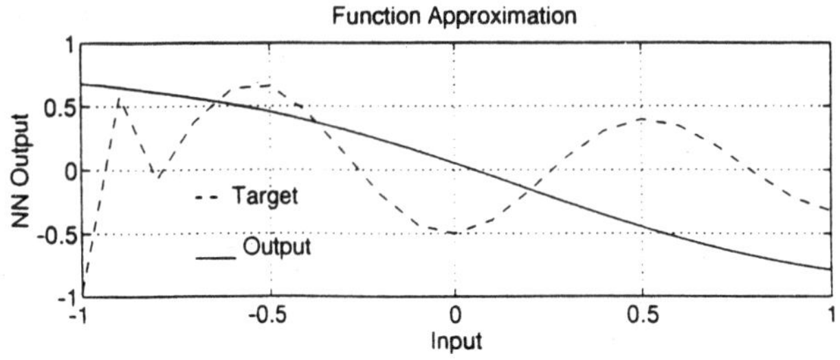

Figure 3 : Target function F(X) to be learned (case 2) and NN output (before training)

Case2 : Complex Case

In this case, the NN (having one hidden layer with 5 neurons) is trained to learn a more difficult function [7]. The training set used (consisting of 21 points) is shown in Table 1. Figure 3 shows the the target to be learned and the NN output (before training).

Table 1 : The training set for case 2

X	F(X)	X	F(X)	X	F(X)	X	F(X)
-1.0	-0.96	-0.5	0.66	0.0	-0.50	0.5	0.39
-0.9	0.57	-0.4	0.46	0.1	-0.39	0.6	0.34
-0.8	-0.07	-0.3	0.13	0.2	-0.16	0.7	0.18
-0.7	0.37	-0.2	-0.20	0.3	0.10	0.8	-0.03
-0.6	0.64	-0.1	-0.43	0.4	0.31	0.9	-0.22
						1.0	-0.32

First, the NN was trained with a constant learning rate. A large value of $\eta = 0.2$ resulted in oscillations and no training (Figure 4.a) while a low value of $\eta = 0.01$ led to a stable but slow learning (Figure 4.b). Figure 4.c shows the output of the NN (after training) as compared to the target.

Second, starting from the same initial values of the weights, the NN was retrained with a momentum term [4] (Figure 5). Again, large values of the learning rate $\eta = 0.2$ and the momentum $\alpha = 0.8$ caused oscillations and led to no learning (Figure 5a). However, low values of η and α result in a stable but slow learning (Figure 5.b). Recall operation of the NN (after training) is shown in Figure 5.c.

Third, the NN was trained (always starting from the same initial conditions) with an adaptive learning rate [7]. In this algorithm, the value η is increased as long as the error is not increasing. Otherwise, the value of η is reduced. Figures 6.a and 6.b show the error and the learning rate during the training process. Although a faster training was obtained, this algorithm caused oscillations which may lead to problems for on-line training.

Finally, the NN was trained with the proposed optimum, time varying learning rate. Figures 7.a and 7.b show the error and the learning rate during training. With this method fast training is obtained, and the weight adjustments are always in the direction of minimizing the error i.e. no oscillations resulted even with large, but optimum values of η. Figure 7.c shows the NN output (recall operation) after training.

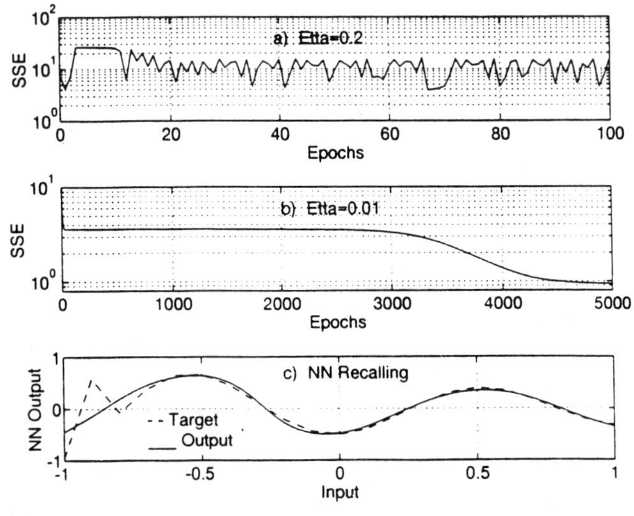

Figure 4 : Training with fixed η (case 2)

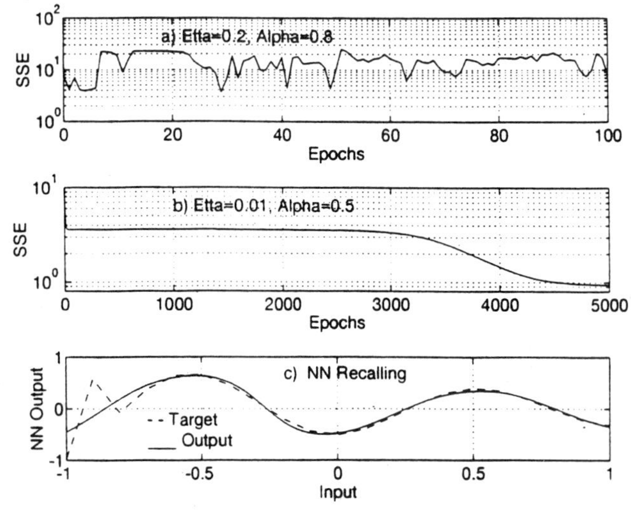

Figure 5 : Training with momentum (case 2)

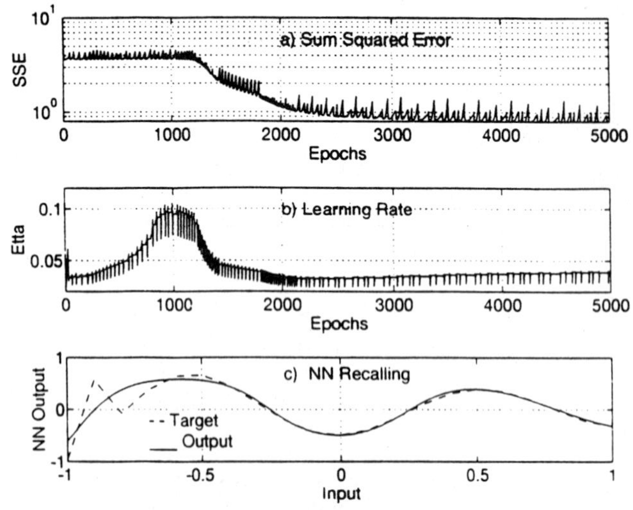

Figure 6 : Training with adaptive learning rate [7]

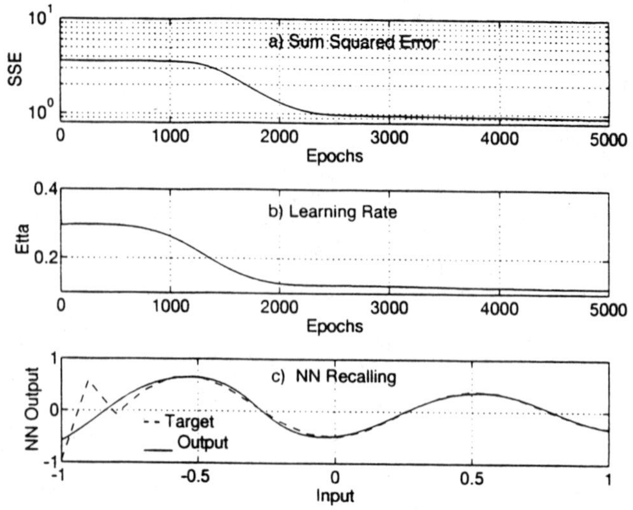

Figure 7: Training with optimum learning rate(proposed method)

Comparison Results obtained in the two cases studied show clearly that low values of η lead to slow learning (Figure 2.a) while large values may cause divergence and oscillations which lead to no learning (Figure 4.a). Adding a momentum term may help in preventing these oscillations (Figure 5.a); however, the choice of the value of this momentum may become a new problem in itself. Using an adaptive learning rate [7] results in a faster training but causes small oscillations (Figure 6.a) which may create problems in the case of on-line training. The proposed method, however, with an optimum, time-varying learning rate, a faster training can be obtained while not causing any oscillations during the training process (Figures 2.c and 7.a). The weight changes are always in the direction of minimizing the error even with large (but optimum) values of η (Figures 7.a and 7.b).

CONCLUSIONS

Test results show that the training time is reduced significantly with an optimum time-varying learning rate. The changes are always in the direction of minimizing the error even with large values of η. Fast learning with no oscillations is a very important feature in on-line training and system stability. The proposed method provides both fast and stable learning.

APPENDIX

In Figure 1, the inputs, outputs, and connecting weights of the NN layers are represented by the vectors and matrices defined below:

The output layer, Y: This layer has n_y neurons. Their outputs are denoted by a column vector $\mathbf{O}_y = [O_1\ O_2 \ldots O_{ny}]_y^t$ given by $\mathbf{O}_y = F(\mathbf{Net}_y)$ where $\mathbf{Net}_y = [net_1\ net_2 \ldots net_{ny}]_y^t$ and is given by

$$\mathbf{Net}_y = \mathbf{W}_y^t\,\mathbf{O}_a + \mathbf{B}_y \qquad (A.1)$$

W_y, with dimensions (n_a,n_y), is the weight matrix connecting the output layer to the first hidden layer, layer A,

$$\mathbf{W}_y = \begin{bmatrix} W_{11}\ W_{12}\ \ldots\ldots & W_{1ny} \\ W_{na1}\ W_{na2}\ \ldots & W_{nany} \end{bmatrix}_y \qquad (A.2)$$

and $\mathbf{B}_y = [B_1\ B_2 \ldots B_{ny}]_y^t$ is the weight vector connecting the output layer to the bias. $\mathbf{O}_a$ is the output vector from the first hidden layer.

The delta vector at this layer is a column vector denoted by $\mathbf{Dy} = [\delta_1\ \delta_2 \ldots \delta_{ny}]^t$ and given by $\mathbf{Dy} = F'(\mathbf{NET}_y)\,\mathbf{e}$ where $\mathbf{e}$ is the error vector given by $\mathbf{e} = [e_1\ e_2 \ldots e_{ny}]^t = \mathbf{T} - \mathbf{O}_y$, and T is the target vector to be learned. $F'(\mathbf{Net}_y)$ is defined to be a square diagonal matrix with dimensions (n_y,n_y). Its diagonal elements are obtained by computing $dF(\mathbf{Net}_y)/d\mathbf{Net}_y$.

The first hidden layer, layer A, has
- A weight matrix, $\mathbf{W}_a(n_a,n_b)$, connecting it to layer B,
- A weight column vector $\mathbf{B}_a(n_a,1)$ connecting it to the bias,
- A net column vector given by $\mathbf{Net}_a(n_a,1) = \mathbf{W}_a^t\,\mathbf{O}_b + \mathbf{B}_a$,
- An output column vector given by $\mathbf{O}_a(n_a,1) = F(\mathbf{Net}_a)$,
- A square diagonal matrix $F'(\mathbf{Net}_a)$ giving derivatives of $\mathbf{O}_a$,
- A delta column vector at this layer $D_a(n_a,1) = F(\mathbf{Net}_a)\,\mathbf{W}_y\,\delta_y$.

Vectors and matrices for the other layers are similarly defined.

The input layer, layer **X**, has n_x neurons. It is just a fan-out layer; i.e. its neurons serve as distributing points. The output vector of this layer is equal to its input vector **X**.

REFERENCES

[1] D.A. Wismer and R.Chatterji, "Introduction to Non-linear Optimization", North Holland, New York 1978.

[2] V.K Sood, N. Kandil, R.V. Patel, and K. Khorasani, "Comparative Evaluation of Neural Network Based Current Controllers for HVDC Transmission", Power Electronics specialists Conf., PESC'92, June 29–July 3, 1992, Toledo, Spain.

[3] D.B. Parker, "Optimal algorithm for Adaptive Networks: Second Order Back Propagation, Second Order Direct Propagation, and Second Order Hebbian Learning", Proc. 1st JICNN, San Diego, 1987, Vol. 2, pp. 593 - 600.

[4] D.E. Rumelhart, et al, "Learning Internal Representations by Error Propagation", Parallel Distributed Processing - Explorations in the Microstructure of Cognition, Vol. 1, MIT Press, Cambridge, MA, 1986, pp. 318–364.

[5] R.A. Jacobs, "Increased Rates of Convergence Through Learning Rate adaptation", Neural Networks., 1988, Vol.1,.

[6] D.J. Park, B.E. Jun, and J.H. Kim, "Novel Fast Training Algorithm for Multilayer Feedforward Neural Network", Electronics Letters, March 12, 1992, Vol.28, No.6.

[7] H. Demuth and M. Beal, "Neural Network ToolBox for Use with MATLAB", The Math Works Inc., Natick, MA, 1992.

[8] M.K. Weir, "A Method for Self-Determination of Adaptive Learning Rates in BackProagation", Neural Netw, Vol.4.

[9] Y-H Poa, "Adaptive Recognition and Neural Networks", Addison-Wesley, Reading, MA, 1989.

On the Convergence of Feed Forward Neural Networks Incorporating Terminal Attractors

Colin R. Jones
colin@cs.uwa.edu.au

Chi Ping Tsang
tsang@cs.uwa.edu.au

Logic & AI Laboratory
Department of Computer Science
The University of Western Australia
Crawley, Western Australia, 6009.

***Abstract*—This paper examines feed forward networks and the backpropagation algorithm from the point of view of dynamical systems theory. We investigate a modification to the learning dynamics using the notion of a terminal attractor - a stable equilibrium solution that is guaranteed to be reached in finite time.**

We find that, even though in theory convergence to a terminal attractor can be achieved within a very short span of the resulting trajectory, computing the trajectory in practice often requires higher numerical accuracy (than the standard algorithm) and thus smaller steps are taken along the trajectory at each iteration. We show that comparable improvements in convergence can be obtained by a simpler and computationally less expensive variant of the standard backpropagation algorithm which incorporates a dynamically varying learning rate.

I. INTRODUCTION

The *backpropagation* algorithm, due to Rumelhart and McClelland [6], is an iterative learning algorithm for neural networks that has received widespread attention. It is a type of gradient descent algorithm that is applicable to a particular class of network, the so called *layered* networks, in which the computational units are grouped in layers, and the only connections are between units in adjacent layers.

While backpropagation has been successfully employed to solve many problems, it has several drawbacks. Firstly, the rate of convergence of the algorithm is generally very slow. Another, perhaps more serious problem, is that, like all gradient descent algorithms, backpropagation is prone to becoming trapped in local minima and can fail to find the global minimum representing the solution.

In this paper we examine gradient descent algorithms in general, and backpropagation in particular, from the viewpoint of dynamical systems theory. We show that, under fairly weak conditions, a class of dynamical systems which includes backpropagation has a theoretically infinite *relaxation time*. Thus the backpropagation algorithm will only reach the point at which the global error is minimised in the limit as $t \to \infty$. We then examine a particular modification to the learning *dynamics*, first suggested by Wang and Hsu [9], incorporating the notion of a *terminal attractor* which guarantees convergence in finite time.

The performance of the resulting (terminal attractor) algorithm is then compared with a variant of the standard backpropagation algorithm, incorporating an adaptive learning rate. We show that, in terms of the number of iterations required, the simple mechanism of choosing a (near) optimal learning rate at each iteration is at least as efficient as the terminal attractor algorithm.

II. THE STANDARD BACKPROPAGATION ALGORITHM

We consider a (fully connected) layered network consisting of n layers. A weight w_{ij}^k is associated with the connection from the output of the jth unit in the $(k-1)^{th}$ layer to the input of the ith unit in the kth layer. The behaviour of the network is governed by the equations

$$net_i^{\nu k} = \sum_j w_{ij}^k u_j^{\nu,k-1} \tag{1}$$

$$u_i^{\nu k} = \sigma\left(net_i^{\nu k}\right) \tag{2}$$

0-7803-0999-5/93/$03.00

$u_i^{\nu k}$ represents the output of the ith unit in the kth layer when the νth pattern is presented to the network.

$net_i^{\nu k}$ represents the total (summed) input to the ith unit in the kth layer (for the νth pattern).

σ is the non-linear threshold function.

The input layer (although not strictly a layer as such) is represented as the 0th layer, while the nth layer is the output layer. The bias for each unit is also represented as w_{i0}^k (or equivalently we assume that the 0th *output* from the previous layer is always clamped to 1).

The performance of the network is measured by an error function E which measures the total error between the output $u_i^{\nu n}$ calculated by the network and the target output y_i^ν for all input/output pairs. The standard choice for E is usually the following

$$E = \frac{1}{2}\sum_{\nu,i}\left(u_i^{\nu n} - y_i^\nu\right)^2 \tag{3}$$

The essential idea behind the backpropagation algorithm is to view the error E as a function of the parameters w_{ij}^k and to perform *gradient descent* in this *weight space* to search for a minimum in the value of the (total) error E.

Gradient descent is a standard technique in which the parameters are updated incrementally so that, at each iteration, a *small* step is taken in the direction in which E is decreasing the most rapidly. This gives rise to the following update rule

$$\Delta w_{ij}^k = -\eta\frac{\partial E}{\partial w_{ij}^k} \tag{4}$$

The parameter $\eta > 0$, called the *learning rate*, controls how large a step we should take. It should be noted that this approach is so far typical of any gradient descent algorithm and not specific to backpropagation. What is distinctive about backpropagation is the manner in which the partial derivatives in the above equations are calculated. By restricting the topology of the network to include only connections between adjacent layers,[1] and assuming that the transfer function σ is *differentiable*, it is possible to recursively calculate the partial derivatives above via the chain rule. Specifically, if we define

$$\delta_i^{\nu k} = -\frac{\partial E}{\partial net_i^{\nu k}} \tag{5}$$

[1] This restriction is somewhat more severe than is actually necessary. It is in fact possible to have connections between layers that are not necessarily adjacent, provided that the output of a unit is not connected to the input of any *previous* layer (lateral connections between units within the same layer are also prohibited). Most networks in use however usually only have connections between adjacent layers.

then, upon application of the chain rule, one obtains

$$\Delta w_{ij}^k = -\eta\frac{\partial E}{\partial w_{ij}^k} = \eta\sum_\nu \delta_i^{\nu k} u_j^{\nu,k-1} \tag{6}$$

where each $\delta_i^{\nu k}$ is obtained recursively via the so called *generalised delta rule*[2]

$$\delta_j^{\nu n} = \sigma'\left(net_j^{\nu n}\right)\left(y_j^\nu - u_j^{\nu n}\right) \tag{7}$$

$$\delta_j^{\nu k} = \sigma'\left(net_j^{\nu k}\right)\sum_i \delta_i^{\nu,k+1} w_{ij}^{k+1} \tag{8}$$

where σ' denotes the derivative of the threshold function.

The rate at which this process will converge is heavily dependent on the value of the learning rate η. Too large a value can lead to instability and oscillation, while too small a value can drastically reduce the rate of convergence. A common modification, with the aim of improving stability, is to include a *momentum* term so that, at the mth iteration, the update rule becomes

$$\Delta w_{ij}^k(m) = \eta\sum_\nu \delta_i^{\nu k} u_j^{\nu,k-1} + \alpha\,\Delta w_{ij}^k(m-1) \tag{9}$$

where $0 \le \alpha < 1$. Thus, in effect, a portion of the correction at the current iteration is retained and not applied until the next iteration. The effect is to dampen any oscillations in the weight changes, resulting in improved convergence. However, the optimal values for η and α are highly problem dependent. One possibility to be considered is that convergence might be improved overall if the learning rate is allowed to vary dynamically, to give the optimal value at each iteration.

III. GRADIENT DESCENT VIEWED AS A DYNAMICAL SYSTEM

We can view the standard backpropagation algorithm (without momentum) as a *discrete* approximation to the *continuous* dynamical system governed by the following system of differential equations

$$\frac{dw_{ij}^k}{dt} = \sum_\nu \delta_i^{\nu k} u_j^{\nu,k-1} \tag{10}$$

This system corresponds essentially to backpropagation with a fixed learning rate.[3] We shall, however, consider the slightly more general system

$$\frac{dw_{ij}^k}{dt} = -\phi_i^k\frac{\partial E}{\partial w_{ij}^k} = \phi_i^k\sum_\nu \delta_i^{\nu k} u_j^{\nu,k-1} \tag{11}$$

[2] The recurrence relation for $\delta_i^{\nu k}$ is obtained by a further application of the chain rule. The reader is referred to [6] for details.

[3] If we identify the learning rate η with the time step Δt then the standard back propagation algorithm (without momentum) is precisely the first order Euler approximation for the differential equations (10)

Each (function) ϕ_i^k should be thought of as the continuous analogue of a dynamically varying learning rate.[4] The dynamics of the error function E is then given by

$$\frac{dE}{dt} = \sum_{i,j,k} \frac{\partial E}{\partial w_{ij}^k} \frac{dw_{ij}^k}{dt} = -\sum_{i,k} \phi_i^k \Gamma_i^k \quad (12)$$

where the functions Γ_i^k , introduced as a notational convenience, are defined via

$$\Gamma_i^k = \sum_j \left(\frac{\partial E}{\partial w_{ij}^k} \right)^2 = \sum_j \left(\sum_\nu \delta_i^{\nu k} u_j^{\nu, k-1} \right)^2 \quad (13)$$

Provided the functions ϕ_i^k are constrained to be non-negative, the total error E will be a non-increasing function of time. We wish to investigate under what circumstances E can be made to decrease as fast as possible.

IV. ALTERNATIVE DYNAMICS FOR THE TOTAL ERROR

A. Motivation

White [10] suggests that, in the discrete form of the back-propagation update rule, we should choose an effective learning rate so that, at each iteration (m), the resulting change in the total error ΔE satisfies the following

$$\Delta E(m) = -c\, E(m) \quad (14)$$

In the case of the continuous dynamical system, the analogous requirement is that the total error E satisfies a dynamics specified by a differential equation of the form

$$\frac{dE}{dt} = -a\, E \quad (15)$$

(for some constant $a > 0$). The solution of this equation is a decaying exponential, which shows that the total error E will converge to the solution 0. In terms of dynamical systems theory, we say that $E = 0$ is an *attractor* of the system.

The solution of (15) also shows that it theoretically takes infinite time to reach the attractor. This may not necessarily be a problem in practice, since we may get sufficiently close to the attractor in a reasonable time. However, for ill-conditioned systems, it can still take a long time to get even close to the attractor. Unfortunately many (feed forward) neural networks do result in dynamical systems that are ill-conditioned or mathematically *stiff* (Owens and Filkin [5]), and thus convergence is generally very slow.

The next section attempts to overcome such difficulties by investigating the possibility of obtaining solutions which can be reached in *finite* time.

[4] Note that this system allows a different learning rate for each unit in the network (excluding of course input units).

B. Terminal Attractors

Consider a general (autonomous) dynamical system characterised by the differential equation

$$\frac{dx}{dt} = f(x(t)) \quad (16)$$

A sufficient condition that guarantees the existence and uniqueness of solutions to (16), is that f satisfy the *Lipschitz* condition; namely, there is some $K > 0$ for which f satisfies the inequality

$$\|f(x_1) - f(x_2)\| \leq K\, \|x_1 - x_2\| \quad (17)$$

(for all x_1, x_2 in the domain of f). It is a standard theorem from elementary analysis that a differential equation of the form (16) satisfying the Lipschitz property *locally*[5] at a point x will admit a unique solution in some neighbourhood of x.

Thus trajectories representing solutions to (16) cannot intersect (since this would violate the uniqueness of the solution). In particular, since an attractor represents a singular solution, a regular solution (trajectory) can only converge to an attractor *asymptotically*, only reaching it in the limit as $t \to \infty$.

Zak [11] was the first to consider dynamical systems which possess (stable) equilibrium points at which the *Lipschitz* condition (17) no longer holds. Such a point, a so called *terminal attractor*,[6] is thus a singular solution to (16), which is intersected by all the regular solutions (transients). In particular, each regular solution approaches the attractor in finite time.

One of the simplest systems that exhibits a terminal attractor is that defined by the differential equation

$$\dot{x} = \frac{dx}{dt} = -x^\beta \qquad (0 < \beta < 1) \quad (18)$$

This equation has an equilibrium point at $x = 0$. It is an *attractor* if, in particular, β is of the form $(2n+1)^{-1}$ for some positive integer n. It is also straight forward to show that the *Lipschitz* condition (17) is violated at $x = 0$. Now integrating (18) directly gives the solution

$$x = \left[{x_0}^{1-\beta} - (1-\beta)\, t \right]^{1/(1-\beta)} \quad (19)$$

from which it is readily seen that the attractor at $x = 0$ becomes terminal, being reached after a finite relaxation time t_f given by

$$t_f = \frac{{x_0}^{1-\beta}}{1-\beta}$$

[5] The function f is said to be *locally Lipschitz* at a point x iff it satisfies the Lipschitz condition (17) on some compact neighbourhood of x.

[6] Although not discussed here, there is also the analogous concept of a *terminal repellor.* The interested reader is referred to [12]

C. *A modified Backpropagation Algorithm Incorporating Terminal Attractors*

Analogous to §IV.A, Wang and Hsu [9] suggest that the dynamics of the backpropagation algorithm should be modified so that the total error E satisfies the differential equation

$$\frac{dE}{dt} = -E^{\beta} \tag{20}$$

so that, in view of the results of the previous section, the the minimum value for the error E will correspond to a terminal attractor. Now equation (20) will be satisfied if we set

$$\phi_i^k = \frac{E^{\beta}}{N\Gamma_i^k} \tag{21}$$

in equation (12). Here N is the number of units (excluding input units) in the network. Note that equation (20) will remain valid provided that the functions ϕ_i^k remain finite for $E \neq 0$. Unfortunately this can not always be guaranteed since, at extremal points of the error E, the value of Γ_i^k will have the value 0. Even in the case when E is not at a genuine local minimum, it is still quite common for the values of Γ_i^k to become extremely small, such as the case where many units are operating well outside their linear regions and the resulting error surface is extremely flat. In such cases, the values of ϕ_i^k can become extremely large, causing difficulties when solving the differential equations (11) numerically.

In order to overcome these problems, we make a slight modification to (21) as follows

$$\phi_i^k = \frac{E^{\beta}}{N}\left(\epsilon + \Gamma_i^k\right)^{-1} \tag{22}$$

where the parameter ϵ is introduced to ensure that ϕ_i^k remains finite at local extrema.

It is worth considering further what happens when equations (11) are solved numerically. In the case when $\epsilon = 0$ then, at points of local extrema or regions where the error surface is extremely flat, the large values of ϕ_i^k that arise can result in a very large jump in weight space, even for a relatively small step size. Thus the value of Δt needs to be carefully chosen in order to avoid overshooting and the resulting unstable behaviour. This of course has to be reconciled with the fact that choosing a step size too small significantly increases the number of iterations that need to be performed.

This problem is less severe if we choose an appropriate $\epsilon > 0$. However, as we approach the *global* minimum of the error surface, the presence of the ϵ term changes the dynamics of the system near the attractor, significantly reducing the rate of convergence if ϵ is chosen to be too large. Thus, ideally, we should require the following:

When the error E is close to 0 we require that the Γ_i^k term dominates, so that the dynamics of E is similar to that of equation (29) near the attractor.

However, when E is still relatively large and $\Gamma_i^k \to 0$ (i.e. at points of local extrema and relatively flat regions of the error surface) we require that the ϵ term dominates so that the value of ϕ_i^k does not become infinitely large.

In order that both the above requirements are met, we propose replacing the parameter ϵ with a function $\lambda(E)$ with the property that $\lambda(E) \to 0$ as $E \to 0$.

We must also be careful to ensure that $\lambda(E)$ does not become too large for large values of E , since this would make the resulting value of ϕ_i^k very small, leading to unnecessarily slow convergence.

With these heuristics in mind, the form of the function $\lambda(E)$ was chosen to be

$$\lambda(E) = min\{\mu, E^m\} \tag{23}$$

for appropriate values for the parameters μ and m (see tables). Thus we arrive finally at the equations

$$\frac{dw_{ij}^k}{dt} = -\phi_i^k \frac{\partial E}{\partial w_{ij}^k} = \phi_i^k \sum_{\nu} \delta_i^{\nu k} u_j^{\nu,k-1} \tag{24}$$

where the functions ϕ_i^k are defined via

$$\phi_i^k = \frac{E^{\beta}}{N}\left(min\{\mu, E^m\} + \Gamma_i^k\right)^{-1} \tag{25}$$

$$\Gamma_i^k = \sum_j \left(\sum_{\nu} \delta_i^{\nu k} u_j^{\nu,k-1}\right)^2 \tag{26}$$

V. BACKPROPAGATION USING AN ENTROPY ERROR MEASURE

There is no a priori reason for choosing the quadratic measure (3) as the appropriate measure of the performance of the network. Baum and Wilczek [2] have shown that, by identifying (output) units in the network with a particular set of hypotheses, and interpreting the output of each unit as the probability that its hypothesis is true, the problem can now be thought of as one of learning a target probability distribution. The appropriate measure of the difference beteen the target distribution and the one calculated by the network is the *relative entropy* measure (Kullback [4]) given by

$$E = \sum_{\nu,i}\left[y_i^{\nu}\, log\left(\frac{y_i^{\nu}}{u_i^{\nu n}}\right) + (1-y_i^{\nu})\, log\left(\frac{1-y_i^{\nu}}{1-u_i^{\nu n}}\right)\right]$$

The gradient descent equations are easily modified to accommodate this new error function. In fact, in the case that the logistic function

$$\sigma(x) = \left(1 + e^{-\gamma x}\right)^{-1} \tag{27}$$

is used as the threshold function, the only modification required is in equation (7); namely[7]

$$\delta_i^{\nu n} = \gamma \left(y_i^{\nu} - u_i^{\nu n}\right) \tag{28}$$

Thus the only significant difference between using the relative entropy measure and the, more traditional, quadratic error measure is the absence of the factor $\sigma'(net_i^{\nu n})$ in the expression for $\delta_i^{\nu n}$.

Note, however, that this only applies to the output layer. The expressions for $\delta_i^{\nu k}$ in the remaining hidden layers remain unchanged. Even so, the presence of this factor in the output layer can have a significant effect on the rate of convergence. When a unit is driven into saturation, the value of $\sigma'(net_i^{\nu n})$ becomes extremely small, and thus only a small correction in the weights is achieved. This corresponds to very flat regions in the error surface. If the factor is not present, then the error surface tends to be less flat and convergence more rapid. Solla et al [8] have shown in fact that use of the relative entropy measure (with the standard backpropagation algorithm) can result in improved convergence of up to several orders of magnitude for some problems.

In the present case, the absence of the factor $\sigma'(net_i^{\nu n})$ in the expression for $\delta_i^{\nu n}$ will have a significant effect on the values of Γ_i^n, and hence also ϕ_i^n, in (24). In view of the results of Solla et al, one would expect improved convergence in this case. It is hoped however, that the improvements in convergence are even greater than those obtained using the standard backpropagation algorithm.

VI. SIMULATING THE DYNAMICS: AN ADAPTIVE LEARNING ALGORITHM

A. The Algorithm

Note that differential equations (24) above, with $\phi_i^k = 1$, correspond to the standard backpropagation algorithm (without momentum) when integrated numerically via the standard Euler approximation, and when the fixed time step Δt is identified with the learning rate η.

In the following simulations it was decided to use a higher order *Runge-Kutta-Fehlberg*[8] integration scheme. This involves using, in the present case, both a 4th and 5th order integration scheme. The difference between the two values calculated is used as a measure of the truncation error at each step, which is then used to control the size of the time step Δt; namely, Δt is always increased where possible while still ensuring that the (truncation) error stays within an acceptable tolerance. This gives rise to the following *adaptive* algorithm

1. Initialise t to 0 and Δt to 1. Set $w_{ij}^k(0)$ to values chosen randomly from the interval $[-0.5, 0.5]$
2. Integrate the equations

   $$\frac{dw_{ij}^k}{dt} = \phi_i^k \sum_{\nu} \delta_i^{\nu k} u_j^{\nu, k-1}$$

   forward in time, using the Runge-Kutta-Fehlberg (RKF) integration scheme, to calculate $w_{ij}^k(t + \Delta t)$
3. If the RKF truncation error is greater than the specified tolerance then reduce the step size via

   $$\Delta t := \tfrac{1}{2}\Delta t$$

   and return to step 2. Otherwise, update t via

   $$t := t + \Delta t$$
4. If the total error E is sufficiently close to 0 (i.e. within the specified accuracy) then HALT.
5. If the total error E is decreasing very slowly[9] (i.e. if E has decreased by less than 5 % since the previous iteration) then increase the step size for the next iteration via

   $$\Delta t := \tfrac{3}{2}\Delta t$$
6. Go to step 2 and repeat.

There is an important distinction to be made between the *continuous time* t, which essentially parameterises the trajectory in weight space, and the time it takes to actually compute the trajectory, measured in either iterations or cpu seconds. Note that, throughout this paper, the symbol t always denotes the former.

However, it is important to note that, in an integration scheme where the time step Δt remains fixed, the time t is proportional to the number of iterations actually performed. In the adaptive algorithm above, this is no longer the case. The time t instead gives a measure of the number of iterations that would have been required had a fixed time step been used throughout. The number of iterations required in this case is given simply by $\frac{t}{\Delta t}$.

[7] The reader is referred to [3] for details.

[8] See [7] for example.

[9] What counts as slow convergence in step 5 above is more or less an arbitrary choice. A reduction rate of more than 5 % per iteration is somewhat ambitious and, since this is rarely attained in practice, it may be advisable to experiment with different values. Also, while it has not been done presently, it is probably worth trying values other than $\frac{3}{2}$ in the update of Δt as well.

B. Results

The standard benchmark problem used in all simulations was the standard XOR problem. The network was configured to have 2 layers (i.e. one hidden layer and the one output layer) and was fully connected in the sense that every unit was connected to all other units in the adjoining layers. Initial weights and bias were chosen randomly from the interval $[-0.5, 0.5]$

The tolerance for the RKF truncation error was set to 1.0×10^{-6}, and each trial was stopped once the total error E reached below 1.0×10^{-5}. Each experiment was performed 20 times. For each trial the following was calculated

- The *continuous time t* taken by the dynamical system to reach the attractor representing the solution.
- The actual number of *iterations* (of the above algorithm) required to compute the resulting trajectory.
- The total cpu time (in seconds) required to compute the trajectory.[10]

In each case a comparison was made between the standard backpropagation algorithm ($\phi_i^k = 1$) and the dynamical system obtained by setting

$$\begin{aligned} \phi_i^k &= \frac{E^\beta}{N}\left(\lambda(E) + \Gamma_i^k\right)^{-1} \\ \lambda(E) &= min\{\mu, E^m\} \end{aligned}$$

for various values of the parameters μ and m. Also, a fixed value of $\frac{1}{3}$ was chosen for the parameter β.

For the first series of trials, μ was fixed at the value 0.1, while m ranged through the values shown in table 1. Each test was carried out using both the standard quadratic error measure and the relative entropy measure. The average[11] values for t, the number of iterations, and cpu time are given for each case in tables 1 and 2 respectively.

In the second series of trials, the parameter m was fixed at the value 3, while μ was allowed to vary according to table 3. As before, each test was carried out using both the standard quadratic error measure and the relative entropy measure, and the results are shown in tables 3 and 4 respectively.

[10] Note that, as one should expect, the cpu time is roughly proportional to the number of iterations.

[11] The values given in the above tables are averages over successful trials, where a trial was deemed unsuccessful if it had failed to converge after 3000 iterations. There were 2 cases out of the 20 sets of initial starting weights, in which the system failed to converge. With one exception, the system failed to converge for both these sets of weights in every case - i.e. for the standard algorithm and the terminal attractor algorithm, and for all permutations of the choice of error function and the values of μ and m.

μ	E^m	**time** (t)	**iterations**	**cpu time**
standard		2.892×10^9	660	261
0.1	E	6.014×10^6	646	353
0.1	E^2	3.795×10^2	686	374
0.1	E^3	1.110×10^2	855	467
0.1	E^4	6.007×10^1	1032	563

Table 1: Convergence times using $\lambda(E) = min\{\mu, E^m\}$ for varying values of m. (E calculated using the quadratic error measure.)

μ	E^m	**time** (t)	**iterations**	**cpu time**
standard		1.157×10^6	490	183
0.1	E	4.582×10^3	481	257
0.1	E^2	1.018×10^2	529	283
0.1	E^3	7.797×10^1	627	335
0.1	E^4	7.279×10^1	719	384

Table 2: Convergence times using $\lambda(E) = min\{\mu, E^m\}$ for varying values of m. (E calculated using the relative entropy error measure.)

μ	E^m	**time** (t)	**iterations**	**cpu time**
standard		2.892×10^9	660	261
1.0	E^3	1.273×10^2	856	467
0.1	E^3	1.110×10^2	855	467
0.01	E^3	1.688×10^1	851	464
0.001	E^3	4.352	826	451

Table 3: Convergence times using $\lambda(E) = min\{\mu, E^m\}$ for varying values of μ. (E calculated using the quadratic error measure.)

μ	E^m	**time** (t)	**iterations**	**cpu time**
standard		1.157×10^6	490	183
1.0	E^3	6.535×10^2	635	339
0.1	E^3	7.797×10^1	627	335
0.01	E^3	1.408×10^1	595	318
0.001	E^3	6.501	540	288

Table 4: Convergence times using $\lambda(E) = min\{\mu, E^m\}$ for varying values of μ. (E calculated using the relative entropy error measure.)

VII. DISCUSSION

As noted above, the computed time t, and the actual number of iterations (i.e. gradient evaluations) are effectively measured in different units.[12] Thus, while the value of the *continuous time* t is not meaningful by itself in absolute terms, it does give a relative measure of the rate of convergence as we progress down each row of each of the tables above. In this context, the decreasing values of t, as we progress down the rows of each table, shows that the relative performance of the *terminal attractor* algorithm is considerably superior (by several orders of magnitude) to the standard backpropagation algorithm in a case where a fixed time step (learning rate) Δt is used.

Consider now an integration scheme in which the time step Δt can be varied at each iteration. In this instance, the continuous time is no longer a meaningful measure of the rate of convergence, in either relative or absolute terms. If we consider the required number of iterations for each algorithm shown in the tables above then, in most cases, the rate of convergence for the terminal attractor algorithm is actually worse than the standard backpropagation algorithm. Although, overall, the relative variation in convergence rates is also considerably smaller.

Furthermore, when we also take in to consideration the fact that each iteration of the terminal attractor algorithm is computationally more expensive than for the standard algorithm, the performance of the terminal attractor is significantly inferior to the standard algorithm (with adaptive learning rate). This can be easily seen by comparing the actual cpu time required in each case.

Thus, while the terminal attractor algorithm clearly wins over a *fixed learning rate* algorithm, the standard backpropagation algorithm, in combination with a scheme for adaptively changing the learning rate, seems the most efficient - both in terms of the total number of iterations required, and the computational cost of each iteration.

It should also be noted that, even though the Runge-Kutta methods used in the simulations are more accurate than the standard first order approximation normally associated with backpropagation, they can still behave badly for ill-conditioned systems (Sewell [7]). However, while even more accurate numerical methods may require still fewer iterations, it is our belief that any computational speedup will apply equally to the terminal attractor algorithm and to the standard backpropagation algorithm with an adaptive learning rate.

VIII. CONCLUSION

In this paper we have sought to apply the techniques of (non-linear) dynamical systems theory in analysing the performance of gradient descent algorithms in general, and the backpropagation algorithm in particular. It has been shown that, the modification of the dynamics to incorporate terminal attractors, leads theoretically to quicker convergence times. Experimental results on the other hand show that, in general, the numerical precision required necessitates smaller time steps and thus tends to work against the gains made.

Computer simulations seem to support the fact that a scheme for dynamically adapting the learning rate is both computationally inexpensive and makes the standard algorithm at least as efficient, in terms of the rate of convergence, as more sophisticated algorithms such as the terminal attractor algorithm.

[12] We may think of t measuring the number of iterations, where 1 unit of time corresponds to $\frac{1}{\Delta t}$ iterations (for a **fixed** time step Δt).

REFERENCES

[1] BARHEN, J. and GULATI, S. and ZAK, M. (1989), Neural Learning of Constrained Nonlinear Transformations, *Computer* June pp67-76

[2] BAUM, Eric B. and WILCZEK, Frank (1988), Supervised Learning of Probability Distributions by Neural Networks *Neural Information Processing Systems* pp52-61

[3] HERTZ, John and KROGH, Anders and PALMER, Richard G. (1991), *Introduction to the Theory of Neural Computation*

[4] KULLBACK, S. (1959), *Information Theory and Statistics*

[5] OWENS, A. J. and FILKIN, D. L. (1989), Efficient Training of the Backpropagation Network by Solving a System of Stiff Ordinary Differential Equations, *Proc. Int. Joint Conf. Neural Networks* II pp381-386

[6] RUMELHART D.E. and McCLELLAND, J.L. (1986), Learning Internal Representations by Error Propagation, *Parallel Distributed Processing (Vol 1)* ch 8. pp319-361

[7] SEWELL, Granville (1988), *The Numerical Solution of Ordinary and Partial Differential Equations*

[8] SOLLA, S.A. and LEVIN, E. and FLEISHER, M. (1988), Accelerated Learning in Layered Neural Networks, *Complex Systems* **2** pp625-639

[9] Sheng-De WANG and Ching-Hao HSU (1991), Terminal Attractor Learning Algorithms for Back Propagation Neural Networks, *Proc. Int. Joint Conf. Neural Networks* III pp182-189

[10] WHITE, H. (1990), The Learning Rate in Backpropagation Systems: an Application of Newton's Method, *Proc. Int. Joint Conf. Neural Networks* I pp679-684

[11] ZAK Michail (1988), Terminal Attractors for Addressable Memory in Neural Networks, *Physics Letters A* pp18-22

[12] ZAK Michail (1989), Terminal Attractors in Neural Networks, *Neural Networks Vol 2* pp259-274

A Comparison of Recurrent Neural Network Learning Algorithms

Antonette M. Logar[1], Edward M. Corwin[1], and
William J.B. Oldham[2]

***Abstract*— This work describes selected recurrent network training algorithms and compares their performances with respect to speed and accuracy for a given problem. Detailed complexity analyses are presented to allow more accurate comparison between training algorithms for networks with few nodes. In addition, network performance for predicting the Mackey-Glass equation is reported for each of the recurrent networks as well as for a back propagation network. Using networks of comparable size, the recurrent networks produced significantly better prediction accuracy. The accuracy of the back propagation network was improved by increasing the size of the network, but the recurrent networks continued to produce better results for the larger prediction distances. Of the recurrent networks considered, Pearlmutter's off-line training algorithm produced the best results.**

I. Introduction

Recurrent neural networks have received increasing attention in recent publications. A recurrent network is one in which self loops and backward connections between nodes are allowed. One of the consequences of this fact is that dynamic behaviors not possible with strictly feed-forward networks, such as limit cycles [10] and chaos [1], can be produced with recurrent networks. The diversity of dynamic behaviors suggests that recurrent networks may be well suited to the problem of time series prediction. Another possible benefit of recurrent networks is that smaller networks may provide the functionality of much larger feed-forward networks. Traditional complexity analysis, however, assumes a large number of nodes. Both of these issues are addressed in subsequent sections.

The training algorithms used in our experiments are the Williams and Zipser algorithm [14], Pearlmutter's algorithm [10], and Sun, Chen and Lee's algorithm [11]. All three learning algorithms attempt to minimize the total error along a trajectory. Pearlmutter's method takes the most direct approach and uses the total error between the network output and the desired trajectory as the error function to be minimized. Thus, this is an off-line method, that is, updates are done after the entire trajectory has been processed. Williams and Zipser present an on-line training algorithm. The error is computed and the weights are changed at each step in the trajectory. As will be seen below, there is a significant time penalty for this change to an on-line algorithm. Sun, Chen, and Lee have given a method for speeding up the calculation involved in a Williams and Zipser style on-line network. Using a Green's function approach, they were able to obtain an order of magnitude increase in training speed for moderately large networks.

II. Speed Complexity Analyses

The standard measure of speed or space complexity of an algorithm is its "Big O." Big O is defined as : $f(x)$ is $O(g(x))$ if there exists an n_0 and a $c > 0$ such that for all $n > n_0$, $f(n) < cg(n)$. This definition does not guarantee a least upper bound, although most authors will endeavor to find one when presenting an algorithm. The real problem is that in determining the Big O of an algorithm, lower order terms and constants are ignored and the analysis is

[1] Department of Mathematics and Computer Science South Dakota School of Mines and Technology

[2] Computer Science Department, Texas Tech University

0-7803-0999-5/93/$03.00 ©1993 IEEE

only considered valid for large values of n. However, none of the research published to date has presented results for recurrent networks with a large number of nodes. "Large" is an admittedly vague term, but it is almost certainly larger than 12, the largest network reported so far. In addition, it is hoped that recurrent networks will perform tasks with fewer nodes than are required by equivalent feed-forward networks. Therefore, a detailed analysis which would allow comparisions between networks with a small numbers of nodes appeared warranted.

Some assumptions have been made in the following analysis. First, initialization and accounting procedures which are common to all of the algorithms have been ignored. Second, only operations involved in non-sequential segments were considered significant. That is, the operations found inside loop structures were counted and those not in loops were omitted. Finally, the analysis assumes that addition and multiplication are roughly the same speed but that division is a factor of two and one half times slower than multiplication. These assumptions were incorporated as a result of instruction timing experiments on a 486 based PC. The coefficients of the expressions presented below would change slightly if the assumptions were not valid for a specific machine. It is common to assume a generic instruction in complexity analyses, but the difference in speed between the divide instruction and the multiply instruction seemed to require that divisions be counted separately. Also, calculating the sigmoid or its inverse required approximately thirty times longer than the calculation of a single multiply. Therefore, these calculations were also treated separately.

Assume that the time interval $0 \rightarrow T$ is discretized into k steps. Each iteration of Williams and Zipser's algorithm contains a loop from 1 to k and for each k a network response is calculated and the weights are updated. The network response requires $2N^2 + 2NI + 30N$ operations, where I is the number of inputs. Recall that Williams and Zipser allow for any number of weighted inputs. The weights are adjusted during training in the same manner as weights connecting processing nodes. The weight update procedure, which involves the calculation of a three dimensional matrix of partials requires $(N + I)(N^3 + 5N^2 + 4N)$ operations. The final expression is :

$$(N^4 + 5N^3 + 6N^2 + 30N + 2N^3I + 5N^2I + 6NI) * k$$

The complexity of this algorithm is given in the literature as $O(kN^4)$, which agrees with the expression presented above.

Pearlmutter's algorithm is different from the approaches proposed by Williams and Zipser and Sun, Chen and Lee in that it requires off-line training. All of the data must be available when training begins. The advantage is that a much faster training algorithm can be used. A network response is calculated for each time step $1 \rightarrow k$, followed by a backward integration performed from $k \rightarrow 1$. Finally, a single weight update is computed. The batch weight update is responsible for the considerable decrease in training time per iteration when compared to the other algorithms. The forward integration requires $2N^2 + 35N$ operations and the backward integration requires $3N^2 + 35N$ operations. These two routines are done k times each. The weight update, done only once per epoch, requires $2kN^2 + 2kN^2 + kN$. The final expression is then :

$$7kN^2 + 71kN + 2N^2$$

Thus, the speed complexity of this algorithm is generally given as $O(kN^2)$. Note that this algorithm does not allow for input weights that are adjusted during training. The advantage of this approach is that the number of weights adjusted during the weight update procedure is smaller than that required by an equivalent Williams and Zipser network. The disadvantage is that the network may be harder to train for some problems.

The Sun, Chen and Lee algorithm possesses the same structure as the Williams and Zipser algorithm. For each of k time steps a network response is calculated and the weights are updated. As in Pearlmutter, inputs with trainable weights are not part of the algorithm. The network response requires $2N^2+35N$ operations. The weight update, which includes a matrix inversion, requires $6N^3+10N^2+30N$ operations. Note that to invert an arbitrary matrix requires $O(N^3)$ operations, but a more exact count of an LU decomposition algorithm yields $\frac{2}{3}N^3 + N^2 + 13N$. The final expression is :

$$(\frac{20}{3}N^3 + 13N^2 + 79N) * k$$

Sun, Chen and Lee give the complexity of their algorithm as $O(N^3)$ [11] but a better expression would be $O(kN^3)$. Although k is constant for a particular application, it is likely that k will be much larger than N, as was the case in Sun, Chen and Lee's experiments, and should not be ignored for small networks.

The effects of the lower order terms and constants can be seen in Table II. The results assume $k = 400$, and $I = 2$ to allow comparison with the Mackey-Glass results reported below. The number of operations was divided by the number of multiplies per second to give a theoretical estimate of time in seconds for one epoch. The table demonstrates that for small N, the difference between methods, particularly between Williams and Zipser's algorithm and that of Sun, Chen and Lee, is not very large. It also shows rather clearly that Sun, Chen and Lee's algorithm can save a substantial amount of time for even modest networks. Finally, if off-line training is possible, Pearlmutter's algorithm is very efficient.

A considerable amount of time was spent creating implementations of these algorithms which were optimized for speed. Tests were conducted to determine how well the theoretical estimates agreed with observed timings. The timings presented in the table are for the Mackey-Glass data set using 400 training samples. As expected, the actual timings are larger than the estimates since the estimates ignored operations not contained in loops as well as memory loads. However, the relative sizes of the numbers are close to those projected by the estimates.

Timing Results			
# Nodes	Pearl-mutter	Williams & Zipser	Sun, Chen, Lee
2	0.1360	0.1888	0.2107
3	0.2208	0.4752	0.4272
4	0.3169	1.0048	0.7605
5	0.4241	1.8880	1.2427
8	0.8131	8.0512	3.9019
10	1.1284	16.8160	7.0053
12	1.4886	31.2768	11.4720
15	2.1129	68.1840	21.2880

Table 1: Estimated times from algorithm analysis

Timing Results			
# Nodes	Pearl-mutter	Williams & Zipser	Sun, Chen, Lee
5	0.495	2.10	1.6
8	1.04	8.35	4.0
10	1.54	17.72	8.3
15	2.99	70.22	24.3

Table 2: Timings, in seconds, for the three networks

III. Comparison of Performance

Time series analysis and prediction is an established branch of mathematics. Recently, time series prediction has also become a topic of interest in neural network literature. [3] [4] [5] [6]. Several studies have demonstrated that feed-forward networks can produce good prediction accuracy [7] [13] [8] [9] but little has been written about the applicability of recurrent neural networks to time series prediction. [2]

A commonly studied time series is the sequence of values produced by the Mackey-Glass equation :

$$\frac{dx(t)}{dt} = \frac{ax(t-1)}{1 + x^{10}(t-\tau)} - bx(t)$$

In these experiments $\tau = 17$, $a = 0.2$ and $b = 0.1$. These values produce a chaotic time series. Accuracy of prediction is measured by the arv :

$$arv = \frac{\sum_k (target_k - prediction_k)^2}{\sum_k (target_k - mean)^2}$$

The accuracy of prediction is affected by the number of previous data points, or the lag, used in making a prediction. The accuracy is also a function of the number of steps into the future the network must predict. Generally, the greater the lag the higher the prediction accuracy and the greater the prediction distance, the lower the accuracy. For these experiments, a lag of three was used and results are presented for a variety of prediction distances.

The back propagation network was composed of 3 input nodes, 10 hidden nodes and a single output node. The recurrent networks each contained 5 nodes making the number of weights, forty, equal to that of the feed-forward network. Note that if a recurrent network with n nodes is fully connected and each node receives m weighted inputs, $n^2 + nm$ weights must be updated. A feed-forward network with a total of n nodes, and assuming one output node and m input nodes, has a total of $(n-m-1)(m+1)$ weights. For $n = 5$ and $m = 3$, a fully connected network would have 40 weights, while the feed-forward network would have only 4. Since a network stores its "knowledge" in the weights, the number of weights was kept equal for all networks rather than the number of nodes.

The results of the experiments are presented in Table 3 and Table 4. Teacher forcing was used in all of the recurrent network experiments. In the recurrent networks studied here, each node produces an output at each time t and the error is calculated as the difference between the actual and desired outputs. Using teacher forcing the desired output value is fed back to the nodes rather than the actual output. Teacher forcing was used by Williams and Zipser in [14] but

Performance on Training Data				
Steps	Back Prop	Williams & Zipser	Pearl- mutter	Sun, Chen, Lee
1	0.0071	0.0054	0.0022	0.0165
2	0.0323	0.0177	0.0107	0.0654
4	0.2192	0.0909	0.0544	0.2515
8	1.3401	0.2125	0.1782	0.8632

Table 3: One, two, four and eight step prediction of the Mackey-Glass equations. Four hundred points were used for training.

Performance on Testing Data				
Steps	Back Prop	Williams & Zipser	Pearl- mutter	Sun, Chen, Lee
1	0.0092	0.0077	0.0031	0.0244
2	0.0441	0.0163	0.0147	0.0985
4	0.3173	0.0915	0.0721	0.3938
8	2.0074	0.2242	0.2951	1.3756

Table 4: One, two, four and eight step prediction of the Mackey-Glass equations. One hundred points were used for testing.

Back Propagation : lag 17		
Steps	arv (train)	arv (test)
1	0.0052	0.0052
2	0.0201	0.0196
4	0.1084	0.0977
8	0.5249	0.3964

Table 5: One, two, four and eight step prediction of the Mackey-Glass equations for a back propagation network with 17 inputs and 20 hidden nodes.

not by Pearlmutter or Sun, Chen and Lee. Our experiments indicate that teacher forcing is very effective in a Pearlmutter network for time series prediction. However, in other experiments, such as generating limit cycles without input, teacher forcing was not necessary. The Sun, Chen and Lee net also produced improved performance with the addition of teacher forcing. The results reported also assume weighted inputs for each of the networks. The algorithm as described by Williams and Zipser contains weighted inputs but modifications had to be made to the other two algorithms to accomodate the additional weights. The disadvantage of weighted inputs is the increase in the time required for the updates, but our experiments showed a significant improvement in prediction accuracy with the addition of trainable input weights.

Tables 3 and 4 show that with the same number of network connections, recurrent networks perform considerably better on this problem than the back propagation network. One reason is that, as noted above, a larger lag tends to improve performance. The recurrent connections allow the networks to retain information about previous states producing an implicitly larger lag. Table 5 shows that the performance of the back propagation network is greatly improved by increasing the lag to 17. However, the recurrent network results are still superior, particularly for the larger lags.

IV. Conclusion

The networks discussed here are just a sample of the possible recurrent network training algorithms. Additional algorithms continue to appear in the literature. In particular, a recent paper by Toomarian and Bahren [12] presents an on-line training rule and an interesting approach to teacher forcing. For the selected networks, two aspects of recurrent neural network performance were addressed here : speed and accuracy. A more thorough speed complexity analysis was presented to allow comparison between training algorithms for networks with a small number of nodes. In addition, it was demonstrated that for predicting the chaotic Mackey-Glass time series, all of the recurrent networks produced better results than that of the comparably sized back propagation network, especially for multi-step prediction. Of the networks studied, the Pearlmutter architecture appears best suited to the task and it is also the least expensive recurrent algorithm. The disadvantage to that approach is that the algorithm is not on-line, but many tasks do not require on-line learning.

References

[1] Aihara, K., T. Takabe and M. Toyoda, "Chaotic Neural Networks," *Physics Letters A*, Volume 144, Number 6,7, March 12, 1990.

[2] Connor, Jerome, Les Atlas and Doug Martin, "Recurrent Neural Networks and Time Series Prediction," *Neural Information Processing Conference*, Denver, December 1991.

[3] Farmer, J. Doyne and John Sidorowich, "Exploiting Chaos to Predict the Future and Reduce Noise," LA-UR-88-901 (1988).

[4] He, Xiangdong and Alan Lapedes, "Nonlinear Modeling and Prediction By Successive Approximation Using Radial Basis Functions," Technical Report LA-UR-91-1375, Los Alamos National Laboratory (1991).

[5] Jones, R.D., Y.C. Lee, C.W. Barnes, G.W. Flake, K. Lee, P.S. Lewis, and S. Qian, "Function Approximation and Time Series Prediction with Neural Networks," LA-UR-90-21 (1989).

[6] Jones, R.D., Y.C. Lee, S. Qian, C.W. Barnes, K.R. Bisset G.M. Bruce, G.W. Flake, K. Lee, L.A. Lee, W.C. Mead, M.K. O'Rourke I.J. Poli, and L.E. Thode, "Nonlinear Adaptive Networks

: A Little Theory, A Few Applications," LA-UR-91-273 (1990).

[7] Lapedes, Alan and Robert Farber, "Nonlinear Signal Processing Using Neural Networks : Prediction and System Modeling," Technical Report LA-UR-87-2662, Los Alamos National Laboratory (1987).

[8] Logar, Antonette, Edward Corwin and William J.B. Oldham, "Predicting Acid Concentrations in Processing Plant Effluent : An Application of Time Series Prediction Using Neural Networks," to appear in the *Conference Proceedings of the ACM SAC '92 Conference*, March 1992.

[9] Mead, W.C., R.D. Jones, Y.C. Lee, C.W. Barnes, G.W. Flake, L.A. Lee M.K. O'Rourke, "Prediction of Chaotic Time Series Using CNLS-Net - Example: The Mackey-Glass Equation," LA-UR-91-720, 1991.

[10] Pearlmutter, Barak, "Dynamic Recurrent Neural Networks," Technical Report CMU-CS-90-196, December 1990.

[11] Sun, Guo-Zheng, Hsing-Hen Chen and Yee-Chun Lee, "Green's Function Method for Fast On-Line Learning Algorithm of Recurrent Neural Network," Advances in Information Processing Systems 4, John E. Moody, Steven J. Hanson and Richard P. Lippmann, editors, 1992.

[12] Toomarian, Nikzad, and Jacob Barhen, "Learning a Trajectory Using Adjoint Functions and Teacher Forcing," Neural Networks, Vol. 5, pp. 473-484, 1992.

[13] Weigend, Andreas, Bernardo Huberman and David Rumelhart, "Predicting the Future : A Connectionist Approach," *International Journal of Neural Systems*, Vol. 1 (1990) p193.

[14] Williams, R.J. and D. Zipser "Experimental Analysis of the Real-Time Recurrent Learning Algorithm," *Connection Science*, Vol. 1, No. 1, 1989.

A Theory of Over-Learning in the Presence of Noise

Kazutaka Yamasaki Hidemitsu Ogawa
Department of Computer Science
Tokyo Institute of Technology
2-12-1 Ookayama, Meguro-ku
Tokyo 152, Japan

Abstract—We discuss the over-learning problem for multilayer feedforward neural networks. A framework was proposed by the present authors for the over-learning problem with noise free training data. In this paper, first we show that the framework is still valid in the case of noisy training data. It is applied to the case where the *rote memorization criterion* is used as a substitute for the Wiener criterion. Necessary and sufficient conditions for two kinds of *admissibility* of the rote memorization criterion by the Wiener criterion are obtained. These conditions lead us to a method for choosing a training set which prevents *Wiener-over-learning.*

I. Introduction

When the error back-propagation (BP) learning algorithm [13] is applied to multilayer feedforward neural networks, it is observed that a decrease in errors over the training data does not mean a decrease over novel data and in fact may lead to lower generalization. This phenomenon is called *over-learning.*

The BP algorithm is an algorithm which can solve the criterion which asks for correct responses to training inputs. This criterion is called the *memorization criterion.* In the context of the generalization problem, we can say that the memorization criterion is used as a substitute for some 'true' criterion which describes errors over all inputs. The essential point of over-learning lies in the relation between those two criteria. Based on this observation, a general framework for the over-learning problem which describes the relation between a true criterion J and its substitute criterion J' was proposed in [9] and [12]. Also introduced were the concepts of *J-over-learning* and various kinds of *admissibility* of J' by J. For example, if J *always admits* J', then *J'-learning* does not cause J-over-learning.

These concepts were originally given for the case of noise free training data. However, there are cases where noisy training data are used. For example, such data may even be intentionally introduced to improve generalization ability [4][5][14]. Although other research considers noisy data taken by some measurement equipment to be one of the causes of over-learning.

In this paper, we discuss mathematically the over-learning problem when we use noisy training data. First we show that the framework proposed in [9] and [12] is still valid in the case of noisy training data. In this case, the BP algorithm is an algorithm which can solve the criterion which generally asks for the same responses as these given by the noisy training data. We shall call this criterion the *rote memorization criterion.* The framework is applied to the case where the rote memorization criterion is used as a substitute for the Wiener criterion. Necessary and sufficient conditions for two kinds of admissibility are obtained. These conditions lead us to a method for choosing a training set which prevents

This research was partially supported by the Grant-in-Aid for Scientific Research in Priority Areas #03244101 and #04236105.

0-7803-0999-5/93/$03.00 ©1993 IEEE

over-learning.

II. Neural network learning as an inverse problem

This paper follows the mathematical framework for the learning problem given in [7]-[9][11]. That is why we shall review it briefly in this section.

We are concerned with a multilayer feedforward neural network whose number of input and output units are L and 1, respectively. Assume that its output unit has a linear activation function. In this case, a neural network can be regarded as a real valued function. It is denoted by $f_0(x)$ with x an L-dimensional real vector. The learning problem is to construct a neural network by using training data so that the neural network expresses the best approximation $f_0(x)$ to a desired function $f(x)$.

Let H be the set of all functions f to be approximated by the neural network. Assume that H is a Hilbert space with the reproducing kernel[1] $K(x, x')$.

The training data are given as a set of M input vectors, say $\{x_m\}_{m=1}^M$, and corresponding desired output values, say $\{y_m\}_{m=1}^M$. Assume that y_m includes an additive noise n_m, i.e.,

$$y_m = f(x_m) + n_m. \qquad (1)$$

Once a set $\{x_m\}_{m=1}^M$ of training inputs is fixed, the set $\{f(x_m)\}_{m=1}^M$ of corresponding outputs is uniquely determined from f. Then we can introduce an operator A which transforms f to the vector consisting of $\{f(x_m)\}_{m=1}^M$. Note that the operator A becomes a linear operator even when we are concerned with nonlinear neural networks. Indeed, it is expressed by

$$A = \sum_{m=1}^{M} e_m \otimes K(x, x_m), \qquad (2)$$

[1]The reproducing kernel $K(x, x')$ of a functional Hilbert space H is a bivariate function which satisfies the following two conditions [3]: (i) For any fixed x', $K(x, x')$ is a function in H. (ii) For any f in H and for any x', it follows that $(f(x), K(x, x')) = f(x')$, where $(\cdot,\cdot)$ denotes the inner product in H.

where $\{e_m\}_{m=1}^M$ is the so-called natural basis, i.e., e_m is the M-dimensional vector consisting of zero elements except the element m equal to 1. The notation $(\cdot \otimes \cdot)$ is the Schatten product[2]. Let us denote the M-dimensional vectors consisting of $\{y_m\}_{m=1}^M$ and $\{n_m\}_{m=1}^M$ by y and n, respectively. From (1), we have

$$y = Af + n. \qquad (3)$$

Now we can say that our learning problem is the problem of obtaining an estimate, say f_0, to f from y in the model (3). It is equivalent to the problem of obtaining an operator B, which provides f_0 from y:

$$f_0 = By. \qquad (4)$$

This problem belongs to the general class of inverse problems, e.g., signal and image restoration. To solve it we can use general results obtained from the field of inverse problems [1][6].

There exist in general many functions f which provide the same vector y. Hence, we need a criterion for choosing an operator B. Such a criterion is called a *learning criterion.*

When an operator B is discussed in the context of a learning criterion J, B is called a *J-learning.* An operator B satisfying J is called a *proper J-learning* and denoted by A_J. Since A_J is not always unique, let $A\{J\}$ be the set of all A_J. The function f_0 given by an A_J is called a *J-optimally generalizing neural network* (J-OGNN) or a *J neural network* for short.

Two examples of learning criteria are listed below.

(i) J_{RM}: Find B which minimizes the following objective function for each $y = Af + n$,

$$J_{RM}[B] = \|ABy - y\|^2, \qquad (5)$$

where $\|\cdot\|$ is the norm in $\boldsymbol{R}^M$.

This criterion is called the rote memorization criterion, which is discussed in detail in IV.

[2]Let H and K be Hilbert spaces. For $f \in H$ and $g \in K$, the Schatten product $f \otimes g$ is an operator from K to H, which is defined by $(f \otimes g)h = (h, g)f$, where h is an arbitrary element of K.

(ii) J_W: Find B which minimizes the following objective function,

$$J_W[B] = E_{f,n}\|By - f\|^2, \tag{6}$$

where $\|\cdot\|$ is the norm in H and $E_{f,n}$ is the expectation taken over $\{f\}$ and $\{n\}$.

This criterion is called the Wiener criterion [1][6]. In practice, the suitable criterion should be chosen based on the requirements of the problem.

III. Over-learning in the presence of noise

As mentioned in the Introduction, the memorization criterion used by the BP algorithm is a substitute for some true criterion. Based on this observation, the present authors introduced in [9] and [12] a mathematical definition of over-learning and the concept of various kinds of admissibility as follows:

Definition 1 *(J-over-learning) If a proper J'-learning $A_{J'}$ does not satisfy a criterion J, i.e., if $A_{J'} \notin A\{J\}$, then $A_{J'}$ is said to cause J-over-learning.*

Definition 2 *(Admissibility)*
(i) *Non admissibility: If all proper J'-learnings cause J-over-learning, i.e., if it follows that*

$$A\{J\} \cap A\{J'\} = \phi, \tag{7}$$

then it is said that J does not admit J'.
(ii) *Partial admissibility: If there is at least one proper J'-learning which does not cause J-over-learning, i.e., if it follows that*

$$A\{J\} \cap A\{J'\} \neq \phi, \tag{8}$$

then it is said that J partially admits J'.
(iii) *Admissibility: If all proper J'-learnings do not cause J-over-learning, i.e., if it follows that*

$$A\{J\} \supset A\{J'\}, \tag{9}$$

then it is said that J always admits J', or briefly said that J admits J'.
(iv) *Complete admissibility: If J always admits J' and vice versa, i.e., if it follows that*

$$A\{J\} = A\{J'\}, \tag{10}$$

then it is said that J completely admits J'.

These concepts were originally given for the case of noise free training data. The concepts, however, do not depend on the choice of the criteria J and J'. Hence, the concepts are still valid in the case where, for example, J_W and J_{RM} are used as J and J', respectively. That is, we can apply the concepts to the present learning model given by (3) and (4), where noisy training data are used.

IV. Memorization learning

A. *Memorization learning from noisy training data*

In this section we shall discuss the case where the substitute criterion J' is the memorization criterion. When we are concerned with noisy training data, we can consider two kinds of memorization learnings. The first is the learning which gives the same outputs as the training outputs even when the training outputs are noisy. We shall call this the *rote memorization learning.* That is why J_{RM} in (5) is called the rote memorization criterion. The suffix '*RM*' of J_{RM} refers to 'rote memorization'. The second is the learning which gives the true outputs to the training inputs even when the training outputs are noisy. We shall call this the *error correcting memorization learning.* The BP algorithm is an algorithm which can solve J_{RM}. Hence, we shall discuss the properties of the rote memorization learning in detail in the next subsection.

B. *Rote memorization learning*

Let A^* and A^- be the adjoint operator and a 1-inverse[3] of A, respectively. Let $\mathcal{R}(A)$ and $\mathcal{N}(A)$ be the range and the null space of an operator A, respectively. Let $S^\perp$ be the orthogonal complement of a subspace S and $S \ominus T$ be $S \cap T^\perp$ for subspaces S and T such that $S \supset T$. Let $P_{S,T}$ and

[3] An operator X which satisfies $AXA = A$ is called a 1-inverse of A [2]. If X is non-singular, then a 1-inverse becomes the usual inverse of A. Otherwise there exist an infinite number of 1-inverses of A. The set of all 1-inverses of A is denoted by $A\{1\}$.

P_S be the projection operator onto a subspace S along a subspace T and the orthogonal projection operator onto S, respectively.

Let Q be the correlation matrix of the set $\{n\}$ of noises. Let S be the subspace spanned by the set $\{y\}$ of vectors $y = Af + n$. Assume that the operator B in (4) is linear hereafter. Note that the linear operator B can provide nonlinear neural networks f_0.

Theorem 1 *An operator B satisfies the rote memorization criterion J_{RM} if and only if*

$$ABP_S = P_{\mathcal{R}(A)}P_S. \tag{11}$$

The minimum value of $J_{RM}[B]$ is given by

$$\min J_{RM}[B] = \|P_{\mathcal{R}(A)^\perp}n\|^2. \tag{12}$$

(Proof) Eq.(11) is equivalent to

$$ABy = P_{\mathcal{R}(A)}y \qquad : y \in S. \tag{13}$$

Assume that B_0 satisfies (13). It follows for any B that

$$\|ABy - y\|^2 = \|ABy - P_{\mathcal{R}(A)}y\|^2 + \|P_{\mathcal{R}(A)^\perp}y\|^2, \tag{14}$$

so that

$$J_{RM}[B]-J_{RM}[B_0] = \|ABy-P_{\mathcal{R}(A)}y\|^2 \geq 0. \tag{15}$$

Eq.(15) implies that B_0 minimizes $J_{RM}[B]$. Conversely, when $J_{RM}[B]$ is minimum, the equality in (15) holds, so that B satisfies (13). Eq.(12) is clear from (14), (13) and (3). □

Theorem 1 yields

Example 1 *For any fixed 1-inverse A^- of A, the operator $A^-P_{\mathcal{R}(A)}$ becomes a proper rote memorization learning.*

Theorem 1 yields

Lemma 1 *It follows for any proper rote memorization learning A_{RM} that*

$$AA_{RM}A = A, \tag{16}$$

$$I - A_{RM}A = P_{\mathcal{N}(A),\mathcal{R}(A_{RM}A)}, \tag{17}$$

$$AA_{RM}Q = P_{\mathcal{R}(A)}Q. \tag{18}$$

Eqs.(3) and (4) yield that

$$f_0 = A_{RM}Af + A_{RM}n. \tag{19}$$

We shall call $A_{RM}Af$ and $A_{RM}n$ in (19) the signal component and the noise component of f_0, respectively. Eq.(17) yields for any f that

$$f - A_{RM}Af = P_{\mathcal{N}(A),\mathcal{R}(A_{RM}A)}f. \tag{20}$$

Eq.(20) yields

Corollary 1 *It follows for the signal component $A_{RM}Af$ that*

$$A_{RM}Af = f \tag{21}$$

if and only if

$$f \in \mathcal{R}(A_{RM}A). \tag{22}$$

Corollary 1 implies that $A_{RM}Af$ does not agree with f in general. However, they have the same values at $\{x_m\}_{m=1}^M$. That is, (16) yields

Corollary 2 *It follows for the signal component $A_{RM}Af$ that*

$$A(A_{RM}Af) = Af. \tag{23}$$

Now we shall discuss the response characteristics of a rote memorization neural network f_0 to $\{x_m\}_{m=1}^M$. Eq.(13) yields

$$AA_{RM}n = P_{\mathcal{R}(A)}n. \tag{24}$$

Eqs.(19), (23) and (24) yield

$$Af_0 = Af + P_{\mathcal{R}(A)}n. \tag{25}$$

Eqs.(25) and (3) yield

Corollary 3 *It follows for any rote memorization neural network f_0 that*

$$Af_0 = y \tag{26}$$

if and only if

$$n \in \mathcal{R}(A). \tag{27}$$

Corollary 3 implies that if (27) holds, then f_0 has the same values as these given by the noisy training output $\{y_m\}_{m=1}^M$ at $\{x_m\}_{m=1}^M$. However, if it follows that $n \in S \ominus \mathcal{R}(A)$, f_0 has the same values as these given by f itself at $\{x_m\}_{m=1}^M$. That is, (25) yields

Corollary 4 *It follows for any rote memorization neural network f_0 that*

$$Af_0 = Af \tag{28}$$

if and only if

$$n \in S \ominus \mathcal{R}(A). \tag{29}$$

V. Wiener Learning vs. Rote Memorization Learning

For further discussion of over-learning problem in the presence of noise, let us consider the case where the rote memorization criterion J_{RM} is used as a substitute for the Wiener criterion J_W. J_W is widely used in the fields of signal and image restoration [1][6]. Let R be the correlation operator of the set $\{f\}$ of desired functions. Assume that n appears independently from f and the expectation of n is 0.

A. Admissibility

The following Lemma 2 is used for discussing admissibility of J_{RM} by J_W.

Lemma 2 *An operator B satisfies the Wiener criterion J_W if and only if*

$$B(ARA^* + Q) = RA^*. \tag{30}$$

Lemma 2 and Theorem 1 yield

Theorem 2 *(Partial admissibility) J_W partially admits J_{RM} if and only if*

$$\mathcal{R}(A) \perp \mathcal{R}(Q). \tag{31}$$

(Proof) Assume that there exists a proper rote memorization learning A_{RM} which satisfies J_W. It follows from (30) that

$$A_{RM}(ARA^* + Q) = RA^*. \tag{32}$$

Eqs.(32) and (17) yield

$$A_{RM}Q = P_{\mathcal{N}(A),\mathcal{R}(A_{RM}A)}RA^*. \tag{33}$$

Multiplying A from the left-hand side of (33) yields

$$AA_{RM}Q = 0. \tag{34}$$

Then (18) yields

$$P_{\mathcal{R}(A)}Q = 0, \tag{35}$$

so that (31) holds.

Conversely, assume that (31) holds. We shall give an operator which satisfies both J_W and J_{RM}. Since subspaces $\mathcal{R}(RA^*)$ and $\mathcal{N}(A)$ are mutually disjoint [10], $\mathcal{R}(RA^*)$ is a subspace of a complement subspace of $\mathcal{N}(A)$. Hence, there exists a 1-inverse A^- which satisfies

$$\mathcal{R}(A^-A) \supset \mathcal{R}(RA^*). \tag{36}$$

For this 1-inverse A^-, it follows that

$$A^-P_{\mathcal{R}(A)}ARA^* = P_{\mathcal{R}(A^-A),\mathcal{N}(A)}RA^* = RA^*,$$

so that

$$A^-P_{\mathcal{R}(A)}ARA^* = RA^*. \tag{37}$$

Eq.(31) yields

$$A^-P_{\mathcal{R}(A)}Q = 0. \tag{38}$$

Eqs.(37) and (38) yield

$$A^-P_{\mathcal{R}(A)}(ARA^* + Q) = RA^*. \tag{39}$$

From (39), Lemma 2 and Example 1, $A^-P_{\mathcal{R}(A)}$ satisfies both J_W and J_{RM}. □

Corollary 5 *If the correlation matrix Q is non-singular, then J_W admits J_{RM} if and only if $A = 0$.*

The fact that $A = 0$ implies that $Af = 0$ for all $f \in H$. Hence, this condition is not practical from the point of view of learning. If Q is non-singular, therefore, we can say that J_W does not admit J_{RM}.

Now we discuss one more case of admissibility of J_{RM} by J_W.

Theorem 3 *(Admissibility) J_W always admits J_{RM} if and only if*

$$\mathcal{N}(A) \supset \mathcal{R}(R) \text{ and } Q = 0 \tag{40}$$

or

$$\mathcal{N}(A) = \{0\} \text{ and } \mathcal{R}(A) \perp \mathcal{R}(Q). \tag{41}$$

The first equation in (40) implies that $Af = 0$ for all $f \in \mathcal{R}(R)$. Roughly speaking, $\mathcal{R}(R)$ is a set of f which appear frequently. Hence, (40) is not practical from the point of view of learning.

If (41) holds, then (17) yields

$$A_{RM}A = I. \tag{42}$$

Eqs.(42), (18) and (41) yield that

$$A_{RM}Q = A_{RM}AA_{RM}Q = A_{RM}P_{\mathcal{R}(A)}Q = 0,$$

so that

$$A_{RM}Q = 0. \tag{43}$$

Eqs.(42) and (43) yield for any $f \in H$ and any $n \in \mathcal{R}(Q)$ that

$$A_{RM}(Af + n) = f. \tag{44}$$

Eq.(44) implies that if (41) holds, then A_{RM} provides the exact f from the corresponding training vector y even when y contains noise $n \in \mathcal{R}(Q)$.

B. A method for choosing a training set

Eq.(41) provides a method for choosing a training set $\{x_m\}_{m=1}^{M}$ which prevents over-learning. The first equation in (41) is equivalent to

$$\mathcal{R}(A^*) = H. \tag{45}$$

The dimension of the subspace $\mathcal{R}(A^*)$ is less than or equal to the number M of training data. Hence, in the case where H is of infinite dimension, we cannot satisfy (45) by using finite number of training data. In the case where H is of finite dimension, we can choose a training set $\{x_m\}_{m=1}^{M}$ as follows.

Let $\boldsymbol{K}$ be the $M \times M$ matrix whose m,n-th entry is given by $K(x_m, x_n)$, where $K(x, x')$ is the reproducing kernel of H.

Theorem 4 *Eq.(41) holds if and only if we choose a training set* $\{x_m\}_{m=1}^{M}$ *so that*

$$\operatorname{rank} \boldsymbol{K} = \dim H \quad \text{and} \quad \boldsymbol{K}Q = 0. \tag{46}$$

We can say from (46) that the number M of training data should be taken such that

$$M \geq \dim H + \operatorname{rank} Q. \tag{47}$$

VI. Conclusion

For the discussion of over-learning problem with noise free training data, a general framework was proposed in [9] and [12]. In this paper, first we showed that the framework is still valid in the case of noisy training data. It was applied to the case where the rote memorization criterion is used as a substitute for the Wiener criterion. Necessary and sufficient conditions for two kinds of admissibility were obtained. Finally, based on these conditions, we gave a method for choosing a training set which does not cause over-learning.

References

[1] H. C. Andrews and B. R. Hunt, *Digital Image Restoration*, Englewood Cliffs, New Jersey: Prentice-Hall, 1977.

[2] A. Ben-Israel and T. N. E. Greville, *Generalized Inverses: Theory and Applications*, New York: John Wiley & Sons, 1974.

[3] S. Bergman, *The Kernel Function and Conformal Mapping*, 2nd ed., Providence, Rhode Island: American Mathematical Society, 1970.

[4] L. Holmström and P. Koistinen: "Using additive noise in back-propagation training", *IEEE Trans. Neural Networks*, vol.3, pp.24-38, Jan.1992.

[5] K. Matsuoka: "Noise injection into inputs in back-propagation learning", *IEEE Trans. Systems, Man, Cybernetics*, vol.22, pp.436-440, May 1992.

[6] H. Ogawa: "A tutorial review: Image and signal restoration [I]~[IV]", *J. IEICE*, Japan, vol.71, pp.491-497, 593-601, 739-748, 828-835, May-August 1988 (in Japanese).

[7] H. Ogawa: "Inverse problem and neural networks", in *Proc. IEICE 2nd Karuizawa Workshop on Circuits and Systems*, May 1989, pp.262-268 (in Japanese).

[8] H. Ogawa: "Neural network theory as an inverse problem", *J. IEICE*, Japan, vol.73, pp.690-695, Feb.1990 (in Japanese).

[9] H. Ogawa: "Neural network learning, generalization and over-learning", in *Proc. ICIIPS'92-Beijing*, Int. Conf. Intelligent Information Processing & System, Beijing, Oct.-Nov.1992, vol.2, pp.1-6.

[10] H. Ogawa and S. Hara: "Properties of partial projection filter", *Trans. IEICE*, Japan, vol.J71-A, pp.527-534, Feb.1988 (in Japanese).

[11] H. Ogawa and E. Oja: "Optimally generalizing neural networks", in *Proc. IJCNN'91-Singapore*, IEEE & INNS Int. Joint Conf. on Neural Networks, Nov.1991, vol.3, pp.2050-2055.

[12] H. Ogawa and K. Yamasaki: "A theory of over-learning", in *Artificial Neural Networks 2*, I. Aleksander and J. Taylor, Eds. Amsterdam: North-Holland, 1992, vol.2, pp.215-218.

[13] D. E. Rumelhart, G. E. Hinton, and R. J. Williams: "Learning representations by back-propagating errors", *Nature*, vol.323, pp.533-536, Oct.1986.

[14] J. Sietsma and R. J. Dow: "Creating artificial neural networks that generalize", *Neural Networks*, vol.4, pp.67-79, July 1991.

Practical Considerations for Kalman Filter Training of Recurrent Neural Networks

G. V. Puskorius and L. A. Feldkamp
Research Laboratory, Ford Motor Company
Suite 1100, Village Plaza
23400 Michigan Avenue
Dearborn, Michigan 48124
Email: gpuskori@smail.srl.ford.com lfeldkam@smail.srl.ford.com

***Abstract*— Although the potential of the powerful mapping and representational capabilities of recurrent network architectures is widely recognized by the neural network research community, general recurrent neural networks for application studies have not been widely used, possibly due to the relative ineffectiveness of existing gradient-based training algorithms. Recent developments in the use of extended Kalman filter algorithms for training recurrent networks may provide a mechanism by which these architectures will prove to be of practical value. This paper presents an overview of a decoupled extended Kalman filter (DEKF) algorithm for training of recurrent neural network architectures with special emphasis on application to control problems. We discuss qualitative differences between the DEKF algorithm, which only performs updates to a recurrent network's weight parameters, and a recent EKF formulation by Williams [1, 2] that performs parallel estimation of both the network's weights and recurrent node outputs.**

I. Introduction

The extended Kalman filter (EKF) has served as the basis for a number of recent neural network training algorithm studies. The EKF can be thought of as a gradient-based, on-line information processing algorithm that is used for smoothing, filtering or predicting the states of a nonlinear dynamical system. Singhal and Wu [3] demonstrated that the global EKF (GEKF) could be used to train layered feedforward networks by treating the weights of the network as an unforced nonlinear dynamical system with stationary states. Alternatively, an identical algorithm is derived by using the method of linearized recursive least squares to infer the weights of a static feedforward network [4]. Although this global approach demonstrates fast learning as a function of number of presentations of training data, the training time per instance scales as the square of the number of weights in the network, hence rendering the algorithm impractical for many problems. A number of researchers have investigated simplifications to GEKF for the training of multilayer perceptrons [5, 6]. In [5], we show that an effective and efficient training algorithm can be achieved by ignoring the interdependencies of mutually exclusive groups of weights, thereby leading to lower computational complexity and storage per training instance. This decoupled EKF (DEKF) algorithm was demonstrated to exhibit faster training, both in terms of number of presentations of training data and in total training time on a serial processor, than a standard implementation of backpropagation for problems in pattern classification and function approximation. Furthermore, the classification and mapping performance of DEKF-trained networks was usually found to be substantially superior to that of networks trained by standard backpropagation.

Current research efforts have focussed on the use of the EKF as a training algorithm for recurrent neural network architectures. Training of recurrent network architectures by either real time recurrent learning (RTRL) [7] or backpropagation through time (BPTT) [8] usually requires that very low learning rates be employed due to the inherent correlations between successive node outputs that lead to an underlying eigenvalue structure that is ill conditioned. On the other hand, the EKF is a second order algorithm that in effect processes and uses information about the shape of the training problem's error surface for updating the states of the system, thereby providing an effective mechanism for dealing with temporal and spatial correlations in input signals and successive node outputs in recurrent neural networks.

The use of EKF as a training algorithm for recurrent neural networks was first explored by Matthews [9] with application to signal processing problems. Williams [1, 2] provides a detailed analytical treatment of EKF training of recurrent neural networks, and suggests that a ten-fold decrease relative to RTRL in the number of presentations

0-7803-0999-5/93/$03.00 ©1993 IEEE

of training data is achieved for some simple finite state machine problems. In contrast to the EKF formulation of Singhal and Wu for feedforward layered networks, the training problems as treated by Matthews and Williams provide for parallel estimation of both network states (i.e., recurrent node outputs before they are used as inputs at the next time step) and parameters (i.e., the network's trainable weights). This approach is one of many ways of performing simultaneous state and parameter estimation for dynamical systems (e.g., see Anderson and Moore [10]). Livstone et al. [11] have also explored the use of parallel state and parameter estimation for radial basis function networks with feedback connections. Although this development appears promising, we restrict the remainder of our discussion to recurrent networks with sigmoidal or linear node output functions.

In earlier work, independently of Matthews and Williams, we had extended the DEKF formulation for feedforward layered networks to network architectures with recurrent connections [12, 13]. The DEKF formulation for recurrent neural network architectures differs from that of the parallel EKF formulation in two fundamental ways. First, the DEKF formulation assumes that the interdependence of disjoint weight groups can be ignored. This simplification has the effect of reducing the computational and storage requirements for the measurement update portion of DEKF relative to the parallel EKF. The second difference is that state estimation is **not** performed in our DEKF formulation, although weights of the recurrent network architecture are trained. We discuss below what we perceive to be the relative advantages and disadvantages of performing parallel state and parameter estimation, as opposed to performing parameter estimation alone, by EKF-based training algorithms.

We are primarily interested in using recurrent neural networks for control applications, both for identification of nonlinear dynamical systems and for the synthesis of nonlinear dynamical feedback controllers. The use of recurrent neural networks as system identification networks and feedback controllers offers a number of potential advantages over the use of static layered networks. Recurrent neural networks provide a means for encoding and representing internal or hidden states, albeit in a potentially distributed fashion, which leads to capabilities that are similar to those of an *observer* in modern control theory. Recurrent network architectures provide increased flexibility for the filtering of noisy inputs. Recurrent neural network feedback controllers may be less sensitive (i.e., more robust) than static feedforward controllers to changes in plant dynamics and parameters. A recurrent neural network controller can be trained to simultaneously provide state-space control and observer capabilities within a homogeneous architecture. We have observed all of these benefits in our application-oriented studies, and believe that these behaviors emerged largely due to the use of an effective recurrent neural network training procedure based on an extended Kalman filter algorithm. We elaborate below on some of the practical issues involved in the use of EKF methods for the training of recurrent neural networks.

II. EKF Algorithms for Parameter Estimation

Derivation of an EKF algorithm for the estimation of a feedforward layered network's weights was first provided by Singhal and Wu [3]. Later, a recursive linearized least squares derivation was developed by Douglas and Meng [4]. Since the resulting algorithms are essentially equivalent, we will simply refer to these algorithms as parameter-based EKF training algorithms. We view the neural network training problem as a parameter estimation problem, and treat the training of purely feedforward networks and recurrent network architectures in a uniform fashion. The major difference in applying parameter-based EKF algorithms for the training of weights in feedforward and recurrent network architectures lies in the computation of the ordered derivatives of network outputs with respect to the trainable weights. Once the derivatives are computed, as we describe below, the same parameter-based EKF training algorithm applies to either class of network architecture.

Assume a general neural network architecture with arbitrary interconnectivity, potentially including both feedforward and feedback connections. The neural network training problem is formulated as a weighted least squares minimization problem, where the error vector is the difference between differentiable functions of the network's node outputs and target values for these functions. Let the target vector at time step n be given by $\mathbf{d}(n) = [d_1(n)\, d_2(n) \cdots d_{N_c}(n)]^T$, and let the vector $\mathbf{h}(n) = [h_1(\mathbf{y}(n))\, h_2(\mathbf{y}(n)) \cdots h_{N_c}(\mathbf{y}(n))]^T$ denote a vector of differentiable functions (potentially nonlinear) of the network's outputs $\mathbf{y}(n)$. N_c is the number of components of the cost function which is given by $E(n) = \frac{1}{2}\boldsymbol{\xi}(n)^T\mathbf{S}(n)\boldsymbol{\xi}(n)$, where $\mathbf{S}(n)$ is a user-specified nonnegative definite weighting matrix, and where $\boldsymbol{\xi}(n) = \mathbf{d}(n) - \mathbf{h}(n)$. The network's trainable weights are arranged into a M-dimensional vector $\mathbf{w}(n)$, and the estimate of the weight vector at time step n is denoted by $\hat{\mathbf{w}}(n)$. The Kalman recursion requires that, in addition to maintaining and updating estimates of the network's weight vector $\hat{\mathbf{w}}(n)$, it is also necessary to maintain and update a matrix that is called the *approximate error covariance* matrix, given by $\mathbf{P}(n)$, which is used to model the correlations or interactions between each pair of weights in the network. At the beginning of training (time step $n = 0$), the weight vector is initialized to small random values (e.g., of magnitude less than 0.1), and the matrix $\mathbf{P}(0)$ is initialized as a diagonal matrix with component values on the order of 10^2. At the nth time step, the input signals and recurrent node activations are propagated through the network, and the functions $\mathbf{h}(n)$ are computed. The error vector $\boldsymbol{\xi}(n)$ is calculated, and the gradients of each component of $\mathbf{h}(n)$ are formed with respect to the weights of the network, evaluated at the current weight estimates $\hat{\mathbf{w}}(n)$; these derivatives are arranged into the M-by-N_c matrix $\mathbf{H}(n)$. Then the weight vector and approximate error covariance matrix are updated by the following GEKF recursion:

$$\begin{aligned}
\mathbf{A}(n) &= \left[(\eta(n)\mathbf{S}(n))^{-1} + \mathbf{H}(n)^T\mathbf{P}(n)\mathbf{H}(n)\right]^{-1}, &(1)\\
\mathbf{K}(n) &= \mathbf{P}(n)\mathbf{H}(n)\mathbf{A}(n), &(2)\\
\hat{\mathbf{w}}(n+1) &= \hat{\mathbf{w}}(n) + \mathbf{K}(n)\boldsymbol{\xi}(n), &(3)\\
\mathbf{P}(n+1) &= \mathbf{P}(n) - \mathbf{K}(n)\mathbf{H}(n)^T\mathbf{P}(n) + \mathbf{Q}(n). &(4)
\end{aligned}$$

This formulation includes a scalar learning rate parameter $\eta(n)$ whose role is similar to that of the learning rate in gradient descent training. The overall learning rate of this EKF algorithm is determined by the scalar $\eta(n)$ and the relative scaling of the components of the weighting matrix $\mathbf{S}(n)$. The EKF recursion also requires the computation of an intermediate matrix $\mathbf{A}(n)$, for which a matrix of size N_c must be inverted at each time step, and of the Kalman gain matrix $\mathbf{K}(n)$, which determines the extent to which the weight estimates and approximate error covariance matrix are changed. Finally, $\mathbf{Q}(n)$ is a diagonal matrix which provides a mechanism by which the effects of process noise are included in the Kalman recursion. The use of a nonnegative $\mathbf{Q}(n)$ matrix tends to increase the training algorithm's effective learning rate and helps the algorithm avoid local minima, as demonstrated in [5].

The matrix $\mathbf{S}(n)$ is described above as a nonnegative definite matrix. For problems in neural controller training, it may be desirable to impose constraints on the desired behavior of the overall system. Jordan [14, 15] describes how the effects of constraints are included in the cost function $E(n)$ for gradient-descent training of neural controllers by allowing $\mathbf{S}(n)$ to be a function of the evaluations of the functions $\mathbf{h}(n)$. In general, if a *configurational* constraint is satisfied at time step n (e.g., the value of $h_i(\mathbf{y}(n))$ falls within a desired range), then the corresponding component of the error vector and derivatives of the function $h_i(\mathbf{y}(n))$ should not contribute to the updates of $\hat{\mathbf{w}}(n)$ and $\mathbf{P}(n)$. The constraint is imposed by introducing zero values into the appropriate columns and rows of the weighting matrix $\mathbf{S}(n)$ for time step n. However, since equation (1) requires the inverse of $\mathbf{S}(n)$, we reformulate the Kalman recursion to remove this mathematical difficulty. Defining $\boldsymbol{\xi}^*(n) = \mathbf{S}(n)^{\frac{1}{2}}\boldsymbol{\xi}(n) = \mathbf{S}(n)^{\frac{1}{2}}\mathbf{d}(n) - \mathbf{S}(n)^{\frac{1}{2}}\mathbf{h}(n) = \mathbf{d}^*(n) - \mathbf{h}^*(n)$ yields the cost function $E(n) = \frac{1}{2}\boldsymbol{\xi}^*(n)^T\boldsymbol{\xi}^*(n)$. Then the GEKF algorithm is given by

$$\begin{aligned}
\mathbf{A}^*(n) &= \left[\eta(n)^{-1}\mathbf{I} + \mathbf{H}^*(n)^T\mathbf{P}(n)\mathbf{H}^*(n)\right]^{-1}, &(5)\\
\mathbf{K}^*(n) &= \mathbf{P}(n)\mathbf{H}^*(n)\mathbf{A}^*(n), &(6)\\
\hat{\mathbf{w}}(n+1) &= \hat{\mathbf{w}}(n) + \mathbf{K}^*(n)\boldsymbol{\xi}^*(n), &(7)\\
\mathbf{P}(n+1) &= \mathbf{P}(n) - \mathbf{K}^*(n)\mathbf{H}^*(n)^T\mathbf{P}(n) + \mathbf{Q}(n), &(8)
\end{aligned}$$

where the scaling matrix $\mathbf{S}(n)$ is now distributed into both the scaled error vector $\boldsymbol{\xi}^*(n) = \mathbf{S}(n)^{\frac{1}{2}}\boldsymbol{\xi}(n)$ and the scaled derivative matrix $\mathbf{H}^*(n) = \mathbf{H}(n)\mathbf{S}(n)^{\frac{1}{2}}$. Although the two formulations are mathematically equivalent, the latter formulation gracefully handles the effects of configurational constraints.

The computational requirements of the GEKF recursion are dominated by the need to store and update the approximate error covariance matrix $\mathbf{P}(n)$. GEKF's computational complexity is $O(N_cM^2)$ and its storage requirements are $O(M^2)$. The DEKF recursion is easily derived from the global recursion by assuming that the interactions between different weight estimates can be ignored. This simplification introduces many zeroes into the global approximate error covariance matrix. Furthermore, if we assume that the weights can be decoupled so that the weight groups are mutually exclusive of one another, then the matrix $\mathbf{P}(n)$ can be arranged into block diagonal form. Let g refer to the number of such weight groups. Then, the vector $\hat{\mathbf{w}}_i(n)$ refers to the estimated weight parameters of group i, $\mathbf{H}_i^*(n)$ is the submatrix of ordered derivatives of the functions $\mathbf{h}^*(n)$ with respect to the weights of group i, $\mathbf{P}_i(n)$ is the approximate error covariance matrix modeling the interactions between the weights of group i, and $\mathbf{K}_i^*(n)$ is the Kalman gain matrix for the ith weight group. Note that the concatenation of the vectors $\hat{\mathbf{w}}_i(n)$ forms the vector $\hat{\mathbf{w}}(n)$, and the global matrix $\mathbf{H}^*(n)$ is composed of the individual submatrices $\mathbf{H}_i^*(n)$. With this convention and simplifying assumption, the DEKF recursion is given by

$$\begin{aligned}
\mathbf{A}^*(n) &= \left[\eta(n)^{-1}\mathbf{I} + \sum_{j=1}^{g}\mathbf{H}_j^*(n)^T\mathbf{P}_j(n)\mathbf{H}_j^*(n)\right]^{-1}, &(9)\\
\mathbf{K}_i^*(n) &= \mathbf{P}_i(n)\mathbf{H}_i^*(n)\mathbf{A}^*(n), &(10)\\
\hat{\mathbf{w}}_i(n+1) &= \hat{\mathbf{w}}_i(n) + \mathbf{K}_i^*(n)\boldsymbol{\xi}^*(n), &(11)\\
\mathbf{P}_i(n+1) &= \mathbf{P}_i(n) - \mathbf{K}_i^*(n)\mathbf{H}_i^*(n)^T\mathbf{P}_i(n) + \mathbf{Q}_i(n). &(12)
\end{aligned}$$

One should immediately note the striking similarity of the decoupled and global recursions. Note that a single global matrix $\mathbf{A}^*(n)$ is computed based on contributions from all of the approximate error covariance submatrices and ordered derivatives. It is also noteworthy that in the limit of a single weight group ($g = 1$), the decoupled Kalman recursion reduces exactly to the GEKF algorithm.

The computational complexity and storage requirements for the DEKF algorithm can be significantly less than those of the GEKF recursion. For g disjoint weight groups, the computational complexity of DEKF becomes $O(N_c^2 M + N_c \sum_{i=1}^{g} M_i^2)$, where M_i is the number of weights in group i, while the storage requirements become $O(\sum_{i=1}^{g} M_i^2)$. Note that this complexity analysis does not include the computational and storage requirements for the matrix of ordered derivatives. In particular, in the case of recurrent network architectures, the computational complexity of the derivative computations can be significant, as we describe below. For the purposes of this paper, we are interested in a DEKF algorithm for which the weights are grouped by node (i.e., the weights connecting inputs to a node are grouped together). We call this node-decoupled EKF (or NDEKF for short).

III. Recurrent Networks and Derivative Computations

We consider neural network architectures that are specified by a generalized version of the *recurrent multilayer perceptron* (RMLP) architecture described in [16]. A general RMLP architecture consists of layers of nodes arranged in a feedforward fashion, where the nodes of a given layer may be connected to one another through trainable feedback connections with a unit time delay. Network architectures ranging from purely feedforward multilayer networks without recurrent connections to a recurrent network consisting of a single layer of nodes, all completely interconnected, can be specified by a generalized RMLP architecture. Between these extremes are network architectures consisting of layers of nodes, with some feedback connections between nodes within a given layer.

The following notation is employed in order to describe the derivative computations for RMLP architectures. A RMLP network is assumed to consist of L layers of nodes, with N_i processing elements in layer i (N_0 is the length of the input vector). Each processing element of the network is characterized by two indexes, one referencing the layer to which the node belongs and the other referencing the node number within the layer. A vector of input signals or node outputs is denoted by $\mathbf{y}_i(n) = [y_{i,1}(n)\ y_{i,2}(n)\ \cdots\ y_{i,N_i}(n)]^T$, where $0 \le i \le L$. Provisions for a bias input are made by constructing an augmented representation for the vectors $\mathbf{y}_i(n)$: $\tilde{\mathbf{y}}_i(n) = [y_{i,0}(n)\ \mathbf{y}_i(n)]^T$, where the bias input $y_{i,0}(n)$ is usually set to unity. Two vectors of weights are generally associated with each processing element of the network, corresponding to the feedforward connections (including the bias weight) and to the feedback connections. Weight vectors are denoted by ${}^h\mathbf{w}_{i,j}$, where the subscript i refers to the layer to which the node belongs ($1 \le i \le L$), the subscript j refers to the node number within layer i ($1 \le j \le N_i$), and the superscript h refers to the layer from which the connection is made. The superscript h takes on only one of two values for the RMLP architectures considered here: $h = i-1$, for which the weight vector consists of feedforward weights that connect the previous layer's augmented output vector $\tilde{\mathbf{y}}_{i-1}(n)$; and $h = i$, for which the weight vector consists of recurrent weights that connect the ith layer's time-delayed output vector $\mathbf{y}_i(n-1)$. The form of the feedforward weight vector for the jth node of the ith layer is given by ${}^h\mathbf{w}_{i,j} = [{}^h w_{i,j,0}\ {}^h w_{i,j,1}\ \cdots\ {}^h w_{i,j,N_h}]^T$, where $h = i-1$; similarly, the form of the recurrent weight vector for the jth node of the ith layer is given by ${}^i\mathbf{w}_{i,j} = [{}^i w_{i,j,1}\ {}^i w_{i,j,2}\ \cdots\ {}^i w_{i,j,N_i}]^T$. With this notation, assuming complete interconnectivity, the weighted input to the jth node of the ith layer at time step n is given by

$$\begin{aligned} x_{i,j}(n) &= {}^{i-1}\mathbf{w}_{i,j} \cdot \tilde{\mathbf{y}}_{i-1}(n) + {}^{i}\,\mathbf{w}_{i,j} \cdot \mathbf{y}_i(n-1) \\ &= \sum_{k=0}^{N_{i-1}} {}^{i-1}w_{i,j,k}\, y_{i-1,k}(n) + \sum_{k=1}^{N_i} {}^{i}w_{i,j,k}\, y_{i,k}(n-1)\ , \end{aligned} \tag{13}$$

and the output of the jth node of the ith layer at time step n is given by $y_{i,j}(n) = F_{i,j}(x_{i,j}(n))$, where $F_{i,j}(\cdot)$ is the node's output function.

A general rule for computing the ordered derivatives (or *total* partial derivatives) of the outputs of a RMLP network with respect to its trainable weights can be formulated based upon three fundamental observations. First, the ordered derivative of the output of a node in the ith layer with respect to a weight in the gth layer (either recurrent or feedforward) is zero when the gth layer follows the ith layer: $\bar{\partial} y_{i,j}(n)/\bar{\partial}\ {}^h w_{g,u,v} = 0$ for $g > i$. Second, the ordered derivative of the output of a node in the ith layer with respect to a weight in the same layer is obtained by a generalization of the RTRL rule for a recurrent network with complete interconnectivity. Third, the ordered derivative of the output of a node in the ith layer with respect to a weight in the gth layer when the gth layer precedes the ith layer is a function of the ordered derivatives of the outputs of nodes from both the $(i-1)^{th}$ and i^{th} layers with respect to the same weight. From these observations we derive the following general formula for computing the ordered derivative of an arbitrary node's output with respect to an arbitrary weight for RMLP architectures:

$$\begin{aligned} \frac{\bar{\partial} y_{i,j}(n)}{\bar{\partial}\ {}^h w_{g,u,v}} &= \left(\frac{1 + \delta_{i,g} + \mathrm{signum}(i-g)}{2}\right) \\ & F'_{i,j}(x_{i,j}(n)) \left\{ (1-\delta_{i,g}) \sum_{k=1}^{N_{i-1}} {}^{i-1}w_{i,j,k} \frac{\bar{\partial} y_{i-1,k}(n)}{\bar{\partial}\ {}^h w_{g,u,v}} \right. \\ & \left. + \gamma(n) \sum_{k=1}^{N_i} {}^{i}w_{i,j,k} \frac{\bar{\partial} y_{i,k}(n-1)}{\bar{\partial}\ {}^h w_{g,u,v}} + \delta_{i,g}\delta_{j,u} y_{h,v}(n+i-h-1) \right\}\ , \end{aligned} \tag{14}$$

where $\gamma(n)$ is a derivative discount factor that exponentially decays the effects of recurrent derivatives from time long past. The value of $\gamma(n)$ is usually set equal to or slightly less than unity. This equation is a compact representation of the derivative formulation as derived by Parlos et al. [17] for RMLP architectures.

The derivative computations as described above assume RMLP architectures of multiple layers of nodes, where all nodes within a layer are interconnected with one another. If an RMLP architecture consists of both recurrent and purely feedforward layers, then the derivative computations can be performed more efficiently by performing backpropagation of derivatives through the feedforward layers, and combining this information with the feedforward derivative computations through the recurrent layers. One can visualize the form that these calculations would require by considering the sensitivity circuits for systems consisting of both feedforward layered networks and models of linear dynamical systems as described by Narendra and Parthasarathy [18, 19].

Our principal interest is in the use of recurrent neural networks for control applications where a RMLP network is used in a feedback loop to control a nonlinear dynamical system. In this case, in addition to the internal recurrence within the RMLP controller, there is also external recurrence in the form of plant outputs used as controller inputs. Because of this external feedback loop, the ordered derivative of a node's output with respect to any weight of the RMLP network is generally nonzero. For RMLP architectures used as feedback controllers, the derivative computations of equation (14) become

$$\frac{\bar{\partial} y_{i,j}(n)}{\bar{\partial}\, {}^{h}w_{g,u,v}} = F'_{i,j}(x_{i,j}(n)) \left\{ \sum_{k=1}^{N_{i-1}} {}^{i-1}w_{i,j,k} \frac{\bar{\partial} y_{i-1,k}(n)}{\bar{\partial}\, {}^{h}w_{g,u,v}} + \gamma(n) \sum_{k=1}^{N_i} {}^{i}w_{i,j,k} \frac{\bar{\partial} y_{i,k}(n-1)}{\bar{\partial}\, {}^{h}w_{g,u,v}} + \delta_{i,g}\delta_{j,u} y_{h,v}(n+i-h-1) \right\}. \tag{15}$$

The vector $\mathbf{y}_0(n)$ consists of the unit time delayed dynamical system's outputs, for which derivatives with respect to controller weights are generally nonzero, and optionally external reference inputs. Note that the derivative computations for an RMLP architecture for which there are feedback paths from system outputs to network inputs generally require increased computational resources, since storage and computation of the ordered derivatives of the outputs of all recurrent nodes with respect to all trainable weights of the network are required.

IV. Parallel State and Parameter Estimation with EKF

The EKF formulations of Matthews [9] and Williams [1, 2] perform both state and weight updates for recurrent network architectures. The parallel estimation of states and parameters leads to an EKF algorithm that has a number of significant differences from the parameter-based EKF algorithm described above. We summarize some of these differences for a recurrent network architecture consisting of a single layer of completely interconnected nodes, and discuss implications of these differences for practical applications. We concentrate on Williams' EKF formulation for comparative purposes.

The parallel EKF algorithm treats the state vector as the concatenation of the recurrent node outputs with the weight parameter vector. Thus, it is convenient to decompose the approximate global error covariance matrix into four distinct blocks: $\mathbf{P}_1(n)$ models the interactions between the recurrent node outputs, $\mathbf{P}_4(n)$ models the interactions between the weights of the network, and $\mathbf{P}_2(n) = \mathbf{P}_3(n)^T$ models the cross correlations between the network's weights and recurrent node outputs. The submatrices $\mathbf{P}_1(n)$ and $\mathbf{P}_4(n)$ lie along the diagonal of $\mathbf{P}(n)$, while $\mathbf{P}_2(n)$ and $\mathbf{P}_3(n)$ fill the off-block diagonal parts of $\mathbf{P}(n)$. The submatrix $\mathbf{P}_4(n)$ is equivalent to the entire matrix $\mathbf{P}(n)$ in the parameter-based EKF recursion defined above.

In applying the parallel EKF recursion, there are two distinct steps, the *time* and *measurement* updates. The time update step involves propagating input signals and time-delayed recurrent node outputs through the recurrent network, computing the linearized dynamics, and propagating the error covariance. The linearized dynamics are provided by computing the *partial* derivatives of recurrent node outputs with respect to both the recurrent node outputs from the previous time step and the network's weight estimates. These partial derivatives, which are **not** recursively defined as a function of ordered derivatives from the previous time step, are then used to propagate the error covariance matrix. The net effect of these steps is that the ordered derivatives of recurrent node outputs with respect to the network's weight parameters (i.e., the RTRL data structure) become embedded in the submatrices $\mathbf{P}_2(n)$ and $\mathbf{P}_3(n)$. However, these ordered derivatives are coupled with the evolution of the error covariance matrix and do not appear to be directly accessible. On the other hand, for the parameter-based EKF formulation, the ordered derivatives of network outputs with respect to network weights are computed by the RTRL algorithm as a function of these derivatives from the previous time step. Thus, the parameter-based and parallel formulations effectively compute the same ordered derivatives, but these derivatives become embedded in the approximate error covariance matrix for the parallel formulation.

There are a number of potential advantages to performing the full parallel EKF formulation as opposed to only estimating the parameters. First, the additional computational cost for state estimation is negligible, since the computational complexities and storage requirements of the two global EKF formulations along with the corresponding derivative computations are identical (for N nodes, $O(N^4)$). In addition, it may also be convenient to perform some decoupling of the weights in either formulation. This would involve ignoring the interdependencies of mutually exclusive groups of weights, thereby leading to a block-diagonal structure for the submatrix $\mathbf{P}_4(n)$ in the parallel formulation. Although weight decoupling does not reduce the order of the computational time complexity for either formulation, the grouping of weights by node has the effect of reducing the storage requirements to $O(N^3)$. The parallel EKF formulation may also exhibit superior performance to the parameter-based formulation because of the cross coupling of estimated states and parameters. Furthermore, the parallel EKF formulation has additional user-settable training parameters such as initial diagonal values for the covariance submatrix $\mathbf{P}_1(0)$ and the corresponding noise covariance matrix $\mathbf{Q}_1(n)$ that can be used to tune the training algorithm. Finally, Williams points out that the parallel formulation has theoretical appeal since it provides a principled generalization of the *teacher forcing* mechanism that is often employed in recurrent network training by gradient descent.

Although the parallel EKF formulation has a number of appealing characteristics, we have identified some apparently unresolved difficulties in its practical application. The first difficulty arises for those training problems in which there are multiple trajectories or sequences, as opposed to a single continuous trajectory of training signals. With each new trajectory, the submatrices $\mathbf{P}_2(n)$ and $\mathbf{P}_3(n)$ are initialized to null matrices, which has the effect of initializing to zero values the ordered derivatives of node outputs with respect to network weights. On the other hand, there is generally no need to reinitialize the submatrix $\mathbf{P}_4(n)$ (although occasional reinitializations may be useful for escaping poor local minima). The major difficulty arises in deciding how to reinitialize the submatrix $\mathbf{P}_1(n)$ at the beginning of a new sequence of inputs. Upon the completion of training with the parallel formulation, if the submatrix $\mathbf{P}_1(n)$ has not converged to a matrix that is nearly zero, then the question arises as to whether it is necessary in deployment to perform some aspect of Kalman filtering of the recurrent node outputs to achieve the same level of mapping performance as observed during training.

Perhaps the most critical obstacle in the practical application of the parallel EKF formulation for real-time training of recurrent neural networks is the coupling of the RTRL data structure with the approximate error covariance matrix. This coupling appears to preclude the use of computationally efficient methods for approximating or computing the necessary ordered derivatives in real time. A potentially useful alternative to computing the ordered derivatives in the forward direction as described by equations (14–15) for the parameter-based EKF algorithms is to approximate these derivatives by truncated backpropagation through time [20]. In addition, Sun et al. [21] describe a promising new algorithm for computing the necessary ordered derivatives based upon a Green's function method that has $O(N^3)$ complexity, which is the same order of complexity as the weight and covariance update portions of a node-decoupled EKF algorithm for recurrent network architectures. The derivatives computed by either of these two methods could be directly used by the parameter-based EKF formulations, while it is not obvious how the parallel EKF formulation would be able to take advantage of these efficiencies.

V. Summary and Conclusions

The parameter-based DEKF algorithm offers a superior alternative to simple gradient descent algorithms such as RTRL and BPTT for training of recurrent neural networks. We have demonstrated that the parameter-based DEKF algorithm is capable of training the weights of recurrent neural networks for a wide range of problems, including simple finite state machines, system identification and control problems, often with results superior to those achieved with the simpler gradient descent methods [12, 13]. We have also shown in simulation that recurrent neural network feedback controllers can be trained to provide excellent control for a variety of automotive subsystems, including control of active suspension [22], anti-lock braking [23], and engine idle speed [24]. These control problems exhibit a number of troublesome characteristics such as process nonlinearities, nonstationary dynamics, unobserved disturbances, time-varying time delays, hidden states, and asynchronous sampling. Interestingly, recurrent neural control architectures of modest complexity (on order of 10 nodes and 100 weights) were found to be sufficient for providing good control for these problems. We have also been able to apply the same training procedure to recurrent networks of larger size [13]. We have found that the imposition of *smoothness* constraints [14, 15] on the computed control signals during training can be conveniently handled in the parameter-based DEKF formulation by including additional terms in the cost function. This constraint is particularly useful for preventing oscillatory behavior in the control signals for dynamical systems with significant time delays.

We have provided here a qualitative comparison of parameter-based EKF algorithms with a parallel state and parameter EKF formulation for the training of recurrent network architectures. Although we have found that the parameter-based EKF algorithms exhibit good performance for many problems, we acknowledge that some classes of problems may benefit from a parallel EKF estimation scheme. Further work is required to address some of the apparently unresolved difficulties described above for practical application of the parallel EKF formulation.

REFERENCES

[1] R. J. Williams (1992a). *Some Observations on the Use of the Extended Kalman Filter as a Recurrent Network Learning Algorithm*, (Technical Report NU-CCS-92-1). Boston: Northeastern University, College of Computer Science.

[2] R. J. Williams (1992b). Training Recurrent Networks Using the Extended Kalman Filter. In *International Joint Conference on Neural Networks* (Baltimore 1992), vol. IV, 241–246.

[3] S. Singhal and L. Wu (1989). Training Multilayer Perceptrons with the Extended Kalman Algorithm. In *Advances in Neural Information Processing Systems 1*, (Denver 1988), ed. D. S. Touretzky, 133–140. San Mateo, CA: Morgan Kaufmann.

[4] S. C. Douglas and T. H.-Y. Meng (1991). Linearized Least-Squares Training of Multilayer Feedforward Neural Networks. In *International Joint Conference on Neural Networks* (Seattle 1991), vol. I, 307–312.

[5] G. V. Puskorius and L. A. Feldkamp (1991). Decoupled Extended Kalman Filter Training of Feedforward Layered Networks. In *International Joint Conference on Neural Networks* (Seattle 1991), vol. I, 771–777.

[6] S. Shah, F. Palmieri and M. Datum (1992). Optimal Filtering Algorithms for Fast Learning in Feedforward Neural Networks. *Neural Networks* **5**, 779–787.

[7] R. J. Williams and D. Zipser (1989). A Learning Algorithm for Continually Running Fully Recurrent Neural Networks. *Neural Computation* **1**, 270–280.

[8] P. J. Werbos (1990). Backpropagation Through Time: What It Does and How to Do It. *Proceedings of the IEEE* **78**, no. 10, 1550–1560.

[9] M. B. Matthews (1990). Neural Network Nonlinear Adaptive Filtering Using the Extended Kalman Filter Algorithm. In *Proceedings of the International Neural Networks Conference* (Paris 1990), vol. I, 115–119.

[10] B. D. S. Anderson and J. B. Moore (1979). *Optimal Filtering*. Englewood Cliffs, NJ: Prentice-Hall.

[11] M. M. Livstone, J. A. Farrell, and W. L. Baker (1992). A Computationally Efficient Algorithm for Training Recurrent Connectionist Networks. In *Proceedings of the 1992 American Control Conference* (Chicago 1992), vol. II, 555–561.

[12] G. V. Puskorius and L. A. Feldkamp (1992). Recurrent Network Training with the Decoupled Extended Kalman Filter Algorithm. In *SPIE Vol. 1710 Science of Artificial Neural Networks* (Orlando 1992), 461–473.

[13] G. V. Puskorius and L. A. Feldkamp (1992). Model Reference Adaptive Control with Recurrent Networks Trained by the Dynamic DEKF Algorithm. In *International Joint Conference on Neural Networks* (Baltimore 1992), vol. II, 106–113.

[14] M. I. Jordan (1989). Supervised Learning and Systems with Excess Degrees of Freedom. In *Proceedings of the 1988 Connectionists Summer School* (Pittsburgh 1988), eds. D. Touretzky, G. Hinton and T. Sejnowski, 62–75. San Mateo, CA: Morgan Kaufmann.

[15] M. I. Jordan (1989). Generic Constraints on Underspecified Target Trajectories. In *International Joint Conference on Neural Networks* (Washington D.C. 1989), vol. I, 217–225.

[16] B. Fernandez, A. G. Parlos, and W. K. Tsai (1990). Nonlinear Dynamic System Identification Using Artificial Neural Networks (ANNs). In *International Joint Conference on Neural Networks* (San Diego 1990), vol. II, 133–141.

[17] A. G. Parlos, A. Atiya, K. T. Chong, W. K. Tsai, and B. Fernandez (1991). Dynamic Learning in Recurrent Neural Networks for Nonlinear System Identification. Submitted for publication.

[18] K. S. Narendra and K. Parthasarathy (1990). Identification and Control of Dynamical Systems Using Neural Networks. *IEEE Transactions on Neural Networks* **1**, no. 1, 4–27.

[19] K. S. Narendra and K. Parthasarathy (1991). Gradient Methods for the Optimization of Dynamical Systems Containing Neural Networks. *IEEE Transactions on Neural Networks* **2**, no. 2, 252–262.

[20] R. J. Williams and J. Peng (1990). An Efficient Gradient-Based Algorithm for On-Line Training of Recurrent Network Trajectories. *Neural Computation* **2**, 490–501.

[21] G.-Z. Sun, H.-H. Chen and Y.-C. Lee (1992). Green's Function Method for Fast On-line Learning Algorithm of Recurrent Neural Networks. In *Advances in Neural Information Processing Systems 4*, (Denver 1991), eds. J. E. Moody, S. J. Hanson and R. P. Lippmann, 333–340. San Mateo, CA: Morgan Kaufmann.

[22] L. A. Feldkamp, G. V. Puskorius, L. I. Davis. Jr., and F. Yuan (1992). Neural Control Systems Trained by Dynamic Gradient Methods for Automotive Applications. In *International Joint Conference on Neural Networks* (Baltimore 1992), vol. II, 798–804.

[23] L. I. Davis, Jr., G. V. Puskorius, F. Yuan and L. A. Feldkamp (1992). Neural Network Modeling and Control of an Anti-Lock Brake System. In *Proceedings Intelligent Vehicle '92 Symposium* (Detroit 1992), 179–184.

[24] G. V. Puskorius and L. A. Feldkamp (1993). Automotive Engine Idle Speed Control with Recurrent Neural Networks. To appear in *Proceedings of the 1993 American Control Conference* (San Francisco 1993).

NEW FORMS OF REINFORCEMENT LEARNING: APPLICATIONS AND BRAIN-LIKE CAPABILITIES

Paul J. Werbos
National Science Foundation*
Washington D.C. 20550

ABSTRACT

Reinforcement learning systems are control systems which learn how to maximize or minimize any user-specified measure of utility over time. Their capabilities are very general, in theory, because users may specify utility measures such as errors in tracking a reference model, energy costs, profit, the degree of task completion, etc. There is good reason to believe that the brains of higher animals are reinforcement learning systems[1,2].

Simple reinforcement learning systems[3] perform well on difficult and dirty problems, like backgammon, but learn slowly in many engineering applications. Based on that experience, many believe that reinforcement learning is slower or less capable than several alternatives (like the backpropagation of utility, which I described in 1974[4]) in many applications. But animals brains do not show such stringent limitations! Newer forms of reinforcement learning demonstrate greater capabilities, and very real aerospace applications, as well as closer parallels to biology.[5].

OVERVIEW OF NEUROCONTROL

Hundreds of papers have appeared which apply artificial neural networks (ANNs) to control in a useful way. Many papers overstress their originality or uniqueness, but they all use ANNs to perform one or more of four basic tasks: (1) subsystem tasks, like diagnostics or pattern recognition, where the ANN itself does not emit anything like a control signal; (2) cloning tasks, where the ANN learns to emulate (at low cost and high speed) an existing controller, such as a human expert; (3) tracking tasks, similar to classical adaptive control, where the ANN makes a plant follow a prespecified reference model, setpoint, or trajectory; (4) optimization over time, as in reinforcement learning or in direct methods based on derivatives of utility. Backpropagation here is simply a general technique for calculating derivatives at minimum cost in any large, sparse nonlinear system[4,5]. In [5], these learning systems are described from the viewpoint of classical control theory, which has contributed a great deal to recent research.

A comprehensive review of all this is given in [5], but many readers will find the simpler material in [4,6,7] important as background material (though oversimplified) in understanding [5]. Cloning is often a good first step in developing a controller, but one can usually improve that controller by using tracking or optimization methods. In tracking, Narendra[5] has shown that the most general and most powerful methods (not the easiest!) are based on an indirect approach, in which optimization designs are used to minimize tracking error over time. (Kawato et al[6] have shown that human arm movement control also seems to be based on an optimization system.) The greatest capabilities in neurocontrol therefore come from two families of optimization methods -- the backpropagation of utility, and "reinforcement learning."

The backpropagation of utility is much easier to use than the newer forms of reinforcement learning. When the plant to be controlled is known exactly, and there is no noise, it yields a more accurate controller. Even then, there is a choice of only two consistent approaches for controlling dynamic plants: (1) backpropagation through time[4], which is essentially a batch or offline method, though tricks have been found to apply it in real time[5], at some cost; (2) forwards perturbation or "dynamic backpropagation" [5], which becomes very expensive to implement as the number of system variables grows. Reinforcement learning is inherently real-time and rooted in stochastic mathematics; therefore it is the only approach in the ANN literature with any hope as a theory of the brain. Even simple forms of reinforcement learning have sometimes outperformed the backpropagation of utility, because of problems in learning a good model of the plant to be controlled; however, chapter 10 of [5] describes new adaptation methods (and research opportunities) which reduce those problems. Reinforcement learning may also offer a way to "learn" a Liapunov function, proving stability after the fact in the zero-noise limit, for an arbitrary well-behaved nonlinear plant; however, research into the details of this has only just recently begun.

BASICS OF REINFORCEMENT LEARNING

Classical reinforcement learning maximizes a utility or reward measure, U(t), observed by the learning system. Both in engineering and in biology, it is usually more efficient to maximize a utility function, $U(\underline{R}(t),\underline{u}(t))$, where $\underline{R}(t)$ is the state of the external plant or environment at time t, and $\underline{u}(t)$ represents the actions taken by the controller or animal at time t. (The former is a special case of the latter[1,5].) Modern designs do this.

*This paper gives my personal views, not the views of NSF.

0-7803-1377-1/93 $3.00 ©1993 IEEE

All of the known useful designs for reinforcement learning can be understood as novel, general-purpose approximations to dynamic programming. Many researchers say they do "approximate dynamic programming" (ADP) rather than "reinforcement learning," in part because they maximize U(R) instead of U(t).

Dynamic programming is the only exact and efficient method to maximize a utility function U(R) over future time, in the general case, in a noisy, nonlinear environment. Dynamic programming proceeds as follows: first it solves for a secondary or strategic utility function, J(R); then it picks (or adapts) a controller (or Action network) which chooses u(t) so as to maximize the expected value of U(u(t))+J(R(t+1)). In neurocontrol and in reinforcement learning, we have focused on a particular type of ADP design: the adaptive critic type, which includes a special neural network (or other learning module) called a Critic network. The job of the Critic is to approximate the function J(R) or something very similar to it.

The term "Critic" was coined by Widrow, who implemented the first ANN adaptive critic network in 1973. His 1973 design is now obsolete. In 1977, I published two alternative designs -- Heuristic Dynamic Programming (1977) and Dual Heuristic Programming (DHP) -- which developed the link between neural net designs and dynamic programming for the first time. (The neural aspects were discussed more explicitly, however, in a 1981 conference paper on backpropagation, reprinted with [4].) In 1983[3], Barto, Sutton and Anderson(BSA) published an implementation of a simpler design -- containing only a Critic network and an Action network -- which has been widely imitated, and is still the best-known design by far; the "TD" methods used to adapt the Critic there turn out to be a special case of HDP[5].

The BSA design has statistical problems, when there is more than one control variable present, which can lead to slow learning. My 1977 designs -- explained briefly in [6] but more consistently in [5], along with new consistency results -- aimed at eliminating these problems, by exploiting backpropagation. In one variation -- Action-Dependent HDP (ADHDP) -- one backpropagates the derivatives of J through a Critic directly to an Action network, and uses derivatives to adapt the Action network. In other approaches, one uses a model of the plant as an intermediate stage. A complex version of the latter (in [8]) first established contact between the BSA stream of activity and my own. Only in 1990 (through [6]) did the neural net community as a whole become aware of the "advanced adaptive critics," the critic designs which exploit the backpropagation of J.

CURRENT STATUS AND APPLICATIONS

In 1990, the advanced adaptive critic designs existed only on paper. By now, three to six groups have demonstrated success with these methods. Two of the three core groups (and two of the uncertain three) have demonstrated real-world applications of much greater significance than the toy problems favored by many theoreticians. As an example, White and Sofge[5], then at McDonnell-Douglas, attempted to use neurocontrol on an important practical problem: the real-time continuous production of high quality composite parts. Millions had been spent trying to solve this using AI and classical problems, to no avail. Direct tracking neurocontrol did not work either. BSA worked only on a reduced version of the problem, but learned too slowly. Advanced adaptive critics worked, and are in the pipeline to a major application.

Notice that these applications use backpropagation (as defined above) in a fast real-time learning system. The same basic design[5] has been used to retrain an F15 controller, to adapt to new conditions (e.g. shot-off wing) in two seconds, in real-time learning.

Advanced adaptive critics have now been written into the baseline plans for the National Aerospace Plane -- the first airplane intended to reach earth orbit as an airplane, at airplane-like cost -- through AAC, which is now a prime contractor on that program, based on success in work so far.

These applications only begin to scratch the surface; new theory [5, chapter 13] suggests that more advanced designs, in the same family, could truly reproduce human-like planning abilities. There is a huge number of untried but well-defined new opportunities here, waiting for those able to understand at least one or two of them. Likewise, there are new opportunities for crucial new experiments linking this to biology -- especially to the cerebellum and the hippocampus[1,2] -- beyond the scope of this paper.

REFERENCES

1.P.Werbos, The cytoskeleton: why it may be crucial to human learning and neurocontrol,Nanobiology, 1(1), 1992.

2.P.Werbos, The brain as a neurocontroller:new hypotheses and experimental possibilities, in P.G.Madhavan et al (eds), Neuroscience and Neural Networks: Efforts Towards an Empirical Synthesis, INNS Press/Erlbaum, forthcoming.

3.A.Barto, R.Sutton & C.Anderson,Neuronlike elements that can solve difficult learning control problems,IEEE Trans. Systems, Man and Cybernetics,13:835-846,1983.

4.P.Werbos,Beyond Regression(1974 PhD thesis), in P.Werbos,The Roots of Backpropagation: From Ordered Derivatives to Neural Networks and Political Forecasting,Wiley, 1993.

5.D.White & D.Sofge(eds), Handbook of Intelligent Control: Neural, Fuzzy and Adaptive Approaches, Van Nostrand, 1992.

6.W.Miller , R.Sutton & P.Werbos(eds),Neural Networks for Control,MIT Press,1990.

7.P.Werbos,Neurocontrol and elastic fuzzy logic: capabilities, concepts and applications, IEEE Trans. Industrial Electronics, April 1993.

8.P.Werbos,Building and understanding adaptive systems: a statistical/numeric approach to factory automation and brain research,IEEE Trans. SMC, Jan.-Feb. 1987.

On the Learning and Convergence of the Radial Basis Networks

Fu-Chuang Chen Mao-Hsing Lin
Department of Control Engineering
National Chiao Tung University
Hsinchu, Taiwan

Abstract

Although the radial basis networks have been shown to be able to model any "well behaved" nonlinear function to any desired accuracy, there is no guarantee that the correct networks weights can be learned using any existing training rule. This paper reports a convergence result for training radial basis networks based on a modified gradient descent training rule, which is the same as the standard gradient descent algorithm except that a deadzone around the origin of the error coordinates is incorporated in the training rule. The result says that, if the deadzone size is large enough to cover the modeling error and if the learning rate is seleted within certain range, then the norm of the parameter error will converge to a constant, and the output error between the network and the nonlinear function will converge into a small ball. Simulations are used to verify the theoretical results.

1 Introduction

The multilayer neural networks (with sigmoid hidden neurons) have been very popular for various applications since the error-backpropagation algorithm was publicized in 1986 [1]. However, it becomes clear that training multilayer networks is usually a time-consuming process [5]. Network nonlinearities also add considerable difficulties to theoretical analyses of network behaviors [2]. The radial basis neural networks functionally resemble the multilayer neural networks (both are general modeling tools for nonlinear functions), but they have replaced the multilayer neural networks in many applications, at least because the radial basis networks greatly reduce the training time [5] and make related analyses much easier [3].

Radial basis networks consist of a linear input layer, a linear output layer, and a nonlinear hidden layer. The relation between the input vector $\mathbf{x}$ and an output node y_i can be expressed by

$$y_i = \sum_{j=1}^{N} c_{ij} g_{\sigma_j}(\mathbf{x}, \xi_j) \tag{1}$$

where $\mathbf{g}$ is a radially symmetric kernal function of a nonlinear hidden neuron, with ξ_j and σ_j denoting the centroid and width of the jth nonlinear neuron. The output of $\mathbf{g}$ depends on the distance between $\mathbf{x}$ and ξ, and on the size of σ. Usually a larger output is obtained when $\mathbf{x}$ is closer to ξ; for example, if the Gaussian radial basis function is used,

$$g_{\sigma_j}(\mathbf{x}, \xi_j) = e^{\frac{-\|\mathbf{X}-\xi_j\|^2}{\sigma_j^2}}$$

Similar to the multilayer neural networks, the radial basis neural networks have been shown to be universal approximators of nonlinear functions. In [6], the Stone-Weierstrass theorem [8] is used to verify that the Gaussian radial basis network can approximate any continuous function to any desired accuracy over convex, compact sets of R^n. Park and Sandberg [4] showed the more general result that radial basis networks (not necessarily Gaussian, with uniform width σ) can approximate any L^p function to any desired accuracy. However, these results did not comment on how efficient the existing network learning rules can reduce the approximation errors.

In this paper we study the learning and convergence issues in training radial basis networks to approximate nonlinear functions. In section 2, we describe the learning problem and the modified gradient descent learning law. The convergence theorom and proof will be given in section 3. Simulation results follow in section 4.

0-7803-0999-5/93/$03.00 ©1993 IEEE

2 The Radial-Basis Network Learning with DeadZone

Let $\mathbf{f} : A \in R^n \longrightarrow R^m$ be a continuous function defined on the compact set A. The task is to train a radial-basis network, with the same number of inputs and outputs as $\mathbf{f}$, to approximate $\mathbf{f}$ over A. Based on the results of [4] and [6], it can be assumed that

assumption

Given any $\epsilon > 0$, there exists a radial basis network $\bar{\mathbf{f}}$, with constant width σ in all hidden neurons, such that the output errors between $\bar{\mathbf{f}}$ and $\mathbf{f}$ are less than ϵ, i.e.,

$$\max |\bar{y}_i - y_i| \leq \epsilon, \;\; \forall\, \mathbf{x} \in A, \;\; for\; i = 1, \ldots, m \quad (2)$$

where $\bar{y}_i$ and y_i are the ith element of $\bar{\mathbf{y}} = \bar{\mathbf{f}}(\mathbf{x}, \mathbf{c})$ and $\mathbf{y} = \mathbf{f}(\mathbf{x})$, respectively. We further assume that the centers ξ_i and the width σ of hidden neurons of $\bar{\mathbf{f}}$ which satisfies (2) are known and fixed. In practice, the centers can be determined through a pretraining process described in [7], or be uniformly distributed over A. The later approach has been studied via frequency domain techniques in [3]. There are also practical ways to determine the width σ [3],[7]. The assumptions stated above imply that there exists a parameter matrix $\mathbf{c} = (c_{ij})$ in $\bar{\mathbf{f}}$ such that (2) holds. Since $\mathbf{c}$ is unknown, a network $\mathbf{f}^*(\mathbf{x}, \mathbf{c}(k))$, with the same architecture as $\bar{\mathbf{f}}(\mathbf{x}, \mathbf{c})$, is trained to approximate $\mathbf{f}(\mathbf{x})$, where $\mathbf{c}(k)$ denotes the estimates of $\mathbf{c}$ at the kth training iteration. Note that the ith row of $\mathbf{c}$, denoted by $\mathbf{c}_i$, are the weights associated with the ith output $\bar{y}_i$. Since the network outputs (and the weights associated with each of them) are independent, the discussion of learning and convergence issues can be focused at a particular output y_i (and the related weights $\mathbf{c}_i$).

The training process is described as follows : At the kth training iteration, an input vector $\mathbf{x}$ is generated according to a probability distribution function over A, and applied to both f and f^*. The error function associated with the ith output is defined as

$$E_i(k) = \frac{1}{2}(y_i^* - y_i)^2 = \frac{1}{2}e_i^2(k) \quad (3)$$

where $e_i = y_i^* - y_i$. The gradient descent rule is used to update the network weights in order to reduce $E_i(k)$

$$\mathbf{c}_i(k+1) = \mathbf{c}_i(k) - \mu_k \left.\frac{\partial E_i(k)}{\partial \mathbf{c}_i}\right|_{\mathbf{c}_i(k)} \quad for\; all\; i \quad (4)$$

where $\mu_k\,(> 0)$ represents the learning rate for the kth training iteration. The gradient $\frac{\partial E_i(k)}{\partial \mathbf{c}_i}$ in (4) can be expressed by

$$\begin{aligned} \left.\frac{\partial E_i(k)}{\partial \mathbf{c}_i}\right|_{\mathbf{c}(k)} &= e_i(k) \left[\frac{\partial y_i^*}{\partial \mathbf{c}_i}\right] \\ &= e_i(k)\, [\mathbf{g}_\sigma(\mathbf{x}, \xi_1) \ldots \mathbf{g}_\sigma(\mathbf{x}, \xi_N)]^T \\ &= e_i(k)\, \mathbf{G}(\mathbf{x}) \quad (5) \\ \text{where } \mathbf{G}(\mathbf{x}) &= [\mathbf{g}_\sigma(\mathbf{x}, \xi_1) \ldots \mathbf{g}_\sigma(\mathbf{x}, \xi_N)]^T \quad (6) \end{aligned}$$

The training is an iterative process.

Although the gradient descent training (4) has proved to be useful in many applications, there is no theoretical guarantee that the correct weights $\mathbf{c}$ can be learned using (4). In order to achieve a convergence result, we propose to add a deadzone in the traditional gradient descent learning rule. To do this, (5) is modified as

$$\begin{aligned} \left.\frac{\partial E_i(k)}{\partial \mathbf{c}_i}\right|_{\mathbf{c}(k)} &= D(e_i(k)) \left[\frac{\partial y_i^*}{\partial \mathbf{c}_i}\right] \\ &= D(e_i(k))\, \mathbf{G}(\mathbf{x}) \quad (7) \end{aligned}$$

where D is the dead-zone function defined as

$$D(e) = \begin{cases} 0 & if\; |e| \leq d_0 \\ e - d_0 & if\; e > d_0 \\ e + d_0 & if\; e < -d_0 \end{cases} \quad (8)$$

The meaning of (7) is that, if the absolute error of an output component is no larger than d_0, then there is no weight updates associated with that output component. Therefore, the updating rule for ith subvector of $\mathbf{c}$ (see (4)) can be modified as

$$\begin{aligned} \mathbf{c}_i(k+1) &= \mathbf{c}_i(k) - \mu_k D(e_i(k)) \left[\frac{\partial y_i^*}{\partial \mathbf{c}_i}\right] \\ &= \mathbf{c}_i(k) - \mu_k D(e_i(k))\, \mathbf{G}(\mathbf{x}) \quad (9) \end{aligned}$$

3 The Convergence Result

With the network learning problem and the modified learning rule described in the previous section, we provide a convergence theorem in this section. Before the statement of the theorem, assume that $B_1 \leq \mathbf{G}^T(\mathbf{x})\mathbf{G}(\mathbf{x}) \leq B_2$ over the domain A, B_1 and B_2 being postive constants.

Theorem

Given any modeling error ϵ (see (2)) , if

1. the deadzone size d_0 (see (8)) is large enough such that $d_0 \geq \epsilon$,
2. the learning rate μ_k (see (9)) is selected such that $0 < \delta_1 \leq \mu_k \leq \frac{2}{\mathbf{G}^T(\mathbf{x})\mathbf{G}(\mathbf{x})} - \delta_2$, where δ_1 and δ_2 are small positive constants.

then

1. $|\tilde{\mathbf{c}}_i(k)| = |\mathbf{c}_i(k) - \mathbf{c}_i|$ will monotonically decrease and converge to a constant, for $i = 1, \ldots, m$.
2. $|\mathbf{c}_i(k+1) - \mathbf{c}_i(k)|$ will converge to zero, for $i = 1, \ldots, m$.
3. The error between y_i^* and y_i will converge to a ball of radius d_0 centered at the origin, for $i = 1, \ldots, m$.

proof:

At iteration k, the error between the ith neural network output and the ith function output is

$$\begin{aligned} e_i(k) &= y_i^*(k) - y_i(k) \\ &= y_i^*(\mathbf{x}, \mathbf{c}(k)) - y_i(\mathbf{x}) \\ &= y_i^*(\mathbf{x}, \mathbf{c}(k)) - \bar{y}_i(\mathbf{x}, \mathbf{c}) + \bar{y}_i(\mathbf{x}, \mathbf{c}) - y_i(\mathbf{x}) \\ &= \sum_{I \in A} \tilde{c}_i(\mathbf{k})\, g_\sigma(\mathbf{x}, \xi_I) + \bar{\epsilon}(\mathbf{x}) \\ &= \tilde{\mathbf{c}}_i^T(k)\, \mathbf{G}(\mathbf{x}) + \bar{\epsilon}(\mathbf{x}) \qquad (10) \end{aligned}$$

where $|\bar{\epsilon}(\mathbf{x})| \le \epsilon$, according to (2).

Next, some analysis related to the deadzone function is provided.

- If $|e_i(k)| \le d_0$, then $D(e_i(k)) = 0$, and the updating rule (9) becomes

$$\begin{aligned} \mathbf{c}_i(k+1) &= \mathbf{c}_i(k) - \mu_k D(e_i(k))\, \mathbf{G}(\mathbf{x}) \\ &= \mathbf{c}_i(k) \qquad (11) \end{aligned}$$

  Subtracting $\mathbf{c}_i$ from both sides of (11), one obtains

$$\tilde{\mathbf{c}}_i(k+1) = \tilde{\mathbf{c}}_i(k) \qquad (12)$$

  and

$$\tilde{\mathbf{c}}_i^T(k+1)\tilde{\mathbf{c}}_i(k+1) - \tilde{\mathbf{c}}_i^T(k)\tilde{\mathbf{c}}_i(k) = 0 \qquad (13)$$

- If $e_i(k) > d_0$, then

$$\begin{aligned} D(e_i(k)) &= e_i(k) - d_0 \\ &= \tilde{\mathbf{c}}_i^T(\mathbf{k})\, \mathbf{G}(\mathbf{x}) + \bar{\epsilon}(\mathbf{x}) - d_0 \qquad (14) \end{aligned}$$

  where $\bar{\epsilon}(\mathbf{x}) - d_0 \le 0$.

  Therefore,

$$\begin{aligned} &\tilde{\mathbf{c}}_i^T(k+1)\tilde{\mathbf{c}}_i(k+1) - \tilde{\mathbf{c}}_i^T(k)\tilde{\mathbf{c}}_i(k) \\ &= \tilde{\mathbf{c}}_i^T(k)\tilde{\mathbf{c}}_i(k) - 2\mu_k D(e_i(k))\tilde{\mathbf{c}}_i^T(k)\mathbf{G}(\mathbf{x}) \\ &\quad + \mu_k^2 D^2(e_i(k))\mathbf{G}^T(\mathbf{x})\mathbf{G}(\mathbf{x}) - \tilde{\mathbf{c}}_i^T(k)\tilde{\mathbf{c}}_i(k) \\ &= -2\mu_k D(e_i(k))\tilde{\mathbf{c}}_i^T(k)\mathbf{G}(\mathbf{x}) \\ &\quad + \mu_k^2 D^2(e_i(k))\mathbf{G}^T(\mathbf{x})\mathbf{G}(\mathbf{x}) \\ &= -2\mu_k D(e_i(k))\,[D(e_i(k)) + d_0 - \bar{\epsilon}(\mathbf{x})] \\ &\quad + \mu_k^2 D^2(e_i(k))\mathbf{G}^T(\mathbf{x})\mathbf{G}(\mathbf{x}) \\ &= -\mu_k D^2(e_i(k))\,\left[2 - \mu_k \mathbf{G}^T(\mathbf{x})\mathbf{G}(\mathbf{x})\right] \\ &\quad + 2\mu_k D(e_i(k))\,[\bar{\epsilon}(\mathbf{x}) - d_0] \\ &\le -\delta_1\delta_2 B_1 D^2(e_i(k)) < 0, \\ &\quad \text{if } 0 < \delta_1 \le \mu_k \le \frac{2}{\mathbf{G}^T(\mathbf{x})\mathbf{G}(\mathbf{x})} - \delta_2 \qquad (15) \end{aligned}$$

- If $e_i(k) < -d_0$, then

$$\begin{aligned} D(e_i(k)) &= e_i(k) + d_0 \\ &= \tilde{\mathbf{c}}_i^T(\mathbf{k})\, \mathbf{G}(\mathbf{x}) + \bar{\epsilon}(\mathbf{x}) + d_0 \qquad (16) \end{aligned}$$

  where $\bar{\epsilon}(\mathbf{x}) + d_0 \ge 0$.

  Then

$$\begin{aligned} &\tilde{\mathbf{c}}_i^T(k+1)\tilde{\mathbf{c}}_i(k+1) - \tilde{\mathbf{c}}_i^T(k)\tilde{\mathbf{c}}_i(k) \\ &= \tilde{\mathbf{c}}_i^T(k)\tilde{\mathbf{c}}_i(k) - 2\mu_k D(e_i(k))\tilde{\mathbf{c}}_i^T(k)\mathbf{G}(\mathbf{x}) \\ &\quad + \mu_k^2 D^2(e_i(k))\mathbf{G}^T(\mathbf{x})\mathbf{G}(\mathbf{x}) - \tilde{\mathbf{c}}_i^T(k)\tilde{\mathbf{c}}_i(k) \\ &= -2\mu_k D(e_i(k))\tilde{\mathbf{c}}_i^T(k)\mathbf{G}(\mathbf{x}) \\ &\quad + \mu_k^2 D^2(e_i(k))\mathbf{G}^T(\mathbf{x})\mathbf{G}(\mathbf{x}) \\ &= -2\mu_k D(e_i(k))\,[D(e_i(k)) - \bar{\epsilon}(\mathbf{x}) - d_0] \\ &\quad + \mu_k^2 D^2(e_i(k))\mathbf{G}^T(\mathbf{x})\mathbf{G}(\mathbf{x}) \\ &= -\mu_k D^2(e_i(k))\,\left[2 - \mu_k \mathbf{G}^T(\mathbf{x})\mathbf{G}(\mathbf{x})\right] \\ &\quad + 2\mu_k D(e_i(k))\,[\bar{\epsilon}(\mathbf{x}) + d_0] \\ &\le -\delta_1\delta_2 B_1 D^2(e_i(k)) < 0, \\ &\quad \text{if } 0 < \delta_1 \le \mu_k \le \frac{2}{\mathbf{G}^T(\mathbf{x})\mathbf{G}(\mathbf{x})} - \delta_2 \qquad (17) \end{aligned}$$

The analysis in (13), (15) and (17) implies that

$$\begin{aligned} & \tilde{\mathbf{c}}_i^T(k+1)\tilde{\mathbf{c}}_i(k+1) - \tilde{\mathbf{c}}_i^T(k)\tilde{\mathbf{c}}_i(k) \le 0 \\ \Longrightarrow\ & \tilde{\mathbf{c}}_i^T(k)\tilde{\mathbf{c}}_i(k) \text{ is } \textit{monotonically decreasing} \\ & \text{and } \tilde{\mathbf{c}}_i^T(k)\tilde{\mathbf{c}}_i(k) \longrightarrow C(\text{ a constant}), \\ & \text{as } k \longrightarrow \infty \quad \text{for all } i = 1, \ldots, m \qquad (18) \\ \Longrightarrow\ & D(e_i(k)) \longrightarrow 0 \quad as\ k \longrightarrow \infty \\ & \text{for all } i = 1, \ldots, m \qquad (19) \\ \Longrightarrow\ & \text{The errors } e_i(k) \text{ converge to a ball of} \\ & \text{radius } d_0, \text{ as } k \longrightarrow \infty \\ & \text{for all } i = 1, \ldots, m \qquad (20) \end{aligned}$$

Combining (9) and (19), we can show that

$$|\mathbf{c}(k+1) - \mathbf{c}(k)| \longrightarrow 0, \quad as\ k \longrightarrow \infty \qquad (21)$$

Thus, the results (18), (21) and (20) show our claims 1, 2 and 3, respectively. □

Remark : If a constant learning rate μ is used, and if $\mu < \min_{\mathbf{x} \in A}[\frac{2}{\mathbf{G}^T(\mathbf{x})\mathbf{G}(\mathbf{x})}]$, the same results can be obtained.

4 Simulation

In this section, some simulations are designed to verify our theoretical results. In **4.1**, we illustrate the effect of the learning rate on the convergence of weight error square. In **4.2**, the learnings with and without deadzone are compared.

4.1 The Effect of Learning Rate on the Weight Error Convergence

A two-input/one-output neural network $\mathbf{f}^*$, with 5×5 Gaussian hidden neurons uniformly distributed over the domain $\mathbf{A} = [-2.0, 2.0]^2$ and σ selected to be 1.0, is trained to approximate a nonlinear function $\mathbf{f}$ (*which appears to be the same network as* $\mathbf{f}^*$). The weight vector $\mathbf{c}$ of the neural network $\mathbf{f}$ are randomly selected between [0,1]. The initial weight vector $\mathbf{c}(0)$ of the neural network $\mathbf{f}^*$ are 0.0 . In each training iteration, the input vector is randomly selected from A.

For this simulation example, there is no modeling error; thus, no deadzone is used in the updating rule (i.e. $d_0 = 0$). When $e_i \neq 0$, the analysis (see(15) and (17)) suggests that

$$\tilde{\mathbf{c}}^T(k+1)\tilde{\mathbf{c}}(k+1) - \tilde{\mathbf{c}}^T(k)\tilde{\mathbf{c}}(k) \begin{cases} < 0 & if\ \mu_k < \frac{2}{\mathbf{G}^T(\mathbf{x})\mathbf{G}(\mathbf{x})} \\ = 0 & if\ \mu_k = \frac{2}{\mathbf{G}^T(\mathbf{x})\mathbf{G}(\mathbf{x})} \\ > 0 & if\ \mu_k > \frac{2}{\mathbf{G}^T(\mathbf{x})\mathbf{G}(\mathbf{x})} \end{cases} \tag{22}$$

This simulation is designed to verify (23). The weight error square $\tilde{\mathbf{c}}^T(k)\tilde{\mathbf{c}}(k)$, for the cases $\mu_k = \frac{1}{\mathbf{G}^T\mathbf{G}}, \frac{2}{\mathbf{G}^T\mathbf{G}}\ and\ \frac{2.01}{\mathbf{G}^T\mathbf{G}}$, are shown in Figure 1. When $\mu_k = \frac{1}{\mathbf{G}^T\mathbf{G}}$, $\tilde{\mathbf{c}}^T(k)\tilde{\mathbf{c}}(k)$ is monotonically deceasing and converges to zero. When $\mu_k = \frac{2}{\mathbf{G}^T\mathbf{G}}$, $\tilde{\mathbf{c}}^T(k)\tilde{\mathbf{c}}(k)$ is a constant. And when $\mu_k = \frac{2.01}{\mathbf{G}^T\mathbf{G}}$, it diverges.

4.2 The Effect of deadzone on Output Error Convergence

The networks $\mathbf{f}$ and $\mathbf{f}^*$ defined in **4.1** are again used here, except that the term $0.02cos(100x_1)$ is added to the output of $\mathbf{f}$ as noise. The network $\mathbf{f}^*$ is trained to appoximation $\mathbf{f} + 0.02cos(100x_1)$ over the domain A. The learning rate used is $\mu_k = \frac{1.0}{\mathbf{G}^T\mathbf{G}}$.

Two cases are studied. In the first case, with results shown in Figure 2, a deadzone of size 0.025 is incorporated in the training rule (see(9)) in order to cover the noise term of magnitude 0.02. The second case, with results shown in figure 3, uses the standard learning rule (without deadzone). In both cases, $\mathbf{f}^*$ is trained for 0.25 million iterations, and whenever $|e_1|$ or $|e_2|$ is larger than 0.025, the training step is recorded and the error size is also recorded as $\max(|e_1|, |e_2|)$.

A comparison of Figure 2 and Figure 3 shows that, when deadzone is used,

1. the number of registered errors is much fewer, and the error occurrence frequency decreases significantly.
2. the output error magnitude decreases towards the deadzone.

5 Conclusion

In this paper, we report a convergence theorem for radial basis network learning problems. We also clearly demonstrate, through analysis and simulation, how the size of the learning rate and the deadzone would affect the learning process.

References

[1] D. Rumelhart, G. E. Hinton, & R. J. Williams, " Learning Internal Representations by Error Propagation," In Rumelhart and McClelland (Ed), *Parallel Distributed Processing*, Vol. 1, MIT Press, 1986.

[2] C. M. Kuan and K. Hornik, "Convergence of Learning with Constant Learning Rates", *IEEE Transactions on Neural Networks*, Vol. 2, No. 5, pp. 484–489, 1991.

[3] R. M. Sanner & J. -J. E. Slotine, "Stable Adaptive Control and Recursive Identification Using Radial Gaussian Networks," *Proceedings 1991 IEEE Int'l Conf. on Decision and Control*, pp. 2116–2123.

[4] J. Park, I. W. Sanderg, " Universal Approximation Using Rdaial-Basis-Function Networks", *Neural Comp.* 3, 1991, pp. 246–257.

[5] R. P. Lippmann, "Pattern Classification Using Neural Networks ", *IEEE Communications Magazine*, November 1989 , pp. 47–46.

[6] E. J. Hartman, & J. D. Keeler, "Layered Neural Networks with Gaussian Hidden Units as Universal Approximations ", *Neural Comp.* 2, 1990, pp. 210–215.

[7] J. Moody, & C. J. Darken, "Fast learning in Networks of Locally-Tuned Processing Units ", *Neural Comp.* 1, 1989, pp. 281–284.

[8] W. Rudin, 1976. *Principles of Mathematical Analysis*, 3rd edition, McGraw-Hill, New York.

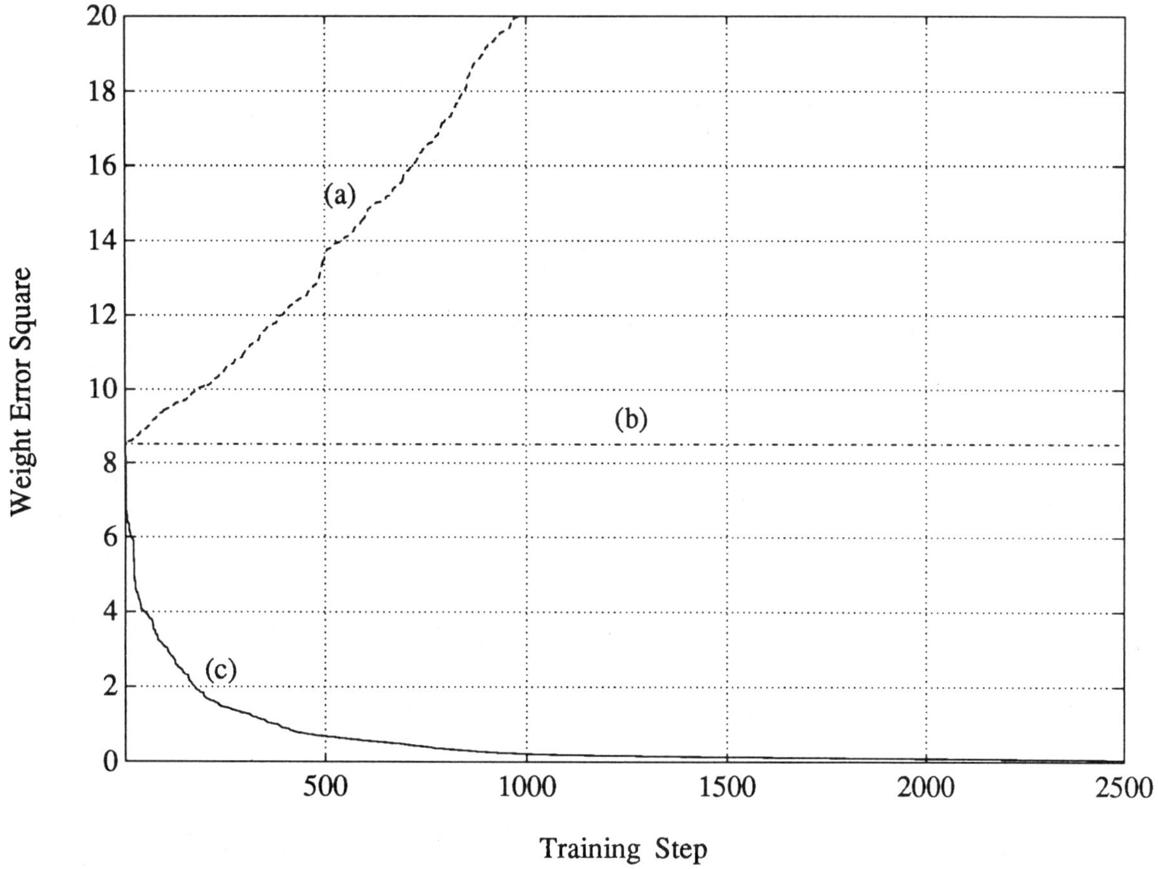

Fiqure 1 : Effect of learning rate. (a) $\mu_k = \frac{2.01}{\mathbf{G}^T\mathbf{G}}$. (b) $\mu_k = \frac{2.0}{\mathbf{G}^T\mathbf{G}}$. (c) $\mu_k = \frac{1.0}{\mathbf{G}^T\mathbf{G}}$.

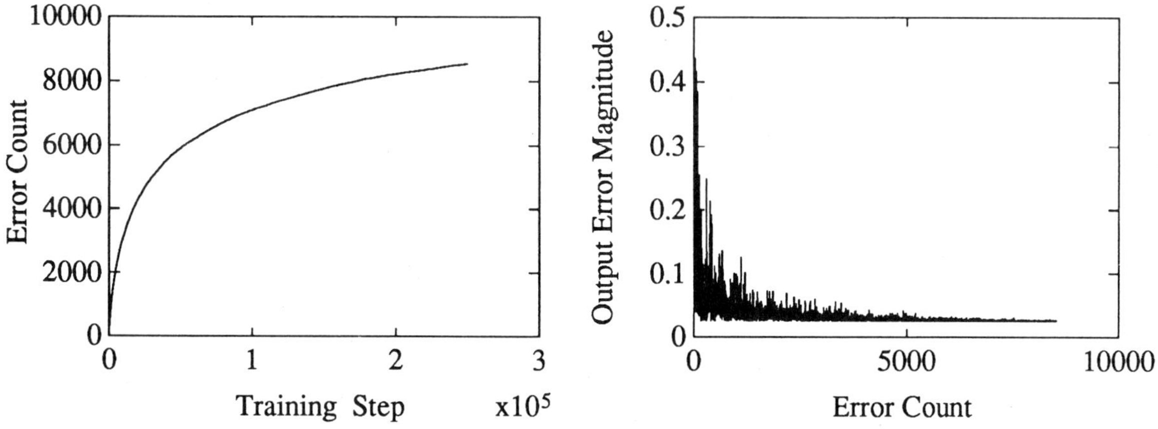

Figure 2 : Learning with deadzone $d_0 = 0.025$.

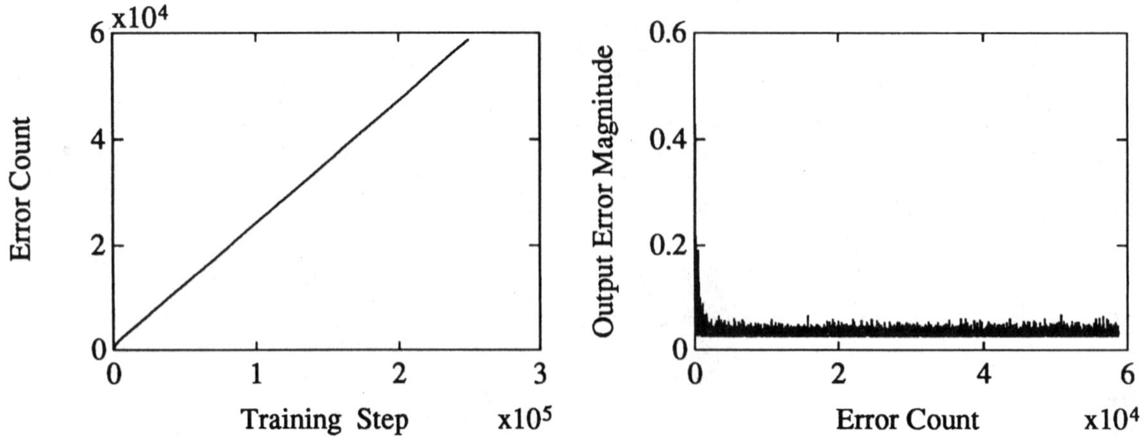

Figure 3 : Learning without deadzone, i.e. $d_0 = 0$.

NONLINEAR APPROXIMATIONS USING ELLIPTIC BASIS FUNCTION NETWORKS

Jooyoung Park and Irwin W. Sandberg*

Department of Control & Instrumentation Engineering
Korea University
Jochiwan, Chungnam, Korea

*Department of Electrical and Computer Engineering
University of Texas at Austin
Austin, TX 78712, USA

Abstract

Sharp conditions are given under which real-valued functions of several real variables can be approximated arbitrarily well by finite linear combinations of elliptic basis functions. Also given is a related result concerning the representation of functions as a limit in the mean of integrals involving elliptic basis functions.

1. Introduction

Studies of properties of memoryless nonlinear networks are playing an increasingly important role in control problems in connection with modelling, identification, and control of dynamic systems. Often interest centers around questions concerning the degree to which memoryless maps can be adequately approximated by certain classes of nonlinear networks. Here we consider questions of this kind for classes of networks that simulation studies have shown to be particularly useful.

In [1, 2] results are given concerning the approximation of functions of an arbitrary finite number of real variables using radial-basis-function (RBF) networks. Attention is focused on two widely used families of RBF networks. The theorems given provide conditions under which finite sums of the form

$$\sum_i w_i K\left(\frac{\cdot - \mathbf{z}_i}{\sigma}\right) \quad (\text{with } \sigma > 0,\ w_i \in \Re, \text{ and } \mathbf{z}_i \in \Re^r)$$

or

$$\sum_i w_i K\left(\frac{\cdot - \mathbf{z}_i}{\sigma_i}\right) \quad (\text{with } \sigma_i > 0,\ w_i \in \Re, \text{ and } \mathbf{z}_i \in \Re^r)$$

are capable of approximation in the sense of the L^p metric or the uniform metric on compact subsets of $\Re^r$. Of course, results of this kind are of interest in connection with the important question of whether a satisfactory network solution can be obtained by using some member of a given family.

In Section 2 of this paper, related results are given for variants of the RBF networks considered in [1, 2]. Here the hidden nodes are described by elliptic basis functions where the smoothing factors need not be the same for each coordinate.

Another purpose of this paper is to consider a connection between the study of EBF (i.e., elliptic basis function) networks and the study of wavelets (for an overview of wavelet theory, see [3, 4]). In wavelet theory attention is often focused on a transform called the continuous wavelet transform. For a real-valued square-integrable function f on $\Re$, this transform of f with respect to a square-integrable $\psi : \Re \to \Re$ is the function $W_\psi f : (\Re \setminus \{0\}) \times \Re \to \Re$ defined by

$$(W_\psi f)(a, b) = \frac{1}{\sqrt{|a|}} \int_{-\infty}^{\infty} f(x)\psi\left(\frac{x-b}{a}\right)dx.$$

Roughly speaking, the main goal of the transform is to decompose a function $f : \Re \to \Re$ into locally concentrated elements in the frequency and time domains. When the function ψ satisfies certain conditions, the original function f can be recovered from $W_\psi f$ through a recovery formula.

0191-2216/93/$3.00 © 1993 IEEE

In Section 3, it is shown that an inversion formula can be obtained for certain functions defined on $\Re^r$. The formula is closely related to the one-dimensional formal recovery formula used in wavelet theory.

Throughout this paper, we use the following definitions and notation, in which $\mathcal{N}$ and $\Re$ denote the natural numbers and the set of real numbers, respectively, and, for any positive number r, $\Re^r$ denotes the normed linear space of real r-vectors (viewed as row vectors) with norm $\|\cdot\|$. $L^p(\Re^r)$ denotes the usual space of $\Re$-valued maps f defined on $\Re^r$ such that f is pth power integrable. The usual inner products in $\Re^r$ and the Hilbert space $L^2(\Re^r)$ are both denoted by $<\cdot,\cdot>$. With $W \subset \Re^r$, $C(W)$ denotes the space of continuous $\Re$-valued maps defined on W. The usual L^p and uniform norms are denoted by $\|\cdot\|_p$ and $\|\cdot\|_\infty$, respectively. The convolution operation is denoted by " $*$," and the characteristic function of a Lebesgue measurable subset A of $\Re^r$ is written as 1_A. The Fourier transform [5] of a function f is written as $\hat{f}$.

2. EBF networks and approximations

There have been several recent studies concerning feedforward neural networks and the problem of approximating arbitrary functionals of a finite number of real variables. Some of these studies deal with cases in which the nonlinear elements in hidden layers are not sigmoidal functions cascaded with affine maps. The RBF networks are one of the most interesting alternatives along these lines.

The block diagram of a typical RBF network with one hidden layer is shown in Fig. 1. Each unit in the hidden layer of this RBF network has its own centroid, and for each input $\mathbf{x} = (x_1, x_2, \cdots, x_r)$, it computes the distance between $\mathbf{x}$ and its centroid. Its output (the output signal at one of the kernel nodes) is some nonlinear function of that distance. Thus, each kernel node in the RBF network computes an output that depends on a radially-symmetric function, and usually the strongest output is obtained when the input is at the centroid of the node. Each output node gives a weighted sum of the outputs of kernel nodes.

In [1, 2] two families of RBF networks are addressed. One family $S_0(K)$ consists of all functions $q : \Re^r \to \Re$ represented by

$$q(\mathbf{x}) = \sum_{i=1}^{M} w_i K(\frac{\mathbf{x} - \mathbf{z}_i}{\sigma})$$

where $M \in \mathcal{N}$ is the number of kernel nodes in the hidden layer, $w_i \in \Re$ is the weight from the ith kernel node to the output node, $\mathbf{x}$ is an input vector (an element of $\Re^r$), and K is the common radially-symmetric kernel function of units in the hidden layer. Here $\mathbf{z}_i \in \Re^r$ and $\sigma > 0$ are the centroid and smoothing factor (or width) of the ith kernel node, respectively. Note that the networks in this family have the same positive smoothing factor in each kernel node.

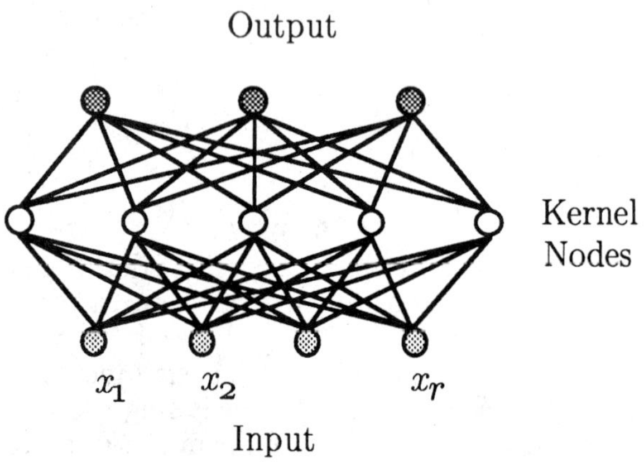

Fig. 1. A radial-basis-function network.

The other family $S_1(K)$ is a vector space whose general element $q : \Re^r \to \Re$ is given by

$$q(\mathbf{x}) = \sum_{i=1}^{M} w_i K(\frac{\mathbf{x} - \mathbf{z}_i}{\sigma_i})$$

where $\mathbf{x} \in \Re^r$, $M \in \mathcal{N}$, $\sigma_i > 0$, $w_i \in \Re$, and $\mathbf{z}_i \in \Re^r$ for $i = 1, 2, \cdots, M$.

For the sake of clarity and convenience, only a one-dimensional output space is considered here instead of outputs represented by multiple nodes as in Figure 1. Note that the kernel function K characterizes the families $S_0(K)$ and $S_1(K)$, and that each kernel node has its output derived from $K : \Re^r \to \Re$ indexed by two parameters (the centroid and smoothing factor), one for position and the other for scale. Ordinarily, the kernel function K of RBF networks is radially symmetric with respect to the norm $\|\cdot\|$ in the sense that $\|\mathbf{x}\| = \|\mathbf{y}\|$ implies $K(\mathbf{x}) = K(\mathbf{y})$.

Simulation results [6] show that the performance of networks can often be improved by relaxing the radial constraint and allowing a different smoothing factor for each coordinate. The resulting networks comprise the family of elliptic basis function (EBF) networks. Given the kernel function $K : \Re^r \rightarrow \Re$, the family of EBF networks $E(K)$ is represented by the set of all functions $q : \Re^r \rightarrow \Re$ of the form

$$q(\mathbf{x}) = \sum_{i=1}^{M} w_i K(\frac{x_1 - z_{i1}}{\sigma_{i1}}, \frac{x_2 - z_{i2}}{\sigma_{i2}}, \cdots, \frac{x_r - z_{ir}}{\sigma_{ir}})$$

$$= \sum_{i=1}^{M} w_i K((\mathbf{x} - \mathbf{z}_i)\mathrm{diag}[\sigma_{i1}, \cdots, \sigma_{ir}]^{-1})$$

where $M \in \mathcal{N}$, $\mathbf{x} \triangleq (x_1, \cdots, x_r) \in \Re^r$, $w_i \in \Re$, $\mathbf{z}_i \triangleq (z_{i1}, \cdots, z_{ir}) \in \Re^r$, and $\sigma_{i1}, \cdots, \sigma_{ir} > 0$ for $i = 1, \cdots, M$. Of course, if the input space is one dimensional (i.e. if $r = 1$), then $E(K)$ is the same as $S_1(K)$. Also, we shall use the observation that $E(K)$ has a translation invariant vector space structure.

A natural choice of the kernel function K of EBF networks is the simple gaussian [6, 7], for which

$$K(\mathbf{x}) = K(x_1, \cdots, x_r) = \exp(-\sum_{j=1}^{r} x_j^2/2),$$

and the output of the ith hidden unit is

$$\exp[-\sum_{j=1}^{r} \frac{(x_j - z_{ij})^2}{2\sigma_{ij}^2}].$$

Since $S_0(K)$ and $S_1(K)$ are subsets of $E(K)$, the "if" parts of the results in [2] hold with $S_0(K)$ or $S_1(K)$ replaced with $E(K)$. This observation led to the following theorems concerning the approximation capabilities of $E(K)$. It will become clear that our proofs are similar to those in [2]. As we shall see, radial symmetry of the kernel function $K : \Re^r \rightarrow \Re$ is needed in the development of only one of the approximation results in this study. Except where indicated to the contrary, radial symmetry of the kernel function K is not assumed.

Theorem 1 *Assuming that $K : \Re^r \rightarrow \Re$ is integrable, $E(K)$ is dense in $L^1(\Re^r)$ if and only if*

$$\int_{\Re^r} K(\mathbf{x})d\mathbf{x} \neq 0.$$

Proof:

When K satisfies the indicated conditions, the denseness of $E(K)$ is a corollary of [2, Theorem 1]. Also, since $\int_{\Re^r} K(\mathbf{x})d\mathbf{x} = 0$ implies that

$$\int_{\Re^r} K(\frac{x_1 - z_1}{\sigma_1}, \frac{x_2 - z_2}{\sigma_2}, \cdots, \frac{x_r - z_r}{\sigma_r})d\mathbf{x} = 0$$

the "only if" part of the proof of the same theorem shows that $E(K)$ is dense in $L^1(\Re^r)$ only if $\int_{\Re^r} K(\mathbf{x})d\mathbf{x} \neq 0$.

Theorem 2 *Assuming that $K : \Re^r \rightarrow \Re$ is square-integrable, $E(K)$ is dense in $L^2(\Re^r)$ if and only if for any $M \subset \Re^r$ with positive measure there is a diagonal matrix $D \triangleq diag[\sigma_1, \cdots, \sigma_r]$ with $\sigma_1, \cdots, \sigma_r > 0$ such that $\hat{K}(\cdot\, D) \neq 0$ almost everywhere on some positive measure subset of M.*

Proof:

Consider any K satisfying the indicated conditions, and suppose that the closure of $E(K)$ is not $L^2(\Re^r)$. Then, since this closure is translation-invariant, by [2, Lemma 2], there is a measurable subset M of $\Re^r$ having positive measure such that

$$\hat{f} = 0 \quad \text{almost everywhere on } M$$

for any f in the closure of $E(K)$. In particular, $\det D \exp(-2\pi i < \mathbf{z}, \cdot >)\hat{K}(\cdot\, D) = 0$ almost everywhere on M for any $\mathbf{z} \in \Re^r$ and any $D \triangleq \mathrm{diag}[\sigma_1, \cdots, \sigma_r]$ with $\sigma_1, \cdots, \sigma_r > 0$. This implies that $\hat{K}(\cdot\, D) = 0$ almost everywhere on M for all diagonal matrices D with positive diagonal elements, which contradicts our supposition.

To show the "only if" part, we prove the contrapositive: Assume that there is a measurable set $M \subset \Re^r$ with positive measure such that $\hat{K}(\cdot\, D) = 0$ almost everywhere on M for all diagonal matrices $D \triangleq \mathrm{diag}[\sigma_1, \cdots, \sigma_r]$ with $\sigma_1, \cdots, \sigma_r > 0$. Then for any $f \in L^2(\Re^r)$ with $J \triangleq \|\hat{f}\, 1_M\|_2 > 0$[1], there is no $g \in E(K)$ satisfying $\|f - g\|_2 < J/2$, because

$$\|f - \sum_i w_i K((\cdot - \mathbf{z}_i)\mathrm{diag}[\sigma_1, \cdots, \sigma_r]^{-1})\|_2$$

$$= \quad \|\hat{f} - \sum_i w_i \sigma_1 \cdots \sigma_r \exp(-2\pi i < \mathbf{z}_i, \cdot >)$$

[1]Here we use $\|\cdot\|_2$ to denote also the usual norm on the space of *complex-valued* square-integrable functions.

$\cdot\hat{K}(\cdot\ \mathrm{diag}[\sigma_1, \cdots, \sigma_r])\|_2 \geq \ \|\hat{f}\ 1_M\|_2 \ = \ J.$

This completes the proof.

The class of maps K for which the conditions of Theorem 2 are met is large. For example, notice that the conditions are satisfied by square-integrable maps $K : \Re^r \to \Re$ for which $\hat{K} \neq 0$ in a neighborhood of the origin.

Theorem 3 *With $p \in (1, \infty)$, let $K : \Re^r \to \Re$ be an integrable function such that*

$$\int_{\Re^r} K(\mathbf{x}) d\mathbf{x} \neq 0$$

and

$$\int_{\Re^r} |K(\mathbf{x})|^p d\mathbf{x} < \infty.$$

Then $E(K)$ is dense in $L^p(\Re^r)$.

Theorem 3 is a corollary of [2, Proposition 1].

Theorem 4 *Let $K : \Re^r \to \Re$ be an integrable function such that K is continuous and such that $\hat{K}^{-1}(0)$ includes no axis $\mathbf{l}_i \triangleq \{(x_1, \cdots, x_r) \in \Re^r : x_j = 0 \text{ for all } j \neq i\}$, $i = 1, \cdots, r$. Then $E(K)$ is dense in $C(W)$ with respect to the norm $\|\cdot\|_\infty$ for any compact subset W of $\Re^r$.*

Proof:

The proof is omitted in this version of the paper.

The hypotheses of Theorem 4 are met if, for example, K is continuous and integrable with a nonzero integral. Concerning Euclidean-radially-symmetric K, we have the following:

Theorem 5 *Let $K : \Re^r \to \Re$ be a nonzero integrable function such that K is continuous and radially symmetric with respect to the Euclidean norm. Then $E(K)$ is dense in $C(W)$ with respect to the norm $\|\cdot\|_\infty$ for any compact subset W of $\Re^r$.*

Theorem 5 is a corollary of [2, Theorem 5].

All of the theorems given above provide conditions under which functions can be approximated by elements of $E(K)$. Since the members of $E(K)$ are finite linear combinations of elliptic basis functions, a natural related question is whether it is possible to give an (exact) integral representation for a large class of functions along the lines of an inversion formula for continuous wavelet transforms.

In other words, it is natural to consider the capabilities of "distributed" elliptic-basis-function networks, and to do this from the perspective of continuous wavelet transforms. In the next section we show that the elements of $L^1(\Re^r) \cap L^2(\Re^r)$ can be expressed as a limit in the mean of integrals of an elliptic basis function over the domain of the centroid and smoothing factor. Our result bears on the matter of providing an algorithm for constructing approximations in $L^2(\Re^r)$ using elements of $E(K)$, but except for a brief remark in Section 4 this is not pursued here.

3. The elliptic basis function as a wavelet in multidimensional spaces

Wavelet theory is a body of results concerning the study of signals, in which attention is focused on bases called wavelets (for an overview, see [3, 4]). The theory covers a large area, and is especially useful in dealing with "non-stationary" signals [4]. In wavelet theory interest is centered on transforms called wavelet transforms, each of which makes use of a family of functions generated by a single function through the operations of dilation and translation. Roughly speaking, this transform provides a signal decomposition onto a set of basis functions which are called wavelets. There are different types of wavelet transforms: the continuous wavelet transform, the wavelet series expansion and the discrete wavelet transform. Below we consider only the continuous wavelet transform.[2]

When a function ψ in $L^2(\Re)$ satisfies the so-called "admissibility" condition

$$0 < c_\psi \triangleq \int_{-\infty}^{\infty} \frac{|\hat{\psi}(w)|^2}{|w|} dw < \infty,$$

ψ is called a "basic wavelet". Consider the following family of functions $\psi^{(a,b)} : \Re \to \Re$ defined by the translation and dilation of a basic wavelet $\psi : \Re \to \Re$:

$$\psi^{(a,b)}(x) = \frac{1}{\sqrt{|a|}} \psi\left(\frac{x-b}{a}\right), \qquad a \in \Re \backslash \{0\},\ b \in \Re.$$

The continuous wavelet transform[3] of $f \in L^2(\Re)$ with respect to the basic wavelet ψ is the function

[2] In particular, we do not consider in this paper material in the wavelet literature concerning, for example, representations with discrete dilation and translation parameters.

[3] This transform was introduced by J. Morlet et. al. [16].

$W_\psi f : (\Re \setminus \{0\}) \times \Re \rightarrow \Re$ defined by

$$(W_\psi f)(a,b) = \int_{-\infty}^{\infty} f(x)\psi^{(a,b)}(x)dx. \quad (1)$$

In [11] an inversion formula is presented for $r = 1$: If $\psi : \Re \rightarrow \Re$ satisfies the admissibility condition, then for any $f \in L^2(\Re)$ and each $x \in \Re$ at which f is continuous,

$$f(x) = \frac{1}{c_\psi}\int_{-\infty}^{\infty}[\int_{-\infty}^{\infty}(W_\psi f)(a,b)\psi^{(a,b)}(x)\frac{da}{a^2}]db. \quad (2)$$

Similar formulas are given without proofs in other studies (e.g. [12, 13]).

Below we give a limit-in-the-mean representation of arbitrary $f \in L^1(\Re^r) \cap L^2(\Re^r)$ closely related in form to the right side of (2).[4]

Before stating our next theorem, we introduce some additional definitions: For $\mathbf{w} \triangleq (w_1, \cdots, w_r) \in \Re^r$, $\Delta(\mathbf{w})$ denotes $w_1 w_2 \cdots w_r$. For any real-valued function K defined on $\Re^r$ and any ordered pair

$$(\mathbf{a},\mathbf{b}) \triangleq ((a_1,\cdots,a_r),(b_1,\cdots,b_r)) \in (\Re \setminus \{0\})^r \times \Re^r,$$

$K^{(\mathbf{a},\mathbf{b})} : \Re^r \rightarrow \Re$ is defined by

$$K^{(\mathbf{a},\mathbf{b})}(\mathbf{x}) = \frac{1}{\sqrt{|\Delta(\mathbf{a})|}}K(\frac{x_1-b_1}{a_1},\cdots,\frac{x_r-b_r}{a_r}).$$

Finally, U_ϵ denotes $(-\infty,-\epsilon)\cup(\epsilon,\infty)$ for $\epsilon > 0$.

Theorem 6 *Let $K : \Re^r \rightarrow \Re$ be a square-integrable function that satisfies*

$$0 < c_K \triangleq \int_{\Re^r}\frac{|\hat{K}(\mathbf{w})|^2}{|\Delta(\mathbf{w})|}d\mathbf{w} < \infty.$$

Then for any f in $L^1(\Re^r) \cap L^2(\Re^r)$:

(i) $< f, K^{(\mathbf{a},\cdot)} > K^{(\mathbf{a},\cdot)}(\mathbf{x})$ *is integrable over $\Re^r$ for each $\mathbf{a} \in (\Re \setminus 0)^r$ and each $\mathbf{x} \in \Re^r$,*

(ii) $\frac{1}{\Delta^2(\cdot)}\int_{\Re^r} < f, K^{(\cdot,\mathbf{b})} > K^{(\cdot,\mathbf{b})}(\mathbf{x})d\mathbf{b}$ *is integrable on U_ϵ^r for each $\epsilon > 0$ and each $\mathbf{x} \in \Re^r$,*

(iii) $\int_{U_\epsilon^r}\int_{\Re^r} < f, K^{(\mathbf{a},\mathbf{b})} > K^{(\mathbf{a},\mathbf{b})}(\cdot)d\mathbf{b}\frac{1}{\Delta^2(\mathbf{a})}d\mathbf{a}$ *belongs to $L^2(\Re^r)$ for each $\epsilon > 0$, and*

(iv) *we have*

$$\lim_{\epsilon\rightarrow 0} \|f - \frac{1}{c_K}\int_{U_\epsilon{}^r}\int_{\Re^r} < f, K^{(\mathbf{a},\mathbf{b})} >$$
$$\cdot K^{(\mathbf{a},\mathbf{b})}(\cdot)d\mathbf{b}\frac{1}{\Delta^2(\mathbf{a})}d\mathbf{a}\|_2 = 0.$$

Proof:

The proof is omitted in this version of the paper.

4. Concluding remarks

In this paper, we address problems concerning the approximation of functions in certain general spaces with elliptic basis function (EBF) networks. The approximation theorems in Section 2 show that under certain sharp conditions on the kernel K the family of EBF networks $E(K)$, whose members have just one hidden layer, is broad enough for universal approximation. An inversion formula is given in Section 3 for recovering $f \in L^1(\Re^r)\cap L^2(\Re^r)$ from the transform $W_K f$. Provided that K satisfies the conditions indicated and the integrand is sufficiently smooth, the inversion formula can be discretized to give an approximate inverse. In applications, K often satisfies the condition that

$$K(x_1,\cdots,x_r) = K(|x_1|,\cdots,|x_r|)$$

[4]For material related in a general sense, see, for example [13, 17, 18, 19]. In particular, in [18] a related limit-in-the-mean recovery relation is given for $r = 1$ involving approximate identities. There the limit is with respect to the integrand rather than with respect to a range of integration (as it is in Theorem 6). A more closely related study is [19, pp. 24-26, 33] in which the focus is on representing f as a limit in the mean of L^2-function representations of certain linear functionals, under a symmetry assumption on K that is not needed here. In this connection, the proof of Proposition 2.4.1 of [19] seems to require an additional hypothesis. Specifically, if f and g there belong to L^1 (or, alternatively, if ψ there belongs to L^1) then, by the fact that the convolution of an L^1 function with an L^2 function is in L^2, G_a and F_a in [19] are in L^2, which is used. Also, it appears that the proof of the convergence relation (2.4.5) of [19] is incomplete in that the infinite double integral referred to at the end of the proof was not shown to converge. (We are referring to what is called the "infinite integral" on p. 26 of [19]. ["infinite integral" appears just before "This establishes (2.4.5)."] The "infinite integral" seems to us to mean the double integral corresponding to the iterated integral that appears on the left side of (2.4.2) of [19] when $f = g$, but this double integral is not shown to converge. [Recall that the convergence of an iterated integral does not imply the convergence of the corresponding double integral.])

for all $(x_1, \cdots, x_r) \in \Re^r$. (e.g. kernel functions that are radially symmetric with respect to the Euclidean norm have this property) For such kernels, the approximating functions obtained by the discretization will be elements of $E(K)$.

The full-length version of this paper is to appear in the Journal of Circuits, Systems, and Signal Processing, vol. 13, no. 1., 1993.

References

[1] J. Park and I. W. Sandberg. Universal approximation using radial-basis-function networks. *Neural Computation*, 3(2):246–257, 1991.

[2] J. Park and I. W. Sandberg. Approximation and radial-basis-function networks. *Neural Computation*, 5(2):305–316, 1993.

[3] C. K. Chui. An overview of wavelets. In C. K. Chui, editor, *Approximation Theory and Functional Analysis*, pages 47–71, Boston, 1991. Academic Press.

[4] O. Rioul and M. Vetterli. Wavelets and signal processing. *IEEE Signal Processing Magazine*, 8(10):14–38, 1991.

[5] E. M. Stein and G. Weiss. *Introduction to Fourier Analysis on Euclidean Spaces.* Princeton University Press, Princeton, 1971.

[6] S. V. Chakravarthy. Capabilities of Adaptive Networks with Gaussian Basis Functions. Master's thesis, The University of Texas at Austin, 1991.

[7] N. Weymaere and J. Martens. A fast and robust learning algorithm for feedforward neural networks. *Neural Networks*, 4(3):361–370, 1991.

[8] W. Rudin. *Real and Complex Analysis.* McGraw- Hill, New York, third edition, 1987.

[9] W. Rudin. *Fourier Analysis on Groups.* Interscience Publishers, New York, 1962.

[10] B. E. Petersen. *Introduction to the Fourier Transform and Pseudo-Differential Operators.* Pitman Publishing Inc., Marshfield, Massachusetts, 1983.

[11] C. K. Chui. *An Introduction to Wavelets.* Wavelets Analysis and Its Applications. Academic Press, Boston, 1992.

[12] A. Grossmann and J. Morlet. Decomposition of Hardy functions into square integrable wavelets of constant shape. *SIAM Journal of Mathematical Analysis*, 15(4):723–736, 1984.

[13] I. Daubechies. The wavelet transform, time-frequency localization and signal analysis. *IEEE Transactions on Information Theory*, 36(5):961–1005, 1990.

[14] D. C. Champeney. *A Handbook of Fourier Theorems.* Cambridge University Press, Cambridge, UK, 1987.

[15] G. Cybenko. Approximation by superpositions of a sigmoidal function. *Mathematics of Control, Signals, and Systems*, 2(4):303–314, 1989.

[16] J. Morlet, G. Arens, I. Fourgeau, and D. Giard. Wavelet propagation and sampling theory. *Geophysics*, 47(2):203–236, 1982.

[17] R. Murenzi. Wavelet transforms associated to the n-dimensional Euclidean group with dilations: Signal in more than one dimension. In J. M. Combes, A. Grossmann, and Ph. Tchamitchian, editors, *Wavelets: Time-Frequency Methods and Phase Space*, pages 239–246, Springer-Verlag, New York, 1989.

[18] C. E. Heil and D. F. Walnut. Continuous and discrete wavelet transforms. *SIAM Review*, 31(4):628–666, 1989.

[19] I. Daubechies. *Ten Lectures on Wavelets.* The Society for Industrial and Applied Mathematics, Philadelphia, 1992.

THE BEST APPROXIMATION PROPERTIES AND ERROR BOUNDS OF GAUSSIAN NETWORKS

Binfan Liu and Jennie Si

Department of Electrical Engineering
Arizona State University
Tempe, AZ 85287-5706

Abstract

The best approximation of any C^2 function with support on the unit hypercube I_m in R^m is considered in the present paper. We prove that a Gaussian radial basis network with centers defined on a regular mesh in R^m has the best approximation property. Moreover, an upper bound $(O(N^{-2}))$ of the approximation is obtained for a network having N^m units.

1. Introduction

There are many papers on the representation ability of multilayer feedforward networks over the past few years. These include Cybenko [4], Funahashi [5], Hornik [9][10], Gorosi and Poggio[6][16] and many others. Their results show that any continuous functions can be approximated arbitrarily well by a layered network with one hidden layer, where the hidden nodes represent either sigmoidal functions [4][5][9][10] or radial basis functions [6][7]. This conclusion holds under the condition that there are a sufficiently large number of hidden units.

Various approaches have been taken to show that a linear combination of continuous sigmoidal functions are universal approximators under the condition of sufficiently many units in the hidden layer. Cybenko [4] applied the Hahn-Banach theorem to prove his result. From Irie-Miyake's integral formula [11], Funahashi [5] showed that the set of linear combinations of bounded and monotone increasing functions is complete in the space of real-valued continuous functions defined on a compact subset of R^n. In [9][10], Hornik, Stinchcombe, and White applied the Stone-Weierstrass Theorem and they obtained that standard multilayer feedforward networks with one hidden layer can be used to approximate not only Borel measurable functions but also their derivatives.

Other approximation schemes implement the hidden units by radial basis functions, for example, Gaussian functions. Lapedes and Farber [12] pointed out that any "reasonable" function can be represented by a linear combination of localized "bumps" that are each nonzero only in a small region of the neighborhood of their centers. Such "bumps" can be constructed by two hidden layers. Moody and Darken [13][14] developed a learning scheme for the network composed of a linear combination of "local bumps". In their network each hidden unit has its own receptive region in the input space with size proportional to the deviation of the input vectors. They demonstrated the learning capability of this network by solving the Mackey-Glass equation.

Girosi and Poggio [6][16] proved that both networks derived from regularization theory and radial basis function networks shared the property of best approximation. Furthermore, every continuous function on a compact subset of R^n can be approximated arbitrarily well by regularization networks with Green's functions as self-adjoint differential operators. In [7], Hartman, Keeler and Kowalski proved that a neural network with a single layer of hidden units of Gaussian-type is an universal approximator for any real-valued mapping defined on a convex, compact subset of R^n.

In mathematical terms, the representation ability of a network means that the set of functions which can be represented by the networks is dense in the space of continuous functions. An important aspect of the approximation problems by artificial neural networks is how well a function can be approximated by a feedforward network with a *finite* number of hidden neurons. Some results have been obtained in this regard. In [1], it is shown that a sigmoid network can uniformly approximate a function. Moreover, the squared error of the approximation is of $O(N^{-1})$. The result holds if the Fourier Transform $F(\omega)$ of the function to be approximated exists and $|\omega|F(\omega)$ is integrable.

This paper is concerned with the problem of approximating a C^2 function by a Gaussian radial basis network with centers defined on a regular mesh in R^m. The variances of the Gaussians are given as σ^2. In this paper, we show that such a network has the best approximation property and the approximation error is of $O(N^{-2})$ for a network composed of N^m Gaussians. A network has the best approximation property if in a set of functions there exists at least one that has minimum distance from a given function. Empirical results obtained in [15, 17] have indicated that the size of a Gaussian network with centers on a regular mesh grows exponentially with the dimension (m) of the input space for large m. Our results provide a theoretical verification

0191-2216/93/$3.00 © 1993 IEEE

of the above observation.

2. Preliminary

In this section, we introduce the general background of best approximation theory and some basic facts (from, e.g., [3][18]) which will be used in the derivation of our results.

Definition 2.1: Let E be a normed linear space with norm $\|\cdot\|$ and G be a subset of E. For each $f \in E$, d(f,G), the distance from f to G, is defined by

$$d(f,G) = \inf \{\|f-g\|: g \in G\}.$$

If there exists an element $g_0 \in G$ for which $\|f-g_0\| = d(f,G)$, then g_0 is a *best approximation* to f from G.

Since it is generally impossible to obtain explicitly the expression of d(f, G), our effort has been devoted to the approximation ability for specific choices of G as convex hull of regular-center Gaussians in $C^2(I_m)$. Problems of existence, uniqueness, and characterization of the best approximation are of essential importance in approximation theory.

Definition 2.2: A set G is called an *existence set* (*uniqueness set*) if for each $f \in E$, there exists at least (at most) one best approximation to f from G. G is a *Chebyshev* set if it is both an existence set and a uniqueness set.

Property 2.1: Let G be a linear subspace of a normed linear space E and g_0 be a best approximation to $f \in E$ from G. Then $\|g_0\| \le 2\|f\|$.

Proof. Suppose that $\|g_0\| > 2\|f\|$. Since $0 \in G$, $\|g_0-f\| \ge \|g_0\|-\|f\| > \|f\| = \|f-0\| \ge d(f,G)$.
This contradicts the fact that g_0 is a best approximation to f. ∎

Property 2.2: An existence set is a closed set.

Proof. Let $G \subset E$ be an existence set. If $f \in \overline{G}$, where $\overline{G}$ is the closure of G, then d(f,G) = 0 and thus f is the only best approximation to f. Since G is an existence set, $f \in G$. Hence $G = \overline{G}$. G is closed. ∎

Property 2.3: Each compact set is an existence set.

Proof. Suppose that G is a compact subset of E. For a given $f \in E$ and an element $g \in G$, the distance $d(f,g) = \|f-g\|$ is a continuous function defined on the compact set G. Then it attains its minimum value at some point $g = g_0$ on the compact set G. By Definition 2.1, g_0 is a best approximation to f. ∎

Property 2.4: Let G be a finite dimensional subspace of a normed linear space E. Then G is an existence set.

Proof. For a given element $f \in E$, consider the closed ball $S = \{g \in G: \|g\| \le 2\|f\|\}$. By Property 2.1, if a best approximation to f exists, it must belong to S. Since S is closed and bounded and G is finite dimensional, it follows that S is compact. Hence, $\|f-g\|$ is a continuous functional of g. Consequently this implies that there exists a $g_0 \in S$ such that $\|f-g\|$ has a minimum at $g = g_0$. By Definition 2.1, g_0 is a best approximation to f. ∎

Definition 2.3: A normed linear space E is *strictly convex* if for any $x \neq y$ in E, $\|x\| \le r$, $\|y\| \le r$ imply $\|x+y\| < 2r$.

Property 2.5: A convex set in a strictly convex space is a uniqueness set.

Proof. Suppose there are two distinct best approximations to $f \in E$, denoted by g_0 and h_0, respectively. Then $\|f-g_0\| = \|f-h_0\| = \delta$. Note however that $f-g_0$ and $f-h_0$ are different. Hence by strict convexity, $\|(f-g_0)+(f-h_0)\| < 2\delta$. This is equivalent to the expression $\|f-\frac{1}{2}(g_0+h_0)\| < \delta$, which is a contradiction of the fact that g_0 and h_0 are the distinct best approximations to f. ∎

Theorem 2.1: Let G be a subspace of the Hilbert space E and let $f \in E-G$, then $g_0 \in G$ is a best approximation to f from G if and only if $f-g_0$ is orthogonal to G. Moreover, g_0 is a Chebyshev set.

Proof. Suppose that there exists an element $h \in G$ such that

$$(f-g_0,h) = \alpha \neq 0.$$

Let

$$h_0 = g_0 + \frac{\alpha h}{\|h\|^2}.$$

Then, $h_0 \in G$, and

$$\|f-h_0\|^2 = \|f-g_0\|^2-2(f-g_0, \frac{\alpha h}{\|h\|^2}) + \frac{\alpha^2}{\|h\|^2}$$

$$= \|f-g_0\|^2 - \frac{\alpha^2}{\|h\|^2} < \|f-g_0\|^2,$$

which contradicts the fact that g_0 is a best approximation to f. We now show that g_0 is unique. It follows from Pythagorean theorem that for any $g \in G$,

$$\|f-g\|^2 = \|(f-g_0)+(g_0-g)\|^2 = \|f-g_0\|^2+\|g_0-g\|^2.$$

Hence,

$$\|f-g\| > \|f-g_0\|, \quad \forall g \neq g_0. \quad ∎$$

3. Main Results

In this section, we present our major results on the representation problems by Gaussian radial basis functions with the centers of the Gaussians defined on a regular mesh. We intend to investigate how to use such a network to represent any C^2 function on R^m in the sense of best approximation. In the present paper we consider Gaussians of the form $g_k = \exp(-\|x-x^{(k)}\|^2/\sigma^2)$, where $x^{(k)}$ are the centers of the Gaussians. The index k is defined on the set $\Omega=\{(k_1, ..., k_m)\in Z^m, k_i\in\{1,...,N\}$ for $i=1,...,m\}$. We use K to denote the total number of elements in Ω. Each of these K Gaussian radial basis functions is "nonzero" only in a small neighborhood $\Delta^{(k)} = \{x: \|x-x^{(k)}\| < \delta\}$ of the center $x^{(k)}$ for some $\delta>0$. The hidden units will be activated only when input value x lies in the set $\Delta^{(k)}$. This local tunability of the Gaussian radial basis networks is considered to be particularly suited for fast learning [13, 14].

However, note that when these "local" functions are used in representation networks, the receptive fields generated by the hidden units may overlap one another. This consequently adds significant difficulty to the analysis of the representation capability of a linear combination of local receptive fields. Since the well established approaches based on orthogonal representation theory do not apply any more.

In the following, our first result is concerned with the best approximation property by Gaussian networks.

Theorem 3.1: Let E be a Hilbert space whose elements are real-valued functions defined on a unit hypercube I_m, and let $G = \text{span}\{g_1, g_2, \cdots, g_K\}\subset E$ where g_i's are linearly independent. Then, for any given continuous function $f\in E$, there exists a best approximation g_0 to f. Moreover, g_0 has the form of $g_0 = c_1g_1+c_2g_2+\cdots+c_Kg_K$, where c_i's are given by

$$C = A^{-1}Y,$$

and where,

$$C = [\, c_1 \; c_2 \; ... \; c_K \,]^T,$$

$$Y = [(f, g_1)(f, g_2)...(f, g_K)]^T,$$

$$A = \begin{bmatrix} (g_1, g_1) & (g_1, g_2) & \cdots & (g_1, g_K) \\ (g_2, g_1) & (g_2, g_2) & \cdots & (g_2, g_K) \\ \cdots & \cdots & \cdots & \cdots \\ (g_K, g_1) & (g_K, g_2) & \cdots & (g_K, g_K) \end{bmatrix}.$$

Proof. Since G is spanned by $\{g_1, g_2, \cdots, g_K\}$, the dimension of G is finite. By Property 2.4, G is an existence set, i.e. there exists a best approximation $g_0(x)\in G$ to any given $f(x)\in E$. Suppose that g_0 has the form of $g_0 = c_1g_1+c_2g_2+\cdots+c_Kg_K$. From Theorem 2.1, $(f-g_0, g) = 0$ for any $g\in G$. Since $\{g_1, \cdots, g_K\}$ is a basis of G, it is equivalent to $(g_0-f, g_i) = 0$ where $i = 1, 2, \cdots, K$. We have a system of equations

$$\sum_{j=1}^{K} c_j(g_j, g_i) = (f, g_i), \qquad i = 1, 2, ..., K.$$

In matrix form AC = Y. Since A is nonsingular (refer to the proof of Theorem A.1 in Appendix 1), the coefficient vector C is given by $C=A^{-1}Y$. This completes the proof of theorem. ∎

The above result shows that the Gaussian networks have the best approximation property. Theorems 3.2 and 3.3 in the following are concerned with the error bound on the best approximation to C^2 functions $(R^m\rightarrow R)$ by Gaussian radial basis networks with N^m hidden units.

Theorem 3.2: Let $G = \text{span}\{g_1, g_2, \cdots, g_K\}$ be a subspace of the Hilbert space E over the unit hypercube I_m. For any given C^2 function f over I_m in E, the distance between f and g_0 is

$$d^2(f, g_0) = \|f\|^2 - Y^TA^{-1}Y,$$

where g_0 is determined by Theorem 3.1.

Proof. By Definition 2.1,

$$d^2(f, g_0) = \|f-g_0\|^2 = (f, f)-(f, g_0)$$

$$= \|f\|^2-Y^TC = \|f\|^2-Y^TA^{-1}Y. \quad ∎$$

Corollary 3.1: Let $G = \text{span}\{g_1, g_2, \cdots, g_K\}$ be a subspace of the Hilbert space E over unit hypercube I_m. For any given C^2 function f over I_m in E, if g_0 is the best approximation to f, then

$$d^2(f, g_0) \le \|f\|^2 - \frac{1}{\lambda_{max}}\sum_{i=1}^{K}(f, g_i)^2,$$

where λ_{max} is the largest eigenvalue of matrix A in Theorem 3.1.

Proof. Because $1/\lambda_{max}$ is the smallest eigenvalue of A^{-1}, by Rayleigh-Ritz Theorem [8], for any vector Y, we have $Y^TA^{-1}Y \ge Y^TY/\lambda_{max}$. The corollary follows from Theorem 3.2. ∎

Theorem 3.3: Let E be a Hilbert space whose elements are real-valued functions defined on $C^2(I_m)$. Let $G = \text{span}\{g_1,\cdots,g_K\}$, where $g_k = \exp(-\|x-x^{(k)}\|^2/\sigma^2)$, and $x^{(k)} = \{(\frac{2k_1-1}{2N}, \frac{2k_2-1}{2N}, \cdots, \frac{2k_m-1}{2N})\in I_m : k\in\Omega\}$ and $\Omega = \{(k_1,k_2,\cdots,k_m)\in Z^m: k_i\in\{1,\cdots,N\}$ for $i = 1,\cdots,m\}$. For any given C^2 function f over unit hypercube I_m in E, there exists a best approximation g_0 to f from G. Moreover, the error between f and g_0 is bounded by

$$\|f(x)-g_0(x)\|^2 \le \frac{m\sigma^2MM_2}{2} + \frac{M_1^2+MM_2}{4N^2},$$

where $M = \sup\{|f(x)|: x\in I_m\}$, $M_1 = \sup\{|f'(x)|: x\in I_m\}$ and $M_2 = \sup\{|f''(x)|: x\in I_m\}$.

Proof. Refer to Appendix 2. ∎

Remark 3.1: 1) Theorem 3.3 shows that Gaussian networks with centers defined on a regular mesh can approximate any C^2 function over I_m in R^m with an error bound of $O(N^{-2})$ for a network having N^m Gaussian units, if σ is of $O(N^{-1})$.

2) Let K denote the total number of Gaussian units, i.e., $K=N^m$. The approximation error bound obtained from Theorem 3.3 is rewritten as $O(K^{-2/m})$. If m=1, this bound is $O(K^{-2})$. If m=2, this bound is $O(K^{-1})$. This observation indicates that Gaussian networks defined on a regular mesh can achieve better or similar approximation results comparing to sigmoid networks (see [1]) when m<3.

4. Concluding Remarks

In this paper we have discussed the best approximation properties of a feedforward Gaussian network with a hidden layer over a regular mesh in R^m. We have shown first that networks considered in the present paper can represent any continuous function in the sense of best approximation (Theorem 3.1). We also show that the approximation error bound is of $O(N^{-2})$ for a network with N^m hidden nodes (Theorem 3.3). Our results provide a theoretical verification of the observations made in [15, 17], i.e., the size of a Gaussian network defined on a regular mesh grows exponentially with the dimension (m) of the input space for large m (Remark 3.1).

5. References

[1] Barron, A. R., "Universal Approximation Bounds for Superpositions of a Sigmoidal Function", Technical Report #58, Dept. of Statistics, Univ. of Illinois at Urbana-Champaign, Champaign, IL. Feb. 1991.

[2] Bartle, R. G., *The Elements of Real Analysis*. John Wiley & Sons, Inc., 1976.

[3] Braess, D., *Nonlinear Approximation Theory*, Springer-Verlag, 1986.

[4] Cybenko, G., "Approximation by Superpositions of a Sigmoidal Function". *Mathematics of Control, Signals, and Systems*, 2, 303-314, 1989.

[5] Funahashi, K, "On the Approximate Realization of Continuous Mappings by Neural Networks". *Neural Networks*, 2, 183-192, 1989.

[6] Girosi, F. and Poggio, T., "Networks and the Best Approximation Property". *Biological Cybernetics* 63, 169-176, 1990.

[7] Hartman, E. J., Keeler, J. D., and Kowalski, J. M., "Layered Neural Networks with Gaussian Hidden Units as Universal Approximations". *Neural Computation*, 2, 210-215, 1990.

[8] Horn, R. A., and Johnson, C. R., *Topics in Matrix Analysis*. Cambridge University Press, 1991.

[9] Hornik, K., Stinchcombe, M., and White, H., "Multilayer Feedforward Networks are Universal Approximators". *Neural Networks*, 2, 359-366, 1989.

[10] Hornik, K., Stinchcombe, M., and White, H., "Universal Approximation of an Unknown Mapping and its Derivatives Using Multilayer Feedforward Networks". *Neural Networks*, 3, 551-560, 1990.

[11] Irie, Bunpei and Miyake, Sei, "Capabilities of Three-layered Perceptrons". *IEEE International Conference on Neural Networks*, 1, 641-648, 1988.

[12] Lapedes, A. and Farber, R., "How Neural Nets Work". In *Neural Information Processing Systems*. 442-456, 1988.

[13] Moody, J., and Darken, C., "Learning with Localized Receptive Fields". *Proceedings of the 1988 Connectionist Models Summer School*, 1988.

[14] Moody, J. and C. Darken, "Fast Learning in Networks of Locally-Tuned Processing Units". *Neural Computation*, 1, 281-294, 1989.

[15] Narendra, K. S., "Adaptive Control of Dynamical Systems Using Neural Networks" in *Handbook of Intelligent Control*, Edited by White, D. A. and Sofge, D. A., Van Nostrand Reinhold, New York, 1992.

[16] Poggio, T. and Girosi, F., "Networks for Approximation and Learning". *Proceedings of the IEEE*, 1481-1497, Sept. 1990.

[17] Sanner, R. M. and Slotine, J-J. E., "Irregular Sampling Theory and Scattered-Center Radial Gaussian Networks". *Proceedings of the 31st Conference on Decision and Control*, Tucson, Arizona, Dec. 1992.

[18] Singer, I., *Best Approximation in Normed Linear Spaces by Elements of Linear Subspaces*. Springer-Verlag, Berlin, 1970.

Appendix 1 (Preliminary)

Theorem A.1: Let $g_1, g_2, \cdots, g_K$ be linearly independent. Then the K×K matrix A, defined in theorem 3.1, is positive definite.

Proof. For any nonzero vector $W = [\ w_1\ w_2\ ...\ w_K\ ]^T$, we have

$$W^TAW = \sum_{i=1}^{K}\sum_{j=1}^{K} w_iw_j(g_i, g_j)$$

$$= \left(\sum_{i=1}^{K} w_ig_i, \sum_{j=1}^{K} w_jg_j\right) = \left|\left|\sum_{i=1}^{K} w_ig_i\right|\right|^2 \geq 0$$

Since $g_1, g_2, \cdots, g_K$ are linearly independent, we have $w_1g_1+w_2g_2+\cdots+w_Kg_K \neq 0$ for some nonzero w_i's. It follows that A is positive definite. ∎

Appendix 2 (Proof of Theorem 3.3)

A2.1. Preliminaries.

In order to prove Theorem 3.3, we need the following results, Theorem A.2, Theorem A.3, and Corollary A.1.

Theorem A.2: $\lambda < (N\sigma^2\pi)^m$, where λ is an eigenvalue of the K×K matrix A defined in Theorem 3.1.
Proof. By Gersgorin theorem [8],

$$\lambda \le \max_{i\in\Omega}\left\{\sum_{j\in\Omega}(g_i, g_j)\right\}$$

$$= \max_{i\in\Omega}\left\{\sum_{j\in\Omega}\int_{\Delta(j)} \exp\{-\sigma^{-2}\|x-x^{(i)}\|^2\}\cdot\exp\{-\sigma^{-2}\|x-x^{(j)}\|^2\}dx\right\}$$

$$= \max_{i\in\Omega}\left\{\sum_{j\in\Omega}\exp\left\{-\frac{1}{2}\sigma^{-2}\|x^{(i)}-x^{(j)}\|^2\right\}\cdot\int_{\Delta(j)}\exp\left\{-2\sigma^{-2}\left\|x-\frac{1}{2}(x^{(i)}+x^{(j)})\right\|^2\right\}dx\right\}$$

$$< \left(\sigma\sqrt{\frac{\pi}{2}}\right)^m \max_{i\in\Omega}\left\{\sum_{j\in\Omega}\exp\left\{-\frac{1}{2}\sigma^{-2}\|x^{(i)}-x^{(j)}\|^2\right\}\right\}.$$

Note that Gaussians are separable nonlinearity, i.e.,

$$\exp\{-\sigma^{-2}\|x^{(i)}-x^{(j)}\|^2\} = \prod_{p=1}^{m}\exp\{-\sigma^{-2}(x_p^{(i)}-x_p^{(j)})^2\},$$

where $x_p^{(i)}$ is the pth component of $x^{(i)}$. Also recall that $x^{(i)}$ and $x^{(j)}$ are uniformly distributed over I_m. Thus

$$\lambda < \left(\sigma\sqrt{\frac{\pi}{2}}\right)^m \max_{i\in\Omega}\left\{\prod_{p=1}^{m}\left[\sum_{j=1}^{N}\exp\left\{-\frac{1}{2}\sigma^{-2}(x_p^{(i)}-\bar{x}^{(j)})^2\right\}\right]\right\},$$

where $\bar{x}^{(j)}=\frac{2j-1}{N}$ for $j=1, \cdots, N$. Since

$$\sum_{j=1}^{N}\exp\left\{-\frac{1}{2}\sigma^{-2}(x-\bar{x}^{(j)})^2\right\}$$

reaches its maximum at x = 0.5, we have

$$\lambda < \left(\sigma\sqrt{\frac{\pi}{2}}\right)^m\left[\sum_{j=1}^{N}\exp\left\{\frac{1}{2}\sigma^{-2}\left(\frac{1}{2}-\bar{x}^{(j)}\right)^2\right\}\right]^m$$

$$\le \left(\sigma\sqrt{\frac{\pi}{2}}\right)^m\left[N\cdot\int_R \exp\left\{-\frac{1}{2}\sigma^{-2}\left(\frac{1}{2}-z\right)^2dz\right\}\right]^m$$

$$= (N\sigma^2\pi)^m. \quad ∎$$

Theorem A.3: Let f(x) be any C^2 function over I_m and $M_2 = \sup\{|f''(x)|: x\in I_m\}$. Then,

$$\int_{I_m} f(x)dx \le \frac{1}{N^m}\sum_{k\in\Omega} f(x^{(k)}) + \frac{M_2}{8N^2},$$

where $x^{(k)}$ is defined in Theorem 3.3.

Proof. Let

$$J^{(k)} = \int_{S_k}[f(x)-f(x^{(k)})]dx,$$

where $S_k = \{x\in I_m: |x_i-x_i^{(k)}|<\frac{1}{2N} \text{ for } 1\le i\le m\}$. We have, by Taylor's Theorem,

$$J^{(k)} = \int_{S_k}\left\{(f'(x^{(k)}))^T(x-x^{(k)}) + \frac{1}{2}(x-x^{(k)})^T f''(\xi^{(k)})(x-x^{(k)})\right\}dx,$$

where $\xi^{(k)}\in S_k$ and x^T is the transpose of x. Note that $\int_S (f'(x^{(k)}))^T z dz = 0$. Thus,

$$J^{(k)} = \int_S\left[(f'(x^{(k)}))^T z + \frac{1}{2}z^T f''(\xi^{(k)})z\right]dz$$

$$\le \frac{M_2}{8N^2}\int_S dz$$

$$= \frac{M_2}{8N^2}\left(\frac{1}{N}\right)^m,$$

where $S = \{x\in I_m: |x_i|<\frac{1}{2N} \text{ for } 1\le i\le m\}$. If we add these inequalities for all $k\in\Omega$ and note first that

$$\sum_{k\in\Omega} J^{(k)} = \int_{I_m} f(x)dx - \frac{1}{N^m}\sum_{k\in K} f(x^{(k)}),$$

we obtain that

$$\int_{I_m} f(x)dx - \frac{1}{N^m}\sum_{k\in\Omega} f(x^{(k)}) \le \frac{M_2}{8N^2}.$$

This completes the proof of the theorem. ∎

Corollary A.1: Let f(x) be a C^2 function over I_m and let $M = \sup\{|f(x)|: x\in I_m\}$, $M_1 = \sup\{|f'(x)|: x\in I_m\}$ and $M_2 = \sup\{|f''(x)|: x\in I_m\}$. Then

$$\int_{I_m} f^2(x)dx \le \frac{1}{N^m}\sum_{k\in\Omega} f^2(x^{(k)}) + \frac{M_1^2+MM_2}{4N^2},$$

where $x^{(k)}$ is defined in Theorem 3.3.

Proof. Since $\frac{d^2}{dx^2}f^2(x) = 2[f'(x)]^2+2f(x)f''(x)$, it follows that

$$\sup\{|(f^2(x))''|: x\in I_m\} \le 2\sup\{|f'(x)|^2: x\in I_m\} + 2\sup\{|f(x)|: x\in I_m\}\sup\{|f''(x)|: x\in I_m\}$$

$$= 2(M_1^2+MM_2).$$

The corollary holds by theorem A.3. ∎

A2.2. Proof of Theorem 3.3.

Now we are in a position to prove Theorem 3.3.

Proof. By Theorem 3.1, there exists a best approximation g_0 which is a linear combination of g_k, $k\in\Omega$. Let $e = d(f, g_0)$. Apply Corollary 3.1 and Theorem A.2, we have

$e^2 <$

$$\int_{I_m} f^2(x)dx - \frac{1}{(N\sigma^2\pi)^m}\sum_{k\in\Omega}\left[\int_{\Delta(k)} f(x)\exp\{-\sigma^{-2}\|x-x^{(k)}\|^2\}dx\right]^2.$$

Using Corollary A.1,

$$e^2 \le \frac{1}{N^m}\sum_{k\in\Omega} f^2(x^{(k)})$$

$$-\frac{1}{(N\sigma^2\pi)^m}\sum_{k\in\Omega}\left[\int_{\Lambda(k)} f(x)\exp\{-\sigma^{-2}\|x-x^{(k)}\|^2\}dx\right]^2$$

$$+\frac{M_1^2+MM_2}{4N^2}$$

$$=\frac{1}{(N\sigma^2\pi)^m}\sum_{k\in\Omega}\Big\{(\sigma^2\pi)^m f^2(x^{(k)})$$

$$-\left[\int_{\Delta(k)} f(x)\exp(-\sigma^{-2}\|x-x^{(k)}\|^2)dx\right]^2\Big\}$$

$$+\frac{M_1^2+MM_2}{4N^2}$$

$$=\frac{1}{(N\sigma^2\pi)^m}\sum_{k\in\Omega}\Big\{\left[\int_{\Delta(k)} f(x^{(k)})\exp(-\sigma^{-2}\|x-x^{(k)}\|^2)dx\right]^2$$

$$-\left[\int_{\Delta(k)} f(x)\exp(-\sigma^{-2}\|x-x^{(k)}\|^2)dx\right]^2\Big\}$$

$$+\frac{M_1^2+MM_2}{4N^2}$$

$$=\frac{1}{(N\sigma^2\pi)^m}\sum_{k\in\Omega}\Big\{\int_{\Delta\times\Delta}\left[f^2(x^{(k)})-f(z_1+x^{(k)})f(z_2+x^{(k)})\right]$$

$$\cdot\exp(-\sigma^{-2}(\|z_1\|^2+\|z_2\|^2))dz_1dz_2\Big\}$$

$$+\frac{M_1^2+MM_2}{4N^2},$$

where $\Delta = \{x: \|x\|<\delta\}$. Let H be the value of the first term. Applying Taylor's Theorem at $(x^{(k)}, x^{(k)})$, we get

$$H=\frac{1}{2(N\sigma^2\pi)^m}\Big|\sum_{k\in\Omega}\int_{\Delta\times\Delta}\left[(z_1)^T f''(\xi^{(k)})f(\xi^{(k)})z_1\right.$$

$$\left.+(z_2)^T f''(\xi^{(k)})f(\xi^{(k)})z_2\right]$$

$$\cdot\exp(-\sigma^{-2}\|z_1\|^2+\|z_2\|^2))dz_1dz_2\Big|$$

$$\le\frac{MM_2}{2(\sigma^2\pi)^m}\int_{\Delta\times\Delta}(\|z_1\|^2+\|z_2\|^2)\exp\{-\sigma^{-2}(\|z_1\|^2+\|z\|^2)\}dz_1dz_2$$

$$\le\frac{m\sigma^2MM_2}{2}.$$

We obtain $e^2 \le \frac{m\sigma^2MM_2}{2}+\frac{M_1^2+MM_2}{4N^2}$. This completes the proof of the theorem. ∎

Fuzzified RBF Network-based Learning Control: Structure and Self-construction

D. A. Linkens and Junhong Nie

Department of Automatic Control & Systems Engineering
University of Sheffield, Sheffield S1 3JD, U.K.

Abstract: This paper describes an example of how fuzzy systems can intergrate with neural networks and what benefits can be obtained from the combination. In particular, by drawing some equivalence between a simplified fuzzy control algorithm (SFCA) and radial basis function networks (RBF), we conclude that the RBF network can be interpreted in the context of fuzzy systems and can be naturally fuzzified into a class of more general networks, referred to as FBFN. Next, the FBFN is used as a multivariable rule-based controller with the ability of self-constructing its own rule-base by using a fuzzified competitive self-organizing scheme and incorporating an iterative learning control algorithm into the system. We have applied the approach to a problem of multivariable blood pressure control with a FBFN-based controller having 6 inputs and 2 outputs, representing a complicated control structure.

I. INTRODUCTION

As a useful alternative to well-known backpropagation networks, the Radial Basis Function network (RBF) has gained increasing popularity in many practical areas. A basic viewpoint concerning a three layered RBF network is that it can represent a specific nonlinear function reasonably well by linearly combining a set of nonlinear and localized basis functions which span a space containing a class of functions to be approximated. Instead of deriving a RBF network from the utilization of the function approximation technique [1], this paper takes a new approach by viewing the RBF network as a mechanism for representing the rule-based fuzzy knowledge and performing the associated fuzzy reasoning. In particular, starting from drawing some equivalence between a simplified fuzzy control algorithm (SFCA) developed by the authors [6] and a RBF network, we have naturally arrived at a position at which the SFCA appears to represent a class of more general basis function networks, referred to as FBFN for short, in the sense that a variety of basis functions with different operators but with clear conceptual interpretations can be used. Since we are interested in using the FBFN as a multivariable controller without relying on control experts to provide the rule-base, considerable effort must be devoted to constructing such a controller in a self-learning manner under real-time control environments. Following Moody's two stage idea, we propose an approach to accomplishing this task by using a fuzzified competitive self-organizing scheme and the incorporation of an *iterative learning control* algorithm into the system. As an illustration, the proposed scheme has been applied to a problem of multivariable blood pressure control.

II. DESCRIPTION OF THE SFCA ALGORITHM

Fuzzification, inference algorithm, and defuzzificztion are the three basic computing procedures of a fuzzy controller. Furthermore the reasoning algorithm usually comprises three further substages, namely, computing the matching degrees between the current fuzzy inputs with respect to each rule's IF part, determining which rules should be fired, and combining these fired rule's THEN parts with different strengths into final fuzzy sets [2]. By taking the nonfuzzy property regarding the numerical input/output of the fuzzy controller into account, we have derived a very simple but efficient fuzzy control algorithm SFCA which consists of only two main steps, pattern matching and weighted averaging, thereby eliminating the necessity of fuzzifying and defuzzifying procedures [6].

Assume that the controlled process is multivariable with m inputs and m outputs and the input and the output of the controller consist of n and m variables denoted by u_i and v_k respectively. Furthermore, assume that there are P rules in the rule-base, each of which has the form:

$$IF\ \bar{U}_1\ is\ A_1^j\ AND\ \cdots\ AND\ \bar{U}_n\ is\ A_n^j$$

$$THEN\ \bar{V}_1\ is\ B_1^j\ AND\ \cdots\ AND\ \bar{V}_m\ is\ B_m^j$$

where $\bar{U}_i$ and $\bar{V}_k$ are linguistic variables corresponding to the numerical variables u_i and v_k, A_i^j and B_k^j are fuzzy subsets and are defined on the corresponding universes of discourse U_i and V_k. Suppose that A_i^j and B_k^j in the rules are normalized fuzzy subsets whose membership functions are so defined that each of them is characterized only by two parameters, $M_{u,i}^j$ and $\delta_{u,i}^j$, or $M_{v,k}^j$ and $\delta_{v,k}^j$ with the notation that $M_{u,i}^j$ ($M_{v,k}^j$) is the center element of the support set of A_i^j (B_k^j), and $\delta_{u,i}^j$ ($\delta_{v,k}^j$) is the half width of the support set. Hence the jth

0-7803-0999-5/93/$03.00 ©1993 IEEE

rule may be written as

$$IF\ \ (M_{u,1}^j, \delta_{u,1}^j)\ AND\ ......\ (M_{u,n}^j, \delta_{u,n}^j)$$

$$THEN\ \ (M_{v,1}^j, \delta_{v,1}^j)\ AND\ ......\ (M_{v,m}^j, \delta_{v,m}^j)$$

Let input space $\Omega = (U_1 \times U_2 \times ...... \times U_n) \in R^n$ be a compact product space, and $M_u^j = (M_{u,1}^j, M_{u,2}^j, ..., M_{u,n}^j) \in \Omega$ and $\Delta_u^j = (\delta_{u,1}^j, \delta_{u,2}^j, ..., \delta_{u,n}^j)$ be two n-dimensional vectors. Then the IF part of the jth rule may be viewed as creating a subspace $\Omega^j \in \Omega$ whose center and radius are M_u^j and Δ_u^j respectively, or as defining a *rule pattern*. Similarly n current inputs $u_{0i} \in U_i$ (i=1, 2, ..., n), with u_{0i} being a singleton, can also be represented as a n-dimensional vector u_0 in Ω, and will be referred to as an *input pattern.*

It is very useful to split the whole reasoning procedure involved in the fuzzy control algorithm into two phases: pattern matching and weighted averaging. The first operation deals with the IF part for all rules, whereas the second one involves an operation on the THEN parts of the rules. From the pattern concept introduced above, we need to compute the matching degrees between the current input pattern (a point in Ω) and each rule pattern (a set of points in Ω).

Distance Measure. Denote the current input by $u_0 = (u_{01}, u_{02}, ..., u_{0n})$. Then the matching degree denoted by $s_d^j \in [0, 1]$ between u_0 and the jth rule pattern $M\Delta_u(j)$ can be measured by the relationship

$$s_d^j = 1 - D^j(u_0, M\Delta_u(j)) \tag{1}$$

where $D^j(u_0, M\Delta_u(j)) \in [0, 1]$ denotes *relative distance* from u_o to $M\Delta_u(j)$. D^j can be specified in many ways. With the assumption of an identical width δ being used for all fuzzy sets A_i^j, the computational definition of D^j is given by

$$D^j = \begin{cases} \|M_u^j - u_0\|/\delta & \text{if } \|M_u^j - u_0\| \le \delta \\ 1 & otherwise \end{cases} \tag{2}$$

where $\|\ .\ \|$ denotes distance metrics which can be Euclidean, Hamming, or Maximum.

Possibility Measure. In a less geometrical manner, the similarity can be evaluated by a more general means called *possibility measure* [12] given by

$$s_p^j = \Phi_{i=1}^{n} poss(C_i / A_i^j) \tag{3}$$

where Φ stands for the *AND* connective defined usually either as a product or as a minimum operation. In our case, since C_i are singletons u_{0i}, (3) reduces to (4)

$$s_p^j = \Phi_{i=1}^{n} A_i^j(u_{0i}) \tag{4}$$

Two common definitions for A_i^j are triangle and exponential forms given by

$$A_i^j(u_i) = 1 - |M_{u,i}^j - u_i|/\delta \quad (5) \qquad A_i^j(u_i) = \exp(-|M_{u,i}^j - u_i|^2/\delta^2) \quad (6)$$

We note that the above definitions have some meaningful interpretations for linguistic terms A_i^j. Four different s_p^j can be obtained by combining (5) or (6) with *product* or *minimum* operators of *AND*.

Once the matching process is completed, whereby a matching degrees vector $s = (s^1, s^2, ..., s^P)$ is obtained for a specific input u_0 and P rules, then the kth component of the deduced control action v_k is given by

$$v_k = \left(\sum_{j=1}^{P} s^j \cdot M_{v,k}^j\right) / \left(\sum_{j=1}^{P} s^j\right) \tag{7}$$

It is worth noting that because only the centers of the THEN parts of the rules are utilized in the above algorithm and they are the only element having the maximum membership grade 1 on the corresponding support sets, the algorithm can be understood as a modified *maximum membership* decision scheme in which the global center is calculated by the *center of gravity* algorithm. Accordingly the rule form can be simplified further as

$$IF\ M\Delta_u(j)\quad THEN\quad M_v^j \tag{8}$$

where $M_v^j = [M_{v,1}^j, M_{v,2}^j, ..., M_{v,m}^j]$ is a center value vector of the THEN part.

III. CONNECTING SFCA TO RBF

A. *RBF network*

Simply stated, a RBF network is intended to approximate a continuous mapping f: $R^n \to R^m$ by performing a nonlinear transformation at the hidden layer and subsequently a linear combination at the output layer. More specifically, this mapping is described by

$$\hat{f}_k(u) = \sum_{j=1}^{N} \pi_k^j \cdot \phi^j(\|u - \omega^j\|) \tag{9}$$

where N is the number of the hidden units, $u \in R^n$ is an input vector, $\omega^j \in R^n$ is the center of the jth hidden unit and can be regarded as a weight vector from the input layer to the jth hidden unit [1], ϕ^j is the jth radial basis function or response function, and π_k^j is the weight from the jth hidden unit to the kth output unit.

Although there exist many possibilities to choose ϕ^j, as observed by Moody [5], Gaussion type functions given by

$$\phi^j(u) = \exp[-\|u - \omega^j\|^2/(\sigma^j)^2] \tag{10}$$

offer a desirable property making the hidden units to be locally-tuned, where the locality of the ϕ^j is controlled by σ^j. Thus, each hidden unit is associated with a center vector ω^j and an width σ^j. As pointed out by Moody [5], the locality of the unit response functions is a vital factor for attaining fast learning speeds. This is because, for any given input, only a small fraction of hidden units close enough to the input will be excited and therefore only those weights associated with the activing units will be evaluated and trained. By noting the factorable property of the Gaussian, Poggio [8] discussed some intriguing analogies of the RBF to the the neurobiological counterpart. Moody also proposed a normalized algorithm given by

$$\hat{f}_k(u)=\left(\sum_{j=1}^{N}\pi_k^j\cdot\phi^j(\|u-\omega^j\|)\right)/\left(\sum_{j=1}^{N}\phi^j(\|u-\omega^j\|)\right) \quad (11)$$

B. *FBFN: generalized RBF networks*

It is remarkable that the SFCA bears some intrinsic similarities with the RBF network, although they originated from two apparently independent fields: fuzzy logic theory and function approximation theory. From the knowledge representation viewpoint, the RBF network is essentially a net representation of IF-THEN rules. Each hidden unit reflects a rule: *IF* ω^j *THEN* π^j, where $\pi^j=(\pi_1^j,..., \pi_m^j)$. The rationale behind fuzzy reasoning in the SFCA and interpolative approximation in the RBF seems to be the same: to create a similar action with respect to a similar situation or to produce a similar output in response to a similar input. By comparing (7) with (9) or (11), we see that the two systems have almost identical computational procedures i.e matching degrees corresponds to response function values and the resemblance of two approaches in the final combination step is evident. The following parameter correspondences are identified: $M\Delta_u(j)$ to ω^j, M_v^j to π^j, δ to σ, and P to N.

Once a formal connection between these two paradigms is made, we can derive a hybrid system taking the advantages of both. One of the possibilities is to generalize the RBF network, by fuzzifying it, into a class of more general networks, referred to as FBFN. This can be done by simply replacing the radial basis function ϕ^j with matching degree s^j. It is easy to verify that the Gaussion basis function (10) is exactly recovered if the exponential membership function (6) with *product* operator for *AND* is used. While the s_d (1) and s_p in the above maintain the *radial* property, the other selections of s_p are no longer n-D radial, instead 1-D radial. However, the similarity measurement interpretation of the basis function reveals that the global radiality is in fact not necessarily a prerequest. What is important is to sustain the locality of ϕ^j in such a way that the similarity measure is reasonable and meaningful. In this regard, ϕ^j can be made not only factorable, but also synthesizable, in a logical sense, as a result of the fuzzy operator *AND* on n independent ϕ_i^j by *product* or *minimum*. It is surprising to note that the factorized ϕ_i^j are nothing but membership functions! Thus we are led to an extremely controversial issue relevant to the basis of fuzzy theory, i.e the subjectivity of the membership function, one of the sources of objection to fuzzy theory. Nevertheless, this subjectivity may provide an alternative explanation of why the choice of ϕ is not crucial.

IV. SELF-CONSTRUCTION OF FBFN CONTROLLER

In what way can the FBFN be benefited from the RBF? Certainly, it would be of great benefit if the FBFN could be made to be self-constructed without relying on the control rules provided by human experts. In terms of FBFN, parameters ω^j, σ^j, π^j, and N must preferably be self-determined. By prespecifying N, Moody [5] developed a hybrid learning scheme to learn ω unsupervisedly, σ^j heuristically, and π^j supervisedly. Since the FBFN-based controller must be operated in real-time, there are some difficulties in applying Moody's method. In particular, it is hard to specify N in advance due to the uncertain distribution of on-line incoming data, and more seriously, there are in general no teacher signals available to guide the learning of π^j. We approach the problem by using a fuzzified dynamical self-organizing scheme and by incorporating an iterative learning control strategy to supply the teacher signals on-line.

By using a prespecified identical width σ, our problems are how to partition a specific region of the input space into N subregions without knowing N in advance and how to learn N representative vector ω^j. We adopt the competitive learning approach of Kohonen with the following modifications. Instead of using absolute minimum distance as the winner selection criteria and a unique learning rate, we employ the matching degree given by (1) or (4) to determine the winner and N local learning rates are used. If one of the existing hidden units is able to win the competition, the corresponding ω^j is modified; otherwise, a new unit is created and $N(t+1)=N(t)+1$. In this manner, the required N and ω are dynamically learned in response to the incoming controller input u. The algorithm is described as follows, where t and T denote the sampling instant and maximum sampling time respectively. In addition, α^j is the local gain controlling the speed of the adaptive process for ω^j and is inversely proportional to the active frequency n^j of the jth unit up to present time instant, $N(t)$ stands for the number of units at time t, and $0\le\phi_0<1$ is a threshold controlling the unit number created.

a) Calculate the ϕ vector by (1) or (4), where

$$\phi=(\phi^1,\phi^2,...,\phi^{N(t)})$$

b) Find the unit J having the maximum response value:

$$\phi^J=\max_{j=1,N}\phi^j \quad (12)$$

c) Determine the winner using the following rule:

$$\begin{cases} \text{if } \phi^J \geq \phi_0 & \rightarrow J \textit{ is winner} \\ \text{if } \phi^J < \phi_0 & \rightarrow \textit{create a new unit} \end{cases} \quad (13)$$

d) Modify or intialize parameters:

If J is the winner:

$$n^J(t) = n^J(t-1) + 1;\ \alpha^J(t) = 1/n^J(t);\ N(t) = N(t-1)$$
$$\omega^J(t) = \omega^J(t-1) + \alpha^J \cdot [u(t) - \omega^J(t-1)] \quad (13)$$

If a new unit is created:

$$N(t) = N(t-1) + 1;\ \omega^{N(t)} = u(t)\ \ n^{N(t)} = 1;\ \phi^{N(t)} = 1 \quad (14)$$

e) Output the ϕ vector.

At each time instant, upon the response vector ϕ being derived, the next step is to modify the weight vector π. Assuming that the kth desired network output v_k^* corresponding to the current FBFN input u is known, the learning rule for π_k^j can be derived easily following the standard instantaneous gradient procedure with respect to (7) or (11) and is given by

$$\Delta\pi_k^j = \beta \cdot [(v_k^* - v_k(u)) \cdot \phi^j)] / [\sum_{j=1}^{N} \phi^j] \quad (15)$$

where $0<\beta<1$ is a learning rate and $v_k(u)$ is the actual output of the FBFN. As mentioned previously, the major difficulty in applying (15) lies in the unavailability of teacher signals v_k^* guiding the supervised training. Here we propose a simple but efficient approach to carrying out the task. The required teacher signals v_k^* are explicitly constructed first by an iterative learning approach [4]. Then the v_k^* are supplied to the FBFN so as to update the π_k^j using (15).

Fig 1 shows the learning system consisting of a reference model and a learning mechanism. The desired performance requirements are specified by the reference model which is assumed to be non-interacting with second-order linear transfer functions. The overall goal of the learning system is to force the learning error $e_L(t)$, defined as the difference between the output y_d of the model and the output y_p of the process, asymptotically to zero or to a predefined tolerant region ε within a time interval of interest [0, T] by repeatedly operating the system.

By taking the process time delay into account, the learning law is given by

$$v^{*l+1}(t) = v^{*l}(t) + P_L \cdot e_{L,l}(t+\lambda) + Q_L \cdot c_{L,l}(t+\lambda) \quad (16)$$

where $v^{*l}, v^{*l+l} \in R^m$ are on-line learning teacher vector-valued functions at the lth and the $(l+1)$th iterations respectively, $e_{L,l}$, $c_{L,l} \in R^m$ are learning error and change of learning error defined by $c_{L,l}(t) = e_{L,l}(t+1) - e_{L,l}(t)$, λ is an estimated time advance

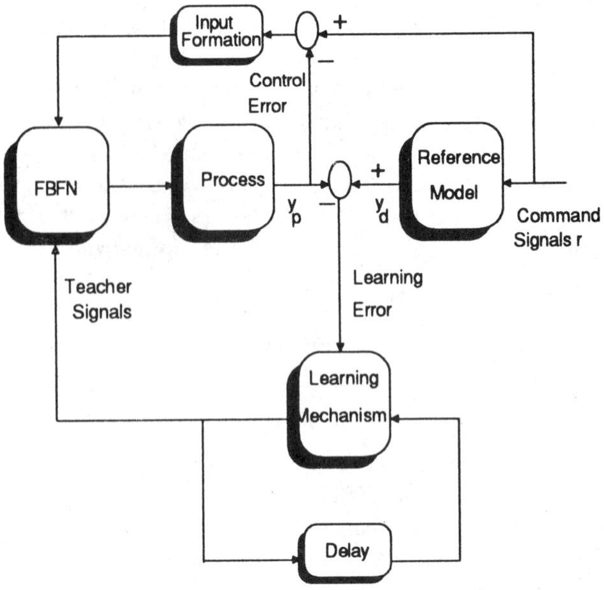

Fig 1 The FBFN-based learning control system

corresponding to time delay of the process, and $P_L, Q_L \in R^{m \times m}$ are constant learning gain matrices.

V. SIMULATION RESULTS

It is often required to regulate simultaneously the cardiac output (CO) and the mean arterial pressure (MAP) of a patient in hospital intensive care using various drugs. Two typical drugs used are dopamine (DOP), an inotropic drug, and sodium nitroprusside (SNP), a vasoactive drug. For the purpose of this simulation study, we adopt the same model as used before in [3,7] which is given by

$$\begin{bmatrix} \Delta CO \\ \Delta MAP \end{bmatrix} = \begin{bmatrix} 1.0 & -24.76 \\ 0.6636 & 76.38 \end{bmatrix} \begin{bmatrix} \frac{K_{11} e^{-\tau_1 s}}{sT_1+1} & \frac{K_{12} e^{-\tau_2 s}}{sT_1+1} \\ \frac{K_{21} e^{-\tau_2 s}}{sT_2+1} & \frac{K_{22} e^{-\tau_2 s}}{sT_2+1} \end{bmatrix} \begin{bmatrix} I_1 \\ I_2 \end{bmatrix}$$

where ΔCO (ml/s) and ΔMAP (mmHg) are the changes in cardiac output and in mean arterial pressure due to I_1 and I_2 ; I_1 (μg /Kg/min) and I_2 (ml/h) are the infusion rates of dopamine and nitroprusside; K_{11}, K_{12}, K_{21} and K_{22} are steady-state gains with typical values of 8.44, 5.275, − 0.09 and −0.15 respectively; τ_1 and τ_2 represent two time delays with typical values of τ_1 = 60s and τ_2 = 30s; and T_1 and T_2 are time constants typified by the values of 84.1s and 58.75s respectively.

The objectives of the simulation were to show the feasibility of the proposed FBFN-based control scheme when applied to this multivariable problem, to compare numerically various response functions ϕ, and to examine the self-construction behaviour of the system. Throughout the simulation, the controller was composed of 6 input and 2 output variables. 6 input variables are two errors, two change-in-errors, and two sum-errors.

With the controller parameters set as follows: learning matrices P_L=diag{0.05,-0.05} and Q_L=0, learning rate β=0.1, threshold ϕ_0=0.1, and width $\sigma(\delta)$=5, we carried out a set of simulations with four different basis functions:

$$\phi_{tp}^j = \prod_1^6 [1 - (|u-\omega^j|)/\sigma] \qquad \phi_{tm}^j = \bigwedge_1^6 [1 - (|u-\omega^j|)/\sigma]$$

$$\phi_{ep}^j = \prod_1^6 \exp[- \frac{|u-\omega^j|^2}{\sigma^2}] \qquad \phi_{em}^j = \bigwedge_1^6 \exp[- \frac{|u-\omega^j|^2}{\sigma^2}]$$

subject to step commands, where Π and Λ denote algebraic product and minimum operator respectively. Corresponding to ϕ_{tp}^j, ϕ_{tm}^j, ϕ_{ep}^j, and ϕ_{em}^j, the squared sum of learning errors e_L (SSR) after 15 iterations were 60.42, 60.51, 60.76, and 60.77 and the number of created hidden units were 8, 8, 7, and 7 respectively. The results indicated that the control performance is not sensitive to the choice of the basis function and therefore it can be designed in various ways. This agrees well with our previous conclusion. This property may have some significant implications. For example, synthesizing the global function from 1-D functions with the minimum operation is much easier to implement using hardware than any others. In what follows, only ϕ_{ep} was adopted.

Fig 2 shows the output responses of the process after 15 iterations together with the desired responses indicated by dashed lines, where the measured process outputs were assumed to be corrupted by random noise with an amplitude of 10% at the setpoints. It can be seen that the process outputs follow the desired responses satisfactorily although both controller inputs and learning inputs were contaminated by noise.

To investigate the adaptive ability of the system to various situations, we conducted the following simulations using the above fixed controller parameters. Fig 3 shows the results when four different desired responses (obtained by changing some parameters in the reference model) were required, whereas Fig 4 gives the results with different process parameters being changed by 10% from their nominal values. It can be seen that after a few iterations, the normalized SSR (NSSR) tend to be stable at small values, indicating that the controller is able, in a uniform manner, to follow different performance requirements and to adapt to the different process parameters.

Finally, we examined the learning convergence property of the system with respect to various controller parameters P_L, β, σ, and ϕ_0. As shown in Fig 5, the learning gain matrix P_L affects the learning speed more than the learning rate β. As would be expected, while the learning convergence is not very sensitive to the choice of the width σ and threshold ϕ_0, the number of created hidden units, however, is directly related to these parameters. Fig 6 shows the created hidden units vs. iteration with different σ and ϕ_0. We see that starting from a large number of units, convergence is small to stable values. A general conclusion is that the bigger σ, the fewer units, and the bigger ϕ_0, the more units, conclusions which are identical with that from conceptual considerations.

VI. CONCLUSIONS

By viewing the RBF network as a mechanism for representing rule-based fuzzy knowledge and performing the associated fuzzy reasoning, we have described a class of generalized basis function networks. The matching degree interpretation of the basis function together with the simulation results have suggested that the basis function can be made not only factorable, but also can be readily synthesized from n independent localized functions by fuzzy logic operators. This property has some significant implications, particularly for hardware implementations. The proposed control system structure and corresponding learning algorithms provide a simple and systematic approach to self-organizing the control knowledge with arbitrary performance requirements in a real-time manner. Simulation results have demonstrated that the proposed method is very efficient in terms of fast learning speed, high capacity to deal with complicated control problems, and, more attractively, little prior knowledge about the controlled process being required.

REFERENCES

[1] D.S. Broomhead and D. Lowe, Multivariable functional interpolation and adaptive networks, *Complex Syst.*, Vol 2, PP 321-355, 1988.

[2] D. A. Linkens and Junhong Nie, A unified real time approximate reasoning approach for use in intelligent control. Part 1: theoretical development, *Int. J. Control*, Vol 56, pp 347-364,1992.

[3] D. A. Linkens and Junhong Nie, A unified real time approximate reasoning approach for use in intelligent control. Part 2: application to multivariable blood pressure control , *Int. J. Control*, Vol 56, pp 365-398,1992.

[4] D. A. Linkens and Junhong Nie, Constructing rule-bases for multivariable fuzzy control by self-learning. Part 1 : system structure and learning algorithms, *Int. J. System Science* , to appear.

[5] J. Moody and C. Darken, Fast-learning in networks of locally-tuned processing units, *Neural Comput.*, Vol 1, pp 281-294, 1989.

[6] Junhong Nie, A class of new fuzzy control algorithms, *Proc. IEEE Int. Conf. on Control and Applications*, Israel, 1989.

[7] Junhong Nie, *Fuzzy-neural control: principles, algorithms and applications*, Ph.D thesis, Department of Automatic Control and Systems Engineering, The University of Sheffield, 1992.

[8] T. Poggio and F. Girosi, Networks for approximation and learning, *Proc IEEE*, Vol 78, pp 1481-1497, 1990.

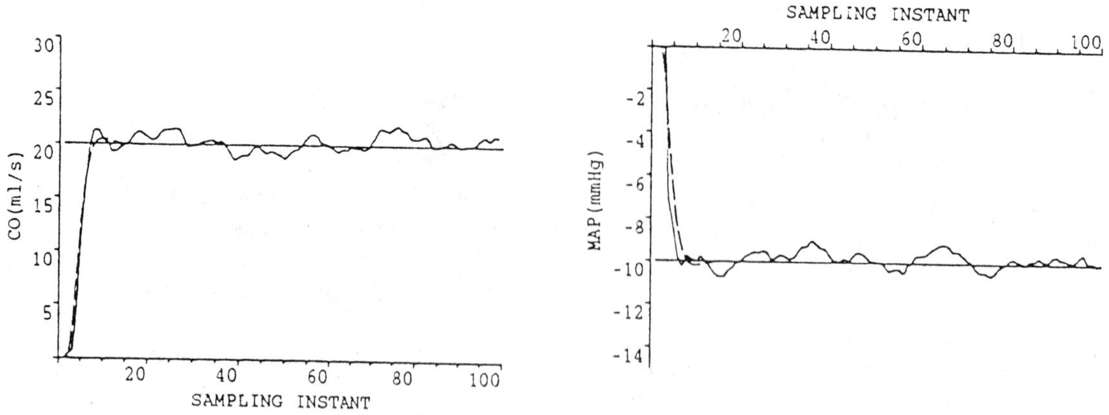

Fig 2 Output responses of the process under noise measurements

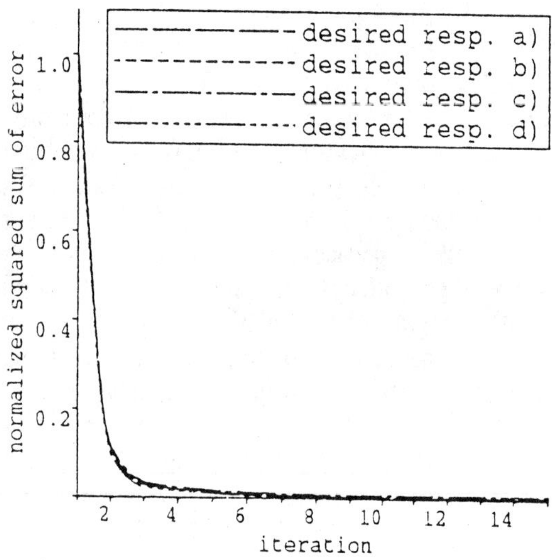

Fig 3 Adaptive ability to desired responses

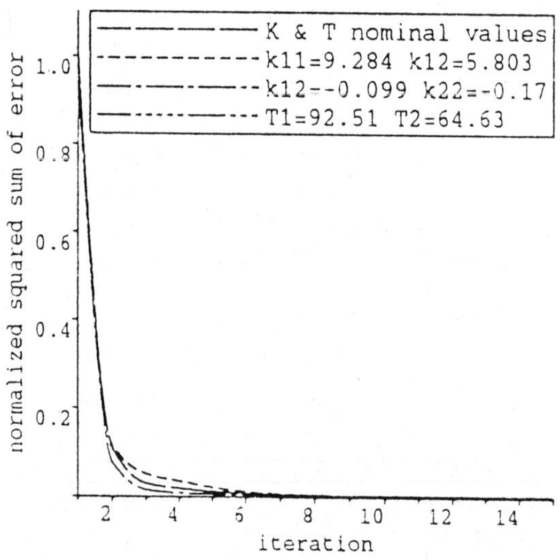

Fig 4 Adaptive ability to process parameters

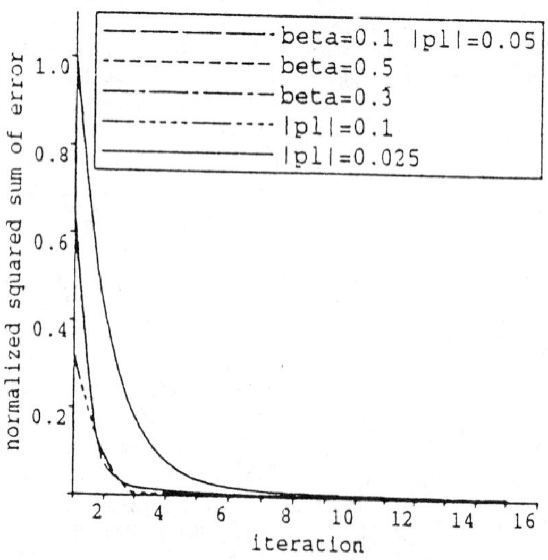

Fig 5 Convergence to learning rates

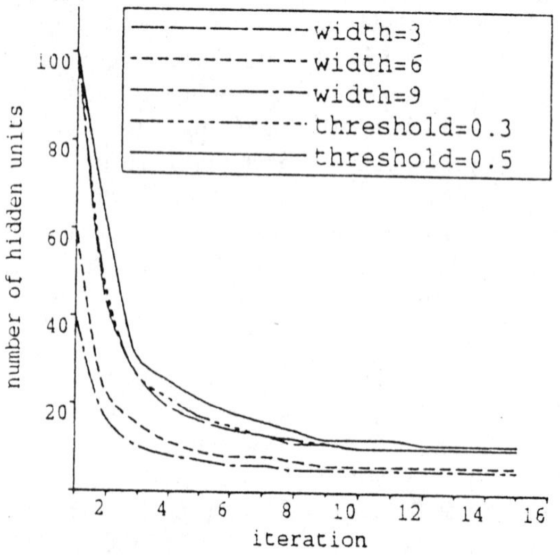

Fig 6 Created hidden units vs iterations

CMAC Learning is Governed by a Single Parameter

Yiu-fai Wong*
Department of Electrical Engineering, 116-81
California Institute of Technology
Pasadena, CA 91125
wong@systems.caltech.edu

***Abstract*— This paper presents a Fourier analysis of the learning algorithm in the Cerebellar Model Articulation Controller (CMAC) proposed by Albus. We prove that CMAC is capable of learning any discrete input-output mapping by Fourier analysis. We obtain the convergence rates for the different frequencies, which are governed by a single parameter M—the size of the receptive fields of the neurons. This complements an earlier result that CMAC always learns with arbitrary accuracy. The approach here offers new insights into the nature of the learning mechanism in CMAC, which may not be obvious from the earlier approach. The analysis provides mathematical rigor and structure for a neural network learning model with simple and intuitive mechanisms.**

I. Introduction

Albus's CMAC [1] is a three-layer feedforward network for learning input-output mappings. Its ideas and applications can be found in associative memory and learning schemes using locally tuned neurons [2, 3, 4, 5, 6, 7, 8, 9, 10]. There have been some investigations into the convergence properties of CMAC [11, 12, 13, 14]. Extensive analysis has been done by Parks and Militzer. In [12], the authors correctly recognized that CMAC learning is equivalent to iteratively solving a linear system and derived the solution the weights converge to. However, they had to assume that the system is invertible for convergence to occur. Wong and Sideris [13] independently showed that CMAC learning is equivalent to Gauss-Seidel iteration and that the linear system is invertible. Thus, CMAC always converges to give zero-error on any training set.

This work presented an even stronger result proved in [15]: *CMAC learning is governed solely by the size of the receptive field of the neurons.* The key idea is to study the Gauss-Seidel iteration in the Fourier domain. Linear techniques can indeed give rigor to such a simple, yet nonlinear, neural network.

The paper is organized as follows: We will present a brief description of CMAC. We then summarize an earlier result that CMAC learning can be treated as Gauss-Seidel iteration of a linear system. A new proof is obtained by using Fourier analysis, leading to a complete characterization of the convergence in the frequency domain.

II. Mechanisms of CMAC

A schematic sketch of CMAC is shown in Figure 1. We will next describe briefly the building blocks of CMAC. Although we can cast the model in the framework of connectionist multi-layer feedforward networks, the description we adopt here is closer to the original version because conceptually both versions are similarly easy to visualize.

For simplicity, let us start with CMAC for one-dimensional mapping, say $R \mapsto R$. But both the description and analysis can be easily extended to the multi-dimensional case. The input interval $[a, b]$ is discretized into a fixed number of levels. Each input x can then be identified by its discretization level x_d. There is a mapping between the discretized input space and a set $\mathcal{S}$ of neurons which is also indexed by integers. For each input x, we first compute its discretization level x_d. Then M consecutive neurons are excited starting at x_d, i.e. the size of the receptive field of a neuron is M. The output of a neuron is 1 if excited, 0 otherwise. A weighted sum of the outputs of these neurons is taken to be the CMAC output.

If the discretization is very fine, there will be too many neurons so that it is physically impossible to implement them (this is especially true for multi-dimensional inputs). Albus solved this problem by hash coding the set of neurons into a smaller, manageable memory $\mathcal{A}_p$ with A_p mem-

*Work supported by Pacific Bell through a grant to Caltech and by NASA through the Caltech Jet Propulsion Laboratory, as well as a Charles Lee Powell Foundation Graduate Fellowship.

0-7803-0999-5/93/$03.00 ©1993 IEEE

ory locations. Collision occurs when two different neurons are mapped to the same address. The question of collision due to hashing was addressed in [13] and it was argued there that its effect on CMAC learning is minimal. In fact, hashing does not cause a problem in simulations reported so far. From now on, we will assume that we have a big enough memory for the neurons so that there is no need for hashing.

Having described the mapping from input to output, we now describe the learning algorithm for CMAC. Let d_i be the desired output for the ith training sample. The network output is $g_i = \sum w_j$ where w_j is the weight for the excited neuron j. The error signal $\delta_i = d_i - g_i$. For each neuron excited by the input, $\delta w_j = \delta_i / M$. This rule can be derived from back-propagation [16] learning rule with learning rate $1/M$.

III. Key Results

Theorem 1 *Given a set of training samples composed of input-output pairs from $\mathcal{R}^n \mapsto \mathcal{R}^m$, CMAC always learns the training set with arbitrary accuracy if the input space is discretized such that no two distinct training input samples excite the same set of neurons. Furthermore, M completely specifies the learning convergence.*

Proof: We now transform CMAC learning to a linear system for the case of $m = n = 1$. We represent the neurons each input sample excites by a vector of characteristic function $\Theta_i(t)$ where

$$\Theta_i(t) = \begin{cases} 1 & \text{if } t^{th} \text{ neuron is excited by input sample } x_i \\ 0 & \text{otherwise.} \end{cases}$$

Let us call this vector the *indicator*. Form the matrix $A = [\Theta_1(t)\ \Theta_2(t) \cdots \Theta_P(t)]^t$ where P is the number of training samples. The goal of CMAC learning is to find a set of weights W such that

$$AW = D \tag{1}$$

where D is the vector of the desired outputs.

The key idea behind the proof in [13] is to identify the CMAC learning rule as Gauss-Seidel iteration of the linear system

$$C\Delta = D \tag{2}$$

where $C = AA^t$. An element c_{ij} of C is just the correlation between the indicators for i^{th} and j^{th} training sample. Thus, learning reduces to the convergence of the Δ. It turns out that C is symmetric and positive definite by noting that Θ_i's are linearly independent. Hence, the iterations always converges [17]. The weights W can be recovered from the accumulated output errors by the operation $W = A^t\Delta$. Putting all the equations together, the weights are given by $W = A^t(AA^t)^{-1}D$. Note that $A^t(AA^t)^{-1}$ is the pseudo-inverse A^+ of A [18]. It is quite remarkable that Albus's intuitive scheme is actually a numerical implementation of this inversion procedure.

Having proved the learning convergence, we want to know how fast the learning converges. Write C as $C = L + R$ where L is the lower diagonal part of C and R is the upper offdiagonal part of C. From matrix theory [17], the convergence of Gauss-Seidel iteration is governed by the spectral radius of $(-L^{-1}R)$. However, the largest eigenvector is not clear analytically. The convergence can be very slow if the spectral radius is close to 1.

We can do better than this. The trick here is to use techniques from digital signal processing to analyze Gauss-Seidel iteration. Before we do that, we note that the linear system in equation (1) is underspecified. That is, it has more unknowns (weights) than equations (one equation for each training sample). Therefore, there are an infinite number of solutions. Any vector of weights which lies in the null space $\mathcal{N} = ker(A)$ of A will produce zero output. We will now try to characterize this null space.

IV. Fourier Analysis of the Convergence

To make the Fourier analysis approach more manageable, we restrict the input space to be one-dimensional. Let N be a number such that all the training samples have their discretization levels between 0 and N. Since we only present training samples x_i for some selected points on the interval, we have the known values of d_i and the unknown values of Δ_i^* for these i's. The rest of Δ_i^* and d_i are don't cares[1]. The number of neurons needed is therefore $N + M - 1$ and the dimension of matrix A is $N \times (N + M - 1)$. Since C is positive definite, we see that the dimension of the null space $\mathcal{N}$ is $M - 1$. It is not difficult to see that $\mathcal{N}$ consists of all sinusoids of frequency $2\pi k/M$ where $k = 1, \ldots, M - 1$. This is because a sum of M consecutive weights will produce a zero output. Note that these frequencies are also the zeros of the spectrum of a rectangular box of length M.

The Gauss-Seidel relaxation takes the form

$$\Delta_i^{(l+1)} = \Delta_i^{(l)} + \frac{1}{M}(d_i - \sum_{j<i} C_{ij}\Delta_j^{(l+1)} - \sum_{j \geq i} C_{ij}\Delta_j^{(l)}) \tag{3}$$

where

$$C_{ij} = \begin{cases} M - |i-j| & \text{if } |i-j| < M \\ 0 & \text{otherwise} \end{cases}$$

and l indexes iteration. Let $e_i^{(l)} = \Delta_i^{(l)} - \Delta_i^*$, where Δ_i^* is one of the desired values. (Note that because of the

[1] It matters when we consider the generalization of CMAC to untrained points, which we do not consider here.

don't-cares in Δ_i, Δ^* is not unique.) Let $e^{(l)}$ be the vector composed of $e_i^{(l)}$'s, At desired solution,

$$\Delta_i^* = \Delta_i^* + \frac{1}{M}(d_i - \sum_{j<i} C_{ij}\Delta_j^* - \sum_{j\geq i} C_{ij}\Delta_j^*) \quad (4)$$

Subtracting equation (4) from equation (3), one finds that the error evolve according to

$$e_i^{(l+1)} = e_i^{(l)} - \frac{1}{M}\Big(\sum_{j<i} C_{ij}e_j^{(l+1)} + \sum_{j\geq i} C_{ij}e_j^{(l)}\Big). \quad (5)$$

This system can be viewed as a linear shift-invariant system on an infinite grid. To take care of the boundary conditions when we replicate the interval over the infinite grid, the index i now runs from $-(M-1)$ to $N+M-2$. Thus, the period is $N_1 = N+2M-2$. It can therefore be analyzed in the Fourier domain. That is, techniques from digital signal processing can be used to analyze this numerical problem [19] provided that we present the inputs in a sequential order.

We now expand e in a Fourier series of the form

$$e_n = \sum_{k=0}^{N_1-1} \tilde{e}_k \exp(j\frac{2\pi}{N_1}kn). \quad (6)$$

Then in the Fourier domain, equation (5) becomes [19]

$$\tilde{e}_k^{(l+1)} = H(e^{j\frac{2\pi}{N_1}k})\tilde{e}_k^{(l)} \quad (7)$$

where

$$H(z) = \frac{-\sum_{n=1}^{M}(M-n)z^n}{M+\sum_{n=1}^{M}(M-n)z^{-n}}. \quad (8)$$

The weights are obtained by the operation $W^{(l)} = A^t\Delta^{(l)}$. Let W^* be one of the desired solutions. If we denote $W^{l+1} - W^*$ by $\delta W^{(l)}$, then $\delta W^l = A^t e^l$. It is clear that in the frequency domain, $\tilde{\delta W}^{(l+1)} = H(e^{j\omega})\tilde{\delta W}^{(l)}$. If CMAC is capable of learning any input-output mapping, we desire that $|H(e^{j\omega})| < 1$.

Note that $H(z)$ can be written as:

$$H(z) = \frac{-h(z)}{1+h(-z)} \quad (9)$$

where $h(z) = \frac{(M-1)z - Mz^2 + z^{M+1}}{M(1-z)^2}$. With $h(z) = a(z) + jb(z)$, the magnitude of $H(z)$ is given by

$$|H(z)|^2 = \frac{1}{1+\frac{1+2a(z)}{a(z)^2+b(z)^2}}. \quad (10)$$

It is obvious that $|H(z)| < 1$ if and only if

$$1 + 2a(z) > 0. \quad (11)$$

Equating the real and imaginary parts of $H(e^{j\omega})$, we find that $a(e^{j\omega}) = \frac{\sin^2\frac{M\omega}{2}}{2M\sin^2\frac{\omega}{2}} - \frac{1}{2}$ and $b(e^{j\omega}) = \frac{M\sin\omega - \sin M\omega}{4M\sin^2\frac{\omega}{2}}$. Thus,

$$1 + 2a(e^{j\omega}) = \frac{\sin^2(\frac{M\omega}{2})}{M\sin^2(\frac{\omega}{2})}. \quad (12)$$

It is seen that $1+2a(e^{j\omega}) > 0$ except at $\omega = 2\pi k/M, k = 1, \ldots, M-1$, where it vanishes. But these harmonics belong to the null space of A. They have no effect on the CMAC output. Thus W and Δ do converge, proving that the Gauss-Seidel iteration converges in the frequency domain. It should come as no surprise that these errors have the same dimension as the null space of the matrix A. The Fourier analysis obviously generalizes to the CMAC with n-dimensional inputs since the kernel $\exp(-jkx)$ separates. The case of m-dimensional output space is taken care by replicating the 1-dimensional output system m times.

Now, let us investigate the rate of convergence for the different frequencies by utilizing the properties of the filter $H(z)$. After considerable algebraic manipulations, we get

$$|H(e^{j\omega})|^2 = \left(1 + \frac{\frac{4}{M}\sin^2(\frac{M\omega}{2})}{(1-p(\omega))^2 + 2p(\omega)(1-\cos(\frac{M-1}{2})\omega)}\right)^{-1} \quad (13)$$

where $p(\omega) = \sin(\frac{M\omega}{2})/M\sin\frac{\omega}{2}$. In Figure 2, we plot the squared magnitude of $H(e^{j\omega})$ for two choices of M and we see that larger M means slower overall convergence, as observed in the last section. The magnitude is 1 at frequencies $2k\pi/M, k = 1, \ldots, M-1$. Hence, the convergence is slow for frequencies near the harmonics of $2\pi/M$. As M increases, there will be more of these harmonics. This in turn means that learning will be slower. Note that $H(e^{j\omega})$ is periodic with period$=2\pi/M$ and its minimum value is $\frac{M/2-1}{M/2+1}$. We also note that the d-c gain of the filter is at the minimum. Thus CMAC can learn smooth mappings quite effortlessly.

That e_i contains frequency components which cannot be reduced does not imply that CMAC cannot learn these frequencies. Remember that when we replicate d_i on an infinite grid, we introduce $M-1$ don't cares in d_i. It is these don't cares which give extra degrees of freedom enabling CMAC to represent any mapping. However, since learning is local, it takes a long time for CMAC to learn these particular frequency components.

To conclude, it is very satisfying that M, the size of the receptive fields of the neurons, governs the learning in CMAC. $H(e^{j\omega})$ gives the rate of convergence for the various frequencies components. Combining some of the conclusions in [13], we now summarize what we know about CMAC:

1. CMAC learning is essentially solving a linear system with known matrix algorithm which converges; this explains why
    - CMAC learning is highly accurate and;
    - CMAC converges exponentially fast.
2. CMAC is doing some kind of interpolation for inputs it has not been trained on; this gives it a certain generalization ability;
3. CMAC learning is slow for frequencies near harmonics of $2\pi/M$ and fast otherwise;
4. CMAC learning is very robust to the noise added in the learning process.

V. Summary

Using Fourier analysis to examine the learning algorithm in the original CMAC, we have presented a new proof that CMAC learning always converges. The approach gives additional insight to the learning process. It shows the convergence rates for the different frequency components of the desired solution. It also clearly shows the relationship between M, which is the size of the receptive field of the neurons, and the overall convergence rate. The results obtained give us a better understanding of CMAC. It is very satisfying that linear techniques can be utilized to rigorously analyze this simple neural network model. This is some encouragement for those who try to build mathematical models of simple neural networks. But it remains to be seen if similar rigor can be brought to bear on more complicated neural networks.

VI. Acknowledgements

I am deeply indebted to Edward C. Posner for his encouragement and advice.

References

[1] J. S. Albus, "A New Approach to Manipulator Control: The Cerebellar Model Articulation Controller (CMAC)," *Trans. ASME, J. Dynamic Syst. Meas. Contr.*, vol 97, 220-227, 1975.

[2] Pentti Kanerva, "Parallel Structures in Human and Computer Memory,", in *Neural Networks for Computing*, J.S. Denker, (Ed.), AIP Conf. Proc. *151*, Snowbird, 1986, 247-258.

[3] D.S. Broomhead and D. Lowe, "Multivariable Functional Interpolation and Adaptive Networks," *Complex Systems*, 2, 321-355, 1988.

[4] John Moody, "Fast Learning in Multi-Resolution Hierarchies," in *Advances in Neural Information Processing Systems 1*, D.S. Touretzky, (Ed.), Morgan Kaufmann Publishers, 1989, 29-39.

[5] W. Thomas Miller, "Real-Time Application of Neural Networks for Sensor-Based Control of Robots with Vision," *IEEE Trans. Syst. Man and Cyb.* vol SMC-19, 825-831, 1989.

[6] Tomaso Poggio and Federico Girosi, "Networks for Approximation and Learning," *Proceedings of the IEEE*, vol 78, 1481-1497, 1990.

[7] Michael Hormel, "A Self-organizing Associative Memory System for Control Applications," in *Advances in Neural Information Processing Systems 2*, D.S. Touretzky, (Ed.), Morgan Kaufmann Publishers, 1990, 332-339.

[8] M. J. Carter, F. J. Rudolph and A. J. Nucci, "Operational Fault Tolerance of CMAC Networks, " in *Advances in Neural Information Processing Systems 2*, D.S. Touretzky, (Ed.), Morgan Kaufmann Publishers, 1990, 340-347.

[9] L. G. Kraft and D. P. Campagna, "A Comparison between CMAC Neural Network Control and Two Traditional Adaptive Control Systems," *IEEE Contr. Syst. Mag.*, 36-43, April, 1990.

[10] C.-S. Lin and H. Kim, "CMAC-based adaptive critic self-learning control," *IEEE Trans. Neural Networks*, 2, 530-533, 1992.

[11] P.C. Parks and J. Militzer, "Convergence Properties of Associative Memory Storage For Learning Control Systems," in *IFAC Symposium on Adaptive Syst. in Control and Signal Processing*, Glasgow, UK, 1989.

[12] P.C. Parks and J. Militzer, "Convergence Properties of Associative Memory Storage For Learning Control Systems," in *Automation and Remote Control*, Plenum Press, New York, vol. 50, No. 2, 254-286, 1989.

[13] Yiu-fai Wong and A. Sideris, "Learning Convergence in the Cerebellar Model Articulation Controller," *IEEE Trans. Neural Networks* , 3, 115-121, 1992.

[14] N.E. Cotter and T.J. Guillerm, "The CMAC and a Theorem of Kolmogorov," *Neural Networks*, 5, 221-228, 1992.

[15] Yiu-fai Wong, *Towards a Simple and Fast Learning and Classification System*, Ph.D Thesis, Caltech, Electrical Engineering, January, 1992.

[16] D.E. Rumelhart, et al., *Parallel Distributed Processing*, vol 1, MIT Press, Cambridge, Mass., 1986.

[17] Joel Franklin, *Matrix Theory*, Prentice-Hall, 1968.

[18] D.E. Catlin, *Estimation, Control, and the Discrete Kalman Filter*, Springer-Verlag, New York, 1989.

[19] C.-C. Jay Kuo and B. C. Levy, "Discretization and Solution of Elliptic PDEs —A Digital Signal Processing Approach," *Proc. IEEE*, 78, 1808-18 42, 1990.

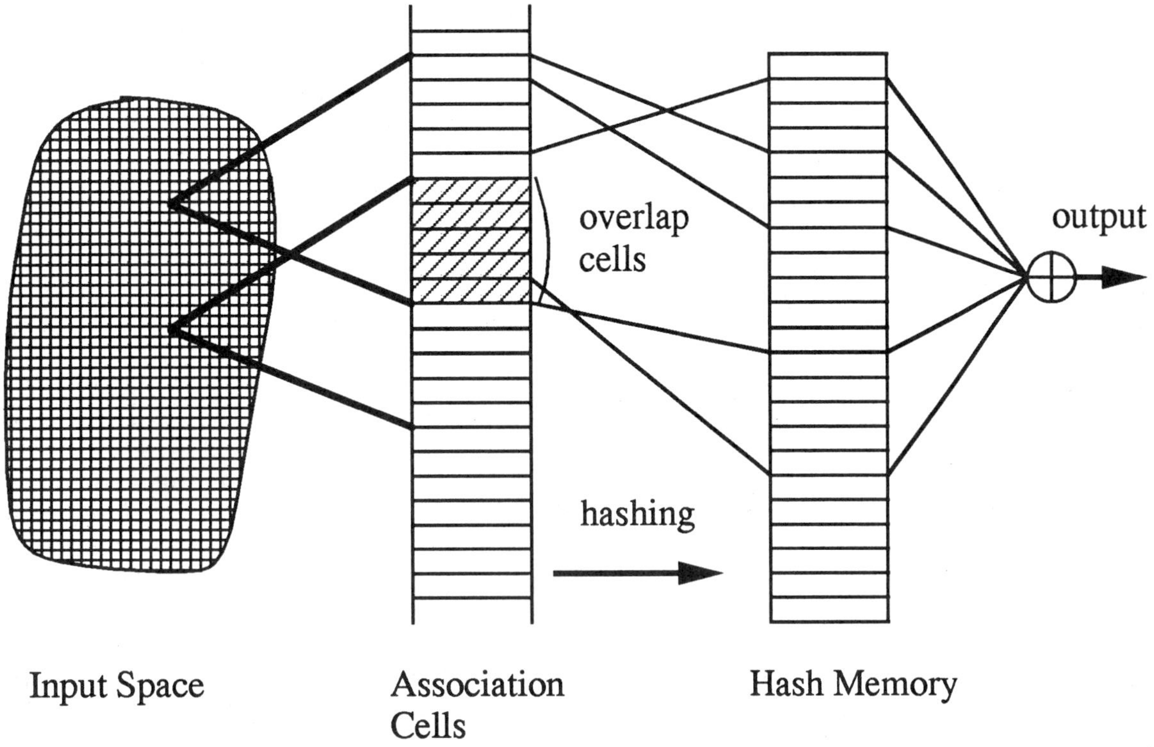

Figure 1: Basic skeleton of CMAC: the input excites M association cells which are coded to produce the output.

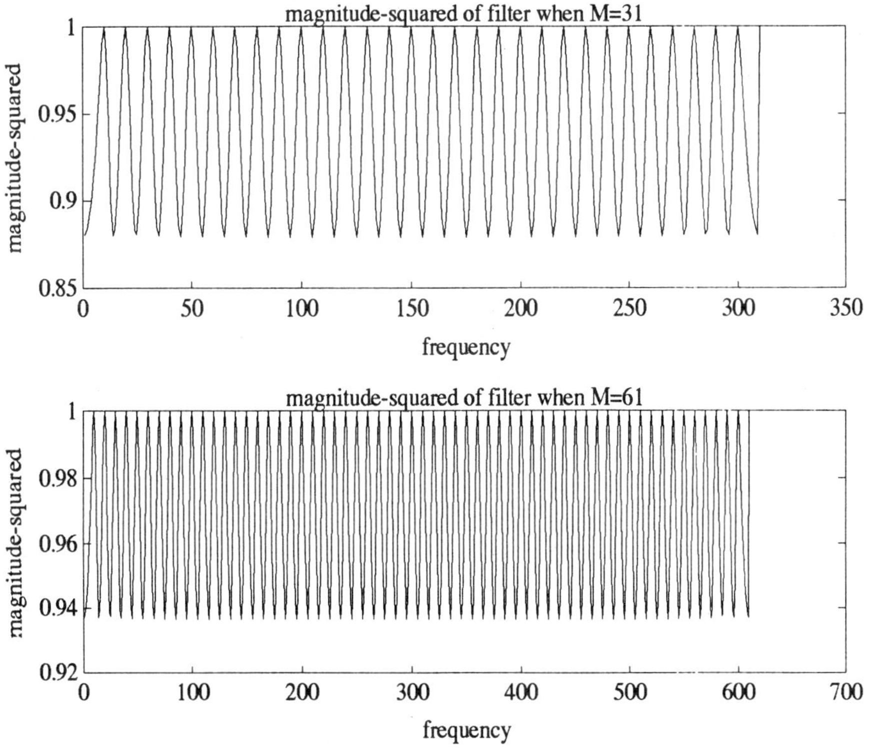

Figure 2: Comparison of the filters for two choices of M. It shows that the convergence is governed by M.

How Lateral Interaction Develops in a Self-Organizing Feature Map

Joseph Sirosh and Risto Miikkulainen
Department of Computer Sciences
The University of Texas at Austin, Austin, TX-78712
sirosh,risto@cs.utexas.edu

***Abstract*— A biologically motivated mechanism for self-organizing a neural network with modifiable lateral connections is presented. The weight modification rules are purely activity-dependent, unsupervised and local. The lateral interaction weights are initially random but develop into a "Mexican hat" shape around each neuron. At the same time, the external input weights self-organize to form a topological map of the input space. The algorithm demonstrates how self-organization can bootstrap itself using input information. Predictions of the algorithm agree very well with experimental observations on the development of lateral connections in cortical feature maps.**

I. Introduction

Two-dimensional topological maps of sensory input are present in various cortices of the brain. They are believed to develop in a self-organizing process based on cooperation and competition between neurons [4, 13, 14]. The Self-Organizing Feature Map (SOFM) algorithm [5, 6] is a computational model of this process. The SOFM algorithm has been applied, for example, into modeling the development of retinotopy, ocular dominance and orientation preference in the visual cortex and somatotopy in the somatosensory cortex [9, 10, 11].

The SOFM algorithm is an abstraction, though biologically inspired. At each step of training, the algorithm finds the neuron whose input synaptic weights are closest to the current input vector and changes the input weights of all neurons in its neighborhood towards the input vector. The size of the neighborhood starts out large, but gradually decreases towards the end of training. The algorithm relies on an external supervisor to find the maximally active unit, and invokes an ad-hoc schedule for decreasing the neighborhood size.

To be biologically realistic, the SOFM algorithm should be reduced to local computations and interactions among neurons of the map. Proposed low-level models of SOFM assume cooperative and competitive lateral interactions through excitatory and inhibitory connections [5, 8]. The lateral connections are non-modifiable and distinct from the external input connections. The connection weight profile in these models is shaped like a "Mexican hat", with short-range excitation and long-range inhibition. Similarly shaped lateral interaction is commonly found in many biological neural networks [5].

How does such lateral interaction arise? Enormous amounts of genetic information would be required to specify each synaptic weight of every neuron in a cortical map. Therefore, it is unrealistic to expect lateral interaction in such networks to be predetermined. All connections of a neuron should be modifiable, and there is no reason why the lateral interaction should have a uniform shape everywhere in the map. It makes sense to assume that the connections initially have random initial weights within a predetermined range. The question is, can these connections self-organize to form global order? Do the random-weight lateral connections develop a biologically realistic profile?

In this paper, we demonstrate through simulations that lateral connections can self-organize simultaneously with external input connections. In the process, the lateral interaction profile becomes a smooth "Mexican hat"-shaped function. The shape varies smoothly from neuron to neuron in the map depending on location. All connections can start out with random weights, and all connections are modified through a version of the Hebb learning rule.

II. The Self-organizing Process

The computations for a self-organizing feature map with lateral connections are described below. The algorithm computes the activity of each neuron in a network as a weighted sum of the external input and refines the activity through lateral interactions between neurons. When the activity stabilizes, all connection weights are modified. The process is repeated for each input. Section A explains and motivates our neuron model. Sections B and C describe the network and the input, and section D delineates

0-7803-0999-5/93/$03.00 ©1993 IEEE

the equations and the computations.

A. The Neuron Model

Each neuron in the network is assumed to have three sets of inputs:

- excitatory input connections that supply external input to the neuron,
- short-range lateral excitatory connections from close neighbors in the map,
- long-range lateral inhibitory connections from within the map.

A connection has a characteristic strength (or weight), which may be any value between zero and a prescribed limit. In a real neuron, these limits would be a property of the synapse.

External inputs to primary cortical areas of the brain synapse differently from intracortical lateral connections [15]. It is possible that the external and lateral connections of the same neuron obey two different rules of weight modification. In our model, the two rules differ only in the normalization. The external connections are normalized to hold the sum of squares of the input weights constant, and the lateral (excitatory/inhibitory) connections are normalized to keep the sum of lateral (excitatory/inhibitory) weights constant.

In the primary cortices, most extrinsic afferents synapse in the dendritic spines of neurons [15]. The dendritic shafts sum the input from the spines approximately linearly. A rule of weight modification proposed by [12] appears realistic when applied to theses synapses. Oja's rule is an approximation of a Hebbian rule in which the synaptic weights are normalized to hold the sum of squares of the weights constant. We use the more general Hebbian rule (5) to modify the external input connections.

In a real neuron, excitatory and inhibitory synaptic transmission are mediated by different neurotransmitters and receptors. The two sets of synapses also have different morphology [15]. A neuron processes each set at different sites with different receptors and secondary messengers, and these resources are limited. It is reasonable to assume that the total synaptic weight for each set is fixed. When lateral connection weights are modified in our model, they are normalized so that the total excitatory weight and the total inhibitory weight are constant (refer to equation 3).

B. The Network

The feature map is a two dimensional $N \times N$ grid of neurons (Fig. 1). Each neuron connects to its neighbors within distance d with excitatory lateral connections and

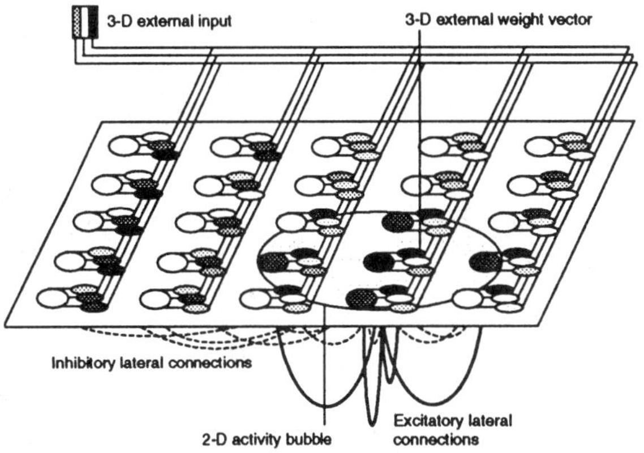

Fig. 1: **The laterally connected self-organizing feature map architecture.** Each neuron receives the same 3-dimensional input vector and computes an initial response based on the similarity with its external weight vector. The response then evolves through propagation along the lateral connections (only a few connections of the most strongly active unit are shown). After a stable activity bubble has formed, weights of the active units are adapted.

to all neighbors within $3d + 1$ with inhibitory connections. Lateral excitation weights are uniformly randomly distributed in the interval $(0,\gamma_e)$ within the excitation radius and are zero outside. Similarly, negative inhibition weights are distributed uniformly in the interval $(\gamma_i,0)$ within the inhibition radius and are zero outside.

C. The Inputs

The input vectors must be normalized to prevent vectors with large norms from dominating the self-organizing process [8]. For this reason, the 2-D square area used as input in the simulations was laid on the surface of a unit sphere and represented in spherical coordinate system. In effect, such inputs are still 2-dimensional because the radius is constant. Each spherical input vector $(x_1, x_2, 1)$, $(-0.5 \le x_1, x_2 \le 0.5)$ was then transformed into a 3-dimensional cartesian vector $x = (\xi_1, \xi_2, \xi_3)$:

$$\begin{cases} \xi_1 = 1 \cdot \cos(x_1)\cos(x_2), \\ \xi_2 = 1 \cdot \sin(x_1)\cos(x_2), \\ \xi_3 = 1 \cdot \sin(x_2). \end{cases} \tag{1}$$

Corresponding to the three input components, each neuron (i,j) has three external input weights $\mu_{ij,h}$, $h = 0, 1, 2$.

D. The Computations

The external and lateral weights are organized through a purely unsupervised learning process. Input items are randomly drawn from the input distribution and presented to the network one at a time. At each training step, the neurons in the network start out with zero activity. The

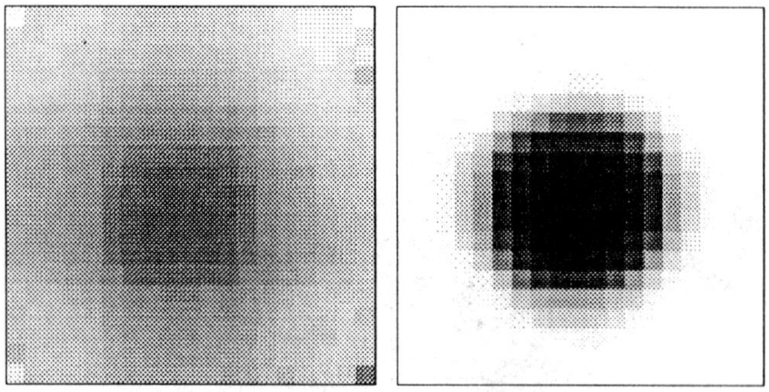

(a) Initial response (b) Final bubble

Fig. 2: **Focusing the response through lateral inhibition.** The darkness of each square indicates the activity level of the corresponding unit in a 20 × 20 map.

initial response of each neuron η_{ij} in the map is based on a scalar product of the input and weight vectors:

$$\eta_{ij} = \sigma\left(\sum_h \mu_{ij,h}\xi_h\right), \qquad (2)$$

where the function σ is the familiar sigmoid activation function. The response evolves over time through lateral interaction. At each time step, the neuron combines external activation with lateral excitation and inhibition according to

$$\begin{aligned}\eta_{ij}(t) = \sigma\,(&\textstyle\sum_h \mu_{ij,h}\xi_h + \\ &\textstyle\sum_{k,l} E_{kl,ij}\eta_{kl}(t-\delta t) + \\ &\textstyle\sum_{k,l} I_{kl,ij}\eta_{kl}(t-\delta t)\,),\end{aligned} \qquad (3)$$

where $E_{kl,ij}$ is the excitatory lateral connection weight on the connection from unit (k,l) to unit (i,j), $I_{kl,ij}$ is the inhibitory connection weight, and $\eta_{kl}(t-\delta t)$ is the activity of unit (k,l) during the previous time step. The activity pattern starts out as diffuse spread over a substantial part of the map and converges iteratively into a stable focused patch of activity, or activity bubble (Fig. 2). After the activity has settled, typically in a few iterations, the connection weights of each neuron are modified.

The lateral weights are modified by a Hebb rule, keeping the sum of weights constant:

$$\gamma_{ij,kl}(t+\delta t) = \frac{\gamma_{ij,kl}(t) + \alpha_L\eta_{ij}\eta_{kl}}{\sum_{kl}\left[\gamma_{ij,kl}(t) + \alpha_L\eta_{ij}\eta_{kl}\right]}, \qquad (4)$$

where η_{ij} stands for the activity of the unit (i,j) in the settled activity bubble, the γs are the lateral interaction weights ($E_{ij,kl}$ or $I_{ij,kl}$) and α_L is the learning rate for lateral interaction (α_E for excitatory weights and α_I for inhibitory). The larger the product of pre- and post-synaptic activity $\eta_{ij}\eta_{kl}$, the larger the weight change.

The external input weights are modified according to the normalized Hebbian rule:

$$\mu_{ij,h}(t+\delta t) = \frac{\mu_{ij,h}(t) + \alpha\eta_{ij}\xi_h}{\left\{\sum_h\left[\mu_{ij,h}(t) + \alpha\eta_{ij}\xi_h\right]^2\right\}^{1/2}}, \qquad (5)$$

which is otherwise similar to (4), but maintains the sum of squares of external weights constant.

Note that each computation is local to an individual neuron and its connections. The algorithm carries out local computations to achieve global self-organization of the map network. It does not require an external supervisory process.

III. Simulation Results

The algorithm was applied into learning the 2-D structure of a uniform distribution on a square area. The simulations were performed on the Cray Y–MP 8/864 at the University of Texas Center for High-Performance Computing. Fig. 3 illustrates the external input weights of the neurons transformed back to the original spherical coordinates. The weight vectors are initially uniformly distributed on the input square. As the simulation progresses, the network unfolds, and the weight vectors spread out to form a regular topological map and to cover the input space. The course of this process is very similar to the standard SOFM algorithm. After a while, the network reaches a stable equilibrium. Further training causes small fluctuations about the stable equilibrium if the learning rate α is nonzero.

The lateral interconnection weights started random, but evolved into a very smooth "Mexican hat" profile around each neuron. Figures 4 and 5 show the lateral weights before and after training for a neuron at the center of the map. The lateral weights converged faster than the input weights, leading the self-organization. Both the input weights and lateral weights reached a stable dynamic equilibrium after sufficient training.

Interestingly, the lateral interaction profile is not uniform throughout the map, but exhibits boundary effects (Fig. 6). Because the units near the boundary do not have full neighborhoods, normalization of lateral weights results in profiles that are taller and asymmetric. The asymmetry is important because it affects the shape and location of activity bubbles. In simulations with uniform, predetermined interaction [8], activity bubbles formed away from the boundary even for input best stimulating a boundary neuron. In other words, the bubbles were representing the location of the best stimulus on the map incorrectly. In the new model, maximally active areas of the bubble correspond to best input response areas of the map even at the boundary. The shape of the activity bubble resembles the initial input activity, and the profile of

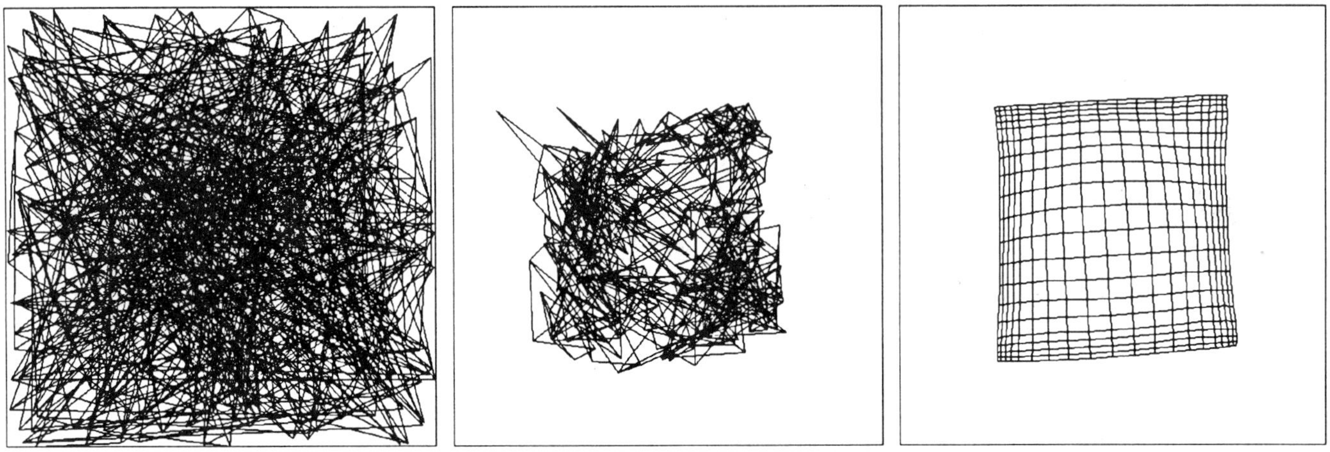

(a) 0 inputs: Random (b) 500 inputs: Unfolding (b) 3000 inputs: Organized

Fig. 3: **Self-organization of external input weights of a** 20×20 **map.** The square areas correspond to the input space. Each neuron is represented by its input weight vector plotted in 2D as a point inside the input square. Each neuron is connected to its four immediate neighbors, and the resulting grid depicts the topological organization of the neurons. An equilibrium is reached in about 3000 inputs. Additional inputs cause little change.

activity is very smooth within the bubble. The lateral interaction adapted to capture the smooth distribution of activity patterns on the map.

In the abstract feature map algorithm, metastable states such as twisted maps can form if the neighborhoods are initially too small [1]. The size of the activity bubble corresponds to the neighborhood size. The bubble size is determined by the radius and amount of lateral interaction. If these parameters are not large enough to make initial activity bubble sizes comparable to the size of the map, metastable states may form. The algorithm is robust within a fair range of parameters, and appropriate values can be easily determined.

IV. Discussion

The new self-organization process described above has several important implications. It is a simulation of a realistic physical system that self-organizes based on purely local rules. If we were to actually construct "neurons" with properties described above and form a network as explained, the map would self-organize completely in parallel, without global supervision. This is in contrast to the abstract SOFM process, where the maximally responding unit is chosen through global supervision, and adaptation neighborhoods are reduced according to a preset schedule.

The shape of the lateral interaction is automatically extracted from the statistical properties of the external input. At each input presentation, the input vector is analyzed by the current state of the input weights and represented as an activity bubble on the map. The distribution of bubbles over time shapes the lateral weights, which in turn results in tighter and smoother activity bubbles and facilitates the self-organization of the external weights. The self-organization thus "bootstraps" by using external input information to establish the necessary cooperative and competive interactions.

Standard feature maps represent the topology of the input space by the network's grid-like layout. Units close by in the map represent input vectors nearby in the input space, and vice versa. In our model, the neighborhood relations are mediated by the lateral connections, and the model is not limited to strictly 2-dimensional topology. Units that are far apart on the map grid may still belong to the same neighborhood if they are strongly connected laterally. Such topologies are automatically learned as part of the self-organizing process. If several areas of the map are simultaneously active, long range connections between such areas will remain strong. These connections cause the units to behave as if they were neighbors on the map. This property is potentially very significant in representing complex high-dimensional input spaces. While lower-level sensory representation in the brain seems to be organized in 2-dimensional maps (such as retinotopic maps), it is possible that higher representations make use of long-range lateral connections to represent more complex similarity relationships [13]. The laterally connected feature map is a potential computational model for formation of such representations.

Standard SOFM has been used to model the development of input connections to neurons in the primary sensory cortices [9, 10, 11]. With the new algorithm, it should be possible to model the development of both lateral and external input connections in sensory cortices.

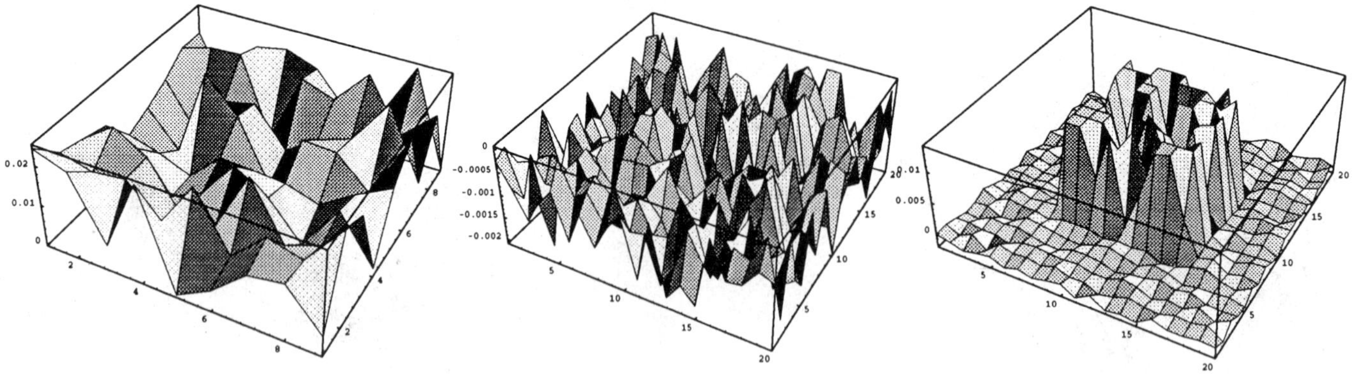

(a) Excitation (b) Inhibition (c) Combined interaction

Fig. 4: **Initial lateral interaction.** The lateral excitation and inhibition weights and the combined interaction profile are plotted for the neuron at position (10, 10) in the 20 × 20 map.

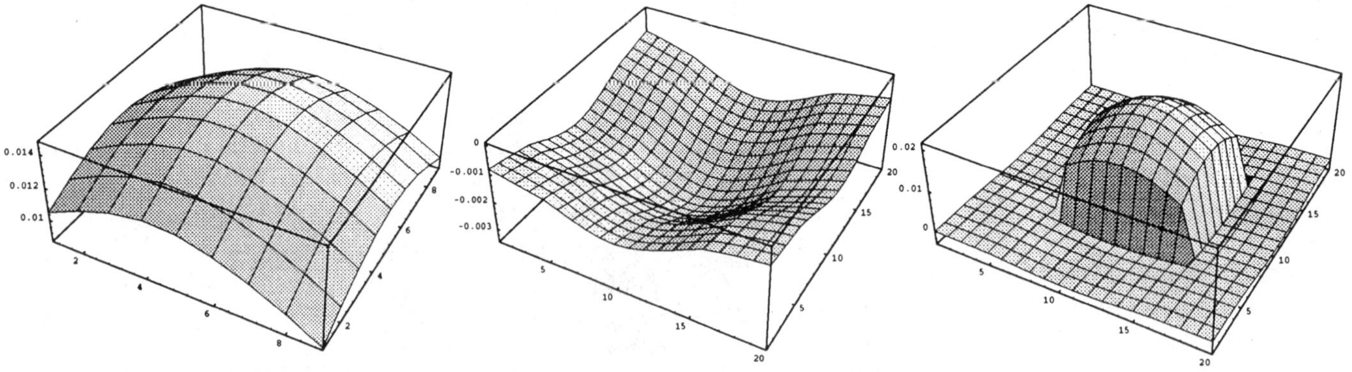

(a) Excitation (b) Inhibition (c) Combined interaction

Fig. 5: **Final lateral interaction.** A smooth pattern of excitation and inhibition weights has evolved, resulting in a smooth interaction profile.

It has recently been found that horizontal connections in the primary visual cortex mainly connect areas with similar functional properties, such as the same orientation sensitivity or ocular dominance [2, 3]. Assuming that average visual input excites similar feature detectors simultaneously, our model could give a computational account to this phenomenom. Specifically, (1) lateral connections between similar feature detectors strengthen due to correlated activity and (2) connections between dissimilar feature detectors weaken due to limited synaptic resources (through normalization). If weak connections are assumed to die off, the surviving connections would be those that link areas with similar functional properties.

The survival of horizontal connections in the primary visual cortex depend on correlated neuronal activity. If visual input to the cortex from both eyes of the cat is decorrelated by artificially introducing strabismus (squint-eye) during development, lateral connections preferentially connect ocular dominance columns of the same eye [7]. In normal cats however, the connections prefer orientation columns of the same orientation specificity (as explained above). These results could be explained by the laterally connected model. In strabismic visual input there are more correlations among inputs from the same eye than between eyes. Ocular dominance columns representing the same eye would have highly correlated activity, and connections between them should strengthen. Other lateral connections should weaken due to normalization and eventually die off. Normally, images in the two eyes are very similar on the average, and have significant correlations. Similar orientation detectors in the cortex would have highly correlated activity irrespective of their ocular dominance. The stronger connections should then run between orientation columns of similar specificity.

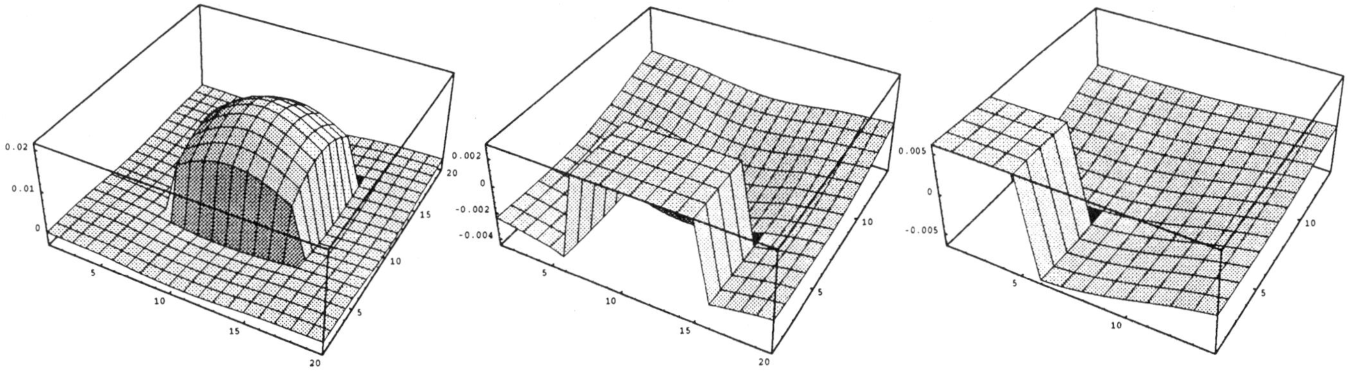

(a) Center unit (b) Edge unit (c) Corner unit

Fig. 6: **Lateral interaction profiles at various locations of the** 20×20 **map after training:** The profiles of neurons at $(10, 10)$, $(0, 10)$, and $(0, 0)$ are plotted. The profiles are tallest at the corner, shorter at an edge and shortest at the center. This is due to redistribution of synaptic weight by normalization.

V. Conclusion and Future Work

Self-organizing models of cortical map development assume lateral interactions to be predetermined. We are not aware of other published work modelling the development of lateral connections in feature maps, biological or abstract. The algorithm presented here demonstrates simultaneous development of lateral interaction and self-organization of input weights. It is biologically motivated, and its predictions tie in very well with experimental observations in visuo-cortical maps.

Currently, the algorithm does not incorporate a mechanism to reduce the extent of lateral connections. The lateral connections of each neuron cover a substantial part of the map. This keeps the neuronal activity correlated over large distances and only the most significant variances in input (the ones that overcome the threshold of correlation; [9]) become represented. To capture features with lower variance, the extent of lateral connections must decrease gradually. We are currently working on an unsupervised mechanism for pruning lateral connections automatically. Research is also underway into constructing general models of cortical map development based on our algorithm.

References

[1] E. Erwin, K. Obermayer, and K. J. Schulten. "Convergence properties of self-organizing maps," *Proceedings of the International Conference on Artificial Neural Networks* (Espoo, Finland). Amsterdam; New York: North-Holland, 1991, pp. 409–414.

[2] C. D. Gilbert, J. A. Hirsch, and T. N. Wiesel. "Lateral interactions in visual cortex," *Cold Spring Harbor Symposia on Quantitative Biology, Volume LV.* Cold Spring Harbor Laboratory Press, 1990, pp. 663–677.

[3] C. D. Gilbert and T. N. Wiesel. "Columnar specificity of intrinsic horizontal and corticocortical connections in cat visual cortex," *Journal of Neuroscience*, 9:2432–2442, 1989.

[4] D. H. Hubel and T. N. Wiesel. "Receptive fields and functional architecture in two nonstriate visual areas (18 and 19) of the cat," *Journal of Neurophysiology*, 28:229–289, 1965.

[5] T. Kohonen. *Self-Organization and Associative Memory*, 3rd ed. New York: Springer, 1989.

[6] T. Kohonen. "The self-organizing map," *Proceedings of the IEEE*, 78:1464–1480, 1990.

[7] S. Lowel and W. Singer. "Selection of intrinsic horizontal connections in the visual cortex by correlated neuronal activity," *Science*, 255:209–212, 1992.

[8] R. Miikkulainen. "Self-organizing process based on lateral inhibition and synaptic resource redistribution," *Proceedings of the International Conference on Artificial Neural Networks* (Espoo, Finland). Amsterdam; New York: North-Holland, 1991, pp. 415–420.

[9] K. Obermayer, G. G. Blasdel, and K. J. Schulten. "Statistical-mechanical analysis of self-organization and pattern formation during the development of visual maps," *Physical Review A*, 45:7568–7589, 1992.

[10] K. Obermayer, H. J. Ritter, and K. J. Schulten. Large-scale simulation of a self-organizing neural network. In *Proceedings of the International Conference on Parallel Processing in Neural Systems and Computers (ICNC)*. New York: Elsevier, 1990.

[11] K. Obermayer, H. J. Ritter, and K. J. Schulten. "A principle for the formation of the spatial structure of cortical feature maps," *Proceedings of the National Academy of Sciences, USA*, 87:8345–8349, 1990.

[12] E. Oja. "A simplified neuron model as a principal component analyzer," *Journal of Mathematical Biology*, 15:267–273, 1982.

[13] C. von der Malsburg and W. Singer. "Principles of cortical network organization," P. Rakic and W. Singer, Eds., *Neurobiology of Neocortex*, New York: Wiley, 1988, pp. 69–99.

[14] C. von der Malsburg. "Self-organization of orientation-sensitive cells in the striate cortex," *Kybernetik*, 15:85–100, 1973.

[15] E. L. White. *Cortical Circuits: Synaptic Organization of the Cerebral Cortex—Structure, Function, and Theory*, 1989. Boston: Birkhauser.

A Self Organizing Neural Net with Three Functions Related to Principal Component Analysis

Kiyotoshi Matsuoka and Mitsuru Kawamoto
Department of Control Engineering
Kyushu Institute of Technology
Sensui 1-1, Tobata, Kitakyusyu, 804 Japan

Abstract **The most remarkable property of our model is that the three mathematical functions related to principal component analysis (principal component analyzer, orthogonal projection operation, and novelty filter) are acquired by the same network but with different learning parameters.**

I. INTRODUCTION

Principal component analysis is an essential technique in data analysis. Recently, a lot of neural net models have been proposed which are connected with principal component analysis and related mathematical operations. Oja [5], Földiák [1], Lean [3], and others showed that some linear networks can self-organize such that each output unit of the network learns to provide the magnitude of a principal component contained in a given input data. Matsuoka [4] showed that the orthogonal projection operator can be created by an unsupervised learning in a similar network but with a different learning rule. The characteristic point in these models is that an anti Hebbian learning rule is used (as well as normal Hebbian rules) for the modification of the connection weights between neural units. Essentially the same anti Hebbian rule is also used for novelty filter proposed by Kohonen [2].

In this paper a linear, single-layer neural network that self organizes with Hebbian and anti-Hebbian learning rules is mathematically analyzed. The structure of the network itself is similar to that of the models of Földiák [1] and Leen [3], but has two different features. (i) The learning rule for the feedforward connections is different from the one used by Földiák and Leen, in which the well known Oja's rule is adopted. (ii) The output units have inhibitory self-connections.

The most remarkable result of this paper is that three mathematical functions related to principal component analysis (principal component analyzer, orthogonal projection operator, and novelty filter) are acquired by giving three different sets of learning parameters to the same network.

II. PRINCIPAL COMPONENT ANALYSIS

Let $s = [s_1,\dots,s_N]^T$ be a random vector which is provided by a stationary stochastic process,where super-script T denotes transpose. The correlation matrix $\mathbf{R}$ of the signal distribution is defined by

$$\mathbf{R} = \langle s\, s^T \rangle,$$

where $\langle * \rangle$ indicates the ensemble average. Let $\mathbf{u}^{(i)}$ and λ_i $(i = 1,\dots,N)$ be the unit eigenvectors and the corresponding eigenvalues of $\mathbf{R}$, respectively, and we define the following matrices

$$\mathbf{U} = [\mathbf{u}^{(1)},\dots, \mathbf{u}^{(N)}],$$
$$\Lambda = \mathrm{diag}\,\{\lambda_1,\dots, \lambda_N\},$$

where diag{...} represents a diagonal matrix with diagonal elements {...}. Eigenvectors $\mathbf{u}^{(i)}$ $(i = 1,\dots,N)$ of $\mathbf{R}$ are sometimes referred to as principal components. Throughout this paper we assume that λ_i $(i = 1,\dots,N)$ are all positive and are different from each other. Then, $\mathbf{u}^{(i)}$ $(i = 1,\dots,N)$ become orthogonal to each other, namely $\mathbf{U}$ is an orthogonal matrix; $\mathbf{U}^T\mathbf{U} = \mathbf{I}$, where $\mathbf{I}$ is the identity matrix. The correlation matrix can be decomposed in terms of the eigenvalues as (eigenvalue decomposition)

$$\mathbf{R} = \sum_{i=1}^{N} \lambda_i \mathbf{u}^{(i)} \mathbf{u}^{(i)T} = \mathbf{U}\Lambda\mathbf{U}^T. \qquad (1)$$

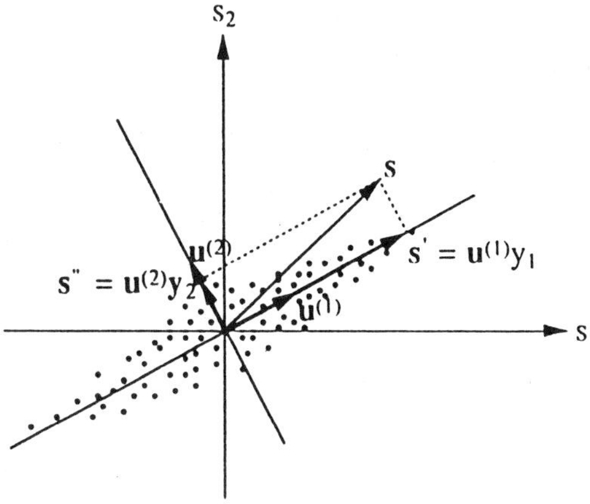

Fig 1. Three operations associated with principal component analysis.

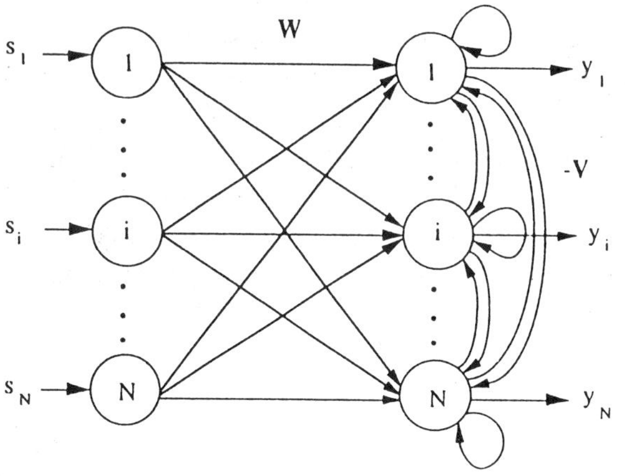

Fig 2. The network model.

By using $\mathbf{u}^{(i)}$ ($i = 1,\ldots,N$) as new basis vectors (Fig. 1), a given signal $\mathbf{s}$ can be expressed as

$$\mathbf{s} = \sum_{i=1}^{N} \mathbf{u}^{(i)} y_i = \mathbf{U}\mathbf{y},$$

where $\mathbf{y} = [y_1,\ldots,y_N]^T$. Coefficient y_i is the magnitude of component $\mathbf{u}^{(i)}$ contained in $\mathbf{s}$, and is calculated by $y_i = \mathbf{u}^{(i)T}\mathbf{s}$ or

$$\mathbf{y} = \mathbf{U}^T \mathbf{s}. \tag{2}$$

We call a network executing the above calculation as *principal component analyzer*.

Now suppose that some eigenvalues of $\mathbf{R}$, say $\lambda_1,\ldots,\lambda_M$, are much greater than the others, $\lambda_{M+1},\ldots, \lambda_N$, and consider the following operation:

$$\mathbf{s}' = \sum_{i=1}^{M} \mathbf{u}^{(i)} y_i = \sum_{i=1}^{M} \mathbf{u}^{(i)}\mathbf{u}^{(i)T}\mathbf{s} = \tilde{\mathbf{U}}\tilde{\mathbf{U}}^T \mathbf{s}, \tag{3}$$

where $\tilde{\mathbf{U}} = [\mathbf{u}^{(1)},\ldots,\mathbf{u}^{(N)}]$. This operation is nothing but the *orthogonal projection* onto the subspace spanned by the principal components with the M largest eigenvalues. This operator can be considered a kind of noise filter if the components in the directions of $\mathbf{u}^{(M+1)},\ldots,\mathbf{u}^{(N)}$ are regarded as abnormal signals. On the other hand, we call the following complementary operation

$$\mathbf{s}'' = \mathbf{s} - \mathbf{s}' = \sum_{i=M+1}^{N} \mathbf{u}^{(i)} y_i = (\mathbf{I} - \tilde{\mathbf{U}}\tilde{\mathbf{U}}^T)\,\mathbf{s} \tag{4}$$

as *novelty filter*.

In the following sections we shall show that the above three operations, (2) (3) (4), can be realized by a self-organizing network with three different sets of learning parameters.

III. NEURAL NET MODEL

The neural net considered here is a single-layer linear network consisting of N input units and N output units (Fig.2). Input unit j sends an external input $s_j(t)$ to every output unit. Output unit i receives these input signals $s_j(t)$ ($j = 1,\ldots N$) and the outputs $y_k(t)$ ($k = 1,\ldots,N$) of the output units (including its own output) as well, and produces their weighted sum $y_i(t)$ with some time lag. Specifically, the network's dynamics is represented by

$$\tau \frac{d\mathbf{y}(t)}{dt} + \mathbf{y}(t) = \mathbf{W}(t)\mathbf{s}(t) - \mathbf{V}(t)\mathbf{y}(t), \tag{5}$$

where $\mathbf{s}(t) = [s_1(t),\ldots,s_N(t)]^T$, $\mathbf{y}(t) = [y_1(t),\ldots, y_N(t)]^T$, $\mathbf{W}(t) = [w_{ij}(t)]$, and $\mathbf{V}(t) = [v_{ik}(t)]$. $w_{ij}(t)$ is the strength of the connection from input unit j to output unit i, and $-v_{ik}(t)$ is the one from output unit k to output unit i. Note that each output unit of the present network has a self-connection weighted by $-v_{ii}(t)$, as opposed to the model proposed by other authors (for example Földiák [1]; Leen [3]).

As for the property of $\mathbf{s}(t)$, we assume that $\mathbf{s}(t)$ is constant in each of successive time intervals of length τ_0 which is much longer than the time constant τ of the network dynamics. Moreover it will be shown in our learning model that $\mathbf{W}(t)$ and $\mathbf{V}(t)$ are slowly varying and all eigenvalues of matrix $\mathbf{V}(t)$ are always positive or close to zero. Then, the network dynamics is stable because all the eigenvalues of $\mathbf{V}(t) + \mathbf{I}$ are nearly equal to or greater than unity. More specifically, output $\mathbf{y}(t)$ of the network settles down to a stationary state for a constant input $\mathbf{s}(t)$ at least in a time of order τ ($<< \tau_0$). So, we can consider that the following static input-to-output relation holds almost always.

$$\mathbf{y}(t) = (\mathbf{I} + \mathbf{V}(t))^{-1}\mathbf{W}(t)\,\mathbf{s}(t) \tag{6}$$

IV. LEARNING RULE

For the adaptation of $w_{ij}(t)$ and $v_{ik}(t)$ we consider the following Hebb-type learning rules, which are completely local rules and therefore seem biologically plausible,

$$T\frac{dw_{ij}(t)}{dt} = c_i y_i(t) s_j(t) - w_{ij}(t) + \varepsilon \quad (c_i \geq 0\,,\, \varepsilon \geq 0), \tag{7}$$

$$T\frac{dv_{ik}(t)}{dt} = d_i y_i(t) y_k(t) - v_{ik}((t) \quad (d_i > 0). \tag{8}$$

where T is the time constant of the learning dynamics which should be much larger than τ_0 and ε is a bias constant. Actually, (9) embodies an anti-Hebbian learning because the strengths of the mutual connections between the output units are represented by $-v_{ik}(t)$, not by $v_{ik}(t)$. Terms $-w_{ij}(t)$ and $-v_{ik}(t)$ in the above equations are introduced to implement a decay (or forgetting) effect. It should be noted that the decay term in (7) is different from that of Oja's model, in which $-c_i y_i^2 w_{ij}(t)$ is used instead of $-w_{ij}(t)$ to prevent instability of the learning dynamics. The bias constant ε is essential in the networks for orthogonal projection and novelty filtering discussed in §6 and §7. Equations (7) and (9) can be expressed in matrix form as

$$T\frac{d\mathbf{W}(t)}{dt} = \mathbf{C}\mathbf{y}(t)\mathbf{s}(t)^T - \mathbf{W}(t) + \varepsilon\,\mathbf{I}, \tag{9}$$

$$T\frac{d\mathbf{V}(t)}{dt} = \mathbf{D}\mathbf{y}(t)\mathbf{y}(t)^T - \mathbf{V}(t), \tag{10}$$

where $\mathbf{C} = \mathrm{diag}\{c_1,...,c_N\}$ and $\mathbf{D} = \mathrm{diag}\{d_1,...,d_N\}$.

We can see that all the eigenvalues of $\mathbf{V}(t)$ become nearly zero or positive after a time has elapsed and therefore the network dynamics (5) becomes stable even if it is unstable at the start of the learning process, as follows. (10) leads to

$$\mathbf{V}(t) = \exp(-t)\mathbf{V}(0) + \mathbf{D}\int_0^t \exp(t' - t)\mathbf{y}(t')\mathbf{y}(t')^T dt'.$$

After a sufficiently long time has elapsed, the first term of the right-hand side in the above equation substantially vanishes, so we have

$$\mathbf{V}(t) \approx \mathbf{D}\int_0^t \exp(t' - t)\mathbf{y}(t')\mathbf{y}(t')^T dt'$$

$$= \mathbf{D}^{1/2}\{\mathbf{D}^{1/2}\int_0^t \exp(t' - t)\mathbf{y}(t')\mathbf{y}(t')^T dt'\mathbf{D}^{1/2}\}\mathbf{D}^{-1/2}, \tag{11}$$

where $\mathbf{D}^{1/2} = \mathrm{diag}\{\sqrt{d_1},...,\sqrt{d_N}\}$. Since the inside of {...} in (12) is a positive semi-definite matrix, the eigenvalues of its similarity transform $\mathbf{D}^{1/2}\{...\}\mathbf{D}^{-1/2}$ become all non-negative.

Substituting (6) into (9) (10) leaves

$$T\frac{d\mathbf{W}(t)}{dt} = \mathbf{C}(\mathbf{I} + \mathbf{V}(t))^{-1}\mathbf{W}(t)\mathbf{s}(t)\mathbf{s}(t)^T - \mathbf{W}(t) + \varepsilon\,\mathbf{I},$$

$$T\frac{d\mathbf{V}(t)}{dt} = \mathbf{D}(\mathbf{I}+\mathbf{V}(t))^{-1}\mathbf{W}(t)\mathbf{s}(t)\mathbf{s}(t)^T\mathbf{W}(t)^T(\mathbf{I}+\mathbf{V}(t)^T)^{-1} - \mathbf{V}(t).$$

If $\mathbf{s}(t)$ (constant in each time interval) is given by a stationary random signal source and T is sufficiently large, then $\mathbf{s}(t)\mathbf{s}(t)^T$ in the above equations can be replaced by its ensemble average $\mathbf{R} = \langle \mathbf{s}(t)\mathbf{s}(t)^T \rangle$,

$$T\frac{d\mathbf{W}(t)}{dt} = \mathbf{C}(\mathbf{I} + \mathbf{V}(t))^{-1}\mathbf{W}(t)\mathbf{R} - \mathbf{W}(t) + \varepsilon\,\mathbf{I}, \tag{12}$$

$$T\frac{d\mathbf{V}(t)}{dt} = \mathbf{D}(\mathbf{I}+\mathbf{V}(t))^{-1}\mathbf{W}(t)\mathbf{R}\mathbf{W}(t)^T(\mathbf{I}+\mathbf{V}(t)^T)^{-1} - \mathbf{V}(t). \tag{13}$$

We refer to these equations as learning equations.

V. PRINCIPAL COMPONENT ANALYZER

As a special case, we set the parameters in (13) (14) as $\mathbf{C} = \mathbf{D} = \mathrm{diag}\{c_1,...,c_N\}$ ($c_i > 0$, $c_i \neq c_j$ for $i \neq j$) and $\varepsilon = 0$. The condition of $c_i \neq c_j$ ($i \neq j$) is essential in this section. Here, we moreover assume $c_i > 1/\min_j\{\lambda_j\}$ ($i = 1,...,N$), i.e., $c_i\lambda_j > 1$ for any i and j.

We can obtain the equilibrium (but not necessarily stable) solution for $\mathbf{W}(t)$ and $\mathbf{V}(t)$ by equating the right-hand sides of (12) and (13) with the zero matrix,

$$\mathbf{W} = \mathbf{C}(\mathbf{I} + \mathbf{V})^{-1}\mathbf{W}\mathbf{R}, \tag{14}$$
$$\mathbf{V} = \mathbf{C}(\mathbf{I} + \mathbf{V})^{-1}\mathbf{W}\mathbf{R}\mathbf{W}^T(\mathbf{I} + \mathbf{V}^T)^{-1} \tag{15}$$

By solving these equations, we can show that an equilibrium solution for **W** and **V** takes the following form if the numbering of the eigenvectors and the output units (i.e., $^{(i)}$ in $\mathbf{u}^{(i)}$ and $_i$ in w_{ij}) are appropriately chosen:

$$\mathbf{W} = \mathrm{diag}\{\sqrt{c_1^2\lambda_1^2 - c_1\lambda_1}, \ldots, \sqrt{c_L^2\lambda_L^2 - c_L\lambda_L}, 0, \ldots, 0\}\mathbf{U}^T, \tag{16}$$
$$\mathbf{V} = \mathrm{diag}\{c_1\lambda_1 - 1, \ldots, c_L\lambda_L - 1, 0, \ldots, 0\}, \tag{17}$$

where number L of the nonzero diagonal elements of the diagonal matrices in (16) and (17) is an arbitrary integer between 0 (meaning $\mathbf{W} = \mathbf{V} = \mathbf{0}$) and N. Conversely, we can easily assure that any expressions taking the form of (16) and (17) are solutions of (14) and (15).

By investigating the stability of the equilibria given by (16) and (17), we can prove that only the following equilibrium (L = N) is stable:

$$\mathbf{W} = \mathrm{diag}\{\sqrt{c_1^2\lambda_1^2 - c_1\lambda_1}, \ldots, \sqrt{c_N^2\lambda_N^2 - c_N\lambda_N}\}\mathbf{U}^T, \tag{18}$$
$$\mathbf{V} = \mathrm{diag}\{c_1\lambda_1 - 1, \ldots, c_N\lambda_N - 1\}, \tag{19}$$

Substituting (18) (19) into (6), we have

$$\mathbf{y}(t) = \mathrm{diag}\{\sqrt{1 - \frac{1}{c_1\lambda_1}}, \ldots, \sqrt{1 - \frac{1}{c_N\lambda_N}}\}\mathbf{U}^T \mathrm{s}(t) \tag{20}$$

If c_i's are given large values compared to $1/\lambda_i$, i.e., $c_i\lambda_i >> 1$, then (18) (19) (20) can be approximated as

$$\mathbf{W} \approx \mathrm{diag}\{c_1\lambda_1, \ldots, c_N\lambda_N\}\mathbf{U}^T = \mathbf{C}\Lambda\mathbf{U}^T,$$
$$\mathbf{V} \approx \mathrm{diag}\{c_1\lambda_1, \ldots, c_N\lambda_N\} = \mathbf{C}\Lambda,$$
$$\mathbf{y}(t) \approx \mathbf{U}^T\mathbf{s}(t),$$

implying that the resultant network works approximately as a principal component analyzer which we have termed in §II.

VI. ORTHOGONAL PROJECTION OPERATOR

Next, we investigate the case that the parameters of the learning rule are set as $\mathbf{C} = \mathbf{D} = c\mathbf{I}$ ($c > 0$) and $0 < \varepsilon << 1$. Namely the learning rates, c_i and d_i, are all identical, and a small positive bias constant is added for the evolution of $w_{ii}(t)$, which is essential for self-organization of the orthogonal projection operator. We moreover assume that $\lambda_1, \ldots, \lambda_M$ are much greater than $\lambda_{M+1}, \ldots, \lambda_N$ and c is chosen to satisfy $\lambda_1, \ldots, \lambda_M >> 1/c >> \lambda_{M+1}, \ldots, \lambda_N$. Then we can show that the following is an equilibrium of (12) (13),

$$\mathbf{W} = \mathbf{U}\mathrm{diag}\{\phi_1, \ldots, \phi_N\}\mathbf{U}^T, \tag{21}$$
$$\mathbf{V} = \mathbf{U}\mathrm{diag}(\psi_1, \ldots, \psi_N)\mathbf{U}^T, \tag{22}$$

Diagonal elements ψ_i are given by the following algebraic equation.

$$(1 + \psi_i - c\lambda_i)^2\psi_i - \varepsilon^2 c\lambda_i = 0$$

It has three or one real roots, depending on $c\lambda_i > 1$ ($i = 1, \ldots, M$) or $c\lambda_i < 1$ ($i = M+1, \ldots, N$), respectively. Diagonal elements ϕ_i are given by

$$\phi_i = \varepsilon\,(1+\psi_i) / (1+\psi_i - c\lambda_i).$$

It can be shown that, when ε is small, ϕ_i and ψ_i for $i = 1, \ldots, M$ can be approximated by either of

$$\phi_i \approx \sqrt{c^2\lambda_i^2 - c\lambda_i} + \varepsilon\{1 + c\lambda_i/(2\,(c\lambda_i - 1))\}$$
$$\psi_i \approx c\lambda_i - 1 + \varepsilon\sqrt{c\lambda_i/(c\lambda_i - 1)} \tag{23}$$

$$\phi_i \approx -\sqrt{c^2\lambda_i^2 - c\lambda_i} + \varepsilon\{1 + c\lambda_i/(2\,(c\lambda_i - 1))\}$$
$$\psi_i \approx c\lambda_i - 1 - \varepsilon\sqrt{c\lambda_i/(c\lambda_i - 1)} \tag{24}$$

$$\phi_i \approx -\varepsilon/(c\lambda_i - 1), \quad \psi_i \approx \varepsilon^2/c\lambda_i \tag{25}$$

and those for $i = M+1, \ldots, N$ are approximated as

$$\phi_i \approx \varepsilon/(1 - c\lambda_i), \quad \psi_i \approx \varepsilon^2/c\lambda_i. \tag{26}$$

By investigating the stability of these equilibria, we can prove that there exists only one stable equilibrium given by

$$\mathbf{W} \approx \mathbf{U}\mathrm{diag}\{\sqrt{c^2\lambda_1^2 - c\lambda_1} + \varepsilon\{1 + c\lambda_1/2\,(c\lambda_1 - 1)\}, \ldots, \sqrt{c^2\lambda_M^2 - c\lambda_M} + \varepsilon\{1 + c\lambda_M/2\,(c\lambda_M - 1)\}, \varepsilon/(1 - c\lambda_{M+1}), \ldots, \varepsilon/(1 - c\lambda_N)\}\mathbf{U}^T$$

$$V \approx U\mathrm{diag}\{c\lambda_1 - 1 + \varepsilon\sqrt{c\lambda_1}/(c\lambda_1 - 1), \ldots, c\lambda_M - 1 + \varepsilon\sqrt{c\lambda_M}/(c\lambda_M - 1), \varepsilon^2/c\lambda_{M+1}, \ldots, \varepsilon^2/c\lambda_N\}U^T.$$

Substituting these equations into (6) we obtain the following network function.

$$y(t) = U\,\mathrm{diag}\{\sqrt{1-1/c\lambda_1}+\varepsilon/2(c\lambda_1-1), \ldots, \sqrt{1-1/c\lambda_M}+\varepsilon/2(c\lambda_M-1), \frac{\varepsilon\, c\lambda_{M+1}}{(c\lambda_{M+1}+\varepsilon^2)(1-c\lambda_{M+1})}, \ldots, \frac{\varepsilon\, c\lambda_N}{(c\lambda_N+\varepsilon^2)(1-c\lambda_N)}\}U^T s(t).$$

By letting ε be very small and taking into account $c\lambda_i >> 1$ for $i = 1,\ldots,M$, W and V can be approximated as

$$W \approx U\mathrm{diag}\{c\lambda_1,\ldots,c\lambda_M,0,\ldots,0\}U^T = c\tilde{U}\tilde{\Lambda}\tilde{U}^T,$$
$$V \approx U\mathrm{diag}\{c\lambda_1,\ldots,c\lambda_M,0,\ldots,0\}U^T = c\tilde{U}\tilde{\Lambda}\tilde{U}^T,$$

where $\tilde{\Lambda} = \mathrm{diag}\{\lambda_1,\ldots,\lambda_M\}$, and the network function becomes

$$y(t) \approx U\mathrm{diag}\{\sqrt{1-1/c\lambda_1}, \ldots, \sqrt{1-1/c\lambda_M}, 0,\ldots,0\}U^T s(t) \approx U\mathrm{diag}\{1,\ldots,1,0,\ldots,0\}U^T s(t) = \tilde{U}\tilde{U}^T s(t), \quad (27)$$

implying that the resultant network acts approximately as an orthogonal projection operator onto the subspace spanned by the dominant M principal components.

VII. NOVELTY FILTER

Finally let us investigate the case of $C = 0$, $D = dI$ and $\varepsilon = 1$. In this case $W(t)$ ultimately converges to I; after the training of the network there survive feedforward connections only between the input units and the counter-parts in the output layer with their weights fixed at unity. Therefore, the present model is virtually equivalent to the novelty filter model proposed by Kohonen [2]. Again we assume that $\lambda_1,\ldots,\lambda_M$ are much greater than $\lambda_{M+1},\ldots,\lambda_N$ and the magnitude of d is set as $\lambda_1,\ldots,\lambda_M >> 1/d >> \lambda_{M+1},\ldots,\lambda_N$. Then we can prove that following state is the only stable equilibrium of (13),

$$V(t) = U\mathrm{diag}(\xi_1,\ldots,\xi_N)U^T \quad (28)$$

where ξ_i is the solution of the follwing algebraic equation,

$$(1+\xi_i)^2\xi_i = d\lambda_i.$$

It is easy to show that this has only one real solution which can be approximated as

$$\xi_i \approx \sqrt[3]{d\lambda_i} >> 1 \quad \text{for } \lambda_i >> \frac{1}{d} \quad (i = 1,\ldots,M),$$
$$\approx d\lambda_i << 1 \quad \text{for } \lambda_i << \frac{1}{d} \quad (i = M+1,\ldots,N). \quad (29)$$

By investigating the stability of the equilibrium and taking account into (29), we can prove that the connection matrix V of the trained network becomes

$$V \approx U\mathrm{daig}\{\sqrt[3]{d\lambda_1},\ldots,\sqrt[3]{d\lambda_M},0,\ldots,0\}U^T = d^{1/3}\tilde{U}\tilde{\Lambda}^{1/3}\tilde{U}^T,$$

where $\tilde{\Lambda}^{1/3} = \mathrm{diag}\{\lambda_1^{1/3},\ldots,\lambda_M^{1/3}\}$. Then, the input-to-output function of the network becomes

$$y(t) = (I+V)^{-1}s(t) = U\mathrm{diag}\{1/(1+\xi_1),\ldots,1/(1+\xi_N)\}U^T s(t)$$
$$\approx U\mathrm{diag}\{0,\ldots,0,1,\ldots,1\}U^T s(t) = (I-\tilde{U}\tilde{U}^T)\,s(t). \quad (30)$$

Thus, we have found that the trained network behaves as a novelty filter.

VIII. DISCUSSION

We assumed in §V that the learning rates c_i $(i = 1,\ldots,N)$ of the output units were different from each other. Due to this assumption the stable equilibrium of the learning dynamics became unique (if $u^{(i)}$ and $-u^{(i)}$ are considered essentially the same). If c_i's are identical, i.e., $c_i = c$ $(> 1/\max_k\{\lambda_k\}$, $i = 1,\ldots,N)$, then the stable equilibrium takes the following form,

$$W = E\mathrm{diag}\{\sqrt{c^2\lambda_1^2 - c\lambda_1}, \ldots, \sqrt{c^2\lambda_N^2 - c\lambda_N}\}U^T,$$
$$V = E\mathrm{diag}\{c\lambda_1 - 1, \ldots, c\lambda_N - 1\}E^T,$$

where E is an arbitrary orthogonal matrix. So, the input-to-output function of the resultant network becomes

$$y(t) = E\,\mathrm{diag}\{\sqrt{1-\frac{1}{c\lambda_1}},\ldots,\sqrt{1-\frac{1}{c\lambda_N}}\}U^Ts(t).$$

E depends on the initial values of **W**(t) and **V**(t). In §**5**, in order to break the arbitrariness of **E**, we introduced the condition that c_i's are different, and obtained a principal component analyzer, i.e., **E** = **I**. An alternative for breaking the uncertainty of **E** is to add a small bias term $\varepsilon\mathbf{I}$ to the learning equation for **W**(t), which was done in §VI. There we obtained the orthogonal projection operator; $\mathbf{E} \approx \mathbf{U}$.

A similar model to the one described in §**5** is analyzed by Földiák [1] and Leen [3], but their model is different from our model in the mechanism by which the learning dynamics is stabilized. Their model is based on Oja's well-known algorithm; the divergence of the weights of the feed-forward connections is suppressed by decay term $-c_iy_i^2w_{ij}$, which implicitly works to normalize the weights of the feedforward connections as $\sum_j w_{ij}^2 = 1$. In our model, on the other hand, the decay term takes a simpler form, $-w_{ij}$, and the stability of the learning dynamics is achieved in another fashion. As the connection weights from the input units to an output unit increase and hence the activity of the output unit is enhanced, then the negative weight of the self-connection, which does not exist in Oja's model, grows large. Due to this growth of the inhibitory self-connection, the activity of the output is suppressed at a level and as a result the strengths of the feedforward connections are saturated.

It should be noted that the network consisting of symmetrically interconnected Oja's neurons (Leen [3]) learns to achieve a perfect principal component analyzer; $\mathbf{y}(t) = \mathbf{U}^T\mathbf{s}(t)$. Due to this very property, however, he learning dynamics becomes unstable when some eigenvalues of **R** are very small, for example in the special case of $\mathbf{R} = \mathbf{0}$. In our model, on the other hand, the relation $\mathbf{y}(t) = \mathbf{U}^T\mathbf{s}(t)$ is achieved only in an approximate sense; it is acquired only as a limit of $c_i\lambda_i \to \infty$. Thanks to the incompleteness, however, the learning process of our model is stable for any input.

IX. CONCLUSION

We have discussed a single-layer neural network that self-organizes with Hebbian and anti-Hebbian learning rules. The equilibria of the learning dynamics and their stability are completely analyzed. It has been shown that three typical operations associated with principal component analysis can be acquired by giving three different sets of learning parameters to the same model.

ACKNOWLEDGEMENT

This work was supported by the Grant-in-Aids for the Scientific Research by the Ministry of Education, Science and Culture of Japan, No.02248104.

REFERENCES

[1] P. Földiák, "Adaptive network for optimal linear feature extraction," *Proceedings of the International Joint Conference on Neural Networks*, pp 401-405, 1989.

[2] T. Kohonen, *Self-organization and associative memory*, Springer-Verlag, 1984.

[3] T.K. Leen, "Dynamics of learning in linear feature-discovery networks," *Network*, vol. 2, pp. 85- 105, 1991.

[4] K. Matsuoka, "A novel model of autoassociative memory and its self-organization," *IEEE Transactions on Systems, Man, and Cybernetics*, vol. 21, pp. 678-683, 1991.

[5] E. Oja, "Neural networks, principal components, and subspaces," *International Journal of Neural Systems*, vol. 1, pp. 61-68, 1989.

[6] E. Oja, "Principal components, minor components and linear neural networks," *Neural Network*, vol. 5, pp. 927-935, 1992.

[7] J. Rubner and K. Schulten, "Development of feature detectors by self-organization," *Biological Cybernetics*, vol. 61, pp. 193-199, 1990.

[8] T. D. Sanger, "Optimal unsupervised learning in a single-layer linear feedforward neural network," *Neural Network*, vol. 2, pp. 459-473, 1989.

Dynamics and Stability of Multilayered Recurrent Neural Networks

Liang Jin, Peter N. Nikiforuk, Madan M. Gupta
Intelligent Systems Research Laboratory
College of Engineering, University of Saskatchewan
Saskatoon, Saskatchewan, Canada S7N 0W0

ABSTRACT

The dynamical analysis of a novel multilayered recurrent neural network (MRNN) is addressed in this paper. The dynamics of the MRNN are represented by a multi-input and multi-output nonlinear difference equation. The existence and stability of the equilibrium points of the MRNN are then discussed, and sufficient conditions of absolute stable are derived.

I. INTRODUCTION

The brain-state-in-a-box (BSB) neural model was conceived by *Anderson* and coworkers [2], and the stability and implementation of associative memories of it with symmetric or nonsymmetric weight matrices were recently discussed by *Hui* and *Zak* [4], and *Michel*, *Si*, and *Yen* [5], respectively. The main difference between the BSB neural model and the usual nonlinear difference equation is that the former is defined on the closed hypercube by a *symmetric ramp function* [1-3], while the latter is defined on R^n. Most recently, the stability of the fixed points was studied for a discrete-time recurrent network by *Li* [6], and the changes in the stable region of the fixed points due to the changing of the neuron gain were obtained.

The problem of the dynamics and stability of the multilayered recurrent neural networks (MRNNs) is discussed in this paper. In Section II, a novel architecture of the discrete-time MRNN is proposed, and the dynamics of the MRNN are described by means of a nonlinear difference equation. The existence and stability of the equilibrium points of the dynamics are shown, and the new absolute stability conditions are given in Section III and Section IV.

II. MULTILAYERED RECURRENT NEURAL NETWORKS (MRNNs)

An artifical neural network consists of many interconnected identical simple processing units called neurons or nodes. An individual neuron sums its weighted inputs and yields an output through a nonlinear activation function with a threshold. A novel multilayered recurrent neural network (MRNN) architecture is proposed in this section. The MRNN is a hybrid feedforward and feedback neural network, with the feedback represented by recurrent connections and cross-talk, appropriate for approximating the dynamic system. The MRNN is composed of an input layer, a series of hidden layers, and an output layer. It allows for feedforward and feedback among the neurons of neighboring layers, and cross-talk and recurrency in the hidden layers.

A basic structure of the multilayered recurrent neural networks (MRNNs) with feedforward and feedback connections is shown in Fig. 1. Let M be total number of hidden layers of the MRNN, the $i-th$ neuron in the $s-th$ layer be denoted by

0-7803-0999-5/93/$03.00 ©1993 IEEE

$neuron(s,i)$, N_s be total number of neurons in the $s-th$ hidden layer, u_i be the $i-th$ input of the MRNN, $x_{s,i}(k)$ be the state of the $neuron(s,i)$, y_i be the i–th output of the MRNN, $w_{s,j}^{s,i}$ be the intra-layer linkweight coefficient from the $neuron(s,j)$ to the $neuron(s,i)$, $w_{s-1,j}^{s,i}$ be the feedforward linkweight coefficient from the $neuron(s-1,j)$ to the $neuron(s,i)$, $w_{s+1,j}^{s,i}$ be the feedback linkweight coefficient from the $neuron(s+1,j)$ to the $neuron(s,i)$, and $w_T^{s,i}$ be the threshold of the $neuron(s,i)$. Mathematically, the operation of the $neuron(s,i)$ is defined by following dynamic equations

$$\begin{aligned} x_{1,i}(k+1) &= \sigma[\sum_{j=1}^{N_2} w_{2,j}^{1,i} x_{2,j}(k) \\ &+ \sum_{j=1}^{N_1} w_{1,j}^{1,i} x_{1,j}(k) \\ &+ \sum_{j=1}^{l} w_{0,j}^{1,i} u_j(k) + w_T^{1,i}] \end{aligned} \quad (1)$$

and

$$\begin{aligned} x_{s,i}(k+1) &= \sigma[\sum_{j=1}^{N_{s+1}} w_{s+1,j}^{s,i} x_{s+1,j}(k) \\ &+ \sum_{j=1}^{N_s} w_{s,j}^{s,i} x_{s,j}(k) \\ &+ \sum_{j=1}^{N_{s-1}} w_{s-1,j}^{s,i} x_{s-1,j}(k) + w_T^{s,i}] \quad (2) \\ &= \sigma[\sum_{h=-1}^{1} \sum_{j=1}^{N_{s+h}} w_{s+h,j}^{s,i} x_{s+h,j}(k) + w_T^{s,i}] \end{aligned}$$

$$s = 2,3,...,M$$

where $w_{M+1,j}^{M,i} \equiv 0$. If the activation function $\sigma(.)$ is a *symmetric ramp function*, the MRNN is then a special type of the BSB model with a nonsymmetric weight matrix. The nonlinear activation function $\sigma(.)$ is assumed to be an arbitrary nonlinear activation function in the range $[a,b]$ in this paper. The terms on the right side of above equation represent respectively the feedback from the upper hidden layer, the intra-layer connections, and the feedforward from the lower layer. It is to be noted that there are no feedback actions from the output layer in the $M-th$ hidden layer. Indeed, the output equations of the MRNN are derived as

$$y_i(k) = \sum_{j=1}^{N_M} w_{M,j}^{M+1,i} x_{M,j}(k), \quad (3)$$

$$i = 1,2,...,m$$

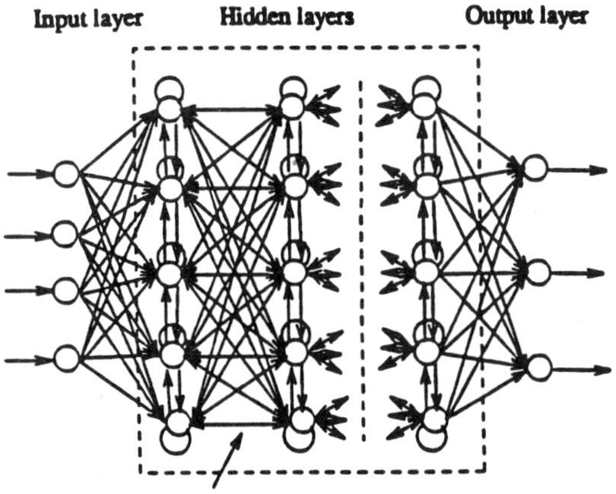

Fig. 1a The network structure

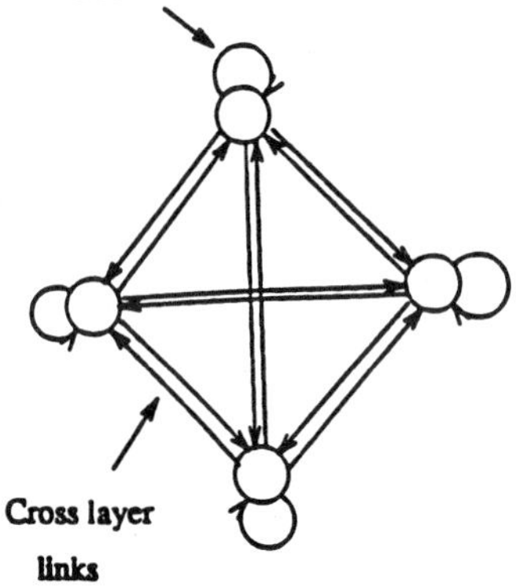

Fig. 1b The intra-layer connections

Fig. 1 The multilayered recurrent neural network

In order to obtain the vector form of Eqs.(1)-(3), let the total number of the neurons of the MRNN be n, and $x = [x_{1,1},...,x_{1,N_1},...,x_{M,1},...,x_{M,N_M}]^T$, $u = [u_1,...,u_l]^T$, and $y = [y_1,...,y_m]^T$ be respectively the state, input and output vectors of the MRNN. The input-output relationship of the MRNN may be then represented by following discrete-time nonlinear equations

$$\begin{cases} x(k+1) &= \sigma[W_H x(k) + W_I u(k) + w_T] \\ y(k) &= W_O x(k) \end{cases} \tag{4}$$

where $\sigma(x) = [\sigma(x_1), ..., \sigma(x_n)]^T$ is a vector value function, the matrices W_H, W_I and W_O are respectively the weight matrices of the hidden, input, and output layers, and w_T is the threshold vector. The expressions of the W_H, W_I, W_O, and w_T are easily implied from Eqs. (1)-(3). Since the function $a \leq \sigma(.) \leq b$, the state vector $x(k)$ of the system (4) exists in the "box" $H^n = [a,b]^n$, which is the closed n-dimensional hypercube, and the output $y(k)$ is uniformly bounded for the bounded input $u(k)$.

III. ANALYSIS OF THE EQUILIBRIUM POINTS

The basic goal of the dynamical analysis is to understand the eventual or asymptotic behavior of the MRNN. For a discrete process of the MRNN, one hopes to understand the eventual behavior of the points $x \equiv \sigma^0(x)$, $\sigma(x) \equiv \sigma^1(x)$, $\sigma(\sigma(x)) \equiv \sigma^2(x)$,...,$\sigma^n(x)$ as n becomes large. The discussion of the stability or instability of a point or a stored pattern in associative memory can be proceed only if the point is an *equilibrium point* of the system.

Definition 1. *The pair $(x^*, u^*) \in [a,b]^n \times R^l$ is an equilibrium point of the dynamical system (4) if $x^* = \sigma(W_H x^* + W_I u^* + w_T)$.*

The *fixed points* of the nonlinear function $f(x)$ are points x which satisfy $f(x) = x$. The following application of the *Intermediate Value Theorem* gives an important criterion for the existence of a fixed point.

Lemma 1. (Brouwer's Fixed Point Theorem) [7] *Let $H^n = [a,b]^n$ be a closed set of R^n and $f: H^n \longrightarrow H^n$ be a continuous vector value function. Then f has at least one fixed point in H^n.*

For the discrete-time nonlinear system (4), it is easy to understand that the fixed points of the function $f(x) \equiv \sigma(W_H x + W_I u^* + w_T)$ are the equilibrium points of the system (4) for the given input u^* and the connect weight matrices W_H, W_I, and w_T. The existence of the equilibrium points of the system (4) is then obtained as follows based on the above lemma.

Theorem 1. *Let the vector activation function $\sigma(x)$ have the range $[a,b]^n$. For any given input u^* and the connection weight matrices W_H, W_I, and w_T, there exists at least one equilibrium point (x^*, u^*), $x^* \in [a,b]^n$ of the dynamical system (4); that is $x^* = \sigma[W_H x^* + W_I u^* + w_T]$.*

Proof. Since the vector activation function $\sigma(x)$ is bounded by $[a,b]^n$, let the initial starting point $x(0) \in [a,b]^n$, then $x(k) = \sigma[W_H x(k-1) + W_I u^* + w_T] \in [a,b]^n$. For any given input u^* and the connection weight matrices W_H, W_I, and w_T, $f(x) = \sigma[W_H x + W_I u^* + w_T]$ is a continuous vector value function because σ is continuous. Thus, f has a fixed point $x^* \in [a,b]^n$ by the Brouwer's fixed point theorem; that is, (x^*, u^*) is an equilibrium point of the system (4). □

In order to analysis the stability of the equilibrium points, the Jacobian of the function $f(x)$ is given by

$$\frac{df}{dx} = f'(x) = \Sigma W_H \tag{5}$$

where Σ is a diagonal matrix with $\Sigma_{h,h} \equiv \sigma'_h(x) = \sigma'(\sum_{m=1}^{n} w_{h,m} x_m + s_h)$. The function $f(x)$ has a unique equilibrium point if all the eigenvalues of the Jacobian are inside the unit circle, which means that f is a contraction mapping. In this case, system (4) is called *absolutely stable* and f has a unique global attractor x^*. Hence, the arbitrary initial state converges to x^* for given input s. For local asymptotically stability, the eigenvalues of the Jacobian at the equilibrium point x^* are examined. If all the eigenvalues of the Jacobian at x^* have absolute values less than one, then x^* is a local asymptotically stable equilibrium point of the system (4), and is called a *sink*. If all the eigenvalues of the Jacobian at x^* are outside the unit circle, it is a *source*. If some eigenvalues are inside the unit circle and some are outside the unit circle, it is a *saddle* or unstable equilibrium point. The work of this paper will concentrate on absolute stability of system (4).

IV. ABSOLUTE STABILITY CONDITIONS

In order to discuss the positions of the eigenvalues of the Jacobian $f'(x)$ in complex plane, the following Lemma is required.

Lemma 2. (Ostrowski's theorem)[8] *Let* $W = [w_{i,j}]_{n\times n}$ *be a complex matrix,* $\gamma \in [0,1]$ *be given, and* R_i *and* C_i *denote the deleted row and column sums of* W*, respectively :*

$$\begin{cases} R_i = \sum_{j=1, j\neq i}^{n} |w_{i,j}| \\ \\ C_i = \sum_{j=1, j\neq i}^{n} |w_{j,i}| \end{cases} \tag{6}$$

Then all the eigenvalues of W *are located in the union of* n *closed discs in the complex plane with center* $w_{i,i}$ *and radius* $r_i = R_i^{\gamma} C_i^{1-\gamma}$, $i = 1, 2, ..., n$.

Corollary 1. *Let* $W = [w_{i,j}]_{n\times n}$ *be a complex matrix,* $\gamma \in [0,1]$ *be given, and* R_i *and* C_i *be defined by (6). If*

$$|w_{i,i}| + R_i^{\gamma} C_i^{1-\gamma} < 1, \qquad i = 1, 2, ..., n \tag{7}$$

Then all the eigenvalues of W *are located in the unit circle in the complex plane.*

Proof. The result is obtained using Ostrowski's theorem. □

Theorem 2. *Let* $0 < \sigma'(.) < c$ *in Eq.(4) and* $\gamma \in [0,1]$ *be given, and*

$$\begin{cases} R_i^H = \sum_{j=1, j\neq i}^{n} |w_{i,j}^H| \\ \\ C_i = \sum_{j=1, j\neq i}^{n} |w_{j,i}^H| \end{cases} \tag{8}$$

If the connection weight matrix $W_H = [w_{i,j}^H]_{n\times n}$ *satisfies*

$$|w_{i,i}^H| + (R_i^H)^{\gamma} (C_i^H)^{1-\gamma} < \frac{1}{c}, \qquad i = 1, 2, ..., n \tag{9}$$

Then system (4) is absolutely stable.

Proof. The Jacobian is $f'(x) = [f'_{i,j}(x)]_{n\times n} = \Sigma W_H$, and $\Sigma = diag[\sigma_1(x), \sigma_2(x), ..., \sigma_n(x)]$. Since

$$|f'_{i,i}(x)| + (\sum_{j=1, j\neq i}^{n} |f'_{i,j}(x)|)^{\gamma} (\sum_{j=1, j\neq i}^{n} |f'_{j,i}(x)|)^{1-\gamma}$$

$$= |\sigma_i'(x) w_{i,i}^H|$$

$$+ |\sigma_i'(x)|^{\gamma} (\sum_{j=1, j\neq i}^{n} |w_{i,j}^H|)^{\gamma} (\sum_{j=1, j\neq i}^{n} |\sigma_j'(x)||w_{j,i}^H|)^{1-\gamma}$$

$$< c|w_{i,i}^H| + c(R_i^H)^{\gamma} (C_i^H)^{\gamma-1}$$

$$< 1 \tag{10}$$

By means of Corollary 1, system (4) is absolutely stable. □

Corollary 2. *Let* $0 < \sigma'(.) < c$ *in Eq.(4). If the connection weight matrix* $W_H = [w_{i,j}^H]_{n\times n}$ *satisfies*

$$\sum_{j=1}^{n} |w_{i,j}^H| < \frac{1}{c}, \qquad i = 1, 2, ..., n \tag{11}$$

or

$$\sum_{i=1}^{n} |w_{i,j}^H| < \frac{1}{c}, \qquad j = 1, 2, ..., n \tag{12}$$

Then system (4) is absolutely stable.

Proof. The results are obtained by setting $\gamma = 1$ and $\gamma = 0$ in Theorem 2, respectively. □

The results of Corollary 2 may be also obtained using well-known Gerschgorin's theorem [8] which can be implied by setting $\gamma = 1$ and $\gamma = 0$ in Ostrowski's theorem. since $(R_i C_i)^{1/2} \leq (R_i + C_i)/2$, that is; when $\gamma = 1/2$, the Ostrowski radius r_i is located in between the Gerchgorin radii R_i and C_i. Consequently, in case some of R_i^H and C_i^H satisfy the conditions of Theorem 2, and others do not, Theorem 1 may give a better estimation of the absolute stability region of system (4).

If the activation function $\sigma(x)$ is the *hyperbolic tangent sigmoidal function* $\sigma_1(x) = tanh(x) = (e^x - e^{-x})/(e^x + e^{-x})$, the range of the function $\sigma_1(x)$ is then $[-1, 1]$, and the derivative of $\sigma_1'(x)$ satisfies $\sigma_1'(x) = sech^2 x = 4/(e^x + e^{-x})^2 < 1$. Therefore, if $\sum_{j=1}^{n} |w_{i,j}^H| < 1$, system (4) has a unique globally asymptotically stable equilibrium point $x^* \in [-1, 1]$. If the activation function $\sigma(x)$ is chosen as $\sigma_2(x) = 1/(1+e^{-x})$, $\sigma_2(x)$ is bounded in [0,1], and the derivative of $\sigma_2(x)$ is given by $\sigma_2'(x) = \sigma_2(x)(1-\sigma_2(x)) < 1$.

Then for $\sum_{j=1}^{n} |w^H_{i,j}| < w^H_{i,i} < 1$, system (4) has a unique globally asymptotically stable equilibrium point $x^* \in [0,1]$.

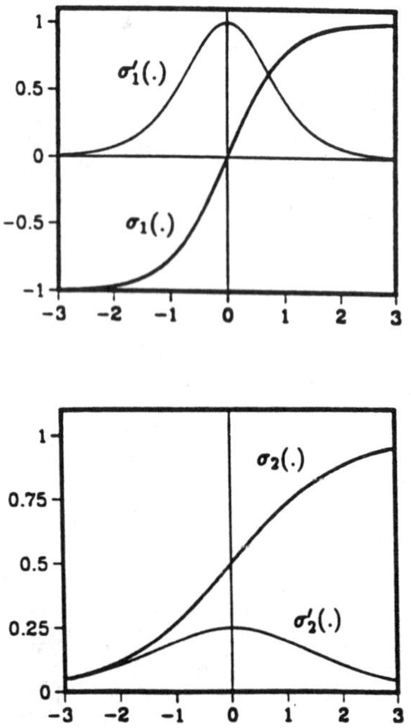

Fig. 2 The activation functions and their derivatives

Since $P^{-1}WP$ has the same eigenvalues as W whenever P is a nonsingular $n \times n$ matrix, the estimation of the union of eigenvalues of $P^{-1}AP$ can be yielded applying Gerschgorin's Theorem. In fact, for some choice of P the bounds obtained may be sharper. A particularly convenient choice is $P = diag[p_1, p_2, ..., p_n]$ with all $p_i > 0$ and system (4) may be then represented using the new coordinate $z(k) = Px(k)$ as follows

$$z(k+1) = P^{-1}\sigma[W_H P z(k) + s] = \bar{f}(z(k)) \quad (13)$$

The Jacobian is

$$\begin{aligned} \bar{f}'(z) &= [\bar{f}'_{i,j}(z)]_{n\times n} \\ &= P^{-1}\Sigma W_H P = P^{-1} f'(x) P \quad (14) \end{aligned}$$

where $\Sigma = diag[\sigma_1(z), \sigma_2(z), ..., \sigma_n(z)]$. Therefore, the Jacobians $\bar{f}'(z)$ and $f'(x)$ have the same eigenvalues, that is; the system (13) has the same stability as the original system (4).

Theorem 3. *Let $0 < \sigma'(.) < c$, $p_1, p_2, ..., p_n$ be positive real numbers, and $\gamma \in [0,1]$ be given, and*

$$\begin{cases} \bar{R}^H_i = \sum_{j=1, j\neq i}^{n} p_j |w^H_{i,j}| \\ \bar{C}^H_i = \sum_{j=1, j\neq i}^{n} \frac{1}{p_j} |w^H_{j,i}| \end{cases}$$

If the connection weight matrix $W_H = [w^H_{i,j}]_{n\times n}$ satisfies

$$|w^H_{i,i}| + \frac{1}{p_i^{\gamma}} (\bar{R}^H_i)^{\gamma} (\bar{C}^H_i)^{1-\gamma} < \frac{1}{c}, \qquad i = 1, 2, ..., n \quad (15)$$

Then system (4) is absolutely stable.

Corollary 3. *Let $0 < \sigma(.) < c$ and $p_1, p_2, ..., p_n$ be positive real numbers. If the connection weight matrix $W_H = [w^H_{i,j}]_{n\times n}$ satisfies*

$$|w^H_{i,i}| + \frac{1}{p_i} \sum_{j=1, j\neq i}^{n} p_j |w^H_{i,j}| < \frac{1}{c} \quad (16)$$

$$i = 1, 2, ..., n$$

or

$$|w^H_{j,j}| + p_j \sum_{i=1, i\neq j}^{n} \frac{1}{p_i} |w_{i,j}| < \frac{1}{c} \quad (17)$$

$$j = 1, 2, ..., n$$

Then system (4) is absolutely stable.

V. AN EXAMPLE

Consider a two-neuron network system described by

$$\begin{cases} x_1(k+1) = & (\frac{1}{2})x_1(k) + tanh((\frac{1}{4})x_1(k) \\ & +(\frac{1}{8})x_2(k) + s_1) \\ x_2(k+1) = & -(\frac{1}{2})x_2(k) + tanh((\frac{1}{3})x_1(k) \\ & -(\frac{1}{4})x_2(k) + s_2) \end{cases} \quad (18)$$

One can easily obtain that $\delta_i = 1/2$, $i = 1, 2$ and

$$\begin{cases} R_1 = 1/8 \\ R_2 = 1/3 \end{cases}, \qquad \begin{cases} C_1 = 1/3 \\ C_2 = 1/8 \end{cases}$$

Let $\gamma = 1/2$ in Theorem 2, then

$$\begin{cases} |w_{1,1}| + R_1^{1/2}C_1^{1/2} = 1/4 + 1/(26)^{1/2} < 1/2 \\ |w_{2,2}| + R_2^{1/2}C_2^{1/2} = 1/4 + 1/(26)^{1/2} < 1/2 \end{cases}$$

Therefore, using Theorem 2, the absolute stability of the neural network (18) is ensured. Now, the absolute stability of system (18) is examined using the results of Corollary 2 as follows

$$\begin{cases} |w_{1,1}| + |w_{1,2}| = 3/8 < 1/2 \\ |w_{2,1}| + |w_{2,2}| = 7/12 > 1/2 \end{cases}$$

and

$$\begin{cases} |w_{1,1}| + |w_{2,1}| = 7/12 > 1/2 \\ |w_{1,2}| + |w_{2,2}| = 3/8 < 1/2 \end{cases}$$

The absolute stability of system (18) can not be determined using Corollary 2. In fact, the absolute stability of system (18) is indicated by the simulation results as shown in Figure 3, where the state $x = (x_1, x_2)^T$ converges to a unique equilibrium point $x^* = (-1.97153, 0.19117)^T$ regardless o f the initial state $x(0)$ as shown in Figure 3.

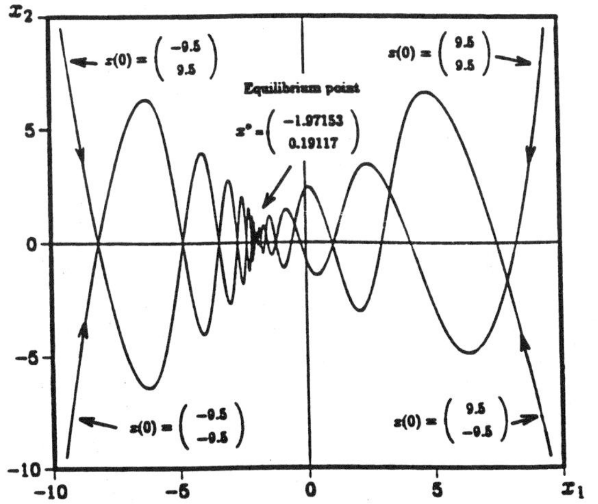

Fig. 3 The phase plane diagram of the states x_1 and x_2 of the neural network (18) with inputs $s_1 = -2$ and $s_2 = 1$. In this case, the unique absolutely stable equilibrium point is $x^* = (-1.97153, 0.19117)^T$

VI. CONCLUSIONS

A novel architecture of the discrete-time MRNN has been proposed in this paper for the potential applications of learning control, computer vision, and pattern recognition; and the dynamics of the MRNN have been described by a system of first-order nonlinear difference equations. The stability of the equilibrium points of the dynamics were studied by means of the discrete-time system analysis approach, and some absolute stability criterions were established.

References

[1] S. Grossberg, " Nonlinear neural networks: Principles, mechanisms and architectures", *Neural Networks*, Vol. 1, No. 1, pp. 17-61, 1988.

[2] J.A. Anderson, J.W. Silverstein, S.A. Ritz and R.S. Jones, "Distinctive features, categorical perception, and probability learning: Some applications of a neural model", in *Neurocomputing: Foundations of Research*, J.A. Anderson and E. Rosenfeld, Eds. Cambridge, MA: MIT Press, 1988.

[3] P.K. Simpson, *Artifical Neural Systems*, Pergamon Press, 1990.

[4] S. Hui and S.H. Zak, , "Dynamical Analysis of the Brain-State-in-a-Box (BSB) Neural Models ", *IEEE* Trans. on Neural Networks, Vol. 3, No. 1, pp. 86-94, 1992.

[5] A.H. Michel, J. Si and G. Yen, "Analysis and Synthesis of a Class of Discrete-Time Neural Networks Described on Hypercubes", *IEEE* Trans. on Neural Networks, Vol. 2, No. 1, pp. 32-46, 1991.

[6] L.K. Li, "Fixed Point Analysis For Discrete-Time Recurrent Neural Networks", Proc. *IJCNN*, Vol. IV, pp. 134-139, June, 1992.

[7] R.L. Devaney, *An Introduction to Chaotic Dynamical Systems*, Addison-Wesley Publishing Company, Inc. 1989.

[8] M.Marcus and H. Minc, *A Survey of Matrix Theory and Matrix Inequalities*, Boston, MA: Allyn and Bacon, 1964.

ANALYSIS OF A SIMPLE HYSTERESIS NETWORK AND ITS APPLICATION FOR AN EFFECTIVE ASSOCIATIVE MEMORY

Kenya JIN'NO *Toshimichi SAITO*

Electrical Engineering Department , HOSEI Univercity , TOKYO , 184 , JAPAN
e-mail : jinno @ toshi . hosei . ac . jp

Abstract

This article analyses the stable equilibria and stable periodic outputs for a simple hysteresis network. The simplified network includes binary hysteresis function and has only three parameters. We show that the number of stable equilibria and that of stable periodic output sequences can be controlled by the three parameters. The domain of attraction of stable equilibria is completely clarified and the local domain of attraction of periodic outputs is given. And we propose an application for an effective associative memory. This associative memory guarantees storing of all desired memories, it has no spurious stable output and it recalls the closest desired memory from an input vector.

1 Introduction

This article analyses a simplified version of our original continuous time piecewise liner hysteresis neural network[1]~[5]. And we propose an application for an effective associative memory. The simplified network includes binary hysteresis function and has only three parameter. Then we discuss the following:

1. We prove the necessary and sufficient condition for the system to have stable equilibria. The number of the attraction and its domain of attraction is completely clarified.

2. We give the sufficient condition for the system to have stable periodic outputs. The outputs consist of binary vectors. The number of the periodic outputs is completely clarified and the local domain of attraction is given.

Applying a part 1), we can construct an efficient associative memory which has three layers. The three layers are hysteresis layer, output layer and initial state generation layer. This network has the following properties.

I. This network guarantees storing of all desired memories.

II. This network has no spurious stable output.

III. This system guarantees to retrieve the closest desired memory from any input.

IV. The implementation is easy. Especially, storing of desired memories can be realized by controlling two terminal switches.

Also we emphasize that the properties I) and II) depend on a hysteresis effect.

In our previous works on the hysteresis associative memories, I) is guaranteed and II) and III) are suggested by practical numerical data, but theoretical discussion on the spurious stable output generation and the domain of attraction of desired memories are not sufficient.

2 Analysis

The objective network is governed by the following dimensionless equation:

$$\begin{aligned} \dot{u}_i &= -u_i + \sum_{j=1}^{m} y_j + T\,y_i, \\ y_i &= h(u_i), \end{aligned} \tag{1}$$

where $\boldsymbol{u} \equiv (u_1, \ldots, u_m)^t$, $u_i \in R$ is a state variable, $\boldsymbol{y} \equiv (y_1, \ldots, y_m)^t$, $y_i \in \{0, 1\}$ is an output and m is the number of the cell. T is a self feedback parameter and $h(u_i)$ is a binary hysteresis function defined by (see Fig. 1)

$$h(u_i) = \begin{cases} 0 & \text{,if } u_i > a \\ 1 & \text{,if } u_i < b, \end{cases} \tag{2}$$

where $h(u_i)$ is switched from 0 to 1 [from 1 to 0] if u_i hits threshold.

For any $\boldsymbol{y}$, the corresponding equilibrium point $\boldsymbol{p}(\boldsymbol{y})$ is given by

$$\begin{aligned} \boldsymbol{p}(\boldsymbol{y}) &= (p_1(y), \ldots, p_m(y))^t, \\ p_i(\boldsymbol{y}) &= q(\boldsymbol{y}) + T\,y_i \qquad , q(\boldsymbol{y}) = \sum_{j=1}^{m} y_j \end{aligned} \tag{3}$$

$q(\boldsymbol{y})$ is the number of "1" in $\boldsymbol{y}$ and is independent of i.

[Definition 1] y_i is said to be stable if

$$\begin{cases} q(\boldsymbol{y}) > a & \text{for } y_i = 0 \\ q(\boldsymbol{y}) + T < b & \text{for } y_i = 1\,. \end{cases} \tag{4}$$

0-7803-1254-6/93$03.00 © 1993 IEEE

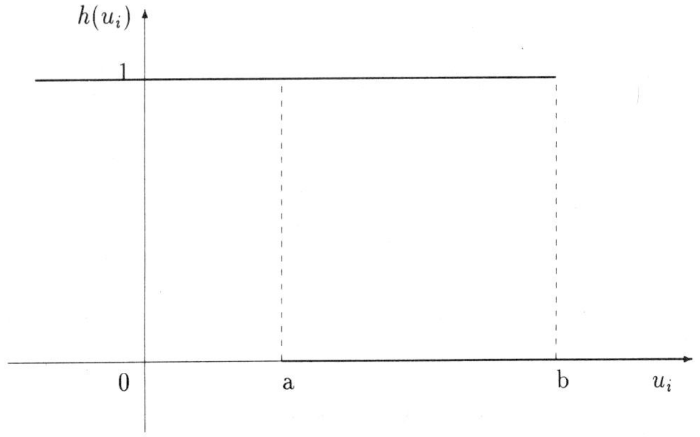

Figure 1: Binary Hysteresis Function

Inversely, y_i is said to be unstable if

$$\begin{cases} q(\boldsymbol{y}) \leq a & \text{for } y_i = 0 \\ q(\boldsymbol{y}) + T \geq b & \text{for } y_i = 1. \end{cases} \tag{5}$$

[Definition 2] $\boldsymbol{y}$ is said to be stable if

$$y_i \text{ is stable for all } i\,. \tag{6}$$

In this case, $\boldsymbol{y}$ is time invariant. Inversely, $\boldsymbol{y}$ is said to be unstable if

$$y_i \text{ is unstable for some } i\,. \tag{7}$$

Then we have:

[Theorem 1] Let K and l be non-negative integer such that $K \leq m$ and $l \leq m - K$ and let

$$\begin{cases} K - 1 < a < K < b < K + 1 \\ b - K - l - 1 < T < b - K - l\,. \end{cases} \tag{8}$$

Then the following is satisfied:

1. $\boldsymbol{y}$ is stable iff $K \leq q(\boldsymbol{y}) \leq K + l$.
2. Any initial output $\boldsymbol{y}(0)$ converges to some stable $\boldsymbol{y}$ for almost all initial state $\boldsymbol{u}(0)$.
3. The number of stable $\boldsymbol{y}$ is $\sum_{r=K}^{K+l} {}_mC_r$.

Remark

1. The probability of more than one element switching simultaneously at the same precise instant is zero. Then we omit such case hereafter. Such switching is impossible in real physical systems.
2. Since K is an integer, perturbed a and b give the same results if the stability condition (8) is held.

[Theorem 2] We assume (8). If initial state satisfy

$$a \leq u_{r(1)}(0) \leq \ldots \leq u_{r(K)}(0) < u_j(0), \quad j \neq r(\cdot), \tag{9}$$

where $r(\cdot)$ is K numbers which are arbitrary selected from 1 to m. Then $\boldsymbol{y}(0)$ converges to a stable $\boldsymbol{y}$ such that $y_{r(\cdot)} = 1$ and $y_j = 0$.

(Example.1)

We consider the case of $m = 4$, $K = 1$ and $l = 0$.

$$a = 0.5, \quad b = 1.5, \quad T = 0\ . \tag{10}$$

It satisfies condition (8). In this case, both $y_i = 1$ and $y_i = 0$ are time invariant if $q(\boldsymbol{y}) = 1$ (see Fig.2).

Then, the stable outputs are

$$(1,0,0,0), (0,1,0,0), (0,0,1,0) \text{ and } (0,0,0,1). \tag{11}$$

Next we assume

$$b < u_3(0) < u_j(0), \quad j \neq 3. \tag{12}$$

Referring (9), the initial output $\boldsymbol{y} = (0,0,0,0)$ converges to $(0,0,1,0)$.

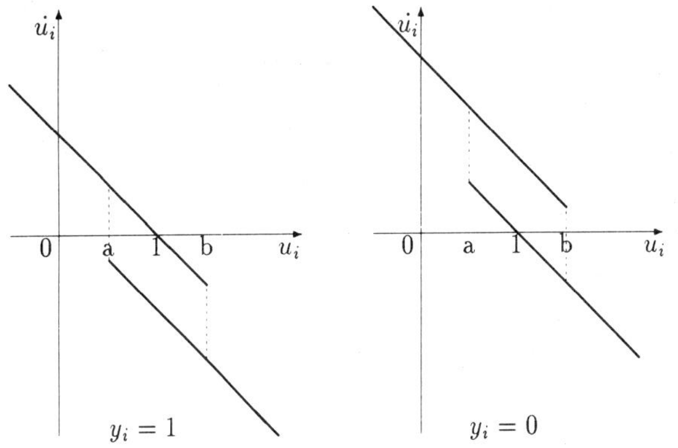

Figure 2: Equilibrium Point

[Theorem 3] Let K be positive integer such that $K \leq m$ and let

$$\begin{cases} K - 1 < a < K < b < K + 1 \\ b - K < T < b - K + 1 \end{cases} \tag{13}$$

Then the following is satisfied:

1. If $q(\boldsymbol{y}) \geq K$ then $y_i = 1$ is unstable and $y_i = 0$ is stable. If $q(\boldsymbol{y}) \leq K - 1$ then $y_i = 1$ is stable and $y_i = 1$ is unstable.
2. Any initial output $\boldsymbol{y}(0)$ converges to some stable periodic outputs sequences such that $q(\boldsymbol{y})$ varies between K and $K - 1$.
3. The number of such periodic outputs is $m\,!$.

(**Example.2**)

We consider the case of $m = 3$ and $K = 1$.

$$a = 0.5, \quad b = 1.5, \quad T = 1\,. \tag{14}$$

Referring definition 1, the stability of each element is as following:

For the case of $q(\boldsymbol{y}) = 1$,

$$\begin{cases} y_i = 0 & \text{is stable.} \\ y_j = 1 & \text{is unstable.} \end{cases}$$

For the case of $q(\boldsymbol{y}) = 0$,

$$\begin{cases} y_i = 0 & \text{is unstable.} \\ y_j = 1 & \text{is stable.} \end{cases}$$

Therefor $\boldsymbol{y}$ oscillates between $q(\boldsymbol{y}) = 1$ and $q(\boldsymbol{y}) = 0$. The stable periodic outputs are

$(0,0,1) \to (0,0,0) \to (0,1,0) \to (0,0,0) \to (1,0,0) \to (0,0,0) \to (0,0,1)$

and

$(0,0,1) \to (0,0,0) \to (1,0,0) \to (0,0,0) \to (0,1,0) \to (0,0,0) \to (0,0,1)$.

Next we consider the case of $q(\boldsymbol{y}) = 2$. Referring the condition (13), y_i is time variant if $y_i = 1$, but y_i is time invariant if $y_i = 0$. Then this output converges to some $\boldsymbol{y}$ such that $q(\boldsymbol{y}) = 1$.

Then we notice that all initial output $\boldsymbol{y}(0)$ converges to one of the stable periodic outputs.

3 Associative Memory

In this section, we propose a layer type associative memory as an application of the hysteresis system. We propose an auto-associative memory. This system has three layers : the hysteresis layer, the output layer, and the initial state generation layer :

(Hysteresis Layer)

$$a = 0.5, \quad b = 1.5, \quad T = 0, \quad K = 1, \quad l = 0\,. \tag{15}$$

$$\begin{aligned} \dot{u}_i &= -u_i + \sum_{j=1}^{m} y_j\,, \\ y_i &= h(u_i)\,. \end{aligned} \tag{16}$$

Since (15) satisfies the condition (8), $\boldsymbol{y}$ is stable iff $q(\boldsymbol{y}) = 1$.

(Output Layer)

$$\boldsymbol{z} = \boldsymbol{B}\boldsymbol{y}, \tag{17}$$

where $\boldsymbol{z} \equiv (z_1, \ldots, z_N)^t$, $z_i \in \{-1, 0, 1\}$ is an output of the associative memory and it corresponds to an information. $\boldsymbol{S}^r \equiv (S_1^r, \ldots, S_N^r)^t$, $S_i^r \in \{-1, 1\}$ is a desired memory, and $\boldsymbol{B} \equiv [\boldsymbol{S}^1, \ldots, \boldsymbol{S}^m]$ is the desired memories matrix. N is a number of cells of the output and m is a number of desired memories. If $y_r = 1$ and $y_j = 0$ for $j \neq r$, the output $\boldsymbol{z}$ is $\boldsymbol{S}^r$.

(Initial State Generation Layer)

The initial state $u_i(0)$ in the hysteresis layer is given by

$$u_i(0) = D_H(\boldsymbol{S}^i, \boldsymbol{x}) + 2 \quad , \quad \boldsymbol{u}(0) \equiv (u_1(0), \ldots, u_m(0))\,, \tag{18}$$

where $\boldsymbol{x} \equiv (x_1, \ldots, x_N)^t$, $x_i \in \{-1, 1\}$is an input vector and $D_H(\boldsymbol{S}^i, \boldsymbol{x})$ is the hammig distance between $\boldsymbol{S}^i$ and $\boldsymbol{x}$.

Referring theorem 2, $y_i(0) = 0$ for all i and first switching cell is the closest cell to threshold a.

Based on theorem 1 for $K = 1$ and $l = 0$, this system guarantees storing all desired memories and not to generate the spurious stable output. And this system guarantees to retrieve the closest desired memory from an input $\boldsymbol{x}$.

[**Lemma.1**] For $\min_{j \neq i} | u_i(0) - u_j(0) | = 2\epsilon$, this network gives the same result if the initial value $u_i(0)$ is replaced by $\tilde{u}_i(0)$ such that is $| \tilde{u}_i(0) - u_i(0) | < \epsilon$.

Then this system is robustness for initial values.

An implementation example of this system is shown in Fig.3. In this figure, left part is the unit element of hysteresis layer and the right part is the unit element of initial state generation layer. Note that storing of desired memory can be realized by controlling two terminal switches.

4 Conclusion

For a simplified version of our original continuous time piecewise liner hysteresis network, we have analysed the stable equilibria and the stable periodic outputs. The number of stable equilibria and stable periodic outputs is controlled by the three parameter a , b and T. And we analyse the domain of the attraction. We have also proposed a novel associative memory. This associative memory has no spurious stable output and guarantees to retrieve the closest desired memory from an input vector. We note that this efficient performance is caused by hysteresis characteristic. Such performance is hard in the case where $h(\cdot)$ is sigmoid function or step function. Then this associative memory is only one example in expected applications. If the initial state setting or the output layer is changed, this system could be used as hetero-associative memory, clustering machine and so on.

We note that such continuous time hysteresis system exhibits various interesting phenomena, for example chaos and fractals. Then we synthesize efficient multi functional nets controlling such rich phenomena.

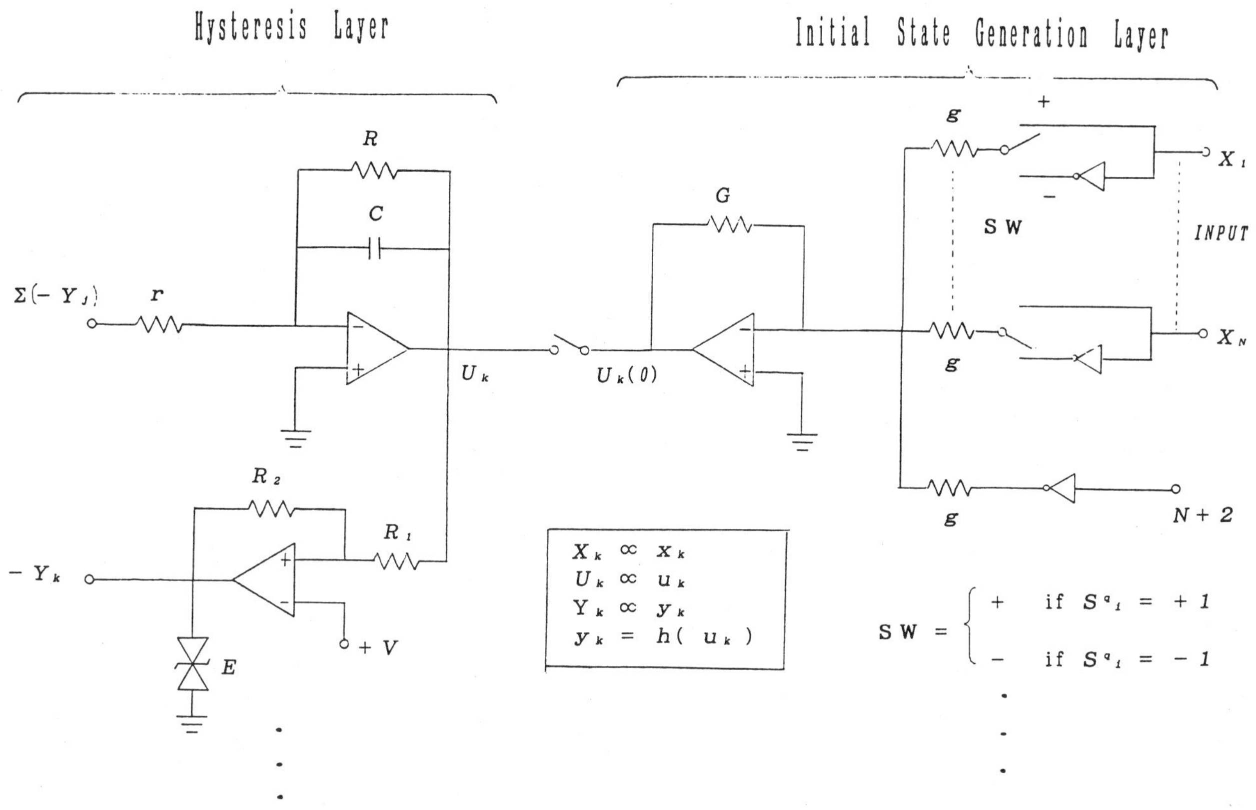

Figure 3: Circuit

References

[1] K.Jin'no and T.Saito : "Analysis and Synthesis of Continuous Time Hysteretic Neural Networks" , *Trans., IEICE Japan J75-A , 3* , pp.552-556 (1992)

[2] T.Saito, M.Oikawa and K.Jinno : "Dynamics of Hysteretic Neural Networks" , *in Proc., IEEE/ISCAS'91* , pp.1469-1472 (1991)

[3] K.Jin'no and T.Saito : "Analysis and Synthesis of a Continuous Time Hysteresis Neural Network" , *in Proc., IEEE/ISCAS'92* , pp.471-474 (1992)

[4] T.Saito, K.Jin'no and K.Kishiro : "On Inner Connection of Artificial Neural Systems",*in Proc., IEEE/ISCAS'92* , pp.2769-2772 (1992)

[5] T.Saito and M.Oikawa : "Chaos and Fractals from a Forced Artficial Neural Cell", *IEEE Trans., Neural Networks* , (in press)

[6] J.J.Hopfield : "Neural Networks and Physical Systems with emergent collective Computational Abilities", *in Proc. Nat. Acad. Sci. USA* , pp.2554-2558 (1982)

[7] J.H.Li and A.N.Michel : "Analysis and Synthesis of a Class of Neural Networks : Variable Structure Systems with Infinite Gain", *IEEE Trans., CAS36-5* , pp.713-731 (1989)

[8] J.A.Farrell and A.N.Michel : "A Synthesis Procedure for Hopfield's Continuous Time Associative memory", *IEEE Trans., CAS37-5* , pp.877-884 (1990)

[9] J.Hao and J.Vandewalle : "A New Model of Neural Associative Memories", *in Proc. IJCNN'92 Baltimore* , Vol.2 , pp.166-171 (1992)

[10] H.Mizutani : "PANN: Neural Network to Associate the Fundamental Memory Nearest in Hamming's Distance", *Trans., IEICE Japan J73-DII , 3* , pp.437-444 (1990)

[11] H.Ueda, Y.Anzai, M.Ohta and S.Yoneda : "An Associative Neural Network Using PDN", *Thechnical Report, IEICE Japan, NL-10* (1992)

[12] M.Morita, S.Yoshizawa and K.Nakano : "Analysis and Improvement of the Dynamics of Autocorrelation Associative Memory", *Trans., IEICE Japan J73-DII , 2* , pp.232-242 (1990)

Minimum-Seeking Properties of Analog Neural Networks with Multilinear Objective Functions

M. Vidyasagar
Centre for AI & Robotics
Raj Bhavan Circle, High Grounds
Bangalore 560 001, India
E-mail: sagar@yantra.ernet.in

August 30, 1993

Abstract In this paper, we study the problem of minimzing an objective function over the discrete set $\{0,1\}^n$. It is shown that one can assume without loss of generality that the objective function is a multilinear polynomial. A gradient type neural network is proposed to perform the optimization. A novel feature of the network is the introduction of a bias vector. The network is operated in the high-gain region of the sigmoidal nonlinearities. The following comprehensive theorem is proved: For all sufficiently small bias vectors except those belonging to a set of measure zero, for all sufficiently large sigmoidal gain, for all initial conditions except those belonging to a set of measure zero, the state of the network converges to a local minimum of the objective function. This is a considerable generalization of earlier results for quadratic objective functions.

1 Introduction

Most of the current research into feedback neural networks is concentrated on networks with *linear* interconnections and *quadratic* energy functions. In his trend-setting paper [1], Hopfield considers two-state networks described by

$$x_i(t+1) = \text{sign}\left[\sum_{j=1}^{n} w_{ij}x_j(t) + \theta_i\right], \; i = 1, \ldots, n, \tag{1.1}$$

where n is the number of neurons, $x_i(t) \in \{-1,1\}$ is the state of neuron i at time t, w_{ij} is the weight of the interconnection from neuron i to neuron j, and $-\theta_i$ is the firing threshold of neuron i. Hopfield [1] defines the energy of the network as

$$E = -\frac{1}{2}\sum_{i=1}^{n}\sum_{j=1}^{n} w_{ij}x_ix_j - \sum_{i=1}^{n} x_i\theta_i, \tag{1.2}$$

and proves the following the property: Suppose $w_{ji} = w_{ij}$ for all i,j (symmetric interactions), $w_{ii} = 0$ for all i (no self-interactions), and the neural states are updated *asynchronously*. Then

$$E[\mathbf{x}(t+1)] \leq E[\mathbf{x}(t)], \tag{1.3}$$

where $\mathbf{x} = [x_1 \ldots x_n]^t$. Thus, in an asynchronous mode of operation, the neural network will eventually reach a fixed point of the network. Hence, if it is desired to optimize a quadratic objective function over the discrete set $\{-1,1\}^n$, one can use a neural network of the form (1.1). Such a network will, within a finite number of time steps, reach a local minimum of E. Some practical problems that can be translated as the minimization of a quadratic objective function include the Travelling Salesman Problem [2], and linear programming [3].

While the above results are very impressive, the asynchronous mode of operation is vulnerable to the criticism that the convergence to a local minimum will be slow, because out of the n neurons, ony one neuron changes its state at a time; that is, the state vector $\mathbf{x}(t+1)$ is *adjacent* to the state vector $\mathbf{x}(t)$.

In an attempt to speed up the operation of the network, Hopfield [4] considers *analog* neural networks, where the constituent neurons have *graded* responses.

0191-2216/93/$3.00

Such networks are described by

$$C_i\dot{u}_i = -\frac{1}{R_i}u_i+\sum_{j=1}^{n} w_{ij}v_j+\theta_i,\ v_i = g_i(\lambda u_i),\ i = 1,\ldots,n, \tag{1.4}$$

where n is the number of neurons; v_i is the neural current and u_i is the neural voltage; θ_i is the external current input to the i-th neuron; C_i is the membrane capacitance and R_i is the neural resistance; λ is a scaling parameter, and w_{ij} is the weight of the interconnection from neuron j to neuron i. The function $g_i : \Re \rightarrow (0,1)$ is continuously differentiable, strictly increasing, $g_i(x) \rightarrow 1$ as $x \rightarrow \infty$, and $g_i(x) \rightarrow 0$ as $x \rightarrow -\infty$. Note that, as the scaling parameter $\lambda \rightarrow \infty$, the function $x \mapsto g_i(\lambda x)$ approaches the "saturation" function sat(x), which equals 0 if $x < 0$ and equals 1 if $x > 0$. In [4], Hopfield assumes that $w_{ij} = w_{ji}$ for all i, j, and that $w_{ii} = 0$ for all i. He then proposes the energy function

$$E_c(\mathbf{v}) = \sum_{i=1}^{n} \left[\frac{1}{\lambda R_i} \int_0^{v_i} g_i^{-1}(v)\, dv - \theta_i v_i - \frac{1}{2} \sum_{j=1}^{n} w_{ij} v_i v_j \right], \tag{1.5}$$

and shows that

$$\frac{d}{dt} E_c[\mathbf{v}(t)] \leq 0 \tag{1.6}$$

along trajectories of the system (1.4). Hirsch [5] shows, using the relationship (1.6), that the system (1.4) is *totally stable*; that is, every solution trajectory approaches an equilibrium. Salam *et al.* [6] fix a small technical flaw in the reasoning of [5] by establishing that no solution trajectory of (1.4) escapes to infinity (in the $\mathbf{u}$-space).

The results of [5, 6] combined show that every solution trajectory of (1.4), irrespective of the initial condition, approaches *an* equilibrium. Thus it becomes important to analyze the location and stability status of the equilibria of the system (1.4). Such an analysis is carried out in [7] for a very general class of neural networks *in the high gain limit*, i.e., as $\lambda \rightarrow \infty$. The analysis of [7] applies also to the neural network (1.4). It shows that, if $w_{ii} = 0$ for all i, $w_{ij} = w_{ji}$ for all i, j, and certain additional assumptions hold, then "almost all" solution trajectories of the network approach a corner of the unit hypercube $[0,1]^n$. Note that, as $\lambda \rightarrow \infty$, the energy function E_c of (1.5) approaches the energy function E of (1.2). Hence, by operating the analog network (1.4) near the high gain limit, it is possible to minimize E over the corners of the hypercube $[0,1]^n$. Note that the operation of the analog network (1.4) is "synchronous" in the sense that the states of all neurons are changing at the same time. It can therefore be argued that the analog implementation combines the speed of synchronous operation with the minimum-seeking property of asynchronous operation.

Thus, in the case where the objective function to be minimized is a quadratic, the situation is quite well-understood. However, there are situations in which it is more natural to use an objective function which is a polynomial of degree three or higher. Two such examples are given in [8] (solution of the satisfiability problem) and [9] (algebraic block-decoding).

The objective of the present paper is to generalize the system description (1.4) to the case of an energy function that is not necessarily quadratic. It can be shown that one can assume, without loss of generality, that the objective function is a multilinear polynomial. The generalized neural network dynamics are analyzed in this case. The main conclusions of the paper are that (i) the network is totally stable, and (ii) "almost all" trajectories of the network converge to a local minimum of the energy function. Though the generalization of (1.4) to a higher order energy function is rather natural, the analysis of the resulting network, based on the approach of [7], is not so straight-forward.

2 Main Results

Throughout the paper, the problem under study is that of minimizing a function $E(\mathbf{x})$ over the *discrete* set $\{0,1\}^n$. Suppose the function $E : [0,1]^n \rightarrow \Re$ is continuously differentiable on the open hypercube $(0,1)^n$, and that it is desired to minimize $E(\mathbf{x})$ as $\mathbf{x}$ varies over the discrete set $\{0,1\}^n$. Thus the exact expression for $E(\mathbf{x})$ is unimportant, and only the set of values of E at the 2^n points in $\{0,1\}^n$ is relevant. In other words, we are free to replace $E(\mathbf{x})$ by another function $F(\mathbf{x})$, so long as

$$E(\mathbf{x}) = F(\mathbf{x}) \text{ for all } \mathbf{x} \in \{0,1\}^n. \tag{2.1}$$

It is easy to show that, given any function $E : \Re^n \rightarrow \Re$, there exists a unique multilinear polynomial $F : \Re^n \rightarrow \Re$ such that (2.1) holds. Thus it can be assumed without loss of generality that the problem at hand is to minimize a *multilinear polynomial* E over the discrete set $\{0,1\}^n$. For this purpose, we propose an analog neural network described by

$$\dot{u}_i = -\frac{u_i}{\alpha_i} - [\nabla E(\mathbf{x})]_i + b_i,\ x_i = g_i(\lambda u_i),\ i = 1,\ldots,n. \tag{2.2}$$

Comparing (2.2) with (1.4), we can observe two important differences: First, the two "physical" constants C_i

and R_i have been combined into a single time constant α_i. This is a very minor difference. Second, a "bias" input b_i introduced into each of the differential equations. This is a substantial difference, and is a novel feature of the network proposed here. Note that the function $E(\mathbf{x})$ of (1.2) is multilinear if and only if $w_{ii} = 0$ for all i, i.e., there are no self-interactions.

Proposition 2.1 *The neural network (2.2) is totally stable.*

To proceed further, we introduce an assumption on the sigmoidal functions $g_i(\cdot)$.

(A1) *For each i, the function $g_i(\cdot) : \Re \rightarrow (0,1)$ is continuously differentiable, strictly increasing, and satisfies*

$$g_i(u) \rightarrow 0 \text{ as } u \rightarrow -\infty, \; g_i(u) \rightarrow 1 \text{ as } u \rightarrow \infty, \tag{2.3}$$

and

$$\lim_{\lambda \rightarrow \infty} \lambda \, g_i'(\lambda u) = 0, \tag{2.4}$$

uniformly in u over the complement of any open neighborhood of 0.

Now we come to the main result of the paper.

Theorem 2.2 *Suppose E is a multilinear polynomial on $\Re^n$, and that Assumption (A1) is satisfied. Let $\{\lambda_j\}$ be any sequence of positive numbers approaching infinity. Under these conditions, there exists an $\epsilon > 0$ such that, for all $\mathbf{b}$ with $\|\mathbf{b}\| < \epsilon$ except for those belonging to a set of measure zero, for all sufficiently large indices j, for all initial conditions $\mathbf{u}(0)$ except for those belonging to a set of measure zero, the solution trajectory $\mathbf{x}(t)$ converges to a vector $\mathbf{e} + o(1/\lambda_j)$, where $\mathbf{e} \in \{0,1\}^n$ and $\mathbf{e}$ is a local minimum of E over $\{0,1\}^n$.*

Remarks

1. Informally, Theorem 2.2 can be stated as follows: For almost all sufficiently small bias vectors $\mathbf{b}$, for all sufficiently large sigmoidal gains λ, solution trajectories of (2.2) starting from almost all initial initial conditions converge to a corner of the hypercube $[0,1]^n$. Moreover, any such corner is a local minimum of the objective function E over the *discrete* set $\{0,1\}^n$.

2. The bias vector $\mathbf{b}$ is very important. Theorem 2.2 states that *almost all* sufficiently small bias vectors will do the job. But it can happen that the "natural choice" $\mathbf{b} = \mathbf{0}$ belongs to the exceptional set. It is can be shown that the problem of minimizing $E(\mathbf{x}) = x_1x_2x_3$ over the corners of the cube $\{0,1\}^3$, which is one of the easiest problems imaginable, requires a nonzero bias vector.

3. In practice, one would use Theorem 2.2 as follows: In order to minimize E over $\{0,1\}^n$, one would choose a "small" bias vector $\mathbf{b}$, a "large" sigmoidal gain λ, a "random" initial condition $\mathbf{u}(0)$, and set the network (2.2) in motion. When the vector $\mathbf{x}(t)$ appears to be approaching some corner of the hypercube $[0,1]^n$, this vector is rounded off to the nearest binary vector $\mathbf{e}$. Then one would check whether $\mathbf{e}$ is a local minimum of E by applying a simple "parity" condition. If the parity condition is *not* satisfied, then the process is repeated by increasing λ, and only as a last resort, changing the bias vector $\mathbf{b}$. Thus, in practice, the neural network (2.2) generates *candidate* local minima, which must then be tested to determine whether they really are local minima. It may be pointed out that this is a common feature of almost all "interior point" methods of discrete optimization.

The proof of Theorem 2.2 proceeds through several stages, some of which are valid for a much more general class of neural networks than (2.2), and are therefore of independent interest. Section 3 contains some such "general" results, and we get back to the specific network (2.2) in Section 4.

3 Some General Results

Throughout this section, we study a very general class of nonlinear neural networks described by

$$\dot{u}_i = -\frac{u_i}{\alpha_i} - f_i(\mathbf{x}) + b_i, \; x_i = g_i(\lambda u_i), \; i = 1, \ldots, n, \tag{3.1}$$

where $\mathbf{f} : [0,1]^n \rightarrow \Re^n$ is continuously differentiable.[1] Note that $\mathbf{f}$ need not be the gradient of any function. Thus the above class of networks is much more general than the gradient neural networks studied in earlier papers, and than (2.2). The object of the study is to determine what happens to the *location of the equilibria* of the network as the sigmoidal gain λ approaches infinity. The same issue is studied in [7], but with lots of "hand waving." In contrast, the development here is completely rigorous.

The objective of this section is to examine the behavior of the equilibria of the neural network (3.1) as $\lambda \rightarrow \infty$. Clearly, a vector $\mathbf{u}$ is an equilibrium of the network (3.1) if and only if

$$\mathbf{0} = -\mathbf{A}^{-1}\mathbf{u} - \mathbf{f}(\mathbf{x}) + \mathbf{b}, \; \mathbf{x} = \mathbf{g}(\lambda \mathbf{u}), \tag{3.2}$$

[1]This means that $\mathbf{f}$ is continuously differentiable over some open set containing $[0,1]^n$.

where $\mathbf{A} \in \Re^{n \times n} = \text{Diag}\,\{\alpha_1, \ldots, \alpha_n\}$, and the maps $\mathbf{f} : [0,1]^n \rightarrow \Re^n$, $\mathbf{g} : \Re^n \rightarrow (0,1)^n$, and the vector $\mathbf{b} \in \Re^n$ are defined in the obvious way.

Proposition 3.1 *There exists a number μ such that, if $\mathbf{u} \in \Re^n$ satisfies (3.2) for some λ, then $\|\mathbf{u}\| \leq \mu$.*

For purely technical reasons, we focus on the case where $\lambda = \lambda_j$ for some index j, and $\{\lambda_j\}$ is a sequence of positive numbers approaching infinity. Define $\mathcal{E}_j$ to be the set of solutions $\mathbf{u}$ of the equation

$$0 = -\mathbf{A}^{-1}\mathbf{u} - \mathbf{f}[\mathbf{g}(\lambda_j \mathbf{u})] + \mathbf{b}, \qquad (3.3)$$

and define

$$\mathcal{E} = \bigcup_j \mathcal{E}_j. \qquad (3.4)$$

The sets $\mathcal{E}_j$ and $\mathcal{E}$ pertain to the $\mathbf{u}$-space and are subsets of $\Re^n$. It is actually more convenient to work in the $\mathbf{x}$-space. Define $\mathcal{S}_j$ to be the set of solutions $\mathbf{x}$ of the equation

$$0 = -\lambda_j^{-1}\mathbf{A}^{-1}\mathbf{g}^{-1}(\mathbf{x}) - \mathbf{f}(\mathbf{x}) + \mathbf{b}, \qquad (3.5)$$

and define

$$\mathcal{S} = \bigcup_j \mathcal{S}_j. \qquad (3.6)$$

Proposition 3.2 *For all $\mathbf{b} \in \Re^n$ except those belonging to a set of measure zero, each set $\mathcal{S}_j$ contains only a finite number of points.*

Proposition 3.2 shows that, for almost all $\mathbf{b} \in \Re^n$, the set $\mathcal{S}$ is countable. Let us now study the cluster points of the set $\mathcal{S}$. Note that a countable set can have an uncountable number of cluster points. The objective of the remainder of the section is to show that, for the set $\mathcal{S}$ of equilibria of the neural network (3.1), such a thing does not happen. In fact, for almost all bias vectors $\mathbf{b}$, there are only a *finite number* of cluster points, and these can be described explicitly. Moreover, as λ_j becomes large, the network (3.1) has exactly as many equilibria as the number of cluster points, and each equilibrium of (3.1) is "close" to the corresponding cluster point. To arrive at this comprehensive characterization of the behavior of the equilibria of (3.1), we go through several intermediate steps. The first step is to categorize the cluster points of the set $\mathcal{S}$ into three groups. Note that, since $\mathcal{S} \subseteq [0,1]^n$, all cluster points of $\mathcal{S}$ must belong to $[0,1]^n$.

Definition 3.1 *Suppose $\mathbf{v} \in [0,1]^n$ is a cluster point of $\mathcal{S}$. Then $\mathbf{v}$ is said to be an* **interior point** *if $\mathbf{v} \in (0,1)^n$, a* **corner point** *if $\mathbf{v} \in \{0,1\}^n$, and a* **face point** *otherwise.*

The next three propositions give explicit characterizations of each of the three types of cluster points.

Proposition 3.3 *Suppose $\mathbf{b}$ is a regular value of the function $\mathbf{f}$. Then $\mathbf{v} \in (0,1)^n$ is a cluster point of $\mathcal{S}$ if and only if*

$$\mathbf{f}(\mathbf{v}) = \mathbf{b}. \qquad (3.7)$$

Proposition 3.4 *Suppose $\mathbf{e} \in \{0,1\}^n$, and define*

$$\mathbf{z} = \mathbf{b} - \mathbf{f}(\mathbf{e}). \qquad (3.8)$$

Choose $\mathbf{b}$ such that no component of $\mathbf{z}$ is zero. Then $\mathbf{e}$ is a cluster point of $\mathcal{S}$ if and only if the vector $\mathbf{z}$ satisfies the parity condition

$$z_k < 0 \text{ if } e_k = 0,\ z_k > 0 \text{ if } e_k = 1,\ k = 1, \ldots, n. \qquad (3.9)$$

Thus far we have examined the cluster points of $\mathcal{S}$ in the interior of $[0,1]^n$ and in the corners of $[0,1]^n$. Next we examine the cluster points in the faces of $[0,1]^n$. As one would expect, the conditions for a vector $\mathbf{v}$ belonging to a face of $[0,1]^n$ to be a cluster point of $\mathcal{S}$ are a combination of Propositions 3.3 and 3.4. But the notation is a little cumbersome. Suppose $\mathbf{v}$ belongs to a face of $[0,1]^n$. Then some components of $\mathbf{v}$ lie in the open interval $(0,1)$, while the rest equal either 0 or 1. Let $I \subset \{1, \ldots, n\}$ denote the set of those indices i such that $v_i \in \{0,1\}$. Define the vectors

$$\mathbf{v}_1 = \{v_i, i \notin I\} \in (0,1)^{n-|I|}, \qquad (3.10)$$

$$\mathbf{v}_2 = \{v_i, i \in I\} \in \{0,1\}^{|I|}. \qquad (3.11)$$

Proposition 3.5 *Suppose $\mathbf{v}$ belongs to a face of $[0,1]^n$, and define $\mathbf{v}_1$ as in (3.10). Partition $\mathbf{f}$ and $\mathbf{b}$ commensurately with $\mathbf{v}$. Suppose the bias vector $\mathbf{b}$ has two properties: (i) $\mathbf{b}_1$ is a regular value of the map $\mathbf{x}_1 \mapsto \mathbf{f}_1(\mathbf{x}_1, \mathbf{v}_2)$, and (ii) the vector*

$$\mathbf{z}_2 = -\mathbf{f}_2(\mathbf{v}_1, \mathbf{v}_2) + \mathbf{b}_2 \qquad (3.12)$$

has all nonzero components. Under these conditions, $\mathbf{v}$ is a cluster point of $\mathcal{S}$ if and only if (i) $\mathbf{v}_1$ is a solution for $\mathbf{x}_1$ of the equation

$$\mathbf{f}_1(\mathbf{x}_1, \mathbf{v}_2) = \mathbf{b}_1, \qquad (3.13)$$

and (ii) the vector $\mathbf{z}_2$ satisfies the parity condition

$$(\mathbf{z}_2)_i < 0 \text{ if } (\mathbf{v}_2)_i = 0,\ (\mathbf{z}_2)_i > 0 \text{ if } (\mathbf{v}_2)_i = 1. \qquad (3.14)$$

All of the above preceding results are now combined into a single statement.

Theorem 3.6 *Suppose $\mathbf{b} \in \Re^n$ satisfies the following conditions:*

1. *$\mathbf{b}$ is a regular value of the map $\mathbf{u} \mapsto \mathbf{A}^{-1}\mathbf{u} + \mathbf{f}[\mathbf{g}(\lambda_i \mathbf{u})]$ for all i.*

2. $\mathbf{b}$ *is a regular value of the map* $\mathbf{x} \mapsto \mathbf{f}(\mathbf{x})$.

3. *For each binary vector* $\mathbf{e} \in \{0,1\}^n$, *the vector* $\mathbf{b} - \mathbf{f}(\mathbf{e})$ *has all nonzero components.*

4. *For each nonempty proper subset* I *of* $\{1, \ldots, n\}$ *and each binary vector* $\mathbf{v}_2 \in \{0,1\}^{|I|}$, *the vector* $\mathbf{b}_1$ *is a regular value of the map* $\mathbf{x}_1 \mapsto \mathbf{f}_1(\mathbf{x}_1, \mathbf{v}_2)$.

5. *For each solution* $\mathbf{v}_1$ *of the equation* $\mathbf{f}_1(\mathbf{v}_1, \mathbf{v}_2) = \mathbf{b}_1$, *the vector* $\mathbf{b}_2 - \mathbf{f}_2(\mathbf{v}_1, \mathbf{v}_2)$ *has all nonzero components.*

Under these conditions, the following conclusions hold:

A. *The cluster points of* $\mathcal{S}$ *in* $(0,1)^n$ *are precisely the vectors* $\mathbf{v}$ *that satisfy the equation* $\mathbf{f}(\mathbf{v}) = \mathbf{b}$, *and these are finite in number.*

B. *The cluster points of* $\mathcal{S}$ *in* $\{0,1\}^n$ *are precisely the binary vectors that satisfy the parity condition (3.9).*

C. *The cluster points of* $\mathcal{S}$ *in the faces of* $[0,1]^n$ *are precisely those vectors* $(\mathbf{v}_1, \mathbf{v}_2)$ *that satisfy (3.13) and (3.14), and these are finite in number.*

D. *Let* $\mathbf{v}_1, \ldots, \mathbf{v}_r$ *denote the cluster points of* $\mathcal{S}$. *Then there exists an integer* N *and a* $\delta > 0$ *such that, for each* $j > N$, *(3.3) has precisely* r *solutions; call them* $\mathbf{x}_1, \ldots, \mathbf{x}_r$. *Moreover, these solutions can be numbered in such a way that* $\|\mathbf{x}_k - \mathbf{v}_k\| < \delta$ *for all* k.

Remarks Observe that the five hypotheses of Theorem 3.6 hold for all $\mathbf{b} \in \Re^n$ except those belonging to a set of measure zero. The last conclusion of the theorem states that, for sufficiently large λ (and almost all $\mathbf{b}$), the number of equilibria of the network (3.1) equals the number of cluster points, and that there is a one-to-one correspondence between them.

4 Proof of the Main Result

The results of Section 4 are applicable to *arbitrary* neural networks, not just gradient networks of the form (2.2). In this section, we specialize to the network (2.2). The proof of Theorem 2.2 is achieved through a series of propositions. Due to space limitations, only the propositions are presented without proof. However, the proof of Theorem 2.2, based on the set of propositions, is given.

Theorem 3.6 forms the starting point of our study. The bias vector $\mathbf{b}$ is chosen so as to satisfy all five hypotheses of this theorem, with $\mathbf{f}(\mathbf{x}) = \nabla E(\mathbf{x})$. By dropping a finite number of terms from the sequence $\{\lambda_i\}$ if necessary, we make the following assumptions:

1. The set $\mathcal{S}$ has exactly r cluster points, $\mathbf{v}_1, \ldots, \mathbf{v}_r$. These are divided into three groups: $\mathbf{p}_1, \ldots, \mathbf{p}_s \in (0,1)^n$, $\mathbf{e}_1, \ldots, \mathbf{e}_c \in \{0,1\}^n$, and $\mathbf{q}_1, \ldots, \mathbf{q}_f$ belong to the faces of $[0,1]^n$.

2. The balls $B(\mathbf{v}_k, \delta)$ are pairwise disjoint, and each ball contains exactly one solution of (3.3), for each j.

Before proceeding further, a few standard concepts are recalled. For further details, see [10].

Definition 4.1 *A matrix* $\mathbf{M}$ *is said to be* **hyperbolic** *if it has no eigenvalues with a zero real part.*

Definition 4.2 *Consider a differential equation*

$$\dot{\mathbf{x}}(t) = \mathbf{h}[\mathbf{x}(t)], \tag{4.1}$$

where $\mathbf{h}$ *is continuously differentiable. Suppose* $\mathbf{x}_0$ *is an equilibrium of (3.1), i.e., that* $\mathbf{h}(\mathbf{x}_0) = \mathbf{0}$. *Then the equilibrium* $\mathbf{x}_0$ *is said to be* **hyperbolic** *if the matrix*

$$\mathbf{H} := \nabla \mathbf{h}(\mathbf{x}_0) \tag{4.2}$$

is hyperbolic.

Hyperbolic equilibria have several advantageous features, one of which is that their stable and unstable manifolds have complementary dimensions and intersect transversally.

The next result is at the level of a homework problem, but it does not seem to be stated in this form anywhere.

Proposition 4.1 *Suppose* $\mathbf{P}$, $\mathbf{Q}$ *are symmetric matrices, with* $\mathbf{Q}$ *positive definite. Then* $\mathbf{PQ}$ *has only real eigenvalues. If* $\mathbf{P}$ *is nonsingular, then* $\mathbf{PQ}$ *is hyperbolic.*

Proposition 4.2 *For all* j *sufficiently large, the solution of (3.3) in the ball* $B(\mathbf{p}_k, \delta)$ *is a hyperbolic equilibrium of the network (2.2) with* $\lambda = \lambda_j$, *and it is unstable.*

Remarks The proposition states that the equilibria that cluster in the interior of $[0,1]^n$ are hyperbolic and unstable for λ_j sufficiently large.

Proposition 4.3 *For all* i *sufficiently large, the solution of (3.3) in the ball* $B(\mathbf{e}, \delta)$ *is an exponentially stable equilibrium of the neural network (2.2) with* $\lambda = \lambda_j$.

Proposition 4.4 *For all* j *sufficiently large, the solution of (3.3) in the ball* $B(\mathbf{q}_k, \delta)$ *is a hyperbolic equilibrium of (2.2) with* $\lambda = \lambda_j$, *and it is unstable.*

Proof of Theorem 2.2 Propositions 4.2, 4.3 and 4.4 show that, for sufficiently large j, the equilibria of the neural network (2.2) are finite in number, are all hyperbolic, and can be divided into three categories: (i) Those in the ball $B(\mathbf{p}_k, \delta)$, (ii) those in the ball $B(\mathbf{q}_k, \delta)$, and (iii) those in the ball $B(\mathbf{e}, \delta)$. Of these, the equilibria in the first two categories are unstable. Hence the only trajectories that converge to these equilibria are those starting on the stable manifolds of these equilibria. Because these equilibria are unstable, the stable manifold of each such equilibrium is a manifold of dimension less than n, and hence has measure zero as a subset of $(0,1)^n$. Therefore the union of these stable manifolds, call it V, also has measure zero as a subset of $(0,1)^n$. Because the network is totally stable, all solution trajectories must converge to *some* equilibrium; therefore, the solution trajectories starting at all initial conditions not in V must converge to an equilibrium in category (iii). By item (B) of Theorem 3.6, these equilibria are precisely the local minima of the objective function E.

5 Conclusions

In this paper, we have shown that an analog neural network can be used to find a local minimum of *any* multilinear polynomial over the discrete set $\{0,1\}^n$. Comparing the present paper with earlier results, we can claim the following advantages: First, the treatment here is comprehensive and rigorous. Second, it has been shown that it is necessary to introduce a so-called "bias" vector, which is not done in earlier work. Without the bias vector, some of the claims of the earlier papers may not be valid.

The results presented here guarantee only convergence to a *local* minimum. In order to build a network that is guaranteed to converge to a *global* minimum, a natural guess would be to mimic the simulated annealing algorithm, by replacing the *deterministic and constant* bias vector by a *stochastic and time-varying* bias vector, and slowly reduce the variance of the bias vector to zero. The analysis of such networks is bound to be extremely complicated, and is left to those more competent than the author in such matters.

At the current state of evolution of the theory of neural computation, it is no longer enough to show that some problems can (also) be solved using a neural network – it is necessary to analyze the *complexity* of the computation. The contents of the present paper highlight the need to develop a theory of complexity for computation using differential equations.

Finally, the reader is invited to contact the author for a complete version of the paper containing the proofs, various illustrative examples, and an application to the so-called weighted MAX-SAT problem.

References

[1] J. J. Hopfield, "Neural networks and physical systems with emergent collective computational capabilities," *Proc. Nat'l. Acad. Sci. (U.S.A.)*, Vol. 79, pp. 2554-2558, 1982.

[2] J. J. Hopfield and D. W. Tank, " 'Neural' computation of decision optimization problems," *Biological Cybernetics*, Vol. 52, pp. 141-152, 1985.

[3] D. W. Tank and J. J. Hopfield, "Simple 'neural' optimization networks: An A/D converter, signal decision circuit, and a linear programming circuit," *IEEE Trans. on Circ. and Sys.*, Vol. CAS-33, pp. 533-541, 1986.

[4] J. J. Hopfield, "Neurons with graded response have collective computational capabilities like those of two-state neurons," *Proc. Nat. Acad. Sci. (U.S.A.)*, Vol. 81, pp. 3088-3092, 1984.

[5] M. W. Hirsch, "Convergence in neural nets," *Proc. Intl. Joint Conf. on Neural Networks*, Vol. II, pp. 115-125, 1987.

[6] F. M. A. Salam, Y-W Wang and M-R Choi, "On the analysis of dynamic feedback neural networks," *IEEE Trans. on Circ. and Sys.*, Vol. CAS-38, pp. 196-201, 1991.

[7] M. Vidyasagar, "Location and stability of the high-gain equilibria of nonlinear neural networks," *IEEE Transactions on Neural Networks*, (to appear).

[8] C. L. Masti and M. Vidyasagar, "A stochastic high-order connectionist network for solving inferencing problems," *Proc. Int. Joint. Conf. Neural Networks*, Singapore, pp. 911-916, Nov. 1991.

[9] J. Bruck and M. Blum, "Neural networks, error-correcting codes, and polynomials over the binary *n*-cube," *IEEE Trans. on Info. Thy.*, Vol. 35, No. 5, pp. 976-987, Sept. 1989.

[10] M. W. Hirsch and S. Smale, *Differential Equations, Dynamical Systems, and Linear Algebra*, Academic Press, New York, NY, 1974.

HOPF-LIKE BIFURCATION IN CELLULAR NEURAL NETWORKS

Fan Zou and Josef A. Nossek

Institute for Network Theory and Circuit Design
Technical University of Munich, Germany
e-mail: fazo@nws.e-technik.tu-muenchen.de

Abstract — **In this study bifurcation phenomena in cellular neural networks are investigated. In a two-cell autonomous system, Hopf-like bifurcation has been found, at which the flow around the origin, an equilibrium point of the system, changes from asymptotically stable to periodic. As the parameter grows further, by reaching another bifurcation value, the generated limit cycle disappears and the network becomes convergent again.**

1. INTRODUCTION

Cellular neural networks are complex nonlinear dynamical system. One can expect interesting phenomena ("bifurcations") and complex ("chaotic") dynamics to occur in such networks.

An important step in analyzing such dynamics is to recognize the topologically distinct types of behavior that can occur in the systems. This leads us to focus attention on those members of the family at which topological changes, or "bifurcations", are possible.

More precisely, let $F : \mathbb{R}^n \times \mathbb{R}^m \rightarrow \mathbb{R}^n$ be an m-parameter, C^r-family of vector fields on $\mathbb{R}^n$, i.e. $\dot{x} = F(x, \mu)$, $x \in \mathbb{R}^n$, $\mu \in \mathbb{R}^m$. The family F is said to have a *bifurcation point* at $\mu = \mu^*$ if, in every neighborhood of μ^*, there exist values of μ such that the corresponding vector fields $F(\cdot, \mu) = F_\mu(\cdot)$ exhibit topologically distinct behavior.

In this paper representative a small network only two cells is taken as objects for analyzing the bifurcation phenomena in the CNN.

We have discussed the stability of CNNs with opposite-sign templates in [8], where we have shown that as a parameter is changed to a critical value, a CNN with opposite-sign template may change from *stable* to *unstable*. This phenomenon, the loss of stability and the birth of a limit cycle occurs as a parameter passes through a critical value, is usually caused by a Hopf bifurcation, which is now widely used to model the sudden appearance of a limit cycle and consequent destabilization of an equilibrium point. We will give a thorough analysis of this type of bifurcation in a two-cell autonomous system in Section 3. We will also give a global bifurcation value, at which the system changes from periodic to convergent again.

These investigations are important for the proper design of CNNs, either excluding chaotic behavior or explicitely making use of it for generating special signals [1].

2. BIFURCATIONS IN CNN

Consider a cellular neural network described by the normalized system equation

$$\frac{dx(\tau)}{d\tau} = -x(\tau) + A\,y(\tau) + B\,u + i = F(x). \qquad (1)$$

The cell *state* vector x is produced by lining up every row of cell states in sequence (lexicographical order). The dimension of the vector is $M \cdot N$. For sake of convenience we set $n = M \cdot N$, then we have $x \in \mathbb{R}^n$. The relation x_k to v_{xij} can be given by

$$x_k = \frac{v_{xij}}{V_{sat}}, \qquad i = ((k-1)\,\mathrm{div}\,M) + 1,$$

$$\text{and} \quad j = ((k-1)\,\mathrm{mod}\,M) + 1$$

where V_{sat} is some reference voltage, e.g. the saturation voltage of the cell, div means here the integer division, and mod the modular division (it results the remainder of integer division). The *input* vector u and the *offset* of cells i are usually set to be constant.

The vector $y \in \mathbb{R}^n$ is the cell *output*, whose elements satisfy

$$y_k = f(x_k) = \frac{1}{2}(|x_k + 1| - |x_k - 1|), \quad 1 \le k \le n. \qquad (2)$$

A cellular neural network is said to be symmetric, if its feedback matrix A is symmetric, i.e. $A = A^T$.

Some constraints are also given as follows:

$$|x_k(0)| \le 1, \qquad |u_k| \le 1, \qquad \text{for} \quad 1 \le k \le n, \qquad (3)$$

and

$$a_{ii} > 1 \quad \text{for} \quad 1 \le i \le n. \qquad (4)$$

0-7803-1254-6/93$03.00 © 1993 IEEE

In the following we denote D_0 the linear region, D_s one of the 2^n saturation regions, and D_p one of the $3^n - 2^n - 1$ partial saturation regions.

One of the most powerful methods for studying periodic solutions in autonomous nonlinear systems is the theory which is based on a proof by Hopf. He showed that oscillations near an equilibrium point can be understood by looking at the eigenvalues of the linearized equations for perturbations from equilibrium [5]. Since then the Hopf bifurcation has been widely studied and has enjoyed considerable success in many applications [7],[6]. For convenience, the Hopf Bifurcation Theorem of planar vector field is outlined in the following without proof [2].

Theorem 1 (Hopf Bifurcation Theorem) : *Suppose the system $\dot{x} = F(x, \mu)$, $x \in \mathbb{R}^2$, $\mu \in \mathbf{R}$, has an equilibrium point at the origin for all values of the real parameter μ. Furthermore, suppose the eigenvalues, $\lambda_1(\mu)$ and $\lambda_2(\mu)$ of $J_0 = DF(0, \mu)$ are purely imaginary for $\mu = \mu^*$. If the real part of the eigenvalues, $\Re\{\lambda_1(\mu)\}$ $(= \Re\{\lambda_2(\mu)\})$, satisfies*

$$\frac{d}{d\mu}\left(\Re\{\lambda_1(\mu)\}\right)\bigg|_{\mu=\mu^*} > 0 \tag{5}$$

and the origin is an asymptotically stable equilibrium point for $\mu = \mu^*$ then :
(a) *$\mu = \mu^*$ is a bifurcation point of the system;*
(b) *for $\mu \in (\mu_1, \mu^*)$ some $\mu_1 < \mu^*$ the origin is a stable focus;*
(c) *for $\mu \in (\mu^*, \mu_2)$ some $\mu_2 > \mu^*$ the origin is an unstable focus surrounded by a stable limit cycle, whose size increases with μ.*

The Hopf bifurcation cannot take place in linear dynamical systems because of the nonexistence of limit cycle. Even the piece-wise linear vector field cannot cause a rigorous Hopf bifurcation, because with the pure imaginary eigenvalues at $\mu = \mu^*$ the equilibrium point is always a center and, therefore, cannot be asymptotically stable. Furthermore, in almost all proofs of the Theorem 1 the vector field $F(x, \mu)$ has been assumed to be C^k with $k \geq 4$. So any CNN cannot undergo a Hopf bifurcation in its rigorous sense. But in a generalized sense the Hopf bifurcation has become now a representative term for the sudden loss of stability with emergence of a limit cycle. In the following such a bifurcation in the two-cell CNN will be described, although it does not meet all conditions in the Theorem 1. Nevertheless the Hopf-like bifurcation in this small CNN will be rigorously proved. The bifurcation is related to the parameter of the cell self-feedback. As it changes from $1-\delta$ to $1+\delta$ $(\delta \geq 0)$ the origin, which is always an equilibrium point of the system, will change from being asymptotically stable to unstable. This is very similar with the Hopf bifurcation. Later we will show that as the cell self-feedback coefficient increases further and gets greater than some critical value the generated stable limit cycle will disappear and the network will become again convergent, even though the origin remains still a source before and after this second bifurcation.

A two-cell autonomous CNN with opposite-sign template can be described by

$$\begin{aligned} \dot{x}_1 &= -x_1 + pf(x_1) - sf(x_2) \\ \dot{x}_2 &= -x_2 + sf(x_1) + pf(x_2) \end{aligned} \tag{6}$$

where $p > 1$, and $s > 0$.

Let us recast this two-cell system defined above, in which we give up the condition that the self-feedback coefficients should be always greater than $+1$.

$$\begin{aligned} \dot{x}_1 = F_1(x_1, x_2, \mu) = -x_1 + (1+\mu)f(x_1) - sf(x_2) \\ \dot{x}_2 = F_2(x_1, x_2, \mu) = -x_2 + sf(x_1) + (1+\mu)f(x_2) \end{aligned} \tag{7}$$

where we assume that $p - 1 = \mu \in (-\Delta, \Delta)$ with $\Delta > 0$, and $s > 0$.

Obviously the system has always an equilibrium point at $x = \mathbf{0}$. The Jacobian matrix is given as

$$J_0 = DF(\mathbf{0}, \mu) = \begin{bmatrix} \mu & -s \\ +s & \mu \end{bmatrix} \tag{8}$$

For $\mu = \mu^* = 0$, it is clear that the system (7) almost meets all conditions of Theorem 1 except that the equilibrium point $x = \mathbf{0}$ is not asymptotically stable. In fact it is a center and it gives rise to undamped simple harmonic motion of period $2\pi/s$. So Theorem 1 cannot be applied directly. In order to show that in spite of its piece-wise linear vector field system (7) has a Hopf-like bifurcation at $\mu = \mu^* = 0$, we have the following theorem.

Theorem 2 : *For system defined in* (7)
(a) *$\mu = \mu^* = 0$ is a bifurcation point of the system;*
(b) *for $\mu \in (\mu_1, \mu^*)$ some $\mu_1 < \mu^*$ the origin is a stable focus;*
(c) *for $\mu \in (\mu^*, \mu_2)$ some $\mu^* < \mu_2 < s$ the origin is an unstable focus surrounded by a stable limit cycle.*

Proof: From (8) we have the eigenvalues of the system at the origin (and everywhere in D_0) $\lambda_{1,2} = \mu \pm js$, so if $\mu < 0$, the origin is a stable focus (spiral sink) and every trajectory starting in D_0 converges asymptotically into the origin.

If $\mu > 0$, the origin becomes an unstable focus (spiral source). But if $\mu < s$ holds, then $s > p - 1$, from Theorem 1 in [8] we know that the system has no stable equilibrium point. After a check for the four partial saturation regions, we know that there is also no equilibrium point in them, thus the origin is in fact the unique equilibrium point of the system. According to Poincaré-Bendixson Theorem [4], there must be at least one stable limit cycle Γ, and there must be at least one equilibrium point in the region bounded by Γ. Now we have proved (c).

After (b) and (c) have been proved, (a) follows immediately. Obviously there is a substantial change of the phase portrait at $\mu = \mu^* = 0$. □

Remark 1: In the proof of (b) only the local convergence property of the equilibrium has been discussed. What about the global convergence property? We can claim that if $\mu < 0$ then the system is convergent and cannot possess any limit cycle. To show this is true, we need the Bendixson's Negative Criterion, which can be formulated as follows:

Theorem 3 (Bendixson's Negative Criterion) : *Suppose that the divergence* $\text{div}\boldsymbol{F} = \partial F_1/x_1 + \partial F_2/x_2$ *of the vector field of* (7) *has a fixed sign in a simply connected region* V. *Then* (7) *has no limit cycle that lies entirely in* V.

We can calculate the $\text{div}\boldsymbol{F} = \partial F_1/x_1 + \partial F_2/x_2$ in each of the nine regions. For $\mu < 0$, we have in D_0: $\text{div}\boldsymbol{F} = 2\mu < 0$; in every D_s: $\text{div}\boldsymbol{F} = -2 < 0$; in every D_p: $\text{div}\boldsymbol{F} = \mu - 1 < 0$. So in the total region of $\mathbb{R}^2$, the divergence is always negative. It follows that there is no limit cycle possible.

Remark 2: This bifurcation of two-cell CNN has many similar features with the Hopf bifurcation, even the features about size and period of the limit cycle, which is not included in the above theorem because of its cumbersome proof, are almost identical.

From the theory of the Hopf bifurcation we know that the amplitude of the limit cycle increases proportionally with $|\mu - \mu^*|^{1/2}$ (In our case, $r \approx |1 + \mu - \mu^*|^{1/2}$). On the other hand, the states of a CNN are bounded. As the size of the limit cycle can not increase infinitely, one may ask, after the system bifurcates at $\mu = \mu^* = 0$, how large can μ grow without a change of topologically distinct behavior? To answer this question we have the following theorem.

Theorem 4 : *For the system defined in* (7)
(a) $\mu = \mu^* = s$ *is a bifurcation point of the system;*
(b) *for* $\mu \in (\mu_1, \mu^*)$ *with* $0 < \mu_1 < \mu^*$ *there is a stable limit cycle surrounding the origin;*
(c) *for* $\mu \in (\mu^*, \mu_2)$ *with* $\mu_2 > \mu^*$ *although the origin is an unstable focus the network is completely stable (convergent).*

For the case $\mu > s$, we have in each of nine subspaces one equilibrium. Fig. 1 shows an example of the position of them in the phase plane.

More precisely, the nine equilibria can be given as follows: in D_0 : the origin $(0,0)$; in four D_s's: they are $(p-s, p+s)$, $(p+s, -p+s)$, $(-p+s, -p-s)$, $(-p-s, p+s)$; and in four D_p's: they are $(p+\frac{s^2}{p-1}, \frac{-s}{p-1})$, $(\frac{-s}{p-1}, -p-\frac{s^2}{p-1})$, $(-p-\frac{s^2}{p-1}, \frac{s}{p-1})$, and $(\frac{s}{p-1}, p+\frac{s^2}{p-1})$.

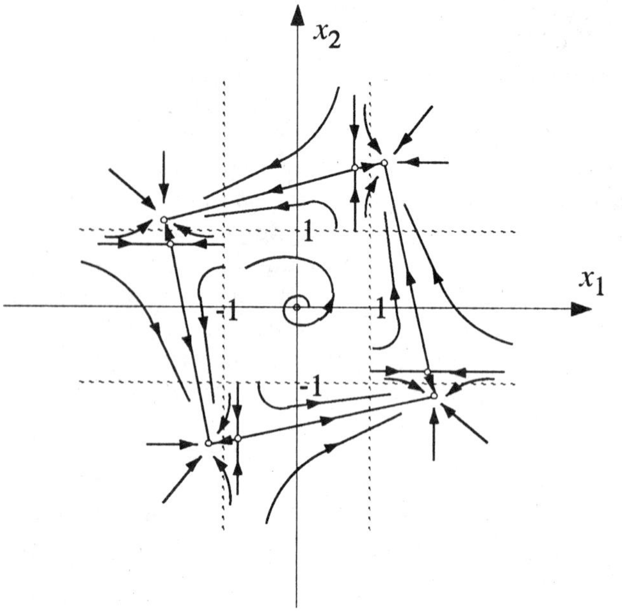

Figure 1: The equilibria and the vector field of the two-cell autonomous system with $\mu > s$. Where $\mu = 0.5$, $s = 0.4$

We may notice that each of the equilibria in D_p's has one stable eigenspace and one unstable eigenspace. For example, the equilibrium $(\bar{x}_1, \bar{x}_2) = (p + \frac{s^2}{p-1}, \frac{-s}{p-1})$ has the stable eigenspace $x_1 - \bar{x}_1 = 0$ and the unstable eigenspace $\frac{x_1 - \bar{x}_1}{p} = \frac{x_2 - \bar{x}_2}{s}$. Based on this knowledge, the corresponding vector field of the example two-cell system is also depicted in the Fig. 1.

Now we can start to prove the Theorem 4.

Proof: The statement (b) is true because of (c) of Theorem 2. We need only to prove (c). After this (a) is obvious.

The proof of (c) can can be carried out in the same way like the proof of Theorem 2 in [8]. First, every trajectory in D_0 will exit the region and never return. Second, every trajectory in any D_p will also inevitably exceed the region and arrive at a neighboring D_s. Because there is an equilibrium point in each of D_s's, and every trajectory entering a D_s will be attracted to the corresponding equilibrium point. Hence, all trajectories starting anywhere except some points of measure zero will converge to one of four stable equilibria, the steady state of the network is stable. This completes the proof. □

Remark 3: While Theorem 2 deals with the local bifurcation, Theorem 4 has treated a problem of global bifurcation. The local dynamics around the origin is not changed before and after this global bifurcation, (the origin remains to be a spiral source).

Remark 4: If $\mu = s$, there are totally five equilibria. One is the origin, other four are located on the border of partial saturation regions and saturation regions. They are $(1, 1+2s)$, $(1+2s, -1)$, $(-1, -1-2s)$ and $(-1-2s, 1)$. We can also observe heteroclinic orbits connecting these four unstable equilibria.

Another way to treat the Hopf bifurcation in CNN is to approximate the piece-wise linear output function by a continuous differentiable function. A reasonable approximation for $f(\cdot)$ is the sigmoid function with the gain parameter $\lambda = 2$, i.e.

$$g(x_i) = \frac{1 - e^{-2x_i}}{1 + e^{-2x_i}} = \tanh(x_i) \quad \text{for} \quad 1 \leq i \leq 2. \tag{9}$$

Under this approximation the system equation of the two-cell network (7) can be expanded to the following normal form by using Taylor's formula:

$$\begin{aligned} \dot{x}_1 &= \mu x_1 - s x_2 + \frac{1}{2} F^1_{11} x_1^2 + F^1_{12} x_1 x_2 \\ &+ \frac{1}{2} F^1_{22} x_2^2 + \frac{1}{6} F^1_{111} x_1^3 + \frac{1}{2} F^1_{112} x_1^2 x_2 \\ &+ \frac{1}{2} F^1_{122} x_1 x_2^2 + \frac{1}{6} F^1_{222} x_2^3 + O(||x||^4) \\ \dot{x}_2 &= s x_1 + \mu x_2 + \frac{1}{2} F^2_{11} x_1^2 + F^2_{12} x_1 x_2 \\ &+ \frac{1}{2} F^2_{22} x_2^2 + \frac{1}{6} F^2_{111} x_1^3 + \frac{1}{2} F^2_{112} x_1^2 x_2 \\ &+ \frac{1}{2} F^2_{122} x_1 x_2^2 + \frac{1}{6} F^2_{222} x_2^3 + O(||x||^4) \end{aligned} \tag{10}$$

where

$$\begin{aligned} F_1(x_1, x_2, \mu) &= -x_1 + (1+\mu) g(x_1) - s g(x_2) \\ F_2(x_1, x_2, \mu) &= -x_2 + s g(x_1) + (1+\mu) g(x_2) \end{aligned}$$

and

$$F^i_{pq} \triangleq \left. \frac{\partial^2 F_i}{\partial x_p \partial x_q} \right|_{x=0} \quad \text{and} \quad F^i_{pqr} \triangleq \left. \frac{\partial^3 F_i}{\partial x_p \partial x_q \partial x_r} \right|_{x=0}. \tag{11}$$

This system satisfies all conditions of Theorem 1. But to prove the origin is asymptotically stable at $\mu = \mu^* = 0$ is not a trivial task. One simple method is due to Mees and Chua [7]. They have shown that in order to check whether (10) has a *supercritical* Hopf bifurcation at $\mu = 0$, we need only to check whether the following quantity is negative:

$$\begin{aligned} \sigma_0 &= \frac{1}{16s} \{ F^1_{11}(F^2_{11} - F^1_{12}) + F^2_{22}(F^2_{12} - F^1_{22}) \\ &+ (F^2_{11} F^2_{12} - F^1_{12} F^1_{22}) \} \\ &+ \frac{1}{16}(F^1_{111} + F^1_{122} + F^2_{112} + F^2_{222}). \end{aligned}$$

If we set the Taylor expansion $g(x_i) = \tanh(x_i) = x_i - \frac{x_i^3}{3} + O(||x_i||^5)$ into the equation (10), we get a $\sigma_0 = -0.25 < 0$. So the system (10) has a supercritical Hopf bifurcation at $\mu = \mu^* = 0$. The word *supercritical* means here a normal Hopf bifurcation as defined in Theorem 1. There is another degenerate case ($\sigma_0 > 0$), where the equilibrium point (the origin) is unstable at $\mu = \mu^* = 0$. It is referred to as a *subcritical* Hopf bifurcation.

3. CONCLUSION

We have presented some bifurcation phenomena in cellular neural networks. For the analysis of these complex dynamics we introduced a few very useful theorems, which deal with the stability properties of equilibrium points in a cellular neural network. There seem to be very rich dynamical behavior even in small-sized networks. It is important to gain an extensive knowledge about these dynamics. For example, the Hopf-like bifurcation in the two-cell autonomous system can be used to generate almost harmonic oscillatory signals.

4. REFERENCES

[1] Y. Andreyev, Y. Belsky, A. Dimitriev and D. Kuminov, "Inhomogeneous Cellular Neural Networks: Possibility of Functional Device Design", Proceeding of CNNA' 92, Munich, 1992

[2] D. K. Arrowsmith, and C. M. Place, *Dynamical Systems*, Cambridge University Press, Cambridge, 1990

[3] L. O. Chua and L. Yang, "Cellular Neural Networks: Theory", IEEE Trans. CAS, vol. 35, No.10, pp 1257-1272, Oct.1988.

[4] M. W. Hirsch and S. Smale, *Differential Equations, Dynamical Systems, and Linear Algebra*, Academic Press, San Diege, 1974

[5] E. Hopf, "Bifurcation of a periodic solution from a stationary solution of a system of differential equations", *Berichten der Mathematischen Physikalischen Klasse der Saechsischen Akademie der Wissenschaften*, (Leipzig, Germany), vol.XCIV, pp. 3-22, 1942.

[6] J. Marsden, and M. McCracken, *The Hopf Bifurcation and its Applications* (Appl. Math. Sci.), vol. 19, New York, Springer Verlag, 1976

[7] A. I. Mees, and L. O. Chua, "The Hopf Bifurcation Theorem and Its Applications to Nonlinear Oscillations in Circuits and Systems", IEEE Trans. CAS, vol. CAS-26, No. 4, pp. 235-254, April, 1979

[8] F. Zou and J. A. Nossek, "Stability of Cellular Neural Networks with Opposite-Sign Templates", IEEE Trans. on CAS, vol. 37, June, 1991

A METHOD FOR TRAINING FEED FORWARD NEURAL NETWORK TO BE FAULT TOLERANT

H. Elsimary*, S. Mashali*, S. Shaheen**
* Electronincs Research Inst., Cairo, Egypt
** Faculty of Engineering,Cairo University, Cairo, Egypt
Email : Hamed@EGFRCUVX.Bitnet

Abstract

This paper describes a method for training feed forward neural network to be fault tolerant against the weight perturbation. Our measure for fault tolerance is the deviation of the network's output after training, when each interconnection weight is perturbed, from that output without perturbation. In our method we try to maintain that deviation as minimum as possible. We have used this measure because it can represent that kind of error arises when neural networks are implemented in hardware.

Introduction

As Artificial Neural Networks (ANNs) has shown great performance in many fields, and has shown its abilities in solving problems difficult to be solved by conventional methods of computation, as it is continually progressing and its application is wide spreading, it is important to study and insure the reliability of its function under different working conditions.

One of the advantages of ANNs is that the processing is distributed among many nodes, this provides a good degree of fault tolerance and graceful degradation to the system even if some of its nodes or interconnection fails to function properly. But this features needs to be emphasized, improved, and maximized through different techniques. Many researches has been done to study, analyze, and improve the fault tolerance of ANNs in the functional level, but little however have not been adreesed that fault related to the hardware implementation [2]. There are many reliability modeling and improvement techniques exist for conventional computers, these models are developed to predict the reliability and fault tolerance characteristics of each functional block of the system such as redundancy and self checking. But the issue is different in ANNs than that of conventional computer architecture, therefore a different approach is required. In this work we will introduce a method for Improving the fault tolerance of ANNs, in the form of a feed forward model, since the feed forward model with the very famous backpropagation algorithm has become very popular and has been used in different engineering applications [3]. We have used a suitable definition and criteria for fault tolerance measurement that can deal with faults that arise when the ANNs implemented in hardware [4,5], and by using this measure an algorithm for training the ANN subject maximizes the fault tolerance has been developed.

Modeling faults in ANNs

Taking into considerations the hardware implementation of ANNs, whether this implementation is analog or digital [4,5] with limited numerical precision [6,7], we should have a model that can deal with faults that comes from each way of implementation.

0-7803-1363-1/93 $3.00 © 1993 IEEE

specific number of iterations, and in fig (3b) represents the percentage deviation of the network's output when the particular weight or threshold is perturbed by a value of +/- ΔW (in this case ΔW=10%). for example the number in the connection from the first unit 3 in the hidden layer to the unit 5 in the output layer, means that the output will be changed by a factor of 47% if this interconnection weight is perturbed by ΔW and averaged all over the training exemplars. The average network sensitivity to the weight perturbation is 35 in this case.

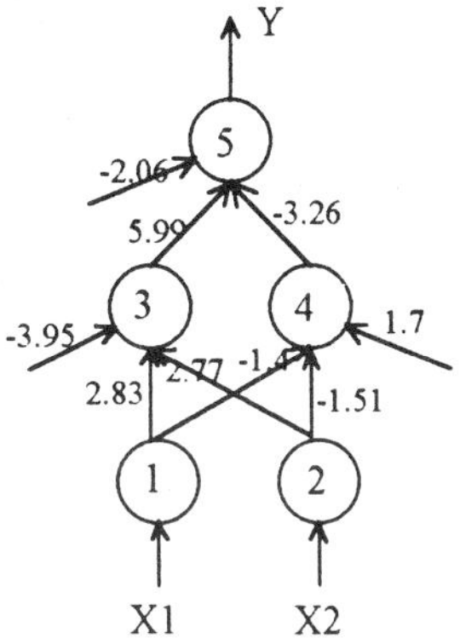

Fig(4a)

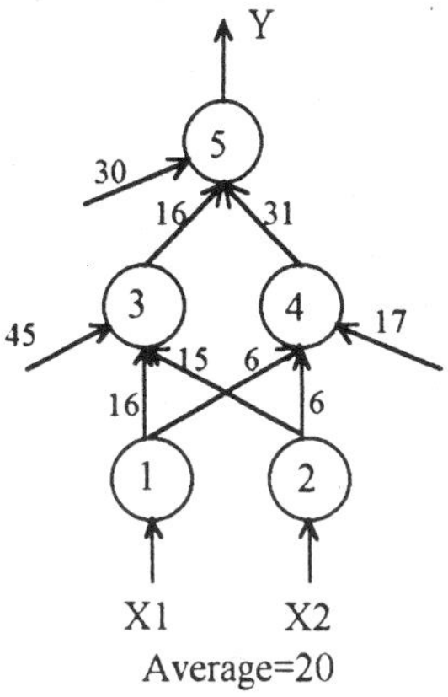

Fig(4b)

On the other hand the network of fig(4) has been trained with initial weight set W2 (not shown also) which leads to a final state shown in fig(4a), the percentage output change when each individual weight or threshold is perturbed by Δw is shown in fig(4b) the average fault tolerance figure has been improved but we don't know yet whether this is the optimum or not, so the main concern right now is to find the optimum weight set that maximizes the fault tolerance. the following example will explain in more details the idea of the fault tolerance improvement.

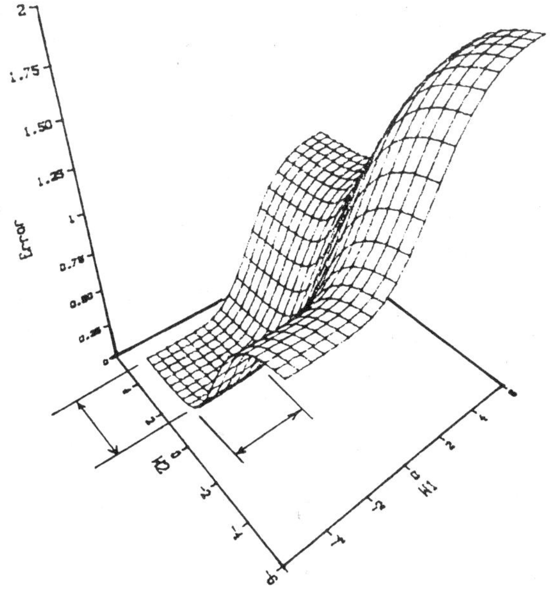

Fig (5a)

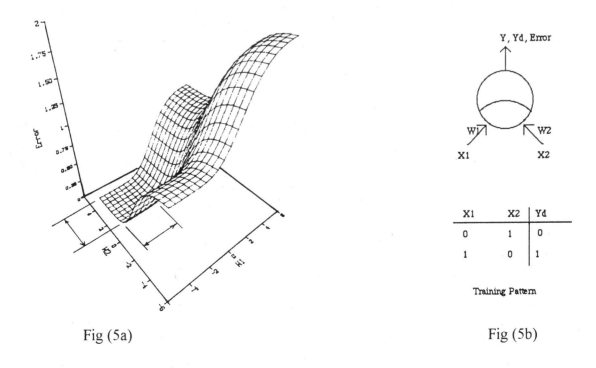

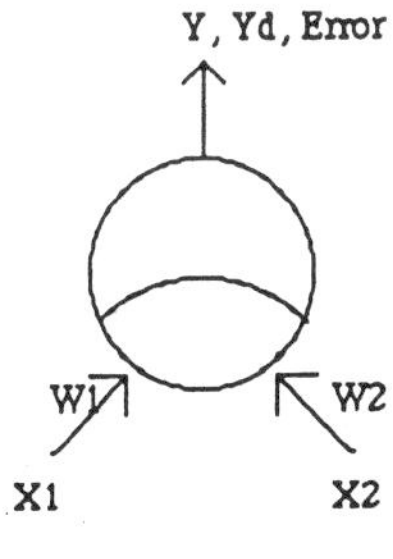

X1	X2	Yd
0	1	0
1	0	1

Training Pattern

Fig (5b)

A single neuron is being trained using them training pattern shown in fig(5b), the output of the neuron is determined by the equation:

$$Y = \frac{1}{1+e^{-Net}} \quad ; \text{Where } Net = \sum w_i x_i$$

And resulting Error over all the training patterns is determined by:

$$E = 1/T \sum (Y - Y_d)^2 \quad ; \text{Where T is the number of training patterns}$$

This example has been considered for the sake of the ability to imagine and draw the error as a function of weight vector. The error surface in our example as a function of w1, and w2 is shown in fig (5a). The objective of any training algorithm is to find the point that minimizes the error function, in this specific case there are many points that can achieve minimum error as shown in the marked region in fig (5b). Selecting one of these points is the role of our algorithm, among these points there is one that can improve the fault tolerance characteristics of the neuron, i.e., decreases its sensitivity to the weight perturbation.

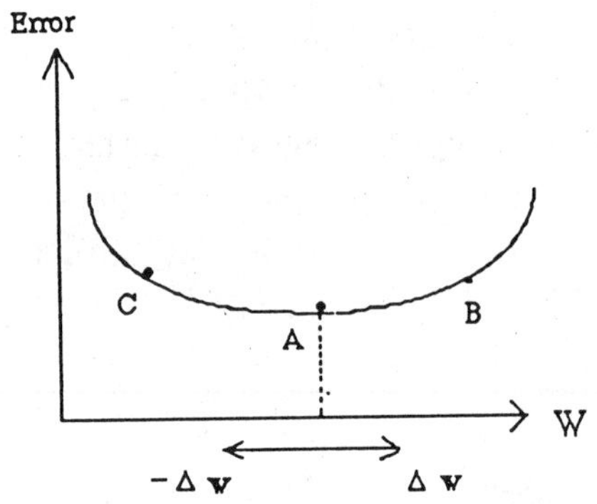

Fig (6a)

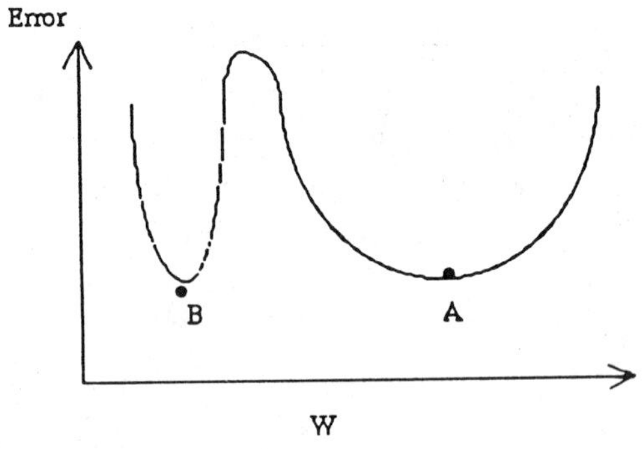

Fig (6b)

As shown in fig (6a), point A is considered better than point B or C in the sense of fault tolerance, as the resulting error will not be much affected if the weight is perturbed by ΔW. Also there may be, in other cases, many minima but one of them may be better than the other in the sense of fault tolerance, as shown if fig (6b) point A is considered better than point B for the same reason. In multidimensional surfaces where the number of variables is more than two, it will be difficult to imagine or draw the error surface, but there may be many minima, where one of them could be better than the other in the sense of our measure of the fault tolerance.

From previous discussion we have shown that the same network can have different fault tolerance characteristics if with different initial conditions, this will lead us to develop an algorithm for training the ANN not only to minimize the output error but also to maximize the fault tolerance capability. We did not discuss in the previous discussion whether the output change will affect the desired output values or not, so we will come to a formal definition of the problem for fault tolerance maximization that will be discussed in the following section.

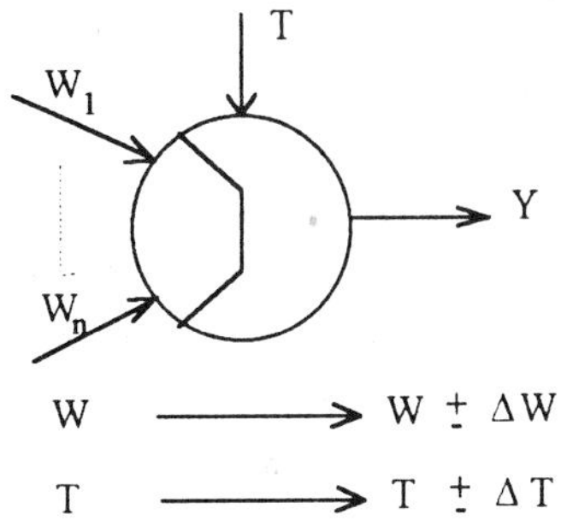

Fig(1)

A possible method to model the faults for ANNs could be the deviation from the original if the interconnection weights and threshold values have been perturbed after the network has been trained. Roughly speaking the ANN should still give correct or at least near correct results even with the existence of fault, the interconnection weight is being perturbed by an amount +/- ΔW as shown in figure (1), this will be illustrated by an example.

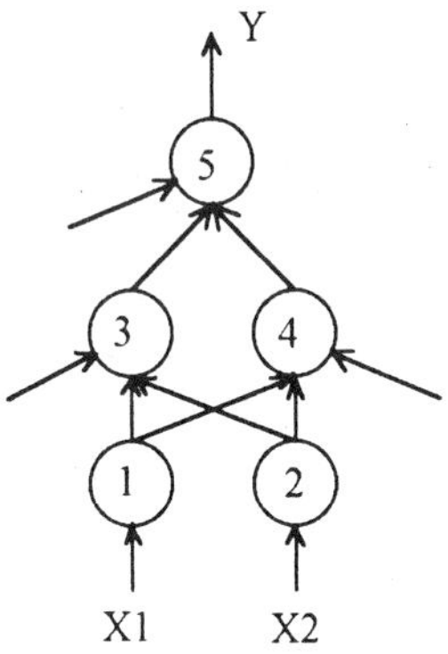

X1	X2	Yd
0	0	0
0	1	0
1	0	0
1	1	1

Training Pattern

Fig (2)

Consider the ANN of fig (2) trained to simulate the logic AND function. It has been noticed that when the network is trained with the same algorithm (Backward Error Propagation), but starting from different initial weight set and allowed to train until certain error limit, it will settle down at different final states that leads to different fault tolerance degrees.

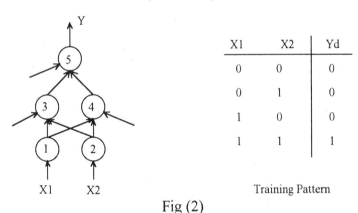

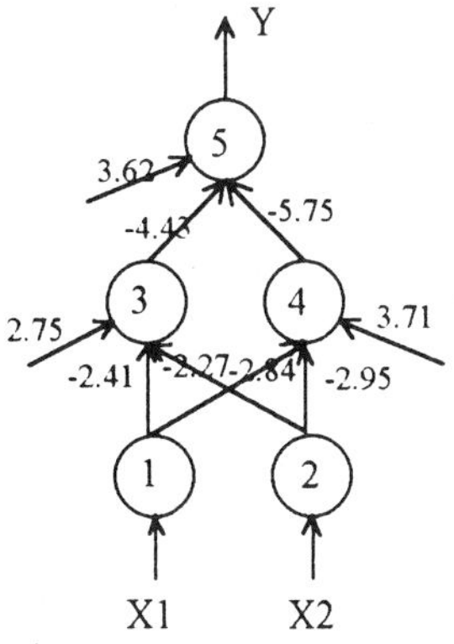

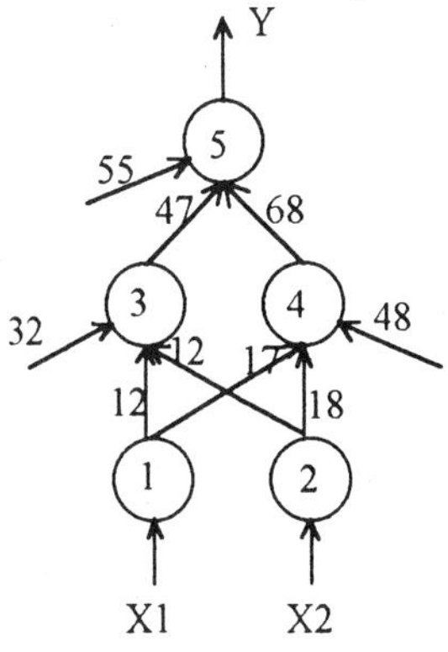

Average=35

Fig(3a) Fig(3b)

For example the final state of a network trained at initial weight set W1(only the final state is shown) shown in fig (3a, 3b), each number in fig(3a) represents the weight values after a

Problem Definition and Solution Approach

The problem we are addressing is to find the weight matrix for a fully connected network, each neuron has a sigmoid transfer characteristics that will minimize the total error and lead to a better fault tolerance characteristics. In our definition to the fault tolerance, the network should still give correct or near correct result even with the interconnection weights are perturbed with $+/-\Delta W$.

ANN is fault tolerant if the computations performed by N', which is a network derived from N by perturbing the interconnection weights by $+/-\Delta W$ is close to the computations performed by N.

E(W) ; Error function, deviation of the actual output of network N from the desired

E'(W') ; Error function of network N' with weight matrix W' Error is being computed for single weight perturbation and averaged all over the interconnection weight

The problem will be formulated as :

$$\min_{w} E(W)$$

subject to : $E'(W')-E(W) < \varepsilon$ where ε is a relatively small number

This a nonlinear optimization problem with multivariants and nonlinear constraints. The problem has been solved using a standard subroutine from the math library which uses successive quadratic programming and finite difference method for solving such optimization problems [8]. Simulation result for training a network to map the logical 'AND' function will be shown next. The training program has been allowed to search for the optimum weight matrix that minimizes the total error subject to be fault tolerant against perturbation in the interconnection weights of +/- 10%, and allowed to search for the weight values in the range -10 to 10, and allowed for a maximum error deviation of 0.000005, the results are summarized as follows:

ε : 0.00005

Perturbation : 10%

Weight matrix:

T3	W31	w32	T4	w41	w41	T5	w53	w54
-0.43	-9.58	3.25	8.92	-4.34	-9.63	4.90	-9.63	-9.96

This means that this network will withstand to a weight change up to 10% with maximum deviation from the actual output of 0.00005.

Conclusion

It has been shown that the same network has different fault tolerance characteristics depends on the way the network is trained. We has used a suitable fault model that can deal with faults that arises with hardware implementation. We have used this fault model to develop a training method for the ANNs to improve its fault tolerance capabilities and demonstrated by examples.

References:

[1] Eva Koscienly-Bunde, "Effect of Damage in Neural Networks", Journal of statistical Phys., Vol. 58, Mar. 1990.

[2] R. K. Chun, L. P. McNamee, "Immunization of Neural Networks Against Hardware Faults", IEEE Int International Symposium on Circuits and Systems, vol 1 pp. 714-718, 1990.

[3] James L. McClelland, and David E. Rumelhart, "Exploration in Parallel Distributed Processing", MIT Press 1988.

[4] Carver Mead, "Analog VLSI and Neural Systems", Addison Wesley, 1989.

[5] Ulrich Ramucher, Ulrich Ruckert, "VLSI Design of Neural Networks", Kluwer Academic Publisher, 1991.

[6] Markus Hoefeld and Scott E. Fahlman, "Learning with limited Numerical Precision Using the ascade-Correlation Algorithm", IEEE Trans. on Neural Networks, Vol. 3, No. 4, pp. 602-611, July 1992.

[7] P.W. Hollis, J.S. Harper, and J.J. Paulos, "The effect of Precision Constraints in Backpropagation learning network", Neural Computation, vol. 2, pp. 363-373, 1990.

[8] Schittkowski, K. , "Nonlinear Programming Codes, Lecture Notes in Economics and mathematical Systems", Springer-Verlag, Berlin, Germany, 1980.

Robustness of Feedforward Neural Networks*

Ching-Tai Chiu, Kishan Mehrotra, Chilukuri K. Mohan, and Sanjay Ranka†
4-116 CST, School of Computer and Information Science
Syracuse University, Syracuse, New York 13244-4100
315-443-2368, *email: cchiu/kishan/mohan/ranka@top.cis.syr.edu*

Abstract— **Many artificial neural networks in practical use can be demonstrated not to be fault tolerant; this can result in disasters when localized errors occur in critical parts of these networks. In this paper, we develop methods for measuring the sensitivity of links and nodes of a feedforward neural network and implement a technique to ensure the development of neural networks that satisfy well-defined robustness criteria. Experimental observations indicate that performance degradation in our robust feedforward network is significantly less than a randomly trained feedforward network of the same size by an order of magnitude.**

I. INTRODUCTION

Artificial neural network applications with no built-in or proven fault tolerance can be disastrously handicapped by localized errors in critical parts. Many researchers have assumed that neural networks that contain a large number of nodes and links are fault tolerant. This assumption is unfounded because networks are often trained using algorithms whose only goal is to minimize error. Classical neural learning algorithms such as backpropagation make no attempt to develop fault tolerant neural networks. The existence of redundant resources is only a precondition and does not ensure robustness. Little research has focused explicitly on increasing the fault tolerance of commonly used neural network models of non-trivial size, although the importance of this problem has been recognized [2, 3, 6, 9].

In this paper, we propose techniques to ensure the development of feedforward neural networks [7] that satisfy well-defined robustness criteria. Faults occurring in the training phase may increase training time but are unlikely to affect the performance of the system, because training will continue until faulty components are compensated for by non-faulty parts. If faults are detected in the testing phase, retraining with the addition of new resources can solve the problem. Such a repair would not be possible after system development is complete or if faults occur in a neural network application that has already been installed and is in use. This necessitates robust design of neural networks, for graceful degradation in performance without the need to retrain networks.

Different evaluation measures may be needed for neural networks intended to perform different tasks. Karnin [4] suggests the use of a sensitivity index to determine the extent to which the performance of a neural network depends on a given node or link in the system; for a given failure, Carter et al. [3] measure network performance in terms of the error in function approximation; and Stevenson et al. [8] estimate the probability that an output neuron makes a decision error, for "Madalines" (with discrete inputs).

Our methodology can be briefly summarized as follows. Given a well-trained network, we first eliminate all "useless" nodes in hidden layer(s). We retrain this reduced network, and then add some redundant nodes to the reduced network in a systematic manner, achieving robustness against changes in weights of links that may occur over a period of time.

In Section II, we describe our terminology and measures of robustness. Methods to achieve a robust network are described in Section III. Section IV contains experimental results, and conclusions are discussed in the final section.

*This research was supported by AFOSR contract F30602-92-C-0031.

†Supported in part by NSF Grant CCR-9110812.

II. Definitions

We consider feedforward $I-H-O$ neural networks, with I input nodes, H nodes in one hidden layer, and O output nodes. The vector of all weights (of the trained network) is denoted by $W=(w_1,\ldots,w_K)$. If the ith component of W is modified by a factor α (i.e., w_i is changed to $(1+\alpha)w_i$) and all other components remain fixed, then the new vector of weights is denoted by $W(i,\alpha)=(w_1,\ldots,(1+\alpha)w_i,\ldots,w_K)$. For a given weight vector W, $E(W)$ denotes the mean square error of the network over the training set, and $E_R(W)$ denote the mean square error over the test set R. The effect on MSE of changing W to $W(i,\alpha)$ is measured in terms of the difference

$$s(i,\alpha)=E(W(i,\alpha))-E(W) \qquad (1)$$

or in terms of the partial derivative of MSE with respect to the magnitude of weight change

$$\hat{s}(i,\alpha)=\frac{E(W(i,\alpha))-E(W)}{|w_i\times\alpha|}. \qquad (2)$$

If $E(W(i,\alpha))<E(W)$, then a better set of weights must have been accidentally obtained by perturbing W, and retraining can occur for $W(i,\alpha)$. The relative change, α, is allowed to take values from a nonempty finite set A containing values in the range -1 to 1.

Definition 1 Link sensitivity: *Two possible definitions for the sensitivity of the ith link ℓ_i are:*

$$S_\ell(i)=\frac{1}{|A|}\sum_{\alpha\in A}s(i,\alpha) \qquad (3)$$

$$\hat{S}_\ell(i)=\frac{1}{|A|}\sum_{\alpha\in A}\hat{s}(i,\alpha). \qquad (4)$$

To compute the sensitivity of each link in a network, all weights of the trained network are frozen except the link that is being perturbed with a fault. $E(W)$ is already known and $E(W(i,\alpha))$ can easily be obtained in one feedforward computation with faulty links.

Definition 2 Node sensitivity: *Let $\mathcal{I}_I(j)$ denote the set of all incoming links incident on the jth hidden node, n_j, from the input nodes; let $\mathcal{I}_O(j)$ denote the set of outgoing links from n_j, and let $\mathcal{I}(j)=\mathcal{I}_I(j)\cup\mathcal{I}_O(j)$. Two definitions are possible for node sensitivity:*

(i) A-sensitivity (average sensitivity) of a node, n_j, is

$$S_n(j)=\frac{1}{|\mathcal{I}(j)|}\sum_{i\in\mathcal{I}(j)}S_\ell(i). \qquad (5)$$

$$\hat{S}_n(j)=\frac{1}{|\mathcal{I}(j)|}\sum_{i\in\mathcal{I}(j)}\hat{S}_\ell(i). \qquad (6)$$

(ii) M-sensitivity (maximal sensitivity) of a node, n_j, is

$$S_n^*(j)=\max_{i\in\mathcal{I}(j)}S_\ell(i). \qquad (7)$$

$$\hat{S}_n^*(j)=\max_{i\in\mathcal{I}(j)}\hat{S}_\ell(i). \qquad (8)$$

Definition 3 *The sensitivity S_N of a network N is $\max_{j\in\mathrm{HL(N)}}\{S_n(j)\}$, where $HL(N)$ is the set of hidden layer nodes in N.*

III. Addition/Deletion Procedure

In this section, we present a procedure (Figure 1) to build robust neural networks that withstand individual link weight changes: we eliminate unimportant nodes, retrain the reduced network, then add redundant nodes. These three steps are repeated until the desired robustness is achieved.

A. Elimination of Unimportant Nodes

In practice, many of the nodes in a large network serve no useful purpose, and traditional network training algorithms do not ensure that redundant nodes improve fault tolerance. Once a network has been trained, the importance of each hidden layer node can be measured in terms of its sensitivity. Given a reference sensitivity ϵ, node n_j is removed from the hidden layer if $S_n(j)\le\epsilon$. The value of ϵ can be adjusted such that elimination of all such nodes makes little difference in the performance of the reduced network compared to the original network. In our experiments, we have used $\epsilon=10\%$ of the maximum node sensitivity. The deletion of 'unimportant' nodes (with a small sensitivity) results in an I-H^*-O network that should perform almost as well as the original network. We have observed that H^* is sometimes considerably smaller than H.

Let $\mathcal{TR}$ be the training set and $\mathcal{TS}$ be the test set. Obtain a well-trained weight vector $\mathcal{W}_0$ by training an I-H-O network $\mathcal{N}_0$ on $\mathcal{TR}$.

$i = 0$, and $H^* = H$.
while *terminating-criterion* is unsatisfied **do**
  $\varepsilon = S_N(\mathcal{N}_i) \times 0.1$
  $\mathcal{N}_{i+1} = \mathcal{N}_i - \{n_j | S_n(n_j) < \varepsilon\}$
  $\mathcal{W}_{i+1} = \mathcal{W}_i -$ {all links connected to n_j}
  Retrain the network $\mathcal{N}_{i+1}$.
  $H^* = H^* + 1$
  $\mathcal{N}_{i+1} = \mathcal{N}_i \cup \{n_{H^*}\}$
  $\mathcal{W}_{i+1} =$ Setting the weights of links incident on the new node n_{H^*}, and modifying those connected to the most sensitive node in $\mathcal{N}_i$.
  $i = i + 1$
end while

Figure 1: Addition/Deletion procedure for improved fault tolerance. The *terminating-criterion* is described in section III-C. $S_N(\mathcal{N}_i)$ is the worst case node sensitivity of the network $\mathcal{N}_i$. The procedure for updating the second $\mathcal{W}_{i+1}$ is described in section III-C.

B. Retraining of Reduced Network

Removal of unimportant nodes from the network is expected to make little difference in the resulting MSE. But the MSE of the resulting network with fewer weights may not be in a (local) minimum. In general, if $(x_1, ..., x_n)$ is a local minimum of a function $f^{(n)}$ of n arguments, there is no guarantee that $(x_1, ..., x_{n-i})$ is a local minimum of a function $f^{(n-i)}$ defined as $f^{(n-i)}(x_1, ..., x_{n-i}) \equiv f^{(n)}(x_1, ..., x_{n-i}, 0, ..., 0)$. For our problem, $f^{(n)}$ and $f^{(n-i)}$ are the MSE functions over networks of differing sizes, where the smaller one is obtained by eliminating some parameters of the larger network.

Retraining the reduced network will change the MSE to a (local) minimum. In our experiments, we have observed that the number of iterations needed to retrain the network to achieve the previous level of MSE is usually small (< 10 in most cases).

C. Addition of Redundant Nodes

To enhance robustness, our method is to add extra hidden nodes, in such a way that they share the tasks of the critical nodes—nodes with "high" sensitivity.

Let $w_{i,k}$ denote the weight from the kth input node to the ith hidden layer node, and let $v_{i,k}$ denote the weight from the kth hidden node to the ith output node. Let the jth hidden node have the highest sensitivity, in a I-H^*-O network. Let $h = H^*$. Then the new network is obtained by adding an extra $(h+1)^{th}$ hidden node. The duties of the sensitive node are now shared with this new node. This is achieved by setting up the weights on the new node's links as defined by:

(1) First layer of weights: $w_{h+1,i} = w_{j,i}, \forall i \in I$, {the new node has the same output as the jth node}

(2) Second layer of weights: $v_{k,h+1} = \frac{1}{2} v_{k,j}, \forall k \in O$, {sharing the load of the jth node}

(3) Halving the sensitive node's outgoing link weights $v_{k,j}, \forall k \in O$.

In other words, the first condition guarantees that the outputs of hidden layer nodes n_j and n_{H^*+1} are identical, whereas the second condition ensures that the importance of these two nodes is equal, without changing the network outputs.

After adding the node n_{H^*+1}, node sensitivities are re-evaluated and another node, n_{H^*+2}, is added if the sensitivity of a node is found to be 'too' large. On the other hand, a node is removed if its sensitivity is 'too' low. Our primary criteria for sensitivity of a link and a node are equations (3) and (7). In our experiments, we have found that there is not much difference in the results obtained using the other definitions of sensitivity. A node is deleted if its sensitivity is less than 10% of the sensitivity of the most critical node.

We continue to add nodes until the termination criterion is satisfied, i.e., the improvement in the network's robustness is negligible. We have experimented with two termination criteria. The first criterion is adding extra nodes until the sensitivity of the current most critical node is less than some proportion of the sensitivity of the initial most critical node. The second criterion is adding extra nodes until the number of nodes is equal to the original number of nodes, in order to compare two networks of the same size.

Notation: Let $E(N_{mn}^{\alpha})$ denote the error obtained when the link weight ν_{mn} in the network N is replaced by $(1+\alpha)\nu_{mn}$. Similarly, let $E(N_k^{\alpha})$ denote the average error obtained when each of the link weights ν_{mk} in the network N is replaced by $(1+\alpha)\nu_{mk}$. Note that ν_{ij} denotes the weight on the link from the jth hidden node to the ith output node.

Theorem: Let N be a well-trained[1] I-h-O network in which link ν_{ij} is more sensitive than every other link in the second (ν) layer, where sensitivity is defined as the additional error resulting from perturbation of any ν_{mn} to $(1+\alpha)\nu_{mn}$, for some α (i.e., with the singleton perturbation set $A = \{\alpha\}$) such that these perturbations degrade performance, (i.e., the error $E(N) < \max_{m,n}\{E(N_{mn}^{\alpha})\}$. Let M be the network obtained by adding a redundant $(h+1)^{st}$ hidden node to M and adjusting weights of links attached to this new node and to the jth hidden node, as specified in the addition/deletion algorithm given earlier. Then M is more robust than N, i.e., the sensitivity of M is lower than that of N.

The above theorem pertained to the special case where A was a singleton set. This result extends to the case when A contains many elements, and for node faults; these additional results and proofs are omitted due to lack of space. The theorem holds even with minor variations in the definitions of the sensitivity. A premise of the above theorem is that perturbations should degrade performance: if such is not the case, i.e., if network error actually decreases as a result of introducing "faults" into the system, then we replace the network by the new 'perturbed' network with better performance, which is then retrained.

IV. Experimental Evaluation

We evaluate our algorithm by comparing the sensitivity of the original network (with redundant nodes, randomly trained using the traditional backpropagation algorithm) with that of the network evolved using our proposed algorithm. Robustness of a network is measured in terms of graceful degradation in MSE and MIS(fraction of misclassification errors) on the test set and the training set. In the average cases, we plot the sets AC_{mse} and AC_{mis}, whereas in the worst cases we plot the sets WC_{mse} and WC_{mis}, which are defined as follows, where $\mathcal{I}$ is the set of all links and $C_R(W)$ is the fraction of misclassification errors on test set.

[1] "Well-trained" means that the network error is almost 0.

- $AC_{mse} = \{(x,y) | -100 \le x \le 100, x \bmod 5 \equiv 0, y = \frac{1}{|\mathcal{I}|}\sum_{i\in\mathcal{I}} E_R(W(i, \frac{x}{100}))\}$,
- $WC_{mse} = \{(x,y) | -100 \le x \le 100, x \bmod 5 \equiv 0, y = \max_{i\in\mathcal{I}} E_R(W(i, \frac{x}{100}))\}$,
- $AC_{mis} = \{(x,y) | -100 \le x \le 100, x \bmod 5 \equiv 0, y = \frac{1}{|\mathcal{I}|}\sum_{i\in\mathcal{I}} C_R(W(i, \frac{x}{100}))\}$,
- $WC_{mis} = \{(x,y) | -100 \le x \le 100, x \bmod 5 \equiv 0, y = \max_{i\in\mathcal{I}} C_R(W(i, \frac{x}{100}))\}$.

We performed four series of experiments for each problem using the following combinations of sensitivity definitions, where A is the set of values by which a weight is perturbed, when testing sensitivity.

Combination 0: Eq. (7) and $A = \{-1\}$.

Combination 1: Eq. (8) and $A = \{-1\}$.

Combination 2: Eq. (8) and $A = \{+0.1, -0.1\}$.

Combination 3: Eq. (8) and $A = \{\pm 1, \pm\frac{1}{2}\}$.

Combinations 0, 1, and 3 have almost identical performance, and also perform better than combination 2, possibly because the former measure performance for large changes in weights. Experimental results are shown only for combination 0, and only for one classic 3-class classification problem: Fisher's Iris data, with a four-dimensional input vector for each pattern, input values being rescaled to fall between 0 and 1. A third of the data points were not used for training, and were used as a test set. To start with, we trained a 4-10-3 neural network. Algorithm 1 reduced it to a 4-4-3 network in the first deletion step and then it was built up, successively, to a 4-10-3 network. There were 10 hidden nodes in the original network; our criterion reduced it to 4, then increased it to 10 as described in Table 1. When a 9-node network was obtained in this manner and retrained, two nodes could again be removed due to the sensitivity criteria, and more nodes were then added following our algorithm in Figure 1. The original 10-node network was roughly as robust as a 6-node network for high perturbations, and worse than all other cases for small perturbations.

Performance degradations of the initial and final 4-10-3 networks are shown in Table 1, and Figures 2 and 3 for the test set. Our robustness procedure achieved 83% improvement on average sensitivity and 81% improvement on worst sensitivity for this problem.

	Initial Net	Final Net
Hidden nodes	10	10
Training MSE	0.005130	0.005129
Testing MSE	0.025139	0.022123
Training Correctness(%)	99.00	99.00
Testing Correctness(%)	94.00	96.00
Avg. Sensitivity	0.025686	0.004314
Wst. Sensitivity	0.110977	0.021464

Table 1: Results of Fisher's Iris data on Combination 0. Deletion/addition process is $10 \to 4 \to 5 \to 6 \to 7 \to 8 \to 9 \to 7 \to 8 \to 9 \to 10$.

V. Discussion

We have developed a procedure for improving the robustness of feedforward neural networks, and shown that our algorithm results in significantly large improvements in the fault tolerance of networks trained for two multiclass classification problems. Minor variants of the algorithm, e.g., in using additional retraining steps in the body of the while-loop, resulted in no significant improvement.

Another possible approach to improve robustness is to build into the training algorithm a mechanism to discourage large weights: instead of the mean square error E_0, the new quantity to be minimized is of the form E_0+ (a penalty term monotonically increasing with the size of weights). We implemented three different possibilities, modifying each weight w_i by the quantities $-\eta(\frac{\partial E_0}{\partial w_i}+cw_i)$, $-\eta\frac{\partial E_0}{\partial w_i}(1+cw_i)$, and $-\eta\left(\frac{\partial E_0}{\partial w_i}(1+\frac{1}{2}c\sum_i w_i^2)+cw_iE_0\right)$, respectively, for many different values of c. This approach does improve robustness slightly, when compared to plain backpropagation, but the results are much less impressive than with our addition/deletion procedure. We also performed experiments combining both approaches, and this resulted in very slight improvements over the addition/deletion procedure.

References

[1] T.Anderson and P.A.Lee, Fault Tolerance: Principles and Practice, Prentice-Hall, 1981.

[2] L.A.Belfore, Fault Tolerance of Neural Networks, Ph.D. Dissertation, Univ. of Virginia, 1989.

[3] M.J. Carter, F.J.Rudolph and A.J. Nucci, *Operational Fault Tolerance of CMAC Networks*, Proc. Workshop on Neural Info. Proc. Systems, 1989, 340-347.

[4] E.D. Karnin, *A Simple Procedure for Pruning Back-Propagation Trained Neural Networks*, IEEE Trans. Neural Networks 1 (2), June 1990, 239-242.

[5] A. Krogh, J.A. Hertz, *A Simple Weight Decay Can Improve Generation.*

[6] T. Petsche and B.W. Dickinson, *Trellis Codes, Receptive Fields, and Fault Tolerant, Self-Repairing Neural Networks*, IEEE Trans. Neural Networks 1 (2), June 1990, 154-166.

[7] D.E.Rumelhart, J.L.McClelland, and the PDP Research Group, *Parallel Distributed Processing*, Vol.1, 1986.

[8] M.Stevenson, R.Winter and B.Widrow, *Sensitivity of Layered Neural Networks to Errors in the Weights*, Proc. Int'l. Joint Conf. Neural Networks, San Diego, June 1990, vol.I:337-340.

[9] G. Swaminathan, S. Srinivasan and S. Mitra, *Fault Tolerance in Neural Networks*, Proc. Int'l. Joint Conf. Neural Networks, San Diego, June 1990, vol.II:699-702.

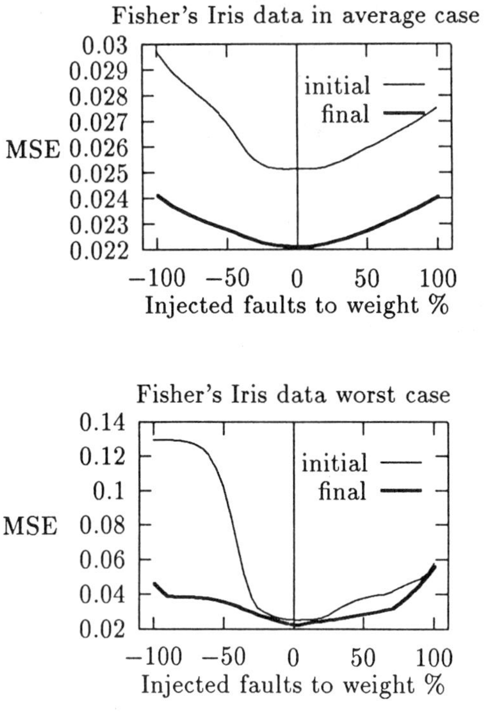

Figure 2: Degradation in mean square error for the test set, using networks with 10 hidden nodes, trained on Fisher's Iris data.

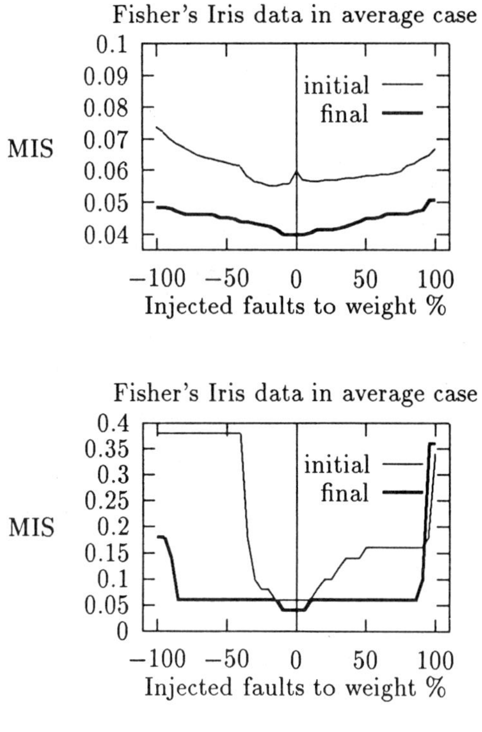

Figure 3: Degradation in the number of misclassified samples for the test set, using networks with 10 hidden nodes, trained on Fisher's Iris data.

CHARACTERIZATION OF NETWORK RESPONSES TO KNOWN, UNKNOWN, AND AMBIGUOUS INPUTS

Benjamin Hellstrom*
Analysis & Technology, Inc.
Century Building, Suite 1250
2341 Jefferson Davis Highway
Arlington, VA 22202
Tel: (703) 418-8617,
e-mail: hellstrm@access.digex.com

Jim Brinsley
Mailstop 417
Westinghouse Electronic Corporation
P.O.B. 746
Baltimore, Maryland 21203
Tel: (410) 993-7005

Abstract – Neural networks typically classify patterns by mapping the input feature space to the corners of the *m*-dimensional unit hypercube where *m* is the number of output classes. When classifier networks of graded threshold neurons are presented with patterns that are strong, ambiguous, or unknown, characteristic responses are emitted. A second tier network can be used to characterize the decision of the classifier network. By using a class count-independent mapping as an intermediary, a training set of unknowns can be generated for training the second tier. In this paper, we describe the two-tiered approach and analyze the internal function of the second tier.

The customary application of neural networks to the m-class pattern recognition problem produces a mapping from the feature space to the interior of the m-dimensional unit hypercube. A network is decisive when its outputs are close to one of the standard basis vectors, (1,0,...,0), (0,1,...,0), ..., (0,0,...,1). The index of the largest network output is then taken to represent the class to which the input vector maps[1]. The precise analog output values together with their relationship is commonly ignored.

We presume that network outputs assume characteristic forms when presented with input vectors that are (1) Strongly characteristic of a trained class, (2) Ambiguous with respect to two or more classes, or (3) Distant from any vector in the training set (i.e., "never seen" or "unknown"). For instance, one would expect a network output of (0.9, 0.1, 0.1) to represent greater certainty than an output of (0.65, 0.62, 0.2). To explore this idea, we use a secondary neural network, a "decision characterizer" (**DC**), to examine transformed outputs from the primary "classifier" network (**CL**). The **DC** network classifies **CL** network outputs as "strong," "ambiguous," or "unknown."

Meaningful characterization of the classifier network response indicates the degree to which the result should be trusted. In addition, the ability to identify **CL** network outputs as "unknown" is extremely important for those problems in

---

* This study conducted and documented by B. Hellstrom while employed by Westinghouse Electric Corporation.

[1] We refer to this as the maximum index decision criterion.

0-7803-0928-6/93$03.00

which it is impossible to adequately represent the feature space due to the cost of, or severe constraints on data collection. Although measures of classification certainty have been derived from radial-basis networks, these networks assume that classes are composed of collections of compact spherical or ellipsoidal clusters and that within each cluster, the distribution of vectors is Gaussian. For many types of data, these assumptions are unjustified.

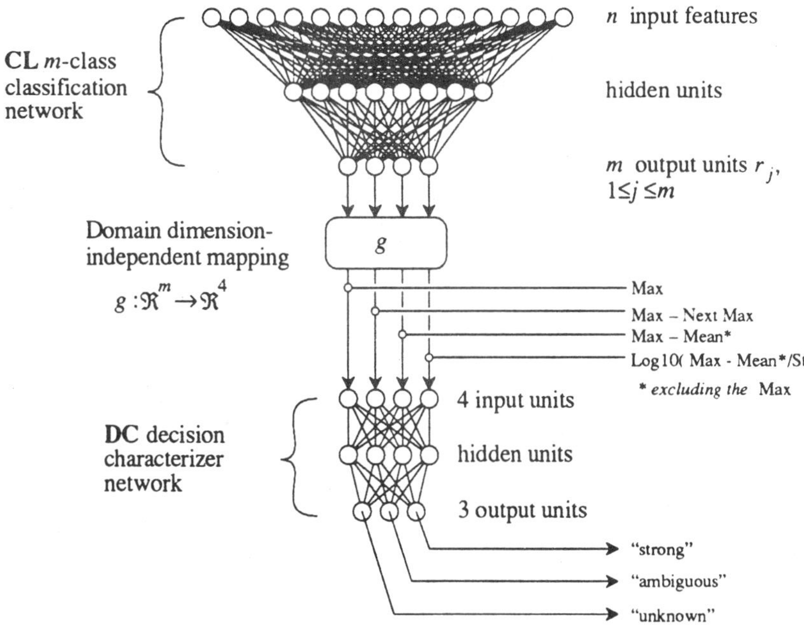

Figure 1

Overall network architecture. The output of the classifier network (**CL**) is mapped by class count-independent mapping, g, to a space of 4 features. The decision characterizer (**DC**) receives the mapped **CL** outputs and determines how the **CL** output should be interpreted.

In real-world applications, training the **DC** network is particularly tricky since the class of "unknowns" is infinitely varied. Rather than tackling all possible unknowns, we assume that outrageous inputs are intercepted by a filter preprocess. We therefore limit our attention to unknown inputs that resemble, to some degree, previously seen inputs. For an m-class decision problem, we start by training m classifier networks, CL_i, $1 \leq i \leq m$. Each classifier network, CL_i, is constructed to address the $m-1$ classification problem where data from class i is excluded. For example, if we have three classes of training data, tr_1, tr_2, and tr_3 classifier network CL_1 is trained to separate classes tr_2 and tr_3 , CL_2 is trained to separate classes tr_1 and tr_3, and CL_3 is trained to separate classes tr_1 and tr_2. When network CL_i is presented with data from class tr_i the network response is labeled as "unknown." If network CL_i responds incorrectly, by the maximum-index criterion described above, to any vector in $\boldsymbol{tr}_j$, $j \neq i$, the network response is labeled as "ambiguous." Otherwise, the response is classified as "strong." By presenting the complete training set to each of the (m –1)-classifier networks, we collect a complete set of "strong", "ambiguous", and "unknown" responses.

Since our final objective is a single m-class classifier network, we map each (m–1)-class classifier network response, $\boldsymbol{r}$, into a class-independent space with mapping $\boldsymbol{g}$. Let r_j be the response of the jth output node of one of the **CL** networks, $1 \leq j \leq m-1$. We define

$$g_1(\boldsymbol{r}) = \max_{1 \leq j \leq m-1} \{r_j\},$$

$$g_2(\boldsymbol{r}) = \max_{1 \leq j \leq m-1} \{r_j\} - \max_{\substack{1 \leq k \leq m-1 \\ k \neq j}} \{r_k\},$$

$$g_3(\boldsymbol{r}) = \max_{1 \leq j \leq m-1} \{r_j\} - \text{mean}\{r_k \mid 1 \leq k \leq m-1, k \neq j\},$$

$$g_4(\boldsymbol{r}) = \log_{10}\left(\max_{1 \leq j \leq m-1} \{r_j\} - \frac{\text{mean}\{r_k \mid 1 \leq k \leq m-1, k \neq j\}}{\text{std}\{r_k \mid 1 \leq k \leq m-1, k \neq j\}} \right), \text{ and}$$

$$\boldsymbol{g}(\boldsymbol{r}) = (g_1(\boldsymbol{r}), g_2(\boldsymbol{r}), g_3(\boldsymbol{r}), g_4(\boldsymbol{r})).$$

When the output of the **CL** network is $\boldsymbol{r}$, the input to the **DC** network is the 4 dimensional vector $\boldsymbol{g}$ ($\boldsymbol{r}$). After training the **DC** network on transformed responses derived from (m–1)-class networks, a single m-class **CL** network is trained on the complete set of training data, $\boldsymbol{tr}_i$, $1 \leq i \leq m$. An independent set of test cases, $\boldsymbol{ts}_1, \boldsymbol{ts}_2, \ldots, \boldsymbol{ts}_m$, from different classes together with unknowns, $\boldsymbol{ts}_0$ is then presented to the m-class **CL** network. The responses are transformed and the resulting 4 components presented to the **DC** network. Experiments with overlapping Gaussian clusters clearly reveal that the **DC** network is able to characterize the response of the **CL** network with a high degree of accuracy.

The first question we asked was whether the **CL/DC** network hierarchy, shown below, places closed decision boundaries around known data. Additional insight was also sought regarding the exact placement of the decision boundaries between "known" ("strong" or "ambiguous") and "unknown" points. Finally, the factors that control the placement of decision boundaries between "strong" and "ambiguous" points were characterized.

In order to visualize the placement of decision surfaces, we consider the problem of 9 overlapping Gaussian clusters in 2-space. For each class (i.e., cluster), $\boldsymbol{tr}_i$, $1 \leq i \leq 9$, 300 vectors were generated. A bank of 9 2-8-8 feedforward networks[2], $CL_1 \ldots CL_9$, was constructed and trained via error-propagation. Network CL_i was trained on 2,400 vectors from all classes except tr_i, i.e. $\bigcup_{1 \le j \le 9, j \ne i} tr_j$. Consequently, when presented with vectors from tr_i, network CL_i would exhibit a characteristic "unknown" response. Because of class overlap, no trained **CL** network was able to classify more than 97% of its training vectors correctly. The entire training set of vectors, $\bigcup_{1 \le i \le 9} tr_i$, was presented to each of the nine 8-class **CL** networks. After presentation of each vector to each **CL** network, the network output was mapped with g and labeled. If the selected **CL** network responded correctly to the input[3], the mapped output, $g(r)$ was labeled as "strong." If the selected **CL** network responded incorrectly to the input the mapped output was labeled as "ambiguous." Whenever any **CL** network, CL_i, was presented with an input in tr_i, the mapped output was always labeled as "unknown." A set of 24,300 labeled vectors was produced. A variety of **DC** network configurations was tested, and a 4-8-3 configuration was found to perform no worse than any other. A single 9-class **CL** network, CL_0, was trained on all vectors $\bigcup_{1 \le i \le 9} tr_i$ and tested on a 2-D grid of 441 evenly-spaced points over $x,y \in [-3,10]$. It should be noted that the range of the training data was roughly [-0.5,6.0] so that network CL_0 was subjected to a considerably larger range of test data than that upon which it was trained. The CL_0 responses were collected, mapped with g, and fed into the previously-trained **DC** network which clearly identified "ambiguous" and "unknown" responses.

The derivatives of the **DC** network outputs W.R.T. the network inputs were computed and weighted by the difference between average out-of-class input features and average in-class input features. This weighting is necessary to compensate for variation in the scale of individual features. Otherwise, we might be misled to believe that certain input features are very important simply because they are very small and the network must significantly scale them with large connection weights. We concluded that only 2 of the 4 **DC** input features, g_1 and g_3 were important. To verify our conclusion, the **DC** network was reconfigured as 2-8-3 and retrained solely on g_1 and g_3. There was no deterioration in performance during training[4].

With only 2 important input features, the labeled vectors, (g_1, g_3), are easily visualized and a **DC** network "rule" is derived. This simple decision rule requires only 2 decision surfaces

---

[2] We refer to a network with *I* inputs, *H* hiddens, and *O* outputs as an "*I-H-O* network."

[3] by the max index criterion.

[4] Both the 2-input and 4-input DS networks trained to 88.6% before stalling.

If the maximum output of the **CL** network is "large"
and the mean† output, is "small"
then a "strong" classification has been made by the **CL** network. (C1)

If the maximum **CL** output is small
then an "ambiguous" classification has been made. (C2)

If the maximum **CL** output is "large"
and the mean output† is also "large"
then the **CL** network has seen an "unknown." (C3)

Since the entire feature space, excluding the cluster region, was accurately being classified as "unknown" by the **DC** network, the cluster region was effectively bounded.

In order to explore the mechanism behind this boundedness, we examined the individual **CL** network outputs over the 2-D grid input domain. Each output node responded "high" over a convex region with its associated target cluster the focus and extending away from other clusters into the "unknown" region (figure 2).

As the **CL** network input deviates from the cluster regions, the amount of overlap of output node responses, i.e., $\sum_{i=1}^{m} r_i$, increases producing an increase in the mean† output response (g_3 decreases). The large g_1 value indicates that we are not in-between clusters within the cluster region. The combination of a large maximum **CL** output together with a large mean† **CL** output signal the location of the input vector in the "unknown" region (condition C3). The precise placement of the cutoff between "known" and "unknown" vectors depends on subtle factors such as the rapidity of the fan-out of the **CL** output responses (which depends on the size and proximity of the original clusters), as well as the proximity of simulated[5] "unknowns" to vectors within clusters.

† The mean output is computed excluding the maximum output, i.e., the second term of g_3.

[5] A vector, t, is a simulated "unknown" W.R.T. a classifier CL_i if $t \in tr_i$ and classifier CL_i has not been trained on any vectors in tr_i.

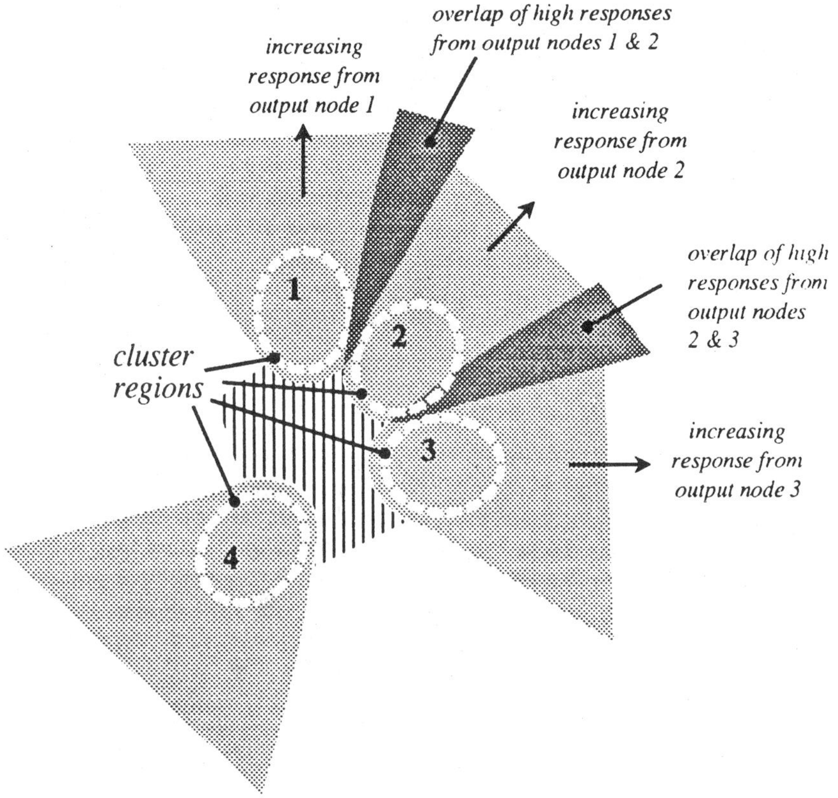

Figure 2

Qualitative response of **CL** output nodes. The regions for which unit output is > 0.5 fan out and overlap with those of adjacent regions as we leave the each unit's specific target cluster. Consequently, the maximum unit output can be used as a thresholded to signal deviation from the space of "known" training points.

The mechanisms behind the **DC** network's classification of "ambiguous" (condition **C2**) and "strong" (condition **C1**) vectors are much simpler. In the ambiguous regions between clusters, the maximum **CL** output is small since these regions (shown above with a vertical hatch) do not provoke a strong response from any **CL** output unit. As expected, a "strong" response stems from a large maximum output (g_1) and a small mean[†] output (large g_3) which indicates that the input vector is in the response region for exactly one **CL** output node.

In addition to employing **CL/DC** networks to artificial problems, we have been successful in applying the technique to a variety difficult real-world problems for which "unknowns" are not available.

Comparative Fault Tolerance of Generalized Radial Basis Function and Multilayer Perceptron Networks

Bruce E. Segee
Department of Electrical and Computer Engineering
University of Maine
Orono, ME 04469
segee@watson.eece.maine.edu

Michael J. Carter
Intelligent Structures Group
Department of Electrical and Computer Engineering
University of New Hampshire
Durham, NH 03824
mj_carter@unhh.unh.edu

Abstract—A method for measuring fault tolerance was developed which provides the means to quantify the effect of large numbers of network faults without explosive computational complexity. The fault tolerance of two types of neural networks used for analog function approximation, the multilayer perceptron (MLP) and the generalized radial basis function (GRBF) network, has been assessed. When standard gradient descent learning was employed, the GRBF was considerably more fault tolerant than an MLP of the same size. Furthermore, when a fault tolerance enhancing training method was employed, the fault tolerance of the GRBF improved substantially while the fault tolerance of the MLP improved only marginally.

INTRODUCTION

Fault tolerance is frequently ascribed as an inherent property of artificial neural networks. The assertion of fault tolerance in artificial neural networks stems from the loose analogy between the architecture of such networks and the organization of biological neural networks. The implication is that if the number of network processing elements can be made large, then fault tolerance would be imbued in the network automatically by virtue of the gross similarity with biological neural networks. The folk theorem of implicit fault tolerance has been further reinforced by a number of papers in which anecdotal reports of fault tolerance properties appeared (see references cited in [3] and [1]), and by repeated incantation in journal and conference papers too numerous to cite here. However, several studies of artificial neural networks have shown that they are not inherently fault tolerant. [2,4,5,9,10,11,12,14]

Since fault tolerance is critical in many applications (e.g., flight control systems), it is important to understand the fault tolerance properties of artificial neural networks. In this paper we investigate the impact of weight faults in networks used for analog function approximation. This paper addresses three key issues. First, we propose a means of quantifying the fault tolerance of a neural network to the loss of an arbitrary number of weights. Next, using this method we assess and compare the fault tolerance of two types of neural networks that have been trained using standard gradient descent methods: the multilayer perceptron (MLP), which is globally generalizing, and the generalized radial basis function (GRBF) network, which is locally generalizing [7]. Finally, we assess the improvement in fault tolerance for both types of networks that results from a fault tolerance enhancing training algorithm [13].

The networks tested were single-input single-output networks composed of one hundred processing elements arranged in a single hidden layer. Since the sigmoidal processing elements have weights associated with the inputs and outputs and the generalized radial basis function processing elements have weights only on their outputs, the multilayer perceptrons tested had two hundred weights while the generalized radial basis function networks had one hundred weights. These networks were trained to produce the sine of the input value in the range [-6,6]. The training set was composed of thirty evenly spaced samples. The networks were trained for 100,000 epochs.

MEASURING FAULT TOLERANCE

Essentially, the problem of measuring fault tolerance consists of two parts. The first is to formulate a reasonable error measure. The second is to formulate a suitable faulting method. Measuring fault tolerance then becomes an exercise in applying the faulting method and observing the effect on the measured error.

The selection of an appropriate error measure depends on the application at hand. For many tasks that involve learning a continuous function, the average squared error or the root mean squared (RMS) error is commonly used. The RMS error is defined as:

$$\text{RMS Error} = \left[\frac{1}{N}\sum_{i=1}^{N}(\mathrm{F}(x_i) - y_i)^2\right]^{\frac{1}{2}} \tag{1}$$

where F(x) is the network approximation to the learned function and y is the corresponding true value of the learned

0-7803-0999-5/93/$03.00 ©1993 IEEE

function. The number of sampling points N and their locations are left unspecified for the moment.

One problem inherent in the RMS error measure is that it doesn't account for differences in scale of the function to be learned. Thus, one must be extremely careful in comparing networks trained to the same approximation error on functions with differences in scale.

It is important to somehow normalize the RMS approximation error with respect to the RMS value of the function to be learned. It is for this reason that the following error measure which is called AQ (standing for approximation quality) is proposed.

$$AQ = \frac{\text{Function RMS}}{\text{Function RMS + RMS error}} \quad (2)$$

This dimensionless measure is always between zero and one, with the value one corresponding to no error, and the value zero corresponding to infinite error. Furthermore, for a value of 0.5, the function RMS and the RMS error are equal.

Once an appropriate error measure has been decided upon, the next step is to choose an appropriate faulting method. It is the authors' belief that to fully characterize network fault tolerance, one must consider worst case degradation in the face of multiple faults. Unfortunately, this is also the most difficult situation to evaluate. The number of ways that one can get N weight faults of a single type in a network having W weights is ${}_W C_N$, where:

$${}_W C_N = \frac{W!}{N!\,(W-N)!} \quad (3)$$

Unfortunately, this expression grows very rapidly. For instance, the curve below shows the combinatorial growth in the number of weight fault combinations for a network having fifty weights.

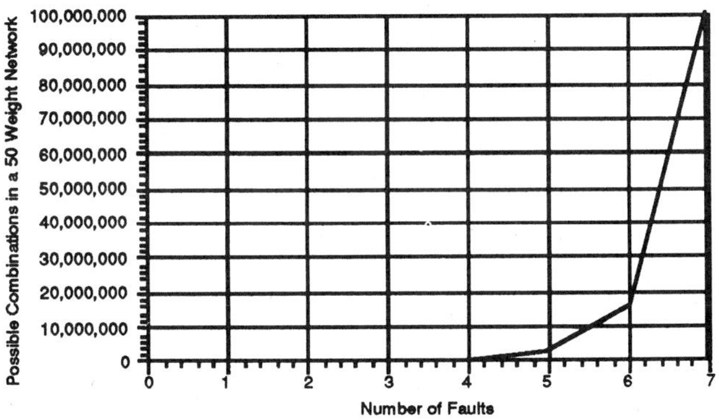

Figure 1: Graph showing the number of combinations of multiple weight faults (up to seven) for a network having fifty network weights.

As can be seen, evaluating even a modest number of weight fault combinations can rapidly lead to an exorbitant number of calculations. Of course, if one has a larger network, the growth is even faster! This leads to a dilemma. One can only characterize the worst case fault condition by evaluating all of the possible combinations; however, evaluating all of the combinations is simply not practical for typical network sizes. Some type of trade-off must be made to ease the computational burden.

A sequential worst case fault selection (worst case path) approach for evaluating multiple faults was employed which avoids combinatorial growth entirely. The assumptions made are that faults occur one at a time, and at each step the fault causing the largest incremental performance degradation is selected. For instance, one first evaluates all single weight faults to find the weight that causes the maximum performance degradation. This weight is then constrained to be one of the weights used in subsequent multiple fault evaluations.

This method has the advantage of eliminating the combinatorial growth in evaluating multiple faults. Additionally, it finds a worst case failure path assuming that faults occur one at a time. The disadvantage is that one cannot be sure that there are not multiple faults which cause larger degradation than the worst case path. For instance, there may exist three weights which when lost together cause a larger performance degradation than the loss of the first three weights in the worst case path. Nevertheless, the worst case path approach should give a reasonable approximation to worst case performance and is much less computationally expensive, being of order N^2.

COMPARING THE FAULT TOLERANCE OF THE MLP AND GRBF NETWORKS

The AQ metric with the worst case path fault selection method was used in evaluating the fault tolerance of the GRBF network and the MLP trained using ordinary gradient descent. The number of processing elements in the two networks was the same. The AQ values were plotted as a function of number of weights removed in the worst case path.

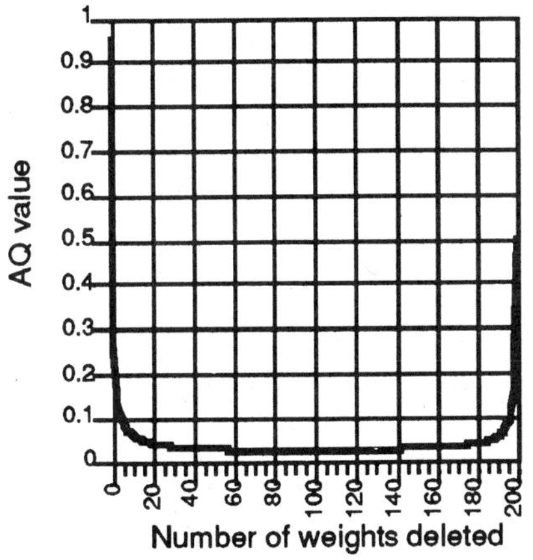

Figure 2: Approximation Quality (AQ) measure versus number of weights removed from the worst case path for the multilayer perceptron trained with ordinary backpropagation.

Figure 2 shows the results for the multilayer perceptron trained with ordinary backpropagation [8]. It is important to note two very striking features of this graph. The first is that even in a large network, the loss of the single most critical weight is sufficient to cause the RMS error to increase to a value much larger than the RMS value of the learned function. Thus, losing the single most critical weight is sufficient to render the network useless. The second feature to note is that as one follows the worst case fault path, the network error can increase by many times the RMS value of the learned function (for instance, an *AQ* value of 0.05 corresponds to the RMS error being about 20 times as large as the function RMS). Thus, with only the loss of a few weights the network becomes "actively bad", producing errors in excess of that which would result from having no network at all.

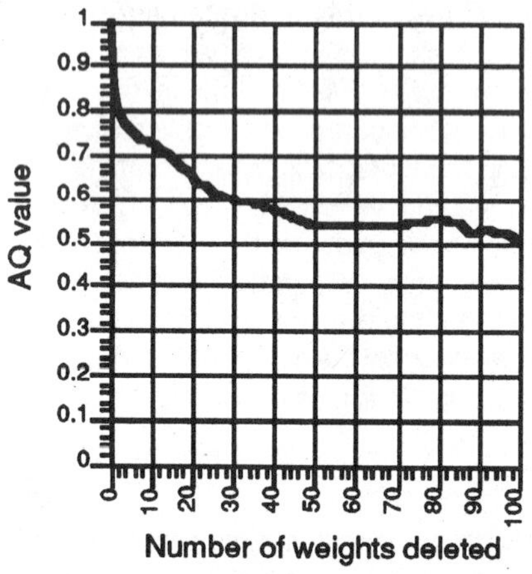

Figure 3: Approximation Quality (*AQ*) measure versus number of weights removed from the worst case path for the GRBF network.

A graph showing the worst case path performance for the generalized radial basis function network is shown in Figure 3. Note the qualitative change in character of the *AQ* curve relative to that found for the multilayer perceptron network. The radial basis function network is much more fault tolerant than the multilayer perceptron. As the worst case path is followed, the normalized approximation error measure slowly approaches a value of 0.5. The normalized error value never drops below 0.5, and thus the GRBF network always performs better than no network even in the face of an extreme number of faults.

It is interesting to note that after 100,000 training passes the MLP had an RMS approximation error of approximately 0.04 while the GRBF network had an RMS approximation error of approximately 0.01. Thus, the GRBF network outperforms the MLP not only in terms of fault tolerance but also in terms of fault free performance.

THE EFFECT OF FAULT TOLERANCE ENHANCING TRAINING METHODS

Given that we have established a baseline for fault tolerance performance for these two networks, it is natural to ask if the fault tolerance can be improved. Toward this end we investigated the effect of a training method that has been found to enhance fault tolerance. This method of improving fault tolerance was proposed by Séquin and Clay [14]. The method is very simple. During training, some number of randomly chosen nodes are disabled temporarily. These intermittent failures are generated throughout the training phase. The number of disabled nodes usually remains the same, but the particular choice of the affected nodes is changed periodically during the training interval. This method helps prevent highly critical units from forming, for if such a unit was disabled, the error would be large and the weights in the remainder of the network would be adjusted to compensate for the loss. This method has been found to improve the network fault tolerance at the expense of some degradation in fault-free approximation performance.

The graphs in Figure 4 show the effect on the normalized approximation error when weight faults in the worst case path are introduced into the multilayer perceptron after being trained by Séquin and Clay's technique. The number of randomly disabled nodes was varied between one and twenty.

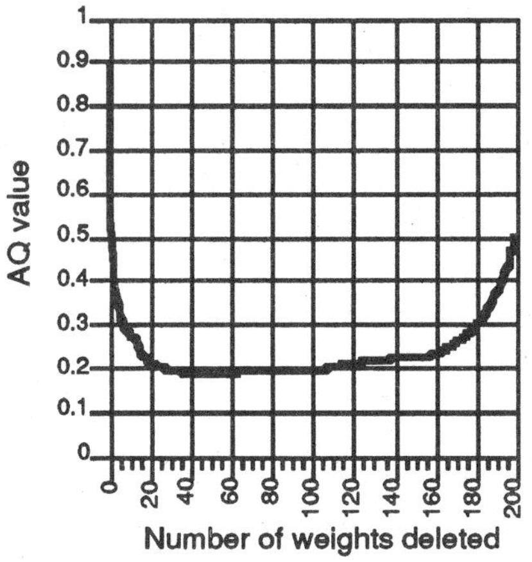

Backpropagation With One Intermittently Failing Unit

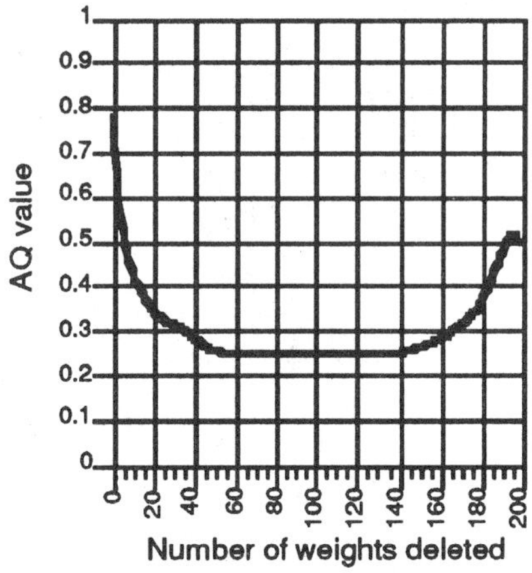

Backpropagation With Twenty Intermittently Failing Units

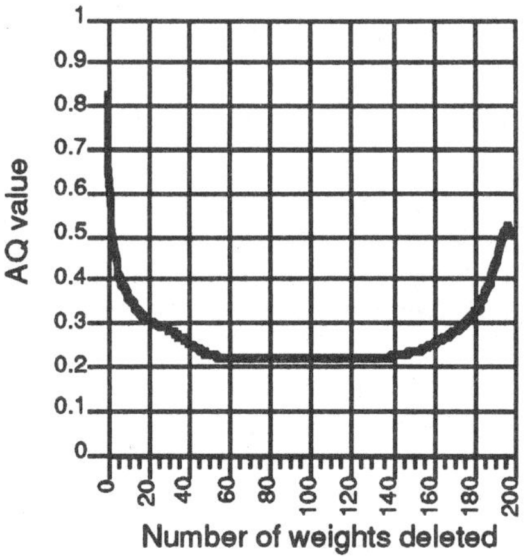

Backpropagation With Five Intermittently Failing Units

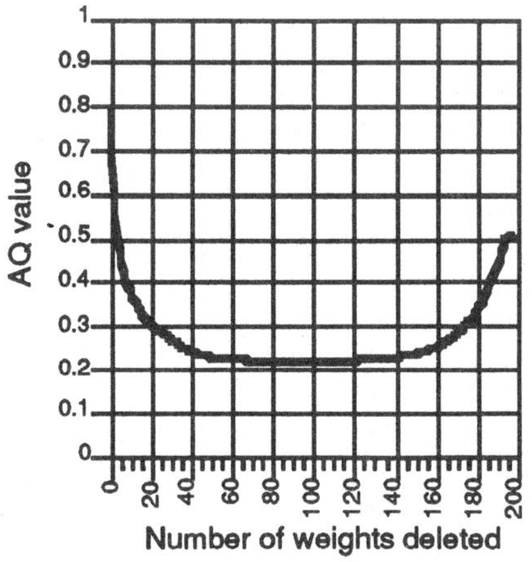

Backpropagation With Ten Intermittently Failing Units

Figure 4: Approximation Quality (*AQ*) measure versus number of weights removed from the worst case path for a multilayer perceptron trained by Séquin and Clay's intermittent node failure technique, (a) one intermittently failing node, (b) five intermittently failing nodes, (c) ten intermittently failing nodes, (d) twenty intermittently failing nodes.

Even when the number of intermittent failures was limited to one randomly chosen unit per training pass, the accuracy to which the multilayer perceptron could learn the function was significantly degraded. Nevertheless, the fault tolerance was improved. The network could tolerate the loss of several weights in the worst case path before the normalized approximation error value dropped below 0.5. Furthermore, the lowest value to which the normalized error dropped on the worst case path increased as more intermittent faults were introduced during training.

When the method of introducing intermittent faults during training was applied to the Gaussian radial basis function network, the results were more impressive. The general trend was again toward improved fault tolerance, albeit at the loss of fault-free performance. However, the relative effect on both fault tolerance and fault-free performance was much different than for the multilayer perceptron. The results for the Gaussian radial basis function network are shown in Figure 5.

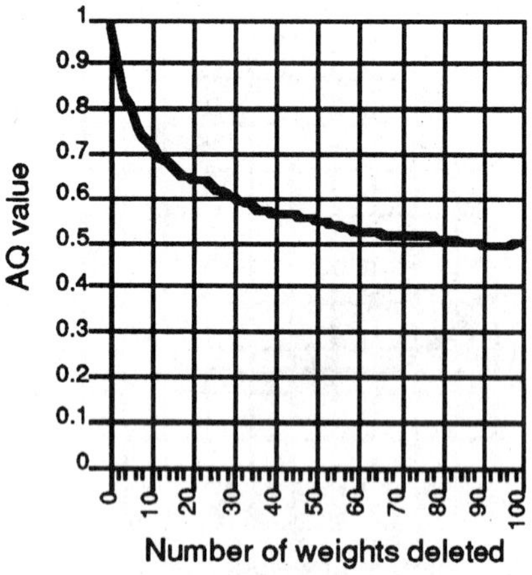

Generalized Radial Basis Function Network
With One Intermittently Failing Unit

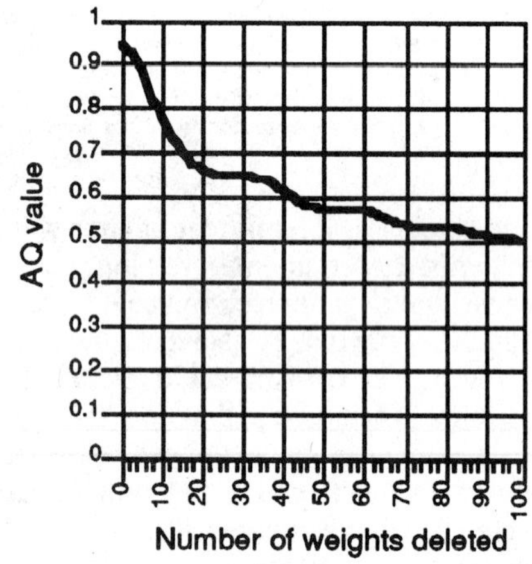

Generalized Radial Basis Function Network
With Five Intermittently Failing Units

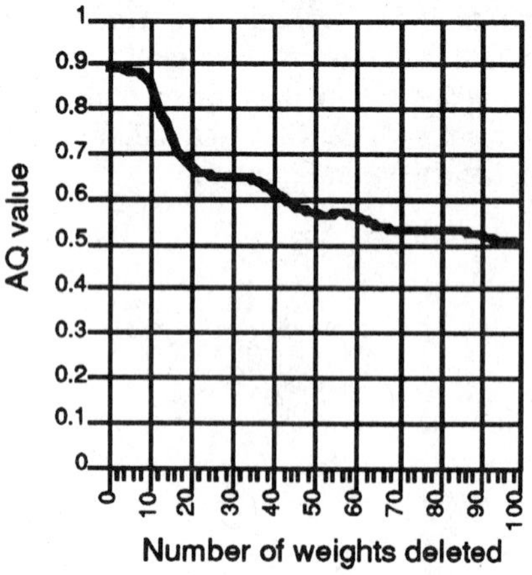

Generalized Radial Basis Function Network
With Ten Intermittently Failing Units

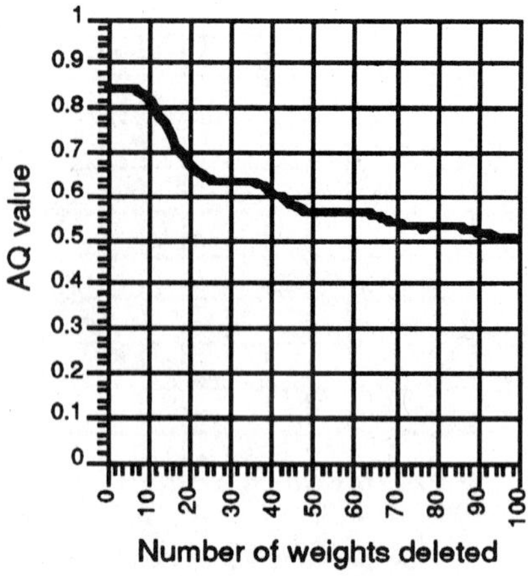

Generalized Radial Basis Function Network
With Twenty Intermittently Failing Units

Figure 5: Approximation Quality(AQ) measure versus number of weights removed from the worst case path for a Gaussian radial basis function network trained with Séquin and Clay's intermittent node failure technique, (a) one intermittently failing node, (b) five intermittently failing nodes, (c) ten intermittently failing nodes, (d) twenty intermittently failing nodes.

Having a single intermittent failure during training had very little impact on the fault-free performance of the radial basis function network. Furthermore, the normalized approximation error dropped off somewhat more slowly than it did in the case of the multilayer perceptron as the worst case weight loss path was followed.

Increasing the number of intermittently failing units during training caused the fault-free performance to worsen, although this effect was much less than was observed with the multilayer perceptron. As more intermittent failures were introduced, something remarkable happened. The normalized approximation error curve became essentially flat for some number of weights (nearly 10% of the network weights). Thus, for the loss of a small number of weights, *the weight which causes the maximum degradation causes essentially no degradation from the nominal fault-free performance.*

SUMMARY

In determining the fault tolerance of neural networks in function approximation applications, it is necessary to first choose a faulting method and an error criterion. Then one can insert faults into the network and observe the effect on the error.

If one is interested in comparing the fault tolerance of different networks, or of the same network trained to perform different tasks, it is important that the error measure be normalized by the RMS value of the function to be learned. We proposed the measure given in Equation 2, which we call the approximation quality. This measure is always in the range (0,1] and is based on the relative sizes of the function RMS value and the network's RMS approximation error.

There are several important considerations when choosing a faulting method. Perhaps the most important is the tradeoff between exhaustively testing all possible faults (and thereby completely characterizing the network) and limiting the testing to a computationally feasible level (and thereby risk missing important information). It is clearly important to study the effect of multiple faults, since it is highly unlikely that a network will experience exactly one fault throughout its operating lifetime. However, the number of possible multiple fault combinations in a network grows explosively.

In order to get a reasonable representation of the network's fault tolerance in the face of multiple faults, while avoiding the combinatorial growth associated with evaluating all possible multiple fault conditions, we chose to use a worst case path approach. Thus, we first removed the network weight which caused the maximum degradation in performance, and then we removed the weight which caused the maximum degradation in the resulting network, and so forth. We believe that the worst case path approach is a good predictor of the true worst case performance.

A method for quantifying the fault tolerance of neural networks has been developed that is applicable to a wide range of network architectures and topologies. This method employs the normalized performance measure which we call *AQ* and a worst case path fault insertion scheme. Fault tolerant networks should have large *AQ* values for as many faults in the worst case path as possible, and then should slowly degrade toward an *AQ* of 0.5. We have applied this method to GRBF networks and MLP networks trained using standard gradient descent procedures, and to the same networks trained with a fault tolerance enhancing learning algorithm. For the GRBF networks, the *AQ* values slowly dropped toward 0.5 with increasing number of faults. For the MLP, on the other hand, the value of *AQ* resulting from the loss of the single most damaging fault was typically below 0.5, and the *AQ* values would drop substantially below 0.5 with increasing number of faults.

In both types of networks, the fault tolerance enhancing learning method tended to improve the network fault tolerance with respect to that observed with conventional gradient descent learning. In every case tested, the GRBF networks outperformed the MLP networks in terms of fault tolerance. This can be explained using frequency domain methods [12,13]. The Gaussian function provides a much better fit to the function to be learned and consequently the GRBF produces a solution that is both lower in error and more fault tolerant than the MLP approximation.

REFERENCES

[1] G. Bolt, , J. Austin, and G. Morgan, " Fault Tolerance in Neural Networks", Technical Report, Computer Science Department, University of York, Heslington, York, YO1 5DD, U.K., 1990

[2] D. Carrara, "Investigating and Improving the Fault Tolerance of the Multilayer Perceptron", Master's Thesis (In Preparation), University of New Hampshire, 1992

[3] M.J. Carter, "The Illusion of Fault Tolerance in Neural Networks for Pattern Recognition and Signal Processing", *Proceedings Technical Session on Fault-Tolerant Integrated Systems*, University of New Hampshire, Durham, NH, 1988

[4] Y. Izui, and A. Pentland, "Analysis of Neural Networks with Redundancy", Neural Computation, Vol. 2, Number 2, pp. 226-238, Summer, 1990

[5] C. Neti, M. Schneider, and E. Young, "Maximally fault tolerant neural networks and nonlinear programming", *Proceedings IJCNN*, pp II-483:496, 1990

[6] D.S. Phatak, and I. Koren, "Fault Tolerance of Artificial Neural Nets", submitted for publication, 1990

[7] T. Poggio, and F. Girosi, "Networks for Approximation and Learning", *Proceedings of the IEEE*, v78, pp1481:1497, September, 1990

[8] D.E. Rumelhart, and J.L. McClelland (eds.), Parallel Distributed Processing, Explorations in the Microstructure of Cognition, MIT Press, Cambridge, 1986

[9] B.E. Segee, and M.J. Carter "Fault Sensitivity and Nodal Relevance Relationships in Multi-Layer Perceptrons", UNH Intelligent Structures Group Report ECE.IS.90.02, March 9, 1990

[10] B. E. Segee, and M. J. Carter, "Fault Tolerance of Pruned Multilayer Networks", *Proceedings IJCNN*, pp. II-447-452, Seattle, WA, 1991

[11] B. E. Segee, and M. J. Carter, "Comparative Fault Tolerance of Parallel Distributed Processing Networks (Debunking the Myth of Inherent Fault Tolerance)", UNH Intelligent Structures Group Report ECE.IS.92.07, February 24, 1992

[12] B. E. Segee, "Characterizing and Improving the Fault Tolerance of Artificial Neural Networks", PhD Dissertation, University of New Hampshire,1992

[13] B. E. Segee, "Using spectral techniques for improved performance in artificial neural networks", Proceedings ICNN (in press), 1993

[14] C. Séquin, and R. Clay, "Fault Tolerance in Artificial Neural Networks", *Proceedings IJCNN*, pp I-703:708, 1990

Extension of Approximation Capability of Three Layered Neural Networks to Derivatives *

Yoshifusa Ito
Toyohashi University of Technology
Tempaku-cho, Toyohashi, 441 JAPAN

Abstract - We consider the problem of approximating arbitrary differentiable functions defined on compact sets of $\mathbf{R}^d$, as well as their derivatives, by finite sums of the form $a_0 + \sum_{i=1}^{p} a_i g(W_i \cdot x + b)$, where W_i are vectors of $\mathbf{R}^d$ and g is an arbitrary non-polynomial C^∞-function fixed beforehand. If f is a polynomial of order n, the upper bound of p is ${}_{n+d-1}C_n$. The linear combinations can be realized by three layered neural networks.

1. Introduction

Hornik, Stinchcombe and White [16] and Hornik [5] have shown that three layered feedforward neural networks are capable of simultaneously approximating continuous functions in several variables and their derivatives if the input-output function of hidden layer units is differentiable. In other words, they have proved that differentiable functions in several variables and their derivatives can be approximated simultaneously by linear combinations of scaled shifted rotations of a differentiable function in one variable. In their articles, the approximation is in the sense of the supremum norm on compact sets or L^p-norm or others.

Although they have used functional analytic methods, we show, in this article, that the simultaneous approximation capability of three layered neural networks can be proved by an elementary method and the parameters in the approximation formulas can be obtained explicitly, if the input-output function of the hidden layer units is nonpolynomial and sufficiently many times differentiable. Moreover, if the function to be approximated is a polynomial, the upper bound of the number of hidden layer units can be estimated by our method. Our result is useful as an algorithm for implementing simultaneous approximation of derivatives by a three layered neural network because our method is concrete and constructive. We treat only approximations on compact sets in this article. Simultaneous approximation of derivatives on the whole space $\mathbf{R}^d$ is discussed in Ito [12].

Related topics to the present problem are simple approximations of continuous functions in various topologies by three layered neural networks having sigmoid units on the hidden layers. This simple case has been investigated by many authours: Carroll and Dickinson [1], Cybenko [2], Funahashi [3], Hecht-Nielsen [4], Hornik, Stinchcombe and white [6], Stinchcombe and White [15],[16], Ito [8], [9], [10] and others. Ito [9] has shown that the simple approximation capability of three layered neural networks can be proved by a very elementary method if the function to be approximated is defined on a compact support and the sigmoid function can be scaled. We shall describe this result in the last section in order to compare it with the present result.

Stinchcombe and White [16] proved by a recursive method that a linear sum of the form $\sum_{i=0}^{n} a_i g(\delta_i t)$ can approximate t^n uniformly on any compact set of $\mathbf{R}$ if $g^{(i)}(0) \neq 0$, $i = 0, \cdots, n$, where $g(t)$ is a function analytic at the origin of $\mathbf{R}$. Kreinovich [13] used a similar formula for $n = 2$ as a tool for approximating continuous functions. We first extend these results to simultaneous approximation of derivatives. Then, using Lemma 3.1 in Ito [9], we extend it to simultaneous approximation on compact sets of a higher dimensional space. The approximation formula we obtain is of the form $a_0 + \sum_{i=1}^{p} a_i g(W_i \cdot x + b)$, where $\cdot$ stands for the inner product of two vectors. It is well known that this formula can be realized by a three layered feedforward neural network having hidden layer units with the input-output function g.

Most part of this article is a curtailed version of Ito [11]. Hence, the proofs of theorems and lemmas are briefed or omitted as they are fully described in the paper.

2. Main theorem

We write $\partial_t^m = \partial^m/\partial t^m$, $t \in \mathbf{R}$, and $\partial^\alpha = \partial^{|\alpha|}/\partial^{\alpha_1} x_1 \cdots \partial^{\alpha_d} x_d$, where α is the multi-index, $x =$

*This article was written with the support of Grant No. 0426221 from the Ministry of Education and Culture, Japan.

0-7803-0999-5/93/$03.00 ©1993 IEEE

$(x_1, \cdots, x_d) \in \mathbf{R}^d$ and $|\alpha| = \alpha_1 + \cdots + \alpha_d$. We call a function f differentiable on a compact set $\mathbf{K} \subset \mathbf{R}^d$ if it is differentiable in an open set which contains $\mathbf{K}$. We denote by $C^m(\mathbf{K})$ the space of functions m-times continuously differentiable on $\mathbf{K}$.

The extended polynomial approximation theorem below is well known and follows from Nachbin's theorem (Nachbin, [14]).

Theorem 1. Let $\mathbf{K}$ be a compact set of $\mathbf{R}^d$. Then, for any $f \in C^m(\mathbf{K})$ and any $\varepsilon > 0$, there is a polynomial P in x for which

$$|\partial^\alpha f(x) - \partial^\alpha P(x)| < \varepsilon \quad \text{on} \quad \mathbf{K} \tag{1}$$

for all α, $|\alpha| \leq m$.

By virtue of this theorem, our purpose can be reduced to the simultaneous approximation of polynomials and their derivatives. The theorem below is pivotal in this article.

Theorem 2. Let g be an N times differentiable function defined in a neighbourhood of the origin of $\mathbf{R}$. Then, for any finite interval $\mathbf{K}_1 \subset \mathbf{R}$, any $\varepsilon > 0$ and any integer n such that $0 \leq n \leq N$, there are constants a_i and δ_i, $i = 0, \cdots, n$, for which

$$v_n(t) = \sum_{i=0}^{n} a_i g(\delta_i t) \tag{2}$$

satisfies

$$|\partial_t^m (\frac{1}{n!} g^{(n)}(0) t^n - v_n(t))| < \varepsilon \quad \text{on} \quad \mathbf{K}_1 \tag{3}$$

for all $m \leq N-1$. If $tg^{(N)}(t)$ converges to 0 as $t \to 0$, (3) holds for $m = N$, too. The $\delta_i's$ can be arbitrarily small and at least one of them can be zero.

If $m < N$ and $n < N$, we have that

$$\varepsilon = O(\max(|\delta_0|, \cdots, |\delta_n|). \tag{4}$$

Further, if $g^{(N)}$ is bounded and $n < m = N$, or if $g^{(N)}$ satisfies the Lipshitz condition and $m \leq n = N$, then we have (4).

Idea of the proof. Suppose that $0 \leq m \leq N$. By Maclaurin's theorem, we have that if $0 \leq m \leq i \leq N$,

$$\partial_t^m g(\delta_i t)$$

$$= \sum_{j=0}^{i-1} \frac{1}{j!} g^{(j)}(0) \delta_i^j \partial_t^m t^j + \frac{1}{i!} g^{(i)}(\theta_i \delta_i t) \delta_i^i \partial_t^m t^i \tag{5}$$

in a neighbourhood of the origin for sufficiently small values of $\delta_i's$, where $\theta_m = 1$ and $0 < \theta_i < 1$ for $i > m$. Hence, for all i, $0 \leq i \leq N$,

$$\partial_t^m g(\delta_i t) = \sum_{j=0}^{i-1} \frac{1}{j!} g^{(j)}(0) \delta_i^j \partial_t^m t^j + \eta_i(t) \delta_i^i, \tag{6}$$

where

$$\eta_i(t) = \begin{cases} \delta_i^{m-i} g^{(m)}(\delta_i t), & i < m, \\ \frac{1}{i!}\{g^{(i)}(\theta_i \delta_i t) - g^{(i)}(0)\} \partial_t^m t^i, & i \geq m. \end{cases} \tag{7}$$

Note that (6) are trivial equalities for $i < m$. Set

$$z_j^{(m)}(t) = \frac{1}{j!} g^{(j)}(0) \partial_t^m t^j, \quad 0 \leq j \leq m.$$

Then, regarding (6) for $i = 0, \cdots, n$ as simultaneous equations with respect to $z_j^{(m)}$, $j = 0, \cdots, n$, we have that

$$z_n^{(m)}(t)$$

$$= \prod_{i=0}^{n} \delta_i^{-i} A(\delta_0, \cdots, \delta_n, t) - \prod_{i=0}^{n} \delta_i^{-i} B(\delta_0, \cdots, \delta_n, t), \tag{8}$$

where

$$A(\delta_0, \cdots, \delta_n, t)$$

$$= \begin{vmatrix} 1 & 0 & 0 & \cdots & 0 & \partial_t^m g(\delta_0 t) \\ 1 & \delta_1 & 0 & \cdots & 0 & \partial_t^m g(\delta_1 t) \\ \cdots & \cdots & \cdots & \cdots & \cdots & \cdots \\ 1 & \delta_{n-2} & \delta_{n-2}^2 & \cdots & 0 & \partial_t^m g(\delta_{n-2} t) \\ 1 & \delta_{n-1} & \delta_{n-1}^2 & \cdots & \delta_{n-1}^{n-1} & \partial_t^m g(\delta_{n-1} t) \\ 1 & \delta_n & \delta_n^2 & \cdots & \delta_n^{n-1} & \partial_t^m g(\delta_n t) \end{vmatrix},$$

and

$$B(\delta_0, \cdots, \delta_n, t)$$

$$= \begin{vmatrix} 1 & 0 & 0 & \cdots & 0 & \delta_0^0 \eta_0(t) \\ 1 & \delta_1 & 0 & \cdots & 0 & \delta_1^1 \eta_1(t) \\ \cdots & \cdots & \cdots & \cdots & \cdots & \cdots \\ 1 & \delta_{n-2} & \delta_{n-2}^2 & \cdots & 0 & \delta_{n-2}^{n-2} \eta_{n-2}(t) \\ 1 & \delta_{n-1} & \delta_{n-1}^2 & \cdots & \delta_{n-1}^{n-1} & \delta_{n-1}^{n-1} \eta_{n-1}(t) \\ 1 & \delta_n & \delta_n^2 & \cdots & \delta_n^{n-1} & \delta_n^n \eta_n(t) \end{vmatrix}.$$

In the equation (8), δ_i, $i \geq 1$, must be nonzero but can be arbitrarily small and δ_0 can be zero with the convention $\delta_0^0 = 1$. The essential part of the proof is the estimation of the second term of (8) (see Ito [11] for details). □

Note that if g is N times continuously differentiable, both (3) and (4) hold for all $n \leq N$ and $m \leq N$.

Example. For $g(t) = e^t$, set $n = 2$, $\delta_0 = 0$, $\delta_1 = \delta^2$ and

$\delta_2 = \delta$. Then, we have that

$$v_2(t) = \frac{1}{\delta^4}\begin{vmatrix} 1 & 0 & 1 \\ 1 & \delta^2 & \exp(\delta^2 t) \\ 1 & \delta & \exp(\delta t) \end{vmatrix} = \frac{1}{2}t^2 + O(\delta),$$

$$v_2'(t) = \frac{1}{\delta^4}\begin{vmatrix} 1 & 0 & 0 \\ 1 & \delta^2 & \delta^2\exp(\delta^2 t) \\ 1 & \delta & \delta\exp(\delta t) \end{vmatrix} = t + O(\delta),$$

$$v_2''(t) = \frac{1}{\delta^4}\begin{vmatrix} 1 & 0 & 0 \\ 1 & \delta^2 & \delta^4\exp(\delta^2 t) \\ 1 & \delta & \delta^2\exp(\delta t) \end{vmatrix} = 1 + O(\delta),$$

and $v_2^{(m)}(t) = O(\delta^{m-2})$ for $m \geq 3$.

We write $(n) = {}_{n+d-1}C_n = \binom{n+d-1}{n}$. This is the number of independent monomials of order n in $x \in \mathbf{R}^d$. Denote by $\mathbf{S}^{d-1}$ the unit sphere in $\mathbf{R}^d$ and by $w \cdot x$ the inner product of two vectors $w \in \mathbf{S}^{d-1}$ and $x \in \mathbf{R}^d$. For almost all sets of vectors $\{w_j \in \mathbf{S}^{d-1}, j = 1, \cdots, (n)\}$, the $(w_j \cdot x)^n$ are linearly independent as polynomials in x. The lemma below, which was used in Ito [9], is obvious.

Lemma 3. For almost all sets of vectors $\{w_j \in \mathbf{S}^{d-1}, j = 1, \cdots, (n)\}$ and any homogeneous polynomial P_i in $x \in \mathbf{R}^d$ of order $i \leq n$, there are coefficients a_j, $j = 1, \cdots, (i)$, for which an equality

$$P_i(x) = \sum_{j=1}^{(i)} a_j (w_j \cdot x)^i \tag{9}$$

holds.

The proposition below follows from this lemma.

Proposition 4. Let g be an N-times differentiable function defined in a neighbourhood of the origin of $\mathbf{R}$ such that $g^{(i)}(0) \neq 0$ for $i = 0, \cdots, N$. Then, for any polynomial P in x of order up to N, say n, any compact set $\mathbf{K} \subset \mathbf{R}^d$ and any $\varepsilon > 0$, there exist constants a_0, a_{jk}, arbitrarily small constants δ_k and vectors $w_j \in \mathbf{S}^{d-1}$, $j = 1, \cdots, (n)$, $k = 1, \cdots, n$, for which

$$\overline{P}(x) = a_0 + \sum_{j=1}^{(n)} \sum_{k=1}^{n} a_{jk} g(\delta_k w_j \cdot x) \tag{10}$$

satisfies

$$|\partial^\alpha P(x) - \partial^\alpha \overline{P}(x)| < \varepsilon \quad \text{on} \quad \mathbf{K} \tag{11}$$

for all α, $|\alpha| \leq N - 1$.

If $g^{(N)}$ is continuous, (11) holds for all, $|\alpha| \leq N$. Further, if $g^{(N)}$ satisfies the Lipschitz condition, $\varepsilon = O(\max(|\delta_0|, \cdots, |\delta_n|)$ for all α, $|\alpha| \leq N$.

Remark. Note that the number of the summands on the right hand side of (10) is $n(n) = n_{n+d-1}C_n$. Suppose that this number of hidden layer units are provided. Then, any polynomial of order up to n can be approximated by a three layered neural network even if the vectors $w_j's$ are fixed beforehand. In the case where the vectors can be chosen after observing the polynomial, the number can be of course decreased. For example, if $d = 2$ and $P(x) = x_1 x_2$, the number can be as small as 4 (Toda, Funahashi and Usui [17]).

In Proposition 4, it is required that $g^{(n)}(0) \neq 0$ for all $n = 0, \cdots, N$. We can prove that if g is an N-times differentiable function and $g^{(N)}(t) \neq 0$ on a dense subset $\mathbf{D}$ of an open set $\mathbf{G} \subset \mathbf{R}$, there is a point $b \in \mathbf{D}$ for which $g^{(n)}(b) \neq 0$ for $n = 0, \cdots, N$. In fact, if $g^{(N-1)}(t) = 0$ on $\mathbf{G}$, $g^{(N)}(t) = 0$ on $\mathbf{G}$. Hence, there is a point $b_1 \in \mathbf{G}$ on which $g^{(N-1)}(b_1) \neq 0$. Since $g^{(N-1)}$ is continuous, there is a nonempty open set $\mathbf{G}_1$ such that $b_1 \subset \mathbf{G}_1 \subset \mathbf{G}$ and $g^{(N-1)}(t) \neq 0$ on $\mathbf{G}_1$. Similarly, there is a nonempty open set $\mathbf{G}_2 \subset \mathbf{G}_1$ on which $g^{(N-2)}(t) \neq 0$. Repeating this procedure, we obtain a series of open subsets $\phi \neq \mathbf{G}_N \subset \mathbf{G}_{N-1} \subset \cdots \subset \mathbf{G}_1 \subset \mathbf{G}$. Then, $g^{(n)}(t) \neq 0$ on $\mathbf{G}_N$ for $n = 0, \cdots, N-1$. Hence, $g^{(n)}(t) \neq 0$ on $\mathbf{D} \cap \mathbf{G}_N$ for $n = 0, \cdots, N$. We can therefore use a shift $g(t + b)$, $b \in \mathbf{D} \cap \mathbf{G}_N$, as the function g in Proposition 4. If g is a nonpolynomial C^∞-function, there is an open set for any n such that any number of the set can be used as the shifter b.

Constants including zero are special polynomials. Hence, nonpolynomial functions cannot be zero or constants.

Theorem 5. Let g be any nonpolynomial infinitely differentiable function defined in an open set of $\mathbf{R}$, and let $\mathbf{K}$ be a compact set of $\mathbf{R}^d$. Then, for any $f \in C^n(\mathbf{K})$ and any $\varepsilon > 0$, there are an integer p, constants a_0, a_{jk} and b, arbitrarily small constants δ_k and vectors $w_j \in \mathbf{S}^{d-1}$, $j = 1, \cdots, (p)$, $k = 1, \cdots, p$, for which

$$\overline{f}(x) = a_0 + \sum_{j=1}^{(p)} \sum_{k=1}^{p} a_{jk} g(\delta_k w_j \cdot x + b) \tag{12}$$

satisfies

$$|\partial^\alpha f(x) - \partial^\alpha \overline{f}(x)| < \varepsilon \quad \text{on} \quad \mathbf{K} \tag{13}$$

for all α, $|\alpha| \leq n$. The bound ε can be as small as $O(\max(|\delta_0|, \cdots, |\delta_p|)$ for all α, $|\alpha| \leq p$.

Proof. By Theorem 1, there is a polynomial P in x which simultaneously approximates f and its derivatives on $\mathbf{K}$. Let p be the order of P. Since g is nonpolynomial, there is a point b for which $g^{(i)}(b) \neq 0$ for $i = 0, \cdots, p$ as described above. By Proposition 4, the polynomial P and its derivatives can be simultaneously approximated on $\mathbf{K}$ by a finite sum $\overline{f}$ of the form (12) and its derivatives respectively. The rest of the theorem is obvious. □

The formula (12) can be written

$$\overline{f}(x) = a_0 + \sum_{i=1}^{q} a_i g(W_i \cdot x + b), \tag{14}$$

where the W_i are vectors in $\mathbf{R}^d$. Although this expression is simpler, it lacks some information contained in the precise expression (12).

In neural network theory, analytic functions are often used as input-output functions of units. Let g be a nonpolynomial analytic function defined in an open set of $\mathbf{R}$. Then, the set $\mathbf{E}_i$ of zeros of $g^{(i)}$ is countable at most. Hence, except for a subset $\mathbf{E} = \cup_{i=0}^{\infty} \mathbf{E}_i$, which is countable at most, $g^{(i)}(t) \neq 0$ for all $i = 0, 1, \cdots$. This implies that almost all points of the open set can be used as b in (12) and, moreover, it can be fixed beforehand.

The logistic function $(1 + e^{-t})^{-1}$ is often used in neural network theory.

Example. Let $g(t) = (1 + e^{-t})^{-1}$. Although g is analytic, $g^{(2i+1)}(0) = 0$ for all $i \geq 0$. As described above, $g^{(i)}(b) \neq 0$ for all $i \geq 0$ for almost all b. We can easily find such a b. If b is a nonzero rational number, e^{-b} is transcendental. Since

$$g^{(i)}(b) = q_i(e^{-b})(1 + e^{-b})^{-i-1},$$

where q_i is a polynomial whose coefficients are integers, $g^{(i)}(b) \neq 0$ for all $i \geq 0$ for any rational number $b \neq 0$. For example, all derivatives of $(1 + e^{-t \pm 1})^{-1}$ do not vanish at $t = 0$.

3. Discussion

Theorem 2 is an extension of Lemma 4.1 in Stinchcombe and White [16] to the approximation of derivatives and Lemma 3 is the lemma originally used in Ito [9]. Combining these results, we have obtained the main theorem. The statement of Lemma 3 is obvious without proof, but it is very useful in neural network theory. Ito [9] has used the lemma to prove the well known classical neural approximation theorem. Let us recall the classical theorem with Ito's proof of the theorem and compare them with Theorem 5 and its proof.

Theorem 6. Let h be any monotone increasing bounded function, and $\mathbf{K}$ be a compact set of $\mathbf{R}^d$. Then, for any $f \in C(\mathbf{K})$ and any $\varepsilon > 0$, there are an integer p, constants a_i and t_i, and vectors $W_i \in \mathbf{R}^d$, $i = 1, \cdots, p$, for which

$$\overline{f}(x) = \sum_{i=1}^{p} a_i h(W_i \cdot x - t_i) \tag{15}$$

satisfies

$$|\partial^\alpha f(x) - \partial^\alpha \overline{f}(x)| < \varepsilon \quad \text{on} \quad \mathbf{K}. \tag{16}$$

Proof. Any power t^n can be uniformly approximated on a finite interval by a staircase function which can be substituted by a finite sum of scaled shifts of h. Combining this fact, Lemma 3 and the extended polynomial approximation theorem, we obtain can the theorem. □

In this proof, Lemma 3 is used in the same way as in the proof of Theorem 5 for converting approximate representations of monomials in one variable into such representations of polynomials in several variables. In the approximate representation, the number of the terms cannot be restricted even if the function f is a polynomial. This type of approximation will be useful if the neural units become less expensive. A three layered neural network with many hidden layer units has a merit that it is robust against failures of a small number of units. On the contrary, if one or two summands are removed from the right hand side of (12), it may be catastrophical to the approximate representation. Another difference between the two approximate representations is that the input-output function g in (12) must be sufficiently many times differentiable even in the case of approximation of non-differentiable continuous functions. In Theorems 5 and 6, approximations are on compact sets and the input-output functions (g or h) must be scalable. This is the reason that these theorem can be proved straightforwardly. Under this condition, Theorem 6 can be easily extended to approximation of derivatives (see Discussion of Ito [12]), where Lemma 3 again plays an important role. However, we need functional analytic method to extend Theorem 6 to approximations of derivatives on the whole space $\mathbf{R}^d$, or to approximations of derivatives without scaling of the input-output function (see the main part of Ito [12]).

This article is different not only from Ito [12] but also from Hornik, Stinchcombe and White [7], Hornik [5], which are concerned with simultaneous approximation of derivatives, because the number of hidden layer units of neural networks based on Theorem 5 can be estimated if the polynomial approximation of the function to be approximated is obtained. In these three papers, the number cannot be estimated. Our result can be regarded as a partial solution of the problem of estimating numbers of hidden layer units of three layered feedforward neural networks.

Kreinovich [13] has obtained an inequality similar to (3) for $n = 2$ and $m = 0$, assuming that the function g is at least three times differentiable. However, as implied by Theorem 2, this is unnecessary. By Theorem 2, a linear sum of g can approximate the square t^2, if g is two times differentiable and $g^{(2)}$ is nonzero. Note that the inequality (3) holds for all m such that $0 = m < n$, if g is exactly n times differentiable. It is obvious that this article has remarkably extended his result.

Stinchcombe and White [16] defined superanalytic functions as useful input-output functions of hidden layer units for approximation of continuous functions by three layered neural networks. However, as shown in Section 2, every nonpolynomial analytic functions are superanalytic in their sense everywhere except on a countable set. We have further proved that really useful, as the input-output functions, are infinitely differentiable nonpolynomial functions. Moreover, they are useful for simultaneous approximation of derivatives as shown in this article.

Since the proofs in this article are all constructive, they can be regarded as an algorithm for constructing three layered neural networks which can implement the simultaneous approximation of derivatives on compact sets. The classical theorem, Theorem 6, and its extension to derivatives can also be proved constructively under the condition of compactness of the domain and the scalability of the input-output function. Hence, these are all useful as algorithms. Thus, we have provided convenient algorithms for approximation of functions and its derivatives, which can be chosen depending on the circumstances.

Many natural phenomena are governed by differential equations. Hence, we may sometimes need approximate quantities and their derivatives simultaneously for treating them by neural networks. As an example, the necessity of such a simultaneous approximation in robotics is mentioned in Hornik, Stinchcombe and White [7]. The concrete method of obtaining parameters of neural networks, described in this article, may be useful for such applications.

Acknowledgement

The work was done while the author was visiting the Department of Statistics and Applied Probability, UC Santa Barbara, in July 1991. The author wishes to thank Professor J. Gani for his encouragement and helpful discussion on the topics.

References

[1] Carroll, B.W. and B.D. Dickinson. *Construction of neural nets using the Radon transform*, '89IJCNN Proceedings, 1989, I-607-611.

[2] Cybenko, G. *Approximation by superpositions of a sigmoidal function*, Math. Control Signal System, **2**, 1989, 303-314.

[3] Funahashi, K. *On the approximate realization of continuous mapping by Neural networks*, Neural Networks, **2**, 1989, 183-192.

[4] Hecht-Nielsen, R. *Theory of the back propagation neural network*, 89IJCNN Proceeding, 1989, I-593-605.

[5] Hornik, K. *Approximation capabilities of multilayer feedforward networks*, Neural Networks, **4**, 1991, 251-257.

[6] Hornik, K., M. Stinchcombe and H. White. *Multilayer feedforward networks are universal approximators*, Neural Networks, **2**, 1989, 359-366.

[7] Hornik, K., M. Stinchcombe and H. White. *Universal approximation of an unknown mapping and its derivatives using multilayer feedforward networks*, Neural Networks, **3**, 1990, 551-560.

[8] Ito, Y. *Representation of functions by superposition of a step or sigmoid function and their applications to neural network theory*, Neural Networks, **4**, 1991, 385-394.

[9] Ito, Y. *Approximation of functions on a compact set by finite sums of a sigmoid function without scaling*, Neural Networks, **4**, 1991, 817-826.

[10] Ito, Y. *Approximation of continuous functions of* $\mathbf{R}^d$ *by linear combinations of shifted rotations of a sigmoid function with and without scaling*, Neural Networks, **5**, 1992, 105-115.

[11] Ito, Y. *Approximations of differentiable functions and their derivatives on compact sets by neural networks*, The Mathematical Scientist. in press.

[12] Ito, Y. *Differentiable approximation by means of the Radon transformation and its applications to neural networks*, Applied Analysis and Stochastics. in press.

[13] Kreinovich, V.Y. *Arbitrary nonlinearity is sufficient to represent all functions by neural networks: A Theorem*, Neural networks, **4**, 1991, 381-383.

[14] Nachbin, L. *Elements of Approximation Theory*, Princeton, New Jersey. 1967.

[15] Stinchcombe, M. and H. White. *Universal approximation using feedforward networks with non-sigmoid hidden layer activation functions*, '89IJCNN Proceedings, 1989, I-613-617.

[16] Stinchcombe, M. and H. White. *Approximating and learning unknown mappings using multilayer feedforward networks with bounded weights*, '90IJCNN Proceeding IJCNN, 1990, III-7-16.

[17] Toda, N., K. Funahashi and S. Usui. *Analytic Realization of Polynomial Functions by Feedforward Neural Networks*, 91IJCNN Proceedings, 1991, IIA-966.

Noninvertibility in Neural Networks *

Ramiro Rico-Martínez and Ioannis G. Kevrekidis
Department of Chemical Engineering, Princeton University, Princeton NJ 08544
Raymond A. Adomaitis
Institute for Systems Research, University of Maryland, College Park, MD 20742

***Abstract*— We present a method for assessing certain validity aspects of predictions made by neural networks used to approximate continuous (in time) dynamical systems. This method searches for noninvertibility (non-uniqueness of the reverse time dynamics) of the fitted model, an indication of breakdown of "proper" dynamical behavior. It is useful for computing bounds on the valid range of network predictions.**

I. Introduction

Input/output maps in the form of neural networks trained on experimental or simulation data are useful for predicting dynamical behavior, both in the short and in the long term (structure of the system attractors). When an operating parameter is one of the inputs to the network, instabilities and transitions (both local and global bifurcations) can be analyzed by varying the parameter in the resulting model.

When we study the predictions of a neural network as a function of the input parameter(s), we expect that not only the short term predictions, but also the long term attractors, their nature and bifurcations, should reflect those of the original system. For example, if a physical system can be described by a set of ordinary differential equations in time, and the states of the system, measured at discrete time intervals, are used as training data for the neural network, we should expect the trained network to be *uniquely invertible*. In other words, given some point in time, we should be able to find a unique preimage of that point, since this is equivalent to integration of the differential equations backwards for the appropriate time interval.

It is easy to see that inverting a discrete time neural network (using the output to find what values of the input are consistent with it) involves solving a complicated set of nonlinear equations (transcendental in the case of tanh-type activation functions). Such equations can, and often will, have multiple solutions, depending on the parameter values and on the output values. In principle, any neural network allowing multiple preimages of any state at any parameter value is inconsistent with a continuous time dynamical system (a set of ODEs). It may be, as we will demonstrate below, that only one of these multiple preimages "makes sense," and the other ones are far away in phase space. In this case, when only one "relevant" preimage can be singled out, we can still claim the network predictions to be valid in a restricted region of phase space. When, however, multiple preimages fall in the relevant range of phase space, the dynamics of the iterated network take on features exclusively found in noninvertible maps producing transitions and types of behavior qualitatively impossible for invertible dynamical systems.

Studying the role noninvertibility plays in complicating the dynamics of a neural network is made less transparent by not being able to explicitly compute the inverse (one step backward in time) mapping. To facilitate the discussion of these dynamical features, we will study a system which provides a good analogy to the problem at hand. Noninvertible phenomena displayed by a system which should only demonstrate invertible behavior occur often when numerical integrators are used, since they essentially attempt the same thing as the neural network–obtaining an approximation to the true dynamics of a set of ODEs by replacing them with a discrete-time map. It is well known that this approximation may break down as the integration time step is increased (numerical instabilities). What is interesting is that sometimes the breakdown involves noninvertibility [1], precisely as it happens for neural networks: dynamical features are generated which are impossible in the original system.

To illustrate the mechanism by which noninvertibility gives rise to dynamical behavior not possible in the original system, consider the Brussellator, a system familiar to those working in chemical dynamics:

$$\begin{aligned}\frac{dx}{dt} &= x^2y-(b+1)x+a,\\ \frac{dy}{dt} &= -x^2y+bx. \qquad (1)\end{aligned}$$

*This work was partially supported by DARPA/ONR and an NSF PYI award (CTS-8957213). RAA acknowledges the support of the ISR through NSF grant ECD-8803012-06.

0-7803-0999-5/93/$03.00 ©1993 IEEE

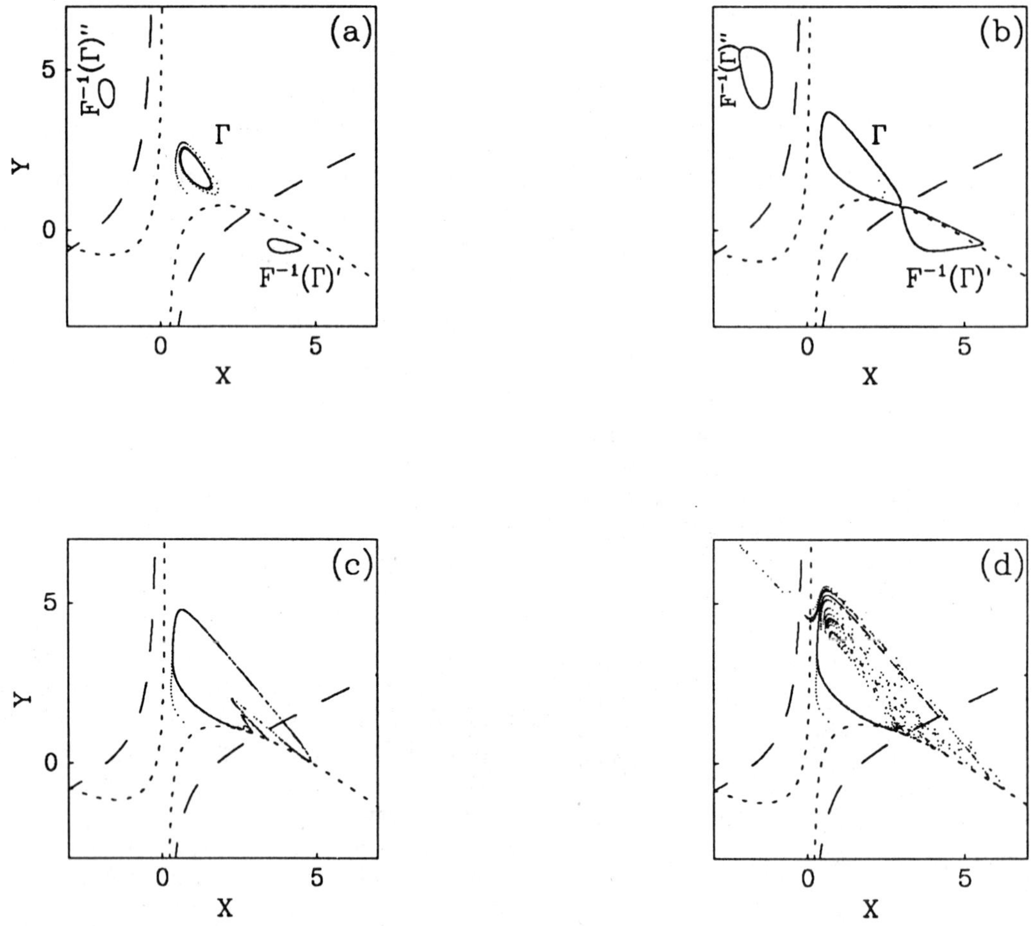

Figure 1: A sample of attractors and J curves for the discretized version of the Brussellator (2). The plots are obtained with $a = 1$, $\tau = 0.15$, and b as follows: (a) 2.0, (b) 2.5, (c) 3.0, and (d) 3.2. The long dash curves represent the J_0 curves and the short dash the J_1 curves. In (a) and (b), Γ is the invariant circle and $F^{-1}(\Gamma)'$ and $F^{-1}(\Gamma)''$ its extra preimages.

Using a one step explicit Euler method, we obtain $F : \mathcal{R}^2 \mapsto \mathcal{R}^2$

$$\begin{aligned} x_n &= x_{n-1} + \tau[x_{n-1}^2 y_{n-1} - (b+1)x_{n-1} + a], \\ y_n &= y_{n-1} + \tau[b x_{n-1} - x_{n-1}^2 y_{n-1}] \end{aligned} \qquad (2)$$

where τ is the time step size, and the subscript $(n, n-1)$ refers to the sequence of time steps. We can explicitly see that this is a noninvertible system, since given some point (x_n, y_n) we find that the inverse map determining (x_{n-1}, y_{n-1}) is a cubic equation whose number of real roots depend on the location (x_n, y_n) in phase space. In other words, some points will have three *real* preimages, and others only one, with the boundaries (called the J_1 curves) between regions of different preimage number having two identical roots plus one distinct root.

Fixing $a = 1$ in (1), we find that the sole fixed point is $(x = 1, y = b)$ and that it undergoes a supercritical Hopf bifurcation at $b = 2$ giving a stable limit cycle which grows in amplitude with increasing b for $b > 2$. For $\tau = 0.15$ in (2), we find the same fixed point, but the Hopf bifurcation occurs at $b = 1.85$ and gives rise to a stable invariant circle. When the invariant circle is small in amplitude (see curve Γ in Fig. 1(a)), the discrete-time, noninvertible representation (2) of the original system (1) appears successful in mimicking the correct dynamical behavior. Taking the preimages of the entire invariant circle, we find that one preimage falls back onto the invariant circle (and at least one *must* since it is invariant forward in time), one (marked $F^{-1}(\Gamma)'$) falls to the right and just across the long-dash curve (this is a J_0 curve, and it is defined by the points where the determinant of the Jacobian of the linearization of (2) vanishes), and the third preimage (marked $F^{-1}(\Gamma)''$) lies far to the left across the "other" J_0 curve. When iterating forward in time, the phase space

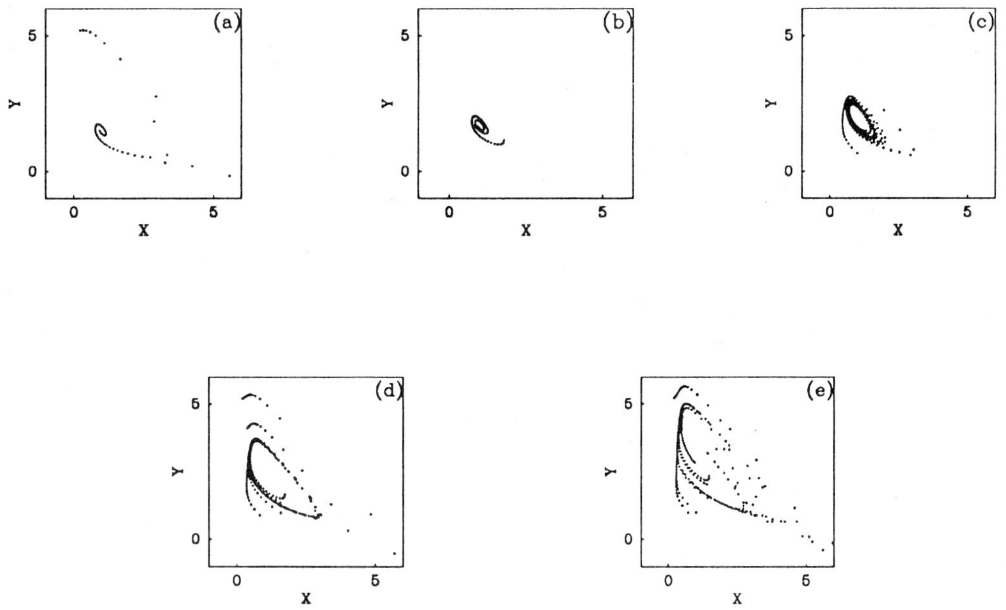

Figure 2: Trajectories for five different b values used in the training set of the neural network. The data were generated by the discretized Brussellator (2) with $a = 1$, $\tau = 0.15$, and b as follows: (a) 1.5, (b) 1.7, (c) 2.0, (d) 2.5, and (e) 3.1. All the trajectories are transient (i.e., are approaching, but have not converged to the attractors).

is "folded" along the J_0 curves and the edges of regions with more than one preimage (the J_1 curves) can be constructed by iterating once, forward in time, points on the J_0 curves [2].

As b is increased (Fig. 1(b)), the invariant circle grows closer to one of its "extra" preimages (the one just to the right), and they ultimately begin to overlap. As pointed out by Lorenz [1], when the tangent of the invariant circle at the point where it crosses J_0 is parallel to the eigenvector associated with the zero eigenvalue of the linearization of (2), the image of that segment of the invariant circle forms a sharp-pointed cusp (see also [3]). As the parameter b is increased past this point, the cusps become self-crossing loops, with the result that in two points *on the attractor* getting mapped to *the same* point on the attractor, a clear "observable" sign of noninvertibility. These transitions result in a complicated attractor (Fig. 1(d)) and produce what Lorenz considered another route to chaos.

II. A Noninvertible Neural Network

In order to illustrate the role of noninvertible dynamics on approximations using neural networks, a three input (the two states (x_{n-1}, y_{n-1}) and the parameter b), two output (x_n, y_n) neural network was trained on data generated by the discrete-time system (2) with values of b and training data shown in Fig. 2. The training set contained one thousand training vectors from five different b values. Only transient trajectories (i.e., not converged *on* the attractors) were used in the training set in an attempt to test the capabilities of the neural network to infer the effects of noninvertibility on the structure of the predicted long term attractors. A large proportion of the training data is composed of apparently "regular" trajectories that do not hint the presence of the noninvertible dynamics (this is more evident in Figs. 2(b) and 2(c)). A standard neural network configuration [4] was used; it included two hidden layers with seven nonlinear neurons (with sigmoidal activation function) each. Convergence was achieved after $O(10^1)$ complete conjugate gradient iterations.

The goal of this experiment was not so much to reproduce the complicated attractors, but to see if it was feasible to locate the important underlying phase space structures (the J_0 and J_1 curves) by only training the network with forward-time data. We were very successful in both aspects: Fig. 3 shows the predicted long term attractors and J curves (calculated numerically) for four different values of b (compare with Fig. 1). The network correctly captures the relevant noninvertible dynamics (compare the location of J curves in the bottom right corner of Fig. 3 with their counterparts on Fig. 1) including the transitions leading to the complex attractors at high b values (Fig. 1(d) and 3(d)). Furthermore, the network also predicts the supercritical Hopf bifurcation of the fixed point with reasonable accuracy at $b = 1.885$ (for system (2) the Hopf occurs at $b = 1.85$).

Not surprisingly (since virtually no data was supplied

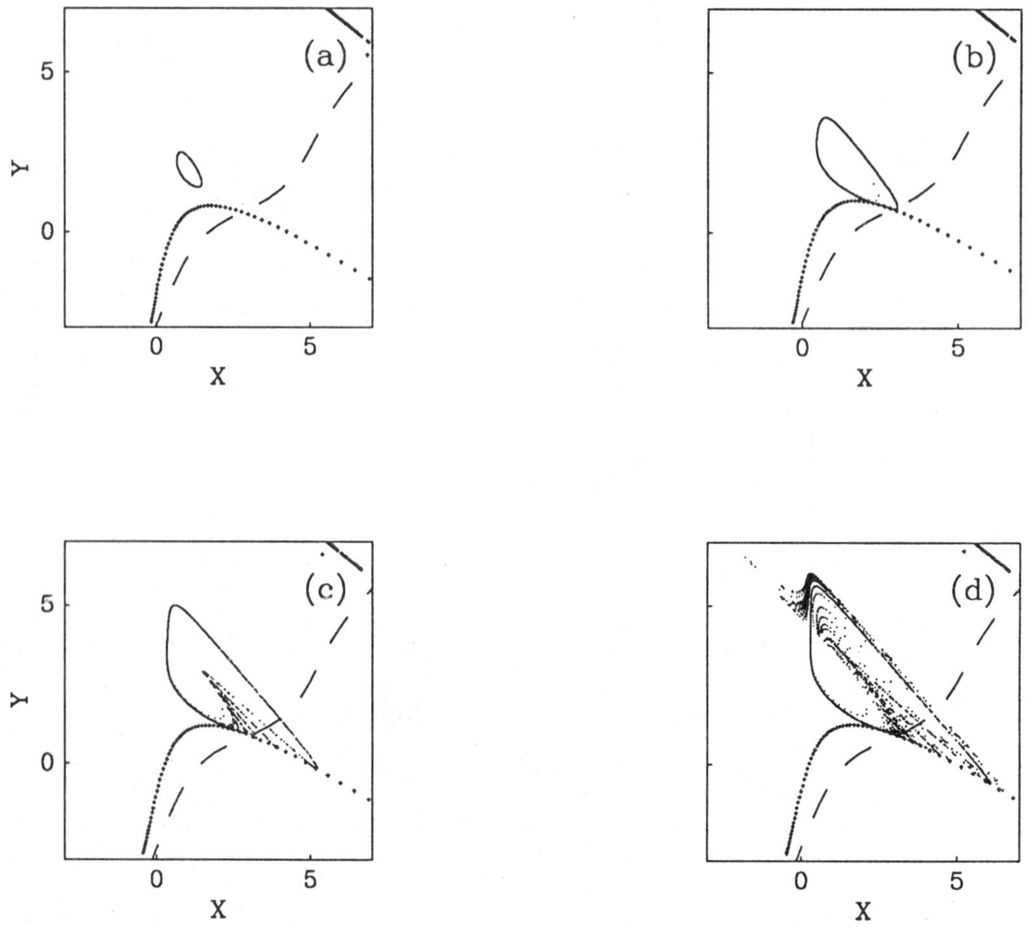

Figure 3: The attractors and J curves predicted by the neural network trained using the data of Fig. 2. The following values of b were used to obtain the depicted phase portraits: (a) 2.0, (b) 2.5, (c) 3.0, and (d) 3.2. The dashed curve represents the J_0 curve and the crosses the J_1 curves.

from that region), the network does not extrapolate the presence of the J curves to the left of the attractors depicted in Fig. 1. On the other hand, the network predicts a larger number of J_0 curves (beyond the range of the plots in Fig. 3) and perhaps a larger number of preimages than the original system (2). In principle, the noninvertible dynamics displayed by the network could be of far greater complexity than the "simple" polynomial system that it approximates. However, it is more difficult to analyze in detail the neural network, because of the lack of explicit expressions for the J curves; now, even the number of preimages in any particular region of phase space cannot be determined without probing $\mathcal{R}^2$ in its entirety.

III. Discussion

We have made use of the noninvertible dynamics exhibited by a continuous dynamical system discretized by an explicit numerical integrator to illustrate the implicit capabilities of neural networks to infer the relevant noninvertible features from a training set. Our goal, rather than elaborate on the complexity of noninvertible dynamics, is to draw attention to the possibility of obtaining noninvertible approximations from neural networks.

Even when the original data are uniquely invertible backward in time, it is possible that a neural network fitted to them may be noninvertible. This noninvertibility can be "latent" when there exists an obviously relevant preimage, or be obvious if the predicted attractors contain self-crossing loops due to their interaction with the J curves. This "obvious" noninvertibility may set in as we try to extrapolate dynamics for parameter values beyond the ones used in training; it may also be caused by noise, insufficient training, or corruption of the training data. In all cases, one could use the simple noninvertible dynamics concepts illustrated here to validate the quality of the approximation given by the neural networks and probe its extrapolation/interpolation range. Another "signature" of obvious noninvertibility that can be used for such validation purposes is the existence of basins of attraction with complicated, disconnected structure [5].

It is important to note that the role played by the noninvertible dynamics, displayed by neural network based approximations, becomes increasingly important when one is interested in more than the mere short term prediction capabilities of such networks. For example, consider studying the bifurcation scenario of an invertible experimental system by numerical bifurcation analysis of the neural network based map trained using data at different parameter values. If the trained neural network is noninvertible, it may predict bifurcations impossible for invertible systems and hence is simply incorrect. Noninvertibility may also create problems when (noninvertible) neural networks are used in nonlinear discrete-time model-predictive control schemes.

References

[1] E. N. Lorenz, Computational chaos—A prelude to computational instability, *Physica D*, vol. 35, pp. 299–317, 1989.

[2] C. Mira, *Chaotic Dynamics. From the One-Dimensional Endomorphism to the Two-Dimensional Diffeomorphism*, World Scientific, 1987.

[3] C. E. Frouzakis, *Dynamics of systems under control: quantifying stability*, Ph.D. Thesis, Princeton University, Department of Chemical Engineering, 1992.

[4] A. S. Lapedes, and R. M. Farber, Nonlinear signal processing using neural networks: prediction and system modeling, *Los Alamos Report LA-UR 87-2662*, 1987.

[5] R. A. Adomaitis, C. E. Frouzakis, and I. G. Kevrekidis, On the dynamics and global stability characteristics of adaptive systems, *Systems Research Center Technical Report TR91-100*, 1991.

Using Spectral Techniques for Improved Performance in Artificial Neural Networks

Bruce E. Segee
Department of Electrical and Computer Engineering
University of Maine
Orono, ME 04469
segee@watson.eece.maine.edu

Abstract— Artificial neural network learning may be viewed as choosing appropriate weightings of basis functions to arrive at a satisfactory function approximation. By examining the frequency domain characteristics of commonly used activation functions one can gain valuable insight into the which basis functions are the most applicable to a given problem. Activation functions which are spectrally similar to the function to be learned give improved performance over activation functions which are spectrally dissimilar to the function to be learned. Using frequency domain information in choosing a basis function based on information of the function to be learned can lead to artificial neural networks which learn more rapidly, with lower approximation error and improved fault tolerance.

INTRODUCTION

Function approximation using an artificial neural network is a process of function synthesis using a (potentially) non-orthogonal set of basis functions[14]. The approximation consists of the weighted sum of the individual basis functions. "Learning" in the neural network usage, is the process of choosing the weights and in some cases choosing the basis functions as well.

For the sake of simplicity, the discussions in this paper will be limited to single-input, single-output systems, although the ideas extend naturally to multiple input networks. Additionally, any multiple-output network can be realized by multiple single-output networks. Considering a single layer of processing elements is also sufficient for the purposes of this paper, since the methods described extend easily to multiple layers of processing elements. Indeed, for virtually any multilayer network, there is a realization in terms of a single layer of (potentially) different complex processing elements that create virtual basis functions in the input domain. The methods of this paper may also be extended to networks having a squashing function (such as a sigmoid) after the summation.

An important observation to make is that the network output is the linear superposition of the individual activation functions (which then may or may not be passed through a final nonlinearity). Thus, important properties of linear superposition can be exploited to both explain previous findings and more importantly to intelligently choose network parameters for a given learning task. Additionally, mathematical tools developed for the analysis of linear systems may be exploited. This paper makes use of one such tool, namely frequency domain analysis.

Frequency domain analysis provides a means for characterizing a signal in terms of the frequency components that it contains. Frequency domain analysis is useful for analyzing the effect of a linear system, such as a filter, on a given signal. In the frequency domain, the filter output is the product of the filter transfer function and the frequency domain representation of the input signal.

One very important fact is that in a linear system, if a frequency or range of frequencies is not present in the input signal, then it cannot appear in the output signal, regardless of the filter transfer function. Similarly, if the filter transfer function is zero at some frequency or range of frequencies, then that frequency or range of frequencies cannot appear in the output signal.

Using frequency domain analysis for neural networks is slightly different. In this case one is not filtering a signal to get a different signal, instead one is linearly summing a collection of different functions in order to synthesize some desired function. The network input is not an input signal in a filtering sense, rather it is the independent variable of the output signal. For instance, if the network input represents length, then the network activation functions and output will be functions of length.

The frequency domain representations of the network output, desired output, and activation functions contain a great deal of information. Here the term "frequency" is being used loosely. If the network input represents time then the frequency domain is truly frequency in the sense of radians per second. If the network input represents some other quantity, then the interpretation of "frequency" must be altered to mean radians per unit measure of input quantity.

One observation that can be made is that if the desired output function has frequency content in regions where the activation functions have little or no frequency content, then learning will be very difficult (but not impossible, since the network only provides an approximation to the desired function). One would expect that the network in this case

0-7803-0999-5/93/$03.00

would learn slowly, if at all, and that the network will also be less fault tolerant.

The rationale for the above statement is as follows. The activation functions have significant energy in some frequency bands (since a zero activation function would be of no use in an artificial neural network). Thus, learning not only requires that one enhance desired frequency components that are very small in the activation function, but also cancel out unwanted frequency components that are large. This requires a very carefully chosen set of network parameters, the loss of any of which will destroy the delicate balance of the network. This is consistent experimental results of studies in the fault tolerance of artificial neural networks [11,12,14]. Additionally, it explains why some researchers claim that neural networks are fault tolerant [cf. references cited in 3 and 5] while others claim that neural networks are not fault tolerant. [cf., 7,9,13,15]

SPECTRA OF COMMON BASIS FUNCTIONS

In this section, spectra for several functions commonly used as activation functions will be derived. These spectra provide valuable insight for explaining properties observed in networks. They also allow one to choose a basis function based on the required spectral properties of the desired network output.

The Sigmoid Function

Members of the sigmoid family of functions are unquestionably the most commonly used network activation function for artificial neural networks. The formula for the sigmoid family of curves is given in Equation 1.

$$Sigmoid(t) = \frac{1}{1 + e^{-at}} \qquad (1)$$

The sigmoid family may be thought of as a generalized step function, however the transition from zero to one is not abrupt and the function is differentiable everywhere. The sigmoid function approaches the unit step function as the parameter 'a' approaches infinity.

Performing a Fourier transform directly on the sigmoid function would be difficult. Furthermore, this approach would not strictly be valid since the sigmoid function is not a finite energy signal [4]. The Fourier transform for the sigmoid function does exist in the limit however. The approach taken is to find a suitable series representation of the sigmoid function and transform this series.

If one performs simple long division on the sigmoid equation, it is readily verified that the infinite series shown in Equation 2 is the result.

$$Sigmoid(t) = 1 - e^{-at} + e^{-2at} - e^{-3at} \ldots \qquad (2)$$

Also, by long division, one can obtain the infinite series shown in Equation 3.

$$Sigmoid(t) = e^{at} - e^{2at} + e^{3at} \ldots \qquad (3)$$

Equation 2 is more well behaved for positive t (i.e., all terms are constant or approach zero as t becomes large), while Equation 3 is more well behaved for negative t. For convenience let $v(t)$ be defined as shown in equation 4.

$$v(t) = - e^{-at} + e^{-2at} - e^{-3at} \ldots \qquad (4)$$

Then the Sigmoid equation can be written as:

$$Sigmoid(t) = u(t) + v(t)\,u(t) - v(-t)\,u(-t), \qquad (5)$$

where u(t) is the unit step function.

Once the equation is written in this form, it is possible to exploit the following Fourier transform relationship [4].

If:

$$z(t) = a_1 v(t) u(t) + a_2 v(-t) u(-t) \qquad (6)$$

then:

$$Z(j\omega) = (a_1 + a_2) V_e(j\omega) + j(a_1 - a_2) V_o(j\omega) \qquad (7)$$

Where: $V_e(jw)$ is the real part of the Fourier transform of $v(t)$ and $V_o(j\omega)$ is the imaginary part of the Fourier transform of $v(t)$.

In the case of the Sigmoid function, $a_1 = 1$ and $a_2 = -1$. Thus, the Fourier transform of the Sigmoid function becomes:

$$Z_{Sigmoid}(j\omega) = \mathcal{F}(u(t)) + j2\left(\mathrm{Im}\left(\mathcal{F}\left(\sum_{i=1}^{\infty} (-1)^i e^{-iat}\right)\right)\right), \qquad (8)$$

where $\mathcal{F}$ represents the Fourier transform operator and Im represents the imaginary part.

Since the Fourier transform is a linear operation, the order of the summation and Fourier transform may be interchanged. Thus, the Fourier transform of the sigmoid becomes:

$$Z_{Sigmoid}(j\omega)=\pi\delta(t)+\frac{1}{j\omega}+j2(\mathrm{Im}(\sum_{i=1}^{\infty}\frac{(-1)^i}{(i*a+j\omega)})) \quad (9)$$

Figure 2 shows a plot of the spectrum represented by Equation 9 when the first one hundred terms of the series are evaluated[1]. The equation was evaluated for a=1.0. For the sake of comparison the spectrum of a unit step function is also plotted. Only positive frequencies are shown, since the magnitude of the transform is an even function of frequency. Also the impulse at the origin is omitted.

As the parameter *'a'* becomes larger, the spectrum of the sigmoid function approaches that of the step function. Also, for any finite value of *'a'* the magnitude of the spectrum falls off more rapidly with increasing frequency for the sigmoid function than for the unit step function.

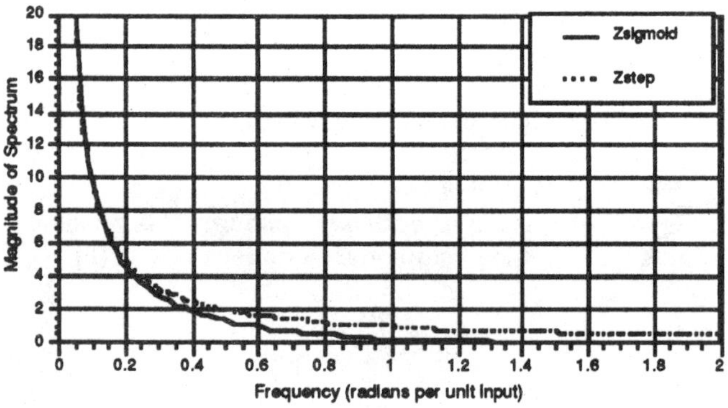

Figure 2 Magnitude of the frequency content of the sigmoid function. This data was generated by evaluating the first 100 terms of Equation 9 with the value *'a'* set to 1.0. The impulse at the origin is not shown. The Fourier transform of the unit step function is plotted for comparison.

Gaussian Curves

The Fourier transform of the Gaussian function is commonly included in tables of Fourier transforms and thus will be presented here without derivation. Given a Gaussian function of the form

$$g(t)=e^{-\frac{t^2}{w^2}}, \quad (10)$$

its Fourier transform is given by:

$$G(j\omega)=w\sqrt{\pi}\,e^{-\frac{\omega^2 w^2}{2}} \quad (11)$$

Thus, the spectrum for a Gaussian function of time is a Gaussian function of frequency. A Gaussian of width w in the time domain transforms to a Gaussian (scaled by a factor of $w\sqrt{\pi}$) of width $\frac{\sqrt{2}}{w}$ in the frequency domain. Gaussian spectra for three different values of w are shown in Figure 3.

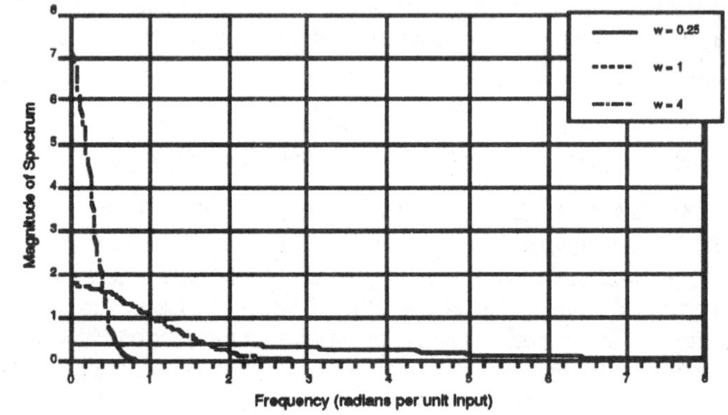

Figure 3 Magnitude of the Fourier transform of the Gaussian function for w = 0.25, w = 1, and w = 4.

The Rectangular Pulse Function

Rectangular pulses are commonly used basis functions in the CMAC neural network[1,8]. The rectangular pulse function $\Pi\left(\frac{t}{\tau}\right)$ is defined as shown in Figure 4. It has height A and width τ.

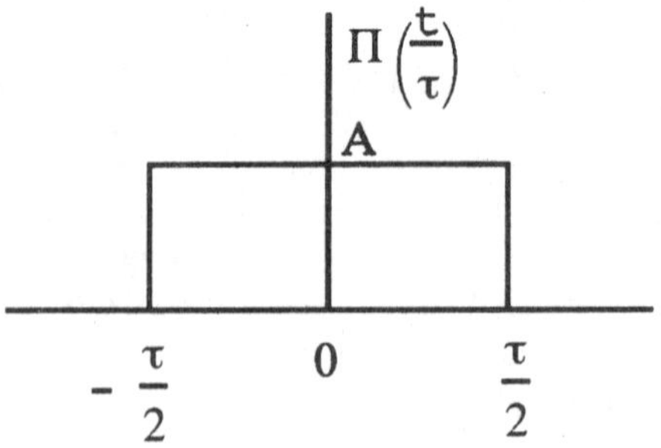

Figure 4 A plot of the rectangular pulse function $\Pi\left(\frac{t}{\tau}\right)$.

The Fourier transform of this function is given by:

1In order to verify convergence the first fifty, one hundred and five hundred terms were evaluated. The differences in the results were far too small to be observed on the scale of the plots.

$$F\left(\Pi\left(\frac{t}{\tau}\right)\right)=\frac{2A}{\omega}\sin\left(\frac{\omega\tau}{2}\right) \qquad (12)$$

A plot of the magnitude of this transform is shown in Figure 5.

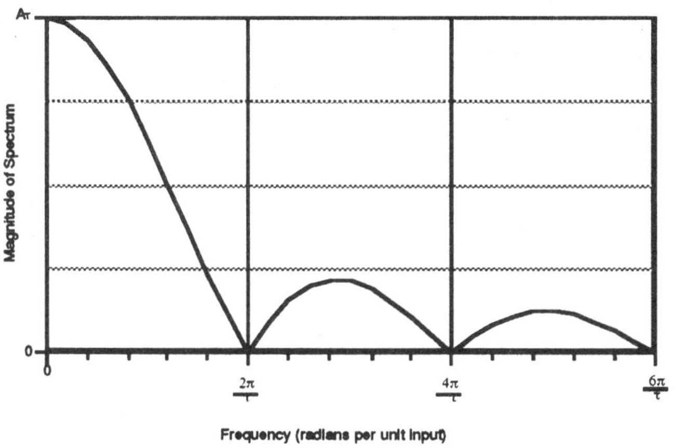

Figure 5 Magnitude of the Fourier transform of the rectangular pulse function shown in Figure 4.

The Triangular Pulse Function

Triangular pulses are also used (though not as commonly as square pulses) as basis functions for the CMAC artificial neural network. The triangular pulse function $\Lambda\left(\frac{t}{\tau}\right)$ is defined as shown in Figure 6. Notice that this function has height B and width 2τ.

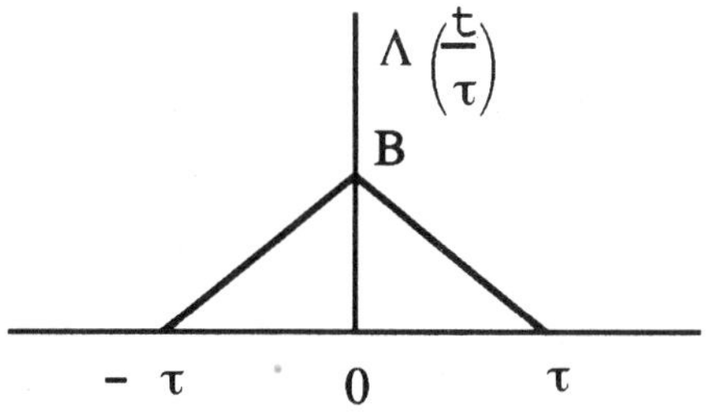

Figure 6 A plot of the triangular pulse function $\Lambda\left(\frac{t}{\tau}\right)$.

The Fourier transform of this function is given by:

$$F\left(\Lambda\left(\frac{t}{\tau}\right)\right)=\frac{4B}{\omega^{2}\tau}\sin^{2}\left(\frac{\omega\tau}{2}\right) \qquad (13)$$

A plot of the magnitude of this transform is shown in Figure 7.

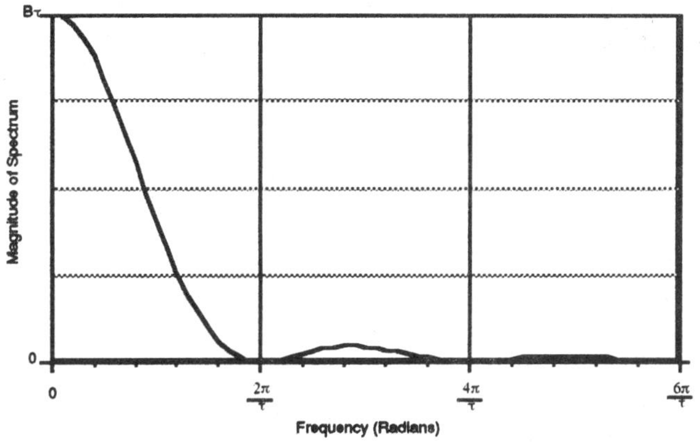

Figure 7 Magnitude of the Fourier transform of the triangular pulse function shown in Figure 6.

As can be seen, the frequency content of the triangular pulse is very similar to the frequency content of the rectangular pulse. Indeed, the zeros of these functions are identical. The magnitude of the spectrum for the triangular pulse drops off more rapidly than that of the rectangular pulse. This may be readily explained by noting the relationship between the rectangular pulse and the triangular pulse. Namely, if one convolves a rectangular pulse of height A and width τ with itself, one would get a triangular pulse of height $A^2\tau$ and width 2τ. Thus, if one lets $B = A^2\tau$, then the triangular pulse shown in Figure 6 is simply the convolution of two rectangular pulses as shown in Figure 4. A nice property of convolution is that the Fourier transform of the convolution of two signals is the product of the Fourier transforms of the two signals. In this case, as may be readily verified, the signal represented in Equation 13 and plotted in Figure 7 is the square of the signal represented in Equation 12 and plotted in Figure 5, provided that $B = A^2\tau$.

CMAC SLOW LEARNING

During experiments with the CMAC neural network it was found [2,6] that when learning sinusoidal functions, certain frequencies were very difficult to learn. These critical frequencies corresponded to the situation where the width of the rectangular receptive field (the region in which a particular weight is active) was equal to an integer multiple of the sinusoid's wavelength. Furthermore, it was found that if triangular basis functions were used, then the first critical frequency was approximately twice as high as that for rectangular basis functions with the same width and the learning speed at this critical frequency was markedly slower than at the first critical frequency when rectangular windows were employed.

All of these findings make perfect sense in the context of frequency analysis. For instance, the critical frequencies occur at frequencies where there are zeros in the basis function spectrum. Furthermore, for a given width, the triangular basis function has twice the bandwidth (between first spectral nulls) of the rectangular window; however, the frequency content of the triangular window drops off more rapidly above the first spectral null.

It is no surprise that the network has difficulty learning at the critical frequencies. It is almost more surprising that the network can learn at all at these frequencies. However, the neural network has several things going for it. The most important fact is that the network need only produce an output that is *close* to the desired output. Furthermore, this approximation need only hold for some finite interval in the input space where the network has been trained, and network behavior outside this interval is left unspecified.

Thus, CMAC slow learning is caused by attempting to learn frequencies which are absent in the network basis function. The fact that learning can occur at all can be explained by the fact that the function to be learned is a finite length segment of a sine wave, and that the network need only produce an approximation to this function. Thus, learning is much more difficult than at lower frequencies, but not impossible.

The simplest "solution" to the CMAC slow learning problem is simply to choose the receptive field width to be narrow enough that the frequencies of interest are below the first critical frequency[2]. In this way, learning can easily converge to the desired output while naturally rejecting any high frequency noise that may be present in the training data.

SPECTRAL FITTING AND FAULT TOLERANCE

Many neural networks perform function approximation using the linear superposition of activation functions or compositions of activation functions. These activation functions will always favor some frequencies over others (unless delta functions are used as activation functions, and thereby reducing the neural network to a lookup table). Essentially, the process of learning requires two simultaneous constraints involving the network weights be satisfied. The first is that a set of weights must be found which accentuates frequencies which are found in the training set. Simultaneously, a set of weights must be found which causes cancellation of frequencies which are present in the activation function, but are not found in the training set. Obviously, the single set of network weights must satisfy both of these goals in order to attain a good function approximation.

When there is a strong spectral match between the activation function and the function to be learned, both tasks become easier. Smaller weights are also necessary, since frequencies present in the training set are well represented in the activation function, and frequencies to be canceled are relatively poorly represented in the activation function. While these characteristics cannot guarantee fault tolerance, they do not actively hinder its achievement as in the case of spectral mismatch.

When there is a strong spectral mismatch between the activation function and the training set, then both learning tasks become much more difficult. Since the frequency components which must be accentuated are very small, large weights are necessary. However, these large weights must be very carefully chosen to cancel out the resulting large, undesirable, frequency components. Such a network cannot be fault tolerant, since the loss of a weight (particularly a large weight) can destroy this delicate balance.

Thus, one can conclude that although a good spectral match between the activation function and the function to be learned is not sufficient to guarantee fault tolerance, a spectral mismatch is sufficient to guarantee that a network will not be fault tolerant unless special steps are taken to control the impact of faults on the approximation. [14] This conclusion is supported by experimental results which found that when learning a unit frequency sine function, a radial basis function network [10] employing unit width Gaussian functions could significantly outperform a sigmoidal network in terms of learning speed, approximation error, and fault tolerance [13], while radial basis function network using a width of 4, performed no better than the sigmoidal network [14].

SUMMARY

This paper derives the spectra for many common network activation functions, including members of the sigmoid family, the Gaussian function, rectangular pulses and triangular pulses. It is found that the sigmoid curves are very ill behaved in the frequency domain and thus almost always provide a strong mismatch between the spectrum of the activation function and the spectrum of the function to be learned. This does not imply that networks using the sigmoid activation function cannot learn good approximations. It does imply, however, that networks using the sigmoid activation function will learn more slowly and will be more sensitive to the loss of parameters than networks using more suitable activation functions. For instance, experimental evidence shows that a network employing well chosen (based on spectral data) Gaussian activation functions can outperform a network employing sigmoid activation functions by more than an order of magnitude, both in terms of learning speed and fault tolerance. On the other hand, networks employing poorly chosen Gaussian functions behave very similarly to networks employing sigmoidal activation functions.

Learning in a neural network can be thought of as function approximation using the linear superposition of activation

[2] Of course, as the receptive field width becomes narrower, the required number of training exemplars for good generalization becomes larger.

functions. These activation functions will always favor some frequencies over others (unless delta functions are used as activation functions, reducing the neural network to a lookup table). Essentially, the process of learning involves two simultaneous activities involving the network weights. The first is that a set of weights must be found which accentuates frequencies that are found in the training set. Simultaneously, a set of weights must be found which causes cancellation of frequencies that are present in the activation function but not found in the training set. Obviously, the single set of network weights must satisfy both of these goals in order to attain a good function approximation.

When there is a strong spectral match between the activation function and the function to be learned, both tasks become easier. Smaller weights are also necessary, since frequencies present in the training set are well represented in the activation function, and frequencies to be canceled are relatively poorly represented in the activation function. While these characteristics cannot guarantee fault tolerance, they do nothing to prevent fault tolerance.

When there is a strong spectral mismatch between the activation function and the training set, then both learning tasks become much more difficult. Since the frequency components that must be accentuated are very small, large weights are necessary. However, these large weights must be very carefully chosen to cancel out the resulting large, undesirable, frequency components. This makes learning a very difficult task. Furthermore, such a network cannot be fault tolerant, since the loss of a weight (particularly a large weight) can destroy this delicate balance.

REFERENCES

[1] J.S. Albus, "A Theory of Cerebellar Functions", Mathematical Biosci*ences*, Vol. 10, pp. 25-61, 1971

[2] P.E. An, "An Improved Multi-Dimensional CMAC Neural Network: Receptive Field Function and Placement", PhD Dissertation, University of New Hampshire, 1991

[3] G. Bolt, , J. Austin, and G. Morgan, " Fault Tolerance in Neural Networks", Technical Report, Computer Science Department, University of York, Heslington, York, YO1 5DD, U.K., 1990

[4] A.B. Carlson, *Communication Systems-An Introduction to Signals and Noise in Electrical Communication*, Third edition, New York, NY, McGraw-Hill Book Company, 1986

[5] M.J. Carter, "The Illusion of Fault Tolerance in Neural Networks for Pattern Recognition and Signal Processing", *Proceedings Technical Session on Fault-Tolerant Integrated Systems*, University of New Hampshire, Durham, NH, 1988

[6] M.J. Carter, A. J. Nucci, W.T. Miller, P.E. An, F. Rudolph, "Slow Learning in CMAC Networks and Implications for Fault Tolerance", 24th Annual Conference on Information Sciences and Systems, Princeton University, March 1990

[7] Y. Izui, and A. Pentland, "Analysis of Neural Networks with Redundancy", Neural Computation, Vol. 2, Number 2, pp. 226-238, Summer, 1990

[8] W.T. Miller, F.H Glanz, and L.G. Kraft, "CMAC: An Associative Neural Network Alternative to Backpropagation", *Proceedings of the IEEE*, Vol. 78, pp. 1561-1567, October, 1990

[10] C. Neti, M. Schneider, and E. Young, "Maximally fault tolerant neural networks and nonlinear programming", *Proceedings IJCNN*, pp II-483:496, 1990

[11] T. Poggio, and F. Girosi, "Networks for Approximation and Learning", *Proceedings of the IEEE*, v78, pp1481:1497, September, 1990

[12] B.E. Segee, and M.J. Carter "Fault Sensitivity and Nodal Relevance Relationships in Multi-Layer Perceptrons", UNH Intelligent Structures Group Report ECE.IS.90.02, March 9, 1990

[13] B. E. Segee, and M. J. Carter, "Fault Tolerance of Pruned Multilayer Networks", *Proceedings IJCNN*, pp. II-447-452, Seattle, WA, 1991

[14] B. E. Segee, and M. J. Carter, "Comparative Fault Tolerance of Parallel Distributed Processing Networks (Debunking the Myth of Inherent Fault Tolerance)", UNH Intelligent Structures Group Report ECE.IS.92.07, February 24, 1992

[15] B. E. Segee, "Characterizing and Improving the Fault Tolerance of Artificial Neural Networks", PhD Dissertation, University of New Hampshire,1992

[15] Séquin, and R. Clay, "Fault Tolerance in Artificial Neural Networks", *Proceedings IJCNN*, pp I-703:708, 1990

Performance Comparison Issues in Neural Network Experiments for Classification Problems

Ramesh Sharda
Rick L. Wilson

Oklahoma State University
College of Business Administration
Stillwater, OK 74078

Abstract

This paper focuses on the methodological aspects of neural network experiments in business applications. A number of papers have attempted to study the comparative performance of neural nets and time series forecasting methods, regression, and classification methods such as multiple discriminant analysis and logistic regression. Many studies report on the superior performance of neural networks on an anecdotal basis, leading to much skepticism. Our paper emphasizes the need for a more statistically rigorous comparison of neural nets with other traditional techniques. Specifically, we identify several measures for estimating the performance of a classification technique. We illustrate these ideas through a comparison of neural nets and discriminant analysis. The results show that a much better picture of the performance capabilities of a technique emerges as a result of this additional analysis.

1. Introduction

Neural networks have been extensively investigated for potential applications in business and engineering problems by many researchers in the last few years. Even without a detailed history and description of how neural networks compute, it can be safely stated that business researchers view neural nets as biologically inspired statistical methods. As such, a number of papers have attempted to study the comparative performance of neural nets and time series forecasting methods, regression, and classification methods such as multiple discriminant analysis and logistic regression. However, many of these studies report on the superior performance of neural networks on an anecdotal basis, leading to much skepticism. The objective of our paper is to emphasize the need for more statistically rigorous comparisons of neural nets with other traditional techniques. Specifically, we identify several measures for estimating the performance of a classification technique such as discriminant analysis or a neural network approach. These ideas are illustrated through a comparison of neural nets and discriminant analysis that we have conducted. The measures identified in this paper are not necessarily new, but have not yet been used in most of the neural net comparison papers of which we are aware.

This paper is organized as follows. Section 2 reviews some of the neural network statistical application papers. Section 3 describes the classification measures that we propose to use in comparison of techniques. Section 4 describes our application of these measures in a bankruptcy prediction problem. Section 5 concludes the paper with a discussion of our results.

2. Some Statistical Applications of Neural Nets

As stated before, neural networks can be viewed as biologically inspired statistical methods. White (1989) lays a mathematical foundation for this argument. The stated advantages of neural nets in statistical applications include robustness to probability distribution assumptions, the ability to classify where nonlinear separation surfaces may be present, and their ability to work with incomplete data. The three major statistical areas where neural networks have been tried are regression analysis, time series prediction, and classification. One of the first reported "applications" was a comparison of neural networks with regression in predicting bond ratings (Shekhar and Dutta 1988). Several other papers (Surkan and Singleton 1990, Utans and Moody 1991) have attempted to verify that neural networks perform better in this task. A recent dissertation by Marquez (1992) is the most complete comparison thus far of neural nets and regression analysis. His results confirm that the neural nets can do fairly well in comparison to regression analysis.

The prediction capability of neural nets has been studied by a number of researchers. Early papers (Lapedes and Farber 1987, Sutton 1988) offered evidence that the neural models were able to predict time series data fairly well. Many comparisons of neural nets and time series forecasting techniques such as the Box-Jenkins approach (Box and Jenkins 1976) have been reported. Such studies include work by Tang *et al.* (1991), Sharda and Patil (1992), and Hill *et al.* (1992). These papers represent a statistically rigorous comparison of neural nets and at least one forecasting technique. For example, Sharda and Patil (1992) attempted to model the appropriate subset of the 111 series employed in other forecasting tests using an automated Box-Jenkins procedure (AFS 1988) and a backpropagation model. The results show that the neural approach performs about as well as the Box-Jenkins approach. A more complete simulation of the performance of the two techniques was conducted by Kang (1991) in her dissertation, with essentially similar results.

The most commonly cited applications of neural networks can generally be termed as classification problems. A number of papers have studied the performance of neural networks in bankruptcy prediction problems. These include the papers by Bell *et al.* (1990), Odom and Sharda (1990), and Raghupathi *et al.* (1991). Other classification problems studied include mortgage underwriting (Collins *et al.* 1988), commodity trading (Collard 1990), and country risk rating (Roy and Cosset 1990). Several authors have attempted to use neural networks for stock market prediction. Examples include Fishman *et al.* (1991), Kimoto and Asakawa (1990), and Yoon and Swales (1991).

While many of the papers cited above report that the neural network models achieved equal or better performance than a statistical technique, most of these results are subject to criticism on two grounds. First, as far as we can tell from the papers, the results are not based on a comprehensive, statistical comparison of techniques. Many studies used one training sample and one validation sample to compare the two techniques. Results based on one comparison are subject to sample biases, and no statistical significance can be attached to such tests. A second concern with most of the studies cited above is that the performance is reported in terms of correct percentage classification rate. However, researchers using discriminant analysis for classification problems have argued for using several other measures to identify the classification power of the model (Huberty 1984). To our knowledge, no published studies of neural networks and statistical techniques have reported the performance using these techniques. A recent dissertation by Gordon (1992) uses many of these measures, but it did not use a sampling approach to achieve statistically significant results. A paper by Wilson and Sharda (1993) used some of the measures discussed in this paper, but not all. We submit that the use of these additional measures is critical to objectively comparing the performance of any classification techniques. Studies reporting the results of technique comparisons using these measures will offer much richer information as compared to the earlier studies.

3. Performance Measures

The classification problem of interest can be described as follows. An entity with n attributes can be a member of one of g classes, based upon the values of its attributes. A classification procedure is trained by showing it several entities with different attribute combinations and the known (desired) classification. The classification procedure builds a discrimination function that can then be used to classify a new entity with some combination of the values of the attributes into one of the g groups.

Let o_g be the observed correct predictions for group g, and f_g be the observed false predictions for group g. For the bankruptcy problem where we apply the performance measures, there are two classes: bankrupt (b) and non-bankrupt (n). Thus, o_b would be the number of firms correctly classified as bankrupt, and f_b would represent the number of firms falsely classified as bankrupt. Similarly, o_n and f_n denote the number of firms correctly and falsely classified as non-bankrupt. Let n_g be the number of test cases in each group and N be the total number of cases in the test set (sum of n_g).

Most of the studies summarized in the earlier section report the performance of a technique in terms of success rates in classifying the test cases. While it is not explicitly defined in many of the papers, it appears to be computed as:

$$S = (o_b + o_n)/N \tag{1}$$

While this is a reasonable measure of the success of a classification technique, some additional measures would present an even better picture of a technique's performance. The first measure is referred to as separate group hit rate by Huberty (1987). This is essentially a conditional probability of being correct in classifying an entity to be in any group: p (corr|g). For the bankrupt and nonbankrupt groups, it is computed as:

$$p_{1b} = o_b/(o_b + f_n) \quad (2)$$

$$p_{1n} = o_n/(o_n + f_b) \quad (3)$$

The measure p_{1g} indicates the percent success in identifying correctly classified entities in each group. This gives a better indication of a technique's performance than S alone. Further, it also allows us to evaluate the performance of a technique in predicting the group of more interest, e.g., bankrupt firms.

Another measure, p_{2g}, can be used to determine the success in predicting entities in group g that actually were in group g. For example, p_{2b} would give the percentage of firms classified as bankrupts that were actually bankrupt. This measure would also serve as a surrogate measure for evaluating a technique's performance as compared to a simple chance-based approach. The measure p_{2g} for our example would be computed as:

$$p_{2b} = o_b/(o_b + f_b) \quad (4)$$

and

$$p_{2n} = o_n/(o_n + f_n) \quad (5)$$

A third metric p_{3g} that can be used is an "inefficiency" measure. This is just a ratio of incorrect (false) to correct classifications. A good classification scheme would not only maximize correct classification, it would also minimize false grouping. For our example, this is computed as:

$$p_{3b} = f_b/o_b \quad (6)$$

$$p_{3n} = f_n/o_n \quad (7)$$

A good classification procedure would achieve the highest possible values of p_{1g} and p_{2g} and would minimize p_{3g}.

Classification Techniques and Chance Criteria

The underlying concept in comparing a classification or prediction technique to pure chance is to consider what one could do by simply guessing at the predictions. A proportion of interest in any population is sometimes referred to as the base rate. For instance, if the base rate was 50 percent for a two group problem, guessing would result in an average of 50 percent correct predictions. Similarly, if the base rate was skewed (80 percent - 20 percent), one could blindly predict with 80 percent accuracy by predicting all cases to belong to the more frequent class (Meehl and Rosen 1955). It has been shown that to achieve significant levels of predictive validity, the proportion of correct positive predictions (bankrupt firms, in our case) to all positive bankrupt predictions must exceed the base rate of the more frequent class (Meehl and Rosen 1955). This is known as the maximum chance criterion. The performance measure p_{2g} serves as a surrogate measure of this criterion. Thus this statistic will indicate whether predictive results obtained by neural networks and discriminant analysis differ greatly from those that can be obtained by chance. The maximum chance criterion does not consider the cost of false negative predictions, and it could be quite expensive to adopt a classification technique solely because it beats the maximum chance criterion. An alternative prediction system based on chance would be to assign a proportional number of entities to each of the two classes based on the observed base rates. This system would detect some entities in each group. A classification technique should be able to do better than this proportional classification scheme. The following standard normal test statistic is calculated as

$$\frac{(O - E) \cdot N^{1/2}}{(E \cdot (N - E))^{1/2}} \quad (8)$$

where

g = groups (bankrupt and non-bankrupt),
n_g = number of test cases in group g,
b_g = training base rate of group g,
o_g = observed correct predictions for group g,
e_g = expected correct predictions for group g by chance ($n_g \cdot b_g$),
O = total correct prediction (Σo_g),
E = total correct predictions obtainable by chance (Σe_g), and
N = total number of cases (Σn_g).

Equation (8) computes the proportional chance criterion for the total classification problem. One can also calculate a similar statistical measure for each separate classification group. Using the same notation as above, the standard normal test statistics for each group (illustrating whether the predictive results obtained by a classification technique significantly differs from chance) is

$$\frac{(o_g - e_g) \cdot n_g^{1/2}}{(e_g \cdot (n_g - e_g))^{1/2}} \qquad (9)$$

The proportional chance criterion is considered to be a more realistic yardstick when the groups have different proportions (Huberty 1984).

Another approach useful in assessing a prediction method is determining how much better a classification approach predicts compared to chance assignment. An index useful in such a setting is the improvement-over-chance or reduction-in-error index (Huberty 1984, Klecka 1980),

$$I = \frac{H_o - H_e}{1 - H_e} \qquad (10)$$

where H_o is the observed rate of correct predictions and H_e is the correct prediction rate expected by chance. Using the previous notation, H_e is defined as $(\Sigma(b_g * n_g))$ / N for the aggregate case and b_g for each separate group. The index I represents a reduction-in-error statistic in that $100 \cdot I$ percent fewer prediction errors result using the classification rule than would be expected by chance.

Thus the classification capability of any technique can be tested using the criteria described in this section. A classification technique may do well on the overall performance, but it may not work well in classifying groups with very small bases rates. Criteria p_{1g}, p_{2g}, and p_{3g} attempt to assess this capability. The proportional chance criterion and the reduction in error index estimate the performance of a technique over a simple proportion-based classification scheme. These measures have been recommended for testing the performance of discriminant models (Huberty 1984), but are just as applicable for comparing neural networks with other techniques.

4. An Illustrative Example

We next describe the application of these criteria in an experiment to compare neural nets with discriminant analysis for bankruptcy prediction. The reader is referred to Wilson and Sharda (1993) for more details of the study. Some of the results reported here are also presented in the other paper.

The basic intent of this study was to compare and contrast the predictive performance of classical multivariate discriminant analysis to that of neural networks for firm bankruptcy. Most of the studies that have compared neural networks with statistical techniques report the results on the basis of either a single experiment or in an anecdotal form. There is a need for a thorough comparison using sound statistical procedures. Our study is based on a resampling technique to assess the effectiveness of neural networks on a statistical basis.

The Altman study (1968) has been used as the standard of comparison for subsequent bankruptcy classification studies using discriminant analysis. Most follow-up studies have identified several other attributes to improve prediction performance. In this exploratory study, we wanted to see if the neural networks can come close to the traditional techniques. More sophisticated inputs to the neural network model should not worsen its performance. Thus, this could establish a lower bound on neural network performance in bankruptcy prediction. For these reasons, we used the same financial ratios as Altman (1968). These ratios were:

X_1 : Working Capital/Total Assets
X_2 : Retained Earnings/Total Assets
X_3 : Earnings before Interest and Taxes/Total Assets
X_4 : Market Value of Equity/Total Debt
X_5 : Sales/Total Assets

The sample of firms for which these ratios were obtained consisted of firms that either were in operation or went bankrupt between 1975 and 1982. The sample, obtained from *Moody's Industrial Manuals*, consisted of a total of 129 firms, 65 of which went bankrupt during the period and 64 nonbankrupt firms matched on industry and year. Data used for the bankrupt firms is from the last financial statements issued before the firms declared bankruptcy. Thus the prediction of bankruptcy is to be made about one year in advance.

The results of this study could be affected by the proportion of non-bankrupt firms to bankrupt firms in both the training and testing sets. That is, the population of all firms contains a certain proportion of firms on the verge of bankruptcy. This base rate may have an impact on a prediction technique's performance in two ways. First, a technique may not work well when the firms of interest (bankrupt) constitute a very small percentage of the population (low base rate). This would be due to a technique's inability to identify the features necessary for classification. A second effect of the base rate is in terms of differences in base rates between training samples and testing samples. If a classification model is built using a training sample with a certain base rate, does the model still work when the base rate in the test population is different? This issue is important for one more reason. If a classification model based on a certain base rate works across other proportions, it may be possible to build a model using a higher proportion of cases of interest than actually occur in the population.

To study the effects of this proportion on the predictive performance of the two techniques, we created three proportions (or base rates) for each of the training and testing set compositions. The first factor level (or base rate) was a 50/50 proportion of bankruptcy to nonbankrupt cases, the second level was a 80/20 proportion (80 percent non-bankrupt, 20 percent bankrupt), and the third factor level was an approximate 90/10 proportion. We do not really know the actual proportion of firms going bankrupt. The 80/20 and 90/10 cases should be close. The 50/50 scenario was utilized to investigate the possibility of a better model by using a high base rate in the training set.

Utilizing a full two-factor design, there were nine different experimental cells. Within each cell, 20 different training-testing set pairs were generated via Monte Carlo resampling from the original 129 firms. Thus a total of 180 distinct training and testing data set pairs were generated from the original data. In each case, the training set and test set pairs contained unique firms, i.e., no overlap was allowed. This restriction provides a stronger test of a technique's performance. Results reported here are only for the 50/50 training set combination. Thus neural networks and DA used training sets of equal proportion of firms to determine the classification function, but were evaluated with test sets containing 50/50, 80/20, and 90/10 base rates. Other results are available in Wilson and Sharda (1993).

BRAINMAKER (Stanley and Bak 1989), a personal computer-based neural network software package that implements the aforementioned back propagation training algorithm, was used to construct and test trained neural network models. For each network trained in the study, a structure of 5 input neurons (one for each financial ratio), 10 hidden neurons, and 2 output neurons (one indicating bankrupt firm, the other indicating nonbankrupt firm) was used. Such a network structure was chosen on the basis of previously espoused heuristic guidelines. In training the networks, a heuristic back propagation algorithm was used to ensure convergence (all firms in the training set classified correctly). A stringent training tolerance was initially used in training the network (a small value of 0.1) and gradually relaxed until such a point when all training cases satisfied the training tolerance criteria. Then the training tolerance was incrementally lowered (made more stringent) and the network was trained until convergence occurred at this level. This was repeated until no further reductions of the training tolerance could occur. In all 180 subsamples generated, the neural network models were able to obtain 100 percent classifications of the training set cases. By using a relaxed tolerance, memorization or overtraining should have been avoided.

Table 1 represents the average percentage of correct classifications, S (irrespective of type of firm), when utilizing the two different techniques to evaluate the 20 holdout samples for each of the three different test set base rates. When the testing sets contained an equal number of the two cases, neural networks correctly classified 97.5 percent of the holdout cases, while multivariate discriminant analysis was correct 88.25 percent of the time. Similarly, when the testing sets contained 20 percent bankrupt firms, neural networks classified at a 95.6 percent correct rate, while discriminant analysis correctly classified 91.8 correct.

A non-parametric test, the Wilcoxon test for paired observations, was undertaken to assess whether the different correct classification percentages for the two different techniques were significantly different. The critical values of this test are also reported in Table 3. Those experimental cells that are statistically significant are highlighted by asterisks. In general, neural networks were statistically significant better predictors of firm bankruptcies in the holdout sample than discriminant analysis.

Other measures in Table 1 provide a more detailed look at the classification results, breaking down the correct percentages in terms of bankrupt firm predictions and nonbankrupt firm predictions. It is apparent from Table 1 that it is in the classification of bankrupt firms (p_{1b}) where neural networks significantly out-perform discriminant analysis. This is important since it is widely accepted in terms of predicting bankrupt firms that it is more costly to classify a failed firm as non-failing than the converse (Watts and Zimmerman 1986).

As with the overall aggregate classification data, the Wilcoxon paired observation test was used to assess the significance of the differences of the two prediction techniques. The critical values of this test are given, and those significant are noted by asterisks. Again, for predicting bankrupt cases, note that neural networks

Table 1

Performance Comparison of Neural Nets and Discriminant Analysis

Criteria/Test Proportions	50/50			80/20			90/10		
	NN		DA	NN		DA	NN		DA
S	97.5	** ($p < .001$)	88.25	95.6	** ($p = .005$)	91.8	95.68	* ($p = .046$)	93.32
p_{1b}	97.0	** ($p < .001$)	79.75	92.0	** ($p = .025$)	82.0	92.5	($p = .282$)	90.0
p_{1n}	98.0	* ($p = .029$)	96.75	96.5	($p = .071$)	94.25	96.0	* ($p = .038$)	93.5
p_{2b}	98.0	** ($p = .006$)	94.9	86.8	($p = .055$)	78.1	69.8	($p = .068$)	58.1
p_{2n}	97.0	** ($p < .001$)	82.7	98.0	* ($p = .016$)	95.4	99.2	($p = .135$)	98.9
p_{3b}	2.1	** ($p < .001$)	4.1	15.2	* ($p = .023$)	28.1	43.2	($p = .282$)	72.2
p_{3n}	3.1	* ($p = .033$)	20.9	2.1	** ($p = .002$)	4.8	0.8	* ($p = .029$)	1.1

* $p < .05$
** $p < .01$

Table 2

Predictive Validity of Classifications

Criteria	NN	DA	NN		DA	NN		DA
	Bankrupt		Nonbankrupt			Total		
Proportional Chance Criterion	2.88 ($p = .002$)	1.86 (p - .031)	4.19	($p < .001$)	4.00	5.19	($p < .001$)	4.36
Reduction-in-Error of Classification	91.5	61.8	63.7		89.7	93.0		81.0

predicted better than discriminant analysis at every level of the test set base rates. For instance, where the test set composition was equal among the two different classes of firms, neural networks correctly predicted 97.0 percent of the bankrupt firms, while discriminant analysis predicted only 79.75 percent. Similar results are shown in the table for the prediction of nonbankrupt cases by the two techniques. Significance is tested and reported, as mentioned previously. Both methods appear to predict nonbankrupt firms quite well.

In Table 1, the measure p_{2g} is also calculated for both neural networks and discriminant analysis. Thus, when the testing sets contained a balanced number of bankrupt and nonbankrupt firms (base rate of 50 percent), a neural network model forecasting a bankrupt firm was correct 98 percent of the time, while discriminant analysis was correct 94.9 percent. Note that neural networks outperformed discriminant analysis irrespective of the base rates. Also note that, with the exception of measuring prediction with test sets having 90 percent nonbankrupt firms, neural networks also exceeded the base rate of the most frequent class, indicative of good predictive validity. Significant differences between the two techniques are reported as mentioned with the previous measures.

Table 1 also includes the third measure, p_{3g}, which gives the inefficiency of a technique. This ratio indicates the percentage of incorrect classifications to correct classifications. Again, the neural network outperforms the discriminant analysis approach in every case. However, this analysis does show that the performance of both neural nets and discriminant analysis degrades drastically when the base rate is 90 percent nonbankrupt and 10 percent bankrupt in the test set. While the errors in predicting nonbankrupt cases were small, the errors in predicting bankrupt firms are rather large, and more so for DA than for the neural model. This measure indicates the "efficiency" of the neural model very well. Again, significant differences between the two techniques for this measure are reported in the same manner as before.

While the results have clearly shown that neural networks outperformed discriminant analysis in predicting firm bankruptcies, our study must now address whether the neural network prediction results are better than can be expected by pure chance (Huberty 1984, Morrison 1969). We employ tests originally proposed by Meehl and Rosen (1955) and further clarified by Huberty (1984) for studying discriminant analysis classification rates. Because our study uses cross-validation (i.e., testing sets) for measuring classification success and utilizes different base rates for the testing set, we will further modify these tests to fit our study.

A classification system will only learn the base rate of the training set. It will have no knowledge about the base rate of the test set. Thus, a pure chance technique, exposed to 90 percent nonbankrupt cases in training, would randomly declare 90 percent of testing cases to be nonbankrupt, irrespective of the testing set composition. Therefore, in further investigating the value added by discriminant analysis and neural networks to the classification problem, our previously identified standard normal test statistics will be based on only information known to the classification techniques (base rate of the training sets, which is 50/50 in our example). The test statistic utilized is then based upon the proportional chance criterion (Huberty 1984). This criterion implies that prediction by guessing can achieve a correct rate for each group involved equal to the proportion of that group (base rate) in the training set. Thus for those training sets with a balanced number of bankrupt and nonbankrupt firms, 50 percent correct predictions could be achieved by chance, while if there are 90 percent nonbankrupt firms, 90 percent correct predictions of nonbankrupt firms could be achieved by chance.

As Table 2 indicates, the predictive validity of neural networks and discriminant analysis is extremely significant. Aggregately, both methods are significantly better than pure chance. Not surprisingly, as previous results have already shown, neural networks are judged more statistically significant than chance as compared to discriminant analysis in every case. Note that the test set base rate has no effect on the determination of predictive validity. Therefore, the table has collapsed the three different experimental cells into one aggregated cell for result presentation.

Table 2 also provides the reduction-in-error index for the neural network and discriminant analysis predictions aggregately for all firms total, as well as the improvement-over-chance index for both bankrupt and nonbankrupt cases. Again, since test set base rates do not affect the calculation of this statistic, results are aggregated across the base rates. Thus the neural network model provides 93 percent fewer classification errors than would occur by blind guessing. Similarly, the improvement-over-chance for the prediction of bankrupt firms with neural networks is 91.5 percent.

5. Discussion and Conclusions

This paper has identified several performance measures to be used in comparing classification techniques, including neural networks. Some of these measures have been previously applied in the psychology literature. These additional measures give a better indication of the power of a classification technique. These measures were applied to a bankruptcy prediction problem. The prediction capability of neural networks becomes even clearer with the use of these additional measures. At the same time, these measures also indicate that the success of classification in the 90 percent range is not necessarily all that superb. Further analysis of this performance is necessary, as indicated by the chance criteria. We propose that at least a subset of these measures should be reported in classification investigations in the future.

References

1. Altman, E.I., "Financial Ratios, Discriminant Analysis, and the Prediction of Corporate Bankruptcy," *The Journal of Finance*, (September 1968), 589-609.

2. *AUTOBOX Software User Manual*, AFS Inc., Hatboro, PA, 1988.

3. Bell, T., G. Ribar, and J. Verchio, "Neural Nets vs. Logistic Regression: A Comparison of Each Model's Ability to Predict Commercial Bank Failures," working paper, Peat Marwick Co., (May 1990).

4. Box, G.E.P., and G.M. Jenkins, *Time Series Analysis: Forecasting and Control*, Holden-Day, San Francisco, CA, 1976.

5. Collard, J.E., "Commodity Trading with a Neural Net," *Neural Network News*, Vol. 2, No. 10 (October, 1990).

6. Collins, E., S. Ghosh, and C. Scofield, "An Application of a Multiple Neural Network Learning System to Emulation of Mortgage Underwriting Judgments," working paper, Nestor, Inc. (1989).

7. Denton, J., M. Hung, and B. Osyk, "A Neural Network Approach to the Classification Problem," *Expert Systems With Applications*, Vol. 1, (1990), 417-424.

8. Dutta, S. and S. Shekhar, "Bond-Rating: A Non-Conservative Application of Neural Networks," *Proceedings of the IEEE International Conference on Neural Networks*, San Diego (1988), 443-450.

9. Fishman, M., D. Barr, W. and Loick, "Using Neural Networks in Market Analysis," *Technical Analysis of Stocks and Commodities* (April 1991), 18-25.

10. Gordon, J.S., *A Neural Network Approach to the Prediction of Violence*, Unpublished Ph.D. Dissertation, Oklahoma State University, Stillwater, OK, 1992.

11. Hill, T., L. Marquez, M. O'Connor, and W. Remus, "Neural Network Models for Forecasting and Decision Making," Working Paper - University of Hawaii, 1992.

12. Hill, T., M. O'Connor, and W. Remus, "Neural Network Models for Time Series Forecasts," Working Paper, University of Hawaii, 1991.

13. Huberty, C.J., "Issues in the Use and Interpretation of Discriminant Analysis," *Psychological Bulletin*, Vol. 95 (1984), 156-171.

14. Kang, S., *An Investigation of the Use of Feedforward Neural Networks for Forecasting*, Unpublished Ph.D. dissertation, Kent State University, Kent, OH, 1991.

15. Kimoto, T., and K. Asakawa, "Stock Market Prediction Systems with Modular Neural Networks," in *International Joint Conference on Neural Networks* at San Diego, CA, Vol. 1, pp. 1-6, 1990.

16. Klecka, W.R., *Discriminant Analysis* (Sage Publishing: Beverly Hills, CA, 1980).

17. Lapedes, A. and R. Farber, "Nonlinear Signal Prediction Using Neural Networks: Prediction and System Modeling," *Los Alamos National Laboratory Report*, Vol. LA-UR-87-2-662, 1987.

18. Marquez, L.O., *Function Approximation Using Neural Networks: A Simulation Study*, Unpublished Ph.D. dissertation, University of Hawaii, 1992.

19. Meehl, P.E. and A. Rosen, "Antecedent Probability and the Efficiency of Psychometric Signs, Patterns or Cutting Scores," *Psychological Bulletin*, 52 (1955), 194-216.

20. Morrison, D.G., "On the Interpretation of Discriminant Analysis," *Journal of Marketing Research*, Vol. 6 (1969), 156-163.

21. Odom, M., and R. Sharda, "A Neural Network Model for Bankruptcy Prediction," in *International Joint Conference on Neural Networks, San Diego, Ca*, Vol. 2 (1990), 163 - 168.

22. Raghupathi, W., L. Schkade, and R. Bapi, "A Neural Network Application for Bankruptcy Prediction," in *Proceedings of the 24th Hawaii International Conference on System Sciences*, Vol. 4 (1991), 147-155.

23. Roy, J., and J. Cosset, "Forecasting Country Risk Ratings Using a Neural Network," in *Proceedings of the 23rd Hawaii International Conference on System Sciences*, Vol. 4 (1990), 327-334.

24. Sharda, R., and R.B. Patil, "Connectionist Approach to Time Series Prediction: An Empirical Test," *Journal Of Intelligent Manufacturing*, forthcoming, 1992.

25. Stanley, J., and E. Bak, *Introduction to Neural Networks*. (California Scientific Software, Sierra Madre, CA, 1989).

26. Surkan, A., and J. Singleton, "Neural Networks For Bond Rating Improved by Multiple Hidden Layers," *International Joint Conference on Neural Networks*, San Diego, (June 1990).

27. Sutton, R.S., "Learning to Predict by the Method of Temporal Differences," *Machine Learning*, Vol. 3 (1988), 9-44.

28. Tang, Z., C. de Almieda, and P.A. Fishwick, "Time Series Forecasting Using Neural Networks vs. Box-Jenkins Methodology," *Simulation*, Vol. 57, No. 5 (November 1991), 303-310.

29. Utans, J., and J. Moody, "Selecting Neural Network Architectures via the Prediction Risk: Application to Corporate Bond Rating Prediction," in *Proceedings of the First International Conference on Artificial Intelligence Applications on Wall Street*, 1991.

30. Watts, R.L., and J.L. Zimmerman, *Positive Accounting Theory*, Prentice Hall, 1986.

31. White, H., "Learning in Artificial Neural Networks: A Statistical Perspective," *Neural Computation*, Vol. 1 (1989), 425-464.

32. Wilson, R.L., and R. Sharda, "Bankruptcy Prediction Using Neural Networks," *Decision Support Systems*, forthcoming, 1993.

33. Yoon, Y., and G. Swales, "Predicting Stock Price Performance," in *Proceedings of the 24th Hawaii International Conference on System Sciences*, Vol. 4 (1991), 156-162.

RBF Networks vs. Multilayer Perceptrons for Sequence recognition

Michele Ceccarelli
Istituto per la Ricerca sui Sistemi Informatici Paralleli, IRSIP-CNR,
Via P. Castellino 111, 80131 Napoli, ITALY

Jöel T. Hounsou
International Institute for Advanced Scientific Studies, IIASS
Via G. Pellegrino 19, 84018 Vietri sul Mare (SA), ITALY, and
Institut de Mathématique et de Sciences Physiques,
Université Nationale du Benin, Porto-Novo, BENIN

Abstract. **In this paper we consider several learning procedures for Radial Basis Function Networks applied to a problem of speech recognition. The dynamic nature of speech is considered by adding delayed connection and integration units to the network. Our study shows that supervised learning of the centroids of the basis functions gives appreciable results at a significantly small cost. The results thus obtained are compared with the generalization performance of multilayer perceptrons. The possibility to include recurrent connections into RBF networks is also investigated.**

I. INTRODUCTION

Theoretical results in the field of functional approximation and automata theory can estimate the potential of a given Artificial Neural Network (ANN) model and, at the same time, suggest training procedures for it. However, the efficiency and realiability of such learning algorithms is often not *a priori* known. In order to consider significant applications of ANNs, suitable compromises between training costs and expected results must be found. Therefore, the comparison of learning algorithms for a given model in terms of computational costs and generalization results on landmark applications is often the only way to address this problem.

Neural networks with Radial Basis Function (RBF) hidden units [1, 2] present several attractive properties. They are a powerful tool for constructing nonlinear mappings and seem suitable to be applied in many classification tasks. RBF networks have the advantage of easy and effective learning algorithms: the main idea is the construction of complex decision regions by superposition of simple kernel functions. The centers and widths of the kernel functions are the main parameters to be estimated during the learning phase. The typical choice of kernel function is a Gaussian which gives the highest ouput when the input is near to its center and monotonically decreases as the distance from the center increases. Therefore, the network architecture consists of one hidden layer of kernel nodes and one output layer of linear decision nodes.

In this paper, we shall consider time delayed radial basis neural network for sequence recognition. It is our aim to compare the learning procedures of RBF networks in terms of generalization abilities and learning time on a specific speech recognition task. Moreover, we give some experiments with sigmoid activation function in the hidden layer for the same task. These experiments show that the simplicity of the learning rules available for Radial Basis Neural networks makes them preferable.

The paper is organised as follows: the section II describes RBF neural networks, section III deals with neural networks for speech recognition and, details of the experiments are given in section IV. The last section introduces an extension of RBF networks for the inclusion of recurrent connections.

II. RADIAL BASIS FUNCTION NETWORKS

Each output unit of an RBF network computes the following function

$$f_i(\mathbf{x}) = \sum_{j=1}^{L} w_{ij}\phi_j(\mathbf{x}) \quad 1 \leq i \leq M \tag{1}$$

where M is the number of output units and the ϕ_j's are L kernel functions computed by the hidden units. Their

*This work was supported by MURST 40% unita' INFM Univ. di Salerno, contratto quinquennale IIASS-CNR and by CNR PF 'Robotica' grant n. 91.02014.67.

form is generally a Gaussian:

$$\phi_j(\mathbf{x}) = k\exp\left(-\frac{1}{2}(\mathbf{x}-\mathbf{m}_j)^T\Sigma_j^{-1}(\mathbf{x}-\mathbf{m}_j)\right)$$

where k is a constant and Σ_j is a covariance matrix which describes the contour of a multidimensional ellipsoid. The vector $\mathbf{m}_j$ represents the input stimulus to which the unit j is maximally receptive, *i.e.* it is the centroid of the kernel function ϕ_j.

A number of results established in the field of multidimensional interpolation and neural network theory [3, 4, 5] can be used either to show the properties of this kind of networks and to develop new training algorithms. The results obtained by Cybenko [6], for sigmoid hidden units, can be easely extended to RBF networks. He rigorously proved that two-layer perceptrons can uniformly approximate any continuous function. Park and Sandberg [7] and Hartman *et al.* [5] independentely extended these results to RBF networks with $\Sigma_j = \sigma I$, where σ is a constant smoothing factor equal for all hidden units which measures the radius of a multidimensional sphere, and I is the identity matrix.

Another important peculiarity of RBF neural networks is their use in maximum likelhood classification. Indeed, as the Parzen Window analogy suggests, the role of the function f_i is the approximation of the class conditional probability density function by means of the potential functions method. With this classification scheme an unknown input sample is classified according to the index of the potential function which has the maximum value.

In order to achieve a given goal several learning procedures can be used. The main points to be addressed are the number and the locations of the kernel centers. Some authors propose to have a number of kernels equal to the number of training patterns [8], but this approach often leads to excessive memory wasting for their implementation and to the so-called *overfitting* problem as regards their generalization abilities [9, 10].

An immediate approach to reduce the number of hidden units is the clustering of input data sets and the selection of kernel centers as the cluster code vectors [1, 2, 11, 12, 13]. Apart from the algorithm adopted, the most important question is whether the clustering must be super- or unsuper-vised. In the first case the clusters will contain data points belonging to the same class and the kernel centers will be "representative samples" of a given class. Whereas, for the second case the clustering method produces a kind of self-organizing quantisation of the input space. This process tries to automatically discover the features inside the input data, and the class-membership information is used only in the upper layer.

The last step of the learning procedure for RBF networks involves the computation of the hidden-to-output weights. This can be done in several ways. A typical choice is the LMS estimation:

$$(2)\qquad w_{i,j}(t+1) = w_{i,j}(t) + \eta[d_i - f_i(\mathbf{x}(t))]\phi_j(\mathbf{x}(t))$$

where d_i is the desired activation of the i-th output unit for the pattern $\mathbf{x}(t)$. Other methods, based on pseudo-inverse, can also be used.

A. *Unsupervised learning of center locations*

Classical unsupervised clustering algorithms can be used for the computation of center locations. The K-means algorithm and the Self-Organizing Feature Map (SOFM) [14] are commonly used for this task. The SOFM algorithm has the property of creating a topologically ordered codebook, *i.e.* the spatial proximity between units implies proximity between the corresponding code vectors. Moreover, it has a natural supervised counterpart and from the functional point of view it is strictly related to the K-means algorithm. The SOFM algorithm can be outlined as follows: given a set of L neural cells, organized as a bidimensional grid, with weight vectors $\mathbf{m}_1(t), \mathbf{m}_2(t), \ldots, \mathbf{m}_L(t)$, for each input sample $\mathbf{x}(t)$ select the nearest weight vector to it, $\mathbf{m}_l(t)$, and apply the following rule:

$$(3a)\qquad \mathbf{m}_i(t+1) = \mathbf{m}_i(t) + \alpha(t)[\mathbf{x}(t) - \mathbf{m}_i(t)] \quad \text{if} \quad i \in N_l(t)$$

$$(3b)\qquad \mathbf{m}_i(t+1) = \mathbf{m}_i(t) \quad \text{if} \quad i \notin N_l(t)$$

where $0 < \alpha(t) < 1$ is the learning rate and $N_l(t)$ is the neigbourhood of the neuron l of radius $\gamma(t)$. The learning rate $\alpha(t)$ and the neigbourhood radius $\gamma(t)$ are slowly decreasing functions. The distance used for the selection of the "winner" cell l is often the Euclidean distance but other metrices can also be used. The SOFM model is inspired by the cortical maps of animal brains and has been widely studied both from the analytical point of view and from the application point of view. As regards the choice of the parameters $\alpha(t)$ and $\gamma(t)$, it must be remarked that they play an important role for the convergence of the algorithm and the topological ordering. Typical choices are $\alpha(t) = \alpha_0 e^{-t/\alpha_1}$ and $\gamma(t) = \gamma_0 e^{-t/\gamma_1}$ with $\alpha_0, \alpha_1, \gamma_0, \gamma_1$ suitable constants. For example, in order to guarantee the topological ordering, the value of γ_0 must be greater than the size of the grid and γ_1 must ensure a slow decrease in the initial phase and a faster decrease once the map is ordered, $500 \leq \gamma_1 \leq 2000$ is a good range of values. Similar consideration apply for the parameters α_0 and α_1. A value of α_0 too small could excessively slow down the learning process, whereas a too high value could lead the the divergence of the algorithm; the range of values $0.05 \leq \alpha_0 \leq 0.5$ is appropriate for many real applications.

B. Supervised learning of center locations

The supervised version of SOFM is known as Learning Vector Quatization (LVQ): it does not take into account the neigbourhood interaction, *i.e.* the updating is carried out just for the winner neuron except that the class membership of the input pattern is used to enstabilish the sign of the updating term in (3b). Specifically, each hidden unit is labeled with a class, and the updating rule for the training pattern $\mathbf{x}(t)$ is the following:

$$l = arg\min_i\{||\mathbf{x}(t) - \mathbf{m}_i(t)||\}$$

if $Class(\mathbf{m}_l) = Class(\mathbf{x}(t))$

(4a) $$\mathbf{m}_l(t+1) = \mathbf{m}_l(t) + \alpha(t)[\mathbf{x}(t) - \mathbf{m}_l(t)]$$

if $Class(\mathbf{m}_l) \neq Class(\mathbf{x}(t))$

(4a) $$\mathbf{m}_l(t+1) = \mathbf{m}_l(t) - \alpha(t)[\mathbf{x}(t) - \mathbf{m}_l(t)]$$

(4b) $$\mathbf{m}_i(t+1) = \mathbf{m}_i(t) \quad \text{for} \quad i \neq l$$

The learning rate $0 < \alpha(t) < 1$ may be constant or a slowly decreasing function as before. The above algorithm and its variants have been successfully applied to many classification tasks.

The asymptotic values of vectors $\mathbf{m}_i(t)$ resulting from this procedure will be the center locations of the RBF hidden nodes; they can be considered as representative vectors of the classes to be discriminated.

C. Generalized Radial Basis Function

Another learning scheme for RBF networks is the so called Generalized Radial Basis Functions [15, 16], *i.e.* the use of gradient descent method for supervised learning of center locations. Given an input vector $\mathbf{x} = (x_1, \ldots, x_N)$ and the corresponding desired output vector $\mathbf{d} = (d_1, \ldots, d_M)$ the updating formulae for this algorithm look like:

(5a) $$\Delta w_{ij} = \eta(d_i - f_i(\mathbf{x}))\exp\frac{||\mathbf{x} - \mathbf{m_j}||}{\sigma_j}$$

(5b)

$$\Delta m_{jk} = \eta\frac{2(x_k - m_{jk})\exp\frac{||\mathbf{x}-\mathbf{m}_j||}{\sigma_j}}{\sigma_j}\sum_{m=1}^{M}(d_m - f_m(\mathbf{x}))w_{mj}$$

This method has been applied to speech recognition by Wu and Chan [17] obtaining no appreciable improvement of performance with respect to classical multilayer perceptrons with sigmoid activation for hidden units. Indeed, the long learning times do not allow large networks to be used, and the advantages of easy learning procedures carried out layer by layer are completely lost.

III. ANNs FOR SPEECH RECOGNITION

Current best speech recognisers use Hidden Markov Model (HMM) techniques for the statistical modelling of data. A supervised training algorithm (the Baum-Welch algorithm) allows to build the Markov Model of the training data and the Viterbi decoding algorithm is then used for the classification of unknown patterns. Neural network approaches for speech recognition recentely received great interest as they could overcome some limitations of HMM systems. Indeed, the distributed knowledge representation and data processing make them easily implementable in hardware. In addition neural network models seem more suitable for multistage recognisers combining coarticulation modelling and high-level sematinc information. Moreover, many works (see for example [18]) show that the combination of HMM and connectionist models can greatly improve the performance of current classifiers.

The neural network models used for speech recognition can be subdivided into three main categories: Static Neural Networks (SNNs), Time Delay Neural Networks with delays (TDNNs) and Recurrent Neural Networks (RNNs). In the first case a neural network classifier is applied to a fixed lenght segment of the speech waveform. SNNs present the serious drawback of needing a critical and complex preprocessing phase for input alignment and lenght normalization. In the second case the net incorporates short delays and the input is provided one frame at time, the last layer of the net performs an integration of the class-membership scores assigned to each frame. The situation is similar for recurrent networks except that together with delays there are recurrent connections. These last networks obtained very promising results but have the drawback of complex learning schema.

For most of the above models the training procedure is an extremely slow process. Indeed, the gradient descent method is often able to discover the hidden structure of data but it requires extensive computation. On the other hand, it is common belief that RBF networks can provide comparable results with a limited training effort.

IV. EXPERIMENTAL RESULTS.

In this section we compare the results obtained by using the training procedures outlined in section II. As mentioned before, the parameters to be used as basis for the comparison are the computational cost and the generalization performance, *i.e.* the percentage of recognition obtained with the same, or almost the same, computational effort due to the training procedure. The computational complexity of a learning algorithm comes from two factors. The first is the complexity of a single learning step, whose estimation is a simple exercise; the second is the rate of convergence of the algorithm, which can be formally defined as the order of the global error reduction at each learning step. This last parameter measures the number of iterations needed to decrease the error of a given factor. The analytical estimation of the convergence rate of an non-linear iterative procedure is often a complex task and some upper bounds are derived making use of functional analysis methods [19]. Such bounds give a theoretical characterisation of a learning scheme, however the performance of a given neural network model on a specific pattern recognition task must be experimentally measured.

The experiments below try to evidence the differences between the considered learning schemata on a speech recognition task. In all considered networks the kernel nodes are provided with a sequence of overlapping segments of the speech waveform. The last hidden layer performs a window by window classification by using sigmoid neurons, whereas the output layer integrates over time the partial classification performed.

The task we faced is the recognition of the ten Italian digits spoken by 64 Italian native speakers of both sexes (28 speakers for training and 36 speakers for test). The speech waveform is sampled at 8 KHz rate, and a spectral representation of the vocal input is obtained by a bank of 14 bandpass filters spaced on the Mel scale. Successively, every 20ms nine 16-bit mel-ceptral parameters are extracted. Training speakers spoke three times the ten digit, whereas the test speakers produce 10 sets of pronunciations of all the digits, consequently the whole database consists of about 4440 isolated words. Therefore, 840 pronunciations were used for training and about 3600 pronunciations for the test. The considered networks have a first RBF hidden layer, a second layer for input data categorization built with sigmoid-activation nodes, and last an output layer which just performs an integration of the activation of the last hidden layer over all the snapshots windows of an input pattern. The classification criterion is the choice of the unit with the maximum activation at the output layer and the target patterns are 10-component binary vectors with a component corresponding to the class of the input set to one, all others are set to zero. The units in the first hidden layer look at 10 consecutive frames at time, *i.e.* a 90 dimentional input; consecutive snapshots are shifted of 4 frames. The second hidden layer is fully connected to the first hidden layer with three delays (0, 1, 2), *i.e.* it receives the action of the RBF layer through a 3 snapshots window.

A. *Unsupervised clustering of data*

In the first experiment (Exp. I) the kernel centroids, $\mathbf{m}_i$, were first computed with unsupervised clustering by using the SOFM algorithm, and then the weights w_{ij} were adjusted with the LMS algorithm. The parameters σ_i were considered constant, this is justified by the fact that with the adopted learning rules the code vectors tend to be uniformly distributed [14], and by the fact that in a related work [16] it has been shown the the learning of the kernel widths does not improve the generalization performances of the resulting network.

It is evident that as the number of hidden units increases the performace gets better. On the other hand, the centroid computation and LMS estimation of the hidden to output weights can lead to unaccettable computational requirements when too large networks are used. The second column of Table 1 shows the recognition performance on 3600 test utterances for a network with 256 hidden units. The convergence and consequentely the learning times strictly depend on the adopted parameters $\alpha(t)$, $\gamma(t)$, η. For our experiments we used $\alpha(t) = 0.2e^{-t/2000}$ and $\gamma(t) = 5e^{-t/1000}$. With these choices, the learning procedure for the whole network approximately required 4200 complete adaptive steps for the first hidden layer and 2500 iteration for the LMS computation the weights w_{ij}. To have an idea of the amount of computation required by the first learning step let n be the number of hidden neurons, d the input dimensions, N the number of training vectors (in our case 6494) and $\tilde{\gamma}$ the average neighbourhood radius. It is easy to show that each iteration of the learning procedure requires about $N(2nd + 3\tilde{\gamma}^2 d)$ floating point operations. Let be o the number of output nodes then, once that the activations of hidden nodes have been computed, the computational requirements of the second step are given by $4Nno$ floating point operations.

B. *Supervised clustering of data*

Thereafter, as suggested in [12, 16], we tried to set the center locations with supervised learning by using the LVQ algorithm (Exp. II). Specifically, the patterns corresponding to consecutive windows of the utterances were grouped depending on the class they belong. In this case the first hidden layer performs a raw classification of the input speech snapshots which is later refined at the second stage. The hidden units were uniformly divided among the ten classes. When the number of such units did not perfectly divide 10 the remaining units were assigned to the class "three". The LVQ layer itself is able to cassify the training frame-vectors with an accuracy of 46 %. The tird column of Table 1 summarizes the recognition percentages of the RBF network with supervised learning of center location. The computational requirements of this learning schema are similar to the previous: $N(2nd + 2d)$ for each learning epoch in the hidden layer and $5Nno$ for the LMS estimation at the second stage. It is important to emphatise that only 50 iterations of the algorithm were needed for the convergence. This is a general property of LVQ, and is due to the fact that the class-membership information allows a faster positioning of the code vectors.

C. Generalized RBF

The next experiment is based on GRBF, (formulae (5a) and (5b)). Previous works [16] show that this method can attain considerably better results than the previous ones. The performance achieved are summarized in the fourth and fifth columns of Table 1. The network of Exp. III has 16 hidden neurons whereas the network of Exp. IV has 64 hidden neurons. The complexity of this learning procedure is easely shown to be proportional to $N(ndo + no + o)$ which is significatively greater than that of the learning methods considered above; such complexity does not allow to use large networks. In order to give an idea of the amount of computation needed by this scheme let us mention that the learning process for the network of Exp. IV takes about three weeks of running time on a scientific workstation, this is about 10 times greater than the layer by layer learning of the previous experiments.

D. Multilayer Perceptron.

The last experiment (Exp. V) makes use of a different kind of neural network which presents sigmoid hidden units. This model is commonly known as Time Delay Neural Network [20]. The direct comparison with the previous results is not immediate; indeed, in this case the hidden units have a completely different behaviour and therefore it is possible that the sizing adopted before does not apply well in this case. For example, an input pattern of length 90, corresponding to 200 mseconds, is too large and several experiments have shown that the convergence to good minima of the error surface is very difficult to be reached. For these reasons we applied to the considered task a network structure which seems to give the best results. The hidden nodes look at a window of three consecutive frames (27 input nodes), and consecutive windows are shifted one frame at time. Moreover, the second hidden layer is fully connected to the first hidden layer with five delays (0, 1 , 2, 3 and 4). The Exp. V column of Table 1 summarizes the obtained recognition rates for a network with 64 neurons in the first hidden layer and 10 neurons in the second hidden layer. Once again we underline the amount of computing resources needed by this schema with respect the first two considerd experiments. In fact, the computational complexity of this scheme is the same as GRBF and physically requires running times which are an order of magnitude

TABLE 1

Table 1: The recognition performance of the five experiments described in the text on the test set. Exp. I uses unsupervised clustering for centroid computation while Exp. II uses supervised clustering. The Exp. III and Exp. IV correspond to GRBF with respectively 16 and 64 hidden nodes. The last column reports the recognition performance of a TDNN network with 64 neurons in the first hidden layer and 10 neurons in the second hidden layer.

Class	Exp. I	Exp. II	Exp. III	Exp IV	Exp. V
0	94.4	97.2	92.7	89.1	94.7
1	96.6	96.1	91.3	94.1	94.4
2	97.8	97.8	93.6	94.4	86.4
3	96.6	85.2	59.1	79.7	80.2
4	94.2	94.7	88.9	88.3	92.5
5	96.4	98.6	98.3	95.3	99.4
6	94.2	95.3	86.6	81.1	76.0
7	97.5	90.0	95.0	97.8	86.9
8	98.6	98.6	88.9	96.7	95.8
9	92.1	95.5	92.7	96.0	92.1
Total	94.8	95.5	89.1	91.2	89.8

greater than those required by the LVQ-LMS scheme. In addition, this major computational effort is not supported by increased generalization performance.

V. DISCUSSION

It is commonly believed that RBF networks have poorer generalization abilities than sigmoid neural networks, however this belief is based on comparisons which do not take into account the cost of the training procedure. In this paper we have shown that it is possible to obtain better recognition performance at a significantly lower cost by using time delayed RBF networks. Moreover, the supervised clustering of data is a very efficient method to obtain good generalization performance at a low computational cost.

In addition, a promising field of research consists in the extension of RBF networks to incorporate recurrent connections. In fact, the existing gap between RBF networks and recurrent networks can be overcomed by considering hidden units simultaneously locally-tuned on the input space and on the activation space. Specifically, the activation of the hidden nodes is the combination of two radial basis functions: the first centered on spatially localised regions of the input space and the second localised on regions of the activation space. In formulae:

$$\phi_j(t) = \theta_0 \exp(-\frac{1}{2\sigma_j^0}(\mathbf{x}(t) - \mathbf{m}_j)^T(\mathbf{x}(t) - \mathbf{m}_j)) +$$

$$\theta_1 \exp\left(-\frac{1}{2\sigma_j^1}(\mathbf{\Phi}(t-1)-\mathbf{M}_j)^T(\mathbf{\Phi}(t-1)-\mathbf{M}_j)\right)$$

where $0 \leq \theta_0, \theta_1 \leq 1$, $\theta_0 + \theta_1 = 1$ and $\mathbf{\Phi}(t-1) = (\phi_1(t-1), \ldots, \phi_L(t-1))$. Even if this model is slightly more complex, it is possible to show that it can be trained with layer by layer procedures as those described in this paper. The inclusion of the recurrent weights $\mathbf{M}_j$ produces an improvement of the performance of RBF networks for sequence recognition. As a preliminary experiment, we generated a set of 1000 patterns of variable lenght containing three kinds of shapes: a sin wave, a square wave and a triangular wave. These shapes were randomly shifted and time scaled. We observed that the recurrent connections produce an average improvement of 10 % in the discrimination between the three classes. The results reported in section IV are a necessary propedeuditic step towards investigating models of this kind.

AKNOWLEDGMENTS

We would like to thank dr. Alfredo Petrosino for his constant help. The authors are indebted with Alcatel FACE for the provision of the speech data.

REFERENCES

[1] D. S. Broomhead, D. Lowe (1988), Multivariate Functional Interpolation and Adaptive Networks, *Complex Systems* 2 (1988) 321-355.

[2] J. Moody and C. J. Darken, Fast Learning in Networks of Locally Tuned Processing Units, *Neural Computation* 1 (1989) 281-294.

[3] M.J.D. Powell (1987), Radial Basis Functions for Multivariate Interpolation: A Review, in: J. C. Mason and M. G. Cox, eds, *Algorithms for the Approximation of Functions and Data* (Clarendon Press, Oxford, 1987) 143-167.

[4] X. Sun, On the Solvability of Radial Function Interpolation, *Approximation theory* 2 (1989) 643-646.

[5] E. J. Hartman, J. D. Keeler and J. M. Kowalsky, Layered neural Networks with Gaussian Hidden Units as Universal Approximators, *Neural Computation* 2 (1990) 210-215.

[6] G. Cybenko (1989), Approximation by Superposition of Sigmoidal Functions, *Mathematics of Control, Signal and Systems* 2 (1989) 303-314.

[7] J. Park and I. W. Sandberg, Universal Approximation Using Radial Basis Function, *Neural Computation* 3 (2) (1991) 246-257.

[8] D. F. Spect (1990), Probabilistic Neural Networks, *Neural Networks* 3 (1990) 109-118.

[9] C. Bishop, Improving the Generalization Properties of Radial Basis Function Neural Networks, *Neural Computation* 3 (1991) 579-588.

[10] S. Geman, E. Bienenstock and R. Dousart (1992), "Neural Networks and the Bias/Variance Dilemma", *Neural Computation* 4 (1) (1992) 1-58.

[11] J. Reynolds and L. Tarassenko, Spoken Letter Recognition with Neural Networks, *International Journal of neural Systems* 3 (3) (1992) 219-235.

[12] J. Bengio, Radial basis Function for Speech Recognition, in: P. Laface and R. de Mori, eds. *Speech Recognition and Understanding: Recent Advances, trends and Applications* (NATO ASI Series Vol. F 75, 1992).

[13] M. T. Musavi, W. Ahmed, K. H. Chan, K. B. Faris and D. M. Hummels, On the Training of Radial Basis Function Classifiers, *Neural Networks* 5 (1992) 595-603.

[14] T. Kohonen (1990), The Self-Organizing Map, *Proceedings of IEEE* 78 (9) (1990) 1464-1479.

[15] T. Poggio and F. Girosi, Networks for Approximation and Learning", *Proceedings of IEEE* 78 (9) (1990) 1481-1497.

[16] D. Wettschereck and T. Dietterich, Improving the Performance of Radial Basis Function Networks by Learning Center Locations, in: J. E. Moody, S. J. Hanson and R. P. Lippman, eds., *Neural Information Processing Systems 4* (Morgan Kaufman 1992) 1133-1140.

[17] J. X. Wu and C. Chan, Recognition of Phonetic Labels of the Timit Speech Corpus by Means of an Artificial neural Network, *Pattern Recognition* 24 (11) (1991) 1085-1091.

[18] E. Singer and R. Lippman, Improved Hidden Markov Model Speech Recognition Using Radial Basis Function Networks, in: J. E. Moody, S. J. Hanson and R. P. Lippman, eds., *Neural Information Processing Systems 4* (Morgan Kaufman, 1992) 159-166.

[19] A. Krzyżak, Learning, Radial Basis Function Nets and Nonparametric Regression, Concordia University internal report, 1993.

[20] A. Waibel, T. Hanazawa, G. Hinton, K. Shikano and K. J. Lang, Phoneme Recognition Using Time-Delay Neural Networks, *IEEE Transaction on ASSP* 24 (11) (1991) 1085-1091.

MINIMUM DESCRIPTION LENGTH PRUNING AND MAXIMUM MUTUAL INFORMATION TRAINING OF ADAPTIVE PROBABILISTIC NEURAL NETWORKS

Waleed Fakhr and M.I. Elmasry
VLSI Research Group, Elect. & Comp. Eng. Dept.
University of Waterloo, Waterloo, Ontario, Canada, N2L 3G1

Abstract-The major problem in implementing artificial neural networks is their large number of processing units and interconnections. This is partly because their architectures are not optimal in size, where too many parameters are usually used when only few would suffice. In this paper we apply an approximated version of the minimum description length criterion "MDL" to find optimal size adaptive probabilistic neural networks "APNN" by adaptively pruning Gaussian windows from the probabilistic neural network "PNN". We discuss and compare both stochastic maximum likelihood "ML" and stochastic maximum mutual information "MMI" training applied to the APNN, for probability density estimation "PDF" and pattern recognition applications. Results on four benchmark problems show that the APNN performed better than or similar to the PNN, and that its size is optimal, and much smaller than the PNN.

1. INTRODUCTION

The backpropagation "BP" trained multilayer perceptron "MLP" estimates the Bayes decision boundaries between classes by estimating their posterior probabilities in the mean-square sense [1,2]. Although proved very successful in many classification applications, the BP trained MLP has several drawbacks. The Most serious drawback is that the MLP has the tendency to overfit training data when its architecture has more degrees of freedom, i.e., more free parameters, than necessary. Recently, many researchers have proposed various techniques to reduce the overfitting problem of the MLP [3-6]. Most of these techniques are based on the Bayesian inference approach, where smoothing priors for the model parameters are used during training. Even though employing smoothing priors, produces reduced variance estimates of the weights, there is no guarantee that any of the weights will actually go to zero so that it can be removed. In other words, the actual size of the MLP may remain unaltered.

On the other hand, the probabilistic neural network "PNN" [7], estimates the probability density function "PDF" for each class, then uses these estimates to implement the Bayes rule. The PNN, however, suffers from two major drawbacks. Firstly, all the training data must be stored, making the PNN unattractive for implementation, as well as making it an inefficient representation of the data [8,9]. Secondly, the PNN lacks any form of corrective training, which is very useful in many classification applications.

In this paper we propose an adaptive neural network architecture which we call the adaptive probabilistic neural network "APNN" [10,11]. The initial APNN architecture is the PNN, and we adaptively reduce its size by removing Gaussian windows according to an approximated version of the minimum description length criterion "MDL" [8,9,12]. Doing this size reduction, we seek to find a minimum complexity PDF estimate for each data set, in the stochastic complexity sense [12]. After the pruning process is completed, stochastic maximum likelihood "ML" training is used to estimate the location and width of each Gaussian window for each class PDF separately. After the ML training the APNN can be used for both density estimation and classification. In many situations, however, the sum-of-Gaussian PDF model is not accurate, e.g., when the data clusters are not Gaussian in shape. To overcome this drawback, we propose to use stochastic maximum mutual information "MMI" corrective training to enhance the classification performance of the APNN.

2. MDL PRUNING OF THE APNN

Each class PDF in the APNN is modeled by:

$$F(X|C_j) = \frac{1}{\sum_{i=1}^{N_j} a_i} \sum_{i=1}^{N_j} a_i \, \Phi_i \tag{1}$$

$$\Phi_i = \left(\frac{2\pi}{\alpha_i^2}\right)^{-p/2} \exp -\alpha_i^2 \sum_{n=1}^{p} (x_n - w_{ni})^2 \tag{2}$$

where N_j is the total number of training patterns for class C_j, p is the input pattern dimensionality, α_i is a width parameter for the ith window and a_i are integer parameters that take only {0,1} value, where 0 indicate that the corresponding window Φ_i is removed and 1 indicates that it is included. In this paper we employ the Kullback-Leibler leave-one-out criterion [13] to find a suitable width for the windows of each class separately. For each class we assume equal α for all windows. The KL leave-one-out criterion is given by:

0-7803-0999-5/93/$03.00

$$KL = \frac{1}{N_j} \sum_{i=1}^{N_j} Log\, F(X_i) \quad (3)$$

where $F(X_i)$ is the probability density function when the window centered at the pattern X_i is not included:

$$F(X_i) = \frac{1}{N_j - 1} [\sum_{n=1}^{N_j} \Phi_n] - \Phi_i \quad (4)$$

A plot is made between the KL and α, and α value corresponding to maximum KL is taken. The KL criterion is used since it is a simple cross-validation criterion, which enhances the generalization capability of the network by making each Gaussian window extends its influence to its neighbors.

To prune the APNN, we apply an approximated version of the minimum description length criterion, as given by Rissanen [8,9]. The approximated MDL criterion for the APNN is given by:

$$-MDL = M = \frac{1}{N_j} [\sum_{i=1}^{N_j} LogF(X_i | C_j) - \frac{k_j}{2} LogN_j] \quad (5)$$

where the first term between brackets is the log-likelihood, the second is the complexity-penalizing term, and k_j is the number of existing windows. In this paper we use the MDL criterion in (5) for pruning the APNN until a minimum of MDL (i.e. a maximum of M) is reached, and also as a performance criterion which indicates how good the PDF model is. The minimum description length criterion is employed since it can discover the closest probability distribution to the true one among many competing models [12]. During pruning the only adaptive variables are the a_i integer variables, which take only $\{0,1\}$ values, and at each step one window is removed, with the corresponding a_i is put to zero. The pruning steps are summarized in the following:

(1) Start with the KL-trained PNN, with all a_i equal one.

(2) Search for a_i which when put to zero results in the highest increase in M. Put this a_i to zero, i.e., remove the corresponding window.

(3) Re-adjust α value by using the KL criterion.

(4) Repeat steps 2 and 3 as long as M keeps increasing (or constant) at each step.

(5) After we reach the final architecture, we perform maximum likelihood "ML" training to enhance the PDF estimates. At this stage we allow all window parameters to adapt.

In applying the MDL, the window centers and widths are considered as fixed parameters for each competing model, hence the complexity of each model is proportional to the number of windows in that model by employing the factor $\frac{k_j}{2} LogN_j$. The MDL is closely related in that sense to the Akaike criterion which employs a term k_j, however the MDL penalizes the number of parameters asymptotically much more severely [8].

3. STOCHASTIC MAXIMUM LIKELIHOOD TRAINING OF THE APNN

In applying the MDL, we restricted the centers of the windows to be fixed, and their widths to be equal at each pruning step. We also restricted the coefficients a_i to take binary value 0 or 1. These restrictions are tools to simplify the use of the MDL criterion, and to find the minimum number of windows needed in the model. The resultant pruned model's parameters however are not the ML estimates in the parameter space, and ML training can be used to obtain these estimates. Maximizing the Log-likelihood is equivalent to minimizing the Kullback-Leibler probabilistic distance between the modeled probability and the true one. The ML parameters are obtained by maximizing:

$$L = \sum_{C_j} Log\, F(X | C_j) \quad (6)$$

with respect to the parameters of the model $F(X | C_j)$, where $\sum_{C_j}$ indicates the training data set of class C_j. Stochastic gradient-ascent maximization of L version is proposed, where the adaptation equations are:

$$\Delta a_i = \mu_a \frac{1}{\sum_{n=1}^{K_j} a_n \Phi_n} [\Phi_i - \frac{\sum_{n=1}^{K_j} a_n \Phi_n}{\sum_{n=1}^{K_j} a_n}] \quad (7)$$

$$\Delta \alpha_i = \mu_\alpha \frac{\Phi_i a_i}{\sum_{n=1}^{K_j} \Phi_n a_n} [\frac{p}{\alpha_i} - \alpha_i \sum_{m=1}^{p} (x_m - w_{mi})^2] \quad (8)$$

$$\Delta w_{mi} = \mu_w \frac{\Phi_i a_i}{\sum_{n=1}^{K_j} \Phi_n a_n} \alpha_i^2 [x_m - w_{mi}] \quad (9)$$

Where μ_a, μ_α and μ_w are learning rates which were chosen experimentally such that the likelihood function increases monotonically. It is to be noted that similar stochastic (Robbins-Monro), ML training was used in [14] for simple Gaussian mixtures, where convergence properties were discussed.

Up to this point we have used the APNN to estimate the PDF of the classes, where the quality of these estimates depend on the quality and quantity of the given data and the accuracy of the sum-of-Gaussians model. In many cases, the ML training is not the best training approach when the APNN is to be used as a classifier, for example, when the training data is poor both in quality and quantity, and/or when the PDF models do not closely approximate the true

PDFs. To enhance the classification performance of the APNN, MMI corrective training is proposed.

4. STOCHASTIC MAXIMUM MUTUAL INFORMATION TRAINING OF THE APNN

A tight upper bound on the Bayes error probability P(e) is given in [15]: $P_u(e)=I/2$, where "I" is the Equivocation. The mutual information "MI" is equal to "-I" plus a constant, hence maximizing MI directly minimizes the P(e) upper bound [10,11]. The MI involves integration over the data space, however to be able to use the criterion for training we rely on the large-sample approximation. The large-sample approximation of the MI for a 2-class case is:

$$MI = \frac{1}{N} \left[\sum_{C1} \frac{p1\, F(X|C_1)}{p1\, F(X|C_1)+p2\, F(X|C_2)} + \sum_{C2} \frac{p2\, F(X|C_2)}{p1\, F(X|C_1)+p2\, F(X|C_2)} \right] \quad (10)$$

Where $\sum_{C_j}$ indicates the training data of class C_j, N is the total number of training data, and p1 and p2 represent the class prior probabilities, which can also be adaptive, subject to p1+p2=1, and we assume here that they are equal for simplicity. Similar to ML, we employ a stochastic gradient-ascent approximation to maximize MI with respect to the model parameters. The jth class model parameters are updated after each pattern according to:

$$\Delta a_i = Z_j \, \mu_a \frac{1}{\sum_{n=1}^{K_j} a_n} \left[\Phi_i - \frac{\sum_{n=1}^{K_j} a_n \Phi_n}{\sum_{n=1}^{K_j} a_n} \right] \quad (11)$$

$$\Delta \alpha_i = Z_j \, \mu_\alpha \frac{\Phi_i a_i}{\sum_{n=1}^{K_j} a_n} \left[\frac{p}{\alpha_i} - \alpha_i \sum_{m=1}^{p} (x_m - w_{mi})^2 \right] \quad (12)$$

$$\Delta w_{mi} = Z_j \, \mu_w \frac{\Phi_i a_i}{\sum_{n=1}^{K_j} a_n} \alpha_i^2 \left[x_m - w_{mi} \right] \quad (13)$$

Where for a 2-class case, Z_j is equal to:

$$Z_j = + \frac{F(X|C_k)}{F(X|C_j)\,(F(X|C_j)+F(X|C_k))} \quad (14)$$

if the data pattern is from class C_j and the parameter is from the model $F(X|C_j)$, i.e., the same class, where $F(X|C_j)$ is that class PDF, and $F(X|C_k)$ is the other class PDF, and:

$$Z_j = - \frac{1}{F(X|C_j)+F(X|C_k)} \quad (15)$$

if the data pattern is from the opposite class.

5. BENCHMARK PROBLEMS RESULTS

We have applied our proposed framework on four benchmark problems: 1.1 and 1.2 are 1-dimensional, and 2.1 and 2.2 are 2-dimensional. The training data used for the 1-dimensional case is 40 pattern/class, and for the 2-dimensional is 50 pattern/class. For testing, 10,000 pattern/class is used so that the verification results are statistically valid. For each problem we show the PDF estimation results by the PNN and the ML-trained APNN, compared to the true PDFs used. We then show the classification results of the PNN, the ML-trained APNN and the MMI-trained APNN compared to the theoretical optimal Bayes classifier performance. We also show the size of the PNN and the APNN compared to the optimal size in terms of the number of Gaussian windows required for the optimal Bayes classifier. We compared the PDF estimates by using the 10,000/class data points for testing, and calculating the average Euclidean distance between the estimated and the true PDFs, which we denote here by DPDF1 and DPDF2 for classes 1 and 2 respectively. In each table, "#error" denotes the number of misclassified patterns out of 20,000 test patterns, "%recog." denotes the % recognition rate, "%opt." denotes the % recognition relative to the optimal (included only if the optimal is not 100%), size1 and size2 are the number of windows in class-1 and class-2 networks respectively, and "NOT" denotes that this result is not included.

5.1. BENCHMARK PROBLEM 1.1

In this problem, each class PDF is composed of 2 uniform clusters of width=4, and centers at 2 & -6 for C1 and -2 & 6 for C2, i.e., the two classes are completely separable. The optimal size is 2 Gaussian windows per class, and a 100% recognition.

TABLE I: RESULTS OF PROBLEM 1.1

	PNN	ML-APNN	MMI-APNN	Optimal
Size1	40	2	2	2
Size2	40	2	2	2
DPDF1	0.0026	0.003	NOT	0.0
DPDF2	0.0028	0.0031	NOT	0.0
#error	565	611	347	0
%recog.	97.175	96.95	98.27	100

5.2. BENCHMARK PROBLEM 1.2

In this problem, each class PDF is composed of 2 Gaussian clusters, with centers at 2 & -6 for C1 and -2 & 6 for C2, and with different widths, where the two classes are highly overlapped with optimal recognition of only 86.8%, and optimal size of 2 Gaussian windows per class.

TABLE II: RESULTS OF PROBLEM 1.2

	PNN	ML-APNN	MMI-APNN	Optimal
Size1	40	2	2	2
Size2	40	2	2	2
DPDF1	0.0002441	0.0000674	NOT	0.0
DPDF2	0.000521	0.000387	NOT	0.0
#error	2723	2698	2700	2640
%recog.	86.39	86.51	86.5	86.8
%opt	99.53	99.67	99.65	100

5.3. BENCHMARK PROBLEM 2.1

This problem is a 2-dimensional generalized XOR, where the data values range between {-1,1}, class-1 is composed of 2 uniformly distributed clusters centered at (0.5,-0.5) and (-0.5,0.5) and class-2 is also composed of 2 uniform clusters at (0.5,0.5) and (-0.5,-0.5). This problem is completely separable, with an optimal recognition of 100% and optimal size of 2 Gaussian windows per class.

TABLE III: RESULTS OF PROBLEM 2.1

	PNN	ML-APNN	MMI-APNN	Optimal
Size1	50	2	2	2
Size2	50	2	2	2
DPDF1	0.0063	0.0059	NOT	0.0
DPDF2	0.0088	0.0089	NOT	0.0
#error	1331	1113	926	0
%recog.	93.35	94.44	95.37	100

5.4. BENCHMARK PROBLEM 2.2

This problem is a 2-dimensional generalized XOR, where class-1 is composed of 2 Gaussian distributed clusters centered at (0.5,-0.5) and (-0.5,0.5) and class-2 is also composed of 2 Gaussian clusters at (0.5,0.5) and (-0.5,-0.5). In this problem the classes are highly overlapped with an optimal recognition of only 75.5%, and the optimal size is also 2 Gaussian windows per class.

TABLE IV: RESULTS OF PROBLEM 2.2

	PNN	ML-APNN	MMI-APNN	Optimal
Size1	50	2	2	2
Size2	50	2	2	2
DPDF1	0.0036	0.00035	NOT	0.0
DPDF2	0.00322	0.00189	NOT	0.0
#error	5159	5070	5072	4900
%recog.	74.2	74.65	74.64	75.5
%opt.	98.28	98.87	98.86	100

6. CONCLUSIONS

(1) In all problems considered the optimal size is reached with the MDL pruning, starting from the PNN. The resulted APNN are much smaller in size than the PNN, which means a tremendous saving in implementation costs, and computational time.

(2) The APNN also has a much smaller stochastic complexity than the PNN, in other words, it is a more efficient representation of the data, or a more compact form of coding the data.

(3) Since the MDL criterion is based on asymptotic approximation of the stochastic complexity [8], it performs better for large data sets. We expect that it might fail to find the optimal number of clusters for more complex problems, with small data sets. In such cases, other approximations for the stochastic complexity should be used [16].

(4) On the other hand, if the data set is large, the MDL works well, and the optimal model for the given data is most likely found with the minimum number of windows, unlike the PNN, which increases in size with larger data sets.

(5) In classification, ML training was superior to MMI when the sum-of-Gaussians model matched the true class distributions, i.e., in problems 1.2 and 2.2, while the MMI training was superior in the other two cases when the true distributions were uniform not Gaussian.

(6) In PDF estimation, the ML-APNN is much better than the PNN when the true distributions are Gaussian sums, and they are almost equivalent in the other cases.

REFERENCES

[1] Robert Schalkoff; "Pattern Recognition, Statistical, Structural, and Neural Approaches", John Wiley & Sons, Inc., 1992.

[2] John Makhoul; "Pattern Recognition Properties of Neural Networks", IEEE-SP Workshop on Neural Networks for Signal Processing, Princeton, NJ, 1991, pp.173-187.

[3] Steven J. Nowlan, Geoffrey E. Hinton; "Adaptive Soft Weight Tying using Gaussian Mixtures", In J.E. Moody, S.J. Hanson and R.P. Lippmann (Eds.), Advances in Neural Information Processing Systems 4, Morgan Kaufmann, San Mateo CA 1992.

[4] Wray L. Buntine, Andreas S. Weigend; "Bayesian Back-Propagation", Complex Systems 5, 1991, pp.603-643.

[5] Mackay, D.J.C.; "A Practical Bayesian Framework for Backprop Networks", submitted to Neural Computation, 1991.

[6] John E. Moody; "Note on Generalization, Regularization, and Architecture Selection in Nonlinear Learning Systems", IEEE-SP Workshop on Neural Networks for Signal Processing, pp.1-10, 1991

[7] Donald F. Specht; "Probabilistic Neural Networks", Neural Networks, Vol.3, pp.109-118, 1990.

[8] Jorma Rissanen; "Stochastic Complexity in Statistical Inquiry", Series in Computer Science-Vol.15, World Scientific.

[9] Jorma Rissanen; "Density Estimation by Stochastic Complexity", IEEE Trans. on Information Theory, Vol.38, No.2, pp.315-323, March 1992.

[10] Waleed Fakhr and M.I. Elmasry; "Mutual Information Training and Size Minimization of Adaptive Probabilistic Neural Networks", ISCAS'92, San Diego CA, May 1992.

[11] Waleed Fakhr, M. Kamel and M.I. Elmasry; "Probability of Error, Maximum Mutual Information, and Size Minimization of Neural Networks", IJCNN, Baltimore MD, June 1992.

[12] Andrew R. Barron and Thomas M. Cover; "Minimum Complexity Density Estimation", IEEE Trans. on Information Theory, Vol.37, No.4, pp.1034-1054, July 1991.

[13] Keinosuke Fukunaga; "Introduction to Statistical Pattern Recognition", 2nd Ed., Academic Press, Inc. 1990.

[14] Tzay Y. Young and T. Calvert; "Classification, Estimation and Pattern Recognition", American Elsevier, 1974.

[15] Martin E. Hellman and Josef Raviv; "Probability of Error, Equivocation, and the Chernoff Bound", IEEE Trans. on Information Theory, Vol.16, No.4, pp.368-372, July 1970.

[16] Waleed Fakhr, M. Kamel and M.I. Elmasry; "Unsupervised Learning by Stochastic Complexity", Unpublished.

Is LVQ Really Good for Classification? – An Interesting Alternative

W. Poechmueller, M. Glesner, H. Juergs
Darmstadt University of Technology
Institute for Microelectronic Systems
Karlstrasse 15
D-6100 Darmstadt, Germany

Abstract — Nearest neighbor classifiers are well-known classifiers in the world of application oriented engineers. Their benefits are simplicity, model free classification and good performance. Learning vector quantization (LVQ) developed by Kohonen is a neural network based method to find a good set of reference vectors to be stored as a nearest neighbor classifier's reference set. In this paper an efficient method of finding reference vectors along class boundaries instead of finding vectors representing class distribution, as LVQ does, will be described. A quantitative comparison with LVQ is done.

I. INTRODUCTION

Nearest neighbor classifiers are simple model free classifiers that are easy to handle an show good classification results even compared with neural network methods [1]. Thereby, a set of vectors with wellknown class affiliation serves as a reference set to classify unknown vectors.

In the following, two tests will be used to benchmark algorithm performance. *Test 1* consists of linearly distributed two-dimensional vectors belonging to two nonoverlapping classes. *Class 1* (500 vectors) lies in area $(0.1, 0.1) \times (0.4, 0.9)$ with a small satellite in area $(0.8, 0.7) \times (0.9, 0.8)$ (see Fig. 1 left). Gaussian distributed vectors belonging to two classes, however, are used in *Test 2*. Thereby, 150 vectors of *Class 1* are restricted to a rather small area around center $(0.6, 0.6)$ with a variance of $\sigma_1^2 = 0.2$, whereas vectors of *Class 2* (1500 vectors) are spread widely around center (0.4,0.4) with variance $\sigma_2^2 = 8.0$ (see Fig. 1 right). Thus, both classes are overlapping with *Class 1* being completely embedded in *Class 2*. In subsequent figures vectors belonging to *Class 1* are represented by small crosses and vectors from *Class 2* are indicated by small rectangles.

II. LEARNING VECTOR QUANTIZATION

Learning Vector Quantization (LVQ) is an adaptive algorithm proposed by Kohonen [4] to find an optimal set of reference vectors for classification purposes. Thereby, during learning, reference vectors are shifted into an optimal position, whereas during recall a nearest neighbor classification technique is used. In the original approach from Kohonen, reference vectors are shifted from a random initial distribution to a final position that describes the probability density function $p(\vec{x})$ of the set X of n-dimensional training vectors $\vec{x} \in \mathbb{R}^n$. Thus, an optimal placement of reference vectors is a placement such that the local point density of reference vectors $\vec{w}^k$ (i.e. the number of $\vec{w}^k$ falling in a small volume $\mathbb{R}^n$ centered at the observed point $\vec{x}$) is as close as possible to the probability density function of the vectors in the training set [4]. Derived from this idea, with the modification of punishing wrong classifications, an algorithm for reference vector adaptation is given by

$$\vec{w}_{t+1}^k = \begin{cases} \vec{w}_t^k + \alpha 1_t \left[\vec{i}_t - \vec{w}_t^k\right] \\ \qquad \text{if } \|\vec{i}_t - \vec{w}_t^k\| \text{ min. and } cl(\vec{w}_t^k) = cl(\vec{i}_t) \\ \vec{w}_t^k - \alpha 2_t \left[\vec{i}_t - \vec{w}_t^k\right] \\ \qquad \text{if } \|\vec{i}_t - \vec{w}_t^k\| \text{ min. and } cl(\vec{w}_t^k) \neq cl(\vec{i}_t) \\ \vec{w}_t^k \qquad \text{else} \end{cases} \tag{1}$$

with k-th reference vector $\vec{w}_t^k$, learning parameters $\alpha 1_t$ and $\alpha 2_t$ (which may be constants or functions of time indicated by index t), and currently applied input vector $\vec{i}_t$ [4] ($cl(\vec{w}_t^k)$ returns the class vector $\vec{w}_t^k$ is belonging to). Several main disadvantages can be observed by applying this algorithm:

1. The fact that a winning reference vector moves away leaving other reference vectors back which thus will never get a chance to win.
2. Using an LVQ-algorithm, the number of reference vectors for each class has to be defined in advance (no adaption of number of reference vectors to actual needs).
3. LVQ-algorithms place reference vectors to copy the probability distribution of training vectors. However, this is not a very efficient method in combination with a nearest neighbor classification method

0-7803-0999-5/93/$03.00

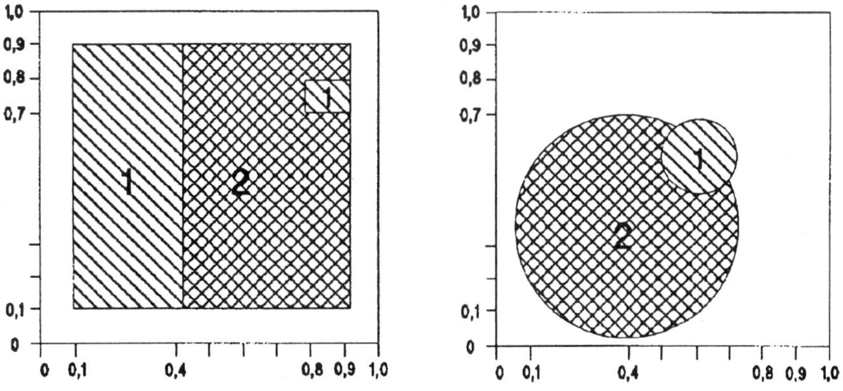

Fig. 1: *Test* 1 (left) and *Test* 2 (right) used as benchmarks for algorithm performance

during recall phase. The more reference vectors are used to represent a class with sufficient accuracy, the more reference vectors will be placed in the class center especially if training vectors are distributed similar to a gaussian distribution (which seems to be a realistic assumption for many practical problems) and only few at class boundaries.

4. The LVQ-algorithm is computational intensive.

In the following, these problems will be referenced as *Problem 1* through *Problem 4*. All these effects may be found in the two tests sketched in Fig. 2. *Test 1* was performed with all 16 reference vectors (8 per class) initialized near the origin. *Problem 1* is obvious since only one reference vector belonging to *Class 2* moved through *Class 1* area into *Class 2* and no reference vector of *Class 1* was able to cross *Class 2* area to reach the small satellite of *Class 1*. Not more than 3 *Class 1* reference vectors moved into *Class 1* area. A total of 12 reference vectors remains in the origin and does not contribute to form class boundaries as accurate as possible. Even a random initialization of reference vectors before learning cannot solve this problem since most of the vectors in wrong class areas after initialization will either be forced to leave the input vector space or remain in wrong class areas. For *Test 2* an initialization with random distributed reference vectors was chosen (right part of Fig. 2). Reference vectors moved into correct positions, however, 8 reference vectors are too many to represent *Class 1* but too few to represent *Class 2* (*Problem 2*). All reference vectors of *Class 1* are forced together but cannot be placed in one point due to respective repulsion (thus, *Class 1* area becomes too large). To cope with this problem, Kohonen recommends to form classification boundaries by using a weighted Voronoi tesselation (vector distances are weighted by average inverse distances of reference vectors at class borders). Then, class borders are formed by Appollonian hyperspheres but this means more complex computations during recall [4].

The mentioned drawbacks are wellknown and deviations of the basic LVQ-algorithm emerged trying to compensate some of the most severe problems. To cope with *Problem 1* deSieno proposed to include a punishment for reference vectors winning too often [3]. Thereby, a punishment of winning reference vector is done by adding a punishment distance b_k to distance $d_k = d(\vec{i}_t, \vec{w}_t^k) = ||\vec{i}_t - \vec{w}_t^k||$ between currently applied training vector $\vec{i}_t$ and neareast reference vector $\vec{w}_t^k$. This punishment is calculated as

$$b_k = \epsilon_t \cdot d_{kmax} \cdot (N \cdot p_k - 1) \tag{2}$$

with ϵ_t influencing punishment strength, d_{kmax} an estimated normalization factor, N the number of reference vectors per class, and p_k the winning frequency of reference vector k. Winning frequency p_k is calculated by

$$p_{k,t+1} = \begin{cases} (1-\gamma) \cdot p_{k,t} & \text{if } cl(\vec{w}_t^k) \neq cl(\vec{i}_t) \\ (1-\gamma) \cdot p_{k,t} + \gamma & \text{if } cl(\vec{w}_t^k) = cl(\vec{i}_t) \end{cases} \tag{3}$$

with γ a constant. The adaptation of the winning reference vector is then done according to

$$\vec{w}_{t+1}^{inclass} = \begin{cases} \vec{w}_t^{inclass} + \alpha 1_t \cdot (\vec{i}_t - \vec{w}_t^{inclass}) \\ \quad \text{if } \vec{w}_t^{inclass} = \vec{w}_t^{glob} \\ \vec{w}_t^{inclass} + \alpha 2_t \cdot (\vec{i}_t - \vec{w}_t^{inclass}) \\ \quad \text{if } \vec{w}_t^{inclass} \neq \vec{w}_t^{glob} \end{cases} \tag{4}$$

and

$$\vec{w}_{t+1}^{glob} = \vec{w}_t^{glob} - \alpha 3_t \cdot (\vec{i}_t - \vec{w}_t^{glob}) \text{ if } cl(\vec{w}_t^{glob}) \neq cl(\vec{i}_t). \tag{5}$$

Thereby, $\alpha 1_t$, $\alpha 2_t$, and $\alpha 3_t$ are learning rates, $\vec{w}_t^{inclass}$ is the nearest reference vector to input vector $\vec{i}_t$ belonging to the same class ($cl(\vec{w}_t^{inclass}) = cl(\vec{i}_t)$), and $\vec{w}_t^{glob}$ is the nearest vector to $\vec{i}_t$ regardless its class affiliation.

This algorithm reduces *Problem 1*, now all 16 reference vectors are used to represent classes, but cannot avoid the other problems as may be seen from the examples sketched in Fig. 3. Still the satellite area of *Class 1* is not found

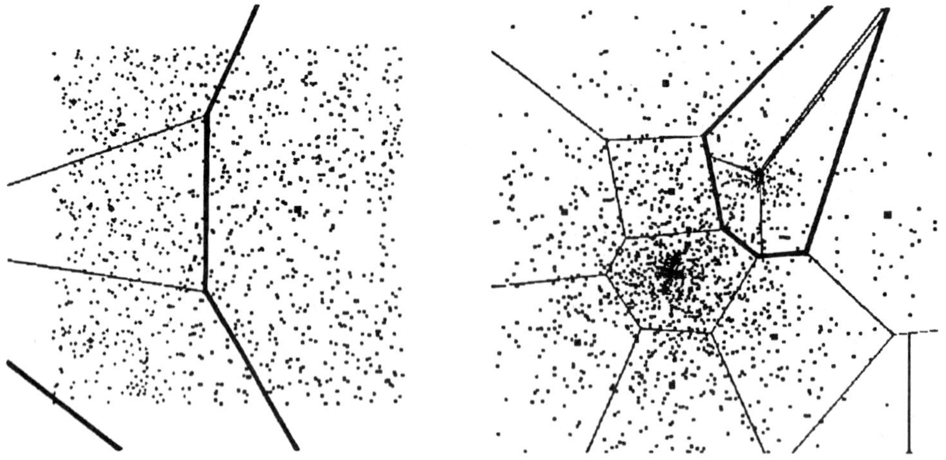

Fig. 2: Behaviour of original LVQ-algorithm on *Test 1* (reference vectors initialized near the origin) and *Test 2* (random initialization of reference vectors)

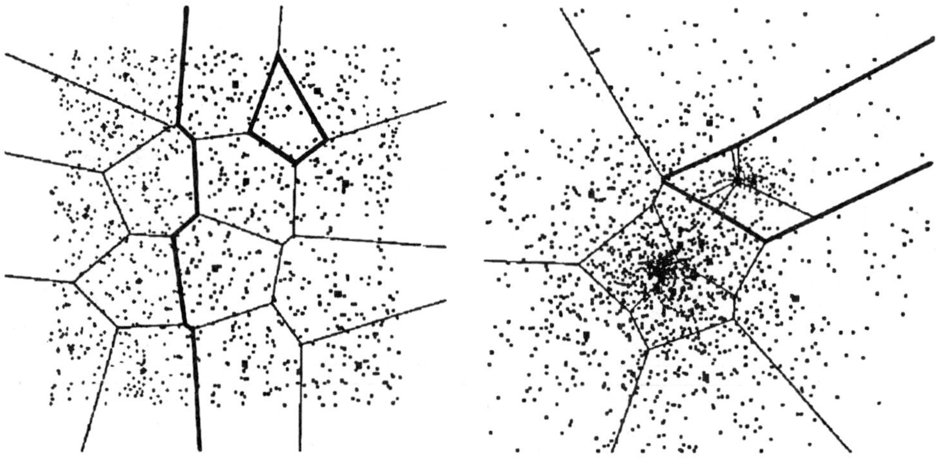

Fig. 3: *Test 1* (left) and *Test 2* (right) with deSieno's algorithm

in *Test 1* and *Class 1* area is too much extended in *Test 2* (*Problem 2*). Furthermore, in both, *Test 1* and *Test 2*, some reference vectors do not contribute in building class boundaries. This is the case if a vector's Voronoi cell does not touch the class boundary. After learning this vector does not affect classification and thus is an unnecessary load (*Problem 3*).

To comply more with Bayes' philosophy, Kohonen proposed a refinement of the LVQ-algorithm called LVQ 2 [4], [2]. Thereby, a window of certain width is defined around the midplane between two class distinct reference vectors $\vec{w}^i$ and $\vec{w}^j$. If $cl(\vec{w}^i)$ is the nearest class but $\vec{i}$ belongs to $cl(\vec{w}^j) \neq cl(\vec{w}^i)$ where $cl(\vec{w}^j)$ is the next-to-nearest class and if $\vec{i}$ falls into the window around midplane, reference vector adaptations are then made according to

$$\vec{w}^i_{t+1} = \vec{w}^i_t - \alpha 1_t \cdot \left(\vec{i}_t - \vec{w}^i_t\right) \tag{6}$$

$$\vec{w}^j_{t+1} = \vec{w}^j_t + \alpha 1_t \cdot \left(\vec{i}_t - \vec{w}^j_t\right) \tag{7}$$

$$\vec{w}^k_{t+1} = \vec{w}^k_t. \tag{8}$$

However, this algorithm results only in a refinement of reference vector placement and thus in a refinement of class boundaries. Furthermore, applying it for many iterations, the placement may become even worse. Therefore, in practical applications a combination of LVQ with punishment (Equations 2-5) and LVQ 2 is used. Such a combination of 20000 learing steps of LVQ proposed by de Sieno followed by further 10000 training steps of LVQ 2 were applied to benchmarks *Test 1* and *Test 2* (with random initialization before learning). The results were similar to those depicted in Fig. 3.

To cope with problems caused by a predefined fixed number of reference vectors for each class (*Problem 2*) Poirier et al. proposed a modified LVQ algorithm that dynamically increases the number of used reference vectors if the closest reference vector $\vec{w}^{inclass}$ belonging to the same class as the currently applied input vector $\vec{i}$ is too far away ($d(\vec{w}^{inclass}, \vec{i}) \geq \sigma$) [5]. This reduces *Problem 2* since the number of reference vectors per class or class cluster is adapted as requested by local demand. Furthermore, it is more efficient with respect to the nearest neighbor classification philosophy since more reference vectors will be placed near class boundaries. The reason for that is that most wrong classifications causing the creation of a new reference vector will occur near class boundaries, thus reducing *Problem 3*. However, the creation of a new reference vector can make previously generated vectors superfluous which then should be deleted. This is not done by the algorithm so it will not work optimally with respect to *Problem 3*. Dynamic Vector Quantization (DVQ) is reported to work better than LVQ 2 [5].

III. DATA REDUCED NEAREST NEIGHBOR PHILOSOPHY

In this section we want to present a "learning method" for nearest neighbor classification which is well suited for this type of classifier. Since the nearest neighbor of a vector to be classified decides about its class affiliation, it would be an unnecessary load to store vectors in a nearest neighbor classifier's reference set that are far away from class boundaries. To store only vectors near to class boundaries, we took the algorithm described subsequently. As in the LVQ simulations we used the Euclidean distance as metric. Vectors near class boundaries are then found by the following simple algorithm:

```
 1:  copy all training vectors in training list
 2:  initialize reference vector list (empty)
 3:  set training list pointer on first element in
       training list
 4:  take element where training list pointer is
       pointing to and classify it
 5:  if classification is correct goto 6
     else insert training vector into
       reference vector list
 6:  increase training list pointer (now pointing on
       next element)
 7:  if not end of training list goto 4
 8:  set reference list pointer on first element in
       reference list
 9:  remove the vector where reference list pointer
       is pointing at and classify removed vector
10:  if vector is not classified correctly it
       must be reinserted in reference list
11:  increase reference list pointer (now pointing
       on next element)
12:  if not end of reference list goto 9
13:  if no reference list change and no training list
       change between lines 2 and 12 goto 14
     else goto 3
14:  end
```

This algorithm is similar to DVQ in that way that reference vectors are dynamically created (inserted in reference list) in steps 4 through 7 if wrong classifications occur but we are generating a new reference vector in any case regardless of a threshold distance $d(\vec{i}, \vec{w}^k) \neq \sigma$. However, during steps 9 through 11 we delete old reference vectors which became unnecessary by the creation of new reference vectors. This is a very efficient method to avoid unnecessary reference vectors placed in class centers. Fig. 4 shows the application of this algorithm to *Test 1*. With a simple reduction many vectors near to class boundaries are found (19 vectors belonging to *Class 1* and 18 belonging to *Class 2*) which then may be stored as a nearest neighbor classifier's reference vectors (left part of Fig. 4). Through this procedure not only a data reduction is obtained but also generalization effects since the class boundary is now formed by fewer vectors. However, the number of reference vectors to be stored may further be decreased by exploiting a feature of the reduction algorithm. The more separated two classes are (the larger the distance between them is) the less will be the number of remaining vectors after reduction. Now in *Test 1*, classes may be separated by eliminating vectors in the boundary region by a cleaning algorithm.

```
1: copy all training vectors in training list
2: set training list pointer on first element
     of training list
3: look for k nearest neighbors of vector where
     training list pointer is pointing at
4: if j (majority) of k nearest neighbors belong
     to other class than observed vector, then
     mark vector
5: if not end of training list then increase
     training list pointer and goto 3
6: delete all marked vectors
```

We eliminated all vectors which are not having at least 8 neighbors belonging to their own class in the scope of their next 10 nearest neighbors. Applying the reduction algorithm to the remaining, cleaned vector set results in the situation depicted in the right part of Fig. 4. Only 5 vectors belonging to *Class 1* and 6 vectors belonging to *Class 2* represent the classes. Very good generalization is obtained. The Voronoi tesselation shows only some few vectors of the underlying training set on the wrong side of the formed class boundaries, which is a result of generalization. Also the test with a recall set shows nearly the same classification performance as the reference vectors in the left part of Fig. 4 (see Table 1).

Unfortunately, problems with simple pure reduction occur if classes overlap. Then, many vectors in the overlapping region will be stored as may be seen from the left image of Fig. 5, forming a complexly shaped class boundary. There, the reduction algorithm was applied to benchmark *Test 2*. Again the previously described cleaning method helps to solve the problem.

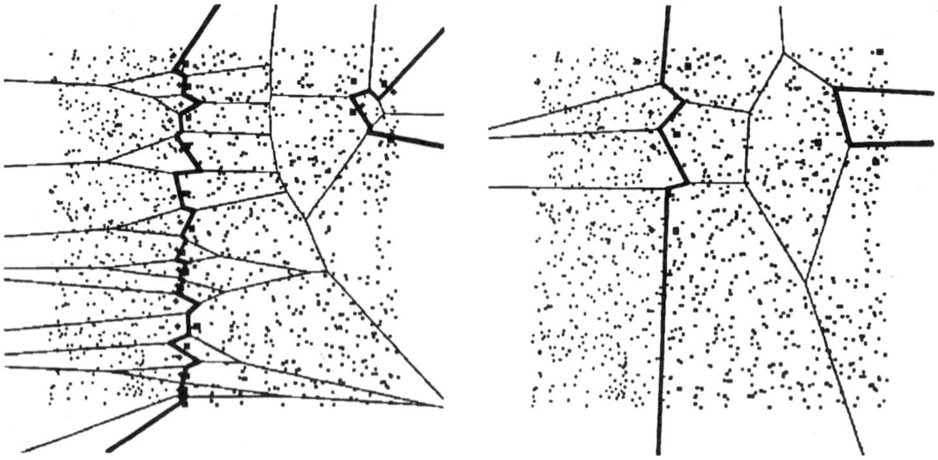

Fig. 4: Reference vector reduction algorithm (left) and combined cleaning/reduction algorithm (right) applied to *Test 1*

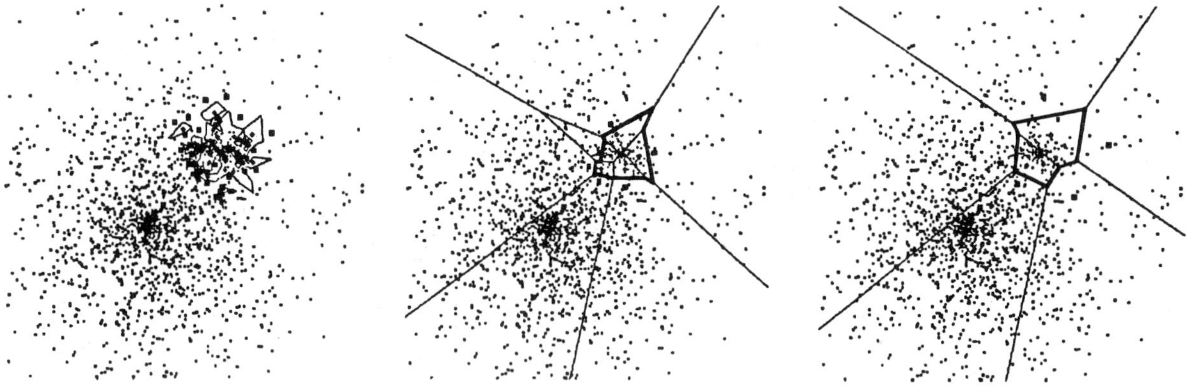

Fig. 5: Application of cleaning and reduction algorithms on data from *Test 2*

By first applying this cleaning algorithm and then the reduction algorithm very good results may be obtained. Fig. 5 shows in its center image the result obtained by first cleaning (all vectors eliminated which do not have at least 3 neighbors belonging to their class within their next 5 nearest neighbors) and then reducing training data from *Test 2*. The result are 5 reference vectors belonging to *Class 1* and 6 reference vectors belonging to *Class 2*. Generalization and the number of reference vectors finally found may be influenced by cleaning parameters. In the right part of Fig. 5 we eliminated all vectors that did not have at least 12 neighbors of the same class within the scope of their next 15 nearest neighbors during the cleaning phase. This results in a wider cleaning of the overlapping area with a wider separation of remaining vector classes. After applying the reduction algorithm there remained only 2 vectors of *Class 1* and 5 vectors of *Class 2*. The numerical classification results of the recall set can be taken from Table 1.

IV. A QUALITATIVE AND QUANTITATIVE COMPARISON TO LVQ

The proposed reduction algorithm generates reference vectors only if needed and locates them near to class boundaries. If classes are widely separated only few vectors will be stored up to an extreme of only one reference vector per class if there is a large distance between classes, whereas the class boundary is built up with fine granularity by many vectors if the classes are facing each other with very short distance. By means of the cleaning algorithm the distance between classes may be increased or overlapping areas erased, thus reducing the number of reference vectors (compare left and right part of Fig. 4) to be stored and thus increasing generalization. Only two parameters must be chosen in the "cleaning" procedure, namely the majority proportion in the k-nearest neighbor search whether to mark or not a vector, which will be deleted later and the size of the environment where the algorithm is looking for neighbors. This is a big difference

Algorithm	Clean	Initialization	Test	References *Class 1*	References *Class 2*	Correct *Class 1*	Correct *Class 2*	Correct total
LVQ	-	origin	1	8	8	96.0	76.4	86.7
LVQ	-	random	2	8	8	99.3	91.0	91.8
LVQ (de Sieno)	-	origin	1	8	8	94.2	92.0	91.0
LVQ (de Sieno)	-	random	2	8	8	99.3	92.6	93.2
LVQ (d.S.)/LVQ 2	-	random	1	8	8	95.3	93.8	94.5
LVQ (d.S.)/LVQ 2	-	random	2	8	8	96.6	92.5	92.9
Reduction	-	-	1	19	18	98.7	98.4	98.5
Clean/Red.	8-10	-	1	5	6	99.6	97.2	98.3
Clean(few)/Red.	3-5	-	2	5	6	87.2	97.4	96.5
Clean(much)/Red.	12-15	-	2	2	5	93.3	97.2	96.8

Table 1: Numerical simulation results

to more elaborate LVQ-algorithms as LVQ from deSieno or LVQ 2, where many parameters influence algorithm behaviour. Furthermore, the described reduction and cleaning algorithms were much faster than LVQ in our simulations. Convergence of reduction was always obtained after few iterations (4-8 iterations). In our simulations we used the NeuralWorks Professional II/Plus environment with the following parameters to simulate LVQ networks:

LVQ: $\alpha 1 = \alpha 2 = 0.05$, 20000 learning steps
LVQ (deSieno): $\alpha 1 = 0.05$, $\alpha 2 = \alpha 3 = 0.04$, $\gamma = 0.001$, $\epsilon = 0.3$, 20000 learning steps
LVQ 2: $\alpha 1 = \alpha 2 = 0.02$, window width $0.4 \cdot ||\vec{w}^i - \vec{w}^j||$, 10000 learning steps

For numerical results we independently generated a training and a recall set of vectors with the same statistical parameters, each.

In the following we will regard numerical simulation results obtained by applying previously described algorithms to data from *Test 1* and *Test 2*. Recall sets generated independently from training sets served to obtain recall results stated in Table 1. Column *Clean* of this table gives the cleaning parameter if cleaning was used. A parameter of e.g. *8-10* means that each vector, which does not have at least 8 neighbors belonging to its class in its 10 neighbors comprising vicinity, will be deleted.

In all cases total classification accuracy of LVQ-algorithms was inferior to that obtained by our simple algorithms. We also changed the number of reference vectors of LVQ networks, however this did not improve results. Major problem of LVQ in *Test 2* is that the rather small *Class 1* area becomes too large if represented by several reference vectors adapted by LVQ technique (which may easily be recognized from good *Class 1* recognition but very bad *Class 2* results compared with our approach). Even LVQ simulations with 30 reference vectors per class did not yield better results but showed clearly a wasteful placement with many reference vectors located in class centers or far away from class boundaries. In addition we evaluated the total correct classifiction rates of some conventional classifiers. We obtained 91.7% (*Test*1) and 82.7% (*Test*2) with an Euclidean distance classifier, 91.8% (*Test*1) and 82.5% (*Test*2) with a Mahalanobis classifier, 93.0% (*Test*1) and 90.9% (*Test*2) with a linear polynomial classifier and 95.4% (*Test*1) and 90.5% (*Test*2) with a quadratic polynomial classifier.

All described algorithms may work on data of arbitrary dimensions using an arbitrary metric for vector comparison.

REFERENCES

[1] C. Windsor (editor), *The Performance of Neural Network and Conventional Algorithms in the Classification of Generic Representations of some Real Problems*, Internal Report ANN90R02 of ESPRIT Project 2092 "ANNIE", January 1990

[2] T. Kohonen, J. Kangas, J. Laaksonen, K. Torkkola, *LVQ-PAK: The Learning Vector Quantization Program Package*, Technical Report from the LVQ Programming Team of the Helsinki University of Technology, Laboratory of Computer and Information Science, Rakentajanaukio 2 C, SF-02150 Espoo, Finland, 31 January 1992

[3] D. DeSieno, "Adding a Conscience to Competitive Learning", *Proceedings of the Second Annual IEEE International Conference on Neural Networks*, Volume 1, 1988

[4] T. Kohonen, *Self-Organization and Associative Memory*, Third Edition, Springer, 1989

[5] F. Poirier, A. Ferrieux, "DVQ: Dynamic Vector Quantization - An Incremental LVQ", *Proceedings of the International Conference on Artificial Neural Networks ICANN'91*, Volume 2, pp. 1333-1336, Helsinky, 1991

TIME SERIES CLASSIFICATION USING THE VOLTERRA CONNECTIONIST MODEL AND BAYES DECISION THEORY

J.J. Rajan and P.J.W. Rayner

Cambridge University Engineering Dept.,
Trumpington St., Cambridge CB2 1PZ, UK

ABSTRACT

This paper describes the development of a new technique for determining the weights of a Volterra Connectionist Model (VCM) applied to the classification of stationary time series. This involves assigning a classification index to each class of time series and developing expressions for the state conditional probability density functions such that the Bayes Risk can be expressed as a function of the weights. The optimal weight values then correspond to the minimum Bayes Risk.

1 INTRODUCTION

The feature of time series analysis that distinguishes it from other types of statistical analysis is the explicit recognition of the importance of the order in which the observations are made. In many time series problems, observations are statistically dependent and the correlation of the data often has a unique structure which can be used to classify the underlying phenomenon. In this paper, we show that the use of correlation terms as discriminatory features for time series classification follows directly from the derivation of the Volterra Connectionist Model (VCM) [1].

The VCM is a linear network that operates on non-linear extended input pattern vectors. Thus, the network implements a general non-linear scalar function of the N-dimensional pattern vector $\mathbf{x}$, but is linear in the weights. Hence, given an input time series vector $\mathbf{x}_m$ from class m (where $m \in \{1, 2, \cdots, M\}$), we can form an extended vector such that the linear discriminator described by

$$d_m = \sum_r w_r \Phi_r(\mathbf{x}_m) = \mathbf{w}^{\mathbf{T}} \mathbf{\Phi}(\mathbf{x}_m)$$

is obtained, where d_m is the classification index for class m, $\Phi_r(\mathbf{x}_m)$ are a set of fixed non-linear basis functions of state vector $\mathbf{x}_m$ and the w_r are weights which may be varied in order to achieve optimal classification. Thus the structure of the network is essentially that of an adaptive finite impulse response digital filter operating on a non-linear extended signal.

The network is trained over a finite set of time series vectors, and thus the statistics over the training set approximate ensemble statistics. Usually the number of training vectors is small and the variance of the parameter estimates will be large. However, if the time series are stationary to order four then it is possible to combine ensemble and time statistical measures to obtain more accurate parameter estimates and hence a more robust classifier.

2 METHOD

Consider a time series of length N. Define the state vector of length 2 of time series observations at $t = i$ and $t = i - 1$ as

$$\mathbf{x}^T = [x(i) \;\; x(i-1)]$$

Taking the (2,2) Volterra series expansion of $\mathbf{x}$, we get an extended time series vector:

$$\Psi^T(\mathbf{x}) = [1 \;\; x(i) \;\; x(i-1) \;\; x^2(i) \;\; x(i)x(i-1) \;\; x^2(i-1)]$$

Let $\Phi(\mathbf{x}) = \hat{\mathrm{E}}\{\Psi(\mathbf{x})\}$ where the estimated expectation operator, $\hat{\mathrm{E}}$, is defined as being the average over the time series. Thus, for a zero-mean process, $\hat{\mathrm{E}}\{\mathbf{x}(i)\} = \hat{\mathrm{E}}\{\mathbf{x}(i-1)\} \approx 0$ and the distinct terms of $\Phi(\mathbf{x})$ are given by

$$\Phi^T(\mathbf{x}) = [1 \;\; \hat{\gamma}(0) \;\; \hat{\gamma}(1)]$$

where $\hat{\gamma}(n)$ is the unbiased sample autocorrelation estimate at lag n and is given by

$$\hat{\gamma}(n) \equiv \frac{1}{N-n} \sum_{i=1}^{N-n} x(i)x(i+n)$$

0-7803-0946-4/93 $3.00 © 1993 IEEE

Hence, the autocorrelation function derives naturally from the Volterra series expansion of the signal. (Note that the second order Volterra extended vector of a state vector of length K would contain autocorrelation function terms up to lag $K-1$).

It is obvious that the use of autocorrelation functions as discriminatory features may not be optimum for all time series, but if no a priori assumptions have been made as to the nature of the data then this would seem reasonable.

The estimated classification index for a time series of class m is given by

$$\hat{\mathrm{d}}_m = w_0 + w_1\hat{\gamma}_m(0) + w_2\hat{\gamma}_m(1)$$

Therefore, the variance of the estimated classification index, $\mathrm{V}(\hat{\mathrm{d}}_m)$, can be written as

$$\begin{aligned}\mathrm{V}(\hat{\mathrm{d}}_m) &= w_1^2\mathrm{V}(\hat{\gamma}_m(0)) + 2w_1w_2\mathrm{Cov}(\hat{\gamma}_m(0),\hat{\gamma}_m(1)) \\ &\quad + w_2^2\mathrm{V}(\hat{\gamma}_m(1)) \\ &= \sum_{r=0}^{1}\sum_{n=0}^{1} w_{r+1}w_{n+1}\mathrm{Cov}(\hat{\gamma}_m(r),\hat{\gamma}_m(n))\end{aligned}$$

The covariance of the autocorrelation function is defined as

$$\mathrm{Cov}(\hat{\gamma}_m(r),\hat{\gamma}_m(n)) = \mathrm{E}\Big\{[\hat{\gamma}_m(r) - \mathrm{E}\{\hat{\gamma}_m(r)\}]\,[\hat{\gamma}_m(r) - \mathrm{E}\{\hat{\gamma}_m(r)\}]\Big\}$$

An expression for $\mathrm{Cov}(\hat{\gamma}_m(r),\hat{\gamma}_m(n))$, for $r \leq n$, can be developed for Gaussian time series (a similar expression was developed by Bartlett [2]):

$$\mathrm{Cov}(\hat{\gamma}_m(r),\hat{\gamma}_m(n)) = \frac{1}{(N-r)(N-n)}\Bigg\{ \sum_{k=-(N-r-1)}^{N-n-1}\Big([N-n-g(k)]\,[\bar{\gamma}_m(|\,k\,|)\bar{\gamma}_m(|\,k+n-r\,|) + \bar{\gamma}_m(|\,k+n\,|)\bar{\gamma}_m(|\,k-r\,|)]\Big)\Bigg\}$$

where

$$g(k) = \begin{cases} k & k > 0 \\ 0 & r-n \leq k \leq 0 \\ r-k-n & -(N-r-1) \leq k < r-n \end{cases}$$

and

$$\bar{\gamma}_m(n) = \frac{1}{N_m}\sum_{i=1}^{N_m}\hat{\gamma}_m^i(n)$$

and $\hat{\gamma}_m^i(n)$ refers to the estimated autocorrelation at lag n of the ith time series of class m in the training set of size N_m.

Similiarly, for non-Gaussian time series the following expression can be used:

$$\mathrm{Cov}(\hat{\gamma}_m(r),\hat{\gamma}_m(n)) = \frac{1}{(N-r)(N-n)}\Bigg\{ \sum_{k=-(N-r-1)}^{N-n-1}\Big([N-n-g(k)]\,\Big[\bar{\mathrm{M}}_m^4(|\,r\,|,|\,k\,|,|\,k+n\,|) - \bar{\gamma}_m(r)\bar{\gamma}_m(n)\Big]\Big)\Bigg\}$$

where $\bar{\mathrm{M}}_m^4$ is the ensemble averaged fourth-order moment of a time series of class m.

Assuming that the training vectors are independent realisations, the Central Limit Theorem will apply and thus both $\hat{\gamma}_m(n)$ and $\hat{\mathrm{d}}_m$ will be Gaussian random variables. Therefore, the state conditional probability density function for the classification index d (that is, the PDF for d given that the class is m) can be written as

$$p(\mathrm{d} \mid m) = \frac{1}{\sqrt{2\pi\mathrm{V}(\hat{\mathrm{d}}_m)}}\exp\left[\frac{-(\mathrm{d}-\hat{\mathrm{d}}_m)^2}{2\mathrm{V}(\hat{\mathrm{d}}_m)}\right]$$

From Bayes decision theory, the Bayes Risk, R, can be defined as the sum of the overlap areas of the state conditional PDFs [3]:

$$\mathrm{R} = \sum_{m=1}^{M-1}\left\{\int_{\mathrm{e}_{m,m+1}}^{\infty} p(\mathrm{d} \mid m)\,d\mathrm{d} + \int_{-\infty}^{\mathrm{e}_{m,m+1}} p(\mathrm{d} \mid m+1)\,d\mathrm{d}\right\}$$

where $\mathrm{e}_{m,m+1}$ is the intersection (that lies between $\hat{\mathrm{d}}_m$ and $\hat{\mathrm{d}}_{m+1}$) of $p(\mathrm{d} \mid m)$ and $p(\mathrm{d} \mid m+1)$. These intersections between the state conditional PDF's define the hyperplane boundaries of the class-conditional decision regions in the feature space. Hence the decision regions are derived solely from the statistical properties of the measurement vectors. The decision rule is optimum in that it minimises the probability of error.

The optimal weight vector in the Bayesian sense, $\mathbf{w}_{opt}$, corresponds to that which gives the minimum value for R. Since R is a function of $\mathbf{w}$ only, an iterative optimisation procedure, such as the BFGS (Broyden-Fletcher-Goldfarb-Shanno) algorithm [4], can be employed to determine the minimum value of R.

2.1 PREDICTING THE MISCLASSIFICATION RATE

The mathematical derivation of the classifier allows us to quantitatively predict the misclassification error as a function of the number of observations of the time series.

The Bayes Risk can be expressed as

$$R = \sum_{m=1}^{M-1} [1 - \Phi(z_m) - \Phi(z_{m+1})]$$

where Φ is the characteristic function of a Gaussian and z_m is given by

$$z_m = \frac{| e_{m,m+1} - \hat{d}_m |}{\sqrt{V(\hat{d}_m)}}$$

$$\Phi(z_m) = \frac{1}{2}\mathrm{Erf}\left(\frac{z_m}{\sqrt{2}}\right)$$

The classifier weight values and mean classification indices are invariant to the number of observations, N, of the time series. The variance of the classification indices is, however, approximately inversely proportional to N.

So, for a given number of time series observations, N_0, calculate $\hat{d}_m$ and $V(\hat{d}_m)$. Then to determine the Bayes Risk (misclassification error) at any value N let

$$V'(\hat{d}_m) = \frac{V(\hat{d}_m)N_0}{N}$$

and recalculate the intersection points $e_{m,m+1}$.

Hence, given the classification indices, $\hat{d}_m$, and their corresponding variances $V(\hat{d}_m)$ for N_0 observations, the misclassification error as a function of the number of observations, N can be written as

$$R(N) = \sum_{m=1}^{M-1} \left[1 - 0.5\mathrm{Erf}\left(\frac{| e_{m,m+1} - \hat{d}_m |}{\sqrt{\frac{2V(\hat{d}_m)N_0}{N}}} \right) - 0.5\mathrm{Erf}\left(\frac{| e_{m,m+1} - \hat{d}_{m+1} |}{\sqrt{\frac{2V(\hat{d}_{m+1})N_0}{N}}} \right) \right]$$

Figure 1 shows the predicted and experimentally determined error rates for the classification of five AR(2) processes using a three weight network (where $N_0 = 200$ observations). The dotted line represents the experimentally determined misclassification error and the full line represents the predicted error.

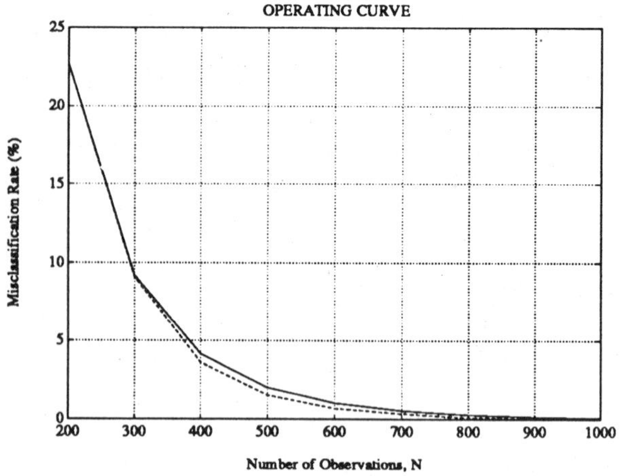

Figure 1: Predicted and Experimentally Determined Error Rates

3 RESULTS

Figure 2 shows the state-conditional PDFs using the VCM applied to the classification of five stationary AR(2) processes driven by Gaussian noise. In this problem a network with four weights was trained using a training set of 10 time series each of length 500 for each class. On applying a test set of 1000 time series for each class, the overall percentage misclassification was 0.08%.

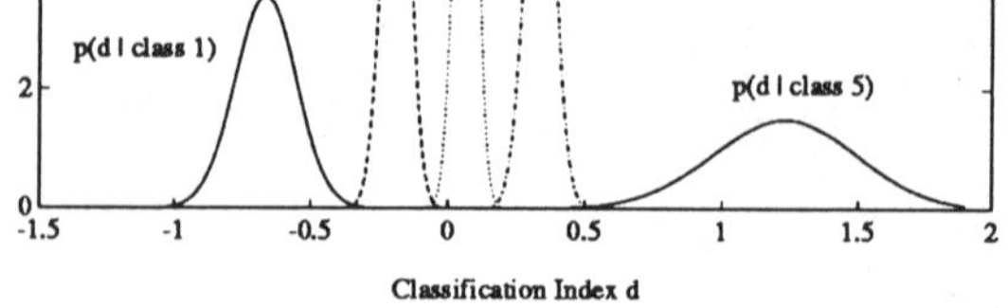

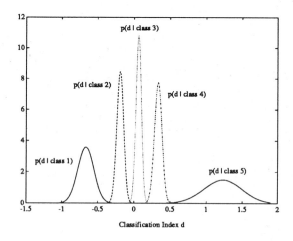

Figure 2: AR(2) Time Series Classification

Figure 3 shows the state-conditional PDFs using the VCM applied to the classification of three AR(1) processes driven by uniform noise and then clipped. The network has three weights and was trained using a training set of 20 time series each of length 500 for each class. A test set of 1000 time series for each class was applied and the overall percentage misclassification was 0.633%.

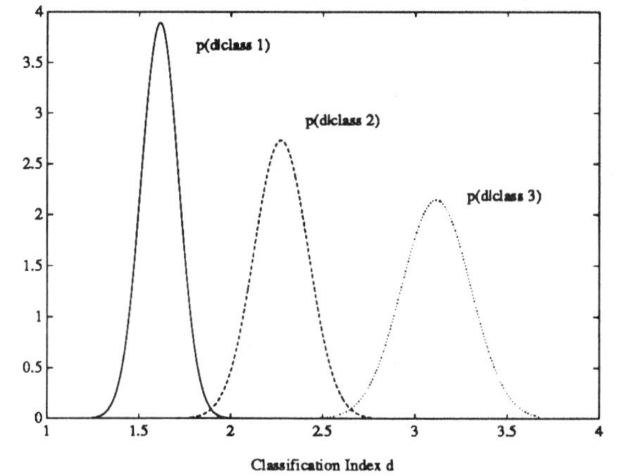

Figure 3: Non-Gaussian Time Series Classification

Figure 4 shows the state-conditional PDFs for the classification of three rock types using acoustic signals obtained at the drill bit of an oil well. The overall percentage misclassification was 0.92%.

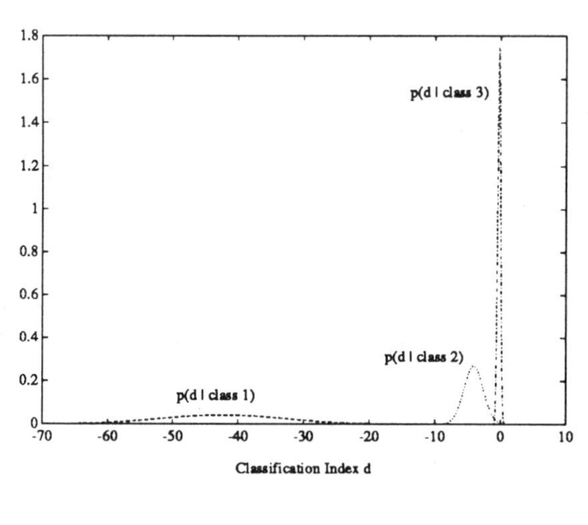

Figure 4: Rock Type Classification

4 CONCLUSIONS

In this paper we have shown that the Volterra Connectionist Model can be used to classify stationary time series within a Bayesian framework. In comparison with other methods for determining the weights of the VCM, such as using the RLS or stochastic gradient algorithm [5, 6], the Bayesian technique has a significantly lower misclassification rate (typically of the order of one magnitude) but suffers from greater computational complexity and a slower rate of convergence.

The firm mathematical basis from which the classifier is developed enables us to formalise the decision making process and allows us to analytically describe the probability of misclassification in terms of the time series parameters.

REFERENCES

[1] P.J.W. Rayner and M.R. Lynch. A new connectionist model based on a non-linear adaptive model. *ICASSP*, pages 1191–1194, 1989.

[2] M.S. Bartlett. On the theoretical specification and sampling properties of autocorrelated time series. *Journal of the Royal Statistical Society*, 8(1):28–41, 1946.

[3] R.O. Duda and P.E. Hart. *Pattern Classification and Scene Analysis.* John Wiley and Sons, 1973.

[4] W.H. Press, S.A. Teukolsky, B.P. Flannery, and W.T. Vetterling. *Numerical Recipes in C - The Art of Scientific Computing.* Cambridge University Press, 1988.

[5] P.J. Rayner and M.R. Lynch. Complexity reduction in Volterra connectionist modelling by consideration of output mapping. *ICASSP*, 1990.

[6] M.R. Lynch and P.J. Rayner. Properties and implementation of the non-linear vector space connectionist model. *1st Int. Conf. on Artificial Neural Networks*, 1989.

DIFFERENTIAL LEARNING LEADS TO EFFICIENT NEURAL NETWORK CLASSIFIERS

J. B. Hampshire II and *B. V. K. Vijaya Kumar*

Department of Electrical and Computer Engineering
Carnegie Mellon University
Pittsburgh, PA 15213-3890

hamps@faraday.ece.cmu.edu kumar@gauss.ece.cmu.edu

ABSTRACT

We outline a differential theory of learning for statistical pattern classification. The theory is based on classification figure-of-merit (CFM) objective functions, described in [9]. We outline the proof that differential learning is *efficient*, requiring the least classifier complexity and the smallest training sample size necessary to achieve Bayesian (i.e., minimum error) discrimination. We conclude with a practical application of the theory in which a simple differentially trained linear neural network classifier discriminates handwritten digits of the AT&T DB1 database with a 1.3% error rate. This error rate is less than one half the best previous result for a linear classifier on this optical character recognition (OCR) task [1].

1. EFFICIENT LEARNING

The objective of all statistical pattern classifiers [2] is to implement the Bayesian discriminant function (BDF — i.e., any set of discriminant functions that guarantees the lowest probability of making a classification error in the pattern recognition task). A classifier that implements the BDF is said to yield Bayesian discrimination. The challenge is to approximate the Bayesian discriminant function *efficiently*, using the fewest training examples and the least complex classifier necessary for the task. By Kolmogorov's theorem [11] there is no algorithm for determining *a priori* the least complex classifier necessary for Bayesian discrimination. Instead we must restrict our search to a particular *hypothesis class*, [1] and focus on selecting and training the member of that class with the minimum sufficient complexity for Bayesian discrimination.

The recent renaissance of connectionism has led to a considerable amount of research regarding generalization in neural network pattern classifiers that are trained in a supervised fashion. Most of this research has attempted to match the functional complexity of the classifier with the size of the training sample in order to follow the maxim of Occam's razor: "the simplest [i.e., minimum complexity] model is the best". Indeed there is a large body of work validating the maxim. We note in particular Valiant's original PAC (probably approximately correct) model of learning deterministic concepts [15], and more recent extensions of this work to learning stochastic concepts (see for example the work of Barron, Baum, Cover, Haussler, Vapnik, and Yamanishi — much of which is summarized in [14]). Yet relatively little attention has been paid to the role that the learning strategy plays in selecting and training a minimum-complexity classifier. We propose a *differential learning strategy*; it is based on the classification figure-of-merit (CFM) objective function,[2] originally described in [9] and recently replicated in [10]. Differential learning

1. **engenders Bayesian discrimination** for asymptotically large training sample sizes.
2. **is monotonic**: that is, the CFM objective function used for differential learning is under all circumstances a monotonic function of the classifier's training sample error rate.
3. **requires the minimum number of training samples** necessary to approximate the Bayesian discriminant function with specified precision.
4. **requires the minimum classifier functional complexity** necessary to approximate the Bayesian discriminant function with specified precision.
5. **yields the lowest probability of error on the training sample** for a classifier with bounded functional capacity (e.g., a multi-layer perceptron with a bounded number of connections and hidden-layer nodes).
6. **yields the lowest probability of error on any/all disjoint test samples** for a classifier with functional capacity that is less than or equal to the minimum complexity necessary for Bayesian discrimination.

In short, differential learning is efficient. Proofs of these assertions are beyond the scope of this conference paper. For this reason, our purpose is simply to convey in more intuitive terms the fundamental concepts upon which the theory is based. Readers interested in mathematical rigor can find it in [5] and the earlier work on which that reference is based [9, 8, 6, 7].

This research was funded by the Air Force Office of Scientific Research (grant AFOSR-89-0551) and supported by a supercomputing grant from the National Science Foundation's Pittsburgh Supercomputing Center (grant CCR920002P). The authors' views and conclusions should not be interpreted as representing the official policies, either expressed or implied, of the U.S. Air Force, the National Science Foundation, or the U.S. Government.

[1] The term *hypothesis class* arises in PAC learning theory. In the statistical pattern recognition context it describes the set of all possible classifiers, given our choice of classifier paradigm and parameter space. As an example, the set of all C-output multi-layer perceptrons with no more than 500 total connections is a hypothesis class.

[2] We assume that the classifier learns by adjusting a set of internal parameters via an iterative search aimed at optimizing an objective function (or empirical risk measure). The objective function is a metric that evaluates how well the classifier's evolving mapping reflects the empirical relationship between the input patterns of the training sample and their class membership, modeled by the classifier's outputs. Optimizing the objective function via iterative search on the classifier's parameter space is therefore a mathematically justifiable approach to machine learning.

0-7803-0946-4/93 $3.00 © 1993 IEEE

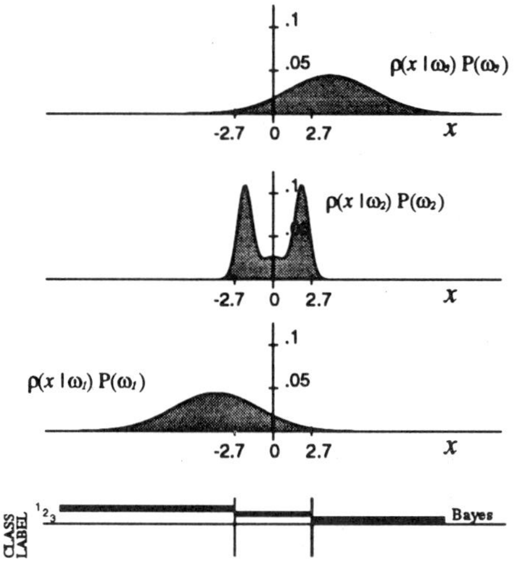

Figure 1: The class-conditional density – class prior probability products $\rho_{\mathbf{x}|\mathcal{W}}(x\,|\,\omega_i)\cdot \mathrm{P}_{\mathcal{W}}(\omega_i)$ for a three-class random scalar x.

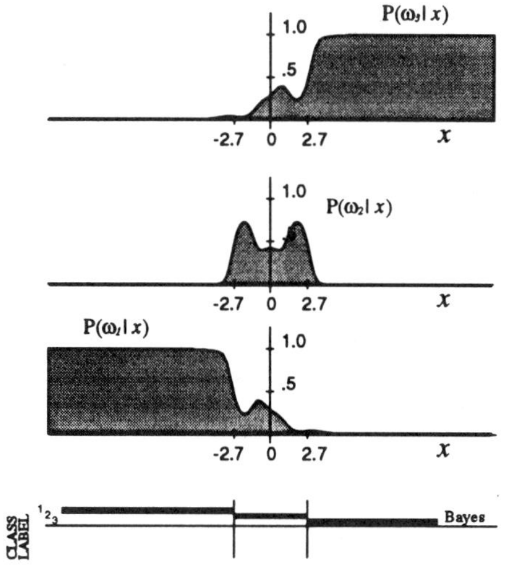

Figure 2: The associated *a posteriori* probabilities $\mathrm{P}_{\mathcal{W}|\mathbf{x}}(\omega_i\,|\,x)$ for each of the three-classes, plotted over the effective domain of x. These constitute the probabilistic form of the Bayesian discriminant function for x.

2. DISCRIMINANT ERROR, EFFICIENCY, AND GENERALIZATION

Let us quantify precisely what we mean by "efficient learning". The post-training error rate of the classifier depends on its initial parameterization and its hypothesis class, the training sample, and the learning strategy. We define *discriminant bias* as the expected difference between the classifier's error rate (i.e., probability of error $\mathrm{P}_e(\cdot)$) and the Bayes error rate:

$$\mathrm{DBias}\left[\mathrm{P}_e\left(\mathcal{G}\mid\{\mathcal{S}^n,\theta_0,\mathbf{G}(\Theta),\Lambda\}\right)\right] \triangleq \mathrm{E}_{\mathcal{S}^n,\theta_0}\left[\mathrm{P}_e\left(\mathcal{G}\mid\{\mathcal{S}^n,\theta_0,\mathbf{G}(\Theta),\Lambda\}\right)\right] - \mathrm{P}_e\left(\mathcal{F}_{Bayes}\right)$$

This bias is always non-negative, since the Bayes error rate is provably minimum (e.g., [2]). The notation $\mathcal{F}_{Bayes}$ indicates the Bayesian discriminant function. $\mathrm{P}_e\left(\mathcal{G}\mid\{\mathcal{S}^n,\theta_0,\mathbf{G}(\Theta),\Lambda\}\right)$ denotes the classifier's ($\mathcal{G}$'s) probability of error, given the set of n training examples $\mathcal{S}^n$, the initial parameterization of the classifier θ_0 (i.e. its parameterization prior to learning), the classifier's hypothesis class $\mathbf{G}(\Theta)$, and the learning strategy Λ. $\mathrm{E}_{\mathcal{S}^n,\theta_0}[\cdot]$ denotes the expectation of this error rate over the set of all possible training samples of size n and all possible initial classifier parameterizations.

We define *discriminant variance* as the second central moment of the classifier's error rate:

$$\mathrm{DVar}\left[\mathrm{P}_e\left(\mathcal{G}\mid\{\mathcal{S}^n,\theta_0,\mathbf{G}(\Theta),\Lambda\}\right)\right] \triangleq \mathrm{E}_{\mathcal{S}^n,\theta_0}\left[\left(\mathrm{P}_e\left(\mathcal{G}\mid\{\mathcal{S}^n,\theta_0,\mathbf{G}(\Theta),\Lambda\}\right) - \mathrm{E}_{\mathcal{S}^n,\theta_0}\left[\mathrm{P}_e\left(\mathcal{G}\mid\{\mathcal{S}^n,\theta_0,\mathbf{G}(\Theta),\Lambda\}\right)\right]\right)^2\right]$$

$$= \mathrm{E}_{\mathcal{S}^n,\theta_0}\left[\mathrm{P}_e\left(\mathcal{G}\mid\{\mathcal{S}^n,\theta_0,\mathbf{G}(\Theta),\Lambda\}\right)^2\right] - \mathrm{E}_{\mathcal{S}^n,\theta_0}\left[\mathrm{P}_e\left(\mathcal{G}\mid\{\mathcal{S}^n,\theta_0,\mathbf{G}(\Theta),\Lambda\}\right)\right]^2$$

We define the *mean-squared discriminant error* (MSDE) as the expected value of the squared difference between the Bayes error rate and classifier's error rate:

$$\mathrm{MSDE}\left[\mathrm{P}_e\left(\mathcal{G}\mid\{\mathcal{S}^n,\theta_0,\mathbf{G}(\Theta),\Lambda\}\right)\right] \triangleq \mathrm{E}_{\mathcal{S}^n,\theta_0}\left[\left(\mathrm{P}_e\left(\mathcal{F}_{Bayes}\right) - \mathrm{P}_e\left(\mathcal{G}\mid\{\mathcal{S}^n,\theta_0,\mathbf{G}(\Theta),\Lambda\}\right)\right)^2\right]$$

$$= \mathrm{DBias}\left[\mathrm{P}_e\left(\mathcal{G}\mid\{\mathcal{S}^n,\theta_0,\mathbf{G}(\Theta),\Lambda\}\right)\right]^2 + \mathrm{DVar}\left[\mathrm{P}_e\left(\mathcal{G}\mid\{\mathcal{S}^n,\theta_0,\mathbf{G}(\Theta),\Lambda\}\right)\right]$$

The learning strategy Λ is efficient if, given a particular hypothesis class $\mathbf{G}(\Theta)$, it generates the minimum MSDE of any learning strategy for each and every training sample size n. Thus, MSDE is a measure of the classifier's ability to generalize, and the efficient learning strategy engenders the classifier with the highest probability of generalizing to unseen test samples.

Note that discriminant bias and variance and MSDE are very different from the *functional* bias, variance, and mean-squared error (along with other related error measures such as the Kullback-Liebler information distance [12]) typically discussed in the neural network and machine/computational learning literature (e.g., [3]).

3. THE DISCRIMINANT FUNCTIONAL MAPPING IS KEY TO EFFICIENCY

The difference between the functional mappings engendered by differential learning (associated with the CFM objective function) and probabilistic learning (associated with more traditional error measure objective functions such as L_R norms and the Kullback-Liebler information distance) is key; it accounts for the efficiency of differential learning, and the inefficiency of probabilistic learning. Figures 1, 2, and 3 illustrate the difference for a three-class random scalar [3] $\mathbf{X}$. Figure 1 illustrates the class-conditional density – class prior probability products for the three classes on $\mathbf{X}$ (i.e.,

[3] We use boldface $\mathbf{X}$ despite the fact that the random variable is a scalar. This is to emphasize that all assertions apply to the more general case in which the entity being classified is a random vector.

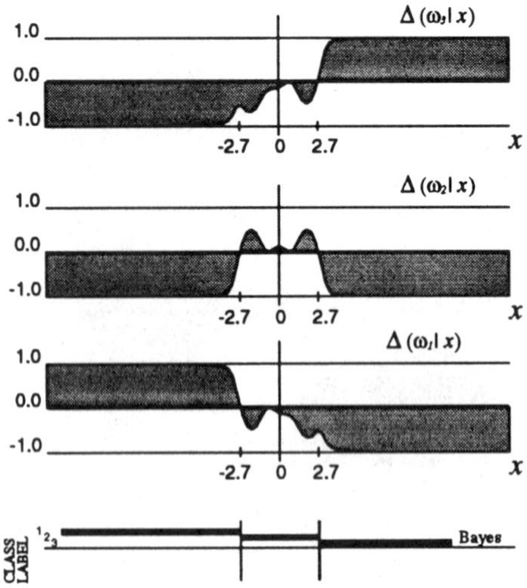

Figure 3: The *a posteriori* differentials $\Delta_{\mathcal{W}|\mathbf{x}}(\omega_i\,|\,x)$ of (3) for the three-class random variable x depicted in figure 1, plotted over the effective domain of x. These constitute the differential form of the Bayesian discriminant function for x, and need only be approximated to one (sign) bit precision in order to achieve Bayesian discrimination of x.

the three concepts that $\mathbf{X}$ can represent). A bar-graph display under these plots shows the Bayes-optimal class for $\mathbf{X}$ over its effective domain. Classes ω_1 and ω_3 have Gaussian densities, and ω_2 has a multimodal density. All class prior probabilities are equal. Figure 2 shows the *a posteriori* class probabilities $P_{\mathcal{W}|\mathbf{X}}(\omega_i\,|\,\mathbf{X})$, $i = 1, 2, 3$ for $\mathbf{X}$. The probabilistically-trained classifier learns the functional mappings [6, 5]

$$\mathbf{X} \rightarrow P_{\mathcal{W}|\mathbf{X}}(\omega_i\,|\,\mathbf{X}), \qquad i = 1, \ldots \mathcal{C} = 3 \tag{1}$$

depicted in this figure, where $\mathbf{X}$ denotes the feature vector of the entity being classified, and ω_i denotes the ith of $\mathcal{C}$ possible classes/concepts with which $\mathbf{X}$ can be associated. In contrast, the differential strategy for identifying the most likely class of a random sample of $\mathbf{X}$ involves identifying the largest *a posteriori* probability $P_{\mathcal{W}|\mathbf{X}}(\omega_{r1}\,|\,\mathbf{X})$ for each point on the domain of $\mathbf{X}$ — note that the subscript i in ω_i is a randomly assigned label, whereas the subscript rj in ω_{rj} denotes a *ranking*; $P_{\mathcal{W}|\mathbf{X}}(\omega_{rj}\,|\,\mathbf{X})$ refers to the jth-ranked *a posteriori* probability, and ω_{rj} is the class associated with that probability. Figure 3 shows the *a posteriori* class differentials $\Delta_{\mathcal{W}|\mathbf{X}}(\omega_i\,|\,\mathbf{X})$ for $\mathbf{X}$, defined in (3). The differentially-trained classifier learns the functional mappings [6, 5]

$$\mathbf{X} \rightarrow \sigma\left[\Delta_{\mathcal{W}|\mathbf{X}}(\omega_i\,|\,\mathbf{X})\right], \; i = 1, \ldots \mathcal{C} = 3 \tag{2}$$

where

$$\Delta_{\mathcal{W}|\mathbf{X}}(\omega_i\,|\,\mathbf{X}) \triangleq P_{\mathcal{W}|\mathbf{X}}(\omega_i\,|\,\mathbf{X}) - \max_{j\neq i} P_{\mathcal{W}|\mathbf{X}}(\omega_j\,|\,\mathbf{X}) \tag{3}$$

and $\sigma(\cdot)$ is a strictly increasing function of its argument, such as the monotonic classification figure-of-merit (CFM) [9]. It can be shown that as $\sigma(\cdot) \Rightarrow \mathrm{sign}(\cdot)$, learning the functional mapping of (2) (i.e., learning the $\mathcal{C}$ functions of (3) to one bit precision) requires the fewest examples and the classifier with the least functional complexity necessary for Bayesian discrimination. In simple terms, the classifier output representing the correct class of x need only be larger than all the other outputs in order to achieve Bayesian discrimination. While the information (i.e., number of training examples) and computational resource (i.e., classifier functional complexity) requirements for differential learning are provably minimal, those for probabilistic learning are almost always greater [6, 5]. Thus, differential learning is efficient, whereas probabilistic learning is not.

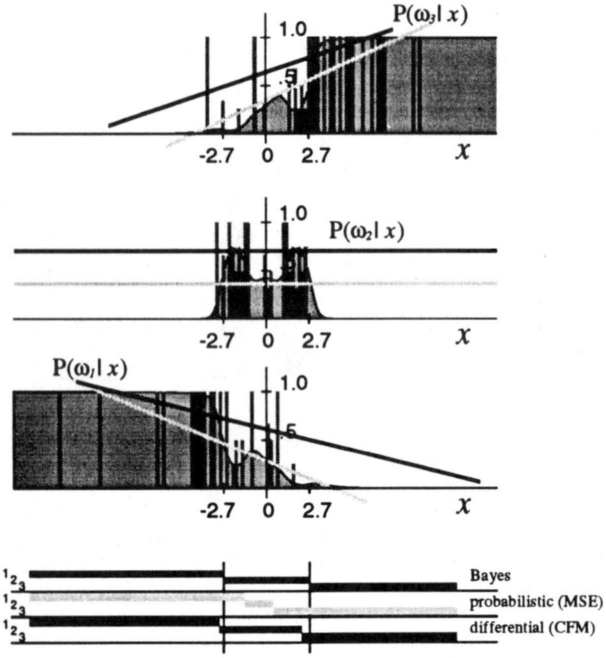

Figure 4: Empirical *a posteriori* class probabilities ($n = 100$) superimposed on the true ones of the random variable depicted in figures 1 – 3. The "optimal" minimum-complexity polynomial discriminant functions: (gray) those obtained via probabilistic learning (MSE) and (black) those obtained via differential learning (CFM). Bar graphs at bottom show how resulting models classify x.

4. AN ILLUSTRATION AND AN OCR APPLICATION OF THE THEORY

Figure 4 illustrates the preceding points for the random scalar depicted by figures 1 – 3. If we choose the set of all polynomial discriminant functions as our hypothesis class, it is straightforward to show that the minimum-complexity classifier necessary to achieve Bayesian discrimination of x has two discriminant functions that are linear functions of x and one discriminant function that is a constant. We assign the linear discriminant functions to classes ω_1 and ω_3, and the constant discriminant function to class ω_2. Next we obtain a training sample containing 100 examples; the empirical *a posteriori* probabilities of this training sample are superimposed in histogram form (dark gray) on the true underlying *a posteriori* probabilities (figure 4). Two sets of discriminant functions are shown. The light gray discriminant functions are obtained by minimizing the mean-squared-error (MSE) between them and the training sample, whereas the black discriminant functions are obtained by maximizing the CFM between them and the training sample. Since the classifier is of very low complexity, probabilistic learning by minimizing MSE (the squared *functional* error) leads to a classifier that exhibits high *discriminant* bias (note the light-gray bar-graph denoting how the probabilistically trained classifier partitions feature space). Clearly, it would take polynomial discriminant functions of higher order (complexity) to reduce the discriminant bias with probabilistic learning. The higher complexity model would, however, result in significantly higher discriminant variance for a given training sample size. The net result would be a classifier with high MSDE, which would generalize poorly to test samples. In contrast, the classifier has sufficient complexity for zero discriminant bias, providing that differential learning is employed. Since the only requirement of the differentially trained classifier is that the output representing the correct class of x be larger than any other output, we achieve low discriminant bias. Since the model has the minimum complexity necessary for Bayesian discrimination, given this hypothesis class and this random variable, it will exhibit the lowest discriminant variance possible. The net result is the most efficient model possible, given our choice of hypothesis class. Reference [7] uses a very similar three-class pattern recognition task, which lends itself to closed-form analysis for infinitely large training samples. It provides a more rigorous illustrative comparison of differential and probabilistic learning.

Recently, we have applied differential learning to the task of hand-printed digit recognition, using the AT&T "little" optical character recognition (OCR) benchmark database (DB1), described and analyzed extensively in [4, 1, 3]. We achieve a 1.3 (+1.1/-0.9)% error rate on this task, using a multi-output perceptron (i.e., an MLP with no hidden layer)[4]. This linear classifier has 650 total weights and operates on 8 × 8 16-ary pixel images, obtained by simple compression of the original 16 × 16 binary pixel images. Further classifier complexity reduction is achieved with weight decay and weight smoothing (e.g., [4]).

If we use traditional probabilistic learning with precisely the same model, learning parameters, etc., our error rate doubles to 3.3 (+1.6/-1.4)% — making it comparable to the best linear classifier results previously achieved. We find that Optimal Brain Damage (OBD) [13] and related complexity reduction techniques [16, 4] are more effective when modified for use and paired with differential learning: the resulting classifier has approximately half the effective parameters of the control model obtained with probabilistic learning and complexity reduction. Clearly, objective functions associated with probabilistic learning are sub-optimal choices both for learning and for learning-directed model complexity reduction. This is consistent with our theory.

The best linear classifier result previously achieved on the DB1 task is 3.2 (+1.6/-1.4)% [1]. The lowest complexity linear classifier we know of [4] has approximately 1.3 times the number of total parameters as our model (a comparison of effective parameter numbers is less clear). The best known result for any model is 0.3 (+0.7/-0.3)%, achieved with a non-linear polynomial classifier operating on filtered input data [1]. Without filtering, the error rate for this polynomial model is 1.5 (+1.1/-1.0)% [1], which is statistically equivalent to our linear classifier result.

Thus, we use a simple linear classifier, train it differentially, and reduce the error rate of the previous best linear classifier by 58%. This finding is consistent with our theoretical claims. Reference [5] shows similar improvements in a diverse collection of pattern recognition tasks related to medical diagnosis/decision support, remote sensing, and digital telecommunications.

[4] All error rates are based on a single benchmark 50/50 split of the database into training and testing sets, used in [4, 1]. 95% confidence bounds are given for each error rate.

5. SUMMARY

If our ultimate objective in training a classifier is estimating the *a posteriori* class probabilities of the feature vector, then we are compelled to use probabilistic learning. This, in turn, compels us to employ a sufficiently complex classifier and obtain a sufficiently large training sample if we are to have confidence in the classifier's probabilistic estimates. However, if the ultimate objective is simply to classify patterns, then differential learning is a better strategic choice, allowing us to achieve the goal of robust pattern classification efficiently. The critical reader will note that differential learning abandons the goal of estimating the feature vector's *a posteriori* class probabilities. While this may seem unreasonable, we believe that it is essential to efficient learning — both in theory and in practice.

6. REFERENCES

[1] B. Boser, I. Guyon, and V. Vapnik. A training algorithm for optimal margin classifiers. In *Proceedings of the Fifth Annual ACM Workshop on Computational Learning Theory (COLT-92)*, pages 144–152, New York, NY, 1992. ACM Press.

[2] R. O. Duda and P. E. Hart. *Pattern Classification and Scene Analysis*. John Wiley & Sons, New York, NY, 1973.

[3] S. Geman, E. Bienenstock, and R. Doursat. Neural Networks and the Bias/Variance Dilemma. *Neural Computation*, 4(1):1–58, January 1992.

[4] I. Guyon, V. Vapnik, B. Boser, L. Bottou, and S. Solla. Structural risk minimization for character recognition. In J. Moody, S. Hanson, and R. Lippmann, editors, *Advances in Neural Information Processing Systems, vol. 4*, pages 471–479, San Mateo, CA, 1992. Morgan Kauffman.

[5] J. B. Hampshire II. *A Differential Theory of Learning for Efficient Statistical Pattern Recognition*. PhD thesis, Carnegie Mellon University, Department of Electrical & Computer Engineering, Hammerschlag Hall, Pittsburgh, PA 15213-3890, expected April 1993.

[6] J. B. Hampshire II and B. V. K. Vijaya Kumar. Shooting Craps in Search of an Optimal Strategy for Training Connectionist Pattern Classifiers. In J. Moody, S. Hanson, and R. Lippmann, editors, *Advances in Neural Information Processing Systems, vol. 4*, pages 1125–1132, San Mateo, CA, 1992. Morgan Kauffman.

[7] J. B. Hampshire II and B. V. K. Vijaya Kumar. Why Error Measures are Sub-Optimal for Training Neural Network Pattern Classifiers. In *IEEE Proceedings of the 1992 International Joint Conference on Neural Networks, Vol. 4*, pages 220–227, June 1992.

[8] J. B. Hampshire II and B. A. Pearlmutter. Equivalence Proofs for Multi-Layer Perceptron Classifiers and the Bayesian Discriminant Function. In Touretzky, Elman, Sejnowski, and Hinton, editors, *Proceedings of the 1990 Connectionist Models Summer School*, pages 159–172, San Mateo, CA, 1991. Morgan Kaufmann.

[9] J. B. Hampshire II and A. H. Waibel. A Novel Objective Function for Improved Phoneme Recognition Using Time-Delay Neural Networks. *IEEE Transactions on Neural Networks*, 1(2):216–228, June 1990. A revised and extended version of work first presented at the 1989 International Joint Conference on Neural Networks, vol. I, pp. 235-241, June, 1989.

[10] B. H. Juang and S. Katagiri. Discriminative Learning for Minimum Error Classification. *IEEE Transactions on Signal Processing*, 40(12):3043–3054, December 1992.

[11] A. N. Kolmogorov. Three Approaches to the Quantitative Definition of Information. *Problems of Information Transmission*, 1(1):1–7, Jan. - Mar. 1965. Faraday Press translation of Problemy Peredachi Informatsii.

[12] S. Kullback. *Information Theory and Statistics*. Wiley, New York, NY, 1959.

[13] Y. LeCun, J. Denker, and S. Solla. Optimal brain damage. In D. S. Touretzky, editor, *Advances in Neural Information Processing Systems, vol. 2*, pages 598–605. Morgan Kauffman, San Mateo, CA, 1990.

[14] B. K. Natarajan. *Machine Learning: A Theoretical Approach*. Morgan Kaufmann, San Mateo, CA, 1991.

[15] L. G. Valiant. A Theory of the Learnable. *Communciations of the ACM*, 27(11):1134–1142, November 1984.

[16] V. Vapnik. Principles of risk minimization for learning theory. In J. Moody, S. Hanson, and R. Lippmann, editors, *Advances in Neural Information Processing Systems, vol. 4*, pages 831–838, San Mateo, CA, 1992. Morgan Kauffman.

Dynamics of Synaptic Transfer in Living and Simulated Neurons

Michael Stiber*
Department of Computer Science
The Hong Kong University of Science and Technology
Clear Water Bay, Kowloon
Hong Kong

José P. Segundo
Department of Anatomy and Cell Biology
and Brain Research Institute
University of California
Los Angeles, California 90024

***Abstract*— Nervous systems and their constituent neurons often display complex dynamics in response to inputs with simple characteristics. Until recently, these behaviors were not even classified, let alone understood. This lack of understanding impedes determination of the utility of dynamical processing elements in artificial neural networks. This paper summarizes a comparison of the responses of an ionic permeability based neural model to periodic inhibitory driving with that of a living preparation. Unlike previous, simpler models, duplication of most neuron response types was excellent, and simulation results led to insights into neuron activities that were subsequently verified by examination of the living data. It is hoped that knowledge of the underlying physiological mechanisms and formal properties of neuron dynamics will lead to advances in artificial neural network computational theory.**

I. Introduction

This paper presents a preliminary comparison of some behaviors found for a dynamic, ionic-permeability-based neural model with those of the crayfish slowly adapting stretch receptor organ (SAO), both receiving periodic, pacemaker inhibitory input trains. The living preparation is of interest as a prototypical inhibitory synapse, an elementary functional unit in nervous systems. The model allows for exploration of the contributions of underlying mechanisms towards overall neural activity. Nonlinear dynamical analysis techniques used throughout are intended to lead to higher-level descriptions of neural dynamics which may be useful for improving understanding of neural computation.

*To whom correspondence should be addressed.

This work was supported by Trent H. Wells, Jr., Inc., the Office of the Dean of the UCLA School of Medicine (BRSG Funds), the UCLA Department of Anatomy and Cell Biology, and by a grant of computer time made possible under a joint study with the IBM Corporation on the IBM 3090/600J Supercomputer at the UCLA Office of Academic Computing. Some analysis was performed using NCSA Image and NCSA Layout, developed at the National Center for Supercomputing Applications at the University of Illinois at Urbana-Champaign.

0-7803-0999-5/93/$03.00

This work has already illuminated some previously misunderstood neural behaviors. For brevity's sake, details of the model, the living preparation, and data capture and analysis methods, are omitted — they can be found in [1, 2]. It seems that this model is capable of reproducing all behavioral forms found in the SAO, unlike simpler ones based on phase transition curves or leaky integrators [2]. These corresponding model forms contain behavioral details that were either obscured by or confused with noise in the SAO. This includes the presence of chaotic dynamics, which reinforces the idea that the SAO is capable of producing chaotic outputs [3].

II. Complex Dynamics in Living Neurons

A neuron produces a series (or *train*) of short lived pulses, called *Action Potentials* (APs) as its most obvious output. The timing of the APs, i.e., the times when they arise, are important. Here, we assimilate the train of APs to a *point process*, with the resultant description the sequence of times of occurrence, $\langle t_0, t_1, \ldots \rangle$. From these, one may extract the ordered series of interspike intervals, $\langle T_1, T_2, \ldots \rangle$, $T_n = t_n - t_{n-1}$.

By way of comparison, the typical output activity of artificial neural network units may be either a real or binary value, considered analogous to a neuron's time-averaged firing frequency, $1/\hat{T}$, where $\hat{T}$ is a mean over some range of T_i, computed for a reasonable time interval. Integration of inputs is performed by a weighted sum (with negative weights signifying inhibition), and the resultant output produced by sending the sum through a squashing function, which is nearly linear through much of its range. As a result, an increase in an inhibitory input causes the neuron's output value to monotonically decrease.

However, the result of periodic inhibition of a live pacemaker neuron at different input rates is much more complex. The output rate versus input rate relation includes paradoxical behavior, with a nonmonotonic response curve containing positive-slope locking regions alternating with regions of negative-sloped, nonlocked responses [4]. Thus, increasing inhibitory input can either increase or decrease a neuron's firing rate, and different inputs can result in changing output behavioral type. Here we concentrate on introducing three major behavioral categories which the

SAO and permeability model have in common.

Any behavior implies telltale relationships between input and output spike timings. *Locked* forms exhibit a fixed, repeating sequence of ϕ_i and T_i; we will call a behavior "locked p:q" if these sequences repeat every q outputs and p inputs, so $\phi_i = \phi_{i+q}$, $T_i = T_{i+q}$.

Intermittent is a descriptive term used for behaviors which might initially seem locked much of the time, but are interrupted at irregular times by wild deviations in output. Upon closer examination, they are revealed to be not quite periodic, only apparently so. This includes *quasiperiodic* behaviors, such as *phase slidings* and *walk-throughs*, in which $T/I \approx p/q$, for T/I irrational and (relatively small) integer p, q. The result is a phase drift or sliding in which phases "walk through" the full range in a non-standard manner.

The third behavior which will be considered has been called "messy" because it can't be summarized briefly or predicted reliably. It includes both *erratic* and *stammering* [1]. The erratic case is now considered *chaotic* [3]. Stammering occurs for high IPSP input frequencies $I < N$, in response to which the SAO is only able to produce outputs during narrow "windows" of time. Whether the SAO does produce an output during a particular window seems to be random, and has been mostly attributed to the influence of noise.

III. Modeling and Analysis

A. The Permeability Model

The model chosen to match the crayfish SAO responses was developed by Edman, Gestrelius, Grampp, and Sjölin for the lobster SAO and FAO (fast adapting stretch receptor organ) [5]. This model, in additional to ion flow *during* APs, emphasizes *between-spike* ionic fluxes, and therefore also includes slow state variables and ionic concentration dependencies. It approximates well the low-frequency spontaneous pacemaker firing seen in the SAO.

A block diagram of a modified version of their model is presented in Figure 1 with the interior of the cell on the right and the exterior on the left. It is a lumped model of the cell membrane, representing ionic concentrations and fluxes explicitly and regulating them by membrane permeabilities P_x (as opposed to the conductances in the Hodgkin-Huxley (H-H) model [6]). From top to bottom, the contributions to trans-membrane current flow are:

- a membrane capacitance (as in the H-H model), C_m,
- active pumping pathways for K^+ and Na^+, which work to maintain internal ionic concentrations,
- three leakage permeabilities, for Cl^-, K^+, and Na^+,
- two voltage-sensitive permeabilities, P_{Na} and P_K,

and an additional two channels added to the model of Edman and collaborators:

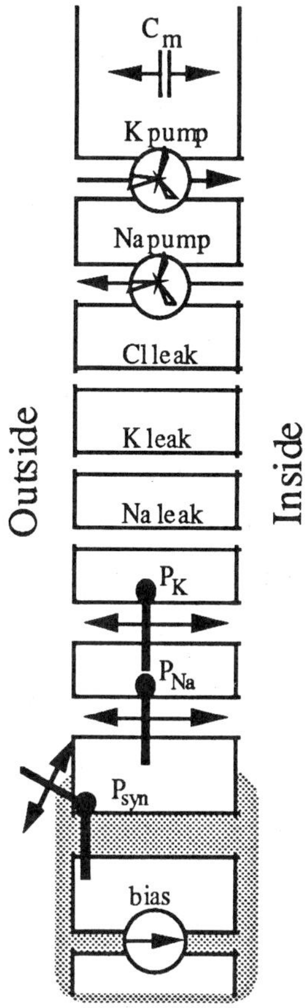

Fig. 1. Block diagram of the permeability model. From top to bottom, ionic channels include active pumps, leakages, voltage controlled, synaptic, and bias.

- a synaptic channel, P_{syn}, used to model the coupling with the driving cell, inputs from the presynaptic cell causing fixed-duration changes in the synaptic permeability to particular ions (Na^+ for EPSPs, Cl^- for IPSPs [7]),
- and a constant bias current, to produce the pacemaking behavior of the living cell.

A key difference from the H-H model is that the ionic fluxes used here are dependent not only on the membrane potential, but also on the transmembrane concentration differential. The internal and external ionic concentrations are state variables, and the internal concentrations are changed by the fluxes, the Na^+-K^+ pump which actively exchanges those two ions to maintain resting potential, and by the bias and synaptic permeabilities.

B. Analysis Methods

We deal here with analysis of data from forced self-oscillators, with the system under study an intrinsic oscillator, producing periodic output APs. When subjected to periodic forcing inputs, the timing of its output changes, and it exhibits new behaviors.

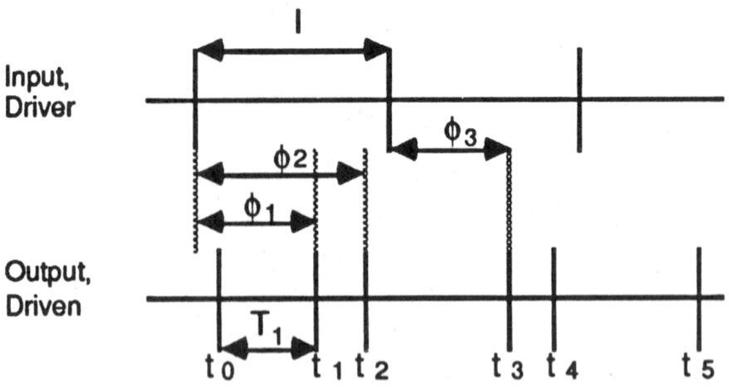

Fig. 2. A schematic view of input (presynaptic) and output (postsynaptic) trains. The input events are regular, with interval I. The output events may be regular of irregular, with the time of event i designated t_i and the interval to preceding one T_i. Phases ϕ_i are measured as the time between an output and the immediately preceding input, normalized to I.

These may differ quantitatively from the unperturbed (regularly spaced APs with different between-AP intervals) or it may differ qualitatively (APs no longer separated by identical intervals). Analyzing these changes is a major focus of this work.

As defined in Fig. 2, the times of the postsynaptic events are $\langle t_0, t_1, \ldots, t_n \rangle$, with the *interval* between two such events $T_i = t_i - t_{i-1}$. The presynaptic events are of fixed interval, I, and are used as reference times for analyses. The relation between the two trains is captured by the *cross interval* between a postsynaptic event and the most recent presynaptic event, ϕ_i, also called the *phase*, and usually normalized as a fraction of I.

A simple (but powerful) way of looking at the relationships between the neuron's current state and a past one is to plot them against each other. In many cases, it is not necessary to use the entire state — one element from it (or some other measured quantity, such as the T_i or ϕ_i) can be used. For instance, by plotting ϕ_i versus ϕ_{i+q}, we obtain a qth order phase *return map*.

There are several characteristics of the return map which will be of interest in diagnosing system behavior. First of all, if all of the plotted points fall within c small, discrete clusters in a first-order map, then locking would immediately be suspected. We would then proceed to generate the return maps of order nc, for some reasonable range of integer n, to see if the clusters fall on the diagonal. Clustering of points along the diagonal in the return map is key to locking detection. If $p{:}q$ locking is exhibited, then the qth order return map will have all points on the diagonal ($\phi_{i+q} = \phi_i$). Additionally, these q outputs will occur in the same amount of time that p inputs do, so that $qT = pI$.

When locking is not present, the points in a first-order return map will typically not fall into discrete clusters. If they form a 1-dimensional curve, then additional techniques can be used to analyze behavior. Quasiperiodicity, an irrational driver to driven ratio, results in the systematic progression of T or ϕ through the

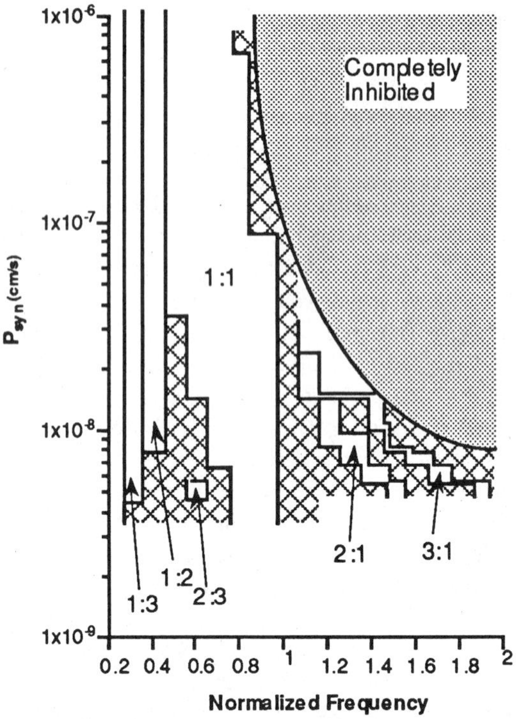

Fig. 3. This graph shows the borders of selected locking behaviors for inhibitory input to the permeability model. Cross-hatched areas correspond to other locking ratios or non-locked behavior. Note the region to the right where inhibition shuts the simulated neuron down.

entire range of values, with current state information sufficient to uniquely determine the future, and the return map will be a 1-1 invertible mapping. If a 1-dimensional curve exists, but it is not 1-1, or there is no 1-D curve, then there are a variety of possibilities, including stochastic, intermittency, and chaos.

Global behavior addresses the question of how behavior changes as we change the input — how the different behaviors of the system are related in the space made up of the input (or other) parameters. Here we will be exploring the effects of input amplitude and frequency, and will therefore be constructing two-dimensional *Arnol'd maps*.

In an Arnol'd map, system behavioral category, such as locked, quasiperiodic, or chaotic, is plotted in the (F, A) plane (where normalized input frequency $F = N/I$, and input amplitude $A = \bar{P}_{syn}$, measured by the maximum synaptic permeability). Lockings tend to occur in relatively tall, narrow regions in this plane, hence they are given the appellation *tongues*. We only diagnosed locking to construct approximate maps, and only for a limited number of ratios. Areas between locking tongues may include other lockings or non-locked behaviors. Ranges of input amplitude and normalized frequency were chosen, such that $A_{min} \le A \le A_{max}$ and $I_{min} \le I \le I_{max}$. A stepsize was

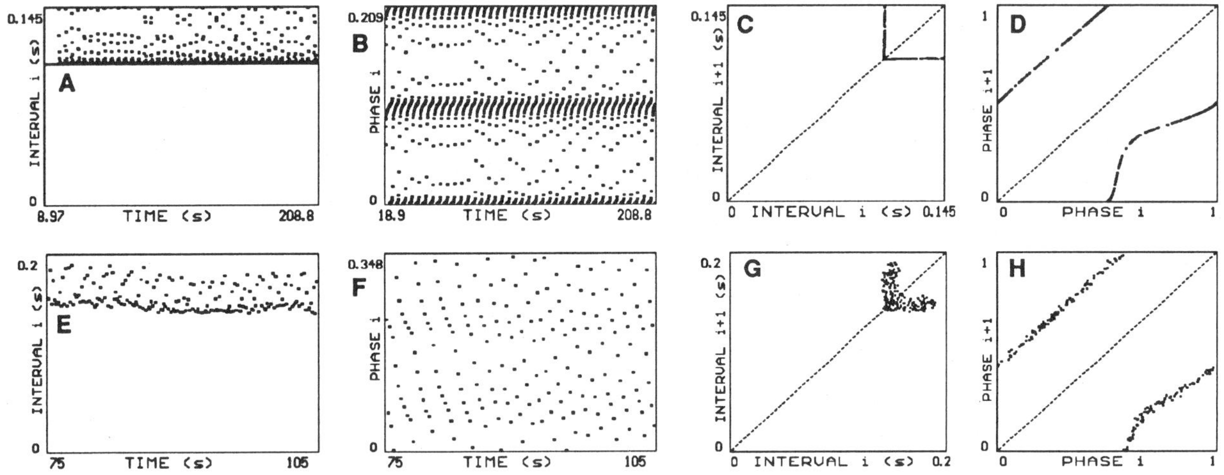

Fig. 4. Walkthrough in simulation and SAO. Intervals (simulation: A, C; SAO: E, G) and phases (simulation: B, D; SAO: F, H). Intime (T_i vs. t_i) plots (A, E) show preferred minimum interval. Phases (B, F) alternate between long and short categories, which walk through the range of values. Interval return maps (C, G) are 'L' shaped with "elbows" on the diagonal. Phase return maps (D, H) shows continuous curves. Simulation parameters: $N/I = 0.5$, $I = 0.209$s, $T = 0.107$s, $\bar{P}_{syn} = 6.0 \times 10^{-9}$cm/s.

used for both A and I, A_{step} and I_{step}, so that a simulation was performed at each amplitude step for each frequency step, within the given ranges.

The map for inhibitory input to the model is Fig. 3. Non-locked behaviors occur in the cross-hatched regions, while only the indicated locked forms arose in the white regions. A sparse exploration of the $(N/I, \bar{P}_{syn})$ space was performed, approximately 20 points across and 30 down, for a total of about 500 simulations. It is important to note that such an Arnol'd map cannot be constructed for the SAO itself, for, apart from inevitable time constraints, the preparation's synaptic strength is not an easily controllable variable.

IV. Results

Several features in the Arnol'd map are immediately apparent. With inhibitory input, the model can be shut down if the input frequency is too high. Additionally, locking tongues tend to narrow at low amplitudes and at high ones (this is noticeable primarily for the 1 : 1 tongue), the former the result of increasing number of non-locked behaviors, and the latter the "squeezing" of the range of frequencies within which the neuron will produce any output at all. With this map as a guide, individual $(N/I, \bar{P}_{syn})$ pairs were explored, and behaviors were found which mimicked well those found in the SAO, i.e. locked (omitted here), intermittent, and messy.

Forcing an oscillator beyond its entrainment limit can result in a type of intermittency called *quasiperiodicity*, in which an almost (but not quite) locked condition exists [8]. In interval and phase return maps, quasiperiodic behavior results in points on continuous, one-dimensional curves. Phase return maps are also invertible and, since phases "walk through" a range of values before (almost) repeating, this behavior is identified with *walkthroughs* [8], noted also in the SAO.

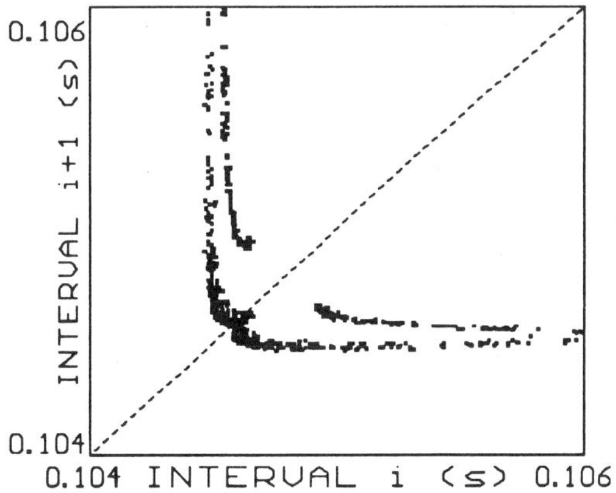

Fig. 5. Expanded view of "elbow" portion of interval return map in Fig. 4(C) indicates fine structure.

In the permeability model, two different type of apparently quasiperiodic behavior were found, though they may represent extremes of a range of behaviors. Fig. 4 shows example graphs for intervals and phases for the model (A-D) and the SAO (E-H). In both cases, the interval return maps (C, G) are 'L' shaped, with the elbow on the diagonal. Additionally, the phase return maps (D, H) contain points which fall along similar one-dimensional, invertible curves.

A magnified view of the elbow in (C) is presented in Fig. 5. We see that the interval return map in Figures 4(C) and 5 is not invertible, and that there is a fine structure associated with

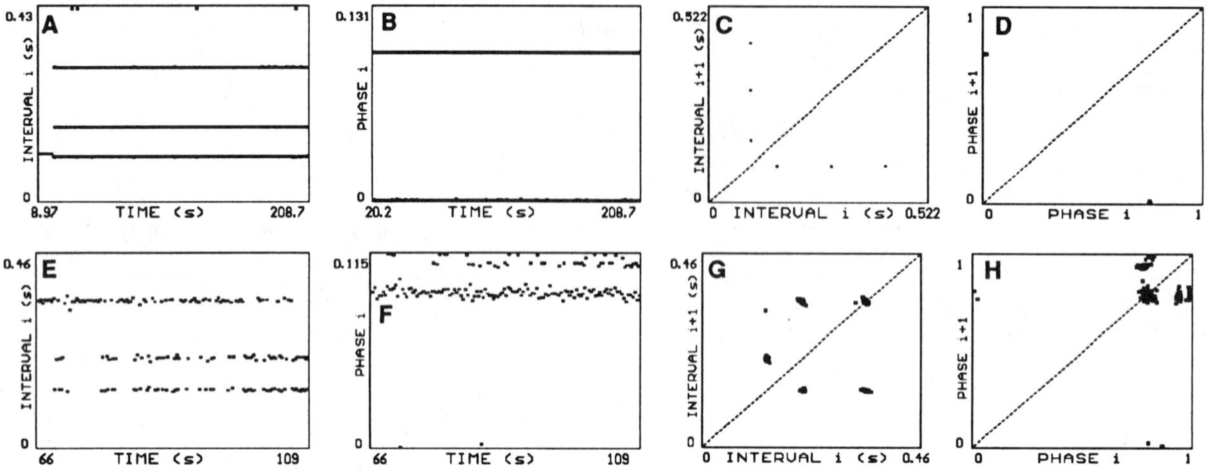

Fig. 6. Stammering in simulation and SAO. Intervals (simulation: A, C; SAO: E, G) and phases (simulation: B, D; SAO: F, H). Intime plot (A) shows acceleratory effect of inhibition and extreme intervals which are multiples of driver. There are two classes of phases (B, F). Phases in the simulation alternate (D). Simulation parameters: $N/I = 0.8$, $I = 0.130\text{s}$, $T = 0.168\text{s}$, $\bar{P}_{syn} = 7.0 \times 10^{-7}\text{cm/s}$.

it. Nearby points fall on topologically distant parts of whatever object is described by the map. This behavior is tentatively assigned to a pathway to chaos called *collapse of the quasiperiodicity*.

In the SAO, two different types of unpredictable (or "messy") behaviors were identified: *erratic* and *stammering* [1, 3]. Erratic behavior occurs at relatively low presynaptic rates below 1 : 1 locking, and stammering occurs at high rates. We shall only comment on stammering here.

In the SAO, after the arrival of an inhibitory spike, there is a period of time when the neuron is unlikely to fire. For low input frequency, it will recover and be able to fire before the next input. As the input frequency is increased, this "recovered interval" is shortened, until it is a narrow "window" just around the input arrival time ($\phi \approx 0$). Higher frequencies than that may cause the neuron to be silenced completely.

This type of discretization occurs in both the SAO and the model, and is called *windowing*. The fluctuation of excitability may be more complex, having multiple windows after an IPSP, separated by silent periods. Fig. 6 corresponds to multiple-window situations (in both cases, with two windows per inhibitory spike). There are two windows visible in the phasetime plots (B, F), one around the time of arrival of the input (note $\phi = 1 \equiv \phi = 0$), and the other longer phase. The behavior is not regular, as evidenced by the interval return maps (C, G). Multiple windows were clear and relatively frequent in simulation data; the latter findings led to recognizing them also in SAO data where they were less apparent and had been missed initially.

Simulation results permit a more discerning dissection of the data, as can be seen in the enlargement of what appear to be points in the return maps (Fig. 7). These "points" have a structure, the result of an underlying deterministic process. These two islands express the same folding and stretching behavior that has been seen in sinusoidally forced autonomously oscillating squid giant axons [9]. Though it had been previously concluded that stammering in the SAO is the result of noise [1, 3], this suggests that there may be an underlying deterministic process which is "washed out" by the noise.

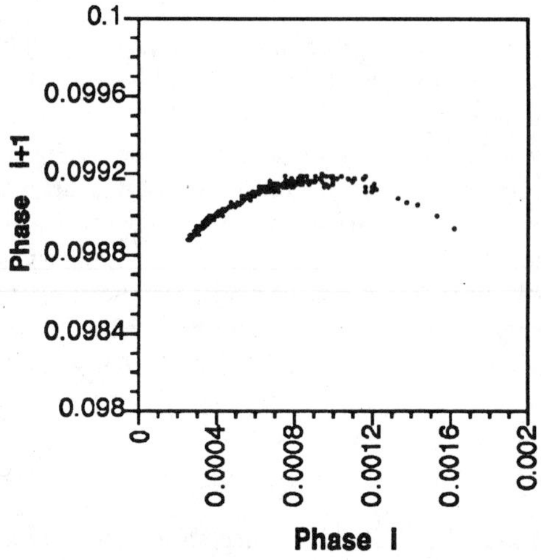

Fig. 7. Enlargement of upper left "point" from Fig. 6(D) show the cluster has fine structure, an extremum, and is not invertible.

V. Conclusions

The permeability model examined here reproduced extensively the variety of behaviors exhibited by the preparation. Only the briefest of comparisons has been included here. This reproduction is important because simpler models, based on phase transition curves (PTCs) or leaky integrators, generate exclusively locked discharges, even when considerably modified [2]. The model was also useful for improving our understanding of the messy behaviors. In erratic forms, it showed how common sliding is, both of intervals and phases (walkthroughs). In stammering, it demonstrated that tight clusters could have special structures suggesting chaotic behaviors within relatively small volumes. Both findings, noticed first in the simulations, were subsequently identified in the SAO data (where they had been missed initially). The presence of chaotic dynamics in a deterministic model is strong evidence for it underlying the corresponding behaviors of the living preparation, reinforcing evidence from other tests [3].

This model is expressed in terms of physiologically relevant entities (e.g., permeabilities, pumps), and therefore allows the exploration of how each basic mechanism contributes to the genesis of each discharge form. Not only can such a model be analyzed more thoroughly, but it can also serve to guide biological experiments in parallel with theoretical investigations. Determining the computational implications of these dynamics can similarly proceed in parallel with experimental investigation of their functional consequences.

While typical ANN models emphasize smooth, continuous transfer functions across synapses, living neurons do not behave accordingly, exhibiting complex input/output relationships, which depend not only on average input frequency, but also on the timing pattern of input spike trains (such as regular, periodic, or aperiodic). This has been amply demonstrated for regularly spaced periodic input [1]. The continuing emphasis of ANN work on simple models entails the risk of the field becoming irrelevant to the underlying neuroscience.

We assert that the dynamics of individual processing elements, and the concommittent complexity of potential behaviors, is essential for the construction of ANNs whose performance is meant to approximate that of biological systems — that "...knowledge of connectivity and synaptic weights alone are not sufficient to account for the operation and capabilities of neural networks..." [10]. The dynamics of individual neurons, and the temporal relationships among groups of them, are essential ingredients.

References

[1] J. P. Segundo, E. Altshuler, M. Stiber, and A. Garfinkel, "Periodic inhibition of living pacemaker neurons: I. Locked, intermittent, messy, and hopping behaviors," *Int. J. Bifurcation and Chaos*, vol. 1, pp. 549–81, September 1991.

[2] M. Stiber, *Dynamics of Synaptic Integration*. PhD thesis, University of California, Los Angeles, 1992.

[3] G. Sugihara, D. Grace, J. Segundo, and M. Stiber, unpublished.

[4] J. Segundo and D. Perkel, "The nerve cell as an analyzer of spike trains," in *The Interneuron: UCLA Forum in Medical Sciences* (M. Brazier, ed.), (Los Angeles), pp. 349–89, University of California Press, 1969.

[5] Å. Edman, S. Gestrelius, and W. Grampp, "Analysis of gated membrane currents and mechanisms of firing control in the rapidly adapting lobster stretch receptor neurone," *J. Physiol.*, vol. 384, pp. 649–69, 1987.

[6] A. Hodgkin and A. Huxley, "A quantitative description of membrane current and its application to conduction and excitation in nerve," *J. Physiol. (Lond.)*, vol. 117, pp. 500–44, 1952.

[7] K. Ozawa and K. Tsuda, "Membrane permeability change during inhibitory transmitter action in crayfish receptor cell," *J. Neurophysiol.*, vol. 36, pp. 805–16, September 1973.

[8] G. Ermentrout and J. Rinzel, "Beyond a pacemaker's entrainment limit: phase walk-through," *Am. J. Physiol.*, vol. 246, pp. R102–R106, 1984. (Regulatory Integrative Comp. Physiol. **15**).

[9] K. Aihara and G. Matsumoto, "Chaotic oscillations and bifurcations in squid giant axons," in *Chaos* (A. V. Holden, ed.), ch. 12, pp. 257–69, Princeton, New Jersey: Princeton University Press, 1986.

[10] N. Azmy, G. Yahiaoui, and J.-F. Vibert, "Critical dependence of neural networks processing on between neuron delays," in *Proceedings ICANN*, (Helsinki), 1991.

Part II: Technology

In the context of this edited volume, technology refers to those aspects of neural networks that are not specific to one application but, rather, represent a generic capability that can be applied in several applications. As an example, nonlinear filtering with neural networks is an example of signal processing technology, and the use of nonlinear filters for adaptive equalization in communications is an example of a specific application.

There are seven technology areas that are covered in this part. A chapter is dedicated to each technology area. The technology areas include Control, Data Fusion, Forecasting, Image Processing & Vision, Optimization, Signal Processing, and Virtual Reality.

Chapter 3: Control

CHAPTER 3
Control

Control is one of the largest technology areas in neural networks (forecasting and pattern recognition are two others). This chapter represents a collection of papers that are focusing on control technology and are not emphasizing a specific application. The trends in control technology are emphasized in three areas:

- **Faster Learning.** Control applications need to be able to respond quickly to changes to be effective. Techniques that provide quicker adaptation of the connection weights that perform the nonlinear operations are still needed.

- **Fuzzy Neural Networks.** Fuzzy logic has been used in a wide variety of control applications. Fuzzy logic control requires domain expertise to develop the rules. In situations where the rules are not available from domain expertise, neural networks are being used to learn the rules. When faster execution is required from existing fuzzy rule bases used for control, the fuzzy rules can be implemented as a neural network that can operate in parallel. In some instances fuzzy rule bases provide a good starting point for a control surface and neural networks can be used to fine tune the rules. All of these are instances of fuzzy neural networks.

- **Recurrent Topologies.** One of the most furtive areas in neural control is the use of recurrent neural networks to capture spatiotemporal relationships. The feedback provided by recurrent topologies provides a great deal more information to the control process.

The papers in this chapter are organized into four areas: survey, system identification, control and identification and control. A review of the papers in each of these sections follows.

1. Survey. Neural networks for control is a diverse area with many results and applications. **Paper 3.1** provides a survey of the work that has occurred in this area.

2. System Identification. System identification attempts to model the plant being controlled. Neural networks used for system identification accept inputs that are parameters extracted from the plant and from the controller at the current time and then maps these to the state of the plant at some predefined time in the future. Once the system is identified, it is possible to utilize more sophisticated control algorithms to control the plant. **Paper 3.2** describes a Kalman-filter based approach to training multilayer perceptrons for nonlinear system identification. Three Kalman-based approaches are compared with backpropagation on a benchmark identification problem. **Paper 3.3** presents a recurrent radial basis function neural network used for nonlinear system identification. Three variants of this approach are compared using a benchmark identification problem. **Paper 3.4** modifies a MLP by replacing the common sigmoid hidden unit transfer functions with Gaussians. Training of this network uses recursive least squares. **Paper 3.5** describes a genetic algorithm approach to training MLPs for the control of complex systems and demonstrates its utility with an aircraft control problem.

3. Control. The use of neural networks for control is straightforward. Parameters (features) are extracted from the environment and from the plant and used as inputs to the neural network. The neural network learns to map these parameters to a set of control values that are used to adjust the state of the plant. **Paper 3.6** presents a neuro-fuzzy controller for phase-lead compensation. The utility of this approach is demonstrated for the control of a two-tank system. **Paper 3.7** describes a fuzzy adaptive controller utilizing reinforcement learning. This approach is analyzed using an inverted pendulum problem. **Paper 3.8** uses a MLP to adjust the Youla parameter in an appropriately parameterized control system.

4. Identification and Control. The previous papers dealt with neural networks that perform identification or control. The following papers describe the combination of both identification and control using neural networks. **Paper 3.9** presents a recurrent higher-order neural network for nonlinear identification and control.

A tracking problem is used to illustrate the effectiveness of the neural network approach. **Paper 3.10** describes combination of MLP identification and control with fuzzy subjective evaluation. This technique is demonstrated for a color correction for high definition television.

Neural Networks in Control Systems

D.H. Rao, M.M. Gupta and H.C. Wood

Intelligent Systems Research Laboratory, College of Engineering
University of Saskatchewan, Saskatoon, Canada, S7N 0W0

ABSTRACT

The purpose of this paper is to provide an overview of neural network structures used for system identification and control. Due to the complexity and diversity of the properties of biological neurons, the task of compressing their complicated characteristics into a model is extremely difficult. Towards this goal, an artificial neuron, also called a 'unit', was developed which receives its inputs from a number of other neurons or from the external world. A weighted sum of these inputs constitutes the argument of an 'activation' function. This is a simple, but useful first approximation of a biological neuron. Using this model, many neural structures usually referred to as feedforward neural networks have been reported in the literature. Many of these networks use only present values of inputs, and are therefore called instantaneous or static systems. A natural extension of static networks is the dynamic or recurrent neural network which incorporates feedback in its structure. No general theory for dynamic neural networks has yet developed like similar to that for static networks. With the parallel growth in the field of fuzzy logic, many neural models encompassing the principles of neural networks and fuzzy set theory are being developed. In this paper we have made an attempt to provide the basic concepts of static, dynamic and fuzzy neural structures.

1. Introduction

The limitations of conventional feedback controllers may be attributed to the fact that the design methods involve the construction of a mathematical model describing the dynamics of the plant to be controlled. In other words, the first step in the design process is to establish the quantities of interest and their relationships. The next step involves the application of analytical techniques to this mathematical model to derive a control law. The control system with this control law in conjunction with the mathematical model of the dynamic plant is expected to give the desired performance. In practice, this may not happen because the exact representative model of the plant is difficult to obtain, may be due to uncertainty and sheer complexity in the plant [1]. Also, the modeling of a physical system for feedback control involves a trade-off between the simplicity of the model and its accuracy in matching the behavior of the physical system.

While adaptive and robust control techniques have shown potential in complex systems, the region of operability of the control systems is rather restricted. This is because the modification of controller parameters is based on convergence and stability constraints and this may place severe limitations on the performance of the adaptive system. Another approach is to use robust stabilizers or robust controllers [2,3,4]. Using this approach, if the actual physical system is contained in a class of systems which are close to the nominal plant, a robust controller is guaranteed to stabilize it. Since one fixed controller is expected to stabilize the whole set, the price might be then the controller thus designed is highly complex compared to the complexity required to stabilize any single plant. Detailed descriptions of robust controllers and adaptive controller techniques may be found in [4,5,6,7] and [8,9,10] respectively.

These limitations can be seen as restrictions on the acceptable operating region of a controller. Control techniques for complex systems will have to be more robust to changes and will need a higher degree of autonomy than the techniques of today. By enhancing conventional controllers with learning capabilities, one can effectively expand the region of operability of a controller and create more robust control mechanisms. The control system can then compensate for a larger number and magnitude of changes in the dynamics of the plant and its environment.

The evolution in the control area has been fueled by two major concerns [11]: the need to deal with increasingly complex systems, and the need to accomplish increasingly demanding design requirements with less precise advanced knowledge of the plant and its environment, that is, the need to control under increased uncertainty. This has made the need for new techniques in the control paradigm quite apparent. The use of neural networks in control systems can be seen as a natural step in the development of control methodology to meet new challenges. Neural networks with their massive parallelism, and their ability to learn, offer exciting possibilities for the design of adaptive systems.

The purpose of this paper is to give an overview of neural networks from the control system perspective. The paper is organized as follows. A brief description of biological neural networks is given in Section 2, followed by the introduction to artificial neural networks in Section 3. This paper describes three neural models, namely static, dynamic and fuzzy, in Sections 4,5 and 6 respectively followed by the conclusions in the last section.

2. Description of Biological Neurons

The basic building block of the animal nervous system is the neuron, the cell that communicates information to and from various parts of the body. The neuron consists of a cell body called the *soma*, several spine-like extensions of the cell body called *dendrites*, and a single nerve fiber called the *axon* that branches out from the soma and connects to many other neurons. The soma is approximately about 30 μm in diameter; the dendrites are 200 to 300 μm in length. The information generated by a nerve cell is transmitted along its axon. The range of lengths of axons is from 50 μm to several meters. The axon is a tubular structure bounded by a typical cell membrane. An axon terminates the synaptic junction of another nerve cell's dendrite. A single axon may be involved with hundreds of synaptic connections. A schematic diagram of a biological neuron is shown in Fig. 1.

All axons near their ends branch many times, often thousands of times. At the end of each of these branches is a specialized axon terminal, called a *synaptic knob* because of its knob-like appearance. The synaptic knob in turn lies on the membrane surface of a dendrite or cell body of another neuron. This contact point between knob end and membrane is called a *synapse*. It is through the synapses that signals are transmitted from one neuron to the next. The synapse is considered as the basic control unit of the nervous system. Impulses traveling over the soma or dendrites of the neuron can not be transmitted backward through the synapses into the synaptic knobs. Thus, only one way conduction occurs at the synapse. This is extremely important to the function of the nervous system, for it allows impulses to be channeled in the desired direction.

Each neuron is activated by the flow of biochemicals across the synapses. The transmission of these biochemicals across the synaptic junction causes a change in the ionic concentration within the neuron, which in turn produces a change in its electro-chemical potential. These inputs may be *excitatory* (positive) and increase the electro-chemical potential of the post-synaptic neuron, or conversely, they may be *inhibitory* (negative) and reduce the electro-chemical potential. If the net potential at the axon hillock is above a certain threshold level then the neuron will 'fire' a sequence of pulses, called the *axon potentials*, along an axon leading to the synaptic junction of another neuron. The electro-chemical activities at these synaptic junctions exhibit complex behavior because each neuron makes

0-7803-1319-4/93/$3.00 © 1993 IEEE

several hundreds of inter connections with other neurons. Each neuron acts as a parallel processor because it receives pulses in parallel from neighboring neurons and then transmits pulses in parallel to all neighboring synapses. All the neurons - interconnected by axons and dendrites that carry signals regulated by synapses - create a neural network.

3. Artificial Neural Networks

The goal of artificial neural network research is to develop mathematical models of its biological counterpart in order to emulate, atleast on a small scale, the capabilities of biological neural structures with a view to the design of intelligent control systems. Artificial Neural Networks (ANNs) or simply neural networks, go by many descriptions, such as connectionist models, parallel distributed processing, and neuromorphic systems [13]. All these models are composed of many nonlinear computational elements operating in parallel and arranged in patterns reminiscent of biological neural nets.

The notion of memory is hypothesized in the biological networks to be in the synaptic connections. Based on this hypothesis, the values or weights, of the connection strengths determine the 'memory', or 'knowledge' of the neural network. Most neural networks undergo a 'learning' procedure during which the network weights are adjusted. Algorithms for varying these connection strengths or weights such that learning ensues are called 'learning rules'. The learning may be 'supervised', in which case the network is presented with target answers for each pattern, or, learning is 'unsupervised' and the neural network adjusts its weights in response to input patterns without the benefit of target outputs. In such networks, the network classifies the input patterns into similarity categories.

There are basically two learning rules, namely, the Hebbian and the delta rule. In the Hebbian rule, the strength of the interconnection between the units or neurons is proportional to the product of the actual activation achieved and the target activation provided in the training set. In the delta rule, however, the weight is proportional to the difference between the activations [13, 14, 15]. Nearly all neural networks incorporate either of these two rules or variations thereof. Some neural networks, however, have fixed weights; these networks operate by changing the activity levels of their neurons without changing the weights. Thus models of artificial neurons are specified by three entities: models of the neurons themselves, models of synaptic connections and structures (that is, net topology and weights), and the training or learning rules (that is, the method of adjusting the weights or connection strengths). Due to differences in either or all these entities, different types of networks are being explored by researchers. They may be categorized into three basic models: static, dynamic and fuzzy neural structures. The taxonomy of neural network structures is shown in Fig. 2.

Although different neural structures have been reported in the literature, the potential benefits of such networks can be summarized as follows:

(i) The neural network models have many neurons (the computational units) linked via the adaptive weights arranged in a massive parallel structure. Because of high parallelism, failures of a few neurons do not cause significant effects on the overall system performance. This characteristic is also called fault - tolerance.

(ii) The main strength of the neural network structures lies in their learning and adaptive abilities. The ability to adapt and learn from the environment means that the neural network models can deal with imprecise data and ill-defined situations. A suitably trained network also has the ability to generalize when presented with inputs not appearing in the trained data.

(iii) The most significant characteristic of neural networks is their ability to approximate any nonlinear continuous function to a desired degree of accuracy. This ability of neural networks has made them useful to model nonlinear systems in the synthesis of nonlinear controllers.

(iv) Neural networks can have many inputs and many outputs; they are easily applicable to multivariable systems.

(v) With the advancements in hardware technology, many vendors have recently introduced dedicated VLSI hardware implementations of neural networks. This brings additional speed in neural computing.

The computational process envisioned with neural networks starts with the development of an 'artificial' neuron based on the understanding of biological neuronal structures, followed by training mechanisms for a given set of applications. In this context, we describe the three main neural models, namely static, dynamic and fuzzy neural structures, in the following sections.

4. Static (Feedforward) Neural Networks

The conventionally assumed structure of an artificial neuron, also called a 'unit', receives its inputs from a number of other neurons or units or from the external world. A weighted sum of these inputs constitutes the argument of an 'activation' function. The weights correspond to the synapses in a biological neuron while the activation function is analogous to its intercellular current conduction mechanism. This activation function is nonlinear and is often a hard or soft limiting threshold. The resulting value of the activation function, if it exceeds an internal threshold w_0 is the neural output as depicted in Fig. 3. This output is distributed through weighted connections to other processing units.

The neuron receives an n-dimension vector of input signals, $\mathbf{x}(t)$, from the axons of neighboring neurons, where

$$\mathbf{x}(t) = [x_1(t), x_2(t), x_i(t), \ldots x_n(t),]^T \in \Re^n, \qquad (1)$$

and yields an axonic output $y(t) \in \Re^1$. Mathematically, this process of mapping from $\mathbf{x}(t) \in \Re^n$ to $y(t) \in \Re^1$ can be expressed by the neuronal mapping function *Ne* as

$$Ne\text{: } \mathbf{x}(t) \in \Re^n \rightarrow y(t) \in \Re^1. \qquad (2a)$$

Thus, Ne provides a nonlinear mapping from n-dimensional space X to one-dimensional space Y. Alternatively, we can write

$$y(t) = Ne\,[\mathbf{x}(t) \in \Re^n] \in \Re^1. \qquad (2b)$$

In the face of the staggering diversity of neuronal properties, the goal of compressing their complicated characteristics into a mathematical model is extremely difficult. It is currently understood that the biological neuron provides two distinct mathematical operations, one distributed over the *synapse* (the junction point between an axon and the dendrite) and one over the *soma*, the main body of the neuron. We will call these two neuronal mathematical operations; (i) *synaptic operation* and (ii) *somatic operation*. From the biological point of view, these two operations are physically separate, however, in the modeling of a biological neuron, these operations have often been combined (for example, thresholding in the soma is transferred to the synaptic operation). A brief description of these operations are give below,

(i) ***synaptic operation*** :

The synapse, the junction point between the axon of the preceding neuron, and the dendrite of the neuron under consideration, provides a storage (memory) to past experience (knowledge). Thus, the synaptic weight w(t) may be considered as a representation of past experience. The *synaptic operation* provides a ***confluence*** between the neural input vector $\mathbf{x}(t) \in \Re^n$ and the synaptic weight vector $\mathbf{w}(t) \in \Re^n$. Thus, these *synaptic confluence operations*, or just the *synaptic operations*, assign a relative weight (significance) to each incoming signal component $x_i(t)$ according to the past experience (knowledge or memory) stored in $w_i(t)$. The synaptic weight $w_i(t)$ is updated occasionally, through learning and adaptation processes in response to the changing environment. The weighted signal $z_i(t)$ can be written as

$$z_i(t) = w_i(t) © x_i(t), i = 1, 2 \dots n \qquad (3a)$$

where © is the confluence operation, The confluence operation © can be modeled by various mathematical and logic (binary or fuzzy) operations. However the dot (inner) product is often used as a confluence operation. Thus,

$$z_i(t) = w_i(t) \cdot x_i(t), i = 1, 2 \dots n \qquad (3b)$$

The *somatic operation* on the dendritic signal $z_i(t)$, $i = 1, 2 \dots n$, is a two step process.

(iia) ***Somatic Aggregation Operation*** :

The first somatic operation provides an aggregation operation on dendritic inputs $z_i(t)$, mapping the dendritic signals $z_i(t)$, $i = 1, 2 \dots n$ to a single value, u(t). Thus,

$$u(t) = \oint_{i=1}^{n} z_i(t) = \oint_{i=1}^{n} w_i(t) © x_i(t). \qquad (4)$$

The generalized aggregation operation, $\oint$, will in general be replaced by summation. Thus,

$$u(t) = \sum_{i=1}^{n} z_i(t) = \sum_{i=1}^{n} w_i(t) \cdot x_i(t) \qquad (5)$$

One can view this aggregation operation as a linear mapping from the n-dimensional dendritic inputs $z_i(t)$ to one dimensional space. This somatic linear mapping operation can be combined with the synaptic operation yielding a linear weighted mapping from n-dimensional neural input space $\mathbf{x}(t) \in \Re^n$ to the one-dimensional space $u(t) \in \Re^1$ as indicated in Equation (5). Expressing u(t) as a scalar product of two vectors,

$$u(t) = \mathbf{w}(t)^T \cdot \mathbf{x}(t) \qquad (6)$$

where

$\mathbf{w}(t) = [w_1(t), w_2(t) \dots w_i(t) \dots w_N(t)]^T \in \Re^n$ is the vector of synaptic weights, and

$\mathbf{x}(t) = [x_1(t), x_2(t) \dots x_i(t) \dots x_N(t)]^T \in \Re^n$ is the vector of neural inputs.

Thus, the combined synaptic weighting operation, and somatic aggregation operation provide a mapping of neural inputs $\mathbf{x}(t) \in \Re^n$ to $u(t) \in \Re^1$.

(iib) ***Non-linear somatic operation with thresholding*** :

A nonlinear mapping operation on u(t) yields a neural output y(t) given by

$$y(t) = f[u(t), w_0] \qquad (7)$$

where $f[\cdot]$ is a nonlinear function with thresholding w_0. Usually, the neural output y(t) is zero if the weighted aggregate u(t) of the neural input signal $\mathbf{x}(t) \in \Re^n$ is less than the threshold value w_0. That is, the neuron will fire only when the weighted aggregate value of the neuronal input vector $n(t) \in \Re^n$ exceeds some threshold w_0. Then, the neural output y(t) increases monotonically with u(t) reaching a saturation value, say 1.

Generalized Mathematical Model of Neuron

From Eqn. (7) and Fig. 8, a new variable v(t) is defined as

$$v(t) = u(t) - w_0, \qquad (8)$$

where u(t) is the weighted aggregate value defined in Eqn. (6) and w_0 is the threshold value. Thus, if the weighted output $u(t) < w_0$, the neural output is zero, implying that the neuron will fire (will provide output) only when the weighted aggregate value u(t) exceeds the threshold w_0. Thus, defining y(t) as

$$y(t) = f[u(t), w_0] = \Psi[v(t)] \qquad (9)$$

and using Eqns. (7) to (9), the neural output may be written as

$$y(t) = \Psi[v(t)] = \Psi[\sum_{i=1}^{n} w_i x_i - w_0]$$

$$= \Psi[\sum_{i=0}^{n} w_i x_i], \quad x_0 = 1 \qquad (10)$$

where, $\Psi[v]$ is a nonlinear function with the threshold (bias) shifted to the origin. In view of Eqn. (9), we define the augmented vectors of the neural input vector $\mathbf{x}_a(t)$ and the weighting vector $\mathbf{w}_a(t)$ by incorporating the threshold (bias) term w_0. Thus,

$$\mathbf{x}_a(t) \triangleq [x_0, \mathbf{x}^T(t)]^T \in \Re^{n+1}, \quad x_0 = 1 \qquad (11a)$$

and

$$\mathbf{w}_a(t) \triangleq [w_0, \mathbf{w}^T(t)]^T \in \Re^{n+1}. \qquad (11b)$$

Thus, using the augmented vectors $\mathbf{x}_a(t)$ and $\mathbf{w}_a(t)$, the neural (synaptic and somatic) operations are defined as follows:

The weighted aggregated value is

$$v(t) = \mathbf{w}_a^T(t) © \mathbf{x}_a(t) : \text{linear operation}, \qquad (12a)$$

and the neural output is

$$y(t) = \Psi[v(t)] : \text{nonlinear operation}. \qquad (12b)$$

Thus, the generalized neural model can be represented as depicted in Fig. 4. The nonlinear function $\Psi[v]$ in Eqn. (12b) usually is some symmetric nonlinear function which can assume any one of a number of shapes. To extend the mathematical operations on both the positive and negative neural outputs, that is, for both the positive (excitatory) and negative (inhibitory) input values of v(t), the nonlinear operator may be defined by the sigmoidal function as

$$\Psi[v] = \frac{e^{\alpha v} - e^{-\alpha v}}{e^{\alpha v} + e^{-\alpha v}} = \tanh[\alpha v] \qquad (13a)$$

where α is a constant controlling the slope of the curve as shown in Fig. 5. In the limit $\alpha \to \infty$, the sigmoid function $\Psi[v] = \tanh[\alpha v]$ tends to become a sign function which is defined as

$$\begin{aligned} \text{sign}[v] &= \tanh[\alpha v] \big|_{\alpha \to \infty} \\ &= 1 \quad \text{for } v \geq 0 \\ &= -1 \quad \text{for } v < 0. \end{aligned} \qquad (13b)$$

Both the sign and the sigmoidal functions have been found to be very useful in learning, optimization and classification problems.

Multilayer Neural Networks

In the preceding subsection the mathematical details of a neuron at the single cell level were described. Although a single neuron can perform certain simple pattern detection functions, the power of neural computation comes from neurons connected in a network structure. Larger networks generally offer greater computational capabilities. Arranging neurons in layers or stages is supposed to mimic the layered structure of a certain portion of the brain. These multi-layered networks have been proven to have capabilities beyond those of a single layer. The most commonly used neural network architecture in applications, such as pattern recognition, system identification and control, is the multilayered neural network (MNN) with an error backpropagation (BP) algorithm.

A typical MNN with an input layer, an output layer, and one hidden layer is shown in Fig. 6a. Its block diagram representation is shown in Fig. 6b where a nonlinear operator with identical sigmoidal elements $\Psi[.]$, shown in Fig. 5, follows each of the weight matrices w^1, w^2, and w^3. Each layer of the network can be represented by the operator

$$N_i[x] = \Psi\left[w^i x\right],\ i = 1, 2, 3, \tag{14}$$

and the input - output mapping of the MNN can then be represented by

$$\begin{aligned} y = N[x] &= \Psi[w^3 \Psi\{w^2 \Psi(w^1 x)\}] \\ &= N_3 N_2 N_1[x]. \end{aligned} \tag{15}$$

The weights of the network w^1, w^2, and w^3 are adjusted based on an error back propagation algorithm to minimize some function of the error between the output y(t) and a desired output $y_d(t)$. This results in the mapping function N[x] realized by the network, mapping vectors into corresponding output classes. From a systems theoretic point of view, MNNs can be considered as versatile nonlinear maps with elements of the weight matrices as parameters. Furthermore, layered neural networks are nonlinear parametric models that can approximate any continuous input-output relation. The quality of approximation depends on the architecture of the network used, as well as on the complexity of the system. The problem of finding a suitable set of parameters that approximate an unknown relation, F, is usually solved using learning algorithms. For networks with certain architectural restrictions, (for example, static networks with feedforward connections only), the back propagation procedure is employed by propagating the error backwards from the output nodes through the hidden layers to adjust the weights by a gradient descent approach. This learning procedure is briefly described below.

For multilayer static neural networks, the most popular learning algorithm in use is backpropagation. Backpropagation is a generalization of the least squares rule for a multilayer neural network. It attempts to reduce the error at each neural node in such a way that it minimizes the disturbance of the weights and degrades the information, previously encoded in the weights the least. The error at each output node is easily determined knowing the target output for each neural node. However, for the hidden layers where outputs are internal to the network and have no explicit target output, the error calculation is much more difficult. The error at a hidden node is literally defined as the amount that its own output contributes to the error in each neuron in the adjacent layer. It is these hidden layers that serve as abstract domains, into which inputs are mapped. These hidden layers emphasize the differences and de emphasis similarities between inputs to allow the network to differentiate between trajectories with only subtle differences. Backpropagation can be applied to networks with any number of hidden layers, by first calculating the output, determining the output error, then recursively propagating the error backwards to each layer, then adapting the weights to minimize the error. A detailed description of the backpropagation learning algorithm is given in [14].

Extension of the backpropagation algorithm to more general network environments, specifically to neural networks with dynamical elements, has recently been of interest in the field of artificial neural networks.

The MNN model described above has no signal feedback connections, that is, connections through weights extending from the outputs of a layer to the inputs of the same or the previous layers. This class of models is called feedforward or non recurrent networks. These networks have no dynamic memory; their output is solely determined by the current inputs and the values of the weights. The lack of feedback ensures that the networks are conditionally stable [15].

5. Dynamic Neural Networks

Feedback, also known as recurrent, neural networks, introduced by Hopfield [16], provide an alternative neural network model. This model consists of a single layer Network N_1, included in a feedback configuration with a time delay as shown in Fig. 7a. Figure 7b depicts the state-model representation of the feedback neural network. This feedback network represents a discrete-time dynamical system and can be described by the following equation

$$x(k+1) = N_1[x(k)],\ x(0) = x_0 \tag{16}$$

where $N_1[x] = \Psi\left[w^1 x\right]$ from Eqn. (14).

Given an initial value x_0, the dynamical system evolves to an equilibrium state if N_1 is suitably chosen. The set of initial conditions in the neighborhood of x_0 which converge to the same equilibrium state is then identified with that state. The term "associative memory" is used to describe such systems. Feedback networks with or without constant inputs are merely nonlinear dynamical systems and the asymptotic behavior of such systems depends both on the initial conditions and the specific input used. In both cases, the behavior depends critically on the nonlinear map represented by the neural network used in the feedback loop [17].

For mathematical tractability, it is assumed that the feedback networks contain only a single layer of neurons. Furthermore, inputs when they exist are assumed to be constant. In spite of the interesting applications that the feedback neural networks have been used for, the basic architecture of the neuron is static; that is, the neuron simply provides a weighted integration of the synaptic inputs over a period of time. In general, the limitations of the conventional neural network models, the feedforward and the feedback networks, are summarized as follows:

(i) The artificial neural network can not keep on learning as it is performing. Biology, of course, combines learning with functioning. Most artificial neural algorithms at present have a learning phase that makes all the connections and is entirely separate from the performing phase, which uses the connections and does not change them.

(ii) The structure of the artificial neuron has to be much more dynamic in nature and must perform much more mathematical operations than just summation.

(iii) The static neuron models do not take into account the time delays that affect the dynamics of the system; inputs produce an instantaneous output with no memory involved.

(iv) They do not include the effects of synchronism or the frequency modulation function of biological neurons [15].

Therefore, any new feedback architectures will not only result in significant developments in neural networks but also bring about greater insights into biological neural structures. The dynamics in neural networks or neural computing do appear to provide some functional basis of the cerebellum and its associated circuitry. Also, dynamic neural networks can offer significant computational advantages over purely static neural networks. For some problems, a small feedback system is equivalent to a large and possibly infinite feedforward system. By analogy, it is well known that an infinite order FIR (Finite Impulse Response) filter is required to emulate a single pole IIR (Infinite Impulse Response) filter. Systems with feedback are particularly appropriate for system modeling (identification) , control and filtering applications. The node equations in dynamic networks are usually described by differential or difference equations. Neural networks are important because many of the systems that we wish to model in the real world are non-linear dynamical systems. This is true, for example, in the controls area in which we wish to model the forward or inverse dynamics of systems such as airplanes, rockets, spacecraft and robots [18]. However, due to the complexity of dynamic neural structures, no general theory, such as for static neural networks, has yet developed.

To overcome some of the limitations of the conventional feedforward and feedback neural networks, we have proposed a new dynamic neural network structure for robotics and control applications [19].

5.1 The Dynamic Neural Processor (DNP)

Motivation: The basic component of a biological information processing system is the neuron which is activated by the flow of biochemicals across the dendrite junctions, called the synapses. As described above, these biochemical inputs may be *excitatory* (positive) and increase the electro-chemical potential of the post-synaptic neuron, or conversely, they may be *inhibitory* (negative) and reduce the electro-chemical potential. The transmission of these biochemicals causes a change in the ionic concentration within the soma of the neuron which results in a change in its electro-chemical potential. The total neural activity is supposed to result from a collective assembly of neurons called the *neural population*. Each neural population may be further divided into several coexisting *subpopulations*. A subpopulation contains a large class of similar neurons that lie in close spatial proximity.

Models of neural networks described in the existing literature often consider the behavior of a single neuron as the basic computing unit for describing neural information processing operations. Each computing unit in the network is based on the concept of an *idealized* neuron. An ideal neuron is assumed to respond optimally to the applied inputs. However, experimental studies in neurophysiology show that the responses of a biological neuron appear random, and only by averaging many observations is it possible to obtain predictable results. This observed variability in the response of a neuron is a function of uncontrollable or extraneous signals that affect the activations of neurons. As well, this variability may also be enhanced by the intrinsic fluctuations of the electrical membrane potential within the neuron.

In general, a biological neuron is an unpredictable mechanism for processing information, however, mathematical analysis has shown that these random cells can transmit reliable information because of substantial redundancy and connectivity. It is postulated, therefore, that the collective activity generated by large numbers of locally redundant neurons is more significant in a computational context than the activity of a single neuron [16, 20, 21].

In view of the above remarks, we have developed a dynamic neural structure called the *dynamic neural processor* (DNP) for robotics and control applications. This structure emphasizes the aggregate dynamic properties of two subpopulation of neurons. For analytical simplicity only two subpopulations are assumed to coexist. The first subpopulation contains only excitatory neurons which project a positive influence when they fire. The second coexisting subpopulation contains only inhibitory neurons which project a negative influence when they fire.

The DNP, presented in this section, comprises of two dynamic neural units; one functioning as an excitatory neuron and the other as an inhibitory neuron is illustrated in Fig. 8. In this DNP structure, $s_\lambda(k)$ and $u_\lambda(k)$ represent respectively the stimulus (input) and state response (output) of the neural computing unit where the subscript λ indicates either an excitatory, E, or inhibitory, I, state. $s_{t\lambda}(k)$ denote the total input to the neural units, $w_{\lambda\lambda}$ represent the strength of self-synaptic connections (w_{EE}, w_{II} in Fig. 8), and $w_{\lambda\lambda'}$ represent the strength of cross synaptic connections from one neural unit to another (w_{IE}, w_{EI} in Fig. 8). The two state variables that describe the dynamic activity exhibited by the neural computing units are defined as the proportion of active excitatory (positive) neurons, $u_E(k+1)$, and active inhibitory (negative) neurons, $u_I(k+1)$.

The state variables $u_E(k+1)$ and $u_I(k+1)$ generated at time (k+1) by the excitatory and inhibitory neural units of the proposed neural processor are modeled as:

$$u_E(k+1) = f_E\,[u_E(k)\,,\ v_E(k)] \tag{17a}$$

$$u_I(k+1) = f_I\,[u_I(k)\,,\ v_I(k)] \tag{17b}$$

where $v_E(k)$ and $v_I(k)$ represent the proportion of neurons in the neural unit that receive inputs greater than an intrinsic threshold, and f_E and f_I represent the excitatory and inhibitory actions of the neuron. The neurons that receive inputs greater than a threshold value are given by a nonlinear function $\Psi\left[v^\lambda(k)\right]$. This nonlinear function is related to the distribution of neural thresholds within the neural unit [20, 22].

As shown in Fig. 9, the two dynamic neural units (DNUs) are coupled in excitatory and inhibitory modes. The DNU, which is described in the next section, comprises of delay operators, and feedforward and feedback paths forming the dynamic structure whose output forms an argument to a time-varying nonlinear function $\Psi[.]$ with threshold θ. The total inputs incident on the excitatory and inhibitory neural units are respectively, Fig. 8,

$$s_{tE}(k) = \left[w_E\, s_E(k) + w_{EE}\, u_E(k) - w_{IE}\, u_I(k)\right], \text{ and} \tag{18}$$

$$s_{tI}(k) = \left[w_I\, s_I(k) - w_{II}\, u_I(k) + w_{EI}\, u_E(k)\right] \tag{19}$$

where w_E and w_I are scaling factors of the excitatory and inhibitory neural inputs respectively, w_{EE} and w_{II} represent the self-synaptic connection strengths, and w_{IE} and w_{EI} represent the inter-neuron synaptic strengths. The above equations may be written in matrix form as:

$$\begin{bmatrix} s_{tE}(k) \\ s_{tI}(k) \end{bmatrix} = \begin{bmatrix} w_E & 0 \\ 0 & w_I \end{bmatrix} \begin{bmatrix} s_E(k) \\ s_I(k) \end{bmatrix} + \begin{bmatrix} w_{EE} & -w_{IE} \\ w_{EI} & -w_{II} \end{bmatrix} \begin{bmatrix} u_E(k) \\ u_I(k) \end{bmatrix} . \tag{20}$$

A direct analytical solution for determining the steady-state and temporal behavior exhibited by the DNP may not be possible because of the inherent nonlinearities in Eqns. (17a) and (17b). However, these nonlinear equations can be analyzed qualitatively by obtaining the phase trajectories in the u_E - u_I phase-plane [20, 22]. These trajectories enable the system characteristics to be observed without solving the nonlinear equations. One may observe from Fig. 1 that the response of the neural processor not only depends on the inputs and the synaptic connections, but also on the structure of the DNU. An analysis of the dynamic activity generated by a spatially distributed dynamic neural processor is extremely complex because of the immense number of inherent nonlinearities and spatial feedback interactions involved. The investigation of such a complex process, therefore, would begin by examining a spatially isolated DNU. A brief description of the DNU is given below.

5.2 Dynamics of an isolated Dynamic Neural Unit (DNU)

The DNU is a dynamic model of a neuron which was proposed by the authors [23, 24, 25]. It comprises of two basic components: the dynamic structure which contributes to the synaptic learning, and a time-varying nonlinear activation function which contributes to the somatic learning. The dynamic structure consists of two delay elements and two feedforward and feedback paths weighted by the synaptic weights a_{ff} and b_{fb} respectively. These dynamics lead to a second-order structure which can be described by the following difference equation

$$v_1(k) = - b_1 v_1(k-1) - b_2 v_1(k-2) + a_0 x(k) + a_1 x(k-1) + a_2 x(k-2), \quad (21)$$

where $x(k) \in \Re^n$ is the input vector, $v_1(k) \in \Re^1$ is the output of the dynamic structure, $u(k) \in \Re^1$ is the neural output, k is the discrete-time index, and $\mathbf{a}_{ff} = [a_0, a_1, a_2]$ and $\mathbf{b}_{fb} = [1, b_1, b_2]$ are the vectors of the adaptable feedforward and feedback weights respectively.

The nonlinear mapping operation on $v_1(k)$ yields a neural output u(k) given by

$$u(k) = \Psi[g_s v_1(k)] \quad (22)$$

where $\Psi[\cdot]$ is some nonlinear activation function, and g_s is the somatic gain which controls the slope of the activation function. In order to extend the mathematical operations on both the positive and negative neural outputs, and to expand the neural activity of both the excitatory and inhibitory inputs, the activation function can be chosen to be a *sigmoidal* function defined as

$$\Psi[v(k)] = \tanh [g_s v_1(k)] = \tanh [v(k)] \quad (23)$$

where $v(k) = g_s v_1(k)$. The adaptable parameters of the DNU, namely the feedforward weights $\mathbf{a}_{ff}$, the feedback weights $\mathbf{b}_{fb}$ and the somatic gain g_s are adjusted based on the following equations:

$$a_{ff_i}(k+1) = a_{ff_i}(k) + \mu_{a_i} E\left\{e(k)\, g_s \operatorname{sech}^2[v_1(k)]\, s_{\phi_{a_{ff_i}}}(k)\right\}, \quad i = 0,1,2, \quad (24a)$$

$$b_{fb_j}(k+1) = b_{fb_j}(k) + \mu_{b_j} E\left\{e(k)\, g_s \operatorname{sech}^2[v_1(k)]\, s_{\phi_{b_{fb_j}}}(k)\right\}, \quad j = 1,2 \text{ and} \quad (24b)$$

$$g_s(k+1) = g_s(k)\left[1 + \mu_{g_s} E\left\{e(k) \operatorname{sech}^2[v_1(k)]\, v_1(k)\right\}\right] \quad (24c)$$

where E is an expectation operator and $s_{\phi(\mathbf{a}_{ff},\mathbf{b}_{fb})}(k) = \dfrac{\partial v(k)}{\partial \phi_{(\mathbf{a}_{ff},\mathbf{b}_{fb})}}$ represents a vector of parameter-state (or sensitivity) signals. The parameter-state signals for the feedforward and the feedback weights are given by:

$$s_{\phi_{a_{ff_i}}}(k) = g_s [x(k-i)], \quad i = 0, 1, 2, \quad (25a)$$

and

$$s_{\phi_{b_{fb_j}}}(k) = - g_s [v(k-j)], \quad j = 1, 2. \quad (25b)$$

Equations (24a) and (24b) correspond to the synaptic learning and Eqn. (25c) to the somatic learning of the DNU. Detailed derivation of Eqns. (24) and (25) are given in [23].

The dynamic neural processor discussed in this section has been successfully used to learn inverse kinematic transformations for two- and three-linked robot and to control unknown nonlinear dynamic systems [19].

6. Fuzzy Neuron

Fuzzy Logic: Introduction

The concept of fuzzy sets was introduced by Zadeh [26] in order to represent and manipulate data that were not precise but rather fuzzy. Fuzzy set theory provides a mechanism for representing useful linguistic constructs such as "many", "low", "medium", "often", "few" [27]. In general, fuzzy logic provides an inference structure that facilitates appropriate human reasoning capabilities [28]. On the contrary, the traditional binary set theory describes crisp events, events that either do or do not occur. It uses probability theory to explain if an event will occur, measuring the chance with which a given event is expected to occur. The theory of fuzzy logic is based upon the notion of relative graded membership and so are the functions of mentation and cognitive processes [29]. The utility of fuzzy sets lies in their ability to model *uncertain* or ambiguous data so often encountered in real life.

Fuzzy Set Definition: [26, 27, 30]

Let X be a space of points (or objects) with a generic element of X denoted by x. [X is often referred to as the universe of discourse]. A fuzzy set (class) A in X is characterized by a membership (characteristic) function $\mu_A(x)$ which associates with each point in X a real number in the interval [0,1], with the value of $\mu_A(x)$ representing the "grade of membership" of x in A. Thus, the nearer the value of $\mu_A(x)$ to unity, the higher the grade of membership of x in A. A fuzzy set A is a subset of the universe of discourse X that admits partial membership. The fuzzy set A is defined as an ordered pair

$$A = \{(x, \mu_A(x)\} \quad (26)$$

where $x \in X$ and $0 \le \mu_A(x) \le 1$. The membership function $\mu_A(x)$ describes the degree to which the object x belongs to the set A where $\mu_A(x) = 0$ represents no membership and $\mu_A(x) = 1$ represents full membership.

To enable a system to track real-life situations in a manner more like humans, one may incorporate the concept of fuzzy sets into the neural network. Although fuzzy logic is a natural mechanism for propagating uncertainty, it may involve in some cases an increase in the amount of computation required (compared with a system using classical binary logic). This can be readily offset by using fuzzy neural network models having the potential for parallel computation with high flexibility [31].

The Fuzzy Neural Model

If we express input signals, Eqn. (11a), in terms of their membership functions each over the interval [0, 1], rather than in their absolute amplitudes, then we can write the augmented vector of neural inputs as

$$\mathbf{x}_a(t) = [x_0(t), x_1(t) \ldots x_i(t) \ldots x_n(t)]^T \in [0, 1]^{n+1}$$

where these neural signal (including the bias term, x_0) are bounded by the (n + 1) dimensional hybercube $[0, 1]^{n+1}$. Similarly, the augmented synaptic weighting vector $\mathbf{w}_a(t)$ can be expressed over the unit hybercube $[0, 1]^{n+1}$.

We perform mathematical operations on these signals using logical operations (connectives) such as **OR**, **AND** (or their generalized form based upon triangular norm or T-operators) and **negation**.

Let us express x_1 and x_2 over [0, 1], then we define, the AND (T-operation) as a T mapping function:

$$T: [0, 1] \times [0, 1] \rightarrow [0, 1] \text{ given by}$$

$$y_1 = [x_1 \text{ AND } x_2] \triangleq [x_1 \,T\, x_2] = T[x_1, x_2] \quad (27)$$

Similarly, we define the generalized OR, (T-conorm) as an S mapping function

$$S: [0, 1] \times [0, 1] \rightarrow [0, 1] \text{ given by}$$

$$y_2 = [x_1 \text{ OR } x_2] \triangleq [x_1 \, S \, x_2] = S[x_1, x_2] \tag{28}$$

Negation N on $x_1 \in [0, 1]$ is defined as a mapping:

N: $[0, 1] \rightarrow [0, 1]$ with the following properties:

$$y_3 = N[x_1] = 1 - x_1 \tag{29}$$

Thus, $N(0) = 1$, $N(1) = 1$, and $N(N(x)) = x$.

Now, we give some important properties of the T and S operators.

$$T(0, 0) = 0,\ \ T(1, 1) = 1,\ T(1, x) = x,\ \ T(x, y) = T(y, x) \tag{30}$$

$$S(0, 0) = 0,\ \ S(1, 1) = 1,\ \ S(0, x) = x,\ \ S(x, y) = S(y, x). \tag{31}$$

Also, De'Morgan's Theorems are stated as follows:

$$T(x_1, x_2) = 1 - S(1 - x_1, 1 - x_2) \text{ and}$$

$$S(x_1, x_2) = 1 - T(1 - x_1, 1 - x_2) \tag{32}$$

In the development of fuzzy logic based neural morphology, we will use the following combined synaptic and somatic operations.

Let the augmented vector of neural inputs and synaptic weights be represented by

$$x_a(t) \in [0, 1]^{n+1}, \text{ and } w_a(t) \in [0, 1]^{n+1}$$

respectively, Then, in Eqn. (12a), by replacing the © - operation by the T - operation, and the $\oint$ - operation by the S - operation, we get

$$v(t) = \underset{i=0}{\overset{n}{S}} [w_i(t) \, T \, x_i(t)) \in [0, 1] \tag{33a}$$

and

$$y(t) = \Psi[v(t)] \in [0, 1] \tag{33b}$$

where Ψ is the usual sigmoidal nonlinear function.

Unipolar to Bipolar Transformation

The logical operations defined in the preceding section are unipolar signals over the positive unit interval [0, 1]. Such logical operations provide only the neural state corresponding to the excitatory (positive) interactions. In order to consider both the excitatory (positive) and the inhibitory (negative) interactions, of the neural input vector, we must consider both $x_a(t)$ and its negated values $N[x_a(t)]$, thus making the neural inputs of dimensions (2n + 2).

Alternatively, we may express the neural inputs and synaptic weights as bipolar signals and weights over the interval [-1, 1] and redefine the logical operations over this interval. We will provide a brief description of this transformation from unipolar, [0, 1], to bipolar [-1, 1] signals.

Let $x(t) \in [0, 1]$ be a unipolar signal. The corresponding bipolar signal z(t) is defined as

$$z(t) = 2\,x(t) - 1. \tag{34}$$

The negation is defined as

$N[x] = 1 - x$, for unipolar signals,

$N[z] = -z$, for bipolar signals.

The T and S functions defined in the interval [0,1] can be transformed to the interval [-1,1] using Eqn. (34).

Learning and Adaptation in Fuzzy Neuron

Figure 9 shows a fuzzy neuron for bipolar signals and bipolar synaptic weights. The augmented neural input signals $x_a(t)$ are defined over the unit hypercube $[0, 1]^{n+1}$. Using the transformation given in (22), we transform the unipolar neural inputs $x_a(t)$ into bipolar signals $z_a(t) \in [-1, 1]^{n+1}$.

The logical operation of this neuron is summarized as follows

$$v(t) = \underset{i=0}{\overset{n}{S}} [w_i(t) \, T \, z_i(t)] \tag{35a}$$

which is equivalent to

$$v(t) = w_a^T(t) \text{ AND } z_a(t) \in [-1, 1] \tag{35b}$$

(a logical scalar product operation), where $w_o(t)$ and $z_o(t)$ correspond to the bias terms and $z_o = 1$. The neural output is defined as

$$y(t) = \Psi(v(t)) \in [-1, 1] \tag{36a}$$

where $\Psi[v]$ is defined as

$$\Psi v] = |v|^{\alpha} \cdot \text{sgn}[v],\ \alpha > 0. \tag{36b}$$

Let us define an error signal with respect to the desired neural output, $y_d(t) \in [-1, 1]$, as $e(t) = y_d(t) - y(t) \in [-1, 1]$.

The objective of learning and adaptation in neural networks is to adapt the parameters of the neural structures, in this case $w_a(t)$ and α in Eqns. (36a) and (36b), in order to minimize an error function. The adaptive rules to modify $w_a(t)$ and $\alpha(t)$ are as follows:

$$w_a(t+1) = w_a(t) \text{ OR } \Delta w_a(t) \tag{37a}$$

and

$$\alpha(t+1) = \alpha(t) \text{ OR } \Delta\alpha(t) \tag{37b}$$

where

$$\Delta w_a(t) = z_a(t) \text{ AND } e(t) \tag{38a}$$

and

$$\Delta\alpha(t) = v(t) \text{ AND } e(t). \tag{38b}$$

Applications and different structures of fuzzy neural networks may be found in [27, 28, 32, 33].

7. Discussion and Conclusions

In this paper we have briefly described static, dynamic and fuzzy neural structures. The theory of static (feedforward) neural networks has been well developed. These networks have no feedback paths in their structures which is in some contrast with biological neural networks. This may be one of the reasons why these networks take enormous time in learning associated patterns and for interpolations between the trained data. Furthermore, there is no evidence that biological networks incorporate the backpropagation learning algorithm which is very commonly used in static networks. The feedforward neural model is a simple, but useful first approximation of biological neuron.

Dynamic (feedback) neural networks have feedback paths from their outputs to the inputs. These dynamic networks are a simple extension of static networks with feedback. Both the static and the dynamic networks are developed based on the assumption that each neuron is an ideal unit which responds optimally to the applied inputs. This assumption is in contrast with the physiological evidence that a neuron is an unpredictable element. It is postulated, therefore, that the collective activity generated by large numbers of locally redundant neurons is more significant in a computational context than the activity of a single neuron. Based on this hypothesis, a new neural structure, proposed by the authors, called the *dynamic neural processor* (DNP) which emphasizes the dynamic properties of subpopulations of neurons was described. A general theory, like for static networks, with regard to functional approximation, learning algorithms and stability analysis of dynamic neural networks has yet to be developed.

It is interesting to note that fuzzy logic is another powerful tool for modeling phenomena associated with human thinking and perception. In fact, the neural network approach fuses well with fuzzy logic and some research endeavors have resulted in 'fuzzy neural networks' which are believed to have considerable potential in the areas of expert systems, medical diagnosis, control systems, pattern recognition and system modeling.

References

[1] Handelman, A.D., Stephen, H.L. and Gelfand, J.J., "Integrating Neural Networks and Knowledge -Based Systems for Intelligent Robotic Control", *IEEE Control System Magazine*, pp. 77-87, April 1990.

[2] Ortega, R. and Tang, Y., "Robustness of Adaptive Controllers - a Survey", *Automatica*, Vol. 25, No. 5, pp. 651-677, 1989.

[3] Vidyasagar, M., Control Systems Synthesis: a Factorization Approach, *MIT Press Cambridge*, Massachusetts, 1985.

[4] McFarlance, D.C. and Glover, K., Robust Controller Design Using Normalized Coprime Factor Plant Descriptions, in Thoma, M. and Wyner, A., Eds., Lecture Notes in Control and Information Sciences, No. 138, *Springer-Verlag, Berlin*, 1989.

[5] Abdallah, C., Dawson, D. and Jamshidi, M., "Survey of Robust Control for Rigid Robots", *IEEE Control System Magazine*, pp. 24-30, February 1991.

[6] Bhattacharya, S.P., Robust Stabilization Against Structured Perturbations, in Thoma, M. and Wyner, A., Eds., Lecture Notes in Control and Information Sciences, No. 99, *Springer-Verlag, Berlin*, 1989.

[7] Dorato, P., Robust Control, Ed., *IEEE Press*, New York, 1987.

[8] Gupta, M.M., Adaptive Methods for Control System Design, Ed., *IEEE Press*, New York, 1986.

[9] Astrom, K.J., "Adaptive Feedback Control", *Proceedings of the IEEE*, Vol. 75, No. 2, pp. 185-217, February 1987.

[10] Narendra, K.S. and Annaswamy, A.M., Stable Adaptive Systems, *Prentice Hall*, Englewood, Cliffs, New Jersey, 1989.

[11] Antsaklis, P.J. and Passino, K.M., "Towards Intelligent Autonomous Control Systems: Architecture and Fundamental Issues", *International Journal of Intelligent and Robotic Systems*, pp. 315-342, 1989.

[12] Fu, K.S., "Learning Control Systems - Review and Outlook", *IEEE Trans. on Automatic Control*, pp. 210-221, April 1970.

[13] Simpson, P.K., Artificial Neural Systems: Foundations, Paradigms, Applications, and Implementations, *Pregamon Press*, New York, 1990.

[14] Werbos, P.J., [1990], "Backpropagation Through Time: What It Does and How to Do It", *Proceedings of the IEEE*, Vol. 78, No. 10, pp. 1550-1560, October.

[15] Wasserman, P.D., Neural Computing: Theory and Practice, *Van Nostrand*, New York, 1989.

[16] Hopfield, J.J., "Neurons with Graded Response Have Collective Computational Properties Like of Those Two-State Neurons", *Proceedings of the National Academy of Sciences*, Vol. 81, pp. 3088- 3092, 1984.

[17] Narendra, K.S. and Parthasarathy, K., [1990], "Identification and Control of Dynamical Systems Using Neural Networks", *IEEE Transactions on Neural Networks*, Vol. 1, No. 1, pp. 4-27.

[18] Hush,, D.R. and Horne, B.G., "Progress in Supervised Neural Networks", *IEEE Signal Processing Magazine*, pp. 8-39, Jan. 1993.

[19] Rao, D.H. and Gupta, M.M., "A Multi-Functional Dynamic Neural Processor for Control Applications", *American Control Conference*, San Francisco, June 2-4, 1993[Accepted].

[20] Wilson, H.R. and Cowan, J.D., "Excitatory and Inhibitory Interactions in Localized Populations of Model Neurons", *Biophysical Journal*, Vol. 12, pp. 1-24, 1972.

[21] Freeman, W.J., *Mass Action in the nervous System*, Academic Press, New York, 1975.

[22] Gupta, M.M., and Knopf, G.K., "A Multitask Visual Information Processor with a Biologically Motivated Design", *Journal of Visual Communication and Image Representation*, Vol. 3, No. 3, pp. 230-246, Sept. 1992.

[23] Gupta, M.M. and Rao, D.H., "Dynamic Neural Units With Applications to the Control of Unknown Nonlinear Systems", *The Journal of Intelligent and Fuzzy Systems*, [In Press].

[24] Gupta, M.M., Rao, D.H. and Wood, H.C., "Learning and Adaptive Neural Controller", *IJCNN*, pp. 2380-2385, Singapore, November 18-21, 1991.

[25] Rao, D.H. and Gupta, M.M., "Dynamic Neural Units and Function Approximation", *IEEE Conf. on Neural Networks*, San Francisco, March 28-April 1, 1993 [Accepted].

[26] Zadeh, L.A., "Fuzzy Sets", *Information and Control*, Vol. 8, pp. 338-353, 1965.

[27] Simpson, P.K., "Fuzzy Min-Max Neural Networks - Part I: Classification", *IEEE Trans. on Neural Networks*, Vol. 3, No. 5, pp. 776-786, Sept. 1992.

[28] Gupta, M.M., and Knopf, G.K., "Fuzzy Neural Network Approach to Control Systems", *Proc. of First Int. Symposium on Uncertainty Modeling and Analysis*, Maryland, pp. 483-488, Dec. 3-5, 1990.

[29] Gupta, M.M., "Uncertainty and Information The Emerging Paradigms", *International Journal of Neuro and Mass-Parallel Computing and Information Systems*, Vol. 2, pp. 65-70, 1991.

[30] Kaufmann, A. and Gupta, M.M., "Introduction to Fuzzy Arithmetic: Theory and Applications", *Van Nostrand Reinhold*, New York, Second Edition, 1991.

[31] Pal, S.K. and Mitra, S., "Multilayer Perceptron, Fuzzy Sets, and Classification", *IEEE Trans. on Neural Networks*, Vol. 3, No. 5, pp. 683-697, Sept. 1992.

[32] Special Issue on Fuzzy Logic and Neural Networks, *IEEE Trans. on Neural Networks* , Vol. 3, No. 5, Sept. 1992.

[33] Gupta, M.M. and Rao, D.H., "Virtual Cognitive Systems (VCS): Neural-Fuzzy Logic Approach", *IFAC Conference*, Sydney, Australia, July 19-23, 1993 [Accepted].

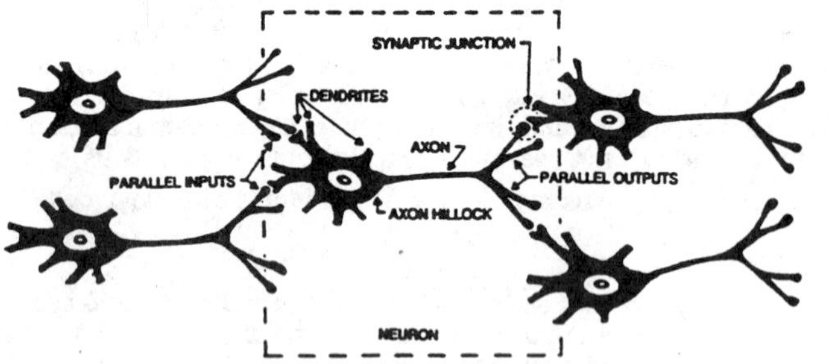

Fig. 1: A schematic view of several interconnected neurons which forms a neural network.

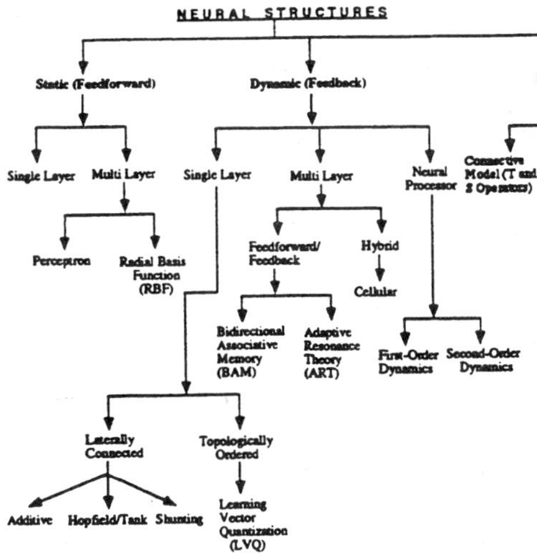

Fig. 2: The taxonomy of neural network structures.

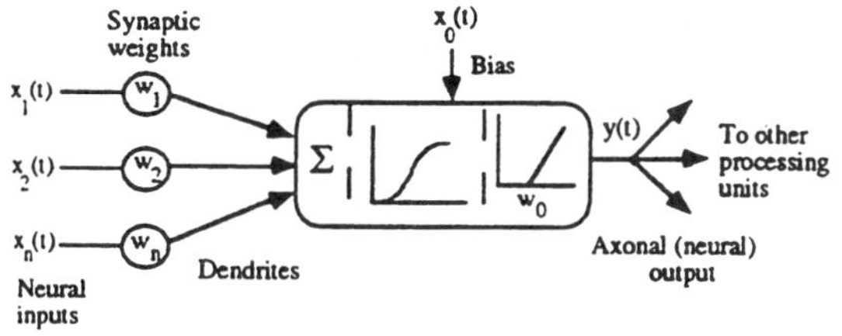

Fig. 3: The simple model of biological neuron in which the weighted sum of the neural inputs forms an argument to a nonliniear activation function. This results, if the weighted sum exceeds a threshold w_0, in the neural output which is fanned out to other neurons.

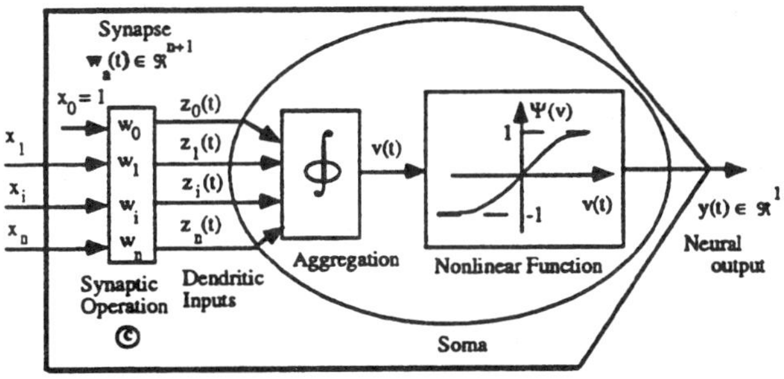

Fig. 4: Generalized neural model. Generalized neural model with threshold shifted to the origin and with augmented vectors $x_a(t) \in \Re^{n+1}$, $w_a(t) \in \Re^{n+1}$ producing an output: $v(t) = \oint_{i=0}^{n} w_i(t)$ © $x_i(t)$, $y(t) = \Psi[v(t)]$.

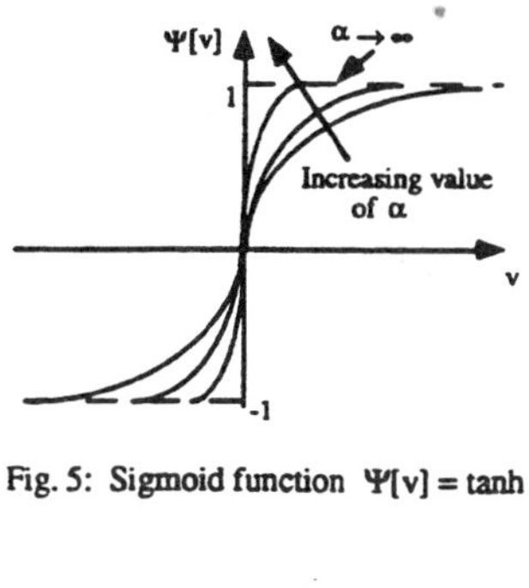

Fig. 5: Sigmoid function $\Psi[v] = \tanh[\alpha v]$.

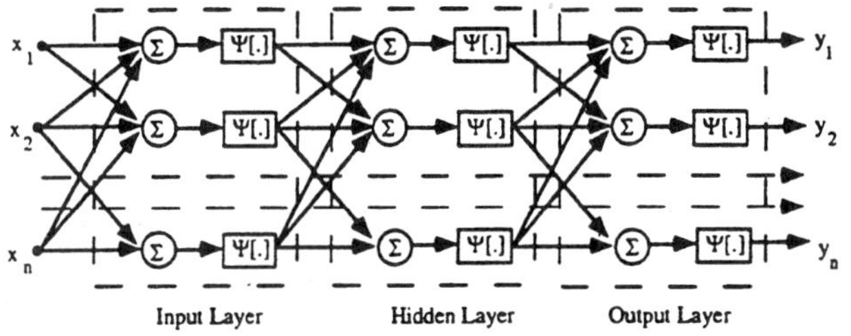

(a)

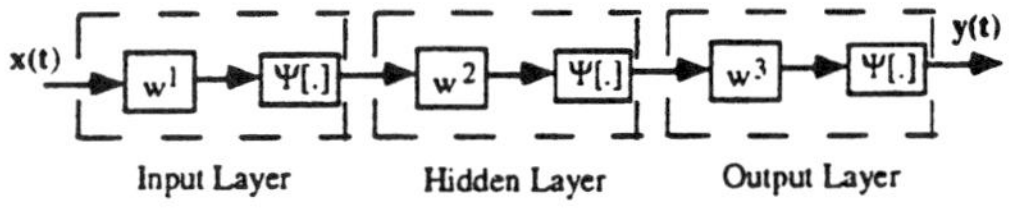

(b)

Fig. 6a: A three-layered neural network having input-, hidden-, and output layers. $\mathbf{x}(t) = [x_1, x_2, ..., x_n]^T$ and $\mathbf{y}(t) = [y_1, y_2, ..., y_n]^T$ represent input and output vectors respectively.

Fig. 6b: The block diagram representation of a three-layered neural network.

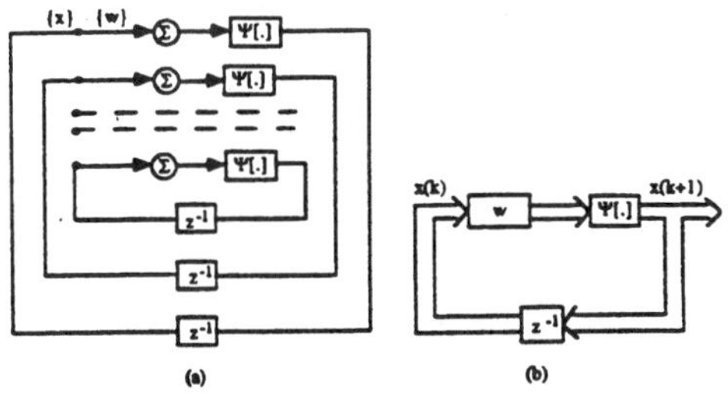

Fig. 7(a): The feedback (recurrent) neural network model. $\{x\}$ represents the set of inputs, $\{w\}$ the set of neural weights, Ψ is some nonlinear activation function, and z^{-1} the unit delay operator.

Fig. 7(b): The state-model or block diagram representation of the feedback network. k represents the discrete-time index, and x(k) and x(k+1) represent the state vectors at k and (k+1) instants.

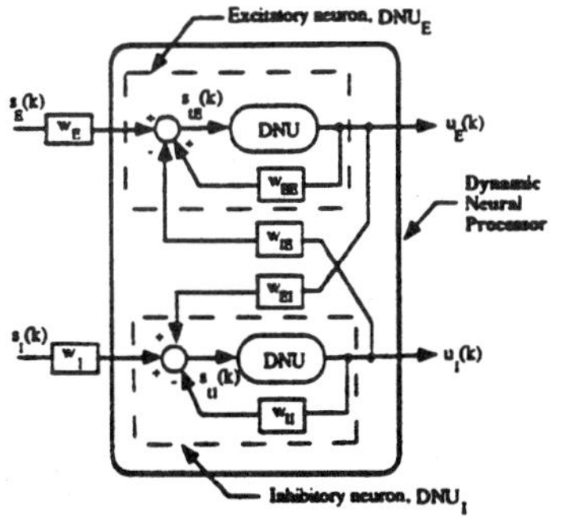

Fig. 8: The dynamic neural processor with two dynamic neural units coupled as excitatory and inhibitory neurons represented as DNU_E and DNU_I respectively.

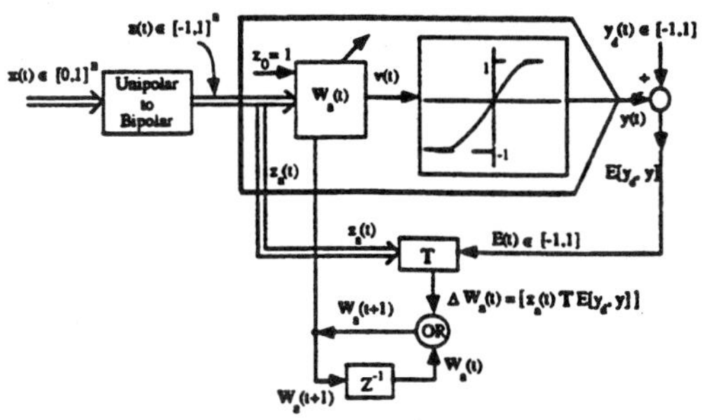

Fig. 9: Fuzzy neuron with learning and adaptation scheme.

Kalman Based Artificial Neural Network Training Algorithms For Nonlinear System Identification

Timothy L. Ruchti, Ronald H. Brown, and Jeffrey J. Garside
Department of Electrical and Computer Engineering
Marquette University
Milwaukee, WI 53233

Abstract - The utility of artificial neural networks (ANN) in nonlinear system identification and control is intimately linked with the ability to parameterize the ANN structure on the basis experimental observations. This paper reviews four existing training algorithms under a parameter estimation framework and extends the method of target state backpropagation previously proposed by the authors. The new algorithm follows a different approach to the generation of error signals in embedded layers by backpropagating target or desired states rather than partial derivatives. The target states are used in conjunction with a linear Kalman based update algorithm and transients associated with initial conditions are eliminated through a time-varying method of covariance modification. Comparisons of the five algorithms are made through a system identification problem and the error convergence associated with each algorithm versus actual training time is presented. The results demonstrate an increased rate of convergence in comparison with backpropagation.

1. Introduction

Although ANNs have been recognized as a suitable structure for representing unknown nonlinearities in dynamic systems [8,18], the method of parameterizing ANNs on the basis of observable information is not fully developed and currently restricts the utilization of this technology in system identification and control applications.

A number of researchers have recently proposed advanced training techniques which are applicable to system identification and control problems. Those considered in this paper include: gradient-descent backpropagation [14], the extended Kalman algorithm [2,4,5,9,16,17], the decoupled extended Kalman algorithm [11], the recursive least-squares method [1,6,15,11], and the recently proposed linear Kalman algorithm [12, 13].

In addition to a comparative analysis of the algorithms listed above, the results reported in [12, 13] are extended and compared through a nonlinear system identification example with the other methods. Sections 1.A. and 1.B. introduce the general notation and estimation framework used by the remainder of the paper. Subsequently, each of the five training algorithms listed above is introduced. Finally, Section 3 presents the experimental results for the purpose of comparison.

A. Feedforward ANNs

This paper considers feedforward ANNs as static mappings from an input vector space $U \subset \mathbb{R}^m$ to an output vector space $Y \subset \mathbb{R}^n$. The input layer of an ANN will be denoted the *1*st layer and each subsequent layer will be referred to as the $(L+1)$th layer. A given layer, L, consists of a set of weights or synapses $\{ w_{ij}^L(k) : i=1 \text{ to } n^L, j=1 \text{ to } n^{L-1} \}$ contained in the matrix $W^L(k)$ and n^L neurons or processing elements. Each weight, $w_{ij}^L(k)$, is an adjustable parameter that propagates and scales the output of the *j*th neuron in the previous layer to the *i*th neuron in the *L*th layer. The summation of these weighted inputs for a particular neuron is the activation level $x_i^L(k)$, that is transformed through a nonlinear activation function $\mathbf{f}:\mathbb{R}\rightarrow\mathbb{R}$ to generate the output:

$$o_i^L(k) = \mathrm{f}[\sum_{j=1}^{n^{L-1}} w_{ij}^L(k)\, o_j^{L-1}(k)] = \mathrm{f}[x_i^L(k)]$$

where $\mathbf{f}(\cdot)$ is the sigmoidal nonlinearity.

B. Estimation framework

In general, after initialization an ANN contains no information reflecting the system it is to approximate. Therefore, at each time instant when new observations are made available, it is desirable to incorporate the additional information into the current parameter estimate. A highly desirable update algorithm which efficiently performs this task for a parameter weight matrix, $W^L(k)$, takes the following general recursive form

$$W^L(k) = W^L(k-1) + \alpha e^L(k) M(k)^T \tag{2}$$

where $M(k) \in \mathbb{R}^{n^{L-1} x 1}$ is the algorithm gain matrix, $y_d^L(k) \in \mathbb{R}^{n^L x 1}$ is the desired or observed output, $y^L(k) \in \mathbb{R}^{n^L x 1}$ is the predicted output, α is a scalar constant modifying the step size, and $e^L(k)$ is the prediction error given by

$$e^L(k) = y_d^L(k) - y^L(k) \tag{3}$$

Typically, $M^L(k)$ is related to prior observations and/or the gradient of $y^L(k)$ with respect to $W^L(k)$. While (2) is actually a subclass of a more general recursive parameter estimation algorithm [7], it is sufficient to serve as a framework for the ANN training algorithms discussed subsequently.

2. Algorithm Summaries

A. Gradient Descent Backpropagation [14]

Gradient descent backpropagation fits the parameter estimation framework provided in (2) by updating the ANN weights according to

$$w_{ij}^L(k) = w_{ij}^L(k-1) + \alpha\, e^{N^T}(k) \frac{\partial y^N(k)}{\partial w_{ij}^L(k)} \tag{4}$$

where α is the step size. The widely used method of

This work was supported in part by grant no. MSS-9216462 from the National Science Foundation.

backpropagation, attributed to [14], is an efficient technique for calculating the partial derivatives of (4) through the weight update equation

$$w_{ij}^{L}(k+1) = w_{ij}^{L}(k) + \alpha\,\delta_i^{L}(k)\,u_j^{L}(k) \tag{5}$$

where in the output layer

$$\delta_i^{L}(k) = e(k)^T \frac{df^{L}(x_i^{L}(k))}{dx_i^{L}(k)} \tag{6}$$

while for any other layer

$$\delta_i^{L}(k) = \frac{df(x_i^{L}(k))}{dx_i^{L}(k)}\, W_i^{L+1}(k)\delta^{L+1}(k)\,. \tag{7}$$

Hence, the partial derivatives of (4) are implicitly calculated in (6) and (7) as part of a recursive error propagation algorithm.

Although this technique is powerful, it suffers from the typical limitations of gradient methods, namely, inefficient step size selection causing slow rates of convergence and the inability to distinguish global from local minimal points. This is elucidated by examining the update law in (4) which modifies the previous weight estimate on the basis of the current observation alone, ignoring all possibly relevant historical information.

B. Extended Kalman Algorithm [2,4,5,9,16,17]

As discussed above, backpropagtion methods estimate the parameters of a layer independent of all other network layers and all prior observations. An alternate approach is to concatenate the weights of all layers into a single vector $\theta(k)$ and to define an operator, NET(·), which performs the complete mapping function of a multilayer feedforward ANN on the basis of this parameter vector and the input, $u(k)$, according to

$$\mathrm{NET}(\theta, u) = f^{N}(W^{N} f^{N-1}(W^{N-1} \cdots f^{1}(W^{1} u)\cdots))$$

where k has been omitted for notational simplicity. The parameter estimation problem is then defined as the determination of $\theta(p)$ which minimizes the criterion function

$$J(p) = \frac{1}{2}\sum_{k=1}^{p}\left(y_d(k) - \mathrm{NET}(\theta(p), u(k))\right)^2 \tag{9}$$

where $y_d(k)$ is the observed output vector and p denotes the number of training samples. Assume that the nonlinearities of (8) are sufficiently smooth and that the observation is

$$y_d(k) = \mathrm{NET}(\theta^*(k), u(k)) + v(k) \tag{10}$$

where $\theta^*(k)$ is the desired parameter vector that minimizes (9) and $v(k)$ is the measurement noise with zero mean and a covariance matrix $R(k)$. Then, the first order Taylor series expansion of (10) about the estimate $\theta(k)$ is given by

$$y_d(k) \cong \mathrm{NET}(\theta(k)) + H(k)(\theta^*(k) - \theta(k)) \tag{11}$$

where

$$H(k) = \frac{\partial \mathrm{NET}(\theta^*(k), u(k))}{\partial \theta(k)}\Big|_{\theta(k)=\hat{\theta}(k)} \tag{12}$$

is the matrix containing the partial derivative of the network output with respect to each individual weight. With these assumptions the suboptimal extended Kalman filter can be applied directly to the estimation problem through the equations:

$$\begin{aligned} \theta(k) &= \theta(k-1) + K(k)\left(y_d(k) - y(k)\right) \\ K(k) &= \frac{P(k-1)H(k)}{\lambda(k)R(k) + H^T(k)P(k-1)H(k)} \\ P(k) &= \frac{1}{\lambda(k)}\left(\mathrm{I} - K(k)H^T(k)\right)P(k-1) \end{aligned} \tag{13}$$

where $P(k)$ is the approximate error covariance matrix and $\lambda(k)$ is a time-varying forgetting factor.

This technique has been found to converge quickly in comparison with gradient-descent techniques, is insensitive to uncorrelated noise, and has a better success rate than does the gradient algorithm [2,16]. However, the computational overhead is significantly increased since the covariance matrix is the same dimension as the number of adjustable weights in the network.

C. Decoupled Extended Kalman [9, 10, 11]

The approach followed by Shah and Palmeiri [9] is fundamentally similar to the extended Kalman algorithm. However, to reduce the computational complexity a decoupled extended Kalman filter is proposed in which the weights are grouped (by neuron) and the extended Kalman filter is applied to each individual sub-group. As a result, the algorithm is computationally expedient and demonstrates significant improvement in specific examples.

Puskorius and Feldman [10, 11] assert that the algorithm above has a tendency towards instability and local minima due to the possibility of large Kalman gains in individual groups. By simplifying the extended Kalman algorithm, they propose an approximation which can be implemented in a decoupled manner and which does not exhibit the same significant increase in the number of computations.

The Kalman based algorithm applied to each sub-grouping of weights is identical to the standard extended Kalman filter with the addition of a global scaling matrix which limits the gain of the individual subgroups. The algorithm assumes the form:

$$\begin{aligned} A(n) &= \left[\, R(n) + \sum_{i=1}^{g} H_i^T(n)P_i(n)H_i(n)\,\right]^{-1} \\ K_i(n) &= P_i(n)H_i(n)A(n) \\ w_i(n+1) &= w_i(n) + K_i(n)e(n) \\ P_i(n+1) &= P_i(n) - K_i(n)H_i^T(n)P_i(n) + Q_i(n) \end{aligned}$$

where $A(n)$ is N_p by N_p global scaling matrix, g_a refers to the number of groups, $Q_i(n)$ is artificially added noise, $H_i(n)$ is the Jacobian of a particular subgroup, $w_i(n)$ is the estimated weight matrix, and $e(n)$ refers to the prediction error. The groupings of the weights can be arbitrary set although natural groupings such as by neuron or by layer are reported to result in more efficient computational structures. The learning rate is small initially and is gradually increased to a value of one.

D. Recursive-Least Squares [1,6,15]

The recursive-least squares (RLS) method partitions the layers of an ANN into a linear set of input-out equations and applies the common RLS algorithm to update the weights in each layer. The RLS algorithm for a weight matrix update in a single layer is given by

$$\begin{aligned} W(k) &= W(k-1)+\alpha\, e(k) K^{T}(k) \\ K(k) &= \frac{P(k-1)u(k)}{\lambda + u^{T}(k)P(k-1)u(k)} \\ P(k) &= \frac{1}{\lambda}\left(I - K(k)u^{T}(k)\right)P(k-1) \end{aligned} \tag{15}$$

where λ is the forgetting factor, $K(k)$ is the gain matrix, $P(k)$ is the covariance matrix, $u(k)$ is the input to the layer, α is the step size, and $e(k)$ is the error associated with the output of the layer. The error signal used to make the update in the output layer is determined according to

$$e^{N}(k) = f^{-1}(y_d^{N}(k)) - x^{N}(k) \tag{16}$$

where N is the number of layers in the ANN, $\mathbf{f}(\cdot)$ is the sigmoidal nonlinearity, $y_d(k)$ is the desired output, and $x^N(k)$ is the activation level of the output layer. All other layers are updated according to the backpropagated error defined by (7). Clearly these equations are similar to (13) and in the form of the general recursive update law (2). The major difference between this law and the extended Kalman is that the estimation problem is partitioned into subsections dependent upon signals propagated through one another.

E. The Linear Kalman Filter [12, 13]

The linear Kalman technique is a generalization of the recursive-least squares method with a different approach to target state propagation. The basic approach is similar to that of the RLS technique previously discussed which prescribes a layer by layer application of the recursive least squares (RLS) estimator. The salient feature of this design is an innovative method of backpropagating target states to embedded layers which facilitates the utilization of a linear Kalman filter.

The design methodology provided consists of three steps: the design of a linear estimation algorithm, the determination of suitable desired or target input and output states for embedded layers, and the formation of techniques to eliminate transients resulting from the initial conditions.

1. Kalman Based Parameter Estimation

The problem of determining the weights of a particular feedforward layer was introduced as a parameter estimation problem in Section 1B by viewing the network as a cascade of separate layers. As noted by [26], the selection of the weights in each layer can be further transformed into a *linear* parameter estimation problem by partitioning individual layers into linear and nonlinear sub-components and solving each linear estimation problem individually. The principle difficulty is the determination of target states with which to train each linear sub-section.

For the moment, assume that appropriate target input-output states, denoted $u_d^L(k)$ and $y_d^L(k)$ are available. Additionally, define $W_d^L(k)$ as the desired linear transformation of the Lth layer such that the measurement or observation of $x_d^L(k)$ given the input $u_d^L(k)$ is found through

$$x_d^{L}(k) = W_d^{L}(k)u_d^{L}(k) + v(k) \tag{17}$$

where $v(k)$ is the measurement noise with zero mean and a covariance matrix $R(k)$. Then the optimal solution for the estimate $W^L(k)$ which minimizes the error criterion function

$$J(p) = \frac{1}{2}\sum_{k=1}^{p}\left(x_d^{L}(k) - W^{L}(p)u_d^{L}(k)\right)^2 \tag{18}$$

is the linear Kalman filter defined below:

$$\begin{aligned} W(k) &= W(k-1)+\alpha\left(x_d(k) - x(k)\right)K^{T}(k) \\ K(k) &= \frac{P(k-1)u_d(k)}{\lambda(k)R(k) + u_d^{T}(k)P(k-1)u_d(k)} \\ P(k) &= \frac{1}{\lambda(k)}\left(I - K(k)u_d^{T}(k)\right)P(k-1) \end{aligned} \tag{19}$$

where $P(k)$ is the covariance matrix, $K(k)$ is the Kalman gain, $\lambda(k)$ is a time-varying forgetting factor, α is the step size, and the layer index L has been omitted for notational simplicity. This defines a linear recursive estimation algorithm with same form as (2) and similar to (15) for determining the weights of an ANN layer by layer. Since this algorithm assumes that the estimated matrix is nonstationary, it is expected that it will allow the tracking of a time-varying system.

2. Error Propagation

As shown in the last section, the application of the Kalman filter to the estimation of weight parameters is straight forward if the appropriate target states are available. Unfortunately, this is not the case. In the input layer, the applied vector input $u_d(k)$ is clearly available. However, the desired input state into each subsequent layer is unavailable since $u_d(k)$ is propagated through untrained or partially trained layers.

Similarly, assuming that the inverse of the nonlinear activation function exists, $x_d^L(k)$, in the output layer can be calculated via

$$x_d^{N}(k) = f^{-1}(y_d(k)) \tag{20}$$

All other target outputs are not prescribed and alternate strategies must be developed. This paper presents a fundamentally different approach than past studies by defining a pseudo or suboptimal target input-output pair for each linear subsection of a given layer as ($\tilde{u}^L(k)$, $\tilde{x}^L(k)$). Then the pseudo target states for the input to the first layer and the output of the output or Nth layer are defined by

$$\tilde{u}(k) = u_d(k)\,, \qquad \tilde{x}^{N}(k) = f^{-1}\left(y_d(k)\right) \tag{21}$$

The suboptimal input target vector to each linear element is defined according to the forward propagated signal resulting from the application of $u_d(k)$:

$$\tilde{u}^{L}(k) = u^{L}(k) \qquad \text{for } L = 2, 3, \cdots, N \tag{22}$$

For the selection of $\tilde{x}^L(k)$ assume that $\tilde{x}_{L+1}(k)$ has been found and it is desired to determine an optimal selection for

$\tilde{x}^L(k)$ considering the weights of the subsequent layer and the current activation level of the Lth layer. The first step is to determine $\tilde{y}^L(k)$ such that $\tilde{x}^L(k)$ can be calculated through the inversion of $\mathbf{f}^L(\cdot)$ described by (20). With this in mind the following criteria are proposed:

1. Select $\tilde{y}^L(k)$ such that the inverse in (21) exists.
2. The selection of $\tilde{y}^L(k)$ must be made to closely approximate $\tilde{x}_{L+1}(k)$ through the current matrix estimate $W^{L+1}(k)$:

$$\tilde{x}^{L+1} \cong W^{L+1}(k)\tilde{y}^L(k) \tag{23}$$

3. In general there may be a family of solutions or there may be no solution which satisfies (21) and (23). In either case, select the pseudo vector $\tilde{y}^L(k)$ that is close to $y^L(k)$.

These criteria are embodied in the following cost function:

$$\begin{aligned} J^L &= \frac{1}{2}(y^L - \tilde{y}^L)^T(y^L - \tilde{y}^T) \\ &+ \frac{\beta}{2}(x^{L+1} - W^{L+1}\tilde{y}^L)^T(x^{L+1} - W^{L+1}\tilde{y}^L) \end{aligned} \tag{24}$$

where $\beta>0$ is chosen such that criterion (1) is satisfied and the index k is neglected for notational simplicity. The suboptimal selection for $\tilde{y}^L(k)$ is defined as that vector which minimizes (24). Therefore, set the partial derivative of (24) with respect to $\tilde{y}^L(k)$ to zero

$$\frac{\partial J^L}{\partial \tilde{y}^L} = -(y^L - \tilde{y}^L) - \beta(x^{L+1} - W^{L+1}\tilde{y}^L) = 0$$

Solving this for $\tilde{y}^L(k)$ yields

$$\tilde{y}^L = \left[I + \beta W^{L+1^T} W^{L+1}\right]^{-1}\left[y^L + \beta W^{L+1^T} x^{L+1}\right] \tag{26}$$

By proper choice of β a solution can always be found that satisfies (21). Intuitively it can be seen that large values of β will cause (26) to approximate the pseudo inverse of (23) while small values of β will make (26) approximately equal to $y^L(k)$. Finally, the desired state $\tilde{x}^L(k)$ can be calculated through (21).

While the matrix inversion of (26) is a drawback of this approach there are several inherent properties that can be exploited. First, the inverse in (26) is guaranteed to exist and the matrix is positive definite symmetrical. Therefore, numerical methods can be applied which will reduce the number of computations significantly. Secondly, if $W^L(k)$ is n^L by n^{L-1} and $n^L<n^{L-1}$, the matrix-inversion lemma can be applied to (26) to produce

$$\begin{aligned} \tilde{y}^L = &\left[I + \beta W^{L+1^T}(I + \beta W^{L+1} W^{L+1^T})^{-1} W^{L+1}\right] \\ &\left[y^L + \beta W^{L+1^T}\tilde{x}^{L+1}\right] \end{aligned} \tag{27}$$

which involves a n^L by n^L matrix inversion rather than a n^{L-1} by n^{L-1} inversion. In an ANN layer with a single output, this results in a scalar division.

3. Covariance Modification

The forgetting factor, $\lambda(k)$, is used to prioritize more recent observations by scaling $P(k)$ in the following manner

$$P^{-1}(k) = \lambda(k)P^{-1}(k-1) + u(k)u^T(k) \tag{28}$$

where $\lambda(k)\varepsilon(0,1]$. A smaller value for $\lambda(k)$ gives better responsiveness to changes but a larger variance in parameter estimates. However, when the input is not persistently exciting or when $\lambda(k)$ is kept small for many samples, $P(k)$ will grow exponentially which can lead to the temporary instability of the estimator. This phenomena is avoided by determining $\lambda(k)$ as follows

$$\lambda(k) = 1 - \gamma\tilde{e}(k) \tag{29}$$

where

$$\tilde{e}(k) = \frac{e^2(k)}{1 + u^T(k)P(k-1)u(k)} \tag{30}$$

and γ is a constant which is inversely proportional to the expected covariance of the prediction error, $e(k)$ [3]. As a result, $\lambda(k)$ remains close to one when $P(k)$ is already large and the estimator is sensitive to parameter variations. A lower bound, λ_0, on $\lambda(k)$ is used to prevent the forgetting factor from becoming excessively small (or even negative), resulting in large estimate fluctuations in spite of small prediction errors.

3. System Identification Example

In this section simulation results from a nonlinear system identification problem are presented in which a feedforward ANN is utilized to approximate a highly nonlinear mapping. The nonlinear function, chosen due to its demanding characteristics, is given by

$$y_d(k) = \frac{u_d(k)}{1 + u_d^2(k)} \tag{31}$$

where $y_d(k)\in[-.05\ 0.5]$ when $u_d(k)\in[-10\ 10]$ as shown in Figure 1. All five of the previously discussed parameter estimation techniques were employed to train an ANN with an architecture of 1-8-4-1. To demonstrate the average rate of convergence, weights were selected randomly as described in each of the following subsections for ten different random initializations. The training set was a different sequence of random points on the function for each experiment, generated with $u_d(k)\in[-10\ 10]$ uniformly distributed. The test set, used to evaluate the performance of each ANN during training through a mean square error (MSE) measurement, consisted of a constant set of 134 points evenly spaced on the range of the input, $u_d(k)$.

Figures 2 and 3 show the ten seed average test set error versus normalized training time and training iteration respectively. The training constants of each algorithm were selected to provide the greatest rate of convergence through trial and error. However, only the 10 seed average of the best set of results from each algorithm are presented in Figures 2 and 3. Details regarding the implementation of each algorithm are provided below.

A. Gradient Descent Backpropagation

The gradient descent algorithm was applied with a constant step size, α, of 2.0 in each layer. Initially the weights were set uniformly in the interval [-1,1]. Convergence in each experiment to a MSE near 1.0E-4 occurred after approximately about 10,000 training iterations which corresponds to a time of about 45 in Figure 2. As will be shown by the subsequent experiments, lower error rates are possible for the same network architecture.

B. Extended Kalman Algorithm

The extended Kalman parameter estimation technique was implemented with a step size of 0.5 and a forgetting factor, described by (30), with γ=0.5. Initially the weights were uniformly distributed in the interval [-0.1, 0.1] and the covariance matrix was set to 1000·**I**. The convergence plots of the ten experiments were averaged and are provided in Figures 2 and 3 revealing a fast convergence in terms of training iterations when compared to backpropagation. In terms of training time the extended Kalman algorithm also demonstrates an improved rate of convergence for this particular size network as shown in Figure 2.

C. Decoupled Extended Kalman Algorithm

The decoupled extended Kalman algorithm was applied with a constant learning rate of 0.5 throughout the entire experiment and in contrast to the details provided in the literature generated noise was not added to the algorithm. The initial covariance matrices were set to 1000·**I** and a constant forgetting factor of 0.99 was employed. The actual rate of convergence was slightly slower in terms of both training time and training iterations than the extended Kalman algorithm.

D. Recursive Least Squares

The recursive least squares method was employed with learning rates $\alpha\mathbf{1}$ = 10, $\alpha\mathbf{2}$ = 5, and $\alpha\mathbf{3}$ = 1 corresponding to the first, second and third layers and a global forgetting factor set to 0.975. Initially, the covariance matrices were set to 100·**I** and the weights were uniformly distributed in the interval [-1 1]. Although the initial rates of convergence were rapid, as shown if Figures 2 and 3, the algorithm did not achieve a final error as low as the other algorithms. The reason for this may be the need for a decreased learning rate.

E. Linear Kalman with Target State Backpropagation

The linear Kalman technique with error signal backpropagation was implemented with a step size of 0.5 for each of the three layers and a measurement error covariance, $R(k)$, of 1. The constant, β, of equation (26), was set to 0.01 and γ was initially set to 10000 and later decreased to 1 after the initial transients subsided. The covariance matrices were initialized to 100,000·**I** and the weights were initially set as follows: in layer 1 the weights were uniformly distributed in the interval [-10 10], in layer 2 the weights were uniformly distributed between [-1, 1], and in layer three the weights were uniformly distributed between [-0.1, 0.1]. When the condition in (21) was not met during training, the particular sample was discarded rather than iteratively generating a new value for β.

The results from the linear Kalman experiments, shown in Figures 2 and 3, demonstrate an improved rate of convergence over the existing algorithms. The use of the error dependent forgetting factor was instrumental in driving the MSE low during the first few hundred training iterations until the bias caused by the initial conditions was eliminated. Different initial weight matrices, particularly in the first layer caused some experiments, not shown in this paper, to remain in local minima well above the final MSE of the experiments.

E. Comparison

The five algorithms exhibited comparable rates of convergence when plotted versus actual computing time. In Figure 2, the linear Kalman technique with target state backpropagation appeared to be the least computationally intensive in terms of actual computing time. However, this conclusion is only valid for this particular example and a more general conclusion cannot be made until additional experimentation is performed using other input sources and nonlinearities. Each of the newer algorithms converged, at least initially, faster in terms of both computing time and training iterations than backpropagation.

4. Conclusions

The rates of convergence demonstrated by the ANN training algorithms described in this paper testify to the suitability of multilayer feedforward ANNs in nonlinear system identification and control. The new technique, described as a linear Kalman algorithm employing target state backpropagation, was shown in the nonlinear identification example to be at least comparable in speed with the other Kalman based techniques and perhaps faster is certain applications than the existing techniques. Each of the more recent training algorithms appeared to converge quicker, in terms of computing time and training iterations than the backpropagation.

5. References

[1] M. R. Azimi-Sadjadi and Ren-Jean Liou, "Fast learning process of multilayer neural networks using recursive least squares method," IEEE Trans. Signal Proc., vol. 40, no. 2, pp. 446-450, Feb. 1992.

[2] S. Chen, C. F. Cowan, s. A. Billings, and P. M. Grant,"Parallel recursive prediction error algorithm for training layered neural networks," Int. J. Control, vol. 51, no. 8, pp. 1215-1228, 1990.

[3] T. R. Fortesque, L. S. Kershenbaum, and B. E. Ydstie, "Implementation of Self-tuning Regulators with Variable Forgetting Factors," Automatica, vol. 17, no. 6, pp. 831-835, 1981.

[4] T. Huang, M. Tsuyuki, and M. Yasuhara, "A learning algorithm of the neural network based on kalman filtering," IEICE Trans., vol. E 74, no. 5, pp. 1059-1065, May 1991.

[5] Y. Iiguni, H. Sakai, and H. Tokumaru, "A real-time learning algorithm for a multilayer neural network based on the extended kalman filter," IEEE Trans. Signal Proc., vol. 40, no. 4, pp. 959-966, April 1992.

[6] S. Kollias and D. Anastassiou, "An adaptive least squares algorithm for the efficient training of artificial neural networks," IEEE Trans. Cir. Sys., vol. 36, no. 8, pp. 1092-1101, Aug. 1989.

[7] L. Lung, System Identification Theory For the User. Englewood Cliffs, New Jersey: Prentice Hall, 1987.

[8] K. S. Narendra and K. Parthasarathy, "Identification and Control of Dynamic Systems Using Neural Networks," IEEE Trans. Neural Networks, vol. 1, no. 1, pp. 4-26, March 1990.

[9] F. Palmieri and S. A. Shah, "A new algorithm for training multilayer perceptron," IEEE Int. Conf. Sys. Man Cybernetics, vol.2, pp. 427-428, 1989.

[10] G. V. Puskorius and L. A. Feldkamp, "Decoupled extended kalman filter training of feedforward layered networks," IJCNN (Baltimore, MD), vol. I, pp. 771-777, 1991.

[11] G. V. Puskorius and L. A. Feldkamp, "Model reference adaptive control with recurrent networks trained by the dynamic dekf algorithm," IJCNN (Baltimore, MD), vol. II, pp. 106-113, 1992.

[12] T. L. Ruchti, R. H. Brown, and J. J. Garside, "A parameter estimation approach to artificial neural network weight selection for nonlinear system identification," 1st IEEE Conference on Control Applications (Dayton, OH), Sept. 1992 pp. 571-576.

[13] T. L. Ruchti, R. H. Brown, and J. J. Garside, "Estimation of artificial neural network parameters for nonlinear system identification," Proc.: 31st IEEE Conference on Decision and Control (Tucson, AZ), Dec. 1992, pp. 2728-2733.

[14] Rumelhart, D. E., Hinton, G. E., and R. J. Williams, "Learning internal representations by error propagation," Parallel Distributed Processing: Explorations in the Microstructure of Cognition, vol. 1, MA: MIT Press, pp. 318-362.

[15] R. S. Scalero and N. Tepedelenlioglu, "A fast new algorithm for training feedforward neural networks," IEEE Trans. Signal Proc., vol. 40, no. 1, pp. 202-210, Jan. 1992.

[16] S. Singhal and L. Wu, "Training feed-forward networks with the extended kalman algorithm," Proc. ICASSP, pp. 1187-1190, 1989.

[17] K. Watanabe, T. Fukuda, and S. G. Tzafestas, "Learning algorithms of layered neural networks via extended kalman filters," Int. J. of Sys. Sci., vol. 22, no. 4, pp. 753-768, April 1991.

[18] P. J. Werbos, "Neural Networks for Control and System Identification," Proc. of the 28th Conf. CDC., Tampa, FL, WA10, pp. 260-265, Dec. 1989.

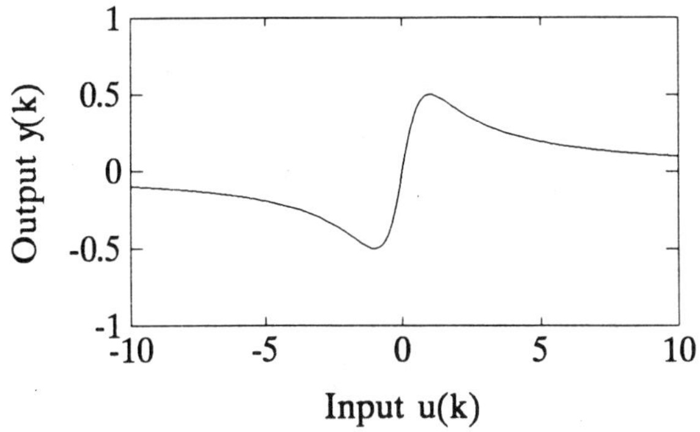

Figure 1. *The nonlinear mapping used in the system identification example.*

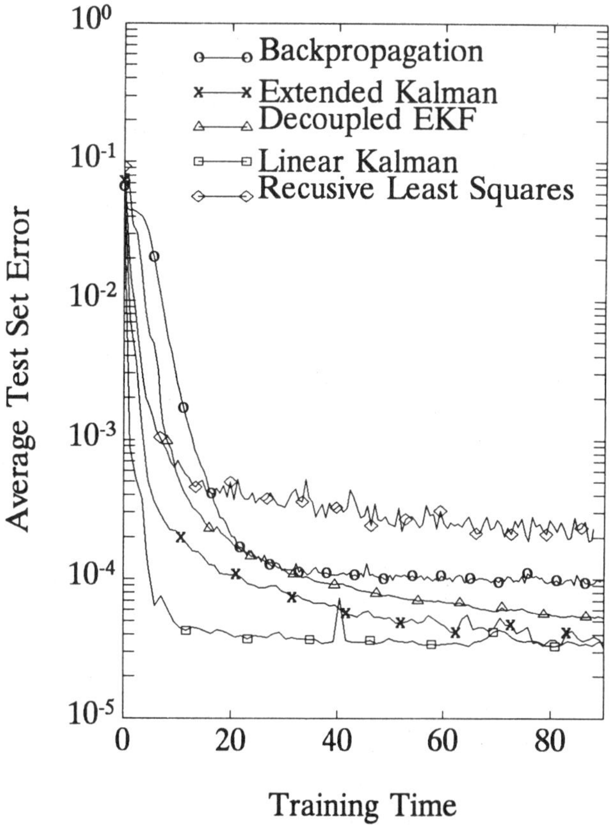

Figure 2. *Comparison of the mean square error versus actual training time of the five ANN training algorithms.*

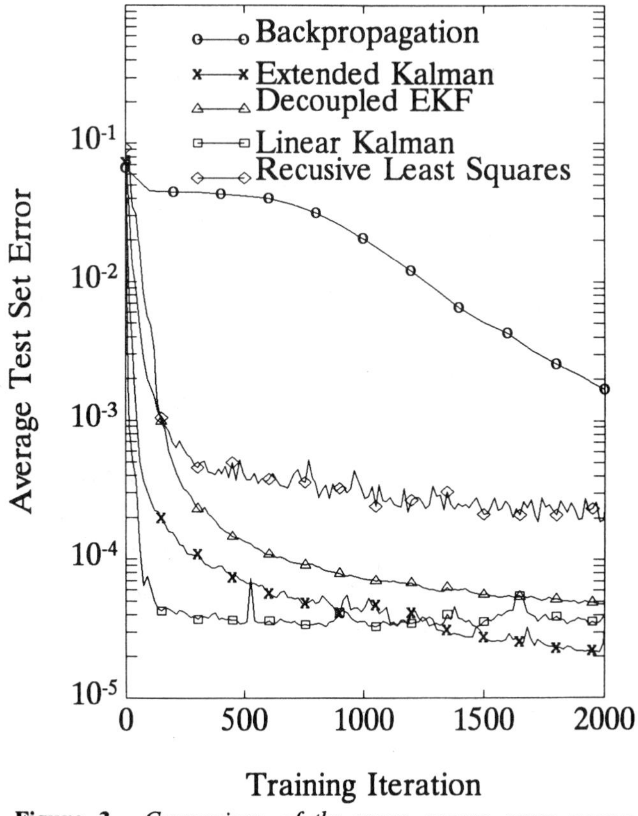

Figure 3. *Comparison of the mean square error versus training iteration of the five ANN training algorithms.*

DYNAMIC SYSTEM IDENTIFICATION USING RECURRENT RADIAL BASIS FUNCTION NETWORK

X. Ye and N.K. Loh

Center for Robotics and Advanced Automation

Oakland University, Rochester MI 48309

ABSTRACT

This paper presents a local neural network structure called *spatiotemporally* local network by combining the radial basis function network (RBFN) and the local recurrent networks. Three local structures are proposed and the algorithms are compared for nonlinear dynamic system identification. System dynamics can be fully modeled with the fast learning of the proposed neural network structure.

1. INTRODUCTION

Artificial neural networks have been widely studied and applied to a variety of areas. One of the successful areas is the nonlinear function approximation or mapping. Feedforward neural networks are often used for this purpose due to their universal approximate property. According to the neural dynamics or node transfer function in the network, feedforward networks are usually classified as the global network and the local network. In a global network, all the network weights are active to any given point in the input space and they are updated with each training exemplar. This global nature of weights updating, however, tends to blur the details of local structure, slows the rate of learning and results in the existing of local minimum. The well known multilayer perceptron (MLP) with back-propagation (BP) algorithm is a global network. Although it has been studied intensively, the problems of slow convergency and local minimum make it hard for practical use without the various speedup algorithms or improvements in the hardware. In a local network, however, only a small subset of weights are active at each point in the input space. The training of the network in one part of the input space does not corrupt what has already been learned in more distant regions. Thus the learning speed of the local network is much fast than the global network. Further more, no local minima exists in the local network. The radial basis function network[1]-[10] and CMAC [20]-[22] are the typical examples of local networks. A speedup over BP by a factor of 1000 has been reported of RBFNs [6]. Because this kind of locality happens due to the topological arrangement of the network, we call it *spatially local* network.

Although it is demonstrated recently that MLP with two hidden layers trained by BP algorithm can perform the same role as one hidden layer RBFN [5], the increase number in weights and the randomness of their arrangement should account for the problems of slow convergence and local minimum in BP.

The feedforword networks mentioned above are static networks and they do not explore the temporal nature of a dynamic system. So they can only be trained to learn static mappings. To model nonlinear dynamic systems, dynamic networks are needed. A usual way to make the network behavior dynamically is to add feedback or recurrent loops between neurons or itself. By doing so, recurrent networks have the abilities to deal with time-varying input or output through their own natural temporal operation.

Recurrent networks can be structured in different ways. According to the arrangement of the recurrent loop, there are mainly three methods to achieve this. The first method is to feedback the delayed output of the network to its input space along with the delayed input. This is referred to as tapped delay line or external recurrent[16], a common practice in system identification and control using neural network approaches. The second method is to connect every neuron in the network to the every other one, thus resulting a fully recurrent network. The fully recurrent networks have been used to learn a state trajectory and other time dependent applications[13] . However, due to the increasing connections in the fully recurrent networks, the learning is computational expensive. The third method is to feedback locally. In this method, every neuron only feedbacks to itself as in diagonal recurrent network[19] or adds an adaptive linear filter after each neuron as FIR and IIR synopsis network[17]. By doing so, it is hoped that the local recurrent nature is enough to capture the system dynamics. We call it *temporally local* network in comparison with the spatially local network.

Most of the recurrent networks mentioned above are based on MLP and have been used successfully in many areas. But answers to the problems raised as how the temporally nature of recurrent structure affects RBFNs and how it will help modeling nonlinear systems are still unknown. In this paper, a new structure is proposed by combining the temporally local nature of recurrent network with spatially local nature of RBFs. The double local network architecture has the benefits of fast learning and fast convergence without loss of modeling abilities. The paper is organized as follows. Brief description of system and RBFs are given in section 1. In section 2, Three different local recurrent structures are discussed and the algorithms are derived. Those algorithms are compared in section 3. Finally in section 4, simulation results are given for a typical nonlinear system.

2. SYSTEM REPRESENTATION AND RBFs

2.1 System Representation

A discrete-time nonlinear dynamic system can be described by a set of difference equations as follows:

$$y(k+1) = f(y(k), ..., y(k-m), u(k), ..., u(k-n)), \quad (1)$$

where $y(k)$ and $u(k)$ are system output and input respectively, $f(\cdot)$ is some nonlinear function. m and n are the maximum lags in the output and input.

The problem of system identification is to build a mathematical or neural network model which has the same characteristic of the real system. Thus the identified model has the form

$$\hat{y}(k+1) = f(\hat{y}(k), ..., \hat{y}(k-m), u(k), ..., u(k-n)). \quad (2)$$

Equation (2) is referred to as parallel model in the literature. While the conditions under which the parallel model parameters will converge are still unknown at present, series-parallel model is often used in system identification. In the series-parallel model the output of the plant (rather than the output of the identified model) is fed back into the identification model which gives the following form for the series-parallel model

$$\hat{y}(k+1) = f(y(k), ..., y(k-m), u(k), ..., u(k-n)). \quad (3)$$

2.2 Gaussian Radial Basis Function

A radial basis function network is the same as multilayer perceptron network with one hidden layer except that the sigmoid function is replaced by a radial basis function, usually Gaussian function:

$$x_j = e^{\left(-\frac{\sum_{i=1}^{n0}(I_i - c_{i,j})^2}{w_j^2}\right)}, \quad (4)$$

where $j = 1, ..., n$, I_j is the jth component of the input to the network. x_j is the output of the jth unit in the hidden layer. $c_{i,j}$ is the center of the jth unit in the input space, and w_j is the width of the jth unit. n is the number of units in the hidden layer. $n0$ is the dimension of input space. For the single output case, the output of the network is given by

$$y = \sum_{j=1}^{n} h_j x_j, \quad (5)$$

where h_j is the weight or height of the jth unit. We see from equ. (4) and (5) that the input layer is only a fan-out layer, the output layer is linear as with the standard MLP. When the structural information is available a priori, i.e., the number of delayed input and output is known, the inputs to the network are those delayed signals. If the parallel identification scheme is used, the structure is the same as external recurrent networks.

3. RECURRENT ALGORITHMS FOR RBFN

For a given network, define the output error for a training cycle as

$$E(k) = \frac{1}{2}(d(k) - y(k))^2, \quad (6)$$

where $d(k)$ is the desired output of the plant and $y(k)$ is the output of the neural network. For the RBFN defined by (4) and (5), the gradient method can be used to derive the updating rule of the parameters. The update of the centers is given by

$$c_{i,j}^{k+1} = c_{i,j}^k + \Delta c_{i,j}^k, \quad (7)$$

where

$$\Delta c_{i,j}^k = 2\mu e(k) x_j^k h_j^k (I_i^k - c_{i,j}^k)/w_j^2, \quad (8)$$

and

$$e(k) = d(k) - y(k),$$

μ is the learning rate.

The update of the weights (heights) is given by

$$h_j^{k+1} = h_j^k + \Delta h_j^k, \quad (9)$$

where

$$\Delta h_j^k = -\mu e(k) x_j^k. \quad (10)$$

The width of the RBFs can be updated too using the same gradient algorithm. But care must be taken in doing so in some cases where the width of the RBFs becomes larger in updating, thus loss its local property. A usual way to avoid this is to set a reasonable overlap between the RBFs and keep the width fixed.

Based on the RBFNs described above, there are three different ways to construct a spatiotemporal local network according to the way the feedback is taken. The update equations (7)-(10) for original parameters in the RBFN, i.e., centers and heights, are still valid for all three proposed local recurrent structures and the error is still defined as (6). The basic structure of a spatiotemporally local network is shown in Fig. 1.

3.1 Center Recurrent

By analogy to the input of the unit, the output of the unit can be fed back to its input space, i.e., the feedback loop is treated as the same as the other input by augmenting another dimension of radial basis function. Thus the recurrent synopsis has the same form as the feedforward synopsis. The extra dimension represents the effect of the feedback loop in a nonlinear way. The center recurrent structure is shown in Fig. 2 (a). The output of the network is same as (5). The output of the jth hidden unit is then

$$x_j^k = e^{\left(-\frac{\sum_{i=1}^{n0}(I_i - c_{i,j})^2}{w_j^2} - \frac{(x_j^{k-1} - c_{i+1,j})^2}{w_j^2}\right)} \quad (11)$$

The gradient method and chain rule can be used to derive the update equation of the recurrent synopsis. Thus the update equation for the additional dimension of the RBFs center (additional recurrent synopsis) is given by

$$c_{i+1,j}^{k+1} = c_{i+1,j}^k - \mu \frac{\partial E}{\partial c_{i+1,j}^k}. \quad (12)$$

The gradient in above equation can be further expanded

$$\frac{\partial E}{\partial c_{i+1,j}^k} = \frac{\partial E}{\partial y} \frac{\partial y}{\partial c_{i+1,j}^k}$$

$$= -e(k)\frac{\partial y}{\partial c_{i+1,j}^k}, \quad (13)$$

where

$$\frac{\partial y}{\partial c_{i+1,j}^k} = \frac{\partial y}{\partial x_j}\frac{\partial x_j}{\partial c_{i+1,j}^k}$$
$$= h_j \frac{\partial x_j}{\partial c_{i+1,j}^k}$$
$$= -2h_j^k x_j^k (x_j^{k-1} - c_{i+1,j}^k)/w_j^2. \quad (14)$$

Substitute (13) and (14) into (12) the update equation becomes

$$c_{i+1,j}^{k+1} = c_{i+1,j}^k + 2\mu e(k) x_j^k h_j^k (x_i^{k+1} - c_{i+1,j}^k)/w_j^2. \quad (15)$$

The above equation is similar to (8). This constitutes a consistent system both in feedforward path and in recurrent path. This also helps to extend the local recurrent network to the fully recurrent networks.

3.2 Linear Recurrent

The second method is to feedback the output of the unit through a connection weight as usually did in the recurrent MLP networks. The recurrent unit structure is shown in Fig. 2 (b). The output of the network is still same as (5). The output of jth hidden unit at time k becomes

$$x_j^k = e^{\left(-\frac{\sum_{i=1}^{n0}(I_i - c_{i,j})^2}{w_j^2} + m_j x_j^{k-1}\right)}. \quad (16)$$

Using the gradient method, the update equation for the linear connection weights is given by

$$m_j^{k+1} = m_j^k - \mu\frac{\partial E}{\partial m_j}. \quad (17)$$

In a similar fashion, the gradient in above equation can be further expanded using chain rule

$$\frac{\partial E}{\partial m_j} = \frac{\partial E}{\partial y}\frac{\partial y}{\partial m_j}$$
$$= e(k)\frac{\partial y}{\partial m_j}, \quad (18)$$

where

$$\frac{\partial y}{\partial m_j} = \frac{\partial y}{\partial x_j}\frac{\partial x_j}{\partial m_j}$$
$$= h_j\frac{\partial x_j}{\partial m_j}$$
$$= -h_j^k x_j^k x_j^{k-1}. \quad (19)$$

Substitute (18) and (19) into (17), we get the final update equation for m_j

$$m_j^{k+1} = m_j^k - \mu e(k) h_j^k x_j^k x_j^{k-1}. \quad (20)$$

3.3 IIR Recurrent

The third method for constructing a local recurrent network is to add an adaptive linear filter after each unit as is called IIR synopsis[17] or dynamic network[16]. The recurrent unit structure is shown in Fig. 2 (c). The output of the network now becomes

$$y = \sum_{j=1}^{n} x_j. \quad (21)$$

The output of the unit is given by

$$x_j^k = h_j^k o_j^k + \sum_{l=1}^{M} a_{j,l}^k o_j^{k-l} + \sum_{l=1}^{N} b_{j,l}^k x_j^{k-l}, \quad (22)$$

where

$$o_j^k = e^{-\frac{\sum_{i=1}^{n0}(I_i^k - c_{i,j})^2}{w_j^2}},$$

a and b are the connection weights or the coefficients of the linear filters, M and N are the number of delays in the input and output of the unit respectively.

The updating equation for the connection weight a and b are

$$a_{j,l}^{k+1} = a_{j,l}^k - \mu\frac{\partial E}{\partial a_{j,l}}, \quad (23)$$

and

$$b_{j,l}^{k+1} = b_{j,l}^k - \mu\frac{\partial E}{\partial b_{j,l}}, \quad (24)$$

where the gradients in above equations can be computed using chain rule

$$\frac{\partial E}{\partial a_{j,l}} = e(k)\frac{\partial y}{\partial a_{j,l}}$$
$$= -e(k)h_j^k\frac{\partial x_j}{\partial a_{j,l}}$$
$$= -e(k)h_j^k o_j^{k-l}, \quad (25)$$

and

$$\frac{\partial E}{\partial b_{j,l}} = e(k)\frac{\partial y}{\partial b_{j,l}}$$
$$= -e(k)h_j^k\frac{\partial x_j}{\partial b_{j,l}}$$
$$= -e(k)h_j^k x_j^{k-l}. \quad (26)$$

4. COMPARISON OF THE THREE APPROACHES

Equ. (11) can be further expanded as follow

$$x_j^k = e^{\left(-\frac{\sum_{i=1}^{n0}(I_i - c_{i,j})^2}{w_j^2}\right)} \cdot e^{\left(-\frac{(x_j^{k-1} - c_{i+1,j})^2}{w_j^2}\right)}$$
$$= e^{\left(-\frac{\sum_{i=1}^{n0}(I_i - c_{i,j})^2}{w_j^2}\right)} \cdot e^{-\frac{(x_j^{k-1})^2}{w_j^2}}$$
$$\cdot e^{\frac{2x_j^{k-1}c_{i+1,j}}{w_j^2}} \cdot e^{-\frac{(c_{i+1,j})^2}{w_j^2}} \quad (27)$$

We see from above equation that the effect of center recurrent is multiplying the output of the unit with the nonlinear delayed terms. In a same way, Equ. (16) can also be expanded as

$$x_j^k = e^{\left(-\frac{\sum_{i=1}^{n0}(I_i - c_{i,j})^2}{w_j^2} + m_j x_j^{k-1}\right)}$$
$$= e^{-\frac{\sum_{i=1}^{n0}(I_i - c_{i,j})^2}{w_j^2}} \cdot e^{m_j x_j^{k-1}}. \quad (28)$$

Compare (27) and (28) we see that in both cases the recurrent loop of the unit affects the output in a nonlinear way. This will help modeling nonlinear dynamic systems. The center recurrent case is, however, more complicated. It is more sensitive to the recurrent loop than the linear recurrent case. The linear recurrent structure is a special case of (27) when only the linear term is presented in (28). Because "the curse of dimensionality" problem in RBFNs, the center recurrent method tends to be more computational expensive. While the linear recurrent method provides a good compromise as can be seen from the simulation results in the next section.

Now observe that in IIR synopsis network equation (22), the total output of the unit is only the linear combination of the current output, the delayed input and the delayed output. So the recurrent loop affect the network in a linear way.

5. SIMULATION RESULTS

Three spatiotemporal local networks are tested for the example 4. in [16].

The plant is assumed to be the form

$$y(k+1) = \frac{y(k)y(k-1)y(k-2)u(k-1)(y(k-2)-1)+u(k)}{1+y^2(k)+y^2(k-1)}. \tag{29}$$

The parallel approach is adopted for both identification and testing. The input to the networks is $u(k)$, the output is $y(k)$. The number of hidden units is 10 in all three networks. The networks are trained using a random input signal uniformly distributed in the interval [-1, 1] and a step size (learning rate) of $\mu = 0.25$. The widths of the Gaussian units are fixed, while the centers and heights are updated according to the algorithms in the previous section. The centers and heights are initialized randomly in [-1, 1]. The identification processes were carried out for 1000 steps compared to the 100000 steps in[16]. The testing input to the plant and the identified model is given by $u(k) = sin(2\pi 250)$ for $k < 500$ and $u(k) = 0.8sin(2\pi 250) + 0.2sin(2\pi 25)$ for $k > 500$ for 800 steps.

1. Center recurrent: the total adjustable parameters in the network are 30. The responses of the plant and the identified model are shown in Fig. 3. The solid line is the response of the plant and the dashed line is the response of the identified neural network model. The network learns very coarsely in given steps.

2. Linear recurrent: the total adjustable parameters in the network are 30. The responses of the plant and the identified model are shown in Fig. 4. From the figure, we can see that the network learns satisfactory in given steps.

3. IIR recurrent: the first order linear IIR filter is added after each hidden unit. The total adjustable parameters in the network are 40. The responses of the plant and the identified model are shown in Fig. 5. In this case, the network also gives correct response after training.

6. CONCLUSIONS

We have presented a spatiotemporally local neural network by combining the recurrent network and the radial basis function network. Three proposed algorithms are all fast than the MLP while still keeping the modeling abilities. The linear recurrent and the IIR synopsis networks showed great improvements over the MLP and therefore are good modeling tools for the nonlinear dynamic systems. The center recurrent case can be generalized to fully recurrent RBFNs, but it tends to be more computational expensive than the other two approaches.

REFERENCES

[1] D. S. Broomhead and D. Lowe "Multivariable functional interpolation and adaptive networks", *Complex Systems*, vol. 2, pp. 321-355, 1988.

[2] T. Poggio and F. Girosi "Networks for approximation and learning", *proc. of IEEE*, vol. 78, pp. 1481-1496, September 1990.

[3] J. Park and I. W. Sandberg "Universal approximation using radial-basis function", *Neural Computation*, vol. 3, pp. 246-256, 1991.

[4] S. Chen, S. A. Billings, C. Cowan and P. M. Grant "Practical identification of NARMAX models using radial basis function", *Int. J. Control*, vol. 52, pp. 1327-1350, 1990.

[5] S. Geva and J. Sitte " A constructive method for multivariate function approximation by multilayer perceptrons", *Neural Networks*, vol. 3, pp. 621-624, July 1992.

[6] J. Moody and C. Darken, " Fast learning in networks of locally-tuned processing units", *Neural Computation*, vol. 2, pp. 281-294, September 1990.

[7] J. Moody and C. darken, "Fast learning in multiresolution hierarchies", in *Advances in neural information processing system 1* , I. D. Touretzky, ed., pp. 29-39, Morgan-Kaufmann, 1990.

[8] J. Platt, " A resource-allocating network for function interpolation", *Neural Computation*, vol. 3, pp. 213-225, 1991.

[9] E. Hartman and J. D. Keeler, "Semi-local units for prediction", *International Joint Conference on Neural Networks*, vol. 2, pp. 561-566, 1991.

[10] Y. Wong, "How Gaussian radial basis functions work", *International Joint Conference on Neural Networks*, vol. 2, pp. 133-137, 1991.

[11] F. J. Pineda, "Generalization of Back Propagation to recurrent neural networks", *Physical Review Letter*, vol. 59, No. 19, pp. 2229-2232, 1987.

[12] F. J. Pineda, "Dynamics and architecture for neural computation", *Journal of Complexity*, vol. 4, pp. 216-245, 1988.

[13] B. A. Pearlmutter, "Learning state space trajectories in recurrent neural networks", *Neural Computation*, vol. 1, pp. 263-269, 1989.

[14] R. J. Williams and D. Zipser, "A learning algorithm for continually running fully recurrent neural networks", *Neural Computation*, vol. 1, pp. 270-280, 1989.

[15] P. J. Werbos, "Backpropagation through time: what it does and how to do it", *Proc. of IEEE*, vol. 78, No. 10, October 1990.

[16] K. S. Narendra and K. Parthasarathy, "Identification and control of dynamical systems using neural network", *IEEE Transitions on Neural Networks*, vol. 1, No. 1, pp. 4-27, March 1990.

[17] A. D. Back and A. C. Tsoi, "FIR and IIR synapses: a new neural network architecture for time series modeling", *Neural Computation*, vol. 3, pp. 375-385, 1991.

[18] R. R. Leighton and B. C. Conrath, "The autoregressive backpropagation algorithm", *International Joint Conference on Neural Networks*, vol. 2, pp. 369-377, 1991.

[19] C. Ku and K. Y. Lee, "System identification and control using diagonal recurrent neural networks", *America Control Conference*, pp. 545-549, 1992.

[20] J. S. Albus, "A new approach to manipulator control: the cerebellar model articulation controller(CMAC)", *Trans. ASME, J. Dynamic Syst. Meas. Contr.*, vol 97, pp. 220-227, 1975.

[21] S. H. Lane, D. A. Handelman and J. J. Gefand, "High-order CMAC neural networks–theory and practice", *American Control Conference*, pp. 1579-1585, 1991.

[22] L. G. Kraft and D. P. Campagna, "A comparison between CMAC neural network control and two traditional adaptive control systems", *IEEE control systems magazine*, vol. 10, pp. 36-43, April 1990.

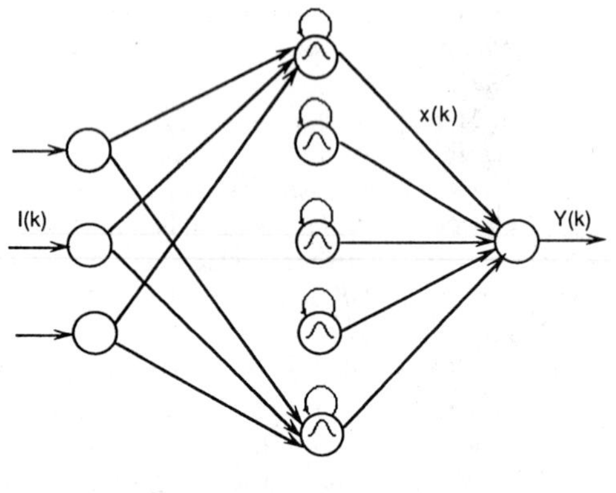

Fig. 1 Spatiotemporal Local Network

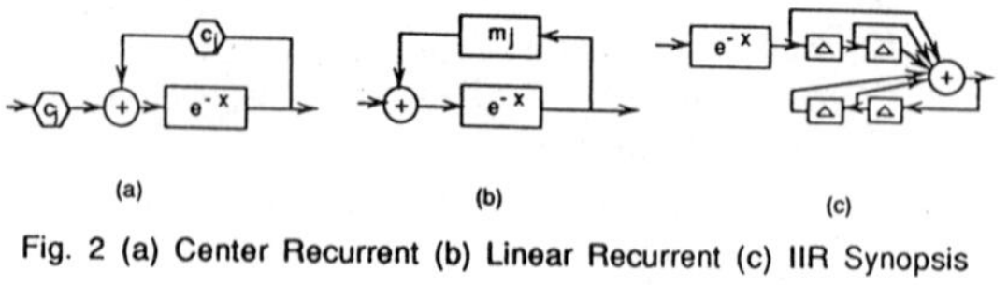

Fig. 2 (a) Center Recurrent (b) Linear Recurrent (c) IIR Synopsis

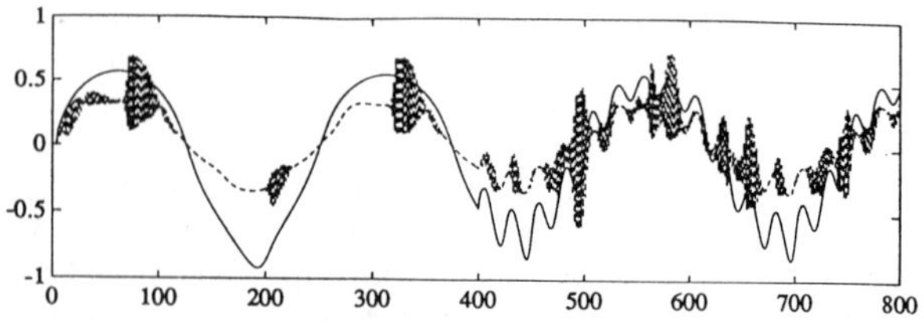

Fig. 3 Center Recurrent Network

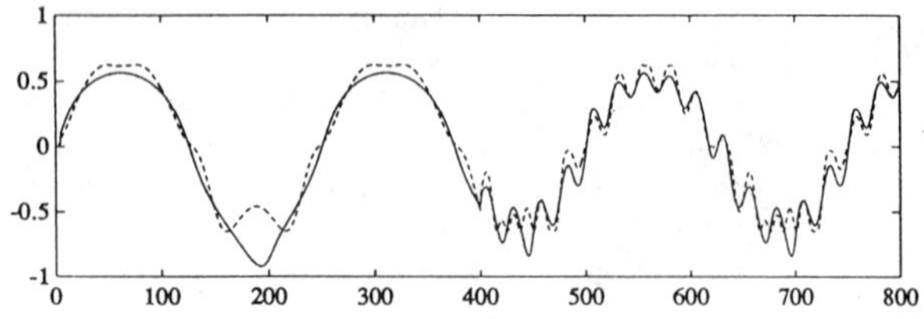

Fig. 4 Linear Recurrent Network

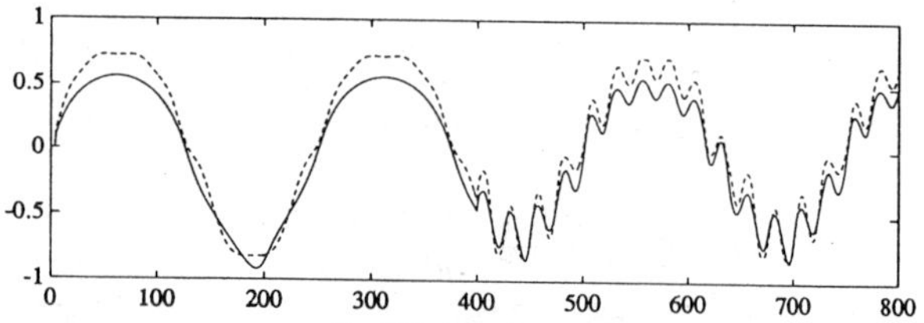

Fig. 5 IIR Synopsis Network

NEURAL-BASED IDENTIFICATION OF CONTINUOUS NONLINEAR SYSTEMS

S. Reynold Chu*, R. Shoureshi
School of Mechanical Engineering
Purdue University

Abstract

In the study presented in this paper, applications of a three-layer feedforward networks with Gaussian hidden units is used to provide the ability to learn nonlinear characteristics of continuous dynamical systems. A new training approach based on the recursive least squares is presented. Results of this expedited learning scheme are compared to those of the more traditional method of gradient descent. Convergence property of the resulting nonlinear identification scheme is derived by applying the Lyapunov stability analysis.

Introduction

The feedforward neural network is the most widely used structure of neural networks and is also the most conventional type of networks. Although the structure of feedforward networks with multiple hidden layers provides the flexibility of learning complex nonlinear mappings, the gradient based learning algorithm such as backpropagation often takes a long time to converge. In a departure from conventional network models, Moody and Darken (1988) have demonstrated that the structure of a three-layer network with highly localized but overlapping receptive fields as the activation functions at the single hidden layer can learn to predict the chaotic time series generated by the Mackey-Glass differential equation. Usually, the radial basis functions (RBF) are used to form the localized receptive fields. The most commonly used RBF is the multi-dimensional Gaussian. Recently, Girosi and Poggio (1990) have shown that a superposition of RBF can approximate continuous functions arbitrarily well. In addition, the number of RBF units required for learning a particular mapping may be less than the number of sigmoid units for the same learning task. This is because some basic convex region in the input space can be formed by a single RBF unit while a superposition of more than one sigmoid unit is required to form any convex region. Sanner and Slotine (1991) have proposed a practical method for designing Gaussian networks where the centers of Gaussian units are located on equally spaced nodes of a grid. The method is based on the multi-dimensional sampling theory and translates given smoothness properties of the nonlinearity into network specifications for a chosen degree of approximation accuracy. With fixed centers and standard deviation, the magnitudes of Gaussian units can be trained by the Recursive Least-squares method where an ever-improving estimate of the inverted Hessian guides the learning process.

The purpose of this paper is to explore the feasibility of applying the feedforward neural model to the identification of continuous-time nonlinear dynamic systems.

Backpropagation Algorithm

The backpropagation algorithm is by far the most popular algorithm for training multilayer neural networks in the supervised learning paradigm. In matrix form, the input-output mapping of the network can be written as

$$y(x) = W_L\Gamma\left\{W_{L-1}\Gamma\left[\cdots\left[W_2\Gamma\left[W_1x+\theta_1\right]+\theta_2\right]\cdots\right] + \theta_{L-1}\right\} + \theta_L \quad (1)$$

where Γ is a diagonal nonlinear operator with g being the activation function of individual neuron, W is the connection weight matrix, and θ is the bias vector. For the training of multilayer networks, the weight adjustment is normally performed by making gradient descent on some error criterion. In this paper, a deterministic criterion, the Least-Squares Error (LSE), is adopted. For continuous-time applications, the LSE with exponential averaging can be written as

$$J(t) = \int_0^t \frac{1}{2}e^T(\tau)e(\tau)\exp\left[-\int_\tau^t \frac{1}{\mu(r)}dr\right]dt \quad (2)$$

where $\mu(t)$ is the time constant of the exponential window at time t. Based on the scheme of gradient descent, the learning law corresponding to the J(t) in (2) is

$$\frac{dw_{ij}^k}{dt} = -\eta\frac{\partial J(t)}{\partial w_{ij}^k} = \eta\int_0^t e^T(\tau)\frac{\partial y(\tau)}{\partial w_{ij}^k}\exp\left[-\int_\tau^t \frac{1}{\mu(r)}dr\right]d\tau \quad (3)$$

Define z_{ij}^k to be $\frac{dw_{ij}^k}{dt}$, then the learning can be determined by the following equation of first order filter, i.e.

* Currently with Navistar Corporation.

$$\frac{dz_{ij}^k}{dt} + \frac{1}{\mu(t)} z_{ij}^k = \eta e^T(t) \frac{\partial y(t)}{\partial w_{ij}^k} \qquad z_{ij}^k(0) = 0 \tag{4}$$

where the input to the filter is $e^T(t)\frac{\partial y(t)}{\partial w_{ij}^k}$ and can be obtained by the backpropagation algorithm. The usefulness of the gradient descent method is often hampered by its slow convergence, particularly in large networks. Various methods have been sought to improve the convergence of backpropagation by utilizing the second order information of the error criterion, i.e., the inverse of the Hessian matrix. However, the added computation complexity of these methods may negate the benefit of faster convergence, particularly in the case of quasi-Newton methods. More importantly, the implementation of these methods requires multiple pass of the same training set and thus are not suitable for on-line training. Therefore, a different method, based on the Recursive Least-Squares (RLS) algorithm, is introduced later to improve the convergence of learning.

Approximation of Nonlinear Functions by Feedforward Networks

It is well known that multilayer feedforward networks can approximate arbitrarily well a continuous nonlinear function, provided that a sufficiently large number of neurons are used (Cybenko 1988,1989; Funahashi,1989; Stinchcombe and White,1989). In order to facilitate the use of linear least-squares, it is desirable to have the following form of network representation

$$y_i(\mathbf{x}) = \sum_{j=1}^{K} w_{ij}\phi_j(\mathbf{x}) + w_{i0}, \quad i = 1,...,M \tag{5}$$

where ϕ_j's belong to some set of basis functions and w_{i0} is the bias. Such form of representation can be easily mapped onto the structure of the feedforward network with only one hidden layer where ϕ_j's are the activation functions of neurons at the hidden layer. A promising set of basis functions, used for multivariable interpolation (Powell 1987), is the radial basis functions (RBF) which has the following form

$$\phi_j(\mathbf{x}) = \phi_j\,(\|(\mathbf{x} - \bar{\mathbf{x}}_j\|_w^2) \tag{6}$$

where $\|\mathbf{x} - \bar{\mathbf{x}}_j\|_w^2$ is a weighted norm defined as $(\mathbf{x} - \bar{\mathbf{x}}_j)^T W^T(\mathbf{x} - \bar{\mathbf{x}}_j)$ and W is a square and positive definite matrix. The most frequently used RBF function is the the multi-dimensional Gaussian function, because it is separable with respect to its variables. Let W be a diagonal matrix with $[W]_{ii} = 1/\sigma$, then the Gaussian function has the form

$$g(\|\mathbf{x} - \bar{\mathbf{x}}\|_w^2) = \prod_{i=1}^{N} \exp[-(x - \bar{x}_i)/\sigma_i^2] \tag{7}$$

A more practical method for designing Gaussian networks where the centers of Gaussian units are located on equally spaced nodes of a grid has been proposed. The following result is based on the study (Sanner and Slotine, 1991), using spatial sampling theory.

The general nonlinear function that $f(\mathbf{x})$ can be represented exactly in terms of the samples of $w(\mathbf{x})$, i.e.,

$$f(\mathbf{x}) = w_s(\mathbf{x}) * g(\mathbf{x}) = \int_{R^N} w(\chi)\delta_h(\chi) g(\mathbf{x}-\chi)\, d\chi$$

$$= \sum_{I\in Z^N} \int_{R^N} w(\chi)\delta(\chi-\mathbf{x}_I) g(\mathbf{x}-\chi)\, d\chi$$

Therefore,

$$f(\mathbf{x}) = \sum_{I\in Z^N} w(\mathbf{x}_I) g(\mathbf{x}-\mathbf{x}_I) \tag{8}$$

Although (8) provides a globally exact representation of a nonlinearity, it is more realistic to consider, instead, the approximation of a much larger class of functions using an extended family of interpolation functions. Here, the purpose is to approximate the actual nonlinearities frequently encountered in dynamic systems. Before investigating the suitable value of the standard deviation, consider the spatial Fourier transform of the Gaussian activation function, i.e.,

$$g(\mathbf{x}-\mathbf{x}_I) = \exp\left[\frac{-\|\mathbf{x}-\mathbf{x}_I\|^2}{\sigma^2}\right]$$

It has been shown that the Fourier transform of $g(\mathbf{x})$ has the following form (the scale factor is not included)

$$G(\mathbf{v}) = \exp\left[-\pi^2\sigma^2\|\mathbf{v}\|^2\right]$$

This indicates that the form of Gaussian function is invariant under the Fourier transformation. Also, it can be observed that a larger value of σ will result in a less localized $g(\mathbf{x})$ with more localized spectrum $G(\mathbf{v})$, and vice versa. From such observation, it can be inferred that, the smoother the function to be approximated (the smaller the value of v_c), the larger the value of σ and thus the larger samples can be used. The following combination of parameters has been suggested by Sanner and Slotine (1991) to yield good results for small number of units.

$$\sigma^2 = \frac{1}{v_c^2\pi^2} \text{ and } h^2 = \frac{\sigma^2\pi}{8} \tag{9}$$

Recursive Least-Squares Method for Weight Training

To introduce the method, first, the optimal weight based on the LSE, equation (2), will be derived. Consider the network representation (5) with Gaussian units, i.e.

$$\phi_j(\mathbf{x}) = \exp\left[\frac{-\|\mathbf{x} - \bar{\mathbf{x}}_j\|^2}{\sigma^2}\right] \triangleq g(\mathbf{x}(t);\bar{\mathbf{x}}_j,\sigma)$$

where $\bar{\mathbf{x}}_j$ and σ have been given a priori. To write the network representation in a matrix form, define

$$\psi^T(t) = [1, g(\mathbf{x}(t);\bar{\mathbf{x}}_1,\sigma), \cdots, g(\mathbf{x}(t);\bar{\mathbf{x}}_K,\sigma)]$$

$$\mathbf{w}_i^T = [w_{i0}, w_{i1}, \cdots, w_{iK}], \quad i = 1, \cdots, M$$

It can be verified that the network output would be

$$y(t)=\begin{bmatrix}\psi^T(t) & 0 & & 0\\ 0 & \psi^T(t) & & \vdots\\ \vdots & & & 0\\ 0 & \cdots & 0 & \psi^T(t)\end{bmatrix}\begin{bmatrix}w_1\\ w_2\\ \vdots\\ w_M\end{bmatrix}=\Phi^T(t)\theta \qquad (10)$$

Substituting (10) into (2) yields

$$J(t)=\int_0^t \frac{1}{2}[d(\tau)-\Phi^T(\tau)\theta(t)]^T[d(\tau)-\Phi^T(\tau)\theta(t)]$$

$$\exp\left[-\int_\tau^t \frac{1}{\mu(r)}dr\right]d\tau$$

Now, if $\theta(t)$ be the optimal solution of J(t), then

$$\theta(t)=\left[\int_0^t \Phi(\tau)\Phi^T(\tau)\exp\left[-\int_\tau^t \frac{1}{\mu r}dr\right]d\tau\right]^{-1}$$

$$\left[\int_0^t \Phi(\tau)d(\tau)\exp\left[-\int_\tau^t \frac{1}{\mu r}dr\right]d\tau\right] \qquad (11)$$

From the definition of Φ, it is easy to verify that

$$\Phi\Phi^T=\begin{bmatrix}\psi\psi^T & 0 & \cdots & 0\\ 0 & \psi\psi^T & & \vdots\\ \vdots & & & 0\\ 0 & \cdots & 0 & \psi\psi^T\end{bmatrix} \qquad \Phi d=\begin{bmatrix}\psi d_1\\ \psi d_2\\ \vdots\\ \psi d_M\end{bmatrix} \qquad (12)$$

Using the above identities, (11) can be simplified to the following

$$w_i(t)=\left[\int_0^t \psi(tau)\psi^T(\tau)\exp\left[-\int_\tau^t \frac{dr}{\mu(r)}\right]d\tau\right]^{-1}$$

$$\left[\int_0^t \psi(\tau)d_i(\tau)\exp\left[-\int_\tau^t \frac{dr}{\mu r}\right]d\tau\right] \quad i=1,\cdots,M \qquad (13)$$

Direct matrix inversion in (13) is the least favorable option due to the computation complexity. Instead, an on-line update of w_i's governed by differential equations is derived in Chu (1992). The results are presented as following: Let $\mathbf{k}(t)$ be the learning gain and W be the weight matrix from the hidden layer to the output layer, i.e.

$$W^T=[w_1 w_2 .... w_M]$$

The derived learning law is

$$\dot{W}(t)=e(t)\mathbf{k}^T(t) \qquad (14a)$$

$$e(t)=\mathbf{d}(t)-\Phi^T(t)\theta(t)=\mathbf{d}(t)-W(t)\psi(t) \qquad (14b)$$

$$\mathbf{k}(t)=P(t)\psi(t) \qquad (14c)$$

$$\dot{P}(t)=\frac{1}{\mu(t)}P(t)-\mathbf{k}(t)\mathbf{k}^T(t) \qquad (14d)$$

Convergence of the above learning algorithm can be studied by using the Lyapunov's direct method. Assume that the desired signals di's can be described as

$$d_i(t)=\phi^T(t)w_i^*, \quad i=1,...,M$$

Let the parameter estimation error be

$$\tilde{w}_i(t)=w_i^*-w_i(t), \quad i=1,...,M$$

From (14), the dynamic equation of the estimation error is described by

$$\dot{\tilde{w}}_i(t)=-P(t)\phi(t)\phi^T(t)\tilde{w}_i(t), \quad i=1,...,M \qquad (15)$$

Theorem : The learning law (14a-d) is exponentially stable if the regression vector $\phi(t)$ is persistently exciting and $\mu_{min}\le\mu(t)\le\mu_{max}$.

Proof: To prove the exponential stability of the estimation scheme, it is sufficient to prove that each $\tilde{w}_i(i=1,...,M)$ approaches zero exponentially fast. Consider the following candidate Lyapunov function:

$$V(\tilde{w}_i,t)=\frac{1}{2}\tilde{w}_i^T(t)P^{-1}(t)\tilde{w}_i(t)$$

Notice that $V(\tilde{w}_i,t)$ is positive definite. It can be shown that

$$P^{-1}(t)\ge\frac{1}{\rho}\exp\left[-\int_0^t\frac{dr}{\mu(r)}\right]I\ge\frac{1}{\rho}\exp\left[-\frac{\delta}{\mu_{min}}\right]I, \quad \text{if } t<\delta$$

$$P^{-1}(t)\ge\gamma\exp\left[-\int_{t-\delta}^t\frac{dr}{\mu(r)}\right]I\ge\gamma\exp\left[-\frac{\delta}{\mu_{min}}\right]I, \quad \text{if } t\ge\delta$$

Therefore,

$$V(\tilde{w}_i,t)\ge\frac{1}{2}\min\left\{\exp(-\delta/\mu_{min})/\rho,\ \gamma\exp(-\delta/\mu_{min})\right\}\|\tilde{w}_i\|^2$$

Now, taking time derivative of $V(\tilde{w}_i,t)$ along the trajectory of $\tilde{w}_i$ yields

$$\dot{V}(\tilde{w}_i,t)=-\frac{1}{\mu(t)}V(\tilde{w}_i,t)-\frac{1}{2}\left[\phi^T(t)\tilde{w}_i(t)\right]^2\le 0\ \frac{1}{\mu(t)}V(\tilde{w}_i,t)<0$$

Clearly, the equilibrium point $\tilde{w}_i=0$ is asymptotically stable. Moreover, due to $\dot{V}\le-\frac{1}{\mu(t)}V$, it can be shown that

$$V(\tilde{w}_i,t)\le V(\tilde{w}_{i0},0)\exp\left[-\int_0^t\frac{1}{\mu(r)}dr\right]\le V(\tilde{w}_{i0},0)\exp(-t/\mu_{max})$$

Therefore

$$\frac{1}{2}\min\{\exp(-\delta/\mu_{min})/\rho,\ \gamma\exp(-\delta/\mu_{min})\}\|\tilde{w}_i\|^2$$

$$\le\frac{1}{2\rho}\exp(-t/\mu_{max})\|\tilde{w}_{i0}\|^2$$

Thus we have

$$\alpha=\{\rho\min[\exp(-\delta/\mu_{min})/\rho,\ \gamma\exp(-\delta/\mu_{min})]\}^{-1}, \qquad \beta=1/\mu_{max}$$

Notice that the above proof is valid for arbitrary initial time t_0.

Therefore, the exponential stability of $\tilde{w}_i = 0$ is established.

Identification of Nonlinear Dynamic System

In this section, the approximation of a single-input/single-output (SISO) nonlinear dynamic system using Gaussian neural network is considered. Extension of the derivation into multi-input/multi-output (MIMO) systems is straightforward. Later, if the nonlinearity is static, state-variable filters will be incorporated into the neural identification scheme such that no derivatives of the output or input are required.

Assume that the nonlinear dynamic system to be approximated has the following form

$$y^{(n)} = f(y^{(n-1)},...,y,u^{(m)},\ldots,u), \quad n>m \tag{16}$$

Let $x = [y^{(n-1)},...,y,u^{(m)},...,u]^T$ and $d(t) = y^{(n)}(t)$. The multivariable function f(.) can be approximated by the Gaussian network, i.e.

$$\hat{f}(y^{(n-1)},...,y,u^{(m)},\ldots,u;w) = \sum_{i=1}^{K} w_i \exp\left[\frac{-\|x-\bar{x}_i\|^2}{\sigma^2}\right] + w_0 \tag{17}$$

where the parameters $\bar{x}_i$'s and σ and the number of hidden units, K, are determined a priori. Then, either the gradient descent method or the RLS based method can be used to train the weight **w**.

Next, consider the following dynamic system with static nonlinearity:

$$\left[p^n + \sum_{j=1}^{n} \alpha_j p^{j-1}\right] y + f(y) = \left[\sum_{j=1}^{m+1} \beta_j p^{j-1}\right] u, \quad n>m \tag{18}$$

where $p^j \triangleq \frac{d^j}{dt^j}$. Here, the Gaussian network is used to approximate f(y) only, i.e.,

$$\hat{f}(y;w) = \sum_{i=1}^{K} w_i \exp\left[\frac{-\|y-\bar{y}_i\|^2}{\sigma^2}\right] + w_0 \tag{19}$$

To generate the required time derivatives of y and u without differentiating the signals, the concept of state-variable filters has been employed (Landau,1979). Define the following

$$\chi_1 = \left[p^n + \sum_{j=1}^{n} \alpha_j p^{j-1}\right] y_f + z_f - \left[\sum_{j=1}^{m+1} \beta_j p^{j-1}\right] u_f$$

Using equations (19), state variable filters, and the definition of χ_1, the following dynamic system is derived

$$\dot{\chi}_1 = \chi_2 = \left[p^n + \sum_{j=1}^{n} \alpha_j p^{j-1}\right] \omega_2 + \zeta_2 - \left[\sum_{j=1}^{m+1} \beta_j p^{j-1}\right] v_2$$

$$\vdots$$

$$\dot{\chi}_{n-1} = \chi_n = \left[p^n + \sum_{j=1}^{n} \alpha_j p^{j-1}\right] \omega_n + \zeta_n - \left[\sum_{j=1}^{m+1} \beta_j p^{j-1}\right] v_n$$

$$\dot{\chi}_n = \left[p^n + \sum_{j=1}^{n} \alpha_j p^{j-1}\right] \dot{\omega}_n + \dot{\zeta}_n - \left[\sum_{j=1}^{m+1} \beta_j p^{j-1}\right] \dot{v}_n = \gamma_1 \cdot 0 - \sum_{i=1}^{n} \gamma_i \chi_i$$

Clearly, the above system is free from external input. Assume that γ_i's are chosen such that the system matrix has a set of eigenvalues with real parts less than $-\sigma(\sigma>0)$. Then, the transients will die out not slower than $\exp(-\sigma t)$. Hence, the following equivalent system is resulted

$$\left[p^n + \sum_{j=1}^{n} \alpha_j p^{j-1}\right] y_f + z_f = \left[\sum_{j=1}^{m+1} \beta_j p^{j-1}\right] u_f \tag{20}$$

And the estimation error of the identification process is

$$e = \left[p^n + \sum_{j=1}^{n} \hat{\alpha}_j p^{j-1}\right] y_f + \hat{z}_f - \left[\sum_{j=1}^{m+1} \hat{\beta}_j p^{j-1}\right] u_f \tag{21}$$

Notice that α_1 is given because it cannot be uniquely identified. Since the Gaussian network is linearly parametrized, i.e.,

$$\hat{f}(y;w) = \sum_{i=1}^{K} w_i \frac{\partial \hat{f}(y;w)}{\partial w_i} + w_0 \frac{\partial \hat{f}(y;w)}{\partial w_0} = \sum_{i=1}^{K} w_i \exp\left[\frac{-\|y-\bar{y}_i\|^2}{\sigma^2}\right] + w_0 \cdot 1$$

With the definition

$$\psi^T(t) = \left[-y_f,...,-y_f^{(n-1)}, -\frac{\partial \hat{z}_f}{\partial w_0}, \frac{-\partial \hat{z}_f}{\partial w_1}, \cdots, -\frac{\partial \hat{z}_f}{\partial w_k}, u_f,...,u_f^{(m)}\right]$$

$$\theta^T(t) = \left[\hat{\alpha}_1,...,\hat{\alpha}_{n-1}, w_0, w_1,..., w_K, \hat{\beta}_0,...,\hat{\beta}_{m+1}\right]$$

the estimation error can be written as

$$e(t) = y_f^{(n)}(t) + \alpha_1 y_f^{(1)}(t) - \psi^T(t)\theta(t) = d(t) - \psi^T(t)\theta(t)$$

Then, the learning algorithms discussed in previous sections can be applied to identify $\theta(t)$.

Results of Computer Simulation

In order to demonstrate the feasibility of training Gaussian networks with RLS algorithm, computer simulations have been performed to identify the nonlinear function of the following mechanical system

$$\ddot{y} + 2\zeta\omega_n\dot{y} + \omega_n^2 + f(y) = \omega_n^2 u$$

where $\omega_n = 2\pi \cdot 2.5$ rad/sec and $\zeta = 0.1$. Several different nonlinear functions have been tested. However, only the results for a cubic nonlinearity, $f(y) = y^3$, is presented here. The input u used in these cases contains two parts: a periodic signal from the sum of four sinusoids with distinct frequencies, i.e.,

$$1.656 \sin 2\pi t - 0.184 \sin 6\pi t + 0.0624 \sin 10\pi t - 0.03796 \sin 14\pi t$$

and a random white noise generated from a uniform distribution over (-0.15,0.15). The addition of white noise is to enrich the frequency content of input so that $\phi(t)$ is persistently excited. Figure 1 shows the network approximation of the nonlinearity at 2.5 sec (dotted line) and the initial network approximation due to random weight initialization (dashed line). Figure 2 shows the result at 5 sec. Notice that the dotted line representing the network approximation coincides with the solid line representing the cubic nonlinearity in both figures. This clearly demonstrates that the learning algorithm achieves significant improvement in network representation in a period less than 2.5 sec. Figure 3 shows the adaptation of the weights. It can be observed that weights from units close to the two ends of interval A = [-2., 2.3] exhibit slower convergence. But, this does not pose significant influence on overall performance of the network. As a comparison to the gradient-based learning, the same network with the same initial weights is trained to approximate the same cubic nonlinearity. The nonlinear dynamic system is excited by the same history of input. Figures 4 and 5 show results of network approximations at 0 sec, 5 sec, 10 sec, 40 sec, and 100 sec. Here, dotted lines represent network approximations, the dashed line represents the initial network approximation, and the solid line is the nonlinearity. Notice that the convergent speed of gradient-based learning tends to slow down significantly as the optimal solution is closing in. The superiority of RLS-based learning in both convergent speed and approximation accuracy is clearly demonstrated in this simulation.

Conclusion

This paper presented a neural-based identification scheme for nonlinear dynamic systems. Radial basis functions in form of Gaussians are used to describe nonlinear behavior of neurons. A recursive least-squares technique for learning was developed. It was shown that nonlinear functions can be learned by the devised network, and because of the RBF and RLS applications better convergence with lower number of neurons can be achieved.

References

Chu, S.R. (1992) "Neural Networks for System Identification and State Observation of Dynamical Systems," Ph.D. Thesis, School of Mechanical Engineering, Purdue University, August.

Cybenko, G.(1988), "Continuous Valued Neural Networks with Two Hidden Layers Are Sufficient," Technical Report, Department of Computer Sciences, Tufts Univ., Medfore, MA.

Cybenko, G.(1989), "Approximation by Superposition of a Sigmoidal Function," Technical Report CSRD 858, Center for Supercomputing Research and Development, Univ. of Illinois, Urbana, IL.

Funahashi K.(1989), "On the Approximate Realization of Continuous Mappings by Neural Networks," Neural Networks, Vol. 2, pp. 183-192.

Girosi, F. and T. Poggio(1990), "Networks and the Best Approximation Property," Biol. Cybernetics 63, pp.169-176.

Landau, I.D. (1979), "Adaptive Control the Model Reference Approach," Marcel Dekker, New York, NY.

Moody, J. and C. Darken(1988), "Learning with Localized Receptive Fields," in Touretzky, Hinton, and Sejnowski, editors, Proceedings of the 1988 Connectionist Models Summer School, Morgan Kaufmann, Publishers.

Powell, M.J.D.(1987), "Radial Basis Functions for Multivariable Interpolation: A review," in J. C. Mason and M.G. Cox, editors, Algorithms for Approximation. Clarendon Press, Oxford.

Sanner, R.M. and J.-J. E. Slotine (1991), "Gaussian Networks for Direct Adaptive Control," Technical Report NSL-910503, Nonlinear Systems Lab., MIT, Cambridge, MA.

Stinchcombe, M.and H. White(1989), "Universal Approximation Using Feedforward Networks with Non-sigmoid Hidden Layer Activation Functions," in Proceedings of the International Joint Conference on Neural Networks, pp. I-607-I-611, Washington, D.C., IEEE TAB Neural Network Committe.

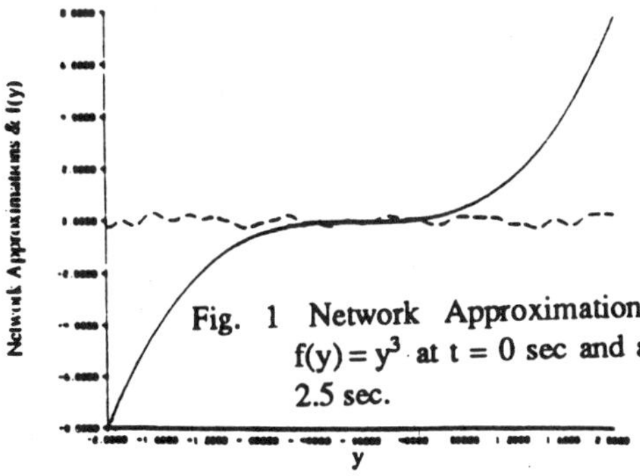

Fig. 1 Network Approximations of $f(y) = y^3$ at t = 0 sec and at t = 2.5 sec.

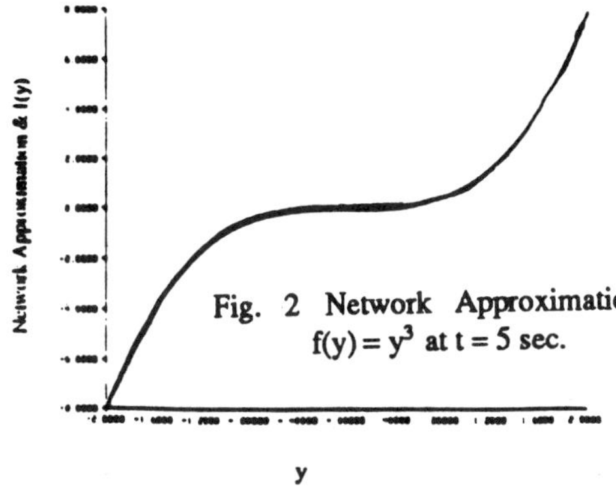

Fig. 2 Network Approximations of $f(y) = y^3$ at t = 5 sec.

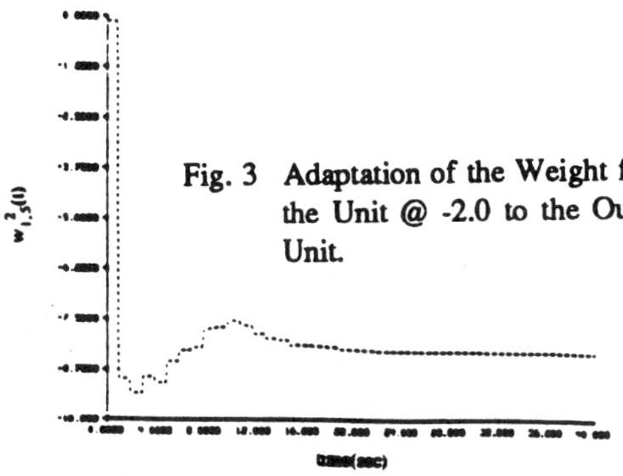

Fig. 3 Adaptation of the Weight from the Unit @ -2.0 to the Output Unit.

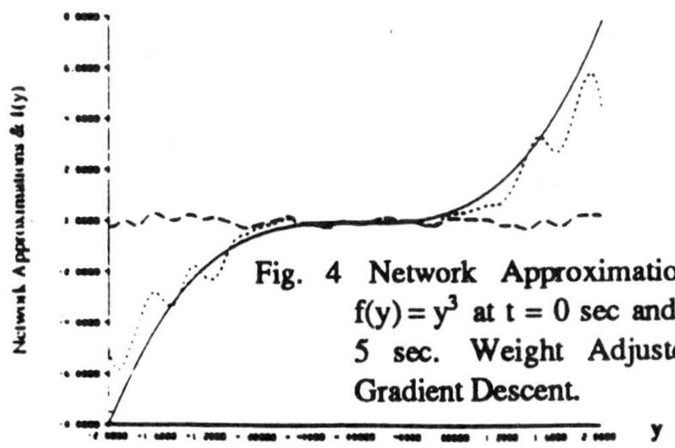

Fig. 4 Network Approximations of $f(y) = y^3$ at t = 0 sec and at t = 5 sec. Weight Adjusted Gradient Descent.

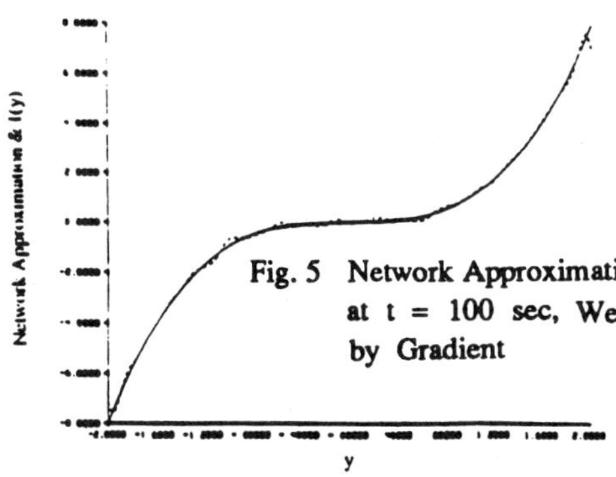

Fig. 5 Network Approximation of $f(y) = y^3$ at t = 100 sec, Weight Adjusted by Gradient

IMMUNIZED NEURAL NETWORKS FOR COMPLEX SYSTEM IDENTIFICATION

J. C. Neidhoefer and K. Krishnakumar

Box 870280, Department of Aerospace Engineering
The University of Alabama, Tuscaloosa, AL 35487

ABSTRACT

This paper addresses the possibility of using artificial neural networks along with concepts from the field of immunology in the modeling of complex dynamic systems. A biological immune system can be thought of as a very robust system. It is capable of dealing with an enormous variety of disturbances. Biological immune systems use a finite number of discrete "building blocks" to achieve this robustness. These building blocks can be thought of as pieces of a puzzle, which must be put together in a specific way to neutralize, remove, or destroy each unique disturbance the system encounters. This paper outlines a technique which attempts to reproduce the robustness of a biological immune system in an artificial neural network.

INTRODUCTION

Since the formalization of the back-propagation technique, there has been a resurgence of interest in the theory, design, and use of neural network (NN) technology. Classical back-propagation nets have been closely scrutinized by the scientific community over the past several years, and many useful and practical applications have been found for them.

In the field of engineering, one of the most common uses of neural networks is that of "model copying" (or system identification, see figure 1). Standard backprop networks have been found to be excellent in the copying of static system models, or input/output models that are stationary. It has been found, however, that mapping very complex time-varying functions, for example, those found in nonlinear, highly coupled, and possibly unstable systems, can be difficult, if not impossible, when using traditional backprop networks.

One of the biggest problems with using standard neural networks to model complex dynamic systems is that such NN models suffer from a lack of robustness. To expand upon this, as a model is made more and more general, it will suffer from an unacceptable loss of accuracy. It is possible to train a standard neural net to give accurate outputs for a static system, or a specific input/output characteristic of a dynamic system. However, a dynamic system can be constantly changing its characteristics. If the system happens to be at the state for which it was trained, the net outputs will be accurate, however, if the system changes its characteristics, erroneous outputs will result. This is due to the fact that there is no provision in a standard static neural network for changing the net model (i.e. the weights and connections) to cope with dynamically changing system characteristics. This can be compared with a biological entity whose immune system is capable of combating only one particular disease (or disturbance). If a new disease is encountered by the immune system, it will be incapable of destroying it, and the system will crash. A biological immune system can be thought of as a very robust system. It is capable of dealing with an enormous variety of disturbances. Biological immune systems use a finite number of discrete "building blocks" to achieve this robustness. These building blocks can be thought of as pieces of a puzzle, which must be put together in a specific way to neutralize, remove, or destroy each unique disturbance the system encounters.

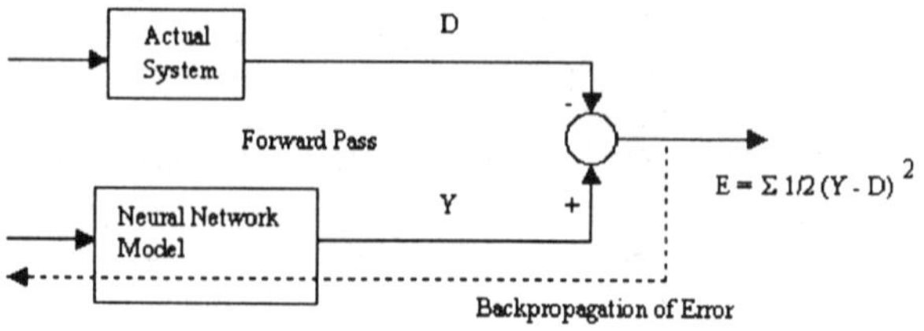

Figure 1. NN with backpropagation of error

In this study, it is attempted to reproduce the robustness of a biological immune system in an artificial neural network (ANN), through use of an

ANN building block scheme. In this paper, a general knowledge of classical neural network theory along with a working knowledge of GA is assumed. Reference [1] presents details of this approach and an application related to a neuro-control problem.

CONCEPTS FROM IMMUNOLOGY

The environment in which we live, along with all other biological creatures, is hostile in the effect that it contains a vast number of infectious agents including viruses, bacteria, fungi, etc. These agents would be deadly to their hosts if it were not for the robustness and adaptability of most biological immune systems. The immune system is made up of two major divisions, the innate immune system, and the adaptive immune system [2]. The innate immune system acts as a first line of defence against infectious agents, most of which are stopped here. If the defenses of the innate immune system are breached, the adaptive immune system is called upon to produce a specific reaction to the infectious agent. The adaptive immune system then remembers the agent, and the reaction, to help prevent a subsequent attack .

When an infectious agent attacks a biological system, the job of the immune system is to remove, neutralize or destroy the hostile agent. The way the immune system carries out this task is by producing molecules called *antibodies*. Antibodies are a class of molecules produced by B lymphocytes (B cells) of the adaptive immune system. These Antibodies bind with the foreign agent to subsequently neutralize them and remove the threat. Antibodies do not bind to the whole infectious agent, but rather to one of the many molecules on the agent's surface. The molecules to which the antibodies adhere are called *antigens*. Antigens each have a set of antigenic determinants called *epitopes*. Epitopes are molecular shapes recognized by the antibodies of the immune system. Antibodies are effectively bifunctional molecules. One part is relatively static, this part binds to receptors of B cells, while the other part is extremely variable, and is responsible for binding to many different infectious agents. It is the second (variable) part which provides the immune system with its amazing robustness and adaptability. Antibodies are produced by randomly recombining specific segments of a DNA molecule. Once a match is found on the epitope level, a signal is given to the specific B lymphocyte which produces that antibody, and more of it is produced. Thus the antibodies overwhelm the foreign agent, and the threat is nullified.

Though the whole process seems complex at first, the underlying principles are simple: identify the antigen, then design and produce antibodies which are capable of destroying them. Mathematically, antigens are recognized by breaking them down into subspaces, and antibodies are created as the inverses of these subspaces. To generate these subspaces, mathematical equivalents of DNA building blocks (which are the fundamental units from which all biological creatures are made) are used.

IMMUNIZED NEURAL NETWORKS

Immunized neural networks use concepts from the field of immunology along with classical neural networks to attempt to reproduce the robustness and adaptability of a biological immune system. Any attempt to mimic the building block process of the immune system in an artificial neural network scheme should contain a definition of the proposed network structure along with a mathematical definition of the subspaces or building blocks.

The following development of the proposed immunized neural network structure will address which types of network partitioning will best mimic the innate immune system, the adaptive immune system, and the antibody-antigen coupling through the epitopes. Figure 2 presents a general block diagram of the proposed neural net structure. The proposed structure has the following attributes:

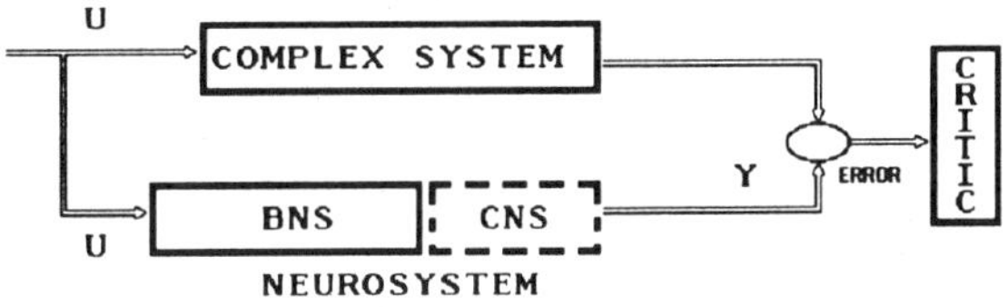

Figure 2. Immunized Neural Network Structure

<u>The Constant Meso-Structure:</u> The solid lines in figure 2 represent the base-line neuro-system model (BNS). This model is designed to represent an average behavior of the uncertain system. Since this design is carried out off-line, any standard technique can be used for its synthesis. The base-line system is analogous the static portion of the antibodies.

<u>The Changeable Meso-Structure:</u> The dashed lines in figure 2 represent the changeable neuro-system model (CNS). This represents the variable region of the antibody and epitope equivalents. This structure must be adapted on-line. To include the

innate immunity equivalence, the changeable neuro-system models that are known a priori can be stored in look-up tables or in another network which can be used to produce the right antibody and CNS models. Similar to the variable region of the antibodies, the changeable neuro-models provide diversity to the immunized neural net structure.

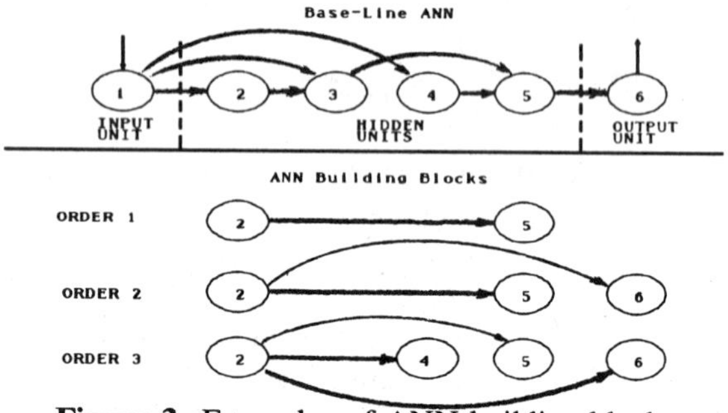

Figure 3. Examples of ANN building blocks

It is necessary at this point to specify exactly what ANN building blocks are, and how they are identified. In this study, ANN building blocks are defined as a neural network connection (or family of connections) along with its associated weight, which contributes in establishing an accurate mapping for a class of input-output characteristics. Building blocks can be of different order. The order of a building block specifies the number of specific connections defined in the building block. Examples of building blocks are shown in figure 3. After obtaining the BNS (the BNS can be thought of as being made up of high order building blocks common to the whole class of input-output characteristics), several new networks are learned using non-average representations of the system and these are then used to define lower order ANN building blocks. These building blocks represent estimates of the system uncertainty and variations that are available.

To identify first order building blocks, we need a priori definitions of the uncertainties. These definitions need not be complete, but should represent the best knowledge the user has on these uncertainties. The identification of ANN building blocks can be summarized as follows:

(1) An average representation of the system is first identified. The end result will be an ANN with optimal connections and optimal weights representing the BNS.

(2) To identify the CNS system, randomly select a set of system uncertainties from the class of uncertainties given.

(3) Code the connections and strengths using the representation given in figure 4, these represent the ANN building blocks.

(4) Repeat the above steps as often as possible for the CNS or until the whole class of uncertainties is covered.

(5) Calculate the statistics (mean and standard deviation) of the weights for these building blocks

Once the ANN building blocks have been identified and coded, they are stored as a long string of concatenated building blocks. This will represent the analogous DNA structure for the given system. For on-line processing, a population of CNS networks are randomly constructed from the available building blocks, forming a population of messy strings (See figure 5). Next we find the best string that will represent the CNS through recombination, selection, and hyper-mutation of these strings.

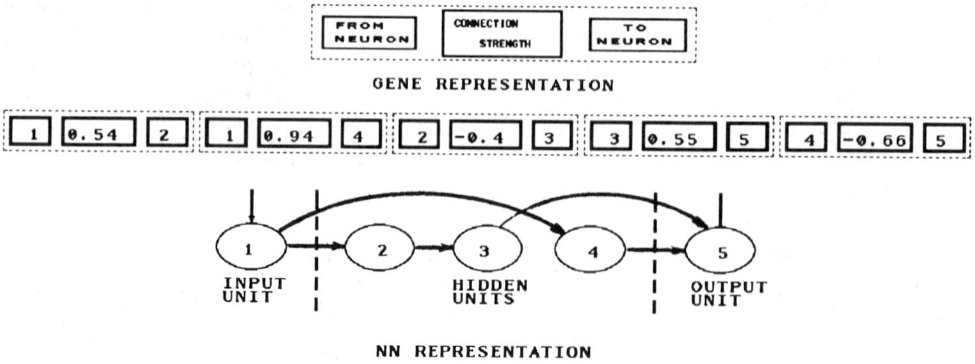

Figure 4. Neural net genetic coding

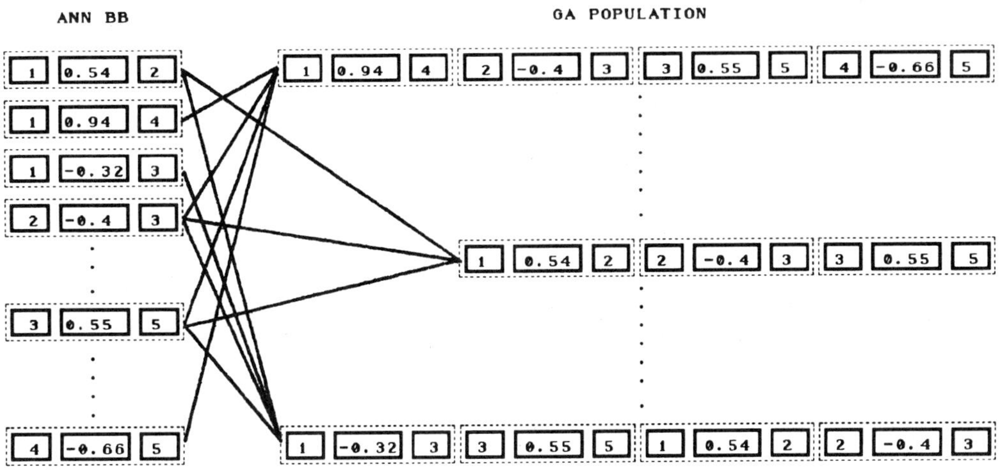

Figure 5. Creation of a population of messy strings

The steps are as follows:

(1) From a population of N messy strings, arrive at a near-optimal CNS network using recombination, mutation, and selection. Optimality will be decided by an on-line critic. Mutation takes place only on the weights assuming a Gaussian probability distribution of these weights.

(2) Ideally, it will be desirable to have a population of all the possible CNS networks. Since this is not possible, we select a finite population of N messy strings and to ensure diversity, in every generation we introduce N/2 new messy strings drawn randomly from the available ANN building blocks.

(3) Once a near-optimal CNS network has been found, hyper-mutation is applied to the weights. In this step, no recombination is conducted, and no new strings are introduced. The selection operator is retained as it increases the number of high-affinity (or highly fit) CNS networks in the population.

The actual on-line processing is done using genetic algorithms and, in particular, messy genetic algorithms [3]. Unlike any other technique, the genetic algorithm (GA) achieves its objective through a mix of random swapping and copying guided by a Darwinistic "survival of the fittest" strategy. GA possess great similarities to biological evolution and also uses the idea of building blocks. The operators used for the recombination phase are similar to those used by Goldberg et al [3]--cut, splice, and mutation. The cut operation is conducted with a specified gene-wise cut probability, p_k, such that the actual probability, $p_c=\min\{p_k(L-1),1\}$, where L is the current string length. The splice operator concatenates two strings at random with specified probability, p_s. Mutation is conducted only on the connection strengths (weights) using a small mutation rate. Figure 6 presents a sample sequence of operators in action. After each cut and splice operation, the strings can grow longer or shorter. Selection is carried out using a binary tournament selection scheme. In the hyper-mutation phase, the connection strengths are mutated using a probability of mutation p_m. The probability distribution for the mutation operator is assumed to be Gaussian and is derived using step 6 as presented above..

APPLICATIONS

It is often desirable to model dynamic systems using some form of a neural network scheme and architecture. As stated earlier, standard backprop NN are almost useless in cases where a system has rapidly changing characteristics. The on-line adaptiveness of the immunized neural networks method actually makes the neural net a dynamic system, thus providing the net with the capability to cope with changing system characteristics. Examples of problems in which this method would be useful include: on-line control of uncertain systems; adaptive control in problems involving system failure; and control of systems with continually changing system characteristics.

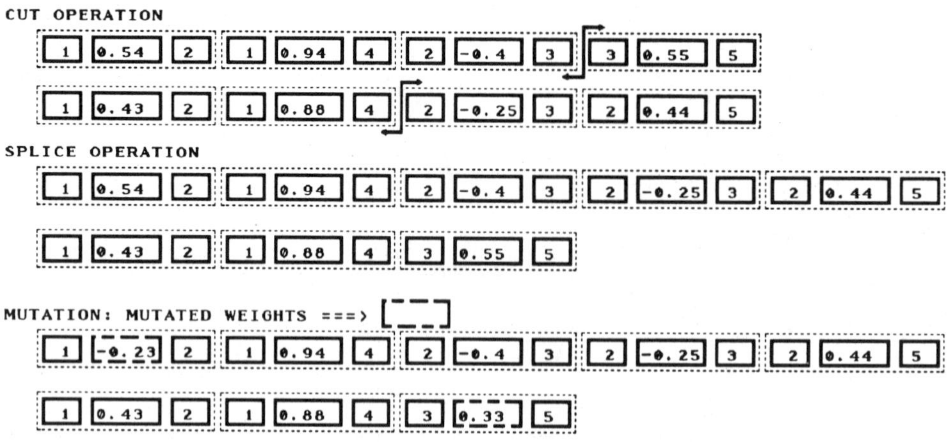

Figure 6. Cut, splice, and mutation operators

At the time of this writing these concepts have been tested on a UH-1 helicopter longitudinal hover system with positive results [1]. Also, research is presently being conducted in the area of high performance aircraft control using immunized neural networks. Since the characteristics are changing rapidly and continuously in such a system, a highly adaptive control system is necessary. Immunized neural networks should provide the desired adaptability. It is also postulated that an aircraft control system designed using immunized neural networks should be adaptable enough to provide positive control throughout certain system failures. The above research issues are currently under investigation.

ACKNOWLEDGEMENT

This material is based upon work supported by the National Science Foundation under Grant No. ECS-9113283.

REFERENCES

[1] KrishnaKumar, K., Immunized Neuro-Control: Concepts and Initial Implementation Results, The University of Alabama, Tuscaloosa, BER Report No. 513-177, AL., 1992.

[2] Roitt, I., Brostoff, J., and Male, D. Immunology, Gower Medical Publishing Company, Inc, 1989.

[3] Goldberg, D.E., Deb, K., and Korb, B. An Investigation of Messy Genetic Algorithms (TCGA Report No. 90005), The University of Alabama, The Clearinghouse for Genetic Algorithms, 1990.

[4] Freeman, J.A. and Skapura, D.M. Neural Networks Algorithms, Applications, and Programming Techniques, Addison Wesley Publishing Company, Inc., 1991.

On Learning Properties of Neuro-Fuzzy Phase-Lead Compensators

Kazuo TANAKA and Manabu SANO

Department of Mechanical Systems Engineering
Kanazawa University
2-40-20 Kodatsuno Kanazawa 920 Japan
Tel. +81-762-61-2101 (ext.405)
Fax. +81-762-63-3849
Email tanaka@kicews2.ms.t.kanazawa-u.ac.jp

Abstract - This paper discusses learning properties of neuro-fuzzy phase-lead compensator which is a self-learning fuzzy controller by neural network. The compensator is constructed by introducing frequency characteristics such as gain crossover frequency and phase margin. We apply the neuro-fuzzy phase-lead compensator to an unknown nonlinear plant and consider its learning properties.

1. Introduction

Fuzzy control was first introduced in the early 1970's by Mamdani [1]. However, we lack at present systematic controller design methods although fuzzy control has been applied to many real industrial processes. We proposed a method of fuzzy phase-lead compensation based on frequency characteristics [6]. This paper discusses its self-learning properties by neural networks. The main feature of the compensator is to have parameters for effectively improving frequency characteristics. We will show the validity of the self-learning properties by considering the learning process in simulation experiments.

Let us define symbols which will be used in this paper.

G(s):A transfer function of a controlled object.
Gc(S):A transfer function of a linear PI controller (a+b·s)/s.
Gc*(S):A transfer function of a linear PI controller (a*+b*·s)/s.
wCG:A gain crossover frequency of open loop transfer function Gc(s)G(s).

2. Phase-lead Compensation

Some papers [2]~[5] dealt with phase-lead compensations in fuzzy control systems. However, we pointed out in [6] that the phase-lead compensations are not sufficient from theoretical viewpoints. We derived an important theorem, which is related to an effective phase-lead compensation, by introducing concept of frequency characteristics such as gain crossover frequency and phase margin [6]. The theorem is given below.

[Theorem] [6]

If we use

$$G^*c(s)=(a^*+b^*\cdot s)/s$$

instead of

$$Gc(s)=(a+b\cdot s)/s,$$

where

$$[a^* \; b^*] = [a \; b]\cdot \mathbf{T}(\theta_c, w_{CG}), \qquad (1)$$

$$\mathbf{T}(\theta_C, w_{CG}) = \begin{bmatrix} \cos(-\theta_C) & -\dfrac{1}{w_{CG}}\sin(-\theta_C) \\ w_{CG}\sin(-\theta_C) & \cos(-\theta_C) \end{bmatrix}, \qquad (2)$$

then the gain crossover frequency and the phase margin of open loop transfer function of G*c(s)G(s) *become* wCG *and* θm+θc, *respectively.*

A fuzzy phase-lead compensator can be constructed by using the transformation matrix of Eq.(2);

Rule 1:IF Φ is about "-π or 0 or π"
THEN

$$\dot{u}_1 = [a \; b]\cdot\begin{bmatrix} e \\ \dot{e}\end{bmatrix}, \qquad (3)$$

Rule 2: IF Φ is about "-π/2 or π/2"
THEN

$$\dot{u}_2 = [a \; b]\cdot \mathbf{T}(\theta_C, w_{CG})\cdot\begin{bmatrix} e \\ \dot{e}\end{bmatrix} = [a^* \; b^*]\cdot\begin{bmatrix} e \\ \dot{e}\end{bmatrix},$$

where $\Phi = \tan^{-1}(\dot{e}/e)$. The final output of this controller is calculated as

$$\dot{u} = \frac{w_1\dot{u}_1 + w_2\dot{u}_2}{w_1 + w_2}, \qquad (4)$$

where w_1 is the membership value of the fuzzy set, about "-π or 0 or π", of Rule 1 and w_2 is the membership value of the fuzzy set, about "-π/2 or π/2", of Rule 2. Fig.1 shows the fuzzy sets.

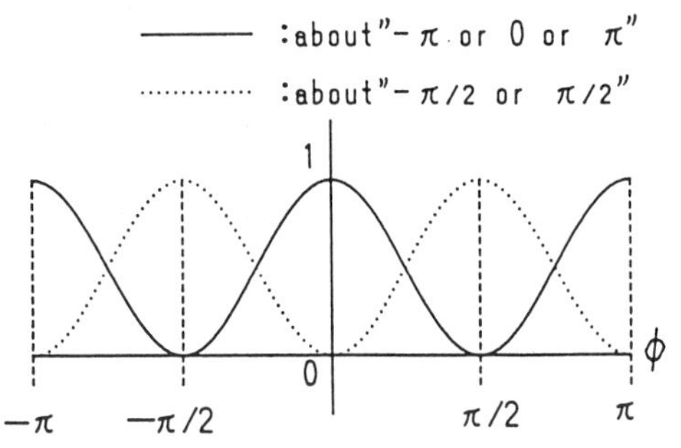

Fig.1 Fuzzy sets.

The parameters of the fuzzy compensator are a, b, wCG and θc in Eq.(3). The controller design is to determine these parameters.

0-7803-0891-3/93$03.00

3. Learning algorithm

In this section, a self-learning control for the fuzzy phase-lead compensation is realized by Widrow-Hoff learning rule which is a basic learning method in neural networks. Fig.2 shows the self-learning control system. The block, which consists of fuzzy controller and learning block (Widrow-Hoff learning rule), is called "Neuro-Fuzzy compensator".

The idea, which optimizes parameters of fuzzy model by using Widrow-Hoff learning rule, was first introduced by Ichihashi [7]~[10].

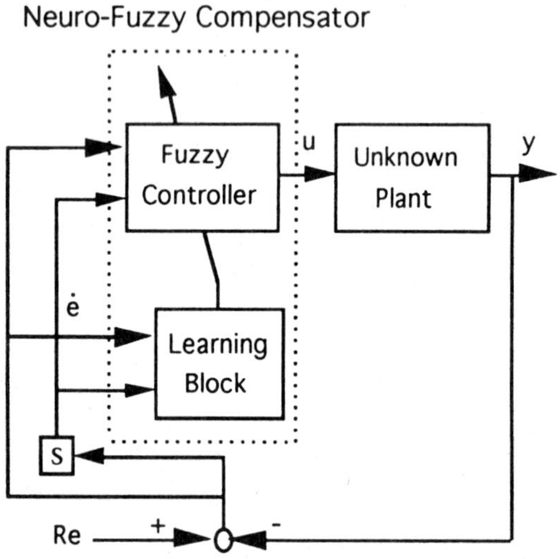

Fig.2 Self-learning control system.

From Eqs.(2), (3) and (4), we can obtain

$$\dot{u} = K\cdot\left[\left(w_1\cdot T+w_2\cdot\{T\cdot\cos(-\theta_c)+\sin(-\theta_c)\}\right)\cdot e + \left(w_1+w_2\cdot\{\cos(-\theta_c)-T\cdot\sin(-\theta_c)\}\right)\cdot\dot{e}\right], \quad (6)$$

where

K=b, T=a/b and wCG=1.

Let us define performance function as follows.

$$J(K, T, \theta_C) = \int_0^{t_0} (Re - y)^2\, dt, \quad (5)$$

where Re is setpoint and y is the output of the unknown plant.

The learning laws can be defined as follows [7]-[10].

$$K(n+1) = K(n) - \varepsilon_1 \cdot \frac{\partial J(K, T, \theta_C)}{\partial K}, \quad (7)$$

$$T(n+1) = T(n) - \varepsilon_2 \cdot \frac{\partial J(K, T, \theta_C)}{\partial T}, \quad (8)$$

$$\theta_C(n+1) = \theta_C(n) - \varepsilon_3 \cdot \frac{\partial J(K, T, \theta_C)}{\partial \theta_C}, \quad (9)$$

where n denotes the number of learning. ε_1, ε_2 and ε_3 are the learning coefficients. Ichihashi applied the learning method based on Widrow-Hoff learning rule to design of open loop optimal fuzzy control and used an exact model of non-linear plant to optimize a given performance function [9]-[10]. It is, however, difficult to apply open loop controller to real plants and to obtain an exact model of the plant in advance. Therefore, we assume in this paper that

(1)plant is unknown, and

(2)we use a feedback controller as shown in Fig.2.

To realize the learning laws in (7)~(9), we have to calculate the gradients, that is, the values of

$$\frac{\partial J(K, T, \theta_C)}{\partial K}, \quad \frac{\partial J(K, T, \theta_C)}{\partial T} \quad \text{and} \quad \frac{\partial J(K, T, \theta_C)}{\partial \theta_C}$$

The gradients are defines as

$$\frac{\partial J(K,T,\theta_C)}{\partial K} \approx \frac{J(K(n)+\Delta K, T(n), \theta_C(n)) - J(K(n), T(n), \theta_C(n))}{\Delta K}, \quad (10)$$

$$\frac{\partial J(K,T,\theta_C)}{\partial T} \approx \frac{J(K(n), T(n)+\Delta T, \theta_C(n)) - J(K(n), T(n), \theta_C(n))}{\Delta T}, \quad (11)$$

$$\frac{\partial J(K,T,\theta_C)}{\partial \theta_C} \approx \frac{J(K(n), T(n), \theta_C(n)+\Delta\theta_C) - J(K(n), T(n), \theta_C(n))}{\Delta\theta_C}, \quad (12)$$

where $J(K(n)+\Delta K, T(n), \theta_C(n))$ denotes the value of performance function when the controller parameters are $K(n)+\Delta K$, $T(n)$ and $\theta_C(n)$, where ΔK is a small value.

We construct a learning algorithm for the compensator.

[Learning algorithm]

[step 1]

Determine the values of ΔK, ΔT and $\Delta\theta_C$. Determine the values of $\varepsilon 1$, $\varepsilon 2$ and $\varepsilon 3$. n=0, where n denotes the number of learning. Determine the initial values of K(n), T(n) and $\theta_C(n)$.

[step 2]

Calculate the gradients, Eqs.(10)~(12).

[step 3]

Calculate the controller parameters, K(n+1), T(n+1) and $\theta_C(n+1)$, from Eqs.(7)~(9).

[step 4]

Control the plant by using the compensator with the parameters, K(n+1), T(n+1) and $\theta_C(n+1)$. Calculate the values of the performance index J form Eq.(5).

[step 5]

If the value of J converges then end else n=n+1 and go to [step 2].

Next, we apply the neuro-fuzzy compensator to level control of a two-tank system which is a non-linear plant. It is assumed in the simulation that the plant is unknown. Fig. 3 shows the two-tank system. The dynamics of the plant can be described as

$$\dot{h}_1(t) = \{q_1(t) - q_2(t)\} / D_1, \quad (13)$$

$$q_2(t) = A_1 \sqrt{2 \cdot g \cdot h_2(t)}, \quad (14)$$

$$\dot{h}_2(t) = \{q_2(t) - q_3(t)\} / D_2(h_2(t), \quad (15)$$

$$q_3(t) = A_2 \sqrt{2 \cdot g \cdot h_2(t)}, \quad (16)$$

$$D_2(h_2(t)) = D_{20} / \{0.5 \cdot log\left(h_2(t) + 1.0\right) + 1.0\}, \quad (17)$$

where D_1 and D_2 are the cross sectional areas of each tank. D_2 changes according to the value of $h_2(t)$ as shown in (17). This means that dynamics of the plant is different according to the value of $h_2(t)$. The tank system becomes more sensitive when the value of $h_2(t)$ is higher. D_{20} denotes the cross sectional area of bottom of Tank 2. A_1 and A_2 are the cross sectional areas of each pipe.

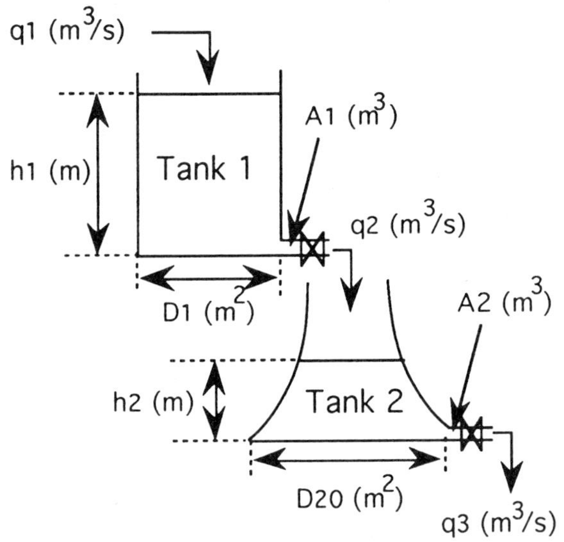

Fig.3 Two-tank system

Table 1 shows two simulation conditions of initial values of controller parameters. Other simulation conditions are as follows;t_0=80 (sec.), ε_1=0.0001, ε_2=0.000001, ε_3=0.0001, D_1=2.0, D_{20}=1.0, A_1=0.1, A_2=0.1, ΔK=0.01, ΔT=0.01 and $\Delta\theta_c$=0.01.

Table 1 Conditions of initial parameters

	K	T	θ_c (deg.)
Condition 1	0.01	0.01	0
Condition 2	2	0.3	0

Figures 4 and 5 show the self-learning control results. It can be found that the self-learning controller works well. Figures 6 and 7 show the controller parameters for Conditions 1 and 2, respectively. Figures 8 and 9 show the values of performance function for Conditions 1 and 2, respectively.

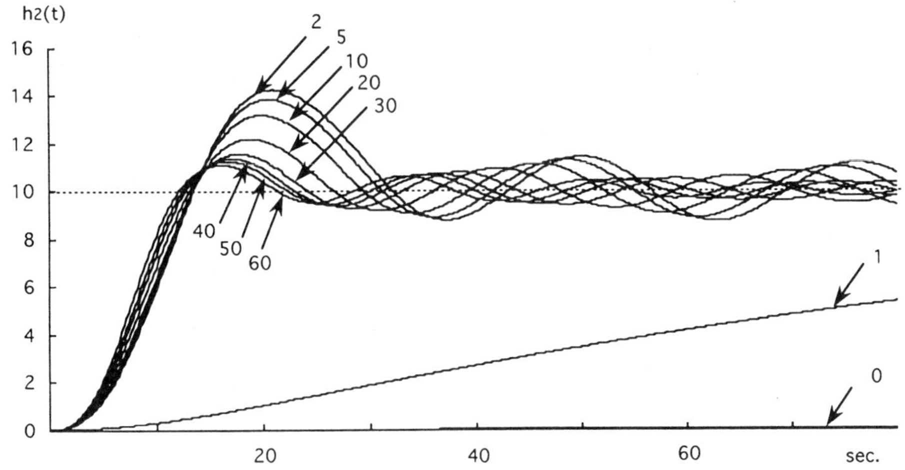

(1) Self-learning control result.

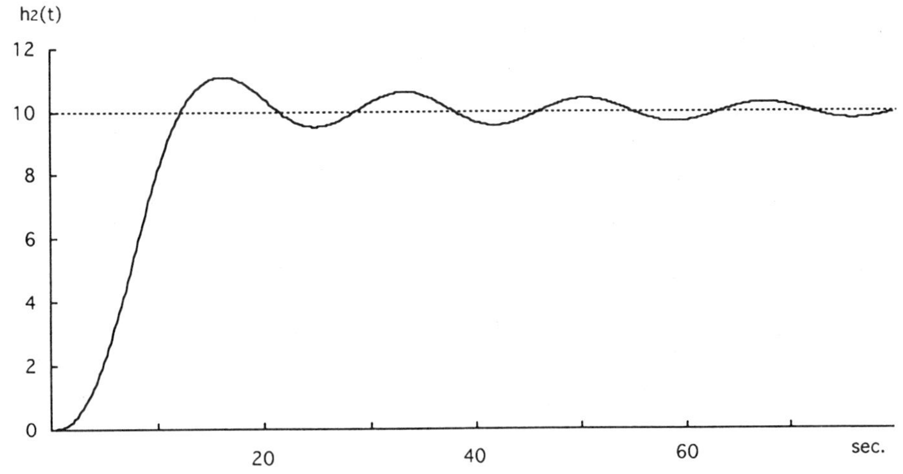

(2) Final result (n=68).

Fig.4 Control result. (Condition 1)

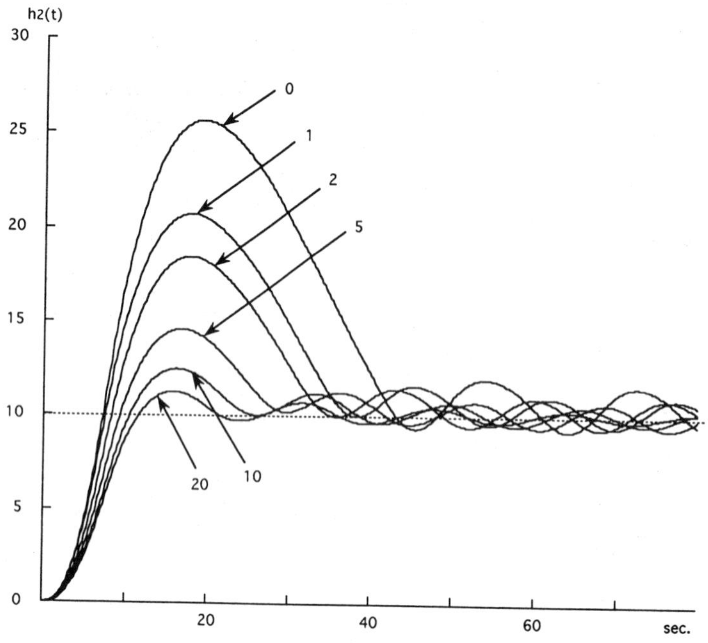

(1) Self-learning control result.

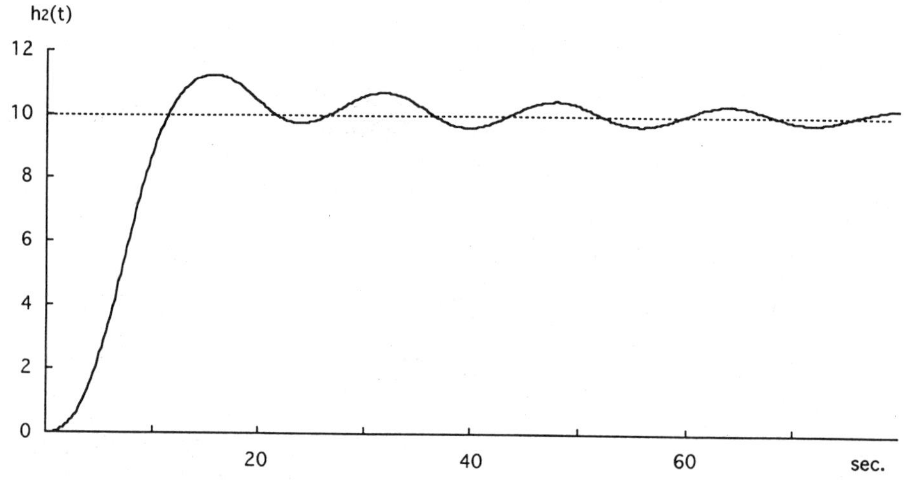

(2) Final result (n=21).

Fig.5 Control result. (Condition 2)

The main feature of the compensator is to have parameters for effectively improving frequency characteristics. We will show the validity of the self-learning properties by considering the learning process of the controller parameters in the simulation experiments. The purpose of controller design in this paper is to successively adjust controller parameters so as to minimize the given performance function, Eq.(5). To minimize the performance function, the speed of response and the damping characteristics (overshoot) have to be improved. We can improve the speed of response and the damping characteristics by increasing gain and phase margin, respectively. The parameter, K, is strongly related to gain characteristics. By increasing the value of K, we can improve the speed of response. On the other hand, θ_C is strongly related to phase characteristics. By increasing the value of θ_C, we can improve the damping characteristics, that is, overshoot. In Condition 1, the initial values of K(0) and T(0) are so small. Therefore, to obtain good speed of response, the value of K must be increased. However, overshoot is caused by increasing gain because phase margin decreases by increasing gain. To improve overshoot, the values of θ_C must be increased. It can be seen from Figure 6 that the self-learning compensator increases the values of K and θ_C. In Condition 2, there is a large overshoot when n=0, because the initial value of K are not small value. Therefore, the value of K dose not have to be increased. Only θ_C must be increased in this condition. It can be seen in Figure 7 that the compensator increases only θ_C. Thus, we can say from consideration of such frequency characteristics that the neuro-fuzzy phase-lead compensator realizes an effective self-learning.

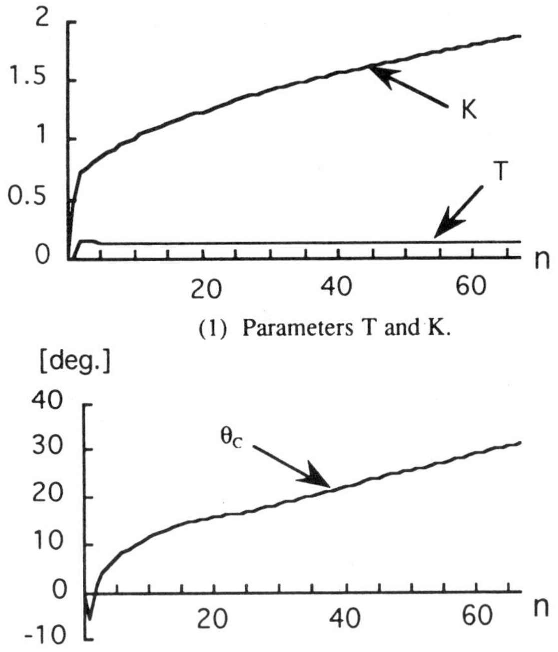

(1) Parameters T and K.

(2) Parameter θ_C.

Fig.6 Parameters T K and θ_C. (Condition 1)

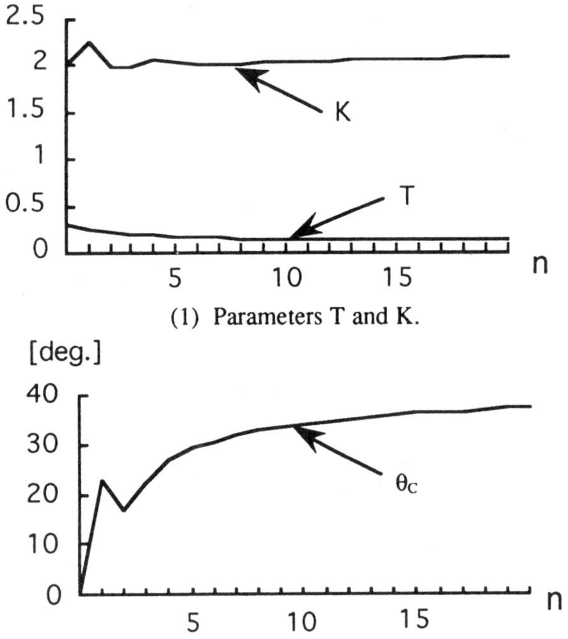

(1) Parameters T and K.

(2) Parameter θ_C.

Fig.7 Parameters T K and θ_C. (Condition 2)

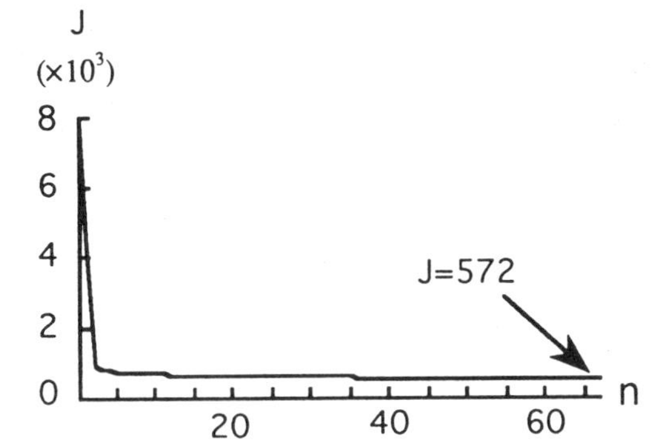

Fig.8 Values of performance function. (Condition 1)

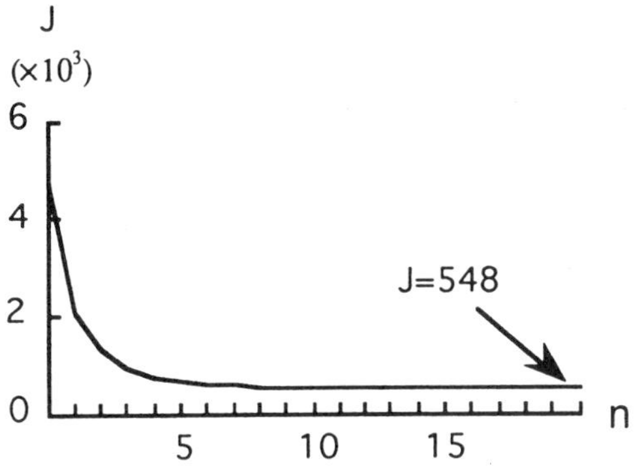

Fig.9 Values of performance function. (Condition 2)

Next, we change the value of D_{20} to 2 for Condition 1. Fig.10 shows the control result. Even in this case, the neuro-fuzzy phase-lead compensator works well.

4. Conclusion

This paper has discussed learning properties of neuro-fuzzy phase-lead compensator which is a self-learning fuzzy controller by neural network. The compensator was constructed by introducing frequency characteristics. We applied the neuro-fuzzy phase-lead compensator to an unknown nonlinear plant and considered its learning properties.

The authors wish to thank Mr. Murakami of Yokogawa Electric Corporation for his useful comments on this study.

References

[1]E.H.Mamdani:Applications of Fuzzy Algorithms for Control of Simple Dynamic Plant, Proc. IEE, vol.121, no.12, pp.1585-1588 (1974).

[2]M.Sugeno:Fuzzy Control, Nikkankogyou Publ.Co., (1988).

[3]K.Tanaka and M.Sano : A New Tuning Method of Fuzzy Control, Proceeding of 4th IFSA World Congress, vol.1, pp.207-210 (1991)

[4]A.Ishigame et al.:Design of Electric Power System Stabilizer Based on Fuzzy Control Theory, IEEE International Conference on Fuzzy Systems, pp.973-980 (1992).

[5] A.Fujii, T.Ueyama and N.Yoshitani:Design of Fuzzy Controller using Frequency Response, Proceeding of 5th Fuzzy System Symposium, pp.115-120 (1989) (in Japanese).

[6]K.Tanaka, M.Sano:Design of Fuzzy Controllers Based on Frequency and Transient Characteristics, 2nd IEEE International Conference on Fuzzy Systems, vol.1,

pp.111-116. (1993)
[7]H.Ichihashi and T.Watanabe:Learning Control by Fuzzy Models Using a Simplified Fuzzy Reasoning, vol.2, no.3, pp.429-437 (1990). (in Japanese)
[8]H.Ichihashi:Iterative Fuzzy Modeling and a Hierarchical Network, Proceedings of IFSA'91, pp.49-52.
[9]M. Tokunaga and H. Ichihashi: Back-Upper Control of a Trailer Truck by Neuro-Fuzzy Optimal Control, Proc. of 8th Fuzzy Systems Symposium, May 1992, pp.49-52 (in Japanese).
[10]H. Ichihashi and T. Wakamatsu:Neuro-Fuzzy Minimum Torque Change Control of DD Manipulator, Proc. of 9th Fuzzy Systems Symposium, May 1993, pp.461-464 (in Japanese)

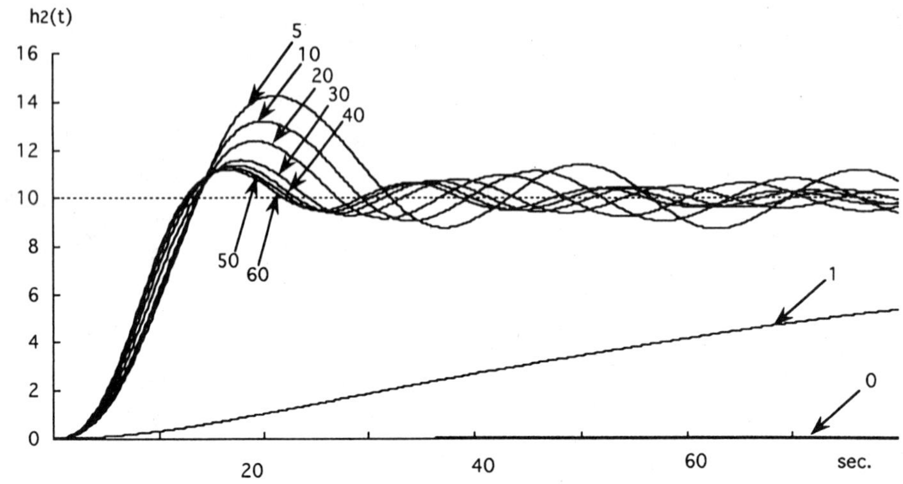

(1) Self-learning control result.

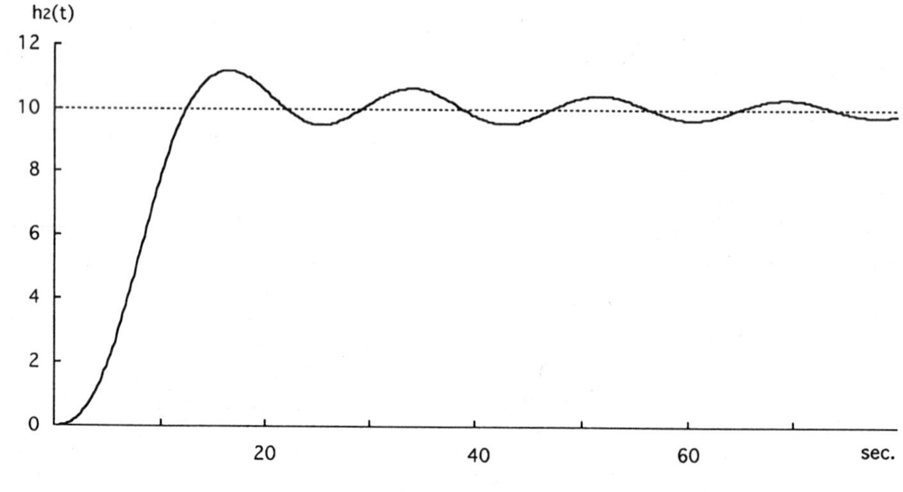

(2) Final result (n=61).

Fig.10 Control result.

A Fuzzy Adaptive Controller Using Reinforcement Learning Neural Networks

Augustine O. Esogbue
James A. Murrell
School of Industrial and Systems Engineering
Georgia Institute of Technology
Atlanta, Georgia 30332-0205

***Abstract*—This paper describes an adaptive controller for complex processes which is capable of learning effective control using process data and improving its control through on-line adaptation. The controller is applicable to processes with multivariable states and with uncertain or nonlinear dynamics for which analytical models or standard control algorithms are either impractical or cannot be derived. This controller performs a fuzzy discretization of the process state and control variable spaces and implements fuzzy logic control rules as a fuzzy relation. The membership functions of the fuzzy discretization are adjusted on-line and the fuzzy control rules are learned using a performance measure as feedback reinforcement. The fuzzy discretization procedure employs a data compression technique permitting multivariable state vector inputs. The controller is implemented with neural networks. Simulation results with the controller applied to a simple dynamical system demonstrate the effectiveness of the controller.**

I. INTRODUCTION

Fuzzy control has proven effective for complex, nonlinear, imprecisely-defined processes for which standard models and controls are impractical or cannot be derived. However, deriving fuzzy control rules is often difficult and time-consuming. Furthermore, problems of high-dimensionality are incurred in the implementation of controls for systems with multiple inputs and outputs. More efficient and systematic methods for knowledge acquisition and fuzzy controller synthesis are needed, such as adaptive fuzzy controllers capable of learning from process data to automatically generate a set of fuzzy control rules and improve on them over time.

Considerable work has been done in this area [1], [2], [3], [4], [5], [6], [7]. The controller proposed here has a unique combination of features and capabilities. It is an adaptive fuzzy controller capable of learning from process data on-line. This controller performs a fuzzy discretization of the process state and control variable spaces and implements fuzzy logic control rules as a fuzzy relation. The membership functions of the fuzzy discretization are adjusted on-line and the fuzzy relation is learned using a performance measure as feedback reinforcement, requiring little prior knowledge about the process; no training data sets nor any error signal derived from knowledge of the desired plant trajectory are needed. The fuzzy discretization procedure employs a statistical data compression technique permitting multivariable state vector inputs. Additional plant variables can be added without a geometric increase in the complexity of the controller structure. This procedure extracts the essential information from each variable needed to form fuzzy subsets of the process state space. While it adapts both the membership functions and the control rule state-control association, the controller primarily learns the control rule associations, unlike many other methods which fix the rule relationships and adjust the membership functions. The controller is implmented with neural networks, featuring a self-organizing neural network, a reinforcement learning neural network, and an associative memory network.

II. THE CONTROLLER OPERATION

The operation of the controller is summarized here. At each interval of a discrete time sequence, the current process state vector is input to the controller. Its membership in each of several reference fuzzy subsets of the input space is calculated in terms of its similarity to the ideal, prototype member of each fuzzy set. Initially the locations of the prototype vectors in the state space are uniformly distributed. Throughout the time sequence, an adaptive algorithm adjusts these locations to reflect the actual clustering of the state vectors into fuzzy sets. The dispersion of the corresponding membership functions are also adapted to the state vector inputs by a similar algorithm. Once an input state has been given its fuzzy characterization in terms of the reference fuzzy sets, the appropriate control fuzzy set is selected. Initially, the selection is arbitrary, but a learning algorithm based on the reinforcement of a performance measure is used to increase the frequency with which good controls are selected. In the process, the controller learns a fuzzy relation between the input state vector and output control vector which embodies the fuzzy control rules. After the learning phase, the fuzzy relation is used to calculate fuzzy control in terms of the reference fuzzy sets of the control space. From this, a crisp control vector is computed.

The controller has five subsystems: the Statistical Fuzzy Discretization Network (SFDN), Fuzzy Correlation Network (FCN), Stochastic Learning Correlation Network (SLCN), Control Activation Network (CAN), and the Performance Evaluation System (PES) . A block diagram of these and the plant is shown in Fig. 1.

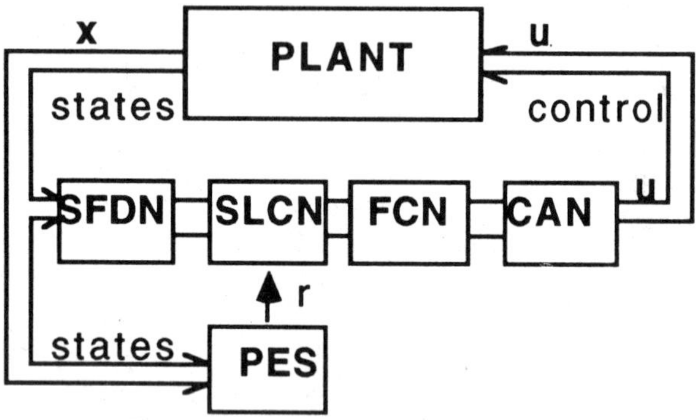

Fig. 1. Controller subsystems and plant

A. Statistical Fuzzy Discretization Network (SFDN)

This subsystem consists of a network of automata nodes ("neurons") arranged in a grid (see Fig. 2). Each node receives as its input the current process state vector. Every time a vector is input, each node computes an output that represents the degree of membership in the fuzzy subset of the input space that corresponds to that node. This output, called the node activation, is a measure of the degree of similarity of the input state vector to the ideal or prototype member of that fuzzy set. It is computed as some combination of the state vector and a location parameter vector associated with that node which represents the prototype process state for the corresponding fuzzy set. Also associated with each node is a parameter that encodes the degree of dispersion or spread of its fuzzy set membership function used to calculate the node activation. For a particular membership function form, the location parameters and spread parameter together define a fuzzy set. The SFDN thus performs a fuzzy discretization, inducing a fuzzy partition of the state space X into reference fuzzy subsets $X_1, X_2, \ldots, X_r$, each represented by a node in the grid (see [8]).

If the measure of similarity is closeness in terms of Euclidean distance, the location of any vector in the state space should result in the corresponding location on the node map being most activated. Similar inputs should result in large activations of nodes which are close to each other in the grid. In the case of a 2-dimensional state space and 2-dimensional grid, the node grid forms a fuzzy map of the input space. The topological ordering and distances among vectors in the state space are preserved in the ordering and proportional distances among the location vectors of the nodes in the map. The process state is then characterized by its fuzzy location on this 2-dimensional fuzzy map based on its similarity to the prototypes of the fuzzy sets defined by the nodes of the map. This can be generalized for a state space of more than two dimensions and for similarity measures other than the Euclidean metric. If the state space were more than 2-dimensional, order and distance could not both be preserved in a 2-dimensional map, but the relative order and closeness (i.e., the topological ordering) could be preserved. (For discussion, see [9].) The choice of similarity measure depends on the nature of the particular process to be controlled. For example, measures such as the normalized inner product (correlation) emphasize the relationships among the components, i.e., the "shape" or pattern in the vector rather than the actual magnitudes of each component. While other fuzzy discretization methods often rely on clustering algorithms that use only a distance metric as a measure, the network described may use alternative similarity measures.

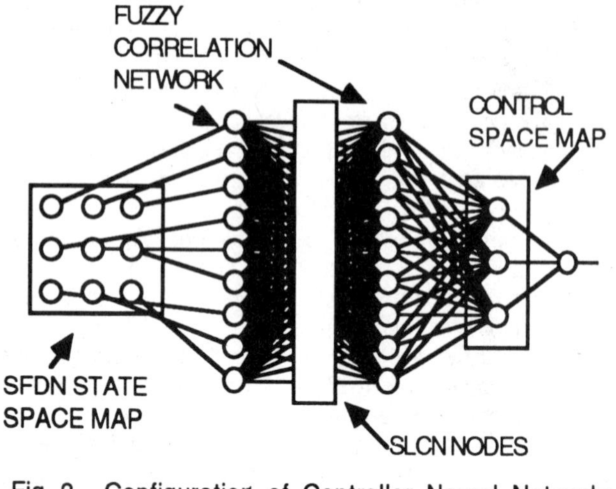

Fig. 2. Configuration of Controller Neural Networks

The state space must be restricted by setting upper and lower bounds in each dimension. The precision of the fuzzy discretization is determined by the number of nodes in the grid relative to the number of state space dimensions and the size of the bounded intervals in each dimension. Other fuzzy discretization schemes generate a complete set of fuzzy subset terms for each dimension of the space, thereby increasing geometrically the potential number of fuzzy rules as the dimension increases. In this method, there is one set of fuzzy terms whatever the dimension of the state space. Whether the number of nodes needs to be increased as the dimension increases is a matter of discretion involving a trade-off between the precision of the fuzzification and a polynomial (rather than geometric) increase in the number of nodes.

It is assumed that little is known a priori about the process, so a meaningful aggregation of the process states into fuzzy sets is not known. Thus, the location parameter vectors are initially distributed throughout the state space so that they are in order and uniformly spaced according to the similarity measure. With the Euclidean distance similarity measure, the initial distribution would be the usual uniform distribution.

The network described here is an extension of Kohonen's self-organizing feature map to fuzzy characterization of dynamic plant states [9]. The output of the ith node in the map is

$$a_i = \exp(-\|\boldsymbol{x} - \boldsymbol{m}_i\| / s_i) \tag{9}$$

where $\boldsymbol{x}$ is the state vector input, $\boldsymbol{m}_i$ is the vector of location parameters and s_i the spread parameter for the ith node, and it is assumed that the choice of similarity measure is the Euclidean metric and the functional form of the membership functions is a gaussian function. Thus, the vector $\boldsymbol{a}$ of node activations is the fuzzy hyperstate due to input state vector $\boldsymbol{x}$:

$$\boldsymbol{a} = (\pi_{X_1}(\boldsymbol{x}), \ldots, \pi_{X_r}(\boldsymbol{x}))^{\mathrm{T}} \tag{10}$$

where $\pi_{X_i}(\bullet)$ is the membership function for fuzzy set X_i given by (9).

A sequence of state vectors is input to the network over time, and an adjustment algorithm adapts the location parameters to reflect the actual clustering of the state vectors by which the aggregation into fuzzy subsets is determined. A simplified version of the update rule of the jth component of $\boldsymbol{m}_i$ for this example is

$$m_{ij,k+1} = \begin{cases} m_{ij,k} + \alpha_k(x_{j,k} - m_{ij,k}) & \text{for } i \in T_{c_k} \\ m_{ij,k} & \text{otherwise} \end{cases} \tag{11}$$

where k indexes the time step of the algorithm, T_{c_k} is a small neighborhood of nodes in the grid within a radius c_k around the node most activated by $\mathbf{x}_k$, and α_k and c_k are decreasing functions of k. The basic concept for updating the spread parameter is given by

$$s_{i,k+1} = \begin{cases} s_{i,k} + \eta_k(|x_{j,k} - m_{ij,k}|^2 - s_{i,k}) & \text{for } i \in T_{c_k} \\ s_{i,k} & \text{otherwise} \end{cases} \tag{12}$$

where η_k is also a decreasing function of k.

The usual Kohonen algorithm requires an uncorrelated time sequence of inputs, whereas the sequence of states from a dynamical process is usually highly correlated. To employ the above algorithm, it is necessary to avoid the correlated sequence by one of several possible methods. For example, the sequence could be infrequently sampled, i.e., the algorithm time step k is larger than the time step t of the input sequence. Alternatively, the data could be collected together in a batch which is then randomized before it is applied to the inputs.

The SFDN provides a means of aggregating similar plant states, thus permitting implementation of the control as a discrete relation. The adaptation update equations are of the simple delta-rule type, which is more easily implemented in real time than clustering algorithms and permits the parallel distributed computation of neural networks.

B. Fuzzy Correlation Network (FCN)

The Fuzzy Correlation Network implements the fuzzy control rules as a fuzzy relation $\boldsymbol{G}$ (learned by the SLCN) which associates the collection of fuzzy sets $X_1, \ldots, X_r$ for input vectors $x \in X$ with the fuzzy sets $U_1, \ldots, U_s$ for the controls $u \in U$. This is accomplished with a fuzzy associative memory (FAM) or correlation network [10], [11]. This can be illustrated as two parallel strings of nodes (see Fig. 2). The ith node on one side represents the degree to which X_i has been selected, given by the SFDN node output a_i for state x. Each of these is linked to every node on the other side. The output b_j of the jth node on the other side indicates the degree to which fuzzy output set U_j is the correct choice given the activations of the X_i's, or the "firing strength" of each rule for which that fuzzy control is the consequent. The connection weight parameter g_{ij} indicates the degree to which X_i relates to U_j. The control rule "If $\boldsymbol{x}$ is X_i then $\boldsymbol{u}$ is U_j" is represented by a strong link g_{ij} between node X_i and node U_j. The network connection weight matrix $\boldsymbol{G} = \{g_{ij}\}$ specfies a fuzzy relation on $\{X_1,\ldots,X_r\} \times \{U_1,\ldots,U_s\}$. Thus, given input activation $\boldsymbol{a}$, the fuzzy hyperstate, the fuzzy control vector is given by

$$\boldsymbol{b}^{\mathrm{T}} = \sigma(\boldsymbol{a}^{\mathrm{T}}\boldsymbol{G}) \tag{13}$$

where σ is a vector-valued function whose components are $b_j = \sigma_j(\boldsymbol{a}^{\mathrm{T}}\boldsymbol{G}_{\bullet j})$, $\boldsymbol{G}_{\bullet j}$ is the jth column of $\boldsymbol{G}$, and each σ_j is some type of limiting function, (i.e., σ_i satisfies $\sigma_i(\alpha)\to 0$ as $\alpha \to -\infty$ and $\sigma_i(\alpha)\to 1$ as $\alpha \to \infty$), such as a sigmoid function. Thus, this implementation uses the product and limited-sum logic operators instead of the common min-max logic (see [12]). The product/limited-sum logic is easily implemented with a neural network associative memory.

C. Stochastic Learning Correlation Network (SLCN)

The purpose of this subsystem is to test and learn the effectiveness of pairing a particular control vector fuzzy set with each given state vector fuzzy set, using the performance evaluation provided by the Performance Evaluation System (PES), then use this knowledge base to generate the fuzzy control relation used by the FCN. Both the SLCN and the FCN receive as input the fuzzy hyperstate $\boldsymbol{a}$ output by the state map grid of the SFDN. The first phase of operation of the controller is a learning phase in which the fuzzy control vector $\boldsymbol{b}$ is generated by the SLCN. In the second phase of operation, the fuzzy relation learned by the SLCN is used by the FCN to generate $\boldsymbol{b}$.

Initially, nothing is known about what control vector gives the best response when the process is in a given state. So, a fuzzy output is just picked and the performance measure indicates how good the selection was. If it was not that good, the controller will be less inclined to pick that control again the next time the system enters that fuzzy state. If the selection was good, that control action is reinforced, so that it is more likely to be selected next time. The network that implements this is akin to stochastic learning automata described by Narendra [13], [14].

The Stochastic Learning Correlation Network consists of a matrix of nodes where each row corresponds to a particular fuzzy input state and each column to a particular fuzzy control action. The degree of activation of a node indicates the fuzzy degree to which it selects the control fuzzy subset to which it is assigned. Each node has a spread parameter h_{ij} for the ith fuzzy state and the jth fuzzy control. The location parameters λ_{ij} (scalar) are adjusted so that they always fall at the center of the spread function. In this case, a box-shaped function defined on a bounded interval is used. Thus, the output of the node for the ith fuzzy state and the jth fuzzy control is given by

$$c_{ij,t} = \begin{cases} 1 & \text{if } \lambda_{ij,t} - h_{ij,t} < \xi_t < \lambda_{ij,t} + h_{ij,t} \\ 0 & \text{otherwise} \end{cases} \tag{14}$$

$$\lambda_{ij,t} = \sum_{k=1}^{j-1} h_{ij,t} + \frac{1}{2} h_{ij,t} \tag{15}$$

where $h_{ij,t}$ and $\lambda_{ij,t}$ are location and spread parameters, respectively, at time t for node (i,j), and $\xi_t \in [0,1]$ is generated by a chaotic or pseudo-random process and serves as the input to the node. The node with the largest spread parameter is then the one that will have the maximum activation most often. The fuzzy control vector **b** is given by

$$b_{j,t} = \begin{cases} c_{ij,t} & \text{for } i = \text{argmax}(a_i) \\ 0 & \text{otherwise} \end{cases} \tag{16}$$

When i is the index of the most activated input fuzzy set, then the most activated node in the ith row of the SLCN node matrix selects the control fuzzy set.

The update algorithm for h_{ij} is given as

$$h_{ij,t+1} = (h_{ij,t} + r_t\, a_{i,t}\, b_{j,t}\, \gamma_{ij,t}) \,/\, (1 + \textstyle\sum_j r_t\, a_{i,t}\, b_{j,t}\, \gamma_{ij,t}) \tag{17}$$

$$\gamma_{ij,t} = \begin{cases} h_{ij,t} & \text{if } r_t < 0 \\ 1 - h_{ij,t} & \text{if } r_t \geq 0 \end{cases} \tag{18}$$

where r_t is the reinforcement which is a function of the performance measure p_t, and $a_{i,t}$ and $b_{i,t}$ are the input and output activations, respectively, for the ith fuzzy state and j^{th} fuzzy control at time t. The product $a_{i,t}\, b_{j,t}$ is the association or correlation between the state and control fuzzy sets. The quantities p_t and r_t are computed by the PES described in Sct. II.E. Initially $h_{ij} = 1/|U|$ for $j = 1$ to $|U|$, i.e., the spread parameters of the nodes for fuzzy state i are set equal to each other, so one control would be picked as often as any other. Then this procedure maintains the sets $C_{i,t}=\{g_{ij,t}\,; j=1, 2, ..., |U|\}$ and $D_{i,t}=\{h_{ij,t}\,; j=1, 2, ..., |U|\}$ each as a unit simplex. Thus, the control is stochastically selected by using the set $D_{i,t}=\{h_{ij,t}\,; j=1, 2, ..., |U|\}$ as a probability distribution over the fuzzy discretization of control set U.

The update algorithm of (17)-(18) weights most heavily the connection between a given (fuzzy discretized) state and the applied control which resulted in the best performance measure. This is essentially the same heuristic that is often used when fuzzy control rules are developed off-line by human experts rather than by on-line adaptive control. Each spread parameter indicates the level of performance for the corresponding fuzzy action when at a particular fuzzy state. The best action is the prototype of good performance and the other parameters indicate how close to that the other choices are. As the SLCN matrix learns which fuzzy control gives the best results for each fuzzy state, the parameters of the fuzzy relation can be computed using the spread parameters. The fuzzy relation parameters g_{ij} are given as follows:

$$g_{ij,t+1} = \phi(h_{i1,t}, h_{i2,t}, \ldots, h_{is,t}) \tag{19}$$

where $\phi(\bullet)$ is a high pass filter function; a simple and adequate implementation would be

$$g_{ij,t+1} = \frac{\sigma(h_{ij,t})}{1 + \sum_j \sigma(h_{ij,t})} \tag{20}$$

$$\sigma(\alpha) = \begin{cases} \alpha - 1/|U| & \text{if } \alpha > 1/|U| \\ 0 & \text{otherwise} \end{cases} \tag{21}$$

Thus, in the second phase of operation, rather than stochastically selecting the fuzzy control using using the SLCN nodes, the fuzzy control $\boldsymbol{b}$ is calculated by the FCN as $\boldsymbol{b}^T = \sigma(\boldsymbol{a}^T \boldsymbol{G})$. The second phase can begin as the learning process of the spread parameters becomes mature. If the process is time-varying and has shifted enough so that the existing control policy of the fuzzy relation is no longer adequate, then the learning mode can be shifted back to the initial phase to learn a new control policy. This second phase is a forcing of a fixed policy as opposed to the random policy given by the SLCN. The two phases can be interspersed, so that the fixed policy phase increases in frequency as the uncertainty decreases. Continued occasional use of the learning phase allows the controller to continue to improve. This mixing of randomized policies with the forcing of fixed policies is useful for those plants which have only a small random component. The level of learning or certainty in the relation parameters can be measured with an entropy measure on $C_{i,t}$, $D_{i,t}$ or the components of $\boldsymbol{b}$. For example,

$$e_i = -\sum_{k=1}^{|U|} g_{ik} \ln(g_{ik}) \quad \text{or} \quad e = -\sum_{k=1}^{|U|} b_k \ln(b_k) \tag{22}$$

and the forcing frequency can be set to be a decreasing function of e or of all the e_i.

The adaptive control described here is dual control in which the dual objectives are achieving good control and obtaining sufficiently variable inputs to make good statistical estimates. The stochastic selection of the controls provides the persistent excitation and randomization needed for consistent estimation of the relation $\boldsymbol{G}$ via the estimated quantities p_t, the performance.

D. Control Activation Network (CAN)

The input to the Control Activation Network is the fuzzy control vector $\boldsymbol{b}$. This fuzzy control is defuzzified to produce a crisp output quantity $\boldsymbol{u}$, which is a vector for multivariable control processes. Each CAN node has its location parameter vector set to the desired control vector prototype levels. Its input is the vector $\boldsymbol{b}$, and its output is a crisp control vector

u. The nodes can be set up as a map network to adapt the fuzzy sets according to the control vectors that are actually being output from the controller.

Using the max criterion defuzzification method, the B_i node with the largest activation (degree of truth) triggers the activation of the CAN node whose output is the prototype value $\overline{u}_j$ corresponding to the fuzzy set B_j. Alternatively, in the center of area method, u is calculated as the normalized weighted sum over the fuzzy sets B_i in which the weights are the activations b_j, given as

$$u = \left(\sum_{k=1}^{|U|} b_k s_k \overline{u}_k \right) \Bigg/ \sum_{k=1}^{|U|} b_k \qquad (23)$$

where s_k are the spread parameters for the output fuzzy set membership functions. If the membership function form is symmetrical, then the effect of the spread is trivial.

E. Performance Evaluation System (PES)

The particular nature of the plant or process to be controlled and the characterization of the desired performance dictate the details of how the performance evaluation network is configured. When a performance measure is available which is an analytical function of the plant states or output, then the reinforcment signal r_t is simply a normalization of the performance measure p_t to lie in the interval [—1,1] or [0,1]. It is often the case, however, that complex processes which have no known well-defined plant model also do not have a well-defined formula for computing performance. Rather, there is a certain qualitative goal or objective to be reached, but it is not known what the values of the plant variables should be when that goal is reached. Even when a formula in terms of the variables is known, there is often an unknown delay between the control action taken and the effect on the plant variables, so that the result of the current control is not known until some future time. In such cases, various methods of estimating the performance evaluation function must be used. Our investigation into performance function estimation methods will be reported elsewhere.

The most straight-forward approach to the situation in which a qualitative determination of reaching the goal is given only after a period of many time intervals is described here. Reaching the goal is indicated by $p_t = 1$ (success) and reaching forbidden states (such as plant shutdown due to variables out-of-bounds) is indicated by —1 (failure). For each state entered at each time, a control action is taken. The average performance over time of this state-control pair is computed and updated whenever there is a success or failure. The reinforcement signal r_t can then simply be the current value of this average for the current state-control pair that just occurred.

III. RESULTS AND PROJECT STATUS

The ability of the controller to learn effective control has been tested through simulations in which the controller is applied to the inverted pendulum problem [15] with two state variables and one control variable. The dynamic equations and parameters are the same as those used in [2]. In these experiments, the controller uses a 5 by 5 node state map, a 1 by 5 node control map, the Euclidean metric and gaussian membership functions for similarity, and adapts the state space fuzzy sets but not the control fuzzy sets. The performance measure is the cumulated average method described in Sct. II.E., where failure is the pole angle exeeeding +12 or —12 degrees from vertical, or angular velocity exceeding +25 or —25, and success is achieving a membership degree of at least 0.9 in a gaussian membership function centered at the 0 degree, 0 angular velocity point (for the set "near zero"). A new trial begins after every failure with randomly selected initial states within the above ranges.

Each run uses a different inital seed for the pseudo-random generator. There is a high degree of variability in the learning phase, so rather than test how many trials it takes to balance the pole, the test is to determine how well the controller learned the control surface after fixed numbers of trials. The controller was run in the learning phase for 25, 50 and 100 trials. At these intervals, the controller was switched to the second phase and its response tested for initial states (10,0), (—10,0), (7,7), (—7,7), (7,—7), (—7,—7), and (0,0). If the controller did not drive the state directly to a point near (0,0), with small final acceleration, then the second phase trial was stopped. The points (0,0), (—7,7) and (7,—7) are easy, and the controller was sometimes able to drive the state to (0,0) after 25 trials. At 50 trials, the controller was sometimes able to drive the controller to near (0,0) for inital state (—10,0) or (10,0). In all but a few cases, 100 trials were required to learn a control surface that could drive all of the inital points to near (0,0) within about 1000 time steps (1 second of real time). Fig. 3 shows the time response of the angle and angular velocity, and Fig. 4 shows the phase space trajectory for initial state (10,0) using the relation weights learned after 100 trials. The distorted grid in Fig. 4 shows the locations of the state space map node vectors.

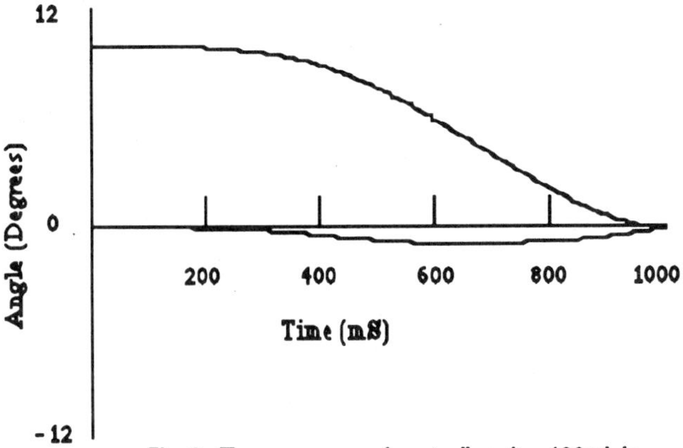

Fig. 3. Time response of controller after 100 trials

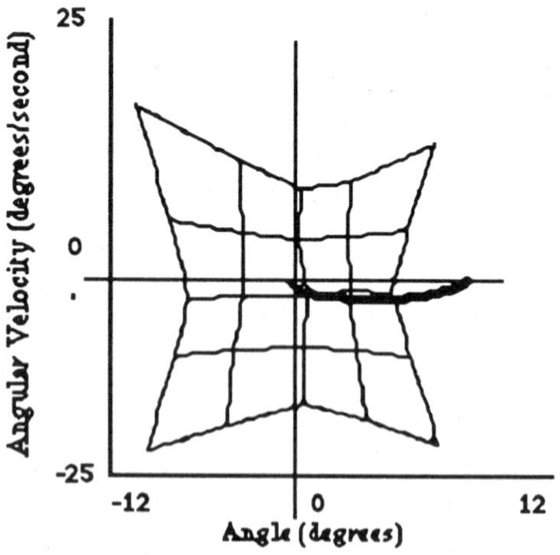

Fig. 4. Phase space plot of control response

IV. CONCLUDING REMARKS AND FUTURE WORK

A new fuzzy adaptive controller using reinforcement learning neural networks has been described. The basic capability to learn effective control has been demonstrated for a simple dynamical system. It learns this control on-line using only the input of the process state and a scalar feedback signal that gives a measure of the performance by whatever criteria can be determined from observation of the process. It does not need to be trained with examples of correct state-control pairs. It does not need an explicit error signal which either requires a priori knowledge of what the correct control vectors are or some type of plant model that is used to estimate them. It holds the promise of handling multi-dimensional systems without a proliferation of fuzzy subsets or discretized values. Also, the relation itself is learned rather than simply adapting the fuzzy sets to fixed rules.

Software test beds are currently under development which will permit studies of the system performance with larger numbers of state and control variables, testing of the data compression properties, and testing the effects of using different alternative similarity measures and various performance measures. Additional study of random/fixed policy schedules will be made also.

The type of control that this controller can provide is potentially applicable in many settings. It can be used in control situations in which there are multiple sensor measurements which may be noisy or imprecise or which require sensor fusion to generate a coherent picture of the process state. It can be used for high-level decision-making or control of data processing, intelligent system reconfiguration in response to changing conditions, or to direct flow in networks. Control of highly nonlinear dynamical systems (e.g., robot arms, etc.) for which it has been difficult to apply standard control theory methods is another application area where adaptive fuzzy controllers have proven effective. It can be used for failure detection and diagnosis or in a statistical process monitoring and control mode. Wherever intelligent decision-making in real-time is required for coping with an uncertain, noisy and/or changing environment, this type of automatic controller may be useful. In future work, we plan to explore the capabilities of this controller in some of these application areas.

ACKNOWLEDGEMENT

This research was sponsored in part by the National Science Foundation under Grant ECS-9216004.

REFERENCES

[1] Lin, C.T. and Lee, C.S.G., “Reinforcement structure/parameter learning for neural-network-based fuzzy logic control systems,” this conference.

[2] Jang, J.S. R., 1992, "Fuzzy controller design without domain experts," *Proc. of IEEE Int. Conf. on Fuzzy Systems 1992*, pp. 289-296.

[3] Berenji, H.R., "A reinforcement learning-based architecture for fuzzy logic control," *Int. J. of Approximate Reasoning*, vol. 6, pp. 267-292, 1992.

[4] Lee, C.C., "Intelligent Control Based on Fuzzy Logic and Neural Net Theory," *Proc. Int. Conf. Fuzzy Logic and Neural Networks*, Iizuka, Japan 1990, pp. 759-764.

[5] Patrikar, A. and Provence, J., "A self-organizing controller for dynamic processes using neural networks," *Int. Joint Conf. on Neural Networks IJCNN 1990*, vol. 3, pp. 359-364.

[6] Procyk, T.J. and Mamdani, E.H., "A linguistic self-organizing process controller," *Automatica*, vol. 15, pp. 15-30, 1979.

[7] Xu, Chen-Wei and Lu, Yong-zai,"Fuzzy model identification and self-learning for dynamic systems," *IEEE Tran. Syst., Man, Cybern.*, vol. 17, pp. 683-689, 1987.

[8] Pedrycz, W., "An identification algorithm in fuzzy relational systems," *Fuzzy Sets and Systems*, vol. 13, pp. 153-167, 1984.

[9] Kohonen, T., *Self-Organization and Associative Memory*, Springer-Verlag, 1988.

[10] Pedrycz, W., Hirota, K. and Takagi, T., "Fuzzy associative memories: concepts, architectures and algorithms," *Proc. of IFES Conf.* 1991, pp. 163-174.

[11] Kosko, B., *Neural Networks and Fuzzy Systems*, Englewood Cliffs, NJ: Prentice Hall, 1992.

[12] Pedrycz, W., *Fuzzy Control and Fuzzy Systems*, Taunton, England: Research Studies Press, Ltd., 1979.

[13] Narendra, Kumpati and Thathachar, M. A. L., *Learning Automata; An Introduction*, Englewood Cliffs, NJ: Prentice-Hall, 1989.

[14] Murrell, J.A., "Stochastic Learning Automata in Adaptive Control Problems," Master's expository, Operations Research Dept., University of N. Carolina at Chapel Hill, 1988.

[15] Barto, A. G., Sutton, R. S., Anderson, C. W., "Neuron-like adaptive elements that can solve difficult learning problems", *IEEE Trans. on Systems, Man and Cybern.*, vol. 13, pp. 834-846, 1983.

Neurocontrol and the Youla Parameterization

R. Saeks, J. Kaiser, and C. Cox
Accurate Automation Corp.
7001 Shallowford Rd.
Chattanooga, TN 37421

Abstract **This paper presents a hybrid frequency domain / neurocontrol algorithm. Neural network techniques are used to adjust the Youla parameter in an appropriately parameterized control system. The resulting neurocontroller is stable, robust, and reconfigurable. The learning algorithm is capable of choosing the order of the Youla parameter. Results are given to validate the concept.**

I. INTRODUCTION

We have developed a hybrid frequency domain / neurocontrol algorithm in which neural network techniques are used to adjust the Youla parameter in an appropriately parameterized control system. This yields a neurocontroller which is guaranteed to be stable and can implement any of the (asymptotic) design criteria derived from the Youla parameterization; tracking and/or disturbance rejection, pole placement, robust tracking and/or disturbance rejection, simultaneous design, initial value design, etc[1][2][3][4][5][6]. The adaptivity and robustness intrinsic to neurocontrol is integrated into the frequency domain controller [7][8][9][10][11][12][13]. Powerful (ontogenetic) neural network training techniques may be brought to bare on the control system design problem allowing one to design a controller without a-priori restrictions on its order[14][15]16]. A reconfigurable control architecture is developed where the controller is trained to deal with multiple scenarios; alternative trajectories for a flight controller, varying loads on a robot arm, alternative current waveshapes in a power system, etc; generalizing to new scenarios beyond the training set where necessary.

The approach is directly applicable to linear multivariate systems and extendable, via the various generalizations of the Youla parameterization, to the time-vary and nonlinear cases[3][17][18].

Manuscript received July 15, 1993. This research is sponsored by the National Science Foundation under Phase I Small Business Innovation Research Grant III-9261450.

II. NEUROCONTROL ARCHITECTURE

The architecture employed in our neurocontroller is illustrated in Figure 1. The feedback loop is a standard configuration in which a plant is driven by a compensator whose input is the error between the

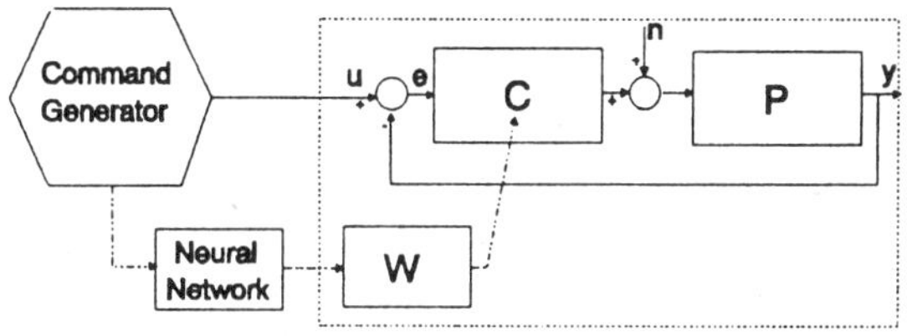

Figure 1. Reconfigurable Neurocontrol Architecture.

plant output and a prescribed reference input (while n represents an external noise source). W represents the stable Youla design parameter and the portion of the system indicated by the "box" is the standard configuration associated with the Youla parameterization. In our reconfigurable system, however, the Youla parameter is determined by a neural network based on inputs from the command generator. Hence, the Youla parameter changes from command to command with neural network training techniques employed to choose the Youla parameter; and, indirectly, the compensator. Indeed, by integrating neurocontrol with the Youla parameterization in this manner the system is guaranteed to meet the powerful stability and asymptotic design constraints associated with the Youla parameterization even when the neural network is required to generalize beyond its training set.

To achieve this end we must design a neural network in such a way to guarantee that W be stable independently of the network weights and / or inputs. To this end we assume that W is parameterized as W(**a**,**b**) where **a** is a vector of arbitrary positive parameters and **b** is a vector of arbitrary real parameters. For instance, **a** might represent the eigenvalues of a state transition matrix and **b** the remaining parameters of the state matrices. Alternatively, **a** might represent the real-part of the poles of (the MacMillan Canonical Form of) a transfer function matrix and **b** its remaining parameters, etc. We then work with a neural network such as that illustrated in Figure 2. Although we have used a feedforward network for the illustration any architecture can be employed. What is important is that the output neurons which define **a** only produce positive outputs while the output neurons which define **b** are allowed to produce both positive and negative outputs. This is readily achieved by choosing the transfer functions for the neurons which define **a** to be sigmoids and the transfer functions for the neurons which define **b** to be hyperbolic tangents.This architecture permits one to incorporate the robustness, adaptivity, and reconfigurability of a

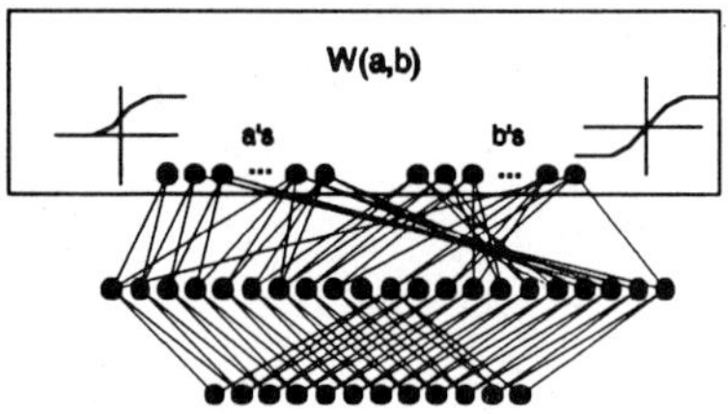

Figure 2. Neural Network for Youla Parameterization.

neurocontroller into our system while simultaneously preserving the full analytical power of the Youla parameterization. In particular, by properly choosing the transfer functions for the output neurons of the network, W is guaranteed to be stable for all possible commands, including those which generalize beyond the training set.

III. A BROADBAND TRACKING PROBLEM

As an example application of our neurocontrol architecture, a controller for a *broadband tracking problem* was simulated. Our goal is to design a feedback system which tracks all inputs in a prescribed band except for a prescribed group delay. The problem differs significantly from the classical tracking problem where one desires to asymptotically track a single feedback system input without delay. The problem is more closely allied to the broadband matching problem of circuit theory where one desires to match all signals in a prescribed band to a load (antenna, hi-fi speaker, etc.) without distortion.

The utility function for this problem is

$$f(h) = \int_{-B}^{B} |h(j\omega) - e^{j\omega T}|^2 d\omega$$

where B denotes the bandwidth in radians and T is the desired group delay. Here, the utility function simply attempts to force the feedback system gain to approximate an ideal delay over the prescribed bandwidth.

For this example we took a simple first order plant

$$p(s) = \frac{1}{(s+1)}$$

and worked with a Youla parameter of the form:

$$w(s) = b_0 + \frac{b_1}{(s+a_1)} + \frac{(b_2 s + b_3)}{(s^2 + a_2 s + a_3)}$$

Our neural network was trained to automatically reconfigure the controller for bandwidths in the range $.1 \leq B \leq 2$ while the coefficients of W(s) were bounded by ±4 (by scaling the output of the neural network transfer functions). For this example, a neural network with 1 input neuron, 7 output neurons and 11 hidden neurons was used and training was done by backpropagation of the utility function.

Figure 3 shows the magnitude curves for the transfer function produced by the neurocontroller for bandwidths B = .25, .75, 1.75 and 2. In these curves, the desired bandwidth is indicated by a pair of vertical lines and, as can be seen from the data, the

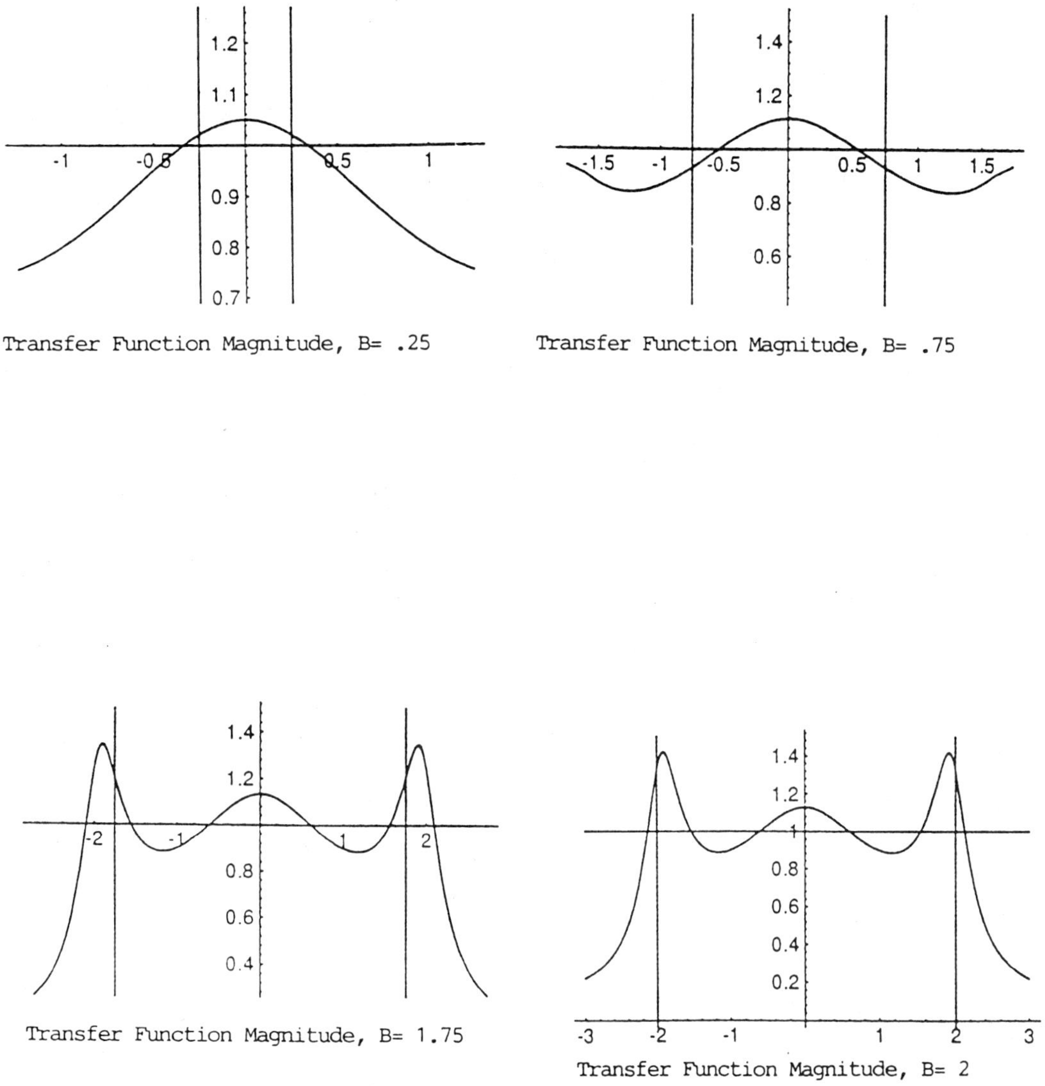

Figure 3. Transfer function magnitude for reconfigurable neurocontroller with B = .25, .75, 1.75 and 2.0.

frequency response closely approximates an ideal delay in the prescribed bandwidth deviating as soon as the bandwidth limit is reached. For low bandwidths, the neurocontroller uses the real pole in the Youla parameter to smoothly approximate the desired frequency response, slowly bringing in the complex conjugate poles to broaden the frequency response as the bandwidth increases.

REFERENCES

[1] Youla, D.C., Bongiorno, J.J., and H.A. Jabr (1976), "Modern Wiener-Hopf Design of Optimal Controllers: Part I", *IEEE Trans. on Auto. Cont.*, (Vol. AC-21, pp. 3-15).

[2] Youla, D.C., Bongiorno, J.J., and H.A. Jabr (1976), "Modern Wiener-Hopf Design of learning by self-organization", Optimal Controllers: Part II", *IEEE Trans. on Auto. Cont.*, (Vol. AC-21, pp. 319-338).

[3] Desoer, C.A., Murray, J.J., Liu, R.-W., and R. Saeks (1980). "Feedback System Design: The Fractional Representation Approach to Analysis and Synthesis", *IEEE Trans. on Auto. Cont.*, (Vol. AC-25, pp. 399-412).

[4] Saeks, R., Murray, J.J., Chua, O., Karmokolias, C., and A. Iyer" (1982). "Feedback System Design: The Single-Variate Case", Part I, *Circuits, Systems, and Signal Processing*, (Vol. 1, 137-169).

[5] Saeks, R., Murray, J.J., Chua, O., Karmokolias, C., and A. Iyer" (1983). "Feedback System Design: The Single-Variate Case", Part II, *Circuits, Systems, and Signal Processing*, (Vol. 2, 2-34).

[6] Vidyasagar (1985). *Control System Synthesis: A Factorization Approach*, Cambridge, MIT Press.

[7] Barto, A.G., Sutton, R.S., and C.W. Anderson (1983). "Neuronlike Adaptive Elements that can Solve Difficult Learning Control Problems", *IEEE Trans. on Systems, Man, and Cybernetics*, (Vol. SMC-13, pp. 834-846).

[8] Bhat, N. and T. McAvoy (1990). "Use of Neural Networks in Dynamic Modeling and Control of Chemical Processes", *Proc. of the 1990 American Control Conference*, (pp. 2466-2471), San Diego.

[9] Miller, W.T., Hewes, R.P., Glanz, F.H., and L.G. Kraft (1990). "Real-Time Dynamic Control of an Industrial Manipulator using a Neural Network Based Learning Controller", *IEEE Journal on Robotics and Automation.*

[10] Narendra, K.S., and K. Parthasarathy (1990). "Identification and Control of Dynamical Systems Using Neural Networks", *IEEE Trans. on Neural Networks* (Vol. NN-1, pp. 4-27).

[11] Levin, A.V, and K.S. Narendra, (1993). "Control of Nonlinear Dynamic Systems", IEEE Trans. on Neural Networks, Vol. NN-4, pp. 192-206.

[12] Werbos, P.J. (1989). "Neural Networks for Control and System Identification", *Proc. of the IEEE Conf. on Decision and Control.*

[13] Werbos, P.J. (1990). "Neurocontrol and Related Techniques", in Handbook of Neural Computing Applications, (ed. Maren, A.J., Harston, C.T., and R.M. Pap, pp. 345-380), New York, Academic Press.

[14] Carpenter, G. & Grossberg, S. (1987), "ART2: self-organization of stable category recognition codes for analog input patterns", Applied Optics, Vol 26, 4919-4930.

[15] Hrycej, T. (1992), "Supporting supervised Neurocomputing, Vol 4, 17-30.

[16] Oja, E. (1992), "Principal Components, Minor Components, and Linear Neural Networks", Neural Networks, Vol 5, Number 6, 927-935.

[17] Hammer, J., (1987). "Fractional Representations of Nonlinear Systems: A Simplified Approach", Inter. Jour. of Cont., Vol. 46, pp. 455-472.

[18] Hammer, J., (1986). "Stabilization of Nonlinear Systems", Int. Jour. of Cont., Vol. 44, pp. 1349-1381.

Robust Adaptive Control of Unknown Plants using Recurrent High Order Neural Networks — Application to Mechanical Systems

George A. Rovithakis, Elias B. Kosmatopoulos, and Manolis A. Christodoulou

Dept. of Electronic & Computer Engineering
Technical University of Crete
73100 Chania, Crete, GREECE

Abstract

In this paper, we extend our previous results on control of unknown dynamical systems using dynamic neural networks. The proposed algorithm is divided into two phases. First a recurrent high order neural network (RHONN) identifier is employed to perform "black box" identification and then a dynamic state feedback is developed to appropriately control the unknown system.

1 Introduction

Adaptive control of dynamical systems has been an active area of research since the 1960's. At the beginning, research was focused on the problem of controlling and identifying linear time invariant plants. But it was not until the last decade, that the problem was solved for both continuous and discrete LTI systems [1].

Recent advances in nonlinear control theory and in particular feedback linearization techniques [2], have inspired the development of adaptive control schemes for nonlinear plants [3]-[5]. A common assumption made in the above works, is that either all or part of the system dynamics are known. Although sometimes it is quite realistic, it constraints considerably the applications field. Furthermore, the most general problem of controlling a totally unknown plant, cannot even be discussed under these control schemes and assumptions.

An obvious solution to overcome the problem, is to introduce identification techniques in the control algorithm. The problem of identification consists of choosing an appropriate identification model and adjust its parameters such that the response of the model to an input signal approximates the response of the plant under the same input. It has been clear that in control systems theory, a mathematical description of a plant is often a prerequisite to analysis and controller design.

Furthermore, it is well known that global stability properties of model reference adaptive systems [6], are guaranteed under the "matching assumption", that the model order is not lower than that of the unknown plant. This restrictive assumption is likely to be violated in applications. Hence, it is important to determine the stability and robustness properties of adaptive schemes with respect to modeling errors.

Ioannou and Kokotovic [7], assumed a separation of time scales between the modeled and unmodeled phenomena and examined the performance of various types of identifiers and adaptive observers, when the order of the model is equal to the slow part of the plant.

Taylor *et al.* [3] and Kanelakopoulos *et al.* [4], examined the stability and robustness properties of nonlinear systems with parametric and dynamic uncertainties. In their work, the true plant is allowed to be of higher order due to unmodeled dynamics. Only the states appearing in the reduced order model were assumed to be available for measurment. Hence, their work appeared as an extension of the robustness analysis of Ioannou and Kokotovic [7], to nonlinear adaptive control.

Recently two of the authors has proposed a dynamical neural network approach for the identification and control of unknown dynamical systems [8, 9]. They have shown, using Lyapunov stability theory and singular perturbation analysis, that if the unknown system satisfies some certain assumptions it can be effectively identified and controller by the dynamical neural network. In this work we extend the results of [8, 9] by replacing the dynamical neural network by recurrent high order neural network (RHONN); the advantage of RHONN over the dynamical neural network of [8, 9] is that the former one is capable of approximating any nonlinear dynamical system [10, 11, 12].

Although the method is applicable to many classes of nonlinear systems, in this paper we will concentrate our attention to the case where the unknown system is a mechanical system. This is since the control of mechanical systems is of great importance in many areas of engineering (e.g. robotics); moreover mechanical systems possess special properties that can be appropriately utilized in order to establish a very efficient identification and control scheme.

2 Identification

In this section we consider the problem of identifying a continuous time mechanical system of the form

$$\dot{x}^{(2)} = f(x^{(1)}, x^{(2)}) + g(x^{(1)})u \qquad (2.1)$$

where $x^{(1)}, x^{(2)} \in \Re^n$ are the system generalized configuration coordinates (position) and the system generalized momenta (velocity); without loss of generallity we assume that $\dot{x}^{(1)} = x^{(2)}$ and that $x := [x^{(1)}, x^{(2)}] \in \mathcal{M}$, where $\mathcal{M}$ is a smooth and compact manifold. The control inputs $u \in \mathcal{U} \subset \Re^n$, where $\mathcal{U}$ is the class of admissible inputs, f is a smooth vector called the drift term, g is a matrix with columns g_i , $i = 1, 2, \ldots, n$ $g = [g_1 \; g_2 \; \ldots \; g_n]$, where g_i are smooth vector-fields and $x(0) = x_0$ is the initial condition in $\mathcal{M}$. It is a well-known fact that $g(x^{(1)})$ is positive definite (and thus invertible) for all $x^{(1)}$.

In examining the identification problem , we will impose the following assumptions on the system (2.1).

(A1) Given a class $\mathcal{U}$ of admissible inputs, then for any $u \in \mathcal{U}$ and any finite initial condition, the state trajectories are uniformly bounded for any finite $T > 0$. Hence, $| x(T) | < \infty$.

(A2) f, g are continuous with respect to their arguments and satisfy a local Lipschitz condition so that the solution $x(t)$ to the differential equation (2.1) is unique for any finite initial condition and $u \in \mathcal{U}$.

The above assumptions are required to guarantee the existence and uniqueness of solution of (2.1), for any finite initial condition and $u \in \mathcal{U}$.

In order to identify the nonlinear dynamical system (2.1), we employ RHONNs [10, 11, 12]. RHONNs are recurrent, fully interconnected nets, containing dynamical elements in their neurons. They are described by the following set of differential equations

$$\dot{\hat{x}}^{(2)} = A\hat{x}^{(2)} + BWS(x) + BW_{n+1}S'(x^{(1)})u \quad (2.2)$$

where A, B are $n \times n$ diagonal matrices with elements the scalars a_i, b_i for all $i = 1, 2, 3, \ldots, n$ and W, W_{n+1} are $n \times L_1$ and $n \times L_2$ matrices containing the adjustable parameters (synaptic weights) of the RHONN. Finally $S(x), S'(x^{(1)})$ are L_1, L_2 respectively vector functions whose elements are given by

$$[S(x)]_k = \prod_{j \in I_k^{(1)}} s(x_j)^{d_j(k)}$$

$$[S'(x_1)]_k = \prod_{j \in I_k^{(2)}} s(x_j^{(1)})^{d_j(k)}$$

where $\{I_1^{(i)}, \ldots I_{L_i}^{(i)}\}, i = 1, 2$ are not-ordered subsets of the sets $\{1, \ldots, 2n\}$ and $\{1, \ldots, n\}$, respectively.

The scalar function $s(\cdot)$ is monotone increasing functions which are usually represented as follows

$$s(x_i) = \frac{k}{1 + e^{-lx_i}} + \epsilon$$

for all $i = 1, 2, 3, \ldots, n$, where $k, l > 0$ are parameters representing the bound, (k) and slope, (l), of sigmoid's curvature. We note here that the small positive constant ϵ is used in order to ensure that the function $s(\cdot)$ is strictly positive. Moreover, using the previous definitions it is not difficult to show that the elements of the vectors $S(\cdot)$ and $S'(\cdot)$ are strictly positive.

The key idea in this paper is to assume that there exist weight values $W^\star$, $W^\star_{n+1}$ such that the system (2.1) can be completely described by a *singularly perturbed RHONN* of the form

$$\begin{aligned} \dot{x}^{(2)} &= Ax^{(2)} + BW^\star S(x) + BW^\star_{n+1}S'(x_1)u \\ &\quad + F(x, W, W_{n+1})(A_0^{-1}B_0W_0u + z) \\ \mu\dot{z} &= A_0 z + B_0 W_0 u \quad , \quad z \in \Re^r \end{aligned} \tag{2.3}$$

where z is the state of the unmodeled dynamics and $\mu > 0$ a small singular perturbation scalar. We mention here that such an assumption seems to be quite realistic: at first as it has been shown in [10, 11] the vector fields of the RHONNs of the form (2.2) are capable of approximating the vector-fields of dynamical systems of the form (2.1) to any degree of accuracy; therefore it is straigthforward to verify that the unknown system (2.1) vector fields are equal to some RHONN vector-fields plus a disturbance term. Regarding now the disturbance term, it is quite natural to assume that this term is related to a dynamical system possessing fast dynamics. In fact, due to the inherent stability and robust stability properties of the mechanical systems, we may assume that this disturbance term becomes negligible as far as the system has reached some equilibrium point.

If we define the error between the identifier states and the real system states as

$$e = \hat{x}^{(2)} - x^{(2)}$$

then from (2.2) and (2.3) we obtain the error equation

$$\begin{aligned} \dot{e} &= Ae + B\tilde{W}S(x) + B\tilde{W}_{n+1}S'(x_1)u \\ &\quad - F(x, W, W_{n+1})(A_0^{-1}B_0W_0u + z) \\ \mu\dot{z} &= A_0 z + B_0 W_0 u \quad , \quad z \in \Re^r \end{aligned} \tag{2.4}$$

where $F(\cdot), B_0W_0u, B\tilde{W}S(x), B\tilde{W}_{n+1}S'(x_1)u$, are bounded and differentiable with respect to their arguments for every $\tilde{w} \in B_{\tilde{w}}$ a ball in $\Re^{n \times n}$, $\tilde{w}_{n+1} \in B_{\tilde{w}_{n+1}}$ a ball in $\Re^n$ and all $x \in B_x$ a ball in $\Re^n$. We further assume that the unmodeled dynamics are asymptotically stable for all $x \in B_x$. In other words we assume that there exist a constant $\nu > 0$ such that

$$Re\ \lambda\{A_0\} \leq -\nu < 0$$

Note that $\dot{z}$ is large since μ is small and hence the unmodeled dynamics are fast. For a singular perturbation from $\mu > 0$ to $\mu = 0$ we obtain

$$z = A_0^{-1}B_0W_0U$$

Since the unmodeled dynamics are asymptotically stable the existence of A_0^{-1} is assured. As it is well known from singular perturbation theory, we express the state z as

$$z = h(x, \eta) + \eta \tag{2.5}$$

where $h(x, \eta)$ is defined as the quasi-steady-state of z and η as its fast transient. In our case

$$h(x, \eta) = A_0^{-1}B_0W_0u$$

Substituting (2.5) into (2.4) we obtain the singularly perturbed model as

$$\begin{aligned} \dot{e} &= Ae + B\tilde{W}S(x) + B\tilde{W}_{n+1}S'(x_1)u \\ &\quad - F(x, W, W_{n+1})\eta \\ \mu\dot{\eta} &= A_0\eta - \mu\dot{h}(e, \tilde{W}, \tilde{W}_{n+1}, \eta, u) \end{aligned} \tag{2.6}$$

where we define

$$\dot{h}(\cdot) = \frac{\partial h}{\partial e}\dot{e} + \frac{\partial h}{\partial \tilde{W}}\dot{\tilde{W}} + \frac{\partial h}{\partial \tilde{W}_{n+1}}\dot{\tilde{W}}_{n+1} + \frac{\partial h}{\partial u}\dot{u}$$

Suppose now that the adjustable parameters are adapted through the follwoing learning law

$$\begin{aligned} \dot{w}_{ij} &= -b_i p_i s(x_j) e_i \\ \dot{w}_{in+1} &= -b_i s(x_i) p_i u_i e_i \end{aligned}$$

for all $i, j = 1, 2, 3, \ldots, n$

Notice now, that in control case, u is a function of $e, \tilde{W}, \tilde{W}_{n+1}$ therefore making $\dot{h}(e, \tilde{W}, \tilde{W}_{n+1}, \eta, u)$ to be equal to

$$\dot{h}(e,\tilde{W},\tilde{W}_{n+1},\eta,u) = \frac{\partial h}{\partial e}\dot{e}+\frac{\partial h}{\partial \tilde{W}}\dot{\tilde{W}}+\frac{\partial h}{\partial \tilde{W}_{n+1}}\dot{\tilde{W}}_{n+1}$$

Before proceeding any further we need the following Lemma.

Lemma 2.1 *It is true that* $\dot{h}(e,\tilde{W},\tilde{W}_{n+1},\eta,u)$ *is bounded by*

$$\|\dot{h}(e,\tilde{W},\tilde{W}_{n+1},\eta,u)\| \le \rho_1\|e\| + \rho_2\|\eta\|$$

provided that the following inequalities hold

$$\begin{aligned}
\|h_w\dot{\tilde{W}}\| &\le k_0\|e\| \\
\|h_{w_{n+1}}\dot{\tilde{W}}_{n+1}\| &\le k_1\|e\| \\
\|h_e B\tilde{W}_{n+1}S'(x_1)u\| &\le k_2\|e\| \\
\|h_e B\tilde{W}S(x)\| &\le k_3\|e\| \\
\|h_e F(x,\tilde{W},\tilde{W}_{n+1})\| &\le \rho_2 \\
\|h_e Ae\| &\le k_4\|e\| \\
\|h_u\dot{u}\| &\le k_5\|e\|
\end{aligned}$$

and

$$\rho_1 = k_0 + k_1 + k_2 + k_3 + k_4 + k_5$$

□

We are now able to prove the following Theorem

Theorem 2.2 *The equilibrium of the singularly perturbed model is asymptotically stable for all*

$$\mu \in (0, \frac{1}{c_1c_2 + 2c_3})$$

and an estimate of its region of attraction is

$$S = \{e,\tilde{W},\tilde{W}_{n+1},\eta : \mathcal{V}(e,\tilde{W},\tilde{W}_{n+1},\eta) \le c\}$$

where c *is the largest constant such that the set* $\{e,\tilde{W},\tilde{W}_{n+1} : \mathcal{V}(e,\tilde{W},\tilde{W}_{n+1},0) \le c\}$ *is contained to* $B_e \times B_w \times B_{w_{n+1}}$*. Furthermore, the following properties are guaranteed*

- $e, \hat{x}, \eta, W, W_{n+1} \in L_\infty$, $e, \eta \in L_2$
- $\lim_{t\to\infty} e(t) = 0$, $\lim_{t\to\infty}\eta(t) = 0$
- $\lim_{t\to\infty}\dot{\tilde{W}}(t) = 0$, $\lim_{t\to\infty}\dot{\tilde{W}}_{n+1}(t) = 0$

□

Where in the above theorem $\mathcal{V}(e,\tilde{W},\tilde{W}_{n+1},\eta)$ is the following Lyapunov function

$$\begin{aligned}
\mathcal{V}(\cdot) &= \frac{1}{2}c_1e^TPe + \frac{1}{2}c_2\eta^TP_0\eta + \frac{1}{2}c_1tr\{\tilde{W}^T\tilde{W}\} \\
&\quad + \frac{1}{2}c_1tr\{\tilde{W}_{n+1}^T\tilde{W}_{n+1}\}
\end{aligned}$$

where $P, P_0 > 0$ are chosen to satisfy the Lyapunov equation

$$PA + A^TP = -I$$

$$P_0A_0 + A_0^TP_0 = -I$$

3 Control

In this section we investigate the tracking problem. The unknown nonlinear dynamical system is identified by a dynamic neural network and then it is driven to follow the response of a known system. The purpose of the identification stage is to provide adequate initial values for the control stage, therefore leading to better transient response of the error.

To analyze the problem, the complete singular perturbation model (2.6) is used. Therefore, the control scheme is now described by the following set of nonlinear differential equations

$$\begin{aligned}
\dot{e} &= Ae + B\tilde{W}S(x) + B\tilde{W}_{n+1}S'(x_1)u - \\
&\quad F(x,W,W_{n+1})\eta \\
\dot{e}_c &= Ae_c \\
\mu\dot{\eta} &= A_0\eta - \mu\dot{h}(e,\tilde{W},\tilde{W}_{n+1},\eta) \\
u &= -[BW_{n+1}S'(x_1)]^{-1} \times \\
&\quad [Ax_m + BWS(x) - A_mx_m - B_mr]
\end{aligned} \tag{3.1}$$

In the tracking problem we want the real system states to follow the states of a reference model. Let the reference model be described by

$$\dot{x}_m = A_mx_m + B_mr$$

where $x_m \in \Re^n$ are the model states, $r \in \Re^n$ are the model inputs and A_m, B_m are constant matrices of appropriate dimensions. Define the error between the identifier states and the model states as

$$e_c = \hat{x}^{(2)} - x_m \tag{3.2}$$

Let the control input u be equal to

$$\begin{aligned} u &= -[BW_{n+1}S'(x)]^{-1} \times \\ & \quad [Ax_m + BWS(x) - A_m x_m - B_m r] \end{aligned} \tag{3.3}$$

To apply the control law (3.3), we have to assure the existence of $(BW_{n+1}S'(x))^{-1}$. However, it can be shown that we can always find a particular selection of $I_k^{(2)}$'s such that there exists a convex set $\mathcal{C}$ such that the term $(BW_{n+1}S'(x))$ is positive definite and (thus invertible) for all $W_{n+1} \in \mathcal{C}$. We mention here that the restriction of W_{n+1} into the convex set $\mathcal{C}$ does not destroy the approximation capabilities of the RHONN; this is due to the special properties of the mechanical system (2.1), namely, due to the fact that $g(\cdot)$ is positive definite.

Hence $W_{n+1}(t)$ is confined through the use of a projection algorithm [1], to the set $\mathcal{W} = \{W_{n+1} : \|\tilde{W}_{n+1}\| \leq w_{max}\}$ where w_{max} is a positive constant. Furthermore, $\tilde{W}_{n+1} = W_{n+1} - W^{\star}_{n+1}$ and $W^{\star}_{n+1}$ contains the initial values of W_{n+1} that identification provides. In particular, the standard adaptive laws are modified to

$$\begin{aligned} \dot{W} &= -EBPS_0 \\ \dot{W}_{n+1} &= \mathcal{P}\{-BPS'UE\} \end{aligned} \tag{3.4}$$

where all matrices are defined as follows

$$\begin{aligned} P &= diag[p_1, p_2, \ldots, p_n] \\ B &= diag[b_1, b_2, \ldots, b_n] \\ E &= diag[e_1, e_2, \ldots, e_n] \\ U &= diag[u_1, u_2, \ldots, u_n] \\ S_0 &= \begin{bmatrix} s(x_1) & \ldots & s(x_n) \\ \vdots & & \vdots \\ s(x_1) & \ldots & s(x_n) \end{bmatrix} \end{aligned}$$

and $\mathcal{P}(\cdot)$ is the projection mapping into the convex set $\mathcal{C}$.

Therefore, if the initial weights are chosen such that $\|\tilde{W}(0)_{n+1}\| \leq w_{max}$, then we have that $\|\tilde{W}_{n+1}\| \leq w_{max}$ for all $t \geq 0$. This can be readily established by noting that whenever $\|\tilde{W}(t)_{n+1}\| = w_{max}$ then

$$\frac{d\|\tilde{W}(t)_{n+1}\|^2}{dt} \leq 0 \tag{3.5}$$

which implies that the weights W_{n+1} are directed towards the inside or the ball $\{W_{n+1} : \|\tilde{W}_{n+1}\| \leq w_{max}\}$.

Before proceeding any further, we need the following Lemma.

Lemma 3.1 *It is true that* $\dot{h}(e, \tilde{W}, \tilde{W}_{n+1}, \eta, u)$ *is bounded by*

$$\|\dot{h}(e, \tilde{W}, \tilde{W}_{n+1}, \eta, u)\| \leq \rho_1\|e\| + \rho_2\|\eta\|$$

provided that the following inequalities hold

$$\begin{aligned} \|h_w\dot{\tilde{W}}\| &\leq k_0\|e\| \\ \|h_{w_{n+1}}\dot{\tilde{W}}_{n+1}\| &\leq k_1\|e\| \\ \|h_e B\tilde{W}_{n+1}S'(x_1)u\| &\leq k_2\|e\| \\ \|h_e B\tilde{W}S(x)\| &\leq k_3\|e\| \\ \|h_e F(x, W, W_{n+1})\| &\leq \rho_2 \\ \|h_e Ae\| &\leq k_4\|e\| \end{aligned}$$

and

$$\rho_1 = k_0 + k_1 + k_2 + k_3 + k_4$$

□

We are now able to prove the following theorem

Theorem 3.2 *The control scheme (3.1), is asymptotically stable for all*

$$\mu \in (0, \mu_0)$$

where $\mu_0 = \frac{1}{2}(\frac{1}{2\gamma_1\gamma_2+\gamma_3})$.
Furthermore, the learning law (3.4) guarantees the following properties

- $e, e_c, \eta, \hat{x}, \tilde{W}, \tilde{W}_{n+1} \in L_\infty$, $\quad e, e_c, \eta \in L_2$
- $\lim_{t\to\infty} e(t) = 0$, $\quad \lim_{t\to\infty} e_c(t) = 0$, $\lim_{t\to\infty} \eta(t) = 0$
- $\lim_{t\to\infty} \dot{\tilde{W}}(t) = 0$, $\quad \lim_{t\to\infty} \dot{\tilde{W}}_{n+1}(t) = 0$

□

4 Simulations

Due to the space limitations, we do not include simulation results that we have performed in our laboratory. The simulations are to be presented during the paper presentation.

5 Conclusions

The purpose of this paper is to adaptively control unknown nonlinear dynamical systems, using RHONNs. Since the plant is unknown, a two step algorithm is considered. In step one, a RHONN identifier is employed to perform "black box" identification. Many cases that lead to modeling errors, ie. parametric and dynamic uncertainties, are taken into consideration. Convergence of the identification error and weights, (under a sufficiency of excitation condition), to zero and to a constant value respectively, is proved. Since our main concern lies on the control problem, only a rough estimation of the region where the weights should belong is needed to proceed to the control phase of our algorithm, in which a dynamic state feedback is developed such that the outputs of the unknown plant follow the outputs of a reference model. Convergence of the error to zero and boundedness of all signals in the closed loop, is again proved.

References

[1] K.S. Narendra and A.M. Annaswamy, *Stable Adaptive Systems*, Englewood Cliffs, Prentice Hall, 1989.

[2] H. Nijmeijer and A.J. van der Schaft, *Nonlinear Dynamical Control Systems*, New York, NY, Springer-Verlag, 1989.

[3] D.G. Taylor, P.V. Kokotovic, R. Marino and I. Kanellakopoulos, "Adaptive Regulation of Nonlinear Systems with Unmodeled Dynamics", *IEEE Trans. Automat. Contr.*, vol. 34, no. 4, pp. 405-412, 1989.

[4] I. Kanellakopoulos, P.V. Kokotovic and R. Marino, "An Extended Direct Scheme for Robust Adaptive Nonlinear Control", *Automatica*, vol. 27, no. 2, pp. 247-255, 1991.

[5] I. Kanellakopoulos, P.V. Kokotovic and A.S. Morse "Systematic Design of Adaptive Controllers for Feedback Linearizable Systems", *IEEE Trans. Automat. Contr.*, vol. 36, no. 11, pp. 1241-1253, 1991.

[6] K.S. Narendra, *Stable Identification Schemes in System Identification : Advances and Cases Studies*, New York: Academic, 1976.

[7] P.A. Ioannou and P.V. Kokotovic, *Adaptive Systems with Reduced Models*, New York: Springer-Verlag, 1983.

[8] G.A. Rovithakis and M.A. Christodoulou, "Dynamical neural networks for control of unknown dynamical systems," *Proc. of the International Symposium on Implicit and Nonlinear Systems*, pp. 87-95, Texas, 1992.

[9] G.A. Rovithakis and M.A. Christodoulou, "Adaptive control of unknown plants using dynamical neural networks," to appear in *IEEE Transactions on Systems, Man, and Cybernetics.*

[10] E.B. Kosmatopoulos, P.A. Ioannou, and M.A. Christodoulou, "Identification of nonlinear systems using new dynamic neural network structures," *IEEE Conference on Decision and Control 1992.*

[11] E.B. Kosmatopoulos, M.M. Polycarpou, M.A. Christodoulou, and P.A. Ioannou, "High-order neural network structures for identification of dynamical systems," to appear in *IEEE Transactions on Neural Networks.*

[12] E.B. Kosmatopoulos and M.A. Christodoulou, "Filtering, prediction, & learning properties of ECE neural networks," to appear in *IEEE Transactions on Systems, Man, and Cybernetics.*

Model-Reference Neural Color Correction for HDTV Systems based on Fuzzy Information Criteria

Po-Rong Chang, and C. C. Tai
National Chiao-Tung University,
Hsin-Chu, Taiwan, R.O.C.

***Abstract*—This paper presents a new adaptive color correction process for High Definition Television (HDTV) system based on human color perception model. To achieve the high-fidelity color reproduction, it requires eliminating the color error sources resulted from camera, monitor, intermediate color image processing and their mutual interaction. The intermediate processing may include the coding/decoding, quantization, and modulation/demodulation. And, the mutual interaction denotes the color gamut mismatch and resolution conversion between camera and monitor. It can be shown that those color error sources of unknown form are highly nonlinear. Hence, a cost-effective indirect adaptive control scheme consisting of both back-propagation neural net controller and forward model is proposed to overcome the difficulty of dealing with both nonlinearity and model-identification of the HDTV systems. The forward model is used to convert the plant output error (color difference) into control signal error for training the back-propagation controller. Furthermore, the values of derivative-related parameters of the forward model are determined by Hornik's multi-layer neural net identification process. In addition, it is noted that the measure of the color difference (plant output error) in human color perception space should be quantified by fuzzy information in order to perform the system control. Finally, the effectiveness of our method is being verified by a number of experiments.**

I. Introduction

The colorimetry of current 525 line NTSC television system is vaguely defined in terms of its display–i.e. , the receiver/monitor. The standard simply states that the signals should be suitable for an NTSC display. Future television systems should be designed to take advantage of future display technologies, which may have different, perhaps improved color characteristics than current CRT based displays. High Definition Television (HDTV) offers the potential for a vastly improved television service. In addition to higher resolution and a wide aspect ratio, it provides an opportunity to improve color reproduction. Its color improvements include complete definitions of color characteristics and a large color gamut which is addressed by the SMPTE Ad- Hoc Group on HDTV production[1][2]. Meanwhile, there are several color error sources which will degrade the quality of color reproduction. The color errors may be caused by the deviation from the ideal image taking characteristics and the nonlinearity of the color camera. Because of the nonlinear gamma-correction used with all color camera, the division of luminance and chrominance in the transmitted signals is imperfect. Therefore, the chrominance signal, which should transmit only chrominance, carries a considerable amount of luminance information too. In other words, the constant luminance principle does not work precisely. As a result, luminance errors that occur are greater in an area with high saturation figures. Therefore, contour in the high saturated image area is somewhat blurred because of the addition of the converted narrow-band chrominance signal to the luminance signal. In contrast to camera, the second kind of color errors is caused by deviation of the primary colors of monitor due to such factors as inadequate luminous efficiency and light residues. Obviously, the noisy channel and the nonlinearity involved in the coder and decoder would also degrade the reproduction quality. This kind of color errors caused by transmission is identified as the third color error source. Additionally, the color gamut mismatch and resolution conversion between the camera and monitor may also lead to be a the fourth color error source to the entire system. Finally, the last color error source comes from the deterioration of the color-rendering properties of illuminating light. It is desired to render correct colors under a varity of lighting conditions.

Figure 1, shows how a neural-based color correction processor can be used to eliminate those undesired color errors based on human perceptual color space. In order for colors to be reproduced desirably, it is necessary to analyze what colors people feel or sense to be desirable. Usually,

0-7803-0614-7/93/$03.00 ©1993 IEEE

it is lack of a quantitative definition of subjective image quality and human color perception. Nevertheless, the psychological color difference perceived by human can be characeterized by the fuzzy information measure[8]. The details of our adaptive fuzzy neural-based correction will be described in the next two section.

II. Fuzzy Neural based Control for Color Correction

Recently, Jordan[3], Psaltis, Sideris, and Yamanura[4] have proposed a promising adaptive control by using the back-propagation neural network as the plant's controller. Meanwhile, it requires propagating the errors between actual and desired plant outputs back to produce the error in the control signal which can be used to train the back-propagation controller. To achieve the goal, their idea is essentially to treat the plant as an additional back-propagation network which is connected to the back-propagation controller directly. This additional network is called the forward model. In Figure 2, this back-propagation process is illustrated by the dashed line passing back through the forward model and continuing back through a second layered network that uses it to learn a control rule. In additon, Jordan[3] showed that the Jacobian or derivative of plant is required in performing the back-propagation process. Next, we will describe how the traditional error back-propagation rule can be applied to convert the plant output error into the control signal error.

For the traditional multilayered back-propagation network shown in Figure 3, error back-propagation rule would modify the weight, ω_{ab}^{m} between neurons a and b of the m-th and $(m-1)$-th layers, in order to minimize the summed squared output error, $||\vec{\epsilon}||^2$, respectively, as follows:

$$\Delta\omega_{ab}^{m} = -\eta\frac{\partial||\vec{\epsilon}||^2}{\partial\omega_{ab}^{m}} \quad (1)$$

$$= \eta\delta_a^m q_b^{m-1} \quad (2)$$

where $\vec{\epsilon}$ is the error vector between the actual output vector $\mathbf{u}(=\mathbf{q}^n)$ and the desired output vector $\mathbf{u}^*(=\mathbf{q}^{n*})$, and η is an acceleration constant. In equation(2), the output of the a-th neuron is q_a, its input is p_a, and δ_a is the back-propagation error given for the output layer, n, by

$$\delta_a^n = G_n'(p_a^n)(u_a - u_a^*) \quad (3)$$

and for all other layers, $1 \le m \le n-1$, by

$$\delta_a^m = G_m'(p_a^m)\sum_i \delta_i^{m+1}\omega_{ia}^{m+1} \quad (4)$$

where u_a and u_a^* are the a-th component of $\mathbf{u}$ and $\mathbf{u}^*$ respectively, and $G_i'(p_a^i)$ is the derivative of the sigmodal activation function for the a-th neuron at the i-th layer.

For a cascade system shown in Figure 4 consisting of the back-propagation controller and the feedforward model, we can apply error back-propagation rule directly to the system with the following modifications. For simplicity, the feedforward model is thought of as an additional,although unmodifiable layer. Obviously, the i-th plant output y_i is identical to the i-th neuron output q_i^{n+1} located at the output layer of the $(n+1)$ layer cascade system. Therefore, the squared error of the cascade system can be given by

$$E = \frac{1}{2}\sum_i(y_i^* - y_i)^2 = \frac{1}{2}\mathbf{e}^T\mathbf{e} \quad (5)$$

where y_i^* is the desired i-th component of the desired reference output vector $\mathbf{y}^*$, and $\mathbf{e}$ is the error vector between $\mathbf{y}^*$ and $\mathbf{y}$.

Since the weights of the forward model or the output layer are unmodified, our objective is to adjust the weights of the preceeding n-layers in order to minimize E. Next, we would like to derive the relationship between the back-propagated errors for the output layer and the n-layer denoted by δ_i^{n+1} and δ_i^n respectively. According to equation (1), the weight increment between neurons a and b of the n-th and $(n-1)$-th layer is given by

$$\Delta\omega_{ab}^{n} = -\eta\frac{\partial E}{\partial\omega_{ab}^{n}} \quad (6)$$

Substituting (5) into (6) and by chain rule, one may obtain

$$\Delta\omega_{ab}^{n} = -\eta\frac{\partial E}{\partial u_a}\frac{\partial u_a}{\partial\omega_{ab}} \quad (7)$$

$$= \eta\{\sum_i(y_i^* - y_i)\frac{\partial y_i}{\partial u_a}\}\frac{\partial u_a}{\partial\omega_{ab}}$$

Furthermore, by using the fact that $u_a = q_a^n$, $\partial q_a^n/\partial p_a^n = G_n'(p_a^n)$, $p_a^n = \sum_j \omega_{aj}q_j^{n-1}$ and chain rule, (7) becomes as follows

$$\omega_{ab}^{n} = \eta q_b^{n-1}\{G_n'(p_a^n)[\sum_i(y_i^* - y_i)\frac{\partial y_i}{\partial u_a}]\} \quad (8)$$

Compared to (2), δ_i^{n+1} and δ_i^n may be defined as

$$\delta_i^{n+1} = y_i^* - y_i \quad (9)$$

and

$$\delta_a^n = G_n'(p_a^n)\sum_i \delta_i^{n+1}\frac{\partial y_i}{\partial u_a} \quad (10)$$

As shown above, the error propagation rule requires computing the partial derivatives or Jacobian of the plant. If the plant is a function of unkown form, the evaluation of its Jacobian becomes a difficult job. Fortunately,

Hornik, Stnchcombe, and White [5][6] proposed a systematic method to identify the Jacobian of the plant. They showed that their multilayer back-propagation-like networks with appropriately smooth hidden layer activation functions are capable of arbitrary accurate approximation to an arbitrary function and its derivatives. As a result, the Jacobian of a plant can be identified by Horink's method. This determined plant Jacobian is then applied to the model-reference indirect adaptive control when the plant is a plant of unknown form. The system architecture of this adaptive control is shown in Figure 5.

It is known that the controller placed in front of plant acts as a pre-equalizer for the plant and forces the plant output be equal to the desired output. The proposed model-reference indirect adaptive control (MIAC) with back-propagation controller is not restricted in performing the control process described in Figure 5. Since the back-propagation neural network [7] has the capability to equalize the second plant placed in front of itself, one may easily show that the MIAC can be extended to perform the control process shown in Figure 6.

Clearly, the generalized MIAC can be applied to the color correction for HDTV system directly. The detailed function diagram is shown in Figure 7. It should be noted that plant 1 includes the HDTV monitor and human evaluation model. Usually, it requires quantifying human evaluation model in order to perform system control. Therefore, we use the Xie's fuzzy information measure [8] in our system and given by

$$\begin{aligned} H_T &= H_s(P_1^R, P_0^R) + H_f(\mu_R) + H_s(P_1^G, P_0^G) \\ &\quad + H_f(\mu_G) + H_s(P_1^B, P_0^B) + H_f(\mu_B) \qquad (11) \end{aligned}$$

As mentioned previously, μ_R, μ_G,and μ_B denote the membership functions for R (Red), G (Green) and B (Blue) respectively. And P_1^X and P_0^X represent the X having grade of membership 1 and membership 0, respectively, where X = R or G or B . $H_s(\cdot)$ and $H_f(\cdot)$ are called the shannon information and fuzzy information, respectively. In contrast to plant 1, plant 2 consists of the HDTV camera and communication channel model. To verify the effectiveness of our model, a number of experiments is being tested.

III. Conclusion

In this paper, we have developed a cost-effective color correction algorithm based on a generalized neural-based indirect adaptive control which consists of both back-propagation controller and forward model. The back-propagation controller is placed between plant 1 and plant 2 which denote a combination of HDTV monitor and human color perception model and a combination of HDTV camera and communication channel respectively. It has been pointed out that this particular controller has two different functions. In other words, it acts as a equalizer to plant 2 and also the pre-equalizer (or controller) to plant 1 simultaneously. To be a controller (or pre-equalizer) for plant 1, it requires propagating the output error of plant 1 througth a converter called the forward model to control signal error for training the back-propagation controller. In addition, the color difference (or the plant output error) evaluated in human perception space is characterized by the Xie's fuzzy information measure.

References

[1] L. E. DeMarsh "HDTV production colorimetry," *SMPTE J.*, pp.796–805 Oct. 1991.

[2] LeRoy DeMarsh "Colorimetry for HDTV," *IEEE Trans. on Consumer Electronics,* pp.1–6, vol. 37, No. 1, 1991.

[3] Jordan, M. " Generic constraints on underspecified target trajectories," In *Proceedings of the 1989 International Joint Conference on Neural Networks,* pp. 217–225 1989 New York: IEEE Press.

[4] D. Psaltis, A. Sideris, and A. A. Yamamura, "A Multilayered Neural Network Controller," *IEEE Contr. Syst. Mag.*, vol 4, pp.17–21 1988

[5] Horink, K., Stinchcombe, M., and White, H. "Multilayer feedforward nteworks are universal approximators," *Neural Networks* vol 2, pp.359–366. 1989

[6] Horink, K., Stinchcombe, M., and White, H. "Universal approximation of an unknown mapping and its derivatives using multilayer feedforward networks." *Neural Networks,* vol 3, pp.551–560. 1990

[7] S. Siu, G. J. Gibson, and C. F. N. Cowan "Decision feedback equalisation using neural network structures and performance comparison with stand architecture," *IEE Proceedings,* vol 137, No 4, 1990.

[8] XIE Wei-Xin "An information measure for color space," *Fuzzy sets and system,* pp157–165 1990 Elsever Science Publishers

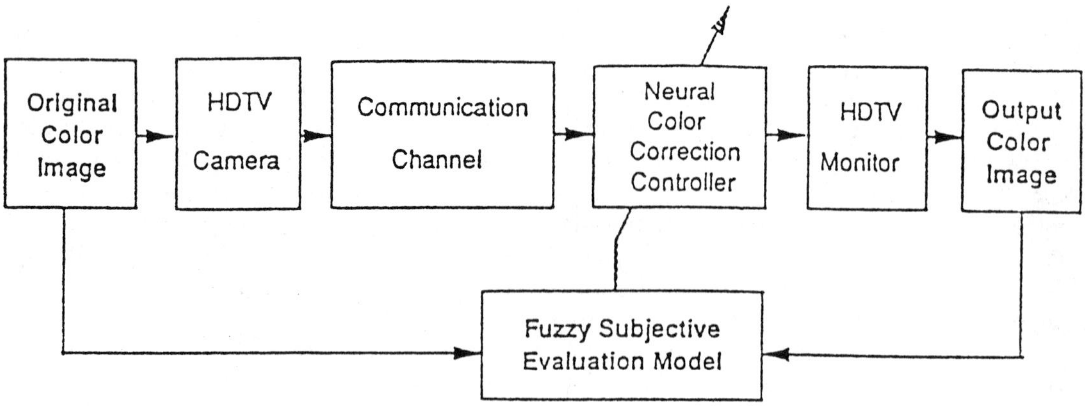

Fig. 1 Color reproduction system

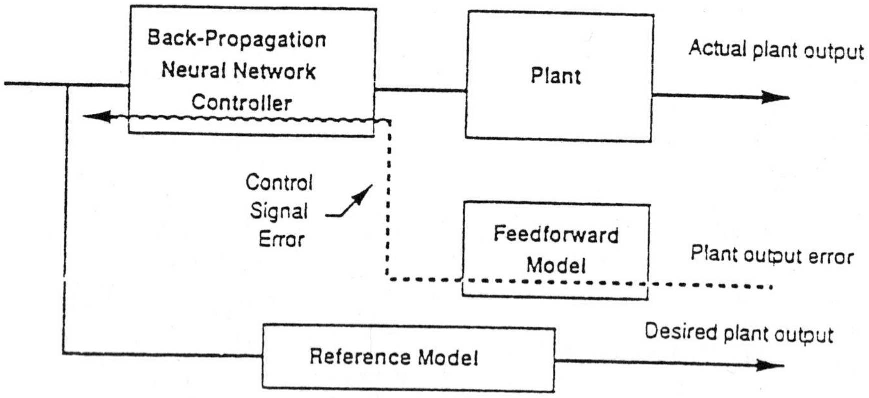

Fig. 2 Model-reference neural network control with backpropagating through a forward model of the plant to determine control signal error

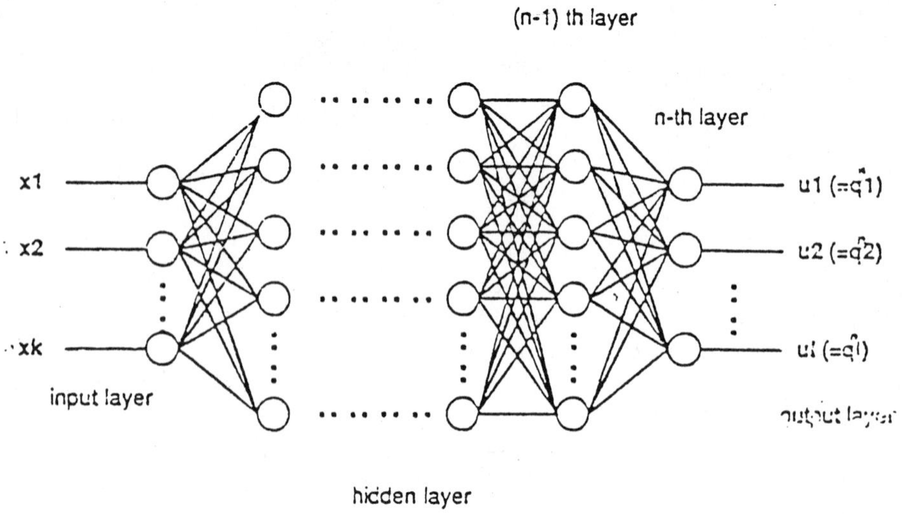

Fig. 3 Traditional n-layer back-propagation

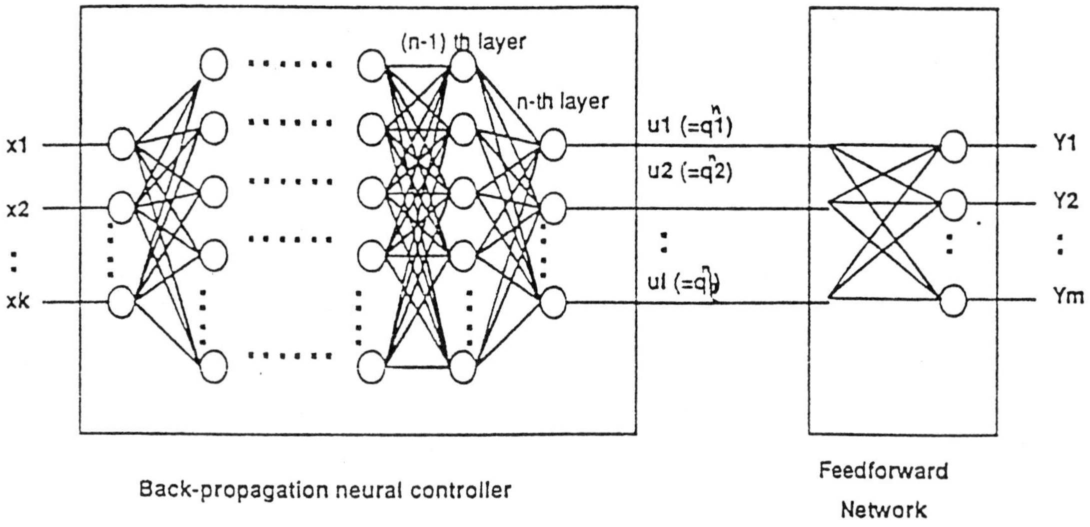

Fig. 4 A cascade system as a (n+1)-layer

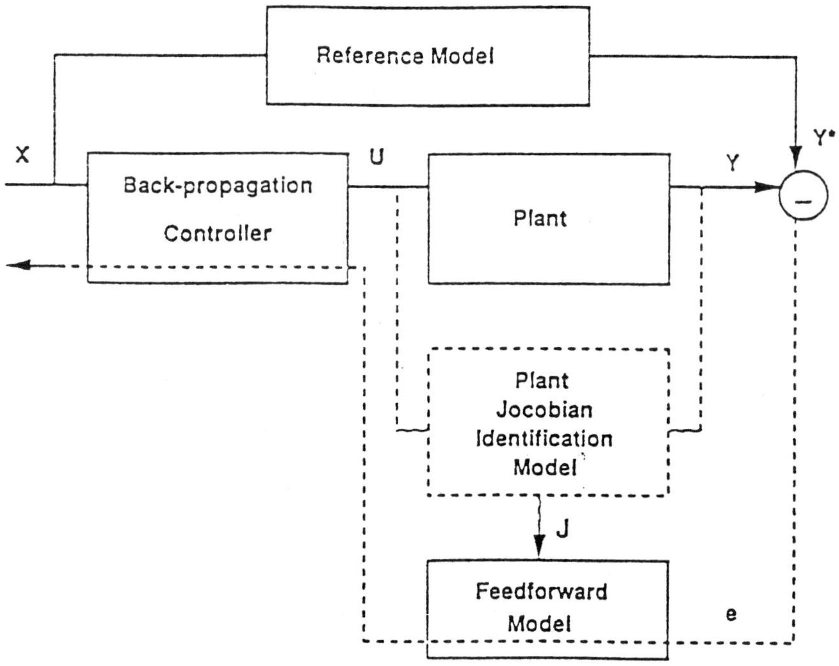

Fig. 5 The system architecture when the plant is unknown

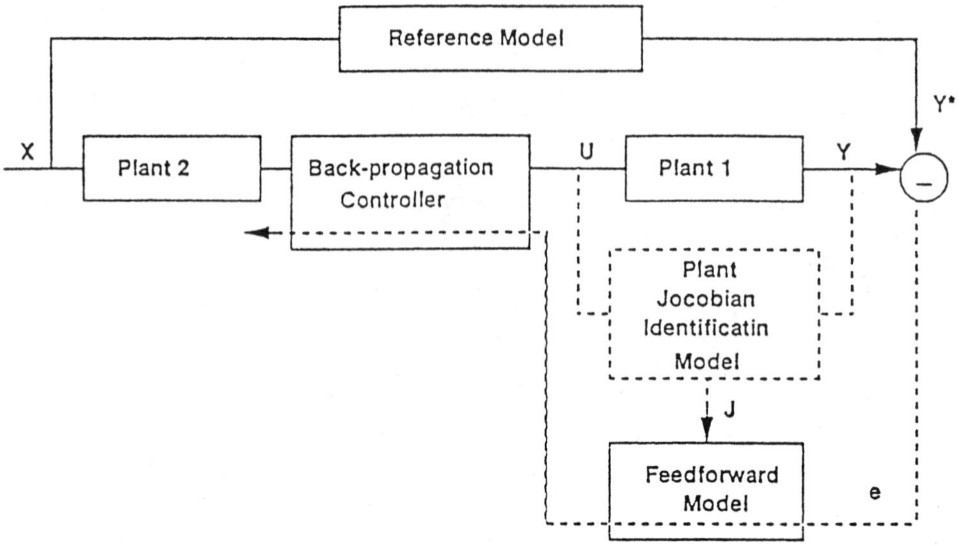

Fig. 6 Generalized MIAC with back-propagation controller

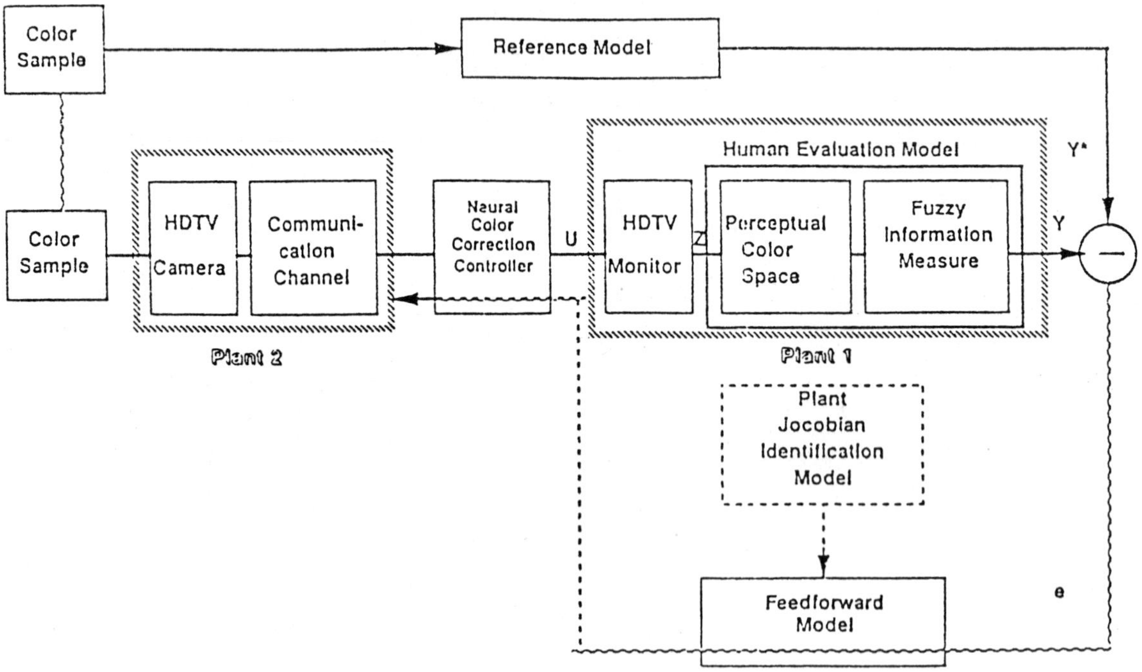

Fig .7 Model-Reference Color Correction Architecture

Chapter 4: Data Fusion

CHAPTER 4
Data Fusion

Data fusion is the synergistic combination of several different data types from several different sources (often sensors) for a single task. Data fusion is used in applications where a single stream of data is insufficient for the task at hand. As an example, in defense systems there are several different sensors that provide data concerning a given area. This data is "fused" together to perform the detection of hostile missiles. Other application areas that might employ data fusion include: information retrieval, medical diagnostics, environmental monitoring, and condition-based machine diagnostics. Several examples of neural network data fusion will be included in a second volume of "Neural NetworksTechnology and Applications".

Data fusion is a growing technology area. The engineering world continues to find new and innovative ways to sense the world with greater precision and at higher data rates. Furthermore, the scientific and engineering community are developing new methods of extracting information from data. As an example, a single time-series can use statistics, higher-order spectra, Fourier spectra, wavelets, chaos theory, and mathematical morphology to extract different aspects of the data. Combining these various data sources and their representations quickly becomes a tremendous task, especially when considering both spatial and temporal alignment, weighting and prioritization, and real-time decision making. Because neural networks learn from data, their application can simplify the design and development of data fusion systems will be included in a second volume of "Neural Networks Technology and Application."

Two trends that have emerged in data fusion with neural networks have emerged recently. First, hierarchical neural networks are being used more frequently and their results continue to be promising. Second, fuzzy neural networks are being used to combine *a priori* data and adaptation in a single system. The papers in this section describe results using both of these approaches.

The following four papers emphasize the development of neural network data fusion technology. **Paper 4.1** utilizes a fuzzy neural network (Fuzzy ARTMAP) for data fusion and demonstrates its capability using a quadruped database. **Paper 4.2** describes a sequence of filter and feature extraction operations that are combined with an MLP classifier to perform multisensor target recognition. **Paper 4.3** presents the Maximum Likelihood Adaptive Neural System (MLANS) and its application to passive sensor fusion. **Paper 4.4** shows how image processing, expert systems, and Adaptive Resonance Theory (ART) neural networks can be combined to perform automatic target recognition.

Fusion ARTMAP: An Adaptive Fuzzy Network for Multi-channel Classification

Yousif R. Asfour*, Gail A. Carpenter †, Stephen Grossberg ‡, Gregory W. Lesher §

Center for Adaptive Systems and
Department of Cognitive and Neural Systems
Boston University,
111 Cummington Street
Boston, Massachusetts 02215 USA

Abstract – Fusion ARTMAP is a self-organizing neural network architecture for multi-channel, or multi-sensor, data fusion. Fusion ARTMAP generalizes the fuzzy ARTMAP architecture in order to adaptively classify multi-channel data. The network has a symmetric organization such that each channel can be dynamically configured to serve as either a data input or a teaching input to the system. An ART module forms a compressed recognition code within each channel. These codes, in turn, become inputs to a single ART system that organizes the global recognition code. When a predictive error occurs, a process called parallel match tracking simultaneously raises vigilances in multiple ART modules until reset is triggered in one of them. Parallel match tracking hereby resets only that portion of the recognition code with the poorest match, or minimum predictive confidence. This internally controlled selective reset process is a type of credit assignment that creates a parsimoniously connected learned network.

I. MULTI-CHANNEL DATA FUSION

Fusion ARTMAP is a neural network architecture designed to adaptively classify objects using multiple sources of information, regardless of its source or type. An example of the fusion problem is the classification of trucks based on inputs from different types of sensors such as range, doppler, and camera. Alternatively, multiple input sources could represent different views of the truck, such as top, front, and side views. Trucks can also be classified using different spatial scales by combining information from cameras that zoom in on the tires and information from cameras that provide a view of the whole truck. In general, Fusion ARTMAP is designed to classify objects using information from multiple sources of any type.

One straightforward approach to the fusion problem is vector concatenation. That is, inputs from each channel are joined to form one large vector that then becomes the input to a single-channel supervised learning system. This approach is used, for example, by Chu and Aggarwal [7] to train a back-propagation neural network on inputs from infrared, range, and visual sensors.

Whenever the classifier makes a wrong prediction during training, it is desirable to modify some system parameters in order to improve the total system performance. Deciding which parameters to modify is known as the the *credit assignment problem*. Since the information from the different sensors is concatenated into a single feature vector, the predictive power of each individual sensor is unknown to the classifier. Therefore, the credit assignment problem is solved by assigning blame non-specifically to all input channels. Failure to account for the individual channels' predictive power leads to connectivity that tends to grow multiplicatively with the size of the input vector.

Fusion ARTMAP utilizes a modular approach to sensor fusion. Each sensor is assigned an indi-

*Supported in part by ARPA (ONR N00014-92-J-401J), the National Science Foundation (NSF IRI 90-00530), and the Office of Naval Research (ONR N00014-91-J-4100).

†Supported in part by British Petroleum (BP 89-A-1204), ARPA (ONR N00014-92-J-4015), the National Science Foundation (NSF IRI-90-00530), and the Office of Naval Research (ONR N00014-91-J-4100).

‡Supported in part by ARPA (ONR N00014-92-J-401J), the National Science Foundation (NSF IRI-90-24877), and the Office of Naval Research (ONR N00014-91-J-4100).

§Supported in part by the Air Force Office of Scientific Research (AFOSR F49620-92-J-0334), a National Science Foundation Graduate Fellowship, and the Office of Naval Research (ONR N0014-91-J-4100).

0-7803-1485-9/93$03.00 © 1993 IEEE

vidual classifier, the outputs of which serve as the inputs to a global classifier which makes a global prediction. For example, information from a range sensor is first classified into depth codes while information from a doppler sensor is classified into speed codes. The compressed depth and speed codes become inputs to a global classifier, which predicts the type of truck. By assigning an individual classifier to each sensor channel, blame can be assigned selectively to the channels with lowest predictive confidence. Such an approach retains system predictive accuracy while reducing total network connectivity by maximizing compression within each channel.

Fusion ARTMAP uses the multi-channel structure of the input data to streamline the network design. One intra-channel code can contribute to several global codes, leading to reduced network connectivity. In addition, teacher and data input channels are dynamically defined via gain control, so each channel can play either the role of a teacher or the role of an input at different times. Gain control also allows the system to function correctly even if input data to certain channels is missing at various times. Thus, faulty sensors may be deleted or new sensors added as the need arises.

II. FUZZY ARTMAP: A FUSION BUILDING BLOCK

Fuzzy ARTMAP is a supervised neural network classifier that learns to classify inputs by a fuzzy set of features, or a pattern of fuzzy membership values between 0 and 1 indicating the extent to which each feature is present. Fuzzy ARTMAP differs from many other fuzzy pattern recognition algorithms [2],[9] in that it learns each input as it is received on-line, rather than by performing an off-line optimization of a criterion function.

Each fuzzy ARTMAP system consists of a pair of fuzzy ART classifiers (ART_a, and ART_b) that create stable recognition categories in response to arbitrary sequences of input patterns (Fig. 1). During supervised learning, ART_a receives a stream $\mathbf{a}^{(p)}$ of input patterns, and ART_b receives a stream $\mathbf{b}^{(p)}$ of input patterns, where $\mathbf{b}^{(p)}$ is the correct prediction given $\mathbf{a}^{(p)}$. These modules are linked by an associative learning network and an internal controller that ensures autonomous system operation in real time. The controller is designed to create the minimal number of ART_a recognition categories, or "hidden units", needed to meet accuracy criteria. It does this by realizing a minimax learning rule that enables the fuzzy ARTMAP system to learn quickly, efficiently, and accurately as it conjointly *minimizes* predictive error and *maximizes* predictive generalization. This scheme automatically links predictive success to category size on a trial-by-trial basis using only local operations. It works by increasing the vigilance parameter ρ_a of ART_a by the minimal amount needed to correct a predictive error at ART_b.

When the ART_a classifier is presented with an input vector $\mathbf{a}$, the bottom-up activation from F_1^a causes the F_2^a layer to choose a category node based on the input's fuzzy membership in that category's fuzzy set. The chosen category then sends information back to the F_1^a layer which is compared to the input vector $\mathbf{a}$. The fuzzy intersection of top-down activation with the input vector produces a *match value* that indicates the classifier's confidence in its category choice. Parameter ρ_a calibrates the minimum confidence that ART_a must have in a recognition category, or hypothesis, activated by an input $\mathbf{a}^p$ in order for ART_a to accept that category, rather than search for a better one through an automatically controlled process of hypothesis testing. Lower values of ρ_a enable larger categories to form leading to broader generalization and higher code compression. A predictive failure at ART_b increases ρ_a by the minimum amount needed to trigger hypothesis testing at ART_a, using a mechanism called *match tracking* [5]. Match tracking sacrifices the minimum amount of generalization necessary to correct a predictive error. Hypothesis testing leads to the selection of a new ART_a category, which focuses attention on a new cluster of $\mathbf{a}^{(p)}$ input features that is better able to predict $\mathbf{b}^{(p)}$.

Fuzzy ARTMAP can itself be used for multisensor fusion, by concatenating the information from all sensors into a single input vector. However, whenever a predictive error occurs during training, the match tracking signal resets the ART_a classifier without regard to the predictive confidence in the individual channel information.

III. FUSION ARTMAP GENERALIZES FUZZY ARTMAP

Fusion ARTMAP extends the fuzzy ARTMAP classifier by incorporating an individual sensor classifier for each input channel, and by extending the match tracking technique in a manner that assigns blame only to the channels with least confidence in their predictions (Fig. 2).

Before a global recognition code is activated in

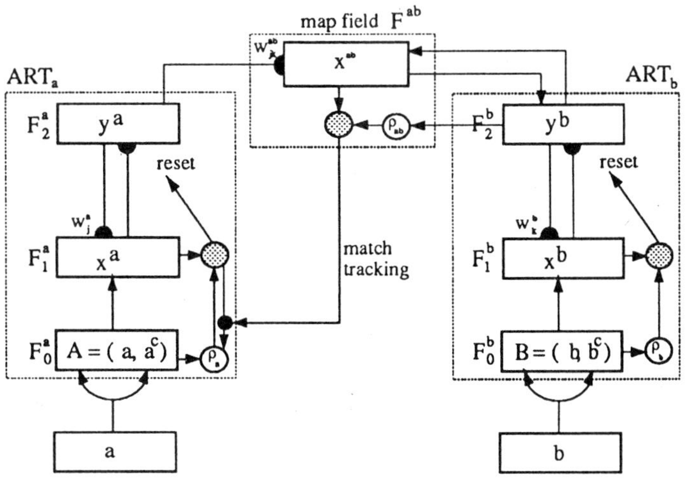

Figure 1: Fuzzy ARTMAP architecture. The ART_a complement coding preprocessor transforms the vector $\mathbf{a}$ into the vector $\mathbf{A} = (\mathbf{a}, \mathbf{a}^c)$ at the ART_a field F_0^a. $\mathbf{A}$ is the input to the ART_a field F_1^a. Similarly, in the supervised mode, the input to the ART_b field F_1^b is the vector $(\mathbf{b}, \mathbf{b}^c)$. When a prediction by ART_a is disconfirmed at ART_b, inhibition of the map field F^{ab} induces the match tracking process. Match tracking raises the ART_a vigilance (ρ_a) to just above the ART_a match value $|\mathbf{x}^a|/|\mathbf{A}|$. This triggers an ART_a search, which leads to activation of either an ART_a category that correctly predicts $\mathbf{b}$ or to a previously uncommitted ART_a category node.

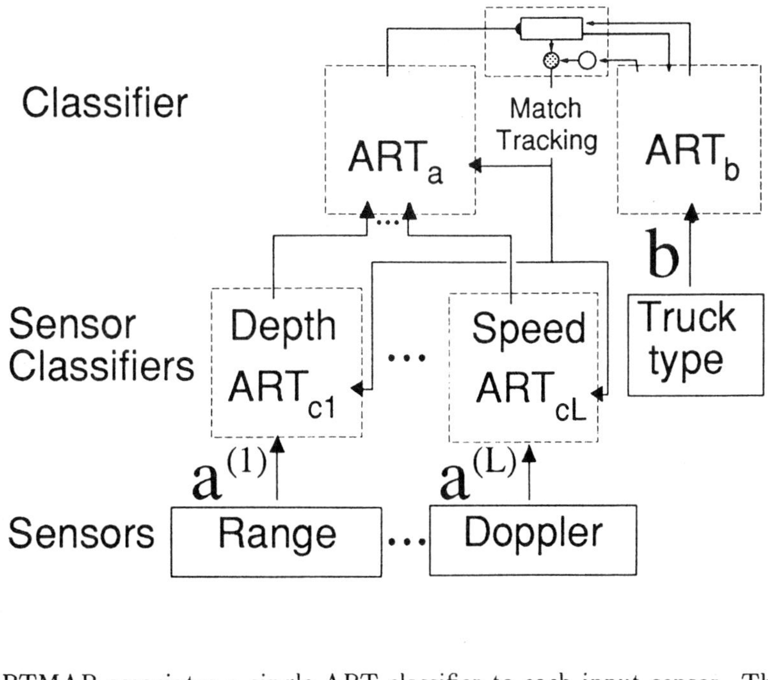

Figure 2: Fusion ARTMAP associates a single ART classifier to each input sensor. The outputs of these classifiers are used as inputs to a fuzzy ARTMAP system that makes a global prediction. Parallel match tracking raises the vigilance of all sensor classifiers simultaneously until the module with the least predictive confidence is reset.

Fusion ARTMAP, input to each channel activates a compressed recognition code in that channel's own fuzzy ART module. Then, one global fuzzy ARTMAP module, which receives compressed categorical input from each channel separately, organizes the multi-channel recognition code. The fuzzy ARTMAP system internally controls code formation via a nonspecific feedback signal sent in parallel to the ART systems of individual channels. This control process, called *parallel match tracking*, generalizes ARTMAP match tracking.

In Fusion ARTMAP, parallel match tracking simultaneously raises the vigilances of multiple sensor ART modules. A search is thereby triggered in just the one module that has the poorest match between bottom-up input and top-down prototype. It is hereby judged to be the most likely source of the predictive error and is defined to be the channel with the least predictive confidence. Search activates a new code in that module alone, preserving other input channel categories of the previously active pattern. This process of credit assignment efficiently shares code subsets across categories in the learned network, since predictively effective channels are not unnecessarily reset to correct errors caused by ineffective channels. Fusion ARTMAP thus creates more parsimonious codes, than single-channel recognition systems, with fewer paths and weights.

IV. INTRODUCING SYMMETRY

Fusion ARTMAP can be generalized by replacing the inter-ART map field F^{ab} with a modified global ART module (Fig. 3). The outputs of all the sensor and teacher classifiers are used as inputs to a global ART module that self-organizes its inputs into stable categories.

Channels are designated to input or teacher status by a set of parametric biases. Changing the bias on a particular channel can change its function from that of an input sensor to that of a target teacher. This symmetrical approach allows the use of multiple teacher channels.

System analysis shows that the generalized symmetric Fusion ARTMAP architecture reduces functionally to the system described in section III in the case of a "fixed single teacher channel" with multiple input sensors.

V. QUADRUPED MAMMAL DATABASE SIMULATIONS

Single-channel fuzzy ARTMAP and multi-channel Fusion ARTMAP systems were simulated using the Quadruped Mammal database [8], which represents four mammals (dog, cat, giraffe, and horse) in terms of eight components (head, tail, four legs, torso, and neck). Each component is described by nine attributes (three location variables, three orientation variables, height, radius, and texture), for a total of 72 attributes. Each attribute is modeled as a Gaussian process with mean and variance dependent on the mammal and component. For example, the radius of a giraffe's neck is modeled by a different Gaussian from that of a cat's neck or a giraffe's tail.

In the first set of simulations, Fusion ARTMAP was configured to be functionally equivalent to an unsupervised fuzzy ART system, with the entire attribute vector presented to a single channel, without a teacher. Fusion ARTMAP was allowed to self-organize the input vectors in categories. Fusion ARTMAP categorized the inputs into four stable categories corresponding to the four mammals.

In the next set of simulations, each of the eight component vectors was presented to a different ART_a module (Fig. 2), and the target animal's identity was presented to ART_b. Fusion ARTMAP achieved 100% prediction rates on both the training and testing sets within a single presentation when 1000 training exemplars were used. The resulting network was compared with that of a single-channel fuzzy ARTMAP system trained on the same data sets, except with a merged attribute vector. Performance was identical, but the single-channel case required about 1.5 times as many path connections and weights as the multi-channel case.

References

[1] Y.R. Asfour, G.A Carpenter, S. Grossberg, and G.W. Lesher, "Fusion ARTMAP: A neural network architecture for multi-channel data fusion and classification." *WCNN Conference Proceedings*, vol. 2, pp.210-215, July 1993.

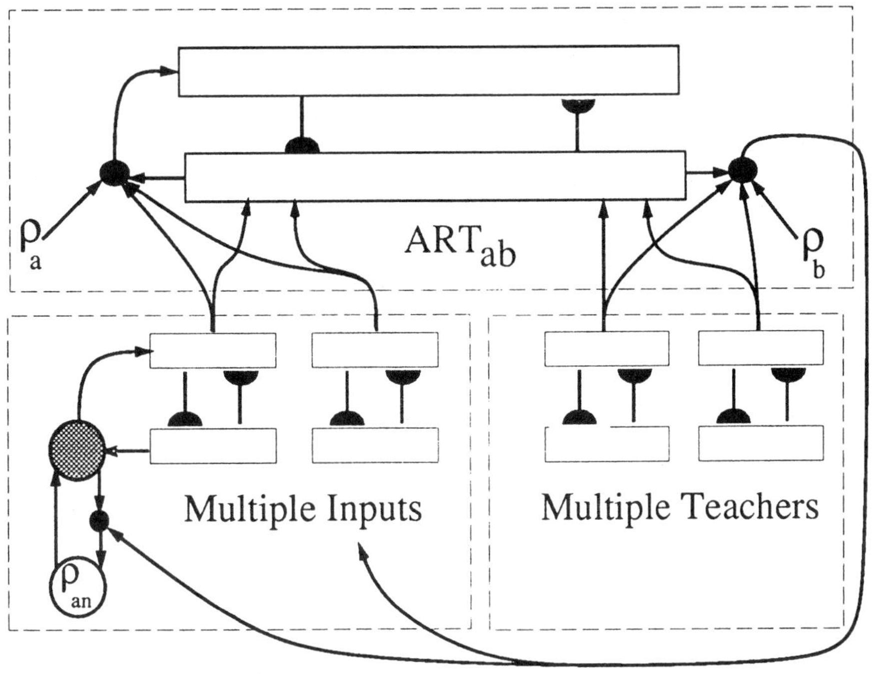

Figure 3: Replacing the inter-ART map field with a global ART module introduces symmetry between input and teacher classifiers, and allows multi-sensory fusion using multiple teachers.

[2] J.C. Bezdek, *Pattern Recognition with Fuzzy Objective Function Algorithms.* New York: Plenum Press, 1981.

[3] G.A. Carpenter, S. and Grossberg, S. "A massively parallel architecture for a self-organizing neural pattern recognition machine," *Computer Vision, Graphics, and Image Processing,* vol. 37, pp. 54-115, 1987.

[4] G.A Carpenter, S. Grossberg, N. Markuzon, J.H. Reynolds, and D.B. Rosen, "Fuzzy ARTMAP: A neural network architecture for incremental supervised learning of analog multidimensional maps." *IEEE Transactions on Neural Networks*, vol. 3, pp. 698-713, 1992

[5] G.A. Carpenter, S. Grossberg, and J.H. Reynolds, "ARTMAP: Supervised real-time learning and classification of nonstationary data by a self-organizing neural network." *Neural Networks*, vol. 4, pp. 565-588, 1991

[6] G.A Carpenter, S. Grossberg, and D.B. Rosen, "Fuzzy ART: Fast stable learning and categorization of analog patterns by an adaptive resonance system." *Neural Networks*, vol. 4, pp. 759-771, 1991.

[7] C.C. Chu, and J.K. Aggarwal, "Image interpolation using multiple sensing modalities." *IEEE Transactions on Pattern Analysis and Machine Intelligence*, vol. 14, pp. 840-846.

[8] J.H. Ginnari, "Quadruped mammals." *UCI Repository of machine learning databases* (Machine-readable data repository at ics.uci.edu:/usr2/spool/ftp/pub/machine-learning-databases). Department of Information and Computer Science, University of California, Irvine, CA, 1992.

[9] S. Pal, and D.K. Dutta Majumder, *Fuzzy Mathematical Approach to Pattern Recognition.* New York: Wiley, 1986.

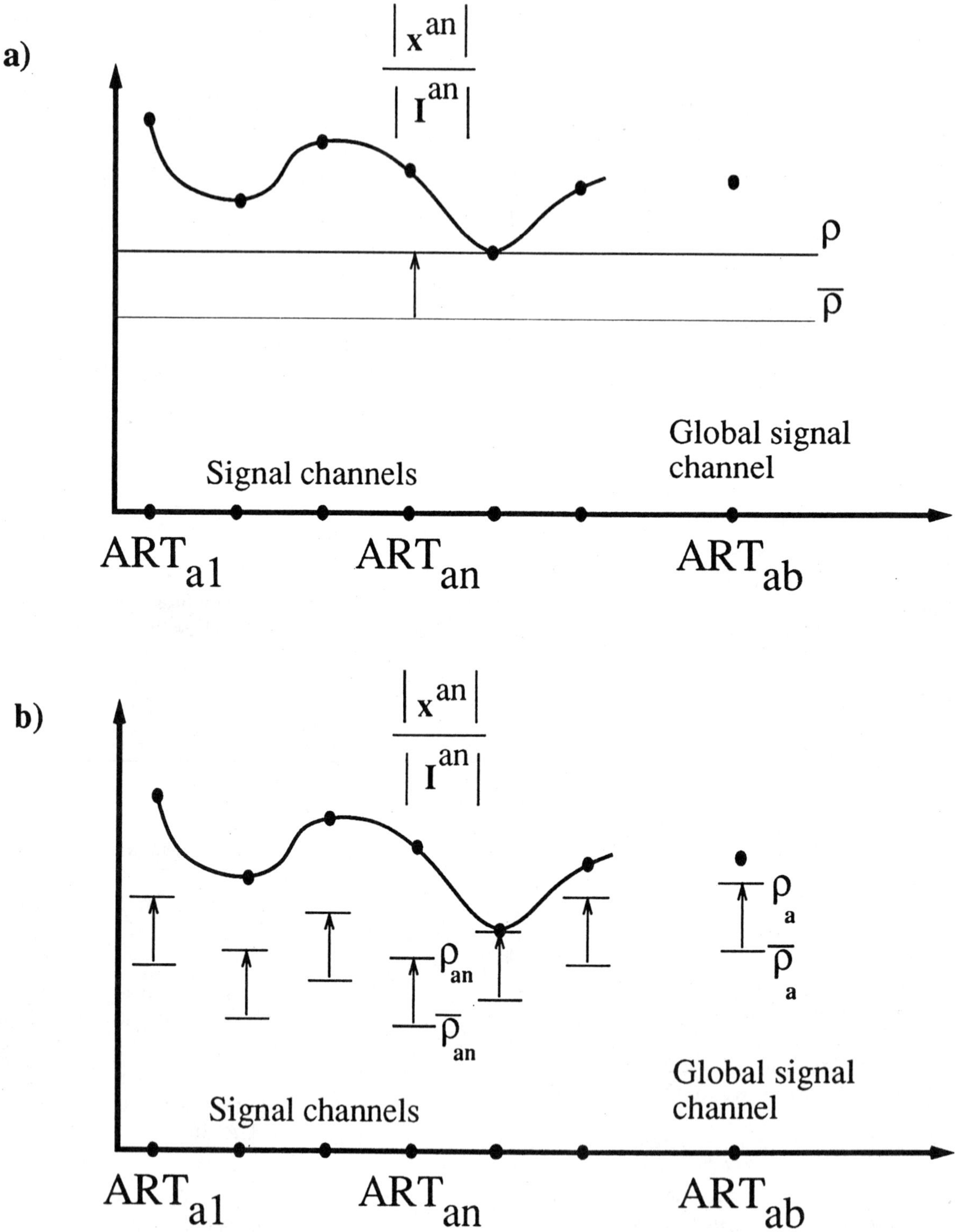

Figure 4: **(a)** When a predictive error occurs, parallel match tracking in Fusion ARTMAP raises multiple vigilance values simultaneously until reset occurs in the ART module most likely to have caused the error. **(b)** Parallel match tracking can simultaneously raise vigilances in independent Fusion ARTMAP modules each with its own initial match criterion value.

Target Recognition Using Multiple Sensors

Y. T. Zhou and R. Hecht-Nielsen
HNC, Inc.
5501 Oberlin Drive
San Diego, CA 92121
Tel.: (619)546-8877
FAX: (619)452-6524

Abstract—This paper presents a novel approach to multi-sensor target recognition. Currently available multi-sensor recognition algorithms/systems have low recognition rates when tested in battlefield conditions. This is mainly due to unrealistic assumptions made during the algorithm/system development. Our approach make no assumptions on either sensors or targets and uses some biologically inspired algorithms to build a multi-sensor target recognition system. It is applicable to many sensors including IR, TV, LADAR, MMW and SAR. The new system has been successfully tested on real TV and IR sensor images.

INTRODUCTION

This paper presents a novel approach to multi-sensor target recognition. Currently available multi-sensor recognition algorithms/systems have low recognition rates when tested in battlefield conditions. This is mainly due to unrealistic assumptions made during the algorithm/system development. Our approach makes no assumptions on either sensors or targets and uses some biologically inspired algorithms to build a multi-sensor target recognition system.

The new target recognition system is designed to recognize potential targets identified by a separated target detection system. The new system consists of two major components: a feature extractor and a target classifier. The inputs to the new systems are gray scale and segmented image patches. Each gray scale image patch contains a full size or partially obscured potential target and its immediate background as shown in Figure 1 (a). The segmented image patch contains the segmented target as shown in Figure 1 (b). (Gray scale and segmented image patches were provided by the U.S. Army Missile Command).

The feature extractor computes translation, rotation and scale (TRS)-variant features from the gray scale image patches. Although TRS-invariant features are often of more interest than TRS-variant features, most of the TRS-invariant features are sensitive to noise. For instance, the orthogonal

0-7803-0928-6/93$03.00 © 1993 IEEE

(a) (b)

Figure 1: A partially obscured tank. (a) The gray scale IR image patch. (b) Its segmentation.

invariant moments which are TRS-invariant can be used for classification to achieve very high recognition rates without noise [1]. When noise is involved, the matching performance will be significantly degraded due to these poorly estimated features. Feature evaluations based on real test data have indicated that the most effective and useful features are noise resistant TRS-variant features [2]. However, matching based on TRS-variant features often requires more computation than that based on TRS-invariant features, To reduce the computation requirements and improve the matching performance, it is common to use transform techniques such as Fourier, logarithmic, log polar, and their combinations to achieve invariance for the TRS-variant features [3, 4, 5]. Since the transform based methods achieve invariance in nonspatial domains, much useful information is discarded during transformation. To preserve information and achieve invariance simultaneously, our feature extractor uses a spatial domain based transform method.

The target classifier uses a multi-layer neural network for multiple sensors and multiple targets. The network can be trained to recognize targets from several classes. It is applicable to many sensors including IR, TV, LADAR, MMW and SAR. Initial tests on real TV and IR sensor images have yielded excellent performance.

FEATURE EXTRACTOR

The feature extractor contains three parts: segmentation refiner, transform network, and Gabor feature extractor. The inputs to the segmentation refiner are segmented image patches. The segmentation refiner finds the boundaries of the target in the patch and clips the target out. It also helps to improve the target's appearance by removing holes and smoothing boundaries. The transform network extracts translation, rotation and scale information from the target and carries out a spatial domain transform for the gray scale image patch to achieve invariance. The Gabor feature extractor computes Gabor features from the transformed gray scale image patch.

Segmentation Refiner

The segmentation refiner is a post segmentation processor. Current automatic target recognition (ATR) segmenters, even those judged to be the best cannot accurately generate target boundaries most of the time [6]. The segmentation problem has been plagued ATR for many years. It is common to use some post segmentation techniques to refine segmented images. The segmentation refiner uses morphological operations to remove holes from the target area and smooth target area boundaries. Figure 2 shows a target segmentation before and after segmentation refinement. It can be seen that the refined segment is better than the original segment. The segmentation refiner can locate multiple targets and refine them individually. However, the segmentation refiner cannot recover missing parts. Nonetheless, our system can function correctly when only small portions of the target are obscured.

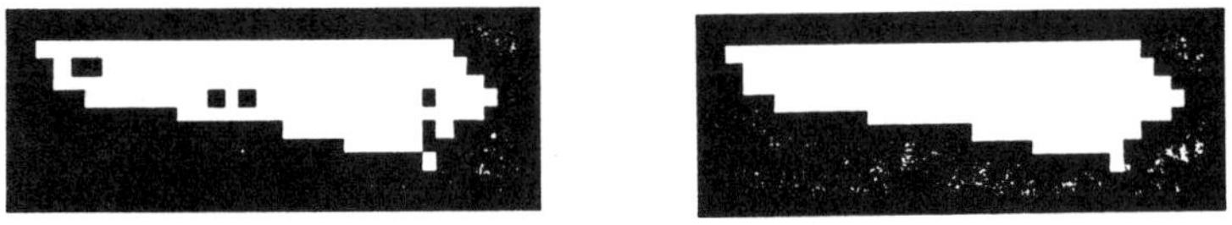

(a) (b)

Figure 2: Target segmentation. (a) Before segmentation refinement. (b) After segmentation refinement

Transform Network

Recently, a what-and-where (WW) neural network has been proposed to generate an invariant representation of the object by using TRS-variant features [7]. The WW neural network is inspired by the the brain's use of parallel cortical streams to simultaneously compute where an object is, and what the object is. It uses multiscale oriented filters to compute the position, boresight-axis orientation, and size of the object. The transform is carried out in the spatial domain by translating, rotating and scaling the object into a standard position. The transformed object finally rests in a specific location at a specific image plane orientation with a specific scale. Features extracted from the transformed object are independent of the position, boresight-axis orientation, and size of the original object. Therefore, considerable invariance has been achieved. The only remaining variance is with object azimuth and elevation.

The transform network is similar to the WW neural network but needs less computation. To solve the translation problem, existing approaches use Fourier transform technique or translate the object back to a standard position in the spatial domain. Instead, the transform network first finds

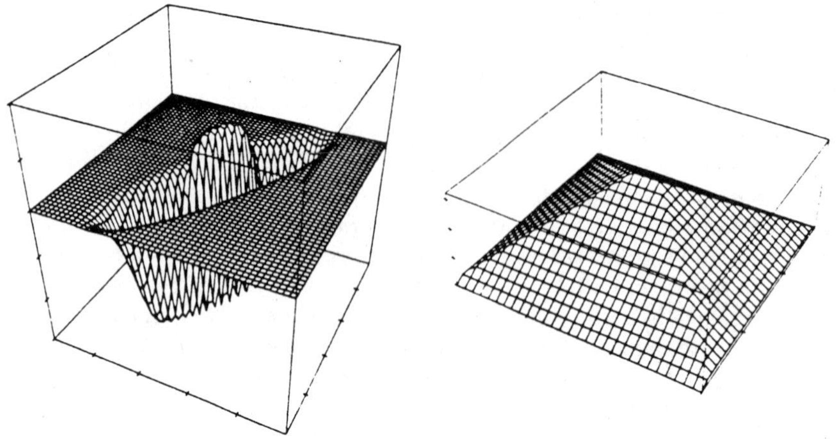

(a) (b)

Figure 3: Filters. (a) An ellipse filter at scale $s = 2$ with orientation $\theta = 120^o$. (b) A 0° oriented pyramid filter

the mass center of segmented target and then estimates its orientation and size.

To solve the scaling and orientation problems, the WW neural network uses ellipse filters to estimate the size and boresight-axis orientation of the segment. However, the transform network uses pyramid filters, which reduces computation considerably and is faster and more efficient than the WW neural network. For comparison purposes, we first introduce ellipse filters and then discuss pyramid filters.

The ellipse filters used by the WW neural network are defined by the kernel [7]

$$W(x, y, \theta, s) = (1 - x^6) \exp(-\frac{r^4}{1 + r^2}) \tag{1}$$

where θ is the orientation, s is the size and r is given by

$$r^2 = (\frac{x \cos\theta + y \sin\theta}{a\, s})^2 + (\frac{y \cos\theta - x \sin\theta}{s})^2$$

with an elongation parameter a. Figure 3 (a) depicts an ellipse filter at scale $s = 2$ with orientation $\theta = 120^o$. The elongation parameter a is set at 2.0. The filter includes a positively weighted oblong center area bordered by a sharp drop-off to negatively weighted surround section which in turn is bordered by an external region of near zero weighting. When a target aligns with and fits within the central region of the filter perfectly, the response reaches the maximum. Due to the highly negatively weighted surround region, the response of the filter starts to drop off sharply when parts of a target fall outside of the center region. To estimate the boresight-axis orientation of an target, the WW neural network uses 108 ellipse filters (18 orientations × 6 scales). The maximal response at each scale represents the optimal boresight-axis orientation and the final decision is determined by direct comparison across scales. Due to the elliptical shape of the negatively weighted surround section, ellipse filters have the double peak problem. Namely, for essentially any target, there always exists a scale such that above the scale, the maximal response occurs at the correct orientation, while below the scale, it occurs at the perpendicular orientation. To overcome the double peak problem, the WW neural network uses another 62 ellipse filters (2 orientations × 31 scales) to estimate the scale [7].

To avoid the double peak problem and reduce the computation requirements, the transform network uses 18 pyramid filters (18 orientations) only. Figure 3 (b) gives a 0° oriented pyramid filter. The pyramid filter has a rectangular base and sloping sides which meet at a top line. In other words, it has a pyramid appearance, hence the name pyramid filter. The orientation of the filter coincides with the orientation of the top line. The maximal response of the pyramid filters in reaction to any oriented target always occurs at the correct orientation, which uniquely determines the boresight-axis orientation of the target. The size of the target is determined by the pyramid level at which it fits best. Once the boresight-axis orientation and size are obtained, the target can be rotated to a specific image plane orientation and scaled to a specific size. However, since features will be extracted from the gray scale image instead of the segmented image, the gray scale image will be rotated and rescaled in the spatial domain based on the information estimated from the segmented image. Figures 4 (a) and (b) show IR tank images before and after transformation. The transformed image is enlarged and oriented in a specific direction. The operation of the transform network is highly insensitive to noise.

(a) (b)

Figure 4: IR tank image. (a) Before transformation. (b) After transformation.

Gabor Feature Extractor

The Gabor feature extractor uses Gabor functions to compute features from the transformed gray scale images. Features extracted by Gabor functions are called Gabor features or Gabor coefficients.

Gabor functions are sinusoidal functions weighted by Gaussian functions. A general form for 2-D Gabor functions can be written as [8]

$$G(x,y) = \exp\{-\pi[(x-x_0)\alpha^2+(y-y_0)\beta^2]-2\pi i[u_0(x-x_0)+v_0(y-y_0)]\} \quad (2)$$

where (x_0, y_0) are position parameters which localize the function to a region in visual space, (u_0, v_0) are modulation parameters which orient the function to a preferred direction and control the size of the perceptive field, and (α, β) are scale parameters which determine spatial dimensions. Whole families of Gabor functions can be derived from (2) by varying the modulation and scale parameters. The real and imaginary parts of the Gabor function are partially decaying cosine and sine waves which respond maximally to bars and edges, respectively. The oscillating portion enables the function to encode spatial frequency and phase information, while the decaying part ensures that spatial frequencies are sampled only from a limited region in visual space.

Since Gabor functions presumably fit the 2-D receptive profiles found in the mammalian brain and their real and imaginary parts can detect perceptually significant features through locating local maxima in their energy at different scales [9], they are useful for feature extraction and pattern recognition [8, 10]. Our feature extractor uses Gabor functions, especially at large scales, to compute features. The large scale Gabor functions resist noise and background clutter effects. In addition, Gabor features computed at large scales are robust against variations in target signatures. At each feature sampling point, Gabor features at multiple orientations and multiple scales are computed. To capture the local structural information, features are computed at multiple sampling points (the mass center and its surrounding points) instead of a single sampling point for each target.

Since the Gabor function is represented as a complex function, each Gabor feature is a complex number. Rather than use the complex number, the feature extractor computes the magnitude of the Gabor feature. The magnitude is invariant to target contrast reversal and is useful for classification [11]. Since all targets are normalized and oriented in the same direction after transformation, Gabor features extracted from the transformed target are independent of the position, boresight-axis orientation, and size of the original target.

TARGET CLASSIFIER

The classifier is a multi-layer feedforward (MLF) neural network [12, 13]. The MLF neural network has been widely used in image and speech recognition since learning algorithms were developed [14, 12]. With learning, the MLF neural network is capable of partitioning the pattern space with appropriate nonlinear decision boundaries [15]. However, many issues concerning the MLF neural network remain to be resolved. For instance, the learning rate, weight initialization, stopping criteria, number of layers and number of PEs in each layer. Fortunately, these issues are only related to the training process and can be experimentally determined, although the solutions may not be optimal. Once the network has been trained, classification is straightforward and takes almost no time.

The input to the MLF neural network consists of Gabor features. Picking good features is the essence of classification. No elaborate formalism will work well for bad features and almost any method will work for very good features. Good features are those which can separate the different classes in feature space based on feature clustering methods. Gabor features have been demonstrated to be good features for classification purposes [8, 10]. However, in practical applications, a limited set of Gabor features is used. As mentioned earlier, multiple feature sampling points are used for each target. The total number of inputs to the MLF neural network is then given by $(M \times N)$, where N is the number of Gabor features computed at each feature sampling point and M is the number of feature sampling points for each target.

The output layer of the MLF neural network contains multiple processing elements (PEs). The number of PEs in the output layer is at least equal to the total number of classes. The number of the inputs and outputs can be predetermined. However, the number of hidden layers and the number of PEs in each hidden layer are variable. They depend on the properties of the features and number of the inputs and outputs, and must be experimentally determined.

The network is trained with a back-propagation learning algorithm [12]. The learning rate for each layer is either fixed or adaptively updated. When features are good, a fixed learning rate works fine if it is not too big. Weights are initialized to small random values to have a safe starting point [16]. To stop the training process, many stopping criteria can be used. For instance, the training can be stopped if the magnitude of the gradient or mean squared error (MSE) is sufficiently small, i.e. smaller than a fixed threshold. The simplest way is to stop the training after a fixed number of iterations have been carried out. However, all of these criteria are sensitive to the choice of parameters, threshold and number of iterations. There is a criterion which dose not suffer from this characteristic. That is the cross-validation method. The cross-validation method essentially splits data into training and test sets. During the training, the performance of the network on both the training and test data is measured after each iteration. When the performance on the test data starts to degrade, i.e., the MSE on the test data increases, the training will be stopped [13].

EXPERIMENTAL RESULTS

A initial test has been carried out for the new multi-sensor target recognition system. We received 242 image patches and their segmentation, statistical features and groundtruth from the U.S. Army Missile Command. The gray scale image patches were from real TV and IR image sequences. They contain full-size or partially obscured targets such as tanks and helicopters, or clutter. Figure 1 shows a partially obscured tank IR image patch and its segmentation. A full-size tank IR image patch is given in Figure 4. Figure 5 shows a full-size tank TV image patch and its segmentation. Figures 6 (a) and (b) show a full-size helicopter IR image patch and a full-size helicopter TV image patch, respectively. Two noise patches are also given in Figure 7. For illustration purposes, images have been enlarged. For instance, the original size of the full-size IR tank image patch is only about 27×20 pixels. The size of the image patches varies from a hundred pixels to a thousand pixels. To extract features from an image patch, the

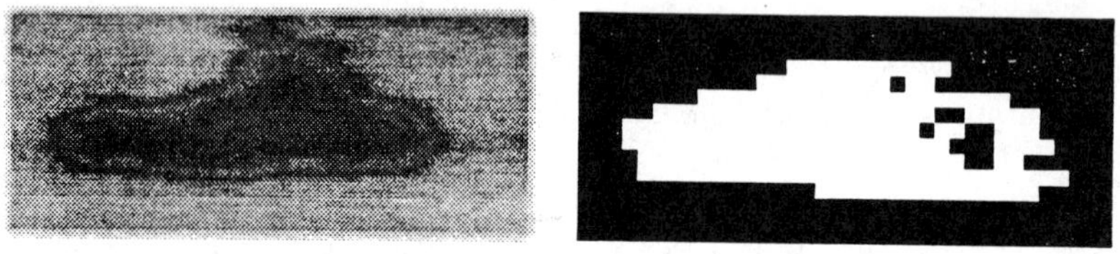

(a) (b)

Figure 5: A full-size tank. (a) The gray scale TV image patch. (b) Its segmentation.

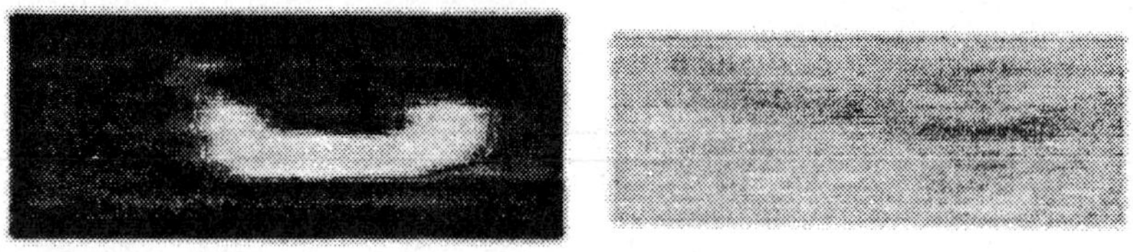

(a) (b)

Figure 6: A full-size helicopter. (a) The gray scale IR image patch. (b) The gray scale TV image patch.

Figure 7: Noise patches.

feature extractor first applies the segmentation refiner to remove holes and to smooth target boundaries, as shown in Figure 2. The module then uses the transform network to transform the gray scale image patch to a standard position as shown in Figure 4. Finally, low resolution Gabor functions are used to compute Gabor features at each feature sampling point. For training purposes, 242 image patches were randomly split into a training set and a test set. The training set had 70% of the image patches and the test set contained 30% of the image patches, i.e., 169 image patches were used for training and 73 image patches were used for test.

The network was first trained for a 3-class problem. Three classes were the tank, helicopter, and noise. The network weights were initialized to small random values between $[-0.1, 0.1]$. Only Gabor features were used as the input. The training set (169 image patches) was used to train the network and the cross-validation method was used to stop the trainging. After every 100 iterations, the performance of the network was measured. Typically, the recognition rate and MSE were first computed for the training set. Then, the test data (73 image patches) were used to test the network and the recognition rate and MSE were computed. For the 3-class problem, a recognition rate of 100% was achieved for both the traing and test sets.

The network was then further trained for a 5-class and a 9-class problems. For the 5-class problem, targets were further divided into full-size tank partially obscured tank, full-size helicopter, and partially obscured helicopter. For the 9-class problem, targets were classified as TV full-size tank, TV partially obscured tank, IR full-size tank, IR partially obscured tank, TV full-size helicopter, TV partially obscured helicopter, IR full-size helicopter, IR partially obscured helicopter, and noise. After training, the network achieved a recognition rate of 100% again for both the 5-class and 9-class problems. In the future we expect to be able to test the system on entirely new test data that was not used for system training termination.

References

[1] M. K. Hu. "Visual Pattern Recognition by Moment Invariants". *IRE Trans. Inofrmation Theory*, pp. 179–187, Feb. 1962.

[2] W. G. Pemberton, A. R. Sanders, and J. M. Sura. "Techniques for Extraction of Mobile Missiles from Infrared Imagery". In *Proc. Conference on Pattern Recognition for Advanced Missile Systems*, Huntsville, AL, Nov. 1988.

[3] P. S. Schenker, K. M. Wong, and E. G. Cande. "Fast Adaptive Algorithms for Low-level Scene Analysis: Application of Polar Exponential Grid (PEG) Representation to High-Speed Scale and Rotation Invariant Target Segmentation". In *Tech. Appl. Image Understanding*, SPIE, vol. 281, pp. 47–57, 1981.

[4] R. A. Messner and H. H. Szu. "Coordinate Transform from an Image Plane Directly to an Invariant Feature Space". In *Proc. Conf. on Computer Vision and Pattern Recognition*, pp. 522–530, Washington, D.C., 1983.

[5] P. Cavanagh. "Image Transforms in the Visual System". In P. C. Dodwell and T. Caelli, editors, *Figural Synthesis*, pp. 185–218. Lawrence Erlbaum Associates, 1984.

[6] F. A. Sadjadi. "Automatic Object Recognition: Critical Issues and Current Approaches". In *Applications of Automatic Object Recognition*, SPIE, vol. 1471, pp. 303–313, Orlando, Florida, April 1991.

[7] G. A. Carpenter, S. Grossberg, and G. W. Lesher. A What-and-Where Neural Network for Invariant Image Processing. Technical Report CAS/CNS-92-006, Center for Adaptive Systems, Boston University, Feb. 1992.

[8] J. G. Daugman. "Complete Discrete 2-D Gabor Transforms by Neural Networks for Image Analysis and Compression". *IEEE Trans. on Acoustics, Speech, and Signal Processing*, vol. ASSP-36, pp. 1169–1179, July 1988.

[9] M. C. Morrone and D. C. Burr. "Feature Detection in Human Vision: a Phase Dependent Energy Model". *Proc. Royal Society of London*, vol. B-235, pp. 221–245, 1988.

[10] Y. Y. Zeevi and R. Ginosar. "Neural Computers for Foveating Vision Systems". In R. Eckmiller, editor, *Advanced Neural Computers*, pp. 323–330. Elsevier Science Publishers B.V., North-Holland, 1990.

[11] Y. T. Zhou and R. Crawshaw. "Contrast, Size and Orientation Invariant Target Detection in Infrared Imagery". In *Applications of Automatic Object Recognition*, SPIE, vol. 1471, pp. 404–411, Orlando, Florida, April 1991.

[12] D. E. Rumelhart, G. E. Hinton, and R. J. Williams. "Learning Internal Representations by Error Propagation". In D. E. Rumelhart and J. L. McClelland, editors, *Parallel Distributed Processing*, vol. 1, pp. 318–362. MIT Press, 1986.

[13] R. Hecht-Nielsen. *Neurocomputing*. Addison-Wesley, Reading, MA, 1991.

[14] D. B. Parker. Learning-Logic. Technical Report TR-47, Center for Computational Research in Economics and Management Science, 1985.

[15] J. Makhoul, A. El-Jaroudi, and R. Schwartz. "Formation of Disconnected Decision Regions with a Single Hidden Layer". In *Proc. Intl. Joint Conf. on Neural Networks*, vol. I, pp. 455–460, Washington, D.C., June 1989.

[16] D. Hush, J. M. Salas, and B. Horne. "Error Surfaces for Multi-layer Perceptions". *IEEE Trans. Syst.,Man and Cybern.*, vol. 22, 1992.

MLANS NEURAL NETWORK FOR SENSOR FUSION

Leonid I Perlovsky

Nichols Research Corporation
251 Edgewater Drive, Wakefield, MA 01880

ABSTRACT

Information fusion from multiple sources is an increasingly important area of research and application. This problem is often complicated by various sensors having different limitations and fields of view. Further complications result from the absence of prior knowledge. In addition to fusing diverse information, it is also necessary to manage multiple sensors with various limitations efficiently for optimal overall system performance. We have solved this set of problems using the MLANS neural network that employs model based approach and fuzzy decision logic.

Fusion of information from multiple sensors and other sources is becoming an increasingly important area of research and application. In many cases the information to be fused originates from sources of different types, having different coverage or field-of-views (FOV), and operated asynchronously. This results in incomplete data sets: while many objects are observed by a single sensor, only a few may be observed by all the sensors. Fusion of such incomplete data sets, a complicated problem that has not previously been solved is the first issue this paper addresses.

Standard Bayesian inference leads to optimal fusion. Often it is not applicable, however, because the statistical distributions of the data are not known exactly. The absence of knowledge of the prior probabilities has been long recognized as a difficulty for the Bayesian approach. In reality, however, the problem is not limited to the absence of knowledge of the priors, but in fact all the distribution parameters are usually unknown, and the common assumption of Gaussian distributions is not usually valid. The second issue addressed in the paper is optimal fusion without prior knowledge of the distributions.

The optimal management of limited sensory and other information resources is a third issue addressed in this paper. For example, a visual sensor observes an entire scene, while tactile and other active sensors are used to obtain additional information on only a few objects in the scene; these additional objects should be selected so that the overall system performance is optimized. In another example, a large amount of data is available for training of a neural network recognizer; however, providing true classification labels is a time consuming procedure involving a human expert. It is desirable to minimize human "teacher" involvement by (a) combining self-learning with supervised learning; and (b)

CH3306-8/93/0000-0880 $1.00 © 1993 IEEE

selecting samples for teacher examination in such a way that will provide for the most improvement in combined neural network learning. All the available information should be used to direct limited sensory resources.

An approach to solving this set of sensor and information fusion problems is developed using the Maximum Likelihood Adaptive Neural System (MLANS)[1,2], Figure 1. This neural network combines a model based approach[3] with optimal statistical techniques to achieve adaptivity in the fusion of the data. In this neural network, the weights are fuzzy measures associating each piece of information with various decision classes. This permits the fusing of data from various sources, and on various levels. These levels include measurements, features, decisions such as subjective probabilities obtained from external sources, or other fuzzy measures of association[4]. The weights are parameterized in terms of a relatively small number of model parameters. These parameters are estimated by the Minimum Entropy (ME) neuron and Maximum Likelihood neurons (N,M,C) shown in Figure 1. The Maximum Likelihood neurons permit extremely fast learning of data distributions so that MLANS achieves the information-theoretic bounds on speed of adaptation and learning[5]. Another related advantage of a model-based approach is the MLANS capability to combine self-learning with any available information, including a priori and a posteriori information[6].

Based on these capabilities of the MLANS, we have developed a Decision Directed Learning (DDL) approach which is illustrated in the following example. In this application, a small number of defective parts (Class 1) have to be found among good parts (Class 2) and other objects (Class 3). Three available sensors are shown in Figure 2: a passive sensor, an active sensor, and an inspection/interrogation sensor. The active sensor provides more accurate classification information than the passive sensor, but its capacity is limited to observing only one third of all the objects. An inspection sensor can unambiguously identify the objects, however, inspection is time consuming and expensive and its utilization should be limited only to the most important objects (Class 3). In our approach, the passive data are used for preliminary clustering and classification of all the observed objects. Based on this preliminary result, the active sensor is pointed at the most important objects and the active sensor data are then used to update the classification of *all* the objects. Based on this improved classification, the inspection is directed at a few of the most important objects and, again, its results are used to update the classification of *all* the objects.

Figure 3 shows the results of this DDL approach. A passive sensor feature space is shown in Figure 3a. A total number of 216 objects are observed by the passive sensor. From these data, the MLANS learns in real time the distributions of three classes of objects. These learned distributions are shown using dotted lines. The true distributions are shown using solid lines for comparison. It is seen, that the distributions for two classes of objects are estimated very closely to the true ones: these are relatively

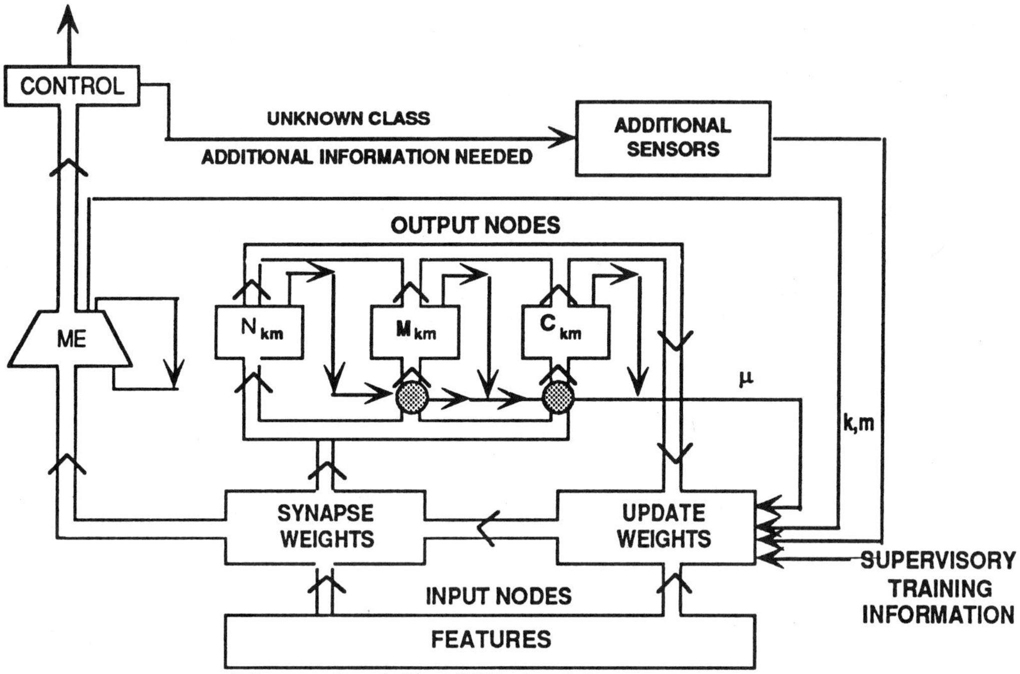

Figure 1. MLANS Architecture

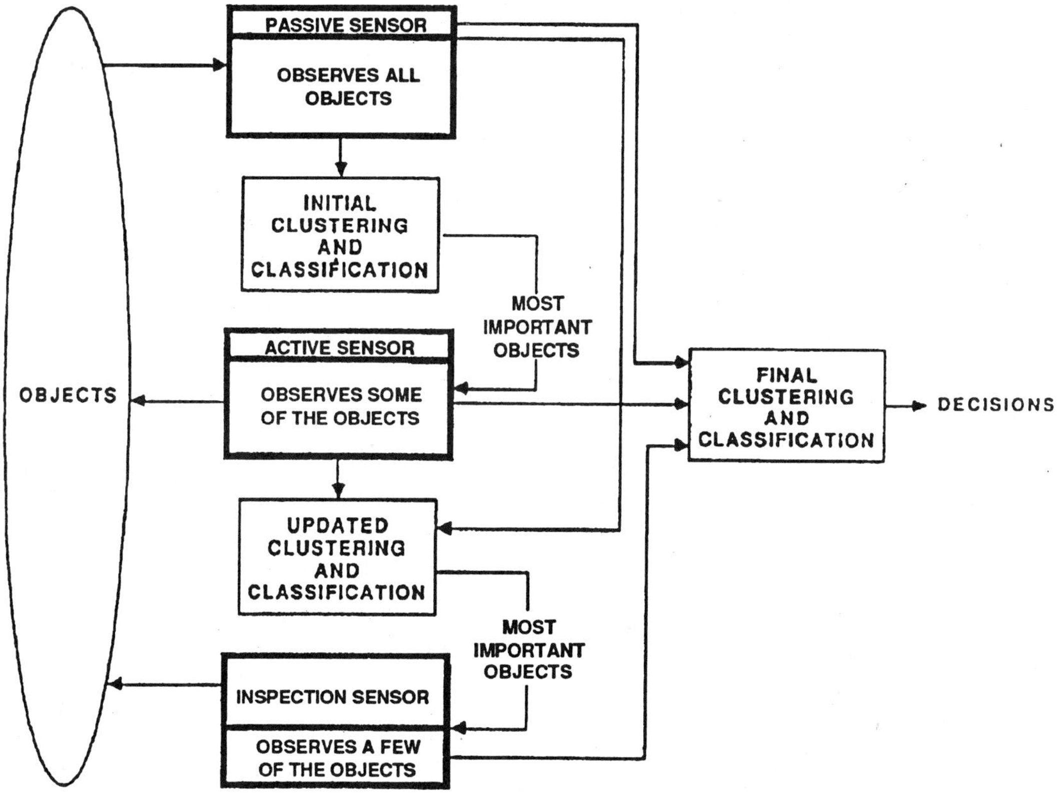

Figure 2. Decision directed learning scenario

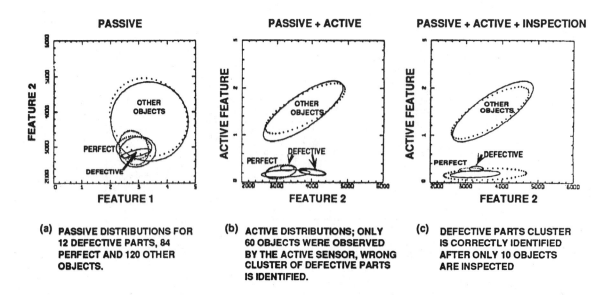

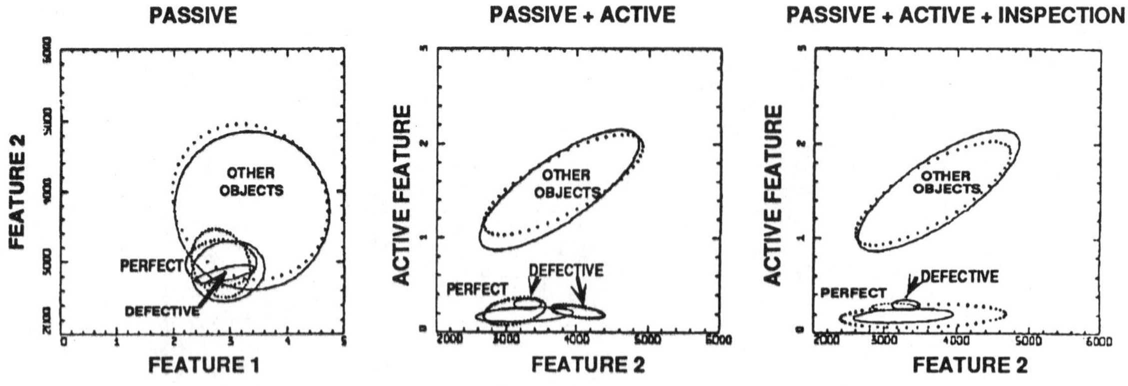

(a) PASSIVE DISTRIBUTIONS FOR 12 DEFECTIVE PARTS, 84 PERFECT AND 120 OTHER OBJECTS.

(b) ACTIVE DISTRIBUTIONS; ONLY 60 OBJECTS WERE OBSERVED BY THE ACTIVE SENSOR, WRONG CLUSTER OF DEFECTIVE PARTS IS IDENTIFIED.

(c) DEFECTIVE PARTS CLUSTER IS CORRECTLY IDENTIFIED AFTER ONLY 10 OBJECTS ARE INSPECTED

Figure 3. Decision directed learning example.

large groups of Class 2 and 3 objects. However, the defective part distribution (Class 1) is not estimated very accurately due to the fact that only a few (12) defective parts are among the observed objects. Classification labels are not yet learned by the neural network.

These learned distributions are used for directing the active sensor which observes only about one third of all the objects, and measures a single additional feature. The MLANS clusters all the available data in the new 3-dimensional feature space comprised of the passive and active sensor features. This result is shown in Figure 3b. The Class 2 and 3 distributions are accurately estimated, although for most of the objects the active sensor measurements are not available. However, the Class 1 distribution is still misidentified. The reason for this is that most of the objects do not have their active feature measured, and the MLANS places them in the active feature coordinate according to their clustering in 2-dimensional passive feature space. Then, based on this incorrect classification, ten most likely Class-1 objects are inspected. None of them turn out to be a defective part. Nevertheless, this "negative" information is used by the MLANS to look for another most likely Class-1 cluster. This cluster is now accurately found in Figure 3c, and all the 12 Class-1 objects (defective parts) are then selected without an error for inspection. All the defective parts, therefore, are found among 216 objects with only 22 being inspected.

In summary, a novel approach has been developed to fuse information from diverse sources and for the optimal direction of sensors with limited resources and fields-of-view has been developed. This approach is implemented in a MLANS neural network and it is applicable to a large number of problems in diverse areas.

REFERENCES

1. Perlovsky, L.I. (1987). *Multiple Sensor Fusion and Neural Networks,* DARPA Neural Network Study, MIT/Lincoln Laboratory, Lexington, MA.

2. Perlovsky, L.I. (1988). *Neural Networks for Sensor Fusion and Adaptive Classification,* First Annual International Neural Network Society Meeting, Boston, MA.

3. Perlovsky, L.I. (1990). *Application of Neural Networks to Transient Signal Classification*, Government Neural Network Application Workshop, NOSC, San Diego, CA.

4. Burdick, B. J., and Perlovsky, L. I. (1991). *Application of MLANS to Real-Time Learning of Targets.* Presidential Scientific Advisory Group Meeting, Washington, DC.

5. Perlovsky, L.I. (1989). *Cramer-Rao Bounds for the Estimation of Normal Mixtures*, Pattern Recognition Letters, **10**, 141-148.

6. Perlovsky, L.I. & McManus, M.M. (1991). *Maximum Likelihood Neural Networks for Sensor Fusion and Adaptive Classification*, Neural Networks **4**(1), pp. 89-102.

USING SELF-ORGANIZED AND SUPERVISED LEARNING NEURAL NETWORKS IN PARALLEL FOR AUTOMATIC TARGET RECOGNITION

Magnús Snorrason & Alper K. Caglayan
Charles River Analytics Inc.
55 Wheeler St.
Cambridge, MA 02138
phone: (617)491-3474
fax: (617)868-0780
email: mss@crasun.cra.com

Bruce T. Buller
Department of the Air Force
WL/MNGS
Eglin AFB, FL 32542-5434
phone: (904)882-2838, ext 2374
fax: (904)882-4034
email: buller@eglin.af.mil

Abstract - In this paper, we present a hybrid approach to automatic target recognition (ATR) combining the complementary strengths of conventional image processing algorithms, artificial neural networks, and knowledge based expert systems. The architecture employs parallel feature and pixel processing channels, the former using a self-organizing neural network and the latter using a supervised learning neural network. The feasibility of the hybrid ATR approach to target detection, classification and recognition is demonstrated using LADAR data.

INTRODUCTION

Automatic target recognition (ATR) is the processing and understanding of an image in order to recognize targets [1]. This problem carries with it most of the complexity of general scene analysis, which has been studied for decades by researchers in animal and machine vision. The present state-of-the-art machine vision systems do not even approach the performance of human vision in general scene analysis, so there is still much to be learned from biological vision systems. We have kept this in mind in our research on ATR and used biomorphic engineering approaches where possible.

0-7803-0928-6/93$03.00 © 1993 IEEE

Neural networks are commonly considered a biomorphic solution and we chose to use two neural network paradigms in parallel, to incorporate the complementary advantages offered by self-organized and supervised learning neural networks. The primary use for neural networks in ATR has typically been as pattern classifiers. There are many reasons why neural networks tend to perform well as classifiers, but the main reason is that they learn by example and therefore do not need to know the *a priori* probability distribution of the underlying classes, unlike Bayesian and many other statistical pattern classifiers. In ATR, this is critical because the probability distribution of the underlying classes is continuously changing.

Operational speed is a critical issue in an ATR system which must perform in real time and possibly with large numbers of target and clutter objects in each frame. This is another reason for choosing neural networks, in particular the feedforward paradigms, over analytic algorithms.

SELF-ORGANIZED VS. SUPERVISED LEARNING

Recognition by supervised learning is clearly applicable to ATR. A neural network can be trained to recognize canonical views of known targets. The trained network can then be expected to recognize those targets even if they are not presented exactly in one of the canonical views due to the inherent abilities of neural networks to generalize. Alternatively, a neural network can be trained on extracted features of known targets which are invariant to scale, rotation, perspective angle, etc. Due to generalization, such a network can also be expected to recognize the training targets even if the extracted features do not match exactly with the learned ones.

The fundamental problem with this approach is that the set of all canonical views or invariant features for all known targets is huge. Both the markings and shape of a target such as a military vehicle changes substantially with the load or weapons being carried, the type of camouflage, etc. This is a well known problem in general scene analysis, for example recognizing the same person wearing different clothes.

Humans are clearly not limited to the use of supervised learning paradigms in their pattern recognition abilities. We learn on-line and we do not need to be told how to classify all novel patterns. Self-organized neural networks, such as Adaptive Resonance Theory networks [3,4], attempt to capture these abilities by not requiring separate training and performance phases and by building new output clusters for novel patterns which do not match any previously learned patterns.

The tradeoff is that self-organized neural networks cannot perform true classification because all the category labels are not known *a priori*. Instead they perform clustering where the output clusters require additional analysis in order to receive symbolic labels. Our solution is to use an expert system to perform this analysis, it allows domain specific knowledge to be incorporated into the decision process without compromising the self-organizing network's ability to handle novel patterns.

OVERVIEW OF SYSTEM ARCHITECTURE

One of the major known facts about the human visual system is the existence of separate parallel processing pathways for form and depth, color, and motion, which are only combined at a late stage of processing [2]. Similarly, our system has parallel processing channels where each processing stream produces a decision based on its own discriminant and the decisions are combined through an expert system voting process to produce the final decision and accompanying certainty measure. Our reasoning for using parallel channels is that is allows us to make use of the complimentary nature of self-organized and a supervised learning neural networks without significantly slowing down the total system throughput.

Through our research on ATR using laser radar (LADAR) sensor data, we have developed the system architecture shown in figure 1. It consists of two channels: one using a self-organizing neural network for feature processing and the other using a supervised learning neural networks for direct pixel processing. Each channel gets inputs from both data streams, LADAR range and intensity data, through initial preprocessing modules. Both channels also get information from the *Parameter Control* knowledge base (KB) which controls parameters of the neural network classifiers using environmental information provided by the *Exogenous Information* block.

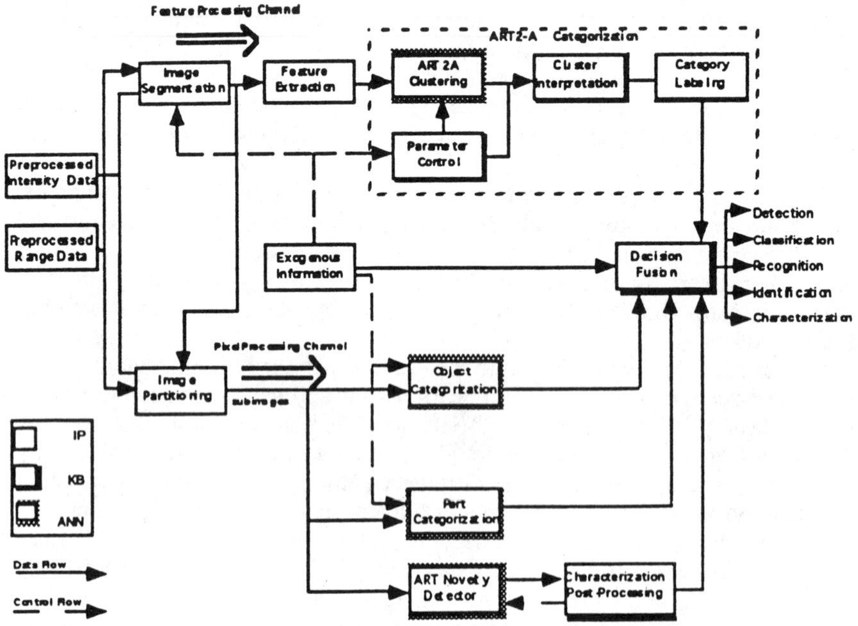

Figure 1: Hybrid Target Classifier Block Diagram

The *Feature Processing Channel* consists of a series of modules which segment the objects in one image, extract features from those objects, cluster the objects based on those features, interpret the clusters, and finally label each cluster to specify the category of each object. The *Pixel Processing Channel* first partitions the intensity image into subimages based on the segmentation from the *Feature Processing Channel*, and then splits into three parallel subchannels which classify the subimages, classify parts of the subimages, and detect novel parts of the subimages. The *Feature Processing Channel* and the *Pixel Processing Channel* then combine in the *Decision Fusion* module which combines the decision from the *Feature Processing Channel* with the three decisions from the *Pixel Processing Channel* into a final decision and a measure of certainty for each object.

There is a risk of losing information that is valuable for discrimination when the dimensionality of the input data is compressed. Feature extraction is a form of data compression and since it is not always clear what information is needed for discrimination in ATR, it is very difficult to produce a set of features which guaranties no degradation in the discrimination process. For this reason, we have chosen to use *both* extracted features and direct pixel representation, in parallel channels.

We have developed working prototypes of the *Feature Processing Channel* and accompanying *Parameter Control*, and the *Object Categorization* component of the *Pixel Processing Channel.* More parallel channels are easily added, their output would go to the *Decision Fusion* component and be included in the voting process which generates the categorization of each object detected in a segmented LADAR image. Additional channels might be added both to increase the certainty of categorization and to expand the usage of *Exogenous Information*, for example to choose different channels based on *a priori* knowledge about the terrain.

THE FEATURE PROCESSING CHANNEL

The first module in the *Feature Processing Channel* is the *segmentation* module. In the present implementation of our architecture no neural networks are used in this module, instead classical region based (such as density slicing) and edge based (such as Sobel and gradient directional) segmentation methods are used. Our initial results have shown those methods to be capable of segmenting all target objects in the LADAR images when both range and intensity data is used. Figure 2 shows a sample segmented LADAR intensity image.

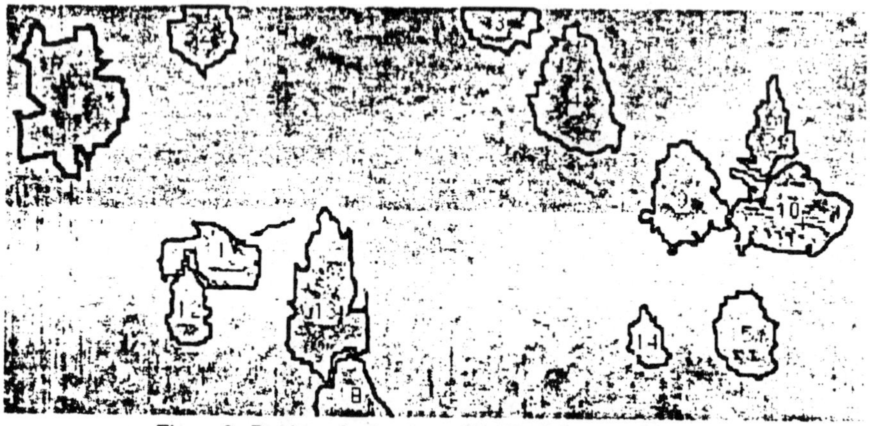

Figure 2: Portion of a Segmented LADAR Intensity Image

Invariant Feature Extraction

Once objects have been segmented a great variety of features can be computed from each object with standard image processing routines. If each feature is a positive scalar value then it is divided by the expected maximum value for that feature (over all objects) to normalize all feature values to the range [0,1]. The input vector for the neural classifier is then simply constructed by copying each feature into one element of the input vector.

Table 1 shows feature values (before normalization) corresponding to the objects shown in figure 2. This is just a demonstrative subset of the features which are potentially important. The set consists of *area* (in pixels), *mean density* (of gray values), *standard deviation density* (of gray values), *orientation* (of major axis of best-fitting-ellipse), *(major axis length)/(minor axis length)*, and *major axis length* (of best-fitting-ellipse). Using just the first three features gave very good results for some images, but the second three features were added as a form of domain specific knowledge: trees tend to be tall and thin and tanks tend to be short and wide (seen from side). Note that it is enough to include the relevant features, it is not necessary to explicitly teach the network that "trees tend to have the longer axis oriented vertically and tanks horizontally". The network clusters inputs based on similarity and adding these three features tends to make an input vector representing a tree less similar to an input vector representing a tank.

Our system architecture is particularly well suited for researching the relative benefits of different choices of features. Not only can more features be added to increase the dimensionality of input vectors to one channel, it is also possible to add a new channel in parallel which uses input vectors built from a different set of features. By monitoring decisions from the two channels and comparing to ground truth during training, it can be determined which feature set does better, or if they have complementary or redundant advantages.

TABLE 1: FEATURE VECTORS

Object No	Target	Area	Mean Density	Std. Dev.	Orientation	Major/Minor	Major Axis
1		3767	95.8	29.7	1.0	1.2	38.9
2		1373	87.6	20.0	3.2	1.2	23.6
3		913	94.0	24.0	84.4	2.0	24.5
4		2702	84.9	23.3	12.0	1.7	38.4
5		1140	109.0	35.5	3.7	2.0	27.3
6	tank	2032	82.6	56.8	77.3	1.6	32.7
7	truck	1035	184.9	66.8	80.6	2.4	28.1
8	miss. launcher	1662	189.	59.8	67.8	1.2	25.6
9		1337	84.6	26.0	12.7	1.2	23.1
10	tank	2471	93.9	57.8	78.6	1.4	33.3
11	tank	2300	77.6	54.9	86.3	1.6	34.3
12		1136	88.7	26.1	9.7	1.8	26.2
13		3431	94.4	36.7	4.8	2.0	47.8
14		440	92.5	22.4	6.0	1.7	15.7
15		1489	91.6	25.1	13.9	1.6	27.8
16		742	113.2	31.7	6.6	2.6	24.9
17		3408	92.8	28.2	7.0	1.5	41.5
18		1366	100.0	24.9	78.1	1.1	21.8
19	tank	1972	136.9	57.7	85.0	1.7	33.0

ART2-A Clustering

ART2-A [3] is an algorithmic version of ART2 [4] which is a dynamical system that can perform unsupervised classification of an arbitrary number of analog spatial patterns. ART2 is a three layer network, where layer F0 performs preprocessing, F1 is a feature representation field, and F2 is a category representation field with competitive learning. In ART2-A, the problem of implementing ART2 on a sequential digital computer is approached by capturing the essential computational steps in an algorithm, rather then in a layered neural network.

After preprocessing (normalization and thresholding), the *best match* category node is chosen by taking the inner product of the preprocessed input vector **I** with each of the weight vectors $\mathbf{Z}_j$ which gate the signal to the category nodes:

$$T_J = \max_j \{\sum_i I_i Z_{ji} : j = 1 \ldots N\} \quad (1)$$

where J is the index of the best *match* node. Note that because $\|\mathbf{I}\| = \|\mathbf{Z}_j\| = 1.0$, equation (1) simplifies to:

$$T_J = \max_j \{\cos(\mathbf{I}, \mathbf{Z}_j) : j = 1 \ldots N\} \quad (2)$$

Since T_J is used in determining whether the match is *good enough*, the measure of *goodness* is simply the angle between the preprocessed input vector and the weight vector of the best match category node. Then to determine whether this *best match* is in fact *good enough*, T_J is compared to the *vigilance* parameter ρ. If $T_J \geq \rho$, then node J is considered *committed* and it learns the given input vector. However, if $T_J < \rho$, then the value of J is reset to the index of an arbitrary *uncommitted* node which then learns the input vector. Learning is done in a single iteration: if J is an uncommitted node, then the weights on pathways connecting to that node are set equal to the input vector, such that $\mathbf{Z}_J = \mathbf{I}$. If J is committed, a convex combination of previous learning and the preprocessed input is learned.

The network parameters, such as ρ, can be varied by a knowledge base (called *Parameter Control* in figure 1) which looks at the overall image statistics. For example, ρ can be automatically varied based on the overall standard deviation of gray levels in a given image compared to the same measure in other images. Ideally, this approach should provide the optimum parameter settings for each image individually, rather than just the best average across all training images.

There is one inherent disadvantage in using an ART type network in ATR: since the network has no *a priori* knowledge of the label for each category (i.e. clutter, building, tank, etc.), the network is in fact clustering rather then categorizing the objects. Hence, it is necessary to examine each cluster to characterize (or "interpret") it, and then based in this characterization to choose a predetermined label for the cluster to turn it into a category.

Cluster Interpretation Knowledge Base

Based on the minimum, maximum and average values within each cluster, the *Cluster Interpretation* KB determines the symbolic significance of the ART2-A clusters. Table 2 shows examples of the empirical rules used in interpreting a cluster. The constants shown in these empirical rules are heuristics determined from analyzing a set of LADAR images.

TABLE 2: SAMPLE RULES FROM THE CATEGORY INTERPRETATION KNOWLEDGE BASE

IF average Mean Density < 90	THEN ASSERT "Low Density"(LD)
IF average Mean Density ≥ 90 AND average Mean Density < 150	THEN ASSERT "Medium Density"(MD)
IF average Orientation < 45 AND min Orientation < 45 AND max Orientation < 45	THEN ASSERT "Vertical" (V)
IF average Orientation ≥ 45 AND min Orientation ≥ 45 AND max Orientation ≥ 45	THEN ASSERT "Horizontal" (H)

Category Labeling Knowledge Base

Just as the *Interpretation* KB, the *Category Labeling* KB is based on a dynamic collection of expert rules which can easily be modified when new interpretations are discovered, and existing interpretations modified. Table 3 lists three of the rules needed to properly label the categories produced in the example shown in tables 4 and 5. (MA and LA denote "Medium Area" and "Large Area", MD and HD denote "Medium Density" and "High Density", NU denote "Not Uniform", and H and V denote "Horizontal" and "Vertical", respectively).

TABLE 3: CATEGORY LABELING KNOWLEDGE BASE

IF interpretation = "LA, MD, NU, H"	THEN ASSERT "Tank"
IF interpretation = "MA, HD, NU, H"	THEN ASSERT "Other Vehicle"
IF interpretation = "LA, MD, HU, V"	THEN ASSERT "Large Tree"

ART2-A Categorization: Sample Results

In the following sample results, we used the network parameter values for "vigilance" $\rho = 0.8$ (table 4) and $\rho = 0.7$ (Table 5), "thresholding" $\theta = 0.5773$ (default value), "initial weights" $\alpha = 0.1$, and "learning rate" $\beta = 0.01$.

TABLE 4: ART2-A CLUSTERING WITH $\rho = 0.8$

Class	Object	Label
1	1 4 13 17	Large Tree
2	2 5 9 12 15	Small Tree
3	3	Small Tree
4	6 10 11 19	Tank
5	7 8	Other Vehicle
6	14 16	Small Tree
7	18	Small Tree

TABLE 5: ART2-A CLUSTERING WITH $\rho = 0.7$

Class	Object	Label
1	1 4 13 17	Large Tree
2	2 5 9 12 14 15 16	Small Tree
3	3 18	Small Tree
4	6 7 8 10 11 19	Tank

The results, as shown in tables 4 and 5, are very good: For the lower value of the vigilance parameter all the vehicles are clustered together and all other objects put in other clusters. For the higher value of the vigilance parameter, the vehicles are clustered into two groups, tanks and non-tank vehicles, and all other objects into other groups.

Six other LADAR intensity images have been processed the same way. The ART2-A categorization was "perfect" in the sense that there were no false alarms or misdetections of targets. The two remaining images produced a few false alarms in addition to the correct classification of targets; these two images also had significantly more clutter objects then any of the other images. Only one misdetection of a target occurred, probably caused by the very small image area of the object. The small area automatically makes the features of that object less reliable due to the statistics of small numbers.

THE PIXEL PROCESSING CHANNEL

Subimage Based Categorization

In the *Pixel Processing Channel*, and in the *Object Categorizer* in particular, we wanted complementary advantages to the ART2-A Categorizer:

a) Use subimages as input data. Valuable information may be lost in feature extraction, therefore it is important to also use image data directly as input. However, this leads to very long input vectors, 5000 elements for a subimage of 50×100 pixels. This requirement precludes the use of back propagation (or any other gradient-descent error correction method) due to extreme training time.

b) Tolerance to noise and occlusion. It is important to cover cases where an ART network would create a new category rather then pick one of the existing ones, to verify that this is not misclassification due to noise or occlusion.

c) Supervised learning. Using a forced decision between a small number of predetermined categories allows *a priori* knowledge about the possible target types to be incorporated. Also, that allows the use of many sets of learned weights, where the appropriate one is chosen based on exogenous information and on the level of discrimination required.

Based on the desired requirements, Linear Associative Memory [5] was chosen as the paradigm for classifying subimages. The approach taken in LAM is deceptively simple. Rather than training the network to adjust the weights, the weights are constructed directly from the input / output pairs by taking the sum of the outer products:

$$W = \sum_{l=1}^{n} \left[\sum_{k=1}^{m} A_k^T B_l \right] \tag{3}$$

where A_k and B_l are row vectors representing the k'th input and the l'th output vectors, m is the number of input vectors used as examples for one category, and n is the number of categories. (i.e. the total number of vectors in the "training set" is $m \times n$). Recall from the LAM is equally simple, just multiply the given input vector A with the weight matrix W to produce the vector B, which is a linear combination of the encoded patterns. In the general case recall will therefore not be perfect, in fact the only case which leads to perfect recall is when the A_k's are orthonormal. However, even with random A_k's as can be assumed for a general image, the resulting B will still point in a direction close to the direction of the desired B_l. Through further research we determined some improvements to the LAM paradigm, producing good recall with just normal, rather then orthonormal inputs.

LAM CATEGORIZATION OF SUBIMAGES

A LAM was trained on input vectors representing the subimages seen in figure 3. The vectors were created by scanning each subimage row by row (from top to bottom and left to right) and reading the gray level values. Since the images are 50 by 100 pixels each input vector is 5000 elements. The size of a subimage was chosen to fit the average object size in the 7 LADAR images. This prevented cases of excessive scaling: the largest of the 20 objects had to be scaled by 65% and the smallest by 150%. Even with bilinear interpolative scaling, such as we used, scaling large objects down removes some of the information content. On the other hand, using the size of the biggest object as the standard increases the computational cost significantly.

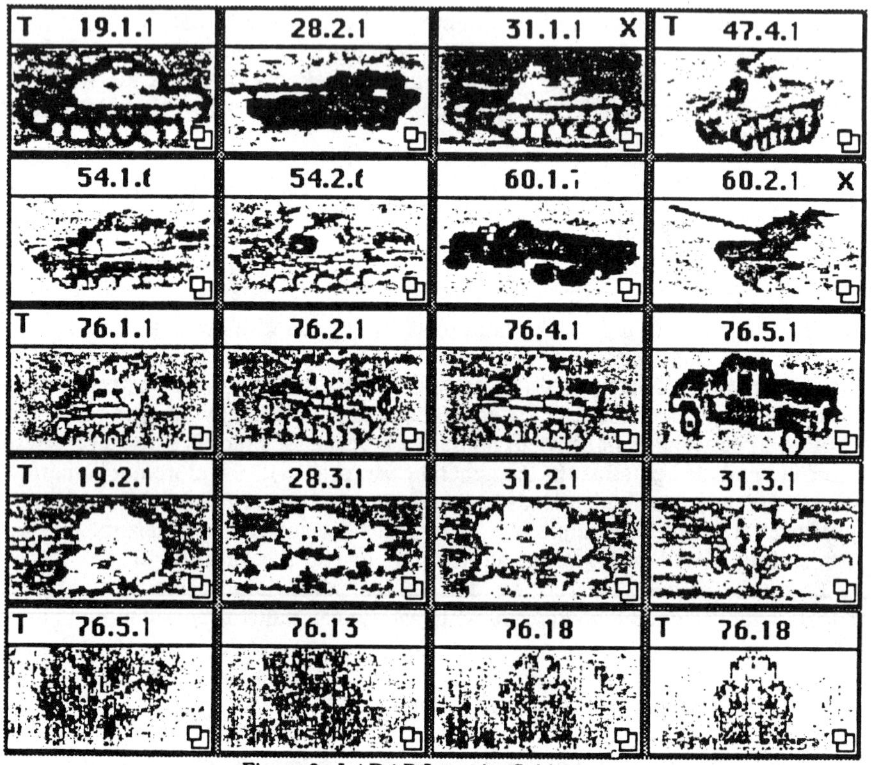

Figure 3: LADAR Intensity Subimages

Six subimages (marked "T" in figure 3) were used to build the memory matrix, three tanks: 19.1, 47.4, and 76.1; and three trees: 19.2.ec, 76.5.ec, and 76.18. When tested on all 20 subimages 2 were incorrectly categorized (marked "X" in figure 5.4-1): tank 31.1 as tree and obscured tank 60.2 as tree. Tank 60.2 is hard to classify with any paradigm due to the level of obscuration. The subimage which contains tank 31.1 has a significantly darker background then the others. We are exploring the use of range based segmentation to delete the background from all subimages. This may prevent misclassification of the kind seen in subimage 31.1.

CONCLUSIONS

We have developed a hybrid ATR architecture where conventional image processing algorithms are used for image segmentation and feature extraction, neural networks are used for target classification and recognition, and knowledge based systems are used for interpreting neural network outputs and fusing parallel decisions. We have demonstrated that ART2-A based neural classifiers perform well in clustering targets by processing the features of segmented objects in LADAR images whereas LAM based neural classifiers perform well in recognizing targets by processing the pixel intensities of subimages.

REFERENCES

[1] Bhanu, B. 1986. "Automatic Target Recognition: State of the Art Survey." IEEE Transactions on Aerospace and Electronic Systems, Vol. AES-22, No. 04: pp. 364-379.

[2] Kandel, E.R. 1991. "Perception of Motion, Depth, and Form." in Kandel, Schwartz, and Jessel (ed.) Principles of Neural Science, 3rd Edition, New York: Elsevier

[3] Carpenter, G., Grossberg, S. and Rosen, D.B. 1991. "ART2-A: An Adaptive Resonance Algorithm for Rapid Category Learning and Recognition." Neural Networks, Vol. 4.

[4] Carpenter, G. and Grossberg, S. 1987. "ART2: Self-Organization of Stable Category Recognition Codes for Analog Input Patterns." Applied Optics, Vol. 26: pp. 4919-4930.

[5] Simpson, P.K. 1990. Artificial Neural Systems, Pergamon Press, Elmsford, N.Y.

Chapter 5: Forecasting

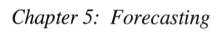

CHAPTER 5
Forecasting

Forecasting the future is an exciting area. Predicting next week's football winner, or the horse on the track, or the stock price, or the next earthquake are all notions that quickly get people's attention. Applications that have a rich set of historical data, such as financial forecasting, are prime candidates for the use of neural networks for forecasting. Like system identification in control, forecasting is modeling. Parameters are extracted from a time-series and used as the inputs to the neural network. The output of the neural network is the forecasted value.

Neural networks have taken the financial world by storm. Neural networks are being used to forecast stocks, bonds, commodities, currency, real estate, credit fraud, and retail prices. Unfortunately, much of this activity has been reported in hallway conversations and during phone conversations, not in the free literature. This is beginning to change. In April 1995 the IEEE Neural Networks Council will be co-sponsoring (with the International Association of Financial Engineers) a meeting entitled Computational Intelligence for Financial Engineering (CIFEr) that focuses on this area.

In addition to financial forecasting, neural networks are also being used to forecast (model) natural phenomena such as stream flow from precipitation and oil spill movement from wind speed and direction These applications offer a great deal to the environmental monitoring community because they provide this data-rich community with a set of tools that can automatically sort through a massive amount of data and perform decision making tasks.

In the future, I would expect to see applications in medicine (e.g., forecasting life expectancy under different drug regimes) and condition-based maintenance (e.g., forecasting the replacement life for components in an automobile based upon driving conditions and operator behavior). Economic behavior, political actions, and other social phenomena might also be forecasted.

The first paper in this chapter, **Paper 5.1**, reviews the results of a competition amongst several different forecasting techniques, including: linear mean square error modeling, Cascade Correlation, MLP, k-d trees, recurrent MLP, and local linear approximations. Six time-series data sets were used in the comparisons, including: laser data, random data, currency exchange, astrophysical data, physiological data (sleep apnea), and music. **Paper 5.2** uses a MLP to reconstruct a crime scene from suspicious factors. **Paper 5.3** uses an MLP to derive stream flow from precipitation data and compares the MLP's performance with existing models. **Paper 5.4** compares existing models with neural network models for oil spill tracking.

Accepted by '1993 IEEE International Conference on Neural Networks, San Francisco, CA'

Results of the Time Series Prediction Competition at the Santa Fe Institute

Andreas S. Weigend
Xerox PARC
3333 Coyote Hill Road
Palo Alto, CA 94304
phone: (415) 812–4765
fax: (415) 812–4241
weigend@cs.colorado.edu

Neil A. Gershenfeld
Media Lab and Department of Physics
MIT / E15-425
Cambridge, MA 02139
phone: (617) 253–7680
fax: (617) 258–6264
neilg@media.mit.edu

Abstract. From August 1991 onward, a set of time series was made generally available at the Santa Fe Institute. Several prediction tasks were specified and advertised. We here analyze the the submissions that we received before the deadline when the true continuations were revealed. One result is that connectionist networks, trained with error back-propagation, outperformed the other methods on all series. Among the architectures that performed best was a time delay neural network (also called finite impulse response network) and a recurrent network, designed to capture the multiple time scales present in currency exchange rates.

1 Motivation

Most observational disciplines, including physics, biology and finance, try to infer properties of an unfamiliar system from the analysis of a measured time record of its behavior. There are mature techniques associated with traditional time series analysis. During the last decade, new approaches such as neural networks have emerged, promising insights not available with these standard methods. However, the evaluation of this promise has been difficult. Adequate benchmarks were lacking, and most of the literature has been fragmentary and anecdotal.

Global computer networks enabled these disjoint communities to attack these problems through the widespread exchange of data and information. In order to foster this process, we organized the *Time Series Prediction and Analysis Competition* under the auspices of the Santa Fe Institute during the fall of 1991. With the assistance of an advisory board from the relevant disciplines, we selected a group of data sets that cover a broad range of interesting attributes. The data was made generally available at `ftp.santafe.edu` (and will remain publicly accessible there).

The participants in the competition were asked to submit:

- Forecasts of the continuation of the data sets (that were withheld).
- Analyses of the number of degrees of freedom, the noise characteristics, and the nonlinearity of the system.
- Models of the governing equations.
- Descriptions of the algorithms employed.

In order to explore the results of the contest, we organized a *NATO Advanced Research Workshop* in the spring of 1992. Workshop participants included members of the advisory board, representatives of the groups that had collected the data, participants in the contest, and some interested observers. Although the participants came from a broad range of disciplines, the discussions were framed by the analysis of common data sets and hence it was usually possible to find a meaningful common ground. In this paper, we focus on the first two data sets; more details can be found in the book edited by Weigend and Gershenfeld [WG93].

2 Datasets and Tasks

We selected the following data sets for the competition and workshop:

- A clean physics laboratory experiment (NH_3 laser).
- A computer generated series designed for this competition.
- Tick-by-tick currency exchange rate data (Swiss Franc – US Dollar).
- Astrophysical data from a variable white dwarf star.
- Physiological data from a patient with sleep apnea.
- J. S. Bach's last (unfinished) fugue from *Die Kunst der Fuge.*

Figure 1 shows 1,000 points of the first three series each as a function of time. Some of the characteristics of the four sets with prediction tasks are summarized in *Table 1.* The remaining sets were only used in the analysis category, not in the prediction category.

	laser	synthetic	exchange rates	music
origin	physics laboratory	computer	a Swiss bank	human
characterization	low-dim det chaos	high-dim det chaos	stochastic (?)	fugue
noise	clean	some	noisy	
stationarity	stationary	small drift	several time scales	
length	1,000	100,000	30,000	3,808
predict:	100 values & errors	500 values	60 values (total)	*ad lib*

Table 1: Attributes of the sets with prediction tasks.

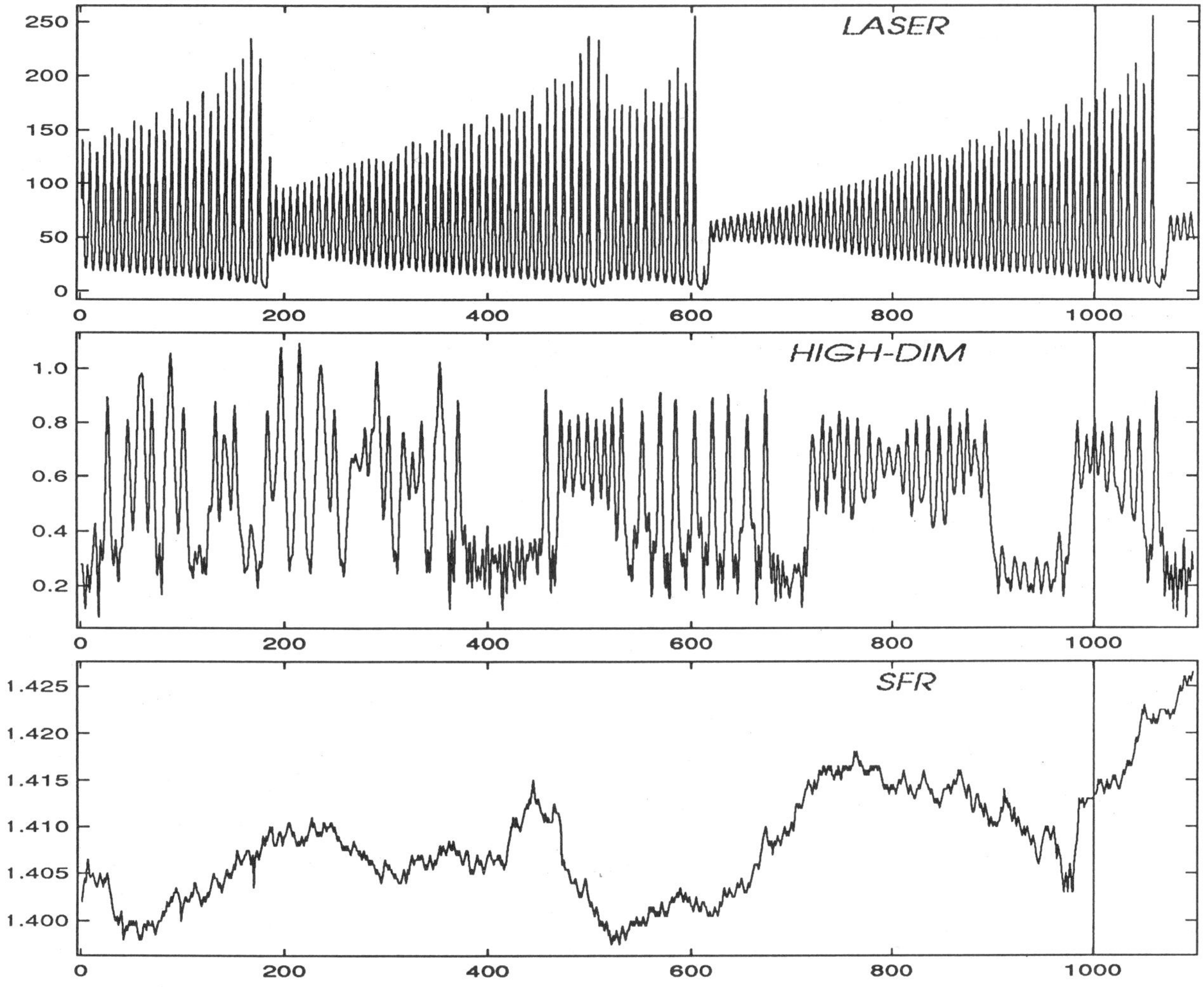

Figure 1: Graphs of the laser series, the high-dimensional synthetic series and the tickwise exchange rate data, plotted on the same time scale. The 1000 points for the Swiss Franc data correspond to March 21 to March 25, 1991.

2.1 Error measures

A standard measure to evaluate the quality of predictions is the **normalized mean squared error,**[1]

$$\mathtt{NMSE}(N) = \frac{\sum_{k \in \mathcal{T}} \left(\text{observation}_k - \text{prediction}_k\right)^2}{\sum_{k \in \mathcal{T}} \left(\text{observation}_k - \text{mean}_{\mathcal{T}}\right)^2} \approx \frac{1}{\hat{\sigma}_{\mathcal{T}}^2} \frac{1}{N} \sum_{k \in \mathcal{T}} (x_k - \hat{x}_k)^2 \qquad (1)$$

$k = 1 \cdots N$ enumerates the patterns in the held-back test set $\mathcal{T}$. $\text{mean}_{\mathcal{T}}$ and $\hat{\sigma}_{\mathcal{T}}^2$ denote average and variance of the target values in $\mathcal{T}$. A value of $\mathtt{NMSE} = 1$ thus corresponds to the value obtained by simply predicting the average.

For the laser data, we also asked to submit an estimate of the uncertainty of the predictions. The contributions were evaluated according to a likelihood criterion: Assuming a Gaussian error distribution for the observed data, and given

[1] We use **NMSE** as abbreviation rather than an abbreviation for relative mean squared error in order to avoid confusion with its square root, the rms or root-mean-squared error.

that the experimental resolution was one count, [2] the probability that an observation $x_k \pm 0.5$ was generated by a Gaussian with center $\widehat{x}_k$ and width $\widehat{\sigma}_k$ is given by the likelihood

$$p(x_k|\widehat{x}_k, \widehat{\sigma}_k) = \frac{1}{\sqrt{2\pi\widehat{\sigma}_k^2}} \int_{x_k-0.5}^{x_k+0.5} \exp - \frac{(\xi - \widehat{x}_k)^2}{2\widehat{\sigma}_k^2} \, d\xi \quad . \tag{2}$$

In other words, k's contribution to the overall likelihood is given by the area between $x_k - 0.5$ and $x_k + 0.5$ under a Gaussian of the estimated width, centered at the prediction value. If the uncertainty is underestimated and the predicted value is not very close to the observed value, the value is very small. If the width is overestimated, the normalization (the factor in front of the integral) suppresses the contribution with $1/\widehat{\sigma}_k$. Hence, both too small and too large estimates of the uncertainty reduce the likelihood that the observation was "generated" by the prediction, or the "model".

To obtain the likelihood of the entire test set, we assume independence of each test point. The individual likelihoods can then be multiplied to obtain the probability of the data given the model,

$$p(\mathrm{D}|\mathrm{M}) = \prod_{k=1}^{N} p(x_k|\widehat{x}_k, \widehat{\sigma}_k) \quad . \tag{3}$$

To avoid too small numbers, we take the negative logarithm. In order to get a quantity that is independent of the size of the test set, we normalize by the number of points N in set $\mathcal{T}$, and thus finally obtain the **negative average log-Likelihood, `nalL`**

$$-\frac{1}{N}\sum_{k=1}^{N} \log p(x_k|\widehat{x}_k, \widehat{\sigma}_k) = \frac{1}{N}\sum_{k=1}^{N} -\log\left[\mathtt{pnorm}(x_k + 0.5; \widehat{x}_k, \widehat{\sigma}_k) - \mathtt{pnorm}(x_k - 0.5; \widehat{x}_k, \widehat{\sigma}_k)\right] \tag{4}$$

where $\mathtt{pnorm}(\xi; x, \sigma)$ denotes the cumulative probability of a Gaussian centered at x with standard deviation σ,

$$\mathrm{pnorm}(\xi; x, \sigma) = \frac{1}{\sqrt{2\pi\sigma^2}} \int_{-\infty}^{\xi} \exp - \frac{(\xi - x)^2}{2\sigma^2} \, d\xi \quad . \tag{5}$$

Having defined the error criteria, we now turn to the submissions we received.

3 Entries and Evaluation

3.1 Laser data

Table 2 lists the methods applied to the laser data, the computers and CPU time required, as well as the relative mean square error the negative average log-likelihood. The submitted continuations of the laser are shown in *Figure 2*.

In *Figure 2* and *Table 2*, the letter *W* refers to the entry by Eric Wan. This architecture was presented at the 1990 Connectionist Models Summer School [Wan90] and is also desribed in [WG93]. The key idea is that each weight gets replaced by a tapped delay line. This architecture is equivalent to a time delay neural network.

[2] The signal to noise ratio is 300:1, and the data was quantized to 8 bits and given as integers.

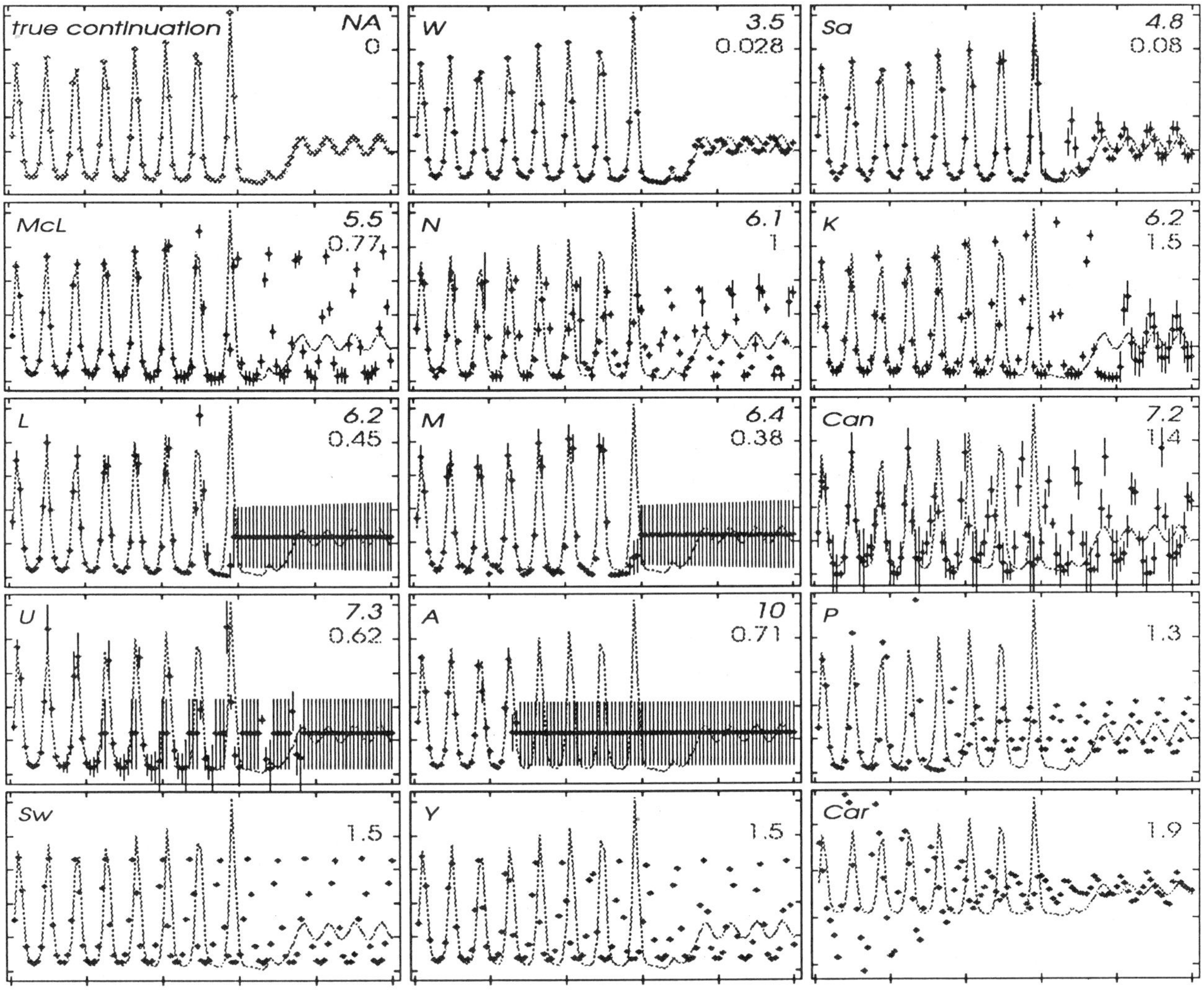

Figure 2: Predicted continuations of the laser data. The letters correspond to the code of the entrant, the upper figure measures (the averaged negative logarithm of) the likelihood that the data were generated by the model, the lower number is the averaged normalized sum squared error.

3.2 Synthetic data

We now turn to the second data set, the high-dimensional data that we generated for the competition. *Table 3* lists the entries received. Since all of the contributions deteriorate fairly quickly, we give the normalized sum squared error only averaged over the first 15 and the first 30 predictions. The first 30 points of the submitted predictions are shown with the true continuation in *Figure 3.*

In *Figure 3* and *Table 3,* the code *ZH* refers to the entry by Zhang and Hutchinson (in [WG93]), who trained a total of 108 different networks, each of which estimated predictions for different numbers of steps ahead. Two distinct network architectures were used, one type for the first 10 predictions, and the second for the remaining 490 predictions; all networks had 100 hidden units. The first type of network predicted some number of temporal positions using the last 20 data points from the data set, plus the predictions from "earlier" networks. The second type of network predicted five temporal positions, using the last 20 data points from the data set, plus 10 more sparsely sampled data

	method		computer	time	NMSE(100)	nalL
W	conn	1-12-12-1; lag 25,5,5	SPARC 2	12 hrs	0.028	3.5
Sa	loc lin	low-pass embd, 8 dim, 4nn	DEC 3100	20 min	0.080	4.8
McL	conn	feedforward, 200-100-1	CRAY Y-MP	3 hrs	0.77	5.5
N	conn	feedforward, 50-20-1	SPARC 1	3 weeks	1.0	6.1
K	visual	look for similar stretches	SG Iris	10 sec	1.5	6.2
L	visual				0.45	6.2
M	conn	feedforward, 50-350-50-50	386 PC	5 days	0.38	6.4
Can	conn	recurrent, 4-4c-1	VAX 8530	1 hr	1.4	7.2
U	tree	k-d tree; AIC	VAX 6420	20 min	0.62	7.3
A	loc lin	21 dim, 30 nearest neighb's	SPARC 2	1 min	0.71	10.
P	loc lin	3 dim time delay	Sun	10 min	1.3	-
Sw	conn	feedforward	SPARC 2	20 hrs	1.5	-
Y	conn	feedforward, weight-decay	SPARC 1	30 min	1.5	-
Car	linear	Wiener filter, width 100	MIPS 3230	30 min	1.9	-

Table 2: Entries received before the deadline for the prediction of the laser. `NMSE` *gives the normalized sum squared error (or relative mean square error),* `nalL` *gives the negative logarithm of the likelihod of the data given the predicted values and predicted errors, averaged over the prediction set.*

points extending further back in history. They found that direct predictions (a different network for each position) worked better than iterated predictions.

3.3 Money, Music, the Stars and the Heart

In this paper, space limited us to focus on only two out of the six data sets. The remaining results are discussed in the book edited by Weigend and Gershenfeld [WG93]. It consists of of three parts:

1. **Overview.** In the first part, we present the results of the competition and the workshop and analyze the advantages and disadvantages of the various techniques both in time series prediction and in characterization. In the area of prediction, recurring themes include the importance for careful assessments of the statistical reliability of the results, and the need to match the level of description of the model to the system being studied (from deterministic low-dimensional dynamics to stochastic processes). In the area of characterization, several techniques are presented that try to estimate the number of degrees of freedom of the system or the rate at which the system loses memory of its state. A common feature here is the desire to reduce the sensitivity to geometrical artifacts abundant in standard methods (such as correlation dimensions and Lyapunov exponents). The methods discussed include information-based measures as well as estimators based on evaluating the reliability of the embedding.
2. **Details.** In the central part, fifteen scientists who applied their methods to the data, motivate and describe their ideas in individual chapters. Although from a wide variety of different disciplines (statistics, experimental and

	method		computer	time	NMSE(15)	NMSE(30)
ZH	conn	...-30-30-1 and 30-100-5	CM-2 (16k)	8 days	0.086	0.57
U	tree	k-d tree; AIC	VAX 6420	30 min	1.3	1.4
C	conn	recurrent, 4-4c-1	VAX 8530	n/a	6.4	3.2
W	conn	1-30-30-1; lags 20,5,5	SPARC 2	1 day	7.1	3.4
Z	linear	36 AR(8), last 4k points	SPARC	10 min	4.8	5.0
S	conn	feedforward	SPARC 2	20 hrs	17.	9.5

Table 3: Entries received before the deadline for the prediction of the high-dimensional, synthetic data.

computational physics, electrical and mechanical engineering, economics and finance, biology and medicine, musicology and others), all contributors focus on the same sets of data. Their strictly refereed contributions are as self-contained as possible.

3. **Data.** In the third part, the scientists who contributed the time series describe the scientific questions behind their data and the kinds of models typical in their home disciplines. They then analyze their data with the current methods in their respective fields, and finally gauge what they have learned from the new techniques that were applied to their data in the competition and at the workshop.

4 Discussion

In this competition and subsequent workshop, we brought together scientists from different disciplines predicting and analyzing temporal sequences: statistics, experimental and computational physics, electrical and mechanical engineering, economics and finance, music, etc. Quite to our surprise, it turned out that connectionist networks consistently outperformed all other methods received, ranging from visual predictions to sophisticated noise reduction techniques.

Although all the networks that did well used some form of error back-propagation, its blind application did clearly not guarantee success. The successful architectures all tried to capture some of the specific temporal issues for temporal sequences. In particular, among the architectures that performed best was a time delay neural network (also called finite impulse response network), a large set of feed-forward network for each sub-task, and a recurrent network designed to capture multiple time scales.

Acknowledgements. We thank Udo Hübner from the *Physikalisch-Technische Bundesanstalt* in Braunschweig, Ary Goldberger and David Rigney from *Beth Israel Hospital and Harvard Medical School* in Boston, Don Winget, James Dixon and Chris Clemens from the *Department of Astronomy and McDonald Observatory, University of Texas at Austin*, a member of a Swiss bank, and Johann Sebastian Bach from the *Thomaskirche zu Leipzig* for the data. We also thank all competition entrants for their submissions.

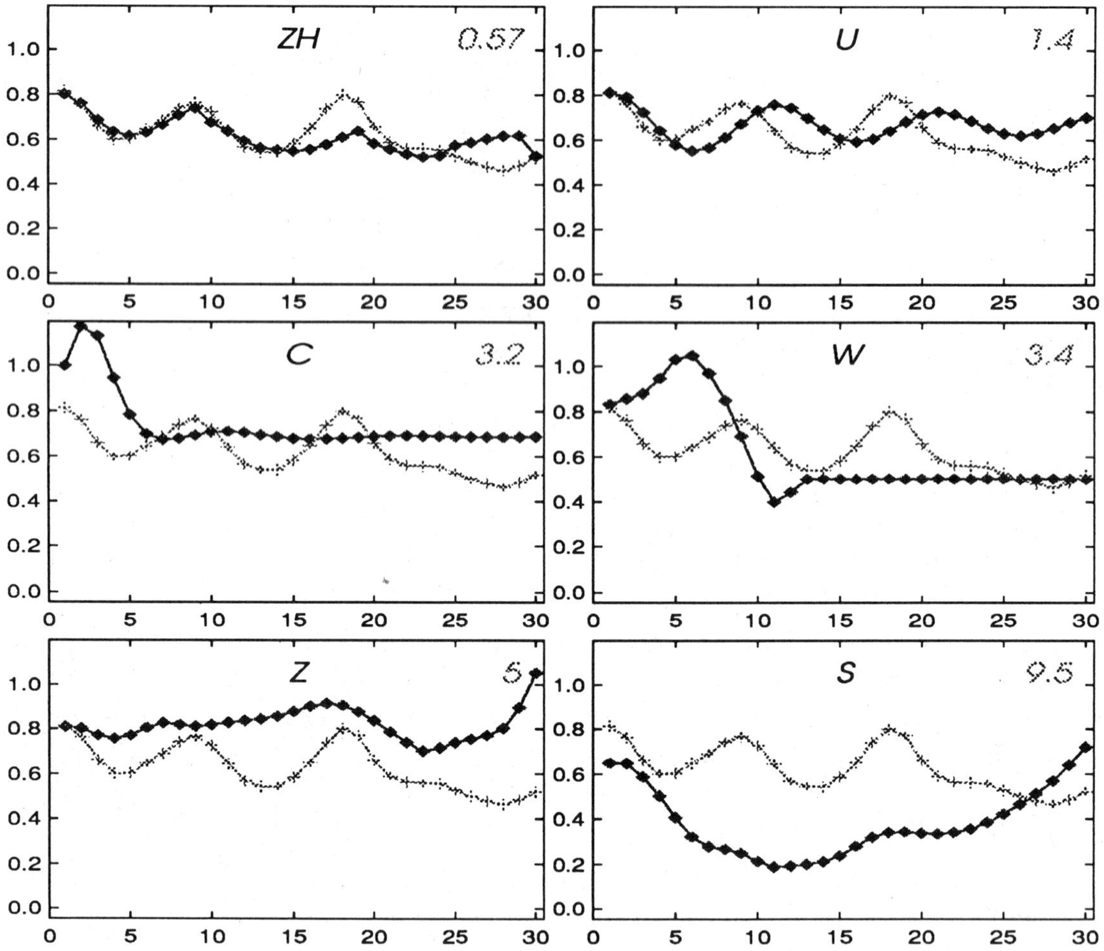

Figure 3: Predicted continuations of the synthetic data. The numbers are the normalized sum squared errors, averaged over 30 steps.

References

[Wan90] Wan, Eric A. *Temporal backpropagation: An efficient algorithm for finite impulse response neural networks.* In Touretzky, D. S., Elman, J. L., Sejnowski, T. J., and Hinton, G. E., editors, *Proceedings of the 1990 Connectionist Models Summer School*, pages 131–137. Morgan Kaufmann, 1990.

[WG93] Weigend, Andreas S. and Gershenfeld, Neil A., editors. **Predicting the Future and Understanding the Past: a Comparison of Approaches.** *(Proceedings of the NATO Advanced Research Workshop on Time Series Analysis and Forecasting held in Santa Fe, New Mexico, May 1992)*, Santa Fe Institute Studies in the Sciences of Complexity. Addison-Wesley, 1993.

An Application of Neural Networks to Reconstruct Crime Scene based on Non-Mark Theory---Suspicious Factors Analysis†

Chenyuan Kou[1], Jih-Mao Shih[2], Chi-ho Lin[3], and Zen-Dah Lee[4]

ABSTRACT

There are three stages to Criminal Behavior(CB) :(1) Pre-CB (2) In-CB (3) Post-CB. [K92] Figure one gives you an explanation of transition state of occurring a crime. The criminal tries to hide his behavior during the stages of committing crime, but, still unveiling the signs of crime. We call it Non-Mark Theory evidence of crime investigation[LCK92]. We may infer it via using 5Ws[who,which,when,where, and what] to understand the level of suspect. This research does a contribution to the investigator to dig up the crime and to watch out the first two stages. The last stage is based on Mark Theory's evidence to reconstruct crime scene.[LCK92]

The development of Neural Network simulates the brain of the human being. It offers capabilities as follows : (1). Powerful Calculation (2). Parallel Processing (3). Learning (4). Fault Tolerance. We prefer Back-Propagation Networks(BPN) to this research. As to the aggregation of research on Neural Network, both Pattern Recognition and Classification benefit from BPN. We establish the BPN of Crime Suspicous Factors Analysis, to scale the suspect of crime, and to differentiate Pre-CB from In-CB.

Expert System fits the requirements of static knowledge(Mark Theory), and Neural Net solves the problem of dynamic knowledge[Non-Mark Theory] which needs the capability of learning.[LCK92] This research tries to establish the methodology of Non-Mark Theory's evidence of crime scene to help the investigator to investigate the crime before the Post-CB happens, especially, it is possibly to prevent from occurring the crime and saving citizen's life.

Keywords: Neural Networks, Criminal Sign, Non-Mark Theory, BPN, CB Model

I. Motivation

There are two characteristics of criminal behavior: (a). Hidden and (b). Vanishment. The first one means that the criminal tries to hide his behavior while he is preparing or committing a crime[Pre-CB]. The other one shows that the criminal is in CB, crime behavior is unveiling and will be recognized. It causes the criminal to vanish the behavior as soon as possible. But, according to our research, there are three stages for a criminal to commit a crime: (a). Pre-CB (b). In-CB and (c). Post-CB[K92]. The criminal even tries to hide his behavior, but, still unveiling the suspicious signs. Those suspicious signs are different from the physical evidence we found on the crime scene, so, we call it Non-Mark Theory evidence. Because they are essential to the whole criminal behavior, and can be treated as evidence[K92]. Although the investigator has lots of experiences in the recognition of crime signs, they sometimes will not be very well to dig up the crime by the heavy work load, emotional stress, and pressure, etc. By the way, we want to establish the knowledge of crime investigation for police. We already set up 200 rules via using the statistics method[LCK92]. The technology of neural network has been rapidly developing in learning the behavior of the human beings since the last decade. In our research, we conclude that the knowledge of learning belongs to dynamic knowledge, and the physical evidence is a kind of static knowledge[K92]. Dynamic knowledge needs to be solved by fuzzy set theory or neural network, and static knowledge is suitable to be established by expert system[K92]. There are lots of successful experiences in applying the technology of neural network. It simulates the thinking model of the human beings, and has the following characteristics: (a). Powerful Calculation (b).Parallel Processing (c).Learning and (d). Fault Tolerance which is benefited to solve the compound problem. We propose Back Propagation Network(BPN) Model in this research, BPN has been implemented in lots of successful research. Pattern Recognition and Classification benefit from BPN. It will be suitable to our research for analyzing the suspicious factors in order to setup the dynamic knowledge base to help investigators to dig up the crime.

II. Non-Mark Theory Evidence

Strictly speaking, there are no theory for conventional crime investigation. But, we proposed and classified two main trends in crime investigation which are Mark Theory andNon-Mark Theory[K921,K92,KLS921,KLS92,LCK92]. Mark Theory towards the physical evidence of crime scene, and Non-Mark Theory does not focus on the physical evidence. The investigator insists that the principle of "Committing Crimes Leaves Marks", which is based on Mark Theory. Its basic concept follows the steps of

† This research was supported in part by the fund. of National Science Council under its Grant-ID:NSC 82-0111-S-015-001

1 Instructor and Chief of AP team, Computing Service,Central Police University, Taoyuan, Taiwan,R.O.C
2 Maj. General, LL.M., Commissioner of Chiayi County Police Department,Taiwan, R.O.C.
3 Professor and Director, Dept. of Crime Investigation,Central Police University, Taoyuan, Taiwan, R.O.C
4 Graduate Student, Graduate School, Central Police University

evidence collection, skills and rules of analysis via the concept to dig up the facts, to make connection, to stimulate inference, and to summarize the whole crime behavior.

---Mark Theory Evidence

There are three key points in conventional methods to do crime investigation: (a). Evidences in Crime Scene: focusing on the evidence collection, identification, individualization, explanation, evaluation and crime scene reconstruction

(b). The left evidences of the criminal: following the characteristics of the left evidence, the smell, the documents, and the individual writing habit on letters, etc.

(c). The stolen stuff: according to the characteristics of the stolen stuff of the scene, to find out the owner, the theft and/or the dealer, etc.

---Non-Mark Theory Evidence

It is possible that the investigator has not enough experience in solving the specific case or he does not have a kind of specific knowledge, or the forensic scientist does not have enough professional knowledge, or the de-facto technology does not fit our requirement. It causes the investigator not to dig up the crime. That is why we propose neural network to this research to focus on the Non-Mark Theory to analyze the criminal, the victim, and the suspect. It includes the criminal's psychology, the society phenomenon, and the factor of environment. There are two key points for Non-Mark Theory:

(a). Caused to investigate: The investigator is caused to dig up the crime such as the victim, the suspect, and the specific case.

(i). The victim: the descriptions of the criminal and his behavior, the family situation, the relationship, economic income or payment of the victim.

(ii). The suspect: the psychology and the **modus operandi(MO)** of the criminal, and to retrieve the police records to investigate.

(iii). The characteristics of the crime: to analyze and to setup the **MO** such as murder with gunshot, or with knife, etc.

(iv). The society broadcasting medium: to investigate the crime according to the news, papers, etc.

(b). To investigate: according to the interview, inspection, surveillance, and undercover investigation to investigate criminal activities.

(i). Interview: to interview the witness or the relational people of crime, and to dig out clues to investigate.

(ii). Inspection: to inspect suspicious characters surrounding the crime scene, and to inspect the the special place such as bar, and casino, etc. to dig out clues.

(iii).Surveillance: according to specific people, specific location surveillance to investigate crime.

(iv). Undercover Investigation: according to the inside connection from questionable groups to dig out clues for investigation.

(c). Crime Scene Reconstruction

To reconstruct crime scene based on the Mark Theory evidence, and to infer the whole situation via using 5Ws[K92]. According to the above concepts, the duty of the investigator is to recombine, to analyze, to evaluate, and to explain the whole crime behavior.

Our research focuses on the crime scene reconstruction which is based on Non-Mark Theory. It fits the Pre-CB and In-CB of the transitive diagram of committing a crime. This research may help the investigator to differentiate the suspect level of a criminal, and to decide what should he do in time.

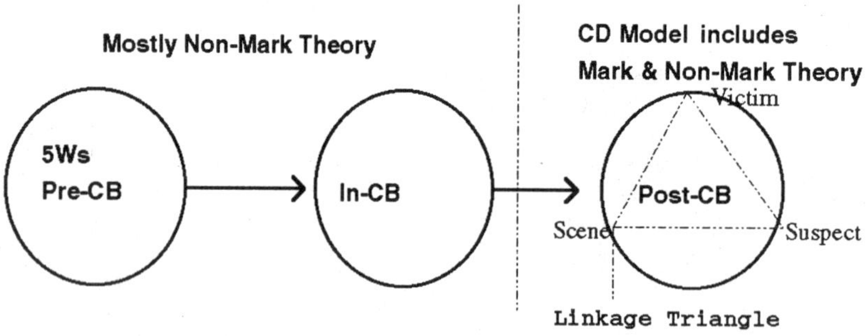

Figure 1. Transitive State Diagram for Criminal Behavior

III. Neural Network

(a). What is Neural Network

From the research of biology and anatomy, we understand that our brain system is composed of tremendous neural cells which constructs highly connected neural network. And the human brain system to process the input information is via using the above neural networks. There are about 10^{11} neural cells which has 10^3 connection to other neural cells in each neural cell. It causes to establish 10^{14} connections to a big network, which has the capabilities of processing tremendous information and high speed communication.

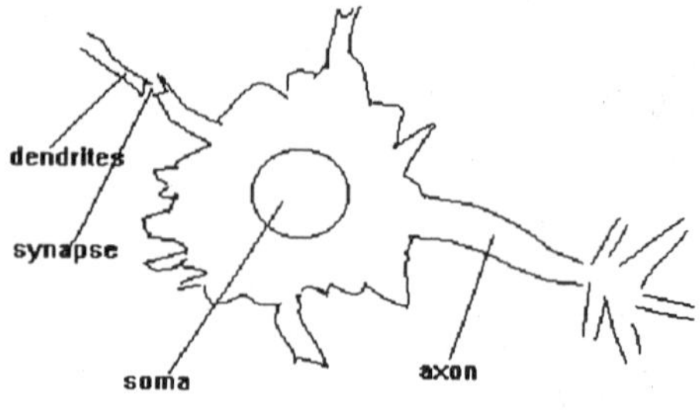

Figure 2. Structure of Neural Network simulates the human brain

Neural Network has the synonym of Artificial Neural Network which simulates the capability of processing information of biological neural network. We may give definition as follow:[Kosko92] Neural network is a calculation system which includes hardware, software, and large volumes of simply, cross-connected processing elements(PEs) to simulate the capability of biological neural network. PE is the simply simulated element of Neuron, which accepts information via the external environment or other PEs. It also simply does calculation and outputs the result to the external environment or other PEs.

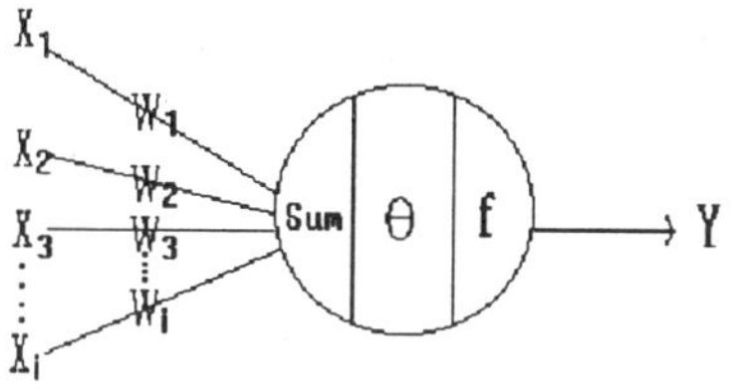

Figure 3. The Processing Element(PE) of Neural Network

The expression for input and output of PE be expressed as follow:

$$Y = f\left(\sum_{i=1}^{n} W_i X_i - \theta\right)$$

Y: Output
f :transfer function
Wi: connection weights
Xi: Inputs
θ:threshold value

We know that a neural network is composed of many cross-connection PEs which constructs Network model or topologies of Network paradigm. We may categorize many Neural Network models to be four types:
(1). Supervised learning network
(2). Unsupervised learning network
(3). Associate learning network
(4). Optimization application network

(b). Why Build a Neural Network

Von Newmann machine is suitable to execute high speed calculation on nowadays computer system, and also contains the accuracy of the result. But, there are still many problems have not yet been solved, for example, Pattern Recognition, Classification and the process of decision-making, etc. For example, a three years old child may recognize his parents among a group of people without any teaching. Nowadays Von Newmann machine cannot reach this goal. Nevertheless, the human beings try to establish the capability of the biology brain to the nowadays computer. They incorporate the technology of computer hardware and software to simulate biological neural network to achieve or to excess the advantages of biological neural network. We also understand that the neural network is to simulate the capability of the brain of biology to process information. It is a kind of computer system to contain the following characteristics:

(1). Powerful Calculation
(2). Parallel Processing
(3). Learning
(4). Fault Tolerance

The investigator finds out the crime suspect via the experience of the criminal to differentiate the levels of crime suspect, which is a kind of thinking model to do parallel and distributive thinking via the aggregation of learning about the crime. Although the coming data is not always complete, but the investigator still makes decision finally. By the way, the neural network contains the above characteristics, therefore, we count on it to analyze the criminal suspicious factors analysis.

(c). Back Propagation Network---BPN

There are many neural network models, BPN is one of the famous and fabulous among them which may be expressed as follow:

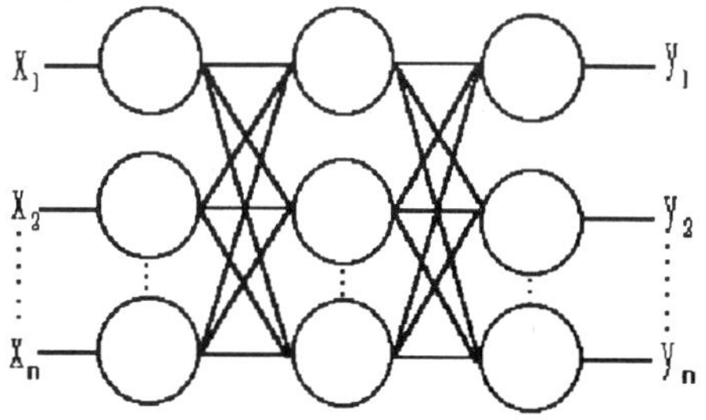

Figure 4. Back Propagation Network Model

The principle of BPN is implemented in the concept of "gradient steepest descent method", to minimize the error function which is to put hidden layer between input layer and output layer, to process those inputted data, and to differentiate learning algorithm from Forward Propagation[FP] and Backward Propagation[BP]. In the process of FP, to process the inputted data from input layer to output layer via experiencing the hidden layer. The status of the former PEs only effects the status of the latter PEs, which is connected PEs by PEs. Supposed that the user does not get the expected output at output layer, then the system reverses to Back Propagation, and returns the error message via the original path to adjust the weights of connections, in order to minimize the error function and to get the optimized output data. However, we hope to analyze the factors of crime suspects via using the characteristics of BPN, to establish the BPN's Crime Suspicous Factors Analysis System, and to help the investigators to dig up the crime.

IV. System Development

There are many recommendations to develop Neural Network system, we here propose 6 steps [Y93] to develop our system of suspect factors analysis. These steps are as follows:

1. Feasibility Analysis

Is it feasible to solve our problem via using Neural Network ? There are five guidances to this proposition as follows:(a). Are there any connections between factors in our proposed problem;(b).Is it possible to solve our problem via using conventional methods to get optimal solution; (c). Are there any successful cases in using neural network which are similar to our problem;(d).Are there any sufficient cases to train our neural network system;(e).The scope or our problem may be solved by nowadays hardware. The answers of (a) through (e) should be positive to solve our problem via using neural network. As to our research, the propositions to the feasibility analysis are (1a) through (1e) which correspond to the guidances of (a) to (e) as follows: (1a). The investigator needs to use 5Ws to analyze and to differentiate the levels of crime suspect. Therefore, there are connections between the factors of 5Ws. (1b).The conventional analysis for crime investigation depends on the experienced investigator's knowledge to dig up the crime, but, he is not always to fit practical requirement in our real world. (1c). The differentiation level of crime suspect belongs to the category of Pattern Recognition and Classification. However, the application of Neural Network to BPN has been doing well. It is possibly to do analysis on crime suspect via using the BPN model. (1d). Owing to the research on the category of criminal sign[LCK92], we have sufficient cases to support this research for Neural Network's learning and training. (1e). This research will be implemented in using Neural Networks Professional II/PLUS software as our development tool. Through (1a) to (1e), we understand that it is possible to use the BPN model to do our research.

2. Cases for training and testing

We include 180 items to categorize to three levels such as **"the most significant"**, **"the significant"**, and **"non-significant"** on the differentiation's of crime sign. Those 180 items will be separated to 55 items for training, and 30 items for testing.

3. Data Preprocessing and Representation

Frankly speaking, the investigator usually recognizes the crime suspect via using 5Ws. According to the above explanation, we may scope 5Ws to be five input PEs to be processed by the network to get output. This output value differentiates the level of crime suspect. The ranges of inputted PE value are between [-1,+1]. These values will be expressed as follows:

-1: represents non-significant suspect[It is possibly not to include 5Ws for each criminal behavior]
0: represents significant suspect
+1: the most significant suspect

As to the ranges of output values are between[-1,+1], and will be expressed as:

-1: non-significant suspect
0: significant suspect
+1: the most significant suspect

Our proposition to real case:

For example, when the murder is occurring, the suspect is holding the knife around the scene with bloodspot on his clothes. Let us express this case with 5Ws and 5 input PEs:

PEs:	Input1	Input2	Input3	Input4	Input5	Output
5Ws:	who	which	when	where	what	result
	1	1	1	1	1	1

The digitized technique for this system includes 6 fields, the former five fields are Input PEs, and the last one is output field.

4. Network Establishment

We have to consider the following items when we want to construct our own network as follows:[Y93]

(a). What kind of tool we will use
(b). Which is the network model we are going to include
(c). How many hidden layers will be picked
(d). How many PEs will be chosen

Propositions to Network Establishment

Propositions to network establishment of our system are as follows:(4a). Neuralworks Professional II/PLUS software will be our tool to construct network. (4b). This research belongs to Pattern Recognition and Classification which benefit from BPN model, therefore, we decide to use BPN to do our research. (4c). The hidden layer is to solve the connections between inputted PEs. We usually need one hidden layer only, except for those complicated cases which need two hidden layers. We pick one hidden layer only in this research. (4d). As to our network, there are five PEs in Input layer(5Ws), and one PE for Output layer(to scope the level of crime suspect). The hidden layers are calculated as :(Input layer PEs+Output layer PEs)/2=(5+1)/2=3 to our research[Y93].

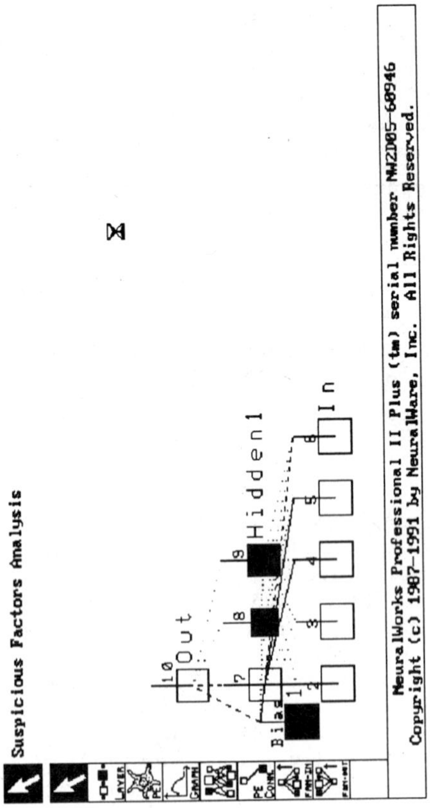

Figure 5. Structure Diagram for BPN of our Neural Network System

5. Learning

This network includes BPN model, and accepts Delta-Rule as learning rule[N91]. By the way, the ranges of Input and Output are between [-1,+1], and the transfer function is TanH which is offered by NeuralWorks Professional II/PLUS software[N91]. The total learning cases are 55 which are expressed as follows:

```
1.0 -1.0  1.0 -1.0  1.0  1.0
-1.0 -1.0 -1.0  1.0  1.0  1.0
1.0 -1.0  0.0  1.0 -1.0  1.0
-1.0 -1.0  0.0  1.0  1.0  1.0
1.0 -1.0  1.0 -1.0  1.0  1.0
1.0 -1.0  0.0  1.0  1.0  1.0
0.0 -1.0  1.0 -1.0  1.0  1.0
0.0 -1.0  1.0 -1.0  1.0  1.0
1.0 -1.0 -1.0  1.0  1.0  1.0
1.0  1.0 -1.0 -1.0  1.0  1.0
0.0 1.0  1.0  1.0  0.0  1.0
-1.0 1.0 -1.0  0.0  1.0  1.0
-1.0 1.0 -1.0  0.0  1.0  1.0
0.0 -1.0 -1.0  1.0  1.0  1.0
-1.0 -1.0 -1.0  1.0  1.0  1.0
0.0 1.0 -1.0 -1.0  1.0  1.0
-1.0 -1.0 -1.0  0.0  1.0  1.0
1.0 -1.0 -1.0 -1.0  1.0  1.0
0.0 -1.0  0.0 -1.0  1.0  1.0
-1.0 0.0  0.0  0.0  1.0  1.0
-1.0 1.0 -1.0 -1.0  1.0  1.0
0.0 -1.0 -1.0  1.0  1.0  1.0
-1.0 0.0 -1.0  1.0  1.0  1.0
0.0 1.0  1.0 -1.0  0.0  1.0
0.0 -1.0 -1.0  1.0  1.0  1.0
0.0 -1.0  1.0 -1.0  1.0  1.0
-1.0 -1.0  1.0 -1.0  1.0  1.0
0.0 -1.0 -1.0 -1.0  1.0  1.0
1.0 1.0 -1.0 -1.0  0.0  1.0
0.0 -1.0  0.0 -1.0  1.0  1.0
0.0 -1.0  0.0 -1.0  0.0  0.0
-1.0 -1.0 -1.0  0.0  0.0  0.0
-1.0 -1.0  0.0 -1.0  0.0  0.0
-1.0 0.0 -1.0 -1.0  0.0  0.0
0.0 0.0 -1.0 -1.0  0.0  0.0
0.0 -1.0 -1.0 -1.0  0.0  0.0
-1.0 -1.0  0.0 -1.0  0.0  0.0
0.0 0.0 -1.0 -1.0  0.0  0.0
-1.0 0.0 -1.0 -1.0  0.0  0.0
-1.0 0.0 -1.0  0.0  0.0  0.0
0.0 -1.0  0.0 -1.0 -1.0  0.0
0.0 -1.0 -1.0 -1.0  0.0  0.0
0.0 -1.0  0.0 -1.0 -1.0  0.0
-1.0 -1.0  0.0  0.0 -1.0  0.0
-1.0 -1.0  0.0  0.0 -1.0  0.0
0.0 -1.0 -1.0  0.0 -1.0  0.0
0.0 0.0 -1.0 -1.0  0.0  0.0
-1.0 -1.0  0.0 -1.0  0.0  0.0
0.0 -1.0 -1.0  0.0 -1.0  0.0
0.0 0.0  0.0 -1.0 -1.0  0.0
0.0 -1.0 -1.0 -1.0 -1.0 -1.0
-1.0 0.0 -1.0 -1.0 -1.0 -1.0
-1.0 -1.0  0.0 -1.0 -1.0 -1.0
-1.0 -1.0 -1.0  0.0 -1.0 -1.0
-1.0 -1.0 -1.0 -1.0  0.0 -1.0•
```

Table 1. The total learning cases of our neural network system

6. Testing

After the learning, the practical output and desired output converges well are expressed as follows:

Training result	Testing result
1.000000	0.999362
1.000000	0.999511
1.000000	0.999217
1.000000	0.999217
1.000000	0.999474
1.000000	0.999112
1.000000	0.999035
1.000000	0.999504
1.000000	0.999388
1.000000	0.998798
1.000000	0.998947
1.000000	0.997484
0.000000	-0.130541
0.000000	0.031722
0.000000	-0.066677
0.000000	-0.024896
0.000000	0.031722
0.000000	-0.130541
0.000000	0.167340
0.000000	-0.053674
0.000000	-0.066677
0.000000	-0.053674
-1.000000	-0.907570
-1.000000	-0.935487
-1.000000	-0.929012
-1.000000	-0.939816
-1.000000	-0.892452
-1.000000	-0.992700

Table 2. The testing result of our neural network system [Comparisons between training and testing]

The values of testing result are similar to the training values, which means that our network model converges well to show it is a good neural network.

7. Finish

After the completion of step 1 through step 6, the network is finished. We offer the following output data to show our system structure.

```
Title:
   Display Mode: Network              Type: Hetero-Associative
   Display Style: default
  Control Strategy: backprop       L/R Schedule: backprop
    4950 Learn          0 Recall          0 Layer
     16 Aux 1           0 Aux 2           0 Aux 3
L/R Schedule: backprop
  Recall Step          1        0        0        0        0
   Input Clamp      0.0000   0.0000   0.0000   0.0000   0.0000
   Firing Density 100.0000   0.0000   0.0000   0.0000   0.0000
   Temperature      0.0000   0.0000   0.0000   0.0000   0.0000
   Gain             1.0000   0.0000   0.0000   0.0000   0.0000
   Gain             1.0000   0.0000   0.0000   0.0000   0.0000
  Learn Step        5000        0        0        0        0
   Coefficient 1    0.9000   0.0000   0.0000   0.0000   0.0000
   Coefficient 2    0.6000   0.0000   0.0000   0.0000   0.0000
   Coefficient 3    0.0000   0.0000   0.0000   0.0000   0.0000
   Temperature      0.0000   0.0000   0.0000   0.0000   0.0000
IO Parameters
    Learn Data: File Rand. (lee_tra) Binary Load
    Recall Data: File Seq. (lee_tes) Binary Load
    Result File: Desired Output, Output
   UserIO Program: leeio
     I/P Ranges:   -1.0000,    1.0000
     O/P Ranges:   -0.8000,    0.8000
    I/P Start Col:      1       MinMax Table: default
    O/P Start Col:      6       Number of Entries: 0
MinMax Table <default>:
Layer: 1
    PEs: 1     Wgt Fields: 2              Sum: Sum
  Spacing: 5     F' offset: 0.00          Transfer: Linear
   Shape: Square                          Output: Direct
   Scale: 1.00   Low Limit: -9999.00   Error Func: standard
   Offset: 0.00  High Limit: 9999.00      Learn: --None--
  Init Low: -0.100  Init High: 0.100    L/R Schedule: (Network)
  Winner 1: None                        Winner 2: None
  PE: Bias

  1.000 Err Factor    0.000 Desired
  0.000 Sum           1.000 Transfer     1.000 Output
    0 Weights         13.470 Error       0.000 Current Error
Layer: In
   PEs: 5     Wgt Fields: 1             Sum: Sum
 Spacing: 5     F' offset: 0.00        Transfer: Linear
  Shape: Square                        Output: Direct
  Scale: 1.00   Low Limit: -9999.00   Error Func: standard
  Offset: 0.00  High Limit: 9999.00      Learn: --None--
 Init Low: -0.100  Init High: 0.100   L/R Schedule: (Network)
 Winner 1: None                       Winner 2: None
PE: 2
  1.000 Err Factor   -1.000 Desired
 -1.000 Sum          -1.000 Transfer    -1.000 Output
    0 Weights         0.000 Error        0.000 Current Error
PE: 3
  1.000 Err Factor   -1.000 Desired
 -1.000 Sum          -1.000 Transfer    -1.000 Output
    0 Weights         0.000 Error        0.000 Current Error
```

```
PE: 4
  1.000 Err Factor   -1.000 Desired
  -1.000 Sum         -1.000 Transfer     -1.000 Output
     0 Weights        0.000 Error         0.000 Current Error
PE: 5
  1.000 Err Factor   -1.000 Desired
  -1.000 Sum         -1.000 Transfer     -1.000 Output
     0 Weights        0.000 Error         0.000 Current Error
PE: 6
  1.000 Err Factor   -1.000 Desired
  -1.000 Sum         -1.000 Transfer     -1.000 Output
     0 Weights        0.000 Error         0.000 Current Error
Layer: Hidden1
   PEs: 3     Wgt Fields: 2              Sum: Sum
  Spacing: 5      F' offset: 0.00        Transfer: TanH
   Shape: Square                         Output: Direct
   Scale: 1.00   Low Limit: -9999.00    Error Func: standard
  Offset: 0.00   High Limit: 9999.00       Learn: Delta-Rule
 Init Low: -0.100  Init High: 0.100    L/R Schedule: hidden1
 Winner 1: None                        Winner 2: None
L/R Schedule: hidden1
 Recall Step          1        0        0        0        0
  Input Clamp      0.0000   0.0000   0.0000   0.0000   0.0000
  Firing Density  100.0000  0.0000   0.0000   0.0000   0.0000
  Temperature      0.0000   0.0000   0.0000   0.0000   0.0000
  Gain           1.0000   0.0000   0.0000   0.0000   0.0000
  Gain           1.0000   0.0000   0.0000   0.0000   0.0000
 Learn Step        10000    30000    70000    150000   310000
  Coefficient 1    0.3000   0.1500   0.0375   0.0023   0.0000
  Coefficient 2    0.4000   0.2000   0.0500   0.0031   0.0000
  Coefficient 3    0.1000   0.1000   0.1000   0.1000   0.1000
  Temperature      0.0000   0.0000   0.0000   0.0000   0.0000
PE: 7
  1.000 Err Factor    0.000 Desired
  -2.107 Sum         -0.971 Transfer     -0.971 Output
     6 Weights        0.000 Error         0.000 Current Error
PE: 8
  1.000 Err Factor    0.000 Desired
  1.126 Sum           0.810 Transfer      0.810 Output
     6 Weights        0.000 Error        -0.000 Current Error
PE: 9
  1.000 Err Factor    0.000 Desired
  6.536 Sum           1.000 Transfer      1.000 Output
     6 Weights        0.000 Error        -0.000 Current Error
Layer: Out
   PEs: 1     Wgt Fields: 2              Sum: Sum
  Spacing: 5      F' offset: 0.00        Transfer: TanH
   Shape: Square                         Output: Direct
   Scale: 1.00   Low Limit: -9999.00    Error Func: standard
  Offset: 0.00   High Limit: 9999.00       Learn: Delta-Rule
 Init Low: -0.100  Init High: 0.100    L/R Schedule: out

 Winner 1: None                        Winner 2: None
L/R Schedule: out
 Recall Step          1        0        0        0        0
  Input Clamp      0.0000   0.0000   0.0000   0.0000   0.0000
  Firing Density  100.0000  0.0000   0.0000   0.0000   0.0000
  Temperature      0.0000   0.0000   0.0000   0.0000   0.0000
  Gain           1.0000   0.0000   0.0000   0.0000   0.0000
  Gain           1.0000   0.0000   0.0000   0.0000   0.0000
 Learn Step        10000    30000    70000    150000   310000
  Coefficient 1    0.1500   0.0750   0.0188   0.0012   0.0000
  Coefficient 2    0.4000   0.2000   0.0500   0.0031   0.0000
  Coefficient 3    0.1000   0.1000   0.1000   0.1000   0.1000
  Temperature      0.0000   0.0000   0.0000   0.0000   0.0000
PE: 10
  1.000 Err Factor   -1.000 Desired
  -2.165 Sum         -0.974 Transfer     -0.974 Output
     4 Weights       -0.026 Error        -0.026 Current Error
```

Table 3. Detail System Descriptions of our neural network

V. Discussion and Conclusion

(1). Discussion

The learning result converges well or not is the key point to influence the success of neural network. Supposed it does not converge well, we need to consider the following propositions to improve our system:

(a). Is it loaded well from a file as the network's I/O; and is the data read correctly or not

(b). To improve the learning rule and the transfer function ,and to adjust the learning coefficient.

(c). To change the network structure such as the numbers of layers, and PEs, etc.

(d). To improve Data Preprocessing or Data Representation such as the digitized technique for inputted PEs, and output values, etc.

(e).To improve the quality and quantity of data, such as the characteristics of data input choice

(f). To include special methodology such as Jog or Purge to improve the convergence.

(2). Conclusion

The development of Neural Network simulates the brain of the human being. It offers capabilities as follows : (1). Powerful Calculation (2). Parallel Processing (3). Learning (4). Fault Tolerance. We prefer Back-Propagation Networks[BPN] to this research. As to the aggregation of research on Neural Network, both Pattern Recognition and Classification benefit from BPN. We establish the BPN of Crime Suspicious Factor Analysis, to scale the suspect of crime, and to differentiate Pre-CB from In-CB. This research includes BPN model which fits mostly on the characteristics of classification.

Expert System fits the requirements of static knowledge[Mark Theory], and Neural Net work solves the problem of dynamic knowledge[Non-Mark Theory] which needs the capability of learning.[LCK92]. This research tries to establish the methodology of Non-Mark Theory's evidence of crime scene to help the investigator to investigate the crime before the Post-CB happens, especially, it is possibly to prevent from occurring the crime and saving citizen's life. This system may be applied to train the investigator to input 5Ws(PEs) to network, to show the result to the investigator, and to differentiate the **significant suspect** from **non-significant suspect.** But, we still have to do the following improvements in the future:(a). This system offers English text, we need to incorporate Chinese text to our system; (b). The ranges of input PEs are -1, 0, and +1, it is possible that our real world information contains uncertainty factors, for example, to a specific crime suspect, it is only 80% or 70% positive for an investigator to make sure that the criminal is going to commit a crime. We allow the user to input these kind of values. Fuzzy set theory could be included in our future research; (c). We had enough experiences and achievements in the applications of Expert System[K92,K921,KLS92,KLS91,LLC92], the whole system should be combined with the police investigation system in the future.

References

[B82] Bellor, N.J.,"Information and Artificial Intelligence in the Lawyer's Office", In Artificial Intelligence and Legal Information Systems, Amsterdam:North-Holland, 1982

[B91] Tom Bevel, "Crime Scene Reconstruction", Journal of Forensic Identification, Vol.41, No.4, July/August,1991. pp.249

[BE84] Bruce G. Buchanan and Edward H. Shortliffe, "Rule-Based Expert Systems:The MYCIN Experiments of the Standford Heuristic Programming Project", Reading Mass.:, Addison- Wesley Publishing Company, 1984

[BF82] Avron Barr and Edward A. Feigenbaum Ed.,The Handbook of Artificial Intelligence, Vol.2,3, William Kaufman, Inc.,Los Altos, California, 1982

[C71] Culliford, B.J.,"The Examination and Typing of Blood Stain in the Crime Laboratory",D.S.Government Printing Office, Washington D.C., 1971

[CN64] B.J.Culliford and L.C. Nickols,"The Benzidine test: A critical review", Journal of Forensic Science, 9(1964), 175 pp.

[CT92] China Times, March 3, 1992

[D70] Herbert Leon MacDonnell "Blood Stain Interpretation", Laboratory of Forensic Science, Corning, New York, 1970

[E88] EXSYS PROFESSIONAL, Exsys Inc., 1988

[FK85] Richard Fikes and Tom Kehler, "The Role of Frame-Based Representation Reasoning",Communications of the ACM, Sep.1985, Vol.28, pp.904-920

[HKM80] Hayes-Roth, F., Klahr, P., and Mostow, D.J. Knowledge Acquisition, Knowledge Programming, and Knowledge Refinement. Washington, DC:Rand Report R-2540-NSF, May 1980

[HK85] Harmon, P., and King, D., Expert Systems: Artificial Intelligence in Business, New York, Wiley, 1985

[HLW83] Hayes-Roth, F. Lenat, D.B., and Waterman, D.B.(Eds.), "Building Expert Systems", Reading Mass.:, Addison-Wesley, Inc., 1983

[IACP75] International Association of Chiefs of Police, Criminal Investigation:Specific Offenses, the International Association of Chiefs on Police, Inc.,Vol.2, 1975

[IEEE91] IEEE Proc. of IJCNN'90, Washington D.C., Jan, 19-22, 1990
IEEE Proc. of IJCNN'90, San Deigo, June, 19-22, 1990
IEEE Proc. of IJCNN'91, Seattle, June 19-22, 1991

[J86] Peter Jackson,"Introduction to Expert Systems", Addison-Wesley, 1986

[JDD89] Jay Liebowitz, Daniel A. De Salvo,"Structuring Expert Systems, Domain, Design, & Development ", Yourdon Press 1989

[K92] Chenyuan Kou, "A Heuristic Approach to Reconstruct Crime Scene based on Mark Theory", The Proceedings of Symposium on Optical Disk and Micrographic Systems, pp.93-110,Dec.21-22, 1992, National Taiwan University Alumni Center

[K921] Chenyuan Kou, Chi-ho Lin, and Frederick Springsteel, "An Adaptive Expert System for Bloodstain Interpretation", Journal of Police Science,Central Police University, Jan. 1992, pp. 87-99

[KLS92] Chenyuan Kou, Chi-ho Lin, and Frederick Springsteel, " HABSI:An Expert System to Reconstruct Crime Scene based on Bloodstain Interpretations", IEEE Carnahan Conference 1992, Oct.14-16, 1992, Atlanta, Georgia, U.S.A.

[KLS91] Chenyuan Kou, Chi-ho Lin, and Frederick Springsteel, "A Heuristic Approach on Bloodstain Interpretations---HABSI", National Computer Symposium, Dec.18-19, 1991, National Central University, Chung-li, Taoyuan, R.O.C.

[Kosko92] Bart Kosko, "Neural Networks and Fuzzy Systems", Prentice-Hall, 1992

[LCK92] Chi-ho Lin, Li-hsin Chen, and Chenyuan Kou, "A Study on the Category of Criminal Signs",IEEE Carnahan Conference 1992, Oct.14-16, 1992, Atlanta, Georgia, U.S.A

[LLC92] Chi-ho Lin, Zen-chen Liu, and Chenyuan Kou, "An Intelligent Expert System to Provide Suitable Comment for the Judge---PSCJ", The 3rd National MIS conference,May 29--May 31, 1992, National Chiao-Tung Univeristy

[N91] NEURAL WORKS PROFESSIONAL II/PLUS REFERENCE GUIDE, NEURALWARE, INC. 1991

[P77] David Powis, "The Signs of Crime", MCGRAW-HILL Book Company(UK), 1977

[P84] J.Pearl, "Heuristics:Intelligence Search Strategies for Computer Problem Solving", Reading MA:Addison-Wesley, 1984

[P87] R.P. Lippman, "An introduction to computing with neural nets",IEEE ASSP magazine, Vol.4.,PP.4-22, 1987.

[R85] Frederick Hayes-Roth, "Rule-Based Systems",Communications of the ACM, Sep.1985, Vol.28, pp.921-932

[RHW86] D. E. Rumelhart and G.E. Hinton and R.J. Williams, "Parallel Distributed Processing (PDP): Exploration in the Microstructure of Cognition(Vol.1),"MIT Press, Cambridge, Massachusetts, Editor:D.E. Rumelhart and J.L.McClelland and the PDP Research Group, Chapter 8, PP.318-362, "Learning Internal Representations by Error Propagation",1986

[S77] LeMoyne Snyder, Homicide Investigation, Charles C. Thomas Publisher, 3rd ed. May, 1977

[SCT84] Charles R. Swanson, Jr, Neil C. Chamelin, and Leonard Territo, Criminal Investigation, Random House, New York, 1984

[TZ12] M.Takayama, Kokka Igakkai Zasshi, no.306(1912), 15.

[W84] P.H.Winston, "Artificial Intelligence, 2nd ed.", Addison-Wesley Publishing Company, 1984

[W86] Donald A. Waterman, A Guide to Expert System, Reading MA:Addison-Wesley, 1986

[Y93] Yi-Cherng Yeh, "Application and Implementation of Neural Networks", Shin-jwu, R.O.C.1993

Estimation Performance of Neural Networks

J. L. Crespo
E. Mora
Dpto. Matematica Aplicada y Ciencias de la Computaciòn
E.T.S.I. de Caminos C. y P.. Universidad de Cantabria
Avda. de los Castros, s/n - 39005 Santander, SPAIN

J. Peire
Dpto. Ingeniería Eléctrica, Electrónica y Control
E.T.S.I. Industriales. UNED
Ciudad Universitaria s/n
28040 Madrid. SPAIN

***Abstract*-In order to test neural network abilities as estimators of engineering value, a network is presented to derive streamflow from precipitation data. Validation tests show good performance, hence increasing confidence in these methods. Monthly mean squared errors remaining after adjustment are presented and compared with those of deterministic methods, since these are other options for the estimation problem.**

A possible caveat of artificial neural networks (ANN) is that they are very difficult to interpret. Interpretation of the learnt representation in this case is offered by simulating with selected inputs, showing reasonable results and providing some insight in the hydrologic process being modeled. This is a generic possibility for dealing with black-box models.

When estimating some system's behavior it is interesting to know whether the qualitative representation is also faithful. In the proposed example, special properties of the flow series with significance in hydrology, such as ranges, are obtained and compared with the sample values, along with other statistical features.

OBJECTIVES

ANN's, which have been successful as estimators, are a recent acquisition of artificial intelligence engineers. In order to test their ability in ordinary engineering problems, we present an example of hydrologic modeling with ANN's.

The purpose of this example is to develop a method for calculating streamflow data from precipitation.

Because of their ability to deal with noisy signals, connectionist models offer an interesting choice for this type of models. Standard feedforward backpropagation networks also offer the possibility of on-line adjustment in a very simple way.

For the particular river chosen, precipitation and streamflow data were available, in the form of 10-day accumulated amounts, for 11 years, and only precipitation for over 40 years. The basin area was 356 Km^2.

NETWORKS SETUP AND ADJUSTMENT

In order to have a referece value for testing the performance of the networks, a usual deterministic model was set up for the dataset, namely a Sacramento model. Since the model predictions are used on a month by month basis, the significant error was obtained by adding all three values of the predicted flows for each month and comparing with the observed total monthly flow, as opposed to the usual one to one comparison. The mean monthly squared error was 21 mm.

Then, 3 feedforward standard nets were set up; two had 23 parameters (the Sacramento model had 22) and the third one had 41 parameters.

Phenomena relevant for streamflow prediction are not only the precipitation history, but also evapotranspiration and infiltration. In order to account for this, the input was: precipitation for the current period, precipitation for the previous period and period within the year (they were numbered starting in October 1st.). So the input layer was to have 3 elements.

They were all 4-layer networks feedforward and with full interconnection between adjacent layers; 3-3-2-1 (23 parameters) the first and second ones and 3-4-4-1 (41 parameters) the third one. The structure of the models can be seen in fig. 1, where the lines represent connections.

The activation function was the hyperbolic tangent in all cases, with the exception of one of the 23-parameter nets, which had a linear element in the output layer. The idea behind this is that, the streamflow being a continuous variable, the fitting will be better if there is not a upper saturation level. It should be noted that if the linear output network produces a negative flow, 0 will be taken instead.

The data were scaled to fit in the [-1,1] range.

First the nets were trained with the whole data series, in order to compare with the deterministic model.

The 23-parameter fully non-linear net gave 25 mm residual mean monthly squared error and the 41-parameter one, 20 mm.

0-7803-1227-9/93/$3.00© 1993 IEEE

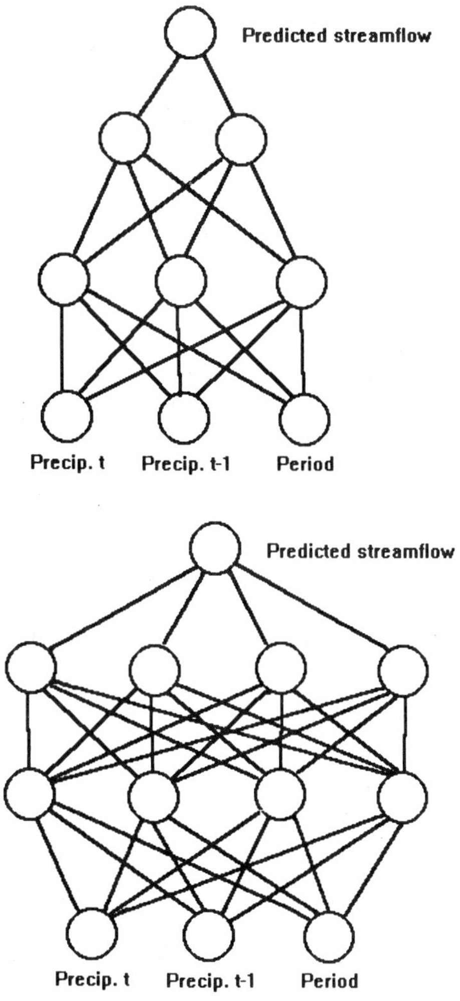

Fig 1: Networks schematic

The 23-parameter net was able to get to 20 mm residual error when using linear output, so the 23-parameter network with nonlinear output was dropped. It should be noted that if the linear output network produces a negative flow, 0 will be taken instead.

The improvement over the network with non linear output shows that, whenever possible, a priori knowledge should be embedded in the network models.

The errors that remained after adjusting the networks with the whole series were acceptable, as is shown in figs. 2 and 3 for one of the years of the training set.

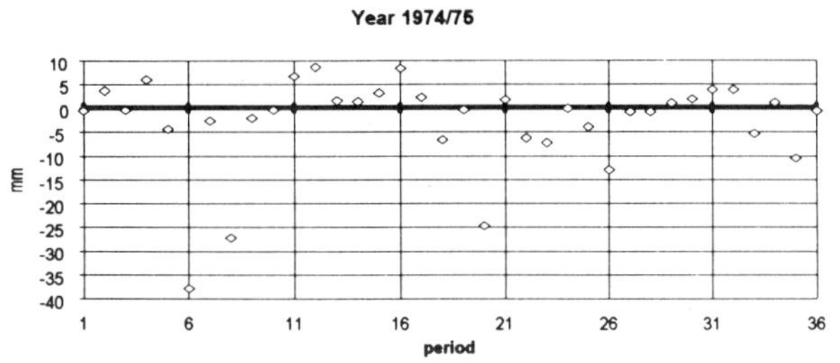

Fig 2: Residual errors in the network with 41 parameters

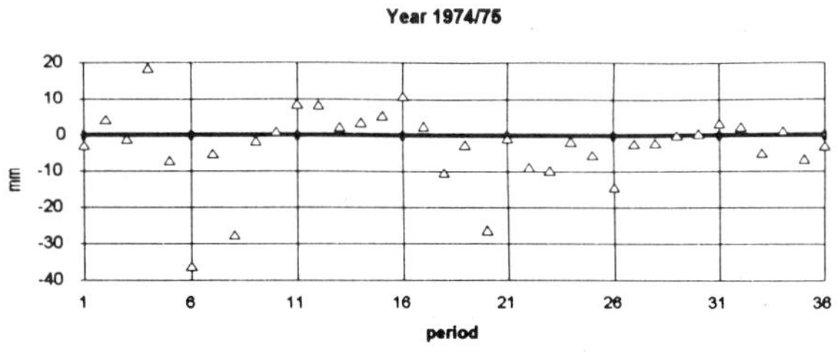

Fig 3: Residual error in the network with 23 parameters

In order to further investigate possible deficiencies of the model, the error-flow relationship was investigated by plotting these values for each point of the 11 year set after using the whole dataset for training (see figs. 4 and 5).

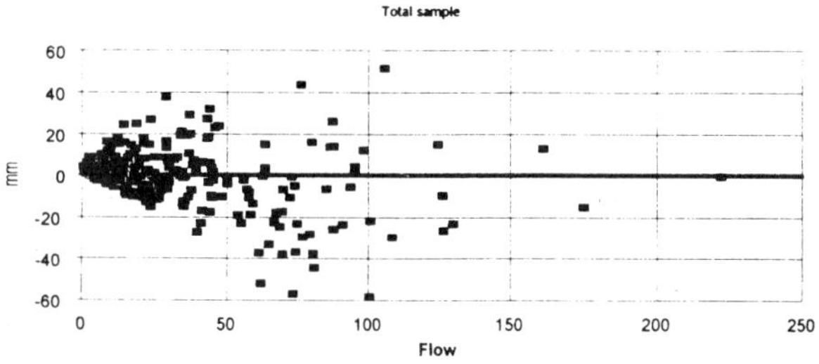

Fig. 4: Residual error vs. flow for the network with 41 parameters

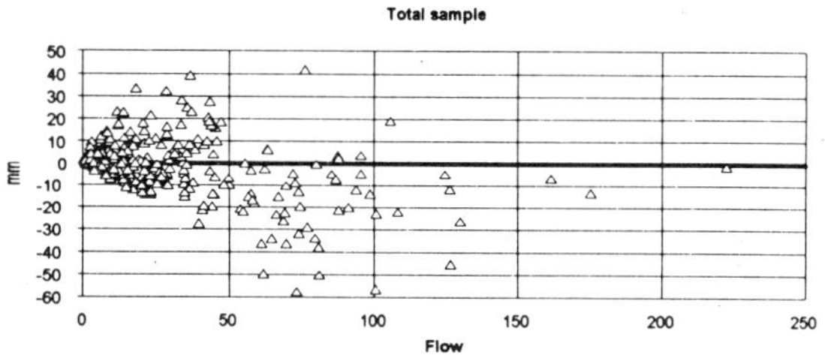

Fig. 5: Residual error for the 23-parameter network

As can be seen in the previous figures, the predicted flows are too low when the observed flow is larger than 50 mm.

VALIDATION

In order to test the generalization ability of the networks, which is a very important feature for engineering work, they were adjusted with the first half of the data and tested with the second half. The mean squared error for the generalization set can be seen in Table I for the less complex network.

TABLE I:
Generalization Errors

Generalization error (mm)	23-parameter; linear output
generalization set	14.03743
training set	10.80127

The model learnt by the networks was good, with the effect of reducing noise, mainly noted in extreme values, as can be seen in fig. 6, where the networks are compared with observed flows for 1 year of the generalization set.

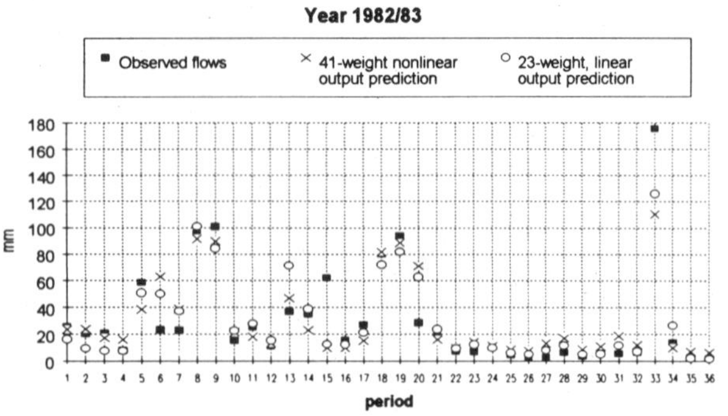

Fig. 6: Generalization errors

The best net was considered to be the one with linear output since it had a low generalization error with only 23 parameters. In the following sections, only this net is considered.

INTERPRETATION

In order to extract the information the net had learned, at least to some extent, it was tested with selected input data. This is needed because of the black-box nature of ANN's.

The first influence to be extracted is that of the period within the year. To isolate its effect, the precipitation was held constant (any value is acceptable, since its influence was not being investigated) and the time of the year was varied. So, the net was run for a year, with a 10 mm/10 days constant precipitation. The result is shown in fig. 7.

It can be seen how the net predicts the storage and evapotranspiration variations throughout the year. The cycle shown by the network is basically what any model or expert would have drawn.

It is usually assumed that storage variation can be neglected if the time interval under study spans for a year. Then, the difference between total precipitation and total runoff is the annual evapotranspiration. The predicted evapotranspiration is 25 mm for this 365 mm precipitation year. So far this figure has not been compared, since this kind of year is not usually assumed when studying evapotranspiration, but it does not look bad.

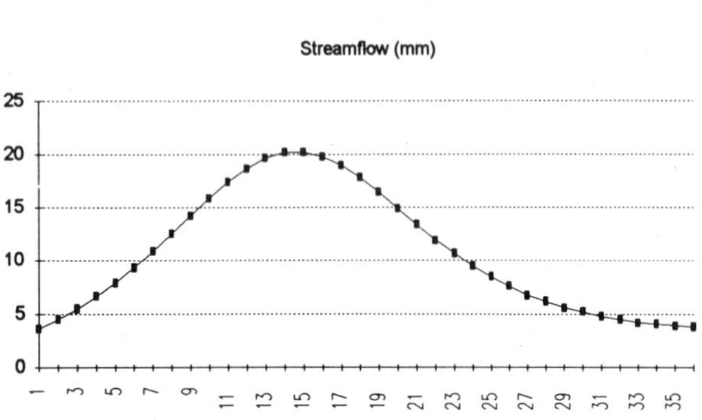

Fig. 7 Streamflow with constant 1 mm/day precipitation

Next, the precipitation influence was deducted by keeping the date constant (namely the 10th. period) and the net was tested for that given period, varying the previous precipitation only when its influence was being tested or varying the current precipitation, and keeping the previous one constant when the current precipitation's influence was to be found. In either case, the constant precipitation was 10 mm. Results can be seen in figs. 8 and 9.

The relationships are linear for high precipitation, since the evapotranspiration and storage variation are negligible. For low precipitations, this does not hold and the network reflects it. It should be noted again that these assumptions were not "programmed" in the network, but rather "extracted" from the sample.

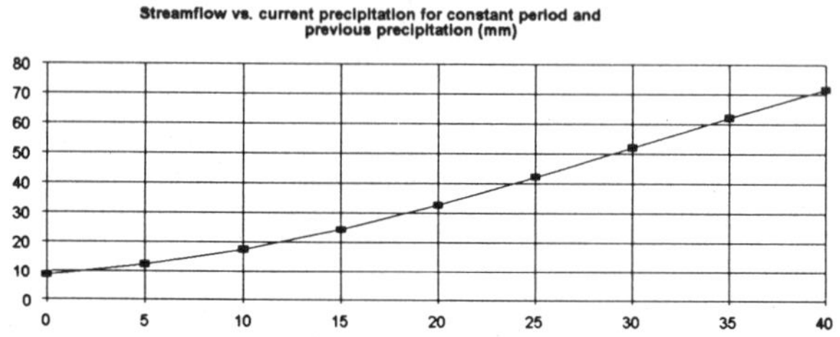

Fig 8: Current precipitation influence

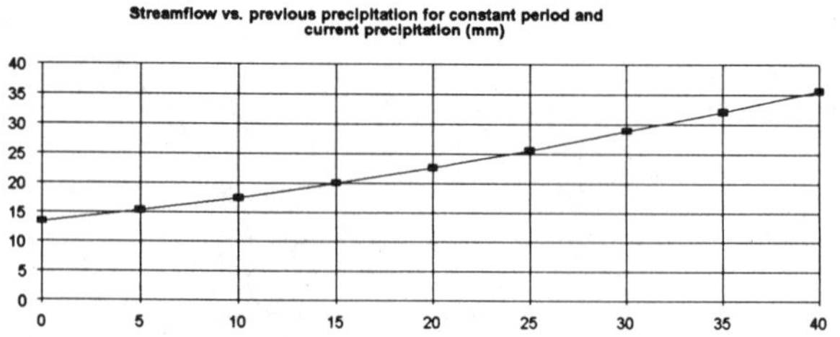

Fig 9: Previous precipitation influence

Finally, the flow with 0 precipitation at the beginning of October and the end of September was obtained. The network gave 0.8 mm. This should be considered a minimum flow, since the storage should be quite depleted at that time of the year. This was a clear extrapolation, since that kind of situation was not in the sample.

STATISTICAL FEATURES

So far, only residual errors have been investigated. In this section, we look for the general features of the model, to see its accuracy. Table II shows the comparison between observed and predicted adjusted and adjusted rescaled ranges, which are useful in the context of reservoir design. It can be seen that the prediction is quite close to the data.

TABLE II
Ranges

	Observed	Predicted
Adjusted range	750 mm	712 mm
Adj. resc. range	25 mm	26 mm

Next, the flow-precipitation observed and predicted covariance matrices and correlation coefficients are presented.

Observed covariance matrix:

$$\begin{vmatrix} 866.3105 & 351.5151 \\ 351.5151 & 210.3011 \end{vmatrix}$$

Predicted covariance matrix:

$$\begin{vmatrix} 733.6761 & 353.2639 \\ 353.2639 & 210.3011 \end{vmatrix}$$

Observed correlation coefficient:

$$0.8235$$

Predicted correlation coefficient:

$$0.8993$$

It can be seen that the predicted flow variance is smaller; this accounts for the difference in correlation coefficients, since the covariance is practically the same; the smaller variance shows that the network has filtered the response, bringing the extreme values closer to the average.

CONCLUSIONS

The results show that relatively simple neural networks, with an adequate choice of the input data, can achieve an accuracy comparable with that of specific models, having a similar number of parameters. The model setup process (learning) can be done very fast (interactively in a standard workstation). This supports the feasibility of ANN models as estimators in common engineering work.

In the proposed example, it can be seen that there is a certain degree of correlation between error and flow, suggesting that the net has focused mainly on low flows. This shows how the backpropagation learning algorithm concentrates on most frequent data.

Out of sample testing shows that accuracy is not degraded significantly.

The network is capable of extracting the annual variation of streamflow, and the relationship between this and precipitation without any a-priori knowledge. In this case, ANN's are more useful than standard parametric methods, which require a very qualified approach.

The averaging effect of the networks produces a more uniform series than the data series used in the learning process. This noise reduction effect should be taken into account when using the ANN in other analysis.

REFERENCES

[1] A. G. Barto. "Connectionist Learning for Control: An Overview". COINS 89. 1989

[2] E. M. Shaw. "Hidrology in practice". Chapman and Hall. 1990

[3] G. C. Goodwin and K.S. Sin. "Adaptive Filtering Prediction and Control". Prentice-Hall, Inc., Englewood Cliffs, N.J., 1984

[4] J. Hertz, A. Krogh, R.G. Palmer, "Introduction to the teory of Neural Computation", Addison-Wesley. 1991

[5] N.T.Kottegode, "Stochastic Water Resources Technology", MacMillan Press. 1980

[6] R.K.Linsley, M.A.Kohler, J.L.H.Paulhus; "Hydrology for Engineers". McGraw-Hill. 1975

[7] J.L.McLelland, D.E.Rumelhart; "Explorations in Parallel Distributed Processing", The MIT Press. 1989

[8] R. J. C. Burnash, R. L. Ferral, R. A. McGuire; "A generalized streamflow simulation system. Conceptual modeling for digital computers", 1979

[9] T.J.Sejnowski, and C.R. Rosenberg . "Parallel Networks that Learn to Pronounce English Text". Complex Systems 1, 145-168. 1987

Model-based Understanding of Uncertain Observational Data for Oil Spill Tracking

Jungfu Tsao, Jan Wolter, and Haojin Wang
Department of Computer Science
Texas A&M University
College Station, TX 77843-3112 USA

Abstract—**Oil spill tracking is essential in oil spill clean-up. Usually, the oil spill tracking is treated by employing a mathematical oil spill model which describes the fate and transport behavior of an oil spill. Before a model can predict where the spilled oil will go in the future, it must have a reasonably accurate understanding about what happened in the past. Typically, the input to the model such as wind, current, etc. is unreliable or sometimes not completely available so that interpolating the past behavior of an oil spill becomes extremely difficult. In this paper, we regard the oil spill tracking as a control problem in which we reduce the errors between the oil observations and the model's outputs by iteratively adjusting the model's inputs and cope with the uncertainty of the model's inputs by using fuzzy logic techniques. Through the process, we can construct a plausible history of the oil spill that is consistent with our observations and can be effectively extrapolated into the future.**

I. Introduction

Before decision makers can determine how to respond to a marine oil spill, they must have a clear picture of the situation, including the oil type, quantity, location, wind, current, etc. Usually, the trajectory of an oil spill is tracked and predicted by a mathematical oil spill model which formulates the fate and transport behavior of the spill. Past research has been aimed largely at developing such oil spill models [1, 3, 8, 9, 10, 12] and they have been widely used to generate simulated oil spill scenarios for training and evaluation of response capabilities [6, 7]. Their use as an aid in planning the clean-up of real world oil spills has, however, been less wide spread. This is because so much of the input data, such as wind and current, is not reliably known, making it difficult to synchronize the modeled scenario with what is happening in the real world. Users must constantly manipulate the input data to try to get the past behavior of the modeled oil spill to match the observed behavior of the real spill so that it can be effectively extrapolated into the future [11].

Our work is aimed at automating such a process. Basically, the idea is to construct a plausible history of the oil spill that is consistent both with the knowledge of oil spill behavior encapsulated in the model and with all the available observations of the real spill. We are not at this point attempting to improve the oil spill models, or suggest clean-up strategies. We are simply trying to fit the model to a set of real world observations in the recent past so that it can be used to better predict what will happen in the future. In this paper, we present an approach where we regard the oil spill tracking as a control problem in which we reduce the errors between the oil observations and the model's outputs by iteratively adjusting the model's inputs.

During the last few years, a wide variety of applications of fuzzy set theory on control area have been reported in fuzzy control literature [4, 5] since Zadeh's seminal paper [14] in 1965. Most conventional fuzzy control systems used linguistic rules in which linguistic terms were represented in fuzzy sets. In our approach, we cope with the uncertainty of observational data by expressing them in fuzzy sets. Through conjunction of fuzzy sets, we form the solution base where constraints are satisfied. We then select the desired solution based on criterion which corresponds to the one with the largest membership value in the solution base.

II. Problem Definition

Typically, an oil spill model is given a description of the spill and weather conditions and generates as its output the oil distribution. The set of input consists of location of spill source, type and quantity of oil, surface wind, and surface current. Given all this data, the model will predict where oil will be found at each point in time. In most systems, all inputs and outputs are expected to be crisp values.

In this paper, we will be given a set of observations of an oil spill. These include observations of the location and amount of the oil at various points in time as well as observations of winds and currents. Many of these observations will have large uncertainties attached to them, and some of the data may be missing completely.

We wish to generate a complete history of oil spill that is consistent both with the observations and with the oil spill model. That is, all modeled data values fall within the uncertainty range of the observed values, and if the modeled spill conditions were run through the oil spill

This research was supported by Texas Advanced Technology Program under Grant Number 999903-282.

0-7803-1485-9/93$03.00 © 1993 IEEE

model, the modeled oil behavior would result. If we have done this, then the set of inputs constitute a valid explanation of the oil spill. Naturally there may be a huge number of possible valid explanations. We should prefer explanations that more closely fit the model and the observations.

Clearly the construction of such an explanation will not always be possible. We will be assuming, however, that the oil spill model actually does come close to explaining the actual behavior of the spill, and that the observations reported are correct within their stated error bounds.

Let V_t be the description of an oil spill and weather conditions at time t, including oil type, wind, and current, and D_t the oil distribution at time t. We can regard the oil spill model as a function f such that

$$D_{t+\Delta t} = f(V_t, D_t),$$

where $\Delta t > 0$. Suppose that a set of observed spill descriptions and weather conditions $\bar{\mathcal{V}}$ and a set of observed oil distributions $\bar{\mathcal{D}}$ are represented, respectively, as

$$\bar{\mathcal{V}} = \{\bar{V}_{t_0}, \bar{V}_{t_1}, \bar{V}_{t_2}, \ldots, \bar{V}_{t_n}\},$$
$$\bar{\mathcal{D}} = \{\bar{D}_{t_0}, \bar{D}_{t_1}, \bar{D}_{t_2}, \ldots, \bar{D}_{t_n}\},$$

where $t_0 < t_1 < t_2 < \ldots < t_n$. These are all values with uncertainties attached to them. Therefore, each observation is in effect a set of possible values, which fall within its own uncertainty envelope. Then, the interpolation of the oil spill tracking can be formulated as finding a set of modeled spill descriptions and weather conditions $\mathcal{V}$, represented as

$$\mathcal{V} = \{V_{t_0}, V_{t_0+1}, V_{t_0+2}, \ldots, V_{t_n}\}.$$

These must be crisp values such that they are close enough to the observed values, that is,

$$V_t \in \bar{V}_t,$$
$$D_t \in \bar{D}_t,$$

where $t \in \{t_0, t_1, t_2, \ldots, t_n\}$, and

$$D_{t+1} = f(V_t, D_t),$$

where $t_0 \leq t < t_n$. Please note that we need to use our best guess to select $D_0 \in \bar{D}_0$ as the model's initial oil distribution. At this point we do not require that the $\mathcal{V}$ values agree with any detailed weather/current model. However, we will enforce spatial and temporal continuity constraints.

III. Approach

A. System Architecture

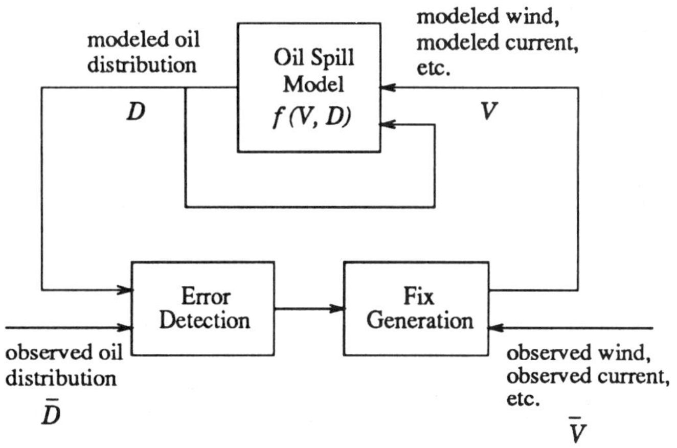

Fig. 1. The system architecture.

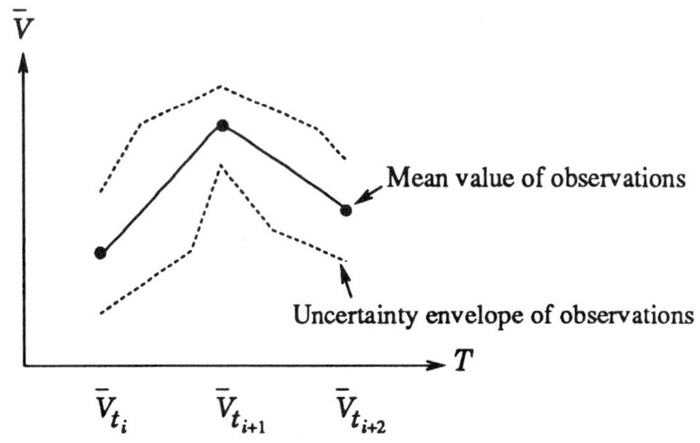

Fig. 2. Example of temporal interpolation of observational input data to fill in gaps in observations.

As previously stated, the problem is essentially to match the modeled oil distribution with the observed oil distribution. The discrepancy between them is simply an indication of error that model has had in tracking the oil spill. Usually, the error is caused by the uncertainty of observational data. To remove the error, we need to adjust some of the model inputs, for example, wind and current, in an iterative fashion. Therefore, the problem resembles a control problem.

In Figure 1, we use an architecture where the *error detection* module compares between the observed and modeled oil distributions to see whether there is any significant error and the *fix generation* module is responsible for resolving it, if one exists.

As a preprocessing stage, we fill in gaps in the observational input data $\bar{\mathcal{V}}$ by interpolating spatially and temporally between observations. Of course, the uncertainty of this interpolated input data will be higher than that of actual observations. Figure 2 shows a simplified example of temporal interpolation between observations.

The system starts at the time of the earliest observation, feeding the best guess of the conditions at that point in time to get the modeled oil distribution for that point in time and comparing it to the observed oil distribution. Once an error is reported by the error detector, the fix generator selects some of the model inputs to adjust in that time step, keeping them within the uncertainty bounds of the corresponding observations. The oil spill model is rerun for that time step, using the new values to generate a new modeled oil distribution. This process repeats until the modeled oil distribution agrees with the observed oil distribution within the range of observational and model errors. If convergence in a time step fails, we backtrack in time to adjust previous time steps.

B. Representing Observations in Fuzzy Sets

A fuzzy set F in a universe of discourse U is characterized by a membership function μ_F which takes values in the interval $[0,1]$, that is, $U \rightarrow [0,1]$. The support of a fuzzy set F is the crisp set of all points u in U such that $\mu_F(u) > 0$. We represent each variable in observations as a fuzzy set F with symmetric triangle membership function. F can be characterized as a pair (α_F, β_F), where α_F is the mean value of F with $\mu_F(\alpha_F) = 1$, $\alpha_F - \beta_F$ the lower limit with $\mu_F(\alpha_F - \beta_F) = 0$, and $\alpha_F + \beta_F$ the upper limit with $\mu_F(\alpha_F + \beta_F) = 0$. We then define the following operations, which will be used later on.

Suppose A and B are two fuzzy sets. We define the addition, subtraction, and multiplication of A and B [2, 13] as

$$A + B = (\alpha_A + \alpha_B, \beta_A + \beta_B),$$
$$A - B = (\alpha_A - \alpha_B, \beta_A + \beta_B),$$
$$A * B = (\alpha_A * \alpha_B, \alpha_A * \beta_B + \alpha_B * \beta_A).$$

We say that a crisp value X is a member of a fuzzy set F if it is a member of the support of F, denoted as

$$X \in F.$$

We define the multiplication of a crisp value X and a fuzzy set F as another fuzzy set

$$XF = (X\alpha_F, X\beta_F).$$

In the following sections, we describe the two modules, error detection and fix generation, in detail.

IV. Error Detection

The error detection module uses a *quadtree spatial partition* approach based on *volume difference* and *centroid difference* to compare the modeled oil distribution with the observed oil distribution. We use an example to describe the algorithm.

Suppose at some point in time we have an observation of the spilled oil distribution and a modeled oil distribution as shown in Figure 3. At the top level, we first look for errors in the total oil volume of the two spill maps. If these agree, then we compare the centroids of the observed and modeled oil distributions. If they disagree, a description of the error is passed to the fix generation module.

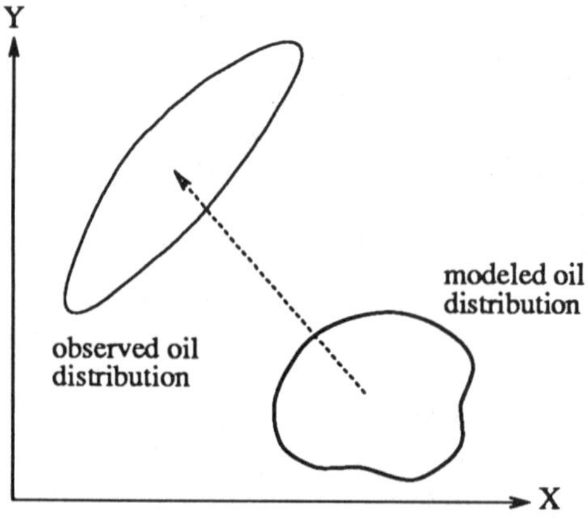

Fig. 3. The centroid difference at the top level is shown as a vector with the initial observed and modeled oil distributions.

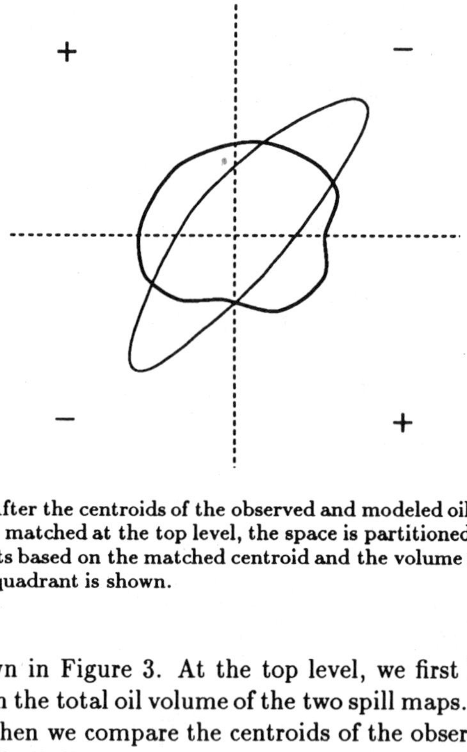

Fig. 4. After the centroids of the observed and modeled oil distributions are matched at the top level, the space is partitioned into four quadrants based on the matched centroid and the volume difference in each quadrant is shown.

From the second level on, we recursively partition the space based on the matched centroid, obtained from the previous level, into four quadrants. In each quadrant, we first calculate the volume difference as shown in Figure 4, where + denotes the volume of the modeled oil distribution is greater than that of the observed oil distribution, − denotes less than, and = denotes equal to. If the volumes in the four quadrants agree, then we compare the centroids of the oil in each of the quadrants, giving rise to an error vector as shown in Figure 5. This recursive error detection procedure continues until both the volumes and the centroids for the modeled oil distribution in each quadrant fall within their uncertainty bounds.

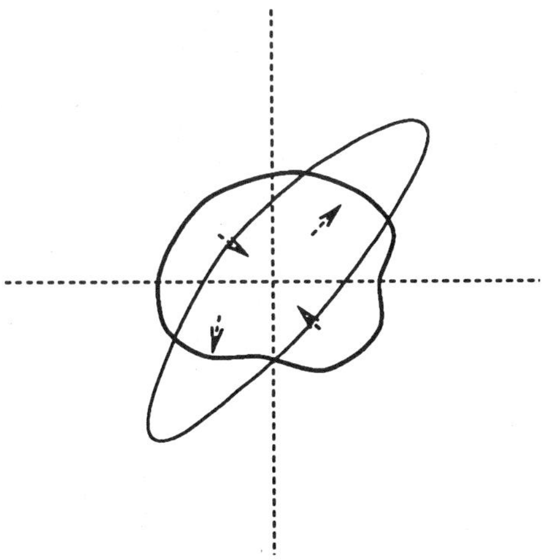

Fig. 5. The centroid difference in each quadrant is shown.

This method of error detection causes the system to first work to get rough agreement between the modeled and observed spills, and then apply finer and finer resolution to the error detection process.

A. Volume Difference

As is commonly done, we assume the map of the sea is divided up into grid squares so that the amount of oil and weather conditions in each grid square can be kept track of. Let the amount of oil at time t in grid square l for the observed oil distribution be $\bar{M}_{t,l}$. Similarly, let the amount of oil at time t in grid square l in iteration i for the modeled oil distribution be $M^i_{t,l}$. Suppose the oil spill area of interest is denoted as L. The total amount of oil at time t in area L for the observed oil distribution, denoted $\bar{M}_{t,L}$, can be expressed as

$$\bar{M}_{t,L} = \sum_{l \in L} \bar{M}_{t,l}.$$

Similarly, the total amount of oil at time t in area L in iteration i for the modeled oil distribution, denoted $M^i_{t,L}$, is expressed as

$$M^i_{t,L} = \sum_{l \in L} M^i_{t,l}.$$

We calculate the volume difference between the observed and the modeled oil distributions at time t in area L in iteration i, denoted $\Delta M^i_{t,L}$, as

$$\Delta M^i_{t,L} = \alpha_{\bar{M}_{t,L}} - M^i_{t,L}.$$

B. Centroid Difference

We calculate the centroid of the observed oil distribution at time t in area L, denoted $\bar{P}_{t,L}$, as

$$\bar{P}_{t,L} = \frac{\sum_{l \in L} \bar{M}_{t,l} l}{\sum_{l \in L} \bar{M}_{t,l}}.$$

Similarly, the centroid of the modeled oil distribution at time t in area L in iteration i, denoted $P^i_{t,L}$ is

$$P^i_{t,L} = \frac{\sum_{l \in L} M^i_{t,l} l}{\sum_{l \in L} M^i_{t,l}}.$$

Then, the centroid difference, denoted $\Delta P^i_{t,L}$, between the observed and the modeled oil distributions at time t in area L in iteration i can be defined as a vector from the centroid of modeled oil distribution at time t in area L in iteration i to that of the observed oil distribution at time t in area L, that is,

$$\Delta P^i_{t,L} = \alpha_{\bar{P}_{t,L}} - P^i_{t,L}.$$

C. Quadtree Spatial Partition

At the top level, we remove the centroid difference by adjusting the model inputs such that the centroids of the observed and modeled oil distributions in terms of the area of interest L could be matched, i.e.

$$P^i_{t,L} \in \bar{P}_{t,L}.$$

At the second level, we partition L into four quadrants, say, $L1$, $L2$, $L3$, and $L4$, based on the matched centroid. We then remove the volume difference and centroid difference in each quadrant at this level such that

$$M^i_{t,Lj} \in \bar{M}_{t,Lj}, \quad (1)$$

$$P^i_{t,Lj} \in \bar{P}_{t,Lj}, \quad (2)$$

where $1 \leq j \leq 4$. We recursively remove the volume difference and centroid difference at each level until we reach a level where the conditions (1) and (2) are satisfied.

Please note that for the case where there's no oil in a quadrant the centroid of that oil distribution is defined to be at the centroid in last partition where the quadrant is derived.

V. Fix Generation

The choice between different fixes for the same error is made based on the certainties associated with different data values. For example, if the modeled spill covers too small an area, we could increase the amount of oil spilled, change the oil type to reduce evaporation and dissolution, or increase the winds to spread it faster. The choice will depend on which of these changes would best fit the observational uncertainties.

Volume differences between quadrants of a quadtree can be corrected by instituting winds or currents in a + quadrant to move oil toward a − or = quadrant. The way we remove volume difference is by moving oil from the quadrant with the largest volume difference to the one with the smallest as the first priority. If it fails to find a fix for it,

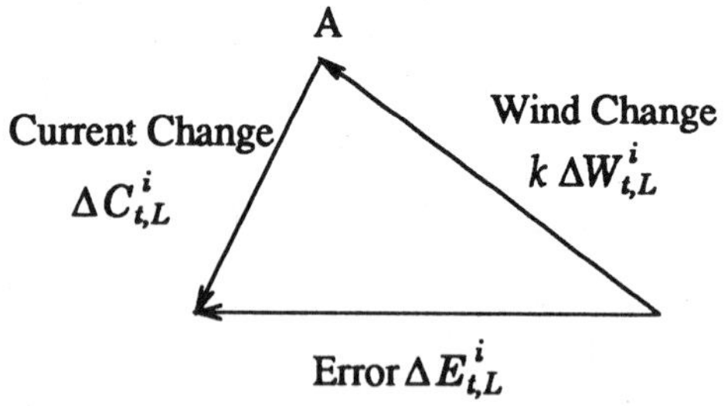

Fig. 6. Error is reduced by the vectorial sum of wind and current changes.

we then try moving oil to the quadrant with the second smallest volume difference, and so on. Centroid differences at all levels can be corrected by adding components of winds or currents in the necessary direction.

The most complex fixes are those involving changes to winds or currents. We will focus our discussion on those types of fixes. In these cases, the system must choose between making the fix by adjusting the wind alone, the current alone, or some combination. In general, the error will be some vector which can be reduced by the vectorial sum of wind and current changes, as shown in Figure 6. Suppose we call the point which forms the wind change and current change into a vectorial sum to reduce the error an *adjustment point*, denoted A in the figure. From the figure, it is obvious that each point in space constitutes a possible adjustment point, in turn, a possible solution to remove the error. If we consider the continuity constraint of wind and current transitions, selecting an adjustment point depends on how we interpolate the present situation of wind and current between two nearest observations.

A. Inputs Adjustment

Since the wind and current are the main factors in oil spill transport, we propose the following adjustment.

Let the wind and current vectors at time t in grid square l in iteration i for the modeled oil distribution be $W^i_{t,l}$ and $C^i_{t,l}$, respectively. We can define the representative wind and current vectors in area L as the averages of winds and currents for those grid squares in L, denoted $W^i_{t,L}$ and $C^i_{t,L}$, as follows

$$W^i_{t,L} = \frac{\sum_{l\in L} W^i_{t,l}}{\|L\|},$$
$$C^i_{t,L} = \frac{\sum_{l\in L} C^i_{t,l}}{\|L\|}.$$

Suppose we define the wind and current changes at time t in area L in iteration i, denoted $\Delta W^i_{t,L}$ and $\Delta C^i_{t,L}$, respectively, as

$$\Delta W^i_{t,L} = W^i_{t,L} - W^{i-1}_{t,L}, \qquad (3)$$
$$\Delta C^i_{t,L} = C^i_{t,L} - C^{i-1}_{t,L}. \qquad (4)$$

Let $\Delta E^i_{t,L}$ represent the error vector either for $\Delta M^i_{t,L}$ or $\Delta P^i_{t,L}$. Then, the error $\Delta E^i_{t,L}$ can be reduced through the vectorial sum of wind and current changes

$$\Delta E^i_{t,L} = k\Delta W^i_{t,L} + \Delta C^i_{t,L}, \qquad (5)$$

where k is the wind effect constant selected in the oil spill model. If we can find such wind and current changes in iteration i, then we make the following adjustments, $\forall l \in L$

$$W^i_{t,l} = W^{i-1}_{t,l} + \Delta W^i_{t,L},$$
$$C^i_{t,l} = C^{i-1}_{t,l} + \Delta C^i_{t,L}.$$

If the error $\Delta E^i_{t,L}$ is not removed in a previous iteration of wind and current changes, the fix generation module will keep proposing new ones until it is resolved.

B. Linear Interpolation of Observations

Let the wind and current vectors at time t in grid square l for the observed oil distribution be $\bar{W}_{t,l}$ and $\bar{C}_{t,l}$, respectively. We define the representative observed wind and current vectors at time t in the area of interest L, denoted as $\tilde{W}_{t,L}$ and $\tilde{C}_{t,L}$, respectively, as

$$\tilde{W}_{t,L} = \frac{\sum_{l\in L} \bar{W}_{t,l}}{\|L\|},$$
$$\tilde{C}_{t,L} = \frac{\sum_{l\in L} \bar{C}_{t,l}}{\|L\|}.$$

Suppose $\tilde{W}_{t_1,L}$ and $\tilde{W}_{t_2,L}$ are two consecutive representative observed wind vectors. We select as the representative observed wind vector at time t, where $t_1 < t < t_2$, denoted as $\tilde{W}_{t,L}$, by linear interpolation

$$\tilde{W}_{t,L} = \tilde{W}_{t_1,L} + \frac{(\tilde{W}_{t_2,L} - \tilde{W}_{t_1,L})(t - t_1)}{(t_2 - t_1)}.$$

Similarly, the representative observed current vector at time t, where $t_1 < t < t_2$, is expressed as

$$\tilde{C}_{t,L} = \tilde{C}_{t_1,L} + \frac{(\tilde{C}_{t_2,L} - \tilde{C}_{t_1,L})(t - t_1)}{(t_2 - t_1)}.$$

C. Adjustment Selection

From equations (3) and (4), we have

$$W^i_{t,L} = W^{i-1}_{t,L} + \Delta W^i_{t,L},$$
$$C^i_{t,L} = C^{i-1}_{t,L} + \Delta C^i_{t,L}.$$

That is, the modeled wind and current vectors in new iteration i are obtained by the modeled wind and current vectors in the previous iteration with the wind and current

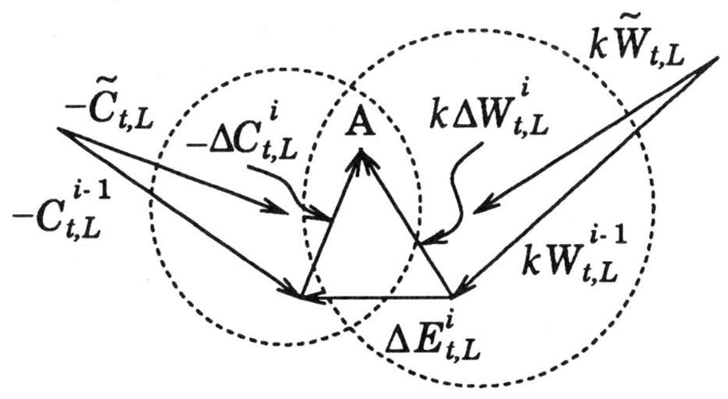

Fig. 7. The adjustment point is selected in the intersected region with the highest membership value.

changes for the new iteration. There are three constraints that have to be satisfied when we select $\Delta W^{i}_{t,L}$ and $\Delta C^{i}_{t,L}$. The equation (5) must be met, and $W^{i}_{t,L}$ and $C^{i}_{t,L}$ must fall within the uncertainty envelopes of the representative observed wind and current vectors, that is, $\tilde{W}_{t,L}$ and $\tilde{C}_{t,L}$. Since the representative observed wind and current are vectors, the uncertainties of them can be represented as fuzzy sets in a universe of points in space characterized by cone membership functions with the centers of the circles having membership value 1 and the perimeters of the circles 0. The radii of the circles are determined by $\beta_{\tilde{W}_{t,L}}$ and $\beta_{\tilde{C}_{t,L}}$.

To satisfy the three constraints, we superimpose three pictures corresponding to the three constraints together as shown in Figure 7. For the continuity constraint, the vectorial sums of $W^{i-1}_{t,L}$ and $\Delta W^{i}_{t,L}$ and $C^{i-1}_{t,L}$ and $\Delta C^{i}_{t,L}$ must lie within the circles representing the uncertainties of $\tilde{W}_{t,L}$ and $\tilde{C}_{t,L}$, respectively. For the equation (5), we must find an adjustment point where $\Delta E^{i}_{t,L}$ can be removed by the vectorial sum of $k\Delta W^{i}_{t,L}$ and $\Delta C^{i}_{t,L}$. Please note that we have multiplied both $\tilde{W}_{t,L}$ and $W^{i-1}_{t,L}$ by the wind effect constant k and negated $\tilde{C}_{t,L}$, $C^{i-1}_{t,L}$, and $\Delta C^{i}_{t,L}$ so that the adjustment point A must lie within the intersected region of the two circles in order to simultaneously satisfy the three constraints. We then see that an adjustment exists if the intersected region is not empty.

After representing the uncertainties of $k\tilde{W}_{t,L}$ and $-\tilde{C}_{t,L}$ as fuzzy sets with cone membership functions, we would desire the adjustment point A to be as close as possible to both the centers of circles of the two cones. Suppose F and G are two fuzzy sets for $k\tilde{W}_{t,L}$ and $-\tilde{C}_{t,L}$, respectively. We then select the adjustment point A to be the one in the intersected region with the highest membership value, i.e.

$$\begin{aligned}\mu_F(A) &= \mu_G(A)\\ &= \sup_{u\in U}(\mu_{F\cap G}(u))\\ &= \sup_{u\in U}(\min\{\mu_F(u),\mu_G(u)\}),\end{aligned}$$

where we follow the Zadeh's interpretation of fuzzy intersection as a min function.

VI. Conclusions

In this paper, we treated the problem of oil spill tracking as a variation of control problem, where we employed a model to interpolate uncertain observational data. We presented a quadtree spatial partition approach to remove the errors between the observed and modeled oil distributions by recursively reducing volume difference and centroid difference between them. Fuzzy logic techniques were used to deal with the uncertainty of the observational data.

References

[1] A. H. Al-Rabeh, H. M. Cekirge, and N. Gunny. A stochastic simulation model of oil spill fate and transport. *Appl. Math. Modelling*, 13:322-329, June 1989.

[2] D. Dubois and H. Prade. *Fuzzy Sets and Systems: Theory and Applications*. Academic Press, New York, 1980.

[3] J. C. Huang and F. C. Monastero. Review of the state-of-the-art of oil spill simulation models. *American Petroleum Institute*, June 1982.

[4] Chuen Chien Lee. Fuzzy logic in control systems: Fuzzy logic controller - part I. *IEEE Trans. on Systems, Man, Cybernetics*, SMC-20(2):404-418, March/April 1990.

[5] Chuen Chien Lee. Fuzzy logic in control systems: Fuzzy logic controller - part II. *IEEE Trans. on Systems, Man, Cybernetics*, SMC-20(2):419-435, March/April 1990.

[6] Harilaos N. Psaraftis, Geverghese G. Tharakan, and Avishai Ceder. Optimal response to oil spills: The strategic decision case. *Operation Research*, 34(2):203-217, March-April 1986.

[7] Harilaos M. Psaraftis and Babis O. Ziogas. A tactical decision algorithm for the optimal dispatching of oil spill cleanup equipment. *MANAGEMENT SCIENCE*, 31(12):1475-1491, December 1985.

[8] Nanda K. Thalasila. Interactive coastal oil spill transport model. Master's thesis, Texas A&M University, Department of Civil Engineering, May 1992.

[9] S. Venkatesh. The oil spill behaviour model of the Canadian Atmospheric Environment Service. part I: Theory and model evaluation. *ATMOSPHERE-OCEAN*, 26(1):93-108, 1988.

[10] S. Venkatesh. Model simulations of the drift and spread of the Exxon Valdez oil spill. *ATMOSPHERE-OCEAN*, 28(1):90-105, 1990.

[11] Haojin Wang, Jan Wolter, and Jungfu Tsao. An intelligent prediction system for oil slick movement. In *Proceedings of The Third International Conference on Industrial Fuzzy Control and Intelligent Systems*, December 1993.

[12] Glen N. Williams, Roy Hann, and Wesley P. James. Predicting the fate of oil in the marine environment. In *Proceedings of Joint Conf. on Prevention and Control of Oil Spills*, pages 567-571, March 1975.

[13] Ronald R. Yager. Connectives and quantifiers in fuzzy sets. *Fuzzy Sets and Systems*, 40:39-75, 1991.

[14] L. A. Zadeh. Fuzzy sets. *Information and Control*, 8:338-353, 1965.

Chapter 6: Image Processing

CHAPTER 6
Image Processing & Vision

Neural networks continue to be used extensively in the areas of image processing and vision. The primary use of neural networks is in the area of object classification and filtering. The application of neural networks to image compression continues to be an area that receives attention, but there have not been any major breakthroughs. A relatively new area where neural networks have been used in image processing is feature extraction. For all of these applications, the inherently parallel operation of neural networks makes them an attractive computational approach to many problems.

Vision is similar to image processing in that the operations performed are manipulation and information extraction, but vision systems are focusing on mimicking biological image processing, attempting to simulate operations such as depth perception, color perception, and temporal processing. Analog circuits continue to be an area of the great promise for the implementation of neural vision processing algorithms because they offer continuous processing and they interface more easily to image sensors than their digital counterparts.

There are several areas where the application of neural networks appears to be growing, including: remote sensing, computer-aided design, and virtual reality. I would expect to see neural networks become more prominent in each of these areas.

The papers in this chapter are organized into five areas as follows:

- **Classification.** Automatically classifying images is of great value to applications ranging from defense to manufacturing. The four papers are examples of this diversity. **Paper 6.1** describes the use of a modified MLP is used to identify user-drawn CAD symbols. **Paper 6.2** describes a hierarchical approach to identifying large images from a collection of smaller images using several MLPs. The approach is applied to the wake detection problem using Synthetic Aperture Radar data. **Paper 6.3** combines texture features, LVQ, and Cascade Correlation neural networks to human face identification. **Paper 6.4** presents the application of MLPs to fingerprint classification. The resulting MLPs are analyzed using principal component analysis. An expert system is used in conjunction with the neural network to make final classification decisions.

- **Compression.** With the explosion of multimedia products and applications, image compression has become increasingly more important to the telephone and broadcast communities. Neural networks offer some opportunities in this area. **Paper 6.5** demonstrates image compression using the LVQ neural network and its counterpropagation extension. **Paper 6.6** combines the LVQ and the MLP in serial to perform image compression.

- **Filtering.** Neural networks can be viewed as powerful nonlinear adaptive filters. Within this framework, there are many image processing operations that can be implemented by a neural network, resulting in a parallel real-time filtering solution. **Paper 6.7** uses an MLP as an image filter for color error reduction in television receivers. **Paper 6.8** employs a MLP as an image filter for edge detection. The performance of the MLP filter is compared with Canny's method to illustrate its effectiveness. **Paper 6.9** presents a two-stage image segmentation system that consists of multiple Daugman Projection neural networks followed by an LVQ network. **Paper 6.10** explores the utility of discrete time cellular neural networks for thinning images.

- **Feature Extraction. Paper 6.11** examines the use of neural networks as feature extractors. The neural networks explored includes ART, LVQ, and MLP. Neural network feature extractors are evaluated using images of sign language hand positions.

- **Vision.** One area where the biological ignorance quotient is lower is the neural network vision applications. Because of the tremendous pay-off in robotics applications, the vision systems of insects and mammals has been studied with fervor. As a testimony to this fact, a volume of edited papers was recently published in this area. Many of the papers found in this chapter represent attempts at modeling the visual processing of various life-forms. **Paper 6.12** presents a hierarchical clustering neural system composed of Hopfield-Tank neural circuits designed to mimic the early visual processing system. **Paper 6.13** describes a neural processing system that models the eye movement used to fixate on a moving object in a scene. **Paper 6.14** investigates the neural pooling of signals generated by the photoreceptors. This approach is considered to be a possible strategy for improving vision at low light levels.

Proc. of the 1993 IEEE
Int.'l Conf. on Tools with AI,
Boston, Massachusetts, Nov. 1993

Management of Graphical Symbols in a CAD Environment: A Neural Network Approach

DerShung Yang[1], Julie L. Webster[2]
Larry A. Rendell[1], James H. Garrett, Jr.[3], Doris S. Shaw[2]

[1]Dept. of Computer Science, University of Illinois at Urbana-Champaign
[2]Div. of Infrastructure Facilities, U.S. Army Construction Eng. Res. Lab.
[3]Dept. of Civil Engineering, Carnegie Mellon University

Abstract

A new neural network called AUGURS is designed to assist a user of a Computer-Aided Design package in utilizing standard graphical symbols. AUGURS is similar to the Zipcode Net by Le Cun et al. in its encoding of transformation knowledge into its network structure, but is much more compact and efficient. Our experiments compare AUGURS with two versions of the Zipcode Net and a traditional layered feed-forward network with an unconstrained structure. The experimental results show that AUGURS can recognize a user-drawn symbol with better accuracy and "plausibility" than the other networks with the least amount of recognition time when the number of training examples is limited.

1 Introduction

Real-world applications usually provide specific requirements and conditions that inspire new technologies and raise new challenges and problems. This research stems from an application in building design using Computer-Aided Design (CAD) systems. Before going into technical detail, this section first describes the application domain.

Advantages of industry standardization

A common architectural symbol is that of a door: commonly a line segment signifying the door itself, and a connected arc signifying its swinging path. This symbol frequently appears in architectural floor plans with modifications in orientation and size. It is often desirable to copy the symbol and place several instances of it in a drawing. The line and arc that compose the door symbol are considered as a unit. It is advantageous to group such primitive drawing entities into a single semantically coherent unit so that the group of entities is manipulated as a whole in a CAD system. Graphical symbols are examples of this grouping idea. Other typical examples of graphical symbols for building design are windows, plumbing fixtures, pieces of furniture, etc., as shown in Figure 1. These symbols can be created in numerous ways, resulting in problems in automated communication. Standardization is a first step in solving this problem.

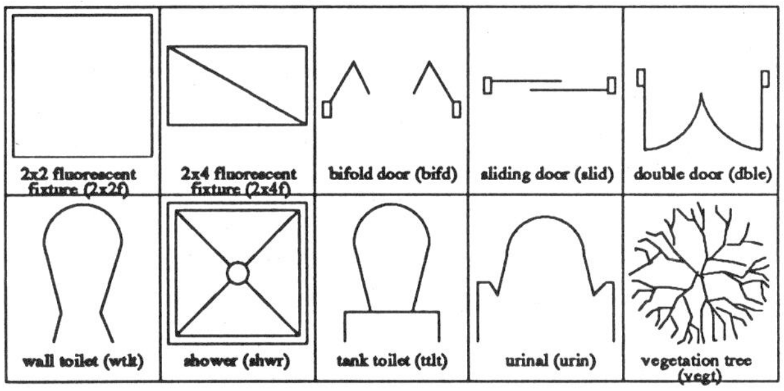

Figure 1: Some example graphical symbols.

The standardization of CAD in the building industry will improve the architectural design process through consistency, precision, simplification, and easier communication. Architects, consultants, contractors, vendors, etc., will all speak the same graphical language. Currently, widespread standardization of CAD in building design is limited to architectural materials/assemblies vendors and centralized organizations such as the U. S. Army Corps of Engineers (USACE). Vendors often supply architecture firms with floppy disks containing graphical symbols and details of their products.

This sounds as if it makes an architect's job easy until one considers the time needed to search numerous vendor libraries and reference binders (printouts of graphical symbols/details on floppy disks) to find the appropriate architectural detail. To add to the symbol and detail management issue, an architect will commonly customize a vendor's detail to fit its particular occurrence in the design. This may result in a new, more personalized standard detail. In addition, a firm may create original standard details and subsequent reference binders. For instance, USACE spends significant effort compiling standard graphical symbols for their organization's use [8]. Over time, collections of standard CAD symbols and details can become large. Navigating such cumbersome bodies of information is time-consuming and costly.

Machine-initiated search

Some tools such as a browser have been developed to assist a CAD user in searching for a desired symbol. However, because of the vast number of graphical symbols in libraries, a CAD user may be unaware of many graphical symbols and fail to initiate a search in the first place. A more effective solution is to develop a usage assistant that volunteers plausible symbols while observing what the user is drawing; this solution is the approach taken for this research. Instead of asking the user to initiate a search, our program, called AUGURS (Assistant for Using GRaphical Symbols), does the search by itself. AUGURS notifies a user when it detects that a portion of her drawing resembles some stored graphical symbols, and then automatically attaches the required libraries and fetches the appropriate symbols.

In Figure 2, the user has drawn a small rectangle and three diagonal line segments outward from the rectangle. AUGURS brings up its graphical symbol window or "Cell Recognizer," within which are four symbols, in the order of `shwr`, `2x4fi`, `dble`, and `tnktlt`, that it considers most similar to what the user is drawing. The user can select the target symbol (`shwr`) and place it in the drawing file.

This searching process consists of two phases. The first phase, the *segmentation phase*, determines where the user is currently working and captures the image of that area. The second phase, the *classification phase*, then uses a neural network to determine what the user is drawing based on the captured image. The description of the segmentation phase is beyond the scope of this paper and can be found in [9]. Here we focus on the classification phase.

The remainder of this paper is organized as follows: Section 2 discusses how this problem differs from other pattern recognition problems. Section 3 details our approach to symbol recognition. Section 4 examines its effectiveness. Conclusions are in Section 5.

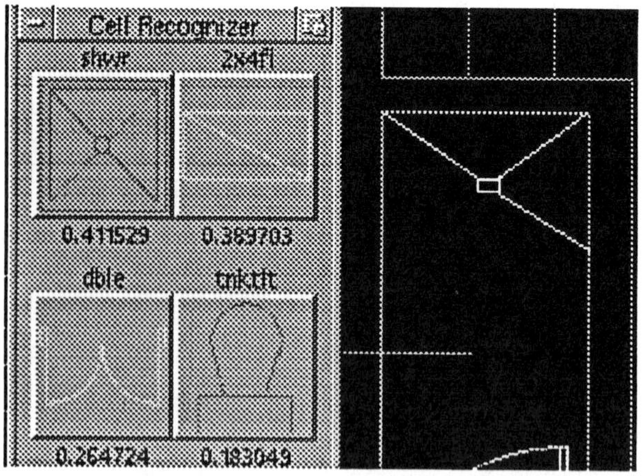

Figure 2: Machine-initiated search.

2 Research issues

Despite its similarity to traditional pattern recognition problems, the task of classifying a user-drawn image has its own distinctive characteristics. First, the network has to learn from a small training set. Most neural networks are statistical models that require a large number of training examples to achieve good results from learning. Some researchers have argued that it might be more cost-effective to spend effort on collecting more training data than on inventing new algorithms [4]. However, in the CAD domain, collecting a large training set can be difficult for several reasons. First, having a person manually create a large training set is time-consuming because of the large number of symbols (more than 1000 in [8]). Second, collecting images of symbols from existing drawings is difficult because of the complexity of typical CAD drawings. Moreover, even if a large training set can be collected, we still prefer a network that can learn from a small training set because the training time is usually proportional to training set size [6].

The second characteristic of this domain is that perfect recognition is unnecessary. AUGURS simply sorts the stored symbols by its assessment of the visual similarity between the input image and each stored symbol. The goal is to make the ordering consistent with human expectations; we could call this "plausible pattern recognition." For example, if a user draws a wall toilet, it is plausible for AUGURS to rank the tank toilet symbol before the wall toilet symbol because the two look similar, while it is implausible to rank the sliding door before the wall toilet (see Figure 1).

The third characteristic of this domain is that AUGURS has to be compact and efficient because it is embedded in a commercial CAD package. A large and slow program would compromise the original goal of accelerating the design process. This special requirement forces us to avoid recurrent networks, which may take an indefinite time to converge, and work solely with feed-forward networks.

3 Approach

The main thrust of our approach is to encode general geometric knowledge into the network structure. The purpose of adding general knowledge is three-fold. First, such knowledge can assist the network to more easily detect regularity in the training data and therefore enable the network to learn reasonably well in spite of the limited number of available training data [7]. Second, such knowledge can guide the generalization of the network by using geometric rules favored by humans and therefore make the generalization more plausible. Third, adding such knowledge can avoid redundant network structure and operations, and thus reduce the network size and improve the efficiency.

The general geometric knowledge, e.g., "a translated object preserves its shape" or "a scaled polygon maintains its included angles," built into the network structure is a form of weak knowledge that can be applied to many different domains (e.g., handwriting recognition). This type of knowledge is different from strong knowledge, e.g., how each symbol is constructed, which cannot be transferred across domains. Therefore, adding weak knowledge does not make the network over-specific to particular symbols and can be considered as a general principle for improving networks in many domains. Before describing our approach in detail, the next section first briefly describes the basic learning procedure.

3.1 The Backpropagation algorithm

The Backpropagation algorithm [5] is a gradient-descent learning procedure suitable for layered feed-forward networks. Because of its popularity, we only list the formulae necessary for replicating our work. Many improvements to the basic Backpropagation algorithm have been proposed. Since our research focuses on the network structure, not on the learning algorithm, we employed the basic Backpropagation algorithm and expected that most of the improvements can be easily applied to AUGURS. The Backpropagation algorithm is composed of a forward phase and a backward phase. Let a_i^l and θ_i^l denote the activation and the bias of node i at layer l, respectively, and let $w_{i,j}^l$ denote the weight of the link from node j at layer $l-1$ to node i at layer l. In the forward phase, the network selects a training example and assigns the input vector to the input nodes. Then it calculates the activation of each node from layer 2 to layer L by:

$$a_i^l = g(\sum_j w_{i,j}^l a_j^{l-1} + \theta_i^l) \tag{1}$$

where

$$g(h) = \frac{1}{1+e^{-h}} \tag{2}$$

In the backward phase, the network modifies the weight of each link from layer L back to layer 1 by:

$$\Delta w_{i,j}^l = \eta \delta_i^l a_j^{l-1} + \rho \Delta w_{i,j}^l \tag{3}$$

where η is the learning rate, ρ is the momentum, and δ_i^l is defined as:

$$\delta_i^l = \begin{cases} (t_i - a_i^L) \cdot a_i^L(1-a_i^L) & \text{if } l = L \\ \sum_k \delta_k^{l+1} w_{k,i}^{l+1} \cdot a_i^l(1-a_i^l) & \text{if } 1 < l < L \end{cases} \tag{4}$$

where t_i is the target activation for output node i. When the network finishes the backward phase, it selects another training example and re-starts the forward phase. This process continues until some stopping criterion is satisfied. Minor modification to the learning procedure is necessary because of the change of network structure and is described later.

3.2 Encoding geometric knowledge

Figure 3 illustrates the structure of our network within AUGURS, which is referred simply as AUGURS for the remainder of the paper. This structure is similar to the Zipcode Net by Le Cun *et al.* [2, 3] and the Neocognitron by Fukushima [1], but is much more compact. Since there are two versions of the Zipcode Net, we use Zipcode Net 1 and Zipcode Net 2 to refer to the earlier version [2] and the later version [3], respectively. AUGURS has five layers. The first layer is the input layer and the fifth is the output layer. The fourth layer is a traditional hidden layer as described above. The second and the third layers are the two layers that distinguish this structure from traditional layered feed-forward network structures.

Pattern maps and weight sharing

Nodes in the second layer of AUGURS are grouped into several *pattern maps* [2], each a two-dimensional array of *pattern detectors*. A pattern detector receives input only from a small region, called a *kernel* [2], in the input layer. In Figure 3, each 3 × 3 shaded area in the input layer is a kernel. Kernels can overlap and may exceed the input area, in which case the kernel assumes that input from outside the input area is

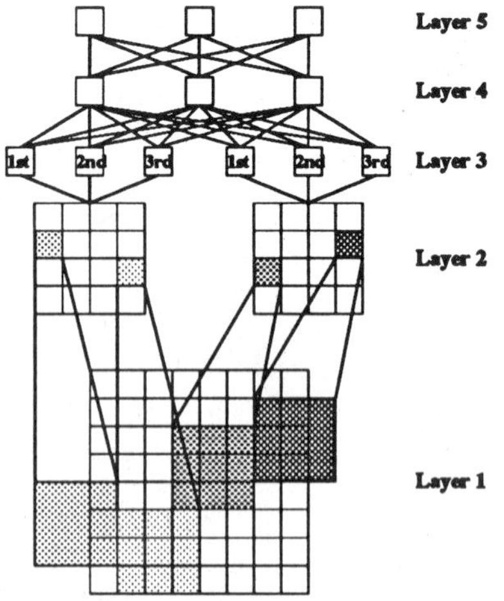

Figure 3: The structure of AUGURS.

the background value. All the pattern detectors in a pattern map share the same set of incoming weights, including the bias. This arrangement allows pattern detectors in the same pattern map to perform the same function over different kernels in the input layer, and ideally enables a pattern map to detect a pattern regardless of the location of the pattern. The concept of a pattern map and weight sharing can be found in other networks [5, 1].

Small pattern maps

Since processing a full-sized pattern map is time-consuming, Zipcode Net 1 employs *under-sampling*, i.e., two adjacent pattern detectors correspond to two kernels that are *two* pixels apart, to reduce the size of a pattern map. This under-sampling reduces the network complexity; however, it also makes a pattern map unable to detect a pattern when the pattern shifts by an odd number of pixels. Zipcode Net 2 and the Neocognitron use another mechanism to manage the network complexity. These two networks use *sub-sampling* to reduce the sizes of pattern maps in higher layers. For example, in Zipcode Net 2, each pattern map p is connected with a sub-sampled pattern map within which each node averages the activations of a 2×2 non-overlapping area in p. The size of a sub-sampled pattern map is thus a quarter of that of the associated pattern map. However, sub-sampling does not alleviate the efficiency problem because the bottleneck is the processing of first level pattern maps, whose sizes are independent of the sub-sampling scheme.

AUGURS maintains small pattern maps by limiting the region covered by each pattern map. The location of the region covered by a pattern map is determined randomly. This design is based on the hypothesis that each pattern moves only locally when the image is somewhat distorted. The "local patterns" hypothesis is especially valid when the image is normalized in size and location. In this way, AUGURS can have small pattern maps while maintaining its translation invariance as long as the pattern does not move out of the area covered by the pattern map.

Selective use of patterns

Both the Zipcode Net and the Neocognitron are built upon the concept that symbol recognition should be performed in multiple layers of pattern maps, with each layer abstracting information from one layer below. This concept may be biologically plausible, but its implementation is inefficient. We believe that a single layer of pattern maps has already extracted more than sufficient information for recognition; we need to filter out unnecessary information, not output all the information to a higher layer. Unnecessary information not only causes extra processing time, but also may confuse higher layers.

The third layer of AUGURS functions to filter out unnecessary information from the second layer. Each pattern map p is associated with m *pattern* nodes in layer 3. These m pattern nodes output the m largest activation values in p. Conceptually, the activation of a pattern detector corresponds to the importance of the pattern detected by it. In other words, the m pattern nodes associated with p represent the m most salient patterns detected in p. For example, in Figure 3, each pattern map outputs the three most important patterns detected in it to layer 3.

3.3 Modified Backpropagation algorithm

Modification to the network structure calls for modification to the Backpropagation algorithm. In the forward phase, nodes in layers 4 and 5 still use (1) to calculate their activation values; whereas the nodes in layers 2 and 3 use different formulae. Let $a^2_{p,(r,c)}$ be the activation of the node at coordinate (r, c) of pattern map p in layer 2, $a^1_{(r,c)}$ be the activation of the node at coordinate (r, c) in layer 1, $w^2_{p,(r,c)}$ be the weight at coordinate (r, c) of the weight matrix for pattern map p, and θ^2_p be the bias value of p. (Notice that the superscripts denote the layers, not the power, of the attached variables.) Then,

$$a^2_{p,(r,c)} = g(\sum_r^k \sum_c^k a^1_{(r+\alpha_p,c+\beta_p)} w^2_{p,(r,c)} + \theta^2_p) \qquad (5)$$

where k is the grid size of a kernel and (α_p, β_p) is the coordinate of the left upper corner of the input area covered by pattern map p. Let $a^3_{p,i}$ be the activation of the i-th pattern node associated with pattern map p. Then $a^3_{p,i}$ is simply the i-th largest activation in p. Also, this pattern node records from which pattern detector it receives the activation.

In the backward phase, nodes in layers 5 and 4 still modify the weights of their incoming links according to (3). Each pattern node in layer 3 simply passes the δ value accumulated at that node, calculated by (4), back to the pattern detector from which it receives the activation in the previous forward phase. Assuming the node at coordinate (a, b) of pattern map p has the maximal δ value, δ_{max_p}, in p, the weight matrix associated with p is modified by:

$$\Delta w^2_{p,(r,c)} = \eta \delta_{max_f} a^1_{(r+a,c+b)} + \rho \Delta w^2_{p,(r,c)} \quad (6)$$

4 Experiments

We designed two sets of experiments to study the effectiveness of our approach. The first experiment set was to validate the two new notions of AUGURS, namely, "selective use of patterns" and "small pattern maps." The second experiment set was to evaluate AUGURS against the other three networks: Zipcode Net 1, Zipcode Net 2, and a traditional layered feed-forward network with an unconstrained structure (fully connected nodes in adjacent layers) in terms of accuracy, efficiency, and plausibility (defined later). We did not experiment with Neocognitron because its gigantic structure is inappropriate for the CAD domain (Fukushima [1] reported a network of more than 34,000 nodes).

4.1 Experimental design

Ten common architectural symbols were chosen from the Army standards [8] and used as the *training* set (Figure 1). To collect symbols containing sufficient distortion, two users were requested to produce these symbols in a CAD system using sketch mode without use of precision aids. Ten sets of such symbols were collected and used as the *testing* set. All the symbol images were extracted from a CAD screen and converted into 24×24-pixel bitmaps, which were centered and scaled to fully occupy the input area.

Each training session stopped when all examples in the training set were recognized. A training example was considered recognized if two conditions were met. First, the target output node had the largest output activation and the activation was larger than 0.6. Second, the difference between the largest and the second largest output activations was at least 0.4. These two values were chosen empirically to avoid over-training. Each datum reported in the following tables and figures represented the average of results from 10 runs, with each run using a different random seed.

4.2 Performance measures

Three measures were used to compare the performance of different networks: predictive accuracy, recognition time, and plausibility. Since *predictive accuracy*, i.e., the number of recognized testing examples over the total number of testing examples, was a common performance measure used in the literature, we followed this tradition so that our results could be compared with other research results. *Recognition time* was measured in CPU time for recognizing 100 symbols. Although this measure was subject to program coding, we tried to equalize by programming all the networks ourselves using the same language and programming style. Fortunately, the differences of speed between different networks were considerable.

The purpose of AUGURS is not to do perfect recognition, but to produce a plausible ordering of stored symbols. Thus, we designed a new measure to account for this ordering information. This *plausibility* was designed to compare the ordering produced by a network with that produced by humans. We asked four users to assign a "similarity value" between 0 and 1 to each pair of symbols, with 1 indicating that the two symbols were indistinguishable. Then, given a target symbol, we could approximate the human-produced ordering by sorting all stored symbols based on the similarity values between stored symbols and the target symbol. In Table 1, each entry is the mean of the four users' similarity values. (See Figure 1 for meaning of abbreviations.) For example, most users considered wall toilet to be most similar to tank toilet (0.90), followed by urinal (0.68).

	2x2f	2x4f	bifd	slid	dble	wtlt	shwr	ttlt	urin	vegt
2x2f	1	.68	0	.11	.11	.11	.90	.11	.11	0
2x4f		1	.11	.23	.23	0	.68	.11	.11	.11
bifd			1	.57	.34	0	.11	0	.23	0
slid				1	.34	0	.11	0	.23	0
dble					1	.23	.49	.11	.11	0
wtlt						1	0	.90	.68	.23
shwr							1	0	.11	.23
ttlt								1	.68	0
urin									1	0
vegt										1

Table 1: Similarity values between symbols.

Given an output sequence (an ordering) $\mathcal{S}$ sorted by decreasing activation values and a target symbol $\mathcal{T}$, we defined the plausibility of $\mathcal{S}$ as the weighted average of the similarity values between the target symbol and the symbols in $\mathcal{S}$. The weight for each symbol in $\mathcal{S}$ was determined by the activation value of its corresponding output node. Let $S(r)$ be the symbol at rank r in $\mathcal{S}$, $V(s_i)$ be the activation value of the output node representing symbol s_i, and $Sim(s_1, s_2)$ be the similarity value between symbols s_1 and s_2. Then the plausibility measure, $\mathcal{P}(\tau)$, was defined as:

$$\mathcal{P}(\tau) = \sum_{i=1}^{\tau} Sim(S(i), \mathcal{T}) \frac{\lceil V(S(i) \cdot 10.0 \rceil}{\sum_{j=1}^{\tau} \lceil V(S(j)) \cdot 10.0 \rceil} \quad (7)$$

where τ was the number of symbols that AUGURS was allowed to suggest to the user (in Figure 2, $\tau = 4$). For example, suppose the activation values of the first four symbols in the sequence were 0.67, 0.39, 0.35, 0.23, and the similarity values between these symbols and the target symbol were 0.80, 0.28, 1.00, 0.40, respectively. Then the plausibility of this sequence was:

$$\mathcal{P}(4) = 0.80 \cdot \frac{7}{18} + 0.28 \cdot \frac{4}{18} + 1.00 \cdot \frac{4}{18} + 0.40 \cdot \frac{3}{18} \simeq 0.66$$

For a "perfect" sequence, i.e., the desired symbol is ranked as the first and the activation for the desired symbol is much larger than that of other symbols, the plausibility value should be 1.00. The "worst" sequence, i.e., a symbol that is very different from the desired symbol is ranked as the first and has a very large activation, should have a plausibility 0.00. In practice, neither the perfect nor the worst sequence is likely to happen because the distortion in input image usually makes a network unable to sharply distinguish between two different symbols. When the plausibility of an output sequence is calculated, most symbols may thus have equal weights. A more realistic way to assess the range of the plausibility measure is to assume that all the symbols are equally weighted in (7). Based on Table 1 and assuming $\tau = 4$, a network that always ranks the four symbols *most* similar to the target symbol the top four symbols in its output sequences should have a plausibility 0.61 (the average of the four largest similarity values of all symbols). Similarly, a network that always ranks the four symbols *least* similar to the target symbol the top four symbols in its output sequences should have a plausibility 0.15 (the average of the four smallest similarity values of all symbols). In general, the plausibility of any output sequence normally falls in this range.

4.3 Experiment set 1

Experiment Set 1 was designed to validate the two new characteristics of AUGURS. First, we tried to verify our selective use of patterns by experimenting on how many patterns should be output from a pattern map. Second, we tried to justify our use of small pattern maps by studying the effect of the pattern map size on the performance of AUGURS.

pattern maps	patterns per pattern map				
	8	t-score	16	t-score	32
8	.53	-0.82	.54	0.31	.54
t-score	-2.79 (***)		-1.98 (*)		-1.78 (**)
16	.56	-0.24	.56	0.29	.56
t-score	-1.46 (*)		-0.71		-1.77 (**)
32	.57	0.45	.57	-0.63	.57

Table 2: Plausibility varying number of patterns and pattern maps (***: significant at 99%, **: significant at 95%, *: significant at 90%).

Selective use of patterns

Table 2 shows the plausibility of AUGURS varying the numbers of pattern maps and patterns per pattern map (the number of pattern nodes associated with each pattern map). The t-scores were the results of t-tests which determined whether the difference between entries in adjacent columns or rows were statistically significant. The *significance level* of a t-test roughly indicates the confidence in the test result. Four parameters needed to be determined for AUGURS: the kernel size, the pattern map size, the number of pattern maps, and the number of patterns output from a pattern map. We first set the kernel size and the pattern map size as 7 and 6, respectively, to determine the values of the other two parameters. We then performed another experiment to validate our choices of the kernel size and the pattern map size.

In Table 2, most t-scores between rows were negative with a significance level at least 90%, meaning that adding more pattern maps usually improved plausibility significantly; whereas most of the t-scores between columns were insignificant, indicating that allowing a pattern map to output more patterns was unnecessary. In other words, the plausibility improvement caused by using more pattern maps was greater than that produced by using more patterns per pattern map, supporting the selective use of patterns. The results suggested that AUGURS could achieve reasonably good plausibility if each pattern map output only the top 3% patterns to layer 3.

Small pattern maps

Conceptually, the kernel size is the size of a pattern and the pattern map size is how far a pattern can move and still be detected by that pattern map. To validate the use of small pattern maps, Table 3 shows the plausibility of AUGURS varying the kernel size and the pattern map size. The table is organized similarly to Table 2. As suggested in the previous

Pattern map grid size	Kernel grid size				
	4	*t*-score	7	*t*-score	10
3	.56	2.28 (**)	.55	-0.40	.55
t-score	0.46		-2.72 (***)		-1.06
6	.56	-1.08	.57	0.85	.56
t-score	-0.35		-0.27		-0.68
9	.56	-1.11	.58	0.24	.57

Table 3: Plausibility varying kernel and pattern map sizes (***: significant at 99%, **: significant at 95%, *: significant at 90%).

experiment, we chose to have 35 pattern maps, each having 8 patterns output to layer 3.

By comparing the *t*-scores between rows and columns, we found that when both the kernel size and the pattern map size were large enough, the *t*-scores became insignificant, indicating that patterns important for recognition were small and would not move too far when the input image was distorted. Large kernels or pattern maps wasted the computational resource. This observation validates the "local patterns" hypothesis, which allows AUGURS to have an economic structure while maintaining its plausibility.

4.4 Experiment set 2

Experiment Set 2 was designed to compare the performance of these four networks in terms of accuracy, plausibility, and efficiency. For AUGURS, the number of patterns allowed for each pattern map, the pattern map size, and the kernel size were 8, 6, and 7, respectively. These values were determined according to the results in the first experiment set. The kernel sizes for Zipcode Nets 1 and 2 were 7 and 5, respectively. The number of first level pattern maps in Zipcode Net 2 was 4, as suggested in [3].

Predictive accuracy versus recognition time

In Figure 4, we plotted the predictive accuracy, i.e., the accuracy on testing set, of each network along the axis of recognition time to study which network can perform most accurately with the least amount of time. For each network, the curve in Figure 4 was produced by varying one parameter for the network structure. For the unconstrained network, we varied the number of hidden nodes to be 16, 32, 64, and 128. For Zipcode Net 1, we varied the number of pattern maps to be 2, 4, and 8. For Zipcode Net 2, we varied the number of the second level pattern maps to be 4, 8, and 16. For AUGURS, we varied the number of pattern maps to be 8, 16, 32, and 64.

Among the four networks, AUGURS achieved best predictive accuracy (77.50%) with the least amount of recognition time (14.9 seconds per 100 symbols).

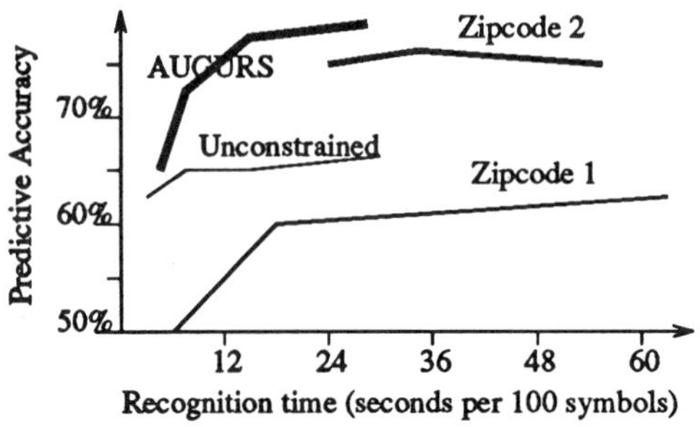

Figure 4: Comparison of predictive accuracy.

Zipcode Net 2 could achieve similar level of predictive accuracy (76.00%); but required a longer recognition time (34.5 seconds). The other two networks could not compete with AUGURS and Zipcode Net 2 in terms of predictive accuracy. Zipcode Net 2 was slow because of its two levels of large pattern maps. The grid size of a first level pattern map in Zipcode Net 2 was 28, while that of a pattern map in AUGURS was only 6. The time used to process one first layer pattern map in Zipcode Net 2 could be used to process 22 ($28^2/6^2$) pattern maps in AUGURS. AUGURS avoided the bottleneck of computing large pattern maps by employing the concept of "local patterns."

Notice that these accuracy values were all less than 80%, while similar research has reported results as good as over 90% [2]. The reason for this low accuracy was because of the size of the training set. In this research, each network was trained on the standard symbols only, i.e., one training example for each symbol, as opposed to hundreds of training examples for each symbol used in other research. With a limited number of training examples, our results indicated a strong correlation between the network structure and its accuracy. For domains where the supply of training examples could be a problem, an appropriate network structure is essential to the success of the network.

Another way to interpret Figure 4 is to consider the time axis as the capacity axis (the recognition time is proportional to the network size, which is proportional to the network capacity, i.e., how many symbols a network can accommodate). AUGURS demonstrated an ideal learning curve with two phases. In the first phase, AUGURS rapidly improved its accuracy when slightly more capacity was allowed, indicating the network could learn the symbols (with lower predictive accuracy) in spite of its insufficient capacity. In the second phase, AUGURS improved its predictive accuracy at a slower rate when even more capacity was given, meaning that extra network capacity was unnecessary since AUGURS had approached its maximal accuracy. The curves of the other three networks showed their inability to learn in situations where the networks had insufficient capacity (we tried some smaller structures and found the networks could not learn the symbols at all, i.e., failed to converge). In this regard, AUGURS was more robust in difficult learning situations.

Plausibility versus recognition time

Figure 5 was constructed as Figure 4 except the measure was plausibility. The basic patterns of these two figures are alike: AUGURS performed best with the least amount of recognition time, Zipcode Net 2 performed reasonably well but was slow, and the other two networks performed the worst. However, we found some interesting patterns not appearing in Figure 4. For example, we could observe a significant improvement of plausibility for the last data point in the curve of the unconstrained network, although the corresponding accuracy increased only by less than 1%. A similar case could also be observed for Zipcode Net 2. These patterns suggested that the measure of plausibility indeed revealed extra information about ordering and could not be substituted by the simple measure of predictive accuracy.

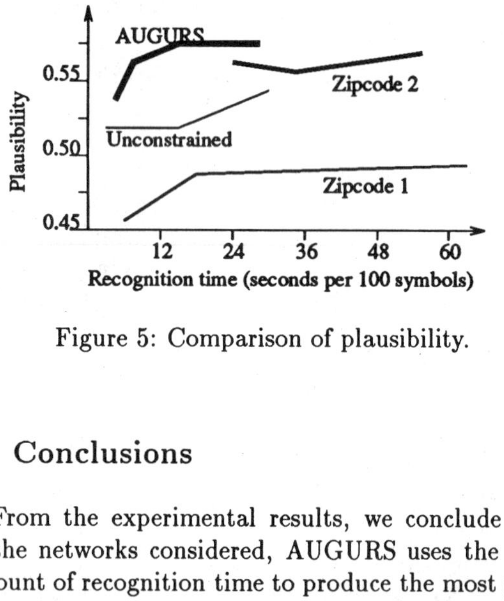

Figure 5: Comparison of plausibility.

5 Conclusions

From the experimental results, we conclude that of the networks considered, AUGURS uses the least amount of recognition time to produce the most plausible results. The superiority of AUGURS comes from the two new characteristics of the network structure: small pattern maps and selective use of patterns. These two characteristics remove redundant network structure and operations, and thus significantly accelerate the recognition process without sacrificing its recognition capability. Because of its compact structure and efficiency, AUGURS can be embedded in any systems that require an intelligent graphical input interface, such as pen-based systems.

Our continuing research focuses on the scalability of this approach. Since there are more than a thousand symbols used in Army standards, how the network scales up is a major concern. Our preliminary results indicate that AUGURS scales up better than Zipcode Net 2. We are conducting more experiments to confirm this observation.

It has taken two decades for CAD to be useful to the architecture profession. The goals of automated analyses on CAD drawings and effective communication between participants have never been fulfilled. This is partly because of the lack of CAD standardization. AUGURS monitors a CAD user's drawing process and unintrusively volunteers standard graphical symbols most resembling her drawing, and thus facilitates the standardization of CAD graphical language.

References

[1] K. Fukushima. Neocognitron: a hierarchical neural network capable of visual pattern recognition. *Neural Networks*, 1(2):119–130, 1988.

[2] Y. Le Cun, B. Boser, J. S. Denker, D. Henderson, R. E. Howard, W. Hubbard, and L. D. Jackel. Backpropagation applied to handwritten zip code recognition. *Neural Computation*, 1:541–551, 1989.

[3] Y. Le Cun, O. Matan, B. Boser, J. S. Denker, D. Henderson, R. E. Howard, W. Hubbard, L. D. Jackel, and H. S. Baird. Handwritten zip code recognition with multilayer networks. In *Proceedings of the Tenth International Conference on Pattern Recognition*, volume 2, pages 35–40, 1990.

[4] G. L. Martin and J. A. Pittman. Recognizing handprinted letters and digits using backpropagation learning. *Neural Computation*, 3:258–267, 1991.

[5] D. E. Rumelhart, G. E. Hinton, and R. J. Williams. Learning internal representations by error propagation. In *Parallel Distributed Processing, Vol. 1*, pages 318–362. MIT Press, Cambridge, MA, 1986.

[6] G. Tesauro. Scaling relationships in back-propagation learning: dependence on training set size. *Complex Systems*, 1(2):367–372, 1987.

[7] G. G. Towell. *Symbolic knowledge and neural networks: insertion, refinement and extraction.* PhD thesis, University of Wisconsin at Madison, 1991.

[8] United States Army Corps of Engineers. *Standards manual for U.S. Army Corps of Engineers computer-aided design and drafting (CADD) systems*, 1990.

[9] Dershung Yang, James H. Garrett, and Doris S. Shaw. Cell management using neural network approaches. In *Proceedings of the 3rd Government Neural Network Applications Workshop*, pages 19–23, Wright-Patterson AFB, Ohio, 1992.

DETECTION OF OCEAN WAKES IN SYNTHETIC APERTURE RADAR IMAGES WITH NEURAL NETWORKS

Gregg Wilensky, Narbik Manukian, Joe Neuhaus, John Kirkwood
Logicon/RDA
6053 W. Century Bl., L.A., Ca. 90045
(310) 645-1122, FAX: (310) 645-0070

Abstract: Two neural networks are combined to detect wakes in Synthetic Aperture Radar (SAR) images of the ocean: The first network detects local wake features in smaller subportions of the image, and the second network integrates the information from the first network to determine the presence or absence of a wake in the entire image. The networks train directly using the gradient descent method on either real SAR images or on synthetic images and are designed to detect wakes in images with low signal-to-noise ratios. When trained on real images, the network detector recognizes the wake in any translation and is robust with respect to rotations. With synthetic images, the network model is able to recognize wakes with all possible translations, rotations and over a wide range of opening angles. The performance of the neural network is measured as a function of the signal-to-noise ratio in synthetic images and as a function of a parameter related to the signal-to-noise ratio in real images. The network outperforms the human eye in detecting wakes in both real and synthetic images.

INTRODUCTION

Detection of low signal-to-noise synthetic aperture radar (SAR) images of wakes on the ocean surface is a difficult problem, and existing template matching techniques suffer from large computational expense and the difficulty of developing realistic templates. Neural networks have been very successful in solving pattern recognition and classification problems particularly when the rules for classification are either unknown or difficult to specify. In image recognition, neural networks have proven to be robust with respect to the degradation of the signal-to-noise ratio and distortions of the image such as translations, scaling, and rotations. In this paper we demonstrate the construction and performance of a neural network designed to detect ship wakes in low signal-to-noise SAR images of the ocean surface. We train and test the network model on both real SAR images and synthetic images generated to provide a larger statistical sampling as well as greater control over the signal-to-noise ratio.

THE IMAGES

Real SAR images and the addition of noise

The real SAR images are produced from a single digital image of a wake obtained from experiments at Loch Linnhe, Scotland. From this single image, we construct smaller 512 x 512 sections of the image such that about half the images contain the wake and the other half contain only noise. An example of a wake containing section is shown in Fig. 1a. The starting pixels of the sections are chosen randomly so that the wake images may contain the wake in any position (translation) within the image.

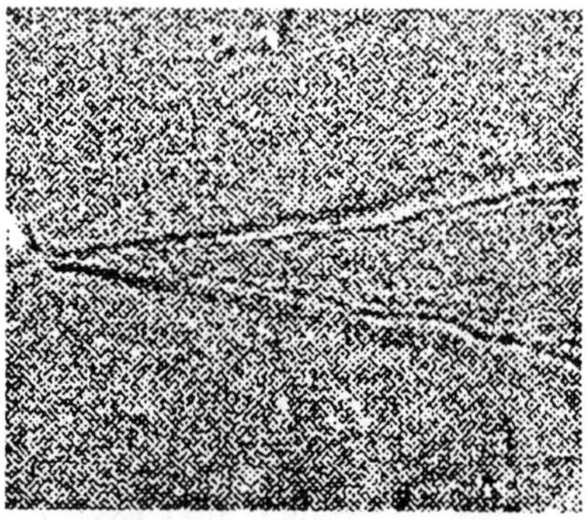

a

b

Figure 1. a) Example of a wake image without added noise obtained from original image and b) Example of a wake image with added noise at a noise level of 3.0.

The distribution of pixel intensities in one-look SAR images in the pure noise and the wake regions of the image is approximately exponential:

$$p_n(I_i) = (1/I_n)\exp(-I/I_n) : \text{noise}$$

$$p_s(I_i) = (1/I_{si})\exp(-I/I_{si}) : \text{wake (signal)} \qquad (1)$$

With such distributions, it is difficult to add noise and reduce the signal-to-noise ratio without disturbing the exponential form of either distribution. But, it is possible to add noise to the entire image and preserve the exponential distribution of the noise sections which comprise the majority of the image. Since the wake distribution is close to that of the noise, its exponential character will be altered only slightly.

To do so, let the distribution of the additional noise ΔI be

$$p(\Delta I) = (I_n / I_n')\,\delta(\Delta I) + (1 - I_n / I_n')(1 / I_n')\exp(-\Delta I / I_n'),$$

where I_n is the average pixel intensity in the noise region of the image and $\delta(\Delta I)$ is the Dirac delta function. Then the final distribution will preserve the exponential form, since at $\Delta I \neq 0$, the first term is zero and only the exponential term survives, and when $\Delta I = 0$, no noise is added. However, the additional noise is always greater than or equal to zero, and thus the overall average intensity of the noise pixels is increased so that $\langle I' \rangle$ is greater than $\langle I \rangle$. By adding to each pixel the difference between the initial and final average pixel intensities, (I_n - I_n'), the average intensity of the pixels will be preserved, i.e.

$$\langle I'' \rangle = \langle I' \rangle + (I_n - I_n') = I_n = \langle I \rangle .$$

The "noise level" is defined by the ratio

$$r = I_n' / I_n$$

and its relationship to the signal-to-noise ratio is shown in the Appendix. An example of an image containing a wake with added noise of noise level of 3.0 which is near or beyond human detection capabilities is shown in Fig. 1b.

Synthetic wakes and the signal-to-noise ratio

The synthetic images allow us to train and test the network on a statistically significant number of images with a controlled signal-to-noise ratio and all possible translations, rotations and opening angles of the wake. The synthetic images are 256x256 pixel images where each pixel intensity in a noise or wake region is generated from the exponential noise and signal distributions found in real images so that the resulting distribution of pixel intensities is similar to that of real images (1). A smaller image size of 256x256 is chosen in order to speed up the training time, and each wake image is constructed with random variations in the position, and orientation of the wake and with opening angles varying randomly from 7 to 28 degrees. With a known distribution of intensities for both signal and noise pixels, the signal-to-noise ratio can be determined in terms of the ratio of average signal to average noise pixel intensities I_{si}/I_n as derived in the Appendix. Therefore, by choosing an average noise pixel intensity I_n for all images, any desired signal-to-noise ratio can be produced by an appropriate choice of the local wake pixel intensity I_{si}.

THE MODEL

A single back-propagation neural network wake detection model with the entire SAR image as its input vector is time consuming to train and does not have built-in translational or rotational invariance. Instead, we have constructed a two-neural network wake detector as illustrated in Figure 2. Both networks are 3 layer (1 hidden layer) back-propagation networks trained with gradient descent. The first neural network (nn1) processes smaller 32 x 32 pixel "templates" of the image and detects the presence of some portion of a wake arm within the template. Its outputs are the probability that some part of the wake arm is present within the template and the most probable angle of the wake with respect to the horizontal. Since the templates can be chosen from any part of the image, nn1 is capable of translationally invariant detection of local features. Dividing the entire image into templates and operating nn1 on each template effectively transforms the entire image into a "reduced template image", where all the pixel values within a template are replaced by the outputs of the first network. The second neural network (nn2) takes the reduced template image output by nn1 as input and determines whether or not a wake is present in the entire image. It integrates the information from nn1, i.e. the presence of the wake and its orientation within each template is correlated with that of other templates.

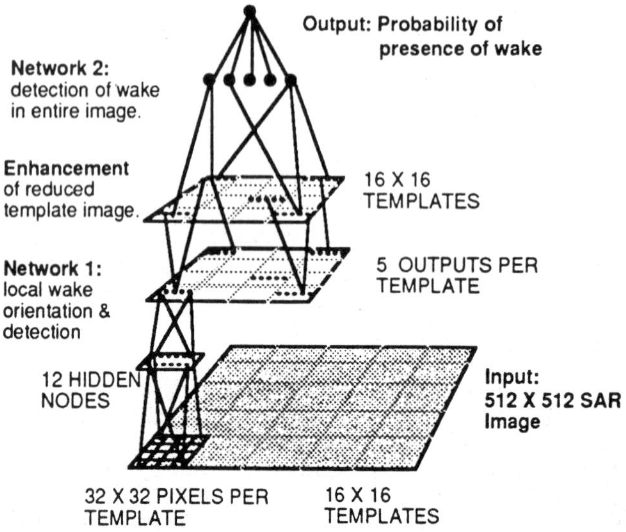

Figure 2: Two neural network model operating on a SAR image

The first neural network

As illustrated in Fig. 2, nn1 is trained to detect local wake features (a portion of a wake arm) in a template. The intensity of each pixel is fed directly as input into the first layer of nn1. Since local features of the wake consist mainly of a band or bands of pixels with intensities which are either higher or lower than the background noise, nn1 must be trained to recognize a light or dark band of pixels with an appropriate distribution of pixel intensities in many positions and orientations within the template. The weights to the intermediate layer nodes can be initially set to be sensitive to such bands at various angles and positions within the template. This initialization saves much computation time, otherwise, with a random initial setting of the weights, the training time of nn1 will be unreasonably long.

When training on real images, nn1 has one intermediate layer of 12 nodes whose weights are initially set to detect bands which are 8 pixels wide, oriented in 4 different directions, 0, $\pi/4$, $\pi/2$, and $3\pi/4$ and in three different positions for each orientation, as shown in Fig. 3. After initialization, the weights and thresholds of all the nodes are allowed to vary during training in order to reach a minimum of the error in the outputs. However, the essential band structure of the intermediate layer weights for both the synthetic and real image problems is not lost, although there are some changes which include the curving of the bands, the creation of double banded templates, and the appearance of considerable heterogeneity in the pixel intensity across the templates. The picture of some of the weights after training on synthetic images is shown in Fig. 4 and illustrates that the band character of the weight templates is maintained through the training process.

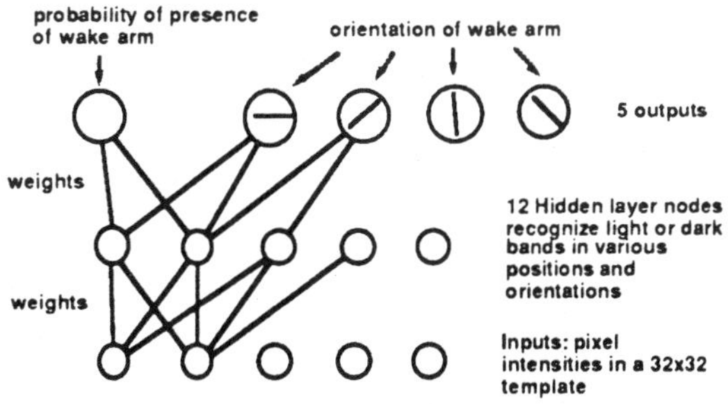

Figure 3. Feature detection neural network (nn1).

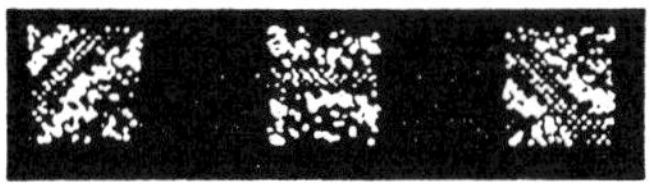

hidden node 1 2 3

Figure 4. Weights to some hidden layer nodes after training.

As illustrated in Fig. 2 and 3, nn1 processes each template as a separate input and reduces it to 5 outputs per template. The first output corresponds to the probability that the template includes the wake as determined by nn1. If the template includes any portion of the wake, the desired output of the first output node (n=1) is 1.0, and if the template includes only pure noise, it is 0.0. The next four outputs, n=2-5, are designed to give the direction of the wake in the template. For each template, the angle of the wake, with respect to the horizontal within the template, θ, is determined, where $0< \theta <\pi$. The maximum values of the 4 angular outputs are equal to 1.0 and occur when $\theta = \theta_n$, where θ_n is 0, $\pi/4$, $\pi/2$, and $3\pi/4$, for n = 2,3,4, and 5, respectively. Given θ, the desired output p_n for each angular node is

$$p_n = (1 - | \theta - \theta_n | / d\theta) \quad \text{if } | \theta - \theta_n | < d\theta ,$$

$$p_n = 0 \qquad \text{otherwise,}$$

where $d\theta$ is the angle between successive node maxima, i.e. $\pi/4$. Note that when θ is between θ_n and θ_{n+1}, the desired values p_n and p_{n+1} of the angular output nodes n and n+1 will be between 0 and 1 according to how close θ is to θ_n and θ_{n+1}. All other angular nodes will have a desired value of zero.

When training on real images, the templates are chosen at random, starting from any pixel in the image, and care is taken to avoid starting points which would result in templates extending beyond the image boundary. This random template choosing process maximizes the variety of templates, and forces nn1 to recognize a portion of the wake with varying widths in any position and orientation within the template. When training on synthetic images, a new noise or wake template is constructed at each training step, with a random position and orientation of the wake for wake-containing templates. When training on real or synthetic images, nn1 is trained with equal frequency on wake and noise templates.

The second neural network

The second neural network (nn2) is trained on the outputs from nn1 for an entire real or synthetic image. With real images, a different image is chosen for each training trial. With synthetic images, a new image is generated for each trial. Then, each real or synthetic image is fed into nn1 in the testing mode. The templates are chosen in order from the upper left to the lower right covering the entire section with no gaps, and they are fed into nn1 one at a time. The combined output of nn1 for all the templates is then fed into nn2. There is just one output for nn2 and its desired value is 1 if the image includes a wake, and it is 0 if it only consists of noise.

Image enhancement techniques

Image enhancement methods applied to the original image or to the "reduced template" image can improve the performance of the neural network and provide a clearer picture of the wake for human observers. An iterative template enhancement technique can be used to improve images of wake arms in the reduced template image. As shown in Figure 2, the reduced template image produced by nn1 can be enhanced through an iterative scheme which updates each template according to the state of its neighboring templates in the following manner: Let p be he probability that template i,j contains part of the wake as predicted by nn1. Of the eight nearest neighboring templates of i,j, examine only the two neighbors which are closest to the y direction with respect to i,j. Let p_+ and p_- be the probabilities of the presence of a wake in these two neighboring templates. Then, enhance the probability of the presence of a wake in i,j to p', where

$$p' = p + p\,(1-p)\,(\,|p_+ - p| + |p_- - p|\,)/2\,,$$

The second term on the right is the enhancement of p, and is designed to have stable points at p=0, p=1, and $p_+ = p_- = p$. Thus, successive enhancements of the probability will tend to converge to either extreme, 0 or 1, or when all three neighbors have equal probabilities.

RESULTS

Performance on real images with added noise

For each iteration in the training of nn1, a new template is chosen randomly from a real image with a noise level r=2.0. Then, nn2 is trained and tested on wake and noise sections of the real image with variable noise levels, r=1.5, 2.0, 2.5, 3.0, 3.5, and 4.0. In a more thorough study nn1 can be trained on a range of noise levels.

The fraction of wake and noise images missed as a function of the noise level r is shown in Fig. 5. The neural network model outperforms the average performance of 5 persons at every noise level. Note that the neural network detector did not miss any wake or noise images when tested at or below a noise level of 1.5. At a noise level of 3.0 (example in Fig. 1b), the neural network correctly identifies between 80% and 85% of the wake and noise images, and i performs well below this level with 75% correct at a noise level of 3.5, and between 60% and 70% correct at a noise level of 4.0 as shown in Fig. 5.

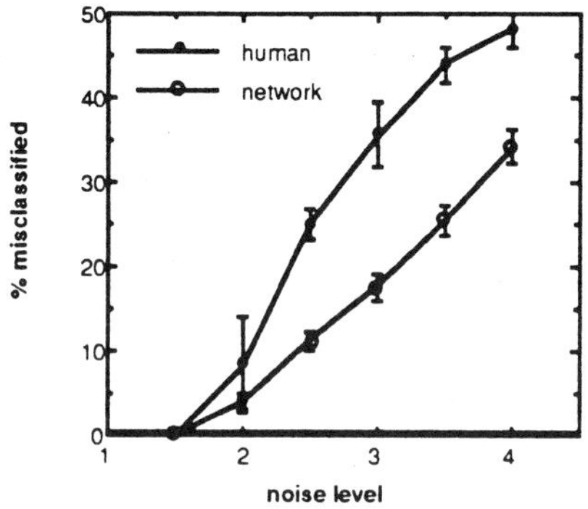

Figure 5: Detection capability of the neural network model vs. the human eye as a function of the noise level on real SAR images.

The single output of nn2 corresponds to the probability that the image section being tested contains a wake. However, we are free to choose the cutoff probability p_c according to our emphasis, and trade between the fraction of the noise and wake sections misclassified. The misclassification of wake and noise sections as a function of p_c at a noise level of 3.0 is shown in Fig. 6, where the tradeoff between false alarms and missed wakes is evident as p_c is varied from 0 to 1.

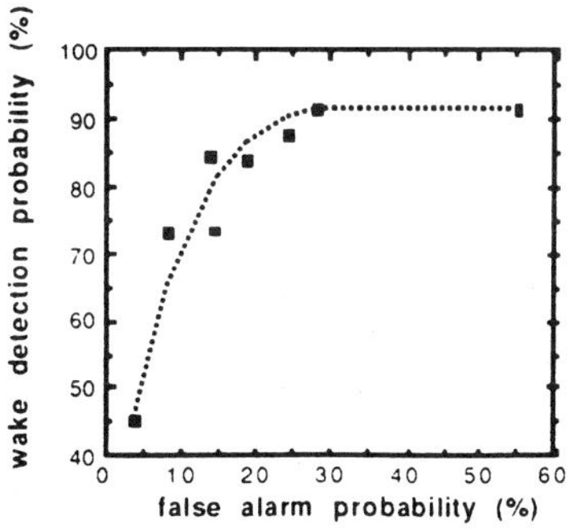

Figure 6: Performance of the network as a function of the cutoff p_c on real images at a noise level of 3.0.

Performance on synthetic images

With synthetic images, a new 256x256 wake or noise image is constructed for each iteration of the training process. Since the synthetic images contain wakes in any position and orientation and a range of opening angles, a neural network trained on these images is capable of translationally and rotationally invariant wake detection and must be robust with respect to opening angles of the wake. nn1 is trained on images at one signal-to-noise ratio (s/n = 20 dB), but nn2 is trained separately on a range of signal-to-noise ratios, namely s/n = 15, 20, 25, and 30 dB.

Its performance is compared to the average performance of 5 persons on the same images and is shown in Fig. 7. The neural network outperforms humans at the lower signal-to-noise ratios, 15 and 20 dB, but not at the higher signal-to-noise ratios, 25 and 30 dB. This results from training nn1 only on one signal-to-noise ratio, and it can be improved by training nn1 separately at each signal-to-noise level. However, in this study, the emphasis was on demonstrating the network's detection capability at signal-to-noise ratios below that of human detection capabilities.

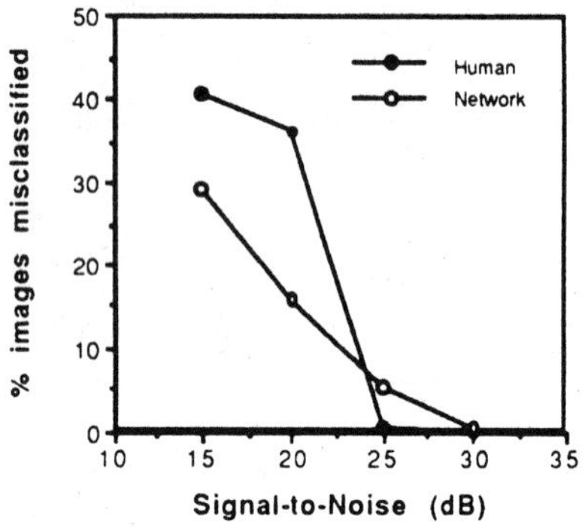

Figure 7: Detection capability of the neural network model and the human eye on synthetic images as a function of signal-to-noise ratio.

CONCLUSIONS

A neural network model for automated detection of wakes on the ocean surface in SAR images has been developed. It can detect wakes in both real and synthetic images which are beyond the detection capabilities of human vision. It has also proven to be insensitive to rotations and translations of the wake and robust with respect to a range of opening angles of the wake. The performance of the network has been measured as a function of the signal-to-noise ratio in synthetic images and as a function of the noise level which is related to the signal-to-noise ratio in real images. The tradeoff between false negatives and false positives has been measured as a function of the threshold which can be set to any desired value.

positives has been measured as a function of the threshold which can be set to any desired value.

Appendix: The Signal-to-Noise Ratio in an Image with Exponential Distribution of Pixel Intensities

The pixel intensities in noisy SAR images are found to follow an exponential distribution. In a "one-look" image, the probability that a particular pixel i will have an intensity I_i is

$$p_s(I_i) = \frac{1}{I_{si}} e^{-I_i/I_{si}} \quad , \qquad p_n(I_i) = \frac{1}{I_n} e^{-I_i/I_n}$$

for images which contain a signal or only noise, respectively. I_{si} is the local average intensity in the neighborhood of the ith site in an image-containing portion, and I_n is the average pixel intensity over the noise only part of an image. For a "four-look" image,

$$p_n(I_i) = \frac{4^4 I_i^3}{3!\, I_n^4} e^{-I_i/I_n} \quad , \quad p_s(I_i) = \frac{4^4 I_i^3}{3!\, I_{si}^4} e^{-I_i/I_{si}} .$$

All the above probabilities are normalized so that their integral over I_i from 0 to ∞ is 1. The probability that a particular set of intensities $\{I_i\}$ will occur is the product of the single site probabilities over the entire image:

$$p_n\{I_i\} = \Pi_i p_n(I_i) \qquad p_s\{I_i\} = \Pi_i p_s(I_i).$$

Since the SAR image used in this paper is a four-look image, we shall evaluate the signal-to noise ratio for a four-look image. The average intensities over an ensemble of noise and signal images are I_n and I_{si} which can be verified by integrating Ii over the distributions. The average of I_iI_j over an ensemble of noise images is

$$\langle I_i I_j \rangle_n = \int_0^\infty \Pi_k dI_k I_i I_j p_n\{I_k\}.$$

For i≠j, $$\langle I_i I_j \rangle_n = \int_0^\infty dI_i I_i p_n(I_i) \int_0^\infty dI_j I_j p_n(I_j) = I_n^2 .$$

For i=j, $$\langle I_i I_j \rangle_n = \int_0^\infty dI_i I_i^2 p_n(I_i) = \frac{5}{4} I_n^2 .$$

The standard deviation of the pixel intensities in pure noise images is

$$\langle I_i I_j \rangle_n = \langle I_i \rangle_n \langle I_j \rangle_n = \frac{1}{4} I_n^2 \delta_{ij} .$$

The signal-to-noise ratio is defined in terms of χ, the log of the ratio of the signal to noise probability distributions:

$$\chi = \log \frac{p_s\{I_i\}}{p_n\{I_i\}} = 4 \sum_i \left[\left(\frac{1}{I_n} - \frac{1}{I_{si}} \right) I_i - \log \frac{I_{si}}{I_n} \right] .$$

The ensemble average of χ over the noise images and the signal images is

$$\langle \chi \rangle_{n,s} = 4 \sum_i \left[\left(\frac{1}{I_n} - \frac{1}{I_{si}} \right) \langle I_i \rangle_{n,s} - \log \frac{I_{si}}{I_n} \right]$$

and the standard deviation of χ over the noise images is

$$\sigma_n^2 = \langle \chi^2 \rangle_n - \langle \chi \rangle_n^2 = 16 \sum_{i,j} \left[\left(\frac{1}{I_n} - \frac{1}{I_{si}} \right) \left(\frac{1}{I_n} - \frac{1}{I_{sj}} \right) \langle I_i I_j \rangle_n - \langle I_i \rangle_n \langle I_j \rangle_n \right]$$

$$= 4 \sum_{i,j} \left(\frac{1}{I_n} - \frac{1}{I_{si}} \right)^2 I_n^2 .$$

The signal-to-noise ratio s/n is defined as

$$s/n = \frac{\langle \chi \rangle_s - \langle \chi \rangle_n}{\sigma_n} = \frac{2 \sum_i \left(\frac{I_{si}}{I_n} + \frac{I_n}{I_{si}} - 2 \right)}{\left(\sum_i \left(\frac{1}{I_n} - \frac{1}{I_{si}} \right)^2 I_n^2 \right)^{1/2}} .$$

which is identical except for the factor of 2 to the expression of s/n for one-look images.

This research was supported by Logicon RDA internal research and development funding (9001-0004), and the extensions to compare with human visual capabilities were sponsored by DARPA/ONR contract N00014-89C-0257. This paper also appears in Government Microcircuit Applications Digest of Papers, vol. 18, Nov. 1992.

Identification of Human Faces through Texture-Based Feature Recognition and Neural Network Technology

Marijke F. Augusteijn and Tammy L. Skufca
Department of Computer Science
University of Colorado at Colorado Springs
P.O. Box 7150, Colorado Springs, CO 80933

Abstract - A method is presented to infer the presence of a human face in an image through the identification of face-like textures. The selected textures are those of human hair and skin. The second-order statistics method is used for texture representation. This method employs a set of co-occurrence matrices from which features can be calculated that can characterize a texture. The cascade-correlation neural network architecture is used for supervised classification of textures. The Kohonen self-organizing feature map shows the clustering of the different texture types. Classification performance is generally above 80% which is sufficient to clearly outline a face in an image.

INTRODUCTION

The identification of a human face in a digital image is among the most challenging tasks in computer vision. A major difficulty is the wide variety of faces in the human population and the many characteristics determining facial appearance. Age is an important factor. The face of an old person often shows little resemblance to that of a small child. In addition, racial features may lend a face its characteristic appearance. But even within the same age group and race many differences can be found in shape, expression, skin tone, and hair color and texture. This large variety complicates the formulation of a general feature set that may enable the discrimination of a face from other objects present in an image.

Most of the existing research has concentrated on the recognition of a particular face. Characteristic measurements, like the distance between the eyebrows and a person's hairline and the distance between the eyes have been used to recognize the face of a particular person [1]. A human face can also be characterized by a set of eigenfunctions [2]. Neural network technology has been used to recognize a person's face [3]. In this case, a neural network is trained on a set of photographs of a small group of people. The trained network is able to correctly classify other pictures of these same people. This work has been extended to classify facial expression [4]. Neural networks have also been used to classify a face as male or female [5]. All of these investigations require that a person is in a particular position at a given distance of the camera. Thus, the location and size of the face are known *a priori*. The problem is not the identification of the presence of a face but the recognition of a particular person or the classification of certain facial attributes.

The goal of the project described in this paper is face identification. The problem is to find a face (or faces) in a picture or conclude that the picture does not contain a face. Identification is important when images must be sorted based on their contents. It may be advantageous to be able to retrieve all images showing a person's photograph from an image database. Identification may also be a first step towards face recognition. The specific technique employed is texture classification. A texture may be described as an observed pattern on the surface of an object. These patterns may appear regular or repetitive, or they may seem more stochastic in nature. They may often be described by properties like smoothness, coarseness, and grain. Every object exhibits some type of texture. Therefore, it is surmised that objects may be detected through the identification of their characteristic textures. In particular, the presence of a face could be inferred from the identification of human skin and hair texture in an image.

Before texture identification can proceed, a texture representation must be determined. The simplest representation is to use the actual gray levels of the pixels of a textured image segment. However, these pixel values may show large variations within a particular texture. Features derived from these pixel values may provide a more condensed and homogeneous texture representation. Many feature extraction methods exist; a comparative study is provided by [6]. In this study, features derived from gray level statistics are compared with those obtained from a Fourier transform of image segments. The second-order statistics features, introduced in [7], were found to supply a powerful feature representation. This texture representation has been used extensively. For example, it was used in the characterization of different types of clouds in satellite images [8], to distinguish different cloud densities [9], and to estimate the amount of fat in beef [10]. This project also employs a subset of the features defined in [7].

Texture identification is performed by a classifier. There are essentially two types of classifiers, those that provide supervised and those that supply unsupervised classification. Supervised classification distinguishes a training and an application phase. During training, a set of patterns and their correct classifications are presented to the classifier. The system is expected to extract the distinguishing features

0-7803-0999-5/93/$03.00 ©1993 IEEE

between the various classes from these exemplars. This knowledge is used in the application phase to classify a different set of patterns from the same population as the training patterns. In unsupervised classification, the system is expected to cluster patterns based on similarity. The various clusters can then be labeled according to their classification.

NEURAL NETWORK ARCHITECTURES FOR PATTERN CLASSIFICATION

Both supervised and unsupervised pattern classification can be performed by neural networks. The appeal of neural networks as pattern classification systems is based upon several considerations. They appear to perform as well or better than other classification techniques and require no assumptions about the nature of the distribution of the pattern data. A comparison of neural networks to classical methods, like K-nearest neighbor and discriminant analysis, has shown that neural networks can achieve equal performance using a much smaller set of training data [8]. An important task is the selection of the actual neural network architecture. This architecture will be different depending on the kind of training (supervised or unsupervised) selected.

Supervised pattern classification is often accomplished by means of a feedforward architecture, like a back-propagation network [11]. However, back-propagation learning tends to be slow and may lead to a sub-optimal solution (local minimum). Also, this architecture requires the investigator to guess the number of hidden units that will be adequate to solve the problem. The architecture selected for supervised texture classification is cascade-correlation [12]. This architecture was designed to improve the slow learning characteristics of back-propagation. Its main distinguishing feature is its dynamic character: the network builds its internal structure incrementally, during training. The initial network consists of only two layers: an input and an output layer which are completely connected. These connections are trained until no significant changes occur anymore. If, at that point, the total error is still unacceptably high, a hidden node will be allocated to further reduce the total error. Each hidden node is trained in isolation. Its input connections are adjusted such that the correlation between the unit's output and the remaining output error of the network (calculated over all training patterns) is maximized. Upon insertion into the network, these input connections are frozen so that the hidden node becomes a permanent feature detector, whose performance will not be corrupted by subsequent allocation and training of hidden nodes. Each hidden node is placed in a separate layer above all previously allocated hidden nodes. In this manner, a cascade of hidden units is built until the total error falls below a preset limit. All output connections are trained with the quickprop algorithm [12] after each insertion of a hidden unit. Training in cascade-correlation is fast because there is no back-propagation of errors. Another advantage is the separate training of each hidden node. When a layer of nodes is trained together, they all independently attempt to minimize the same errors. Training is more efficient when each node successively tries to minimize the residual error.

Unsupervised clustering of similar patterns is often achieved with a Kohonen self-organizing map [14]. This map facilitates a better understanding of the underlying structure of the classification problem. The Kohonen network provides a means to project a high dimensional vector space onto a lower (usually two) dimensional space which is simple to represent graphically. It creates a topology preserving map in which units that are physically located next to each other will respond to input patterns that are likewise next to each other. In this manner, the Kohonen map will show the clustering of the various categories in the classification problem. This information is complementary to that obtained from a supervised classifier. The supervised classifier will indicate the actual misclassifications, while the Kohonen map may reveal the difficulty of the classification task. If the different categories do not show distinct clusters when graphed on this map, then the representation used as input to the classifier does not discriminate these categories very well. It may then be advantageous to research alternative representations which may lead to improved classification performance.

THE SECOND-ORDER STATISTICS METHOD

The second-order gray level statistics method, as introduced by [7], has been successfully used by many researchers. This method is defined in the spatial domain of the image and takes the statistical nature of the texture into account. A set of co-occurrence matrices is calculated. Each one measures the frequency of the simultaneous occurrence of two specified gray levels at two designated relative positions in an image segment. Generally, four different matrices are used. They compute the frequency of gray level co-occurrence at neighboring positions in four different directions (horizontal, vertical, and along the two diagonal directions of the image segment).

Reference [7] defines fourteen features that are derived from these matrices. Some of them are computationally involved. Most researchers do not use the complete set. For example, [8] only uses four of these measures. For the face identification project, it was found that eight measures could adequately represent the textures of hair and skin. The following measures were used: *Angular Second Moment* (measures the homogeneity of the texture), *Contrast* (measures local variation in the texture), *Correlation* (measures the linear dependencies of the intensity values), *Inverse Difference Moment* (another measure of contrast), *Entropy, Sum Entropy, Difference Entropy* (all three entropy measures are an indication of the amount of randomness in the texture), and *Sum Average*. The mathematical formulas for these measures are given in [7]. Each measure was calculated four times using each one of the four directional co-occurrence matrices. Since the textures used in this project did not show directional preference, each set of directional measures was averaged. These average values were used as a non-directional texture representation.

HUMAN FACE IDENTIFICATION

Data Collection

A set of photographs of faculty members and students of the University of Colorado at Colorado Springs was obtained. Pictures were taken of forty-five people. Figure 1 shows a representative subset. Each person contributed three poses. This group consisted of twenty-eight males and seventeen females. The subjects varied in age, hair coloration, and skin tone. The lighting varied slightly as did the distance at which the pictures were taken. These images were digitized for computer processing but were not preprocessed or standardized in any other way.

Image segments of size 16 x 16 pixels, containing hair, skin and other textures were extracted. Anything appearing in these images that was not hair or skin was classified as "other". Thus, the "other" category was used as a default classification. Segments for this category were extracted from the rather uniform background and the few pieces of clothing visible in these pictures. Three samples of each texture class were selected from each picture. These samples were all homogeneous in the sense that they did not cross borders between textures. The eight second-order statistics features were calculated for each sample. The mean and standard deviation of the gray values were also obtained. These ten numbers, appropriately scaled, were collected in a feature vector. Thus, each segment was represented by a ten-dimensional vector. These vectors serve as a characterization of the textures, and their clustering properties will determine classification performance.

Classification by the Cascade-Correlation Architecture

Several classification experiments were performed with the cascade-correlation neural network. Since this architecture uses supervised training, a training and a test set must be constructed for each experiment. In each case, the network was trained five times on the same set of data. Each invocation of the network allocates a new set of random initial weights. Thus, different invocations (trials), trained on the same data, will find different solutions and may show different classification performance. Therefore, performance should not be measured by means of a single trial but should be the result of several trials. The minimum and maximum performance, observed within each set of five trials, as well as the average performance is reported in the tables.

When comparing the performance of the different experiments, it is not sufficient to merely note the difference in average values. A statistical analysis must be performed to decide if the observed differences are merely statistical fluctuations or represent actual differences in performance. The statistical method used in the comparisons is Analysis of Variance (ANOVA), as described by [14]. This method starts from a null hypothesis which states that there is no difference between the means of the groups that take part in the comparison. Based on the individual performance measurements, this hypothesis will be accepted with a predeter-

Fig. 1. A representative set of photographs of the people database used for training the neural networks.

mined probability. This probability is generally set at 0.05, indicating that there is a 5% chance that the hypothesis will be accepted erroneously. If the null hypothesis is rejected then there is a significant difference between the means not caused by statistical fluctuations.

The first experiment tested the feasibility of face identification. A small set of segments was extracted from a single image. A training set was constructed from the feature vectors calculated from these segments combined with the correct classification into three different classes (skin, hair, and other). The test set was based on segments extracted from a different set of photographs of the same person. Classification was decided by comparing the output values of the neural network after presentation of a test pattern. The output unit with the highest activation determined the category of that pattern. Correct classification varied from 83.3% to 100% with an average of 94.4%. This test showed that cascade-correlation could learn the texture features from one image and successfully apply this knowledge to different photographs of the same person.

In the following experiments, the persons providing pictures for the training set and those supplying photographs for the test set were always different. One experiment used groups of four people to provide training data. Three different groups were used. One of them was relatively homogeneous consisting of four dark-haired females. The other two groups were more varied, consisting of males, females, brunettes and blondes. Each person contributed the same number of training patterns taken from all three poses. The training sets consisted of 108 patterns equally distributed among the three classes. The classification accuracy was measured with a large set of test data (630 patterns), collected from the remaining photographs. The performance of each group is shown in Table 1. The first set shown in this table (set 1) is the one consisting of dark-haired females. It is interesting to note that this set showed the best performance when tested on a heterogeneous group of people. Most likely, this result is just a statistical fluctuation. The difference in performance between set 1 and set 2 is not statistically significant. When comparing the results of set 1 with those obtained from set 3 (which showed the worst performance) a small, statistically significant difference was noted.

The next experiment tested the influence of the size of the group used for training on test performance. Two additional groups, one consisting of eight people and a third one including twelve people were formed. The photographs used for these training sets are shown in Figure 1. The four pictures in top left part of this figure form the group of four. This is the group of dark-haired females that showed the best performance in Table 1. The four pictures directly below this set were added to this group to form the group of eight, and all pictures shown in Figure 1 form the group of twelve. The classification performance on test segments, extracted from photographs of people that were not part of the training set, is shown in Table 2. It is seen that performance increases slightly as more people are incorporated in the training group. This is to be expected since a larger training group will have a better chance of representing the various skin and hair types present in the test group. However, the differences are small. Only the classification difference between the four and twelve person groups is statistically significant.

All experiments discussed thus far involve tests with isolated segments showing a uniform texture. The real test, which will show if this method can find a face in a picture, is to scan an image which may or may not contain a face. In scanning, a photograph is segregated into overlapping segments of size 16 x 16. Each segment is processed and classified. The problem is that an arbitrary image database will contain many textures unknown to the neural network; that is, these textures were not represented in the training set. These textures should be categorized as "other". However, if the maximum activation of an output node is used as the classification criterion, this will often not happen. Figure 2a shows a photograph from the people database, and Figure 2b shows the output of the scanner. The scanned image shows hair segments in black and skin segments in white. The pixel values of segments classified as "other" are not changed. Note that the eyes, nostrils and mouth are all classified as hair. The network was never trained on these facial features and does not automatically put them into the "other" category. Figure 3a shows a picture of a piece of cloth with a flower pattern. The textures in this image are very different from any training patterns used for the neural network. The scanned image clearly shows many misclassifications. This problem can be reduced by changing the classification criteria. The new criteria do not simply classify a pattern according to the highest activation of the output units. A segment will only be labeled as hair or skin if the entire output pattern is sufficiently similar to the "ideal

TABLE 1.
CLASSIFICATION RESULTS OF DIFFERENT TRAINING GROUPS

Training Set	Range of Correct Classifications in %	Average Percentage of Correct Classifications
Set 1	80.2 - 84.6	82.4
Set 2	76.8 - 84.6	80.7
Set 3	74.4 - 78.4	77.3

TABLE II.
CLASSIFICATION RESULTS OF DIFFERENT SIZED TRAINING GROUPS

Training Set	Range of Correct Classifications in %	Average Percentage of Correct Classifications
4 Person	80.2 - 84.6	82.4
8 Person	81.5 - 84.4	83.6
12 Person	82.4 - 85.6	84.4

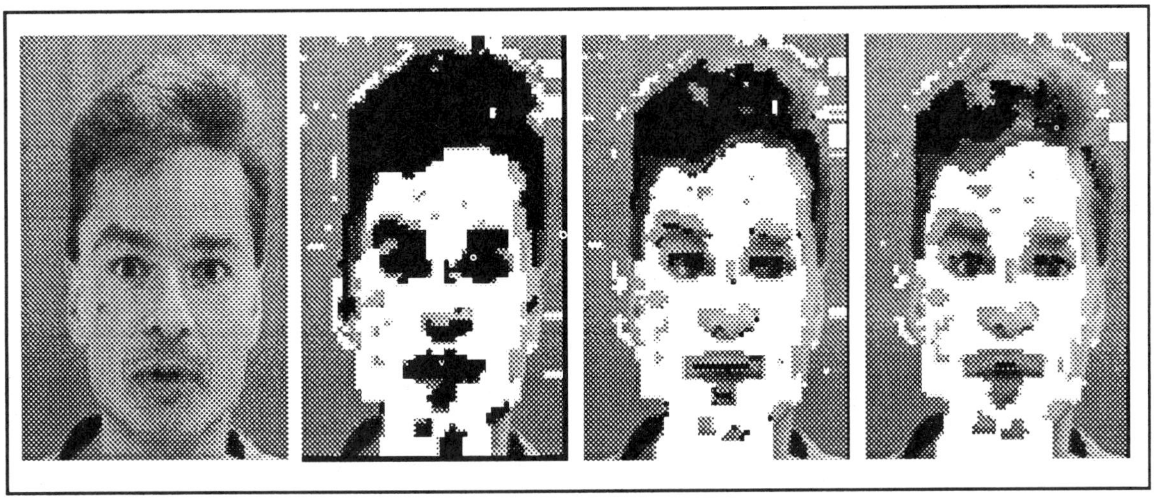

a b c d

Fig. 2. The results of scanning a photograph of the people database. a) The original photograph b) Scanner output, showing hair segments in black and skin segments in white c) Scanner output with loose restrictions imposed on the classification d) Scanner output with more stringent restrictions imposed on the classification

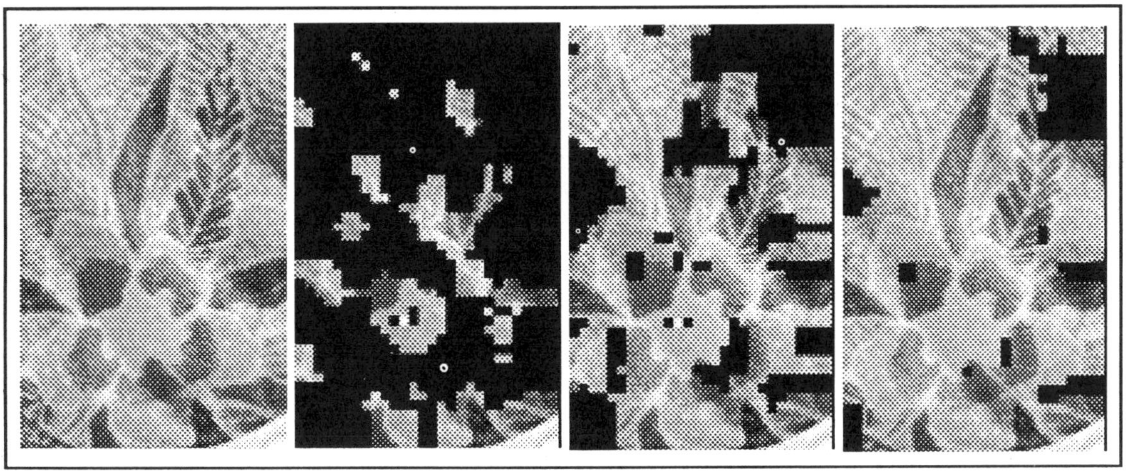

a b c d

Fig. 3 The results of scanning an arbitrary photograph with a network trained on the people database. a) The original photograph b) Scanner output, output with no additional restrictions on the classification c) Scanner output with loose restrictions imposed on the classification d) Scanner output with more stringent restrictions imposed on the classification

TABLE III

Confusion matrices showing the nature of the misclassifications when maximum activation is used as a classification criterion (left) and when the more stringent similarity measure is applied (right).

	skin	hair	other
skin-class	137	3	9
hair-class	3	136	33
other-class	10	11	108

	skin	hair	other
skin-class	133	2	8
hair-class	0	105	7
other-class	17	43	135

pattern" of that category used during training. If a pattern is not sufficiently similar it will be classified as "other". The degree of similarity, required to classify a pattern as skin or hair, will depend on the image database and the investigator's objectives. With more stringent similarity requirements, fewer segments of class "other" will be misclassified but more hair and skin segments will be missed.

Figures 2c and 3c show the effect of scanning with a weak similarity restriction, while Figures 2d and 3d show the result when a stricter similarity constraint is enforced. The stricter requirements seem to work in the current situation. A sufficiently large patch of hair is still left on the person's head, and the misclassifications of the skin texture have not increased by much. When these stricter requirements are also applied to the 12-person test case shown in Table 2, the resulting performance range is 82.4% - 84.0% with an average value of 83.2%. Thus, the decrease in performance is insignificant. Table 3 shows the classification performance in the form of confusion matrices. A confusion matrix has the number of correctly classified patterns on the diagonal and shows the number of misclassifications of each category in the off-diagonal elements. For example, the matrix on the left indicates that 33 patterns in category "other" were mislabeled as category hair. Table 3 shows that the shift in misclassification types, caused by the change in classification criteria, is essentially between patterns labeled as hair and "other". This is not surprising since the patterns labeled as skin form a more homogeneous group and are easier to recognize than the patterns labeled as hair. Note that in Figures 2c and 2d the voids in the skin texture now show the eyes, nostrils and mouth. These voids may facilitate the identification of these facial features in an image. For example, in [14] a deformable eye template was developed for feature extraction. This method assumes knowledge of the approximate location of human eyes in an image, which may be provided by the location of these voids. However, the problem of misclassification, especially of textures not learned by the network during training, is a severe limitation which may be reduced but cannot be eliminated.

The Kohonen Feature Maps

The Kohonen feature maps were trained with the same training sets that were presented to cascade-correlation. The network was trained for 15,000 iterations with an initial learning rate of 0.2 and an initial neighborhood size of 4. A large test set was then presented to the trained network. Figure 4 shows a representative example of the resulting maps. A distinct clustering of hair and skin patterns is observed. The patterns classified as "other" do not cluster because they represent many different backgrounds.

CONCLUSION

This project has shown that it is possible to identify the textures of hair and skin in an image. It was found that the second-order statistics method, introduced by [7], could represent the skin and hair textures in a general way. The cascade-correlation neural network could be trained with this representation and showed a classification rate of over 80% on homogeneous segments extracted from the people database. When a photograph of this database was scanned, a significant clustering of skin and hair textures could be observed. The main problem with the approach is that the neural network is essentially trained on hair and skin textures and not on the many other textures that will also be present in an arbitrary database. The network must classify all textures that are not hair or skin as belonging to the default category "other". Certain similarity criteria must be imposed on the output of the neural network in order to correctly filter out the hair and skin textures and deposit all other textures in this default category.

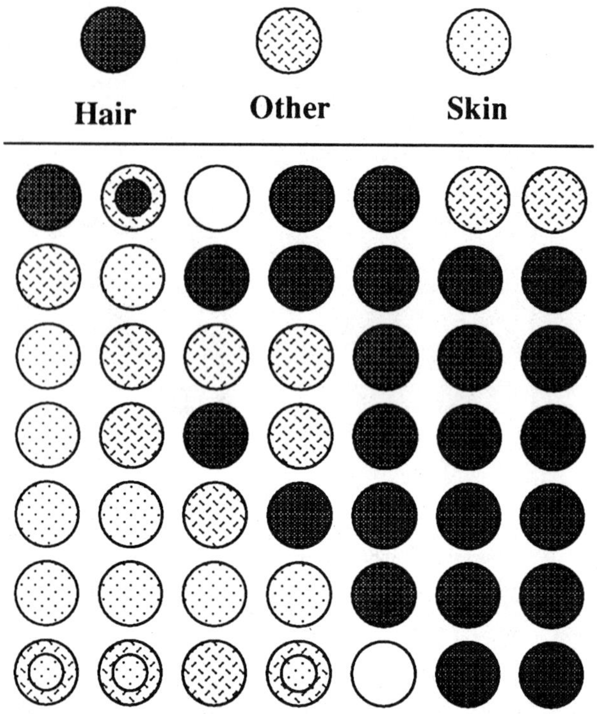

Fig. 4. A Kohonen feature map showing the clustering of the units that respond to the same texture category.

In order to infer the presence of a face from the texture identification, simple counters of the occurrence of hair and skin textures could be implemented. It should be noted that the identification of skin is necessary for this inference while the presence of hair is not. However, occurrence by itself may not be sufficient evidence and will not discriminate between the presence of a single face and the occurrence of several faces in the same image. In order to strengthen the conclusion, geometrical information concerning the location of the skin and hair segments will be helpful. Isolated hair and skin segments are likely to be misclassifications and should be ignored. On the other hand, if hair segments surround a skin area or are found above a skin area then the likelihood of the presence of a face is increased. Additionally, voids in the skin area may indicate the location of eyes, nostrils and mouth which may then be identified with other methods. Once a face has been found in an image, the next step could be recognition. With the size and location of the face approximately known, existing recognition procedures could be applied.

The methodology developed in this project goes well beyond the identification of the presence of faces. Other objects may be identified through their textures. For example, household objects may be classified through the identification of the materials of which they are made (wood, plastic, metal, glass, etc.). An important drawback of the method is a lack of speed. Co-occurrence matrices must be calculated for every image segment, and a set of features must be calculated from these matrices. Because of this overhead, scanning of an image takes considerable CPU time. The use of other texture representations need to be investigated. Alternative methods are first-order statistics features, features derived from the Fourier transform and Gabor filters. If a large number of images need to be processed, more efficient algorithms will need to be developed.

ACKNOWLEDGMENTS

The authors thank Scott Fahlman and Scott Crowder III for making the cascade-correlation code available.

REFERENCES

[1] S. R. Cannon, G. W. Jones, R. Campbell, and N. W. Morgan, "Identification of Individuals by Computer Vision," *First Annual Rocky Mountain Conference on Artificial Intelligence*, Univ. of Colorado, Boulder, June 1986.

[2] M. Kirby and L. Sirovich, "Application of the Karhunen-Loeve Procedure for the Characterization of Human Faces," *IEEE Transactions on Pattern Analysis and Machine Intelligence*, Vol. 12, pp. 103-108, 1990.

[3] G. W. Cottrell and M. Fleming, "Face Recognition Using Unsupervised Features Extraction," *Proceedings of the International Joint Conference on Neural Networks, Vol. I*, 1990.

[4] G. W. Cottrell, "Extracting Features from Faces Using Compression Networks: Face, Identity, Emotion, and Gender Recognition Using Holons," in *Connectionist Models: Proceedings of the 1990 Summer School*, Morgan Kaufmann, San Mateo, pp. 328-337.

[5] B. A. Golomb, D. T. Lawrence, and T. J. Sejnowski, "Sexnet: A Neural Network Identifies Sex from Human Faces," in: *Advances in Neural Information Processing 3*, pp. 572- 577, 1991.

[6] J. S. Weszka, C. R. Dyer, and A. Rosenfeld, "A Comparative Study of Texture Measures for Terrain Classification," *IEEE Transactions on Systems, Man, and Cybernetics*, Vol. 6, pp. 269-274, 1976.

[7] R. M. Haralick, K. Shanmugam, and I. Dinstein, "Texture Features for Image Classification," *IEEE Transactions on Systems, Man and Cybernetics*, Vol. 3, pp. 610-621, 1973.

[8] J. Lee, R. C. Weger, S. K. Sengupta, and R. M. Welch, "A Neural Network Approach to Cloud Classification", *IEEE Transactions on Geoscience and Remote Sensing*, Vol. 28 pp. 846-855, 1990.

[9] M. F. Augusteijn and A. S. Dimalanta,. "Feature Detection in Satellite Images Using Neural Network Technology," *1992 Goddard Conference on Space Applications of Artificial Intelligence*, NASA Conference Publication 3141, pp. 123-136.

[10] J. D. McCauley, B. R. Thane, and A. D. Whittaker, "Fat Estimation in Beef Ultrasound Images Using Texture and Adaptive Logic Networks", in press.

[11] D. E. Rumelhart, G. E. Hinton, and R. J. Williams, "Learning Internal Representations by Error Propagation," in *Parallel Distributed Processing: Explorations in the Microstructure of Cognition, Vol. 1: Foundations*, D. E. Rumelhart and J. L. McClelland, Eds . MIT Press, Cambridge, Mass., pp. 318-364, 1986.

[12] S. E. Fahlman and C. Lebiere, "The Cascade-Correlation learning Architecture," in *Advances in Neural Information Processing Systems 2*, D. Touretzky, Ed., Morgan Kaufmann, pp. 524-532, 1990.

[13] S. E. Fahlman, "Faster-Learning Variations on Back-Propagation: An Empirical Study," in *Connectionist Models: Proceedings of the 1988 Summer School*, Morgan Kaufmann, pp. 38-51.

[14] T. Kohonen, "The Neural Phonetic Typewriter," *Computer*, Vol. 21, pp. 11-22, 1988.

[15] G. Keppel, *Design and Analysis: A Researcher's Handbook.* Prentice Hall, Englewood Cliffs, NJ, 1982.

[16] A. L. Yuille, D. S. Cohen, and P. W. Hallinan, "Feature Extraction from Faces Using Deformable Templates", *CVPR*, pp. 104-109, 1989.

Classifying Fingerprint Images using Neural Network : Deriving the Classification State

Masayoshi KAMIJO
The Science University of Tokyo, Suwa College
Department of Management and System Science
5000-1,Toyohira,Chino,Nagano,391-02 Japan
Phone : +81-266-73-1201, Fax : +81-266-73-1230
E-mail:MASA@JPNSUT60(BITNET)

Abstract—In our study we have constructed a neural network for a classification of fingerprint images as an expert system which can classify the complicated fingerprint images. And we have proposed the so called *two-step learning method* as a learning process and the four-layered neural network which has one subnetwork for each category. The classification results for 500 unknown samples were 86.0 percent classification rate for the first candidate and 99.0 percent classification rate including the second candidate. Moreover, we carried out the principal component analysis with respect to the unit values of the second hidden layer and studied the fingerprint classification state represented by the internal state of the network. Consequently, we confirmed that the fingerprint patterns are roughly classified into each category in the second hidden layer and the effectiveness of the two-step learning process.

I. INTRODUCTION

The purpose of our study is to develop an automatic fingerprint classification system to create an efficient database for fingerprint matching. We thereby proposed a four-layered neural network which can extract feature from two-dimension data such as complicated fingerprint images. The neural network has one subnetwork for each category as the automatic classification system of the fingerprint images. To realize in one subnetwork the pattern information of one category, the networks are trained by supervised learning in the usual manner by the back propagation algorithm with a so called two-step training method.

Further, to demonstrate the reliability and effectiveness of our system, we carried out the principal component analysis with respect to the unit values of the second hidden layer and studied the pattern classification state represented by the internal state of the network. This was useful to improve the network structure and the training process.

The automatic processing of fingerprints can be roughly divided into fingerprint input equipment and fingerprint pattern recognition, and the latter is further divided into fingerprint classification and fingerprint matching. Among these, there is still room for improvement in fingerprint input equipment and fingerprint matching, but they have been made practical. On the other hand, it is still the case that fingerprint classification is a specially field and is generally performed by hand. As the number of fingerprints collected increases, problems in classification efficiency and reduction in reliability due to long run times still remain. For these reasons, the development of a fast, accurate automatic fingerprint classification system is desired, with the goal of creating an effective database for fingerprint comparison. However, It is difficult to establish an algorithm. Neural networks are ideally suited for the construction of an expert system for fingerprint classification which mimics the recognition capabilities of an expert handling the complicated fingerprint patterns, and recognize inaccurate and distorted patterns; they also make it possible to realize recognition capabilities with human-like adaptability.

II. CLASSIFICATION SYSTEM OF FINGERPRINT IMAGES

A. Fingerprint Images

Among fingerprint patterns, there are the following four types: Arch, Loop, Whorl, and Accidental. The Arch type can be divided into Normal Arch and Tented Arch types. The Loop type can be divided into Left Loop and Right Loop types.

0-7803-0999-5/93/$03.00 ©1993 IEEE

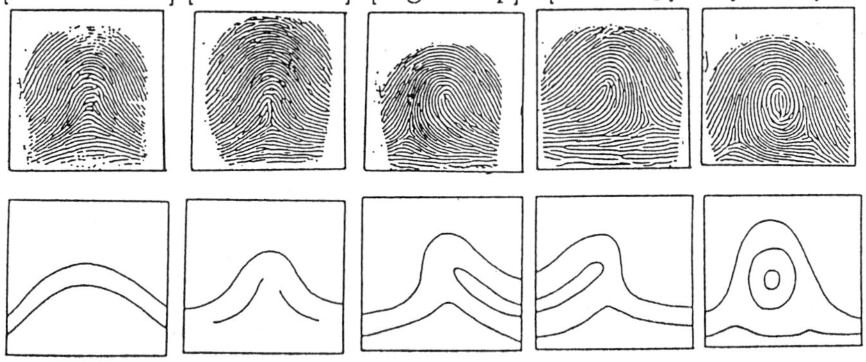

Fig. I. Categories and characteristics of fingerprint images.

In this paper, we do not concern ourselves with accidental fingerprints and experiment only with the following five categories: Normal Arch, Tented Arch, Right Loop, Left Loop, and Whorl. Fig. I shows fingerprint images and their characteristic patterns.

Fingerprint classification can be divided into methods which key on feature points and methods that in turn key on ridge line orientations. In this paper, since features are easily extracted from complex print types, we use ridge line orientations as the features of a fingerprint pattern and employ this for classification. Since the fingerprint image data contains variations due to noise and variations in contrast, direction extraction is difficult. However, by combining projection and relaxation method and a so-called *ridge-tracing algorithm*, the feature ridge pattern is extracted from fingerprints which does not require additional preprocessing. Fig. II shows examples of the feature ridge patterns(16×16 pixels, 256 gray levels) which are actually used to classify the patterns. For detailed explanation, please refer to [2][3].

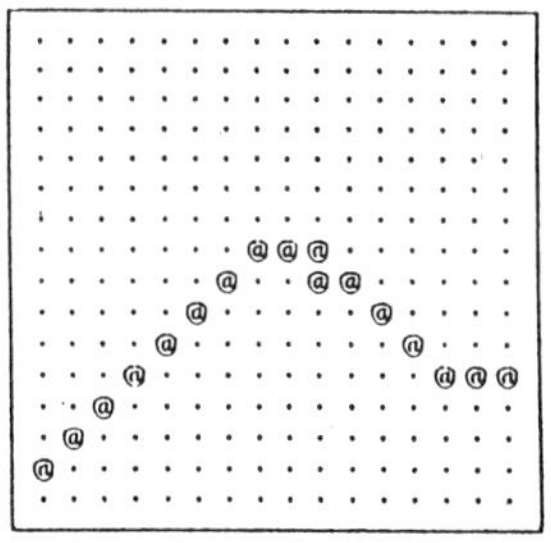

Fig. II. Characteristics fingerprint pattern (Normal arch). This pattern is a example of actual data.

B. The Network Architecture

To effectively extract the feature of a two-dimensional fingerprint pattern, we propose a four-layered network which has one subnetwork for each category and has connections from each horizontal and vertical band in the input layer to the inputs of the first hidden layer (Fig. III). Each subnetwork is independent, and there are no connections within layers – only between them. Also, there are no weights on the connections from the third hidden layer to the output layer. The output layer is a layer used to display the outputs of the subnetworks. Many methods can be considered in order to form units in the hidden layers that classify spatial information in a fingerprint pattern. However, to reduce the number of links and the processing time, the forementioned extraction method using horizontal and vertical bands to effectively extract spatial information from the pattern can be thought to extract feature which are more local than every input unit being connected to every unit in the hidden layer. Further, if a network goes into saturation due to too much information being taught to one network, the learning state for each category falls into a local minimum and there is the possibility that the recognition rate will be reduced. However, with respect to this problem, given the interpretation that "an output which is biased toward some category will become the output state," if we consider applying this in reverse, we prepare one subnetwork corresponding to each category and have a structure that obtains an output using subnetwork cooperation. In this method, each subnetwork can be trained inde-

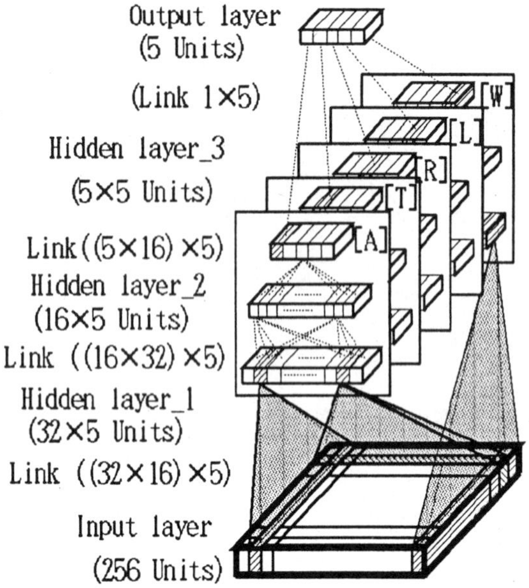

Fig. III. Network architecture

pendently; and since learning can proceed in categories other than one which suffers from shortened learning time and low recognition rate without being affected by it, we can expert an increase in learning accuracy.

C. Learning rule

Link weights and unit thresholds are adjusted using back error propagation learning rule, and the subnetwork are taught the characteristics of a category. Then, by using one subnetwork for each category, we expect to raise the recognition accuracy; to realize this, however, each subnetwork must respond correctly to every output to some extent and must perform compression between the input and the output while possessing the properties of parallelism, abstraction, and extensibility. To fulfill these conditions, all of the learning symbols must be presented to each subnetwork and each subnetwork trained as an expert in one category. To realize in one subnetwork the pattern information of one category, we use a two-step training method.

During learning, the training examples are presented in the order: Normal Arch, Tented Arch, Right Loop, Left Loop, and Whorl. The training patterns for each subnetwork consisted of setting to 1 just the output corresponding to the category of the pattern being input, and the outputs of the remaining units were set to zero. Ten patterns were given for each category, making a total of 50.

First, when each of the subnetworks is being trained, the most important patterns are identified and only those patterns are learned. Then learning is done by presenting all of the training patterns in the normal order. The termination condition for training is when the output error E_L at iteration L is less than ϵ_0 during the first step; and during the second step it is when the error becomes less than ϵ_1 and when the difference in the errors at steps L and $L-1$ becomes less than ϵ_2. The values $\epsilon_i (i = 0, 1, 2)$ determine convergence of the error to a stopping condition using the mean of the squared symbol. From the results of many experiments, appropriate values which did not fall into overtraining were determined to be $\epsilon_0 = 0.001, \epsilon_1 = 0.8, \epsilon_2 = 0.01$.

D. Classification Experiment

Using the internal state obtained through learning, we classified 100 fingerprints per category, for a total of 500 fingerprints. Since the neural network output is based on similarity with the learning data, classification is evaluated with the second candidate included in the classification result. The results of the classification experiment are given here. A recognition accuracy of 100 percent was obtained for the training samples; and as shown in Table I, the classification results for 500 unknown samples were 86.0 present for the first candidate and 99.0 present including the second candidate. Values in the table are numbers of discriminations; values in parentheses are classification rates with respect to 500.

III. Evaluation of the Internal State Using Principal Component Analysis

We found the effectiveness of the two-step learning process using the principal component analysis by deriving the fingerprint pattern classification state represented by the internal state of the networks. We performed the principal component analysis with respect to the unit values of the second hidden layer and studied the fingerprint classification state represented by the internal state of the network. This second layer contains 16 independent units and the values of these units are a partial transformation of the inputs.

A. Pattern classification state

As a result of applying principal component analysis to the values of the units of the second hidden layer in a case of classifying the training patterns by the network which is trained in the two-step

Table I. Classification results for 500 unknown pattern data

	Normal arch	Tented arch	Right loop	Left loop	Whorl	Total (%)	
Number of First candidate patterns	88 (17.6)	52 (10.4)	97 (19.4)	98 (19.6)	95 (19.0)	430 (86.0)	495 (99.0)
Number of second candidate patterns	12 (2.4)	47 (9.4)	0 (0.0)	2 (0.4)	4 (0.8)	65 (13.0)	
Number of misclassified patterns	0 (0.0)	1 (0.2)	3 (0.6)	0 (0.0)	1 (0.2)	5 (1.0)	
Totals (%)	100 (20.0)	100 (20.0)	100 (20.0)	100 (20.0)	100 (20.0)	500 (100.0)	

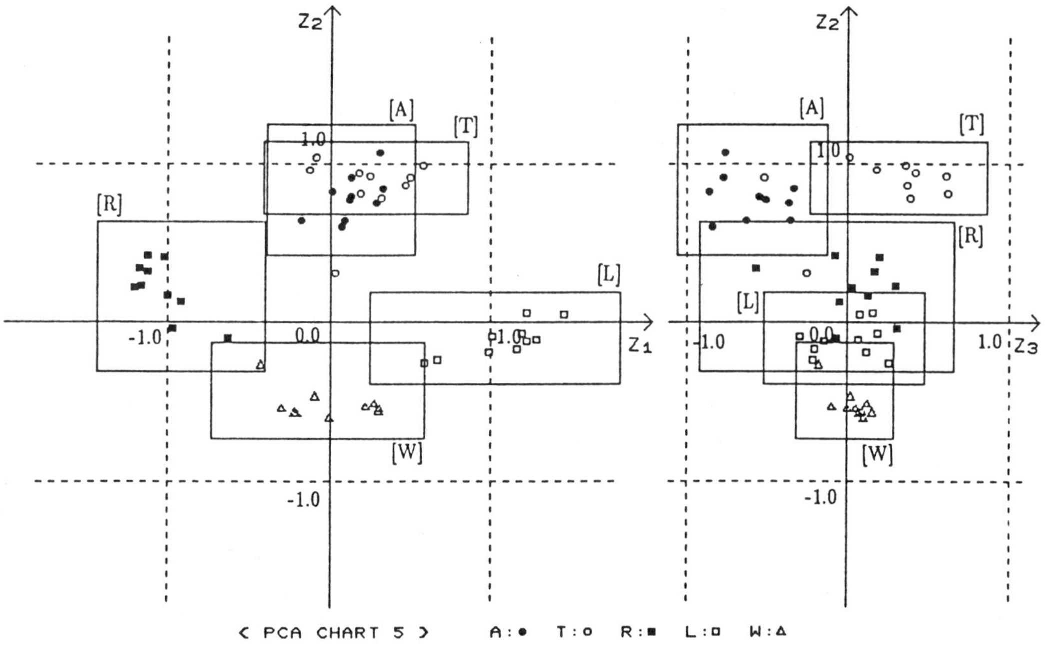

Fig. IV. Results of a principal component analysis of the unit values in the second hidden layer

learning process, Fig. IV shows a plot of the results with respect to these three principal components, i.e., with the first, second and third principal components as the axes. These principal components are shown as Z_1, Z_2, and Z_3 respectively. For each category, we let 40 percent of the distance between the maximum and minimum values represent the same category and enclosed that region with a rectangle. When an input pattern is summarized in the second hidden layer, we verified that it can be categorized to some extent. The similarity between Normal Arch [A] and Tented Arch [T] is strong in patterns up to here, and an overlap between those regions in Fig. IV is not a problem.

B. *Effectiveness of the learning process*

We considered two training processes : the so called two-step training process stated in the previous section and the so called one-step training process. The one-step training process means that the network is trained in the error back propagation learning rule using the fifty patterns of all categories in order, normal arch, tented arch, right loop. left loop and whorl. We compared the two classification state by the respective networks trained in the two different training process. The pattern classification state represented by the internal state of the network is evaluated by carrying out the principal component analysis with respect to the unit values of the second hidden layer. The link weight and threshold values were initialized by using normal random numbers because both the networks start to train from the same initial condition. In the previous section, the link weight and threshold values were initialized by using uniform random numbers.

Table II shows the classification results for the 50 training patterns by the networks initialized the normal random numbers with the mean value $Ave = 0$ and the variance $V = 0.001$. Values in parentheses are classification rates with respect to 50. We can see that the classification rate for the network trained in the one-step training process was 96.0 %; and since this is quite poor compared to the network trained in two-step training process.

Fig. V shows the pattern classification state when the training patterns are classified using the network trained by the one-step training process. Fig. VI shows the pattern classification state of the network by the two-step training process.

IV. Conclusion

Using the neural network proposed in this paper, we demonstrated that classification of two-dimensional fingerprint data is possible and we obtained classification rates of 86.0 percent for the first candidate and the high values of 99.0 percent by adding the second candidate. Since a classification rate of around 95 percent is reported previous work on fingerprint classification [4], our system can be said to be an exceptionally effective system for automatic fingerprint classification.

Further, in a comparison of the classification rate with other networks and from a principal component analysis in the second hidden layer, it is established that our network is effective at classifying fingerprint patterns.

The principal component analysis is useful to indicate the pattern classification state represented by the internal state of the network. The effectivity of the two step training method used here is confirmed by the principal component analysis.

Furthermore, we suggested that the principal component analysis is exceptionally useful to choose training data[1]. When high classification ratio is obtained, each category is separated well into the network. When low classification ratio is obtained each category is hardly separated.

References

[1] M. KAMIJO and H.MIENO et.al. Internal representation of neural networks addlied to classification of fingerprint images. *The Congress of The International Fuzzy System Association*, 73–76, 1991.

[2] M. Kamijo, K. Kojima, and H. Mieno. Classification of fingerprint images by the neural networks. *Trans. I.E.C.E., Japan*, J74-D-II(2):199–209, 1991.

[3] M. Kamijo, K. Kojima, and H. Mieno. Classification of fingerprint images using a neural network. *Systems and Computers in Japan*, 23(3), 1992.

[4] O.Nakamura, K. Gotoo, and S. Minami. Classification of fingerprint images using direction patterns. *Trans. I.E.C.E., Japan*, J65-D(10):1286–1293, 1982.

Table II. Classification results for the learning pattern $Ave = 0$, $V = 0.001$.

	Number of First Candidate Patterns	Number of Second Candidate Patterns	Number of misclassified Patterns
Two-step learning	50(100)	0 (0)	0 (0)
One-step learning	47(96)	3 (6)	0 (0)

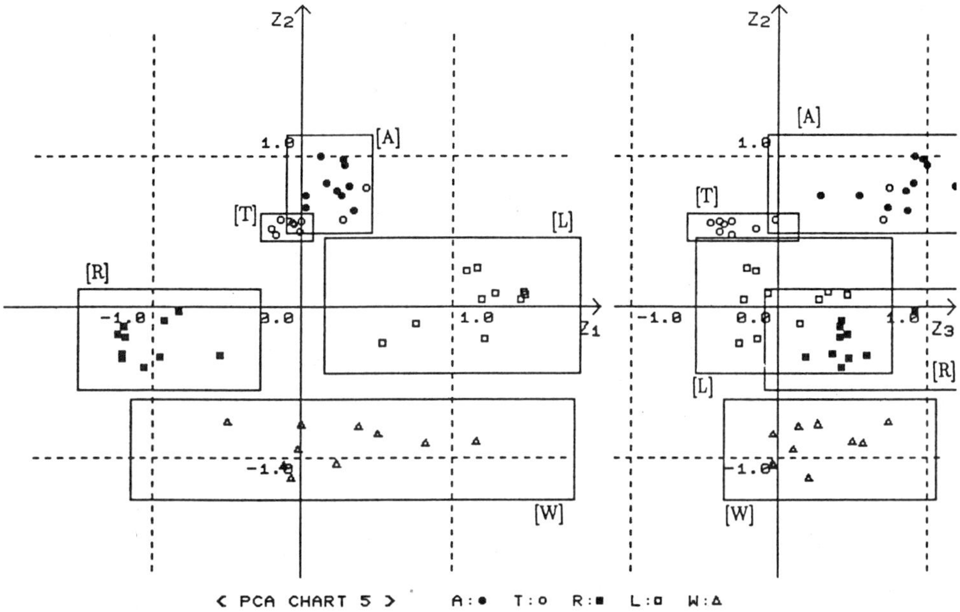

Fig. V. Results of a principal component analysis of the unit values in the second hidden layer for the network trained in the one-step training process.

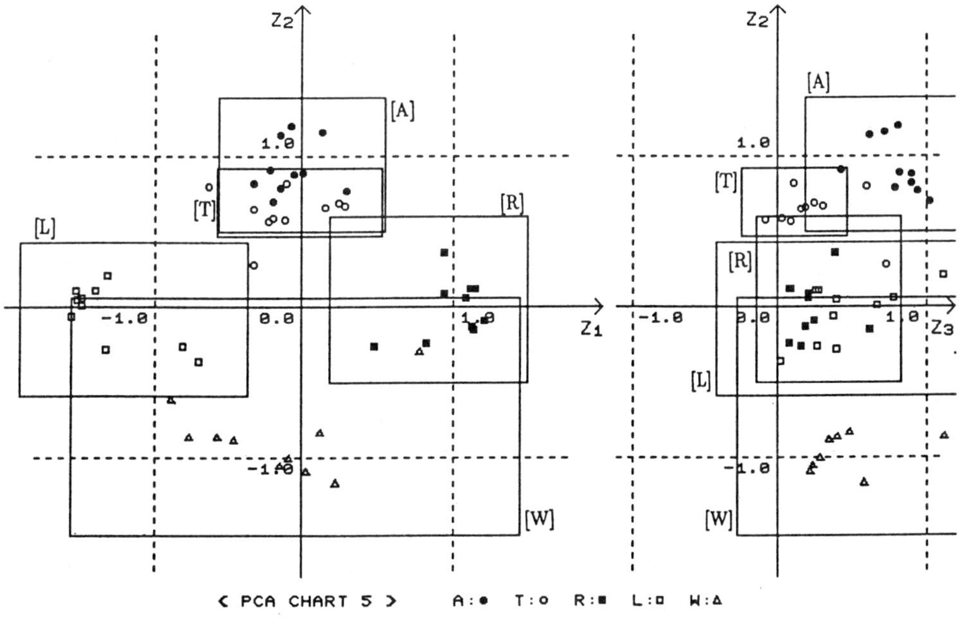

Fig. VI. Results of a principal component analysis of the unit values in the second hidden layer for the network trained in the two-step training process.

Preserving Visual Perception by Learning Natural Clustering

W. Chang, H. S. Soliman & A. H. Sung
New Mexico Institute of Mining and Technology
Computer Science Department
Socorro, NM 87801-4682
E-mail: changw@nmt.edu

Abstract – **In natural-clustering learning, the similarity of two patterns is indicated by the distance of their representing vectors in the pattern space. The existence of pattern classes is exhibited by the clustering of the representing vectors. The natural clustering behavior of self-organizing neural networks enables the learning of perceptually meaningful pattern features and makes it possible to store pictorial data in an effective way. Our experiments show that the storage of perceptual features requires a fraction of the size of the original data, and still renders little or no difference comparing with the original. Experimental results of natural clustering and non-trivial clustering from Counter-propagation Networks using Feature Map and Frequency-Sensitive variations of Kohonen Network are shown and discussed in this paper.**

I. Introduction

Data compression methods have been well studied and developed. They can be accomplished on the basis of the existence of the redundancy in data. The data entropy is then calculated to find the compression rate [1]. In cases where there is no redundancy, compression can be made with loosing some detail as a *lossy* method. When processing pictorial data, the target picture is usually first separated into orthogonal frames of subareas for finding common patterns. The worst case is when these sub-pictures are all different with the same *Mean-Square Error* (MSE), i.e., they are evenly distributed in their pattern space, the compression efficiency will be reciprocal (if lossiness is allowed) to the quality of the decompressed result.

Pictorial or acoustic data patterns are rarely evenly distributed in the pattern space with the same occurrence frequency. They are usually not free from redundancy. Hence, either a *lossless* or *lossy* method can be applied. Some self-organizing artificial neural networks can extract, in a lossless or lossy fashion, repeated data patterns in the weight learning process and thus achieve compression with little MSE or none. The lossless method has a fixed redundancy entropy for each compression target while the lossy method reveals an issue of finding natural clusters in data patterns.

II. Finding Natural Clustering

Since finding pattern classes is the crux of data compression and feature extraction, a neural network that perceives classes without supervision is conceivably more useful.

A. Natural Clustering

Let the training vector set be T, and let y_i be the centroid of a natural cluster S_i. A natural clustering is

$$S_i = \{\, x \in T \mid (\forall j)[\, j \neq i \Rightarrow \|x - y_i\| < \|x - y_j\| \,]\,\}.$$

Each vector in S_i is closer to y_i than to any other centroid y_j, and $\bigcup S_i = T$. Each region where a natural cluster resides is tend to be isotropic.

B. Learning Pattern Clustering

The classification learning is adjusting weights to the centroids of natural clusters so that each training vector becomes closer to its respective clustering weight than to other weights. The ideal learning result is the number of centroids found is minimal (in order to minimize the number of weights needed); and the MSE is still tolerable (i.e., the total distance between each training vector and its centroid is within a given tolerance). Since the problem appears to belong to the class *NP*, networks that give close to optimal solutions within feasible learning time are considered satisfactory (Fig. 1).

The partitioning of a training set into pattern classes is based on the closeness of pattern vectors. It is easier for the network to learn the clustering when each cluster is tight. Some artificial neural networks can find natural clusters with unsupervised learning. In certain situations when human perceives pattern classification differently

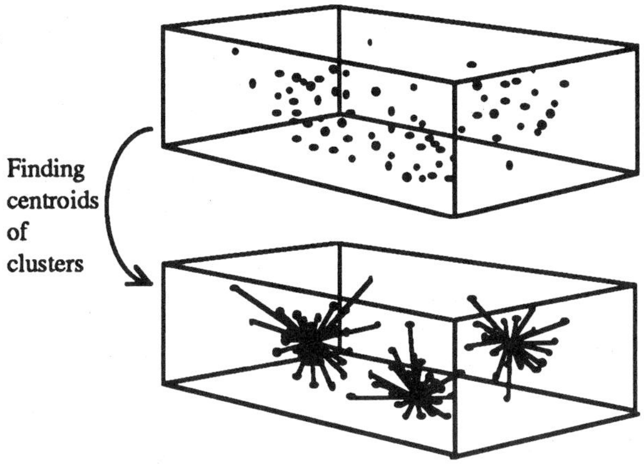

Fig. 1 Upper is a distribution of patterns (of three-dimensional vectors) in their pattern space. Lower is the patterns clustered into three classes by learning the three centroids.

from natural clustering (Fig. 2), a network must be guided through training to achieve the non-natural or *non-trivial* clustering classification. Feed-forward networks such as the *Kohonen Feature Map* (KFM) can be guided with biased teaching patterns [2], [3].

III. Natural Clustering Networks

In recent neural network studies, researchers have begun to apply neural computation techniques on pictorial data compression by using the supervised *Back Propagation Network* (BPN) [4] and a *Frequency-Sensitive Self-organizing* (FSSO) network [5]. They found that the synaptic adaptation of artificial neural networks interprets visual perception in terms of synaptic weights which are themselves compact forms of pictorial knowledge [6]. Using *Counterpropagation Network* (CPN) of Hecht-Nielsen ([7],[8]) is a plausible approach

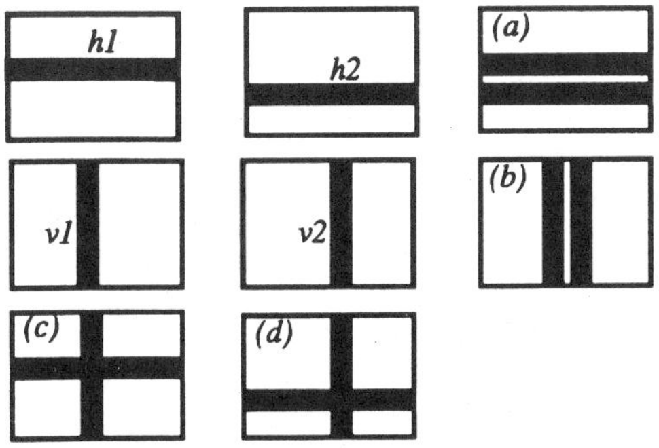

Fig. 2 Images *h1* and *h2* seem to be of the same class but in the pattern space they have no common area (a). *h1* is closer to *v1* or *v2* than to *h2* since they have common points (c); and *h2* is closer to *v1* or *v2* than to *h1* (d).

for finding natural clusters in pictorial data. In our experiments, an FSSO network is used for achieving lossless data compression. Two different CPNs are also used for lossy compressions: one is an outstar layer with an FSSO layer, and the other is an outstar layer with a KFM.

A. Frequency-Sensitive Self-Organizing Network

A simple version of FSSO networks is a competitive learning network of one dimension. Each vector of training set X, where $|X| = s$, is given to the network for a full adaptation in weight w_i during training:

$$w_i^{new} = w_i^{old} + \| x_i - w_i^{old} \| \qquad 1 \le i \le s$$

The idea is to capture repetitive data patterns, and the compression can be made (in the lossless fashion) without introducing any error. The drawback is the resulting number of classes can be large and the compression ratio can be impaired. In our experiments, the compression ratio is at most 2.68. An improvement can be made by discarding the weights that handle less occurring data patterns and assigning other weights to adapt these patterns. Hence, with some error introduced, the compression ratio can be improved (in the lossy fashion). In another version of the FSSO, a gain term η is introduced and initial weights are random:

$$w_i^{new} = w_i^{old} + \eta \| x_j - w_i^{old} \| \qquad 1 \le j \le p \cdot r$$

where w_i^{old} has the smallest difference to x_j and the target data is divided into p training vectors, and each vector is presented r times. Similar training vectors tend to shape a weight to their average. However, the repetition r has to be large to reach a sufficiently accurate average. Still, this FSSO network can be used as a classifier similar to a KFM.

B. Forward-Only Counterpropagation Network (CPN)

The *forward-only* CPN of Hecht-Nielsen [7] is a combination of Kohonen layer which clusters training vectors by *Adaptive Vector Quantization* (AVQ) [7]-[9], and Grossberg's outstar structure which adapts the associated vectors through supervision [8]-[14]. When the supervision set equals the training set, the learning can be regarded as a "non-supervised" one (Fig. 3).

IV. Compression Method

By decomposing a large pictorial data into subpictures as the input, the Kohonen layer identifies the picture classes by winning nodes. The outstar layer then averages the corresponding class vectors in the weights emanating from the winners. Only the class numbers generated by the Kohonen layer and the winners-connected part of the outstar weights are needed to restore the subpictures [6].

A. Training Set and Supervision Set

No supervision is required when using the single-layered FSSO network for a lossless compression. However, when using the FSSO network or the KFM as the classifier layer of a CPN for a lossy compression, a supervision set is required for the outstar layer.

In CPN's grayscale learning, a predetermined supervision set and a training set are provided. For unsupervised learning, the following method is used. For each training vector x of class c, incorporate an identity function φ to generate the supervision vector $y=\varphi(x)=x$, the CPN learns y_c, the centroid of c.

B. Compression Operation

Once the class c_i containing a subpicture x is identified, the index i is stored or transmitted. When restoring x, the outstar vector that carries the average of the vectors of class c_i is used as a replacement for x. The class index of x is the winner's index w in the Kohonen layer, and the representative subpicture of the class c_w is stored in weights $u_{w1}, u_{w2}, \ldots, u_{wm}$ (m pixels per subpicture) of the outstar layer or simply y' produced at the output of the outstar layer.

C. Compression Ratio

The picture I to be compressed is split into N subpictures of m pixels. $I = (m, N)$. The indices generated by the Kohonen layer requires $N \cdot \lg_2 h$ bits for storage (h is the number of classes or winning nodes after the training stage.) The weight matrix U (the part

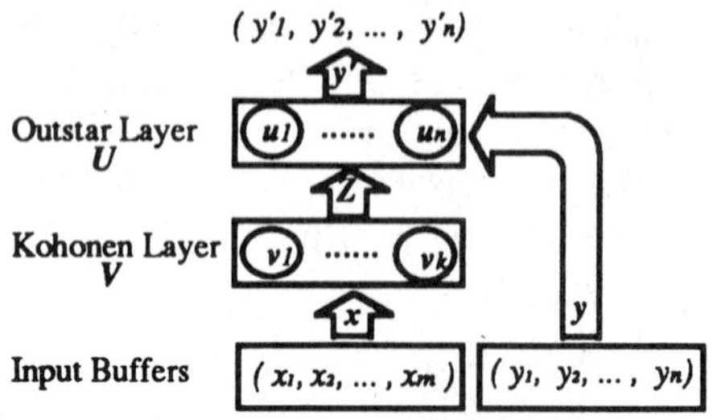

Fig. 3 *Forward-only* CPN: Kohonen layer self-organizes by applying AVQ on x. Outstar layer adjusts weights with z and supervision y.

emanating from winner nodes to outstar nodes) of the outstar layer is also needed. The compression rate is

$$Q = \frac{b \cdot m \cdot N}{N \cdot \lg_2 h + c \cdot h \cdot m}$$

where b is the number of bits needed to store a pixel value (e.g., a grayscale real), c is the number of bits needed to store the value of a connection weight in U, and m is both the number of outstar nodes and the input dimension [6].

D. Decompression Process

Class indices given by the classifier layer are stored to recall subpictures which, in turn, are put together to reconstruct the picture. The pixel values of the subpictures are stored in the weights connected from Kohonen winners to outstar nodes [6].

E. Distortion Ratio

The compression error is the sum of the differences between each pixel in the original picture I and the corresponding one in the restored picture I'. The lossy compression has the *error* E distributed over the picture [4], [6]: $E = abs(I - I')$.

V. Experimental Results

The experiments were performed on one computer drawing (Bear) of 256^2 black-and-white pixels and two black-and-white (actually grayscale) photographs (Boy and House). The photographs were scanned and converted into picture files with a resolution of 300 dots (scanning pixels) per inch, in two different modes: the extra fine half-tone (bit map) mode and the 16 gray-level (grayscale) mode. Three different sizes (in pixels) were obtained from scanning: 256^2, 512^2, and 1024^2 pixels. The grayscale-supervised CPN compression results are discussed in [6]. The subpicture sizes are 2^2 pixels and 4^2 pixels. The distortion percentage is E, the total difference, over the size of the original data size. Table 1 shows the error-free FSSO network results. Note that the compression rate increases (but only up to some limit) with larger pictures since more subpictures are repeated. In Table 2, selective entries from the results of using the grayscale-supervised CPN are compared with the best results (selected from a large set of test cases with different training parameters) obtained from the non-supervised CPNs using KFM or FSSO layer. Note that although the general purpose grayscale-supervised CPN seems to achieve higher compression rates with smaller errors the restored pictures of the non-supervised CPNs convey better visual perception due to the learning of meaningful features such as line segments (Fig. 4).

VI. Discussion

Though the Kohonen classifier approximates the centroids, the trained Kohonen weights are not used for picture restoration. This is because the nearest-neighbor method of AVQ cannot sufficiently approximate centroids without massive computation. Instead of taking the Kohonen weights as pixel values, an outstar layer is used to average the pixel values in the learning process.

TABLE 1.
FSSO Network (E=0, D=Network Dimension)

Subpicture Size	4^2	8^2	16^2	32^2	64^2
Bear (256^2)					
Q	1.23	1.76	1.82	1.59	0.999
Classes	1022	455	134	40	16
D	64^2	32^2	16^2	8^2	4^2
Boy (512^2)					
Q	1.33	2.23	1.48	1.04	0.99
Classes	11	170	2072	944	256
D	256^2	128^2	64^2	32^2	16^2
Boy (1024^2)					
Q	1.33	2.65	1.94	1.13	0.99
Classes	9	121	5378	3463	1024
D	1024^2	256^2	128^2	64^2	32^2
House (512^2)					
Q	1.33	2.24	1.92	1.17	1
Classes	12	161	1494	836	253
D	256^2	128^2	64^2	32^2	16^2
House (1024^2)					
Q	1.33	2.65	**2.68**	1.32	1.03
Classes	9	124	3307	2916	983
D	1024^2	256^2	128^2	64^2	32^2

TABLE 2.
Comparison of Supervised and "Non-Supervised" CPNs on Processing Bear (256^2)

	Q	E(%)	Picture #
GrayScale-Supervised CPN (with KFM layer)			
Subpicture Size = 2^2	1.99	4.6	
Subpicture Size = 4^2	7.88	**6.5**	(2)
"Non-supervised" CPN (with KFM layer)			
Subpicture Size = 2^2	1.33	1.44	(3)
Subpicture Size = 4^2	2.86	**12.89**	(4)
"Non-supervised" CPN (with FSSO layer)			
Subpicture Size = 2^2	1.33	0.5	(5)
Subpicture Size = 4^2	3.82	**12.02**	(6)

When using an FSSO layer as the classification layer of CPN, the effective radius for weight adjustment over a winner's neighborhood is 1. Hence, only the winner adapts. When using a KFM, the pattern classes perceived after training is attributed to the effects of the starting adaptation radius, the radius retardation, and the dimension of the KFM. In general, if the starting radius is a large fraction of the network dimension, the network is inclined to produce fewer winners that represent more generalized classes. If the chosen radius retardation is small, the examination of such generalization intensifies in the AVQ process.

Determining the minimal dimension of the classifier layer to achieve an MSE smaller than a given tolerance is an *NP* problem and there are solutions proposed in [15]. By giving a small layer we guarantee the compression ratio by forcing the network to utilize at most all the available nodes as class indices. An FSSO layer is more suitable than a KFM for this purpose.

The experimental results meet most of the expectation but also reveal a few issues. We have little to measure the perception conveyance; and MSE does not always indicate how well features are preserved.

Till now, the recognition of similar patterns of variant scales, translations, and rotations can be done either by preprocessing the data and transforming them into a different representation [16], or by using other complex neural networks ([17], [18]) for delivering normalized vectors.

Conventional training methods dictate a uniform dimension in the training vectors. If the Euclidean distance between two vectors of different dimensions can be calculated, the network can benefit from such and perceive pattern features of variant scales. Dimensions of vectors can be magnified or reduced by a smart preprocessing layer (Fig. 5a, b). The result is the Euclidean distance between two vectors originally having different dimensions can be compared for natural clustering. An additional network structure (usually a network layer) is required to learn the *magnification* or *reduction* function (Fig. 5c). Acoustic data are usually one-dimensional, hence, the *scaling* is done by distributing or averaging vectors on a single-dimension basis (Fig. 5d); while pictorial data require rescaling in two dimensions. Other preprocessing functions are *translation*, *rotation*, *mirroring*, and *focusing*. Their descriptions are similar to *scaling*. These functions must be learned by preprocessing apparatus in order to achieve a collaborated applicational capability in a neural network.

Future work will be focused on the formalization of these preprocessing functions, the learning rules of the function approximation, and the structures of the preprocessing network layers.

(1)

(2)

(3)

(4)

(5)

(6)

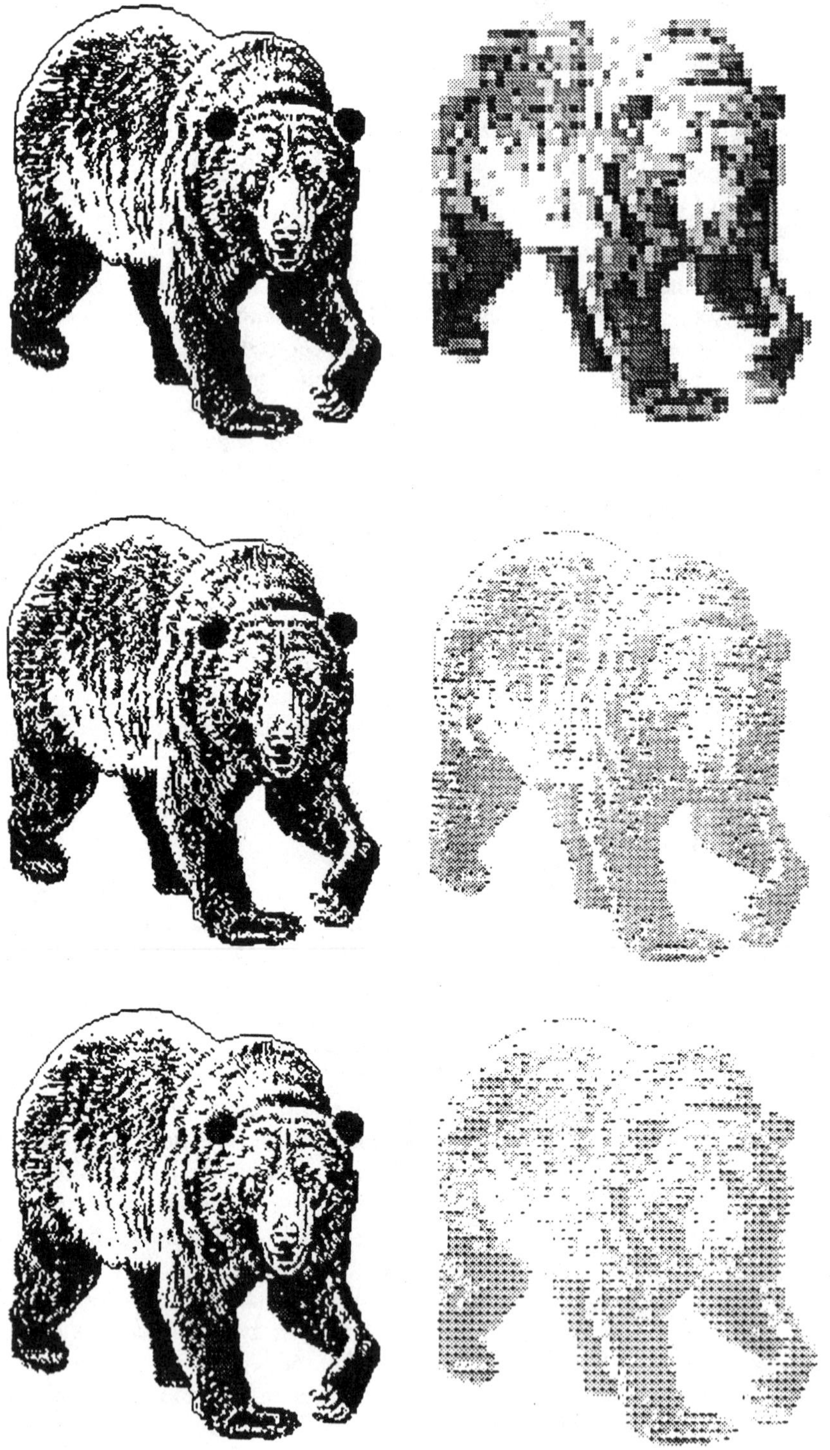

Fig. 4. The original is (1) and others (2-6) have the same numbering as in Table 2:

(2) has higher compression and smaller MSE but not much detail.

(3) shows the learning of edges and lines on the back of the bear.

(4) has larger MSE but pertains more detail than (2) (CPN with KFM layer.)

(5) is almost identical to the original.

(6) has almost twice MSE than (2) but pertains more detail (CPN with FSSO layer.)

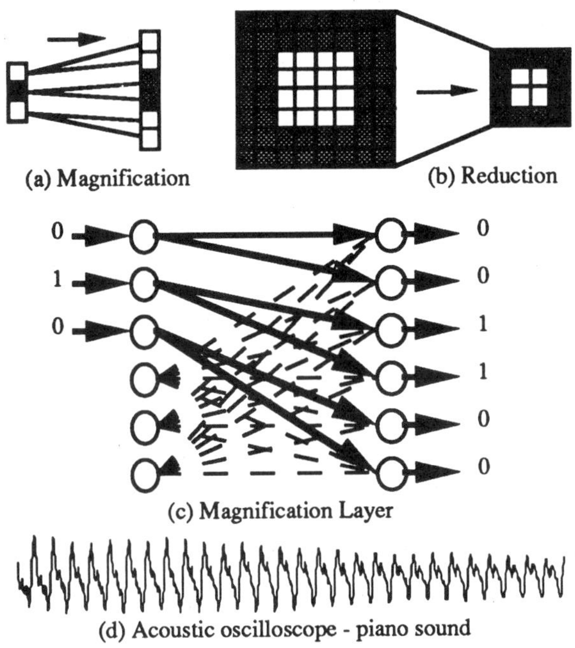

Fig. 5 One-dimensional vector magnification (a) and two-dimensional vector reduction (b). The preprocessing layer learns the magnification (c). Acoustic data compression can benefit from rescaling the repeated patterns (sound waves) (d).

ACKNOWLEDGMENTS

We would like to thank the National Center for Supercomputing Applications (NCSA) at Champaign, Illinois for providing us the computing resources on their supercomputers (Connection Machine and Cray YMP). The authors also acknowledge the support from BDM International.

REFERENCES

[1] D. Lelewer, and D. Hirschberg, "Data compression," *ACM Computing Surveys*, vol. 19, pp. 261-292, 1987.

[2] D. E. Rumelhart and D. Zipser, "Feature discovery by competitive learning," *Parallel Distributed Processing: Explorations in the Microstructure of Cognition*, vol. 2, pp. 151-193, MIT Press, 1986.

[3] V. R. de Sa and D. H. Ballard, "Top-down teaching enables non-trivial clustering via competitive learning," *University of Rochester, Computer Science Department*, Technical Report 402, 1991.

[4] M. Mougeot, R. Azencott, and B. Angeniol, "Image compression with back propagation: improvement of the visual restoration using different cost functions," *IEEE Trans. Neural Networks*, vol. 4, pp. 467-476, 1991.

[5] W.-C. Fang, B. J. Sheu, O. T.-C. Chen, and J. Choi, "A VLSI neural processor for image data compression using self-organization networks," *IEEE Trans. Neural Networks*, vol 3, pp. 506-518, 1992.

[6] W. Chang, H. S. Soliman, and A. H. Sung, "Image data compression using counterpropagation network," *IEEE Systems, Man, and Cybernetics*, vol. 1, pp. 405-409, 1992.

[7] R. Hecht-Nielsen, "Counterpropagation networks," *Applied Optics*, vol. 26, pp. 4979-4984, 1987.

[8] R. Hecht-Nielsen, "Applications of counterpropagation networks," *IEEE Trans. Neural Networks*, vol. 1, pp. 131-141, 1988.

[9] T. Kohonen, *Self-Organization and Associative Memory*,2nd ed. New York, NY: Springer-Verlag, 1988.

[10] S. Grossberg, "Some networks that can learn, remember, and reproduce any number of complicated space-time patterns," *Journal of Mathematics and Mechanics*, vol. 19, pp. 53-91, 1969.

[11] G. Carpenter and S. Grossberg, "A massively parallel architecture for a self-organizing neural pattern recognition machine," *Computer Vision, Graphics and Image Processing*, vol. 37, pp. 54-115, 1987.

[12] R. Beale & T. Jackson, *Neural Computing*, Adam Hilger, 1990.

[13] R. J. T. Morris, L. D. Rubin, and H. Tirri, "Neural network techniques for object orientation detection: solution by optimal feedforward network and learning vector quantization approaches," *IEEE Trans. Pattern Anal. Machine Intell.*, vol. 12, pp. 215-223, 1990.

[14] B. Kosko, *Neural Networks and Fuzzy Systems*, Prentice-Hall, 1992.

[15] Y. Lirov, "Optimal dimensioning of counterpropagation neural networks", *International Joint Conference on Neural Networks*, vol. 2, pp. 455-459, 1991.

[16] J. A. Starzyk and S. Chai, "Vecor contour representation for object recognition in neural networks," *IEEE Systems, Man, and Cybernetics*, vol. 1, pp. 399-404, 1992.

[17] K. Fukushima, S. Miyake, and T. Ito, "Neocognitron: a neural network model for a mechanism of visual pattern recognition," *IEEE Trans. Systems, Man, and Cybernetics*, Sept/Oct, pp. 826-834, 1983.

[18] S. J. Perantonis and P. J. G. Lisboa, "Translation, rotation and scale invariant pattern recognition by high-order neural networks and moment classifiers," *IEEE Trans. Neural Networks*, vol. 3, pp. 241-251, 1992.

Image Compression using Topological Maps and MLP

Gilles BUREL & Jean-Yves CATROS
Thomson CSF, Laboratoires Electroniques de Rennes
Avenue de Belle Fontaine, 35510 Cesson-Sévigné, France

***Abstract*— Image compression is an essential task for image storage and transmission. We propose a compression technique in which an MLP predictor takes advantage of the topological properties of the Kohonen algorithm. The Kohonen algorithm creates a code-book which is used for Vector Quantization of the source image. Then, an MLP is trained to predict references to code-book, allowing further compression. Even with difficult images, the result is a reduction of 15% to 20% of the bit rate compared with classical Vector Quantization techniques, for the same quality of decoded images.**

***Keywords*— Image Compression, Multi-Layers Perceptron, Backpropagation, Topological maps, Prediction.**

I. Introduction

Image compression is an essential task for image storage and transmission. As these domains have become increasingly important, the theory and practice of image compression have received increased attention. Since the bandwidth of many communication systems, or mass memory storage capacities are relatively inextensible, some kind of data compression is required to face the growing amount of information that people want to transmit or store.

Existing compression techniques dedicated to static images can be grouped in 3 great families, on the basis of their specific nature :

1. **Predictive techniques** take profit of image redundancy to predict the luminance of a pixel according to its neighbourhood.

2. **Vector Quantization** takes advantage of image redundancy to define a code-book for image blocks.

3. **Transform Coding** performs compression of image blocks by energy preserving transformations that pack maximum information on a minimum number of samples.

A good review of image compression techniques can be found in [5] [7]. Predictive techniques are the easiest to implement, but they show some lack of robustness and do not achieve high compression rates (generally, they only take profit of redundancies between adjacent pixels). Transform Coding or Vector Quantization techniques are preferently used when higher compression rates are required. Their better performances are mainly due to the fact that they take into account large image blocks, taking profit this way of a larger amount of redundancies. A comparative study is provided in [4]. It shows the interest of Vector Quantization techniques when high compression rates are required (bit rate under 1 bit per pixel). For smaller compression rates (bit rate above 2 bits per pixel), transform coding performs better.

In the neural network field, Cotrell, Munro, and Zipser [3] have proposed a method for image compression that lies in the Transform Coding family. It is based on a 3-layers perceptron, that performs identity mapping of image blocks via a small hidden layer. Its performances are the same as those of the classical Discrete Cosinus Transform technique. Hence, it should be used preferently for small compression rates. For high compression rates, techniques of the VQ family should be prefered.

The method we propose [2] lies in the Vector Quantization family. We use Kohonen's topological maps [8] for block compression of digital images by Vector Quantization, and an MLP trained by backpropagation [10] to perform further compression by prediction of references to code-book. The paper is organized as follows. In section 2, we shortly describe the principle of VQ techniques, and compare the performances of neural and non-neural VQ algorithms. In section 3, we explain the proposed approach, that takes advantage of topological properties of Kohonen algorithm to design an MLP predictor for further compression. We also describe the structures of corresponding coder and decoder, and we discuss experimental results.

II. Principle of Vector Quantization techniques

Vector Quantization is a compression technique that has been widely used ([1], [6] for instance). The method consists in dividing the image in small blocks, and replacing each block by an index. The index is a reference to a code-book of standard blocks: it indicates which block of the code-book is the closest to the image block. The code-book is generally built using the LBG algorithm [9].

Let us note K the number of pixels in a block, and M the size of the code-book. Assuming the availability of the code-book on the decoder side, the compression achieved is $(log_2 M)/K$ bits per pixel. To maintain a small distortion on a lot of images, a huge code-book is required. Furthermore, it is necessary to use large blocks sizes in order to take profit of a large number of redundancies. That's why we prefer an approach in which the code-book is adapted to each image (or to each group of images). Such a point of view has already been suggested in [6]. It allows to use small code-books, and quite small block sizes. For the experiment described below, we use a code-book of 256 blocks of 3x3 pixels.

The counterpart is the need to transmit or store the code-book with each image, or each group of similar images. But we will show below that it isn't very costly. There is also the need to adapt the code-book for each image, or group of images. This may be a drawback for TV applications, due to real time constraints. Hence, our method is more dedicated to image storage, and transmission of satellite images or aerial images (more generally transmission of individual images rather than video sequences). Furthermore, whithin the context of compression of TV images, it is better to use techniques based on movement estimation.

We describe in the next section experiments done with a data-base of 4 difficult images, often used to evaluate compression algorithms: "foot", "Kiel", "calendar", and "boat" (figure 1).

To compare the performances of VQ algorithms, we have built a data-base of 15716 blocks of 3x3 pixels, randomly extracted from images "foot", "Kiel", and "calendar".

Figure 2 shows the mean square error of each algorithm versus the number of iterations. KH stands for the Kohonen algorithm [8]. It is clear that all these algorithms reach approximately the same performances in terms of mean-square error. The exception is the k-means algorithm, which is likely to be trapped in a local minimum. Hence, we want to emphasis the idea that the advantage of Kohonen algorithm over LBG is not its performances as a Vector Quantizer, but its hability to preserve topology. The objective of the next section is to show how an MLP can take profit of these topological properties to increase the compression rate without degradation of the decoded image.

III. Taking profit of topological properties

A. Basic ideas

Figures 3 shows the images of indexes obtained using code-books built by Kohonen algorithm (KH), and LBG. The topological properties of the Kohonen algorithm clearly appear: The image obtained with KH is very coherent, while the image obtained with LBG looks like noise.

To take profit of preservation of topology, we propose to compress the image of indexes itself. The idea is to use a predictor to provide an estimation of an index knowing its causal neighbourhood. An MLP [10] trained by backpropagation seems to be a good candidate to achieve that task. If we obtain a good prediction, it will be possible to compress the image of indexes itself by transmitting only the prediction error. We will perform reversible compression of the image of indexes, because we don't want to degrade it. So, the reconstructed original image will be exactly the same whether we use the predictor or not. This will allow to measure the gain provided by use of prediction simply by comparing the resulting bit rates.

The MLP receives on input the causal neighbourhood $\mathcal{N} = \{C_1, C_2, C_3, C_4\}$ of the index C to predict, and provides on output an estimation $\widehat{C}$ of C.

C_1	C_2	C_3
C_4	$C?$	

We have evaluated the performances of various MLP architectures. 2-layers MLP offer generally quite poor performances. A good compromise between performances and complexity is obtained with a 4-layers MLP (4+12+8+1 neurons). The neuron model is a linear summator (with bias) followed by a non-linear function (hyperbolic tangent), exept for the output neuron which is linear, and the input neurons which do nothing.

The interest of topology preservation can be easily justified on a mathematical point of view. The best possible predictor according to a quadratic criteria is the predictor which minimizes the mean square prediction error $E\{(\widehat{C} - C)^2\}$, where E designs the mathematical expectancy.

$$E\{(\hat{C}-C)^2\} = E_{\mathcal{N}} E_{C|\mathcal{N}}\{(\hat{C}-C)^2|\mathcal{N}\}$$

but

$$E_{C|\mathcal{N}}\{(\hat{C}-C)^2|\mathcal{N}\} = (\hat{C}-\bar{C})^2 + var_{C|\mathcal{N}}\{C|\mathcal{N}\}$$

Where $\bar{C}$ designs $E_{C|\mathcal{N}}\{C|\mathcal{N}\}$. So the best predictor is:

$$\hat{C}(\mathcal{N}) = E_{C|\mathcal{N}}\{C|\mathcal{N}\}$$

and its mean square error is:

$$E\{(\hat{C}-C)^2\} = E_{\mathcal{N}}\left\{var_{C|\mathcal{N}}\{C|\mathcal{N}\}\right\}$$

Hence, it is obvious that no good prediction can be obtained if topology isn't preserved, because $var_{C|\mathcal{N}}\{C|\mathcal{N}\}$ would always be high. And, of course, since we have shown that $E_{\mathcal{N}}\left\{var_{C|\mathcal{N}}\{C|\mathcal{N}\}\right\}$ is the theoretical lower bound of mean square prediction error, neither the MLP nor any other predictor can provide a better prediction than that.

On the contrary, if topology is preserved, $var_{C|\mathcal{N}}\{C|\mathcal{N}\}$ will generally be small, hence there is no theoretical obstacle to good prediction.

B. *The structure of the coder and the decoder*

Figures 4 and 5 show the structure of the coder and decoder, and the messages format. To compress a source image (SI), the coder computes a topological code-book using Kohonen algorithm (to achieve very fast convergence, the Kohonen network is initialized with a codebook computed on a large set of images). Then, it computes the image of indexes (II). It computes the weights of the MLP predictor (again, to achieve very fast convergence, the MLP is initialized with weights computed on a large set of images of indexes). It computes the prediction errors (PE), then the corresponding optimum Huffman code, and computes the message. The message contains a header: bit P indicates if the predictor is used or not, bits UC, UM, UH indicate respectively if the code-book, the MLP, and/or the Huffman follow (for update). Then, if P=1, the prediction errors follow, else the image of indexes follows.

The decoder reads the header, updates the code-book, the predictor, and/or the Huffman codes if UC, UM, and/or UH is/are set. Then, if P=1, it reconstructs the image of indexes using the predictor and the prediction errors, else it reads directly the image of indexes. The image (RI) is then reconstructed from the image of indexes thanks to the code-book.

C. *Experimental results*

The table below shows some results obtained on the previously mentioned images. These images, often used to test compression algorithms, are difficult images. So, these results provide a lower bound of expected results on more classical images.

image	foot	Kiel	calendar	boat
header	3071	3063	3053	3080
data	32567	38440	33247	21547
message	35668	41503	36300	24667
source	358425	414720	358425	254016
bpp (P=0)	0.94	0.93	0.94	0.96
bpp(P=1)	0.79	0.80	0.81	0.77
gain	16%	14%	14%	20%

Lines 2 to 4 indicate respectively the size (in bytes) of the header, the data field, and the message (header+data), when the predictor is used. The size of the header correspond to the worst possible case (UC=UM=UH=1, which means that everything is updated), in order to indicate the lower bounds of possible performances. Line 5 reminds the size in bytes of the source image. Lines 6 and 7 indicate respectively the bit rate in bits per pixel when VQ is used alone, and when both VQ and prediction are used. The last line shows the gain in bit rate provided by use of the MLP predictor (we remind that it corresponds to the worst possible case because we have assumed that UC=UM=UH=1).
Photographies of the reconstructed images are not provided here, because differences with source images can be visually detected only on high quality video screens.

IV. Conclusion

We have proposed an approach for image compression that takes profit of both Vector Quantization properties and topological properties of Kohonen algorithm. An MLP predictor is used to compress the image of indexes provided by Vector Quantization, and that is possible only because topology has been preserved. Even in the worst possible configurations (difficult images plus need to update all the internal parameters), the benefit of that approach over classical Vector Quantization is a reduction of 15% to 20% of the bit rate.

Further work could include definition of a variant of the MLP model to achieve better prediction (this model will use non-linear synapses), extensive tests on large bases of images, and sudy of potential for image perception as well as compression/communication.

REFERENCES

[1] R. ARAVIND, Allen GERSHO, "Image compression based on Vector Quantization with finite memory", Optical Engineering, July 1987, vol 26, $n^o 7$

[2] Gilles BUREL, "Procédé de compression d'images", French patent n° 91-11609, september 20th, 1991

[3] G.W.COTTREL, P.MUNRO, D.ZIPSER, "Image compression by backpropagation", ICS Report 8702, February 1987, University of California, San Diego

[4] Thomas R. FISCHER, Mary E. BLAIN, "A comparison of Vector Quantization Subband and Tranform Coding of Imagery", International Symposium on Circuits and Systems, 1989, pp 1520-1523

[5] Robert FORCHHEIMER, Torbjörn KRONANDER, "Image coding - From waveforms to animation", IEEE trans. on ASSP, vol 37, $n^o 12$, December 1989

[6] Morris GOLDBERG, Paul R. BOUCHER, "Image compression using adaptative Vector Quantization", IEEE trans. on Communications, vol COM-34, $n^o 2$, February 1986

[7] A.K. JAIN, "Image Data Compression : A Review", Proceedings of the IEEE, vol 69, $n^o 3$, March 1981

[8] Teuvo KOHONEN, "Self-Organization and Associative Memory", Springer-Verlag, 1984

[9] Y. LINDE, A. BUZO, R.M. GRAY, "An algorithmm for Vector Quantizer design", IEEE Trans. on Communications, vol COM-28, $n^o 1$, January 1980

[10] D.E. RUMELHART, G.E. HINTON, R.J. WILLIAMS, "Learning internal representations by error backpropagation", Parallel Distributed Processing, D.E. RUMELHART and J.L. Mc CLELLAND, Chap8, Bradford book - MIT Press - 1986

Figure 1: From left to right and top to bottom: images "boat", "foot", "Kiel", and "calendar"

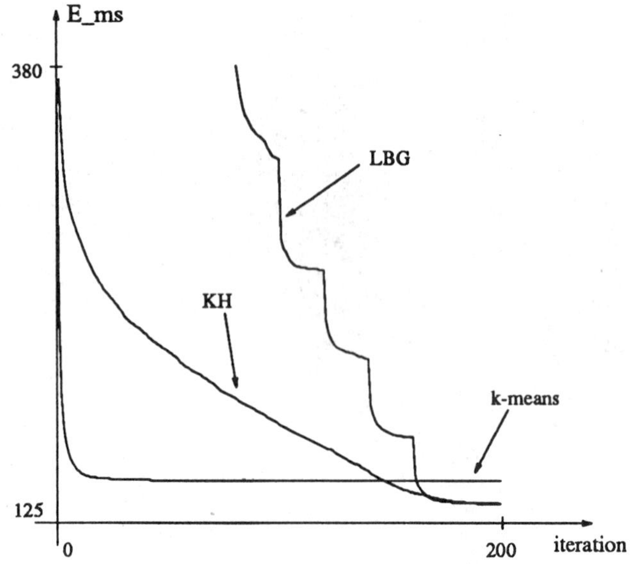

Figure 2: Comparison of algorithms KH, LBG and k-means

Figure 3: images of indexes of "foot" obtained by LBG (top) and KH (bottom)

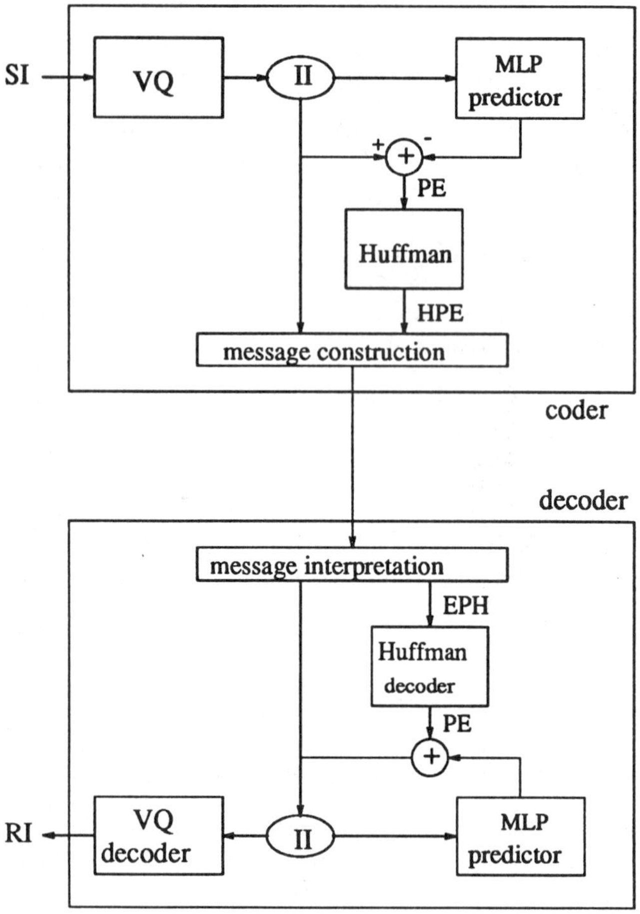

Figure 4: Structure of the coder and the decoder

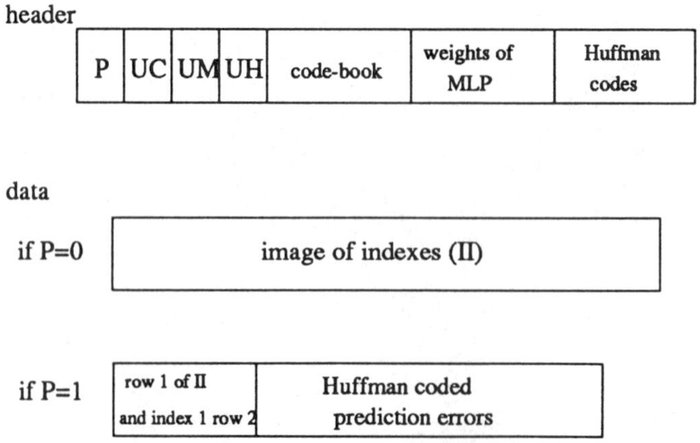

Figure 5: Format for compressed image

THAM 18.5

APPLICATION OF NEURAL NETWORKS ON COLOR ERROR REDUCTIONS IN TELEVISION RECEIVERS

Shaofan Xu, Paul B. Crilly

Electrical & Computer Engineering Dept.
The University of Tennessee, Knoxville

ABSTRACT

The application of neural network on color error reductions in television receivers was investigated. A backpropagation neural network with one hidden layer of seven processing elements gave the best result. About 70% of color errors was reduced. The color error reduction was displayed with a CIE chromaticity diagram and tested with a video graphics system set-up.

INTRODUCTION

Presently most of the color television manufacturers have changed the display White set-up from the NTSC (National Television System Committee) standard to a more bluish-white set-up. In addition, different display primaries from those of the NTSC standard were used for a brighter display. In doing these, many other colors significantly differed from the NTSC standard.

To illustrate the color errors, a CIE chromaticity diagram [1] was produced as shown in Figure 1 with a computer simulation program. In a CIE chromaticity diagram, any color is represented with its (x, y) coordinates. The triangle encloses all the colors a TV receiver can display, with Red, Green, and Blue at the vertices. In Figure 1, the little squares represent source colors, while the diamonds represent display colors. The distances between the squares and diamonds indicate the color errors.

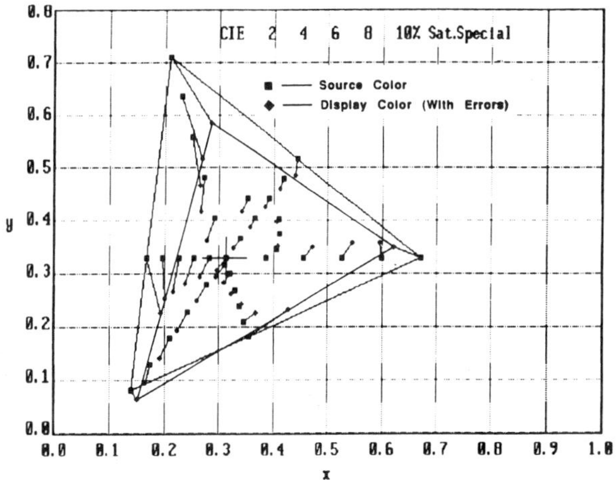

Figure 1 Chromaticity Diagram Showing Color Errors. (White Set-up at 8200^0 K)

NEURAL NETWORK SOLUTION

Neural network method was proposed. Neural Networks have been extensively studied during the last decade [2]. A neural network is a computing system which is useful for complicated problems where an exact mathematical model is hard to establish. The basic processing element in an artificial neural network is the neuron. Neurons, or processing elements (PEs), are organized into layers.

Neural Network Design

In the application of the color error reductions, there are three inputs, the color difference signals $(R\text{-}Y)_d$, $(G\text{-}Y)_d$ and $(B\text{-}Y)_d$, and three outputs, the desired color difference signals $(R\text{-}Y)_r$, $(G\text{-}Y)_r$ and $(B\text{-}Y)_r$. The number of PEs for input layer and output layer is fixed at 3. Only the number of PEs for the hidden layer is to be determined. The neural network for this application should be like that in Figure 2. This

0-7803-0843-3/93 $3.00

is a supervised back-propagation neural network that uses the sigmoid transfer function. Many neural networks have been built with different numbers of hidden layers and different PE numbers in the hidden layers.

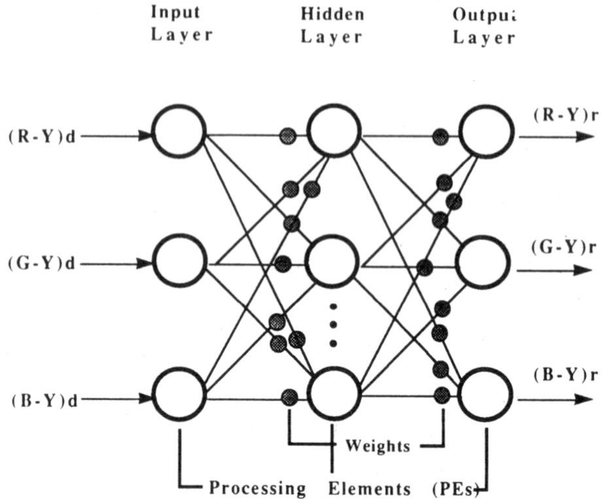

Figure 2 Neural Network for Color Difference Signal Processing.

Neural Network Training, Testing and Improvement

Training and testing were made to those networks. It turned out that optimum results were obtained with one hidden layer of seven PEs. The neural network (RGB_Y) with 7 PEs in the hidden layer was chosen for training with the color difference data. After training, the neural network was tested. The test result indicated that this network needed some improvement. One way was to train the neural network with more uniform data.

Results

To compare the large number of input and output data, some computer programs were needed and created. The input, output and desired data were compared using one of these programs. Approximately 70% of the output data were closer to the desired data than the input data. It was found that a large majority of the data with large errors, for example, the (B-Y) data, had been improved.

Then, these data were inputted to a program to plot a chromaticity diagram, Fig. 3. The comparison of this diagram with that diagram before color error corrections, Fig. 1, verified that most of the color errors were greatly reduced.

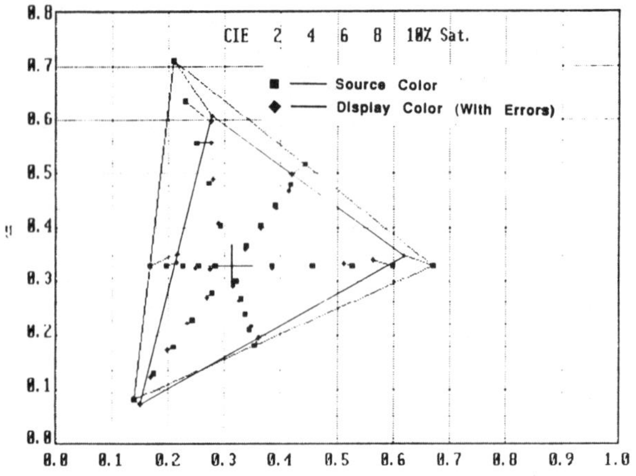

Figure 3 Chromaticity Diagram after Error Correction.

COLOR TEST SYSTEM SET-UP AND COLOR ERROR REDUCTION EVALUATION

To see on a monitor how the color errors are reduced, a color test and evaluation system was designed and assembled. Color bar patterns and frames of video with and without neural network processing were generated and displayed on this system. Color measurements of the color bars were taken. Subjective viewing scenes. The color bar and video scene evaluation verified the effect of the neural network.

CONCLUSIONS

Neural networks for reduction of color errors in color TV receivers were designed, built and tested. The results of the networks were examined with computer programs and verified with a color test and evaluation system.

REFERENCES

[1] John T. Cahill, Robert L. Werner, Petition of Radio Corporation of America and National Broadcasting Company, Inc. for Approval of Color Standards for the RCA Color Television System, June 25, 1953.

[2] Maureen Caudill, "Neural Networks PRIMER Part I", AI Expert, December 1987, pp. 46-52.

A Neural Network Based Edge Detector

Kamran Etemad and Rama Chellappa
Department of Electrical Engineering
University of Maryland
College Park, Maryland

Abstract:
A new approach to the edge detection problem based on the nonlinear mapping and generalization capabilities of multilayer feed forward neural networks is proposed. The task of edge detection is broken into two parts: (1) Mapping typical gray levels in primitive small image blocks (e.g. 3 x 3 windows) to their corresponding most likely edge patterns using a simple neural network. (2) Combining this locally derived information (including presence, orientation and strength of edge) in a consistent way. Some edge detection experiments based on this scheme are provided. The suggested scheme, because of its parallel structure is fast and can be easily implemented using analog VLSI hardware.

I. Introduction

Edges in an image are the results of rapid changes of intensities which in turn reflect changes in some physical and surface properties of the objects in the scene such as illumination, orientation and reflectance. They contain very useful structural information about objects' boundaries in a compact form. Thus edge detection serves to simplify the analysis of images by dramatically reducing the amount of data to be processed. Edge information is useful in many image understanding problems such as segmentation, registration, feature and line extraction, and stereo matching. During the last 20 years many algorithms have been developed for edge detection among which the most important ones are: The Marr-Hildreth [1] method based on detecting zero crossings at the output of Laplacian- Gaussian operators of different widths, Haralick's [2] facet model based method that uses the zero crossings of a second directional derivative of Gaussian edge operator; and Canny's [3] computational approach to edge detection by formulating the task as a numerical optimization problem. There are also other algorithms for refining step edges derived from Gaussian operators [4], and also some linear feature extraction and line finding methods based on two-dimensional autoregressive random field models [5].

There are also other edge and line detection schemes in which neural networks are either implicitly or explicitly involved. Grant and Page [6] have compared Hopfield associative memory with matched filter implementation for detecting line patterns in images corrupted by Gaussian noise. Their result show that the performance of associative memory is inferior but can at best be close to that of matched filter. On the other hand, Meer, Wang and Wechsler[7] have described the problem of univariance between goodness of fit and the strength of an edge which occurs in most template matching edge operators. To solve this problem they have developed a new set of edge operators based on a vector space analysis, and suggested that detection of an edge be based on a proposed confidence measure of the goodness of fit to a template. Although they have not mentioned anything about neural network implementation of their method, almost all of their computations can be done in parallel using neural network models.

Recently Moura[8] and Lepage[9] have developed, independently, a so called competitive-cooperative network to refine edge patterns obtained from simple gradient operators, e.g. Sobel's or Prewitt's operators. In both methods the networks consist of several neurons corresponding to pixels in a small neighborhood of image. These neurons have competitive/cooperative effect(due to exitory and inhibitory connections) on each other. In Moura's method gradient magnitude and direction for image intensity (derived from Sobel operators) are given to the network and based on that the network enforces edge patterns normal to gradient and weakens edge patterns along gradient direction. In Lepage's method however the competitive cooperative network idea is used in a multi-scale scheme. The network consists of several layers corresponding to different resolution levels, and at each layer edges are detected using lateral connections and Sobel's operator. Edges at coarser scales will then reinforce corresponding edge patterns at finer scale through competitive/cooperative connections, so those edges in finer scales

0-7803-0999-5/93/$03.00

which are not reinforced will tend to disappear.

Also Bhatia[10] has recently suggested a single layer edge detector with competitive unsupervised learning, in which the strength and direction of the edge can then be roughly estimated using four outputs of this network.

In this paper an alternative approach to the problem based on neural networks is presented. The proposed method has features such as:

a) High speed and simplicity; since it only relies on the non-linear mapping capability of a simple neural network that directly provides the binary edge pattern as well as edge strength.

b) Edge detection independent of edge strength.

c) Incorporating contex in edge detection without going to lower resolutions.

d) Robustness to noise.

e) Extendability to corner and line detection as well as multi-resolution methods.

As image data are typically massive in nature, it is always desirable to devise methods that involve parallel processing of data or methods that can easily be implemented using parallel algorithms. On the other hand, due to massive amounts of image data, except for a small number of applications where image sizes are small, it is not feasible to process the whole image concurrently. An important characteristic of typical images is that there is a large amount of local spatial correlation among pixels; thus we are looking for efficient local processing schemes that have as much parallel computational structure as possible. But local processing of image data(i.e. block by block) raises the question of how to combine information extracted from the local processing to arrive at consistent global results, so every local processing approach must give some method of achieving this consistency.

II. Formulation of the Edge Detection Problem

The basic idea is the following: if for each primitive image block (say 3 x 3 or 5 x 5) one can correctly distinguish the edge (if there is an edge) and can properly combine the edge information (e.g. existence, orientation and strength) extracted from adjacent blocks, then a set of consistent boundaries for the whole image can be obtained.

So the problem can be broken into two parts;

1) Given any gray level pattern in a small block (e.g. 3 x 3 or 5 x 5 pixel) of an image find the corresponding "most likely" edge pattern.

2) Combine the information derived from neighboring blocks in a consistent way.

Step 1 : Edge Detection in Primitive Blocks

The problem is basically to find a nonlinear mapping from typical gray level patterns at the input to their "most likely" edges at the output. In order to solve this problem we employ the nonlinear mapping and generalization properties of multilayer feed forward neural networks.

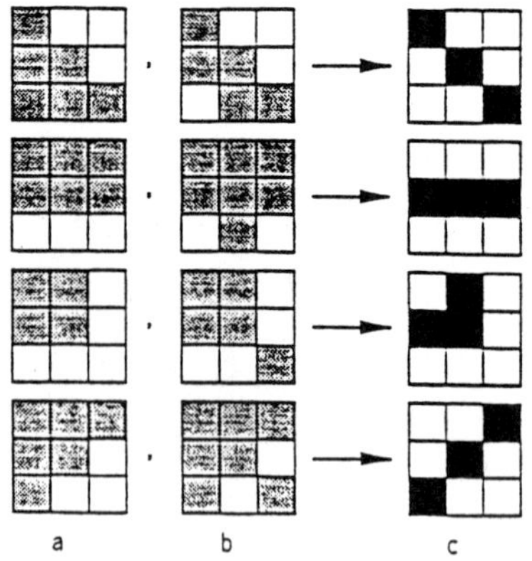

Figure 1: a. Perfect input patterns b.Imperfect input patterns c.The corresponding most likely edge patterns

The network is trained in a supervised mode, i.e. for each pattern presentation (patterns like those in the first and second columns of Fig.(1)) at the input we require the target output to be the most likely edge pattern (e.g. edge patterns like those in the third column in Fig.(1)). What we mean by "most likely" here is simply what humans may claim about the presence and orientation of the edge in the given input. The so-called completeness of the training set is of great importance since it must include almost all typical cases for a small number of gray levels(say 8 different levels between 0 and 256).

The network consists of at least three (i.e. input, hidden and output) layers. Fig.(2) shows such a network with most of the neurons having sigmoidal nonlinearity. Considering the complexity of the mapping one could expect that just two layers are not enough and our experiments have shown that even with three layers convergence of the training algorithm is fairly slow.

In any edge detection scheme in addition to edge presence and orientation one has to give a relative measure of edge strength which can be used in discarding weak as well as parasitic edges at the output. In order to extract edge strength we can again consider the problem as a nonlinear mapping which can be implemented easily using the same network with some additional (and perhaps linear) units in hidden and output layers. In our experimental network there is a special and separate linear unit at the output layer for which upon any presentation of input patterns we require the output value to be a number proportional to the edge strength. This normalized number, say between 0 and 1. is of course zero for all non-edge patterns. There are also a few linear units in the hidden layer(s) which are connected to this output only.

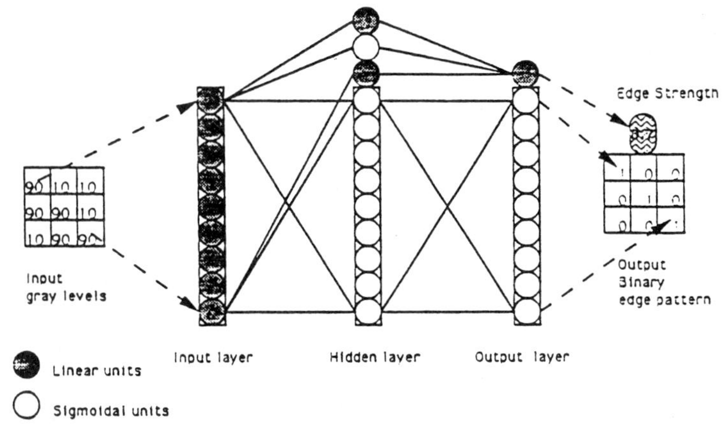

Figure 2: A simple three layer neural network that can provide the required mapping to edge patterns as well as edge strength

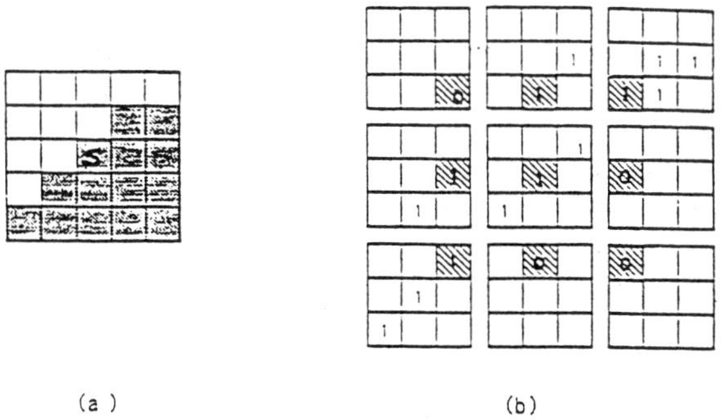

Figure 3: a) A typical gray level pattern b) Each pixel S appears in 9 blocks including its principal block; for each of these blocks a "1" means a vote for S as an edge point

Having defined the network architecture and specified input and target output pairs for a "complete" set of training data, our objective would be to minimize the difference(normally in the Euclidean sense) between the actual output of the network and the target outputs. In order to minimize this objective function one can use one of the popular training algorithms e.g. back error propagation [11] or other optimization methods like conjugate gradient or BFGS[12].

In our experiment we used all three methods and the last two methods gave us the fastest convergence. Also one can take advantage of the symmetric structure of edge detection at this level to reduce the number of free parameters(i.e. weights) to simplify training [13].

In order to consider more "typical" input patterns after some iterations of training based on perfect gray level patterns (patterns like the first column in Fig. (1)), some imperfect patterns (patterns like second column in Fig. (1)) and some noisy versions of the training data were added to them and the rest of the training was done based on both perfect and noisy patterns.

Finally, irrespective of the training algorithm used, as long as the objective error is negligible and the training data used is a good representation of typical input patterns, the resulting network gives us the required mapping. This continuous nonlinear map, at least at those points corresponding to the training data, coincides with our objective mapping and due to continuity and the so called generalization property of the resulting map we expect to obtain reasonable edge patterns on any given block of image data. Assuming that this objective is achieved, which is almost done in our experimental network, we are ready for the next step.

An alternative may be just to map the output of the network directly to the corresponding block of the output image and do this for all non-overlapping blocks. Actually this can be done only for images with very simple and straight edges and with high signal to noise ratios. In that case using non-overlapping blocks and skipping the next step would result in a method that is faster by at least a factor of 9 (for our example of 3 x 3 blocks), but in general for more complex shapes and noisy images the next step is necessary.

Step 2: Combining Edge Information

After the required mapping is achieved we need to combine the edge information derived from adjacent blocks to get boundaries that are as consistent and smooth as possible and to decrease the effect of noise and spurious edges.

There are several ways of doing this combination; for example, one simple way is to use the following observation;

As we sweep across the image each pixel appears in several window blocks. In our example of 3 x 3 windows each pixel at s=(i,j) appears in its own "principal block", which has that pixel S at its center,as well 8 surrounding blocks. Of course pixels on the boundaries are contained in fewer number of windows but we concentrate on interior pixels.

If a pixel is along an edge and if our proposed network performs its job correctly it will assign a one (corresponding to "part of an edge") to that pixel several times; see Fig.(3). In this Figure pixel S is on the edge and therefore assigned to be on the edge by five windows consistently; but on real images where noise is present, it makes sense to use a majority of votes based on the accumulated vote given by all such windows compared to a threshold. Also it is reasonable that in this majority voting policy we give more weight to the so called principal block because logically it is the window that is most informative about its central pixel. Suppose we want to claim that S is an edge point if the principal block and one other block or at least three out of five blocks except for the principal block assign one to this pixel and not an edge point otherwise. In order to implement this rule, we add up the votes given by all nine windows that contain pixel S, with two votes for the principal block, and then compare the accumulated number to three and claim an edge point only if the number is greater than three. The weight given to the principal block, minimum number of votes and threshold are parameters that depend on our choice of training data and can be obtained after several simulations. In our experment we gave 2.5 votes to principle block and 1.0 to others and compared the combined vote to 3.0, of course we need to consider blocks that are on the border separately.

Also one can use two or three windows of different sizes(e.g. 3x3, 5x5 ...) around each pixel and do the same local processing as step 1 for all of them using the same neural network approach, and then combine the results again using a majority of votes with emphasis on smaller windows. Generally the more independent votes we consider in our majority decision, the less is the number of errors and higher is the level of robustness of our results to noise. One can also consider this majority voting policy as incorporating the context information into our final decision about the edge points, which is in the same spirit as that proposed by Haralick[14].

Edge strength should also be considered in our decision process either in step 1 or in step 2. In other words, one can ignore all weak edge patterns with strengths less than a threshold and just consider strong edges in step 2, i.e. each window votes for a pixel to be an edge point only if our local edge detection in that window gives a "1" at the corresponding output neuron and the edge strength output is above some threshold. This is more like a hard decision approach. On the other hand one can multiply the vote of each window for each pixel by the edge strength derived at that window and add up all the combined votes and strengths for a pixel and compare the result to a final threshold. In this "soft decision mode", an edge is declared if this combined result is more than a preset threshold. Normally the later approach namely soft decision has a better result in terms of lower number of erroneous edge points.

III. Results and Discussion

In order to test the performance of the proposed method, we have used it to extract edges in several synthetic and real images; some of the results are shown in Fig.4. As one can see in Fig.4 (a) edges in all directions are extracted. It has been observed that the correct choice of training set as well as thresholds will affect the result significantly.

One can also use some simple pre/post processing like gray level quantization, histogram equalization or line finding algorithms to simplify the training data or to enhance the resulting edge boundaries and also to remove some fine and texture edges. Note that in this scheme we reduce the effect of noise in two steps:

First, within each primitive block, since our final training set contains noisy versions of perfect patterns and due to the generalization property of our nonlinear but continuous mapping, for small amounts of noise the output is still the most likely edge pattern. This kind of training improves the generalization, robustness and fault tolerance of the network[15,16]. Secondly, in combining information of adjacent blocks majority voting reduces the effect of noise further, as long as noise in these blocks are independent. Note that this is the only assumption we need about the noise for reliable results.

Also note that in our network edge presence and orientation are detected independent of edge strength, i.e. we have two separate networks to map gray levels to edge pattern and its strength. It may seem to be kind of redundant, but noting that we assign zero strength to all non edge patterns, we see that it provides us with more reliability (i.e. less error probability), and also a better measure for thresholding.

Another important feature of this method is that there are no iterative or complex computations involved and once the network is properly trained, the derived connection weights can be saved and used. All the computations are also parallel. Therefore compared to most analytical approaches to edge detection including Canny's and Haralick's methods our method is much faster and simpler. It is also faster than edge detectors based on sequential template matching. Some of these template matching methods can be implemented using parallel algorithms and structures like neural networks. However, their drawback is that their complexity increases as we add the number of templates (e.g. to obtain better resolution in edge orientation and/or to include corners). Whereas in our scheme the same network can be trained to satisfy all mapping requirements including ability to extract corners and edge patterns in any direction or discard all isolated lines,etc. The only difference would be the training set which could be modified in any application.

Considering Moura's and Lepage's methods, we see that they have actually used neural network to enhance edge patterns, not to detect them. Their competitive/cooperative network, and especially Lepage's multiresolution idea can be combined with our method to give a completely neural network based edge detection scheme.

Finally if we compare our results with those derived by Bhatia using competitive unsupervised learning, we see

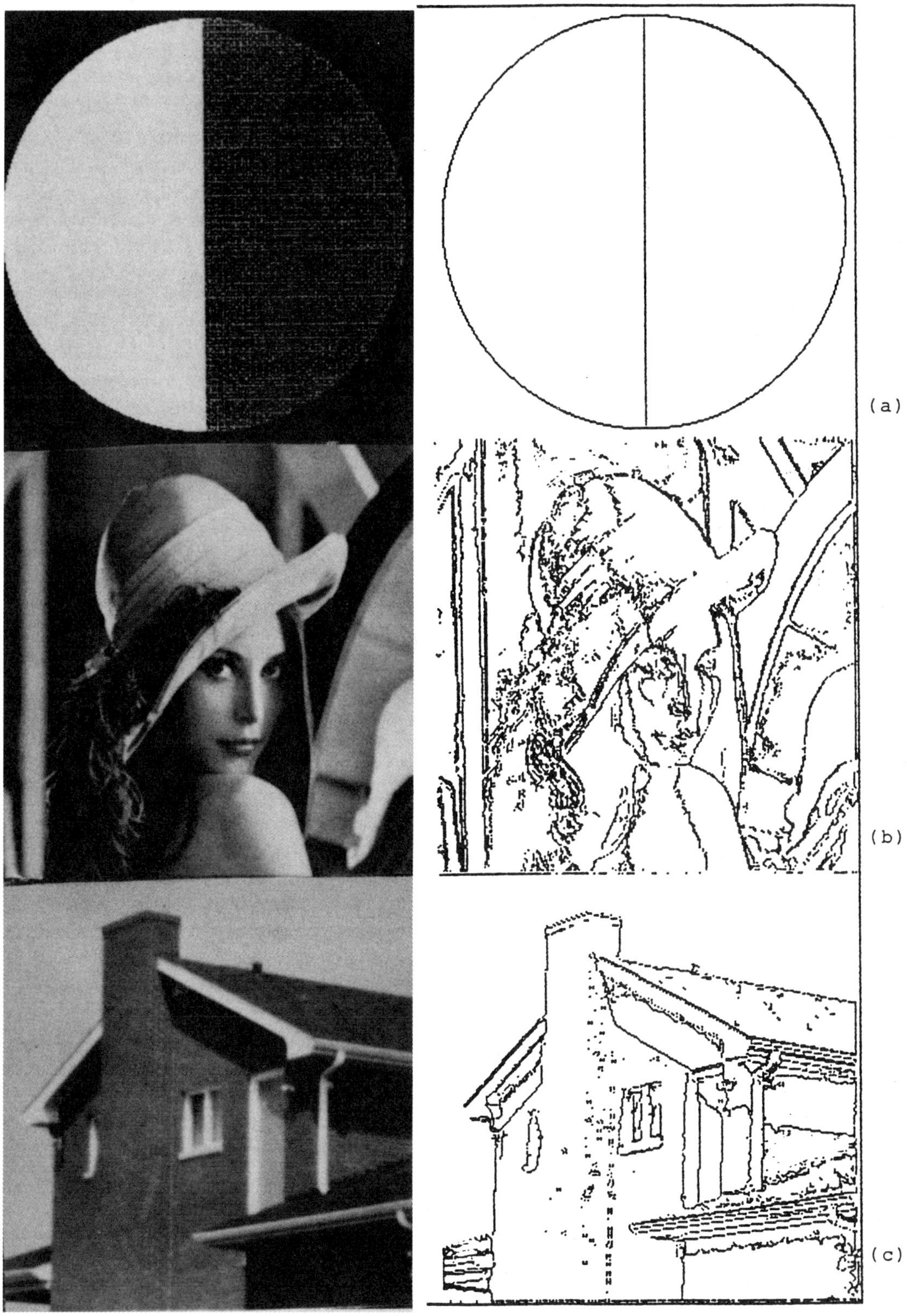

Figure 4. Examples of some synthetic and real images with their corresponding extracted edge patterns.

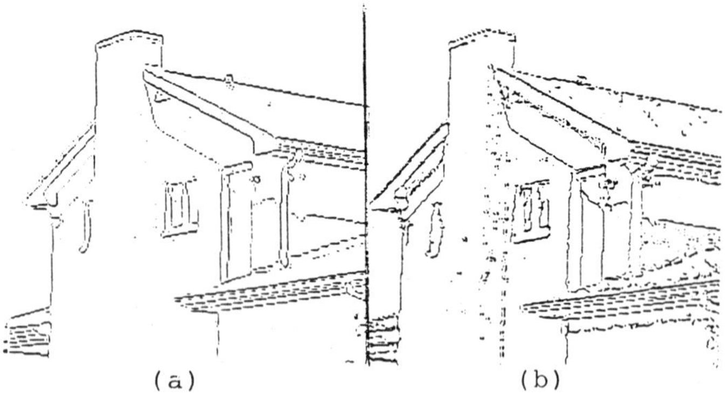

Figure 5: a) An example of edge patterns obtained using Canny's method b) our result without any pre/post processing

that as in most other cases where networks with supervised learning give better results, edge patterns extracted by our method are finer, more accurately localized, and more resistant to noise.

Figure 5. shows the edge patterns obtained from Canny's edge detector (available in KBVision package) and the result that we have obtained with our simple network. Unlike the implementation of Canny's operatorin KBVision, we have not used any post processing, and the results clearly show the potential capabilities of the suggested approach. Also, as we mentioned before, our method can be easily extended to incorporate multiresolution idea's without significantly increasing the complexity of the system.

Of course, further experiments can be done based on our proposed method with larger training sets, windows with different sizes and overlaps; also combining this method with multi-resolution and multiscale approaches improves the performance.

IV. Conclusion

Edge detection problems can be solved in two steps: edge detection in small primitive blocks of 3 x 3 or 5 x 5 pixels, which can be considered as a non-linear mapping and solved using a simple 3 or 4 layer feed-forward neural network; and then combining information derived from neighboring blocks. By setting an appropriate threshold, edge strength can be incorporated in the first or second step to discard parasitic and weak edges, we recommend the later. Since most of the computations are done by a neural network in parallel, this algorithm seems to be fast and can easily be implemented using analog VLSI hardware.

V. Bibliography

[1] D.C. Marr and E.Hildreth, "Theory of edge detection," Proc. Roy. Soc. London., Vol. B207, pp. 187-217, 1980.

[2] R.M.Haralick, " Digital step edges from zero crossings second directional derivative," IEEE Trans. Pattern Anal. Mach. Intell., Vol. PAMI-6, pp. 58-68 Jan. 1984.

[3] J.F.Canny, "A computational approach to edge detection," IEEE Trans. Pattern Anal. Mach. Intell., Vol. PAMI-8, pp. 679-698, Nov. 1986.

[4] F. Ulupinar and G.Medioni, " Refining edges detected by a LoG operator," Proceedings IEEE Conf. on Comp. Vision and Pattern Recog., pp. 202-207, June 1988.

[5] Y.T.Zhou, V. Venkateswar and R.Chellappa, " Edge detection and linear feature extraction using a 2-D random field model," IEEE Trans. Pattern Anal. Mach. Intell., Vol. 11,Jan 1989.

[6] P.M.Grant and J.P.Sage,"A comparison of neural network and matched filter processing for detecting lines in images", AIP Conf. Proceedings 151, Neural Networks for Computing, pp.194-199, Snow Bird, UT, 1986.

[7] P.Meer, S.Wang and H.Wechsler, "Edge detection by associative mapping", Tech. Rep. CAR-TR-281, CFAR, University of Maryland, College Park, Maryland,March 1987.

[8] L.Moura and F.Martin,"Edge detection through cooperation and competition", Proc. IJCNN 1991, Singapore, Vol. 3, pp. 2588-2593.

[9] R.Lepage and D.Poussart,"Multi-resolution edge detection", Proc. IJCNN 1992, Baltimore, Vol. 4, pp. 438-443.

[10] P.Bhatia, V.Srinivasan and S.H.Ong,"Single layer edge detector with competitive unsupervised learning", Proc. IJCNN 1991, Singapore, Vol. 1, pp. 634-639.

[11] D.E. Rumelhart and J.C.McClelland, Parallel Distributed Processing, Vol.1, Ch.8, pp. 318-362, Cambridge, Mass., MIT Press, 1986.

[12] R. L. Watrous, "Learning algorithms for connectionist networks: applied gradient methods of nonlinear optimization." Proc. First ICNN, pp. 619-627, June 1987.

[13] H.S. Na and Y. Park, "Symmetric neural networks and its examples." Proc. IJCNN 1992, Baltimore, Vol.1, pp.413-418

[14] R.M. Haralick and J.S.Lee, "Context dependent edge detection", Proceedings IEEE Conf. on Comp. Vision and Pattern Recog., pp. 202-207, June 1988.

[15] R.D. Clay and C.H. Sequin,"Fault tolerance training improves generalization and robustness." Proc. IJCNN, 1992, Baltimore, Vol.1, pp. 769-774.

[16] J.I. Minnix, "Fault tolerance of the back propagation neural networks trained on noisy inputs." Proc. IJCNN, 1992, Baltimore, Vol.1, pp. 847-852.

A Two-Stage Neural Net for Segmentation of Range Images *

S. Ghosal (ghosal@ms.uky.edu) and R. Mehrotra (rajiv@ms.uky.edu)
Center for Robotics & Manufacturing Systems
University of Kentucky
Lexington, KY 40506

***Abstract*— A new two-stage neural network is proposed in this paper for segmentation of range images. Range images carry viewpoint dependent depth information and are being used extensively for 3-D scene analysis and interpretation. This work concentrates on a novel NN-based system that integrates edge and surface information to generate robust surface maps in the range data. The proposed architecture has two stages - the first stage extracts the surface information through "self-learning" least-square surface fitting along a set of nonorthogonal basis functions. Daugman's projection NN stage locally computes the surface normals in the image. In the second stage, the surface and edge information compete with each other to perform region growing. The edge information is obtained using a set of Zernike moment-based operators. Kohonen's self-organizing NN is used to implement the competitive region-growing. Experimental results with real range images are shown to demonstrate the effectiveness of the proposed NN architecture.**

I. Introduction

NNs are basically connectionist machines where many hypotheses are performed in parallel and connection weights (synaptic strengths) are adapted to form nonlinear decision boundaries. Also, NN algorithms are nonparametric and make less assumptions about the underlying probability distributions. Thus it is expected that NN-based techniques would perform better in nonstationary image analysis and pattern recognition problems [8].

Recent studies in the NN field have opened up potential alternatives to conventional computer vision and pattern recognition problems. Examples include classification of images represented by translation, scale and rotation-invariant geometric and Zernike moments [7], transformation of images into generalized nonorthogonal 2-D Gabor representations for image analysis, segmentation and compression [1], texture segmentation [3, 2], range image segmentation by clustering of Zernike moment-based surface features [10], surface representation [11], dynamic image segmentation and occlusion-finding [4], spatial contrast enhancement [6], 3-D motion detection [5] etc. In this paper, we propose an integrated "self-learning" two-stage neural net (NN) architecture for extracting regions corresponding to different visible surfaces of an input range image.

Range images carry viewpoint dependent depth information about the physical scenes and are typically formed by time-of-flight range-finders. Direct interpretation of range images is not practical because of high dimensionality and huge storage requirements. Instead, it is more convenient to segment them into features that are useful for higher-level interpretation and recognition tasks. The focus of this work is on a novel two-stage NN-based approach for range image segmentation, where surface and edge information compete with each other to provide automatic segmentation of range images. In the first stage, the Daugman's projection NN is used to extract local surface features. Most of the surfaces present in range images are either planar or quadratic. Thus, biquadratic surface fitting is performed in every local neighborhood in the range data using the projection neural net. It is found that "synaptic strengths" are directly related to the surface normal components once the self-organization of the net is over. In the second stage, the surface features and edge features compete with each other to perform region-growing. Edge features are obtained using a set of Zernike moment-based detectors [12]. The Kohonen's self-organizing neural net (KSNN) is employed to implement the competitive region-growing process.

The rest of the paper is organized as follows. Some recent important work in range image segmentation is pre-

*Partially supported by the NASA-Langley Research Center Grant NAG-1-1276, and by the NIH Biomedical Research Support Grant BRSG S07 RR07114-21.

0-7803-0999-5/93/$03.00 ©1993 IEEE

sented in Section 2. Section 3 deals with the two-stage integrated NN architecture for range image segmentation. Surface feature extraction using Daugman's projection neural network and competitive region-growing using Kohonen's NN are also described. Experimental results are shown in Section 4 to demonstrate the excellent performance of the proposed technique. We present the conclusions of the present investigation in Section 5 and mention some future research activities.

II. Related Work

Range image segmentation techniques can be broadly classified into three categories: (i) Edge-based, (ii) Region-based, and (iii) Hybrid segmentation techniques.

Edge-based segmentation techniques detect boundaries between different regions. These boundaries are formed by points, called edges, where discontinuity of some surface property is detected. There are at least three types of edges in a range image: step edges, roof edges and smooth or ramp edges. Step edges are the points, where range value is discontinuous. Roof edges are the points where surface normals are discontinuous. Smooth or ramp edges are the points where surface curvature is discontinuous. Step edges are easy to detect, whereas roof and smooth edges are very difficult to detect because they can be easily corrupted by the noise. Usually in real range images, edges formed by the composition of two or more of these primitive edges are also present.

There are two main classes of region-based range image segmentation techniques. Region-growing techniques obtain a connected set of pixels to form a region by repeatedly merging neighboring regions based on the similarity of the surface properties. On the other hand, clustering methods partition the pixels of an input image into several clusters of connected pixels based on the similarity of surface properties.

The hybrid (or integrated) method refers to the combination of region-based and edge-based methods. Region-based segmentation attempts to group pixels into surface regions based on the homogeneity or similarity of surface properties. On the other hand, edge-based approach, which is also referred to as edge detection, attempts to extract discontinuities in properties that form the closed boundaries of components. Since both the edge-based and region-based methods suffer the problem of oversegmentation and undersegmentation, it is expected to use the combination of the two to solve the segmentation problem. Among the recent integrated segmentation techniques, Yokoya and Levine [13] used the combination of edge detection and curvature clustering to segment a range image. In their approach the range image of an object is divided into surface primitives which are homogeneous in their intrinsic differential geometric properties and do not contain discontinuity in either depth or surface orientation. The method employs a selective surface fit and is based on the computation of first and second partial derivatives determined by locally approximating object surfaces using biquadratic polynomials. Then by computing the Gaussian and mean curvatures and examining their signs, an initial region-based segmentation is obtained in the form of a curvature sign map. Two initial edge-based segmentations are also computed from the partial derivatives and depth values. The three initial image maps are then combined to produce the final range image segmentation. Jain and Nadabar [14] proposed an integrated method by using both the edge-based segmentation and region based segmentation to obtain robust surface segmentation. The main contribution of this paper is to model the *a priori* knowledge of edge labels in range images by a Markov random field (MRF) and to derive the *a posterior* probability of edge labels in a Bayesian framework. A simple hybrid segmentation method which combines the initial region-based boundary detection method of global clustering and MRF model-based boundary detection method has been developed. The hybrid method shows better segmentations than the individual approaches. The focus on this paper is on a "self-learning" NN-based integrated technique for generating surface maps in range images.

III. Integrated NN Architecture for Range Image Segmentation

In this section, a two-stage NN architecture for integrated range image segmentation is described. These two stages are implemented using the Daugman's projection NN (DPNN) and the Kohonen's self-organizing NN (KSNN), as illustrated in Figure 1. A DPNN is used to reliably estimate the surface normals associated with each of the adjacent neighborhoods in the image through least-square biquadratic surface fitting. These features along with the edge information obtained using a set of Zernike moment-based detectors [12] are fed to the KSNN for region growing. Two image pixels belong to the same "class" (or physically surfaces) if the normal vectors at those points are close to each other and edginess between them is small. Otherwise, they belong to different classes. The following sections describe the normal vector extraction and region growing stages in detail.

A. Surface Feature Extraction

In real-world range images, most of the underlying surfaces can be approximated by biquadratic surfaces. The parameters in the biquadratic surface function uniquely describe the surface characteristics of a range image-point. Robust estimation of surface parameters is important for generating accurate surface maps of the range image.

Consider the optimization problem of projecting an im-

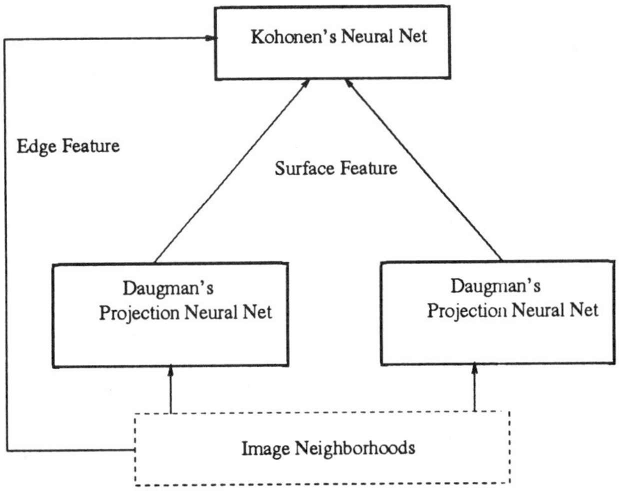

Figure 1: Two-stage NN architecture for range image segmentation

age $g(x,y)$ in optimal sense onto a chosen set of elementary functions $\{G(x,y)\}$. This requires minimization of the error,

$$E = ||g(x,y) - H(x,y)||^2 \tag{1}$$

where

$$H(x,y) = \sum_{i=i}^{n} f_i G_i(x,y)$$

f_i's are optimal projection coefficients onto the set of elementary functions $\{G(x,y)\}$. Thus,

$$\begin{aligned} E &= ||g(x,y) - \sum_{i=1}^{n} f_i G_i(x,y)||^2 \\ &= \sum_{i=1}^{N}\sum_{j=1}^{N}\left(g(i,j) - \sum_{k=1}^{n} f_k G_k(i,j)\right)^2 \end{aligned} \tag{2}$$

If f_k's are optimal then for all f_k's,

$$\frac{\partial E}{\partial f_k} = 2\sum_{i,j}\left[g(i,j)G_k(i,j) - \sum_{l=1}^{n} f_l G_l(i,j)G_k(i,j)\right] = 0 \tag{3}$$

Satisfying this condition for all f_k generates a system of n simultaneous equations with n unknowns:

$$\sum_{i,j}[g(i,j)G_k(i,j)] = \sum_{i,j}[(\sum_{l=1}^{n} f_l G_l(i,j))G_k(i,j)] \tag{4}$$

If G_k's are orthogonal then each of these n equations has a single unknown and can be solved easily. However, if these are not orthogonal as it is in general case, the solution technique by popular algebraic means is not at all trivial. In fact, the time complexity of the solution process is $O(n!)$ for n simultaneous equations. However, methods based on iterative improvements of f_k's are much faster for large n. Also, the error measure E is quadratic in every f_k and so a unique global minimum for E exists. Thus, it is unlikely that the iterative adjustments of f_k's would result in local minima. This motivates the application of a gradient descent type of NN for extracting surface features in the range data.

Consider the three-layer NN shown in Figure 2. It has a middle-layer of adjustable weights and two fixed-weight layers. The first fixed-weight layer computes the product of $[G_i(x,y)]$ and $[g(x,y)]$. The middle layer is basically constituted of the projection coefficients $\{f_i\}$. The final layer computes the sum of cross-correlations $\{G_iG_j\}$, weighted by f_i's. The ith neuron in the first layer computes the inner product of $G_i(x,y)$ with the input image $g(x,y)$ in the local neighborhood. This is based on the neurophysiological concept of a linear neuron's receptive field profile, which refers to the spatial weighting function by which a local region of the retinal image is multiplied and integrated to generate the neuron's response strength [1]. The adaptive control signal adjusts each of the f_i's by an amount δ_i, proportional to the difference between a feedforward signal and a feedback signal. The feedforward signal is the level of activity of the neuron from the first layer, and the feedback signal is the inner product of the weighing function of the corresponding neuron in the third layer with the weighed sum of all the other neighboring neurons in that layer with which it is connected. However, it may be possible to reduce the effect of the neighboring neurons by defining a neighborhood shrinking function, similar to that in the Kohonen's self-organizing neural net. The weight adjustments can be written as,

$$\delta_k = \alpha\sum_{i,j}\left[G_k(i,j)g(i,j) - G_k(i,j)\sum_{l=1}^{n} f_l G_l(i,j)\right] \tag{5}$$

where α is the learning rate. A moderate value of α is preferable to prevent "overshooting" of error. The adaptive control signal δ_k arises only from interlaminar network representations and thus it is a unsupervised system.

Let us return to the problem of computing surface features. Assume a biquadratic surface function,

$$g(x,y) = a_0 + a_1x + a_2y + a_3x^2 + a_4y^2 + a_5xy \tag{6}$$

If $g(x,y)$ is shifted by (c,r) then we can write,

$$\begin{aligned} g'(x,y) &= g(x+c, y+r) - a_0 \\ &= a_0' + a_1'x + a_2'y + a_3x^2 + a_4y^2 + a_5'xy \end{aligned} \tag{7}$$

where

$$a_1' = a_1 + ra_5 + 2a_3c \quad a_2' = a_2 + ca_5 + 2a_4c$$

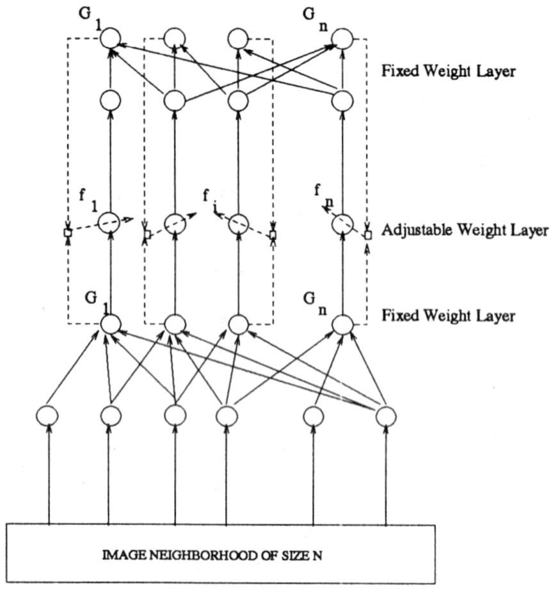

Figure 2: Daugman's projection neural network

$$a'_0 = a_1 c + a_2 r + a_3 c^2 + a_4 r^2 + a_5 rc$$

and a'_0 is a constant. a'_i is the connection weight associated with the i-th elementary function G_i, after the network stabilizes. An interesting observation is that the surface normal components are trivially related to the connection weights $\{a'_i\}$ of the 3-layer NN after it stabilizes. The horizontal and vertical components of the surface normal vector can be written as,

$$\eta_x(c,r) = \left.\frac{\partial g(x,y)}{\partial x}\right|_{x=c,y=r} = a'_1 \qquad (8)$$

$$\eta_y(c,r) = \left.\frac{\partial g(x,y)}{\partial y}\right|_{x=c,y=r} = a'_2 \qquad (9)$$

Hence, for the chosen biquadratic function, the connection weights a'_1 and a'_2 basically represents the optimal normal vector-components. The robustness of this approach is experimentally demonstrated in [11].

In real-world range images, most of the surfaces can be approximated by

$$f(x,y) = a_0 + a_1 x + a_2 y + a_3 x^2 + a_4 y^2 + a_5 xy.$$

Thus if the elementary functions $\{G_i(x,y)\}$s are chosen to be $\{1, x, y, x^2, y^2, xy\}$, then the optimal a_is can be obtained by linear combinations of connection weights a'_is, after the network stabilizes. The biquadratic surface parameters are quite small and do not seem to vary quite significantly for dissimilar surfaces. It is our belief that biquadratic surface parameters cannot be effectively used as surface descriptors, unless large neighborhood size is used. Large neighborhood size in turn results in higher computational complexity. Thus, we have concentrated on use of surface normals, which have strong "discriminatory" power as surface features. The optimal surface normal-components can be obtained directly from a'_1 and a'_2. These surface features calculated in local neighborhoods of the input range are used along with edge information extracted by means of a set of Zernike moment-based operators to create a descriptor of a randomly sampled range image point. This descriptor is used in the region-growing phase described in the next section.

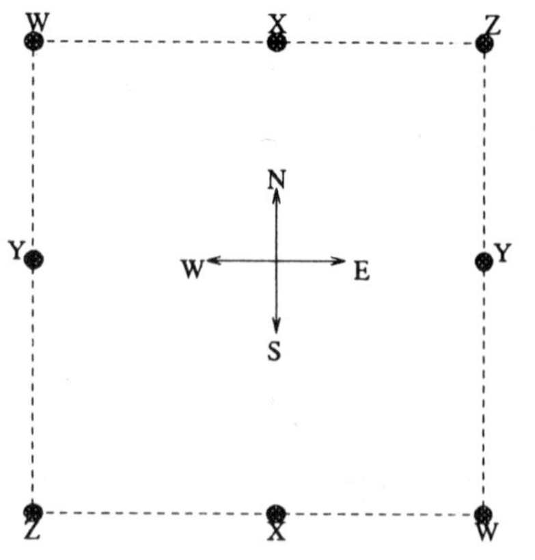

Figure 3: Training point selection in an image neighborhood. Dark circles having same labels are training point-pairs.

B. Competitive Region-growing

As mentioned earlier, an integrated approach that utilizes both the edge and surface information, combines strengths of both the region-based and the edge-based approaches and eliminates their weaknesses. An NN-based technique that simultaneously uses the edge and surface information to segment a range image is described in this section. This technique allows local competition between surface and edge features which result in robust segmentation of range data. The KSNN is used to perform region growing. This technique is implemented in two phases: (1) Training phase and (2) Connectivity detection stage.

Training Phase

Given randomly sampled points in a range image, two points are chosen in a sufficiently large neighborhood in N-S, E-W, NE-SW and NW-SE directions, as shown in Figure 3. A descriptor is formed with normal vectors associated with each pair of points and the maximum "edginess" between those points (i.e., maximum of the edginess associated with points on the straight line joining them). These training descriptors are fed to the KSNN with 7 input nodes (6 nodes for two normal vectors, 1 node for the maximum edginess) and two output nodes. Each output node denotes if the two input points belong to the same "class" (physically surface) or different classes. If the edge strength is high and two normal vectors are significantly different, then the points lie on different surfaces. If the edginess is not significant but the disparity between the surface normals is sufficiently significant, then also the points belong to different surfaces. In fact, this condition corresponds to a missing edge between two adjacent surfaces. Two points belong to the same surface if the two normal vectors are similar, and the edginess is small. Also, two points belong to the same surface when normal vectors are nominally different and edginess is high - this precisely corresponds to the presence of a spurious edge point. Thus, the surface and edge information compete with each other to grow regions.

Simple modification is made to the existing training algorithm to simulate the competition between the edge and surface information. The modified training algorithm can be summarized as follows:

Step 1 Initialize weights from N inputs to M output nodes to small random values. Set the initial radius of the neighborhood around each node.

Step 2 Present new input vector.

Step 3 Compute distances d_j between the input and each output node j using the relation $d_j = \sum_{i=0}^{N-1} \alpha_i(x_i - w_{ij}(t))^2$, where $x_i(t)$ is the input to node i at time t, α_i is the weighing associated with the i-th component of the feature vector, and $w_{ij}(t)$ is the weight from input node i to output node j at time t.

Step 4 Select output node j^* with minimum distance.

Step 5 Weights are updated for node j^* and all nodes in the neighborhood defined by NH_{j^*} according to the relation $W_{ij}(t+1) = w_{ij}(t) + \eta(t)\alpha_i(x_i(t) - w_{ij}(t))$ for $j \in NH_{j^*}$ and $0 \leq i \leq N-1$. The gain term $\eta(t)$ decreases in time provided that $0 \leq \eta(t) \leq 1$.

The training set is presented to the network until the gain term η becomes equal to zero. Sufficient number of epoches is allowed for self-organization of the network. In all our experiments, reasonably accurate segmentation is achieved in 40 epoches. Once the training is over, given each training vector, one or the other node would be active, denoting if the pair of pixels belong to the same surface or not. Thus, the network "learns" the distribution of the feature space associated with the training set.

It is obvious that proper weights must be associated with the edginess and the surface normal information to ensure the success of this region-growing technique. If the edginess is given too high a weight, the presence of a spurious edge would disturb the region-growing and two points would be classified to belong to different surfaces even if they actually lie on the same surface. If the surface information is given low emphasis, then a weak edge point would result in merging of two points, which actually belong to different surfaces. In our experiments, 60% weight is given to the edginess feature and the rest 40% to the other features. There is trade-off involved with the size of the neighborhood required for the estimation of surface characteristics. If too small a neighborhood is used, fewer points are available for estimating surface features. In this case, estimates may not be very reliable. On the other hand, if a large neighborhood is used, points from adjacent surfaces may be enclosed. Again, the surface feature estimates would be incorrect. In our experiments, neighborhoods of size 5 x 5 are used.

In the connectivity detection stage, test vectors are created with surface and edge information of every adjacent pair of pixels in the neighborhood (within the square area shown in Figure 3) and presented to the net. The net classifies each pair to be connected or not. Thus a connected mesh is created between the pixels belonging to the same surface. Pixels belonging to different surfaces are not connected. Next the connected components are labeled and appropriate surfaces are fit to provide the final segmentation of the input range image.

IV. Experimental Results

Figure 4(Top) shows one of the 128 x 128 range images used in our experiments. Figure 4(Middle) shows the connected pixels of input images obtained using the proposed NN architecture. It can be observed that regions corresponding to different surfaces are connected by a "narrow" connection (i.e., one or two pixel wide) near corners of the boundaries between adjacent surfaces. The object is completely separated from the background; but the top and front surfaces are connected through two "narrow" connections. This is caused by the fact that at corner points the estimates of both the edge and the surface information are not very reliable because the underlying assumptions are not met. This problem can be corrected by a postprocessing step which locates and eliminates "narrow" connections between large regions. The final segmented image is shown in Figure 4(Bottom). In the proposed approach, it takes approximately 200 msto extract the surface features using the DPNN, 20 msto train the KSNN and 100 msof system time to detect the connectivity on a Sun Sparc 2 workstation.

V. Conclusions

A novel two-stage NN architecture is proposed in this paper for segmentation of real-world range images into a set of surfaces. In the first stage, a projection NN is used to extract local surface features in the range data.

These surface features along with the edge features compete with each other in the second stage to grow regions pixel-by-pixel. A modified Kohonen's self-organizing NN is employed to implement the competitive region-growing. The entire architecture is "self-learning" and requires no supervision. Experimental results with real images are shown to demonstrate the excellent performance of the proposed architecture. We are presently investigating similar approaches to gray-level image segmentation, superquadratic surface fitting and spatio-temporal feature extraction.

REFERENCES

[1] J.G. Daugman, "Complete discrete 2-D Gabor transforms by neural networks for image analysis and compression," *IEEE Trans. on Acoustics, Speech and Signal Processing*, Vol. 36, No. 7, pp. 1169-1179, 1988.

[2] B.S. Manjunath, T. Simchony, and R. Chellappa, "Stochastic and deterministic networks for texture segmentation," *IEEE Trans. on Acoustics, Speech and Signal Processing*, Vol. 38, pp. 1028-1049, 1990.

[3] B.S. Manjunath and R. Chellappa, "A computational approach to boundary detection," *Proc. IEEE CVPR*, pp. 358-363, Hawaii, 1991.

[4] H. Tunley, "Dynamic image segmentation and optic flow extraction," *Proc. IJCNN*, Vol. 1, pp. 599-604, Seattle, 1991.

[5] I.K. King, J. Liaw, and M.A. Arbib, "A neural network for the detection of rotational motion," *Proc. IJCNN*, Vol. 1, pp. 707-712, Seattle, 1991.

[6] D.A. Fay and A.M. Waxman, "Real-time early vision neurocomputing," *Proc. IJCNN*, Vol. 1, pp. 621-626, Seattle, 1991.

[7] A. Khotanzad and J.H. Lu, "Classification of invariant image representations using a neural network," *IEEE Trans. on Acoustics, Speech and Signal Processing*, Vol. 38, no. 6, pp. 1028 -1038, 1990.

[8] R.P. Lippman, "An introduction to the computing with neural nets," *IEEE ASSP Magazine*, pp. 4-22, 1987.

[9] T. Kohonen, *Self-organization and Associative Memory*, Springler-Verlag, 1988.

[10] S. Ghosal and R. Mehrotra, "Application of neural networks in range image segmentation," *Proc. IJCNN*, pp. 392-397, Baltimore, 1992.

[11] S. Ghosal and R. Mehrotra, "Neural network-based surface representation," *Proc. IJCNN*, Beijing, China, 1992.

[12] S. Ghosal and R. Mehrotra, "Detection of generalized step edges," *Technical Report* # 202-92, Dept. Comp. Sc., Univ. of KY, 1992.

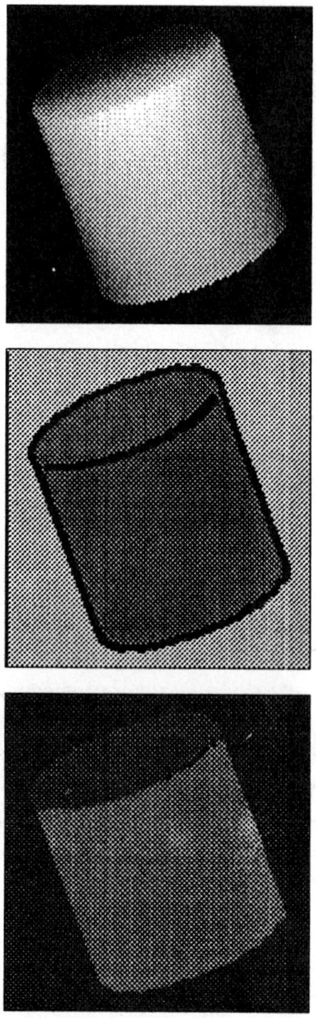

Figure 4: Segmentation of a 128 × 128 range image of a cylindrical object.

[13] N. Yokoya and M.D. Levine, "Range Image Segmentation Based on Differential Geometery: A Hybrid Approach," *IEEE Trans. on Pattern Analysis and Machine Intelligence*, Vol. 11, pp. 643-649, 1989.

[14] A.K. Jain and S. Nadabar, "MRF Model-Based Segmentation of Range Image," *Proc. ICCV*, pp. 667-671, Osaka, Japan, 1990.

Discrete-Time Cellular Neural Network for Thinning: A Compound Synthesis

Chun-ying HO†, Tsz-kin CHU‡ and Shinsaku MORI†
email: murphy@mori.elec.keio.ac.jp
†Dept. of Electrical Engineering, Keio University
‡Dept. of Computer Science, Keio University

***Abstract*—The paper depicts a novel thinning method by using discrete-time cellular neural network. By extracting the inherent topographical properties, namely the midpoints of every line segment of the input image, thinning is shown to be attainable without clumsy 7-neighbor test and stopping condition check. Circuit simplication is achieved by eliminating the usage of time-variant templates, and thus the only control signal in the network is the system clock. Overall performance of the thinning system is evaluated and is compared with previous studies.**

I. INTRODUCTION

Discrete-time cellular neural networks (DTCNNs) [1] are a new type of array computation paradigm which despite confined contiguous interconnections, they exhibit the capability of solving global problems in image processing through signal propagation between adjacent cells. The features of nearest neighborhood connections and translation-invariant templates highly facilitate VLSI implementation. Applications including thinning, connected component detection, etc. have been reported [2-3]. However, designs of templates for a prescribed problem to date have to rely on exhaustive search and/or intuition (trial-and-error). In [4], the feasibility of applying the mathematical tools in threshold logic to the design of DTCNNs has been addressed. By writing the rules which govern the evolution dynamics of DTCNN as a Boolean function, and then transforming it into a threshold function, the required cloning templates are calculated.

The realization of thinning by extracting the mid-points of the input image in the horizontal (H) and vertical (V) directions has been studied in [5]. By utilizing the inherent topographical properties (mid-points) of every line segment of the input image *per se*, thinning is shown to be attainable without 7-neighbor test. However, all overlapping sections that exist between the horizontal and the vertical lines of the image are disconnected. In this paper, by first extracting the horizontal and vertical lines of the image, overall connectivity of the thinning algorithm is improved. A compound synthesis, which implements the local Boolean functions of the proposed thinning algorithm, is adopted from the mathematical tools of threshold logic, and the results are compared with previous studies. Most important, a two-clock scheme is introduced which enables:

a. *the elimination of the clumsy 'stopping' condition check required in conventional designs, and*
b. *time-multiplexing of neurons for compound synthesis of the dynamics of thinning.*

A. Discrete-Time Cellular Neural Networks

The dynamics of DTCNN [1] are governed by the following equation:

$$x_c(t) = \sum_{d\in \Xi_r(c)} A_c^d y^d(t) + \sum_{d\in \Xi_r(c)} B_c^d u^d + I_c, \tag{1a}$$

$$y_c(t+1) = f(x_c(t)) = \begin{cases} 1 & for\ x_c > 0 \\ -1 & for\ x_c < 0 \end{cases}. \tag{1b}$$

The summation term in (1a) is limited to a r-neighborhood $\Xi_r(c)$, which is defined as the set of neighboring cells within a distance r of the cell c in a two-dimensional or three-dimensional sense. The weights in the feedback $\boldsymbol{A}$ and feedforward $\boldsymbol{B}$ templates, and the offsets I_c are supposed to be continuous values, while the input binary image $\boldsymbol{u}$ and the output states $\boldsymbol{y}$ take on a binary value of either 1 or -1. All neurons are assumed to be synchronously updated. This paper will deal exclusively with the designs of DTCNN based on rectangular grid topology. In the following discussion, only 8-connected binary input images with objects being represented by '+1' and the background by '-1' are considered.

Note that (1), albeit consists of variables in a two-dimensional or three-dimensional sense, one can concatenate the cell state and input variables (y^d, u^d) into an ordered n-tuple X where $X = (y^d, u^d)$, $d \in \Xi_r(c)$, and n is the number of variables in (y^d, u^d). Obviously n is dependent on the radius of neighborhood r in the DTCNN. Now, (1) can be rewritten as

$$y_c(t+1) = 1,\ \text{if}\ f(X) = \sum_{d\in \Xi_r(c)} A_c^d y^d(t) + \sum_{d\in \Xi_r(c)} B_c^d u^d > -I_c, \tag{2a}$$

$$y_c(t+1) = -1,\ \text{if}\ f(X) = \sum_{d\in \Xi_r(c)} A_c^d y^d(t) + \sum_{d\in \Xi_r(c)} B_c^d u^d < -I_c, \tag{2b}$$

where (2) is a function which takes on the weighted sum of the inputs $X = (y^d, u^d)$ and compares it with an internal offset $-I_c$. If it is greater than $-I_c$, the output is 1, and -1 otherwise. The programming task amounts then to finding a set of weights and offset $[\boldsymbol{A}, \boldsymbol{B}, -I_c]$ that satisfies (2).

B. Threshold Logic

Threshold functions are a restricted class of switching functions of binary variables. For a given switching function F of n variables, as the number of variables n increases, the fraction of attainable threshold functions dramatically decreases. Following [6], a Boolean or switching function $F(X)$ of n binary variables is said to be a threshold function if the following conditions are satisfied:

$$F(X) = 1,\ \text{if}\ f(X) = \sum_{j=1}^{n} w_j x_j \geq I_u,\ \forall X \in F, \tag{3a}$$

$$F(X) = -1,\ \text{if}\ f(X) = \sum_{j=1}^{n} w_j x_j \leq I_l,\ \forall X \in \bar{F}^1 \tag{3b}$$

where x_j = a binary variable assuming a value of either -1 or 1, for j = 1, 2, ..., n.
$X = (x_1, x_2, ..., x_n)$ = an ordered n-tuple.
w_j = a real coefficient called the weight of x_j, for j = 1, 2, ..., n.
$F(X)$ = a Boolean function of X.
$f(X)$ = an algebraic function (a summation function) of X.
I_u = the upper boundary of the offset I.
I_l = the lower boundary of the offset I.
Note that one can choose any offset I with $I_l < I \leq I_u$. However, we assert here without providing proof that in a direct-R realization method [7], the optimum choice of I for maximum overall sensitivity of a network is $I = (I_l + I_u)/2$, if the sensitivities of the weights and the offset are proportional [6, pp. 162]. Comparing (2) and (3), the dynamics of a DTCNN can be considered as a threshold function with $X = (y^d, u^d) \equiv (x_1, x_2, ..., x_n)$ and $-I_c = I$. The realization $[w_1, w_2, ..., w_n]$ is thus equivalent to the cloning template parameters $[\boldsymbol{A}, \boldsymbol{B}, -I_c]$ [4]. Given a switching function of n input variables, there are 2^n vertices in the n-dimensional space where (3) have to be satisfied. However, it is plain to see that only two vertices X_j and X_k

[1] Any value of 0 is assumed to be converted into -1 before algebraic summation, and a -1 is converted back into a 0 before Boolean operation.

0-7803-1254-6/93$03.00 © 1993 IEEE

$\left(X_j \in F \text{ and } X_k \in \overline{F}\right)$ which correspond to the minimum and maximum values of $f(X_j)$ $(=I_u)$ and $f(X_k)$ $(=I_l)$, respectively, are needed to be considered in (3). For the sake of completeness, the synthesizing techniques developed in [4] are summarized in the following subsection.

C. Pre-assignment of Signs and Grouping of Weights

As the number of variables n in the switching function F increases, it becomes difficult, if not possible, to determine the corresponding realization $[w_1, w_2, \ldots, w_n, I]$. However, due to the symmetrical properties, which is quite common, in the switching functions of the image processing problems, the number of weights (unknown template parameters) can greatly be reduced beforehand.

Theorem 1: *If a switching function F of n variables is positive (negative)* [6] *but not negative (positive) in x_i, then the corresponding threshold function, if implementable, should have a weight $w_i > 0$ $(w_i < 0)$.*

Proof: Without loss of generality, let $[w_1, w_2, \ldots, w_n, I]$, where $I_l < I \le I_u$, be the set of weights and offset that realizes the switching function F, since F is positive in x_i, then $\forall X \in F$,

$$f(X) = \sum_{j=1}^{n} w_j x_j \ge I_u,$$

$$\Rightarrow \sum_{j \ne i}^{n} w_j x_j + w_i \ge I_u,$$

if $w_i < 0$, then it follows that

$$\sum_{j \ne i}^{n} w_j x_j - w_i > \sum_{j \ne i}^{n} w_j x_j + w_i \ge I_u. \tag{4}$$

Since $w_i \ne 0$, or F is independent of w_i. (4) implies F is also negative in x_i. This is a contradiction and hence $w_i > 0$. The proof for the negative case is trivial and is left to the reader.

Theorem 2: *If a switching function F of n variables is symmetrical in x_i and x_k, it is admissible that the corresponding threshold function has the weight $w_i = w_k$.*

Proof: Without loss of generality, let $X = x_1 x_2 \ldots \overline{x}_i \ldots x_k \ldots x_n$ be a vertex in F. Since F is symmetrical in x_i and x_k, then $X'' = x_1 x_2 \ldots x_i \ldots \overline{x}_k \ldots x_n$ is also a vertex in F. If we impose $w_i = w_k$, then

$$f(X'') = f(X) - 2w_k + 2w_i = f(X) \ge I_u \tag{5}$$

and there exists no contradiction. Hence $w_i = w_k$ is admissible. In the *Appendix*, we shall use *theorems* 1 and 2 to calculate the required cloning templates for the realization of our proposed thinning system.

II SYSTEM STRUCTURE

Thinning is one of the fundamental preprocessing procedures in image processing where the most important features of the input image are captured and are represented by simple lines of one or two pixels thickness. However, the skeleton and the overall connectivity of the input image must be retained.

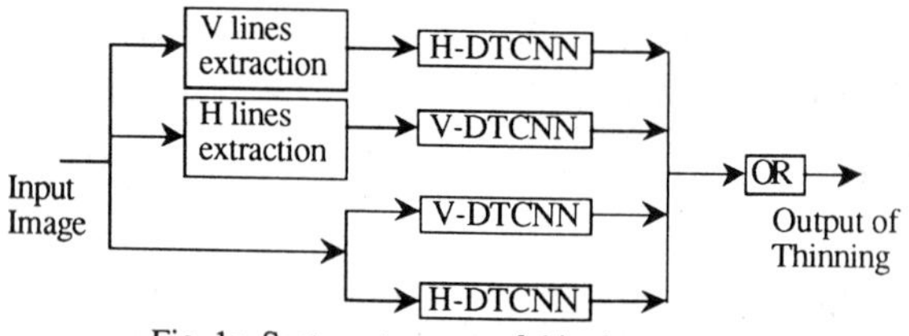

Fig. 1a System structure of thinning.

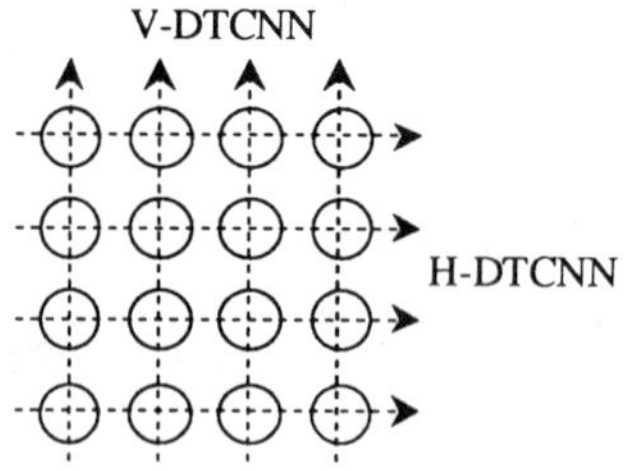

Fig. 1b Partitioning of the two-dimensional binary input image into 2 one-dimensional sub-problems.

Fig. 1a depicts the system structure of the proposed thinning algorithm which is quite different from conventional approaches. The horizontal (H) and vertical (V) lines of the input image are first extracted, then the mid-points of *i.* the horizontal and vertical lines; and *ii.* the original image in the V, and H directions are extracted. Empirical results show that it suffices to logical OR the extracted mid-points of all the line segments on the V and H axes in order to accomplish the thinning of the image. Fig. 1b shows the partitioning of the network into 2 one-dimensional sub-problems along the H and V axes.

III. DTCNN REALIZATION

A. Lines Extraction

Since the input lines may have a thickness even wider than the length of a line in the other axial direction, one must define the minimum length of a 'line'. Without loss of generality, let the minimum length of a line be 5 pixels[2]. Initialize the image with $\mathbf{y} = 0$, and consider $r = 2$ in the horizontal direction, the procedure of extracting the horizontal lines is as follows:

a. if u_i and all its four neighbors u_{i-2}, u_{i-1}, u_{i+1} and, u_{i+2} are '1's, then $y_i^t = 1$;

b. if u_i = '1' and y_{i-1}^{t-1} or $y_{i+1}^{t-1} = 1$, then $y_i^t = 1$.

The procedure is iterated until no further change of the neurons occurs. The Boolean function is rendered as

$$y_i^t = u_i \cdot \left(u_{i-2} \cdot u_{i-1} \cdot u_{i+1} \cdot u_{i+2} + y_{i-1}^{t-1} + y_{i+1}^{t-1}\right), \tag{6}$$

where $\boldsymbol{u}$ is the input image and $\mathbf{y}$ is the output state. Following [4], the procedures of calculating the cloning template parameters for the realization of (6) are summarized in the *Appendix*. With an input image of size NxN pixels, the number of neurons required is N^2. Cloning templates for the extraction of the vertical lines are at a 90° rotation of those for the horizontal lines. Note that convergence for (6) is assured due to a limited size of the input image.

B. Mid-points Extraction

Consider the sub-problem in the horizontal direction H-DTCNN, with a NxN input rectangular image. In each row, denote the cells as number (0, 1, 2, ..., N-1). Without loss of generality, assuming even cells (0 included) are updated at (1, 3, ..., t+1, ...)-th time steps while odd cells at (2, 4, ..., t+2, ...)-th time steps, where $t = 2k$, and k is an integer. Every row is assumed to be independent with dynamics governed by the following Boolean function

$$\begin{aligned} F = y_i^{t+1} &= y_i^{t-1} \cdot \left(\overline{y}_{i-1}^t \cdot \overline{y}_{i+1}^t + y_{i-1}^t \cdot y_{i+1}^t\right) \\ &= y_i^{t-1} \cdot \left(y_{i-1}^t \ominus y_{i+1}^t\right), \end{aligned} \tag{7}$$

where y_{i-1}^t and y_{i+1}^t are the states of the adjacent neighboring cells of cell i (i even) at the t-th time step, and $\ominus$ is the Equivalence operation. The truth table of (7) is shown in Table I, and its evolution characteristics are depicted in Fig. 2. This update strategy prevents the erasure of two connected '1' pixels simultaneously in a single update which leads to error in conventional designs [8]. For an input

2 To extract lines of length other than 5 pixels, one will have to modify the rules *a* and *b* above.

TABLE I
TRUTH TABLE OF BOOLEAN FUNCTION F

y_{i-1}^{t}	y_{i}^{t-1}	y_{i+1}^{t}	$F = y_{i}^{t+1}$
-1	1	-1	1
-1	1	1	1
1	1	-1	-1
1	1	1	1
-1	-1	-1	-1
-1	-1	1	-1
1	-1	-1	-1
1	-1	1	-1

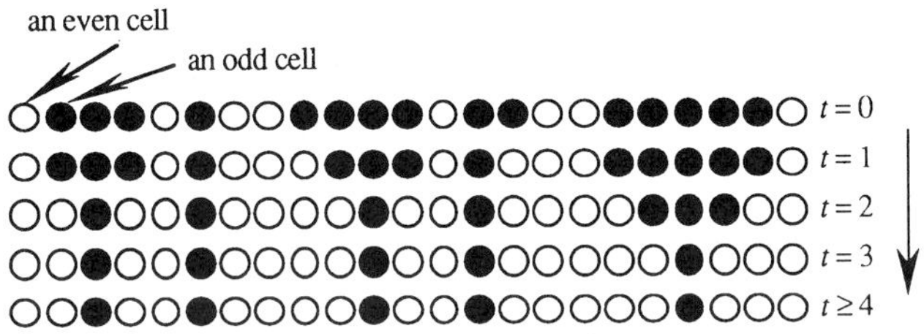

Fig. 2 Evolution characteristics of H-DTCNN.

pattern that has two or an even number of '1' pixels, the retaining of an even cell or an odd cell depends on the order of the update. However, there will remain one and only one '1' pixel for every connected component in the same row of the H-DTCNN. The procedures of calculating the cloning template parameters of F for DTCNN realization are summarized in the *Appendix*.

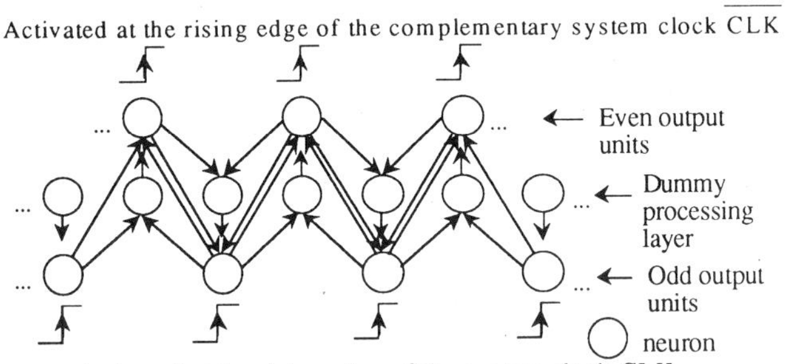

Fig. 3 System structure of H-DTCNN.

Fig. 3 shows the structure of F realized by DTCNN. Odd and even output cells are updated at every rising edge of the original and complementary clocks, CLK and $\overline{CLK}$, respectively. It is assumed that the settling time of the neurons is less than half a cycle of the system clock CLK, and adjacent cells can be triggered by the rising edges of CLK and $\overline{CLK}$, respectively. A dummy processing layer, which serves as the hidden layer to solve the Equivalence operation, is also inserted into the network. With an input image of size NxN pixels, the total number of neurons required for the realization of H-DTCNN is $2N^2$ where only N^2 neurons are connected to the external.

The structure of V-DTCNN is almost the same as H-DTCNN with the exception that interconnections are made in the vertical direction. Due to a limited size of the input binary image and only peeling steps are iterated in the proposed thinning algorithm, convergence is automatically assured.

IV. SIMULATION RESULTS

The simulation results of the proposed thinning algorithm are shown from Fig. 4 to Fig. 6. In Fig. 4, a regular printed character 'H' is considered, the mid-points along different axes of the original image and its horizontal and vertical lines are extracted, and are logical-ORed together to give the final result. Fig. 5 shows a highly irregular handwritten character 'A' adopted in [2]. The final outcome shows that connectivity is preserved by using the proposed thinning algorithm. In Fig. 6, the simulation result of a calligraphic Chinese character of size $32x32$ pixels is shown. Although the overall skeleton of the character is retained, one of the strokes fails to maintain the connectivity of the thinned image.

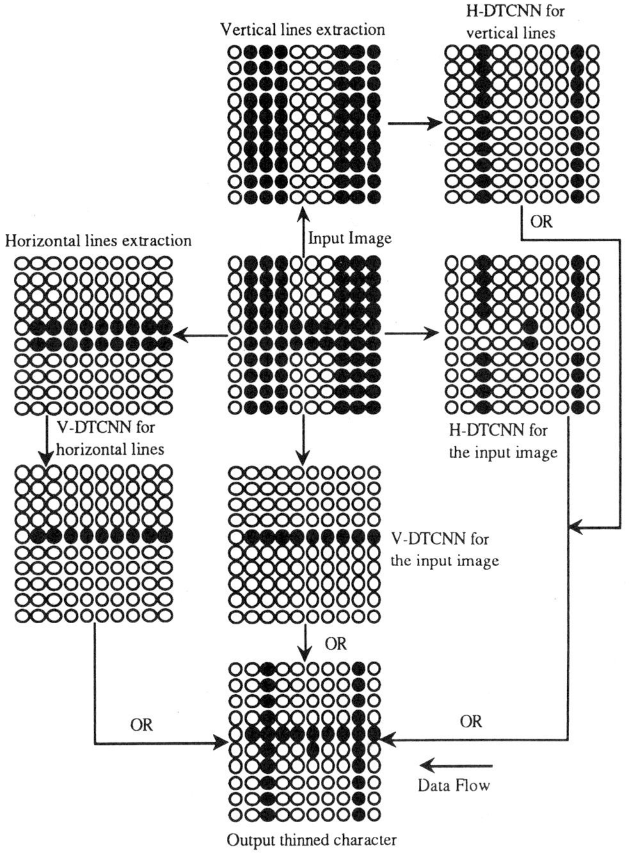

Fig. 4 Simulation results of an input printed character 'H'

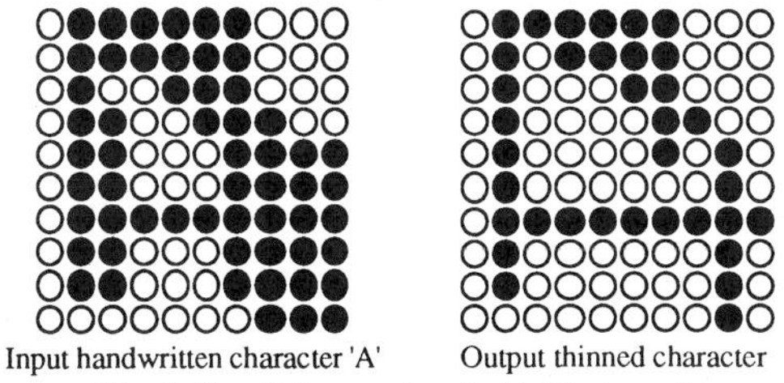

Fig. 5 Simulation results of a highly irregular handwritten character 'A' after [2].

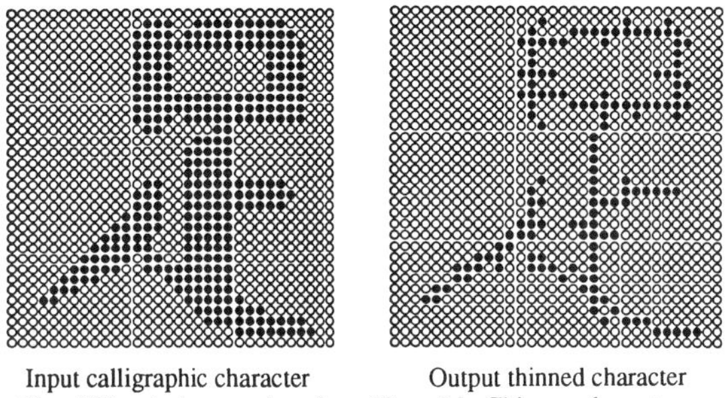

Fig. 6 Simulation results of a calligraphic Chinese character.

In general, for an input binary image of a size NxN, line

extraction can be accomplished within 3 cycles, and the overall thinning operation can be attained within (3+N/4) cycles of the system clock.

V. DISCUSSIONS & CONCLUSIONS

In this paper, a novel thinning algorithm is proposed. By partitioning the original two-dimensional problem into one-dimensional sub-problems, the overall circuit realized by DTCNN is simplified. A solution of the cloning template parameters is also given for DTCNN realization of the proposed algorithm. In particular, since no time-variant template is used in the system, the only control signals in the network are the system clock, CLK and $\overline{\text{CLK}}$, which are usually available in conventional CMOS designs. Although a two-clock scheme is used to partially serialize the dynamics of the network, the proposed thinning algorithm is nevertheless parallel. This approach, albeit has the disadvantage of more redundant pixels in the final thinned image, the one-dimensional DTCNNs with r = 1 or 2 and time-invariant templates highly facilitates VLSI implementation. It is worth pointing out that the circuit in Fig. 3 is robust to clock skews between CLK and $\overline{\text{CLK}}$ due to its properties of nearest neighbor inter-connections.

Compared with the 8-plane approach in [9], the algorithm adopted in this paper enables a simpler hardware design at the expense of more neurons (hardware) executed in parallel. Note that six networks are needed to realize the proposed thinning algorithm by comparison with three layers adopted in [2]. However, the implementation of layer 3 in [2] is more difficult than it looks like. In particular, the overall convergence speed has been improved by a factor of $\approx 16N$ $(=4N^2/(3+N/4)$ if $N \gg 12)$. Most important, empirical results show that connectivity can also be preserved if the input image is not too irregular. It is expected that the overall connectivity of the thinned input image can be further improved by the addition of more feature extraction layers akin to diagonal lines to the network.

REFERENCES

[1] H. Harrer, J. A. Nossek, and F. Zou, "A Learning Algorithm for Time-Discrete Cellular Neural Network," *IJCNN '91 Singapore*, pp. 718-722, 1991.

[2] H. Harrer, and J. A. Nossek, "Skeletonization: A New Application for Discrete-Time Cellular Neural Networks Using Time-Variant Templates," *ISCAS'92*, pp. 2897-2900, 1992.

[3] H. Harrer, J. A. Nossek, and R. Stelzl, "An Analog Implementation of Discrete-Time Cellular Neural Network," *IEEE Trans. on Neural Network*, pp. 466-476, 1992.

[4] C. Ho, et al, "Synthesis of Discrete-time Cellular Neural Networks for Binary Image Processing," *to appear in IEICE Trans. on Fund.*.

[5] D. Yu, C. Ho, X. Yu and S. Mori, "On the Application of Cellular Automata to Image Thinning with Cellular Neural Network," *to appear in CNNA'92*.

[6] C. Sheng, "Threshold Logic," *Academic Press*, 1969.

[7] B. Lee and B. Sheu, "Hardware Annealing in Analog VLSI Neurocomputing," *Kluwer Academic Publishers*, 1991.

[8] E. S. Deutsch, "Thinning algorithms on rectangular, hexagonal and triangular arrays," *Commun. ACM* 15, pp. 827-837, 1972.

[9] T. Matsumoto, L. O. Chua, and T. Yokohama, "CNN Cloning Template: Image Thinning with a Cellular Neural Network," *IEEE Trans. on CAS*, vol. 37, no. 5, pp. 638-640, 1990.

APPENDIX

A. Line Extraction

Consider Boolean function (6),

$$F_1 = y_i^t = u_i \cdot \left(u_{i-2} \cdot u_{i-1} \cdot u_{i+1} \cdot u_{i+2} + y_{i-1}^{t-1} + y_{i+1}^{t-1}\right). \quad \text{(A1)}$$

Following *theorems* 1 and 2, the threshold function F_1, if realizable, should be in the form of

$$Qu_i + R(u_{i-2}+u_{i-1}+u_{i+1}+u_{i+2}) + S\left(y_{i-1}^{t-1}+y_{i+1}^{t-1}\right) \ge I_u,\ \forall u,\ y^t \in F_1, \text{ and}$$

$$Qu_i + R(u_{i-2}+u_{i-1}+u_{i+1}+u_{i+2}) + S\left(y_{i-1}^{t-1}+y_{i+1}^{t-1}\right) \le I_l,\ \forall u,\ y^t \in \overline{F}_1, \quad \text{(A2)}$$

where $Q, R, S > 0$. By the substitution of the minimum and maximum values of the summation function, the inequalities reduce to

$$Q + 4R - 2S = I_u \text{ or } Q - 4R = I_u, \text{ and}$$

$$-Q + 4R + 2S = I_l \text{ or } Q + 2R - 2S = I_l. \quad \text{(A3)}$$

Assuming a value of R = 1, the solution becomes

$$Q = 9,\ R = 1,\ S = 4, \text{ and } I_u = 5,\ I_l = 3. \quad \text{(A4)}$$

Choosing a value of $-I_c = I = (I_u + I_l)/2 = 4$ gives the maximum sensitivity. Thus the cloning templates are

$$A = 4\ \ 0\ \ 4;\ B = 1\ \ 1\ \ 9\ \ 1\ \ 1;\ I_c = -4. \quad \text{(A5)}$$

B. H-DTCNN

Consider Boolean function (7), the equivalence operation is not linearly separable, and hence at least two threshold elements are needed to implement F. Now, rewrite F as

$$F = y_i^{t+1} = y_i^t \cdot \left(F_2 + y_{i-1}^t \cdot y_{i+1}^t\right), \text{ and}$$

$$F_2 = \overline{y}_{i-1}^t \cdot \overline{y}_{i+1}^t. \quad \text{(A6)}$$

Following *theorems* 1 and 2, the threshold function F_2, if realizable, should be in the form of

$$-M\left(y_{i-1}^t + y_{i+1}^t\right) \ge I_u,\ \forall y^t \in F_2, \text{ and}$$

$$-M\left(y_{i-1}^t + y_{i+1}^t\right) \le I_l,\ \forall y^t \in \overline{F}_2, \quad \text{(A7)}$$

where $M > 0$. By the substitution of the minimum and maximum values of the summation function, the inequalities reduce to

$$2M = I_u \text{ and } I_l = 0. \quad \text{(A8)}$$

Assuming a value of M = 1, the solution becomes

$$M = 1,\ I_u = 2 \text{ and } I_l = 0. \quad \text{(A9)}$$

Choosing a value of $-I_c = I = (I_u + I_l)/2 = 1$ gives the maximum sensitivity.

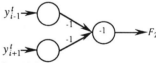

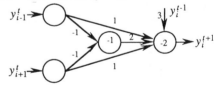

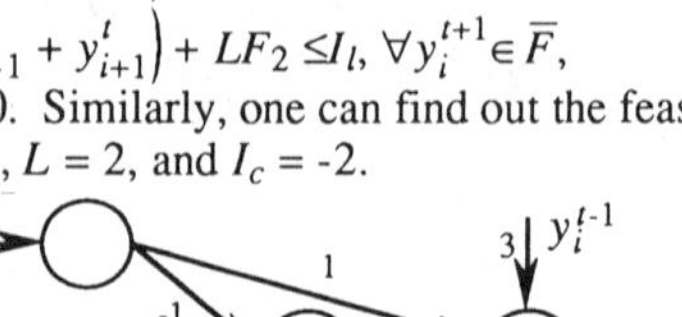

For Boolean function (A6)

$$F = \left(F_2 + y_{i-1}^t \cdot y_{i+1}^t\right) \cdot y_i^{t-1}, \quad \text{(A10)}$$

the threshold function should be in the form of

$$Jy_i^{t-1} + K\left(y_{i-1}^t + y_{i+1}^t\right) + LF_2 \ge I_u,\ \forall y_i^{t+1} \in F, \text{ and}$$

$$Jy_i^{t-1} + K\left(y_{i-1}^t + y_{i+1}^t\right) + LF_2 \le I_l,\ \forall y_i^{t+1} \in \overline{F}, \quad \text{(A11)}$$

where $J, K, L > 0$. Similarly, one can find out the feasible solution is

$$J = 3,\ K = 1,\ L = 2, \text{ and } I_c = -2. \quad \text{(A12)}$$

Applying Neural Network Developments to Sign Language Translation

Elizabeth Wilson and Gretel Anspach
Raytheon Company *

May 1993

Abstract

Neural networks are used to extract relevant features of sign language from video images of a person communicating in American Sign Language or Signed English. The key features are hand motion, hand location with respect to the body, and handshape. A modular design is under way to apply various techniques, including neural networks, in the development of a translation system that will facilitate communication between deaf and hearing people. Signal processing techniques developed for defense-related programs have been adapted and applied to this project. Algorithm development and transition using neural network architectures has been encouraging and the results of the feasibility study for this project are described.

1 Introduction

Neural networks have been applied successfully to a number of difficult signal processing problems and the project described here is attempting to transfer some of these developments to sign language translation. There has already been work completed that shows that English words can be represented in sign language in terms of three features: location, movement, and handshape [8]. The focus of this project is the automatic acquisition of these parameters directly from the video image of the signer.

To address this, we have adapted advanced signal processing techniques and neural network algorithms that are applied to other pattern recognition problems. Figure 1 shows an example of how sensor techniques used for other target recognition tasks are being applied to this problem. The use of infrared imagery emphasizes the heat related features in a number of defense-related programs and has been applied with measurable success to the sign language

*This work was supported by the Raytheon Company Miccioli Scholarship Program and the Raytheon IR&D Program

0-7803-0928-6/93$03.00 © 1993 IEEE

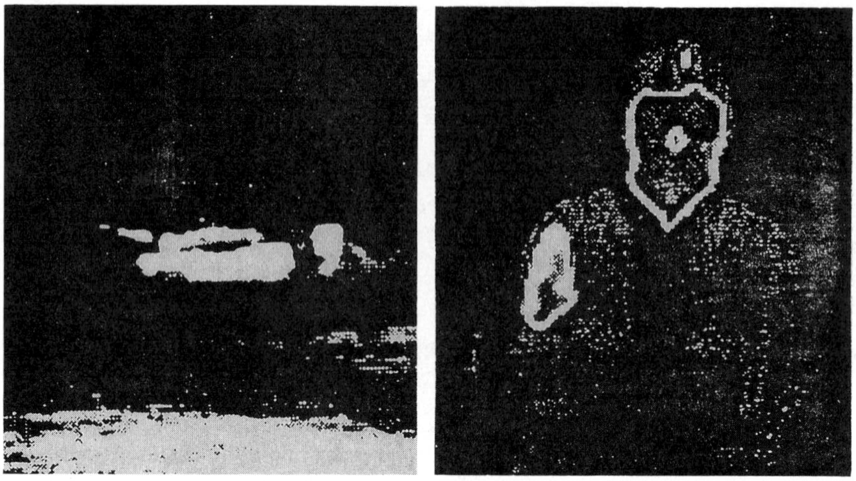

Figure 1: Infrared sensors used to recognize tanks are applied to locating and tracking the hand

project. As shown in the figure, the hand and face exhibit the greatest amount of heat when compared to the rest of the body and the background. This sensor choice simplifies the tracking of the hand movement and provides valuable clues for location labeling.

The motivation to use neural networks for this problem came first from an analysis of where neural networks have been applied in other programs within our company. In particular, neural network algorithms have been developed for a number of image feature extraction applications including the use of Laser Radar imagery for target recognition [1]. By applying target tracking algorithms to follow the hand *movement*, using image segmentation and classification algorithms for labeling the *location*, and converting silhouette classification algorithms to *handshape* classification, the necessary features can be extracted.

A number of neural network architectures have been used for extracting similar features. Multilayer Perceptrons (MLP) are used to interpret handshape signals transmitted by a specially designed glove [4] and for scene segmentation [9]. The Learning Vector Quantization (LVQ) network has been used for face recognition [2]. An Adaptive Resonance Theory (ART) architecture has been used for silhouette classification [3]. Time Delay Neural Networks (TDNN) have been used to identify the movement of an object [6].

2 Problem Description

There are many situations where an interpreter is not currently used such as in a restaurant, hotel, bank, or small business. These are areas where the deaf are consumers of a common service, but unless they bring an interpreter they must communicate by gestures and written notes. The recent passage of the American Disabilities Act (ADA) requires that more establishments be accessible. For those that have a somewhat standard vocabulary (such as a restaurant or hotel), such a unit would provide this accessibility when conditions prevent scheduling the use of an interpreter. For places such as a police station or hospital, the unit could serve to facilitate communication until the interpreter arrived.

The ideal end-item would be a small, portable, inexpensive unit that would provide full sign language to voice conversion for any user using any variation of American Sign Language (ASL). A venture such as this requires extensive processing and very advanced techniques. There exists equipment to convert the three sign parameters into spoken English [10]. This equipment, *Vois-Shapes*, contains a keyboard to input the three parameters in a sequence, and a speech synthesizer to voice the associated English word in the age- and gender-appropriate synthetic voice. The problem, then, is to automate the acquisition of these three sign parameters directly from a video image of the signer.

The extraction of the necessary parameters is a difficult task for humans and is no easier for the computer. In fact, the receptive skills associated with sign language communication are the most difficult part of this language. Conventional image processing techniques are unable to utilize language concepts to clarify ambiguous signs and correct improper parameters used in sign production. The computer will have trouble knowing when one word ends and another begins and will not know the difference between signs and gestures. The computer will not be able to use cues of body movement and positioning or facial expressions to augment the understanding. These factors coupled with the need to accommodate different signing styles, speed, and production makes this translation system a significant technical challenge.

3 Overall Approach

The problem of sign language translation is a difficult one. Features must be extracted for many users with a variety of hand sizes (e.g. adults and children) who each use different signing styles, speed, and clarity. The reality is that sign to voice conversion is very difficult for human interpreters to accomplish. Further, technical approaches to processing images are very different from that of humans.

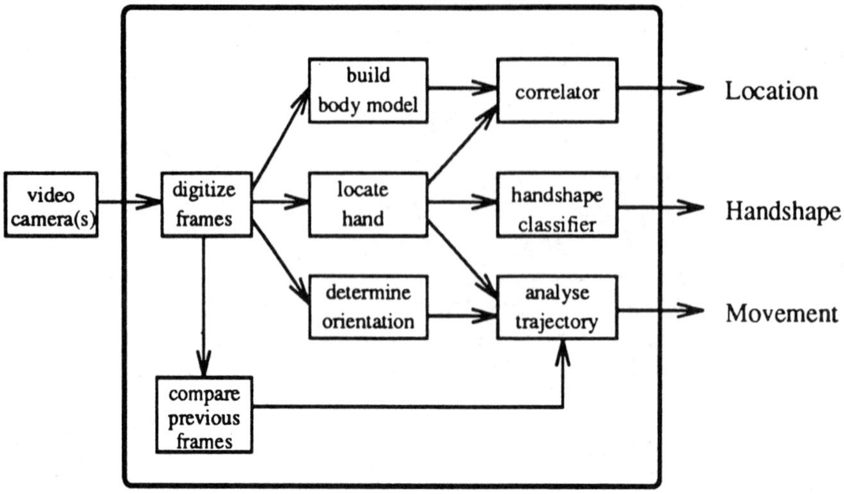

Figure 2: Block Diagram of Sign Language Parameter Extraction System

The approach currently being developed involves the interaction of many advanced techniques. In addition to neural network algorithms, the design involves the integration of numerous image processing techniques, infrared and CCD sensor technology, wavelet analysis, fuzzy logic, and expert systems. The interaction of these technology areas provides a means of addressing this difficult problem and the results of our feasibility study has shown that these techniques are viable for this application.

A modular hybrid design approach allows the best suited algorithm to be applied at each conceptual stage of the processing and provides for their integration at each development stage. This modular approach begins with a limited vocabulary and a restricted environment. The concept design we have constructed allows for increasing this vocabulary and removing restrictions as the development progresses. The first stage of development provides location and movement labels and coarse handshape descriptions. The beginning features have been chosen to allow early implementation of a limited unit that has the largest vocabulary possible for such a stage.

The translation system requires the use of at least one camera to capture the images of the signer. Our development work has been with CCD and infrared cameras. Both cameras have advantages at different areas of analysis and complement each other well. Sensor fusion techniques are being applied to allow for the integration of both camera types.

The second stage of the system converts the running video into sequences of digitized frames. The video must be processed in real time, so compression techniques are employed at this stage. Some of the algorithms require less resolution, so it is not necessary to present every frame to every part of the process. Real time computation can be achieved by capturing high resolution frames at a high frame rate and dropping a number of frames in between processes to reduce the effective rate.

The computer implements a number of image processing and signal processing algorithms to parse the image data into sign parameters. The algorithms interact with each other at various levels of complexity to produce a sign parameter triplet of location, movement, and handshape.

Figure 2 shows the interactions of various stages of computation in the system. The coarsest level of processing identifies the hand and its relation to the body. The "head" and "body" are identified as locations first. The next level of location labels builds on the "head" description to include the difference between "forehead" and "chin" and builds on the "body" to provide "shoulders" and "waist" as labels.

People use their sign space differently and produce signs differently, so location labels will not be exact. In the early development stages, consistent sign production is necessary, but in later stages context and other sign features can help to clarify the parameters. The design goal is to not only produce a decision on the parameter triplet, but to also assign probabilities or likelihood values to the parameters so that alternatives can be readily produced when the most likely does not make sense. This will allow the use of expert systems and fuzzy logic at later development stages.

The information about the hand placement in a single image used to correlate the hand with its location label will also be used to define movement. Successive hand placements will be used for the movement algorithm. Early development stages will detect and track simple movements such as "up," "down," "in," "out," and "side-to-side." Later stages will identify "rotation" and "shake" movements.

Comparison between sequential frames will provide much of the information needed for the movement classification. It will also label the dominant hand as opposed to the non-dominant hand and the face. In standard or infrared video images, the hands and face exhibit the same contrast to the background. As a result, the first level of image processing will identify both hands and the face as the potential dominant hand to track. This hand, however, moves significantly more than the head and more than the other hand. The only case where both hands are moving as much is where the two hands are interacting in a complimentary sign. In this case choosing the wrong hand as dominant will not affect the location, movement, or handshape classifications and therefore will not produce an incorrect triplet.

The hand placement information will also be used to segment the hand portion of the image for use by the handshape classification algorithm. At the coarsest level, the handshapes will be grouped into similar shapes. Because the handshape will require the highest level of resolution and is statistically the least accurate part of sign production, the early development stages will de-emphasize the use of handshape for feature extraction. Later stages will need to be invariant to handshape ambiguities and mistakes.

4 Feasibility Study Results

Preliminary work on algorithm development has been encouraging [12]. We have successfully digitized video images of three signers in addition to some pilot still photographs. The video images were recorded using a number of different cameras to examine the aspects of camera angle, contrast (hands, body, clothing, background), frame rate, speed limitations, memory constraints, and the amount of blurring for faster sign sequences. The resulting images were studied to determine how much pre-processing was required and to test potential feature extraction algorithms. The image processing complexity was evaluated for sign location identification (i.e. head versus waist), hand identification and segmentation from remainder of image, and tracking the hand movement.

4.1 Camera Experiments

We have conducted trials with a number of different cameras including some prototype development hardware. Our goal was to identify hardware that would allow for data capture from a native signer under minimal restrictions. We evaluated equipment that did not require special lighting and favored that which would not require special clothing or cues (i.e. reflective bracelets).

The most promising experiments were with an infrared camera. Although the shape outlines are not as defined as in the CCD experiments, the contrast is excellent. Under ideal conditions, the hand can be segmented from the rest of the image with little or no pre-processing. At the extreme scale of the temperature contrast, only the hands and face are visible making the movement of the hand clear and easy to track. At a less extreme scale the hands and face are visible with the general shape of the body providing ideal images for location classification.

4.2 Location Feature Extraction

Identifying the location requires detecting the hand and correlating it with the part of the body the hand is near to designate its sign. The challenge in this area is in identifying the various regions of the body that are partially obstructed by the moving hand and discriminating the signer from the background. For the feasibility study the various images were studied for consistent templates. The head and torso could be identified and the algorithms were implemented from the hand-segmented images.

Preliminary results have been encouraging using wavelets to attain scale-invariant segmentation [7][13]. The three features of interest in the image have very different processing requirements. The successive approximations that result from application of the scaling function to both the rows and columns provides a much desired data reduction for some of the feature extraction algorithms that can operate at lower resolution. The accuracy required for the location feature varies with more precision being needed in the face region to distinguish ambiguous signs and less precision acceptable in the waist region. The wavelet techniques provide the necessary details at different scales and allow for coarse or fine resolution analysis where required.

4.3 Movement Feature Extraction

There are a number of conventional methods that are used to track motion of an identified object. In addition to these automatic tracking methods, the successive frames of video can also provide some clues as to the movement.

The dominant hand provides the most movement and exhibits the greatest difference when frames are compared with one another. The speed of the hand may be an important factor in later stages for word parsing, so potential velocity estimation was a consideration in the camera studies. The infrared images can be calibrated to reveal only the hand and face for easy segmentation and measurement.

The wavelet analysis with varying scales provides the flexibility for comparing selected frames. The signs that are made in the face region where more detail is required are typically made slower than those in the waist region where coarse resolution can be used. As a result, where the movement analysis requires a higher frame rate, the frame can have less information for simplier processing. Where more detail is required for location discrimination, the slower sign rate allows for the additional processing because every frame in the sequence is not necessarily required for movement analysis.

4.4 Handshape Feature Extraction

Accurate handshape classification is the most difficult part of the feature extraction because this requires the highest resolution and so many handshapes are similar. The design goal is to de-emphasize the need for accurate handshape classification for the overall understanding because this is also the parameter that yields the most sign production errors. Because signers are able to understand one another even when wearing mittens or gloves that restrict the clarity of the handshapes, it is not unreasonable to make the handshape the least important aspect of the final word choice.

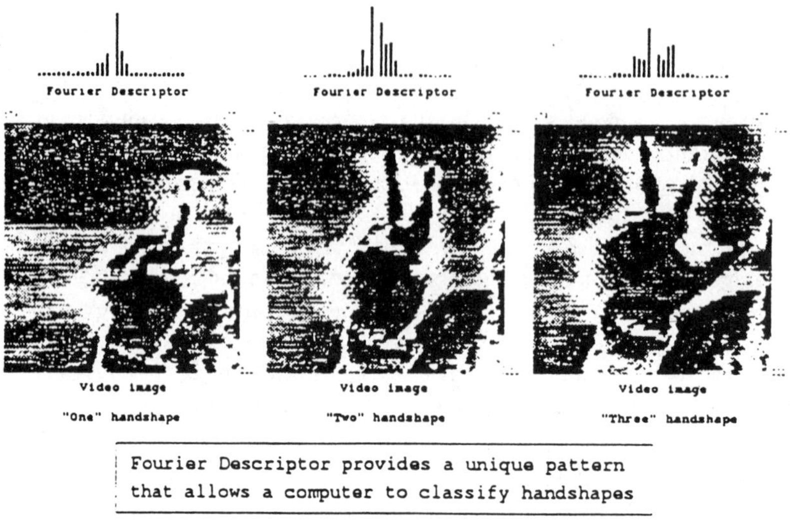

Figure 3: Handshape Fourier Descriptor Examples

The work so far in this area uses shapes that are very different from one another, such as "a," "b", and "2." Successive stages will build on the shapes and provide a more detailed estimate as to the exact shape, but will retain an understanding of the groupings.

For each camera trial and for each signer a number of isolated words and connected sentences were recorded. Each signer was then asked to fingerspell the alphabet and the numbers one through ten. These test images were used to explore the complexity of handshape classification.

To evaluate potential algorithms, the test images were hand-segmented to isolate the area of the dominant hand. Smoothing algorithms were applied to produce a silhouette of the hand. Fourier descriptors were extracted to convert the image into a set of features suitable for a neural network. Different types of neural networks were trained with some of the sample feature sets and tested with new examples. For the initial three handshapes the networks classified the groups perfectly among different signers on different trials. The preliminary studies were successfully completed [12] using a Learning Vector Quantization (LVQ) network [5] and work is currently be done using the Multilayer Perceptron design algorithm [11]. This algorithm utilizes the correlation matrix computations of the data and this is being used to expand the groupings and to determine the structure and starting weights of the necessary networks.

5 Summary

An effort has begun to design a system that will eventually serve as an automated Sign Language to English conversion system. Our focus is on the extraction of hand motion, location, and shape from video images of a person communicating in sign language. A feasibility study has been completed addressing the complexity of designing such a system. This study included an understanding of the linguistic and technical aspects of the problem, research into available and promised hardware, and experimentation with signal processing algorithms including the use of neural networks. The completion of this study indicates that the development of a comprehensive translation system is difficult yet achievable.

References

[1] G. Anspach and T. Kostizak, "Target Recognition: Optimal Feature Selection Using Neural Networks," *Raytheon Electronic Progress*, Vol. 32, No. 1, 1992, pp. 45-49.

[2] H. Bouattour, F. Fogelman-Soulie, and E. Viennet, "Neural Nets for Human Face Recognition," *Proceedings of the IEEE International Joint Conference on Neural Networks*, Vol. 3, 1992, pp. 700-704.

[3] G.A. Carpenter, S. Grossberg, and G.W. Lesher, "A What-and-Where Neural Network for Invariant Image Preprocessing," *Proceedings of the IEEE International Joint Conference on Neural Networks*, Vol. 3, 1992, pp. 303-308.

[4] S.S. Fels and G.E. Hinton, "Glove-Talk: A Neural Network Interface Between a Data-Glove and a Speech Synthesizer," *IEEE Transactions on Neural Networks*, Vol. 4, No. 1, 1993, pp. 2-8.

[5] T. Kohonen, "The Self-Organizing Map," *Proceedings of the IEEE*, Vol. 78, No. 9, September 1990, pp. 1464-1477.

[6] D.T. Lin, J.E. Dayhoff, and P.A. Ligomenides, "Trajectory Recognition with a Time-Delay Neural Network," *Proceedings of the IEEE International Joint Conference on Neural Networks*, Vol. 3, 1992, pp. 197-202.

[7] S.G. Mallat, "A Theory for Multiresolution Signal Decomposition: The Wavelet Representation," *IEEE Transactions on Pattern Analysis and Machine Intelligence*, Vol. 11, No. 7, July 1989, pp. 674-693.

[8] H.C. Shane and R.B. Wilbur, "Potential for Expressive Signing Based on Motor Control," *Sign Language Studies*, Vol. 29, 1980, pp. 331-340.

[9] E. Viennet and F. Fogelman, "Multiresolution Scene Segmentation Using MLPs," *Proceedings of the IEEE International Joint Conference on Neural Networks*, Vol. 3, 1992, pp. 55-59.

[10] *VoisShapes* product in use at the Children's Hospital in Boston, Massachusetts (Communication Enhancement Center)

[11] E. Wilson, S. Umesh, and D.W. Tufts, "Designing a Neural Network Structure for Transient Detection Using the Subspace Inhibition Filter Algorithm," *Proceedings OCEANS*, Newport, RI, Vol. 1, 1992, pp. 120-125.

[12] E. Wilson and G. Anspach, "Neural Networks for Sign Language Translation," to appear in *Applications of Neural Networks, SPIE Conference 1965*, April 1993.

[13] E. Wilson and G. Anspach, "Wavelets for Sign Language Translation," submitted to *Visual Communications and Image Processing '93, SPIE Conference*, November 1993.

A Unified Neural Framework for Early Visual Information Processing

Ling Guan
Department of Electrical Engineering
University of Sydney
Sydney NSW 2006 Australia

Abstract **This paper proposes a unified neural network framework for the modeling and process of early visual information. The proposed framework is based on a neural network with hierarchical cluster architecture (NNHCA) which nicely simulates the regionally coordinated locally parallel processing structure embedded in image formation process. The internal structure of NNHCA is quite flexible so that a large number of processing techniques can be accommodated within the framework. Examples on restoration and enhancement will be provided to demonstrate the performance of the proposed method.**

I. INTRODUCTION

In early visual information processing, the classical techniques are based on either pure mathematical models or *ad hoc* heuristics. The pure mathematical models take lightly the image formation process, and complicate the intended task; the dominance of global processing techniques in image restoration is a typical example [1, 2]. On the other hand, *ad hoc* heuristics tend to oversimplify the scenarios to be dealt with; the majority of image enhancement filters fall into this category [2]. To some extend, both models ignore the regionally coordinated locally parallel processing (RCLPP) structure enbedded in image formation process.

In this work a unified neural network framework for the modeling and process of early visual information is proposed. The modeling scheme is based on a neural network with hierarchical cluster architecture (NNHCA) proposed in [3, 4]. Instead of employing a global or a *ad hoc* criterion, the proposed method processes images in a RCLPP fashion. Naturally, the proposed framework suggests a massive hierarchical real-time parallel processing architecture.

Compared with the conventional techniques, the proposed framework possesses some unique properties:

1. In digital processing, the effect of optical imaging system is local. However, the local processing must be coordinated in order to achieve global optimality. The optimization procedure simulated by NNHCA takes this fact into account, and thus closely reflects the image formation process without losing generality.
2. Statistical processing techniques assume that the image to be processed is an ensemble from a stationary process so that the algorithms can be designed computationally practical. This assumption is rarely true for even an image of medium size where nonstationarity is easily identified. Since NNHCA is based on local information, the stationarity assumption is easily satisfied in most cases. Thus the mechanism of NNHCA adaptively and closely simulates the underlining stochastical process.
3. Space domain processing has always been a formidable task for many conventional image processing techniques, especially for restoration, because of the size of the image involved, let alone real-time parallel processing. However, there is no problem for NNHCA in this regard since the computation involved is inherently local.

The parallelism of NNHCA is natural and efficient. By the term – hierarchical clustered architecture, it is meant that there are several information processing levels existing simultaneously in the neural network model. Each level contains one or more clusters of processing units. For image processing, NNHCA consists of four levels of clusters, representing individual units, local processing model, information exchange and coordination, and overall control, respectively.

Although NNHCA provides a unified framework, processing strategies must be independently designed for different processing techniques; that is each particular processing technique should correctly reflect the underlying image formation structure.

To illustrate the usefulness of NNHCA as a unified framework in modeling early visual information processing, two processing tasks, restoration and enhancement, will be presented in terms of NNHCA. In particular:

- It will be shown that, due to the local nature of point spread functions, restoration can be nicely fit into the RCLPP structure of NNHCA.

- A good image model and reasonable estimates of local noise statistics are vital to the success of image enhancement. By utilizing an adaptive image model with local noise statistics as constraints, solving image enhancement problem is equivalent to minimizing the energy function of an NNHCA.

Real-time processing features of NNHCA will be presented. Numerical examples will be provided to illustrate the quality of restoration and enhancement.

II. NEURAL NETWORKS WITH HIERARCHICAL CLUSTERED ARCHITECTURE

NNHCA is a multi-leveled neural network consisting of nested clusters of units capable of hierarchical memory and learning tasks. The architecture has a fractal-like structure, in that each level of organization consists of interconnected arrangements of neural clusters. Individual units in the model form the zeroth level of cluster organization. Local groupings among the units *via* certain types of connections, produce first level clusters. Other connections link first level clusters at second level, while the coalescence of second level clusters yields third level clusters, and so on. There are considerable data suggesting that networks of this type are abundant in the cerebral cortex.

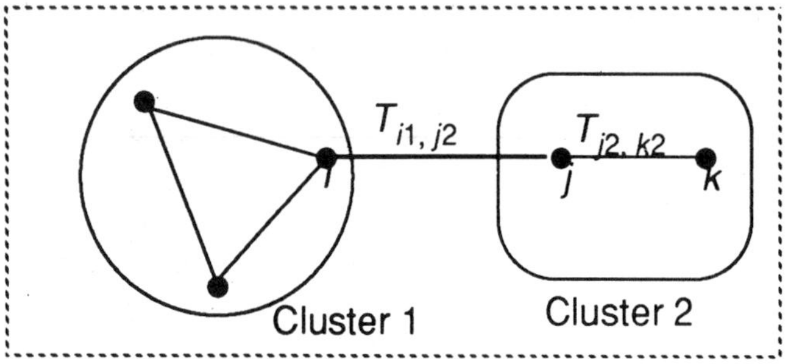

Figure 1: Schematic Representation of An NNHCA

A typical three level NNHCA with 2 first level clusters is illustrated in Fig 1. In general, the energy function of such a system is complicated. For example if NNHCA has a second level structure, and Hopfield network is used for each of the first level clusters, then its energy function is given by

$$E = -\frac{1}{2}\left[\sum_{k=1}^{K}\sum_{i=1}^{P_k}\sum_{j=1}^{P_k} T_{ik,jk}S_{ik}S_{jk} + \sum_{k\neq l}\gamma_{kl}\sum_{i=1}^{P_k}\sum_{j=1}^{P_l} T_{ik,jl}S_{ik}S_{jl}\right] \qquad (1)$$

where K is the number of first level clusters, P_k is the number of units in cluster $k, k = 1, 2, \ldots K$. $S_{ik} = \pm 1$ is a state variable representing firing and resting states of unit (i, k), $T_{ik,jk}$ represents the intra-cluster connection between units (i, k) and (j, k) in the same cluster, and $T_{ik,jl}$ represents the inter-cluster connection between units (i, k) and (j, l) in two different clusters k and l.

The equilibrium, or optimal state of NNHCA is achieved by means of a mean field theory (MFT) learning approach proposed by Sutton [5].

The MFT derived for NNHCA treats the model as a separable Spin-glass like system and the performance of MFT shows that self-organizing features in the hierarchical model resemble aspects of the generalized Hopfield model [6].

In the next section, NNHCA will be modified and used to realize the forementioned framework which handles the local information processing and the information exchange mechanism amongst the adjacent group of processing units in a hierarchical fashion.

III. Early Visual Information Processing Framework by NNHCA

The proposed framework consists of four levels of information processing, namely the zeroth level, the first level, the second level, and the third level. The zeroth level represents individual information units, the first level simulates optimization which governs local processing, the second level acts as a link for information exchange between local clusters in the first level, and the third level coordinates the complete process.

The number of the second level units is equal to the number of first level clusters. Initially, each first level cluster registers a false status at its corresponding second level unit, indicating that the clusters are in unoptimized states.

Corresponding to such a processing structure, NNHCA also have an architecture of four levels of processing units. The three upper processing levels in terms of NNHCA will be discussed in separate subsections. But first, it should be pointed out that the original NNHCA is only partially utilized in the framework for the following reasons:

1. In Sutton's model [3, 4], each unit only belongs to one cluster. However, the image formation procedure requires that the units representing image pixels on the boundaries of clusters belong to, at least, two adjacent clusters.
2. Instead of applying MFT learning to (1), the optimization procedure is broken into several stages. For intra-cluster (the first level), a modified Hopfield learning scheme is applied. A simple but effective heuristic approach is used to execute inter-cluster (the second level) information exchange.

3A The First Level - Local Image Processing

The general image formation model is given by

$$\mathbf{g} = \mathbf{\Phi f} + \mathbf{n} \qquad (2)$$

where $\mathbf{g}$ represents the recorded image of size $M \times M$, $\mathbf{f}$ represents a square array of size $M \times M$, carrying information of the original image, $\mathbf{n}$ represents additive noise array of size $M \times M$, and $\mathbf{\Phi}$ represents transformation operation underlying the modeling of image formation.

To utilize NNHCA the recorded image $\mathbf{g}$ is first partitioned into small regions or clusters to justify the requirement of locality. There are a few points which should be followed in partition:

1. From the the viewpoint of NNHCA, the shapes of the regions can be arbitrary. However, image formation process suggests that squares be preferred.
2. The size of a region is also arbitrary. So let it be $M_* \times M_*, 1 \leq M_* \leq M$. If $M_* = 1$, the most localized partition is achieved. On the other hand, if $M_* = M$, there is no locality in the partition.
3. The partition is overlapped because the boundary pixels must be used by adjacent regions.

The optimization criterion used at the processing level is arbitrary as well. A group of good candidates is the the global processing criteria mentioned in the last section. In this work, the global neural network approach proposed by Zhou *et al* [7] and Paik [8] is chosen because it also follows the network structure of Hopfield's.

For simplicity, 1-D analysis is used in the following. The generalization of the result to 2-D is straight forward. In 1-D analysis, $\mathbf{g}, \mathbf{f}$ and $\mathbf{n}$ are vectors of length M, and $\mathbf{\Phi}$ is a matrix of size $M \times M$.

In each of the partitioned region, the recorded subimage is given as

$$\mathbf{g}_m = \mathbf{\Phi}\mathbf{f}_m + \mathbf{n}_m \tag{3}$$

where $m = 1, 2, ..., M/M_*$. For simplicity, the subscript $_m$ will be dropped in the following.

Based on the formation model (3), the network to be considered has the following topology. It consists of $M_* \times L$ mutually interconnected neurons where L is the maximum value of the grey level function. Let $S = \{s_{ik}$ where $1 \leq i \leq M_*$, $1 \leq k \leq L\}$ be a set of binary states of the neural network with $s_{i,k}$ (1 for firing and 0 for resting) denoting the state of the (i,k)th neuron. Let $T_{i,k;j,l}$ denote the strength of the interconnection between neuron (i,k) and neuron (j,l). Symmetry is required:

$$T_{ik,jl} = T_{jl,ik}, \quad 1 \leq i,j \leq M_*, \quad 1 \leq k,l \leq L$$

Neurons are permitted to have self-feedback, i.e., $T_{ik,ik} \neq 0$. In this model each neuron receives input from all neurons and a bias input term I_{ik}:

$$t_{ik} = \sum_j^{M_*} \sum_l^{L} T_{ik,jl} s_{jl} + I_{ik} \tag{4}$$

Each t_{ik} is fed back to corresponding neurons after thresholding:

$$s_{ik} = Z(t_{ik}). \tag{5}$$

where

$$Z(x) = \begin{cases} 1 & \text{if } x \geq 0 \\ 0 & \text{otherwise} \end{cases} \tag{6}$$

In a digital image, each pixel is described by a finite set of grey level function f_i with f_i denoting the grey level of the pixel. The grey level function can be represented by a simple sum of the neuron state variables as

$$f_i = \sum_{k=1}^{L} s_{ik} \tag{7}$$

The neural network model parameters, the interconnection strength and bias inputs can be determined in terms of the energy function of the neural network. The energy function is given by

$$E = -\frac{1}{2} \sum_{i=1}^{M_*} \sum_{j=1}^{M_*} \sum_{k=1}^{L} \sum_{l=1}^{L} T_{ik,jl} s_{ik} s_{jl} - \sum_{i=1}^{M_*} \sum_{k=1}^{L} I_{ik} s_{ik} \tag{8}$$

This function can be naturally reformulated as an error-minimizing function with constraints. The function is defined as

$$E = \frac{1}{2}(\mathbf{C}\hat{\mathbf{f}})^T(\mathbf{C}\hat{\mathbf{f}}) + \frac{1}{2}\lambda[(\mathbf{g} - \mathbf{\Phi}\hat{\mathbf{f}})^T(\mathbf{g} - \mathbf{\Phi}\hat{\mathbf{f}}) - \mathbf{n}^T\mathbf{n}] \tag{9}$$

where λ is a constant, and $\mathbf{C}$ is a second order difference operator. By comparing equation (8) and (9), it can be seen that, except for a constant term, the interconnection strengths and the bias inputs are given by

$$T_{ik,jl} = -\lambda \sum_{p=1}^{M_*} \phi_{pi} \phi_{pj} - \sum_{p=1}^{M_*} c_{pi} c_{pj} \tag{10}$$

and

$$I_{i,k} = \lambda \sum_{p=1}^{M_*} g_p \phi_{pi} \tag{11}$$

respectively. The quantities ϕ_{ij} and c_{ij} are the (i,j)th elements of the matrices $\mathbf{\Phi}$ and $\mathbf{C}$, respectively.

From (10) and (11), one can see that the interconnection strengths and the bias inputs are completely determined by known quantities. Therefore they can be computed *a priori*.

Image processing is carried out by neuron evaluation. Once the parameters are computed, each neuron can randomly and asynchronously evaluate its state and adjust accordingly. The recorded image is taken as the initial state. When one minimum energy point (either global or local) is reached, a signal is sent to its corresponding second level unit. The status of the cluster is changed to true, and the energy at equilibrium E_e is recorded. At the same time, processing in this region (cluster) is suspended.

3B The Second Level Information Exchange

The previous subsection described the processing procedure carried in each first level cluster, which is the major information processing part. This subsection is concerned with information exchange amongst clusters in the first level.

If the original NNHCA model can be utilized without modification, optimization procedure in the first level is performed simultaneously in all the clusters. Thus maximum parallelism in processing is achieved. However, as pointed out earlier, the boundary pixels (units) have to be included in at least two adjacent clusters. This fact introduces confusion if two adjacent clusters are processed simultaneously because the states representing the boundary pixels in the two clusters might be conflict. So a scheme has to be instrumented to avoid such conflicts.

In the following a method is introduced which achieves the maximum possible parallelism without causing conflicting boundary conditions. The solution is to split the first level processing into phases. In each phase, only clusters without common boundaries are processed simultaneously. Fig 2 shows one such solution containing four phases. In Fig 2, each square represents a cluster. Clusters in the four phases are marked 1, 2, 3, and 4, respectively. Clearly, this strategy eliminates the confusion. In the following, a serial execution of the four phases is called a sweep.

1	2	1	2	1	2
3	4	3	4	3	4
1	2	1	2	1	2
3	4	3	4	3	4
1	2	1	2	1	2
3	4	3	4	3	4

Figure 2: Four first Level Processing Phases

A sweep is executed as follows.

1. In phase 1, units in group 1 evolve. The initial states of the units corresponds to initial pixel values.
2. After group 1 reaches equilibrium, phase 2 begins. The units belonging to both group 1 and group 2 assume initial states as those reached by phase 1.
3. After group 2 reaches equilibrium, phase 3 begins. The units belonging to at least two of the three groups assume initial states as those reached by phase 1 or phase 2, whichever are later.
4. After group 3 reaches equilibrium, phase 4 begins. The units belonging to at least two of the four groups assume initial states as those reached by phase 1, phase 2, or phase 3, whichever are the latest.

At the end of each phase, the status of the clusters in the phase are changed to true, and the corresponding E_e's are recorded. Since the processing of the later phases might change the results of the earlier phases, the energy E_e will be used to check consistency. After a sweep. The energy E for each cluster is calculated again and compared with its respective E_e. For any cluster the difference $E - E_e$ is greater than a predefined constant, it is said that the optimal status for that cluster is violated. The status for that cluster is changed back to false. If the optimal status of one or more clusters is violated, another sweep will be executed for those clusters, utilizing the current states as initial states. The procedure carries on until a globally stable status is achieved.

3C The Third Level - Global Coordination

The third level processing is straightforward. It has only one unit. The inputs of the unit are the status of the first level clusters stored at the second level. After each first level processing phase is finished, the status are summed at the third level unit (1 for true and 0 for false). The sum S_c is compared with a predefined threshold $T = N_c$, the number of first level clusters. If

$$T - S_c < \epsilon \qquad (12)$$

where ϵ is a predefined positive constant, the processing is complete. Otherwise, the first level processing continues.

Note that since the status for all the clusters will be true right after the last phase is finished, the summation at this stage should be performed after $E - E_e$ is checked for each first level cluster and the status are adjusted.

When all the clusters achieve equilibrium simultaneously (equation (12) is satisfied), the third level unit emits a signal indicating that the optimization process is complete. Then the image can be constructed using (7).

IV. APPLICATIONS

The processing framework introduced in the previous sections has been applied to some early visual information processing tasks. In this section, two application examples will be given. restoration and enhancement.

4A Image Restoration

It is universally accepted that the energy of the point spread function of an optical system is restricted in a finite spatial area. The fact is particularly true for digital systems due to truncation errors. The application of NNHCA to restoration is straightforward. In equation (2). $\mathbf{f}$ is the original image, and the transformation operator $\mathbf{\Phi}$ becomes a Toeplitz matrix $\mathbf{H}$ underlying the effect of the point spread function. The support for $\mathbf{H}$ is $N \times N$; $N << M$. Hence only N^2 pixels in $\mathbf{f}$ contribute to the formation of a particular pixel in $\mathbf{g}$, and image formation is a local process. Therefore only a finite number of pixels in the recorded image **g** contains relevant information to restore a particular pixel in the original image **f**. Hence image restoration techniques with local structures should perform as well as, if not better than, those with global structures.

An example is used to demonstrate the performance of the RCLPP approach implemented by NNHCA. The result is summarized in Fig 3.

Image Lenna shown in Fig 3a) is of size 256×256. The image was degraded by convolving with a 5×5 uniform point spread function. 20 dB white Gaussian noise was added after convolution. Fig 3b) shows the distorted image. The method proposed in the previous sections was applied to this example. The size of a region was 32×32, so the first order cluster contains $32 \times 32 \times 256$ units. An average of three iterations was needed for the first sweep. It was found that only 9 out of the 64 first level clusters need a second sweep. After the second sweep, the overall network enters stable condition. The restored image was constructed then, which is given in Fig 3c).

Compared with the approach introduced by [7], the most significant practical feature of the proposed method is that with the RCLPP structure in terms of NNHCA, restoration is sped up drastically. In [7], over 200 iterations were required in order to reach satisfactory restoration.

4B Image Enhancement

In enhancement the meaning of **g**, **f**, and **n** in (2) are kept unchanged. However, the transformation operator $\mathbf{\Phi}$ represents adaptive piecewise modeling of the recorded image. The modeling scheme in a linear sense was described in [9]. In the 1-D case, the local model is composed of connected ramps that may vary in length and number. For a smooth image section, the model is one single ramp; for an edge, the model will be a set of three ramps. In particular, the estimate of the grey scale value of the current pixel is based on the values of the previous pixels. Then the estimated value is compared with the measured value of the current pixel to predict the position of the boundary pixels of "reasonably smooth" intervals. The nonzero entries in $\mathbf{\Phi}$ indicate the boundary points of the intervals, and the slops of the piecewise linear segments. The generalization of the modeling scheme to 2-D is theoretically straightforward. The boundary pixels of "reasonably smooth" regions and the slops of piecewise linear areas are critical parameters which should be searched in modeling. Apparently this modeling scheme agrees to the RCLPP structure with some subjectivities.

Image Lenna in Fig 31a) was again used in the numerical example. The original image was corrupted by 15 dB white Gaussian noise which was shown in Fig 4a). The corrupted image was modeled by the forementioned adaptive scheme. Then the method proposed in the previous sections was applied. The size of a region was again 32×32, so the first order cluster contains $32 \times 32 \times 256$ units. An average of five iterations was needed for the first sweep. It was found that 12 out of the 64 first level clusters need a second sweep. After another two sweeps, the overall network enters stable condition. The enhanced image was constructed then, which is given in Fig 4b).

V. CONCLUSIONS

A neural network with hierarchical cluster architecture (NNHCA) is used to realize a unified early visual information processing framework. Because the model correctly simulates the underlying image formation process, satisfactory processing result is achieved. However, because of the local and hierarchical structure, this approach provides a natural parallel processing architecture in image processing, and is computationally inexpensive compared with the globally connected neural models.

References

[1] H.C. Andrews, and B.R. Hunt, *Digital Image Restoration*, Prentice-Hall, Englewood Cliffs, New Jersey , 1977.

[2] W.K. Pratt, *Digital Signal Processing,* John Wiley & Sons, New York, 2nd Edition, 1991.

[3] J.P. Sutton, J.S. Beis, and L.E.H. Trainor, "Hierarchical model of memory and memory loss," *J. Phys. A: Math. Gen.* 21, pp.4443-4454, 1988.

[4] J.P. Sutton, J.S. Beis, and L.E.H. Trainor, "A hierarchical model of neucortical synaptic organization," *Mathl. Comput. Modeling,* 11, pp.346-350.

[5] J.P. Sutton, "Mean field theory of nested neural clusters," *Proc. The First AMSE International Conference on Neural Networks,* San Diego, USA, May, 1991.

[6] J.J. Hopfield and D.W. Tank, "Neural computation of decisions in optimization problems," *Biol. Cybern.*, vol. 52, pp. 141-152, 1985.

[7] Y.-T. Zhou, R. Chellappa, A. Vaid, and B.K. Jenkins, "Image restoration using a neural network," *IEEE Trans. on ASSP*, vol. ASSP-36, pp. 1141-1151, Jul. 1988.

[8] J.K. Paik, and A.K. Katsaggelos, "Image restoration using a modified Hopfield network," *IEEE Trans. on Image Processing*, vol. 1, pp. 49-63, Jan. 1992.

[9] L. Guan, "A neural network approach to adaptive image enhancement," *SPIE Proceedings* vol. 1658, pp. 258-266, Feb. 1992.

a)

b)

c)

Figure 3: Restoration: a) The original image; b) The distorted image; c) The restored image

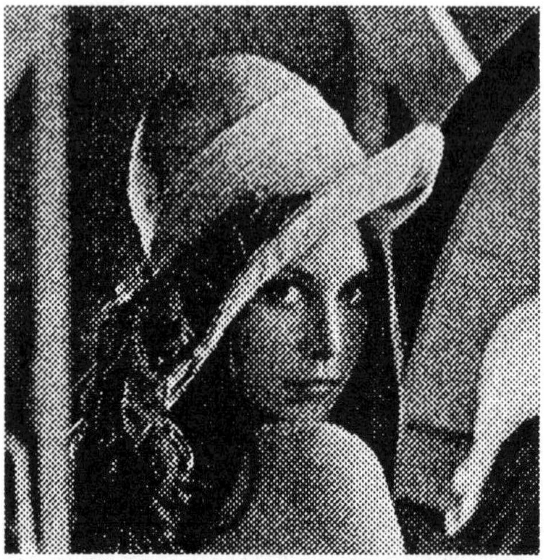

a)

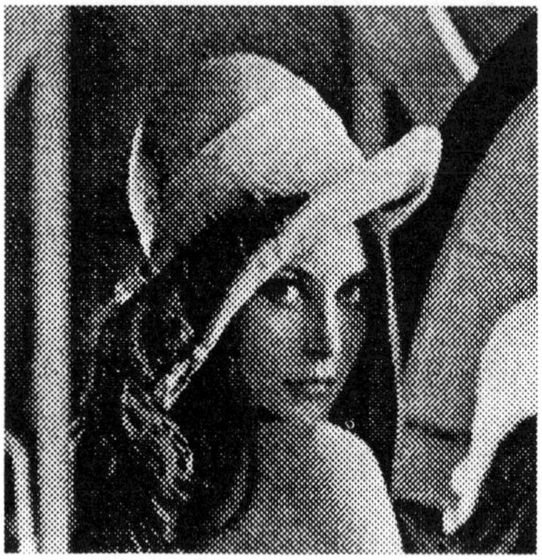

b)

Figure 4: Enhancement: a) The noise corrupted image; b) The enhanced image

An Algorithm of Eye Movements in Selective Fixation

Tohru Yagi[a] Kazutoshi Gouhara[b] Yoshiki Uchikawa[c]
[a,c]School of Engineering, Nagoya University, Nagoya 464-01, Japan
[b]School of Engineering, Chubu University, Kasugai 487, Japan

Abstract—*Fixation*, which is the visual behavior to focus any region in a scene on the fovea, is very important for the recognition processes. Since the retinal structure seems to play the main role of the fixation, we simplified its structure to make a mathematical model on the retinal signal processing, and implemented it to an algorithm of eye movements. After the computer simulation using this algorithm on the simple displayed images, we compared its computed eye movements with the actual human eye movements observed in a cognitive experiment. Analysis of both results revealed that they were very similar eye movements.

I. INTRODUCTION

Since most living creatures have much higher resolution in the focal visual area than the peripheral, eye movements are required for *fixation* [7], which is the visual behavior to focus any region in a scene on the fovea. In fixation, eyes are considered to move toward "attractive" regions in a scene selectively rather than at random. Because the factors which guide eye movements vary [1], eye movements seem to be complicated. For our purpose to make an algorithm of eye movements in fixation, it is necessary to sort out several criteria which cause eye movements. Therefore, we started observing the human eye movements on very simple scenes to confirm one of the already-known criteria, *the proximity of stimulus* [1]. It is the factor that something located close to the fovea are more likely to be detected.

According to the reference [8], the detection position seems to be processed at the lower level of the visual systems and independent of the recognition processes which are made at the higher level. We have hypothesized that the retinal signal processing plays the main role of the detection position in fixation. In the retina [5][6][9], the visual signals are transferred topologically from the photo receptor layer to the retinal ganglion cell layer. Each ganglion cell connects several photo receptor cells through several kinds of neurons, and makes a receptive field. Neighboring receptive fields are considered to be overlapping to process the input visual signals. Two features of the retinal structure seems to cause differences in the resolution between the focal visual area and the peripheral in vision. One is the distribution of cells in the retina. Cells are located more densely in the fovea than in the peripheral region [11]; therefore, the focal visual area is more highly resolved than the peripheral. The other feature to cause the non-uniform resolution is the size of the receptive field. The size of the receptive fields in the central region is relatively small and increasingly larger towards the periphery of the retina [2]. Because the input visual signals are converged less in the fovea and more in the peripheral region, this feature makes for fine coding in the fovea and coarse coding [3] in the peripheral region.

In this paper we assumed the non-uniform distribution of cells, and focused on the latter feature. Moreover the photo receptor cells and the retinal ganglion cells only were considered when making a mathematical model of the signal processing in the retina. Using this model we made an algorithm of eye movements in fixation, and then simulated it in the computer. The computed results were compared with the actual human eye movements examined in a cognitive experiment to evaluate the algorithm.

II. HUMAN EYE MOVEMENTS

A. A cognitive experiment

To record the actual human eye movements, we executed a cognitive experiment using the ophthalmography "Eye Camera" produced by NAC Co. In this Eye Camera, an infrared ray is irradiated towards a cornea, and its reflection is detected with a CCD camera. Eye movements are detected as movements of its reflection. According to the specification of this ophthalmography, temporal resolution is 1/600th of a second, and spatial resolution 0.17 of a degree. Spatial resolution which we measured in our experiment, however, was 3.0 degrees. It might have resulted from the head motion of the test persons, even though their heads were kept relatively stable.

The experiment was performed in a dark room. Fig. 1 shows the facilities for the experiment. The screen was set 1.5m away from the test person. We used the

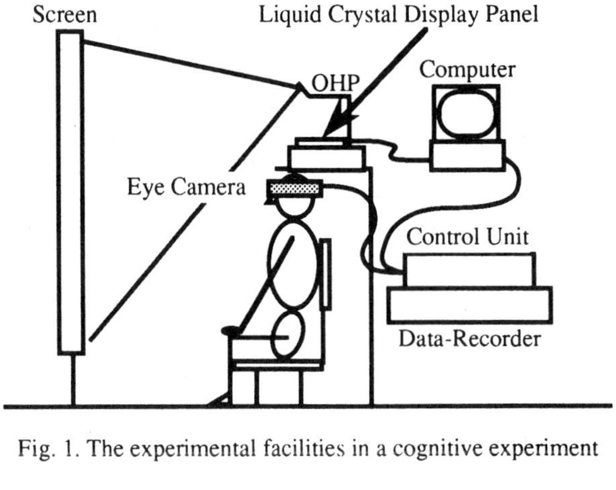

Fig. 1. The experimental facilities in a cognitive experiment

0-7803-0999-5/93/$03.00 ©1993 IEEE

computer graphic images as the displayed scenes. It was displayed on the screen from an overhead projector and a liquid crystal display that were located behind the test person.

The experimental procedure is as follows. After we calibrated Eye Camera, a test person was told to stare at the center of the screen, then the experiment was started. The images were displayed for only a few short seconds since the aim is to prevent the test person from recognizing the objects in the displayed image. During the display of the image, the position of both eyes was recorded as the x-y spatial data every 1/600th of a second. Finally we calibrated Eye Camera again to measure how accurately eye movements were recorded. After the experiment, the eye scanpaths of each test person were obtained from the data and imposed into the displayed image. It enables us to observe eye movements on the displayed image.

B. Displayed image

For our purpose, the displayed images must be suitable to produce eye movements to the nearest object. Reducing other factors which guide shifts in the image, the images were specially designed in some ways. First, we have chosen the meaningless images as the displayed scenes in our experiment. Something important for understanding the meaning of the scene, called "higher-level visual features", are more likely to be selected as targets [1]; however, it is ambiguous which the physical stimulus of the target, or the meaning of the target caused eye movements. Eliminating the factor of the meaning, we recorded eye movements caused by the physical stimulus. Second, every target in the images was identical in color, brightness, shape and size, and differs only in position. As each target has equal stimulus, only the position affects human eye movements. Above all, we have chosen dots as targets and placed them at randam in a scene.

Since the detection range of the Eye Camera is limited to 40x40 degrees both horizontally and vertically, the projected size of the whole image was set within such a range. Moreover, the size of each object was determined within a 4x4 degree area corresponding to the size of the human focal visual area. Fifteen different images were made for the computer simulation. In the experiment, five of them were chosen at random for use.

C. Experimental results

In the experiment, 10 test persons who have good eye sight were selected. Four selected images were displayed twice to each person. The displaying time was two seconds which was not enough time for him/her to recognize all the objects in the image. Fig. 2 indicates the locus of eye movements, so called "eye scanpaths" [7], on the displayed images. Symbol "S" denotes the initial fixation point of the eye scanpath. Starting from position "S", eyes scan most targets in the image. Because eye scanpaths were not overlapping in most results, eyes may not move towards the scanned targets within two seconds. On the basis of these results, we have analyzed 1) the relative position between the fixation point and the target and 2) the speed of eye movements between each fixation point.

1) The relative position between the fixation point and the target: Some parts of the locus in Fig. 2 make the blotches. This seems to be caused by the eyes pausing momentarily at one point before proceeding to the next. Therefore we picked up the x-y spatial data which stayed within three degrees for 25 (*msec*) or longer, and showed such points on the displayed images with white dots (Fig. 3). According to this analysis, the blotches were the fixation points. Moreover 82% of all 862 fixation points included the targets within four degrees. Because each fixation point was often located on or close to the object, the object was detected with only one eye movement from the fixation point. It implies that the peripheral low resolution vision has enough ability to detect the next target.

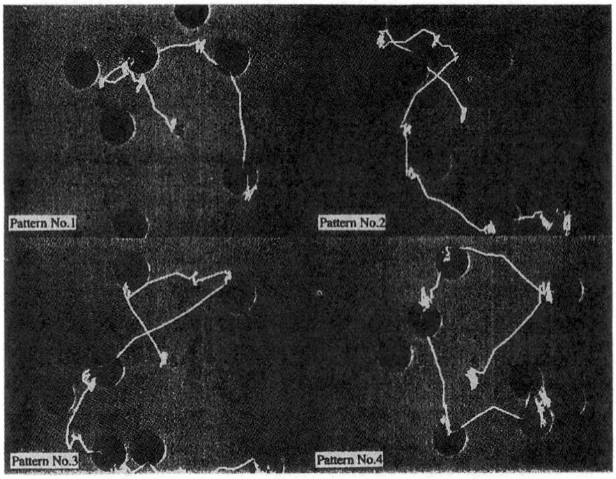

Fig. 2. Human eye scan paths

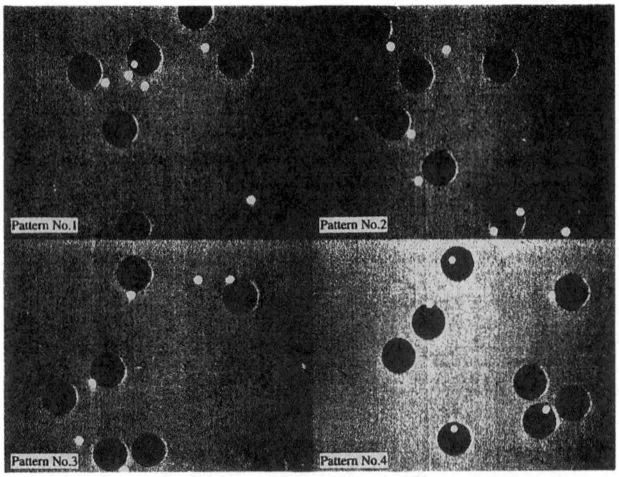

Fig. 3. Fixation points

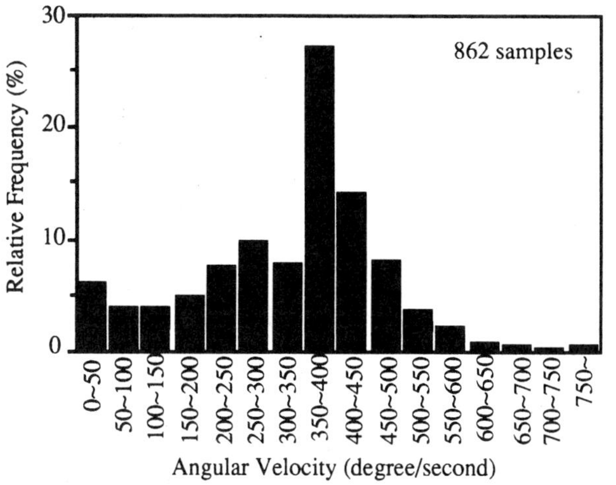

Fig. 4. The speed of each eye movement

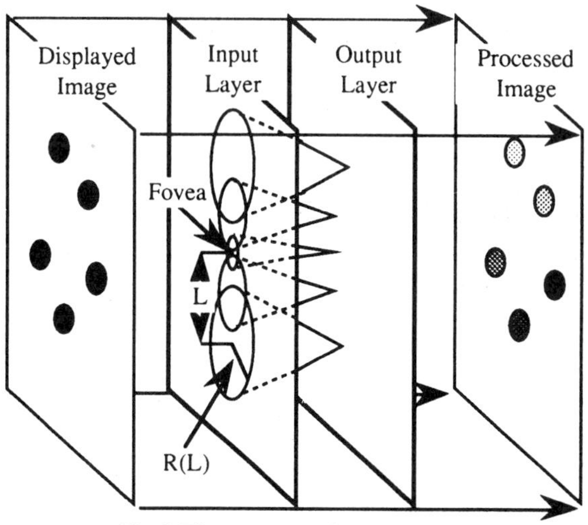

Fig.5. The structure of Retinal Model

2) The speed of eye movements between each fixation point: Fig. 4 indicates the angular velocity of eye movements among any two consecutive fixation points. 74% of all eye movements had the speed of 250 (*degrees/msec*) or faster. Therefore most eye movements were certainly *saccadic eye movements* [4], and the human vision might be suppressed during eye movements, so called *saccadic suppression* [10].

III. COMPUTED EYE MOVEMENTS

A. Structure on an algorithm of eye movements

On the ground of several features in the human fixation, we presented an algorithm of eye movements in fixation. The algorithm consisted of four steps:

1) Taking a image.
2) Processing the image.
3) Relocating of the fovea.
4) Excluding the detected objects.

These steps were repeated until all objects are detected.

1) Taking the image: Because our experiment showed that the human vision might be suppressed during eye movements, the image was not processed while eyes were moving. Therefore the images were taken during the fixation period of eyes. It is easier to process the stable images than those which are taken during eye movement period because an image is flowing during the period.

2) Processing the image: In our algorithm an image was processed with a mathematical model of the retinal structure called "Retinal Model" (Fig. 5). Retinal Model consisted of two layers. Assume that the first layer corresponds to a layer of photo receptor cells, and the second, retinal ganglion cells. In both layers, cells were distributed uniformly. Each retinal ganglion cell connected several photo receptors to make a circular receptive field. The radius of the receptive field $R(L)$ increases corresponding to the distance from the fovea L. Define the strength of connection between the photo receptors and the retinal ganglion cell as the connection value. The spatial distribution of its value can be considered as the spatial filter. Therefore, the signal process in the retina is expressed as the local operation of the image using the spatial filters. Define $I(x,y)$ as input visual signals, $F_{x,y}(\xi,\eta)$ as the spatial filters, and $A_{x,y}$ as the integral area. Hence the processed image $O(x,y)$ is as follows:

$$O(x,y)=f\left[\int\int_{A_{x,y}} F_{x,y}(\xi,\eta)\cdot I\,(x+\xi,y+\eta)d\xi d\eta\right]$$

$A_{x,y}$ is the group of ξ and η which suffices the following equation, $|\xi^2+\eta^2|\leq R(L)$. $f[\ ]$ is the output function of the ganglion cells.

3) Relocating of the fovea: The fovea was directly relocated on the target immediately after the image has been processed. We defined the relocation of the fovea as an eye movement. We assumed that the target contained the pixel that had the maximum signal value among the pixels in the processed image. The position of such a pixel was defined as the fixation point calculated with the algorithm. Afterwards, the fovea was relocated on that position, and the relocation process was completed.

4) Excluding the detected objects: To prevent the model from continuing to detect the same objects, it is necessary to exclude every detected object from further selection. In this algorithm, we masked the determined area to eliminate the detected object, after the fovea was relocated on the detected target.

B. Processed images by Retinal Model

In this section, we show how the images are processed by Retinal Model. In following processed images (Fig. 6), we used pillbox function as $F_{x,y}(\xi,\eta)$. This function have a cylindrical shape. In this simulation its height was 1, and the radius of the cylinder R was proportional to the square root of the distance L between the fovea and the center of the receptive field. The darkest area has the maximum signal value in the pixel of the output layer which is denoted by symbol "□". Symbol "x" denotes the position of the fovea. This figure shows that each object has been classified corresponding to the distance between the object and the fovea.

C. Computer simulation using the proposed algorithm

Fig. 7 is the computed eye scanpaths. Symbol "□" denotes the fixation points, "S" the starting position of the fovea. After the image was processed, the fovea was

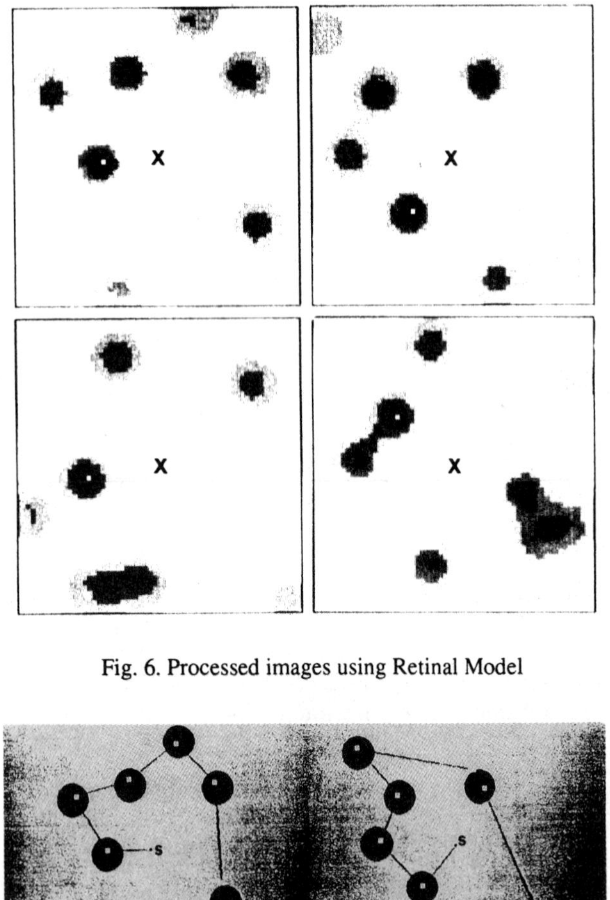

Fig. 6. Processed images using Retinal Model

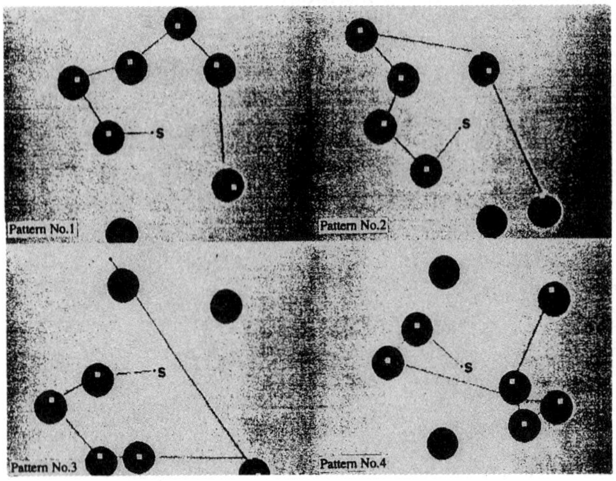

Fig. 7. Computed eye movements

relocated on the position which had the maximum signal value, then we masked in a 6 degree area which is slightly larger than the size of each object. This process was repeated for 6 times on each displayed image. This figure shows that the fovea was relocated on the object, and each object was detected one by one.

IV. EVALUATION OF RESULTS

Both results in the computer simulation and the experiment showed quite similar eye movements. They were alike in five points:

1) 82% of 431 human fixation points and 100% of 51 computed fixation points included the objects within four degrees.
2) The objects which had already been detected were not detected again.
3) Usually only one eye movement accomplished movement between fixation points.
4) Images might not be extracted during human eye movements because of saccadic suppression.
5) Eye movements occurred towards the closest object from each fixation point.

We have already shown the similarity from 1) to 4); therefore, we shall discuss the fifth feature here.

We confirmed that our experimental results were "idiosyncratic" [7]. It seems that there were no particular rules in detecting orders. Each eye movement between fixation points, however, tended to occur towards the closest object from the present fixation point. We shall show this proximity of the stimulus using a quantitative method.

To analyze this tendency quantitatively, we need to evaluate the distance between each fixation point. L, L_{max} and L_{min} indicate the distance between each fixation point, the maximum and the minimum distance between the present fixation point and the objects, respectively. We defined the distance index a as the following:

$$a = \frac{L_{max} - L}{L_{max} - L_{min}}$$

Figure 8, for example, indicates the distance index from one fixation point to each object. The fixation point is adjusted to the center of the closest object. If eyes move towards the object "B" from the fixation point "A", the distance index a is 0.590 on this eye movement. Likewise, all simulated and experimental eye movements were analyzed in the same way, and then the frequencies of each value were graphed as a histogram in Figure 9. This denotes that most computed and human eye movements occurred towards the object that is closely located from the present fixation point.

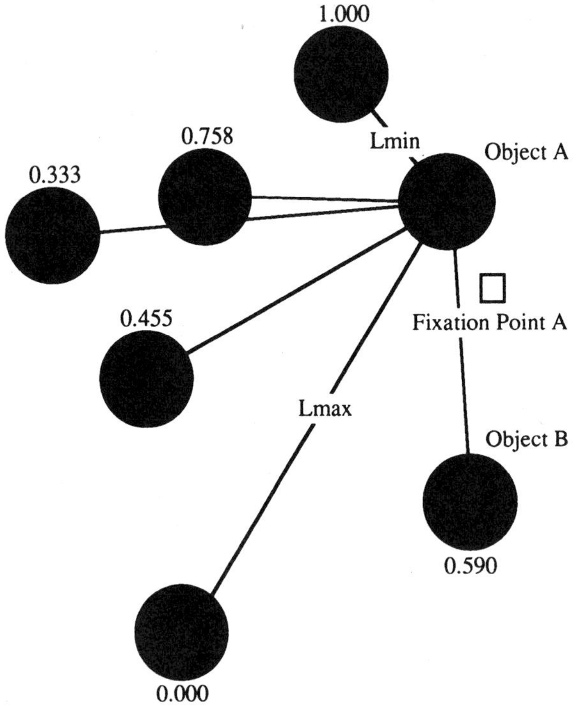

Fig. 8. The distance index between the object and the fixation point

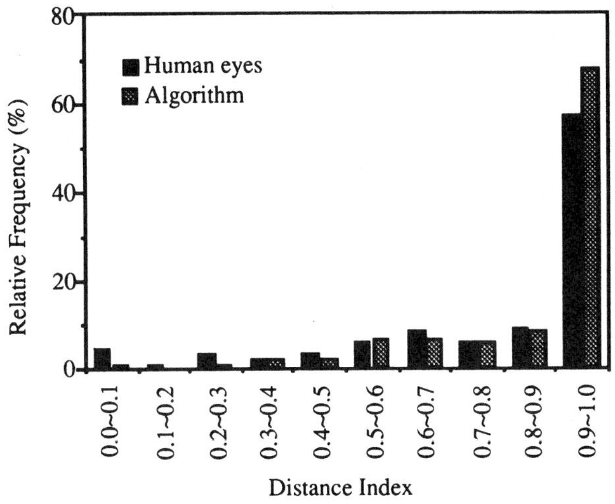

Fig. 9. The histogram of the distance index

V. CONCLUSIONS

In this paper we made a mathematical model of the retinal signal processing. The size of the receptive field was small in the fovea and gradually became larger towards the periphery. Using this model we proposed an algorithm of eye movements in fixation. Its computer simulation showed that each object in the image was detected one by one with eye movements. This result was compared with the actual human eye movements that were recorded with ophthalmography in a cognitive experiment. Comparison revealed that both results were basically identical. It implies the algorithm proposed in this paper realized eye movements in fixation.

The ability of the proposed algorithm might depend on the two mathematical functions: the function which causes the size of the receptive field to change, and the function which defines the spatial distribution of the connecting value between input and output layers. These functions, as well as the procedure to mask every detected object in the image, will be investigated in a further study.

REFERENCES

[1] Abbott, A.L. : "A survey of selective fixation control for machine vision," *IEEE Control Systems*, Vol. 12, No. 4, pp. 25-31, 1992

[2] Hitchcock, P.F. and S.S. Easter, Jr., : "Retinal ganglion cells in gold fish : A qualitative classification into four morphological types, and a quantitative study of the development of one of them," *J. Neurosci.*, Vol. 6, No. 4, 1986

[3] Hinton, G.E., J.L. MaClelland and D.E. Rumelhart : "Distributed Representation," *Parallel Distributed Processing* Vol.1, MIT Press, 1986

[4] Komatsuzaki, A., Y. Shinoda and T. Maruo : Neurology of the oculomotor system, Ikaku-shoin Ltd., Tokyo, 1985

[5] Lindsay, P.H. and D.A. Norman : *Human Information Processing, An Introduction to Psychology, 2nd Edition*, Academic Press, New York, 1977

[6] Marr, D. :*Vision*, W.H.Freeman and Company, New York, 1982

[7] Noton, D. and L.W. Stark : "Scanpaths in eye movements during pattern perception," *Science*, Vol. 171, pp. 308-311, 1971

[8] Schneider, G. E. : "Two visual systems," *Science*, Vol. 163, pp.895-902, 1969

[9] Sterling, P., M. Freed and R.G. Smith : "Microcircuitry and functional architecture of the cat retina," *Trends in Neuro Science*, Vol. 9, No. 5, pp. 186-192, 1986

[10] Volkmann, F. C., A. M. L. Schick and L. A. Riggs : "Time course of visual inhibition during voluntary saccades," *J. Opt. Soc. Am.*, 58, pp. 562-569, 1968

[11] Wassle, H., U. Grunert, J. Rohrenbeck and B. Boycott : "Cortical magnification factor and the ganglion cell density of the primate retina," *Nature*, Vol. 341, pp. 643-646, 1989

Can neural pooling help insects see at night?

Eric J. Warrant
Department of Zoology, University of Lund
Helgonavägen 3, S-22 362 Lund, SWEDEN

Abstract **Neural pooling of signals generated in the photoreceptors of neighbouring ommatidia is investigated as a possible strategy for improving vision at low light levels in compound eyes. Theoretical calculations of the maximum spatial frequency detectable by an eye suggest that neural pooling greatly improves vision in dim light. This strategy is particularly useful for an insect such as the locust which is primarily day-active, has an eye design more suited to bright light (the apposition design), but often flies in the evening. Nevertheless, compound eyes primarily designed for nocturnal vision (superposition eyes) are found to out-perform neurally pooled apposition eyes in dim light, a situation which is most likely reversed in bright light when the apposition eye ceases to pool, thereby greatly improving spatial resolution.**

I. INTRODUCTION

Insects active at dusk, dawn or night are faced with the problem of extracting reliable information from an environment whose mean light intensity may be up to 10^8 times lower than during the day. In such insects this problem can be significantly reduced if the visual system can somehow improve photon capture. This can be achieved by one of two methods: (1) *optically*, by widening the aperture through which light enters relative to the eye's focal length, and/or (2) *neurally*, by summing, or *pooling*, signals from neighbouring visual channels, thus increasing the number of photons perceived per channel. However, the improvements to vision at low light levels afforded by both of these strategies are usually offset by simultaneous and unavoidable losses in spatial resolution. These losses result from image blurring due to aberrations associated with a widened aperture in the optical method, and from a coarsening of the visual sampling array associated with pooling in the neural method. This trade-off between spatial resolution and light capture (or *sensitivity*) highlights the strategies employed by eyes for extracting the maximum visual information from scenes at different light intensities (Fig. 1): during the day, when light is plentiful, more emphasis can be placed on improving resolution at the expense of sensitivity, and *vice versa* during the night. In compound eyes, part of this trade-off is already fixed in the physical design of the eye (Fig. 2). In *apposition* eyes (Fig. 2A), the design most common in day-active insects, the structural units (the *ommatidia*) are optically isolated, which preserves resolution but limits photon capture by each photoreceptor (or *rhabdom*) because of a limited aperture. On the other hand, in *superposition* eyes (Fig. 2B), the design most common in nocturnal insects, an internal clear zone removes optical isolation between ommatidia and allows a wide aperture to provide light to a single rhabdom: this improves photon capture, but incurs losses in resolution due to aberrations and other optical imperfections [2].

Manuscript received July 6th 1993. This work was supported by the Swedish Natural Science Research Council.

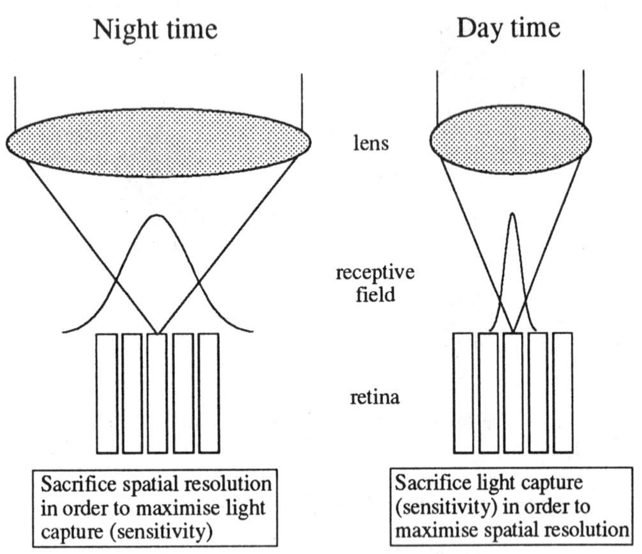

Fig. 1. Strategies for extracting maximum visual information from scenes at different mean light intensities

However, there are some insects with apposition eyes which are primarily active during the day but also have some activity at night. A good example is the locust *Locusta*, which may undertake long flights at night, but has eyes whose designs are much better suited to diurnal intensities. One may wonder how well locusts can see at night compared to their truly nocturnal counterparts with superposition eyes. This is the question investigated in this paper. In particular, can a locust's vision be improved at night by neural pooling, and if so, can the locust thereby see just as well as insects with superposition eyes? To answer these questions simple calculations were made to estimate the maximum spatial frequency (ν_{max}) the locust can perceive at each light intensity using pooling, and what kind of pooling is optimal to achieve this value of ν_{max}.

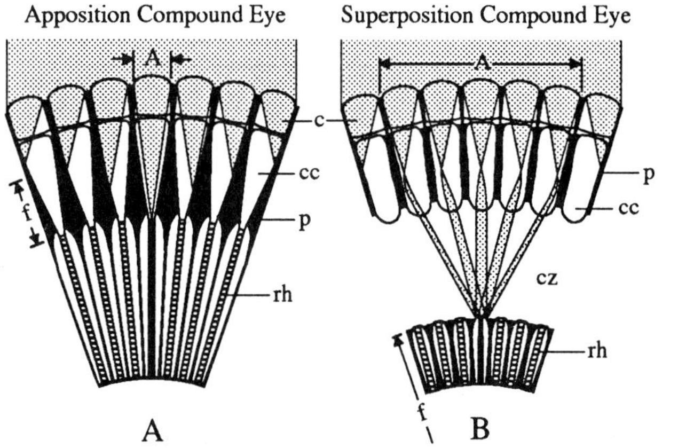

Fig. 2. Schematic longitudinal sections through the two major classes of compound eyes. A. Apposition eyes, typical in diurnal insects. B. Superposition eyes, typical in nocturnal insects. c = cornea, cc = crystalline cone, p = screening pigment, A = aperture, f = focal length, rh = rhabdom, cz = clear zone.

II. THEORY

Imagine a compound eye is viewing a regular grating of equally spaced black and white stripes which has a spatial frequency ν and contrast m, and from this grating is receiving an average light intensity I (photons/cm^2/sec/sr). The quantity of photons (N) absorbed by a rhabdom of diameter d and quantum capture efficiency ε during one integration time of the eye (Δt), per steradian solid angle of the grating, is given by [3]

$$N = 0.89\, n\, \varepsilon\, \Delta t\, d^2\, I\, (D/f)^2, \tag{1}$$

where n is the number of ommatidial facets contributing light to a single rhabdom (one in apposition eyes, several hundred or even over 1000 in superposition eyes - see Fig. 2), f is the focal length and D is the diameter of a single corneal facet lens. Associated with this absorption of N photons is an uncertainty or *noise* which, in the Poisson statistics governing photon absorption, is simply equivalent to $\sqrt{N}$ [2,3], that is

$$\text{Noise} = \sqrt{N}. \tag{2}$$

This formulation of Noise is really only valid at lower light levels: in bright light it is photoreceptive transduction noise which dominates [4]. One can also define a *Signal*, and this depends not only on N but also on the modulation transfer function (MTF) of the eye, M(ν), and the grating contrast m [3]:

$$\text{Signal} = m\, N\, M(\nu). \tag{3}$$

The MTF describes the potential range of spatial frequencies that an eye can perceive. Very conveniently, the MTF is simply the Fourier transform of the photoreceptor's spatial receptive field profile (or *angular sensitivity* function), which can be measured electrophysiologically from the insect retina.

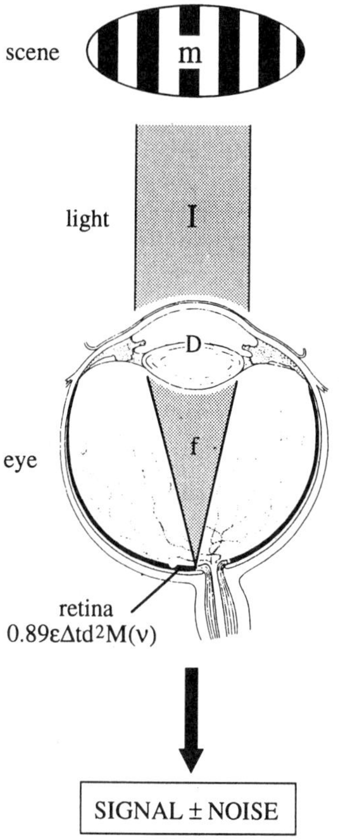

Fig. 3. A schematic representation of the parameters used to calculate Signal and Noise. m = grating contrast, I = light intensity (Photons / μm^2 / sec / sr), D = pupil diameter (μm), f = focal length (μm), ε = photoreceptor capture efficiency, Δt = photoreceptor integration time (sec) d = rhabdom diameter (μm), M(ν) = modulation transfer function (MTF), ν = spatial frequency (cycles / deg).

Signal and Noise (Fig. 3) both have units of photons, but more importantly, it is only the Signal that has a dependency on spatial frequency: the Noise has a constant amplitude.The effects of Noise on the range of perceivable spatial frequencies are easily seen by plotting Signal and Noise together (Fig.4). Only those spatial frequencies which have a Signal greater than the Noise will be perceived by the eye: those with a lower signal will be 'lost' in the Noise. The spatial frequency at which the signal becomes equal to the noise is the *maximum detectable spatial frequency* of the eye, ν_{max} (Fig.4). Only spatial frequencies lower than ν_{max} will be perceived: all those above have a Signal lower than the amplitude of the Noise and will be lost.

For a given eye design and angular sensitivity function, one can use (1) to (3) to calculate ν_{max} at each light intensity. This approach was taken to compare the apposition eye of the day-active locust *Locusta* and the superposition eye of the dusk-active dung beetle *Onitis* for a range of light intensities equivalent to the normal range of the daily cycle (Figs. 5-7). The values of parameters used in the equations are (respectively for the beetle and the locust): n = 180 and 1, Δt = 50 and 58 msec, d = 14 and 4 μm, D = 32 and 37 μm, and f = 352 and 160 μm. For

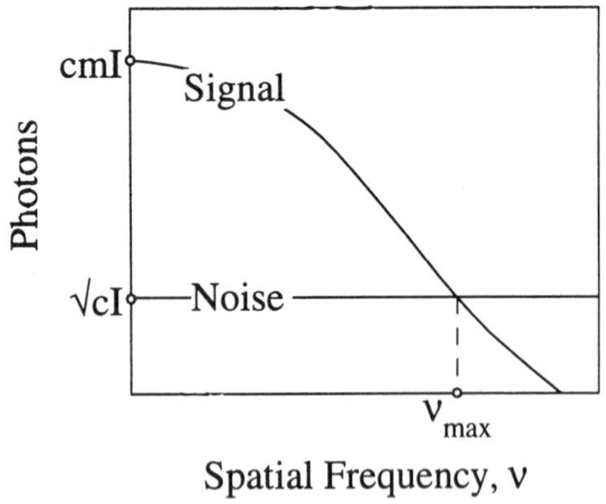

Fig. 4. Signal and Noise represented graphically as function of spatial frequency (ν). Assume we know the contrast of the scene (m) and the eye's light gathering constant ($c = 0.89\, n\, \varepsilon\, \Delta t\, (D\, d\, /\, f)^2$). For each intensity ($I$), Signal becomes equal to Noise when the spatial frequency reaches a value ν_{max}, the maximum detectable spatial frequency.

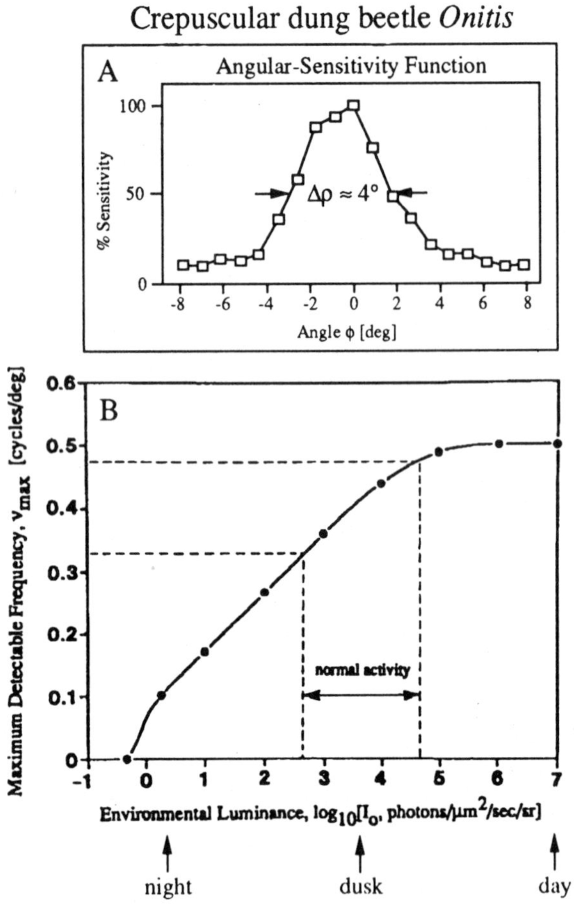

Fig. 5. A. The spatial receptive field (or angular sensitivity function) of a single photoreceptor in the retina of the dusk-active dung beetle *Onitis*. The receptive field's half-width is its acceptance angle, Δρ. B. The maximum detectable spatial frequency as a function of light intensity, calculated using the receptive field profile in A. During its normal activity, is able to detect spatial frequencies up to around 0.4 cycles/deg.

both species, $m = 0.5$ and $\varepsilon = 0.5$. A similar approach was used to calculate improvements in ν_{max} which may result from neural pooling in the locust, but an exact description of the procedure will be reserved until neural pooling is first discussed (see below).

III. RESULTS AND DISCUSSION

We will begin the analysis by comparing the dusk-active (i.e. crepuscular) dung beetle superposition eye with the night dark-adapted apposition eye of the day-active (i.e. diurnal) locust. Then we will introduce a model of neural pooling to see whether this improves vision for the locust at low light levels, and whether this improvement can match the performance of the superposition eye in the absence of pooling.

A. Can a locust see as well at night as a dung beetle?

In the dung beetle superposition eye an aperture of about 200 ommatidial facets focuses light onto each single rhabdom. Electrophysiological recordings reveal the eye to have high sensitivity to light [5] and quite reasonable resolution [6], with receptive fields of half-width (i.e. acceptance angle, Δρ) around 4° (Fig. 5A), which is only about twice as wide as in the locust (see below). Using the receptive field of Fig. 5A and (1) to (3), we find that in *Onitis* ν_{max} remains non-zero down to an intensity of - 0.3 log units (dark night; Fig. 5B). Below this intensity *Onitis* is unable to distinguish spatial details in its environment (pooling mechanisms assumed absent). During its normal activity at dusk, *Onitis* is able to resolve spatial frequencies up to around 0.4 cycles/deg (Fig. 5B) which is more than adequate to negotiate the smaller branches of trees on the open African veldts where it normally flies [6].

Locusts, despite being day-active, have certain adaptations which improve their vision at night by increasing photon capture [1,7]. The receptive field of the rhabdom more than doubles in width between the light-adapted day state and the dark-adapted night state (Fig. 6A), this change mainly being due to a doubling of the rhabdom's diameter (Fig. 6B). Using the receptive field of Fig. 6A and (1) to (3), we find that in *Locusta* ν_{max} remains non-zero down to an intensity of 2.3 log units (dusk; Fig. 7), which is 2.6 log units brighter than the equivalent intensity for *Onitis*. In fact, at all intensities dimmer than dusk, the beetle superposition eye performs significantly better than the locust apposition eye. This is mostly because the dung beetle has the potential to capture up to 200 times as much light as the locust, but by doing so only halve its resolution. It is only at brighter intensities, when photons are plentiful, that the locust eye probably out-performs the beetle eye, mostly because of the locust's narrower angular sensitivity function.

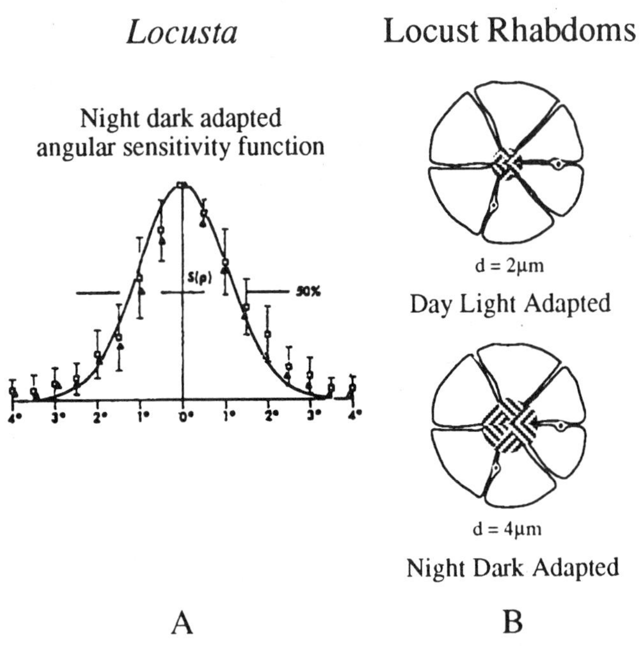

Fig. 6. A. The night dark-adapted receptive field of a photoreceptor in the locust *Locusta*, which has $\Delta\rho$ = 2.5°.(adapted from [1]). B. As an adaptation for capturing more photons at night, the rhabdom diameter, *d* (rhabdom shown in schematic cross-section), doubles from 2 μm during the day to 4 μm during the night.

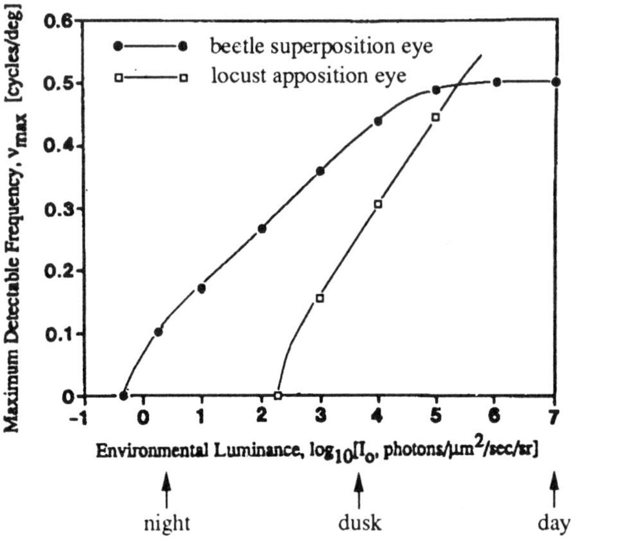

Fig. 7. Maximum detectable spatial frequency as a function of light intensity in the dung beetle (filled circles) and the locust (open squares) calculated using the receptive fields shown in Figs. 5 and 6 respectively. The beetle is able to detect spatial details at much lower intensities than the locust.

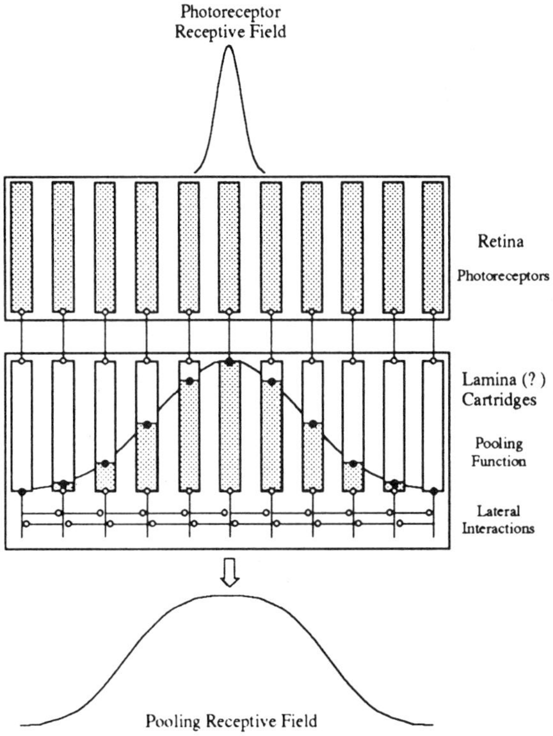

Fig. 8. A neural pooling strategy in compound eyes. The retina contains neurally isolated photoreceptors each of which views a particular region of space within its receptive field. At some higher region of the optic lobe (possibly the lamina) lateral connections between these spatial channels may allow pooling of signals according to some pooling function, whose shape represents the strength of the interaction with distance. The action of the pooling function on each pooled photoreceptive signal leads to a receptive field due to pooling. There is one such pooling receptive field per spatial channel (only one spatial channel's pooling receptive field is shown).

B. Can neural pooling help the locust see better at night?

Obviously, to see adequately at night the locust cannot rely on its eyes alone. The only other option remaining for the locust is to utilise neural pooling (Fig.8), a strategy which has been inferred in crabs and flies [8,9,10], but never directly demonstrated. Imagine a retina with a sampling array of neurally isolated photoreceptors, each of which supplies a signal to the brain which is proportional to the average light intensity it receives from the solid angle of visual space defined by its own receptive field. For neural pooling to function, these signals have to be summed together neurally, via lateral connections between neighbouring visual channels in some higher optic neuropil in the insect brain, such as the lamina or the medulla. Prime candidates for the cell types involved in such lateral interactions are amacrine cells, which are known to interconnect neighbouring visual channels, but whose function is unclear. Experimental work, investigating the neural basis of pooling, is currently underway (Warrant, unpublished). If the strength of the pooling interaction decreases with distance from each central channel according to some *pooling function*, then the interaction of this function with the signal from each photoreceptor produces a *pooling receptive field*. Each visual channel (there are as many channels as rhabdoms) has an identical pooling receptive field: when pooling is taking place this represents a substantial oversampling of the visual scene. In this way, each channel receives a greatly increased photon catch, but only at the expense of a

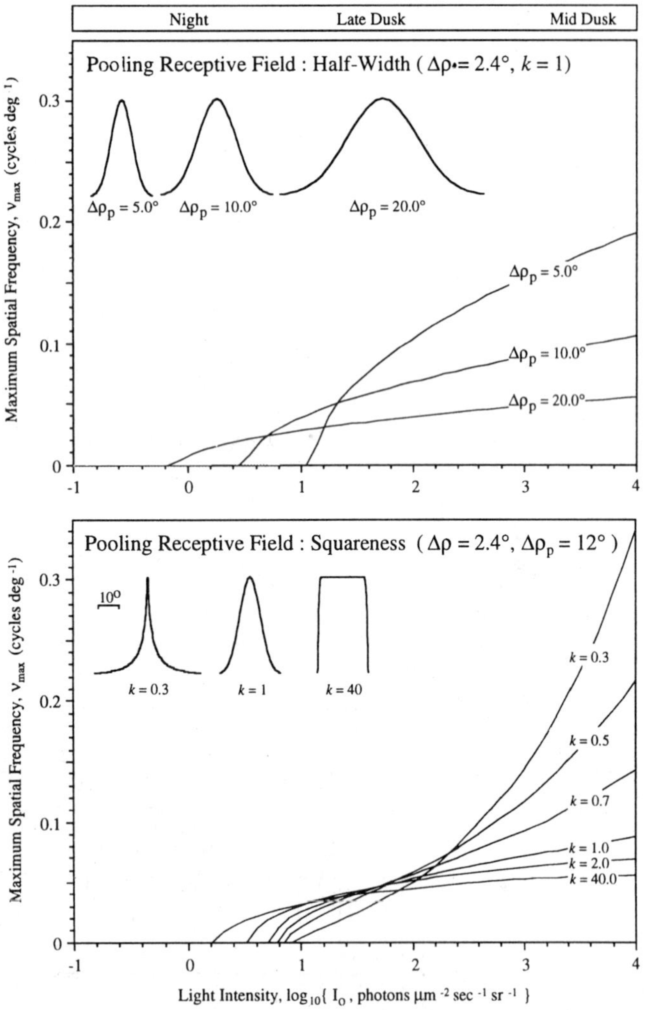

Fig. 9. Maximum detectable spatial frequency as a function of light intensity for various combinations of A. pooling receptive field half-width ($\Delta\rho_p$) and, B. squareness (k). Wider, squarer receptive fields (larger $\Delta\rho_p$ and k) allow detection of spatial details at lower intensities, but only at the expense of spatial resolution at higher intensities. The photoreceptor's acceptance angle ($\Delta\rho$) was held constant at 2.4° in this example.

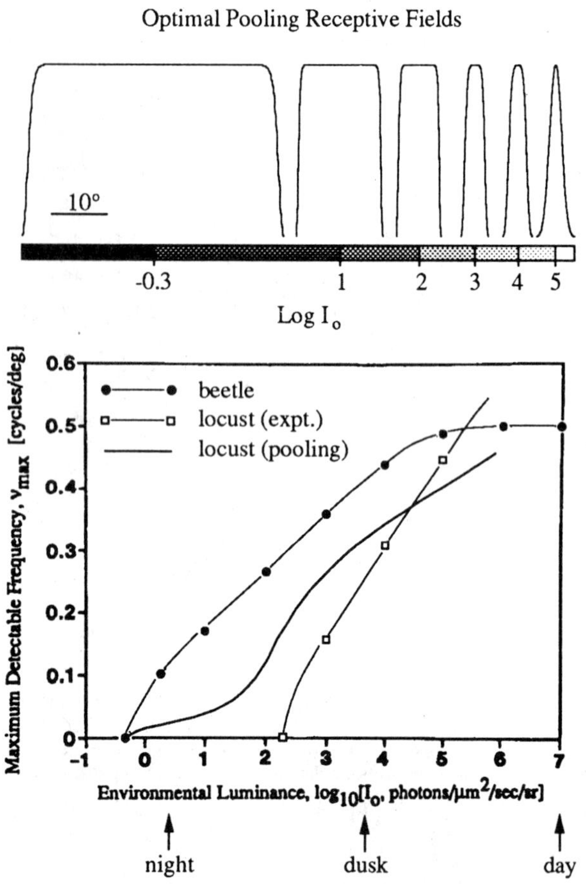

Fig. 10. The optimum pooling receptive field shape in locusts at each light intensity (top) and the corresponding maximum detectable spatial frequency (solid line without symbols, bottom). The optimum receptive field is wider and squarer at lower light intensities and becomes narrower and more Gaussian at higher intensities. Despite pooling, the locust is unable to detect the same spatial detail at each intensity as the beetle (which is not pooling).

substantial loss in spatial resolution. Nevertheless, the resulting balance may still improve vision.

According to the model, at high light intensities pooling is unnecessary and the lateral pooling interactions are 'turned off'. As the light intensity drops, the interactions are gradually 'turned on' according to the pooling function that best matches the particular intensity being experienced. If the light intensity drops further, the neural connections are assumed sufficiently plastic to widen the pooling accordingly.

A simple approach to explore the benefits of pooling is to calculate ν_{max} using (1) - (3) just as before, but instead of using the photoreceptor's receptive field in the calculation, we use the pooling receptive field. The number of photons absorbed by a rhabdom during one integration time (i.e. N ; (1)) is actually equivalent to the volume of the photoreceptor's receptive field in 3 dimensions. Thus, we can replace N in (2) and (3) by the volume of the 3 dimensional pooling receptive field. In addition, the MTF of the pooling receptive field can be used in (3). The most physiological approach to the problem is to generate the pooling receptive field from a known pooling function working on known receptive field profiles. This, however, is computationally very involved and is the subject of a current study (Warrant, in preparation). A simpler, and slightly less physiological approach, is to propose a particular pooling receptive field profile, and assume that a pooling function exists neurally that can generate it (which may not always be true). The pooling receptive field profile used in the calculations that follow has the form

$$f(\phi) = 0.79\, n\, \varepsilon\, \Delta t\, D^2 I \exp\{ -2.77 (\phi / \Delta\rho_p)^{2k} \} \qquad (4)$$

where ϕ is an angular variable, $\Delta\rho_p$ is an angular constant, k is a constant and all other symbols have their usual meanings. When $k = 1$, $f(\phi)$ is a Gaussian function of half-width $\Delta\rho_p$. When $k < 1$,

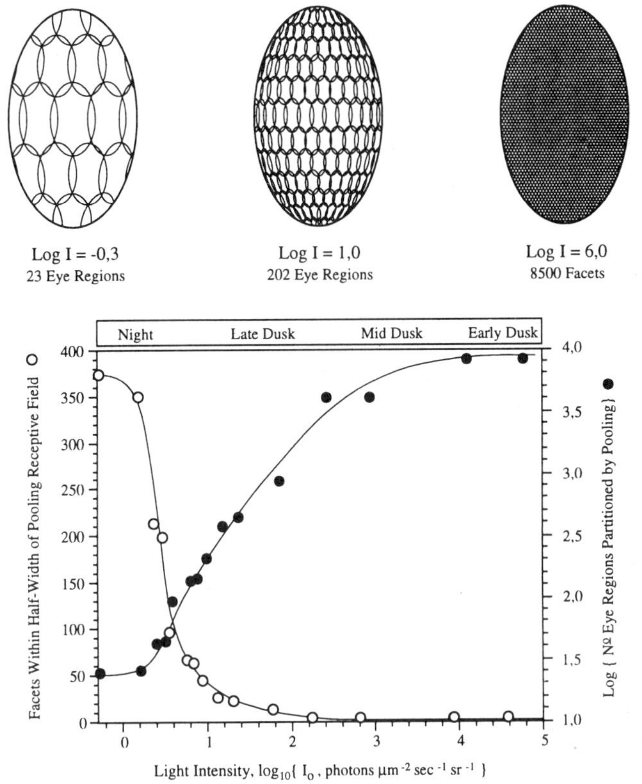

Fig. 11. The effect of optimum pooling receptive field on the spatial sampling mosaic of the locust apposition eye at various light intensities. We can define the half-width of the pooling receptive field as the minimum angular separation which two point objects require in order for both to be resolved separately in the pooling eye. The eye, shown schematically (top), is partitioned into a number of regions by the pooling receptive field half-width: because the half-width is wider at lower light intensity, there are fewer regions. In bright daylight, when pooling is absent, the 8,500 facets of the eye act in isolation. The number of eye regions (filled circles) and the number of facets in each of these regions (open circles) is shown as a function of light intensity below.

$k = 1$, $f(\phi)$ is a Gaussian function of half-width $\Delta\rho_p$. When $k < 1$, $f(\phi)$ becomes cusp-shaped, and when $k > 1$, $f(\phi)$ becomes squarer (Fig. 9, insets). An increase in $\Delta\rho_p$, at any value of k, makes $f(\phi)$ wider.

Widening $f(\phi)$ (Fig. 9A) and/or making $f(\phi)$ squarer (Fig. 9B) reduces the light intensity at which the eye is still able to discriminate spatial detail in a scene, but only at the expense of spatial resolution at higher intensities. One could imagine a strategy of pooling whereby the lateral neural interactions widen the pooling receptive field, and make it squarer, at lower intensities, and then narrow it and make it more cusp-shaped at higher intensities. In this way, ν_{max} could be kept as high as possible at all intensities, thereby greatly improving vision. If one calculates the optimum pooling receptive field shape at each intensity, this is exactly the strategy one finds (Fig. 10, top). The optimum value of ν_{max} obtained at each intensity indicates that vision in the locust is greatly improved at low light levels by neural pooling (Fig. 10, bottom): not only is the minimum intensity for which the eye is useful reduced by 2.5 log units, but ν_{max} is elevated significantly at all other evening intensities. This is despite the fact that in real terms the sampling mosaic of the eye becomes much coarser at low light levels (Fig. 11): as the light intensity falls, so too do the number of regions of the eye viewing the world with clarity (as defined by a partitioning of the eye by the half-widths of neighbouring pooling receptive fields). Nevertheless, the increased photon catch per visual channel more than counteracts the loss of resolution due to a coarsening of the sampling mosaic, and thus vision is improved.

Despite the benefits bestowed by neural pooling, the locust apposition eye is unable to match the performance of the beetle superposition eye (which is not pooling) at any intensity (Fig. 10). This indicates the evolutionary advantage for a truly nocturnal animal to develop an eye that catches as many photons as possible *optically* whilst maintaining as good an image quality as possible. If even better vision is needed, then pooling may be employed in addition. Nevertheless, in an insect like the locust, which needs to see at night but which evolution has deemed to have a day-design eye, neural pooling represents an impressive strategy for nocturnal vision.

ACKNOWLEDGEMENTS

I am extremely grateful to my friend and colleague Dr. Dan-Eric Nilsson for his encouragement and stimulating discussions, and also for the ongoing support I receive form the Swedish Natural Science Research Council.

REFERENCES

[1] M. Wilson, "Angular sensitivity of light and dark adapted locust retinula cells," *J. Comp. Physiol.* vol. 97, pp. 323-328, 1975.

[2] E.J. Warrant and P.D. McIntyre,"Arthropod eye design and the physical limits to spatial resolving power," *Prog. Neurobiol.* vol. 40 (4), pp. 413-461, 1993.

[3] A.W. Snyder, "Acuity of compound eyes: physical limitations and design," *J. Comp. Physiol.* vol. 116, pp. 161-182, 1977.

[4] J. Howard, B. Blakeslee and S.B. Laughlin, "The intracellular pupil mechanism and photoreceptor signal:noise ratios in the fly *Lucilia cuprina*," *Proc. R. Soc. Lond. B* vol. 231, pp. 415-435, 1987.

[5] E.J. Warrant and P.D. McIntyre, "Screening pigment, aperture and sensitivity in the dung beetle superposition eye,"*J. Comp. Physiol. A* vol. 167, pp. 805-815, 1990.

[6] E.J. Warrant and P.D. McIntyre, "Limitations to resolution in superposition eyes," *J. Comp. Physiol. A* vol. 167, pp.785-803, 1990.

[7] D.S. Williams, "Changes of photoreceptor performance associated with the daily turnover of photoreceptor membrane in the locust," *J. Comp. Physiol.* vol. 150, pp. 509-519, 1983.

[8] A. Dubs, S.B. Laughlin and M.V. Srinivasan, "Single photon signals in fly photoreceptors and first order interneurons at behavioural threshold," *J. Physiol.* vol. 317, pp. 317-334, 1981.

[9] F.E. Doujak, "Can a shore crab see a star?," *J. exp. Biol.* vol 116, pp. 385-393, 1985.

[10] B. Pick and E. Buchner, "Visual movement detection under light- and dark-adaptation in the fly, *Musca domestica*," *J. Comp. Physiol.* vol. 134, pp. 45-54, 1979.

Chapter 7: Optimization

CHAPTER 7
Optimization

For many years the primary method of neural network optimization was the technique proposed by Hopfield and Tank. This approach cast the optimization problem in the form of a cost function that could be implemented as a one-layer feedback associative memory. The biases and weights of the associative memory represent the constraints and the node values represent the solutions. An initial state is passed to the nodes, feedback ensues, and when stability is reached we read the node values to determine the solution.

The Hopfield-Tank approach has been studied in great detail. It has many good properties, including parallel execution for fast solutions to computationally intensive optimization problems. One of the drawbacks to this approach is that the resulting solution is not guaranteed to be optimal. In fact, it is almost a guarantee that it is not optimal. Nonetheless, for many optimization problems close is good enough and the execution speed more than makes up for the lack in solution accuracy.

Over the past few years, the MLP and LVQ neural networks have also been shown to be capable of performing optimization tasks. Results in these areas are found in the papers in this chapter.

Today, most of the applications of neural network optimization networks is in the area of scheduling or routing. Design has emerged recently as a new area, and one paper is included in this chapter that describes this application. This application has some exciting possibilities, especially in the construction, automotive, and airlines communities. Also, with the emergence of neural networks in financial forecasting (see Chapter 5), I would expect more applications of neural network optimization in market analysis and optimization to surface soon. Finally, the integration of evolutionary computation (genetic algorithms, evolutionary programming, and evolutionary strategies) and neural networks will undoubtedly lead to new optimization techniques.

The papers included in this chapter fall into two areas: scheduling/routing and design. A description of each papers is as follows:

- **Scheduling/Routing.** It is well known that the computational complexity of finding optimal solutions to scheduling and routing problems increases exponentially with the number of constraints. Seemingly simple problems such as finding the shortest route from one city to another can quickly become computational nightmares when there are over 20 cities involved in the solution. The following papers describe some fresh neural network approaches to this age-old problem. **Paper 7.1** describes a self-organization procedure that can solve arbitrarily large cell placement problems. **Paper 7.2** uses the counterpropagation neural network (an LVQ extension) to predict the number of no-shows for airline flights. The resulting predictions are used to optimize seat allocations on flights. **Paper 7.3** employs a Hopfield-Tank neural circuit to produce near optimal schedules in a manufacturing plant. **Paper 7.4** combines a Hopfield-Tank neural circuit and an expert system to optimize robotic assembly sequences. **Paper 7.5** uses a Hopfield-Tank neural circuit to optimally place heat sources in hybrid power circuits. **Paper 7.6** describes how a MLP can be used to estimate the trip O-D matrix when trip generation and trip attraction counts are approximate (fuzzy).

- **Design.** As mentioned above, the use of neural networks for design optimization is an exciting new application area. **Paper 7.7** shows how a MLP and an expert system can be combined to design bridges that are aesthetically pleasing within the environment in which they will be constructed.

Arbitrarily Sized Cell Placement by Self-Organizing Neural Networks

Ray-I Chang and Pei-Yung Hsiao
Department of Computer and Information Science
National Chiao Tung University
Hsinchu, Taiwan, R.O.C.

Abstract - This paper describes a new self-organizing neural network which can solve arbitrarily sized cell placement problem with various constraints on their connection and dimension. The presented solution procedure modifies the Kohonen's self-organization algorithm to adapt to the sub-class of self-organization problems in which the sample vectors are not easily available, as well as in the case of cell placement problem. For the arbitrarily sized cell placement, the *overlap penalty function* and the *cell growing-up algorithm* are introduced to our solution model where sizes of the cells are considered during the self-organization process to reduce overlaps among the cells. Our procedure is convergent in a reasonable number of iterations and the resulting total wire lengths are at least the same as the previous results.

I. Introduction

Cell placement has been proven to be NP-hard [14]. Although a number of heuristic algorithms have been proposed in the literature [7], they are inherently sequential and unable to efficiently exploit massively parallel architecture. The neural nets which can solve optimization problems [5][6] have been suggested as new ways to solve the cell placement problems [1][3-4][8-9][12]. This paper proposes a self-organizing neural network to solve the arbitrarily sized cell placement problem. Cell placement using a self-organizing net consists in finding the positions of cells within the specified region such that the closely related cells are placed near one another, or, loosely speaking, the whole interconnection wire length is minimized. Opposing to Kohonen's self-organizing feature maps, in cell placement, the sample vectors are not easily available. In this paper, we use the topological relation to produce these sample vectors. Fig. 1 shows the difference between the proposed method and the Kim's method [12]. Kim's self-organization assisted placement (SOAP) generates these sample vectors randomly. Unless enormous amounts of random data are generated, the quality of results would not be guaranteed. Experimental results show that the total wire lengths obtained are at least the same as the previous results. As the proof of convergence for this model is lengthy, the details will not be apperaed in the submission summary.

II. Summarized modeling of cell placement and self-organization

Definition 2.1.

Given the connectivity cm_{ij} between cell i and cell j. Let d_{ij} be the distance between cell i and cell j. The *cell placement problem* is defined as to minimize the following cost function

$$C_{WL} = \sum_{i=1}^{m} \sum_{j=i+1}^{m} cm_{ij} \times d_{ij}$$

Definition 2.2.

Given the similarity sm_{ij} between output neuron i and output neuron j. Let d_{ij} be the distance (difference) between output neuron i and output neuron j. The *self-organization problem* can be defined as to minimize the following cost function

$$C_{SO} = \sum_{i=1}^{m} \sum_{j=i+1}^{m} sm_{ij} \times d_{ij}$$

Theorem 2.1.

Let the output neurons and their similarities be corresponding to the cells and their connectivities, respectively. Then the cell placement problem can be solved if the related self-organization problem is solvable.

Proof:

To prove that the cell placement problem can be solved if the related self-organization problem is solvable, it must be shown that $C_{SO} = C_{WL}$. Under the assumption that the output neurons and their similarities are corresponding to the cells and their connectivities, respectively, it then can be concluded that $C_{SO} = C_{WL}$. Therefore, the total wire length is minimized if the output neurons are self-organized. The cell placement problem then can be solved if the related self-organization problem is solvable. **Q.E.D.**

III. Arbitrarily sized cell placement algorithm

In this paper, the force directed concept [11] is used to simulate the lateral interactions among the neighboring neurons and to produce the sample vectors. Fig. 2(a) shows a selected neuron, *i.e.*, neuron 3, and the forces come from its neighbors. The summation of forces is computed and the sample vector V_3

0-7803-1254-6/93$03.00

Table I presents the detailed experimental results of total wire length. Our experience indicates that our algorithm is competitive with the other approaches mentioned above. In our future works, we intend to use ellipse istead of circle to model a cell. We foresee that it will give us better results.

V. Conclusion

A novel self-organizing neural network has been presented in the context to solve the arbitrarily sized cell placement. The experimental results are quite encouraging. It was found that this proposed approach is competitive with the previous state-of-the-art algorithms. The modelling of a cell by a circle is disadvantageous in case of narrow, rectanglar cells. In our future works, we intend to use ellipse or rectangular instead of circle to improve the modeling of a cell.

VI. Acknowledgments

We thanks Dr. K. Doerffer, Dr. P. Kraus (univ. of Karlsruhe) and especially Dr. F. M. Fohannes (univ. of Munich) for their valuable comments and sugestions.

REFERENCES

[1] A. Hemani and A. Postula, "Cell placement by self-organisation," *Neural Networks*, Vol. 3, pp. 377-383, 1990.

[2] G. Odawara, T. Hamuro, K. Iijima, T. Yoshino, and Y. Dai, "A rule-based placement system for printed wiring boards," In *Proc. DAC*, 1987, pp. 777-785.

[3] G. Persky, "Experiments in cell placement with a simulated neural network," In *Proc. Int. Workshop on Placement and Routing*, May 1987, pp. 10-13.

[4] H. Date, M. Seki, and T. Hayashi, "LSI module placement methods using neural computation networks," In *Proc. Int. Conf. Neural Networks*, 1990, pp. 831-836.

[5] J. J. Hopfield and D. W. Tank, "Neural computation of decisions in optimization problems," *Biological Cybernetics*, Vol. 52, pp. 141-152, 1985.

[6] J. Naft, "Neuropt: Neurocomputing for multiobjective design optimization for printed circuit board component placement," in *Proc. IJCNN* 1989, pp. I/321-325.

[7] K. Shahookar and P. Mazumder, "VLSI cell placement techniques," *ACM computing surveys*, Vol. 23, No. 2, June 1991.

[8] M. L. Yu, "A study of the applicability of Hopfield decision neural nets to VLSI CAD," in *Proc. 26th Design Automa. Conf.*, 1989, pp. 412-417.

[9] M. Sriram and S. M. Kang, "A modified Hopfield network for two-dimensional module placement," in *Proc. IEEE ISCS*, 1990, pp. 1664-1667.

[10] R. P. Lippmann, "An introduction to computing with neural nets," *IEEE ASSP Mag.*, April 1987.

[11] S. Goto, "An efficient algorithm for the two dimensional placement problem in electrical circuit layout," *IEEE Trans. C&S*, Vol. 28, pp. 12-18, Jan. 1981.

[12] S. S. Kim and C. M. Kyung, "Circuit placement in arbitrarily-shaped regions using the self-organization principle," *IEEE Trans. CAD*, vol.11, no.7, pp.844-854, 1992.

[13] T. Kohonen, Self-organization and associative memory, 3rd ed. New York: Springer-Verlag, 1989.

[14] W. E. Donath, "Complexity theory and design automation," In *Proc. 17th Design Automat. Conf.*, 1980, pp. 412-419.

[15] C. C. Tsai, S. J. Chen, P. Y. Hsiao and W. S. Feng, "New iterative construction approach to routing with compacted area," *IEE Proc. E*, Vol. 138, No. 1, pp. 57-72, 1991.

TABLE I.
Experimental results for the test examples.

Examples	Regions	Ours	[1]	[12]
[1] Fig. 2	4 × 4	15.31*	16	21.66
	4 × 2	16*	16*	16*
	2 × 2 × 2	12*	12*	12*
[12] Fig. 15	4 × 4	24*	24*	24*
mblk-2 [15]	100 × 85	1207.83	-	-
ALU [12]	30 × 30	608.14	949.26	837.75
ALU+	30 × 30	524.42	-	-

* Optimal solutions.
\+ The size of cells are random numbers.

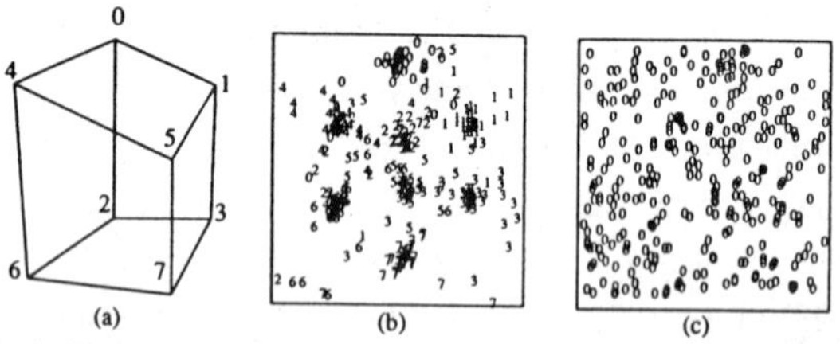

Fig. 1. Example to illustrate the difference between force directed method and random method with 300 generated sample vectors in a 480 x 480 region. (a) Topological relation of input nodes. (b) Force directed sample vectors. (c) Random generated sample vectors.

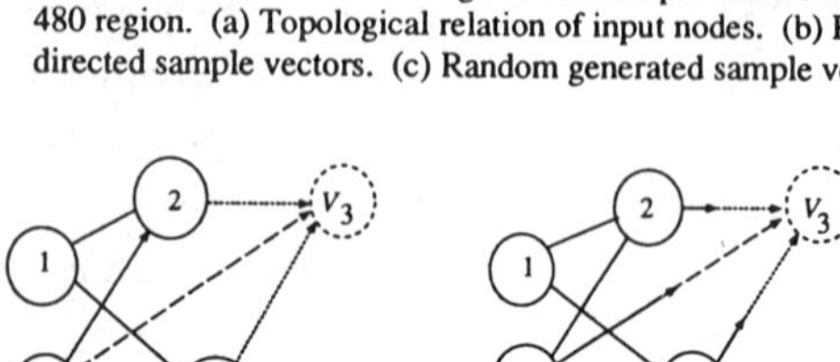

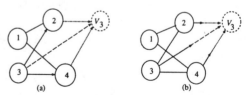

Fig. 2. (a) Calculate the summation of forces and select the sample vector. (b) The selected node and its neighbors are moving toward V3 with some weights.

is produced. In Fig. 2(b), the selected neuron and its neighbors move toward V_3 in association with the movement vectors. Fig. 3 shows the neighborhood $NE_j(t)$ of a neuron j at time t is a set of neurons lying within the topological distance $\delta(t)$ from the neuron j. Here the $\delta(t)$ determining the size of the neighborhood is a time-decreasing function. The size of neighborhood is initially large and will decrease slowly and gradually decreases over time.

The overlap penalty function is modeled by the repulsive force. The repulsive forces are calculated between cells to reduce the overlaps between cells. Arbitrarily sized cells are modeled as circles. This model is reasonable to reflect the connection and overlaps between cells directly. Cells' growing up is a useful technique proposed to improve the placement result. The sizes of cells are increased gradually to preserve the current placement configuration and to reduce the overlaps of cells in the final result. It is generally not desirable that an abrupt change of cell sizes will result in a significant distortion of the current placement. The system is convergent if the position weights have no distinct changes.

Step 1. Initialization: $t = 0$.

Set the working radius r_i' of each cell i as a small value. Set the position weights as bounded random values. The predefined bounding functions $f_x()$ and $f_y()$ are

$$f_x(x) = \begin{cases} 0 & x \le 0 \\ w & x \ge w \\ x & \text{others} \end{cases}$$

$$f_y(y) = \begin{cases} 0 & y \le 0 \\ h & y \ge h \\ y & \text{others} \end{cases}$$

Step 2. Randomly (or with some priority) select a cell, say b_i.

Step 3. Compute the sample vector $V_i = (vx_i, vy_i)$ by the self-organizing principle.

$$vx_i = x_i(t) + \frac{dx_i}{D_i}, \qquad vy_i = y_i(t) + \frac{dy_i}{D_i}$$

$$D_i = \sqrt{dx_i^{\,2} + dy_i^{\,2}}$$

$$dx_i = \sum_{j=1}^{m} f(d_{ij}) \times dx_{ij} \,/\, d_{ij},$$

$$dy_i = \sum_{j=1}^{m} f(d_{ij}) \times dy_{ij} \,/\, d_{ij}$$

where $dx_{ij} = x_j - x_i$, $dy_{ij} = y_j - y_i$ and

$$d_{ij} = \sqrt{dx_{ij}^{\,2} + dy_{ij}^{\,2}},$$

$$f(d_{ij}) = cm_{ij} \times \frac{d_{ij}}{r_i' + r_j'} - \frac{(r_i' + r_j')^2}{d_{ij}^{\,2}}.$$

Step 4. Update the position of cell i and its neighbors within $NE_i(t)$. For all such cells, b_k, perform

$$x_i\,(t + 1) = f_x(x_i\,(t) + \eta(u, t) \times (vx_i - x_i\,(t)))$$

$$y_i\,(t + 1) = f_y(y_i\,(t) + \eta(u, t) \times (vy_i - y_i\,(t)))$$

where $\eta(u, t)$ is a gain term and u is the topological distance between b_k and b_i. The moving distances of the cells are decreased as the iteration is increased or as u is increased.

Step 5. Increase t. Increase r_i'. If $(r_i' > r_i)$ then $r_i' = r_i$.

Step 6. If (system not convergent) then go to *Step 2*.

IV. Experimental results

The proposed algorithm has been implemented in C language on a SUN SPARC IPC station running UNIX. The results of running this algorithm on various examples of placement problem are given below.

The first example is an artificial, but difficult, problem from Fig. 4 of Ref. [12]. This circuit has 16 cells connected in a 4 × 4 mesh-connected pattern. The proposed algorithm was able to achieve the optimal solution (shown in Fig. 4) in approximately 5 seconds. In addition, the result is free from overlap and has been minimized the wire length and the area used. The second example consisting 29 cells and 82 nets, called mblk-2, was reproduced from Ref. [15]. Fig. 5 presents the solution of placing mblk-2 within a 100 × 85 region. The total wire length obtained was 1207.83. The third example from Fig. 2 of Ref. [1] has eight cells. Each cell was connected to three closest neighbors. Fig. 6 presents solutions of this problem under various constraints on the shape and dimension of the region. The final corresponding optimal solutions were achieved. We have illustrated that the proposed method can be used under different constraints.

The last example consisting 67 cells and 81 nets, called ALU, was reproduced from Ref. [12]. Each cell in this example is a 3 × 3 rectangle and has to be placed within a 30 × 30 region. The total wire length obtained was 608 units. We did get a better result than that achieved in Kim's SOAP [12], where it used approximately 838 units. Fig. 7(a) presents the time behavior during the process. The initial position weights are random values around the center of the given region, as shown in 1), and finally are spread out over the given region, as shown in 6). The plots shown in Fig. 7(b) demonstrate the changes of the total wire length versus the iteration number during the placement of ALU. Both Euclidean and Manhattan distance are shown. It is seen that the wire length variation at the early stage is high and gradually convergent to a constant value. The large variation of wire length at the early stage is due to the large size of the neighborhood and the large gain term. As the process continues, the changes are reduced. Because that the size of the neighborhood and the magnitude of the gain term are decreased. Fig. 8 presents solution of placing ALU within a 30 × 30 region in which the size of cells come from the generated random numbers between 1 × 1 and 5 × 5. The total wire length achieved was 524.42.

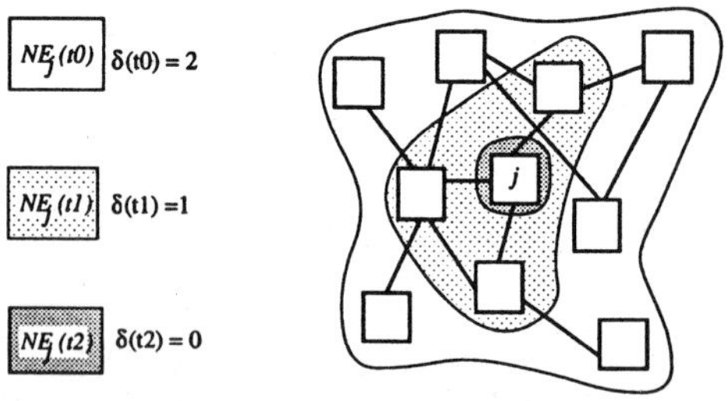

Fig. 3. Node j is represented as the selected node. Regions with different fill pattern are represented as the neighborhood at difference time, t0 < t1 < t2.

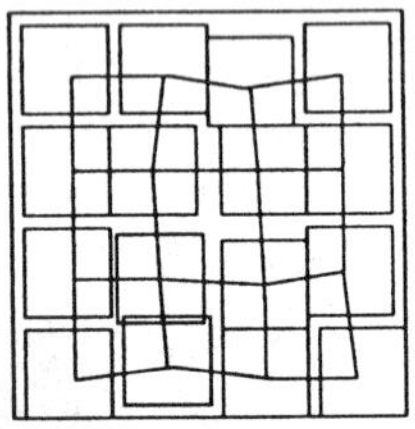

Fig. 4. An example from Fig. 15 of [12] having 4x4 mesh connected cells.

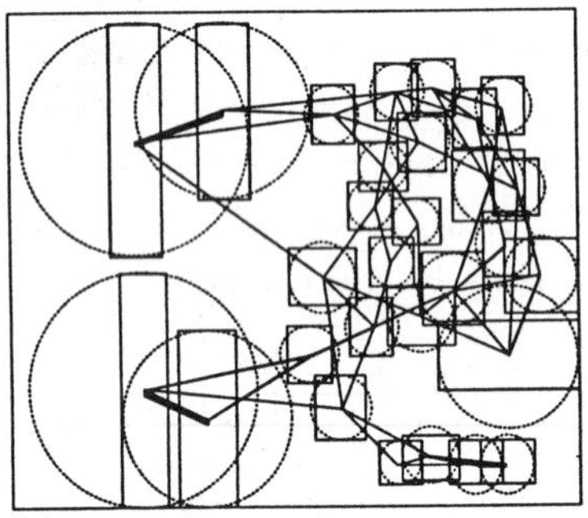

Fig. 5. The mblk-2 example from [15]. Place 29 cells within a 100 x 85 region, then the obtained result has a total wire length of 1297.83.

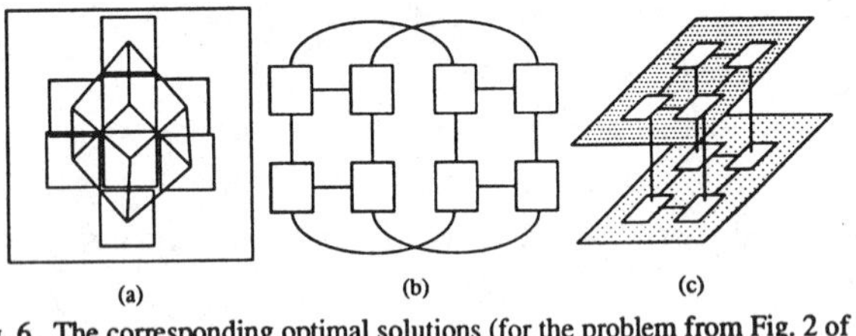

Fig. 6. The corresponding optimal solutions (for the problem from Fig. 2 of [1]) are achieved under following constraints: (a) 2-D 4x4 region, (b) 2-D 4x2 region, and (c) 3-D 4x4x2 region.

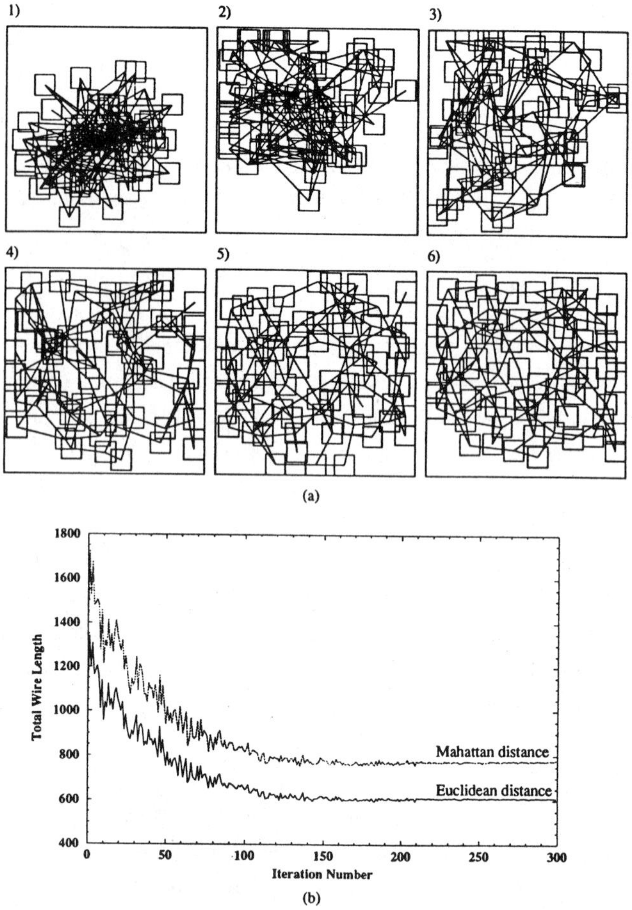

Fig. 7. The ALU example from [12]. (a) The initial positions are randomly generated within the given region and finally are spread out over the given region. (b) The change of wire length versus the iteration number.

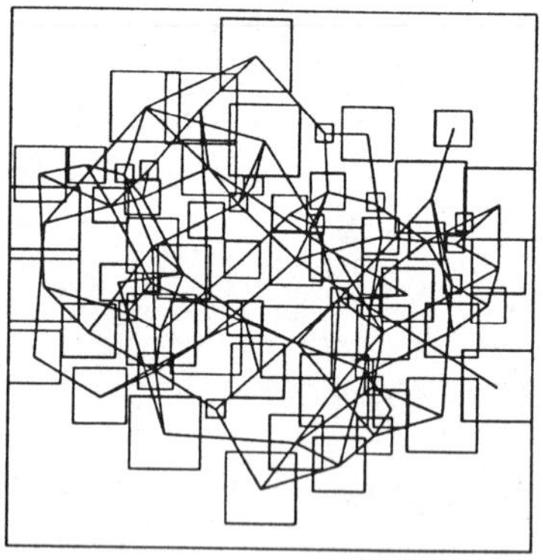

Fig. 8. Solution of placing ALU within a 30 x 30 region in which the size of cells come from the generated random numbers between 1 x 1 and 5 x 5. The total wire length achieved was 524.42.

---

* *This work was supported in part by the National Science Council, Rep. of China, under contract number: NSC 82-0404-E009-129.*

Controlling Airline Seat Allocations with Neural Networks

Bernd Freisleben

Dept. of Computer Science (FB 20)
University of Darmstadt
Alexanderstr. 10
D–6100 Darmstadt, Germany

Gernot Gleichmann

Deutsche Lufthansa AG
System Vertrieb und Verkauf
Im Taubengrund 6
D–6092 Kelsterbach, Germany

Abstract

In this paper we present a neural network that is intended to support airline marketing specialists in controlling seat allocations on flight departures. The focus of our investigation is the prediction of overbooking rates in order to avoid that an aircraft departs with empty seats when passengers who have booked seats do not participate in the flight. The neural network proposed to solve the problem is an extension of the forward–only counterpropagation model. The network learns to approximate the mapping between the input data (the number of booked seats for each reservation class at distinct time periods prior to departure) and the desired output (the number of no–shows). The trained network is then used to make the predictions for the future. The feasibility of our approach is demonstrated by an efficient implementation. Experimental results obtained on real–life booking data for a particular flight indicate that the proposed neural network model is superior to the standard forward–only counterpropagation model and quite competitive to traditional, non–neural methods applied to the overbooking prediction problem.

1 Introduction

Seat inventory management is a very important economical task for airline companies, because it is aimed at balancing the number of seats sold for each reservation class to maximize total passenger revenues. In order to achieve this goal, airline marketing specialists must be able to forecast the expected market demand and the passenger behaviour as precisely as possible. The task is to determine optimal limits on the number of bookings that may be accepted in a particular reservation class, with the intention to avoid selling low cost seats to passengers who would have been willing to pay a high cost or to avoid selling too many discounted seats which at the end could have been sold to full–fare customers. The complexity of the problem is further increased by the fact that some passengers who have booked seats do not show up (*no–shows*). In order to solve this problem, it has become common practice among airline marketers to accept more bookings than physically available on an aircraft (*overbookings*). Since the number of no–shows is highly variable, despite overbooking there will quite often still be empty seats that could have been sold, while at other times so many ticket holders will show up that some will be denied boarding. The task of the marketing specialist is to accurately predict the demand and the number of no–shows for each class of ticket and each flight under various conditions, in order to make the optimal tradeoff between aircrafts departing with some empty seats and costs for compensating customers who have been denied boarding.

Such predictions are usually supported by elaborate statistical program packages, but the final decision is made by the airline marketer and thus mainly depends on his or her experience. Statistical tools suffer from the highly interrelated economical, political and psychological factors which must be considered to make the predictions as accurate as possible. Since most of these relationships seem to be probabilistic and therefore cannot be expressed as deterministic rules, market predictions are among the most well suited and promising applications of artificial neural networks. Several proposals have been made to use neural network models for prediction and forecasting problems in business–related tasks, such as locating sources of forecast uncertainty in a recurrent gas market model [25], corporate bond rating [4], currency exchange rate analysis [8, 18], economical modelling [13], mortgage delinquency prediction [7], chaotic timeseries prediction [24], prediction of IBM daily stock prices [26], prediction of three selected German stock prices [22], prediction of the FAZ–Index [6] and prediction of the weekly Standard & Poor 500 index [17]. In some of these proposals, the neural networks performed better than regression techniques [4, 22] or as good as the Box–Jenkins technique [24], while in others the results were disappointing [7, 26].

The possibility of using neural techniques for airline market control has been sketched by Hutchison and Stephens [14]. However, their paper neither describes the neural network model used, nor the steps taken to enable a network to make predictions for airline seat allocations.

Most neural network approaches to prediction problems described in the literature are based on the well known backpropagation architecture [21]. The basic idea is to let the network learn an approximation of the mapping between the input and output data in or-

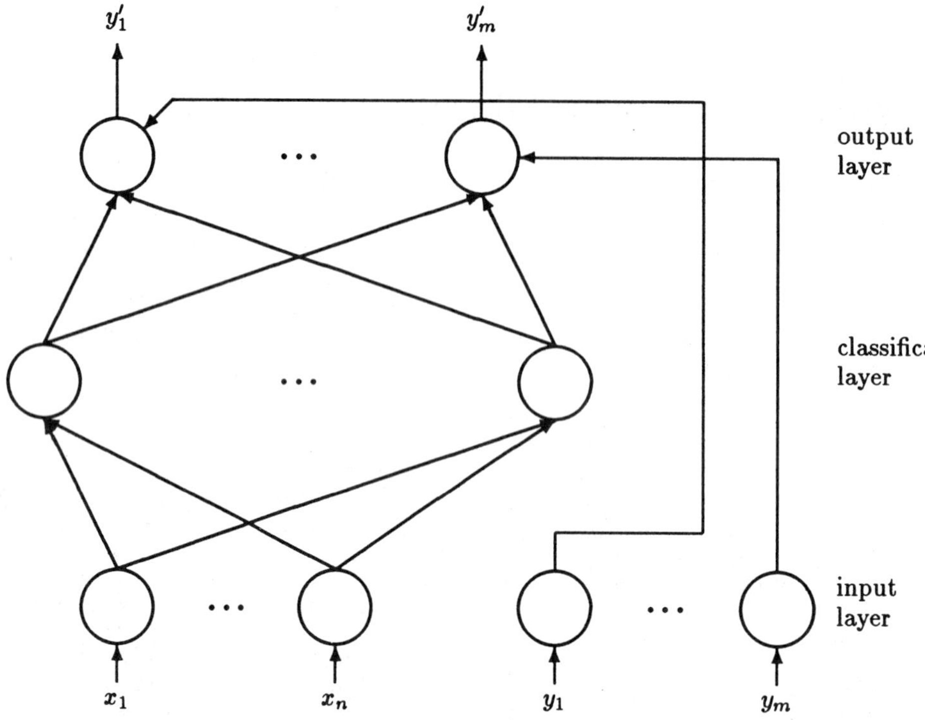

Figure 1: Architecture of the forward–only counterpropagation network

der to discover the implicit rules governing the development of the timeseries considered. The training set typically consists of input vectors with N components, where the N components represent N successive values of the timeseries. The desired output "vector" has exactly 1 component, namely the timeseries value at time $N + 1$. Thus, the training set is processed in a sliding window fashion, with N being the size of the window (typically $N = 10$). The network is supposed to learn the mapping between the pairs of input/output vectors, and the recall phase starts with the current value (the last known desired output) together with the last $N - 1$ values in the training set in order to predict the first unknown value at time $N + 1$. The real value at time $N + 1$ is then used in conjunction with the last $N - 1$ known values to predict the value for time $N + 2$. This is repeated for the prediction period desired, i.e. the size of the test set. The prediction quality is measured by comparing the network outputs to the known real values of the test set.

In this paper we present an extension of the forward–only counterpropagation neural network proposed by Hecht–Nielsen [10, 11] that is used to predict airline seat allocations. The counterpropagation architecture is an attractive alternative to backpropagation, because it offers significant advantages in terms of learning speed without considerably degrading the results. The extension is based on elements from Carpenter and Grossberg's *adaptive resonance theory* [3] in order to improve the network's approximation ability. Its benefits will be demonstrated by presenting experimental results obtained for real–life booking data.

The paper is structured as follows. In section 2 we briefly review the properties of the standard forward–only counterpropagation network. Section 3 presents the architecture of the extended counterpropagation network. In section 4 we describe how the booking data is made available to the network and how the predictions are obtained. The experimental results obtained are presented in section 5. Section 6 concludes the paper and discusses areas for future research.

2 The counterpropagation network

In this section we present the relevant features of the forward–only counterpropagation network (FCPN) [10, 11]. The network combines a portion of Kohonen's self–organizing map [15] with the outstar structure of Grossberg [9]. In its forward–only variant, it consists of an input, a hidden and an output layer with full connections between the layers (see figure 1). It functions as a statistically near–optimal key–value lookup table and organizes itself to implement an approximation to a function. The keys are encoded in the input–to–hidden weights and the values are in the hidden–to–output weights. Since the former are established by unsupervised competitive learning and the latter are found in a supervised learning manner, the counterpropagation architecture is an example of a hybrid learning network.

In order to approximate a function $\varphi : X \to Y$, pairs of example vectors ($X = (x_1, \ldots, x_n)$, $Y = (y_1, \ldots, y_m)$) are presented to the network at the input layer. The vector X then propagates through the network to yield an output vector Y' that is intended to be an approximation of Y. The approximation is based on letting the network assign X to one of the *winner-take-all* units in the classification layer, the weight vector of which is closest to X. The associated classification unit effectively represents the average prototype of a particular class of similar inputs.

The (initially random) weight vectors U_j (the weights of all incoming connections) of each unit j in the classification layer and W_j of each unit j in the output layer are assumed to be of unit length. This also holds for the pairs of example vectors presented to the network, i.e.

$$\begin{aligned} ||U_j|| &= u_{1j} * u_{1j} + \cdots + u_{nj} * u_{nj} &= 1 \quad \forall j \\ ||W_j|| &= w_{1j} * w_{1j} + \cdots + w_{pj} * w_{pj} &= 1 \quad \forall j \\ ||X|| &= x_1 * x_1 + \cdots + x_n * x_n &= 1 \\ ||Y|| &= y_1 * y_1 + \cdots + y_m * y_m &= 1 \end{aligned} \tag{1}$$

The activations $C_j, j \leq p$ of each unit j in the classification layer are computed by

$$C_j = \begin{cases} 1 & \text{if } \sum_{i=1}^{n} u_{ij} * x_i > C_k \quad \forall k \leq p \\ 0 & \text{otherwise} \end{cases} \tag{2}$$

and the activations $O_j, j \leq m$ of each unit j in the output layer are computed by

$$O_j = \sum_{i=1}^{p} w_{ij} * C_i \tag{3}$$

In the learning mode, the weight vector U_j of the winning classification unit j ($C_j = 1$) (ties are broken on the basis of the smallest unit index), is adjusted according to

$$U_j' = U_j + \alpha * (X - U_j) \tag{4}$$

where α is a learning parameter. The other weight vectors U_k, $k \neq j$ remain unaffected. In addition, the weights w_{ji} of all connections between the winning classification unit j ($C_j = 1$) and the output layer are updated by

$$w_{ji}' = w_{ji} + (\delta y_j - \gamma w_{ji}) * C_j \quad \forall i \leq m \tag{5}$$

where δ, γ are learning parameters.

Again, all other weights w_{ki}, $k \neq j$ do not change.

Thus, the classification layer uses Kohonen's learning rule [15] to employ some form of *competitive learning* and the output layer is identical to Grossberg's outstar structure [9] which learns the average Y vector values in response to the winner of the competition.

3 Vigilant counterpropagation

Since the standard FCPN described in the previous section will, after statistical equilibration, always try to find the classification unit with the best matching weight vector in response to the presentation of the input vector X, similar X vectors will be assigned to the same category. This is what the network should do as long as similar input vectors have similar desired outputs. However, if the desired output of some of these similar inputs diverges significantly from the desired outputs of the others, then the average output values for that class learned by the output units will get out of shape and thus might not represent *any* of the members of the class adequately. This is a major drawback of the standard FCPN when applied to classification problems where vector pairs (X, Y) of the kind described above are present, leading to a serious degradation of the network's approximation quality.

In order to avoid the distortions of the classification created by such inputs, it is necessary to recognize them and prevent that they are being mapped to the same category. This is achieved by an extension of the standard FCPN, called *vigilant* FCPN [5], as shown in figure 2.

There are two differences between the vigilant FCPN and the standard FCPN. First, in addition to the units competing for the input vectors, the classification layer has been extended by a number of units (indicated by the double circles) which initially do not participate in the competition, i.e. their weight vectors are initialized to 0. Second, an additional unit (the *vigilance* unit) is provided which monitors and evaluates the quality of the network output produced. It has receives information from the output units (both the desired and produced outputs) and influences the the initially non-competing classification units. The vigilance unit computes the squared error Q between the desired output vector Y and the produced output vector Y', where

$$Q = (y_1 - y_1')^2 + \cdots + (y_m - y_m')^2 \tag{6}$$

If the squared error is above a predefined threshold, the standard FCPN learning procedure will not be applied to the input vector X that produced Y'. Instead, a hitherto unused unit j is selected from the set of initially non-competing units provided in the classification layer and its weight vector U_j is set to the input vector X, i.e.

$$u_{ij} = x_i \quad \forall i, \ 1 \leq i \leq n \tag{7}$$

This causes unit j to join the set of competing units in the classification layer and ensures that unit j will win the competition when X is presented the next time, because

$$\begin{aligned} C_j &= \textstyle\sum_{i=1}^{n} u_{ij} * x_i \\ &= \textstyle\sum_{i=1}^{n} x_i * x_i \\ &= 1 \end{aligned} \tag{8}$$

As a consequence, the vector X does not disturb the classification already obtained. Moreover, since it

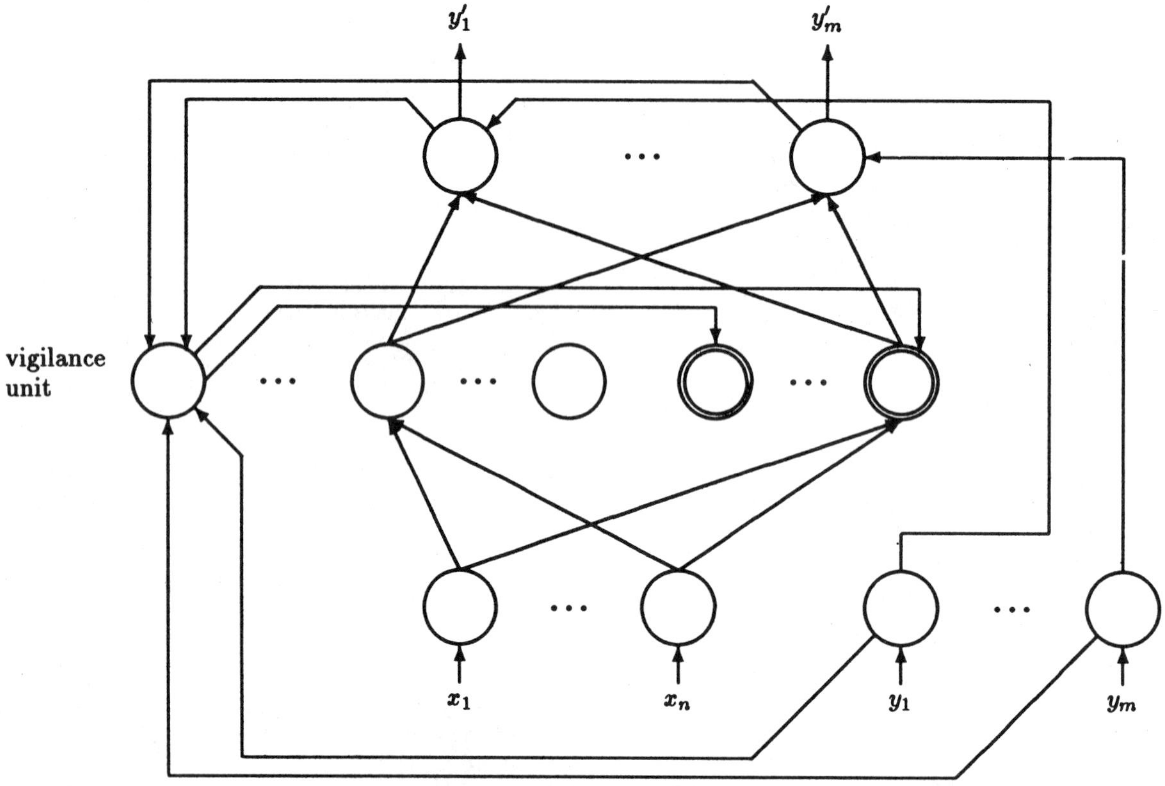

Figure 2: Architecture of the vigilant forward–only counterpropagation network

is the only exemplar in its class, it may be perfectly learned in a ***one–shoot*** manner by making the weights w_{ji}, $1 \leq i \leq n$ of the connections from the classification unit j to the output layer equal to the desired output vector Y, i.e.

$$w_{ji} = y_i \quad \forall i, \ 1 \leq i \leq m \qquad (9)$$

Thus, the vigilance unit acts as a filter for inputs with insufficiently similar desired outputs as compared to the average desired outputs of the exemplars in the class. It allows to treat such inputs separately and therefore preserves the quality of the approximation.

If all initially non–competing units in the classification layer are occupied, then the capacity of the network is exceeded. There are two apparent possibilities to deal with this situation: either the learning phase is restarted with an increased number of initially idle classification units, or X will simply be not learned at all. Since these "strange" X vectors are considered as exceptions, the latter possibility appears to be a legitimate approach, particularly when taking into account that the majority of inputs is classified with high accuracy.

In order to give the network time to self–organize its classification, it is reasonable that the monitoring unit starts operating after the input data has been presented to the network some number of times. It closely resembles the ***vigilance neuron*** employed in Carpenter and Grossberg's ***adaptive resonance theory*** [3], hence the name ***vigilant*** FCPN. The proposed architecture maintains the operational features of the standard FCPN, but beyond that it is capable of significantly improving the classification quality and the learning speed (for "strange" inputs). Its advantages over the standard FCPN will be demonstrated in the next section where both networks are applied to the task of making predictions for airline seat allocations.

4 Predicting airline seat allocations

Our investigation is based on real–life booking data for one particular, daily operating flight (Lufthansa flight LH 3589, Rome–Frankfurt), collected over a period of six months. The data set contains 16 equally structured collections of entries for each day within the six months period; each of these collections holds information about the bookings for 5 fare classes known at one out of 16 distinct time frames prior to the corresponding day of departure. Since the collections also contain data required for the statistical package that is currently in use, we have extracted the relevant items from the data set and have converted them to a format amenable for using them in our counterpropagation environment.

The input vector X consists of 7 components $(x_1, \ldots, x_7)$, where
x_1: weekday of departure $(1 \leq x_1 \leq 7)$
x_2: number of days prior to departure $(-1 \leq x_2 \leq 90)$
x_3: number of booked seats for class 1 $(0 \leq x_3 \leq 200)$
x_4: number of booked seats for class 2 $(0 \leq x_4 \leq 200)$
x_5: number of booked seats for class 3 $(0 \leq x_5 \leq 200)$
x_6: number of booked seats for class 4 $(0 \leq x_6 \leq 200)$
x_7: number of booked seats for class 5 $(0 \leq x_7 \leq 200)$

The desired output vector Y consists of 5 components $(y_1, \ldots, y_5)$, where $y_j, 1 \leq j \leq 5$ is the number of no-shows for class j at the day of departure. The network consequently produces an output vector Y' with $y'_j, 1 \leq j \leq 5$ representing the number of seats to overbook for class j x_2 days prior to departure. The different values for each class j in conjunction with particular time frames prior to departure (x_2) are used in order to take the different no-show behaviours and the different cancellation rates per class and days until departure into account. Both X and Y have been normalized to unit length. From the approximately 2500 data collections that were available, we used 2400 as the training set and the remaining 100 as the test set.

In the learning mode, the network is trained to approximate the mapping between the input and the desired output. In order to achieve this, an input/desired pair is taken from the training set, presented to the network and the described connection update equations are applied. All input/desired output pairs in the training set are processed in the same manner. The whole procedure is repeated until the network has seen the complete training set several times. In the recall mode, the input is propagated through the trained network without modifying the connection weights.

The format of the input data is a crucial factor for determining the quality of the approximation when the data is processed by a FCPN. A classification unit which has won the competition for a particular input vector X will concentrate on all inputs that are similar to X. However, if a particular component of X is present in a large number of inputs, the adjustment of the weight vector of the winning classification unit will heavily depend on this particular feature in the X vectors. This means that the other components of X are almost fully neglected and therefore do not make a contribution to the classification process, resulting in a classification where the input vectors are assigned to only a few classes. This effect was observed when we initially started the experiments with a larger number of input components, some of which were relatively static and therefore part of most of the input vectors. Examples of such input components are the identifier for a class, the number of seats available in each compartment and several mean values of booked/occupied seats in the past.

The original input data set was successively reduced to the format presented above; the only "critical" vector components are x_1 and x_2, because x_1 can adopt only 7, and x_2 16 distinct values ($x_2 \in \{90, 60, 42, 35, 28, 21, 17, 14, 11, 8, 6, 5, 4, 2, 0, -1\}$), because we have selected these 16 time frames from the time periods the airline has determined for checking the demand for tickets and making the predictions (the value -1 is used to determine the number of really occupied seats one day after the aircraft has departed). In order to avoid that these two components dominate the classification process, we randomly selected the input vectors from the data set, instead of presenting, for example, the sequence of all fligths departing on a monday to the network, then the flights departing on a tuesday and so on.

5 Experimental results

In this section we present the results of the standard FCPN and the proposed vigilant FCPN applied to the problem of predicting the number of seats to overbook for each reservation class. The simulations of the networks were implemented in the programming language *C* on a SUN Sparcstation [23]. The prediction quality was measured in terms of the squared error Q between the desired output vector Y and the output vector Y' produced by the network (see equation (6)). The test set was presented after the networks had been trained with the whole learning set for a different number of iterations. The number of units in the classification layer was set to 50 for the standard FCPN and 30 plus 20 initially non-competing units for the vigilant FCPN. Figure 3 shows the results of the standard FCPN for particular values of α, γ, δ (see equations (4) and (5)).

Network Parameters			
hidden units: 50,	$\alpha = 0.2, \gamma = 0.05, \delta = 0.05$		
Squared Error Q			
presentations	min	max	average
1	0.000005	0.653349	0.213456
3	0.000000	0.437531	0.164530
5	0.000000	0.539413	0.144065
10	0.000000	0.699137	0.133705
30	0.000000	0.698235	0.129455

Figure 3: Prediction quality of the standard FCPN

Figure 4 shows the results of the vigilant FCPN applied to the overbooking problem. The vigilance unit started operating after the learning set had been presented two times and its threshold value was set to 0.5 (see equation (6)).

Network Parameters			
hidden units: 30 + 20,	$\alpha = 0.2, \gamma = 0.05, \delta = 0.05$		
Squared Error Q			
presentations	min	max	average
3	0.010399	0.634748	0.172696
5	0.000000	0.529803	0.093962
10	0.000000	0.200979	0.057941
30	0.000000	0.094497	0.031117

Figure 4: Prediction quality of the vigilant FCPN

Figure 3 and figure 4 demonstrate that the vigilant FCPN is superior to the standard FCPN, because the average squared error of the vigilant FCPN after 30 learning iterations is smaller than the corresponding value for the standard FCPN (0.031117 compared to 0.129455). The difference is more drastic when the values for the maximum squared error are considered (0.031117 vs. 0.698235).

In order to illustrate these results, we have conducted a further experiment with the vigilant FCPN where the normalization of the output vector to unit length has been switched off. The components of the produced output vector have then been rounded to obtain natural numbers for the predicted seats to overbook. Figure 5 shows 20 out of the 100 predictions produced by the network (the Y' values) when applied to the test set together with the correct output values (Y).

y'_1	y'_2	y'_3	y'_4	y'_5	y_1	y_2	y_3	y_4	y_5
1	7	8	3	0	0	5	7	3	1
0	7	8	4	1	1	6	9	5	2
1	7	8	6	1	1	8	8	8	1
0	8	6	4	0	0	9	5	2	0
0	7	6	4	1	1	7	6	2	1
0	13	3	2	1	0	15	2	1	0
0	7	9	7	1	1	7	11	7	2
0	7	7	8	0	0	9	7	10	1
0	6	5	4	0	0	6	3	3	0
0	5	3	7	0	0	4	4	9	0
0	5	6	7	1	0	7	7	5	1
0	4	6	4	0	1	3	7	3	1
0	5	3	7	0	0	6	3	9	0
0	7	5	5	1	0	5	3	4	0
0	13	3	2	1	0	12	4	2	0
1	8	8	3	0	1	8	7	3	1
0	5	3	7	0	0	6	2	6	0
0	8	3	6	0	0	8	1	5	0
1	8	8	3	0	0	8	7	2	0
0	7	6	7	1	1	7	8	5	0

Figure 5: Predicted number of seats to overbook for class i (y'_i) vs. real number of no-shows for class i (y_i)

A direct comparison between our results and and the predictions produced by non–neural, statistical methods [1, 2, 19, 20] usually applied to the overbooking problem is difficult to perform, and we would like to point out three major reasons to explain why.

First, the statistical methods developed for the sophisticated seat inventory management systems used by the major airlines are primarily aimed at maximizing the expected total revenues under the given capacity constraints, instead of merely attempting to keep the differences between the number of overbooked seats and the number of no–shows as small as possible. The forecast models employed typically require estimates of the expected demand densities (estimates of mean and standard deviation) and estimates of the average prorated revenue associated with a passenger booking for the different reservation classes on future flights. The estimates are derived from historical data for the flight in discussion (or a similar one), and they are assumed to remain valid for future operations of that flight, at least in the short run and in the absence of changes to exogenous factors. The estimation methods used are usually based on the assumptions of a normal distribution around the expected values, an independence among the reservation classes and an independence between existing and future bookings. In all statistical approaches, the accuracy of the estimates is clearly of primary importance for the prediction quality. This is in sharp contrast to neural network approaches, because unlike statistical estimators, they estimate a function without a mathematical model of how outputs depend on inputs. They are *model-free* estimators [16] which learn from experience with sample data.

Second, whenever a prediction has been made by a seat inventory management system, it is inspected by the airline marketing expert responsible for the particular flight considered. A prediction that he or she identifies as contradictory to his or her experience will inevitably lead to manual modifications in order to improve the prediction quality. Since these manual interventions affect the parameters associated with the statistical model, it is hardly possible to guarantee equal prerequisites for a comparison with the neural network (which bases its predictions only on the raw booking data).

Third, the prediction quality obtained by the statistical packages is intimately related to the time when a forecast is made prior to departure. It is pretty obvious that the prediction quality increases with increasing proximity to the departure day. This particular kind of temporal dependence does not hold for the trained neural network, because its predictions are solely based on the pairs of input/desired output vectors presented during the learning mode; the number of days prior to departure is just one out of several components of the input vectors, and all of these are treated alike. Nevertheless, empirical investigations conducted with the statistical package available have shown that the majority of predictions made at large time frames prior to departure deviate more than 30% from the number of boarded passengers, whereas the majority of predictions made shortly before departure exhibit differences of up to 10%. For the particular flight considered, the latter value is equivalent to about 4 wrongly predicted seats per class. As shown in figure 5, the neural network produces predictions where the predicted number of seats to overbook for each class are not smaller or larger than 2 seats compared to the correct values. This seems to suggest that the neural network solution is superior to the statistical approach, but when interpreting the results in this manner the points we made above about the comparison should be taken into account.

It should be mentioned that the results obtained are based on a single data set and are thus certainly not generalizable. However, our work is hopefully sufficient to illustrate the potential value of using neural networks for airline seat allocation applications.

It is also worth mentioning that our results were obtained without taking into consideration the detailed relationships between the individual components of the full data set. A careful analysis of these relationships would probably reveal other important parameters to be encoded as inputs to the network and therefore might possibly further improve the prediction quality.

The prediction results are relatively immune to changes of the learning parameters α, γ and δ, because when values between 0.05 and 0.3 were used, no significant differences could be observed. The best results were obtained for $\alpha = 0.2$ and $0.05 \leq \gamma, \delta \leq 0.1$.

The experiments have shown that the vigilance unit should start operating after $3 - 5$ presentations of the learning set. If its threshold value is small (between 0.05 and 0.2), the network will permanently open new classes. In our application example, a threshold of $0.4 - 0.5$ turned out to be most appropriate. An approach worth considering is to start with a relatively large value and then successively reduce it during each (or every k-th) learning iteration.

6 Conclusions

In this paper we have presented a neural network approach to the problem of predicting overbooking rates for airline seat allocations. The network used was an extension of the forward-only counterpropagation network, developed to avoid the disadvantages of the latter when applied to classification problems where similar inputs yield significantly different desired outputs. The extension employed an additional vigilance unit which was introduced to monitor and evaluate the produced network output during the learning phase in order to prevent distortions in the categories already built up. It was demonstrated that the proposed vigilant counterpropagation network maintains the simple competitive learning mechanisms of the standard forward-only counterpropagation model, but additionally improves the classification quality and increases the learning speed for insufficiently similar inputs.

The network was trained to approximate the mapping between the input data (the number of booked seats for each reservation class at distinct time periods prior to departure) and the desired output (the real number of no-shows). It was then used to make predictions for the future. The feasibility of our approach was demonstrated by presenting experimental results obtained for real-life booking data for one particular flight. The results have indicated that the proposed neural network model is superior to the standard forward-only counterpropagation model and quite competitive to traditional, non-neural methods applied to the overbooking prediction problem.

There are several issues for further research which we plan to investigate in the future. Among these are: the use of the vigilant counterpropagation network in further airline seat allocation predictions, the development of a sophisticated neural prediction tool that can handle a large number of flights in an efficient manner and a detailed comparison of the results obtained with those achieved by backpropagation and non-neural methods.

References

[1] P.P. Belobaba. Air Travel Demand and Airline Seat Inventory Management. Technical Report R87-7, Flight Transportation Laboratory, Department of Aeronautics and Astronautics, Massachusetts Institute of Technology, Cambridge, Massachusetts, 1987.

[2] Boeing Commercial Airplane Company. Boeing Promotional Fare Management System: Analysis and Research Findings. Sales Technique Department, Boeing Commercial Airplane Company, Seattle, Washington, 1982.

[3] G.A. Carpenter and S. Grossberg. The ART of Adaptive Pattern Recognition by a Self-Organizing Neural Network. *IEEE Computer*, 3, 77–88, 1988.

[4] S. Dutta and S. Shekkar. Bond Rating: A Non-Conservative Application of Neural Networks. In *Proceedings of the 1990 International Joint Conference on Neural Networks*, Washington, D.C., vol. 2, 443–450, 1988.

[5] B. Freisleben. Pattern Classification with Vigilant Counterpropagation. In *Proceedings of the 2nd IEE International Conference on Artificial Neural Networks*, Bournemouth, UK, 252–256, 1991.

[6] B. Freisleben. Stock Market Prediction with Backpropagation Networks. In *Proceedings of the 5th International Conference on Industrial and Engineering Applications of Artificial Intelligence and Expert Systems*, Paderborn, Germany. *Lecture Notes in Artificial Intelligence*, vol. 604, 451–460, Springer-Verlag, Berlin, 1992.

[7] S. Gosh, E.A. Collins, and C.L. Scofield. Prediction of Mortgage Loan Performance with a Multiple Neural Network Learning System. In *Abstracts of the First Annual INNS Meeting*, vol. 1, 439–440, 1988.

[8] C. de Groot and D. Würtz. Forecasting Time Series with Connectionist Nets: Applications in Statistics, Signal Processing and Economics. In *Proceedings of the 5th International Conference on Industrial and Engineering Applications of Artificial Intelligence and Expert Systems*, Paderborn, Germany. *Lecture Notes in Artificial Intelligence*, vol. 604, 461–470, Springer-Verlag, Berlin, 1992.

[9] S. Grossberg. Embedding Fields: A Theory of Learning with Physiological Implications. *Journal of Mathematical Psychology*, 6, 209–239, 1969.

[10] R. Hecht-Nielsen. Counterpropagation Networks. *Applied Optics*, 26, 4979–4984, 1987.

[11] R. Hecht-Nielsen. Applications of Counterpropagation Networks. *Neural Networks*, 1, 131–139, 1988.

[12] J. Hertz, A. Krogh, and R.G. Palmer. *Introduction to the Theory of Neural Computation.* Addison–Wesley, Reading, Massachusetts, 1991.

[13] R.G. Hoptroff. The Principles and Practice of Time Series Forecasting and Business Modelling Using Neural Nets. *Neural Computing & Applications*, 1(1):59–66, 1993.

[14] W.R. Hutchison and K.R. Stephens. The Airline Marketing Tactician (AMT): A Commercial Application of Adaptive Networking. In *Proceedings of the IEEE International Conference on Neural Networks*, San Diego, 753–756, 1987.

[15] T. Kohonen. *Self-Organization and Associative Memory.* Springer-Verlag, Berlin, 1989.

[16] B. Kosko. *Neural Networks and Fuzzy Systems.* Prentice–Hall, Englewood Cliffs, 1992.

[17] A. Lapedes and R. Farber. Nonlinear Signal Processing Using Neural Networks: Prediction and System Modelling. Technical Report LA–UR–87–2662, Los Alamos National Laboratory, Los Alamos, NM, 1987.

[18] A.N. Refenes and M. Azema–Barac and L. Chen and S.A. Karoussos. Currency Exchange Rate Prediction and Neural Network Design Strategies. *Neural Computing & Applications*, 1(1):46–58, 1993.

[19] M. Rothstein. An Airline Overbooking Model. *Transportation Science*, 5, 180–192, 1971.

[20] M. Rothstein. OR and the Airline Overbooking Problem. *Operations Research*, 33(2):237–248, 1985.

[21] D.E. Rumelhart, G. Hinton and R.E. Williams. Learning Internal Representations by Error Propagation. In *Parallel Distributed Processing: Explorations in the Microstructures of Cognition*, vol. 1, 318–362, MIT Press, 1986.

[22] E. Schöneburg. Stock Price Prediction Using Neural Networks: An Empirical Test. *Neurocomputing*, 2, 1, 1991.

[23] O. Seipp. Competition and Competitive Learning in Neural Networks (in German). Master's Thesis, Dept. of Computer Science, University of Darmstadt, Germany, 1991.

[24] R. Sharda and R.B. Patil. Neural Networks as Forecasting Experts: An Empirical Test. In *Proceedings of the 1990 International Joint Conference on Neural Networks*, Washington, D.C., vol. 2, 491–494, 1990.

[25] P.J. Werbos. Generalization of Backpropagation with Application to a Recurrent Gas Market Model. *Neural Networks*, 1:339–356, 1988.

[26] H. White. Economic Prediction Using Neural Networks: The Case of IBM Daily Stock Returns. In *Proceedings of the IEEE International Conference on Neural Networks*, vol. 2, 451–458, 1988.

Near Optimal Jobshop Scheduling Using Neural Network Parallel Computing

Akira Hanada and Kouhei Ohnishi
Keio University
Dept. of Elec. Eng., 3-14-1 Hiyoshi, Kohoku, Yokohama, 223 Janpan
E-mail: hana@sumgwy.sum.elec.keio.ac.jp

Abstract

A parallel algorithm based on the neural network model for jobshop scheduling problem is presented in this paper. In the manufacturing system, it is becoming more complex to manage operations of facilities, because of many requirements and constraints such as to increase product throughput, reduce work-in-process and keep the due date. The goal of the proposed parallel algorithm is to find a near-optimum scheduling solution for the given schedule. The proposed parallel algorithm requires N x N processing elements (neurons) where N is the number of operations. Our empirical study on the sequential shows the behavior of the system.

I. Introduction

In recent years, as the diversification of consumers' demand and the progress of production technology result in a wider variety of products, the necessity of effective scheduling is increasing. Jobshop scheduling is one of the most important issues in the planning and operation of manufacturing systems. There was many papers about this area in resent years[1],[2],[3]. The scheduling problem is NP-complete problem [4]. It takes huge times to compute optimal scheduling generally. It is necessary to develop the method to find near optimal scheduling. Nishikawa [10] proposed branch-and-bound method and solved partial problems which are arranged in a time-sequence. Morikawa [5] and Nishikawa [4] used genetic algorithm to solve the problem. Ichikawa [9] used special neural network theory called "Boltzmann Machines" to develop "production scheduling system". It is difficult to compose the energy function in this type of problem. They proposed the method to compose the energy function to compute time table. This paper presents a parallel algorithm based on the neural network model for the problem. The proposed parallel algorithm requires N x N processing elements (neurons), where N is the number of operations. The key idea of the neural network model is to use "2-maximum maximum neuron" to satisfy the two dimensional constraint and "binary neuron" to stable the two dimensional neural system in the same times. The proposed method can find the near optimal solution quickly with N x N processing elements.

II. Jobshop Scheduling Problem

The following three conditions are considered on our jobshop scheduling problem, which should not be violated in the problem.
1) Machine can be applied to many processing, but machine can't process the same processing in the same time.
2) Processing time is constant.
3) The priority of the operations of processing, processing time and used machine is decided in advance.
Table 1 shows an example [5] of jobshop scheduling. The case on the table has three jobs J1-J3 and three machines M1-M3. The operations of the jobs should be done in the sequence given by Table 3. The job J1 consists of two operations O1, O2. The operation O1 should be done by the machine M1 and take 3 unit time. Then the operation O2 is to be done by M2 taking 6 units of time. Fig. 1 (b) [5] shows an example of scheduling. The scheduling in the figure is inefficient. The total elapsed time (C_{max}) should be made minimal.

Table 1. Jobshop scheduling problem (total 6 operations)

Job	Operation (Machine, Time)
J1	(O1) M1,3 (O2) M2,6
J2	(O3) M2,5 (O4) M3,4 (O5) M1,3
J3	(O6) M1,2

III. Optimization Computation with Nerual Network

In 1985 John J. Hopfield and David Tank proposed an artificial neural network for optimization problems [11] which has attracted many new investigators to get involved in neural computing. However in 1988 G. V. Willson and G. S. Pawley strongly criticized the neural network for optimization problems [12]. Since 1988 it has been widely believed that the artificial neural network is not suitable for optimization problems. This paper is intended to demonstrate the capability of the artificial neural network for solving jobshop scheduling problem (JSP).
The mathematical model of the artificial neural network consist of two components; neurons and synaptic links. The output signal

0-7803-0891-3/93$03.00

transmitted from a neuron propagates to other neurons through the synaptic links. The state of the input signal of a neuron is determined by the linear sum of weighted input signal of a neurons where the respective weight is the strength of the synaptic links. Every artificial neuron has the input U and the output V. The output of the ith neuron is given by;

$$V_i = f(U_i) \qquad (1)$$

where f is called the neuron's input/output function. The interconnections between the ith neuron and other neurons are determined by the motion equation. The change of the input state of the ith neuron is given by the partial derivatives of the computational energy function E with respect to the output of the ith neuron where E follows an n-variable function: $E(V_1,V_2,...,V_n)$. The motion equation [6] is given by:

$$\frac{dU_i}{dt} = -\frac{\partial E(V_1,V_2,...,V_n)}{\partial V_i} \qquad (2)$$

The goal of the artificial neural network for solving optimization problem is to minimize the fabricated computational energy function E in Eq. (2). It is usually easier to build the motion equation than the energy function. From Eq. (2) the energy function E can be obtained:

$$E = \int dE = -\int \frac{dU_i}{dt} dV_i \qquad (3)$$

IV. Neural Network Approach

Job shop scheduling problem is generally NP-complete problem [4]. The number of possible sequences grow exponentially as the problem size increases [8]. The artificial neural network for optimization problem may solve the problem more quickly and easily. The proposed parallel algorithm is based on two dimensional artificial neural network model which is composed of a large number of massively interconnected simple processing elements (neuron). The system uses an N x N neural network array where N is the number of operations. Fig. 1 (a) and Fig. 2 (a) shows the neural representation of Fig.1 (b) and Fig. 2 (b) respectively. Each squares indicate processing elements and black squares shows fired neuron which output is one and the output of other squares is zero. The i-j-th fired neuron means ith operation should be operated in the jth oder. The operations of a schedule is numbered by the sequence of Job number and the priority of the operations. For example, The operation number should be numbered from left to right and from the top to the bottom in Table 1 problem. The i-th number in Fig. 1 (a) and Fig. 2 (a) indicate that the operation number. the j-th number means that the order of operations.

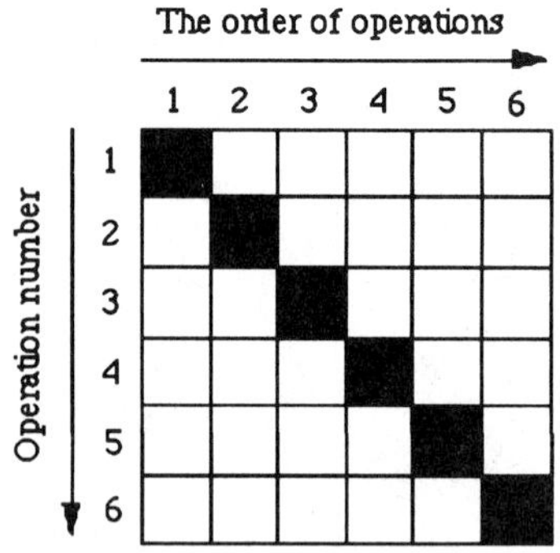

(a) Neural representation
Oder (O1,O2,O3,O4,O5,O6)

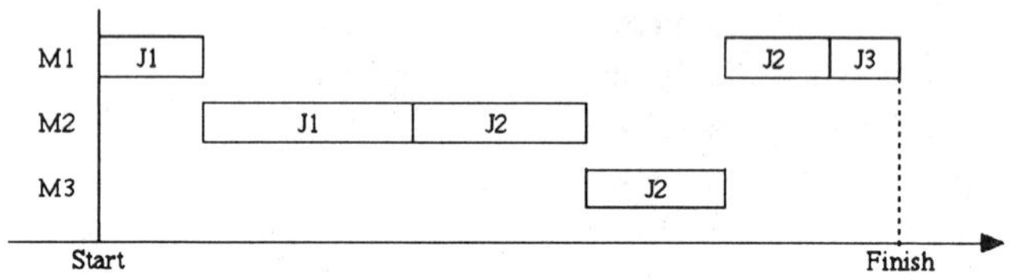

(b) time table

Fig. 1 Neural Representation and time table

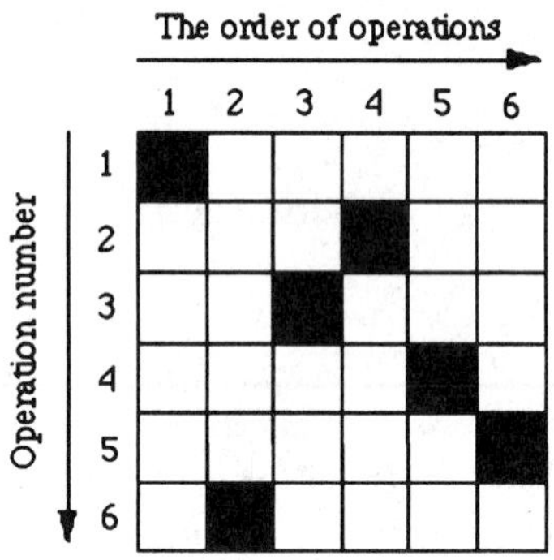

(a) Neural Representation
Oder(O1,O6,O3,O2,O4,O5)

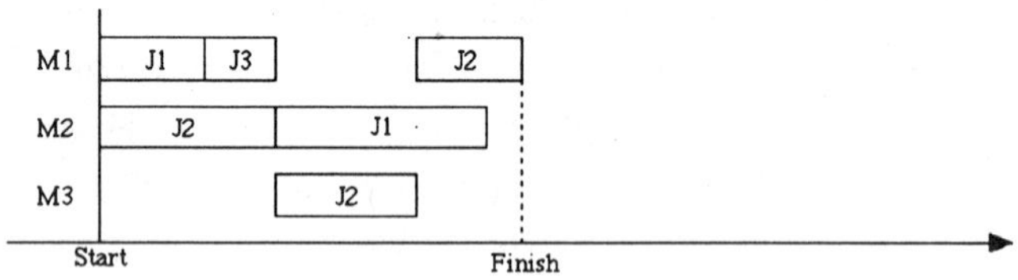

(b) time table

Fig. 2 Neural Representation and time table

The oder of operation in Fig. 1 (a) and Fig. 2 (a) is O1-O2-O3-O4-O5-O6 and O1-O6-O3-O2-O4-O5 respectively. This type of representation is famous City-Oder 2-dimensional neural network like a Traveling Salesman Problem (TSP). It is easy to compute time table like a Fig. 1 (b) or Fig. 2 (b) from the oder of operations. To assign a operation number to a oder, one and only fired neuron must be fired in a row and column. We call the constrain as operation-oder constrain. The constrain is famous as 2-dimensional problem such as traveling salesman problem (TSP) [12].

This paper presents two neural input/output function, one is binary function (McCullch-Pitts neuron), the other is 2-maximum neuron function. The binary input/output function (McCullch-Pitts neuron) [13] is given by:

$V_{ij}'=1$ if $U_{ij}>0$

0 otherwise (4)

where V_{ij}' and U_{ij} are the output and the input of the i-j-th neuron respectively. Using the neuron model, the motion equation to satisfy the condition in which one and only one neuron in a column and a row must be fired is given by:

$$\frac{dU_{ij}}{dt} = -A\cdot\left(\sum_{p=1}^{N} V'_{ip} - 1\right) - A\cdot\left(\sum_{p=1}^{N} V'_{pj} - 1\right) \qquad (5)$$

where A is a coefficient. The first term gives the row constraint such that one and only one neuron should be fired in the ith row. The second term described the column constraint such that one and only one neuron should be fired in the jth column. Using Eq. (5), the time table can not be made when no neurons are fired on the ith row or the jth column. The real outputs always satisfy the condition to compute time table and total cost. To satisfy the condition, the 2-maximum neuron model is introduced where the input/output function of the ij-th neuron is given by;

$$V_{ij} = 1 \quad \text{if} \quad U_{ij} = \max\{U_{is} \mid s \in s(m_i)\} \quad \text{and 0 otherwise} \qquad (6)$$

where $s(m_i)$ is a set to satisfy the row and column condition. The effect of Eq. (6) is to fire the neurons having the strongest input in $s(m_i)$. Using the function, the system is always satisfied the row and column condition. We used 'binary neuron' to stable the system and '2-maximum neuron' to satisfy the row and column condition in the same time.

It is difficult to make the energy function in oder to minimize total elapsed time. Our method is to compute time table from neuron map.

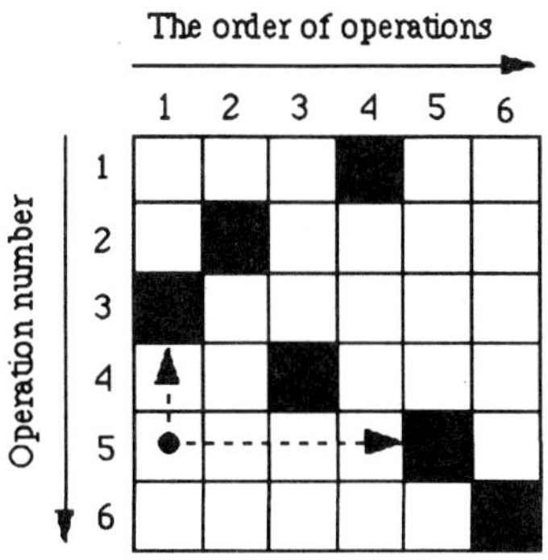

(a) The computation of (i,j)=(5,1) neuron

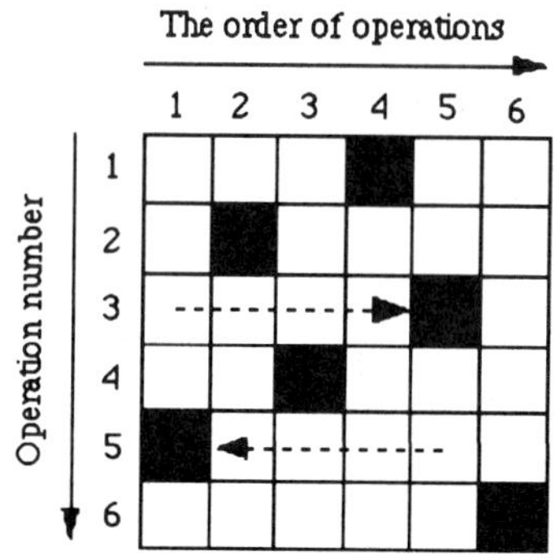

(b) Exchange

Fig. 3 Compute Energy

Fig. 3 shows the method to compute Cost(5,1) of (i,j)=(1,5) neuron. Fig. 3 (a) indicate a state of the system. Computing Cost(5,1), the same column and row neurons are exchanged and compute the total cost using time table.

The operations of the jobs should be done in the sequence of the scheduling in advance. the condition for the i-j-th processing element is given by:

$$\sum_{\substack{p=1\\p\neq i}}^{N} \sum_{\substack{q=1\\q\neq j}}^{N} V_{pq} f(p,i,q,j) J(p,i) \qquad (7)$$

where $f(p,i,q,j)=1$ if ($p>i$ and $q<j$) or ($p<i$ and $q>j$)

=0 otherwise.

and $J(p,i)=1$ if (pth job number) = (ith job number)

=0 otherwise.

Eq. (7) is the sum of the number of fired neurons which is not satisfy the priority of operations. This condition is zero if the priority of operations is the same jobs are satisfied.

The motion equation of the i-j-th processing element for the N-operations problem is given by:

$$\frac{dU_{ij}}{dt} = -A\cdot\left(\sum_{p=1}^{N} V'_{ip} - 1\right) - A\cdot\left(\sum_{p=1}^{N} V'_{pj} - 1\right) - B\cdot \mathrm{Cost}(i,j) - C\cdot \sum_{\substack{p=1\\p\neq i}}^{N} \sum_{\substack{q=1\\q\neq j}}^{N} V_{pq} f(p,i,q,j) J(p,i) + D\cdot h\left(\sum_{p=1}^{N} V'_{ip}\right) + D h\left(\sum_{p=1}^{N} V'_{pj}\right) \qquad (8)$$

where U_{ij} is the input of i-j-th neuron on the two dimensional neural network array. V_{ij} is the output of 2-maximum neuron. V_{ij}' is the sub-output of the i-j-th neuron. $V_{ij}'=1$ if $U_{ij}>0$, 0 otherwise. $h(x)=1$ if $x=0$, 0 otherwise. A, B, C and D are constant coefficients. In Eq. (8) the first term and second term are the row constraint and the column constraint respectively. The first term forces one and only one neuron to be fired per row. The second term forces one and only one neuron to be fired per column. The third term (B-term) forces total elapsed time to be minimize. The forth term (C-term) is always inhibitory which describe the priority of the operation in the same job. The fifth and the last term (D-term) are the row hill-climbing term and the column hill-climbing term respectively. The hill-climbing terms are activated only when local conflicts are detected. In other words, The D-terms encourages the sub-output of i-j-th processing element (V_{ij}') to be nonzero if the sub-output of all the processing elements in the i-row or j-th column.

The following procedure describes the proposed algorithm based on the first order Euler method.

0. Set t=0.

1. The initial values of $U_{ij}(t)$ for i=1,...,N j=1,...,N are randomized.

2. Evolute value of Vij(t) based on the 2-maximum function.

3. Evolute value of $V_{ij}'(t)$ based on binary function.

$V_{ij}'(t)=1$ if $U_{ij}(t)>0$

$=0$ otherwise for i=1,...,N j=1,...,N.

4. Use the motion equation in Eq. (8) to compute $\Delta U_{ij}(t)$.

$$\Delta U_{ij}(t) = -A\cdot\left(\sum_{p=1}^{N} V'_{ip}(t) - 1\right) - A\cdot\left(\sum_{p=1}^{N} V'_{pj}(t) - 1\right) - B\cdot Cost(i,j)$$
$$- C\cdot\sum_{\substack{p=1\\p\neq i}}^{N}\sum_{\substack{q=1\\q\neq j}}^{N} V_{pq}(t) f(p,i,q,j) J(p,i) + D\cdot h\left(\sum_{p=1}^{N} V'_{ip}(t)\right) + Dh\left(\sum_{p=1}^{N} V'_{pj}(t)\right)$$

5. Compute $U_{ij}(t+1)$ based on the first oder Euler method:

$U_{ij}(t+1)=U_{ij}(t)+\Delta U_{ij}(t)$ for i=1,...,N j=1,...,N.

6. If $U_{ij}(t+1)>U_{max}$ then $U_{ij}(t+1)=U_{max}$

If $U_{ij}(t+1)<U_{min}$ then $U_{ij}(t+1)=U_{min}$

7. Increment t by 1. If t=T terminate this procedure else go to step 2.

It is important that the values of the inputs are always kept in the certain range where they are computed by Step 6 because of reducing searching space.

V. Simulations and Results

The simulator has been developed on a SUN-SP/2 workstation, although the algorithm is executable both in a sequential machine and a parallel one. We have examined the same problem of a paper [5]. The simulator is to simulate the synchronous parallel neural network model. Table. 2 is the problem which has 28 operations and 8 jobs. The problem has $28!=3\times10^{29}$ possible states. We solved the problem to demonstrate our method and see the behavior of the system. Fig. 4 shows the relationship between the number of iteration steps and frequency. Our method can find optimum solution within 70 iteration steps in any initial random value of $U_{ij}(0)$.

Table 2 28 operations and 8 jobs [8] (exam. 1)

Job	Operation (Machine, Time)
J1	(5,9) (6,12) (3,11) (2,6)
J2	(4,3) (2,10) (6,7) (6,10)
J3	(1,4) (3,6) (3,2)
J4	(4,5) (6,5) (1,7) (4,7)
J5	(6,12) (1,10) (3,11)
J6	(4,4) (5,12) (6,2) (4,12)
J7	(6,4) (3,11) (6,12)
J8	(6,3) (5,11) (2,8)

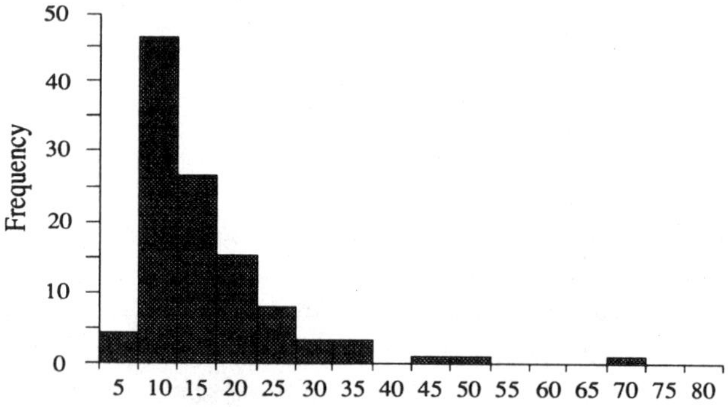

Fig. 4 The relationship between the number of iteration steps and frequency

Table 3 shows the the problem where there are 10 jobs, 5 operations and 8 machines in each job, and total 50 operations. Fig. 5 shows the relationship between the error and the frequency. The error is computed by subtracting most minimal time from obtained total time. The obtained near optimal total elapsed time in the scheduling are C_{max}=69-80 within 300 iteration steps. Total 84 % converge to the near optimal solution within 10 % error.

Table 3 50 operations and 10 jobs (exam. 2)

Job	Operation (Machine, Time)
J1	(5,9) (2,6) (7,12) (1,3) (4,7)
J2	(2,4) (8,6) (1,10) (4,7) (3,10)
J3	(6,3) (5,7) (3,12) (8,6) (1,4)
J4	(1,5) (8,10) (4,3) (3,11) (4,6)
J5	(6,12) (7,6) (1,5) (7,12) (2,4)
J6	(4,5) (6,7) (5,3) (3,2) (5,11)
J7	(1,4) (7,7) (8,4) (3,10) (2,12)
J8	(6,4) (5,5) (3,9) (2, 12) (7,3)
J9	(7,6) (4,5) (8,12) (3,7) (1,5)
J10	(5,12) (4,7) (7,11) (6,8) (7,8)

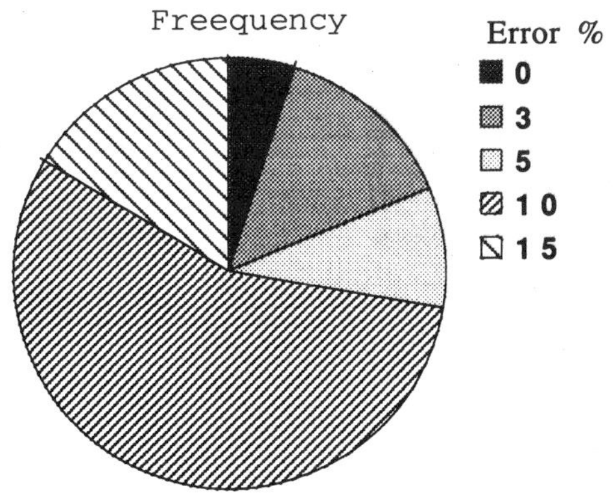

Cmax=69-80

error<10% is total 84%

Fig. 5 The relationship between solution error and frequency (exam. 2)

Table 4 70 operations and 10 jobs (exam. 3)

J1	(9,8) (8,6) (6,7) (1,6) (2,12) (4,8) (3,7)
J2	(5,9) (2,6) (7,12) (1,9) (4,7) (8,5) (2,5)
J3	(1,5) (8,10) (4,3) (3,11) (4,6) (3,7) (4,2)
J4	(6,3) (5,7) (3,12) (8,6) (1,4) (5,8) (1,7)
J5	(6,12) (7,6) (1,5) (7,12) (2,4) (1,4) (4,8)
J6	(4,5) (6,7) (5,3) (3,2) (5,11) (9,10) (6,5)
J7	(1,4) (7,7) (8,4) (3,10) (2,12) (8,4) (7,8)
J8	(6,4) (5,5) (3,9) (2, 12) (7,3) (1,6) (6,7)
J9	(7,6) (4,5) (8,12) (3,7) (1,5) (4,5) (9,6)
J10	(5,12) (4,7) (7,11) (6,8) (7,8) (8,5) (1,12)

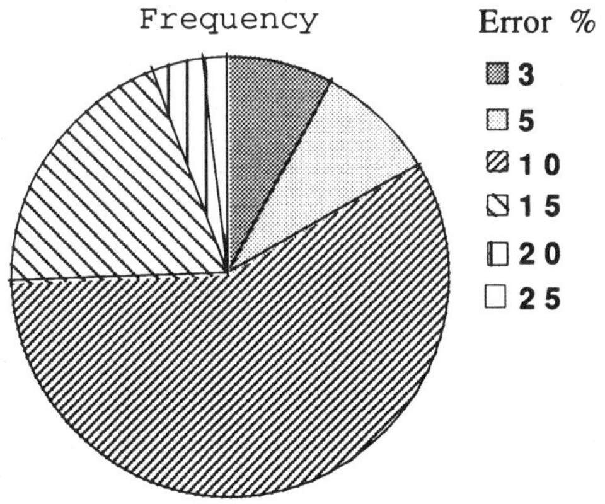

Cmax=88-108

error< 10% is total 75%

Fig. 6 The relationship between solution error and frequency (exam. 3)

Table 4 shows the the problem where there are 10 jobs, 7 operations and 9 machines in each job, and total 70 operations. Fig. 6 shows the relationship between the error and the frequency. Total 75 % converge to the near optimal solution within 10 % error. The obtained near optimal total elapsed time in the scheduling are C_{max}=88-108 within 300 iteration steps.

Comparing exam. 1, exam. 2 and exam. 3, the ratio of converge to the optimal solution is decrease in increasing the problem size. But using our method, the system always converge to the optimal solution in exam. 1 [5] within a few iteration steps, and converge to the near optimal solution in exam. 2 and exam. 3.

VI. Conclusions

A parallel algorithm using neural network for jobshop scheduling problem is introduced in this paper. The proposed algorithm requires N x N neurons, where N is the number of operations. Using "binary neuron" and "2-maximum neuron", the system always satisfy 2-dimensional conditions and allows to compute time table. The goal of using the neural network is to minimize fabricated computational energy function where it is given by 2-dimensional condition and priority condition and total elapsed time. By observing the behavior of the simulator in small size problem (exam. 1), the state of the system converge to the optimal solution in a few iteration steps. Increasing the problem size, the quality of the obtained solutions are decrease, but the system can find the near optimal solution.

Appendix 1

Convergence property of the maximum neural network is determined by the time derivatives of the energy of the system, $\frac{dE}{dt}$. Lemma 1 and lemma 2 are introduced to prove that the proposed system is always allowed to converge to the equilibrium state or the optimal (near-optimum) solution.

Lemma 1:

$\frac{dE}{dt} \leq 0$ is satisfied under two conditions such as $\frac{dU_i}{dt} = -\frac{\partial E}{\partial V_i}$ and $V_i = f(U_i)$ where $f(U_i)$ is a nondecreasing function.

Proof :

$$\frac{dE}{dt} = \sum_i \frac{dU_i}{dt}\frac{dV_i}{dU_i}\frac{\partial E}{\partial V_i}$$

$$= -\sum_i \left(\frac{dU_i}{dt}\right)^2 \frac{dV_i}{dU_i} \quad \text{where } \frac{\partial E}{\partial V_i} \text{ is replaced by } -\frac{dU_i}{dt} \text{ (condition 1)}$$

$$\leq 0 \quad \text{where } \frac{dV_i}{dU_i} > 0 \text{ (condition 2)}$$

Q.E.D.

Lemma 1 states that the state of the system finally reaches an equilibrium state. The input/output function must follow a nondecreasing function. In lemma 2, the convergence of the priority maximum neural network is given.

Lemma 2:

$\frac{dE}{dt} \le 0$ is satisfied under two conditions such as

(1) $\frac{dU_{ij}}{dt} = -\frac{\partial E}{\partial V_{ij}}$ and

(2) $V_{ij} = 1$ if $U_{ij} = \max\{U_{is} \mid s \in s(m_i)\}$ and 0 otherwise

Proof: Consider the derivatives of the computational energy E with respect to time *t*.

$$\frac{dE}{dt} = \sum_i \sum_j \frac{dU_{ij}}{dt} \frac{dV_{ij}}{dU_{ij}} \frac{\partial E}{\partial V_{ij}}$$

$$= -\sum_i \sum_j \left(\frac{dU_{ij}}{dt}\right)^2 \frac{dV_{ij}}{dU_{ij}} \quad \text{where } \frac{\partial E}{\partial V_{ij}} \text{ is replaced by } -\frac{dU_{ij}}{dt} \text{ (condition 1)}$$

Let $\frac{dU_{ij}}{dt}$ be $\frac{U_{ij}(t+dt)-U_{ij}(t)}{dt}$. Let $\frac{dV_{ij}}{dU_{ij}}$ be $\frac{V_{ij}(t+dt)-V_{ij}(t)}{U_{ij}(t+dt)-U_{ij}(t)}$. Let us consider the term $\sum_j \left(\frac{dU_{ij}}{dt}\right)^2 \frac{dV_{ij}}{dU_{ij}}$ for each operation of scheduling separately. Let $U_{i,a}(t+dt)$ be the maximum at time *t+dt* and $U_{i,b}(t)$ be the maximum at time t for the job *i*.

$U_{i,a}(t+dt) = \max\{U_{i,s}(t+dt) \mid s \in s(m_i)\}$

$U_{i,b}(t) = \max\{U_{i,s}(t) \mid s \in s(m_i)\}$

It is necessary and sufficient to consider the following two cases :

1) a = b

2) a ≠ b

If the case 1) is satisfied, then there is no state change for the scheduling. Consequently, $\sum_j \left(\frac{dU_{ij}}{dt}\right)^2 \frac{dV_{ij}}{dU_{ij}}$ must be zero.

If the case 2) is satisfied, then

$$\sum_j \left(\frac{dU_{ij}}{dt}\right)^2 \frac{dV_{ij}}{dU_{ij}}$$

$$= \left(\frac{U_{i,a}(t+dt)-U_{i,a}(t)}{dt}\right)^2 \frac{V_{i,a}(t+dt)-V_{i,a}(t)}{U_{i,a}(t+dt)-U_{i,a}(t)} + \left(\frac{U_{i,b}(t+dt)-U_{i,b}(t)}{dt}\right)^2 \frac{V_{i,b}(t+dt)-V_{i,b}(t)}{U_{i,b}(t+dt)-U_{i,b}(t)}$$

$$= \left(\frac{U_{i,a}(t+dt)-U_{i,a}(t)}{dt}\right)^2 \frac{1}{U_{i,a}(t+dt)-U_{i,a}(t)} + \left(\frac{U_{i,b}(t+dt)-U_{i,b}(t)}{dt}\right)^2 \frac{-1}{U_{i,b}(t+dt)-U_{i,b}(t)}$$

$$= \frac{U_{i,a}(t+dt)-U_{i,a}(t)}{(dt)^2} - \frac{U_{i,b}(t+dt)-U_{i,b}(t)}{(dt)^2}$$

$$= \frac{1}{(dt)^2}\{ U_{i,a}(t+dt) - U_{i,a}(t) - U_{i,b}(t+dt) + U_{i,b}(t) \}$$

$$= \frac{1}{(dt)^2}\{ U_{i,a}(t+dt) - U_{i,b}(t+dt) + U_{i,b}(t) - U_{i,a}(t) \}$$

$$> 0$$

because $U_{i,a}(t+dt)$ is the maximum at time *t+dt* and $U_{i,b}(t)$ is the maximum at time *t* for the oprration i.

The contribution from each term is either 0 or positive, therefore

$$\sum_j \left(\frac{dU_{i,j}}{dt}\right)^2 \frac{dV_{i,j}}{dU_{i,j}} \ge 0 \text{ and } -\sum_i \sum_j \left(\frac{dU_{ij}}{dt}\right)^2 \frac{dV_{ij}}{dU_{ij}} \le 0 \Rightarrow \frac{dE}{dt} \le 0$$

Q.E.D.

Lemma 1 guarantees the convergence of the system. Lemma 2 states that the solution quality improves as time elapses until no further improvement can be achieved.

References

[1] Dileepan, P. and Sen, T. ; Bicriterion jobshop scheduling with total followtime and sum of squared lateness., Engineering costs and production economics., JUL 01 1991 v 21 n 3, Page: 295

[2] Ramesh, R. and Cary, J. M.; An efficient approach to stochastic jobshop scheduling: algorithms and empirical investigations., Computers & industrial engineering., 1990 v 18 n 2,Page: 181

[3] D. Whitley, T.Starkweather and D.Fuquary; Scheduling Problem and Traveling Salesman: The Genetic Edge Recombination Operator, Proceedings of the 3rd International Conference on Genetic Algorithms, 133/140, 1989.

[4] Y. Nishikawa and H. Tamaki; A genetic Algorithm As Applied to the Jobshop Scheduling., Transactions of the society of instrument and control engineers, 1991 v27 n 5,Page: 593

[5] K.Morikawa, T.Furuhashhi, Y.Uchikawa; Single Populated Genetic Algorithm and its Application to Jobshop Scheduling; IECON'92, 1014/1019,1992.

[6] Yoshiyasu Takefuji: Neural Network Parallel Computing, Kluwer Academic publishers, 1992.

[7] K. C. Lee and Y. Takefuji, "A Generalized Maximum Neural Network for The Module Orientation Problem," *Int. J. Electronics*, 72, 3, pp 331 (1992).

[8] D. J. Hoitomt, P. B. Luh, and Krishna R. Pattipati, "A Practical Approach to Job-Shop Scheduling Problems," IEEE Tran. on Robotics and Automation, 1993 v9 n1. Page:1

[9] H. Ichikawa, H. Inoue and H. Yoshida, "Development and Application for Scheduling System Using Neuralnetwork",Simulation Technology conf., 1993, pp239/240.

[10] Y. Nishikawa, H. Tamaki and Atsuto Maki, " A Decomposition Method for Jobshop Scheduling", Transactions of the society of instrument and control engineers, 1991 v27 n 5,Page: 607

[11] Hopfield J. J., and Tank D. W., "Neural Computation of Decisions in Optimization Problems.", Biological Cybernetics, 52, 141-152 (1985).

[12] Wilson G. V. and Pawley G. S., "On stability of the Travelling Salesman Problem Algorithm of Hopfield and Tank. Bio. Cybern., 58, 63-70 (1988).

[13] McCulloch W. S., and Pitts W. H., " A logical caliculus of ideas immanent in nervous activity.", Bulletin of Mathematical Biophysics,5,115, (1943).

OPTIMIZATION OF ROBOTIC ASSEMBLY SEQUENCES USING NEURAL NETWORK

D. S. Hong and H. S. Cho
Department of Precision Engineering and Mechatronics
Korea Advanced Institute of Science and Technology
373-1 Kusong-dong, Yusong-gu, Taejon, 305-701, Korea

Abstract

This paper presents a neural network based computational scheme to generate the optimized robotic assembly sequence for an assembly product consisting of a number of parts. An assembly sequence is considered to be optimal when it meets a number of conditions: it must satisfy assembly constraints, keep the stability of in-process subassembly, and minimize assembly cost. Currently, various search algorithms have been reported for the purpose, but as the number of the parts increases they often fail to generate assembly sequences due to the explosion of the search space. As an alternative solution to overcome this problem, we propose a scheme using both the Hopfield neural network and the expert system [1], previously proposed method. Based upon the inferred precedence constraints and the assembly costs obtained from the expert system, we derive the evolution equation of the network, and finally obtain an optimal assembly sequence resulting from the evolution of the network. To illustrate the suitability of the proposed scheme, case study is presented for an electrical relay. The result is compared with that obtained by the expert system.

1. Introduction

It is known that, on the average, assembly cost accounts for 10 to 30 percent of total cost of most industrial products [4], and thus reducing the assembly cost may significantly reduce total cost of a product. Consequently, much research efforts are made on enhancing assembly system performances either by investigating into DFA (Design for Assembly) [5], [6] or through in-depth study on assembly sequence itself [1], [7]-[16], whereas in some research efforts assembly sequence planning is used for an evaluation tool of DFA [7]. Assembly sequence has a direct influence on the productivity of the process, product quality, and the fixed cost involving with the assembly machines and other equipment. Currently, the plannings of assembly sequences in most industries are left to the experiences and intuitions of production engineers. However, as the number of the parts consisting of a product becomes larger, the number of feasible sequences increases explosively, so that the engineers often fail to find the optimal sequence. Therefore, it is necessary to develope tools to provide them technical assistances.

Up to now, most researchers tackled the problem based on well-known tree search or graph search methods. By using most of the search methods, feasible assembly sequences can be generated [7]-[14], and optimal sequence generations are given in Mello and Sanderson [10] and Huang and Lee [12]. The search methods have some drawbacks that they use cumbersome questions and answers or time consuming geometric reasoning. Also, as the number of the parts becomes larger, the search space increases explosively, so that the examples of the product having more than 20 parts seldom appear in literature.

To cope with the former problems, Cho and Cho [15] proposed a method of inference on assembly precedence constraints using part contact level graph, and the inferred constraints were successively applied to the expert system [1] previously proposed system, for generating feasible sequences and the optimal ones. But, the method also has the problem of the explosion of search space as the number of the parts increases.

To overcome the problem of search space explosion, Chen [16] proposed a method to generate optimal assembly sequence of the liaisons using a neural network. He adopted the Hopfield network [2], [3] consisting of rxr neurons, where r is the number of the liaisons in a product. In this method, the AND/OR precedence constraints are inferred from the answers to a series of questions about precedence relation between liaisons. The assembly costs between liaisons are obtained prior to the determination of the sequence. A limitation of this method is that the number of the liaisons r in a product must be smaller than that of the parts n by one to generate the sequence of the liaisons. In general, the number of the liaisons r is known to be a value between n-1 and $(n^2\text{-}n)/2$ [9], but the method did not consider the general case. Another drawback of the method lies in that it is difficult to find the assembly cost between liaisons prior to the determination of the assembly sequence, for the cost is generally dependent upon the sequence to be generated.

In this paper, to overcome the above shortcomings, we propose a scheme to generate optimal assembly sequence in a product using both the Hopfield network [2], [3] and the expert system [1] previously developed. Here, the optimal sequence is defined as the one having the minimum value of the assembly cost as well as satisfying assembly constraints. The assembly cost is defined to be proportional to the number of the direction changes and the degree of the instability of the in-process subassemblies associated with the sequence, for they result in the increase of the fixed cost involved with the equipment. From the assembly cost and the energy associated with neural network, we derive the evolution equation of the network, and finally obtain an assembly sequence resulting from the evolution of the network. Specifically, in the expert system, assembly constraints are inferred from the liaisons data of a product. Then, for any sequence expressed in the network, the assembly constraints are checked, and the assembly cost is evaluated. While, in the network composed of nxn neurons with initial random values, the neurons are evolved according to the above checking and evaluation results obtained from the expert system. As a result, the network finally gives a converged pattern from which we can find an optimal sequence.

To illustrate the suitability of the proposed scheme, case study is presented for an electrical relay. The simulation result obtained for the relay shows that we can obtain an optimal sequence or at least a suboptimal sequence by using the proposed scheme. This paper is organized as follows: representation of assembly sequences, optimization of the assembly sequences, case studies and discussions, and conclusions.

0-7803-0823-9/93/$3.00 (C) 1993 IEEE

2. Representation of Assembly Sequences

As a prerequisite of the subsequent assembly planning, the assembled states of the parts in a product must be represented. Such representation should contain the connection method and assembly directions of the parts, and the geometrical relations between the parts. In the previous works, a product has been modeled by : (1) topological relations between parts [1], [7]-[10], [15] (2) extracted features by a geometric reasoning from CAD or CSG data [11]-[14]. In this paper, we adopt the modeling method, previously proposed by Cho and Cho [15], which utilizes liaisons data between the parts to describe the assembled states of the parts.

2-1. Product Modeling

A product is assumed to be suitable for robotic assembly: it is composed of rigid parts interconnected with each other in mutually orthogonal directions. Each part can be assembled by a simple insertion or a fastening such as screwing operation. An example of such a product is shown in Fig. 1. Let a mechanical assembly A = (P, L) consist of n parts

$$P = \{p_1, p_2, \ldots, p_n\} \tag{1}$$

interconnected by r liaisons

$$L = \{\ell_{jk} \mid j,k = 1,2,\ldots,n,\ j \neq k\} \tag{2}$$
$$(n-1) \leq r(=|L|) \leq n(n-1)/2$$

where |L| means the number of the elements of a set L. The liaison ℓ_{jk}, representing the connective relations between a pair of part p_j and p_k, includes the information on the connecting states and assembly directions. The connective relations are divided into a contact type connection and a fit type connection. The assembly directions are defined with respect to 6 directions $x, y, z, \bar{x}, \bar{y}, \bar{z}$ as shown in the figure. Then, a liaison ℓ_{jk} is expressed by a predicate as follows:

$$\ell_{jk} = (p_j, C_{jk}, F_{jk}, p_k) \tag{3}$$

where $p_j, p_k \in P$ are two interconnected parts. The C_{jk} is called the contact type connection matrix and the F_{jk} is the fit type connection matrix, expressed by 2x3 matrix as follows:

$$C_{jk} = \begin{pmatrix} c_x & c_y & c_z \\ c_{\bar{x}} & c_{\bar{y}} & c_{\bar{z}} \end{pmatrix}, \quad F_{jk} = \begin{pmatrix} f_x & f_y & f_z \\ f_{\bar{x}} & f_{\bar{y}} & f_{\bar{z}} \end{pmatrix} \tag{4}$$

where the elements of C_{jk} are given by

$$c_d = \begin{cases} 0 : \text{no contact in the } d \text{ direction between } p_j \text{ and } p_k \\ rc : \text{real contact in the } d \text{ direction between } p_j \text{ and } p_k \\ vc : \text{virtual contact in the } d \text{ direction between } p_j \text{ and } p_k \end{cases}$$

and the elements of F_{jk} are given by

$$f_d = \begin{cases} 0 : \text{no fit in the } d \text{ direction between } p_j \text{ and } p_k \\ sw : \text{screwing in the } d \text{ direction between } p_j \text{ and } p_k \\ rf : \text{round peg-in-hole fit in the } d \text{ direction between } p_j \text{ and } p_k \\ mp : \text{multiple round peg-in-hole fit in the } d \text{ direction between } p_j \text{ and } p_k \end{cases}$$

and $d \in \{x, y, z, \bar{x}, \bar{y}, \bar{z}\}$. More detailed descriptions on connective relations can be found in Cho and Cho [15]. Fig. 2 shows an example of a liaison ℓ_{jk} chosen from product A shown in Fig. 1. The liaison ℓ_{jk} is then expressed by

$$\ell_{jk} = \text{liaison}\left(p_j, \begin{pmatrix} 0 & rc & rc \\ rc & rc & 0 \end{pmatrix}, \begin{pmatrix} 0 & 0 & rf \\ 0 & 0 & 0 \end{pmatrix}, p_k\right).$$

This predicate expresses the fact that part p_j has the real contacts in directions $\bar{x}, y, \bar{y}, z$ and the round peg-in-hole fit with part p_k in z direction. Similarly, the liaisons of subproduct A' constituting the product A shown in Fig. 1 are expressed by

$$\ell_{13} = \text{liaison}\left(p_1, \begin{pmatrix} 0 & rc & rc \\ 0 & 0 & 0 \end{pmatrix}, \begin{pmatrix} 0 & mp & 0 \\ 0 & 0 & 0 \end{pmatrix}, p_3\right),$$

$$\ell_{14} = \text{liaison}\left(p_1, \begin{pmatrix} 0 & 0 & vc \\ 0 & rc & 0 \end{pmatrix}, \begin{pmatrix} 0 & 0 & 0 \\ 0 & 0 & 0 \end{pmatrix}, p_4\right),$$

$$\ell_{15} = \text{liaison}\left(p_1, \begin{pmatrix} 0 & 0 & vc \\ 0 & 0 & 0 \end{pmatrix}, \begin{pmatrix} 0 & 0 & sw \\ 0 & 0 & 0 \end{pmatrix}, p_5\right),$$

$$\ell_{21} = \text{liaison}\left(p_2, \begin{pmatrix} 0 & 0 & 0 \\ rc & 0 & rc \end{pmatrix}, \begin{pmatrix} 0 & 0 & 0 \\ 0 & 0 & 0 \end{pmatrix}, p_1\right),$$

$$\ell_{23} = \text{liaison}\left(p_2, \begin{pmatrix} 0 & rc & rc \\ 0 & 0 & 0 \end{pmatrix}, \begin{pmatrix} 0 & 0 & 0 \\ 0 & 0 & 0 \end{pmatrix}, p_3\right),$$

$$\ell_{24} = \text{liaison}\left(p_2, \begin{pmatrix} 0 & 0 & rc \\ 0 & rc & 0 \end{pmatrix}, \begin{pmatrix} 0 & 0 & 0 \\ 0 & 0 & 0 \end{pmatrix}, p_4\right).$$

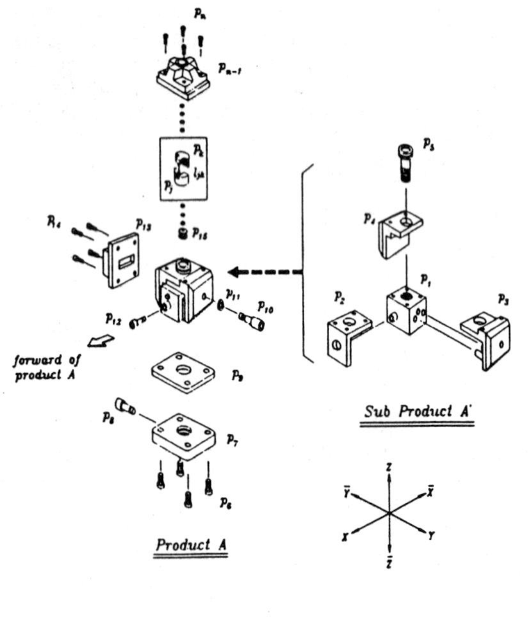

Fig. 1 An example of a product

$$\ell_{25} = \text{liaison}\left(p_2, \begin{pmatrix} 0 & 0 & vc \\ 0 & 0 & 0 \end{pmatrix}, \begin{pmatrix} 0 & 0 & rf \\ 0 & 0 & 0 \end{pmatrix}, p_5\right),$$

$$\ell_{34} = \text{liaison}\left(p_3, \begin{pmatrix} 0 & 0 & rc \\ 0 & rc & 0 \end{pmatrix}, \begin{pmatrix} 0 & 0 & 0 \\ 0 & 0 & 0 \end{pmatrix}, p_4\right),$$

$$\ell_{35} = \text{liaison}\left(p_3, \begin{pmatrix} 0 & 0 & vc \\ 0 & 0 & 0 \end{pmatrix}, \begin{pmatrix} 0 & 0 & rf \\ 0 & 0 & 0 \end{pmatrix}, p_5\right),$$

$$\ell_{45} = \text{liaison}\left(p_4, \begin{pmatrix} 0 & 0 & rc \\ 0 & 0 & 0 \end{pmatrix}, \begin{pmatrix} 0 & 0 & rf \\ 0 & 0 & 0 \end{pmatrix}, p_5\right).$$

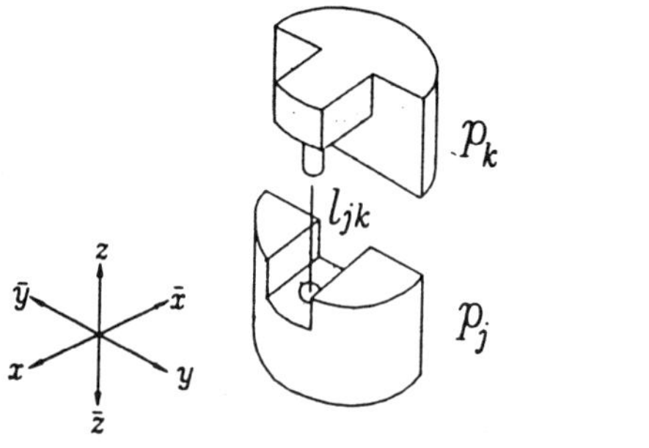

$$l_{jk} = liaison(p_j, C_{jk}, F_{jk}, p_k)$$

Fig. 2 An example of representing liaison ℓ_{jk}

2-2. Feasible assembly sequences

Another important concept in describing an assembly sequence is assembly constraints which can be classified into assembly precedence constraint and avoidance of plural in-process subassemblies. Here, assembly precedence constraint of a part is represented by a set consisting of a number of parts that must be connected to the in-process subassembly prior to the part. The detailed procedure of the inference is described in Cho and Cho [15]. Let $BA = \{p_{j_1}, p_{j_2}, \ldots, p_{j_q}\}$ be an in-process subassembly, and p_f be a part to be assembled to the subassembly. Then, the precedence constraint $PC(p_f)$ of the part p_f is expressed by

$$PC(p_f) = \bigcup_{j=j_1}^{j_q} P(\ell_{jf}) \tag{5}$$

where $P(\ell_{jf})$, the precedence constraint of liaison ℓ_{jf}, is directly inferred from the liaisons data by using a part contact level graph [15]. Equation (5) states that the part precedence constraint $PC(p_f)$ is the union of liaison precedence constraint $PC(p_f)$ for all liaisons which exist between p_f and the parts assembled on the in-process subassembly. Let us take an example of the part precedence constraint for the subproduct A' shown in Fig. 1. Suppose that parts p_1, p_2 and p_3 have been assembled to form an in-process subassembly BA. Then, the precedence constraints for parts p_4 and p_5 are inferred by

$$PC(p_4) = \{p_2, p_3\}, \qquad PC(p_5) = \{p_1, p_2, p_3, p_4\}.$$

The above results of the part precedence constraints mean that, in order to assemble part p_4 to the BA, the BA must contain parts p_2 and p_3. Similarly, to assemble part p_5 to the BA, the BA must contain parts p_1, p_2, p_3 and p_4. Since the BA is composed of parts p_1, p_2 and p_3, part p_4 can be assembled but part p_5 cannot be assembled.

Another constraint, avoidance of plural in-process subassemblies, states that a part p_f to be assembled must have at least a real contact or a fit with any part assembled onto the in-process subassembly, so that there exists only one in-process subassembly from the start to the end of the assembly work. In the above example, part p_4 has the real contacts with parts p_1, p_2 and p_3 as shown in the liaisons data ℓ_{14}, ℓ_{24} and ℓ_{34}. Part p_5 has the screwing fit with part p_1 and the round peg-in-hole fits with parts p_2 and p_3 as shown in the liaisons data ℓ_{15}, ℓ_{25} and ℓ_{35}. Thus, parts p_4 and p_5 satisfy the constraint of avoidance of plural in-process subassemblies.

Feasible assembly sequences are the ones satisfying the assembly constraints such as the precedence constraints and the avoidance of plural subassemblies. The precedence constraints were inferred from the liaisons data by using a part contact level graph, and the avoidance of plural subassemblies was checked by examining whether there exists at least a real contact or a fit between a part to be assembled and the parts constituting the in-process subassembly. In the above example of the subproduct A', the feasible sequences inferred are $p_1 \rightarrow p_2 \rightarrow p_3 \rightarrow p_4 \rightarrow p_5$ and $p_2 \rightarrow p_1 \rightarrow p_3 \rightarrow p_4 \rightarrow p_5$ [15].

2-3. Stable Assembly Sequences

Although feasible assembly sequences are found, they do not always guarantee the parts to be fixed on the subassembly; parts may be loosely connected, and come apart when the subassembly is rotated or moved. In the assembly sequence planning, the movement of a subassembly must be avoided if the state of the subassembly is unstable. Such assembly sequences keeping stability of the in-process subassembly movement are called the stable sequences by which all the parts are successfully assembled to form an end product. As can be expected, if we use a large degree-of-freedom robot instead of using the one having smaller degree of freedom motion, we can find the increased number of stable sequences, for the robot motion may reduce the necessary movement of the subassembly itself. Stable sequences, therefore, are related not only to the state of the subassembly but also to the degree-of-freedom of the robot motion.

We define the normalized degree of the instability C_{as} of the in-process subassemblies for an assembly sequence $TSEQ_{\alpha i} = \{p_{\beta_1}, p_{\beta_2}, \ldots, p_{\beta_i}\}$ as follows:

$$C_{as} = \frac{1}{12i}\sum_{j=1}^{i} S(BA_j), \qquad 0 \le S(BA_j) \le 12 \tag{6}$$

where $p_{\beta_i} = p_\alpha$, $1 \le i \le n$, and $S(BA_j)$ represents the degree of the instability of each subassembly BA_j at the jth assembly step when a degree-of-freedom of the robot is chosen. The instability is divided into a translational instability and a rotational instability, and each instability is composed of six degree of freedom of movements, i.e., x, y, z, $\bar{x}$, $\bar{y}$ and $\bar{z}$. The degree of the instability of the $S(BA_j)$ means the number of the degree of freedom of translational and rotational movements of the $S(BA_j)$, so its maximum value becomes 12. The detailed procedure of finding $S(BA_j)$ is referred to Cho [1]. The C_{as} will be given to consideration when we will train the neural network to obtain an optimal assembly sequence.

3. Optimization of Assembly Sequences

To obtain the optimal assembly sequence, we will define the assembly cost, and accordingly determine the condition of the optimal sequence. Next, we will relate the assembly cost with the network energy, and consequently obtain the modified evolution equation of the network.

3-1. *Optimal Sequence*

Among the stable sequences, we can find the optimal sequence whose value of the cost function associated with the sequence is the minimum. Here, the cost function $J_{\alpha i}$ is defined to reflect the normalized degree of the instability of in-process subassemblies C_{as} of (6) and the normalized number of the direction changes of the subassemblies C_{nt} when a degree-of-freedom of the robot is chosen. The cost function $J_{\alpha i}$ for an assembly sequence $TSEQ_{\alpha i} = \{p_{\beta_1}, p_{\beta_2}, \ldots, p_{\beta_i}\}$ is given by

$$J_{\alpha i} = \begin{cases} 1 & : \text{if the } TSEQ_{\alpha i} \text{ does not satisfy the assembly constraints} \\ \rho_s C_{as} + \rho_t C_{nt} & : \text{otherwise} \end{cases} \quad (7)$$

where $p_{\beta_i} = p_\alpha$, $1 \le i \le n$, and the C_{nt} is defined by

$$C_{nt} = \frac{1}{i}\sum_{j=1}^{i} g_j, \quad (8)$$

where

$$g_j = \begin{cases} 1: \text{if the direction change of each in-process subassembly } BA_j \text{ occurs at the jth assembly step} \\ 0: \text{otherwise.} \end{cases}$$

The ρ_s and the ρ_t are the weighting factors determined by the type of assembly system and the assembly cycle time [1], and $\rho_s+\rho_t=1$, $0 \le C_{as} \le 1$, $0 \le C_{nt} \le 1$.

To find the optimal assembly sequence based on the cost function $J_{\alpha i}$ of (7), we adopt the Hopfield neural network model [2], [3] whose energy function is related to the cost function. The model is characterized by the energy function associated with the network, which is defined by the output values of the neurons, the interconnection weights between neurons, and the external input bias to the neurons. As the network evolves, the energy function tends to decrease and reach an equilibrium state. Since the assembly cost is related to the network energy, we can find the optimal assembly sequence having the minimum assembly cost when the network energy reaches the global minimum.

3-2. *Neural Network Model*

Utilizing the above evolution characteristics for the assembly sequence optimization, the network, composed of nxn neurons, is expressed in an n by n matrix. Fig. 3 shows an example of such an expression for an assembly sequence illustrated for a product consisting of four parts. In the figure, the row index α represents the part p_α and the column index i is the ith step of an assembly sequence. Then, a neuron output value $V_{\alpha i}$ can be represented as an assemblability, that is, possibility for the part p_α to be assembled at the ith step. In this case, $V_{\alpha i}$ having a value close to 1 implies that the part p_α can be assembled at the ith step of a sequence. In Fig. 3, the sequence expressed by the pattern is $p_4 \rightarrow p_1 \rightarrow p_3 \rightarrow p_2$. By adopting this representation, the evolution equations of the network are expressed by:

$$\frac{dU_{\alpha i}}{dt} = -U_{\alpha i} + \sum_{\beta}^{n}\sum_{j}^{n} w_{\alpha i,\beta j}V_{\beta j} + I_{\alpha i} \quad (9)$$

$$V_{\alpha i} = \text{Sigmoid}(U_{\alpha i}) = \frac{1}{1+e^{-U_{\alpha i}/U_0}} \quad (10)$$

where $U_{\alpha i}$: total input to neuron $X_{\alpha i}$. The value is related to the assemblability of the part p_α at the ith assembly step.

$V_{\alpha i}$: output of neuron $X_{\alpha i}$ having an analog value between 0 and 1. It implies the assemblability of the part p_α at the ith assembly step.

$w_{\alpha i,\beta j}$: interconnection weight between two neurons $X_{\alpha i}$ and $X_{\beta j}$.

$I_{\alpha i}$: external input bias. It will be derived in section 3-3 to be a value proportional to the number of the parts n.

U_0 : threshold value determining the slope of the sigmoid function.

Fig. 4 depicts a neuron $X_{\alpha i}$ evolved by (9) and (10). The

α \ i	1	2	3	4
1	0	1	0	0
2	0	0	0	1
3	0	0	1	0
4	1	0	0	0

Fig. 3 Neural network repesentation for 4 parts assembly sequence

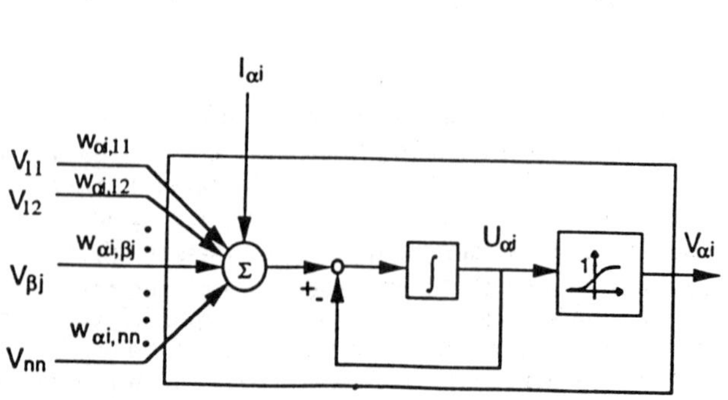

Fig. 4 Schematic diagram of a neuron Xαi in the network

energy function E_h associated with the network is defined as follows:

$$E_h = -\frac{1}{2}\sum_{\alpha}^{n}\sum_{i}^{n}\sum_{\beta}^{n}\sum_{j}^{n} w_{\alpha i,\beta j}V_{\alpha i}V_{\beta j} - \sum_{\alpha}^{n}\sum_{i}^{n} I_{\alpha i}V_{\alpha i}. \quad (11)$$

3-3. *Energy function Related to Optimal Sequence*

To derive the relation between the network energy and the optimal sequence, let us define the energy function related to the optimal sequence by

$$E_{os} = E_A + E_B + E_C + E_D \quad (12)$$

where E_A, E_B and E_C are the terms to be increased for abnormal sequence. That is, E_A is the energy term for a part belonging to more than one assembly step, E_B is the one for a step having more than one part. The third term E_C is increased when the number of the parts expressed in the network is different from that of a product. Then, the energy terms are expressed by

$$E_A = \frac{A}{2}\sum_{\alpha}^{n}\sum_{i}^{n}\sum_{j\neq i}^{n} V_{\alpha i}V_{\alpha j} \quad (13)$$

$$E_B = \frac{B}{2}\sum_{\alpha}^{n}\sum_{i}^{n}\sum_{\beta\neq\alpha}^{n} V_{\alpha i}V_{\beta i} \quad (14)$$

$$E_C = \frac{C}{2}\left(\sum_{\alpha}^{n}\sum_{i}^{n} V_{\alpha i} - n\right)^2 \quad (15)$$

where A, B, C are positive constants. The other energy term E_D for assembly constraints and assembly cost is derived hereinafter.

Let us consider the evolution of a neuron $X_{\alpha i}$ whose output $V_{\alpha i}$ represents the possibility for the part p_α to be assembled at the ith step. When the assembly cost $J_{\alpha i}$ in (7) of a sequence in which the part p_α is assembled at the ith step is relatively high, the neuron output $V_{\alpha i}$ should be decreased so that the network energy term E_D related to the assembly cost $J_{\alpha i}$ decreases, and vice versa. In this case, to evaluate the assembly cost it is necessary to find all the sequences in which the part p_α is assembled at the ith step. For example, Fig. 5 shows all the sequences for neuron X_{33}. As a result, (n-1)! sequences must be evaluated per one evolution of the neuron $X_{\alpha i}$, which results in the explosive increase of the computational burden as the number of the parts increases. The example of Fig. 5 shows that (4-1)! = 6 sequences are produced for a neuron in four parts assembly.

To overcome this difficulty, we choose a representative

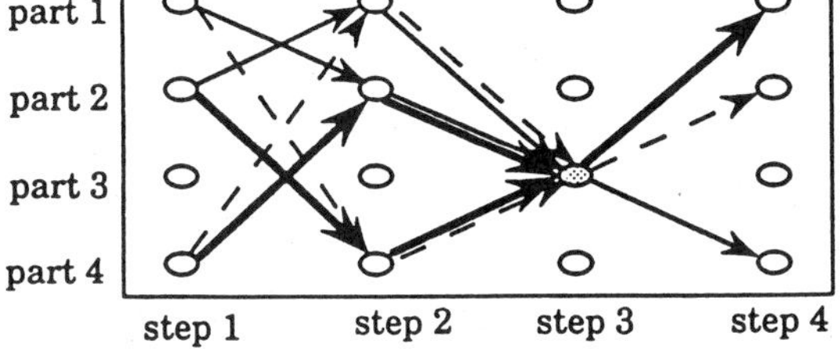

Fig. 5 Representation of all the sequences for neuron X_{33}

sequence in which the part p_α is assumed to be assembled at the ith step. The representative sequence is chosen to consist of the parts having a relatively high assemblability in the network. Then we can check the precedence constraints and evaluate the assembly cost for the representative sequence only, so that a fair amount of the computational burden decreases. According to the results of the checking and evaluation, neuron $X_{\alpha i}$ will evolve. Here, the chosen representative sequence is called the temporary sequence specified for a neuron $X_{\alpha i}$, and is denoted as $TSEQ_{\alpha i}$ which consists of i parts. The $TSEQ_{\alpha i}$ is expressed by

$$TSEQ_{\alpha i} = \{p_{\beta_1}, p_{\beta_2}, \ldots, p_{\beta_i}\} \quad (16)$$

where p_{β_j}, j = 1, 2, ..., i, represents the part to be assembled at the jth assembly step in accordance with the $TSEQ_{\alpha i}$. An example of the steps finding a temporary sequence $TSEQ_{24}$ for α=2 and i=4 is shown for five parts assembly in Fig. 6, and the steps for a neuron $X_{\alpha i}$ are summarized as follows:

step 1. The last part p_{β_i} of $TSEQ_{\alpha i}$ in (16) is chosen to be the part p_α, and the neuron output value $V_{\alpha i}$ is denoted by $V_{\beta_i i}$. (In Fig. 6(a), $p_{\beta_4} = p_2$, and $V_{\beta_4 4} = V_{24} = 0.3$)

step 2. It proceeds to find the first part p_{β_1} to be assembled. In the first column of the network, we select a neuron output $V_{\beta_1 1}$ having the maximum value among the neurons except the previously chosen row α. That is, $V_{\beta_1 1} = \max_{\beta\neq\alpha}^{n}(V_{\beta 1})$, and accordingly p_{β_1} becomes the first part to be assembled. (In Fig. 6(b), $V_{\beta_1 1} = \max(V_{11}, V_{31}, V_{41}, V_{51}) = \max(0.3, 0.5, 0.1, 0.3) = V_{31} = 0.5$, and $p_{\beta_1} = p_3$.)

step 3. It proceeds to find the second part p_{β_2} in the second column of the network. In the same manner as illustrated in step 2, $V_{\beta_2 2} = \max_{\beta\neq\alpha,\beta_1}^{n}(V_{\beta 2})$, and p_{β_2} becomes the second part to be assembled. (In Fig 6(c), $V_{\beta_2 2} = V_{12} = 0.8$, and $p_{\beta_2} = p_1$.)

step 4. We continue to find the remaining parts p_{β_3}, p_{β_4}, ..., $p_{\beta_{i-1}}$ to be assembled in the same manner. (In Fig. 6 (d), $V_{\beta_3 3} = V_{43} = 0.5$, and $p_{\beta_3} = p_4$.)

In the above example shown in Fig. 6, we can obtain $TSEQ_{24}$ = {3, 1, 4, 2} according to the above steps.

In order that the network energy increases when the obtained temporary sequence does not satisfy the assembly constraints or has a high assembly cost , we define the energy function E_D as follows:

$$E_D = \frac{D}{2}\sum_{\alpha}^{n}\sum_{i}^{n}\sum_{j}^{i} J_{\alpha i}V_{\alpha i}V_{\beta_j j} \quad (17)$$

where D is a positive constant and

$J_{\alpha i}$: assembly cost in (7) for the obtained $TSEQ_{\alpha i}$ in (16),

x \ i	1	2	3	4	5
1	0.3	0.8	0.2	0.4	0.2
2	0.2	0.3	0.1	0.3	0.9
3	0.5	0.1	0.6	0.5	0.3
4	0.1	0.2	0.5	0.2	0.1
5	0.3	0.3	0.2	0.8	0.2

(a)

x \ i	1	2	3	4	5
1	0.3	0.8	0.2	0.4	0.2
2	0.2	0.3	0.1	0.3	0.9
3	0.5	0.1	0.6	0.5	0.3
4	0.1	0.2	0.5	0.2	0.1
5	0.3	0.3	0.2	0.8	0.2

(b)

x \ i	1	2	3	4	5
1	0.3	0.8	0.2	0.4	0.2
2	0.2	0.3	0.1	0.3	0.9
3	0.5	0.1	0.6	0.5	0.3
4	0.1	0.2	0.5	0.2	0.1
5	0.3	0.3	0.2	0.8	0.2

(c)

x \ i	1	2	3	4	5
1	0.3	0.8	0.2	0.4	0.2
2	0.2	0.3	0.1	0.3	0.9
3	0.5	0.1	0.6	0.5	0.3
4	0.1	0.2	0.5	0.2	0.1
5	0.3	0.3	0.2	0.8	0.2

(d)

Fig. 6 An example of the steps finding the temporary sequence $TSEQ_{42}=\{3,1,4,2\}$ for neuron X_{42} in five parts assembly

○ : currently selected ◎ : previously selected

$V_{\beta,j}$: output value of the neuron associated with the $TSEQ_{\alpha i}$ in (16).

Thus, the energy functions obtained in (13), (14), (15) and (17) are summed to give the next energy function associated with the optimal sequence

$$E_{os} = E_A + E_B + E_C + E_D$$

$$= \frac{A}{2}\sum_{\alpha}^{n}\sum_{i}^{n}\sum_{j\neq i}^{n} V_{\alpha i}V_{\alpha j} + \frac{B}{2}\sum_{\alpha}^{n}\sum_{i}^{n}\sum_{\beta\neq\alpha}^{n} V_{\alpha i}V_{\beta i} \tag{18}$$

$$+ \frac{C}{2}\left(\sum_{\alpha}^{n}\sum_{i}^{n} V_{\alpha i} - n\right)^2 + \frac{D}{2}\sum_{\alpha}^{n}\sum_{i}^{n}\sum_{j}^{i} J_{\alpha i}V_{\alpha i}V_{\beta_j j}.$$

From the network energy function E_h in (11) and the optimal sequence energy function E_{os} in (18), we can derive the interconnection weight $w_{\alpha i,\beta j}$ and the external input bias $I_{\alpha i}$ as follows:

$$w_{\alpha i,\beta j} = -A\delta_{\alpha\beta}(1-\delta_{ij}) - B\delta_{ij}(1-\delta_{\alpha\beta}) - C - DJ_{\alpha i}\delta_{\beta_j \beta}u(i-j) \tag{19}$$

$$I_{\alpha i} = Cn \tag{20}$$

where

δ_{pq} : Kronecker delta function $= \begin{cases} 1 : \text{for } p = q \\ 0 : \text{otherwise} \end{cases}$

$u(k)$: unit step function $= \begin{cases} 1 : \text{for } k \geq 0 \\ 0 : \text{otherwise.} \end{cases}$

Substituting the interconnection weight $w_{\alpha i,\beta j}$ of (19) and the external input bias $I_{\alpha i}$ of (20) into the evolution equation (9) gives the modified evolution equation of the network at next stage.

$$\frac{dU_{\alpha i}}{dt} = -U_{\alpha i} - A\sum_{j\neq i}^{n} V_{\alpha j} - B\sum_{\beta\neq\alpha}^{n} V_{\beta i} - C\left(\sum_{\beta}^{n}\sum_{j}^{n} V_{\beta j} - n\right) - D\sum_{j}^{i} J_{\alpha i}V_{\beta_j j} \tag{21}$$

In the next section, we will illustrate case studies using the proposed neural network based computational scheme evolved by (21) and (10).

3-4. Comments on the Convergency

In the Hopfield network, the network energy always decreases, remains unchanged, or reaches an equilibrium state as the network evolves. This convergency is guaranteed only if the interconnection weights are symmetric between any two neurons, that is, $w_{\alpha i,\beta j} = w_{\beta j,\alpha i}$. However, as shown in (19) the proposed model does not have fully symmetric interconnections due to the last term related to assembly cost. Therefore, the network energy related to the assembly cost may increase as the network evolves. But it tends to globally decreases although the network energy increases slightly at some moments as the network evolves.

4. Case Study and Discussions

4-1. Simulation procedure

To implement the proposed scheme, we compose the network of nxn neurons. Initially, each neuron output has a random value between $(1.0 \pm 0.5)/n$ so that the summation of all the neurons output is close to n. The evolution equation (21), expressed in a first order differential equation, is solved by Euler's method which is subject to significant round-off errors but gives quick convergency. To improve the speed of the network convergency, the first part to be assembled may be assigned in the simulation. Fig. 7 shows the simulation flow system. The system has two divisions: one division is part of an expert system which infers precedence constraints directly from the liaisons data, and check the precedence constraints and evaluate the assembly cost for temporary sequences. The other is a neural network which is evolved by (21) and (10). The simulation steps are summarized in the followings:

step1. Initialize the network composed of nxn neurons by assigning random values.
step2. Select an arbitrary neuron.
step3. Find the temporary sequence for the selected neuron.
step 4. Check the precedence constraints and evaluate the assembly cost for the temporary sequence.
step 5. The neuron evolves according to the result of step 4.
step 6. Check if the pattern of the network is converged. If it is converged, the optimal sequence is found, and accordingly the simulation stops.
step 7. Go to step 2.

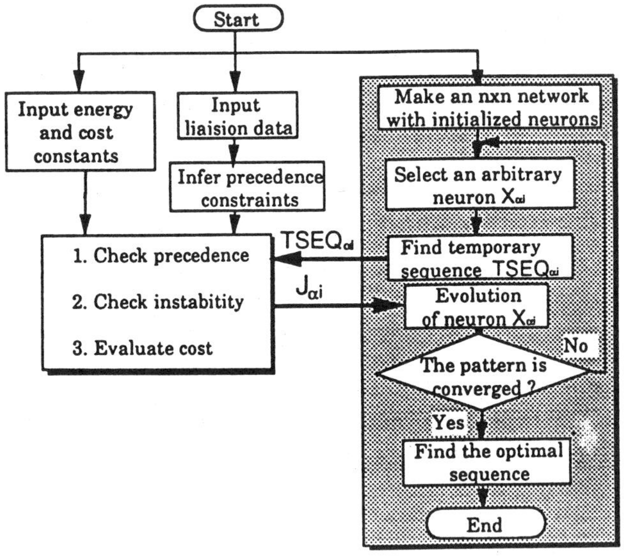

Fig. 7. The simulation flow chart

Table 2. The result of simulation for an electrical relay

	Sequences obtained	$\sum_{\alpha=1}^{n} J_{\beta\alpha\gamma}$	No. of solutions
Optimal sequences	6,1,2,3,5,9,10,4,7,8	1.154	3
	6,1,2,3,5,10,9,4,7,8	1.154	1
	6,1,2,3,5,10,4,9,7,8	1.233	1
	6,1,2,3,10,5,9,4,7,8	1.233	1
	6,1,2,3,9,5,10,4,7,8	1.233	2
	6,1,2,3,10,5,4,9,7,8	1.353	1
	6,1,2,3,5,4,10,9,7,8	1.353	2
	6,1,2,3,10,9,5,4,7,8	1.420	1
Stable sequences	6,1,3,2,5,10,9,4,7,8	1.275	1
	6,1,3,2,10,9,5,4,7,8	1.323	1
	6,1,3,2,5,10,4,9,7,8	1.353	1
	6,1,2,10,3,5,9,4,7,8	1.455	1
	6,1,3,2,10,9,5,4,7,8	1.481	1
	6,1,3,2,5,4,9,10,7,8	1.520	1
	6,1,10,3,2,5,9,4,7,8	1.781	1
	6,1,3,10,9,2,5,4,7,8	1.897	1
Total			20

4-2. Results and Discussions

To illustrate the suitability of the proposed scheme, the scheme was applied for determining the optimal sequences of an electrical relay. The relay consists of 10 parts as shown in Fig. 8. The simulation conditions are listed in Table 1, and the simulation result is shown in Table 2. The energy constants in the Table 1 (A, B, C, D in (13), (14), (15) and (17)) are determined during the

Table 1. The simulation Conditions

Product	Energy constants						Cost constants		The base part	Assembly direction of robot
	A	B	C	S	P	D	ρs	ρt		
Relay	10	10	10	10	12	12	0.5	0.5	6	$\bar{z}$ only
Alternator	8	8	10	20	10	5	0.5	0.5	6	z and $\bar{z}$

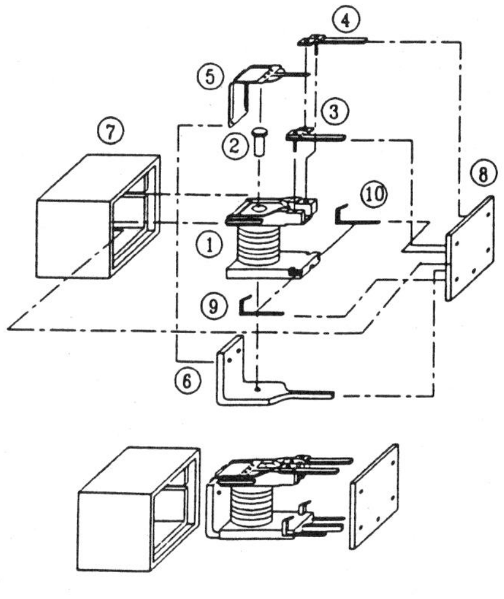

Fig. 8 An exploded view of an electrical relay

simulation by observing the convergency tendency. If the constants are balanced adequately, the network is converged to give a proper pattern. Otherwise, the network fails to give a proper pattern.

To evaluate the performance of the proposed scheme, we compare the simulation result with that obtained from the expert system. The expert system result is shown in Table 3. To compare the result reveals that 10 trials out of 20 simulations give the optimal sequences, and the remaining 10 trials give non-optimal but stable ones. Fig.9 shows examples of network convergency for the product.

The above results show that we can obtain an optimal sequence or at least suboptimal stable one using the proposed scheme. The reason for obtaining the suboptimal sequence is that the network energy related to the assembly cost often reaches a local minimum [2], [3].

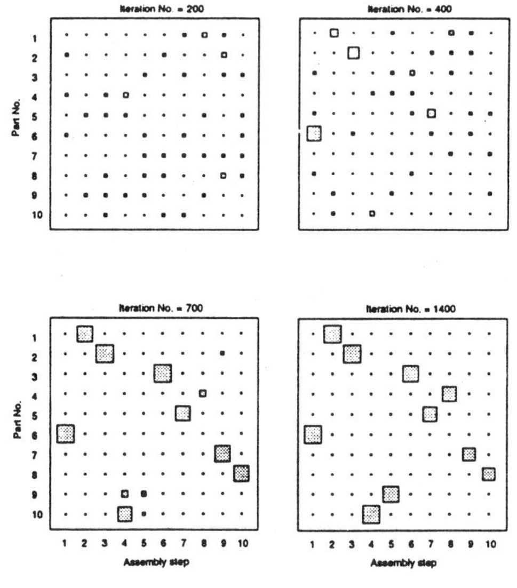

Fig. 9 Network convergency during a simulation for a relay

Table 3. Optimal Sequences for a relay obtained from the expert system

Optimal sequences
6 1 2 3 9 10 5 4 7 8
6 1 2 3 9 5 10 4 7 8
6 1 2 3 9 5 4 10 7 8
6 1 2 3 10 9 5 4 7 8
6 1 2 3 10 5 9 4 7 8
6 1 2 3 10 5 4 9 7 8
6 1 2 3 5 9 10 4 7 8
6 1 2 3 5 9 4 10 7 8
6 1 2 3 5 10 9 4 7 8
6 1 2 3 5 10 4 9 7 8
6 1 2 3 5 4 9 10 7 8
6 1 2 3 5 4 10 9 7 8

In the neural network, assembly cost is evaluated for a representative sequence, the temporary sequence, of a neuron. By introducing the temporary sequence, the burden of computation has been decreased, but asymmetry interconnections between neurons has occurred. Owing to the asymmetry interconnections, the network energy related to the assembly cost does not always decrease but it increases slightly at some moments as the network evolves. Fig.10 shows the change of network energy for the relay. Observing from the figure, we draw a conclusion that the assembly cost associated with the network tends to globally decrease in spite of its momentary increase.

5. Conclusions

In designing an assembly system it is essential to determine optimal assembly sequence for increasing productivity and reducing cost. In this paper, we have proposed a scheme to find the optimal assembly sequence of a product using both the expert system and neural network. Through case study for an electrical relay, we have illustrated the suitability of the scheme, evaluating the performance. The summary of the results obtained from the simulation is as follows:

(1) We have defined a network energy function which adequately reflects the factors associated with optimal assembly sequence, such as assembly constraints, stability of in-process subassembly, and direction change of in-process subassemblies. Also, using the fact that the network energy related to assembly cost tends to decrease and reach an equilibrium state, we have found an optimal sequence resulted from the evolution of the network.

(2) The results of the case studies have shown that we can obtain an optimal sequence or at least suboptimal stable one using the proposed scheme. The reason for obtaining the suboptimal sequence is that the network energy related to the assembly cost often reaches a local minimum.

(3) Since this scheme can cope with the problem of the search strategy usually suffering from the explosion of the search space, the scheme can be applied to the case when the number of the parts are too large to obtain a sequence using conventional search methods.

Acknowledgment

The authors wish to thank the Korea Science Engineering Foundation for sponsoring this research.

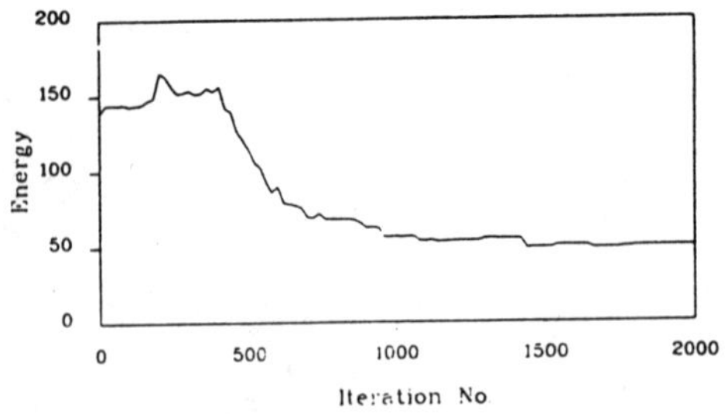

Fig. 10 Change of network energy related to assembly cost for a relay

References

[1] D. Y. Cho, "An expert system approach to the generation of robotic assembly sequences," Ph. D. dissertation, Korea Advanced Institute of Science and Technology, Korea, Feb. 1992.

[2] J. J. Hopfield, "Neural networks and physical systems with emergent collective computational ability," *Proc. Natl. Acad. Sci.* , Vol.79, pp.2254-2258, 1882.

[3] J. J. Hopfield and D. W. Tank, "Neural computation of decisions in optimization problems," *Biol. Cyber.* , Vol.53, pp.141-152, 1985.

[4] J. L. Nevins and D. E. Whitney, "Assembly research," *Automatica* , Vol.16, pp.78-94, 1980.

[5] G. Boothroyd, "Design for Assembly - The key to design for manufacture," *Int. J. Adv. Manuf. Tech.*, Vol.2, pp.3-11, 1987.

[6] M. M. Andreasen, C. Poli and L. E. Murch, *Design for assembly.* IFS Pub. Ltd., U. K., 1983.

[7] D. F. Boldin, T. E. Abell, M. C. M. Lui, T. L. D. Fazio and D. E. Whitney, "An integrated computer aid for generating and evaluating assembly sequences for mechanical products," *IEEE Tran. Rob. Auto.* , Vol.7, No.1, pp.78-94, 1991.

[8] A. Bourjault, "Contribution a une approche méthodologique de l'assemblage automatisé: Elaboration automatique des séquences opératiories," Ph. D. dissertation , L'Université de Franche-Comté, Nov. 1984.

[9] T. L. D. Fazio and D. E. Whitney, "Simplified generation of all assembly sequences," *IEEE J. Rob. Auto.* , Vol.RA-3, No.6, pp.640-658, Dec. 1987.

[10] L. S. H. Mello and A. C. Sanderson, "AND/OR representation of assembly plans," *IEEE Tran. Rob. Auto.* , Vol.6, No.2, pp.188-199, April 1990.

[11] K. Sekiguchi, T. Kojima, K. Inoue and H. Takeyama, "Study on Automatic determination of assembly sequences," *Annals of the CIRP* , Vol.32, No.1, pp.371-374, 1983.

[12] Y. F. Huang and C. S. G. Lee, "A framework of knowledge-based assembly planning,". *Proc. IEEE Int. Conf. Rob. Auto.*, pp.599-604, April 1991.

[13] Y. Liu and R. J. Popplestone, "Planning for assembly from solid models," *Proc. IEEE Int. Conf. Rob. Auto.* , pp.222-227, 1989.

[14] R. Hoffman, "Automated assembly in a CSG domain," *Proc. Int. Conf. Rob. Auto.* pp.210-215, 1989.

[15] D. Y. Cho and H. S. Cho, "Inference on robotic assembly precedence constraints using part contact level graph," *Robotica* (to appear).

[16] C. L. P. Chen, "Neural computations for planning AND/OR precedence-constraint robot assembly sequences," *Proc. Int. Conf. Neural Net.* , Vol.1, pp.127-142, 1990.

An Approach to Thermal Placement in Power Electronics Using Neural Networks

Andrzej Kos
University of Mining and Metallurgy
Institute of Electronics
Czarnowiejska 78, 30-054 Kraków, Poland

Abstract **- The paper deals with the optimum thermal placement of heat sources in hybrid power circuits. The combination of original heuristic method and the Hopfield neural net is presented. Because of the introduced hierarchical approach, the significant reduction of the computational effort is achieved.**

I. INTRODUCTION

Hybrid circuits are the focus of considerable interest nowadays. A hybrid power circuit is simply a rectangular substrate which has rectangular heat sources - Fig.1. The cooling is wholly from the surface and proportional to the temperature. Such circuits must meet two quite conflicting requirements: high integration density and high power dissipation. This condition is a result of the physical proximity of surface mounted integrated circuits, resistors, and high - power elements. The temperature distribution of hybrid power circuits greatly influences the parameters of the components involved.

One of the most important problems in hybrid microcircuits design is an optimum thermal placement. "Optimum" means here that all thermally significant electronic devices are expected to work in the possibly lowest temperatures. Such an idea implies that the temperature in every point of a substrate should not differ considerably from the average temperature. Traditional optimization techniques, e.g. gradient or Powell methods, need a lot of computational effort. To avoid this disadvantage a heuristic method has been proposed [1]. In this method the substrate is divided into n equal subareas. If P_c is the total dissipated power, $P_c = P_1 + P_2 + ... + P_N$, N – the number of heat sources, then an amount P_c / n is attributed to each subarea. n should be sufficiently large to let the powers $P_1, P_2, ..., P_N$ be the integer multiplies of P_c / n. For example if $P_c = 9\text{W}$, $P_1 = 1\text{W}$, $P_2 = 8\text{W}$, then one subarea is assigned to the resistor P_1 and 8 neighbouring subareas grouped together into one coherent area, so called c-area, are assigned to the resistor P_2 (see Fig.2). P_2 is placed in the centre of gravity of this c-area. For this simple example there are only two possible various layouts. In more complicated cases with more heat dissipating devices the number of possible placements quickly increases.

The solutions with c-areas resembling circles are considered as quasi-optimum. It means that a substrate should be divided into c-areas with minimal perimeters. Fig. 3 shows some possibilities of the heuristic placement of four heat sources (screen-printed resistors) with powers $P_1 = 0.4\text{W}$, $P_2 = 0.6\text{W}$, $P_3 = 1.0\text{W}$, $P_4 = 2.0\text{W}$. The substrate in this case has to be divided into four c-areas. Because they have to be proportional to the power dissipated in the resistors P_1, P_2, P_3, P_4, they will consist of 4, 6, 10, 20 subareas respectively. Table I shows various possibilities of such a division. An important parameter is there $S = S_1 + S_2 + S_3 + S_4$, S_i – perimeter of the i-th c-area. It has already been mentioned that only the solutions with small S should be taken into consideration.

Sometimes, when the number of heat devices is great, it is difficult to choose the best division of a substrate into appropriate c-areas. To facilitate the choice it is suggested to use a Hopfield neural net.

II. NEURAL COMPUTATIONS

A. Hopfield Neural Net

Successful application of neural networks to N-P complete problems, such as the travelling salesman problem, are becoming increasingly bright. Hopfield applied a Lyapunov function for a network of some neurons. Hopfield and Tank [2] laid the groundwork for the progress in this area. They recognized that it was possible to use the energy function to make optimization. Because a network of neurons will seek to minimize the energy function, one may design a neural network for function minimization by associating variables in an optimization problem with variables in the energy function. The net is presented in Fig.4. It looks like a n x n matrix. Coordinates *(i, k)* determine the presence of the i-th subsource in the k-th subarea. A subsource is a conventionally introduced source with a power P_c / n being a part of a total dissipated power. Every subsource is assigned to one and only one heat source. In the network weights are symmetrical, i.e. $w_{ik,jl} = w_{jl,ik}$ and no self-feedback exists, $w_{ik,ik} = 0$. The behaviour of a processing element is characterised by its activation level u_{ik} which is governed by the differential equation

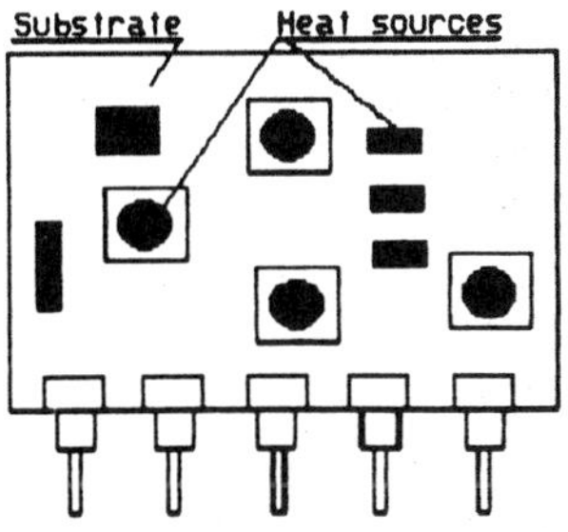

Fig.1. A hybrid circuit

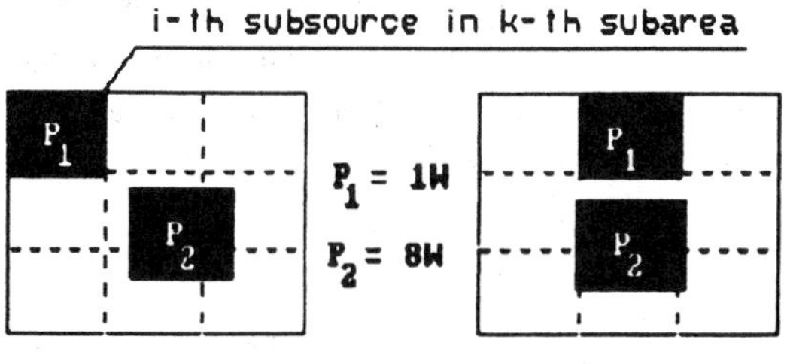

Fig. 2. Heuristic placement of two thick-film resistors

0-7803-1254-6/93$03.00

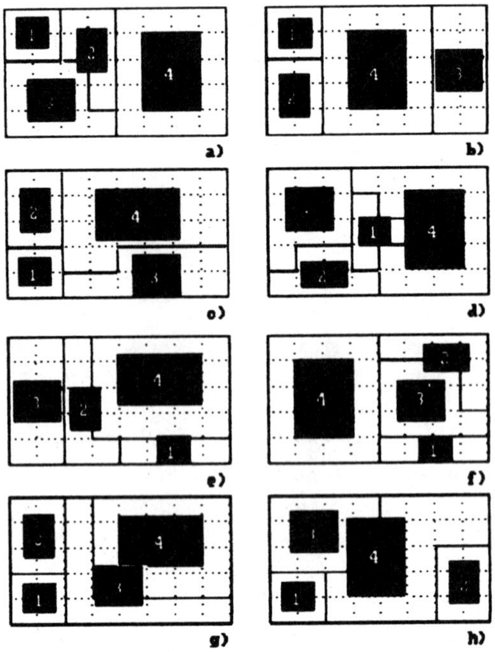

Fig. 3. Some possibilities of placement of four heat sources
P1 = 0.4 W, P2 = 0.6 W, P3 = 1.0 W, P4 = 2.0 W

$$\frac{du_{ik}}{dt} = -\frac{u_{ik}}{\tau} + \sum_{j,l=1}^{n} w_{jl,ik} x_{jl} + I_{ik} \qquad (1)$$

$$i, k = 1,\dots,n$$

where: t - time,
τ - time constant,
n - number of subareas = number of subsources,
$w_{jl,ik}$ - weight of a synapse between unit (j, l) and unit (i, k),
I_{ik} - external input to each neuron,
x_{ik} - output of (i, k) neuron.

The activation function is typically a smooth sigmoid as illustrated in Fig. 4b

$$x_{ik} = 1/\left[1+\exp(-u_{ik})\right] \qquad (2)$$

Let the energy function of the neural network be given by the formula

$$E = -\,0.5\,\mathbf{x}^{\mathrm{T}}\mathbf{W}\mathbf{x} - \mathbf{R}^{\mathrm{T}}\mathbf{x} \qquad (3)$$

where $\mathbf{x}$ - m-th variable vector, $m = n^2$
$\mathbf{R}$ - m-th vector
$\mathbf{W}$ - m x m weighting matrix

The energy function consists of four components

$$E = E_1 + E_2 + E_3 + E_4 \qquad (4)$$

E_1 – specifies that one subarea must have one and only one subsource, E_2 – specifies that all neuron outputs converge to one or zero, E_3 – states explicitly that each c-area has to be coherent, E_4 – represents the objective function F

$$F = 0.5\sum_{i,j}\sum_{k,l} d_{kl} e_{ij} x_{ik} x_{jl} \qquad (5)$$

where d_{kl} – distance between subarea k and subarea l,
e_{ij} – coefficient proportional to the power of this source which contains both subsource i and subsource j.

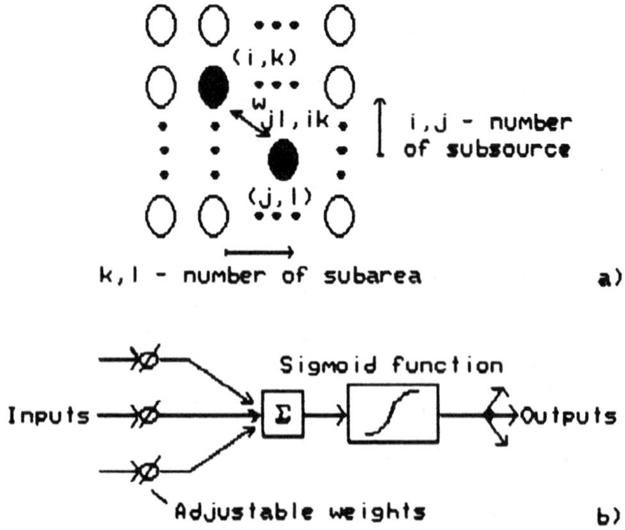

Fig.4. a) Hopfield neural net b) Key elements of a neuron

If subsources i and j belong to different sources then $e_{ij} = 0$. The components of the energy function are following

$$E_1 = A_1\left[\sum_i\left(\sum_k x_{ik} - 1\right)^2 + \sum_k\left(\sum_i x_{ik} - 1\right)^2\right] \qquad (6)$$

$$E_2 = A_2\sum_i\sum_k x_{ik}(1 - x_{ik}) \qquad (7)$$

$$E_3 = A_3\sum_{i,j}\sum_{k,l} c_{kl} e_{ij} x_{ik} x_{jl} \qquad (8)$$

$$E_4 = A_4\sum_{i,j}\sum_{k,l} d_{kl} e_{ij} x_{ik} x_{jl} \qquad (9)$$

$$A_1, A_2, A_3, A_4 \in \mathbf{R}$$

$c_{kl} = 0$ if subareas k and l belong to the coherent c-area, otherwise $c_{kl} = 1$.

B. Optimization Using Neural Networks

The neural network simulated with a digital computer was used to solve our optimization problem.

Our power microcircuit consists of a substrate made of ceramics with dimensions 50 x 80 x 0.6 mm and four screen-printed resistors $P_1 = 0.4$W, $P_2 = 0.6$W, $P_3 = 1.0$ W, $P_4 = 2.0$W, see Fig.3. The circuit was cooled by free air, convection coefficient $\alpha = 15\mathrm{W/m^2 °C}$. The substrate was divided into 5 x 8 square subareas. The value of total dissipated power was 4W, so the subsource 0.1W was attributed to each subarea. Resistors should be placed in the centres of gravity of the appropriate c-areas consisting of the adequate number of subareas. Constants for equations were set as follows: $A_1 = A_2 = 3$, $A_3 = 1$, $A_4 = 0.1$, $\tau = 10$. The following initial values were assumed

(iv1) $u_{ik}(0) = -\log_e(n-1)$, for $i, k = 1,\dots, n$ (10)

(iv2) $u_{ik}(0) = 0$ (11)

(iv3), (iv4) $u_{ik}(0) =$ randomly chosen values (12)

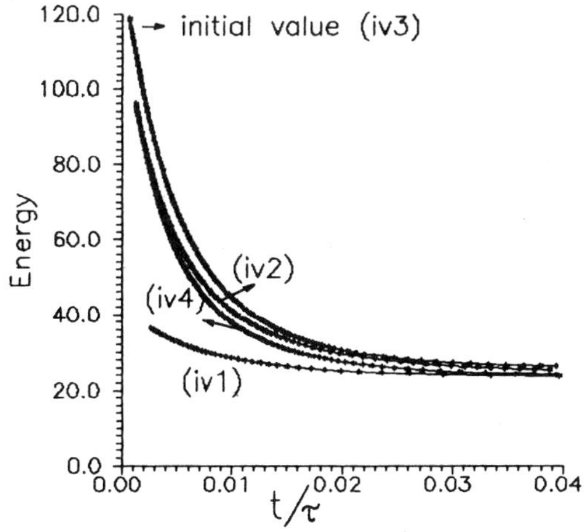

Fig. 5. Function of energy

The first condition $(iv1)$ causes $x_{ik}(0) = 1/n$. When this condition is fulfilled the component E_1 of the energy function equals zero at the initial state. The condition $(iv2)$ sets every neuron output to 0.5. Conditions $(iv3)$ and $(iv4)$ represent different randomly chosen values. The Equation (1) has been solved using fourth-order Runge - Kutta method with various step h. h was initially equal to 0.0001.

For different initial conditions $(iv1 \div iv4)$ four solutions has been obtained. They are presented in Fig. 3b, 3d, 3h and 3a respectively. The solutions differ both in the shape of c-areas and in the number of iterations *ITER*, needed to achieve the local minimum of the energy function, see Table I and Fig.5. For each of the obtained results the temperature distribution was found with the use of an eigenfunction expansion [3], [4] - Fig.6. Then using the following formula the temperature deviation D was calculated, which represents the mean square difference between the temperature in which each resistor works and the average temperature.

$$D = \sqrt{\frac{1}{N}\sum_{i=1}^{N}(T_i - T_m)^2} \tag{13}$$

where T_m - average temperature, N - number of heat sources. The results can be found in Table I. Analysing them, we can notice that although different solutions concern different local minima of the energy function, they have practically the same deviation D, and therefore should be treated as equally good. However the case $(iv1)$ deserves our special attention because of its minimum number of iterations.

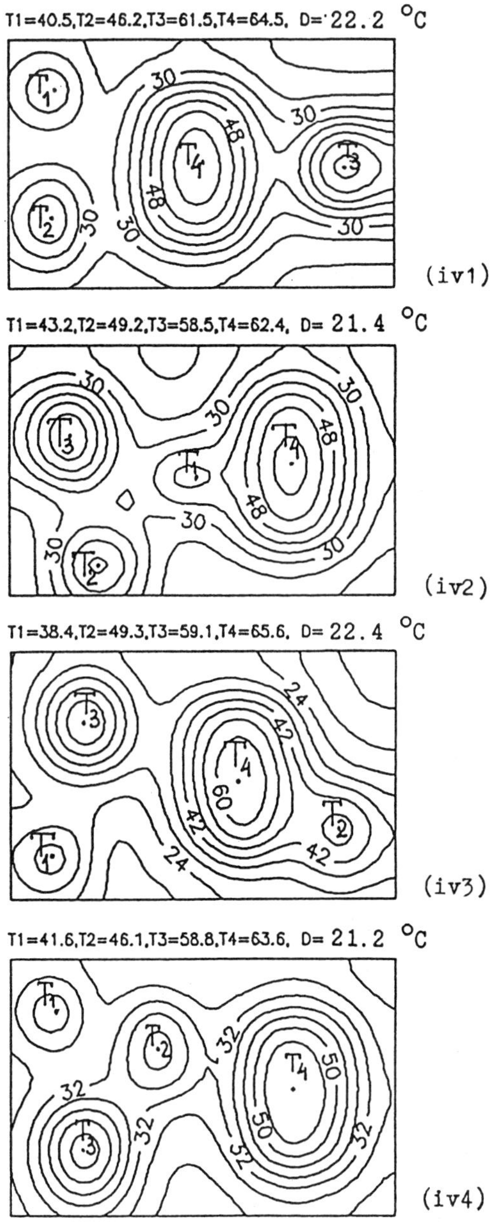

Fig. 6. Temperature distribution

TABLE I
VARIOUS POSSIBILITIES OF DIVISION OF THE SUBSTRATE

Fig3	*S1*	*S2*	*S3*	*S4*	*S*	D,°C	*iv*	*ITER*
a	8	12	14	18	52	21.2	4	146
b	8	10	14	18	50	22.2	1	46
c	8	10	16	20	54			
d	10	12	14	22	58	21.4	2	172
e	10	14	14	18	56			
f	10	14	14	18	56			
g	8	10	22	18	58			
h	8	10	14	22	54	22.4	3	190

C. *Hierarchical Approach*

When the number of heat sources increases, the number of neurons in the Hopfield network increases too. To simplify the analysis the hierarchical pre-placement is proposed. Each level of the hierarchy contains only three or four parts, see Fig.7. Some heat sources are gathered into groups, treated as new imaginary sources. It enables to reduce the total number of elements and leads to the new task - searching the optimum placement for the new situation. When the solution of the highest level is found we can go further, one level lower, which means solving the problem of the particular group, i.e. finding the placement of its elements. If the number of elements in any of the groups is still large the procedure can be used once more, making an additional level and so on.

In our problem the following groups were assumed: $P_1 + P_2 = 1.0\text{W}$, $P_3 = 1.0\text{W}$, $P_4 = 2\text{W}$. In this case the substrate was divided into three c-areas (see Fig.8). "*1+2*" c-area was then divided into two parts, when the problem of the lower level was considered. Thanks to such a two-level hierarchical division of the problem, the significant shortage of the computational time was achieved. The first level required only 16-neuron net, and the second one (lower) required the net with 100 neurons. The computational time was over 100 times shorter than the time needed by the non-hierarchical method. The obtained results are shown in Table II. The initial values (10) and (12) were used. Values of the estimator D were only a little bit worse than the ones obtained with the non-hierarchical method.

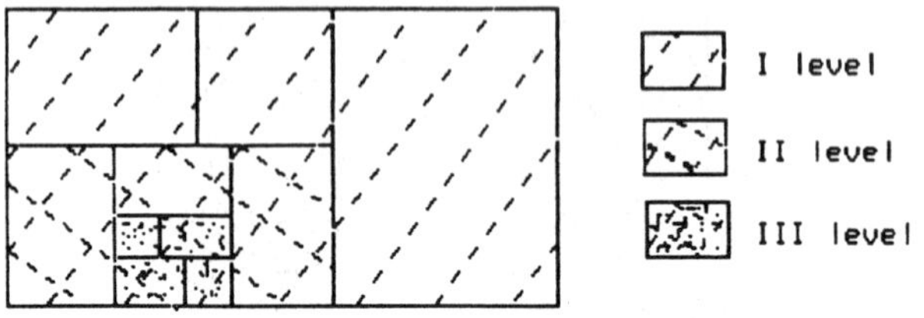

Fig. 7. Three level hierarchy

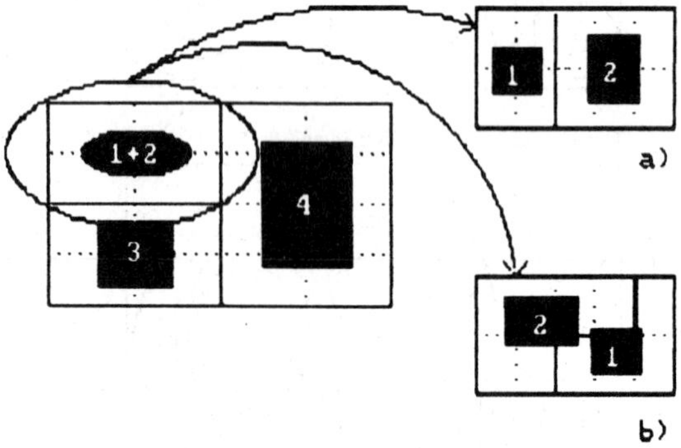

Fig.8. Hierarchical placement of four resistors

TABLE II

DIVISION OF THE SUBSTRATE FOR HIERARCHICAL TECHNIQUE

Fig.8	*S1*	*S2*	*S 1,2*	*D*°C	*iv*	*ITER*
a	12	14	26	22.5	1	42
b	14	16	30	22.8	3	98

III. CONCLUSION

The paper deals with the idea of optimization of the topology of hybrid power circuits using combination of the heuristic method and the Hopfield neural net. Local minima of Lyapunov function lead to various placements of heat sources. Each of the obtained solutions can be treated as well and satisfactory because the differences of the temperature deviations are negligible. For the reduction of computational effort, even several hundred times, the heuristic approach is proposed. In this case, before starting the optimization procedure the number of heat sources is reduced by grouping some of them into new imaginary sources. It causes the cardinal decrease of the number of processing elements and synapses in the neural net what results in finding the solution in a relatively short time. The optimization technique is being successfully used in practice.

REFERENCES

[1] A. Kos, G. De Mey, "Thermal placement in hybrid circuits - a heuristic approach", in press

[2] J.J. Hopfield, D.W. Tank, "Neural computation of decisions in optimization problems", *Biol. Cyber.* 52, 1985, pp.141-152

[3] A. Kos , "Temperature analysis of hybrid circuits - steady state model", *Elektrotechnika* (Science Bulletin of the University of Mining and Metallurgy), vol.4, no. 1, 1985, pp.57-74.

[4] A. Kos, "Accuracy of temperature computation in hybrid microelectronics", *Hybrid Circuits,* no.27, January 1992, pp.25-27.

[5] A. Kos, " Hopfield neural network approach in quasi-optimum thermal placement" *Proc. of the XV National Conference on Circuit Theory and Electronic Circuits",* Szczyrk, Poland, October 1992, pp.607-613.

[6] T. Shimamoto, A. Sakamoto, "Neural computation for channel routing using Hopfield neural network model", *Trans. of the IEICE,* vol. E 72, no.12, 1989, pp.1360-1366.

[7] M. Vellanki, C.H. Dagli, "Artificial neural network approach in printed circuit board assembly", University of Missouri-Rolla, Working Paper Series # 90-19-44.

[8] R.P. Lippman "An introduction to computing with neural nets" , *IEEE ASSP Magazine,* April 1987, pp. 4-22.

Estimation of Trip O-D Matrix When Input and Output are Fuzzy

Raman Nanda

Department of Civil Engineering
University of Delaware
Newark, DE 19711

Shinya Kikuchi

Department of Civil Engineering
University of Delaware
Newark, DE 19711

Abstract

A method to estimate the trip O-D matrix when trip generation and trip attraction counts are approximate is presented. This is a two step process. In the first step the existence of a consistent travel pattern is examined. If a pattern is found to exist, in the second step, a backpropagation neural network is used to identify the O-D matrix. This method can be used to estimate the input-output relationship for any general system problem.

1 Introduction

An O-D table represents the travel pattern of a region in a matrix form as seen in Figure 1. This table provides a planner with the basic information for planning a transportation system. An element ij of the table represents the volume of travel originating at zone i and terminating at zone j. The O-D table can be interpreted as the cause-effect relationship between trip generation and trip attraction. The trip generation is the total number of trips generated from a zone and the trip attraction is the total number of trips attracted to a zone. They are functions of socio-economic factors of the zone. The trip generations are presented in the right hand side column vector **B** and the trip attractions in the bottom row vector **A**.

An O-D matrix can be obtained by an extensive traffic survey; this is not only a cumbersome process but also very expensive. Consequently, several models have been suggested to estimate the O-D matrix when only the trip generation and the trip attraction counts are known.

The underlying assumption of such models is that a consistent travel pattern exists in the region under consideration. This pattern cannot be identified if only one set of **B** and **A** values are known. However, if many sets of **B** and **A** are available then a consistent travel pattern may emerge, as repeated occurence of similar pattern is indicative of the existence of a pattern. None of the existing models include mechanisms to confirm the existence of a pattern before estimating the O-D matrix.

This paper presents a method to determine the elements of the O-D matrix when the information on trip generation (input) and trip attraction (output) for each zone is approximate. This is a practical problem faced by transportation planners because the data used to estimate trip generation and trip attraction are usually not precise. The approximate trip generation and trip attraction counts are denoted by $\tilde{\mathbf{B}}$ and $\tilde{\mathbf{A}}$. In this paper, the individual elements of $\tilde{\mathbf{B}}$ and $\tilde{\mathbf{A}}$ are assumed to be triangular fuzzy numbers.

This paper consists of six sections of which the introduction is the first section. The second section describes the problem and the third section briefly reviews the past work. The fourth section presents a detailed explanation of the proposed methodology and also the working of the backpropagation neural network. The fifth section presents an example which determines the O-D matrix based on this proposed model, and the final section presents the conclusions and findings.

2 Problem Statement

The problem is to complete an O-D matrix as shown in Figure 1, given right-hand side and bottom vectors in fuzzy numbers. Since the values of these vectors are fuzzy, the individual cell elements ($\tilde{w}_{ij}$'s) are also fuzzy.

A cell $\tilde{w}_{ij}$ in the matrix indicates the volume of trips (vehicular or people) to zone j as a proportion of trips originating at zone i: thus $0 < w_{ij} \leq 1$. The following notation will be used in reference to the fuzziness of $\tilde{w}_{ij}$ assuming that it is a triangular fuzzy number.

0-8186-3850-8/93 \$3.00

			Destination zones						
		1	2	.	$\tilde{J}$	.	.	.	n	
	1	0	$\tilde{w}_{12}$	.	.	.	.	.	$\tilde{w}_{1n}$	$\tilde{B}_1$
	2	$\tilde{w}_{21}$	0	.	.	.	.	.	.	
	.	.	.	0	.	.	.	.	.	
	.	.	.	.	.	.	.	.	.	
	i	.	.	.	$\tilde{w}_{ij}$	0	.	.	.	$\tilde{B}_i$
	.	.	.	.	.	.	.	.	.	
	.	.	.	.	.	.	.	.	.	
	n	$\tilde{w}_{n1}$	.	.	.	.	.	.	0	$\tilde{B}_n$
		$\tilde{A}_1$	.	.	$\tilde{A}_j$	.	.	.	$\tilde{A}_n$	

(Origin zones label along left side)

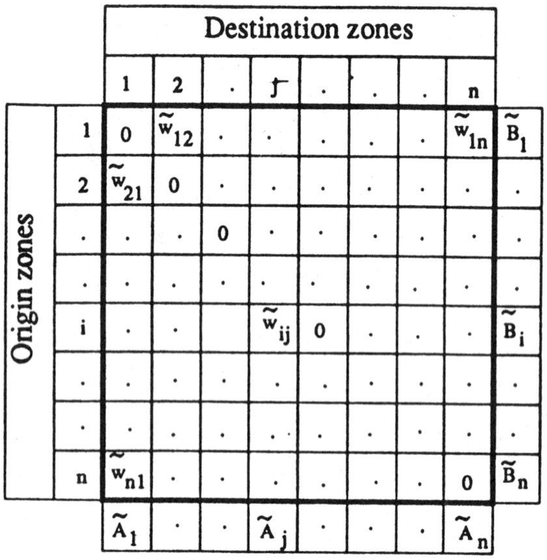

Figure 1: An O-D Matrix

$w_{ij,\,l}$ = lower bound of $\tilde{w}_{ij}$
$w_{ij,\,m}$ = intermediate value of $\tilde{w}_{ij}$
$w_{ij,\,u}$ = upper bound of $\tilde{w}_{ij}$

Let the trip generation at the i th zone and the trip attraction at the j th zone be denoted by fuzzy numbers $\tilde{B}_i$ and $\tilde{A}_j$, respectively. $\tilde{B}_i$ can be designated by $B_{i,l}$, $B_{i,m}$, $B_{i,u}$ and $\tilde{A}_j$ by $A_{j,l}$, $A_{j,m}$, $A_{j,u}$, respectively:
$B_{i,l}$ = lower bound of input at the i th zone
$B_{i,m}$= middle value of input at the i th zone
$B_{i,u}$= upper bound of input at the i th zone
$A_{j,l}$= lower bound of output at the j th zone
$A_{j,m}$= middle value of output at the j th zone
$A_{j,u}$= upper bound of output at the j th zone

Assuming that the input and output counts in fuzzy numbers have been rationally assigned by the experts, the flow conservation equations can be written as

$$\sum_j w_{ij,\,l} = 1 \qquad \forall i = 1\,to\,n \qquad (1)$$

$$w_{ij,\,l} = 0 \qquad when\; i = j \qquad (2)$$

$$\sum_i w_{ij,\,l} A_{j,l} = B_{i,l} \qquad \forall j = 1\,to\,n \qquad (3)$$

$$\sum_j w_{ij,\,m} = 1 \qquad \forall i = 1\,to\,n \qquad (4)$$

$$w_{ij,\,m} = 0 \qquad when\; i = j \qquad (5)$$

$$\sum_i w_{ij,\,m} A_{j,m} = B_{i,m} \qquad \forall j = 1\,to\,n \qquad (6)$$

$$\sum_j w_{ij,\,u} = 1 \qquad \forall i = 1\,to\,n \qquad (7)$$

$$w_{ij,\,u} = 0 \qquad when\; i = j \qquad (8)$$

$$\sum_i w_{ij,\,u} A_{j,u} = B_{i,u} \qquad \forall j = 1\,to\,n \qquad (9)$$

This system of equations has $3n(n-1)$ unknowns and $3(2n-1)$ equations. For n greater that 2, the system is indeterminate and an infinite number of possible solutions exist.

Though, the above system of equations cannot be solved algebraically, the fact that repeated occurrences of comparable $\tilde{B}$'s and $\tilde{A}$'s suggest the existence of a pattern should not be overlooked. The pattern may not be exactly the same for each data set for $\tilde{B}$ and $\tilde{A}$ but may be a somewhat vague pattern which more or less satisfies all the data sets. Thus, the O-D problem reduces to the problem of identifying and determining the relationship between $\tilde{B}$ and $\tilde{A}$ when many such sets are given. The identification of the relationship, which is in effect the O-D travel pattern, and its determination is described in the following sections.

3   Review of Past Work

Several researchers have studied the problem of the O-D matrix estimation under different settings. These settings include travel demand forecasting, transit line station-to-station travel estimation, parking lot utilization, by-pass traffic estimation of a city etc. Furth[1], Hendrickson and McNeil[2], Landau et al.[3], Geva et al.[4] proposed models which assume an initial seed matrix and revise it iteratively such that the flow conservation equations are satisfied.

Van Zuylen[5] estimated the most-likely O-D matrix from traffic counts based on the principles of information theory. Willumsen[6] used the maximum entropy principle to estimate O-D elements. Recently, linear programming method of estimating O-D matrix has been proposed by Kikuchi and Perincherry[7].

All the above models estimate the O-D matrix from a single set of observations. This single set of observations may not be representative of the travel pattern.

Neural networks have been successfully used for image recognition problems. Von der Malsburg and Bienenstock[8] have studied the use of neural networks for pattern retrieval, Lubin et al.[9] used neural networks to assess several image representation schemes for object recognition. Since the idea of recognizing travel patterns is similar to what has been done by researchers of neural networks, such networks may offer an alternative to identify travel patterns.

4 The Methodology

A two step methodology is proposed in estimating the O-D matrix. In the first step, it is tested if the travel pattern is consistent among the given data sets. This is done by first constructing possibility distributions for each element of the matrix. Next, using the shapes of the possibility distributions the consistency of the pattern is examined. This step is described in Section 4.1.

In the second step, a backpropagation neural network is constructed. The input for this neural network is the trip generation data and the output is the trip attraction data. The O-D matrix is determined such that the input-output relationship is satisfied to specified levels for all the data sets. Because the input and the output are triangular fuzzy numbers, the training of the neural network is repeated three times such that the input-output relationship for the lower, the middle and the upper values of the trip generation and the trip attraction data are satisfied. Hence, the value of each O-D element is obtained as a triangular fuzzy number.

4.1 Step 1 : Testing of the existence of a pattern

This step tests the existence of a travel pattern for each cell of the O-D matrix. First, we develop possibility distributions for each element of the O-D matrix. From each set of $\tilde{\mathbf{B}}$ and $\tilde{\mathbf{A}}$ the maximum and the minimum values of $\tilde{w}_{ij}$, designated by r_{ij}^{max} and r_{ij}^{min}, are computed.

$$r_{ij}^{max} = min\,(\frac{A_{j,u}}{B_{i,l}},\, 1) \tag{10}$$

where,
$A_{j,u}$ = upper bound of trip attraction at the j th zone
$B_{i,l}$ = lower bound of trip generation at the i th zone

$$r_{ij}^{min} = max\,(1 - \sum_{j=1,j\neq i}^{n} r_{ij}^{max},\ 1 - \sum_{i=1,i\neq j}^{n} r_{ij}^{max},\ 0) \tag{11}$$

Thus, if we have m sets of data for $\tilde{\mathbf{B}}$ and $\tilde{\mathbf{A}}$, we will have m ranges of possible values $[r_{ij}^{max}, r_{ij}^{min}]$ for

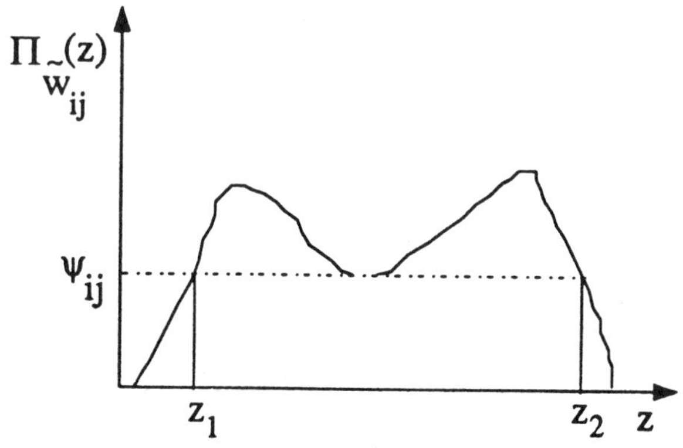

Figure 2: Testing the uniqueness of the pattern

each element. Superimposing these m ranges, in other words, stacking these ranges one on top of another, a possibility distribution could be obtained. The possibility that a value z represents the true value of an element $\tilde{w}_{ij}$ is found to be

$$\Pi_{\tilde{w}_{ij}}(z) = \frac{p}{m} \tag{12}$$

where
$\Pi_{\tilde{w}_{ij}}(z)$ = possibility that z is the true value of $\tilde{w}_{ij}$
p = number of times z cuts the range $(r_{ij}^{max}, r_{ij}^{min})$
m = number of data sets

The shapes of the possibility distributions are used to determine the uniqueness and the sharpness of the patterns. The uniqueness of the pattern is tested by a somewhat relaxed form of uni-modality measure. For a particular element ij this measure is denoted by ψ_{ij}. This is shown in Figure 2. The value of ψ_{ij} is based on the maximum value of Ω which allows for the existence of z_1 and z_2 satisfying the following conditions

$$\Pi_{\tilde{w}_{ij}}(z_1) = \Pi_{\tilde{w}_{ij}}(z_2) = \Omega \tag{13}$$

$$\Pi_{\tilde{w}_{ij}}(z) \leq \Omega\ \ for\{z|z \leq z_1,\ \ z \geq z_2\} \tag{14}$$

$$\Pi_{\tilde{w}_{ij}}(z) \geq \Omega\ \ for\{z|z_1 \leq z \leq z_2\} \tag{15}$$

where Ω is a value between 0 and 1.

The average value for all the elements denoted by Ψ can be used as a measure of existence of a unique pattern. The average value is given by

$$\Psi = \frac{\sum \psi_{ij}}{3n(n-1)} \tag{16}$$

Apart from the uniqueness of the pattern, the sharpness of the pattern can be measured in terms of non-specificity measure. This measure is usually computed as the area under the possibility distribution curve. In this paper, it is designated by β. Smaller values of β are indicative of a sharper pattern. For a cell ij it is expressed by:

$$\beta_{ij} = \int \Pi_{\tilde{w}_{ij}}(z)dz \tag{17}$$

The average value of β_{ij} for all the elements is denoted by η and it can be used as a measure of sharpness of the pattern. The average value is given by

$$\eta = \frac{\sum \beta_{ij}}{3n(n-1)} \tag{18}$$

In summary, the shapes of the possibility distribution can be used to examine the existence of a consistent pattern among the given data sets, and also to ascertain how crisp the pattern is. Higher values of ψ_{ij} and lower values of β_{ij} indicate a consistent and sharp pattern.

4.2 Step 2 : Determination of the pattern

An artificial neural network (ANN) is a parallelly distributed network comprising of many interconnected processing elements, each of which process information in a pre-determined manner. According to Rumelhart et al.[10] such networks should contain

- a set of input units
- a set of output units
- a set of processing units
- a pattern of connectivity among the units
- a learning rule whereby the patterns of connectivity are modified so as to satisfy the input output relationship

A typical backpropagation neural network is shown in Figure 3. In the figure, the nodes designated 1,2 etc. are the input units and **B** = (B_1, B_2, ..., B_n) is the input to the network. The node designated O is the output unit and A_j is the desired output. In this network, there is only one processing unit designated by P. The processing unit processes the input and develops output. In this case, the processing unit computes the weighted sum of inputs (NET), weighted by the strength (weight) of interconnections between the input nodes and the processing unit. NET is compared to A_j and if there is no satisfactory match, the weights are adjusted by a learning rule in successive iterations until a satisfactory match is obtained.

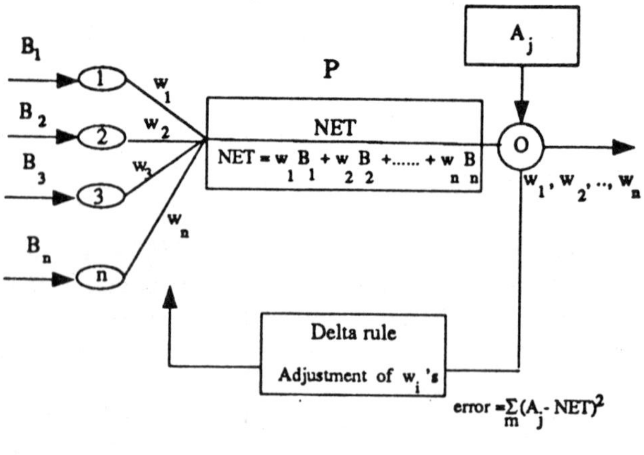

Figure 3: A typical backpropagation neural network

4.2.1 Working of a simple backpropagation neural network

In Figure 3, $\mathbf{B} = \{B_1, B_2, ..., B_n\}$ is the input vector, P is the processing unit, NET is the computed output and A_j is the corresponding target value. The values of weights, designated by weight vector $\mathbf{w} = \{w_1, w_2, ..., w_n\}$ are initially randomly assigned and NET is computed.

The backpropagation neural network works on the idea of correcting the randomly assigned weight vector $\mathbf{w} = \{w_1, w_2, ..., w_n\}$ in such a manner that the input-output relationship is satisfied as much as possible for most of the data sets.

For m data sets, $NET^{(q)}$ is compared with $A_j^{(q)}$ for all q = 1 to m, and the error ($A_j^{(q)}$ - $NET^{(q)}$) is computed. If the sum of the squared errors with respect to these m data sets exceeds a specified level γ, then the weights of the network are iteratively adjusted until the sum of squared errors becomes less than or equal to γ. The weight correction process is done by using the Delta rule.

The Delta rule, also known as the gradient descent rule is used to determine the correction vector $\Delta\mathbf{w}$ to $\mathbf{w}$ such that the error is reduced at the fastest possible rate. A way of doing this is to set the correction vector proportional to the negative gradient of the error with respect to the weight.

For a simple neural network as shown in Figure 3, the correction vector can be derived as follows. Let us denote 2E to be the sum of squared errors for all the data sets. Then

$$E = \frac{\sum_{q=1}^{m}(A_j^{(q)} - NET^{(q)})^2}{2} \tag{19}$$

From the above discussion, we know for a particular weight w_i

$$\Delta w_i \propto -\frac{\partial E}{\partial w_i} \quad (20)$$

Also, from chain rule we can write

$$\frac{\partial E}{\partial w_i} = \frac{\partial E}{\partial NET^{(q)}} \times \frac{\partial NET^{(q)}}{\partial w_i} \quad (21)$$

Now

$$\frac{\partial E}{\partial NET^{(q)}} = -(A_j^{(q)} - NET^{(q)}) \quad (22)$$
$$= -\delta^{(q)} \quad (23)$$

Also, from Figure 3 we know

$$NET^{(q)} = w_1 B_1^{(q)} + w_2 B_2^{(q)} + \ldots + w_n B_n^{(q)} \quad (24)$$

Thus,

$$\frac{\partial NET^{(q)}}{\partial w_i} = B_i^{(q)} \quad (25)$$

Hence, from Eq(21), Eq(23) and Eq(25) we have

$$-\frac{\partial E}{\partial w_i} = \delta^{(q)} B_i^{(q)} \quad (26)$$

Therefore,

$$\Delta w_i = \alpha \delta^{(q)} B_i^{(q)} \quad (27)$$

where α is a constant between 0 and 1. The value of α determines how finely the training process is to take place.

Thus, for each weight a correction term can be determined. Written in vector form the correction term can be written as

$$\Delta \mathbf{w} = \alpha \delta \mathbf{B} \quad (28)$$

The weight correction vector is applied at every iteration. At the (k+1) st iteration the vector $\mathbf{w_{k+1}}$ can be written as

$$\mathbf{w_{k+1}} = \mathbf{w_k} + \Delta \mathbf{w_k} \quad (29)$$
$$= \mathbf{w_k} + \alpha \delta \mathbf{B} \quad (30)$$

The process represented by Eq(30) is continued until the condition $2E \leq \gamma$ is met.

An important feature of the neural networks is that all the weights need not be corrected. This helps incorporate subjective information. For example, if information of a particular cell w_{ij} is known, then the corresponding weight which is tied to that information can be fixed and all the other weights can be corrected as explained earlier. Provision of such subjective information further reduces solution space and the existing pattern is more closely identified.

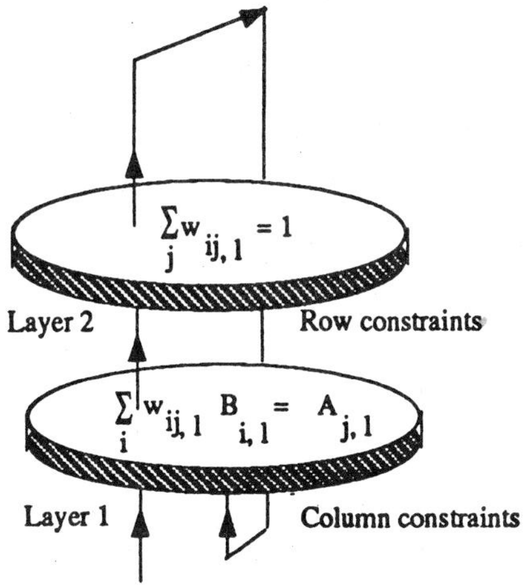

Figure 4: Training process for lower bound values

4.2.2 O-D pattern determination by neural networks

The simple backpropagation network described above can be used to determine the elements of the O-D matrix. Let the trip generation $\tilde{\mathbf{B}}$ (= $\{\mathbf{B_l}, \mathbf{B_m}, \mathbf{B_u}\}$) be the input to the network and the trip attraction $\tilde{\mathbf{A}}$ (= $\{\mathbf{A_l}, \mathbf{A_m}, \mathbf{A_u}\}$) be the output. The input output relation is satisfied when the equations dictated by Eq(1) and Eq(3) are satisfied for the lower bound, Eq(4) and Eq(6) are satisfied for the middle value and Eq(7) and Eq(9) are satisfied for the upper bound of the input and output values, respectively.

The process of determining the weight vector involves the training of three separate networks, each satisfying conditions for the lower bound, the middle value and the upper bound of the input and output values. The process of training for the lower bound values is illustrated in Figure 4. In the figure, the first step is to adjust the weights $w_{ij,l}$ (j= 1 to n) such that Eq(3) is satisfied for every column for all the m data sets.

The next step is to satisfy Eq(1) for all rows, for all the m data sets. In this case the input is assumed to be 1 and the output is also 1. These two steps are sequentially and repeatedly performed until Eq(3) and Eq(1) are satisfied to a specified level γ. The weights at the end of the iterations are the lower bounds of the O-D cell elements. In a similar manner the middle values and the upper bounds of each O-D cell element are obtained.

		Destination zones					
		1	2	3	4	5	6
Origin zones	1	0	0.2	0.3	0.1	0.3	0.1
	2	0.4	0	0.1	0.1	0.2	0.2
	3	0.1	0.3	0	0.2	0.3	0.1
	4	0.2	0.2	0.1	0	0.2	0.3
	5	0.1	0.2	0.1	0.3	0	0.3
	6	0.2	0.4	0.1	0.2	0.1	0

Figure 5: An assumed O-D matrix

5 An Example

The proposed model was used to generate an O-D matrix for hypothetical sets of values of input and output. Since it is difficult to validate the results, an O-D table was assumed and for a particular set of values of trip generation the corresponding trip attraction values were computed. Assuming that the trip generation counts is normally distributed, different sets of trip generation (**B**) and corresponding trip attraction (**A**) counts were generated. Using these values of **B** and **A**, fuzzy trip generation $\tilde{\mathbf{B}}$ and trip attraction $\tilde{\mathbf{A}}$ counts were generated around the actual **B** and **A**. These values of $\tilde{\mathbf{B}}$ and $\tilde{\mathbf{A}}$ are the input to the model and the O-D table is reconstructed, and then it is compared with the original O-D table.

Consider a six-zone O-D matrix as shown in Figure 5. Let the trip generation count for this matrix be represented by $\mathbf{B} = \{ 3000, 2250, 1800, 2400, 1800, 1500\}$. Assuming the trip generation values to be normally distributed around these values, 10 to 70 sets of input and output counts (with standard deviation σ=50) were generated. Using these values, triangular fuzzy numbers were generated for $\tilde{\mathbf{B}}$ and $\tilde{\mathbf{A}}$.

In the first step, the data sets were used to see whether a pattern existed. Based on the procedure described in Section 4.1, the values of Ψ and η were computed. As the trip generation and trip attraction counts were assumed to be normally distributed it was expected that the O-D cell elements also exhibit a pattern. The average value of Ψ was found to be 1.0. The value of η was found to be 0.833. The value of η indicates how fluid a pattern is. These values of Ψ and η indicate that a pattern exists but it is not very sharp.

Next, the neural network was used to determine the O-D pattern as explained Section 4.2. In this example, α was set to be 0.01 and γ was set to be 0.001. Table 1 shows the results for m=10 and m=70.

The results in Table 1 validate our expectations of the O-D pattern being more closely identified when more number of data sets are available. As seen, the elements of the matrix are closer to the actual values for $m = 70$ than for $m = 10$.

For a given number of data sets (in this case m=10), Table 2 shows the comparison of elements of the O-D matrix with increasing scatter of the input-output data sets. This scatter is achieved by changing the value of variance of the distribution from which **B**, **A**, and correspondingly $\tilde{\mathbf{B}}$, $\tilde{\mathbf{A}}$ were generated. The table seems to indicate that for a given number of data sets, a greater scatter identifies the pattern more closely to the original pattern. This feature can be expected because with greater variation, the pattern must be more specific to satisfy all the input-output data sets, and if a pattern is more specific then it can be more closely identified.

6 Conclusions

This paper presented a model to identify the O-D trip pattern and to determine the O-D matrix when only trip generation and trip attraction data are available, but in fuzzy values. For a given trip generation-trip attraction scenario, the proposed model can generate the maximum and minimum values of trips between any two zones. Such information is useful in order to examine the worst case loading of the networks.

This model is a general model and can be used without much modification in any situation wherein an input-output relationship has to be determined.

References

[1] Furth, Peter, G., "Updating Ride Checks with Multiple Point Checks", *Transportation Research Board*, 1209, pp. 49-57, 1989.

[2] Hendrickson, Chris and McNeil, Sue., "Estimation of Origin-Destination Matrices with Constrained Regression", *Transportation Research Board*, 976, pp. 25-32, 1984.

[3] Landau, U., Hauer, E. and Geva, I., "Estimation of Cross-Cordon Origin-Destination Flows from

Table 1: O-D Matrix for m=10 ($\sigma = 50$) and m=70 ($\sigma = 50$)

		Zone 1	Zone 2	Zone 3	Zone 4	Zone 5	Zone 6
Act.		0	0.2	0.3	0.1	0.3	0.1
m=10	Zone 1	0	0.260-0.290-0.300	0.090-0.100-0.130	0.090-0.093-0.112	0.254-0.282-0.282	0.225-0.226-0.228
m=70		0	0.260-0.267-0.271	0.133-0.154-0.160	0.069-0.071-0.115	0.256-0.270-0.285	0.190-0.199-0.230
Act.		0.4	0	0.1	0.1	0.2	0.2
m=10	Zone 2	0.196-0.198-0.201	0	0.180-0.185-0.203	0.186-0.190-0.199	0.206-0.231-0.233	0.194-0.199-0.200
m=70		0.199-0.204-0.210	0	0.175-0.177-0.178	0.180-0.187-0.190	0.199-0.231-0.232	0.199-0.202-0.207
Act.		0.1	0.3	0	0.2	0.3	0.1
m=10	Zone 3	0.192-0.195-0.199	0.210-0.216-0.227	0	0.147-0.193-0.195	0.205-0.209-0.222	0.190-0.192-0.204
m=70		0.178-0.188-0.199	0.223-0.223-0.227	0	0.146-0.198-0.201	0.205-0.209-0.221	0.197-0.200-0.204
Act.		0.2	0.2	0.1	0	0.2	0.3
m=10	Zone 4	0.142-0.154-0.157	0.256-0.258-0.311	0.092-0.136-0.138	0	0.241-0.243-0.245	0.206-0.209-0.215
m=70		0.128-0.154-0.161	0.252-0.253-0.293	0.128-0.142-0.145	0	0.242-0.246-0.252	0.206-0.209-0.215
Act.		0.1	0.2	0.1	0.3	0	0.3
m=10	zone 5	0.189-0.191-0.222	0.208-0.211-0.257	0.124-0.223-0.227	0.167-0.189-0.191	0	0.186-0.188-0.230
m=70		0.186-0.193-0.222	0.229-0.232-0.257	0.123-0.168-0.174	0.167-0.202-0.207	0	0.202-0.207-0.230
Act.		0.2	0.4	0.1	0.2	0.1	0
m=10	Zone 6	0.188-0.189-0.190	0.179-0.198-0.203	0.222-0.224-0.247	0.190-0.195-0.197	0.187-0.194-0.196	0
m=70		0.186-0.202-0.209	0.205-0.233-0.236	0.150-0.164-0.199	0.210-0.212-0.220	0.173-0.192-0.202	0

Table 2: O-D Matrix for m=10 : σ=10 and σ=100

		Zone 1	Zone 2	Zone 3	Zone 4	Zone 5	Zone 6
Act.		0	0.2	0.3	0.1	0.3	0.1
σ=10	Zone 1	0	0.265-0.299-0.302	0.096-0.097-0.126	0.090-0.092-0.112	0.254-0.282-0.284	0.226-0.227-0.235
σ=100		0	0.262-0.289-0.292	0.119-0.132-0.133	0.086-0.090-0.116	0.255-0.282-0.284	0.226-0.227-0.235
Act.		0.4	0	0.1	0.1	0.2	0.2
σ=10	Zone 2	0.196-0.197-0.198	0	0.180-0.185-0.203	0.189-0.190-0.199	0.206-0.231-0.233	0.194-0.199-0.202
σ=100		0.197-0.198-0.201	0	0.177-0.178-0.179	0.186-0.190-0.199	0.200-0.231-0.232	0.200-0.200-0.205
Act.		0.1	0.3	0	0.2	0.3	0.1
σ=10	Zone 3	0.192-0.192-0.199	0.210-0.216-0.227	0	0.147-0.193-0.195	0.205-0.209-0.222	0.190-0.192-0.204
σ=100		0.192-0.192-0.199	0.215-0.223-0.227	0	0.146-0.192-0.193	0.208-0.209-0.223	0.190-0.192-0.204
Act.		0.2	0.2	0.1	0	0.2	0.3
σ=10	Zone 4	0.142-0.154-0.157	0.256-0.257-0.311	0.091-0.136-0.138	0	0.240-0.243-0.245	0.206-0.209-0.215
σ=100		0.142-0.153-0.157	0.255-0.256-0.293	0.125-0.139-0.140	0	0.242-0.246-0.245	0.198-0.204-0.207
Act.		0.1	0.2	0.1	0.3	0	0.3
σ=10	zone 5	0.189-0.191-0.222	0.208-0.211-0.257	0.124-0.223-0.224	0.167-0.189-0.190	0	0.186-0.187-0.230
σ=100		0.186-0.193-0.222	0.218-0.219-0.257	0.126-0.139-0.140	0.167-0.192-0.195	0	0.190-0.194-0.230
Act.		0.2	0.4	0.1	0.2	0.1	0
σ=10	Zone 6	0.188-0.189-0.190	0.179-0.198-0.199	0.223-0.224-0.247	0.190-0.195-0.197	0.187-0.194-0.196	0
σ=100		0.195-0.198-0.201	0.202-0.206-0.211	0.181-0.198-0.202	0.199-0.203-0.211	0.178-0.201-0.202	0

Cordon Studies", *Transportation Research Board*, 891, pp. 5-10, 1982.

[4] Geva, I., Hauer, E. and Landau, U., "Maximum Likelihood and Bayesian Methods for the Estimation of O-D Flows", *Transportation Research Board*, 944, pp. 101-105, 1983.

[5] Van Zuylen, Henk, J. and Willumsen, Luis, G., "The most likely trip matrix estimated from traffic counts", *Transportation Research*, 14 B, pp. 281-293, 1980.

[6] Willumsen, L., "Estimation of O-D matrix from traffic counts: a review", *Institute of Transport Studies Working Paper 99*, Leeds University, 1978.

[7] Kikuchi, S. and Perincherry, V., "A Model to Estimate the Passenger Origin-Destination Pattern on a Rail Transit Line," *Transportation Research Board* 1349, pp. 54-61, 1992.

[8] Von der Malsburg, C. and Bienenstock, E., "A neural network for the retrieval of superimposed connection patterns", *Europhysics Letters*, Vol. 3, pp. 1243-1249, 1987.

[9] Lubin, J., Jones, K. and Kornhauser, A. (1990),"Using backpropagation networks to assess several image representation schemes for object recognition", *Proceedings of International Joint Conference on Neural Networks (IJCNN)*, Vol. 2, p 618, 1989.

[10] Rumelhart, D.E., McClelland, J.L., and the PDP Research Group *Parallel Distributed Processing*, MIT Press, Cambridge, Massachusetts, 1986.

Application of Neural Network to Aesthetic Design of Bridges

K.Yasuda
NEWJEC, Inc.

H.Furuta
Kyoto University

H.Yamanishi
Pacific Consultants, Co.

Abstract

In the recent years, the importance of the landscape in the environmental design of bridges is being greatly acknowledged. The present study concerns with the development of a method which, by applying the learning ability of the neural network to the data of past bridge designs, attempts to quantify and assess the landscape design. The data, totaling over 100 bridges, were collected from the "Bridge Annals" [1] and include both objective and subjective data of continuous girder and arch bridges.

1.Introduction

Despite of the wide recognition of the importance of landscape design, the complexity and uncertainty attributed to undefinable elements of the environment have not yet allowed the technology to assess quantitatively the environmental design in the actual projects. Bridge design factors include economy, workability, maintenance and the environment (i.e. harmony with the surroundings). The latter, being composed by both objective and subjective elements, depends on the person who assesses and/or the circumstances, making the quantification of the assessment difficult. Consequently, creating rules for an expert system to assess the landscape design is not an easy task.

The present paper describes a study on a quantitative method of assessing the landscape design. This method makes use of the data of past bridge designs by applying the learning ability of the neural network. These data include, besides the element color, important in the environmental design of bridges, the criteria of the bridge harmony with the environment. The main feature of the neural network is the pattern recognition, which allows to learn from the input-output response patterns of the sample data and imitates them. This ability provides useful information for landscape design. For example, information on the necessary elements for parameters such as "sense of stability" would be of great use in the actual landscape design.

2.Present Status of Landscape Design

Among the many factors considered in bridge design, the total environmental design is now gaining importance, specially from the social point of view. However, including factors such as aesthetics and the bridge harmony with the surrounding environment, the optimization of the landscape design of bridges is not simple.

Due to its complexity and subjectiveness, there is no definite rules for the landscape design and its assessment tends to be in nature, more qualitative than quantitative. On the other hand, the landscape design being time- and labor-consuming, it is current to select the most adequate alternative among previously selected ones, rather than search for the optimum solution in order to save time.

As shown in the flow chart in Fig.1, the environmental factors are

0-8186-3850-8/93 $3.00 © 1993 IEEE

considered in every design stage, from the initial design concept to the final finishing detail. Therefore, the bridge design has to start with a solid image of the bridge final shape, after which the economy, workability, maintenance and the environmental features is to be considered to decide upon its structure. The environment, unlike the economy, includes both objective and subjective elements, making it difficult to perform a quantitative assessment. Moreover, its results may differ from person to person and/or depending on circumstances. For example, deck bridges, as a rule, apparently seem to be more stable than through deck bridges. However, this is because in most of cases only the elevation view is considered. This opinion may change if no supports could be seen. Also, the color of the bridge and/or the surrounding landscape may affect the results of the assessment.

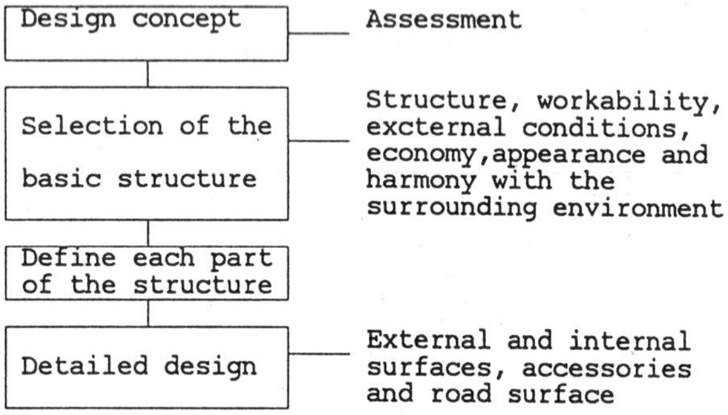

Fig.1 Landscape Design Flow

The present study proposes to investigate whether the currently accepted criteria for assessing the bridge aesthetics and harmony with the environment are appropriate or not and to define the factors relevant for the landscape design.

3.Questionnaire

The appearance of a bridge is the result of a complex combination of form, color and environment. However, the concepts of the assessment parameters such as "beauty", "vigorousness" and "sense of stability" differ from person to person. Therefore, as it is not easy to select the key factors affecting the bridge appearance and its harmony with the surroundings, almost all possible factors were taken into consideration as input and output data.

Tables 1 and 2 show factors to be considered in the landscape design, including the superstructure, infrastructure, piers, accessories, composition and proportion. These objective data were collected from available literatures for 104 girder bridges and 113 arch bridges, among the ones completed during the period of 1987-1991.

Table 3 shows the questionnaire sheet with 27 assessing items. The assessors were asked to answer it based on the photograph of bridges chosen from "Bridge Annals" [1]. Figs. 2 and 3 show examples these photographs.

Fig.2 Example of the Photographs (Girder)

Fig.3 Example of the Photographs (Arch Bridge)

Table 1 Assessment Parameters for the Environmental Design of Girder Bridges

			Bridge A	Bridge B	Bridge C
Classifiction					
Year			H3	H3	H3
Page			71	72	74
Bridge Name			Bridge A	Bridge B	Bridge C
Super structures	Structural Type	Number of spans	3	2	3
		Structural Type	Continuous box girder	Continuous box girder	Continuous box girder
	Number of Bridges		3	4	2
	Color	Railing	Gray	Gray	Black
		Girder	Green	Blue	Yellow
		Curb	Red	Gray	Gray
	Brightness	Railing	High	Low	Low
		Girder	Low	High	Medium
		Curb	High	Medium	Medium
	Chroma	Railing	Medium	Medium	Low
		Girder	Low	High	Medium
		Curb	High	Medium	Medium
Sub structures	Structural Type		Single T-shape column	Single wall column	Single wall column
	Cross-section		Ellipse	Ellipse	Ellipse
Accessories	Railing		Vertical stripe	Vertical stripe	Vertical stripe
	Lighting		Normal	Non	Normal
	Sound insulating wall		Non	Non	Non
	Drain pipe		Virtical	Virtical	Virtical
Composition	Viewing distance		Medium	Near	Medium
	View point	Incident angle	30°	30°	30°
		Height	Side	Lower	Upper
	Background		River	River	River
	Background color	Upper part	Brue	Brue	Green
		Lower part	Green	Brue	Gray
	Background brightness	Upper part	High	Medium	Medium
		Lower part	Medium	Medium	Medium
Proportion	Span ratio		1.0～1.5	～1.0	1.0～1.5
	Span/pier height ratio		15～20	20～25	5～10
	Girder height change ratio		1.5～2.0	1.5～2.0	1.5～2.0
	Span/girder height ratio		25～30	20～25	25～30
	Width/girder height ratio		80～10	2～4	4～6

Table 2 Assessment Parameters for the Environmental Design of Arch Bridges

					Bridge X	Bridge Y	Bridge Z
Classification							
Year					H3	H3	H3
Page					10	12	91
Bridge Name					Bridge X	Bridge Y	Bridge Z
Super structure	Structural Type	Structural Type			Lohse	Nielsen	Langer
		Deck position			Deck	Through	Deck
		Arch rib inclination			Basket handle	Basket handle	Parallel
	Road width (m)				9.2	9.0	9.2
	Members	Arch	Span (m)		190.0	183.4	55.0
			Rise (m)		35.0	28.0	14.0
			Distance between main girders (m)		6.5	2.0	7.2
			Member height	Crown	2.2	1.8	0.5
				Support	2.2	1.8	0.5
			Cross-section		Box	Box	Box
		Girder	Cross-section		Box	Box	"I"
			Girder height		1.6	1.2	1.4
		Hangers	Cross-section		Box	Circular	"I"
			Interval (m)		10.0	11.3	6.9
	Color	Arch, girder, hanger			Brown	Red	Red
Sub structure	Clearance (m)				91.0	60.0	29.0
Accessories	Railing				Virtical grid	Virtical grid	Horizontal rail
	Lighting				None	None	None
	Drain pipe				Horizontal	None	Vertical
Composition	Viewing distance				Medium	Near	Medium
	View point	Incident angle			Side, oblique	Side, oblique	Side
		Height			Horizontal	Horizontal	Horizontal
	Background				Mountain	Mountain	Mountain
	Background color	Upper part			Green	Dark green	Green
		Lower part			Green	Dark green	Dark green
Proportion	Span/arch rise ratio				5.43	6.55	3.93

Table 3 Assessment Results of the Landscape Design

		2	1	0	-1	-2		
1	Beautiful	○					Ugly	Neutral
2	Attractive			○			Unattractive	Subjective
3	Like		○				Dislike	Subjective
4	Friendly		○				Unfriendly	Neutral
5	Remarkable				○		Not remarkable	Objective
6	Unique					○	Ordinary	Neutral
7	Impressive			○			Not impressive	Neutral
8	Vigorous		○				Weak	Objective
9	Dynamic				○		Static	Objective
10	Functional				○		Not functional	Neutral
11	Stable			○			Unstable	Objective
12	Calm			○			Uneasy	Neutral
13	Natural			○			Unnatural	Neutral
14	Harmonious	○					Mismatching	Objective
15	Consistent		○				Inconsistent	Objective
16	Rythmical			○			Monotonous	Neutral
17	Clear		○				Cramped	Objective
18	Refresh			○			Dull	Objective
19	Freedom				○		Restraint	Neutral
20	Soft				○		Hard	Objective
21	Modern			○			Old fashioned	Objective
22	Sophisticated			○			Not sophisticated	Objective
23	Well balanced			○			unbalanced	Objective
24	Bright				○		Dark	Objective
25	Light				○		Heavy	Objective
26	Grave		○				Mean	Objective
27	Cold			○			Warm	Neutral

4.System Configuration

4.1 System Configuration by Neural Network

The neural network is composed by multiple units, each consisting of multiple input (Ik) and a specific output (Q), a weight for each input (Wk) and a threshold value (h). Q is defined as:

$$Q = f(\ Wi\ Ii-h) \quad (1)$$

where, the function f is normally the sigmoid function:

$$F(x) = 1/(1+\exp(-x)) \quad (2)$$

A number of units similar to the above mentioned one are combined to form the neural network.

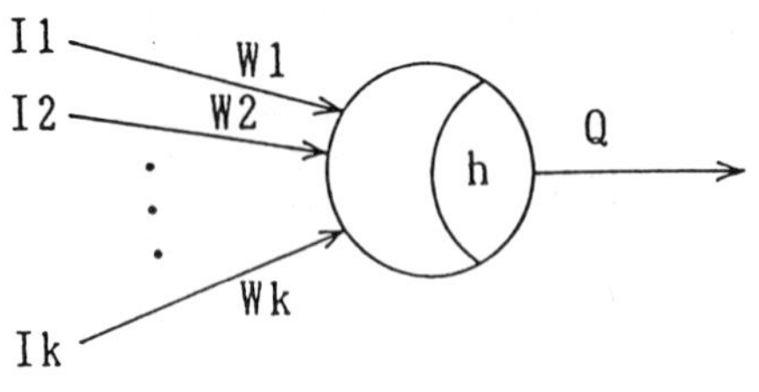

Fig.4 Structure of the Unit

The system applies a neuro-computing software with learning ability, the "CRC RHINE", and the neural network used herein is a three-layer hierarchical model comprising an intermediate layer. The number of units in each layer is as it shown in Table 4.

Table 4 Number of Units in Each Layer

	Girder bridge	Arch bridge
Input layer	78	84
Intermediate layer	40	40
Output layer	5	5

The learning process uses back propagation and the numbers of layers and intermediate layers were determined by comparing the average errors in the learning convergence. The system has as input data the values of parameters for assessing landscape design, from which, the numerical ones were input as they were and the ones representing options were expressed as follows:

For instance, in case of a through deck bridge, the input parameter "bridge deck position" having options is expressed as:

$$(A,\ B,\ C) = (0,\ 0,\ 1)$$

where A: upper (deck bridge)
B: middle (half-through)
C: lower(through))

In the output, the assessment results are expressed by 5 ranks: 2, 1, 0, -1, -2. For example, when a result is 1, the output is expressed as:

$$(2,\ 1,\ 0,\ -1,\ -2) = (0,\ 1,\ 0,\ 0,\ 0)$$

The learning process in the above lines was repeated for 104 girder bridges and 113 arch bridges. In each learning, the process ended when the error was considered small enough for the process to stabilize, that is, there was no specific limitation for the mean square errors.

4.2 System Configuration by Expert System

It is not easy to create rules for an expert system oriented for landscape design, in which a variety of factors are involved. Thus an attempt was made to construct a system using a tool, the XPT, with which rules can be inductively extracted from past events (samples for judgment), and knowledge can be automatically acquired by inputting the data in the form of a table. This inductive method for obtaining rules is an enhanced ID3 algorithm of J. Ross Quinian. This method can derive a rule (determination tree) to provide the fastest way to reach a result from given past events, through a process,in which branching can be minimized. In this method, the entropy (information amount) of each element is calculated, and the element having the minimum entropy is then assigned as the trunk of the determination tree. Values of parameters for assessing the landscape design are input as elements, giving as output the assessment results, expressed by the 5 ranks. Numerical data such as span length and road width were input as logical numbers, after classifying them into convenient groups.

Fig.5 presents the rule-induction results for arch bridges. This figure shows some determination trees marked with "insufficient" due to the lack of samples for judgment. This phenomenon is attributed to the characteristic of the ID3 algorithm, which tries to classify every sample into the determination tree, creating an excessive number of branches. To solve this problem, the Pessimistic Pruning algorithm, by J.Ross.Quinian, was applied to replace the branches considered as insufficient. Fig.6 and Fig.7 show that, by applying this method, branches marked "insufficient" can be eliminated from the determination tree.

Fig.5 Rules for the "Beauty" Assessment of Arch Bridges

```
XpertRule            Subject name  yas20_01       Rule printing

Color/bridge
|--------- Red:Arch rise
|          |------ 25~: Member height/support
|          |           |-- 1.6~1.9: 2              (2,1.00)
|          |           |-- 1.0~1.3: 2              (1,1.00)
|          |           |-- 0.0~0.4: (Insufficiency)
|          |           |-- 0.4~0.7: 1              (1,1.00)
|          |           |-- 0.7~1.0: 2              (1,1.00)
|          |           |-- 1.3~1.6: 1              (2,1.00)
|          |           `----- 1.9~: 2              (1,1.00)
|          |---- 10~13: Girder height
|          |           |-- 1.2~1.4: 1              (2,1.00)
|          |           |-- 1.4~1.6: 1              (2,1.00)
|          |           |----- 2.0~: 1              (1,1.00)
|          |           |-- 1.8~2.0: (Insufficiency)
|          |           |-- 1.0~1.2: Bridge type
|          |           |           |-----      Nielsen:(Insufficiency)  (0)
|          |           |           |------       Lohse: 0               (1,1.00)
|          |           |           |-----       Langer:(Insufficiency)  (0)
|          |           |           |--  Langer truss:(Insufficiency)    (0)
|          |           |           |- Trussed langer:(Insufficiency)    (0)
|          |           |           `-------       Arch: -1              (1,1.00)
|          |           |-- 1.6~1.8: (Insufficient)
|          |           `-- 0.0~1.0: (Insufficient)
|          |---- 13~16: 1         (9,1.00)
|          |---- 22~25: 0         (2,1.00)
|          |---- 16~19: Girder height
|          |           |-- 1.2~1.4: 1              (2,1.00)
|          |           |-- 1.4~1.6: 0              (1,1.00)
|          |           |----- 2.0~: Bridge type
```

Fig.6 Rules for the "Beauty" Assess-
      ment of Girder Bridges
      (with Pruning)

```
XpertRule              Subject name     c7j02        Rule printing
 1 Color/girder
 2 |--------- Blue:Background
 3 |           |------- Urban area:Lower background color
 4 |           |          |------     Red: -2        (1,1.00)
 5 |           |          |------   Green:  1        (1,1.00)
 6 |           |          |------    Brue: -1        (1,1.00)
 7 |           |          |------    Gray: -1        (0,0.34)
 8 |           |          |------   White: -1        (0,0.34)
 9 |           |          |------   Black: -1        (0,0.34)
10 |           |-- Flat area: -1      (1,1.00)
11 |           |------- Mountain:Girder height ratio
12 |           |          |-----   20-25:  1         (1,1.00)
13 |           |          |-----   15-20: -2         (3,1.00)
14 |           |          |-----   30-35:  1         (1,1.00)
15 |           |          |-----   35-40: -1         (0,0.34)
16 |           |          |-----   25-30:  0         (1,1.00)
17 |           |          |--------  -15: -1         (0,0.34)
18 |           |          |--------  40-: -1         (0,0.34)
19 |           |------- Sea:Span/pier height ratio
20 |           |          |------    5-10: -1        (0,0.34)
21 |           |          |---------   -5: -1        (0,0.34)
22 |           |          |-----    15-20:  1        (1,1.00)
23 |           |          |-----    10-15:  0        (2,1.00)
24 |           |          |--------   30-: -1        (1,1.00)
25 |           |          |------   20-25: -1        (0,0.34)
```

Fig.7 Rules for the "Beauty" Assess-
      ment of Arch Bridges
      (with Pruning)

```
XpertRule              Subject name     yas20_01      Rule printing
 1 Color/bridge
 2 |--------- Red:Arch rise
 3 |           |------- 25~: Member height/support
 4 |           |          |-- 1.6~1.9: 2         (2,1.00)
 5 |           |          |-- 1.0~1.3: 2         (1,1.00)
 6 |           |          |-- 0.0~0.4: 1         (0,0.53)
 7 |           |          |-- 0.4~0.7: 1         (1,1.00)
 8 |           |          |-- 0.7~1.0: 2         (1,1.00)
 9 |           |          |-- 1.3~1.6: 1         (2,1.00)
10 |           |          |------ 1.9~: 2        (1,1.00)
11 |           |----- 10~13: 1      (7,0.50)
12 |           |----- 13~16: 1      (9,1.00)
13 |           |----- 22~25: 0      (2,1.00)
14 |           |----- 16~19: Girder height
15 |           |          |-- 1.2~1.4: 1         (2,1.00)
16 |           |          |-- 1.4~1.6: 0         (1,1.00)
17 |           |          |------ 2.0~: Bridge type
18 |           |          |          |------      Nielsen: 1   (0,0.36)
19 |           |          |          |-------       Lohse: 0   (2,1.00)
20 |           |          |          |------       Langer: 1   (0,0.36)
21 |           |          |          |-- Langer truss: 1        (0,0.36)
22 |           |          |          |- Trussed langer: 2       (1,1.00)
23 |           |          |          |-------         Arch: 1   (0,0.36)
24 |           |          |-- 1.8~2.0: 1         (1,1.00)
25 |           |          |-- 1.0~1.2: 1         (1,1.00)
26 |           |          |-- 1.6~1.8: 2         (1,1.00)
```

5. Application

An assessment system was developed using a neural network together with an expert system, applying the data of 104 girder bridges and 113 arch bridges (constructed during 1987-1991) to create the rules automatically, by learning. The system suitability was then check with the data of not-learned bridges constructed during 1992.

Tables 5 and 6 show the results of the actual assessment and the ones resulting from the RHINE and XPT assessments. For RHINE, the assessment rank is represented by the values 2, 1, 0, -1 or -2, in each column. For instance, the arch bridge 1, having the largest value (0.964) for the possibility of belonging to the rank 1 ("fairly beautiful"), can be considered as fairly beautiful.

Table 5 Results of the System Assessment for Girder Bridges

Bridge	Actual	RHINE 2 Beautiful	RHINE 1	RHINE 0 Average	RHINE −1	RHINE −2 Ugly	XPT
1	−1	0.005	0.002	0.126	◎ 0.796	0.003	○ 0
2	1	0.169	0.001	○ 0.936	0.002	0.005	× −1
3	0	0.000	0.025	◎ 0.992	0.003	0.001	○ 1
4	1	0.005	◎ 0.422	0.410	0.000	0.020	○ 0
5	0	0.021	0.000	0.050	○ 0.815	0.024	○ −1
6	0	0.002	○ 0.797	0.001	0.469	0.093	◎ 0
7	0	0.024	0.007	◎ 0.929	0.065	0.022	◎ 0
8	1	0.003	0.144	○ 0.870	0.072	0.002	○ 0
9	0	0.020	0.187	◎ 0.918	0.018	0.010	◎ 0
10	0	0.002	0.080	◎ 0.819	0.003	0.027	◎ 0

◎ : Coincident
○ : Different by one rank
△ : Different by two ranks or more
× : Inverted signs

Table 6 Results of the System Assessment for Arch Bridges

Bridge	Actual	RHINE 2 Beutiful	RHINE 1	RHINE 0 Average	RHINE −1	RHINE −2 Ugly	XPT
1	2	0.075	○ 0.946	0.000	0.002	0.002	◎ 2
2	0	0.011	0.080	◎ 0.987	0.001	0.000	◎ 0
3	−1	0.001	× 0.990	0.002	0.003	0.012	◎ −1
4	2	◎ 0.710	0.015	0.047	0.015	0.044	◎ 2
5	0	0.001	○ 0.585	0.032	0.286	0.000	○ 1
6	1	0.001	◎ 0.563	0.100	0.281	0.013	◎ 1
7	1	0.029	◎ 0.958	0.005	0.024	0.000	◎ 1
8	0	0.000	0.011	◎ 0.993	0.112	0.005	◎ 0
9	1	0.006	◎ 0.961	0.040	0.003	0.000	◎ 1
10	0	0.000	○ 0.714	0.138	0.011	0.002	○ −1
11	0	0.000	0.008	◎ 0.963	0.032	0.002	○ 1
12	1	0.003	◎ 0.978	0.004	0.020	0.002	◎ 1
13	0	0.040	○ 0.946	0.018	0.008	0.006	○ 1
14	1	0.037	◎ 0.944	0.080	0.004	0.001	◎ 1
15	1	0.021	◎ 0.925	0.012	0.004	0.006	○ 0
16	0	0.001	0.009	◎ 0.953	0.383	0.017	◎ 0
17	1	0.006	◎ 0.680	0.234	0.089	0.138	◎ 1
18	1	0.044	◎ 0.805	0.327	0.010	0.049	○ 0
19	0	0.030	○ 0.803	0.467	0.004	0.002	△ 2
20	−1	0.000	0.653	0.540	0.002	0.011	○ 0
21	0	0.006	0.185	◎ 0.859	0.020	0.000	○ 1
22	0	0.001	0.271	◎ 0.889	0.087	0.001	◎ 0
23	1	0.697	◎ 0.716	0.003	0.000	0.000	◎ 1
24	1	0.092	◎ 0.831	0.036	0.063	0.052	◎ 1
25	−1	× 0.543	0.089	0.259	0.091	0.031	○ 0
26	2	0.467	○ 0.808	0.004	0.001	0.000	◎ 2
27	−2	0.000	0.028	0.484	○ 0.495	0.073	× 1
28	1	0.072	◎ 0.559	0.005	0.002	0.006	◎ 1

◎ : Coincident
○ : Different by one rank
△ : Different by two ranks or more
× : Inverted signs

In case of girder bridges, the actual assessment, carried out by bridge designers, presented significantly different results from the ones of the assessment by the neural network and the expert system, for the subjective parameter "beauty". As for the arch bridges, both assessments seem to agree well, except for some patterns which were not well learned. The discrepancy among the girder bridges assessment result indicates that there are more assessment parameters to be considered other than those considered in this study and, that girder bridges, having simpler structures, may be subjected to changes in the assessment weights. Other possible causes for the discrepancy include the problem of the data quality due to the time factor, that is, this type of assessment is associated with intrinsic ambiguity and/or errors, not to mention that the assessment criteria may change from time to time. For arch bridges, in most case, RHINE and XPT assessments agree to the actual one and the few cases with discrepancy may also be attributed to the quality of the data, that is, the number of samples may have been insufficient for judgment. Also, if the number of assessment ranks were reduced from five to three, this agreement would certainly improve.

Discrepancy between the neural network (RHINE) and the expert system (XRT) mainly depends on the difference in the methodology: the expert system produces the rules automatically, by event learning, providing a production system with reduced number of rules, this, being different from the weights one might attribute to the rule. To solve the above problem, weights has be attributed to the assessing parameters of the neural network and the rules should be created manually, combining the neural network with the expert system.

Assessment with subjective factors naturally differs from person to person. Thus, to investigate the influence of personal opinion on the assessment, graphic data base including bridge photographs is now being developed, so that a great number of persons can assess the landscape design using the same data.

6.Conclusion

A method for the quantitative assessment of landscape design of girder and arch bridges was developed, by applying a general purpose knowledge acquisition assistance tool to a neural network, which made it possible to obtain good results from the input of sample events, without having to use complex models or rules. In addition, the method can be improved to be more practical by using a refined neural network and combining it with an expert system.

To solve problems existing in the black-box part of the neural network, the weight of each assessing parameter has to be investigated in a 2-layer model to define the degree of their effects. Besides, in deleting or adding assessment parameters, its effects on the rules produced automatically by learning have to be carefully investigated, so as keep its compatibility with the results. Another point to be noted is the problem concerning the method for collecting learning data, as well as the quality and quantity of the data. Since the number of data for girder and arch bridges totaled over 100 each, the problem of quantity seems not to be the point. As for the quality, the data have to be revised in some way, by means, for instance, of site surveys.

References

[1]Japan Society for Bridge Construction: Bridge Annals, No. 1987 to 1991.

[2]M. Kato, S. Tanaka, K. Ooba: A Study on Landscape Design Based on Questionnaires, Journal of Structural Engineering, Vol.36A, pp. 535-542, March 1990.

[3]Report by Hanshin Expressway Corporation: Application of Expert System to Bridge Design (No.3), March 1990.

[4]H. Furuta, H. Ootani, S. Nakabayashi, N.Shiraishi: Application of Neural Network to Landscape Design of Bridge, Journal of Structural Engineering, Vol.37A, pp.669-675, March 1991.

[5]W. Shiraki, S. Matsuho, N. Takaoka: Assessing System for Landscape Architecture for Bridge Design by Neural Network: Journal of Structural Engineering, Vol.37A, pp. 687-697, March 1991.

Chapter 8: Signal Processing

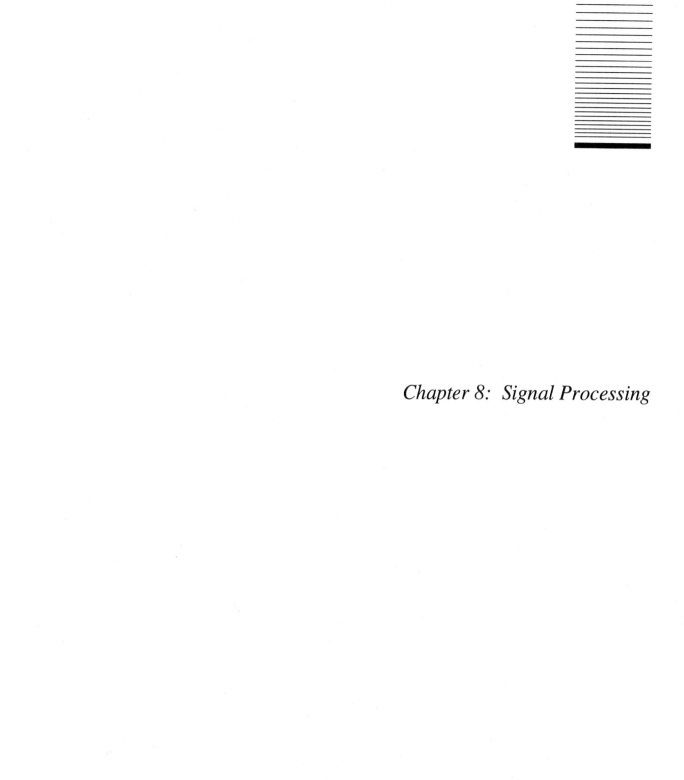

CHAPTER 8
Signal Processing

Digital signal processing (DSP) has matured significantly over the past three decades. DSP chips are now common to many sound boards found in personal computers, they are used in fax machines, copy machines, telephones, televisions, and many other areas. In most instances, the signal processing operations performed are linear. As such, neural networks provide the signal processing community with the ability to extend many of these existing applications into a nonlinear domain. In some instances, this extension provides significant improvements over existing linear techniques. In other instances, the extension is not as advantageous.

Neural networks are used in four signal processing areas:

- **Signal Decomposition.** Feature extraction decomposes a signal into a set of parameters that describe different aspects of the signal. In some cases, such as the Fourier transform, the parameters can be used to completely reconstruct the signal. In other instances this is not possible. Like in image processing (Chapter 6), neural networks can implement some of these techniques in parallel, hence making them significantly faster. As an example of this, **Paper 8.1** shows how a MLP can be used to compute the wavelet decomposition of discrete time signals.

- **Radar Signal Processing.** There are many areas within radar signal processing where neural networks are showing promise. In radar there is a need to improve resolution without increasing power. In addition, in the absence of an Identify Friend or Foe (IFF) transponder, radar systems need to have the ability to identify targets from their backscatter. The following two papers are examples of how neural networks are being used to address these problems. **Paper 8.2** shows how a MLP can be used to resolve ambiguity in medium Pulse Repetition Frequency (PRF) radar systems. **Paper 8.3** shows how a recurrent cascade correlation neural network is used for radar pulse detection.

- **Filtering.** Filtering in signal processing can be used to perform many functions. As an example, in an upcoming volume of "Neural Networks Technology and Application" there will be several communications and speech papers that describe filters that are used for channel equalization and noise removal, respectively. In this chapter, the emphasis is more toward generic filtering operations. **Paper 8.4** presents a cascaded recurrent neural network that performs adaptive nonlinear filtering in real-time. **Paper 8.5** shows that neural network filters provide equivalent detection performance in the presence of Gaussian noise and superior performance in non-Gaussian noise when compared to traditional linear detection approaches. **Paper 8.6** analyzes the detection performance of the MLP using performance measures derived from Johnson distributions. **Paper 8.7** introduces a generalized adaptive neural filter and compares its performance with other nonlinear filters.

- **Instrumentation and Measurement.** One area within engineering that has not applied neural networks to a great extent is instrumentation and measurement. **Paper 8.8** is a survey of several possible applications of neural networks in this area.

- **Localization and Tracking.** It once was true that most of the localization and tracking applications existed within defense and air traffic control. With the proliferation of satellites and the recent mandates for more intelligent highways, this has changed. Now localization and tracking within Global Positioning System (GPS)-driven navigation systems both on and off shore are becoming more commonplace. Like data fusion, localization and tracking involves the combination of several pieces of information. In this instance, the task is the determination of location and heading. Neural networks offer some potential to enhance several aspects of localization and tracking. **Paper 8.9** uses several independently operating neural networks (one per sensor) for direction of arrival (DOA) estimation and shows that this approach provides better performance than maximum likelihood estimation. **Paper 8.10** describes a Hopfield-Tank neural circuit that computes the noise subspace for the MUSIC bearing estimation algorithm. **Paper 8.11** presents a system that employs multiple MLP neural networks for contact tracking in an oceanic environment. **Paper 8.12** combines a fast adaptive Hopfield-Tank neural circuit with the Joint Probabilistic Data Association (JPDA) filter for tracking multi-maneuvering targets.

A FEEDFORWARD NEURAL NETWORK FOR THE WAVELET DECOMPOSITION OF DISCRETE TIME SIGNALS

Sylvie Marcos and Messaoud Benidir
Laboratoire des Signaux et Systèmes, E.S.E.
Plateau de Moulon, 91192 Gif–sur–Yvette, France
Phone : (33) 1 69 41 80 40, Fax : (33) 1 69 41 30 60
E-mail : Marcos@marine.lss.supelec.fr

Abstract - **In this paper a feedforward neural network with sigmoïdal activation functions is proposed to perform the wavelet decomposition of a discrete time signals.**

1 INTRODUCTION

The problem of representing a signal as an expansion of elementary functions is very important in signal processing. The aim of such a representation is often to reveal temporal and frequential properties of a signal in order to characterize and process this signal. For example, the Fourier expansion of a signal with respect to a trigonometric system has been widely used for the frequency analysis of a signal. The distribution of coefficients appearing in the Fourier expansion provides information about the frequency composition of the original signal. However, in a non stationary context, the Fourier expansion fails in providing information. It is then useful to be able to obtain an expansion of a signal in terms of elementary functions which are well localized both in time and frequency. The wavelet expansion of a signal has appeared to be a good way to study this problem [1]. In this case, the elementary functions are obtained by dilating and translating the single function $\psi(t)$ referred to as the mother-wavelet. Recent works, see for example [2] [3] [4] [5] [6] [7], have shown the existence of orthonormal bases of wavelets in which any signal of $L^2(\mathbb{R})$ can be expanded. The coefficients appearing in this expansion are given by the scalar products of the signal to be analysed and the components of the orthonormal basis.
Many real life applications, however, deal with discrete time signals. The scalar products abovementioned can be replaced by Riemann approximations requiring the discretization of the wavelets in relation with the signal sampling. In practice, several difficulties arise. Wavelets forming an orthonormal basis with well localisation properties are constructed numerically and have not an explicit formulation. It follows that it is not trivial to obtain, for each scale and each delay, the discretization corresponding to the signal sampling. These difficulties are usually solved via the multiresolution analysis [3] [5] [7] and the determination of conjugate quadratic filters.

0-7803-0928-6/93$03.00 © 1993 IEEE

As an alternative to the solution proposed via the multiresolution analysis, we here present a feedforward neural network with sigmoïdal activation functions capable of dealing with these difficulties.
Note that some recent works relating neural networks to wavelet expansion recently appeared in the litterature (see, for example, [8] [9]). Their aims, however, are different from ours. The authors of [8] use the time-frequency localization properties of some cluster of three sigmoïdal neurons to determine the number of neurons necessary to approximate a function with a given accuracy. In [9], the classical universal approximator feedforward neural network with sigmoïds is replaced by a wavelet neural network with the Morlet wavelet as activation function (note that the Morlet wavelet does not yield an orthonormal basis).
The following section presents the main results concerning the continuous and discrete wavelet transforms and the multiresolution analysis. In Section 3, we propose a feedforward neural network capable of performing the discrete wavelet transform and we discuss the advantages of this approach. In Section 4, the performances of the proposed network are illustrated.

2 WAVELET DECOMPOSITION VIA THE MULTIRESOLUTION ANALYSIS

2.1 Continuous and discrete wavelet transforms

The continuous wavelet transform (CWT) (see for example [3] [4] [6]) is an operator which associates to any function $x(t)$ of $L^2(\mathbb{R})$ a function of $L^2(\mathbb{R}^2)$ defined by

$$C(a,b) \triangleq \int_{\mathbb{R}} x(t)\sqrt{|a|}\psi(a(t-b))dt. \qquad (1)$$

Under the hypothesis

$$I_\psi \triangleq \int_0^\infty \frac{|\widehat{\psi}(a\omega)|^2}{a} da < \infty \qquad (2)$$

where $\widehat{\psi}(\omega)$ is the Fourier transform of $\psi(t)$, the CWT is an isometry (up to a constant) which is invertible and the original signal is given by [6] :

$$x(t) = \frac{1}{I_\psi}\int_{\mathbb{R}^2} \sqrt{|a|}C(a,b)\psi(a(t-b))dadb. \qquad (3)$$

In the recent work [6], it is shown that it is possible to build functions $\psi(t)$ and to choose a and b such that, by the natural discretization of the parameters $a = 2^j$ and $b = 2^{-j}i$, the family

$$\{\psi_{i,j}(t)\}_{i,j\in\mathbb{Z}} \triangleq \{2^{j/2}\psi(2^jt - i)\}_{i,j\in\mathbb{Z}} \qquad (4)$$

is an orthonormal basis of $L^2(\mathbb{R})$. Then the following expansion exists for any signal $x(t)$ of $L^2(\mathbb{R})$:

$$x(t) = \sum_{i,j \in \mathbb{Z}} c_{i,j} \psi_{i,j}(t) \tag{5}$$

where the coefficients $c_{i,j}$, referred to as the wavelet coefficients, are given by the scalar products

$$c_{i,j} = \int_{\mathbb{R}} x(t) \psi_{i,j}(t) dt. \tag{6}$$

2.2 Orthonormal bases of compactly supported wavelets

The construction of the base $(\psi_{i,j})_{(i,j)\in\mathbb{Z}^2}$ is directely related to the concept of multiresolution analysis developped in [3] [4] [5] [6] [7]. The procedure consists of the two following steps.

1. Construction of a scale function ϕ of $L^2(\mathbb{R})$ according to the identity :

$$\frac{1}{2}\phi(\frac{t}{2}) = \sum_{k=-\infty}^{\infty} h_k \phi(t-k) \tag{7}$$

where the h_k satisfy general conditions [4] [6].

2. Construction of a wavelet function ψ according to

$$\frac{1}{2}\psi(\frac{t}{2}) = \sum_{k=-\infty}^{\infty} g_k \phi(t-k) \tag{8}$$

where the coefficients g_k are such that the sequences h_k and g_k, $k \in \mathbb{Z}$ define the inpulse responses of *Quadrature Mirror Filters* (QMF). For example, the coefficients g_k can be constructed from the h_k as :

$$g_k = (-1)^{1-k} h_{1-k}. \tag{9}$$

The construction of the scale function ϕ, associated with the sequence h_k, is based on the relation (7). According to this relation, ϕ can be seen as a fixed point of the operator T from $L^1(\mathbb{R})$ into $L^1(\mathbb{R})$, defined by

$$T[\phi(t)] = 2\sum_{k=-\infty}^{\infty} h_k \phi(2t-k). \tag{10}$$

Under some assumptions on the sequence (h_k), the fixed point of T exists and is unique [6]. One can numeriquely determine ϕ as a limit, when n tends to the infinity, of the sequence of functions ϕ_{n+1} defined by

$$\phi_{n+1}(t) \triangleq T[\phi_n(t)] \tag{11}$$

starting with ϕ_0 equal to the characteristic function of the interval [-1/2, 1/2]. The wavelet ψ can then be deduced from ϕ using (8). In general, the sequence h_k is assumed to be of finite lengh, i.e., $h_k = 0$ for $k < 0$ or $k > N$. In this case, ϕ and ψ are compactly supported functions [7]. The derivation of the basis elements $\psi_{i,j}$ is then straightforward.

2.3 Decomposition of the signal

The problem consists in recursively determining the coefficients $c_{i,j}$ appearing in (6). For this, one can establish from relations (7) and (8) the following recursions

$$\phi_{i,j}(t) = 2 \sum_{n=-\infty}^{\infty} h_{n-2i}\phi_{n,j-1}(t) \tag{12}$$

and

$$\psi_{i,j}(t) = 2 \sum_{n=-\infty}^{\infty} g_{n-2i}\phi_{n,j-1}(t) \tag{13}$$

where $\phi_{i,j}(t) \triangleq 2^{j/2}\phi(2^j t - i)$. Introducing the coefficients

$$\bar{c}_{i,j} = \int_{\mathbb{R}} x(t)\phi_{i,j}(t)dt \tag{14}$$

and taking into account relations (12) and (13), we can establish the following recursions.

$$\bar{c}_{i,j} = 2 \sum_{n=-\infty}^{\infty} h_{n-2i}\bar{c}_{n,j-1} \tag{15}$$

and

$$c_{i,j} = 2 \sum_{n=-\infty}^{\infty} g_{n-2i}c_{n,j-1} \tag{16}$$

The coefficients $c_{i,j}$ can thus be recursively computed if, for a fixed $j = j_0$, the sequence $(c_{i,j_0})_{i\in\mathbb{Z}}$ is known. Taking for example $j_0 = 0$, one has to compute the scalar products for $i \in \mathbb{Z}$:

$$c_{i,0} \triangleq 2 \int_{\mathbb{R}} x(t)\phi_{i,0}(t)dt. \tag{17}$$

It is thus necessary to know the scale function ϕ.

3 THE PROPOSED NEURAL NETWORK

Our aim is to design a feedforward neural network with sigmoïds capable of decomposing any discrete time signal into an orthonormal wavelet expansion. The proposed network, exhibited in Figure 1, is made of two parts, the main network and the auxiliary network. The learning of the auxiliary network is achieved off-line, in a prior phase, in order to identify the desired wavelet $\psi(t)$. This identification is possible due to the well known properties of a neural network with one hidden layer to approximate any continuous function with a desired accuracy [10]. It comes that we obtain the following representation of the wavelet

$$\psi(t) = \sum_k \gamma_k \sigma(\alpha_k t - \beta_k) \tag{18}$$

where $\sigma(t)$ is a sigmoïdal function and where the parameters α_k and γ_k are the weights of the first and last layers, respectively, and where β_k is the bias terms. The main neural network which is proposed to achieve the wavelet expansion consists of the auxiliary network having fixed parameters which is duplicated at every scale 2^j and delay $2^{-j}i$. The scales and delays appear as fixed weights 2^j and bias i on the first layer (see Fig.1). The coefficients $c_{i,j}$ of the expansion (5) appear as the weights of the last layer.

The advantages of such a structure are the following.

1. The auxiliary network is optimized before being integrated to the main network and gives the derivable and explicit formulation (18) of a wavelet which can be translated, dilated and sampled as wanted.
2. Once a wavelet is chosen for its regularity or its time-frequency properties, its explicit and derivable approximation given by the auxiliary network can be used indefinitely for every signal to be analyzed.
3. Since the scale and delay parameters ensuring that the wavelets form an orthonormal basis are being fixed, the learning of the main network consists in minimizing a quadratic and convex function of the coefficients $c_{i,j}$ of the wavelet expansion only. The learning of the main network then achieves the desired scalar products.
4. As a consequence of the previous point, the optimization of the main network with a gradient or a quasi-Newton algorithm is guaranted to converge to the unique minimum.
5. The wavelet decomposition is then obtained with sigmoïdal function which, as it is well-known, are easily implementable.
6. Finally, we also mention as an advantage of the proposed structure that the scale a and delay b parameters can be optimized by learning instead of keeping them fixed to 2^j and $2^{-j}i$, respectively. Whereas

in this case the wavelets do no longer form a orthonormal basis, this way of working the network can be of interest in some applications (for example, in order to minimize the number of representative coefficients in the wavelet expansion). The cost function to be minimized however is no longer quadratic with respect to the parameters. Nevertheless, a good initialization would first consist in performing the network with fixed scales and delays and would then consist in optimizing the scales and delays by backpropagation.

For all these reasons, the proposed neural network can be viewed as an interesting implementation of the wavelet expansion of a signal. A further comparison between this approach and the multiresolution analysis approach is under consideration. The following section illustrates the performances of the proposed neural network.

4 AN ILLUSTRATION

Figure 2 exhibits the wavelet $\psi(t)$ under consideration (solid line). It was constructed through the multiresolution analysis with the CQF coefficients $\{h_k\}$ defined in [7] so that the $\{\psi_{i,j}(t)\}$ is an orthonormal basis of compactly supported wavelets. This mother-wavelet $\psi(t)$ is then approximated (+ lines) by an auxiliary network of 36 neurons, using a quasi-Newton algorithm. The relative error corresponding to the wavelet and its approximation in Fig.2 is less than -40 dB. The number of neurons in this network has not been optimized. Less neurons would have been used, for example, with a two hidden layers network.

The parameters α_k, β_k and γ_k, appearing in (18) and obtained in the preliminary phase, are fixed and the auxiliary network is integrated in the main network. The coefficients $c_{i,j}$ of the main network are optimized by a LMS algorithm (backpropagation on the last layer only). According to (5), these coefficients are also the wavelet transform coefficients, and the output of the main network is an approximation of the signal to be analyzed. In order to illustrate the performances of the network, we have chosen the following signal to be analyzed :

$$x(t) = 1.3\psi(t-1) - 1.5\psi(t+1) + 0.5\psi(4t) + \psi(2t-3) + \psi(2t+3) + \psi(4t-2) \quad (19)$$

Figure 3 exhibits the signal to be analyzed (solid lines) and its approximation (+ lines). Figure 4 exhibits the learning curves of the wavelet coefficients $c_{i,j}$. One can see the very good performances obtained at convergence.

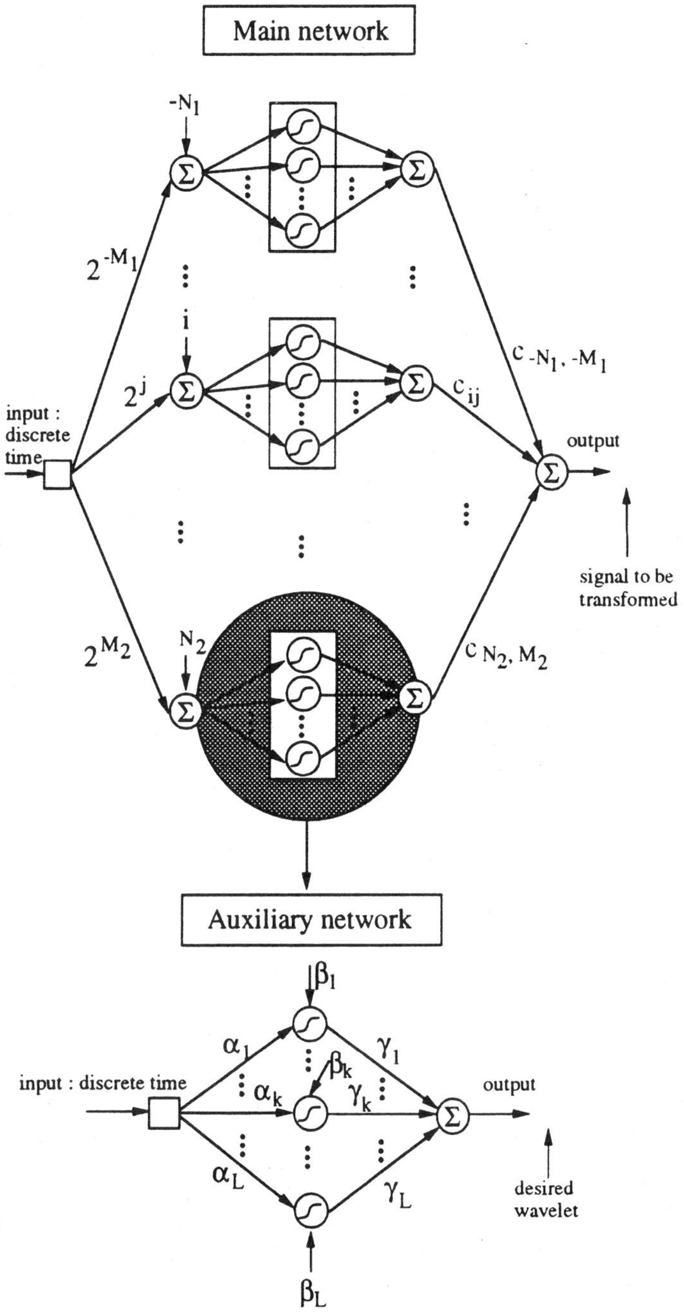

Figure 1 : The main network consists of an auxiliary network with fixed parameters, duplicated for every scale and delay. The auxiliary is optimized off-line to give an explicit approximation of a desired wavelet.

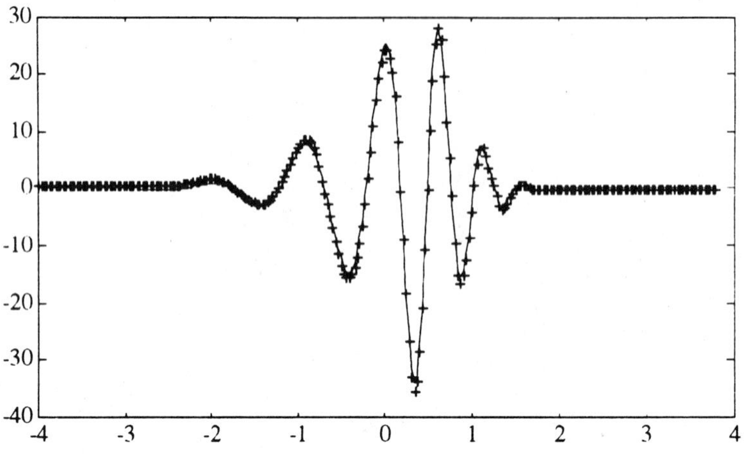

Figure 2 Mother-wavelet constructed in [5] and its approximation (+) by the auxiliary network in Fig.1.

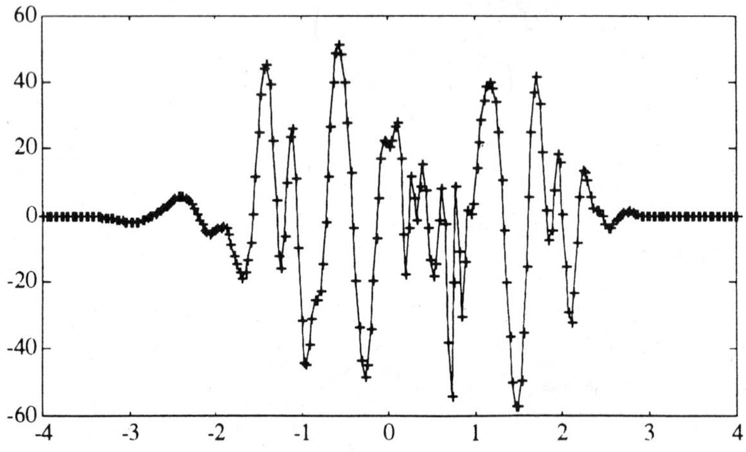

Figure 3 Actual signal and its approximation (+) by the neural network in Fig.1.

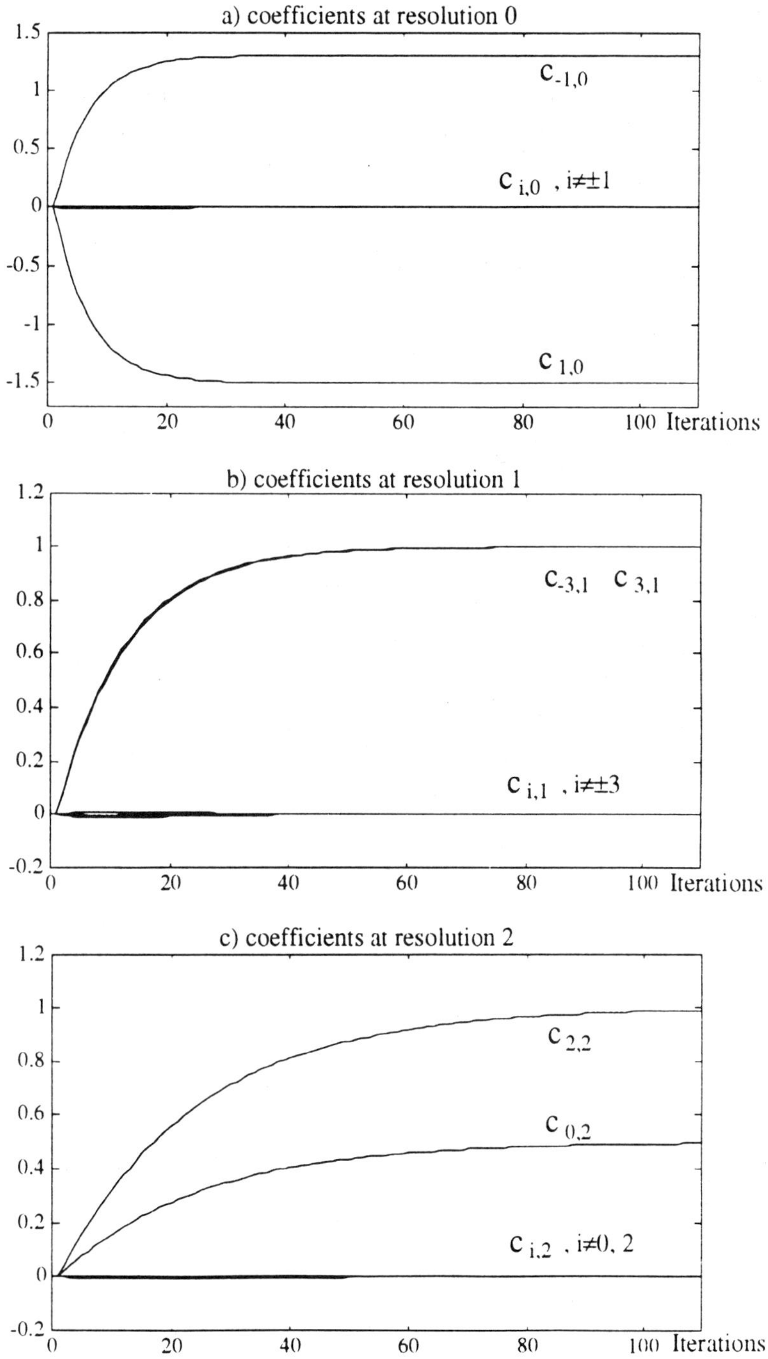

Figure 4 : learning curves of the wavelet coefficients at resolution : a) 0; b) 1; c) 2.

References

[1] O. Rioul and M. Vetterli, "Wavelets and signal processing", *IEEE SP-Magazine*, pp. 14-38, Oct. 1991.

[2] Y. Meyer, "Ondelettes, fonctions splines, et analyses graduées", *Univ. of Torino*, 1986.

[3] Y. Meyer, "Ondelettes et opérateurs", Tome 1, *Hermann, Paris*, 1990.

[4] S. Mallat, "A theory for multiresolution signal decomposition: the wavelet representation", *IEEE Trans. on PAMI*, Vol. 11, pp. 674-693, Jul. 1989.

[5] S. Mallat, "Multiresolution approximation and wavelet orthonormal bases of $L^2(\mathbb{R})$", *Trans. Amer. Math. Soc.*, Vol. 315, pp. 69-87, Sep. 1989.

[6] I. Daubechies, "The wavelet transform, time-frequency localization and signal analysis", *Trans. IT*, Vol. 36, pp. 961-1005, Sep. 90.

[7] I. Daubechies, "Orthonormal bases of compactly supported wavelets", *Com. Pure and Appl. Math.*, Vol. XLI, pp. 909-996, 1988.

[8] Y.C. Pati and P.S. Krishnaprasad, "Analysis and synthesis of feedforward neural networks using discrete affine transformations", *Technical Research Report at University of Maryland*, 1990.

[9] Q. Zhang and A. Benveniste, "Wavelet networks", *IEEE Trans. on Neural Networks*, Vol. 3, No.6, pp. 889-898 Nov. 1992.

[10] G. Cybenko, "Approximation by superposition of a sigmoidal function", *Mathematics of control, signals and systems*, Vol. 2, pp. 303-314 1989.

Analog Neural Networks Solve Ambiguity Problems in Medium PRF Radar Systems

Chia-Jiu Wang
Electrical and Computer Eng. Dept.
University of Colorado
Colorado Springs, CO 80933

Chwan-Hwa "John" Wu
Electrical Engineering Department
Auburn University
Auburn, AL 36849

Abstract - Medium PRF radars are designed to combine the desirable features of high PRF radars and low PRF radars. Both range and Doppler (range rate) ambiguities exist in medium PRF radars. In this paper we demonstrate that the ambiguity problems in medium PRF radars can be solved efficiently using the neural network approach. A multilayer feedforward network is designed to solve the ambiguity problems. Both the simulation results and the analog electronics implementation are presented. A theory is developed and proven to facilitate a modular approach, dividing a significantly large number of stored patterns into modules, for making analog neural chip implementation feasible for a real-world problem. Compared to the method used in modern radars, an iterative algorithm, the analog electronic feedforward neural network is two orders faster than the algorithmic approach. The intel ETANN 80170NX analog neural VLSI chips are used in the analog electronic implementation.

1. Introduction

Pulse radars measure distance between the radar and the target by transmitting a pulse and timing the returned pulse from the target. The elapsed time between transmit and receive pulses may be measured by placing range gates all along the receive time. In order to obtain an unambiguous range, low pulse-repetition frequency (PRF) is preferred. Using the Doppler effect (frequency), rather than timing of transmit-receive pulses, allows one to measure the range rate as a function of the transmit-receive frequency shift. High PRF is used to detect the frequency shifts of moving targets without ambiguity. Medium PRF radars are designed to combine the desirable features of high PRF radars (long range, accurate range rate, clutter discrimination) and low PRF radars (accurate range, beam, and tail target detection) [1,2].

Both range and Doppler (range rate) ambiguities exist for signals of interest in medium PRF radars. To overcome this difficulty, the method of multiple PRF has been used successfully. Hovanessian [3] proposed an algorithm for the calculation of the target range in a multiple PRF radar. In modern radars, range and range rate (Doppler) are combined and solved through a computer search and selection process [3,4].

Since the conventional method uses computer programs to search for the correct answer, it is essentially a sequential process. Neural networks however, can solve problems in a parallel fashion due to the simultaneous operations of many neurons. In this paper, we investigate the feasibility of using neural networks to solve the ambiguity problem in real time in a multiple PRF radar. In this paper, the basic principles used in the multiple PRF are presented in Section 2. Neural solutions to the range and frequency ambiguity problem are presented in Section 3. Section 4 contains the analog implementation of a multilayer feedforward neural network trained for solving the ambiguity problem. Discussions and concluding remarks are given in Section 5.

2. Multiple PRF Method

The principles involved in the multiple PRF method are based on the Chinese Remainder Theorem [3,10]. To construct an effective multiple PRF radar system, the basic PRF f_b, which determines the maximum unambiguous target range and Doppler shift, is decided first, then a set of PRF's can be calculated, for example, by

$$f_1 = M_1 f_b \quad (1)$$
$$f_2 = M_2 f_b \quad (2)$$
......
$$f_n = M_n f_b \quad (3)$$

where the multipliers $(M_i, M_j)=1$, $i \neq j$. (a, b) denotes the greatest common divisor of a and b. Theoretically, a large number of PRF's can be used to approach the unambiguous range of the basic PRF of a multiple PRF ranging system. The true target range can be calculated using the Hovanessian's algorithm [1] as described briefly in the following.

Hovanessian's algorithm

Z: target unambiguous range {variable to be solved}
D: maximum target detection range
x: range cell no of PRF 1
y: range cell no of PRF 2
....
z: range cell no of PRF n
p: the unambiguous range of PRF 1 in range cells

```
q: the unambiguous range of PRF 2 in range cells
.......................
r: the unambiguous range of PRF n in range cells
initial a=0, b=0, c=0
temp1 = x + ap
temp2 = y + bq
..........
tempn = z + cr
if temp1 = temp2 = tempn
then
     Z = temp1
     Exit {target range has found}
else
     do a = 0, D/p
     do b = 0, D/q
     ...........
     do c = 0, D/r
     temp1 = x + ap
     temp2 = y + bq
     ............
     tempn = z + cr
     if temp1 = temp2 = tempn then
             Z = temp1
             Exit; {true range has found}
     end if
     end do
endif
```

Clearly, this is an iterative algorithm which therefore requires some iterations to converge to the final solution.

The above method also applies to the true Doppler shift of a target. The only difference is that the radar returns will appear in different filters rather than in range cells.

3. Neural Solution to Ambiguity Problems

Neural computing is a fundamentally new and different approach to information processing. It is concerned with non-programmed adaptive information processing systems, and it processes data in a parallel fashion. Neural network applications emphasize areas where they appear to offer a more appropriate approach than does traditional computing. Neural networks offer possibilities for solving problems that require pattern recognition, dealing with noisy data, pattern completion, associative look-ups, and systems that learn or adapt during use [5,6]. Some optimization problems can also be addressed with neural networks [7].

Many neural network architectures have been proposed and implemented for commercial and industrial applications. Multilayer feedforward networks can form arbitrarily complex decision regions. Multilayer feedforward networks with backpropagation training have been successfully used to discriminate speech sounds, underwater sonar returns and many other applications [8,9]. The capabilities of multilayer feedforward networks stem from the nonlinearities used within neurons, i.e. processing elements. A trained multilayer feedforward neural network often produces surprising results and generalizations in applications where explicit derivation of mappings and discovery of relationships is almost impossible.

3.1 A three-layer feedforward neural network

A three-layer feedforward neural network is selected to solve the ambiguity problem because of the availability of intel ETANN (Electrical Trainable Analog Neural Network) chip, 80170NX. The intel Neural Network Training System (iNNTS) is used to train the analog neural network chips in this research. The iBrainMaker software, provided by iNNTS, is chosen to perform the off-line training and chip-in-loop optimization [11].

The architecture and backpropagation training algorithm are briefly reviewed in the following. The three-layer feedforward neural network has an input layer, a hidden layer, and an output layer. Each input feeds up through the hidden layer to the output layer. Each neuron forms a weighted sum of the inputs from the previous layer to which it is connected, adds a threshold value, and produces a nonlinear function of this sum as its output value. Each neuron output serves as an input to the next layer to which it is connected. The process is repeated until output values are obtained for all neurons in the output layer. Thus, each neuron performs

$$y_j = f\{\Sigma_i W_{ij} x_i + \theta_i\} \quad (4)$$

where W_{ij} is the positive or negative real number weight from neuron i to neuron j, and θ_i is the threshold of the ith neuron. The function f(x) is a nonlinear function that often is chosen to be a sigmoid form. In this work, f(x)=tanh(ax), where tanh is the hyperbolic tangent function. Let d_i be the desired output and y_i the actual output from the output layer. The neural network is trained by minimizing the error function

$$E=\Sigma_i(d_i-y_i)^2 \quad (5)$$

where index i is over the output layer neurons. The error E is summed over all training patterns. The weights W_{ij} are found by using the steepest descent procedure to minimize E. The commonly used procedure minimizes E by changing W_{ij} and θ_j by ΔW_{ij} and $\Delta\theta_j$, where

$$\Delta W_{ij} = -\eta \partial E/\partial W_{ij} \quad (6)$$

$$\Delta\theta_j = -\eta \partial E/\partial \theta_j \quad (7)$$

and η is a positive constant called the learning constant. After simplification ΔW_{ij} and $\Delta\theta_j$ can be expressed as

$$\Delta W_{ij} = \eta \delta_j y_i \quad (8)$$

$$\Delta\theta_j = \eta \delta_j \quad (9)$$

where $\delta_j=(d_j-y_j)y_j(1-y_j)$ for output layer neurons; $\delta_j=y_j(1-y_j)\Sigma_k\delta_k W_{jk}$ for hidden layer neurons and the index k taken over all neurons in the layer above neuron j. A momentum α is often used to speedup convergence in training as shown in equation 10.

$$\Delta W_{ij}(t) = -\eta \nabla E(t) + \alpha \Delta W_{ij}(t-1) \quad (10)$$

3.2 Training the feedforward network

We present two real medium PRF radar examples in the following two sections to illustrate the construction of the training data set and to demonstrate the performance of the feedforward neural network through simulation. Since the amount of training data is large, a modular training approach is proposed and used successfully.

3.2.1 Training to solve the range ambiguity problem

Assuming that a medium PRF radar is designed to have a detection range = 150 Km and to use two PRF's, PRF 1 = 24K Hz, PRF 2 = 25K Hz. A range cell is defined to be 0.1 Km. The unambiguous range of PRF 1 is 6.25 Km, i.e. from range cell 1 to range cell 63. (Range cell 1 covers [0, 0.1)Km, Range cell 2 covers [0.1, 0.2)Km, etc.) The unambiguous range of PRF 2 is 6.0 Km, i.e. from range cell 1 to range cell 61. But the true unambiguous detection range in this radar system is 150 Km, i.e. from range cell 1 to range cell 1501. Any radar returns from PRF 1 or 2 will fall into the corresponding range cells. The true range cell in which the target is residing is derived from the returns of PRF 1 and PRF 2.

Training data representation and generation

There are 1501 different outputs corresponding to 1501 target locations. Hence there are 1501 output patterns. The input pattern contains the returns from PRF 1 and PRF 2, by concatenating them. Both inputs and outputs are binary encoded. As such there are 11 bits used for outputs and 12 bits (6 bits required by each PRF) for inputs. For example, a target situating at 99.95 Km, (i.e. inside range cell 1000), away from the radar site, the return of PRF 1 will be in range cell 55 (= 1000 mod 63), and the return of PRF 2 will be in range cell 24 (= 1000 mod 61). The input pattern for this specific target is constructed by concatenating the binary encoded 55 and 24, resulting in a 12-bit binary number 110111011000. The corresponding output pattern is 00001100100 for this target 99.95 Km away. In total, there are 1501 patterns to be learned by the neural network. A program based on the Chinese Remainder Theorem is written to generate the whole training data covering the entire 150 km range. Table 1 presents some representative training data for targets at short, medium, and long distance. Since we use the bipolar data format, 0 in the following table is converted to -1 during training.

There are 1501 unique patterns for the neural network to learn. The number of patterns is too large and time-consuming to be learned by the analog feedforward neural network chip using backpropagation training to achieve a reasonable noise immunity between the output levels 1 and 0. In order to facilitate training and implementation, we adopt the modular training approach to divide the 1501 stored patterns into 8 modules. The following describes a theory which provides the mathematical foundation for the approach.

Modular approach for training

The input pattern can be expressed as a vector I=(A, B), where A is the radar return of PRF 1; B is the radar return of PRF 2.

Theorem 1: Let X be a set of integers and $X = \{ X_i = i, 0 < i \le yz \}$. ($X_i = i$ indicates that the target appears in range cell i). Let y be the maximum unambiguous range cell of PRF 1, and z be the maximum unambiguous range cell of PRF 2. Both y and z are relatively prime integers. For every $X_i \in X$, there exists a unique $I_i = (A_i, B_i)$ where $X_i \equiv A_i \bmod y$, $X_i \equiv B_i \bmod z$. $\equiv$ denotes the congruence and A_i and B_i are integers.

Proof: First we prove that there exists a X_i satisfying $X_i \equiv A_i \bmod y$, and $X_i \equiv B_i \bmod z$ simultaneously. Since the greatest common divisor of y, z, denoted as (y, z), is (y,z)=1 and $y \neq 0$, $z \neq 0$, there exist integers p and q such that yp+zq=1. Multiplying this equation by $(B_i - A_i)$, we have $yp(B_i-A_i) + zq(B_i-A_i) = B_i-A_i$. Then by setting $X_i = A_i + py(B_i-A_i)$, we have $X_i-A_i = y(p(B_i-A_i))$ and $X_i-B_i = z(q(B_i-A_i))$, by the definition of congruence, $X_i \equiv A_i \bmod y$, $X_i \equiv B_i \bmod z$.

Secondly we prove that if $X_i \neq X_j$, then $I_i \neq I_j$. Since the maximum value of X_i is less than yz which is the least common multiple, the duplication of I_i appears only when $X_i > yz$. As such, there exists an unique I_i for every $X_i \in X$.□

Based on Theorem 1, it shows that X can be partitioned into several smaller regions as shown in Table 2, and no each region can be processed independently. It is desired to have an approximately equal number of patterns in each group. Here $|A_i-B_i|$ is used as an index to each group, mainly is for simple hardware implementations. Each group has a corresponding feedforward network to learn all the patterns in the group.

All patterns in the same group are used to train a feedforward network. Since data in different groups are independent, eight feedforward neural networks can be trained at the same time. A feedforward neural network with 12 input neurons, 64 hidden neurons, and 11 output neurons is used for each group. All together eight neural networks are trained and tested through computer simulation. The learning rate has to be adjusted properly for the neural network to learn all the patterns. In other words, the learning rate is reduced as more patterns are learned. Table 3 presents the learning rate change versus the percentage of correct outputs.

After training, the feedforwad network is tested by another 800 inputs with different noise distribution. These 800 testing inputs are generated by adding different white Gaussian noise to the 200 input patterns. All test inputs are recognized successfully by the network. In all of the test cases, the signal to noise ratio (SNR) ranges from 5 db to 10 db.

3.2.2 Training for solving the frequency ambiguity

It is assumed that a medium PRF radar uses two PRF's, PRF 1 = 24K Hz, PRF 2 = 25K Hz, and has a bank of filters placed every 1000 Hz in hardware, i.e. the doppler frequency resolution is 1 KHz. The maximum target Doppler shift is 100K Hz. Because the maximum target Doppler shift is higher than any PRF, the frequency ambiguity exists.

Training data representation

There are 100 different output patterns corresponding to 100 target Doppler frequencies respectively. The input pattern is constructed by concatenating the target Doppler frequencies of PRF 1 and PRF 2. Both outputs and inputs are binary encoded. The output pattern requires 7 bits and the input pattern requires 10 bits (5 bits for PRF 1, another 5 bits for PRF 2). For example, if the target Doppler shift = 70K Hz, then this target falls into filter 22 (=70 mod 24) in the 24 kHz PRF, and into filter 20 (=70 mod 25) in the 25 kHz PRF. The input pattern for this specific target is 1011010100, and the output pattern is 1000110. Table 4 presents part of the training data.

Training procedures

A three-layer (one hidden) feedforward network is trained to learn these 100 patterns. The hidden layer has 64 neurons, the output layer 7 neurons, and the input layer 10 neurons. In order to learn these 100 patterns, the learning parameter η is dynamically changed according to learning rate shown in Table 5. The momentum used during training is kept as a constant (=0.9). The constant a, in equation $f(x)=\tanh(ax)$, to determine the slopeness of the sigmoid function is 3.3. Using the above parameters, the neural network has learned 100 patterns successfully. After training, the feedforward network is tested by 200 inputs generated by adding white Gaussian noise to the 100 input patterns. The network recognizes all 200 test patterns with SNR between 5 db to 10 db.

4. Analog Electronics Implementation

The simulation results indicate that the three-layer neural network solves the ambiguity problem. In this section, we describe the implementation of this feedforward neural network using intel's 80170NX analog neural chips [11]. Intel's 80170NX is a 64-neuron, 10240 synapse electrical trainable analog neural network which offers fully parallel processing performance in excess of 2 billion multiply-accumulate operations. This performance level can not be achieved by conventional computing techniques [7]. Training the 80170NX involves a chip-in-loop optimization process, as shown in Figure 1, which modifies the weights download to the chip on the off-line simulation according to the backpropagation learning algorithm. This chip-in-loop optimization process is essential to tune an analog device for high performance because of fabrication variations.

4.1 Analog neural system to solve range ambiguity

To design an electronic neural network to solve the range ambiguity problem, or other real problems of the same size, it is necessary to adopt the modular approach. There are 1501 patterns for the range ambiguity problem. These 1501 patterns are partitioned into 8 groups. A feedforward network is designed and trained for each group. Figure 2 shows the configuration of eight feedforward neural networks for solving the range ambiguity problem. Table 6 shows the learning rate of the chip-in-loop optimization process. The learning rate has to be adjusted dynamically in order to make the 80170NX learn all of the patterns; otherwise the 80170NX learns new patterns by sacrificing some of the patterns learned earlier. The momentum is not used during chip-in-loop training. The testing of the trained 80170NX shows that the noise immunity between the two levels of outputs, corresponding to 1 and 0 in Table 1, is 2.04V. The noise immunity is calculated as follows:

$$\text{noise immunity} = V_{HW} - V_{LW}$$

where V_{HW}, and V_{LW} are defined as the worst case output voltages for outputs corresponding to 1 and 0 respectively; whereas perfect output voltages for 1 and 0 are 3V and 0V.

4.2 Analog neural network for frequency ambiguity

Since there are only 100 patterns for the feedforward network to learn, one 80170NX is sufficient. Figure 3 presents the circuit diagram. The learning rate of the chip-in-loop optimization process for solving the frequency ambiguity problem is shown in Table 7. The momentum used in chip-in-loop training is kept constant (α=0.9). The testing of the trained 80170NX shows that the noise immunity between the two levels of outputs corresponding to 1 and 0 in Table 4 is 1.77V.

5. Discussions and Concluding Remarks

In modern radars range and range rate (Doppler) PRFs are combined through a computer search and selection process [4]. This is a sequential operation and takes some iterations to solve the ambiguity problem. The neural network approach is a parallel operation. Using the intel 80170NX, it takes 6 microseconds from receiving the input data to generating output data available on the output pins. The Sun3 Sparc workstation needs about 500 microseconds to find the solution based on Hovanessian's algorithm. This difference in speed is nearly a two order improvement in processing time. For time-critical defense applications where real-time response is highly desired, the feedforward multilayer neural network should provide a viable alternative to existing algorithmic approaches for this specific problem.

A modular approach is used in training and implementation in this research. The modular approach makes it possible to integrate several multilayer feedforward neural networks to solve a large scale real world problem. A theory is developed to support the mathematical foundation of the modular approach for this specific application problem. The problem size used in this research is the same as the real radar systems operating in the field. Both the simulation results and electronics implementation are presented in this paper.

References

[1] S.A. Hovanessian, "Medium PRF Performance Analysis," IEEE Trans. on Aerospace and Electronics Systems, Vol. ASE-18, No.3 May 1982, pp. 286-296.

[2] M.E. Skolnik, Radar Handbook, Mcgraw-Hill book company, 1970.

[3] S.A. Hovanessian, "An Algorithm for Calculation of Range in a Multiple PRF Radar," IEEE Trans. on Aerospace and Electronics Systems, Vol AES-12, No. 2, pp. 287-290, March. 1976.

[4] S.A. Hovanessian, Radar System Design and Analysis, Artech House, Inc. 1984.

[5] R.P. Lippmann, "An Introduction to Computing with Neural Nets," IEEE ASSP Magazine, pp. 4-22, April 1987.

[6] T. Kohonen, Self-Organization and Associative Memory, Second Edition, Springer-Verlag, 1988.

[7] J.J. Hopfield and D.W. Tank, "Neural Computation of Decisions in Optimization Problems," Biolog. Cybernetics. 52: 141-154, 1985.

[8] T. Sejnowski and C. Rosenberg, "Parallel Networks that Learn to Pronounce English Text," Complex Systems 1(1):145-168, 1987.

[9] R. P. Gorman and T.J. Sejnowski, "Analysis of Hidden Units in a Layered Network Trained to Classify Sonar Targets," Neural Networks vol. 1 pp. 75-89, 1988.

[10] T.W. Hungerford, Abstract Algebra An Introduction, Saunders College Publishing, 1990.

[11] Intel, 80170NX Electical Trainable Analog Neural Network, 1990.

Table 1. Part of the training data

Range	Input Pattern	Output Pattern
0.95km	001010001010	00000001010
9.95km	100101100111	00001100100
24.95km	111101000110	00011111010
54.95km	101110000001	01000100110
76.95km	001110100110	01100000010
94.95km	000101100011	01110110110
102.95km	010110110110	10000000110
124.95km	110101011110	10011100010
136.95km	101111011100	10101011010
148.95km	101001011010	10111010010

Table 2 Partition of the training data

group #	$\|A_i-B_i\|= K$	no. of patterns
group 1	$0\le K\le 4$	179
group 2	$4<K\le 7$	166
group 3	$7<K\le 12$	205
group 4	$12<K\le 17$	185
group 5	$17<K\le 23$	204
group 6	$23<K\le 30$	202
group 7	$30<K\le 38$	158
group 8	$38<K\le 60$	202

Table 3. Learning rate vs % of correct outputs

Learning rate η	% of correct outputs
0.1	0 - 50%
0.05	50% - 75%
0.025	75% - 90%
0.023	90% - 100%

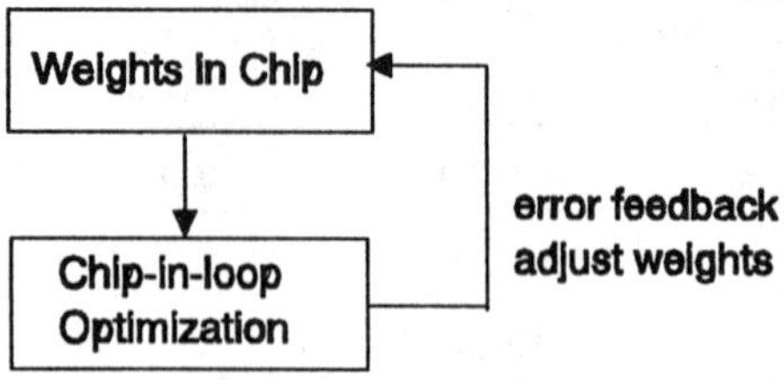

Figure 1. Chip-in-loop optimization

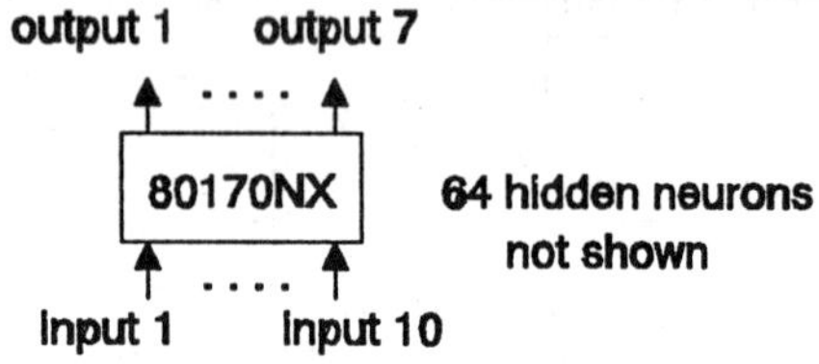

Figure 3. An analog neural chip to solve the frequency ambiguity problem

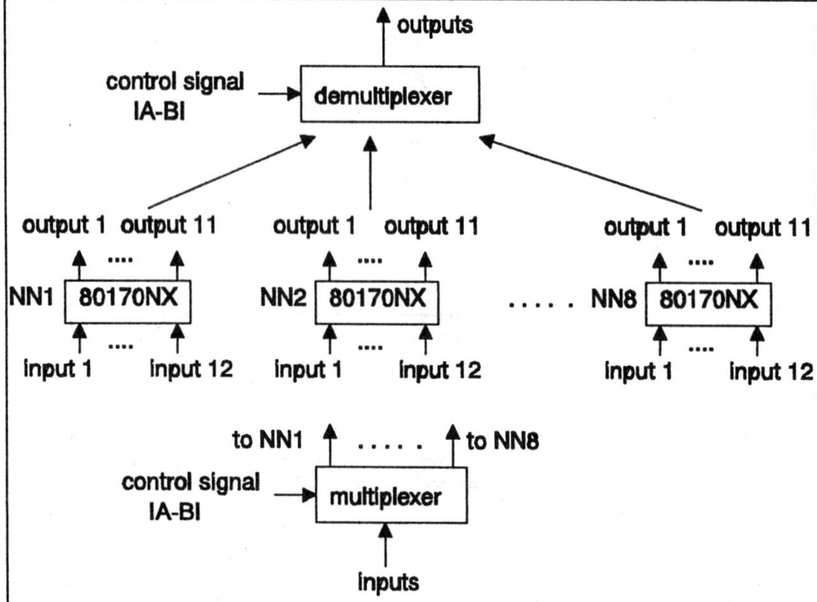

Figure 2. Configuration of eight neural networks to solve range ambiguity problem (64 hidden neurons not shown in the figure)

Table 4. part of the Doppler shift training data

Doppler Shift	Input Pattern	Output Pattern
10khz	0101001010	0001010
27khz	0001100010	0011011
45khz	1010110100	0101101
67khz	1001110001	1000011
84khz	0110001001	1010100
100khz	0010011001	1100100

Table 5. Learning rate vs. % of correct outputs

Learning rate η	% of correct outputs
0.05	0 - 50%
0.04	50% - 75%
0.03	75% - 90%
0.013	90% - 100%

Table 6. Learning rate used in chip optimization

Learning rate η	% of correct outputs
0.05	0 - 50%
0.04	50% - 75%
0.03	75% - 90%
0.01	90% - 100%

Table 7. Learning rate used in chip optimization

Learning rate η	% of correct outputs
0.04	0 - 50%
0.04	50% - 75%
0.03	75% - 90%
0.011	90% - 100%

A MODIFIED RECURRENT CASCADE-CORRELATION NETWORK FOR RADAR SIGNAL PULSE DETECTION

N. Karunanithi
2E-378, Bellcore
445, South Street
Morristown, NJ 07960
karun@faline.bellcore.com

D. Whitley
Computer Science Dept.
Colorado State Univ.
Fort Collins, CO 80523
whitley@cs.colostate.edu

D. Newman
Texas Instruments
5825 Mark Dabling Blvd.
Colorado Springs
CO 80919

Abstract: A Jordan-style cascade-correlation architecture is developed for radar signal pulse detection. Pulse detection is difficult for non-recurrent nets because signals are of varying length and networks using tapped delay lines to obtain inputs often fail to maintain an output signal during mid-pulse. Also, the cascade-correlation learning architecture was modified to facilitate hardware implementation of the network. The network was constructed using only two hidden layers, with nodes added to the layers in a lateral fashion. Comparisons to networks trained using back-propagation and genetic algorithms indicates that the cascade-correlation architecture trains approximately 50 times faster and produces much better generalization.

1 PROBLEM STATEMENT

The signal detection problem that we studied involves identifying radar signal pulses in one of several channels that span a frequency range. The signals are such that a valid signal causes "false signals", or "splatter" to appear in surrounding channels. These "false signals" should not be detected. Also it is necessary that there should not be a "false alarm" whenever there is no signal. The problem is further complicated by the fact that more than one valid signal may simultaneously exist across multiple channels.

The input signal for the detector is a logarithmic envelope of the amplitude of prefiltered outputs of radar returns. The actual pulse may occur anywhere within the envelope and can be of variable duration. There are 24 basic "signal events" in our data set and each signal event can occur somewhere across 21 channels (labeled 1 through 21). Of the 24 basic signal events, 10 are multiple pulse cases while the remaining 14 are single pulse cases. A signal event is called a *single pulse* (SP) if the pulse occurs on only one of the 21 channels at any given instance. A signal event is said to be a *multiple pulse* (MP) case if the useful pulses occur simultaneously on more than one channel. All

0-7803-0928-6/93$03.00

signal events are of equal duration and each signal event is represented in terms of approximately 2000 equally spaced samples that are 1 nanosecond apart. (However, the actual pulses within the signal events can be of variable duration.) If all 21 channels are considered then all signal events can be represented in terms of 1.008 million time slices. The signal space can be further characterized as highly sparse because: 1) not all signal events contain target pulses, and 2) only a small fraction of the samples within a channel contain useful information (i.e., those samples that represent the region where the pulse is present). The problem requires not only identifying whether the pulse is present (amplitude detection) in the signal event but also to locate the position as well as the duration of the pulse within the channel. There are several outputs in the signal detector corresponding to the width of the pulse, time of arrival and frequency information. The outputs from the detector are then fed to a postprocessing unit for further analysis. The objective of this study was to develop a connectionist network that can detect the presence of pulse(s) in signal events.

Over the past 3 years we have trained neural networks for the radar signal pulse detection problem using 1) traditional back-propagation [5], 2) a genetic hill-climbing algorithm [8], 3) a non-recurrent Cascade-Correlation learning architecture algorithm [2] and 4) a variant of Jordan-style recurrent net [3] developed by the Cascade-Correlation algorithm. Our empirical data indicate that the Cascade-Correlation algorithm produces superior results compared to the other two algorithms, both in terms of learning speed (approximately 50 times faster that the backpropagation) and in terms of generalization [6,7]. Here we present results from only the Cascade-Correlation correlation algorithm.

2 EXPERIMENTAL APPROACH

2.1 A Training Data Selection Method

In this study, it is assumed that all 24 signal events occur on either channel 10 or channel 11. Thus, it became necessary to test for all 24 signal events on both channels 10 and 11 (i.e., there are 48 signal events in the test set). Among 24 signal events on each channel, only 8 were used for selecting training data because they typify most of the peculiarities present in the signal space. Of these 8 selected signal events 6 were single pulse cases and the remaining 2 were multiple pulse cases. Selecting samples from these selected signal events at random may not produce a meaningful training set because majority of the samples belong to noninformative regions. In order to study the influence of training data selection method, five training sets (of sizes 364, 434, 546, 634 and 815 respectively) were constructed by manually selecting samples from both transition and nontransition regions. Furthermore, the number of samples from each signal event was also varied depending on the duration and nature of the pulse as well as the noise characteristics of the signal events.

Since the signals occurring on a particular channel can be affected by the interference from the adjacent channels, an equal number of samples from the two side channels (one above and one below) were also included in the training set. These samples could be helpful in identifying "splatters". In the single pulse case, channel 11 was considered as the main channel and channels 10 and 12 as the side channels whereas in the multiple pulse case, both channels 10 and 11 were considered as the main channels. (In the multiple pulse case, if channel 10 was considered as the main channel then channels 9 and 11 would act as the side channels; on the other hand, if channel 11 was the main channel then channels 10 and 12 would be the side channels.) Some of the signal events are shown in solid lines at the top of Figures 1 through 4. The dash lines at the bottom of these figures represent the target pulses.

2.2 Network Models Used

In order to evaluate the generalization performance of connectionist networks, both feedforward networks and a variant of Jordan style recurrent networks were examined. The input layer of the feedforward network had 8 inputs (1 signal + 7 delays) corresponding to the main channel and 4 inputs (1 signal + 3 delays) for each side channel. The output layer of the networks had six units corresponding to the width of the pulse, time of arrival and frequency information. The tapped delay line was added to the input because the actual hardware implementation of the signal detector would incorporate delay lines on the input terminals.

Since the training sets have more samples from the transition regions, the feedforward network was successful in detecting both the rising and falling edges of the pulse but had difficulty in recognizing the middle of the pulse, especially if the pulse had a long duration. This problem can partially be addressed by using a training set that has a large number of midpulse samples. However, if the network has to detect pulses based only on amplitude information and if there are two or more inputs that are similar but their outputs are opposite then it is possible for the network to produce an incorrect output. Increasing the size of the training set is of no avail because the feedforward networks cannot perform one-to-many mapping. To address this situation, the network must develop contextual information in the form of memory based on the previous state (or, output) values. The recurrent network models can be used to address this issue.

One logical choice for the recurrent network model would be to use Elman's recurrent network [1] which is simple and is capable of developing memory based on hidden unit activations of the previous time steps. However, the Elman network can produce meaningful result only when the samples are presented in a continuous fashion. Hence the sampling strategy used for constructing the training sets precludes the use of Elman network because samples were selected only from a subset of discrete locations. So, as an alternative we used a variant of Jordan style recurrent networks with "teacher forced" training outputs. In this network the recurrent connections from the output layer were fed to the hidden units. All the recurrent connections had a fixed weight of strength 1.0. Under teacher forced training, the teacher outputs at the time $t-1$ were used as the feedback at time t. The output of the network at time t was a function of the current input and the previous output. Thus, training this style of Jordan network is equivalent to training a feedforward network in which the input consists of both the actual input at time t and the target output at time $t-1$. The resulting Jordan network had 16 input units for the tapped delay inputs and 6 additional input units for the feedback from the output layer. However, when a Jordan network is tested for generalization the actual output of the network (not the target output) are recirculated as the input to the feedback input units. In this study, both the feedforward network and the Jordan style networks were developed and trained using Fahlman et al's Cascade-Correlation algorithm [2].

2.3 Hardware Implementation Consideration

Since the Cascade-Correlation algorithm adds one unit for each hidden layer and each hidden unit receives fan-in connections from all the earlier hidden units as well as the input layer the resulting networks can be very deep and may not be appropriate for analog hardware implementation because of the noise problem. To facilitate hardware implementation, a modification was made to the Cascade-Correlation algorithm such that it builds a 2 hidden layer network instead of a deep multilayer network [4]. The modified algorithm constructs networks by adding a predefined number of hidden units to the first hidden layer and as many units in the second hidden layer as needed. In the experiments reported here, approximately 20 hidden units were added to the first hidden layer. (The size of the first hidden layer was empirically determined by trial-and-error.) While constructing hidden layers, the algorithm adds hidden units only in a lateral fashion. Thus, the hidden units in the first hidden layer receive fan-in connections only from the input layer and the units in the second hidden layer receive fan-in connections from both the input and the first hidden layers. (We also experimented with an another version of the Cascade-Correlation algorithm which developed nets with 1 hidden layer. However, the resulting generalization and the size of the network were not satisfactory.)

3 RESULTS

In order to evaluate the generalization performance of different network models it is necessary to use a proper test set. Since the networks were trained using a very small subset of signals on the main (channel 11) and the side channels, it would be appropriate to test the networks by using the remaining samples that were not part of the training set. So a test set containing 96,000 samples from all 48 signal events (24 signal events on channels 10 and 11 respectively) was constructed.

To evaluate the influence of different training sets, the generalization performance of feedforward networks trained using 5 training sets were compared. The results reported here are from the networks that produced the best results. In order to compare the performance of the networks, the outputs are classified into different categories such as "Correct +", "Correct -", "Noisy +", "Noisy -", "False +" and "False -".

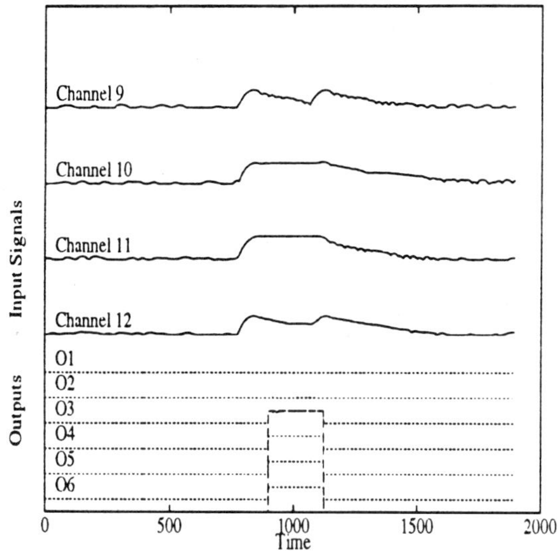

Figure 1: Generalization result of a multilayer FFN network trained with 815 samples for SP1-CH11.

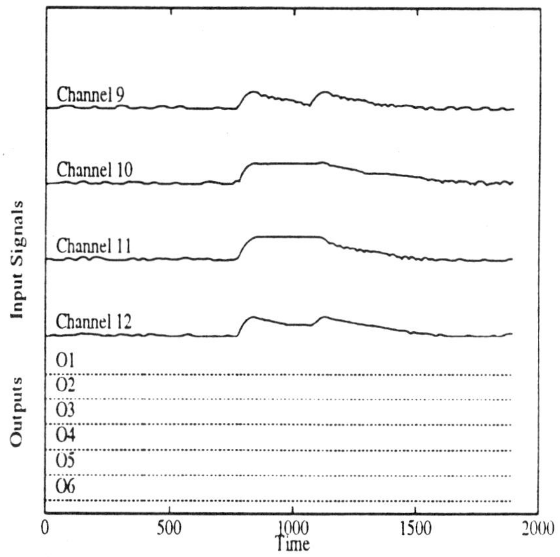

Figure 2: Generalization result of a multilayer FFN network trained with 815 samples for SP1-CH10.

A response is classified as "Correct +" if the network's output matches the target pulse in terms of its location, amplitude and duration. A "Correct -" response occurs if the output of the network is low for the entire duration

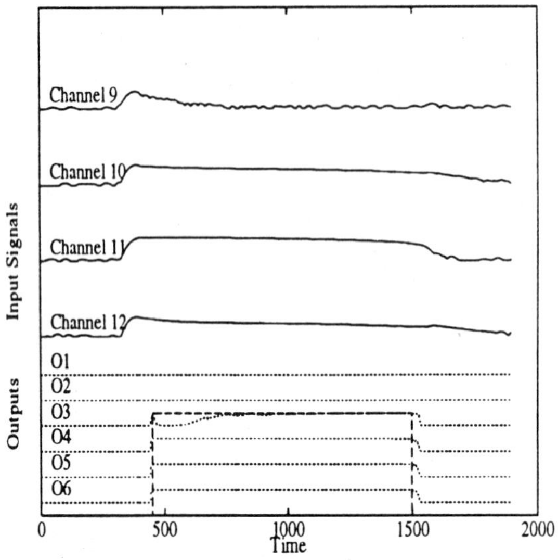

Figure 3: Generalization result of a multilayer FFN network trained with 815 samples for SP7-CH11.

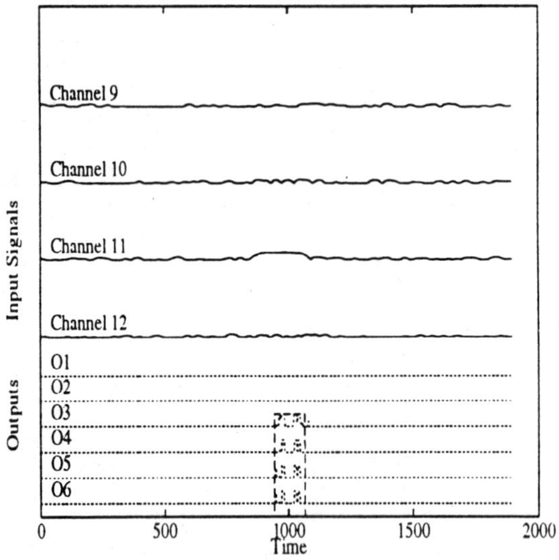

Figure 4: Generalization result of a multilayer FFN network trained with 815 samples for SP8-CH11.

of the signal event in the absence of a pulse. Responses that are positive, but either the duration is wrong or turns on and off during the signal are indicated as "Noisy +". "Noisy -" responses occur when the network very briefly indicates a signal; these responses appear to be brief enough that they can be identified and ignored. A "False +" response occurs when the network comes on for a sufficient duration at places where there is no target pulse. A "False -" occurs if the network does not indicate a signal at places where there is a pulse. Some typical outputs of a multilayer feedforward network trained using 815 samples are illustrated in Figures 1 through 4. The topmost 4 graphs in each figure (solid lines) represent the actual signals that appeared on channels 9 through 12. The "dotted" lines represent the six outputs of the network and the "dashed line" represent the envelope of the target events.

Figure 1 represents the output of the network for the single pulse signal event 1 on channel 11 (SP1-Ch11). This is one of the single pulse signal events from which training samples were selected. Of 2000 samples in SP1-Ch11, only 42 were selected for training. This illustrates how well the network learned to detect the entire pulse only from limited training samples. In this case, the response of the network was "Correct +". The output of the network for one of the side channels (SP1-CH10) is illustrated in Figure 2. Even though the side channel signal also has similar amplitude as that of the main channel, the network was successful in detecting the signal event as a single pulse case in an adjacent channel. Figure 3 illustrates the "Correct +" response of the network for a single pulse signal event (SP7-CH11) that was not part of the training set. Figure 4 represents another test case (SP8-CH11) in which the network produced a "Noisy +" response. SP8-CH11 is one of the difficult cases because the amplitude of the signal was not high.

Figures 1 through 4 illustrate the response of the network only for 4 of 48 test cases. A summary of the network response for all 48 signal events is presented in Table 1. In this table, the signal events that are marked ⊗ were sampled for training data. The "X" in each row denotes the response of the network for that particular signal event. Table 2 shows the effect of training size. The first column represents the signal types and the channels on which the network was tested. (For example, SP*-Ch11 indicates that *all* SP signal events on channel 11 were considered in obtaining these results.) The values in each row represents the number of times the network classified the signal events into that particular category and were obtained by combining both the + and - responses. By comparing the values across each column, the following observations can be made: i) the network response in majority of the test cases were correct, and ii) as the training set size was increased the generalization performance of the network has also increased considerably across all signal types. This trend can be seen not only across different pulses but also across the channels. Thus, these results suggest that generalization can be improved by properly selecting training samples from the regions in which the actual pulses occur.

In order to study the generalization performance of the two hidden layer network another learning experiment was conducted using feedforward nets constructed by the modified Cascade-Correlation algorithm. A summary of comparative test results are shown Table 3. The results in Table 3 suggests that the difference in performance between the multilayer feedforward network and the 2 hidden layer feedforward network is not significant. The 2 hidden

Table 1: GENERALIZATION RESULTS OF A MULTILAYER FEEDFORWARD NET TRAINED WITH 815 SAMPLES.

Signal Event	Classification						Signal Event	Classification					
	Correct		Noisy		False			Correct		Noisy		False	
	+	−	+	−	+	−		+	−	+	−	+	−
SP1-CH11 ⊗	X						SP1-CH10 ⊗		X				
SP2-CH11 ⊗	X						SP2-CH10 ⊗				X		
SP3-CH11	X						SP3-CH10				X	X	
SP4-CH11				X			SP4-CH10		X				
SP5-CH11			X	X			SP5-CH10				X		
SP6-CH11 ⊗	X						SP6-CH10 ⊗				X		
SP7-CH11	X						SP7-CH10				X	X	
SP8-CH11			X				SP8-CH10		X				
SP9-CH11 ⊗	X						SP9-CH10 ⊗		X				
SP10-CH11⊗	X						SP10-CH10⊗		X				
SP11-CH11		X					SP11-CH10		X				
SP12-CH11			X				SP12-CH10					X	
SP13-CH11⊗		X					SP13-CH10⊗				X		
SP14-CH11		X					SP14-CH10		X				
MP1-CH11		X					MP1-CH10		X				
MP2-CH11		X					MP2-CH10		X				
MP3-CH11			X				MP3-CH10		X				
MP4-CH11				X	X		MP4-CH10		X				
MP5-CH11 ⊗	X						MP5-CH10⊗	X					
MP6-CH11			X				MP6-CH10				X		
MP7-CH11 ⊗	X						MP7-CH10⊗		X				
MP8-CH11		X					MP8-CH10		X				
MP9-CH11		X					MP9-CH10		X				
MP10-CH11		X					MP10-CH10		X				

layer feedforward network has improved its performance over the multilayer network in terms of the number of "Correct" and "Noisy" classifications for Sp*-Ch11, SP*-Ch10 and MP*-Ch11. However, the 2 hidden layer network did not reduce the number of "False" classifications in all cases. On the other hand, the multilayer network's performance is slightly better than the 2 hidden layer network in all categories of MP*-CH10. Thus, these results suggest that one could use a 2 hidden layer feedforward network to get almost the same performance as that of a deep network.

To evaluate how well the modified Jordan network performs, another experiment was conducted using modified Jordan nets constructed by the modified Cascade-Correlation algorithm. The modified Jordan network also had the almost same number of hidden units as that of the feedforward networks with 2 hidden layers. The performance of the two hidden layer Jordan network is shown in the last column of Table 3. It is clear that the performance of the two hidden layer Jordan network is better than both the multilayer feedforward network and the two hidden layer feedforward network in SP*-CH10, SP*-CH11 and MP*-CH11 and as good as that of the best feedforward network (i.e., the multilayer feedforward network) in MP*-CH10. The number of "Correct" classifications of the modified Jordan network has considerably increased in single pulse cases (on both channel 10 and 11) as well as in multiple pulse cases on channel 11. Also, the number of "False" and "Noisy" classifications has been considerably reduced in all signal events. Thus, these

Table 2: GENERALIZATION RESULTS OF MULTILAYER FEEDFORWARD NETS TRAINED WITH DIFFERENT TRAINING SETS.

Signal Event	Classification	Training Set Size				
		364	434	564	634	815
SP*-CH11	Correct	7	8	9	10	10
	Noisy	8	7	5	5	5
	False	0	1	0	1	0
SP*-CH10	Correct	5	5	6	7	7
	Noisy	8	7	6	6	6
	False	5	5	5	5	3
MP*-CH11	Correct	6	7	7	7	7
	Noisy	5	4	2	3	3
	False	1	1	2	1	1
MP*-CH10	Correct	5	7	7	7	9
	Noisy	5	3	3	2	1
	False	1	1	1	1	0

Table 3: GENERALIZATION RESULTS OF DIFFERENT NETWORK MODELS TRAINED WITH 815 SAMPLES.

Signal Event	Classification	Network Model Used		
		Multilayer FFN	FFN with 2 hid. layer	JN with 2 hid. layer
SP*-CH11	Correct	10	11	13
	Noisy	5	2	1
	False	0	1	1
SP*-CH10	Correct	7	11	12
	Noisy	6	1	1
	False	3	3	1
MP*-CH11	Correct	7	7	9
	Noisy	3	2	1
	False	1	1	0
MP*-CH10	Correct	9	8	9
	Noisy	1	2	1
	False	0	1	0

results suggest that the modified Jordan network model is better than the feedforward networks in this signal detection application. This improvement in performance of the modified Jordan network may be due to the fact that the network is able to maintain the output signal until it detects the trailing edge of the pulse using the previous state information. The use of the previous state information is helpful not only in identifying correct duration of the pulse but also in suppressing noisy inputs.

4 SUMMARY

This paper demonstrated the applicability of training data selection methods for improving generalization in connectionist networks using a problem that is closely related to a real world application. The results presented here show that the performance of the connectionist networks can be improved by increasing the training set size with samples from regions in which useful information is available, Thus selecting training data according to their importance should be preferred over a random sample. However, this data selection method can be applied only to domains in which the problem space is known and where the data is readily available.

It is also demonstrated how different network models can be used to improve generalization in connectionist networks. The results from the modified Jordan style recurrent network suggested that a simple feedback from the output layer can be valuable in developing a limited contextual information for the network. Furthermore, this style of recurrent network is simple to implement and allows the network to process inputs that are temporally discontinuous.

The applicability of the modified Cascade-Correlation algorithm is also demonstrated. One main advantage with the modified Cascade-Correlation algorithm is that it can produce a two hidden layer network which is easy to implement in hardware. Furthermore, the 2 hidden layer networks have simpler layered connections than the multilayer networks developed by the standard Cascade-Correlation algorithm. One drawback of the modified algorithm is that the number of hidden units in a 2 hidden layer network may be larger than an equivalent multilayer network. However, it is quite straight forward to identify the redundant units in such networks and prune them without too much additional effort.

REFERENCES

[1] Elman, J. L., "Finding Structure in Time", *Cognitive Science*, no. 14, pp. 179-211, 1990.

[2] Fahlman, S. E., and Lebiere, C., "The Cascaded-Correlation Learning Architecture". School of Computer Science, Carnegie Mellone University, Tech. Rep. CMU-CS-90-100, Feb. 1990.

[3] Jordan, M. I., "Attractor Dynamics and Parallelism in a Connectionist Sequential Machine", *Proc. 8th Annual Conf. of the Cognitive Science*, pp. 531-546, 1986.

[4] Karunanithi, N., "Generalization in the Cascade-Correlation Architecture: Some Experiments and Applications". *Ph.D. Dissertation*, Computer Science Dept., Colorado State Unive rsity, Fort Collins, CO, Fall 1992.

[5] Rumelhart, D., Hinton, G., and Williams, R., "Learning Internal Representations by Error Propagation", **Parallel Distributed Processing, Vol. I**, MIT Press, pp. 318-362, 1986.

[6] Whitley, D., "Solving Signal Detection and Sonar Problems Using Neural Networks". Final Report, *The Colorado Institute of Artificial Intelligence*, 1992.

[7] Whitley, D., and Karunanithi, N., "Generalization in Feedforward Neural Networks". *Proc. Int. Joint Conf. on Neural Networks, Seattle, WA.*, Vol. II, 77-82, July 1991.

[8] Whitley, D., Starkweather, T., and Bogart, C., "Genetic Algorithms and Neural Networks: Optimizing Connections and Connectivity", *Parallel Computing*, vol. 14, pp. 347-361, 1990.

A Cascaded Recurrent Neural Networks for Real-Time Nonlinear Adaptive Filtering

Liang Li *and* Simon Haykin
Communications Research Laboratory
McMaster University
Hamilton, Ontario, Canada L8S 4K1

Abstract—A new form of recurrent neural network, referred to as a cascaded recurrent neural networks (CRNN), is described. This network can perform temporally extended tasks. A learning procedure is described for adjusting the weights in the network in order to produce a desired input-output relation in the time-domain. An important feature of CRNN is that it can perform real-time nonlinear adaptive filtering. This application is illustrated by exploring the nonlinear prediction of chaotic signals.

1 Introduction

Recurrent neural networks are important because they can perform temporally extended tasks, giving them considerable power beyond the static mapping performed by the now-familiar multilayer feedforward networks. This ability to perform highly nonlinear dynamic mapping makes these networks particularly useful in tasks that have an important temporal component not easily handled through the use of simple tapped delay lines[1].

In this paper, we describe a new neural network, referred to as a **Cascaded Recurrent Neural Networks (CRNN)**. The operation of the new network is based on two principles: modularity, and recurrent processing.

The CRNN is well suited for real-time nonlinear adaptive filtering. The operation of the network involves the combined use of three operations: (1) real-time learning and nonlinear filtering performed by a recurrent neural network, (2) linear recursive least squares estimation, and (3) linear least square prediction.

2 Cascaded Recurrent Neural Networks

Artificial neural network theory is motivated by biological considerations. In this context, it appears that modularity is an important principle in the architecture of the vertebrate neural system. Houk and Wise[2] point out that in such a system there are a few basic types of information processing modules, and that these modules are used iteratively to process information bearing signals. A module consists of several neurons and their interconnections.

From the viewpoint of biological modularity, a recurrent neural network model can be treated as an information module. Such a network model, consisting of several neurons that are fully connected, offers a rich set of possibilities for representing the internal state of a dynamic system. In a manner similar to the biological module, one recurrent neural network can iteratively process information bearing signals, and several recurrent neural networks can be cascaded to construct a larger neural network.

With modularity and recurrence as the guiding principles, we show in Figure 1 the structure of a neural network consisting of the cascaded connection of M_c modules with overall feedback from module 1 to module M_c. Each module consists of a recurrent neural network with a few neurons, which is shown in Figure 2. In addition to the M external inputs, there are N other inputs, representing the outputs of a previous module. Let $\mathbf{y}(n-i)$ denote the N-tuple output vector of the ith module at n^{th} time point, and let $\mathbf{u}(n-i)$ denote the M-tuple external input signal vector to the module at time n. We define $\mathbf{u}_{bf}(n-i)$ to be the M-tuple feedback input vector, which is the output of the previous module. The network weight matrix $\mathbf{W}$ of every module is chosen to have the same

0-7803-0999-5/93/$03.00

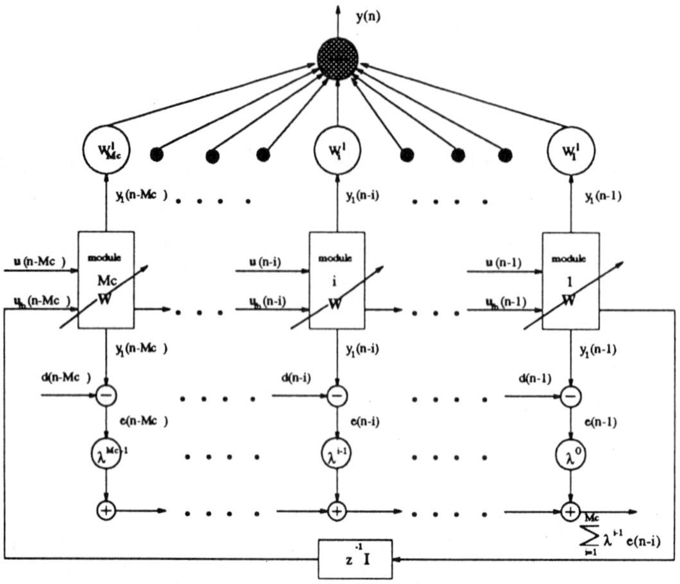

Figure 1: Cascaded Recurrent Neural Networks (CRNN)

value. Note further that to accommodate a bias for each note, beside the M input lines, we include one input whose value is always 1.

Further, biological considerations indicate that proper coordinations between the various connected modules is likely to produce a global learning mechanism in addition to the module-specific mechanisms. We also use this principle in the new neural network. A linear system is used to combine the outputs of the different recurrent neural networks. The overall output of the cascaded neural networks is the weighted sum of the outputs of the individual modules. The weight vector of the linear output network is denoted by $\mathbf{w}^l$.

3 Real-Time Learning of the New Neural Network

Here we consider an algorithm for training the cascaded recurrent networks to perform supervised temporal learning tasks.

The real-time learning algorithm of recurrent neural network is described by Williams and Zipser [3]. It is assumed that there is only one output node in every recurrent neural network, which is connected to the linear output network. The input layer is made up of M external input nodes and N feedback nodes. The upper layer is the computational layer of the network, consisting of N neurons. So, there are N feedback paths (including the output of the network). Let $\mathbf{u}(n)$ denote the $M-by-1$ external input vector, and $\mathbf{y}(n)$ denote the output vector at time n. The basic building block of the filter is a "neuron", which performs a weighted sum of the inputs and computes an "activation function", described by:

$$\begin{aligned} \hat{y}_k(n) &= \Phi[\hat{v}_k(n)], \qquad (1) \\ \hat{v}_k(n) &= \sum_{l=1}^{M} w_{kl}(n-1)u_l(n) + \\ & \sum_{l=M+1}^{M+N} w_{kl}(n-1)\hat{y}_l(n-1) \end{aligned}$$

where $w_{kl}(n-1)$ is the weight on the link between input node l and neuron k calculated at $(n-1)^{th}$ time point, $u_l(n)$ is the extra input scalar at l^{th} node$(1 \le l \le N)$, and $\hat{y}_k(n)$ denotes the output of neuron k at the nth time point in the ith module, where $1 \le k \le N$, and $1 \le l \le M+N$.

From the viewpoint of an adaptive filter, the recurrent neural network is a nonlinear recursive filter. At the nth time point, the input-output relation of the neural network may also be written as

$$\hat{\mathbf{y}}(n) = \Phi[\mathbf{W}(n-1), \mathbf{u}(n), \hat{\mathbf{y}}(n-1)] \qquad (2)$$

where $\mathbf{W}(n-1)$ is the weight matrix of the recurrent neural network at the $(n-1)^{th}$ time point, $\mathbf{u}(n)$ is the input vector at n^{th} time point, and $\hat{\mathbf{y}}(n)$ is prediction vector at the same time point. The function $\Phi(\cdot)$ is a nonlinear function.

The CRNN consists of M_c recurrent neural networks. At the nth time point, suppose that

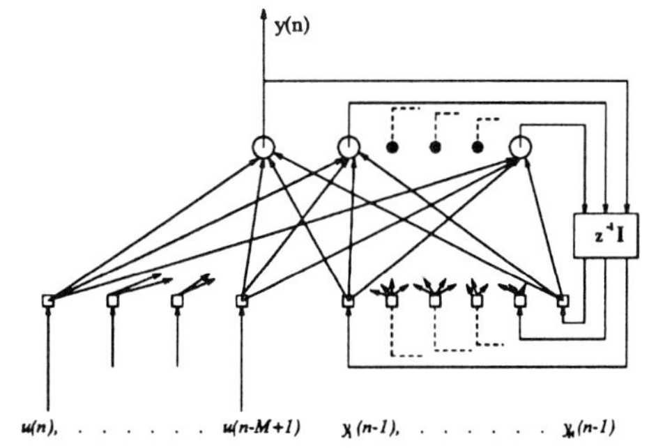

Figure 2: Recurrent Neural Network with a Single Output; z^{-1} denotes the Unit-delay Operator, and $\mathbf{I}$ denotes the Identify Matrix.

the time series is made up of the observations $u(1), u(2), \cdots, u(n)$. For real time learning, M successive sample points of the time series are used as the external inputs of every recurrent neural network sequentially.

For convenience of notation, we define the $M-by-1$ input vector of the ith module as

$$\begin{aligned} \mathbf{u}(n-i) &= [u_1(n-i), \cdots, u_M(n-i)]^T \qquad (3) \\ &= [u(n-i), \cdots, u(n-i-M+1)]^T \end{aligned}$$

where M is the number of external input nodes.

Consider next the contribution made by the feedback signals, which is the output of the previous module. With each recurrent neural network containing N output neurons, we may define an $N-by-1$ "feedback input vector" $\mathbf{u}_{fb}(n-i)$ of the ith module as:

$$\begin{aligned} \mathbf{u}_{fb}(n-i) &= \hat{\mathbf{y}}(n-i-1) \qquad (4) \\ &= [u_{bf_{M+1}}(n-i), \cdots, u_{bf_{M+N}}(n-i)]^T \\ &= [\hat{y}_1(n-i-1), \cdots, \hat{y}_N(n-i-1)]^T \end{aligned}$$

where $\hat{\mathbf{y}}(n-i-1)$ is the output vector of $(i+1)^{th}$ module.

The composite data matrix $\mathbf{A}$ formed by combining every external input data vector and feedback input data vector for the M_c modules at the nth time point, can be rewritten as:

$$\mathbf{A}(n-1) = \begin{bmatrix} \mathbf{u}(n-1) & \cdots & \mathbf{u}(n-M_c) \\ \mathbf{u}_{fb}(n-1) & \cdots & \mathbf{u}_{fb}(n-M_c) \end{bmatrix} \qquad (5)$$

For real time learning, the corresponding desired response vector of the M_c modules at the same time point is

$$\mathbf{d}(n-1) = [d(n-1), \cdots, d(d-M_c)]^T \qquad (6)$$

The real-time recurrent learning algorithm is used on every neural network module in the cascaded structure. For convenience of computation, we assume that the weight matrix $\mathbf{W}(n-1)$ has the same value for each module.

For the ith module, the output and error signals are defined by, respectively,

$$\begin{aligned} \hat{y}_k(n-i) &= \Phi(\hat{v}_k(n-i)) \qquad (7) \\ \hat{v}_k(n-i) &= \sum_{l=1}^{M} w_{kl}(n-1)u_l(n-i) + \\ &\quad \sum_{l=M+1}^{M+N} w_{kl}(n-1)u_{bf_l}(n-i) \\ e(n-i) &= d(n-i) - \hat{y}_1(n-i) \qquad (8) \end{aligned}$$

where $\hat{y}_k(n-i)$ is the output of the kth neuron$(1 \leq i \leq M_c)$.

We use the stochastic gradient estimation algorithm to update the weight matrix of the recurrent neural network. The sum of squared errors for the individual recurrent modules is the cost function of the cascaded array. Also, it is customary to introduce a forgetting factor λ $(0 < \lambda \leq 1)$ into the definition of the cost function $E(n)$. We thus write

$$E(n) = \sum_{i=1}^{M_c} \lambda^{i-1} e^2(n-i) \qquad (9)$$

We take as objective the minimization of the cost function $E(n)$. So, the gradient estimation algorithm is used to calculate the $\triangle \mathbf{W}$ along the negative of the gradient $\nabla_{\mathbf{W}} E(n)$. The weight change for the kl^{th} element in the weight matrix can be written

$$\begin{aligned}\triangle w_{kl} &= -\eta \frac{\partial}{\partial w_{kl}} (\sum_{i=1}^{M_c} \lambda^{i-1} e^2(n-i)) \\ &= -2\eta \sum_{i=1}^{M_c} \lambda^{i-1} e(n-i) \frac{\partial e(n-i)}{\partial w_{kl}} \end{aligned} \tag{10}$$

where η is a fixed learning rate parameter.

Using the real-time recurrent learning algorithm, we write

$$\frac{\partial e(n-i)}{\partial w_{kl}} = -\sum_{\beta=1}^{N} \frac{\partial \hat{y}_\beta(n-i)}{\partial w_{kl}} \tag{11}$$

$$\begin{aligned}\frac{\partial \hat{y}_\beta(n-i)}{\partial w_{kl}} &= \Phi'_\beta(v_\beta(n-i)) * \\ & [\sum_{\alpha=1}^{N} w_{\beta\alpha}(n-1) \frac{\partial \hat{y}_\alpha((n-1)-i)}{\partial w_{kl}} + \\ & \delta_{k\alpha} u_l(n-i)]\end{aligned}$$

where $\delta_{k\alpha}$ denotes the Kronecker delta, $\Phi'_\beta(v_\beta(n-i))$ is the derivative of the nonlinear function Φ_β for i^{th} module at n^{th} time point, and $\hat{y}_\alpha((n-1)-i)$ is the output of neuron α in the ith module at the $n-1^{th}$ time point.

Finally, we write

$$\mathbf{W}(n) = \mathbf{W}(n-1) + \triangle \mathbf{W} \tag{12}$$

and the modified output

$$\begin{aligned} y_1(n-i) &= \Phi(v_1(n-i)) \\ v_1(n-i) &= \sum_{l=1}^{M} w_{1l}(n) u_l(n-i) + \\ & \sum_{l=M+1}^{M+N} w_{1l}(n) u_{bf_l}(n-i) \end{aligned} \tag{13}$$

The outputs of the M_c cascaded modules form an $M_c - by - 1$ output vector:

$$\mathbf{y}_o(n-1) = [y_1(n-1), y_1(n-2), \cdots, y_1(n-M_c)]^T \tag{14}$$

This output vector is used as the input to the linear output part of the CRNN.

At the nth time point, we obtain the prediction output of the CRNN

$$\hat{y}(n) = \mathbf{w}^{l^T}(n-1)\mathbf{y}_o(n-1) \tag{15}$$

The weight vector $\mathbf{w}^l$ is updated in accordance with the Least-Mean-Square(LMS) algorithm[4]:

$$\begin{aligned} e(n) &= d(n) - \hat{y}(n) \quad (16) \\ \mathbf{w}^l(n) &= \mathbf{w}^l(n-1) + \mu \mathbf{y}_o(n-1) e(n) \quad (17) \end{aligned}$$

where μ is another positive learning rate parameter.

The operation described herein constitutes a real-time training of the neural network.

From the viewpoint of an adaptive filter, the last step of this real-time learning algorithm is similar to the regular LMS algorithm. The vector $\mathbf{y}_o(n-1)$ is calculated using the nonlinear recurrent neural modules. The cascaded recurrent neural networks provide pre-processing for the linear prediction part. Moreover, every recurrent neural network provides a local interpolation for M time-series points. The M_c modules process the time series $u(n), u(n-1), \cdots, u(1)$ and provide M_c local interpolations sequentially. The final linear prediction thus presents a "global" interpolation with good localization properties.

4 Algorithm of Real-Time Nonlinear Adaptive Prediction

An important attribute of the CRNN is that it is suitable for nonlinear adaptive filtering. Moreover, network training and prediction are performed on line. In other words, the parameters are adjusted continually while the filter is being used; thus "training" never stops during processing the time series.

For real-time training and prediction, one of the key problems is to know how to determine the initial values of $\mathbf{W}$ and $\mathbf{w}^l$. The initial weights may influence the convergence speed and accuracy of the real-time learning and adaptive prediction.

We introduce a prior training method to determine suitable values for initial weights before the real-time training and prediction calculations begin. The traditional epochwise training method is a time-consuming training method. But it is a stable and reliable training method. So, before using the cascaded recurrent neural network, the epochwise training method is used to train the individual modules and the linear output network with some sample points of the time series.

For a given time series, the algorithm of the real-time nonlinear adaptive prediction proceeds as follows:

1. Determine the number of external inputs M at the input level, and the number of neurons N

at the upper lever for every module. Choose a suitable number of modules, M_c.

2. With a few time series points, initial values of the weights $\mathbf{W}$ for each module are determined by using the epochwise training method. The outputs of the trained recurrent neural networks are used to train the weight vector $\mathbf{w}^l$ of the linear output network.

3. Begin the adaptive training and prediction calculation at $n = C$, where C is the first point of real-time adaptive processing.

4. Input time series point $u(n)$ and construct the data matrix $\mathbf{A}(n-1)$ and desired data vector $\mathbf{d}(n-1)$.

   For one-step prediction, $\mathbf{d}(n-1)$ is

   $$\mathbf{d}(n-1) = [u(n), u(n-1), \cdots, u(n-M_c+1)]^T \tag{18}$$

5. Using the real-time recurrent neural network algorithm, calculate the prediction and error for every module: $\hat{y}_1(n-i)$ and $e(n-i)$ $(1 \leq i \leq M_c)$; hence, update the weight matrix $\mathbf{W}_{n-1}$ to $\mathbf{W}_n$ and calculate the modified prediction of every module $y_1(n-1), \cdots, y_1(n-M_c)$.

6. Using the linear LMS algorithm, obtain the prediction $\hat{y}(n)$ and update the weight vector $\mathbf{w}^l(n)$. $\hat{y}(n)$ is the prediction value of $u(n+1)$ based on the time series $u(1), u(2), \cdots, u(n)$.

7. Let $n = n+1$ and return to 4.

The computational requirement for the real-time learning of the CRNN consists of both the computation of the M_c recurrent neural networks and the computation of the LMS algorithm. The computational requirement of the LMS algorithm is only $2M_c + 1$ multiplications and $2M_c$ additions per iteration, where M_c is the number of cascaded modules. The computational requirement of every recurrent neural network is $O(N^4)$ arithmetic operations, where N is the number of neuron in every neural module. So, the computational requirement of the CRNN is about $O(M_c * N^4 + 4M_c)$ arithmetic operations per time step. Simulation results with the CRNN model to solve a prediction problem show that we can choose a small size for each module, with only a few neurons N in every module. On the other hand, to solve the same problem with a single real-time recurrent neural network, N_r neurons are needed in the upper layer with $N_r \gg N$. The computational requirement of the latter structure is about $O(N_r^4)$. Therefore, ignoring the term $4M_c$ compared to $M_c N^4$, the computational requirements of training the new neural network is less than that for a single recurrent neural network, provided that $N < N_r M_c^{-\frac{1}{4}}$.

5 Calculations and Analysis

In this section, we calculate and analyze the real-time adaptive prediction for a chaotic time series and sea clutter time series. Chaos poses a significant challenge for time series analysis, since the structure in strange attractors tends to be very intricate and nonuniform[5]. Chaotic time series analysis is a relatively new discipline concentrating on the peculiarities of characterizing and modeling chaotic systems. In fact, chaotic systems have become an interesting test for researchers developing new architectures and training algorithms for neural networks.

In particular, we consider the Mackey-Glass chaotic time series[6], generated by a delay differential equation of the form

$$\frac{du(t)}{dt} = \frac{au(t-\tau)}{1+u(t-\tau)^{10}} - bu(t) \tag{19}$$

with values $a = 0.2$ and $b = 0.1$. We choose the Mackey-Glass delay-differential equation with a parameter $\tau = 17$, and an embedding dimension greater than four. For every module, the number of external inputs is chosen to be five ($M = 5$). We choose two neurons ($N = 2$) in the upper layer. The cascaded array is a combination of 5 recurrent neural networks ($M_c = 5$). The real-time prediction result for the Mackey-Glass chaotic time series may be summarized as follows: the average mean square prediction error is about 0.01% of the average mean square value of 1000 chaotic series sample points.

Another example is the the real-time prediction of sea clutter. Sea clutter is a complex time series. In 1989, Haykin and Lenug [7] presented experimented results showing that sea clutter is chaotic. To model the sea clutter, we use the CRNN consisting of 15 modules ($M_c = 15$). For every module, the number of external inputs is chosen to be seven ($M = 7$), which is slightly greater than the correlative dimension of the sea clutter used in this study (estimated to be 6.3-6.7). We use three neurons in the upper layer ($N = 3$). The real-time nonlinear prediction results for sea clutter, using the CRNN, are shown on Figure 3(a). The value of every point is normalized with respect to the maximum valve of the sea clutter.

Figure 3(b) presents the corresponding prediction result for sea clutter using the linear LMS algorithm

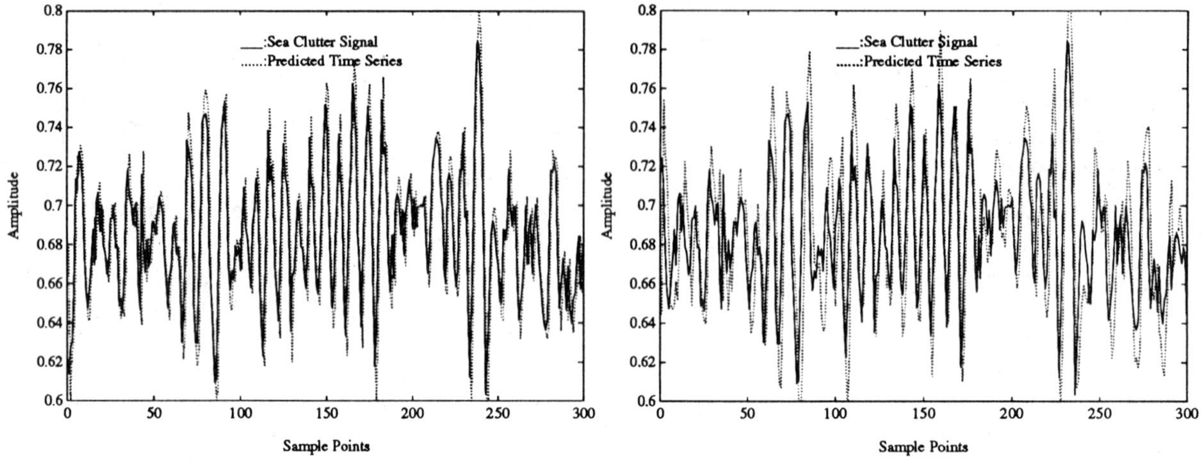

(a) Cascaded Recurrent Neural Network Algorithm (b) LMS Algorithm

Figure 3: Real-Time Prediction of Sea Clutter

under similar conditions. The results shown in Figure 3 were computed using real-life data collected by means of an instrument quality radar at a site on the East Coast of Canada. Comparison of Figure 3(a) and 3(b) shows that the use of the nonlinear filtering is superior to the linear filtering for this application. In quantitative terms, we can use the average mean-square error to evaluate the performance of the prediction. In processing 1000 sea clutter samples, the average mean square value of the prediction error is $7.6 * 10^{-4}$ using the nonlinear prediction algorithm of the CRNN, and $20.0 * 10^{-4}$ using the linear LMS prediction algorithm.

6 Conclusion

In this paper, we have proposed a new kind of neural network model and analyzed its behavior. We have shown that the neural network can be used as a general nonlinear filter that is trainable adaptively. Simulation results show that this real-time adaptive algorithm can process a complex chaotic time series, and sea clutter data just as well. Presently, we are exploring the use of this real-time nonlinear prediction in speech waveform coding, involving the use of adaptive differential pulse-code modulation(ADPCM). Preliminary results appear to be promising.

References

[1] R.J.Williams *and* D.Zipser, *Gradient-Based Learning Algorithm for Recurrent Connectionist Networks* (Technical Report NU-CCS-90-9). Northeastern University, College of Computer Science.

[2] J.C.Houk, *Learning in Modular Networks. Proceeding of Adaptive and learning Systems.* Yale University. pp.80-84, May,1992.

[3] R.J.Williams *and* D.Zipser, *A Learning Algorithm for continually Running Fully Recurrent Neural Networks.* Neural Computation 2, pp270-280, 1987.

[4] S. Haykin, *Adaptive Filter Theory.* Englewood Cliffs, NJ07632 Prentice Hall -2nd, 1991.

[5] John j. Sidorowich, *Modeling of Chaotic Time Series for Prediction, Interpolation, and Smoothing. Proc. 1992 IEEE ICASSP.*IV-121.

[6] Martine CASDAGLI, *Nonlinear Prediction of Chaotic Time series.* Physica D 35 , pp.335-356, 1989.

[7] S.Haykin *and* H.Leung, *Model Reconstruction of Chaotic Dynamics: First Preliminary Radar Results. Proc. 1992 IEEE ICASSP.*IV-125.

NEURAL DETECTORS FOR SIGNALS IN NON-GAUSSIAN NOISE

Viswanath Ramamurti, Sathyanarayan S. Rao and Prashant P. Gandhi *

Department of Electrical and Computer Engineering
Villanova University, Villanova, PA 19085

Abstract

In this paper, we train a neural network for the purpose of detecting a known signal corrupted by additive Gaussian as well as non-Gaussian noise of impulsive type. In the presence of Gaussian noise, we show that performance of a properly trained neural network is very similar to that of the optimum matched filter detector. In the presence of non-Gaussian noise, however, neural detectors are shown to perform better than both matched filter and locally optimum detectors.

1 Introduction

Detection of signals from noisy observations is an important area of statistical signal processing with direct applications in fields such as radar, sonar and communications. Many linear and nonlinear detectors have been studied to detect signals embedded in noise. Generally, detectors that are optimum in some sense, such as the ones that are *uniformly most powerful* (UMP) or the less restrictive ones that are *UMP unbiased* or *UMP invariant*, are often desired [1]. Unfortunately, such optimum detectors do not exist for many practical noise distributions.

Linear detectors, which are in many cases optimum under the assumption of additive Gaussian noise, have been thoroughly investigated due to their simple and easily implementable structure [1]. In the presence of non-Gaussian noise, a class of *locally optimum* detectors has been studied under the assumptions of vanishingly small signal strength, large sample size and independent observations [2]. In many practial cases of interest, however, signal strengths are moderate-to-large, and sample sizes are generally finite. In such cases, performance of a locally optimum detector degrades considerably, and therefore its use is generally limited to some very specific situations.

Neural networks have been extensively studied in the last few years in many areas of signal processing. One of the appealing features of a neural network is that it can be trained to operate, with acceptable performance, in a situation for which an optimum signal processor is not available. Hence, given a sufficiently large training sequence and a neural network with enough degrees of freedom, one would expect this nonlinear neural network to adapt to the situation under consideration.

In this paper, we employ a neural network to detect the presence or absence of a known signal corrupted by Gaussian and non-Gaussian noise components. Because signal detection can be viewed as a pattern recognition problem (i.e. recognizing a specific signal pattern from an all-zero pattern) and because neural networks have been successfully used in signal classification problems, it is natural to consider them for the purpose of signal detection as well.

The use of neural networks for signal detection is a recent one [3]-[5]. To improve performance of the matched filter in the presence of impulsive noise, Lippmann and Beckman [4] employed a neural network as a preprocessor to reduce the influence of impulsive noise components. Michalopoulou *et al* [5] trained a multilayer neural network to identify one of M orthogonal signals embedded in additive Gaussian noise. They showed that, for $M = 1$, operating characteristics of the neural detector were quite close to those obtained by using the optimum matched filter detector.

When using a neural network for signal detection, it is not clear how the network can be designed to operate at a specific false alarm probability. In matched filter and other traditional approaches, one simply changes the detector threshold in order to obtain the desired false alarm probability. In this paper, we consider one reasonable approach in which the bias of output node of the neural detector is varied to yield the desired false alarm probability. The algorithm to properly train a neural network so that it can function as a detector is also described.

The main contribution of this paper is the study of operating characteristics of neural detectors in the presence of additive *non-Gaussian* noise. For many non-Gaussian noise distributions such as double exponential, Cauchy, contaminated Gaussian, etc., optimum detectors generally

*Supported in part by 1992 Villanova Summer Research Grant.

0-7803-0946-4/93 $3.00 © 1993 IEEE

do not exist. A linear matched filter detector, which is optimum for detecting a known signal in additive Gaussian noise, often performs poorly when additive non-Gaussian noise is encountered. We demonstrate via computer simulations that, for several different non-Gaussian noise distributions, properly trained neural detectors outperform both matched filter and locally optimum detectors.

2 Preliminaries

The commonly used additive observation model is described below followed by a brief description of the matched filter and locally optimum detectors.

Let $\mathbf{X} = (X_1, X_2, \ldots, X_n)^T$ be the size-n vector of real-valued independent and identically distributed (IID) observations X_i, and let $f_X(x)$ be the marginal probability density function (pdf) of X_i, $i = 1, 2, \ldots, n$. Assuming the additive observation model, we have

$$\mathbf{X} = \theta \mathbf{s} + \mathbf{N} \tag{1}$$

where $\mathbf{s} = (s_1, s_2, \ldots, s_n)^T$ and $\mathbf{N} = (N_1, N_2, \ldots, N_n)^T$ are the signal (which is known *a priori*) and noise vectors, respectively, and $\theta \geq 0$ is the signal-strength parameter. Noise components N_i, $i = 1, 2, \ldots, n$, are IID zero-mean random variables with a common variance $E[N_i^2]$ and a symmetric marginal probability density function $f_N(x)$. The case $\theta > 0$ implies the presence of a signal versus the case $\theta = 0$ which implies the noise-only situation.

We study performance characteristics of neural detectors for several noise distributions and compare them with those of matched filter and locally optimum detectors. The pdfs that we consider are (1) Gaussian pdf with $f_N(x) = e^{-x^2/2\sigma^2}/\sqrt{2\pi\sigma^2}$ and $E[N_i^2] = \sigma^2$, (2) double exponential pdf with $f_N(x) = e^{-|x|/\sigma}/2\sigma$ and $E[N_i^2] = 2\sigma^2$, (3) contaminated Gaussian pdf with $f_N(x) = (1-\epsilon)e^{-x^2/2\sigma_0^2}/\sqrt{2\pi\sigma_0^2} + \epsilon e^{-x^2/2\sigma_1^2}/\sqrt{2\pi\sigma_1^2}$ where σ_0^2 is the nominal variance, σ_1^2 ($> \sigma_0^2$) is contaminated variance, $0 \leq \epsilon \leq 1$ is the degree of contamination and $E[N_i^2] = (1-\epsilon)\sigma_0^2 + \epsilon\sigma_1^2$, and (4) Cauchy pdf with $f_N(x) = \sigma/[\pi(\sigma^2 + x^2)]$ and $E[N_i^2] = \infty$.

Block diagram of a traditional detector is shown in Figure 1 where test statistic $T(\mathbf{X})$ is compared to a threshold τ. A signal is declared to be present if $T(\mathbf{X}) > \tau$. Operating characteristics of the detectors that we consider here are given in terms of probability of false alarm P_{fa} and probability of detection P_d. They are defined as, respectively,

$$\begin{aligned} P_{fa} &= P[T(\mathbf{X}) > \tau | \theta = 0] \\ P_d &= P[T(\mathbf{X}) > \tau | \theta > 0]. \end{aligned} \tag{2}$$

For a matched filter detector, the test statistic assumes a linear form:

$$T_{MF}(\mathbf{X}) = \sum_{i=1}^{n} s_i X_i. \tag{3}$$

It is obtained by maximizing the signal-to-noise ratio (SNR) at the detector output (prior to thresholding) or by maximizing P_d for a fixed P_{fa} under the assumption of additive Gaussian noise [1]. For a locally optimum detector, the test statistic is given by [2]

$$T_{LO}(\mathbf{X}) = -\sum_{i=1}^{n} s_i \frac{f_N'(X_i)}{f_N(X_i)}. \tag{4}$$

For f_N a Gaussian pdf, for instance, we have $T_{LO}(\mathbf{X}) = \sum_{i=1}^{n} s_i X_i$ ($= T_{MF}$) while, for a double exponential pdf, we have $T_{LO}(\mathbf{X}) = \sum_{i=1}^{n} s_i \operatorname{sgn}(X_i)$ where $\operatorname{sgn}(x)$ is the sign of x.

3 Neural Networks for Signal Detection

Training the network

The multilayer neural detector structure that we use in this paper is shown in Figure 2. Excluding the bias nodes, the network has n input nodes, one hidden layer of m nodes and one output node. A bias term is included in the hidden layer and also at the output node. The network is trained using the backpropagation algorithm [6]. During each epoch, both noise-only and signal-plus-noise values are presented to the network. During the noise-only inputs, the network is trained to produce an output zero while, during signal-plus-noise inputs, it is trained to produce unit output.

Once the network is trained and is employed as a detector, a signal is declared to be present if the network output exceeds 0.5. In order to operate the neural detector at a specific false alarm probability, it is necessary to change the output threshold so that the desired P_{fa} is achieved. Increasing the threshold from the value 0.5 will clearly lead to a decrease in the false alarm probability and vice versa. Alternatively, one can also vary the bias weight applied to the output node and leave the threshold at 0.5. This is because any variations in the bias term will directly affect the threshold, and hence lead to variations in the P_{fa}. We use the latter approach to obtain performance characteristics of a neural detector.

We note, however, that a neural detector is trained to obtain the largest detection probability and the smallest false alarm probability a specific bias value (at the output node) which is obtained during training. If this bias term is changed to achieve a desired P_{fa}, the neural detector may exhibit some loss of performance as it is no longer "optimum" at this new operating point. If this performance loss is more than that obtained by employing a matched filter, then clearly the neural detector is not a useful detector.

Simulation Results

To illustrate the potential of this new class of detectors, we now present simulated performance characteristics of neural detectors trained in several different noise environments. The neural detector has $n = 10$ input nodes and $m = 5$ hidden nodes. It is trained for 20,000 epochs. Both constant and triangular signals are considered. In Examples 1-3, θ is chosen so that the SNR $= [\theta^2 \sum_{i=1}^{n} s_i^2]/E[N_i^2] = 10$ for one case and $= 3.16$ for the other case (i.e. SNR = 10 dB or 5 dB).

Example 1. (Gaussian Noise) Performance characteristics of the neural detector and the matched filter are depicted in Figures 3(a)-3(c). For both signal profiles, the neural detector performance is close to that of the matched filter, as one would expect.

Example 2. (Double exponential noise) Performance characteristics of the three detectors are given in Figures 4(a)-4(c). Note that neural detector performs better that both matched filter and locally optimum detector in all three cases.

Example 3. (Contaminated Gaussian noise) In this case, we choose $\epsilon = 0.2$ and $\sigma_1^2/\sigma_0^2 = 16$. Figures 5(a)-5(c) illustrate performance characteristics of the three detectors. The matched filter and locally optimum detectors performance similarly in all three cases. The neural detector clearly yields the best performance.

Example 4. (Cauchy noise) As we noted in Section 2, the variance of a Cauchy random variable is not finite, and therefore, definition of SNR is meaningless in this case. In Figures 6(a) and 6(b), we consider the case where signal energy is 250, and the parameter σ of the Cauchy pdf is set to 1.0. In Figure 6(c) we consider the case where signal energy is 10 and $\sigma = 0.2$. Detector performance characteristics are depicted in Figures 6(a)-6(c). For relatively high P_{fa} values, either the matched filter or the locally optimum detector (or both) perform slightly better than the neural detector in some instances. For low P_{fa} values which are of interest in most practical cases, the neural detector outperforms the other two detectors.

4 Conclusions

We demonstrated that a neural network can be trained to function as a detector in non-Gaussian noise, yielding considerable performance improvement over matched filter and locally optimum detectors. Further investigation is needed to fully understand the behavior of neural detectors. One promising area of future research is the study of robustness characteristics of neural detectors in mixed noise environments. Performance of neural detector in dependent noise is another area that requires careful investigation.

References

[1] H. V. Poor, *An Introduction to Signal Detection and Estimation*, Springer-Verlag, 1988.

[2] S. A. Kassam, *Signal Detection in Non-Gaussian Noise*, Springer-Verlag, 1988.

[3] J. W. Watterson, "An optimum multilayer perceptron neural receiver for signal detection," *IEEE Trans. on Neural Networks*, Vol. 1, No. 4, pp. 298-300, 1990.

[4] R. P. Lippmann and P. Beckman, "Adaptive neural net preprocessing for signal detection in non-Gaussian noise," In *Advances in Neural Information Processing Systems*," Vol. 1, 1989.

[5] Z. Michalopoulou, L. Nolte and D. Alexandrou, "ROC performance evaluation of multilayer perceptrons in the detection of one of M orthogonal signals," In *Proc. of ICASSP*, 1992.

[6] D. E. Rumelhart and J. L. McClelland, editors, *PDP: Explorations in the Microstructure of Cognition*, Vol. 1, MIT Press, 1986.

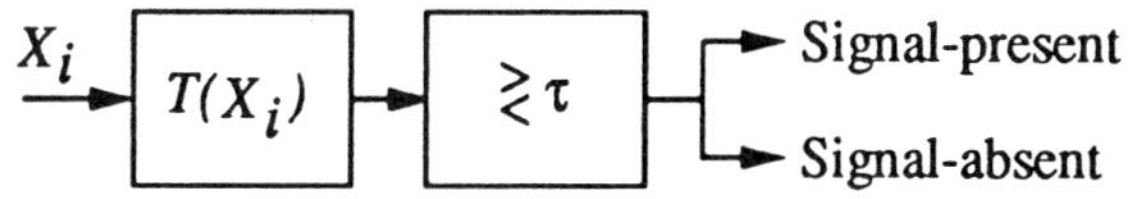

Figure 1. Block diagram of a traditional detector.

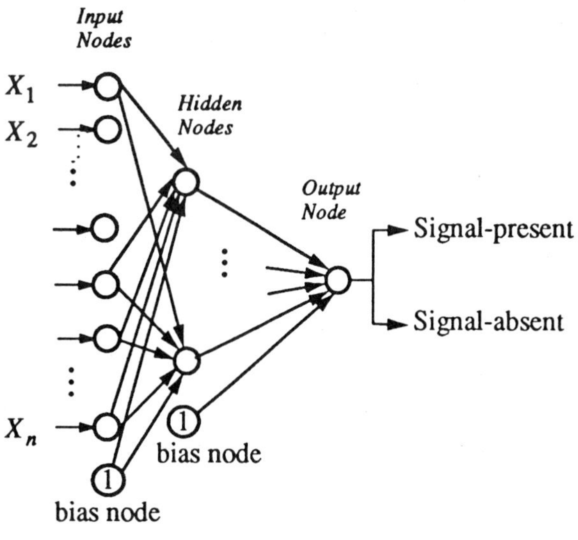

Figure 2. Block diagram of a neural detector.

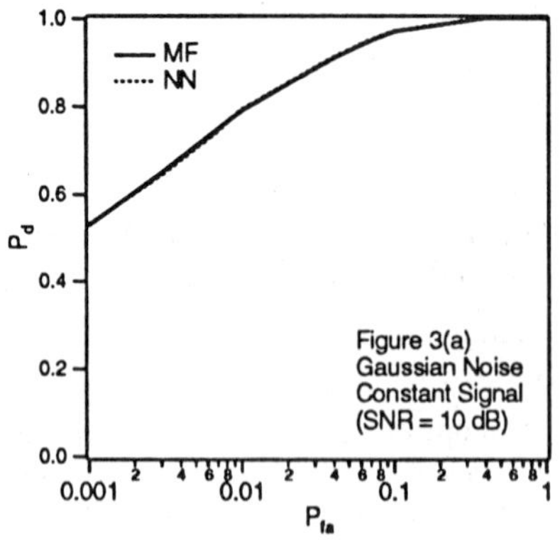
MF
NN
Figure 3(a)
Gaussian Noise
Constant Signal
(SNR = 10 dB)
P_d
P_{fa}

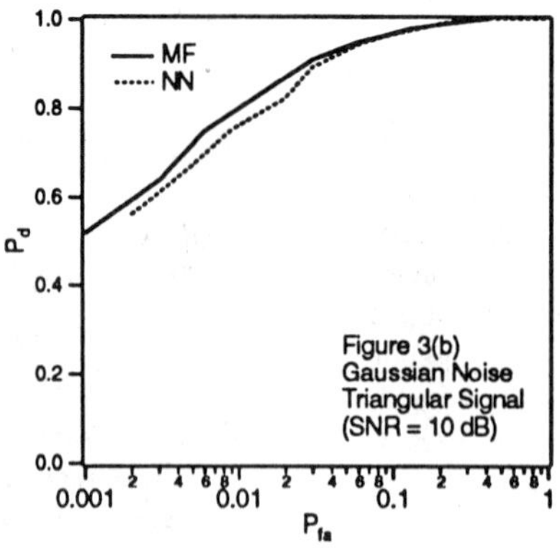
MF
NN
Figure 3(b)
Gaussian Noise
Triangular Signal
(SNR = 10 dB)
P_d
P_{fa}

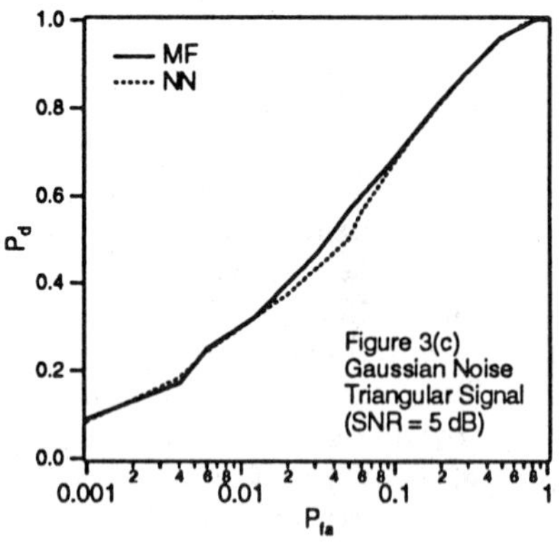
MF
NN
Figure 3(c)
Gaussian Noise
Triangular Signal
(SNR = 5 dB)
P_d
P_{fa}

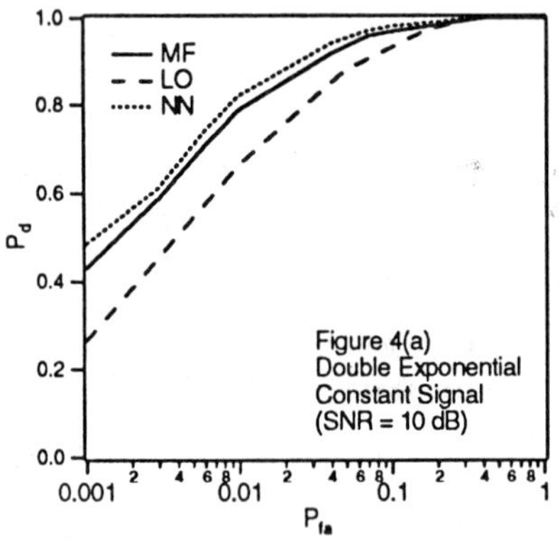
MF
LO
NN
Figure 4(a)
Double Exponential
Constant Signal
(SNR = 10 dB)
P_d
P_{fa}

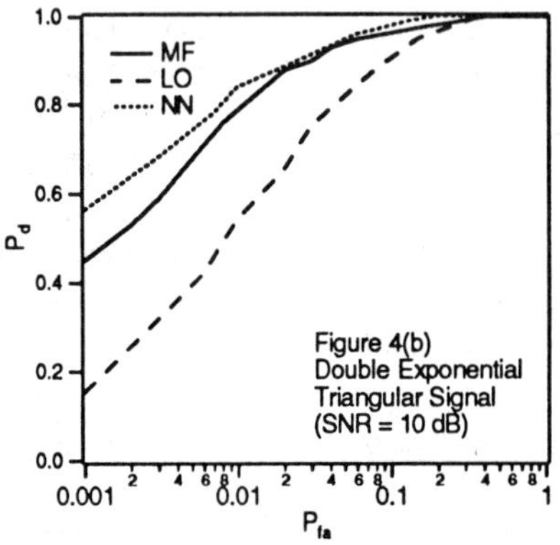
MF
LO
NN
Figure 4(b)
Double Exponential
Triangular Signal
(SNR = 10 dB)
P_d
P_{fa}

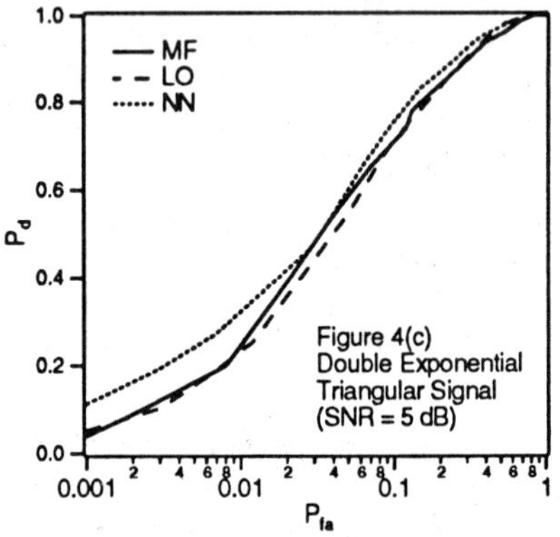
MF
LO
NN
Figure 4(c)
Double Exponential
Triangular Signal
(SNR = 5 dB)
P_d
P_{fa}

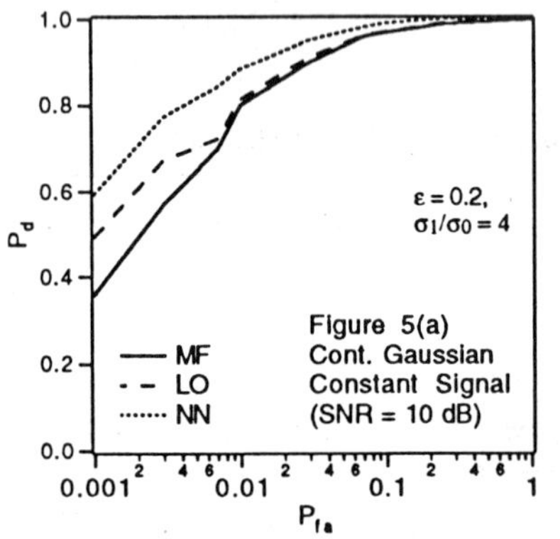
$\varepsilon = 0.2$,
$\sigma_1/\sigma_0 = 4$
MF
LO
NN
Figure 5(a)
Cont. Gaussian
Constant Signal
(SNR = 10 dB)
P_d
P_{fa}

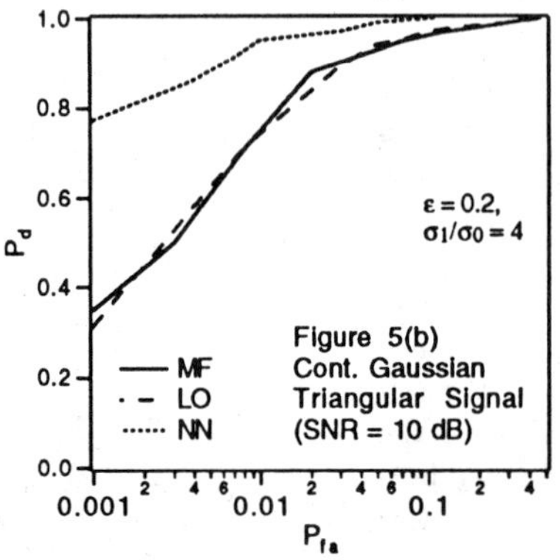
$\varepsilon = 0.2$,
$\sigma_1/\sigma_0 = 4$
MF
LO
NN
Figure 5(b)
Cont. Gaussian
Triangular Signal
(SNR = 10 dB)
P_d
P_{fa}

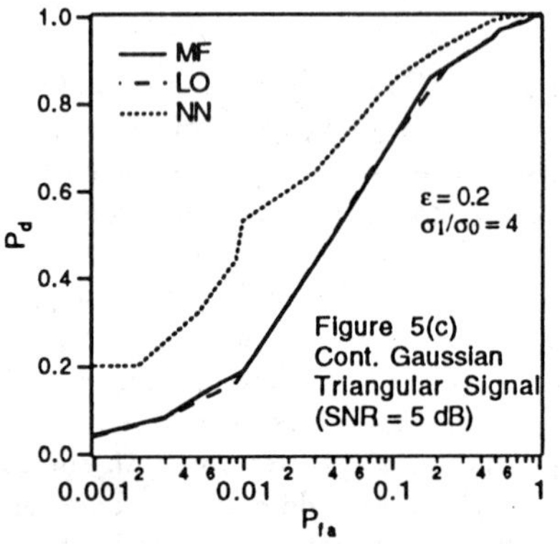
MF
LO
NN
$\varepsilon = 0.2$
$\sigma_1/\sigma_0 = 4$
Figure 5(c)
Cont. Gaussian
Triangular Signal
(SNR = 5 dB)
P_d
P_{fa}

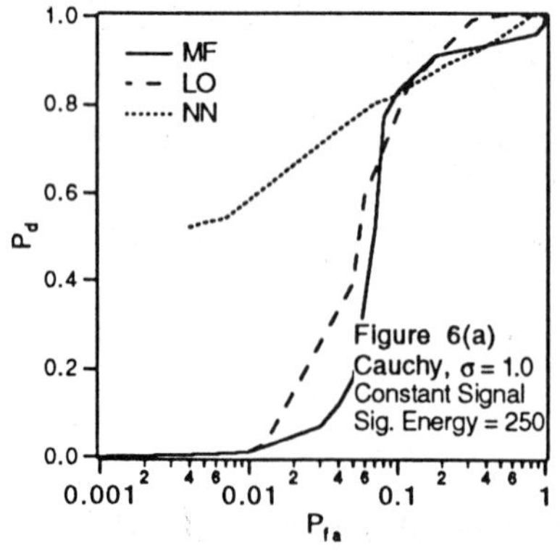
MF
LO
NN
Figure 6(a)
Cauchy, $\sigma = 1.0$
Constant Signal
Sig. Energy = 250
P_d
P_{fa}

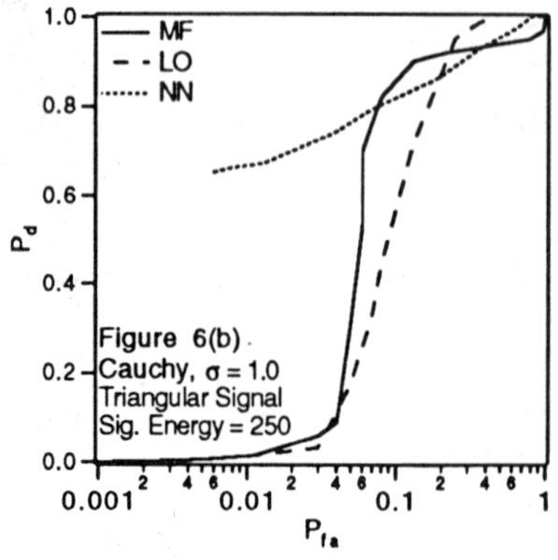
MF
LO
NN
Figure 6(b)
Cauchy, $\sigma = 1.0$
Triangular Signal
Sig. Energy = 250
P_d
P_{fa}

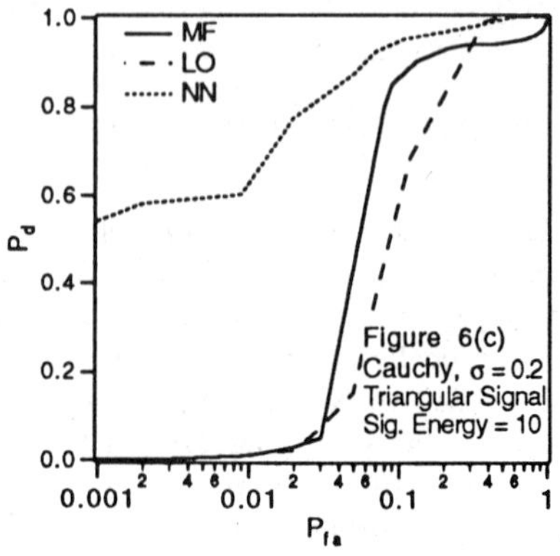
MF
LO
NN
Figure 6(c)
Cauchy, $\sigma = 0.2$
Triangular Signal
Sig. Energy = 10
P_d
P_{fa}

Performance Measures for Neural Nets Using Johnson Distributions

William C. Torrez and Jayson T. Durham
Signal and Information Processing Division
NCCOSC RDT&E Division

Richard D. Trueblood
ORINCON Corporation
San Diego, CA

***Abstract*— A probability distribution for multilayer perceptron artificial neural net outputs is derived assuming a sigmoidal activation function. This distribution is known to be a member of the Johnson system of distributions. Using this distribution, theoretical receiver operating characteristic curves can be developed to obtain recognition differential values for corresponding values of the probability of false alarm. Application of these techniques for the detection of broadband signals is presented.**

I. Introduction

In this paper, we consider a feedforward multilayer perceptron trained with back propagation of error. The output nodes in one layer are transmitted to nodes in another layer through links that amplify or attenuate such outputs through weighting factors. Except for the input layer nodes, the net input to each node is the sum of the weighted outputs of the nodes in the prior layer. Each node is activated in accordance with the input and bias to the node, and the activation function of the node. The typical activation function for the nodes in the hidden layers is the common sigmoid or logistic function,

$$f(a) = \frac{1}{1 + e^{-(a-\theta)/\theta_o}}. \tag{1}$$

This function is also known, in neural net terminology, as the squashing function. In (1), the parameter θ serves as a threshold or bias and the parameter θ_o modifies the shape of the sigmoid. It is the objective of this paper to evaluate the performance of the neural net by modeling the class conditional probability density functions $p_{c_i|\mathbf{x}}, i = 0, 1$, for noise alone and for signal plus noise, respectively, using the sigmoidal squashing function. Although the detection and false alarm statistics are unchanged, it will be seen that the bias and shape parameters characterize these distributions. Here $\mathbf{x}$ is the input feature vector to be classified, and the output class c_0, represents the noise alone case, while class c_1 represents the signal plus noise case. The performance metric presented in this paper is based on the class conditional pdf's and is known as the receiver operating characteristic (ROC) curve, which presents the probability of detection $P_d = \int_t^{\infty} p_{c_1|\mathbf{x}}(\tau)d\tau$ as a function of detection threshold t, where t is chosen to achieve some prescribed level of probability of false alarm, $P_{fa} = \int_t^{\infty} p_{c_0|\mathbf{x}}(\tau)d\tau$.

In II, it will be shown that under certain conditions the pre-sigmoided hidden layer input is an approximate normal random variable. It follows that, in these cases, the sigmoided output is a logistic transformation of an approximate normal random variable. In III, the distribution of this transformation will be derived and will be identified as a member of the Johnson system of distributions. Using this model identification, ROC curves can be plotted as a function of detection threshold t and parameterized by signal-to-noise ratio (SNR). Another metric of practical utility is the recognition differential (RD), which is the SNR which guarantees probability of detection equal to 1/2 for a prescribed level of false alarm probability; in practical applications, this may in fact be the preferred metric. This point will be made in IV for the detection of certain broad-band transient signals generated by simulation in our laboratory.

II. Sums as Gaussian Distributions

We consider now a multilayer perceptron with M continuous valued inputs $\mathbf{x} = (x_1, \ldots, x_M), x_k \epsilon(-\infty, \infty)$, and two layers of hidden nodes. Taking the Bayesian approach allows us to consider x_k as a random variable; we will assume that its mean μ_k and variance σ_k^2 are finite. Without loss of generality, we assume that $\mu_k = 0$. The net input

0-7803-0999-5/93/$03.00 ©1993 IEEE

to hidden node j may be expressed as

$$X_j = \sum_{k=1}^{M} w_{kj} x_k,$$

for real-valued weights, $\{w_{kj}\}$.

The requirement that the terms $w_{kj} x_k$ be uniformly small, which is known as the Lindeberg condition [1], is a sufficient condition to insure that the sums X_j, properly normalized, converge to the normal distribution. We have made the empirical observation in the laboratory that, in certain cases, the independent random variables $w_{kj} x_k$ do, in fact, have a uniformly small effect on the sum X_j. Thus, our contention that, in these cases, the sums X_j follow a normal distribution is borne out by the application of the central limit theorem as described above.

For the present application, M is sufficiently large (on the order of 1440) and the x_k are sufficiently decorrelated to insure a high degree of statistical independence in the collected samples, so we may, in fact, invoke the central limit theorem to assert normality when the Lindeberg condition holds. To insure independence, if x_k is a portion of continuous time series, then we assume that x_k has been sampled at a rate which is higher than the decorrelation time of the time series. We could also pre-whiten the time series by Gram-Schmidt orthogonalization techniques to insure a high degree of independence.

III. Sigmoidal Squashing Function and the Johnson Distributions

Recall the squashing function, $f(a)$, defined in (1),

$$f(a) = \frac{1}{1 + e^{-(a-\theta)/\theta_o}}, -\infty < a < \infty.$$

Assuming that X_j has an approximate normal distribution with mean 0 and variance $\overline{\sigma}_j{}^2 = \sum_{k=1}^{M} w_{kj}{}^2 \sigma_k{}^2$ as asserted in the previous section, the probability density function, $p_{c|\mathbf{x}}(s)$, of $f(X_j)$ can be easily derived. In fact by the change of variables formula,

$$p_{c|\mathbf{x}}(s) = \phi\left(\theta + \theta_o \ln \frac{s}{1-s}\right) \frac{dz}{ds}, 0 < s < 1, \quad (2)$$

where $\phi(z) = \frac{1}{\overline{\sigma}_j \sqrt{2\pi}} e^{-z^2/2\overline{\sigma}_j{}^2}, -\infty < z < \infty$ and $z = \theta + \theta_o \ln\left(\frac{s}{1-s}\right)$. After differentiating z with respect to s in (2), we obtain

$$p_{c|\mathbf{x}}(s) = \frac{\eta_j}{\sqrt{2\pi}} \frac{1}{s(1-s)} e^{-\frac{1}{2}\{\gamma_j + \eta_j \ln \frac{s}{1-s}\}^2}, 0 < s < 1, \quad (3)$$

where, $\eta_j = \theta_o / \overline{\sigma}_j, \gamma_j = \theta / \overline{\sigma}_j$. The density in (3) is a member of the Johnson system of distributions and its properties are well-known [2]. In fact, maximum likelihood estimates of γ_j and η_j, are given by

$$\hat{\gamma}_j = -\overline{X}_j / s_j, \hat{\eta}_j = 1/s_j, \quad (4)$$

where $\overline{X}_j = \frac{1}{n} \sum_{i=1}^{n} X_{ji}$ and $s_j^2 = \frac{1}{n} \sum_{i=1}^{n} (X_{ji} - \overline{X}_j)^2$, where $\{X_{ji} : i = 1, \ldots, n\}$ are sampled from the hidden layer at node j.

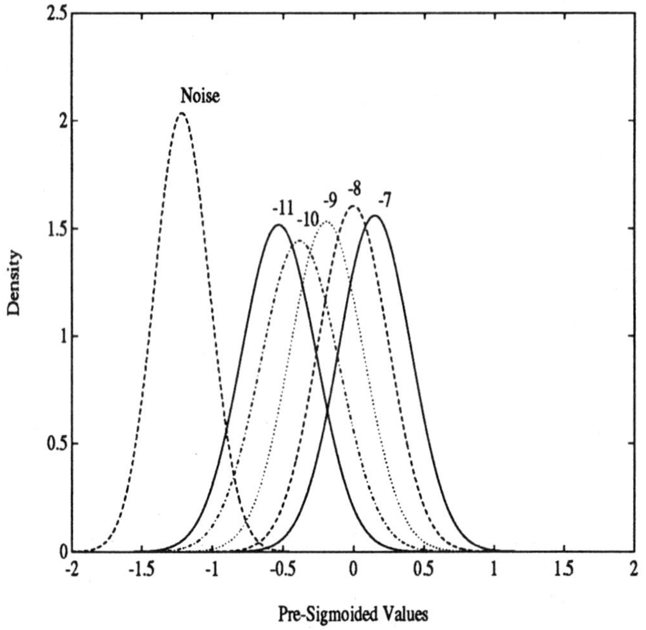

Figure 1: Fitted Normal Density Plots for Pre-Sigmoided Values Indexed by Signal Level Offsets (in dB) Including the Case of Noise Only.

IV. Receiver Operating Characteristic Curves for Broad-Band Signals

The pre-sigmoided values were collected from the data sets described in the Appendix for the five cases of signal mixed with noise at various levels offset in 1 dB increments from a reference signal and for the noise alone case. Fitted normal density plots for these values are shown in Fig. 1. In each of these cases, the observed pre-sigmoided values passed the Kolmogorov-Smirnov (K-S) and the chi-square goodness of fit tests for normality at the 5 % level of significance as we had asserted in II.

Fig. 2 shows the corresponding fitted Johnson density plots, where the form of the pdf is given by (3). The fits were based on the parameter estimates, $\hat{\gamma}_j$ and $\hat{\eta}_j$ given in (4). The signal-to-noise ratio (SNR) in dB offset is noted on each density curve. The SNR values given have been calculated for the simulated broad-band transient signals according to recent work described in [3]. The reader is

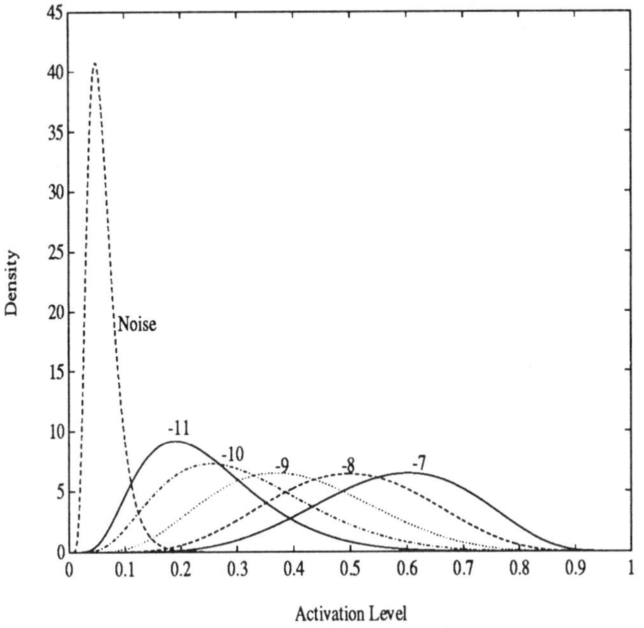

Figure 2: Fitted Johnson Density Plots for Sigmoidal Outputs Indexed by Signal Level Offsets (in dB) Including the Case of Noise Only.

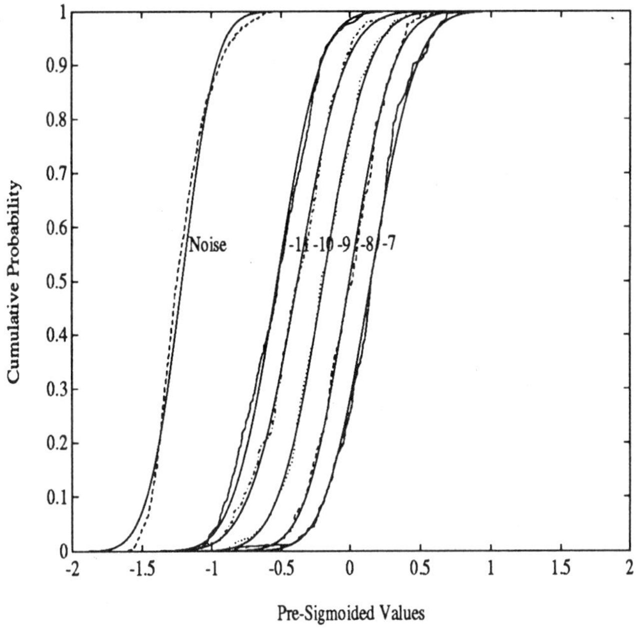

Figure 3: Empirical Distribution Functions for Pre-Sigmoided Values Overplotted with Semi-empirical Normal Cumulative Distribution Functions.

referred to that source for the technical details for the SNR calculations.

Fig. 3 shows the fitted normal cumulative distribution functions overplotted with the empirical distribution function for the pre-sigmoided values. Fig. 4 shows the corresponding semi-empirical fits of the Johnson cumulative distribution functions (smooth curves) to the empirical distribution functions of the sigmoided outputs (i.e., activation levels) for the five levels of signal power considered as well as the noise alone case. These semi-empirical fits using the Johnson distribution were deemed statistically close to the empirical observations as measured by the K-S goodness of fit test performed at the 5 % level of significance.

Finally Fig. 5 gives the ROC curves for the various signal level offsets based on the semi-empirical (i.e., fitted) Johnson distributions. These plots show P_d as a function of P_{fa}. One sees that for a prescribed level of P_{fa} of 10^{-5} and $P_d = \frac{1}{2}$, the signal level offset is very close to -10 dB. This value is known as the recognition differential offset or RD offset (for the prescribed level of P_{fa}).

Also Fig. 6 below shows a plot of the means and standard deviations of the five signal levels considered as a function of the level offset. Beyond allowing a straightforward interpolation, the fitted least squares line also allows us to extrapolate the mean and standard deviation of non-

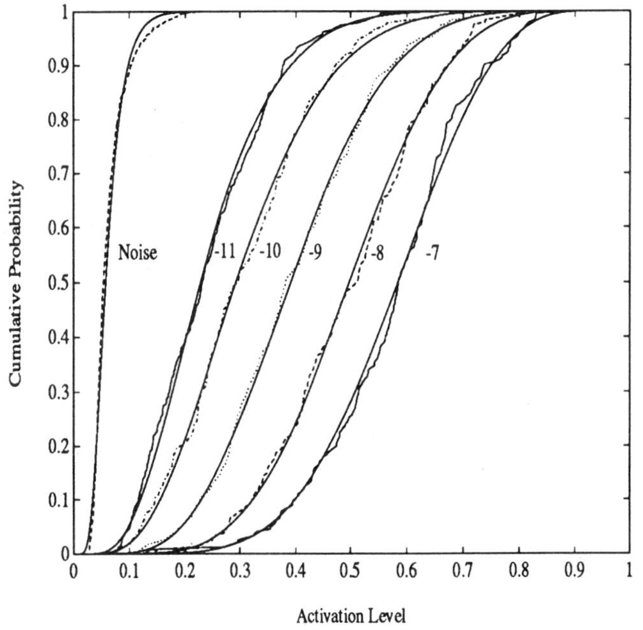

Figure 4: Empirical Distribution Functions for the Sigmoidal Outputs Overplotted with Semi-empirical Johnson Cumulative Distribution Functions.

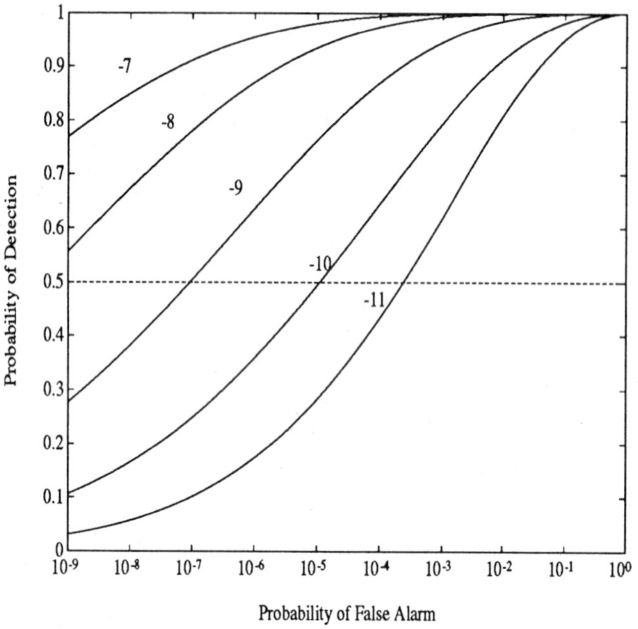

Figure 5: Semi-empirical Receiver Operating Characteristic Curves Using Johnson Distributions for the Sigmoided Outputs Indexed by Signal Level Offsets (in dB).

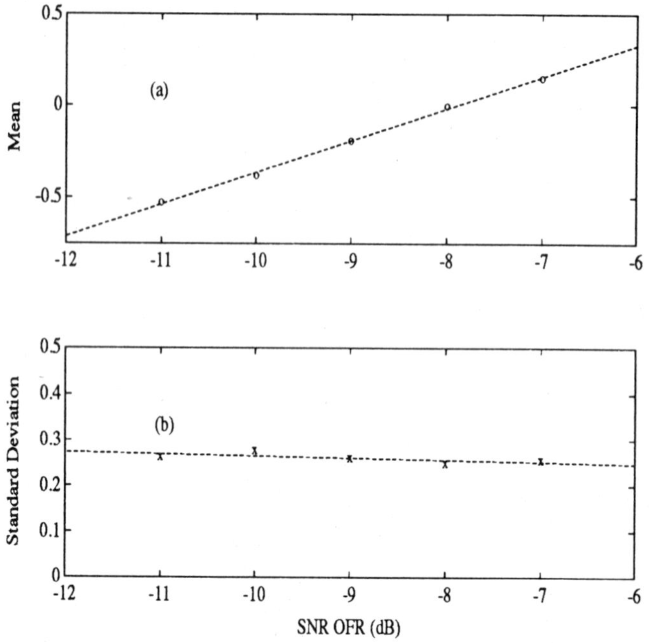

Figure 6: (a) Means and (b) Standard Deviations of Five Cases with Linear Fits.

simulated signal levels. The equations for the mean and standard deviation fits are respectively,

$$y = 1.3722 + 0.17381x, \tag{5}$$

$$y = 0.22241 - 0.004246x. \tag{6}$$

Now to obtain the RD given any prescribed level of P_{fa}, we observe that the detection threshold, $t_d(\alpha)$, is given by

$$t_d(\alpha) = s_o\Phi^{-1}(1-\alpha) + m_o, \tag{7}$$

where $m_o = -1.21474$ and $s_o = 0.196038$ are the mean and standard deviation,respectively, of the noise, and Φ^{-1} is the inverse of the unit normal cumulative distribution function. Using (5), it is easy to see that the RD at level α must satisfy

$$RD = \frac{t_d(\alpha) - m_1}{m_2},$$

where $m_1 = 1.3722$ and $m_2 = 0.17381$. Together with (7), we have finally,

$$RD = \frac{s_o\Phi^{-1}(1-\alpha) + m_o - m_1}{m_2} \tag{8}$$

Finally, Fig. 7 plots RD as function of P_{fa} given by (8).

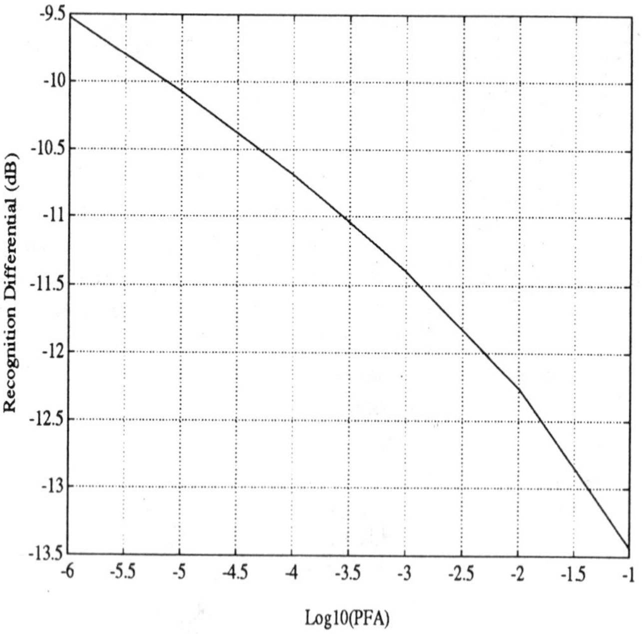

Figure 7: Recognition Differential as a Function of P_{fa}.

V. Conclusions

For a prescribed level of P_{fa} of 10^{-3}, the RD may be extrapolated by noting a functional relationship of the means and variances of the normal distributions of the pre-sigmoided values as a function of the signal level offset (cf. Fig. 1). Extrapolating this value gives an RD of approximately -11.4 dB (cf. Fig. 7) offset from the reference signal.

As mentioned in II, the invocation of the central limit theorem for establishing the normality of the weighted sums of sigmoided neuron outputs is only applicable when the Lindeberg condition holds. Our most recent work [4] demonstrates that we can, in fact, fit the Johnson system of distributions to empirical distributions of various shapes and that, like the results described in this paper, these generalized fits can also describe the location and shape of the distributions in terms of the input SNR levels.

Acknowledgment

We wish to thank Mr. Lou Griffith, Project Manager at NRaD for his support and encouragement during the preparation of this report.

References

1. B. V. Gnedenko, *The Theory of Probability*, 4th ed., New York, N. Y.: Chelsea, 1968, p. 305.

2. N. L. Johnson, "Systems of frequency curves generated by methods of translation," *Biometrika*, vol. 36, 1949, pp. 149-176.

3. J. T. Durham, W. C. Torrez, and E. W. VonColln, "Performance analysis of the Air Defense Initiative neural network processor using data sets from the E1 test," *NRaD Tech. Document*, in press.

4. W. C. Torrez and J. T. Durham, "Johnson distributions for fitting weighted sums of sigmoided neuron outputs," unpublished.

Appendix: Experimental Methodology

A strong SNR broadband transient event was digitized from a recorded data tape. A 30 second interval, which contained the signal with a trailer of noise, was then repeatedly played to a tape recorder for two hours. There were no gaps between the beginning and ending noise samples of the captured interval. Edge effects were an initial concern but none have been observed. The recorded tape of repeated events was designated as the signal master tape. Using an analog signal attenuator, bandpass filtered output from the signal master was then recorded to a series of tapes with the analog attenuator offset one dB from the reference signal, per recorded tape. The initial tape, which was consequently recorded at the strongest signal level, was designated as the reference signal level. Each two hour tape stored 240 repetitions of the same event.

Finally, all the signal tapes were analog mixed with a two hour period of ambient ocean noise. For a given time on the noise tape, the time of occurrence of the events varied up to within a few seconds. None of the events were mixed with the noise to within the same sampling interval. By not playing a signal tape, a noise only tape was recorded. For all the test recordings, the two-hour noise interval was simply repeated for each signal tape with all other system parameters fixed.

Each tape was played into a realtime classification system which utilizes in- house developed artificial neural networks. For noise only, the output activation levels were blocked into contiguous signal length durations and the maximum activation level was recorded for each block. Those values were used to calculate the empirical distribution of noise only. For each signal tape, the maximum activation plus or minus the signal duration was then recorded. Those values were used to calculate the signal present distributions.

COMPARATIVE STUDY ON THE GENERALIZED ADAPTIVE NEURAL FILTER WITH OTHER NONLINEAR FILTERS

Henry Hanek, Nirwan Ansari and Zeeman Z. Zhang

Center for Communications and Signal Processing
Department of Electrical and Computer Engineering
New Jersey Institute of Technology
University Heights
Newark, New Jersey 07102
USA

ABSTRACT

The Generalized Adaptive Neural Filter (*GANF*) is a new type of adaptable filter. The GANF relies upon neural functions to set up a filtering operation. This paper looks at a few of the possible neural operators which can be used in a GANF. The capabilities of the neural nets are examined and the filtering abilities of the GANF are obtained through simulation. While the GANF structure used here is somewhat simplified, the filter is also compared to other non-adaptive filters. These filters provide a reference so that relative performance can be more realistically judged.

1. INTRODUCTION

There are situations encountered in signal processing where nonlinear filtering is required. Included in these are the recovery of signals corrupted by non-Gaussian noise [1]. One class of filters, called stack filters, are known to suppress non-AWG (Additive White Gaussian) noise well. Stack filters [1] are defined by the two properties which they possess: the threshold decomposition property and the stacking property. These properties allow the stack filter to break a filtering operation down into a group of parallel binary operations. However, just as with other nonlinear filters, optimal stack filters often cannot be practically designed. As a result, a few methods of adaptive stack filtering have been proposed [2] -[4]. Recently, a new type of adaptive filter, based on the stack architecture has emerged. The Generalized Adaptive Neural Filter (*GANF*), developed by Ansari *et al* [5], uses artificial neural elements in place of the stack filter's Boolean function. Figure 1 shows a stack filter. Here, an input signal of integers from the set {0,1,..,M} is filtered. To determine each output sample, the filter processes only a finite window of input samples, denoted by $\underline{r}$. Let $r(n)$ denote the nth element of $r(n)$. The stack structure dictates that the filter consists of M-1 levels. For each of these levels, the windowed section of the input signal is threshold decomposed according to $T^{level}_{(n)} = \begin{cases} 1 & if \ \ r(n)\geq level \\ 0 & if \ \ r(n)<level \end{cases}$. This has the effect of producing a "stack" of 0's on top of a "stack" of 1's for each of the windowed integers. Adding a complete column produces the decomposed integer. In a stack filter, there are M-1 identical binary filters, each processing the binary information on their own level to produce M-1 bits of output. These bits are added to yield the filter output for a given index. It should be noted that identical, positive Boolean functions on each level produce output bits which always stack (i.e.- 1's never above 0's in the column).

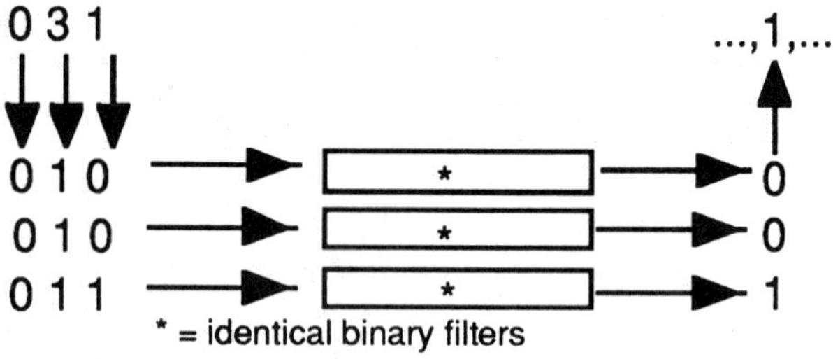

Figure 1. Stack Filter

Figure 2 shows a section of the GANF. Its structure is borrowed from that of the stack filter, but the filtering has been modified in two important ways. First, the identical fixed binary operators of the stack filter are replaced by independent neural operators. Second, the GANF structure allows the neurons on individual levels to receive inputs from adjacent levels on the stack. These changes allow the filter to be adaptive and have more capabilities, but the stacking property may no longer be preserved. (With different Boolean functions implemented on each of the levels, the binary outputs may not necessarily stack anymore.) As discussed in [5], the GANF has been shown to be quite effective in the suppression of non-AWG noise.

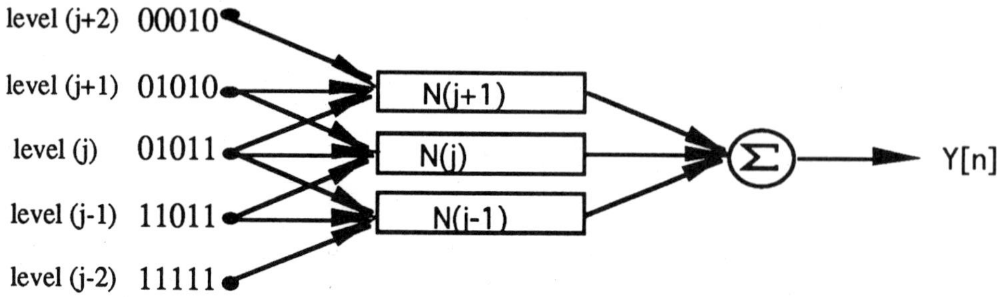

Figure 2. A section of the GANF.

0-7803-0946-4/93 $3.00 © 1993 IEEE

2. NEURAL OPERATORS

The neural operators on each level of the GANF perform a classification of the binary input data. Certain binary patterns produce a level output of "1," while others produce a "0" output. The classification operation of each neural element determines the overall filtering operation of the GANF. These neural elements are, of course, configured through an adaptive training procedure. There are many choices of neural operators and training schemes. We will consider a few possibilities.

In the simplest case, a single neuron can be used to implement a Boolean function. This scheme was used for stack filter adaptation in [2]. However, a single neuron cannot implement all possible Boolean functions for a given input vector length. For example, let b equal the window size of the GANF. This will result in a total input vector length of N=b(2I+1), where I equals the number of adjacent levels fed in. There are then 2^{2^N} possible Boolean functions or classifications which the neuron could be called upon to perform. However, only a fraction of these can be realized by a single neuron [6]. As a result, if complicated classifications are required, such a neural operator will limit the capabilities of the GANF.

To develop a neural network capable of implementing any Boolean function, first consider the case where there are two inputs (N=2). Two binary inputs specifies four possible input combinations. Most of the class assignments for these four possibilities can be realized with a single neuron. The only difficulty arises when XOR functions must be implemented. A solution to this involves using an additional neuron. Two hyperplanes can be used to separate both of the product terms in the XOR Boolean function. The outputs of each neuron can then be ORed together (by a third neuron) to produce the final class assignment. It can be easily proved that the third neuron can perform the OR operation. Therefore, a two layer, three neuron network can implement any Boolean function in 2 variables. Now, if we want to classify an input vector of length 3 or more, the number of possible classifications get squared. Adding an input to a network with N-1 inputs yields two independent classifications of the N-1 inputs – one set of class assignments for the Nth input high and another for the Nth input low. So the solution can be implemented by doubling the structure that already exists. Each independent structure can be ANDed with x_N and $\bar{x}_N$.

PROPOSITION: A single neuron which implements a particular Boolean function can be made to implement the ANDing of this function with a particular state of an added (Nth) input. That is, for one state of x_N the neuron output will always be low, while the other state of x_N will allow a certain classification of the other N-1 inputs. (proof omitted due to lack of space.)

Using this idea, Figure 3 shows the structure needed to classify a 3 bit input. Generally, a two layer net with 2^{N-1} neurons on the first layer and 1 neuron in the second layer can implement any Boolean function of N variables.

Another possibility for implementing any Boolean function is to pre-process the input data in a fixed manner. One way of doing this can be seen by considering a one input case. A linear discriminant function (LDF) capable of arbitrarily classifying this input is:

$$g_1(x_1) = w_0 + w_1 x_1$$

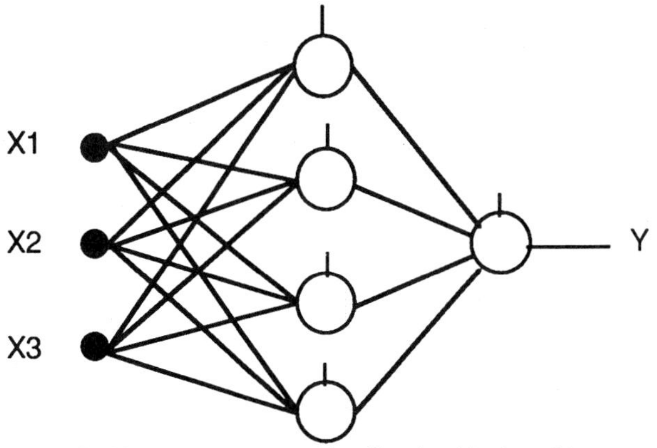

Figure 3. Two layer net to arbitrarily classify three binary inputs

Another classification can be represented by

$$g_2(x_1) = w_A + w_B x_1$$

Now, combining these as

$$g(\underline{x}) = (1 - x_2) g_1(x_1) + x_2 g_2(x_1)$$

any classification in 2 variables can be achieved. Here, we are letting $\underline{x}$ represent the input vector (x_1, x_2). $\underline{x}$ is classified according to $g_1(x_1)$ if $x_2 = 0$ and by $g_2(x_1)$ if $x_2 = 1$. Simplifying yields the expression,

$$g(\underline{x}) = w_0 + w_1 x_1 + w_2 x_2 + w_3 x_1 x_2$$

where $w_2 = w_A - w_0$ and $w_3 = w_B - w_1$. Each time a new input is added, the new LDF has the form of the old LDF plus the old LDF times the new input. From this, it can be seen that a single neuron with 2^N pre-processing functions can implement any Boolean function of N variables.

A third possibility is to use a 3 layer network [7][8], which can implement any function defined on $[0,1]^N$. Such a network would have N first layer neurons, (2N+1) second layer neurons and 1 output neuron.

Finally, a compromise between the single neuron and the more complicated arrangements can be examined. One possibility is to use pre-processing in a limited sense. That is, the input vector can be processed by something such as a quadric function. Then the neural classification abilities would be better than that of a single perceptron, but less than that of the other 3 networks discussed.

3. EXPERIMENTAL RESULTS AND CONCLUSIONS

For simulation, the clean image shown in Figure 4a was corrupted with an ε-mixture of Gaussian noise to create the image in Figure 4b. Four separate GANFs were set up to filter the image. Each of these GANFs used one of the neural networks previously discussed. The 3 layer and Quadric networks were used in GANF structures with both 3x3 and 5x5 window sizes. Due to their complexity, the 2 layer and complete pre-processing networks were simulated only for a 3x3 window. All the GANFs used independent neural functions on each of the 255 levels and no adjacent level information was used. Backpropagation was used to train the 2 and 3 layer nets, while the LMS rule was used for the two pre-processing nets. The filters were trained on the lower right hand corner of the image. Then the weights were fixed and the remaining section of the image was filtered.

In addition, the noisy image was filtered with conventional, non-adaptive nonlinear filters. All of the filtering results are shown in Table 1, where only the upper left hand three-quarters of the images were considered. The non-adaptive filters were taken from [9]. However, to clarify the Wilcoxon, ver. 1 allowed the indexes j and l (as shown in [9]) to be equal while ver. 2 did not.

The GANFs performed rather well, both in terms of error and in subjective impression. Figure 4c shows the image after filtering by the quadric GANF, while Figure 4d shows it for the 2 layer GANF. Figures 4e and 4f show the best results for the non-adaptive filters. Theoretically, the 2 layer, complete pre-processing and 3 layer nets all had the same capabilities, which were greater than that of the quadric. However, the network with the least separation abilities (the quadric) produced the best results. This suggests that for the more complicated networks, the training algorithms did not allow convergence to a minimum error solution. While complex networks can handle more precise pattern classification, they must be trained properly to take advantage of this.

In conclusion, the effectiveness of the GANF was demonstrated. However, it was also shown that the structure of the neural operators need not be overly complex to achieve good results. Complicated networks should do better in terms of error, but they really slow down the operation of the filter. In addition, inadequate learning can easily cancel the benefits of complete separation. GANF structure may therefore be dependent on such things as window size, amount of training data and expected usage. Future work could involve improvements in training schemes along with GANF structure improvements. These improvements will be necessary to increase performance both in terms of error and filtering speed.

4. REFERENCES

[1] P. D. Wendt, E. J. Coyle and N. C. Gallagher, "Stack filters," *IEEE Trans. ASSP*, vol. ASSP-34, pp. 898-911, Aug. 1986.

[2] N. Ansari, Y. Huang and J. Lin, "Configuring stack filters by the LMS algorithms," *First IEEE-SP workshop on neural networks for signal processing*, Sept. 29 - Oct. 21, 1991, Princeton, NJ, pp. 570-579.

[3] B. Zeng, H. Zhou and Y. Neuvo, "FIR Stack hybrid filters," *Optical Engineering*, vol. 30, pp. 965-975, July 1991.

[4] J.H. Lin, T.M. Sellke and E.J. Coyle, "Adaptive Stack Filtering Under the Mean Absolute Error Criterion," *IEEE Trans. ASSP*, vol. 38, no. 6, pp. 938-954, June 1990.

[5] Z.Z. Zhang, N. Ansari and J. Lin, "On Generalized Adaptive Neural Filters," *Proc. IJCNN'92*, June 7-11, 1992, Baltimore, MD, pp. IV.277-282.

[6] N.J. Nilsson, *"The Mathematical Foundations of Learning Machines,"* Morgan Kaufmann Publishers, CA, 1990.

[7] R. Hecht-Nielson, "Kolmogorov's Mapping Neural Network Existence Theorem," *Proc. IEEE Internat. Conf. of Neural Networks*, June 21-24, 1987, San Diego, CA, pp. III.11-13.

[8] R. Hecht-Nielson, "Theory of the Backpropagation Neural Network," *Internat. Joint Conf. on Neural Networks*, June 18-22, 1989,Washington, DC, Vol. 1, pp. 593-605.

[9] Y.S. Fong, C.A. Pomalaza-Raez, X.H. Wang, "Comparison study of nonlinear filters in image processing applications," *Optical Engineering*, vol. 29 no. 7, July 1989.

FILTER	3X3 WINDOW SIZE			5X5 WINDOW SIZE		
	MAE	MSE	SNR [dB]	MAE	MSE	SNR [dB]
Clean Image	0	0	∞	0	0	∞
Noisy Image	44.46	5067.89	0.98	44.46	5067.89	0.98
GANF (2 layer)	20.56	742.60	9.32	---	---	---
GANF (Complete pre-processing)	22.89	1104.38	7.60	---	---	---
GANF (3 layer)	30.55	1477.29	6.33	15.63	480.86	11.21
GANF (Quadric pre-processing)	15.74	602.51	10.23	13.04	427.31	11.72
Alpha-trimmed mean, alpha=0.4	19.64	932.70	8.33	14.97	464.17	11.36
Modified trimmed mean, q=10	18.58	946.74	8.26	14.30	456.28	11.44
K-nearest neighbor v.1, K=6 (3x3), 18 (5x5)	25.89	1653.16	5.84	21.39	1082.42	7.68
K-nearest neighbor v. 2, K=4, 12	25.20	1707.14	5.70	24.59	1584.61	6.03
Modified K-nearest neighbor, v.1, K=3, 9	18.04	952.70	8.24	12.88	382.30	12.20
Modified K-nearest neighbor, v.2, K=2, 6	18.27	1006.61	8.00	13.36	410.88	11.89
Wilcoxon v.1	25.30	1364.70	6.68	22.09	966.60	8.18
Wilcoxon v.2	27.19	1524.23	6.20	23.61	1092.05	7.64
Adaptive Mean, C=100	33.24	1524.23	6.20	23.61	1092.05	7.64
Adaptive Median, C=100	31.02	3864.55	2.16	27.62	3578.59	2.49
Conventional Median	18.51	929.47	8.34	14.50	450.70	11.49
Separate Median	20.02	1106.39	7.59	15.45	530.88	10.78
Max/median	52.87	6013.65	0.24	45.31	4283.38	1.71

Table 1.

(a) Clean Image

(b) Noisy Image

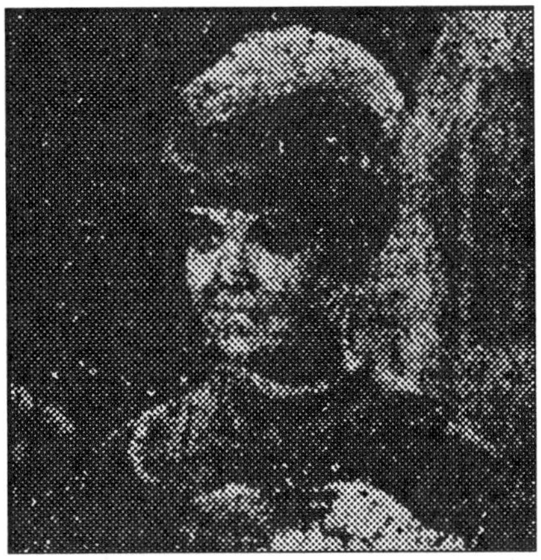

(c) GANF (Quadric Neuron)

(d) GANF (2 Layer)

(e) Alpha-trimmed Mean

(f) Conventional Median

Figure 4: Experimental results with 3×3 window.

INTRODUCTION AND OVERVIEW OF ARTIFICIAL NEURAL NETWORKS IN INSTRUMENTATION AND MEASUREMENT APPLICATIONS

William B. Hudson
Department of Electrical and Computer Engineering
Kansas State University
Manhattan, KS 66506-5105

Abstract

The use of artificial neural networks in instrumentation and measurement applications has been increasing. Many areas of instrumentation and measurement may benefit from the application of artificial neural network computational techniques. This paper will describe some neural network implementations as well as provide the reader with basic artificial neural network theory and references to allow them to explore the applicability of neural network technologies for their specific applications.

Introduction

To the skeptics, of whom I was one not many years ago, artificial neural networks do provide computational advantages in certain cases over more traditional computational strategies. Artificial neural networks have been constructed that have learned to talk when presented standard text input[1], identify kinship patterns[2] and correctly recognize hand written text and other patterns[3]. Examples of artificial neural networks used in instrumentation and measurement applications can be found in past Instrumentation and Measurement Transaction articles. Specifically neural network computational techniques have been used for "Detection and Classification of Buried Dielectric Anomalies..."[4] and for "A PC-Based Tissue Classification System..."[5] These research articles have demonstrated the computational abilities of such systems.

Do these alternate computer structures "think"? I think not, but that is my opinion. Many individuals have strong opinions and justification for declaring that these highly interconnected computing structures are capable of thought. The determination of whether artificial neural systems are capable of intelligence, or defining what intelligence is, presents an interesting question. However, this question does not need to be answered to make use of the computational power of artificial neural networks. The question of why we should use methods of computing other than conventional programs is a question that is frequently asked. Research conducted by Turing has described the digital computer as the "Universal Machine" capable of simulating any digital or analog computer or any other task that is explicitly defined.[6] Turing's work has defined the computational properties of the basic Turing machine but does not address the resolution of incompletely defined or specified problems. Further the time or computational space required may preclude the convectional "Turing Machine" solution of a problem. For example if two similar spirals are constructed using discrete points such that the spirals are intertwined a conventional program to separate the points as to whether they belong to spiral one or two would be very involved. However it has been shown that this problem can be easily resolved with a neural network computational structure which has two inputs, two hidden layers, and an output layer of only one processing element (node). The hidden layers are each constructed with five processing elements. This problem solution structure is then able to determine after training by use of x and y coordinate inputs which spiral the point belongs to.[7] This computation technique is far superior to conventional coding in my opinion. To the skeptics who feel that artificial neural networks can be replaced with statistical analysis and curve fitting I encourage you examine the divide by three problem presented by Sigillito and Eberhart.[8] This problem involves determining if the eight bit binary input value is evenly divisible by three. If the number is divisible by three the network is to indicate this by generating a signal output level of one. Otherwise the output is to be zero. If a plot is developed to show the desired output as a function of input it can be seen that neither curve fitting or statistical properties will give us results comparable to the artificial neural network solution.

This paper is not intended as an exhaustive literature review or an all encompassing tutorial on neural network technology rather it is intended as a starting point, a point from which ideas may evolve. Ideas that will allow inclusion of neural network computational strategies in instrumentation and measurement applications.

Terminology

A common problem in the understanding and usage of new technologies is the terminology used to explain and demonstrate necessary concepts. To alleviate this difficulty the author is providing a list of commonly used artificial neural network terms.

Activation Function: The function associated with the smallest functional unit in a network in which the unit's output is determined by the combination of all inputs and the transfer characteristic of the functional unit the present output may or may not be included in determining the future output.[9]

Auto-Associative memory or system: "A process in which the system has stored a set of information repeatedly presented to it. ... When a similar pattern is presented to the system, it can recall the information from a degraded or incomplete version of the original." In many texts and research articles this type of memory is referred to by is acronym "BAM" (Bidirectional Associative Memory).[10]

Back-propagation: "A learning algorithm for a multilayer network in which the weights are modified via the propagation of an error signal "backward" from the outputs to the inputs."[11]

Connection: A pathway or connection between processing elements or units. The strength of the connection is conveyed by the magnitude of a weight value assigned to the connection.

Delta Rule: A training method for a two-layer network in which the amount of learning is proportional to the difference between the actual output and the desired output.[12,13]

Error: The difference between the desired output and the actual

0-7803-1229-5/93/$3.00 © 1993 IEEE

output of a node.

Feedback Loop: A path which allows transfer of the output back as an input to the network.

Generality: The ability of networks of different structures to produce equal outputs for equivalent inputs.

Hidden Layer: "A third layer of units between input and output layers..."[14] that have no connection to the outside systems. All inputs and outputs to and from hidden layer elements must come from other units in the system.[15]

Knowledge Surface: An abstract concept describing, the energy surface formed by a network of a given configuration, the connection weights and the node transfer functions. It is the knowledge surface which dictates the system response to input stimulus.

Learning: The process whereby data are presented to a network and the interconnection weights are modified to better approximate the desired response to the presented inputs.

Neural Network or Simulated Neural Network: A highly interconnected simulation system of simple processing elements and connection weights, characterized by connection and processing element transfer characteristics.

Network Paradigm: "A network architecture that specifies the interconnection structure of a network."[16]

Node: The portion of a network which exhibits a transfer function.

Parallel Distributed Processing (PDP): A method of calculation using artificial neural networks or simulated neural networks.

Perceptron: "A large class of simple neuron-like networks with only an input and an output layer. Developed in 1957 by Frank Rosenblatt, this class of neural network had no hidden layer."[17] "A perceptron is a device capable of computing all predicates which are linear in ... set of partial predicates."[18]
Sigmoid: A mathematical function which asymptotically approaches a maximum and a minimum.

Summation Function: A function that combines multiple input signals and produces a single output value.

Threshold Function: A function in which a minimum level must be exceeded prior to obtaining an output change.

Training: The process in which a network is modified so that it associates an appropriate output pattern with a given input pattern.

Weight: The value by which an input signal is multiplied prior to summation with other node inputs. The magnitude and sign of this value indicate strength of interconnection and inhibitory or excitatory effects of the input signal being presented to the node.

Training Methods

To effectively use artificial neural networks the networks must be either configured or trained to realize the desired system response when provided an input. This training (learning) can be accomplished using various techniques. The technique used will depend on network topology and problem type. To provide the reader with an appreciation of network training strategies a listing of common training methods is provided with references which provide a detailed discussion of the training method. As you will see training can be broadly grouped in supervised and unsupervised methods. Methods of training that use examples of the desired outputs are supervised training methods, training methods which do not provide "target" outputs are referred to as unsupervised training methods.

Hebb's Rule: as developed by Donald Hebb states simply that "If a processing element receives an input from another processing element, and if both are highly active, the weight between the processing elements should be strengthened."[19] This method of supervised training is the basis for many other training strategies. Application of this rule involves altering the connection strength joining neurodes together in proportion to the product of the activation values. The necessary equations to implement Hebbian learning can be found in Neural Computing Theory and Practice.[20]

The Delta Rule (also referred to as Widrow - Hoff Learning Rule, and Least Mean Square Learning Rule): this rule is based on the premise that modification of connection strengths to reduce the difference between the desired output and actual output in a single layer network will cause the network to learn the desired relationships. This modification of weights does reduce the mean square error of the system. This learning algorithm is described by many authors one of the clearer explanations of this technique is presented by Wasserman.[21]

Gradient Descent: is a technique which uses the derivative of the function to direct the changing of values associated with the function to achieve a minimum solution. Good examples of gradient decent minimization can be found in the book authored by Luenberger.[22] There are problems associated with gradient descent methods. A gradient descent method can not guarantee a solution except under very restricted conditions.

Kohonen's Learning Law: was developed by Teuvo Kohonen. This law was developed to simulate the learning process that occurs in biological systems. Using this method the output layer node which has the largest output value is declared the winner. The positive connection strengths to this node are increased while inhibitory connections are amplified to further decrease the other nodes output levels. Using this form of unsupervised learning results in network configurations with only one output node being active at a time. This method of training can be best understood using the code supplied in the book edited by Eberhart and Dobbins.[23]

Back Propagation Learning: this method of network training is one of the most widely used supervised training methods. The use of this training method allows networks with multiple layers to be trained using the concept of "local error". Using this training method first requires determining an error at each output layer node. This error is used to adjust the connection strengths at each output layer node. This error value is then "back propagated" to hidden layer nodes. By the "back propagation" of the error from the output layer, each of the hidden layer nodes is then assigned limited responsibility for incorrect outputs. There are many variations of this technique some use momentum terms, others only adjust weights after a complete training cycle. However, it is important to note that this method still suffers from the weakness of a gradient descent based method. That is, it is possible for this method to be trapped in local minima. One of the clearest descriptions of back propagation learning can be found in the NeuralWorks Networks II[24] reference manual. The description provided uses very clear notation and describes many of the possible variations on the standard back propagation algorithm.

Grossberg Learning: this learning strategy was developed by Stephen Grossberg and uses concepts of Hebbian learning, Pavlovian conditioning and biological forgetting. Discussions on Grossberg training can be found in the book Neural Networks and Fuzzy Systems.[25]

Conclusions

Neural networks will find additional usage in instrumentation and measurement applications. These networks can simplify and accomplish many tasks not feasible using conventional techniques. The readers are cautioned that neural networks are not the solution to all problems. Neural network system validation is difficult some would say impossible and as such must be used with care in critical applications. Many differing view exist as to how, why and where neural networks should be used. You the potential user is encouraged to explore the use of this fascinating technology. Excellent starting points for literature reviews of existing neural network implementations would include "Neural Source"[26] the overview article on artificial neural network technology by Lippmann[27] and a follow up article by Hush and Horne entitled "Progress in Supervised Neural Networks, What's New Since Lippmann?"[28] In addition to the previous references IEEE Transactions on Neural Networks and the AI Expert magazine can provide both theoretical and applied information to those wishing to develop artificial neural network applications. Other references that may be of use to those of you looking for more information about neural networks would be Neurocomputing[29], Analog VLSI and Neural Systems,[30] Optical Signal Processing, Computing and Neural Networks,[31] Foundations of Neural Networks,[32] Artificial Neural Networks: Theoretical Concepts,[33] Artificial Neural Networks Electronic Implementations,[34] and Artificial Neural Networks Concept Learning.[35]

REFERENCES

[1] T. J. Sejnowski and C. Rosenberg, Parallel Networks that Learn to Pronounce English Text, Complex Systems, Vol. 1, pp. 145-168, 1987.

[2] G. E. Hinton and T. Sejnowski, Edited by D. E. Rumelhart, J. McClelland and the PDP Research Group. Learning and Relearning in Boltzmann Machines, Parallel Distributed Processing Explorations in the Microstructure of Cognition, Vol. 1 Foundations, The MIT Press, pp. 299-301, 1988.

[3] K. Fukushima, S. Miyake and T. Ito, Neocognitron: A Neural Network Model for a Mechanism of Visual Pattern Recognition, IEEE Trans. on Systems, Man and Cybernetics, Vol. 13, No. 5, pp. 826-834, Sept/Oct 1983.

[4] M. R. Azimi- Sadjadi, D. Poole, S. Sheedvash, K. Sherbondy, and S. Stricker, Detection and Classification of Buried Dielectric Anomalies Using a Separated Aperture Sensor and a Neural Network Discriminator, IEEE Trans. on Instrumentation and Measurement, Vol. 41, No. 1, pp. 137-143, Feb. 1992.

[5] N. M. Botros, A PC-Based Classification System Using Artificial Neural Networks, IEEE Trans. on Instrumentation and Measurement, Vol. 41, No. 5, pp. 633-638, Oct. 1992.

[6] H. C. Anderson, Neural Network Machines, IEEE Potentials, Vol. 8, No. 1, pp. 13, Feb. 1989.

[7] K. K. Obermeier and J. Barron, Time to Get Fired Up, Byte, Vol. 14, No. 8, pp. 219, Aug. 1989.

[8] V. G. Sigillito and R. Eberhart, Edited by R.C. Eberhart and R. Dobbins, Neural Network PC Tools, Academic Press, pp. 178-182, 1990.

[9] R. J. Williams, Edited by D. E. Rumelhart, J. McClelland and the PDP Research Group, Parallel Distributed Processing Explorations in the Microstructure of Cognition, Vol. 1: Foundations, The MIT Press, pp. 425, 1986.

[10] K. K. Obermeier and J. Barron, Time to Get Fired Up, Byte, Vol. 14, No. 8, pp. 219, Aug. 1989.

[11] K. K. Obermeier and J. Barron, Time to Get Fired Up, Byte, Vol. 14, No. 8, pp. 219, Aug. 1989.

[12] P. D. Wasserman, Neural Computing Theory and Practice, Van Nostrand Reinhold, pp. 40-41, 1989.

[13] D. E. Rumelhart, G. Hinton and J. McClelland, Edited by D. E. Rumelhart, J. McClelland and the PDP Research Group, Parallel Distributed Processing Explorations in the Microstructure of Cognition, Vol. 1: Foundations, The MIT Press, pp. 48, 1986.

[14] K. K. Obermeier and J. Barron, Time to Get Fired Up, Byte, Vol. 14, No. 8, pp. 219, Aug. 1989.

[15] D. E. Rumelhart, G. Hinton and J. McClelland, Edited by D. E. Rumelhart, J. McClelland and the PDP Research Group, Parallel Distributed Processing Explorations in the Microstructure of Cognition, Vol. 1: Foundations, The MIT Press, pp. 48, 1986.

[16] K. K. Obermeier and J. Barron, Time to Get Fired Up, Byte, Vol. 14, No. 8, pp. 219, Aug. 1989.

[17] K. K. Obermeier and J. Barron, Time to Get Fired Up, Byte, Vol. 14, No. 8, pp. 219, Aug. 1989.

[18] M. L. Minsky and J. Papert, Perceptrons, The MIT Press,pp. 12, 1988.

[19] M. M. Nelson and W. Illingworth, A Practical Guide to Neural Networks, Addison-Wesley Publishing, pp. 137, 1990.

[20] P. D. Wasserman, Neural Computing Theory and Practice, Van Nonstrand Reinhold, pp. 212-214, 1989.

[21] P. D. Wasserman, Neural Computing Theory and Practice, Van Nonstrand Reinhold, pp. 216-218, 1989.

[22] D. G. Luenberger, Linear and Nonlinear Programming, Addison Wesley, pp. 214-231, 1984.

[23] R. C. Eberhart and R. Dobbins, Neural Network PC Tools, Academic Press, pp. 347-366, 1990.

[24] C. C. Klimasauskas, NeuralWorks Networks II, Neural Ware Inc., 103 Buckskin Court, Pittsburgh, PA., 15143, pp. 440- 446, 1988.

[25] B. Kosko, Neural Networks and Fuzzy Systems, Prentice Hall, pp. 94-99, 1992.

[26] P. D. Wasserman and R. M. Oetzel, Neural Source, Van Nostrand Reinhold, 1989.

[27] R. P. Lippmann, An Introduction to Computing With Neural Networks, IEEE Acoustics, Speech, and Signal Processing, Vol. 3, No. 4, pp. 17f, April 1987.

[28] D. R. Hush and B. G. Horne, Progress in Supervised Neural Networks, What's New Since Lippmann, IEEE Signal Processing Magazine,Vol. 10, No. 1, pp.8-39, Jan. 1993.

[29] R. Hecht-Nielsen, Neurocomputing, Addison Wesley, 1990.

[30] C. Mead, Analog VLSI and Neural Systems, Addison Wesley, 1989.

[31] F. T. S. Yu and S. Jutamulia, Optical Signal Processing, Computing, and Neural Networks, Wiley Interscience, 1992.

[32] T. Khanna, Foundations of Neural Networks, Addison-Wesley, 1990.

[33] V. Vemuri, Editor, Artificial Neural Networks: Theoretical Concepts, IEEE Computer Society Press, 1988.

[34] N. Morgan, Editor, Artificial Neural Networks Electronic Implementations, IEEE Computer Society Press, 1990.

[35] J. Diederich, Editor, Artificial Neural Networks Concept Learning, IEEE Computer Society Press, 1990.

Neural Networks for Array Processing: From DOA estimation to Blind Separation of Sources

Gilles BUREL[†] & Nadine RONDEL[†‡]
[†]Thomson CSF/LER, Av. Belle Fontaine, 35510 Cesson-Sévigné, France
[‡]SEFT, 18 rue du Dr Zamenhof, 92130 Issy-Les-Moulineaux, France

Abstract— **In many signal processing applications, signals are received on an array of sensors, and the problem consists in estimating the Directions Of Arrival (DOA) of the signals, and/or in estimating the sources. Basically, the techniques proposed for its solution use either information about the geometry of the array, or information about the statistics of the sources.**
Efficient neural-based approaches for both kinds of situations are proposed in this paper. When geometrical knowledge is available, the weights and structure of the neural networks are constrained according to the geometry of the array. When statistical information is available, neural networks which optimize a statistical criterion (namely the measure of dependence) are developed. Furthermore, neural networks provide the opportunity to fuse both approaches in a unified framework, and to take profit simultaneously of both kind of information.

Keywords— **Array Processing, Blind Separation of Sources, Higher Order Moments, Neural Networks, Backpropagation.**

I. Introduction

The localization or estimation of radiating sources by passive sensor arrays has received considerable attention in the last 30 years because it is one of the central problems in radar, sonar, radio-astronomy, and seismology [7]. Depending on the kind of a priori knowledge, two classes of approaches have been proposed: when the geometry of the array is known, a Maximum Likelihood Estimator (MLE) can be used [5]; when the sources are statistically independent, blind separation methods can be employed [1] [2], without need of geometrical knowledge (e.g. long underwater antennas which are being deformed by streams).

In this paper, neural based approaches are developed. The formulation of the problem is recalled in section 2, and the principles of neural networks are summarized in section 3. In section 4, it is shown that use of geometrical information can be realized via constraints on the weights of the neural network. The neural approach provides a dramatic reduction of computation time for the same precision than MLE. In section 5, an unsupervised neural network which minimizes a statistical measure of dependence is proposed. This neural network is able to realize blind estimation of the sources, without any geometrical knowledge. Then, in section 6, it is shown that both approaches can be fused in a unified framework, and the interest of taking profit simultaneously of geometrical and statistical information is stressed. Finally, section 7 provides some experimental results.

II. Problem formulation

Consider an array composed of m sensors with arbitrary locations and arbitrary directional characteristics [7], and assume that n narrow-band sources centered around a known frequency ν_0 impinge on the array from locations $\theta_1, ..., \theta_n$. Let us note:

- $\rho_i(\theta_k)$ the amplitude response of the ith sensor to a wavefront impinging from location θ_k
- $\tau_i(\theta_k)$ the propagation delay between a reference point and the ith sensor for a wavefront impinging from location θ_k
- $b_i(t)$ the complex envelope of the noise at the ith sensor
- $x_k(t)$ the complex envelope of the signal emitted by the kth source and received at the reference point
- $y_i(t)$ the complex envelope of the signal received at the ith sensor

The signal emitted by the kth source and received at the ith sensor is:

$$Y_{ik}(t) = \mathrm{Re}\left\{x_k(t - \tau_i(\theta_k))\rho_i(\theta_k)e^{j2\pi\nu_0(t-\tau_i(\theta_k))}\right\}$$

Because of the narrow-band assumption $x_k(t - \tau_i(\theta_k)) \simeq x_k(t)$, hence:

$$y_i(t) = \sum_{k=1}^{n} \rho_i(\theta_k) e^{-j2\pi\nu_0\tau_i(\theta_k)} x_k(t) + b_i(t)$$

Using matrix notation, we can write:

$$\begin{pmatrix} y_1 \\ \cdot \\ \cdot \\ \cdot \\ \cdot \\ \cdot \\ y_m \end{pmatrix} = \begin{pmatrix} a_1(\theta_1) & \ldots & a_1(\theta_n) \\ \cdot & & \cdot \\ \cdot & & \cdot \\ \cdot & & \cdot \\ \cdot & & \cdot \\ \cdot & & \cdot \\ a_m(\theta_1) & \ldots & a_m(\theta_n) \end{pmatrix} \begin{pmatrix} x_1 \\ \cdot \\ \cdot \\ \cdot \\ x_n \end{pmatrix} + \begin{pmatrix} b_1 \\ \cdot \\ \cdot \\ \cdot \\ \cdot \\ \cdot \\ b_m \end{pmatrix}$$

or more compactly:

$$y = A(\Theta)x + b$$

The problem is to estimate the sources $x(1), ..., x(N)$ and/or the directions of arrival Θ, on the basis of a set of snapshots $y(1), ..., y(N)$. In the following, it will be assumed that the number of sources has been determined (see [6]).

III. Principles of neural networks

Neural networks have gained popularity among the scientific community during the last decade because of their success as non-linear adaptative systems [3]. Many neural networks models can be described as a non-linear parametric function $s = G_w(e)$, where e is the input vector, s the output vector, and G_w a function parameterized by a vector w. The entries of w are the weights of the network.

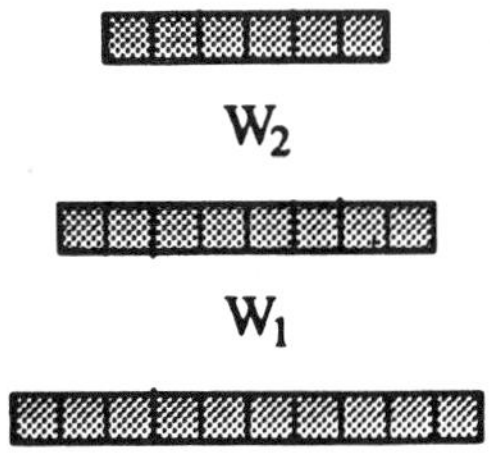

Figure 1: *A 3-layer perceptron*

Let us consider for instance the well known multilayer perceptron (MLP). The output vector of the 3-layer perceptron depicted on figure 1 is given by:

$$s = f\left[W_2 f\left(W_1 e + b_1\right) + b_2\right]$$

where f is a function, W_1 and W_2 are matrices, and b_1 and b_2 are bias vectors. The learning algorithm, known as "backpropagation" [4], updates the components of the matrices and of the bias vectors according to the gradient of the mean-square error $e_{MS} = E\{||s - s_{desired}||^2\}$.

IV. Taking profit of geometrical information

The first class of techniques uses information about the geometry of the array. By way of illustration, let us consider the case of a uniform linear array (fig 2). Let us note c the celerity of the wave, and λ the wavelength. The array is composed of n sensors equispaced by $d = \lambda/2$, and the sensors have uniform directional response.

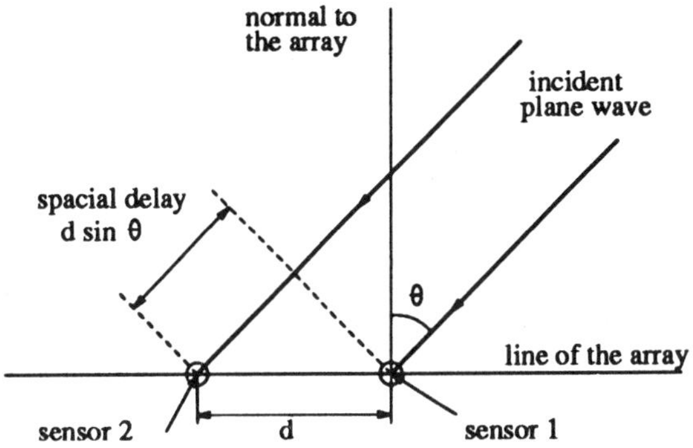

Figure 2: *Uniform Linear Array*

Taking the first sensor as the reference point, the delay is:

$$\tau_i(\theta_k) = \frac{(1-i)d\sin\theta_k}{c}$$

Hence, $a_i(\theta_k) = e^{j(i-1)\omega_k}$ with $\omega_k = \pi \sin\theta_k$

Usually, the noise is assumed to be a white gaussian noise with zero mean and correlation matrix $E\{b(t)b^H(t)\} = \sigma^2 I$, where H stands for the hermitian transpose, and I stands for the identity matrix. The noise is also assumed to be independent from the sources. The log-likelihood function of the observations is then:

$$L = const - mN \ln\sigma - \frac{1}{2\sigma^2} \sum_{t=1}^{N} ||y(t) - A\hat{x}(t)||^2$$

Maximizing the log-likelihood function is equivalent to minimizing

$$C_{MLE} = \sum_{t=1}^{N} ||y(t) - A\hat{x}(t)||^2$$

For a given A, the best choice for $A\hat{x}(t)$ is the orthogonal projection of $y(t)$ on the subspace spanned by the columns of A. Hence:

$$\hat{x}(t) = (A^H A)^{-1} A^H y(t)$$

The MLE of Θ is then given by the $\hat{\Theta}$ which minimizes

$$\sum_{t=1}^{N} ||(I - P_{\hat{A}(\hat{\Theta})})y(t)||^2$$

where $P_{\hat{A}(\hat{\Theta})}$ is the projection operator. It should be pointed out that estimation of Θ can be performed only if $m \geq n+1$ (otherwise, $P_{\hat{A}(\hat{\Theta})}$ would be always equal to identity).

Let us consider the MLP depicted on figure 3 (mlp2). It receives on input a snapshot $y(t)$, and it tries to minimize $e_{MS} = \sum_{t=1}^{N} ||y(t) - \hat{y}(t)||^2$. The structure of the MLP is such that $\hat{x}(t) = By(t)$ and $\hat{y}(t) = \hat{A}\hat{x}(t)$

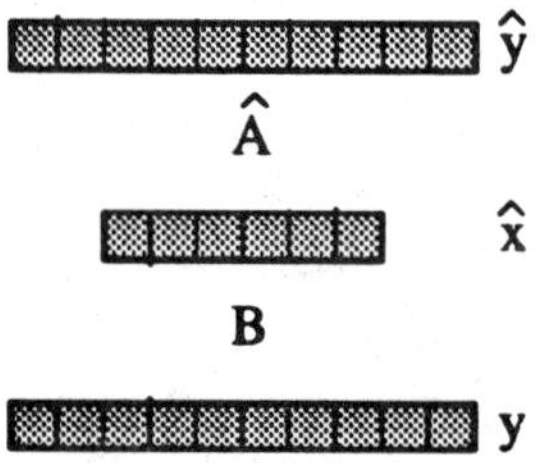

Figure 3: *MLP constrained by geometrical information*

Matrix $\hat{A}$ is constrained by geometrical information:

$$\hat{A} = \begin{pmatrix} 1 & \cdots & 1 \\ e^{j\hat{\omega}_1} & & e^{j\hat{\omega}_n} \\ \cdot & & \cdot \\ \cdot & & \cdot \\ \cdot & & \cdot \\ e^{j(m-1)\hat{\omega}_1} & \cdots & e^{j(m-1)\hat{\omega}_n} \end{pmatrix}$$

The result is an implicit constraint on matrix B, because, for any $\hat{A}$, the matrix B which minimizes e_{MS} is the pseudo-inverse $B = (\hat{A}^H\hat{A})^{-1}\hat{A}^H$. Hence, it becomes obvious that the neural network minimizes the same criterion as MLE.

The interest of the neural network in comparison with MLE is its speed. MLE requires the computation of C_{MLE} for each possible value of Θ (with some quantification step) in order to find the minimum. Since Θ is multi-dimensional, the number of possible values is huge. The neural network directly goes to the minimum via gradient descent. However, it should be stressed that the neural network might be trapped in a local minimum. To avoid this problem, a rough estimation of DOA is computed before activation of this MLP.

The rough estimation is provided by another neural network, depicted on figure 4 (mlp1). It receives on input the normalized correlation matrix R^{nor} whose entries are

$$R_{ij}^{nor} = \frac{\text{Re}(R_{ij})}{\sum_{i=1}^{m} R_{ii}}$$

with $R = \frac{1}{N}\sum_{t=1}^{N} y(t)y^H(t)$. The objective of the normalization is invariance w.r.t. the energy of the sources. Providing only correlation information to this neural net can be justified by the fact that MLE itself uses only correlation information as shown in appendix A. In this network, the function f is the hyperbolic tangent. This rough estimation MLP must be trained previously on a large number of signals. The rough estimation is then used to initialize the weights of the constrained MLP.

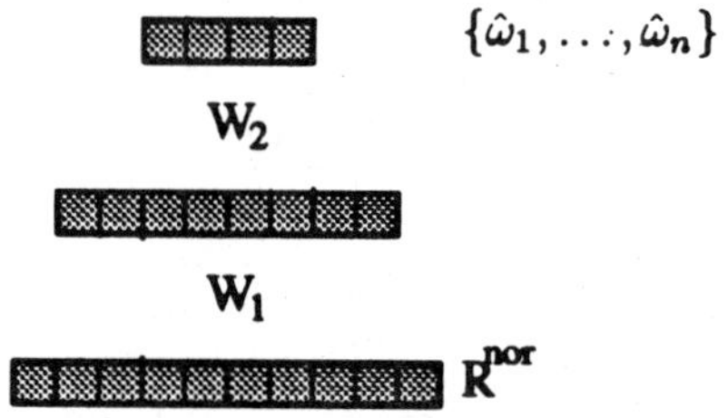

Figure 4: *MLP for rough estimation of DOA*

Computation time is low, because it only requires one propagation through the rough estimation MLP, and a few learning iterations on the fine estimation MLP. Since the fine estimation MLP starts from an initial state close to the solution, it is not trapped in a local minimum, and it reaches quickly the global minimum.

V. Taking profit of statistical information

Without information about the geometry of the array, it is impossible to estimate the directions of arrival. Anyway, the sources still can be estimated if statistical information is available. The methods based on statistical information are usually called "Blind Separation Methods". The information is generally the statistical independence of the sources. Assume that:

$$\forall x_1^R, x_1^I, \ldots, x_n^R, x_n^I,$$
$$p(x_1^R, x_1^I, \ldots, x_n^R, x_n^I) = p(x_1^R)p(x_1^I)\ldots p(x_n^R)p(x_n^I)$$

where p is the density of probability, and z^R and z^I stand for the real and imaginary part of z.

A neural network which minimizes a measure of the statistical dependence of its outputs $e_D(s)$ has been proposed in [1]. The algorithm is based on the minimization of a quadratic form of high order moments. Assume that the number of sensors is equal to the number of sources (if it is not the case, one may perform a principal component analysis on the snapshots, and keep the n most significant directions). Let us consider a linear neural network ($s = Be$) whose input is $e = y(t)$ and whose output is $s = \hat{x}(t)$. Then, we have:

$$\hat{x}(t) = BAx(t) + Bb(t)$$

If the SNR is high enough, $\hat{x}(t) \simeq BAx(t)$, and a minimum of $e_D(\hat{x})$ is obtained when BA is the product of a diagonal matrix by a permutation matrix (because, in that case, the entries of $\hat{x}$ are statistically independent).

It should be underlined that such a blind separation method works even if the number of sources is equal to the number of sensors, while the MLE requires more sensors than sources. But it does not work with gaussian sources, because in that case, it suffices that BA be pseudo-orthogonal (see appendix B for more details) to provide independence of the entries of $\hat{x}$. Hence $\hat{x}$ is not an estimation of the sources any more. Another way to understand why blind separation does not work with gaussian variables is to notice that gaussian variables are totally defined by their moments up to order 2. Hence, the higher order moments employed in [1] become useless.

VI. Fusion

Let us go further by noticing that neural networks provide a framework to combine geometrical and statistical information. Consider the network of figure 3 again, and let us replace the mean square error e_{MS} by a mixed error:

$$e_{mixed}(\hat{y}, \hat{x}) = e_{MS}(\hat{y}) + \gamma e_D(\hat{x})$$

One may retort that e_{MS} is useless when $m = n$ because there is always a matrix ($B = \hat{A}^{-1}$) which provides a null mean square error for any $\hat{A}$. But in fact, the mean square error is still usefull because, as stressed previously, it imposes an implicit constraint on matrix B.

The table below shows what the condition is to obtain an estimation with respect to the information taken into account and to the nature of the sources (gaussian or not). The mixed approach is able to estimate the sources and the DOA for any kind of sources, even if the number of sensors is not greater than the number of sources.

cost function	$e_{MS}(\hat{y})$	$e_D(\hat{x})$	$e_{mixed}(\hat{y}, \hat{x})$
gaussian	$m > n$	does not work	$m \geq n$
non gaussian	$m > n$	$m \geq n$	$m \geq n$

Let us consider for instance the case of gaussian sources when $m = n$. Because the sources are gaussian, minimizing $e_D(\hat{x})$ does not provide enough equations to correctly determine the $2n^2$ real unknowns of matrix B (see appendix B). But, with the addition of $e_{MS}(\hat{y})$, B is implicitely constrained to be close to the pseudo-inverse of $\hat{A}$. Since $\hat{A}$ contains only n unknowns, the system becomes over-determined.

VII. Experimental results

Experimental results obtained with two gaussian sources and a SNR of 20dB are presented in this section.

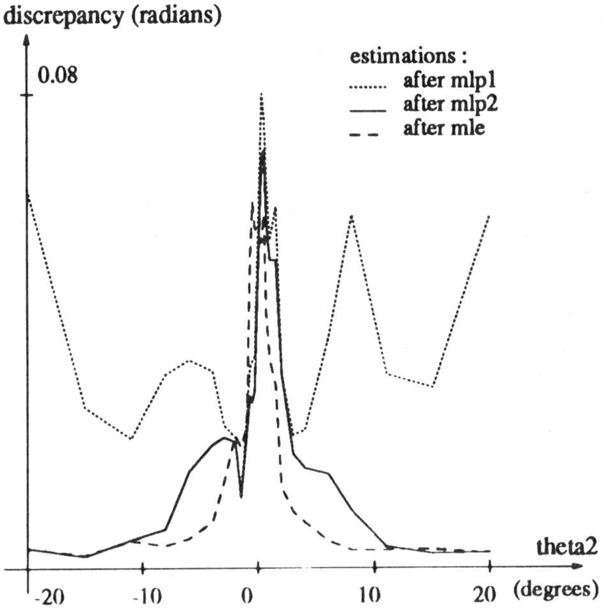

Figure 5: *Estimation error with 2 sources and 10 sensors*

Figure 5 shows the discrepancy $\sqrt{E\{(\hat{\omega}_2 - \omega_2)^2\}}$ as a function of θ_2, when the number of sensors is $m = 10$ and the number of snapshots is $N = 20$. The other source is at $\theta_1 = 0^o$. As expected the MLE and the fine estimation MLP provide comparable results. Cases where MLE is better can be explained by the fact that the MLP has not performed enough iterations to reach exactly the minimum by gradient descent. When the MLP is better, it may be due to the limit imposed by the quantization of the MLE, or to the inversion of an almost singular matrix (near $\theta_2 = 0^o$) in the computation of C_{MLE}.

The rough estimation MLP comprises $m^2 = 100$ inputs, 42 hidden units, and 2 outputs. It has been previously trained on 3071 examples (various combinations of ω_1 and ω_2). The fine estimation MLP comprises 10 complex inputs, 2 complex hidden units and 10 complex outputs. For

MLE, the criterion C_{MLE} is computed for each combination of angles ($-60^o \leq \theta_1 \leq 60^o$ and $-60^o \leq \theta_2 \leq 60^o$) with steps of 0.0047rad on ω_1 and ω_2. Hence C_{MLE} must be evaluated around 1.3x10^6 times for each set of 20 snapshots. On a Sun workstation, the MLE requires 11 hours for each set of 20 snapshots, while the neural networks require only 1.5 second. Figure 6 shows the value of e_{MS} for a particular set of snapshots. The true DOA are $\theta_1 = 0^o$ and $\theta_2 = 20^o$. As mentioned in section 3, there is no spurious local minimum near the solution.

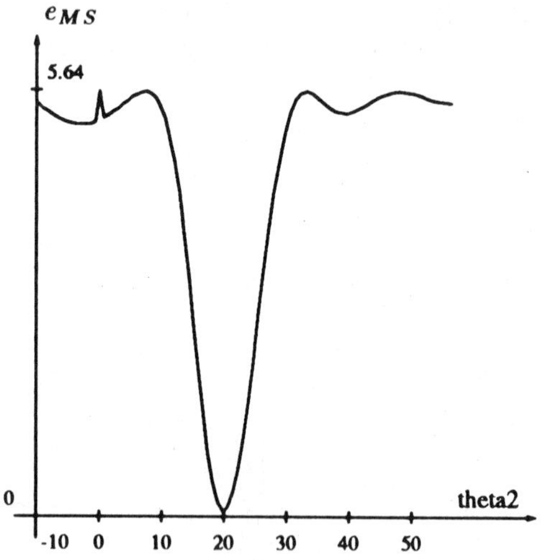

Figure 6: *value of the mean square error as a function of the estimated angle, for a particular set of snapshots*

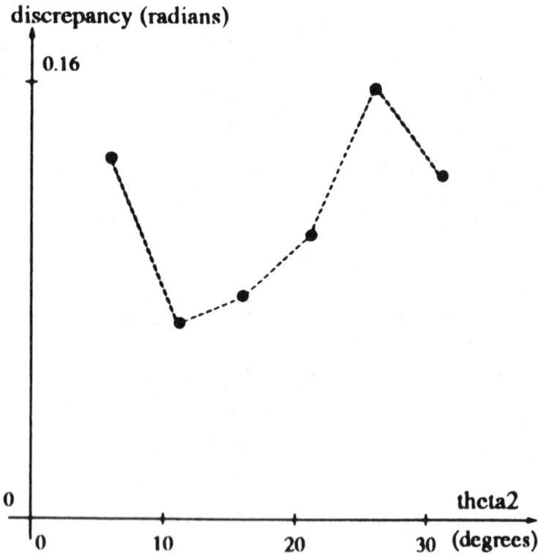

Figure 7: *Estimation error with 2 sources and 2 sensors*

Figure 7 shows $\sqrt{E\{(\hat{\omega}_2 - \omega_2)^2\}}$ when the number of sensors is $m = 2$ and the number of snapshots is $N = 200$. Since the number of sources is equal to the number of sensors, classical methods such as MLE do not work. Here, a MLP using e_{mixed} (see section 6) has been used. Figure 8 shows the value of e_{mixed} for a particular set of snapshots. It can be seen from this figure that there is no spurious local minimum in the neighbourhood of the solution. The true DOA are $\theta_1 = 0^o$ and $\theta_2 = 20^o$. As expected, the minimum is close to the true value of θ_2.

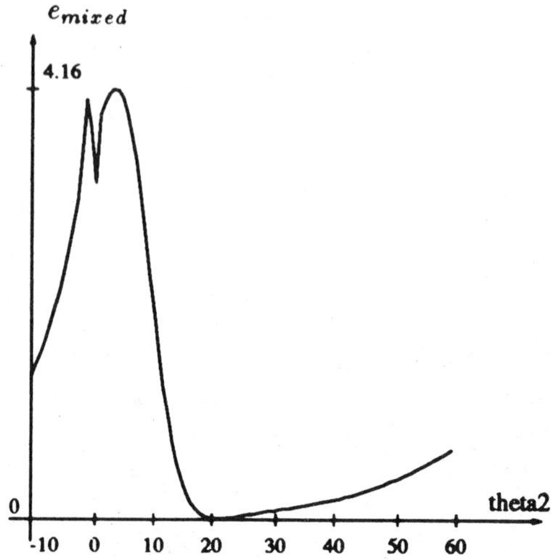

Figure 8: *value of the mixed error as a function of the estimated angle, for a particular set of snapshots*

VIII. Conclusion

Neural approaches for DOA Estimation and Blind Separation of Sources have been developed in this paper. Furthermore, neural networks allow to combine in an efficient way geometrical and statistical a priori information. The result is the possibility to estimate the sources and the DOA, even with gaussian sources and with as many sources as sensors. It has also been shown that (when the MLE works) the neural approach provides almost the same precision than MLE with less computation time. Taking into account that some potentialities of this approach still remain unexploited, we are currently studying the possibility to estimate more directions of arrival than sensors.

References

[1] G. Burel, "Blind Separation of Sources: a Nonlinear Neural Algorithm", Neural Networks, vol. 5, pp. 937–947, 1992

[2] C. Jutten, J. Hérault, "Blind Separation of Sources, part I: an adaptative algorithm", Signal Processing, vol. 24, n°1, July 1991

[3] R.P. Lippmann, "Pattern Classification using Neural Networks", IEEE Communication Magazine, November 1989

[4] D.E. Rumelhart, G.E. Hinton, R.J. Williams, "Learning internal representations by error backpropagation", Parallel Distributed Processing, D.E. Rumelhart and J.L. Mc Clelland, Chap8, Bradford book - MIT Press - 1986

[5] P. Stoica, A. Nehorai, "MUSIC, Maximum Likelihood, and Cramer-Rao Bound", IEEE ASSP, vol 37, $n^0 5$, May 1989

[6] M. Wax, T. Kailath, "Detection of signals by information theoretic criteria", IEEE ASSP, vol 33, $n^o 2$, pp 387-392, April 1985

[7] I. Ziskind, A. Wax, "Maximum Likelihood Localization of Multiple Sources by Alternating Projection", IEEE ASSP, vol 36, $n^o 10$, October 1988

Appendix A: Interest of the correlation matrix

It is proved below that the MLE uses only information contained in the correlation matrix:

$$\begin{aligned} C_{MLE} &= \sum_{t=1}^{N} \|(I - P_{\hat{A}})y_t\|^2 \\ &= \sum_{t=1}^{N} tr\left\{(I - P_{\hat{A}})y_t y_t^H (I - P_{\hat{A}})^H\right\} \\ &= tr\left\{(I - P_{\hat{A}})\left[\sum_{t=1}^{N} y_t y_t^H\right](I - P_{\hat{A}})^H\right\} \end{aligned}$$

Appendix B: Particularity of gaussian sources

Let us consider a blind separation of sources problem, and let us note x the sources, A the mixture, B the separator, and $\hat{x}$ the output of the separator. The vectors are of dimension n, and the matrices are nxn. By noting $C = BA$, we have:

$$\hat{x} = Cx$$

The ideal would be to obtain a matrix C equal to identity. In fact, we can expect only $C = \Gamma P$, where Γ is a diagonal matrix, and P a permutation matrix. This is not a problem because the sources are estimated modulo a permutation and a dilatation. But, with gaussian sources, we show below that C can be any pseudo-orthogonal matrix, hence the separation may fail. Let us consider the characteristic function:

$$\begin{aligned} \Psi_{\hat{x}}(v) &= \ln E\{e^{jv^H \hat{x}}\} \\ &= \ln E\{e^{jv^H Cx}\} \\ &= \ln E\{e^{j(C^H v)^H x}\} \\ &= \Psi_x(C^H v) \\ &= \sum_{j=1}^{n} \Psi_{x_j}(C_j^H v) \end{aligned}$$

where C_j is the jth column of C. The last equation is due to the independence of the sources. After convergence of the separator, the entries of $\hat{x}$ are independent, hence we can write:

$$\begin{aligned} \Psi_{\hat{x}}(v) &= \sum_{i=1}^{n} \Psi_{\hat{x}}(..., 0, v_i, 0, ...) \\ &= \sum_{i=1}^{n}\sum_{j=1}^{n} \Psi_{x_j}(C_{ij}^* v_i) \end{aligned}$$

Thus, we obtain:

$$\sum_{j=1}^{n}\sum_{i=1}^{n} \Psi_{x_j}(C_{ij}^* v_i) = \sum_{j=1}^{n} \Psi_{x_j}(\sum_{i=1}^{n} C_{ij}^* v_i)$$

And using Taylor expansion:

$$\sum_{j=1}^{n}\sum_{i=1}^{n}\sum_{k=1}^{\infty} b_{jk}(C_{ij}^* v_i)^k = \sum_{j=1}^{n}\sum_{k=1}^{\infty} b_{jk}(\sum_{i=1}^{n} C_{ij}^* v_i)^k$$

where b_{jk} is proportional to the cumulant of order k of x_j. Since the equation above must be true for any v, we can equal the terms of the same order:

$$\forall k, \quad \sum_{j=1}^{n}\sum_{i=1}^{n} b_{jk}(C_{ij}^* v_i)^k = \sum_{j=1}^{n} b_{jk}(\sum_{i=1}^{n} C_{ij}^* v_i)^k$$

Then, by developing the right hand side term, we obtain:

$$\forall k, \quad \sum_{j=1}^{n} b_{jk} \sum_{\substack{i_1,\dots,i_k \\ (not\ all\ equal)}} C_{i_1 j}^* ... C_{i_k j}^* v_{i_1} ... v_{i_k} = 0$$

Since the equation above must be true for any v, all the coefficients of the polynomial must be null:

$$\forall k, \ \forall(i_1, ..., i_k)\ (not\ all\ equal), \quad \sum_{j=1}^{n} b_{jk}^* C_{i_1 j} ... C_{i_k j} = 0$$

One can easily verify that any matrix $C = \Gamma P$ is a solution. For gaussian sources, the b_{jk} are null for $k > 2$, hence the equations system reduces to:

$$\forall(i_1, i_2)\ (not\ equal), \quad \sum_{j=1}^{n} b_{j2}^* C_{i_1 j} C_{i_2 j} = 0$$

This is some kind of pseudo-orthogonality condition, hence, any pseudo-orthogonal matrix C is a solution, and, consequently, separation of sources may fail. On the contrary, non-gaussian sources have at least one cumulant of order greater than 2 which is non zero. Hence, the number of equations becomes large enough to constraint C as wanted.

Real–Time Neural Computation of the Noise Subspace for the MUSIC Algorithm

Luo Fa–Long Li Yan–Da
Department of Automation, Tsinghua University
Beijing, 100084, P. R. China

Abstract

A neural network approach to computing in real–time the noise subspace for the MUSIC bearing estimation algorithm is proposed. We show analytically and by simulation results that the proposed neural network is guaranteed to provide the solution arbitrarily close to the accurate noise subspace during an elapsed time of only a few characteristic time constants of the circuit.

1. Introduction

The estimation of the directions of arrival of sources is a significant problem in array signal processing. MUSIC algorithm is of high–resolution performance and has been come to be regraded as one of the best bearing estimation methods. However, it is not easy to implement the MUSIC algorithm in real–time mainly because of its intensive computational complexity for computing the noise subspace which involves the eigen–decomposition of the spatial covariance matrix. For the purpose of providing the MUSIC bearing estimation in real–time, it is desired to compute the noise subspace as fast as possible. Although many schemes based on the digital computational methods [2–4] have been proposed, it is still difficult to deliver the desired real–time performance.

As an alternative, this paper proposes a neural network approach to computing the noise subspace in real–time, the key features of this proposed computational approach are the asynchronous parallel processing, continuous–time dynamics and the high–speed computational capability. We show analytically and by simulation results that the proposed neural network is guaranteed to be stable and to provide the solution arbitrarily close to the accurate noise subspace during an elapsed time of only a few characteristic time constants of the circuit (on the order of hundreds nanoseconds). In addition, the parameters of the proposed neural network are obtained from the spatial covariance matrix without any computations (or say, without any programming complexity). As a result, this neural network approach for computing the noise subspace is much more powerful than the many existing methods [2–4].

This paper is organized as follows: Section 2 gives a brief description of the MUSIC algorithm. In Section 3, we deal with the proposed neural network approach to computing the noise subspace in real–time. Simulation results are given in Section 4. Finally, we give some conclusions.

2. The MUSIC Bearing Estimation Algorithm

Let us consider a linear array of N omnidirectional sensors illuminated by P narrow–band signals (P<N). At the n'th snapshot the output of the i'th sensor can be described by

$$X_i(t_n) = \sum_{l=1}^{P} s_l(t_n) exp\{jk(i-1)d sin(\theta_l)\} + n_i(t_n) \qquad (1)$$

where the various quantities are described as follows: $k = 2\pi / \lambda$ is the wavenumber associated with the central wavelength λ, d is the space between two adjacent sensors, θ_1 is the angle of arrival of the l'th signal, $s_l(t_n)$ is the complex envelope of the l'th signal of arrival and $n_i(t_n)$ is the additive white noise at the i'th element.

Using vector notation, Eqn.(1) can be written as

$$X(t) = AS(t) + n(t) \qquad (2)$$

where the vectors $X(t)$, $S(t)$, and $n(t)$ are defined as

$$X(t) = \begin{bmatrix} X_1(t) \\ X_2(t) \\ \cdots \\ X_N(t) \end{bmatrix}, \quad S(t) = \begin{bmatrix} s_1(t) \\ s_2(t) \\ \cdots \\ s_P(t) \end{bmatrix}, \quad n(t) = \begin{bmatrix} n_1(t) \\ n_2(t) \\ \cdots \\ n_N(t) \end{bmatrix}$$

respectively, and the $N \times P$ matrix A is defined as $A = [a_1, a_2, \cdots, a_P]$, where the a_i is column vector defined by

$$a_i = [1,\ exp(jkd\ sin(\theta_i)),\ exp(j2kd\ sin(\theta_i)), \cdots, exp(jkd(N-1)sin(\theta_i))]^T$$
$$for\ i = 1,2 \cdots, P$$

0-7803-0946-4/93 $3.00

and is called a signal direction vector. The ensemble average spatial covariance matrix R is given by

$$R = E[X(t)X^H(t)] = AR_sA^H + \sigma^2 I = \sum_{i=1}^{N} \lambda_i e_i e_i^H \quad (3)$$

where $E(\cdot)$ denotes the expectation operator, "H" is used to denote the matrix complex conjugate transpose, R_s is the signal covariance matrix assumed to be a full rank-matrix, σ^2 is the noise variance, $\lambda_1 \geqslant \lambda_2 \geqslant \cdots \lambda_P > \lambda_{P+1} = \cdots \lambda_N = \sigma^2$ are the eigenvalues of R, and e_i are its orthonormal eigenvectors.

The eigenvectors corresponding to the first P largest eigenvalues are referred to as the signal eigenvectors, and those corresponding to the minimum eigenvalues are referred to as the noise eigenvectors. The subspace spanned by the signal eigenvectors is called the signal subspace, and its orthogonal complement spanned by the noise eigenvectors is called the noise subspace [1]. The matrix $R - \sigma^2 I = AR_sA^H$ has the same eigenvectors as R, and has eigenvalues $\lambda_i - \sigma^2$ for $i = 1,2,\cdots,P$ and $\lambda_i = 0$ for $i > P$. Thus it follows that

$$AR_sA^H = \sum_{i=1}^{P} (\lambda_i - \sigma^2) e_i e_i^H \quad (4)$$

Equation (4) shows that the signal direction vectors $\{a_k; k = 1,\cdots,P\}$ and the signal eigenvectors $\{e_i, i = 1,\cdots,P\}$ span the same subspace. This implies that all signal direction vectors are orthogonal to the noise subspace. Accordingly, the MUSIC algorithm estimates the directions of the P arrivals by finding the values of $\theta's$ corresponding to the P maxima of the following function

$$f(\theta) = \frac{1}{T(\theta)} = \frac{1}{\|Q^H a(\theta)\|^2} \quad (5)$$

where

$$a(\theta) = [1, exp(jkdsin(\theta)),\ exp(j2kd\ sin(\theta)), \cdots, exp(jkd(N-1)sin(\theta))]^T$$

is the projection vector, and

$$Q = \sum_{i=P+1}^{N} e_i e_i^H \quad (6)$$

is the orthogonal projection operator on the noise subspace and $T(\theta)$ is the noise subspace projection, which can be written as follows:

$$T(\theta) = \sum_{i=P+1}^{N} \left| a^H(\theta) e_i \right|^2 \quad (7)$$

Note that Eqn.(7) involves computing the noise eigenvectors (or say, noise subspace) of the spatial covariance matrix R, and therein lies a great computational burden and makes it difficult to implement the MUSIC algorithm in real–time. To tackle this problem, we present in the next section a neural network approach to computing the noise eigenvectors in real–time.

3. Neural Network Approach to Computing the Noise Eigenvectors

The schematic architecture of the proposed neural network is shown in Figure 1, which has four layers and can be represented by the following equations

$$\frac{dV(t)}{dt} = K\{LT[V(t)DV^T(t)]V(t) - V(t)D\} \quad (8)$$

where $V(t)$ is the output matrix of the last layer with the M × N elements which consists of adders and integrators; LT denotes on operator which make its matrix argument lower triangular by setting all entries above the diagonal to zero; D is the interconnection strength matrix which is selected to be non–negative definite. The multiplications in Eqn.(8) can be implemented by employing the CMOS analog multipliers as shown in Reference [5], K is a positive constant concerning with the adders, integrators and multipliers.

According to the convergence analysis of generalized Hebbian algorithm (GHA) introduced by Sanger [6], we have the following theorem for the proposed neural network represented by the dynamic differential Equation (8).

Theorem: The proposed neural network is stable and the stable output matrix V_f of the last layer can be obtained by letting $\frac{dV(t)}{dt} = 0$ and

$$V_f = [d_{N-M+1}, d_{N-M+2}, \cdots, d_N]^T \quad (9)$$

where d_i is the orthonormal eigenvector corresponding to the eigenvalues λ_i of interconnection strength matrix D ($\lambda_1 \geqslant \lambda_2 \geqslant \cdots \geqslant \lambda_{N-M} \geqslant \lambda_{N-M+1} \cdots \geqslant \lambda_N \geqslant 0$).

This theorem can be easily proved by use of the proof of the convergence theorem of generalized Hebbian algorithm [6], and is also generalized for the case in which matrix D takes complex values, in this case, two elements are needed in the network architecture to provide the real and imaginary parts for a complex value, and the dynamic differential equation of the network becomes

$$\frac{dV(t)}{dt} = K\{LT[V(t)DV^H(t)]V(t) - V(t)D\} \quad (10)$$

In order to use the neural network to compute the noise eigenvectors, we choose D = R, that is, the spatial covariance matrix is directly take as the interconnection strengths of the network. Because R is nonnegative definite, we may know, according to the above theorem, that the neural network is guaranteed to be stable and to provide a output matrix in stable state:

$$[e_{P+1}, e_{P+2}, \cdots, e_N]^T$$

that is, the noise eigenvectors.

About this neural network approach for computing the noise subspace, we make the following comments:

(1) Because this approach is based on the analog circuit architecture which has continuous–time dynamics, the convergence time (the time to reach closely to the stable state) is during an elapsed time of only a few characteristic time constants of the circuit, which means that the neural network can provide the noise eigenvectors in real–time with arbitrarily small error.

(2) The matrix R is directly taken as the interconnection strengths of the neural network without any computations, in other words, the complexity invested in computing the parameters of the network from the matrix R is zero. As a result, we do not encounter the problem of programming complexity pointed out in [7].

(3) This neural network approach is easily generalized for computing in rea time the noise subspace required in the other high–resolution bearing estimation methods [8].

4. Simulation Results

We have simulated the proposed neural network approach for computing the noise subspace of the MUSIC algorithm. Two sets of simulation results are given in this paper.

In the first simulation example, four planar–wave signals are considered with directions of arrival being −55°, −45°, 3°, 25°, and their associate signal–to–noise ratios being 7 dB. The array is uniform and linear with 6 elements with a half wavelength apart, the number of snapshots is 30. Table 1 and Figs.2 and 3 show the simulation results, where Q_R and Q_I are the real and imaginary parts of the accurate orthogonal projection operator on the noise subspace computed by Eqn.(6), and Q_{fR} and Q_{fI} are the real and imaginary parts of the projection operator computed by use of the output matrix V provided by the neural network after the time 100ns, obviously, $Q_R + jQ_I \doteq Q_{fR} + jQ_{fI}$, Figs.2 and 3 are the estimated spatial spectrum of Eqn.(5) by use of the accurate noise eigenvectors and the output matrix V of the neural network, respectively.

In the second simulation example, two signal sourceswith the directions being −5° and 5° are considered, the array is uniform and linear with five elements, other parameters are the same as in the first example. Table 2 shows results of bearing estimation for ten Monte–Carlo runs by use of the proposed neural network.

5. Conclusions

We have proposed a neural network approach to computing in real–time the noise subspace for the MUSIC bearing estimation algorithm. The theoretical analyses and the simulation results are also given in this paper. Compared with the available digital and sequential methods for computing the noise subspace[2–4], this neural network approach is much more powerful because this network can provide the desired solution within an elapsed time of only a few characteristic time constants (on the order of hundreds nanoseconds). As a result, this proposed neural network approach is satisfactory for the real–time applications of the MUSIC algorithm.

Acknowledgements

This work is part of a project supported by the National Natural Science Foundation of China.

References

〔1〕 M.Kaveh and A.J. Barabell, "The statistical performance of the MUSIC and the minimum–norm algorithms in resolving plane wave in noise", IEEE Trans. on ASSP. Vol.34, No.4, pp.331–341, 1986.

〔2〕 W.Robertson and W.J.Philips, "A system of systolic modules for the MUSIC algorithm, IEEE Trans. on SP, Vol.39, pp.2524–2534, No.11, 1991.

〔3〕 A.H.Abdallah and Y.H.Hu, "Parallel VLSI computing array implementation for signal subspace updating algorithm, "IEEE Trans. on ASSP, Vol.37, pp.742–749, No.5, 1989.

〔4〕 W.Phillips and W.Robertson, "A systolic architecture of the symmetric tridiagonal eigenvalue problem, "Proce, of Int. Conf. Systolic Arrays, pp. 145–150, 1988.

〔5〕 R.Unbehauen and A. Cichocki, MOS switched–capacitor and continuous–time integrated circuits and systems–analysis and design. New York, Springer–Verlag, 1989.

〔6〕 T.D. Sanger, "Optimal unsupervised learning in a single–layer linear feedforward neural network", Neural Networks, Vol.2, pp459–473, 1989.

〔7〕 M.Takeda and J.W.Goodman, "Neural networks for computation: numerical representation & programming complexity", Applied Optics, Vol.25, No.18, pp.3033–3052, 1986.

〔8〕 G.Bienvenu and L.Kopp, "Optimality of high resolution array processing using the eigensystem approach", IEEE Trans. on ASSP, Vol.31, No.5, pp.1235–1247, 1983.

Table I

Q_R =

+0.258489	+6.28191−2	+6.84121−3	−4.60454−2	−0.252478	−2.95639−2
+6.28191−2	+0.270058	−3.61319−2	−1.52006−3	−9.47644−2	−0.254078
+6.84121−3	−3.61319−2	+0.474691	−0.126503	+6.3284−4	−4.08077−2
−4.60454−2	−1.52006−3	−0.126503	+0.475472	−0.037899	+1.22484−2
−0.252478	−9.47644−2	+6.3284−4	−0.037899	+0.266104	+6.15871−2
−2.95639−2	−0.254078	−4.08077−2	+1.22484−2	+6.15871−2	+0.255185

Q_I =

+5.6954e−14	−0.056791	+0.341879	−0.028773	−2.33854e−3	−2.77093e−5
+0.056791	+3.58824e−13	+2.11803e−2	+0.31821	−0.115776	+1.00689e−3
−0.341879	−2.11803e−2	+4.75175e−14	+0.112655	+0.315792	−2.43505e−2
+0.028733	−0.31821	−0.112655	+5.52447e−13	+1.84259e−2	+0.338482
+2.33854e−3	+0.115776	−0.315792	−1.84259e−2	−1.44373e−12	−0.062159
+2.77093e−5	−1.00689e−3	+2.43505e−2	−0.338482	+0.062159	+4.1744e−13

Q_{rR} =

+0.258663	+6.28672e−2	+6.51918e−3	−0.045759	−0.252443	−2.97312e−2
+6.29295e−2	+0.269792	−3.57869e−2	−1.85092e−3	−9.48866e−2	−0.253722
+6.70331e−3	−0.036042	+0.47974	−0.126505	+7.50639e−4	−4.09461e−2
−4.58500e−2	−1.59458e−3	−0.126765	+0.4758835	−3.81955e−2	+1.23877e−2
−0.252352	−9.48607e−2	+8.51114e−4	−3.81419e−2	+0.26623	+6.15014e−2
−2.97663e−2	−0.253845	−4.099735e−2	+1.23716e−2	+6.15317e−2	+0.255080

Q_{rI} =

+2.04332e−4	−5.69196e−2	+0.341844	−2.87862e−2	−2.5272e−3	+3.00338e−4
+0.056486	+9.54057e−5	+0.021507	+0.31787	−0.115518	+8.20695e−4
−0.341868	−2.11394e−2	−2.09527e−4	+0.112851	+0.315791	−2.43919e−2
+2.89543e−2	−0.318522	−0.112338	−2.77355e−4	+1.84024e−2	+0.338665
+2.20579e−3	+0.115919	−0.315778	−1.84647e−2	+1.21765e−4	−6.21942e−2
+1.40785e−5	−1.02484e−3	+2.42153e−2	−0.38823	+0.06193	+6.58953e−5

Table II

	1	2	3	4	5	6	7	8	9	10
∂	−5.4	−4.8	−4.8	−4.8	−5.2	−5.2	−5.2	−5	−5.4	−5.1
∂_2	5.2	5.1	5	4.8	4.8	4.7	5.2	5.4	4.8	5.2

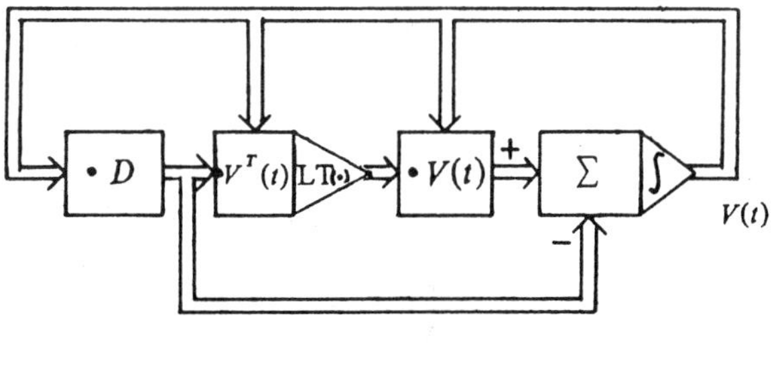

Figure 1

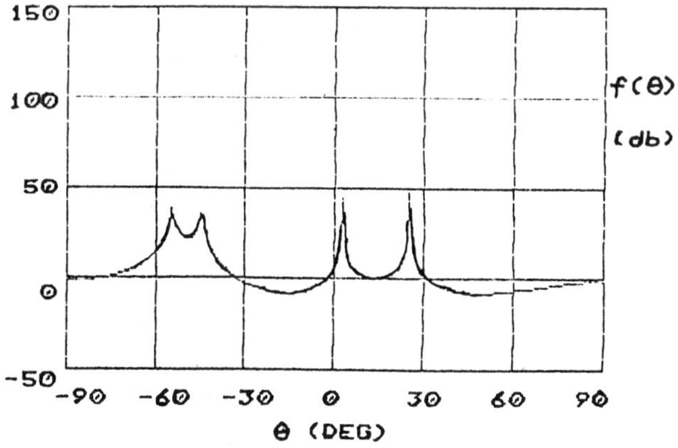

Figure 2

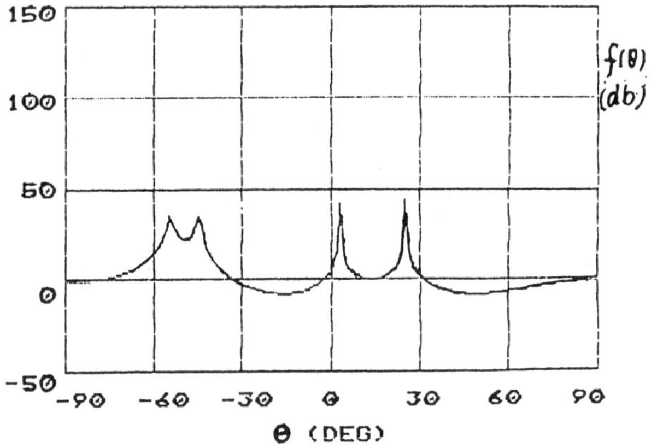

Figure 3

Performance Characterization Of Artificial Neural Networks For Contact Tracking

David J. Ferkinhoff, Chung T. Nguyen, Sherry E. Hammel, Kai F. Gong

Naval Undersea Warfare Center Division Newport
Newport, Rhode Island 02841

Abstract - *Artificial neural networks (ANN's) can be exploited in a variety of information processing applications because they offer simplicity of implementation, possess inherent parallel processing characteristics and are nonlinear and less reliant on modeling of the real process. This paper is concerned with the problem of determining performance of ANN's trained to provide estimates of contact state variables given a time series of measurements. A method is presented for determining ANN performance. Specifically, performance is shown to be intrinsically related to system observability. A performance analysis of ANN's under various observability conditions is presented along with a methodology for selecting the appropriate ANN-generated solution with a system architecture comprised of multiple clusters of ANN's.*

I: INTRODUCTION

Tracking in the ocean environment involves determining the position and velocity, or state, of a contact using a sequence of noise corrupted measurements. In most undersea tracking problems, the measurements are nonlinearly related to the contact state. Consequently, linearized or nonlinear estimation techniques using various modeling assumptions must be employed.

Performance of these techniques is known to be intrinsically related to system observability [1-3]. Here, observability is a measure of the information content of the data, and is influenced by signal-to-noise ratio and the geometric and kinematic relationship between the observer and the contact. In conditions of poor system observability, linearization can introduce large estimation errors [4,5]. Uncertainties associated with the data and system models further encumber the estimation process [6-8]. Consequently, stability is a major concern in traditional tracking methods, such as the extended Kalman filter and maximum likelihood estimator (MLE). Grid-based search methods, which partition the contact state space and then compute and evaluate the corresponding conditional density values, can overcome this instability but are very computationally expensive.

The inherent simplicity, computational speed and stability of artificial neural networks (ANN's) may provide performance gains and alleviate many of the difficulties associated with nonlinear tracking. However, their appropriateness will depend on the allowable system complexity and realizable performance. Factors impacting performance include pattern selection, training time and system architecture.

In a previous analysis, issues associated with training and applying ANN's have been explored [9]. That analysis, which used patterns obtained from segmenting the state space, revealed the importance of observability on ANN training. This paper extends that investigation to a more rigorous examination of the relationship between ANN performance and observability.

In the sections that follow, the formulation of the tracking problem and traditional solutions are presented. The ANN approach is then briefly described. Next, a method for characterizing and analyzing performance is presented which relates the Cramer-Rao lower bound (CRLB), pattern distributions and ANN estimation errors to system observability. Experimental results using this method are presented for angle-of-arrival measurements.

II: TRADITIONAL PROBLEM FORMULATION AND SOLUTION

Trajectory estimation entails relating a time series of measured data to contact parameters. The quantities measured by many sensor systems are angles-of-arrival, which are azimuthal bearing or conical bearing depending on the sensor employed. In this paper, we consider the conical bearings-only tracking problem. As shown in Figure 1, conical bearing is the angle between the sensor array axis and the direction of signal arrival. With rotational symmetry about the array axis, the contact under observation can be located anywhere on the surface of revolution, which is a cone. Thus, the measurement-to-contact state relation is highly nonlinear.

Let $\underline{x}(t) = [r_x(t), r_y(t), v_x(t), v_y(t), z]^T$ define the Cartesian state vector, comprised of 3-dimensional contact position, $[r_x(t), r_y(t), z]^T$, and 2-dimensional contact velocity, $[v_x(t), v_y(t)]^T$, relative to the observer. The parameter z represents the relative depth between the contact's image and the observer and is assumed constant. It can be seen from Figure 1 that the conical bearing, $\beta_c(t)$, is related to $\underline{x}(t)$ by

0-7803-1385-2/93/$3.00

$$\beta_C(t) = \cos^{-1}(\cos[\beta(t)-O_C(t)] \cos[\theta(t)]) \tag{1}$$

where $O_C(t)$ is observer course, and the azimuth bearing $\beta(t)$ and D/E angle $\theta(t)$ are given by

$$\beta(t) = \tan^{-1}[r_x(t) / r_y(t)] \ , \tag{2}$$

$$\theta(t) = \tan^{-1}[z / r(t)] \tag{3}$$

with r(t) the horizontal range given by $(r_x^2(t) + r_y^2(t))^{1/2}$.

Assuming constant contact velocity, the unknown state vector $\underline{x}(t^*)$, defined at some arbitrary time t^*, can be propagated to measurement time t via the system dynamics described by

$$\underline{x}(t) = A(t,t^*)\, \underline{x}(t^*) - \underline{a}_O(t,t^*) \tag{4}$$

where

$$A_{5x5}(t,t^*) = \begin{bmatrix} I_{2x2} & (t-t^*)I_{2x2} & 0 \\ 0 & I_{2x2} & 0 \\ 0 & 0 & 1 \end{bmatrix} \ , \tag{5}$$

and $\underline{a}_O(t, t^*)$ is a deterministic vector depicting observer acceleration. Hence, the contact trajectory most representative of the sensor data sequence can be ascertained from estimating $\underline{x}(t^*)$.

The noisy measurement at time t_i is given by

$$\beta_C(t_i) = h_i(\underline{x}) + \eta_i \ ; \ \eta_i \sim N(0,\sigma_i^2) \tag{6}$$

where $h_i(\underline{x})$ is the function defined by equation (1) and where explicit delineation of the reference time t^* for $\underline{x}$ has been omitted for convenience. Denoting

$$\underline{Z} = [\beta_{Ct1}, \beta_{Ct2}, \beta_{Ct3}, \ldots, \beta_{Ctk}]^T \ , \tag{7}$$

$$H(\underline{x}) = [h_1^T(\underline{x}), h_2^T(\underline{x}), h_3^T(\underline{x}), \ldots, h_k^T(\underline{x})]^T , \tag{8}$$

$$\underline{U} = [\eta_1, \eta_2, \ldots, \eta_k]^T , \qquad E[\underline{U}\, \underline{U}^T] = W \tag{9}$$

the measurement sequence can be expressed as

$$\underline{Z} = H(\underline{x}) + \underline{U} \ . \tag{10}$$

As shown in [10], determining the maximum likelihood estimate is equivalent to finding

$$\hat{x} = \min_{\hat{x}}\{ \| \underline{Z}-H(\underline{x}) \|^2_{W^{-1}} \} \ . \tag{11}$$

Performing the above operation yields

$$\hat{x} = [A^T M^T W^{-1} M A]^{-1} A^T M^T W^{-1/2} \tag{12}$$

where

$$M = \partial H(\underline{x}) / \partial \underline{x} \ , \ \underline{x} = \hat{x} \tag{13}$$

The term $[A^T M^T W^{-1} M A]$ in (12) is the Fisher Information Matrix (FIM). The FIM must be non-singular for $\hat{x}$ to be uniquely determinable, or observable, from the data [11,12].

Inherent to the problem formulation are assumed system models. However, in many situations the models may not be known exactly. Traditional methods of solving the nonlinear tracking problem are not only sensitive to mismodeling, but also to errors introduce by linearization and initialization. As such, they may be prone to ill-conditioning and instability [4,5,7].

To enhance the estimation process, ANN's can potentially be applied because they not only can infer unknown relationships from data, but they are inherently nonlinear and can respond properly to patterns that are only broadly similar to the training patterns [13]. In the remainder of this paper, we will describe ANN implementation and explore performance to determine their appropriateness for nonlinear contact tracking.

III: ARTIFICIAL NEURAL NETWORK IMPLEMENTATION

Segmentation of the Problem Domain

A critical step in developing a neural network is the selection, analysis and representation of the training patterns. From equations (1-7), it is seen that Z is a function of spatial and temporal variables and noise. Specifically, for a contact traveling at a constant velocity, the spatial and temporal variables include: initial range and bearing, observer and contact speed, course and depth, observer acceleration, and time-on-leg which represents a period of constant observer motion. In addition, there may be other parameters including the length of data gaps, signal propagation conditions and sensor orientation. When the problem domain is viewed in terms of all of these variables, the number of training patterns required to cover the problem space is unwieldly. It was previously found that training a single ANN using patterns that span the entire problem space is intractable [9].

In order to obtain acceptable levels of performance with practical training sets, a segmentation strategy was derived. As shown in Figure 2, the observer is constrained such that it can end anywhere in the shaded areas. The contact can begin in the shaded area W1 and end in W2. Range, bearing and depth are also constrained between times t_1 and t_2 [9]. To generate patterns with this strategy, both observer and contact parameters were derived from uniform distributions with limits given in Table 1.

ANN Architecture, Data Representation and Training

For each segment of the problem domain, a separate ANN cluster is proposed as shown in Figure 3. Within each cluster, individual ANN's are trained to provide estimates of the contact parameters: range, r, bearing, β, speed, S, course, C and D/E angle, θ. This enhances ANN estimation accuracy through the separation of parameters being estimated within each cluster.

The five individual ANN's are fully connected back propagation networks using the sigmoid function. Each ANN has fifteen inputs, thirty neurons for the first hidden layer, ten neurons for the second layer, and one output.

The measurement data is represented as the input by eight compressed parameters, obtained from a third order regression fit to each of two data legs of the conical bearings. Other inputs include: observer speed and time on each leg and the change in the components of observer's heading with the corresponding length of any data gaps.

With the problem segmentation strategy and the ANN architecture defined, training patterns can be generated with geometries randomly chosen from a pre-defined segment. Training is accomplished via a Quasi-Newton back propagation method [14].

IV: PERFORMANCE CHARACTERIZATION

One index of performance commonly employed for traditional estimation techniques is the CRLB, which specifies the best performance achievable for unbiased estimators. Assuming constant noise level, σ^2, the CRLB can be denoted as

$$\mathbf{R} = E\,[(\underline{x} - \hat{\underline{x}})(\underline{x} - \hat{\underline{x}})^T] \geq (\mathbf{F}_o \sigma^2)^{-1}\,, \tag{14}$$

where $\mathbf{R}$ is the error covariance and $\mathbf{F}_o$ is the normalized FIM representing the information content in the observation model given by

$$\mathbf{F}_o = -E\{\partial^2 \ln P \,/\, \partial \underline{x}^2\} \,/\, \sigma^2 \tag{15}$$

where

$$P = P[\underline{\mathbf{x}} \mid \underline{Z}] = K \exp\{-\tfrac{1}{2}\ \| \underline{Z} - H(\underline{\mathbf{x}}) \|^2_{W^{-1}}\}\ . \tag{16}$$

The quadratic form of $\mathbf{R}$ defines a hyper-ellipsoid depicting the distribution of errors with the one sigma volume expressed as

$$V_{1\sigma} = \pi\, |\mathbf{R}|^{1/2}\,, \tag{17}$$

where $|\cdot|$ denotes determinant [11,12]. As indicated by (14), the error covariance matrix and FIM are inversely related. Hence, the uncertainty can also be expressed by

$$V_{1\sigma} \geq \pi\, |1/\mathbf{F}_o|^{1/2} \tag{18}$$

In nonlinear estimation problems, the CRLB can be realized by linearizing the error covariance matrix about the true states; i.e., by replacing $\hat{x}$ in (13) with the true state vector, $\underline{x}$ [15]. Using (18), theoretical aspects of algorithm performance can be also be discerned by incorporating error free states in the FIM. The ability to achieve an accurate solution from the data is thereby intrinsically related to system observability. For nonlinear estimation problems, the geometric and kinematic relation between contact and observer appears in the covariance matrix via the linearization term (13).

Specific impacts of observer motion on estimation accuracy have been examined in previous studies for traditional estimation techniques [1]. In general, the relative geometric and dynamics in a scenario becomes an intrinsic factor in characterizing algorithm performance through system observability.

An analogous relation is examined in this paper with regard to ANN system performance. To this end, two distinct segments of the state space were selected and the corresponding ANN clusters were trained. The allowable ranges were bounded such that a scenario could be either classified as a short- or long-range encounter (segment) with relatively high or low dynamics, respectively. As will be seen in the next section, the observability characteristics of each encounter are different.

Using $\log_{10}|\mathbf{F}_o|$ as the index of system observability , histograms for both training and testing patterns for each segment can be plotted to reflect the degree of system observability. Then, performance of each ANN cluster can be examined relative to the CRLB via Monte Carlo simulation for test patterns within each segment.

To obtain performance parameters, the observability index axis was partitioned and experiments with N_s noise sequences were executed for all patterns within each bin. The mean error and variance of the bearing and inverse range estimates for the lth observability bin were computed via:

$$m_{pl} = \frac{1}{K_l} \sum_{k=1}^{K_l} \frac{1}{N_s} \sum_{j=1}^{N_s} (p_{kj} - \hat{p}_{kj}) \tag{19.a}$$

$$\sigma^2_{pl} = \frac{1}{K_l} \sum_{k=1}^{K_l} \frac{1}{N_s} \sum_{j=1}^{N_s} (p_{kj} - \hat{p}_{kj} - m_{pl})^2 \tag{19.b}$$

where p represents either β or $1/r$ and K_l is the number of geometries in the lth bin. The averaged ANN variances were then plotted as a function of observability and performance compared to the respective averaged CRLB as an indication of relative performance.

In addition, to evaluate performance of the multiple-clusters system architecture of Figure 3 we employed the method of feature detection and non-detection for identifying and selecting the ANN cluster which provides the correct solution for arbitrary geometries [6-8].

V: EXPERIMENTAL RESULTS AND DISCUSSION

ANN training and performance analysis were conducted using the two segments defined in Table 1. Both training and testing patterns were generated for each geometry with a data rate of 20 seconds. An ANN cluster was constructed for each segment.

For illustration purposes, we trained the azimuth bearing and range ANN's for each cluster using 1000 noise free patterns. Using the method described in Section IV, performance analysis was conducted using 10,000 test patterns corrupted with zero mean Gaussian noise with standard deviations of 0.05° and 0.10°.

The distributions of both training and testing patterns are shown in Figure 4 as a function of observability . To obtain the performance parameters, we partitioned the distribution into 80 bins. The equivalency of the training and test distributions in the figure indicates that the performance results obtained were meaningful. Monte Carlo experiments with N_s=200 were executed for all patterns within each bin. The mean errors and variances are computed via (19). Since the results for both ANN clusters are similar, only those of the short-range ANN's are shown.

For the measurement noise levels considered, the mean errors obtained in both bearing and range were small within the interval of observability studied. The average azimuth bearing and range errors were 0.18° and 137m, respectively.

The ANN variances as a function of observability are plotted in Figure 5 along with the corresponding CRLB. In addition, the ratios of ANN variance to CRLB are illustrated in Figure 6 and are shown to be always greater than one. Therefore, the ANN's were not efficient estimators. It was also observed that while the CRLB varies directly with the input noise variance, increasing the ANN input noise by a factor of four increased the output noise variance only by a factor of 3.4. More experiments need to be conducted to determine the appropriate functional relationship of ANN variance to the input noise level.

Inspection of these figures shows that the minimum ANN-based variances occur at approximately the distribution peak. The variances decrease or increase with increasing observability depending on the location of bins that are to the left or right of the peak, respectively. This behavior is due to three contributing factors of the ANN-based variance: the observability, the number of training patterns, and the convergence threshold or achievable level of convergence during training. The monotonically increasing ratio to the right of the peak shown in Figure 6 is due to the combination of this behavior and the monotonically decreasing CRLB.

To illustrate the performance of the system architecture with multiple ANN clusters, we used a conical bearing sequence of a randomly selected geometry from the short-range segment and applied to both ANN clusters. Residuals generated using the estimated range and bearing from both with assumed known velocity and depth are shown in Figure 7. These results suggest that the validity of the short-range ANN solution can be ascertained based on the residual signal and existence of features in the long-range ANN residual signal.

VI: SUMMARY AND CONCLUSION

Performance of ANN systems for tracking in the undersea environment was addressed . Both traditional statistical and ANN methods for solving the tracking problem along with factors affecting performance were presented. Central to both is system observability which generalizes all parameters characterizing the tracking scenarios used in generating the training and testing pattern sets. A method for characterizing and analyzing ANN system performance was presented. The method relates ANN estimation errors and CRLB to observability. Performance analysis using ANN clusters trained with conical bearings-only tracking scenarios was presented.

Experimental results showed that the method proposed for assessing ANN tracking system performance is very effective. First, the analysis provides insights into achievable solution accuracy, relative to the CRLB for unbiased estimators, as a function of observability. Second, it provides knowledge of solution behavior. Because the analysis showed that the ANN system examined followed the expected performance trend when viewed in the context of observability and pattern distribution, it can provide a guide to the level of suitability of ANN's for tracking. Third, it suggests that observability can be exploited to enhance segment definition and pattern manipulation, as well as improving the training and testing process.

The level of accuracy achieved by the ANN's for the highly nonlinear conical bearings-only tracking problem indicates they may be useful for initializing traditional tracking algorithms. However, for the ANN clusters considered, performance could be improved by training with noise, increasing the number of training patterns, adjusting the segment parameters, overlapping the distributions, and/or by weighting the training patterns, all as a function of observability.

Acknowledgment: This work was supported by the Office of Naval Research, program manager D. Houser ONR-T-232. The authors would like to thank the technical contributions of the people at Code 2211 NUWC Division Newport, and of Dr. N. A. Pendergrass of the University of Massachusetts Dartmouth.

Segment	β_{max}	β_{min}	z_{max}	z_{min}	r_{max}	r_{min}
Short-Range	60°	20°	2.5 km	0 km	10km	5km
Long-Range					30km	25km

Table 1: Sample Segments of the State Space

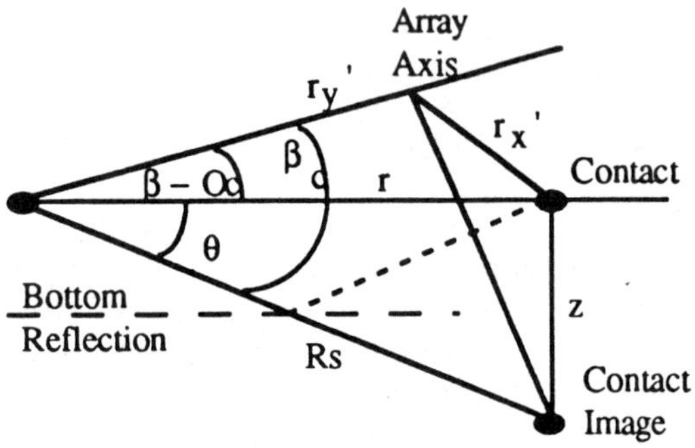

Figure 1: Conical Bearing

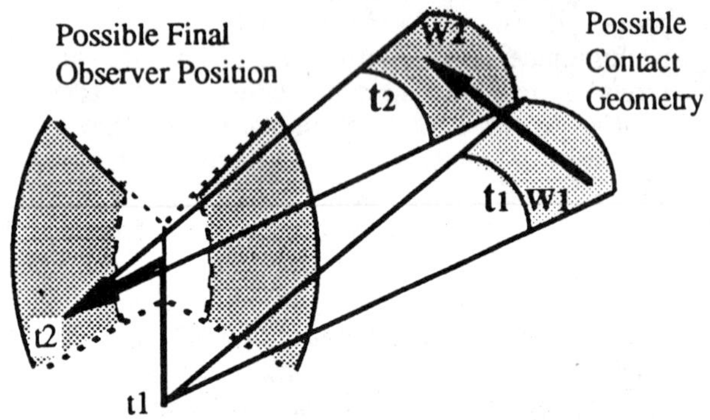

Figure 2: Segmentation Strategy

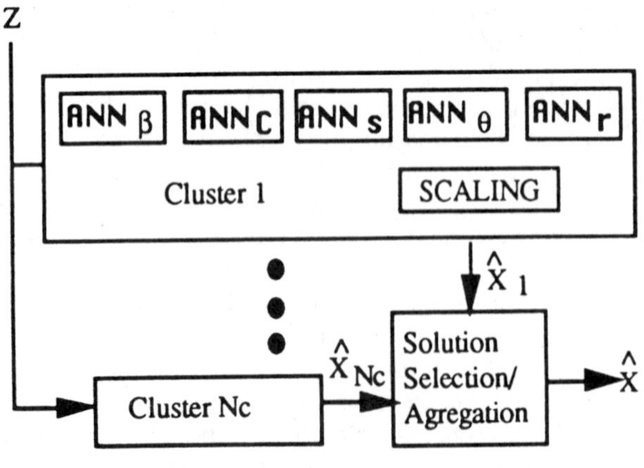

Figure 3: ANN Clusters for N_c Segments

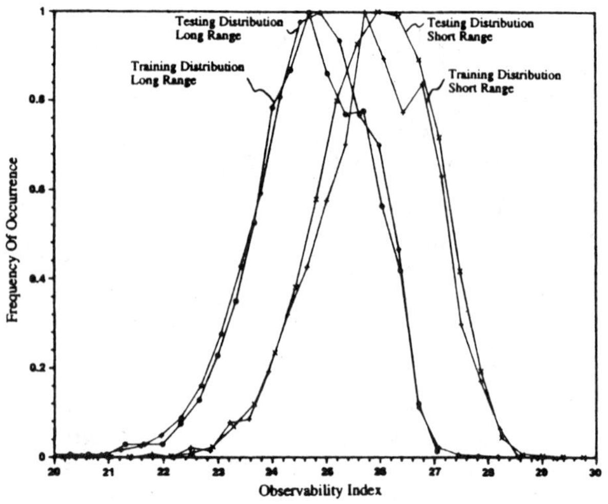

Figure 4: Pattern Distribution vs. Observability

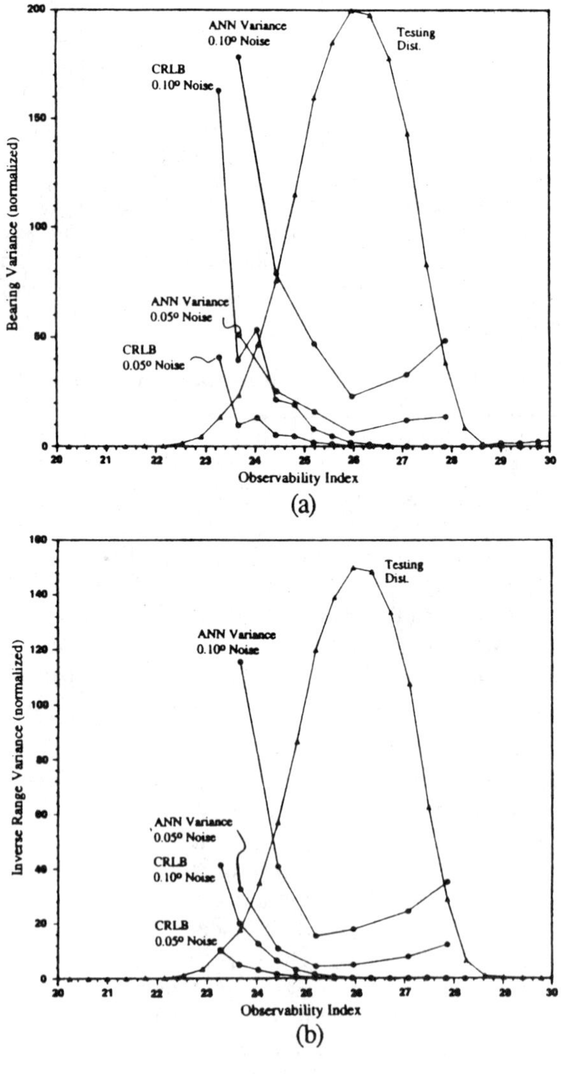

Figure 5: ANN Variance and CRLB for
(a) Bearing (b) Inverse Range

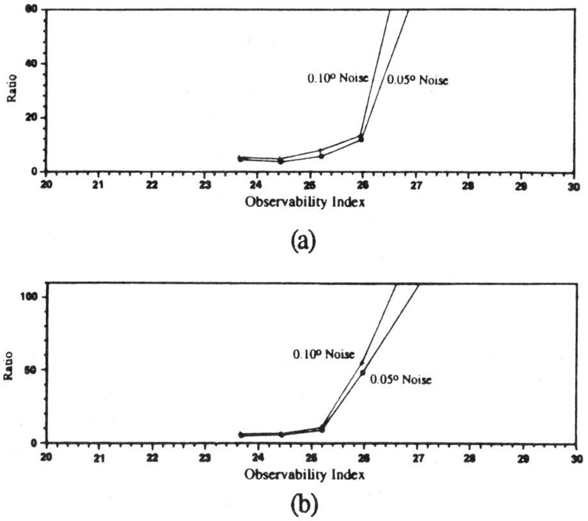

Figure 6: Ratio of ANN-based Variance to CRLB
(a) Azimuthal Bearing (b) Inverse Range

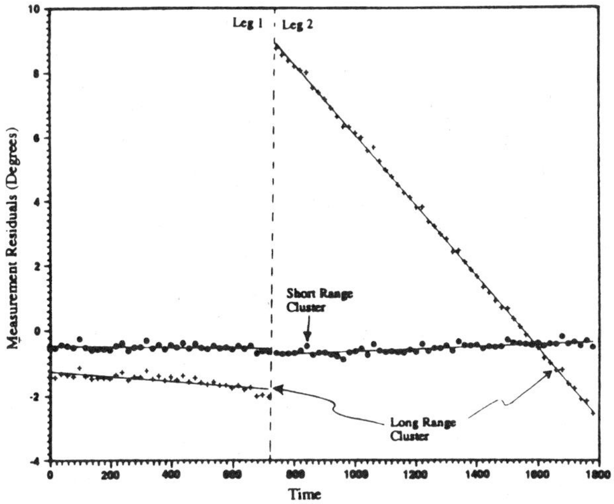

Figure 7: Residual Sequences

REFERENCES

1. S. E. Hammel, "Optimal Observer Motion for Bearings-Only Localization and Tracking," Ph.D. Dissertation, Mathematics Dept., University of Rhode Island, R.I., 1988.

2. S.E. Hammel and V.J. Aidala, "Observability Requirements for 3-Dimensional Tracking via Angle Measurements," IEEE Trans. on Aerospace and Electronic Systems, Vol. AES-21, Mar. 1985.

3. V. J. Aidala and S. E. Hammel, "Utilization of Modified Polar Coordinates for Bearings-Only Tracking, " IEEE Transaction on Automatic Control, Vol. AC-28, Feb. 1983.

4. V. J. Aidala, "Kalman Filter Behavior in Bearings-Only Tracking Applications,"IEEE Trans. on Aerospace and Electronic Systems, Vol. AES-15, No. 1, Jan. 1979.

5. S. E. Hammel, V. J. Aidala, K. F. Gong and A. Lindgren,"Recursive vs. Batch Processing Algorithms forBearings-Only Tracking," Proc. of the 1983 International Ocean Engineering Conf., Aug. 1983.

6. K. F. Gong, J. G. Baylog and A. A. Magliaro, "A Decision-Directed Approach to Solution Integration for Tracking in An Underwater Environment," Proc. of the 18th Asilomar Conf. on Signals, Systems and Computers, Nov. 1984.

7. J. G. Baylog, A. A. Magliaro, S. M. Zile and K.F. Gong, "Underwater Tracking in the Presence of Modeling Uncertainty," Proc of the 21st Asilomar Conf. on Signals, Systems and Computers, Nov. 1987.

8. D. J. Ferkinhoff, J.G. Baylog, K. F. Gong and S.C. Nardone, "Feature Extraction and Interpretation for Dynamic System Model Resolution," Proc. of the 24th Asilomar Conf. on Signals, Systems and Computers, Nov. 1990.

9. D. J. Ferkinhoff, C. DeAngelis, K. F. Gong, S E. Hammel and R. Green, "On Training Artificial Neural Networks for Tracking in the Ocean Environment," Proceeding of the 1992 International Conference on Ocean Engineering, Oct. 1992.

10. H. Sorenson, Parameter Estimation Principles and Problems, Vol. 9, Marcel Dekker, Inc., New York, NY, 1980.

11. A. H. Jazwinski, Stochastic Processes and Filtering Theory, Academic Press, N.Y., 1970.

12. H. L. Van Trees, Detection, Estimation, and Modulation Theory, Part I, John Wiley and Sons, Inc., N.Y., 1968.

13. D. Hammerstrom, "Working with Neural Networks," IEEE Spectrum, July 1993.

14. R. Fletcher, Practical Methods of Optimization John Wiley and Sons, Inc., N.Y., 1990.

15. J. H. Taylor, "The Cramer-Rao Estimation Error Lower Bound Computation for Deterministic Nonlinear Systems," IEEE Trans. Automatic Control, Vol. AC-24, April 1979.

A FAST ADAPTIVE NEURAL NETWORK SCHEME FOR MULTI-MANEUVERING TARGET TRACKING

Jing Zhongliang Zhang Guowei Zhou Hongren

Department of Automatic Control
Northwestern Polytechnical University
Xi' an, 710072, PRC

Abstract

In this paper, a new fast adaptive neural network scheme (FANNJPDAF) based on joint probabilistic data association filter (JPDAF) for multi-maneuvering target tracking (MMTT) is presented. The computational burden of MMTT can be reduced drastically by stochastic neural network. Computer simulations show that the scheme has high convergence performance, good accuracy and robustness to the uncertainty of target and clutter environments.

1. Introduction

The theory and applications of multi-maneuvering target tracking (MMTT) have been received considerable attention in recent years. How to track multi-maneuvering targets fast and precisely has always been the main object of designing MMTT system [1]. Since it was presented by Bar-shalom in 1974 [2], JPDAF has been regarded as a powerful and reliable tool without any priori information about targets and clutters for MMTT. However, the number of possible hypotheses associating different returns to targets under consideration increases rapidly with the number of returns, the presence of clutters increases the complexity further. The complexity proves to be significant for a number of targets in moderately dense clutter and results in the combinatorial explosion of computation. This situation limits the wide applications of JPDAF. Though there have been efforts to approach the performance of JPDAF, the effectiveness of these approximations in tracking many targets in the presence of clutter is not guaranteed.

The investigation on neural network brings about a streak of light to this problem. In this paper, by means of stochastic neural network, a new fast adaptive neural network scheme FANNJPDAF is presented. Simulations show that the scheme not only can solve the combinatorial explosion of computation of joint probabilistic data association (JPDA), but also is an effective and reliable method for MMTT.

2. Hopfield neural network and gain annealing algorithm

The general Hopfield network is commonly described by a set of first-order differential dynamic equations [3]

$$C_i \frac{dU_i}{dt} = \sum_j T_{ij} V_j - \frac{U_i}{R_i} + I_i \tag{1}$$

$$V_i = g(U_i) \tag{2}$$

where U_i is the state, V_i is the output, I_i is the input bias current, $T_{ij}\,(=T_{ji})$ is the conductance connecting neuron i and j, R_i and C_i are the resistance and capacitance of neuron i, respectively. $g(U_i)$ is a monotonically increasing sigmoid function. To have a gradient system, the *Lyapunov* energy function for this network is

$$E = -\frac{1}{2} \sum_i \sum_j T_{ij} V_i V_j + \sum_i V_i I_i + \sum_i \frac{1}{R_i} \int_0^{V_i} g^{-1}(V)\, dV \tag{3}$$

The network can converge to one of the stable equilibria (minimum states of the associated energy function) if the initial conditions are sufficiently close to the stable equilibrium. The stable equilibria can be regarded as the near-optimal so-

0191-2216/93/$3.00 © 1993 IEEE

lutions to the problem.

Hopfield neural network has attracted considerable attention as candidates for solving the typical combinatorial optimization problem-TSP [4,6]. Chose g(•) to be

$$V_i = g(U_i) = \frac{1}{1+\exp(-U_i/\lambda_0)} \qquad (4)$$

The state trace of Hopfield neural network is associated with the gain (λ_0) of the neuron. If λ_0 is large, some local equilibria can be avoided. However, the rate of convergence is slow and not suitable for real-time processing. If λ_0 is small, the rate of convergence is fast and suitable for real-time processing, but the equilibrium reached may only be a local minimum. So, at the beginning of convergence, a large value for λ_0 is chosen, than λ_0 is lowered gradually. This is called gain annealing algorithm [7]. It allows the neural network to converge to good solutions.

3. JPDA and its combinatorial explosion of computation

The dynamic equations for targets in dense clutter environments are

$$X^t(k+1) = \Phi^t X^t(k) + G^t w^t(k), t \leqslant T \qquad (5)$$

the measurement models are as follows

$$z^t(k) = \begin{cases} HX^t(k)+v(k), & \text{when from } t\text{th target,} \\ Y(k), & \text{when from clutter} \end{cases} \qquad (6)$$

where $X(k)$ is target state vector, $z(k)$ is measurement vector, $w(k)$ is a vector of zero-mean Gaussian noise uncorrelated with any such noise vector at a different instants of time, $v(k)$ is a zero-mean Gaussian noise vector independent of $w(k)$, the vectors $v(k)$ at different time instants are assumed to be independent of each other. The covariance matrices $Q(k)$ and $R(k)$ of $w(k)$ and $v(k)$, respectively, are known. Φ and G are known matrices describing the dynamics of targets, H is the measurement matrix. The measurement due to clutter $Y(k)$ is uniformly distributed over the validation region. The innovation vector is introduced

$$d(k) = z(k) - H\hat{X}(k|k-1) \qquad (7)$$

its covariance is

$$S(k) = HP(k|k-1)H^T + R(k) \qquad (8)$$

where $\hat{X}(k|k-1)$ and $P(k|k-1)$ are the predicted state and error covariance, respectively. Define the distance function as

$$g(k) = d^T(k)S^{-1}(k)d(k) \qquad (9)$$

in order to track T targets in dense multi-return environments, all the received returns should be correlated to T targets respectively. By designing the tracking threshold or correlation region for each target, $V_u^t(k)$, T sets of validated return are produced:

$$Z^t(k) = \{z_{r^t}(k)\}_{r^t=1}^{m^t(k)} \quad t=1,2,\cdots T \qquad (10)$$

where $m^t(k)$ denotes the number of returns in the validation region of tth target. The set of all the validated returns is:

$$Z(k) = \{Z_r(k)\}_{r=1}^{m(k)} \qquad (11)$$

where $m(k)$ denotes the number of all validated returns at instant k. The validation matrix can be formed in the following way:

$$[\Omega(k)]_{r,t} = \begin{cases} 1, & Z_r(k) \in V_u^t(k) \\ 0, & Z_r(k) \notin V_u^t(k) \end{cases} \qquad (12)$$

the number of "1" in the tth column of $[\Omega(k)]$ equals to $m^t(k)$

Define the following event:

$\theta_r^t(k) = \{z_r(k)$ comes from the tth target$\}$

$\theta_0^t(k) = \{$no valid return comes from tth target$\}$

The state estimate of tth target can be derived to be

$$\hat{X}^t(k|k) = E[X^t(k)|Z(k)] = \sum_{r=0}^{m(k)} \beta_r^t(k)\hat{X}_r^t(k|k) \qquad (13)$$

where $\hat{X}_r^t(k|k)$ is the state estimate under the hypothesis that the rth validated return comes from the tth target. The weight $\beta_r^t(k)$ corresponds to the probability that the rth return comes from the tth target and

$$\beta_r^t(k) = \begin{cases} P\{\theta_0^t(k)|Z(k)\}, & \text{if } r=0 \\ P\{\theta_r^t(k)|Z(k)\}, & \text{if } r\neq 0, \text{ and } [\Omega(k)]_{r,t}=1 \\ 0, & \text{otherwise} \end{cases} \qquad (14)$$

$\beta_r^t(k)$s satisfy $\sum_{r=0}^{m(k)} \beta_r^t(k) = 1$.

In order to calculate $\beta_r^t(k)$, consider the feasible joint events defined as

$$\varepsilon(n,k) = \bigcap_{r=1}^{m(k)} \theta_r^{t_r}(k) \qquad (15)$$

where n indexes the set of such joint events, $\{t_r$:

$r=1,2,\cdots,m(k)\}$ is a permutation of targets and clutter points. The case $t_r \neq 0$ corresponds to targets and $t_r=0$ to clutter. The feasible hypotheses matrix $\odot(k)$ $(N\times T)$ is formed as follows, its every row corresponds to a feasible hypothesis

$$[\odot(k)]_{n,t}=\begin{cases} r, \text{if the } t\text{th target is associated with the } r\text{th return under the hypothesis } \varepsilon(n,k) \\ 0, \text{if the } t\text{th target is not associated with any return under the hypothesis } \varepsilon(n,k) \end{cases}$$

Then

$$\theta_r^t(k)=\bigcup_{\{n:[\odot(k)]_{n,t}=r\}} \varepsilon(n,k), \quad t=1,2,\cdots,T \tag{16}$$

And

$$P\{\varepsilon(n,k)\,|\,Z(k)\}=\frac{1}{C}P\{Z(k)\,|\,\varepsilon(n,k),Z(k-1)\} \tag{17}$$

where C is a normalizing constant. The joint likelihood function is represented as

$$\begin{aligned} P\{Z(k)\}\,|\,\varepsilon(n,k),Z(k-1)\} &= \prod_{r=1}^{m(k)} P\{Z_r(k)\,|\,\varepsilon(n,k),Z(k-1)\} \\ &= \lambda^{m(k)-T} \prod_{t=1}^{T} p^t_{[\odot(k)]_{n,t}}(k) \end{aligned} \tag{18}$$

where

$$p_r^t(k)=\begin{cases} \lambda(1-Pd), \text{if } r=0 \\ \frac{1}{(2\pi)^{M/2}|S^t(k)|^{1/2}}\exp[-\frac{1}{2}g_r^t(k)]Pd, \quad \text{if } r\neq 0 \text{ and } [\Omega(k)]_{r,t}=1 \\ 0, \quad \text{otherwise} \end{cases} \tag{19}$$

λ is the clutter density, Pd is the probability of accepting correct returns, M is the order of the measurement vector, $g_r^t(k)$ is the distance between rth return and tth target defined by (9), $S^t(k)$ is the innovation covariance matrix. The joint probability of JPDA is derived as

$$\beta_r^t(k)=\sum_{\{n:[\odot(k)]_{n,t}=r\}} P\{\varepsilon(n,k)\,|\,Z(k)\},$$
$$t=1,2,\cdots,T.\ r=0,1,\cdots,m(k) \tag{20}$$

The number N of the feasible joint events is

$$N=\prod_{t=1}^{T} m^t(k) \tag{21}$$

It is obvious that the number N of possible hypotheses associating different returns to targets under consideration increases repidly with the clutter density λ and the target number T. Therefore, the increase of complexity in computing association probabilities may be significant for a number of taregts in moderately dense clutter and results in the combinatorial explosion of computation. This situation limits the wide applications of JPDA.

4. Analyses of the features of JPDA and introduction of neural network

JPDA has two distinguishing features [5,8] which make it to be excellent in MMTT compared with other methods. Define the event $G(X)$ as

$G\{X\}=\{$variable X possesses large value$\}$

Then the two distinguishing features of JPDA are

Feature 1 $\quad G\{\beta_r^t(k)\}\cap G\{\beta_r^\tau(k)\}=0, \text{if } t\neq\tau$

Feature 2 $\quad G\{\beta_r^t(k)\}=G\{p_r^t(k)\}\cap G\{\prod_{\substack{t\neq\tau \\ j\neq r}} p_j^\tau(k)\}$

JPDA has the following constraints

1. $\sum_{r=0}^{m(k)} \beta_r^t(k)=1, t=1,2,\cdots,T$
2. $G\{\beta_r^t(k)\}\cap G\{\beta_r^\tau(k)\}=0$ if $t\neq\tau$: it is impossible for two or more targets to generate a return
3. $G\{\beta_r^t(k)\}\cap G\{\beta_{r'}^t(k)\}=0$ if $r\neq r'$: every target can generate one and only one return
4. $G\{\beta_r^t(k)\}=G\{p_r^t(k)\}\cap G\{\prod_{\substack{t\neq\tau \\ j\neq r}} p_j^\tau(k)\}$: to find the best association probabilities

Now, we form a $(m(k)+1)\times T$ neural network matrix, the columns represent targets and the rows indicate returns. The zeroth row corresponds to the special event that no return comes from a given target. If the output voltages $V_r^t, r=0,1,\cdots,m(k), t=1,2,\cdots,T$, of neurons are defined to be the association probabilities $\beta_r^t(k)$, the energy function is

$$\begin{aligned} E_{DAP}=&\frac{A}{2}\sum_r\sum_t\sum_{t\neq\tau} V_r^tV_r^\tau+\frac{B}{2}\sum_r\sum_t\sum_{j\neq r} V_r^tV_j^t+\frac{C}{2}\sum_t(\sum_r V_r^t-1)^2 \\ &+\frac{D}{2}\sum_r\sum_t(V_r^t-\rho_r^t)^2 \\ &+\frac{E}{2}\sum_r\sum_t\sum_{t\neq\tau}(V_r^t-\sum_{j\neq r}\rho_j^\tau)^2 \end{aligned} \tag{22}$$

The $\rho_r^t(k)$ are the normalized versions of the $p_r^t(k)$. In (22), the first term corresponds to the constraint 2, the second term corresponds to the constraint 3, the third term corresponds to the constraint 1, the fourth and fifth terms correspond to the constraint 4. Formula (22) can be rewriten as

$$E_{DAP}=-\frac{1}{2}\sum_r\sum_j\sum_t\sum_\tau W^{t\tau}_{rj}V^t_rV^\tau_j-\sum_r\sum_t V^t_rI^t_r \tag{23}$$

where

$$W^{t\tau}_{rj}=-[A\delta_{rj}(1-\delta_{t\tau})+B\delta_{t\tau}(1-\delta_{rj})+C\delta_{t\tau}+D\delta_{t\tau}\delta_{rj}+E(T-1)\delta_{t\tau}\delta_{rj}] \tag{24}$$

$$I^t_r=C+(D+E)\rho^t_r+E(T-1-\sum_\tau\rho^\tau_r) \tag{25}$$

It is very obvious that the strengths of connection $W^{t\tau}_{rj}$ given by (24) do not depend on ρ^t_r and are formed completely by the coefficients A,B,C,D and E. Thus a new network need not be designed every a new set of likelihood functions are available. Instead, the input currents I^t_r described by (25) can be controlled easily by these functions. This makes parallel processing very convenient for the neural network: once the ρ^t_rs received, the network starts its dynamic evolution process and reaches one of the stable equilibria. At this moment, the output voltages of V^t_rs correspond to association probabilities β^t_rs. In this way, the complexity in computing association probabilities in MMTT under dense multi-return environments can be reduced drastically. The superior performance of the neural network method have been shown fully when the clutter density and the target number increase.

5. FANNJPDAF scheme

Based on the "Current" Statistical Model [1], JPDAF and stochastic neural network, We can give the FANNJPDAF scheme for MMTT as follows:

Under the hypothesis that the rth validated return comes from the tth target, the state update is

$$\hat{X}^t_r(k|k)=\hat{X}^t(k|k-1)+P^t(k|k-1)H^T(k)S^t(k)^{-1}[z_r(k)-H(k)\hat{X}(k|k-1]$$
$$r=1,2,\cdots,m(k) \tag{26}$$

The covariance update is

$$P^t_r(k|k)^{-1}=P^t(k|k-1)^{-1}+H^T(k)R^t(k)^{-1}H(k) \tag{27}$$

The zeroth return corresponds to the special event that the correct return is not among the validated set of returns in which case

$$\hat{X}^t_0(k|k)=\hat{X}^t(k|k-1) \tag{28}$$

$$P^t_0(k|k)=P^t(k|k-1) \tag{29}$$

The overall state estimate is given by a weighted combination of all the estimates under different hypotheses

$$\hat{X}(k|k)=\mathrm{E}[X^t(k)|Z(k)]=\sum_{r=0}^{m(k)}\beta^t_r(k)\hat{X}^t_r(k|k) \tag{30}$$

The weight $\beta^t_r(k)$ corresponds to the probability that the rth return came from the tth target, which can be obtained by stochastic neural network. The overall covariance update is

$$P^t(k|k)=\sum_{r=0}^{m(k)}\beta^t_r(k)[P^t_r(k|k)+\hat{X}^t_r(k|k)\hat{X}^t_r(k|k)^T]-\hat{X}^t(k|k)\hat{X}^t(k|k)^T \tag{31}$$

Finally, the state and covariance predictions are

$$\hat{X}(k+1|k)=\Phi^t(k)\hat{X}^t(k|k)+U^t(k)\bar{a}^t(k) \tag{32}$$

$$P^t(k+1|k)=\Phi^T(k)P^t(k|k)\Phi^t(k)^T+Q^t(k) \tag{33}$$

The innovation covariance is

$$S^t(k)=H(k)P^t(k|k-1)H^T(k)+R^t(k) \tag{34}$$

If we consider the one-step-ahead prediction $\hat{\ddot{x}}^t(k+1|k)$ of $\ddot{x}^t(k)$ as the current acceleration and also as the mean value of randomly maneuvering acceleration at the instant k, an acceleration mean value adaptive algorithm can be obtained. So let

$$\bar{a}^t(k)=\hat{\ddot{x}}^t(k+1|k) \tag{35}$$

Now, the acceleration variance adaptive algorithm can be accomplished. That is, we let

$$\sigma_a^{2(t)}=\frac{4-\pi}{\pi}[a_{max}-\hat{\ddot{x}}^t(k+1|k)]^2=\frac{4-\pi}{\pi}[a_{max}-\hat{\ddot{x}}^t(k|k)]^2 \tag{36a}$$

when the current acceleration $\hat{\ddot{x}}^t(k|k)$ is positive, or

$$\sigma_a^2(t)=\frac{4-\pi}{\pi}[-a_{-max}+\hat{\ddot{x}}^t(k|k)]^2 \tag{36b}$$

when the current acceleration $\hat{\ddot{x}}^t(k|k)<0$.

and

$$Q^t(k)=2a\,\sigma_a^{2(t)}Q^t_0 \tag{37}$$

where, a_{max} and a_{-max} are the known positive and negative acceleration limits of the targets, respectively; a is the reciprocal of the maneuver time constant, Q^t_0 is a known matrix.

6. Computer simulation

The equations of motion for the energy function defined as (22) are

$$\frac{dU_r^t}{dt}=-\frac{U_r^t}{to}-A\sum_{\substack{\tau=1\\ \tau\neq t}}^{T}V_r^{\tau}-B\sum_{\substack{j=0\\ j\neq r}}^{m(k)}V_j^t-C(\sum_{j=0}^{m(k)}V_j^t-1)$$
$$-[D+E(T-1)]V_r^t+(D+E)\rho_r^t$$
$$+E(T-1-\sum_{\tau=1}^{T}\rho_r^{\tau}) \quad (38)$$

and

$$V_r^t=g(U_r^t)=\frac{1}{2}(1+\tanh\frac{U_r^t}{2\lambda_0} \quad (39)$$

In order to examine the effectiveness of FANNJPDAF, computer simulation is done. The difference equation for (38) is

$$U_r^t(i+1)=\frac{s_0-\xi}{s_0}U_r^t(i)-\xi A\sum_{\substack{r=1\\ r\neq t}}^{T}V_r^T(i)-\xi B\sum_{\substack{j=0\\ j\neq r}}^{m(k)}V_j^t(i)$$
$$-\xi C(\sum_{j=0}^{m(k)}V_j^t(i)-1)-\xi[D+E(T-1)]$$
$$V_r^t(i)+\xi(D+E)p_r^t+\xi E(T-1-\sum_{r=1}^{T}\rho_r^T) \quad (40)$$

s_0 and ξ were selected to be 1s and 0.00001s, respectively. An experimentally determined limit of 400 iterations was imposed on the recursive equation (40). The 400th iterates $V_r^t(400)$, $r\leqslant m(k)$, $t\leqslant T$ are expected to be close to the steady state solutions of (38) and considered as $\beta_r^t(k)$. The values of the parameters are chosen as follows: $A=5$, $B=38$, $C=950$, $D=32$, $E=6$, $\lambda=0.2km^{-2}$. The computer simulations indicate that a suitable operating point can be obtained for a range of target and clutter densities. In order to get high convergence performance, good accuracy and high robustness, the gain annealing algorithm is used. So let

$$\lambda_0=0.01*0.995^k$$

k is the iteration times.

Figure 1 gives the tracking traces of ten maneuvering targets. Table 1 lists the root-mean-square (RMS) errors of tracking. The results show that FANNJPDAF has very satisfactory performance for MMTT.

7. Conclusion

The analyses and computer simulation results confirm that the FANNJPDAF scheme proposed in this paper does indeed track highly multi-maneuvering targets, has high convergence performance, good accuracy and high robustness to the uncertainty of targets and clutter environments, and is an effective and reliable method for MMTT.

8. References

[1] Zhou Hongren, Jing Zhongliang, Wang Peide. "Tracking of Maneuvering Targets." *Beijing, China: National Defence Industry Press*, 1991.

[2] Fortmann T E, Bar-Shalom Y, Scheffe M. "Multitarget Tracking Using Joint Probabilistic Data Association." *Proceedings of 19th IEEE Conference on Decision and Control*, 1980: 807—812.

[3] Hopfield J J, Tank D W. "Computing with Neural Circuits: A Model." *Science*, 1986; 233: 625—633.

[4] Wilson G V, Pawley G S. "On the Stability of the Traveling Salesman Problem Algorithm of Hopfield and Tank." *Biological Cybernetics*, 1988; 58: 63—70.

[5] Bar—Shalom Y, Fortmann T E. "Tracking and data association." *Oriando: Academic Press*, 1988.

[6] Hopfield J J. Tank D W. " 'Neural' Computation of Decisions in Optimization Problems." *Biological Cybernetics*, 1985; 52: 141 — 152.

[7] Kirkpartick S, Gelatt C, Vecchi M(1983). "Optimization by Simulated Annealing." *Science* 220: 671—680.

[8] Debasis Sengupta, Ronald A. Iltis, "Neural Solution to the Multitarget Tracking Data Association Problem." *IEEE Trans. AES*, 1989, 25(1): 96-108.

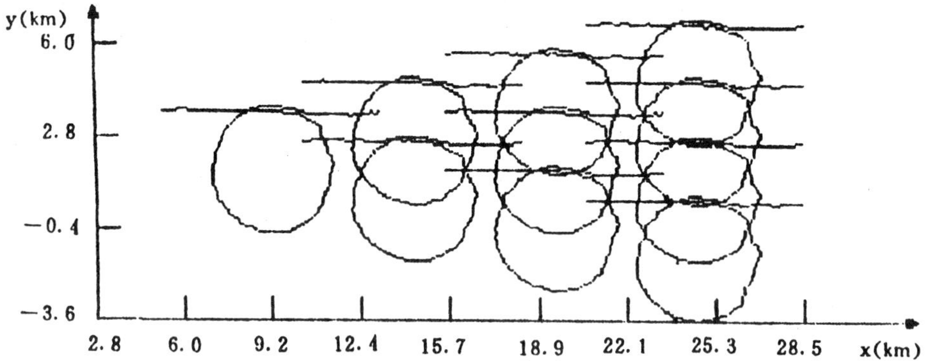

Fig. 1 Tracking traces of ten maneuvering targets

Table 1 RMS Errors of Tracking

Target	Position (km)	Velocity (km/s)	Acceleration (km/s^2)
1	9.773430E−002	7.744120E−002	1.954616E−002
2	1.047592E−001	8.074360E−002	2.148012E−002
3	1.009956E−001	8.011974E−002	2.087224E−002
4	1.133226E−001	8.457156E−002	2.392528E−002
5	1.101342E−001	8.396661E−002	2.332949E−002
6	1.071354E−001	8.347872E−002	2.282547E−002
7	1.230582E−001	8.867351E−002	2.673586E−002
8	1.201659E−001	8.821356E−002	2.616481E−002
9	1.175078E−001	8.781704E−002	2.566210E−002
10	1.150884E−001	8.752530E−002	2.525668E−002

Chapter 9: Virtual Reality

CHAPTER 9
Virtual Reality

Virtual reality has ignited a great deal of excitement over the past few years. Virtual environments for shopping, exercising, learning, and playing are seen as large revenue applications of the future. One key consideration that must be made in virtual reality is the man-machine interface. In some instances the interface is an extension of current technology (e.g., vision and hearing systems), but other interfaces will pose tremendous difficulty.

Neural networks are being used in virtual reality to facilitate the interface between the machine and the human. Examples of these interfaces include mapping voice to facial expressions, mapping human motion to video motion, and mapping video motion to human feedback effectors.

The use of neural networks as an enabling technology has only begun. In the coming years I envision this will be a major application area for neural networks in the area of communications, speech processing, image/vision processing, and control.

This chapter contains two papers on neural network technology in support of virtual reality. **Paper 9.1** describes the use of a MLP to generate facial animation models for use in virtual reality telecommunications. **Paper 9.2** presents shows how a MLP can be used to map voice to facial expressions.

Neural Modeling of Face Animation for Telecommuting in Virtual Reality

THOMAS P. CAUDELL, ADAM L. JANIN, AND SEAN K. JOHNSON[†]
Boeing Computer Services
MS 7L-66
P.O. Box 24346
Seattle, WA 98124-0346

Abstract

Neural networks are used to generate facial animation models for use in virtual reality telecommuting systems. 2D face silhouettes are used to train and test multilayer perceptrons with backpropagation learning. This approach overcomes the problems encountered with the integration of face sensing devices and visual displays.

1. Introduction

The term "Telecommuting" was originated by Jack Nilles in 1975 [1] to describe the concept of people working together in remote physical locations using personal computers and telephones. The socioeconomical advantages and disadvantages of telecommuting have been studied by many researchers ([2], [3]). The prime advantages are higher quality work output, lower worker stress, longer uninterrupted work sessions, reduced ware on the transportation infrastructure, reduced use of petrochemicals, and improved worker job satisfaction. The prime disadvantages are management fear of control loss, lack of personal face-to-face interactions leading to a feeling of isolation by telecommuting workers and supervisors, and the basic cost of telecommuting hard- and software. Although several companies have started telecommuting programs on a voluntary bases for jobs that involve information processing or management, such as secretarial and computer programmers, the practice is not widely used in industry. The perceived need for face-to-face workplace interactions verses the trend towards more "cocooning" in the home [4], has lead to a dilemma in the effective use of the telecommuting paradigm.

Immersive virtual reality (VR) provides a technological solution to the "face-to-face/cocooning" dilemma in telecommuting. The idea is to equip the telecommuter with a VR system that is connected through the telephone system to other telecommuters with similar equipment. With head-mounted graphical displays, body-suit interaction systems, 3D sound systems and a microphone, the worker will perceive and interact with coworkers in a natural way, as if they are in each other's physical presence. The coordinates of the person's body components, such as his head, arms, torso, and legs, as well as audio signals would be transmitted to the receiving station, where a graphics engine animates a polygonal human model of the transmitter. The receiver views this in his local head-mounted display. With suitable compression techniques, the signal bandwidth for near real time communication is well within that found in standard telephone transmission lines. Several people could simultaneously work together within this virtual workplace, forming a strong team spirit, while never leaving home.

The dilemma is not solved completely by the above scenario. A critical missing component is the transmission of facial information. Although "body language" conveys much, the face is the primary conveyor of personal feelings and attitudes. Face transmission poses a practical problem in VR telecommuting systems -- unobstructed view of the users face. If not for the fact that part of the face is covered with a video display system, a standard video camera could image the face in motion, compress the video, transmit it over the telephone lines to the receiver's graphics engine, which could superimpose it on the human model. Unfortunately, this is not possible with the current generation of VR head mounted displays.

[†] Morehouse College, Atlanta, GA

0-7803-1363-1/93 $3.00 © 1993 IEEE

The solution known to several researchers ([5], [6], [7], [8]) is to model the dynamics of the face in motion using either interpolation techniques or anatomical face muscle models. With such a model, a reduced number of parameters of the model needs to be transmitted to the receiving station for animation. Colors and textures can be added to the face models to add realism. Real time models based on facial anatomy have been developed in the last few years that execute on graphics workstations [9]. Other researchers have developed a system that tracks special features on the face from which they control texture maps for the animation of face models [10]. There are three primary disadvantages of these approaches: 1) it is difficult to rapidly customize the model for each individual telecommuter's face, 2) one must develop methods to sense facial features under the graphics video display, and 3) a great deal of processing power is necessary to execute anatomical models.

In this paper, we present the preliminary results in the application of artificial neural networks to the automatic generation of face animation models. The network "learns" the complex nonlinear mapping between position sensor readings on the face and the position of graphical polygons that best fit the real face. The following section describes the neural approach in some detail. The third and fourth sections discuss the data collection and preprocessing of 2D face silhouettes. The fifth section gives the results of the neural modeling of the face silhouettes, and the sixth section draws conclusions and discusses future work.

2. The Neural Solution

Artificial neural networks have been used in many applications to form highly nonlinear mappings between high dimensional feature spaces [11]. Although several different types of neural architectures can perform this function ([12], [13]), we focus in this paper on a class of networks called multilayer perceptrons. The architecture is characterized by a "feed forward" layered structure, where weighted signals from the outputs of neurodes (neuron node) in one layer flows into the inputs of the next layer. Such an architecture in shown in the central portion of Fig. 1.

The layers not directly accessible to the inputs or outputs are called hidden layers. The constituent neurodes are called hidden nodes. The network learns through a weight adjustment algorithm called, in this case, backpropagation ([14], [15], [16]). The training data consists of a set of example input/output pairs of vectors representing the mapping between the input space and the output space. A vector from the input set is presented to the input neurodes. The signals forward propagate through the network until they reach the output neurodes where they are compared to the associated output vector. Backpropagation learning performs an error reducing correction to the weights in the network for each presentation. The error is defined as the root-mean square difference between each neurodal output in the output layer and a vector of target output values, summed over all example input/output vector pairs in the training set. The training set is presented to the system multiple times in what are called presentation epochs, until the total error has reduced to an acceptable level. The number of hidden nodes determines the degree of generalization produced by the trained network when it is applied to a testing set of input/output vector pairs not previously presented to the network for learning. Too many hidden nodes and the system will memorize the data, too few hidden nodes and the system will poorly generalize previously unused pattern classifications.

Fig.1 illustrates how such a network learns a personal face model. A set of training data is collected from the person by a 3D scanner (such as the laser scanner of Cyberware) while they are talking and making a wide range of facial expressions. This data is then preprocessed (Sec 4.) and a small set of sampling points on the face is extracted. Distances from the sample points to nearby fixed points on a rigid reference surface are computed in software and are used as the input parameters to the model. The full set of face polygons is used as target values for the outputs of the model. This forms one example mapping in the training set composed of (input parameter, output polygons) pairs. Many such pairs are presented to the network in random order to constitute one training epoch. Many such epochs are performed to reduce the total error to an acceptable level. At this point, the network is trained and ready for production use. In production, the network weights are frozen and the network is used in forward propagation mode only.

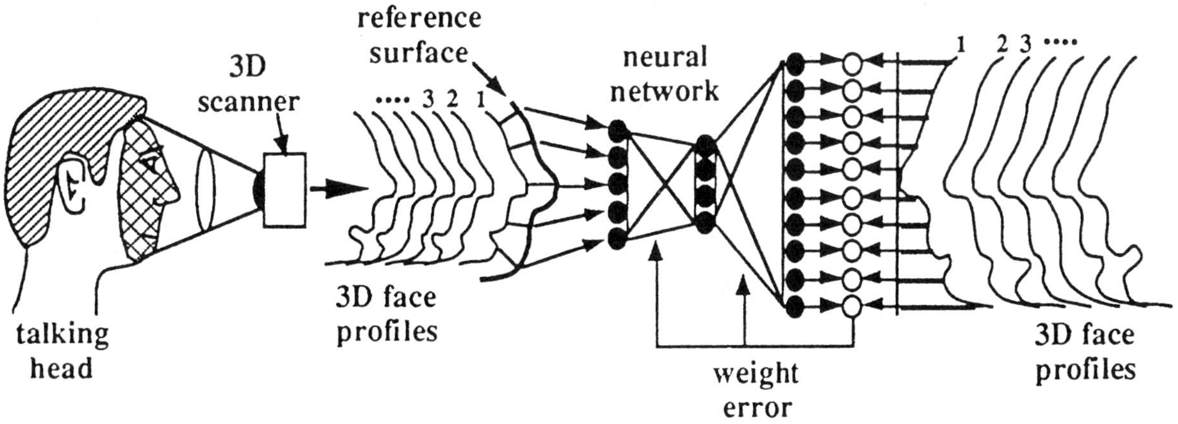

Figure 1. Diagram of training of network with face data.

Fig. 2 shows how the network is used in a telecommuting system. At startup time, after a telephone connection has been made, the face model is downloaded into the receiver's graphics engine. The transmitting individual dons a face mask that contains, in addition to the displays, a grid of gap sensors as seen in Fig. 3. The grid forms the physical counterpart of the reference surface used during training. Distance measurements are made in real time between the same selected sample points on the face used during training. As illustrated in Fig. 2, these distances are relayed to the inputs of the remote neural network over the telephone lines. At the other end, the network forward propagates the inputs to produce and display in real time an animated polygonal estimate of the original face. The gap sensors are not addressed in this paper, although either optical, acoustic, or electromagnetic technology may be used for their implementation.

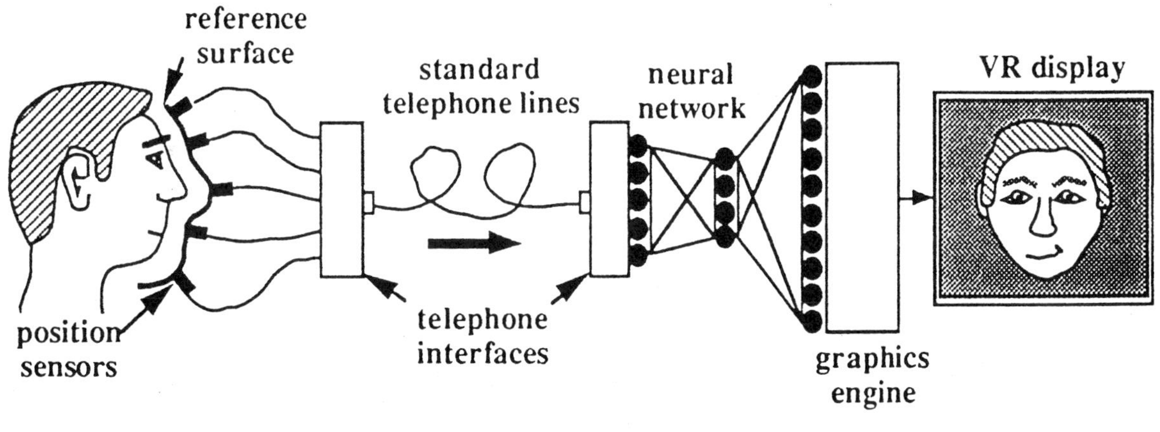

Figure 2. Diagram of neural network operational system

Several issues need to be resolved before this system can be implemented. First, the ability of a neural network to capture and generalize the expressions and conformations of facial expressions needs to be proved. Second, a procedure for the selection of the smallest set of sampling points must be devised. To begin addressing these two issues, we used a somewhat simpler set of face data in a prototype system.

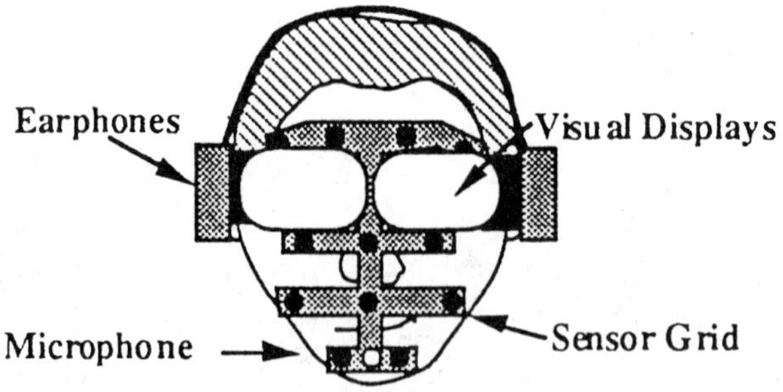

Figure 3. Example sensor points and a close up of Face Mask / Display

3. Face Silhouette Data Collection

To demonstrate the feasibility and to study the practical issues in the generation of neural face models, we generated models of 2D face silhouettes. Fig. 4 shows a diagram of the experimental setup for data collection. The subject stands with her shoulder against a wall near a convex corner. The room behind the corner is brightly illuminated, forming a high contrast scene. A black and white video camera mounted on a tripod and interfaced to a standard VHS video recorder is trained on the head of the subject as seen in Fig.4. The scale of the image is adjusted to leave a sharp baseline edge above and below the talking head. While holding as still as possible, the subject talks and makes facial expressions as the session is taped. No attempt has been made to control what is said or the expressions made.

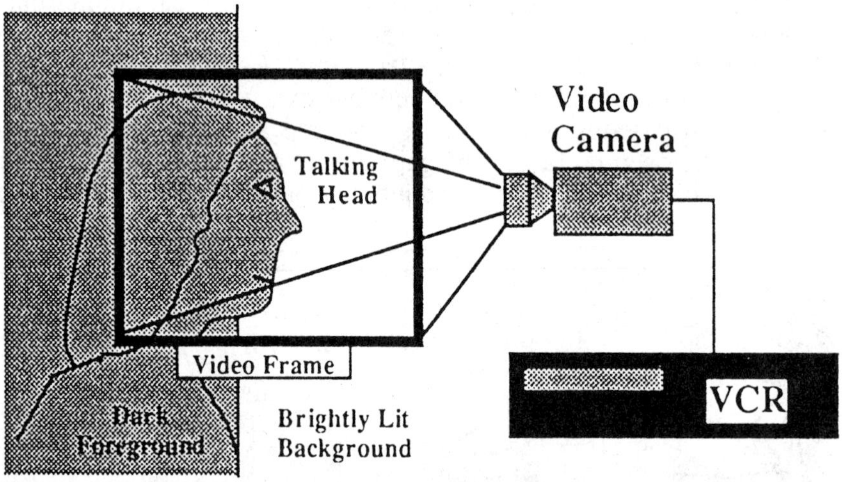

Figure 4. Configuration of high contract video silhouette collection system

For this pilot study, approximately five minutes of tape were produced. The tape was taken to a computer with a video frame grabber card for digitization. There, the tape was played into the computer and frames were grabbed as fast as possible. For this system, the grab rate was approximately once per second, leading to 299 face silhouettes. The eight-bit deep digitized 640x480 pixel image was converted into an edge list by a simple thresholding technique. Each row was searched from the right to find the column number where the intensity dropped to half its maximum value. A set of 480 edge column numbers was generated for each of the 299 faces. Following this, an average baseline edge was subtracted from each edge list and the result was stored for subsequent analysis.

4. Data Preprocessing

It is necessary to preprocess the data before presentation to the neural network for two reasons. First, glitchy or bad digitization scans must be removed. Second, the data must be transformed into a uniform location and scale because it is difficult for this type of network to learn "invariances" from a small set of data. After deglitching and rejecting bad edge lists from the face data, 229 sillhuettes remained.

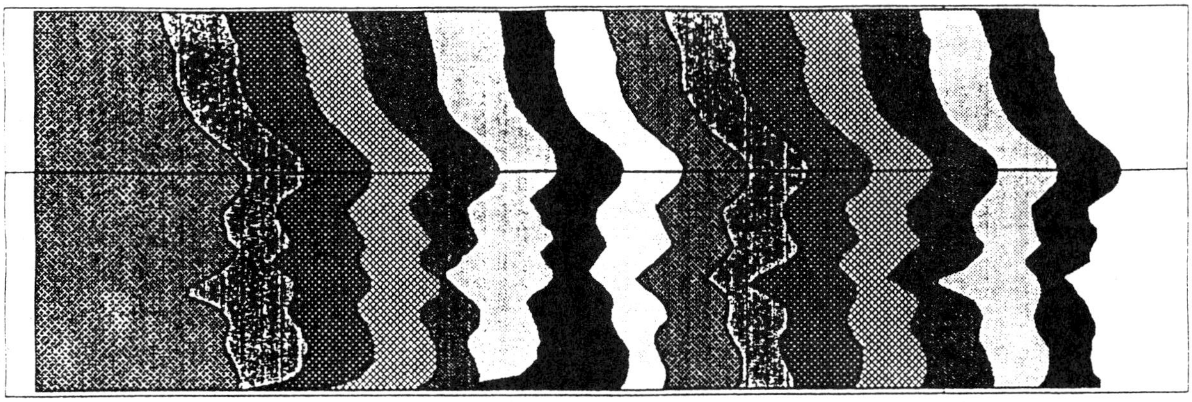

Figure 5. Processed, smoothed, and translated face edge profiles for a short sequence .

The transformation to a uniform position provided an interesting challenge. After perusing the data a number of times, we discovery the nose invariant -- the tip of the nose in this subject did not change shape significantly throughout the data set. We therefore adopted this point as an invariant, and translated all edge lists both in row and column number to a standard nose tip location. After translation, the edge lists were truncated at the top and bottom to include the largest number of rows common in all lists, reducing the number of rows from 480 to 240. A few examples from the sequence of processed data are shown in Fig. 5 after smoothing with a five point triangle convolution filter and normalization to the [0,1] interval. The mean and standard deviation for the final set of face edge profiles are given in Fig. 6.

Since the edge positions vary smoothly along the face profile, and there exist sizable linear regions in most face samples, we conclude that not all of the edges in the list are necessary. We therefore applied a thinning filter which amounted to an automatic piecewise linear segmentation of the edges based on a population variance test on the linear pieces. Basically, this procedure forms the largest linear pieces, or 1D polygons, that tessellate the edge profile without exceeding a maximum error over the entire data set. Similar algorithms exist for 2D polygons. In this case, we set the error to be 0.3 times the original quantization error in the raw edge data, reducing the number of edges from 240 to 39. These larger 1D polygons were used in the training of the neural model.

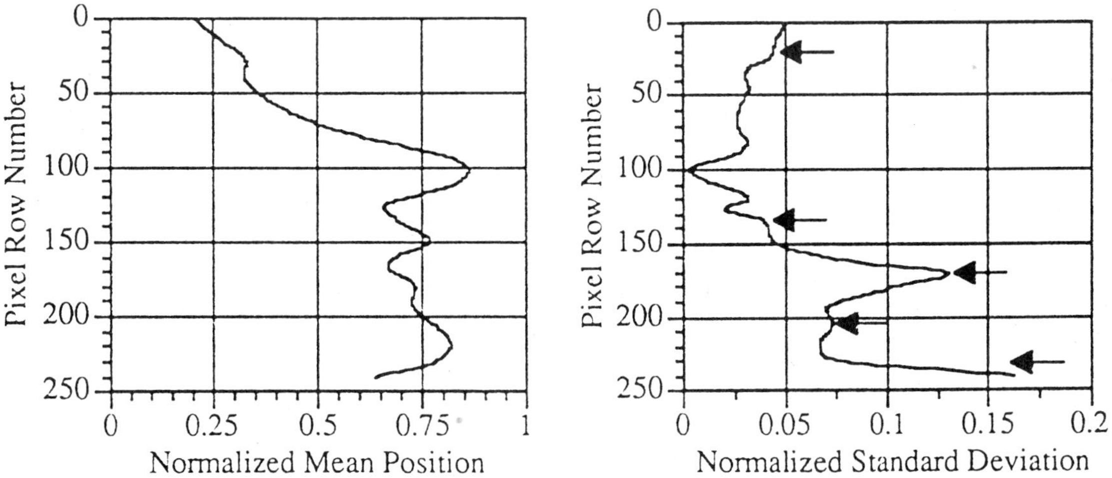

Figure 6. The mean and standard deviation face edge profile computed over the complete data set.

Before the network can be trained, the sample points must be selected. For this pilot study, the sample number and locations were manually picked based on the locations of the largest standard deviations plotted in Fig. 6 The arrows in the figure indicate their locations. More sophisticated optimization techniques based on maximizing regions of linear correlations have been designed, but were not necessary for this preliminary demonstration.

Trial	Hidden Units	Number of Epochs	% in Testing Set	RMS Error Training	RMS Error Testing
1	2	1000	25%	0.0406	0.0395
2	5	1000	25%	0.0296	0.0341
3	5	3000	50%	0.0284	0.0310
4	8	900	25%	0.0299	0.0272
5	10	1000	25%	0.0268	0.0287
6	15	2000	25%	0.0264	0.0307
7	20	175	25%	0.0379	0.0353

Table 1. Specific network parameters and fitting results for several network configurations.

5. Results of Neural Modeling

The multilayer perceptron used for this study had five input and 39 output neurodes. The number of hidden nodes was varied empirically. Training was performed with the vanilla backpropagation algorithm [17]. The learning rate was 0.05 and the momentum term was 0.01 with asynchronous weight updates. The weights were initialized with uniform random numbers between ±0.2. The data set was randomly divided into different training and testing subsets for each trial. During a trial, at intervals of 25 epochs, a validation test was performed with the testing subset. Training was terminated when either the validation error began to increase or a maximum epoch limit was reached.

The results of several trials are given in Table 1. Column 1 lists the number of hidden nodes, column 2 lists the maximum allowable number of epochs, column 3 lists the percentage of the data set used for testing validation, column 4 lists the final root-mean-square error summed over all 39 output values and all training samples, and column 5 lists the final root-mean-square error summed over all 39 output values and all testing samples.

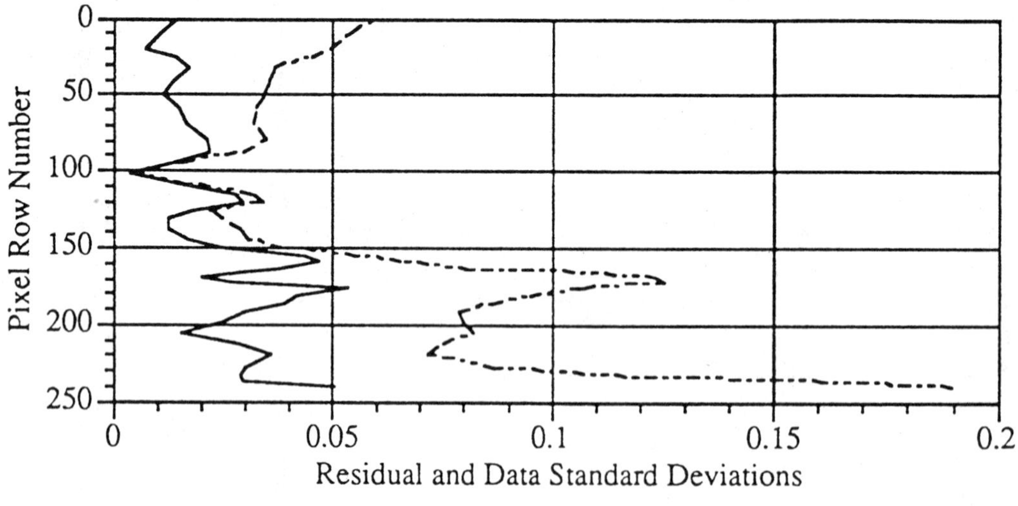

Figure 7. Testing data errors for Trail #5 in Table 1. Solid curve RMS residuals, dashed curve edge standard deviations.

To get a feeling for the goodness of these models, we plot in Fig. 7 the individual residual RMS errors for each output polygons along with the edge standard deviations for the testing data of Trial #5 in the table. The solid curve is the RMS error for the outputs while the dashed curve is the preprocessed data.

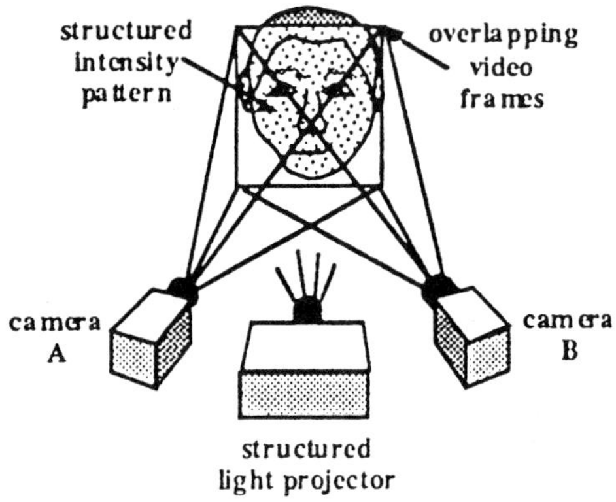

Figure 8. Configuration of stereo video face profiling using structured light

6. Discussion and Conclusions

The results given in Table 1 and Fig. 7 indicate that this simple neural model is to a large extent capturing the dynamics and deformations of this subject's facial expressions. In Fig. 7, the residuals are almost all significantly smaller than the variation found in the original edge data, showing that the network learned to generalize the nonlinear mapping between the sampled input measurements and the output face polygons. As a further demonstration of the performance of neural models, a video is being prepared for submission to the video proceedings.

Future work will involve larger 2D data sets, optimization of sampling points, experimentation with other neural architectures such as ARTMAP [12] and LAPART [13], and true 3D face data. Fig. 8 shows one possible method of collecting 3D face data currently under development using projected structured light and stereo metrology using video camera pairs [18].

Based on these experiments, we believe that neural networks have a potentially significant role to play in telecommunting and face model generation.

Acknowledgments

We would like to thank the subject talking head, Dr. Kathryn Ann Caudell, for facing up to this study and Drs. David Mizell and Henry Sowizral for many helpful comments and support.

References

1. J. M. Nilles, "Telecommuting and Organizational Decentralization", IEEE Trans. on Communications, Vol. 23, No. 10, pp. 1142-1147, 1975.
2. J. Fraser, "U.S. Telecommuting: Has Its Time Come", SRI International Technical Reprot #D91-157, 1991.
3. M. Quaid and B. Lagerberg, "Puget Sound Telecommuting Demonstration, Executive Summary", Washington State Energy Office Report #92-138, 1992.
4. M. Rose, "The Cocooning of America", Direct Marketing, pp.55-61, Feb. 1990.
5. F. I. Parke, "Computer Generated Animation of Faces", Proc. ACM Natil Conf., 1:451-457, 1972.
6. J. Kleiser, "A Fast, Efficient, Accurate Way to Represent the Human face", SIGGRAPH '89 Tutorial Notes: State of Art in Facial Animation, No 22, pp. 37-40, 1989.
7. M. Platt and N. I. Badler, "Animating Facial Expressions", Proc. SIGGRAPH '81, Computer Graphics, Vol. 15, No 3, pp. 245-252, 1981.
8. K. Waters, "A Muscle Model for Animating Three-Dimensional Facial Expressions", Proc. SIGGRAPH '87, Computer Graphics, Vol. 21, No 3, pp. 17-24, 1987.

9. B. deGaf, Notes on Facial Animation, SIGGRAPH '89 Tutorial Notes: State of Art in Facial Animation, No 22, pp10-11.

10. L. Williams, 'Performance Driven Facial Animation", Proc. SIGGRAPH '90, Computer Graphics, Vol. 24, No 3, pp.235-242.

11. R. D. Lipmann, "An Introduction to Computing with Neural Networks", IEEE ASSP, Vol. 4, No.22, 1987.

12. G. Carpenter, S. Grossberg, and J. Reynolds, "ARTMAP: Supervised Real-Time Learning and Classification of Non stationary Data by a Self-Organizing Neural Network", Neural Networks, Vol. 4, pp. 565-588, 1991.

13. J. Healy, T. P. Caudell, and S. D. G. Smith. "A Neural Architecture for Pattern Sequence Verification Through Inferencing", IEEE Transactions on Neural Networks, Vol. 4, No. 1, 1993.

14. E. Rummelhart and J. L. McClelland, Parallel Distributed Processing -- Explorations in the Microstructure of Cognition, Vol 1, Ch. 8, MIT Press Cambridge, Mass., 1986.

15. D. Parker, "Learning Logic", Invention report, S81-64, File 1, Office of Technology Licensing, Stanford University, 1982.

16. P. Werbos, "Beyond Regression: New Tools for Pridection and Analysis on the Behavioral Sciences", Ph.D. Dissertation, Harvard University, 1974.

17. K. Simpson, "Artificial Neural Systems -- Foundations, Paradigms, Applications, and Implementations", Pergamon Press, Ch. 5, p. 115, 1990.

18. S. K. Johnson, A. L. Janin, and T. P. Caudell, "See-thru Virtual reality Registration", Boeing Computer Services, Research and Technology Tech. Report #BCS-CS-ACS-92-006, 1992.

Facial Expression Synthesis Based on Natural Voice for Virtual Face-to-Face Communication with Machine

† Shigeo MORISHIMA and ‡ Hiroshi HARASHIMA
† Seikei University and ‡ University of Tokyo

† Faculty of Engineering, Seikei University
3-3-1 Kichijoji-kitamachi, Musashino Tokyo 180, Japan
Phone:+81-422-37-3726 Fax:+81-422-37-3871
E-mail:shigeo@tansei.cc.u-tokyo.ac.jp
‡ Faculty of Engineering, University of Tokyo
7-3-1 Hongo Bunkyo-ku Tokyo 113, Japan

Abstract -- Basic research to a virtual face-to-face communication environment between an operator and a machine is presented. In this system, human natural face appears on the display of machine and can talk to operator with natural voice and natural face expressions. Especially in this paper, face expression synthesis scheme driven by natural voice is presented. Voice is including not only linguistic information but also emotional features. So we proposed expression control scheme driven by both features. We express a human head with 3D wire frame model. The surface model is generated by texture mapping with 2D real image. All the motions and expressions are synthesized and controlled automatically by the movement of some feature points on the model.

1. INTRODUCTION[1][2][3][4][5][12]

A user friendly human-machine interface using Multi-media are focused recently. Our goal is to realize very natural human-machine communication environment by giving a face to computer terminal or communication system. It is virtual face-to-face communication system between user and machine. For this purpose, we have already proposed basic schemes including a 3D modeling of face, face expression synthesis and coding technique, media conversion schemes, modeling and rendering method of hair, and modeling method of emotional aspect of facial expression based on the parameter mapping using neural network. A real-time animation synthesizer based on Pixel Machine is constructed for the interface prototype system. In these schemes, *Facial Action Coding System (FACS)* is selected as the efficient criteria to describe delicate face expression and motion.

Voice is essential to multi-media interface. It's including linguistic information, speaker information, emotional information and so on. If these information can be extracted automatically, natural voice can be an information source of human-machine communication. Moreover, media conversion and media integration of multi-media can be realized in the semantic level.

This paper presents a facial expression synthesis scheme driven by natural voice. Especially, two aspects of voice are utilized to express face image. Mouth shape and its motion are controlled by the linguistic information of voice. Full face expressions are controlled by the basic emotional information included in natural voice.

In this paper, some basic schemes to synthesize natural face expression, synchronization method between synthesized motion image and natural voice, scenario making tool to express delicate face expressions and animation scenes and quantitative emotion model based on neural network are presented. The basic research of emotion extraction from natural voice is reported at last.

0-7803-1363-1/93 $3.00 © 1993 IEEE

2. *EXPRESSION SYNTHESIS*[8][13]

2.1. Modeling of Human Face

A 3-D generic model which approximately represents a human face, is composed of about 600 polygonal elements and was constructed by measuring a mannequin's head. This generic model is including the teeth's model inside the head. The generic model is 3-D affine-transformed to harmonize its several feature point positions with those of given 2-D full-face image. This point adjustment is done by semi-automatical procedures. Some feature points' positions around face, lip, eyes and eyebrows are recognized roughly using the results of color information analysis of original image. Some corrections of each feature point can be done manually if necessary.

RGB intensity for a 2-D full-face surface image is then projected and mapped onto an adjusted generic model, following which a 3-D personal facial model is created. This model has a set of points which have 3-D oblique coordinate values and intensity in every polygon.

Once the 3-D facial model is gotten from the 2-D original image, it's easy to rotate the 3-D model in any arbitrary direction or to give many delicate facial actions for lips, jaws, eyes, and eyebrows by controlling lattice points in the wire frame.

2.2. Facial Expression Synthesis

Facial image synthesis is composed of deforming the wire frame model through facial expression parameters and mapping the texture in every polygon of the original image onto the surface of the deformed wire frame model. The deforming rules are formulated to simulate the facial muscular actions. Ekman and Friesen decomposed the facial muscular actions into 44 basic actions called *"Action Units" (AUs)* and described the facial expressions as combinations of *AUs* .

We express each *AU* with the combination of the movements of some specific feature points in the wire frame model. We quantize the movement in each AU into 100 levels between maximum change and no change. So any intermediate expression can be synthesized by combination of *AUs* and their levels.

2.3. High Definition Model

Now, we have a high definition wire frame model (HD model) which is measured by 3D digitizer (Cyberware) and has 24000 polygons and surface texture all around the head. Figure 1 shows both generic model (600 polygons version) and HD model. However, HD model doesn't have every feature point explicitly, so HD model has to be controlled hierarchically using generic model after adjustment between generic model and HD model. This adjustment is done by analysis of front view texture synthesized by HD model.

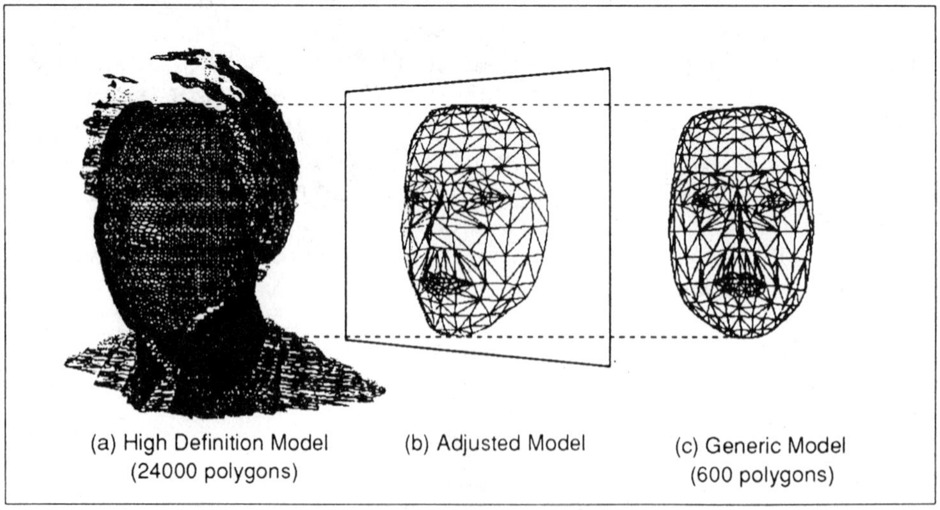

Figure 1. Hierarchical control of HD model with generic model

3. *MEDIA CONVERSION SCHEMES*[3][6][7][10][11]

When one is speaking, the motion around mouth can be predicted and synthesized only by text or voice. We have already proposed two types of media conversion schemes. They are Text-to-Image conversion and Voice-to-Image conversion. In the former system, mouth shape and motion are synthesized automatically by given Japanese or English text sentence. As the Voice-to-Image conversion system, we proposed two systems. These are frame by frame style conversion system based on neural network for real-time communication and recognition based conversion system for voice storage or voice mail. In the multi-media e-mail system, there may be both natual voice and mail text, so high quality mouth shape control and synchronization of voice and image can be achieved.

3.1. Text to Image Conversion

When each phoneme of sentences is analized to the *Allophone* code, a standard mouth shape and duration time are decided by the table of this allophone symbol. The number of typical mouth shapes are 17 categories in Japanese and 65 categories in English. In some consonants, the mouth shapes should be decided by an interpolation of the parameters between the preceding and following phonemes. Typical mouth shapes are located on the keyframes decided by the standard duration of each phoneme.

The motion between keyframes is decided upon by 3-D basis Spline interpolation of feature points. So, lip motions change very smoothly and naturally. In English, pronunciation is more complicated than Japanese and phonetic symbol and its duration time change according to word and accent. So, our dictionary much more categories for English.

To construct a Multi-media interface using this scheme, speech synthesis system is indispensable to make voice synchronize with synthesized motion image. Phonetic symbol and its duration are used at both image synthesis system and speech synthesis system.

3.2. Voice to Image Conversion for Communication System

For the voice communication system, real-time processing of speech and synthesis of image are essencial. Here, mouth shape is generated frame by frame basis with speech spectrum analysis. The window size is 32 msec. and frame rate is 1/30 second same as the video rate, so synchronization can be done simultaneously when there is no delay between video output and speech playback. Media conversion is progress based on three layer feedforward neural network. The input layer has 16 units, corresponding to the dimensions for LPC Cepstrum parameters. The output layer units correspond to lip control parameters. The mapping is learned by only a few training sequence, but the motion can be generated very delicately because the interpolation effect of neural network appears.

We have already construced a prototype voice communication system based on pipe line processing using Pixel Machine of AT&T. When one speaks in front of the microphone, the processes from speech analysis to image synthesis go at the speed of 10 frames per second with few delay time.

3.3. Voice to Image Conversion for Voice Storage System

In case of a media conversion from stored voice to image, the processing delay time isn't so important. So, complicated algorithms like speech segmentation and vowel recogintion can be available to improve the conversion performance. In this system, focused on the spectrum change and power shift between successive frames, segmentation boundaries are founded and keyframes are located based on this result. Mouth shape of each segment is decided by template matching of vowel. So only 8 categories are included in the templates. Interpolation of keyframes are 3D Spline function. Subjective evaluations of this synthesized motion image show higher conversion performance than the neural network version. When speech analysis and image synthesis can proceed in off-line condition, prototype system can be implemented on low-cost workstation .

3.4. Voice and Text to Image Conversion for Advanced Mail System

In this section, synchronization method of animation and natural voice using both stored voice and text is introduced. Voice recognition for long sentence is difficult problem now. So vowel recognition using template matching and voice sequence segmentation are performed as bottom-up process. After that process, text of sentence is entered and time scale matching between recognized vowels and entered vowels is performed. At last, consonant position is decided by entered text and standard duration table of phoneme. In this system, mouth shapes can be generated accurately by text information and duration of each phoneme can be decided by segmentation result. In the advanced multi-media e-mail system, text input and voice input may be possible.

3.4.1. Vowel Recognition and Segmentation

Vowels in the long Japanese sentence is detected here. Recognition categories are five Japanese vowels that are /a/, /i/, /u/, /e/, /o/, nasals /N/ and voiceless. At first, voice sequience is stored and devided into many segments according to power change and spectrum distance between successive two frames. Each segment is classified into a vowel category by template matching. This result includes more numbers of segments than real phoneme numbers in voice and it has some vowel recognition errors too.

3.4.2. Time Scale Matching

When text sentence is entered, the order and number of phoneme become clear. DP based time scale matching proceeds by comparing a recognized vowel sequence and a correct vowel sequence of input text. Correct vowel sequence is located on the vertical axis and recognized vowel sequence is located on horizontal axis. Matching path takes zigzagging line. The distance between each phoneme category is pre-determined as normalized Cepstrum distance using training data of specific speaker. The optimum path is decided to minimize the total distance between correct sequence and recognized sequence using DP Matching method. The vowel recognition result includes many errors, but these errors can be restored and more accurate segment position of each phoneme of text are decided by this matching.

Each consonant position is located in front of this vowel position and its length is selected by standard duration table. The keyframes for standard mouth shape are located at the start point of each phoneme segment. The shape of mouth between keyframes is interpolated by 3D Spline function. Mouth closing moments can be re-generated as well as original motion.

4. *SCENARIO MAKING TOOL*[13][14]

Delicate face expression and facial animation synthesis scenario can be generated by scenario making tool. This tool gives an animation making environment to user.

Facial expression and motion around mouth are controlled by several media conversion schemes selected. The other expression is controlled manually in this tool. The face expression can be chosen from the database and put it into time axis window by mouth operation. Standard expressions are stored as the combination of AU's numbers and its intensities. If necessary, user can preview and check the motion image on wire frame model.

After choice of original 2-D face image and execution of texture mapping processes, all frame motion pictures can appear on the window. The *Facial Action Coding System (FACS)* is a well-known method to describe facial actions. However, *FACS* doesn't provide a numeric representation. In this system, any kinds of face expressions can be realized by combination of *Action Units* of *FACS* and these intensities quantized by 100 levels.

This scenario making tool includes *AU* editor. In this *AU* editor, several kinds of expression can be generated by assigning the *Action Units'* numbers and their intensities in the window. The relation between AU parameters and human's emotion condition is expressed in *Emotion Space* in this system. An extraction of emotional features in several media is future problem.

5. *ANALYSIS OF EMOTIONAL FEATURE OF VOICE*[9]

Emotional feature of voice have not been studied so well until now. Even if the target of classification is limited only to typical emotional patterns, advanced media conversion from voice to face expression is possible. For example, when one is speaking with angry voice, face in the display gets angry. When one is speaking with sad voice, face appears to be sad. Emotion analysis and generation are important problem in speech synthesis too. In this section, we try to do a quantative analysis of voice including only five basic emotions.

5.1. Voice Sample with Emotion

Real actors speak some sentences and words with basic emotions and we recorded them as voice samples. These sentences and words don't include emotional meaning. Basic emotions are anger, sadness, happiness, disgust and neutral. Typical samples which are considered as representing basic emotions are selected by subjective test.

5.2. Voice Feature of Emotion

For the first trial, average power spectrum of octave band and histogram of pitch period are analized with emotional voice samples. Figure 2 indicates average power spectrums in octave band comparing with the power in 125 to 250[Hz] band. In both cases, there is an order of emotion according to the strength of high frequency power. This order appears to be *anger, happiness, disgust, neutral, sadness*. Figure 3 shows histograms of pitch period in voice. In both cases, there is the order of peaks. *Sadness* is longer than neutral, *Disgust* is shorter and *happiness/anger* are much shorter. However, the order of *happiness and anger* can not be decided by this result.

Now we are trying to analize all of the other acoustical feature parameters of sample voices too and it's our goal to find speaker- and sentence-independent parameters of emotional features.

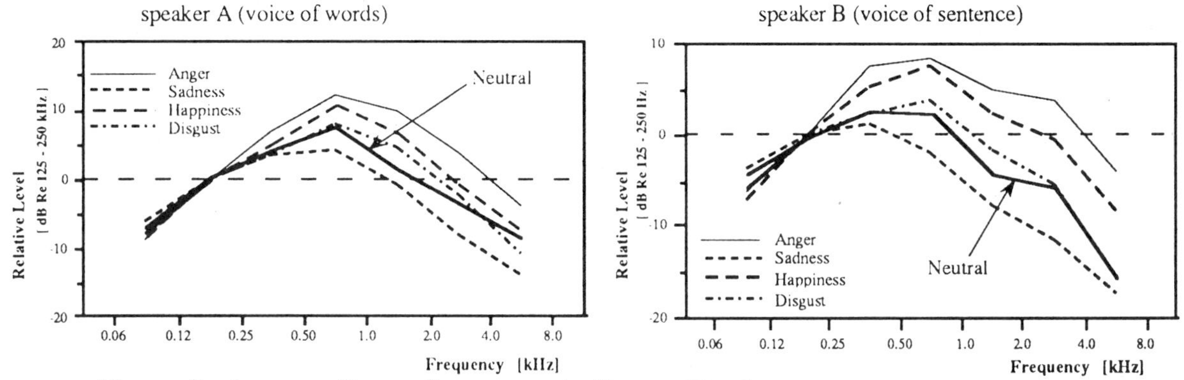

Figure 2. Average Power Spectrums in Octave Band

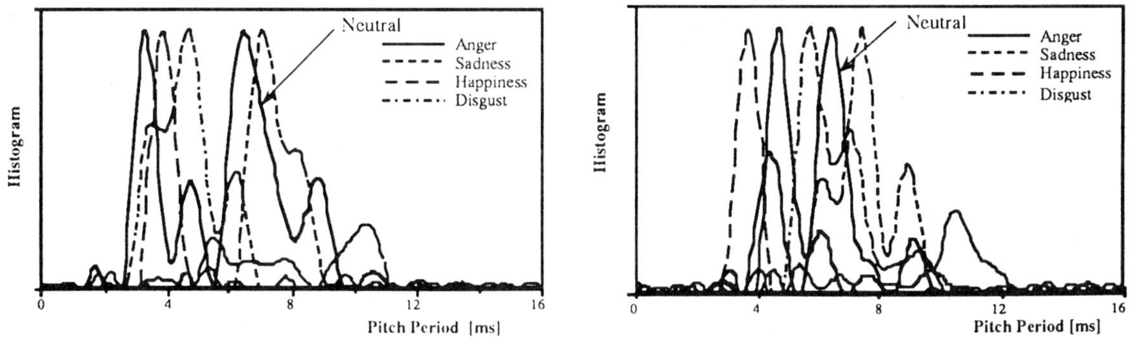

Figure 3. Histograms of Pitch Period in a Voice Samples

6. CONCLUSION

This paper presents a prototype of multi-media interface with face based on several kinds of media conversion schemes. Mouth shape and its motion can be synthesized by analysis of voice and sentence naturally. Scenario making tool gives the user friendly expression synthesis environment. In future, expression control based on the emotional feature in voice will be possible. For the first trial, some experimental results of voice feature analysis with basic emotion are presented. This technique will contribute to the advanced voice communication system and user-friendly human-machine interface.

References

[1] P.Ekman and W.Friesen, "Facial Action Coding System", Consulting Psychologists Press, 1977.

[2] S.Morishima and H.Harashima, "A Media Conversion from Speech to Facial Image for Intelligent Man-Machine Interface", IEEE Journal on Selected Areas in Communication, Vol.9, No.4, 1991.

[3] S.Morishima and H.Harashima, "Speech-to-Image Media Conversion Based on VQ and Neural Network", Proceedings of ICASSP91, M10.11, pp.2865-2868, 1991.

[4] S.Kobayashi, S.Morishima et.al, "Representation of Feel and Motion of the Thread-like Objects", Proc. of NICOGRAPH90, pp.29-36, 1990.

[5] Y.Fukuda and S.Hiki, "Characteristic of the mouth shape in the production of Japanese - Stroboscopic Observation", Journal of Acoustical Society of Japan (E), 3.2, pp.75-91, 1982.

[6] M.Potmesil and E.M.Hoffert, "A Pixel Machine: A Parallel Image Computer", ACM Computer Graphics, vol.23, No.3, pp.69-78, 1989.

[7] S.Morishima and H.Harashima, "A Proposal of a Knowledge Based Isolated Word Recognition", Proc. ICASSP, 14.5, 1986.

[8] C.S.Choi, H.Harashima and T.Takebe, "Analysis and Synthesis of Facial Expressions in Knowledge Based Coding of Facial Image Sequences", ICASSP91, M9.7, pp.2737-2740, 1991.

[9] C.E.Williams and K.N.Steven,: "Emotions and Speech: Some Acoustical Correlates", JASA, 52(4), pp.1238-1250, 1972.

[10] S.Morishima and H.Harashima,"Human Machine Interface Using Media Conversion and Model-Based Coding Schemes", Visual Computing, CG International Series, Springer-Verlag, pp.95-105, 1992.

[11] S.Morishima, T.Sakaguchi, H.Harashima, "A Facial Image Synthesis System for Human-Machine Interface", IEEE International Workshop on Robot and Human Communication, pp.363-368, 1992.

[12] E. Ono, S.Morishima and H.Harashima, "A model based shade estimation and reproduction schemes for rotational face", Picture Coding Symposium '93, 2.2, 1993.

[13] S.Morishima, T.Sakaguchi and H.Harashima, "Face animation scenario making system for model based image synthesis", Picture Coding Symposium '93, 13.19, 1993.

[14] S.Morishima and H.Harashima, "Facial Animation Synthesis for Human-Machine Communication System", HCI International, 1993.

Part III: Implementations

The third part of this edited volume addresses the implementations of neural networks. There have been many different strategies adopted to take advantage of the inherently parallel structure of neural networks. One strategy uses existing array processors as an implementation medium. Another strategy is the design and development of integrated circuits that implement a specific class of neural networks. Yet another strategy is the development of software systems that can operate on a wide range of computer architectures.

There are three chapters in this last part . Chapter 10 covers array processor implementations. Chapter 11 describes integrated circuit implementations. Chapter 12 reviews some of the existing software simulators that are available.

Chapter 10: Array Processor Implementations

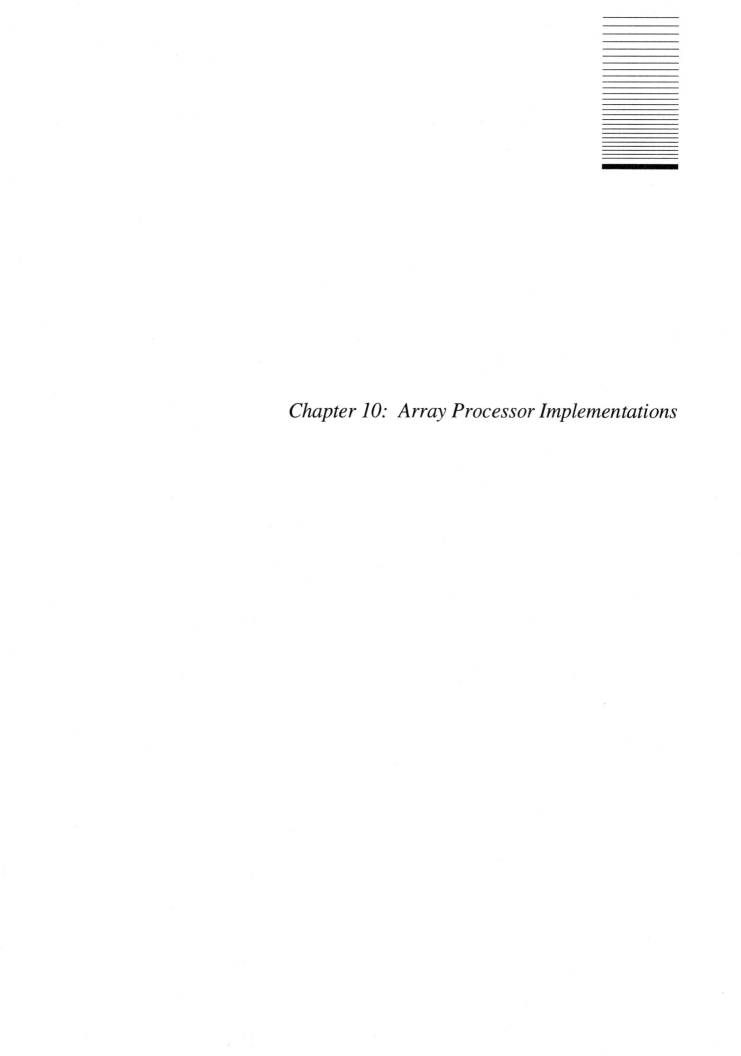

CHAPTER 10
Array Processor Implementations

There are many array processors available for mathematically intensive computing. The most prevalent example of this class of processors is the Digital Signal Processor. The papers in this chapter describe the implementation of neural networks with existing array processors. Some of the processors were designed specifically for neural network operations, but most were not.

Paper 10.1 describes a neural network accelerator (MANTRA I) that uses a systolic array of dedicated processing elements (GENES IV chips). Several neural network implementations are defined for MANTRA I. **Paper 10.2** presents a massively parallel array processor (PAN IV) for simulating large neural networks such as the SOFM and MLP. Several different topological mappings from the neural network to the array processor are analyzed for computational and throughput efficiency. **Paper 10.3** describes a neurocomputer system (SYNAPSE) that uses a VLSI array processor (MA16). The MLP is given as an example of a neural network that can be implemented by using SYNAPSE. **Paper 10.4** presents implementations of the MLP and SOFM on an 8-neighbor processor array (MasPar). Analysis of the computational requirements of each implementation is provided. **Paper 10.5** describes the implementation of the MLP using a neural network chip (ETANN). The implementation emphasizes the application to emitter identification. **Paper 10.6** describes how an accelerator board with a DSP (TMS 320C30) provides an environment for teaching the applications of various neural networks. **Paper 10.7** introduces the hardware design for the K/N neural network. Simulations of the hardware design are presented to confirm feasibility of the design. **Paper 10.8** presents the Integrated NeuroComputing Architecture (INCA) which uses the Neural Processing Unit (NPU).

GENES IV: A Bit-Serial Processing Element for a Multi-Model Neural-Network Accelerator

Paolo Ienne and Marc A. Viredaz
Swiss Federal Institute of Technology
Microcomputing Laboratory & Centre for Neuro-Mimetic Systems
IN-F Ecublens, CH-1015 Lausanne
E-mail: Paolo.Ienne@di.epfl.ch

Abstract

A systolic array of dedicated processing elements (PEs) *is presented as the heart of a multi-model neural-network accelerator. The instruction set of the PEs allows the implementation of several widely-used neural models, including multi-layer Perceptrons with the backpropagation learning rule and Kohonen feature maps. Each PE holds an element of the synaptic weight matrix. An instantaneous swapping mechanism of the weight matrix allows the implementation of neural networks larger than the physical PE array. A systolically-flowing instruction accompanies each input vector propagating in the array. This avoids the need of emptying and refilling the array when the operating mode of the array is changed.*

Both the GENES IV *chip, containing a matrix of 2 × 2 PEs, and an auxiliary arithmetic circuit have been manufactured and successfully tested. The* MANTRA I *machine has been built around these chips. Peak performances of the full system are between 200 and 400 MCPS in the evaluation phase and between 100 and 200 MCUPS during the learning phase (depending on the algorithm being implemented).*

1: Introduction

The field of *neural-networks (NNs)* is now extending above the boundaries of academic research. Applications to real-life problems tend to become competitive with well-established traditional techniques. Recent experiences (as the Santa Fe Institute's competition on *Time Series Prediction and Analysis* [5]) show the maturity of some NN algorithms and the importance of their intrinsic non-linearity contrasted to classical linear approaches. Unfortunately, real applications tend to require large networks and/or large data sets for the learning phase. This makes implementation on conventional hardware platforms extremely inefficient. The four best connectionist entries in [5] took between three hours and three weeks to run, the quickest one being programmed on a CRAY Y-MP. Difficulties in experimenting with large networks also prevent researchers from exploring the field. Often a good result is obtained by repeatedly learning the problem prototypes with different parameters to search for an optimal tuning. This empirical but nevertheless necessary process becomes prohibitive for sufficiently large networks. Hardware accelerators and host-attached computers represent a cost-effective alternative to supercomputers.

In this paper, an NN accelerator, based on a systolic square array of *processing elements (PEs)*, is presented. It is not dedicated to a single algorithm but supports several connectionist models and learning rules. In the next section, a survey of the targeted neural

0-8186-3492-8/93 $3.00 © 1993 IEEE

algorithms is proposed. The following section is devoted to the array architecture and deals with the mapping of the NN algorithms on the array. The PE structure and implementation choices are exposed in section 4, followed by details on the system architecture in section 5. Finally, performance evaluation is analyzed in the last section.

2: Neural-networks algorithms

This section briefly introduces the algorithms addressed by the architecture presented in this paper. A more detailed description can be found in a classic introductory book, such as [6]. The typical artificial neuron model represents a device with n inputs and a single output. The output y_i of the i-th neuron of the network is computed as:

$$y_i \;=\; \sigma(p_i) \;=\; \sigma\Big(\sum_{j=1}^{n} W_{i,j}\cdot x_j\Big) \qquad \text{for } i = 1,2,\ldots,m; \tag{1}$$

where $W_{i,j}$ represents a coefficient or ***synaptic weight*** associated with the j-th input x_j and the i-th neuron. The weighted sum p_i is called ***potential***. Equation (1) can be rewritten in a matrix form as $\vec{\mathbf{y}} = \sigma(\vec{\mathbf{p}}) = \sigma(\mathbf{W}\cdot\vec{\mathbf{x}})$. Usually, the ***activation function*** σ represents some saturating non-linear function. Neurons are often organized in layers, all neurons in a layer sharing the same inputs and having their outputs connected to the inputs of the next layer. The weight matrixes are then shown as $\mathbf{W}^{[q]}$, where q is the layer number.

Neural networks usually undergo a learning process. The synaptic-weight matrixes are iteratively updated according to a *learning rule*. One of the simplest one is the *Hebb rule*:

$$\mathbf{W} \;:=\; \mathbf{W} + \alpha\cdot(\vec{\mathbf{y}}\cdot\vec{\mathbf{x}}^{\mathrm{T}}); \tag{2}$$

where α is a *learning factor*. Though this rule is seldom used as stated, most of the commonly-used learning rules are slight modifications of equation (2).

Multi-layer networks make it possible to implement any arbitrary function $\vec{\mathbf{y}} = \mathbf{\Phi}(\vec{\mathbf{x}})$, $\vec{\mathbf{x}}$ being the input of the first layer and $\vec{\mathbf{y}} = \vec{\mathbf{y}}^{[L]}$ representing the output of the last layer L. Often, the activation function σ is a hyperbolic tangent. The function $\mathbf{\Phi}$ is learned by repeated presentation of input-output pairs $\{\vec{\mathbf{x}}, \vec{\mathbf{d}}\}$, called *prototypes*. The *backpropagation (BP) learning rule* is a gradient-descent algorithm that updates the weights to minimize the square-error on the learning prototypes. For that purpose an error signal is computed for each layer:

$$\delta_i^{[L]} \;=\; \left(d_i - y_i^{[L]}\right)\cdot\sigma'(p_i^{[L]}) \tag{3}$$

$$\delta_i^{[q]} \;=\; \left(\sum_{k=1}^{m_{q+1}} W_{k,i}^{[q+1]}\cdot\delta_k^{[q+1]}\right)\cdot\sigma'(p_i^{[q]}) \qquad \text{for } q = 1,2,\ldots,L-1; \tag{4}$$

where $\sigma'(v) = d\sigma(v)/dv$. Equations (3) and (4) are valid for all neurons $i = 1,2,\ldots,m_q$ of layer q. Once the errors have been back-propagated, the weights are updated as:

$$\mathbf{W}^{[q]} \;:=\; \mathbf{W}^{[q]} + \alpha\cdot\vec{\delta}^{[q]}\cdot\vec{\mathbf{y}}^{[q-1]\mathrm{T}} \qquad \text{for } q = 1,2,\ldots,L; \tag{5}$$

where $\vec{\mathbf{y}}^{[0]} = \vec{\mathbf{x}}$.

Fully-connected recurrent networks, as the *Hopfield model*, can memorize and detect input patterns. Given an initial input, the output is computed and fed back until a stable pattern is reached. A possible learning rule for this model is the Hebb rule of equation (2) with $\vec{y} = \vec{x}$.

A different neural network model is the *Kohonen self-organizing map*. Several variations of the algorithm exist. Neurons are organized as regular meshes where some topological relations are defined (e.g., distance). They all share the same inputs. For every input vector $\vec{x}$, its distance from each neuron i is measured in the n-dimensional input space. Common distances are the scalar product of equation (1) or the Euclidean distance:

$$y_i = \Delta_{\text{in}}(\vec{x}, \mathbf{W}_i) = \sqrt{\sum_{j=1}^{n} (x_j - W_{i,j})^2} \quad \text{for } i = 1, 2, \ldots, m; \tag{6}$$

where $\mathbf{W}_i$ indicates the i-th row of matrix $\mathbf{W}$. Often, the input space has a much higher dimensionality than the topological space of the map. The winner neuron $I \in \{1, 2, \ldots, m\}$, whose weight vector is the closest to the input vector, is identified by:

$$\Delta_{\text{in}}(\vec{x}, \mathbf{W}_I) \leq \Delta_{\text{in}}(\vec{x}, \mathbf{W}_i) \quad \forall i \in \{1, 2, \ldots, m\}. \tag{7}$$

The weights are then modified as:

$$\mathbf{W}_i := \mathbf{W}_i + \alpha \cdot \lambda(\Delta_{\text{topo}}(i, I)) \cdot (\vec{x}^{\mathrm{T}} - \mathbf{W}_i) \quad \text{for } i = 1, 2, \ldots, m; \tag{8}$$

where $\Delta_{\text{topo}}(i, I)$ is the distance of neuron i from the winner neuron I in the topological space. The *neighbourhood function* λ restricts the update to neurons close to the winner. The result, after repeated presentation of the input vectors, is a population of neurons whose selection through equation (7) is equiprobable. In another version of the algorithm, instead of detecting the winning neuron I and updating the weights with $\lambda(\Delta_{\text{topo}}(i, I))$, these operations are replaced with the output after convergence of a fixed recurrent network. The latter network is described by equation (1) with the input $\vec{x}$ of one iteration being set to the output $\vec{y}$ of the previous one.

3: Array architecture

It has been shown by Blayo [3] that some common connectionist algorithms can be decomposed in simple operations that can be conveniently implemented on a 2-D mesh of PEs. This has been demonstrated with the implementation of a recurrent network in VLSI [9]. The *GENES IV* PE extends the basic scheme to include on-chip learning and to address more connectionist models. Figure 1 (a) shows the basic architecture, together with all the operands: (1) the matrix $\mathbf{W}$, resident in the $N \times N$ PEs; (2) the sequence of input vectors $\vec{\mathbf{I}}^{\text{v}}$ on the top side; (3) the sequence of input vectors $\vec{\mathbf{I}}^{\text{h}}$ on the left side. The result is produced in the vectors $\vec{\mathbf{O}}^{\text{h}}$ or $\vec{\mathbf{O}}^{\text{v}}$, or by modifying the resident matrix $\mathbf{W}$.

The evaluation of the function σ in equation (1) is performed with a look-up table outside the mesh. Similarly, the subtraction and the multiplication of equation (3) are performed externally by a linear array of auxiliary arithmetic units.

3.1: Feed-forward data flow

The first class of operations produces its results in $\vec{\mathbf{O}}^{\text{h}}$ or $\vec{\mathbf{O}}^{\text{v}}$ but does not modify the weight matrix. The operations performed by the PE of indexes i, j are:

$$h_{i,j} := \psi(W_{i,j}, v_{i-1,j}, h_{i,j-1}) \tag{9}$$

$$v_{i,j} := v_{i-1,j} \quad \text{for } i, j = 1, 2, \ldots, N. \tag{10}$$

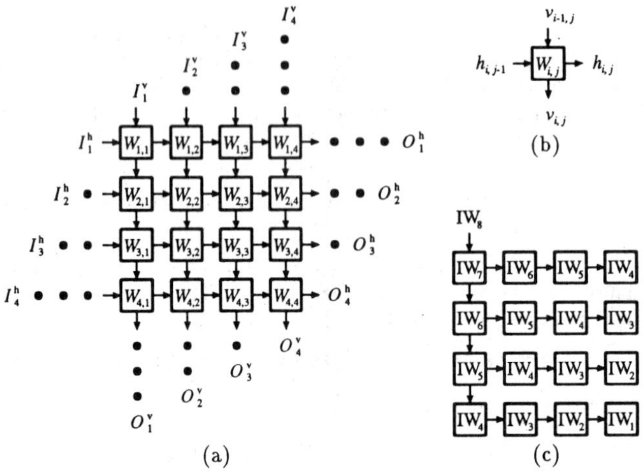

Figure 1. (a) GENES IV systolic array architecture. (b) Definition of the input/output path of a PE. (c) Systolic flow of instruction words (IWs).

Boundary conditions at the edges of the array are:

$$h_{i,0} := I^h_i \qquad (11)$$
$$v_{0,j} := I^v_j \qquad (12)$$
$$O^h_i := h_{i,N} \qquad (13)$$
$$O^v_j := v_{N,j} \quad \text{for } i,j = 1,2,\ldots,N. \qquad (14)$$

Table 1 shows the functions ψ required for each operation that uses this data flow. The symbols $+\infty$ and $-\infty$ indicate respectively the maximum and minimum representable numbers. The mprod operation implements a classic matrix-vector multiplication scheme. The euclidean operation is very similar, the product being replaced by a squared difference. It computes the squared Euclidean distance between a vector and each row of the matrix $\mathbf{W}$. As the resulting vector of distances is used only in equation (7) to identify the minimum, there is no need to perform a square root. The presence of the additive term $\vec{\mathbf{I}}^h$ in both

Operation	$\psi(a,b,c)$	Result in normal mode	Reference
mprod	$a \cdot b + c$	$\vec{\mathbf{O}}^h = \mathbf{W} \cdot \vec{\mathbf{I}}^v + \vec{\mathbf{I}}^h$	Eq. (1)
euclidean	$(b-a)^2 + c$	$O^h_i = \sum_{j=1}^{N} (I^v_j - W_{i,j})^2 + I^h_i$	Eq. (6)
min	c if $c \leq b$ $+\infty$ if $c > b$	if $I^h_I = \min_i (I^h_i)$ then $O^h_I = I^h_I$, all other elements in $\vec{\mathbf{O}}^h$ being $+\infty$	Eq. (7)
max	c if $c \geq b$ $-\infty$ if $c < b$	if $I^h_I = \max_i (I^h_i)$ then $O^h_I = I^h_I$, all other elements in $\vec{\mathbf{O}}^h$ being $-\infty$	Eq. (7)

Table 1. Feed-forward operations in normal mode.

the mprod and euclidean operations is fundamental for cumulating the result over different matrixes as required when the physical array is smaller than the implemented network.

The searches for the minimum and the maximum element of a vector are provided. The algorithm requires the input vector to be entered at both $\vec{\mathbf{I}}^{\mathrm{v}}$ and $\vec{\mathbf{I}}^{\mathrm{h}}$. The basic idea is—e.g., in the case of the min operation—to let propagate horizontally an element only if it is smaller than the one entering the PE vertically. If it is not, it is saturated to the maximum representable value. As each element meets all the others before reaching the right side of the array, only the smallest element is output unsaturated. This operation (min) should be used for Euclidean distance while the max operation is appropriate for normalized weights and the scalar product (the minimum angle between the input vector and the neuron weight producing the maximum scalar product).

It can be noted that the error backpropagation requires a matrix-vector multiplication in equation (4), but, compared to equation (1), the weight matrix is transposed. The computation on the transpose matrix can be performed simply by exchanging the role of the horizontal and vertical data flows:

$$h_{i,j} := h_{i,j-1} \tag{15}$$

$$v_{i,j} := \psi(W_{i,j}, h_{i,j-1}, v_{i-1,j}) \quad \text{for } i,j = 1,2,\ldots,N. \tag{16}$$

The role of the inputs is also exchanged, and the output is now:

$$\vec{\mathbf{O}}^{\mathrm{v}} = \mathbf{W} \cdot \vec{\mathbf{I}}^{\mathrm{h}} + \vec{\mathbf{I}}^{\mathrm{v}}. \tag{17}$$

Though all other operations can be executed in the *transpose mode*, this has hardly any practical use.

3.2: Weight update data flow

The second class of operations modifies the weight matrix $\mathbf{W}$ without producing any result in $\vec{\mathbf{O}}^{\mathrm{h}}$ or $\vec{\mathbf{O}}^{\mathrm{v}}$. The operations performed by the PE of indexes i, j are:

$$h_{i,j} := h_{i,j-1} \tag{18}$$

$$v_{i,j} := v_{i-1,j} \tag{19}$$

$$W_{i,j} := \psi(W_{i,j}, v_{i-1,j}, h_{i,j-1}) \quad \text{for } i,j = 1,2,\ldots,N. \tag{20}$$

Boundary conditions at the edges of the array are given by equations (11) and (12). Table 2 shows the weight updating operations. In both cases, the input vector $\vec{\mathbf{I}}^{\mathrm{h}}$ has already been multiplied, in auxiliary arithmetic units, by the coefficient α. The term $\lambda(\Delta_{\mathrm{topo}}(i, I))$ in equation (8) is computed as follows:

1. The vector containing the m distances (m being the number of neurons) is processed by the min or max operation. An external look-up table is used to convert all the $+\infty$ or $-\infty$, respectively, to 0's and any other value (i.e., the usually single minimum or maximum) to 1.

Operation	$\psi(a,b,c)$	Result in normal mode	Reference
hebbian	$a + c \cdot b$	$\mathbf{W} = \mathbf{W} + \vec{\mathbf{I}}^{\mathrm{h}} \cdot \vec{\mathbf{I}}^{\mathrm{v}\mathrm{T}}$	Eq. (2), (5)
kohonen	$a + c \cdot (b - a)$	$\mathbf{W}_i = \mathbf{W}_i + I_i^{\mathrm{h}} \cdot (\vec{\mathbf{I}}^{\mathrm{v}\mathrm{T}} - \mathbf{W}_i)$	Eq. (8)

Table 2. Learning operations.

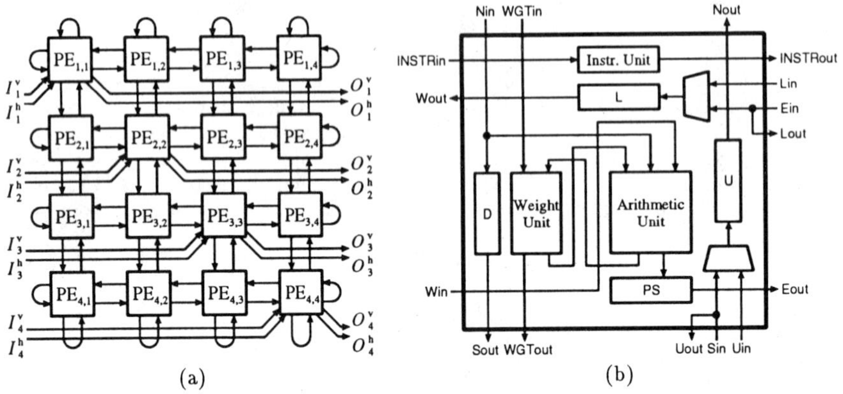

Figure 2. (a) 4 $\times$ 4 array architecture. (b) Processing element basic structure.

2. This vector is then multiplied (mprod operation) by an $m \times m$ matrix Λ expressing at the same time the topological distance of the neurons and the neighbourhood function. The elements of this symmetric matrix are $\Lambda_{i,j} = \lambda(\Delta_{\text{topo}}(i,j))$. This matrix formulation of the topological distance has the advantage of allowing to compute any type of network (e.g., multi-dimensional orthogonal arrays or 2-D hexagonal arrays).

3.3: Systolic instruction flow

The number of stages T of the 2-D mesh together with the look-up table and the auxiliary arithmetic units impose to process a minimum of T input vectors at a time to optimize the utilization rate. If an *epoch* (batch) of T vectors is used, the first result becomes available the cycle after the last input vector has been injected in the mesh. The latter is thus still processing the old vectors while a new operating mode would be required to process the results. A conventional *single instruction flow, multiple data flow (SIMD)* approach would require the array to be emptied before the new computation phase can be started. To improve the throughput, an *instruction word (IW)* can be associated with each input vector and systolically propagated with it, as shown in figure 1 (c). This allows the operation mode to be changed progressively and avoids intermediate inactive cycles.

4: Processing Element (PE) structure and implementation

The architecture of the implemented array and the structure of the PEs are illustrated in figure 2. Unlike the basic architecture shown in figure 1 (a), the access to the processing array is done through input and output ports located on the top-left to bottom-right diagonal. These inputs (Uin and Lin) and outputs (Uout and Lout) are present on all PEs for modularity but are used only on diagonal cells. They are always bypassed or left unconnected on non-diagonal cells. As figure 2 (b) shows, two further registers (U and L) are required for this path. The advantage is that no external hardware is required to *diagonalize* the inputs or *un-diagonalize* the outputs to and from the array (see figure 1 (a)). All the components of a vector are entered or read at the same time.

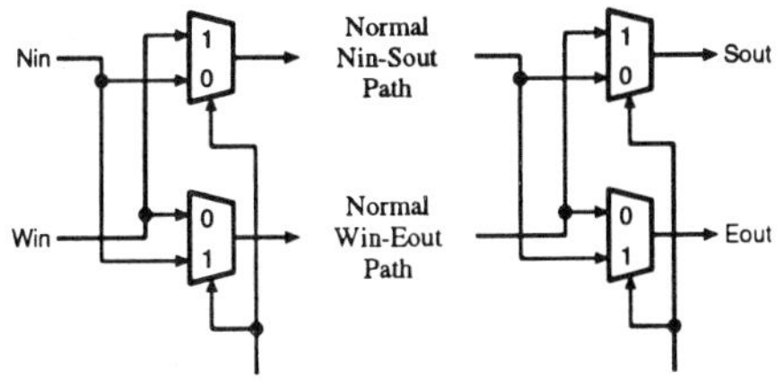

Figure 3. Circuit to operate on the transpose matrix.

The transposition mechanism, described by equations (15) and (16), is added to the PE by providing two control signals from the systolic instruction unit. A first signal exchanges the roles of Nin and Win, while the other exchanges Sout and Eout, as shown in figure 3. When a computation on the transpose matrix begins, the inputs are exchanged. The quantities in the PE registers, belonging to the previous computation are output on the regular path. On the next computation step, the outputs are also exchanged. The same applies when the operation mode reverts to the direct matrix.

The inter-PE communication is bit-serial LSB-first. The bit-serial protocol is imposed by the silicon area of a parallel multiplier (preventing multiple PEs on a single die) and by the number of pads required for the parallel communication (about 400). Of course, the performance is reduced by a factor equal to the number of bits of the longest data word in the PE.

4.1: Double weight-register unit

Figure 2(b) also shows two inter-PE connections not seen in figure 2(a): the weight path and the instruction path. The latter one has already been discussed in connection with figure 1(c). The *weight units* are loaded through a dedicated vertical data path independent from the two standard data inputs. A key feature of a general-purpose NN accelerator is the ability to support problems larger than the physical array available. The weight unit contains two weight registers, one connected on the weight data path, and the other used for the computation. The multiplexers shown in figure 4 allow the two registers to be exchanged in between two instructions. This way, a new weight matrix can be loaded in the background while an epoch of input vectors is being processed with another one. Figure 5 shows the timing of the exchange, supposing that every epoch a new weight

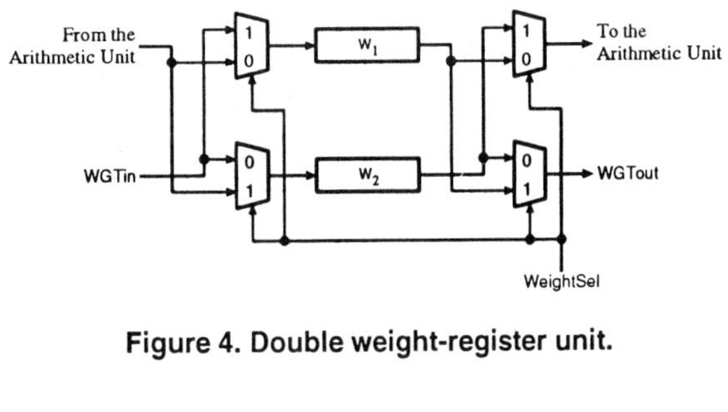

Figure 4. Double weight-register unit.

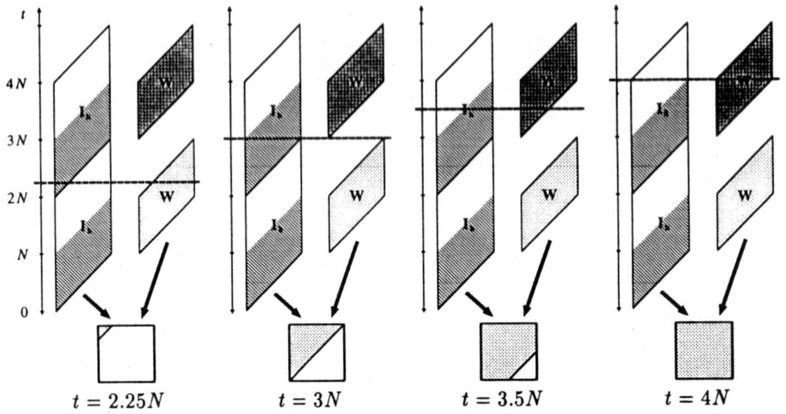

Figure 5. Background weight exchange mechanism.

matrix has to be used. The square at the bottom represents the $N \times N$ array of PEs and the shaded areas indicate which of the weight matrixes is currently in use by the PEs in that zone. The groups of $2N$ input vectors, each composed of N elements, are depicted as parallelograms injected from the top side even if the inputs are actually on the diagonal. At $t = 2.25N$, most of the N PEs in the first column are still using an old matrix. By $t = 3N$, thus after N vectors have been entered, until just before a new epoch is started (N cycles later, i.e., at $t = 4N$ in the figure), all the PEs in the first column use the first matrix shown in figure 5. During this time, the column of weights can be shifted in the background without affecting the current computation. The whole process requires an epoch length of at least $2N$ vectors, which happens to be compatible with the latency of the whole array. It can be noted that this process applies to the other columns but one cycle later for each column, thus requiring the weight matrix to be injected diagonalized. Three registers could have allowed a non-diagonalized download at the expenses of a slightly larger PE structure.

4.2: Arithmetic precision

The choice of the arithmetic precision of the hardware is quite delicate. A first, typical choice, motivated by hardware simplicity, is to represent all variables in two's complement fixed point. As for the required number of bits for each element, theoretical analysis usually leads to absolute minimum boundaries that, on themselves, cannot guarantee convergence [13]. In the absence of strong analytical grounds, simulation usually provides the designer with the required information. In [2] and [7] simulations are performed to determine the needs of typical backpropagation applications. These have been completed by simulations of the Kohonen model in the application that prompted the development of the present system. This resulted in the following choices:

- The weights for the forward operations (mprod and euclidean) are stored on $N_W =$ 16 bits. Simulations show that more than 9–10 bits are required for real-world applications of the Kohonen network. The closest larger multiple of 8 was therefore chosen. Similarly, input data are stored on $N_D = 16$ bits. $N_W = N_D$ because in the

Kohonen network the weights and the inputs belong to the same space.

- The minimum number of bits to avoid overflow in the accumulation register PS for the mprod operation (in two's complement) is:

$$N_{PS} = N_W + N_D + \lfloor \log_2(n) \rfloor \qquad (21)$$

where n is the number of inputs of the network being simulated (independently from the size of the physical array on which the computation is performed). 39 bits (plus one overflow bit) have been chosen, allowing networks with up to 255 inputs to be computed with no overflow, in mprod mode (somewhat less in euclidean mode). Much larger networks can be simulated if occasional overflows can be tolerated.

- The results of weight-update computations hold on about $2N_W$ bits. To avoid truncation (whose negative effects are shown in [2]) and to keep the maximum information, a hidden fractional part, consisting of 16 bits more, is added to the weight registers. It is hidden in the sense that this part is not used in the forward mode but it accumulates the fractional part of successive updates. This has the important consequence of allowing convergence to continue also when α becomes small enough that single updates no longer reach unity.

In practice, due to the requirements for the min and max operands, and because of the transposition mechanism, all the data registers are composed of 40 bits and the weight registers have a total of 33 bits each (all registers include an overflow bit).

4.3: Arithmetic unit

The arithmetic unit (computing the functions $\psi(a, b, c)$ listed in tables 1 and 2) requires three building blocks: a multiplier, an adder, and a subtracter. The choice of the multiplier is a delicate one. The mprod operation is not critical, a compact serial-parallel multiplier could be used since the weight comes from an internal register and can easily be read in parallel while the other factor comes from the vertical data channel in serial form. Unfortunately this scheme could not be used for the weight update (hebbian or kohonen) and for the square in the euclidean operation, where both factors serially arrive from external inputs. A solution could be to wait for the arrival of one of the elements, and then multiply by the other, delayed as required. Unfortunately, this is only possible with a loss in performance (additional cycles for operand transmission) or an increase in the pipelined nature of the array (requiring an even more complex control logic). Typical serial-serial multipliers have some cycles of latency between the first input bit and the first output one [4]. This would again lead to additional delay cycles in operations like euclidean, where the accumulation is performed on the longest data word of the system. An improved multiplication scheme was therefore developed for two's complement numbers [8]. A 17-bit multiplier has been implemented in the PE. Apart from presenting only a combinational delay, this design has the additional advantage of indefinitely sign-extending the output as long as the inputs remain correctly sign extended. This is useful in many situations, e.g., when adding a 34-bit result to a 39-bit word.

It can be noted in figure 2 (b) that the arithmetic unit gets the external operands directly from the input channels and that the registers are placed after it. This simplifies the implementation of the min and max search and allows, on the last clock cycle, when the comparison has been performed, to saturate to $+\infty$ or $-\infty$ the value propagating in the PS register. Similarly, this allows to saturate the result of other operations, when an overflow is detected. The saturation should allow the convergence of algorithms even in presence of

Operation	Condition	Sign
mprod	$\psi(a,b,c) \notin [-2^{38}, 2^{38}-1]$	$\mathrm{sgn}(\psi(a,b,c))$
euclidean	$\psi(a,b,c) \notin [0, 2^{38}-1]$	$+$
hebbian	$\psi(a,b,c) \notin [-2^{31}, 2^{31}-1]$	$\mathrm{sgn}(\psi(a,b,c))$
	$c \notin [-2^{16}, 2^{16}-1]$	$\mathrm{sgn}(c \cdot b)$
kohonen	$\psi(a,b,c) \notin [-2^{31}, 2^{31}-1]$	$\mathrm{sgn}(\psi(a,b,c))$
	$c \notin [-2^{16}, 2^{16}-1]$	$\mathrm{sgn}(c \cdot (b-a))$

Table 3. Overflow conditions.

occasional overflows. A sticky-bit is nevertheless added to the PS register (and consequently to all the other data registers) and to the weight registers. This flag informs the user that an anomalous situation occurred and the network may require attention. Table 3 list the saturation sign under the possible overflow conditions. In the table, a, b and c are the inputs to the arithmetic unit and $\psi(a,b,c)$ is its full-precision result. Operand b is never checked to hold on 16 bits, because this is already imposed by the external hardware. When $c \notin [-2^{16}, 2^{16}-1]$ in weight update operations, the product cannot be determined with the 17-bit multiplier and it is therefore assumed that it always dominates over the additive term a.

5: System architecture

The *MANTRA I* system [14] is shown in figure 6. The computational heart is a GENES IV array of 40 × 40 PEs. The sequencing of the systolic array is performed by a TMS320C40 *digital signal processor (DSP)* from Texas Instruments. It also handles the communications with a host workstation and between different MANTRA I machines connected through the dedicated communication links of the DSP.

Two look-up tables (indicated as σ and σ' in figure 6) are used to compute the evaluation function and its derivative. A double look-up table scheme allows a coarse-grain table to map the whole input space with reduced precision and a fine-grain one to map a small window with high precision (up to one entry per input value). It is possible to zoom the fine-grain window in or out by trading window width for precision. As already mentioned, a linear array of auxiliary arithmetic units (*GACD1*) computes the error for the

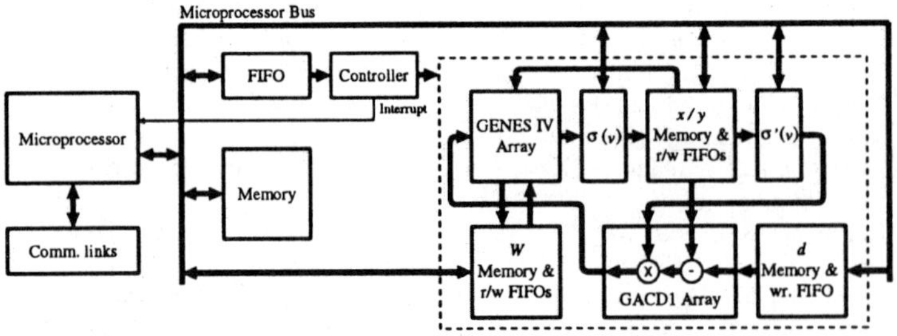

Figure 6. General architecture of the MANTRA I machine.

Model	Evaluation phase		Learning phase	
	Operations	MCPS	Operations	MCUPS
Perceptron, ADALINE, Delta rule, and BP rule (output-layer)	mprod	400	mprod + hebbian	200
Backpropagation (BP) rule (all layers but the last)	mprod	400	2 × mprod + hebbian	133
Kohonen with Euclidean distance and minimum	euclidean + min	200	euclidean + min + mprod + kohonen	100

Table 4. GENES IV peak performance.

backpropagation rule. Some memory banks locally store inputs, outputs, desired outputs, and weights, to minimize transfers from and to the DSP memory.

6: Performance

Two VLSI chips were designed in CMOS 1μm technology using VLSI Technology standard cells: the first one integrating three GACD1 cells and the second one housing an array of 2×2 GENES IV PEs. The latter chip contains 71,690 transistors (3,179 standard cells) on a die measuring $6.3 \times 6.1\,\text{mm}^2$. Both chips have been successfully tested. The MANTRA I system has been built and debugged. It is composed of four different printed-circuit boards and will host about 900 integrated circuits in the largest configuration.

No comprehensive benchmark has been run so far, but a peak performance can be calculated using the two classic metrics for neuro-computers: (1) the number of *connections per second* or *CPS* (evaluation phase) and (2) the number of *connection updates per second* or *CUPS* (learning phase). The expected performance of GENES is given by:

$$P = \frac{N^2 \cdot f}{n_{\text{op}} \cdot N_{\text{PS}}} \cdot U \tag{22}$$

where N^2 is the total number of PEs, f is the clock frequency, n_{op} is the number of operations required to compute a connection (evaluation phase) or to update it (learning phase), $N_{\text{PS}} = 40$ is the number of clock cycles per operation, and U is the utilization rate. Using the maximum supported array in the MANTRA I system (40×40) at a clock frequency of $f = 10\,\text{MHz}$, the peak performance ($U = 100\,\%$) of GENES IV is shown in table 4. Delta rule algorithm tests on the prototype show that a utilization rate $U \approx 95\,\%$ can easily be sustained if the problem data are already in the DSP memory.

These values compare well to those reported for supercomputers (e.g., 130 MCUPS on the NEC SX-3 [12]). The results show that, all differences taken into account (such as the fixed or floating point), neuro-computers can efficiently and cost-effectively compete with larger general-purpose systems. The performance is also expected to be comparable or superior to most other NN-dedicated systems (e.g., the RAP, 45 MCUPS on a backpropagation problem [11]) or VLSI accelerators (Lneuro 1.0, 32 MCUPS [10]). The CNAPS Server/512 [1] has a higher peak performance of 1,460 MCUPS (at a lower precision) thanks to a higher clock rate, parallel PE communication, and a more advanced VLSI technology. Its PE on-chip memory may however severely limit the size of the networks that can be simulated.

7: Conclusions

Neural-network accelerators connected to scientific workstations are appealing alternatives to large computers, when very large computational power is required and reduced cost is at a premium. The described architecture represents an acceptable compromise between simplicity and regularity of design (thus implying a reduced cost) and generality of use. Primitives are implemented to provide most of the typical neural-network algorithm building blocks. Future evolution may attempt to improve generality even more by slightly regularizing the processor structure (general purpose registers, wider instruction word, etc.) and obtain a reduced system complexity by simplifying the array interface. Finally, the small PE size, the reduced inter-PE connectivity and the high regularity make this architecture a good candidate for a wafer scale integration implementation.

Acknowledgements

This work is supported from the Swiss National Fund for Scientific Research through the SPP-IF program and from the Swiss Federal Institute of Technology through the MANTRA project. The authors wish to thank Prof. Jean-Daniel Nicoud for his constant support. The original works of François Blayo and Christian Lehmann provided the bases of the present project.

References

[1] Adaptive Solutions, Inc., Beaverton, Oreg. *CNAPS Server.* Preliminary datasheet.

[2] Krste Asanović and Nelson Morgan. Experimental determination of precision requirements for back-propagation training of artificial neural networks. In *1st International Conference on Microelectronics for Neural Networks*, pages 9–15, Dortmund, 1990.

[3] François Blayo. *Une implantation systolique des algorithmes connexionnistes.* PhD Thesis N° 904, École Polytechnique Fédérale de Lausanne, Lausanne, 1990.

[4] Luigi Dadda. Fast multipliers for two's-complement numbers in serial form. In *IEEE 7th Symposium on Computer Arithmetic*, pages 57–63, 1985.

[5] Neil A. Gershenfeld and Andreas S. Weigend. The future of time series: Learning and understanding. In A. S. Weigend and N. A. Gershenfeld, editors, *Time Series Prediction: Forecasting the Future and Understanding the Past*, pages 1–70. Addison-Wesley, Reading, Mass., 1993.

[6] John Hertz, Anders Krogh, and Richard G. Palmer. *Introduction to the Theory of Neural Computation.* Santa Fe Institute Studies in Sciences of Complexity. Addison-Wesley, Redwood City, Calif., 1991.

[7] Jordan L. Holt and Thomas E. Baker. Back propagation simulations using limited precision calculation. In *International Joint Conference on Neural Networks*, Seattle, Wash., July 1991.

[8] Paolo Ienne and Marc A. Viredaz. Bit-serial multipliers and squarers. *IEEE Transactions on Computers*, To appear.

[9] Christian Lehmann. *Réseaux de neurones compétitifs de grandes dimensions pour l'auto-organisation: analyse, syntèse et implantation sur circuits systoliques.* PhD Thesis N° 1129, École Polytechnique Fédérale de Lausanne, Lausanne, 1993.

[10] Nicolas Mauduit, Marc Duranton, Jean Gobert, and Jacques-Ariel Sirat. Lneuro 1.0: A piece of hardware LEGO for building neural network systems. *IEEE Transactions on Neural Networks*, 3(3):414–22, May 1992.

[11] Nelson Morgan, James Beck, Phil Kohn, Jeff Bilmes, Eric Allman, and Joachim Beer. The Ring Array Processor: A multiprocessing peripheral for connectionist applications. *Journal of Parallel and Distributed Computing*, 14:248–59, 1992.

[12] Urs A. Müller, Bernhard Baümle, Peter Kohler, Anton Gunzinger, and Walter Guggenbül. Achieving supercomputer performance for neural net simulation with an array of digital signal processors. *IEEE Micro*, pages 55–65, October 1992.

[13] Patrick Thiran, Vincent Peiris, Pascal Heim, and Bertrand Hochet. Quantization effects in digitally behaving circuit implementations of Kohonen networks. *IEEE Transactions on Neural Networks*, To appear.

[14] Marc A. Viredaz. MANTRA I: An SIMD processor array for neural computation. In *Proceedings of the Euro-ARCH'93 Conference*, München, October 1993. In press.

Implementation of Large Neural Associative Memories by Massively Parallel Array Processors

Alfred Strey

Department of Neural Information Processing
University of Ulm
Oberer Eselsberg, 89069 Ulm, Germany
E-mail: strey@neuro.informatik.uni-ulm.de

Abstract

This paper discusses the use of massively parallel array processors for simulating large neural associative memories. Although based on standard matrix operations the simulation of neural associative memories requires special parallel algorithms because a sparse coding of the input and output information is needed. Four different implementations with different mapping strategies and different array processor topologies are presented and illustrated by examples. The theoretical performance of all implementations is compared and the architecture of the massively parallel array processor PAN IV, designed for the efficient simulation for large neural associative memories is shortly described.

1 Introduction

During the last few years some special-purpose parallel architectures for the simulation of neural networks have been realized (see e.g. [4] [9]). They are mainly designed for the very high speed simulation of neural networks with full interconnection networks between different neuron layers (like the multilayered backpropagation network [11]), or with full interconnection networks between the inputs and neurons (like the Kohonen's self-oraganizing feature map [2]). The underlying matrix-vector operations are implemented by fast (signal) processors operating mostly in a systolic mode [3].

Another important neural network model is the neural associative memory [5], in which the correlations between pairs of corresponding input and output vectors are stored by Hebbian learning. It is also based on standard matrix-vector operations but relies on a sparse coding of the input and output vectors for achieving a large storage capacity. For the use of neural associative memories with large correlation matrices in real-time applications (e.g. speech recognition) a fast array processor is required for the matrix calculations. This paper focuses on the theoretical aspects of implementing neural associative memories on array processors. Especially the influence of the sparse coding of the input and output patterns on the architecture of the array processor and on the parallel algorithms is studied.

In the next section the most important aspects of neural associative memories are shortly resumed. Section 3 defines the underlying array processor model. Different parallel implementations of neural associative memories on the array processor model are explained in

0-8186-3492-8/93 $3.00 © 1993 IEEE

sections 4 to 8 and compared in section 9. In the last section the architecture of a massively parallel array processor called PAN IV designed for simulating neural associative memories is briefly described.

2 Neural associative memories

A neural associative memory provides a mapping between a binary input pattern $x \in \{0,1\}^k$ and a binary output pattern $y \in \{0,1\}^m$. It consists of m neurons, each neuron $j \in \{0,\ldots,m-1\}$ connected to some or all of the k input signals $x_i, i \in \{0,\ldots,k-1\}$ by weighted links (synapses) w_{ij}. The elements of the weight matrix W represent the correlation between input and output pairs of x and y. In the retrieval phase each neuron performs the operation

$$s_j = \sum_{i=0}^{k-1} x_i \cdot w_{ij} \,. \tag{1}$$

The sum s_j is compared with a threshold value Θ_j to produce the binary output signal y_j of the neuron:

$$y_j = \begin{cases} 1 & \text{if } s_j \geq \Theta_j \\ 0 & \text{if } s_j < \Theta_j \end{cases} \tag{2}$$

The neural synapses w_{ij} may have binary or integral values. Correct associations (x, y) are learned by presenting the inputs x and outputs y to the associative memory and updating the weights by a learning rule. Assuming integer synapses and p distinct pairs of input vectors x and output vectors y the update of the weights can be described by the equation:

$$w_{ij} = \sum_{\mu=0}^{p-1} x_i^\mu y_j^\mu \text{ with } w_{ii} = 0 \tag{3}$$

For binary synapses the following learning rule is used:

$$w_{ij} = \max x_i^\mu y_j^\mu \tag{4}$$

Input and ouput patterns may be identical (*auto-association*, e.g. of disturbed patterns) or may have different dimensions (*hetero-association*).

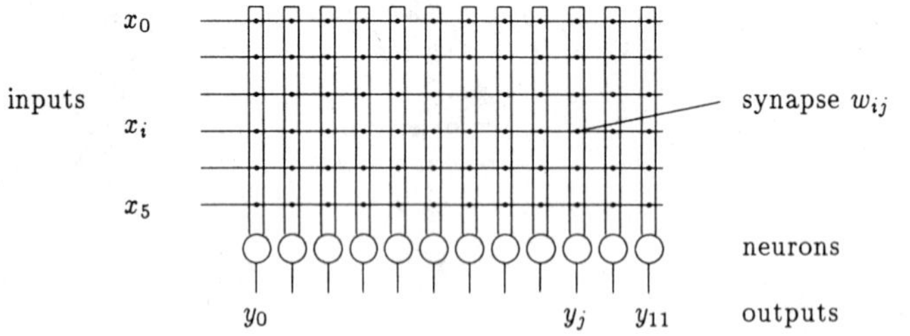

Figure 1: A neural associative memory with $k = 6$ inputs and $m = 12$ neurons

For further details, especially on the information storage capacity of such neural associative memories, see [5]. A sparsely coded input and output vector should be used for achieving a large storage capacity. The storage capacity reaches its maximal value if only ld k of the k input and output vector elements are active [6]. In the rest of the paper only the retrieval phase is considered.

3 Array processor model

The underlying array processor model consists of $N = 2^n$ processing elements (PEs), indexed 0 through $N - 1$. Each PE has an arithmetical and logical processing unit, some registers and a sufficient amount of local memory. All PEs are controlled by a special processor (CP = Control Processor) which broadcasts instructions, addresses and data to the PEs and performs operations on scalar data. The PEs can be enabled/disabled by a mask, and all enabled PEs perform the same instruction *synchronously* on (different) data. Each PE has a special register containing the unique index $id \in \{0, \ldots, N-1\}$.

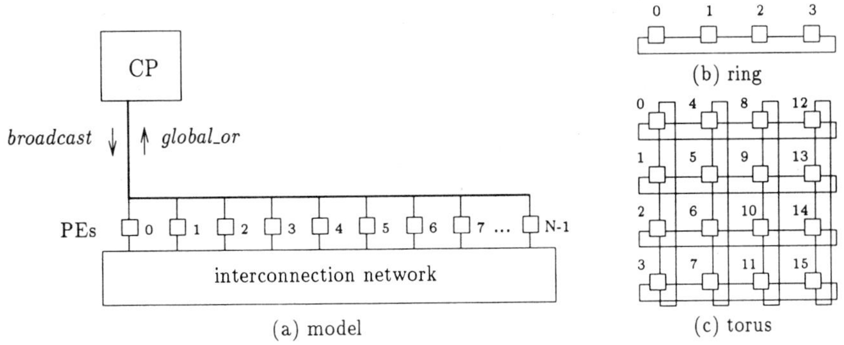

Figure 2: The array processor model

The global bus is the main communication medium of the array processor. Only the CP is allowed to *broadcast* data via the global bus to all PEs. The bus can also be used for gathering data from the PEs by a *global_or* operation. All active PEs put some local data on the bus and the CP receives a scalar value which represents the bitwise logical disjunction of all data values. If all but one PE are disabled by a mask the CP can *read* the data of a single processing element. In the following two different array processor models are introduced which have different additional communication networks:

1. **ring**: Each of the N PEs at location A(x), $x \in \{0, \ldots, N-1\}$ is connected to the left and right neighbor PEs at locations A($x \pm 1 \bmod N$). In one time step, all PEs can transmit some local data only to their nearest neighbor in the *same* direction. This operation is called a *cyclic shift* to the *left* or *right*.

2. **torus**: The PEs are arranged in a 2-dimensional array with $\sqrt{N}$ PEs in each dimension. The PE at location A(x, y), $x, y \in \{0, \ldots, \sqrt{N}-1\}$, has the index $id = y + x\sqrt{N}$ and is connected to the four PEs at locations A($x \pm 1 \bmod \sqrt{N}, y$) and A($x, y \pm 1 \bmod \sqrt{N}$). The corresponding communication operations are called cyclic shifts to one of the directions *north, south, west* and *east*.

4 Simulation of neural associative memories

Due to the sparse coding of the binary input vector x there are only some vector elements x_i that have the value one. In the following, these elements are called *relevant* input vector elements, the corresponding vector indices are called *addresses*. Thus, an input vector x with p relevant elements can shortly be described by an *address vector* a_x containing only the p addresses in ascending order. This vector is generated by the control processor and represents a request for an association to be performed by the neural associative memory.

It is assumed that at the beginning of the simulation on the parallel computer the p addresses of the active vector elements x_i are stored in the CP memory. During the simulation of the neural associative memory the following operations must be realized on the array processor model:

1. Distributing the p addresses of the active input vector elements x_i to all those PEs where the corresponding synapses w_{ij} are stored
2. Multiplying the input values x_i with all nonzero synapse values w_{ij} for all relevant input vector elements x_i and all neurons j in parallel (due to the binary data type of x_i the multiplication is a simple parallel *masking* operation)
3. Summing the products $x_i w_{ij}$ of all relevant input vector elements x_i and all nonzero weights w_{ij} for all neurons j in parallel
4. Comparing the sums s_j with the the thresholds Θ_j for all neurons j in parallel
5. Collecting the q addresses of the newly active neurons (i.e. of those neurons j for which $s_j \geq \Theta_j$)

The new q addresses are returned to the control processor and may be used again for a further association in the case of hetero-association or for a further iteration in the case of auto-association.

Depending on the number of available PEs N, the number of neurons m and the sparseness of the weight matrix W a *neuron parallel* or a *synapse parallel* implementation can be chosen. In the first case each neuron is mapped onto one processing element. All operations listed above are performed in parallel for N neurons but sequentially for all p relevant input vector elements. Thus the summing phase takes $\Omega(p)$ time steps. In the second case each neural synapse with a weight value $w_{ij} \neq 0$ is assigned to one PE so that the summing operation can be realized in parallel as well and the maximal theoretical degree of parallelism is achieved.

Whereas the neuron parallel implementation is applicable for *dense* matrices W, the synapse parallel implementation is especially suited for *sparse* associative matrices. In the following two sections both implementations are described for an array processor model with a sufficient number of PEs. If, however, the number of neurons m or the number of nonzero weight elements e exceeds the number of available PEs N, a virtual mapping strategy must be implemented which is illustrated in section 7. The basic algorithms *COLLECT* and *SEGMENT_SUM* used in the next two sections depend on the topology of the additional interconnection network of the array processor model and are explained in section 8.

5 Dense matrix implementation

Each neuron j is mapped to PE j according to the unique PE index id. All k weight values w_{ij} that belong to neuron j are stored in the local memory of PE j at consecutive addresses starting at some address α. Thus, the CP can address a row i of the matrix W by broadcasting the corresponding physical address $\alpha + i$ to all PEs. Besides the column j of the matrix W the neuron index j and the threshold value Θ_j are available in each PE.

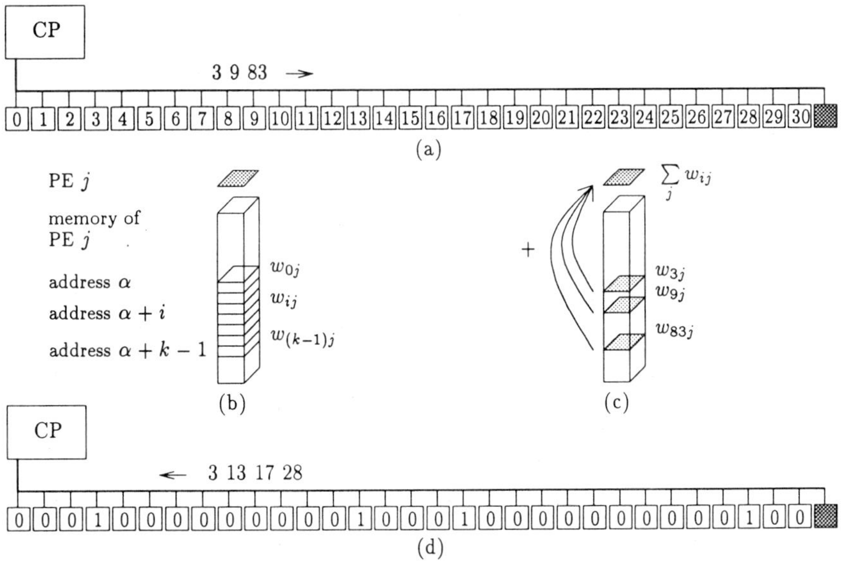

Figure 3: Dense matrix implementation

The distribution of the p addresses of active input vector elements x_i is realized by the CP which broadcasts the p addresses via the global bus. Thereafter, the corresponding weight values w_{ij} are summed in PE j in p time steps. The distributing phase can be overlapped with the summing phase, thus avoiding a local storage of the broadcasted addresses in each PE. All PEs j compare their calculated sums s_j with the threshold values Θ_j and generate a boolean value y_j which is true only if $s_j \geq \Theta_j$. All values y_j together represent a boolean mask y which marks all active neurons. The gathering of the q addresses of the active neurons represents an enourmous problem in a synchronous array processor architecture. It cannot be solved efficiently by using only the global bus and the *global_or* bus operation. In section 8.3 three different implementations of a *COLLECT* procedure are presented that use the additional interconnection network of the parallel computer model for gathering the q addresses.

Figure 3 illustrates the implementation for an associative memory with 31 neurons on an array processor with 32 PEs. In figure 3a the starting configuration is shown. The 31 neurons are mapped to the PEs according to the unique PE indices. The PEs with the highest index 31 is not used in this example. The addresses of 3 active input vector elements are stored in the CP and are broadcasted to all PEs. Figures 3b illustrates the storage of the synapses w_{ij} in the local memory of each PE j. The weights w_{ij} belonging to the 3 broadcasted addresses i are summed in each PE j (see figure 3c). After the comparison of the calculated sums with the threshold values a certain number of neurons are in an active state. The output vector y and the gathering of the addresses of active neurons by the CP via the global bus are shown in figure 3d.

6 Sparse matrix implementation

If the same algorithm is used in the case of a sparse correlation matrix W, a lot of PE memory space and computation time would be wasted for the storage and addition of zero weights. Whereas a pointer data structure could be used on a sequential computer for the efficient implementation of a sparse associative matrix, no adequate method exists on a massively parallel array processor. In the case of an extremly sparse matrix however, each PE can efficiently simulate one neural synapse. Because a zero weight value has no influence on the neuron activity only those synapses with $w_{ij} \neq 0$ are mapped onto the array processor. If the number of synapses with nonzero weights connected to neuron j is designated as e_j, then all synapses of neuron j are mapped to a *segment* of e_j PEs with indices in the range from $\sum_{\mu=0}^{j-1} e_\mu$ to $\sum_{\mu=0}^{j-1} e_\mu + e_j - 1$. Thus, all segments are mapped consecutively onto the array processor according to the unique PE index *id*. All together, $e = \sum_\mu e_\mu$ PEs are used for the simulation. The neuron index j, the input index i and the threshold value Θ_j are stored in the local memory of each PE.

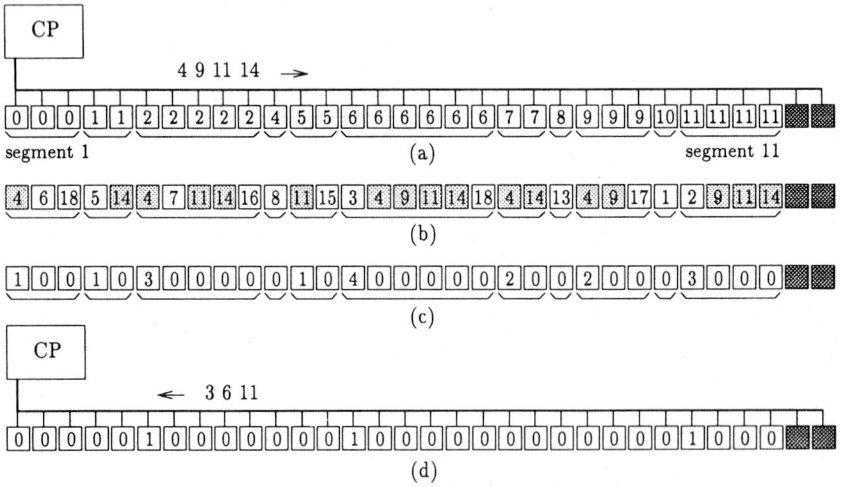

Figure 4: Sparse matrix implementation

As an example for the mapping strategy and the implementation described below a neural associative memory with $m = 12$ neurons, $k = 20$ inputs and $e = 30$ nonzero synapses is used. Figure 4a presents the mapping of all nonzero weight values onto the array processor with 32 PEs. All PEs simulating the e_j synapses of neuron j represent the segment j and are marked with the label j (e.g. neuron 1 has 3 nonzero weights which are mapped onto the first 3 PEs, neuron 2 has 2 nonzero weights which are mapped onto the next 2 PEs ...). At the beginning of a retrieval phase the CP broadcasts the p addresses of the active input vector elements stored in its local memory to all PEs via the global bus. All PEs in parallel compare the broadcasted addresses with the indices i of their locally stored synaptical weights w_{ij} (see figure 4b). As result a vector of integers (or booleans in the case of binary synapses) is generated which is zero except for those weight values w_{ij} that belong to active input vector elements x_i. In figure 4b all vector elements with nonzero elements are shaded. The summing phase is performed by the *SEGMENT_SUM* algorithm which sums the values of the generated vector for all segments in parallel. Thereafter, the resulting sums s_j are stored in the first PE of each segment j (see figure 4c, binary synapses are assumed here). The remaining operations are the same as those described already in the last section for dense matrices: The procedure *COLLECT* (see section 8.3) gathers the q addresses of all neurons with values $s_j \geq \Theta_j$ which is illustrated in figure 4d for $\Theta = 3$.

7 Virtual mapping

If in the case of a dense weight matrix the number m of neurons or in the case of a sparse weight matrix the number e of nonzero matrix elements exceeds the number N of available PEs, a *virtual* mapping strategy consisting of two steps is used:

At first, the synapses or neurons are mapped onto a virtual one-dimensional array processor with $d \cdot N$ PEs by using the mapping strategies already described in sections 5 and 6. The factor d should be the smallest integral value for which $m \leq d \cdot N$ or $e \leq d \cdot N$ holds, respectively. Thereafter, d PEs of the virtual one-dimensional array are mapped to one PE of the physical processing array by using one of the following mapping strategies:

- **crinkling:** d *neighboring* virtual PEs are mapped onto *one* physical PE.
- **slicing:** The virtual array is cut into d slices, each consisting of N neighboring PEs. The i-th virtual PE of each slice is mapped onto the physical PE with index i.

All parallel operations on the virtual processor array must be performed d times on the physical array, each time with a different PE memory address. Also the communication functions of the ring or torus network can be simulated in d steps on the physical array.

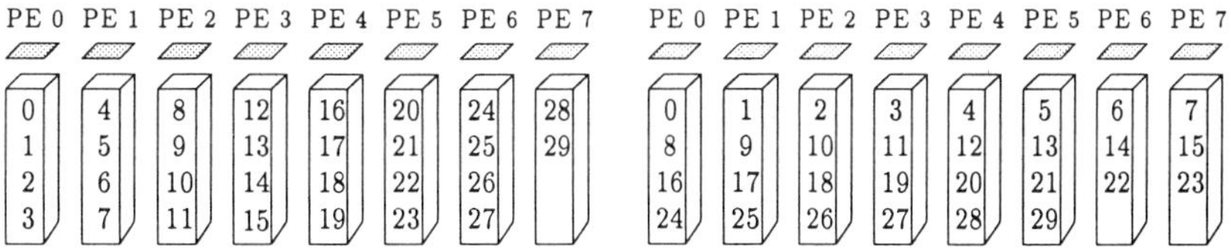

(a) crinkling (b) slicing

Figure 5: Virtual mapping strategies

Figure 5 illustrates both virtual mapping strategies for the case of 30 virtual PEs that are mapped onto an array processor with 8 PEs.

8 Basic algorithms

All basic algorithms are described in the following for a sufficent large (virtual) processor array with $N = 2^n$ (virtual) PEs. The data elements stored at a certain memory address of *all* PEs can be considered as a *vector*, using the PE index as vector index.

8.1 VECTOR_SHIFT

The following basic algorithm specifications often rely on a vector shift by a certain distance k to the left (or right). This shift can be realized directly on the ring interconnection network or by the following three steps on the torus interconnection network of the array processor model (see figure 6):

1. All vector elements that are mapped onto the torus according to the one-dimensional index *id* are cyclically shifted by k div $\sqrt{N}$ to the west (east).
2. All PEs perform a cyclic shift by k mod $\sqrt{N}$ to the north (south).
3. Thereafter, in the last (first) k mod $\sqrt{N}$ rows of the array processor a correction shift by 1 to the west (east) must be done.

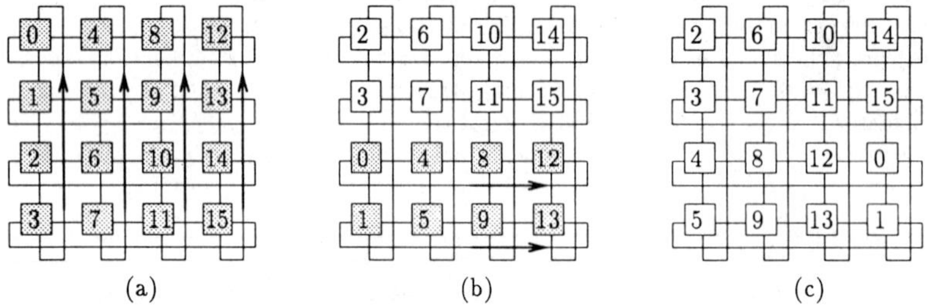

Figure 6: Right shift of a vector by the distance 2 on a torus with 4×4 PEs

8.2 SEGMENT_SUM

A number m of different data segments are consecutively mapped onto the array processor according to the unique indices of the PEs. The following algorithm computes in parallel the sums s_j of all m segments, each with e_j, $j = 0, \ldots, m-1$ data elements. The m segments to be summed constitute a vector v with $e = \sum e_j$ elements.

At first all elements of the vector v and the neuron (segment) indices j are shifted a distance of 1 to the left by the algorithm *VECTOR_SHIFT* described above. If the vector element received from the neighbor PE belongs to the same segment (i.e. if it has the same neuron index j) it is added to the local vector element, thus forming a new intermediate sum vector v. Next, all elements of v and the segment indices j are shifted a distance of 2 to the left. The shifted elements of v are added to the local vector elements only if they belong to the same segment. These two steps are repeated for all distances $4, 8, 16, \ldots$ until the shift distance exceeds the maximal segment length $\max_j e_j$. At the end the first PE in each segment contains the sum of all segment data elements. The shift and the comparison of the neuron indices in each step can be replaced by using *precomputed* masks.

The total number of steps taken by the algorithm *SEGMENT_SUM* depends on the maximal segment length $\max_j e_j$. In the worst case (i.e. if $\max e_j \geq N/2$) in total $N - 1$ communication steps on the ring network or $2(\sqrt{N} - 1) + \frac{1}{2} \operatorname{ld} N$ communication steps on the torus, and $\operatorname{ld} N$ computation steps are required.

8.3 COLLECT

A vector v containing relevant data only in some PEs marked by a logical mask vector m is given ($m = 1$ if the element is relevant, $m = 0$ in all other PEs). All relevant vector elements must be sent to the CP via the global bus. Although this seems to be a rather trivial problem it is very difficult to realize it efficiently on the array processor model; this is because the PEs are allowed to put data on the global bus only if the CP issues a *global_or* command. In the following, three different algorithms that solve this problem are described:

Algorithm 1: The CP broadcasts in order the indices $0, 1, \ldots, N - 1$ of all PE via the global bus. After the broadcast of each index i all PEs in parallel compare the received value with their locally stored index id and generate a logical mask which is true only if both are identical and if $m = 1$. The CP disables all PEs where the computed mask bit is false and executes a *global_or* command on all enabled PEs. So the CP receives either the next relevant vector element $v(i)$ or a special value indicating that all PEs are disabled (i.e. that PE i contains no relevant vector element).

This algorithm takes $3N$ time steps ($2N$ bus operations and N comparisons). It has the advantage that it needs only the global bus and not the additional interconnection network of the array processor.

Algorithm 2: It is assumed that at the beginning in all PEs a logical mask is available which is true for the PE with index $id = 0$ and false for all other PEs. This mask is used for enabling/disabling the PEs and it is shifted in N steps through all PEs of the array processor by using the *VECTOR_SHIFT* operation described above. Thus after each vector shift by a distance of 1 to the right another PE is enabled. If $m = 1$ the enabled PE puts its relevant vector element on the global bus and the CP issues a *global_or* command.

The algorithm takes N elementary vector shifts on the ring, N bus operations and N comparison steps. Only boolean values are moved to the neighbor PEs, so that the interconnection network only needs a data path width of 1 bit. The use of the torus topology is not profitable here.

Algorithm 3: The following algorithm consists of two phases. In the first phase a unique enumeration index $1, 2, \ldots, q$ is generated for all q relevant vector elements. In the second phase the CP gathers the relevant elements by using the calculated enumeration index.

The generation of unique indices for all active neurons can be realized by a parallel *prefix* operation. The logical mask m marks all (virtual) PEs containing relevant vector elements with the value one, in all other PEs the mask value is zero. At first, all partial sums $s_j = \sum_{\mu=0}^{j} m_\mu$ are calculated for all PEs j in parallel by the *PARTIAL_SUM* algorithm described below. Now in each PE j the value s_j represents the number of relevant vector elements with indices lower than or equal to j. By resetting the partial sums to zero in all PEs with $m = 0$, a unique index $s_j = 1, 2, \ldots, q$ is generated.

In the second phase the CP broadcasts in order the numbers $i \in \{1, 2, \ldots\}$ via the global bus. All PEs in parallel compare the received value i with their locally stored enumeration index of phase 1 and set a local mask bit if both are identical. The CP disables all PEs with a false mask bit and receives the relevant vector element of the only enabled PE by issuing a *global_or* command. The second phase is terminated if the *global_or* result indicates that all PEs were disabled in the last step.

All together, q comparison steps, ld N additions, $q + 1$ global bus operations and N ring communication steps or $2(\sqrt{N} - 1) + \frac{1}{2}\,\mathrm{ld}\,N$ torus communication steps are required.

8.4 PARTIAL_SUM

All partial sums $s_j = \sum_{\mu=0}^{j} x_\mu$ of a vector x mapped onto the array processor according to the one-dimensional PE indices can be computed in parallel. All elements are first shifted a distance of $\Delta = 1$ to the right by using the *VECTOR_SHIFT* algorithm described above. In all PEs with index $id \geq 1$ the shifted elements are added to the local data elements. These two steps are repeated for all distances $\Delta = 2, 4, \ldots, N/2$: The already computed intermediate sums are shifted a distance of Δ to the right and are added to the local sums if the index id is greater than or equal to Δ. The parallel computation of all partial sums is also called the parallel *prefix* operation and takes ld N addition and $2(\sqrt{N} - 1) + \frac{1}{2}\,\mathrm{ld}\,N$ communication steps on the torus topology or $N - 1$ communication steps on the ring.

9 Results

The following tables summarizes the total counts of computation steps t_{op} and communication steps t_{comm} needed for the different phases of both implementations (with N = number of PEs, p = number of active input vector elements and q = number of active output neurons). For each of the topologies ring and torus the implementation of *COLLECT* with the smallest time complexity is used.

Dense matrix implementation:

		distribute	sum	compare	collect
t_{op}	(ring)	0	p	1	N
t_{comm}	(ring)	p	0	0	$2N$
t_{op}	(torus)	0	p	1	$\mathrm{ld}\ N + q + 1$
t_{comm}	(torus)	p	0	0	$2\sqrt{N} + \frac{1}{2}\,\mathrm{ld}\,N + q - 1$

Sparse matrix implementation:

		distribute	sum	compare	collect
t_{op}	(ring)	p	$\leq \mathrm{ld}\,N$	1	N
t_{comm}	(ring)	p	$\leq N - 1$	0	$2N$
t_{op}	(torus)	p	$\leq \mathrm{ld}\,N$	1	$\mathrm{ld}\,N + q + 1$
t_{comm}	(torus)	p	$\leq 2\sqrt{N} - 2 + \frac{1}{2}\,\mathrm{ld}\,N$	0	$2\sqrt{N} + \frac{1}{2}\,\mathrm{ld}\,N + q - 1$

Considering that p und q should be of order $\mathcal{O}(\log \mathcal{N})$ for achieving a large storage capacity, the most time consuming operation for all neural associative memory implementations is the collection of the addresses of the active neurons. Due to the global communication operations of the *COLLECT* algorithm the total time complexity is $\mathcal{O}(N)$ for the ring topology and can be reduced to $\mathcal{O}(\sqrt{N})$ by using the torus topology and algorithm 3. In the summing phase of the sparse matrix implementation also $\mathcal{O}(\sqrt{N})$ communication steps are needed. But the high step count for this phase only applies to the the worst case in which the number e_{max} of nonzero synapses connected to *one* neuron exceeds $N/2$. Normally only a small number of steps is needed here to calculate the segmented sums so that the *COLLECT* complexity is the dominating term for the total time complexity of the implementation. A further improvement of the time steps needed for the implementation is only possible by using a faster (hardware) mechanism for collecting the addresses of the active neurons (see section 10). Also a balanced communication/operation ratio is more important for the simulation of associative memories on massively parallel computers than the usage of PEs with very fast addition capabilities.

10 The PAN IV

Some special-purpose neural associative memory chips which can be used as a processing element of an massively parallel array processor have already been realized. They are based either on a standard cell design [8] or Field Programmable Logic Arrays [10].

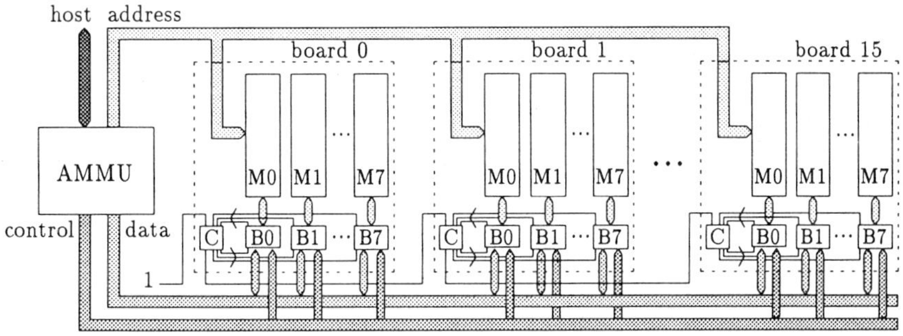

Figure 7: The system architecture of the PAN IV system

Recently, a massively parallel array processor architecture called PAN IV especially designed for the simulation of very large associative memories has been completed [7]. The overall architecture of the PAN IV is shown in figure 7. It is based on a VLSI standard cell design called BACCHUS III developed in a joint project sponsered by the BMFT at the Institute of Microelectronics in Darmstadt [1]. The hardware of 32 simple neurons is included in this chip. One printed circuit board contains 8 BACCHUS chips (designated as B0 to B7 in figure 7), each equipped with 1 MByte local memory (M0 to M7). The prototype of the PAN IV consists of 16 boards physically located in a VME-Bus rack. Thus, the overall number of neurons is 4096 with a total memory of 128 MByte. The control processor (called AMMU = Associative Memory Management Unit) resides on an additional board and is based on a 68030 CPU. It provides communication with a Unix SPARCstation via a bidirectional FIFO interface and generates the instructions and addresses for all memory boards. Only the algorithms described in section 5 for the case of a dense correlation matrix can be implemented on the PAN IV system because the distributed implementation of the summing phase (cf. section 8.2) is not supported by the

BACCHUS chips. If the number of required neurons exceeds the number of available PEs, the partitioning strategy *slicing* (cf. section 7) is used. All address modifications that are necessary for the partitioned implementation are computed by the AMMU.

For the time consuming collection of the addresses of the active neurons after a retrieval phase a special hardware acceleration has been developed. Basically, the algorithm 2 explained in section 8.3 is used. But the slow shift of a mask bit is implemented only between different boards. Each board is provided with a controller (designated as C in figure 7) that receives a special signal from all BACCHUS chips indicating that they contain active neurons. Depending on this information either some BACCHUS chips are allowed to put the addresses of the active neurons in order on the data bus, or the mask bit is shifted to the next board. Thus, the number of time steps required in the collecting phase could be reduced drastically.

A more detailed description of the PAN IV hardware can be found in [7].

Acknowledgement

This work was partially supported by the German Ministry for Research and Technology (BMFT).

References

[1] Huch, M., Poechmueller, W., and Glesner, M. BACCHUS: A VLSI Architecture for a Large Binary Associative Memory. In *Proceedings of the International Neural Network Conference, Paris* (1990), Kluwer Academic Publishers.

[2] Kohonen, T. The Self-Organizing Map. *Proceedings of the IEEE* **78**, 9 (1990), 1464–1480.

[3] Kung, S., and Hwang, J. A Unified Systolic Architecture for Artificial Neural Networks. *Journal of Parallel and Distributed Computing* **6** (1989), 358–387.

[4] Morgan, N., Beck, J., Kohn, P., Bilmes, J., Allman, E., and Beer, J. The RAP: A Ring Array Processor for Layered Network Calculations. In *Proceedings of the International Conference on Application Specific Array Processors* (Princeton, 1990), IEEE Computer Society Press, pp. 296–308.

[5] Palm, G. On Associative Memory. *Biological Cybernetics* **36** (1980), 19–31.

[6] Palm, G. Associative Networks and Cell Assemblies. In *Brain Theory*, G. Palm and A. Aertsen, Eds. Springer-Verlag, 1986, pp. 211–228.

[7] Palm, G., and Palm, M. Parallel Associative Networks: The PAN-System and the Bacchus-Chip. In *Proceedings of the 2nd international Conference on Microelectronics for Neural Networks* (Munich, 1991), Kyrill & Method.

[8] Pöchmüller, W., and Glesner, M. A Cascadable VLSI Architecture for the Realization of Large Binary Associative Networks. In *International Workshop on VLSI for Artificial Intelligence and Neural Networks* (Oxford, 1990).

[9] Ramacher, U. Synapse – A Neurocomputer that Synthesizes Neural Algorithms on a Parallel Systolic Engine. *Journal of Parallel and Distributed Computing* **14** (1992), 306–318.

[10] Rückert, U., Funke, A., and Pintaske, C. Acceleratorboard for Neural Associative Memories. *Neurocomputing* **5**, 1 (1993), 39–49.

[11] Rumelhart, D., Hinton, G., and Williams, R. Learning Internal Representations by Error Propagation. In *Parallel Distributed Processing, Volume 1: Foundations*, D. Rumelhart and J. McClelland, Eds. MIT Press, 1986, ch. 8, pp. 318–362.

A VLSI ARRAY PROCESSOR FOR NEURAL NETWORK ALGORITHMS

J. Beichter, N. Brüls, U. Ramacher, E. Sicheneder, H. Klar[1]

Siemens AG, Corp.R&D, W-8000 Munich 83, Germany

[1] Technical University of Berlin, W-1000 Berlin 12, Germany

Abstract: **A VLSI array processor is presented which especially supports the compute-bound algorithmic primitives used for search and learning in neural networks. The architecture combines high performance with a high grade of flexibility for all types and sizes of neural networks. The processor chip can be connected to form one and two dimensional arrays. 16 bit block floating point data are used for the weights and signal input. The chip was realized in 1.0μm CMOS (610k transistors) and achieves $800*10^6$ connections/s at 50MHz.**

1. INTRODUCTION

A VLSI array processor (MA16) is presented which is the main building block of the neurocomputer system SYNAPSE [1]. In order to serve a vast variety of neural networks, a versatile VLSI architecture must absorb in silicon the algorithmic compute-intensive primitives shared by all neural networks. These neural primitives can be described by the following matrix operations:

- matrix-matrix-multiplication:

$$S^*_{i,k} = \Sigma_j A_{i,j} * B_{j,k}$$

- matrix-matrix addition/substraction:

$$S^*_{i,j} = A_{i,j} \pm B_{i,j}$$

- matrix-matrix computations using transposed matrices: A^T, B^T, S^T
- squares, absolute values of the S^* sums:

$$S_{i,j} = |S^*_{i,j}|^q, \quad q=1,2$$

- search for the maximal/minimal matrix component, also including the index
- controllable rounding effects
- normalization of weights
- statistics of weight saturation

Besides, the chip architecture must stress parallelism to offer sufficient processing power to speed up the learning phase. It must also support scalability to build larger systems by connecting several processor chips to adapt easily to applications in terms of computing power and memory size. All weight memory must then be placed off-chip, because of lack of chip area.

2. PROCESSING NODE

2.1 Functional Architecture

To achieve a high computing power the matrix operations are distributed among parallel processing nodes (PN). Each PN works on 4*4 submatrices. A PN architecture with the following features has been defined (figure 1).

Four 16bit integer multipliers and adders are connected to form a systolic multiplier-adder chain which performs 4 multiplications in each clock cycle. Running a 4*4 matrix-matrix multiplication on the PN takes 16 cycles, exactly the time to load another 4*4 matrix to each of the two input channels Xin, Yin. It is necessary to store the incoming 4*4 matrices temporarily in buffers because each matrix element has to be used 4 times for multiplication. These buffers allow preloading and multiplication at the same time. Transpostion of the 4*4 matrices is also solved using the buffers. This way, a high computing rate can be combined with a moderate I/O. Addition and subtraction of 4*4 matrices is done in the adder chain.

The partial results S^* from these matrix-matrix operations are sent first to a fifth multiplier for scaling and computing squares and absolute values. The resulting values S flow into a multifunctional accumulator loop where the final sums are computed and stored in the S-buffer. A min/max search can also be done for running Kohonen or competitive networks. A barrel shifter enables the circuit to handle double precision 32bit input data and to normalize weight data. The PN has integrated a programmable weight saturation circuit. A noise generator is included to avoid local minima during the learning steps. Statistics of the occurence of weight overflows help monitoring the development of values in large weight matrices. The local loop of the accumulator which is based on an adder

 0-7803-0826-3/93 $3.00

and the S-buffer can be reconfigured to form a global loop by connecting the adders of all PNs in the systolic array. This distributed accumulation supports the computation on the transposed weight matrix without physically transposing it.
These versatile operations are realized with a minor need of silicon area by making multiple use of the implemented functional blocks (adders, shifter, registers).

2.2 Design of the functional blocks
The multipliers are designed for high throughput and layout density. A regular array of partial product gates and 24-transistor carry-save-adder cells are pipelined by pass-gate latches. A pipeline stage includes a partial product gate or two adder cells. The carry-save data format is used throughout the multiplier-adder chain. The cell area of a 16*16bit multiplier is $0.6mm^2$ in $1.0\mu m$ CMOS.
The buffers keeping the matrix data are realized by small dynamic memory cells which all are refreshed by the cyclic read of the matrix data.
In order to save chip area the carry save data have to be converted to binary format before being stored in the S-buffer or multiplied by data from the α-buffer. Carry-select-adders are used which offer low latency as well as moderate chip area. Because of this, a delayed pipelining is used to allow 22ns delay for the carry-select-adders under worst case conditions.
The functional blocks are layouted by a cell based full-custom design style.

2.3 Data formats
The accuracy of the PN is 16 bit for the Xin, Yin inputs, 32 bit for the multipliers and 47 bit for the accumulator path. This is sufficient for weights updates during the learning phase and processing of very large matrices as well. The multiplier-adder chain adds 4 products of input data to form a correct 34 bit sum. After the scalar multiplication of the 34 bit data by the 16 bit data from the α-buffer, only the upper 36 bits are kept for use inside the accumulator loop. For large neural nets the width of the accumulator is set to 47 bit to sum at least 3.2e4 weighted inputs for each neuron. If an overflow occurs, a flag will be set and passed along with the bounded data (47 bit data + 1 bit flag).
32 bit data can also be handled with a time penalty. The product of 32 bit multiplications will be 32 bit numbers.

2.4 Control
The operations of the PN are selected by loading a 96bit wide opcode word. These opcode bits can be transmitted to the PN in a multiplexed manner by using

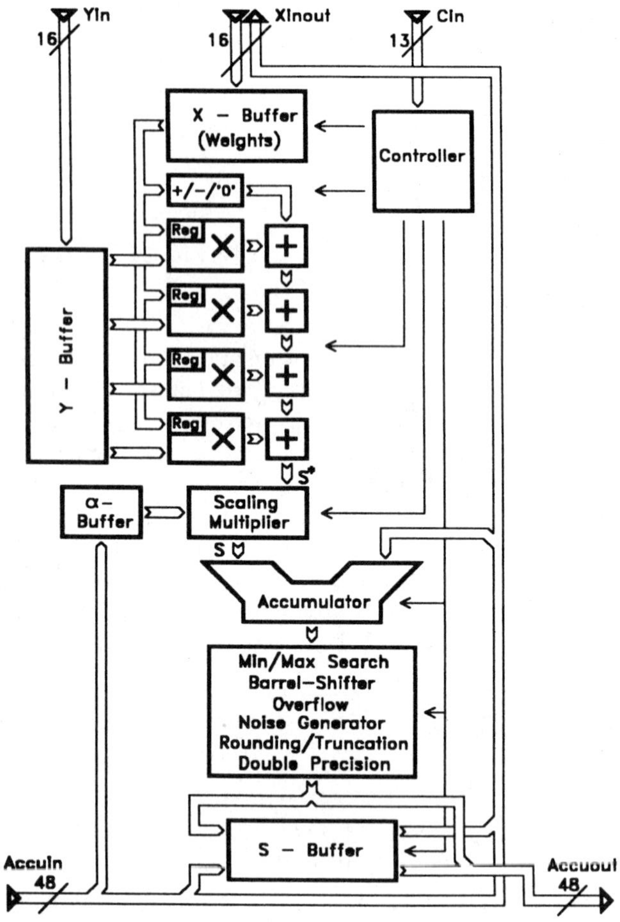

Figure 1: The functional block architecture of the processing node

only 13 control lines, because a new matrix operation will start earliest every 16 clock cycles. In addition, the PN remembers the old opcode word. Hence, only a few opcode bits have to be reloaded for selecting a new operation. An operation is started by sending a trigger pulses which signals the I/O of new 4*4 matrices.
A token mechanism is used to selectively program, load or download PNs along the systolic chain. A token is passed along the array that enables the receiving PN to open its buffers. The buffers of the other PNs are bypassed meanwhile.

2.5 Test and Redundancy
Functional testing is used for the PNs throughout the chip. The simple control and dataflow of the PN is exploited to test the functional blocks and routines seperately. Pseudo-random and specific test pattern are applied from the input pins to all 4 PNs in parallel. The observability of internal blocks is improved to faciliate testing. I.e. the min/max logic is built on the accumulator's carry-select adder where the intermediate

carry states can be controlled easily. The multipliers and adders can also be bypassed.
Inside the systolic neurocomputer array whole PNs can be disabled by software to test selected PNs and chips seperately. After testing, extra redundant PNs can be enabled as defect PNs can be kept disabled from the operations in the systolic array. Defect PNs will degrate the performance of the array gracefully.
The whole MA16 chip was tested by 21000 test vectors.

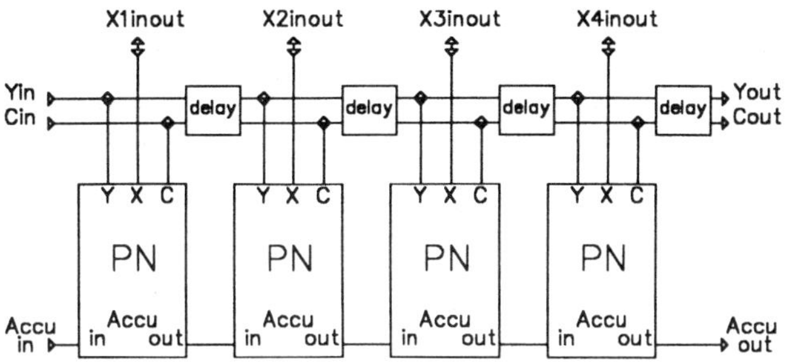

Figure 2: The MA16 chip architecture

3. THE MA16-CHIP

The PNs can be connected easily to form a linear systolic array of arbitrary length (figure 2). The resulting accumulator path lines up all processing nodes while the input (Yin) and the control path (Cin) reach them along bypasses. Along these pathes the data can either be broadcasted or loaded to selected PNs. The bidirectional data pathes (X1inout to X4inout) connect the processing nodes to the local off-chip memories. The data bandwidth to the local memory is 400MB/s.
A linear array of 4 processing nodes is implemented in the MA16 chip and is realized in 1.0μm CMOS technology (figure 3). The technical data are shown in table 1. The chip shows full functionality at 50MHz which is the worst case frequency.
In future submicron technologies the architecture of the chip and the processing node can easily be adapted under moderate I/O bandwidth to offer more processing power by enlarging the multiplier-adder chain and the number of PNs on a chip.

4. APPLICATIONS

A system built of eight MA16 chips performs 5.12GCONS/s (forward path @40MHz) on running the backward-error propagation algorithm for a multi-layer perceptron.
By exploiting its flexibility the chip can also be used to perform preprocessing and filtering tasks like the discrete Fourier and cosine transformations and convolutions.

5. CONCLUSIONS

A chip based on a new scalable parallel systolic VLSI architecture is presented for executing the compute-bound algorithmic primitives used by search and learning algorithms in neural networks and low level signal processing.
The architecture combines high performance with a high grade of flexibility for all types and sizes of neural networks. By offering an accuracy of 16 bit for input and 47 bit for output data the chip achieves 800Mconnections/s at 50MHz. It is realized in 1.0μm CMOS (610k transistors on 13.7*13.7mm^2) and has a total data bandwidth of 10.9 Gbit/s.

6. REFERENCES

[1] Ramacher U.; "SYNAPSE - A Neurocomputer That SYnthezises Neural Algorithms on a Parallel Systolic Engine"; Journal of Parallel and Distributed Computing, vol 14., pp306-318; 1992

Technology	1.0 μm CMOS
Transistors	610 k
Chip Area	13.7mm*13.7mm
Clock Frequency (worst case)	50MHz
Supply voltage	3.5 - 7 V
peak power dissip. @5V, 50MHz	
core	3.5W
Pads (30pF)	2.7 W
# Pads: total/data	342/228
Peak performance@50MHz	800*10^6 MAC/s

Table 1: Technical Data of the MA16 chip; MAC/s = multiplications & accumulations per second

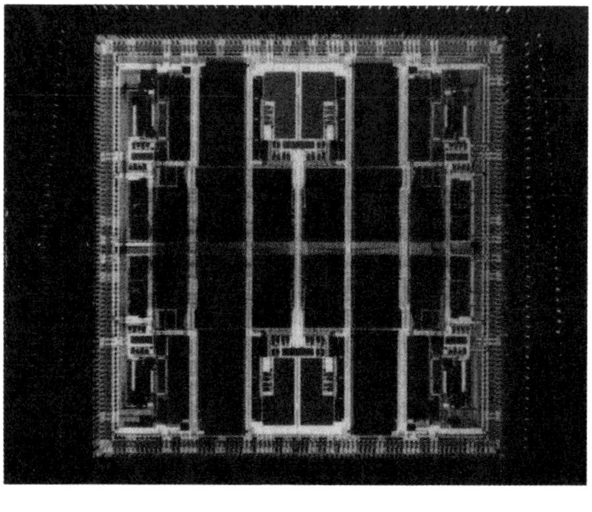

Figure 3: Photography of the MA16 chip

PARALLEL COMPUTING ALGORITHM OF NEURAL NETWORKS ON AN EIGHT-NEIGHBOR PROCESSOR ARRAY

Toshihiro TAKEDA, Akiyoshi TANAKA and Kuninobu TANNO
Department of Electrical and Information Engineering
Yamagata University
Yonezawa, Yamagata 992, JAPAN

E-mail:takeda@eie.yz.yamagata-u.ac.jp

ABSTRACT Neural network technologies have been promoted in wide application fields such as pattern recognition, image processing, control. Since neural networks require an enormous of time in learning, various kinks of parallel computers, for examples the connection machine, the n-cube machine and so no, have been developed. In this paper, we describe parallel computing algorithm to simulate the back propagation (BP) model and Kohonen's self-organizing feature map (SOFM) upon an 8-neighbor processor array. Taking account of the parallelism intrinsically found in the neural networks, we develop algorithms which minimizes the transmission overhead among processors, so that we obtain high-speed simulation of neural networks. This algorithm may be applicable to the MasPar parallel computer which has capability to communicate among eight neighbor processing elements.

1. INTRODUCTION

Various types of neural networks have been proposed and their fundamental researches and analyses have been made for years. At the same time, neural network technologies have also been vigorously promoted in wide application fields such as pattern recognition, image processing, control and so on [1][2]. In the study of neural networks, simulation techniques using digital computers is one of the most important research strategies because mathematical analysis seems to be very hard. However, since neural networks require an enormous of time in learning, we need faster simulators, especially for larger scale neural networks. To attain high-speed processing rate, a number of software/hardware simulators utilizing general/special purpose parallel computers have been developed [5].

In this paper, we describe parallel computing algorithm to simulate the back propagation (BP) model and Kohonen's self-organizing feature map (SOFM) upon an 8-neighbor processor array. Taking account of the parallelism intrinsically found in the neural networks, the algorithm minimizes communications overhead among processors so that it obtain high-speed simulation of neural networks.

2. NEURAL NETWORK MODELS

2.1 BP model

BP model [1][2] applies the back-error propagation learning rules to a multilayer neural network as illustrated in Fig. 1. The learning is conducted by repeating the two phases: the forward propagation processing and back-error propagation processing. In the forward propagation processing, output signal is obtained after input data at input layer are propagated to the middle and output layers in turn. In the back-error propagation processing, the error between the output on the output layer are compared with teaching signal at first. Then the error between them is propagated in inverse directions from the output layer to the input layer, and the weights and threshold values are renovated to reduce the error. The processing equations of the BP model with L layers are given by (1) through (7).

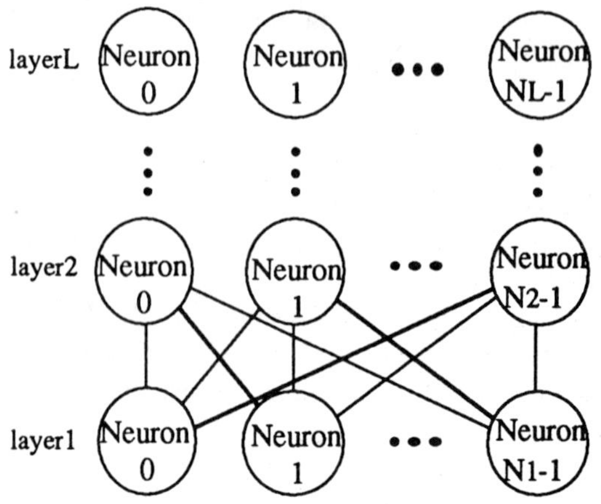

Fig.1 A multilayer neural network with L layers.

0-7803-0922-7/93$03.00 1993©IEEE

$$y_i(k+1)=\sum_j x_j(k)w_{ij}(k) \quad (1)$$

$$x_i(k+1)=f(y_i(k+1),\theta_i(k+1)) \quad (2)$$

$$\delta_i(L)=(T_i-x_i(L))f'(y_i(L),\theta_i(L)) \quad (3)$$

$$\sigma_i(k)=\sum_j \delta_j(k+1)w_{ji}(k) \quad (4)$$

$$\delta_i(k)=\sigma_i(k)f'(y_i(k),\theta_i(k)) \quad (5)$$

$$w_{ij}(k)=w_{ij}(k)+\alpha\delta_i(k+1)x_j(k) \quad (6)$$

$$\theta_i(k)=\theta_i(k)+\beta\delta_i(k+1) \quad (7)$$

where x_i: outpit of unit i, y_i: product sum of uniti, w_{ij}: weight connecting layer k to layer k+1, θ_i: threshhold of unit i, δ_i: error of unit i, α, β: learning rate of weight and threshold, f: a sigmoid function, f': the derivation of the function f, and k: layer No..

2.2 Kohonen's SOFM

In Kohonen's model, each neuron is arranged in two-dimensional plane as shown in Fig. 2. All neurons are given the identical input vector x. Each neuron has a reference vector m_i, which is the same dimension as the input vector x [3].

Learning is referred to as the unsupervised learning. It proceeds by repeating the distance calculation, competition, and renovation for the input vectors given one by one. The distance calculation produces the distance (differences) between the input vector x and the reference vector m_i. Then with the competition, a neuron with the nearest distance (smallest distance) is chosen. Finally, the reference vectors of the chosen neuron and the neurons in its neighborhood are renovated. A series of the above processing is shown below.

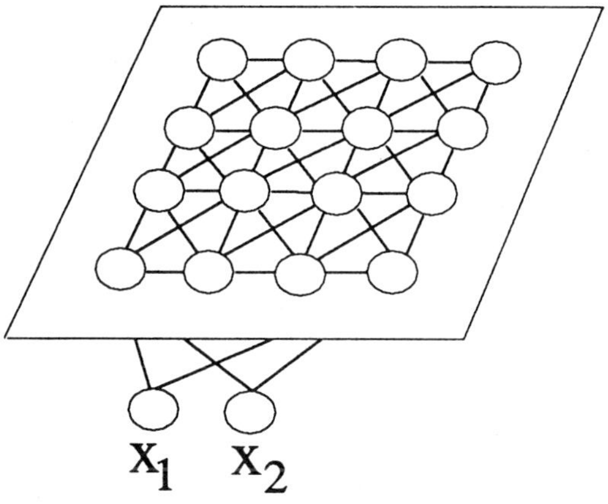

Fig2 Kohonen's model.

Distance calculation

$$d_i=\|x(t)-m_i(t)\| \quad (8)$$

Competetion

$$d_c=\min_i d_i \quad (9)$$

Renovation

$$\begin{cases} m_i(t+1)=m_i(t)+\alpha(t)[x(t)-m_i(t)] & \text{if } i\in N_c(t) \\ m_i(t+1)=m_i(t) & \text{if } i\notin N_c(t) \end{cases} \quad (10)$$

where a(t) is a scaler-valued "adoption gain" $0<a(t)<1$, which should decrease with time.

3. PARALLEL COMPUTING ON 8-NEIGHBOR PROCESSOR ARRAY

3.1 Structure and function of 8-neighbor processor array

The 8-neighbor processor array dealt with in this paper is of the torus structure having communication route among nearest 8-neighbor processing elements (Fig. 3). Each processing element (PE) has a function of addition/distraction, multiplication, and input/output function operation together with local memory to hold the data required for the operation. Also each PE has half-duplex and bi-directional communicasion capability as illustrated

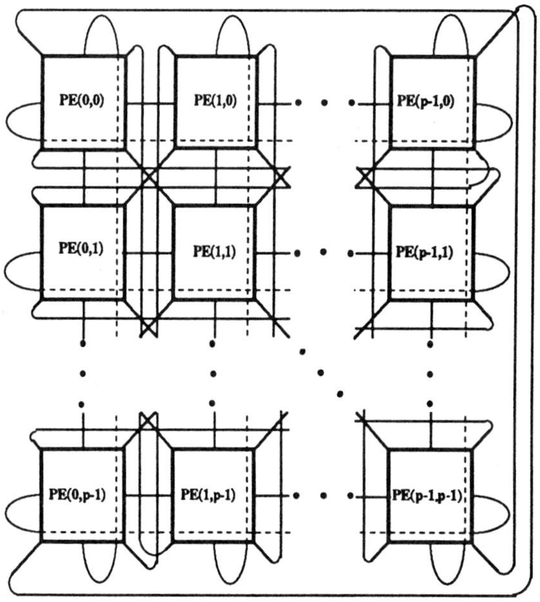

Fig. 3 Structure of an eight-neighbor processor array.

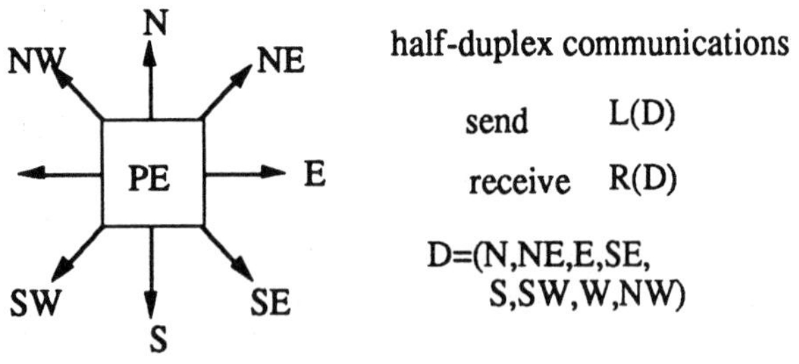

Fig. 4 Communication links of a PE.

in Fig. 4. Data transmission is designated by L(D), where D indicates transmission direction on a link. Receiving is designated by R(D), where D indicates one of eight-registers in PE. Let P (=p$\times$p) be the number of processors, and let each PE be expressed in a form of PE(i, j) (i, j=0, 1, ..., p-1).

3.2 Implementation of BP model

Eqs. (1) through (7) present the learning for BP model, but they are classified into the two processing types depending on communication discipline. That is, communications among PEs are unnecessary in (2), (3), (5) and (7) because they are completed in each neuron without communications. However, (1), (4) and (6) require communications among neurons. Consequently, it is important for parallel simulator of neural networks to minimize communication time as possible. A way to reduce communications time is to distribute and to map the processing in a neuron to plural PEs. It means not only we develop parallel processing algorithm of neural networks, but also we efficiently derive parallelism embedded in neural networks.

We explain mapping method of neural networks to the 8-neighbor processor array, and then consider processing and communications times required in each PEs with respect to (1), (4) and (6). Let L be the number of the layers of the multilayer neural network, and let N_k(k=1, ..., L) be the number of neurons of each layer. Although N_k and P are not equal to each other in general, we assume that P=N_k (k=1,...,L) for the sake of simplification in explanation.

3.2.1 Mapping of neurons

The neurons on each layer is mapped to each PE one by one. Then each PE is mapped L neurons, which equal to the number of the layers. We denote a value of the input to a neuron i on the input layer as $x_i(1)$, and the weight between a neuron i on the k-th layer and a neuron on the (k+1)-th layer as $w_{ij}(k)$. Also the threshold values of the neurons on each layer are expressed as $\theta_i(k)$, and the teaching signal for a neuron i on the output layer is expressed as

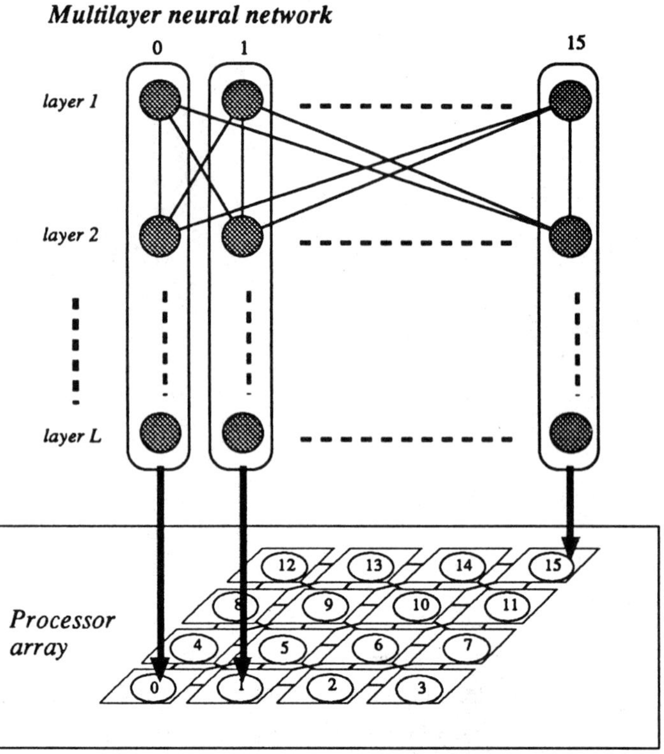

Fig. 5 Mapping of neurons to processor array.

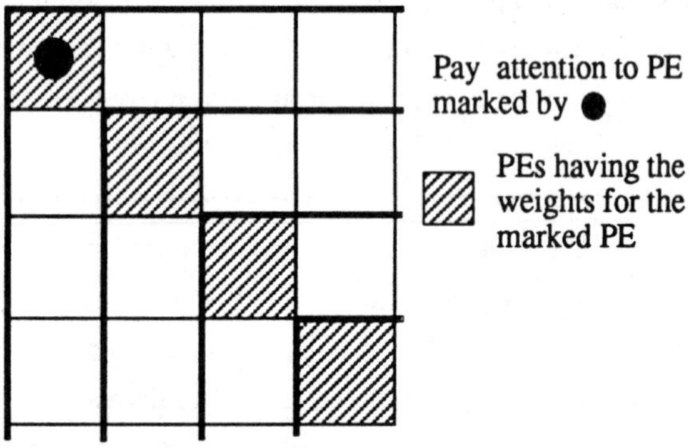

Fig. 6 Mapping of weights for the PE marked by ●

T_i. A mapping example for P=16 is illustrated in Fig. 5.

The weights of the neurons mapped onto PE(i,j) are distributed and stored upon PE(l, m) (l=i, i+1, .., 0, .., i-1, m=j, j+1, ..,0, .., j-1) on the diagonal line. Consider the forward propagation processing between the (k-1)-th and the k-th layers. We focus on the first neuron in the k-th layer which is mapped onto PE(0,0). The weights connecting the neurons on the (K-1)-th layer are distributed and stored upon PE(i,j) (i=j=0, 1, .., p-1) on a diagonal line as illustrated as in Fig. 6. That is, each neuron (hatched) upon a diagonal line contains the weights with respect to the $x_j(k-1)$ (j=1,2,...,N), which are derived from the neurons allocated in the counter-L-shaped PEs including each PE on the diagonal line. The counter-L-shaped PEs mean PE(0, j) (j=0, 1, .., p-1) and PE(i, 0) (i=0, 1, .., p-1)for PE(0, 0), PE(1, j) (j=1, 2, .., p-1) and PE(i, 1) (i=1, 2, .., p-1) for PE(1, 1), and so on. We can also say that the weights from the N_k-th neuron of the (k-1)th layer to neurons of the k-th layer are mapped upon the PE(i,p-1) (i=0,1,2,...,p-1) and PE(p-1,j) (j=0,1,2,...,p-1). The solid arrows in Fig. 7 indicate the transfer of output from the neuron mapped on PE(3, 3), and the PEs (hatched) with the weights produce the partial product sum with respect to the output. The dotted arrows indicate the transfer of the partial product sum.

Because the processor array used in this algorithm is the torus type, the all N_k neurons of the k-th layer are mapped on the array in the same manner.

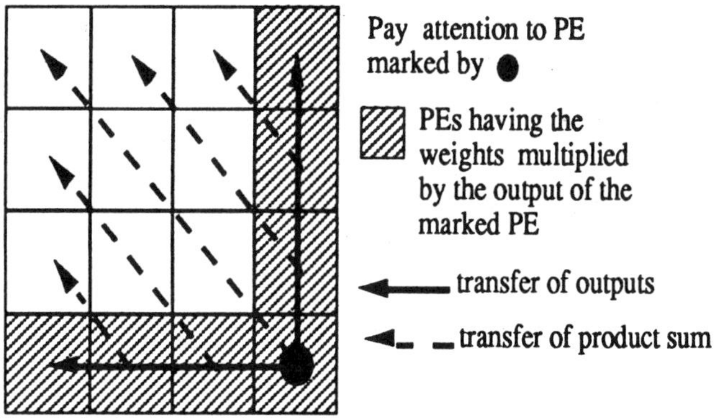

Fig. 7 Mapping of weights multiplied by output of the marked PE.

3.2.2 Processing in each PE

Eq. (1) shows that the forward-propagation processing requires all output $x_j(k-1)$ from the (k-1)-th layer to compute output of a neuron on the k-th layer. Taking account of the weights allocation and the transfer of product sum in Figs. 6 and 7, we can see that a product sum is obtained by repeating the following two steps: (1)transferring the output $x_j(i-1)$ and making products on the neurons upon the corresponding diagonal lines, (2) gathering them . As illustrated in Fig.8, the output $x_j(k-1)$ is transmitted in the directions of N and/or W. Concurrently the partial product sum are transmitted one by one in a direction of NW in order of remote PEs. On the other hand,the received output $x_j(k-1)$ is sent out for final PE in an opposite direction to the input link.

Transmission is occurred in 3 directions, i.e. N, W, and NW. Thus no conflict is caused even with the half-duplex transmission. Furthermore since the arrangement of PEs is symmetric, the same processing can be made at all PEs in parallel. The algorithm is formally presented in Fig.9, where the "send" in the algorithm indicates the transmission destained by a link with L(D), and the "receive" indicates the receipt by the receiving register with R(D). NE(i,j) represents the neurons No. mapped onto PE(i,j).

In the back propagation processing equation (4), the data are transmitted in the contrary directions for the forward processing of (1). Accordingly the processing proceeds by transmitting the error δ in SE direction, making the product sum with the weights placed on PEs in counter-L-shaped areas, and transmitting product sum in S and E directions.

To update the weights of the k-th layer, the back propagation equation (6) requires the errors of the (k+1)-th layer and $x_j(k)$. The errors are transmitted to PEs upon diagonal lines, and $x_j(k)$ are transmitted in directions of S and E (Fig. 10).

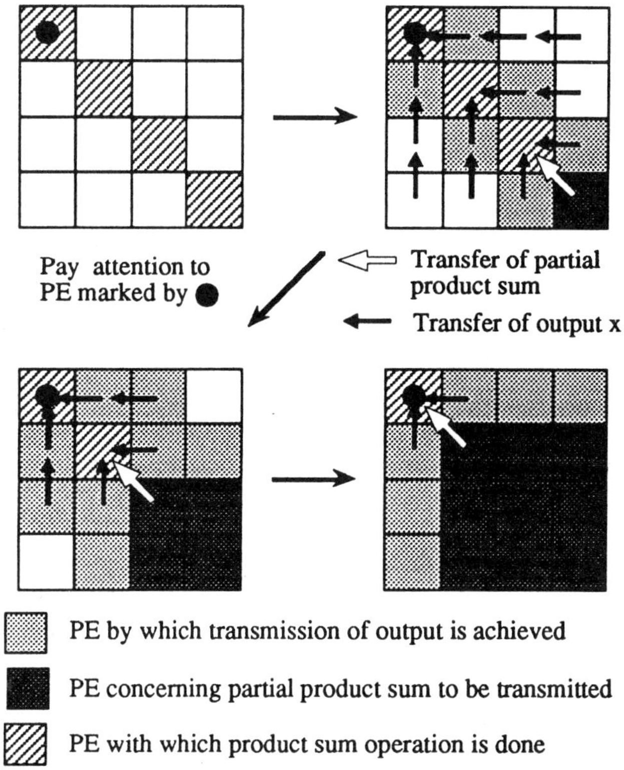

Fig. 8 Forward propagation algorithm on 4x4 processor array.

3.2.3 Enhancement to general BP model

Let us enhance the above algorithm to the general BP model, where the number of neurons in each layer and processors do not necessarily coincide with each other, that is, $P \neq N_k$ (k=1,2,3,...,L).

Eq.(1), the forward propagation processing equation, is rewritten as follows:

a) $P \geqq N_k$ (k=1, 2, .., L): By adding redundant neurons which always output 0, we get the equality $P=N_k$. Redundant neurons do not affect the behavior of the original neural networks.

```
begin
  (do in parallel)
 for i,j=0 to n-1 do
  for u=0 to n-1 do
   M(u):=w_NE(i-u,j-u)NE(i,j) × x_NE(i,j)
  end for
  send M(n-1) to L(NW)
  send x_NE(i,j) to L(N) and L(W)
  receive R from L(E) and L(S) and L(SE)
  for step=1 to n-2 do
   for u=0 to n-step-1 do
    M(u):=M(u)+w_NE(i-u,j-u)NE(i+step,j) × R(E)
       +w_NE(i-u,j-u)NE(i,j+step) ×R(S)
   end for
   M(n-step-1):=M(n-step-1)+R(SE)
   send R(E) to L(W)
   send R(S) to L(N)
   send M(n-step-1) to L(NW)
   receive R from L(E) and L(S) and L(SE)
  end for
  y_NE(i,j):=M(0)+w_NE(i,j)NE(i+n-1,j) ×R(E)
      +w_NE(i,j)NE(i,j+n-1) × R(S)
      +R(SE)
 end for
  (end parallel)
end
```

Fig. 9 Algorithm to compute eq. (1).

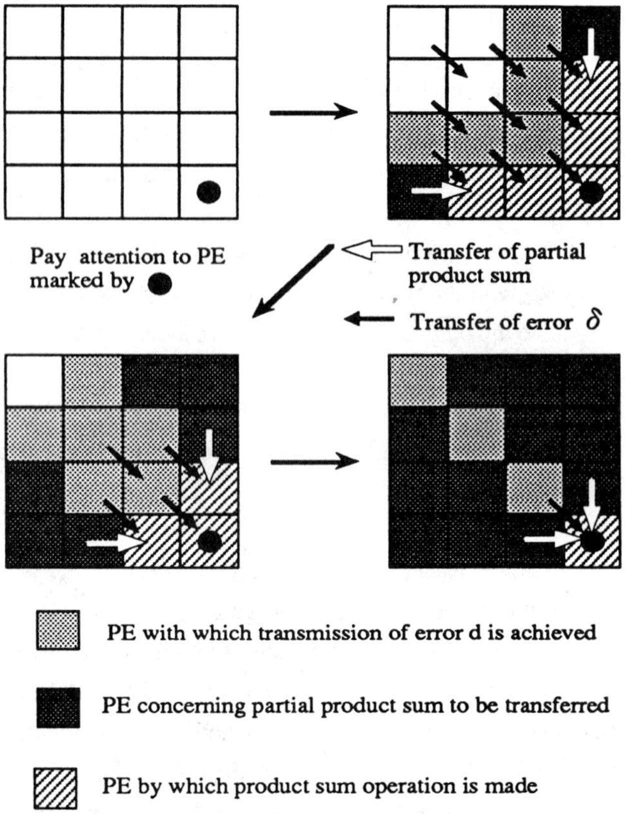

Fig. 10 Back propagation algorithm on 4x4 processor array.

b) $P<N_k$: By adding neurons so that $m_k P=N_k$ (m_k is natural number), then the neurons are divides into m_k pieces with the amount of $P=p\times p$. We allocate each piece onto the PE array so that m_k neurons are stored in a PE.

Since each portion does not require $w_{ij}(k)$ and $x_j(k)$ of other portions in the same layer, each portion can calculate (1) independently. To calculate the output on the (k+1)-th layer, we repeat the operation for each portion (totally $m_k \times m_{k+1}$ times), and finally acquire the product sum. By the same manner, (4) and (6) can also be dealt with.

3.3 Kohonen's SOFM

3.3.1 Mapping of neurons

Since Kohonen's SOFM uses 2-dimensional neuron arrangement as illustrated in Fig.2, it is directly mapped onto the 8-neighbor processor array.

Two algorithms are considered depending on input data allocation methods: 1) all neurons have all the same input data individually, 2) each neuron has a part of data. The former need not communicate to other neurons to determine the distance between x and m_i, whereas each neuron need to provide enough memory to store the entire input vector x. The latter requires communication in obtaining the distance, whereas memory is just sufficient for the dimension size of x / the number of neurons. This is advantageous when the number of PEs and the dimension size are close with each other. The algorithm to determine the distance is omitted because it is realized as the same processing of (1) of the BP model.

Hereafter, the algorithm to determine a winner by means of a competition is described. For the simplification of the explanation, we assume P=N, where N is the number of neurons.

3.3.2 Processing of PE

A winner by means of a competition can be determined by using the broadcast, which is very suitable for the 8-neighbor processor array. That is to say, a PE(i,j) compares its distance with distances of three neighbor PEs (E, S, SE directions), and selects and sets the minimum one as its new distance d(i, j). Then the PE(i, j) transfers the d(i, j) to tree neighbor PEs (N, W, NW directions). After p times repetitions of those operations, the finally remaining d(i, j) is the minimum distance $d_c(i,j)$. At this time, all PEs have the same minimum distance, then the PE which initially has the same distance with the final minimum $d_c(i,j)$ is a

```
begin
  (do in parallel)
  for i,j=0 to n-1 do
   C=min(all d in this PE)
   for step=1 to n-1 do
    send C to L(N) and L(W) and L(NW)
    receive R from L(E) and L(S) and L(SE)
    C=min(C,R(E),R(S),R(SE))
   end for
  end for
  (end parallel)
end
```

Fig. 11 Algorithm to compute eq. (9).

new winner. The algorithm is as illustrated in Fig.11, where C is a structure having two members, neuron No. and a minimum distance, and the function min is a function to set the neuron No. and the minimum d(i, j) to the structure C.

4. EVALUATION OF PROCESSING TIME

Processing time required for one learning of BP or Kohonen's SOFM for one input vector is estimated. Some assumptions described in the section 3 is held here.

4.1 BP model

Let T_2, T_3, T_5, and T_6 be the time required for the operations of Eqs.(2), (3), and (5), respectively. Let T_t, T_m, and T_a be the times for communication between PEs, a multiplication and a addition in (1), (4) and (6), respectively. Then the time T needed for the forward and the back propagation processing is given as shown below.

$$\begin{aligned} T = {} & (n^2(3L-4)+2(L-1))T_m+(n^2(3L-4) \\ & +n(3L-5)-2(L-2))T_a \\ & +(n-1)(3L-4)T_t \\ & +(L-1)T_2+(L-2)T_5+T_3 \end{aligned} \tag{11}$$

It is comprehended that the time complexity of the product sum processing is $O(n^2L)$. Also the time complexity of the communication is O(nL).

4.2 Kohonen's SOFM

Let T_d and T_c be the time for distance calculation and the comparison time in the competition, respectively. Also let T_t and T_u be the communication time and the update time for the reference vector m_i. The processing time T is given by

$$T=T_d+(T_c+T_t)(n-1)+T_u \tag{12}$$

From this equation, the time complexity of both the competition and the communication is O(n).

Now we consider the case of P<N. In this case, because plural neurons are allocated in one PE, in the competition, just the steps to obtain the minimum distance increase proportional to the number of neurons allocated in one PE. But no communication is increased. Accordingly the processing time T is a little changed below

$$T=mT_d+T_c'+(T_c+T_t)(n-1)+mT_u \tag{13}$$

where m=(N/P) and T_c' are the comparison time to determine d(k,j) for neurons in a PE.

5. CONCLUSIONS

We have discussed parallel processing algorithm to simulate the back propagation (BP) model and Kohonen's Self-organizing Feature Map(SOFM) upon an 8-neighbor processor array.

The algorithm realized the parallel processing to minimize the overhead of the communication time by distributing the processing among PEs. The algorithm can be easily implemented onto a state-of-the-art commercial machine [4], which can communicate between eight neighbor PEs. A problem of the algorithm is that efficiency is degraded when the number of the neurons to be mapped onto the processor array is not the multiple amount of the number of PEs.

References

[1]R. P. Lippmann, "An Introduction to Computing with Neural Nets, " IEEE ASSP Magazine, April(1987).

[2]"Fundamental Theory of Neurocomputing (in Japanese)," Kaibundou(1990).

[3]T. Kohonen, "The Self-Organizing Map," Proc. of IEEE, vol. 78, no. 9, pp.1464-1480, September(1990).

[4]MasPar Computer Corporation, "MasPar Parallel Application Language (MPL) reference Manual," Document Part No. 9302-0000, Revision A4, March(1991).

[5]S. Koike, "Hardware for Neurocomputing (in Japanese)," Trans. IEICE D-II, vol. J73-D-II, no. 8, pp. 1132-1145, August(1990).

NEURAL NETWORK HARDWARE IMPLEMENTATION FOR EMITTER IDENTIFICATION

D. Zahirniak, J. Calvin, S. Rogers
Wright Laboratory, Avionics Directorate, WPAFB, OH 45433
Air Force Institute of Technology, Wright-Patterson AFB, OH 45433

Abstract

This paper presents the results of a neural network hardware implementation for emitter identification. In future electronic warfare environments, pulse densities on the order of hundreds of thousands of pulses per second can be expected in any given mission. To identify hostile radar systems, a processor must be able to store enough signatures for emitters of interest that proper identifications of unknown emitters can be made. Furthermore, the processor must make this identification in "real-time". One method of performing this identification is to use neural networks. Neural networks are computing systems composed of simple processing elements called nodes; each node produces a single output from a combination of inputs from other nodes or the environment. Neural networks have been simulated performing complex pattern recognition tasks. However, these simulations were completed on serial computers, such as Sun Workstations, using high resolution, 16 to 32 bit, numbers. This paper presents the results obtained when the Electronically Trainable Neural Network (ETANN) hardware is used to perform emitter identification from time-sampled emitter waveforms. The ETANN is a low (4-6 bit) resolution, high speed(2 billion operations/sec) parallel processor implementing sigmoidal-based backpropagation networks. This hardware was chosen due to minimal interlayer processing times, 3us per layer, which can allow threat identifications to be made in a matter of microseconds. For this paper, a sigmoidal- based neural network was developed, via simulation on a DEC VAX station, to discriminate between 30 emitters. The network weights were loaded on the ETANN for performance comparisons. Due to resolution constraints, the accuracy of the ETANN was typically 10%-12% lower. However, the ETANN was able to make classifications in less than 6us. This significant processing speed, with only slight degradations in performance, makes neural network architectures viable alternatives for emitter identification.

1 INTRODUCTION

The primary mission of an electronic warfare threat identification system is to detect the presence of hostile emitters and identify the emitters as quickly and accurately as possible.[1] Since pulse densities on the order of hundreds of thousands of pulses per second will be expected in any given mission, future threat identification systems must be able to make their identifications in real-time. One method of accomplishing this goal is to use a pattern recognition processing scheme based on neural network technology. This paper begins by covering some of the background associated with pattern recognition techniques and neural network processing in general. The state of the art in neural network hardware is briefly covered, followed by a discussion of the experiments used to demonstrate the hardware. After presenting the results of the hardware classification accuracies, the paper concludes by discussing the applicability of this hardware to threat identification systems.

2 BACKGROUND

The process of classifying an unknown emitter as one of several known emitters is a standard concept of pattern recognition. That is, for most pattern recognition tasks, samples of the environment, such as samples of the emitter's waveform, are sent as a K-dimensional feature vector, $\bar{x} = [x_1, x_2, \ldots x_K]$ to a pattern recognition machine which classifies $\bar{x}$ as one of the M possible emitters. Such a pattern recognition machine makes an error whenever it identifies $\bar{x}$ as emitter J, E_J, when $\bar{x}$ is actually from emitter I, E_I [2]. One method of minimizing classification errors is to assign $\bar{x}$ to E_I if $P(E_I|\bar{x}) > P(E_J|\bar{x})$. Here, $P(E_I|\bar{x})$ is the a posteriori probability of emitter I given sample $\bar{x}$[3]. As is usually the case, $P(E_I|\bar{x})$ isn't known directly, but can be estimated from the probability distribution of $\bar{x}$ for each of the M possible emitters and, using Bayes' rule, calculated as

$$P(E_I|\bar{x}) = \frac{p(\bar{x}|E_I)\,P(E_I)}{p(\bar{x})} \qquad (1)$$

Here, $p(\bar{x}|E_I)$ is the state conditional probability density function of $\bar{x}$ and $P(E_I)$ is the a priori probability of emitter I. The decision rule now becomes to identify the samples as being from E_I if $p(\bar{x}|E_I)P(E_I) > p(\bar{x}|E_J)P(E_J)$. Thus, by estimating the conditional densities from a set of P known data samples, we can develop pattern recognition machines, for emitter classification, which makes minimum numbers of classifications errors from a given set of known samples.

One type of pattern recognition system receiving a great deal of interest is the artificial neural network (ANN). These networks are composed of simple computing elements called nodes. Each node in the network computes a single output, based upon a single transfer function, from a weighted combination of inputs from other nodes or from the environment. With a proper combination of weights and transfer functions, ANNs have been constructed to perform many types of pattern recognition tasks. One particular ANN investigated thoroughly is the backpropagation network. Each node in this type of network computes a sigmoidal output from a linear combination of its inputs, $\bar{x}$, weights, $\bar{w}$, and biases, $\boldsymbol{\theta}$ as shown in equation 2.

$$y_{out} = 1/(1+e^{-(\bar{w}\bar{x}+\theta)}) \qquad (2)$$

These networks perform as Bayes' Optimal Discriminants [5], implementing equation 1, by partitioning the feature space into decision regions with hyperplanes. Classification is then accomplished by determining which decision region the unknown waveform is located. These networks have been extensively analyzed through simulations on main frame computers using high resolution (16-32 bit) floating point values for the inputs, weights and outputs. Only recently, in the form of Intel's Electronically Trainable Analog

Neural Network, has VLSI circuitry been commercially produced implementing this ANN.

3 ETANN HARDWARE

The ETANN is Intel's analog neural network on a single chip. Each chip contains 64 neurons and 10240 modifiable synapses. This configuration allows each neuron to have 128 weights and 12 biases. As implemented by Intel[6] the 10240 weights and biases are stored as analog transconductance values. Each weight or bias produces an analog output from an analog input voltage and a stored "synaptic" voltage. As shown in figure 1, the currents generated from these input/synapse combinations are summed, converted to a voltage and passed through a sigmoid function which outputs the following [7]

$$y_{out}=\frac{1.83}{1+e^{-1.74(\overline{w}\cdot\overline{x}+\theta)}}-.94 \qquad (3)$$

This analog configuration allows each neuron in the ETANN to process the input data in parallel, bypassing the serial processing bottleneck inherent in single instruction, serial processing Von Neuman conventional computers. Through this parallel processing scheme, the ETANN is specified to operate at 3 us for each layer of neurons. Since all pattern recognition techniques can be accomplished with a two-layer network of this type [8], the ETANN could provide a classification in 6 us.[6] This increase in processing speed has been at the expense of the resolution capabilities of the inputs, outputs and weights of the network. According to Intel[6], typical resolution of the weights and inputs is 6-bits. Furthermore, the weights are limited to values of +/- 2.5 and the inputs to +/- 1. Finally, each chip is not yet "interchangeable", there is some slight variations in the operating characteristics between chips.

4 EXPERIMENTS

The procedure to determine the classification accuracy of the ETANN was to collect "real" data, simulate a neural network on a main frame, determine the classification accuracy of this simulation, download the network weights to the ETANN and determine the classification accuracy of the ETANN.

The data patterns used to train and test the neural network are from a set of time-sampled waveforms collected from 30 known emitters. Each training and test pattern was a 16-dimensional feature vector representing measurements of the emitters waveform at intervals along the pulsed waveform. Each feature of this data was then limited to values of +/-1 through a statistical normalization technique. Figure 2 shows typical composite waveforms from three emitters.

Several neural networks were constructed using the Neural-Graphics simulator, developed by the Air Force Institute of Technology, on a NEXT computer. The neural network topology chosen was the single hidden-layer network with 16 inputs, one for each waveform measurement, in the first layer, a variable number of nodes in the middle, or hidden layer, and 30 nodes, one node representing each emitter, in the last or output layer. Since previous research indicated the number of hidden nodes needed, with no constraints, ranged from 16 to 35 [7], the simulations consisted of networks with 16, 20, 25, 30 and 35 hidden-layer nodes and 30 output layer nodes. Each node in the network computed its output based on equation 3; each weight was constrained to remain between +/- 2.5. With one output node for each class, the classification rule was to choose the class as the highest output node.

Neural network architectures, with the same topologies of the simulations, were implemented using the ETANN hardware. The network weights, as determined by each simulation, were downloaded to the chip for analysis of the hardware. Again, the classification rule was to choose the class as the highest output node.

5 RESULTS

Table 1 shows the results, for various configurations, obtained from the neural network simulations and the networks implemented on the ETANN. From this table, it's evident the best average performance of the ETANN occurred with 35 nodes in the hidden layer. With this architecture, we then analyzed the performance of the ETANN after the networks were optimized via extensive training.

Table 2 shows the ETANN results for various simulator training times. The increase in accuracy of the ETANN from 75% to 83%, while the simulation increased only from 93% to 94%, was probably due to overcoming some of the loss in resolution of the weights from the simulation to the ETANN. Once this resolution loss had been overcome, the network performances "leveled-out" for both the simulation and the ETANN.

Finally, we evaluated the performance of five different ETANN chips configured with 35 nodes in the hidden layer and the weights obtained by 177 training iterations. These results are shown in Table 3. Though each ETANN chip was configured the same, and downloaded with the same set of weights, the accuracy of the ETANN network varied significantly from chip to chip. This effect is probably due to both the analog architecture and developmental nature of the chips. The analog architecture of the chips, in which currents and voltages are used to perform the calculations, are, in part, a function of the characteristics of individual chips. This makes the processing less predictable, from chip to chip, than equivalent digital architectures. The chip's developmental status indicates the initial manufacturing processes aren't yet be stable enough to allow production of identical chips.

6 CONCLUSIONS

These tests show the ETANN could be a promising implementation of the ANN architecture in hardware. The processing speed of 6us for pattern recognition tasks makes the ETANN ideal for real-time applications such as emitter identification. However, two drawbacks need to be overcome before the ETANN architecture could be implemented in military systems. First, the ETANN's classification accuracy is not yet able to match accuracies obtained through simulations. This is probably due to the loss in resolution of the inputs and weights associated with the ETANN chip and the chips analog nature in general. A method needs to be found to increase the classification accuracies without resorting to "on-chip" training. Finally, the ETANN chips are not yet interchangeable. This lack of consistency from chip to chip is probably due to the fact that "first-generation" chips were used in this experiment. Once these two problems are overcome, the ETANN could prove a viable method of identifying emitters in real-time.

7 REFERENCES

1. Filippo Neri, *Introduction to Electronic Defense Systems*. Norwood, MA: Artech House, Inc. 1991

2. Duda and Hart, *Pattern Classification and Scene Analysis*. New York: Wieley and Sons Inc, 1973.

3. J. T. Tou And R. C. Gonzalez, *Pattern Recognition Principles*, Reading MA: Addison-Wesley Publishing Co. 1974.

4. Wasserman, Philip D. *Neural Computing, Theory and Practice*. New York: Van Nostrand Reinhold, 1989.

5. Ruch, D and others. "The Multilayer Perceptron as an Approximation to a Bayes' Optimal Discriminant Function." *International Joint Conference on Neural Networks*, pages 863-873.

6. Intel Corporation. *80170NX Electronically Trainable Analog Neural Network*. Product Manual, Order Number: 290408-002, Intel Corporation, Santa Clara CA (June 91).

7. Calvin, James B. *ETANN Hardware Implementation for Radar Emitter Identification,* Masters Thesis, School of Engineering, Air Force Institute of Technology (AU), Wright-Patterson AFB OH, Dec 1992.

8. Cybenko, G. "Approximation of Superpositons of a Sigmoidal Function", *Mathematics of Control, Signals and Systems*, 2:303-314 (March 1989)

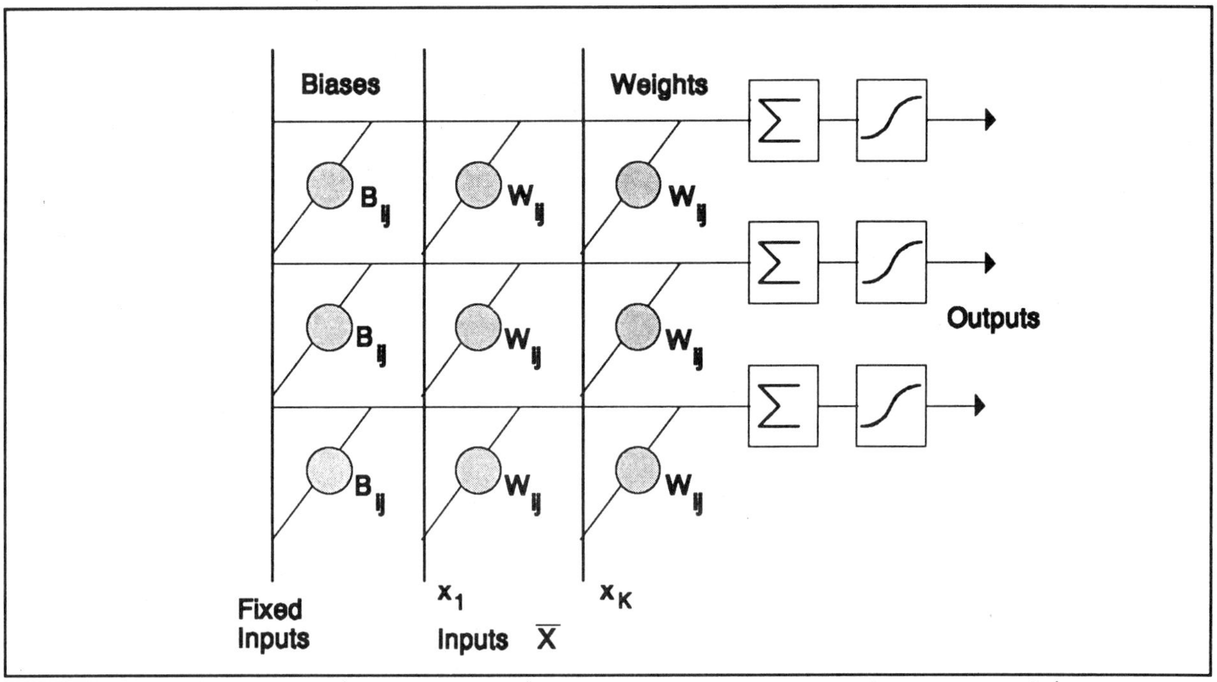

Figure 1: Electronically Trainable Analog Neural Net Architecture

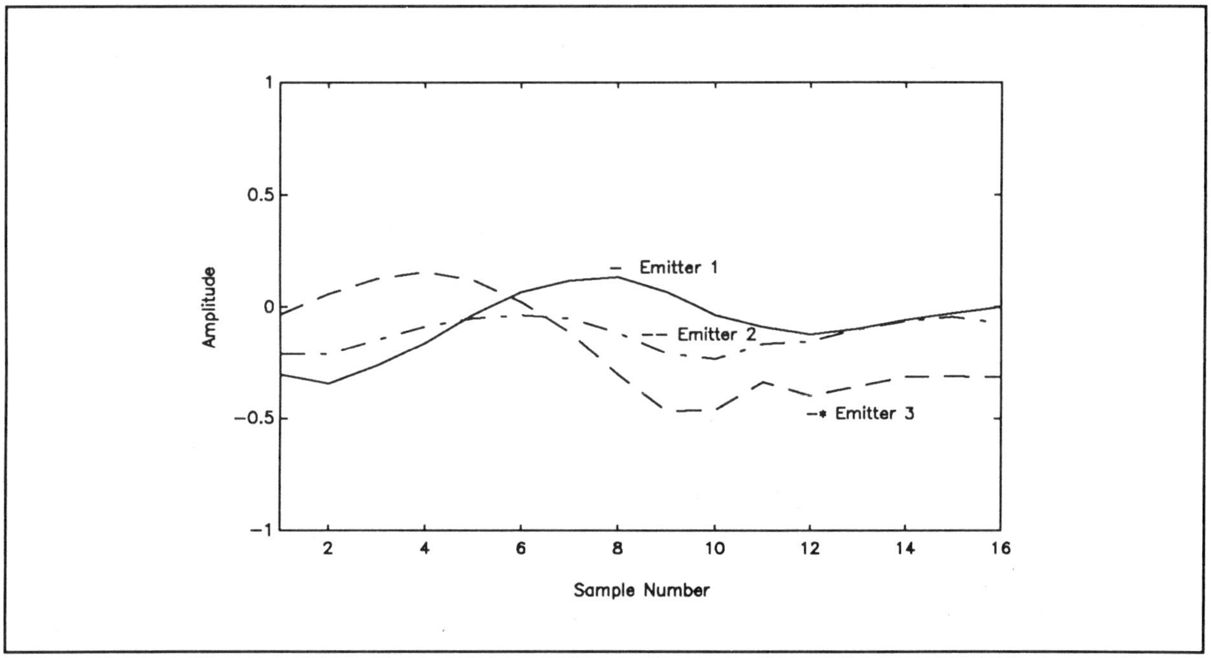

Figure 2: Composite Normalized Waveforms for Three Emitters

Iterations (x1000)	Network Size (in-hid-out)	Simulator Train/Test	ETANN Test Only
200	16-16-30	82%/81%	76%
200	16-20-30	86%/85%	81%
200	16-25-30	92%/90%	77%
200	16-30-30	91%/91%	72%
200	16-35-30	92%/92%	83%

Table 1: Simulation vs ETANN Results for Various Network Sizes

Number of Epochs	Network Size	Simulator Train/ Test	ETANN Test Only
44	16-35-30	95%/93%	75%
89	16-35-30	96%/94%	83%
133	16-35-30	96%/95%	81%
177	16-35-30	96%/95%	82%

Table 2: Simulation vs ETANN Results for "Optimal" Network Size

Chip #	Classification Performance	Average Accuracy
1	572/750	76.27%
2	644/750	85.87%
3	601/750	80.13%
4	622/750	82.93%
5	607/750	80.93%
Avg	609/750	81.22%
Std	28.46/750	3.78%

Table 3: ETANN Results for Five Different Chips, Same Weight Set

A Digital Signal Processor Based Accelerator for Artificial Neural Network Simulations in a Personal Computer Environment

A. Proctor, W.B. Hudson
EECE Department
Kansas State University
Manhattan, KS 66506
913-532-5600

Abstract

A method to accelerate artificial neural network calculations on personal computers for an educational environment is presented. The method utilizes the advanced architecture of Digital Signal Processors (DSP) in the Texas Instruments (TI) TMS320 family to conduct network simulations. Network performance is greatly enhanced due to the efficiency with which the DSPs accomplish the necessary computations relative to conventional processors. To further enhance performance a look-up table of precalculated transfer function values is used with the DSPs. The advantages of DSP with artificial neural network simulations are given. Also, a detailed description of the design is presented.

Introduction

Artificial neural network simulations can be enhanced using digital signal processors (DSP) to implement the network. The efficiency with which DSPs accomplish the many necessary calculations can provide greatly increased performance relative to conventional processors. Because the system is being developed for educational purposes, improved performance at a low cost is important. This system will provide students an exposure to neural networks and DSP devices.

A neural network is a highly parallel tool that when implemented in a serial computer, it becomes slow. It would not be uncommon for a graduate researcher to wait three or more hours for the results of a single neural network simulation. Long simulation times make research tedious. Also, for students learning about artificial neural networks in a classroom the time required for simulation is prohibitive and prevents real-world simulations. Because of these limitations, an accelerator board has been designed to greatly decrease simulation time and to be affordable to the academic community.

This paper first provides an overview of feed forward back-propagation neural networks. It then describes the advantages of using DSP products with artificial neural network simulation, specifically with the TI TMS320C25 processor. Next, a description of a simple, but flexible design for the accelerator board is given.

Feed Forward Back-Propagation Neural Networks

A "thinking machine," one that is capable of "learning" is the current objective of many scientists. Artificial intelligence or the "thinking machine " has been envisioned, attempted and evaluated by many, with substantial ranges of success [1]. Past research would imply that the artificial neural networks are capable of extracting rules for a wide variety of purposes. Simulated neural networks have been constructed that are capable of learning to talk [2], identifying kinship patterns [3], and correctly recognizing handwritten patterns [4].

The idea of computing machinery similar in structure to the human brain is reported to have begun in the 1940s. Interest and research continued on these brain like machines into the 1960s. Yet, why is a learning machine necessary? Frequently when algorithmic search becomes too complex or time consuming or when continuous output levels are desired, it may become beneficial to tap the richness of the structure of the human brain to provide alternate computational solutions to the problem [5].

A major consideration in the use of artificial neural networks as a computational tool has been the long training and response times required. The TMS320 family of devices can be used to reduce these training and response times. Using a single TMS320 device can provide performance gains over many conventional simulation platforms.

The use of artificial neural networks allow approximations and representations that contain implied abstractions. The classical system of thought views the simulation network as a system which operates on an energy landscape. The energy landscape or knowledge space in response to the input stimulus, generates an output which should be the minimum energy point of the system, corresponding to the present input and represents a desired system response [7].

The simulation of an artificial neural network on a conventional computer system requires the simulation of four major components: 1) interconnection pathways between processing units, 2) summation functions for combining all connecting inputs to a node, 3) transfer characteristic of each neuron, mapping inputs to outputs, and 4) a network connection scheme describing how nodes are interconnected.

The operation of the biological "thinking machine," the human brain is not fully understood. The simplified neural network model works based on the premise that knowledge exists in the interconnection strengths and transfer functions of the nodes. To prevent saturation or cutoff in node outputs, the transfer function of the simulation neuron is many times chosen to be sigmoidal, which again mimics the biological response. By using a sigmoidal response, the output of the neurons can be observed to asymptotically approach maximum and minimum extremes.

One of the common transfer functions used in artificial neural networks is defined by a nonlinear mapping that has an output that asymptotically approaches 0 and 1 and provides a continuous response. These characteristics are necessary for back-propagation learning to work successfully. It was previously stated that "knowledge" in an artificial neural network exists in the transfer functions and connection strengths. Having defined a transfer characteristic for the system it is now necessary to define appropriate connection strengths.

Neural Network Training Using Back-Propagation

The lack of understanding of the biological learning system requires artificial strategies to be developed for modification of the network connection weights to create the knowledge surface of the system. Presently, the delta rule or back-propagation is one of the most widely used methods of modifying connection weight values,

0-7803-1229-5/93/$3.00 © 1993 IEEE

allowing the network to learn. The back-propagation algorithm uses a gradient "steepest descent" algorithm to allow the network to converge to a self-organized knowledge representation [7], [8].

The standard back-propagation algorithm has been described by many authors. In the most general sense back-propagation requires creation of a non-uniform energy landscape, presentation of a training set input pattern, propagation of the pattern through the network to obtain an output pattern, computation of the error at the output layer, calculation of the local error at each hidden layer node, and adjustment of the weight values to minimize the error [9], [10], [11]. The back-propagation algorithm involves the following steps:

1. Present the input pattern to the network and propagate the signal through the network to the output.

2. For each processing element (node) in the output layer calculate output error and calculate the change in weights.

3. Calculate local error of hidden nodes and then calculate the delta weights.

4. Update all connecting weights.

5. Repeat process until adequate level of learning has occurred [12].

As these operations are examined it is found that back-propagation requires the floating point operations of addition, subtraction, multiplication, division and logarithmic transformation.

Advantages of DSP

There are many advantages of DSPs relative to conventional processors for neural network simulation. A digital signal processor is a specialized microcomputer that was designed for real-time number crunching applications. These applications include digital audio, image processing, speech recognition and many others. Therefore, the processor was optimized to perform algorithms such as FFTs or FIR/IIR filtering efficiently. These algorithms called for extremely fast execution of multiplication, addition, and shifting. Due to this, the operations were integrated in hardware on the chip. Also, DSPs were designed with the ability to perform several non-conflicting operations in parallel. These designs were made to perform limited numbers of operations very quickly instead of performing many operations more slowly.

The operations that are performed by a digital signal processor are compatible with the calculations required to implement artificial neural networks. An artificial neural network can be implemented in several manners, but most algorithms include some sort of thresholding, weighting, and non-linear transformation process. For a conventional back-propagation algorithm the input is propagated through a transfer function such as $1/1+e^{-x}$. This function may take several hundred clock cycles to complete in a conventional processor. Using a DSP there are several methods to increase the efficiency of this calculation. First, the calculation can be carried out with 'brute force' with the fast multiplies and additions. The second method is to use a Laurent Series Approximation of the function which also utilizes the fast multiplies and additions [13]. Because of the flexibility of the DSP, the last method is to use the large memory space as a look-up table of precalculated values for the transfer function. This is possible because the transfer function only gives unique answers for a small range of input values.

Another feature of a neural network is its high interconnectivity. A typical neural network may have three layers with several input, hidden, and output nodes all connected. With each connection an appropriate weight is associated. This information must be stored for future retrieval because the neural network continues to update the weight associations depending on the overall results of the threshold functions. To accomplish this, the large memory space can again be used. The TMS320C25 has three separate and distinct memory locations for program memory, data memory, and I/O memory space. For example, the Texas Instruments TMS320C25 has 64k word external memory space for each of these three blocks along with ample on-chip memory space for program and data memory. Each of these blocks can be accessed by separate bus signals thereby improving transfer speed and creating a high memory bandwidth. Also, the continued update of connection weights is again enhanced by the fast multiples and additions in the hardware of the DSP.

A fourth feature of neural networks that is compatible with DSPs is its massive parallelism. One of the ideas about artificial neural networks that has provided an interest in its development is that they simulate brain activity. While current implementations are a long way from obtaining that goal, their development has been influenced by research about the brain. One conclusion that most people agree with is that the brain is a massively parallel computing device. Therefore, to be an effective tool for problem solving, the artificial neural network could be implemented in a parallel fashion. This can be accomplished to an extent with a DSP. The DSP allows multiprocessor support and also has parallel execution units to process several non-conflicting operations at the same time. The idea of using multiprocessors can be extended so that each processor is a single node of the network with a main processor controlling the operation. This feature could greatly enhance artificial neural network simulation.

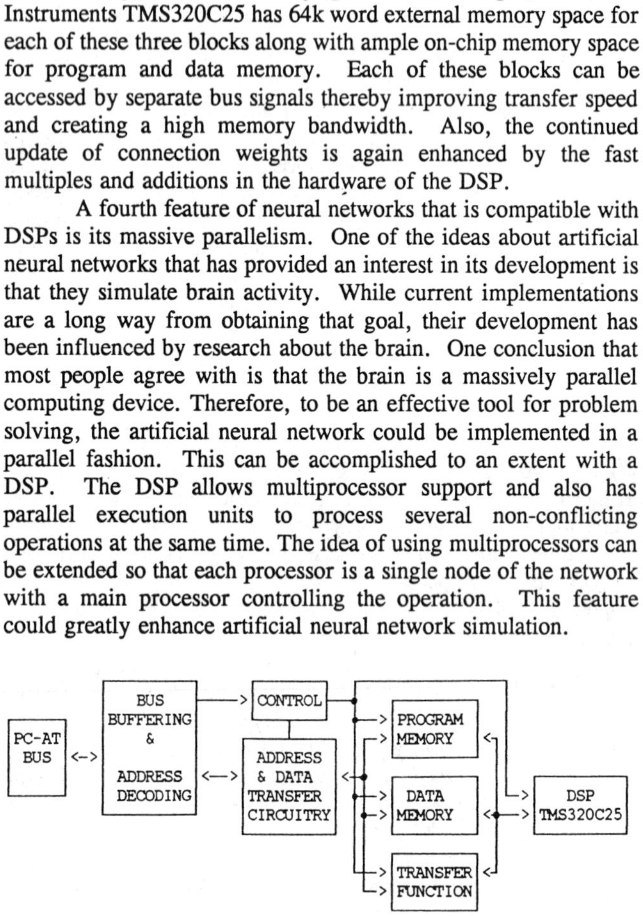

Fig. 1 - Block Diagram of the Accelerator Board Design

Design

To utilize the features of digital signal processors for artificial neural network simulation, a prototype system was created. This system was designed for a personal computer platform using an IBM-AT interface for use in student laboratories and/or home use. The design begins with a simple interface to the host CPU and continues with programming the DSP to optimumally execute the neural network computations. To begin the design, a block diagram of the system components was made (see Fig. 1). This consisted of an interface block, a control block, and a processor/memory block. The interface block was created so information could be sent in both directions without timing restraints. For example, to download the program into memory an address is decoded to select the transfer circuit, then when the appropriate control bit is set the data is latched to memory. This process must be reversed to send data back to the host CPU in a manner that avoids bus conflicts. Therefore, a signal that is controlled by the DSP, allows the data to be latched back into the appropriate transfer circuit. Then when the CPU is ready, it sends a decoded address to this circuit to grab the data. This method allows the host CPU to continue executing without concern of when the data is ready to come back. The transfer is accomplished with 16-bit values and for each transfer an address must be decoded and a control bit set. This means that the process will take some time to completely move a block of data to the DSP. However, the process is a one-time start-up procedure, so the speed of the transfer is not a major concern.

To complete the transfer, the appropriate memory space for the data must be selected. The external memory was divided into three separate and independent sections for program, data, and I/O memory spaces. All of these spaces were 64k memory blocks, and to achieve this, 32k x 8 static RAMs were used. Typically, small, fast memories are used with DSPs for a fast transfer and the static RAMs were chosen to eliminate the need of refresh circuitry. To select the three memory banks, three separate signals are used by the DSP to choose between them. This is necessary because each of the 64k blocks are mapped to the same location in memory. To avoid the timing constraints of transferring between the three blocks every time a different block is needed, the on-chip memory is utilized for the program and some of the data. The external data memory block is used to contain the interconnection weights and possibly some intermediate hidden node values. While the I/O memory space is used for the look-up table of the transfer function. This method allows the look-up table to be accessed by way of 'IN' and 'OUT' instructions.

The look-up table will contain real-valued numbers between 0 and 1 and has a limited range of input values because of the transfer function. Also, due to the transfer function a fixed-point representation is adequate for the data. This is because the relative magnitude of all the numbers will be close to each other so that the precision errors introduced by fixed-point arithmetic will not be a factor. However, overflow must be controlled, therefore a numerical representation for the data was used with the TMS320C25 that had a sign bit, i integer bits, and 15-i fractional bits. For the design, a Q8 format (8 fractional bits) was used [14]. This format has a range of values between -128 <-> 127.996 with a fractional accuracy of .004. These limitations are adequate for neural network calculations. Most weight values will not be larger than 128 and an error of .004 introduced by the transfer function should not effect network convergence. The design presented provides a great deal offlexibility. For example, if it is decided thata different transfer function should be used, it can just be changed in memory. Also, ifthe accuracy of the Q8 format is not enough, theformat can be changed in the program and evena floating-point routine could be implemented. Another change that could be made isthe program itself. Any number a paradigms could be used for the program, including back- propagation, Kohonen, Adaptive Resonance, etc. Afourth variation that is allowed, is the accommodation of many different network configurations with varying number of nodes. Thisagain can be accomplished by changing the contents of memory. Therefore, this design provides a simple yet flexible system for use inmany different artificial neural network simulations.

Future Developments

Although, the current design will provide an enormous speed improvement over conventional processors, there are still items that could be added to further enhance performance. One of these items would be to run several of these boards in parallel to emulate the nodes themselves. This would reduce the number of calculations per processor and improve the overall performance.

Conclusions

Due to the need to provide fast artificial neural network simulations in a student environment, an accelerator board was designed for a personal computer. This accelerator uses the many features of the TI TMS320C25 to enhance performance for artificial neural network calculations. The performance was further enhanced by the use of a look-up table of precalculated transfer function values. Using these techniques, the time for a artificial neural network calculation to be processed has been reduced. In a conventional floating-point processor such as the 80287- 16Mhz, these calculations may take over 500 clock cycles [15]. However, this system will reduce the number of clock cycles per calculation to approximately ten for the 40Mhz processor. Therefore, this design has allowed for a fast, simple, and flexible procedure to accelerate the simulations.

References

[1] W.P. Jones and J. Hoskins, Back- Propagation A Generalized Delta Learning Rule, Byte, Vol. 12, No. 11, pp. 155, Oct. 1987.

[2] T.J. Sejnowski and C.R. Rosenberg, Parallel Networks that Learn to Pronounce English Text, Complex Systems, Vol. 1, pp. 145-168, 1987.

[3] G.E. Hinton and T.J. Sejnowski, Edited by D.E. Rumelhart, J.L . McClelland and the PDP Research Group. Learning and Relearning in Boltzman Machines, Parallel Distributed Processing Explorations in the Microstructure of Cognition, Vol. 1 Foundations, the MIT Press, pp. 328-330, 1988.

[4] K. Fukushima, S. Miyake and T. Ito, Neocognitron: A Neural Network Model for a Mechanism of Visual Pattern Recognition, IEEE Trans. on Systems, Man and Cybernetics, Vol. 13, No. 5, pp. 826-834, Sept/Oct 1983.

[5] G. Josin, Neural-Network Heuristics Three heuristic algorithms that learn from experience, Byte, Vol. 12, No. 11, pp. 183, Oct. 1987.

[6] N.H. Farhat, Optoelectronic Neural Networks and Learning Machines, IEEE Circuits and Devices Magazine, Vol. 5, No. 5, pp. 32-41, Sept. 1989.

[7] H.C. Anderson, Neural Network Machines, IEEE Potentials, Vol. 8, No. 1, pp. 14, Feb. 1989.

[8] W.P. Jones and J. Hoskins, Back- Propagation a Generalized Delta Learning Rule, Byte, Vol. 12, No. 11, pp. 155, Oct. 1987.

[9] D.E. Rumelhart, G.E. Hinton and R.J. Williams, Edited by D.E. Rumelhart, J.L. McClelland and the PDP Research Group. Learning and Relearning in Boltzman Machines, Parallel Distributed Processing Explorations in the Microstructure of Cognition, Vol. 1 Foundations, The MIT Press, pp. 328-330, 19 88.

[10] R.P. Lippmann, An Introduction to Computing With Neural Networks, IEEE Acoustics, Speech, and Signal Proc., Vol. 3, No. 4, pp. 17, April 1987.

[11] J.P. Guiver and C.C. Klimasauskas, NeuralWorks Networks II, Neural Ware Inc., 103 Buckskin Court, Pittsburgh, PA., 15143, pp. 440-446, 1988 .

[12] J.P. Guiver and C.C. Klimasauskas, NeuralWorks Networks II, Neural Ware Inc., 103 Buckskin Court, Pittsburgh, PA., 15143, pp. 438-447, 1988 .

[13] E.B. Saff and A.D. Snider, Fundamentals of Complex Analysis, Prentice-Hall Inc., Englewood Cliffs, New Jersey, pp.203- 209, 1976.

[14] Third-Generation TMS320 User's Guide, Digital Signal Processor Products, Texas Instruments, pp. 1-3 and 3-5, 1988.

[15] Microsystem Components Handbook, Microprocessors, Volume 1, Intel, pp. 4-79, 1986.

[16] TMS32010 User's Guide, Digital Signal Processor Products, Texas Instruments, pp. 5-2, 1985.

[17] Digital Signal Processing Applications with the TMS320 Family, Theory, Algorithms, and Implementations, Texas Instruments, pp. 371-373, 1986.

A New Digital Neural Network And Its Application

J. O. Tuazon , K. Hamidian and L. Guyette
Electrical Engineering Department
California State University, Fullerton,
Fullerton, California 92634

Abstract

A new digital model of the neuron, called K/N gate, is presented. The K/N neural networks have important potential application in such areas as pattern recognition and image processing.The proposed model is applied to pattern recognition, like the decimal digits in presence of random noise, and comparison is made with its analog counter part perception model.The results show that the K/N net performs better than the perceptron net.The advantages of the proposed model over the analog model are reported as follows: 1) No time consuming training is needed. 2) The desired pattern can be easily distinguished from possible noise inputs given the fact that the distance between the two has been predetermined and included in the design. 3) The implementation can be achieved with memory and register architecture.

I. INTRODUCTION

In the past several decades our nervous system has been studied, analyzed and modeled in the hope of achieving human-like intelligence. It is a complex network of about 10^{11} neurons with 10^{16} inter-connections. Neurons are nonlinear, analog systems responding to chemical and biological stimuli.

There are various types of neural network models. These models can be broken down into classifications of binary input or continuous input. A further classification is accomplished by designating the way a neural network "learns". For supervised learning, the system may use external feedback or desired response signal to shape its behavior. In an unsupervised learning scenario, the net itself may generate these desired response signals [2]. Although this paper concerns two specific neural net models, there are five basic neural network models that should be mentioned: Hopfield net (binary input, supervised learning), Hamming net (binary input, supervised), Carpenter / Grossberg Classifier (binary input, unsupervised), Multi-level perceptron (continuous input, supervised) and Kohonen self organizing feature maps (continuous input unsupervised), [6],[7],[10],[11] .

Because of the analog nature of neurons, they are modeled with analog operational amplifiers set up as an integrator as well as a summer. The operation amplifier is forced into saturation to mimic the firing of the neuron. Variable input resistors are placed in series for every input of the summer, to control the contribution of each input. Recently, Mead[3] applied analog VLSI techniques to achieve massive parallelism.

The main difficulties in the analog VLSI is the implementation and setting of the variable input resistance, normally called weights. Also, operational amplifier requires precise component values and analog signals are more susceptible to noise.

In this paper, we present a novel digital model of the neuron, K/N gate, which possesses the key features of neural network and has important potential application in such areas as pattern recognition and image processing. The proposed model is applied to pattern recognition and its advantages over the analog counter part, perceptron, are presented in section V. Digital VLSI implementation of the model is suggested, since this is a more mature process where 10^6 transistors could be produced in a single chip and digital circuits are insensitive to component accuracy and noise.

II. ARTIFICIAL NEURAL NETWORKS AND PERCEPTRONS

A commonly used model for the neuron is the threshold gate. A threshold gate consists of n-inputs (x_i), n-variable weights (w_i), and a threshold level T, as shown in Figure 1. The input stimuli x_i represent the neural impulse from the ith neuron. The output (z) is defined as:

$$z = 1 \ \text{if} \ \sum x_i w_i > T \qquad (1)$$

$$z = -1 \ \text{if} \ \sum x_i w_i < T \qquad (2)$$

While the inputs and output are discrete values of +1 or -1, the weights are real numbers, and can have negative value. A positive value indicates a supplementary contribution to the firing (+1 output) of the neuron while a negative value indicates inhibitory

Extensive research have been conducted in modeling the human nervous system. These artificial neural networks consist of massively connected simple computing element (threshold gates), "trained" to recognize image patterns and speeches. "Training" consists of setting the connection weights of the threshold device. Algorithms serve in varying the weights to improve the performance of the network.

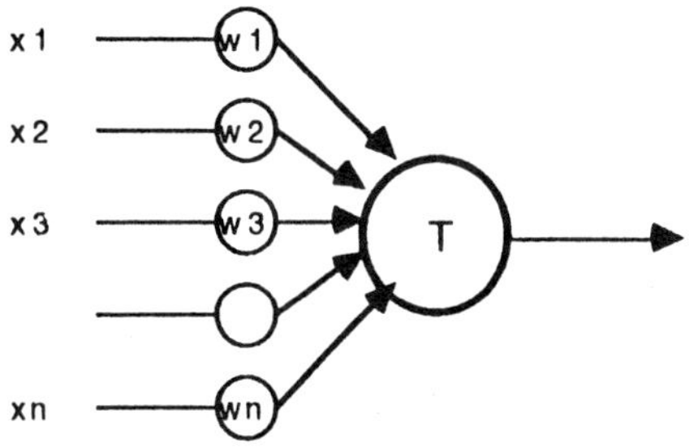

Figure 1

A preceptron is an n-input threshold device "trained" to recognize a set of input pattern belonging to a class. Figure 2 shows the training set up and the corresponding algorithm. Training is accomplished by providing the test input patterns to the device and the weights are adjusted to get the correct response. The weight adjustment procedure is basically an approximate method to find a hyperplane equation in an n-dimensional space which separates the class of patterns [10]. This equation is given by :

$$\sum x_i w_i = 0 \qquad (3)$$

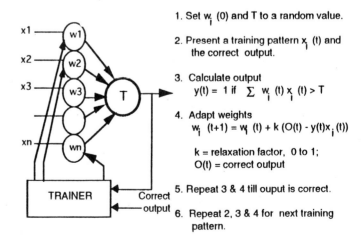

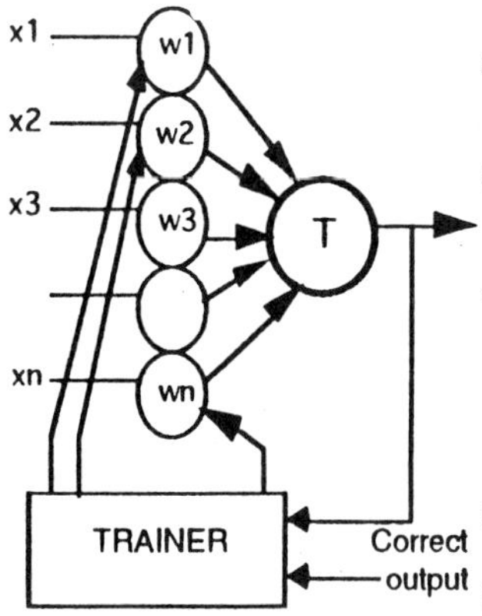

1. Set w_i (0) and T to a random value.
2. Present a training pattern x_i (t) and the correct output.
3. Calculate output
   $y(t) = 1$ if $\sum w_i(t) x_i(t) > T$
4. Adapt weights
   $w_i(t+1) = w_i(t) + k\,(O(t) - y(t)x_i(t))$
   k = relaxation factor, 0 to 1;
   O(t) = correct output
5. Repeat 3 & 4 till ouput is correct.
6. Repeat 2, 3 & 4 for next training pattern.

Figure 2

An actual pictorial representation of this hyperplane is difficult to illustrate. Figure 3 shows a simplified illustration of a Boolean space with the x's as the input patterns. The x's can be visualized as peaks of a mountain that is cut by a hyperplan such that all x's are above the cutting plane.

0-7803-1443-3/93 $3.00

A single perceptron can recognize only patterns that are contiguous in the hyperspace. For example, patterns positioned as in Figure 3B cannot be recognized by a single perceptron, because there is a valley in between the clustered region. For such cases, we need more perceptrons in parallel, each recognizing a contiguous area. For more sophisticated classifications, multiple layers of perceptrons may be connected, and the Back Propagation algorithm could be used to calculate the weights [10], [12].

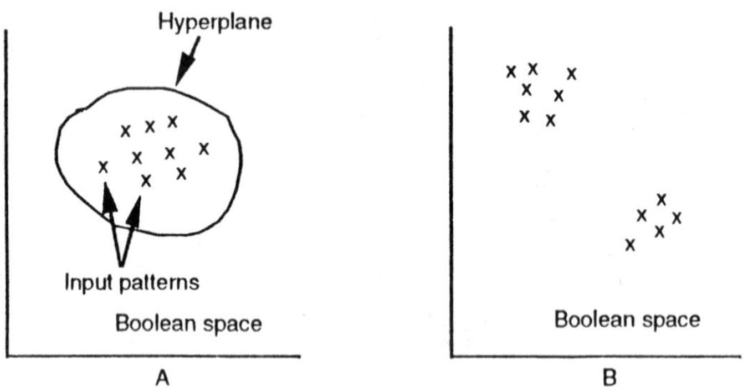

Figure 3

There are actually several topologies that have been used within the framework of the perceptron [1]. The perceptron is not only a stand- alone neural network, but it can also be used as a basic building for other complex networks.

III. K/ N GATES

The major problem of using the perceptrons or the threshold gate in the implementation of neural nets is the tedious way of determining the weights of each node. For a single threshold, the weights could be determined mathematically by solving the inequality equations (1) and (2). However, this method is impractical for a large number of inputs, and impossible to use on neural nets.

Another disadvantage of perceptrons is that its functionality cannot be quickly determined, making it difficult to analyze and design a network of perceptrons. It is imperative that in order to construct and analyze more complex neural nets, their functions must be obvious like the logic gates used in digital circuits. Hence we are proposing a gate that may be as flexible as a perceptron but can be implemented immediately. This gate will be called as K of N (K/N) gate.

The weights of K/N network are modelled as -1, 0 and +1 . The zero weight is assigned to those inputs that do not affect the outcome. N is the total number of inputs with +1 and -1 weights assigned to represent the pattern . K is the minimum number of matches from N comparisons between the input and the pattern. N - K is the Hamming distance between the unknown input and the known pattern. Figure 4 shows the implementation of basic K/N gates Although, it may take several of these gates to function like a single preceptron, it will be easier to design a network of these gates than implementing it through the use of perceptrons.

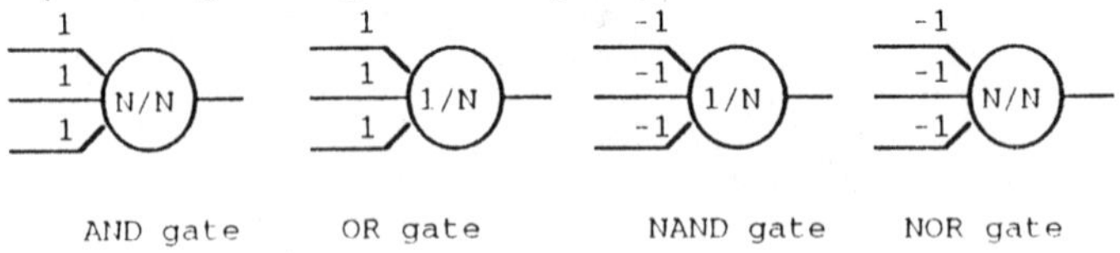

Figure 4

The K/N gates could be used in digital logic . Consider the four variable K-map shown in Figure 5. A four variable function is chosen to simplify and easily map the functions, which will be generalized to n-variables in the following discussion. Observe also that the k-maps use + and - to imply +1 and -1 logic instead of the 1 and 0 logic level. Recall that a 0-weight is used to mask out the input.

The 3/4 gate in Figure 5a will recognize the minterm (pattern) whose x1, x2, x3 and x4 inputs are -1, +1, -1, and +1 respectively, and all other 4 minterms which differ only by one bit position from the above minterm. The 3/4 gate shows how to use the 0-weight on x4 to disregard this input and implement a 3-input AND gate. These two groups of patterns can be combined through 1/2 gate used as OR gate.

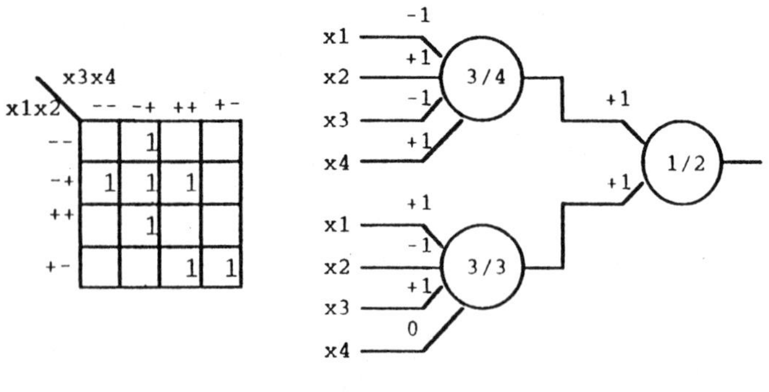

a. Logical OR of two K/N gates

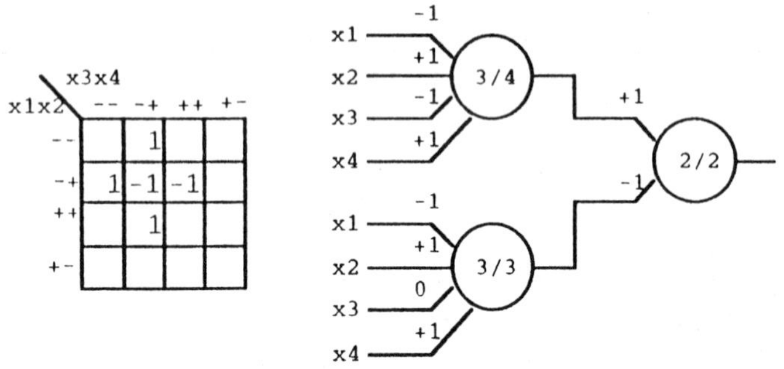

b. Exclusion function of K/N gate

Figure 5

Figure 5b shows a more interesting property of the K/N gate. We can easily exclude a set of points that are initially included in the first K/N gate. The first 3/4 gate includes all five minterms marked as +1 as well as -1. If we want to exclude the two -1s, then we need to cover them with the 3/3 gate and exclude them with the 2/2 gate and weigh of -1. These two properties of the K/N gate will be used in classifying application of neural nets.

VI. K/N NEURAL NETWORK FOR PATTERN RECOGNITION

In the world of neural nets, the number of inputs are exceedingly large and it will be impossible to draw a map as in Figure 5. We know certain items or patterns belong to a class but not all the patterns belonging to that class. Therefore, we 'train' a neural nets to recognized the known patterns and hope that it also cover all the unknown patterns belonging to that class.

Let us pause here to differentiate the classical approach and our technique in this application. In the classical technique, we use a multi-layer of threshold gates and 'train' the network to recognize the patterns. The known patterns are applied and the weights are adjusted according to the Back Propagation method, until the network respond correctly to these patterns [13]. At the end of this process, we apply unknown patterns and the network will classify these inputs. We expect that inputs in the neighborhood of the input patterns will be classified as belonging to the class, however we don't have a general idea of the pattern coverage of the network.

In the K/N gate approach, we design the network instead of training it to recognize all the known patterns. We, however, know the pattern coverage by the network and in fact it could be designed to cover only the known patterns or include patterns in the neighborhood of the known patterns. The shape and size of the neighborhood can be designed accordingly using the inclusion and exclusion functions of the gate. Figure 6 shows how to design such coverage, noting that the K/N gate always covers a circular area in an n-dimensional Boolean space. Figure 6a shows how to cover patterns that are not in one neighborhood, where each circular coverage corresponds to a K/N gate. The output of these gates will go to a final gate implemented as an OR gate. Figure 6b shows the exclusion function discussed in the previous section, where one big K/N gate covers all the necessary patterns. However in doing so we also covered a large area that does not belong to the class. This area can be excluded by several small K/N gates.

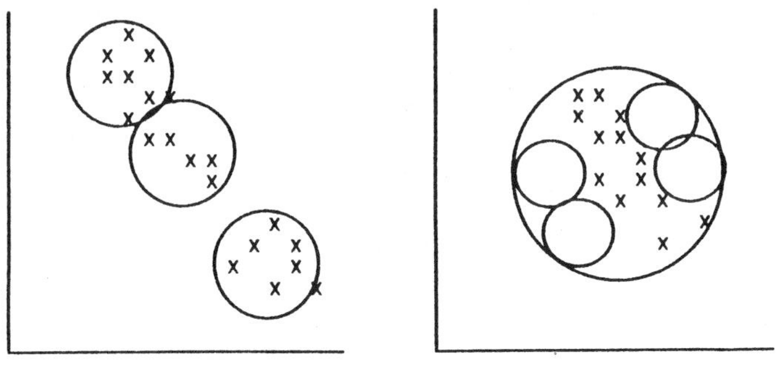

a. Inclusion function b. Exclusion function

Figure 6

For pattern classification, where we have numerous samples that are known to be within a class and another set of samples which are not in that class, a multi-layer neural network may be used. Figure 7 shows a multi-layer K/N neural net for pattern classification. The corresponding algorithm is as follows:

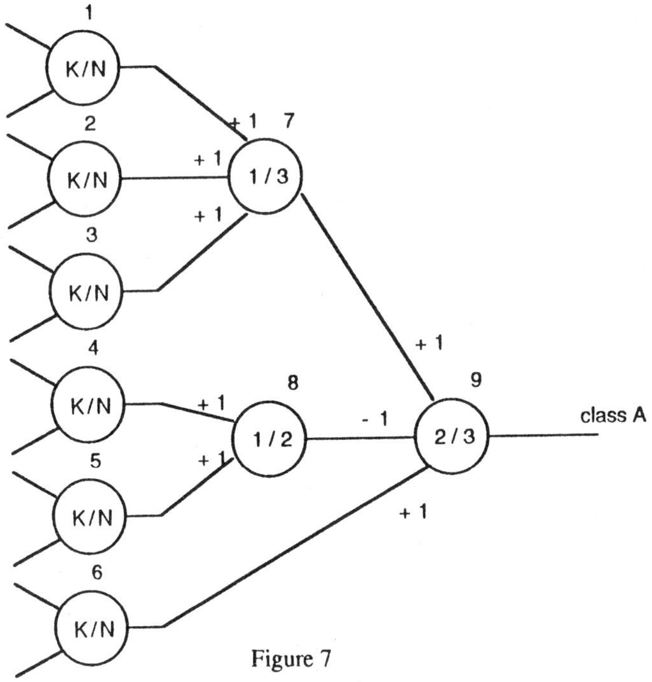

Figure 7

Step 1. Consider all the known patterns belonging to the class and design a network to cover all these inputs. The network may be a single K/N gate if all inputs are clustered together or several gates if inputs are spread out. In Figure 7, we use three gates (gate number 1, 2 and 3) to cover these inputs and gate number 7 is to collect them together. If we are certain that these are the only inputs belonging to the class, then we can design a very tight coverage; on the other hand we can implement a loose coverage when there is uncertainty over the inputs.

Step 2. Initialize the weights of the output gate 9 to be +1 from covering gate 7 and zeros from other gates. Now apply the known input patterns that does not belong to the class and record all cases where the output is +1. These patterns must be excluded from the initial coverage.

Step 3. Depending upon the number of patterns to be excluded, we can redo step 1 or design an exclusion network. If the number of excluded patterns is small, design a tight exclusion network. Gates 4, 5 and 8 in Figure 7 is the exclusion network.

Step 4. Assign a -1 to the input of the output gate 9 from the excluding network gate 8, and set the threshold to 2/2. At this point we have designed a network not to recognize all patterns belonging to the other classes, however, it is possible that we may have excluded patterns that belong to the group. Hence, we re-apply all pattern belonging to the group and check it if some were excluded. If there were none then the design is completed otherwise continue to step 5.

Step 5. Consider all the excluded patterns and design an exact coverage of them. This is accomplished by gate 6 in Figure 7. Finally, change the 3rd input weight to the output gate 9 to +1 and the threshold to 2/3.

V. IMPLEMENTATION OF K/N NEURAL NETS USING MEMORY CHIPS

The proposed digital threshold device is a K/N gate which will recognize a pattern that will match all N inputs and all other patterns that will mismatch no more than k inputs. Figure 8 shows the proposed digital circuit.

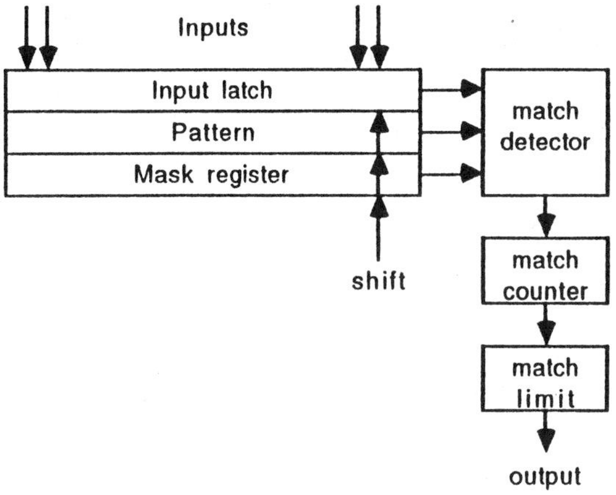

Figure 8

In this circuit, we latched the inputs and the pattern to be recognized. The mask register will mask out bit positions that are not relevant. We shift these three registers and compare the unmasked bits of the input and the pattern. The match counter will only increment if the bits are matched . The match limit detector is programmable such that if the match count is greater than the preset, (K), value, the output will be true.

The advantages of this circuit over the analog counter part are: (1) no time-consuming training is needed, (2) the Hamming distances of the noisy inputs from the desired pattern is predetermined, (3) the implementation can be achieved through register architecture and finally (4) neural nets implemented in analog can be converted to this digital circuit.

Figure 9 is the suggested implementation of 256 neurons each with 128-input K/N gates. In this circuit, we both do serial as well as parallel operations in determining the number of matches. The degree of parallelism can be increased by duplicating the circuit.The EPROM memories are used to store the patterns, masks and match count of every K/N gate to minimize chip counts and shift registers to latch the outputs and inputs.

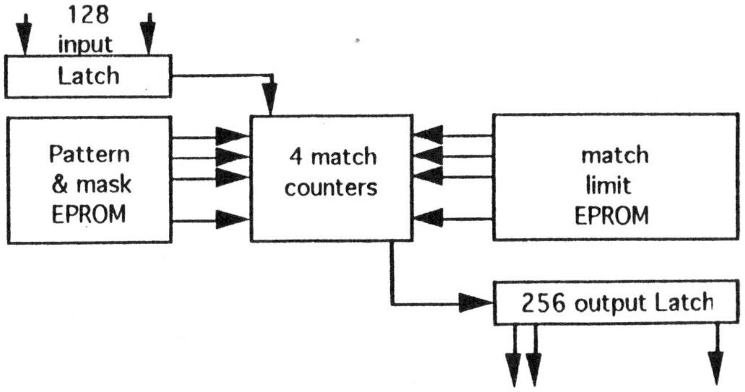

Figure 9

Initially the inputs are latch at the input register. The EPROM contains the known patterns and mask vectors which are serially stored by word, i.e. the first set of bits are stored in word 0 and the 128th set of bits are in word address 127. If the EPROM is 8-bit wide, we can process 4 gates in parallel . after 128 comparison the first 4 limit count in the other EPROM will be compared with the 4 match counters and set the value to the output latch. In this example, we need an 8k EPROM to store all the 256 patterns and mask vectors.

Depending upon the mask vector bit, an exclusive-or operation between the input bit and the pattern bit for the 4 gates is performed. The input is then recirculated and the next bits are considered. After 128 shifts and read the counter contains the number of matches which are to be compared with match limits in the second EPROM and the correct output is latched accordingly. Since the match limit count can not be greater than 128, the second EPROM is only 256 x 8.

If we want to speed up the process, we can increase the width of the first EPROM to 16 or 32 and the number of comparators will also be doubled or quadrupled. A sequencer (not shown) is assumed to control the processing.

To form a network, we can cascade these 256 neurons into multiple layers. Modification can be made to be able to cascade within the 256 neuron set and vary the number of outputs neurons. Since memories and shift register can be easily implement in VLSI, the VLSI implementation of this circuit will be straight forward.

VI. EXAMPLE OF APPLICATION OF K/N NEURAL NETS TO PATTERN RECOGNITION

Now that the algorithm for both the perception network and the K/N network have been explored, lets get on with the application. The task is to create a 7 by 9 template for each of a possible 10 digits, 0 through 9. Then model two selected neural networks, a single layer perception network and a K/N network, to recognize the exemplar patterns. In our experiment, we trained ten analog neurons using the algorithm given in the preceding section with the final weights stored in a file. In the K/N network, we provide an exemplar pattern to each neuron and determine the optimum K. To find the value of K of the nth neuron, the nth exemplar pattern with noise is applied to the network and recorded the number of matches on each gate. As the noise is increased, the number of matches in the nth gate decreases while the other gates match count increases. We increase the noise level up to a point where the matches by the nth neuron is barely greater than the rest, and took this number of matches as the K value.

Once the weights and the K values are determined, the remainder of the task is to subject both network with the same noisy patterns and collect data. There are large amounts of data that can be generated from such a task. The decision was made to concentrate on data that has been induced with noise. More specifically, as noise is increased at what point is the perception network and K/N network functional and at what point do either of the networks break down. Noise has been established as:

% noise = (number of incorrect bits)/(number of possible bits)
or
% noise = (toggled exemplar bits)/(63)

The results are established on a pattern basis,and sample of example are shown in Figures 10 through 12.These results are gathered while keeping in mind that various assumptions have been made. One of the assumptions is that if a network is functional at a certain noise level, it is also functional at a lower noise levels. A similar assumption made is that if a failure occurs at a given noise level, the network will fail at larger induced noise levels.

When comparing the perception approach to that of the K/N method, the results could be studied on a pattern basis, which is summarized in Figure 13, or examined as overall data. This may include research into the types of failures for a given neural network. The perception net rarely failed by solely classifying a class B pattern a class A. However, the remainder of the failures are equally split between finding no comparable exemplar pattern or by designating too many exemplar patterns (Figure 11). By better understanding the failure, possible methods for network improvements can be found. Overall, the K/N algorithm performed strongly, while the perception net was merely satisfactory. In fact, the perception network is preferred in only 10% of the cases, whereas the K/N network operated better than the perception network in 70% of the cases (Figure 14).

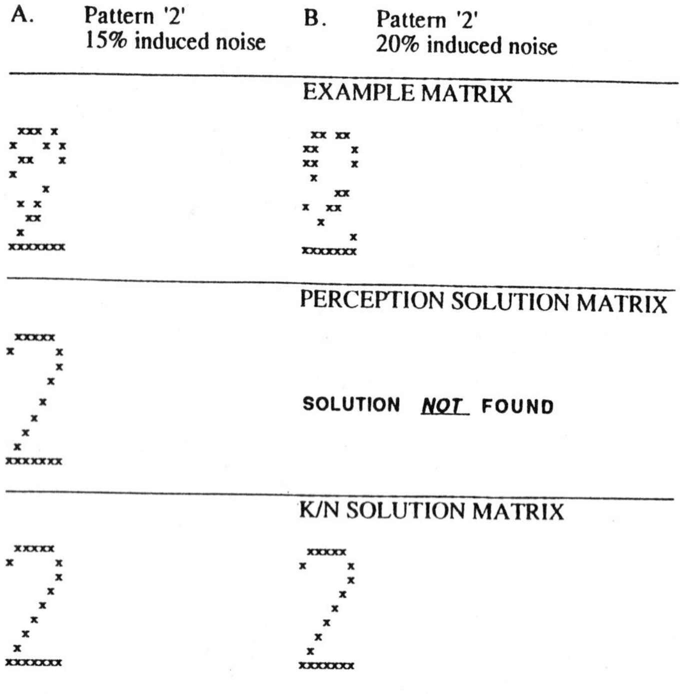

Figure 10

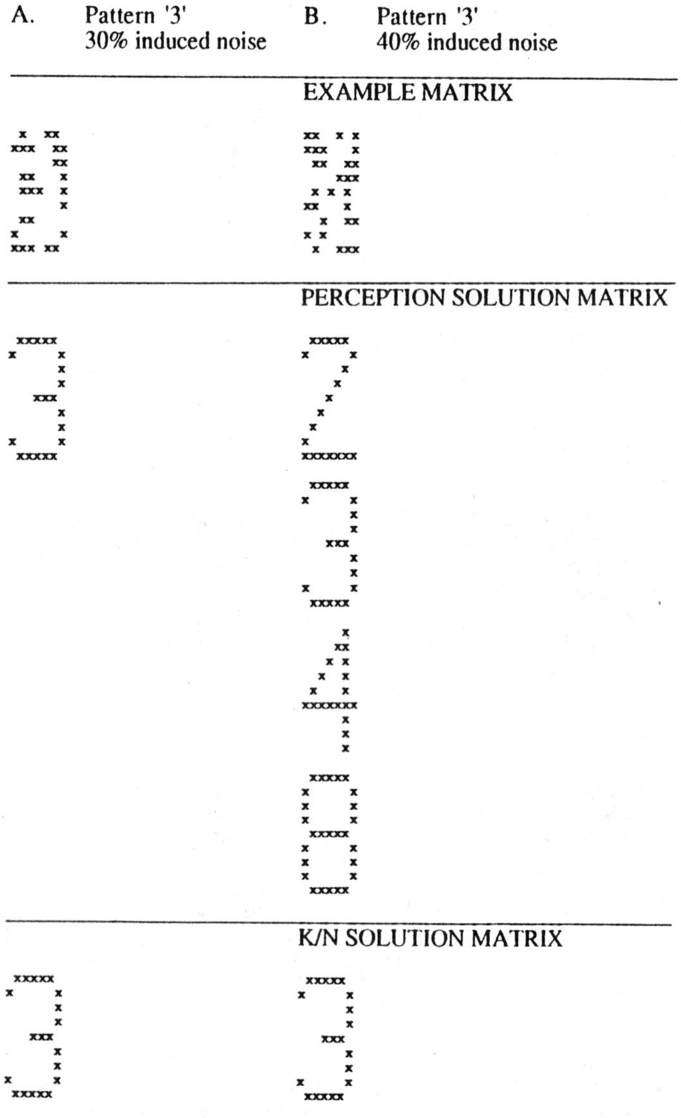

Figure 11

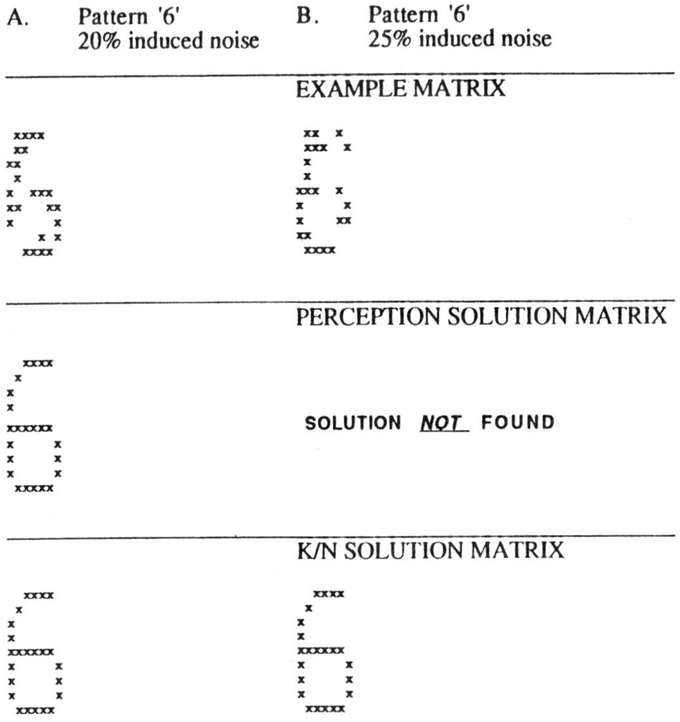

Figure 12

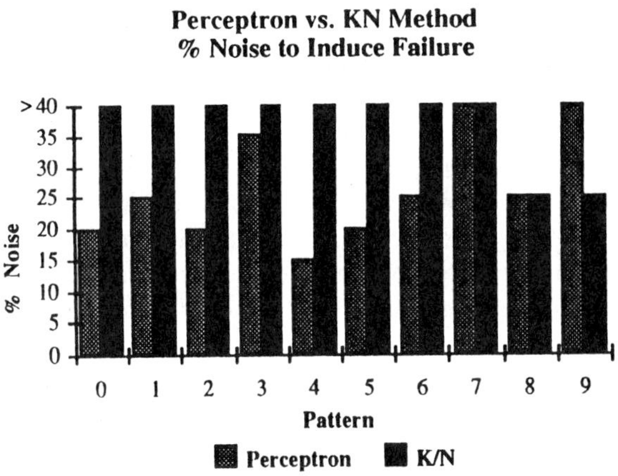

Figure 13

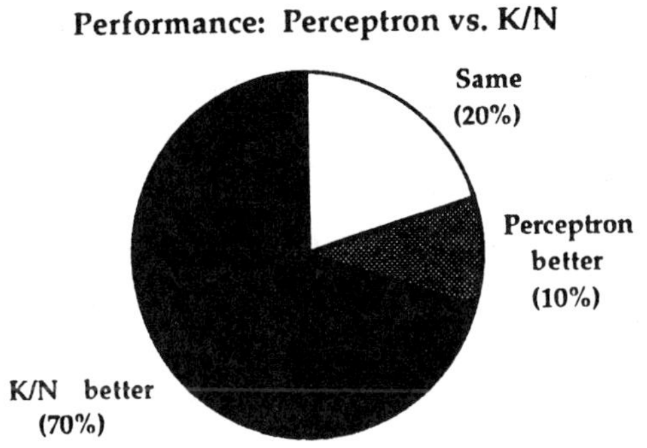

Figure 14

VII. SUMMARY AND CONCLUSION

In this paper, a new digital model of the neuron called K/N gate is presented. The weights of K/N neural networks are modeled as +1, 0 , and -1. The proposed model is applied to pattern recognition with the following algorithm:

1) Inclusion function: given the patterns in class A, design a K/N network to provide a complete coverage of the patterns in class A.

2) Exclusion function: step 1 may provide coverage for certain patterns that belong to another class B. The exclusion function enables the network to exclude the class B patterns from the pattern coverage.

3) Inclusion function: step 2 may have eliminated specific class A patterns from pattern coverage. The inclusion function will relocate the excluded class A patterns and include them into the pattern coverage. This process will continue until the network provides only the complete coverage of patterns in class A.

We simulated a single layer of perceptron and K/N gates, and compare their performances on 7x9 templates of digit 0 to 9. Noise is injected by randomly toggling several bits of the exemplar pattern. .

From the results, we found out that in most cases the K/N network performed better than the perceptron. On the average the perceptron recognize patterns with 25% noise induce while the N/K accurately identifies with 35% noise.Noise level is increase until a network fails to recognize that pattern. The reason is that the perceptrons were trained to recognize only noise-free patterns while the K/N gates were designed to recognized patterns with maximum noise induced.

REFERENCES

[1] Simpson, P.,"Artificial Neural Systems: Foundations, Paradigms, Applications, and Implementations", Pergamon Press (pp. 100-106), 1990.

[2] Klimasauskas, C.,"What Neural Networks Really Do?", Engineering Design News, Special Supplement (pp. 540-545), December , 1989.

[3] Mead, C.,"Analog VLSI and Neural Systems", Addison-Wesley Publishing Company,1989.

[4] Shipley, C.,"What Happened to AI?", PC Computing (pp. 64-74), March , 1989.

[5] Graf, H., "VLSI Implementation of a Neural Network Model", IEEE Computer (pp. 41-49), March , 1988.

[6] Grossberg, S., "Nonlinear Neural Networks: Principles, Mechanisms, and Architectures", Neural Networks, Vol. 1 (pp. 17-61), 1988.

[7] Kohonen, T., "An Introduction to Neural Computing", Neural Networks, Vol. 1 (pp. 3-16), 1988.

[8] Jackel, L., "Electronic Neural Network Chips", Applied Optics (Vol. 26, No. 23, pp. 5077-5084), December , 1987.

[9] Thakoor, A. P., "Electronic Hardware Implementations of Neural Networks", Applied Optics (Vol. 26, No. 23, pp. 5085-5091), December, 1987.

[10] Lippmann, R. , "An Introduction to Computing with Neural Nets", IEEE ASSP. Magazine (pp. 4-22), August ,1986.

[11] Hopfield, J., "Computing with Neural Circuits: A Model", Articles (pp. 625-633), August ,1986.

[12] Naccade, N. J. & Shinghal, R., "SPTA: A Proposed Algorithm for Thinning Binary Patterns", IEEE Transactions on Systems, Man, and Cybernetics. SMC-14, 409, 1984.

[13] Duda, R. O., "Pattern Classification and Scene Analysis", John Wiley & Sons (pp. 130-182), 1973.

[14] Mendel, J. M., "Adaptive, Learning and Pattern Recognition Systems: Theory and Applications", Academic Press (pp. 115-133), 1970.

Solving the Serializability Problem by a Connectionist Machine

Mert SUNGUR[a] Uğur HALICI[b]

Department of Electrical and Electronics Engineering
Middle East Technical University
06531 Ankara, Turkey

E-mail : [a]mert@trmetu.bitnet, [b]halici@trmetu.bitnet

***Abstract*— The serializability problem, which is NP-complete, is to decide on the existence of a total order consistent with a given ordering constraint. In this paper, a connectionist machine is proposed for finding an 'almost sure' solution to the serializability problem such that a feasible final configuration implies that the set is serializable with the given ordering constraint but an infeasible final configuration does not mean that it is not serializable. Therefore, the machine is not able to recognize all the serializable constraints, however the experiments show that the machine seems to converge to a stable configuration in polynomial time and the performance of the machine is quite high, i.e. for most of the time, it is able to find the correct answer.**

I. INTRODUCTION

In connectionist models, information processing takes place through the interactions of a large number of simple processing elements called *units*, each sending excitatory and inhibitory signals to other units ([1], [2]). Some application areas are associative memory, pattern recognition, combinatorial optimization, constraint satisfaction.

Given a set and an ordering constraint on how to order the elements in the set, it may or may not be possible to find a total order consistent with the given ordering constraint on the set. A set is said to be *serializable* with a given ordering constraint if it is possible to find a total order on the set which is consistent with that constraint. *Serializability problem* is to decide on whether a given set with an ordering constraint is serializable or not. If the constraints are restricted to contain information of only in the form 'A precedes B', then the problem reduces to simply finding an answer to whether the given constraint is a partial order and this problem is in P. However, it becomes an NP-complete problem for the ordering constraints containing information also in the form 'A precedes B, and C does not appear in-between' ([3]).

In [4], a connectionist machine to find a total order for the restricted case is proposed. In that machine, $|\mathcal{S}|^2$ units are used for the representation of the problem, where $\mathcal{S}$ is the set on which the ordering constraints are given. It has been observed that the convergence time of the machine depends on $|\mathcal{S}|$ and on the number of total orders consistent with the given ordering constraint and it increases exponentially.

If we simply have to solve an NP-complete problem, then a very long computation may be needed for an exact solution. Thus, in some cases, approximate algorithms are developed [5]. In this paper, a connectionist approach is used for the '*almost sure*' solution of the serializability problem. The proposed machine has a structure different from the classical approaches such as those trying to achieve row-column feasibility [6],[7]. The machine sometimes cannot decide on whether the set is serializable with the given constraint or not because it may not converge to a feasible configuration in spite of serializability. However, the simulation results show that such situations are very rare and the performance of the machine is quite high, so such decisions may be considered as the sacrifice for the short convergence time for an NP-complete problem.

Section II includes the necessary definitions related to the serializability of a set. Section III describes some basic concepts in connectionist models. Section IV describes the structure of the proposed machine and explains how the machine works. Simulation results are given in Section V. Section VI concludes the study.

II. SERIALIZABILITY OF SETS

In the following, the necessary definitions related to the serializability of a set with a given ordering constraint [3] are given:

0-7803-0999-5/93/$03.00

Definition 1 An *ordering constraint* (or shortly a *constraint*) $\mathbb{C}$ on a set $\mathcal{S}$ is a relation on $\mathcal{S} \times \mathcal{S} \times \mathcal{S} \cup \{\varphi\}$ such that $(a, b, l) \in \mathbb{C}$ implies that $(a, b, \varphi) \in \mathbb{C}$ for all $a, b \in \mathcal{S}$ and $l \in \mathcal{S} \cup \{\varphi\}$. If $(a, b, l) \in \mathbb{C}$ where $l = \varphi$ then it is said that *a precedes b* in the constraint $\mathbb{C}$; when $l \neq \varphi$ then it is said that *a precedes b and l does not appear between a and b* in the constraint $\mathbb{C}$. □

Definition 2 *Image* of a total order TO, denoted by Im(TO), is the relation on $\mathcal{S} \times \mathcal{S} \times \mathcal{S} \cup \{\varphi\}$ and is defined by the following rules:

1. $(a, b, \varphi) \in \text{Im(TO)} \Leftrightarrow (a, b) \in \text{TO}$
2. $(a, b, c) \in \text{Im(TO)}$ and $(b, c, a) \in \text{Im(TO)}$ $\Leftrightarrow (a, b) \in \text{TO}$ and $(b, c) \in \text{TO}$

□

Definition 3 A total order TO on $\mathcal{S}$ is said to be *consistent* with a constraint $\mathbb{C}$ on set $\mathcal{S}$ if and only if the constraint $\mathbb{C}$ is a subset of the image of the total order TO, i.e. $\mathbb{C} \subseteq \text{Im(TO)}$. The set $\mathcal{S}$ is said to be *serializable* with $\mathbb{C}$, if and only if a total order consistent with $\mathbb{C}$ exists. □

In [3], it has been proven that deciding on the serializability of a set is an NP-complete problem and special cases for which the serializability problem of sets is in P have been investigated. The restricted case, for which $(a, b, l) \in \mathbb{C}$ if and only if $l = \varphi$, is a subcase for which the problem is in P.

III. CONNECTIONIST APPROACH

A connectionist machine considered in this paper is a network consisting of a number of two-state units (either 1 or 0 corresponding to 'on' or 'off' respectively), that are connected in some way. Some basic concepts related to a such a machine are given below [7]:

The network can be represented by a simple, undirected, weighted graph, $\mathcal{B} = (\mathcal{U}, \mathcal{C})$, where $\mathcal{U}$ denotes the finite set of units and $\mathcal{C}$ is a set of unordered pairs of elements of $\mathcal{U}$ denoting the connections between the units. A *connection* $\{u, v\} \in \mathcal{C}$ joins the units u and v and it is said to be *activated* if both the units u and v are 'on'.

Definition 4 A *configuration* k of a connectionist machine is given by a global state of the connectionist machine and is uniquely defined by a sequence of length $|\mathcal{U}|$, whose u^{th} component $k(u)$ denotes the *state* of unit u in configuration k. The *configuration space* $\mathcal{R}$ is given by the set of all possible configurations. Clearly $|\mathcal{R}| = 2^{|\mathcal{U}|}$. □

Definition 5 With a connection $\{u, v\} \in \mathcal{C}$, a *connection strength* $s_{\{u,v\}} \in \Re$ is associated. The connection strength is a quantitative measure for the *desirability* that $\{u, v\}$ is activated. By definition, $s_{\{u,v\}} = s_{\{v,u\}}$. If $s_{\{u,v\}} > 0$ then it is desirable that $\{u, v\}$ is activated; if $s_{\{u,v\}} < 0$ it is undesirable. Connections with a positive strength are called *excitatory*; connections with a negative strength are called *inhibitory*. Furthermore, the strength $s_{\{u,u\}}$ is called the *bias* of unit u. A bias with a negative strength is sometimes called *threshold*. □

Definition 6 The *consensus function* $C : \mathcal{R} \to \Re$ assigns to each configuration k a real number that is given by the sum of the strengths of the activated connections, i.e.

$$C(k) = \sum_{\{u,v\} \in \mathcal{C}} s_{\{u,v\}} k(u) k(v) \quad (1)$$

□

The objective of a connectionist machine is to reach a globally maximal configuration, i.e. a configuration with maximal consensus.

IV. DESCRIPTION OF THE MACHINE

In the following, the units and the connections used in the connectionist machine proposed for the serializability problem are described and the algorithm defined for this machine is given.

A. Units

For a given constraint $\mathbb{C}$ on a set $\mathcal{S}$, we have the following units:

- *Ordering Units*
  The set of ordering units is denoted by $\mathcal{U}_o$. For each pair $a, b \in \mathcal{S}$, we have the ordering units $u_{a<b} \in \mathcal{U}_o$ and $u_{b<a} \in \mathcal{U}_o$ where $a \neq b$. If the unit $u_{a<b}$ is 'on', this means "a is less than b" and vice versa for $u_{b<a}$. The units $u_{a<b}$ and $u_{b<a}$ constitute a pair such that it is provided that they cannot be simultaneously 'on'. The shorthand notation u_{ab} will be used to indicate the pair $(u_{a<b}, u_{b<a})$. Note that there exist a total of $|\mathcal{S}|(|\mathcal{S}|-1)$ ordering units and $|\mathcal{S}|(|\mathcal{S}|-1)/2$ ordering pairs.
- *Transitiviy Units*
  The set of transitivity units is denoted by $\mathcal{U}_{tr}$. For each $u_{a<b} \in \mathcal{U}_o$ and $u_{b<c} \in \mathcal{U}_o$, we have a transitivity unit $u_{a<b<c} \in \mathcal{U}_{tr}$, indicating whether both "a is less than b" and "b is less than c". $u_{a<b<c}$ is 'on' if and only if both $u_{a<b}$ and $u_{b<c}$ are 'on'. The transitivity units are assumed to respond very fast so that their states are always consistent with the states of the related ordering units. Note that there exist a total of $|\mathcal{S}|(|\mathcal{S}|-1)(|\mathcal{S}|-2)$ transitivity units.

B. Connections

The set of connections is taken as the union of the following disjoint sets :

- *Bias connections*

$$\mathcal{C}_b = \{\{u_{a<b}, u_{a<b}\}|\ u_{a<b} \in \mathcal{U}_o\} \quad (2)$$

These are the bias connections for the ordering units.

- *Check connections*

$$\begin{aligned}\mathcal{C}_{check} = & \{\{u_{a<b}, u_{a<b<c}\}|\ u_{a<b} \in \mathcal{U}_o, u_{a<b<c} \in \mathcal{U}_{tr}\} \\ \bigcup & \{\{u_{b<c}, u_{a<b<c}\}|\ u_{b<c} \in \mathcal{U}_o, u_{a<b<c} \in \mathcal{U}_{tr}\}\end{aligned} \quad (3)$$

These excitatory connections are used to check whether any two ordering units implying a transitive relation are simultenaously 'on'.

- *Support connections*

$$\mathcal{C}_{support} = \{\{u_{a<c}, u_{a<b<c}\}|\ u_{a<c} \in \mathcal{U}_o, u_{a<b<c} \in \mathcal{U}_{tr}\} \quad (4)$$

These excitatory connections are used to provide support for an ordering unit to be 'on' if this is implied by a transitive relation through other ordering units.

- *Threshold connections*

$$\mathcal{C}_{th} = \{\{u_{a<b<c}, u_{a<b<c}\}|\ u_{a<b<c} \in \mathcal{U}_{tr}\} \quad (5)$$

These inhibitory connections are used to guarantee that a transitivity unit is 'on' if and only if both of the check connections incident on it are activated.

- *Exclusion connections*

$$\mathcal{C}_{exc} = \{\{u_{a<c}, u_{c<b}\}|\ (a,b,c) \in \mathbb{C}\} \quad (6)$$

These inhibitory connections are used to handle 'does not appear in-between' constraints such that if $(a,b,c) \in \mathbb{C}$ then, due to these connections, it will be undesirable that units $u_{a<c}$ and $u_{c<b}$ are simultaneously 'on'.

If two connections are in the same set, then they have the same strengths. Furthermore, the strengths of check, support and threshold connections are chosen such that

$$2s_{\{u_{a<b}, u_{a<b<c}\}} > |s_{\{u_{a<b<c}, u_{a<b<c}\}}| \quad (7)$$

$$s_{\{u_{a<c}, u_{a<b<c}\}} + s_{\{u_{a<b}, u_{a<b<c}\}} < |s_{\{u_{a<b<c}, u_{a<b<c}\}}| \quad (8)$$

where $\{u_{a<b}, u_{a<b<c}\} \in \mathcal{C}_{check}$, $\{u_{a<c}, u_{a<b<c}\} \in \mathcal{C}_{support}$, $\{u_{a<b<c}, u_{a<b<c}\} \in \mathcal{C}_{th}$. These two constraints guarantee that a transitivity unit is 'on' if both of the check units incident on it are activated and that a support and a check connection are not enough to force a transitivity unit to be 'on'.

ALGORITHM

- For each constraint $(a,b,c) \in \mathbb{C}$, clamp the units $u_{a<b}$ to 'on' and $u_{b<a}$ to 'off'.
- Set all unclamped units to 'off'.
- While $(\max(\Delta C_{u_{a<b}}) > 0)$ and $(t \le t_{max})$
  - Select an unclamped unit $u_{a<b}$ causing maximum change in the consensus, i.e.,

    $$\Delta C_{u_{a<b}} \ge \Delta C_{u_{c<d}} \quad \forall u_{c,d} \in \mathcal{U}_o$$
  - $k(u_{a<b}, t+1) \leftarrow 1 - k(u_{a<b}, t)$

    $k(u_{b<a}, t+1) \leftarrow 1 - k(u_{a<b}, t+1)$
  - Update the states of all transitivity units in $N_{tr}(u_{ab})$ by considering $k(u_{a<b}, t+1)$ and $k(u_{b<a}, t+1)$
- Check the resultant configuration and decide on the answer (*YES* or *NO*)

Figure 1: The algorithm of the proposed machine

C. Algorithm

In this paper, a connectionist approach is used for the 'almost surely' solution of the serializability problem such that [5]

a) it always reaches a decision in polynomial time,

b) whenever it responds *YES*, the final configuration of the machine represents a total order consistent with the given constraint $\mathbb{C}$,

c) when it says *NO*, the machine is not able to find a total order consistent with the given constraint C in the predetermined time interval; the set may or may not be serializable with that constraint.

The proposed algorithm is summarized in Figure 1 and explained in the following:

The ordering unit pairs used in the machine obeys the following state transitions : Each unit pair initially has state 0–0. However, due to the consensus difference, there may be a transition from 0–0 to 1–0 or to 0–1. After this point on, it is never possible to return back to state 0–0 but, due to the consensus difference, transitions between the states 0–1 and 1–0 may appear. It is never possible to enter state 1–1.

For each ordering unit, the consensus difference is calculated by considering the changes due to the related ordering unit pair and also due to the transitivity units in their neighbourhood, which is defined in the following:

Definition 7 The *transitive neighbourhood*, N_{tr} of $u_{a<b}$ is defined as

$$\begin{aligned} N_{tr}(u_{a<b}) &= \{u_{i<a<b} \mid u_{i<a<b} \in \mathcal{U}_{tr}\} \\ &\bigcup \{u_{a<b<i} \mid u_{a<b<i} \in \mathcal{U}_{tr}\} \end{aligned} \tag{9}$$

The transitive neighbourhood of pair u_{ab} is given by

$$N_{tr}(u_{ab}) = N_{tr}(u_{a<b}) \cup N_{tr}(u_{b<a}) \tag{10}$$

□

Figure 2 shows the transitive neighbourhood of pair u_{ab}. Note that $|N_{tr}(u_{a<b})| = 2(|\mathcal{S}|-2)$ and $|N_{tr}(u_{ab})| = 4(|\mathcal{S}|-2)$.

Definition 8 The consensus difference due to a state change of $u_{a<b}$ together with its neighbourhood, $\Delta C_{u_{a<b}}$, is given by

$$\Delta C_{u_{a<b}} = C(k_{u_{a<b}}(t+1)) - C(k(t)) \tag{11}$$

where $k_{u_{a<b}}$ satisfies

$$\begin{aligned} k_{u_{a<b}}(u_{a<b}, t+1) &= 1 - k(u_{a<b}, t) \\ k_{u_{a<b}}(u_{b<a}, t+1) &= 1 - k(u_{a<b}, t+1) \\ k_{u_{a<b}}(u_{i<j<k}, t+1) &= f(k_{u_{a<b}}(u_{a<b}, t+1)) \\ & \quad \forall u_{i<j<k} \in N_{tr}(u_{a<b}) \\ k_{u_{a<b}}(u_{i<j<k}, t+1) &= f(k_{u_{a<b}}(u_{b<a}, t+1)) \\ & \quad \forall u_{i<j<k} \in N_{tr}(u_{b<a}) \end{aligned}$$

and $k(t)$ is the configuration of the network at time (iteration) t and $k_{u_{a<b}}(t+1)$ is the configuration to be obtained at the next step due to the state change of $u_{a<b}$ and its neighbourhood. $k(u,t)$ represents the state of unit u at time t. $f()$ is the transitivity function such that $u_{a<b<c} \in \mathcal{U}_{tr}$ is 'on' if and only if $u_{a<b}$ and $u_{b<c}$ are both 'on', and 'off' otherwise. □

For a distributed calculation, each ordering unit calculates the consensus difference due to its state change and the unit which causes the maximum consensus difference is selected for a state change. Note that $|N_{tr}(u_{a<b})| = 4(|\mathcal{S}|-2)$ is much less than the total number of units, $|\mathcal{S}|(|\mathcal{S}|-1)^2$, used in the structure. This is a local calculation including only u_{ab} and $N_{tr}(u_{ab})$.

Although it seems that finding the unit which causes maximum improvement in the consensus requires a global calculation, this problem may be overcome by assigning a delay to each ordering unit such that the state change occurs after a time period proportional to $\frac{1}{\Delta C_{u_{a<b}}}$ and by assuming that the units continuously check the consensus difference so that, as soon as a unit changes state, the previous calculations are no more valid. No two units are allowed to change their states simultaneously. These eliminate any problem which may occur due to synchronous parallelism.

When the algorithm terminates, we say that the final configuration of the machine is *feasible* if and only if the following conditions are satisfied:

1. Exactly one ordering unit of each ordering pair is 'on'.
2. None of the exclusion connections is activated.
3. For each support connection, if the related transitivity unit is 'on', then the supported ordering unit should also be 'on'.

If a final configuration is feasible, the decision for the serializability of the set is *YES* and the total order represented by this configuration can be deduced as explained in the following:

Consider the following ordering constraint:

$$\mathbb{C} = \{(a,c,b), (b,c,\varphi), (b,d,a)\}$$

which leads to the unique total order $b < d < a < c$. The ordering units are topologically arranged in a two dimensional array as shown in Figure 3.a. For this constraint, when the network converges, we expect the states of the ordering units to be as shown in Figure 3.b where the filled circles correspond to 'on' units. Note that, if an element $a \in S$ is assigned the order i, then in the corresponding row, exactly $|\mathcal{S}| - i$ units should be 'on', indicating that i elements are assigned orders before a. This appears as a result of the feasibility of the network.

If the final configuration is not feasible, then the decision is *NO* indicating that the set may or may not be serializable with the given constraint.

V. EXPERIMENTAL RESULTS

Although the proposed machine is highly parallel in nature, simulations have been carried out on a sequential personal computer, emulating the parallel structure. In the following, an *iteration* includes all the computation required for a state change, i.e. *in one iteration*, all the ordering units locally (including their neighbourhoods) compute the consensus change that they will cause and the one yielding the maximum change in the consensus changes its own state and the units in its neighbourhood updates their states according to this state change.

Simulations have been carried out for various set sizes and for different experimental constraints at each set size. Experimental constraints are chosen randomly so as to guarantee serializability, for different combinations each including different numbers of (a,b,c) and (a,b,φ) informations. Nonserializable constraints are not considered because such constraints can never yield a feasible configuration. Since the algorithm checks the resultant configuration, the machine will always respond with *NO* for such constraints. A possible cycle is prevented by the fact that an upper limit (t_{max}) exists for the number of iterations.

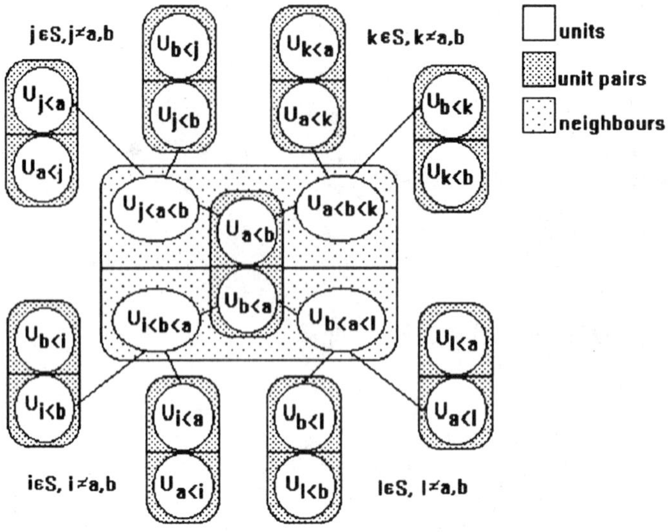

Figure 2: Transitive neighbourhood of pair u_{ab}

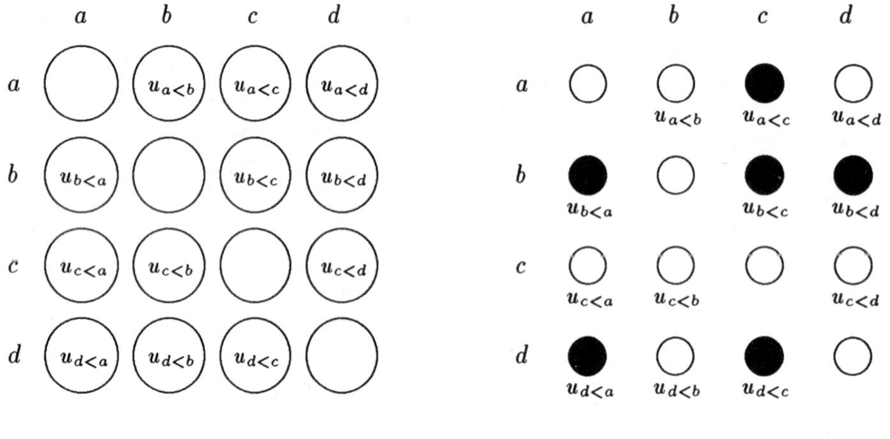

(a) (b)

Figure 3: a) The topological arrangement of the ordering units used in the representation for $|S| = 4$ b) The final configuration of the network representing the total order $b < d < a < c$

TABLE I

EXPERIMENTAL RESULTS FOR VARIOUS SET SIZES

$\|S\|$	# of experimental constraints	*YES*	*YES/NO*	*NO*	# of iterations Min	Max	Avg
4	9	9	0	0	2	5	3.11
5	14	14	0	0	1	8	4.21
6	21	20	1	0	2	15	6.16
7	21	21	0	0	4	21	12.22
8	21	20	1	0	3	26	14.45
9	33	32	1	0	4	32	14.00
TOTAL	119	116	3	0			

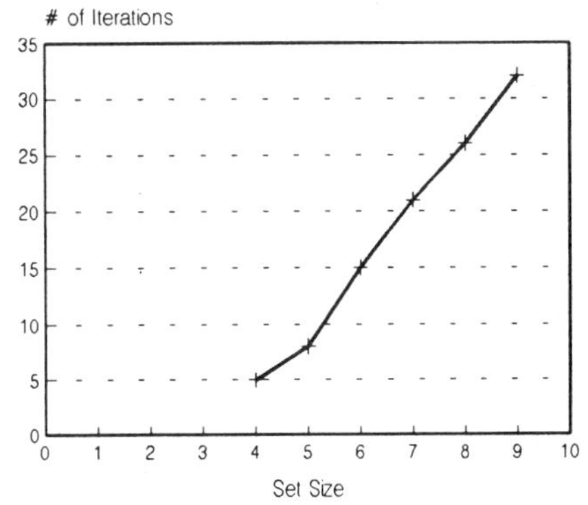

Figure 4: Set size vs maximum number of iterations

Experimental results are summarized in Table I. $|S|$ is the set size; *# of experimental constraints* gives how many different random serializable constraints have been tried. For each random constraint, 10 experiments have been performed. The *YES* column gives the number of constraints which have ended up with *YES* answer in all the 10 trials. The *YES/NO* column gives the number of constraints which have ended up with both *YES* and *NO* answers although the set is serializable with the constraint. Finally, *NO* column shows the number of constraints which have never ended up with *YES* answer in any of the 10 trials. The maximum number of iterations is plotted as a function of the set size in Figure 4.

Note that, if the answer is *YES* for any experiment, it is enough for the decision that the set is serializable with the given constraint. It has been observed that it is very rare that the machine responds with *NO* in spite of serializability. As can be seen from the table, only $\frac{3}{119} = 2\%$ of the constraints lead to such wrong decisions. However, we have observed no serializable constraints which always yield a *NO* answer. The constraints which have sometimes caused wrong decisions have yielded *YES* answers in at least 50% of the 10 trials performed for these constraints.

Whether the answer is correct or not, it has been observed that the network converges to a final configuration in a small number of iterations. The iterations listed in the table indicate the actual time for convergence without being stopped by an upper limit (t_{max}) as suggested by the algorithm. This fact and the above discussion suggest that an extension of the algorithm to running the machine up to a specified number of times as long as a *NO* answer is yielded, will increase the performance of the machine because if the set is serializable with the given constraint, it is probable that the machine will find a total order in at least one of these runs, which is enough to decide that the set is serializable.

VI. CONCLUSION

In this paper, a connectionist machine is proposed to solve the NP-complete serializability problem in accordance with an 'almost sure' policy. Two types of units are used in the machine: the ordering units and the transitivity units. The connections between these units are chosen such that if a final configuration is feasible then the 'on' elements of the ordering units represent a total order consistent with the given ordering constraint and the 'on' elements of the transitivity units are those implied by this total order. In the simulations of this machine, it has been observed that the machine seems to converge to a stable configuration in polynomial time. If the set is serializable with the given ordering constraint, the machine rarely converges to infeasible configurations. To increase the performance of the machine, the algorithm may be extended to run the machine for a number of times in case of a *NO* answer since it is probable that the machine will find a total order in at least one of these runs and a single *YES* answer is enough to decide that the set is serializable. It should also be noted that the proposed structure is quite different from the classical row-column approaches and it may be interesting to apply such a structure to some other combinatorial optimization problems such as the travelling salesman problem.

REFERENCES

[1] K. Knight, "A gentle introduction to subsymbolic computation : Connectionism for the AI researcher," Tech. Rep. CMU-CS-89-150, Carnegie-Mellon University, May 1989.

[2] D. E. Rumelhart and J. L. McClelland, eds., *Parallel Distributed Processing : Explorations in the Microstructure of Cognition.* MIT Press, 1986.

[3] U. Halici, *Contributions to the Theory of Database Concurrency Control.* PhD thesis, Dept. of Electrical and Electronics Eng., Middle East Tech. Univ., 1988.

[4] U. Halici and M. Sungur, "A Boltzmann machine for restricted total ordering problem," in *Proc. of the 6th Int'l Symp. on Computer and Information Sciences*, pp. 907–916, Elsevier Science Publishers, Nov. 1991.

[5] H. S. Wilf, *Algorithms and Complexity.* Prentice Hall, 1986.

[6] J. Hopfield and D. Tank, ""Neural" computation of decisions in optimization problems," *Biological Cybernetics*, vol. 52, pp. 141–152, 1985.

[7] E. Aarts and J. Korst, *Simulated Annealing and Boltzmann Machines.* John Wiley and Sons Ltd., 1989.

Chapter 11: Integrated Circuit Implementation

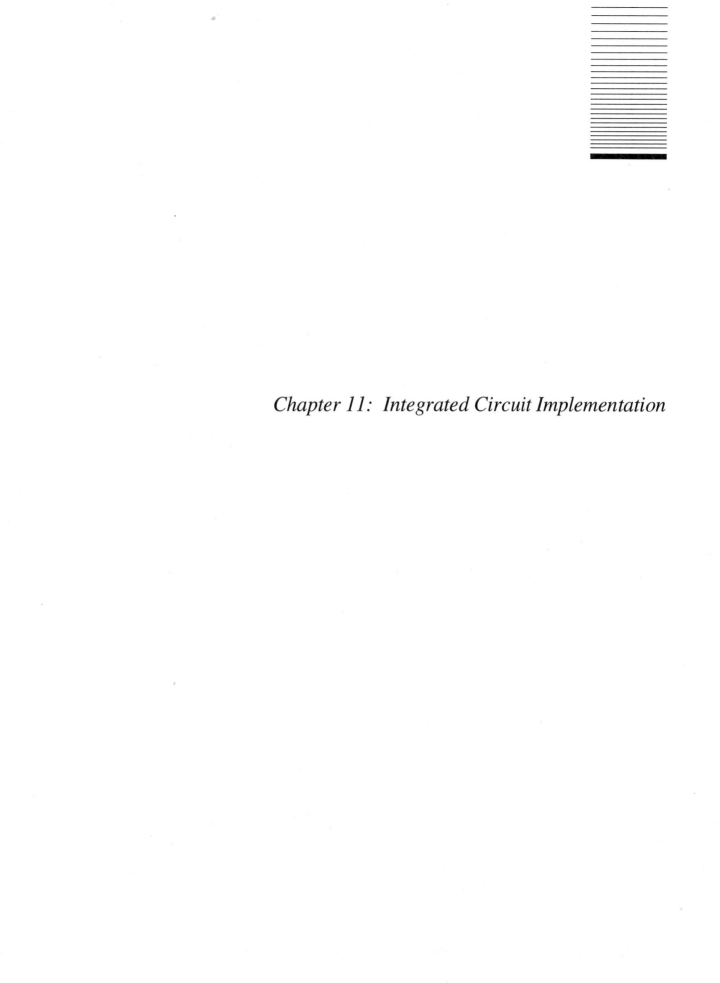

CHAPTER 11
Integrated Circuit Implementations

Unlike the previous chapter, which looked at more of a board-level implementation of neural networks, the papers in this chapter emphasize the development of integrated circuit (IC) implementations of neural networks. The growth in IC implementations of neural networks appears to have leveled off. The increased availability of very high speed DSP chips has been largely responsible for the slowed growth.

The papers in this chapter are organized into four areas:

- **Survey.** IC neural network implementations requires many aspects to be considered. **Paper 11.1** provides a survey of various IC implementations of neural networks with an emphasis on these design issues and trade-offs. **Paper 11.2** provides an additional survey and tutorial of VLSI implementation, with more emphasis on the neural network architectures.

- **On-Chip Learning.** Adaptation of weights on the chip offers a tremendous improvement in the training time of neural networks. **Paper 11.3** describes the design and test results of an analog processing chip capable of on-chip learning. **Paper 11.4** presents the design of an analog neural network chip with on-chip learning using the backpropagation algorithm.

- **Neural Network IC Implementations.** There have been several IC implementations of specific neural networks. **Paper 11.5** describes a neural network fuzzy logic chip designed for control applications. **Paper 11.6** describes the design and simulation of a winner-take-all neural network chip capable of implementing LVQ neural networks. **Paper 11.7** presents a 3-D Wafer Scale Integration for implementing a wide variety of neural network operations. **Paper 11.8** describes a CMOS digital retina chip with multi-bit output for analog to digital coding.

- **Neural Network IC Support.** One important area in all neural network IC implementations is the throughput for the chip. **Paper 11.9** emphasizes the point in its discussion of a CMOS device designed for data transfer for the CNAPS IC for high-speed massive throughput processing.

- **Biological ICs.** Because of the dramatic improvement in processing speeds for DSP chips the demand for specialized digital neural network chips has decreased. However, neural network ICs will continued to emphasize analog sensor processing. One example of this is **Paper 11.10**, which describes an analog IC implementation of the cochlea.

Evaluation of Electronic Artificial Neural Network Implementations

Raj P. Malhotra and Dr. Raymond Siferd
Wright State University, Department of Electrical Engineering
Dayton, Ohio 45435

Abstract--*Artificial Neural Networks (ANNs) have recently gained recognition as a valuable tool to aid in the solution of difficult computing problems. Despite an abundance of work in the application and mathematical foundations of ANNs there currently exists no consensus on how to implement ANNs in hardware. The goal of this paper is to provide an analytical perspective on electronic ANN implementation by addressing issues and design tradeoffs.*

INTRODUCTION

Present day computers exhibit essentially the same underlying structure as those first proposed by John Von Neuman nearly forty years ago. The Von Neuman Architecture features separate logic and arithmetic units, memory units,and a centralized interconnection structure and control unit. Perhaps the key limitation results from the *control flow* nature of these machines; the computer must be controlled by a stream of instructions which are presented in a sequential fashion. For many tasks a procedural solution is inefficient or impossible to find.

Although computers have increased performance by an order of magnitude every five to ten years since their inception many obstacles remain in applying them in real-world situations. Conventional computers must be programmed (an expensive proposition) and cannot deal well with new, unforseen inputs. Further, these devices cannot easily recognize patterns (such as speech or handwriting) causing them to interface with humans in an unnatural manner. These inadequacies, together with our inability to sustain the rapid growth in performance of conventional computer hardware has motivated the study of alternative methods.

Artificial Neural Networks represent an unusual, biologically-inspired strategy to do computing. Although ANNs are not a new development, born in the work of McCulloch and Pitts in the 1940s and 1950s, only recently (1980s) have important breakthroughs been made to allow them to become an effective computational paradigm. These systems work well in many areas where traditional computers fail: ANNs are particularly promising in *artificial perception* tasks such as speech recognition and machine vision. They have found increased use in adaptive signal processing and adaptive control theory as well.

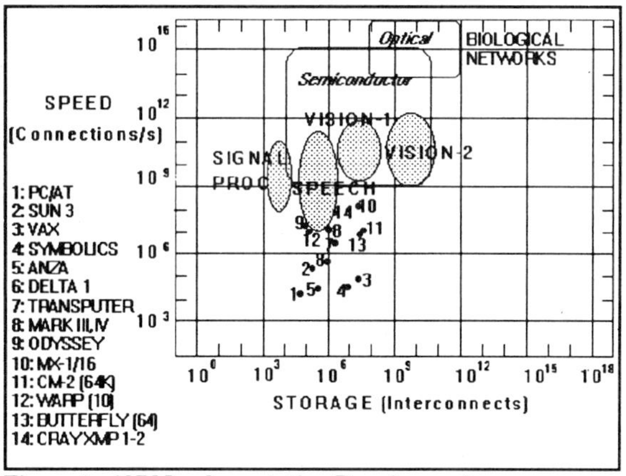

Figure 1 - ANN Implementation Requirements

The response and characteristics of present models of artificial neural networks are primarily investigated by simulation on conventional computers or parallel processing machines. Figure 1 shows the performance obtainable with commercially available simulators in terms of interconnections (storage) and interconnections per second (speed). This must be compared with application requirements. It becomes obvious that today's hardware capabilities are limiting the development of neural network research. The fundamental drawback of these simulators is that much of the spatial and temporal parallelism, inherent to ANNs, is lost and that the computing time of the simulated net, especially for large associations of neurons, grows to such orders of magnitude that a timely response may not be achievable. If the real-time requirement cannot be satisfied by software simulation it makes sense to think about designing specialized hardware.

There currently exists no consensus on how to implement ANNs into hardware. Optical technologies may hold the most promise in the long term, but electronics are currently favorable because of the maturity of the technology and the level of integration. However there remain many largely unaddressed questions with regard to electronic ANN implementation: How do we deal with the massive number of interconnections required (the *connectivity problem*) ? What are the advantages and disadvantages of continuous vs. discrete time, analog vs. digital valued, and literal vs. virtual, implementations ? What metrics can be applied to compare different realizations ?

The goal of this paper is simply to provide some perspective on the implementation of ANNs. This will be done by discussing issues and examples. Although it is assumed that the reader is familiar with the pertinent aspects of ANNs, they will be briefly reviewed in the next section.

NEURAL NETWORK FUNDAMENTALS

Neural Networks primarily operate in two modes; *learning* mode and *recall* or *relaxed* mode. These may both be running concurrently. *Learning* involves the update of weights to strengthen or weaken network connections while *recall* involves processing inputs to produce outputs. As we propagate signals through the network we require two basic operations: *processing* and *communication*. We shall see that these may be mathematically represented as a matrix-vector multiplication.

The basic component of a neural network is the neuron model. A number of models have been constructed to describe the behavior of neurons in biological nervous systems. These have been inspired by different goals. Some describe the operation of neurons in great mathematical detail, usually to study them from a neuropsychology standpoint. Others assume some simplifications for ease of implementation, making them more amenable to performing computations. Since we are interested in performing computations, we will discuss the latter type of model.

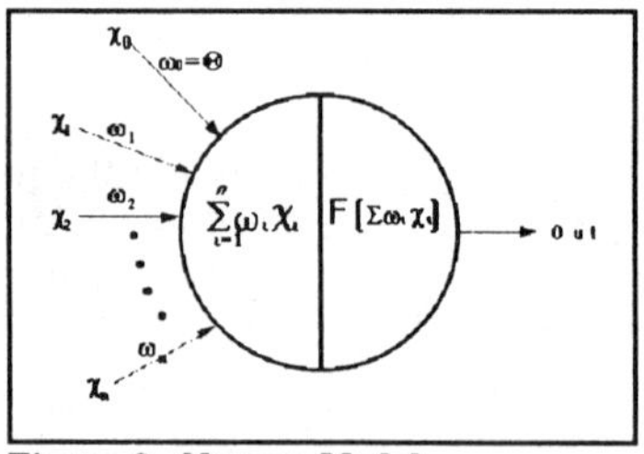

Figure 2 - Neuron Model.

Figure 2 shows the general structure of most simplified neuron models. The neuron receives a set of input signals, x_i, which are multiplied by a corresponding set of weighting factors, w_i. All of the weighted input signals are added up to produce n, the complete input to the neuron. An *activation function*, F, operates on the neuron input, transforming it into an output signal which is transmitted to other neurons. The weight w_0, is the threshold value Θ which biases the firing of the neuron. By convention the input x_0 is set to unity.

The weighting factors play an important role in the neuron model. A positive weighting factor tends to increase the level of activation of the neuron, this is called an *excitatory connection*. A negative weight tends to decrease the output of the neuron, this is called an *inhibitory connection*. The magnitude of the weights effect the relative importance of the connections between neurons. Some neurons are more responsive to particular inputs coming from other neurons. In this way associations may form.

The activation function F determines the overall behavior of the neuron. Several types of activation functions are shown in figure 3. Typically, some type of nonlinear function is used. Early neuron models often used some type of hard-limiting (sgn or step) function which is discontinuous at the origin and produces a two-valued output analogous to a digital system. The discontinuity in the Hard-limiter is undesirable since learning procedures for multi-layer networks often require the neuron transfer function to be differentiable. The sigmoidal function ($f_s(y) = (1 + e^{-\beta y})^{-1}$) and the hyperbolic tangent, tanh(y), are common choices today.

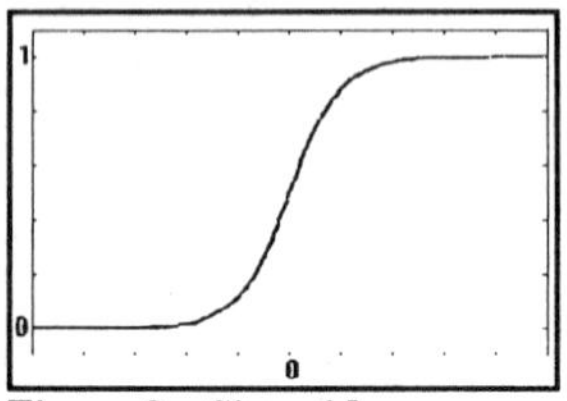
Figure 3a. Sigmoid

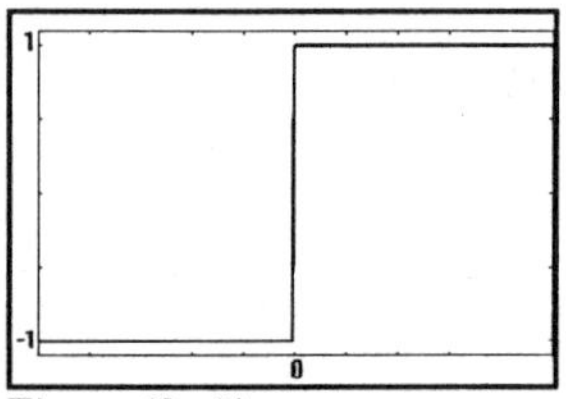
Figure 3b. Signum

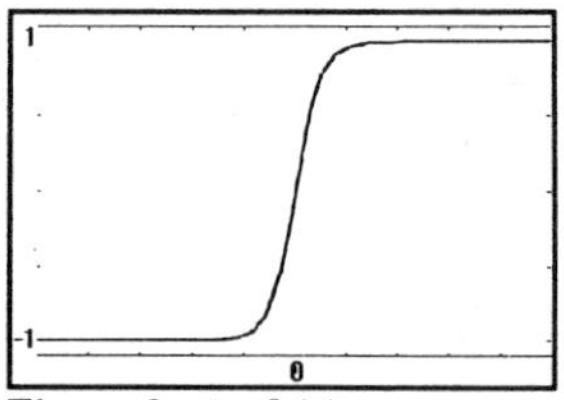
Figure 3c. tanh(y)

The real power of a Neural Network emanates in from it's connections and it's consequent ability to form associations. The vast majority of network models are variations on two principal topologies; *feedback (recursive)* and *feedforward* networks. The latter is shown in figure 4. This network has an input layer, two hidden layers, and an output layer. The

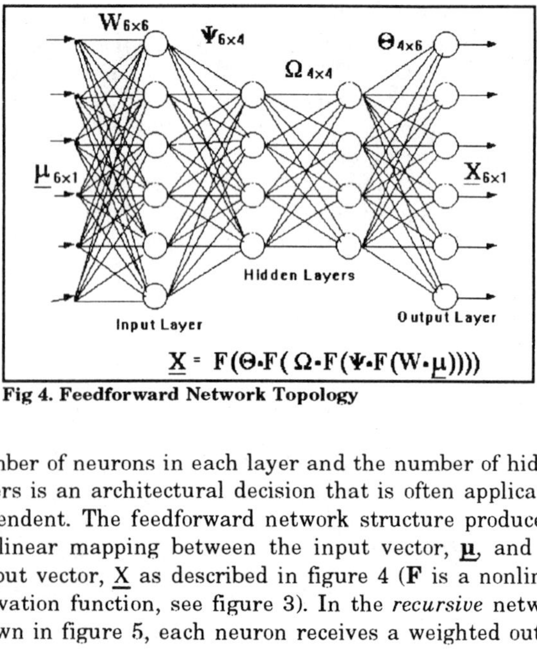

$$\underline{X} = F(\Theta \cdot F(\Omega \cdot F(\Psi \cdot F(W \cdot \underline{\mu}))))$$

Fig 4. Feedforward Network Topology

number of neurons in each layer and the number of hidden layers is an architectural decision that is often application dependent. The feedforward network structure produces a nonlinear mapping between the input vector, $\underline{\mu}$, and the output vector, $\underline{X}$ as described in figure 4 (F is a nonlinear activation function, see figure 3). In the *recursive* network shown in figure 5, each neuron receives a weighted output from all the neurons in the single-layer net. This system receives and input vector of u_is and iterates according to the equation $x_i = F(\Sigma w_{ij} x_j + u_i)$. This operation is used to implement an associative memory; the network is supplied with a partial input pattern and after iterating it converges to the complete and closest pattern. The output of a recursive ANN is described by a trajectory of vectors over time rather than a single vector as in the feedforward case.

The weights of a network define the nonlinear mappings or the associations to be implemented. These weights are adjusted when the network is in a *training mode* by some *learning laws*. There are a great many learning laws and much attention is focused on this area. Two general classes of learning procedures exist. In *unsupervised learning*, network models are first presented with an input vector from the set of possible network inputs. The network rule adjusts

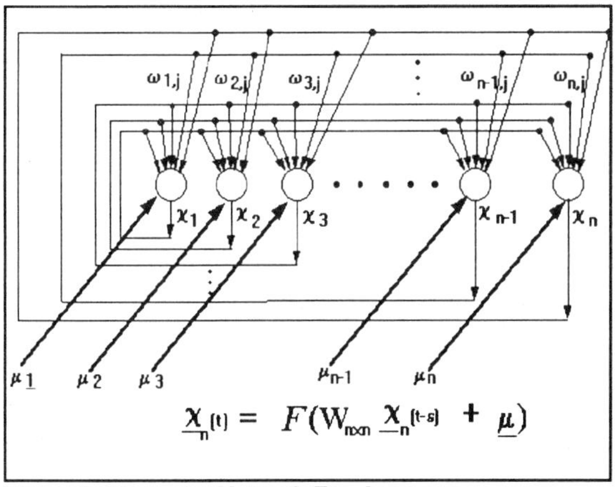

Figure 5 - Recursive Network Topology

the weights so that input examples are grouped into classes based upon their statistical properties. In *supervised learning* the network is presented with a set of training examples (inputs and desired outputs). The output error is then minimized by modifying the weights. Efficient learning is one of the primary focuses of ANN research.

DESIGN ISSUES

We have discussed the large number of neurons and connections required to apply a network to problems in machine vision and speech recognition (see figure 1). The task of the hardware developer, then, is generally to pack as many connections and neurons as possible on a chip for a particular application; the pattern storage capacity increases with the number of neurons while the computation time decreases linearly with the number of connections [3]. The amount of space required by this massive number of connections (10^6 to $>10^9$) amounts to a major problem. It appears that only VLSI or ULSI technologies are capable of achieving the required density. ANNs for applications like vision and speech appear to overtax the single chip integration potential of present technology as well as that of future submicron (0.1 - 0.3μm) technologies [10]. It seems apparent that we must stretch the capabilities of current technology to implement ANNs. This gives rise to the issues and tradeoffs documented below.

Literal vs. Virtual Implementation and The Connectivity Problem

One fundamental question in ANN hardware design is whether to implement the network literally or not. In other words, how many virtual neurons should be hosted on each physical processor ? The extreme cases are the serial implementation of an ANN algorithm on a general-purpose uniprocessor (full virtualization), and the fully parallel implementation of one processing element per algorithmic neuron (no virtualization).

The feasibility of literal implementation depends partially upon the size of the network. To realize a fully connected recursive network (see figure 5) of n nodes requires n^2 connections. While the realization of a multi-layer feedforward network (see figure 4) containing ℓ layers with N_i nodes in each layer requires $\Sigma_{i=1}^{\ell} N_{i-1} N_i$ connections. Literal realizations of larger networks may not be plausible because of the overwhelming number of connections and the amount physical space they would require. The size of the network and the ability of the technology to accommodate this massive communication burden are key to the decision on literality.

The *speed* of a network is always an important consideration. It affects the propagation time (time to pass signals through the network) in both the learning and relaxed modes. We compare the forward (relaxed mode) propagation time of a literal implementation, t_{lit}, with that of a virtual implementation, t_{vir}, for the multi-layer feedforward network of figure 4. We assume that the network has N neurons in ℓ layers, and C connections. The virtual realization of this network contains P physical processors (analog or digital) connected by B hardware buses. We see that for the literal case

$$t_{lit} = \ell t_{proc} + (\ell - 1) t_{com}$$

where t_{proc} is the neuron's processing time and t_{com} is the communication time representing the latency time of connections between layers. The virtual net requires a forward propagation time given by

$$t_{vir} = \frac{N}{\mu P}\hat{t}_{proc} + C(\hat{t}_{bus} + \lambda_B)\,\rho[P_{send} \neq P_{recv}] + C\hat{t}_{local}\,\rho[P_{send} = P_{recv}]$$

where $\hat{t}_{proc}$, $\hat{t}_{bus}$, and $\hat{t}_{local}$ represent the neuron processing time, the transmission delay of the bus, and the transmission delay to send a signal over a local bus internal to a processor (this may be a memory access). We include μ as a processor utilization factor. The term λ_B symbolizes the overhead in communication from bus request collisions (usually $\lambda_B \gg \hat{t}_{bus}$). λ_B can be expressed as

$$\lambda_B = \frac{C}{\alpha B} t_{bus}$$

where α represents bus utilization. We note that the overhead factors, μ and α, are increasing functions of P and C - for simplification we shall assume both to be unity (best case for literal implementation). A virtual neuron may signal another neuron in either the same or a different host processor, denoted as $P_{send}=P_{recv}$ and $P_{send}\neq P_{recv}$ respectively. Assuming that virtual neurons are uniformly distributed across all the processors the probabilities for these two cases is given by

$$\rho[P_{send}=P_{recv}] = \frac{1}{P} \quad and \quad \rho[P_{send}\neq P_{recv}] = \frac{P-1}{P}$$

We will assume the virtual implementation incurs no penalty in processing or communication times, that is $t_{proc} = \hat{t}_{proc}$ and $t_{com} = \hat{t}_{bus} = \hat{t}_{local}$. With these simplifications we may express the forward propagation time as

$$t_{vir} = \frac{N}{P} t_{proc} + \left[\frac{C^2(P-1)+CBP}{BP}\right] t_{com}$$

It becomes obvious what we loose in virtualization when we compare t_{lit} and t_{vir}: The propagation time of the ideal, literal implementation does not increase with network size (*N* or *C*); ℓ (usually between 2 and 4, [3]) is an architectural decision, independent of *N* and *C*. The virtual implementation's communication time increases quadratically with *C* or roughly as a function of N^4 since $C = \Sigma_{i=1}^{\ell} N_{i-1} N_i \approx O(N^2)$ and the processing time increases linearly with *N*. For large networks t_{vir} becomes excessive, particularly if *P* and *B* are small.

Of course there are practical considerations. How many processors or busses should we use ? This often becomes a question of efficiency and cost. Suppose we have *N* virtual nodes with *C* connections out of each of them (now $C = N_{i+1}$, the number of nodes in the next layer). If there are *P* physical processors, then the probability that a particular connection will not be directed to any one processor (causing it to go idle) is

$$\rho\,(miss/conn) = \frac{P-1}{P}$$

and the probability that none of the *C* connections made in a single broadcast step are implemented on this processor is

$$\rho\,(miss) = \left[\frac{P-1}{P}\right]^C$$

This probability is essentially an inefficiency factor. For *P* = *C* this is approximately equal to $1/e$, since

$$\lim_{x\to\infty}\left[\frac{x}{x-1}\right]^x \approx \lim_{x\to\infty}\left[\frac{x+1}{x}\right]^x = e$$

Thus, asymptotic performance (total useful computation within 37% of the maximum achievable by an infinite number of processors) is reached for a number of processors comparable to the number of connections out of each unit. Much fewer than *C* processors, however, would imply significantly reduced computational throughput.

Digital vs. Analog Implementation

Historically, ANN simulation has favored digital devices while dedicated ANN implementations have used primarily analog devices. The motivation for these areas is slightly different. Simulation investigates ANN properties and must be done on a general-purpose *digital* computer. Dedicated ANNs, which work in one application area, have followed the most successful model known, the biological (*analog*) model. Both of these paradigms have particular advantages and as a result, somewhat of a controversy has developed. Analog supporters point to the fact that analog devices can process more than one bit (of accuracy) per transistor leading to greater levels of integration which is key to the ability to support literal implementations. Analog devices perform the pervasive multiply-accumulate operations in parallel as a result of physics, making them potentially quicker. Those that advocate digital devices have pointed to the superior noise immunity, more sophisticated time multiplexing techniques (which better support virtualization), and better fabrication processes associated with digital VLSI. Further, digital devices are more easily programmed and more capable of supporting the large dynamic range that network weights require to implement gradient learning algorithms.

We may observe the slower execution times for digital networks by re-examining the forward propagation time discussed above. In particular we investigate the processing time, t_{proc}. For a single neuron with **n** inputs, as shown in figure 2, the computations required include **n** multiplications, (**n**-1) additions, and a nonlinear activation function approximation. We write the execution time for a single neuron as

$$t_{proc}(neuron) = n\,t_{mult} + (n-1)\,t_{add} + t_{act}$$

Realizing that a fully-connected feedforward network (as shown in figure 4) provides each neuron of layer **i** with $\mathbf{n}_{i-1}$ + 1 input connections (we account for the threshold weight) we can easily derive an expression for the processing time:

$$t_{proc}(network) = \sum_{i=1}^{\ell} \left[(n_{i-1}+1)\,n_i\,(t_{mult}+t_{add}) + t_{act}\right]$$

where ℓ is the number of layers and $\mathbf{n}_i$ denotes the number of nodes in layer **i**. It is clear that the processing time for the digital case increases quadratically ($O(\mathbf{n}^2)$) with network size. Analog implementations do not generally suffer from this problem because additions, multiplications, and even the activation function may result directly from the device and circuit characteristics.

Another consideration is cost. To investigate this we first reflect upon ANN structure; there are two basic operations, computation and communication. These can be dissected into three fundamental architectural tenets; processing, memory, and communication. One approach to a cost analysis would compare the price of performing these three functions in the analog and the digital case. We follow that approach.

The cost of interconnecting points in analog and digital technology is essentially the same assuming the "wiring" process and material to be identical for both cases. It becomes a question of the amount of interconnection required and the space it consumes. We will assume that after taking noise margins into account a particular analog device provides us with β bits of accuracy which, for analog implementations, is propagated over a single interconnect. For equivalent accuracy we will then require β digital interconnects for each analog interconnect. We can establish a simple relationship between the relative costs as

$$C_{interconnect}(digital) = \beta \cdot C_{interconnect}(analog)$$

where $\beta \geq 1$ and β is assumed to be independent of network size. Following the same argument for the processing costs (two cases differ in quantity of processing devices required for equivalent accuracies) we can assert

$$C_{processing}(digital) = \beta \cdot C_{processing}(analog) .$$

We now must compare the relative costs to store the weights in memory. Fortunately, an applicable analysis exists in Wiener [9] which we shall site.

Normally we would expect a more accurate device to cost more than a less accurate one and we assume, for the purposes of this argument that the cost, C_{memory}, is proportional to accuracy. In fact, if one thinks of the device as a meter with a pointer that must finish in one of n well defined regions, it is clear that having just one region would not convey any information and should not contribute to the cost. Therefore the cost of the device should be counted only for regions in excess of 1 and may be written as $C_{memory} = (n - 1)A$, where A is some arbitrary constant which depends upon the method of manufacture. The amount of information, β, contained in n messages is $\beta = log_2 n$ bits hence the cost equation may be written as $C_{memory} = (2^\beta - 1)A$. The key question here is: 'Is it better to distribute the information over several less accurate devices or keep it all in one highly accurate device ?'. If we were to divide the information β over two devices the total cost will be $C_{memory} = 2(2_{\beta/2} - 1)A$. Similarly by dividing β over N devices the cost becomes $C_{memory} = N(2^{\beta/N} - 1)A$. It may be shown that this function decreases as N increases. For example, with $A = 1$ and $\beta = 16$, we have:

N	C_{memory}
1	65,535
2	510
4	30
8	24
16	16

We observe that the cost function is minimized when each memory device has only two states (when $N = \beta$). This implies that if information is to be stored at all, it can be done most cheaply in binary code with digital devices. We can derive the relative costs as

$$C_{memory}(analog) = \frac{2^\beta - 1}{\beta} C_{memory}(digital)$$

using $N = 1$ for the analog case and $N = \beta$ for the digital case. The total cost can now be found by summing the component costs;

$$C_{total}(analog) = \sum_{i=proc,intrcon,mem} C_i(analog)$$
$$= \frac{1}{\beta}\left[C_{processing}(digital) + C_{interconnect}(digital)\right] + \frac{2^\beta - 1}{\beta} C_{memory}(digital) .$$

We may assume that $C_{processing}(digital)$, $C_{interconnect}(digital)$ and $C_{memory}(digital)$ are all linearly related (differing only by a constant factor) and they are independent of the signal accuracy β. We can say that

$$C_{processing}(digital) = \alpha \cdot C_{interconnection}(digital) = \sigma \cdot C_{memory}(digital) \quad (\alpha, \sigma \geq 0)$$

For simplicity we shall assume $\alpha, \sigma = 1$. It then becomes clear that as our precision requirements increase the cost ratio of analog memory over digital memory increases exponentially:

$$C_{total}(analog) = \frac{2^\beta + 1}{3\beta} C_{total}(digital)$$

where β represents network accuracy requirements (as well as the number of bits for the digital case). We may also observe that

$$\frac{Cost\ of\ analog}{Cost\ of\ digital} = \frac{2^\beta + 1}{3\beta} \quad and \quad \lim_{\beta\to\infty} \frac{Cost\ of\ analog}{Cost\ of\ Digital} = \infty$$

We conclude that digital implementations are generally more cost-efficient for any given precision.

Continuous vs. Discrete Implementation

Literality and the number of quantization levels (as discussed above) are *spatial* decisions for ANN implementors. We have not yet considered the *temporal* aspect. The issue of whether to use asynchronous, continuous time devices or synchronous, discrete implementation involves efficiency and optimization in time. Although the question is often entangled with the issues discussed above, it need not be. It is true that analog implementations tend to operate in continuous time and digital devices are usually discrete but hybrids abound. Asynchronous-digital ANNs (see the pulse stream implementation below) and synchronous-analog realizations do exist.

Continuous operation is more biologically accurate and almost essential in many of the recursive networks often used as associative memories [3]. But discrete implementations may simulate continuous time by stochastically firing the neurons [6]. Discrete implementations tend to have larger network delay time due to the overhead in synchronization mechanisms (these mechanisms carry a penalty in terms of chip area). The tradeoff made here is between smaller, faster, more biologically accurate implementation and slower, more flexible, operation.

DESIGN EXAMPLES

Literal Neural Systems in Analog VLSI

Carver Mead's work, including the SeeHear Chip and Electronic Cochlea [4], is perhaps the most well-known and best received in the field of ANN Implementation. Mead attempts to mimic biology through continuous time, analog circuits. This work is important, not as a result of innovation at the network level, but because of the establishment of analog VLSI building blocks for the neuron (device) level.

We have previously discussed some of the limitations imposed by the *Connectivity Problem* but not from a device perspective. For neuron devices it is the issue of *fan-in* rather than fan-out that encumbers us. The number of inputs a node must accommodate grows with the total number of neurons in the network; $C = O(N)$ as discussed above. Digital devices tend to execute the many needed multiply-accumulate operations slowly and inefficiently. We shall examine the analog neuron described in Mead's book [4].

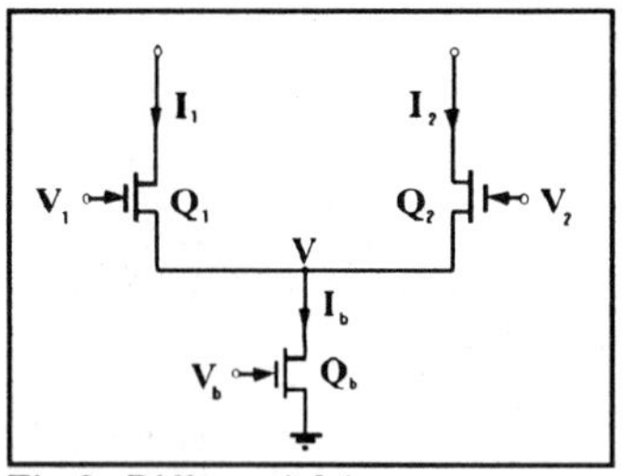

Fig 6 - Differential Amp

The CMOS circuit shown in figure 6 is a differential pair. Using the equation relating drain current to gate and source voltages, $I_{sat} = I_0 \exp(\kappa V_g - V_s)$ we write

$$I_1 = I_0 e^{\kappa V_1 - V} \qquad I_2 = I_0 e^{\kappa V_2 - V}$$

The sum of the two drain currents must be equal to I_B:

$$I_b = I_1 + I_2 = I_0 e^{-V}(e^{\kappa V_1} + e^{\kappa V_2})$$

We can solve this equation for the voltage V:

$$e^{-V} = \frac{I_b}{I_0} \frac{1}{e^{\kappa V_1} + e^{\kappa V_2}}$$

Substituting this into the equations for I_1 and I_2 we obtain an expression for the two drain currents

$$I_1 = I_b \frac{e^{\kappa V_1}}{e^{\kappa V_1} + e^{\kappa V_2}} \qquad I_2 = I_b \frac{e^{\kappa V_2}}{e^{\kappa V_1} + e^{\kappa V_2}}$$

Then we may take the difference between currents as

$$I_1 - I_2 = I_b \frac{e^{\kappa V_1} - e^{\kappa V_2}}{e^{\kappa V_1} + e^{\kappa V_2}}$$

By multiplying both the numerator and denominator by exp[-(***V1*** + ***V2***)/2] we get

$$I_1 - I_2 = I_b \tanh \frac{\kappa(V_1 - V_2)}{2}$$

The device is able to produce a *tanh* activation function. The differential amplifier is the primary component of Mead's neuron. Inputs are presented as voltage differences which ultimately produce output currents. By combining the differential amplifier and other simple analog circuits, Carver Mead is able to *economically* imitate neuron functions.

Reconfigurable CMOS Neural Network

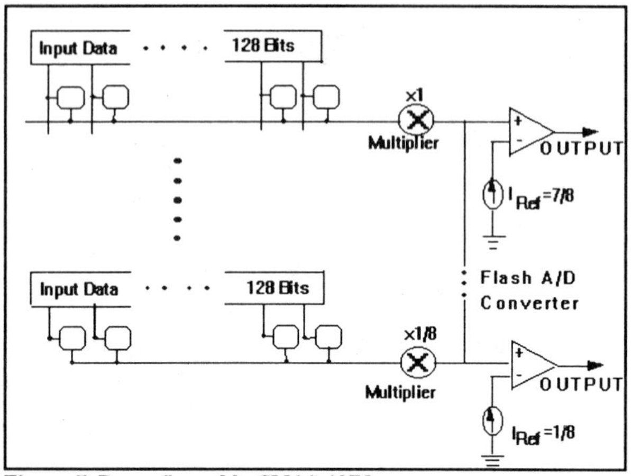

Figure 7. Reconfigurable CMOS ANN

An example of a mostly digital, virtual design is presented in the reconfigurable CMOS neural network chip described by H.P. Graf [8] (See figure 7). The chip provides 256 functional blocks to implement neurons, each of which has 128 binary inputs. The ternary weights (-1,0,1) are stored in 6-transistor cells and the multipliers are realized as inverted XORs. Graf calls these 'synaptic blocks', together these multiply the inputs by appropriate weights. The sum of products is then accumulated in an analog fashion. The resulting current is operated on by a subsequent multiplier and comparator. The additional multiplier is set to one of the values 1, 1/2, 1/4, or 1/8. Aside from the wire that connects the output of the partial products the comparator is the only analog unit, all other components are digital. This provides the flexibility of the chip. Reconfiguration is possible with regard to the number $\boldsymbol{B}$ (≤ 8) of synaptic blocks attributed to a neuron and the word width $\boldsymbol{W}$ (1 to 4 bits) of the input data. For example with $\boldsymbol{B} = 4$ and $\boldsymbol{W} = 1$ a neuron possesses 4x128 = 512 binary synapses and there are 256/4 = 64 such neurons implementable at single instant. Since the chips bus width is 128 bits, 4 clock cycles are necessary to present the 512 binary signals to the 64 neurons. If $\boldsymbol{B} = 4$ and $\boldsymbol{W} = 4$ had been chosen, a neuron would have 512 synapses each of which consist of 4 1-bit multipliers. Consequently the number of neurons would be cut to 64/4 = 16. The price of increasing precision is to reduce the number of neurons realizable in a single instant consequently driving up execution time.

Asynchronous Hybrid ANN Using Pulse Stream Arithmetic

As a final design example we investigate an interesting hybrid approach [7]. A.F. Murray has managed to combine the advantages of digitally stored weights with analog processing. This allows for the flexibility required for learning and the speed and accuracy afforded by analog devices.

Neurons may be viewed as signalling their states, $\mathbf{X}_j$, into a regular array of synapses (performing multiply-accumulate operations), which then gate these presynaptic states to increment or decrement the total activity of the receiving neuron. In a pulse stream implementation, a neuron is a switched oscillator. The level of accumulated activity is used to control the oscillator's firing rate. As a result, the neuron's output state, $\mathbf{X}_j$, is represented by a pulse frequency $\mathbf{v}_i$, such that for $\mathbf{x}_i=0$, $\mathbf{v}_i=0$, and for $\mathbf{x}_i=1$, $\mathbf{v}_i=\mathbf{v}_{max}$. Each synapse stores a weight, $\mathbf{w}_{ij}$, which is used to determine the proportion of the input pulse stream $\mathbf{v}_j$ that passes to the summation.

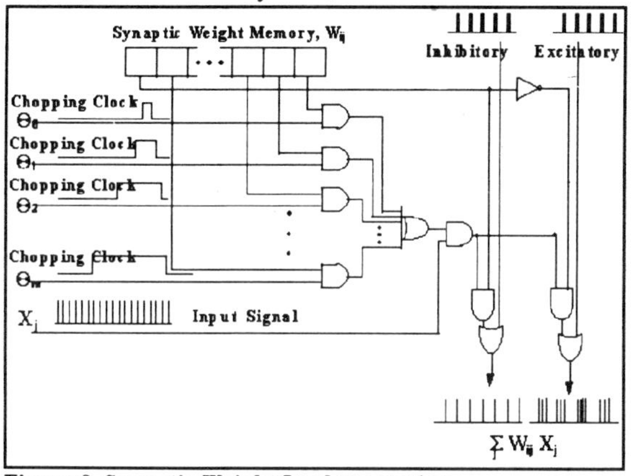

Figure 8. Synaptic Weight Implementation

The weighting is performed by several "chopping" clocks (asynchronous to all neural firing) which gate the pulse stream input, allowing only the appropriate fraction of the input pulses through (as determined by $\mathbf{w}_{ij}$). This is shown in figure 8. The output is then passed to the neuron block (figure 9) which integrates (sums) all of the incoming pulse stream signals and sinks or drains the activity capacitor's voltage as appropriate. The activity capacitor's voltage is used to drive the voltage-controlled ring oscillator which produces the neuron's output pulse stream.

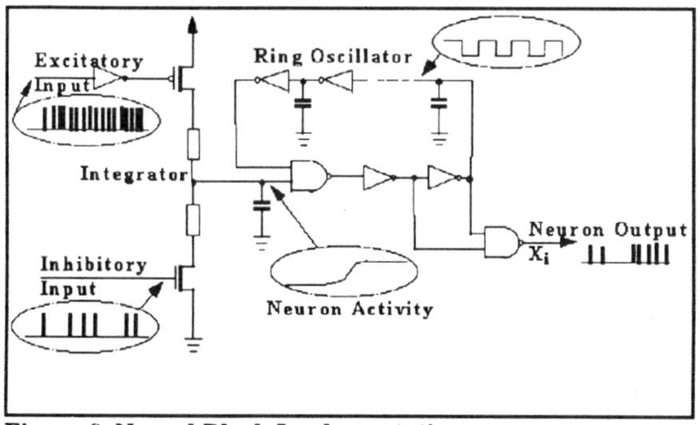

Figure 9. Neural Block Implementation

CONCLUSION

Several of the principal issues, challenges, and tradeoffs for the implementation of neural networks have been discussed. These include the question of analog vs. digital implementation, virtual vs. literal realizations, as well as speed and cost considerations in implementing a network. We have seen that there is a large range of possible implementation strategies, from simulation to literal physical imitation, each with its own strength and weaknesses. Ultimately, design tradeoffs will be made for the problem at hand. Several generalizations have been made which will hopefully help to filter the 'clutter' in the field. Hopefully the scientific community will continue to search for efficient neural network implementations: The potential rewards are very great.

REFERENCES

[1] R.P. Lippman, "An Introduction to Computing with Neural Nets", *IEEE ASSP Magazine*, April 1987, pp. 4-22

[2] Don R. Rush, "Progress in Supervised Neural Networks: What's New Since Lippman ?", *IEEE Signal Processing Magazine*, January 1993, pp. 8-39

[3] Philip D. Wasserman, *Neural Computing, Theory and Practice*, 1989, Van Nostrand Reinhold, New York.

[4] Carver A. Mead, *Analog VLSI and Neural Systems*, 1989, Addison-Wesley, Massachusetts.

[5] *Silicon Architectures for Neural Nets*, Ed. by M. Sami and J. Calzadilla-Daguerre, 1991, North-Holland, New York.

[6] Matthew S. Melton, "The TInMANN VLSI Chip", *IEEE Trans. on Neural Networks*, May 1992, pp. 375-383

[7] A.F. Murray, "Asynchronous VLSI Neural Networks Using Pulse-Stream Arithmetic", *Journal of Solid State Circuits*, June 1988, pp. 688-697

[8] H.P. Graf, "A Reconfigurable CMOS Neural Network", *Digest of Technical Papers of the Int. Solid State Circuits Conf.*, vol 33, pp. 144, San Francisco, February 1990

[9] Norbert Wiener, *Cybernetics*, 1986, MIT Press, Massachusetts.

[10] *Darpa Neural Network Study*, November 1988, AFCEA International Press

VLSI Neural Network Architectures

Ramalingam Sridhar and Yong-Chul Shin

Department of Electrical and Computer Engineering
The State University of New York at Buffalo
Buffalo, NY 14260

Abstract – VLSI architectures for neural networks is presented. Neural networks have wide-ranging applications in classification, control and optimization. With the need for real-time performance, VLSI neural networks have gained significant attention. Digital, analog and mixed-mode designs are used for this application. Modular and reconfigurable designs are necessary so that various neural network models can be easily configured.

Introduction

This tutorial presents the VLSI implementation aspects of various Neural Network Architectures. Artificial Neural Networks were modeled as simple computing elements with appropriate connection strength [1]. Many models have been developed over the years for the Neural Networks. These have wide ranging applications in Image classification, Fault detection, Various Image Processing operations including Character recognition, Prediction and in Optimization.

One of the drawbacks of the neural networks has been the extraordinary amount of time required for training the network and in the testing. Various faster models are being developed to overcome this problem. This is particularly needed because of the real-time requirement of many applications. In the recent past, there has been a number of efforts in the realization of these networks in VLSI to achieve faster and efficient use of the networks. These efforts include many digital and analog implementations of the synaptic weights and the neurons. In this tutorial, the strategies used in the implementation is presented. The analog or digital choices (which sometimes depends on the types of applications) will be discussed. Discussion of the design and use of reconfigurable neural network architecture is also presented. A simple compact design of an analog neural network is described. Issues on on-chip learning are discussed. An efficient and modular implementation of the second-order neural networks is developed using multi-dimensional weights.

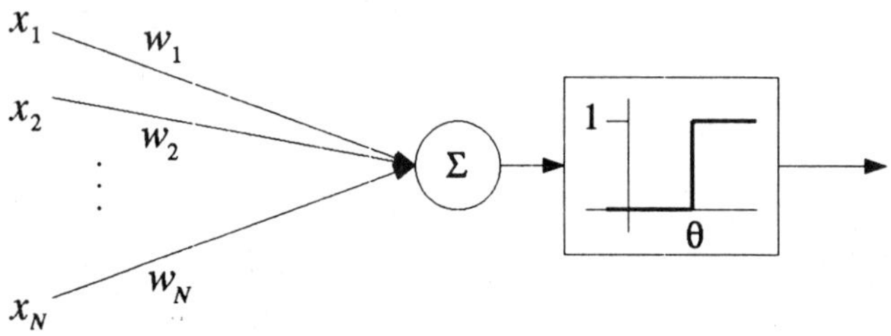

Figure 1: McCulloch and Pitts Neuron Model

Neural Network Models

The function of the first neuron model proposed by McCulloch and Pitts is to add up its inputs, and to produce an output, after the sum is compared to a value, known as the *threshold* value. The McCulloch and Pitts model is shown in Figure 1. The inputs to the neuron is fed through dendrites, which are connected to the outputs of other neurons by special junctions called *synapses.* These junctions change the effectiveness with which the signal is transmitted. Some junctions can pass through a large signal, while others allow very little flow. The neuron receives all these inputs, and fires if the total input exceeds the threshold value. The output of the neuron is either *on* or *off*. The efficiency of the synapse is modeled by a multiplicative factor on each of the inputs, which is called *weight.*

If there are N inputs to the neuron, there are N weights on the input lines. The total input to the neuron can be represented as

$$\begin{aligned} \text{total input} &= \text{weight on input } 1 \times \text{input } 1 + \\ &\quad\ \text{weight on input } 2 \times \text{input } 2 + \\ &\quad\ \cdots + \\ &\quad\ \text{weight on input } N \times \text{input } N \\ &= w_1 x_1 + w_2 x_2 + \cdots + w_N x_N \end{aligned}$$

0-7803-1375-5/93$03.00 © 1993 IEEE

$$= \sum_{i=1}^{N} w_i x_i.$$

This sum is compared to the threshold value of the neuron. If the sum is greater than the threshold value (often represented as θ), then the neuron outputs a "1". Otherwise, the output is "0". This thresholding operation can equivalently be stated that θ is subtracted from the sum, then compared to zero.

Alternatively, one can achieve the same effect by adding an extra input that has connected to a fixed value, "1". The weight between the fixed input and the neuron is defined as $-\theta$. The value of $-\theta$ is sometimes called *bias* or *offset* of the neuron. Both can be used interchangeably. The neuron output, z, can be represented as

$$z = H\left(\sum_{i=1}^{N} w_i x_i - \theta\right),$$

where H is a step function (or *Heaviside function*) and θ is a threshold. This can also be represented as

$$z = H\left(\sum_{i=0}^{N} w_i x_i\right),$$

where w_0 is $-\theta$ and $x_0 = 1$.

This simple model can be useful in the approximation of the underlying continuous processes in some special case of real neurons. However, the biological neurons, except in the special case, are not simple computing devices realizing the proportions of formal logic [2].

In 1949, Hebb postulated a learning process in the following way [3]. If the axon of an "input" neuron is close enough to excite a "target" neuron, and if it persistently takes part in firing the target neuron, some growth process takes place in one or both cells to increase the efficiency of the input neuron's stimulation. Synapses that behave according to this postulate became known as Hebb synapses [4]. Although it was only his speculation, this was the most clear and formal statement at that time [4].

Perhaps the first attempt to test the neural theory with computer simulation was presented by Rochester *et al.* in 1956 [5]. They made few changes to the simple model based on their test results. First, they incorporated *inhibition*: weights of synapses could range from [-1, +1], instead of [0, +1]. Secondly, the neuron model was modified: the output of a neuron was graded from 0 to 15, based on the activity measure of neuron represented as the average frequency of immediate past discharge [2]. The Hebb learning rule was also modified so that if the frequencies of pre- and post-synaptic activities were correlated, the weight of the synapse increased. This was a generalization of the Hebb synapse that is commonly used in many different forms.

In 1958, Rosenblatt proposed a set of new models called Perceptrons [6]. One of the simple perceptron consists of three layers of units based on his definition[1]. The units in the first layer called a retina on which the inputs are projected. The connections between the retina and the second layer of units called A-units (Association-units) form random local connectivity. The units at the third layer are called R-units (Response-units). The A-units and the R-units are connected reciprocally through the inhibitory or excitatory connections. The perceptron models lacked a proper efficient learning rule. One of the simple learning rules known as "self-organizing", reinforces the activities in A-units by activating the appropriate R-unit. Although the perceptrons had such a limitation, they had demonstrated the capability of generalization and could respond appropriately to patterns they had never seen before.

The limitation of the perceptron lies also in its generalization. Too much generalization gives a problem in classification. Although this was mentioned at the end of Rosenblatt's book, the study of computational limitations of perceptron was pointed by the book titled *Perceptrons* by Minsky and Papert in 1969, based on solid foundation [7].

In 1972, Kohonen [8] and Anderson [9] presented what has become known as *linear associator* model for associative memory. This is a generalization of both the perceptron used by Rosenblatt and the logical predicates used by Minsky and Papert, using a *linear* model of neuron. The learning rules proposed for both models of neuron networks are generalization of the Hebb synapse.

In most later research, however, the neuron model built on the linear associator has nonlinearities on large signal. One of the most common nonlinearity is *sigmoid* [10] [11] [12]. The sigmoid function is shown in Figure 2. At low and high activation levels, changes in activation produce small changes in output, while at intermediate level, changes in activation produce large changes in output. This reflects the limited dynamic range of a cell.

Backpropagation Training Method

In 1985 and 1986, a new learning rule called error back-propagation (or *backpropagation*, in short) [13] [14] [15] [16] was established and applied to multiple-layer networks as well as single-layer networks. The backpropagation method uses repetition of the chain rule for partial derivatives. The error is propagated through the network backward from the output layer, then to the *hidden layer* (if exists), and finally to the input layer.

[1] However, sometimes it is called two-layer network, since it has two set of connections between the units. This terminology is more often used than three-layer network. In this tutorial, such a network is called two-layer network.

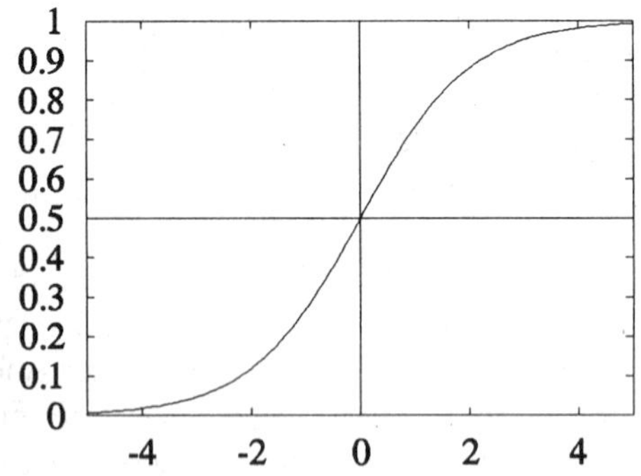

Figure 2: Sigmoid Function

The weights in each layer are modified by the learning process. It is noted that the algorithm was discovered independently in 1974 by Paul. J Werbos [17].

The following is a summary of the backpropagation method. The weighted net input to the jth neuron from N other neurons is

$$\text{net}_j = \sum_{i=0}^{N} w_{ij} x_i,$$

where w_{ij} denotes the synaptic weight connection from neuron i to neuron j. The output, x_j, of the jth neuron is obtained as

$$x_j = f_j(\text{net}_j) = \frac{1}{1 + e^{-\text{net}_j}},$$

where f_j is a sigmoid transfer function. The amount of weight update of a particular weight over the training should be

$$\Delta w_{ij} = \alpha\, \delta_j\, x_i,$$

where α is a learning rate. The δ_j is determined as follows. If the jth node is an output node, δ_j becomes

$$\delta_j = (t_j - x_j) f_j{}'(\text{net}_j),$$

where t_j is a target output for the jth neuron. If the jth neuron is a hidden neuron, then

$$\delta_j = f_j{}'(\text{net}_j) \sum_{k=1}^{K} \delta_k\, w_{jk},$$

where $k = 1, \cdots, K$ are indices of neurons to which the jth neuron is connected.

The training is based on error (or energy) function, $E = -1/2(t_j - x_j)^2$. This represents the amount by which the output of the network differs from the target output. Large differences correspond to large energies, while small differences correspond to small energies. Since the output of the network is related to the weights and inputs, the energy is a function of the weights and inputs. We can draw a graph of the energy function showing how varying the weights affects the energy for a fixed input pattern. If N weights are considered, the energy versus weights graphs form landscape in N space. If the landscape is simple, this training method can find the global minimum easily. In general, however, the local minima can trap the training and prevent it from reaching the deeper point.

To avoid the local minima and to improve the convergence time, an *inertia* (or momentum) can be added. The weight change equation is modified to include an inertia (γ) ranging from [0, +1) as

$$\Delta w_{ij}(t) = \alpha \delta_j(t) x_i(t) + \gamma \Delta w_{ij}(t-1).$$

Higher-Order Neural Networks

The network models discussed in the previous sections are referred to as linear networks in which the net input to the neuron is given by $\sum w_{ij} x_i$. Sometimes, however, two or more inputs are multiplied before entering the neuron resulting in higher-order neural networks. Hence the net input to a neuron of a higher-order neural network can be represented by

$$\sum_i w_{ij} x_{i_1} x_{i_2} \cdots x_{i_k} = \sum_i w_{ij} \prod_k x_{i_k},$$

which is called Sigma-Pi ($\sum - \prod$) Unit [14]. Such a multiplicative connection forms basis of the higher-order neural networks. The multiplications of inputs, such as $x_1 x_2 x_3$, are called *conjuncts*. The number of inputs in a conjunct is called a *the size of a conjunct*. Therefore, the size of the conjunct $x_1 x_2 x_3$ is three. If the size of conjunct is two, it can be shown that one input is to *gate* another. In other words, if an input is 1, the other input is passed to the neuron without any change. On the other hand, if an input is zero, the other input has no effect on the neuron, no matter how strong the input value is. The sigma-pi unit with arbitrary order can solve any classification problem [18]. However, the number of Pi-elements (multiplier) and the number of interconnections required increase considerably as the size of conjunct and the number of total inputs increase. Therefore, it is a non-trivial problem to find an efficient method for implementation of such a network in software as well as in hardware. If the size of the conjunct is limited to 2, the sigma-pi unit becomes the second-order neural network. A set of new network models that is presented in this tutorial is fundamentally different from the sigma-pi units, although it forms a subset of the second-order neural networks. In this tutorial, these non-fully configured neural networks are compared to the conventional fully configured second-order neural networks.

Other Neural Network Models

So far, we have restricted ourselves to *feedforward* networks. There are many other network configurations. In general, the network models can be classified into feedback or feedforward networks based on their connection schemes. Also, the networks can be classified into two categories based on the training method; (a) unsupervised model and (b) supervised model. Each model can be further classified into [19]:

- Unsupervised Models
  - Feedforward Associative Memory Model (Hamming Networks)
  - Feedback Associative Memory Model (Hopfield Networks)
  - Competitive Learning Networks (Self-organizing Feature Map)
- Supervised Models
  - Perceptron Networks
  - Multi-Layer Perceptron Networks

VLSI Architectures

In the recent past, special-purpose hardware has become available to replace the general processors that include microprocessors and digital signal processors for neural network implementation [20]. Hence, there has been a lot of research in the realization of neural networks in VLSI to achieve faster and efficient use of the networks. The effectiveness of a neural network algorithm mainly depends on the hardware that executes it. One obstacle to implementing neural network into hardware is its huge connectivity. A biological neuron is typically connected to several thousand other neurons. In order to implement the massive connectivity, neural network IC needs a large number of synaptic elements.

A major step in the hardware implementation of neural network is the design of interconnection weights as well as the neurons represented as a processing elements in most hardware design. The number of neurons which can be implemented on a chip is limited by the area required for the interconnections. Depending on the application requirements, fixed (resistive), digital or analog memory elements have been used [21]. Also some special methods have been applied such as the use of impulse dynamics [22].

If the function of a network is known in advance and there is no need to change the synaptic weight during operation, resistive weights give reasonable solution. An A/D converter based on neural network approach is a good example of resistive network [23]. The advantage of resistive weight is in its area efficiency. But in general, with standard CMOS process technology, it is hard to achieve precise value of resistance, and due to the fixed value, it loses adaptive features of the neural networks.

Currently, there are some digital and/or analog neural network hardware products available or announced as follows [20].

- Connected Network of Adaptive Processors (CNAPS), by Adaptive Solutions, Inc.
- Analog Neural Network Architecture (ANNA), by AT&T Bell Lab.
- Electrically Trainable Analog Neural Network (Etann), by Intel Corp.
- Ni1000, by Nestor Inc.
- SIMD Neurocomputer Array Processor (SNAP), by HNC
- NR-200, yy Richo
- MA-16, by Siemens Corp.

Analog Implementation: Most learning techniques require several bits of weight resolution (adjustable steps of weight value) which needs considerable circuitry and is difficult to implement in a small area. For these requirements and the massive connectivity, an analog approach is area efficient over the digital implementation with a moderate resolution.

For the same functionality, analog basic cells are much smaller than those of digital neural networks. Among the analog approaches, one method is to use MOS capacitor as storage device where amount of charge stored in the capacitor represents continuous value of synaptic weight [24]. But in a single capacitor approach with standard processing technology, precision of the weight cannot be guaranteed due to leakage current through substrate unless there are refreshing cycles to compensate. Precise CMOS capacitors can be obtained by special processes but result in significant increase in the cost. Use of two capacitors can solve this problem, which however, needs additional circuitry to detect the voltage difference between the capacitors as well as for refreshing cycles unless the system is constantly adapting [24]. Yet another digital and analog approach uses RAM cells for the storage and uses analog circuitry for converting stored weights to proportional amount of current [25]. The floating gate MOSFET has received a lot of attention in analog implementations. One drawback is that it needs a special processing technique to obtain ultra thin oxide between floating gate and control gate [26] [27] [28]. Recently, Thomsen and Brooke proposed a layout technique which enables tunneling effect with the 2-μm double-polysilicon CMOS process through MOSIS [29]. Also similar technique which utilizes bump area between overlapped polysilicon 1 and polysilicon 2 to enhance the electric field has been reported by Lee *et al.* [30].

Analog Synapse: Some of the properties required of an analog synaptic element can be summarized as follows.

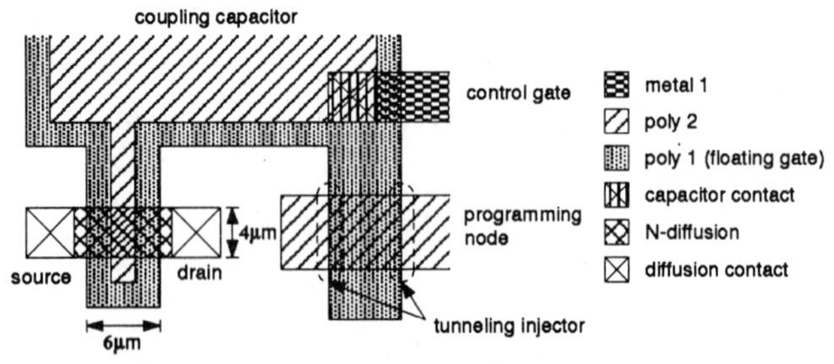

Figure 3: A Floating-Gate MOSFET.

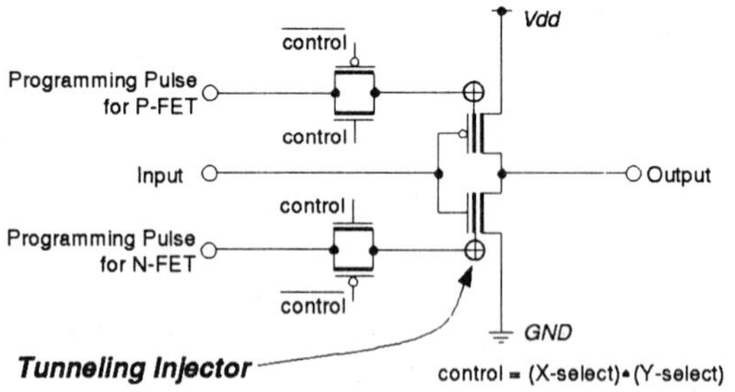

Figure 4: Synapse Architecture.

- Massive connectivity: small geometry of synaptic element
- Fine control over the synaptic weight: small weight change Δw
- Adaptiveness: programmability of many writing and/or erasings

To implement an analog synapse with these properties, a complementary floating-gate MOSFET pair with individual programmability of P-transistor and N-transistor has been developed [31]. The structure of the synaptic element is similar to that of a conventional inverter and it has a small geometry. Programming of the floating-gate MOSFET is performed using tunneling effect on both P and N-transistors independently. Weight change Δw is controlled by the amplitude and the duration of the programming pulse. Therefore, finer control of synaptic weight is possible. The analog synapse has been fabricated by the double-polysilicon CMOS process through MOSIS. Figure 3 shows the structure of the floating-gate. Fully connected array implementation of the analog synapse is also shown.

The floating gate MOSFET acts as a non-volatile storage cell and the electrical charge on the floating gate represents a connection weight. It has been reported that tunneling electrons into the floating gate shifts the threshold voltage V_{th} of the connection transistor [29]. Tunneling effect can be achieved by applying a programming pulse. The amplitude and the duration of the programming pulse determines the amount of charge injected and in turn the threshold voltage shift(ΔV_{th}). The voltage shift is

$$\Delta V_{\text{th}} = \frac{\Delta Q}{C_f},$$

where ΔQ is the injected charge due to Fowler-Nordheim tunneling [32] and C_f is the capacitance between the floating gate and the control gate. The effective gate input voltage $V_{G\text{eff}}$ is

$$V_{G\text{eff}} = V_G - V_{\text{th}0} + \Delta V_{\text{th}},$$

where V_G is the control gate input voltage and $V_{\text{th}0}$ is the initial threshold voltage before programming. The amount of drain current of a transistor can be controlled by the effective gate input voltage. The synapse uses two P-type and N-type floating gate MOSFETs as shown in Figure 4. Hence output current of a synapse, I_d is

$$I_d = I_{dp} - I_{dn},$$

where I_{dp} and I_{dn} are the drain currents of the P-transistor and the N-transistor, respectively.

Since floating gate of either P-type or N-type MOSFET is programmed separately with different duration of programming pulses, finer control of the output current can be achieved.

Digital Implementation: In spite of the area efficiency of analog circuits in realizing neural networks, they are prone to problems like noise, offsets and gain errors, arising due to device mismatches and inaccuracies in device models [33]. Digital design technologies have been well studied and hence provide stable means for neural network hardware design. Digital circuits are especially suitable for large-scale neural networks, since they do not require high-precision components and they are less affected by electrical noise than analog circuits [34]. The existing digital design technology can be used without much efforts. Digital wafer-scale integration has also been used for implementation of neural networks [34]. The conventional DRAM cells can be used for the storage elements and a million synapses have been integrated on a single chip [35]. Also, testability is an advantage of the digital design over the analog design. The issues on testability in the analog design has not been studied rigorously.

Reconfigurability

The need to have a reconfigurable network topology was realized by many researchers [33] [36] [37]. Due to the variety of neural network architectures that need to be considered, reconfigurable implementation of a neural network has advantage over a fixed design. Reconfigurability is defined as the ability to alter the topology of the neural network [33]. In [33], reconfiguration switches inserted in the interconnection between synapses and neurons allows one to change the network topology. In [36] and [37], linear systolic array (also called toroid) is used. These networks have been used for feedforward networks with arbitrary number of layers and hidden units or feedback networks such as Hopfield Networks.

On-Chip Learning

In general, the operation of the multi-layer feedforward networks can be characterized by two phases: feedforward and feedbackward. During the feedforward phase, the network receives a set of inputs and produces a set of output values that is determined by the inputs and the weights. During the feedbackward phase, the network outputs are evaluated against the target outputs. The errors are propagated backward from the output to the input and the weights are changed accordingly, if the network employs a typical backpropagation training method. Hence, the backward phase is also called a training or learning phase. Learning capability is a fundamental aspect of artificial neural networks. The on-chip learning allows high speed training and hence the real-time application where continuous training is required can be exploited.

Prior to the implementation of the on-chip learning capability in VLSI, one may have to decide the network topologies and the training methods to use in the application. The design complexity of the neurons, the synapses, the interconnection and the control logic is dependent on the required on-chip learning capability.

Example Architecture

In this section, example architectures on various network configurations are presented.

Associative Memory: Biological information processing systems outperform modern digital machines in problems that require processing large amounts of fuzzy, noisy, real-world data, such as pattern recognition and classification. One of the such a biological paradigm is the associative memory [8] [9]. In general, the basic operation of an associative memory is a certain mapping between two finite sets A and B at the input and the output layers, respectively. In the *store* mode, the current state of each layer is stored, forming the association of (A, B). In the *recall* mode, the network converges to the stored state (A, B) nearest to its initial state (X, Y) [38].

The important aspect for VLSI implementation of the associative memory model is the close relationship to conventional memory structure. Based on the network model of the associative memory, single-instruction-multiple-data (SIMD) architecture is a promising compromise between flexible modeling and a complete parallel processing of large network [38].

Toroidal Architecture: The toroidal architecture is also called the linear systolic array architecture. This

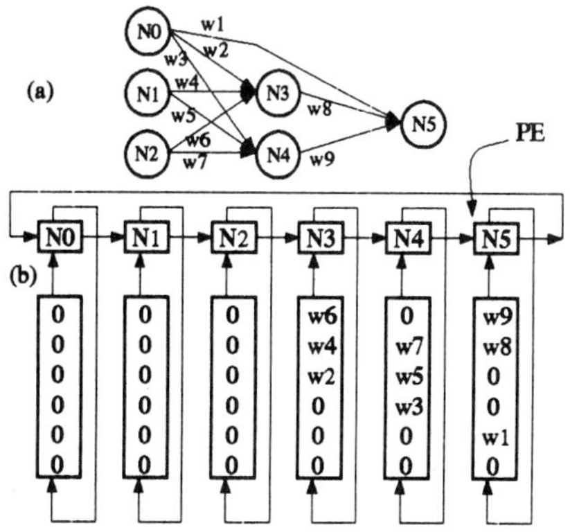

Figure 5: Typical Use of the Linear Systolic Array for the Implementation of Conventional Linear 2-2-1 Network

was developed to compute the matrix-vector multiplication in parallel [39] with modular structure and hence high-concurrency. Since the computation involved in neural networks can be characterized by a set of multiplications of weight matrices and input vectors, the toroidal architecture can efficiently achieve the desired parallelism in the application to the neural network computations.

The typical use of toroidal architecture in neural networks is briefly explained in Figure 5. The linear systolic array configuration shown in the figure represents a network that implements a conventional linear 2-2-1 (2-input, 2-hidden and one output) network.

Self-Timed Architecture: It has been attempted to implement self-timed asynchronous neural networks [36]. The operations of self-timed circuits are determined by their average processing times rather than their worst case as in synchronous circuits. Hence a high speed processing can be obtained. Also, large scale synchronous neural networks have shown problems in clock loading and current spikes. Using the self-timed circuits avoids the clock loading and distribution problems. Although the self-timed architectures have advantages over the synchronous design, the interface to the memory elements that require synchronous operation is an issue to be investigated further [36].

Non-Fully Configured Quadratic NN

In general, it is a non-trivial problem to implement the quadratic (or second-order) networks in VLSI, due to global interconnection problem. Hence the implementation of these neural networks has not been investigated vigorously. This section presents issues related to the network configurations and training speeds of the various quadratic neural networks. This section summarizes the work by authors [40] [41] [42]. A complete set of novel network configurations developed [42] using multi-dimensional weights is presented, that not only speeds up training, but also simplifies the VLSI architecture.

The output of a neuron, z, of conventional second-order neural networks can be described as

$$z = s\left(W_0 + \sum_{j=1}^{n} W_j x_j + \sum_{j,k=1}^{n} T_{jk} x_j x_k\right),$$

where s is a sigmoid transfer function, W_0 is an offset term, W_j is weight for first-order input, T_{jk} is weight for second-order input [43] [44] [45]. The weights in conventional neural networks are defined as scalar values. In contrast, the proposed second-order network uses multi-dimensional vectors in addition to the scalar weights. The output of a neuron in layer k is represented as a vector $\mathbf{z}^k = [z_1^k\, z_2^k \cdots z_N^k]^T$. The output $\mathbf{z}^k$ is fed to the layer l as an input vector $\mathbf{x}^l = [z_1^k\, z_2^k \cdots z_N^k]^T = [x_1^l\, x_2^l \cdots x_N^l]^T$. Considering a bias as a part of the weight, $\mathbf{X}^l$ is defined as $[1\; x_1^l\, x_2^l \cdots x_N^l]^T$, where 1 is a fixed input. The weight $\mathbf{w}_{k_n l_p}$ determines the connection strength from the n-th neuron of the k-th layer to the p-th neuron of the l-th layer and is defined as

$$\mathbf{w}_{k_n l_p} = [w^0_{k_n l_p}, w^1_{k_n l_p}, w^2_{k_n l_p}, \cdots, w^R_{k_n l_p}]^T.$$

If only one output neuron is in consideration, we will ignore the unnecessary subscripts and superscripts. Hence, we will denote the weights as $\mathbf{w}_n$. For simplicity, the inputs are represented as $\mathbf{X} = [1\; x_1\, x_2 \cdots x_N]^T$. Similarly, the output is denoted as y and defined by $g(\text{net})$, where *net* is a net input to the neuron and g is a conventional sigmoid function. Now, the weight $\mathbf{w}_n$ is represented as combination of scalar and multi-dimensional vector as

$$\overbrace{w_n^0}^{\text{scalar}},\ \underbrace{w_n^1,\ w_n^2,\ \cdots,\ w_n^R,}_{R\text{-dimensional vector}}$$

where $R \leq N$. Each input is multiplied by the weight and the resulting value is a combination of scalar and vector. Since the input and the output of the network is defined as scalar, a mapping from vector space to scalar space is required and defined by the square of the magnitude of the vector sum. Hence the net input to the output neuron is defined as

$$\begin{aligned} \text{net} \;=\; & (w_0^0 + w_1^0 x_1 + w_2^0 x_2 + \cdots w_N^0 x_N) + \\ & (w_0^1 + w_1^1 x_1 + w_2^1 x_2 + \cdots w_N^1 x_N)^2 + \\ & (w_0^2 + w_1^2 x_1 + w_2^2 x_2 + \cdots w_N^2 x_N)^2 + \\ & \cdots \\ & (w_0^R + w_1^R x_1 + w_2^R x_2 + \cdots w_N^R x_N)^2. \quad (1) \end{aligned}$$

As shown in (1), it is noted that the *net* input can be alternatively represented by a linear summation (the first line of the equation) and multiple use of square of the linear summation (the rest R lines of the equation). This indicates that a linear summation is a basis of the proposed network configuration. A complete set of the proposed network configurations are listed in Table 1. The backpropagation method was used to train various non-fully configured quadratic neural networks with Aspirin/Migraines [46] with minor modifications.

Table 1: Non-Fully Configured Quadratic Neural Networks

rank1	$w_0^0 + \left(w_0^1 + \sum_{i=1}^{N} w_i^1 x_i\right)^2$
⋮	
rank$R$	$w_0^0 + \sum_{r=1}^{R}\left(w_0^r + \sum_{i=1}^{N} w_i^r x_i\right)^2$
lank1	$\left(w_0^0 + \sum_{i=1}^{N} w_i^0 x_i\right) + \left(w_0^1 + \sum_{i=1}^{N} w_i^1 x_i\right)^2$
⋮	
lank$R$	$\left(w_0^0 + \sum_{i=1}^{N} w_i^0 x_i\right) + \sum_{r=1}^{R}\left(w_0^r + \sum_{i=1}^{N} w_i^r x_i\right)^2$

$R \leq N$, where N is the number of inputs

Significance of the Work: Based on the results obtained through an exhaustive tests for all the possible 256 3-input functions [42], it has been noted that the proposed network configurations can be trained much faster than the conventional linear or quadratic networks by the same backpropagation method for solving linear separable functions as well as quadratic separable functions.

Also, with the proposed network configurations, network designer can have more choices to choose from. For a given problem, one can find an optimum network by exploring various configurations. If an actual implementation is in consideration such as in VLSI, the comparison should take into account the complexity of each component and the routing.

There is an advantage of the **rank$n$** or the **lank$n$** networks over the conventional quadratic network. These networks have modular structure of $(a_0 + a_1 x_1 + \cdots + a_N x_N)$ that forms the basis of the conventional linear networks. Therefore, highly utilizable modular structure can be obtained for the second-order networks using the existing hardware technology developed for the conventional linear networks [47].

Discussion: It has been established that there is a topological equivalence between the non-fully configured and the conventional quadratic equations for a give problem [42]. In many applications, it has been noted that the dimension of vector component, R, can be $1 \leq R \ll N$. For example, 2-dimensional vector weights have been used for handwritten digit recognition problem using a two-layer network with 16 x 16 inputs, 5 x 5 hidden units and 10 outputs [42]. The training has been done within 18 epochs and a success rate of 94.99% has been obtained with another set of test data different from training set. A conventional linear network with the same configuration was compared with and the training took 125 epochs with a success rate of 93.95%.

Another difference between the non-fully configured and the conventional quadratic network in implementation is summarized in Table 2. The table compares the networks for single-layer configuration with N inputs and M outputs. R is the dimension of weights.

Figure 6 shows the difference in the configurations in implementing a 3-input 1-output network in (a) the conventional quadratic structure and (b) in the proposed structure of **lank3**. Although the figure visualizes the differences very well, the actual design complexity is dependent on the complexity of each component, the connection strategies and the network architecture chosen.

Conclusion

In summary, various neural networks and VLSI architectures were presented. Reconfigurability, on-chip learning, analog and digital design aspects are dominant issues in the design of specialized neural network processors. Neural network ASICs are expected to play an important role in the future.

References

[1] W. S. McCulloch and W. Pitts, "A Logical Calculus of the Ideas Immanent in Nervous Activity," *Bulletin of Mathematical Biophysics*, vol. 5, pp. 115–133, 1943.

[2] J. A. Anderson and E. Rosenfeld, *Neurocomputing: Foundations of Research.* The MIT Press, 1988.

[3] D. O. Hebb, *The Organization of Behavior*, ch. 4, pp. 60–78. New York, NY: Wiley, 1949.

[4] P. M. Milner, "The Mind and Donald O. Hebb," *Scientific American*, vol. 268, pp. 124–129, January 1993.

[5] N. Rochester, J. H. Holland, L. H. Haibt, and W. L. Duda, "Tests on a Cell Assembly Theory of the Action of the Brain, using a Large Digital Computer," *IRE Transactions on Information Theory*, vol. IT-2, pp. 80–93, 1956.

[6] F. Rosenblatt, "The perceptron: a probabilistic model for information storage and organization in the brain," *Psychological Review*, vol. 65, pp. 386–408, 1958.

[7] M. Minsky and S. Papert, *Perceptrons: An Introduction to Computational Geometry.* Cambridge, MA: The MIT Press, 1969.

[8] T. Kohonen, "Correlation Matrix Memories," *IEEE Transactions on Computers*, vol. C-21, pp. 353–359, 1972.

[9] J. A. Anderson, "A Simple Neural Network Generating an Interactive Memory," *Mathematical Biosciences*, vol. 14, pp. 197–220, 1972.

[10] S. Grossberg, "Adaptive Pattern Classification and Universal Recoding: I. – Parallel Development and Coding of Neural Feature Detectors," *Biological Cybernetics*, vol. 23, pp. 121–134, 1976.

[11] J. L. McClelland and D. E. Rumelhart, "An Interactive Activation Model of Context Effects in Letter Perception: Part 1," *Psychological Review*, vol. 88, pp. 375–407, 1981.

[12] J. J. Hopfield, "Neural Networks and Physical Systems with Emergent Collective Computational Abilities," *Proceedings of the National Academy of Sciences*, vol. 79, pp. 2554–2558, 1982.

[13] D. Parker, "Learning logic," tech. rep., Center for-Computational Research in Economics and Management Science, MIT, Cambridge, MA, 1985.

[14] D. E. Rumelhart, G. E. Hinton, and R. J. Williams, "Learning Internal Representations by Error Propagation," *Parallel Distributed Processing: Explorations in the Microstructure of Cognition,* vol. 1, ch. 8, pp. 318–362, Cambridge, MA: The MIT Press, 1986.

[15] D. E. Rumelhart, G. E. Hinton, and R. J. Williams, "Learning Representation by Back-Propagating Errors," *Nature*, vol. 323, pp. 533–536, 1986.

[16] Y. LeCun, "Learning processes in an asymmetric threshold network," in *Disordered Systems and Biological Organization* (E. Bienenstock, F. F. Souli, and G. Weibuch, eds.), (Berlin, Springer), 1986.

[17] P. J. Werbos, *Beyond Regression: New Tools for Prediction and Analysis in the Behavioral Sciences.* PhD thesis, Harvard University, Cambridge, MA, 1974.

[18] D. E. Rumelhart and J. McClelland, *Parallel Distributed Processing: Explorations in the Microstructure of Cognition.* Cambridge, MA: The MIT Press, 1986.

Table 2: Configuration Details per Layer with N-Inputs and M-Outputs.

	# of weights and biases	# of fixed connections	# of input multipliers	# of square sum	# of linear sum
Conventional	$M(N^2+N+1)$	$N(2N-1)$	N^2	0	1
Proposed	$M(R+1)(N+1)$	$R+1$	0	R	2

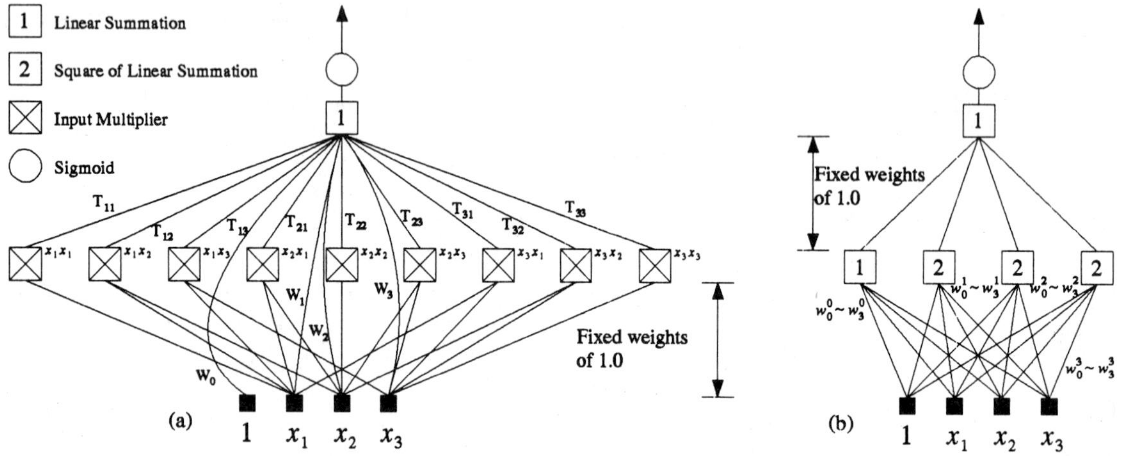

Figure 6: Example Showing the Network Configurations of a 3-input 1-output network implemented in (a) Conventional Quadratic Network and (b) Proposed Second-Order Networks **lank3**

[19] S. Y. Kung, *Digital Neural Networks.* Englewood Cliffs, NJ: Prentice Hall, 1993.

[20] D. Hammerstrom, "Neural Networks at Work," *IEEE Spectrum*, pp. 26–32, June 1993.

[21] H. P. Graf and L. D. Jackel, "VLSI Implementations of Neural Network Models," in *Concurrent computing* (S. K. Tewksbury *et al.*, ed.), (New York, NY), pp. 33–46, Plenum, 1988.

[22] Jack L. Meador and Angus Wu and Novat Nintunze and Pichet Chintrakulchai, "Programmable Impulse Neural Circuits," *IEEE Transaction on Neural Networks*, vol. 2, pp. 101–109, January 1991.

[23] B. W. Lee and B. J. Sheu, "Design of a Neural-Based A/D Converter Using Modified Hopfield Network," *IEEE Journal of Solid-State Circuits*, vol. 24, pp. 1129–1135, August 1989.

[24] D. B. Schwartz, R. E. Howard, and W. E. Hubbard, "A Programmable Analog Neural Network Chip," *IEEE Journal of Solid-State Circuits*, vol. 24, pp. 313–319, April 1989.

[25] P. W. Hollis and J. J. Paulos, "Aritificial Neural Networks Using MOS Analog Multipliers," *IEEE Journal of Solid-State Circuits*, vol. 25, pp. 849–855, June 1990.

[26] E. Säckinger and W. Guggenbuehl, "An Analog Trimming Circuit based on a Floating-gate Device," *IEEE Journal of Solid State Circuits*, vol. 23, pp. 1437–1440, December 1989.

[27] M. Holler, S. Tam, H. Castro, and R. Benson, "An electrically trainable artificial neural network(ETANN) with 10240 floating gate synapses ," in *Proceedings of IJCNN*, vol. II, (Washington, D.C.), pp. 191–196, June 1989.

[28] T. C. Ong, P. K. Ko, and C. Hu, "The EEPROM as an analog memory device," *IEEE Transaction on Electron Devices*, vol. 36, pp. 1840–1841, September 1989.

[29] A. Thomsen and M. A. Brooke, "A Floating-Gate MOSFET with Tunneling Injector Fabricated Using a Standard Double-Polysilicon CMOS Process ," *IEEE Electron Device Letters*, vol. 12, pp. 111–113, March 1991.

[30] B. W. Lee, B. J. Sheu, and H. Yang, "Analog Floating-Gate Synapses for General-Purpose VLSI Neural Computation," *IEEE Transactions on Circuits and Systems*, vol. 38, pp. 654–658, June 1991.

[31] S. Kim, Y.-C. Shin, N. R. C. Bogineni, and R. Sridhar, "A Programmable Analog CMOS Synapse for

Neural Network," *Journal Analog Integrated Circuits and Signal Processing*, vol. 2, pp. 345–352, 1992.

[32] Z. A. Weinberg, "On Tunneling in Metal-Oxide-Silicon Structures," *Journal of Applied Physics*, vol. 53, pp. 5052–5056, July 1982.

[33] S. Satyanarayana, Y. P. Tsividis, and H. P. Graf, "A Reconfigurable VLSI Network," *IEEE Journal of Solid-State Circuits*, vol. 27, January 1992.

[34] M. Yasunaga, N. Masuda, M. Yagyu, M. Asai, K. Shibata, M. Ooyama, M. Yamada, T. Sakaguchi, and M. Hashimoto, "A Self-Learning Digit Neural Networks Using Wafer-Scale LSI," *IEEE Journal of Solid-State Circuits*, vol. 28, pp. 106–114, February 1993.

[35] T. Watanabe, K. Kimura, M. Aoki, T. Sakata, and K. Ito, "A Single 1.5-V Digital Chip for a 10^6 Synapse Neural Network," *IEEE Tr. on Neural Networks*, vol. 4, pp. 387–393, May 1993.

[36] S. Jones, K. Sammut, C. Nielsend, and J. Staunstrup, "Toroidal Neural Networks: Architecture and Process Granularity Issues," in *VLSI Design of Neural Networks* (U. Ramacher and U. Rückert, eds.), (Boston, MA), pp. 229–254, Kluwer Academic Publishers, 1991.

[37] P. Y. Alla, G. Dreyfus, J. D. Gascuel, A. Johannet, L. Personnaz, J. Roman, and M. Weinfeld, "Silicon Integration of Learning Algorithms and Other Auto-Adaptive Properties in a Digital Feedforward Network," in *VLSI Design of Neural Networks* (U. Ramacher and U. Rückert, eds.), (Boston, MA), pp. 168–186, Kluwer Academic Publishers, 1991.

[38] U. Rückert, "VLSI Design of an Associative Memory based on Distributed Storage of Information," in *VLSI Design of Neural Networks* (U. Ramacher and U. Rückert, eds.), (Boston, MA), pp. 153–168, Kluwer Academic Publishers, 1991.

[39] C. Mead and L. Conway, *Introduction to VLSI systems*. Readng, Mass.: Addison - Wesley, 1980.

[40] Y.-C. Shin and R. Sridhar, "Artificial Neural Network with Complex Weight and Its Training," in *1992 RNNS/IEEE Symposium on Neuroinformatics and Neurocomputing, Rostov-on-Don, Russia*, vol. 1, pp. 354–361, 1992.

[41] Y.-C. Shin and R. Sridhar, "Network Configurations and Training Speeds of Second-Order Neural Networks," in *World Congress on Neural Networks*, 1993.

[42] Y.-C. Shin, *Non-Fully Configured Second-Order Neural Networks using Multi-Dimensional Weights*. PhD thesis, The State University of New York at Buffalo, June 1993.

[43] C. L. Giles and T. Maxwell, "Learning, Invariance, and Generalization in Higher-Order Neural Networks," *Applied Optics*, vol. 26, pp. 4972–4978, 1987.

[44] D. Psaltis, C. H. Park, and J. Hong, "Higher Order Associative Memories and Their Optical Implementations," *Neural Networks*, vol. 1, pp. 149–163, 1988.

[45] T. Maxwell, C. L. Giles, Y. C. Lee, and H. H. Chen, "Nonlinear Dynamics of Artificial Neural Systems," in *AIP Conference Proceedings, Neural Networks for Computing* (J. S. Denker, ed.), pp. 299–304, 1986.

[46] R. R. Leighton, *The Aspirin/MIGRAINES Software Tools*, 1991.

[47] U. Ramacher and U. Rückert, eds., *VLSI Design of Neural Networks*. Boston, MA: Kluwer Academic Publishers, 1991.

A Neural Processing Node with On-Chip Learning

James Donald and Lex A. Akers
Center for Solid State Electronics Research
Arizona State University
Tempe, AZ 85287-6206

Abstract:-Real-time control requires adaptive, analog VLSI chips. We describe the design and test results of an adaptive analog processing chip. These chips use pulse coded signals for communication between processing nodes and analog weights for information storage. The adaptive rule is implemented on chip. Experimental results demonstrate that the network produces unsupervised linearly separable outputs that correspond to dominant features of the inputs.

I. INTRODUCTION

Many applications exist for real-time control systems that can adapt to changing control environments. Neural networks can provide solutions for some of these applications. Several researchers have simulated the performance of neural network control systems using various types of input-output mapping units [1,2]. These systems use multi-layers of neurons with various learning rules that modify the weights to reduce error in the output. Our application interest is real-time adaptive control. Therefore, we are concentrating on the VLSI implementation of an adaptable processing node.

An adaptive system must continuously adjust to the nonstationary statistics provided by the controlled environment. To maintain an optimal representation of the input requires a leaning rule that continuously adapts through weight modification. We implement a variation of the weight modification rule proposed by Oja [3]. Oja rule extracts the principle components of the input vector, and uses negative feedback to control the magnitude of the weights. We combined our rule with a variable lateral inhibition mechanism which forces each node to extract a different feature from the inputs while learning. The learning rule in the processing node is unsupervised and these nodes act as a pre-processing stage to a supervised neural network. Rows of such nodes reduce the dimension of the inputs while generating efficient representations for additional processing in later layers.

II. DIMENSIONAL REDUCTION LAYER

The dimensional reduction layer consists of 3 parts: feed-forward, learning rule, and inhibition. In our system, the dimensional reduction layer performs a linear sum-of-products computation. Nonlinearities producing a decision are provided by the next processing layer. The problem of inter-processor communication is addressed using digital pulses. Pulse coded information allows both robust information transfer and space efficient computation [4]. Inputs and outputs of a processing node are represented by a sequence of pulses. Analog inputs have values proportional to the duration of the pulse divided by the period between pulses. Additional details and circuit diagrams may be found in Ref [5].

A. Feed-forward

The feed-forward function in most synthetic neural systems consists of a sum of products between an input vector and weight vector. This provides a measure of the match between the weight vectors and input. Summation of the product of the weight and input occurs by injecting a current, proportional to the synaptic weight, into a summing node for the duration of each input pulse. The summing node receives the current produced by a complete row of synapses producing summation through Kirchhoff's current law. An integrating capacitor converts the current pulses to a voltage change at the summing node. The neuron output function compares the voltage on the summing node to a threshold voltage and produces an active high digital output if the threshold voltage is exceeded. The output increases the summing node voltage by positive feedback while a current sink discharges the summing node to the threshold voltage.

B. Learning Algorithm

We implement a modified unsupervised learning algorithm using concepts developed by Oja [3] to determine the change in the weights to best represent the input statistics. For a single synapse element, Oja's weight modification rule is:

$$w_i(t+\tau)=w_i(t)+\lambda\, y(t)(x_i(t)-y(t)\,w_i(t)) \quad (1)$$

where, $x_i(t)$ is the input, $w_i(t)$ is the weight, $y(t)$ is the output from the linear sum of products function, and λ is the learning rate or weight increment size.

One of the main advantages of Oja's weight modification rule is the utilization of feedback from the neuron output to normalize the weights. This has several significant advantages in a VLSI hardware implementation. First, if the system is stable, the weight equilibrium is independent of the weight increment size (λ). Second, negative feedback reduces the effects of nonlinearities in the weight to output transfer-function resulting from the implementation. We take advantage of

0-7803-1254-6/93$03.00 © 1993 IEEE

the insensitivity to the forward weight transfer function to simplify circuit design and allow continuous adaptation.

The weight modification circuit operates as follows. The weight update is calculated in two stages. The argument (x - yw) is calculated by using pulses to enable current sources to charge and discharge the statistical sampling capacitor. The charging is proportional to x, and the discharging is proportional to yw. Then, a switch capacitor system produces the multiplication of the output, y, with the argument (x - yw).

We use a switched capacitor approach to calculate the final multiplication. This allows us to use pulse computation to simplify the design. During the learning phase, each output pulse transfers charge from the statistical sampling capacitor to a weight capacitor. The size of charge transfer must be as small as possible so the time constant of the weight filter is as long as possible (λ small). Since y is proportional to output pulse frequency, when the output operates in the linear region, the output can be used to set the frequency of the switched capacitor system.

C. Inhibition

An array of neurons using a modified Hebbian weight modification rule requires a mechanism to force each neuron to extract a different feature from the inputs. We use a variable lateral inhibition mechanism to force the outputs to be uncorrelated during learning and allow overlap between outputs during recall.

Pulse computation allows a simplified inhibition circuit. Our lateral inhibition circuit uses a global wire-or signal and a gate circuit to allow the neuron with the greatest sum of products to inhibit all other neurons in the array without inhibiting itself. This inhibition occurs only during the high output pulse of the active neuron. When the output pulse is high it resets all nonfiring neuron summing node voltages to the inhibition voltage. After the active neuron's pulse occurs, synapses attached to each neuron charge the summing node capacitor at a rate that depends on the sum of products between the weights and inputs.

III. EXPERIMENTAL RESULTS

Tests of the chip presented here show how an array of these processing elements extract important features from continuous time signals. Figure 1 shows the test fixture used. Four second-order bandpass filters, with a center frequency of 23, 59, 159, and 408 Hz, generate four training waveforms from a single periodic triangle wave input. The positive part of these four training waveforms control the frequency of the four pulse generators that supply inputs to the chip. To allow our digital oscilloscope to record pules at the inputs and outputs of the chip, the pulses were averaged with a 8 kHz lowpass filter. This provides a signal that was proportional to the pulse density. Figures 2 and 3 show the triangle generator waveform and the four resulting waveforms as measured from the low-pass filter. Note the relative positions of the two inputs from the higher frequency bandpass filters. To generate the output waveforms shown in Figs. 4 and 5, the synaptic weights were first set to nearly equal values and learning was enabled. Figure 4 shows the outputs when learning inputs from Fig. 3, and Fig. 5 shows the outputs when learning inputs from Fig. 2. Figure 6 shows the output when the network was first trained with the inputs from Fig. 2 and the inputs were changed to those of Fig. 3. This shows how the network adapts to varying statistics in the inputs.

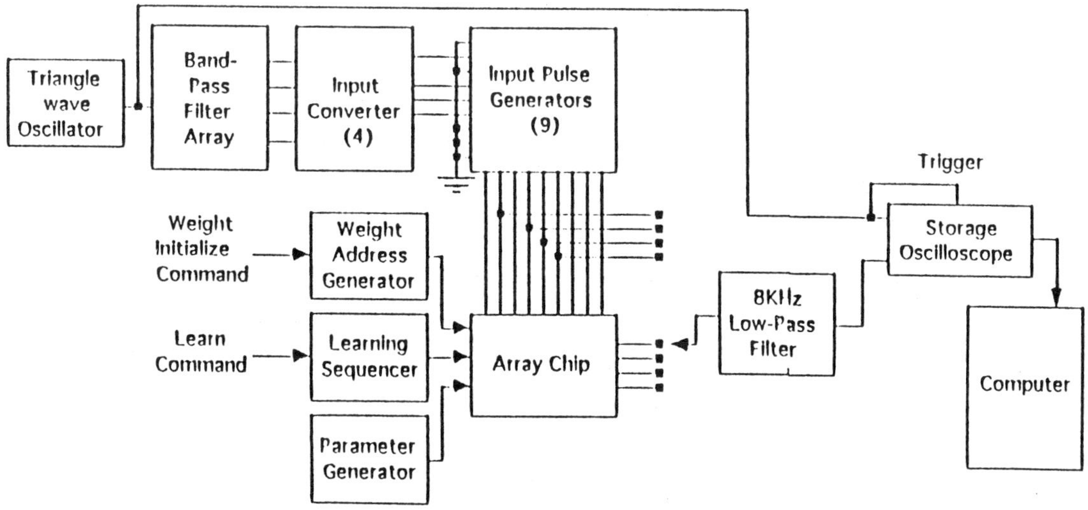

Fig. 1 Array Chip Test Fixture

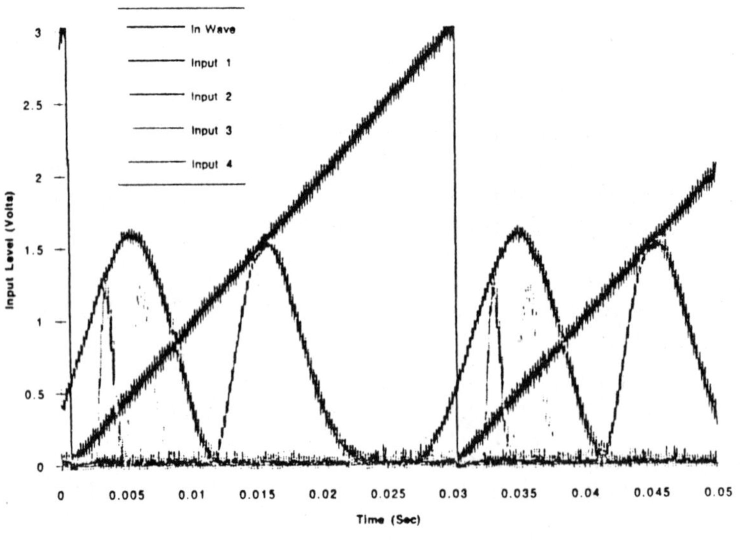

Fig. 2: Training Set with 33Hz Triangle Input

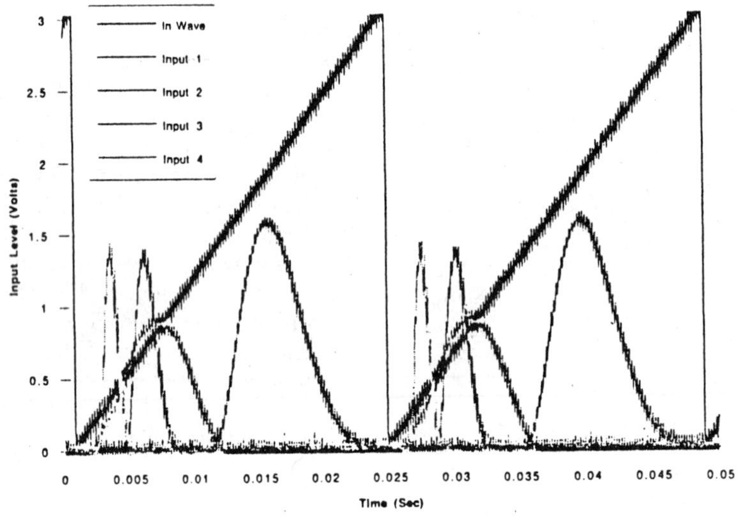

Fig. 3: Training Set with 40Hz Triangle Input

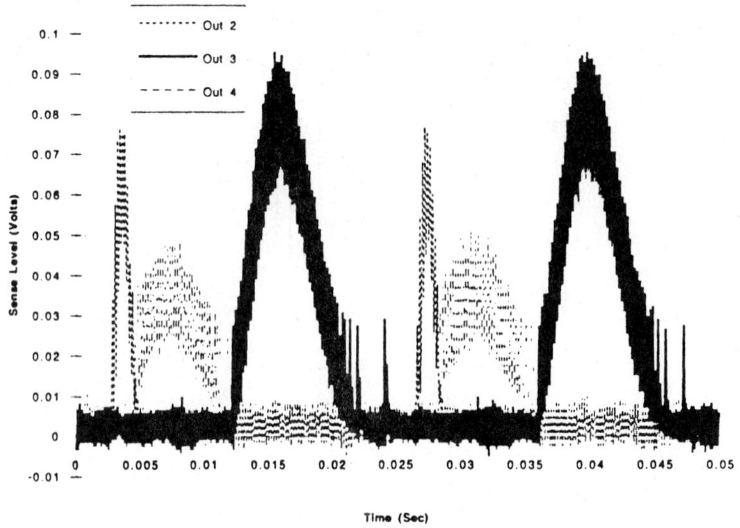

Fig.4: Measured Outputs after Learning 40Hz Training Set

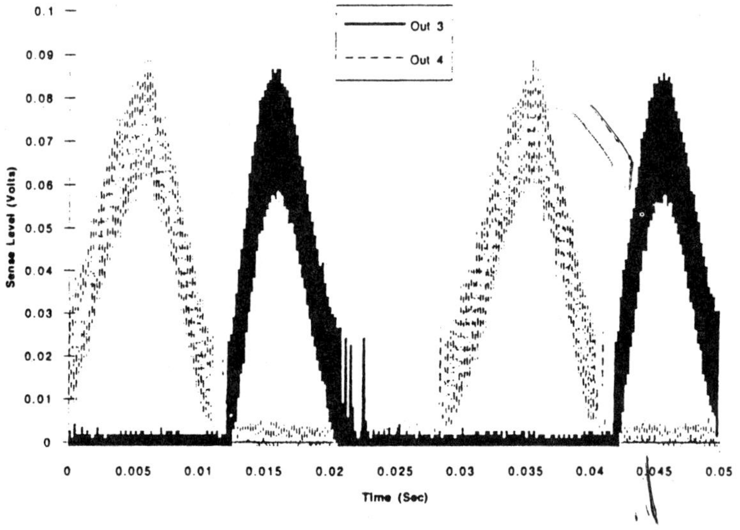

Fig. 5: Measured Outputs after Learning 33Hz Training Set

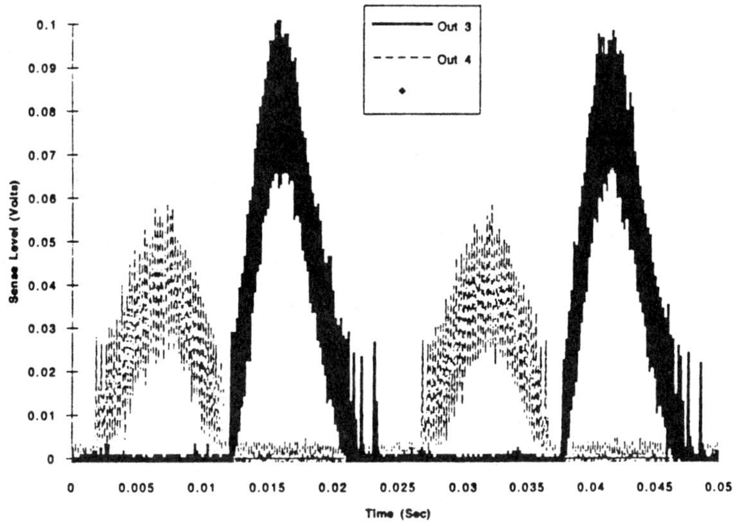

Fig. 6: Measured outputs after Learning 40Hz Training Set when Learning Started with the 33Hz Training Set

IV. CONCLUSIONS

We have constructed a VLSI test chip to explore the operation of a processing node using pulsed communication, analog weights, and on-chip adaptation. We have implemented a variation of the modified Hebbian algorithm presented by Oja. To complete the learning rule, we have added a lateral inhibition mechanism that makes the output representation useful for a final layer of neurons for output mapping. The chip allowed us to test a complete classifier system implementation and explore the ability of the array to distinguish between two similar features. Future work will include tests of the chip using features with larger numbers of inputs, and finally implementation of a complete input-output mapping system.

REFERENCES

[1] K. Hunt, and D. Sbarbaro, "Neural Networks for Nonlinear Internal Model Control," IEE Proceedings, vol. 138, no. 5, September 1991
[2] K. S. Narendra, and K. Parthasarathy, "Identification and Control of Dynamical Systems Using Neural Networks," IEEE Transactions on Neural Networks, Vol. 1, no. 1, pp 4-26, March 1990
[3] E. Oja, "A Simplified Neuron Model as a Principal Component Analyzer," Journal of Mathematical Biology vol.15, pp.267-273, 1982
[4] A. F. Murray, "Pulse Arithmetic in VLSI Neural Networks," IEEE Micro, pp. 64-74, December 1989
[5] J. Donald and L. A. Akers, "An Adaptive Neural Processing Node," IEEE Transactions on Neural Networks, May 1993 (in press).

The Effects of Analog Hardware Properties on Backpropagation Networks with On-Chip Learning

Brion K. Dolenko* and Howard C. Card
Department of Electrical and Computer Engineering
University of Manitoba
Winnipeg, Manitoba, Canada R3T 2N2

***Abstract*—Artificial neural networks trained using the popular backpropagation algorithm are usually trained either on slow serial computers with floating-point computation, or on dedicated digital hardware, which requires much area in silicon and may hamper backpropagation learning because of the limited resolution in the weight updates. Analog hardware is very compact and allows for very small weight increments, but until now its use in backpropagation networks has been primarily limited to a minority of the computation, the forward computation. The learning computations are usually performed off-chip. In this paper we present results of simulations performed assuming both forward *and* backward computation are done on-chip using analog components. Aspects of analog hardware studied are component variability (variability in multiplier gains and zero offsets), limited voltage ranges, and components (multipliers) that only approximate the computations in the backpropagation algorithm. It is shown that backpropagation networks can learn to compensate for all these shortcomings of analog circuits except for zero offsets. Variability in multiplier gains is not a problem, and learning is still possible despite limited voltage ranges and function approximations. Fixed component variation from fabrication is shown to be less detrimental to learning than component variation due to noise.**

I. Introduction

There has been considerable work on implementing the backpropagation algorithm [2] in dedicated hardware in order to achieve much greater speed than is possible with floating-point computation on serial computers. Many networks use limited-precision digital hardware to perform all or most of the computation. Analysis of these networks usually involves the effect of limited resolution in the computation on learning and/or the network outputs. A typical suggested resolution is 16 bits; this large number of bits results in extensive hardware area.

Analog hardware does not suffer from the same drawbacks as digital hardware. Limited resolution is not an inherent feature of the hardware, and the components typically take up much less area than their digital counterparts. Implementing the entire backpropagation training algorithm in analog hardware is not difficult. Addition operations in analog hardware are easily performed by summing currents on a wire. Multiplications can be done using analog multipliers such as the wide-range Gilbert multiplier [3]. This type of multiplier was recently employed in the implementation of mean-field networks [4]. It was suggested that an extension of the circuits used in that work might be used to implement the backpropagation learning algorithm. The other operations involved in backpropagation, including the sigmoid functions and subtractions, may also be implemented using these multipliers, as will be shown later.

There has been very little previous work done on implementing the backpropagation algorithm in analog hardware. Networks with analog forward-only computation and floating-point reverse computation are presented in [5], [6], and [7]. One must attempt to implement *all* computation on-chip, however, in order to build networks capable of learning new patterns very quickly. The lack of previous implementation of all backpropagation computation in analog hardware is probably due to the non-idealities present in analog hardware, and the fact that it is not obvious that non-ideal backward computation can learn to compensate for non-ideal forward computation (and vice-versa). Different analog components, such as multipliers, will produce different results when presented with the same inputs due to variations in transistor dimensions, etc. between the components. Also, the components all perform computations that are only approximations to the corresponding mathematical operations of the backpropagation algorithm, due to non-ideal device characteristics and limited voltage ranges.

Not surprisingly, given the lack of analog implementations of the full backpropagation algorithm, there is also a lack of systematic studies of the effects of analog hard-

*Supported by grants from Micronet and NSERC and by an NSERC postgraduate scholarship. Much of this work is derived from the thesis [1].

0-7803-0999-5/93/$03.00 ©1993 IEEE

ware properties on backpropagation learning. This paper attempts such a study. The hardware properties analyzed include variations in multiplier gains and zero offsets (both cases: due to fabrication and due to noise are analyzed), and function approximations (due to nonlinearities in the multiplier characteristics and limited voltage ranges).

II. Circuit Description

A schematic view of a single neuron and synapse of the circuits analyzed in this paper is shown in Fig. 1. This circuit is a direct extension of that presented in [4], [8]. "U" is the voltage value corresponding to the abstract value of 1.0 (the maximum neuron output).

There are only two different components in the circuit: Wide-range Gilbert multipliers (components marked with X's in Fig. 1), and simple two-transistor circuits that act as resistors for current-to-voltage conversion (components marked "I/V" in Fig. 1).

The wide-range Gilbert multiplier works by accepting four voltages V_1, V_2, V_3, and V_4 as input and (for small- to moderate-sized inputs), producing a current proportional to $(V_1 - V_2)(V_3 - V_4)$. Note that subtractions can be performed at multiplier inputs by arranging the input signals appropriately. The inputs to the multipliers in Fig. 1 correspond, from the top down, to V_1, V_2, V_3, and V_4 respectively. The multipliers can also be thought of as having two differential inputs, $(V_1 - V_2)$ and $(V_3 - V_4)$.

Typical characteristics of the Gilbert multiplier are shown in Fig. 2. Notice that the output current saturates for sufficient input voltage. The characteristics also become nonlinear as this saturation region is approached. This nonlinearity has at least one advantage. The sigmoid nonlinearity of the neuron can be obtained using one of these multipliers, as will be shown in the next section. The number of types of components required to build the complete backpropagation circuit is therefore reduced.

The current-to-voltage converter characteristics (not shown) are approximately linear.

The circuitry shown can be implemented at any hidden layer in the network. At the output layer the same circuit can also be used except that two of M2's inputs are different: $V_3 = V_i^{desired}$ and $V_4 = V_i^{actual}$, instead of $V_3 = -\partial E/\partial V_i$ and $V_4 = 0$.

Weight changes are performed in the circuit by allowing the current flowing out of multiplier M3 to charge a capacitor (whose voltage represents the synaptic weight) for some length of time that can be thought of as the learning rate. Most of the time for training is due to charging or discharging of the capacitors; very little time is required to compute the weight error derivatives $\partial E/\partial w_{ij}$.

During learning, multiplier M3 must produce a constant current while the voltage across the capacitor is changing. As shown in [4], the multipliers perform this function very well over most of their operating range, acting as near-ideal current sources.

Pattern presentations of sufficient frequency will help to keep the capacitive weights refreshed. Further simulations [1] showed that the weights could not afford to lose more than order 0.01% of their charge between pattern presentations. However, given that modest cooling of the circuits (to about 250K) will result in capacitive charge leakage on the order of 1% every hour, and that each pattern presentation can be done in microseconds, the circuits can still function.

Rough estimates of the variations between multipliers, which were fabricated using a 1.2μm CMOS process, were $\pm 10\%$ for the gains, $\pm 5\%$ of maximum output for intra-chip zero offset variation, and $\pm 10\%$ of maximum output for inter-chip zero offset variation.

III. Circuit Modelling

At the abstract level, each neuron i outputs the value $out_i = \tanh(net_i)$, where net_i is the net input to neuron i (the weighted sum of inputs, including the bias value). The tanh function was used instead of the logistic function because it is natural to fabricate circuits with symmetric activation functions for positive and negative input voltages. The derivative of the sigmoid function, used in the backward error derivative calculation, is then $1 - out_i^2$.

At the circuit level, the equations that generate the characteristic of Fig. 2 are quite complex (see [4] for details). For simplicity of simulation the multiplier characteristic of Fig. 2 is modelled by the approximation

$$Out = \phi^2 \tanh(\sqrt{\theta}\, input_1/\phi) \tanh(\sqrt{\theta}\, input_2/\phi) + O_y \quad (1)$$

where ϕ is used to adjust the function range and θ is used to adjust the multiplier's gain. ϕ roughly corresponds to the maximum value that one of the differential inputs can assume before the multiplier becomes very non-linear. Maximum multiplier output is ϕ^2. O_y is the zero offset of the multiplier — the actual output when one input is zero.

For all simulations and equations in this paper, signal values and parameters such as θ and ϕ are used in abstract terms rather than as voltage values. For example, the neurons have maximum outputs of 1.0 rather than, say, 0.8 volts. This simplifies the simulation process.

Notice that when both inputs are small with respect to ϕ,(1) becomes

$$Out = \theta\, input_1\, input_2 + O_y \quad (2)$$

During simulation, equation (2) was retained for multiplier M1 because in this case the inputs are small (within ± 1.0) with respect to ϕ. The parameter ϕ should obviously be greater than 1.0 to allow the network to respond properly throughout the entire range (-2.0 to +2.0) of the desired output minus actual output signal used at the output neurons.

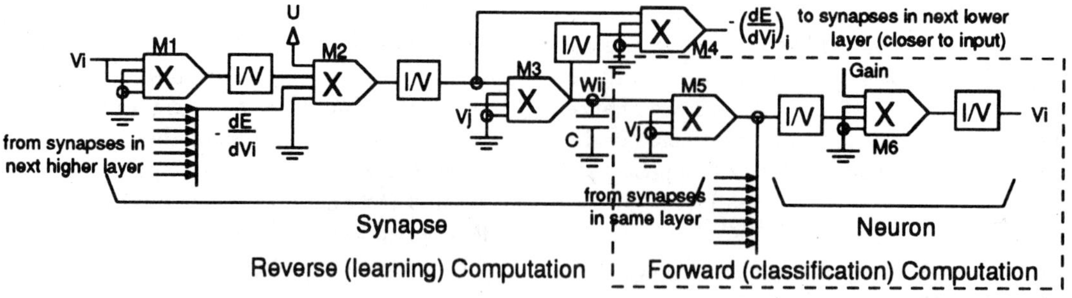

Fig. 1. Schematic of analog circuit for Backpropagation learning

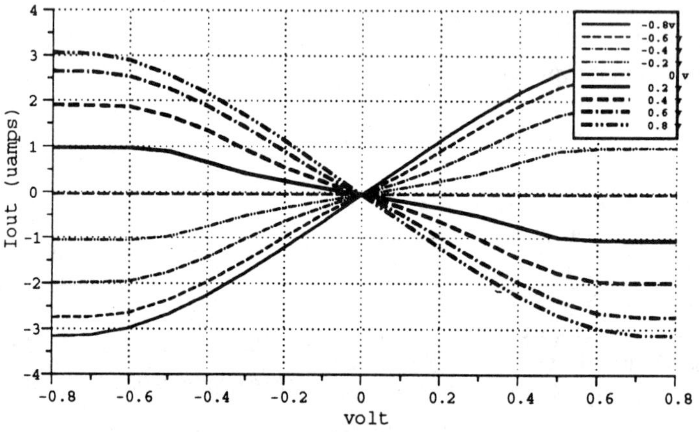

Fig. 2. Measured Gilbert multiplier characteristics (from [4])

In (1), if we let $\theta = \phi^2$ (in reality the circuit designer must design the multiplier, or more simply the I/V converter, to allow for this),

$$Out = \phi^2 \tanh(input_1)\tanh(input_2) + O_y \qquad (3)$$

If $input_2$ is then set to $\tanh^{-1}(1/\phi^2)$, then we are left with the familiar hyperbolic tangent activation function. This shows that the multipliers can serve a dual purpose: multiplication and sigmoid calculation.

For the multiply and sigmoid operations, component variability was simulated by varying the gain of the multiplier (the slope of the multiplier characteristic near the origin). For the multipliers performing the multiply operations this corresponds to varying the θ parameter. For the sigmoids this implies varying the η parameter in (4).

$$Out = \tanh(\eta\, input_1) + O_y \qquad (4)$$

It was assumed that the multiplier gains for various circuits distributed over the chip would have a Gaussian-like distribution:

$$gain = (1.0 + devn)^{pow} \qquad (5)$$

where *pow* is a normal random variable (with Gaussian distribution, mean 0.0 and standard deviation 1.0). *devn* was a parameter in the simulation, to allow one to observe the degree of component variation the circuits could tolerate. Possible values for *gain* are from 0.0 to $+\infty$, but for small values of *devn* the gains are distributed roughly symmetrically around 1.0.

Zero offsets were given Gaussian distributions with mean 0.0. Standard deviation of the offsets was another simulation parameter.

IV. Simulation Environment

The simulations were run using a modified version of the public-domain **Xerion** simulator [9] on Sun workstations. The backpropagation learning equations were modified to support component variation. Each individual multiply and tanh operation in the network could be assigned its own gain and offset term either at the start of simulation (to simulate variability from fabrication) or immediately prior to the multiply or tanh operation being required in the computation (to simulate variability due to noise). The standard deviations of multiplier gains and offsets were user-settable parameters and a feature was implemented to automatically run a network through a number of simulations, each with progressively greater component variation. The user could also select whether or not the weights and other values corresponding to voltage levels in the circuits should be bounded. This allowed for component variation effects to be studied separately from weight saturation effects.

The ϕ parameter was made user-settable, allowing for investigation of effect of limited voltage range on learning.

When weight saturation was in effect, every multiplication operation was simulated using (1). When saturation was not in effect, the multipliers were simulated using (2). The latter corresponds to ϕ (multiplier range parameter) values approaching infinity.

V. Simulations Performed

A number of different problems were used for simulation, both artificial and real. The problems are the following:

1. The 4-bit parity problem. Here the network is presented with 4 binary inputs, 0's and 1's, and must output a '1' if the inputs have an odd number of 1's, and a '-1' if the inputs have an even number of 1's. While the desired output was -1 or +1 (because of the tanh sigmoid used), the inputs remained coded as is usual for binary numbers — 0's and 1's.
2. The eight-input "hard" overlapping Gaussian problem, presented in [10]. Here the network must discriminate between two classes with Gaussian distributions, a task probably similar to that found in many real-world classification problems. For class 1, each input has mean zero and standard deviation one. For class 2, each input has mean zero and standard deviation two. This problem is quite difficult for a backpropagation network — Kohonen reported an error of 18.9% for an 8 hidden unit backpropagation network as compared to the optimal 9.0% achieved by a Gaussian maximum likehihood classifier. Two outputs were used, one for each class.
3. A small version of a real-world classification problem, that of distinguishing between various cereal grain kernels (barley, oats, rye, and amber durum, hard red spring, and soft white spring wheats) using data obtained through optical measurements [11]:
   (a) Light reflectance data: red, green, and blue.
   (b) Size data: length, width, contour length (perimeter), aspect ratios, and area.

   The problem adopted in this paper is simply determining whether or not the input corresponds to an amber durum wheat kernel. This problem is not linearly separable and requires hidden units for a solution. Preliminary simulations showed that at least 2 hidden units are necessary (4 were actually used in the hardware simulations presented here).

Table I shows some simulation parameters for all three problems. All were done using weight updates after each pattern presentation. A training epoch is as usual defined as a pass through all the training data. Target values in all problems were -0.7 and +0.7.

For the grain classifier network, a classification was considered "correct" if the network's output was > 0 for an amber durum kernel, or < 0 for a non-amber durum kernel. For the parity network, a stricter performance measure was used because of the relatively high probability with which the network could correctly classify all patterns. This performance measure was one suggested by Scott Fahlman in [12] where the classification is considered "correct" only if the network's output is greater than 0.2 for odd parity, or less than -0.2 for even parity. For the overlapping Gaussian classifier, a classification was correct if the output of the neuron corresponding to the correct class was greater than the other neuron's output.

VI. Simulation Results

A. Learning with Multiplier Gain Variation

The first results we present are from simulations of circuits such as those of Fig. 1, with saturation effects neglected (ϕ in (1) $= \infty$), and zero offsets also neglected. The standard deviations of multiplier/sigmoid gain (*devn* in (5)) were varied from 0.0 (ideally matched components) to 1.0 in 0.05 increments. The gains were generated using one of ten different random number streams. Two different sets of starting weights were also employed, yielding a total of twenty simulations for each standard deviation studied. In an attempt to distinguish between the effects of noise and of noiseless systematic variation in analog components, the gains were either fixed at the start of simulation (component variation) or allowed to vary (the case of noise-induced variation). Plots of average percent correct classification (over 20 simulations) for both the fixed and variable cases are shown in Figs. 3 and 4 for the 4-bit parity and grain classification problems respectively. The overlapping Gaussians problem was not attempted without saturation in effect.

The networks performed well when standard deviation of multiplier gain was within about 20% and 15% of the ideal for the parity and grain problems respectively. These standard deviations are at least as great as the anticipated values. It is clear that on average the networks did better when the gains were fixed at the start of simulation (the solid lines in Figs. 3 and 4), rather than when they were variable (the dashed lines). This is an encouraging result because it shows that the networks are able to make some sense out of a fixed nonideal environment, and can learn to compensate. They exhibit considerably less tolerance to random variation, or noise. Increases in accuracy for high (and probably unrealistic) standard deviations for the parity network occurred because the network tended

TABLE I. SIMULATION PARAMETERS

Problem	Inputs	Hidden Units	Outputs	Training data points	Test data points	Learning rate	Training epochs
4-bit parity	4	8	1	16	-	0.01	5000
Gaussians problem	8	8	2	2000	2000	0.02	50
Grain classifier	10	4	1	242	485	0.02	1000

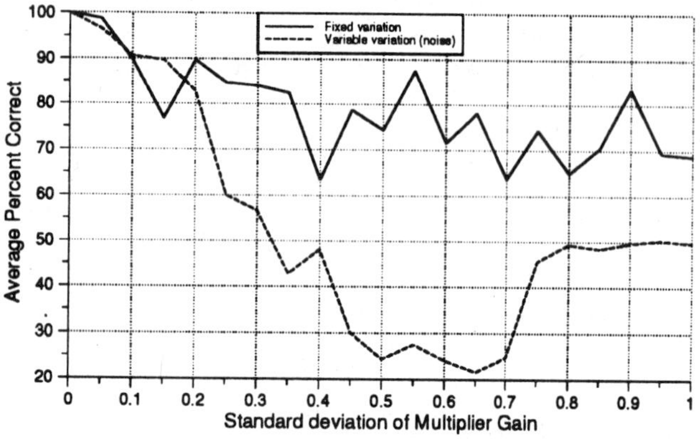

Fig. 3. Performance of 4-bit parity network with multiplier gain variation

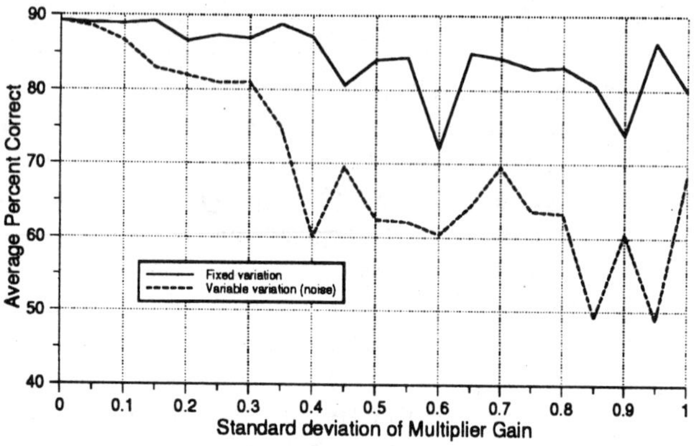

Fig. 4. Performance of grain classifier with multiplier gain variation

to classify the patterns as all even or all odd parity with great confidence (outputs very close to -1 or +1), thereby achieving near 50% accuracy.

B. Learning with Limited Voltage Ranges

The next results presented here are from simulations of the circuits in Fig. 1 with saturation effects (ie: the multipliers obey (1), and produce maximum output ϕ^2). ϕ was varied from 1.0 to $\sqrt{10.0}$ to allow for multiplier ranges from ± 1.0 to ± 10.0. The multiplier gains were maintained at the ideal value (= 1.0). All weights and signals, including summations, were clipped at the maximum multiplier output ϕ^2 because of the voltage limits that would be experienced within an actual circuit. These simulations attempt to determine the required range of the multipliers and weights. Variation in multiplier gain is not expected to have any greater effect when the voltage ranges are limited because for high input values, the multipliers will then produce outputs near the limits of their range regardless of their gains.

Final percent correct classifications, averaged over 4 simulations each with different starting weights, are shown in Table II for the 4-bit parity, grain classification, and overlapping Gaussian problems.

The networks achieved reasonable classification accuracy relative to that achieved with unlimited range, as long as the ranges of the multipliers and weights were within [-5.0, 5.0]. In other words the voltage value corresponding to unity (1.0) in the circuit should be set to about one-fifth that of the multiplier maximum output, which is not unreasonable given that the multiplier maximum output will be several volts. More work must be done on determining whether networks with many outputs will be able to work as well. There may be a problem with the ∂(network error)/∂(neuron output) term for the hidden neurons in this case, because this term involves a summation that may become quite large for a large number of output units.

C. Learning with Zero Offset Variation, Gain Variation, and Bounded Voltages

The final results presented here are from simulations conducted assuming limited voltage ranges, gain variation and offset terms added to each multiplication operation. Results for the 4-bit parity, grain classification, and overlapping Gaussian problem are shown in Table III. A total of 20 simulations were run for the parity and Gaussians problem (2 sets of initial weights and 10 random number streams to generate component variation), and 10 simulations for the grains problem (2 sets of initial weights and 5 random number streams). Each simulation was run using a multiplier maximum output (and weight maximum value) of 5.0. Standard deviation of multiplier gain variation was fixed at 0.15. It is clear that the networks could not learn to overcome the multipliers' additive offsets for degrees of variation near the anticipated values of 5 and 10% of maximum output. This is probably due to the fact that very small weight changes are required by the back-propagation algorithm during learning to achieve smooth

TABLE II. AVERAGE CLASSIFICATION ACCURACIES (%) WITH LIMITED VOLTAGE RANGES

Problem	Maximum weight and signal magnitude										
	1	2	3	4	5	6	7	8	9	10	∞
4-bit parity	0.0	20.3	62.5	89.1	95.3	95.3	96.9	96.9	98.4	98.4	100.0
Grain classifier											
(training data)	80.6	82.5	84.5	85.6	85.9	86.1	86.5	86.8	87.6	87.5	88.9
(test data)	80.4	81.4	83.6	86.3	86.7	86.6	86.8	86.9	87.0	87.0	87.3
Gaussians problem											
(training data)	67.7	80.1	82.7	83.5	84.2	85.6	86.1	86.5	86.9	86.9	88.4
(test data)	64.6	77.6	80.2	80.1	80.1	81.2	81.0	81.2	82.2	82.2	84.2

TABLE III. AVERAGE CLASSIFICATION ACCURACIES (%) WITH ZERO OFFSETS

Problem	Std. Deviation of Multiplier Additive Offset (% of Maximum Output)							
	0.0	0.1	0.2	0.5	1.0	2.0	5.0	10.0
4-bit parity	78.1	96.6	95.9	77.5	77.5	62.2	55.6	49.1
Grain classifier								
(training data)	88.1	84.6	82.9	81.4	80.3	79.8	59.9	62.9
(test data)	87.0	83.5	82.2	80.9	80.5	79.5	59.7	62.8
Gaussians problem								
(training data)	84.4	72.5	60.5	55.5	42.4	44.4	37.6	40.5
(test data)	80.1	68.3	59.3	54.6	41.3	44.4	37.5	40.6

gradient descent, and the additive offsets may not permit these small changes. This problem may be correctable at the expense of more complex analog circuitry.

VII. CONCLUSIONS

The results from simulations of backpropagation training on several difficult problems, with various hardware precision effects, have been presented. It was shown that, for the case of variation in multiplier gain, the networks were learning properly despite mismatched components and in particular, learning to compensate for systematic variation in the circuits which update the synaptic weights. This the circuits are able to do considerably better than they are able to compensate for a comparable degree of random noise. Additive offsets in the multiplication operations continues to be a problem, however. Nevertheless, limited ranges of the weights and multipliers is an acceptable feature of the analog circuits, as is the nonlinear approximation to the true multiplication operation.

ACKNOWLEDGEMENT

We wish to thank C. Schneider for helpful conversations regarding the analog hardware components.

REFERENCES

[1] B. Dolenko, "Performance and Hardware Compatibility of Backpropagation and Cascade Correlation Training Algorithms", MSc thesis, Department of Electrical and Computer Engineering, The University of Manitoba, 1992.

[2] D. E. Rumelhart, G. E. Hinton, and R. J. Williams, "Learning internal representations by error propagation" in *Parallel Distributed Processing: Explorations in the MicroStructure of Cognition*, Vol. 1, D. E. Rumelhart and J. L. McClelland, eds. Cambridge, MA: M.I.T. Press, 1986.

[3] B. Gilbert, "A high-performance monolithic multiplier using active feedback", *IEEE Journal of Solid-state Circuits*, 1974, SC-9, pp. 364–373.

[4] Christian R. Schneider, "Analog CMOS circuits for artificial neural networks", PhD thesis, Department of Electrical and Computer Engineering, The University of Manitoba, 1991.

[5] Robert C. Frye, Edward A. Rietman, and Chee C. Wong, "Back-Propagation learning and nonidealities in analog neural network hardware", *IEEE Transactions on Neural Networks*, Vol. 2, No. 1, January 1991, pp. 110–117.

[6] Jerzy B. Lont and Walter Guggenbühl, "Analog CMOS implementation of a multilayer perceptron with nonlinear synapses", *IEEE Trans. on Neural Networks*, Vol. 3, No. 3, May 1992, pp. 457–465.

[7] Joongho Choi and Bing J. Sheu, "VLSI design of compact and high-precision analog neural network processors", *Proceedings of the 1992 International Joint Conference on Neural Networks, Baltimore*, Vol. 2, pp. 637–641.

[8] Christian R. Schneider and Howard C. Card, "CMOS implementation of analog Hebbian synaptic learning circuits", *Proceedings of the 1991 International Joint Conference on Neural Networks, Seattle*, Vol. 1, pp. 437–442.

[9] Drew van Camp, Tony Plate, and Geoffrey Hinton, "The **Xerion** neural network simulator", Department of Computer Science, The University of Toronto, 1991.

[10] Teuvo Kohonen, György Barna, and Ronald Chrisley, "Statistical pattern recognition with neural networks: benchmarking studies", *Proceedings of the 2nd IEEE International Conference on Neural Networks*, Vol. I, pp. 61–68.

[11] B. Dolenko, H.C. Card, M. Neuman, and E. Shwedyk, "Classifying cereal grains using backpropagation networks", University of Manitoba, Department of Electrical and Computer Engineering Technical Report 91-101.

[12] Scott E. Fahlman, "An empirical study of learning speed in back-propagation networks", Carnegie-Mellon University Technical Report CMU-CS-88-162, 1988.

Single–Chip Realization of a Fuzzy Logic Controller with Neural Network Structure (NNFLC)

WANG Zhenfeng, JIN Dongming and Li Zhijian
Institute of Microelectronics, Tsinghua University,
Beijing, 100084, P.R.China

Abstract: **A NNFLC has been studied and designed employing the technology of current mode multi–value CMOS and analog E^2PROM. The NNFLC applies neural network for knowledge memory instead of IF–THEN knowledge base of ESFLC. This NNFLC behaves more intelligent than any traditional FLCs The single–chip ASIC realization of such NNFLC has been designed. The circuit has a systolic mesh structure with single–clock control, bi–direction data flows and A / D, D / A converting interface.**

Keywords: Fuzzy control; neural networks; multi–value logic; current–mode CMOS; self–learning.

1. Introduction

During the past several years, fuzzy control has emerged as one of the most active and fruitful areas for reserch in the application of fuzzy set theory. Many countries have established special research institutes for the study of Fuzzy Logic Control system. In most real states, it is very difficult to find an exact analytic relation between the controlled values and the observed values so men usually deal with such problems in habits or experience. The fuzzy logic control system in expert system structure (ESFLC) finds its good use in such area and performs superior to the traditional control algorithm (such as PIDs).

The expert system structure is used in the first application of fuzzy logic in control realm[1]. Although the FLC technology has greatly developed in many aspects, its fundamental structure still remains the old type. Fig.1 shows the basic construction of ESFLC.

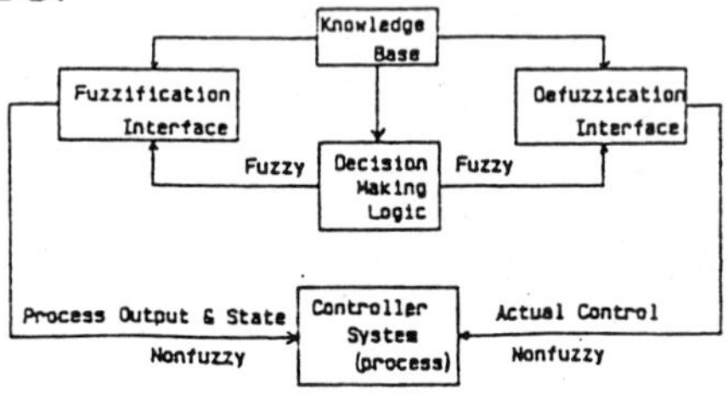

Fig.1 The constitution of ESFLC

In the whole process of ESFLC, the IF–THEN form knowledge base plays an essential role, which reflects the input / output relation of the control systems. So the ESFLCs have the same disadvantages as the expert systems[2]. 1) To many duplicated real–time systems, it is rather difficult to establish suitable IF–THEN rules by expert experience. To the existed IF–THEN rules, their reasonableness is unknown, so the duplicated process of optimization is necessary. 2) The rules in such structure FLC system are fixed. The optimization only can be done in design period. In real–time control process, the fixed rules usually perform not so perfect as designed before because of the disturbance of circumstance and the drafting of the system parameters, so they should be adaptable to fit the demand of real–time application. 3) The rules of the ESFLC are set to deal with certain problem, that is, the rules must be changed in different system.

So the ESFLCs are not in common use. The three drawbacks all come from the innate feature of expert system. That means, using a new structure of knowledge base replacing the expert system structure may bring about new development to the FLC technology.

In part2, a new FLC with neural network structure (NNFLC) will be introduced. In part3, the on chip design of this NNFLC will be discussed employing current–mode multi–valued logic[3].

2. Learnable, Geeral used NNFLC

Neural network theory is a fast developing realm based on the recent research about human brain by current neural science[4]. The theory reveals some features of human thinking. The neural network can serve many human–like fuctions such as knowledge memory, knowledge learning, through the huge amount of interconnection between neurons. Many current developed models and algorithms based on neural network theory make great progress in many traditional science research fields.

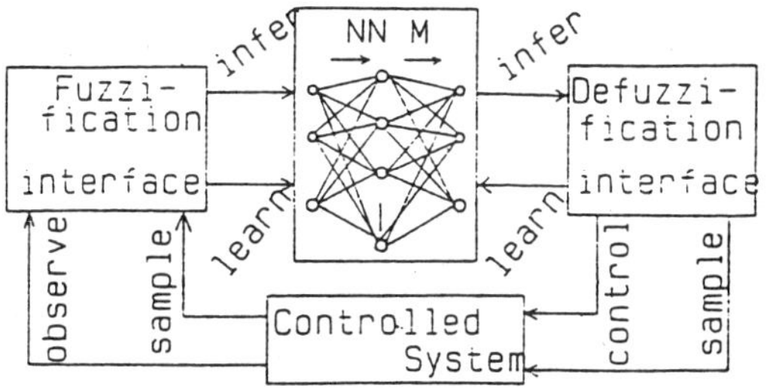

Fig.2 The consitution of NNFLC

The drawback of ESFLC introduced in part1 all can be surmount by the application of neural network strcture. A neural network consists of huge amount of computational elements(neuron) linked with adaptive weights. Each neuron is a MISO unlinear element, $y=f(x_i, w_i, \theta)$, where x_i means input variable, w_i means weight value, θ is threshold value [5]. When a huge amount of neurons constitute a network through links with variable weights, they obtain the capacity of knowledge memory, parallel calculation, etc[6]. The algorithms of learning have many kinds. For the convenience of the on chip realization, the BP algorithm is selected [7].

The development of neural network theory enlightens scientists on the new methods for the reform of the traditional ESFLC. Some papers have put forward several new FLC structures in neural network frame [8] [9]. But in all of these new neural network FLC structure no essential progress has been made to overcome the drawbacks of the ESFLC because they still remain the intrinsic quality of IF–THEN knowledge base, while the IF–THEN knowledge base is just the source of the disavantages of ESFLC. To solve this problem, we establish a three–layer neural network to replace the IF–THEN knowledge base of the FLC. Fig.2 shows the basic constitution of the new NNFLC. This FLC has a three–layer net for knowledge learning and memory suitable for MIMO control system.

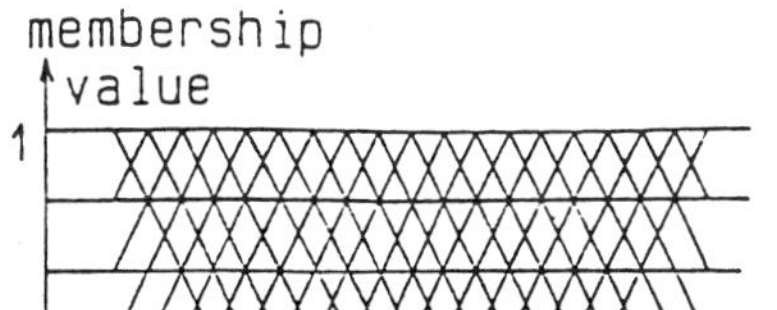

Fig.3 The contour of implicant function

The input vector {input} have N_1 variables. Through fuzzification operation a membership matrix $A(N_1 \times K_1)$ toward K_1 fuzzy sets can be produced, while the implicant function behaves linear which shown in Fig.3[10]. The input of the network

M are the $N_1 \times K_1$ elements of matrix A. On the other hand, the output vector {output} has N_2 variables towords k_2 fuzzy sets. Adopting the implicant function with contour of Fig.3, it is easy to produce the membership matrix $B(N_2 \times K_2)$ of output vector and its $N_2 \times K_2$ elements act as the output of the network M. The node function of M also adopts sigmoid type function. The forward deduction of $A \rightarrow B$ represents the process of the intelligent control system. From the sample {input, output}, the $\{w_{ij}\}$ can be deducted through a learning period.

The NNFLC employs neural network as the medium for knowledge learning and memory, thus behaves good generality. The design of the NNFLC also shows more convenient than the ESFLC because the complex work of optimization can be ignored. Desptite of the difference among the control objects and environment, the only thing consumers should do is to detect the discourses of the input / output variables. According to the actual discourse and the NNFLC–demanded discourse, the ratio calculation can be done for the fuzzification use which produces the implicant matrixes A or B. The operations between A, B and $\{w_{ij}\}$ including inference and learning are not related to the certain control objects.

After the initial whole–scope learning the control system can be used in real–time work, that is, on–line operation. The calculation in the whole process adopt linear operation so a high process speed can be obtained and the VLSI realization become possible. The node function of M employs segmental linear function in sigmoid type.

During the real–time course, the parameters of control system and circumstance often emerge drafting in some degrees and the disturbance also happen. We supply new samples for M to learn during the control course and the learning speed here needs more high because the BP algorithm to whole–scope M is difficult to fit the real–time demand. So a quick algorithm for network learning has been deducted in the child–mesh term.

The NNFLC introduced above employ neural network to replace IF–THEN knowledge base, thus behaves more advantages: 1) Generality and interchangeability. No restrict limit to the control objects and environment. The inner structure of the NNFLC needs no adjustment facing different control problem. 2) Self–learning ability. No rules from expert experience are required. Optimization in design course also becomes unnecessary. The only work the consumer should do is to supply the NNFLC actual examples to learn and definite the certain discourses of the system input / ouput variables. 3) Anti–drafting ability. The NNFLC can adjust M during control course, so NNFLC can deal with the parameters drafting and circumstance disturbance. 4) On–line operation. All the operation of the NNFLC are linear and in parallel form. 5) On–chip realization. The NNFLC has a make–up structure with function blocks. Its on–chip realization are not very complicated compared with other types of intelligent controller.

3. On–Chip Realization of NNFLC current–mode multi–value logic CMOS VLSI single– chip design

The VLSI realization of NNFLC is very important to the general use, because the on–chip hardware can greatly raise the speed of initial learning and on–line adjustment. The key for the design of circuit structure and the technology process is to seek high speed performance.

We adopt the current mode multi–value logic CMOS circuit. This technology has been well developed in our institute [11]. We have designed and fabricated many kinds of 8–value ALU, 16 bit multiplier, etc. The most attractive character of current mode multi–value logic is the ability of simplifying the circuit form, reducing the gate number, especially suitable for the ALU design. The basic algorithm unit in current–mode multi–value CMOS circuit are shown in Fig.4[12].

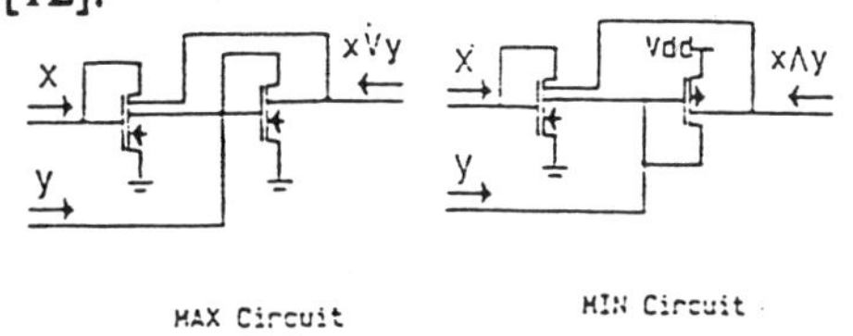

Fig.4 The Basic ALUs of current mode multi–value logic CMOS

The NNFLC circuits consist of three parts: control block, computation block and adaptive weight memory. To realize the high speed parallel computation, the systolic arrays structure is employed in the whole–scope design. The bi–direction data flows are controlled by the single clock and operated in synchronism. Fig.5 show the data flows in two states [13].

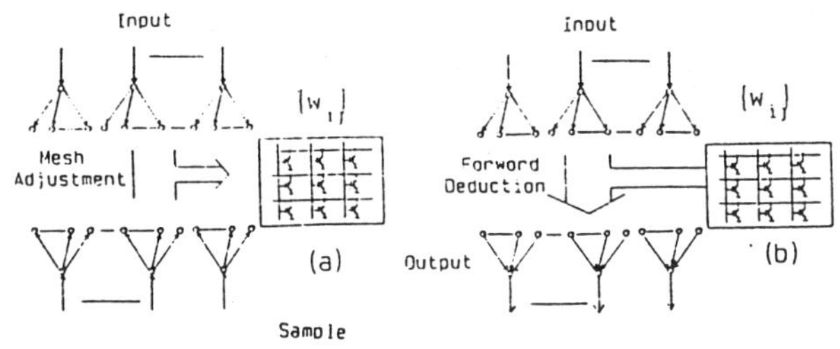

Fig.5 The two states of the data flows

The ALU array is adopted to realize the parallel operations. The scale of ALU is small enough to constitute the array processor, based on the innate superiority of the current mode multi–value circuit structure. The functions of ALUs are varied at the different nodes in the mesh. The ALUs at the frontier area of the systolic mesh behave less complex. They connect I / O nodes and mainly operate fuzzification, defuzzification and the comparison for adjusted weights, while data flows here are relatively narrow. The inner ALUs need more complicated function, including computation of neuron function and weight modification, so they have more elments and more operation steps. In order to accelerate the operation of the inner ALUs we employ child mesh design, that is, adopt systolic mesh structure inside these ALUs with bi–director data flows and parallel operation.

To fit the demands of the data flows with different width, we distinguish the processor arrays in two modes, shown in Fig.6. Stage–wise parallel process mode (Fig.6.a) is employed where data flows are narrow, while the multi–step batch process mode (Fig.6.b) is adopted to deal with the wide data flows. With the aid of the high speed performance of CMOS circuit, the combination of the two modes can realize the on–line operation while greatly decrease the circuit scale and design complication.

To VLSI realization of neural network, the kernel is the adaptive weight design which proposes high flexibility, certain precision and maintain time. After synthesis several circuit modes of neural network, we decide to combine the technology of current–mode multi–value logic and analog value memories.

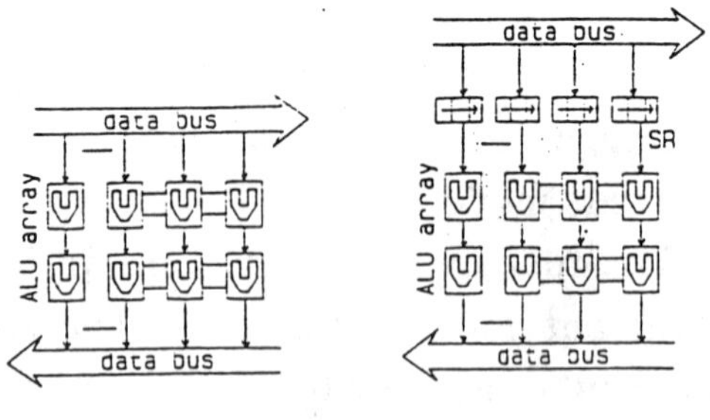

(a) (b)

Fig.6 The connections of processor arrays

In the past design of neural network VLSI realization, the mode of weight memory always defines the other parts of the whole circuits, that is why the chip structure exists innate drawbacks. We decide to adopt E^2PROM as analog value memories with current mode multi–value logic for digital process [14][15].

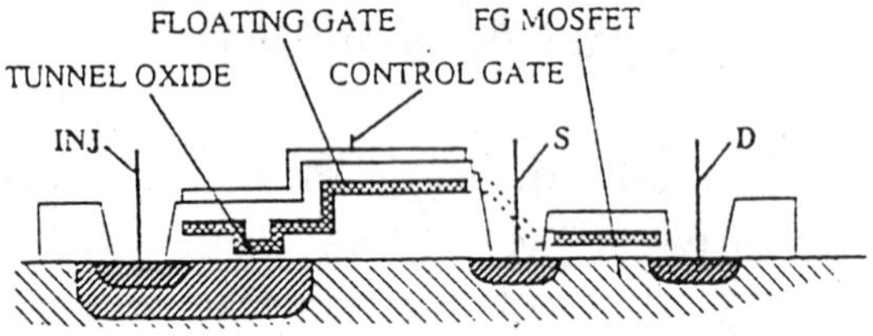

Fig.7 The structure of analog E^2PROM

Fig.7 shows the structure of analog E^2PROM. V–I converter and current quantizer which are shown in Fig.4 form an array as an A / D, D / A interface for the single–chip VLSI realization.

In technology process, the current–mode multi–value logic and analog E^2PROM are compatible, while the matching behaves flexible of computation, decoding, etc. The single–chip realization of ALU arrays, control block and E^2PROM naturally avoid the void tips and time dealy of data transition between chips. Thus the final ASIC chip for consumer is transparent and in common use.

4. Conclusion

A new NNFLC structure is introduced here. An overall comparation has been done between the NNFLC and the ESFLC. The new structure FLCs have learning ability, on–line adjustment ability and generality, so it can deal with varied real–time control process in spite of different objects and environment. A design for the single–chip VLSI realization of this NNFLC has been done, with the combination of current mode multi–value logic and analog E^2PROM technology. It is also a combination of analog circuit mode and digital circuit mode. The systolic mesh structure is applied in circuit design with bi–direction data flows, syntonic circuits and ALU arrays.

Reference

〔1〕 Chuen Chien Lee, "Fuzzy Logic in Control Systems: Fuzzy Logic Controller –Part1," IEEE Trans. on Systems, Man, Cybernetics, pp.404–418, vol.20, no.2, Mar / Apr. 1990;

〔2〕 Floor Van Der Rhee, "Knowledge Based Fuzzy Control of Systems, " IEEE Trans. on Automatic Control, pp.148–155, vol.35, no.2, Feb. 1990;

〔3〕 M.Kameyama, S.Kawahito and T.Higuch, "A Multiplier Chip with Multiple–valued bidirectional current–mode logic circuits, "Computer, Vol.21, pp.43–56, Apr. 1988;

〔4〕 D.O.Hebb, "The organization of Behavior," Wiley, New York, 1949;

〔5〕 S.Grossberg, "Neural Networks and Natural Intelligence," MIT. Press, 1988;

〔6〕 J.J.Hopfield, "Artificial Neural Networks," IEEE Circuit and Devices mag., pp.3–10, Sept. 1988;

〔7〕 D.H.Ackely, G.E.Hinton, "A Learning Algorithm for Boltzman Machines," Cog. Sci., pp.147–169, no.9, 1985;

〔8〕 Ronald R.Yager, "Implementing Fuzzy Logic Controllers using a Neural Network Framework," Fuzzy Sets and Systems, pp.53–64, no.48, 1992;

〔9〕 James M.Keller, "Neural Network Implementation of Fuzzy Logic," Fuzzy Sets and Systems, pp.1–12, no.45, 1992;

〔10〕 Liang Jong Huang and Masayoshi Tomizuka, "A Self–Paced Fuzzy Tracking Controller for Two–Dimensional Motion Control," IEEE Trans. on Systems, Man, and Cybernetics, pp.1115–1123, vol.20, no.5, Sep / Oct. 1990;

〔11〕 Z.Tang, "MOS Current Mode Logic Circuits Studies on a New Type of MOS Integrated Circuits," PhD Thesis, 1988, Tsinghua University.

〔12〕 K.C.Smith, "The Prospects for Multi–valued Logic: a Technology and Applications View," IEEE Trans. Comput, pp.619–634, vol.c–30, Sept. 1981;

〔13〕 R.Davis and D.Thomas, "Systolic Array Chip Matches and Pace of High–Speed Processing," Electronic Design, pp.207–218, vol.32, no.22, Oct. 1984;

〔14〕 David A.Durfee and F.S.Choncair, "Comparison of Floating Gate Neural Network Memory Cells in standard VLSI CMOS Technology," IEEE Trans. on Neural Networks, pp.347–352, vol.3, no.3, May. 1992;

〔15〕 E.Vittoz, H.Oguey, "Analog Storage of Adjustable Synaptic Weights," VLSI Design of Neural Network, Kluwer Academic Publishers, pp.47–63, 1991.

H2.

A NEW ANALOG IMPLEMENTATION OF THE KOHONEN NEURAL NETWORK

Chung-Yu Wu and Wen-Kai Kuo

Integrated Circuits and Systems Laboratory

Department of Electronics Engineering and Institute of Electronics

National Chiao-Tung University

ABSTRACT

In this paper, a new circuit implementation of the Kohonen neural networks is proposed. A novel winner-take-all circuit is developed and digital counters are used to store and update the weights. An experimental chip of this system has been fabricated by 1.2um CMOS technology. A architecture is also proposed for these chips to be combined together to form a larger net.

I. INTRODUCTION

The Kohonen neural network (KNN), also known as self-organizing feature mapping network, has the desirable property of effectively producing spatially-organized presentation of various features of the input signals[1]. There exists the similar structure in human brain as found from some biological experiments. It has been shown that this neural network are efficient in the field of image and vision processing applications such as pattern recognition [2] and vector quantization [3].

The implementation of artificial neural nets may use digital and analog VLSI circuit techniques. However, it has been shown that the analog realization is much more suitable than the digital one [4]. In this paper, the current-mode circuit design technique is used and a new novel winner-take-all (WTA) circuit with simpler circuit structure and other new circuit design technologies are developed to implement the KNN. Besides, a new architecture is also proposed to expand the implemented neural net.

The following text is divided into four sections. Section II will describe the algorithm of the implemented KNN. In Section III, the new novel WTA and other building circuits will be presented. Section IV contains HSPICE simulation and measurement results of the experimental neural chip. The architecture for expanding this chip will be described in Section V. Finally, Section VI will make conclusions.

II. THE KOHONEN NEURAL NETWORK

The general algorithm of the KNN can be described briefly in the following:

Step 1. Initialize the weights w_{ij} to random values and topological neighborhood $N_c(0)$

Step 2. Present new inputs

Step 3. Compute the distance between input vector $X = [x_1, x_2 \ldots x_N]$ and all weight vectors $W_i = [w_{i1}, w_{i2}, \ldots w_{iN}]$ at time t

Step 4. Select the best-matching (Winner) neuron c with minimum distance $D_i = |\boldsymbol{X} - \boldsymbol{W_i}|$

Step 5. Update the weights of the neuron c and its neighbors within N_c

Step 6. Go to *Step 2* repeatedly

It has been proven mathematically that the above algorithm will produce topological ordering of weights [5]. One of the simple system which can produce self-organizing feature is a linear array of functional unit. This kind of the KNN circuit with single input and eight outputs will be implemented in this work. One of the simple topological neighborhood N_c is of a linear array. The neighbors of the best matching neuron (winner) are the previous one and the next one in the linear topology at the beginning of the training. It is the maximum neighborhood during the training process. The winner becomes to have no neighbor when the training time increases. The adaptive equation in the implemented KNN is

$$\begin{cases} W_i(t+1) = W_i(t) + \text{sign}[X - W_i(t)] \cdot \kappa(t) & \text{for } i \in N_c \\ W_i(t+1) = \quad W_i(t) & \text{for } i \notin N_c \end{cases}$$

where

X : Input signal,

W_i : The stored weight of ith neurron,

$\kappa(t)$: An integer which decreases in time,

$$\text{sign}[a] = \begin{cases} 1 & \text{for } a > 0 \\ -1 & \text{for } a < 0 \end{cases}$$

This research is supported by National Science Council, Taiwan, R.O.C under contract NSC 82-0416-E-009-212

Though the above described type of the KNN circuits has only a single input, a new architecture is proposed here to be easily expand it as a larger system with more input nodes.

III. IMPLEMENTATION OF THE KOHONEN NETWORK

In the implementation, the KNN is divided into three layers. In the first layer, the cell computes the distance between the input signal and the stored weights. The second layer is mainly devoted to the detection of the best-matching cell of the first layer. Thus the WTA circuit can be used to realize the function of the second layer. The third layer is the neighbor-choosing circuit that will determine which weights of the non-winner neurons should be adapted.

According to the algorithm and the adaptive equation presented in Section II, the implementation architecture of the KNN with single input and eight outputs is proposed and shown in Fig.1. Each building block is described below.

1. *Winner-Take-All (WTA) Circuit*

The conceptual WTA circuit is shown in Fig.2(a), This circuit is adapted from the bipolar current-mode maximum-follower described in [6]. The corresponding MOS transistors in each cell have the same size and all the transistors are operated in the saturation region. MBX is shared by all cells and its aspect ratio is a small fraction of MB_i in each cell. The WTA circuit receives many current inputs $I_1, I_2 ... I_N$. Only the maximum input current I_i becomes the sum of the mirror currents in MB_i and the shared MBX. The current flow in MBX turns on MA_i. If $(W/L)_{MBi}/(W/L)_{MBX}$ is equal to 100, $1/101 I_i$ flows through MBX whereas $100/101 I_i$ flows through MB_i of the ith cell and MB_j of other cells. If other input currents I_j ($j \neq i$) less than $100/101 I_i$, the mirror current in MB_j exceeds I_j so that MC_j is turned on in other cells. Finally, only the voltage output O_i corresponding to the maximum input current is below the ground (GND), while the other outputs are above the GND. The detail circuit design and it's symbol are shown in Fig.2(b) and Fig.2(c).

2. *Distance Measurement Circuit (DMC)*

The DMC has the function that when receives two input currents, I_x and I_w, output current I_{out} is generated which is the square value of the difference $(I_x - I_w)$. At the same time, an indicator "Udctl" is also generated to indicate which input is larger. The DMC circuit is shown in Fig.3(a) which consists of a current subtractor and a simple current square circuits. MP3, MP4, MN3, MN4, and the inverter are used to indicate whether the input current signal I_x is larger than the stored weight current I_w. If I_x is not larger than I_w, the indicator output "Udctl" becomes saturated toward the negative power supply value. In contrast, if I_x is larger than I_w, the output "Udctl" of the inverter becomes saturated toward the positive power supply value. MN7~MN9 form a simple current square circuit as described is [7]. MP7,MP8, MN10, and MN11 are added to sink current from the next stage. The symbol of the DMC is shown in Fig.3(b).

3. *Synchronous Counter (SYCNT)*

In some implementation of neural net, the synaptic weight value is usually stored on the capacitor and refreshed periodically [8]. A synchronous up-down counter for both storing and updating the weight values is proposed here. The schematic is depicted in Fig.4(a). There are five inputs in total, namely, "Enable", "Pul", "Pr", "Cr" and "Udctl" in this 5-bit up-down counter. "Enable" input is controlled by neuron's output to determine whether the weight value of this neuron will be updated or not. The "Pul" is the pulse stream input for counting. It can regulate the amount of weight to be updated. "Pr" and "Cr" are the inputs to preset and clear the counter. The "Udctl" is controlled by the indicator output of the DMC to determine the counter will count up or down. According to the updating equation, if the input signal is larger than stored weight value, then the weight value should be counted up; otherwise, it should be counted down. There are five outputs in each counter. These outputs are the inputs of the simple 5-bit current-mode digital-to-analog converter (DAC) described in the next section. The symbol of the SYCNT is shown in Fig.4(b).

4. *5-bit Current-Mode DAC (CMDAC)*

This neural circuit does not require the DAC circuit with good linearity. The DAC circuit is shown in Fig.5(a). MN1~MN6 are the MOS transistors (W/L) which ratios ranging from 1/4 to 4 and MN6~MN10 are the MOS transistors used as switches [9]. MN11 and MN12 are necessary to keep the output current being the offset value I_c if the 5-bit inputs are all zero. The output current can be expressed by:

$$I_{out} = I_c + K(D_0 \cdot 2^0 + D_1 \cdot 2^1 + D_2 \cdot 2^2 + D_3 \cdot 2^3 + D_4 \cdot 2^4)$$

The symbol is shown in Fig.5(b) .

5. *Neighbor-Choosing Circuit (NCC)*

There are many papers to describe how to define the neighborhood for the self-organizing neural network in real applications[3][10]. The simple neighborhood function circuit shown in Fig.6(a) is used in the simulation but does not be implemented. Every unit i has the neighbors i-1 and i+1, except the units at the borders of the array. The neighbor unit N_i can be expressed as follows:

$$N_i = \{\max(1, i-1), i, \min(N, i+1)\}$$

For total N neurons, the "Nctl" input closes all switches at the beginning of the training and opens all switches when the time increases to meet the condition that the neighbor unit N_i should decrease with the time. The symbol of this circuit is shown in Fig.6(b).

Using the building block circuits introduced above, the whole KNN circuit with one input node and eight output nodes can be constructed and shown in Fig.7. The operational principles are described below. First, because each synchronous counter has its own "Pul" input for counting, each counter can be preset to different initial values. After presetting the initial value, the "Pul" inputs of all counters are merged together. That is, all the counters have the same "Pul" input. The initial topological neighborhood can also be set to different status by the control input "Nctl" of the NCC. Then the input current signal I_x is compared with five stored weights. The resulting eight distances between I_x and each weight are fed into the inputs of the WTA circuit. The output corresponding to the input with the minimum distance becomes saturated toward the positive supply value, while the other outputs toward the negative power supply value. Then, the outputs of the NCC will indicate which weights should be updated. The "Udctl" output of the DMC will control the synchronous counter to count up or down. The merged "Pul" input can be used to control the counting amount of the counters by feeding the pulse stream with different frequencies. The frequency of the pulse stream for the "Pul" input should be decreased as the time increasing.

When the input signals are presented sequentially, the weights will form the topological ordering. At the end of the training, the frequency of the pulse stream will be zero, that is, no more counting pulse will be fed into the counter. Thus all counters will not count any more and the weight values in the counters are remain unchanged. Therefore, the topological relationship among the weights is fixed, which can be utilized to classify the input signal.

IV. SIMULATION AND MEASUREMENT RESULTS

In this section, the simulation results about the ordering of all synaptic weights will be demonstrated. As shown in Fig.8, in the beginning, all weights are preset to different values and there is no metric ordering relationship among them. Initially, $W_1>W_2>W_4>W_3>W_5$ is the relationship among them. The input current signal is always equal to 16uA from t=0 to t=20usec and the second neuron is the winner all the time. The weights of first neuron, second neuron, and third neuron are adjusted during this time interval. It can been seen that all the weights have metric ordering relationship among them at the end of training, the relationship becomes $W_1> W_2> W_3>W_4>W_5$. After t=20usec, there is no "Pul" counting pulse input, so all the weights will keep their values as the same at t=20usec.

The experimental chip has been fabricated by 1.2um technology and measured. The "Pul" inputs are used to preset different weight values. When the input current varies, the winner is the one whose stored weight current is best-matching with the input current. If the input current is the same as the stored, its output voltage has the maximum value. This shows that the WTA and SYCNT circuits in the experimental chip are functional properly. The stored current values for the 32-level (5-bits counter) weights can be obtained by this way. The result is shown in Fig.9. and a microphotograph of this experimental chip is shown in Fig.10.

V. EXPANDING

Fig.11 shows how to expand this experimental chip. The outputs of the single net are those of the WTA circuit, not those of the NCC circuit. Two of these chips and an AND-gate plan are combined to form a larger net with two inputs, and so on. The number of the outputs of the larger net can be determined by the number of AND gates in the AND plan. If some input signals requires higher resolution, the number of their associated output nodes should be increased. Meanwhile, those of the other one should be decreased if the number of total output nodes is fixed. The configuration can be adjusted to meet different requirement.

VI. CONCLUSION

From the above descriptions, it's shown that the realized KNN has self-organizing capability. The locations of the weight values have spatially stochastic meaning which can describe the structure of the input signal density. The KNN has been implemented in IC chips successfully. The measurement shows each building block works properly. These chips can be combined to form a larger net. That will make the implemented KNN to be more powerful and flexible for different applications.

REFERENCES

[1] T. Kohonen, "Self-Organized Formation of Topological Correct Feature Maps," Biolog. Cybern., Vol.43, pp.59-69, 1982.

[2] T. Kohonen, "The Neural Phonetic Typewriter," IEEE Computer, Vol.21, pp.11-22, Mar., 1988.

[3] T. C. Lee, A. M. Peterson, "Adaptive Vector Quantization Using a Self-Development Neural Networks," IEEE J. Selected Areas Comm., Vol.8, No.8, pp.1458-1471, Oct., 1990.

[4] M. Verleysen, *et al.*, "Neural Networks for High-Storage Content- AddressableMemory: VLSI Circuit and Learning Algorithm," IEEE J. Solid-State Circuits, Vol.25, pp.849- 855, June, 1990.

[5] T. Kohonen, Self-Organization and Associative Memory, 3rd ed. Berlin, Heidelberg, Germany: Springer-Verlag, 1989.

[6] C. Toumazou, F. J. Lidgey, and D. G. Haigh, Analogue IC Design: The Current-Mode Approach, Peter Peredrinus Ltd, pp.84-86, 1990.

[7] K. Bult, H. Wallinga, "A Class of Analog CMOS Circuits Based on The Square-Law Characteristic of an MOS Transistor in Saturation," IEEE J. Solid-State Circuits, Vol.22, No.3, pp.357-365, June, 1987.

[8] B. Hochet *et al.*, "Implementation of a Learning Kohonen Neuron Based on a New Multilevel Storage Technique," IEEE J. Solid-State Circuits, Vol.26, No.3, pp262-267, March, 1991.

[9] P. W. Hollis, J. J. Panlos, "Artificial Neural Networks Using MOS Analog Multipliers," IEEE J. Solid-State Circuits, Vol.25, No.3, pp.849-855, June, 1990.

[10] A. K. Krishnamurthy, *et al.* "Neural Networks for Vector Quantization of Speech and Images," IEEE J. Selected Areas Comm., Vol.8, No.8, pp. 1449-1457, Oct., 1990.

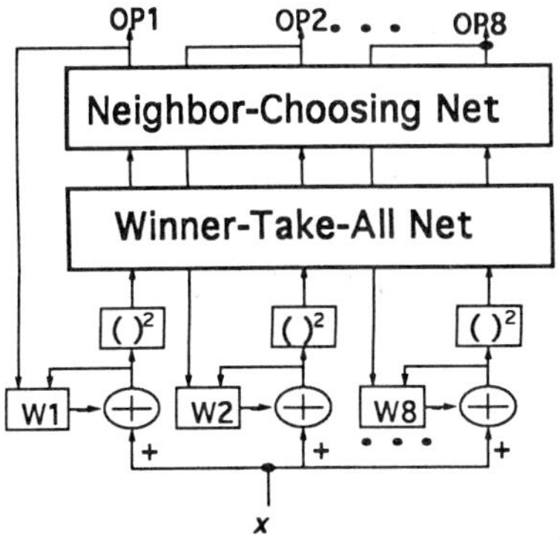

Fig.1 Architecture of the KNN

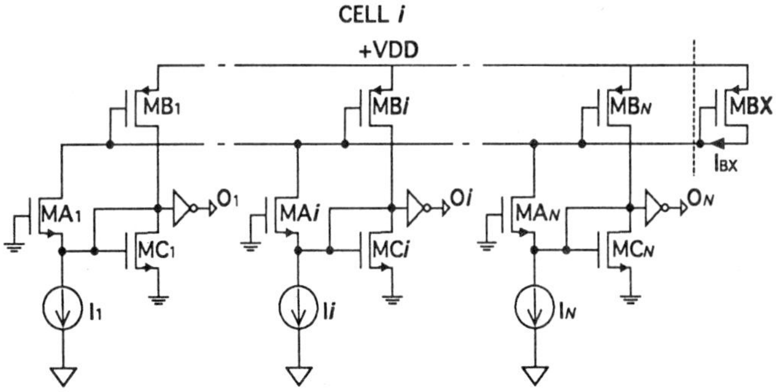

Fig.2(a) Conceptual WTA circuit to indicate maximum input

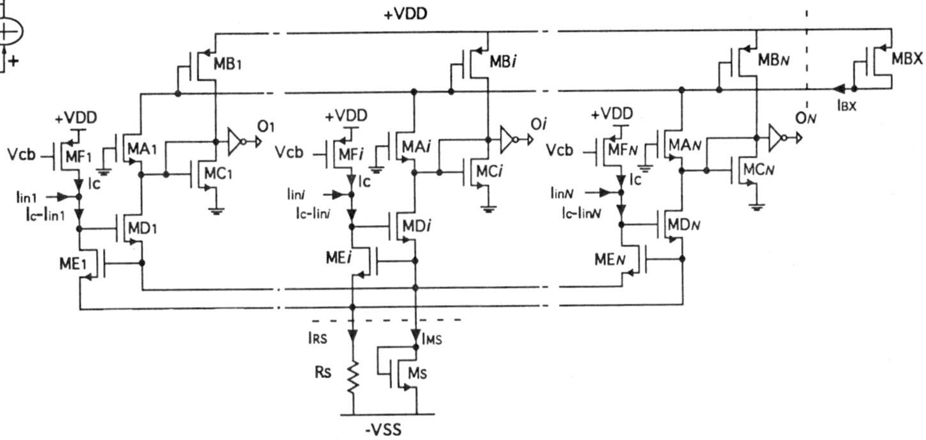

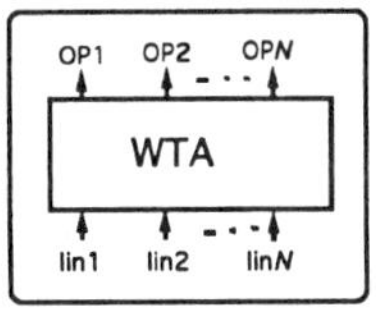

Fig.2(c)) Symbol of the WTA circuit

Fig.2(b) The design of the WTA circuit to indicate minimum input

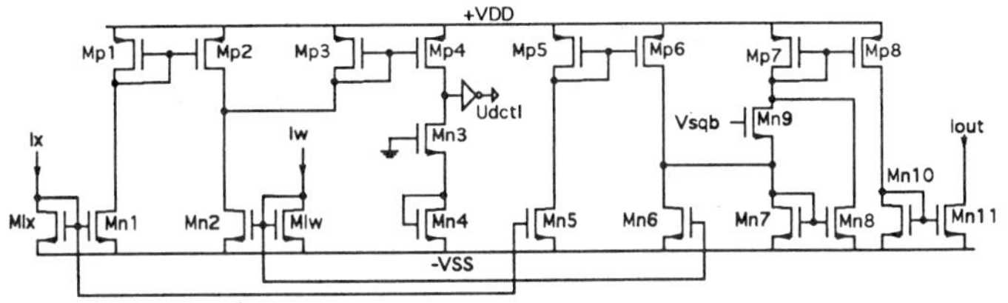

Fig.3(a) Schematic of the DMC

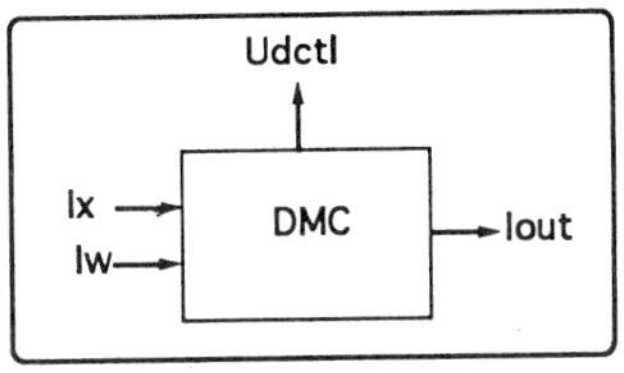

Fig.3(b) Symbol of the DMC

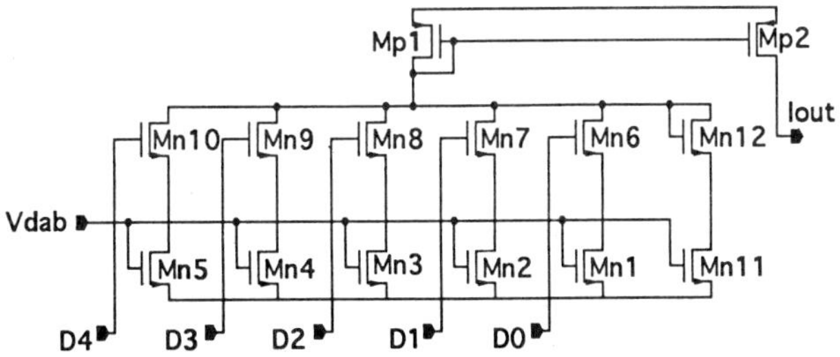

Fig.4(a) Schematic of the CMDAC

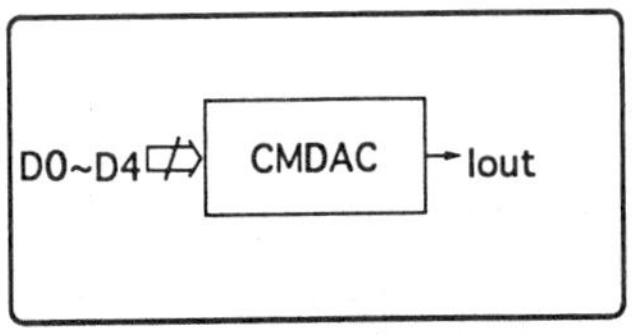

Fig.4(b) Symbol of the CMDAC

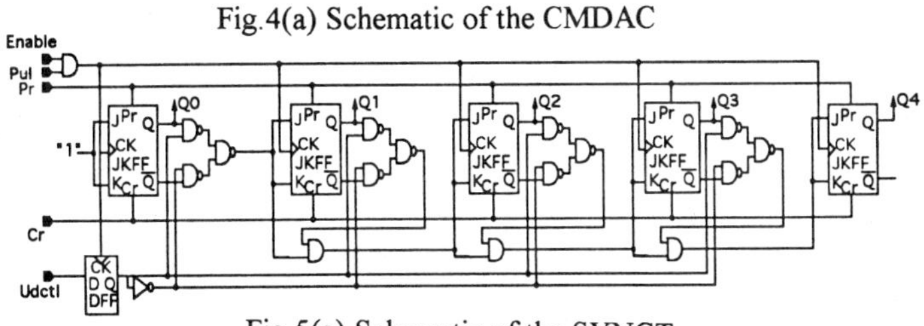

Fig.5(a) Schematic of the SYNCT

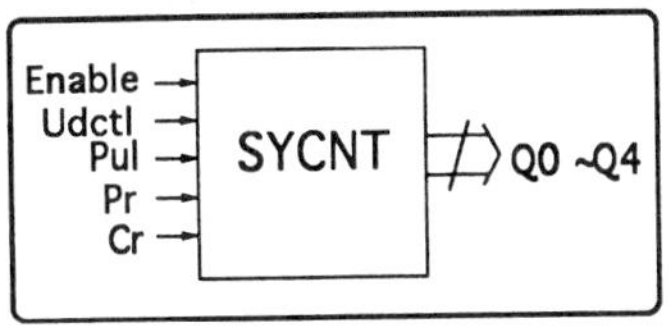

Fig.5(b) Symbol of the SYNCT

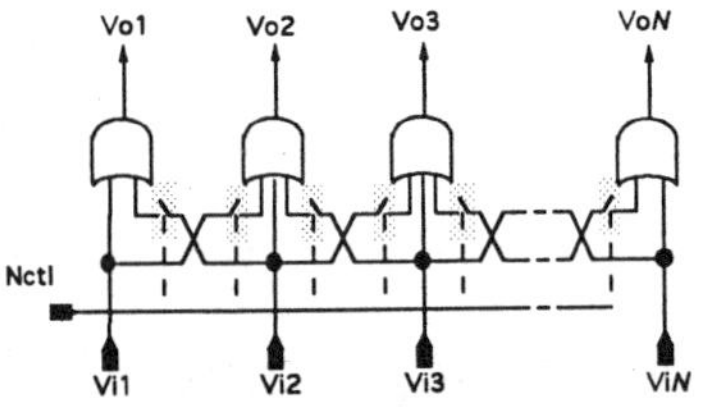

Fig.6(a) Schematic of the NCC

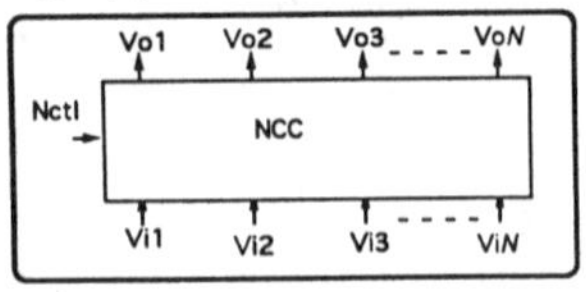

Fig.6(b) Symbol of the NCC

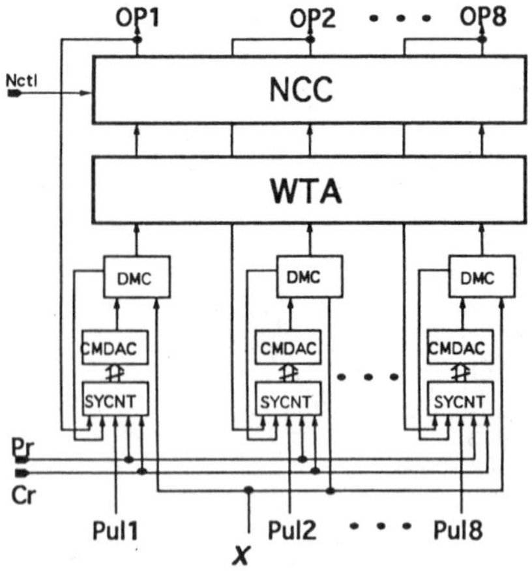

Fig.7 Complete circuit diagram of the KNN

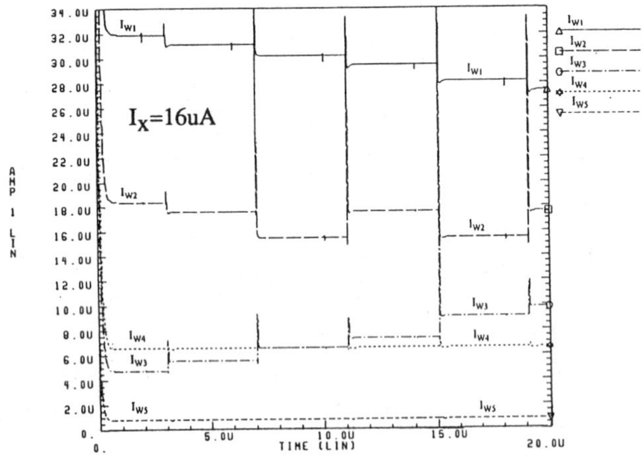

Fig.8 Simulation result of weight updating and ordering process

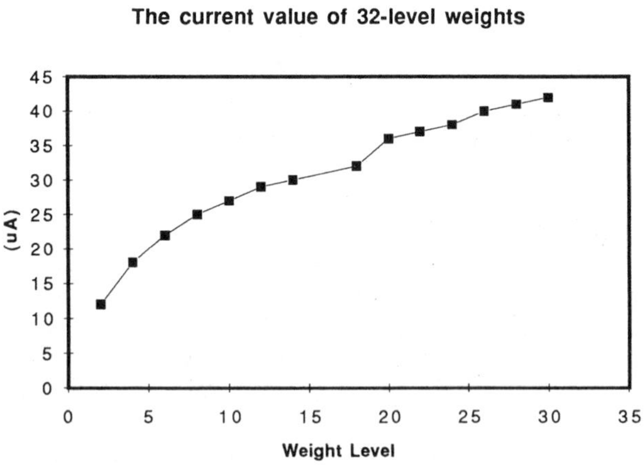

Fig.9 Measured 32-level stored weight current by matching method

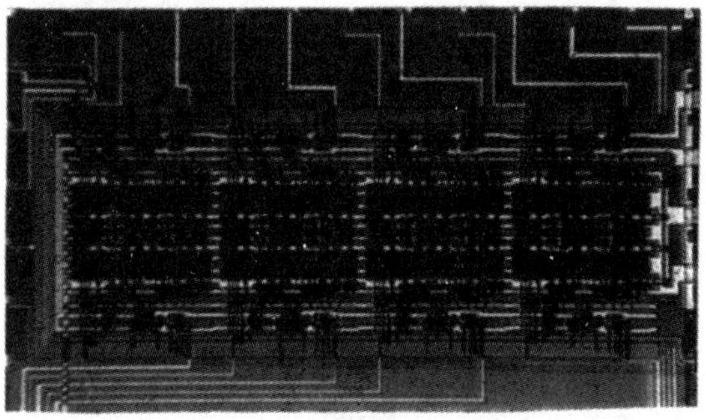
Fig.10 Microphotograph of the fabricated KNN chip

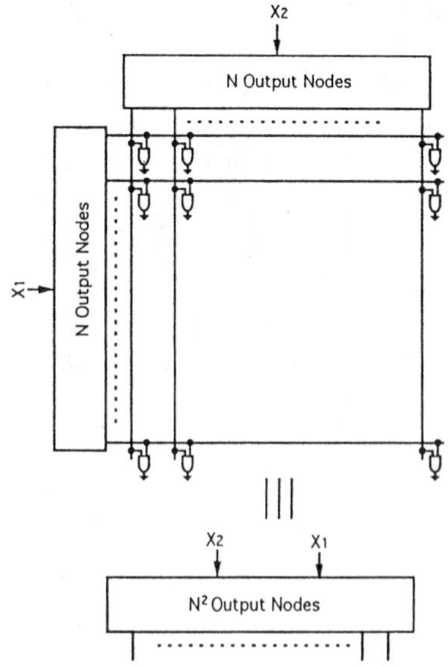

Fig.11 Illustration of expanding the network

3-D Wafer Stack Neurocomputing

Michael L. Campbell, Scott T. Toborg
Hughes Research Laboratories
3011 Malibu Canyon Rd., Malibu, CA 90265
Tel: (310) 317-5974
email: campbell@maxwell.hrl.hac.com

Scott L. Taylor
Hughes Space and Communications Group
P.O. Box 92919
Los Angeles, CA 90009

Abstract

We introduce a family of massively parallel MSIMD architectures which can be configured to efficiently handle a variety of different neural network models. The underlying technology is HRL's Three-Dimensional Wafer Scale Integration (3-D WSI), which provides an ideal medium to construct powerful, compact and low-power hardware tailored for neural network processing. A second generation prototype architecture consisting of a 128 x 128 array of processors formed by stacking 16 four-inch CMOS wafers is nearing completion. The performance of this prototype is compared with enhanced architectures configured with special wafer types to accelerate neural network operations. The design of these specialized resources emphasizes the synergy between neural processing functions and the 3-D WSI architecture & packaging. Detailed microcode emulations are used to assess the impact of different algorithm/architecture modifications. Neural networks for cooperative vision integration and multilayer backpropagation are mapped onto various 3-D wafer stacks. Estimated performance ranges from 2.4 billion connections per second (Giga-CPS) for the vision integration network up to 20.4 Giga-CPS for the backprop network, depending on the mapping technique and the hardware configuration.

1.0 Introduction

Many different types of parallel architectures have been proposed for implementing neural networks. While some of these approaches come close to meeting the computational requirements for neural networks, few meet the needs imposed on weight, size and power mandated by real-time embedded applications. This research focuses on extending the performance limits of neural network implementations on programmable digital computers in order to provide greater understanding of the potential synergy between neural network operations, parallel architecture, and advanced electronic packaging. The emphasis of this paper is on the use of the Three-Dimensional Wafer Scale Integration (3-D WSI) packaging technology, being developed at Hughes Research Laboratories [1]. This technology can be used to construct machines that meet the compact, low-power, high-performance requirements of real-time embedded systems, and allow for the programmable flexibility lacking in most analog approaches.

In this paper, we illustrate the utility of the 3-D WSI approach by describing the design of a family of massively parallel bit-serial Multiple-SIMD (MSIMD) array processors tailored for processing different neural network models. We begin with a description of the 3-D WSI approach and an update on its current status. Then we illustrate the flexibility of 3-D WSI

0-7803-0867-0/93 $3.00 ©1993 IEEE

technology by contrasting two representative examples. First, we describe wafer stacks for processing regularization-based early vision and cooperative integration problems. Next, we show how multilayer backpropagation networks can be efficiently mapped to 3-D WSI. We compare the performance of various architecture options with a baseline architecture currently under construction. Architecture enhancements are also proposed and their impact on performance is evaluated via microcode emulation.

2.0 3-D WSI Approach and Current Status

While 3-D WSI architectures introduced in this research have many features common to other machines for neural network processing, 3-D wafer stacks also provide some unique computational and technological characteristics:

- Elimination of chip packaging, printed circuit boards, backplanes and cables
- Massively parallel communications between wafers (128 x 128 vertical connections)
- Flexibility in PE design (wafers can be swapped in or out depending on application)
- Dynamically Reconfigurable wafer stack partitioning into multiple instruction streams

The essential features of 3-D WSI technology allow stacking of wafers to achieve architectural flexibility, high performance, and very high packaging density. Figure 1a depicts how conventional parallel architectures are constructed by replicating predefined processing elements. On the other hand, Figure 1b shows how the 3-D approach results in a stack of silicon wafers with massively parallel bus lines penetrating each wafer. The number of interconnects between wafers is greater than 16K, which is two orders of magnitude greater than other technologies limited to perimeter connections. A single processing element consists of a single functional cell from each wafer connected by a common bus.

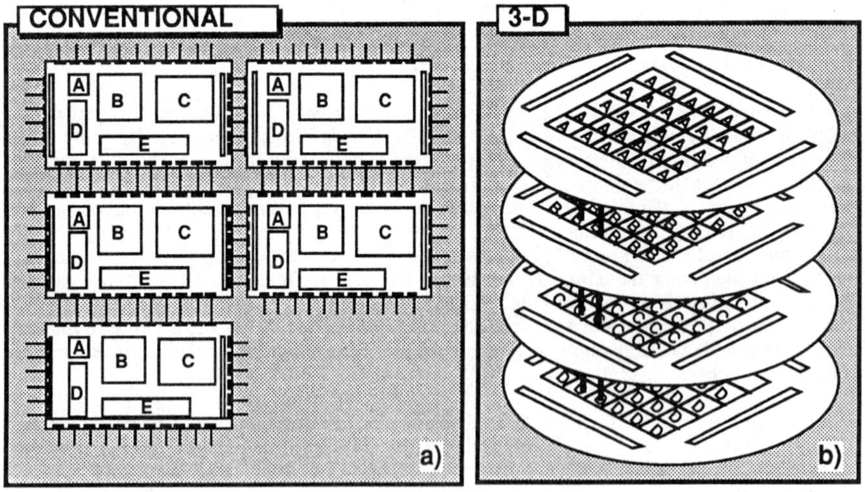

Figure 1. Comparison between conventional VLSI parallel hardware and 3-D WSI

Some of the 3-D wafer types also support communication horizontally between different functional units. Vertical communication paths greatly simplify the signal distribution problem that commonly exists in conventional 2-D WSI technologies. Compared with other digital 3-D packaging and WSI techniques, our approach has by far the highest reported speed per volume-power [2], and the simplified assembly process is expected to significantly reduce manufacturing costs. Of particular relevance to neural processing, the 16K vertical interconnections lead to an inter-wafer communication bandwidth of over 160 Gigabits/second, effectively eliminating the Von Neumann bottleneck that hinders neural processing on conventional computers.

A wafer stack can be constructed from a number of different wafer types, listed in Table 1. The final column indicates different stages of development: **f** = in fab/test, **d** = design and layout, **c** = concept and design. Each wafer contains a array of N x N identical functional units which make up the processors of the stack. A major advantage of 3-D WSI is that the processing element architecture can be tailored to specific applications by simply swapping in or out different wafer types. This is particularly important in a rapidly evolving field such as neural networks.

Table 1. 3-D Wafer types with communication and function capabilities

Wafer Type	Communication	Function	Status
Shifter	Edge, Nearest Neighbor, Vertical	Provides nearest neighbor shifting of data	f
Accumulator	Vertical	Addition and subtraction	f
Replicator	Edge, Vertical Row & Column broadcast	Allows rapid data replication across the array	f
Comparator	Vertical	Performs simple arithmetic comparisons (< > =)	f
Counter	Vertical	Increment and decrement ops	f
Switching plane	Vertical	Stack partitioning for MSIMD, layer-level parallelism	d
Parallel Shifter	Edge, Vertical	16 x increase in performance for neuron weight summation	d
Dense Memory	Edge, Vertical	Increases weight storage 4 x	d
Parallel Multiply/Divide	Edge, Vertical	16-bit parallel multiply Speeds neuron activation update 16 x	c

The Accumulator, Comparator, and Counter wafer types are designed to perform bit-serial arithmetic operations within each PE; whereas the Shifter and Replicator wafer types are designed to perform inter-PE communication. Memory is distributed across each of the wafer types. The Shifter wafer type provides communication via a 4-nearest-neighbor mesh topology. Since each wafer is controlled independently, it is possible to perform several shifts of different sets of data across the array simultaneously, even in different directions. The Replicator wafer type provides communication to and from the array controller unit via 128 row-wise and 128 column-wise busses, which can be used to efficiently broadcast data values from the controller or the array itself along the rows & columns of the array of PEs.

A microcode emulator was developed to verify software and wafer stack designs. The emulator models 3-D electronics at the logic level and allows single stepping or tracing of every clock cycle. Using the software-defined instruction set of the 3-D computer, we can exploit the characteristics of the hardware to optimize designs for maximum performance with minimal wafers. Furthermore, the extreme flexibility of the design due to the horizontally programmed, long instruction word format allows us to tune the arithmetic precision for maximum efficiency. For example, we can perform 8-bit ADDs in 8 clocks and 12-bit ADDs in 12 clocks, and we can perform most 1-bit logical operations in a single clock cycle.

One of the most unique attributes of the wafer stack organization is the ability to execute several different instruction streams simultaneously in different portions of the stack. This is achieved by using the Switching Plane wafer type, currently under development, which provides a 128x128 array of switches along the vertical busses. The switches are under software control, such that when the switches are opened, the vertical busses are disconnected to form multiple independent segments which we call "slices." Each segment of the busses is electrically isolated from the others, so arithmetic operations and vertical data transfers can proceed in different slices simultaneously. When the switches are closed, data can be transferred between slices at the full data rate of 160 Gigabits/second. This Multiple-SIMD capability is extensively used in the mappings of neural processing, below.

The technologies described in this section have been demonstrated by the completion of several 32 x 32 five wafer processor arrays, the first of which became operational in October 1987. A 128x128 sixteen-wafer array is expected to be operating by early 1993. Currently, we are performing the wafer array testing and laser repairs on first silicon for the 128x128 circuits, with very promising initial results. At the time of this writing, two of the wafer types have already demonstrated nearly perfect yield on two 2.5-inch^2 dice. This second generation machine will consist of 16 stacked wafers and will have a stack height of only 0.84 cm. It will weigh 700g, consume 75W of power, and have a peak performance of 10 billion operations per second (BOPS, 16-bit integer ADDs.) Performance estimates relevant to neural processing are given in the next two sections.

3.0 Wafer Scale Architectures for Neural Network Vision

Computer Vision deals with the automatic construction of 3-D scene descriptions from sparse, noisy 2-D image data. Unfortunately, information contained in a 2-D image is generally insufficient to reconstruct a unique set of 3-D surface properties. Recurrent neural networks have been used to minimize "visual cost" functions formulated using regularization theory or Markov Random Fields (MRFs) for solving several important vision problems. Vision integration is one technique for combining constraints from different data sources (e.g. contours, stereo, motion, texture, color) to improve computation of 3-D surface properties. In this approach, information from one vision module is used to guide the calculation of image properties in another module. The process may also be cooperative in the sense that vision modules can mutually and interactively affect each others computations. Using regularization theory or Markov Random Fields (MRFs) this cooperative vision integration process can be conveniently cast as the simultaneous minimization of multiple vision modules.

These algorithms were initially developed using a massively parallel bit-serial SIMD array processor, the AMT DAP 610C. While the DAP typically provides a speed-up of over 300 times the processing time of a serial workstation (Sun4), this is still too slow by over an order of magnitude for real-time processing.

However, 3-D WSI is an alternative hardware technology that allows us to increase performance by more fully exploiting the problem parallelism. Through 3-D WSI, we can take advantage of several different types of parallelism inherent in the vision integration problem. For example, the vision integration problem has three significant levels of parallelism:

1. *Spatial*--Neurons representing image estimates are processed simultaneously.

2. *Procedural*--Neuron update equations can be decomposed and the parts can be computed in parallel.

3. *Modular*--Each vision module may be processed independent of other modules.

We have performed detailed analyses of many different wafer stack configurations for early vision and cooperative vision integration networks. Table 2 summarizes the wafer composition of 5 different architecture designs. The first column lists the wafers being assembled for the baseline 16-wafer machine (3D/16). This machine will be capable of operating at a sustained rate of 204 MCPS for the regularization network. By adding a Switching Plane wafer along with more memory and accumulators we can enhance the baseline machine and take advantage of the procedural parallelism in the algorithm (3D/26).

Table 2. Wafer composition of 3-D WSI architectures

3-D Wafer Type	3D/16 Baseline	3D/26 Enhanced	3D/16-ParDivide	3D/26-ParDivide	3D/60-MultiMod
Replicator	1	1	1	1	3
Comparator	1	1	1	1	3
Shifter	5	12	5	12	9
Accumulator	9	11	7	11	15
Switching	0	1	0	1	2
Parallel Shift	0	2	0	2	6
Par Mul/Div.	0	2	2	2	6
Dense Mem.	0	0	0	0	16
Total Wafers	16	26	16	26	60

New wafers have been designed to speed performance by reducing computational bottlenecks and simultaneously exploiting multiple levels of neural network parallelism (See Table 1). These changes are reflected in the 3D/26-par design and speed processing to over 1.6 Giga-CPS for the regularization network benchmark.

Table 3 summarizes timing estimates for several wafer stack configurations compared with other machines on benchmarks running a single surface reconstruction module. These timings represent significant performance improvements over previously reported estimates for this problem [4].

Table 3. Benchmarks and timing estimates for various serial and parallel machines on 200 iterations of 128^2 regularization network for surface reconstruction.

	Sun 4	DAP 610C	3D/16	3D/26-par
Time (s)	171.34	0.52	0.33	0.042

We have extended the use these wafer stack architectures to the cooperative processing of *multiple* vision modules (3D/60-multi). Table 4 compares the performance of this wafer stack with benchmarks from the DAP. For this case, the neural network performance on the vision integration problem is over 2.4 billion connections per second. The SIMD organization of the 3-D Computer and massively parallel vertical interconnects greatly simplifies the intermodule synchronization required in the multimodule architecture. Figure 2 summarizes other performance estimates for this architecture.

Table 4. Benchmark and timing estimates for vision integration operations

	DAP 610C	3D/60-multi
Time (s)	1.58	0.048

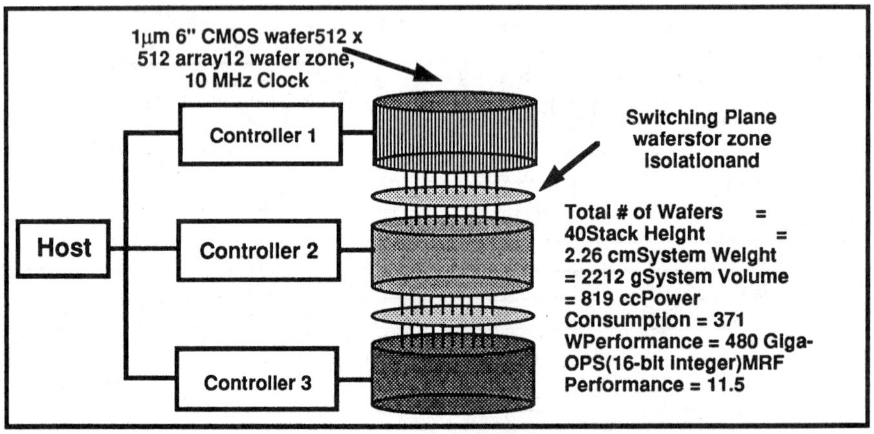

Figure 2. Combined MIMD/SIMD 3-D WSI architecture for cooperative vision integration. Each module is a MSIMD machine with a separate microcontroller.

CMOS Digital Retina Chip with Multi-bit Neurons for Image Coding

Cong-Kha Pham, Munemitsu Ikegami, Mamoru Tanaka and Katsufusa Shono
Department of Electronic and Electrical Engineering, Sophia University
7-1 Kioi-cho Chiyoda-ku Tokyo 102 Japan

Abstract- This paper describes the CMOS digital retina chip with neurons having multi-bit output for the image coding from analog to digital formats. The neuron having 1-bit output model can easily be implemented by the use of CMOS inverters. It has individual digital inputs, a common quantized output and a comparator. The weight vector is given as a fixed numerical value by a channel conductance for pull-up PMOS and pull-down NMOS transistors, respectively. The delayed binary outputs of neurons in the neighborhood are directly connected to the digital inputs. The next state of the network is computed from the current state at some neurons in any time interval. In order to reduce the error between the input analog gray image u and the output digital gray image y, multi-bit dynamics using CMOS neurons having multi-bit output is proposed. The output bit of each neuron can be determined from MSB to LSB bit by bit in analog delay.

I. Introduction

There are many researches for AD and DA conversions. The AD-DA conversion technique is effectively used for the data compression, which is useful for the data storage and transmission in digital format. Recently, it has been very important to develop an AD-DA system simulating the human visual system from the retina to the brain. It is known that the data on the nervous transmission is *digital* though the retina and brain operations are *analog*. Human visual system can be constructed by using the *locally connected neural networks*.

We think that the most important operation of a retina can be represented employing the nonlinear parallel dynamics, in which the set of all analog optical gray images can be mapped into the set of all digital images. This means the image digitalization for the $M \times N$ gray image is done as the following coding mapping $\mathbf{A}^{M\times N} \rightarrow \mathbf{D}^{M\times N}$, where symbols **A** and **D** denote the sets of analog optical or current gray-level and quantized-level value, respectively. It is expected that the number of quantized levels is reduced as possible as we can. If the quantized-level is binary, the output image will be a halftoning image. Although, it is well known that the fully connected *Hopfield neural networks* is able to solve many optimization problems, the digitalization discussed above is usually done with the *sparse Hopfield neural networks* (S-HNN), that is suitable for an integration of the whole system on one chip. Anasatassiou [1] proposed a digital halftoning techniques based on a symmetric error diffusion method with the digital S-HNN having eye characteristics. Crounse et al. [2] proposed that Chua's CNN can perform a natural image halftoning with eye characteristics using only analog process.

This paper describes the CMOS digital retina chip with neurons having multi-bit output for the image coding from analog to digital formats. The well-known formal neuron having 1-bit output model [4] represented by

$$F = \begin{cases} 1 & \sum a_i X_i \geq \sum b_j Y_j \\ 0 & \text{others} \end{cases}, \quad (1)$$

can easily be implemented by the use of CMOS inverters. It has individual digital inputs, a common quantized output and a comparator. The weight vector is given as a fixed numerical value by a channel conductance. For the halftoning image, the delayed binary outputs of neurons in the neighborhood are directly connected to the digital inputs. The next state of the network is computed from the current state at some neurons in any time interval. In order to reduce the error between the input analog gray image **u** and the output digital gray image **y**, multi-bit dynamics using CMOS neurons having multi-bit output is proposed. The output bit of each neuron can be determined from MSB to LSB bit by bit in analog delay. It will be concluded that it is best to use a network with CMOS neuron having 2-bit output to transform an analog natural image to the corresponding digital image.

II. Basic Neuron Circuit

Our study targeting a neuro computer system starts to find neural phenomena in the CMOS digital LSI. Well-known formal neuron model represented by [4] can easily be implemented by the use of CMOS inverters. It has individual digital inputs, a common quantized output and a comparator. The weight vector is given as a fixed numerical value by a channel conductance β_i, assuming $\beta_{pi} = \beta_{ni}$ for pull-up PMOS and pull-down NMOS transistors, respectively. Learning can be done during a design procedure of a set of mask, employing alternatively the simulation and the emulation.

An analog-digital balancing (ADB) inner product circuit which was a part of CMOS variable threshold logic [5] is employed for composing the neuron circuit. An analog input was given to the largest weight CMOS inverter. The chip can be implemented under the conventional Si wafer processing of the CMOS digital LSI.

An ADB circuit with n digital inputs is composed by n+1 CMOS inverters connected in parallel as shown in Figure 1. The channel conductances of pull-up PMOS and pull-down NMOS transistors of each CMOS inverter are

0-7803-1254-6/93$03.00

equivalently designed and weighted by the channel width-to-length ratio (W/L). In order to utilize the analog portion of the DC transfer characteristic of a CMOS inverter operating in the transition region, the ADB circuit has two types of inputs. One is a digital code input (terminals: $D_1, D_2, D_3, \cdots, D_n$) and the other one is an analog voltage input (terminal: U). The analog input voltage U is translated into a quantized voltage level (voltage) between the ground and power supply. For the PMOS and NMOS transistors of the inverters having digital inputs, the given weights are integer numbers (1,2,3,$\cdots$). For the PMOS and NMOS transistors of the inverter having an analog voltage input U, the given weights are the sum of weights which given to the CMOS inverters having digital inputs. The ADB circuit can be treated as a CMOS inverter which has a channel conductance ratio $\frac{\beta_n}{\beta_p}$ as follow:

$$\frac{\beta_n}{\beta_p} = \frac{\eta + \sum_{i=1}^{n} W_i D_i}{\eta + \sum_{i=1}^{n} W_i \overline{D_i}}, \qquad (2)$$

where $\eta = \sum_{i=1}^{n} W_i$. This means the ADB circuit has various transfer characteristic curves which correspond to various values of the digital inputs. Furthermore, if we connect the common output to the Vdd/2 comparator which implemented by two cascaded CMOS inverters, an output F can be obtained as follow:

$$F = \begin{cases} 1 & \text{if} \quad \frac{1}{\eta}\sum_{i=1}^{n} W_i D_i + C \geq U \\ 0 & \text{others} \end{cases}, \qquad (3)$$

where C is a bias to the analog input U. The concept of this ADB circuit can be used for constructing of the neuron for image coding.

In order to confirm the operation of the ADB circuit, we have evaluated as implementation of a 4-bit analog-to-digital converter. Four ADB circuits with Vdd/2 comparator are used for converting each bit, respectively. Each ADB circuit has the binary numbers (1,2,4,8,15) as the weights. In which, the weight 15 is given to the CMOS inverter having the analog input, and the others (1,2,4,8) are given to the CMOS inverters having digital inputs. In this case, the channel conductance ratio $\frac{\beta_n}{\beta_p}$ can be rewritten as follow:

$$\frac{\beta_n}{\beta_p} = \frac{15 + \sum_{i=0}^{3} 2^i D_{i+1}}{15 + \sum_{i=0}^{3} 2^i \overline{D_{i+1}}}, \qquad (4)$$

The ADB circuit in this case has 16 transfer characteristic curves which correspond to 16 values of the digital inputs (0~15), as shown in Figure 2. The 4-bit analog-to-digital converter have fabricated employing a convention CMOS technology. The chip photography is shown in Figure 3 and its dynamic characteristic is shown in Figure 4.

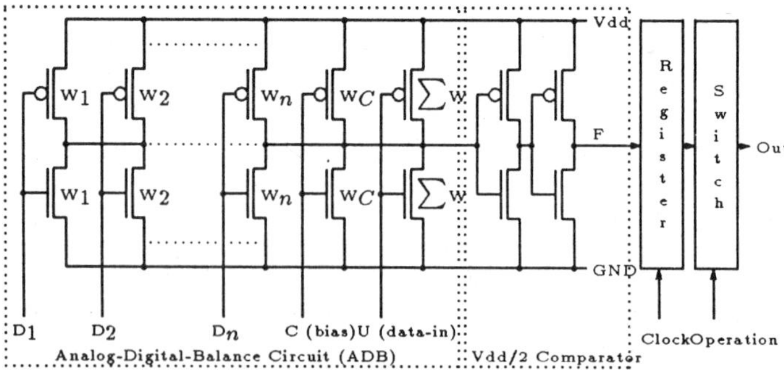

Figure 1: Schematic of the proposed neuron circuit.

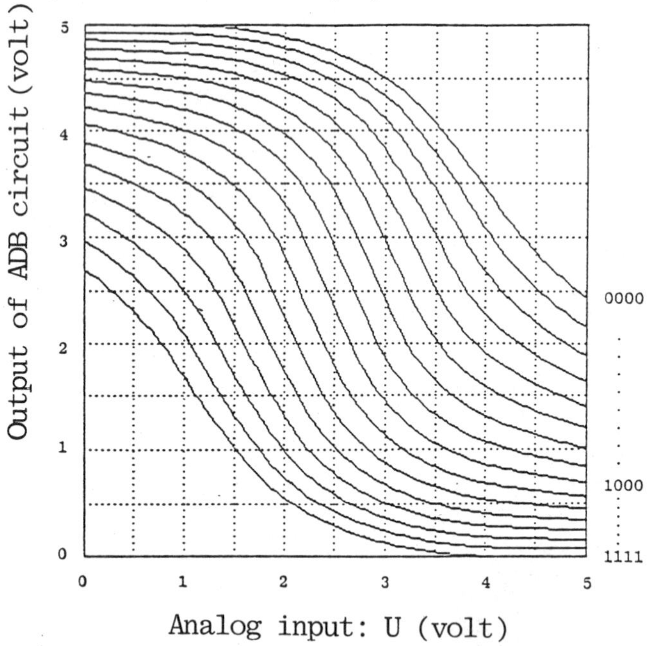

Figure 2: Transfer characteristic of ADB circuit.

III. Image 1-bit coding

The structure of the digital retina chip based on a cellular type. It composed with a simple grid plane on which each neuron having 1-bit output processes one pixel. The neuron receives and holds an input image pixel data. The network is a two-dimensional $M \times N$ array of neurons, which generates the quantized value employing the dynamic quantization method. In which, each analog element $u \in [0,1]$ of an analog sequence is transformed to the corresponding quantized value $y \in \{0,1\}$. The neuron is denoted by $C(i,j)$ $(0 \leq i < M; 0 \leq j < N)$. Each of analog pixel data u_{ij} is given to the corresponding neuron. The neuron computes a difference between the input value and a weighted average of the output values of neighbor neurons. The transition of the neuron $C(i,j)$ through the quantizing function f is done corresponding to equation (3) as follows :

$$y_{ij}(t+1) = f(\sum_{mn} A_{ijmn} y_{mn}(t) - u_{ij} + \frac{\delta}{2}), \qquad (5)$$

$$A_{ijmn} \geq 0, \; A_{ijij} = 0,$$

$$f(x) = \begin{cases} 0 (x \geq 0) \\ 1 (x < 0) \end{cases}. \qquad (6)$$

Figure 3: Chip photography of 4-bit A/D converter.

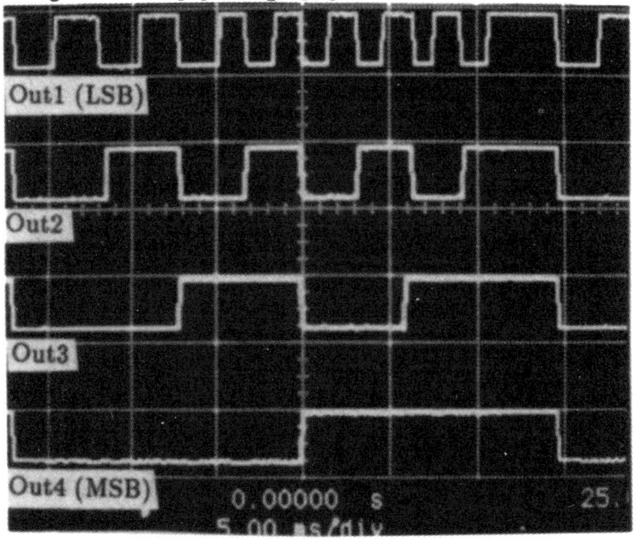

Figure 4: Dynamic characteristic of 4-bit A/D converter.

Here, A_{ijmn} is the weight from neuron $C(i,j)$ to neuron $C(m,n)$, which is a positive value or 0, and $\delta/2=\eta C$. Also, for the network stability, A_{ijij} always takes the value 0. In this case any symmetric template **A** with zero center diagonal elements (i.e., $A_{ijmn} = A_{mnij}, A_{ijij} = 0$) guarantees that the transition is converged to the steady state [3]. At first, the initial value of the neuron is randomly set, and the neurons of the network are randomly and asynchronously activated.

In order to determine the weights for the network, a two-dimensional Gaussian distribution is employed as follows:

$$w_{ijxy} = \frac{1}{2\pi\sigma^2} \exp\{-\frac{(i-x)^2+(j-y)^2}{2\sigma^2}\} \quad (7)$$

$$A^*_{ijxy} = \begin{cases} w_{ijxy} & \text{if } max\{|i-x|,|j-y|\} \le r \\ 0 & \text{otherwise} \end{cases} \quad (8)$$

According to this distribution, the elements which are far form the center take very small values. Therefor, the weights for the neurons outside of the r neighborhood can be approximated to 0, and the network becomes sparse. When a "5×5 neighborhood" (r=2) is took into account, a normalized weights template is calculated as follow:

$$\mathbf{W} = \begin{bmatrix} 0 & 1 & 2 & 1 & 0 \\ 1 & 4 & 5 & 4 & 1 \\ 2 & 5 & 8 & 5 & 2 \\ 1 & 4 & 5 & 4 & 1 \\ 0 & 1 & 2 & 1 & 0 \end{bmatrix} \quad (9)$$

and the template **A** becomes as follow:

$$\mathbf{A} = \begin{bmatrix} 0 & 1 & 2 & 1 & 0 \\ 1 & 4 & 5 & 4 & 1 \\ 2 & 5 & 0 & 5 & 2 \\ 1 & 4 & 5 & 4 & 1 \\ 0 & 1 & 2 & 1 & 0 \end{bmatrix} \quad (10)$$

Here, $\delta/2$ is defined as $\frac{w_{ijij}}{2} = 4$.

For the simulation, the gray image "SIDBA-girl" shown in Figure 5(a) is used. The size of original image is 256 × 256 pixels, and has 8-bit as the gray level. The image got from simulation result employing 1-bit image coding is shown in Figure 5 (b).

The neuron having 1-bit output which will be an important element of the CMOS digital retina chip is proposed. It bases on the concept of the ADB circuit with Vdd/2 comparator as shown in Figure 1. Also, the additional register and switch circuits are appended for controlling of the neuron's operation. The given weights to the CMOS inverters having digital inputs (the outputs from neighborhood neurons) of the ADB circuit are values of the elements of the template **A** (except elements with 0 value). The given weight to the CMOS inverter having the analog input (analog gray image) of the ADB circuit is the sum of all of values of the elements of the template **A** and δ (in this case it is 60). Also, an additional CMOS inverter with $\delta/2$ (in this case it is 4) as a weight is added, for representing of the bias $C=\delta/2$. The input to this CMOS inverter is either high- or low-level. The proposed structure for 1-bit network of the CMOS digital retina chip with 8 × 8 neurons is shown in Figure 6. It includes a 8 × 8 network and a control circuit which operates with an external clock. The control circuit generates control signals for every neuron that derive the dynamic operation for the network. The designed physical layout of the CMOS digital retinal chip is shown in Figure 7.

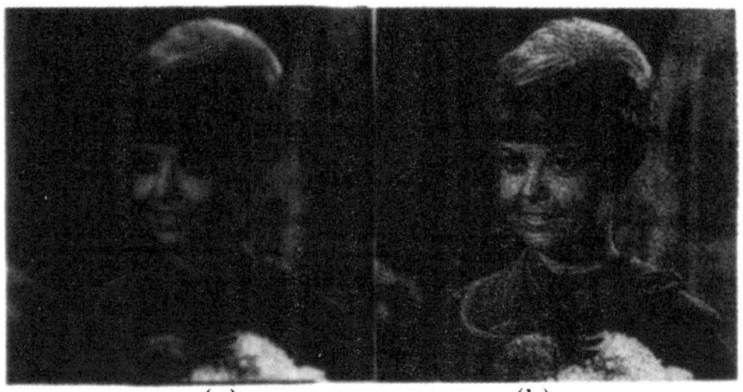

(a) (b)

Figure 5: Simulation image (a) original "SIDBA-girl" (b) result image of 1-bit coding.

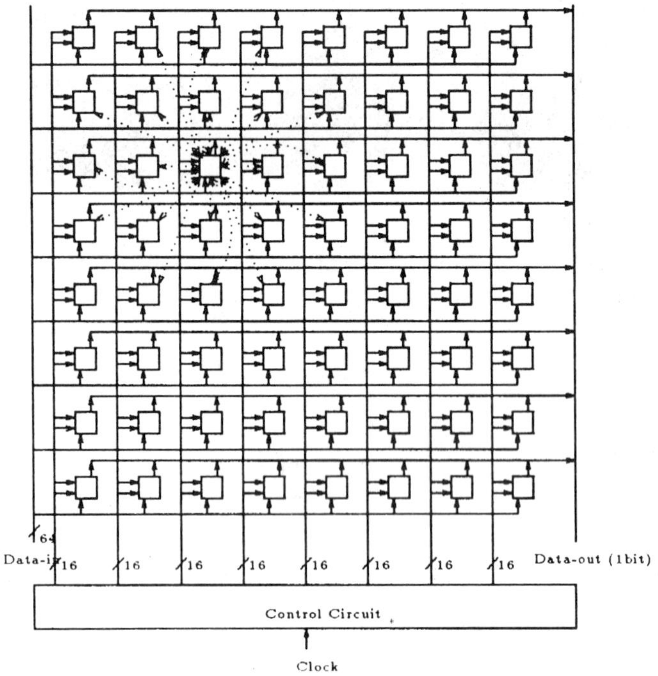

Figure 6: Proposed structure of CMOS digital retinal chip.

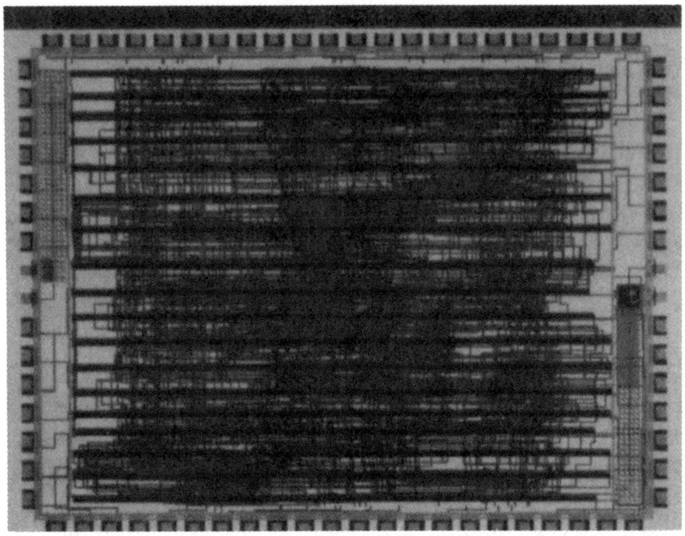

Figure 7: Physical layout of CMOS digital retinal chip.

Figure 8: Result image of 2-bit coding.

IV. Image 2-bit coding

In order to reduce the error between the input analog gray image and the output digital image, we propose 2-bit image coding method. The concept of this method is similar to the 1-bit image coding described above. However, each analog element $u \in [0,1]$ of an analog sequence will be transformed to the corresponding 2-bit of the quantized value y. This means the quantized value y will take 4 levels $\in \{0,1\}$. In this case, the transition of the neuron $C(i,j;k)$ is represented as follows :

$$y_{ij0}(t+1) = f(e_{ij} + \frac{\delta}{2}) \tag{11}$$

$$y_{ij1}(t+1) = f(e_{ij} + \delta y_{ij0}(t+1) + \frac{\delta}{4}) \tag{12}$$

$$e_{ij} = \sum_{ij} A_{ijmn} \sum_{k=0}^{1} \frac{2^{(1-k)}}{3} y_{ijk}(t) - u_{ij} \tag{13}$$

where k is the bit number of neuron $C(i,j)$,

The image got from simulation result employing 2-bit image coding is shown in Figure 8. The design of 2-bit network for the CMOS digital retina chip is in progress. The neuron having 2-bit output can be implemented by expanding of two modules of the neuron having 1-bit output.

V. Conclusion

We have described the digital retina chips with multi-bit dynamics. In the case that the neuron having 1-bit output, some noises have founded on the output halftoning image. The output halftoning image will be improved by using neurons having 2-bit output and the suitable distributed weights.

References

[1] D. Anastassiou, "Neural Net based Digital Halftoning Images", *IEEE International Symposium on Circuits and Systems,* Finland, June 1988, pp. 507-510.

[2] K. R. Crounse, T. Roska, and L.O.Chua, "Image halftoning with Cellular Neural Networks", *Memorandum UCB/ERL* M91/106, November, 1991.

[3] J.J. Hopfield, "Neurons with graded response have collective computational properties like those of two-state neurons" in *Proc. Natl. Acad. Sci, USA,* vol. 81, 1984, pp3088-3092.

[4] W. S. McCulloch, and W. H. Pitts, "A logical calculus of the ideas immanent in neural nets", in *Bull. Math. Biophys.*, vol. 5, pp. 115-133, 1943.

[5] C. Kim, N. Kushiyama and K. Shono, "Variable threshold logic - a highly flexible logic", *IEEE Electron Device Letter,* vol. EDL-6, pp. 390-393, Jul. 1985.

A Neural Network Systems Component

Dean Mueller and Dan Hammerstrom
Adaptive Solutions, Inc.
1400 NW Compton Drive Suite 340
Beaverton Oregon 97006

Abstract - This paper presents a CMOS device designed to interface the CNAPS™-1064 neural processor IC to traditional computing environments. The encapsulation of flexible I/O models and sequencer control into a modular architecture enables the creation of systems across a wide spectrum of performance capabilities.

I. Introduction

Adaptive Solutions' mission is to leverage the combination of state-of-the-art VLSI, and the non-linear, adaptive capabilities of neural networks to provide a quantum leap in our capability to perform pattern recognition and control applications. This objective is met by optimizing a VLSI architecture for the problem domain at hand. The CNAPS (Connected Network of Adaptive Processors) system provides orders of magnitude improvement in performance at the cost of traditional microprocessor-based systems. We believe this performance increase translates directly to vastly improved solutions for pattern recognition (such as speech, OCR, and image processing) and control problems.

We have chosen artificial neural networks (ANN) as our primary model, since the essence of our approach is to provide general applicability for implementing data transformations (such as from an image scan to the ASCII representation of a character). These transformations are extremely complex and often involve time-varying, non-linear functions. The non-linear capabilities and adaptive nature of ANNs make them a natural for these types of tasks. However, for most applications the neural network is a small part of a larger system which generally involves more traditional computations such as Fourier transforms, Markov models, rule-based knowledge, image segmentation, etc.

Consequently, the CNAPS architecture is not limited to neural networks but has been designed to meet the needs of an entire range of associated problems. It is not a general-purpose computer, but it is reasonably general-purpose within the target domain. By restricting the range of applicability, simplifications are possible that allow an inexpensive implementation of a parallel processor system with a significant boost in performance. Low cost, in turn, is essential because of the pervasive nature of the problems we are trying to solve and the situations where such solutions are required.

Crucial to the CNAPS strategy is the ability to provide low-cost program and I/O control of the CNAPS processor array and to encapsulate this functionality efficiently into a single piece of silicon. In addition, a traditional, digital co-processor-like interface to the CNAPS system is essential for the target applications of this processor. This paper presents the design of the CSC — the CNAPS Sequencer Chip — which performs this function.

A common criticism of neural network chips is that their designs often represent local optimizations with little thought given to the larger system context in which these devices must operate. The CSC is a *systems* component and was designed with the larger system in mind. It has two objectives, to control the CNAPS processor array and to interface the array efficiently to the larger digital world. The CSC provides efficient control of CNAPS programs. In addition, it is a powerful I/O processor which simultaneously controls system input and output. The CSC operates as a building-block component and can interface directly to external I/O devices and to other CSCs, allowing large, complex systems to be created. It also can control external input and output devices interfacing directly with the CNAPS processor array chips, increasing the usable I/O bandwidth of the CNAPS system. Finally, and most importantly, integrating the entire I/O control and sequencing functions into a single chip enables low-end CNAPS systems to be created easily and inexpensively.

The CSC functionality and its simple, clean interface is critical to the deployment of real world pattern recognition and neural network applications executing on CNAPS. We believe that the CSC is the first neural network *systems* component. This paper presents the CSC architecture and design methodology.

II. CNAPS System Architecture

To appreciate the functionality of the CSC, an understanding of a general CNAPS system architecture is helpful. A CNAPS application development system consists of a control subsystem and a CNAPS subsystem as shown in Fig. 1. The control subsystem is responsible for downloading programs, data I/O support, debugging services, diagnostics, and interfacing to other hardware peripherals. In this type of full-function environment, the CP could be a microprocessor controller board with RAM, ROM, and various other hardware interfaces to control system-level, real-time functions. However, the control subsystem implementation

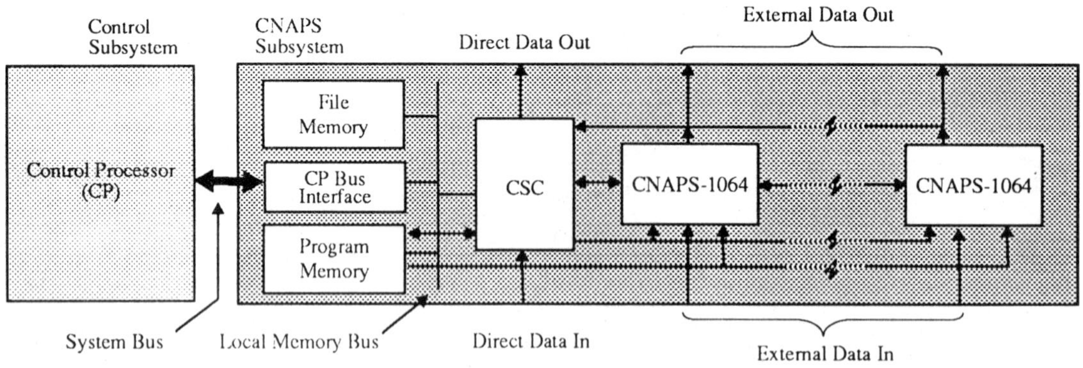

Fig. 1 System Architecture and CNAPS Subsystem Architecture

depends on the extent of the functionality required in the application. For a simple end-use application, the CP may be very simple, or it may not exist at all. With the help of a small state machine and some ROM, the CSC can implement an auto-boot function that tests the system, loads the application program, and begins execution without any external assistance.

The CNAPS subsystem executes the CNAPS program. A block diagram of the basic architecture is shown in Fig. 2. The subsystem consists of three types of interfaces to external systems: the CP interface, the Direct Data interface, and the External Data interface. The CP interface is required to interface to the larger compute system. The Direct and External interfaces access stream data independent of the system memory bus. These interfaces may allow higher access rates than the system bus, as well as the benefits of off-loading system traffic. The architecture of the CNAPS subsystem can be broken down into a few basic modules: an interface to the CP, the DRAM file memory space, a SRAM program memory space, the CSC, and an array of Adaptive Solutions CNAPS-1064 multi-processor ICs.

The CP bus interface links the local bus and the system bus. It is also configured to map the CNAPS subsystem into the larger control and memory space. This interface can be a slave only, or a master/slave depending on the application. Master capability is mandatory if the CNAPS program requires data that is outside the range of local file memory. The CNAPS subsystem can be easily adapted to different compute environments by simply modifying the CP interface block to be compatible with the target system bus.

The various memory spaces in the CNAPS subsystem are connected to a local memory bus. A local, synchronous memory bus was implemented so that the CSC could perform high-speed memory access to the local data memory without contending for the system memory bus. The major units on this bus are: File memory, Program memory, the CSC, and the CP interface. The DRAM file memory is a slave device used to store data locally in the CNAPS subsystem. This memory can hold input or output data files and can be accessed by the CP or the CSC.

The SRAM program memory is a slave device that must be downloaded with programs before execution can begin. It is accessed by the CP over the local memory bus, but when a CNAPS program is executing, it is accessed by the CSC over an independent address and data bus. This lets the CSC access an instruction from the program memory on every clock cycle independent of the traffic on the local memory bus.

The CSC accesses a 64-bit instruction from program memory on every cycle. Thirty-two bits of each instruction are decoded by the CSC to specify sequencer operation and I/O control. The other 32 bits are broadcast to control the CNAPS array processing nodes. As a slave on the local memory bus, the CSC can be accessed by the CP to initialize various state. As a master, it can read or write to local memory while it executes a CNAPS program. The CSC also interfaces to the CNAPS-1064 to supervise the data and instruction flow to/from the array.

Each CNAPS-1064 IC is a VLSI device that contains an array of 64 digital signal processor-like processing nodes (PNs). The processing nodes are arranged in a SIMD (single instruction, multiple data) configuration using broadcast interconnect [1]. The architecture of each PN is general enough for classical digital signal processing and pattern recognition, but is optimized for neural network applications.

One of the major advantages of the CNAPS system is its ability to perform feature extraction [2] as well as pattern recognition on the same system. The CNAPS system has been effectively used for speech recognition [3] as well as for speaker identification applications [4]. The system has also been effective for high speed image processing applications such as Kanji character recognition [5].

The PN architecture, as shown in Fig. 2, has proven to be very suitable for many types of applications. Two input buses are supplied to the array: the PNCMD Bus and the IN Bus. The PNCMD Bus contains the 32-bit instruction and the IN Bus contains the 8-bit data broadcast to all PNs. The OUT Bus allows any PN to output data under the control of the CSC. In addition to the parallel broadcast buses, each processor is interconnected to its nearest neighbor by a one-

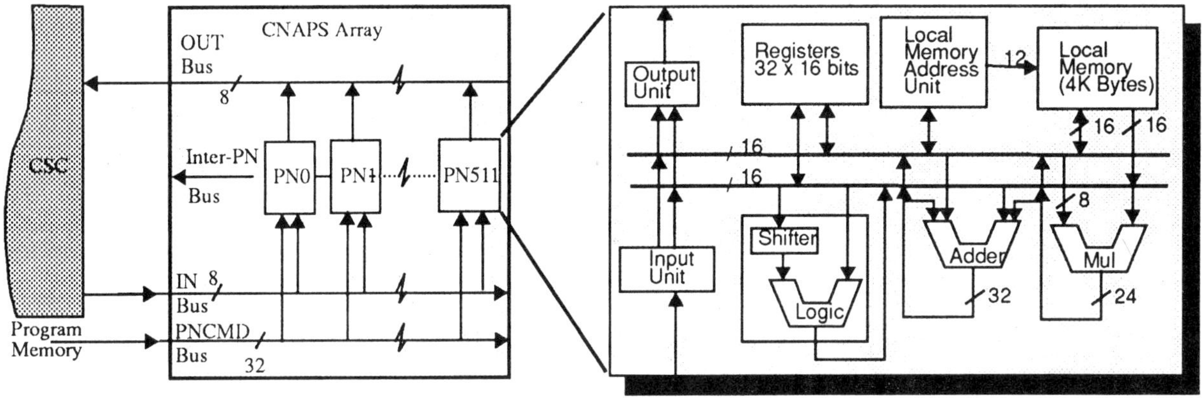

Fig. 2 The CNAPS Array and PN Architecture

dimensional Inter-PN Bus.

Each PN contains 4K bytes of memory and its own address generation logic to access the local memory. The multiplier, ALU, and dual internal buses provide an efficient architecture for high-speed sum-of-products execution. Signed 8-, 16-, or 32-bit integer arithmetic is supported by these units. The input and output units support 8- or 16-bit communication to the rest of the array. When operating at 20MHz, each 64-processor chip is capable of performing 1.28 billion connections per second. When executing the Back Propagation algorithm, each chip performs 210 million updates per second [6]. ANNs are implemented by mapping neurons into physical or virtual PNs. All processors execute a multiply-accumulate in a single cycle. A PN can place its output on the OUT Bus, and the CSC will broadcast this value to the IN Bus where it is available to all PNs in the next network layer. Each PN will broadcast its output in turn implementing n^2 connections in n clocks [1].

The broadcast SIMD structure allows for easy expansion of the array beyond a single chip. Multiple CNAPS-1064 chips can be connected to create larger systems without the concept of distinct chip boundaries. However, the user must know the number of PNs in the system when programming.

III. CSC Operation and Architecture

The master state-machine in the CSC is shown in Fig. 3.

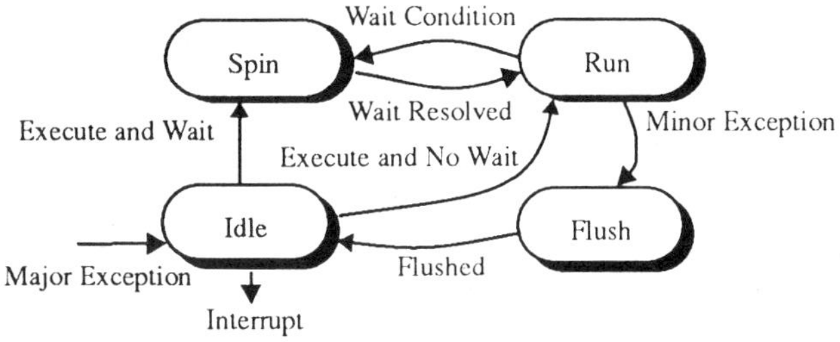

Fig. 3 CSC State Machine

When IDLE, the CSC does not execute a CNAPS program, and the entire internal state is accessible from the local memory bus. When instructed to do so, the CSC moves to RUN mode and begins executing instructions. When RUNning, the CSC may require mastership of the local memory bus. Various wait conditions such as a wait-for-data cause the CSC to SPIN until the wait is resolved. When a minor condition occurs that stops execution, the CSC will first flush the file memory output buffers before entering IDLE. There are also some major exceptions that can occur that will cause the CSC to enter the IDLE state without flushing the buffers. When the CSC returns to IDLE, it issues an interrupt, and the CP can query the status register to determine the cause of termination.

The CSC contains the five major modules shown in Fig. 4. Each of these units has control lines to communicate with each other, as well as a global data bus that connects all blocks and allows instruction-controlled data transfer between the units. In addition to these functions, there are mode registers, profile counters, and other miscellaneous functions that are beyond the scope of this paper. There has been much discussion so far about interfacing to the local bus, sequencing instructions, and I/O processing, the three major blocks in the CSC. In addition to these functions, there is also a 64x32 register file and a 32-bit ALU. These two structures, along with the CSC's ability to perform internal data transfers, enable complex address control and file structure maintenance. Each of the three major functional units will now be discussed.

A. The Control Processor Interface (CPIF)

The interface to the local memory bus functions as a basic master/slave memory interface with interrupt capability. The internals of the CSC are highly accessible and observable by the CP because most CSC internal state is mapped into the bus. The CPIF controls these accesses by acting as a slave on the local bus. In addition to providing a pathway into the internal state, this interface contains command and status

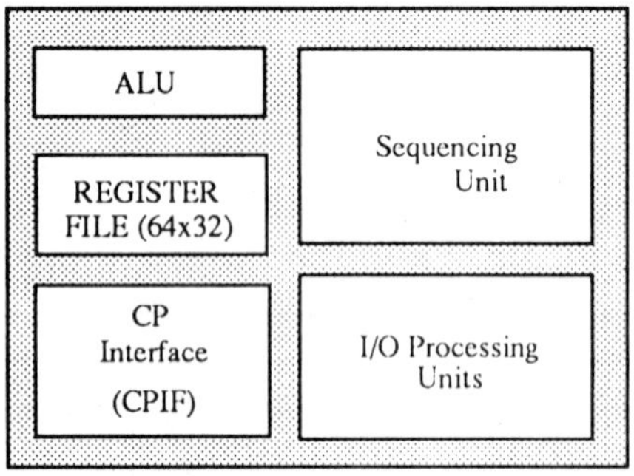

Fig. 4 CSC Block Diagram

registers that allow the CP to start, stop, or query the status of the CSC at any time. Before executing a CNAPS program, the CP sets up the CSC by initializing various state and pointers to file memory data input and output space. The CP then issues a command to the command register and CNAPS execution begins.

When the CSC is executing CNAPS programs, it may become master of the local bus to access file memory or locations in the larger system memory space. The interface is responsible for taking requests from the I/O processing unit, arbitrating for the local memory bus, and controlling the access. This interface is capable of transferring data at the maximum combined I/O rate of the CNAPS-1064. As the program executes, a number of conditions can occur that cause the CSC to halt execution and issue an interrupt. The status registers in this interface can be read at any time to determine the cause of the interrupt or to monitor the internal modes and status of the CSC.

B. Sequencing Unit

The sequencer unit controls the activity of the CNAPS array interface by executing instructions that specify sequencing and I/O control. The 16-bit program counter can address 64K, 64-bit instructions. Thirty-two bits of the instruction are sent to the array, while the other half is sent to the CSC to dictate sequencer and data flow control. The sequencer and I/O control blocks work together to supply synchronized instruction and data flow to the CNAPS array.

There are two distinct types of CSC commands: those that control the program sequencing and data I/O flow (sequencer), and those that cause intra-CSC data transfers (DATAXFR). Sequencer commands support breakpoints, CP system calls, conditional looping with eight different loop registers, literal loading into various sequencer registers, a single level jump and return, and control of I/O source and destination. The various conditional instructions can test the loop register, ALU output tests, CNAPS arbitration, and OUT Bus status.

The DATAXFR instruction group allows the user to specify direct or indirect data transfers within the CSC. This includes access to most internal state, the register file, and the ALU. This instruction type is useful for transferring data that has been loaded from the program into sequencer registers to some other place such as the I/O pointers or the CNAPS array itself. Since the DATAXFR instruction uses some of the fields normally used to control I/O and sequencer operation, default functions are implied.

C. I/O Processing Units

The I/O processing units for the IN Bus and OUT Bus are designed to allow a variety of data flow paths to interact with and be synchronized to the CNAPS array. Each CSC instruction contains fields that specify the I/O type for that specific instruction. These fields, along with some control registers, are used to control the actions of the I/O processors.

In defining the types of I/O support, the primary goal is to use data at the maximum rate allowed by the CNAPS array, to support traditional file and stream data flow from DRAM, and to support stream data flow that is independent of the memory bus. Another integral factor in solving the instruction/data synchronization problem is the ability for the I/O processing units to block instruction flow and pause the array if data is required but not yet available, or if the instruction calls for data output, but there is no room. In this case, the I/O units instruct the master mode control to SPIN on the current instruction until the wait is resolved. When SPINning, even though the sequencer and array are stalled, the I/O units will continue to operate with the CSC-external interfaces to resolve the wait condition.

Fig. 5 shows a block diagram of the I/O datapaths in the CSC. This diagram illustrates the possible sources for the IN Bus and the various destinations for the OUT Bus. A portion of the CNAPS array is also shown for clarity. The IN Bus data on any particular CNAPS chip can come from five possible sources: External, Direct, Constant register, Out-In pipe, or File memory. There are four possible destinations for data on a CNAPS chip's OUT Bus: External, Direct, File memory, and the Out-In pipe. The Out-In pipe actually latches the OUT Bus on every instruction, independent of the use of the other destinations. Only one of the other destinations can be specified at one time. Each I/O processing unit type will now be briefly described.

The 16-byte input and output queues that access file memory can transfer data at 40MByte/sec, which is the maximum combined I/O rate of the CNAPS-1064. In addition to the data buffers themselves, there are also address generation and control functions. This includes address pointers, counters, byte counters, and bounds detection to fully control file memory access. The buffers perform sequential access from a user-defined starting point, which allows auto-increment access to sub-portions of data that randomly exists in a larger data set. This capability is useful in an image application for scanning the region of interest, or for sliding templates or windows in a pattern recognition application. When maintaining file structures, the various pointers can be saved in the register file, manipulated in the ALU, and restored by the program, so the CSC can emulate a large number of *virtual* channels.

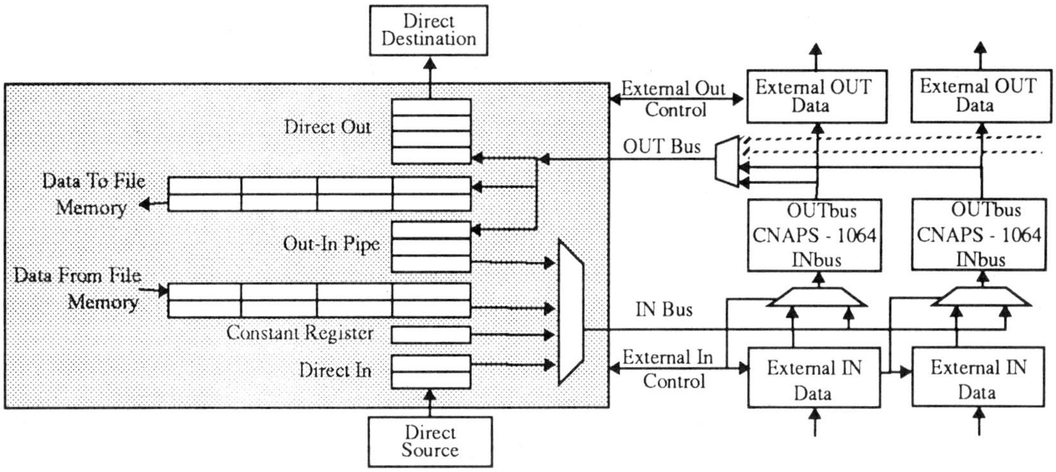

Fig. 5 CNAPS I/O Datapaths

The Direct I/O channels consist of two (one for input, one for output) 8-bit parallel interfaces. These direct data paths are used in applications where data does not come from file memory, but rather from a separate CSC data port. Access to this data by the CNAPS array is synchronized by the CSC. The Directin interface accepts data at 20MBytes/sec and routes it to the IN Bus. The Directout interface takes data from the OUT Bus at 20MBytes/sec and applies it to the Direct output port. A simple synchronous handshake interface allows multiple CSC systems to connect directly and operate in a loosely synchronized, data dependent manner.

The external I/O is a control interface that allows independent, remote data transfer to/from each CNAPS-1064 in the array, thus permitting multiple external datapath channels to/from each CNAPS-1064. Such a system, when used with multiple CNAPS-1064 chips, could provide the data rates required for high-resolution continuous video processing. When instructed to use external data, the CSC asserts the control lines to an external multiplexor that allows the remote device to place data on the IN Bus or take data from the OUT Bus. This is just a control interface; data are not transferred through the CSC. A burst mode supports external data transfers on every clock cycle. Each external channel supports a 20MBytes/sec transfer rate; the total maximum data rate depends on the number of external channels. The maximum rate is (20M * n) where n is the number of external channels. For example, an 8-chip system with 8 external in and 8 external out channels can transfer data at 320MByte/second.

In addition to the three sources listed above, the user can indicate that the IN Bus be driven from the constant register, or that the data on the OUT Bus are fed back around to the IN Bus. This data wrap-around allows recursive neural networks or feedforward neural networks to be implemented efficiently on the CNAPS array. For a feedforward network, one layer transmits its outputs while the next layer in the network computes its outputs.

IV. Design Technology and Methodology

The CSC is implemented in a 240-pin MQFP package using a 95K gate array in a 0.8 micron double-metal CMOS process. The design methodology used to develop the CSC relies heavily on simulation and a top-down design flow. A high-level simulator was written in C that allowed clock-accurate simulation of the architecture. It is fully integrated with Adaptive Solutions' software products, providing the ability to accurately simulate the CP and CNAPS system concurrently. This simulator is used for software and architecture development and is considered the "golden" simulator for the system.

The CSC was designed by creating an RTL-level description in Verilog. A behavioral-level model was created for the CNAPS subsystem so that the CSC could be verified in its native environment. The Verilog CNAPS subsystem was tested by running programs on the C simulator and capturing transactions for application to the Verilog simulation. A run-time comparison technique is used to compare the idealistic realm of architecture simulation against a real hardware implementation. Random "throttles" control the models to allow the transactions to take place randomly. This creates the ability to superimpose asynchronous random data rates, random bus contention, and random halt and restart functions while performing robust validation against the architectural simulator. This technique was instrumental to the success of the CSC design in an environment dominated by unknown data/control rates and distributions.

Synthesis tools were used to create a gate-level implementation from the RTL-level model. This gate implementation was verified in the same system as the RTL-level model. A static timing analyzer was used to verify chip timing with the ASIC vendors library. After the design was complete, automatic test insertion and test pattern generation were used to implement internal serial scan and JTAG.

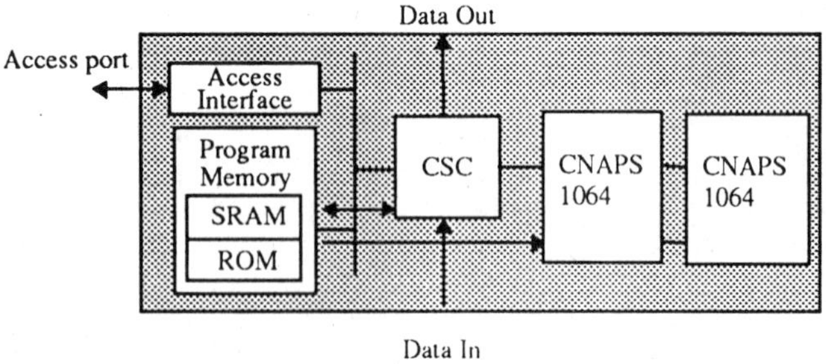

Fig. 6 Low-cost Application Engine

V. A Spectrum of CNAPS System Configurations

The system configuration shown in Fig. 1 is typical of a high-performance application development system. The CSC was designed to support a wide range of systems that could be much bigger, or much smaller than this example. To give the reader a feeling for the flexibility of the system, two different systems will now be described.

The configuration shown in Fig. 6 shows a small system that could be designed for a specific end-use application. It contains 2 CNAPS-1064 chips (128 processors) running at 20MHz. This system is capable of performing 2.56 billion connections (multiply-accumulates) per second and 420 million connection updates per second. Notice that the CP interface has been replaced by a simple access port for special-purpose access only. It is not required for normal operation and could be used for diagnostics or for downloading EPROM software updates. Also notice that there is no File memory in this system. Instead of getting data from a file memory, data is accepted from an acquisition system into the Direct input port of the CSC. Likewise, data is pumped out via the Direct out interface. Each of these ports can maintain a transfer rate of 20MByte/second.

On system power-up, the CSC executes from ROM to perform diagnostics and load the application software into SRAM program memory. The CSC can immediately start performing the application software loop. The program will expect data from the Direct input port and will block on any instruction that requires data if data does not exist. As soon as data is available, the CSC continues execution. This provides the capability to perform real-time computations in a data stream environment. If the Access Interface shown here is replaced with PC bus converter logic or a SCSI interface, an external device could control or interact with the application. A low-cost implementation designed with a popular interface can bring impressive computational power to the consumer market.

The basic architecture can be easily expanded to support large, high-performance systems with flexible dataflow configurations. The system shown in Fig. 7 consists of four CNAPS arrays. Each array contains 8 CNAPS-1064s with direct and external I/O support. Operating at 20MHz, such a system would provide 2048 processors computing 40 billion connections per second. It is useful for compute intensive, high-bandwidth applications where the problem can be broken down into independent programs and process levels with point-to-point data communication between each level.

Each CNAPS array requires a CSC to control the array. This example shows two such arrays per local memory bus. This is just an arbitrary choice, the number of CSCs on any

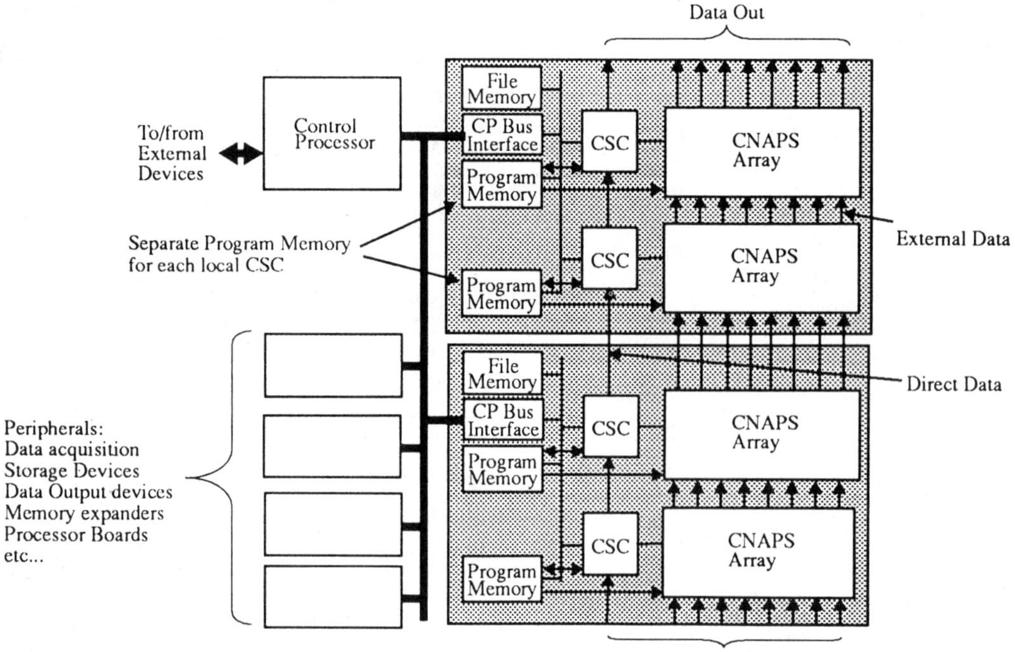

Fig. 7 Complex Multi-level CNAPS Configuration

local bus depends on the memory structure, the bus loading, and the target frequency. Each CSC has its own program memory to allow independent programming in each array. The CSCs that are attached to the same local bus have high-speed access to the same file memory. Such a scenario is useful in applications that require independent processing but share the same data. Semaphores can be used to synchronize access to shared data files.

The CSCs can also initiate transfers across the system bus to allow access to alternate memory spaces, data acquisition boards, or other system devices. Such a configuration is useful when data is shared across the system, as long as the bandwidth/traffic load does not impose an unacceptable limit on the performance of the CNAPS array.

The CSCs are connected to each other via the Direct data ports. These ports allow data to be transferred between CSCs without the use of the system or local bus. Communicating between levels is accomplished by allowing instruction blocking on the data until the communicating neighbor is synchronized, thus allowing data transfer between levels. In addition to communicating between CSCs, these ports could also be used to communicate with a data acquisition system or some other data output device. A similar configuration is used to connect the external interfaces together for high-bandwidth requirements such as high-end image applications.

VI. Summary

Adaptive Solutions has successfully achieved its goal of creating a device to efficiently interface the CNAPS architecture to traditional computing environments. The CSC provides a simple co-processor interface that can be easily adapted to different target environments and, at the same time, utilize the CNAPS architecture at the maximum performance possible. The architecture is simple and modular, with general data I/O support that can be adapted to varied system dataflow models. The architecture modularity allows efficient implementation of a wide range of systems from simple and low-cost, to very complex and high performance applications. This development is a significant step towards the deployment of truly high performance neural networks and other highly parallel algorithms into the computing and application mainstream.

References

[1] Hammerstrom, D., "A VLSI srchitecture for high-performance, low-cost, on-chip learning", Proceedings IJCNN June 1990.

[2] Skinner, T., "Speech signal processing on a neurocomputer", Proceedings of ICSLP 1990.

[3] Holt, J., Skinner, T., and Nguyen, N., "Automating operator services using automatic speech recognition", Proceedings of IEEE Asilomar Conference 1992.

[4] Skinner, T., Holt, J., and Nguyen, N., "Automatic identity confirmation at Adaptive Solutions", *Speech Technology*, Vol. 5, no. 4 1991.

[5] Togawa, F., Ueda, T., Aramaki, T., Tanaka, A., "Receptive field neural network with shift tolerant capability for Kanji character recognition", IJCNN, Singapore, Nov 1991.

[6] McCartor, H., "Back propagation implementation on the Adaptive Solutions neurocomputer chip", Advances in Neural Information Processing Systems, Vol. 3, pp. 1028-1031, Morgan Kaufmann, 1991.

A Sound Localization System Based On Biological Analogy

Neal Bhadkamkar* Boyd Fowler†
Electrical Engineering Department, Stanford University, Stanford, CA 94305
email: neal@milo.stanford.edu fowler@isl.stanford.edu

***Abstract*—**
We have designed, fabricated and tested a low-power analog VLSI system that implements a model of sound localization in the horizontal plane. The model uses the time difference between a sound arriving at each ear to determine the location of the sound source. The system consists of two chips fabricated through MOSIS in a standard 2μm, p-well, CMOS process. One chip contains circuitry to model left and right side cochleas, hair cells and auditory neurons, while the other chip contains circuitry to model the binaural cross-correlation activity of neurons in the superior olive of the brainstem. Measured test results are promising but reveal challenges that must be overcome in order to obtain reliable performance. This is necessary before subthreshold designs can be used in mass-produced products.

I. Introduction

Sound localization is a biologically important function for both predator and prey. It is a complex process involving the joint action of many stages of auditory processing. The location of a sound source in the horizontal plane, that is whether it is to the left or the right, results in a time difference between sounds arriving at each ear. This time difference is believed to be one of the main cues that the auditory system uses to localize sound sources [1]. For a human head this time difference can be as much as one millisecond, while for an elephant's head it is proportionately larger. The processing is believed to start in an evolutionarily old part of the brain called the brainstem. Specifically, a region of the brainstem called the superior olive contains cells that are preferentially responsive to sounds with specific interaural time differences; these cells receive inputs from both the left and right cochleas via their respective hair cells and auditory neurons and can discriminate differences of microseconds in the arrival time of sounds at the two ears [2].

We have designed a set of two CMOS chips that are meant to model the early processing done by the left and right cochlea, hair cells and auditory nerves, and the portion of the brainstem responsive to interaural time differences. Save for buffers for driving the signals off chip, the design is based almost entirely on circuits operating in the subthreshold region [3, 4]. Current flow in this region is governed by diffusion rather than by drift, and is exponentially related to the gate voltage of the transistor. Subthreshold current flows are so small that traditional CMOS designs consider the transistor to be off. The circuits used for the cochlea, hair cells and correlators are novel and differ from implementations by other researchers [5, 6, 7]. At a high level our approach to sound localization is similar to that in [8], but our implementation is radically different.

The remainder of this paper is organized as follows. Section II. provides an overview of the design of the system. Section III. provides more detail on the design of the cochlea-chip and correlator-chip, while Section IV. presents summary results for the two chips. Section V. presents a discussion of the results and the design challenges that arise from the use of subthreshold circuitry, and Section VI. presents our conclusions.

II. System Design

An overview of the two-chip system is shown in Figure 1. The **cochlea-chip**, receives its inputs through two microphones or function generators, representing the left and right ears. It contains two single input multiple output circuits to model the left and right cochleas. These circuits perform a frequency decomposition of the incoming sound, with high frequencies causing maximum excitation at the near end outputs, and low frequencies at the far end. The cochlea-chip also contains left and right circuitry meant to model the rectification and pulsing behavior of the inner hair cells and auditory nerve fibers associated with each cochlea. The output of the cochlea-chip is a set of 20 left signal lines and 20 right signal lines. The signals on these lines are pulses occurring as a function of the left and right

*Supported by NASA under Grant NAGW-419
†Supported by Texas Instruments

0-7803-0999-5/93/$03.00 ©1993 IEEE

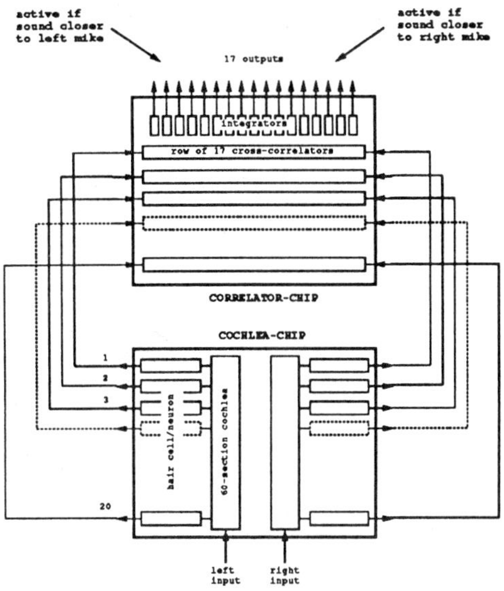

Figure 1: Overview of the two-chip sound localization system.

sounds entering the chip. These provide the input to the **correlator-chip**, which models that portion of the superior olive containing neurons sensitive to interaural time differences. It contains 20 rows of circuitry, each receiving a left and right input from the cochlea-chip. Each row has seventeen cross-correlation circuits that respond to the coincidence of pulses on the left and right input lines, but with different delays. The circuitry on the left side of the correlator-chip responds if the left inputs pulse before the right inputs, and vice-versa for the right side. The outputs of the cross-correlation circuits corresponding to a particular delay are summed and integrated across the twenty rows. These 17 integrated outputs form the output of the correlator-chip. The basic idea is that as a sound source moves from the left to the right, the excitation location of the outputs moves in the same fashion.

III. Analog Circuit Design

A. *Cochlea-chip*

The cochlea-chip contains two major subsystems, a 60-section cochlea and 60 hair-cell/auditory neuron circuits. Every third output of the system is brought to a pin, and a multiplexer allows the output of either the cochlea or the auditory neuron to be viewed. Each of these subsystems has a left and right version. A schematic of one cochlear section connected to one hair-cell and auditory neuron circuit is shown in Figure 2.

A.1. Cochlea circuit

The cochlea circuit is based on a cascade of 60 sections identical in every way save for their characteristic frequencies, which fall exponentially from the near to the far end of the cascade based on a linearly declining voltage along a polysilicon wire that runs the length of the cascade. Each section is meant to model the effect of a small section of the biological cochlea, which is assumed to contain active outer hair cells that enhance the motion of the basilar membrane. Details of the design can be found in [9], though for the current chip we have incorporated some of the techniques described in [10] to achieve larger output signal values.

The approach of cascading sections to model the cochlea was first used in analog VLSI implementations by Lyon and Mead [5], who used a cascade of second order sections. We use a more complex section in the cascade that we believe better approximates the behavior of the real cochlea. In particular, it allows the construction of cochleas of different granularities without imposing a delay penalty on fine grained implementations. Analysis of the other cascade designs reported in the literature [5, 6, 7] suggest that the number of sections in those designs must be limited in order to not incur an excessive delay. Also, since our design is structurally more similar to the biological cochlea, it mimics some of the latter's nonlinear behavior.

A.2. Hair-cell/auditory neuron circuit

The hair-cell circuit shown in Figure 2 rectifies and low pass filters the output of the cochlear section to which it is connected. The filter cutoff frequency is proportional to the bias current set by the *am_tau_bias* voltage and inversely proportional to the associated capacitor. The circuit pumps current into the auditory neuron circuit that follows it during the discharge time of the capacitor. At low frequencies this occurs for approximately half of every input cycle that it sees. At high frequencies, current is pumped in for a much smaller portion of the cycle. At these high frequencies, increases in the amplitude of an input sinusoid cause a sudden but temporary increase in the current pumped into the auditory neuron circuit. The circuit differs from the hysteretic-differentiator hair-cell circuit described in [11], which activates the circuitry that follows it at the peaks of its input waveform.

The auditory neuron circuit is similar in many respects to the self-resetting neuron circuit described in [4], but includes a refractory period control. In the quiescent state, the output voltage is high at V_{dd}. Sufficient time-integration of input current causes the state of the output to flip low to *Gnd*. The *PW_bias* voltage controls the duration of time for which the output stays low. Once the output flips high again, the *TR_bias* voltage controls the refractory period of the neuron, not permitting input cur-

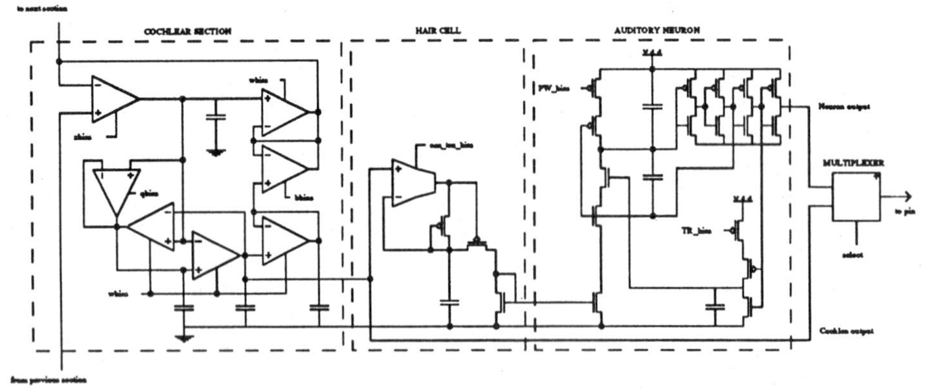

Figure 2: Cochlea-chip circuits. The triangular blocks in the cochlear section are simple transconductance amplifiers, while the snub-nosed triangular block in the hair-cell is a wide-range transconductance amplifier [4].

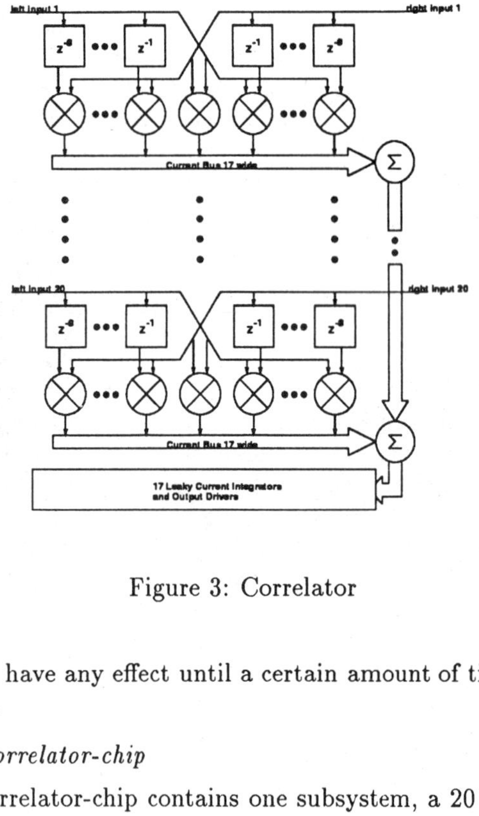

Figure 3: Correlator

rent to have any effect until a certain amount of time has passed.

B. *Correlator-chip*

The correlator-chip contains one subsystem, a 20 section cross correlation circuit. A block diagram of the correlator is shown in Figure 3.

B.1. *Correlator circuit*

The correlator is composed of twenty separate rows each with two digital input voltages and seventeen analog output currents. The set of output currents represent a discrete-time cross-correlation of the input pulses. In other words, each row calculates the time difference between inputs. To perform this task two sets of delay elements are connected to a set of multipliers as shown in Figure 3 . Typically correlators are constructed with serial delay lines [12], but in an attempt to minimize error accumulation we have designed our correlator with parallel delay lines. Each of the seventeen analog output currents are summed over the set of twenty rows and integrated on leaky capacitors. A leaky capacitor is a capacitor with a shunt MOS transistor biased in subthreshold. The seventeen capacitor voltages constitute the outputs of the sound localization system.

As shown in Figure 4, the two building blocks in the correlator are the delay element and the multiplier. The delay circuit builds on the self-resetting neuron circuit described in [4] and has a controllable delay time and output pulse width. The time delay between input pulse and output pulse is determined by the equation

$$t_{delay} = \frac{V_{dd}C_2}{I_{delay}} \quad (1)$$

where V_{dd} is the power supply voltage and I_{delay} is the current through *M4* controlled by the *delay_bias* voltage. The output pulse width of the delay circuit is given by

$$t_{pw} = \frac{V_{dd}C_2}{I_{pw}} \quad (2)$$

where I_{pw} is the current through *M6* controlled by the *pw_bias* voltage. The multiplier is a NAND gate with a bias transistor at the base.

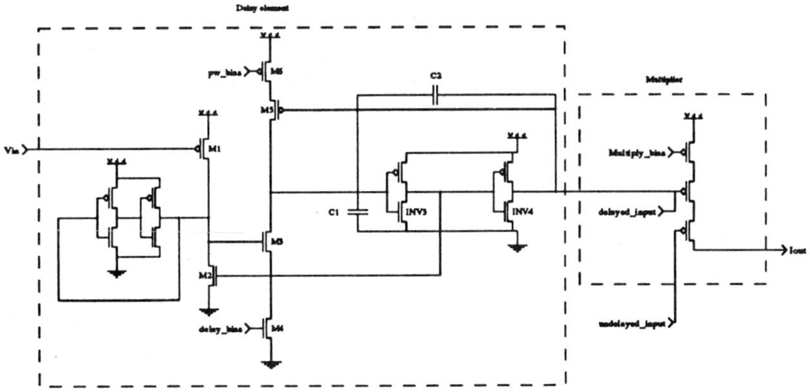

Figure 4: Correlation Delay Section

IV. Experimental Results

All of the testing was performed by an automated GPIB-based testing system controlled by an Apple Macintosh-IIsi with a National Instruments GPIB board. The software was initially developed at Apple Computer and then revised at Stanford in the analog-VLSI laboratory. The main control program ran under Matlab, which was also used for all the data analysis.

The results reported below are for the cochlea and correlator chips separately. Large variances in the correlator-chip, described in B., made the joint testing unfeasible. We are in the process of making extensive measurements on the cochlea-chip in order to simulate what the effect of a "perfect" correlator-chip would have been.

A. Cochlea

The top left, top right and lower left panels of Figure 5 show results from an earlier version of the cochlea in which all 60 taps were accessible for measurement. All three panels show results for the same settings of the bias voltages. The top left panel shows the transfer function at a particular tap (number 45 in this case), the top right panel shows how the peak frequency falls exponentially with tap number, and the lower left panel shows that the group delay flattens out at around 4 cycles of the peak frequency for these particular bias voltages. The lower right panel pertains to the current design, and uses different bias voltage settings. The upper and lower sinusoidal traces in the panel show the responses at the right and left cochlear tap when both cochleas are receiving a 30 mV sinusoidal input at the best frequency of the tap. The pulse like traces show the response of the auditory neurons connected to the cochlear taps, ensemble averaged over 64 cycles of input. The responses have been offset vertically to make the data more readable. Ideally, both left and right responses should be identical, but variations in the chip cause them to be offset in phase.

B. Correlator

The correlator inputs were created by two HP3314A pulse generators, and the seventeen analog outputs were time multiplexed using two MC14051s and displayed on a HP54601A digital oscilloscope. Data from the oscilloscope was acquired and stored using the automated system described above.

The results of a typical correlator row and the sum of all correlator rows are show in Figure 6. The upper two plots show the correlator output results with a single row being excited, while the lower two show the results with all twenty rows being excited. Each of these plots represents the correlator outputs with pulses arriving at the right input before the left. The time delay between the inputs was varied between 2 ms and 0.2 ms. The individual row results show that for a typical row, the peak excitation location is correlated with the time delay; small time delays excite the center, near section 9, and large time delays excite the edge, near section 16. Unfortunately, the sum of row results do not show this desired correlation. This is because subthreshold parameter variation causes the delay time differences of various correlator rows to be large.

V. Discussion

The main problem with this design was the use of nominal analog circuit design methods, by which we mean using the nominal value of circuit and device parameters to complete a design. This works if CMOS devices are operated above threshold, where variations are small. However, devices operated below threshold have much greater varia-

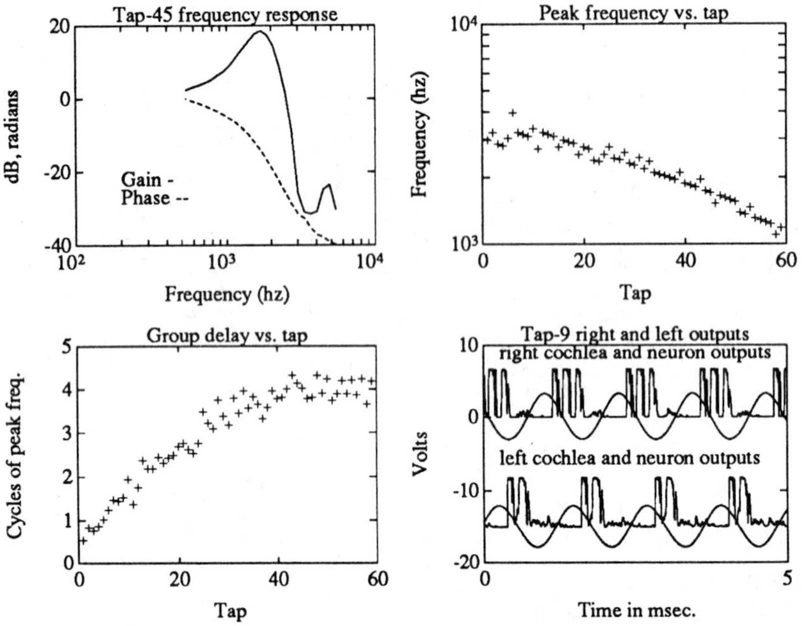

Figure 5: Performance of the cochlea-chip.

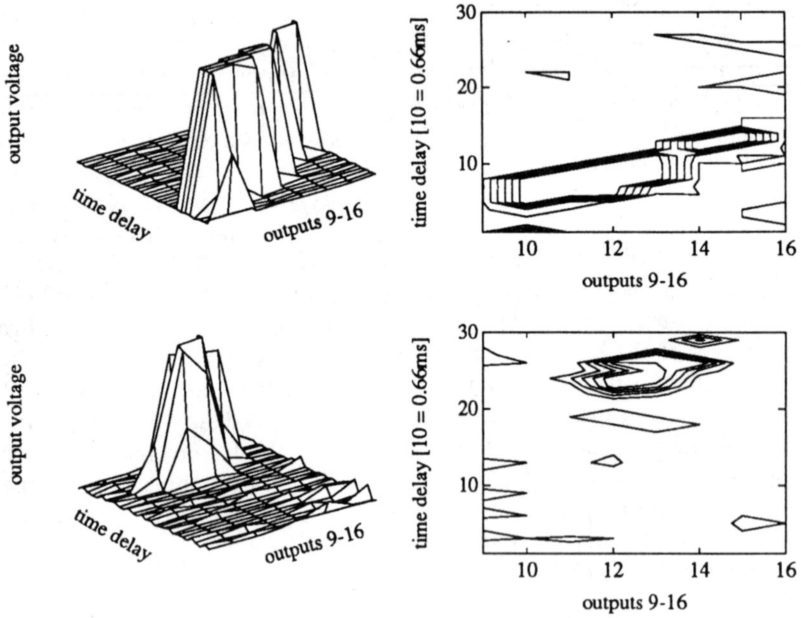

Figure 6: The correlator results were measured at 23.1^0 C with V_{dd}=5 V. The x, y and z axes of the mesh plots represent correlator outputs 9-16, output voltage and time delay between inputs, respectively. The x and y axes of the contour plots represent correlator outputs 9-16 and time delay between inputs respectively. Each contour plot is a top view of the mesh plot on its left.

tion [13, 14] that can make many nominally correct designs non-functional. We believe that in these circumstances a different design approach is called for that specifically takes into account the inherent variations in the transistor building blocks. We are working on approaches to this problem for the cochlea, hair cell, auditory neuron and correlator designs. Approaches that suggest themselves are automatic compensation for device variations, as well as statistical designs that use the law of large numbers to overcome the problem.

Another problem was the mixing of subthreshold and above threshold circuits without adequate isolation. High current circuits can cause small voltage drops in the V_{dd} line, and consequently cause substrate bias plugs to have different potentials at different points in the substrate. This causes potential gradients in the substrate, which change the subthreshold currents in native devices through the back-gate effect. Similarly, wells can have different potentials due to small voltage drops along the Gnd lines. This affects the current through well devices. Because of the exponential effect of substrate and well voltages on subthreshold current, the deviation from the expected current value can be quite high, leading to unwanted variations in the circuit behavior. This is a problem that has been observed in many of the chips designed in the Stanford analog-VLSI lab. We are working on general design approaches to overcome this problem. Some options we are evaluating include isolating low power from high power circuits, or obtaining the substrate and well biases from dedicated V_{dd} and Gnd nets respectively with no power drawn from them.

VI. Conclusions

Subthreshold analog VLSI allows systems with high computation rates to be constructed with very little power drain. Specifically, our construction of a sound localization system has demonstrated the cost, power and reduced complexity advantages of this technology. However, our system also reveals problems and suggests that traditional design methods must be modified if they are to result in reliable and mass-producible products.

VII. Acknowledgement

We would like to thank Professors Michael Flynn and Michael Godfrey of the Electrical Engineering Department at Stanford University for their encouragement. We would also like to thank Apple Computer for providing support and equipment, Hewlett Packard for their test equipment, and MOSIS for their fabrication facilities.

References

[1] J. Blauert. *Spatial Hearing – The Psychophysics of Human Sound Localization.* MIT Press, 1983.

[2] Richard F. Thompson. *The Brain.* W.H. Freeman and Company, 1985.

[3] E. A. Vittoz. Micropower techniques. In Y. Tsividis and P. Antognetti, editors, *Design of MOS VLSI Circuits for Telecommunications*, pages 104–144. Prentice Hall, 1985.

[4] Carver Mead. *Analog VLSI and Neural Systems.* Addison Wesley, 1989.

[5] Richard F. Lyon and Carver Mead. An analog electronic cochlea. *IEEE Transactions on Acoustics, Speech, and Signal Processing*, 36(7):1119–1134, July 1988.

[6] Richard F. Lyon. CCD correlators for auditory models. In *1991 Asilomar Conference on Signals, Systems, and Computers*, 1991.

[7] W. Liu, A. G. Andreou, and M. H. Goldstein, Jr. Voiced-speech representation by an analog silicon model of the auditory periphery. *IEEE Transactions on Neural Networks*, 3(3):477–487, May 1992.

[8] Noboru Sugie, Jie Huang, and Noboru Ohnishi. Localizing sound source by incorporating biological auditory mechanism. In *IEEE International Conference on Neural Networks*, pages II:243–250. IEEE, 1988.

[9] Neal Bhadkamkar. A variable resolution, nonlinear silicon cochlea. Technical Report CSL-TR-93-558, Stanford University, January 1993.

[10] Lloyd Watts, Douglas A. Kerns, Richard F. Lyon, and Carver A. Mead. Improved implementation of the silicon cochlea. *IEEE Journal of Solid-State Circuits*, 27(5):692–700, May 1992.

[11] John Lazarro and Carver Mead. Silicon modeling of pitch perception. *Proceedings of the National Academy of Science, USA*, 86:9597–9601, December 1989.

[12] J. Lazzaro. A Silicon Model of an Auditory Neural Representation of Spectral Shape. *IEEE Journal of Solid State Circuits*, 26(5):772–777, May 1991.

[13] Michael D. Godfrey. CMOS device modeling for subthreshold circuits. *IEEE Transactions on Circuits and Systems,II*, 39:532–539, August 1992.

[14] A. Pavasovic, A. G. Andreou, and C. R. Westgate. Characterization of CMOS process variations by measuring subthreshold current. In R. E. Green and C. O. Ruud, editors, *Nondestructive Characterization of Materials IV.* Plenum Press, 1991.

Chapter 12: Software Simulations

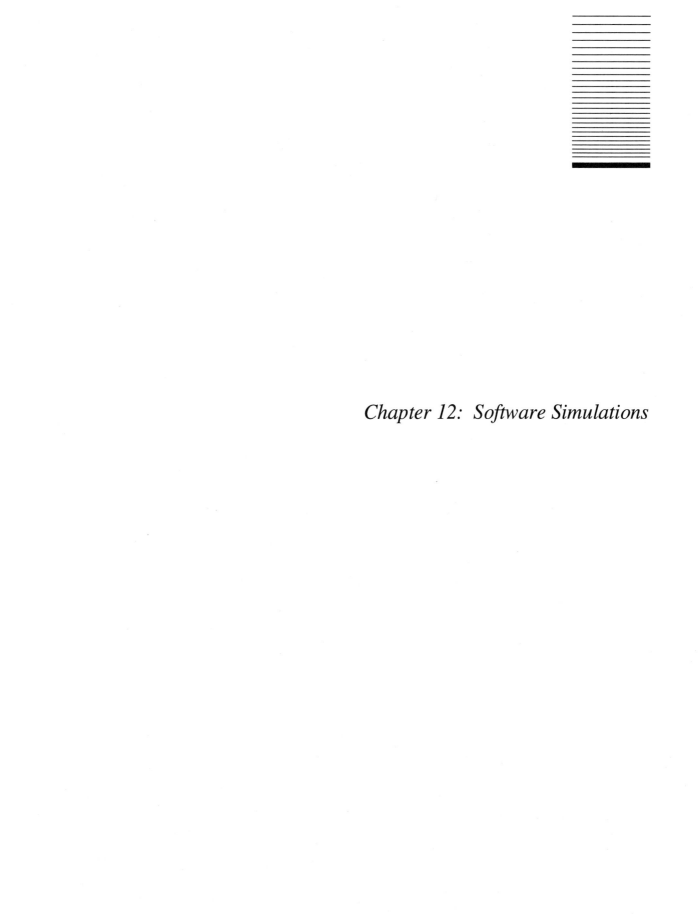

CHAPTER 12
Software Simulations

Processors continue to increase in speed each year. As such, most neural network applications do not require specialized hardware, only a competent software simulation. The last two of the four papers reviews one of the many neural network software simulators that are available to the public via the Internet. Before buying software or specialized hardware, these simulators should be considered. **Paper 12.1** compares several different simulations using the MasPar massively parallel SIMD computer. **Paper 12.2** describes the NeMoSys neural modeling system. This simulator models individual neurons at the level of local membrane currents and voltages. **Paper 12.3** reviews the NeuroGraph neural network simulator. **Paper 12.4** reviews the SESAME object oriented software tool for the design, simulation, and analysis of neural networks is described; SESAME consists of 130 C++ objects that are available free of charge.

Problems of Massive Parallelism in Neural Network Simulation

Andreas Zell, Niels Mache, Michael Vogt, Markus Hüttel
University of Stuttgart,
Institute for Parallel and Distributed High Performance Systems (IPVR),
Breitwiesenstr. 20-22, D-7000 Stuttgart 80, Fed. Rep. Germany
E-mail: zell@informatik.uni-stuttgart.de

Abstract—We here present and compare different massively parallel implementations of multilayer feedforward neural networks on a MasPar MP-1216, a parallel SIMD computer with 16,384 processors. For multilayer feedforward networks we have obtained sustained rates of up to 348 M CPS and 129 M CUPS with backpropagation, a high mark for general purpose SIMD computers. This paper focuses on the problems of mapping neural networks to parallel hardware, on implementation problems in obtaining high propagation rates on a SIMD machine and on problems with the resulting learning algorithms.

Keywords: artificial neural networks, neural network simulators, massive parallelism

I. INTRODUCTION AND MOTIVATION

Our research group wants to understand the advantages and the trade-offs of the various artificial neural network paradigms and learning algorithms, their training efficiency and generalization capabilities and their suitability for massively parallel implementation. We have developed a neural network simulator, SNNS, which has proven well suited for research on learning algorithms, on issues of visualization, training and performance and on parallel implementation of neural networks. SNNS is also used in a number of other university research groups and with growing acceptance in industry as a neural network evaluation and prototyping tool. In this paper we are describing the experiences we gained in developing a massively parallel simulator kernel for SNNS running on our 16 K processor MasPar MP-1216.

II. STUTTGART NEURAL NETWORK SIMULATOR

SNNS (Stuttgart Neural Network Simulator) [1], [2], [3], is an efficient and portable neural network simulation environment for Unix workstations developed at the University of Stuttgart. It is a software tool to generate, train, test and visualize artificial neural networks. The whole network simulator has been developed in C on Unix workstations. The graphical user interface was implemented under X-Windows X11R5 (Athena widget set), for maximal portability.

SNNS now consists of a sequential and a parallel simulator kernel and a graphical user interface (Fig. 1). The simulator kernel operates on the internal representation of the neural networks and performs all operations of the learning and recall phase. It is coupled with the graphical user interface via an interface of function calls. The simulator kernel has already been ported to a number of architectures (Sun, HP, DEC, IBM, etc.).

A. Graphical User Interface of SNNS

The graphical user interface is used to create, visualize and modify the network topology interactively. All display elements are kept in separate windows and thus can be arbitrarily arranged. The user has a powerful set of operations (insertion, deletion, copying, moving) which may be applied to individual units or to selections of units and may affect links as well, like 'copy all selected units with their input links' or 'delete all links into the selected units'. Networks can be modified through the user interface during simulation. Units can be introduced, removed, or have their activation values changed. Connections among the units can be inserted, deleted, redirected, or have their strengths modified. Contrary to many other simulators most modifications can be done directly from the visual display of the network. Fig. 2 gives an overview of the graphical user interface of SNNS.

B. Connectionist Models supported by SNNS

From its design SNNS supports any network that can be specified as a directed graph with weighted links. The concept of sites which has been adapted from RCS [4] even allows multiple links between two units. Although most users of SNNS use simple multilayer feedforward networks with one or two hidden layers and standard sigmoid activation functions (logistic, sine or tanh), some recurrent networks have also been implemented. The following learning algorithms have been implemented: backpropagation [5], backpropagation with momentum, weight decay and flat spot elimination, batch backpropagation, quickprop [6], counterpropagation [7], backpercolation [8], cascade correlation [9], radial basis function networks (RBF) [10], ART1, ART2 and ARTMAP [11], Time-Delay Networks [12] and self organizing feature maps. Not all of them are available in the public distribution, however.

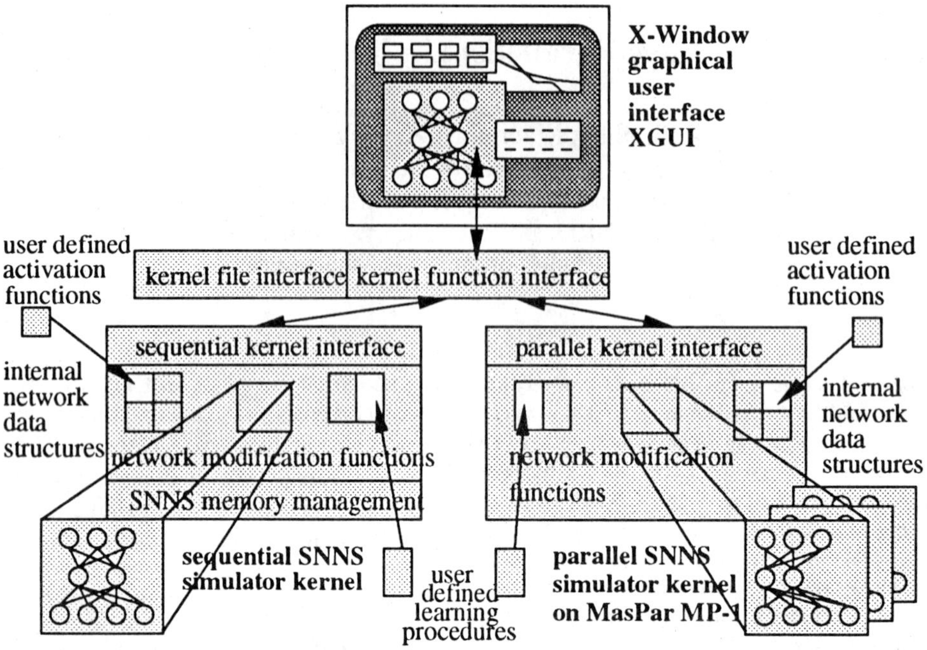

Fig. 1: Structure of SNNS consisting of sequential simulator kernel, parallel kernel and graphical user interface

C. Selected Applications of SNNS

SNNS is currently used in at least 300 installations worldwide, approx. one third of them each in Germany, other Europe and the U.S. Its main use so far is in university research but some commercial research projects use SNNS as a prototyping tool to find optimal learning procedures, network sizes and learning parameters for various neural network applications. Applications include rotation invariant pattern recognition, handwritten character recognition, stock price prediction, recognition and classification of exogenic and endogenic components of event correlated brain potentials, noise reduction in natural language communication in a telecom environment, prediction of secondary structure of proteins and texture analysis.

III. PARALLEL SNNS KERNELS ON THE MASPAR MP-1

Two parallel implementations for the SNNS kernel and one prototype implementation have been developed on our 16 K processor MasPar MP-1216 for multilayer feedforward networks. The goal of the parallelization was to enable the simulation of large neural networks, mainly for the tasks of image processing, feature extraction and pattern and object recognition.The parallel simulator is integrated with the sequential simulator as an alternative simulator kernel. From the X-Windows based graphical user interface it is possible to switch between both kernels at runtime, provided the user restricts itself to multilayer feedforward networks.

A. Architecture of the MP-1

The MasPar MP-1216 is a SIMD machine with up to 16,384 four-Bit processors. 32 processors are integrated on a single chip, 32 chips fit on a processor board. Our full scale model delivers a quoted peak performance of 30,000 MIPS (32 bit addition) and 1,500 resp. 600 MFLOPS (32 bit resp. 64 bit). There exist two separate communication architectures on the MasPar: one is a 3-stage global router which allows up to 1024 simultaneous connections between any two processors, the other is a torroidal two-dimensional 8 neighbour grid (X-net). Communication bandwidth is up to 1.5 GB/s peak global router and up to 24 GB/s peak X-net communication. From this data it can be seen that it is advisable to use the local grid as much as possible since the communication bandwidth is much larger than with the router. Also on our machine we experienced a number of router hardware failures which forced us to avoid it if possible.The MasPar can be programmed with parallel versions of C (AMPL) and Fortran. MPPE (MasPar parallel programming environment), an integrated graphical tool set based on X-Windows, facilitates program development and debugging.

Having investigated the trade-offs of different approaches to parallelization of neural networks, as given in [13], [14], [15] and [16] we decided on an implementation which combines unit parallelism with training vector parallelism. All implementations of our parallel simulator kernel were done in MPL, a parallel extension of C. Two of them have recently been converted to AMPL, the ANSI C extension of MPL.

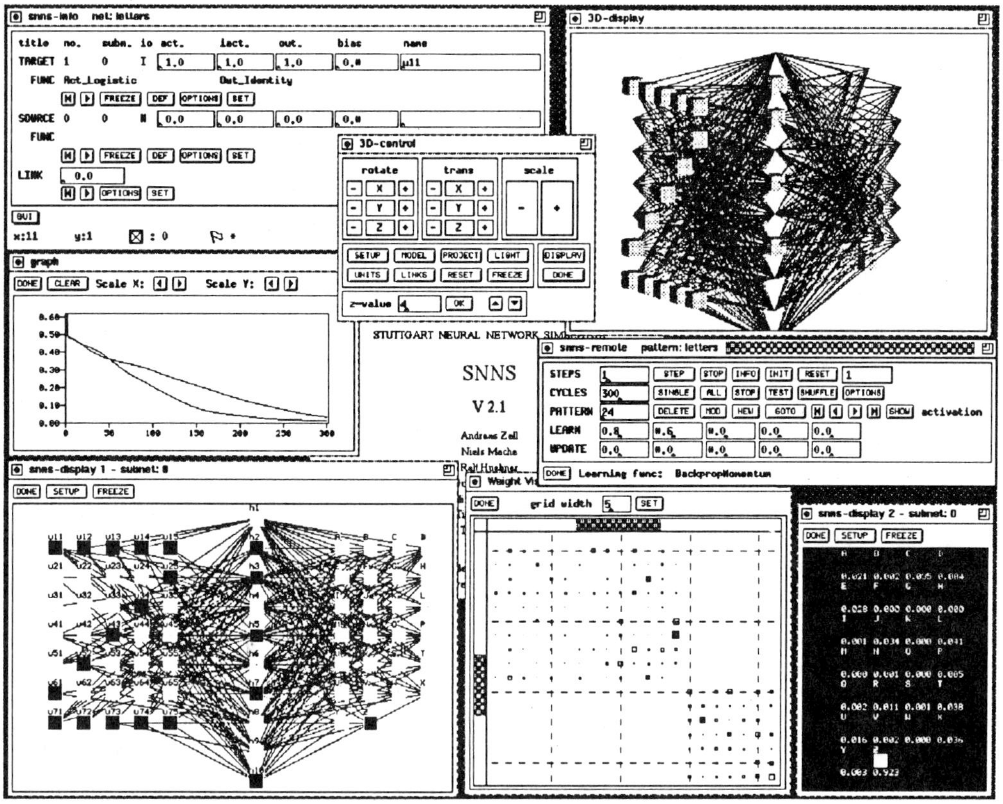

Fig. 2: Graphical user interface of SNNS with a toy letter recognition network: info panel (top left), 3D control panel (top center) and 3D-display (top right), error graph (center left), SNNS banner (center), remote control panel (center right), 2D-display (bottom left), Hinton diagram (bottom center), 2D-display (bottom right).

B. Implementation with Unit-Parallelism and Training Pattern Parallelism

The implementation of Mache [17] uses the following technique (Fig. 3): All hidden and output units of a vertical slice are mapped to a single processing element (PE) of the MasPar. The computation of unit activation is done in parallel for all units of a layer. Thus, a number of processors is needed which equals the largest number of processing elements in a layer, i.e. the width of the network determines the number of processors needed.

If the number of input units is greater than the number of units of the other layers, an additional PE is used to store the remaining components of the input pattern and to send them to its neighbor when they are needed. Each processor stores the weights of all of its input links. The processors are located in a logical ring communication structure which can easily be realized on the X-net grid (with possible copying at the fringes). During forward or backward propagation, the intermediate values for the net input or the accumulated error signal, resp., are shifted cyclically to the left. The weights are stored with a skew factor of 1 in each processor. This allows all units of a layer to perform the computation of the sum of all weighted predecessor units outputs in a number of steps equal to the size of the preceding layer.

Since the width of a feedforward network is usually much smaller than the number of available processors on our MasPar, multiple copies of the network with different input patterns are updated in parallel. In this way weight changes have to be computed in each network individually without actually changing the weights. The sum of the weight changes is then computed and applied to all corresponding weights of the identical network copies. This results in a batech backpropagation algorithm with the batch size at least equal to the number of network copies in the machine or an integer multiple of it.

For an optimal 128-128-128 network which fits into the machine without an additional PE and which does not need copying at the end of a cycle this implementation we obtained 176 M CPS (connections per second) and 67 M CUPS (connection updates per second) for backpropagation training. The Nettalk network [18], a 203-120-26 network, can be trained with 41 M CUPS and operated with 98 M CPS. These times did not include the time for transfer of the input patterns from the frontend to the parallel machine.

One advantage of this approach is, that the numbers of proc-

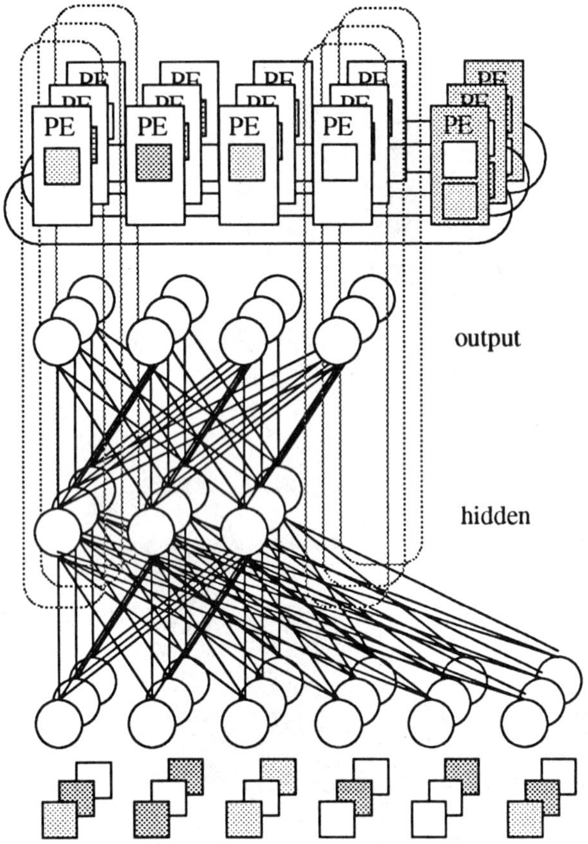

Fig. 3: First parallel SNNS kernel with a 6-3-4 feedforward network: all hidden and output neurons of a column and their input links are mapped onto a single processor. An additional PE holds the remaining input pattern parts. Multiple network copies with different input patterns are trained in parallel (training pattern parallelism).

essors used is not determined by the size of the input layer, which is usually much larger than any hidden or output layer. So a large number of networks can be trained in parallel. A disadvantage is the fact that the one additional PE has to store much more pattern elements than the others. In an SIMD machine with identical memory allocation on all PEs this memory becomes a limiting factor of how many patterns can be stored in parallel on the machine. Since pattern I/O was the limiting factor of our parallel implementation, a second implementation was performed.

C. Second Implementation with Unit-Parallelism and Training Pattern Parallelism

Our second implementation was done to alleviate the pattern I/O bandwidth problem of the first implementation. Its main objective was to store as many patterns as possible in the parallel PE memory, even if the number of PEs needed to store the network is larger. This implementation uses a number of PEs which is equal to the size of the biggest layer, including input layer. If the input layer is the biggest layer, all PEs store a similar number of pattern components, otherwise some PEs may store no components. The mapping of neurons and training patterns to PEs of this implementation is diplayed in Fig. 4.

For an optimal 128-128-128 network we obtain sustained 348 M CPS in recall mode and 129 M CUPS for backpropagation training. The NETtalk network can be recalled with 47 M CPS and trained with 17.6 M CUPS. These times include the time for the transfer of the input patterns and the results. Since the I/O times dominated the learning and recall times in the previous implementation, the speed improvement of the latter version was even greater than the figures tell. It resulted from a new, better compiler and from extensive code optimizations. The fact that in this scheme less networks can be trained in parallel can be seen in the NetTalk benchmarks which yield lower performance results than the first implementation.

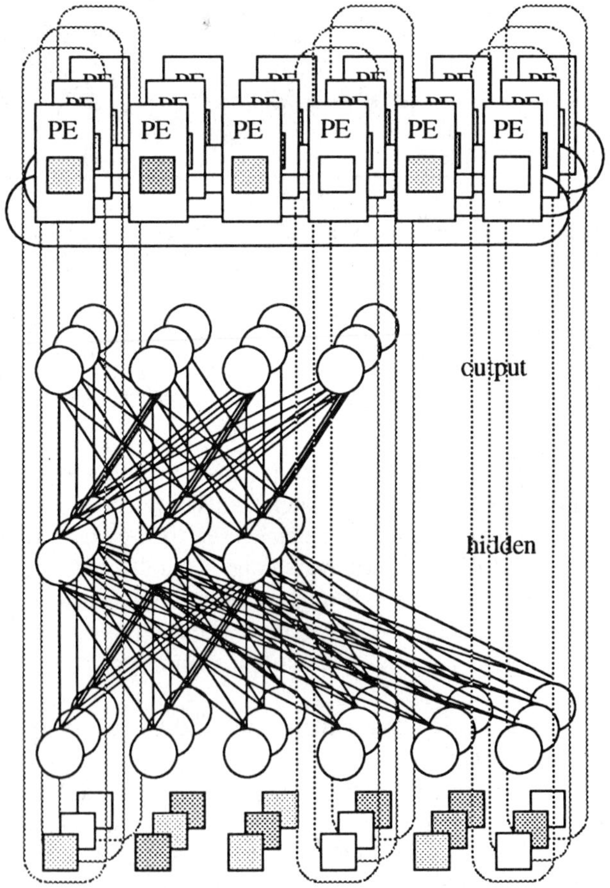

Fig. 4: Second parallel SNNS kernel with a 6-3-4 feedforward network: all neurons of a column and their input links are mapped onto a single processor. The number of processors needed is equal to the size of the biggest layer, usually the input layer. Multiple network copies with different input patterns are trained in parallel (training pattern parallelism).

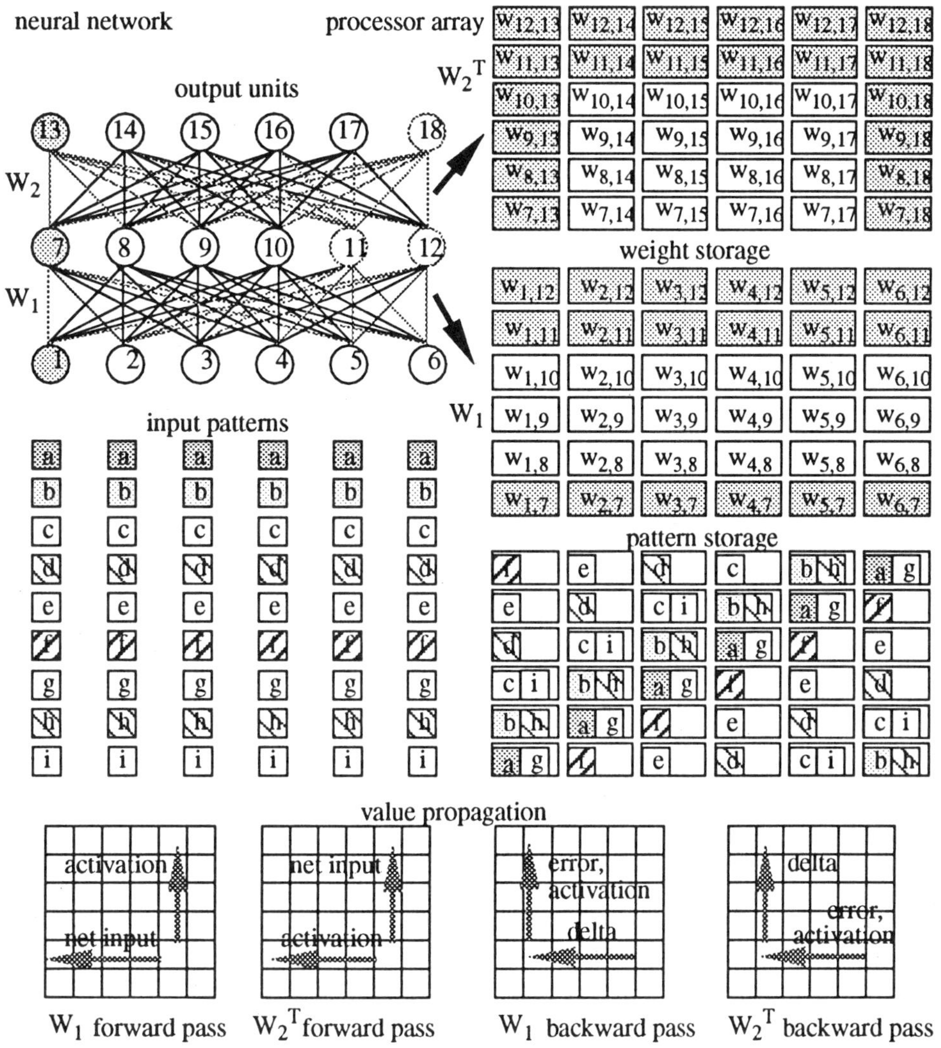

Fig. 5: Link-parallel prototype implementation with a 5-3-4 feedforward network: Each layer is filled up with dummy nodes to the size of the largest layer. There is a bias unit for each layer. The weight matrices are mapped to the processor array directly and in transposed form, in alternating order (W_1, W_2^T, W_3, W_4^T, ...). Dummy weights are set to 0 and prevented from updating with a mask (shown grey). Patterns are mapped to the processor array in diagonal order. The directions of propagation change in each layer according to the weight matrix.

D. Link-Parallel Implementation

The last implementation compared [19] is not a full SNNS kernel but was intended as a prototype implementation. It lacks the support of all SNNS kernel functions but can read SNNS network files. It is graphically displayed in Fig. 5.

First the network is extended with one bias unit for each layer and dummy units to make each layer of equal size n. All units of adjacent layers are connected. The weights to dummy units are initialized to zero and are prevented from being updated by masking them with zero in the last step of weight updates. In our terminology weights from source i to j are denoted by w_{ij}. If the weight matrices connecting adjacent layers are denoted W_1, ...W_m then the mapping of units to PEs of the MasPar follows the rule that if r is odd, the outgoing weights w_{ij} of unit i are mapped to columns of the PE array, with the source unit of lowest index giving the leftmost column, if r is even, the outgoing weights w_{ij} of unit i are mapped to rows of the PE array, with the source unit of lowest index giving the bottom row.

This parallel prototype implementation with link parallelism and training pattern parallelism [19] was measured at 136 M CUPS for a fully connected 127-127-127 network and 160 M CUPS for a 127-127 network on our MasPar MP-1216.

IV. PROBLEMS OF THE PARALLEL SIMULATOR KERNELS

All three parallel SNNS kernels on the MasPar yield impressive performance figures. However, these results have only been obtained after a lengthy period of optimization and several rewrites of the parallel kernel. Our biggest hurdle was the slow communication of the training patterns from the workstation to the parallel backend, which at first took minutes versus milliseconds for the actual training. A lot of effort was therefore spent to load training patterns in large blocks and to keep as many of them as possible in the distributed parallel PE memory.

Another problem concerns the batch backpropagation algorithm necessary for the training pattern parallel implementations: For applications with a large number of similar input patterns this learning algorithm is much slower than online backpropagation. We tested our simulator with handwritten character recognition problems. In this example the slower convergence of batch backpropagation offset most of the performance gain of the parallel architecture. However, some applications need batch backpropagation for convergence and others report better generalization results. Also, other batch learning algorithms like quickprop [3] may be used with better results.

V. CONCLUSIONS

We here have investigated different mappings of neural networks to a massively parallel SIMD computer. These different implementations have shown that it is possible, albeit not at all easy to obtain impressive performance figures for neural network simulation on current SIMD computers. However, these high marks are only obtained for simple network architectures with a network size that fits well into the parallel machine.

We have learned that propagation figures quoted for neural network algorithms are only meaningful if they take communication time from disk or workstation to the parallel machine into account. Overcoming slow pattern I/O took most of the time of the implementations and forced several fundamental changes in the algorithms. Our results can be extended to VLSI neural network hardware in the sense that the time go load training patterns into the parallel hardware must match the speed of forward or backward propagation.

Another lesson learned was that the speed advantage gained by a parallel implementation can be lost for certain applications because of the slower batch backpropagation algorithm. These results have been obtained with precise floating point computations. It would have been even more difficult with fixed point arithmetic or special VLSI hardware with limited precision.

REFERENCES

[1] A. Zell, Th. Korb, T. Sommer, R. Bayer: A Neural Network Simulation Environment, Proc. Applications of Neural Networks Conf., SPIE Vol. 1294, pp. 535-544

[2] A. Zell, N. Mache, T. Sommer. T. Korb: Recent Developments of the SNNS Neural Network Simulator, Applic. of Neural Networks Conf., Proc. SPIE´s 1991 Aerospace Sensing Intl. Symp., Vol. No. 1469, April 1991, Orlando, Florida, pp. 708-719

[3] A. Zell, N. Mache, R. Hübner, M. Schmalzl, T. Sommer, T. Korb: SNNS User Manual, Version 2.1, Universität Stuttgart, Fakultät Informatik, Report No. 8/92

[4] N. H. Goddard, K. .J. Lynne, T. Mintz, L. Bukys, The Rochester Connectionist Simulator: User Manual, Tech Report 233 (revised), Univ. of Rochester, NY, 1989

[5] D. E. Rumelhart, J. A. McClelland, the PDP Research Group: Parallel Distributed Processing, Vol. 1, 2, MIT Press, Cambridge MA, 1986

[6] S. E. Fahlman, : Faster Learning Variations on Backpropagation, in Touretzky et al: Proc. of the 1988 Connectionist Models Summer School, Morgan Kaufmann 1988

[7] R. Hecht-Nielsen: Neurocomputing, Addison-Wesley, 1990

[8] M. Jurik: Backpercolation, (unpublished) paper distributed by Jurik Research and Consulting, PO 2379, Aptos, CA 95001 USA

[9] S. E. Fahlman, C. Lebiere: The Cascade Correlation Learning Architecture, Report CMU-CS-90-100, School of Computer Science, CMU, Pittsburgh, PA 15213, August 1990

[10] T. Poggio, F. Girosi: A Theory of Networks for Approximation and Learning, A.I. Memo No. 1140, A.I. Lab., M.I.T., 1989

[11] G. A. Carpenter, S. Grossberg: The ART of Adaptive Pattern Recognition by a Self-Organizing Neural Network, IEEE Computer, March 1988, 77-88

[12] A. Waibel: Consonant Recognition by Modular Construction of Large Phonemic Time-Delay Neural Networks, in Touretzky (Ed.): NIPS 1, pp. 215-223, Morgan Kaufmann, 1989

[13] A. Singer: Implementations of Artificial Neural Networks on the Connection Machine, Thinking Machines Corp. Tech. Rep. RL 90-2, Jan. 1990 (also in Parallel Computing, summer 1990)

[14] K.A. Grajski, G. Chinn, C. Chen, C. Kuszmaul, S. Tomboulian: Neural Network Simulation on the MasPar MP-1 Massively Parallel Processor, INNC, Paris, France, 1990

[15] G. Chinn, K.A. Grajski, C. Chen, C. Kuszmaul, S. Tomboulian: Systolic Array Implementations of Neural Nets on the MasPar MP-1 Massively Parallel Processor, MasPar Corp. Int. Report

[16] X. Zhang, M. Mckenna, J.P. Mesirov, D. L. Waltz: An efficient implementation of the Back-propagation algorithm on the Connection Machine CM-2, Thinking Machines Corp. TR

[17] N. Mache: Entwicklung eines massiv parallelen Simulatorkerns für neuronale Netze auf der MasPar MP- 1216, Diplomarbeit Nr. 845, Univ. Stuttgart, Fakultät Informatik, Feb. 92 (in German)

[18] T. J. Sejnowski, C.R. Rosenberg: NETtalk: a parallel network that learns to read aloud, in: Anderson, Rosenfeld: Neurocomputing: Foundations, ch. 40, pp. 661-672, MIT Press, 1988

[19] M. Hüttel: Parallele Implementierungen mehrstufiger feedforward-Netze auf einem SIMD-Parallelrechner, Studienarbeit Nr. 1124, Univ. Stuttgart, Fakultät Informatik, Juli 92 (in German)

NeMoSys: A NEURAL MODELING SYSTEM

Frank H. Eeckman[1,2], Frédéric E. Theunissen[1] and, John P. Miller[1]

[1]Dept. of Cell and Molecular Biology, University of California at Berkeley, Berkeley CA 94720
[2]Institute for Scientific Computing Research Lawrence Livermore National Lab, Livermore CA 94550

Design Philosophy

Ne-Mo-Sys (Neural Modeling System) is a program created to model individual neurons at the level of local membrane currents and voltages. It is one part of a series of programs, created in our laboratory for the study of the anatomy and physiology of real neurons. The common denominator for all these programs is a shared file format for the description of the anatomy and physiology of neurons (see below). These shared files are a compact representation of the important coordinates and parameters of neurons in human readable form. To make the program useful to physiologists, we devoted a lot of attention to creating an interface that is easy to use, while at the same time powerful enough to allow one to mimic any possible experimental paradigm. The user interacts with the program as he or she would interact with an experimental preparation and the associated laboratory equipment.

Implementation

Nemosys was written in C using Xlib to provide maximal portability between different Unix platforms. Nemosys has been succesfully ported to the IBM RISC/6000, the SUN SPARC 2, the SGI Personal IRIS and the SGI Indigo. Both source code and executable files for IBM, SUN, and SGI are available. Contact eeckman@llnl.gov.

Nemosys consists of a base code that is compiled and linked to form the executable program. The base code generates a series of tools that allow the user to create modules that can be inserted into the simulation without recompiling. Examples of such modules are: various types of graphs, arbitrary channel kinetics, sub- and super-trees of existing neurons. In this manner, users can change or add new functionality to the program at run time. One can also add new routines to the existing program with only minimal modifications to the existing code.

Representation of neurons

Two crucial issues in data representation that need to be addressed are flexibility and efficiency. Flexibility describes how it easy it is for the user to edit, assign, and modify the local properties of the neuron in the simulator. Efficiency relates to speed of searches and speed of computation. The representation of neurons in Nemosys is an important aspect of the design. The high computational efficiency of Nemosys (see below) is due to both the integration method and the specific representation that is used. Neurons are represented as binary branched tree structures. The neurons exist in three dimensions. Various locations along the neuron arborization are used to divide the cell into "nodes". Each x, y, z position and local diameter defines one node. The first node in the tree is called the root node. All other nodes are either continuation nodes (having one child, also called "right leave"), branch nodes (having two children, right and left leave), or termination nodes (having no children). Complex branching patterns are represented by a series of binary branchings. The tree is traversed in right-handed depth first mode with the root node being node number one.

Interaction and Input-Output (I/O)

We provided 3 specific ways of interaction with the neuron under study: 1) Properties that apply to all compartments can be examined and modified via the set menu. These properties and their parameter values are stored in the parameter file (one per neuron, see below). 2) Individual compartments can be addressed via a menu driven search that uses their unique id number. 3) Users can define arbitrary regions and assign functions to these regions with a two step process. First, the region is defined and stored using a combination of selection and mathematical and logical commands; second, a series of functions and values is assigned to that region using the menu interface.

Inputs: four kinds of input files are required.
a)The *anatomy file* is an ASCII file that describes the neuron by x, y, z position, diameter and compartment type (regular, branching or terminal).
b) The parameter file is an ASCII file. A default file is provided for the first time user.
c) The channel file is a binary file. The conductances are described according to the Hodgkin-Huxley paradigm. A

default file is provided for the first time user.
d) The *parametric file* is an ASCII file that stores the specific information needed for parametric runs. This file has a free format and can be empty.

Outputs: the program generates several types of graphical and numeric output.
a) animation: pseudocolor-coded animation of transmembrane voltage in all compartments.
b) transient analysis (time domain): graphs of voltages, and currents at various locations.
c) bode plots (frequency domain): frequency and phase bode plots.

Calculation methods

In any simulator the accuracy and the relative efficiency (ie., computational speed) of the numerical method used for solving differential equations is a major concern. A superb review by Mascagni (1989) describes all the relevant numerical methods and provides a comparative analysis of the different methods used for different purposes. Nemosys uses a hybrid implicit-explicit integration scheme. The equations are divided into two types: voltage update equations and conductance update equations. The two types of equations will be updated separately, so that voltage changes are assumed to occur while the conductance is held constant and conductance changes are assumed to occur while the voltage is constant. The nonlinear equations are thus treated as conditionally linear equations (Mascagni, 1989).

The integration method is a first-order implicit scheme ("backward Euler"). With such a first order implicit integration method, the evaluation of the state variables at a subsequent point requires the evaluation of their derivative at that next timestep:

$$V_{t+1} = V_t + \Delta t\, F(dV_{t+1}, dt) \qquad (1)$$

where V_{t+1} can be obtained by solving a system of N coupled algebraic equations (see below). An implicit method is used because the equations describing the voltage of a compartmental model of a neuron are said to be "stiff" (for a review on stiff equations see Press *et al.*, 1988). Stiffness in compartmental models is the result of the two different timescales that are present in the simulation: the fast timescale of intracellular events (between compartments) and the slow timescale of membrane events. In the explicit method, one would be required to follow the change in the solution on the fastest scale (microseconds in this case) to maintain stability, even though the events of interest happen on a much slower timescale (milliseconds). Use of the backward Euler integration scheme in a compartmental model involves inverting a matrix K,

where

$$V_t = K\, V_{t+1}\,; \qquad (2)$$

In the case of a binary tree representation K is a sparse matrix resembling a tridiagonal matrix that can be inverted by Gaussian elimination in 2(N-1) steps, instead of the N^3 steps required to invert a full matrix. This calculation scheme was first applied to neural modeling by Michael Hines (Hines, 1984). It has been extended since (Mascagni, 1991).
The main advantage of the implicit method is that it makes it possible to use larger stepsizes while maintaining stability of integration. A second advantage of our hybrid scheme stems from the explicit part of the calculation. By decoupling the voltage and conductance updates, it is easy to incorporate any arbitrary conductances and/or synaptic events.

Network Extension

An extension of NemoSys designed to model networks of neurons has been described in Tromp and Eeckman (1992).

References

Hines, M (1984) Efficient computation of branched nerve equations. *Int J. Biomed. Comput.* 15: 69-75.

Kernighan, B.W. and Pike, R. (1984) The *Unix Programming Environment*. Prentice-Hall, New Jersey.

Mascagni, M. (1989) Numerical Methods. In: *Methods in Neuronal Modelling*. Koch and Segev (eds.) MIT Press, Cambridge, MA. p 439.

Mascagni, M. (1991) A parallelizing algorithm for computing solutions to arbitrarily branched cable neuron models. *J. Neurosci. Methods*. 36: 105-114.

Press, W.H., Flannery, B.P., Teukolsky, S.A. and Vetterling, W.T. (1988). *Numerical Recipes in C.* Cambridge University Press, Cambridge. p. 592.

Tromp, J.W. and Eeckman, F. H. (1992) Efficient modeling of realistic neural networks with application to the olfactory bulb. In: *Analysis and Modeling of Neural Systems*. F.H. Eeckman (ed.) Kluwer Acad. Publishers. Norwell, MA.

THE NeuroGraph NEURAL NETWORK SIMULATOR

Peter Wilke and Christian Jacob
Universität Erlangen-Nürnberg
Lehrstuhl für Programmiersprachen
Martensstr. 3 · D-8520 Erlangen, Germany
E-mail {wilke, jacob}@informatik.uni-erlangen.de

1) The NeuroGraph Neural Network Simulator

NeuroGraph is a neural network simulation environment for UNIX workstations. It is a software tool based on the X-Windows programming libraries and allows interactive design, training, testing and visualization of artificial neural networks. The simulator consists of four major components: a simulator kernel that operates on the internal representation of the neural network models, a graphical user interface to interactively design net topologies and functionality (see fig. 1), and control network dynamics, an analyzation component to get and evaluate performance information during net execution, and a real world interface component for easy integration of the simulated networks into practical application environments.

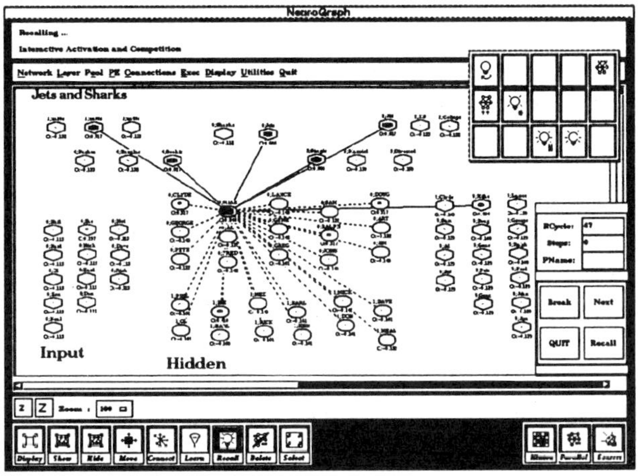

Fig. 1: NeuroGraph's grafical interface

Furthermore, there are two special modules for advanced experimentation with neural nets: an easy to use toolbox for developers of neural nets offering interactive definition of specialized neuron functionality as well as net control strategies, and a parallelization component which is able to divide neural nets into parallely executable modules, and then map these modules to parallel hardware. With the parallelization module, time-consuming net control algorithms can be efficiently performed on multiprocessor platforms or workstation clusters, whereas online visualization of the network dynamics is handled by graphic workstations.

2) The Simulator Kernel

The simulator kernel (see fig. 2) provides a library of functions which are responsible for the management of the internal representation of the neural network topology and functionality. The kernel routines are subdivided into two major parts: routines which offer model-independent manipulation of data structures (installing or deleting layers, adding neurons, defining pools of neurons, installing connections between groups of neurons etc.), and routines which essentially depend on different neural network models, their connectivity and control strategy, i.e. modules containing model-specific learn and recall algorithms and interface routines (e.g., feed-forward backpropagation nets, constraint satisfaction, interactive activation and competition, pattern-associator, competitive learning, for a description of these models see [Rumelhart, McClelland 88]). The whole kernel is written in C for efficiency and portability reasons.

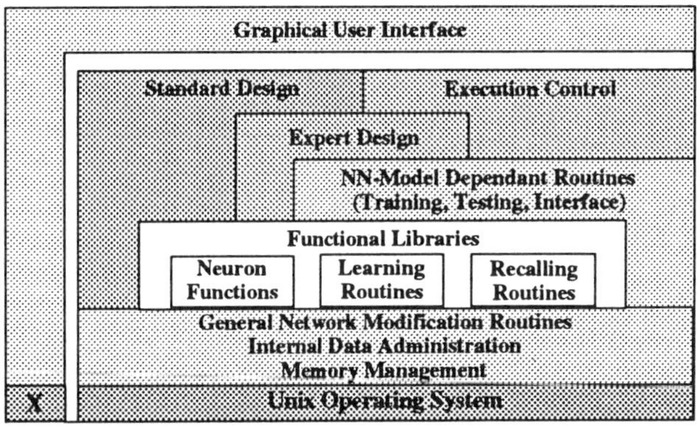

Fig. 2: Design of the NeuroGraph kernel

3) The Graphical User Interface

The graphical user interface (GUI) is based on the X-Windows system together with the OSF/Motif Widget Libraries. The GUI is (see fig. 1) an easy-to-use tool to interactively design different standard net topologies and control strategies; however, it is also possible to define new net architectures as well as neuronal and net-global functional behaviour. There are a number of standard functions (scaled summation/product, linear threshold, sigmoid, stochastic sigmoid, step, linear) available to characterize the learn and recall functionality of each processing element. But there is also a module to define user-specific signal processing andlearning functions for the neurons; description of the functions is done via entering mathematical expressions for these functions.

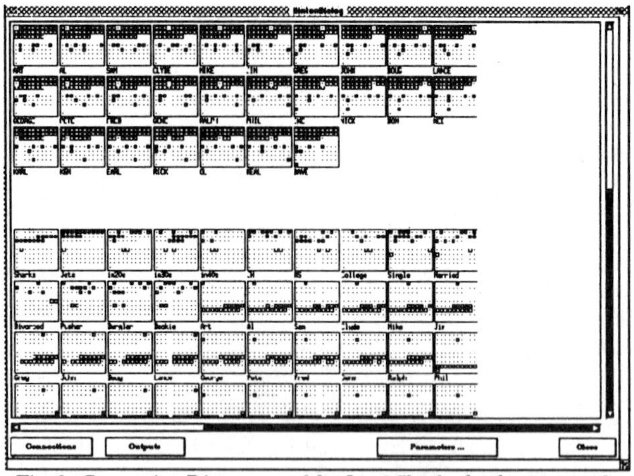

Fig. 3: Connection Diagramm of the Jets&Sharks database network

In order to get different views on a simulated network there are several modes to visualize its topology and/or connection structures, to show only parts of a network, display neuron parameters in graphical and/or textual form etc. One special module presents connection structures in the form of a diagram (see fig. 3), as proposed by Hinton and Sejnowsky ([Rumelhart, McClelland 86], page 24).

4) System components communication

As mentioned before, NeuroGraph is devided into separate modules. Common to all modules is the internal network representation which is a flexible data structure.

Using NeuroGraph on a single workstation this data structure is accessed via shared memory management. In a distributed computing environment NeuroGraph uses the X-Protocol [Young90] for communication between the software modules running on different computer networknodes [Jacob, Wilke 91]. Therefore NeuroGraph is able to visualize a neural net on a personal computer running an X-Server, using network parameters stored on a fileserver while the net is being trained on a multi-processor-system using back-propagation or any other learning rule.

5) Communication with Parallel Hardware

In order to achieve a reasonable speedup in the performance of large and complex networks (with more than 10000 processing elements and more than 100000 connections), the functional network data (i.e., excluding the parameters needed for visualizing the net topology on the screen) is sent to a multi-processor system via X-Protocol mechanisms. Time-consuming learning and recalling is then performed in parallel (as far as possible, depending on the selected control strategy and connectivity) with specially designed algorithms that efficiently use the underlying hardware. Any network data changes of which the user wants to be informed are signaled to the supervising kernel or GUI (Graphical User Interface) module, which then decides whether to reflect the changes on the screen immediately (e.g., to see a refined step by step evaluation of the network) or to wait for a general update signal (e.g., at the end of a training epoch). Alternatively the described data interchange can take place via files if the learning process is to be performed independently of the visualization GUI module (e.g., when learning may last some hours).

6) Analyzing Network Dynamics

During the training and test phases, dynamic network data (neural activity change, variations of the weights, error measures, etc.) can be visualized by several „instruments", which help to analyze network behaviour on-line, and support the user in finding problem-specific parameter values for the simulated networks. A protocol facility enables off-line analyzation of selected network data. In order to alleviate offline analyzation of selected network data, we are currently implementing a protocol module which is first of all able to filter user-defined, specific network data out of the large amount of data that can be observed during learning and recall processes, and secondly provides interfaces to spreadsheet programs or other available software for statistical and/or graphical analyzation and visualization (e.g., Lotus 1-2-3, Mathematica).

7) The Real World Interface

A few „real world interfaces" should help in integrating simulated and trained neural nets into practical application environments. In its simplest form, this means that there is a textual description or ASCII representation of all parameters which influence network performance. Another possibility is to control networks (trained or untrained) without the help of the graphical user interface, but connect the simulation via X-Protocol into other X-based applications. A future extension to the real world interfaces will be provided by a module which is able to generate (e.g.) C-code for trained networks so that nets could be intergrated into programming systems as „black boxes" performing some learnt functions.

8) Related Work

Some ideas in the NeuroGraph simulator were inspired by the PDP-Simulators [McClelland, Rumelhart 88] and Neural Works Professional II [NeuralWare 90]. Recently we obtained the SNNS simulator [Zell et al. 91], which is also based on X-Windows, but (up to now) implements only backpropagation methods. First ideas about the NeuroGraph parallelization modules have been presented at the IJCNN 91 in Singapore [Jacob, Wilke 91].

9) Literature

[Jacob, Wilke 91] C. Jacob, P. Wilke: "A Distributed Network Simulation Environment For Multi-processing Systems", *Proceedings International Joint Conference on Neural Networks, IJCNN 1991*, Singapore, pp. 1178-1183.

[McClelland, Rumelhart 88] J. L. McClelland, D. E. Rumelhart.1988. *Explorations in Parallel Distributed Processing*, MIT Press, Cambridge, .

[NeuralWare 90] NeuralWorks Professional II: 'Neural Computing", Users Guide, Reference Guide, Neural Ware Inc., 1990.

[Rumelhart, McClelland 86] D. E. Rumelhart, J. L. McClelland. 1986. *Parallel Distributed Processing, Vol. 1,2*, MIT Press, Cambridge.

[Young 90] Douglas A. Young: *The X Window System - Programming ans Applications with Xt OSF/Motif*, Prentice Hall, Englewood Cliffs, New Jersey, 1990

[Zell et al. 91] A. Zell, Th. Korb, N. Mache, T. Sommer: "Recent Developments of the SNNS Neural Network Simulator", *Proceedings Applications of Neural Networks Conference*, SPIE Vol. 1294, pp. 535-544.

SESAME – An Object Oriented Software Tool for Design, Simulation and Analysis of Neural Nets

Christoph Tietz Alexander Linden Thomas Sudbrak

AI Research Division, Institute for Applied Information Technology
German National Research Center for Computer Science (GMD)
Schloss Birlinghoven, D-5205 Sankt Augustin 1, Germany

SESAME is a simulation tool that was written for the design, simulation and analysis of complex neural network architectures. Such architectures contain modular neural network structures as well as simulations or other special modules that provide the environment in which the experiments will take place. This includes interfaces to external components of the experiment or even interfaces to real world applications.

We have chosen an object oriented approach to the development of SESAME to build a large but nevertheless maintainable system that supports the development of extensions or even new conceptual ideas without complete knowledge of the system. On the other hand the object oriented approach provides transparency and flexibility for setup and conducting experiments with complex architectures. It is visible to the user through the building blocks of an experiment that represent data manipulation objects and are the basic elements of an experiment setup the user manipulates.

The main design goal was to support large hierarchical and modular network structures that may combine multiple learning paradigms for neural networks in one experiment and augment the neural architectures with conventional function modules to hybrid systems. We have implemented our ideas in the prototype system SESAME (Software Environment for the Simulation of Adaptive Modular SystEms) which consists at this moment of about 130 C++ – classes written in approx. 39.000 lines of code. This prototype is used in our research group for experiments in the areas of pattern recognition, speech recognition and robotics.

Experiments are constructed from building blocks that manipulate data fields (arrays of data elements) and communicate by distributing them over communication channels. The building blocks (called *modules* in the following) for our experiment architectures contain *sites* as the endpoints of communication channels, *data fields* that may be associated with the sites, *action* and *command functions* that perform the data manipulation operations and the user interface that is based on a *symbol table*. The user interface makes the parameters of a module available together with the the action and command funtions the user may call eg. to print values of data fields or trigger special operations. Typically a parameterless action function triggers the main operations of a module, receiving, processing and sending data fields. Command functions may get additional parameters from the user introducing a larger call overhead for operations that are typically used interactively from the user interface. Higher level control is provided through *scripts* that define procedures of action/command functions and script calls.

We classify our building blocks in modules responsible for file i/o, pattern handling and storage, neural basis modules (backpropagation net, feature map, kanerva memory, radial basis function net etc.), data coding, general mathematical operations on data vectors and simulations (eg. for robot arms or autonomous vehicle environments).

An experiment description consists of the topology of the used modules, defining names and types of modules and meta-modules and their connections. A meta-module may contain other modules (and meta-modules) and may define meta-sites that connect external modules with its submodules. Thus large and complex architectures may be structured into modular hierarchies. At the user level modules created from C++ – classes linked to SESAME or modules created from the description of a meta-module are principally handled the same way. The only difference is that meta-modules may contain submodules.

An experiment description also contains parameters for the created modules and the definition of scripts completes the description by defining the control flow. Scripts are always defined locally to a module and thus are part of its functional interface. Control is distributed over the whole module hierarchy to the points where the functionality is provided in the action functions of single modules.

When SESAME constructs an experiment, first the module descriptions are loaded from description files that may be found locally in the experiment directory or along a given path in library directories. The description files contain the experiment description in the form of commands that could also be used interactively to create the experiment. After the construction the experiment modules are configured using the given parameters and a configuration mechanism that propagates data formats over the communication channels. With these data formats it is possible to automatically configure modules like weight layers for neural nets that determine the size of the weight layer from the data formats they receive from their predecessor and successor modules. Using this auto-configuration mechanism it is possible to create library modules for neural nets that automatically adapt to the experiment environment in which they are used. When the experiment configuration is finished the data fields are created using the propagated data formats and initialized loading possibly saved data from the description files.

The experiment is now ready to run. The user can interactively change parameters, add modules eg. for visualization of the simulation or statistical data collections, he can remove modules that are no longer needed and edit or create scripts. The user can save module descriptions together with the data field contents or simply display details about the current configuration. All these operations are possible even in the middle of an experiment run to provide complete interactive control over the experiment.

The user navigates through the structure of an experiment in a similar way as he navigates in the trees of a hierarchical file system. His commands are always interpreted locally to a module and the user interface provides commands to change the current module or define the module which shall provide the scope for a single command execution. Scripts and meta-modules may be parameterized using convenience variables defined locally to a module.

There are a few methods a user of SESAME can use to extend the current library of predefined modules and meta-modules. He can build a new module from already defined ones, combining them in a meta-module that may be added to a library. For such experimental setups a set of primitive modules is provided that perform simple functions on data fields and help control the data flow in an experiment. If a meta-module already exists that performs most of the necessary functions it may be loaded and then modified via description files so that not all of its functionality has to be reconstructed in another meta-module. This may be interpreted as inheritance between meta-modules. The third method is feasible if there was no way to provide the necessary functionality in the form of meta-modules or the unavoidable runtime inefficiency of meta-modules is too much to bear. The user may then write a new C++ – class that he derives from a basic module class or more derived classes that already provide some of the needed functionality. This class may then be linked to the SESAME code to make the new module available. We plan to augment this mechanism by supporting dynamic linking for SESAME which would allow to add new module types even during simulation runs.

Other future developments for SESAME include a graphical user interface that helps the user to graphically define network structures and display the experiment topology. The script language in use now has been redesigned to use more powerful control structures to give the user better control over the experiment and the mechanisms to load experiments from description files have been augmented to allow a quite sophisticated partitioning of experiment descriptions. Many ideas for further development are under consideration as our experimental work with and on SESAME continues.

SESAME is still a prototype system. As a consequence the system changes (hopefully evolves) rapidly and we really do not have the resources to give full support to all external users of SESAME. Nevertheless do we take snapshots of the system from time to time and make them available via anonymous ftp. You will find our ftp server under the address **ftp.gmd.de** where you can log in as user **anonymous** using your mail address as password. In the directory **gmd/as/sesame** you will find a **README** file that should tell you all necessary details. For questions concerning SESAME the mailing address **sesame-request@gmd.de** is provided. A mailing list for users of SESAME is also available.

Author Index

Subject Index

U

V

W

Patrick K. Simpson

Patrick K. Simpson was born in Cordova, AK, a small fishing community on the Prince William Sound. From 1974 to 1986, Mr. Simpson worked with his family on fishing boats, starting as a crew member and working his way up to captain.

Mr. Simpson received his Bachelor of Arts degree in Computer Science from the University of California at San Diego in 1986. Since college, Mr. Simpson has distinguished himself in the application of neural networks, fuzzy systems, and artificial intelligence to difficult defense-related problems in areas such as electronic intelligence, radar surveillance, sonar signal identification, and various aspects of automated diagnostics.

In addition to his career as an engineer, Mr. Simpson has written several archival papers, taught several courses, written a text book that has been used in college courses around the United States, and lectured on the theory and application of neural networks and fuzzy systems world wide.

Recently, Mr. Simpson has combined his past with the present and formed Scientific Fishery Systems, Inc., a small business dedicated to the conversion of defense technologies to the fisheries.